The Dictionary of Art · volume fourteen

The Dictionary of Art

14

Habsburg, §II:
Spanish branch
TO
Hungary, §V:
Interior decoration
and furniture

GROVE

The Dictionary of Art

edited by JANE TURNER, in thirty-four volumes, 1996

Reprinted with minor corrections, 1998, 2002

This edition is distributed within the United Kingdom and Europe
by Macmillan Publishers Limited, London, and within the United States and Canada by
Grove's Dictionaries Inc., New York.

Text keyboarded by Wearset Limited, Sunderland, England
Database management by Pindar plc, York, England
Imagesetting by William Clowes Limited, Suffolk, England
Printed and bound by China Translation and Printing Services Ltd, Hong Kong

British Library Cataloguing in Publication Data

The dictionary of art
  1. Art - Dictionaries 2. Art - History -
    Dictionaries
  I. Turner, Jane
  703

ISBN 1-884446-00-0

Library of Congress Cataloging in Publication Data

The dictionary of art / editor, Jane Turner.
  p. cm.
  Includes bibliographical references and index.
  Contents: 1. A to Anckerman
  ISBN 1-884446-00-0 (alk. paper)
  1. Art—Encyclopedias.
  I. Turner, Jane, 1956–
N31.D5 1996   96–13628
703—dc20   CIP

Contents

List of Colour Illustrations   vi

General Abbreviations   vii

A Note on the Use of *The Dictionary*   xiii

The Dictionary, volume fourteen:
Habsburg, §II: Spanish branch–Hungary, §V:
Interior decoration and furniture   1

Illustration Acknowledgements   911

List of Colour Illustrations

PLATE I. **Hardstones**

1. Black marble table-top inlaid with pietre dure, including lapis lazuli, chalcedonies, agates and jaspers, diam. 1.25 m, made by Jacopo Ligozzi and Bernardino Poccetti at the Opificio delle Pietre Dure, Florence, 1633–49 (Florence, Museo dell'Opificio delle Pietre Dure/ Photo: Scala, Florence)

2. Lapis lazuli piece carved with figures in a mountain landscape, h. 240 mm, from China, Qing dynasty, 18th century (San Francisco, CA, Asian Art Museum of San Francisco/Photo: Asian Art Museum of San Francisco, Avery Brundage Collection; no. B60 J31)

PLATE II. **Hardstones**

1. Moss-agate bowl with gold enamel setting by Ottavio Miseroni, h. 171 mm, made in Prague, *c.* 1600 (Vienna, Kunsthistorisches Museum/Photo: Kunsthistorisches Museum)

2. Five-layered onyx cameo with gold rim, known as the Gemma Claudia, depicting (*left*) Emperor Claudius and Agrippina the younger and (*right*) Germanicus and Agrippina the elder, h. 120 mm, from Rome, AD ?49 (Vienna, Kunsthistorisches Museum/Photo: Kunsthistorisches Museum)

PLATE III. **Heraldry**

1. Memorial plaque to *Ulrich Ketzel* with his coat of arms and badges of orders of knighthood, oil on panel, 680 × 600 mm, 1462 (Nuremberg, Germanisches Nationalmuseum/Photo: Germanisches Nationalmuseum)

2. Coat of arms of Charles the Bold, Duke of Burgundy, detail from the centre of a *millefleurs* tapestry, wool, silk, gold and silver thread, 3.06 (originally *c.* 4.46)×7.05 m, made by Jean Le Haze, Brussels, 1466 (Berne, Historisches Museum/Photo: Historisches Museum)

PLATE IV. **Heraldry**

Armorials of the kings of Aragon, France, Hungary and Scotland showing shields, helms and crests; illustrations from the *Armorial Gelre*, 1370–86 (Brussels, Bibliothèque Royale Albert 1er, B.R. MS. 15.652–6, fols 46*r*, 52*v*, 62*v*, 64*r*/Photo: Bibliothèque Royale Albert 1er)

General Abbreviations

The abbreviations employed throughout this dictionary, most of which are listed below, do not vary, except for capitalization, regardless of the context in which they are used, including bibliographical citations and for locations of works of art. The principle used to arrive at these abbreviations is that their full form should be easily deducible, and for this reason acronyms have generally been avoided (e.g. Los Angeles Co. Mus. A. instead of LACMA). The same abbreviation is adopted for cognate forms in foreign languages and in most cases for plural and adjectival forms (e.g. A.= Art, Arts, Arte, Arti etc). Not all related forms are listed below. Occasionally, if a name, for instance of an artists' group or exhibiting society, is repeated within the text of one article, it is cited in an abbreviated form after its first mention in full (e.g. The Pre-Raphaelite Brotherhood (PRB) was founded...); the same is true of archaeological periods and eras, which are abbreviated to initial letters in small capitals (e.g. In the Early Minoan (EM) period...). Such abbreviations do not appear in this list. For the reader's convenience, separate full lists of abbreviations for locations, periodical titles and standard reference books and series are included as Appendices A–C in vol. 33.

A.	Art, Arts	Anthropol.	Anthropology	Azerbaij.	Azerbaijani
A.C.	Arts Council	Antiqua.	Antiquarian, Antiquaries	B.	Bartsch [catalogue of Old Master prints]
Acad.	Academy	app.	appendix		
AD	Anno Domini	approx.	approximately	*b*	born
Add.	Additional, Addendum	AR	Arkansas (USA)	BA	Bachelor of Arts
addn	addition	ARA	Associate of the Royal Academy	Balt.	Baltic
Admin.	Administration			*bapt*	baptized
Adv.	Advances, Advanced	Arab.	Arabic	BArch	Bachelor of Architecture
Aesth.	Aesthetic(s)	Archaeol.	Archaeology	Bart	Baronet
Afr.	African	Archit.	Architecture, Architectural	Bask.	Basketry
Afrik.	Afrikaans, Afrikaner	Archv, Archvs	Archive(s)	BBC	British Broadcasting Corporation
A.G.	Art Gallery	Arg.	Argentine	BC	Before Christ
Agrar.	Agrarian	ARHA	Associate of the Royal Hibernian Academy	BC	British Columbia (Canada)
Agric.	Agriculture	ARIBA	Associate of the Royal Institute of British Architects	BE	Buddhist era
Agron.	Agronomy			Beds	Bedfordshire (GB)
Agy	Agency	Armen.	Armenian	Behav.	Behavioural
AH	Anno Hegirae	ARSA	Associate of the Royal Scottish Academy	Belarus.	Belarusian
A. Inst.	Art Institute			Belg.	Belgian
AK	Alaska (USA)	Asiat.	Asiatic	Berks	Berkshire (GB)
AL	Alabama (USA)	Assist.	Assistance	Berwicks	Berwickshire (GB; old)
Alb.	Albanian	Assoc.	Association	BFA	Bachelor of Fine Arts
Alg.	Algerian	Astron.	Astronomy	Bibl.	Bible, Biblical
Alta	Alberta (Canada)	AT&T	American Telephone & Telegraph Company	Bibliog.	Bibliography, Bibliographical
Altern.	Alternative			Biblioph.	Bibliophile
a.m.	ante meridiem [before noon]	attrib.	attribution, attributed to	Biog.	Biography, Biographical
Amat.	Amateur	Aug	August	Biol.	Biology, Biological
Amer.	American	Aust.	Austrian	bk, bks	book(s)
An.	Annals	Austral.	Australian	Bkbinder	Bookbinder
Anatol.	Anatolian	Auth.	Author(s)	Bklore	Booklore
Anc.	Ancient	Auton.	Autonomous	Bkshop	Bookshop
Annu.	Annual	Aux.	Auxiliary	BL	British Library
Anon.	Anonymous(ly)	Ave.	Avenue	Bld	Build
Ant.	Antique	AZ	Arizona (USA)	Bldg	Building
Anthol.	Anthology				

Bldr	Builder
BLitt	Bachelor of Letters/Literature
BM	British Museum
Boh.	Bohemian
Boliv.	Bolivian
Botan.	Botany, Botanical
BP	Before present (1950)
Braz.	Brazilian
BRD	Bundesrepublik Deutschland [Federal Republic of Germany (West Germany)]
Brecons	Breconshire (GB; old)
Brez.	Brezonek [lang. of Brittany]
Brit.	British
Bros	Brothers
BSc	Bachelor of Science
Bucks	Buckinghamshire (GB)
Bulg.	Bulgarian
Bull.	Bulletin
bur	buried
Burm.	Burmese
Byz.	Byzantine
C	Celsius
C.	Century
c.	*circa* [about]
CA	California
Cab.	Cabinet
Caerns	Caernarvonshire (GB; old)
C.A.G.	City Art Gallery
Cal.	Calendar
Callig.	Calligraphy
Cam.	Camera
Cambs	Cambridgeshire (GB)
can	canonized
Can.	Canadian
Cant.	Canton(s), Cantonal
Capt.	Captain
Cards	Cardiganshire (GB; old)
Carib.	Caribbean
Carms	Carmarthenshire (GB; old)
Cartog.	Cartography
Cat.	Catalan
cat.	catalogue
Cath.	Catholic
CBE	Commander of the Order of the British Empire
Celeb.	Celebration
Celt.	Celtic
Cent.	Centre, Central
Centen.	Centennial
Cer.	Ceramic
cf.	confer [compare]
Chap., Chaps	Chapter(s)
Chem.	Chemistry
Ches	Cheshire (GB)
Chil.	Chilean

Chin.	Chinese
Christ.	Christian, Christianity
Chron.	Chronicle
Cie	Compagnie [French]
Cinema.	Cinematography
Circ.	Circle
Civ.	Civil, Civic
Civiliz.	Civilization(s)
Class.	Classic, Classical
Clin.	Clinical
CO	Colorado (USA)
Co.	Company; County
Cod.	Codex, Codices
Col., Cols	Collection(s); Column(s)
Coll.	College
collab.	in collaboration with, collaborated, collaborative
Collct.	Collecting
Colloq.	Colloquies
Colomb.	Colombian
Colon.	Colonies, Colonial
Colr	Collector
Comm.	Commission; Community
Commerc.	Commercial
Communic.	Communications
Comp.	Comparative; compiled by, compiler
Concent.	Concentration
Concr.	Concrete
Confed.	Confederation
Confer.	Conference
Congol.	Congolese
Congr.	Congress
Conserv.	Conservation; Conservatory
Constr.	Construction(al)
cont.	continued
Contemp.	Contemporary
Contrib.	Contributions, Contributor(s)
Convalesc.	Convalescence
Convent.	Convention
Coop.	Cooperation
Coord.	Coordination
Copt.	Coptic
Corp.	Corporation, Corpus
Corr.	Correspondence
Cors.	Corsican
Cost.	Costume
Cret.	Cretan
Crim.	Criminal
Crit.	Critical, Criticism
Croat.	Croatian
CT	Connecticut (USA)
Cttee	Committee
Cub.	Cuban
Cult.	Cultural, Culture
Cumb.	Cumberland (GB; old)

Cur.	Curator, Curatorial, Curatorship
Curr.	Current(s)
CVO	Commander of the [Royal] Victorian Order
Cyclad.	Cycladic
Cyp.	Cypriot
Czech.	Czechoslovak
$	dollars
d	died
d.	denarius, denarii [penny, pence]
Dalmat.	Dalmatian
Dan.	Danish
DBE	Dame Commander of the Order of the British Empire
DC	District of Columbia (USA)
DDR	Deutsche Demokratische Republik [German Democratic Republic (East Germany)]
DE	Delaware (USA)
Dec	December
Dec.	Decorative
ded.	dedication, dedicated to
Democ.	Democracy, Democratic
Demog.	Demography, Demographic
Denbs	Denbighshire (GB; old)
dep.	deposited at
Dept	Department
Dept.	Departmental, Departments
Derbys	Derbyshire (GB)
Des.	Design
destr.	destroyed
Dev.	Development
Devon	Devonshire (GB)
Dial.	Dialogue
diam.	diameter
Diff.	Diffusion
Dig.	Digest
Dip. Eng.	Diploma in Engineering
Dir.	Direction, Directed
Directrt	Directorate
Disc.	Discussion
diss.	dissertation
Distr.	District
Div.	Division
DLitt	Doctor of Letters/Literature
DM	Deutsche Mark
Doc.	Document(s)
Doss.	Dossier
DPhil	Doctor of Philosophy
Dr	Doctor
Drg, Drgs	Drawing(s)
DSc	Doctor of Science/Historical Sciences
Dut.	Dutch
Dwell.	Dwelling
E.	East(ern)

EC	European (Economic) Community	figs	figures	Heb.	Hebrew
Eccles.	Ecclesiastical	Filip.	Filipina(s), Filipino(s)	Hell.	Hellenic
Econ.	Economic, Economies	Fin.	Finnish	Her.	Heritage
Ecuad.	Ecuadorean	FL	Florida (USA)	Herald.	Heraldry, Heraldic
ed.	editor, edited (by)	*fl*	*floruit* [he/she flourished]	Hereford & Worcs	Hereford & Worcester (GB)
edn	edition	Flem.	Flemish		
eds	editors	Flints	Flintshire (GB; old)	Herts	Hertfordshire (GB)
Educ.	Education	Flk	Folk	HI	Hawaii (USA)
e.g.	*exempli gratia* [for example]	Flklore	Folklore	Hib.	Hibernia
Egyp.	Egyptian	fol., fols	folio(s)	Hisp.	Hispanic
Elem.	Element(s), Elementary	Found.	Foundation	Hist.	History, Historical
Emp.	Empirical	Fr.	French	HMS	His/Her Majesty's Ship
Emul.	Emulation	frag.	fragment	Hon.	Honorary, Honourable
Enc.	Encyclopedia	Fri.	Friday	Horiz.	Horizon
Encour.	Encouragement	FRIBA	Fellow of the Royal Institute of British Architects	Hort.	Horticulture
Eng.	English			Hosp.	Hospital(s)
Engin.	Engineer, Engineering	FRS	Fellow of the Royal Society, London	HRH	His/Her Royal Highness
Engr., Engrs	Engraving(s)			Human.	Humanities, Humanism
		ft	foot, feet	Hung.	Hungarian
Envmt	Environment	Furn.	Furniture	Hunts	Huntingdonshire (GB; old)
Epig.	Epigraphy	Futur.	Futurist, Futurism	IA	Iowa
Episc.	Episcopal	g	gram(s)	ibid.	*ibidem* [in the same place]
Esp.	Especially	GA	Georgia (USA)	ICA	Institute of Contemporary Arts
Ess.	Essays	Gael.	Gaelic		
est.	established	Gal., Gals	Gallery, Galleries	Ice.	Icelandic
etc	*etcetera* [and so on]	Gaz.	Gazette	Iconog.	Iconography
Ethnog.	Ethnography	GB	Great Britain	Iconol.	Iconology
Ethnol.	Ethnology	Gdn, Gdns	Garden(s)	ID	Idaho (USA)
Etrus.	Etruscan	Gdnr(s)	Gardener(s)	i.e.	*id est* [that is]
Eur.	European	Gen.	General	IL	Illinois (USA)
Evangel.	Evangelical	Geneal.	Genealogy, Genealogist	Illum.	Illumination
Exam.	Examination	Gent.	Gentleman, Gentlemen	illus.	illustrated, illustration
Excav.	Excavation, Excavated	Geog.	Geography	Imp.	Imperial
Exch.	Exchange	Geol.	Geology	IN	Indiana (USA)
Excurs.	Excursion	Geom.	Geometry	in., ins	inch(es)
exh.	exhibition	Georg.	Georgian	Inc.	Incorporated
Exp.	Exposition	Geosci.	Geoscience	inc.	incomplete
Expermntl	Experimental	Ger.	German, Germanic	incl.	includes, including, inclusive
Explor.	Exploration	G.I.	Government/General Issue (USA)	Incorp.	Incorporation
Expn	Expansion			Ind.	Indian
Ext.	External	Glams	Glamorganshire (GB; old)	Indep.	Independent
Extn	Extension	Glos	Gloucestershire (GB)	Indig.	Indigenous
f, ff	following page, following pages	Govt	Government	Indol.	Indology
		Gr.	Greek	Indon.	Indonesian
F.A.	Fine Art(s)	Grad.	Graduate	Indust.	Industrial
Fac.	Faculty	Graph.	Graphic	Inf.	Information
facs.	facsimile	Green.	Greenlandic	Inq.	Inquiry
Fam.	Family	Gr.-Roman	Greco-Roman	Inscr.	Inscribed, Inscription
fasc.	fascicle	Gt	Great	Inst.	Institute(s)
fd	feastday (of a saint)	Gtr	Greater	Inst. A.	Institute of Art
Feb	February	Guat.	Guatemalan	Instr.	Instrument, Instrumental
Fed.	Federation, Federal	Gym.	Gymnasium	Int.	International
Fem.	Feminist	h.	height	Intell.	Intelligence
Fest.	Festival	ha	hectare	Inter.	Interior(s), Internal
fig.	figure (illustration)	Hait.	Haitian	Interdiscip.	Interdisciplinary
Fig.	Figurative	Hants	Hampshire (GB)	intro.	introduced by, introduction
		Hb.	Handbook	inv.	inventory

Inven.	Invention	m	metre(s)	Moldov.	Moldovan
Invest.	Investigation(s)	m.	married	MOMA	Museum of Modern Art
Iran.	Iranian	M.	Monsieur	Mon.	Monday
irreg.	irregular(ly)	MA	Master of Arts; Massachusetts (USA)	Mongol.	Mongolian
Islam.	Islamic			Mons	Monmouthshire (GB; old)
Isr.	Israeli	Mag.	Magazine	Montgoms	Montgomeryshire (GB; old)
It.	Italian	Maint.	Maintenance	Mor.	Moral
J.	Journal	Malay.	Malaysian	Morav.	Moravian
Jam.	Jamaican	Man.	Manitoba (Canada); Manual	Moroc.	Moroccan
Jan	January	Manuf.	Manufactures	Movt	Movement
Jap.	Japanese	Mar.	Marine, Maritime	MP	Member of Parliament
Jav.	Javanese	Mason.	Masonic	MPhil	Master of Philosophy
Jew.	Jewish	Mat.	Material(s)	MS	Mississippi (USA)
Jewel.	Jewellery	Math.	Mathematic	MS., MSS	manuscript(s)
Jord.	Jordanian	MBE	Member of the Order of the British Empire	MSc	Master of Science
jr	junior			MT	Montana (USA)
Juris.	Jurisdiction	MD	Doctor of Medicine; Maryland (USA)	Mt	Mount
KBE	Knight Commander of the Order of the British Empire			Mthly	Monthly
		ME	Maine (USA)	Mun.	Municipal
KCVO	Knight Commander of the Royal Victorian Order	Mech.	Mechanical	Mus.	Museum(s)
		Med.	Medieval; Medium, Media	Mus. A.	Museum of Art
kg	kilogram(s)	Medic.	Medical, Medicine	Mus. F.A.	Museum of Fine Art(s)
kHz	kilohertz	Medit.	Mediterranean	Music.	Musicology
km	kilometre(s)	Mem.	Memorial(s); Memoir(s)	N.	North(ern); National
Knowl.	Knowledge	Merions	Merionethshire (GB; old)	n	refractive index of a medium
Kor.	Korean	Meso-Amer.	Meso-American	n.	note
KS	Kansas (USA)			N.A.G.	National Art Gallery
KY	Kentucky (USA)	Mesop.	Mesopotamian	Nat.	Natural, Nature
Kyrgyz.	Kyrgyzstani	Met.	Metropolitan	Naut.	Nautical
£	libra, librae [pound, pounds sterling]	Metal.	Metallurgy	NB	New Brunswick (Canada)
		Mex.	Mexican	NC	North Carolina (USA)
l.	length	MFA	Master of Fine Arts	ND	North Dakota (USA)
LA	Louisiana (USA)	mg	milligram(s)	n.d.	no date
Lab.	Laboratory	Mgmt	Management	NE	Nebraska; Northeast(ern)
Lancs	Lancashire (GB)	Mgr	Monsignor	Neth.	Netherlandish
Lang.	Language(s)	MI	Michigan	Newslett.	Newsletter
Lat.	Latin	Micrones.	Micronesian	Nfld	Newfoundland (Canada)
Latv.	Latvian	Mid. Amer.	Middle American	N.G.	National Gallery
lb, lbs	pound(s) weight	Middx	Middlesex (GB; old)	N.G.A.	National Gallery of Art
Leb.	Lebanese	Mid. E.	Middle Eastern	NH	New Hampshire (USA)
Lect.	Lecture	Mid. Eng.	Middle English	Niger.	Nigerian
Legis.	Legislative	Mid Glam.	Mid Glamorgan (GB)	NJ	New Jersey (USA)
Leics	Leicestershire (GB)	Mil.	Military	NM	New Mexico (USA)
Lex.	Lexicon	Mill.	Millennium	nm	nanometre (10^{-9} metre)
Lg.	Large	Min.	Ministry; Minutes	nn.	notes
Lib., Libs	Library, Libraries	Misc.	Miscellaneous	no., nos	number(s)
Liber.	Liberian	Miss.	Mission(s)	Nord.	Nordic
Libsp	Librarianship	Mlle	Mademoiselle	Norm.	Normal
Lincs	Lincolnshire (GB)	mm	millimetre(s)	Northants	Northamptonshire (GB)
Lit.	Literature	Mme	Madame	Northumb.	Northumberland (GB)
Lith.	Lithuanian	MN	Minnesota	Norw.	Norwegian
Liturg.	Liturgical	Mnmt, Mnmts	Monument(s)	Notts	Nottinghamshire (GB)
LLB	Bachelor of Laws	Mnmtl	Monumental	Nov	November
LLD	Doctor of Laws	MO	Missouri (USA)	n.p.	no place (of publication)
Lt	Lieutenant	Mod.	Modern, Modernist	N.P.G.	National Portrait Gallery
Lt-Col.	Lieutenant-Colonel	Moldav.	Moldavian	nr	near
Ltd	Limited				

Nr E. Near Eastern
NS New Style; Nova Scotia (Canada)
n. s. new series
NSW New South Wales (Australia)
NT National Trust
Ntbk Notebook
Numi. Numismatic(s)
NV Nevada (USA)
NW Northwest(ern)
NWT Northwest Territories (Canada)
NY New York (USA)
NZ New Zealand
OBE Officer of the Order of the British Empire
Obj. Object(s), Objective
Occas. Occasional
Occident. Occidental
Ocean. Oceania
Oct October
8vo octavo
OFM Order of Friars Minor
OH Ohio (USA)
OK Oklahoma (USA)
Olymp. Olympic
OM Order of Merit
Ont. Ontario (Canada)
op. opus
opp. opposite; opera [pl. of opus]
OR Oregon (USA)
Org. Organization
Orient. Oriental
Orthdx Orthodox
OSB Order of St Benedict
Ott. Ottoman
Oxon Oxfordshire (GB)
oz. ounce(s)
p pence
p., pp. page(s)
PA Pennsylvania (USA)
p.a. per annum
Pak. Pakistani
Palaeontol. Palaeontology, Palaeontological
Palest. Palestinian
Pap. Paper(s)
para. paragraph
Parag. Paraguayan
Parl. Parliament
Paroch. Parochial
Patriarch. Patriarchate
Patriot. Patriotic
Patrm. Patrimony
Pav. Pavilion
PEI Prince Edward Island (Canada)
Pembs Pembrokeshire (GB; old)

Per. Period
Percep. Perceptions
Perf. Performance, Performing, Performed
Period. Periodical(s)
Pers. Persian
Persp. Perspectives
Peru. Peruvian
PhD Doctor of Philosophy
Philol. Philology
Philos. Philosophy
Phoen. Phoenician
Phot. Photograph, Photography, Photographic
Phys. Physician(s), Physics, Physique, Physical
Physiog. Physiognomy
Physiol. Physiology
Pict. Picture(s), Pictorial
pl. plate; plural
Plan. Planning
Planet. Planetarium
Plast. Plastic
pls plates
p.m. post meridiem [after noon]
Polit. Political
Poly. Polytechnic
Polynes. Polynesian
Pop. Popular
Port. Portuguese
Port. Portfolio
Posth. Posthumous(ly)
Pott. Pottery
POW prisoner of war
PRA President of the Royal Academy
Pract. Practical
Prefect. Prefecture, Prefectural
Preserv. Preservation
prev. previous(ly)
priv. private
PRO Public Record Office
Prob. Problem(s)
Proc. Proceedings
Prod. Production
Prog. Progress
Proj. Project(s)
Promot. Promotion
Prop. Property, Properties
Prov. Province(s), Provincial
Proven. Provenance
Prt, Prts Print(s)
Prtg Printing
pseud. pseudonym
Psych. Psychiatry, Psychiatric
Psychol. Psychology, Psychological
pt part

Ptg(s) Painting(s)
Pub. Public
pubd published
Publ. Publicity
pubn(s) publication(s)
PVA polyvinyl acetate
PVC polyvinyl chloride
Q. quarterly
4to quarto
Qué. Québec (Canada)
R reprint
r *recto*
RA Royal Academician
Radnors Radnorshire (GB; old)
RAF Royal Air Force
Rec. Record(s)
red. reduction, reduced for
Ref. Reference
Refurb. Refurbishment
reg *regit* [ruled]
Reg. Regional
Relig. Religion, Religious
remod. remodelled
Ren. Renaissance
Rep. Report(s)
repr. reprint(ed); reproduced, reproduction
Represent. Representation, Representative
Res. Research
rest. restored, restoration
Retro. Retrospective
rev. revision, revised (by/for)
Rev. Reverend; Review
RHA Royal Hibernian Academician
RI Rhode Island (USA)
RIBA Royal Institute of British Architects
RJ Rio de Janeiro State
Rlwy Railway
RSA Royal Scottish Academy
RSFSR Russian Soviet Federated Socialist Republic
Rt Hon. Right Honourable
Rur. Rural
Rus. Russian
S San, Santa, Santo, Sant', São [Saint]
S. South(ern)
s. solidus, solidi [shilling(s)]
Sask. Saskatchewan (Canada)
Sat. Saturday
SC South Carolina (USA)
Scand. Scandinavian
Sch. School
Sci. Science(s), Scientific
Scot. Scottish
Sculp. Sculpture

SD	South Dakota (USA)
SE	Southeast(ern)
Sect.	Section
Sel.	Selected
Semin.	Seminar(s), Seminary
Semiot.	Semiotic
Semit.	Semitic
Sept	September
Ser.	Series
Serb.	Serbian
Serv.	Service(s)
Sess.	Session, Sessional
Settmt(s)	Settlement(s)
S. Glam.	South Glamorgan (GB)
Siber.	Siberian
Sig.	Signature
Sil.	Silesian
Sin.	Singhala
sing.	singular
SJ	Societas Jesu [Society of Jesus]
Skt	Sanskrit
Slav.	Slavic, Slavonic
Slov.	Slovene, Slovenian
Soc.	Society
Social.	Socialism, Socialist
Sociol.	Sociology
Sov.	Soviet
SP	São Paulo State
Sp.	Spanish
sq.	square
sr	senior
Sri L.	Sri Lankan
SS	Saints, Santi, Santissima, Santissimo, Santissimi; Steam ship
SSR	Soviet Socialist Republic
St	Saint, Sankt, Sint, Szent
Staffs	Staffordshire (GB)
Ste	Sainte
Stud.	Study, Studies
Subalp.	Subalpine
Sum.	Sumerian
Sun.	Sunday
Sup.	Superior

suppl., suppls	supplement(s), supplementary
Surv.	Survey
SW	Southwest(ern)
Swed.	Swedish
Swi.	Swiss
Symp.	Symposium
Syr.	Syrian
Tap.	Tapestry
Tas.	Tasmanian
Tech.	Technical, Technique
Technol.	Technology
Territ.	Territory
Theat.	Theatre
Theol.	Theology, Theological
Theor.	Theory, Theoretical
Thurs.	Thursday
Tib.	Tibetan
TN	Tennessee (USA)
Top.	Topography
Trad.	Tradition(s), Traditional
trans.	translation, translated by; transactions
Transafr.	Transafrican
Transatlant.	Transatlantic
Transcarpath.	Transcarpathian
transcr.	transcribed by/for
Triq.	Triquarterly
Tropic.	Tropical
Tues.	Tuesday
Turk.	Turkish
Turkmen.	Turkmenistani
TV	Television
TX	Texas (USA)
U.	University
UK	United Kingdom of Great Britain and Northern Ireland
Ukrain.	Ukrainian
Un.	Union
Underwtr	Underwater
UNESCO	United Nations Educational, Scientific and Cultural Organization
Univl	Universal
unpubd	unpublished

Urb.	Urban
Urug.	Uruguayan
US	United States
USA	United States of America
USSR	Union of Soviet Socialist Republics
UT	Utah
v	*verso*
VA	Virginia (USA)
V&A	Victoria and Albert Museum
Var.	Various
Venez.	Venezuelan
Vern.	Vernacular
Vict.	Victorian
Vid.	Video
Viet.	Vietnamese
viz.	*videlicet* [namely]
vol., vols	volume(s)
vs.	versus
VT	Vermont (USA)
Vulg.	Vulgarisation
W.	West(ern)
w.	width
WA	Washington (USA)
Warwicks	Warwickshire (GB)
Wed.	Wednesday
W. Glam.	West Glamorgan (GB)
WI	Wisconsin (USA)
Wilts	Wiltshire (GB)
Wkly	Weekly
W. Midlands	West Midlands (GB)
Worcs	Worcestershire (GB; old)
Wtrcol.	Watercolour
WV	West Virginia (USA)
WY	Wyoming (USA)
Yb., Y.-b.	Yearbook, Year-book
Yem.	Yemeni
Yorks	Yorkshire (GB; old)
Yug.	Yugoslavian
Zamb.	Zambian
Zimb.	Zimbabwean

A Note on the Use of the Dictionary

This note is intended as a short guide to the basic editorial conventions adopted in this dictionary. For a fuller explanation, please refer to the Introduction, vol. 1, pp. xiii–xx.

Abbreviations in general use in the dictionary are listed on pp. vii–xii; those used in bibliographies and for locations of works of art or exhibition venues are listed in the Appendices in vol. 33.

Alphabetization of headings, which are distinguished in bold typeface, is letter by letter up to the first comma (ignoring spaces, hyphens, accents and any parenthesized or bracketed matter); the same principle applies thereafter. Abbreviations of 'Saint' and its foreign equivalents are alphabetized as if spelt out, and headings with the prefix 'Mc' appear under 'Mac'.

Authors' signatures appear at the end of the article or sequence of articles that the authors have contributed; in multipartite articles, any section that is unsigned is by the author of the next signed section. Where the article was compiled by the editors or in the few cases where an author has wished to remain anonymous, this is indicated by a square box (□) instead of a signature.

Bibliographies are arranged chronologically (within section, where divided) by order of year of first publication and, within years, alphabetically by authors' names. Abbreviations have been used for some standard reference books; these are cited in full in Appendix C in vol. 33, as are abbreviations of periodical titles (Appendix B). Abbreviated references to alphabetically arranged dictionaries and encyclopedias appear at the beginning of the bibliography (or section).

Biographical dates when cited in parentheses in running text at the first mention of a personal name indicate that the individual does not have an entry in the dictionary. The presence of parenthesized regnal dates for rulers and popes, however, does not necessarily indicate the lack of a biography of that person. Where no dates are provided for an artist or patron, the reader may assume that there is a biography of that individual in the dictionary (or, more rarely, that the person is so obscure that dates are not readily available).

Cross-references are distinguished by the use of small capital letters, with a large capital to indicate the initial letter of the entry to which the reader is directed; for example, 'He commissioned LEONARDO DA VINCI . . .' means that the entry is alphabetized under 'L'.

H

[continued]

Habsburg, House of. [continued]

II. Spanish branch.

The Habsburg dynasty in Spain was the result of the marriage alliance arranged by Maximilian I (*see* §I(3) above) between his son Philip the Fair, Duke of Burgundy (1478–1506), and (1) Joanna, Queen of Castile (see fig.). In 1516, their son Charles (later Holy Roman Emperor; *see* §I(5) above) became Charles I of Spain (*reg* 1516–56), and the combined inheritances of his grandparents Ferdinand II, King of Aragon, and Isabella, Queen of Castile (*see* ARAGON, (5) and (6)), gave the Spanish Habsburgs Spain and the New World possessions in addition to the Burgundian territories and the Netherlands. In 1556 Charles abdicated and these extensive and wealthy assets were inherited by his son, (2) Philip II. For the following century Spain was the dominant political power in Europe, and under the patronage of the Spanish Habsburgs the Spanish royal collection was built up by generations of collectors and connoisseurs. Philip II was one of the greatest connoisseurs of the 16th century. His dazzling collection of paintings (including works by Titian, Tintoretto and Veronese), sculpture, arms and armour, books and manuscripts and decorative arts was housed in the various royal residences, notably the monastery at the Escorial. The personal collection of (3) Joanna of Austria was the most extensive contemporary collection of Habsburg family portraits. (5) Philip III continued the family tradition of collecting, purchasing Flemish and Italian paintings. His son (7) Philip IV was one of the greatest collectors and connoisseurs of his times whose patronage was dedicated to the creation of splendour as a demonstration of the wealth of the Crown and the genius of its servants. He was the patron of Diego Velázquez and Peter Paul Rubens; the latter was also commissioned to celebrate the military victories of Philip's brother (9) Ferdinand, Cardinal-Infante. The last Spanish Habsburg, (10) Charles II, died without an heir and bequeathed his dominions to Philip, Duc d'Anjou (*see* BOURBON, §II).

See also SPAIN, §XII, 1.

BIBLIOGRAPHY

J. Lynch: *Spain under the Habsburgs, 1516–1598* (New York and Oxford, 1964)
J. Miguel Morán and F. Checa Cremades: *El coleccionismo en España* (Madrid, 1985)
J. H. Elliott: *Spain and its World, 1500–1700: Selected Essays* (New Haven, 1989)

□

(1) Joanna [Joanna the Mad], Queen of Castile (*b* Toledo, 6 Nov 1479; *reg* 1504–16; *d* Tordesillas, Valladolid, 12 April 1555). She was the daughter of Ferdinand II, King of Aragon, and Isabella, Queen of Castile and León (*see* ARAGON, (5) and (6)). In 1496 she married Philip the Fair (1478–1506), son of Maximilian I (*see* §I(3) above). Queen Isabella died on 26 November 1504, and due to her daughter's mental instability, apparent as early as 1502, and Isabella's distrust in any future political activity of her son-in-law, her will decreed that the government of Castile should remain in Ferdinand's hands until Joanna's first-born son, Charles of Ghent, the future Emperor Charles V (*see* §I(5) above), reached 20 years of age. The death of her husband, Philip, on 25 September 1506, pushed Joanna into insanity, and in 1509 she was confined in the castle of Tordesillas, where she remained until her death. BARTOLOMÉ ORDÓÑEZ designed the recumbent funerary monument to *Queen Joanna* and *King Philip* (*c.* 1520; Granada, Capilla Real). Her person and tragic life inspired many works of art during the 15th and 16th centuries, including a panel by an anonymous artist that shows *Joanna of Castile with her Family and with Cardinal Pedro González de Mendoza before the Virgin* (*c.* 1485; Burgos, Real Monasterio de las Huelgas). She also appears in 19th-century Spanish historical paintings, including *The Madness of Doña Joanna of Castile* by Lorenzo Valles (1830–1910) and *Doña Joanna the Mad* by Francisco Pradilla (1878; both Madrid, Mus. A. Mod.).

BIBLIOGRAPHY

V. Carderera y Solano: *Colección de retratos . . . y demás monumentos inéditos de reyes, reinas . . . desde el siglo XI hasta el XVII* (Madrid, 1855–64)
F. J. Sánchez Cantón: *Los retratos de los reyes de España* (Barcelona, 1948)
Iconografía Hispana: Catálogo de los retratos de personajes españoles de la Biblioteca Nacional, ii (Madrid, 1966), pp. 656–60
I. Altayo and P. Nogues: *Juana I, la reina cautiva* (Madrid, 1985)

TERESA NAVA RODRÍGUEZ

(2) Philip II, King of Spain [Philip I, King of Portugal] (*b* Valladolid, 21 May 1527; *reg* Spain, 1556–98, Portugal 1580–98; *d* El Escorial, 13 Sept 1598). Grandson of (1) Joanna, Queen of Castile. His reputation as a patron derives primarily from his connection with the monastery of the Escorial (begun 1563), although he also deserves to be ranked as one of the greatest connoisseurs of the

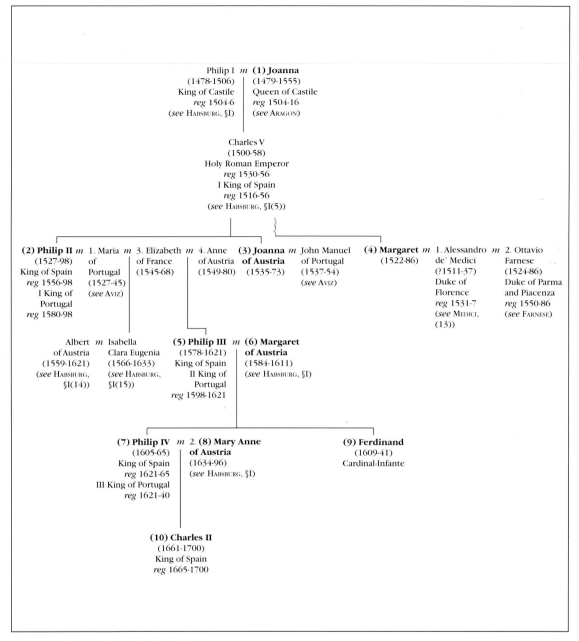

Family tree of the Spanish branch of the Habsburg dynasty

16th century. As a collector, Philip's tastes were eclectic. His library of rare books and manuscripts, deposited gradually in the Escorial, was organized as the *summa* of all human knowledge, secular as well as spiritual, and conceived on a scale intended to rival the Vatican library. Equally impressive were his collections of arms and antiquities, maps and medals, prints and drawings, sculptures and tapestries. Natural 'curiosities', many of them imported from the New World, represented another interest; these collections were displayed in the form of a *Wunderkammer* in the Alcázar, Madrid. The size and diversity of these collections were such that the Italian art critic Giovanni Paulo Lomazzo, commenting solely on those objects housed in the Escorial, wrote in 1590 that 'there are so many paintings, sculptures, jewels, books and arms in his celebrated museum that my mind was dazzled just by looking at it'.

Architecture had fascinated Philip since at least 1545, when the treatises of Sebastiano Serlio and Vitruvius were purchased for his library. In addition to the Escorial, his best-known building project, he built or remodelled ten other residences, which ranged in size from the small country houses of Aceca and la Fresneda to the palaces of Aranjuez, El Pardo and Valsaín (nr Segovia) and the

Alcázares of Madrid and Toledo. He was also responsible for numerous projects of urban reform, including the reconstruction of Valladolid's *plaza mayor* (1561), and his *Ordenanzas de descubrimiento, nueva población y pacificación de las Indias* of 1573 established a blueprint for city planning in the New World.

Philip's collection of more than 1500 pictures, over two-thirds of which were donated to the Escorial, marks the beginning of large-scale picture collecting in Spain. Most of these works were purchased with the help of agents and ambassadors abroad, although some, including an important group of works by Titian and various Netherlandish masters, were inherited, including those from his aunt, Mary, Queen of Hungary (*see* §I (7) above). The masterpieces Philip acquired, notably those by Titian, Tintoretto and Veronese, helped to inspire such 17th-century artists as Diego Velázquez and thus laid the foundations of Spain's Golden Age of painting.

The first reference to Philip's interest in the visual arts appeared around 1540, when he ordered a large book with blank sheets in which he could draw. His taste in art initially appears to have been limited primarily to the Flemish and Hispano-Flemish styles he would have seen in the small royal collection begun by his great-grandparents, Ferdinand II, King of Aragon and Sicily, and Isabella, Queen of Castile and León (*see* ARAGON, (5) and (6)). His artistic preferences gradually widened, but he never lost interest in northern European painting and by the 1570s had developed a passion for the work of Hieronymus Bosch, acquiring many of his paintings including in 1591–3 the famous triptych of the *Garden of Earthly Delights* (Madrid, Prado; *see* BOSCH, HIERONYMUS, fig. 3). Philip also collected works by Rogier van der Weyden, notably his *Descent from the Cross* (*c.* 1435; Madrid, Prado; *see* WEYDEN, VAN DER, (1), fig. 2), van Eyck, Gerard David and Joachim Patinir. Another indication of Philip's admiration of Flemish art was his patronage of Michiel Coxcie, who was specifically commissioned to copy Flemish paintings the King was unable to purchase, among them, in 1557, the van Eyck brothers' *Adoration of the Holy Lamb* (Ghent, St Bavo; Coxcie's copy, Madrid, Prado).

The journey that Philip, then prince, made to Northern Italy, Germany and the Netherlands (1548–51) helped to broaden his taste. Both in Milan and Mantua the Prince was exposed to the work of Leonardo da Vinci, Giulio Romano, Andrea Mantegna and other masters of the Italian Renaissance. In Milan in 1548 he met Titian, who had previously been employed by his father, the Emperor Charles V. Philip subsequently became one of his major patrons and would eventually acquire no fewer than 30 of his paintings.

Philip's relationship with Titian is particularly well-documented (*see* TITIAN, §I, 1(vii)). When they first met, the Prince harboured reservations about Titian's broad manner of painting; he even criticized the full-length portrait of him (*Philip II in Armour*, 1550–51; Madrid, Prado; see fig.) that Titian had executed at Augsburg in November 1550. He wrote in a letter to his aunt, Mary of Hungary (Brown): 'The haste with which he did my portrait can easily be seen, and if there had been more time I would have had him do it again.' In contrast Philip

Philip II in Armour, by Titian, oil on canvas, 1.93×1.11 m, 1550–51 (Madrid, Museo del Prado)

reacted enthusiastically to a *St Margaret* (Madrid, Escorial) and to the so-called *Venus of Pardo* or *Figures in a Landscape* (*c.* 1546–52; Paris, Louvre) that Titian sent him in 1552, suggesting that his taste had meanwhile evolved. Subsequently patron and artist forged exceptionally close ties, with Philip essentially agreeing to purchase whatever paintings Titian elected to send him. Patronage on these terms was unusual for the period and resulted in several of Titian's greatest masterpieces, including the series of mythological paintings, or *poesie*, as the artist described them. The paintings in the series sent to Spain were *Venus and Adonis* (1553; Madrid, Prado), *Perseus and Andromeda* (1554–6; London, Wallace), *Diana and Actaeon* (*see* ITALY, fig. 029823.003) and *Diana and Callisto* (both 1556–9; Duke of Sutherland, on loan to Edinburgh, N.G.) and the *Rape of Europa* (*c.* 1560; Boston, MA, Isabella Stewart Gardner Mus.; *see* TITIAN, fig. 8)).

Despite his growing appreciation for Titian, Philip continued to admire the highly finished style of portraits typical of Flemish artists, particularly that of Antonis Mor, whom he first met in 1550 in Brussels. Mor went with the Prince to Spain on two occasions and accompanied him to England in 1554, where he painted his portrait of Philip's new bride, *Mary Tudor* (Madrid, Prado; *see* MOR, ANTONIS, fig. 1). Mor's understated style of portraiture subsequently became the standard of Philip's court (for example, *Philip II*; *c.* 1557; Madrid, Escorial), which was continued by such artists as Mor's disciple, Alonso Sánchez Coello, and later by Juan Pantoja de la Cruz.

In the 1560s Philip continued to collect Flemish primitives and other masters of northern art; Hans Baldung's *Allegory on the Three Ages of Man* (*c.* 1547; Madrid, Prado) was in the royal collection by 1574. The King's lifelong interest in northern art is also reflected in his preference for the steep, slate roofs he had seen in Flanders. Such roofs were added to the palaces Philip had built or remodelled, as well as the Escorial, and subsequently became a hallmark of the architectural style of the Spanish court.

Otherwise, Philip's artistic tastes became increasingly Italianate. Architecturally this shift was confirmed by the appointment of Michelangelo's former assistant, JUAN BAUTISTA DE TOLEDO, as the principal architect of the Escorial (*see* ESCORIAL, §2) in 1559 as well as by the King's patronage of Alonso de Covarrubias, designer of the imperial staircase in Toledo's Alcázar, Giovanni Battista Castello and JUAN DE HERRERA, all of whom built in a Renaissance style. Similarly, the appointment of GASPAR BECERRA, a Spanish artist who had worked with Vasari as Pintor del Rey in 1562, reflected Philip's growing appreciation for Italian art. Yet Titian remained the King's favoured artist. After completing the *poesie* he supplied Philip with such mythological paintings as *Tarquin and Lucretia* (1568–71; Cambridge, Fitzwilliam) and *Venus with a Mirror* (*c.* 1567; Washington, DC, N.G.A.) along with a number of religious paintings for Philip. These included the *Last Supper* (1558–64) and *St Lawrence* (1564–7; both Madrid, Escorial, Iglesia Vieja), a painting originally intended to decorate the principal retable of the Escorial.

In the 1570s Philip's taste became yet more refined. He expressed new interest in history painting, especially that illustrating Habsburg military triumphs, for example the frescoes (1574–84) in the Sala de Batallas, Escorial, by Nicolás Granello and Fabrizio Castello. Religious and devotional art became another priority. This change was partly the result of the need to decorate the interior of the Escorial, but it also reflected Philip's growing preoccupation with the defence of Catholicism and the reform of the Church. Philip became an exacting patron prepared to reject those artists whose work did not strictly adhere to the artistic guidelines decreed by the Council of Trent. FRAY JOSÉ DE SIGUENZA, librarian of the Escorial, probably expressed the King's view of art when, commenting on the reasons why Philip disapproved of El Greco's artful *Martyrdom of St Maurice* (1580–83; Madrid, Escorial) he wrote, in 1582, that 'the saints must be painted so that they do not remove the desire to pray to them. Instead they should inspire devotion, because this is the principal effect and aim of painting'(Brown). The painting was replaced in 1584 by a dull but doctrinally correct rendition of the same subject by Diego de Rómulo Cincinnato. Similar religious concerns had led Philip to drape the offending portions of Benvenuto Cellini's nude *Crucifixion*

(1562; Madrid, Escorial), a gift from Francesco I de' Medici, Grand Duke of Tuscany, in 1576.

Philip's high standards of patronage are exemplified in his close, personal supervision of the decoration of the church of the Escorial. He originally assigned the altarpieces to JUAN FERNÁNDEZ DE NAVARRETE, a Spanish artist who had studied in Italy, where he was principally inspired by Titian. Following Navarrete's premature death in 1579, Philip turned to a series of Italian painters, starting with LUCA CAMBIASO, who came to Spain in 1583 and decorated the sacristy vault with a fresco of the *Gloria* (1584). Then, having failed to persuade either Tintoretto or Veronese to abandon Venice for Spain, the monarch summoned Federico Zuccaro from Rome. This widely admired but somewhat uninspired late Mannerist artist arrived at the Escorial in 1585 but was dismissed in 1588, after several of his paintings did not meet with the King's approval. In 1586 Philip summoned to Spain another Italian, Pellegrino Tibaldi, whose *Martyrdom of St Lawrence* served as the centrepiece of the high altar in the Capilla Mayor at the Escorial. The imposing three-tiered retable was designed by Herrera and adorned with sculptures by Leone Leoni and Pompeo Leoni, two Milanese sculptors regularly in Philip's employ (*see* LEONI). Tibaldi also decorated the ceiling of the main gallery of the Escorial library with a series of allegorical frescoes (begun 1591–2) of the *Liberal Arts and Sciences*. The iconography of this work and its alleged references to the 'magical' design of the Escorial remain a source of scholarly controversy, but originally the ceiling was intended to complement the 'gallery of illustrious men', a collection of several hundred portraits that included likenesses of famous painters and scholars that Philip also installed in the Escorial library. In this sense the overall programme of the library was probably more humanistic than hermeneutical (*see* ESCORIAL, §3).

If the Escorial served primarily as Philip's museum of devotional art, much of it illustrating late Italian Mannerism, the paintings in the other royal residences were more varied in theme. In Madrid's Alcázar religious and mythological works were displayed beside genre pictures, portraits, scientific instruments and maps. In this palace only the Armoury (now Madrid, Real Armeria), a repository for the military glories of the dynasty, and the Great Hall, a prototypical Hall of Princely Virtue adorned with paintings of Habsburg military triumphs and topographical views of cities under Philip's dominion, can be said to have had a decorative programme. Equally varied was the collection at El Pardo, a small royal residence on the outskirts of Madrid that contained some of the 'jewels' of Philip's collection: Titian's *Venus of Pardo* and the *poesie*, along with paintings by Bosch and Mor and another gallery of Habsburg portraits (*see* PARDO, EL). Elsewhere Titian's *Annunciation* (untraced) adorned the chapel at Aranjuez, an elegant palace on the banks of the Tagus and Jarama that was surrounded with gardens of Flemish design, another of Philip's continuing passions (for discussion and illustration *see* ARANJUEZ PALACE). Meanwhile, van der Weyden's *Crucifixion* (Madrid, Escorial; *see* WEYDEN, VAN DER, (1), fig. 4) was hung in the chapel of the palace at Valsaín.

Philip's large and thematically diverse art collection reflected the fundamental character of his domains: a decentralized and heterogeneous collection of principalities and kingdoms that embraced not only Spain and Portugal, Naples and the Low Countries but also large portions of the New World. Both were imperial in scale, almost universal in scope and conceived in secular as well as spiritual terms.

See also SPAIN, §III, 2.

BIBLIOGRAPHY

G. Lomazzo: *Idea del tempio della pittura* (Milan, 1590); (Florence, 1974), 1, pp. 359–60
Colección de documentos inéditos relativos al descubrimiento, conquista y organización de las antiguas posesiones españolas de América y Oceanía (Madrid, (1854–84), viii; Eng. trans. by D. P. Crouch, D. J. Garr and A. I. Mundigo as *Spanish City Planning in North America* (Cambridge, MA, 1982), pp. 6–19 [contains *Ordenanzas de descubrimiento, nueva población y pacificación de las Indias*]
J. Miguel Morán and F. Checa Cremades: *El coleccionismo en España* (Madrid, 1985), pp. 63–127
IV centenario del monasterio de El Escorial: Las colecciones del rey: Pintura y escultura (exh. cat. by J. Brown and others, Madrid, Escorial, 1986)
J. Brown: 'Philip II as Art Collector and Patron', *Spanish Cities of the Golden Age*, ed. R. L. Kagan (Berkeley, CA, 1989)
F. Checa Cremades: *Felipe II: Mécenas de los artes* (Madrid, 1993)
C. Wilkinson-Zerner: *Juan de Herrera: Architect to Philip II of Spain* (New Haven and London, 1993)
R. Mulcahy: *The Decoration of the Royal Basilica of El Escorial* (Cambridge, 1994)

RICHARD L. KAGAN

(3) Joanna of Austria, Princess of Portugal (*b* Madrid, 24 June 1535; *d* the Escorial, 7 Sept 1573). Daughter of Charles V, Holy Roman Emperor (*see* §I (5) above). Her mother was Isabella of Portugal. She married the Infante John (1537–54), Prince of Brazil, son of John III, King of Portugal (*see* AVIZ, (7)), in Lisbon in December 1552. This dynastic marriage, by which Joanna became known by the title of Princess of Portugal, is recorded by the portrait of *Joanna of Austria* by Alonso Sánchez Coello (1552–3; Vienna, Ksthist. Mus.), who was her official painter from 1557. Her young husband died in January 1554, only a few weeks before the birth of their son, Sebastian, the future King of Portugal. In May 1554 Joanna returned to Spain to act as Regent for her brother Philip II, while he was in England. During the five years of the Regency, Joanna became known for her ability in handling state affairs at the court of Valladolid. Her firmness and resolve are seen in *Joanna of Austria* (*c.* 1560; Madrid, Prado; *see* DRESS, fig. 27) by Antonis Mor, one of the many portraits made of her.

Joanna's religious devotion led to her foundation in 1557 of the discalced Franciscan Order of the Poor Clares, the Descalzas Reales, in the mansion in Madrid in which she had been born. In the late 16th century the convent became the most important centre for artistic patronage in Madrid, and in an order dedicated to the worship of the Eucharist this was the underlying theme for many of the works of art. The church (dedicated 1564) was designed by either Juan Bautista de Toledo, the first architect of the Escorial, or Francesco Paciotto. The high altar, of Renaissance design (destr. 1862), was by Gaspar Becerra and is known from a drawing (Madrid, Bib. N.), which shows a balance of ornament, sculpture and paintings that is Italian in character. The inventory (1573) of Joanna's personal collection lists 104 family portraits, and it formed the most

extensive gallery of Habsburg portraits in Spain at this date. After her death, the paintings were partly absorbed into the royal collection of Philip II, partly dispersed in a sale, and others were hung in the Salón de Reyes at the convent of Descalzas Reales (*in situ*). These last include *Dom Sebastião* (1565) by Cristóvão de Morais, one of five portraits that record his childhood and which were sent from Portugal to his mother in Castile. She was also an active patron of music and literature, and she created and fostered many cultural and diplomatic links between Spain and Portugal during the period just before the crowns were united in 1580. Joanna's funerary monument (1574) by Pompeo Leoni shows her dressed in court mantle and kneeling facing the high altar of the church of the convent of Descalzas Reales, Madrid. This outstanding work (*in situ*) is in a setting of marble and jasper, designed by the Italian Jacopo da Trezzo, who had designed jewellery, cameos and reliquaries for the Princess.

BIBLIOGRAPHY

C. Perez Pastor: *Noticias y documentos relativos a la historia y literatura*, xi (Madrid, 1914), pp. 315–80
E. Tormo y Monzó: *En las Descalzas Reales de Madrid: 33 retratos en las Descalzas Reales*, 2 vols (Madrid, 1915–44)
M. Bataillon: 'Jeanne d'Autriche, Princesse de Portugal', *Études sur le Portugal au temps de l'humanisme* (Paris, 1974), pp. 199–217
Alonso Sánchez Coello y el retrato en la Corte de Felipe II (exh. cat. by Juan Miguel Serrera and others, Madrid, Prado, 1990), pp. 138–9
A. Delaforce: *Juana of Austria, Princess of Portugal as a Patron of the Arts* (in preparation)

ANGELA DELAFORCE

(4) Margaret [Margaret of Austria; Margaret of Parma], Regent of the Netherlands (*b* Oudenarde, 28 Dec 1522; *d* Ortona, 18 Jan 1586). Half-sister of (2) Philip II. She was the illegitimate daughter of Emperor Charles V (*see* HABSBURG, §I(5) above) and the Flemish lady-in-waiting Johanna van der Gheynst. In 1536 she married Alessandro de' Medici, Duke of Florence (assassinated 1537), and in 1538 Ottavio Farnese, later 2nd Duke of Parma and Piacenza. Her brief regency was difficult at the time of the Inquisition and the revolt in the Netherlands, as Philip II left her with little authority.

Her art patronage was undistinguished. Two portraits of a girl, one shown weighing gold (Berlin, Bodemus.), the other playing a clavichord (Worcester, MA, A. Mus.), both *c.* 1530 and by Jan Sanders van Hemessen, are now thought to represent Margaret when young. Her best-known likeness is a representational knee-length portrait by Antonis Mor (Berlin, Gemäldegal.). Titian painted her later (untraced). In 1559 she ordered a commemorative series of 33 etchings by Jan and Lucas van Doetechum of the *Funeral Procession of Charles V* (Florence, Uffizi), designed by Hieronymus Cock and published by Christoph Plantin. Two large tapestries of the *Feast of Ceres* and *Perseus and Atalante* (1559; Rome, Pal. Quirinale) were manufactured for Margaret by the van den Hoeck family of Brussels, and Willem de Pannemaker executed the *Life of Noah* cycle (1563–6; Amsterdam, Rijksmus.) from cartoons by Michiel Coxcie (Kraków, N.A. Cols). From the sculptor Jacques Jonghelinck she commissioned bronze figures for a fountain (*c.* 1559; destr.) in Brussels and a portrait medal (1567). She corresponded with and owned some works by Giulio Clovio. Francesco Paciotti and Francesco de Marchi (1504–77) built for her the

Palazzo Farnese (begun 1558) in Piacenza; they also made designs for fortifications in Tournai and a citadel in Antwerp (both unrealized).

BIBLIOGRAPHY

C. Piot: 'Inventaire des joyaux et autres objets de prix trouvées dans la succession de Marguerite de Parme', *Compte rendu des séances de la commission royale d'histoire*, 5th ser. (1895), pp. 328–56
I. d'Onofrio: *Il carteggio intimo di Margherita d'Austria, Duchessa di Parma e Piacenza* (Naples, 1919)
J. de Jongh: *Madama Margaretha van Oostenrijk, Hertogin van Parma en Piacenza* (Amsterdam, 1965)
R. Lefevre: *Madama Margherita d'Austria, 1522–1586* (Rome, 1986)
B. W. Meijer: *Parma e Bruxelles: Committenza e collezionismo farnesiani alle due corti* (Parma, 1988)

ROSEMARIE BERGMANN

(5) Philip III, King of Spain [Philip II, King of Portugal] (*b* Madrid, 14 April 1578; *reg* 1598–1621; *d* Madrid, 31 March 1621). Son of (2) Philip II. He married Margaret of Austria (*see* (6) below) by proxy in November 1598. In character he was pious and kindly but weak; he neglected his duty, spending his days hunting or attending the theatre and lavish court festivals. After his accession to the throne on 13 September 1598 he left the government in the hands of a favourite (the *privado* or *valido*); first, until 1618, Francisco Gómez de Sandoval y Rojas, Duque de Lerma, and then his son, Cristóbal Sandoval y Rojas, Duque de Uceda (*d* 1624), both of whom instituted a regime based on favours (*see* SANDOVAL Y ROJAS). Domestic policies were marked by social and economic maladministration, which adversely affected government finances, by an increase in public expenditure and by the distribution of offices by Lerma among his own close circle. From 1601 until 1606 the capital was temporarily transferred to Valladolid to promote development of the northern regions. Other significant events of the reign included the expulsion on 9 April 1609 of the Moors (Moriscos), who were accused of complicity with the Turks. A positive action in foreign policy was the signing in 1609 of the Twelve Year Truce with the Netherlands. Conflict with Italy centred on two fronts, the 'Conspiracy of Venice', organized by Pedro Tellez de Girón de Guzmán, Duque de Osuna (Viceroy of Sicily, 1611–16), to seize power from the Republic, and the Milanese War, which culminated in the Peace of Asti in 1617. The attacks by Barbary pirates on the Levantine coast were the cause of war between 1601 and 1616, and attacks by English ships culminated in the Peace of London in 1604. The Thirty Years War, which began in 1618, led to Spain's entry into the Palatinate.

Philip III sought to maintain Spanish hegemony, based on loyalty to the Church and a balance of forces that would defend patrimonial territories. The outcome was a conflict between the official and traditional Spain and the Spain of the people, which would eventually lead to the crises of the 17th century and from 1640 to the disintegration of the Spanish Empire. In literature his reign marks the beginning of the Golden Age and the remarkable works of Miguel de Cervantes (1547–1616), Felix Lope de Vega (1562–1635), Francisco Gomez de Quevedo y Villegas (1580–1645) and the scholars and theologians from the university of Salamanca. Artistically the period was to a certain extent creative. Trends from the 16th century persisted (*see* SPAIN, §III, 2), and the foundation was laid for the important patronage of the arts by Philip IV (*see* (7) below). The capitals of Valladolid and Madrid became the most important centres. Most significant artistically was the school of Madrid and at court the role of the court painter (Pintor de Cámara). Artists such as Bartolomé Carducho and Vicente Carducho, Eugenio Cajés and Patricio Cajés, and the court painter Bartolomé González, Felipe Diricksen, Angelo Nardi and Bartolomé Román worked for the court and nobility with the emphasis on religious themes and court portraiture. The tradition of the Austrian Habsburgs as collectors continued, with the purchase of Flemish and Italian paintings (e.g. Juan van der Hamen y León's *Apotheosis of the Lamb*; Madrid, Convento Encarnación). Religious architecture, financed by the nobility, the Church and the monarchy, retained stylistically a combination of elements derived from Juan de Herrera and from the Counter-Reformation. The court architects Francisco de Mora and Juan Gómez de Mora (*see* MORA, DE (i)) built the royal convents of La Encarnación (founded 1611) and S Isabel la Real (1610), both in Madrid; S José (1607–10), Ávila; the Descalzas (1601), Alcalá de Henares, and the palace of the Duque de Lerma at Lerma. Sculptors continued the tradition of Leone Leoni and Pompeo Leoni at the Escorial and laid the foundation for Baroque statuary, whose precedents are found in the work of Juan de Juni and Alonso Berruguete. The most important of these sculptors were Gregorio Fernández in Valladolid, who realized many commissions for Madrid, and Juan Martínez Montañés in Seville.

BIBLIOGRAPHY

Relación de la muerte de nuestro Catolicísimo y bienaventurado rey y señor D. Felipe III (Seville, 1621)
G. González d'Ávila: *Historia del reinado de Felipe III* (Madrid, 1630)
B. Porreño: *Dichos y hechos del señor Rey D. Felipe III* (Madrid, 1723)
F. Chueca Goitia: 'Sobre arquitectura y arquitectos madrileños del siglo XVII', *Archv Esp. A.*, xv (1945)
A. Pérez Bustamante: *Semblanza de un monarca y semblanza de una privanza* (Madrid, 1950)
F. T. Valiente: *Los validos en la monarquía hispana del siglo XVII* (Madrid, 1963)
L. Cervera Vera: *La época de los Austrias* (Madrid, 1968)
I. Angulo Iñiguez and A. Pérez Sánchez: *Historia de la pintura española: Escuela madrileña del primer tercio del siglo XVII* (Madrid, 1969)
J. Gómez de Mora: *Aparato del túmulo real que se edificó en el convento de San Jerónimo para celebrar las honras del esclarecido rey D. Felipe III* (Salamanca, 1973)
M. Agullo y Cobo: *Noticia sobre pintores madrileños de los siglos XVI y XVII* (Granada, 1978)
J. J. Martin González: *Escultura barroca castellana* (Madrid, 1978)
V. Tovar Martín: *Juan Gómez de Mora, arquitecto y trazador del rey y maestro mayor de obras de la Villa de Madrid* (Madrid, 1986)

(6) Margaret of Austria, Queen of Spain (*b* Gratz, Austria, 25 Dec 1584; *d* El Escorial, 3 Oct 1611). Wife of (5) Philip III. She was the sister of Ferdinand II (*see* §I(16) above). Her marriage was arranged by Philip II and celebrated by proxy by Pope Clement VIII on 13 November 1598. She sailed from Genoa in February 1599 and was received in Vinaroz by the Cardinal of Seville and Francisco Gómez de Sandoval y Rojas (Duque de Lerma from 1599), who escorted her to Valencia to meet Philip III. Her state entry to Madrid in November 1599 was devised by the court architect, Juan Gómez de Mora. The Queen's life was closely supervised by the Duque de Lerma, who replaced her German entourage with people he could trust. She devoted her life to pious foundations and works of charity, including the foundation of the Descalzas Franciscas (c. 1600–15) in Valladolid; a *colegio* for poor soldiers in Salamanca; and in Madrid the Antón Martín Hospital, the convents of S Isabel la Real (1610) and La Encarnación (founded 1611). The last was an important centre for artistic patronage in the second decade of the 17th century and has a *retable mayor* with an *Annunciation* (1614–16; *in situ*) by Vicente Carducho. She had eight children, among them the heir, Philip IV (see (7) below), and Anna, who became the wife of Louis XIII of France. At the Queen's death, the elaborate funerary memorials (*túmulos*) temporarily erected in her honour included one, the most notable, designed by Juan Gómez de Mora in Madrid.

BIBLIOGRAPHY

J. de Florencia: *Sermón que predicó a la Magestad del Rey D. Felipe III, Nuestro Señor, a la serenísima Reina Margarita... en las honras a la serenísima Reina Margarita... en San Jerónimo el Real de Madrid a 18 de noviembre de 1611* (Madrid, 1611)
J. Gómez de Mora: *Relación de las honras funerales que se hizieron para la Reina Margarita de Austria... en esta Villa de Madrid* (Madrid, 1612)
D. de Gúzman: *Vida y muerte de Margarita de Austria, Reina de España* (Madrid, 1617)
E. Florez: *Memoria de las Reinas católicas* (Madrid, 1761)
J. M. Perez Martin: *Margarita de Austria, Reina de España* (Madrid, 1961)
M. Leticia Sánchez Hernández: *El Monasterio de la Encarnación de Madrid* (Salamanca, 1986)
V. Tovar Martin: 'La entrada triunfal en Madrid de Margarita de Austria', *Archv Esp. A.*, ccxliv (1988), pp. 385–403

M. LETICIA SÁNCHEZ HERNÁNDEZ

(7) Philip IV, King of Spain [Philip III, King of Portugal] (*b* Valladolid, 8 April 1605; *reg* Spain 1621–65, Portugal 1621–40; *d* Madrid, 17 Sept 1665). Son of (5) Philip III. He is now generally recognized as one of the greatest patrons and collectors of his time. After an itinerant early childhood with his father, who loved to hunt and make pilgrimages, a serious illness in 1610 forced him to return to a court upbringing in Madrid. There he was portrayed by Rodrigo de Villandrando, official court painter, in *Philip IV and the Dwarf Soplillo* (c. 1620; Madrid, Prado), and studied painting and drawing under Juan Bautista Maíno.

Intelligent but wilful, he came under the influence of Gaspar de Guzmán, Conde Duque de Olivares (*see* OLIVARES), who was appointed as a gentleman of the Prince's chamber in 1615. Olivares continued to direct Philip's education after the latter's succession in 1621 and became a member of the Council of State and subsequently principal minister as well as favourite (*valido*) in 1622. Olivares influenced the King's opinions in politics and the arts and encouraged his involvement in the intellectual life of his native Seville. In politics this centred around the radical neo-Stoic philosophy of Justus Lipsius (1547–1606), a formative element in much of European politics between 1600 and 1650. In literature and painting, too, Andalusian mores and aspirations were imported to court, a process reflected in the appointment of DIEGO VELÁZQUEZ as Pintor del Rey to replace Villandrando in 1623.

As Philip steadily matured into a conscientious and competent ruler, the emotional and intellectual hold of his *valido* weakened. To some extent this process can already be glimpsed in the King's earliest sequence of commissions, the construction of a new main façade for the Alcázar (destr. 1734), by the court architect, Juan Gómez

de Mora (*see* MORA, DE (i), (2)). The council chambers and domestic apartments were remodelled, and an important new stateroom (Salón Nuevo) was created (*see* MADRID, §IV, 2). For their embellishment Philip turned to the collection of his grandfather, Philip II (*see* (2) above). His discovery of Titian and Raphael and other Italian artists led to renewed artistic contact between Spain and Italy. Although Velázquez and VICENTE CARDUCHO were given important commissions, Philip also ordered paintings from many Neapolitan and Roman artists, including Artemesia Gentileschi (*Birth of St John the Baptist, c.* 1635; Madrid, Prado).

The influence of PETER PAUL RUBENS on the King during the painter's visit to Madrid in 1628 was profound and wide-ranging, undoubtedly extending to politics as well as intensifying the monarch's interest in Italian culture. In 1629 Rubens made a sketch of Philip (Bayonne, Mus. Bonnat) still as a young man, with a lightness of demeanour in his face and carriage, the result of their rapidly achieved intimacy. Around this time Philip became fascinated by Renaissance Italy and in the early 1630s began his translation into Castilian of part of the celebrated *Historia d'Italia* by Francesco Guicciardini. In 1629, in the middle of a serious dispute between Spain and the Barberini Papacy precipitated by Olivares's miscalculated attack on Monferrat (Mantuan War, 1628–31), the King sent Velázquez on his first visit to Rome.

The decoration of the Salón Nuevo in the Alcázar, Madrid, established the representational programme in the works created by Philip and Olivares. Celebration of the Church, almost invariably linked with the glorification of Spain's traditional military role in protecting it, formed the basis of the iconographical programme. Subordinate elements were the exalted veneration of saints and martyrs associated with the Iberian world and the hardly less exalted presentation of Philip's kingly predecessors, usually portrayed as defenders of the faith, an ideological message at the heart of Philip's patronage. Olivares likewise had a vivid sense of political mission and an informed interest in the media of its presentation. King and favourite shared the conviction that artistic munificence was a political necessity, that the continuous creation of splendour was an intrinsic element of the Crown's *reputación*—a demonstration to subjects, allies and enemies that the wealth of the Crown and genius of its servants were alike inexhaustible. The building of the Buen Retiro (*see* MADRID, §IV, 1 and fig. 7), an extensive new palace in Madrid's eastern suburbs begun in 1630, was undertaken partly for this reason, partly an attempt to revitalize the friendship and collaboration of Philip and Olivares, but also as a symbol of the ethos of the Spanish monarchy.

The construction and decoration of the Buen Retiro dominated the 1630s. Olivares supervised the associated artistic activity, commissioning on an unprecedented scale and plundering, through threats and promises, collections belonging to friends and enemies alike. Numerous studios in Spain, Italy and the Low Countries were called upon to contribute (Brown and Elliott, 1980). After 1650 Philip concentrated on the decoration of the little hunting-lodge to the west of Madrid known as the Torre de la Parada (*see* PARDO, EL). Commissions were placed for more than 60 paintings, including the series of large mythological and allegorical canvases from Rubens and his studio, such as *Mercury and Argus* and *Rape of Ganymede* (both 1636–8); the surviving canvases from the Torre and some *boceto* (e.g. *Rape of Proserpina*; *see* MYTHOLOGICAL PAINTING AND SCULPTURE and fig. 4) are all in the Prado, Madrid. The paintings also included hunting scenes and animal pieces from Frans Snyders and hunting scenes depicting Cardinal-Infante Ferdinand and Philip IV by Pieter Snayers (examples of 1636–8, Madrid, Prado).

The intense artistic activity at the court of Philip IV is indicated by the *nomina*, drawn from various sections of the General Archive of Simancas; it lists no fewer than 42 painters in receipt of royal payment during the reign. Dozens of apprentices awaited their first commissions by gilding new frames for the old masterpieces being moved from the Escorial to Madrid, decorating the plaster or woodwork surfaces of the new palace or preparing scenery for the dramatic productions at court. Many prospered, including Diego de Velázquez y Silva, *aposentador mayor* in the King's household and Knight of Santiago. The annual salary of court painter Angelo Nardi was 72,000 maravedis, about the earnings of a successful Madrid shopkeeper. The Artists' Guild (*Gremio*) was able to enlist the support of such notables as the dramatist Lope de Vega (1562–1635) and the barrister Juan de Butrón in its campaign for recognition as well as the painters Vicente Carducho, Eugenio Cajés and Francisco Pacheco, Velázquez's father-in-law.

Philip's relationship with Velázquez is perennially fascinating. The paintings reveal the monarch's strong influence, showing that even an ennobled artist and his elevated art still remained—as much as Olivares himself—absolutely in the service of the King. All Velázquez's colleagues too generally accepted the most detailed prescriptions of subject and treatment from their patrons, whether clerical or lay. Throughout their association the King seemed to be engaged in many of Velázquez's productions. Earlier in his reign Philip preferred to be portrayed in armour or—as if interrupted—near the desk of his study, state-paper in hand. But his growing preoccupation with the idea of an active military career, which he regarded as a duty but which was constantly frustrated by Olivares, appears to have dictated much of the work of his favourite painter. Velázquez's hunting and equestrian studies, images of power such as the portrait of *Philip IV on Horseback* (*c.* 1635; Madrid, Prado; *see* VELÁZQUEZ, DIEGO, fig. 3), painted for the Salón de Reinos, the focal point of the Buen Retiro, show the King expertly managing a great war-horse as a symbol of the State. From 1635 to 1644, whether for personal or political reasons is uncertain, the King did not sit for Velázquez, and the artist appears to have executed only one portrait of Philip in the 1640s—*Philip IV of Spain* (1644; New York, Frick; *see* fig.)—the famous one painted during the successful Aragonese campaign against the French at Fraga in which again it is clear that Philip influenced the shaping of his own image and recorded his military triumph. The King's desire to identify the dogma of the Immaculate Conception with Spain's critical struggle for survival in the five years following Olivares's fall in 1643 is, for example, eloquently expressed in Velázquez's *Coronation of the Virgin* (before 1644; Madrid, Prado).

The last great phase of commissioning and acquisition coincided with a period of government bankruptcies, multiple revolts and military desperation. In 1649, against some opposition on the grounds of expense, Velázquez was sent once more to Italy to obtain copies of Classical sculpture for another refashioning of the Alcázar. In 1651 the collection of Charles I was put up for sale by the English Commonwealth. There was widespread resentment over spending on the Buen Retiro, and the King worried about the ethical problems of dealing with heretic regicides. Neither consideration, however, prevented the acquisition of paintings, which was managed by Luis Méndez de Haro y Guzmán, 6th Marqués del Carpio (*see* CARPIO, (2)), ostensibly on his own behalf. It is difficult to believe in this instance that political motives predominated over artistic covetousness. Paintings purchased for the Spanish royal collection included *Madonna and Child with the Infant Saint John and Two Angels* by Andrea Del Sarto and *Holy Family* (*c.* 1518) by Raphael (both Madrid, Prado).

In a painting apparently still extant in a private collection in Madrid, the King himself is shown at work on a representation of the Immaculate Virgin. Most authorities accept the claim made by Carducho, Pacheco and other contemporaries that Philip and his two younger brothers painted as a pastime. Despite the obviously biased nature of these assertions and the absence of tangible evidence, common sense suggests that it was a probable if minor *afición*. However, the investigation by Gallego concludes, in respect of Philip himself, that the case is unproven. That for Don Carlos (1607–32), the prince who was still heir to the throne when painted by Velázquez (*c.* 1626; Madrid, Prado), is accepted by Angulo Iñíguez and Pérez Sánchez (along with other authorities) on the strength of one attribution, a *St Anthony and Child* in the Carmelite convent of Alba de Tormes.

See also SPAIN, §III, 2.

BIBLIOGRAPHY

V. Carducho: *Diálogos de la pintura, su defensa, origen, essencia, definición, modos y diferencias. Al gran monarcha de las Españas y Nuevo Mundo, Don Felipe IIII* (Madrid, 1633; ed. F. Calvo Serraller, Madrid, 1979)

J. María de Azcárate: 'Algunas noticias sobre pintores cortesanos del siglo XVII', *An. Inst. Estud. Madril.*, vi (1970), pp. 43–61

D. Angulo Iñíguez and A. Pérez Sánchez: *Historia de la pintura española: Escuela Madrileña del primer tercio del siglo XVII* (Madrid, 1970)

J. Brown and R. Engass: *Italy and Spain, 1600–1750*, Sources and Documents in the History of Art (Englewood Cliffs, NJ, 1970)

S. Alpers: *The Decoration of the Torre de la Parada* (Brussels and London, 1971)

M. Levey: *Painting at Court* (London, 1971)

M. Crawford Volk: *Vicencio Carducho and 17th-century Castilian Painting* (New York and London, 1977)

J. Brown: *Images and Ideas in 17th-century Spanish Painting* (Princeton, NJ, 1978)

J. Gallego: 'Felipe IV—Pintor', *Estudios en las bellas artes dedicados al profesor Emilio Orozco*, ed. J. Gallego Morell (Granada, 1979), pp. 533–40

J. Brown and J. H. Elliott: *A Palace for a King: The Buen Retiro and the Court of Philip IV* (New Haven and London, 1980)

V. Gérard: 'Philip IV's Early Italian Commissions', *Oxford A. J.*, v (1982), pp. 9–14

J. Brown: *Velázquez, Painter and Courtier* (New York, 1986)

——: 'Enemies of Flattery: Velázquez's Portraits of Philip IV', *J. Interdiscip. Hist.*, xvii (1986), pp. 1–23

S. Orso: *Philip IV and the Decoration of the Alcázar of Madrid* (Princeton, NJ, 1986)

Philip IV of Spain, by Diego Velázquez, oil on canvas, 1298×994 mm, 1644 (New York, Frick Collection)

B. von Barghahn: *Philip IV and the 'Golden House' of the Buen Retiro: In the Tradition of Caesar*, 2 vols (New York and London, 1986)

M. T. Ruiz Alcón and F. Lorrio: *Monasterio de las Dezcalzas Reales* (Madrid, 1987)

——: *Real Monasterio de la Encarnación* (Madrid, 1987)

R. Stradling: *Philip IV and the Government of Spain, 1621–65* (Cambridge, 1988)

ROBERT STRADLING

(8) Mary Anne of Austria, Queen of Spain (*b* 21 Dec 1634; *d* 16 May 1696). Wife of (7) Philip IV. She was the daughter of Ferdinand III (*see* §I(17) above). In 1640 a betrothal was planned between her and Prince Baltasar Carlos (1629–46), son of Philip IV, a match intended to strengthen ties between Spain and the Habsburg empire. The couple were engaged in January 1646, but Baltasar died in that year. In November 1648 a Spanish delegation led by Don Jaime Manuel de Cardenas, Duque de Nájera e Maqueda, was sent to Vienna for the formal betrothal of Mary Anne to her uncle, Philip IV, and the marriage took place in October 1649. The Infanta Margarita was born in 1651 and in 1661 a son, the future Charles II (*see* (10) below). Velázquez painted two portraits of the Queen *c.* 1652 (Paris, Louvre; Madrid, Prado), and Queen Mary Anne also appears in *Las Meninas* (1656; Madrid, Prado; *see* VELÁZQUEZ, DIEGO and fig. 10), the celebrated group portrait of the royal family by Velázquez, in which the King and Queen are portrayed as a reflection in a mirror beyond the painter's self-portrait at the easel. After the death of Philip IV, patronage at court was under the control of the Queen, who ruled as Regent until 1677 when she was temporarily banished to Toledo. In 1669 she appointed JUAN CARREÑO DE MIRANDA as court painter, and he portrayed her in the habit of a nun as a costume of mourning in *Queen Mary Anne of Austria* (version, *c.* 1669; Madrid, Prado).

BIBLIOGRAPHY

J. Lynch: *Spain under the Habsburgs; 1516–1598* (New York and Oxford, 1964)

D. Gies McGuigan: *The Habsburgs* (London, 1966)

(9) Ferdinand, Cardinal-Infante (*b* 1609; *d* 1641). Son of (5) Philip III. He was made Cardinal-Infante and created a role that was more military and diplomatic than ecclesiastical, as indicated in *Cardinal-Infante Don Ferdinando* by Velázquez (*c.* 1632–6; Madrid, Prado), in which he is depicted as a huntsman. During internal problems in Spain while the country was threatened by the revolts of the Catalans from 1626, Ferdinand represented Philip IV in Barcelona as president of the Cortes and Viceroy of Catalonia. He was Viceroy of the Netherlands from 1634 and played an important role in Flanders as agent in acquiring works of art for the Spanish royal collection. In the European conflicts of the 1630s, when the Habsburg empire was threatened by France and attacked by Sweden, Ferdinand assumed command in 1633–4 of a powerful force assembled by the imperial Houses of Vienna and Madrid and defeated the Swedes at the Battle of Nördlingen in September 1634. His defeat of the Dutch army at Calloo was honoured in a Triumphal Entry into Antwerp in 1635, for which Peter Paul Rubens was designer and architect of the elaborate triumphal arches and stages (*see* RUBENS, PETER PAUL, §I, 5). Rubens was assisted in the devising of the political programme—a sophisticated mixture of history and allegory—by Jan Caspar Gavaerts, who also provided the commentary for the commemorative engraving by Theodoor van Thulden of the event, published as the *Pompa introitus Ferdinandi* (1643). Among the preparatory sketches by Rubens that survive are those for the *Stage of Wisdom* and the *Temple of Janus* (both 1634; St Petersburg, Hermitage) and that for the *Triumphal Chariot of the Victory at Calloo* (1635; Antwerp, Kon. Mus. S. Kst.). As agent for Philip IV, Ferdinand was responsible for placing and coordinating the major commissions to Rubens for mythological pictures, as well as commissions to such other artists as Frans Snyders, Pieter Snayers and others for the Torre de la Parada (*see* PARDO, EL and (7) above). Snayers also painted portraits of Ferdinand himself (e.g. *Hunting Scene with the Cardinal-Infante*, *c.* 1636–8; Madrid, Prado). In 1636 Ferdinand made Rubens his court painter.

BIBLIOGRAPHY

J. Lynch: *Spain under the Habsburgs* (London, 1969)

S. Alpers: *The Decorations of the Torre de la Parada* (1971), ix of *Corpus Rubenianum Ludwig Burchard* (Brussels, London and Philadelphia, 1968–)

J. R. Martin: *The Decorations for the Pompa introitus Ferdinandi* (1972), xvi of *Corpus Rubenianum Ludwig Burchard* (Brussels, London and Philadelphia, 1968–)

R. Kann: *A History of the Habsburg Empire* (Berkeley, CA, 1977)

(10) Charles II, King of Spain (*b* 6 Nov 1661; *reg* 1665–1700; *d* 1 Nov 1700). Son of (7) Philip IV. He was a victim of generations of Habsburg inbreeding and was prone to psychological disturbances and acute melancholia with frequent collapses of health, which rendered him incapable of government. There is, however, evidence of his interest in painting, and his role as protector of the arts is indicated by the expansion in the number of royal artists appointed in his reign and his founding of the Cofradía de Escultores (*see* SPAIN, §IV, 3). The vacuum created by the weak incumbent to the throne was filled by the Spanish aristocracy and the Church, who advanced their own interests. A new class of Grandees emerged from the lower ranks of nobility, who used their fortunes to acquire rank and title openly, and the collapse of the Crown's authority led to the rise of the Grandees and their feudal territories centred in Castile, Toledo, Avila, Cuidad Réal and Seville. The Queen Mother Mary Anne of Austria (*see* (8) above) was appointed Regent, and her personal adviser Fernando Valenzuela as prime minister held unprecedented powers. Charles acceded to the throne in November 1675, though his position was largely a passive one. In 1677 Valenzuela was deposed by Don John of Austria, who remained in power until 1679. Neither of Charles's marriages produced an heir, and in October 1700 the King finally endowed his dominions to Philip, Duke of Anjou (*see* BOURBON, §II(1)).

Despite the political situation, there was considerable artistic activity at the court of Charles II. Among the artists active in his reign were Francisco de Herrera the younger, who was royal painter from 1672, Acisclo Antonio Palomino y Velasco (honorary royal painter from 1686) and Francisco Rizi. JUAN CARREÑO DE MIRANDA was appointed Pintor de Cámara in 1671 and painted several remarkable portraits of the King (e.g. *Charles II*, version, 1671; Oviedo, Mus. B.A.). The portrait of *Charles II Receiving the Blessing of the Holy Sacrament* (1683; Ponce,

Mus. A.) by Pedro Ruíz González depicts the King as a devout defender of the Faith, while his rather pathetic personal appearance is recorded in such portraits as *Charles II* (1675–80; Madrid, Prado) by CLAUDIO COELLO. Coello was appointed royal painter in 1683, and his best-known work was the altarpiece the *Sagrada Forma* or *Charles II and his Court Adoring the Eucharist* (1685–90; Madrid, Escorial, Sacristy), a ceremonial group portrait that depicts Charles and the court kneeling in devotion before the miraculous host. In 1692 Charles summoned Luca Giordano to Spain, where he was appointed court painter in 1694. He carried out fresco decoration at the Escorial (1692–4; *see* ESCORIAL, §3 and fig. 4) and also executed decorative work at Buen Retiro (*see* GIORDANO, LUCA).

BIBLIOGRAPHY
J. Langdon-Davies: *Carlos the Bewitched* (Englewood Cliffs, NJ, 1963)
D. Gies McGuigan: *The Habsburgs* (London, 1966)
J. Lynch: *Spain under the Habsburgs* (Oxford, 1969)
J. Brown: *The Golden Age of Painting in Spain* (London and New Haven, 1991), pp. 285–306

Habsburg–Lorraine. Austrian dynasty of rulers, collectors and patrons. Lacking a male heir, Emperor Charles VI (*see* HABSBURG, §I(20)) was succeeded in 1740 by his daughter Maria-Theresa in the Habsburg lands (*see* HABSBURG, §I(21)). Her husband, Francis, Duke of Lorraine, was elected Holy Roman Emperor Francis I in 1745 (*reg* 1745–65), and since 1765 the imperial family has been designated the House of Habsburg-Lorraine. Francis I favoured natural science but enriched the imperial collections with his valuable coin collection. By appointing Jean Nicolas Jadot de Ville-Issey as court architect, he introduced a French element into Viennese architecture. His son, the Holy Roman Emperor Joseph II (*reg* 1765–90), ardently embraced the ideas of enlightened absolutism. Guided by reason and utility, he liberated the arts from the restricting guild system, so that competition could develop. In architecture he favoured a simpler style: the Josephinum (1783–5; *see* AUSTRIA, fig. 7) and the 'Narrenturm' (1783) in Vienna, both by ISIDORO CANEVALE, foreshadow French revolutionary architecture. The Albertina collection built up by the Emperor's brother-in-law Albert, Duke of Saxe-Teschen (*see* WETTIN, (9)), which now incorporates the Imperial Printroom, was inherited by Archduke Charles of Austria (1771–1847); he and his descendants, despite their military positions, faithfully fulfilled the founder's will. Archduke Joseph Antony of Austria, Palatine of Hungary (1776–1847), was actively involved in the foundation (1802) of the Magyar Nemzeti Múzeum [Hungarian National Museum] and founded the Verschönerungskommission (1808) for the renewal of Pest. In 1811 Archduke John of Austria (1782–1859) founded the Steiermärkische Landesmuseum Joanneum in Graz.

(1) Leopold II exerted a beneficial influence on the arts, mainly as Grand Duke of Tuscany before he ascended the throne. His son, the Holy Roman Emperor Francis II (*reg* 1792–1806), took the title Emperor of Austria in 1804 and relinquished the title of Holy Roman Emperor in 1806. He enriched the imperial collections through numerous acquisitions and added old and contemporary works of his own choice to the picture gallery. Privately he collected books and portraits. His patronage is evident in the Franzenburg (1796–1836), a pleasure castle in the Romantic spirit in Laxenburg. Ferdinand I, Emperor of Austria (*reg* 1835–48), although well disposed towards the arts, suffered from ill health, and Chancellor Prince Clemens Lothar Wenzel Metternich (1773–1859) continued to lead the country much as he had in the previous reign. Archduke Leopold of Austria (1823–98) commissioned Hernstein Castle (1856–80) in Lower Austria, an example of historic eclecticism from Theophilus Hansen. Archduke Rainer of Austria (1827–1913) gave his considerable collection of manuscripts to the Court Library. The reign of (2) Francis-Joseph I had a great influence on the arts. His brother Archduke Ferdinand Maximilian of Austria (1832–67), later Emperor of Mexico (*reg* 1864–7), promoted the construction of the Votivkirche (1856–79; for discussion and illustration *see* FERSTEL, HEINRICH VON) in Vienna, built various castles, such as that at Miramare (1856–60) near Trieste, and as governor of Lombardy-Venetia ordered the renovation of important buildings. Archduke Franz Ferdinand of Austria (1863–1914), an avid collector, was influential as protector of the Central Commission for Artistic Monuments and built the War Office (1909–13) in Vienna and remodelled the Schloss Artstetten.

During the age of enlightened absolutism and the 19th century, imperial rule moved from absolutism to constitutional monarchy (1860–61), and the emperors' decisions were increasingly expressed through a highly organized and centralized administration. Patronage was also transformed: instead of amassing art treasures as indispensable signs of monarchical glory, the Habsburgs saw support of the arts less as private fulfilment than as a public and educational service to benefit the people. Inseparably connected with the imperial house were the imperial collections, given by successive emperors to the state and housed in the Kunsthistorisches Museum (1891) in Vienna. By the mid-19th century their stated purpose had become 'primarily to bear witness to the artistic taste and munificence with which Austria's rulers cultivated and supported the arts and sciences' (Lhotsky, p. 569). This purpose found expression not only in the constantly increasing wealth of the collections and in the development of modern museology but also through the publication of the renowned series *Jahrbuch der Kunsthistorischen Sammlungen der Allerhöchsten Kaiserhauses* (from 1883). Although the emperors, especially Francis-Joseph I, were often criticized as not being well disposed towards modern tendencies in the arts, they were nonetheless generous patrons and created a climate under which a prosperous, varied and lively arts community could develop. In long reigns, such as those of Maria-Theresa and Francis-Joseph especially, an imperial style developed that spread to the furthest corners of the empire, showing itself first in churches but in the 19th century in schools, post offices and railway stations. The conservative taste of Charles I, Emperor of Austria (*reg* 1916–18), was well known but did not have much impact, as his brief reign was during World War I. In 1918 the Austro-Hungarian empire ceased to exist.

See also AUSTRIA, §II, 4.

BIBLIOGRAPHY

J. Kertesz: *Bibliographie der Habsburger-Literatur, 1218–1934* (Budapest, 1934)

A. Lhotsky: *Die Geschichte der Sammlungen* (1941–5), ii/2 of *Festschrift des Kunsthistorischen Museums zur Feier des fünfzigjährigen Bestandes*, ii (Vienna, 1941–5)

K. Martin-Weidinger: *Bibliographie der Habsburg-Literatur seit dem Jahre 1934* (diss., U. Vienna, 1985)

B. Hamann, ed.: *Die Habsburger: Ein biographisches Lexikon* (Vienna, 1988)

BEATE STOCK

(1) Leopold II, Holy Roman Emperor (*b* Schönbrunn, nr Vienna, 5 May 1747; *reg* 1790–92; *d* Vienna, 1 March 1792). As the third son of Emperor Francis I (*reg* 1745–65) and Maria-Theresa (*see* HABSBURG, §I(21)) he inherited the grand duchy of Tuscany and in 1765 established his court in Florence. Supported by Austrian counsellors and Tuscan reformers, he made Tuscany a fine example of European Enlightenment. His reforms embraced free internal trade in corn, flour and bread, the abolition of guilds in favour of trade licences, the introduction of hereditary tenure of the peasants' land, municipal organization of police, prisons and hospitals, an exemplary legal code (1786), the liberation of the peasantry and creation of a citizen militia. His ecclesiastic policy was rather restrained.

His patronage of cultural institutions included reorganization of various scientific academies, and he had the Medici collection rearranged; much of it was sold. Hilarius Eckel and Raimondo Cocchi rearranged the coin cabinet according to modern methods. He collected drawings, engravings, coins and Etruscan vases and had the NIOBE GROUP (Florence, Uffizi) moved from the Villa Medici in Rome to Florence. Philipp Hackert and Anton Raphael Mengs were his favourite painters. Gasparo Maria Paoletti was appointed First Engineer to the Royal Works and was commissioned to construct roads and hospitals rather than prestigious buildings, though the Grand Duke continued the conversion of the Palazzo Pitti, begun in 1744 by his father, and had the Boboli Gardens newly arranged.

In 1790 he succeeded his brother Joseph II (*reg* 1765–90) and immediately prevented the outbreak of war with Prussia by the Convention of Reichenbach (27 Jan 1790) and consequently uprisings in Hungary and the Habsburg Netherlands. He concluded peace with the Ottomans at Sistoro in 1791. Initially sympathetic towards the French Revolution, he concluded a defensive alliance with Prussia on 7 February 1792. Many unpopular reforms of the previous reign were cancelled by the 'Prince of Peace' and 'Pastor Emperor'.

BIBLIOGRAPHY

H. Peham: *Leopold II, Herrscher mit weiser Hand* (Graz, 1927)

A. Wandruszka: *Leopold II, Erzherzog von Österreich, Grossherzog der Toskana, König von Ungarn und Böhmen, Römischer Kaiser*, 2 vols (Vienna, 1963–5)

A. GERHARDT

(2) Francis-Joseph I, [Franz-Joseph] Emperor of Austria [King of Hungary] (*b* Vienna, 18 Aug 1830; *reg* 1848–1916; *d* Vienna, 21 Sept 1916). Great-grandson of (1) Leopold II. He ascended the throne after the abdication of his uncle, Ferdinand I, Emperor of Austria (*reg* 1835–48), in the revolutionary year 1848. After the loss of Lombardy (1859) in the course of Italian unification, there was a shift from a neo-absolutist to a constitutional monarchy and subsequently the regime became increasingly liberal. Conflict with Prussia over the nature of the Deutscher Bund culminated in war in 1866; Austria's defeat brought the loss of Venice, and Austria withdrew from the Deutscher Bund. The Emperor's concern to preserve the state with its multiplicity of peoples was challenged by nationalist conflicts in Bohemia, Croatia and the Tyrol. Ethnic tension in Bosnia-Herzegovina led to the assassination in Sarajevo of Archduke Franz Ferdinand of Austria (1863–1914), heir to the throne, and the outbreak of World War I in 1914.

In the fine arts, the Emperor's efforts were geared more towards the management and systematization of the Habsburg collections than to direct patronage. From 1857 Vienna was redesigned and given its Ringstrasse (*see* VIENNA, §II, 3 and fig. 5) and many imposing public buildings. These included, in 1863, the Österreichisches Museum für Kunst und Industrie (now Österreichisches Museum für Angewandte Kunst), to promote the arts and crafts, and, from 1872, the Kunsthistorische Sammlungen des Allerhöchsten Kaiserhauses (now Kunsthistorisches Museum; *see* SEMPER, GOTTFRIED, and AUSTRIA, fig. 8), which brought together the extensive and scattered Habsburg collections (*see* VIENNA, §II, 3). The main works added to the Habsburg collection were family portraits, notably those of the Emperor's wife, Elizabeth of Bavaria, Empress of Austria (1837–98), by Franz Xaver Winterhalter (e.g. of 1865; Vienna, Hofburg-Schauräume), as well as portraits of the Emperor himself.

See also AUSTRIA, §II, 4.

BIBLIOGRAPHY

E. C. Conte Corti: *Kaiser Franz Joseph*, 3 vols (Graz, Vienna, Cologne, 1950–55)

F. Herre: *Kaiser Franz Joseph von Österreich* (Cologne, 1978)

H. Drimmel: *Franz Joseph* (Vienna, 1992)

ELISABETH SCHEICHER

Habuba Kabira. Together with Tell Qannas [Kannas], Habuba Kabira formed the site of the earliest known city in Syria, which flourished in the second half of the 4th millennium BC on the right bank of the middle Euphrates. The sites were excavated by German and Belgian teams led, respectively, by Strommenger and Finet, as part of a rescue programme prompted by the building of a dam; they are now flooded. The eastern side of the city had been eroded by wind but the remaining ruins (see fig.), often referred to as Habuba Kabira South, were excavated south of a mound called Tell Habuba Kabira and in the lowest level of Tell Qannas. The two tells were only formed in the 3rd millennium BC, well after the original city was deserted. The finds are mostly in the National Museum in Aleppo and in the Museum für Ur- und Frühgeschichte in Berlin.

The original city covered between 17 and 18 ha and was surrounded by a mud-brick wall 3 m thick with towers and fortifications; much of the area inside the wall had been built on. The city centre, found in Tell Qannas, was a cult and administrative district consisting of several particularly large buildings with a big niched central room (*Mittelsaal*), which resemble buildings from contemporary

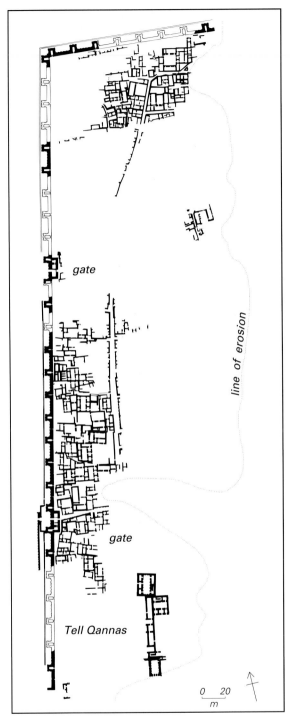

Habuba Kabira, plan of excavated areas of Habuba Kabira South and Tell Qannas, 4th millennium BC

outside the city gates. The city was well organized; its obvious wealth is probably attributable to its role as a commercial depot in the international trade between south Mesopotamia, Anatolia and the Mediterranean.

The house contents remained largely *in situ*, particularly in a few houses that had been destroyed by fire. There is a rich variety of pottery vessels, objects of stone, copper and bone, copper pins and beads. A deposit of slingshots made from sun-dried mud was found inside one of the city gates. The remains of a workshop for the manufacture of gaming-boards with an inlay of square black and white stones is evidence of manufacturing industry.

Some of the most interesting finds at the site were the many cylinder seal impressions; these are in the Uruk and Jemdet Nasr styles, which are therefore shown to have overlapped (*see* MESOPOTAMIA, §I, 2(i)(c)). Some of the seal impressions were on tablets of unbaked clay that also had numerical signs impressed on them. These tablets provided the recipients of goods with information about the quantity sent, and the seal identified the sender, but they gave no information about the type of goods. Since only numbers and no regular script have been found, this city probably belongs to the earliest phase of writing documented in Sumer and Elam (*see* ANCIENT NEAR EAST, §I, 3). More numerous than the clay tablets are oval bullae with pointed ends. These were modelled in soft clay around the knot of a cord and then sealed; occasionally they were impressed with numerical signs. There are also tokens shaped like small balls, eggs, discs and cubes, which were covered with incisions or impressions and baked. Each one stands for a particular commodity (e.g. a sheep, or an oil jar). These tokens, attached to cords and fastened to bullae, would accompany a consignment of goods and be checked by the recipient. Sometimes the tokens were enclosed in hollow balls of clay, the exterior of which was sealed by the sender and occasionally bore impressions of the specific form of the tokens concealed within, the number of impressions corresponding to that of the tokens. The seals and sealings depict scenes of animal husbandry and patterns of animals, scorpions, pots and figures.

The settlement was abandoned after, at most, 150 years, but the reason for this is not known. Where the inhabitants of the city, the surrounding Euphrates Valley and the probable capital on nearby JEBEL ARUDA came from, and the language they spoke, is not known either. Their material remains and their architecture (from the ground-plans to the smallest details) suggest a close connection with the cities of Sumer and Elam more than 1000 km further south in Iraq and Iranian Khuzistan. In addition to a common culture there must have been a common political system, but at present its structure is not known. A few burnt-out houses in Habuba Kabira South, Tell Qannas and on Jebel Aruda may be an indication of violent destruction.

After the city had been abandoned there was probably no permanent settlement in this part of the Euphrates Valley until the beginning of the 3rd millennium BC, when a new period of concentrated settlement began. Houses were built on the raised area of the old city centre (Tell Qannas) and further north, outside the former city, at Tell Habuba Kabira. Successive layers of occupational debris

URUK in south Mesopotamia. Private houses were built to the same plan. The excavations revealed two city gates, several relatively broad main thoroughfares and a network of small alleys. Drains covered with paving stones, pipes or U-shaped gutters carried effluent into pits or to an area formed mounds during the next few centuries and by the early 2nd millennium BC, Tell Habuba Kabira had reached a height of about 10 m. It consisted of a fortified citadel with a surrounding settlement. Apart from a ruler's palace, there were workshops for beads of stone and shell, terracotta figures, pottery and metalworking.

BIBLIOGRAPHY

A. Finet: 'Bilan provisoire des fouilles belges du Tell Kannas', *Annu. Amer. Sch. Orient. Res.*, xliv (1979), pp. 79–97

E. Strommenger: 'Ausgrabungen der deutschen Orient-Gesellschaft in Habuba Kabira', *Annu. Amer. Sch. Orient. Res.*, xliv (1979), pp. 63–79

——: *Habuba Kabira: Eine Stadt vor 5000 Jahren* (Mainz, 1980)

EVA STROMMENGER

Hach'ŏn. *See* KO UN.

Hacılar. Neolithic and Chalcolithic site (*c.* 7000–5000 BC) near Burdur, south-west Turkey. It was excavated by James Mellaart between 1957 and 1960. Two overlapping settlements, separated by a gap of perhaps 750 years, have produced a mound 5 m high and 137 m in diameter. Roughly one quarter of the site was excavated; virgin soil was reached. The objects from the excavations are in the Museum of Anatolian Civilizations in Ankara.

The Early Neolithic (late 8th millennium BC–early 7th) settlement, known only from a small sounding, yielded no complete architectural plans, and no doorways came to light. Exterior mud-brick walls rested on stone foundations, and some lime-plastered floors had a pebble base and were reddened with ochre and burnished; one had a cream band in reserve. Ovens and hearths stood in courtyards. There was no pottery, but there were marble bowls and presumably baskets and woodwork. Two polished axes were of local greenstone, but obsidian for neatly pressure-flaked blades came from the island of Melos and perhaps from central Anatolia. Four human skulls supported by piles of pebbles stood in courtyards.

Levels IX to VI were Late Neolithic (*c.* 6500–*c.* 6300 BC). In this phase, which was built over the previous settlement, houses were rectangular with a doorway in either the long or short side, internal partitions of sticks and plaster, and unpainted, white-plastered floors. Fixtures included clay storage bins, raised square hearths and flat-topped ovens with, perhaps, a chimney in the wall. Cubicles outside the door housed kitchen equipment. Houses adjoined one another, often at right angles, and there is evidence for courtyards—one with a well—but the overall plan of the site is unknown. Most pottery was monochrome in various shades of red-brown to cream, but a few pieces had stripes or network in red. Bowls and jars predominated, and oval shapes were characteristic. Occasional designs in relief depicted bucrania, ram's head, ibex, scorpion or hand-and-arm motifs. Elegant vessels were in the forms of a backward-looking seated doe, a boar, a four-legged duck and a woman's head. White marble was used for large, three- and four-footed bowls and for buttons, greenstone for polished tools, sandstone for mortars and cosmetic palettes, and local limestone and blue or green apatite for beads and jewellery. Most chipped stone blades were of flint or chert. Female clay figurines, mostly unpainted, had exaggerated breasts, stomach and buttocks, bulging upper arms, vestigial hands and feet, and a mouthless head attached by a peg. Young girls were

Hacılar, effigy vase, probably from level I, h. 287 mm, Chalcolithic, *c.* 5900–*c.* 5600 BC (Istanbul, Sadberk Hanim Museum)

shown in bikinis with hair in a coiled pigtail, older women corpulent and nude with hair in a bun (*see* ANATOLIA, ANCIENT, fig. 2(a)). As at ÇATAL HÜYÜK, the principal subjects were birth and fertility, and a female figure, possibly a goddess, as mistress of animals. A wider range of positions was used, but there was no sign of Çatal's interest in bulls and rams. The only male figures were children. Most houses in level VI contained an incised stone slab of uncertain significance.

Levels V to II are Early to Middle Chalcolithic (*c.* 6300–*c.* 5900 BC), but the period is best known from level II. After a possible short gap, a fortification wall, 3 m thick, with small towers and three narrow gates now enclosed the settlement, and three courtyards divided it within. Houses stood side by side, the L-shaped combinations of level VI having disappeared. They had megaron-like plans, with antechamber and main room. Buttresses, platforms and benches were built in, but there were no internal partitions. Kitchen sheds no longer adjoined the houses but were in a separate, eastern quarter of the village. Earlier building traditions survived only in two possible shrines at the north-east and south-west corners. A potter's workshop in the centre of the village provided a rich sample of pottery that, unlike that of levels VI and I, has almost no distribution beyond the site itself. Monochrome wares still predominated, but with better techniques, more stylish shapes and better cream surfaces, the proportion of painted wares increased. Inspiration for their inventive designs may have come from traditional rug and felt work, religious motifs and the geometric linear designs of Late Neolithic wares. Some of the red-on-cream textile-type designs find close comparisons in the Çatal Hüyük wall paintings. A 'fantastic' style seems to have translated earlier, naturalistic motifs of, for example, bucrania, human heads, seated goddesses and attendant animals, into semi-abstract patterns, which are sometimes reversible (*see* ANATOLIA, ANCIENT, fig. 2(b)). The range of statuettes, however, was much more limited than in Hacılar VI, there being only the one type, a standing female figure with string skirt and painted body, usually with pigtail, incised hair, no mouth, small breasts and large buttocks.

A very different settlement (level I, Middle Chalcolithic; *c.* 5900–*c.* 5600 BC) followed the burning of Hacılar II. The only excavated architecture is one sector of a massive, stone-footed, mud-brick structure, which presumably encircled the site. It contained two or more rows of rooms, often with large, internal buttresses; a paucity of doorways suggests that, despite the presence of hearths and sleeping-platforms, these were basements with entry from above. An upper storey was of timber, brushwood and mud. Small courtyards separated one block of rooms from another and also provided access from the narrow, outer gates to the centre of the fortress, possibly an open courtyard. The pottery, typical throughout south-west Anatolia, appears to have developed from Hacılar VI, largely bypassing levels V–II. Clay, paint, slip, technique and most decorative motifs are different from level II. The shapes, including deep bowls with ring bases and shallow bowls with carination, are descended from the deeper shapes of level VI; theriomorphic pots and painted female effigy vases with obsidian eyes reappear (see fig.), as does relief decoration. Painted decoration, almost all red-on-white, is mostly linear geometric, often recalling rushwork. Some of the earlier 'fantastic' motifs, however, are absorbed and quietly incorporated. Clay female statuettes exhibit three postures: standing, sitting or leaning backwards, and recumbent. As before, no mouth is shown; but there is some stylization towards a 'fiddle' body shape, breasts are smaller, genitals more explicit and heavy brows merge into the nose. Eyes are sometimes inlaid with obsidian.

After the close of excavations, many effigy vases and clay statuettes of Hacılar type came on to the antiquities market. Thermoluminescence dating and other physical tests have suggested that most were fakes. Those that are genuine may have been robbed from Hacılar, a related site or a Hacılar cemetery that is otherwise unknown.

BIBLIOGRAPHY
J. Mellaart: *Excavations at Hacılar*, 2 vols (Edinburgh, 1970)
M. J. Aitken, P. R. S. Moorey and P. J. Ucko: 'The Authenticity of Vessels and Figurines in the Hacılar Style', *Archaeometry*, xiii (1971), pp. 89–141

DONALD F. EASTON

Hackaert, Jan [Johannes] (*bapt* Amsterdam, Feb 1628; *d* Amsterdam in or after 1685). Dutch painter, draughtsman and etcher. The earliest information about Hackaert indicates that he visited Switzerland several times between 1653 and 1656; he probably did not go to Italy, as was long supposed. By 1658 he was back in Amsterdam. When in Switzerland, he made several large topographical drawings, for example the *View of the Via Mala* (pen and brown ink and brown wash, 750×560 mm, 1655; Vienna, Österreich. Nbib.). Many of these drawings, which give a

good sense of space but are somewhat dry in execution, were probably made for the multi-volume atlas of LAURENS VAN DER HEM, an Amsterdam lawyer who commissioned topographical views from several artists.

Hackaert's paintings may be broadly divided into two categories: Italianate landscapes and woodland scenes. Both genres were much influenced by the landscapes of the Dutch Italianates Jan Both and Jan Asselijn, especially in the treatment of colour. An example of the first category is the *Lake of Zurich* (*c.* 1660–64; Amsterdam, Rijksmus.); this masterpiece is exceptional in depicting a topographical view in an idealized style. The only comparable work is Hackaert's *View of Cleve* (Groningen, Groninger Mus.), in which the influence of Both and Asselijn is evident in the rendering of the abundant golden light. In the later *Landscape in the Campagna with Cattle* (*c.* 1670; Berlin, Gemäldegal.), the slender, graceful trees, with their light foliage bathed in brilliant southern sunshine, are again reminiscent of Both.

Similar trees and sunlight can be seen in Hackaert's woodland scenes, in which he generally made use of a *sous-bois* composition: painting the underside of the leafy canopy has the effect of drawing the spectator into the forest. The *Deer-hunt in a Wood* (*c.* 1660; London, N.G.), despite the density of the foliation, achieves an impressive sense of space by the depiction of sunlight penetrating the trees. Hackaert's staffage, which in this case was painted by Nicolaes Berchem (who also signed the picture), is often attributed to other artists (e.g. Adriaen van de Velde and Johannes Lingelbach). The *Avenue of Birches* (*c.* 1675–80; Amsterdam, Rijksmus.; see fig.) is an example of Hackaert's more open woodland views. It depicts a hunting

Jan Hackaert: *Avenue of Birches*, oil on canvas, 665×535 mm, *c.* 1675–80 (Amsterdam, Rijksmuseum)

party in an avenue alongside a stretch of water bordered by slender birch trees; a soft golden light suffuses the whole view. Hackaert's forest landscapes with hunting scenes show more originality than his Italianate landscapes and were very popular on the contemporary art market, largely because they reflected the prosperity and affluent leisure pursuits, real or coveted, of the prospective buyers.

Besides the Swiss topographical drawings, Hackaert made several other drawings in the style of Jan Both, some of whose works he owned and copied (e.g. the *Italianate Landscape* by Hackaert, 1661; Groningen, Groninger Mus.). These drawings are sketchier, broader and lighter in execution than his topographical work. Seven etchings by him are also known, all showing northern European landscapes. According to Hofstede de Groot, Hackaert's latest signed work dates from 1685, in which year, or soon after, he is assumed to have died.

BIBLIOGRAPHY

Hollstein: *Dut. & Flem.*

C. Hofstede de Groot: *Holländischen Maler* (1907–28), ix, pp. 1–47

S. Stelling-Michaud: *Unbekannte schweizer Landschaften aus dem XVII Jahrhunderts: Zeichnungen und Schilderungen von Jan Hackaert und anderen holländischen Malern* (Zürich and Leipzig, 1937) [reconstruction of Hackaert's journey through Switzerland; good illus]

G. Solar: *Jan Hackaert: Die schweizer Ansichten, 1653–55; Zeichnungen eines niederländischen Malers als frühe Bilddokumente der Alpenlandschaft* (Zürich and Leipzig, 1981)

Masters of 17th-century Dutch Landscape Painting (exh. cat., ed. P. C. Sutton; Amsterdam, Rijksmus.; Boston, MA, Mus. F.A.; Philadelphia, PA, Mus. A.; 1987–8), pp. 338–42 [complete bibliog.]

LUUK BOS

Hacker, Dieter (*b* Augsburg, 4 Aug 1942). German painter. Between 1960 and 1965 he studied at the Akademie der Bildende Künste in Munich, moving to West Berlin in 1970. Here he found the experimental spirit, the artists' cooperative groups and the proximity of art and politics conducive to his own interests and a year later he opened the 7 Produzentengalerie with a show called *Everybody Could Be his Own Artist*. In this exhibition and subsequent ones he questioned the alienation of art from society and the role of cultural institutions. He sought to control responsibility for making, exhibiting, disseminating and commenting on art. To this end he became editor of *Zeitungen der 7 Produzentengalerie*, a publication that acted as an expansive commentary on exhibitions held at the gallery in 1971–2. In 1974 he became guest professor at the Hochschule der Künste in Hamburg. In the same year he contributed to an exhibition at the ICA, London, called *Art into Society, Society into Art*. The painting was a reproduction of George Stubbs's *Horse Attacked by a Lion*, which Hacker reworked and entitled *Art Must Claw at the Neck of the Bourgeois as the Lion Does at the Horse* (artist's col.). The accompanying text commented on the tensions between art and society caused by differing expectations.

Towards the end of the 1970s Hacker turned to more traditional painting and in 1977 exhibited a canvas entitled the *House Painters Begin to Paint their Own Future* (1976; Munich, Lenbachhaus), in which the artist is portrayed as a workman. The painterly treatment of the subject-matter expressed his increasing interest in the intrinsic qualities of the medium. The 1980s saw a further exploration of different mediums as he worked in clay and iron and continued his discussions on theoretical issues, particularly in the magazine *Volksfoto* (1977–80) in relation to amateur photography.

BIBLIOGRAPHY

Art into Society, Society into Art: Seven German Artists (exh. cat., ed. C. M. Joachimides and N. Rosenthal; London, ICA, 1974)

Dieter Hacker: Paintings and Works on Paper (exh. cat., London, Marlborough F.A., 1985)

DEBORAH NASH

Hackert. German family of painters and printmakers, active in Italy. The Berlin portrait and animal painter Philipp Hackert (*d* Prenzlau, 1768) had five artist sons. The eldest and most famous was (1) Philipp Hackert, a landscape painter whose international experience and views in the tradition of Claude Lorrain proved highly influential when he settled in Naples in the late 18th century. The second son, Carl Ludwig Hackert (*b* Prenzlau, 1740; *d* Morges, 1796), travelled in France and then settled in Rome in 1772 with his older brother, who encouraged him to take up landscape painting in oil and gouache. In 1778 Carl Ludwig went to Geneva and Lausanne, producing a series of coloured engravings of views of Switzerland and Savoy. He committed suicide. The third son, Johann Gottlieb Hackert (*b* Prenzlau, 1744; *d* Bath, 1773), after studying at the Berlin Akademie, worked with Philipp in Paris and Rome from 1766. (Many of his drawings from 1766–9 are in the Kupferstichkabinett, Berlin.) He specialized in landscape and animal studies, producing gouaches in both genres for Lady Hamilton in Naples in 1770. In this year he went to England, where he showed work at the Royal Academy. The fourth son, Wilhelm Hackert (*b* Prenzlau, 1748; *d* St Petersburg, 1780), journeyed in 1772 to Rome, where he worked under Anton Raphael Mengs. In 1774, while working in Tuscany, he met Admiral Orlov, and through this contact he travelled to Russia, where he became a drawing master. The fifth son, (2) Georg Hackert, was a distinguished engraver, turning many of Philipp's paintings into prints.

(1) (Jacob) Philipp Hackert (*b* Prenzlau, 1737; *d* San Pietro di Careggi, 1807). He studied first with his father, Philipp Hackert, then from 1755 with Blaise Nicolas Le Sueur at the Berlin Akademie. There he encountered, and copied, the landscapes of Dutch artists and of Claude Lorrain. The latter influence shows in two works exhibited in 1761, views of the *Lake of Venus in the Berlin Zoological Garden* (versions of 1764 in Stockholm, Nmus.). These much admired paintings retain a rather rigid late Baroque style. Hackert's main interest in these early works was to arrive at a special understanding of a place through alternate views, with reverse directions of observation. This systematic documentation bears witness to his interest in the study of nature.

In 1762 Hackert left Berlin for a study tour in northern Germany. He stopped in Stralsund and the nearby island of Rügen, where he was a guest of Adolph Friedrich von Olthoff, the Swedish councillor in Pomerania. The stimulus these travels provided is reflected in six landscapes in tempera (*c.* 1763; Potsdam, priv. col.), painted for the Olthoffs, and four frescoes (1763) in the great hall of Schloss Boldewitz. In May 1764 Hackert went from Stralsund to Stockholm with Baron von Olthoff, who presented him at court. In Sweden he produced a *View of Karlsberg* (1766; priv. col., see Forsmann, fig. 20) for the King and some drawings for the Queen. In the former all traces of decorative painting have disappeared, and Hackert gives a personal interpretation of the Dutch 17th-century painting and the work of Claude that he had copied. During this time he also produced a series of etchings, *Vues de Suède*, which shows his development, from rather perfunctory beginnings, into a remarkably evocative printmaker.

In 1765 Hackert went to Hamburg, and from there to Paris, where there was a growing interest in the kind of landscape developed by Dutch painters. He modelled his work closely on the work of the most famous exponent of this genre, Jean-Claude Wille, and his small landscape gouaches, well suited to contemporary taste, brought him renown. This enabled him in 1768 to depart for Italy. After visiting Livorno, Pisa and Florence, he arrived at Rome, where he remained until 1786. During this period the colonies of French, German and English artists and scholars in Rome were growing more and more numerous. Hackert brought to the German group, headed by Anton Raphael Mengs and Johann Joachim Winckelmann, an already rich and complex cultural experience. He upheld his classical formula of landscape through sketches made on study tours (to Sicily in 1777, to Switzerland in 1778), through oil paintings and through such prints as the four *Views Sketched in the Kingdom of Naples* (1779; Naples, Capodimonte), which mark a new independence for engraving as a medium for landscape.

In 1782 Hackert met King Ferdinand IV of Naples, and in 1786 he settled in Naples as court painter. During his 13 years in the city he consolidated his European fame, largely through the advocacy of Goethe, whom he met in 1787 and who became his close friend. He also started his own school, propounding his ideas about landscape painting to engravers, including his brother (2) Georg Hackert and W. G. Gmelin (*c.* 1760–1820), and such painters as Christopher Kniep (1755–1825), Michael Wutki (1738–1822), and the Neapolitans Vincenzo Aloja (*fl* 1790–1815) and Salvatore Fergola (1799–1874). Perhaps Hackert's finest Neapolitan works were the *Four Seasons*, luminous Neapolitan *vedute* enlivened by figures in local dress. The originals, intended for King Ferdinand's hunting-lodge on Lake Fusaro, were destroyed by 1799, but smaller copies by Hackert survive (*Spring*, Switzerland, priv. col.; *Summer*, *Winter*, Nuremberg, Ger. Nmus.; *Autumn*, Cologne, Wall-raf-Richartz-Mus.). Hackert's intellectual interests can be seen among the pictures (1792–3) painted for Queen Maria Carolina's bathroom in the Belvedere di S Leucio near Caserta. Some of these use the old encaustic technique and are inspired by objects that came to light during the archaeological excavations at Herculaneum. Hackert did not merely evoke the Antique; he re-lived the tradition in his own personal way, again confirming his acuteness in interpreting the most recent cultural trends of his time. Another work painted at S Leucio, the *Harvest Festival* (1782; Caserta, Pal. Reale; see fig.) is a fine example of his idyllic interpretation of the landscape around him.

Philipp Hackert: *Harvest Festival at S Leucio*, tempera, 470×700 mm, 1782 (Caserta, Palazzo Reale)

When the Revolution of 1799 forced him to leave Naples, Hackert settled permanently at San Pietro di Careggi, near Florence. Here he returned to his old interest in nature with renewed perception, in fact becoming a sort of proto-Romantic landscape artist. After his death his memoirs were edited and published by Goethe.

WRITINGS
J. W. Goethe, ed.: *Philipp Hackert* (Tübingen, 1811/*R* Rome, 1988) [memoirs]

BIBLIOGRAPHY
B. Lohse: *Jacob Philipp Hackert: Leben und Anfänge seiner Kunst* (Emsdetten, 1936)
E. Forsmann: 'Jakob Philipp Hackert und Schweden', *Ksthist. Tidskr.*, xxiv (1955), pp. 17–34
A. Negro Spina: *L'incisione napoletana dell'ottocento* (Naples, 1976), pp. 15–21
——: 'Philipp Hackert incisore', *Atti Accad. Pontaniana*, n.s. 3, xxvii (1978), pp. 181–205
F. Mancini: *Philipp Hackert* (Naples, 1988)

(2) Georg (Abraham) Hackert (*b* Prenzlau, 1755; *d* Florence, 1805). Brother of (1) Philipp Hackert. He trained in Berlin with F. G. Berger and went to Italy in 1776 at the invitation of his elder brother Philipp. Though his training was based mainly on 17th-century Dutch and Flemish art, he was soon influenced by the Neo-classical theories of Winckelmann and Mengs. His work in Rome compromises effectively between a calligraphic approach and the Romantic spirit. In fact, while faithfully rendering his brother's landscapes, he managed to infuse a new sense of nature into his engravings. He had the ability to illustrate a scene as if engraving from life rather than from a painting. Georg did most of his work in Naples, where the Bourbon court appointed him official engraver. In this position he was an upholder and propagator of Neoclassical theories, but his influence on Neapolitan engraving, especially through his renderings of his brother's great canvases of *Ports of the Realm*, remains to be studied. He fled Naples with his brother in 1799.

ANNAMARIA NEGRO SPINA

Hackhofer, Johann Cyriak (*bapt* Wilten, nr Innsbruck, 14 Feb 1675; *d* Vorau, Styria, 9 May 1731). Austrian painter and draughtsman. His early influences were probably from the Tyrolean artists Egid Schor, Kaspar Waldmann and Johann Josef Waldmann (1676–1712) and, in Vienna, from Johann Michael Rottmayr and Matthias Steinl. Hackhofer was in Vienna from 1704 to 1706, where he drew some of the plates for the series of engravings (1705) dedicated to Emperor Joseph I (*reg* 1678–1711) as hereditary ruler. From 1708 until his death he held the post of Official Painter to the Augustine abbey in Vorau. His reputation as one of the most original and progressive Baroque artists in the province of Styria is based on his frescoes, while his panels are less important. His early works, a ceiling fresco depicting the *Trinity* in the Marktkirche at Vorau and the *Holy Order* on the ceiling of the chapter house in the monastery there (both 1708), reveal his Austrian training but also show an influence from High Baroque art in Rome: it is possible that he spent some time in Italy, but there is no proof of this. His major commission was for the complete decoration of the Festenburg near Vorau, carried out in 1709–15, 1720 and 1723. In 1710 he painted the walls, side altars and ceiling of the Katharinenkirche, which had been installed in the medieval building. The ceiling, depicting the *Assumption of St Catherine*, creates the illusion of glimpsing vistas of open sky through clouds and borrows from Rottmayr's ceiling fresco in the Jesuit church of St Matthias, Breslau (now Wrocław, Poland). In six of the chapels that were installed within the Festenburg, Hackhofer's illusionistic techniques were carried to the point of *trompe l'oeil*: he skilfully integrated his frescoes and paintings of the *Martyrdom of St Catherine* and other subjects and the sculptures of the Salzburg wood-carver Johann Fenest into his overall concept. His inspiration for this work may have come from the designs of Viennese theatre painters and from Gaudenzio Ferrari's chapel of the Crucifixion (*c.* 1520–26) in the Sacromonte in Varallo, Italy. Another major commission was for the decoration of the interior of the sacristy of the Stiftspfarrkirche in Vorau with depictions of the *Passion*, the *Last Judgement* and the *Damned* (1715–16). This programme was done in a similar manner to that of the Katharinenkirche in Festenburg. Some of his late ceilings—the Wallfahrtskirche 'Maria Hasel' in Peggau, done in 1718, the Friedhofkapellen in Wenigzell, done in 1721, and his frescoes in Peggau, executed *c.* 1724—show painted, simulated architecture closer in spirit to the work of Andrea Pozzo. His pupil and successor Josef Georg Mayr (1707–44), from Vorau, continued his tradition.

BIBLIOGRAPHY
R. Meeraus: *Johann Cyriak Hackhofer*, Beiträge zur Kunstgeschichte Steiermarks und Kärntens, iv (Graz, 1931)
G. Brucher: *Die barocke Deckenmalerei in der Steiermark* (Graz, 1973)
Johann Cyriak Hackhofer (exh. cat. by F. Hutz, Vorau, Augustine Abbey, 1981)
C. Weeber: *Der Vorauer Stiftsmaler Johann Cyriak Hackhofer, 1675–1731* (diss., Graz, Karl-Franzens-U., 1987)

KURT WOISETSCHLÄGER

Hackney, Rod(erick Peter) (*b* Liverpool, 3 March 1942). English architect. Having studied at the University of Manchester School of Architecture (1961–7), he worked briefly in Montreal, in connection with Expo '67, and in Tripoli, where he was a housing architect for the Libyan government. From 1968 to 1971 he was an assistant to Arne Jacobsen in Copenhagen, for whom he worked on the design of the Kuwait Central Bank (built 1973–6), Kuwait City. His doctoral dissertation (1979) has Jacobsen's work as its subject-matter. In 1972 he formed the practice of Rod Hackney & Associates at Macclesfield, Ches, and soon became known for the refurbishment of several brick-built terrace houses (1972–5) around Black Road in the town. Although intended for demolition, the houses were saved and then improved and altered in accordance with the wishes of the inhabitants. The significant contribution of the residents in determining what alterations were made and assisting in the execution of the work meant that the scheme was subsequently seen as one of the pioneering examples of 'Community architecture', which became increasingly prominent in the 1980s. The practice was involved in similar schemes, for example at Graver Weir Terrace (1981), Macclesfield, and also in some later housing developments where the purchasers could be involved in the building work. A variety of other projects of a community nature, including industrial regeneration schemes in Chesterfield and Burnley, were also undertaken in the 1980s. Hackney was President of the RIBA (1987–9) and of the Union Internationale des Architectes (1988–91), also being significantly involved with bodies that promote community enterprise.

WRITINGS

The Life and Work of Arne Jacobsen: The Complete Design Approach to Architecture, 4 vols (PhD thesis, U. Manchester, 1979)
'New Role for Architects', *Bldg Conserv.*, ii/2 (1980), pp. 17–22
The Good, the Bad and the Ugly (London, 1990)
Contributions to *Architects' J.*, *Archit. Preserv.*, *Bldg Conserv.*

BIBLIOGRAPHY

M. Hook: 'Macclesfield: The Self-help GIA', *Architects' J.*, clxii (1975), pp. 995–1002
C. Knevitt: 'Down your Way: Current Projects by Rod Hackney', *Architects' J.*, clxvi (1977), pp. 630–36
N. Wates and C. Knevitt: *Community Architecture: How People Are Creating their Own Environment* (Harmondsworth, 1987)
ALLAN M. CRAVEN

Hadatu. *See* ARSLAN TASH.

Hadda [Haḍḍa; Hilo]. Site of numerous Buddhist monasteries, 8 km south-west of Jalalabad, Afghanistan. It flourished from the 1st century BC to the 8th century AD. The ancient site, known as Hilo to Chinese pilgrims of the 5th–8th century, is partially covered by a modern village. The earliest archaeological reports were compiled by Claude-Auguste Court (1827), Charles Masson (1834) and William Simpson (1878–9). Masson excavated 14 stupas, primarily at Gundi Kabul (also known as Tepe Kabul and Tepe Safed). He also uncovered the stupa at Tepe Kalan (also known as Tapa-é-Top-é-Kalan, Tope Kelan and Bordji-i Kafariha). A French delegation excavated most of the remaining ruins, including Tepe Kafariha and Bagh Gai, between 1926 and 1928. In 1965 a Japanese mission investigated Lalma, 3 km south-west of Hadda. Tepe Shotor (also known as Tapa-é-Shotor) and Tepe Kalan were excavated by the Afghan Institute of Archaeology between 1965 and 1979.

The principal complexes all comprise a courtyard of stupas and shrines and an adjacent monastery. Walls are of mud or baked brick, coated with clay, plaster or stucco. Most of the stupas are built of schist and limestone mixed together over a clay and rubble core, but in the earliest examples only schist is used for the outer structure, while in the later ones limestone predominates. There is also an evolution in form: the square base and cylindrical drum supporting the dome become increasingly multi-tiered, elongated and ornate. Sculptural decoration consists of pilasters alternating with figures or occasional legendary Buddhist scenes. Similar Buddhist subjects are executed in high relief in the surrounding niches and shrines or as wall paintings in caves. There are few schist or limestone sculptures, the majority of the figural decoration being modelled in stucco or clay on wooden armatures. Pressed moulds were used for certain details. Most notable are a number of naturalistic figures, including some in the round, that exhibit Hellenistic influence.

See also AFGHANISTAN, §II, 1(ii)(b)–(d) and figs 7 and 11.

BIBLIOGRAPHY

C. Masson: 'Memoir on the Topes and Sepulchral Monuments of Afghanistan'; *Ariana Antiqua*, ed. H. H. Wilson (London, 1841), pp. 105–13
J. Barthoux: *Les Fouilles de Haḍḍa*, vols I and III, Mém.: Dél. Archéol. Fr. Afghanistan, iv–v (Paris, 1933, 1930) [Vol. III, pls only, pubd in 1930, followed by vol. I in 1933]
S. Mizuno, ed.: *Durman Tepe and Lalma* (Kyoto, 1968)
C. Moustamindy [S. Mostamindi]: 'La Fouille de Haḍḍa', *Acad. Inscr. & B.-Lett.: C. R. Séances* (1969), pp. 119–28
——: 'Nouvelles Fouilles de Haḍḍa (1966–1967)', *A. Asiat.*, xix (1969), pp. 15–35
Z. Tarzi: 'Haḍḍa à la lumière des trois dernières campagnes de fouilles de Tepe-é-Shotor (1974–76)', *Acad. Inscr. & B.-Lett.: C. R. Séances* (1976), pp. 381–410; Eng. trans. by A. A. Motamedi with C. Grissmann as 'Hadda after the last three seasons of excavations at Tepe Shotor (1974–1976)', *Afghanistan Q.*, xxxii/2 (Sept. 1979), pp. 60–89
W. Ball and J.-C. Gardin: *Archaeological Gazetteer of Afghanistan* (Paris, 1982), no. 404, pp. 116–18
Z. Tarzi: 'Haḍḍa', *Encyclopaedia universalis* (Paris, 1985), pp. 64–6, pl. i–iv
——: *Haḍḍa à la lumière des fouilles afghanes de Tapa-é-Shotor et Tapa-é-Top-é-Kalan* (diss., U. Strasbourg II, 1991)
E. ERRINGTON

Haddad, Tell. *See under* HAMRIN REGION.

Haddon, Robert (Joseph) (*b* London, 25 Feb 1866; *d* Melbourne, 16 May 1929). Australian architect, theorist and writer of English birth. He trained as an architect in London from 1881 and then worked in various architectural offices there. He emigrated to Australia in 1889 and worked in various states before settling in Melbourne in 1899. He designed a number of offices, residences, churches and other public buildings, often for other architects. Through this work and his teachings and writings, he influenced many Australian architects by his strong principles of originality and simplicity in design, harmony and balance in composition, and national sentiment. These principles were closely allied with those of English architects working in the Arts and Crafts Movement; however, his use of nature for inspiration and his relaxation of past rules of composition and decoration also place him within the Art Nouveau movement. Haddon's designs were characterized by plain façades, the careful use of simple ornament and the positioning of elements to produce a distinctive and often delicately balanced composition. Examples of this work include his residence, Anselm (1906), Glenferrie Street, Caulfield; the remodelling of the Fourth Victorian Building Society office (1912), Collins Street, Melbourne, and the Wharf Labourers' building (1915–16; destr.; see *Building*, 11 Nov 1916, p. 55), Flinders Street, Melbourne; and the design of the Swinburne Arts School (1917), Hawthorn. His individualistic approach provoked some hostile criticism, but he was admired as a vocal, dominating figure within his profession.

WRITINGS

'Some Thoughts on Architectural Design', *J. Royal Vict. Inst. Architects* (Nov 1903), pp. 144–51
'Australian Planning and Construction', *Modern Buildings: Their Planning, Construction and Equipment*, ed. G. A. T. Middleton, v (London, 1905–6), pp. 144–97
Australian Architecture: A Technical Manual (Melbourne, 1908)

BIBLIOGRAPHY

R. Hunter: *Robert Joseph Haddon: Architect, 1866–1929* (BArch thesis, U. Melbourne, 1981)
ROSLYN F. COLEMAN

Haden, Sir (Francis) Seymour (*b* London, 16 Sept 1818; *d* Bramdean, Hants, 1 June 1910). English surgeon, etcher and collector. In 1838 he completed his medical studies at the Sorbonne in Paris, where he attended a government art training school and learnt to draw and etch. After travelling in Italy and Switzerland in 1844, he took over his late father's London practice. In 1845 he began to study and collect etchings, becoming a notable Rembrandt specialist. In 1847 he married Deborah Whistler, half-sister of James McNeill Whistler. Haden began to etch seriously in 1858 and a close collaboration with Whistler developed. In 1864 the Paris critic Philippe Burty lauded Haden in an article in the *Gazette des Beaux-Arts* and in 1866 published a portfolio of his landscape etchings, *Etudes à l'eau forte*, which brought international acclaim. Whistler's jealousy of Haden led to a fight in a Paris café in 1867; they never spoke again. Haden's finest plates include such landscape subjects as *Fulham* (Harrington, no. 19) and the *Towing Path* (Harrington, no. 76). He continued to etch intermittently in his later years, but with less vigour. Assuming the role of leader of the British Etching Revival (*see* ETCHING, fig. 6), he founded the Royal Society of Painter–Etchers and Engravers in 1880. He campaigned relentlessly on behalf of etching as a medium of creative artistic expression while railing against reproductive engraving. Haden retired in 1887 and began to sell his superb print collection. His porcelain collection had already been sold (London, Christie's, 28 April 1882). He was knighted in 1894 for his contribution to art.

WRITINGS

Catalogue of the Etched Work of Rembrandt (exh. cat., London, Burlington F.A. Club, 1877)
About Etching (London, 1879)
'Mr Seymour Haden on Etching', *Mag. A.*, ii (1879), pp. 188–91, 221–4, 262–4
The Relative Claims of Etching and Engraving to Rank as Fine Arts, and to Be Presented as such in the Royal Academy of Arts (London, 1890)

BIBLIOGRAPHY

P. Burty: 'L'Oeuvre de M. Francis Seymour Haden', *Gaz. B.-A.*, xvii (1864), no. 3, pp. 271–87; no. 4, pp. 356–66
H. N. Harrington: *The Engraved Work of Sir Francis Seymour Haden* (Liverpool, 1910)
F. Lugt: *Marques* (1921), pp. 216–17, no. 1227
M. C. Salaman: *The Etchings of Sir Francis Seymour Haden PRE* (London, 1923)
J. Laver: 'Seymour Haden and the Old Etching Club', *Bkman's J. & Pr. Colr*, x (1924), pp. 87–91
R. S. Schneiderman: *A Catalogue Raisonné of the Prints of Sir Francis Seymour Haden* (London, 1983)

KATHARINE A. LOCHNAN

Hadëri, Shaban (*b* Palavli, Sarandë, 28 March 1930). Albanian sculptor. He studied sculpture at the Jordan Misja Arts Lyceum in Tiranë (1946–50) and at the Academy of Fine Arts in Leningrad (now St Petersburg; 1953–8). He later taught monumental sculpture at the Higher Institute of Art in Tiranë. Hadëri quickly established himself as a Socialist Realist sculptor specializing in dramatic and narrative figure compositions, for example *Friends* (cement, 1958; Tiranë, A.G.). Inspired mainly by the events of World War II, he aimed at symbolic representations of the heroism of the partisans, as in the monument to the *Heroes of Vig* (bronze, 4.90 m, 1984; Shkodër). Characteristic of Hadëri's figure sculpture is the emphasis on movement and gesture, and the deformation of detail in order to increase psychological tension. When treating individual historical figures, such as *Isa Boletini* (bronze, 4.8 m, 1986; Shkodër), Hadëri modelled the subject more naturalistically. He collaborated with Kristaq Rama and Muntaz Dhrami on numerous monumental sculptures erected in several cities in Albania.

BIBLIOGRAPHY

Përmendore të Heroizmit Shqiptar [Monuments of Albanian heroism: the catalogue of Albanian sculpture] (Tiranë, 1973), pls 30, 46, 59, 62, 76, 84, 133
K. Buza: 'Monumenti Heronjtë e Vigut' [The monument to the heroes of Vig], *Nëntori* (1984), no. 4, pp. 41–2

SULEJMAN DASHI

Hadfield, George (*b* Livorno, Italy, *c.* 1763–4; *d* Washington, DC, 5 Feb 1826). American architect of English origin. After studying architecture with James Wyatt in London, he received the first travelling scholarship in architecture from the Royal Academy (1790). He was, however, frustrated with his progress professionally. On the recommendation of the painter John Trumbull, then serving as Secretary to the American Minister to Great Britain, Hadfield was appointed superintendent of construction of William Thornton's Capitol in Washington, DC. In 1795 he emigrated to the USA. While overseeing construction of the Capitol, Hadfield established a practice in Washington, in 1796 designing the first US Treasury building (destr.), the Ionic order of which was based on that of the Erechtheion, Athens. Hadfield thus shares with Benjamin Henry Latrobe the honour of bringing a true Greek Revival to the USA. Hadfield's boldest Greek Revival design was the emphatic portico he added to the Custis-Lee Mansion (1817–20) in Arlington, VA; the six massive unfluted Doric columns are modelled on those at Paestum. His most important extant buildings show his command of the Greek Revival idiom and include his Ionic Washington City Hall, with its grand Ionic portico (1820–26; now District of Columbia Court House), and his round peripteral mausoleum for John Peter Van Ness in the Oak Hill Cemetery, Georgetown, Washington (1826).

BIBLIOGRAPHY

DAB; *Macmillan Enc. Architects*
H. F. Cunningham: 'The Old City Hall, Washington, DC', *Archit. Rec.*, xxxvii (March 1915), pp. 268–73
G. S. Hunsberger: 'The Architectural Career of George Hadfield', *Columbia Hist. Soc. Rec.*, ci–cii (1955), pp. 46–65
D. D. Reiff: *Washington Architecture, 1791–1861: Problems in Development* (Washington, DC, 1971)
J. M. Goode: *Capitol Losses: A Cultural History of Washington's Destroyed Buildings* (Washington, DC, 1979)

LELAND M. ROTH

Hadid, Zaha (*b* Baghdad, 31 Oct 1950). British architect, designer and teacher, of Iraqi birth. She studied at the Architectural Association, London, from 1972 to 1977 and then joined the Office for Metropolitan Architecture founded by Rem Koolhaas, one of her teachers; there she worked on the Dutch Parliament Building extension (1978), The Hague. In 1979 she opened her own practice in London, designing a flat in Eaton Place that won a gold medal from *Architectural Design* in 1982. She also began teaching at the Architectural Association (1980–87). During the 1980s she entered several architectural competitions, winning those for the Hong Kong Peak (1983), the Kurfürstendamm (1986), Berlin, and for an art and media centre in Düsseldorf (1989). She also designed furniture and interiors (1985) for Bitar, London, and interiors (1990) for the Monsoon Restaurant, Sapporo, Japan. Her work seeks to develop the traditions of Modernism; it is inspired by Cubism, Futurism and Constructivism, but perhaps most profoundly by the Suprematism of Kazimir Malevich: she believed that the possibilities inherent in the work of such figures as Malevich had only begun to be realized. Sometimes described as 'Neo-Suprematist' and as resembling spaceships, her designs are typified by fragmented convex geometrical forms that engage and define the space around them, incorporating a Futurist sense of dynamic movement. Many of her ideas were executed as large oil paintings (e.g. *Night and Day*, *c.* 1985), an urban landscape where space seems to be folding back over itself. While such works often contain an element of fantasy, Hadid insisted on the buildability of her projects, an assessment confirmed by her engineering consultants. Nevertheless few of her major designs of the 1980s were built. Her first significant constructed work was the Vitra fire station (1989–93) at Weil am Rhein, Germany, which has been described as having the appearance of 'an exploding set of parallelograms' (Winter, 1993), containing the sharp angles of her previous designs and including large expanses of glass. From a distance its roof line resembles the wings of a bird; the interior reflects the tension between space and form familiar in her unexecuted designs. Hadid continued to teach in universities around the world, including Harvard University, Cambridge, MA, where she held the Kenzō Tange Chair at the Graduate School of Design. In 1994 she won the important Cardiff Bay Opera House competition.

BIBLIOGRAPHY

D. Dietsch: 'Three Projects by Zaha Hadid, Architect', *Archit. Rec.*, clxxv/7 (1987), pp. 118–29
——: 'A Room of one's Own', *Archit. Rec.*, clxxv/11 (1987), pp. 84–6
P. Patton: 'Zaha Hadid Builds a Building', *NY Times Mag.* (16 May 1993), pp. 32–3
J. Winter: 'Provocative Pyrotechnics', *Archit. Rev.* [London], cxciii/1156 (1993), pp. 44–6
D. Matheou and P. Finch: 'Let's Make an Opera House', *Architects' J.*, cc/11 (1994), pp. 20–21

WALTER SMITH

Haditha region. Area in Iraq lying *c.* 210 km north-west of Baghdad and consisting of a narrow strip of land along both banks of the Euphrates River, running for some 90 km upstream from the town of Haditha (Arab. al-Hadītha, Hadīthat al-Furat). It contains a concentration of approximately 34 archaeological sites predominantly from the first half of the 2nd millennium BC (Isin-Larsa and Old Babylonian periods) and the first half of the 1st millennium BC (Neo-Assyrian period). The region has been extensively investigated as part of the Haditha Dam (renamed the Qadisiya Dam) Salvage Project. Finds are in Baghdad (Iraq Mus.).

The major settlement of the Old Babylonian period was at Khirbet ed-Diniyeh, the ancient name of which, known from texts discovered at the site, was Haradum. This town provides one of the earliest known examples in Mesopotamia of a settlement laid out on a regular plan. It was a fortified square, each side 150 m long. Streets, houses and artisans' workshops were laid out in a grid pattern. The principal gate was in the western wall, and from there the main street led to a central square. On the north side of this was the mayor's house and on the south side a small temple with an entrance protected by two large terracotta lions, painted in red, black and white. The private houses consisted of rooms around a central courtyard, and in these were found private archives of economic texts and letters, which revealed the history of the town. Haradum was a merchant colony founded in the 18th century BC to facilitate trade along the Euphrates from Syria to Babylonia.

At 'Usiyeh, a large and unusual subterranean grave of the earlier part of the 2nd millennium BC was excavated. Five rooms, built and roofed over with large stone slabs, had been constructed below ground. In these were found fifteen cylinder seals, several thousand shell rings, twenty haematite weights (some in the shape of frogs) and a human face carved in ivory. Above ground, the approach to the tomb was dominated by a staircase flanked by life-size terracotta lions. Unusual burial practices of the same period were also attested at Shuweimiyeh, a large cemetery where about 200 graves were excavated. Eleven of these had a circular perimeter wall of stone or mud-brick (*c.* 11 m in diameter) that enclosed a rectangular mud-brick tomb with a corbelled roof. This form of grave architecture is known only in the Haditha region.

In the Neo-Assyrian period a series of heavily fortified sites, located mostly on the east bank of the river and on islands in mid-stream, dominated this stretch of the Euphrates. The most complex defensive system, three walls and a ditch, was found at Sur Jur'eh. The outer wall (with sides *c.* 750 m long) was built of packed clay and had a series of single rooms constructed along the inner face. The middle defensive wall (enclosing an area 300×300 m) was an earth rampart with a deep ditch in front; there was a small fort in the north-east angle. The inner wall of mud-brick enclosed the administrative buildings. An elaborate system of pipes, drains and rock-cut cisterns ensured an adequate water supply in times of siege.

Opposite Sur Jur'eh on the west bank of the river was the small fort of Glei'eh, which was protected by two defensive walls, built of limestone rubble, and a ditch. Further fortifications were found up-river: Bijan Island was artificially extended in this period and surrounded by a stone wall (6 m wide) that protected the fortress and harbour area; Telbis Island was similarly fortified; Sur Telbis, opposite, was surrounded by a stone defensive wall, protecting a fortified palace; and remains of monumental buildings were also found on 'Ana Island.

These fortifications are a prime source of information on the military architecture of the Neo-Assyrian period. Texts and inscriptions suggest that they were constructed in the 8th century BC by the local dynasty of Kudurru. These rulers acted as local but independent governors within the greater orbit of the Assyrian empire. The defences were required to protect their control over trade flowing into Babylonia down the Euphrates. Many of these sites were heavily denuded, and there are few outstanding finds. Some fragments of stone reliefs were found on 'Ana Island; they depict such scenes as horsemen riding over the bodies of the defeated enemy, a scribe writing on a clay tablet and the local governor at worship. These themes and the linear style of the sculpture are Neo-Assyrian in inspiration. At Khirbet ed-Diniyeh a grave of Middle/Neo-Assyrian date yielded a rich collection of grave goods, including weaponry, a bronze goblet and a superb bronze rhyton with a bull's head.

BIBLIOGRAPHY

'Excavations in Iraq, 1979–80', *Iraq*, xliii (1981), pp. 167–98
'Excavations in Iraq, 1981–2', *Iraq*, xlv (1983), pp. 199–224
'Ausgrabungen und Geländebegehungen', *Archv Orientforsch.*, xxix–xxx (1983–4), pp. 207–13
H. Fujii and others: 'Preliminary Report on the Excavations at Area A and Area B of 'Usiyeh', *Al-Rāfidān*, v–vi (1984–5), pp. 111–50

R. G. KILLICK

Hadji Boškov, Petar (*b* Skopje, 1 June 1928). Macedonian sculptor. He graduated from the Academy of Fine Arts in Ljubljana in 1953 as a disciple of the sculptors Boris Kalin (1905–75) and Zdenko Kalin (*b* 1911). On his return to Skopje he began to exhibit sculptures, prints and drawings conceived according to his mentors' poetic interpretation of French Expressionist sculpture. By the end of the 1950s he was working on abstract organic forms, inspired by Hans Arp and Henry Moore. In 1960, after a two-year stay in London, he joined the group Mugri in Skopje and started his series of *Masks* (1961–3), made of welded scrap-metal sheets. From the mid-1960s the influence of Lynn Chadwick and Kenneth Armitage was superseded by that of MINIMALISM. During the 1970s Hadji Boškov sculpted the granite monument to *Kliment Ohridski* in Skopje (1972) and the monument to the *Fallen Combatants* (1977) in Ravne na Koroškem in Slovenia. In this period he produced tall, mineral-like objects in polished metal, as well as massive clay blocks with richly faceted planes glazed in vivid colours. From 1980 to 1993 he was a professor at the Academy of Fine Arts in Skopje.

BIBLIOGRAPHY

Petar Hadji Boškov (exh. cat. by S. Abadjieva Dimitrova, Skopje, Mus. Contemp. A., 1989) [with Eng. summary]
V. Veličkovski: *Sovremena makedonska skulptura* [Contemporary Macedonian sculpture] (Skopje, 1989), pp. 44–51 [with Fr. summary]

BOJAN IVANOV

Hadjimichail, Theophilos. *See* THEOPHILOS.

Hadrian [Publius Aelius Hadrianus], Emperor (*b* Italica, Spain, 24 Jan AD 76; *reg* 117–38; *d* Baiae, 10 July AD 138). Roman emperor and patron. After the death in Spain of his father, he was taken to Rome to be brought up by his grandfather's cousin, the future emperor Trajan, under whose patronage his career prospered. He gained his first military experience in AD 95 under Domitian, and during Trajan's second Dacian campaign (AD 105–6) he commanded a legion. To strengthen his ties to the imperial family, he was married in AD 100 to Vibia Sabina, a niece of Trajan's wife, Plotina. He became consul for the first time in AD 108, was governor of Syria *c.* AD 114 and accompanied Trajan on his Parthian expedition (AD 113–17). The story that Hadrian had been adopted by Trajan on his deathbed was said to have been invented by Plotina, but on his succession Hadrian swiftly consolidated his position by executing four of his most resolute opponents, putting on magnificent displays, distributing largesse and cancelling debts. He skilfully overhauled the imperial bureaucracy, creating a new civil service staffed by Roman knights to implement legal and financial reforms. Throughout his reign he travelled widely, reorganizing the administration of the provinces on the basis of first-hand experience. On his accession, the Roman Empire was at its greatest extent, but to create a safer frontier he abandoned the recently annexed territories beyond the Tigris and Euphrates and redefined the boundaries of other provinces, establishing strong lines of fortifications in Germany, Africa and northern Britain.

Hadrian was an accomplished writer and a great patron of literature and the arts. His reign is often viewed as a period of 'Classical revival', and Hadrian himself was undoubtedly a philhellene. However, Hadrianic sculpture (*see* ROME, ANCIENT, §IV, 2(vi)) did not simply mimic Greek prototypes. Portraits of the Emperor (*see* ROME, ANCIENT, fig. 77) and his wife Sabina projected an image of the Imperial family and established the pattern for depictions of later rulers: they transformed the style of Roman sculpture, creating a taste for fluid forms and ornately curled beards and hair which reached its apogee under the Antonines. In contrast, Hadrian's notorious liaison with Antinous led to the erection of classicizing statues of the youth throughout the Empire. During his official travels Hadrian added new quarters and fine monuments to existing cities and founded several new ones, including Aelia Capitolina, where his attempts to impose Greco-Roman culture caused a serious Jewish revolt (AD 132–5). In Italy he built himself the grandiose villa complex at Tivoli (*see* TIVOLI, §2 and ROME, ANCIENT, fig. 32) with its innovative use of space, and erected or transformed many buildings in Rome itself, including the Pantheon (*see* ROME, §V, 8). His building schemes established a trend towards greater monumentality, though his infelicitous design for the gigantic Greek-style Doric Temple of Venus and Rome was criticized by Trajan's old architect Apollodoros, whom the Emperor thereupon executed in a fit of pique. Hadrian also designed his own elaborate mausoleum, now the Castel Sant'Angelo (*see* ROME, §V, 9 and MAUSOLEUM, fig. 1), where he was eventually buried by his adopted heir Antoninus Pius. Although personality changes had made him unpopular in his last years, Hadrian left behind him a strong, prosperous and well-administered Empire.

BIBLIOGRAPHY

B. W. Henderson: *Life and Principate of the Emperor Hadrian* (London, 1923)
R. Syme: *Tacitus*, 2 vols (Oxford, 1958)
H. W. Benario: *A Commentary on the 'Vita Hadriani' in the 'Historia Augusta'* (Chico, CA, 1980) [includes Lat. text]

J. M. C. BOWSHER

Hadrian's Wall. Roman defensive wall extending 50 km through Northumberland and Cumbria, England, from the Tyne estuary to the Solway. It was built in AD 122–8 to protect the northern frontier of Britain by the three legions of the province's garrison, following a visit from Hadrian (*reg* 117–38). Originally the wall was to be of mortared masonry, about 4.5 m high and 3 m wide, as far west as the River Irthing. From there, where limestone for the mortar was no longer available locally, the wall was to be made of turf. It had a ditch in front, gates through it at intervals of approximately one Roman mile (1.5 km) with small fortified enclosures (mile-castles) behind them to house the patrol guard and two watch-towers (turrets) at intervals of one third of the distance between each mile-castle. Initially the base garrison of auxiliary troops (raised from the provincials, as distinct from the legions of Roman citizen status) remained in forts already existing to the south. Tactically, the wall was a barrier rather than a work to be manned defensively. The gateways allowed the passage of troops for operations to the north and were points where civilian traffic between north and south could be controlled.

The scheme was modified while under construction. The width was reduced to 2.4 m. New forts for the garrison were built across the line of the wall, spaced about 8 km apart. South of the wall, the Vallum, a ditch 6 m wide with banks on both sides and causeways leading across it to the forts, demarcated the military zone. In *c.* 138, while the turf sector was being rebuilt in stone, the wall was abandoned when the frontier was moved north to the Antonine Wall (a turf wall approximately 47 km long) between the Firth of Forth and the Firth of Clyde in Scotland, built under Antoninus Pius (*reg* AD 138–61). After it had been rebuilt *c.* 163, Hadrian's Wall was reoccupied and remained the basis of Britain's northern defences for the rest of the Roman period.

This permanent establishment led to the growth of civilian townships of simple houses outside the fort walls, where temples and bathhouses were situated. The forts, for regiments nominally of 500 or 1000 men, were laid out in a regular manner, with the headquarters building in the centre at the intersection of the two main streets, the commander's house next to it and stores buildings and workshops nearby. There were between six and ten barrack blocks, depending on the size of the unit. The forts at Chester, Housesteads (see fig.), Vindolanda and Corbridge (a legionary stores base a few km south of the wall) are the most fully excavated and displayed. Their site museums and those at Newcastle upon Tyne (U. Newcastle upon Tyne, Mus. Ant.) and Carlisle (Carlisle, Mus. & A.G.) exhibit the many finds, including numerous inscriptions and sculpture (not all of great finesse), which provide a variety of evidence for Roman frontier life, its religious observances and its local versions of Mediterranean urban society.

BIBLIOGRAPHY

D. J. Breeze and B. Dobson: *Hadrian's Wall* (London, 1976, rev. 1987)
E. J. Phillips: 'Corbridge, Hadrian's Wall East of the North Tyne' (Oxford, 1977), I/i of *Great Britain*, Corpus signorum imperii romani (Oxford, 1963–)
J. C. Coulston and E. J. Phillips: 'Hadrian's Wall West of the North Tyne and Carlisle' (London, 1988), VI/i of *Great Britain*, Corpus signorum imperii romani (Oxford, 1963–)

T. F. C. BLAGG

Hadrumetum. *See* SOUSSE.

Haecht, Tobias van. *See* VERHAECHT, TOBIAS.

Haecht, Willem van, II (*b* Antwerp, 1593; *d* Antwerp, 12 July 1637). Flemish painter. He was the son of the

Hadrian's Wall, Housesteads fort from the air, looking north, *c.* AD 122

landscape painter TOBIAS VERHAECHT, the first teacher of Rubens. Willem grew up in a cultivated milieu of art and humanism and was taught to paint by his father. In 1615 he went to Paris, where he stayed until 1619; thereafter he travelled to Italy and in 1626–7 returned to Antwerp, where he became a master in the city's Guild of St Luke. By 1628 he was employed by the patron, collector and amateur CORNELIS VAN DER GEEST as curator of his collection, a post he held until his death.

Willem van Haecht is regarded as one of the earliest and most outstanding painters of *Kunstkammern*, a genre that arose in the first decades of the 17th century in Antwerp (*see* CABINET PICTURE, §2). His signed and dated *Picture Gallery of Cornelis van de Geest* (1628; Antwerp, Rubenshuis; *see* COLLECTING, fig. 1) is a fine example of the type. The painting shows the visit of the Archdukes Albert and Isabella to van der Geest's picture cabinet some 13 years earlier, between 15 and 27 August 1615. It is not only a key work in the artist's small oeuvre but also of great documentary value, since it depicts one of the greatest art collections ever assembled in Antwerp as well as many contemporary connoisseurs and collectors. Other important paintings by van Haecht are his *Alexander the Great Visiting the Studio of Apelles* (1628; The Hague, Mauritshuis; *see* DISPLAY OF ART, fig. 4) and the *Salon of Archduchess Isabella* (Kent, Hawkhurst, Hardcastle priv. col.; *see* Speth-Holterhoff, 1957, pl. 39), with the Archduchess in a *Kunstkammer* in her favourite residence at Tervuren. While van Haecht's paintings are more idealized than accurate in their composition, they are characterized by their sharp powers of observation, particularly of contemporary interiors and the assembled art objects; they contain recognizable portraits and a good sense for realistic detail, with the figures completely integrated into the surroundings.

BIBLIOGRAPHY

L. Van Puyvelde: 'Willem van Haecht en zijn *Galerij van Cornelis van der Geest*', *Belg. Tijdschr. Oudhdknd. & Kstgesch.*, xxiv/3–4 (1955), pp. 159–63
J. S. Held: '*Artis pictoriae amator*: An Antwerp Art Patron and his Collection', *Gaz. B.-A.*, n. s. 5, i (1957), pp. 53–84
S. Speth-Holterhoff: *Les Peintres de cabinets d'amateurs au XVIIe siècle* (Paris and Brussels, 1957), pp. 98–104

——: 'Trois amateurs d'art flamands au XVIIe siècle (Francois Francken II le jeune, Guillaume van Haecht, Gonzales Coques)', *Belg. Tijdschr. Oudhdknd. & Kstgesch.*, xxvii/1–4 (1958), pp. 45–62

F. Baudoin: 'De "constkamer" van Cornelis van der Geest geschildered door Willem van Haecht', *Antwerpen*, xv/4 (1969), pp. 158–73

CHRISTINE VAN MULDERS

Haecken, Joseph van. *See* AKEN, JOSEPH VAN.

Haefeli, Max Ernst (*b* Zurich, 25 Jan 1901; *d* Herrliberg, nr Zurich, 17 June 1976). Swiss architect, furniture designer and writer. He studied architecture (1919–23) at the Eidgenössische Technische Hochschule, Zurich, under Karl Moser; one of his fellow students was Rudolf Steiger, his future partner. His student designs show an interest in the formal idiom of Expressionism. After graduating he worked for Otto Bartning in Berlin before returning to Zurich in 1924 to enter the practice of his father, Max Haefeli (1869–1941), and Otto Pfleghard (*b* 1869). In 1925 he set up on his own and acted until 1927 as Director of the Kollektivgruppe Schweizer Architekten zur Beteiligung an der Werkbundausstellung in Stuttgart, designing furniture and fittings for some of the dwellings on the Weissenhofseidlung (1927), the Deutscher Werkbund's show housing estate in Stuttgart. His work was by this time thoroughly Modernist, and when CIAM was formed at La Sarraz in 1928 he was a founder-member (*see* CIAM, fig. 1).

Haefeli's new approach to design is apparent in the houses he designed (1927–8) at Rottach, Zurich, which are among the earliest examples of Neues Bauen in Switzerland. With his usual concern for adaptation to the existing urban context, he adopted a staggered arrangement of three south-west-facing units. The accommodation is on four levels, with living-rooms unconventionally placed above sleeping areas. Careful functional planning makes the interiors look spacious, although all the living, sleeping and service areas are fitted into an extremely limited space. Priority is given to the need for light, air and sunshine, achieved by means of roof terraces, balconies and an open basement storey. The use of modern materials and fittings, including some prefabricated elements, added to the progressive nature of this development.

From 1928 to 1931 Haefeli was on the planning team of the Zürcher Werkbund's development at Neubühl in Zurich, which established Modernist ideas of housing estate layout and design in Switzerland. He also provided appropriately modern, functional, aesthetically satisfying and often subtle furniture designs, which were produced on an industrial scale. Alongside his practical activity as a designer, Haefeli also wrote and lectured on the theoretical dimension of his work, focusing mainly on furniture and industrial design. In 1935, for example, he set out his ideas on the theme of bathing in the home in an exhibition, *Das Bad von gestern zu heute*, held at the Kunstgewerbemuseum, Zurich. The design of public bathing facilities was also an important part of his work. The Allenmoos Bad (1936–9), Zurich, marked an entirely new departure in the design of open-air swimming-baths in Switzerland. The architecture is totally integrated with the park-like landscaping, and the mushroom-shaped pillars create a motif that is both structurally and visually important.

Haefeli's early work adopted the International style but later designs pay more heed to regional context and the use of local materials. They also manifest a more sculptural quality; detailing becomes a specific design preoccupation and repeating motifs a characteristic feature. This specifically Swiss interpretation of Modernism found its definitive formulation in Haefeli's work with Werner Moser (*see* MOSER(ii), (3)) and RUDOLF STEIGER in the partnership they formed in 1937 to build the Kongresshaus (1937–9), General-Guisan-Quai, Zurich, for the Landesausstellung of 1939 (for illustration *see* STEIGER, RUDOLF). Another large project carried out by the firm was the Kantonsspital (1942–51), Zurich. Haefeli was responsible for the treatment of the exteriors and all the interiors; he was particularly successful in freeing the wards of their usually sterile and unwelcoming atmosphere. In the 1950s and 1960s most of his commissions were for commercial buildings, for example the office block Zur Palme (1959–64) and the Bally shoe store (1966–8), both on important sites in the centre of Zurich. He retired from practice in 1975.

WRITINGS
'Die neue Spitaltoilette', *Werk*, xxxiii/5 (1946), pp. 163–7
'Poliklinik des neuen Kantonsspitals, Zürich', *Werk*, xxxiii/11 (1946), pp. 368–80
'Formgebung sanitärer Apparate', *Werk*, xlvii/11 (1960), pp. 400–03

BIBLIOGRAPHY
P. Meyer: *Moderne Schweizer Wohnhäuser* (Zurich, 1928)
M. Bill: *Moderne Schweizer Architektur* (Basle, 1944)
H. Volkart: *Schweizer Architektur, 1930–1940* (Ravensburg, 1951)
'Haefeli, Moser, Steiger', *Archithèse*, 2 (1980) [whole issue]

FRIEDERIKE MEHLAU-WIEBKING

Haegang. *See* KIM KYU-JIN.

Haeghen, Jan-Baptiste van der (*b* Brussels, 1688; *d* Brussels, 1738 or 1740). Flemish sculptor. He is credited with making statues for the high altar of the cathedral of SS Michel et Gudule in Brussels (untraced) and also with making the sculptures of animals that decorate the staircase of the cathedral's pulpit, itself the work (1708) of Henricus-Franciscus Verbrugghen. Van der Haeghen's *St Joseph and the Infant Jesus* and *St James the Greater* (1723–4) are preserved at the church of Notre-Dame de Bon Secours, Brussels. He also worked (1728–30) at the Onze Lieve Vrouwekerk of the Premonstratensian abbey of Ninove, where he made the high altar and two side altars, three statues of saints, the eight high-relief sculptures for the communion bench and the decoration for the organ case. In 1734 he made, for the Parc de Bruxelles in Brussels, the only two secular statues that are known in his work: *Thetis* (destr. 1830) and *Leda* (*in situ*).

Van der Haeghen's works belong to the current in early 18th-century sculpture that successfully reconciled classical beauty and Baroque power. The restrained poses, the elegance of the figures and the suggestion of inward feeling and of calm and gentleness that they convey, underline the classical ideal; while the Baroque element is marked by the dynamism of the compositions and by the treatment of drapery, with a lively play of light and shade.

BIBLIOGRAPHY
Thieme–Becker
Trésors d'art des églises de Bruxelles (exh. cat., ed. D. Coekelberghs and P. Loze: Brussels, Notre-Dame de la Chapelle, 1979); also in *An. Soc. Royale Archéol. Bruxelles*, lvi (1979), pp. 175–6

DOMINIQUE VAUTIER

Haelwegh, Albert (*b* ?Amsterdam or Deventer, *c.* 1600; *d* Copenhagen, 28 Aug 1673). Danish engraver and etcher, presumably of Dutch origin. Due to the occurrence of his surname in the northern Netherlands and to stylistic parallels between his work and that of the Haarlem engraver Jonas Suyderhoef, it is assumed that Haelwegh was Dutch and trained in the Netherlands. Further evidence for this may lie in his combined use of etching and engraving, the painterly style of his prints and the way they are bordered. Moreover, he contributed *December* (Sthyr, no. 9) to a print series of the *Months* after Joachim von Sandrart, engraved mainly by Dutch artists.

Haelwegh's earliest prints date from 1643–4 and were made in Denmark, where he produced several brilliant portraits of the royal family, for example *Christian IV* (1645; s 6) after Karel van Mander III, before his official appointment in 1647 and 1648. Haelwegh's painterly style was particularly suited to engraving portraits by Karel van Mander III, Abraham Wuchters (his brother-in-law) and, after 1660, Henrich Dittmar (*d* 1677). Suyderhoef's influence is again noticeable in the series of 17 portraits of members of the Rigsraad (Privy Council; s 171–87), made *c.* 1655–9, after paintings by Wuchters. In the 1660s and early 1670s Haelwegh became interested in the portrait engravings of the French artist Robert Nanteuil, evidenced, for instance, in the use of an emphatic, comma-like burin technique in the faces (e.g. *Christian V*, 1670; s 276). Some 290 prints have been attributed to Haelwegh, approximately half of which seem to have been executed by his workshop, particularly the book illustrations; these include the series of Danish kings (Copenhagen, 1646; s 13–116) and the engravings of anatomical studies for a book by Thomas Bartolin (Copenhagen, 6 vols, 1654–61; s 151–67). The quality of impressions of the plates varies.

BIBLIOGRAPHY
Hollstein: *Dut. & Flem.*
J. Sthyr: *Kobberstikkeren Albert Haelwegh* (Copenhagen, 1965) [with bibliog.][s]
CHRISTIAAN SCHUCKMAN

Haenel [Hänel], **Karl Moritz** (*b* Dresden, 27 April 1809; *d* Dresden, 3 Jan 1880). German architect. He studied architecture (1820–28) under Karl August Benjamin Siegel (1757–1832) and Joseph Thürmer (1789–1833) in the Industrie- und Bauschule at the Dresden Kunstakademie. From 1830 he spent his life in the state service of Saxony, becoming Landbaukondukteur (1834) rising ultimately to Oberlandbaumeister (1851). He was especially involved in the rebuilding and enlargement of public buildings in Dresden. His works include the chapel (1839) in the royal vineyard at Wachwitz and the restoration and rebuilding (1847–8) of Schloss Heynitz, near Meissen. The main building of the Forstakademie (also 1847–8) at Tharandt, near Dresden, is built in a restrained Romanesque Revival style. He directed sensitive restorations of a wide range of historic buildings, including the Zwinger (1849–50), adding two single-storey pavilions (1854–7) on the east side, which match the existing buildings; the German Renaissance castles at Döben (1857), near Grimma, and Altrossthal (1858–9), near Dresden, both with additions; the Gothic Schlosskirche (1864–74; jointly with Northoff) at Chemnitz; and, above all, the Late Gothic Albrechtsburg

(1864–*c.* 1870) at Meissen. His own buildings, making free use of the Italian High Renaissance style, include the Tierarzneischule (1859–61), the main building (1861–4) of the old Böhmischer Bahnhof, and the Entbindungsinstitut (1869) in the Seminarstrasse, all in Dresden. Haenel helped to foster an understanding of the architecture of the more recent past. In particular, he exemplifies the attention given to the conservation of monuments in Saxony, a state that showed concern for the buildings of the German Renaissance, and even the Baroque, earlier than the rest of Germany.

BIBLIOGRAPHY
Thieme–Becker
Obituary, *Dt. Bauztg*, xiv (1880), pp. 9–10
Sächsische Herrensitze und Schlösser (Dresden [*c.* 1885])
V. Helas: *Architektur in Dresden, 1800–1900* (Brunswick, 1985), p. 195
VOLKER HELAS

Haentz, Zacharie. *See* HEINCE, ZACHARIE.

Haerdtl, Oswald (*b* Vienna, 17 May 1899; *d* Vienna, 9 Aug 1959). Austrian architect and designer. He studied with Kolo Moser, Oskar Strnad and Josef Frank at the Kunstgewerbeschule in Vienna, graduating in 1922. He then became Josef Hoffmann's assistant at the school and taught architecture and design there until his death in 1959. He also worked for many years in Hoffmann's studio, becoming office manager in 1927, and serving as a joint partner from 1930 to 1939. In 1939 Haerdtl opened his own office, specializing in exhibition buildings and interiors for homes, hotels and restaurants. His early works display the influences of Hoffmann's decorative vocabulary, although he later pursued a stripped modernist style more allied with Neue Sachlichkeit. Among Haerdtl's most important architectural works are a house for two families for the Werkbundausstellung in Vienna in 1932, the Austrian pavilions at the Monza Triennale (1930) and Exposition Universelle in Brussels (1935), and the Historisches Museum der Stadt Wien (1954–9). Haerdtl also designed furniture, glass, lamps, metalwork and fashions for a number of firms, including the Wiener Werkstätte, Deutsche Werkstätten, Bakalowits and Lobmeyr. Although characteristic of the Austrian design of inter-war years, his works display an unusual fusion of elegance, formal inventiveness and simplicity.

BIBLIOGRAPHY
O. Uhl: *Moderne Architektur in Wien von Otto Wagner bis heute* (Vienna, 1966)
Oswald Haerdtl 1899–1959 (exh. cat., ed. J. Spalt; Vienna, Hochsch. Angewandte Kst, 1979)
E. Sekler: *Josef Hoffmann: Das architektonische Werk* (Salzburg, 1982; Eng. trans., 1985; rev. 2/Salzburg, 1986)
A. Gmeiner and G. Pirhofer: *Der österreichische Werkbund* (Vienna, 1985)
CHRISTOPHER LONG

Haes, Carlos de (*b* Brussels, 27 Jan 1826; *d* Madrid, 17 June 1898). Spanish painter of Belgian birth. In 1835 he moved with his parents to Málaga, where he studied under the court portrait painter and miniature painter Luis de la Cruz y Ríos (1776–1853). In 1850 he returned to Belgium and studied with the landscape painter Joseph Quineaux (1822–95). During his studies there and on his travels in France, Germany and Holland, he became acquainted with contemporary Realist trends. He returned to Spain in 1855, becoming a naturalized Spaniard, and the following year he exhibited numerous landscapes at the Exposición Nacional, Madrid, to much acclaim. In 1857 he won the competition for the fourth chair of landscape painting at the Escuela de Bellas Artes in Madrid with *View of the Royal Palace from the Casa de Campo* (1857; Madrid, Real Acad. S Fernando), a work showing characteristics of the Barbizon and Fontainebleau landscape schools. In 1860 he was elected Académico de mérito at the Real Academia de S Fernando in Madrid. By 1861 he was officiating and drawing up the regulations for the landscape competitions for aspiring *pensionnaires*. Consequently *plein-air* works came to be required in place of the previous tradition of submitting historical landscapes executed in the studio, a practice that discouraged the study of nature. De Haes suggested that only final corrections should be made in the studio, an attitude that indicates his timid initiation and acceptance of Realist trends.

In the 1870s de Haes increasingly concentrated on the more rugged landscapes of the Spanish Pyrenees and the Guadarrama mountains of Castile. Henceforth, during numerous journeys in Spain, he captured landscapes ignored by earlier Spanish painters. He used a freer brush, smaller format and painted *en plein air*, as is demonstrated by his many sketches of Mallorca, Elche (e.g. *Palm Trees (Elche)*) and Aragón (e.g. *Sunset (Aragón)*; both Madrid, Casón Buen Retiro). The finished works of these years were very popular and influenced various students, particularly Aureliano Beruete, who joined de Haes on his journeys in 1874. De Haes continued to paint larger format, finished compositions based on *plein-air* studies, among the most famous of which is *Picos de Europa* (1876; Madrid, Casón Buen Retiro; *see* SPAIN, fig. 18). This incorporates theatrical effects of light and crisp descriptive details so as to suggest both the grandeur and sublimity of nature. De Haes was perhaps the most influential landscape artist in Spain in the later 19th century, and his pupils included Beruete, Darío de Regoyos and Agustín Riancho. De Haes bequeathed his paintings to his students, and they were subsequently donated to Spanish museums, the majority now being in the Casón del Buen Retiro, Madrid.

WRITINGS
De la pintura de paisaje antiguo y moderno: Discurso leído 26–II–1860 en la Real Academia de San Fernando (Madrid, 1872)

BIBLIOGRAPHY
M. Ossorio y Bernard: *Galería biográfica de artistas españoles del siglo XIX* (Madrid, 1869, 2/1883/R 1975), pp. 325–6
A. Beruete: 'Carlos de Haes', *Ilus. Esp. & Amer.* (30 June 1888)
B. Pantorba: *El paisaje y los paisajistas españoles* (Madrid, 1943)
C. Cid Priego: *Aportaciones para una monografía del pintor Carlos de Haes* (Lérida, 1955)
F. Calvo Serraller: *Carlos de Haes, pintor belga de paisaje realista en España* (diss., Madrid, U. Complutense, 1971)
Los estudios de paisaje de Carlos de Haes (exh. cat., ed. J. de la Puente; Toledo, Mus.–Pal. Fuensalida, 1971)
M. del Carmen Pena: *Pintura de paisaje e ideología* (Madrid, 1983)
Catálogo de las pinturas del siglo XIX, Madrid, Prado cat. (Madrid, 1985), pp. 90–110
Paisajistas españoles decimónicos: Villaamil, Haes, Beruete, Centro Cultural del Conde Duque (Madrid, 1990)

OSCAR E. VÁZQUEZ

Haese, Günter (*b* Kiel, 18 Feb 1924). German sculptor. After World War II he became a self-taught painter and draughtsman, before attending a private art school in Plön, Holstein (1948–9). The paintings from this period are figurative. When Haese began his studies at the Staatliche Kunstakademie in Düsseldorf (1950–57), he first of all attended Bruno Goller's painting class but soon transferred to Ewald Mataré's sculpture class, joining his master class in 1956. The other students included Joseph Beuys. During his studies he assisted his teacher in public commissions, including doors for the cathedral in Cologne (1947–54).

Stimulated by the appearance of a dismantled clock mechanism, Haese began to form his characteristic language in the early 1960s. As early as 1964 his fragile wire structures were exhibited in a small one-man show at MOMA, New York, including *Rare Type of Cactus* (1963; artist's col.), and in 1966 he was awarded a prize as a West German representative at the Venice Biennale. Thereafter he continued to work on his sculptures with the unchanging precision of the craftsworker. Formally, the beginnings of his works recall the linearity of *Art informel* and bear a slight resemblance to the writing-pictures of Gerhard Hoehme. Haese, however, avoided relying on spontaneous gesture, developing a formal vocabulary based on careful construction. An external and usually stereometric structure is serially filled with slightly varying components made of brass and clockwork parts. Illuminated structures in space cast calculated shadows as graphic, two-dimensional images on the wall. The sculptures stand on delicate wire legs and sway and shake slightly, for example *After the Rain I* (1965; London, Tate). Haese's works appear as interconnected little worlds, and the titles often make references to the universe, but the constructions are never meant figuratively. The forms permit some associations, but these are suggestive rather than direct in a way comparable to the paintings of Paul Klee.

BIBLIOGRAPHY
Günter Haese (exh. cat., Zurich, Marlborough Gal.; Munich, Haus Kst.; 1974)
Günter Haese: Objekte, 1962–1984 (exh. cat., Neuss, Clemens-Sels-Mus., 1984)

EVA MEYER-HERMANN

Haese, Roel d'. *See* D'HAESE, ROEL.

Haffner. Italian family of painters, of Swiss origin. (1) Enrico Giovanni Haffner and (2) Antonio Maria Haffner were renowned *quadraturisti* and fresco painters. They were the sons of a Swiss guard stationed in Bologna. The dynamic, flamboyant quality of their *quadratura* schemes, which they often executed in collaboration, reflected the Genoese Baroque style of the late 17th century and was in sharp contrast with the style of the brothers' Bolognese contemporaries. Opinion appears to credit Enrico with being superior in invention, Antonio Maria with being the better colourist.

(1) Enrico Giovanni Haffner (*b* Bologna, *bapt* 24 Aug 1640; *d* Bologna, 8 Aug 1702). He was trained in the style of Agostino Stanzani Mitelli and followers. After a period of service in the court of Modena in the early 1660s, he joined forces with the painter Domenico Maria Canuti, with whom he executed his finest work, the frescoes in the nave of SS Domenico e Sisto (1674–5), Rome, and the decorations of the vault of the first antechamber on the first floor of the Palazzo Altieri (1675–6), Rome. The *quadratura* of SS Domenico e Sisto constitutes a striking modification of traditional Bolognese schemata, with the conventionally solid surround reduced to an undulant bordure that lends the ensemble a rhythmic quality, liberating rather than constricting the picture field and anticipating the style of the following century. In 1675 Haffner was admitted to the Accademia di S Luca. He moved back to Bologna and there worked with Gian Antonio Burrini and Marcantonio Franceschini, with whom he decorated the ceiling of the Palazzo Ranuzzi (now Pal. Giustizia) with *Fortuna and the Seasons* (1680). His last major work in Bologna was in collaboration with Canuti: frescoes (1677–8) in the library of S Michele in Bosco. In Savona he collaborated with Bartolomeo Guidobono on a vault fresco, *Chariot of the Sun* (*c.* 1680), in the Palazzo Gavotti. Some considerable time later he is known to have gone to Modena, to decorate the main reception hall of the Palazzo Ducale with Franceschini and Luigi Quaini (1643–1717). At an unknown date he moved to join his younger brother, (2) Antonio, in Genoa. They worked together with several noted Genoese painters, decorating palazzi, among them the celebrated Palazzo Rosso.

(2) Antonio Maria Haffner (*b* Bologna, *bapt* 15 Oct 1654; *d* Genoa, 6 July 1732). Brother of (1) Enrico Giovanni Haffner. He studied with Domenico Maria Canuti, his brother's partner in many decorative projects, and travelled with them both to Rome in 1672, afterwards moving to Genoa in 1676. He worked in Liguria and Piedmont for the rest of his life, often for the Order of the Oratorians, and became an honorary brother of that Order in 1704. He collaborated with major artists (e.g. Giovanni Andrea Carlone II, Domenico Piola, Gregorio de' Ferrari), usually as a *quadraturista*, and sometimes in association with Enrico. The work he did with Carlone discloses the influence of his teacher Canuti; otherwise his style was typical of late 17th-century Genoese Baroque.

Thieme–Becker

BIBLIOGRAPHY

R. Soprani: *Vite* (1674); enlarged, ed. C. G. Ratti (1768–9), ii, pp. 345–8 [Antonio Maria]
L. Crespi: *Vite de' pittori bolognesi non descritte nella Felsina Pittrice* (Rome, 1769), pp. 171–2
R. Wittkower: *Art and Architecture in Italy, 1600–1750*, Pelican Hist. A. (Harmondsworth, 1958, rev. 1973)
C. Marcenaro: *Gli affreschi del Palazzo Rosso di Genova* (Genoa, 1966), pp. 28–31
P.-E. Schazmann: 'Les Peintres baroques Enrico et Anton-Maria Haffner', *Versailles*, xxxvii (1969), pp. 122–30
E. Feinblatt: 'A Letter by Enrico Haffner', *Burl. Mag.*, cxii (1970), pp. 229–32
R. Roli: *Pittura bolognese, 1650–1800* (Bologna, 1977)
I. Sjöström: *Quadratura: Studies in Italian Ceiling Painting* (Stockholm, 1978), p. 58

E. FEINBLATT

Hafiz Osman [Ḥāfiẓ 'Uthmān ibn 'Alī] (*b* Istanbul, 1642; *d* Istanbul, 1698). Ottoman calligrapher. Son of a muezzin at the Haseki Sultan Mosque, he memorized the Koran at an early age and became known as Hafiz (Arab.: 'he who knows the Koran by heart'). The Ottoman grand vizier Mustafa Pasha encouraged him to study with the dervish 'Ali Mustafa al-Ayyubi (*d* 1668) and then with Nafaszada Sayyid Isma'il. Hafiz Osman attained his degree at the age of 18 and spent most of his life teaching and writing. His pupils ranged from the sultans Mustafa II (*reg* 1695–1703) and Ahmad III (*reg* 1703–30) to poor students for whom he set aside one day a week. Considered the second most important Ottoman calligrapher after ṢEYH HAMDULLAH, Hafiz Osman evolved a simple, pure style of *naskh* based on that of YAQUT AL-MUSTA'SIMI and Hamdullah (*see* ISLAMIC ART, §III, 2(iv)(a)). This style became the model for later calligraphers such as MUSTAFA RAQIM, Mahmud Jalal al-Din (*d* 1829) and MUSTAFA IZZET. Hafiz Osman was also responsible for the development of *dīvānī jalī*, an ornamental script used in the chancelleries for official documents. In addition to transcribing many copies of the Koran (e.g. Istanbul, U. Lib., A. 6549), single pieces and albums of exercises, he was one of the first to pen large calligraphic descriptions of the Prophet Muhammad (Arab. *ḥilya*; e.g. 1691; Dublin, Chester Beatty Lib., MS. 2). He was paralysed three years before his death and was buried in the Koca Mustafa Pasha cemetery.

BIBLIOGRAPHY

D. James: *Islamic Masterpieces of the Chester Beatty Library* (London, 1981), no. 40
H. Lowry: 'Calligraphy: Hüsn-i hat', *Tulips, Arabesques & Turbans: Decorative Arts from the Ottoman Empire*, ed. Y. Petsopoulos (London, 1982), p. 173; no. 174
The Anatolian Civilisations III: Seljuk/Ottoman (exh. cat., 18th Council of Europe exh.; Istanbul, 1983), no. E.309

NABIL SAIDI

Hafsid. Dynasty that ruled in Tunisia and eastern Algeria from 1228 to 1574. Descended from Abu Hafs 'Umar (*d* 1176), a disciple of the founder of the ALMOHAD movement, Abu Zakariya Yahya I (*reg* 1228–49) was governor of the region for the Almohads. He declared his independence in 1237 and expanded his territory as far as Constantine, Annaba, Algiers and Tlemcen, obliging the MARINID dynasty of Morocco to acknowledge his supremacy and engaging in trade and diplomatic relations with Christian governments. His son Abu 'Abdallah (*reg* 1249–77) assumed caliphal titles, and his court was equally celebrated for its culture and international relations. Violent family rivalries, Christian intervention and independence movements, particularly in the cities of the interior, led to a period of decline at the end of the 13th century. Abu'l-'Abbas (*reg* 1370–94) reunified the country, and during the 15th century the Hafsid empire enjoyed its last period of prosperity and expansion. Spain and the Ottoman empire threatened North Africa in the 16th century, and in 1574 Tunis fell to the Ottomans and the last Hafsid sovereign was taken captive to Istanbul.

The first responsibility of the Hafsids was to repair the damage and neglect to the land that had been devastated by the Hilali bedouin in the 11th century, and such religious buildings as the Great Mosque in KAIROUAN were restored (*see* ISLAMIC ART, §II, 6(iv)(c)). The city of Kairouan, the traditional capital, was supplanted by TUNIS, and Hafsid buildings there show a change from Almohad models, as in the kasba of the 13th century, to Andalusian ones, as at the Bardo Palace of the 15th. Abu Zakariya and his widow, the princess 'Atf, introduced the institution of the MADRASA (e.g. Tunis, Shamma'iyya Madrasa, 1249), and similarly the use of dichromatic masonry in the 14th century seems to have been the result of contacts with Egypt. A distinctive feature of Hafsid architecture is a type of capital ultimately derived from Classical acanthus models and used long after the dynasty fell. The cosmopolitan nature of Hafsid society was enriched by Italian, Spanish and French merchants who founded trading establishments (Arab. *funduq*; *see* CARAVANSERAI) and Muslim craftsmen and intellectuals fleeing the Christian reconquest of Spain. Hafsid decorative arts reflect this Hispano-Moresque heritage: ceramics, for example, continue Almohad techniques of moulding and applied decoration, as well as Andalusian techniques of lustre and *cuerda seca*, particularly after the fall of Granada in 1492. Other examples of this heritage can be seen in silks and coffered ceilings. In sum, Hafsid art synthesizes eastern traditions first introduced by the AGHLABID dynasty and western, Spanish ones already used by the ALMORAVID and Almohad rulers.

BIBLIOGRAPHY

R. Brunschvig: *La Berbérie orientale sous les Hafsides: Des Origines à la fin du XVe siècle*, 2 vols (Paris, 1940–47)

G. Marçais: *L'Architecture musulmane d'occident* (Paris, 1954)

J. Revault: *Palais et demeures de Tunis, I (XVIe et XVIIe siècles)* (Paris, 1967)

——: 'Une Résidence Hafside: L''Abdalliya à la Marsa', *Cah. Tunisie*, xix (1971), pp. 53–65

A. Daoulatli: *Tunis sous les Hafsides* (Tunis, 1976)

MARIANNE BARRUCAND

Haftavan Tepe. Site in the Salmās plain just north-west of Lake Urmia (*see* IRAN, ANCIENT, §I, 1) and one of the largest settlement mounds in the Urmia basin of north-western Iran. A high citadel mound and an extensive lower settlement covering about 20 ha were excavated under the direction of Charles Burney between 1968 and 1978 and produced evidence for markedly different styles of pottery and architecture during a long occupation from the mid-3rd millennium BC until the Sasanian period (AD 240–651), but virgin soil was not reached. Finds are in the Archaeological Museum in Tehran.

The widely distributed red and black burnished Early Trans-Caucasian II-III wares (3rd millennium BC) were found, respectively, in conjunction with a mud-brick round house (Haftavan (H) VIII) and a massive, rectangular public building, also of mud-brick, exposed on the citadel (H VII), of which only the basement rooms were preserved. The first half of the 2nd millennium BC marked the period of maximum settlement. Dark-on-light painted pottery of a brief phase (H VIC) was replaced by distinctive Urmia ware (H VIB) with crosshatched triangles in red and black paint on a buff ground and the occasional use of bird motifs; parallels with the TRIALETI barrows of Georgia are apparent in some of the decoration. The architecture of Haftavan VIB is characterized by wooden beams used as reinforcement. The grey wares of the early Iron Age (H V) are generally associated with the Iranian migrations of the second half of the 2nd millennium BC and were found in buildings constructed of stones set in mud.

Although red polished Urartian wares of the 8th century BC were found in debris fallen from upper rooms of the citadel building of Haftavan III, most of the pottery seems to have been local. This building resembles a government centre rather than a fortress, and its burning can plausibly be attributed to either the Cimmerians or Sargon II of Assyria (*reg* 721–705 BC). Comparisons with Hasanlu to the south suggest that Haftavan Tepe did not share in trade between Mesopotamia and the Iranian plateau: its links were largely with the north. The citadel and probably the whole site were abandoned for about two centuries. When rebuilt in early Achaemenid times (H II, 6th–5th century BC) the citadel wall had at least one square projecting tower, constructed of large square mud-bricks, with a dry defensive ditch at the foot of the slope. Small finds included personal ornaments and burial goods such as earrings and a chain pendant (H IV) and miniature glass scent bottles and mirrors of the Sasanian period (H I).

BIBLIOGRAPHY

Iran, viii (1970), pp. 157–71; x (1972), pp. 127–42; xi (1973), pp. 153–72; xiii (1975), pp. 149–64 [preliminary excavation reports by C. A. Burney]

C. A. Burney: 'Haftavan Tepe and Early Settlement Patterns in North-western Iran', *Problems in Economic and Social Archaeology*, ed. G. de G. Sieveking, I. H. Longworth and K. E. Wilson (London, 1976), pp. 97–100

M. Edwards: *Haftavan: Period VI* (1983), i of *Excavations in Azerbaijan (North-western Iran)*, Brit. Archaeol. Rep. Int. Ser., clxxxii (Oxford, 1983–)

C. A. BURNEY

Haft Tepe [Pers. Haft Tappa; anc. Kabnak]. Site of a large city in south-west Iran that was built by the ELAMITES and flourished *c.* 1505–1350 BC. It is located in Khuzistan Province about 10 km south-east of Susa and comprises 14 major mounds covering an area of approximately 1×1.5 km. From 1964, E. O. Negahban carried out 14 seasons of excavation, uncovering widespread Elamite remains. The finds are in the Archaeological Museum, Tehran.

Haft Tepe may have been a religious centre, and an extensive Tomb Temple Complex and two large terraces or platforms, all built of sun-dried and baked brick, have been uncovered in the small excavated part of the site. The temple contains two large rooms, a portico and a large courtyard, in which were found parts of a dedication stele of King Tepti-Ahar, a little-known Elamite contemporary of the Kassite king of Babylonia Kadashman-Enlil I (*reg c.* 1374–1360 BC). Next to the temple are two baked-brick tombs with vaulted roofs; the larger tomb is connected to the temple and contained a number of skeletons, apparently including those of King Tepti-Ahar and his principal wife, while a subsidiary tomb held 23 tightly packed skeletons, possibly of sacrificial victims. The whole Tomb Temple Complex is enclosed by massive walls of sun-dried brick.

East of this temple is the large Terrace Complex I, consisting of a massive central core or terrace surrounded by halls and courtyards, mostly built of sun-dried brick, with baked brick found in a few floors and pavements and natural bitumen coating used in waterways and basins. On the eastern side of the central core is a workshop divided into sections for various crafts; in front of this is a unique double-winged kiln, one side used for firing pottery and the other for smelting metal. A nearby Terrace Complex II has been only partly uncovered.

The pottery vessels of Haft Tepe are for the most part plain, simple in shape, buff-coloured and sometimes decorated with incised or impressed designs. Large numbers of moulded human figurines, both male and female, were also found, always broken and incomplete. There are some finely made stone vessels, stone tools, weight stones

Haft Tepe, male portrait head, possibly of King Tepti-Ahar, clay, almost life-size, *c.* 1505–1350 BC (Tehran, Archaeological Museum)

and bronze tools and weapons. The site also yielded a large number of cylinder seals and seal impressions of the middle of the 2nd millennium BC, including some with features that are unique to Haft Tepe (e.g. a god on a twisted column). Of particular interest are two almost life-size male and female portrait heads of clay (see fig.), a clay mask, mosaic jewellery and two bitumen roundels, all found in the workshop. A very large collection of cuneiform tablets was also discovered, and the inscriptions reflect the political, economic, social and religious activities of the Elamites and their relations with neighbouring countries during the 14th century BC.

BIBLIOGRAPHY
E. O. Negahban: 'Brief Report on the Excavation of Haft Tepe', *Iran*, vii (1969), pp. 175–9
——: *A Guide to the Haft Tepe Excavation and Museum* (Tehran, 1977)
——: 'Architecture of Haft Tepe', *Archäol. Mitt. Iran* (1979), pp. 9–29
——: 'Haft Tepe Roundels: An Example of Middle Elamite Art', *Amer. J. Archaeol.*, lxxxviii/1 (1984), pp. 3–10
——: *Haft Tepe Excavation* (Philadelphia, 1991)
EZAT O. NEGAHBAN

Hagbolt, Jacob (*b* Uerdingen, nr Duisburg, 17 April 1775; *d* Cologne, 13 June 1849). German sculptor, wax modeller, draughtsman and painter. In Cologne he was a pupil of B. C. Hardy, from whom he learnt the art of modelling in wax. He subsequently travelled to northern Germany and the Netherlands, during which time he produced several wax models. In 1802 he settled in Amsterdam. As well as small wax reliefs of portraits in profile, he executed life-size busts. One of his best-known sitters was Louis, King of Holland and brother of Napoleon I, and several plaster casts (e.g. Leiden, Stedel. Mus. Lakenhal) were taken from the sculpture Hagbolt made

of him (Haarlem, Pav. Welgelegen). In Amsterdam Hagbolt exhibited portrait sculptures and tableaux of historical and religious scenes (e.g. *Christ Blessing the Little Children* and *Virgin and Child*, both after paintings by van Dyck). After moving to London, he did numerous busts of such distinguished British contemporaries as the geographer and antiquary *Major James Rennell* (London, Westminster Abbey) and the medallist and wax modeller *William Tassie* (UK, priv. col.). Between 1826 and 1833 he exhibited at the Royal Academy and while in London he also drew and painted. In 1840 he returned to Cologne. His brother Ludwig Hagbolt (1784–1846) was also a wax modeller.

BIBLIOGRAPHY
Thieme–Becker
G. K. Nagler: *Monogrammisten* (1858–1920) [under 'Hagblot']
J. J. Merlo: *Kölnische Künstler* (Cologne, 1895/*R* 1966)
HANNELORE HÄGELE

Hagborg, (Vilhelm Nikolaus) August (*b* Göteborg, 26 May 1852; *d* Paris, 30 April 1921). Swedish painter. He studied at the Konstakademi in Stockholm (1871–5), then went to Paris in the autumn of 1875, where he lived until 1909. He began to exhibit at the Salon as early as 1876 and became one of its most industrious contributors. In 1877 he showed at the Salon his painting *Waiting* (1877; priv. col., see S. Strömbom: *Konstnärsförbundets historia* [History of the Federation of Artists], i (Stockholm, 1945), pl. 35), developed from a study made in Bohuslän on the west coast of Sweden. It shows a young fisherman's wife, her child on her arm, gazing out over the sea and waiting for her husband. This introduced what was to become Hagborg's favourite subject-matter: the fishing community, mostly in Normandy and Brittany. Typical elements of his paintings are young women, depicted in idealized and heroic manner, in theatrical poses, and a realistic background, usually of shallow beaches at ebb tide; in his later works, he painted in more delicate and exquisite, silvery colours.

Hagborg's interest in painting rural life was probably influenced chiefly by the idealized peasant and fishing scenes of Jules Breton and Jules Bastien-Lepage. Eugène Boudin's coastal landscapes with their silvery colours were also an important source of inspiration.

Hagborg's best works are the paintings from his early years in France, for example *Blessing a Fishing Boat* (1881; preparatory studies in Göteborg, Kstmus.) or the large *Churchyard at Trouville* (1882–3; Göteborg, Kstmus.), which shows a fisherman's wife with her little son grieving by her husband's grave. Hagborg was acclaimed by the critics and general public, but the great demand for his paintings resulted in mannered and stereotyped work.

BIBLIOGRAPHY
N. Olsson: 'Hagborg, Vilhelm Nikolaus August', *Svenskt konstnärslexikon* [Encyclopedia of Swedish artists], ii (Malmö, 1953), pp. 352–4
HANS-OLOF BOSTRÖM

Hagedorn, Christian Ludwig von (*b* Hamburg, 14 Feb 1712; *d* Dresden, 25 Jan 1780). German diplomat, theorist, collector and etcher. The brother of the poet Friedrich von Hagedorn (1708–54), from 1735 he served in the Saxon diplomatic service. Travelling through Germany and Austria, he met and corresponded with several artists and art theorists, including Johann Joachim Winckelmann,

J. G. Sulzer and Salomon Gessner. His collection of paintings and drawings—primarily Dutch and German 17th- and 18th-century work, especially landscapes—became famous, and his advice on art matters was widely appreciated. In 1764 he became director of the Saxon art collections and art schools in Dresden.

Hagedorn's *Lettre à un amateur de la peinture avec des éclairissements historiques . . .* (Dresden, 1755), combining a description of his collection with biographies of 18th-century artists, was, according to its author, a continuation of the *Teutsche Academie* by Joachim von Sandrart; it remains an important source for art history. The *Betrachtungen über die Mahlerey* (Leipzig, 1762) and numerous essays that appeared in the *Bibliothek der schönen Wissenschaften und freien Künste* and its successor, the *Neue Bibliothek*, were highly acclaimed as examinations of the theory of art. Under the influence of British theorists, Hagedorn set emotion against rationality as an aesthetic criterion and thus influenced the *Sturm und Drang* movement as well as Romanticism. Although believing that art should be modelled on antiquity and the Old Masters, he also gave northern artists their due place in art history and distinguished between colourists and artists emphasizing line. His amalgamation of history and bourgeois genre painting is symptomatic of an incipient 19th-century bourgeois approach.

Hagedorn's etchings (some of which may be seen in the Kupferstichkabinett, Dresden) are known only from the years 1743–5 and 1764–6.

WRITINGS

Lettre à un amateur de la peinture avec des éclairissements historiques sur un cabinet et les amateurs des tableaux qui les composent (Dresden, 1755/*R* Geneva, 1972)
Betrachtungen über die Mahlerey, 2 vols (Leipzig, 1762)
Briefe über die Kunst von und an Christian Ludwig von Hagedorn (Leipzig, 1797)

BIBLIOGRAPHY

M. Stübel: *Christian Ludwig von Hagedorn: Ein Diplomat und Sammler des 18. Jahrhunderts* (Leipzig, 1912)
W. Waetzold: *Deutsche Kunsthistoriker*, i (Leipzig, 1921), pp. 94–103
C. S. Cremer: *Hagedorns Geschmack: Studien zur Kunstkennerschaft in Deutschland im 18. Jahrhundert* (diss., U. Bonn, 1989)

ANDREA M. KLUXEN

Hageladas. *See* AGELADAS.

Hagemeister, Karl (*b* Werder, 12 March 1848; *d* Werder, 6 Aug 1933). German painter. He studied from 1871 at the Kunstschule in Weimar under Friedrich Preller, who introduced him to the principles of classical landscape painting. In 1873 he began to develop a more modern approach when he met Carl Schuch at the Hintersee, near Berchtesgaden; he immediately became his pupil and later wrote Schuch's biography. Schuch introduced Hagemeister to the Leibl circle (*see* LEIBL, WILHELM). He travelled to the Netherlands and Belgium (1873–4), Italy (1876) and France (1884–5), often accompanying Schuch and, in the early journeys, Wilhelm Trübner. His approach to landscape changed from classical Naturalism to 'pure painting', a more formalist approach in which purely pictorial qualities were given priority over naturalistic representation, as in *Lake Shore* (*c.* 1900; Schweinfurt, Samml. Schäfer). His brushwork became broader, his depiction of objects became increasingly summary, and

his colours lighter and cooler. Absorbing the influence of Japanese art through the interpretations of the French Impressionists, and following trends in international Art Nouveau, Hagemeister developed an individual variant of *Jugendstil*. His pictures were composed in accordance with decorative rather than naturalistic principles and became primarily ornamental, as in *White Poppy* (1881; Hannover, Niedersächs. Landesmus.).

In 1890 Hagemeister settled in Entenfang in the Brandenburg Marches, where he lived quietly in comparative isolation. Apart from a few still-lifes and figure studies, he produced mainly local landscape paintings; since these were painted at very close range they consisted merely of landscape details, which the artist interpreted solely as elements of colour. He also produced marine paintings in the same style from 1907. Following Courbet, he often focused on a single wave breaking, as in *The Wave* (1911; Hannover, Niedersächs. Landesmus.). In taking this new subject, Hagemeister attempted to free himself from the Leibl circle's static approach to landscape painting and give his paintings a dynamic energy.

WRITINGS
Karl Schuch: Leben und Werke (Berlin, 1913)

BIBLIOGRAPHY
Die Münchener Schule, 1850–1914 (exh. cat., Munich, Haus Kst., 1979)
E. Ruhmer: *Der Leibl-Kreis und die Reine Malerei* (Rosenheim, 1984)

EBERHARD RUHMER

Hagen. City in Nordrhein-Westfalen, Germany, on the edge of the Ruhr industrial area, about 20 km south of Dortmund. First mentioned in the 11th century as belonging to the bishops of Cologne, Hagen passed to the Counts of Mark in 1392. Industry was first established in 1661, when metalworkers from Solingen settled in the area, and Hagen, which then had a population of 1200, was given a charter in 1746. Textile manufacture, brought by an influx of new settlers, soon became the main economic activity. During the 18th century several large merchant commission houses evolved, which began to establish an extensive system of trade relations within Germany and abroad. The most important of these was the Harkorten Company, and the Haus Harkorten (1756–7) in the Haspe district, where the German railway pioneer Franz Harkort (1793–1880) was born, is a good example of a residence built in a regional Baroque style. It is a two-storey house set on a raised foundation and topped by a mansard roof and deep pediment. Its walls are hung with slates and pierced by symmetrical rows of white-trimmed windows and elaborately carved doorframes. In 1845 the first metallurgical plant was founded in Haspe, and rapid expansion followed between 1876 and 1929, principally due to large-scale industrialization and the incorporation of a number of surrounding towns and villages.

In the early 20th century Hagen became an important centre of *Jugendstil* art and architecture through the patronage of the influential banker, art critic and collector Karl Ernst Osthaus (1874–1921). In 1902 Osthaus founded the Folkwang Museum for the purpose of displaying his collection of French Impressionist and Post-Impressionist paintings and early works by the German Expressionists. The works were exhibited in a building remodelled in 1902 by HENRY VAN DE VELDE; only the entrance hall survives. In 1922, after Osthaus's death, the contents of the Folkwang Museum were transferred to Essen, and in 1972–4 the much-altered building in Hagen became the Karl Ernst Osthaus Museum, with new collections including 20th-century paintings, sculpture and prints, as well as Meissen and Fürstenberg porcelain. Osthaus's interest in architecture, urban planning and the garden city movement was reflected in the construction of the garden suburb of Hohenhagen east of the city: from 1906 this project, although never completed, involved such architects as Van de Velde, PETER BEHRENS and J. L. MATHIEU LAUWERIKS. Van de Velde designed the two-storey Hohenhof (1907–8), Osthaus's own home, as the centrepiece of the project. It is an important early work by Van de Velde, who took account of local traditions in his choice of colour and materials. Van de Velde also designed the interior, which includes stained glass and paintings by JOHAN THORN PRIKKER, reliefs by Hermann Haller in the entrance hall and a triptych in tile by Matisse in the conservatory. Lauweriks designed a row of houses on the Stirnband, one of which (no. 38) was Thorn Prikker's house and studio during his stay in Hagen from 1910 to 1919. The artists originally invited by Osthaus also worked elsewhere in Hagen. The Eduard Müller Crematorium (1906–7) in Delstern, with its black-and-white geometric panelling inside and out, is one of the most successful *Jugendstil* buildings by Behrens, who also designed Haus Cuno (1908–11) and Haus Goedecke (1910), both in Eppenhausen. *Trade's Homage to the Artist* (1910), the first stained-glass windows done by Thorn Prikker, are in the monumental entrance hall of Hagen's railway station. At the initiative of Osthaus, Richard Riemerschmid designed an estate of textile workers' housing at Bruchstein in 1910. During World War II nearly three-quarters of the city was destroyed, and the old quarter was subsequently rebuilt as a modern shopping and business centre.

BIBLIOGRAPHY

W. Zimmermann and H. Borger, eds: *Nordrhein-Westfalen: Landesteil Nordrhein*, Handbuch der historischen Stätten Deutschlands, iii (Stuttgart, 1963)
Knaurs Kulturführer in Farbe: Deutschland (Munich, 1976); Eng. trans. as *Germany: A Phaidon Cultural Guide* (Oxford, 1985)
W. Timm: *Hagener Chronik: Über 400 Daten zur Geschichte der Stadt Hagen*, Hagener Hefte, ix (Hagen, 1979)
A. Henze and others: *Nordrhein-Westfalen: Kunstdenkmäler und Museen*, Reclams Kstführer, iii (Stuttgart, 1982)

Hagen, William van der [Vander Hagen, Willem] (*b* The Hague, *fl c.* 1720; *d* Ireland, 1745). Dutch painter and designer, active in Ireland. Having worked in England and on the Continent as a topographical painter, in the early 1720s he left England for Ireland, where he soon became the country's first resident professional landscape painter. In October 1722 Dublin's Theatre Royal opened with a production of *Alexander the Great*, which was advertised as having 'lofty scenes entirely new and Painted by Mr Vander Hagen, lately arriv'd from London' (*Harding's Impartial Newsletter*, 29 Sept 1722). In addition to his theatrical designs, he painted views of ports, idealized landscapes and decorative capriccios in country houses. He benefited from the rising prosperity of Irish cities that occurred in the second decade of the 18th century: Edward

Lovett Pearce's Irish Houses of Parliament were begun in Dublin in 1729, and shortly afterwards van der Hagen was commissioned to design tapestries for the House of Lords (now the Bank of Ireland). Only two were executed; they represent historic moments from military victories by William III, the *Defence and Relief of Londonderry* and the *Landing of King William and his Army at Carrickfergus* (both *in situ*). He was greatly patronized by the aristocracy and decorated a number of country houses (e.g. Curraghmore, Co. Waterford; Beaulieu, Co. Louth). In 1736 he was paid £20 by the Corporation of Waterford to paint a *View of Waterford* (Waterford, Town Hall); this bird's-eye view is one of the earliest extensive views of an Irish city.

BIBLIOGRAPHY

Strickland
L. Stockwell: *Dublin Theatres and Theatre Customs, 1637–1820* (Kingsport, TN, 1938)
A. Crookshank and the Knight of Glin: *The Painters of Ireland, c. 1660–1920* (London, 1978), pp. 55–61

FINTAN CULLEN

Hagenauer, Friedrich (*b* Strasbourg, 1490–1500; *d* after 1546). German wood-carver and medallist. He may have been the son of the sculptor Nikolaus Hagenauer. By his own account, he left Strasbourg soon after 1520 and worked in a number of cities, including Speyer, Mainz, Frankfurt, Heidelberg, Nuremberg and Salzburg, but no works from this period have been found. Between 1525 and 1527, while living in Munich and Landshut, he executed some 20 medals portraying *Duke William IV of Bavaria*, *Duke Ludwig X* (examples in Munich, Bayer. Nmus.) and *Pfalzgraf Philipp, Bishop of Freising* (example in Nuremberg, Ger. Nmus.) and members of the Munich court and bourgeoisie. He next moved to Augsburg, where in 1531 the guilds complained to the City Council that he was working as a wood-carver and *conterfetter* (portrait sculptor) without being one of their members. Hagenauer replied that in other cities his work was recognized as free art and not subject to compulsory guild restrictions.

Hagenauer left Augsburg in 1532, having cast some 85 medals there; the 15 medals he produced of citizens of Strasbourg and Alsace make it seem likely that he spent some part of that year in his native city. In subsequent years he appears to have worked in Baden and Swabia; during the ten years beginning in 1536 he lived in Bonn and then Cologne. It was not difficult for Hagenauer to find commissions in Cologne, as up to that time no important medallist had worked there; nevertheless, he had to change his artistic practice and adapt himself to the taste of the citizens of Cologne, which was influenced by the close proximity of the Netherlands. Notable works from his later years are a medal of the painter *Bartolomaeus Bruyn I* and medals of some important figures in the Reformation controversies, such as *Philipp Melanchthon*, *Martin Bucer*, *Kaspar Hedio* (examples in Berlin, Bodemus.), *Johannes Sturm* (example in Munich, Bayer. Nmus.) and *Johann Pistorius* (all 1543), whom Archbishop Herman von Wied had summoned to Cologne. After 1546 nothing more is known of Hagenauer.

In accordance with his training as a wood-carver, Hagenauer prepared his models out of boxwood or pearwood and then cast them in silver, bronze or lead.

These models, 35 of which are extant (e.g. *Lukas Furtenagel*, limewood, 1527; Munich, Bayer. Nmus.), show that in the course of his career Hagenauer reduced the diameter of his models from *c.* 70 mm to *c.* 45 mm. He marked most of his medals with his monogram; later models from his Cologne period are also marked on the reverse with F. H. C. (C may stand for *Coloniensis* or *Conterfetter*). Hagenauer was active throughout the whole South German area as well as the lower Rhine, but because his work shows so many characteristic idiosyncrasies, it is relatively easy to catalogue. His Munich medals were still exclusively one-sided, and individual medals from his Augsburg period have large simple coats of arms on the reverse, but from 1529 onwards he produced plain, inscribed reverse sides, bearing the device of the person portrayed and the year of production, carefully and clearly composed in Roman capitals. Until 1530 he used only profile views, but subsequently he produced a few full-face and three-quarter profile portraits.

Even Hagenauer's earliest medals show his ability to achieve strong plastic qualities and differentiated modelling of the surface, using strikingly flat relief, particularly in the formation of the heads. His models are distinguished by accuracy and precision; they are exact in the smallest detail. His compositions have balance rather than tension. The artistry of his models aroused the admiration of his patrons, who treasured them as works of art and had them framed and sometimes coloured; this explains why so many of them have survived.

BIBLIOGRAPHY
Forrer; *NDB*; Thieme–Becker
G. Habich: 'Studien zur deutschen Renaissancemedaille: III. Friedrich Hagenauer', *Jb. Preuss. Kstsamml.*, xxviii (1907), pp. 181–98, 230–72
——: *Die deutschen Schaumünzen des 16. Jahrhunderts*, i (Munich, 1929), pp. 70–101
W. Vöge: 'Bildwerke deutscher Medailleure', *Jb. Preuss. Kstsamml.*, liii (1932), pp. 139–43
M. Bernhart: 'Augsburgs Medailleure und Bildnisse Augsburger Kunsthandwerker auf Schaumünzen des 16. Jahrhunderts: Friedrich Hagenauer', *Mitt. Bayer. Numi. Ges.*, lv (1937), pp. 48–52
A. Suhle: *Die deutsche Renaissance-Medaille* (Leipzig, 1950), pp. 136–51
R. Zeitler: 'Frühe deutsche Medaillen, 1518–1527: III. Friedrich Hagenauer', *Figura*, i (1951), pp. 107–19
T. Müller: *Die Bildwerke in Holz, Ton und Stein*, Munich, Bayer. Nmus. cat., xiii (Munich, 1959), pp. 291–3

HERMANN MAUÉ

Hagenauer, Johann Baptist (*b* Strass, nr Salzburg, 14 June 1732; *d* Vienna, 11 Sept 1810). Austrian sculptor. He was apprenticed to Johann Georg Itzlfeldner (?1705–90) in Tittmoning. From 1754 to 1759 he studied at the Akademie der Bildenden Künste in Vienna, where he produced sculptures in the Bavarian Rococo style (e.g. *Christ at the Martyr's Pillar*, gilded bronze, 1756; Cleveland, OH, Mus. A.). The Archbishop of Salzburg, Sigismund, Graf von Schrattenbach, enabled him to continue his studies in Bologna, Florence and Rome. He returned to Salzburg to become official sculptor to von Schrattenbach, and collaborated closely with his brother, the architect Wolfgang Hagenauer (1726–1801), who was also working for the Archbishop. In 1764 he married the Italian painter Rosa Barducci (1743–86). His most important commission in Salzburg was the *Mariensäule* on the Domplatz (lead, 1766–71; *in situ*). In 1773 he moved to Vienna and until 1779 worked with Christian Friedrich Wilhelm Beyer on the sculptural decoration of the park at Schloss Schönbrunn. It was at this time that he moved away from the Rococo style towards late Baroque Neoclassicism (e.g. *Apollo*, marble, 1779; Vienna, Schloss Schönbrunn). In 1774 he was appointed Professor of Sculpture at the Akademie and in 1780 became Director of the Graveurschule. In the 1780s he received several commissions for portraits (e.g. *Abbot Dominikus von Hagenauer*, plaster, 1787; Salzburg, Dommus.). From *c.* 1790 he concentrated on preparing design drawings of arts and crafts objects for the Graveurschule. He also wrote and published *Unterricht von der Proporzion des Menschen*.

WRITINGS
Unterricht von der Proporzion des Menschen (Vienna, 1791)

BIBLIOGRAPHY
Thieme–Becker
I. Wegleiter: *Johann Baptist Hagenauer* (diss., U. Vienna, 1952)
O. Kurz: 'Hagenauer, Posch and Mozart', *Burl. Mag.*, cx (1968), pp. 325–8
E. Baum: *Katalog des Österreichischen Barockmuseums*, i (Vienna and Munich, 1980), pp. 217–25

MARIA PÖTZL-MALIKOVA

Hagenauer [von Hagnow; Hagnower], **Nikolaus** [Niclas] (*b* Hagenau; *fl* 1493; *d* before 1538). In 1493 he became a citizen of Strasbourg, where he is last mentioned in 1526. Although three inscriptions with his name are documented, it is difficult to relate them to existing works, so attributions are based on stylistic analysis. Hagenauer is thought to have made the male half-length figure on the balustrade above the entrance to St Andrew's Chapel in the south transept of Strasbourg Cathedral. In 1500–01 he was commissioned to carve the *Corpus Christi* retable (dismantled 1682) for the high altar of the cathedral. Some parts survive, including the predella figures of a *Lamentation* (Strasbourg, Coll. Episc. St-Etienne) and busts of two prophets (Strasbourg, Mus. Oeuvre Notre-Dame). In 1505 he carved the figures for the altarpiece (Colmar, Mus. Unterlinden) in the Anthonite church at Isenheim, Alsace, for which Matthias Grünewald painted the wings some ten years later. The predella shows half-length figures of *Christ* and the *Twelve Apostles*. In the middle of the shrine is the enthroned figure of *St Anthony* together with the kneeling donor *Jean d'Orliac* flanked by *St Jerome* and *St Augustine*. At the feet of St Anthony there were originally figures (Munich, Julius Böhler) of a country squire and a peasant bearing a cock and a piglet as offerings. The space above the canopies is filled with fine vegetal carvings. The figures are carved in limewood and preserve much of the original polychromy; their relative scale reflects differences in social standing. To a certain degree Hagenauer continued the style of Nicolaus Gerhaert, but the faces of his figures show his penetrating powers of observation and his skill in expressing intellectual and psychological content.

NDB
BIBLIOGRAPHY
O. Schmitt: *Oberrheinische Plastik im ausgehenden Mittelalter* (Freiburg, 1924), pp. 30–35
W. Vöge: *Niclas Hagnower: Der Meister des Isenheimer Hochaltars und seine Frühwerke* (Freiburg im Breisgau, 1931)
A. Feulner and T. Müller: *Geschichte der deutschen Plastik* (Munich, 1953), pp. 297–9

E. Zimmermann: 'Plastik', *Spätgotik am Oberrhein: Meisterwerke der Plastik und des Kunsthandwerks, 1450–1530* (exh. cat., ed. E. Petrasch; Karlsruhe, Bad. Landesmus., 1970), pp. 168–79

R. Recht: 'Les Sculptures du retable d'Issenheim', *Cah. Alsac. Archéol., A. & Hist.*, xix (1975), pp. 27–46

C. Heck and R. Recht: *Les Sculptures de Nicolaus de Hagenau* (Colmar, 1987)

R. Recht: 'Nicolaus de Leyde et la sculpture à Strasbourg (1460–1525)', *Pays d'Alsace*, 142 (1987), pp. 261–325, 380–84 [suppl. issue]

Sculptures allemandes de la fin du moyen âge dans les collections publiques françaises (exh. cat., ed. D. Guillot de Soduiraut; Paris, Louvre, 1991–2), pp. 84–91

VINCENT MAYR

Hagenbund [Künstlerbund Hagen; Hagengesellschaft]. Austrian group of artists formed in 1900 in Vienna and active until 1930. Its most prominent members included Heinrich Lefler and Joseph Urban. The group took its name from Herr Haagen, the landlord of an inn at which artists often met for informal discussion. Originally called the Hagengesellschaft, most of its members left the Künstlerhaus at the same time as the Secessionists in 1897. Three years later they left the Secession to form the Hagenbund. At first the group intended to remain within the Künstlerhaus, and they held their first two exhibitions on its premises. However, between 1902 and 1912, and again from 1920 until 1930, they exhibited independently in a market-hall (the Zedlitzhalle) converted by Urban. The group favoured a distinct Art Nouveau style based on folk art and British antecedents, such as the work of Aubrey Beardsley. Their manner was less extreme than that of the Secessionists, and this contributed to their official success; Lefler and Urban were the major contributors to a pageant held in 1908 in celebration of Francis Joseph's 60 years on the throne. The influence of the Hagenbund was felt largely through their illustrations, which were popular with a younger and less upper-class audience than the Secessionists had. Most notable was the series *Gerlachs Jugendbücherei*, illustrated with lithographs by Lefler, Urban and Karl Fahringer (1874–1952). Among Austrian artists who participated in Hagenbund exhibitions were Robin Christian Andersen, Anton Hanak, Oskar Laske (1874–1951) and, at times, Oskar Kokoschka and Egon Schiele. Although the group was not dissolved until 1930, its importance had faded by the outbreak of World War I.

BIBLIOGRAPHY

H. Bisanz: 'The Visual Arts in Vienna from 1890 to 1920', *Vienna 1890–1920*, ed. R. Waissenberger (New York, 1984), pp. 148–50

□

Hager, Carl [Karl] **Otto** (*b* Dresden, 16 Oct 1813; *d* Stellenbosch, 8 Oct 1898). German architect, builder, painter and photographer, active in South Africa. He showed a talent for drawing at an early age. In 1825 he entered the Akademie der Künste, Dresden, to study architecture, qualifying in 1829. He emigrated to Cape Town in 1838. His first commission in 1840 was the new Roman Catholic Cathedral of St Mary, Cape Town, undertaken with his partner Carel Sparmann, which was an unsuccessful venture. Hager then moved to Stellenbosch living principally by portrait painting (examples in Stellenbosch Mus.). It was not until 1854 that his next building, the Lutheran Church, Dorp Street, Stellenbosch, was built. Only in 1863, however, did he receive his first

major commission, the remodelling of the Dutch Reformed Church, Stellenbosch. This involved the addition of a large nave, aisles and tower to the existing cruciform church. All the additions were strongly Gothic Revival in character, and the rest of the church was given a Gothic appearance. It would be an exaggeration to claim that it was Hager who introduced the Gothic style into Dutch Reformed churches, but it can be said that he introduced a purer strain of the Revival, although this was still far from 'correct'. The church at Stellenbosch differs most from previous attempts to Gothicize Dutch Reformed churches in the tower, which has triple-stage base tracery windows surmounted by a broach spire. The open Gothic trussed roof marks its first appearance in Dutch Reformed churches. In 1858, having learnt the technique of photography from Sparmann, Hager opened his own photographic studio in Cape Town, taking portraits. In 1864 he opened a successful studio in Stellenbosch.

After the Dutch Reformed Church Hager was continuously at work for the next 25 years on at least 14 churches throughout the Cape colony, mostly in the western region. The majority were traditional, simple rectangles, although a few of the larger ones were T-shaped or cruciform in plan. Hager seems never to have attempted to introduce any 'correct' Gothic features and there is no evidence that there was much enthusiasm for Gothic within the Dutch Reformed Church; the ritual of the church demanded a large, unobstructed space, focused on the pulpit.

For the same reason Hager's churches were wider than Gothic planning demanded and he had to adopt a curious triple-bayed front to reduce the apparent width of the building and restore the vertical emphasis of the style. He applied pinnacled buttresses to the middle panel, which contained a large tracery window, and the vertical emphasis was completed by pinnacled corner buttresses. The whole ensemble was often surmounted by a spiky bellcote. There is little evidence of his direct influence on church architecture, probably because during the time that he was working, he virtually monopolized the field and, by the time he stopped, other, better-trained young architects had started practices.

BIBLIOGRAPHY

DSAB

A. M. Hugo and J. van der Bijl: *Die Kerk van Stellenbosch* (Cape Town, 1963)

D. S. Picton-Seymour: *Victorian Buildings in South Africa* (Cape Town, 1977)

D. J. C. Radford: *The Architecture of the Western Cape, 1838–1901* (diss., Johannesburg, U. Witwatersrand, 1979)

DENNIS RADFORD

Hagesandros, Polydoros and Athenodoros (*?fl c.* AD 10–20). Greek sculptors. Though originally from Rhodes, they emigrated to Italy at some time in the early Empire, where they produced the statue of LAOKOON (*see* ROME, ANCIENT, fig. 59), which Pliny (*Natural History* XXXVI.iv.37) called 'superior to all works of both painting and sculpture', and some or all of the groups of sculptures recently discovered in the Sperlonga grotto (*see* SPERLONGA, §2). Tiberius owned the grotto, and the sculptures are in the 'neo-baroque' style that he is known to have favoured, suggesting that he may have commissioned the work from artists whose sculptures he may have admired while exiled on Rhodes from 6 BC to AD 2: the episodes depicted recall works by his favourite poet, Euphorion, and give prominence to his personal hero Odysseus.

While all these works embody the style of the Hellenistic 'neo-baroque', with turbulent surfaces, exaggerated musculature, dramatic expressions and an intense theatricality that recalls the reliefs on the Great Altar at Pergamon (*see* PERGAMON, §3), they contrast strikingly in treatment. The *Laokoon* strives for pathos by including both sons in their father's fate while hinting that one may yet escape: the Sperlonga sculptures represent a rather academic attempt to capture Odysseus' character (his loyalty, courage, ingenuity and craftiness) through four scenes from the hero's life carefully positioned for viewing from the imperial dining-room.

Though anticipated by some Hellenistic works, this contrived use of several different elements to illustrate a single theme is typically Roman and occurs in the groups of mythological scenes in contemporary Pompeian wall painting. Also Roman is the device of grouping episodes widely separated in space and time within a single setting and 'frame': this represents the ultimate development of the 'continuous' narrative method, which reached its highest popularity in early Imperial frescoes, while provision of a single fixed position for viewing is paralleled by the landscaped vistas created for late Republican and early Imperial villas (1st century BC–1st century AD).

Hagesandros, Polydoros and Athenodoros had a crucial impact on the development of both style and presentation in Roman art. Not only did the 'neo-baroque' become one of the main styles of Roman Imperial sculpture, but the Sperlonga groups themselves were repeatedly copied: fragments of a version of the *Polyphemus* group (London, BM, 1860) were even discovered in Hadrian's villa (*c.* AD 120–30) at Tivoli (*see* TIVOLI, §2(ii)).

BIBLIOGRAPHY
B. Conticello, B. Andreae and P. C. Bol: 'Die Skulpturen von Sperlonga', *Ant. Plast.*, xiv (1974)
A. F. Stewart: 'To Entertain an Emperor: Sperlonga, Laokoon and Tiberius at the Dinner-table', *J. Roman Stud.*, lxvii (1977), pp. 76–90
B. Andreae: *Odysseus: Archäologie des europäischen Menschenbildes* (Frankfurt, 1982)
B. Conticello: 'Sul Gruppo di Scilla e della nave nel Museo di Sperlonga', *Alessandria e il mondo ellenistico-romano: Studi in onore di Achille Adriani* (Rome, 1984), pp. 611–24
E. Simon: 'Laokoon und die Geschichte der antiken Kunst', *Archäol. Anz.* (1984), pp. 643–72
B. Andreae: *Plinius und der Laokoon* (Mainz, 1987)
——: *Laokoon und die Grundung Roms* (Mainz, 1988)
A. F. Stewart: *Greek Sculpture: An Exploration* (New Haven, 1990), pp. 96–9, 215–16, 309–10

ANDREW F. STEWART

Hagesias. *See* HEGIAS.

Hägg, Axel Herman. *See* HAIG, AXEL HERMAN.

Haggadah [Heb.: 'story']. Hebrew text recited during the Passover celebrations. The Haggadah (pl. Haggadot) consists of a compendium of blessings, prayers, biblical passages, homiletic commentaries and psalms, and is read during the *Seder* ceremony on the first night (in the Diaspora, first and second night) of Passover. The actions performed during the *Seder*, such as the eating of *matzah* (unleavened bread) and *maror* (bitter herbs), and the drinking of four glasses of wine, are integrated into a banquet or family meal.

The Haggadah was probably first compiled in the 7th or 8th century AD and canonized in the 9th–10th centuries. Most manuscript copies date from the Middle Ages, between the 13th and 15th centuries. It was produced in a small format for family use and was frequently decorated and even illustrated. The 14th and 15th centuries were the golden age of the illuminated Haggadah, the period when the production of illuminated Hebrew manuscripts flourished in Europe (*see* JEWISH ART, §V, 1). Although there were regional variations in the ordering of decorations and illustrations, the programme of the Haggadah was stable, comprising textual illustrations, representations of ritual actions, biblical images and evocations of the Messianic age to come. The textual illustrations of the *matzah*, the *maror* and the paschal lamb form part of the oldest tradition of the illustrated Haggadah, as can be seen from some fragments (9th–10th century) of the *Genizah* (document collection). In the same category are representations of the four sons, who allegorically represent different attitudes with regard to tradition, and of Rabbi Gamaliel expounding the principles of the *Seder*. The illustrations representing the preparation of the *Seder* and its rituals were primarily didactic, ensuring the survival of traditional procedures. These two types of illustration were usually inserted into the text, either in the small panels illuminating the first word of a section or in the margin of the corresponding passage. However, the little scenes depicting the preparations for the festival were usually placed at the front of the volume or following the biblical scenes, when these appeared as complete narratives.

The arrangement of the biblical illustrations varied with the region of origin. In the Ashkenazi Haggadot, those originating in northern France or the Germanic countries (sometimes also in Italian Haggadot, when these were the work of scribes of Germanic origin, such as JOEL BEN SIMEON), the biblical illustrations in the margins opposite the corresponding passages in the text were interspersed with other types of illustration. In the Ashkenazi Haggadot the biblical scenes were usually ones illustrating the event commemorated by the festival. Some 15th-century Ashkenazi Haggadot, such as those called Hileq and Bileq (Paris, Bib. N., Hebrew MS. 1333), the Second Nuremberg Haggadah (Jerusalem, Schocken Lib., MS. 27087) and the latter's copy, the Haggadah Yahuda (Jerusalem, Israel Mus., MS. 180/50), also contain illustrations of various biblical episodes not alluded to in the text.

In the Sephardic (southern European) Haggadot, those originating in Spain, particularly 14th-century Catalonia, the biblical images form uninterrupted sequences occupying whole pages (two or four scenes per page) placed at the front of the volume, before the text. Some of these sequences narrate only the story of the Book of Exodus; for example, the Rylands Haggadah (Manchester, U. Lib., Heb. MS. 6; copy, London, BL, MS. 1404) and the Kaufmann Haggadah (Budapest, Lib. Hung. Acad. Sci., MS. A 422). Other Haggadot, such as the Sarajevo Haggadah (Sarajevo, N. Mus.), began with the Creation, or with the story of Adam (e.g. the Golden Haggadah, London, BL, Add. MS. 27210; see fig.; Or. MS. 2884). Some scholars believe that these long sequences were copied from models that probably dated from late Antiquity; however, the style of the paintings reflects the influence of local contemporary art, and the organization into unbroken sequences was inspired by contemporary Latin psalters. Illustrations alluding to the Messiah included images of the return of the prophet Elijah, the coming of the Messiah and the entry of the Just into Jerusalem. The sacred city was visualized in the form of the Temple, which was to be rebuilt in the Messianic age.

Some printed Haggadot, illustrated with engravings, are as celebrated as the illuminated manuscripts. Only two pages survive of the first illustrated printed Haggadah, produced in Constantinople in 1515. The true prototype of the illustrated Haggadah was that printed by Solomon ha-Kohen in Prague in 1526. In addition to the ornate letters and the triple border that framed the opening of the major sections, the text was accompanied by little scenes placed in the inner and outer margins, illustrating the *Seder* rituals and the departure from Egypt. A second edition was published in 1590 and a third, with some additions and several scenes re-engraved, in 1606; a fourth edition, with the new scenes, was printed in 1624 and a fifth, with the original engravings, in 1706. In Italy, the series of illustrated Haggadot began with that of Mantua in 1550, reprinted in 1560 and 1568. The illustrations followed, with a few variations, those of the Prague Haggadah, but the borders were re-engraved in the Italian style.

A new tradition was inaugurated in the Venice Haggadah, printed in 1609 in Venice by Israel ben Daniel Zifroni. It appeared in three versions: the Hebrew text, printed in the centre of the page, was flanked in the margins by a translation into one of the vernacular languages—Ladino, Yiddish or Italian—transcribed into Hebrew characters. The decoration was identical in all three versions. On each page, the text was framed by monumental decoration— two columns supporting a pediment—and each section of the text opened with a historiated letter. The rectangular vignette that framed the letter also enclosed a little scene illustrating the text. Larger scenes placed at the foot of the page illustrated the biblical narrative.

The Venice Haggadah also marked an important step forward as regards technique: it was printed with movable type, which ensured the flexibility of the layout. The title page was illustrated with an image of Jerusalem at the moment of the Messiah's arrival, and the second and third pages had little scenes showing preparations for the festival and the *Seder* ritual. This edition was reprinted even more often than that of Prague: copies with individualized title-pages appeared throughout the 17th century. In 1629, Gershom Prinz reprinted the three versions of the original edition with the addition of a commentary by Rabbi Judah Arieh of Modena, and with slightly modified illustrations.

The third great series of illustrated Haggadot was inaugurated by the Amsterdam Haggadah, published in Amsterdam in 1695. The title page, which still showed Moses and Aaron between two columns, also displayed seven medallions depicting biblical scenes, which were taken from Matthäus Merian the Elder's *Icones biblicae* (Basle, 1625–6). The Amsterdam Haggadah ended with a map of the Holy Land, the first to be printed in a Hebrew

Joseph and his Brethren, illustration from the Golden Haggadah, 14th century (London, British Library, Add. MS. 27210, fol. 6v)

work. It was reprinted in 1712, with an enriched iconography partly taken from the Venice Haggadah. This edition, too, inspired numerous later editions (e.g. Frankfurt am Main, 1710; Sulzbach, 1711; Offenbach, 1721 and 1755). The illustrations later served as a model for artists who during the 18th century returned to hand-copying and painting illustrations.

Printed Haggadot continued to be produced throughout the 19th and 20th centuries, reflecting in their styles and technique both traditional elements and the influence of modern art movements. Some special editions were created (e.g. for the *kibbutzim*) where even the text was modified to meet the interest of a specific public. Known artists such as Jacob Steinhardt and Ben Shahn illustrated the Haggadah, which was translated into many languages.

BIBLIOGRAPHY

D. H. Müller and J. von Schlosser: *Die Haggada von Sarajevo* (Vienna, 1898)
C. Roth: 'The John Rylands Haggadah', *Bull. John Rylands Lib.*, xliii (1960–61), pp. 132–59
——: *The Sarajevo Haggadah* (Belgrade, 1963)
J. Gutmann: 'The Illuminated Passover Haggadah: Investigations and Research Problems', *Stud. Bibliog. Bklore*, vii (1965), pp. 3–25
B. Narkiss: *The Golden Haggadah* (London, 1970)
M. Metzger: *La Haggada enluminée: Etude iconographique et stylistique des manuscrits enluminés et décorés de la Haggada du XIIIe au XVI siècle* (Leiden, 1973)
Y. H. Yerushalmi: *Haggadah and History* (Philadelphia, PA, 1975)
G. Sed-Rajna: *The Hebrew Bible in Illuminated Manuscripts* (New York, 1987)

GABRIELLE SED-RAJNA

Haghpat Monastery, view from the north-east, founded *c.* 976; the bell-tower (1245) is on the left

Haghpat Monastery. Armenian monastery in the village of Haghpat *c.* 10 km north-east of Alaverdi in the district of T'umanyan, northern Armenia. It is one of the largest and best preserved architectural complexes of medieval Armenia. Its principal buildings are grouped together in a fairly compact manner, surrounded by a vast fortified precinct. Only a small portion of the annexes have survived. Several structures are located outside the complex, including a fort, a hermitage and a fountain (1258).

The monastery was probably founded *c.* 976, at the time the main church of the Holy Sign (Armen. Sourb Nshan) was built by Queen Khosrovanush, wife of King Ashot III of Ani (*reg* 952–77). The church's construction may have been supervised by the Armenian architect Trdat (*fl* 989–1001) and was completed in 991 by the founder's two sons, King Smbat (*reg* 977–89) and Gurgēn, the leader of the small local kingdom of Loṙē. It is a typical example of an Armenian cross-in-rectangle church, with a cylindrical drum surmounted by a conical shaped dome (rest. between the 11th and 13th centuries) and supported by pendentives and arches that spring from piers with engaged columns. The façades are articulated with pairs of tall V-shaped slits. On the east façade, the rectangular recess beneath the gable contains a relief of the two donor brothers holding a model of the church and crowned according to their respective ranks: Smbat wears a voluminous turban presented to the Bagratid kings by the caliphs, whereas Gurgēn wears a sort of helmet.

The narthex (Armen. *gavit* or *zhamatun*; *see* ARMENIA, §II, 2) on the west side of the church was built in 1185 in the form of a rectangular gallery to serve as a mausoleum for the descendants of Gurgēn. In 1210 it was extended westwards, becoming larger than the church and occupying a lower level. It contains the earliest and most accomplished example in Armenia of a vaulted ceiling supported on two pairs of intersecting arches that spring from pillars abutting the walls. The usual dome with a central opening is here replaced by another set of intersecting arches.

The monastery's other buildings are grouped to the north-east of the church. They are all built of basalt and in an austere style. The bell-tower, which stands apart, on a small hill (see fig.), was built in 1245 under the monastery's superior Hamazasp. In an original form, it has two storeys surmounted by a small rotunda; the external squinches at the corners of the cruciform lower storey support the upper octagonal storey. Hamazasp also built the *gavit* (1253–7), which is connected to the north façade of the church by a gallery. It is the largest example in Armenia of a four-piered hall covered by a dome with a central opening; its originality also lies in the fact that it is located in front of a small chapel, not a church. Next to the *gavit*'s south-eastern corner is a library (1262), which was later converted into a storeroom. It has a square plan with a vaulted roof supported by two pairs of intersecting arches that spring from eight pillars abutting the walls. Recesses in its walls were for storing books. A third building is the refectory, which stands the furthest north-east from the church. It is a long hall divided into two square halves, each covered by a vaulted roof resting on intersecting arches.

The monastery also contains several *khatchk'ars* (stone slabs with a cross engraved in the centre), especially in the gallery that bypasses the church and leads to the other buildings. A *khatchk'ar* of particular note is the *Amenap'rkich'* ('All Saviour'; 1273), which depicts in low relief the *Deposition* with *Christ in Majesty* above and the *Apostles* in the border. It was carved for Prince Sadun, a member of the Ardsruni dynasty. The monastery was restored in the 17th century. In 1989 it was returned to the Armenian Church to function again as a place of Christian worship.

BIBLIOGRAPHY
K. Ghafadaryan: *Haghpat: Tjartarapetakan karutsvatzkner yev vimakan ardzanagrutyunner* [Haghpat: architectural constructions and stone inscriptions] (Erevan, 1963)
S. Mnatsakanian and A. A. Novello: *Haghbat* (1970), i of *Documenti di architettura armena* (Milan, 1970–)
O. Khalpakhchian: *Architectural Ensembles of Armenia* (Moscow, 1980)
J. M. Thierry and P. Donabédian: *Les Arts arméniens* (Paris, 1987)
PATRICK DONABÉDIAN

Hagi. Centre of ceramics production in Japan. High-fired Hagi ware was manufactured from the early 17th century in Nagato Province (now Yamaguchi Prefect.; *see* JAPAN, §VIII, 3(ii)). The first Hagi potters, the brothers Yi Suk-wang and Yi Kyŏng (Jap. Sakamoto Sukehachi), were brought to Japan from Korea during TOYOTOMI HIDE-YOSHI's invasions in the 1590s. The older Yi was first brought to Hiroshima to serve the daimyo Mōri Terumoto (1553–1625), a student of the tea master SEN NO RIKYŪ. After the defeat of the Toyotomi family at the Battle of Sekigahara in 1600 and the establishment of Tokugawa hegemony, Terumoto's fief was reduced to Nagato Province alone. The Yi brothers were probably brought together to found an official kiln at the new clan seat, Hagi, when it was established in 1604.

Production began in the village of Matsumoto just east of Hagi. Yi Suk-wang died not long after the opening of the kiln, whereupon leadership was assumed by his younger brother. Yi Kyŏng also trained his brother's son, who received the name Sakunojō in 1625. Official domain records identify six other potters working in Matsumoto in 1645; several of that group opened a second kiln centre at Fukawa (now part of Nagato City), some 30 km to the west, in 1653. Ten years later the clan reinforced the Matsumoto staff with two more potters, Miwa Chūbei Toshisada (later Miwa Kyūsetsu I) and Saeki Hanroku; the former was even sent to Kyoto to study Raku ware techniques. In contrast to the consistent clan support of the Matsumoto kilns, Fukawa operated on a semi-private basis from its inception, and by 1693 the clan surrendered its supervision to the village headman.

The term 'Hagi ware' does not appear in Japanese records until 1668; before that the product was called Matsumoto ware or Fukawa ware. The earliest work, represented by a few securely provenanced heirlooms, consists of Korean-style stoneware bowls for the tea ceremony (*see* JAPAN, §XIV, 1 and 3) known to Japanese connoisseurs as Ido, Komogae and Kohiki. They are characterized by thickly potted forms, flaring from foot to lip, set on a high and sometimes notched foot rim; the granular clay bodies are covered with a semi-transparent feldspathic glaze ranging in colour from warm ivory to salmon pink. Their artless appearance and the tactile qualities of the material placed Hagi teabowls second only to Raku ware in the esteem of tea masters. In the second half of the 17th century, the Miwa potters introduced new shapes and glazes from Kyoto (*see* KYOTO, §III), IGA and SHIGARAKI, contributing to a gradual Japanization of the Hagi repertory. Excavations of mid-17th-century Saka family kilns also show that they produced far more utilitarian wares than articles for the tea ceremony.

The Mōri clan continued its patronage of the official kilns throughout the 18th century. A requisition from the Saka workshop to the fief office in 1733 lists the supplies needed for one production cycle, including a request for Daidō clay, a kaolinic material that imparts the distinctive colour and texture to Hagi ware. The kilns found a particularly fervent supporter in the seventh-generation Mōri clan head, Shigetaka (1725–89); he constructed a tea house at his villa, made his own ceramics and in 1782 invited the Edo tea master Kawakami Fuhaku (1716–1807) to teach at the domain. Seeking a new source of revenue in the burgeoning demand for porcelain, the clan opened a kiln at Obata, just outside Hagi, in the early 19th century. The Fukawa potters built their own porcelain kiln at Kurimoto in 1830. Besides everyday wares, much of the production was devoted to comparatively delicate pieces for *sencha*, a style of steeped-tea ceremony that gained popularity in the late 18th century (*see* JAPAN, §XIV, 1). All the Hagi kilns experienced severe difficulties after the Meiji Restoration (1868). Not until the revival of the tea ceremony in the 20th century did Hagi ware regain its popularity; by then only five of the old families remained, two in Matsumoto and three in Fukawa, supplemented in the post-war period by about 100 workshops making wares for the tourist and teaware trades.

BIBLIOGRAPHY

T. Yoshiga: 'The History and Variety of Hagi Ceramics', *Chanoyu Q.*, xxiv (1980)

R. Kawano: *Hagi, Famous Ceramics of Japan*, xi (Tokyo, 1983)

Nihon no tōji [Japanese ceramics] (exh. cat., ed. Y. Yabe; Tokyo, N. Mus., 1985)

RICHARD L. WILSON

Hague, The [Haag, Den; 's Gravenhage]. City on the North Sea coast of the Netherlands. Originally a small village behind the dunes, The Hague became the main residence of the Count of Holland, William II (*reg* 1234–56), when he was nominated Holy Roman Emperor elect in 1247. The community continued to expand even after 1433 when the 3rd Duke of Burgundy inherited most of the northern provinces and the court moved to Brussels. The High Court of Holland and Zeeland was established in The Hague, and meetings of the Dutch States General were held in the old castle, the Binnenhof (*see* §V, 2 below). Although the early 16th century brought invasion and decline, the successful revolt against the Habsburgs later in the century created new growth, as did the establishment of the independent States General and other permanent legal and administrative institutions around the Binnenhof. With the appointment of successive members of the ORANGE NASSAU family as stadholders and Captains General, the town also became the centre of international court life. By the end of the 18th century, however, political strains had resulted in the dismissal of the last Orange stadholder and only after the defeat of Napoleon I did his son return as William I, the first king of the Netherlands (*reg* 1813–40). The Hague then became the seat of a constitutional monarchy as the Dutch sought to accommodate their institutions to new economic needs and social demands. By the end of the 19th century, having benefited from colonial exploitation, it was the fastest growing urban community in the Netherlands, while in the early 20th century the establishment of the International Court of Justice and the rise of multinational oil companies gave a new impetus to foreign contacts. Although in the late 20th century post-war resurgence brought the strains of large-scale immigration, the city still displays many signs of cosmopolitan ambition.

BIBLIOGRAPHY

's-Gravenhage [monthly council pubn]

Haagsch Jaarboekje [annual, 1889–99]

Die Haghe [annual, 1899–]

J. van der Does: *'s-Gravenhage met de voornaemste plaetsen en vermaeckelijkheden* (The Hague, 1668)

J. de Riemer: *Beschrijving van 's Gravenhage*, 3 vols (The Hague, 1730–39/*R* 1973)

F. Allan: *De stad 's Gravenhage en hare geschiedenis* (1859)

W. P. van Stockum: *'s Gravenhage in de loop der tijden*, 2 vols (The Hague, 1889)

R. van Marle: *Bibliographie van 's-Gravenhage* (The Hague, 1905)

H. E. van Gelder: *'s-Gravenhage in 7 eeuwen* (Amsterdam, 1937)

J. G. Pippel: *In en om de Hofstad: Den Haag in de loop der tijden* (The Hague, 1941)

H. E. van Gelder: *De historische schoonheid van 's Gravenhage* (Amsterdam, 1948)

C. de Wit: *Den Haag vroeger en nu* (The Hague, 1968)

J. P. A. van Ballegoyen de Jong: *Hofjes in de Hofstad* (Baarn, 1975)

P. Don: *Kunstreisboek, Zuid-Holland* (Weesp, 1985)

I. History and urban development. II. Art life and organization. III. Centre of furniture production. IV. Buildings.

I. History and urban development.

1. Before *c.* 1585. 2. *c.* 1585–1813. 3. After 1813.

1. BEFORE *c.* 1585. The oldest buildings in The Hague are in the Binnenhof (*see* §V, 2 below). William II extended

the sober living quarters *c.* 1250, and his son Floris V (*reg* 1256–96) added an imposing ceremonial hall (the Ridderzaal) about a quarter of a century later. The town itself, housing courtiers and suppliers, developed to the south-west. The names of surviving streets, for example the Noordeinde, Westeinde and Zuideinde (now Venestraat), indicate the extent of the ancient centre. At the end of the 14th century when Albert I, Duke of Bavaria (*reg* 1347–1404), became Count of Holland, he expanded the Binnenhof substantially. The court chapel, built *c.* 1280 and dedicated to the Virgin Mary, was endowed with a chapter of 12 canons and a library. After a colourful history, it was dismantled in the 20th century. One of the entrance gatehouses, added to the outer court of the castle complex in the 14th century, survived as a prison and is hence named the Gevangenpoort (Prison Gate). Albert donated large areas of his domain around the Binnenhof to the civic community, and it was then that most of the stately wooded avenues, which still form the idyllic centre of the town, were laid out. The Vijverberg, a bank of earth that had been raised and planted following the excavation of a lake on the west of the Binnenhof, became an elegant shaded walk lined by imposing houses. Roughly parallel to it was the even more prominent wooded Voorhout, where grand residences were also built, as was a Dominican friary, the church of which survives as the Kloosterkerk. Slightly later, between 1420 and 1500, the parish church dedicated to St James, now known as the Grote Kerk (*see* §V, 1 below), was built on an axis extending west from the Binnenhof. In its remarkable hexagonal tower on the west side is the entrance to the nave, flanked by tall chapels. Beyond the nave is a much loftier choir, finished *c.* 1500.

Little building took place in the early 16th century, when the town, which had no walls, was exposed to plunder by the forces of Gelderland, but the hostility felt towards the religious and economic policies of the remote Habsburgs (who controlled Gelderland from 1538 to 1579) awakened a new civic selfconsciousness. This found expression in the construction in 1565 of a new town hall (the Oude Stadhuis), situated on the axis between the parish church and the Binnenhof. Its façade was based on the classicizing forms of the recently finished town hall in Antwerp (*see* ANTWERP, §IV, 2), thus advertising the Protestantism of the regents and the pride they felt for their town and province.

2. *c.* 1585–1813. More building took place from *c.* 1585 onwards, when the meetings of the young independent States General became regular and firmly established in the Binnenhof. The stadholder, Prince Maurice (*see* ORANGE NASSAU, (2)), came to live there and asserted his position by enlarging his official quarters and by constructing a fortified tower that gave emphasis to his military power base. Maurice played an active role in the planning of The Hague, being influential in the expansion of the ring of canals around the old centre between 1613 and 1619, although the fortifications that he had planned earlier did not materialize. His military interests led him to establish an arsenal and a cannon foundry in the former Dominican church on the Voorhout. The official master arms-caster lived next door in a large house. The church was adapted for Calvinist services during the Truce (1609–21), when Calvinism was a violent political weapon.

Maurice's successor, Prince Frederick Henry (*see* ORANGE NASSAU, (3)), was able to build on the military security established by his half-brother. Although he distinguished himself principally as a general, his interest in architecture is demonstrated by his various private and public enterprises. He created two grandiose country houses just outside The Hague, the hunting lodge Honselaarsdijk (*c.* 1620; destr.) and the HUIS TER NIEUBURCH, RIJSWIJK (1630–34; destr.), and in 1640 he commissioned Pieter Post (*see* POST, (1)) to enlarge and embellish his mother's 16th-century house on the Noordeinde (now the Paleis Noordeinde; see fig. 1), after designs of 1639 by

1. The Hague, Paleis Noordeinde (1553), rebuilt 1640 by Pieter Post after designs (1639) by Jacob van Campen; enlarged 1814

JACOB VAN CAMPEN. Post also designed the Huis ten Bosch (*see* §V, 3 below), begun in 1645 and completed after the Prince's death. Frederick Henry was also instrumental in the creation of the stately character of the Plein, just east of the Binnenhof. He donated a building plot to his secretary, Constantijn Huygens (i) (*see* HUYGENS, (1)), and allowed the general audit office of the States of Holland to use the proceeds from the sale of the remaining land, on condition that a few large houses should be built. Several splendid residences were consequently constructed on the Plein during the 1630s. The only one that survives is the Mauritshuis (1633–44), a small palace by van Campen and Post, which was built for Johan Maurits, Count of Nassau-Siegen (now the art museum; for description and illustration *see* CAMPEN, JACOB VAN; *see also* NASSAU, (1) and EGGERS, BARTHOLOMEUS). In acknowledgement of Frederick Henry's financial assistance within the town, the regents placed his name and that of his young male heir on the pediment of the new militia building (St Sebastiaansdoelen), which was erected in 1636 on the Korte Vijverberg from designs by Arent Arentsz. van 's Gravesande (*see* ARENTSZ., (1)). Slightly later, the Prince was instrumental in the development of the town towards the west with the construction *c.* 1640 of the large canal called the Prinsegracht.

While the stadholders had a great influence in shaping the town, the other powerful governmental bodies, the States General, the States of Holland and the Higher Court of Holland, only rarely displayed interest in their material surroundings. The extensive project (1652–7) to renovate the meeting-rooms of the States of Holland in the Binnenhof after designs by Post is thus all the more striking and must reflect the political ambitions (in the absence of an Orange stadholder) of the Grand Pensionary, Johan de Witt (1625–72). Ceiling and chimney decorations emphasize the fruits of world trade under peaceful republican government. The town council, on the other hand, was a constantly active patron. During 1649–56 the large, centralized Protestant Nieuwe Kerk was built by the city architect, Pieter Arensz. Noorwits (*see* ARENTSZ., (2)), and Bartholomeus Cornelisz. van Bassen as part of a project to modernize an overcrowded industrial and harbour area. To the west of this quarter the imposing Prinsegracht was developed, along which many official trade buildings, for example the Groot Boterhuis (Butter weigh-house; 1681), arose next to wealthy private dwellings and a private charitable institution, the grand almshouses known as the Hofje van Nieuwkoop (1658). The effectiveness of the town government was demonstrated in the early 18th century, when the Stadhuis was more than doubled by the addition of a large wing overlooking the old parish church.

Although The Hague was not the richest town of the Dutch Republic, it had the richest inhabitants. The deputies of the United Provinces regularly met in the quarters of the States General in the Binnenhof, while the representatives of the towns of Holland gathered in their own rooms. To acquire stability and prestige, these dignitaries required respectable lodgings in The Hague, and many of its grandest residences were the result of this political pressure. Government officials also developed beautiful country retreats on the borders of the town. Sorghvliet

was the name the Grand Pensionary JACOB CATS (i) gave to the area of dunes that he bought in 1643 and where ten years later he built his country house. Huygens planned his nearby HOFWIJCK in 1639, and it was built in 1641–3 by van Campen and Post. Huygens's son-in-law Philips Doublet developed his estate Clingendael between 1660 and 1685. Their friend, the poet Jacob Westerbaen, resided in Ockenburgh and another friend, Arend van der Dorp, created Arendsdorp.

The 18th century was a period of decorative upgrading rather than one of expansion. The king–stadholder William IV had introduced a strong French taste in buildings when he invited Daniel Marot I (*see* MAROT, (2)) to work in The Hague in 1686. Marot later designed several small palaces including Lange Vijverberg 8 (1715; for Cornelis van Schuylenburch); Kneuterdijk 20 (*c.* 1717–20; for Johan Hendrik van Wassenaar-Obdam); and, with Jan Pieter van Baurscheit (ii), Lange Voorhout 34 (1734–5; for Adriana Huguetan). Later in the century the more sober Louis XVI style was introduced by PIETER DE SWART, architect to the stadholder, and is exemplified by Lange Voorhout 74 (1760; for Anthony Patras, Deputy of the States of Friesland) and in the elegantly curved Korte Voorhout 3 (*c.* 1760–67; for Prince Karl van Nassau-Weilburg), which was almost immediately (1802–4) transformed into the city theatre.

3. AFTER 1813. Between the revolution in 1795 and the return of the stadholder as King William I in 1813, there was little architectural activity, but after 1813 The Hague entered a period of rapid expansion. Following the introduction of the railways in 1843, extensive new residential areas were developed around the stations towards the south. Most of these were built without much town planning: they include a workers' area (Schilderswijk) and two middle-class areas (Zeeheldenbuurt and Archipelbuurt). A different approach was applied to the more aristocratic development, just north of the outer ring of canals, initiated by King William II and hence named Willem's Park. Here, along one side of the Nassaustraat, is a Gothic Revival terrace, built originally for the King's entourage. In the middle arose an enormous stable complex, which was converted into a church soon afterwards and later, in the 20th century, into offices. On the other side of the street are the wooded back gardens of the large villas that surround the impressive oval Plein 1813, laid out in the 1860s to commemorate the year that brought the end of French domination, the return of the Oranges and the inauguration of the Kingdom of the Netherlands. The focal-point is a colossal Neo-classical monument to these events. The grandiose elegance of the Willem's Park makes it unique in the Netherlands. Throughout the 19th century the town continued to expand and several dignified suburbs were created to house the growing numbers of civil servants. A green belt was preserved between the urban centre and the coastal village of Scheveningen, though some elegant villas were constructed there. In contrast to the spacious suburbs created for the affluent, the industrial centre around the Nieuwe Haven, the Spui (Sluice) and the Nieuwe Kerk had become very overcrowded. Many of the canals there became health hazards and had to be closed. In spite of the impression created

2. The Hague, Gemeentemuseum by H. P. Berlage, 1927–35

by the aristocratic boulevards around the Binnenhof, The Hague had a severe housing problem. Between 1800 and 1850 the population nearly doubled (from 42,000 to 71,000) and something had to be done. The Society for the Amelioration of the Housing of the Working Class in The Hague was founded in 1854, and in succeeding years many complexes of small houses around common gardens—*hofjes*—were developed, often between existing rows of houses. Those resulting from private enterprise, which were smaller and more modest, became known as 'exploitation' *hofjes*.

Population increase, democratic movements and the many wars during the 19th century led to various peace movements based on the principles of international law and arbitrage. The Hague hosted two peace conferences (1899 and 1907), and it was decided to build a peace palace to accommodate an international court of justice, a permanent court of arbitration and an academy for international law. Through the gifts of individuals such as Andrew Carnegie and donations from many countries, a richly decorated, eclectic building, the Vredespaleis, was erected (1909–13) in splendid grounds near the Sorghvliet estates between The Hague and Scheveningen.

The population had tripled (to 210,000) by the beginning of the 20th century, and housing became an even more pressing concern. Large-scale projects were developed by H. P. BERLAGE but were only partially realized. His idea was to create satellite towns with their own parks, offices and shopping areas. The Zuiderpark quarter was one of these. Berlage's vision is also evident in his design (1927–9) for the Gemeentemuseum, for which he campaigned over many years (completed posthumously in 1935; see fig. 2). Sensitively integrated with the surrounding garden, the strong horizontal masses of the building are clad in traditional brickwork and abstract tiled ornament. After World War II a plan to reorganize the whole town was developed by the city architect, W. M. Dudok, but few elements were realized. It was only during the prosperous 1970s that large parts of the centre were remodelled. A number of 19th-century quarters near the stations were destroyed and the increasing demand for office space was met by massive new structures surrounded by advanced traffic systems. Huge subsidies also became available for the building and renovation of low-cost housing. In following years there was a revival of the high-level patronage that had once played an important role in urban development. After the coronation of Queen Beatrix (1980), The Hague again became the seat of the monarch and palaces were restored. In the early 1980s the town council constructed a new music theatre next to an area destined to combine a new town hall with a commercial complex, and later in the decade a new building for the lower House of Parliament (Tweede Kamer) was constructed just outside the Binnenhof. These building projects show ambitious new attitudes towards the relationship between society and economy.

BIBLIOGRAPHY

D. S. Zuiden: *Haagse straatnamen en hun afkomst en betekenis* [Street names of The Hague and their origin and meaning] (The Hague, 1909)

D. F. Slothouwer: *De paleizen van Frederik Hendrik* [The palaces of Frederik Hendrik] (Leiden, 1946)

C. de Wit: 'Het ontstaan van het haagse Binnenhof', [The origin of the Binnenhof in The Hague], *Bull. Ned. Oudhdknd. Bond*, 6th ser., vii (1954), cols 1–22

L. Tasseron: *Twaalf eeuwn Binnenhof* [Twelve centuries of the Binnenhof] (The Hague, 1956)

J. J. F. W. van Agt: 'De Sint Jacobskerk te 's Gravenhage', *Bull. Ned. Oudhdknd. Bond*, 6th ser., xiv (1961), cols 153–80

J. Schwencke: *Wandelingen door oud Den Haag* [Walks through old The Hague] (The Hague, 1965)

D. G. Hoek: *Haags leven by de inzet van de Gouden Eeuw* [Life in the Hague at the start of the Golden Age] (The Hague, 1966)

J. M. Galjaard: *Parken en buitenplaatsen in en om Den Haag* [Parks and country houses in and around The Hague] (The Hague, 1967)

J. C. Herpel: *Het oude Raadhuis van 's Gravenhage*, [The old town hall of the Hague], 2 vols (The Hague, 1975)

K. Nieuwenhuyzen: *Den Haag en omstreken in 19de eeuwse foto's* [The Hague and its suburbs in photos from the 19th century] (Amsterdam, 1975)

R. van Pelt, ed.: *Het Binnenhof* (The Hague, 1984)

A. Eyffinger: *Het Vredespaleis* (Amsterdam, 1988)

K. Havelaar and E. Stegeman, eds: *Wonen in 't slop* [Living in the slum] (The Hague, 1988)

H. P. R. Rosenberg, E. C. Vaillant and D. Valentijn: *Architektuur oud Den Haag* (The Hague, 1988)

ELISABETH DE BIÈVRE

II. Art life and organization.

1. Before *c*. 1585. 2. *c*. 1585–1799. 3. 1800 and after.

1. BEFORE *c*. 1585. There is little evidence of a flourishing artistic life in the village of The Hague before the mid-1580s when it became the seat of government for the newly independent northern Netherlands. Yet artistic activity did have some significance during the preceding centuries, particularly during periods when the court of the Dutch counts was actually in residence in The Hague. In the area of precious metalwork, for example, there is already evidence of some activity in archives as early as the 15th century; moreover, the court occasionally attracted painters of repute from other parts of Europe, for example Jan van Eyck from the southern Netherlands, who was active in The Hague in 1422–5 (*see* EYCK, VAN, (2)). After Philip the Good, Duke of Burgundy, obtained the title of Count of Holland in 1433, the centre of court life was once again displaced, though the archives show that some artistic activity persisted. A brotherhood for artists was founded in 1487; it included painters and later functioned as a guild (the Guild of St Luke). However, the most important 16th-century Hague artists settled elsewhere. They included Corneille de Lyon, known until the 19th century as Corneille de la Haye, who is first recorded in Lyon in 1533, and the sculptor Adriaen de Vries, who was in Florence in 1581 and never returned to his native city.

2. *c*. 1585–1799. Artistic activity began to flourish in The Hague in the last quarter of the 16th century and the beginning of the 17th, principally in the fields of portraiture, printmaking and metalwork. In portraiture, from 1598, JAN VAN RAVESTEYN was the leading master; he worked for the Stadholder's court (see fig. 3) as well as for regents in The Hague. The development of printmaking received an impetus from Jacques de Gheyn II (*see* GHEYN, DE, (1)) and Hendrik Hondius I (*see* HONDIUS (ii), (1)), whose arrival, in 1595 and 1597 respectively, was decisive. The town's rising importance as a centre for printers and publishers enabled printmaking to develop both as an independent art form and as a means of book illustration.

Two significant developments in the growth of art life in The Hague in the 17th and 18th centuries were the

3. Jan van Ravesteyn: *Officers of the Civic Guard Leaving the Stadhuis*, 1616 (The Hague, Haags Historische Museum)

increasing importance of the town as a centre of government as its economy continued to expand and the emergence of a courtly culture around the court of Prince Frederick Henry. The court of the exiled 'Winter King' of Bohemia, Frederick V, Elector of the Palatine (*reg* 1610–23), was another cultural centre. The concomitant expanding bourgeois culture of patronage and collecting involved, among others, some of the same artists who worked in court circles. Given this cultural context, The Hague, compared with other Dutch cities, had a rather international character. A sizeable proportion of the artists who settled there were foreigners or Dutch artists who had worked abroad for a time.

Throughout the 17th century portraits were extensively produced, the court and its international contacts being largely responsible for the importance of The Hague in this sphere. As court painter, Gerrit van Honthorst held a commanding place during the second quarter of the century. Adriaen Hanneman, Jan Mijtens and Caspar Netscher were active in the second half of the century. Among other significant painters working in The Hague in the 17th century were the landscape painters Esaias van de Velde, Jan van Goyen and Joris van der Haagen, the history painter Moses van Uyttenbroeck, the architectural painter and architect Bartholomeus Cornelisz. van Bassen, the still-life painter Abraham van Beyeren and the genre painter Adriaen van de Venne (for his illustration of the 'Winter King and Queen' *see* VENNE, ADRIAEN VAN DE). Shortly after the middle of the century there seem to have been about 50 Hague painters who were no longer content to remain in the Guild of St Luke. They left it in 1656 and formed the confraternity Pictura, whose first dean was Adriaen Hanneman. The members of Pictura set up an academy in 1682 where life drawing was done in the evenings.

The art of metalwork was scarcely less important than painting in the 17th and 18th centuries, and the town was regarded as the second Dutch centre in this sphere, after Amsterdam. Jan Gerritsz. Oosterlingh was active as a silversmith in the early 17th century. Among other important 17th-century masters were Andries Grill and Hans Conraet Brechtel, both originally from Germany, and, at the end of the century, Adam Loofs (*see* NETHERLANDS, THE, fig. 54). Pewter and bronze were also produced in The Hague. There were also eminent sculptors in the town at this period, particularly in the second half of the century, notably Rombout Verhulst, Johannes Blommendael and Johannes Hannaert (1683–1709).

In general there were fewer paintings produced in The Hague in the 18th century than in the 17th, and far fewer important artists were active there. However, in the second half of the 18th century, when the Stadholder's court encouraged foreign artists to settle in The Hague, paintings became much more cosmopolitan in style. The Dutch still led the way in portraiture during the first half of the century with such painters as Philip van Dijk and Hendrik van Limborch (1681–1759). Around the middle of the century the leaders in this field included the German Johann Valentin Tischbein (1715–67/8), the Frenchman Jean Fournier (*c.* 1700–95) and, for a short time, the Swiss Jean-Etienne Liotard, who, among others, worked at the court of Stadholder William IV and his wife Anna of Hanover. At the court of their son William V, the Flemish Guillaume Jean Joseph de Spinny (1721–85) and the Swiss Benjamin Samuel Bolomey (1739–1819) were the leading portrait painters. In bourgeois circles foremost were Hendrik Pothoven and Jean Humbert (1734–94), both Dutchmen, and the Frenchman Pierre Frédéric de La Croix (1709–82). In decorative painting Mattheus Terwesten (1670–1757) was the leading artist in the first half of the century, and later the German Heinrich Wilhelm Schweickardt (1746–97) came to prominence. Other painters working in The Hague were the townscape painters Jan ten Compe and Paulus Constantijn La Fargue and the still-life painter Jan van Os. The landscape painter Jan van Gool acquired his lasting reputation not so much for his paintings as for his two-volume book about Dutch painters, in which he wrote extensively about his contemporaries. In 1780 Pictura's academy was reorganized as a drawing school for young artists.

The growth of precious metalworking in The Hague continued in the 18th century. The most prominent masters included Albert de Thomese and members of the van Stapele family, François, his son Martinus (*fl* 1774) and grandson Reynier (*fl* 1788). The Hague also played a part in national developments in other decorative arts, for example porcelain manufacture and glass-engraving, while Jan Baptiste Xavery from Antwerp was active there as a sculptor in the second quarter of the century.

Among the private collections of Old Master paintings in The Hague in the 18th century were those of the van Heteren family, most of which ended up in the Rijksmuseum, Amsterdam, and the small, but exquisite collection of Govert van Slingelandt, which was acquired in 1768 by William V, himself one of the most important collectors of his day (*see* ORANGE NASSAU, (8)), whose gallery of paintings became the core of the Mauritshuis.

BIBLIOGRAPHY

A. Bredius: 'Mededeelingen uit het Haagsche Gemeentearchief' [Information from The Hague municipal archives], *Obreen's Archf Ned. Kstgesch.*, iii (1880–81), pp. 255–98; iv (1881–2), pp. 1–44, 34–221; v (1882–3), pp. 67–94, 129–66
J. Gram: *De schildersconfrerie Pictura* [The artists' confraternity] (Rotterdam, 1882)
J. H. Plantenga: *De Academie van 's-Gravenhage en haar plaats in de kunst van ons land* [The Hague Academy and its place in the art of our country] (The Hague, 1938)
E. Voet: *Merken van Haagsche goud- en zilversmeden* [Trade marks of gold and silversmiths in The Hague] (The Hague, 1941)
A. Staring: *Kunsthistorische verkenningen* [Art historical researches] (The Hague, 1948)
Zeven eeuwen Den Haag [Seven centuries in The Hague] (exh. cat., The Hague, Gemeentemus., 1948)
Haags zilver uit vijf eeuwen [The Hague silver from five centuries] (exh. cat., The Hague, Gemeentemus., 1967)
B. Haak: *The Golden Age: Dutch Painters in the Seventeenth Century* (Amsterdam, 1984)
RUDOLF E. O. EKKART

3. 1800 AND AFTER. In 1800 a Nationale Konstgalerij (National Art Gallery), comprising those parts of the Stadholder's collection that had not been taken to France by Napoleon Bonaparte, was set up in the Huis ten Bosch (*see* §V, 3 below). Here, painters were able to make copies after Old Masters to improve their own technique. In 1808 King Louis Napoleon (*reg* 1806–10) introduced the *Tentoonstellingen van Levende Meesters* (Exhibitions of Living Masters), comparable to the Paris Salon, which took place in major cities on a rotating schedule.

Until the end of the 18th century art education had been left to Pictura (the Painters' Association), but from the time of the French occupation it was considered the responsibility of the French government. In 1839 the Haagsche Teeken-Academie (Hague Drawing School), housed in an imposing Neo-classical building by the city architect Zeger Reyers, was opened, with places for 400 students. Most of the art treasures taken during the Napoleonic wars had been returned to The Hague under state ownership and in 1822 were moved to the Mauritshuis, where such young painters as Wijnand Nuyen, Gerard Builders (1838–65) and Jan Hendrik Weissenbruch would copy the Old Masters. Many artists completed their training in the studio of a master of Romantic landscapes, one of whom was Andreas Schelfhout, whose students worked mostly in the Dutch landscape tradition. However, Schelfhout encouraged Johan Barthold Jongkind to go to Paris to study with Eugène Isabey. French and German Romanticism was slow to penetrate; nevertheless, the work of Nuyen shows the influence of Isabey, Richard Parkes Bonington and the Düsseldorf school.

Sculpture remained largely neglected. The equestrian statue of *William the Silent* (1845) in the Noordeinde was made by the French sculptor Alfred-Emilien O'Hara, Comte de Nieuwerkerke; the monument of *Liberty* (designed by Johan Philip Koelman) in Plein 1813 was executed in 1869, after a long dispute, by the Belgian Joseph Jaquet (1822–98).

The Pulchri Studio (founded 1847), an artists' association, was an important stimulus for artistic life. Life classes and discussions were held, and contacts were made between artists and collectors. The association board was responsible for organizing the exhibitions of living masters whenever they were held in The Hague. The exhibition of

1875 led to the recognition of a distinct HAGUE SCHOOL of painters devoted to landscapes and genre pieces, among them Jozef Israëls, the Maris brothers, Anton Mauve and Jan Hendrik Weissenbruch. In 1876 several of them founded the Hollandsche Teeken-Maatschappij (Dutch Drawing Society).

Painters of the Hague school became well known at international exhibitions, and the demand for their work spread abroad. The Paris dealers Goupil opened a branch in The Hague and absorbed the firm run by an uncle of Vincent van Gogh. Vincent worked there as a junior clerk and later returned to The Hague to study with his cousin, Anton Mauve, absorbing the influence of the Hague school. Piet Mondrian was also taught in The Hague, by his uncle Frits Mondriaan (1853–1932). A view of the beach at Scheveningen, near The Hague, is the subject of H. W. Mesdag's famous *Panorama* (see fig. 4), to which important contribution was made by George Hendrik Breitner, Théophile de Bock, Bernard Blommers and Sientje Mesdag-van Houten (1834–1909).

In 1892 the Haagsche Kunstkring (Hague Art Circle) was founded by Jan Toorop and de Bock. Toorop was also a member of the Belgian group Les XX, who were soon exhibiting in The Hague. The Kunstkring, which organized the first memorial exhibition of the work of van Gogh in 1892, became a meeting-place for painters, musicians, architects and writers, including followers of

various movements such as Neo-Impressionism and Symbolism. The Hague also became the centre of the Dutch Art Nouveau movement. In 1884 the Gemeentemuseum, devoted to the city's history and modern art, was established, though it was not until 1935 that it moved to the purpose-built site by H. P. Berlage (see fig. 2 above).

The influence of the Hague school lingered well into the 20th century. Such painters as Willem Bastiaan Tholen, Willem de Zwart and Willem Adriaan van Konijnenburg perpetuated what had become a somewhat introspective tradition. The Akademie voor Beeldende Kunst (est. 1682), however, introduced a new approach from such teachers as Paul Citroen and Willem Rozendaal (1899–1971).

After World War II the painters' group Verve (1952–7), of which Co Westerik was a member, used figurative painting as their point of departure, sometimes with a Surrealistic aspect. Abstract art was represented in the 1950s by Jaap Nanninga, Willem Hussum (1900–74) and Piet Ouborg. In 1950 the Haagse Salon was founded to exhibit the work of new artists.

Prominent painters of the 1970s and 1980s included Pat Andréa (*b* 1942), Peter Blokhuis (*b* 1938), Walter Nobbe (*b* 1941), Jurjen de Haan (*b* 1936), Maarten van Dreven (*b* 1941) and Arja van den Berg (*b* 1947). Each perpetuated a more or less figurative tradition. De Haan was one of the initiators of the Nieuwe Haagse Salon

4. H. W. Mesdag, George Hendrik Breitner, Théophile de Bock, Bernard Blommers and Sientje Mesdag van Houten: *Panorama of Scheveningen* (detail), oil on canvas, h. 14 m, circum. 120 m, 1881 (The Hague, Panorama Mesdag)

(founded 1984), at which young artists not yet affiliated with an established society could exhibit. Non-figurative artists such as Gerard Verdijk (*b* 1934) and Auke de Vries (*b* 1937) developed independently of the local Hague tradition.

BIBLIOGRAPHY

G. H. Marius: *Dutch Painters of the 19th Century* (Woodbridge, 1973)
Verve, 1952–1957 (exh. cat. by J. Sillevis, The Hague, Gemeentemus., 1974)
M. van Delft: 'Kunstbeschouwingen bij "Pulchri Studio", 1847–1917', *Jb. Die Haghe* (1980), pp. 147–68
J. J. Beljon: *300 jaar Koninklijke Academie van Beeldende Kunsten, 's-Gravenhage, 1682–1982* (The Hague, 1982)
G. Pollock: 'Stark Encounters: Modern Life and Urban Work in Van Gogh's Drawings of The Hague, 1881–3', *A. Hist.*, vi (1983), pp. 330–58
The Hague School (exh. cat. by C. Dumas, R. de Leeuw and J. Sillevis, Paris, Grand. Pal.; London, RA; The Hague, Gemeentemus.; 1983)
L'arte dell'acquerello olandese dell'ottocento (exh. cat. by J. Sillevis, Rome, Gab. N. Stampe, 1985)
M. van der Mast and others: *Vincent van Gogh en Den Haag* (exh. cat., The Hague, Hist. Mus.; Florence, Pal. Medici-Riccardi, 1990–91)
R. de Leeuw and others: *De kunst van het tentoonstellen: De presentatie van beeldende kunst in Nederland van 1800 tot heden* (The Hague and Amsterdam, 1991)
Dutch Drawings from the Age of Van Gogh, from the Collection of the Haags Gemeentemuseum (exh. cat. by J. Sillevis, Cincinnati, OH, Taft Mus., 1992)

JOHN SILLEVIS

III. Centre of furniture production.

During the second half of the 19th century the furniture industry in The Hague became concentrated (to a far greater extent than elsewhere in the Netherlands) in a few large factories, which catered primarily for the prosperous middle classes. These factories enjoyed a reputation for high quality and specialized in providing complete interiors from upholstery to panelling. Three of the factories—HORRIX, H. PANDER & Zonen and H. P. MUTTERS—achieved a nationwide reputation for luxury goods, owing to commissions from the royal family. There were also several smaller workshops that produced noteworthy furniture, among them John Uiterwijk & Co.'s Arts and Crafts workshop (*see* ARTS AND CRAFTS, JOHN TH. UITERWIJK).

BIBLIOGRAPHY

J. M. W. van Voorst tot Voorst: 'Haagse meubelmakers en negentiende-eeuwse meubelstijlen', *Antiek*, iii (1974), pp. 237–62
——: 'Twee Haagse meubelfabrieken' [Two furniture factories in The Hague], *Antiek*, iv (1974), pp. 357–75
J. de Mooy: 'Kunsthandel Arts and Crafts in Den Haag, 1898–1904', *Kunstlicht*, xii (1982), pp. 19–23
M. Teunissen: 'Pander', *Industry and Design in the Netherlands, 1850–1950* (exh. cat., Amsterdam, Stedel. Mus., 1985), pp. 260–63

MONIQUE D. J. M. TEUNISSEN

IV. Buildings.

1. GROTE KERK. A small chapel occupied the site in the 13th century, and was replaced by a church dedicated to St Jacob in the 14th. Of this building, only the three bays along the northern side remain. Apart from these, the church, known more often as the Grote Kerk than as the St Jacobskerk, dates mainly from the 15th century: the hexagonal tower from 1420–24 and the nave, aisle and side chapels, all barrel vaulted in wood, from 1456. Between 1490 and 1500 the large wooden-vaulted choir was built in Brabant Late Gothic style. It is articulated

with slender columns whose capitals are decorated with a double row of leaves and is surrounded by an ambulatory with a stone stellar vault. The church interior is wide, allowing a maximum of light and space. The proportions are large and the impression monumental, but a careful use of vaulting has ensured that the outward pressure of the roof on the walls is reduced to a minimum.

After a major fire in 1539, the church and tower were quickly restored to their original form, except that the tower was given a new top, in the Renaissance style. The vaults of the nave were covered with a wooden ceiling in 1829–30 and those of the choir in 1912–20, when the church was extensively restored by P. J. H. Cuypers. Further restoration took place under Ph. Bolt in 1951–62, including the restoration of the top of the Renaissance tower, which for a period had been replaced with a Gothic Revival cast-iron spire.

The pulpit (1550), surmounted by a small domed baldacchino, is an outstanding example of Dutch Renaissance carving. The stained-glass windows in the choir are attributed to Dirck Crabeth and represent the *Annunciation* (set in the Binnenhof) and the *Virgin and Child with Charles V, the Donor* (1547). There are a marble epitaph (1670) by Rombout Verhulst for the lawyer *Theodorus Graswinckel* (*d* 1666) and a monument made by Bartholomeus Eggers to *Admiral Jacob van Wassenaar Obdam* (1667), who was killed in the sea battle of Lowestoft (1665). The design for this was by the painter Cornelis Moninks (*c.* 1623–66). At the south end of the nave is the Assendelft Chapel with a stone cross vault, probably made after the fire of 1539. Within the chapel are alabaster tombs of *Heer van Assendelft* (*d c.* 1492) and his wife, *Beatrix van Daelem* (*d c.* 1492). There is also a marble tomb to *Philip, Landgraaf van Hessen Philipstal* (*d* 1721), designed by Daniel Marot I. Along the north and south aisles are 34 panels decorated with the coats of arms of the Knights of the Golden Fleece, who met in the church in May 1456, summoned by Philip the Fair, 3rd Duke of Burgundy. The panels are original, but the frames were lost in the fire of 1539.

BIBLIOGRAPHY

H. F. Ambachtsbeer, ed.: 'Grote of St Jacobskerk: De restauratie en aanpassing van de Grote Kerk te 's-Gravenhage', *Ver. Onderzoek Mnmt.*, v (1987) [whole issue]
C. F. C. G. Boissevain and C. M. Nigten, eds: *De Grote of St Jacobskerk van 's-Gravenhage* (Zwolle, 1987)

□

2. THE BINNENHOF. The foundation of the counts' brick building in the Binnenhof is undocumented. The earliest sources are two mid-14th-century chronicles, which state that it was founded by Count William II (*reg* 1234–56), who sought to confirm his status after his election as Holy Roman Emperor in 1248. He allegedly began building a 'princely residence' at the Binnenhof but was killed in battle before the project had been completed. Other sources yield little information. There is a series of accounts, the oldest dating from 1316, but some (1317–43) are missing, and in any case they do not mention events. There are also various paintings, prints and drawings with representations of the Binnenhof, but most of these date from the 16th century and later.

Architectural research, however, has supplied a considerable amount of evidence. While restoring the Ridderzaal (Knights' Hall) *c.* 1900, Cornelis Hendrik Peters deduced, for stylistic reasons, that the Grote Zaal (Great Hall), as it was previously known, and the living quarters behind it dated from 1275–80. This accorded with de Wit's reconstruction of the building's history (1954), which was based on a deed of 1229 that stated that Floris IV (*reg* 1222–34) bought a piece of land where there had once stood an earlier palace (destr. 1204), parts of the foundations of which he incorporated into a small structure; on his death, William II built a residence flanked by a round tower and the remains of a square tower, on the other side of this ruined complex, and a quarter of a century later Floris V (*reg* 1256–96) had the Ridderzaal built, but on a larger ground-plan than his father had visualized. Another theory, based on a comparison between the Binnenhof and part of the nearby abbey church at Loosduinen, was put forward by ter Kuile (1978), who claimed that it was Floris IV who had the original Ridderzaal built. William II then partly demolished his father's building to make room for a larger knights' hall. Ter Kuile dated the Ridderzaal to the mid-13th century. More recently, A. J. J. Mekking, comparing the Ridderzaal with Westminster Hall in London and Salisbury Cathedral, argued that only Floris V could have been responsible for a hall so English in concept, for contact between the Dutch and English courts occurred for the first time in the 1270s when he and the English king Edward I (*reg* 1272–1307) were negotiating a marriage between their children. According to Mekking, 1285–95 is the most plausible date of construction.

The Ridderzaal (see fig. 5) is 38.40 m long, 17.80 m wide and about 27 m high. It is free-standing, except for the east side where it adjoins the other parts of the Binnenhof. In front of the main entrance is a projecting porch, and in the façade is a rose window, 5 m in diameter. At each end of the façade is a round stair tower; these provided access to the cellars and defensive tunnel. The hall is divided into six bays; in each (except for the first on either side) is a tall window with leaded panes. The original floor was of unglazed tiles. The hall's distinctive feature was its timber roof carried by seven trusses, a 13th-century masterpiece. At the time of Albert I of Bavaria (*reg* 1389–1404), a structure was erected for the accountant above the new portal, next to the Ridderzaal. After Albert's death, the Binnenhof was rarely used as the count's residence. Gradually all the open areas were filled in. In the second half of the 17th century the hall became a saleroom and, from the 18th century, national lotteries were held there: it hence became known as the Loterijzaal. In 1806 it was fitted out as a palace for Louis Napoleon, and in 1815 it again became a public assembly room. In 1862 it was closed for restoration. The state architect Willem Nicolaas Rose, mistakenly believing that the roof dated from much later than the 13th century, wanted to replace it with a cast-iron structure on columns. Despite a storm of protest, his plan was carried out. Fortunately the roof had been measured and drawn by J. Cramer in 1859, permitting its restoration in 1898–1905 by C. H. Peters (advised by P. J. H. Cuypers). The hall is now used for social gatherings of the two houses of parliament, which

5. The Hague, the Binnenhof, interior view of the Ridderzaal, 13th century; restored 1898–1905

meet in chambers at the Binnenhof. In addition to the First and Second Chambers of the parliament, there are other rooms at the Binnenhof not normally open to the public: the Rolzaal (1511) where justice was administered, the Lairessezaal (1688) decorated with allegorical paintings by GÉRARD DE LAIRESSE, the Statenzaal (rebuilt 1697) and the Trèveszaal, named from the truce with Spain in 1688.

BIBLIOGRAPHY
C. H. Peters: *De Groote Zaal op het Binnenhof te 's-Gravenhage* [The Great Hall of the Binnenhof of 's-Gravenhage] (The Hague, 1905)
Beschrijving van de grafelijke zalen op het Binnenhof te 's-Gravenhage [Description of the count's halls of the Binnenhof in 's-Gravenhage] (The Hague, 1907)
C. de Wit: 'Het ontstaan van het Haagse Binnenhof' [The origins of the Binnenhof in The Hague], *Kon. Ned. Oudhdknd. Bond: Bull. KNOB* (1954), pp. 2–22
E. H. ter Kuile: 'De bouwgeschiedenis van het grafelijk paleis op het Binnenhof' [The history of the construction of the count's palace in the Binnenhof], *Holland*, x (1978), pp. 313–28
E. H. P. Cordfunke: 'Floris V en de Schotse troon' [Floris V and the Scottish throne], *Holland in wording* (Hilversum, in preparation)
A. J. J. Mekking: 'De "Grote Zaal" van Floris V te Den Haag: Een onderzoek naar de betekenis van het concept' [The Great Hall of Floris V of The Hague: an investigation into the meaning of the concept], *Holland in wording* (Hilversum, in preparation)
INGRID W. L. MOERMAN

3. HUIS TEN BOSCH. Early in 1645 Pieter Post, the newly appointed court architect, was asked to design a house for Princess Amalia von Solms (*see* ORANGE NASSAU, (4)), wife of Prince Frederick Henry, and a few months later she received permission from the States of Holland to use land on the east side of the Hague forest. In September the first stone of the Huis ten Bosch was laid. Situated in the former domains of the Counts of

Holland, it was developed according to different criteria from the country houses built outside of The Hague by the Prince himself. Whereas Honselaarsdijk and the HUIS TER NIEUBURCH, RIJSWIJK, were inspired by the broad layouts of contemporary France, the Huis ten Bosch has a compact, centralized design based on Italian models. Two suites of apartments are balanced symmetrically around a central hall, the Oranjezaal (Orange Hall), which rises through three floors and is crowned by an octagonal cupola. The single-storey entrance porch, approached up a long flight of steps and surmounted by a balustraded balcony, stands proud of the main structure. The Oranjezaal was originally planned as an official reception room, but this changed drastically after Frederick Henry's sudden death in 1647. His widow decided to dedicate the central hall to the glorious memory of her husband and invited Constantijn Huygens (i) to develop a learned programme of paintings to celebrate the heroic deeds of the Prince and propagate the dynastic claims of the Orange Nassau family. The cycle was intended to be akin to that previously commissioned by Charles I in Whitehall Palace, London (destr.).

The decorative scheme of the Oranjezaal (1648–52), coordinated and partly executed by Jacob van Campen, was arranged in four parts. On entering the hall, the visitor sees the largest scene, the *Triumph of Prince Frederick Henry* by Jacob Jordaens, accompanied by allegories of peace. Jordaens represented the *Apotheosis of the Prince* above the main scene symbolizing his military success. Opposite, above the entrance, are panels allegorizing the *Birth of the Prince* (painted by Caesar van Everdingen) and the new era of cultural excellence and military supremacy that it heralded. On the two sides of the hall the two main aspects of the Prince's life are illustrated: his public role as a general and statesman and his private role as a husband and father. The paintings were executed by a team of artists under van Campen's supervision, some from the southern Netherlands—Antwerp (e.g. Jordaens, Thomas Willeboirts Bosschaert, Jan Lievens, and Gonzales Coques) and 's Hertogenbosch (e.g. Theodoor van Thulden)—but the majority from Haarlem (e.g. van Campen, van Everdingen, Salomon de Bray, Pieter de Grebber, Pieter Soutman and Gerrit van Honthorst). All the artists were chosen for their skill in monumental history painting.

Between 1734 and 1737 the palace was substantially enlarged for Stadholder William IV, through the addition of side wings designed by Daniel Marot I. Later it was completely restored (1977–81) to serve as a residence for Queen Beatrix (*reg* 1980–) and her family.

BIBLIOGRAPHY

P. Post: *De sael van Orange, ghebouwt by haere Hooch', Amalie Princesse Douariere van Orange* (Amsterdam, 1655)

D. F. Slothouwer: *De paleizen van Frederik Hendrik* (Leiden, 1946)

H. P. R. Rosenberg, E. C. Vaillant and D. Valentijn: *Architektuur gids Den Haag* (The Hague, 1988)

K. A. Ottenheym and J. J. Terwen: *Pieter Post (1608–1669)* (Zutphen, 1993)

ELISABETH DE BIÈVRE

Hague, William (*b* Cavan, 1840; *d* Dublin, 22 March 1899). Irish architect. The son of a local builder, he had already designed a number of fine churches that were inspired by the Irish work of A. W. N. Pugin, such as that at Ballybay (1859), Co. Monaghan, and Butlers Bridge (1861), Co. Cavan, by the time he moved to Dublin in 1862. His practice, based in Dublin, was primarily in the country and was closely associated with Catholic Church property, including schools, seminaries, hospitals and convents. Among the parish churches he designed for his native diocese of Kilmore are St Brigid's (1862), Killeshandra. This has a spacious nave with two aisles, two short transepts and a shallow chancel. The architectural treatment is simple but not severe, and a sense of lightness is heightened by the clear layout. The large stained-glass window (produced in France) carries figures of Christ, the Virgin and the Four Evangelists; smaller panels incorporate symbols of the Passion. All his buildings display the contemporary interest in polychromy, employing local stones, especially limestone, as well as more costly imported stones and marbles. The parish church at Kingscourt (1872), Co. Cavan, has an exterior of hammered local sandstone and dressed Carrickmacross limestone; the interior incorporates polished Aberdeen granite columns on limestone bases with Bath stone capitals. His large secular buildings include St Patrick's College (1871), Cavan, and Sligo Town Hall (1866–70). Hague supervised the completion of many churches including SS Augustine and John (1898), Thomas Street, Dublin, which was commissioned from E. W. Pugin and George Coppinger Ashlin in 1860. Following the death of J. J. McCarthy in 1882 he completed the spire of the College Chapel, Maynooth, Co. Kildare. He was involved with many professional organizations, becoming a Fellow of the Royal Institute of Architects of Ireland in 1863 and a member of the Society of Antiquaries in 1864.

BIBLIOGRAPHY

J. Sheehy: *J. J. McCarthy and the Gothic Revival* (Belfast, 1977)

HUGH MAGUIRE

Hague school. Group of Dutch artists, mainly living in The Hague between 1870 and 1900. The name was first coined in 1875 by the critic Jacob van Santen Kolff (1848–96). The Hague school painters drew their inspiration from the flat polder landscape and the everyday lives of peasants and fishermen around The Hague and the nearby port of Scheveningen.

The group covers two generations of painters, born roughly between 1820 and 1845. Their headquarters was the artists' society Pulchri Studio. In the mid-1850s some of the younger painters, including the three brothers Jacob, Matthijs and Willem Maris from The Hague, and the Haarlem-based Paul Joseph Constantin Gabriël and Anton Mauve, laid the foundation for a new landscape art based on the close study of nature in the area around Oosterbeek, later styled the 'Dutch Barbizon'. Jozef Israëls, who was still living in Amsterdam at the time, established himself as the leading artist in the depiction of fishing scenes in the early 1860s.

In many ways the Hague school painters built on the achievements of the 17th-century Dutch masters, whose brilliant skies they emulated, but stylistically they were more influenced by the contemporary Barbizon school in France. Like their 17th-century ancestors, they mostly specialized in well-defined areas. Johannes Bosboom painted church interiors. Jozef Israëls and his close followers Adolphe Artz, Philip Sadée (1837–1904), Albert Neuhuys and Bernard Blommers all specialized in figure paintings and interiors showing the life of the fishing communities. Willem Roelofs started by painting Romantic wooded landscapes but then turned to painting cattle, as did his younger colleagues Anton Mauve and Willem Maris. H. W. Mesdag, originally a banker from Groningen and a prominent collector of Barbizon painting, scored a surprising success at the Paris Salon of 1870 with *Breakers in the North Sea* and restricted himself to marine painting subsequently. As painters of land- and townscapes, Jacob Maris and Jan Hendrik Weissenbruch were the most versatile. Matthijs Maris is generally included as a member of the school but his late work is closer to German Romantic illustrators and the Pre-Raphaelites than the rural art of the Hague school; he was an important influence on the Dutch Symbolists. The work of artists of the Hague school is distinguished from most contemporary European landscape and genre painting by an extreme preference for tonal painting, which earned them the nickname of the 'Grey school'. Their aim was to render atmospheric effects. Their work is Realist in style and, though not free from sentiment, generally succeeds in avoiding the anecdotal. The influence of the school, especially Jacob Maris, Mauve and Israëls, was enormous; they dominated the Dutch art world until the end of the 19th century. Some younger artists, such as Willem de Zwart and Willem Bastiaan Tholen, continued their intimate and restrained manner, while the 'Amsterdam Impressionists', such as Floris Arntzenius, George Breitner and Isaac Israëls, developed a more outgoing urban variant of the school in the 1880s and 1890s. Jan Toorop, Vincent van Gogh and Piet Mondrian were all dominated by the Hague school in their early work.

The Hague school was widely shown and collected abroad, particularly in the USA, Canada and Scotland. Some of the most important collectors were Scots by birth, including James Staats Forbes, Alexander Young, John Forbes White (1831–1904) and William Burrell. The main dealers for the Hague school were Goupil (The Hague, Paris), Elbert J. van Wisselingh (London), the French Gallery (London), Knoedler (New York) and Vose (Boston). Paintings and watercolours of the Hague school can be seen in abundance in Dutch museums, such as the Gemeentemuseum and Rijksmuseum Hendrik Willem Mesdag in The Hague, and the Rijksmuseum and Rijksmuseum Vincent van Gogh in Amsterdam.

For illustrations *see* MARIS, (1); MAUVE, ANTON; ROELOFS, WILLEM.

BIBLIOGRAPHY

J. de Gruyter: *De Haagse school*, 2 vols (Rotterdam, 1968–9)
The Hague School: Dutch Masters of the 19th Century (exh. cat., ed. R. de Leeuw; Paris, Grand Pal.; London, RA; The Hague, Gemeentemus.; 1983)
The Age of Van Gogh: Dutch Painting, 1880–1895 (exh. cat., ed. R. Bionda and C. Blotkamp; Glasgow, Burrell Col.; Amsterdam, Rijksmus. van Gogh; 1991)

RONALD DE LEEUW

Ha ha. Landscape barrier in the form of a hidden trench. It is used in country estates as an alternative to fencing to keep livestock confined to their own grazing area and out of the gardens; it has the advantage of not interrupting the view from the house.

□

Hahn [Haan; Han], **Herman** [Hermann] (*bapt* Nysa, Silesia, 20 July 1574; *d* Chojnice, between 18 Dec 1627 and 22 March 1628). Silesian painter. Probably trained by his father of the same name, whose paintings are extant in Brzeg, he lived in Gdańsk from *c.* 1597, and in 1623 he settled in Chojnice, although continuing to work in Gdańsk. In 1609 he renovated a mural, the *Transformation of Actaeon* (destr.), for the Artushof, Gdańsk, and in 1616 he donated an *Agony in the Garden* (destr. 19th century) to the church of St Mary, Gdańsk. He was involved in the founding of the city's painters' guild in 1612 and painted numerous altarpieces in the region; an *Annunciation* (1616) is in the parish church at Kläckeberga, near Kalmar, Sweden. Most of his works, however, were produced for the Cistercian monasteries at Pelplin and Oliwa: besides full-length historical portraits of Polish kings and other notable figures for Oliwa (all 1616; with participation of artists from Hahn's workshop), he painted for the cathedral at each a *Coronation of the Virgin* (Pelplin, 1623–4; Oliwa, after 1624). These two works are undoubtedly his masterpieces; indeed, the one for Pelplin led to Hahn being named *pictor regius*. One drawing by Hahn is known, *Conscientia* (1611; Cologne, Wallraf Richartz-Mus.).

Hahn's art was eclectic. Like the more important Bartholomäus Strobel, he came from a milieu of Silesian painters' guilds influenced by the art of Rudolfine Prague. However, his works show him to be an artist of independent stature, with a highly developed culture of his own. He enhanced Polish religious painting with pictorial schemes in an 'archaizing hieratic "church style"' (Geissler) that was based iconographically on Late Gothic styles. These became a powerful means of expression for Counter-Reformation piety in the area around Gdańsk, as is testified by the large number of altarpieces and devotional paintings that may be credited to Hahn's workshop or 'school' until the end of the 17th century.

BIBLIOGRAPHY

SAP; Thieme–Becker

M. Walicki, W. Tomkiewicz and A. Ryszkiewicz: *Malarstwo Polskie: Manieryzm, Barok* [Polish painting: Mannerism, Baroque] (Warsaw, 1971), pp. 11–14, 27–8, 32, 57, 311, 317, 319, 324–32, 355, 357; nos 36–46
J. St Pasierb: *Malarz gdański Herman Han* (Warsaw, 1974)
Zeichnung in Deutschland: Deutsche Zeichner, 1540–1640 (exh. cat. by H. Geissler, Stuttgart, Staatsgal., 1979–80), ii, p. 162, no. 0.19
Z. Kruszelnicki: *Historyzm i kult przeszłości w sztuce pomorskiej XVI–XVIII wieku* (Warsaw, 1984), pp. 79–148

JÜRGEN ZIMMER

Hahn, Hermann (*b* Kloster-Veilsdorf, nr Rudolstadt, Thuringia, 28 Nov 1868; *d* Munich, 18 Aug 1945). German sculptor. He entered the Kunstgewerbeschule in Munich in 1887 and a year later went to the Akademie where he studied under Wilhelm von Rümann until 1892. In 1896 he took over Rümann's teaching at the Akademie; he became an honorary professor in 1902 and was appointed full professor in 1912, training a whole generation of sculptors who were nicknamed the 'Münchner Archaiker'. Although he became a member of the National Socialist Party, he was compelled to give up his teaching post in

1937. The small bronze statue *Eva* (e.g. Munich, Ver. Bild. Kstler) established Hahn's reputation as a *Jugendstil* artist. It was only in his middle years that he developed into an outstanding representative of neo-classicism, as is demonstrated in particular by his two monuments to *Moltke*, one made in 1899 for Chemnitz, in the Hauptmarkt, and the other in 1909 for Bremen, on the façade of the north tower of the Liebfrauenkirche, and the monument to *Liszt* made in 1900 for Weimar, in the Grossherzoglicher Park. While he still adhered to the portrait figure in these statues, in his monument to *Goethe* for Lincoln Park, Chicago, unveiled in 1914, he turned the poet into a symbolic figure in the guise of a youthful hero from antiquity.

From the end of World War I until the mid-1920s Hahn incorporated Nordic elements in his work. On the other hand, his last monumental sculpture, *The Charioteer* (1931) sited in front of the Technische Universität in Munich, was said to have 'proto-Nazi' features because of its size and subject-matter. He also created full-length portraits, busts and portrait reliefs and medallions, as well as numerous architectural sculptures, fountains and tombs.

BIBLIOGRAPHY

A. Volwahsen: *Der Bildhauer Hermann Hahn (1868–1945)* (Munich, 1987)
M. G. Davidson: *Kunst in Deutschland, 1935–1945* (Tübingen, 1988), p. 444

CLEMENTINE SCHACK VON WITTENAU

Hahn, Wolfgang (*b* Euskirchen, 22 April 1924; *d* Cologne, 5 April 1987). German collector and restorer. After World War II he trained as a restorer of paintings in Cologne, Munich and Vienna. He worked in the Wallraf-Richartz-Museum in Cologne from 1949 and took charge of the restoration department in 1963. He started his collection with paintings by Cologne painters such as Peter Abelen (1884–1962), Joseph Fassbender, Peter Herkenrath (1900–93) and Ludwig Egidius Ronig (1885–1959). Under the stimulus of avant-garde exhibitions in Cologne and Düsseldorf, a keen interest in current events in the world of art and his friendships with artists and gallery owners, Hahn widened the scope of his collection. His advice as a connoisseur of contemporary art was valued not only by his museum colleagues but also by collectors such as Peter Ludwig.

Hahn assembled a remarkably complete collection of works by many artists closely connected with Nouveau Réalisme, including Arman, Christo, César, Jean Tinguely, Niki de Saint-Phalle, Martial Raysse, Raymond Hains and Mimmo Rotella, as well as more than 20 works by Daniel Spoerri. Spoerri's *Hahn's Supper* (Vienna, Mus. Mod. Kst) consists of crockery, cutlery and the remains of a meal for 16 people mounted on a wooden panel; it was prompted by an invitation to Hahn's house in 1964 and shows the tendency of his collection towards object-based art. Among other artistic trends and movements represented in his collection are Fluxus and Happening. Works by George Brecht, Swedish artist Erik Dietmann (*b* 1937), Dieter Roth, Wolf Vostell, German artist Stefan Wewerka (*b* 1928) and Nam June Paik are particularly well represented. The majority of the collection was purchased by the Republic of Austria in 1978 and is housed in the Museum Moderner Kunst, Vienna.

BIBLIOGRAPHY

Sammlung Hahn: Zeitgenössische Kunst (exh. cat., Cologne, Wallraf-Richartz-Mus., 1968)
Museum Moderner Kunst: Sammlung Hahn, Vienna, Mus. Mod. Kst cat. (Vienna, 1979)
Die 60er Jahre: Kölns Weg zur Kunstmetropole, vom Happening zum Kunstmarkt (exh. cat., ed. W. Herzogenrath and G. Lueg; Cologne, Kstver., 1986), pp. 232–61
S. Gohr: 'Epitaph für Wolfgang Hahn', *Bilderstreit: Widerspruch, Einheit und Fragment in der Kunst seit 1960* (exh. cat., Cologne, Mus. Ludwig and Rheinhallen Köln. Messe, 1989), pp. 481–4

ACHIM SOMMER

Hähnel, Ernst Julius (*b* Dresden, 9 March 1811; *d* Dresden, 22 April 1891). German sculptor. He studied architecture in Dresden (1826–30) and in Munich, where Ludwig von Schwanthaler and Ernst Rietschel persuaded him to take up sculpture. He lived in Italy from 1831 to 1832 where he attended the academy in Florence and studied the works of Michelangelo. In Rome he met Joseph Anton Koch, Martin von Wagner and Gottfried Semper, and was influenced by Bertel Thorvaldsen. In 1835 he travelled to Munich, where he became friendly with Bonaventura Genelli and Moritz von Schwind. Works from this period included a bust of *Genelli* (1835; Weimar, Schlossmus.); he also completed statues of *Homer* (1832–43; Munich, Bayer. Staatsbib.), *Perugino* and *Poussin* (both 1832–7; Munich, Alte Pin.), after sketches by Schwanthaler.

Semper persuaded him to return to Dresden in 1838 to help with sculptural decorations for the Hoftheater, for which he produced a *Bacchanalian Procession* (destr. 1869; plaster version, Dresden, Gemäldegal. Neue Meister) and figures of *Aristotle, Sophocles, Shakespeare* and *Molière* for the façade (*in situ*). In 1842 he produced *Flora* and *Pomona* as figures for niches in the façade of the Orangerie in Dresden and a monument to *Beethoven* (1845; Bonn, Münsterplatz). In 1848 he executed a monument to Emperor *Charles IV* (Prague, Karlsbrücke); in the same year he was appointed professor at the Königliche Kunstakademie in Dresden.

The revolution of 1848 and Semper's flight from Dresden to Paris in 1849 interrupted work on the Gemäldegalerie, which had begun in 1847. Working in close collaboration with Rietschel, Hähnel designed a comprehensive programme of contrasting figures for this building. The north side was decorated with characters from Greek mythology and artists from ancient times, and the south side with biblical figures and Christian artists. Hähnel produced the figures on the southern façade, which is dominated by the two life-size figures of *Raphael* and *Michelangelo*; they are two of his most widely admired works (destr. 1945; marble versions, 1871; Leipzig, Mus. Bild. Kst.; 1877; Berlin, Alte N.G.). Hähnel began to develop into a leading monumental sculptor from mid-century and, at the same time, the focus of his activities shifted from Dresden to Vienna. This was partly a reaction to the very slow progress being made on building in Dresden after Semper's departure, which affected architectural sculpture. Apart from minor, largely decorative works, such as the six statues for the Zwingerpavillon (destr. 1849) and the *Evangelists* (destr.) on the tower of the Neustädter Kirche, Hähnel completed only two more important works for Dresden, the monuments to *Frederick*

Augustus II, Elector of Saxony (1866; Dresden, Neumarkt) and *Theodor Körner* (1871; Dresden, Georgsplatz).

Among Hähnel's most important later works produced outside Dresden are the equestrian monument to *Feldmarschall Carl Schwarzenberg* (1864–7; Vienna, Schwarzenberg-Platz), and the allegorical figures, such as the *Pegasus Group*, for the Opera in Vienna (1868–70). Apart from major commissions, such as the equestrian monument to *Duke Frederick William* (1874) in Brunswick and the monument to *Wilhelm Leibnitz* (bronze, 1883; Leipzig, on Kurt-Schumacher-Strasse, August-Platz), during his last two decades he concentrated increasingly on portraits. A few late works reflect the naturalistic and neo-Baroque tendencies of Wilhelmine sculpture; his last works were the personifications of *Architecture* and *Sculpture* (both 1885–94) for the Kunstakademie in Dresden.

BIBLIOGRAPHY
Thieme–Becker
F. Löffler: *Das alte Dresden: Geschichte seiner Bauten* (Dresden, 1955)
F. Otten: 'Ludwig Michael Schwanthaler, 1802–1848: Ein Bildhauer unter König Ludwig I von Bayern', *Stud. Kst 19. Jhts*, xii (1970), pp. 66, 108, fig. 8
H.-E. Mittig and V. Plagemann: 'Denkmäler im 19. Jahrhundert', *Stud. Kst 19. Jhts*, xx (1972)
E. Trier and W. Weyres, eds: *Plastik* (1980), iv of *Kunst des 19. Jahrhunderts im Rheinland* (Düsseldorf, 1979–81)
H. Magirius: *Gottfried Sempers zweites Dresdner Hoftheater: Entstehung, künstlerische Ausstattung, Ikonographie* (Vienna and Cologne, 1985)
PETER SPRINGER

Haid (i). German family of artists. Johann Lorenz Haid (*b* Augsburg, 1702; *d* Augsburg, 1750) and Johann Gottfried Haid (*b* Augsburg, 7 May 1714; *d* Vienna, 5 Sept 1776) were the sons of the Augsburg goldsmith Johann Valentin Haid (1668–1737). Johann Lorenz, a pupil of Georg Philipp Rugendas I, produced primarily engraved portraits, including 22 fantasy heads after Giovanni Battista Piazzetta, of which few have survived. Johann Gottfried studied initially with his brother, then from *c*. 1750 with the Viennese court painter Martin van Mytens II. During a stay in London in the first half of the 1760s he worked as a mezzotint-engraver for John Boydell, producing mezzotints after oil paintings by Rembrandt, Reynolds and Nathaniel Dance, included in the *Catalogue of Plates of John and Josiah Boydell* (London, 1803). He founded a school of mezzotint-engraving in Vienna in 1766, which continued after his death as a specialist school within the Kaiserliche Akademie der Bildenden Künste. He also designed numerous ornamental engravings and made reproductive prints after François de Cuvilliés I.

BIBLIOGRAPHY
NDB; Thieme–Becker

Haid (ii). German family of artists and print publishers. Johann Jakob Haid (*b* Kleineislingen, ?23 Jan or 10 Feb 1704; *d* Augsburg, *bur* 9 Dec 1767) worked initially with the animal painter Johann Elias Ridinger. He then founded a publishing house in Augsburg and became known primarily for the series of large mezzotint portraits after his own and other artists' drawings. Johann Elias Haid (*b* Augsburg, 1737; *d* Augsburg, *bur* 5 Feb 1809) was the son and pupil of Johann Jakob Haid; he was artistically more important than his father, whose publishing house he

continued. Among the important works published by the firm were the 132 coloured engravings in *Britische Tiergeschichten* (Augsburg, 1782), the German translation of Thomas Pennant's *British Zoology* (London, 1768–70), as well as numerous engravings after famous European painters. He was also Protestant Director of the Reichsstädtische Kunstakademie in Augsburg from 1788 to 1809.

PRINTS
J. W. Weimann: *Phytanthoza iconographia . . .* (Regensburg, 1737) [engs by J. J. Haid]
J. J. Haid: *Bilder-sal heutiges Tages lebender und durch Gelahrheit berühmter Schriftsteller . . .* (Augsburg, 1741)
——: *Ehrentempel der deutschen Gelehrsamkeit . . .* (Augsburg, 1747)
C. J. Treu: *Plantae selectae* (Augsburg, 1750) [engs by J. J. Haid]

BIBLIOGRAPHY
NDB; Thieme–Becker
M. Akermann: 'Der Kupferstecher Johann Jakob Haid', *Alt-Württemberg*, ix (1963)
EBBA KRULL

Haida (i). Indigenous people of the Northwest Coast region of North America (*see under* NATIVE NORTH AMERICAN ART). They are divided into two subgroups, the Eagles and the Ravens, and are notable particularly for their canoes, totem poles and richly decorated dwellings.

Haida (ii). *See* NOVÝ BOR.

Haidenreich. *See* HEIDENREICH.

Haider. German family of artists. In the late 15th century and the 16th three generations of the family were active as cabinetmakers, sculptors, painters and masons in Konstanz. Simon Haider (*d c*. 1480) was the most important employer of craftsmen in Konstanz, and his workshop executed commissions for the cathedral. Haider himself prepared the central panel of the high altar (1465; destr.), for which NICOLAUS GERHAERT prepared the figure sculptures. The workshop also executed the choir-stalls (stylistic evidence suggests that Gerhaert may have been the designer) and the main doorway (1470), which has 20 reliefs with scenes from the *Life of Christ* derived from various sources. Haider's two sons, Hans Haider (*d* 1519) and Andreas Haider (i), worked with him, and the sculptors Hans Heckel and Heinrich Iselin were his sons-in-law.

Hans Haider, who became a citizen in 1474, remained in the workshop until his father's death: he is mentioned as independent from 1487 onwards and became mayor and imperial governor in Konstanz. With Heinrich Iselin he worked on the choir-stalls (destr.) for the town church and the altar for the hospice chapel at Überlingen from 1493 onwards. He left the choir-stalls for the Paulikirche, Konstanz, uncompleted at his death. Andreas (i) was a mason, and a younger son, Michael Haider (*d* 1517), was a painter, first mentioned in 1479. In 1485 he was a citizen of Konstanz and became a councillor and a member of the court of magistrates. After 1481 Michael was employed at Konstanz Cathedral, making the new *Stations of the Cross*, gilding the candelabrum in the choir and producing an altarpiece of the *Assumption of the Virgin* in 1503. In 1516 he coloured a free-standing sculptured group of wooden figures dating from 1503. Andreas Haider (ii) (*d* Ravensburg, 1544–5) was the son of Andreas (i) and was a citizen of Konstanz at least by 1522. A painter, he was commissioned by the city to produce a canvas of the *Battle of Milan*, and he produced paintings for the 'Hohes Haus' (1527–8; destr.), Konstanz, Zollernstrasse 29. Among his portraits was one of the *Magistrate of Überlingen* (1528; destr.). Around 1530 he had to leave Konstanz, which had become Protestant, and although Abbot Jakob Murer of Weissenau Abbey near Ravensburg intervened on his behalf with the Council in Konstanz, he was unable to return. In 1539 he became a citizen of Ravensburg, and the drawings in the Weissenau Codex (Schloss Zeil, nr Leutkirch), which had been commissioned by Abbot Murer, possibly date from this period. The only surviving information about a painter, Thomas Haider (*d* 1597), is that he was a 'pictor subtilis et artificiosus' and was buried in Fribourg (Switzerland).

BIBLIOGRAPHY

Thieme–Becker

W. Pinder: *Die deutsche Plastik vom ausgehenden Mittelalter bis zum Ende der Renaissance* (Wildpark-Potsdam, 1929), pp. 361, 364, 388
H. Rott: *Quellen und Forschungen zur südwestdeutschen und schweizerischen Kunstgeschichte im XV. und XVI. Jahrhundert*, i: *Bodenseegebiet* (Stuttgart, 1933), pp. 90, 100, 102–3, 145, 176
H. Wilm: 'Die Kunstsammlung im Schloss zu Berchtesgaden', *Alte Kunstschätze aus Bayern*, ed. H. Wilm (Ulm, 1934), pp. 67–83
C. Gröber: *Das Konstanzer Münster* (Konstanz, 1948), pp. 70, 105
A. Feulner and T. Müller: *Geschichte der deutschen Plastik* (Munich, 1953), p. 304
H. Reiners: *Das Münster Unserer Lieben Frau zu Konstanz*, Die Kunstdenkmäler Südbadens, i (Lindau-Konstanz, 1955), pp. 363–70, 407
G. Dehio: 'Westliches Schwaben', *Handbuch der deutschen Kunstdenkmäler*, rev. E. Gall (Munich, 1956), p. 157
H. Koepf: *Schwäbische Kunstgeschichte* (1963), iii of *Plastik und Malerei der Gotik* (Konstanz, 1962–5), p. 83
H. Huth: *Künstler und Werkstatt der Spätgotik* (Darmstadt, 1967), p. 78
M. J. Liebmann: *Die deutsche Plastik, 1350–1550* (Gütersloh, 1984), p. 176

VINCENT MAYR

Haidt, John Valentine (*b* Danzig [now Gdańsk, Poland], 4 Oct 1700; *d* Bethlehem, PA, 18 Jan 1780). American painter of German birth. Born into a family of goldsmiths, he received his first training in that craft from his father. When his father became a court goldsmith in Berlin, Haidt attended his first drawing lessons at the Akademie der Bildenden Künste in that city. After a 10-year journey around Europe (1714–24) he set up his studio in London, where he joined the Moravian Church. From 1724 to 1738 he worked as a preacher in England and Germany; it was probably *c.* 1746 that he began to paint for the Church. In 1747 he exhibited *First Fruits* (version, Bethlehem, PA, Archv Morav. Church), which contained 25 life-size figures of people converted to Christianity by Moravian missionaries.

In 1752 Haidt was sent to assist in the decorating of Lindsey House, London, owned by the Moravians. In 1754 he and his wife settled in Bethlehem, PA, and then in Philadelphia, where he painted portraits of his American associates and religious scenes for various Moravian churches and missions. His religious pictures are frequently crowded with figures and brightly coloured and exhibit an awkwardness of perspective and scale, for example *Christ before Herod* (Nazareth, PA, Whitefield House Mus.). His portraits of women, all dressed in the Moravian dark garb with tight-fitting white caps tied with ribbons, denoting status (e.g. blue for wives, white for widows), are mannered and pleasantly self-conscious. His portraits of men are realistic depictions, the most successful being his perceptive likeness of *David Nitschmann* (Bethlehem, PA, Archv Morav. Church).

BIBLIOGRAPHY

John Valentine Haidt (exh. cat. by V. Nelson, Williamsburg, VA, Rockefeller Flk A. Col., 1966)
American Colonial Portraits, 1700–1776 (exh. cat. by R. H. Saunders and E. G. Miles, Washington, DC, N.P.G., 1987), pp. 248–9

MONROE H. FABIAN

Haig [Hägg], **Axel Herman** (*b* Katthammarsvik, Gotland, 19 Nov 1835; *d* Southsea, England, 23 Aug 1921). Swedish printmaker, painter and architect. He studied shipbuilding in Karlskrona from 1850 to 1856. The following year he joined the shipbuilders Lawrence Hill & Co. in Glasgow, but soon left to study architecture in London, where he worked with the English architect Ewan Christian (1814–95) and with William Burges. Under the influence of Burges he became especially interested in Gothic architecture. In the late 1870s he began etching, with the intention of illustrating a book on Scotland's medieval architecture (examples in Stockholm, Nmus.). Haig contributed illustrations to numerous English magazines, including *The Architect*. (For Haig's drawing of William Burges's competition entry for the Law Courts, London, *see* COMPETITION, fig. 1.) In 1882 he was awarded a medal for his etchings at the Paris Salon and elected an honorary member of the Swedish Royal Academy. He was also a member of the Royal Academy of Painter-Etchers in London.

BIBLIOGRAPHY

E. A. Armstrong: *Axel Herman Haig and his Work* (London, 1905)

MICHELLE FACOS

Haight, Charles C(oolidge) (*b* New York, 17 March 1841; *d* Garrison-on-Hudson, NY, 8 Feb 1917). American architect. He was the son of a minister at New York's prestigious Trinity Church. Throughout his career, Haight relied on his connections with Trinity and with New York's Episcopal élite for major commissions. After serving in the Civil War, Haight studied with Emlen T. Littell (1840–91), opening his own office in 1867. In the 1870s he became architect for Trinity Corporation and designed many commercial and institutional buildings for that organization. Haight was an early proponent of the English-inspired collegiate Gothic style, which he used initially for Columbia College's mid-town New York campus (1880–84; destr. *c.* 1900). For the Episcopal Church's General Theological Seminary (1883–1902) at Chelsea Square, New York, he planned a pair of adjoining quadrangles enclosed on three sides by collegiate Gothic buildings of brick with stone trim. The ensemble, dominated by the library (destr. 1958), chapel and refectory, was to be reminiscent of an English academic complex. Haight made extensive use of the collegiate Gothic at Yale University, New Haven, CT, designing buildings between 1894 and 1914, most notably Vanderbilt Hall (1894) and Phelps Hall (1896) with their Tudor-inspired gatehouses leading to the main campus. Haight was also responsible for the H. O. Havemeyer Residence (1891–3; destr. *c.* 1948), New York, generally considered to have been one of the finest Fifth Avenue mansions. The building exemplified Haight's preference for simple, bold forms rather than the flamboyant ornament favoured by many of his contemporaries. Haight's most unusual work is the New York Cancer Hospital (1884–6; addition, 1889–90; later the Towers Nursing Home), Central Park West, New York, the first hospital in the USA exclusively for cancer patients. The hospital, with its five round towers, was modelled on the French Renaissance château at Le Lude, Sarthe.

BIBLIOGRAPHY

M. Schuyler: 'Great American Architects Series No. 6—The Works of Charles C. Haight', *Archit. Rec.* (1899); repr. in *Great American Architects: Series Nos 1–6, May 1895–July 1899* (New York, 1977)
——: 'Architecture of American Colleges II: Yale', *Archit. Rec.*, xxvi (1909), pp. 393–416
——: 'Architecture of American Colleges IV: New York City Colleges', *Archit. Rec.*, xxvii (1910), pp. 443–69
A. Githens: 'Charles Coolidge Haight', *Archit. Rec.*, xli (1917), pp. 367–9
Towers Nursing Home [New York Cancer Hospital] Designation Report, New York City Landmarks Preservation Commission (New York, 1976)
Buildings and Grounds of Yale University (New Haven, 1979)

ANDREW SCOTT DOLKART

Haihaya [Chedis; Kalachuris of Chedi; Kalacuris of Tripuri]. Dynasty that flourished in central India from the 8th century AD to the early 13th. Tripuri, the capital of the dynasty, was located at the present village of Tewar, near Jabalpur, Madhya Pradesh. As the large kingdom of the Gurjara-Pratiharas fell apart in the 10th century, the Haihayas vied with the CHANDELLA and PARAMARA dynasties and other powers for supremacy in north India. The last notable king was Gayakarna (*reg c.* 1122–53). The Haihayas lingered until 1211 when the Chandella king Trailokyavarman (*reg c.* 1205–41) overran the greater part of their domain.

The Haihayas were largely patrons of Hindu temples, although Jaina and, to a lesser extent, Buddhist sculptures are found throughout their realm. The earliest sculpture associated with the dynasty is a relief panel depicting a royal couple, with an inscription datable to the 8th century (U. Sagar, Archaeol. Mus.). Stylistically related work is found at Nand Chand, Chhoti Deori and Tigowa, all in the Dahala territory ruled by the Haihayas. A school of Shaiva Siddhanta was introduced into the kingdom in the 10th century: the monastery at Chandrehe, dated by an epigraph to AD 973, and the sites of Bilhari and Gurji belonged to this religious tradition. The temples at Gurji no longer survive; an enormous temple gate was removed to Rewa Palace in the 19th century.

BIBLIOGRAPHY

R. D. Banerji: *The Haihayas of Tripuri and their Monuments*, Mem. Archaeol. Surv. India, xxiii (Calcutta, 1931)
R. C. Majumdar, ed.: *The Age of Imperial Kannauj*, iv of *The History and Culture of the Indian People* (Bombay, 1955, 2/1964), pp. 87–99
V. V. Mirashi, ed.: *Inscriptions of the Kalachuri–Chedi Era*, Corp. Inscr. Indic., iv (Ootacamund, 1955)
R. C. Majumdar, ed.: *The Struggle for Empire*, v of *The History and Culture of the Indian People* (Bombay, 1957, 2/1966), pp. 61–4
D. M. Stadtner: 'Nand Chand and a Central Indian Regional Style', *Artibus Asiae*, xliii/1–2 (1981–2), pp. 129–52
——: 'Kalacuri Art at Singhpur', *Orient. A.*, xxxviii/3 (1982), pp. 270–78

DONALD M. STADTNER

Haincelin de Hagenau. *See* MASTERS, ANONYMOUS, AND MONOGRAMMISTS, §I: BEDFORD MASTER.

Hainhofer, Philipp (*b* Augsburg, 21 July 1578; *d* Augsburg, 23 July 1647). German dealer, collector, writer, political agent and diplomat. Although his father, Melchior Hainhofer (1539–83), a Protestant cloth merchant, was ennobled by Emperor Rudolf II in 1578, the family did not belong to the Augsburg patriciate. After studying in Padua, Cologne and the Netherlands, Philipp founded his own cloth business (1601) in Augsburg and was elected to the Greater Council (1605) of the city. His trade, mainly in Italian silk but also in objects of vertu and luxury articles of all kinds, brought him into contact with German princes. In 1607 he succeeded his uncle, Hieronymus Hörmann (1544–1607), as correspondent to Henry IV, King of France, and later became political agent to several other rulers, including Philip, Duke of Pomerania-Stettin, and Augustus, Duke of Brunswick-Lüneburg. He also undertook diplomatic missions for his patrons, representing them at ceremonial and political gatherings. His urbanity and flexibility, extensive knowledge of languages and profound humanist education made him well suited to such missions. Although a devout Lutheran, he did not hesitate to work for Catholic princes.

Due to his power of observation and attention to detail, Philipp Hainhofer's reports of his travels are of considerable interest for the history of art, as is his correspondence with patrons. The dukes of Pomerania-Stettin and Brunswick-Lüneburg were his most important patrons in matters of the arts and entertainment. He supplied them not only with objects of vertu, books, clocks, tableware, telescopes and spectacles, games and toys but also with sheep, horses and dogs and even musicians and domestic servants. He is, however, known mainly for the multipurpose cabinets, which served as miniature *Kunst- und Wunderkammern*, made after his instructions by many artists and craftsmen. Through his services in gaining such commissions for the craftsmen of Augsburg, they named him the 'Father of all Artists'. Between 1611 and 1616 the Pomeranian Cabinet was made on commission from Philip, Duke of Pomerania-Stettin, after drawings by Johann Mathias Kager. The joiner was Ulrich Baumgartner (*c.* 1580–1652), and almost 30 artists and craftsmen worked on its decoration and contents, among them Anton Mozart and Matthias Walbaum. The cabinet contained a set of instruments and tools for almost every human occupation, symbolizing the triumph of Art and Science over Nature. The cabinet was destroyed in 1945, but the contents are intact (Berlin, Tiergarten, Kstgewmus.).

Another cabinet (*c.* 1619–26; Florence, Pitti), also made by Ulrich Baumgartner, was executed as a speculative venture on the part of Hainhofer. In 1628 he sold it to Leopold V, Archduke of Tyrol (1586–1632), who presented it to Ferdinand II, Grand Duke of Tuscany. The cabinet was delivered, however, without the intended contents of artefacts and natural specimens. Hainhofer described its pictorial programme as 'a compendium of all the sacred scripture', arousing 'beautiful meditations and contemplations' (Wolfenbüttel, Herzog August Bib., Cod. 6.6. Aug. Fol.).

The only cabinet with its original contents intact (*c.* 1625–31; Uppsala U.) was probably manufactured in Ulrich Baumgartner's workshop. It was bought by the Protestant councillors of Augsburg for presentation to

Gustav II Adolf, King of Sweden (*reg* 1611–32), at his entrance into the city after its capitulation to Swedish troops in April 1632, before which Hainhofer had served as mediator between the Protestant majority and Catholic council; when the Swedish king reinstated the Protestant councillors, Hainhofer was elevated to patrician status. In 1633 the cabinet was transported to Sweden and in 1694 was donated to Uppsala University by Karl XI, King of Sweden (*reg* 1660–97). With its richly carved ebony with hundreds of pictures in lapis lazuli, agate, chalcedony and other hardstones, the cabinet is typically Mannerist in style. It is *c.* 2.4 m high and crowned with a ewer consisting of a Seychelles nut given the form of a ship with silver figures of *Venus* and *Neptune* made by the silversmith Johannes Lencker (*c.* 1573–1637) of Augsburg. The figure of *Venus* is linked with the pictorial programme, of which allegories of love form an important part, with biblical scenes and conventional allegories. The artefacts and natural specimens that form the contents represent the natural world and human activities.

Philipp Hainhofer died in poverty, having lost his fortune and been forced to sell most of the works in his collection during the Thirty Years War. He was deprived of his rank as a patrician when imperial troops recaptured Augsburg in 1635. While he lay dying, another of his cabinets (1631–4; Vienna, Ksthist. Mus.) was bought by Augustus, Duke of Brunswick-Lüneburg, who gave it to Carl Gustaf Wrangel (1613–76), supreme commander of the Swedish army in Germany. It was taken to Sweden, but in the early 19th century it was bought by the Austrian minister in Stockholm and moved to Vienna, where it still remains. The Duke also bought Hainhofer's literary remains (Wolfenbüttel, Herzog August Bib.).

BIBLIOGRAPHY
ADB; *NDB*

P. von Stetten: *Lebensbeschreibungen zur Erweckung und Unterhaltung bürgerlicher Tugend*, i (Augsburg, 1778), pp. 269–88

Philipp Hainhofers Reise-Tagebuch, enthaltend Schilderungen aus Franken, Sachsen, der Mark Brandenburg und Pommern im Jahr 1617, Balt. Stud., ii/2 (1834)

C. Häutle: 'Die Reisen des Augsburgers Philipp Hainhofer nach Eichstädt, München und Regensburg in den Jahren 1611, 1612 und 1613', *Z. Hist. Ver. Schwaben & Neuburg*, viii/1 (1881) [whole issue]

A. von Oechelhäuser: 'Philipp Hainhofers Bericht über die Stuttgarter Kindertaufe im Jahre 1616', *Neue Heidelberg. Jb.*, i (1891), pp. 254–335

O. Doering: 'Des Augsburger Patriciers Philipp Hainhofer Beziehungen zum Herzog Philipp II von Pommern-Stettin: Correspondenzen aus den Jahren 1610–1619', *Quellenschr. Kstgesch. & Ksttech.*, n. s., vi (1894) [whole issue]

——: 'Des Augsburger Patriciers Philipp Hainhofer Reisen nach Innsbruck und Dresden', *Quellenschr. Kstgesch. & Ksttech.*, n. s., x (1901) [whole issue]

J. Lessing and A. Brüning: *Der pommersche Kunstschrank* (Berlin, 1905)

J. Böttiger: *Philipp Hainhofer und der Kunstschrank Gustav Adolfs in Uppsala*, 4 vols (Stockholm, 1909–10)

O. Hartig: 'Unbekannte Reisen des jungen Hainhofer nach München und Stuttgart, 1603–1607', *Der Sammler*, cxviii (1924)

T. Hausmann: 'Der pommersche Kunstschrank: Das Problem seines inneren Aufbaus', *Z. Kstgesch.*, xxii (1959), pp. 337–52

D. Heikamp: 'Zur Geschichte der Uffizien-Tribuna und der Kunstschränke in Florenz und Deutschland', *Z. Kstgesch.*, xxvi (1963), pp. 193–268

G. Himmelheber: 'Ulrich und Melchior Baumgartner', *Pantheon*, xxxiii (1975), pp. 113–20

A. Losman: *Carl Gustaf Wrangel och Europa: Studier i kulturförbindelser kring en 1600-talsmagnat* [Carl Gustaf Wrangel and Europe: a study of the cultural circle of a 17th-century magnate] (Stockholm, 1980), pp. 64–71

B. Volk-Knüttel: 'Maximilian I. von Bayern als Sammler und Auftraggeber: Seine Korrespondenz mit Philipp Hainhofer, 1611–15', *Quellen und Studien zur Kunstpolitik der Wittelsbacher vom 16. bis zum 18. Jahrhundert*, i of *Mitteilungen des Hauses der bayerischen Geschichte* (Munich and Zurich, 1980), pp. 83–128

R. Gobiet, ed.: *Der Briefwechsel zwischen Philipp Hainhofer und Herzog August d.J. von Braunschweig-Lüneburg* (Munich, 1984)

H.-O. Boström: 'Philipp Hainhofer and Gustavus Adolphus's *Kunstschrank* in Uppsala', *The Origins of Museums*, ed. O. Impey and A. MacGregor (Oxford, 1985), pp. 90–101

D. Alfter: *Die Geschichte des Augsburger Kabinettschranks* (Augsburg, 1986)

H.-O. Boström: 'Die geheime Verbindung zwischen Kunst und Natur: Der Kunstschrank Gustavs II. Adolf in Uppsala', *Kst & Ant.*, i (1988), pp. 38–51

——: 'Ein wiederentdeckter Hainhoferschrank', *Kst. & Ant.*, iv (1993), pp. 32–6

——: 'Philipp Hainhofer: Seine Kunstkammer und seine Kunstschränke', *Macrocosmos in microcosmo—Die Welt in der Stube: Zur Geschichte des Sammelns 1450 bis 1800*, Berliner Schriften zur Museumskunde, x, ed. A. Grote (Opladen, 1994)

——: 'Philipp Hainhofer als Vermittler von Luxusgütern zwischen Augsburg und Wolfenbüttel', *Augsburg in der frühen Neuzeit: Beiträge zu einem Forschungsprogramm*, ed. J. Brüning and F. Niewöhner (Berlin, 1995), pp. 140–57

——: 'Ein wiederentdeckter Hainhoferschrank', *Ksthist. Tdskr.* (in preparation)

HANS-OLOF BOSTRÖM

Hains, Raymond (*b* St Brieuc, Côtes-du-Nord, 9 Nov 1926). French décollagist, photographer and sculptor. He began taking photographs in 1944 and in the following year, while studying sculpture at the Ecole des Beaux-Arts in Rennes, met the French artist Jacques de la Villeglé (*b* 1926) with whom he worked collaboratively from 1950 to 1953. In 1949 Hains produced his first pictures using the technique of DÉCOLLAGE, ripping off the successive layers of posters found on city walls (for illustration *see* NOUVEAU RÉALISME). Although the emphasis in these works is often on abstract qualities of texture and colour, he had a particular eye for fragments of text and for their political implications, as in *Peace in Algeria* (375×325 mm, 1956; Paris, Ginette Dufrêne priv. col., see 1986 exh. cat., p. 151). These works were first shown in 1957 alongside those of de la Villeglé, in an exhibition, *Loi du 29 juillet 1881* (Paris, Gal. Colette Allendy), named after the law banning the display of posters; they led to his becoming one of the founder members of NOUVEAU RÉALISME in 1960.

A love of word play led Hains in 1965 to exhibit a series of sculptures and reliefs in the form of giant matchboxes, in homage to the gallery's proprietor, IRIS CLERT, who was nicknamed 'la brune incendiaire' (the fiery brunette); she extended the joke by having the gallery invigilated by firemen. In his later photographs produced in specific contexts, such as *Palissade du chantier du Carré d'Art, Nîmes* (1990; see 1990 exh. cat.), he continued to make use of word games and free associations in relation to names and local particularities; he made reference to archaeological curiosities, local history, gastronomic specialities, famous people of different periods and even other exhibitions of contemporary art in the form of photographs, posters, labels, signs, postcards and other found materials.

BIBLIOGRAPHY
Raymond Hains (exh. cat. by J. de la Villeglé and others, Paris, Cent. N. A. Contemp., 1976)

1960: Les Nouveaux Réalistes (exh. cat., ed. B. Cotenson; Paris, Mus. A. Mod. Ville Paris, 1986), pp. 148–61, 232–4

Raymond Hains (exh. cat., Poitiers, Mus. Poitiers, 1989)
Guide des collections permanentes ou mises en plis: Raymond Hains (exh. cat.
  by C. David and others, Paris, Pompidou, 1990)

For further bibliography *see* DÉCOLLAGE and NOUVEAU RÉALISME.

VANINA COSTA

Hainsch, Johann Georg. *See* HEINTSCH, JOHANN
GEORG.

Hainsse, Zacharie. *See* HEINCE, ZACHARIE.

Hainzelmann [Heinzelman]. German family of engravers. Elias Hainzelmann (*b* Augsburg, ?1640; *d* Augsburg, 1693) was in Paris from 1665 to 1675, in the studio of François de Poilly I, but most of his career was spent in Augsburg. His surviving works include 22 religious subjects based on Francesco Albani, Annibale Carracci, Raphael and Tintoretto, several *Thesenblätter* and *c.* 80 realistic portraits, based on Johann Ulrich Mayr, Daniel de Savoye (1654–1716) and Andreas Stech. Although his style is occasionally rather dry, some works are of high quality, such as the over life-size portrait of *Juliana Winckler* (Hollstein, no. 94), presented as a bust on a small pedestal.

His brother Johann [Jean] Hainzelmann (*b* Augsburg, 1641; *d* Berlin, 1693) was in Paris from 1671 to 1688, where he probably also studied with de Poilly or with Guillaume Vallet (1632–1704) and before 1687 bore the title 'Graveur du Roi'. He produced *c.* 15 religious subjects based on Sébastien Bourdon, Simon Guillebault (*c.* 1636/43–1708), Louis Licherie de Beuron (1629–87) and Poussin, book illustrations and *c.* 30 portraits in the style of Robert Nanteuil, generally of small dimensions and based on his own drawings. The most important of these include *J.-B. Tavernier* (Hollstein, no. 29), *M.-F. Le Tellier* (Hollstein, no. 24) based on Ferdinand Voet (1631–1700), *Jean III Sobieski* (Hollstein, no. 28), *F. Lanchenu* (Hollstein, no. 23) and a group of *Siamese Ambassadors* (Hollstein, nos 31, 33). As engraver to Frederick III, Elector of Brandenburg, from 1688, he executed notable portraits of members of his patron's family.

BIBLIOGRAPHY

Hollstein: *Ger.*; Thieme–Becker
Inventaire du fonds français, graveurs du XVIIème siècle, Paris, Bib. N.,
  Dépt. Est. cat., v (Paris, 1968)

VÉRONIQUE MEYER

Hairreddo Senta. *See* HI-RED CENTER.

Haité, George Charles (*b* Bexley, Kent, 8 June 1855; *d* 1924). English designer and painter. He was the son of George Haité, a textile designer. Among his numerous publications on design, the most important is *Plant Studies for Artists, Designers, etc.* (London, 1884). Comprised of 50 plates of plant ornament, the book also contains a detailed life history of each plant. Using conventionalized motifs derived from a study of nature and Japanese art, he created ceiling designs for J. Tollman & Co., wallpapers for Arthur Sanderson & Sons and Essex & Co., and fabrics for G. P. & J. Baker. He designed small decorative objects; for example, his interior fittings (1896) for the studio of Mr E. Davis included metallic electroliers decorated with leaves and flowers, and four copper repoussé grilles representing the *Four Seasons* (for illustrations see White).

Haité was instrumental in founding the Society of Designers in 1896 and served as its first president. He produced landscapes in oil and watercolour, which he exhibited at the Royal Academy, London. An enthusiastic member of the Langham Sketch Club and the London Sketch Club, he was known for his rapid sketching ability.

BIBLIOGRAPHY

G. White: 'The Work of Geo. C. Haité, Designer and Painter', *Archit.
  Rev.* [London], i (1896), pp. 83–98

E. A. CHRISTENSEN

Haiti, Republic of. Country occupying 26,000 sq. km of the western part of the Caribbean island of Hispaniola (see fig. 1). It is volcanic in origin and mountainous. Intense cultivation of mountain slopes has caused severe erosion, and despite attempts at reforestation, Haiti is virtually barren of forest cover. The principal agricultural regions are the lowlands of the northern plain, the central plateau, the valley of the Artibonite River and the Cul de Sac plain in the south. Over 100 rivers and streams flow from mountain headlands into the Atlantic to the north, the Gulf of La Gonâve to the west and the Caribbean Sea to the south. The largest cities are the capital of Port-au-Prince and Cap-Haïtien in the north. The majority of Haitians speak French Creole and practise the religion of Vodoun.

I. Introduction. II. Cultures. III. Architecture. IV. Painting, sculpture and other arts. V. Patronage and art institutions.

I. Introduction.

Christopher Columbus landed on Hispaniola in 1492, making it a Spanish colony. In 1664 Louis XIV placed the territory of Haiti under the control of the French West India Company, and, renamed Saint-Domingue, it was ceded to France in 1697 by the Treaty of Rijswijk; Spain retained control over Santo Domingo (now the DOMINICAN REPUBLIC) in the east of the island. French hegemony over Saint-Domingue created a wealthy colony with a productive plantation economy built on the labours of African slaves, the Amerindian population having proved too recalcitrant and too physically frail for the gruelling work and maltreatment meted out by their Spanish overlords. Ironically, a Dominican priest, Bartolemé de Las Casas, appalled at the dreadful toll suffered by the Amerindians, suggested the importation of African labour. As a result, Africans arrived in ever-increasing numbers from the beginning of the 16th century until the Haitian Revolution of 1791, led by Toussaint L'Ouverture. Slaves were briefly freed following the French Revolution (1789–99), but slavery was subsequently reimposed, and it was not until independence was declared in 1804 that they were finally emancipated. Despite the country's small size, the nature of its terrain has produced a rich variety of regional differences. The north has tended to retain more vestiges of its colonial past.

Since it became the first independent republic in the Caribbean, Haiti has suffered a troubled history, particularly in the 20th century. Between 1915 and 1934 the country was occupied by the USA, and in 1950, following a military coup, Dr François 'Papa Doc' Duvalier became

1. Map of Haiti

president, marking the beginning of a period of dictatorship that lasted until 1991. After another brief period of military rule, Jean-Bertrand Aristide was re-installed as president in 1994.

BIBLIOGRAPHY

J.-B. du Tertre: *Histoire générale des Antilles habitées par les Français* (Paris, 1667)
Le R. Père Labat: *Nouveau voyage aux îles de l'Amérique*, 8 vols (Paris, 1742)
L. E. Moreau de Saint-Méry: *Description topographique, physique, civile, politique et historique de la partie française de l'Ile de Saint-Domingue*, 2 vols (Philadelphia, 1797)
T. Madiou: *Histoire d'Haiti*, 4 vols (Port-au-Prince, 1848–1922)
H. Courlander: *The Drum and the Hoe: Life and Lore of the Haitian People* (Berkeley, 1960)
C. L. R. James: *The Black Jacobins* (New York, 1963)
U. Stebich, ed.: *Haitian Art* (New York, 1978; Ger. trans., 1979)

II. Cultures.

1. AMERINDIAN. The earliest migrants to arrive in the Caribbean were the Amerindians known as Ciboneys. They came from either Venezuela, Yucatán or Florida, or perhaps from all three regions. Motifs carved on their hemispherical stone vessels, axes and other objects resemble those found on stone bowls and early pottery from Florida, particularly in the striations incised on the rims of pots. Forms of flint implements, however, suggest Cuban connections. The finely polished petalloid celts are found throughout the Caribbean, and they appear with clay griddles that coincide with the development of agriculture. When Columbus landed on the north shore of Haiti, most of the inhabitants were Arawak-speaking Tainos, who are believed to have emigrated from the Amazon Basin. Sometimes they are also referred to as 'Ceramic Indians' from the red slip-painted pottery that they produced. They decorated the handles of their vessels with modelled zoomorphic and anthropomorphic figures, probably of religious significance. On his second voyage Columbus brought the Spanish priest Ramón Pané to make a record of the island's culture. Pané noted that these saucer-eyed creatures with relief appliqués represented deities, or *zemis*. *Zemis* were also carved in wood, stone, bone and shell. They presumably served also as amulets or small, personal altars; funeral remains were also packed into baskets elaborated with figures of *zemis*. Such objects were sometimes preserved in caves, which evidently served as shrines; petroglyphs and paintings of *zemis* have also been found in caves. Pané explained the *zemis* as intermediaries to the all-powerful deity. Columbus recorded in his diary that Taino chiefs (*caciques*) had small houses reserved as *zemi* shrines where ceremonies were led by priests in narcotics-induced trances.

Few objects carved in wood have survived, but these exhibit a high level of skill and aesthetic sensibility. The largest, taken from the Ile de La Gonâve, is a squatting figure carved from a hollowed tree trunk, which may have served as the body of a drum. Several examples of *dujos* (squat, four-legged stools with curved seats carved with an animal or human head at the front) are preserved in the Museo del Hombre Domeniciano (formerly the Museo Nacional), Santo Domingo; the Heye Foundation, Museum of the American Indian, New York; the British Museum, London; and the Musée de l'Homme, Paris. One has its gold inlay intact, a rare surviving example of Taino goldwork (see fig. 2). A terracotta vessel in the form of a head, with characteristic discoid eyes (Paris, Mus. de l'Homme), was used to hold *cohoba*, the narcotic powder inhaled through tubes to induce trance during religious ceremonies (*see also* SOUTH AMERICA, PRE-COLUMBIAN, §I, 3(ii)). One curious and common form is the trigonolite, a triangular stone carving that often bears rudimentary human features, whose function is unknown but could relate to the custom recorded by Columbus's son that each *cacique* had three ritual stones for use in ceremonies for fertility or rain.

Columbus instituted a scheme called *repartimientos* or *encomienda*: a system of distributing land to European settlers that included the Amerindians living there. Within decades of European arrival on Hispaniola the Amerindian population was virtually annihilated, but *encomienda* survived and continued as the foundation of the subsequent plantation economy. The influence of Arawak dwelling-types can be seen in the palisaded walls, porches and lashing building techniques still used in some areas of Haiti.

BIBLIOGRAPHY

I. Rouse: *Prehistory in Haiti* (New Haven, 1939)
E. Mangones and L. Maximilien: *L'Art pré-colombien d'Haïti* (Port-au-Prince, 1941)
F. G. Rainey: *Excavations in the Fort Liberté Region, Haiti* (New Haven, 1941)
M. Aubourg: *Haïti préhistorique* (Port-au-Prince, 1951)
H. J. Braunholtz: 'The Oldman Collection: Aztec Gong and Ancient Arawak Stool', *BM Q.*, xvi/2 (1951), pp. 54–5
I. Rouse: 'Areas and Periods of Culture in the Greater Antilles', *SW J. Anthropol.*, vii (1951), pp. 248–65
——: 'Prehistory of the West Indies', *Science*, i (1964), pp. 419–513
J. E. Cruxent and I. Rouse: 'Early Man in the West Indies', *Sci. Amer.* (Nov 1969), pp. 42–69
M. V. Maggiolo: *Arqueología prehistórica de Santo Domingo* (Singapore, 1972)
I. Rouse: 'Roots: Pre-Columbian', *Haitian Art*, ed. U. Stebich (New York, 1978), pp. 22–5
W. Hodges: 'L'Art rupestre précolombien en Haïti', *Conjonction*, cxliii (1979), pp. 5–38

2. AFRO-CARIBBEAN. After the annihilation of the Amerindians it became imperative for the Spanish to find an alternative source of labour to support their evolving colonial regime. Bartolomé de Las Casas's proposal to import Africans, since he believed them more resistant to the tropical climate and more accustomed to fieldwork, was attractive to the Spanish government. Their concurrent incursions into Mesoamerica had absorbed much of their resources, and the prospect of a productive and relatively docile colony was a welcome one. Nicholas de Ovando, the first Governor of Haiti, ordered the importation of the first Africans; by 1520 they constituted almost all of the labour force. By 1521 the Spanish interest in their Caribbean colonies waned, after they had achieved the conquest of Mexico and tapped the gold reserves of South America. The population dwindled and the northern coast fell prey to French and English pirates.

By the 17th century the population of Saint-Domingue was estimated at 6000 adult white and mulatto males and *c.* 50,000 black slaves. By 1775 the slave population had increased to *c.* 250,000, and whites and mulattos numbered *c.* 30,000. These statistics do not, however, include the 'maroons', escapees from slavery or servitude who sought and maintained asylum in isolated mountain valleys, building their own society based on African rather than European models. Although they periodically raided plantations, the maroons were of only peripheral concern until the years preceding the Revolution. Maroon chiefs formed warrior bands in the mountains and established contact with counterparts in the plantations and towns. The revolutionaries considered themselves as Africans, enlisting the aid of spiritual entities derived primarily from the cultures of Dahomey (*see* BENIN REPUBLIC) and the lower Congo Basin. The complex of beliefs, customs and ethical standards that united them was called Vodoun, a term deriving from the Fon language of Dahomey, as does much of the terminology and practice of Vodoun.

2. Amerindian Taino *dujo*, carved 'gayac' wood seat with inlays and engraving, *c.* 1490 (Paris, Musée de l'Homme)

The 18th century was a crucial period in the development of Haitian culture. A rapidly increasing demand for fieldworkers for sugar and indigo plantations coincided with an influx of Congolese immigrants. Afro-Caribbeans of Dahomean origin tended to look down on the more recent, Congolese arrivals, referring to them as *bossale*, a term used in Vodoun to designate an uncontrolled and often violent possession of the spirit. Vodoun is the religion practised by the majority of Haitian people. An essential objective is the invocation of the *loas* (spirits), which constitute a pantheon of 401, all facets of an all-powerful deity referred to as the 'Bon Met' (Fr. Creole: 'Good Master'). During the ritual these spirits are believed to 'mount' their 'horses', that is possess the devotees. The *loas* are divided into groups or 'nations', two of which are dominant: the Rada *loas*, believed wise and essentially beneficent, are named after Alladah, a Dahomean town; the Petro *loas* have linguistic and symbolic connections to the Republic of Congo and to Angola. The Rada spirits reside over such domestic rites of passage as marriage, initiation and naming; the Petro *loas* are spoken of as tough and fiery, ready to meet the demands of a devotee given the appropriate remuneration. The pantheon of Vodoun reflects sources of other African peoples' migrations: Mande, Bamana, Yoruba, Ewe, Igbo and Akan.

The influence of Africa survives in Haiti in manufacturing techniques, cooperative labour and the construction and design of dwellings in *lakous* (traditional compounds). Such social institutions as the decision-making hierarchy, polygamy, kinship ties and obligations, veneration of ancestors, and child-naming have African prototypes. As in some traditional African societies, women play the crucial role in commercial transactions. Certain assumptions are held in common with African ones, including the accessibility to divinity by means of mediating spirits in anthropomorphic form. Music and dance are central to any gathering in Haiti, and both are heavily influenced by Africa in the instruments, dances, songs and ritual objects used, for example the iron standards (*asens*), deriving from Dahomey, and the power objects (*paquets Congo*). Creolized with sequins, ribbons and feathers, these resemble

3. Afro-Caribbean *vèvè*, geometric ground drawing used in Vodoun ceremonies

the *minkisi* medicine bundles of the Congo and Zaïre. The tradition of linked terracotta bowls honouring twins is found in various African societies, especially the Fon and Bamana.

Before most ceremonies, geometric ground drawings (*vèvès*) are executed in flour, brick dust, ashes or coloured powders (see fig. 3). Sifted skilfully on to the earth floor of the temple (*houmfort*) by a priest or priestess, they are intended to invite spirits to attend the ceremony and possess their devotees. Each *loa* has a particular *vèvè*, and the complete ensemble of hundreds of drawings constitutes a symbolic set. Similar drawings are made in Angola, Zambia, Zaïre and Nigeria; some authorities have suggested Amerindian prototypes. The emblems and the ceremonies have appeared in the paintings of Haitians who are also adepts (*see* §IV below). The influence of Vodoun on arts also applies to such colourful ritual objects as the sequinned flags emblazoned with sacred *vèvès*, shrine objects, sacred wall paintings and regalia. The complex symbolism used in the service of the *loas* directs the use of certain colours, musical rhythms, dance movements, odours and tastes. The ceremonies are multi-sensory in their appeal.

BIBLIOGRAPHY
J. Price-Mars: *Ainsi parle l'oncle* (Paris, 1928; Eng. trans., Washington, DC, 1983)
M. Herskovits: *Life in a Haitian Valley* (New York, 1937)
H. Courlander: *Haiti Singing* (Chapel Hill, 1939)
L. Maximilien: *Le Vodou haïtien: Rite Radas-Canzo* (Port-au-Prince, 1945)
M. Deren: *Divine Horsemen: The Living Gods of Haiti* (New York, 1953)
M. Rigaud: *La Tradition voudoo et le voudoo haïtien* (Paris, 1953)
A. Métraux: *Le Vaudou haïtien* (Paris, 1958; Eng. trans., London, 1959 and New York, 1972)
H. Courlander: *The Drum and the Hoe: Life and Lore of the Haitian People* (Berkeley, 1960)
R. Bastide: *Les Amériques noires* (Paris, 1967; Eng. trans. as *African Civilizations in the New World*, London, 1971)
J. B. Romain: *Africanisme haïtien: Compilations et notes* (Port-au-Prince, 1978)
R. F. Thompson: *Flash of the Spirit: African and Afro-American Art and Philosophy* (New York, 1983)

III. Architecture.

Indigenous architectural forms were a composite of available materials and technologies suitable to the climate and life values of the populace. Several types were published by Gonzalez de Oviedo in 1526 (see bibliography). An early type, the caney, was hexagonal in plan with a single door: cane strips or twigs were lashed to heavy corner posts, often trunks of the royal palm; the roof was steeply pitched for drainage. The more common rectangular-plan form with a verandah-like porch, a single doorway and several small windows was probably based on Yoruban prototypes. Like its modern successor, it was thatched with palm leaves or guinea grass, the wattled walls filled with mud, then plastered. It was grouped with storehouses, cookhouses and a community vodoun temple (*houmfort*) in a compound (*lakou*) that stems from African models. Adapted to the Spanish urban grid, this house type, timber-framed, extended three or four rooms deep. High ceilings and heavily shuttered doors and windows with iron fittings reflected a colonial influence. The verandah, providing cool shelter and allowing for social interaction, also evolved in the West Indies.

Columbus ordered earthwork fortifications at once for Hispaniola's vulnerable north coast. Sizeable coastal cities were subsequently protected with more durable fortifications. Typical of the coastal forts was St Louis, constructed in an irregular pentagonal plan around an open court, with five bastions at the corners. It provided a model for subsequent constructions. France was forced to fortify 40 more sites, using designs inspired by Sébastien Leprestre de Vauban, which abandoned easily targeted high walls and towers for a more expansive series of earthen walls surfaced with heavy masonry, taking advantage of topographical features.

Henri Christophe's Citadelle de la Ferrière (inaugurated 1816) remains the ultimate example of West Indian military architecture. Covering one ha atop a mountain, it is a four-sided fort, with a prow-like bastion soaring c. 15 m above ground. Below it, the Palais de Sans Souci (c. 1813; designed by an English officer, Ferrière) is an imposing three-storey Neo-classical edifice (see fig. 4). The pedimented façade is approached by a monumental double stairway. A remarkable water-system supplied the buildings and irrigated the elegant gardens and its fountains.

In the 18th century the designs of residential buildings were based largely on English Georgian traditions. English pattern books provided examples of classically symmetrical façades, with pediments and engaged pilasters that were adapted to urban as well as plantation houses. The

shops and town houses in Jacmel and Cap-Haïtien typify the more modest urban structures. Heavy, masonry ground floors with doors opening on to the street support lighter and often overhanging second storeys, with decorated balconies of iron or turned wood. Exuberantly scrolled ironwork was imported from France and Germany and inspired iron markets to be set up in the major town centres.

Few examples of early churches remain. The Old Cathedral, Port-au-Prince, a timbered barrel-vaulted, slate-roofed, five-aisle example, was built in 1720 and was under restoration until destroyed in 1991. The Baroque pedimented façade, with a central tower flanked by curved volutes, was typical. In the 19th century the simple town-house form in Port-au-Prince exploded in a riot of fanciful towers, fretwork and ornamental colonnades. The development of machines capable of producing decorative multiples challenged Haitian creativity and produced the 'gingerbread' house style. Like the popular louvres and jalousies, fretwork was not only decorative but provided natural ventilation from the prevailing trade winds.

The surviving public buildings in Port-au-Prince exemplify variety and eclecticism. The Roman Catholic cathedral (completed 1915), a confection of pink and white stone, is a Romanesque Revival building. The glistening white Palais National (1918) on the Champ de Mars was designed and built by Georges Baussan during the American occupation (1915–34). ALBERT MANGONES and Robert Baussan (b 1937), as well as the younger Pierre-Richard Villedrouin, have contributed to the development of modernism in Port-au-Prince with blocks of

4. Palais de Sans Souci, Milot, c. 1813

flats, office buildings and restaurants. The Musée du Panthéon National Haïtien on the central Champ de Mars owes its blue-tiled conical roof fantasies to the French architect Alexandre Guichard.

UNPUBLISHED SOURCES

Port-au-Prince, Inst. Sauvegarde Patrm. N. [various documents]

D. Didier, D. Elie and P. E. Lubin: *Evolution du système de défense en Haïti* (1983)

BIBLIOGRAPHY

G. F. de Oviedo: *Natural History of the West Indies* (originally pubd Toledo, 1526; Eng. trans., Chapel Hill, NC, 1959)

A. A. Phillips: *Gingerbread Houses: Haiti's Endangered Species* (Port-au-Prince, 1975)

The Afro-American Tradition in Decorative Arts (exh. cat. by J. Vlach, Cleveland, OH, Mus. A., 1978), pp. 122–38

P. Gosner: *Caribbean Georgian: The Great and Small Houses of the West Indies* (Washington, DC, 1982)

DOLORES M. YONKER

IV. Painting, sculpture and other arts.

Wealthy colonials were eager consumers of art from abroad: the construction and furnishing of plantation houses and town houses created a demand for luxury items and decorative objects. Foreign artists satisfied most of the demand for portraiture; furniture, ceramics, glassware, jewellery and textiles were imported from France and elsewhere. The Revolution, which terminated slavery, and French hegemony marked the founding of a black republic. The history of Haitian painting and sculpture is documented principally from that time. Henri Christophe, crowned King in 1811, set out to build a monarchy modelled on that of England: the creation and appreciation of art was to be the province of royalty. Christophe's portrait was painted by the English painter Richard Evans (1784–1871), whom Christophe had invited to Haiti to begin a programme of art education (*see* §V below). Christophe's pose and the setting are derived from English historical portrait tradition. One of Evans's students, Numa Desroches (?1802–?1880), painted naive but informative renderings of Christophe's Palais de Sans Souci at Milot.

Until well into the 20th century painting was dominated by European styles, mainly French and English Romanticism, and French and Italian Baroque. Alexandre Pétion, President of the southern Haitian Republic (1807–19), was determinedly Francophile, patronizing such French painters as J. Barincou, who arrived in Haiti in 1816 and was listed in the Philadelphia City Directory in 1839. His paintings of generals adorned the Palais National. Thimoleon Dejoie (?1800–65) received commissions from President Boyer (1818–43) for historic paintings celebrating his rule: one of his most notable works represented Boyer entering Cap-Haïtien with his generals. Little more than the names of two sculptors important at the time are documented: the quality of Jayme Guilliod's (1800–70) work can be estimated in a drawing for a figure of Toussaint L'Ouverture in chains, which dates from 1851. Louis Edmond Laforesterie (1837–94), who was also noted for heroic portraits, had studied in Paris and later returned there when political turmoil threatened his livelihood. It was the Emperor Faustin Soulouque who appointed and titled the court painter Baron Colbert de Lochard (1804–74). Seven of his religious paintings (1851–3) hung in the Old Cathedral in Port-au-Prince. For Lochard and others

the French portrait painter Hyacinthe Rigaud (1659–1743) was a model. By the late 19th century the popularity of the new medium of photography had reduced the market for painted portraits, but historic subjects were still depicted. Edouard Goldman (1870–1930) won a medal at the Exposition Universelle in Brussels (1910) for his interpretation of the *Discovery of America*. Unfortunately the destruction of the Palais National in 1912 destroyed the entire national collection of paintings, including the historical series.

Until the advent in the 1920s of the Indigenist movement, which stimulated a new interest in Haitian culture, Haiti's art was based upon academic models; talented students were sent to Paris for instruction in drawing and painting. However, the literary movements of 1890 and 1915 paved the way to a genuinely Haitian art. The excesses of the first years of the American occupation prompted Goldman in 1920 to paint the *caco* (rebel) chief Charlemagne Perrault crucified. The same subject was to be taken up again by the Cap-Haïtien painter PHILOMÉ OBIN, whose aim was to be the creator of a visual history of his country. In 1944 he sent the representation of Roosevelt's lifting of the American occupation to the newly opened Centre d'Art in Port-au-Prince. At this time a flowering of Haitian arts began. Three generations of artists have emerged from the Centre, including Petion Savain (1906–73) and his pupils George Remponeau (*b* 1916) and Maurice Borno (1917–55). Some, such as Luce Turnier (*b* 1924), ANTONIO JOSEPH and Jacques Enguerrand Gourgue (*b* 1930), work in international styles; others known as 'primitives' were essentially self-taught, including Obin, CASTERA BAZILE, WILSON BIGAUD and RIGAUD BENOIT (see fig. 5). The latter were the principal artists selected to contribute murals (executed in tempera) to the project at Sainte Trinité Cathedral in Port-au-Prince. Artists who are also priests of Vodoun, such as HECTOR HYPPOLITE, ANDRÉ PIERRE and LaFortune Félix, and those who claim to be only observers, such as Benoit, Bigaud and GÉRARD VALCIN, have depicted the dramatic ceremonies of their religion, representing *loas* in imaginative forms.

Sculptors in Haiti have developed a unique medium using scrap metal to cut and pound into figure compositions. Oil-drums have also been transformed into decorative, lace-like representations of everyday scenes, Vodoun archetypes or mythical images of African origin. The drums are processed into flat plates, with designs traced in chalk and then cut out with hammer and chisel, and finished by polishing. Artists working with this form include GEORGE LIAUTAUD, Serge Jolimeau (*b* 1952), Murat Brierre (1938–92) and Gary Darius. Several artists have produced notable wood-carvings, but threats of terrible retribution during the centuries of colonial domination effectively stifled the African legacy of carved masks and figures. Other sculptors have produced brightly painted papier-mâché works, including figures with a carnivalesque gaiety.

The collaboration after *c.* 1944 between fine artists and craftsworkers is exemplified by the painted screens and room dividers, the results of a successful union between the local popular painters and cabinetmakers. Most are mass-produced, but some are painted by such artists as

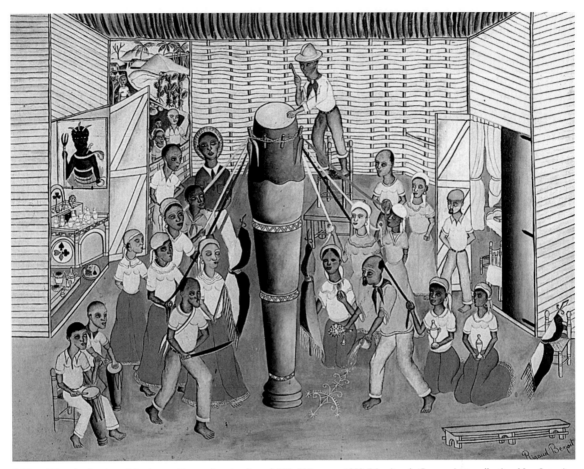

5. Rigaud Benoit: *Baptism of the Assotor Drum*, oil on hardboard, 584×737 mm, *c.* 1950 (Mrs Angela Gross private collection, New Jersey)

Fernand Pierre, Adam Leontus (*b* 1923) and Ghandi Daniel. They depict brilliantly coloured scenes of enchanted landscapes or jungles with fantastic flora and fauna. Wooden storage boxes of various sizes, painted with similar decoration, have become popular with tourists and collectors. Artists who have painted these include Bernard Touissant, Vierge Pierre (*b* 1945) and Jackson Charlot. The painted decoration on 'tap-taps', small open buses used for public transport in Port-au-Prince, includes religious subjects and colourful animals and flowers. Vodoun flags and ritual paraphernalia are also mass-produced for the tourist market, for example painted calabashes or gourds, intended as offerings to *loas*. André Pierre has elevated this medium to an art form. Pottery, weaving and basketwork are also produced by skilled Haitian artists.

BIBLIOGRAPHY

L. E. Moreau de Saint Méry: *Description topographique, physique, civile, politique et historique de la partie française de l'Ile de Saint-Domingue*, 2 vols (Philadelphia, 1797)

P. Thoby-Marcelin: *Art in Latin America Today: Haiti* (Washington, DC, 1959)

Artists of the Western Hemisphere: Art of Haiti and Jamaica (New York, 1968)

S. Williams: *Voodoo and the Art of Haiti* (1969)

P. Apraxine: *Haitian Painting: The Naïve Tradition* (New York, 1973)

S. Rodman: *The Miracle of Haitian Art* (New York, 1973)

J.-M. Drot: *Journal de voyage chez les peintres du vaudou* (Geneva, 1974)

E. I. Christensen: *The Art of Haiti* (New York, 1975)

L. G. Hoffman: *Haitian Art: The Legend and Legacy of the Naïve Tradition* (Iowa, 1975)

U. Stebich: *Haitian Art* (New York, 1978; Ger. trans., 1979)

J. Anquetil: *Haïti, l'artisanat créateur* (Paris, 1982)

M.-J. Nadal and G. Bloncourt: *La Peinture haïtienne: Haitian Arts* (Paris, 1986)

S. Pataki: *Haitian Painting: Art and Kitsch* (Chicago, 1986)

Haïti: Art naif, art vaudou (Paris, 1988)

S. Rodman: *Where Art Is Joy: The First Forty Years* (New York, 1988)

M. P. Lerrebours: *Haïti et ses peintres*, 2 vols (Port-au-Prince, 1989)

A. Fourbet: *Voodoo Blacksmiths* (New York, 1990)

Black Ancestral Legacy (Dallas, TX, Mus. A., 1990), pp. 87–96

DOLORES M. YONKER, EVA PATAKI

V. Patronage and art institutions.

An infrastructure to provide opportunities for training and sale did not develop beyond the rudimentary stage until the second half of the 20th century. During the colonial period the taste of wealthy planters for luxuries and decorative objects created a market for these arts, but most of it was probably from abroad. Fire, pillage and earthquakes have destroyed the evidence to support this belief, however. Foreign artists also often served as teachers. The Church, usually a source of dependable patronage, was entirely absent from Haiti during the 19th century until the Concordat of 1860, which strengthened the bond between Rome and the Haitian government and church. Some political leaders believed that the presence of art and artists was essential as an index of civilization. Henri Christophe summoned the English artist Richard Evans (1784–1871) to establish an academy of painting and drawing at the Palais de Sans Souci, Milot, and to plan for including painting and drawing in the schools. At the same time, in southern Haiti Alexandre Pétion authorized the purchase, from 1807 to 1818, of French works more in keeping with his Francophile taste, and he encouraged French painters, particularly J. Barincou, to establish an art school in Port-au-Prince; he also ordered that the visual arts be included in the school curriculum. Most commissions to Haitian artists were for portraits, although there were a few of historic themes and fewer still of landscapes. From time to time such Haitian painters as Baron Colbert de Lochard (1804–74), appointed court painter to Emperor Faustin Soulouque (reg 1849–59), created grand historic tableaux for public edification. Unfortunately, public buildings were often the victim of the most violent eruptions; when they were destroyed, works of art inside also suffered the same fate.

Developments in the 20th century included the foundation of the Académie de Peinture et de Dessin in 1915 by Archibald Lochard (1837–1923) and Normil Charles (who also opened the Académie de Peinture et Sculpture after 1927). There is little evidence of the existence of an art museum in Haiti previous to the museum attached to the Bureau of Ethnology, founded in 1941 by Jacques Romain (1907–44), Haitian ethnologist, poet, novelist, journalist and diplomat. In 1944 the Centre d'Art was established in Port-au-Prince, offering both exhibition facilities and classes. By 1947 it had mounted forty exhibitions of pictorial art and one of sculpture, two exhibitions in Cap-Haïtien, one in the USA and one in Paris. A branch of the centre, planned as only the first of five in smaller towns in the country, was opened in 1945 under the directorship of the painter Philomé Obin. In 1958 the Ecole des Beaux Arts was set up in Port-au-Prince. In 1962 the Musée d'Art Haïtien opened under the patronage of the Episcopal College St Pierre. Together the Centre and the museum have organized Haitian representation in European and American museums and galleries. A government-supported Institut National de la Culture et des Arts Haïtiens in Port-au-Prince opened in 1983 with an exhibition of the first generation of Haitian naive artists. Ironically the support for production of works representing Haitian themes came largely from the USA and Europe: important collections include the Richard and Anna Flagg Collection at the Milwaukee Art Museum, WI; the Davenport Municipal Art Gallery, IA; and the Astrid and Halvor Jaeger private collection in Neu-Ulm, Germany. The Musée d'Art Haïtien in Port-au-Prince retains a foundation collection, as formed by its late Director, PIERRE MONOSIET.

DOLORES M. YONKER

Hajdúsámson. Site in Hajdu-Bihar county, north-east Hungary. A hoard of bronze objects characteristic of the Hungarian Early Bronze Age metal workshops of the mid-2nd millennium BC was found by farm workers in 1907 and bought by the Déri Múzeum, Debrecen. It consisted of a bronze sword and twelve bronze axes, of which ten passed to the museum. The sword lay in a sand mound with its point to the north, the axes placed over it, their blades to the west.

Eight of the axes are of the 'shaft-hole' variety and undecorated. A ninth, with shaft-hole and disc-butt, is also undecorated. The sword, two disc-butt axes and one shaft-tube axe are decorated, mostly in a curvilinear geometric style, produced by free-hand drawing with a graver between carefully arranged fixed points. The most common motif is a scroll-like design consisting of several concentric lines outlined by small dots, forming a shape like a figure 6. In some cases these are juxtaposed so that an impression of spirals is given. Subsidiary motifs, used to fill in the spaces between the main fields, include arcades and finely hatched triangles. The art is non-representational but perhaps has its origins in the naturalistic depiction of leaves and tendrils. The sword is 530 mm long with a solid bronze hilt and rhomboid pommel decorated with zones of hatched triangles. The semicircular haft has five skeuomorphic rivet heads, with lily motifs, formed of dots, between them. In the semicircle formed by the haft are two rows of four opposed hatched triangles. The blade, swelling in outline, is decorated with scroll motifs in two rows, one either side of the midrib.

Some authorities have considered this art style to be related to that of early Mycenaean Greece, but while some of the motifs do appear similar, the method of execution and the medium itself are quite different.

See also PREHISTORIC ART, §V, 4.

BIBLIOGRAPHY
M. Gimbutas: *Bronze Age Cultures in Central and Eastern Europe* (The Hague, 1965), pp. 57–65, 215–18, fig. 146
A. Mozsolics: *Bronzefunde des Karpatenbeckens* (Budapest, 1967), pp. 139–40, figs 7, 31, pls 9–11

A. F. HARDING

Hajek, Otto Herbert (*b* Kaltenbach, Czechoslovakia, 27 June 1927). German sculptor. He studied at the Staatliche Akademie der Bildenden Künste in Stuttgart (1947–54). His sculptural work began in 1950 with figurative wooden pieces. The non-figurative bronzes (from 1956) were called *Spatial Knots* and *Spatial Layerings.* The spiky forms and the rough and indented surfaces of his sculptures, moulded using the lost-wax technique, demonstrate the close relation of his work to *Art informel*, for example *Spatial Knot 64* (1958; Ravensberg church). In the 1960s the sculptures, while maintaining their large number of joints, were stripped of surface encrustations as Hajek began to move towards geometric constructions. Spaces are created in these works through intermeshing systems of braced concrete beams and articulated through the addition of paint, which takes on certain plastic functions; the tracks of paint drawn over the sculptures—many of which may be walked over—led Hajek to use the term *Farbwege, Paint Paths* for these works, for example *Spring in Frankfurt* (1963–4; Frankfurt; exh. Kassel, *Documenta 3*, 1964). In setting up series, mathematical arrangements of brightly coloured, horizontal, vertical and angled structures alternating with diagonal courses, he achieved a dynamicization of space.

In the 1970s powerful primary colours were augmented by surfaces plated with nickel and chrome. Hajek's articulations of space in urban buildings, at first utopian (in the spirit of urban colour projects by Marc Chagall and Fernand Léger), were executed as formations in space from the 1960s, in particular in *Artificial Gardens* (1973–7) as a realization of the *Art—Landscape—Idea* at the Adelaide Festival in Australia (1977). He sought to humanize the environment and to encourage viewers to become consciously aware of their surroundings. His *Urban Signs*, large sculptures in an urban space, formulate a 'city iconography', which stands programmatically for his cultural-political commitment. From the 1980s painting and coloured reliefs took a more important role in his work. From 1980 he taught at the Staatliche Akademie der Bildenden Künste in Karlsruhe.

BIBLIOGRAPHY
Otto Herbert Hajek—Farbwege, 1963–1971 (exh. cat., Bielefeld, Ksthalle, 1971)
Otto Herbert Hajek: Ikonographien, Zeichen, Plätze, Stadtbilder (exh. cat., Stuttgart, Staatsgal., 1978)
Otto Herbert Hajek (exh. cat., Nuremberg, German. Nmus., 1987)
EVA MEYER-HERMANN

Hajime Yatsuka. *See* YATSUKA, HAJIME.

Hajós [Guttmann], **Alfréd** (*b* Budapest, 1 Feb 1878; *d* Budapest, 12 Nov 1955). Hungarian architect. He graduated from the Hungarian Palatine Joseph Technical University, Budapest, in 1899. He then worked with Ignác Alpár and Ödön Lechner, the former having the greater influence on him. His work can be seen as part of a historicist trend, but from the beginning he also employed audacious construction ideas, through which he became more receptive to modernist design ideas in the 1930s. Although his work was very varied, he is principally remembered for his designs for sports facilities, reflecting his own achievements as a sportsman, including successes as a swimmer at the Olympic Games of 1896 at Athens. His chief preoccupation was the plan (unexecuted) for a Hungarian National Stadium, which he began working on before World War I. In 1919 he published a design for the stadium that was markedly classical, and a more developed version, which he produced in 1924, was a great success winning first prize in the Cultural Olympiad, Paris. This was followed by numerous commissions for sports facilities, notably the National Swimming Pool (1929–31), Margaret Island, Budapest, which is in a modernist style. The interior of the covered pool is dominated by huge, curved iron girders that evoke an imposing sense of space. On the exterior the clinker- and ceramic-faced façade forms a modest composition with nearby trees. His most important residential building, the English-named 'Boarding House' (1938), Budapest, employs similar materials and methods, although in a slightly different way, and its smooth-lined, elegant façade, with a loggia, achieves an impression of grandeur despite its small scale. During the 1930s Hajós produced other designs for the National Stadium, but none of them was realized.

WRITINGS
'A margitszigeti nemzeti uszóstadion' [The national swimming pool on Margaret Island], *Tér & Forma*, iv (1931), pp. 1–7
'Boarding House Budapesten', *Tér & Forma*, xi (1938), pp. 67–70

BIBLIOGRAPHY
F. Merényi: *A magyar épitészet, 1867–1967* [Hungarian architecture, 1867–1967] (Budapest, 1970), p. 170 [detailed bibliog.]
L. Pusztai: 'Száz éve született Hajós Alfréd' [A. Hajós was born a hundred years ago], *Magyar Épitőművészet*, xvii/5 (1978), pp. 56–9
FERENC VADAS

Hakp'o. *See* YANG P'AENG-SON.

Haksan. *See* YUN CHE-HONG.

Hakuin Ekaku [Nagasawa] (*b* Hara, 1685; *d* Hara, 1769). Japanese Zen monk, painter and calligrapher. He was one of the most important painters of the Edo period (1600–1868), creating hundreds of paintings and calligraphies that revolutionized *Zenga* (painting and calligraphy by Zen monks from the 17th century to the 20th; *see* JAPAN, §§VI, 4(vii) and VII, 2(iv)). In earlier centuries, Zen painting and calligraphy had been generally limited to portrayals of famous masters of the past, landscapes and Zen phrases or poems. Under Hakuin's influence, however, a new range of styles and of subjects—including Zen-related subjects, those drawn from other Buddhist sects and from native folklore—made *Zenga* appealing not only to the Zen initiates but also to lay people. In this way Hakuin responded to the Tokugawa government's lack of support for Zen; he reached out to people of all beliefs and levels of education through art that had both humour and dramatic impact. Indeed, his use of art in the service of religion permanently changed the *Zenga* tradition.

1. LIFE. Hakuin was the fifth child of a family of devout Buddhists. According to his own account, he was still a child when he heard a terrifying sermon on the Buddhist hells by the evangelistic Nichiren-sect monk Shōnin (*fl c.* late 17th century) and determined to become a monk himself. He began his Zen Buddhist studies at the age of 14 at the Rinzai-sect temple of Tokugenji in Hara, and later spent many years travelling to different Zen teachers (*angya*) for instruction. As a priest he took the name Ekaku.

In 1718 Hakuin settled at the small Rinzai temple of Shōinji in Hara, declining positions in more famous monasteries to avoid the potential interference of government officials or wealthy patrons. He trained many pupils through strict methods that included *kōan* (Zen conundrums that can be understood only through enlightened vision and after long meditation) taken from Chinese Zen records. He also wrote on various subjects, including writings and lectures on traditional Zen texts and a commentary on the popular Buddhist Heart *sūtra*, a part of the *Daihannya haramittakyō* (Skt *Mahāprajñāpāramitā sūtra*; the greater *sūtra* of the Perfection of Wisdom), which he mischievously called a 'useless collection of junk'.

Around the age of 60 Hakuin began to turn more often to brushwork to express his Zen vision. He had received some training in calligraphy, and perhaps in painting, in his youth, but had abandoned the attempt to become an artist. He discovered in his later years, however, that painting and calligraphy could convey more than words alone, and in his last 25 years he produced a large amount of *Zenga*. Although all of his known works bear his seals, most are unsigned and undated. However, his works are often divided, on stylistic criteria, into early (1745–55), middle (1755–65) and late (1765–9) periods.

2. WORK.

(i) Early period, 1745–55. Hakuin's paintings from his 60s display a wide range of subject-matter, from traditional themes such as the first patriarch of Zen Buddhism, Bodhidharma (Jap. Daruma or Bodaidaruma; see fig.) to entirely new subjects. An example of the latter is *Blind Men Crossing the Bridge* (priv. col.; see Addiss, pl. 55), in which tiny figures can be seen creeping and crawling over a log bridge spanning a chasm. The imagery of blind men crossing a bridge, as explained by the calligraphy on the piece, is a metaphor for a 'mind that can cross over', that is, an enlightened mind. The dominant ink tonality in such early works by Hakuin is usually grey, occasionally with added colours, and the calligraphic inscriptions are in vibrant but rather spidery script.

Another of Hakuin's early subjects is the folk figure Otafuku, the low-ranking, aging courtesan who was the embodiment of the virtuous, hard-working woman. Hakuin depicted her variously as an elegantly dressed geisha, cooking rice cakes, or putting hot moxa on the rear end of a rich old customer with haemorrhoids (e.g. a hanging

Hakuin Ekaku: *Daruma*, hanging scroll, ink on paper, 2.23×0.37 m, 1751 (Aichi, Shōjūji)

scroll, Tokyo, Eisei Bunko). In such paintings Hakuin suggests that compassion and service to others are more important than wealth or high position. Hakuin also depicted subjects and sayings from Confucianism, Shinto and the Esoteric and Pure Land Buddhist sects.

Another theme of his early period was the *ebi* (shrimp). With its bent back and long 'whiskers', the *ebi* was an appropriate if not classical symbol of old age. On some of Hakuin's paintings of this subject, brushed for his monk followers, he wrote, 'If you want to live a long life, moderate your eating and sleep alone'. He would not expect a farmer or shopkeeper to be celibate, so he painted other pictures of *ebi* with the inscription, 'If you want to live a long life, moderate your eating, moderate your eating'.

(ii) Middle and late periods, 1755–69. In his 70s, his middle period, Hakuin continued his wide range of themes but began to use a thicker and heavier calligraphic line, bringing more sense of direct power to his works. He did several portrayals of Kannon (Skt Avalokiteshvara; Chin. Guanyin), the *bodhisattva* of mercy, sometimes adding conventional inscriptions about the compassion of Kannon. On other Kannon paintings, however, he introduced the surprising notion that the deity might be tired and overworked by people's constant entreaties. This was Hakuin's humorous way of attempting to make people think twice about their accepted beliefs.

During this period Hakuin also depicted the rotund monk Hotei (Chin. Budai), one of the seven Gods of Good Fortune, who preferred a life of wandering to that in a temple and enjoyed playing with children more than conducting Buddhist ceremonies. Sometimes, as in the hanging scroll *One Hand Clapping* (priv. col.; see Addiss, pl. 62), Hakuin showed Hotei standing upon his round bag with one hand raised, asking Hakuin's famous *kōan*, 'What is the sound of one hand clapping?' Hakuin believed that if one went beyond hearing, seeing, knowing or perceiving and meditated on this *kōan* at all times, then reason and words would end, discriminations would cease and enlightenment could be found. When any of his followers solved this *kōan*, Hakuin presented him with a painting of a Zen master's staff and whisk as a 'graduation certificate'. He would write the name of the follower and the date, and praise the heroism of the man who had struggled so hard to come to an awakening. Eventually Hakuin changed the painted staff into a dragon form full of energy and vigour.

During his 70s Hakuin began to experiment with ink. Instead of grinding it afresh each day, he used old ink on highly sized paper so that it produced puddling effects rather than being absorbed quickly. In this way he added tonal interest to his works, especially notable in the massive paintings and calligraphies of his final years. During his late period he concentrated on only a few major themes; his portrayals of Bodhidharma from this time are among the most forceful and dynamic in the history of *Zenga*. On these works he usually added inscriptions based on the words of the patriarch himself, as in the hanging scroll *Daruma in Red* (Manjūji, Ōita): 'Pointing directly to the human heart: See your own nature and become Buddha!'

In this riveting painting the powerful image of Bodhidharma has pronounced eyes and a bold red robe, and is set against a stark black background.

In his final years Hakuin also did several single-column calligraphies of phrases drawn from the doctrines of Zen and other Buddhist sects, such as the hanging scroll with the phrase *Namu Amida Butsu* ('Praise to Amida Buddha'; Shin'wa-an priv. col.; see Addiss, pl. 59) from the Esoteric sect of Pure Land (Jōdo) Buddhism. This scroll was written in large blocky characters, easily readable by anyone but the totally illiterate. Using this form of visual sermon, Hakuin was able not only to teach and encourage all those he met but also to convey his own personality and character through brush and ink.

After Hakuin's death, his pupils continued his traditions in Zen practice, teaching and art. Among his most notable students were Tōrei Enji (1721–92) and Suiō Genro (1717–89). The Rinzai sect continues to be dominated by principles promulgated by Hakuin and his followers.

BIBLIOGRAPHY

K. Brasch: *Hakuin und die Zen Malerei* (Tokyo, 1957)
N. Takeuchi: *Hakuin* (Tokyo, 1964)
P. Yampolsky: *The Zen Master Hakuin: Selected Writings* (New York, 1971)
S. Furuta: *Hakuin: Zen to sono geijutsu* [Hakuin's Zen and art] (Tokyo, 1978)
C. Yamanouchi: *Hakuin: Sho to e no kokoro* [The heart of Hakuin's calligraphy and painting] (Tokyo, 1978)
K. Tanahashi: *Penetrating Laughter: Hakuin's Zen and Art* (Woodstock, NY, 1984)
T. Kameyama: *Hakuin Zenshi no e o yomu* [Reading Zen master Hakuin's paintings] (Kyoto, 1985)
S. Kato: *Hakuin Osho nenpu* [Chronology of the monk Hakuin] (Kyoto, 1985)
A. Tanaka: *Hakuin no Zenga* [Hakuin's Zen paintings] (Numazu, 1985)
S. Addiss: *The Art of Zen: Paintings and Calligraphy by Japanese Monks, 1600–1925* (New York, 1989)

STEPHEN ADDISS

Hakurenshi. *See* KANŌ, (11).

Hakuyō Fuchigami. *See* FUCHIGAMI, HAKUYŌ.

Hal, Notre-Dame-de-. Pilgrimage church near Brussels, Belgium. It was constructed between 1341 and 1409, preserving one of the most important ensembles of later Gothic sculpture in the Netherlands. Statues of the Virgin surmount each of the principal entrances to the church: the finest are the elegant Virgin accompanied by music-making angels (*c.* 1380) in the south-west porch portal and the slightly later Virgin of the north entrance (*c.* 1400), both carved by Tournai sculptors working in the manner of ANDRÉ BEAUNEVEU. The statues of the Magi (*c.* 1380) in the south-west portal are in a similar style and by an outstanding sculptor, possibly from Brussels. The sculptural decoration of the west tower, nave and adjoining Virgin chapel, completed in several campaigns, provides an excellent guide to the development of 14th-century Brabantine small-scale sculpture, extending from the regional style in the expressive bust corbels of the tower vault (*c.* 1341–50) to the incipient realism of the historiated bosses and spandrels of the nave and Virgin chapel (*c.* 1370–80). The ornate choir (1399–1409), a superb example of the mature Brabantine style of the early 15th century, harmoniously integrates architecture and sculpture. The imposing life-size Apostles in the triforium and the delicate narrative reliefs of the wall tabernacle (1409) may be attributed to the Brussels MASTER OF HAKENDOVER (*see* MASTERS, ANONYMOUS, AND MONOGRAMMISTS, §I) and his workshop.

Among other notable works in the church may be cited the wooden cult statue of the Black Madonna (*c.* 1220–40); the splendid Triumphal Cross (1420–30), probably of Brussels origin; the bronze baptismal font (1446) signed by the Tournai founder Guillaume Lefèvre (*fl* 1431; *d* 1476); and the early Renaissance alabaster altarpiece (1533) by JEAN MONE.

BIBLIOGRAPHY

R. Hamann: 'Spätgotische Skulpturen der Wallfahrtskirche in Hal', *Belgische Kunstdenkmäler*, ed. P. Clemen, i (Munich, 1923), pp. 203–46
D. Roggen and M. De Vleeschouwer: 'De Apostelen en de Aanbidding der Driekoningen in de St. Maartenskerk te Halle', *Gentse Bijdr. Kstgesch. Oudhdkd.*, i (1934), pp. 149–72
A. Louis: *L'Eglise Notre-Dame de Hal (Saint-Martin)*, Ars Belgica, vi (Brussels, 1936)
R. Lemaire: 'La Chronologie de l'église de Hal', *Belg. Tijdschr. Oudhdkd. & Kstgesch.*, xx (1951), pp. 29–55
I. Geisler: 'Studien zur niederländischen Bildhauern des ausgehenden 14. und frühen 15. Jahrhunderts', *Wallraf-Richartz-Jb.*, xviii (1956), pp. 143–58
R. Didier, M. Henss and J. Adolf Schmoll gen. Eisenwerth: 'Une Vierge tournaisienne à Arbois (Jura) et la problème des Vierges de Hal: Contribution à la chronologie et à la typologie', *Bull. Mnmtl*, cxxviii (1970), pp. 93–113
J. Steyaert: *The Sculpture of St Martin's in Halle and Related Netherlandish Works* (diss., U. Michigan, 1974)
Die Parler und der Schöne Stil, 1350–1400: Europäische Kunst unter den Luxemburgern, i (exh. cat., ed. A. Legner; Cologne, Schnütgen-Mus., 1978), pp. 92–5

J. STEYAERT

Halaf, Tell [anc. Guzana]. Site in north-east Syria, near the source of the River Khabur and the modern town of Ra's al-'Ayn. It is famous for its prehistoric pottery and its 1st-millennium BC palace with sculptured portico and reliefs. It was discovered and excavated by Baron Max von Oppenheim between 1911 and 1929. Objects and sculpture from the site are preserved in the National Museum of Aleppo, the British Museum in London and the Pergamonmuseum in Berlin.

Tell Halaf was already settled during the Neolithic and Chalcolithic periods. It gave its name to a widespread culture of the 6th to 5th millennium BC, characterized by painted pottery of high quality (*see* MESOPOTAMIA, §V, 1). During the Neo-Assyrian period (between *c.* 1000 and 600 BC) the site was known as Guzana. At first it was the capital of one of the petty north Syrian states that developed after the fall of the Hittite empire (*c.* 1200 BC) and the end of Middle Assyrian rule over north Mesopotamia. The name of this state, Bit Bahiani, as well as the names of local rulers known from cuneiform sources, indicate that the Aramaeans were the leading population group. During the 9th century BC Guzana came under the supremacy of the Neo-Assyrian empire, first as a vassal state, then as a province; at that time it lost most of its importance.

The flourishing period of Guzana is thus restricted to about 150 years between 950 and 800 BC. At that time it was a walled city of rectangular shape *c.* 1000×600 m. An inner defensive wall enclosed the citadel (*c.* 400×300 m), where the more important public buildings were concentrated. Part of this citadel, probably again enclosed by a

Tell Halaf, two basalt figures, h. 800 mm, 9th century BC (Aleppo, National Museum of Aleppo)

Museum in Aleppo, which comprises two statues of gods and one of a goddess, mounted on lions and bulls, and carrying the architrave over the entrance, two sphinxes flanking the entrance and a number of orthostats. The gods represented seem to belong to the realm of Teshub, the Hurrian storm god venerated in a large part of northern Syria. His name is mentioned in the bilingual inscription of a ruler of Guzana, written in Aramaic and cuneiform on a statue (Damascus, N. Mus.) dedicated to this god. This statue, made in a more Assyrianizing style, was found on the neighbouring site of Tell Fekheriye. Other sculptures found at Tell Halaf itself are the doorjambs of the 'Scorpion Gate' (the entry to the palace area), and two cuboid sitting figures, probably of members of the royal family, which had been erected on top of their graves (see fig.).

The art of Guzana is the best example of a local school of art, which was independent of the Assyrian tradition to the east and of the Hittite tradition to the west and which might reasonably be called 'ARAMAEAN'.

BIBLIOGRAPHY
M. von Oppenheim: *Der Tell Halaf* (Leipzig, 1931)
J. Friedrich and others: 'Die Inschriften von Tell Halaf', *Archv Orient-forsch.*, vi (Berlin, 1940) [suppl. issue]
H. Schmidt and others: *Tell Halaf*, 4 vols (Berlin, 1943–60)

WINFRIED ORTHMANN

fortification wall, was the palace area. Since only a small part of it has been excavated, its layout can only be reconstructed hypothetically, taking contemporary north Syrian cities as models.

The most important building was the so-called Temple-Palace, a building of the north Syrian porticoed palace type (*bit hilani*), richly adorned with gate sculptures and orthostats made of basalt and red-stained limestone. Many of the orthostats bear inscriptions of a certain 'Kapara, son of Hadiani', who was the builder of this complex. Only scant remains of an earlier building are preserved, but a number of reused orthostats from the rear of the later building has been associated with the earlier building phase. These orthostats, which form a distinctive stylistic group, are characterized by a somewhat crude execution and by a rich repertory of themes: various animals occur frequently, such as lions, stags and boars, as well as hybrid creatures, for instance lion-men, sphinxes or genii. Human beings can be seen in a variety of different scenes, sometimes as hunters or warriors. Some chariot scenes show similarities with Neo-Assyrian representations of the same theme, but in general the imagery has little to do with Assyrian art of the 9th century BC. The few representations of gods show the influence of 2nd-millennium BC prototypes; in this respect the art of Tell Halaf can be compared with that of Neo-Hittite sculptures such as those from Carchemish. The peculiar style and composition of the reliefs are also found in the decorative arts, especially in ivories of the 2nd and 1st millennium BC.

The fully developed Kapara sculptures (those not inherited but made especially for the *hilani* building) are more carefully executed and larger in size, but it is evident that their style is a development from that of the earlier group. To this later style belongs the impressive group from the main entrance, now reconstructed in the National

Hala Sultan Teke. Site of a Bronze Age town by the Larnaca Salt Lake in Cyprus. Its ancient name is unknown; it takes its modern name from an adjacent mosque. It was excavated by British expeditions in 1897 and 1898 and, since 1971, by Paul Åström of Göteborg University. Founded in Middle Cypriot (MCYP) III (*c.* 1600 BC), it flourished throughout the Late Cypriot (LCYP) period (*c.* 1600–*c.* 1050 BC). The MCYP remains consist only of pottery. The LCYP I and II periods (*c.* 1600–*c.* 1200 BC) are represented mainly by rich chamber tombs situated inside the town and by walls underneath a later town (LCYP III, *c.* 1200–*c.* 1050 BC). This new town was laid out on a regular grid system. A central area has been excavated to reveal a street, *c.* 4 m wide, running north–south; houses open on to it, often with a paved area of protecting stones in front of their entrances. The houses are rectangular units with a central court surrounded by three or four rooms like those at Pyla–Kokkinokremnos. One of the rooms was a bathroom, its floor covered with ashlar stones and revetted with thin limestone plaques; it recalls Minoan 'lustral basins'. Some of the house walls were built with regular ashlar blocks, occasionally bound in a header-and-stretcher system, and a number of stepped bases, probably used for pillars, have been found, often near entrances. A rich shaft grave dating from about 1175 BC was sunk into a courtyard; a possible sanctuary has been discovered. A limestone model of a house (580×280×150 mm; 13th century BC; Larnaca, Archaeol. Mus.) was found built into a wall on the site; it has a door with recessed sides and four windows with grilles. Other artefacts include a limestone basin with a bucranium (bull's head) in relief against an indigo blue background (12th century BC), an exquisite engraving of a bull on an ivory disc (LCYP II–III; London, BM) and gold jewellery (LCYP II–III; London, BM, and Nicosia, Cyprus Mus.).

BIBLIOGRAPHY

P. Åström and others: *Hala Sultan Teke*, 9 vols (Göteborg, 1974–89)

P. Åström: 'Excavations at Hala Sultan Teke', *Archaeology*, xxxvii/2 (March–April 1984), pp. 58–9, 77, 81

——: 'Hala Sultan Teke: An International Harbour Town of the Late Bronze Age', *Opuscula Athen.*, xvi (1986), pp. 7–17

PAUL ÅSTRÖM

Halász, Gyula. *See* BRASSAÏ.

Halaward. *See* KHELAVERD.

Halbax [Hallwachs; Halpax; Halwachs], **Michael Wenzel** (*b* Ebenfurth, 1661; *d* St Florian bei Linz, 11 Aug 1711). Austrian painter, active in Bohemia. As a pupil of Johann Carl Loth he inherited the tenebrist legacy of Caravaggio. Between 1685 and 1694 he worked in Prague as a respected and versatile artist. A contract of 1694 to work for St Florian Abbey began a lasting friendship with this Augustine foundation. He set up his workshop in Linz from 1694, and soon became the painter most employed by the abbey, prior to the Altomontes' arrival. His first altarpiece for it, the *Martyrdom of St Vitus* (*c.* 1695; ex-Rohrbach Church; Markt St Florian, Stiftssamml.), shows Halbax not only revelling in contrasts of light and shade but also developing his own style, decorative, picturesque and free.

Again in Prague (1700–09), Halbax attempted, together with František Preiss and František Maximilián Kanka, to found a painting academy. A lack of interest on the part of the authorities thwarted him, however; his strength, in fact, lay in teaching and inspiring others, rather than in his own creative work. Among his followers in Bohemia were Petr Jan Brandl and Václav Vavřinec Reiner (1689–1743). Brandl's achievements far outstripped those of his master. Halbax's paintings of the period include *Touch*, *Hearing* and *Smell*, from a series of the *Five Senses* (1700), and *Four Evangelists* and *Four Church Fathers* (1705; all Prague Castle). From 1709 Halbax again worked for St Florian Abbey. Apart from altarpieces for the altars of SS Augustine and Barbara in the abbey church, he produced many ceiling paintings; the *Four World Monarchies* in the Tafelsaal (begun 1710; completed by Johann Degler, 1666–1729) is considered the finest of these.

BIBLIOGRAPHY

I. Franzl: *Michael Wenzel Halbax: Leben und Werk* (diss., U. Innsbruck, 1970)

HANNES ETZLSTORFER

Halberstadt. City in north-central Germany. It is known for three important locally made tapestries: *Abraham and Isaac* (*c.* 1150; *see* GERMANY, fig. 81), which is the earliest surviving large-scale European wall tapestry, the *Apostles* tapestry of *c.* 1170–75 and the *Charlemagne* of the 1230s (all Halberstadt Cathedral, Treasury). The earliest northern European knotted carpets were made in the same region. A rare surviving example (Quedlinburg, Domschatz) was made by the nuns of the Quedlinburg convent and donated *c.* 1200.

See also GERMANY, §XI, 4.

☐

Halbherr, Frederico (*b* Rovereto, nr Verona, 15 Feb 1875; *d* Rome, 17 July 1930). Italian epigrapher and archaeologist. An important figure in the history of archaeological exploration in Crete, he first visited the island in 1884. His interests at that time were mainly epigraphical, and within four months of his arrival he made the remarkable discovery of the Law Code of Gortyn, one of the most important inscriptions ever found in the Greek world. Halbherr became thoroughly committed to the recovery of Crete's past, broadening his interests from the purely epigraphical to the archaeological; the long list of sites that he explored, excavated or encouraged others to excavate includes Gortyn, Axos, the Idaian Cave, Lebena, Prinias and perhaps the two most important sites dug by Italian archaeologists, the Minoan palace of Phaistos and the neighbouring Minoan villa of Ayia Triadha. From 1889 Halbherr was Professor of Greek Epigraphy and Antiquity in the University of Rome. In 1899 he founded the Italian Archaeological Mission in Crete, and in 1910 he was instrumental in the foundation of the Italian School of Archaeology in Athens. His career in Crete spanned the last years of Turkish rule in the island and the great age of excavation in the first decades of this century. His early work did much to interest scholars of other nationalities in the Cretan heritage, while his encouragement of young Italian colleagues laid firm foundations for the long and fruitful tradition of Italian research in Crete that still continues.

WRITINGS

M. Guarducci, ed.: *Inscriptiones creticae, opera et consilio Friderici Halbherr collectae*, 4 vols (Rome, 1935–50)

BIBLIOGRAPHY

L. Pernier: 'Commemorazione del Socio Frederico Halbherr', *Rendi. Accad. N. Lincei, Cl. Sci. Mor., Stor. & Filol.*, vi (1930), pp. 420–35 [with complete list of writings]

A. Di Vita and others: *Creta antica: Cento anni di archeologia italiana, 1884–1984* (Rome, 1984)

J. LESLEY FITTON

Hald, Edward (*b* Stockholm, 17 Sep 1883; *d* 4 July 1980). Swedish painter, glassmaker and ceramicist. Although he worked as a painter, he was most famous for his work as a designer. From 1917 he worked for the Orrefors Glasbruk, Orrefors, Småland, where he produced high-quality engraved glass (*see* SWEDEN, fig. 27). Together with Simon Gate (1883–1945) he designed 'Graal glass', which involved encasing engraved glass with clear glass. He also produced pottery and porcelain in both classical and more advanced styles, working at the ceramics factory at Rorstrand.

☐

Halebid [Haḷebīḍ; anc. Dōrasamudra, Dvārasamudra]. Indian town and temple site in southern Karnataka that flourished *c.* 1100–1350. It was the capital of the HOYSALA dynasty; remains include four major temples and several irrigation tanks. Two temples were built in the reign of Vishnuvardhana (*reg c.* 1108–42), who consolidated the dynasty's power—the Jaina Parshvanatha (1133) and Shaiva Hoysaleshvara (*c.* 1121–60)—and two in the reign of his grandson Ballala II (*reg c.* 1173–1220)—the Jaina Shantinatha (1196) and Shaiva Kedareshvara (1219). The site was pillaged by Malik Kafur in 1311.

The Hoysaleshvara is the most extensive and mature example of the dynasty's characteristic, ornate style. Built for Ketamalla, an officer of Vishnuvardhana, by the architect Kedaroja, it is a two-shrined (*dvikūṭa*) Shiva temple, resembling a double version of the Chhennakeshava temple at BELUR. The two halves are linked by a complex system of subshrines on the interior, with corresponding projecting offsets on the outside wall. The temple stands on a high platform that serves as an exterior circumambulatory passage (*pradakṣiṇa*) around the shrine and as a base for two dissimilar Nandi halls in the east.

The Hoysaleshvara is characterized by several elements that are typical of the style at Belur: nine-course bases, elaborate 3 m-high pierced screens enclosing the halls (*navaraṅga*) and figure-brackets (Kannada: *madanakai*). A unique feature is the continuous band of figurative panels on its exterior wall with over 400, half life-sized, sensuous, richly bejewelled figures of outstanding quality and detail. There are no superstructures over the shrines, but the miniature temples flanking the entrances give an idea of the form they may have taken.

The interior of the temple is equally ornate. Pillars, ceilings and doorways are carved with intricacy and invention. Two features of special interest are the opening up of interior space through a reduction in the number of pillars and the elaboration of the walls by richly decorated, massive shrine niches.

See also INDIAN SUBCONTINENT, §§III, 6(i)(f) and IV, 7(vi)(c).

BIBLIOGRAPHY

H. Cousens: *Chālukyan Architecture of the Kanarese Districts*, Archaeol. Surv. India, New Imp. Ser., xlii (Calcutta, 1926)
M. H. Krishna: 'Halebid', *Mysore Archaeol. Dept, Annu. Rep. 1930* (Bangalore, 1934), pp. 33–60
S. Settar: *The Hoysaḷa Style of Temple Architecture and Sculpture, Eleventh to Fourteenth Centuries* (diss., Cambridge U., 1970)
R. J. Del Bonta: *The Hoysala Style: Architectural Development and Artists, 12th and 13th Centuries* (diss., Ann Arbor, U. MI, 1978)

GARY MICHAEL TARTAKOV

Halepas [Chalepas]**, Yannoulis** (*b* Tinos, 24 Aug 1851; *d* Athens, 15 Sept 1938). Greek sculptor. The son of a sculptor and born on an island with a considerable artistic tradition, he left Tinos in 1869 to study sculpture at the School of Fine Arts in Athens. He continued his studies (1873–6) at the Akademie der Bildenden Künste in Munich under Max von Windmann. He returned to Athens in 1876 and produced some highly finished classicist marble sculptures, including *Sleeping Girl* (1878; Athens, First Cemetery, Tomb of Sophia Afentakis). In such works as this the classical references are evident in the treatment of anatomical detail and drapery, while in other works (e.g. *Filostorgia*, 1875; Tinos, Mus. Tinian Artists) they are apparent in a more austere form. Mental illness forced him to interrupt his work in 1878, and he did not return to it until 1918. While his themes remained essentially the same after this—'Satyr and Eros', 'Medea' and so on—his style changed dramatically. He produced rough clay moulds and plaster casts and became more interested in conveying the inner strength of works than the surface sculptural qualities, as shown by *Satyr Playing with Eros* (marble, 1877; Athens, N.G.; plaster version, 1918; Tinos, Mus. Tinian Artists) and *Medea and her Children* (1922–3; Tinos, Mus. Tinian Artists; plaster version, 1934, Athens, N.G.; *see* GREECE, fig. 5). This change is best seen in his large series of powerful expressionistic sketches (e.g. Athens, N.G.), which were not always connected to specific sculptures. Casts of Halepas's sculptures were brought to Athens from Tinos, and an exhibition of his work was held in 1925 at the Academy of Athens, which also awarded him the Arts Distinction in 1927. His isolation and illness prevented any real contact with contemporary artists and trends. Despite this, Halepas's romantic use of myth inspired a move towards Expressionism in Greek sculpture.

BIBLIOGRAPHY

M. Kalligas: *Yannoulis Halepas: E zoi kai to ergo tou* [Yannoulis Halepas: his life and work] (Athens, 1972; Eng. trans., 1973)
S. Doukas: *Yannoulis Halepas* (Athens, 1978)
D. Papastamos: *Drawings by Yannoulis Halepas* (Athens, 1981)
Yannoulis Halepas, 1938–1988 (exh. cat. by A. Goulaki-Voutyra, Tinos, Pnevmatiko Kent. Evangel., 1988)

EVITA ARAPOGLOU

Hales, John. *See* HAYLS, JOHN.

Halfpenny, William [Hoare, Michael] (*fl* 1723–55). English architect and writer. He was by trade a carpenter, and his surname and the fact that his first known design was for Holy Trinity Church, Leeds (1723; unbuilt) suggest that he was born in Yorkshire. In the later 1720s he was established at Richmond, Surrey, whence he moved to Bristol, probably *c.* 1730. The list of his known executed designs is a short one, comprising a horse barracks (1732) at Hillsborough, Co. Down, N. Ireland; the altar (1742) in Redland Chapel, Bristol; Coopers' Hall (1743–4), Bristol; a monument to Mrs Ann Dash (*d* 1750) in Isleworth parish church, Middx; and a Chinese bridge (before 1754) at Croome Court, Hereford & Worcs. Of the buildings attributed to him, Upton House (1752), Tetbury, Glos, with a pedimented stone Palladian façade enriched with oeil-de-boeuf windows and rusticated pilaster strips, is the most distinguished survivor.

It was as an indefatigable author of architectural handbooks and pattern books that Halfpenny made his mark. His *Practical Architecture* has been called the first true patternbook of the English Palladian movement. It was soon followed by *The Art of Sound Building, Demonstrated in Geometrical Problems*; in this Halfpenny says that he was motivated by 'the daily Errors that I saw Workmen commit in framing their Works for Buildings, on account of their Want of the Knowledge of the Proportions contain'd in this book', and the Palladian doctrine of the supreme importance of proportions is a theme in most of his books. Yet he had his non-Palladian or even anti-Palladian side. His classical designs often incorporate Baroque or Rococo features; his *New Designs for Chinese Temples* was the first book of Chinese designs to be published, and in *Chinese and Gothic Architecture Properly Ornamented*, written with his son John, 'Invention and Variety of Construction' are given first place, above order and proportion, as indispensable attributes of architecture. By depicting, in *The Country Gentleman's Pocket Companion*, original designs in landscape settings, he scored a first in English architectural literature that may be seen as anticipating the Picturesque. He wrote more books than any other architectural author, and 12 of his 22 books are recorded as having been available in the American colonies before 1776.

WRITINGS
Practical Architecture (London, n.d., 2/1724)
The Art of Sound Building, Demonstrated in Geometrical Problems (London, 1725/R 1968)
New Designs for Chinese Temples (London, 1750)
Twelve Beautiful Designs for Farm-houses (London, 1750)
with J. Halfpenny: *Chinese and Gothic Architecture Properly Ornamented* (London, 1752/R 1968)
——: *The Country Gentleman's Pocket Companion* (London, 1753)

BIBLIOGRAPHY
Colvin [contains a complete writings list]
M. Binney: 'Upton House, Tetbury, Gloucestershire, the Home of Mr and Mrs Malcolm St Clair', *Country Life*, cliii/3947 (1973), pp. 390–94
H. Park: *A List of Architectural Books Available in America before the Revolution* (Los Angeles, 1973)
A. Gomme, M. Jenner and B. Little: *Bristol: An Architectural History* (London, 1979)
J. Archer: *The Literature of British Domestic Architecture, 1715–1842* (Cambridge, MA, 1985)

MARCUS WHIFFEN

Half-tone printing. *See under* PHOTOGRAPHY, §I.

Halich [Rus. Galich]. Town on the River Dniester in Ukraine *c.* 100 km south-east of L'viv. The original town, which is first mentioned in the 12th century, was situated 7 km away, near the present-day village of Krylos: in 1144 it was the centre of the principality of Halich and from 1199 that of Halich and Volyn'. Although the town was destroyed by the Mongols in 1241, the remains show that it was one of the most important centres of old Russian architecture. Excavations in 1939–41 and during the 1950s have revealed the ramparts and ditches of the citadel as well as the walls of several white-stone churches, including the church of Our Saviour (Khram Spasa; 1153), the three-aisled cathedral of the Dormition (Uspenskiy Sobor; 1157) and the church of St Panteleymon (built 1200; reconstructed in the 17th century).

The present-day town of Halich developed during the 14th century. As part of Ruthenia, it was annexed by Poland in 1367 and became an important centre for artisans. After the First Partition of Poland in 1772, it became part of Austria, returning to Poland in 1920, until its annexation to the USSR in 1939. After the declaration of independence in 1991, it became part of Ukraine. Among the town's important buildings are the church of the Nativity (Rozhdestva Khristova; late 14th century–early 15th; rest. 1825) and the remains of the 16th-century castle.

BIBLIOGRAPHY
V. K. Goncharov: 'Drevniy Halich' [Old Halich], *Visnyk Akad. Nauk Ukrainskoy RSR*, i (1956), pp. 61–7
M. N. Tikhomirov: *Drevnerusskiye goroda* [Old Russian cities] (Moscow, 1956)

L. I. POPOVA

Halifax (i). English town in West Yorkshire. The cloth trade thrived in Halifax from the 13th century. The fine Piece Hall, built as a cloth market in 1775 by Thomas Bradley, housed over 315 merchants' rooms; the central open rectangular space is surrounded by two- and three-storey colonnades. The town is now chiefly important as a centre of carpet manufacture.

The firm of J. Crossley & Sons is synonymous with the production of carpets in Halifax and has been responsible for introducing some of the most far-reaching innovations in machine-produced floor coverings. The firm was founded by John Crossley (*d* 1837), a hand-loom weaver who set up his own weaving shed at nearby Dean Clough in 1803. By 1833 the venture was profitable enough to enable the company to purchase from Richard Whytock of Edinburgh, for £10,000, the patents for weaving warp-printed carpets (*see* CARPET, §II, 2(iv)), a technique that became especially associated with Crossley's and which made Halifax the centre for such production in England. The task of printing the design on to the warp threads before weaving was laborious and dirty but made it possible for designers to incorporate up to 150 colours, although in practice a total of 30 to 40 colours was more common. As the entire pile warp was raised to form each row of loops, carpets could be woven at considerable speed. Two qualities of carpet were produced: 'Tapestry Brussels', with uncut loops, and 'Tapestry Velvets', with cut pile (*see* CARPET, fig. 11). Some of the first power looms to be used in the carpet industry were installed at Dean Clough in 1850, and in the following year Crossley's bought the patent for the power loom invented by Erastus Brigham Bigelow (1814–79) for Brussels carpets, which could weave carpeting at the rate of 23 m per day compared with the 6.4 m produced on a hand loom. Crossley's soon dominated the industry and in the second half of the 19th century was the world's largest producer of carpets. The firm amalgamated with the Carpet Trades Group in 1953.

BIBLIOGRAPHY
A. F. Kendrick and C. E. C. Tattersall: *Handwoven Carpets: Oriental and European* (London, 1926)
C. E. C. Tattersall and S. Reed: *British Carpets* (London, 1966)
B. Jacobs: *Axminster Carpets* (Leigh-on-Sea, 1969)
C. Gilbert, J. Lomax and A. Wells-Cole: 'Country House Floors', *Temple Newsam Country House Stud.*, iii (1987)

JENNIFER WEARDEN

Halifax (ii). Capital city of the Canadian province of Nova Scotia. It is situated on the Atlantic coast, on a hill on the eastern slope of a rocky peninsula, and is the largest city in the Maritime provinces. In 1749 the British established a fortified settlement, named after the 2nd Earl of Halifax. Early development consisted of grid-pattern streets rising in neat terraces from the waterfront. Local forests provided abundant wood for the simple, painted clapboard houses. Dominating the top of the hill is the Citadel, originally a star-shaped, stone fortress. The present edifice (1861; now Army Mus., Citadel) is the fourth on the site. The town also thrived as a centre for fishing and shipbuilding and as a port for transatlantic vessels. Its early civil population was made up largely of British and German immigrants, as well as of New Englanders. The timber, Palladian St Paul's Anglican Church (1750; altered), influenced by New England models, is the oldest surviving structure. Palladianism was also the favoured style for large stone buildings, such as Government House (1800) and Province House (1811), and for timber buildings, for example the Naval Commissioner's House (*c.* 1785; destr. 1909), with wooden imitation quoins. Edward, Duke of Kent (1767–1820), who was stationed at Halifax (1794–1800), introduced the Picturesque style for his landscaped estate (mostly destr.), complete with grottoes and a pagoda, at Bedford Basin. He also donated the timber, classical Old Town Clock (1800–03), one of the principal landmarks of Halifax.

In the 19th century Halifax was a handsome, European-style provincial city, whose architecture reflected the prevailing revivals of historical styles. Timber building still predominated, as the supply of stone was haphazard; that for Harrington House (1820; restored 1977), for example, arrived as ships' ballast. Substantial buildings of the late 19th century and the early 20th are the Forrest Building (1887), Dalhousie University, by JAMES DUMARESQ, and the neo-Gothic Anglican Cathedral (1908) by Ralph Adams Cram and Bertram Goodhue. In 1917 the northern section of the city was destroyed in a catastrophic explosion following the collision of two munitions ships. In the late 20th century the city continued to serve as a naval base and important commercial port.

Halifax has a strong tradition of handicrafts, evidenced by the many examples of 18th- and 19th-century scrimshaw executed by seamen (examples in Maritime Mus. Atlantic) and by wood-carving, weaving and calligraphy in Gothic script (Ger. *Fraktur*). Also notable are articles of birchbark quillwork made by Micmac Indians, for example a cradle of painted birchbark (*c.* 1841; Bridgewater, NS, DesBrisay Mus. & N. Exh. Cent.) by Christianne Morris. In 1887 the Victoria School of Art and Design (now the Nova Scotia College of Art and Design) was founded; during the 1970s it became one of the principal focuses for international avant-garde activities in North America, holding exhibitions, seminars and art events attended by painters, sculptors and conceptual artists from many parts of the world, particulary the USA.

BIBLIOGRAPHY
S. Hines: *Halifax* (Halifax, 1981)
M. Bird: *Canadian Folk Art: Old Ways in a New Land* (Toronto, 1983)

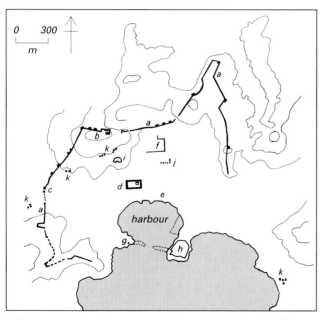

1. Halikarnassos, plan, 4th century BC: (a) outer fortifications; (b) Göktepe; (c) Myndus gate; (d) Mausoleum; (e) supposed site of market-place; (f) large platform; (g) supposed site of Temple of Aphrodite and Hermes; (h) castle of St Peter; (i) theatre; (j) colonnade; (k) tombs

Halikarnassos [now Bodrum]. City on the south-west coast of Caria, now south-west Turkey. It was founded *c.* 900 BC by Dorian Greek colonists from Troezen in the Peloponnese, but by the 4th century BC the population was a mixture of Ionian Greeks, Carians and Lelegians. It is famous for its 4th-century BC Mausoleum. From 546 to 480 BC and again from *c.* 403 to 334 BC the city formed part of the Persian Empire; during the intervening years it was a loyal member of the Athenian alliance. In 334 BC it was stormed by Alexander the Great, and later it was taken over by the Ptolemies of Alexandria, from whom it was freed by the Romans in 190 BC. One of its most famous citizens was the historian Herodotus (*c.* 484–425 BC).

1. ARCHITECTURE. Halikarnassos reached the height of its wealth and importance in the 4th century BC, when MAUSOLOS (*reg* 377–352 BC), a local dynast who was also satrap (governor) of Caria for the Great King of Persia, refounded the city *c.* 370–*c.* 365 BC and moved his capital here from Mylasa, appreciating the strategic significance of its harbours and the possibilities for commercial development. He greatly enlarged the city by forcibly moving in the populations of neighbouring Lelegian hill-towns, and he may have been responsible for its plan, of which remains are visible today. Most impressive of these is the circuit of fortifications some 5.5 km long (see fig. 1a), constructed in fine ashlar masonry and following an irregular line of defence that takes in the principal acropolis Göktepe (1b) and an extended salient in the north-east. Particularly well preserved is the Myndus gate to the west (1c).

There has been no systematic excavation of the city except for the site of the Mausoleum (1d), and we still depend for our knowledge of the main features on a detailed description given by Vitruvius (*On Architecture* II.viii.10–15), apparently based on an eye-witness account. He compared the site to the curving shape of an ancient theatre. At the lowest level beside the harbour was the market-place (1e), still unlocated. At the middle level like a cross gangway ran a broad avenue (*plateia*) in the centre of which was built the Mausoleum, Mausolos' tomb monument. On the top of the acropolis in the middle was a Temple of Ares, the site of which is disputed; some would place it on the summit of Göktepe, others on a large platform lower down (1f) excavated by Charles Newton.

A Temple of Aphrodite and Hermes mentioned by Vitruvius was probably set on the headland to the west of the harbour entrance (1g). The nearby fountain of Salmacis, the waters of which were reputed to afflict its drinkers with venereal disease, may now rise within the harbour, as the land here has sunk almost two metres in the last 2000 years. On the promontory opposite, called Zephyrion, now occupied by the great Crusader castle of St Peter (1h), is the probable site of the palace of Mausolos. According to Vitruvius, its walls were cheaply constructed of sun-dried brick but given an expensive veneer of Proconnesian marble and so highly finished with stucco plaster that they seemed to have the translucency of glass. Foundations of walls have recently been found that may belong to this palace, but its secret harbour, which was linked by canal to the main harbour, remains elusive. The purpose of this was to enable Mausolos to draw up his troops and naval forces unobserved without leaving his palace, and it was from here that Mausolos' sister and wife Artemisia (*d* 351 BC) surprised and captured Rhodian invaders in 352 BC after the death of her husband. The secret harbour was probably to the east of the promontory of Zephyrion, and the canal to the north beneath the centre of the old Turkish town of Bodrum.

Ancient structures not mentioned by Vitruvius include the theatre (1i) set on the slopes of the acropolis, which probably dates from the mid-4th century BC although the façade of its stage building is Roman (1st–2nd century AD), a Doric colonnade (1j) and numerous rock-cut tombs (1k). The splendid castle of St Peter, which dominates the bay, was built by the Knights Hospitallers of Rhodes between 1402 and 1522. In the later phases of its construction after 1494, much building material from the Mausoleum was incorporated in its walls.

BIBLIOGRAPHY

G. E. Bean and J. M. Cook: 'The Halicarnassus Peninsula', *Annu. Brit. Sch. Athens*, l (1950), pp. 85–169 (85–108)

W. Radt: *Siedlungen und Bauten auf der Halbinsel von Halikarnassos* (Tübingen, 1970)

G. E. Bean: *Turkey beyond the Maeander* (London, 1971, rev. 2 by S. Mitchell, 1980)

S. Hornblower: *Mausolus* (Oxford, 1982)

K. Jeppesen and A. Luttrell: *The Written Sources and their Archaeological Background* (1985), ii of *The Maussolleion at Halikarnassos* (Århus, 1981–91)

P. Pedersen: *The Mausolleion Terrace and Accessory Structures* (1991), iii of *The Mausolleion at Halikarnassos* (Århus, 1981–91)

2. MAUSOLEUM. Artemisia is credited by ancient writers with the construction of the tomb monument of Mausolos, and for this reason it has often been dated to 352–351 BC, the two-year period between their deaths. The tomb was too large, however, to have been completed in this short space of time, and it is more likely that it was begun during Mausolos' lifetime, perhaps soon after he refounded Halikarnassos, and finished *c.* 350 BC. All that survives on the site is the rock-cutting for the foundations (sometimes called the Quadrangle) and some blocks of the lowest courses of masonry that once supported the massive tower-tomb. The reconstruction of its original appearance, which has exercised scholars for nearly 500 years, depends on the interpretation of a wide range of fragmentary evidence. This evidence falls into three main categories: accounts and references in ancient writers; sculpture and masonry built into the castle of St Peter at Bodrum by the Knights Hospitallers, who dismantled the remains of the monument; and the finds from two major archaeological excavations, conducted by Charles Newton (1856–8) and by Kristian Jeppesen (1966–76).

(i) Evidence of ancient sources. (ii) Evidence from the castle of St Peter. (iii) Evidence from Newton's excavations. (iv) Evidence from Jeppesen's excavations. (v) Reconstruction. (vi) Character. (vii) Influence.

(i) Evidence of ancient sources. The most detailed ancient source is the partial description of the Mausoleum by Pliny (*Natural History* XXXVI.iv.30–31), written *c.* AD 75. Although there are variant readings in the manuscripts, and the facts and figures do not all quite add up, the following points are generally accepted.

The Mausoleum was rectangular in plan with a perimeter at ground level of 440 Roman feet (141 m), giving sides of 120 and 100 feet (38.4×32.0 m), the longer sides at north and south. It was 140 feet (44.8 m) high and consisted of three main parts: a high podium or base; above this a colonnade of 36 columns, probably arranged 11 by 9; and above this a roof in the form of a pyramid with 24 steps, on top of which was a marble *quadriga* (four-horse chariot). Pliny named four famous Greek sculptors, each responsible for the decoration of one side of the building: Skopas (east), Bryaxis (north), Timotheos (south) and Leochares (west). Of the individual sculptures he mentioned only the *quadriga* on the summit, which he said was by Pythis, who is usually equated with the Pytheos named by Vitruvius (*On Architecture* VII. Pref. 12–13) as one of the two architects of the Mausoleum, the other being Satyros. Vitruvius' short account, written *c.* 30–25 BC, includes the name of Praxiteles among the four sculptors, relegating Timotheos to a possible alternative. This is usually supposed to be an error.

(ii) Evidence from the castle of St Peter. At some time the roof and colonnade of the Mausoleum collapsed in an earthquake, but the ruins remained reasonably intact until 1494, when the Knights Hospitallers used its squared stone to refortify their castle at Bodrum. Long stretches of walling in the castle are constructed from blocks of green volcanic stone (*c.* 900 mm square and 300 mm thick) that formed the core of the Mausoleum. The marble facing of the building and its marble sculptures were mostly smashed and burnt for lime. Research by Luttrell (see Jeppesen and others, ii) shows that this destruction continued until 1522, by which time almost every block had

2. Halikarnassos, Mausoleum, sculpted frieze showing *Amazonomachy*, marble, h. 900 mm, *c.* 370–*c.* 350 BC (London, British Museum)

been removed to the bottom of the foundations, and the subterranean tomb chamber had been opened up and looted. A 16th-century account of the discovery of the tomb chamber (Guichard) has been partially confirmed by excavations. This suggests that the ashes and bones of Mausolos had been wrapped in gold-embroidered cloth and placed in a small gabled sarcophagus of alabaster. Above the tomb chamber was apparently a richly decorated room where offerings could be made.

Between 1505 and 1507 a few sculptures were built into the castle for decoration. At least a dozen slabs of the *Amazonomachy* frieze were thus preserved (see fig. 2), together with a single block of the *Centauromachy* frieze and the foreparts of four standing lions and one running leopard. These were later taken to the British Museum, the friezes in 1846 and the lions and leopard in 1857. The castle walls continue to yield up their treasures. A complete architrave block reused as a lintel over a gateway (see Jeppesen and Zahle) has given us the axial spacing of the columns, while a corner block of the *Amazonomachy*, found in 1975 and not yet published, provides proof that this ran round all four sides of the monument.

(iii) Evidence from Newton's excavations. The most substantial body of material evidence from the Mausoleum derives from the excavations of Newton. Sufficient fragments of architecture were found, including the northwest corner capital, to show that the order was Ionic, and within the area of the foundations he came upon the blocking-stone for the tomb still *in situ*. Fragments of sculptures left by the Knights in the Quadrangle were collected, including several fine slabs of the *Amazonomachy*

3. Halikarnassos, Mausoleum, female (?Artemisia) and male (?Mausolos) portrait statues, marble, h. 2.67 m (female), 3.00 m (male), *c.* 370–*c.* 350 BC (London, British Museum)

frieze reused as drain covers, remains of two further friezes (one with a race of four-horse chariots, the other the *Centauromachy* frieze), fragments of lion statues like those in the castle, and two much-damaged colossal statues, one of a seated male figure, the other of a Persian horseman. His greatest discovery, however, was made in a field to the north of the building: the only large deposit of architectural stones and sculptures missed by the Knights, because they had fallen beyond the peribolus (precinct wall), which here ran close to the tomb. From this relatively limited area came almost all the large sculptures to be seen today in the British Museum: the splendid fore- and hindquarters of horses from the chariot group; the fine male and female portrait statues identified by Newton as *Mausolos* and *Artemisia* (see fig. 3) and wrongly assigned by him to the chariot group; more lion statues; and the head of *Apollo*, the only deity known to have been represented on the Mausoleum. With them were numerous pieces of masonry, including several steps from the pyramid roof that provided important dimensions for this part of the building. This deposit gave the truest indication of how lavish the sculptural decoration of the Mausoleum had really been. Even so, Newton and his architect Richard Popplewell Pullan were unable to come up with a reconstruction that satisfactorily accommodated the many different groups of sculpture, in the round and in relief, to the building. The free-standing sculptures brought back by this expedition were published in full by Waywell.

(iv) Evidence from Jeppesen's excavations. The great achievement of Jeppesen's excavations was to clear the area of the foundations completely and to produce an accurate plan. The monument was set in the north-east part of the huge rectangular peribolus (242.5×105.5 m), entered through a gateway on the east side. The foundations were sited on a former (?royal) burial ground, of which only the south-west staircase survives. Important features are the western staircase, made for the burial of Mausolos, with the ritual deposit of food at its foot, the dromos (passageway) leading to the tomb chamber, and the tomb chamber itself in which were a few gold ornaments left by the looters (Bodrum Mus.). Blocks of green volcanic stone still in place in the south-west and north-east corners of the cutting for the foundations provide the dimensions of the sides of the Mausoleum at ground-level (*c.* 38.5× 32.0 m). This agrees roughly with Pliny's figure for the perimeter (440 feet) if we assume a foot length of 320 mm.

Further architectural blocks recovered from within the foundations furnished new evidence for the Mausoleum's appearance. Fragments of wider pyramid steps with cuttings for statues suggest that the standing lions were placed at the base of the roof. Fragments of statue bases in blue limestone with moulded front edges and cuttings for statues evidently came from the podium and prove that free-standing sculptures were accommodated on ledges against the wall of the podium, probably on more than one level. Facing blocks in blue limestone further suggest that certain parts of the podium were finished in this darker stone to contrast with the white marble of the rest of the architecture and the polychrome painting of the sculptures. Thousands of fragments of architecture and sculpture from these excavations are now in the Bodrum Museum on the site.

(v) Reconstruction. A provisional reconstruction of one of the shorter sides based on that by Waywell illustrates a likely arrangement of the varied sculptures on the building (see fig. 4). The numbers of pyramid steps and columns are taken from Pliny's account. So too is the overall height of 140 feet (44.8 m), of which 60 feet (19.2 m) is allotted to the podium, 37.5 feet (12 m) to the colonnade, 22.5 feet (7.2 m) to the pyramid, and 20 feet (6.4 m) to the chariot group. Known dimensions that fit this scheme are the height and tread of the pyramid steps (h. 300 mm; tread 600 mm for the lowest step, otherwise 430 mm for the longer sides, 540 mm for the shorter), the axial spacing of the columns (3 m), the dimension of the base of the monument (32 m), the projection of the lowest step of the podium (720 mm), and the sizes of statues and friezes. Sculptures whose positions are fixed are the chariot group on the summit, the lions at the base of the roof and the *Amazonomachy* at the top of the podium. There was no frieze in the Ionic entablature, and so, of the other two friezes, the *Centauromachy* may plausibly be placed around the base of the chariot group, while the chariot frieze may have been inserted into the upper part of the wall behind the colonnade. In this way a frieze would have decorated the top of each of the three main parts of the Mausoleum. Within the peristyle the ceiling coffers were sculpted in relief with the exploits of Theseus.

The extensive series of colossal portrait statues (2.7–3.0 m high) representing the ruling dynasty of Caria, of which the so-called *Mausolos* and *Artemisia* are the best preserved, are most reasonably placed between the columns. Most of the other sculptures belonged to groups designed to be viewed from one side, which were evidently set on narrow bases against the wall of the podium like pedimental sculptures. As they are of three different scales, from life-size to one and two-thirds times life-size, there were perhaps three separate ledges to accommodate them (Jeppesen, however, favoured only two steps on the podium). In the reconstruction the heights of the steps on the podium are divided in the proportion 3:4:5 to suit the scale of the sculptures associated with them. Subjects represented included animal hunts, scenes of offering or sacrifice, a battle between Greek and Persian warriors, and numerous standing figures, probably portraits, some male, some female. The sculptures from the podium suffered most severely at the hands of the Knights and survive now only in small fragments.

(vi) Character. The magnificent architecture and sculpture of the Mausoleum are entirely Greek in technique and style and of the highest quality, but the designs incorporate many non-Greek elements, which may be attributed to the taste of the Carian patron. The building's curious form may result from an attempt to combine features from three different civilizations: Lycian, Greek and Egyptian. The high, rectangular podium is characteristic of Lycian tombs, such as the Nereid Monument (*c.* 400 BC; London, BM) from XANTHOS. Above this the peristyle is Ionic Greek of the variety found at Ephesos, with plinths and elaborate bases supporting slender columns with trim capitals, and a relatively low entablature from which a sculpted frieze is deliberately excluded in favour of dentils and rich Ionic mouldings. In proportion and detail the order is closely similar to that of the Temple of Athena Polias at Priene (begun *c.* 345 BC), which supports Vitruvius' attribution of both buildings to Pytheos. Finally, the ingenious stepped pyramid roof is probably Egyptianizing. Little is known of the internal layout of the Mausoleum, but judging from the quantities of green volcanic stone reused in the castle it probably consisted mostly of solid masonry, except for the tomb chamber and the cult room allegedly situated above it.

The sculptures were carved by Greek masons from a variety of Greek marbles. Largest and most important was the chariot group on the summit, the horses of which were sculpted in two parts so that they could be lifted on to the building more easily. The horses' stocky proportions and the large-wheeled chariot suggest that the sculpture was a satrapal ceremonial group. The statue of the chariot's occupant does not survive, but it must surely have represented Mausolos. To a Greek mind such an elevated position for the group would have implied deification, but there is no historical evidence that Mausolos regarded himself as a god. The pose of the walking lions is oriental rather than Greek, and imparts a slightly stylized character to the sculptures of the roof.

Some of the finest sculptures are the colossal male and female portrait statues of the Carian dynasty. The identification of the two most complete statues as *Mausolos* and *Artemisia* is possible but not proven. The *Mausolos*, with his Asiatic features, long hair and proud bearing, is a fine

4. Halikarnassos, Mausoleum, *c.* 370–*c.* 350 BC; reconstructed elevation of one of the shorter sides, based on that by G. B. Waywell

and rare example of realistic Greek portraiture from the 4th century BC. Most of the statues, both male and female, are heavily draped as a concession to Carian sensibilities. Only one naked torso, of a Greek involved in a battle scene, survives among the free-standing sculptures. By contrast the *Amazonomachy* is purely Greek in design and execution: here in magnificently energetic compositions naked Greek warriors battle with lightly clad female opponents. The subject-matter of the groups from the podium is most closely paralleled in the art produced for local rulers in Asia Minor, Lydia, Lycia and Syria. Comparable figure-types are to be seen especially on the fine Greek sarcophagi from the royal necropolis at Sidon (e.g. the Alexander sarcophagus; *c.* 325–*c.* 300 BC; Istanbul, Archaeol. Mus.).

All four sides of the Mausoleum appear to have had similar sculptural decoration. It is possible, therefore, that one sculptor was responsible for each side in the way that Pliny suggested, although most scholars consider this simplistic division to be the invention of the local guides at Halikarnassos. The sculptors named by both Pliny and Vitruvius were all active in the 4th century BC, and there is no reason to doubt their participation in work on the monument, but they must have had many assistants, and it is fruitless to attempt to associate particular sculptures with individual artists.

(vii) Influence. The Mausoleum was one of the most famous buildings of antiquity. By the 3rd century BC it was already counted among the Seven Wonders of the World, and by Roman times its name had become the generic term for any large-scale architectural funerary monument (*see* MAUSOLEUM). Its impact on Greek sculpture and architecture was immediate and profound. Through its immense scale and magnificence, its combination of Greek forms with non-Greek themes and its glorification of a mortal ruler in a manner previously reserved for gods, the Mausoleum marked a turning-point between the restraint of Classical Greek art and the extrovert qualities characteristic of Hellenistic and Roman art. Important changes in taste that were either initiated or promoted by the Mausoleum include: the use of a high podium or base to elevate buildings or sculptures, which led in turn to such developments as the monumental altar, exemplified by the Great Altar of Zeus at Pergamon (*see* PERGAMON, fig. 2) and the introduction of the high raised stage into the ancient theatre; enhanced interest in realistic portraiture and in genealogical portrait groups; and the incorporation of free-standing sculptures into architectural façades on multiple levels, an innovation that greatly influenced Roman Imperial theatres and nymphaea.

In funerary architecture the influence of the Mausoleum can be seen in the many Greek and Roman podium tombs with external orders and pyramidal or conical roofs from Syria, North Africa, Italy, France and Germany, though variations of scale, proportion and decorative detail show that there was no simple line of continuity. Early diversification may have taken place in Attica around 350–320 BC in the grand tombs and victory monuments built beside the roads into Athens. The Tomb of Nikeratos from Kallithea with its Ionic columns, portrait statues and Amazon frieze (*c.* 340 BC; Peiraeus, Archaeol. Mus.) and the Monument of Lysikrates at Athens (335–334 BC) serve to illustrate these flamboyant structures. Military victory monuments in the form of miniature mausolea also occur from the 4th century BC (e.g. lion monuments at Chaironeia and Amphipolis) continuing into the Roman period (e.g. an Augustan trophy monument, the Tropaeum Alpium, at La Turbie in the French Alps, and a Trajanic memorial to the conquest of Dacia at Adamklissi (anc. Tropaeum Traiani) in Romania). Of the many tomb monuments in Asia Minor derived from the Mausoleum, the closest in size and decoration is that at Belevi (the Heroön or Mausoleum; *c.* 281–246 BC; *see* GREECE, ANCIENT, fig. 30), with its square podium and peristyle, pyramidal roof, griffin statues and chariot group. Already here, however, the Corinthian and Doric orders have replaced Ionic, an increasing tendency in Hellenistic tombs (e.g. the Lion Tomb at KNIDOS).

An important structure linking the Mausoleum with later Hellenistic royal tombs is the monument at Limyra in Lycia (*c.* 275 BC), possibly connected with the ruler-cult of Ptolemy II (*reg* 285–246 BC). It has a square Doric podium on which rested an Ionic tholos, apparently modelled on the Philippeion at Olympia (338–335 BC). This combination of square and circular elements, common in later mausolea, may have been further influenced by the circular tomb monument of Alexander the Great at Alexandria. Of the two giant Imperial mausolea built at Rome by Augustus (28–23 BC) and Hadrian (AD 130–39), which in turn influenced Roman private tombs, Hadrian's (the Castel Sant'Angelo; *see* ROME, §V, 9) was closer to the Hellenistic tradition, with its combination of square base, circular superstructure and lavish sculptural decoration.

BIBLIOGRAPHY

Pauly–Wissowa: 'Pytheos'

C. Guichard: *Funérailles et diverses manières d'ensevelir* (Lyons, 1581)

C. T. Newton: *A History of Discoveries at Halicarnassus, Cnidus and Branchidae*, 2 vols (London, 1862–3)

A. H. Smith: *A Catalogue of Sculpture in the Department of Greek and Roman Antiquities, British Museum*, ii (London, 1900), pp. 65–135

J. Formigé: 'Le Trophée des Alpes', *Gallia*, suppl. ii (1949) [whole issue]

K. Jeppesen: *Paradeigmata: Three Mid-4th-century Main Works of Hellenic Architecture Reconsidered* (Århus, 1958), pp. 1–67

J.-C. Richard: ' "Mausoleum": D'Halicarnasse à Rome, puis à Alexandrie', *Latomus*, xxix (1970), pp. 370–88

B. Ashmole: *Architect and Sculptor in Classical Greece* (London, 1972)

K. Jeppesen and J. Zahle: 'Investigations on the Site of the Mausoleum, 1970/1973', *Amer. J. Archaeol.*, lxxix (1975), pp. 67–79

K. Jeppesen: 'Neue Ergebnisse zur Wiederherstellung des Maussolleions von Halikarnassos', *Istanbul. Mitt.*, xxvi (1976), pp. 47–99

——: 'Zur Gründung und Baugeschichte des Maussolleions von Halikarnassos', *Istanbul. Mitt.*, xxvii–xxviii (1977–8), pp. 169–211

G. B. Waywell: *The Free-standing Sculptures of the Mausoleum at Halicarnassus in the British Museum* (London, 1978)

H. Horn and C. Rüger: *Die Numider* (Bonn, 1979)

C. Praschniker and others: *Das Mausoleum von Belevi* (1979), vi of *Forschungen in Ephesos* (Vienna, 1906–)

G. B. Waywell: 'Mausolea in South-west Asia Minor', *Yayla*, iii (1980), pp. 4–11

K. Jeppesen and others: *The Maussolleion at Halikarnassos*, i–iii (Copenhagen and Århus, 1981–91)

M. T. Boatwright: *Hadrian and the City of Rome* (Princeton, 1987), pp. 161–81

J. Borchhardt: 'Löwen am Naos des Ptolemaion in Limya', *Akten des XIII. internationalen Kongresses für klassische Archäologie: Berlin, 1988*, p. 498

T. Linders and P. Hellström, eds: *Architecture and Society in Hecatomnid Caria* (Uppsala, 1989)

G. B. Waywell: 'The Mausoleum at Halicarnassus', *The Seven Wonders of the Ancient World*, ed. P. Clayton and M. Price (London, 1989)

J. Fedak: *Monumental Tombs of the Hellenistic Age* (Toronto, 1990)

I. D. Jenkins: *Archaeologists and Aesthetes in the Sculpture Galleries of the British Museum, 1800–1939* (London, 1992), pp. 168–95

K. Jeppesen: 'Tot operum opus: Ergebnisse der dänischen Forschungen zum Maussolleion von Halikarnass seit 1966', *Jahrbuch des Deutschen Archäologischen Instituts*, 107 (1992), pp. 59–102

G. B. WAYWELL

Hall (i). Building type, usually consisting of a large roofed space with a public or communal function. The term probably derives from the Teutonic *halla* ('covered space') rather than the Latin *aula* ('open court').

I. Ancient Greece and Rome. II. Europe after *c.* AD 500. III. Indian subcontinent. IV. South-east Asia. V. East Asia.

I. Ancient Greece and Rome.

Halls are not generally characteristic of Greek and Roman architecture. In Creto-Mycenaean palaces the hall is the great throne room (*see* HELLADIC, §II, 3). Subsequently this type of building was associated with democratic political organization that necessitated a place for the meetings of the council of the people (*boule*). In its earliest form this room (called the BOULEUTERION) was rectangular and quite wide; it apparently derived from the MEGARON with its axial colonnade, for example those on Delos and Kalauria and at Olynthos. It resembled a closed portico, and for this reason certain deep or long porticos are also called 'halls' by archaeologists, for example the Hall of Votive Gifts in Samothrace (*see* SAMOTHRACE, §I), the north-east hall at Mamurt Kale (Turkey) and the Hypostyle Hall at Delos, called a stoa in the inscriptions (*see* DELOS, §1). Gradually, in particular from the 4th century BC onwards, these rooms tended to have square plans, with interior colonnades arranged radially, for example the Thersilion at MEGALOPOLIS or the bouleuterion at Sikyon. Naturally these large, high rooms posed problems of lighting (solved by windows high up) and of roofing, and in order not to block the view of those inside an attempt was made to decrease the number of columns. From a rectangular plan, with benches arranged in a semicircle (as at Miletos; for illustration *see* BOULEUTERION), these rooms in some instances became round. Although the circular plan was popular in Roman times, it was already known previously under the generic name of tholos (*see* THOLOS).

The Romans built many types of halls, including the curia (senate house) derived from the bouleuterion; the BASILICA, with several aisles; porticos for commerce; groups of vast reception halls that characterized the houses of the rich; and, above all, palaces, such as that of the Emperor Domitian (*reg* AD 81–96) on the Palatine (*see* ROME, §V, 3 and PALACE, §I, 5). These oblong-plan rooms, tending towards square, are characterized by strong axial lines, reinforced by colonnades that are often more ornamental than structural, with apses or rectangular niches and abundant sculptural decoration, while the practice of vaulting solved the problem of roofing (*see* ROME, ANCIENT, §II, 1(ii)).

BIBLIOGRAPHY

B. Tamm: *Auditorium and Palatium: A Study on Assembly Rooms in Roman Palaces* (Stockholm, 1963)

D. Gneisz: *Das antike Rathaus: Das griechische Bouleuterion und die frührömische Curia* (Vienna, 1990)

MARIE-CHRISTINE HELLMANN

II. Europe after c. AD 500.

1. *c.* AD 500–*c.* 1000. 2. After *c.* 1000.

1. *c.* AD 500–*c.* 1000. In medieval northern Europe the hall became the central focus of domestic buildings, whether palaces or farmsteads. There was a social distinction between the hall as the audience chamber or entertaining room of a ruler (e.g. Charlemagne's Palace at Aachen, *c.* AD 800, where the hall formed one part of a large complex; *see* AACHEN, fig. 1) and the house of a lord, where the communal hall was the principal, indeed the only, sizeable room. While the Roman world had abounded with a variety of civic halls (*see* §I above), many of which were probably later reused as the central chamber of private or semi-royal houses, it is the area beyond the northern Roman frontier that provides evidence for the development of the hall from pre-Roman times to its medieval role as the nucleus of the typical house-plan. Excavations at Ezinge, Holland, revealed a succession of timber-framed, aisled halls dating from *c.* 400 BC to *c.* AD 400, and ranging in size from 4×7 m to 11×12 m. All apparently had a hearth, the social and practical focal point. Smaller halls often had sunken floors similar to *Grubenhäuser* ('Sunken featured buildings'; *see* VIKING ART, §III, 1). Such halls were all-purpose, with a communal living space at one end and animal housing at the other. Similar halls existed across north-west Germany, for example Feddersen-Wierde, a hall over 30 m long. All were built of timber with wattle-and-daub infill.

In England, the Anglo-Saxons built halls of many sizes, from 3 m square at West Stow, Suffolk, to 11×25 m at Yeavering, Northumb. The 7th-century royal settlement at Yeavering contained groups of timber halls within timber fortifications. The two largest had aisles, central entrances flanking the hearth and partitions to screen rooms at each end. There are many references to halls in the literature of the period, reflecting their central position in a semi-tribal society. Bede (AD 673–735), in the *Historia Ecclesiastica Gentis Anglorum*, implies that the halls at Yeavering lacked closing exterior doors, but Hrothgar's hall in the Anglo-Saxon poem *Beowulf* (?8th century AD) had ironwork doors. The reconstructed timber hall at Lojsta, Sweden (*c.* 1000), is dominated by the great sloping roof reaching to the ground, supported by timber piers dividing the aisled interior into bays. Other domestic buildings were informally arranged around a court beside the hall.

Excavations at Cheddar, Somerset, have provided evidence for later Anglo-Saxon royal halls, revealing a sequence of timber structures dating from *c.* 850 to 1150. The earliest, an oblong hall some 5.5×24.0 m had bow-shaped sides and may have been a first-floor hall, a type known to have existed at Calne, Wilts, *c.* 978. Bow-sided halls date back to the Neolithic period in north Germany (e.g. Zwenkau-Harth) and bow-sides were also a feature of early Scandinavian halls. Raised, first-floor timber halls may have been a new departure, and were possibly ceremonial rather than domestic. Harold is depicted on the BAYEUX TAPESTRY (Bayeux, Mus. Tap.) banqueting at Bosham in a first-floor hall raised upon a stone arcade.

2. AFTER *c.* 1000. As a communal living, eating and sleeping area for most of the household, the hall long remained the central feature of medieval domestic planning in northern parts of Europe with cold winters, and where the political situation was sufficiently settled to permit lords and kings to move out of stone castles, notably in England. The Mediterranean world, both Christian and Islamic, with a warmer climate and the lingering remnants of a Classical Roman lifestyle, had little use for such protected, semi-barbaric arrangements. Even in war-torn Italy, the hall, where present, was purely for ceremonial or official business, whether in ducal or people's palace. (*See also* PALACE, §II.)

(i) Germany. (ii) France. (iii) England.

(i) Germany. The medieval German emperors were peripatetic, moving from one imperial city to another. The Carolingians had created several 'Roman-style' palace complexes (e.g. at Aachen), but later rulers built simpler residences, based on an arrangement of a central hall with outbuildings. Despite rebuilding, GOSLAR PALACE (*c.* 1050) is the best example of an imperial great hall, in which the Teutonic concept of the single communal living space survives. The raised stone hall (l. 47 m), with an external, public balcony, limited private apartments at one end and a detached chapel, provided living space, audience chamber and court of justice, hence its grand, dominant architectural status. Bishop Meinwerk's palace in Paderborn (*c.* 1020) has a similar layout. Many imperial churches have grand vaulted halls within their multistorey westworks, and the continued association in northern Europe between such halls and the dispensing of justice (e.g. Ste

Gertrude, Nivelles, Belgium) suggests that many were provided to accommodate the emperor and his entourage in the absence of a nearby palace.

The German landowners, however, because of their great numbers and virtual autonomy, were continually fighting each other, which discouraged them from leaving their fortified homes. Many castles stand on precipitous sites, making the provision of a major hall impractical. Those that do exist are usually situated high up within a central, defensive structure. They are generally vaulted and twin-aisled (Marburg is a good 14th-century example), but the strategic planning of such castles tended to favour the provision of many smaller chambers, and the hall was rarely given special architectural emphasis.

(ii) France. Little is known of the lifestyle of the medieval kings of France before the 14th century. Like their English and German counterparts, they were peripatetic, with numerous palaces and castles in their personal domain. The Palais de la Cité, Paris, was rebuilt by Philip Augustus (*reg* 1180–1223) *c.* 1200, with at least one, twin-aisled great hall, illustrated in the *Très Riches Heures* of Jean, Duc de Berry (Chantilly, Mus. Condé). At an early stage, however, and certainly by *c.* 1200, the French kings developed the concept of the palace, a building with perhaps several halls, but used in concert with many other important chambers. This was in contrast to the English and Germans, who long continued the notion of the 'Great Hall', with accompanying secondary buildings. The shift in France away from a single, all-purpose and architecturally dominant royal hall may have been connected with French ideas of kingship—perhaps inspired by the Byzantine tradition—and the increasing tendency towards a remote, almost unapproachable monarchy. A proliferation of rooms, of specialized chambers and a degree of secrecy all helped to inspire awe in the court, the people and visiting notables. The rough-and-tumble of the communal hall could play no part in such a transformation.

Some great halls were built in France, notably before the reign of Louix IX (*reg* 1226–70). Bishop Sully's Parisian palace had a twin-aisled, vaulted hall (*c.* 1160), similar to contemporary hospital or monastic refectories. At Blois a twin-aisled but unvaulted hall was added to the château *c.* 1200. Institutional communal halls continued to be built, such as the vaulted Grande Salle in the crusader castle of KRAK DES CHEVALIERS, Syria (*c.* 1200). Lacking a crucial social function, however, the great hall never dominated French domestic planning. A notable exception, the refurbished great hall of the Palais de Justice at Poitiers (*c.* 1380; see fig. 1; *see also* POITIERS, §1), property of Jean, Duc de Berry, was possibly influenced by his captivity in England, where such communal halls were common. Its tripartite fireplace illustrates the main reason for the general decline of the great hall: inadequate heating. The replacement of open fires by chimney-stacks rendered such huge, draughty halls redundant as living spaces.

In late medieval France, great halls were still occasionally built, mainly for ceremonial or chivalric purposes. The fortified palace of Pierrefonds, built for Louis, Duke of Orléans (*c.* 1380), has a 'Hall of the Heroines' and a 'Hall of the Knights of the Round Table'. Sometimes halls were created to display great tapestry collections, such as those

1. Hall of the Palais de Justice, Poitiers, interior, ?12th century; refurbished *c.* 1380

of Charles V, of Louis, Duke of Anjou, at Angers (*c*. 1375), and of Philip the Bold of Burgundy, who possessed over 200 tapestries. The less aristocratic house-builders of France seem to have copied the concept of the palace rather than that of the ceremonial hall. In addition, the Hundred Years War (1337–1453) so disrupted domestic building that by the time France recovered the great hall was an anachronism. The bourgeois had no need of chivalric display, and the development of fireplaces led to the provision of chambers with low ceilings, not great open halls, for example the Palais Jacques Coeur, Bourges (1443–51; *see* BOURGES, §II, 4).

(iii) England. The medieval hall was most developed in England after the Norman Conquest of 1066. Relative stability and firm centralized power encouraged the king and the land-based aristocracy to build more generous, less fortified houses (*see* COUNTRY HOUSE). The classic English hall was stone, oblong, timber-roofed, with a raised high-table platform or dais at one end and doors to the kitchen offices at the other. The principal entrance to the house was usually at the kitchen end on a lateral wall. A second door might face opposite, later to be screened off as a passage. All access routes throughout the house went via the hall. Heating was by open-hearth fires or by charcoal braziers, the smoke escaping through louvres constructed in the open roof. In general, domestic halls were situated on the first floor until *c*. 1200, and on the ground floor after that.

Although the earliest residences of William the Conqueror (*reg* 1066–87) were castles (London, Colchester, Canterbury), they contained a great hall within the principal, rectangular stone keep. Commonly two-storeys high, the halls served as communal space for the court, though the plan and complexity of the buildings permitted some diversity of room use. Such castles were primarily defensive, however, and unrepresentative of the plans of contemporary royal palaces. William built a new palace hall at Winchester (destr.), presumably as his principal residence. His successor, William II (*reg* 1087–1100), began a hall in the 1090s as part of his new palace at Westminster (*see* LONDON, §V, 3(i)(a)). At approximately 80×22 m, this hall was the largest ever built in England, and at the time, perhaps the largest in Europe, although when William first saw it, he commented that it was too big for a chamber, but too small for a hall. The surviving exterior stone walls are 12 m high, and the original roof was probably supported by timber columns, dividing the interior into three aisles (altered *c*. 1395). Like earlier halls (e.g. Cheddar), the long walls are slightly bowed. All secondary buildings are lost.

Other unfortified palaces were built by leading ecclesiastics. Archbishop Lanfranc's palace at Canterbury (*c*. 1070), known from excavations and from accounts of the murder of Thomas Becket (1170), contained a large stone hall with a private chamber at one end. The Archbishop's household ate and slept in the hall, where visitors were received and business conducted. Presumably, ecclesiastical justice was also conducted there. Like other bishops, Canterbury possessed a string of such palaces throughout the diocese, each centred on a great hall.

English land ownership differed somewhat from most continental systems, with far more minor lords and gentry farming rural estates based on the manor house, the seat of the landlord, headquarters for estate business and, often, the local magistrate's court. The house was centred on the hall, many being named from this feature, for example Chorley Hall, Cheshire. The plans were simple and remarkably consistent, and probably based on royal hunting lodges, such as Clarendon, Wilts, a favourite of Henry II (*reg* 1154–89). This contained a stone, aisled hall (26×17 m), a private king's chamber, a chapel, kitchens and outbuildings. Many, like Woodstock, Oxon, rebuilt by Henry II, were architecturally superb, and set the trend for manorial imitation. Undoubtedly, such grand halls were regarded as status symbols and some were monumental in scale and lavishly decorated. Bishop Hugh of Le Puiset's hall at Bishop Auckland, Durham (*c*. 1190; 26×14 m), is similar to Clarendon but even more splendid. Canterbury (51.25×21.0 m), as rebuilt *c*. 1200, was second in size only to Westminster but far more richly adorned with marble-work and considerable glazing. The best preserved hall of the period, Oakham, Leics (*c*. 1190; 20.0×13.5 m), has four bays of richly decorated stone arcading, plentiful sculpture and many low-level windows. Entirely timber-framed halls were still built, some very fine, for example the Bishop's Palace hall, Hereford (*c*. 1160), which, at 25×18 m, was nearly the size of Clarendon.

The Great Hall of Winchester Castle (1222–36; 34× 17 m; *see* WINCHESTER, §I) is the main surviving royal hall from the 13th century (see fig. 2). A smaller version of the hall at Canterbury, it has marble columns and tall lateral windows. It continued to serve as a law-court until *c*. 1970. By the mid-13th century, however, Henry III (*reg* 1216–72) appears to have adopted a specifically French model at Westminster Palace, the 'Great Chamber' being the focal point of the palace rather than the hall. In this, he was undoubtedly influenced by the court of Louis IX, and no major royal halls were constructed in England for some time.

Later kings constructed chivalric halls in the French manner, notably Edward III's hall at Windsor of the 1340s (destr.). In the 15th century English royal residences were much replenished, though little is known of the earliest: Sheen Palace, Surrey (destr. 1499), and Rouen, Normandy, France. The finest royal example from later in the century, Edward IV's hall at ELTHAM PALACE, near London (*c*. 1475–83), still emphasizes the communal nature of court life though it was surrounded by an elaborate complex of private apartments. The last of the great medieval royal halls, Whitehall Palace in London (destr.) and Hampton Court, were built by Henry VIII (*reg* 1509–47), but by then such structures were superfluous. Even state banquets tended to be held in temporary, specially constructed banqueting houses.

Many early rural stone manor houses survive, with a simple first-floor hall screened at one end to conceal the lord's private chamber, while other buildings, such as kitchens, were probably of timber and kept separate. Some halls, such as Christchurch, Hants (*c*. 1160), and Boothby Pagnell, Lincs (*c*. 1200), had stone chimney-stacks, but most continued to be heated by open fires.

2. Great Hall of Winchester Castle, interior, begun 1222

In the 13th century the classic English manor house plan developed, with a dominant great hall, a two-storey solar block behind the dais, and kitchen offices at the opposite end. Many have surprisingly spacious halls, for example Stokesay, Salop (*c.* 1285; 17×10 m), and Penshurst Place, Kent (*c.* 1341; 20×13 m). Penshurst preserves its original arrangement though now flanked by late medieval, more 'modern' apartments.

Even English town houses adopted a reduced form of the country manor-house plan. Surviving 12th-century stone houses in Canterbury, Lincoln, Bury St Edmunds and Norwich often have first-floor halls, though some had aisled, ground-level halls added after *c.* 1200, for example Cogan House, Canterbury, and the Music House, Norwich. The low density of most English towns permitted considerably more spacious houses than their European counterparts, where 'halls' are generally unknown. In, for instance, Prague, Czech Republic, and Munstereifel, Germany, tower-houses with many rooms are common. Canterbury preserves two exceptional institutionalized versions of the country manor. Eastbridge Hospital (1180) has an aisled first-floor hall of stone above a vaulted crypt, and a two-storey stone street range including an upper chapel. The kitchen block is lost. The Poor Priest's Hospital (*c.* 1220) occupies a larger site, with a ground-floor great hall along the street, kitchens to the south, a two-storey solar block to the north and an attached chapel. Such buildings doubtless reflect richer, early medieval town houses.

Norwich has the best collection of late medieval urban halls (*see* NORWICH, §1). Stranger's Hall (*c.* 1480) has a great hall of flint with an oriel facing the garden, built above 14th-century vaulted cellars and set within a yard, parallel to the street range, probably of shops. Pickerell's House (*c.* 1480) has a two-storey, timber-framed street range, with a stone hall at right angles immediately behind. The flanking yards permitted tall oriels on either side of the hall dais. In both cases, the oriels and the open timber roofs were objects of great architectural display. By the late 15th century the hall doors, still the principal entrance to the house, were usually screened behind a partition or screens passage to minimize the draught.

Such houses were clearly the homes of the urban rich; but even quite modest, timber-framed town houses commonly had a rear hall standing in a yard or garden, generally at right angles to the street range. Examples abound in most English medieval towns. The 'hall house' appeared in southern England. This was a middle-class farmstead of timber, being a reduced and compact version of the stone manor, with a central open hall, flanked by two-storey ranges, kitchen offices at the entrance end with a chamber above, a room behind the high-table and a solar above. Many examples survive, perhaps the best is the re-erected hall of *c.* 1400 at Singleton, W. Sussex.

In large country houses the great hall declined in importance in the 16th century. Efficient heating by brick stacks and draught-proof panelling, together with a desire for more private, intimate accommodation, encouraged the building of more complex houses with smaller rooms at the expense of the communal hall. Halls were still built, but their role was increasingly ceremonial and symbolic. Splendid entrance halls, as for example at Sutton Place, Surrey (1525), were virtually redundant for all but the grandest of occasions. The function of the hall as the centre of the household, providing sole access to all other parts of the house, gradually diminished as two-storey ranges were built at their rear, as at Hengrave, Suffolk (1535), or even above their roofs as at Sawston, Cambs (*c.* 1550), while stair-halls became separate, luxurious additions to many great houses.

In royal palaces the hall continued to fulfil a monumental role, providing a suitably spectacular setting for receptions and official entertainments. Some halls were built specifically for formal banquets (e.g. Hampton Court Palace; Whitehall Palace, London), and this idea was soon adopted by other public, or institutional organizations, such as the London livery companies.

The term hall was given to the headquarters of trade guilds throughout the Middle Ages, expressing the collective nature of such organizations and their custom of communal dining. Guild members conducted their business around the open fire, recalling the Teutonic origin of the hall. The guildhalls could be situated on either the ground or the first floor. Many medieval examples survive throughout Europe, especially in Germany, the Low Countries and England (e.g. Norwich, 1407–11; York, 1448–60). Town halls are simply municipal versions of the guildhalls, the guilds providing the basis for most of Europe's civic government.

The term hall was also applied to some Oxford and Cambridge colleges, for example Clare Hall (later College),

Cambridge (founded 1338), and St Edmund Hall, Oxford (*c.* 1317). In this sense, the word implies a building containing all the facilities necessary for academic life, religion, teaching, eating and sleeping.

BIBLIOGRAPHY

E. Viollet-le-Duc: *Dictionnaire raisonné de l'architecture française du VIe au XVIe siècle* (Paris, 1859)
J. Smith: 'Medieval Aisled Halls and their Derivatives', *Archaeol. J.*, cxii (1955), pp. 76–94
R. Cramp: 'Beowulf and Archaeology', *Med. Archaeol.*, i (1957), pp. 55–77
K. Conant: *Carolingian and Romanesque Architecture, 800–1200*, Pelican Hist. A. (Harmondsworth, 1959, rev. 1978)
H. M. Colvin, ed.: *The History of the King's Works*, i and ii (London, 1963)
M. Wood: *The English Medieval House* (London, 1964/R 1981)
H. Kubach: *Romanesque Architecture* (New York, 1975)
W. Swaan: *Art and Architecture of the Late Middle Ages* (London, 1977/R 1982)
E. Fernie: *The Architecture of the Anglo-Saxons* (London, 1981), pp. 11–22
H. Colvin, ed.: *The History of the King's Works*, iv (London, 1982)

FRANCIS WOODMAN

III. Indian subcontinent.

In South Asia the hall has assumed a variety of forms and functions, both sacred and secular. In the Vedic period (*c.* 1500–*c.* 600 BC) great fire sacrifices were held in temporary halls of wood and thatch, which were burned at the completion of the ritual. In the Maurya period (*c.*321–*c.* 232 BC) the political and ritual activities of the king seem to have necessitated large structures for assembly, such as the 'audience hall' at the palace complex in Pataliputra (*see* PATNA), a multi-columned structure possibly modelled on the palaces of Achaemenid Persepolis.

The building type most often described as a hall, however, is the *maṇḍapa* of the Hindu temple. Usually rectangular, this structure is placed before a square shrine chamber housing the image or emblem of a divinity. While the shrine itself is generally only large enough for a few persons, the size of the *maṇḍapa* suggests a congregational function. Although not all temples have a *maṇḍapa*, by the 7th century AD it seems to have become a canonical element of the temple plan.

The earliest stone temples of the Gupta period (4th–5th centuries AD), such as Temple 17 at Sanchi, have only a simple porch, comprising a roof supported by columns, preceding the shrine. This open type continued in a more elaborate form into the 10th century and later. From the 7th century onwards, *maṇḍapa*s tended to be closed structures with single axial entrances and grillework windows. This type is common in Orissa (e.g. the Parashurameshvara temple at Bhubaneshwar; *see* BHUBANESHWAR, §2(i)), and in the Chalukya regions of the Deccan, for example the Lad Khan temple, AIHOLE, and the Kailashanatha temple, Ellora (*see* ELLORA, §2). In Orissa and the central and western parts of northern India, temple halls were built with elaborate pyramidal roofs, as at the Rajarani temple, Bhubaneshwar (*c.* 1030), and the Udayeshvara temple at Udaipur, Madhya Pradesh (1080). In southern India the Pallava temples were also often preceded by congregational *maṇḍapa*s; in later periods these assumed gargantuan proportions (e.g. the 14th–17th-century Jambukeshvara temple at Srirangam). In the north many Hindu temples feature a series of halls, axially aligned and connected to one another by buffer walls. At

KHAJURAHO the Kandariya Mahadeva temple (*c.* 1025) has three forehalls, which increase in both area and height as they lead towards the shrine. In Orissa temple halls may have specific functions: for example the Lingaraja temple at Bhubaneshwar (*see* BHUBANESHWAR, §2(v)) has, in addition to the main hall (*jagamohan*), a *nāṭamaṇḍapa* (hall of dance) and a *bhogamaṇḍapa* (offering hall), both 13th-century additions. Frequently, the hall of dance is a detached structure, as at the 13th-century Surya temple at KONARAK.

In Buddhist architecture the hall functioned as an assembly area within a monastic dwelling unit. These *vihāra* halls usually consist of a central area, often pillared, surrounded by walls which contain individual monastic cells. By the Gupta period the central cell on the wall opposite the entrance had been enlarged to serve as a shrine containing an image of the Buddha. Numerous remains of *vihāra* halls survive, both rock-cut, as at BHAJA and Ajanta (*see* AJANTA, §2(ii)), and structural, as at Taxila, Takht-i-Bahi and Sanchi.

With the entry of Islam into India, new types of hall, both sacred and secular, were introduced. In Indian mosques, space for congregational prayer was created by a covered space in front of the *qibla* wall, creating a prayer hall (*liwan*). The palaces of Muslim kings contained two types of assembly hall: the Di an-i-'Am (hall of public audience) and the Di an-i-Khas (hall of private audience). The most spectacular examples are those built by the Mughal dynasty (1526–1858) at Delhi (*see* DELHI, §III, 5), Agra (*see* AGRA, §II, 3) and Lahore. Similar reception halls exist in the palaces of Rajput rulers, for example at Chittaurgarh, Jaipur and BIKANER.

In the colonial period many official buildings contained halls for public functions, such as the Durbar Hall in the Viceroy's House at Delhi. Domed, Western-style reception halls were subsequently constructed in public buildings such as the Umaid Bhavan in Jodhpur (1929–44).

BIBLIOGRAPHY

F. Stall: *Agni: The Vedic Ritual of the Fire Altar*, 2 vols (Berkeley, 1983)
S. L. Huntington: *The Art of Ancient India* (New York, 1985)
J. C. Harle: *The Art and Architecture of the Indian Subcontinent*, Pelican Hist. A. (Harmondsworth, 1986)
G. H. R. Tillotson: *The Rajput Palaces* (New Haven, 1987)
C. Tadgell: *The History of Architecture in India* (London, 1990)
G. H. R. Tillotson: *Mughal India* (San Francisco, 1990)

WALTER SMITH

IV. South-east Asia.

Halls in South-east Asia can have a variety of forms and functions. Since as a rule neither Hindu nor Mahayana Buddhist temples were built for assemblies or congregational worship but rather for ceremonial use by rulers and élites, as for example at Angkor, the only halls they contain are generally in the form of entrance pavilions (*gopura*s) (*see* CAMBODIA, §II, 1 and figs 9 and 11). Theravada Buddhist monastic complexes in Burma (*see* BURMA, §II, 1(ii)(b)), Thailand (*see* THAILAND, §II, 1(iv), (v)(a), (vi)(a) and (vii)) and Laos (*see* LAOS, §II, 1(ii)), on the other hand, usually have both assembly halls (Skt *vihāra*; Thai *wihan*) (*see* LAOS, fig. 2 and THAILAND, fig. 6) for monks and laity containing the principal Buddha image and also monks' ordination halls (*bot*, *ubosot*) (*see* THAILAND, fig. 8). The central portion of Burmese monastic complexes (*marabin hsaung*) (*see* BURMA, §II, 1(iii)(c)) often contains two main halls under a single roof divided from each other by a partition—one for the monks and the other for the laity.

Great throne halls (*see* THAILAND, fig. 9) and halls for the reception of foreign envoys are a prominent feature of the palaces of South-east Asian rulers. The pillared, open-sided hall known as *pendopo* in Indonesia and *sala* in Thailand is often an important element both of Hindu temples in Java, such as the 12th-century Candi Panataran (*see* INDONESIA, §II, 1(ii)), and of palaces and traditional houses in Java, Bali and other Indonesian islands (*see* INDONESIA, §II, 4(iii)). It was adopted at an early date after the introduction of Islam in the 15th century as an integral part of the architecture of the mosque in Indonesia, especially in Java.

BIBLIOGRAPHY
P. Strachan: *Pagan: Art and Architecture of Old Burma* (Arran, 1989)
J. Durmarçay: *The Palaces of South-east Asia: Architecture and Customs* (Singapore, 1991)
R. Waterson: *The Living House: An Anthropology of Architecture in South-east Asia* (Singapore, 1991)

JOHN VILLIERS

V. East Asia.

The hall (Chin. *dian* or *tang*; Jap. *ten* or *dō*) is the standard building type in East Asia, but its structure lends it adaptability to the widest range of functions. The East Asian hall is, almost without exception, a timber-frame building of no more than two storeys elevated on a platform and with an elaborately decorated roof. Its context can be imperial, secular or sacred, and within those categories the hall may be used, among other things, for ceremonies, entertainment, residence, worship or dining.

Most information about Chinese halls comes from two sources: literary descriptions or records, the most important being the architectural treatise *Yingzao fashi* ('Building standards'; 34 chapters; 1103, reissued 1145); and the buildings themselves. The *Yingzao fashi* is evidence that halls of profoundly different status were constructed in China up to and including the 12th century, the higher ranking known as *diantang* ('high-ranking hall'; e.g. the main hall of Foguang Temple, Mt Wutai, Shanxi Province, AD 857) and the lower as *tingtang* ('hall'; e.g. Sutra Library of Huayan Temple, AD 1038). Both were constructed of columns, beams and struts (*tailiang*) using the same method and components. Specific elements of the timber frame were determined by a single module, the *cai*, divided into smaller units known as *fen*. Even in Chinese construction of the Qing period (1644–1911), by which time most standard features of the hall had been altered in style, a modular system was used, based on the *doukou* (bracket cluster), and buildings continued to be ranked by specific architectural features.

The platforms on which all East Asian halls are raised may, but need not, be approached by stairs. The wooden column network, which differs from its Western counterpart in that it bears most of the roof's weight, is implanted either directly into the platform or in stone pillar bases. The pillars may be placed in rows, as in a hypostyle hall, sometimes with gaps left in an otherwise complete grid to make room for a throne or altar; or they may be in concentric groups. These arrangements result in a square or rectangular structure, either with a central space and flanking corridors or porches at one or two sides—respectively in Chinese the inner and outer *cao* ('troughs') and in Japanese the *moya* (core) and the *hisashi* (subsidiary space or enclosed aisle)—or a central core surrounded on four sides by an aisle or porches. On top of the columns in either type of hall are beams running along the longitudinal and transverse axes of the building. The number, length and arrangement of beams are reflections of the hall's rank. Bracket sets, also determined by the status of a hall, are interlocked directly into beams or into wider architraves. Roof purlins are joined to the beams, and one or two sets of roof rafters are placed on the purlins, which are then decorated with a tile roof. Ideally, no metal joiners are required. In the Ming period (1368–1644) the Chinese experimented with 'beamless halls', made of brick and derived from more permanent subterranean tomb structures, but only a handful of these halls seem to have been built.

Halls of high and low rank survive in China and Japan. In China the main hall of the Foguang Temple (*see* CHINA, §II, 2(iv) and fig. 20) is a high-ranking hall of which elements prefigure by two and a half centuries those described in the *Yingzao fashi*. Another high-ranking hall is the Hall of the Three Pure Ones (Sanqing dian) of the Yongle gong, Ruicheng, in southern Shanxi Province (Yuan period, 1279–1368; *see* CHINA, §II, 2(vii) and fig. 24). In its architectural details this hall contrasts sharply with a contemporary hall of lower status, the main hall at Guangsheng Lower Temple in Hongzhao County, less than 200 km away in the same province.

In Japan the same sorts of status distinctions in halls are evident, whether or not the architectural styles derive from China. For instance, the main image hall (*kondō*) of the monastery Tōdaiji in Nara, which received imperial patronage, was of highest rank, whereas the Chinese-derivative *kondō* of Tōshōdaiji, also in Nara, had lower status (*see* NARA, §III, 4 and 9). In Japan, however, the structural differences between high- and low-status halls are not outlined in an architectural manual.

BIBLIOGRAPHY
Li Jie: *Yingzao fashi* [Building standards], 34 chaps (1103, reissued 1145)
Liu Zhiping: *Zhongguo jianzhu leixing ji jiegou* [Chinese architectural types and structures] (Beijing, 1957/R 1987)
Liu Dunzhen: *Zhongguo gudai jianzhu shi* [History of traditional Chinese architecture] (Beijing, 1980, rev. 1984, 2/1987)

NANCY SHATZMAN STEINHARDT

Hall (ii). Irish writers, active in England. Samuel Carter Hall (*b* Waterford, Ireland, 9 May 1800; *d* London, 16 March 1889) moved to England in 1821 where he worked as a literary agent (1822), parliamentary reporter (1823) and began to study law (1824), but found more success as a freelance journalist. In 1824 he married Anna Maria Fielding (*b* Dublin, 6 Jan 1800; *d* London, 30 Jan 1881), and the two became a well-known literary couple. Between 1825 and 1839 he edited nine different magazines or papers. In 1839 he was appointed editor of the new *Art Union*, a subscription publication modelled on German societies for the promotion of the arts, which was later renamed the *Art Journal* and became the leading art periodical in Britain. Hall's editorship continued until 1881, when he retired on the death of his wife, during which time he exercised great influence over the British art scene. He also edited a number of illustrated survey books on British and European art.

Anna Maria Hall's career was based firstly on her original writings and secondly on her collaborations with her husband. She published a steady stream of novels as well as children's fiction, plays and memoirs. With her husband she published the illustrated books *Hall's Ireland* (1841–3) and the *Book of the Thames* (1859), both of which covered the history, architecture and other aspects of their respective areas. They both supported the topical causes of women's rights and temperance. Contemporaries judged Samuel Carter worthy but dull, and Anna Maria an overshadowed original.

WRITINGS

SAMUEL CARTER HALL

ed.: *The Book of Gems: The Poets and Artists of Great Britain*, 3 vols (London, 1836–8)
ed.: *Gems of European Art: The Best Pictures of the Best Schools*, 2 vols (London, 1843–5)
ed.: *The Vernon Gallery of British Art*, 3 vols (London, 1849–54)
Retrospect of a Long Life (London, 1883)

ANNA MARIA HALL

Sketches of an Irish Character, 3 vols (London, 1829–31)
Chronicles of a School-room (London, 1830)
Marian, or a Young Maid's Fortunes (London, 1840)

JOINT

Hall's Ireland, 3 vols (London, 1841–3); abridged by M. Scott, 2 vols (London, 1984)
The Book of the Thames from its Rise to its Fall (London, 1859)

BIBLIOGRAPHY
DNB
Obituary, *The Times* (1 Feb 1881)
Obituary, *The Times* (19 March 1889)

PAMELA GERRISH NUNN

Hall, George Henry (*b* Manchester, NH, 21 Sept 1825; *d* New York, 17 Feb 1913). American painter. Brought up in Boston, he began his career as an artist at the age of 16. In 1849 he travelled with his friend Eastman Johnson to Düsseldorf. Hall studied at the Königliche Akademie for about a year, and after a further two years of study in Paris and Rome he returned in 1852 to New York where he settled. However, he remained an enthusiastic traveller and spent a total of more than twenty years abroad.

One of the best-known still-life painters of the mid-19th century, Hall specialized in painting fruit (raspberries were a particular favourite) and flowers. His work of the 1860s has affinities with the highly detailed, naturalistic imagery of the American Pre-Raphaelites, though by 1868 he was concentrating on figure painting and Spanish and Italian themes. In the early 1880s he returned to still-life subjects (e.g. *California Grapes*, 1893; Worcester, MA, A. Mus.) and remained a popular and successful artist until the turn of the century.

The subject-matter of his figure paintings was often inspired by the Mediterranean locations he favoured. His art was distinguished by a dark colour range and highly polished finish and reflected his love of Venetian painting.

After 1870 Hall exhibited regularly at the National Academy of Design, New York.

BIBLIOGRAPHY
W. H. Gerdts: *Painters of the Humble Truth: Masterpieces of American Still-life, 1801–1939* (Columbia, MO, 1981)

LEE M. EDWARDS

Hall, John (*b* Wivenhoe, Colchester, Essex, 21 Dec 1739; *d* London, 7 April 1797). English engraver. Having studied engraving under Simon François Ravenet (1706–74), he engraved small portraits for periodicals but was soon recognized as an able line-engraver and was engaged by John Boydell. He engraved five important plates of history paintings by Benjamin West, beginning with *Pyrrhus* (1769; Erffa and Staley, p. 167). Hall's role in these was sufficiently crucial that he was joint publisher in 1781 of West's *Battle of the Boyne* (Erffa and Staley, p. 71) and in 1789 of *Cromwell Ordering the Mace to Be Taken Away* (Erffa and Staley, p. 76). In 1785 he became Engraver to George III. As well as subject plates after other painters, he also engraved excellent portraits, such as that of his friend *R. B. Sheridan* (1790; Hamilton, p. 68).

BIBLIOGRAPHY
DNB; Thieme–Becker
C. Le Blanc: *Manuel de l'amateur d'estampes*, ii (Paris, 1856), pp. 338–9
E. Hamilton: *The Engraved Works of Sir Joshua Reynolds* (London, 1878, 2/1884/*R* 1973)
A. Graves: *The Society of Artists of Great Britain (1760–1791): The Free Society of Artists (1761–1783)* (London, 1907), p. 111
Gainsborough and Reynolds in the British Museum (exh. cat. by T. Clifford, A. Griffiths and M. Royalton-Kisch, London, BM, 1978), p. 56
H. von Erffa and A. Staley: *The Paintings of Benjamin West* (New Haven and London, 1986)

DAVID ALEXANDER

Hall, Peter Adolf (*b* Borås, Älvsborg, 23 Feb 1739; *d* Liège, 15 May 1793). Swedish painter and collector. In 1753 he attended Uppsala Universitet to study medicine and natural history. In 1755 he went on a study trip abroad, led by his drawing-master Lars Brisman. While in Germany (1756–9) he studied miniature painting with Eichhardt in Berlin and with Karl Friedrich Wilhelm Richard (1725–70) in Hamburg. After this trip, he decided to become a professional portrait painter, and in 1759 he enrolled at the Kungliga Akademi för de Fria Konsterna in Stockholm, studying drawing with the French sculptor Pierre-Hubert Larchéveque (1721–78) and painting with Gustaf Lundberg. He attracted the attention of C. F. Adelcrantz, who in 1766 gained for him a commission for the pastel portrait of *Princes Karl and Fredrik Adolf*. In that year he also executed a miniature portrait of *Crown Prince Gustav* on the occasion of his engagement to Princess Sophia Magdalena of Denmark. Also in 1766 he received a royal travel grant to study in Paris, where he developed a completely new technique of miniature painting using sweeping brushwork and a clear and fresh range of colour that allowed for lively characterization. He made exquisite detailed studies of the backgrounds of his paintings, as well as his sitters' costumes and their attributes and accessories. His new technique involved applying gouache to the ivory in a manner that allowed the ivory to show through, a method that was particularly successful in depicting drapery. The smooth surface of the ivory also allowed freer brushwork associated with full-scale portraits.

With his exhibition in 1768 of the portrait of the *Dauphin Louis Auguste and his Brother, the Comte de Provence and Artois* (ex-Pierpont Morgan priv. col.), Hall became highly fashionable. He received commissions from court nobility, was accepted into the circles of French artists in Paris and counted among his friends Fragonard, Chardin, Greuze, Hubert Robert and Augustin Pajou. After having been admitted to the Académie des Beaux-Arts and to the Konstakademi in Stockholm, he participated in the annual Salons in Paris up to 1789 (e.g. *Johan Tobias Sergel*, 1778–9; Stockholm, Nmus.). Yet in spite of his success he often felt restricted by the genre of miniature painting and often did oil and pastel portraits on a larger scale (e.g. *Marquise Choiseul-Stainville*, 1792; priv. col., see 1943 exh. cat., p. 61). During the 1780s he began to place complementary colours side by side to enhance their luminous properties, further developed his technique of the painting of fabrics and moved away from the rather stiff poses typical of traditional portraits towards more individual and casual arrangements. He completed his compositions with fresh accessories that he felt were suited to the model. He admired Fragonard's work and executed several rather sugary and sensual miniatures in his style.

During the French Revolution, Hall initially sympathized with the opponents of the *ancien régime* and in a *Self-portrait* (1789; Stockholm, Nmus.) he portrayed himself dressed in revolutionary costume. However, he began to suffer a loss of income due to a decline in his clientele and soon switched allegiances. In 1791 he left Paris destitute and travelled to Brussels and then to Liège, where he remained until his death. He was also a collector and owned drawings by Rubens, van Dyck and Watteau, and paintings by his French contemporaries (e.g. Chardin, Fragonard and Robert) and by such earlier artists as Rembrandt, Ruisdael and Velázquez, whose techniques, colours and compositions he studied. Many of these works were donated to the Nationalmuseum in Stockholm by August Hjalmar Wicander (1860–1927).

UNPUBLISHED SOURCES

Uppsala, U. Lib., S. L. Gahm-Persson col., XIV (x219) [copy of autobiography of 1783]

WRITINGS

K. Asplund, ed.: *P. A. Hall: Sa correspondance de famille*, Nationalmusei Skriftserie, ii (Stockholm, 1955)

BIBLIOGRAPHY

SVKL
Fem store Gustavianer [Five great Gustavians] (exh. cat., ed. S. Strömbom; Stockholm, Nmus., 1943)
J. Z. Lofgren: *The Miniatures of Peter Adolf Hall* (diss., Eugene, OR, U. Oregon, 1976)

A.-G. WAHLBERG

Hall church [Ger. *Hallenkirche*]. Term introduced in Wilhelm Lübke's *Die mittelalterliche Kunst in Westfalen* (1853) to define a church in which the aisles are the same, or almost the same, height as the nave, so that the nave is lit indirectly by the aisle windows. The hall church differs from the basilica, the distinguishing characteristic of which is the fact that the nave is higher than the aisles and is lit by a clerestory. A variation of the hall church is the *Staffelkirche* or *Stufenhalle* (Ger.: 'staggered hall'), in which the main vessel is higher than the aisles but there is no clerestory.

In all European countries, from the early Middle Ages (e.g. Bartholomäuskapelle, Paderborn; 1017) to the 20th century (e.g. Erlöserkirche, Cologne-Rath; 1954), the hall church has, with the basilica and the centrally planned church, been one of the basic church types as defined by art historians. The hall church was, however, most widespread in German-speaking countries. French art historians saw the hall church as a modified basilica, expressed by the term *nef sans fenêtres* (Lefèvre-Pontalis, 1922), and most hall churches in south-west France are simplified basilicas (e.g. Saint-Savin-sur-Gartempe, *c.* 1080; Notre-Dame-la-Grande, Poitiers, *c.* 1100). German scholars interpreted the hall church as an indigenous stylistic development, and they established a system of classification whereby the early hall churches, with their prototype in the Elisabethkirche, Marburg (begun 1235), were related to basilicas, with close-set piers and broad arches visibly separating the nave from the aisles, while the later halls ('reine' Halle), such as the nave of Minden Cathedral (begun *c.* 1260), with widely spaced piers, nave and aisles of equal width and identical transverse and arcade arches, were seen to have a unified space no longer related to basilicas. This classification developed with the creation of art-historical terminology in the 19th century. It ignored early hall churches, such as the Liebfrauenkirche at Bremen (begun *c.* 1230), which already had the characteristics of the 'reine' Halle, and such later buildings as St Georg, Dinkelsbühl (1448–99), the nave and aisles of which are closer to the basilican arrangement. Clear distinctions cannot be made, either in the wall structure, which is frequently similar, or in the vaulting. In many hall churches the articulation of the vaulting seems to separate the nave from the aisles, and in some basilicas the vaulting serves to connect the nave and aisles, as in the hall-like double aisles of the cathedrals of Amiens (begun 1220), Cologne (begun 1248) and above all Bourges (begun *c.* 1195). The hall church did not develop in opposition to the basilica, but out of it and with it.

In contrast to the basilica the hall church had greater spatial clarity. Despite the basilican ground-plan, there is a sense of breadth, because the space is defined only by the piers, arcades, transverse arches and vaulting, while in a basilica these are to some extent subordinated to the upper nave walls. Furthermore, the free-standing piers and their arches give an impression of great height, which has encouraged the notion that hall churches in general evolved by raising the height of the aisles. This theory is incorrect because even the tallest hall churches (e.g. Elisabethkirche, Marburg) are not much taller than the side aisles of Cologne Cathedral. The omission of the clerestory is more significant. Moreover, a hall church was cheaper and quicker to build than a basilica because, not needing flying buttresses, the nave could be more simply supported. Finally, because it obviates the need for any architectural articulation of the nave elevation, the hall church provides simpler solutions to formal problems.

Lübke's theory that the hall church was the architectural expression of a bourgeois society, while the basilica was a manifestation of the feudal aristocracy, affected subsequent research into hall churches (Gerstenberg (1913),

Rosemann (1924), Wilhelm-Kästner (1955) and Schade (1963)), but as the hall type was used for cathedrals, monastic, mendicant and collegiate churches all over Europe, while urban parish churches and minsters were often basilicas, this idea is invalid.

It has been thought that the German hall church originated in Westphalia. The character of Westphalian architecture was to a large extent determined by Paderborn Cathedral, built from *c.* 1230 onwards and modelled on Poitiers Cathedral. Even in Westphalia, however, the close relationship of the hall church to the basilica is evident from the fairly extensive group of *Stufenhallen* or hall churches based on the *gebundenes* system whereby two smaller aisle bays flank each square nave bay; examples are the Marienkirche, Lippstadt, and the collegiate church at Bassum (both first half of the 13th century). Similar hall churches are, however, found in north Italy in the second half of the 12th century (e.g. S Lorenzo, Trent; S Marco, Vercelli). Some hall churches in Westphalian towns were models for hall churches in Mecklenburg and Gotland, such as the parish church at Grevesmühlen and the Nikolaikirche, Rostock (both third quarter of the 13th century), and the two-aisled hall churches at Rone (*c.* 1300) and Sanda (*c.* 1300) in Gotland, the last two based on the Nikolaikapelle in Soest. There is also a group of hall churches in north Bavaria (e.g. Karthaus-Prüll, Walderbach) dating from the second half of the 12th century. These hall churches are therefore earlier than the Westphalian examples, and some of them are probably derived from two-storey castle chapels, such as that at Donaustauf (*c.* 1060).

The first Gothic hall church in Germany was the Elisabethkirche at Marburg (for illustration *see* MARBURG), which became the model for a series of dynastic churches (e.g. the parish church of Frankenberg, St Stephen's, Mainz, and the collegiate church in Wetzlar). Earlier scholarship regarded the Marburg hall church as a translation into Gothic forms of Paderborn Cathedral; but it has since been related to the Liebfrauenkirche at Trier, the nave walls of which are supported by tall, slender columnar piers like those planned for the nave at Marburg. The earliest hall ambulatory choir in Germany was built at Verden Cathedral (1274–1323) in the second half of the 13th century, as was the hall nave of Minden Cathedral (begun 1260). The influence of Minden Cathedral is recognizable in parish and collegiate churches such as those of Lemgo (Marienkirche, begun *c.* 1285) and Herford (Marienkirche, completed 1325), while the influence of the choir of Verden Cathedral can be found in the hall churches at Lüneburg, Lübeck, Stendal and Tangermünde. At this time the basilican nave of the Marienkirche, Lübeck, was converted into a hall church on the model of the churches in Brunswick. It was destroyed when the church was rebuilt in basilican form after 1274, but it was the model for the Jakobikirche, Lübeck, and the Marienkirche, Neubrandenburg (both begun *c.* 1270); the influence of the latter is apparent in many Brandenburg and Mecklenburg churches (e.g. at Friedland and Pasewalk).

In central Germany the tall columnar naves of the mendicant churches at Erfurt and Brunswick became a characteristic feature of many town parish churches, such as at Göttingen (Johanniskirche, first quarter of the 14th century; Jakobikirche, 1361–83; see fig. 1), while in the south the Stephansdom in Vienna and the Heiligenkreuzmünster, Schwäbisch-Gmünd (both begun *c.* 1300), considerably affected the character of hall churches. The hall choir ambulatory became particularly significant, and its plan and elevation were developed in ways that were not possible with basilican choirs, as at the Franciscan church, Salzburg (from 1408). Lastly there is the group of late 15th- and early 16th-century hall churches in Saxony: of these the Annenkirche, Annaberg (first quarter of the 16th century; for illustration *see* ANNABERG), is particularly notable for its complicated vaulting.

Some hall churches cannot be regarded as modifications of the basilican form. They include the palace and cathedral chapels that are traceable to the Liebfrauenkirche at Goslar (1034–8; destr.), built by the Salian emperors Conrad II (*reg* 1024–39) and Henry III (*reg* 1039–56). This was a two-storey building on a centralized plan with its vaults supported by four piers on each storey. Of the buildings derived from it the chapels of St Emmeram (*c.* 1080) at Speyer Cathedral and St Godehard (consecrated 1137) at Mainz Cathedral have survived, as well as a number of castle chapels, such as those at Nuremberg and Eger (now Cheb, Czech Republic). The hall churches of similar plan at Bremen, Berne, Osnabrück and especially the Frauenkirche at Nuremberg (*c.* 1350) are also presumably derived from these imperial and episcopal chapels. The Nuremberg Frauenkirche is probably an imitation of the late 12th-century imperial chapel at Nuremberg Castle.

1. Hall church, Jakobikirche, Göttingen, nave facing east, 1361–83; rebuilt 1555

2. Hall church, St Jacques (formerly St Rémy), Lunéville, by Germain Boffrand and Emanuel Héré, nave facing east, 1730–47

There is also a group of hall churches derived from assembly rooms, such as refectories, dormitories and chapter houses. These aisled rooms have arch and vault mouldings of the same profile, so that the spaces seem to be conceived not as an agglomeration of aisles or bays but as an integral space subdivided into aisles or bays. One of the earliest hall churches of this kind is St Serge at Angers (c. 1220), which followed the model of a great hospital hall in the same city, a three-aisled columnar hall built c. 1180. Also probably deriving from secular rooms are such buildings as the retrochoir of Salisbury Cathedral and the choir of the Temple Church, London (both c. 1220); the two-aisled Dominican church at Toulouse (begun after 1229); a group of Spanish hall churches (Melgar de Fernamental, second half of the 16th century; Castrogeriz, c. 1500); and the churches known as *Dreistützenkirchen* (churches with three columns), for example the Spital-kirche, Braunau, consecrated in 1430, and *Einstützen-kirchen* (churches with one column), for example St John the Baptist (c. 1365), Neuhaus (now Jindřichův Hradec, Czech Republic).

The hall church continued to be an important type after the Middle Ages, the choice being determined by the interests of the patron. Thus the town churches of Wolfenbüttel (1608 onwards) and Bückeburg (1611 onwards; for illustration see BÜCKEBURG), which are among the most important Protestant churches in Germany, are aristocratic foundations. Designed as hall churches, they are clearly related to the medieval hall churches of Brunswick and Stadthagen. Other later hall churches are remodellings of medieval ones, for example the Heiliggeistkirche, Munich (c. 1722). The Jesuit adoption of the form was in keeping with the Order's Counter-Reformation task of reviving old church traditions (e.g. the Jesuit church at Coesfeld, begun 1673).

In the early 19th century several churches in parks were built in the form of hall churches, their piers modelled on the tree trunks that were considered by MARC-ANTOINE LAUGIER to be the 'primitive hut', the origins of architecture. Examples are Schinkel's design for the mausoleum of Queen Louise (1810) in Charlottenburg Park, Berlin, and the Helenakirche, the Catholic church built from 1803 to 1809 in the park of the Schloss Ludwigslust, Schwerin, Germany. In the second half of the 19th century, the influence of nationalistic ideology made the medieval hall church, especially the Elisabethkirche, Marburg, the model for many historicist churches, such as the Protestant garrison church at Strasbourg (begun 1892).

There were hall churches in other European countries besides Germany, even in Russia (e.g. the cathedral of SS Peter and Paul, St Petersburg, begun 1733). However, more detailed research is needed to determine the extent to which many hall churches in France, for example St Jacques, Lunéville (begun 1730; see fig. 2), should be regarded as simplified versions of the chapel at Versailles. A hall church even stands at the beginning of modern church architecture: Notre-Dame-du-Raincy (1922–3), near Paris, the masterpiece of Auguste Perret and Gustave Perret (*see* PERRET, fig. 1).

BIBLIOGRAPHY
W. Lübke: *Die mittelalterliche Kunst in Westfalen* (Leipzig, 1853)
K. Gerstenberg: *Deutsche Sondergotik* (Munich, 1913)
E. Lefèvre-Pontalis: 'Les Nefs sans fenêtres dans les églises romanes et gothiques', *Bull. Mnmtl*, lxxxi (1922), pp. 257–309
R. Hamann and K. Wilhelm-Kästner: *Die Elisabethkirche zu Marburg und ihre künstlerische Nachfolge*, i (Marburg, 1924)
H. Rosemann: *Die Hallenkirchen auf germanischem Boden* (diss., Munich, Ludwig-Maximilian-U., 1924)
R. Krautheimer: 'Lombardische Hallenkirchen', *Jb. Kstwiss.*, xii (1928), pp. 176–81
J. Roosval: *Westfälisch-gotländische Beziehungen in der Architektur* (Lübeck, 1928)
L. Stoltze: *Die romanischen Hallenkirchen in Altbayern* (Leipzig, 1929)
L. Zinsel: *Die Hallenkirchen der hessischen Schule* (Darmstadt, 1932)
E. Fink: *Die gotischen Hallenkirchen Westfalens* (Münster, 1934)
W. Rave: 'Die Stufenhalle', *Westfäl. Z.* (1934)
S. Thurm: *Gotische Backsteinhallenkirchen mit dreiapsidialem Chorschluss* (Berlin, 1935)
W. Krönig: 'Hallenkirchen in Mittelitalien, *Kstgesch. Jb. Bib. Hertz.*, ii (1938), pp. 1–142
F. Mühlen: *Die westfälischen Hallenkirchen der romanisch-frühgotischen Übergangszeit* (diss., Münster, Westfäl. Wilhelms-U., 1941)
O. Franke: 'St Nikolai in Rostock, die erste chorlose Hallenkirche in Mecklenburg', *Marburg. Jb. Kstwiss.*, xiv (1949)
H. Peters: *Das Aufkommen der Hallenkirchen in Westfalen* (diss., Tübingen, Eberhard-Karls-U., 1952)
G. Weise: *Die spanischen Hallenkirchen der Spätgotik und Renaissance* (Tübingen, 1953)
K. Wilhelm-Kästner: 'Der Raum Westfalen in der Baukunst des Mittelalters', *Der Raum Westfalen*, ed. H. Aubin and F. Petri, II/i (Münster, 1955), pp. 369–460
H. Thümmler: 'Westfälische und italienische Hallenkirchen', *Festschrift Martin Wackernagel* (Cologne, 1958)
E. Mundt: *Die westfälischen Hallenkirchen der Spätgotik (1400–1550)* (Lübeck, 1959)
G. Schade: *Der Hallenumgangschor als bestimmende Raumform der bürgerlichen Pfarrkirchenarchitektur in den brandenburgischen Städten von 1350 bis zum Ende des 15. Jahrhunderts* (diss., Halle, U. Martin-Luther, 1963)
W. Goetz: *Zentralbau und Zentralbautendenz in der gotischen Architektur* (Berlin, 1968)
C. B. Heller: *Gotische Hallenkirchen in Piemont und der Lombardei* (diss., U. Frankfurt am Main, 1968)

N. Zaske: *Gotische Backsteinkirchen Norddeutschlands zwischen Elbe und Oder* (Leipzig, 1968)

H. J. Kunst: 'Die Entstehung des Hallenumgangschores: Der Domchor zu Verden an der Aller und seine Stellung in der gotischen Architektur', *Marburg. Jb. Kstwiss.*, xviii (1969), pp. 1–104

J. Michler: 'Die Langhaushalle der Marburger Elisabethkirche', *Z. Kstgesch.*, xxxii (1969), pp. 104–32

H. J. Kunst: 'Zur Ideologie der deutschen Hallenkirche als Einheitsraum', *Architectura: Z. Gesch. Archit.*, i (1971), pp. 38–53

H. Magirius: 'Die gotischen Hallenkirchen', *Die Stadtkirchen in Sachsen*, ed. F. Löffler (Berlin, 3/1977), pp. 32–42

H. Hipp: *Studien zur Nachgotik des 16. und 17. Jh. in Deutschland, Böhmen, Österreich und der Schweiz* (diss., Tübingen, Eberhard-Karls-U., 1979)

E. Lehmann: 'Zum Problem der zweischiffigen Kirchen des 13./14. Jh. im Ostseegebiet', *Wiss. Z. Ernst-Moritz-Arndt-U. Greifswald*, ii-iii (1980), pp. 31–5

K. Röckener: *Die münsterländischen Hallenkirchen gebundener Ordnung* (Münster, 1980)

N. Nussbaum: *Spätgotische Dreistützenbauten in Bayern und Österreich* (Cologne, 1982)

H. J. Böker: 'Die spätromanische "Wandpfeilerhalle": Entstehung und Rezeption einer Sonderform des Kleinkirchenbaus im Umkreis des Wittgensteiner Landes', *Westfalen: Hft. Gesch., Kst & Vlksknd.*, lxii (1984), pp. 54–76

H. E. Kubach: 'Der Raum Westfalen in der Baukunst des Mittelalters', *Der Raum Westfalen*, ed H. Aubin and F. Petri, vi (Münster, 1985), pp. 1–24

S. Schünke: *Entwicklungen in den Chorformen englischer Kirchen vom 11. bis ins 13. Jahrhundert* (diss., U. Cologne, 1987)

R. Weidl: *Die ersten Hallenkirchen in Bayern* (Munich, 1987)

R. Nenno: *Die spätgotischen Hallenkirchen in der Südchampagne* (St Ingbert, 1988)

W. Schenkluhn: 'Die Erfindung der Hallenkirche in der Kunstgeschichte', *Marburg. Jb. Kstwiss.*, xxii (1989), pp. 193–202

N. Damrich: *Einstützenkirchen der Spätgotik in Oberösterreich* (Munich, 1990)

U. Bölts: *Die Baugeschichte der Kirche Unser Lieben Frauen zu Bremen* (Hamburg, 1992)

E. Olschewski: *Die Godehard-Kapelle am Mainzer Dom* (Marburg, 1993)

D. Seiler: *Saint-Hilaire in Melle und die romanischen Hallenkirchen des Poitou* (Munich, 1993)

HANS-JOACHIM KUNST

Hallé. French family of artists. (1) Daniel Hallé and his son (2) Claude-Guy Hallé were active in Paris in the 17th century and the early 18th, chiefly as painters of religious scenes, and enjoyed high contemporary reputations. Claude-Guy's son (3) Noël Hallé was one of the major French painters of the 18th century and received many commissions from the Crown, from the Church and from the city of Paris. His sister Marie-Anne Hallé (*b* 15 Nov 1704) married the painter Jean Restout (ii), a nephew of Jean Jouvenet, in 1729. The family was thus part of a network of related artists who dominated the areas of history and religious painting in the early and middle decades of the 18th century.

BIBLIOGRAPHY

Bellier de La Chavignerie–Auvray; Jal; Thieme–Becker

O. Estournel: 'La Famille des Hallé', *Réun. Soc. B.-A. Dépt.* (1905), pp. 71–236

N. Willk-Brocard: *Une Dynastie: Les Hallé Daniel (1614–1675), Claude-Guy (1652–1736), Noël (1711–1781)* (Paris, 1993)

(1) Daniel Hallé (*bapt* Rouen, 27 Aug 1614; *d* Paris, 14 July 1675). Painter. He was the son of a draper and in 1631 became apprenticed for five years to his uncle Raullin Bunel (or Brunel), a painter of religious pictures in Rouen. In 1636 he became a master in the Rouen guild. He subsequently left for Paris and in 1646 was living in the Rue de Buci, near the abbey of St Germain. Here he painted a *Holy Family* (1648; untraced). In 1650 he married Catherine Coquelet; they had 14 children.

Daniel Hallé was best known for his religious paintings: his *Annunciation* (1659; Paris, Notre-Dame de Bercy) shows him as an accomplished artist influenced by Charles Le Brun, Eustache Le Sueur and Jacques Stella. The more individual aspects of his style are to be found in his inclusion of picturesque and sometimes naive details taken from life, such as the strikingly lifelike expressions of his angels or the poses, clearly sketched from nature, of the animals in his landscapes. His religious paintings often have a Mannerist sumptuousness of costume and accessory, while his colouring allies the clear tones of lapis lazuli blue and vermilion with the subtle tints of orange-yellow, mauve-pink and blue-white.

In 1660, together with Charles Poerson, Daniel Hallé executed, from a design by Le Brun, a temporary triumphal arch in the Place Dauphine, for the entry of Louis XIV and Maria-Theresa into Paris. In 1662 the Goldsmiths' Corporation commissioned him to paint as the May of Notre-Dame de Paris the *Martyrdom of St John at the Porta Latina* (Clermont-Ferrand, Mus. Bargoin), the work that established his reputation. In 1663 he executed the *Apparition of the Virgin and Child to St Francis and St Anthony* (Quebec, St Henri). He sent numerous paintings to foundations in and around Rouen, including the *Vision of St Benedict* (1660s; Caudebec, nr Rouen, abbey of St Wandrille) and a *Miracle of the Loaves* (1664; Rouen, St Ouen). Later works include *St Roch's Wounds Dressed by the Angels* (1669; Versailles, St Symphorien), a *Martyrdom of St Symphorian* (1671; Saint Flour Cathedral) and a delicate *Entombment* (*c*. 1670; Tournus, Mus. Greuze). Further works, now lost, are recorded in engravings by François Lescowé (Lescouvé; *d* 1666), F. Roger (*d* 1634), Gérard Edelinck, Pierre Landry (?1630–1701), Louis Cossin (Coquin; 1627–1704) and Jean Lenfant (examples in Paris, Bib. N., Cab. Est.). The expressions and poses of Hallé's figures are sometimes awkward and conventional, but his works nevertheless have a freshness and spontaneity that, combined with his blend of classicism and Mannerism, makes his style both engaging and original.

BIBLIOGRAPHY

N. Willk-Brocard: 'Daniel Hallé', *La Peinture d'inspiration religieuse à Rouen au temps de Pierre Corneille, 1606–1684* (exh. cat., ed. F. Bergot, P. Rosenberg and D. Lavalle; Rouen, St Ouen, 1984), pp. 101–11

(2) Claude-Guy Hallé (*b* Paris, 17 Jan 1652; *d* Paris, 5 Nov 1736). Painter and draughtsman, son of (1) Daniel Hallé. In 1675 he won the Premier Prix at the Académie Royale, Paris, for his painting the *Sin of Adam* (untraced). In 1682 he was received (*reçu*) as a member of the Académie, presenting the *Re-establishment of the Catholic Religion in Strasbourg* (untraced). He had a very successful career within the Académie, rising steadily through the hierarchy to become joint rector and director in 1733, together with Nicolas de Largillierre, Guillaume Coustou (i) and Hyacinthe Rigaud. He also exhibited at the Salons of 1699 and 1704, showing *Moses on the Waters* (France, priv. col., see Estournel, pl. iv) and *Eliezer and Rebecca* (untraced), which was engraved by Louis Desplaces (1682–1739), at the latter. His composition was considered among the finest of his generation by Antoine Dézallier d'Argenville, and his drawing, mannered in his youth, later acquired precision and vigour. His elongated figures have powerful musculature, and his draperies, Baroque at first, gradually became more sober, without losing their dynamism. His colouring is cold but harmonious, tending to contrasts of blue and ochre and of pink, green and mauve.

Among Claude-Guy Hallé's secular works are *Fishing* and *Dog Jumping*, for the Ménagerie at the Château of Versailles (1702; Bonn, Fr. Embassy), and the tapestry cartoon *Surrender of the Doge of Genoa* for the Gobelins (1715; Versailles, Château). He is, however, best known for his religious paintings, among them the May of 1688, *Christ Driving the Moneylenders from the Temple* (Arras, Mus. B.-A.), and an *Annunciation* of 1717 (Paris, Louvre), both painted for Notre-Dame de Paris. His major works include *Christ Giving the Keys to St Peter* (1690; Saint-Riquier Abbey, Somme), a *Presentation in the Temple* (1713; untraced; oil sketch, Rouen, Mus. B.-A.), *St Paul at Lystra* (1717; untraced; oil sketch, Paris, Carnavalet), for St Germain-des-Prés, Paris, and a *Miracle of the Loaves* (1723; Yssingeaux, St Pierre), as well as works now in museums at Orléans and Abbeville. He also painted portraits, including those of the sculptor *Simon Hurtrelle* (Versailles, Château) and *Dom Jean Mabillon* (untraced; engraved by Alexis Loir II). He was a remarkable draughtsman, whose subtle use of chiaroscuro can be seen in such works as *St Martin Dividing his Cloak with a Beggar* (pen and grey ink with grey wash, heightened with white; Stockholm, Nmus.), and was much sought after as an illustrator, especially by the Benedictines of Paris. He executed a large number of precise vignettes, in pen and ink with wash heightened with white on blue paper and enclosed by an outline (e.g. *Constantine Glimpsing a Cross in the Sky*, Rennes, Mus. B.-A. & Archéol.). Among books illustrated in this fashion were the works of St Jerome, published by L. Roulland (5 vols; Paris, 1693) with engravings by Simon Thomassin after Hallé, those of St Gregory, published by C. Rigaud (4 vols; Paris, 1705) with engravings by F.

Ertinger after Hallé, and Dom Michel Félibien's *Histoire de l'abbaye royale de Saint-Denys en France* published by F. Léotard (Paris, 1706) with engravings by P. Simoneau after Hallé. Other engravers who reproduced drawings by Claude-Guy Hallé include Gérard Edelinck, Jacques Jollain (1649–after 1710), Etienne Gantrel (1640–1710), Cornelis Vermeulen (1644–1708) and Pierre Giffard (?1631–1723).

BIBLIOGRAPHY
A.-J. Dézallier d'Argenville: *Abrégé de la vie des plus fameux peintres* (1745–52, 2/1762), iv, pp. 252–7
O. Estournet: 'La Famille des Hallé', *Réun. Soc. B.-A. Dépt.* (1905)
N. Willk-Brocard: 'Some Unpublished Drawings by Claude-Guy Hallé', *Master Drgs*, xxiii–xxiv (1985–6), pp. 363–6

(3) Noël Hallé (*b* Paris, 2 Sept 1711; *d* Paris, 5 June 1781). Painter, draughtsman and printmaker, son of (2) Claude-Guy Hallé. After studying architecture he became the pupil of his father and of his brother-in-law Jean Restout (ii). In 1736 he won the Prix de Rome, and he spent the period from 1737 to 1744 at the Académie de France in Rome. There he made a copy (untraced) of Raphael's *Heliodorus Driven from the Temple* (Rome, Vatican, Stanza d'Eliodoro), which he intended for a tapestry cartoon for the Gobelins, as well as executing drawings and engravings after antique monuments and works of art. On his return to Paris, he was approved by the Académie Royale in 1746 and received (*reçu*) as a full member in 1748 on presentation of the *Dispute of Minerva and Neptune over Choosing a Name for the City of Athens* (Paris, Louvre). He became a professor at the Académie in 1755 and was named Surinspecteur de la Manufacture des Tapisseries de la Couronne at the Gobelins in 1770. In 1775 he was entrusted with the reorganization of the Académie de France in Rome, neglected by its aging director Charles-Joseph Natoire; he was rewarded for his efforts by ennoblement and the Order of St Michel. He was treasurer of the Académie Royale from 1776 to 1781 and became rector in the year of his death.

Noël Hallé was an extremely talented artist who worked in every genre with equal facility. He was, however, primarily a history painter and received numerous royal commissions, including those for *Jupiter and Callisto* (1754; Versailles, Château; see fig. 1), an overdoor for the Trianon, Versailles; the *Justice of Trajan* (1765; Marseille, Mus. B.-A.) for the Château of Choisy, Val-de-Marne; the *Grape Harvest* (1776; Versailles, Petit Trianon) for the Petit Trianon dining-room, and the *Liberality of Cimon the Athenian* (1777; Paris, Louvre). He executed many large tapestry cartoons for the Gobelins, two of which may be considered among the masterpieces of 18th-century French painting: *Hippomenes and Atalanta* (1765; Paris, Louvre; see fig. 2) and *Achilles Recognized at the Court of Deidameia* (1769; Limoges, Mus. Mun.). Among his other patrons were King Stanislas II Augustus of Poland, who commissioned *Scilurus, King of the Scythians, Giving his Dying Advice to his Children* (1767; Warsaw, N. Mus.), and the city of Paris, which commissioned an *Allegory of Peace* (1767; Versailles, Château).

Hallé painted numerous religious pictures, including a *Flight into Egypt* (1759; Orléans, Mus. B.-A.), *St Vincent de Paul Preaching* (1761; Versailles, Cathedral of St Louis), *St Peter Delivered from Prison* (1764; Saint-Chamond, Loire, St Pierre), an *Adoration of the Shepherds* (1771; untraced:

1. Noël Hallé: *Jupiter and Callisto*, oil on canvas, 900×990 mm, 1754 (Musée National du Château de Versailles et de Trianon)

2. Noël Hallé: *Hippomenes and Atalanta*, oil on canvas, 3.20×7.13 m, 1765 (Paris, Musée du Louvre)

engraved by the artist), *St Louis Carrying the Crown of Thorns* (1773; Paris, Ecole Mil.) and *Christ in the Garden of Olives* (1777; Pontoise, Val d'Oise, Notre-Dame). He produced decorative works for private residences, such as the overdoors *Midday*, *Evening* and *Night* (France, priv. col.); large easel paintings, including the pendants of the *Dangers of Love* and the *Dangers of Wine* (both Cholet, Mus. A.), which were exhibited at the Salon of 1759; and some exquisite portraits, including that of his wife and son, *Geneviève Lorry and Jean-Noël Hallé* (1758; France, priv. col., see Estournet, pl. xiii). He also produced some lively, realistic and acutely observed genre paintings, such as the pair *Education of the Rich* and *Education of the Poor* (1765; France, priv. col., see 1984–5 exh. cat., nos 76–7). He tried his hand at wax painting and illustrated numerous books (e.g. J.-A. Guer: *Moeurs et usages des Turcs* (2 vols; Paris, 1746–7) and the *Works* of Remond de Saint-Mard (5 vols; Amsterdam, 1749–50)). His drawings were engraved by Nicolas-Henri Tardieu, Jean-Augustin Patour (*b* 1746), Claude Duflos, Etienne Fessart (1714–77), Jacques Aliamet, Benoît-Louis Prévost (1747–1804) and Pedro Pascual Moles. He also practised as a printmaker, providing, for example, the etching after his early *Antiochus Falling from his Chariot* (1738; Paris, Bib. N.) and an engraving after his untraced *Adoration of the Shepherds* (1770; Paris, Bib. N.).

The atmosphere of Noël Hallé's painted compositions is ethereal and luminous. Carefully studied architectural features play a major part in them, and they have a distinctive sense of movement, with figures captured in action shown as curved and elongated silhouettes, their hands reddish and gnarled. His scenes were constructed with Rococo ease and are rendered in pastel tints blending with sharp and acid tones. His female faces, sometimes plump, characteristically have turned-up noses, hair worn up and a scarf tied high on the head. His touch, often thick in his oil sketches, appears smooth, fluid and free in the completed works. He was a prolific draughtsman, working in red and black chalk heightened with white; with pen and ink and wash; with wash alone (worked with

the point of the brush); and with watercolour. He also had a liking for pastel, particularly for portrait heads. Among his finest drawings is that made after the *Scilurus*, a highly finished sheet in black and red chalk, heightened with white (France, priv. col., see 1984–5 exh. cat., no. 78). Strongly influenced by Jean-François de Troy and by Jean Restout (ii) in his youth, he became increasingly free in his style towards middle age. He did not develop greatly, however, and remained uninfluenced by the beginnings of Neo-classicism in the 1760s and 1770s.

BIBLIOGRAPHY

Eloge historique de feu Mr Noël Hallé . . . par M. son fils (Paris, [1781])

Catalogue des tableaux, dessins, estampes . . . provenans du Cabinet de feu M. Hallé . . . (Paris, 2 July 1781)

J. Locquin: *La Peinture d'histoire en France de 1747 à 1785* (Paris, 1912, rev. 2/1978)

P. Rosenberg: 'Noël Hallé', *French Painting, 1774–1830: The Age of Revolution* (exh. cat., Paris, Grand Pal.; Detroit, MI, Inst. A.; New York, Met.; 1974–5), pp. 481–3

D. Lomax: 'The Early Career of Noël Hallé', *Apollo*, cxvii (1983), pp. 106–9

N. Willk-Brocard: 'Noël Hallé', *Diderot et l'art de Boucher à David* (exh. cat., Paris, Admin. Monnaies & Médailles, 1984–5), pp. 268–76

NICOLE WILLK-BROCARD

Hallen, Hans (Heyerdahl) (*b* Durban, 31 Aug 1930). South African architect, teacher, writer and urban planner. He was trained at the University of Natal, Durban (1949–53), and gained experience in local offices and at the London County Council; he also travelled widely in Europe and lived and studied in Rome for a period. In 1959 he entered into private practice in Durban. His early houses are distinguished by their white modulated surfaces, interior–exterior relationships and the integration of planting, for example the Hattingh House (1962), Kloof. In his low-rise, high-density residential buildings in Durban he introduced the concept of duplex flats with private and semi-private courts; these included Stellenberg (1962) and Musgrave Mews (1963). He developed an architecture of strong geometric form, exploiting a combination of off-form concrete, red brick, glass and metal, in the residences (1964–6) at the University of Natal and the Shaw House

(1968), Durban; geometry was also a strong feature of his early churches such as St Olav's (1967) and St John's Convent (1967), Durban. In the 1970s Hallen built a series of simple, large-span industrial and decentralized office buildings that reinterpreted traditional verandah design; examples include Hulett's head office (1974–6), La Lucia, and the Small Business Development Corporation building (1983–5), Westville. Later work such as the Mangosutho Technikon (1980–81), Umlazi, the Brenthurst Library (1982–3), Johannesburg, and the BMW headquarters (1984–5), Midrand, synthesized geometry and brick construction and incorporated works of art. His buildings remained strongly related to the characteristics of site, with skilled treatment of level changes. One of the most accomplished and versatile architects of his generation, who used technology to generate new formal solutions, Hallen was also acknowledged as a teacher, writer and urban planner. He was President of the Institute of South African Architects (1974–5) and served on the Council of the Union of International Architects (1975–87). He received numerous design awards including the Gold Medal of the Institute of South African Architects (1980) and he became an honorary fellow of the American Institute of Architects (1981). He moved to Australia in 1987.

WRITINGS

Needs and Resources Survey: Durban (Durban, 1977)

BIBLIOGRAPHY

B. E. Biermann: 'Hans Hallen: Gold Medallist ISAA 1980', *Archit. SA*, 13 (1981), pp. 41–9

W. H. PETERS

Haller, Fritz (*b* Solothurn, 1924). Swiss architect, theorist, designer and teacher. He established an independent practice in Solothurn in 1949. His early work, including schools, service, industrial and residential buildings, was designed on the basis of a free geometrical grid. From the early 1960s he introduced his own version of a construction system of modular blocks. Notable examples are the Sparkasse (1963), Kriegstetter, and the Höhere Technische Lehranstalt, Windisch, which consist of cubic blocks of glass and steel, with careful proportioning and detailing that reflect his study of Mies van der Rohe. The three steel building systems developed by Haller, differentiated as Mini, Midi and Maxi, are employed in several houses in the form of crystalline prisms and in the SBB-Ausbildungszentrum (1979–82) in Murten, which consists of integrated units set in parkland. Haller was also active in the field of research, developing quasi-utopian urban projects and the highly regarded USM Haller system of office and domestic furniture, which reflected his unitary conception of the architect as a planner, designer and engineer. Haller's position as an exponent of a school characterized by a cool, technical perfection, seemingly opposed to nature, made him an influential figure in post-war Swiss modernism. He was the leader of the independent Solothurn school, and his influence can also be traced in the works of the Ticino school, particularly those of Livio Vacchini (*b* 1933). In 1977 he was appointed a professor at the Universität Fridericiana, Karlsruhe.

BIBLIOGRAPHY

Fritz Haller—Bauer und Forscher (exh. cat., Solothurn, Kstmus., 1988; Zurich, Mus. Gestalt.; 1989)

ROMAN HOLLENSTEIN

Haller, Hermann (*b* Berne, 24 Dec 1880; *d* Zurich, 23 Nov 1950). Swiss sculptor. He trained first as a painter, studying in Stuttgart and Munich before making his first trip to Rome in 1901 in the company of his friend Paul Klee. He settled there for six years and in 1905 turned to sculpture. He maintained close links with Germany and had his first solo exhibition at the Galerie Cassirer, Berlin, in 1909. He settled in Paris in the same year and had two studios—one in Paris and another in Zurich which he established in 1914—until World War II. In addition to an increasing number of official commissions (e.g. for the university and the Kunsthaus, Zurich, and the Kunstmuseum Winterthur), Haller also produced portraits and, above all, sculptures of the female figure. His work preserved an impression of spontaneity through its suggestion of an infinite variety of incipient movements. This type of work, typical of Swiss sculpture between the World Wars, had both grace and energy; it earned Haller rapid recognition both in Switzerland and in Germany, where several museums bought versions of his *Standing Girls* and *Soaring Girls*, which were exhibited at the major galleries in Berlin (including Galerie Cassirer, Galerie Gurlitt and Galerie Thannhauser) and Düsseldorf (Galerie Flechteim). His successful career was interrupted, however, by his decision to retire when faced with the rise of Nazism. In 1933 he was awarded an honorary doctorate at the University of Zurich and he received a commission to execute an equestrian monument to *Hans Waldmann*, which was unveiled four years later. With Hermann Hubacher (1885–1976), Haller was seen at the time as one of the great forces of renewal in Swiss sculpture: his harmonious modernity, seemingly unconnected with the times in which he lived, was favoured by various institutions when making official selections for such international exhibitions as the Venice Biennale, where Haller received the Grand Prix for sculpture in 1934.

BIBLIOGRAPHY

D. Wild: 'Hermann Haller', *Neujbl. Kstges. Zürich* (1956) [whole issue]
U. Gertz: *Hermann Haller* (St Gall, 1968) [with a complete bibliog.]
P.-A. Jaccard: 'La Sculpture suisse de l'entre-deux-guerres', *La Sculpture*, Ars Helvetica: Arts et culture visuels en Suisse, vii (Disentis, 1992), pp. 231–6

□

Haller, Jost (*b* ?Strasbourg, *c.* 1410; *d* Saarbrücken, before 1485). German painter. He is recorded in 1438 as a master and in 1444 as a member of the guild of painters and goldsmiths in Strasbourg. In 1447, together with Hans Tieffental (*fl* 1391–1448), he undertook to paint and gild a stone crucifix (untraced) in Metz. Probably directly after this he entered the service of Count Johann III of Nassau-Saarbrücken (*d* 1472) as court painter and moved to Saarbrücken. In 1453 he concluded a contract for an extensive series of murals (destr.) showing scenes from the *Lives of SS Ursula and Barbara* (among others) for a newly built chapel in the church of the Carmelite convent in Metz. No further record of his work is known until his death.

Haller has been credited, however, with several panels from altarpieces that were of considerable significance in the evolution of painting in the Upper Rhine area and that influenced the work of Martin Schongauer (*see* SCHONGAUER, (1)): the *Sermon of John the Baptist* and *St George Fighting the Dragon* of the Bergheim Predella (Colmar, Mus. Unterlinden), undoubtedly produced while Haller was still in Strasbourg; and four separated panels of an altarpiece, which may have been produced towards 1455 for the Commanders of the Teutonic Order in Saarbrücken since their portraits, as donors, are included. The panels show the *Nativity* (Nuremberg, Ger. Nmus.), *Salome Receiving the Head of John the Baptist* (Munich, Alte Pin.), the *Annunciation* and the *Visitation* (both France, priv. col., see Sterling, figs 106, 108). Each pair of panels may have formed the front and back of one wing of an altarpiece. They show well-proportioned figures with expressive faces and poses (particularly the *Nativity* and *Salome Receiving the Head of John the Baptist*), deeply tucked and folded drapery (the *Annunciation*) and precisely observed, naturalistic detail (the *Nativity* and the *Annunciation*). Their attribution to Haller permits a clearer definition of the oeuvres of the MASTER OF THE STAUFFENBERG ALTAR and of the HOUSEBOOK MASTER (*see* MASTERS, ANONYMOUS, AND MONOGRAMMISTS, §I), to whom these pictures have occasionally been attributed.

BIBLIOGRAPHY
C. Sterling: 'Jost Haller: Maler zu Strassburg und zu Saarbrücken in der Mitte des 15. Jahrhunderts', *Wien. Jb. Kstgesch.*, xxxiii (1980), pp. 99–126; also in *Bull. Soc. Schongauer* (1979–82), pp. 53–89

DETLEF ZINKE

Haller, Martin (Emil Ferdinand) (*b* Hamburg, 1 Dec 1835; *d* Hamburg, 25 Oct 1925). German architect. While still at school in 1854 he entered the first architectural competition for a new building to replace the Hamburg Rathaus, which had burnt down in 1842, and his entry was shortlisted. He studied in Berlin and at the Ecole des Beaux-Arts, Paris, obtaining his doctorate in 1859, then worked until 1861 in the office of Charles Garnier where he was involved in plans for the successful design for the new Opéra. In 1861 he returned to Hamburg and set up independently. Before long Haller occupied a leading position among Hamburg architects. He collaborated on projects with all the important Hamburg architects of his day, was president of his professional association for ten years, a representative in the Hamburg Bürgerschaft for 14 years, and finally, in 1897, he succeeded in steering the Hamburg architects Grotjan, Hanssen, Wilhelm Hauers (1836–1905), Emil Meerwein (1844–1927), Hugo Stammann (1831–1909) and Gustav Zinnow (1846–1934) towards producing a collaborative design, which formed the basis for the new Hamburg Rathaus (1886–97). This building occupies a central position in Haller's work, but the total of 562 projects executed by him in his long working life also made him the most important Hamburg architect of the second half of the 19th century. His buildings include detached houses and blocks of flats, the rebuilding of the opera house (1873–4), offices such as the Dovenhof (1885–6), the first large office building in Hamburg, splendid villas and imposing country houses, hospitals, sanitoriums, residential institutions and the

Hamburg Musikhalle (1904–6). The variety and scope of his commissions, nearly all of them in Hamburg, left their stamp on the architectural aspect of the city at the turn of the century and caused his influence to extend far beyond its boundaries. He retired in 1914.

BIBLIOGRAPHY
NDB; Thieme–Becker
Hamburg und seine Bauten (Hamburg, 1890)
Hamburg und seine Bauten, 2 vols (Hamburg, 1914)
H. -J. Brandt: *Das Hamburger Rathaus* (Hamburg, 1957)

MICHAEL EISSENHAUER

Haller von Hallerstein, Karl (*b* Hilpoltstein, nr Nuremberg, 10 June 1774; *d* Ampelakia, Greece, 5 Nov 1817). German archaeologist and architect. He studied architecture at the Karls-Akademie in Karlsruhe and with David Gilly at the Bauakademie in Berlin. In 1808 he visited Italy. For a short while he worked as a building official in Nuremberg, but only a small number of his designs were executed. In 1810 he travelled to Greece, where he spent the rest of his life on archaeological expeditions and excavations. In April 1811 he was one of an English and German group, which included C. R. Cockerell, that discovered and excavated the Temple of Aphaia at Aigina. Haller von Hallerstein was able to persuade Crown Prince Ludwig of Bavaria (later King Ludwig I) to acquire the pediment sculptures for Munich (Munich, Glyp.). In August 1811 the same group excavated at Bassai and unearthed the Temple of Apollo, with its now-famous reliefs (London, BM). During his time in Greece, Haller von Hallerstein collated a collection of sketches and notes of great academic value, now held at the University of Strasbourg. As an architect, he is known mainly for his designs (1813) commissioned by Ludwig I for his commemorative temple, the Walhalla, near Regensburg, and the Glyptothek, the sculpture gallery in Munich. Neither of his designs, sent from Greece, was executed for financial reasons, and at the time they were relatively unnoticed. His Walhalla was reminiscent of Friedrich Gilly's proposed monument to *Frederick II* (1797) but introduced the idea of a hill setting, later adopted by Leo von Klenze, who built the Walhalla between 1830 and 1842.

BIBLIOGRAPHY
Thieme–Becker; Wasmuth
K. Frässle: *Karl Haller von Hallerstein (1774–1817)* (diss., U. Freiburg im Breisgau, 1971)   □

Hallmarks. *See under* MARKS, §4.

Hallstatt. Prehistoric site in Salzkammergut, Austria. The site is at the exit of a narrow valley, 450 m above the lake at Hallstatt, in an area rich in natural salt, which has been mined at least from the Iron Age (*c.* 750–*c.*50 BC), if not earlier; there are also copper deposits near by. Excavation of an extraordinarily rich cemetery at the site was conducted unsystematically and with poor recording between 1824 and 1831, but rather more methodically between 1846 and 1863. Graves continued to be excavated until 1939, and more than 2000 burials have been recovered. The Hallstatt cemetery has given its name to a culture that flourished *c.* 750–*c.* 450 BC, spanning the Late Bronze Age (*c.* 1350–*c.* 750 BC) and Early Iron Age (*c.* 750–*c.* 500 BC) (*see also* PREHISTORIC EUROPE, §§V and VI).

The cemetery covers a time from *c.* 800 BC to the beginning of the La Tène period *c.* 450 BC. Because of the lack of method in their recovery and the frequent absence of recording, about half of the graves could not be used satisfactorily for the purposes of constructing a chronology. Nevertheless, many of the tens of thousands of objects found were used to define the two final phases of the European Bronze Age (*c.* 1220–*c.* 750 BC), termed Hallstatt A and B, and the first two phases of the Iron Age (*c.* 750–*c.* 600 BC), termed Hallstatt C and D. Some 45% of the graves contained cremations, the remaining 55% being inhumations, and, though the sexing of the skeletons and burnt remains was highly unreliable, it appears that most burials were of men, although female and child burials were also present. Only a small percentage of the male graves contained weapons, and those that did were almost all cremations. The 19 'warrior graves' containing swords from the Hallstatt C phase yielded almost half of the fine sheet bronze vessels from the cemetery, implying a close relationship between the available wealth and those men entitled to bear arms: even after 600 BC, when swords were replaced by daggers, three-quarters of the graves at the site contained no weapon of any kind.

Apart from swords and daggers, the cemetery yielded a wide range of iron objects: knives, spits, 'spectacle' brooches, arc and serpentiform fibulae, multi-headed pins and ribbed arm-rings. Bronze pieces included stamped belt-plates, pendants, decorated axes and the high-quality beaten vessels—bowls, buckets, containers and stands—found in the richest graves. Grave 507, for example, contained an iron sword with ivory inlay on the hilt, three bronze buckets, a belt plate decorated with bird-shaped stamps and the bronze figure of a bull, together with a highly decorated vessel on a stand (now all Vienna, Nathist. Mus.). This vessel has a stamped frieze of alternating bird and sun motifs—a common combination on Hallstatt metalwork—while the stand has slender legs decorated with individually modelled ducks. Many parts of this magnificent piece are ornamented with hanging rings of unknown function.

Many of the buckets and bowls from other graves have impressed decoration of different kinds of birds, sun motifs and wheel symbols, interspersed with panels of engraved or repoussé ornament in geometric designs. Animal representations most frequently occur in the form of solid castings, which are either free-standing or attached to the handles of bronze containers or the tops of decorated axes. The overall characteristics of the style are geometry and regularity, and apart from the animal models, few curves are seen. Grave 994, an Early La Tène period burial (*c.* 450–*c.* 350 BC), yielded a knife, two spearheads, a bronze cap, a sieve with a pouring spout and an iron sword with an elaborate bronze scabbard inlaid with coral (now all Vienna, Nathist. Mus.). This scabbard is one of the most interesting pieces in a cemetery noted for high-quality metalwork of all types. The finely engraved decoration features a central scene of four mounted soldiers—one dispatching an enemy with his spear—and three foot-soldiers, flanked by pairs of men in pugilistic attitudes, each pair holding a wheel between them; the scene at the tip, enclosed by a chape with bird-headed terminals, shows two men fighting while a third figure with a tendril growing out of his back looks on. All the men wear striped trousers, which marks them out as Celts, and they also have shoes with turned-up points of the type shown on brooches and worn by the body interred at EBERDINGEN-HOCHDORF. Another example of attention to detail is provided by the treatment of the horses' tails: two are long and flowing, the third quite clearly docked short, and the fourth long and decorated, perhaps plaited and bound with ribbon.

BIBLIOGRAPHY

G. Kromer: *Das Gräberfeld von Hallstatt* (Florence, 1959)

SARA CHAMPION

Hallström, Eric (*b* Stockholm, 22 Nov 1893; *d* Södertälje, 17 June 1946). Swedish painter. He studied at the private art school in Stockholm run by Carl Wilhelmson and then travelled to Germany, Austria, England, Italy and France. His early work was influenced by Swedish folk art and was executed in a naive style, as in *New Year's Eve on Skansen* (1918; Stockholm, Mod. Mus.). In 1925 Hallström travelled to Madeira, and in 1927 he was awarded a travel scholarship, which allowed him to visit Italy and France again. In the 1920s his work lost its earlier naivety and became more firmly modelled, as in *View from the South, Stockholm* (watercolour, 1925; Stockholm, Mod. Mus.). While continuing to concentrate on landscapes and town-scapes in the 1930s, his pictures became more expressive and were executed in looser brushstrokes, as in *Hagalund* (1932; Stockholm, Mod. Mus.). His later works were yet more loosely brushed and structured, as in *Trout Stream* (*c.* 1944–5; Stockholm, Mod. Mus.).

BIBLIOGRAPHY

Vollmer

Katalogen: Över Moderna Museets samlingar av Svensk och internationell 1900-talskonst [Cat. of the Moderna Museum's col. of Swed. and int. 20th-century art] (Stockholm, 1976), pp. 57–8

☐

Hallwyl, Count and Countess von. Swedish industrialists, patrons and collectors. Walther, Count von Hallwyl (*b* Berne, 26 Jan 1839; *d* Stockholm, 27 Feb 1921), was from an old Romansch family in Switzerland, named after Hallwil Castle in the Swiss canton of Aargau. He became a Swedish citizen in 1874. His wife, Wilhelmina, Countess von Hallwyl [née Kempe] (*b* Stockholm, 1 Oct 1844; *d* Stockholm, 25 July 1930), was a keen collector whose interests were made possible by the wealth of her father, Wilhelm Kempe, the founder of the wood export firm Ljusne-Woxna Ltd based in northern Sweden. After their marriage in 1865, the couple settled in Sweden, where Walther took over the export business on the death of his father-in-law in 1883. Between 1893 and 1898 they had a private palace built in Stockholm by the architect Isak Gustaf Clason, where the Countess's collection of Dutch and Flemish 17th-century paintings, silver, South-east Asian and European porcelain, ceramics, weapons, furniture and textiles were exhibited. With the intention of it becoming a public museum, in 1920 they donated the house and collection to the Swedish State, together with a sum of money for its maintenance, and it opened as a museum in 1938. During her last years the Countess initiated the cataloguing of the collections, which was completed in 1956. She also made donations to various cultural institutions in Sweden and restored Hallwil Castle, which she and her husband owned.

BIBLIOGRAPHY

Hallwylska Samlingen [The Hallwyl collections], 78 vols (Stockholm, 1926–56)

E. H. Cassel-Pihl: *Hallwylska Museet: Ett privatpalats från sekelskiftet* [The Hallwyl museum: a private palace from the turn of the century] (Stockholm, 1979) [with Eng. summary]

EVA HELENA CASSEL-PIHL

Halmhuber, Gustav (*b* Stuttgart, 23 March 1862; *d* Stuttgart, 28 Aug 1936). German architect and painter. He studied painting and architecture in Stuttgart at the Kunstschule and Technische Hochschule. He went to Berlin in 1886 and for the next three years worked with Paul Wallot. He assisted Wallot on the Reichstag building in Berlin and the experience was formative for his later career. His many competition designs for monuments to Emperor William and to Bismarck showed clearly his skills as a designer of monumental architecture and his mastery of decorative ornament. His first independent work was the Säulenhalle of the monument to Emperor William in Berlin (unveiled 1897), and in 1896 he designed the layout of the Siegesallee, a monument to German glory in Berlin. In 1884 he won the competition for a water tower in the centre of Mannheim, still extant, with a much praised monumental design. This competition had caused certain controversy and became the focus of debates around the values of eclectic historicism. From 1897 to 1906 Halmhuber taught at the Technische Hochschule in Stuttgart. In 1906 he became the director of the Kunstgewerbeschule in Cologne, moving to the Technische Hochschule in Hannover in 1909. There he completed the town hall (designed and begun by Hermann Eggert) and designed for the already half-completed Renaissance building some Art Nouveau interiors painted by such well-known German artists as Fritz Erler and Ferdinand Hodler. He published two collections of architectural and arts and crafts studies and designs. As a painter he concentrated mainly on figurative work and portraits but also produced landscapes and interiors.

WRITINGS

Architektonische Gedanken (Berlin, 1897)
Freie Studien (Leipzig, 1903)

BIBLIOGRAPHY

Thieme–Becker; Wasmuth

V. Hammerschmidt: *Anspruch und Ausdruck in der Architektur des späten Historismus, 1860–1914* (Frankfurt am Main, 1985)

CLAUDIA BÖLLING

Halmstad group [Swed. Halmstadgruppen]. Swedish group of six painters active from 1929. It disbanded only with the death of the various members. The artists were the brothers Axel Olson (1899–1986) and Erik (Arthur) Olson (1901–86), their cousin (Anders) Waldemar Lorentzon (1899–1984), Sven Jonson (1902–83), (Carl) Stellan (Gabriel) Mörner (1896–1979) and Theodor Esaias Thorén (1901–81). All had connections with Halmstad, a town on the west coast of Sweden. In 1919 Egon Östlund, a mechanical engineer working in Halmstad, established contact with the Olsons and Lorentzon. Through Östlund,

they became familiar with the work of Gösta Adrian-Nilsson, and over the years Östlund supported the Halmstad group. Adrian-Nilsson's paintings were important early mutual influences for the group, as were Cubism and Neo-plasticism. In the early 1930s the group began to paint in a Surrealist style, as in, for example, Erik Olson's the *Day through the Night* (1935; Stockholm, Mod. Mus.); they were influenced by such artists as Salvador Dalí and Yves Tanguy. Gradually the painters developed in different directions, but the group remained active, exhibiting together. They were the most significant exponents of Surrealism in Sweden and took part in various Surrealist exhibitions in Europe in the 1930s. Axel Olson became very involved in local art life, while Erik Olson had close contacts with Danish Surrealists and participated in the resistance to the German occupation of Denmark during World War II. In 1950 he converted to Catholicism and had connections with the *art sacré* movement in France. He also painted many religious works. In 1963 he was awarded the Order of Gregory the Great by Pope John XXIII (*reg* 1958–63). Lorentzon joined the Oxford Movement in 1938 and from that time executed mainly religious decorations. Mörner was very versatile, designing sets for various theatres, mostly in Stockholm and Göteborg. He wrote articles on art and several books, including his autobiography *Spegel mot mitt liv* ('Mirror to my life'; Stockholm, 1969) and *Det varma kvällsljuset* ('The warm evening light'; Stockholm, 1976).

BIBLIOGRAPHY

P. Hultén and others: *Halmstadgruppen 50 år* [50 years of the Halmstad group] (Halmstad, 1979)

Halmstadgruppen 60 år: Halmstad-Berlin-Paris-Halmstad (exh. cat., ed. L. Robbert; Stockholm, Liljevalchs Ksthall, 1989)

JACQUELINE STARE

Halonen, Pekka (*b* Lapinlahti, 23 Sept 1865; *d* Tuusula [Swed. Tusby], 1 Dec 1933). Finnish painter. He was born into an artistic peasant family; his cousin was the sculptor Eemil Halonen (1875–1950). Pekka received his initial training at the Finnish Arts Association's School of Drawing in Helsinki (1886–90). Over the next two years he worked in Paris at the Académie Julian, and his work was first exhibited in 1891. Halonen's themes were the Finnish landscape and people, and his artistic approach was always rooted in Realism. *The Mowers* (1891; priv. col., see Lindström, p. 108) is an important example of his Realist *plein-air* painting, which was tinged with Jean-François Millet's brand of idealization, while *The Shortcut* (1892; Helsinki, Athenaeum A. Mus.) is a sombre study of the landscape of eastern Finland. Halonen spent the years 1893–4 in Paris as a pupil of Paul Gauguin; his interest in Symbolism was short-lived, but Gauguin's decorative Synthetism, as well as Japanese woodcuts, made a lasting impression on his work, in particular on his later portrayals of Finnish landscape.

On his return to Finland in 1894, Halonen joined the National Romantic Movement, which favoured themes from the Finnish national epic, the *Kalevala*. Halonen's most important works derived from this source are *At the Cape were Maidens Standing* (1895) and *On the War Path* (1896; both priv. cols, see Lindström, pp. 86, 107), which refer to the *Kalevala* only in terms of their period-setting and atmosphere. Halonen did experiment with portraying heroes from the epic, but he found difficulty adapting such subject-matter to the Realist nature of his art. Halonen's significance lies primarily in his post-1895 paintings of the Finnish winter. The beauty of winter had begun to fascinate Finnish artists such as Eero Nikolai Järnefelt and Victor Westerholm from the late 1880s, but it was not until the second half of the 1890s that the classic image of Finnish winter was created, with Halonen's winter landscapes of eastern Finland. He combined Synthetist colour surfaces with curved outlines inspired by Art Nouveau to create decorative effects at their most striking in his paintings of spruce trees covered in frost and snow (e.g. *Frost*, 1895; Kokkola, K. H. Renlund Mus.). His style was sensitive and delicate, the mood created sometimes sunny, sometimes sombre when the deep grey gloom of a cloudy winter's day predominated. Halonen always worked on his winter landscapes outdoors, even when the temperature was well below freezing; his health suffered as a result.

In 1898 Halonen moved to Tuusula, in the countryside near Helsinki, where many other artists and writers had settled. In 1901, in the spirit of National Romanticism, he constructed a large log-house to serve as his home and studio on the shore of Lake Tuusula (the building is now a museum). In the years immediately afterwards the tranquil scenery of the Tuusula area in all seasons provided him with his main subject-matter. At the beginning of the 20th century, when Finland's autonomy was threatened, Halonen strove to foster a sense of national pride through symbolic interpretations of the Finnish landscape. In 1899 he had painted the monumental *Wilderness, Karelian Landscape* (Turku, A. Mus.; *see* FINLAND, fig. 6), a stylized depiction of Finnish pine trees stretching tall and unbending to confront the storm rising in the east. The patriotic mood of the painting has much in common with that of Sibelius's tone-poem *Finlandia*, composed in the same year. Halonen's figure compositions were often no less monumental than his landscapes, for example *The Meal* (1899; Helsinki, Didrichsen A. Mus.).

By the early 1900s Halonen was widely acknowledged as among Finland's leading artists. During this period monumental compositions dominated his output. His most important paintings of folk life reflect the influence of Pierre Puvis de Chavannes, for example the allegorical *Forging a Road to Karelia* (1900; Helsinki, Athenaeum A. Mus.) and *Return from Work* (1907; Vaasa, Pohjanmaan Mus.). Halonen produced his finest altarpieces for the churches in Mikkeli and Kotka (e.g. the *Adoration of the Magi*, 1900; Kotka, parish church); they both reveal the influence of early Renaissance painting, which he had studied in Italy in 1896–7.

With the decline of the National Romantic Movement around 1907, Halonen abandoned his austere and idealized conception of the common people for the sensuality of heightened colour. Halonen, like many of his generation, experimented with the new trend within the more restrained Impressionist and Neo-Impressionist idioms. In 1908 he developed an intuitive sense of colour, characterized by brilliant tones and the evocation of powerful sunlight. A structured pattern of discernible brushstrokes enlivens the surface of his canvases. From about 1910 and into the 1920s Halonen reverted to a more subdued treatment of colour. It was as a landscape painter that he was most productive and respected in his later years.

BIBLIOGRAPHY
O. Hämäläinen, ed.: *Pekka Halonen* (Porvoo, 1947) [Eng. summary]
A. Lindström: *Pekka Halonen: Elämä ja teokset* [Pekka Halonen: life and works] (Porvoo, 1957)
J. Boulton Smith: *The Golden Age of Finnish Art: Art Nouveau and the National Spirit* (Helsinki, 1975, rev. 2/1985)
Dreams of a Summer Night (exh. cat., ACGB, 1986)

AIMO REITALA

Halprin, Lawrence (*b* New York, 1 July 1916). American architect and urban planner. He studied at Cornell University, Ithaca, NY, the University of Wisconsin, Madison, and at Harvard University (MSc 1941) with Walter Gropius and Marcel Breuer. After serving in the US Navy in the Pacific, he worked with the firm of Thomas D. Church and Associates, San Francisco, from 1945 to 1949. He then established his own office in San Francisco, occasionally accepting partners. In his work he emphasized the role of landscape, a theme he developed from houses and gardens to shopping centres and eventually in urban planning. Notable examples of the latter include the master plan (1957) for the Seattle Center, Seattle World's Fair (1962), portions of the BART (Bay Area Rapid Transit) project, San Francisco (1966), and the Freeway Park, Seattle (1976). His concern with environmental issues led him to design functional projects that seek to balance the demands of man and nature, particularly in areas affected by urban blight. He received several awards for this work, notably the American Institute of Architects Design award seven times between 1954 and 1969. He also taught at a number of universities across the USA, and his workshops and writings attracted a large following. Two of his most important books, *RSVP Cycles* (1970) and *Notebooks* (1972), emphasize the cooperation and creativity necessary for the design team.

WRITINGS
Cities (New York, 1963)
Freeways (New York, 1966)
RSVP Cycles: Creative Processes in the Human Environment (New York, 1970)
Notebooks of Lawrence Halprin, 1959–1971 (Cambridge, MA, 1972)
The Sketchbook of Lawrence Halprin (Cambridge, MA, 1981)

BIBLIOGRAPHY
M. Laurie: 'Lawrence Halprin: A Profile', *Landscape Des.*, i (Feb 1971), pp. 12–13
N. Lindgren: 'Halprin Revisited in 1973: Still Changing to Stay Alive', *Landscape Archit.*, lxiv/3 (1974), pp. 140–47

DARRYL PATRICK

Hals. Dutch family of painters of Flemish origin. The brothers (1) Frans Hals and (2) Dirck Hals were the sons of Franchoys Hals, a clothworker from Mechelen, who moved to Antwerp, where Frans was born. They left Antwerp in 1585 and by 1591 had settled in Haarlem. Frans Hals was one of the first great artists in the new Dutch Republic and is generally regarded as an outstanding portrait painter. His brother Dirck, who, according to Houbraken, trained under him, was noted for small genre paintings. Five of Frans's sons were painters: Harmen Hals (*bapt* Haarlem, 2 Sept 1611; *bur* Haarlem, 15 Feb 1669), Frans Hals the younger (*bapt* Haarlem, 16 May

1618; *d* Haarlem, April 1669) and Reynier Hals (*bapt* Haarlem, 11 Feb 1627; *d* Amsterdam, 1671) were all genre painters, while Nicolaes [Claes] Hals (*bapt* Haarlem, 25 July 1628; *bur* Haarlem, 17 July 1686) specialized in landscape printing, and Johannes [Jan] Hals (*fl* 1635–74) painted portraits, genre and history subjects. (2) Dirck Hals had seven children by his wife, Agneta Jans (*d* 1662), the eldest of whom, Anthonie Hals (*b* Haarlem, 1621; *d* before 25 Aug 1702), became a painter and, like his father, executed genre subjects.

BIBLIOGRAPHY

Thieme–Becker

(1) Frans Hals (*b* Antwerp, 1581–5; *d* Haarlem, 29 Aug 1666). In the field of group portraiture his work is equalled only by that of Rembrandt. Hals's portraits, both individual and group, have an immediacy and brilliance that bring his sitters to life in a way previously unknown in the Netherlands. This effect, achieved by strong Baroque designs and the innovative use of loose brushstrokes to depict light on form, was not to the taste of critics in the 18th century and the early 19th, when his work was characterized as lazy and unfinished. However, with the rise of Realism and, later, Impressionism, Hals was hailed as a modern painter before his time. Since then his works have always been popular.

1. Life and work. 2. Working methods and technique. 3. Character and personality. 4. Patrons and clients. 5. Critical reception and posthumous reputation.

1. LIFE AND WORK. The introduction to the second edition of Karel van Mander's *Schilderboeck* (1618) mentions Hals as one of his pupils. This apprenticeship would have lasted until 1603 at the latest. Hals may have begun his career by painting scenes of merry companies, such as the *Banquet in a Park* (*c*. 1610; ex-Kaiser Friedrich Mus., Berlin; destr.). In 1610 he became a member of the Guild of St Luke in Haarlem and married Annetgen Harmensdr. (*d* 1615); their first son, Harmen, was born in 1611, the year of Hals's earliest dated painting, a portrait of *Jacobus Zaffius* (1534–1618), of which only a portion survives (1611; Haarlem, Frans Halsmus.). Hals's distinctive style can already be seen in this work: the loose brushstrokes, applied 'wet on wet' without erasure, the lively characterization and the strong illumination of the head, the light always coming from the left.

During the second decade of the 17th century Hals painted single and double portraits, a civic guard piece and genre paintings. The portraits adhere strictly to Dutch conventions established by such artists as Cornelis Ketel and Paulus Moreelse. Hals also borrowed from the portrait engraving tradition such motifs as the oval *trompe-l'oeil* stone frame, which he used several times up to 1640. From 1616 to 1625 he was a member of the Haarlem chamber of rhetoric called De Wijngaertrancken. His connection with this organization is reflected in a portrait (1616; Pittsburgh, PA, Carnegie) of *Pieter Cornelisz. van der Morsch* (1583–1628), a rhetorician in Leiden, as well as in genre scenes of Shrove Tuesday revellers. Also in 1616 he painted his first militia piece: the *Banquet of the Officers of the St George Civic Guard Company* (Haarlem, Frans Halsmus.; *see* HAARLEM, fig. 2), of which he himself had become a member in 1612. Its composition is borrowed

from a militia piece by Cornelis Cornelisz. van Haarlem (1599; Haarlem, Frans Halsmus.) and a design for a civic guard banquet in a drawing (*c*. 1600–1610; Amsterdam, Rijksmus.) by Hendrick Goltzius. However, Hals enlivened the effect by giving each of the diners more individual space.

The first of a long list of creditors' claims on Hals dates from 6 August 1616; it relates to purchases of paintings, indicating his activity as a dealer or collector. On that date Hals was in Antwerp, probably on family business; he was back at Haarlem by 11 November. In 1616 his cousin and namesake Frans Hals was in trouble with the Haarlem authorities for being drunk and ill-treating his wife; he afterwards settled in Antwerp. (This cousin was confused with his more famous relative by van der Willigen.) On 12 February 1617 the painter Frans Hals married Liesbeth Reyniers, and in 1621 he and his brother Dirck were mentioned for the first time in a literary source (Ampzing). While in Antwerp, Frans probably came under the influence of Rubens, for his *Portrait of a Married Couple in a Garden* (early 1620s; Amsterdam, Rijksmus.) resembles the latter's *Rubens and his Wife Isabella Brant in the Honeysuckle Bower* (1609–10; Munich, Alte Pin.; *see* DRESS, fig. 37). Hals's sitters were probably the Haarlem diplomat and cartographer Isaac Massa (*b* 1587) and Beatrix van der Laen, who were married in 1622. Other paintings from the 1620s include a *Portrait of a Family in a Landscape* (*c*. 1620; Viscount Boyne, on loan to Cardiff, N. Mus.) and numerous genre pieces of children and young men drinking, smoking and making music. The portrait of *Jonker Ramp and his Sweetheart* (1623; New York, Met.) has been interpreted as representing the Prodigal Son,

1. Frans Hals: *Two Laughing Boys, One with a Fur Hat and Holding a Jug*, oil on canvas, 695×580 mm, *c*. 1627 (Rotterdam, Museum Boymans–van Beuningen)

while the children drinking (see fig. 1) and making music are usually interpreted as standing for the Five Senses or the Cardinal Sins. The prominent role of children is new in Dutch painting. Typical of Hals's genre work is its portrait-like character: most consist of only one or two figures and practically no background (which was emphasized more by other contemporary genre painters). Hals's portraits and genre pictures of the 1620s are also marked by their vivid colouring, *plein-air* effects, shifting contours and foreshortenings. The tonality is lighter than in the previous decade, probably under the influence of the Utrecht Caravaggisti, which affected both Hals's style and his subject-matter: it was Caravaggisti who set the fashion for drinkers, lute-players and life-size, half-length single genre figures. Hals also cut the figures off and used a *di sotto in sù* viewpoint, with strong contrasts of light and dark in the hands and faces, though not in the figures' clothing.

Apart from the supposed scenes of the Prodigal Son, Hals's only other known biblical paintings are his *St Luke* and *St Matthew* (both *c.* 1625; Odessa, A. Mus.), from a series of the Four Evangelists; a third picture from the series, of *St Mark* (priv. col., see 1989–90 exh. cat., p. 193), was discovered in 1974. Sources also mention a *Cain*, a *Magdalene* and a *Denial of St Peter* (all untraced). Hals painted his second and third militia pieces *c.* 1627 (both Haarlem, Frans Halsmus.), depicting the civic guard companies of St Hadrian and St George, and about the same time executed the portrait of *Verdonck Holding a Jawbone* (*c.* 1627; Edinburgh, N.G.). The latter was one of several of Hals's works that were altered at a later date: in this case a hat was added and the jawbone replaced by a wine-glass. The original composition is a unique example of a contemporary sitter portrayed with the attribute of a biblical character (Samson).

Frans also continued to trade in works of art. On 17 May 1627 Dirck stood surety for his purchases at an auction of paintings, and in 1630 Frans paid 89 guilders in Amsterdam for Hendrick Goltzius's painting of *Tityus* (1613; Haarlem, Frans Halsmus.) and sold it through an intermediary to the city of Haarlem for 200 guilders. In 1629, for 24 guilders, he cleaned some canvases for the monastery of St John at Haarlem.

About 1630 Frans painted several outdoor genre scenes of fisher boys and girls (e.g. Dublin, N.G.; these are not accepted by Grimm, 1972), the subjects of which have been interpreted as symbolizing laziness. Dating from about the same period or slightly earlier are the *Malle Babbe* (*c.* 1633–5; Berlin, Gemäldegal.), the *Gypsy Girl* (*c.* 1628; Paris, Louvre), the *Pickled Herring* (*c.* 1628–30; Kassel, Schloss Wilhelmshöhe), '*The Mulatto*' (*c.* 1628–30; Leipzig, Mus. Bild. Kst.) and the *Merry Drinker* (*c.* 1628–30; Amsterdam, Rijksmus.). The 1630s also marked the peak of Hals's career as a portrait painter. The early bright colours have been abandoned in favour of a more mono-chrome effect; the composition is more unified and simple, the poses more frontal (see fig. 2). Besides the many single and double portraits, there is a small family group of *c.* 1635 (Cincinnati, OH, A. Mus.). Hals also painted the civic guard company of St Hadrian again, this time in the open air (*c.* 1633; Haarlem, Frans Halsmus.); in contrast to the earlier version, the officers are not placed in order

2. Frans Hals: *Maritge Vooght Claesdr., Wife of Pieter Jacobsz. Olycan*, oil on canvas, 1280×945 mm, 1639 (Amsterdam, Rijksmuseum)

of rank. In 1633 he received a commission from Amsterdam to paint another militia piece, the *Company of Capt. Reynier Reael and Lt Cornelis Michielsz. Blaeuw* (the '*Meagre Company*'; Amsterdam, Rijksmus.; see fig. 3), for which he was at first offered 60 guilders per person, afterwards 66 guilders. The work led to a dispute, as Hals could not get the group of men to pose together in Amsterdam; subsequently he refused to return there, and they would not go to Haarlem. Consequently Pieter Codde took over the commission, which he completed in 1637. In 1635 Hals was also involved in a dispute with Judith Leyster, who had been his pupil *c.* 1630 and stood god-mother to his daughter Maria in 1631. Contrary to Guild regulations, Hals took over a pupil of hers. Also in 1635 he was in arrears with his Guild contributions. A few years later he painted himself in the background of the *Officers and Sergeants of the St George Civic Guard Company* (*c.* 1639; Haarlem, Frans Halsmus.). This is his only known self-portrait, apart from a painting known only from copies (e.g. Indianapolis, IN, Clowes Fund Inc., priv. col., on loan to Indianapolis, IN, Mus. A.).

After these peak years, the 1640s show a falling-off in commissions. Public taste increasingly favoured the smooth manner of such painters as Ferdinand Bol, Govaert Flinck and Bartholomeus van der Helst, all active in Amsterdam. Probably under their influence, Hals began to paint portraits with a more aristocratic air, and more static and less ostentatious poses. The backgrounds are darker, usually golden-brown or olive-green, and the

3. Frans Hals (and later Pieter Codde): *Company of Capt. Reynier Reael and Lt Cornelis Michielsz. Blaeuw* (the '*Meagre Company*'), oil on canvas, 2.07×4.27 m, completed 1637 (Amsterdam, Rijksmuseum)

clothing is predominantly black. It seems that he no longer painted genre scenes. Large commissions were for the sober portrait of the *Regents of the St Elizabeth Hospital at Haarlem* (*c.* 1641; Haarlem, Frans Halsmus.), the composition of which was probably borrowed from Thomas de Keyser, and two family portraits in a landscape (both *c.* 1648; Madrid, Mus. Thyssen-Bornemisza, and London, N.G.).

In 1642 family problems arose. Hals's feeble-minded son Pieter was locked up as a public danger; and on 31 March the painter's wife tried to have their daughter Sara committed to a workhouse owing to her loose morals. In 1644 Hals became an inspector (*vinder*) of the Guild of St Luke in Haarlem. His last dated works are of 1650. Those ascribed later dates are for the most part dark and sober in coloration, the paint is thin and the brushstrokes loose and broad. The poses are static and frontal, in line with the new classicizing trend. Unique in the portrait iconography of 17th-century Holland are the pendant portraits (both *c.* 1650) of *Stephanus Geraerdts* (Antwerp, Kon. Mus. S. Kst.) and *Isabella Coymans* (Paris, Baronne Edouard de Rothschild priv. col.): the two paintings (for illustration *see* PENDANT) are linked by the wife's gesture, as she hands her husband a rose.

In 1652, on account of an unpaid baker's bill of 200 guilders, a distraint was levied on Hals's furniture and meagre collection of paintings: two of his own works, two by one of his sons, one by van Mander and another by Maarten van Heemskerck. The last documented creditor's demand dates from 1661 and relates to purchased paintings. In the same year Hals was exempted from Guild contributions on account of his age. In 1662 the burgomasters of Haarlem made a lump sum payment of 50 guilders and granted him a pension of 150 guilders a year, which was raised to 200 guilders in 1663. On 22 January 1665 he stood surety for a debt of 458 guilders incurred by his son-in-law, Abraham Hendrix Hulst. He was probably able to do so because of the commissions for two group portraits: the *Regents of the Old Men's Almshouse* and the *Regentesses of the Old Men's Almshouse* (both *c.* 1664; Haarlem, Frans Halsmus.). (It is sometimes supposed that Hals became an inmate of the same old men's home, but there is no documentary evidence for this.) These and other late works are marked by a very summary use of colour, loose brushwork in flowing paint and very imprecise outlines. Some critics see this as the climax of Hals's virtuosity as a painter; others put it down to old age, stiffness and failing sight.

2. WORKING METHODS AND TECHNIQUE. Hals's oeuvre consists of oil paintings on canvas or panel and three small portraits on copper. The works vary in size from very small portraits (145×120 mm) to life-size portrait groups. No drawings or prints can be ascribed to him with certainty. He probably painted directly from the model, and very fast. In correspondence concerning the '*Meagre Company*', he promised that the sittings would not take long. No underdrawing has been detected. No doubt some small portraits were intended as preliminary studies for larger ones. Pigment analysis has shown that, especially in the flesh parts, there is no clear division between the layers of paint, indicating that he painted *alla prima* or 'wet on wet'. Before *c.* 1626, Hals applied a ground of white and grey under the flesh colours. His priming generally consisted of a light-coloured layer, with a thinner, darker one above it, the colour of which varied from one painting to another. His colour schemes, which developed from bright to monochrome, were achieved with a fairly limited palette. In the *Portrait of a Lady* (1627; Chicago, IL, A. Inst.), only six pigments have been identified. The umber-coloured background seen in many of his portraits was achieved with a mixture of lead white, yellow ochre

and black. In his later work, only four colours have been found: black, white, Venetian red and light ochre.

Hals's work derives its specific character from the loose brushwork and thin, flowing paint applied *alla prima*; the texture of the canvas is generally still clearly visible. It is also typical of him that the thickness of the pigment, the amount of detail and the style of brushwork can vary considerably in one and the same work. The faces in the portraits are invariably more carefully painted than the hands and clothing; the brushstrokes often flow so smoothly into one another that the separate strokes can scarcely be perceived. However, the hands and clothing are painted with parallel strokes varying in length and breadth. The somewhat 'frayed' appearance of his outlines, increasingly evident in the late work, is achieved by consecutive overlapping strokes. His genre scenes are much more loosely painted than the portraits of the same period, with clearly visible brushstrokes, although in Hals's later period this looser technique was also found in the portraits. Until *c.* 1626 the colour is generally thin and half transparent, with opaque, wax-like highlights; subsequently, the pigment becomes more opaque and less contrasting. In the 1650s it again becomes more transparent; while the latest works, from the 1660s, are characterized by the use of opaque and transparent colour in a single painting. Although the poses and grouping of figures used by Hals are broadly traditional, nevertheless his portraits make a much livelier impression than those of his contemporaries: this is due not only to his handling of the paint, but also to the sense of unfinished movement: heads turn away and somewhat to one side, half-open mouths seem about to speak, laugh or smile (quite unusual in contemporary portraiture). All of this contributes to the sense of animation, as do the suggestion of movement in hands and the way in which the sitters lean slightly back, forward or sideways.

Hals evidently had apprentices, as is shown by the dispute with Judith Leyster. His son-in-law Pieter van Roestraten stated in 1651 that he had worked with Hals for five years, and during Hals's lifetime copies of his works, perhaps from his own studio, were already in circulation. Sometimes he collaborated with other painters: the female figure in *Fruit and Vegetable Seller* (*c.* 1630; Burwarton Hall, Salop), by Claes van Heussen (*c.* 1600–after 1630), is thought to be by Hals. A document of 1651 states that Willem Buytewech executed the painted borders for two of Hals's portraits, and Slive has ascribed the background of some of Hals's landscapes to Pieter de Molyn.

3. CHARACTER AND PERSONALITY. Since the early 18th century, Hals has been persistently represented as a profligate and toper. The earliest account of his character is given by the German artist Mattias Scheits (see Bode), who claimed Hals was 'somewhat high-spirited in his youth'. His reputation as a drunkard originated with Houbraken, who said he was so drunk every evening that his pupils had to help him home. According to Houbraken, Hals exploited his pupil Adriaen Brouwer; he further related that Hals once met Anthony van Dyck, on which occasion the two artists painted each other's portrait. The many claims for debt, and the grants made to Hals at the end of his life, appeared to confirm this reputation. Due to a confusion of identity with his namesake and cousin, Hals continued to be regarded as an alcoholic, and as a wife-beater. His supposedly unappealing portraits of the regents and regentesses of the old men's home were thought by some to be a form of revenge on the authorities who had treated him callously in his impoverished old age.

The truth is hard to determine. Hals's alleged chronic drunkenness is hardly confirmed by two outstanding bills of 1644, amounting to about 5 guilders altogether, and another of 1650 for 31 guilders, which in any case he refused to acknowledge. The many demands for arrears of rent, provisions and footwear illustrate the regular financial troubles of a large family, but do not prove constant poverty. His output was relatively small, and his income therefore probably irregular. It is unclear whether or not he was impoverished in later life: he received an official grant, but was then suddenly able to stand surety for more than twice the amount. His behaviour over the Amsterdam militia piece seems to show that he had little ambition to extend his clientèle beyond Haarlem. His membership of a militia company and a chamber of rhetoric may testify to his social standing, while, as Scheits observed, the later grants may have been made in recognition of his eminence as a painter.

Hals's artistic connections were evidently limited to his Haarlem colleagues. In 1629, in his capacity as a guild official, together with Pieter de Molyn and Jan van de Velde the younger, he carried out an inspection of the conditions of imprisonment of their fellow artist Johannes Torrentius, and in 1642, with Frans Pietersz. de Grebber (1573–1649), Pieter de Molyn, Cornelis van Kittensteijn (*fl c.* 1600) and Salomon van Ruysdael, he presented a petition concerning a sale of paintings for the benefit of Haarlem artists. His only conflict with the guild was over the dispute with Judith Leyster; he was not its only member to be in arrears or in default over contributions, and this did not prevent his being appointed an inspector in 1644.

4. PATRONS AND CLIENTS. The majority of Hals's portraits were commissioned, but he may have had an intermediary for the sale of his genre paintings; in 1631 his landlord Hendrik Willemsz. den Abt offered a number of pictures for sale, including four of Hals's works and copies of others by him. (These may have been in his possession as a pledge in respect of board and lodging.) In 1634 two equestrian portraits and a *Vanitas* by Hals were offered as lottery prizes. Some of his portraits were engraved at a very early date and may have been painted for that purpose: most of the prints, however, particularly the genre subjects, were not made until after his death. Hals's clients were the wealthiest and most influential people in the city of Haarlem, including the Olycan family of brewers. There were only a few exceptions to this, René Descartes being the most notable; Hals painted his portrait *c.* 1649 (Copenhagen, Ny Carlsberg Glyp., on loan to Copenhagen, Stat. Mus. Kst). Members of the Amsterdam banking family of Coymans were among his faithful customers. Isaac Massa, who had his portrait painted three times by Hals, and perhaps his wedding portrait also, was present at the baptism of Hals's daughter Adriaentgen in 1623. Hals also painted portraits of his fellow-artists,

including *Adriaen van Ostade* (Washington, DC, N.G.A.), *Vincent Laurensz. van der Vinne* (*c.* 1655–60; Toronto, A.G. Ontario) and *Frans Post* (USA, priv. col., see 1989–90 exh. cat., no. 77).

5. CRITICAL RECEPTION AND POSTHUMOUS REPUTATION. Hals's characteristic loose brushwork was imitated only for a time by his son Jan Hals and by Judith Leyster. Houbraken listed as his pupils Frans's brother Dirck, his sons, his son-in-law Pieter van Roestraten, Adriaen Brouwer, Dirck van Delen, Adriaen van Ostade, Vincent van der Vinne and Philips Wouwerman; the last-named was mentioned as Hals's pupil by Cornelis de Bie as early as 1661. Many painters are said to have been influenced by Hals: Jan Miense Molenaer, Hendrick Pot, Thomas de Keyser, Jan Verspronck, Pieter Codde, Pieter Claesz. Soutman, Bartholomeus van der Helst, Jan de Bray, Gabriel Metsu, Gerard ter Borgh and finally Jan Steen, who represented the *Pickled Herring* by Hals in his *Christening Party* (Berlin, Gemäldegal.).

Hals's individual style and the liveliness of his portraits were recognized already in his lifetime. Samuel Ampzing described the *Banquet of the St Hadrian Civic Guard Company* (*c.* 1627) as 'very boldly painted after life'. In 1647 Theodorus Schrevelius (1572–1653), whom Hals painted in 1617 (Ascona, Bentinck-Thyssen priv. col., on loan to Luxembourg, Mus. N. Hist. & A.), drew attention to Hals's forceful manner and declared that his portraits seemed to breathe. De Bie described him as 'miraculous excellent at painting portraits or counterfeits which are rough and bold, nimbly touched and well-ordered. They are pleasing when seen from afar, seeming to lack nothing but life itself.' However, in 1660 H. F. Waterloos (*d* 1664) criticized Hals's portrait of the Amsterdam clergyman *Herman Langelius* (*c.* 1660; Amiens, Mus. Picardie): Hals, he said, was too old, his eyes too weak, his 'stiff hand too rude and artless'; he added, however, that Haarlem was proud of Hals's skill and early masterpieces. It was even said that van Mander himself moved to Amsterdam because his pupil Hals was more famous than he.

Despite such praise, there is reason to doubt Hals's status among his contemporaries, and his fame was fairly localized. Notwithstanding the great demand for portraits, they were regarded as an inferior form of art; Hals signed his full name only on his genre pieces. He received only average sums for his painting: the 66 guilders for each figure he was offered for the *'Meagre Company'* contrasts with the 100 guilders per figure Rembrandt received for the *'Night Watch'* (Amsterdam, Rijksmus.). Until the 19th century Hals's paintings continued to fetch low prices, about 15 guilders on average. He painted few self-portraits, which were an important means of enhancing status. For such a rapid worker, his output seems very slight: even at its peak, fewer than ten portraits a year, although it may be that as his work was undervalued after his death, much of it has been lost.

Hals's rough style of painting did not appeal to 18th-century taste. Joshua Reynolds and Goethe thought his work lacking in finish, and on the few occasions when Hals is mentioned in literature before the 1860s, this lack of finish is blamed on his dissolute way of life. From the 1860s onwards, however, opinions rapidly changed under the influence of Théophile Thoré. Both Hals's style and his way of life were now considered artistic, spontaneous, full of joy and individuality—qualities taken to exemplify the new Dutch Republic of the 17th century. After long neglect, he was ranked next to Rembrandt and hailed as an exponent of modern ideas of painting: 'Frans Hals est un moderne' (*L'Art moderne*, 1883, p. 302). Gustave Courbet copied his *Malle Babbe* (1869; Hamburg, Ksthalle), and van Gogh extolled his sense of colour and lively characterization. The prices paid for his works (and the number of forgeries) rose rapidly; in 1865 the 4th Marquess of Hertford and Baron Rothschild competed at auction for the *Laughing Cavalier* (1624; London, Wallace) and bid up the price to an unprecedented level for a painting. Although the 19th-century estimation still persists, since the 1960s critics have endeavoured to place Hals's work in the 17th-century context as regards both style and iconography. The frequent lack of a signature and date on his works has provoked much dispute: Valentiner ascribed *c.* 290 works to Hals, Trivas 109, Slive *c.* 220, Grimm 168. There is, however, much more agreement on issues of chronology, although the early critics generally dated the genre pieces later than do more recent ones.

BIBLIOGRAPHY

EARLY SOURCES

S. Ampzing: *Het lof der stadt Haerlem in Hollant* [The praise of the city of Haarlem in Holland] (Haarlem, 1621)

——: *Beschrijvinge ende lof der stadt Haerlem in Holland* [Description and praise of the city of Haarlem in Holland] (Haarlem, 1628), iv, p. 383

T. Schreveli: *Harlemias, ofte om beter te seggen, de eerste stichtinghe der stadt Haerlem* [The Harlemiad, or rather the first foundation of the city of Haarlem] (Haarlem, 1648)

H. F. Waterloos: *Hollandsche Parnas* [Dutch Parnassus], i (Amsterdam, 1660)

C. de Bie: *Het gulden cabinet* (1661)

A. Houbraken: *De groote schouburgh*, i (1718–21), pp. 90–95

A. van der Willigen: *Geschiedkundige aanteekeningen over Haarlemsche schilders en andere beoefenaren van de beeldende kunsten voorafgegaan door eene korte geschiedenis van het Schilder- of St. Lucas Gild aldaar* [Historical notes on Haarlem painters and other artists, preceded by a short history of the painters' Guild of St Luke in Haarlem] (Haarlem, 1866), pp. 116–23

MODERN STUDIES

W. Bode: 'Frans Hals und seine Schule', *Jb. Kstwiss.*, iv (1871), pp. 1–66 [p. 64 transcription of Scheits on Hals (1679)]

A. Bredius: 'De geschiedenis van een schuttersstuk' [The history of a militia-piece], *Oud-Holland*, xxxi (1913), pp. 81–4

W. R. Valentiner: *Frans Hals: Des Meisters Gemälde in 322 Abbildungen* (Stuttgart, Berlin and Leipzig, 1923)

A. Bredius: 'Archiefsprokkels betreffende Frans Hals' [Gleanings from the archives concerning Frans Hals], *Oud-Holland*, xli (1923–4), pp. 19–31

N. S. Trivas: *The Paintings of Frans Hals* (London, 1941)

C. A. van Hees: 'Archivalia betreffende Frans Hals en de zijnen' [Archival records concerning Frans Hals and his family], *Oud-Holland*, lxxiv (1959), pp. 36–42

E. de Jongh and P. J. Vinken: 'Frans Hals als voortzetter van een emblematische traditie' [Frans Hals as the continuer of an emblematic tradition], *Oud-Holland*, lxxvi (1961), pp. 117–52

P. J. J. van Thiel: 'Frans Hals' portret van de Leidse rederijkersnar *Pieter Cornelisz. van der Morsch*, alias Piero (1583–1628)' [Frans Hals's portrait of the Leiden rhetoricians' jester *Pieter Cornelisz. van der Morsch*, alias Piero], *Oud-Holland*, lxxvi (1961), pp. 153–72

M. Butler: '*Portrait of a Lady* by Frans Hals', *Mus. Stud.*, v (1970), pp. 6–21

S. Slive: *Frans Hals*, 3 vols (London, 1970–74)

C. Grimm: *Frans Hals: Entwicklung, Werkanalyse, Gesamtkatalog* (Berlin, 1972)

J. van Roey: 'De familie van Frans Hals: Nieuwe gegevens uit Antwerpen' [The family of Frans Hals: new data from Antwerp], *Jb.: Kon. Mus. S. Kst.* (1972), pp. 145–70

C. Grimm: '*St Markus* von Frans Hals', *Maltechnik, Rest.*, 80 (1974), pp. 21–31

F. S. Jowell: 'Thoré-Bürger and the Revival of Frans Hals', *A. Bull.*, lvi (1974), pp. 101–17

S. Koslow: 'Frans Hals's Fisherboys: Exemplars of Idleness', *A. Bull.*, lvii (1975), pp. 418–32

H. Miedema, ed.: *De Archiefbescheiden van het Lucasgilde te Haarlem, 1497–1798*, 2 vols (Alphen aan den Rijn, 1980)

P. J. J. van Thiel: 'De betekenis van het portret van *Verdonck* door Frans Hals' [The significance of Frans Hals's portrait of *Verdonck*], *Oud-Holland*, xciv (1980), pp. 112–37

N. Middelkoop and A. van Grevenstein: *Frans Hals: Leven, werk, restauratie* (Amsterdam and Haarlem, 1988)

Frans Hals (exh. cat., ed. S. Slive; Washington, DC, N.G.A.; London, RA; Haarlem, Frans Halsmus.; 1989–90)

INGEBORG WORM

(2) Dirck Hals (*b* Haarlem, *bapt* 19 March 1591; *d* Haarlem, *bur* 17 May 1656). Brother of (1) Frans Hals. From 1618 to 1624 and again in 1640 he was an amateur of the Haarlem chamber of rhetoric known as De Wijng-aertrancken, to which Frans also belonged. He was en-rolled in the Guild of St Luke in Haarlem from 1627 to his death. As Blade has established on stylistic grounds, Dirck collaborated with the architectural painter Dirck van Delen from that year until 1634, with Hals painting the figures (e.g. *Banquet Scene in a Renaissance Hall*, 1628; Vienna, Gemäldegal. Akad. Bild. Kst.). On 4 April 1634 a lottery of paintings was announced, organized by Dirck Hals (who sent some of his own pictures) and Cornelis van Kittensteijn in the inn De Basterdpijp in Haarlem. The following year, on 20 June 1635, the notary van Leeuwen at Leiden authorized Dirck Hals to collect moneys for Pieter Jansz. van den Bosch of Leiden in connection with the proceeds of paintings sold at Haarlem.

On 2 March 1643 Dirck Hals signed as a witness in the presence of the notary Willem van Vredenburch at Leiden. Although both documents were signed in Leiden, Dirck's residence is given as Haarlem.

Almost all Dirck Hals's paintings are of merry compa-nies in and out of doors, with numerous symbolic motifs. His earliest dated work, *Merry Company out of Doors* (1621; Budapest, Mus. F.A.) was painted two years before his earliest known interior (1623; St Petersburg, Hermitage). The subject-matter of these early works seems to be more influenced by Willem Buytewech than by that of his brother Frans. There is often a table in the centre of the composition, parallel to the picture plane, at or beside which there are amorous couples and figures eating and drinking, smoking and making music. The space is not deep and the perspective is uncertain. Until 1628 Dirck adopted figures from Buytewech literally, as in his *Fête champêtre* (1627; Amsterdam, Rijksmus.; see fig.). The depiction of worldly pleasures is often given added signif-icance by the addition of comic or foolish figures (e.g. Paris, Louvre, 4160; Frankfurt am Main, Städel. Kstinst. & Städt. Gal. 1587), attributes of the Five Senses (e.g. Amsterdam, E. Douwes priv. col., see 1976 exh. cat., no. 26) or a chained monkey (see 1976 exh. cat., no. 27).

After 1630 Dirck's works show a more tonal use of colour. With a broader touch he painted merry companies and also genre pieces with one or two figures, for instance the *Woman Tearing up a Letter* (1631; Mainz, Landesmus.) and the *Seated Woman with a Letter* (1633; Philadelphia, PA, Mus. A.). His later works are very varied in quality. He also painted a number of figure sketches in oil on paper, in the fluent manner of his brother Frans. Engrav-ings after Dirck Hals's work were made by Cornelis van Kittensteijn (e.g. the *Five Senses*; see Hollstein: *Dut. & Flem.*, ix, pp. 246–7), Salomon Savery (Hollstein,

Dirck Hals: *Fête champêtre*, oil on panel, 0.78×1.37 m, 1627 (Amsterdam, Rijksmuseum)

xxiv, p. 25) and Gillis van Scheyndel (Hollstein, xxiv, p. 210).

BIBLIOGRAPHY

NKL; Thieme–Becker

A. Houbraken: *De groote schouburgh* (1718–21), i, p. 322

A. van der Willigen: *Les Artistes de Harlem* (Haarlem, 1870), p. 149

W. Martin: 'Hoe schilderde Willem Buytewech' [How Willem Buytewech painted], *Oud-Holland*, xxxiv (1916), pp. 197–203, 199

A. Bredius: 'Archiefsprokkels betreffende Frans Hals' [Gleanings from the archives concerning Frans Hals], *Oud-Holland*, xli (1923–4), pp. 19–31; xli (1923–4), pp. 60–61

F. Würtenberger: *Das holländische Gesellschaftsbild* (Schramberg im Schwarzwald, 1937), pp. 58–63

E. Plietzsch: 'Randbemerkungen zur holländischen Interieurmalerei am Beginn des 17. Jahrhunderts', *Wallraf-Richartz-Jb.*, xviii (1956), pp. 174–86

E. Haverkamp Begemann: *Willem Buytewech* (Amsterdam, 1959), pp. 49–50

I. Linnik: 'Vnov' otkrytaya kartina Dirka Halsa' [A rediscovered painting by Dirck Hals], *Omagiu lui George Oprescu* (Bucharest, 1960), pp. 327–30 [Rus. text]

S. Slive: *Frans Hals*, 3 vols (London, 1970–74)

P. Schatborn: 'Olieverfschetsen van Dirck Hals' [Oil sketches by Dirck Hals], *Bull. Rijksmus.*, xxi (1973), pp. 107–16

T. T. Blade: *The Paintings of Dirck van Delen* (diss., Minneapolis, U. MN, 1976; microfilm, Ann Arbor, 1980), p. 127

Tot lering en vermaak [For instruction and pleasure] (exh. cat., ed. E. de Jongh and others; Amsterdam, Rijksmus.; 1976), nos 25–7

H. Miedema: *De archiefbescheiden van het St Lukasgilde te Haarlem* [The archives of the Guild of St Luke, Haarlem] (Alphen aan de Rijn, 1980)

Haarlem: The Seventeenth Century (exh. cat. by F. Fox Hofrichter, New Brunswick, NJ, Rutgers U., Zimmerli A. Mus., 1983), no. 65

A. Groot: 'Drank en minne: Een vroeg zeventiende-eeuwse gezelschap van Dirck Hals' [Drink and love: an early 17th-century merry company by Dirck Hals], *Kunstlicht*, xv (1985), pp. 10–16

AGNES GROOT

Hals, Harald (*b* Christiania [now Oslo], 10 May 1876; *d* Oslo, 20 Feb 1959). Norwegian architect, urban planner and writer. After preliminary training at the Royal School of Design in Christiania, he was educated as an architect in Berlin (1898), Stockholm (1900) and Champaign, IL (1906). He worked in the USA and in England until 1911, starting his own practice in Christiania 1912. In 1918 he was appointed Director of the Municipal Housing Office of Christiania, and from 1926 to 1947 he acted as the city's Chief Planning Officer. Hals began in a 'romantic' vein with his buildings for the English-inspired Ulleval Garden City (1915–22), Oslo, laid out by Paul Oscar Hoff (1875–1942), but he soon became an accomplished neo-classicist. Hegermanns plass (1919) is an octagonal open space surrounded by thinly plastered brick blocks of flats. Classical pilasters set off the corner angles, but National Romanticism is suggested by the steep roofs and the colonnettes between the arched openings. The neo-classicism of the two blocks of flats at Hans Nielsen Hauges gate 32 and 34 (1926) is much more literal. The buildings are painted and plastered to resemble stone masonry and separated by a giant, roofed colonnade reminiscent of that designed by C. F. Harsdorff for Amalienborg Plads, Copenhagen, in the late 18th century. Hals's most handsome design is perhaps the stone and concrete Ila steps (1926), Oslo, which form a centrepiece for the Ila housing development (1923–33), laid out with the symmetry characteristic of his work. His unexecuted plans for Oslo (1920s) aimed at transforming the entire city into a composition of regular streets and squares. The many blocks of flats and housing developments he designed for Oslo, as well as his brilliant and often polemic writings, earned Hals the dominant position in Norwegian urban planning and housing between the World Wars. In the 1930s he adopted the new Functionalist ideas.

WRITINGS

Ti aars boligarbeide i Kristiania [Ten years' housing work in Christiania] (Christiania, 1920)

Fra Christiania til Stor-Oslo [From Christiania to Greater Oslo] (Oslo, 1929)

Byen lever [The city lives] (Oslo, 1933)

Generalplan for Oslo: Aker og Baerum [General plan for Oslo: Aker and Baerum] (Oslo, 1934)

BIBLIOGRAPHY

NKL

C. Norberg-Schulz: *Modern Norwegian Architecture* (Oslo, 1986)

CHRISTIAN NORBERG-SCHULZ

Halsbach, Jörg von. *See* JÖRG VON HALSBACH.

Halsband, Frances. *See under* R. M. KLIMENT & FRANCES HALSBAND ARCHITECTS.

Hälsingborg. *See* HELSINGBORG.

Hama [Ḥamā, Ḥamāh; bibl. Hamath; anc. Gr. Epiphania]. City on the River Orontes in inland western Syria. The tell has been occupied almost continuously since Neolithic times.

1. ANCIENT. Hama's location on the Aleppo–Damascus road ensured its prosperity for long periods (*see also* SYRIA-PALESTINE, §I, 1). Its position also exposed it to influence and domination by a wide variety of cultures. In the 9th century BC Hama was ruled by a Neo-Hittite dynasty, which was replaced *c.* 800 BC by an Aramaean one (*see* ARAMAEAN). The city was destroyed by the Assyrians in 720 BC and its population deported, as mentioned in the Bible (2 Kings 17:24); occupation on the tell was limited to an Assyrian garrison. Hama was included in the Roman Empire after the conquest of Syria by Pompey in 64 BC. In 1812 J. L. Burckhardt visited Hama and discovered what later proved to be hieroglyphic Hittite inscriptions (*see* HITTITE). The tell, which dominates the modern town, was excavated in 1931–8 by a Danish expedition led by Harald Ingholt. Finds are in the National Museum of Aleppo.

Although there is possible evidence for occupation in the 'Pre-Pottery Neolithic B' phase (level M; 7th millennium BC), the Bronze Age levels (K–G; *c.* 3000–*c.* 1200 BC) yielded the earliest works of artistic interest. Pottery of the 3rd millennium BC shows Canaanite influence with a distinctive Syrian element in some of the forms (*see* SYRIA-PALESTINE, §I, 2(iv)). Simple human and animal figurines appear, as well as stamp seals; seal impressions (level J; *c.* 2400–*c.* 2000 BC) testify to a thriving Syrian cylinder seal industry.

From the Iron Age I level (F; *c.* 1200–1000 BC) came a beautiful ivory goblet. In shape it is a narrow-waisted cylinder with a handle in the form of an ibex modelled in the round. In the same level was a basalt stele with two registers: at the top a crescent moon above a worshipper offering incense on an altar before the enthroned moon god; at the bottom a large, double-headed eagle, all crudely carved in low relief.

Hama is one of the few sites in the region with significant Iron Age remains, which include the royal ceremonial centre of an Iron Age II city (level E). At the south end of the tell was a massive gateway that led into a large 'plaza' flanked on the south-west by a palace, dated to the 9th century BC, that shows Mesopotamian architectural influence, and on the north-east by a 'temple'. The jambs of the gate and of the 'temple' were flanked by basalt orthostat lions in the Hittite style of the Late Bronze Age. A basalt throne and altar were found in the 'plaza'. It is unclear whether the throne was intended for human use or for the deity. From the palace came two over life-size basalt lions carved in the round. These impressive examples of the Hittite tradition of lion-orthostats, though highly stylized, are remarkably lifelike. In the debris of a building north-west of the palace was found the torso of a basalt male figurine, well modelled in the round, wearing an Egyptian-style kilt.

A remarkable limestone lion was uncovered (level D), carved in the round, dating from c. 161 BC. From the Roman level (C) came a half-size limestone statue of a goddess and a Palmyrene-style female bust.

BIBLIOGRAPHY

Rapport préliminaire sur sept campagnes de fouilles à Hama en Syrie (1932–1938) (Copenhagen, 1940) [excavation report by H. Ingholt]
Hama: Fouilles et recherches de la fondation Carlsberg, 1931–1938, 1948–87 (all Copenhagen, Nmus.) [excavation reports by P. J. Riis and others]

RUPERT L. CHAPMAN

2. ISLAMIC. At the time of the Arab conquest in AD 636 the town was of minor importance. During the period of Umayyad rule (reg 661–750) a congregational mosque (destr. 1982) was constructed on the site of a Byzantine church, which provided some of the materials. The mosque had a court surrounded by vaulted porticos with semicircular arches, a plan inspired by the Great Mosque of Damascus (see DAMASCUS, §13). A free-standing minaret (1135) to the east of the prayer-hall stands on an earlier base. Another minaret abutting the north portico was added under the Mamluks (reg 1260–1517), as was a fine wooden minbar (1302; see ISLAMIC ART, §VII, 2(ii)). By the reign of the Abbasid caliph al-Mu'tadid (reg 892–902), Hama was a large market town protected by walls. It continued to enjoy prosperity under the Ayyubids (reg 1186–1260 in Damascus) and comprised an upper and lower town with houses on both banks of the Orontes. Both towns had congregational mosques: the Umayyad mosque served the upper town, and the Jami' al-Nuri, a mosque founded by the Zangid Nur al-Din (reg 1146–74), served the lower. It contained a contemporary wooden minbar. The lower town also had a hospital, three madrasas and a souk. The citadel, which overlooked the lower town, was probably destroyed by Timur and its stones used for other buildings. From the 14th century Hama was administered by Mamluk governors who brought further prosperity to the town. It was during this time that some large norias (water-wheels) and the large aqueduct were built. The town passed to the Ottomans in 1517; the governor in the first half of the 18th century, As'ad Pasha al-'Azam, built a large residence, which has been converted into a museum. A fine specimen of provincial Ottoman architecture, it was damaged during the 1982 uprising.

BIBLIOGRAPHY

Enc. Islam/2: 'Ḥamāt'
M. van Berchem and E. Fatio: Voyage en Syrie, 2 vols (Cairo, 1913–14)
K. A. C. Creswell: Early Muslim Architecture, i (Oxford, 1932/R 1969)
——: 'The Great Mosque of Hamā', Aus der Welt der islamischen Kunst (Berlin, 1959), pp. 48–53
G. C. Miles: 'A Mamlūk Hoard of Ḥamāh', Amer. Numi. Soc. Mus. Notes, xi (1966), pp. 307–9

□

Hamada, Chimei (b Kumamoto Prefect., 23 Dec 1917). Japanese printmaker. He studied in the department of oil painting at the Tokyo Art School (now Tokyo University of Fine Arts and Music) from 1934 to 1939, when he was conscripted into military service; in 1940 he was dispatched to China. Despite a brief military discharge, he was reconscripted but was sent home in 1945 because of his injuries. In 1949 he became a member of the Jiyū bijutsuka kyōkai (Independent Artists' Association), and he continued to exhibit with them until leaving the group in 1959. He gained recognition with the series Elegy of the New Recruits, which he worked on from 1950. The series was based on the experiences that occurred to one soldier during his military service. Unable to erase the experiences both of military service that paralleled his own suffering and of the absolute obedience and absurdity of the miserable conditions that characterized the war, he expressed these sentiments in his work in monochromatic etchings. In 1956 Hamada exhibited Sentry, a representative piece from the series Elegy of the New Recruits (1951), for which he received a prize. From that time the humanistic strain as illustrated in this series remained part of his work. He continued to create works that are sarcastic and that occasionally are criticisms containing jokes and scathing comments towards society and government. In 1975 the Kitakyushu Municipal Museum of Art opened an exhibition of his etchings, which displayed all 99 of his works produced between 1938 and 1975.

BIBLIOGRAPHY

C. Hamada: Dōbanga sakuhinshū [Collection of the etchings of Hamada Chimei] (1972)
Chimei Hamada Complete (Tokyo, 1993)

ATSUSHI TANAKA

Hamada, Shōji (b Kanagawa, 9 Dec 1894; d Tochigi, 5 Jan 1978). Japanese potter and museum official. In 1916 he graduated from the department of ceramics at the Tokyo Technical College. He then entered the Kyoto Municipal Institute of Ceramics, where he worked with Kanjirō Kawai, who was his senior there. In 1920 he went to England with BERNARD LEACH, who had been staying in Japan, and together they set up the Leach Pottery studio in St Ives, Cornwall. Hamada worked there until 1924, when he returned to Japan. He settled in Mashiko in Tochigi Prefecture, where he continued to produce ceramics using reddish brown iron glaze and black-and-white devitrified glazes and clay from the surrounding region. He absorbed traditional technical methods and emulated the organic beauty of various forms of Korean ceramics and of the folk crafts of Japan, and in particular Okinawa. In 1926 with Muneyoshi Yanagi and others he promoted the MINGEI ('folk crafts') movement. In his later years he established a simple, bold style working with such techniques as salt glazing (e.g. Pitcher, salt glaze on Chinese cobalt, 1960; Ohara, Mus. A.). In 1962, succeeding Yanagi, he became head of the Japan Folk Art Museum (Nihon Mingei-Kan) in Tokyo, and in 1968 he was awarded the

Order of Cultural Merit. In 1977 an exhibition comprising folk objects collected by Hamada and many of his own works was organized to inaugurate the opening of the Mashiko Ceramics Museum (Mashiko Sankōkan).

BIBLIOGRAPHY

S. Peterson: *Shōji Hamada: A Potter's Way and Work* (Tokyo, New York and San Francisco, 1974)
B. Leach: *Hamada: Potter* (Tokyo, New York and San Francisco, 1975)
Hamada Shōji Ten [Retrospective exhibition of Shōji Hamada] (exh. cat. by K. Yoshida, Tokyo, N. Mus. Mod. A., 1977) [in Jap. and Eng.]

MITSUHIKO HASEBE

Hamaguchi, Yozō (*b* Wakayama Prefect., 5 April 1909). Japanese printmaker. He entered the department of sculpture at the Tokyo Art School (now Tokyo University of Fine Arts and Music) in 1927, but left his studies in 1930 to go to France; he returned to Japan in 1939. In 1953 he settled in Paris. During this period he made copperplate prints and from about 1955 began producing his unique colour mezzotints, for example *Paris* (1956; Tokyo, N. Mus. Mod. A.), in which the roof-tops of the city's skyline are treated as a virtually abstract rhythmic pattern. In 1957 he was awarded prizes at the São Paulo Biennale and the first International Biennial Print Exhibition in Tokyo. He moved from Paris to San Francisco in 1981. In 1985 he held his first solo exhibition in Japan at the National Museum of Art in Osaka; the show comprised over 160 prints.

In his works, which are largely colour mezzotints, Hamaguchi used an original technique characterized by areas of colour and light that seemed to appear from dark voids. He particularly favoured the depiction of fruits, vegetables or still-lifes as seen in the print *Nine Shells* (1979). His prints are graceful and colourful, as well as rich in humour.

BIBLIOGRAPHY

Modern Japanese Art: Selected Works from the National Museum of Modern Art, Tokyo (Tokyo, 1984), pp. 13, 138, 219

ATSUSHI TANAKA

Hamamura. *See* ZŌROKU.

Hamann, Johann Georg (*b* Königsberg [Kaliningrad], 27 Aug 1730; *d* Münster, 21 June 1788). German philosopher and theologian. After travels that included sojourns in London and Riga, he based himself in his native city from 1759, occupying minor posts and acting as a Christian gadfly to the German Enlightenment. He separated himself from Kant with the esoteric *Sokratische Denkwürdigkeiten* (1759), which spurned the philosophy and recondite style of the Enlightenment. His differences were further developed in the first, and perhaps most influential riposte to Kant's *Critique of Pure Reason*, the *Metacritik über den Purismum der Vernunft* (1784), which questions how it is possible to criticize reason without assuming its validity, and claims that reason was already abstracted from language.

A similar argument informs Hamann's main work in the philosophy of art, the 'Aesthetica in Nuce', one of the *Kreuzzuge des Philologen* (1762). This essay, subtitled 'a rhapsody in cabbalistic prose', attacks the abstract theories of imitation proposed by German aesthetics: art does not imitate nature, says Hamann, but translates its language

into human language; this activity of translation, described as 'poetry', is the 'adaptation' of nature by human creativity. Hamann's emphasis on creativity over imitation was adopted by the Romantic generation, through whom the most self-consciously esoteric of 18th-century German writers ironically became one of the most influential.

WRITINGS

Sokratische Denkwürdigkeiten (1759); Eng. trans. by J. C. O'Flaherty as *Socratic Memorabilia* (Oxford, 1967)
J. Nadler, ed.: *Sämtliche Werke*, 6 vols (Vienna, 1949–57)
'Aesthetics in a Nutshell', *German Aesthetic and Literary Criticism*, ed. H. B. Nisbet (Cambridge, 1985)

BIBLIOGRAPHY

G. W. F. Hegel: 'Ueber Hamann's Schriften' (1828), *Hegel sämtliche Werke*, ed. H. Glockner (Stuttgart, 1958)
R. Unger: *Hamann und die Aufklärung. Studien zur Vorgeschichte der romantischen Geistes im 18. Jahrhundert*, 2 vols (Halle, 1925/*R* Tübingen, 1963)
J. Nadler: *Johann Georg Hamann. Der Zeuge des Corpus Mysticum* (Salzburg, 1949)
R. G. Smith: *J. G. Hamann, 1730–1788: A Study in Christian Existence. With Selections from his Writings* (London, 1960)
W. M. Alexander: *Johann Georg Hamann: Philosophy and Faith* (The Hague, 1966)
J. C. O'Flaherty: *Unity and Language: A Study in the Philosophy of Johann Georg Hamann* (New York, 1966)
E. Metzke: *J. G. Hamanns Stellung in der Philosophie des 18. Jahrhunderts* (Darmstadt, 1967)
T. J. German: *Hamann on Language and Religion* (Oxford, 1981)

HOWARD CAYGILL

Hamann, Richard (*b* Seehausen, Saxony, 29 May 1879; *d* Immenstadt, Allgäu, 9 Jan 1961). German art historian. In Berlin he studied philosophy, obtaining his doctorate in 1902, and then he read German and art history, qualifying as a lecturer under Heinrich Wölfflin in 1911. The same year he was appointed to a chair at the Königliche Akademie, Posen (now Poznań), and in 1913 at the newly founded Kunsthistoriches Institut, Marburg. There he founded and built up the Foto-Marburg pictorial archive and the Verlag des Kunstgeschichtlichen Seminars Marburg/Lahn (1922), which published the *Marburger Jahrbuch* from 1924; he also established the Jubiläumsbau (1928; now the Ernst-von-Hülsen-Haus) and the Preussisches Forschungsinstitut für Kunstgeschichte (1929). He taught at the Humboldt University, East Berlin, alongside his Marburg duties from 1947 to 1950. In 1949 he was awarded a national prize by the DDR and appointed ordinary member of the Deutsche Akademie der Wissenschaften. In 1954 he founded the Arbeitsstelle für Kunstgeschichte an der Deutschen Akademie der Wissenschaften zu Berlin, a post concerned with art history at the German Academy of Sciences. From 1957 he was joint editor of the *Schriften zur Kunstgeschichte*.

Hamann's research, which emphasized formal analysis, focused primarily on medieval French and German sculpture, Rembrandt, German painting after 1850 and the overall development of art since 1919. He also showed a receptive interest in contemporary Expressionism. He always stressed the function of art as a mirror of society. Among his achievements is a clear delineation between Ottonian and Romanesque (redating the Gero Crucifix in Cologne Cathedral from the 12th century to the 10th), although his regrouping and renaming of individual periods of art history have found little agreement. Characteristic of his approach are his division of art epochs into archaic, classical and baroque phases and his parallel treatment of ancient, medieval and modern art.

WRITINGS

Der Impressionismus in Leben und Kunst (Cologne, 1907, 2/1923)
with F. Rosenfeld: *Der Magdeburger Dom: Beiträge zur Geschichte und Ästhetik mittelalterlicher Architektur, Ornamentik und Skulptur* (Berlin, 1910)
Deutsche und französische Kunst im Mittelalter, 2 vols (Marburg, 1922–3)
Die deutsche Malerei vom Rokoko bis zum Expressionismus (Leipzig and Berlin, 1925)
Die Holztür der Pfarrkirche zu St Maria im Kapitol (Marburg, 1926)
'Die Bonner Pietà', *Festschrift Paul Clemen* (Bonn, 1926), pp. 365–74
ed.: *Die frühmittelalterlichen Bronzetüren*, 4 vols (Marburg, 1926–53)
Die Elisabethkirche zu Marburg und ihre künstlerische Nachfolge: Die Plastik (Marburg, 1929)
'Studien zur ottonischen Plastik', *Städel-Jb.*, vi (1930), pp. 5–19
Geschichte der Kunst von der altchristlichen Zeit bis zur Gegenwart (Munich and Berlin, 1933, rev. 17/1959)
Rembrandt: Leben und Werk (Berlin, 1944)
Geschichte der Kunst: Von der Vorgeschichte bis zur Spätantike (Munich, 1952, 10/1959)
Die Abteikirche von St Gilles und ihre künstlerische Nachfolge, 3 vols (Berlin, 1955, 2/1956)
with J. Hermand: *Deutsche Kunst und Kultur von der Gründerzeit bis zum Expressionismus*, 5 vols (Berlin, 1959–60)
Regular contributions to *Marburger Jb. Kstwiss.* (1924–) and to *Marburger Kunstbücher für jedermann* (Marburg, 1922–4; Leipzig, 1927)

BIBLIOGRAPHY

Festschrift Richard Hamann zu seinem 60. Geburtstage (Burg bei Magdeburg, 1939)
F. Dettweiler: 'Schriften von Richard Hamann', *Marburger Jb. Kstwiss.*, xiii (1944), pp. 271–80; xiv (1949), p. 234
E. Lehmann: *Richard Hamann in Memoriam: Mit zwei nachgelassenen Aufsätzen und einer Bibliographie der Werke Richard Hamanns* (Berlin, 1963)
G. André: 'Richard Hamann (1879–1961)', *Marburger Gelehrte in der ersten Hälfte des 20. Jahrhunderts*, ed. I. Schnack (Marburg, 1977), pp. 124–9
P. H. Feist: *Beiträge Richard Hamanns zur Methodik der Kunstgeschichtsschreibung* (Berlin, 1980)
M. Warnke: 'Richard Hamann', *Marburger Jb. Kstwiss.*, xx (1981), pp. 11–20

ULRIKE LIEBL

Hamaya, Hiroshi (*b* Tokyo, 28 March 1915). Japanese photographer. He joined Oriental Photographic Industries in 1933 where he learnt photographic techniques. In 1939 he met the ethnologist Keizō Shibusawa and, strongly influenced by his positivistic documentary spirit, began to photograph the life, particularly the New Year customs, of the people of the mountain village Tanihama in Niigata prefecture. The photographs, which combine lyricism with documentation, were published as *Yukiguni* ('Snow country'; Tokyo, 1956). After the war he published works in the magazines *Bungei shunjū* and *Chūō kōron* and in 1960, under contract to the Magnum agency, he became active internationally. Representative work includes the photographs of the relationship between the natural features and life of Japanese people in *Ura Nihon* ('Back regions of Japan'; Tokyo, 1957) and *Nihon rettō* ('The Japanese archipelago'; Tokyo, 1964) and the portrait collection *Gakugeishoka* ('Scholars and artists'; Tokyo, 1982).

Contemp. Phots
BIBLIOGRAPHY

Japan: A Self-portrait (exh. cat., ed. C. Capa and S. Yamagishi; New York, Int. Cent. Phot., 1979), pp. 41–5
Hamaya on Hamaya: 50 Years of Photography, 1935–1985 (exh. cat., ed. R. L. Kirschenbaum; New York, Int. Cent. Phot.; Tokyo, Ginza A.G.; 1986)

KOHTARO IIZAWA

Hambling, Maggi (*b* Hadleigh, Suffolk, 1945). English painter. She trained at the Ipswich School of Art, Suffolk (1962–4), and in London at the Camberwell School of Art (1964–7) and the Slade School of Fine Art (1967–9). In 1969 she received a Boise Travel Award to New York. Hambling's reputation was formed by a major series of portraits of the celebrated British comedian Max Wall, produced while she was the first Artist-in-Residence at the National Gallery, London (1980–81), and exhibited at the National Portrait Gallery in 1983. The vivid observation in numerous paintings and charcoal sketches encapsulated her direct and committed engagement with her subject, interpreted in dynamic and bravura impressions. In the mid-1980s she turned to landscape painting, made in her native Suffolk. Her studies of dawn in the Orwell Estuary recall the luminous visions of the 19th-century English masters J. M. W. Turner and John Constable. In works from the early 1990s a violent symbolism disturbs dreamlike compositions; whirlpools of primal colour revolve around the image of a fractured moon in elegies of spectral radiance. Hambling not only worked from life and the model but also drew on memory and her subconscious imagination to escape the limits of documentary realism.

BIBLIOGRAPHY

Maggi Hambling: Paintings, Drawings and Watercolours (exh. cat. by M. Warner and others, London, Serpentine Gal., 1987)
Maggi Hambling: An Eye through a Decade, 1981–1991 (exh. cat. by M. Gooding and G. Melly, New Haven, CT, Yale Cent. Brit. A., 1991)
Maggi Hambling (exh. cat., interview J. Collins; Sunderland, A. Cent., 1993)

Hamburg. German city, port and commercial and industrial centre on the River Elbe, *c.* 110 km from its mouth at its confluence with the Alster and the Bille. It is Germany's second city after Berlin, with a population in 1994 of 1,705,000.

1. History and urban development. 2. Centre of gold and silver production.

1. HISTORY AND URBAN DEVELOPMENT. A Frankish baptismal church and later the Hammaburg were constructed on the orders of Charlemagne *c.* AD 810, over an earlier Saxon settlement at the confluence of the Alster and the Elbe. Merchants and artisans settled in the vicinity and established the first harbour. It was probably Louis the Pious (*reg* 813–40) who established (831) Hamburg as a bishopric and missionary centre under Bishop Ansgar (*d* 865) and it was the latter who built the first cathedral. In 845 the Hammaburg was plundered and destroyed by Vikings. In 848 the bishopric was united with that of Bremen, and Ansgar transferred his residence there with Hamburg remaining de jure an ecclesiastical centre and the bishops' second residence until 1223. Although the settlement rapidly recovered, it suffered repeated attacks by the Slavs.

The first church of St Petri was probably built *c.* 1195. In 1188, under Count Adolf III of Schauenburg (*d* 1225), the Neustadt was laid out around what was to be the church of St Nikolai; it had a separate harbour and was endowed by Frederick I Barbarossa with trading and customs rights and navigation privileges on the lower Elbe. From 1201 to 1227 Hamburg was in the possession of Denmark–Holstein although the old city (parish of St

Petri) remained under archiepiscopal rule. In 1216 the old and new towns were united under a common civic law. In 1218 the archbishop of Bremen transferred his right over the old town to Count Adolf IV (before 1205–1261). By then Hamburg was an important export centre with a steadily growing population. The church of St Nikolai had been begun *c.*1200, and with the development of the parishes of St Katharina (*c.* 1250) and St Jacobi (*c.* 1255) Hamburg reached the size that it maintained until the 16th century. From 1241 alliances with Lübeck played a major role in the rise of the Hanseatic League. The council codified an extended civic law in 1270 and gradually increased the town's independence, attaining rights of legislation and jurisdiction (1292) and the minting of coinage (1325). During the 14th and 15th centuries the churches of St Petri, St Katharina (1380–1426; see fig.) and St Jacobi were rebuilt as Gothic brick hall churches. Around this time the painters MASTER BERTRAM and Master Francke (*fl* first quarter of 15th century) were active in the city.

Hamburg, St Katharina, 1380–1426; restored after World War II

Hamburg not only was an important reloading point between the North Sea and the Baltic but carried on its own vigorous trade with the surrounding region, the upper Elbe and western Europe. Beer was a highly important export commodity: there were more than 500 breweries in Hamburg at the end of the 15th century. From the 14th century, above all to protect its trade routes, Hamburg temporarily acquired extensive territory, claiming control over the lower Elbe in 1359 and receiving appropriate imperial privileges until the staple-right (1482). It was the merchants who formed the upper class of the city and who fully controlled its self-electing council. Civic riots were such as to necessitate peace treaties in 1410, 1458 and 1483. From the 14th century Hamburg's relationship with the Holy Roman Empire had been contentious. In 1510 the Diet of Augsburg declared it an imperial city. The Danish rulers of Holstein, however, also claimed sovereignty, while both claims were resisted by the city. For a long time its status remained unclear. (While the emperor's claim was reasserted in 1618 by the Reichskammergericht, it was not recognized by Denmark until 1768.)

The Reformation was introduced in a gradual, non-violent manner, being confirmed by Johann Bugenhagen (1485–1558) in a ruling of 1529. By the coincident *Langer Rezess*, civic participation increased, and burgher charity commissions set up during this period became a lasting means of representation and control, as against that of the council. The revised civic law of 1497, which adopted many Roman principles, emphasized the authority of the council; it was renewed in 1603. In 1558 the first stock exchange in Germany was founded in Hamburg. The admission of the English Merchants Adventurers (1567–77; from 1611), of religious refugees from the Netherlands (last third of 16th century) and later of Portuguese Jews and other immigrants furthered the growth (1600: almost 40,000) and economic development (e.g. 1619: foundation of the bank) of the city. A new rampart (1616–26), which doubled the area of the city by including the later parish of St Michaelis (1685), afforded protection during the Thirty Years War (1618–48). From the mid-17th century, however, social, political and religious divisions developed, causing violent unrest, which King Christian V of Denmark (*reg* 1670–99) repeatedly tried to exploit (1679, 1686) to achieve the military subjugation of the city. An imperial commission finally resolved the conflict and, in 1712, restored the old constitution (*Hauptrezess*).

From the late 17th century Hamburg experienced a cultural flowering, with the foundation of the opera in 1678 and of the Nationaltheater in 1767, formed from an older theatre. The city attracted poets, scholars and musicians. The church of St Michaelis, one of the most important German Protestant Baroque churches, was built (1751–62) by Johann Leonhard Prey (*d* 1757) and Ernst Georg Sonnin (1713–94) (tower added 1786; rebuilt 1906–12 after a fire). Hamburg also became a centre for the German Enlightenment. The charitable and educational 'Patriotic Society' of 1765 became a model much imitated elsewhere, as did the institute for the poor founded by the Society's members in 1788. Despite an economic crisis in 1763, Hamburg expanded in the later 18th century, and the population grew. The city maintained its independence under the decision of the Reichsdeputationshauptschluss in 1803 but was occupied by French troops in 1806, suffering heavily from Napoleon's continental blockade. During the Romantic period (1804) PHILIPP OTTO RUNGE settled in Hamburg.

From 1811 to 1814 Hamburg was incorporated into the Napoleonic empire and in 1815, after its liberation, it joined the German Confederation a 'Free and Hanseatic City' (1819). The Börse was built 1839–41 (damaged in World War II; rest.). In 1842 a major fire reduced a third of the city's area and most of its historic buildings to ashes. This resulted in the need for major rebuilding. A new church of St Nikolai was built (1846–74) to designs by George Gilbert Scott (only the tower, completed 1880, survived World War II). Although plans to replace the Rathaus were underway in 1843, it was not rebuilt until 1886–97, when a collaborative group of architects under MARTIN HALLER created a new building in the historicist style. Under the constitution of 1860 the old council was replaced by an elected body of citizens who elected the senate. Subsequently the Kunsthalle (1867) and the Museum für Kunst und Gewerbe (1877) were founded. In 1867 Hamburg joined the North German Confederation, and in 1871 it became part of the German Empire. After joining the German Zollverein in 1881–8, it experienced an economic boom, matched by rapid population growth (in 1871: 300,000; in 1913 more than 1 million). A monument to *Bismarck* (1901–2) by Hugo Lederer and Emil Schaudt (*b* 1871) was unveiled on the Elbhöhe in 1906.

Notwithstanding the adverse effects of World War I, a new university was founded in 1919 and a new constitution established in 1921. In 1921–3 the unique Chilehaus (*see* EXPRESSIONISM, fig. 4) was built by FRITZ HÖGER. The war memorial by Ernst Barlach was set up in 1931. In 1933 the citizens' assembly was abolished and replaced by a governor representing the Nazi state. The Gross-Hamburg-Gesetz (1937) extended Hamburg to include the previously Prussian towns of Altona, Wandsbek and Harburg but ceded Cuxhaven and other districts. After World War II (1946) Hamburg was reconstituted as a state within the British occupied zone and became a city state within the Federal Republic of Germany (1949). In 1952 the victims of the air raids were commemorated in a monument by Gerhard Marcks. The constitution of 1952 established an assembly of citizens with the right to legislate and to elect the senate. The appearance of late 20th-century Hamburg is dominated by office blocks and modern commercial and residential buildings.

BIBLIOGRAPHY
K. Detlev Möller and others, eds: *Bücherkunde zur hamburgischen Geschichte*, i–v (Hamburg, 1939–90)
H.-D. Loose and W. Jochmann, eds: *Hamburg: Geschichte der Stadt und ihrer Bewohner*, 2 vols (Hamburg, 1982–6)

RAINER POSTEL

2. CENTRE OF GOLD AND SILVER PRODUCTION. Hamburg was one of the important centres in Germany for the export of gold- and silverwork, but the work produced is less original than that made in Augsburg and Nuremberg. Goldsmiths in Hamburg did not create styles but assimilated external influences. A guild of goldsmiths was established in Hamburg in the 14th century. Notable extant Late Gothic works include a gold chalice (Schleswig,

Schloss Gottorf) by Hinrik Rentzel (*d* 1509) and the *Ilsabenbecher*, a covered cup (Hamburg, Mus. Hamburg. Gesch.) by Dirik Ostorp. Little survives from before the most important period of goldsmithing in Hamburg, which lasted from about 1590 to 1690, when the finest products were sent to the courts of the rulers of north Germany and the Scandinavian countries. During this period the town council ordered substantial commissions as gifts intended to propitiate powerful princes and rulers. About 1600 one of the most prominent goldsmiths was Dirich Utermarke (?1565–1635), to whom the town council gave most of its commissions. His work is varied and includes two censers in the form of mountains with castles (Moscow, Kremlin, Armoury).

Jakob Mores (1540–1612) was also one of the most innovative goldsmiths of this period, as can be seen in his surviving pieces and presentation drawings. His production of silverware, however, gradually declined in favour of his extensive activities as an entrepreneur and dealer, which included acting as supplier to the Danish and Swedish royal courts. The creation of the monumental ebony and silver altar (Hillerød, Frederiksborg Slot church) was supervised by him; it was delivered to King Christian IV of Denmark in 1606 and is one of the most important pieces of its kind. This piece and a later pulpit in the same church, also in ebony and silver, are evidence of the high standard of goldsmithing in Hamburg in the early 17th century.

During the Thirty Years War (1618–48) increased difficulties in transport impeded competition from goldsmithing centres in south Germany, and consequently a large number of goldsmiths were active in Hamburg, although they did not often specialize in particular wares. Four types of drinking vessel were produced in the 17th century: the *Hansekanne*, a tall cylindrical drinking vessel that was developed in the late 16th century but that also remained the most popular type in the first third of the 17th century; the wider, squatter tankard derived from the *Hansekanne* that became the main speciality until *c.* 1700; the standing-cup, especially the Baroque embossed type with a characteristic figured stem; and the tall beaker, usually made *en suite* with a presentation plate, most of which are untraced or have been destroyed. Dutch influence is often evident in the decoration of these pieces: the Auricular style was fashionable for most of the 17th century, while floral motifs were particularly popular from about 1650 to 1700.

Goldsmithing in Hamburg declined at the beginning of the 18th century, as patrons in northern Europe and Russia tended to place important commissions with goldsmiths in Augsburg, who were more progressive in style and had a well-organized trade. As craftsmen in Hamburg could not reach an agreement concerning the division of labour, it was not possible for them to adapt successfully to the production of fashionable matching services. They gradually turned to less expensive and less elaborate goods, for example snuff-boxes and sugarbowls, and their style became provincial. The type of vessel produced only in north Germany and particularly in Hamburg was the *Türkenkopfkanne* ('Turk's head' pot), of which the characteristic feature is the turban-shaped lid.

Despite the gradual decline of goldsmithing, a number of talented goldsmiths were active in the 18th century, for example Jürgen Richels (*fl* 1664–1710), who used late Baroque flower and acanthus decoration, J. W. Heumann (1699–1732), who specialized in gadrooning and classical ornament, Johann Conrad Otersen (1761–90), an exponent of the Rococo style based on that of Augsburg, and Johann Hues (1768–1802), who made high-quality Neoclassical pieces. In the 19th century many master goldsmiths in Hamburg were active only as dealers who put their own maker's mark on imported goods. In 1865 the guild of goldsmiths was dissolved. Alexander Schönauer, who had trained in Munich and who moved to Hamburg in 1895, was one of the leading goldsmiths working in the historicist style. He made municipal silver to replace that destroyed in the early 19th century.

BIBLIOGRAPHY
E. Schliemann, ed.: *Die Goldschmiede Hamburgs* (Hamburg, 1985)

FABIAN STEIN

Ham Che-gŏn (*fl* 17th century). Korean painter. He was born into a family of hereditary painters (*hwawŏn*) at the Bureau of Painting (Tohwasŏ). After he, in turn, entered the Bureau, he became an instructor. It is known that in 1682 he travelled with Korean envoys to Japan, with the job of recording the mission. In its characteristics Ham's Dark Bamboo Drawing, held in Japan, confirms him as an artist active in the mid-Chosŏn period (1392–1910).

BIBLIOGRAPHY
Hong Sŏn-p'yo: '17–18 segi-ŭi han'ilgan hoehwa kyosŏp' [The relationship between Korean and Japanese paintings in the 17th and 18th centuries], *Kogo Misul*, cxliii/cxliv (1929), pp. 22–46

HONG SŎN-P'YO

Hamdi, Osman [Hamdi Bey]. *See* OSMAN HAMDI.

Hamdullah, Şeyh [Shaykh Ḥamdullah ibn Muṣṭafā Dede] (*b* Amasya, 1436; *d* Istanbul, 1520). Ottoman calligrapher. His father, a Suhrawardi shaykh, emigrated from Bukhara to Amasya where Hamdullah studied calligraphy under Khayr al-Din Mar'ashi. Hamdullah's early style imitated that of YAQUT AL-MUSTA'SIMI and his pupil 'ABDALLAH SAYRAFI. While governor of Amasya, the future sultan Bayezid II (*reg* 1481–1512) studied with Hamdullah, and when the prince became sultan he brought Hamdullah to the imperial palace in Istanbul. Bayezid reportedly admired Hamdullah so greatly that the sultan held the inkwell while the master worked. At the beginning of the reign of Selim I (*reg* 1512–20), Hamdullah was forced to leave Istanbul because of political intrigue in the palace and took refuge in his estate at Alemdağ. He died shortly after returning to Istanbul at the beginning of the reign of Süleyman (*reg* 1520–66) and was buried in Üsküdar.

Hamdullah adapted the six scripts canonized by Yaqut and refined the *dīvānī* script used in the Ottoman chancelleries for official documents (*see* ISLAMIC ART, §III, 2(iv)(a)). A prolific scribe, Hamdullah is said to have transcribed almost 50 copies of the Koran. A manuscript of the Koran made for Bayezid (1495–6; Istanbul, Topkapı Pal. Lib., E.H. 72) shows Hamdullah's command of *naskh* script in which the rounded tails swoop rhythmically across the page. Hamdullah also penned hundreds of volumes of prayers, Koranic verses and calligraphic exercises (Arab. *qiṭʿa*), in which a line of large script is juxtaposed with several lines of smaller script and panels of painting and marbled paper (e.g. a page in *muḥaqqaq* and *rayḥān*, Istanbul, Topkapı Pal. Lib., E.H. 2078). He also designed architectural inscriptions, such as those on the entrance portal and mihrab in Bayezid's Mosque in Istanbul (1505). Hamdullah trained many followers, including AHMAD KARAHISARI, and a dozen members of his family became calligraphers.

BIBLIOGRAPHY
Enc. Islam/2: 'Ḳhaṭṭ, iii. In Turkey'; pls XXXIV–XXXV
M. Lings: *The Quranic Art of Calligraphy and Illumination* (London, 1976), pls 29–30
H. Lowry: 'Calligraphy; Hüsn-i hat', *Tulips, Arabesques & Turbans: Decorative Arts from the Ottoman Empire*, ed. Y. Petsopoulos (London, 1982), pp. 172–3; pls 163, 173
The Anatolian Civilisations III: Seljuk/Ottoman (exh. cat., 18th Council of Europe exh.; Istanbul, 1983), nos E.14–16
The Age of Sultan Süleyman the Magnificent (exh. cat. by E. Atıl, Washington, DC, N.G.A.; Chicago, IL, A. Inst.; New York, Met.; 1987–8), pp. 44–5; no. 7

NABIL SAIDI

Hameel, Alart du. *See* ALART DU HAMEEL.

Hamel, Théophile (*b* Sainte-Foy, nr Quebec, 8 Nov 1817; *d* Quebec, 23 Dec 1870). Canadian painter. In 1834 he was apprenticed for six years to the leading Quebec painter Antoine Plamondon. He began his career painting portraits and religious subjects for the Quebec upper classes. In 1843 he went to Europe, staying mainly in Italy. Returning to Canada in 1846, he stayed first in Quebec and then moved to Montreal the following year. His career started to prosper in 1851, when he settled permanently in Quebec. Hamel became affluent, enjoying the patronage and respect of the ruling élite. In 1853 he was made official portrait painter by the government of the United Canadas, an honour that confirmed him as the best painter of the day. He was commissioned to produce portraits of all the presidents, from 1791 onwards, of the Assembly and Legislative Council chambers (e.g. Ottawa, N. Archvs). He also painted a series of historical figures, including the explorer *Jacques Cartier* (1491–1557) (1846; Quebec, Inst. Can. Qué.), and some religious paintings, which were mainly copies.

Hamel's portrait practice encompassed members of the aristocracy, the bourgeoisie and the clergy (e.g. *Abbé Edouard Faucher*, 1855; Lotbinière, St Louis). He also painted children and made three self-portraits *c.* 1841–3 (Quebec, Mus. Sémin.), *c.* 1849–50 (Quebec, Mus. Québec) and 1857. His portraits were generally direct and unrhetorical, giving prominence to the face of the subject through simple composition. His work is characterized by its dignity, verisimilitude, sobriety and precise composition. Described by contemporary critics as a national painter, Hamel had a considerable influence on Canadian artists of the next generation, including his pupil Napoléon Bourassa.

BIBLIOGRAPHY
DCB
Deux peintres de Québec: Antoine Plamondon, 1802–1895, Théophile Hamel, 1817–1870/Two Painters from Quebec: Antoine Plamondon, 1802–1895, Théophile Hamel, 1817–1870 (exh. cat. by R. H. Hubbard, Ottawa, N.G., 1970) [bilingual text]

R. Vézina: *Théophile Hamel*, i: *Peintre national, 1817–1870* (Montreal, 1975); ii: *Catalogue des oeuvres* (Montreal, 1976)

MARIO BÉLAND

Hamen y (Gómez de) León, Juan van der (*b* Madrid, *bapt* 8 April 1596; *d* Madrid, 28 March 1631). Spanish painter and courtier. He served at the courts of Philip III and Philip IV and can be credited more than anyone else with establishing the popularity of the new genre of still-life in Madrid in the 1620s. He was the son of a Flemish courtier, who had moved to Madrid from Brussels before 1586, and a half-Flemish mother of noble Toledan ancestry. Van der Hamen and his two brothers (both of whom were writers) emphasized their Spanish roots by using all or part of their maternal grandmother's family name, Gómez de León. The artist inherited his father's honorary positions at court and also served as unsalaried Pintor del Rey. According to 18th-century sources, the artist's father had also been a painter, but there is no evidence for this. Van der Hamen's artistic activity in the service of the crown is first recorded on 10 September 1619, when he was paid for painting a still-life for the country palace of El Pardo, to the north of Madrid. He painted religious history paintings, allegories, landscapes, low-life subjects, portraits and still-lifes but the last two categories brought him the greatest fame.

Van der Hamen's still-lifes reflect the strong influence of those painted at the beginning of the 17th century in Toledo by Juan Sánchez Cotán, in which fruit and vegetables are often shown suspended from a window frame or arranged along a ledge. However, as can be seen in van der Hamen's elegant *Still-life with Sweets and Glassware* (1622; Madrid, Prado), he adapted Sánchez Cotán's compositional style to the conditions of cosmopolitan life in Madrid, ranging elaborate confections, imported Venetian crystals and ceramic vessels along a simple stone shelf. The objects are silhouetted against a dark background and caught in a powerful light. Their regular, zigzag arrangement and the strong shadows falling on the shelf result in a lucid sense of space that is heightened by the impression given by wafers extending beyond the edge of the shelf towards the viewer. Whether in this format or in a symmetrical composition (e.g. *Basket of Fruit*, 1623; Madrid, Prado), which van der Hamen often used before 1626, his works are bound together by a strict geometry, resulting in a sense of spatial clarity and an abstract interplay of formal elements.

Most of van der Hamen's surviving still-lifes from 1626 onwards reveal a more elaborate arrangement of objects, in three distinct planes, using stepped stone plinths whose plain grey colour offsets the rich detail of the objects, fruit and flowers that are arrayed upon them before an empty

Juan van der Hamen y León: *Still-life with Sweets and Pottery*, oil on canvas, 842×1128 mm, 1627 (Washington, DC, National Gallery of Art)

dark space. *Still-life with Sweets and Pottery* (1627; Washington, DC, N.G.A.; see fig.) comprises circular, spherical and cylindrical shapes whose formal interplay provides a powerful internal structure supporting a skilful description of surface detail.

During the 1620s van der Hamen painted a series of bust-length portraits of the principal intellectuals and writers of his time, including Lope de Vega (1562–1635), Francisco de Quevedo (1580–1645), Luis de Góngora (1561–1627), José de Valdivielso, Juan Pérez de Montalván, Juan Ruiz de Alarcón (*c*. 1580–1639) and Francisco de Rioja. On van der Hamen's death, 20 of these portraits were inventoried as a single item among his belongings. The portrait of his older brother *Lorenzo van der Hamen* (Madrid, Inst. Valencia Don Juan) probably belonged to this series. The series itself was a focal point for philosophic speculation on the art of portraiture by some of the most fertile minds of the time: van der Hamen was one of the most frequently lauded artists in contemporary verse and prose encomiums.

In 1626, when Cardinal Francesco Barberini visited Madrid for five months as papal legate in the company of Cassiano dal Pozzo, van der Hamen was asked to paint the Cardinal's portrait after one executed by Diego Velázquez had failed to please the sitter. Well satisfied with van der Hamen's work (untraced), Barberini acquired three further portraits from him. The *Portrait of a Dwarf* (Madrid, Prado; perhaps Bartolillo, who amused Charles, Prince of Wales, on his visit to the Escorial in 1623 and who served Philip IV until at least 1626) is powerfully naturalistic.

As a painter of religious subjects, van der Hamen worked for several of the major institutions in and around Madrid. Although 18th-century sources such as Palomino, Ponz and Ceán Bermúdez mention the subject-matter of quite a few of them, the only surviving examples are in the cloister of the convent of the Encarnación in Madrid, notably the large *Vision of the Apocalypse* (1625), painted in a naturalistic, tenebrist style.

Two large canvases, perhaps intended as a pair, reveal van der Hamen's application of his skill as a still-life painter to figural compositions: *Pomona and Vertumnus* (1626; Madrid, Banco de España) depicts the goddess of fruit-trees dressed in silks and seated in an autumnal landscape beside a cornucopia that spills a profusion of fruit upon the ground at her feet; the *Offering to Flora* (1627; Madrid, Prado) shows the goddess of flowers seated beside a cornucopia of spring flowers. Both paintings adopt a Flemish compositional type and reveal an interest in the play of light on iridescent fabrics that probably derives from the Caravaggesque style of Juan Bautista Maino.

Ceán Bermúdez

BIBLIOGRAPHY

J. Pérez de Montalván: 'Indice de los ingenios de Madrid', *Para todos, exemplos morales, humanos y divinos* (Huesca, 1633), fol. 11*r*
F. Pacheco: *Arte* (1649); ed. F. Sánchez Cotán (1956), ii, pp. 125–6
A. A. Palomino de Castro y Velasco: *Museo pictórico*, iii (1724/*R* 1947), pp. 886–7
A. Ponz: *Viaje* (1772–94); ed. C. M. de Rivero (1947), pp. 119, 430, 456, 878, 972
J. A. Alvárez y Baena: *Hijos de Madrid, ilustres en santidad, dignidades, armas, ciencias y artes* (Madrid, 1789–91/*R* 1973), iii, p. 212
Conde de la Viñaza: *Adiciones al diccionario* (1889–94), iv, p. 12
E. Tormo y Monzó: 'La clausura de la Encarnación en Madrid', *Bol. Soc. Esp. Excurs.*, xxv (1917), pp. 131–4
F. J. Sánchez Cantón: *Fuentes literarias para la historia del arte español* (Madrid, 1923–41), ii, p. 369; v, pp. 169–70, 399–400, 419
I. Bergström: 'Juan van der Hamen y León', *L'Oeil*, cviii (1963), pp. 24–31
W. B. Jordan: 'Juan van der Hamen y León: A Madrilenian Still-life Painter', *Marsyas*, xii (1964–5), pp. 52–69
——: *Juan van der Hamen y León* (diss., New York U., 1967)
E. Harris: 'Cassiano dal Pozzo on Diego Velázquez', *Burl. Mag.*, cxii (1970), pp. 364–73
J.-R. Triadó: 'Juan van der Hamen, bodegonista', *Estud. Pro A.*, i (1975), pp. 31–76
J. Held: 'Verzicht und Zeremoniell: Zu den Stilleben von Sánchez Cotán und van der Hamen', *Stilleben in Europa* (exh. cat., Münster, Westfäl. Landesmus., 1980), pp. 380–401
Pintura española de bodegones y floreros de 1600 a Goya (exh. cat. by A. E. Pérez Sánchez, Madrid, Prado, 1983), pp. 41–3, nos 15–29
Spanish Still-life in the Golden Age; 1600–1650 (exh. cat. by W. B. Jordan, Fort Worth, TX, Kimbell A. Mus., 1985), pp. 103–46

WILLIAM B. JORDAN

Hamerani. Italian family of engravers and medallists, of Bavarian origin. They worked mainly in the Roman mint from the mid-17th century to the end of the 18th. The medals they made are notable above all for their documentary value relating to the history of Rome and the city's monuments. They were technically skilled but somewhat unimaginative portrait artists. Johan Andreas Hamerani (*b* Adensburg, *c*. 1600; *d* Livorno, 1644) arrived in Rome in 1615 during the pontificate of Pope Paul V. Although he worked in the papal mint, he did not execute annual medals. His son Alberto Hamerani (*b* Rome, 10 Oct 1620; *d* Rome, 21 June 1677) worked for a short time at the mint of Massa Carrara, then, between 1657 and 1669, in Rome, as assistant first to Gaspare Morone Mola and later to Girolamo Lucenti. From 1667 he engraved papal seals. Noteworthy among his medals was one commemorating the entry into Rome of Queen Christina of Sweden (1655).

The most significant member of the family was Giovanni Hamerani (*b* Rome, 10 Feb 1646; *d* Rome, 28 June 1705), son of Alberto Hamerani. After working with his father in the mint at Massa Carrara, he was appointed engraver of the papal mint. From 1681 he was sole medallist to the papacy, in which capacity he worked for popes Innocent XI, Alexander VIII (1689–91) and Clement XI, executing seals for the papal court. He also worked for private citizens: for example, he made a medal of *Livio Odescalchi* (1689), the reverse of which shows the sun with rays emerging from the hemisphere and in which Italy is outlined with its islands and surrounding lands and seas. He had three children who followed the family profession. The oldest was Beatrice Hamerani (*b* Rome, 1675; *d* Rome, 1705), whose best-known medal bears a vigorous portrait of *Pope Innocent XII* and, on the reverse, the pelican opening its breast to nourish its children. Beatrice's brother Ermenegildo Hamerani (*b* Rome, 25 Sept 1683; *d* Rome, 29 Nov 1756) succeeded his father as engraver to the papal mint in 1704; he executed numerous medals for the popes of the first half of the 18th century, from Clement XI to Benedict XIV, and also for private patrons. The reverse sides of some of his medals are distinguished for their complexity, for example the medal of *Clement XI* (1706) with a view of the port of Ripetta, the church of S Rocco and the Palazzo Borghese. In 1730 he worked for Charles-Emanuel III, King of Sardinia, in the Palermo mint. Ermenegildo's brother Ottone Hamerani (*b* Rome, 7 Nov, 1694; *d* Rome, 21 March 1761), also worked in the papal mint, producing medals for popes Clement XI to Clement XIII, as well as for King John V of Portugal and James Stuart, the 'Old Pretender' (1688–1766). In 1716 he made a medal for Clement XI to commemorate Sultan Ahmed III's victory over the Venetians. On the obverse, the rulers of Christian lands, including the Doge of Venice, genuflect before the enthroned pope while in the background the Sultan emerges from his tent. On the reverse the pope is depicted in grandiose style and rich detail, kneeling before the altar of the cathedral in St Peter's, flanked by bishops, soldiers and other figures. Ottone also made various medals for private individuals and prelates, including one for Giuseppe Cervi, the King of Spain's physician, and several for Nicola Coscia, Archbishop of Benevento, and for Cardinal Angelo Maria Quirini, Bishop of Brescia. The reverse sides of many of his medals show monuments of Rome and of other cities, for example the port and the leper hospital of Ancona, the façade of S Giovanni in Laterano, or the cross-section of the Corsini chapel in S Giovanni. Ottone's grandson Gioacchino Hamerani (*b* Rome, 1766; *d* Rome, 1796) worked in the Roman mint during the pontificate of Pius VI. He created medals for the pope and for such private individuals as Marco Antonio Giustinian and Cardinal Henry Benedict Stuart (1725–1807), the son of James Stuart. On the reverse sides of his medals are sober scenes whose coldness of composition reflects the art of the time.

BIBLIOGRAPHY

Thieme–Becker
L. Forrer: *Biographical Dictionary of Medallists*, ii (London, 1904)
F. Bartolotti: *La medaglia annuale dei Romani pontefici* (Rome, 1967), pp. 84–182
F. Panvini Rosati: *Medaglie e placchette italiane dal rinascimento al XVIII secolo* (Rome, 1968), pp. 56–9
Mostra della medaglia barocca (exh. cat. by V. Johnson, Udine, 1976), pp. 213–24
N. T. Whitman: *Roma Resurgens: Papal Medals from the Age of the Baroque* (Chicago, 1983), pp. 128–84
F. Vannel and G. Toderi: *La medaglia barocca in Toscana* (Florence, 1987), p. 24
C. Johnson: *Collezione Johnson di medaglie*, ii (Milan, 1990), pp. 476–513

FRANCO PANVINI ROSATI

Hamerton, Philip Gilbert (*b* Lane Side, Haslingden, Lancs, 10 Sept 1834; *d* Boulogne-sur-Seine, 4 Nov 1894). English critic. He was educated at Burnley and Doncaster grammar schools and later studied painting with Joseph Paul Pettitt (1812–82) in London and William Wyld in Paris. He taught himself art criticism, chiefly by reading John Ruskin. Early efforts to become a photographic landscape painter led him to the English Lake District and the Scottish island of Innistrynich, Loch Awe, resulting in his first books: *The Isles of Loch Awe and other Poems of my Youth* (London, 1855), *A Painter's Camp in the Highlands* (1862) and *Thoughts about Art* (1862). He married Eugénie Gindriez in 1858, and by 1861 they had settled in France, first in Sens, then shortly afterwards in Pré-Charmoy. If Hamerton failed to become a successful artist, he did become a prolific writer whose numerous books were read extensively on both sides of the Atlantic and beyond. He made his début as a critic with a review

of the Paris Salon of 1863 that appeared in the *Fine Arts Quarterly Review* (i, p. 343). Hamerton set forth themes in this review that would reappear throughout his writing career; he argued for greater national efficiency in the circulation of artistic products, advocated conservative aesthetic values and aimed to foster an appreciation of contemporary art through an understanding of its technique. During the 1860s he contributed articles and book reviews to the *Cornhill Magazine*, *Macmillan's Magazine* and the *Fortnightly Review*.

In 1866 Hamerton assumed Francis Palgrave's responsibilities as art critic for the *Saturday Review*, a post he held until 1868, the year that *Etching and Etchers*, arguably his best-known work, was published. The book was quickly acknowledged as a landmark in the revival of etching and remained so through the early years of the 20th century. By turns a synthesis of the history of printmaking, a technical manual and a collector's guide, *Etching and Etchers* found an enthusiastic audience throughout the English-speaking world. With Seymour Haden, Hamerton was a key figure in the revival of etching in England and America. Hamerton edited *The Portfolio* from 1870, its first year of publication, until 1894, the year of his death. Under his editorship *The Portfolio* communicated the aesthetics of the French etching revival and, by publishing the work of English artists, sought to advance the cause of the contemporary artist, particularly the 'painter-etcher'.

Hamerton's books include a biography of J. M. W. Turner, novels, compilations of his essays drawn from *The Portfolio* and other sources, a book of poems and travel literature. He wrote about art for the non-specialist, adopting a clear writing style that was both persuasive and popular. The fact that he practised the crafts of painting and etching lent credibility to his books, as did their simplicity of thought and expression.

WRITINGS

The Isles of Loch Awe and other Poems of my Youth (London, 1855, 2/1859)
A Painter's Camp in the Highlands (London, 1862)
Thoughts about Art (London, 1862)
Contemporary French Painters (London, 1868)
Etching and Etchers (London, 1868)
Painting in France after the Decline of Classicism (London, 1869)
The Intellectual Life (London, 1873)
The Life of J. M. W. Turner (London, 1879)
The Graphic Arts: A Treatise on the Varieties of Drawing, Painting and Engraving in Comparison with One Another and with Nature (London, 1882)
Landscape (London, 1885)
Imagination in Landscape Painting (London, 1887)
Portfolio Papers (London, 1889)
Man in Art (London, 1892)
The Etchings of Rembrandt (London, 1894)
with E. Hamerton: *Philip Gilbert Hamerton: An Autobiography, 1834–1858, and a Memoir by his Wife, 1858–1894* (London, 1896)

MARIE CZACH

Hamesse, Paul (*b* Brussels, 7 April 1877; *d* Brussels, 22 Feb 1956). Belgian interior designer and architect. He was the son of the painter Adolphe Hamesse (1849–1925) and studied architecture at the Académie Royale des Beaux-Arts in Brussels. He then worked successively in the offices of Paul Hankar and Alban Chambon. With the latter he found his true vocation in interior design using numerous ornamental components, manufactured industrially, which he excelled at combining in Art Nouveau compositions. Assisted by his two brothers, the painters Georges Hamesse (*b* 1874) and Léon Hamesse (*b* 1883), he responded to the eclectic tastes of the period by exploiting a very broad range of styles in such commissions as the Cohn-Donnay house (1904), the Ameke department store (1905), a masonic lodge (1909) and the Théâtre des Variétés (1909), all in Brussels. He also worked on a number of cinemas in Brussels, including the Artistic Palace (1913), Pathé Palace (1913; destr.), Queen's Hall (1919) and Agora (1920–21), as well as a project (*c.* 1914; unexecuted) for a grand hotel near a railway station, whose bold design is reminiscent of a city of the future (see exh. cat.). The more austere period following World War I prevented the Hamesse brothers from demonstrating their originality to the full, but with the revival of the taste for decoration in *c.* 1925, the year of the Exposition des Arts Décoratifs et Industriels Modernes in Paris, they were able to design several shop windows in the main commercial streets of Brussels in the Art Deco style, some large villas in the suburbs and some town houses in the second ring of development around Brussels. In 1927 they took part in the competition for the Palace of the League of Nations in Geneva.

BIBLIOGRAPHY

L. Pierard: 'Nos architectes, les frères Hamesse', *Le Home*, ix (1911), pp. 13–15
Antoine Pompe et l'effort moderne en Belgique, 1890–1940 (exh. cat., ed. M. Culot and F. Terlinden; Brussels, Mus. Ixelles, 1969), p. 129
Monumenten en landschappen, 1 (1981) [illus.]
F. Loyer: *Paul Hankar: La Naissance de l'Art Nouveau* (Brussels, 1986) [illus.]

HERVÉ PAINDAVEINE

Hamilton [Douglas-Hamilton], **Alexander**, 10th Duke of Hamilton [7th Duke of Brandon] (*b* Hamilton, 3 Oct 1767; *d* London, 18 Aug 1852). Scottish landowner, diplomat, collector and patron. He developed an interest in art while living in Italy as a young man. In 1802 he was elected to Parliament and in 1806–7 served as Ambassador to St Petersburg. By this time he was buying paintings on the advice of Samuel Woodburn. Among the important Old Masters purchased by him were Poussin's *Lamentation over the Dead Christ* (Dublin, N.G.) and several paintings subsequently acquired for the National Gallery, London: Filippino Lippi's *Adoration of the Magi*, Tintoretto's *Christ Washing the Disciples' Feet* (*c.* 1556) and Rubens's *Birth of Venus* (*c.* 1632–3). In 1810 he married Susan Euphemia, second daughter of William Beckford and, in 1812, commissioned from Jacques-Louis David a painting of *Napoleon in his Study* (Washington, DC, N.G.A.). He also assembled a fine collection of 17th- and 18th-century French furniture, much of which had belonged to Marie-Antoinette, Queen of France, and rare manuscripts and books. In 1844 he inherited Velázquez's *Philip IV in Brown and Silver* (*c.* 1631–5; London, N.G.) from the Beckford estate, as well as Beckford's superb library, for which he added a wing to Hamilton Palace. Works of art from his collection were auctioned at Christie's, London, between 6 June and 21 July 1882, raising the then record total of £397,562. The Beckford holdings were sold by Sotheby, Wilkinson and Hodge in 1882 and 1883 and his own library on 1–9 May 1884.

BIBLIOGRAPHY

G. Waagen: *Treasures of Art in Great Britain*, ii (London, 1854/*R* 1970), pp. 295–309
G. Redford: *Art Sales: A History of Sales of Pictures and Other Works of Art*, 2 vols (London, 1888); i, pp. 319–45
J. Paul, ed.: *The Scots Peerage*, iv (Edinburgh, 1907), p. 395
F. Herrmann: *The English as Collectors* (London, 1972), pp. 238, 345, 348

R. WINDSOR LISCOMBE

Hamilton, Cuthbert (*b* India, 15 Feb 1884; *d* Cookham, Berks, 13 March 1959). English painter, designer, ceramicist and sculptor. He studied at the Slade School of Fine Art between 1899 and 1903, where Wyndham Lewis was a fellow student, and then taught art at Clifton College (1907–10). It seems that Hamilton was in sympathy with avant-garde developments since he was involved *c.* 1912 with the Cave of the Golden Calf, the audacious cabaret club decorated with murals and sculpture by Jacob Epstein, Eric Gill, Charles Ginner, Spencer Gore and Wyndham Lewis. His work was shown in the final month of Roger Fry's *Second Post-Impressionist Exhibition* (January 1913) in London, and later that year he joined the Omega Workshops, designing furniture, clothes and avant-garde interiors. In October 1913, however, he left Omega with Frederick Etchells, Lewis and Edward Wadsworth in protest against Fry's policy.

Hamilton's work was included in the 'Cubist Room' section of the *Camden Town Group and Others* exhibition in Brighton (December 1913–January 1914). Soon afterwards he became an active member of the Rebel Art Centre and then signed the Vorticist manifesto in *Blast* magazine. A work called *Group* (untraced, see *Blast*, 1, 1914) shows an enthusiastic involvement with the most explosive aspects of Vorticism: its angular figures, strongly mechanistic in structure, appear to be thrusting out towards the boundaries of the composition. The loss of Hamilton's Vorticist paintings obstructs a clear assessment of his contribution to the movement. His work did not appear in the Vorticist Exhibition of June 1915 in London, but after World War I he rejoined the former Vorticists when they exhibited together for the last time in Group X at the Mansard Gallery, London, in the spring of 1920. *Reconstruction* (London, Tate), a vigorous Vorticist image, is one of his few surviving works. Hamilton later devoted his energies to pottery and sculpture, founding the Yeoman Potteries, but he is remembered primarily for his work as a Vorticist.

BIBLIOGRAPHY

W. C. Wees: *Vorticism and the English Avant-garde* (Manchester, 1972)
Vorticism and its Allies (exh. cat. by R. Cork, London, Hayward Gal., 1974)
R. Cork: *Vorticism and Abstract Art in the First Machine Age*, 2 vols (London, 1976)

RICHARD CORK

Hamilton, David (*b* Glasgow, 11 May 1768; *d* Glasgow, 5 Dec 1843). Scottish architect. The son of William Hamilton, a mason, he was admitted to the Incorporation of Masons in Glasgow in 1800. Little is known of his early architectural training, although he may have been acquainted with Robert Adam (i) and James Adam (i) since he made many copies of their drawings at a time when they were virtually unknown. Hamilton developed a large practice, mainly confined to Glasgow and the west of

Scotland. He showed a particular feeling for theatricality in his work, which is seen in his sometimes idiosyncratic employment of styles and the inclusion of carving and statues on his buildings. His earliest recorded building of note is the Neo-classical Hutcheson's Hall (1802–5), Ingram Street, Glasgow, which incorporates two 17th-century statues from the former Hutcheson's Hospital. Other commissions included his monument to *Lord Nelson* (1806), Glasgow Green, which was the first to be erected in Britain in memory of Nelson; it consists of an obelisk (44 m) on a plain plinth. Early residential work included a new front (1807) for Airth Castle, Stirlingshire, for T. G. Stirling, where the addition of a battlemented screen to the medieval castle produced an interesting V plan; and in 1809 he designed a domestic Gothic-style addition to Crawford Priory (ruined), Fife, for Lady Mary Lindsay Crawford.

Hamilton used the Greek Revival style for the town steeple at Falkirk (1813–14), Stirlingshire, and for the less successful Port Glasgow Town Buildings (1815–16), Renfrewshire, which are dominated by a tall steeple and Doric tetrastyle portico. For his enlargement (1813) of Kincaid House, Stirlingshire, he used a simple, symmetrical Adam castle style, but he later designed a picturesque, asymmetrical castellated mansion (1820–21) nestling in the trees at Castle Towards, Argyll, for Kirkman Finlay. At Keir, Dunblane, Perthshire, he conceived a circular lodge with an integral Doric gateway (1820), an ingenious design brilliantly executed; he later added a very large drawing room and gallery to the house (1829–34).

The culmination of Hamilton's career was the building of the Royal Exchange (1827–32), Glasgow, when he encased an existing mansion, built in 1778–80 by William Cunninghame of Lainshaw, with a Greco-Roman exterior incorporating a great Corinthian octastyle portico and giant pilasters carrying an elaborate parapet. The newsroom added at the back, with its fluted Corinthian columns and richly coffered ceiling, is considered Glasgow's most magnificent early 19th-century interior. Later residential work included Dunlop House (1831–4), Ayrshire, built for Sir James Dunlop, where Hamilton used a Scottish Jacobean style; and Lennox Castle (1837–41), Lennoxtown, Stirlingshire, built for J. L. Kincaid Lennox, where he designed one of the only Romanesque Revival buildings in Scotland. His competition entry (1836) for the Houses of Parliament in London was another design in Scottish Jacobean and was placed third.

Hamilton's last public work was the Western Club (1840; later enlarged), Buchanan Street, Glasgow, an Italianate palazzo design. In his church architecture he usually followed a simple Gothic Revival style with battlemented towers, as at Erskine Bishopton Church (1813–14), Renfrewshire, and Campsie High Church (1827–8), Lennoxtown, both in Stirlingshire; and at his last work, Ascog Free Church (*c.* 1843), Isle of Bute. About 1840 Hamilton was joined by his son James (1818–61), who continued the practice after his father's death in partnership with his brother-in-law James Smith (1808–63); financial problems inherited from his father led to his early retirement. Among the assistants whose later work was influenced by Hamilton was Charles Wilson.

BIBLIOGRAPHY

Colvin; Papworth

A. Gomme and D. Walker: *Architecture of Glasgow* (London, 1968)

CATHERINE H. CRUFT

Hamilton, Gavin (*b* Murdieston, Lothian, 1723; *d* Rome, 4 Jan 1798). Scottish painter, archaeologist and dealer, active in Italy. He was educated at Glasgow University and in 1748 arrived in Rome to study portrait painting under Agostino Masucci. He lodged with the architects James Stuart and Nicholas Revett; they probably encouraged him to visit Herculaneum and the recently discovered archaeological site of Pompeii, which had a profound effect on his subsequent career. Convinced that 'the ancients have surpassed the moderns, both in painting and sculpture', Hamilton undertook a systematic study of Classical antiquities during the 1750s and 1760s. In 1751 he was briefly in Scotland, where he painted a full-length portrait of *Elizabeth Gunning, Duchess of Hamilton* (Lennoxlove, Lothian), in a conventional style derived from van Dyck. He returned to Rome in 1752 and remained there, with the exception of short visits to England, for the rest of his life. In 1755 he was introduced by Anton Raphael Mengs to Johann Joachim Winckelmann, who was to become one of the leading theorists of Neoclassicism. In the same year Hamilton entertained Robert Adam (i), who studied in Rome from 1755 to 1757. He was to know and encourage almost all the British artists who worked in Rome during the second half of the 18th century. Henry Fuseli, who was not an uncritical admirer, wrote of Hamilton in 1805, 'however eminent his talents or other qualities were, they were excelled by the liberality, benevolence and humanity of his character'.

In 1758 Hamilton painted *Robert Wood and James Dawkins Discovering Palmyra* (U. Glasgow, Hunterian A.G.). The two explorers are shown, incongruously, in Roman togas, although their entourage wear contemporary dress. Two years later, encouraged by Nathaniel Dance, he painted his first true history painting, *Andromache Bewailing the Death of Hector* (untraced; engraved by Domenico Cunego; see fig.). The subject, taken from Greek legend, was praised by Winckelmann and much admired when the picture was shown at the Society of Artists in London in 1762. The composition reveals a debt to Nicolas Poussin and to Classical reliefs, which also provided authentic sources for the architecture, dress and accessories. This was the first painting of Hamilton's 'great plan in life', a series of Homeric subjects executed for different patrons over a period of 15 years during the 1760s and 1770s. This first series (a second was painted in the 1780s) also includes *Hector Taking Leave of Andromache* (Lennoxlove, on loan to U. Glasgow, Hunterian A.G.). Hamilton commissioned an engraving of each picture from Domenico Cunego, which allowed wide circulation and greatly increased his influence. In addition to his Homeric subjects he drew upon Roman history for one of his most influential paintings, *Brutus Promising to Avenge the Death of Lucretia* (1763; London, Theatre Royal, Drury Lane), which was to inspire indirectly Fuseli's *Oath of the Rutli* (1778; Zurich, Rathaus) and Jacques-Louis David's *Oath of the Horatii* (1784; Paris, Louvre). A rare subject from Scottish history, the *Abdication of Mary Queen of Scots* (exh. RA 1776; U. Glasgow, Hunterian

Engraving after Gavin Hamilton by Domenico Cunego: *Andromache Bewailing the Death of Hector*, 457×629 mm, 1764 (London, British Museum)

A.G.), was commissioned by James Boswell. *Il Penseroso* and *L'Allegro* (both untraced; engraved 1768) are the earliest Neo-classical works inspired by the poetry of John Milton.

Hamilton's history paintings were intended to stir noble and universal emotions and exhibit the qualities of calmness (which Winckelmann thought the chief characteristic of Greek art), nobility and lack of the particular so admired by contemporary theorists. Stylistically they owe a compositional debt to Poussin, while Hamilton's palette reveals the influence of 17th-century Bolognese painters. The figures are often smooth to the point of blandness, a quality thought at the time to be typical of Classical art as exemplified in the *Apollo Belvedere*, which Hamilton, in common with Winckelmann and Joshua Reynolds, greatly admired. His second Homeric series, commissioned by Prince Marcantonio IV Borghese, coincided with his decoration in 1782–4 of a room in the Villa Borghese with scenes from the *Story of Paris and Helen*. The ceiling panels remain in the villa, three large wall panels are in the Museo di Roma, Palazzo Braschi.

Hamilton never painted an uncommissioned work, and his prices were high: *Achilles Lamenting the Death of Patroclus* cost Sir James Grant £300 in the early 1760s. He nevertheless augmented his income by dealing. From the early 1760s he acquired and sold Italian paintings, travelling with a copyist to replace the religious works that he bought. His greatest coups were the purchases of Raphael's Ansidei *Madonna* in 1764 and Leonardo's *Virgin of the Rocks* in 1785 (both now London, N.G.). In 1773 he published *Schola italica picturae*, a textless volume of 40 engravings of 16th- and 17th-century Italian paintings, designed to form taste and stimulate trade. From the late 1760s Hamilton also undertook archaeological excavations. The most important and lucrative of these was that of Hadrian's Villa at Tivoli (1769–71), where the finds included the Warwick Vase (Glasgow, Burrell Col.) purchased by Sir William Hamilton, and the Newdigate Candelabrum (Oxford, Ashmolean). The sale of the candelabrum involved the collaboration of Giovanni Battista Piranesi, who restored and published the piece before its purchase in 1775. Hamilton made a profit of £2000 from his three years' work at Hadrian's Villa. Despite the great success of his history paintings he continued to paint the occasional portrait. *The 8th Duke of Hamilton with Dr John Moore and Ensign Moore* (Lennoxlove, Lothian), completed in 1777, is particularly successful. The painting owes a debt to Pompeo Batoni but has an individual naturalism. His other late portraits—*Emma Hart, Lady Hamilton as a Sibyl* (priv. col.) and *Lady Hamilton as Hebe* (priv. col.; version, Burghley House, Cambs), both painted in 1786—were inspired not only by Emma Hart's beauty but also by his own friendship with Sir William Hamilton. In 1779 Hamilton met the Venetian sculptor Antonio Canova newly arrived in Rome and was instrumental in persuading him to abandon Rococo for the more restrained Neo-classical style in which he was to excel. Although Hamilton's only identifiable pupil was David Allan, his encouragement assisted artists in Rome for over 30 years, and the example of his paintings inspired artists of his own and younger generations throughout Europe.

BIBLIOGRAPHY

D. Irwin: 'Gavin Hamilton: Archaeologist, Painter and Dealer', *A. Bull.*, xliv (1962), pp. 87–102

D. Irwin and F. Irwin: *Scottish Painters at Home and Abroad, 1700–1910* (London, 1975)

British Artists in Rome (exh. cat. by L. Stainton, London, Kenwood House, 1975)

DAVID RODGERS

Hamilton, Gawen (*b* nr Hamilton, Scotland, *c.* 1697; *d* London, 28 Oct 1737). Scottish painter. He was the pupil of a bird painter named Wilson (*fl* 1692–1723). From *c.* 1730 he lived in London, where he painted as a member of the St Luke's Club, specializing in conversation pieces and small full-length portraits. His best-known work is a *Conversation of Virtuosi at the Kings Armes* (1734–5; London, N.P.G.; *see* LONDON, fig. 17), a group portrait of the most famous artists of the day, including Michael Dahl, John Wootton, William Kent, James Gibbs, George Vertue and John Michael Rysbrack, but excluding William Hogarth. Other works by him are *Thomas Wentworth, 1st Earl of Strafford and his Family* (*c.* 1732; Ottawa, N.G.) and the *Porten Family* (*c.* 1736; Springfield, MA, Mus. F.A.). Hamilton was considered in his day to be one of the chief rivals of William Hogarth as a painter of conversation pieces.

BIBLIOGRAPHY

H. F. Finberg: 'Gawen Hamilton: An Unknown Scottish Portrait Painter', *Walpole Soc.*, vi (1917–18), pp. 51–8

'The Note-books of George Vertue', *Walpole Soc.*, xxii (1934), p. 71

R. Edwards: *Early Conversation Pictures* (London, 1954)

J. Kerslake: *Early Georgian Portraits*, London, N.P.G. cat., i (London, 1977), pp. 340–42

Manners and Morals: Hogarth and British Painting, 1700–1760 (exh. cat., ed. E. Einberg; London, Tate, 1987–9), nos 62–5

Hamilton, Hugh Douglas (*b* Dublin, *c.* 1740; *d* Dublin, 10 Feb 1808). Irish painter, active in England and Italy. He trained under Robert West at the Dublin Society's Drawing School, after which he moved to London in the early 1760s. There his skilfully executed pastel portraits attracted a large number of commissions from Irish and English sitters. Among his portraits of the royal family is that of *Queen Charlotte* (1769; Berlin, Kupferstichkab.); many others are in the British Royal Collection. In 1779 Hamilton travelled to Italy, where he soon attracted an impressive array of British patrons. These included George John, 2nd Earl Spencer (examples at Althorp House, Northants); Lady Hannah Cowper, for whom he made an oval portrait in pastel: *Countess Cowper* (*c.* 1787; Firle Place, E. Sussex); and the exiled Stuart royal family, for example the portraits in oil of *Charles Edward Stuart* (*c.* 1785; Dundee, Cent. Mus. and A.G.; Edinburgh, N.P.G.).

Hamilton spent 13 years in Rome and Florence. In Rome he became friendly with numerous artists, among them Antonio Canova, John Flaxman, Christopher Hewetson and Henry Tresham, and his portraits included that of the dealer *James Byres of Townley* (*c.* 1785; Aberdeen, A.G.). He had begun to paint in oils in 1783, producing a large, not wholly successful subject piece that year of *Diana and Endymion* (ex-art market, Dublin, 1984). Following his return to Dublin in 1792 he painted almost exclusively in oils. Economic necessity meant that portraiture was his dominant form of production, although the large *Cupid and Psyche in the Nuptial Bower* (*c.* 1793; Dublin, N.G.) proved to be a successful essay in erotic Neo-classicism. He exhibited in Dublin between 1800 and 1804; his quarter-length portraits of prominent figures such as *J. P. Curran* or *R. L. Edgeworth* (*c.* 1798–1800; Dublin, N.G.) received high praise in local reviews.

BIBLIOGRAPHY

Strickland

A. Crookshank and the Knight of Glin: *The Painters of Ireland, c. 1660–1920* (London, 1978), pp. 72–3, 91–5

F. Cullen: 'Hugh Douglas Hamilton in Rome, 1779–92', *Apollo*, cxv (1982), pp. 86–91

——: 'Hugh Douglas Hamilton: Painter of the Heart', *Burl. Mag.*, cxxv (1983), pp. 417–21

——: 'The Oil Paintings of Hugh Douglas Hamilton', *Walpole Soc.*, l (1984), pp. 165–208

——: 'Hugh Douglas Hamilton's Letters to Canova', *Irish A. Rev.*, i/2 (1984), pp. 31–5

FINTAN CULLEN

Hamilton (of Finnart), Sir James (i) (*b c.* 1496; *d* Edinburgh, 15 Aug 1540). Scottish architect. He was the great-grandson of King James II of Scotland (*reg* 1437–60) and the illegitimate son of James, first Earl of Arran; but for his illegitimacy he would have been heir to the throne. One of the key figures in the Scottish Renaissance court of King James V (*reg* 1513–42), he was ambassador to France (1517–18), leader of the Scottish army (1523), Captain of Home Castle, Dumbarton Castle, Blackness Castle and Linlithgow Palace, Lord of the Privy Council, Master of the King's Stables and Master of Works Principal, his remuneration being double that of the highest royal officials. Hamilton may have been Scotland's first architect. Recorded involvement in building includes a fortified villa at Craignethan (from 1532), Linlithgow Palace (from 1534), Boghouse of Crawfordjohn (1535), the state prison of Blackness (1535), the manor house in Greenock (1538) and the royal palace at Stirling (1538–40). It is possible that he was also responsible for the rebuilding of Home Castle (1518–19), Cambusnethan (1523), Cadzow Castle (1525), extensions to his town house in Linlithgow (1531), alterations to the castle of Avendale (1533) and to Dean Castle (1535), Kilmarnock.

Craignethan is Hamilton's masterpiece: a formal geometric composition within a rectangular towered courtyard, to a rigid set of proportions, unique in Scotland. Its defences include the only example in Scotland of a caponier (a defensive device by Francesco di Giorgio Martini). The principal chamber in Craignethan is a double cube with a vaulted roof. The nearest parallel in plan are the designs of Sebastiano Serlio, published five years later. Many of Hamilton's architectural preoccupations can be seen at Craignethan: his fondness for axial entry (also evident at Linlithgow Palace) and symmetry of façade (also at Avendale), his siting of the principal chambers on the ground floor (the only other example in Scotland being the palace of Stirling), and his use of a walled courtyard with high square towers to enfold a lodging. Hamilton was executed on a fabricated charge of treason, after which his enormous riches and landholding went to the King.

BIBLIOGRAPHY

I. MacIvor: 'Craignethan Castle', *Historic Scotland* (Edinburgh, 1993)

C. McKean: 'Hamilton of Finnart', *Hist. Today*, 43 (1993), pp. 43–7

'James Hamilton of Finnart: A Scottish Renaissance Icarus', *Scot. Local Hist.*, xxxii (1994)

CHARLES McKEAN

Hamilton, James (ii) (*b* Entrien, nr Belfast, 1819; *d* San Francisco, 10 March 1878). American painter of Irish birth. He emigrated to the USA and arrived in Philadelphia at the age of 15, where he was encouraged to study art by the engraver John Sartain (1808–97). Hamilton had drawing lessons with local teachers and studied from English artists' manuals including that on oil painting by Samuel Prout; he was also influenced by the English watercolour technique of broad transparent washes. With these stylistic interests and his innate sensitivity to nature, Hamilton's style evolved towards Romantic Impressionism and he became known as 'the American Turner'.

The use of watercolour dominated Hamilton's early career, particularly as the preparatory medium for his designs for book illustration. Most successful were his haunting illustrations of the Arctic based on the sketches made by the explorer Elisha Kent Kane during his voyages to the Arctic in 1850–51 and 1853–5. Some of the illustrations became the subjects of Hamilton's major oil paintings, notably *The 'Rescue' in her Arctic Ice Dock* (1852; Seneca Falls, NY, Hist. Soc. Mus.) and *Breaking up of an Iceberg in Melville Bay* (1852; Healdsburg, CA, I. McKibbin White priv. col.), and inspired such artists as Frederick Edwin Church and William Bradford to make their expeditions to paint polar regions. Although Hamilton enjoyed popular and critical acclaim as an artist during his lifetime, his work was inconsistent; at his best, for instance in *Foundering* (1863; New York, Brooklyn Mus.), he followed his natural inclination to spontaneity and suggestiveness, while the influence of his American contemporaries caused him to produce tighter, more precise lines to which he was less well suited. He died on the first leg of what was to have been a world tour financed by the sale of his paintings in 1875.

BIBLIOGRAPHY

'Arctic Adventure', *Blackwood's Edinburgh Mag.*, lxxxi (1857), pp. 366–79

J. I. H. Baur: 'A Romantic Impressionist: James Hamilton', *Brooklyn Mus. Bull.*, xii/3 (1951), pp. 1–8

E. K. Kane: *Artic Explorations: Second Grinell Expedition in Search of Franklin, 1853, '54, '55* (Philadelphia, 1956) [illus. Hamilton]

James Hamilton, 1819–1878: American Marine Painter (exh. cat. by A. Jacobowitz, New York, Brooklyn Mus., 1966)

James Hamilton: Arctic Watercolours (exh. cat. by C. Martin, Calgary, Glenbow–Alta Inst., 1983–4)

CONSTANCE MARTIN

Hamilton, Philipp Ferdinand de (*b* Brussels, *c.* 1664; *d* Vienna, 15 Sept 1750). Flemish painter. He was the son of the Scottish still-life painter James Hamilton (*c.* 1640–1720), who was active in Brussels. James had two other sons who became painters, Karl Wilhelm de Hamilton, called 'Thistle-Hamilton' (*c.* 1668–1754), and Johann Georg de Hamilton (1672–1737). Although born in Brussels, the three Hamilton sons spent their careers as court painters in central Europe, where they specialized in animal and still-life pictures. The same subjects were also painted by Franz de Hamilton (before 1650–after 1695), presumably a relative.

Philipp Ferdinand de Hamilton was employed in Vienna from 1705 as court painter to the emperor Joseph I, to his brother and successor Charles VI and later to Empress Maria-Theresa. The artist often signed his works with the initials *S.C. et R.M.C.P.* for *Suae Caesareae et Romanorum Maiestatis Curtialis Pictor* ('Court Painter to His Majesty the Holy Roman Emperor'). Early in his career, Hamilton created still-lifes of fruit and insects. His later works often featured dead game, as in *Game with Feather and Fur* (1698; Budapest, Mus. F.A.), which reflects Hamilton's knowledge of Dutch game painters such as Willem van Aelst and Jan Weenix. The ornate hunting bag and colourful birds on the stone slab, together with the precise brushwork and dramatic light, are typical of these artists. Hamilton also painted scenes of live animals and hunts, undoubtedly in response to the demands of his courtly patrons. The more spacious and animated style of these works (e.g. *Wolves and Dead Hind*, 1720; Vienna, Ksthist. Mus.) is in the Flemish tradition of Frans Snyders.

BIBLIOGRAPHY

R. H. Wilenski: *Flemish Painters, 1430–1830*, 2 vols (London, 1960), i, pp. 352, 369, 372, 380, 401, 569

Delights for the Senses: Dutch and Flemish Still-life Paintings from Budapest (exh. cat. by I. Ember, Budapest, Mus. F.A., 1989), nos 17, 18, pp. 74–7

SCOTT A. SULLIVAN

Hamilton, Richard (*b* London, 24 Feb 1922). English painter and printmaker. Three different strands of training and experience contributed to his early life and career after being taught briefly by Mark Gertler at Westminster Technical College in 1936: a traditional training at the Royal Academy Schools (1938–40, 1945–6), from which he was eventually expelled 'for not profiting by the instruction given in the Painting School'; experience in commercial art at the Design Unit (1941–2) and at the record company EMI (1942–5); and an avant-garde, modernist-influenced training at the Slade School of Fine Art (1948–51). These prepared the ground for his subsequent exploration of the means by which received boundaries between 'high' and 'low' art could be eliminated, in order to examine the relationships between diverse forms of expression, styles and currents of taste normally considered mutually exclusive.

As early as 1948 James Joyce and Marcel Duchamp became major influences on his thinking, first in drawings illustrating *Ulysses* and subsequently in his *Reaper* prints (1949–51; see *Richard Hamilton: Prints, 1939–83*, pp. 23–31). He participated in the discussions of the INDEPENDENT GROUP concerning popular culture, advertising, the media and mass art (1952–5), and he adapted elements from these forms in developing his distinctive stance. In the exhibition *Man, Machine and Motion* (U. Newcastle upon Tyne, Hatton Gal., and London, ICA, 1955), which Hamilton devised, he examined ways in which car design made covert statements about status, power and sexuality. These concerns paralleled the semiological analyses of contemporary writers such as Roland Barthes, Umberto Eco and Jean Baudrillard, in which everyday fashions, lifestyles and commodities came to be read as critiques of consumerism, revealing its ethics, its imagination and the way in which it transformed desires, values and expectations into particular styles. Such ideas were among the

Richard Hamilton: *Just What Is it that Makes Today's Homes So Different, So Appealing?*, collage, 260×250 mm, 1956 (Tübingen, Kunsthalle Tübingen)

themes of the collage *Just What Is it that Makes Today's Homes So Different, So Appealing?* (1956; Tübingen, Ksthalle; see fig.), which Hamilton produced for the exhibition *This Is Tomorrow* at the Whitechapel Art Gallery, London, in 1956. In this domestic interior scene a stereo-typed semi-nude couple cut from the pages of mass-circulation magazines disport themselves amid up-to-date accessories of comfortable living. This iconography of modernity, affluence and glamour, while appearing to promise a blissful picture of the forthcoming consumer paradise, is relayed with a questioning and ironic tone that announces the double-edged mode of parody, a character-istic of POP ART.

In a letter of 1957 Hamilton set himself an aesthetic programme based on a definition of consumerist everyday culture as 'Popular, Transient, Expendable, Low Cost, Mass Produced, Young, Witty, Sexy, Gimmicky, Glamor-ous, and Big Business'. In the paintings that followed, such as *£he* (1958–61; London, Tate) and *AAH!* (1962; priv. col., see *Collected Words*, p. 5), excerpts from popular culture are imitated to the letter only the better to depart from their spirit. Media spectacle and advertising mythol-ogy are cited and rendered so faithfully that they do not ring true, and a more circumspect, reflective attitude is evoked. The source material is rephrased and filtered through the conventions of fine art, treated with a cool detachment that neither glorified nor derided it. Hamil-ton's admiration for the skill that went into the artefacts of popular culture and the pleasure they could afford was tempered by his awareness of their manipulative stereo-typing. The 'ironic affirmation' of works such as the portrait of *Hugh Gaitskell as a Famous Monster of Filmland*

(1964; AC Eng), painted in oil over an enlarged black and white photograph of the then recently deceased leader of the British Labour party, not only refuted the period's snobbish dismissal of popular culture but replaced the direct moralizing of satire with a savage humour.

Two lines of stylistic development can be traced in Hamilton's work after 1964. The first emphasized chance and spontaneity within a conceptual approach inspired by Duchamp and Joyce, as in *Epiphany* (1964; artist's priv. col.), a homage to American Pop art conceived as a grossly enlarged badge bearing the message 'slip it to me'. The assisted or rectified readymade became his principal means of expression, particularly in prints such as *People* (screen-print, 1968; see *Richard Hamilton: Prints, 1939–83*, p. 50) and '*I'm Dreaming of a White Christmas*' (1969; for illustration *see* DYE TRANSFER), which were based on photographs retouched by hand in the manner of seaside postcards. *The Critic Laughs* (1971–2; see *Collected Words*, p. 73), a sculptural multiple made in part from an electric toothbrush, and *Palindrome* (1974; see *Prints, 1939–83*, p. 68), a laminated collotype giving the illusion of three dimensions, both used images to convey ideas, in the first case concerning art criticism and in the second in relation to the ambiguity of visual illusion. Other works such as the *Chicago Project Paintings* (1969; London, Brit. Council), which were ordered by telephone, dramatized the drive towards risk and randomness.

The second stylistic current after 1964 entailed a so-phisticated play with Hamilton's own and other art idi-oms—a mannerist tendency involving 'pictures about pictures', announced by the screenprint *A Little Bit of Roy Lichtenstein* (1964; see *Prints, 1939–83*, p. 42). An-other print, *Picasso's Meninas* (1973; see *Prints, 1939–83*, p. 65), elaborated the theme, paying homage to Picasso's variations of the 1950s on Velázquez's original through allusions to Picasso's successive styles. *In Horne's House* (1981–2; see *Richard Hamilton: Prints, 1939–83*, p. 81), based on Joyce's *Oxen of the Sun* parodies, depicted characters from *Ulysses* through a kaleidoscope of styles spanning the history of pictorial representation.

In the series *Collaborations of Ch. Rotham* (1977), Hamilton and Dieter Roth adopted various stylistic masks and voices: each cited, deliberately misquoted and traves-tied the other in pairs of pictures on which they both worked. These joint works confounded the normal bound-aries between the original work of art and its pastiche, implying that copying was not an aberration of Pop art's self-confessed plagiarism but the intrinsic condition of all artistic creation: a notion akin to Jacques Derrida's theories of deconstruction.

From the late 1970s Hamilton's activity was concen-trated largely on investigations of printmaking processes, often in unusual and complex combinations (see SCREEN-PRINTING, §2 and LITHOGRAPHY, §II, 2(ii)(c)). The delib-eration of his working methods, which had always restricted his production as a painter, led to his increasing emphasis on a small number of major canvases painted over a long period. One of the most widely exhibited of these, *The Citizen* (1982; London, Tate), took as its subject the 'blanket protest' of an Irish Republican prisoner in his cell. Divided into two equal sections recalling traditional devotional pictures in diptych form, it contrasts the Christ-like figure of the prisoner in the right-hand panel with an apparently abstract area that describes the cell wall smeared with excrement. While indicating the increased politicization of his work, it thus remains typical of his art in its richly ambiguous multiple readings.

WRITINGS
Richard Hamilton (exh. cat., New York, Guggenheim, 1973)
with D. Roth: Collaborations of Ch. Rotham (Stuttgart, 1977)
Collected Words (London, 1982)

BIBLIOGRAPHY
Richard Hamilton (exh. cat. by R. Morphet, London, Tate, 1970) [retro.]
Richard Hamilton: Studies—Studien, 1937–77 (exh. cat., ed. M. Pausebeck; Bielefeld, Städt. Ksthalle; Tübingen, Ksthalle; Göttingen, Kstver.; 1978)
R. S. Field: Richard Hamilton: Image and Process (London, 1983) [graph. work]
Richard Hamilton: Prints, 1939–83 (London, 1984) [fully illus. cat. rais.]
S. C. Maharaj: The Dialectic of Modernism and Mass Culture: A Historical and Stylistic Study of Pop Art in Britain with Particular Reference to Richard Hamilton's and Eduardo Paolozzi's Work (1940–84) (diss., Reading U., 1985)
D. Leach-Ruhl: Studien zu Richard Hamilton: Das Frühwerk (diss., Bochum, Ruhr U., 1986)
Richard Hamilton (exh. cat. by M. Francis, Edinburgh, Fruitmarket Gal.; Oxford, MOMA; 1988) [installations]
Richard Hamilton (exh. cat., London, Tate; Dublin, Irish MOMA; 1992–3)

S. C. MAHARAJ

Hamilton, Thomas (b Glasgow, 11 Jan 1784; d Edinburgh, 24 Feb 1858). Scottish architect. He was a leading Neo-classical architect of early 19th-century Edinburgh. His father, Thomas Hamilton, was a mason from Edinburgh, temporarily resident in Glasgow when his son was a child. By 1794 the family had returned to Edinburgh, and Thomas Hamilton senior became a successful speculative builder involved in the New Town. Thomas junior received a classical education at the High School in Edinburgh, was apprenticed under his father (1801) and appears to have entered the family business. In 1816 his higher ambitions were demonstrated when he unsuccessfully entered the competition to complete Robert Adam's university buildings. In 1817 he anonymously published an article in the Scots Magazine proposing large-scale road improvements to open up the Old Town. These plans were not immediately adopted but formed the basis for the work later implemented by the Edinburgh Improvements Commission (set up in 1827), for which he was the architect between 1827 and 1834. The Commission was beset with financial difficulties and disputes, but its great achievement was the construction of the George IV and King's bridges and their associated thoroughfares.

Meanwhile, it took some time for Hamilton to establish himself. In 1819 he unsuccessfully attempted to become superintendent of Edinburgh City Works, but in 1820 he won the competition for the Burns Monument at Alloway. The monument, built 1820–23, was based on the choregic monument of Lysikrates published in Stuart and Revett's Antiquities of Athens (London, 1762), and it attracted a great deal of favourable publicity. In 1824 Hamilton was commissioned to design assembly rooms for the British Hotel, Edinburgh (known as the Hopetoun Rooms; destr. 1967). They were Hamilton's best interiors, top lit and with caryatids supporting a central rotunda. The following year he won the competition to design the new

Royal High School (later known as the Old High School), Edinburgh, his best-known building (completed 1829). The splendidly sited school was an adaptation to modern use of the windowless Greek temple; with its careful and correct detailing, it is one of Britain's most important Greek Revival monuments. Furniture that Hamilton designed for the school was dispersed during the last decades of the 20th century. The High School established Hamilton's reputation. In 1827 he designed the Municipal Buildings in Ayr, the neo-Baroque tower and spire of which still dominate the town. His Orphan Hospital, Belford Road, Edinburgh, designed in 1831, is a slightly clumsy essay in John Vanbrugh's monumental manner; in the same year he designed the Burns Monument, Regent Street, Edinburgh, another classical rotunda. Hamilton never travelled abroad but was capable, as in this monument, of using correct Antique details.

Hamilton designed churches in an unremarkable Gothic style. His first commission (unexecuted) was in 1829 for the John Knox Church, Edinburgh. Following an apparently fallow period of his career in the mid-1830s, he designed Alyth Parish Church (1836), the Episcopal Chapel (1842), Dunfermline, and at least five other churches from 1843 to 1850, all in the Romanesque Revival or Gothic Revival styles. He is also known to have designed a handful of country houses and villas, including Kirkhill House (c. 1828), near Gorebridge, Midlothian, but he never enjoyed the success of his contemporary William Burn in this field. Hamilton's last building of importance was the Royal College of Physicians (1844), Queen Street, Edinburgh; his designs for the new Scottish Academy and National Gallery (1847) were turned down in favour of those by William Henry Playfair. Hamilton is known to have taken on only three minor commissions after 1850, in which he was assisted by his son, Peter Hamilton (1817–61).

BIBLIOGRAPHY
Colvin; Macmillan Enc. Architects; Papworth
Obituary: Builder, xvi (1858), p. 146
A. J. Youngson: The Making of Classical Edinburgh (Edinburgh, 1966)
I. Fisher jr: 'Scottish Pioneers of the Greek Revival', Scot. Georg. Soc. Bull., xi (1984), pp. 37–42
Thomas Hamilton, Architect, 1784–1858 (exh. cat. by J. Rock, U. Edinburgh, Talbot Rice Gal., 1984)

DAVID PROUT

Hamilton, Sir **William (i)** (b Henley, Oxon, 13 Dec 1730; d London, 6 April 1803). English diplomat, connoisseur and collector. The youngest son of Lord Archibald Hamilton, he was educated at Westminster School before embarking on a military career. In 1758 he married Catherine Barlow, an heiress, and resigned his commission. He was MP for Midhurst from 1761 until 1764, when he accepted the post of Plenipotentiary to Naples. He arrived there at a time of considerable archaeological and volcanic activity and was thus able to indulge his twin passions of collecting and vulcanology. He wrote several papers on Vesuvius, Etna and Stromboli, and in 1769 published Campi Phlegraei on the volcanoes of the Two Sicilies, finely illustrated by his protégé Pietro Fabris. Hamilton's portrait (1777) by the studio of Joshua Reynolds (London, N.P.G.) shows him seated, with antique vases beside him and a volcano in the background (see fig.).

Sir William Surrounded by Vases, by the studio of Sir Joshua Reynolds, oil on canvas, 2.55×1.75 m, 1777 (London, National Portrait Gallery)

Hamilton, who was by his own admission an avid collector, began to acquire antiquities almost immediately after his arrival in Naples, specializing in Greek vases, then thought to be Etruscan. Much of his collection was bought cheaply, and sometimes illicitly, from Neapolitan excavators, whose methods he deprecated. In 1766 he purchased the important Porcinari collection and, in the same year, commissioned the antiquary Baron d'Hancarville to catalogue his pieces. *The Collection of Etruscan, Greek and Roman Antiquities from the Cabinet of the Honble Wm Hamilton* was published (1766–7) in Naples, in four lavish volumes, with the avowed intention of providing examples and inspiration for contemporary artists and craftsmen. It was widely acclaimed in France and England and influenced the work of David, Ingres, Fuseli and Josiah Wedgwood; the latter celebrated the opening in 1769 of his factory, at Etruria, Staffs, with the production of six black basalt vases, painted in red with three figures from Hamilton's catalogue (Barlaston, Wedgwood Mus.). However, there is no doubt that the catalogue also served the less altruistic purpose of publicizing the collection, negotiations for the sale of which to the British Museum were successfully concluded in 1772, when the museum paid £8400 for 730 vases, 175 terracottas, quantities of glass, bronzes, gems, ivories and over 6000 coins.

Having sold his first collection, Hamilton set out to acquire another. In 1775 he purchased the antique marble Warwick vase (Glasgow, Burrell Col.) from Gavin Hamilton and sold it to the Earl of Warwick; and in 1784 he sold the cameo glass Portland vase (London, BM), which he had purchased for £1000 from James Byres, to the Dowager Duchess of Portland for 1800 guineas. Hamilton's wife died in 1782; the following year, in England, he first met Emma Hart (1765–1815), the mistress of his nephew, Charles Greville. In 1785 Greville, having tired of Emma, despatched her to his uncle in Naples; and, in 1791 the infatuated Sir William Hamilton married her. Goethe, visiting Naples in 1787 with the painter Wilhelm Tischbein, was among the first spectators of Emma's 'Attitudes', a series of Classical *tableaux vivants*, almost certainly devised by Hamilton, which brought her fame and notoriety.

Tischbein stayed on in Naples after Goethe's departure and supervised the engraving, after drawings by Costanzo Angelini, of Hamilton's second collection, for publication in four volumes (Naples, 1791–5) as the *Collection of Engravings from Ancient Vases Mostly of Pure Greek Workmanship Discovered in Sepulchres in the Kingdom of the Two Sicilies.* This work, engraved in outline only, to reduce expenditure, had a profound effect on John Flaxman.

In July 1798 Hamilton, made anxious by Neapolitan unrest and French military activity, drew up a catalogue of his paintings (London, BM, Add. MS 41200 ff 121–6), listing over 200 works by Old Master and contemporary painters, including 14 portraits of his wife. Like his friend Sir Horace Mann, the envoy in Florence, he purchased paintings for English clients and as speculations; in 1772 he attempted to sell *Venus Disarming Cupid* by Correggio, now attributed to Luca Cambiaso (Longford Castle, Wilts) for £3000; and was active in the mid-1770s collecting works for Greville. Hamilton's pictures were packed in October and November 1798 (inventory of the works, Cambridge, Fitzwilliam Mus.) and then loaded on board Admiral Lord Nelson's flagship, the *Foudroyant*. Hamilton's vases were transported on the store ship *Colossus*, which foundered off the Scillies in 1799, much to his distress. However, two-thirds of the collection was eventually salvaged and in 1801 sold to Thomas Hope for £4000. (For further information on Hamilton's collections *see* GREECE, ANCIENT, §V, 10.)

In 1800 Hamilton returned to London with Nelson and Emma, who had become Nelson's mistress. In 1801 she gave birth to a daughter, Horatia; this event brought public ridicule on the elderly diplomat, as recorded in James Gillray's vicious caricature, *A Cognoscenti Contemplating ye Beauties of ye Antique*, 1801 (London, BM). In the same year Hamilton, beset by debt, sold 334 pictures, which fetched £5742. 13s, at Christie's.

BIBLIOGRAPHY
D. Irwin: *English Neo-classical Art* (London, 1966)
B. Fothergill: *Sir William Hamilton: Envoy Extraordinary* (London, 1969, R 1973)
Lady Hamilton (exh. cat. by P. Jaffé, London, Kenwood House, 1972)
G. Wills: 'Sir William Hamilton and the Portland Vase', *Apollo*, cx (1979), pp. 195–201
G. Chigiotti: 'Altri documenti per il giardino inglese della Reggia di Caserta', *Antol. B.A.*, v/19–20 (1981), pp. 193–8
B. Ford: 'The Grand Tour', *Apollo*, cxiv (1981), pp. 390–400
C. Knight: 'I luoghi di delizie di William Hamilton', *Napoli Nob.*, n.s. 2, xx (1981), pp. 180–90

D. Sutton: 'Aspects of British Collecting II', *Apollo*, cxvi (1982), pp. 358 ff
H. Acton: *Three Extraordinary Ambassadors* (London, 1983)
M. A. Cheetham: 'The Taste for Phenomena: Mount Vesuvius and Transformations in Late 18th Century European Landscape Depiction', *Wallraf-Richartz Jb.*, xlv (1984), pp. 131–44
C. Knight: 'La quadreria di Sir William Hamilton a Palazzo Sessa', *Napoli Nob.*, xxiv (1985), pp. 45–59
N. H. Ramage: 'Sir William Hamilton as Collector, Exporter and Dealer', *Amer. J. Archaeol.*, xciv (1990), pp. 469–80
C. Knight: *Hamilton a Napoli* (Naples, 1990)
Vases and Volcanoes: Sir William Hamilton and his Collection (exh. cat. by I. Jenkins and K. Sloan, London, BM, 1996)

DAVID RODGERS

Hamilton, William (ii) (*b* Chelsea, London, 1751; *d* London, 2 Dec 1801). English painter and illustrator. The son of one of Robert Adam's assistants, Hamilton was sent to Rome to be trained as an architectural draughtsman. He studied under Antonio Zucchi (who was later Adam's chief decorative painter), possibly in Rome from 1766 and in London from 1768. At the Royal Academy Schools from 1769, Hamilton developed into a figure painter and exhibited portraits and subject pictures at the Royal Academy from 1774 to 1801. He became ARA in 1784 and RA in 1789.

Hamilton's most interesting work pertains to the theatre, particularly Shakespearean. His most distinguished large pictures are the 23 he painted for John Boydell's Shakespeare Gallery, including *A Scene from 'Love's Labour's Lost'* (Act 4, scene i; London, Drury Lane Theat.). Also in the 1790s he contributed illustrations to Bowyer's *History of England* and Thomas Macklin's Bible and *British Poets*. Nevertheless, his pleasantly plump and youthful figures were better suited to the less pretentious format of book illustration than that of history painting. His attractive romantic scenes appear in many editions of 18th-century poets as well as in John Bell's second editions of *Shakespeare* (1786–8) and *The British Theatre* (1791–7). Hamilton was capable of being an accomplished draughtsman in a variety of styles; his album of drawings (London, V&A) includes work reminiscent of Henry Fuseli and Angelica Kauffman as well as more distinctive compositions nervously constructed with repeated, scratchy strokes of the pen. His portraits are mostly theatrical and include many of Sarah Siddons; they are curiously stilted, although the *John Philip Kemble as Richard III* (exh. RA 1788; priv. col., see G. Ashton: 'Paintings in the Mander and Mitchenson Theatre Collection', *Apollo*, cxiv (1981), p. 88) is a fine dramatic pastiche of Hogarth's portrait of David Garrick in the same role (1745; Liverpool, Walker A.G.).

BIBLIOGRAPHY
H. Hammelmann and T. S. R. Boase: *Book Illustration in Eighteenth Century England* (London, 1975)

GEOFFREY ASHTON

Hamlin. American family of architects and architectural historians.

(1) A(lfred) D(wight) F(oster) Hamlin (*b* Bebek, Turkey, 5 Sept 1855; *d* New York, 21 March 1926). He was the author of the first American textbook survey of Western architecture and of the only American survey of Western architectural ornament. He studied at the Massachusetts Institute of Technology School of Architecture (1876–8), Boston, and the Ecole des Beaux-Arts in Paris (1878–81), where he was a member of the atelier of Julien Azais Guadet. After working for a year with McKim, Mead & White in New York, he joined the staff of the Columbia School of Architecture in 1882, where he remained until the year of his death; he became professor there and was executive director from 1903 to 1912.

Hamlin contributed articles to many architectural journals in New York, including *Building*, in which he published a series devoted to architectural composition (1887–8), one of the earliest composition manuals ever published in the USA. His articles appeared primarily in *Architectural Record*, for which he wrote a lengthy series on the historiography of architectural history (1916–27). His address before the International Congress of Arts and Science (St Louis, MO, 1904) is also notable. Hamlin was a pillar of the City Beautiful movement in New York, serving on many committees concerned with urban growth. In his architectural journalism, he welcomed a broad range of academic historicism; he thought Victorian architecture to be in bad taste, and he disliked Art Nouveau, although he was a champion of Otto Wagner. As an architect, his major work was a set of academic classroom buildings (1889–1913) on the campus of his alma mater, Robert College preparatory school in Bebek, Turkey.

WRITINGS
A Textbook of the History of Architecture, College Histories of Art, ed. J. C. Van Dyke, ii (New York, 1896/*R*1954)
A History of Ornament, 2 vols (New York, 1916–23/*R*1973); vol. i repr. as *A History of Ornament, Ancient and Medieval* (Kennebunkport, ME, 1978)

(2) Talbot F(aulkner) Hamlin (*b* New York, 16 June 1889; *d* Beaufort, SC, 16 Aug 1956). Son of (1) A. D. F. Hamlin. He studied at the Columbia School of Architecture (1910–14), where his father was professor. After graduating from Columbia, Talbot made a brief trip to Europe and then joined the firm Murphy & McGill, becoming a partner in 1921. In 1934 the Depression forced him to seek work outside the practice of architecture, and he became Avery Architecture Librarian at Columbia University: the library's rise to international prominence has been attributed to Talbot. He began *The Avery Index to Architectural Periodicals*, one of the principal reference tools of the profession. From 1946 to the year of his death he was full Professor of Architecture at the school.

In his writings up to about 1935, Talbot advocated creative expressions of academic Modernism such as the work of Bertram Grosvenor Goodhue, rejecting radical, secessionist European Modernism as 'ascetic' and 'impersonal'. After that date he championed the new style as the inevitable product of modern times, with its freedom from the formality of academic strictures and its creative use of new, industrial materials. His *Architecture through the Ages* (1940) was the last American Beaux-Arts survey of Western architecture; *Greek Revival Architecture in America* (1944) is still considered the definitive treatment of its subject-matter. *Benjamin Henry Latrobe* (1955), a biography of America's first professional architect, won the Pulitzer Prize in 1956. His encyclopedic *Forms and Functions of Twentieth Century Architecture* (1952) in four volumes was modelled on Julien Guadet's *Eléments et théorie de l'architecture* (1901–4).

WRITINGS

The Enjoyment of Architecture (New York, 1916/*R* 1929)
The American Spirit in Architecture, The Pageant of America, ed. R. Gabriel, xiii (New Haven, 1926)
Some European Architectural Libraries: Their Methods, Equipment and Administration (New York, 1939/*R* 1967)
Architecture through the Ages (New York, 1940, rev. 1944, 1953)
Greek Revival Architecture in America (London, 1944/*R* New York, 1964)
Architecture: An Art for All Men (New York, 1947/*R* Westport, 1975)
Forms and Functions of Twentieth Century Architecture, i, ii (New York, 1952)
Benjamin Henry Latrobe (New York, 1955)

BIBLIOGRAPHY

K. Frampton: 'Slouching toward Modernity: Talbot Faulkner Hamlin and the Architecture of the New Deal', *The Making of an Architect* (New York, 1981), pp. 149–67
P. S. Kaufman: *American Architectural Writing, Beaux-Arts Style: The Lives and Works of Talbot Hamlin and A. D. F. Hamlin* (diss., Ithaca, NY, Cornell U., 1986)

PETER S. KAUFMAN

Hammam. *See* BATH (ii), §2.

Hamman, Edouard(-Jean-Conrad) (*b* Ostend, 24 Sept 1819; *d* Paris, 31 March 1888). Belgian painter and illustrator. He studied first at the Tekenacademie in Ostend with François Bossuet (1798–1889) and Michel van Cuyck (1797–1875), then from 1837 with Nicaise De Keyser in his private school in Antwerp. He was also influenced by the works of Louis Gallait. From the beginning he painted historical genre scenes with great success. He first exhibited at the Ghent Salon of 1838, but it was his *Last Moments of Francisco de Zurbarán* (untraced), shown at the Brussels Salon in 1842, that first brought him to the notice of the Belgian public. A commission from the Belgian government followed soon afterwards, *Entry of Archduke Albert and Isabella into Ostend after the Fall of the Town in 1604* (destr. 1940; ex-Mus. S. Kst., Ostend). During his Antwerp period he also illustrated books by his friend the novelist Hendrik Conscience (1812–83), including his *Histoire de Belgique* (Antwerp, 1845).

In 1846 Hamman left for Paris to continue his studies with Joseph Nicolas Robert-Fleury and Thomas Couture at the Ecole des Beaux-Arts. His style imitated that of his teachers, but after a visit to Italy in 1849 he became strongly influenced by Titian, Domenico Tintoretto and Veronese. He settled in Paris and specialized in scenes from the lives of famous artists, composers, scientists and monarchs. Among those commemorated were Dante, Albrecht Dürer, Christoph Glück, Josef Haydn, Shakespeare, *Andreas Vesalius* (exh. 1848; Marseille, Mus. B.-A.) and *Erasmus Teaching the Young Karl V* (1865; Paris, Mus. d'Orsay). Many of his works were reproduced by lithographers such as Adolphe Mouilleron (1820–81) and Charles Billoin (1813–69) and were widely disseminated. His portrait drawings of famous composers were sold in photographic reproduction. Among his major works was a series of six paintings (1864–6; Turin, Pal. Reale) depicting scenes from Italian history, commissioned by Victor Emanuel II of Italy.

BIBLIOGRAPHY

NBW; Thieme–Becker
A. P. de Mirimonde: 'Edouard Hamman et l'histoire de la musique en peinture', *Jb.: Kon. Mus. S. Kst.* [Antwerp] (1973), pp. 269–99
N. Hostyn: *Beeldend Oostende* (Bruges, 1993), pp. 14–15, 162

NORBERT HOSTYN

Hamme, Guillaume [Guilielmus] **van** (*b* Brussels, before 1600; *d* Antwerp, 24 May 1668). Flemish cleric and collector. He was appointed canon of the St Catharinakerk of Hoogstraten in 1628 and in 1633 exchanged his canonacy for that of his uncle Godevaart van Hamme (*d* 1641), who was canon of the Onze Lieve Vrouwenkerk in Antwerp. At that time Guillaume was already licensed to practise law. He served as chaplain to the Antwerp Guild of St Luke and was himself an enthusiastic admirer of paintings and sculpture. His friends included the art dealers Herman de Neyt of Antwerp and Matthijs Musson (1598–1678) and P. Christijn of Brussels. Van Hamme owned more than 170 works by artists of the 16th and 17th centuries. According to his wills drawn up in 1646 and 1653, van Hamme stipulated that all his furniture, household goods and silver were to be sold within a month of his death. The auction of books, engravings and paintings was to be delayed until a peace treaty had been signed between the kings of France and Spain. Six to eight months after his death the sale was announced throughout the Netherlands, France and the surrounding areas, and a catalogue of the library and art collection was distributed; no copy has been found to date.

BIBLIOGRAPHY

P. J. Goetschalckx: *Geschiedenis der kannunniken van O. L. V. kapittel te Antwerpen* [History of the canonry of the chapter of Our Lady in Antwerp] (Antwerp, n.d.), pp. 231–2
F. J. Van den Branden: 'Verzamelingen van schilderijen te Antwerpen' [Collections of paintings in Antwerp], *Antwerp. Archvbl.*, xxi (1902–3), pp. 455–8
E. Duverger: *Antwerpse kunstinventarissen uit de zeventiende eeuw*, v (Brussels, 1991), pp. 358–60; vi (1992), p. 460; vii (1996)

ERIK DUVERGER

Hammer, Armand (*b* New York, 21 May 1898; *d* Los Angeles, 10 Dec 1990). American art collector and dealer. He was the eldest son of Julius Hammer, a descendant of Russian Jewish immigrants and a member of the Socialist Labor Party. By the age of 23, Armand had become a millionaire by reviving his father's failing pharmaceutical business and selling it to his own employees; he had also completed medical school. When an epidemic of typhus broke out in the USSR in 1923 he volunteered his services, but once there determined that starvation was the country's most severe problem. He hit on the idea of trading grain with the USSR in exchange for furs. He stayed in Russia for nine years, establishing successful pencil and asbestos concessions and representing 36 American companies there.

Hammer's interest in art was stimulated by finding at flea markets in Moscow vast quantities of tapestries, silver and other goods abandoned by the Russian nobility. With his brother Victor Hammer (1902–85) he bought entire sets of Tsarist china and religious icons and vestments for next to nothing. They also purchased fine art and built up the first of three major collections. By 1928, the brothers had become art dealers and soon opened Hammer Galleries in New York. In 1971 they acquired M. Knoedler & Co. In the USA Hammer sold masterpieces at retail through department stores, dealt in Fabergé Easter eggs, and arranged unprecedented exchanges of art with the Soviet authorities. He bought art on a grand scale and donated generously to the National Gallery of Art and the Corcoran Gallery of Art in Washington, DC, the Metropolitan Museum in New York and the Los Angeles County Museum of Art. In 1988 he withdrew a promised bequest, the bulk of his third collection, to the Los Angeles County Museum of Art and marked it for installation instead in his proposed museum (the Armand Hammer Museum of Art and Cultural Center) in Westwood, CA, on the property of his company, Occidental Petroleum. The collection, which has since been housed in the new museum, contains over 10,000 paintings, drawings, and sculptures, among them works by major 19th-century artists, such as Corot, Vincent van Gogh, Monet and Honoré Daumier. The *Codex Hammer* (now *Codex Gates*), a Leonardo manuscript, was formerly in Hammer's collection but was sold in 1994 (New York, Christie's, 11 Nov).

WRITINGS

with N. Lyndon: *Hammer* (New York, 1987)

BIBLIOGRAPHY

J. Walker, ed.: *The Armand Hammer Collection: Five Centuries of Masterpieces* (New York, 1980)
S. Weinberg: *Armand Hammer: The Untold Story* (Boston, 1989)

KATHRYN BONOMI

Hammer [Hamer; Meyer; Meiger von Werde]**, Hans** (*d* summer 1519). German architect. He is mentioned in the Brotherhood book of the masons' lodge at Strasbourg in 1471 and was apparently brought to Strasbourg that year. He was made a Citizen in 1482, by which time he was a foreman at the masons' lodge of the cathedral (*see* STRASBOURG, §III, 1). In 1486 he became Master of the Works but lost the position in 1490, when he applied unsuccessfully for the job of Master of the Works at Milan Cathedral. Hammer then entered the service of the Bishop of Strasbourg to carry out various works in his residence at Saverne. He was again made Master of the Works at Strasbourg Cathedral in 1513 and kept the position until his death.

The earliest works entrusted to Hammer were the tabernacle (destr.) in the choir of Strasbourg Cathedral and the pulpit for the nave, both made before he became Master of the Works. The pulpit, one of the richest and most beautiful works of the Late Gothic, was made in 1485, and a drawing for it is dated a year earlier (Strasbourg, Mus. Oeuvre Notre-Dame). It has a hexagonal base, the parapet resting on surrounding posts. The form is enriched by moulded arch and tracery forms with applied branch motifs (*Astwerk*) and lavishly decorated with statuettes. The baldacchini over the individual sculptures are joined together to form the higher edge of the pulpit. In the middle of the stair parapet an angel holds a shield with Hammer's mark.

After Hammer became Master of the Works he drew up plans for the south tower of the cathedral (Strasbourg, Mus. Oeuvre Notre-Dame); but although he began to build the tower, it was later pulled down. Hammer's design largely remained faithful to the north tower constructed by Ulrich von Ensingen (*see* ENSINGEN, (1)) and JOHANN HÜLTZ, although he enriched the tracery and added other decorations. In 1488 Hammer also built the 'Small Treasury', a room between the south nave buttresses where the documents and treasures of the masons' lodge were stored.

After 1490 Hammer designed the Holy Trinity Chapel for the church of St Pierre-le-Jeune in Strasbourg, which is dated 1492 and bears his mark. A little later he built the chapel of St Mary at the conventual church at Saverne and vaulted the north aisle there. In 1495 he built the chancel, which is considerably less elaborate than that of Strasbourg Cathedral. Nevertheless it shows his characteristic tracery forms and displays his mason's mark. At the same time he contributed to the construction of the parish church in Finstingen, north-west of Saverne, although one would hardly associate this building, with its simple window tracery, socles and portal, with Hammer, were it not for the frequent appearance of his mason's mark.

In 1515, during Hammer's second period as Master of the Works in Strasbourg, the former St Martin's Chapel (now dedicated to St Lawrence) was built on the north side of the transept to balance St Catherine's Chapel on the south transept. His chapel buildings combine simple exteriors with beautiful interior detailing. Holy Trinity Chapel and St Mary's Chapel are closely related, with the same vault patterns, a type of springing lozenge vault with a row of lozenges down the middle. His delight in decoration and love of carefully executed details are significantly displayed on his last work, St Martin's Chapel, where his ability to create new forms of socle and baldacchino seems to have been unlimited. His architectural details show close knowledge of Strasbourg designs, and it is even possible that he studied under Jodok Dotzinger (*see* DOTZINGER, (2)). There are also significant links to the Swabian architect Alberlin Jörg, with whom he certainly worked for a time: his mark appears on Jörg's churches in Stuttgart (the collegiate church and St Leonard's) and St Bartholomew's, Markgröningen.

Hammer was one of the most inventive designers of the Late Gothic. Despite the luxuriant nature of his decorative architecture his constructions remain clear and geometric, and the execution is precise and of high quality. He was married to Margarethe, the daughter of the stone mason Hans von Erfort, who was active in Strasbourg. He had at least three children, of whom his son Friedrich became a mason.

BIBLIOGRAPHY

A. Adam: 'Hans Hammerer oder Hamer in Zabern', *Mitt. Ges. Erhaltung Gesch. Dkml Elsass*, n. s., xviii (1897), pp. 523–31
M.-L. Hauck: 'Der Bildhauer Conrad Sifer von Sinsheim und sein Kreis', *An. U. Sarav.*, ix (1960), pp. 113–368
H. Reinhardt: La Cathédrale de Strasbourg (Grenoble, 1972)
J. Julier: *Studien zur spätgotischen Baukunst am Oberrhein*, Heidelberg. Kstgesch. Abh., n. s., 13, (Heidelberg, 1978)
B. Schock-Werner: *Das Strassburger Münster im 15. Jahrhundert*, 23, Veröff. Abt. Archit. Ksthist. Inst. U. Köln (Cologne, 1983)

BARBARA SCHOCK-WERNER

Hammerbacher, Herta (*b* Nuremberg, 2 Dec 1900; *d* Starnberg, 25 May 1985). German landscape architect. She studied garden design in Berlin in the 1920s, followed by employment as a garden architect for the famous Ludwig

Späth nursery in Berlin. In 1928 she started a long collaboration with Hermann Mattern (1902–71), a garden architect, and with Karl Foerster (1874–1970), a breeder of herbaceous perennials. She later collaborated also with such architects as Hans Scharoun, Peter Poelzig, Egon Eiermann and Richard Neutra. In the course of her career Hammerbacher created over 3000 gardens, parks and cemeteries, and open spaces for hospitals and schools. She was influenced by the garden architect Willy Lange (1864–1941), who developed concepts of natural garden design that gained particular ideological influence in Germany during the Nazi period. Hammerbacher interpreted the garden as part of the landscape and promoted informal design and the use of so-called native plant associations. Her own garden in Nikolassee, Berlin, planned together with the gardens of Peter Poelzig and the painter Vincent Piper, serves as a characteristic example of her design style: the native pines and oaks are preserved, and the intervening spaces are sown with wild grasses and planted with wild roses, yews, hornbeams and other indigenous species. In 1946 she began teaching garden and landscape design in the department of architecture at the Technische Universität, Berlin. She was a professor from 1950, and in April 1969 became an emeritus professor. She won many awards, including first prize for the Kassel Federal Garden Exhibition in 1955.

WRITINGS

'Die Hausgärten', *Berlin und seine Bauten*, 'Eine Entgegnung', *Bauwelt*, lxviii (1977), pp. 963–4

BIBLIOGRAPHY

A. Jacobshagen and K. Sommer-Kempf: *Festschrift Herta Hammerbacher* (Berlin, 1975)

G. Nagel: 'Professor Herta Hammerbacher', *Das Gartenamt*, xxxiv (1985), pp. 590–91

J. Wolschke-Bulmahn and G. Gröning: 'The Ideology of the Nature Garden: Nationalistic Trends in Garden Design in Germany during the Early Twentieth Century', *J. Gdn Hist.*, xii (1992), pp. 73–80

JOACHIM WOLSCHKE-BULMAHN

Hammershøi. Danish family of artists.

(1) Vilhelm Hammershøi (*b* Copenhagen, 15 May 1864; *d* Copenhagen, 13 Feb 1916). Painter. He attended the Kongelige Akademi for de Skønne Kunster, Copenhagen, under Frederik Vermehren, between 1879 and 1884. He also studied under Frederik Rohde (1816–86), Vilhelm Kyhn and Peder Severin Krøyer. His style matured early in his life and did not change much during the 30 years of his career.

1. EARLY WORKS TO 1901. Hammershøi's first work to be exhibited officially (Copenhagen, Charlottenborg, 1885) was *Portrait of a Young Woman: The Artist's Sister Anna Hammershøi* (1885; Copenhagen, Hirschsprungske Saml.). In this picture the main characteristics of his distinctive manner of painting portraits and interiors are already evident. He concentrated on the sitter's expression and stance and omitted anything not essential. The black gown makes a fine point of departure for the blank face, which contrasts with the expressive, fidgety hands, showing the artist's sympathetic insight into the dreamy world of his younger sister. The simple backdrop—a brownish wall and a white door—emphasizes the image of an isolated figure in an empty room.

The development of Hammershøi's cool, deliberate style is shown in a copy made in the Louvre, *Greek Archaic Relief* (1891; Copenhagen, Ny Carlsberg Glyp.). A procession of three women carved in marble is rendered with a close attention to the wear of time and chipping of the surface, which does not preclude a delicate treatment of the light on the stone and a sense of the spirituality of the subject. The lessons of such studies appear in his ambitious *Artemis* (1893–4; Copenhagen, Stat. Mus. Kst). Three women and one adolescent boy, all nude, form a rhythmical frieze. Every movement and proportion is carefully measured, yet the overall impression is one of great natural ease. In tune with the fashion of the contemporary art world in Denmark and elsewhere he endeavoured to lend the painting symbolic overtones; it depicts a poetic interpretation of Eros, Artemis and Demeter as personifications of female eroticism and fertility. The composition was inspired by Luca Signorelli's *Court of Pan* (*see* SIGNORELLI, LUCA, fig. 2), which he may have seen in Berlin on his way back to Denmark from Paris in 1892.

2. 'FIVE PORTRAITS' AND THE LATER YEARS. In 1901 Hammershøi began work on a monumental painting, *Five Portraits* (Stockholm, Thielska Gal.; see fig.). This group portrait of the artist's friends, including his brother the artist (2) Svend Hammershøi, is one of the most modern, controversial and notable paintings of the decade, not only from a Danish point of view. In this work he reinterpreted a form of portrait that had been practised since the Renaissance. The five men seated around a table are resting, smoking, drinking or thinking but not engaging in conversation. The room is lit by just two candles, which emphasizes the contrast between the white tablecloth and two pitch-dark windows on the back wall, conveying a strange atmosphere of isolation. The picture gives a feeling of solemnity and importance, as if the scene were a Last Supper. Each figure is an individual psychological study, and the composition is meticulously designed, yet the overall effect is wonderfully natural. The figure of Carl Holsøe, for example, sits with his legs resting on a footstool, dramatically foreshortened to reveal the soles of an enormous pair of shoes, thus becoming a measure of the painting's depth.

Hammershøi's distinctive interiors were often based on his own homes, which were simply but beautifully decorated. The choice furniture is carefully arranged, as in *Interior with a Young Man Reading* (1898; Copenhagen, Hirschsprungske Saml.), where a white Hepplewhite chair in front of a dark mahogany card-table balances the youth (Svend Hammershøi) standing by the window. In *Room with Piano and Woman in Black* (1901; Copenhagen, Ordrupgaardsaml.) the artist's wife, Ida, is standing in the middle of the room with her back turned, apparently doing nothing, but she fills the space with her silent existence.

Perhaps Hammershøi's most remarkable interiors are those without any figures or furniture at all. *Dust Motes Dancing in Sunlight* (1900; Copenhagen, Ordrupgaardsaml.) is empty but for a Baroque door and panelling; the sunlight pours through the window, hitting the empty floor. Everything is reduced to architectural lines and a scrupulous gradation of grey tones. With the simplest of means, as in *Open Doors*, also known as *White Doors*

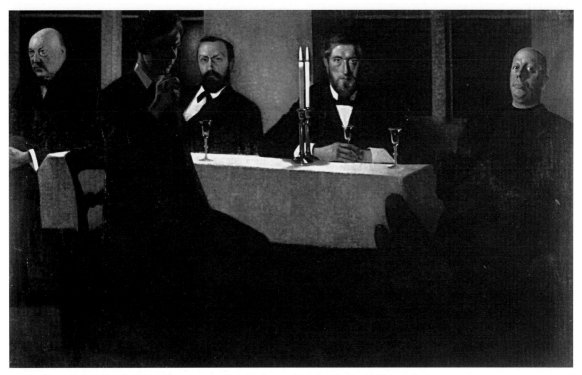

Vilhelm Hammershøi: *Five Portraits*, oil on canvas, 1.9×3.4 m, begun 1901 (Stockholm, Thielska Galleri)

(1905; Copenhagen, Davids Saml.), or the *Four Rooms* (1914; Copenhagen, Ordrupgaardsaml.), he managed to catch the spirit of the place and to give us a hint of its inhabitants: a series of open doors leads the eye through a succession of rooms where people live quiet and undisturbed lives.

This kind of wordless dialogue is also present in Hammershøi's townscapes. *London Scenery: Montague Street with the British Museum* (Copenhagen, Ny Carlsberg Glyp.) was painted during the winter of 1905–6, when he visited London for a couple of months. The dull, foggy weather suited his style well. He chose a wintry day with snow on the roofs when he depicted the *Gateway of the East Asiatic Company* (1902; Copenhagen, Stat. Mus. Kst) in front of his own house in Copenhagen. Here he concentrated on the stark symmetry of the 18th-century building. Even in his landscapes he looked for graphic simplicity, as in *Sunshine and Shower, Lake Gentofte* (1903; Copenhagen, Davids Saml.), with the lake in the foreground, a strip of flat land with a chain of roadside trees, and a cloudy sky dominating the scene. He avoided the more banal subject of a Danish summer day, and more often than not he imbued the landscape with his own melancholy.

Hammershøi's refined works were in tune with his own tastes in art, which ranged from ancient Greek sculpture and Italian 15th-century painting to the Danish Golden Age. The influence of the Dutch Old Masters, especially Vermeer and Rembrandt, on his portraits and interiors is more a matter of feeling and atmosphere than of style and colour, while some of Whistler's works seem to be a closer model. His admiration for Ingres's draughtsmanship is also evident in his pictures. However, Hammershøi's artistic language is unmistakably personal. At a time when art, both in Denmark and abroad, tended towards a more glamorous style, his subdued works did not meet with immediate understanding. He was never the centre of a school, but he did have a few followers, including his brother-in-law Peter Ilsted (1861–1933) and Carl Holsøe.

BIBLIOGRAPHY
Vilhelm Hammershøi: En retrospektiv udstilling (exh. cat., ed. H. Finsen and I. V. Raaschou-Nielsen; Copenhagen, Ordrupgaardsaml., 1981)
Vilhelm Hammershøi: Painter of Stillness and Light (exh. cat., ed. H. Finsen and I. V. Raaschou-Nielsen; New York, Wildenstein's; Washington, DC, Phillips Col.; 1983)
P. Vad: *Hammershøi; Værk og liv* [Hammershøi: work and life] (Copenhagen, 1988); Eng. trans. as *Vilhelm Hammershøi and Danish Art at the Turn of the Century* (London, 1992)

JENS PETER MUNK

(2) Svend Hammershøi (*b* Copenhagen, 10 Aug 1873; *d* Frederiksberg, Copenhagen, 27 Feb 1948). Painter and potter, brother of (1) Vilhelm Hammershøi. He studied at a technical school in Copenhagen in 1889 before being admitted to the Kongelige Akademi for de Skønne Kunster, where he spent 1890–92 studying under Frederik Vermehren. From 1892 to 1897 he was attached to Kristian Zahrtmann's school. He was also taught by his elder brother and Thorvald Bindesbøll. In 1894 he travelled to Berlin for the first time, after which he made numerous journeys to Germany. From 1910 he made annual trips to England.

Svend Hammershøi belonged to the circle of Danish artists gathered around his brother, and he adopted his brother's style for a series of landscapes and architectural paintings. With a limited range of colour and a tight composition, he created a series of evocative motifs for which he sought inspiration partly in England, where he spent much time in Oxford and Wells on his annual trips, and partly in Denmark, by the great Kronborg, Vordingborg and Rosenborg castles, as well as in old Copenhagen. One of his better-known paintings is the *Garden by the Prince's Palace* (before 1906; Copenhagen, Stat. Mus. Kst).

As a potter Hammershøi worked with Thorvald Bindesbøll in the pottery factory in Valby from 1891 to 1904. He was a great admirer of Bindesbøll but was only indirectly influenced by him in his work. His ceramic work is characteristic of the period's interest in Classical form and decoration, and he was in demand at various places, including the Kongelige Porcelænsfabrik, and then the Kähler Ceramic Factory in Næstved (1894), working with the factory's famous lustre glazes. A series of fluted pots in simple and precise forms, modelled by hand in red clay, were produced during this period. Hammershøi fastened voluminous joints to the large, unbroken surfaces and sometimes used embossed patterns. He returned to the Kongelige Porcelænsfabrik in 1904–6. He also produced drawings for a number of major works, among them classicizing dishes and pots for the silversmith Holger Kyster (1872–1944), as well as drawings for a number of elegant bookbindings. He wrote two books about Bindesbøll, and in 1944 he received the Eckersberg Medal.

WRITINGS

with H. Kystel and J. Simonsen: *Thorvald Bindesbøll: Keramiske arbejder 1883–1904, en raekke gengivelser med text* [Thorvald Bindesbøll: ceramic works 1883–1904, a series of reproductions with text] (Copenhagen, 1918)
Thorvald Bindesbøll in memoriam, 1846–1946 (Copenhagen, 1946)

BIBLIOGRAPHY

Svend Hammershøi: Trær og bygninger—12 reproduktioner efter malerier [Svend Hammershøi: trees and buildings—12 reproductions after paintings] (Copenhagen, 1918)
R. Magnussen: *Svend Hammershøis billeder fra Oxford og Wells* [Svend Hammershøi's pictures from Oxford and Wells] (Copenhagen, 1936)
K. Flor: *Svend Hammershøi* (Copenhagen, 1939)
J. Thirslund: *Kähler-Keramik gennem 100 aar* [Kähler ceramics over 100 years] (Copenhagen, 1939)

RIGMOR LOVRING

Hamnett, Nina (*b* Tenby [now in Dyfed], 14 Feb 1890; *d* London, 16 Dec 1956). British painter and illustrator. She studied at the Pelham School of Art (1906–7), the London School of Art (*c.* 1907–10) and at Marie Wassilieff's Academy in Paris (1914), where Fernand Léger taught. In Paris she met most of the leading members of the avant-garde as well as her husband, the Norwegian artist Edgar de Bergen [Roald Kristian] (*b* 1893), with whom she briefly lived (1914–17). Flamboyantly unconventional, she rapidly became a well-known bohemian personality in London and Paris and modelled for many artists. Friends and mentors included Walter Sickert, Roger Fry, Henri Gaudier-Brzeska, Modigliani, Augustus John and Wyndham Lewis. Hamnett worked at the Omega Workshops (1913–19) on decorative art, for example a mural on the theme of contemporary London life at 4 Berkeley Street, London (for the art dealer Arthur Ruck). She exhibited widely during World War I and the 1920s in solo and group shows, including those of the London Group, the New English Art Club and the Salon d'Automne.

Influenced by Fry and modern French art, Hamnett painted portraits, still-lifes, landscapes, café and pub scenes. Her declared ambition was 'to paint psychological portraits that shall represent accurately the spirit of the age' (see Gordon-Stables, 1924). Her portraits, for example *Ossip Zadkine* (1914; priv. col., on loan to Bradford, Cartwright Hall) and *Rupert Doone* (1922–3; Doncaster, Mus. & A.G.), are strong statements of character, combining fine draughtsmanship, well-defined modelling of forms, a robust sense of composition and an often subdued palette to give her figures an almost sculptural solidity. Hamnett excelled as a draughtsman, as may be seen in her illustrations for Osbert Sitwell's *The People's Album of London Statues* (London, 1928); she also illustrated W. S. Leslie's *The Silent Queen* (London, 1927). Her fluent, sensitive, often witty line and simplified forms testify to the lasting influence of Gaudier-Brzeska and Modigliani.

In Paris (1920–26) Hamnett was the best-known British woman painter, and friendly with Cocteau, Satie, Stravinsky and the composers known as Les Six. For the next 30 years she presided over Fitzrovia, London's bohemian district south of Fitzroy Square, despite the decline that marked her work from the mid-1930s.

WRITINGS

Laughing Torso (London, 1932/*R* 1984)
Is She a Lady?: A Problem in Autobiography (London, 1955)

BIBLIOGRAPHY

L. Gordon-Stables: 'Nina Hamnett's Psychological Portraiture', *A. Work*, (Oct 1924), pp. 112–15
D. Hooker: *Nina Hamnett: Queen of Bohemia* (London, 1986) [with illus. and complete bibliog.]
Nina Hamnett and her Circle (exh. cat. by D. Hooker, London, Parkin Gal., 1986)
J. Collins: 'Nina Hamnett', *Five Women Painters*, by T. Grimes, J. Collins and D. Baddeley (Oxford, 1989), pp. 57–81

DENISE HOOKER

Hamon, Jean-Louis (*b* Saint-Loup, near Plouay, Côtes-du-Nord, 5 May 1821; *d* Saint-Raphaël, 29 May 1874). French painter and designer. He was encouraged to practise drawing by the Brothers of the Christian Doctrine at Lannion. Through the intervention of Félicité-Robert de Lamennais (1782–1854), he was made drawing-master at a religious seminary at Ploërmel, Brittany, although at this stage he had received no instruction and had never seen an oil painting. In 1840 he asked his *conseil général* for help and left for Paris the following year with a grant of 500 francs. He went to Delaroche's studio, where he made friends with Picou, Jean-Léon Gérôme, Jean Aubert (1824–1906) and Jean Eugène Damery (1823–53). Charles Gleyre, who took over Delaroche's studio in 1843, encouraged and protected him during years of poverty. *Daphnis and Chloe* (untraced), his first Salon picture, exhibited in 1847, was painted in Gleyre's studio.

In 1848, on Gleyre's recommendation, Hamon was given a post as a designer to the Sèvres factory where he developed a thin, pale, transparent style of figure painting especially suited for decorating vases. He worked at this time with the group at 27 Rue de Fleurus where Gérôme and his friends painted their first Salon pictures inspired by the myths and history of Greece and Rome. Hamon's pictures showed the influence of his work at Sèvres. His vase, *Woman with a Butterfly*, was the forerunner of a series of paintings of women and children with insects that he exhibited in Paris. In 1851 he received payment from Sèvres for the *Human Comedy* (1852; Compiègne, Château), which he sent to the Salon of 1852. Théophile Gautier alone remarked that it was arranged like the decoration of a vase, but, like most critics, he was unduly puzzled by the subject of the picture, which shows a group of famous men of all ages, from Diogenes to Dante, gathered round a puppet-show in which the Goddess of Wisdom sends Cupid to the gallows. In 1854 Hamon was dismissed from Sèvres following long absence from the studio. From 1856 until his departure for Italy in 1863 he worked with a team of artists at the studio of Théodore Deck (1823–91), designing pictures for transfer on to porcelain. However, easel painting was now his chief interest. There is no evidence to connect the picture which he exhibited in 1853, *My Sister Isn't There* (destr. 1871), with his ceramic work, but the types of children, the shallow frieze-like composition and pale colours, noticed by all the critics, recall the decoration of a vase. His style was generally liked by the picture-buying public until a revulsion against the Etruscan style in 1859 made his art less fashionable. Hamon was persuaded by dealers to appease criticism by making his pictures less misty, but by 1861 he was in debt.

Hamon went to Rome in 1863 with a letter of introduction to Jean-Jacques Henner, who invited him to share his studio. There he completed *Aurora Drinking Dew* (destr. 1871), inspired by the sight of an insect sipping from a leaf in the woods at Meudon. The painting revived his reputation and was bought by Empress Eugénie. In 1865 Hamon settled in Capri with Louis Français, Edouard Alexandre Sain (1830–1910) and Jean Benner (1836–1906), convinced that he was going to make a fortune exploiting new subjects. He seems, in fact, to have spent his time there painting replicas of earlier work for American collectors through the intermediary of a Genevan banker, Walter Fol. On one of his frequent visits across the bay to Pompeii he had the idea of *Muses Weeping over Pompeii* (untraced), exhibited at the Salon of 1865, a fantasy like Curzon's *Dreams on the Ruins of Pompeii* (1866; Bagnères-de-Bigorre, Mus. A.) or Gautier's *Arria Marcella*. In 1873 Hamon exhibited his last picture, the *Sad Shores* (untraced), a melancholy, poetic picture that was bought by Fol. His death the following year went almost unnoticed in Paris. His influence, however, survived. Following the reorganization of the Sèvres factory in 1848, he developed a style that lastingly affected the decorative arts in France. His pictures, often disconcerting, sometimes tinged with a darker undercurrent, are always witty and original.

BIBLIOGRAPHY
E. Hoffmann: *Jean-Louis Hamon, peintre* (Paris, 1904)
L'Art en France sous le Second Empire (exh. cat., Paris, Grand Pal., 1979), pp. 368–9

JON WHITELEY

Hampi. Site of the ruined city of VIJAYANAGARA in Bellary District, Karnataka, India. The city was founded in the 14th century at the sacred centre of Hampi. The modern village of the same name occupies part of the site.

1. History and urban layout. 2. The sacred centre. 3. The urban core and royal centre. 4. Suburban centres.

1. HISTORY AND URBAN LAYOUT. Vijayanagara ('City of victory') emerged as the capital of an empire comprising much of peninsular India by the end of the 14th century, a position it maintained throughout the 15th and 16th centuries. While its rulers were Hindu, its society included an influential Muslim minority. Foreign travellers were welcomed; descriptions of the city's grandeur survive in accounts of Persian, Portuguese and Italian visitors; Arab horse-traders also visited the city at this time. Celebrated kings include Deva Raya I (*reg* 1406–22) of the Sangama dynasty and Krishnadeva Raya (*reg* 1510–29) and Achyutadeva Raya (*reg* 1529–42) of the third or Tuluva dynasty. Vijayanagara's rivals for supremacy in the Deccan were the Muslim kingdoms to the north. In 1565, on the death of Rama Raja who had risen to prominence during the reign of Sadasiva (*reg* 1542–*c.* 1570), Vijayanagara's armies were defeated by a coalition formed by the neighbouring Muslim states. The capital was abandoned and eventually much of it destroyed; it was never again occupied.

The ruined city commands a spectacular setting with excellent natural defences. To the north the landscape is dominated by a wild granite gorge through which the Tungabhadra River flows; to the south and west, the landscape opens up, and an extensive plain stretches to the Sandur Hills. The region has strong associations with the great Hindu epic the *Rāmāyaṇa* and is identified in local belief with Kishkindha, where Rama met the monkey chiefs Hanuman and Sugriva and planned the campaign to rescue Sita from Lanka.

The plan of the capital consists of a number of discrete zones spread over a vast area of no less than 25 sq. km. Overlooking the southern bank of the Tungabhadra River is the sacred centre (see fig. 1), incorporating the earlier, pre-Vijayanagara-period settlement of Hampi. The fortified urban core is located to the south, beyond an irrigated valley through which ancient canals still run. A complete ring of massive fortifications defines an elliptical zone, about 4 km along its axis, where the bulk of the city's population lived. At the south-western end of the urban core are the irregular enclosures of the royal centre (see fig. 2 below). Within and around these enclosures are monuments linked with the king, court and military. The city's suburbs extend south and west in the plains beyond the urban core. Fragmentary fortifications indicate a system of concentric protective walls. Gateways are located along the roads leading into the urban core.

2. THE SACRED CENTRE. The most important pre-Vijayanagara-period structures are located on the sloping shelf of Hemakuta Hill, overlooking the village of Hampi from the south. These date from the 9th century to the early 14th, when Hampi was celebrated as a holy spot dedicated to the worship of Shiva. In the 14th century, when the newly established Vijayanagara kings made this their dynastic centre, Hemakuta Hill was fortified; gateways were built and tanks excavated into the rock. The temples illustrate pre-Vijayanagara-period styles in the Deccan (*see* INDIAN SUBCONTINENT, §III, 6(i)(f)). The three largest examples are built on a three-shrine plan (Skt *trikūṭācala*), with each shrine opening off a common hall,

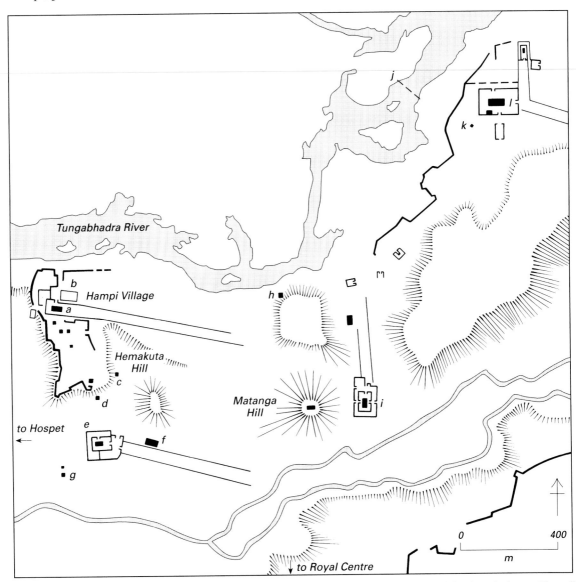

1. Hampi, site of Vijayanagara , plan of sacred centre: (a) Virupaksha Temple; (b) tank; (c) large monolithic Ganesha image; (d) small monolithic Ganesha image; (e) Krishna Temple; (f) tank; (g) monolithic Narasimha image; (h) Kodandarama Temple; (i) Tiruvengalanatha Temple; (j) ruined bridge; (k) 'King's Balance'; (l) Vitthala Temple

part of which serves as an open verandah. There is also a double-shrined temple and several smaller temples. Most have plain exteriors with granite pyramidal roofs and finely finished columns.

The indigenous goddess Pampa and her consort Viru-paksha or Pampapati (an aspect of Shiva) are housed in the Virupaksha Temple (mainly 16th century; see fig. 1a) at the heart of the modern village of Hampi. The complex has two courts, each entered through a *gopura* (towered gateway) on the east. The larger *gopura*, giving access to the outer court, was erected by Krishnadeva Raya in 1512. It is a splendid example of the typical Vijayanagara-period scheme (*see* INDIAN SUBCONTINENT, §III, 6(i)(f)) consisting of nine levels (*tala*) and reaching a height of 52 m. Each level has pilastered walls with sculptures flanking a central opening. The inner court, entered through the smaller *gopura* (*c.* 1510), is surrounded by a colonnaded cloister. At the centre is the principal temple, consisting of the sanctum (*garbhagrha*), enclosed by a narrow am-bulatory (*pradakṣiṇa-prākāra*), preceded by a closed hall (*ardha-maṇḍapa*) and an open hall (*raṅga-maṇḍapa*). The sanctum, which houses a Shiva *liṅga*, has a stepped pyramidal superstructure of three storeys (creating a *tritala vimāna*) with a cupola (*śikhara*) surmounted by a large pot finial (*stūpī*). The open hall has columns arranged in five aisles; the central sixteen columns are carved with *yāli* (rampant leonine mythical creatures) with riders, in the typical 16th-century manner.

The mythological scenes painted on the ceiling of the open hall are probably no earlier than the 17th century.

Large, four-armed door-guardians (*dvārapālas*) flank the entrance of the closed hall. The outer walls have reliefs illustrating Shaiva themes. Facing the *liṅga* within the sanctum is a brass image of Shiva's mount, the bull Nandi.

Built into the north colonnade are two pre-Vijayanagara structures, the Parvati and Bhubaneshvari shrines (*c.* 12th century). Their highly ornate doorways, columns and ceilings, all carved in schist, are typical of the Late Chalukya-period style. Some 20 other less ornate but early shrines, most consisting of a sanctum (*garbhagṛha*), vestibule (*antarāla*) and porch, are crowded around the stepped tank (1b) immediately north of the complex.

Extending eastwards from the principal gateway is a colonnaded street almost 750 m long. Double-storey structures along it were possibly used by the courtiers attending religious festivals. A pavilion at the end of the street houses a monolithic image of Nandi. South-east of Hemakuta Hill is a plain shrine built around a boulder that is carved with a large Ganesha image (1c). Further southwards, an open pavilion shelters another smaller monolithic Ganesha image (1d).

The great Krishna temple complex (1e) further south was erected by Krishnadeva Raya in 1513 to commemorate his successful campaign in Orissa. The temple is badly ruined; the monumental gateways have partly collapsed, and the colonnaded street and tank (1f) to the east are mostly overgrown. A double series of enclosure walls contains the principal shrine. This is provided with both an outer open-columned hall (*mahāmaṇḍapa*) and an inner enclosed hall (*ardhamaṇḍapa*), the latter leading to a narrow ambulatory (*pradakṣiṇa prākāra*) surrounding the sanctum (*garbhagṛha*) and vestibule (*antarāla*). Above rises a triple-storey (*tritala*) superstructure of the *kūṭina* type (with small *kūṭa*s or square elements at the corners as a dominant feature) topped by a cupola (*śikhara*). The complex has numerous sculptures; the fragmentary reliefs of military scenes on the tower of the east gateway with warriors, horses and elephants may depict Krishnadeva Raya's battles. A multi-domed structure in the south court of the temple may have served as a granary. A short distance to the south of the complex is a monolithic sculpture of Narasimha (1g), the man-lion incarnation of Vishnu, dated to 1528. This huge (6.7 m) image is enclosed by walls.

East of Hampi is Matanga Hill, the site's most prominent elevation, named after the sage who protected Sugriva and Hanuman. Despite this *Rāmāyaṇa* association, the hill's main shrine is devoted to Virabhadra, an aspect of Shiva. North of the hill is the Kodandarama Temple (1h), enshrining large standing images of Rama, Sita and Lakshmana. A popular pilgrimage temple, it marks the spot where Rama crowned Sugriva. The Tiruvengalanatha Temple (1i), east of Matanga Hill, was built at the order of a military commander during the reign of Achyutadeva Raya. The layout follows the scheme of the mature Vijayanagara period. There are two walled rectangular enclosures, one within the other. The outer enclosure has a *gopura* on the north, while the inner one has three *gopura* on the east, west and north. Most of the architectural elements are ruined, but some fine sculptures are preserved on the columns in the hall west of the main gateway.

Small shrines, a natural cavern and a pool, all associated with Rama, line a path along the Tungabhadra River. Massive walls indicate that this part of the sacred centre was strongly fortified. Granite pylons in the river are all that remain of a foot-bridge (1j). Facing the ruined bridge is a hall associated with Purandaradasa, the celebrated Vijayanagara-period musician. Near by is an unusual feature known as the 'King's Balance' (1k), where rulers weighed themselves against food, less commonly against gold and jewels, which they then distributed to temple priests.

The nearby Vitthala complex (1l) is, even in its ruined state, one of the outstanding artistic achievements of the mature Vijayanagara period. Most of the complex is generally placed around the first quarter of the 16th century; parts of it may date to the reign of Krishnadeva Raya. An impressive ensemble of structures is set within a large rectangular enclosure (164×94.5 m) with *gopura* on the east, north and south. The main temple, dedicated to Vitthala, a form of Vishnu, consists of a sanctum with stepped pyramidal superstructure (*kūṭina vimāna*) preceded by a closed hall (*ardhamaṇḍapa*) with side porches and an open hall (*mahāmaṇḍapa*). A closed ambulatory (*pradakṣiṇa-prākāra*) with friezes encircles the sanctum (*garbhagṛha*) and its vestibule (*antarāla*). The superstructure, which is capped by a cupola (*śikhara*), appears to be a substitute, as its base does not reach the edges of the sanctum's wall section. The sanctum is now empty.

The glory of the temple is its open hall, which is laid out on a stepped plan. Massive granite piers fashioned with remarkable virtuosity into clusters of colonettes are covered with sculptures. Peripheral piers have rearing animals and riders. Composite brackets support beams spanning large spaces; ceilings are decorated with foliage and geometric designs. Overhanging eaves are double-curved; lotus designs are incised on to the corners, which have stone rings to hold lamps. The socle (*adhiṣṭhāna*) is unusual, with its friezes of lions, elephants and horses, the last accompanied by foreign attendants. Elephant balustrades flank the access steps on the east, while the steps on the north and south are decorated with leonine mythical creatures.

Immediately in front of the temple is a celebrated stone chariot housing an image of Garuda, Vishnu's vehicle (*see* INDIAN SUBCONTINENT, fig. 82). Reproducing in granite the form of a real chariot used in temple festivals, it is fashioned like a miniature shrine, but with wheels. The delicacy of the carved ornament, especially the lotus designs on the wheels, is exceptional. The detached open hall (*kalyāṇamaṇḍapa*) within the court has slender pillars remarkable for the intricacy of their carving.

Running eastwards from the principal gateway is a street (some 1 km long) lined with colonnades. To the north is a large tank with stepped sides and a small pavilion in the middle. Another colonnaded street runs northwards towards a Shiva temple, also of impressive proportions.

3. THE URBAN CORE AND ROYAL CENTRE. Separated from the sacred centre by an irrigated valley, the urban residential area is ringed by massive fortifications. Walls some 6 m high made of gigantic granite blocks with irregular but tightly fitting joints follow the tops of ridges

wherever possible; rectangular bastions preserve look-out posts.

Elaborately constructed defensive gateways are positioned along the ancient roads. Doorways are defined by high walls and roofed with beams on corbelled brackets. 'Bhima's gateway', one of the best preserved of the series, has ornamented corbels. Other examples employ Islamic architectural features, such as a dome raised high on four arches, or façades with arched openings and plaster decoration. Massive walls in front of the gateways define square enclosures with bent entrances where all traffic passing into the capital was controlled.

Within the urban core, mostly ruined or buried beneath accumulated soil, are the remains of habitations, temples, gateways, tanks, wells and other structures. An Islamic quarter, identified by its mosques and tombs, is located at the north-eastern end. Raghunatha Temple (see fig. 2p), on Malyavanta Hill in the eastern zone, has a great boulder forming its core. The side of the boulder within the sanctuary is sculpted with chief personages of the *Rāmā-yaṇa*. The royal centre (see fig. 2) is located at the south-western end of the urban core, within an incomplete circuit of fortification walls with gateways. Monuments associated with the king, court and military are located within and around a number of irregular and partly interlocking enclosures defined by high granite walls. Structures include palaces, temples, ceremonial platforms, columned halls, stables, treasuries, storehouses, watch-towers, tanks and wells.

The Ramachandra ('Hazara Rama') Temple (see fig. 2a) is situated at the core of the royal centre at the boundary between the zones of royal performance (west) and royal residence (east). The cult of Rama was of particular significance for the Vijayanagara rulers, and this temple served as a state chapel. It is contained within a rectangular compound, and its royal character is expressed in the vivid reliefs carved on to the outer face of the enclosure walls. These depict the processions of elephants, horses, militia and dancing girls of the Mahanavami festival, the capital's most important annual celebration. Unadorned gateways lead into the rectangular court. On the inner faces of the enclosure walls are friezes depicting the *Rāmāyaṇa* epic. In the middle stands the principal temple. The sanctum has a multi-storey superstructure (*tritala vimāna*) and is fronted by a closed hall and an open hall. Its socle (*adhiṣṭāna*) is delicately modelled, and the pilastered walls have a complete series of *Rāmāyaṇa* reliefs in three registers. Polished granite columns of the interior are adorned with elaborate images of Vishnu. A smaller shrine near by with a double sanctum has finely carved mouldings

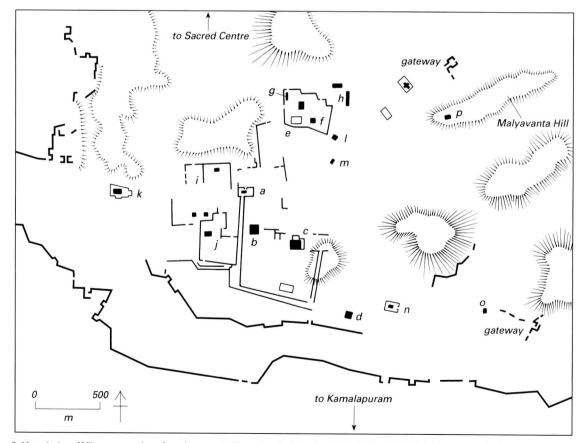

2. Hampi, site of Vijayanagara, plan of royal centre: (a) Ramachandra Temple; (b) 'hall of justice'; (c) 'Mahanavami' platform; (d) 'Queen's Bath'; (e) palace enclosure; (f) 'Lotus Mahal'; (g) 'treasury'; (h) 'elephant stables'; (i) palace enclosure; (j) palace enclosure; (k) Virupaksha Temple; (l) Madhava Temple; (m) Yellamma Temple; (n) Chandrashekhara Temple; (o) Ganagitti Jaina Temple; (p) Raghunatha Temple

and sculpture panels in which the *Rāmāyaṇa* reliefs are concluded.

The enclosures east of the Ramachandra Temple include the remains of structures associated with the ceremonial, administrative and military functions of the Vijayanagara rulers. South-east of the temple is a large enclosure (popularly known as the 'King's Palace') containing two platforms. One is square with 100 column footings and was probably the lower level of a hall of justice (2b). The sides of the second, the 'Mahanavami' platform (2c), which is multi-storey, are covered with lively friezes depicting royal scenes of hunting and state visits, as well as processions of musicians, dancers, elephants and horses. The Vijayanagara kings may have ascended this platform to witness the celebrations of the Mahanavami festival. All around are the remains of smaller columned structures, possibly for officers or guards. A subterranean chamber, now missing its roof, may have served as the state treasury. There is evidence of a substantial hydraulic system with wells, aqueducts and tanks. These include a finely finished tank with stepped stone sides and another almost 75 m long. Outside the enclosure to the south-east is a pavilion, known as the 'Queen's Bath' (2d), with Islamic architectural features. A square water-basin is surrounded by a corridor with ornamented vaults and decorated balconies.

An enclosure (2e) north-east of the Ramachandra Temple was possibly the residence of the king himself or of the military commander. In the middle of the enclosure is a two-storey pavilion built on a stepped plan known as the 'Lotus Mahal' or 'Chitragni Mahal' (2f), which is the finest example of the Vijayanagara courtly style at the capital. On an ornate socle (*adhiṣṭāna*) are 24 pillars supporting recessed, foliated arches. Much of the delicately modelled plaster detail around the arches is still preserved. Nine pyramidal towers with eavelike mouldings rise upon the roof. Three watch-towers in the surrounding walls are in a similar style. A nearby rectangular building with a gabled roof may have served as a treasury (2g).

Outside this enclosure to the east is a parade ground for military displays. Facing on to this are the celebrated 'elephant stables' (2h), the most impressive civic structure at the capital. Eleven chambers are aligned in a row; the central one has a square turret, while the others are roofed with alternating domes and vaults. The double-storey pavilion in the middle may have housed drummers and musicians. The adjacent structure has a raised verandah with multi-lobed arches and an inner colonnaded court. Athletic displays and military contests may have taken place here.

West of the Ramachandra Temple are palace enclosures (2i and 2j)—sometimes known as the 'mint' and the 'danaik's (governor's) enclosure'—constituting the zone of royal residence and associated with the private activities of the king and his household. Several buildings have Islamic architectural features, for example a multi-domed watch-tower, an octagonal two-storey pavilion and a nine-domed reception hall. Near by is an octagonal fountain. The remains of palace structures consist typically of a symmetrical stepped plan with a sequence of rising level in a 'U' formation; private chambers are located at the highest level at the rear. Excavations have revealed the stone basements, plaster floors and fragmentary rubble walls of these structures. Artefacts uncovered include mainly earthenware pottery, coins, figurines and mortars.

West of the palace enclosures is the Virupaksha Temple (2k), which probably served as a private chapel for the kings. Temples to the east of the royal centre include the Madhava (2l), Yellamma (2m) and Chandrashekhara (2n); further east is the Ganagitti Jaina Temple (2o), dated to 1385.

4. SUBURBAN CENTRES. Vijayanagara-period monuments are preserved in the modern villages of Kamalapuram, Kadirampuram, Anantasayanagudi and Hospet, all of which were suburban centres. Spread over more than 10 km, they give an idea of the original extent of the Vijayanagara capital.

Anantasayanagudi is named after its temple, dated to 1524 on the basis of an inscription. It has a double-apsidal vault rising more than 24 m. The long pedestal within the sanctuary was intended to support an image of Vishnu, the deity to whom the temple was dedicated, reclining on the cosmic serpent Ananta. The Pattabhirama Temple on the outskirts of Kamalapuram is set within an unusually large rectangular courtyard. Its principal shrine displays a long elevation; the halls have elegantly proportioned columns. The *gopura* is almost completely preserved in all of its ascending storeys. The village of Kadirampuram has two imposing tombs, one of which retains its masonry dome. Architecturally, the tombs are related to 15th-century Bahmani-style monuments (*see* INDIAN SUBCONTINENT, §III, 6(ii)(f)). They were evidently erected by wealthy Muslim citizens of Vijayanagara outside what must have been an Islamic quarter of the capital.

The nearby town of Anegondi has a longer history than the capital, having been a fortified settlement in pre-Vijayanagara times. It has several temples and also an interesting late Vijayanagara-period example of civic architecture (the Gagan Mahal), now serving as the town hall. Numerous 15th-century shrines are built on the nearby river bank, evidently the local holy spot. Outside the town to the south is a dilapidated two-storey structure with reused earlier columns; little remains of the Vijayanagara paintings that once adorned the ceiling. West of Anegondi is a large rocky outcrop ringed by fortifications. Within this citadel are the remains of military barracks, granaries, wells, tanks and palaces. Elaborate gateways are flanked by circular bastions. Walls and defensive gateways along the road to Gangawati indicate the northernmost extent of the capital.

BIBLIOGRAPHY

R. Sewell: *A Forgotten Empire* (London, 1900)

D. Devakunjari: *Hampi* (New Delhi, 1970)

G. Michell and V. Filliozat, eds: *Splendours of the Vijayanagara Empire: Hampi* (Bombay, 1981)

M. S. Nagaraja Rao, ed.: *Vijayanagara: Progress of Research*, 2 vols (Mysore, 1983–5)

J. M. Fritz, G. Michell and M. S. Nagaraja Rao: *Where Kings and Gods Meet: The Royal Centre at Vijayanagara* (Tucson, 1984)

J. Gollings, J. M. Fritz and G. Michell: *City of Victory, Vijayanagara: The Medieval Hindu Capital of Southern India* (New York, 1991)

A. L. Dallapiccola and others: *The Ramachandra Temple at Vijayanagara* (New Delhi, 1992)

G. Michell: *The Vijayanagara Courtly Style* (New Delhi, 1992)

GEORGE MICHELL

Hampton Court Palace. English palace situated on the north bank of the River Thames, *c.* 23 km upstream from central London. In the building that survives, two main periods of work can be seen: the remains of the Tudor royal palace, begun by Cardinal Thomas Wolsey between 1514 and 1529 and completed by Henry VIII between 1529 and 1547; and the Baroque palace built for William and Mary between 1688 and 1702 by Christopher Wren. The palace has also been continually altered and repaired up to the present day. The Tudor part of the building is probably the most important surviving example of early Tudor domestic architecture in England, and the Wren building contains one of the finest collections of early 18th-century decorative arts *in situ*.

1. TUDOR PALACE. The earliest buildings (destr.) on the site belonged to the Knights Hospitallers of the Order of St John of Jerusalem, although little is known about the nature of these buildings. The first important period of expansion began *c.* 1500, when the Grand Prior of the Order was Thomas Docwra. A manor house of brick and stone was constructed within the original moated enclosure, incorporating the earlier buildings on the site. Excavation has revealed the plan of this building, the courtyard of which is now partly defined by Clock Court. After 1500 the manor house was leased by Henry VII's Lord Chamberlain, Giles, 1st Baron Daubenny (*d* 1509), although Henry continued to have close connections with the property.

The second major phase of expansion began in 1514, when Henry VIII's Lord Chancellor, Cardinal Wolsey, took a lease on the manor house and the surrounding parkland. Wolsey's principal works survive: Base Court, containing double and single lodgings opening off a gallery; the south range (which replaced an earlier south range), with its geometrical ribbed ceiling; the eastern kitchen (much extended by Henry VIII after 1529); and a chapel and cloister, also altered by the King (*see* WOLSEY, THOMAS). The staterooms, which were arranged after the French fashion, with the King's lodgings on the principal floor, those of the Queen above, and Wolsey's long gallery, which projected 100 m into the gardens laid out around the house, were later destroyed.

Wolsey fell from favour in 1529, since when Hampton Court has remained the property of the Crown. The subsequent works of Henry VIII did not differ significantly in style from those of his minister; both he and Wolsey built in red brick with stone dressings, the façades of the buildings articulated by bay windows and by turrets surmounted by lead cappings. The brickwork was generally painted and the heraldic carvings that crowned gables, turrets and cappings held ephemeral vanes and banners. Henry's principal works, the royal lodgings (built on the site of the present Cloister Court), were later destroyed but his Great Hall (1532–4; see fig. 1), with its hammer-beam roof and grotesque decorations, gives some idea of the scale and magnificence of his ideas. The other surviving works of this period are the kitchens, a low range of domestic buildings on the north side of the palace; the indoor tennis-court, which was converted into lodgings in the 17th century; the Prince's Lodgings (built for the future Edward VI), sited on the north of Chapel Court;

1. Hampton Court Palace, interior of the Great Hall, 1532–4

and the ceiling of the chapel, a deep-ribbed structure with antique cherubs clasping the pendants.

The palace was surrounded by elaborate gardens (*see* GARDEN, §VIII, 4(iv)), beyond which stretched extensive parkland. To the north were orchards and to the south a privy garden, pond garden and mount garden. On the west side of the palace was a tilt-yard. Several small, brick banqueting houses and viewing towers were built in the gardens. Although the plan of the royal lodgings is lost, it is clear that Henry's important innovation was the construction of an entirely private wing to the east, in addition to the Queen's and King's sides that lay to the north and south respectively of the earlier inner court (destr.).

2. BAROQUE PALACE. After Henry VIII's death in 1547, Hampton Court remained largely unaltered until the Restoration (1660); in the 1670s Charles II built a new block of privy lodgings on the south-east corner of Henry VIII's inner court, and a canal was dug on an east–west alignment, centred on the middle of the east front. Charles's new lodgings did not survive long, however, since they were demolished with the rest of the inner court to make way for the Baroque palace of William and Mary. The canal was retained, however, and became an important factor in the subsequent designs both of Wren's new building and of William Talman's gardens. William and Mary employed Wren to draw up plans for remodelling the old palace (*see* WREN, CHRISTOPHER, §I, 5 and fig. 3). Two of Wren's early schemes survive; each involved demolishing the Tudor palace, retaining only the Great Hall as the centrepiece of an entrance court, with a court for offices behind and the royal apartments to the east. Both its plan and the surviving sketch of the elevations indicate that Wren's ideas owed much to Louis Le Vau's remodelled Louvre, Paris, which Wren had seen in 1666, a year after its completion. Possibly for reasons of speed,

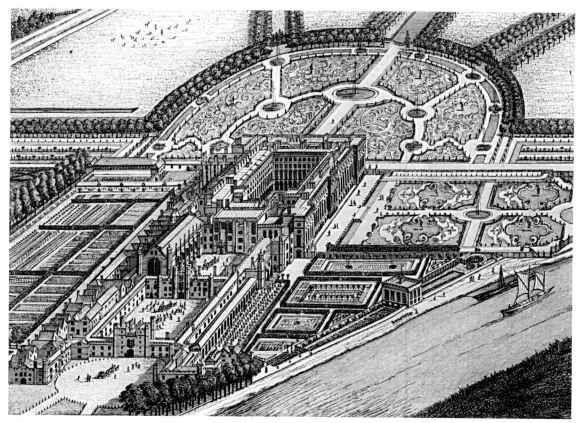

2. Hampton Court Palace from the south-west, begun 1514; detail from Johannes Kip and Leonard Knyff: *Britannia illustrata*, i (London, 1707, rev. 1720), pl. 6

and possibly because William and Mary did not favour Wren's idea, a more modest project replacing only the royal lodgings was undertaken.

In plan, Wren's Cloister Court is essentially a reorganization of the Tudor building. The disposition of accommodation—the King's to the south, the Queen's to the north and the privy lodgings to the east—is identical to Henry VIII's scheme of the 1530s. The elevations of Wren's building screen this plan and bear little relation to it; they resemble the work of Jules Hardouin Mansart at Versailles, the flat, block-like quality of which they share. Wren's elevations are richly decorated with dressings of Portland stone, which sit dazzlingly on the finely jointed scarlet brickwork of the façade. A low ground floor supports the principal floor, above which there is a mezzanine level and an attic. Building work, which began in 1688, came to a halt in 1694 once the shell of the structure had been constructed, owing to the death of Mary. When work resumed in 1699, after a fire had destroyed the principal royal palace at Whitehall, London, it was mostly the interior decoration that was undertaken.

The staterooms are generally panelled in oak from floor to ceiling; some were hung with damask or tapestries. Most of the ceilings were originally left plain, although Antonio Verrio worked on those of the King's staircase and dressing-room and, later, on that of the Queen's

drawing-room (*see* VERRIO, ANTONIO). Lime-wood carvings by Grinling Gibbons adorned fireplaces and door surrounds; the decorative ironwork was undertaken by JEAN TIJOU. The decoration of the royal apartments continued under Queen Anne (*reg* 1702–14) and George I (*reg* 1714–27): James Thornhill undertook the redecoration of the chapel and the ceiling of the Queen's bedchamber, and John Vanbrugh designed the rooms in the north-east corner of the Fountain Court for the Prince of Wales, later George I. It was not until 1735 that the Queen's staircase was painted by William Kent.

The original plan for the gardens had been to execute a parterre to a design by Daniel Marot I in the French style of André Le Nôtre. The gardens were eventually laid out, however, to designs prepared by William Talman and George London (see fig. 2). The main elements of this plan included a new privy garden to the south, the Great Fountain Garden to the east and the wilderness and kitchen garden to the north. The Fountain Garden was a vast semicircle, beyond which were three radiating avenues, each aligned with the central portico of Wren's building to the west and with Charles II's canal to the east. None of these gardens survives in its original form, nor is there any trace of the Thames-side Trianon planned by William Talman for the grounds.

3. LATER WORK. In 1732 the east side of Clock Court was rebuilt in a Gothic Revival style by William Kent, but

this was the last major alteration to the palace; after 1760 it ceased to be used as a residence for the Court. For the next 200 years Hampton Court provided grace and favour residences for impoverished servants of the Crown. Many minor alterations were undertaken in this period for the convenience of the residents, but none seriously altered the 18th-century plan. In 1838 the state apartments were opened to the public, and these now display the Crown's important collection of Renaissance paintings. This includes examples by Titian, Tintoretto and Mantegna (the *Triumph of Caesar* series), as well as by English 16th-century masters. During the 19th and 20th centuries a series of restoration programmes, influenced by the prevailing philosophies of the time, was undertaken. In 1845 the chapel ceiling was restored with advice from A. W. N. Pugin; in 1910 the original moat on the west front, filled in during the 18th century, was redug. In 1986 most of the south wing of the Wren building was destroyed by fire, which led to a new programme of restoration, completed in 1993.

BIBLIOGRAPHY

E. Law: *The History of Hampton Court Palace*, 3 vols (London, 1898)

J. Summerson: *Architecture in Britain, 1530–1830*, Pelican Hist. A. (Harmondsworth, 1953, rev. 7/1983), pp. 24–8, 245–8

H. Colvin, ed.: *The History of the King's Works* (London, 1963–82), iv, pp. 126–47; v, pp. 153–82; vi, pp. 329–39

G. H. Chettle, J. Charlton and J. Allan: *Hampton Court Palace* (London, 1982) [official guidebook]

S. Thurley: 'Henry VIII's Hampton Court: A Reconstruction of the Tudor Palace', *Archit. Hist.*, xxxi (1988), pp. 1–58

——: 'The Building of Wren's Fountain Court: Archaeological Findings after the Fire of 1986', *Apollo* (Aug 1994)

——: *The Genesis of Hampton Court Palace, 1100–1529*, English Heritage Archaeological Monograph (in preparation)

SIMON THURLEY

Hamrin region. Area in Iraq, some 150 km north-east of Baghdad. The Hamrin basin is lozenge-shaped, about 40 km long and 15 km wide. At the southern end the Hamrin Gorge marks where the Diyala River breaks through to the Mesopotamian plain. Here the construction of a dam led to an international project to salvage the archaeological sites in the valley. Approximately 90 ancient mounds were identified, ranging in time from the 6th millennium BC to the Sasanian and Early Islamic periods. The excavations, carried out between 1977 and 1980, produced significant discoveries of the Ubaid, Early Dynastic, Old Babylonian and Neo-Assyrian periods. Finds are in the Iraq Museum in Baghdad.

The Ubaid period (5th millennium BC) produced one of the earliest distinctive forms of vernacular architecture. This is the tripartite house-plan, of which particularly well-preserved examples were found at Tell Madhhur, Tell Abada and Tell Kheit Qasim III. This house type is characterized by a central cruciform hall running the length of the building, and a range of rooms on either side of the long axis. At Tell Madhhur, such a house had burnt down leaving many of the household contents *in situ*. These included 70 pots highly decorated with painted geometric designs and with incision, and typical everyday artefacts such as grindstones, hoes, spindle whorls and over 3800 clay sling bullets. At Tell Abada and Kheit Qasim III (see fig.) larger tripartite houses were found, consisting of up to three interlocking cruciforms.

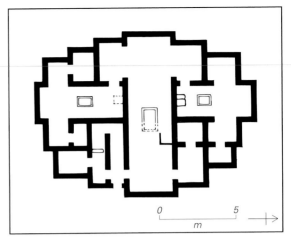

Hamrin region, Tell Kheit Qasim III, plan of building 1, Ubaid period (5th millennium BC)

The Early Dynastic period (*c.* 2900–2340 BC) is also marked by a distinctive architectural form. At four sites in the valley large round buildings were found, built of concentric walls of mud-brick. At Tell Gubba, such a building was made up of a central circular platform, *c.* 5 m in diameter, surrounded by eight ring walls 2 to 4 m thick. The total diameter of the building was *c.* 60 m. Running between the walls were corridors roofed over at a height of 4 m by corbelled arches, and there were four staircases leading to the roof or perhaps to a second storey. Rectilinear houses and storerooms were found built against the external face of the outermost concentric wall. At Uch Tepe there was a round building 27 m in diameter made up of two ring walls encircling an open courtyard. A fortified doorway was the only entrance. Corbelled arches of sun-dried mud-brick spanned the 5-m gap between the two walls—a considerable engineering feat. Around this building lay a town, possibly with a town wall. Five concentric walls were found at Tell Suleimeh, making up a massive solid structure. These walls abutted one another, so that there were no corridors between them as at Tell Gubba and Uch Tepe. In the central area was a mud-brick altar and fire installation. The fourth example was found at Tell Madhhur, where a single curving wall enclosed small rooms built against the inner face.

Not all these buildings necessarily served the same function. It has been suggested that the Uch Tepe building was a fortress, citadel and multi-purpose administrative complex, established by outsiders to secure the area and to protect trade routes; the altar and fire installation at Tell Suleimeh might suggest an additional religious function. Such structures are at the moment unique to the Hamrin area.

The temple or palace built at Tell Haddad during the Old Babylonian period (*c.* 2000–1600 BC) had two large rectangular courtyards with walls of semi-engaged mud-brick columns decorated in date palm and barley sugar designs. These are similar to decorations on the Old Babylonian temples at TELL EL-RIMAH in northern Iraq and at TELL LEILAN in Syria. At Tell Haddad and at Tell Khallaweh extensive areas of the town were excavated.

There were blind alleys, open squares, small shrines and temples, one-room houses (or shops) and larger courtyard houses. As at Ur, there was little planning; structures were built into the available space.

A Neo-Assyrian temple dedicated to the god Nergal was found at Tell Haddad. It had an outer and inner courtyard, with the shrine on the same axis as the entrance—a feature of Neo-Babylonian temples. According to inscriptions on the baked bricks, the temple was built by Assurbanipal (*reg* 668–627 BC). Fragments of the bronze doors decorated with heraldic animals and demigods were found as well as bronze plaques with designs of archers and animals, jewellery and some 250 tablets.

Although many of the objects from the region are rather mundane and of little artistic value in comparison to the architecture, their recovery has provided an unusually complete picture of the material cultures of the Hamrin area.

BIBLIOGRAPHY

'Excavations in Iraq, 1977–1978', *Iraq*, xli (1979), pp. 141–81
'Excavations in Iraq, 1979–1980', *Iraq*, xliii (1981), pp. 167–98
H. Fujii, ed.: 'Preliminary Report of Excavations at Gubba and Songor', *Al-Rāfidān*, ii (1981) [whole issue]
M. Gibson, ed.: *Uch Tepe I*, Hamrin Report, x (Copenhagen, 1981)
M. D. Roaf: 'The Hamrin Sites', *Fifty Years of Mesopotamian Discovery*, ed. J. Curtis (London, 1982), pp. 40–47
S. A. Jasim: 'Excavations at Tell Abada: A Preliminary Report', *Iraq*, xlv (1983), pp. 165–86
Sumer, xl [1983–4] [special issue devoted to the Hamrin excavations]

R. G. KILLICK

Ham Yun-dŏk (*fl* 16th century). Korean painter. Hardly anything is known of his life. What information is available states that he painted well. From this it can be assumed that Ham was a professional painter, as ordinary court painters at the Tohwasŏ (Bureau of Painting) occupied a very lowly position in society, their accomplishments only being mentioned in contemporary sources in cases of extreme merit. *Riding a Donkey* (album leaf, light colour on silk, 155×194 mm; Seoul, N. Mus.), traditionally attributed to Ham Yun-dŏk, depicts a scholar on a donkey. The animal's legs are splayed under the heavy burden as it stoops almost to the ground. Branches and twigs hang down from a rock face leaning obliquely into the picture. In its composition the painting is reminiscent of works produced by the Chinese Ming-period (1368–1644) Zhe school, which was much emulated in 16th-century Korea and the style of which was subsequently assimilated into the Korean tradition of literati painting. The painting is comparable to *Scholar Gazing at the Water* (mid-15th century; Seoul, N. Mus.) by Kang Hŭi-an (for illustration *see* KANG (ii), (1)). In Ham Yun-dŏk's picture, however, there is greater emphasis on the figure of the scholar. Various other devices, such as the extended 'axe-blow' strokes used in the depiction of the rocks, the light pink colouring of the gown and the anecdotal content, suggest a connection with *Landscape with a Boy Pulling a Donkey* (late 16th century; Seoul, Ho-am A. Mus.) by Kim Che (for illustration *see* KIM (i), (1)).

BIBLIOGRAPHY

An Hwi-jun: 'Hanguk chŏlp'a hwap'ung-ŭi yŏn'gu' [A study of Korean painting of the Zhe school style], *Misul Charyo*, xx (1977), pp. 36–7
R. Whitfield and Young-sook Pak [Pak Yŏng-suk], eds: *Korean Art Treasures* (Seoul, 1986), p. 60

B. Jungmann: *Die koreanische Landschaftsmalerei und die chinesische Che-schule* (Stuttgart, 1992), pp. 178–9

BURGLIND JUNGMANN

Han, Hermann. *See* HAHN, HERMAN.

Hana. *See under* TERQA.

Hanabusa Itchō [Taga Shinkō; Chōko, Hokusōō, Ushimaro] (*b* Osaka, 1652; *d* Edo [now Tokyo], 1724). Japanese painter. The second son of a physician, he went to Edo when he was 15 and began his artistic training under Kanō Yasunobu (*see* KANŌ, (13)). Itchō disliked the constraints of the KANŌ tradition, preferring the richer colour of TOSA painting and the lively genre depictions of urban life by such pioneers of *ukiyoe* ('pictures of the floating world'; *see* JAPAN, §VI, 4(iv)(b)) as HISHIKAWA MORONOBU. Itchō's unwillingness to embrace Kanō norms led to his expulsion from Yasunobu's tutelage. He achieved independence through the patronage of individual merchants rather than that of established élites. His art was a distinctive blend of *ukiyoe* subjects and a light, often satirical tone, but in a controlled style still influenced by Kanō brushwork. He enjoyed the pleasures of the world he depicted and participated in the urban intellectual culture of the late 17th century. He studied *haiku* poetry with Matsuo Bashō (1644–94) and perhaps influenced Bashō's painting style. A further dimension of Itchō's art is revealed in his *haiga* (painting illustrating a *haiku*). An example of one such collaboration is Itchō's sketch of a bagworm cocoon, which accompanies Bashō's *haiku* about the insect (Tenri, Cent. Lib.). Itchō occasionally ran foul of the authorities, suffering imprisonment and, in 1698, exile to the island of Miyakejima. He continued to paint in exile, treating rural themes such as *Country Scenes* (six-panel folding screen; Washington, DC, Freer). He was pardoned in 1709 and returned to Edo, where he began to use the name Hanabusa and founded the Hanabusa school, achieving considerable popularity with his works in an *ukiyoe* vein. His importance lies in the bridge he provided between *ukiyoe* and the Kanō school.

BIBLIOGRAPHY

Hanabusa Itchō, 1652–1724 (exh. cat., ed. J. Ostier; Paris, Gal. Jeanette Ostier, 1964)
T. Kobayashi and S. Sakakibara: *Morikage, Itchō*, Nihon bijutsu kaiga zenshū [Complete collection of Japanese painting], xvi (Tokyo, 1978)

JOAN H. O'MARA

Hanada, Kiyoteru (*b* Fukuoka, 29 March 1909; *d* Tokyo, 23 Sept 1974). Japanese writer and critic. He left the English Department of Kyoto University before graduating. In the period of censorship before and during World War II he developed a form of critical writing disguised by a vivid rhetorical style. After the war he wrote criticism based on a Marxist aesthetic theory and took part in many artistic movements. At the same time he wrote drama and fiction full of light humour and wit. He formed the Night Association (Yoru no Kai) in 1948 and the Record Art Society (Kirokugeijutsu no Kai) in 1957, while also advocating audio-visual art. He was also very influential on younger art critics such as Ichirō Haryū (*b* 1925), Yoshiaki Tōno (*b* 1930), Yūsuke Nakahara (*b* 1931) and Shin'ichi Segi (*b* 1928). Hanada believed strongly in the need for a synthesis of abstract art and Surrealism, and he argued that avant-garde art should be accepted as the representation of a personal form of realism.

WRITINGS

Avangyarudo geijutsu [Avant-garde art] (Tokyo, 1954)

SHIGEO CHIBA

Hanak, Anton (*b* Brno, Moravia [now Czech Republic], 22 March 1875; *d* Vienna, 7 Jan 1934). Austrian sculptor. He came from a poor family and moved to Vienna in 1889, becoming an apprentice wood-carver there until 1893. He spent the following years as a journeyman in Austria and southern Germany. In 1898 he began to study sculpture with Edmund von Hellmer at the Akademie der Bildenden Künste in Vienna, completing the course with honours in 1904. From 1901 he lived with his wife at her parents' house in Langenzersdorf, near Vienna. There he came into contact with the Primavesi family, who supported the artists of the Vienna Secession and also gave Hanak generous financial assistance. After the completion of his studies he was awarded the Akademie's Rome scholarship and travelled to Italy in 1904–5. He subsequently became an independent sculptor, carrying out commissions for his patron, the industrialist and banker Otto Primavesi, and taking part in exhibitions by the Vienna Secession, of which he was a member from 1906 to 1910. He became a friend of Gustav Klimt and Josef Hoffmann, with whom he took part in several exhibitions at home and abroad including those in Rome (1911), Dresden (1912) and Cologne (1914). He worked with Hoffmann on several projects, including Robert Primavesi's Vienna villa (1914–15). At the same time he made sculptures for the buildings of the socialist Vorwärts printing works (1910), the Stafa department store (1911) and the Eisenbahn-Versicherungsgesellschaft (1913) in Vienna.

From 1913 to 1932 Hanak ran a sculpture class at the Kunstgewerbeschule in Vienna. Despite a heart condition that impaired his working ability, he carried out major public commissions over the next few years, including the Magna-Mater-Brunnen fountain (1924–6; courtyard of the Viennese institution for homeless children; moved in 1965 to a park near the church of Wien-Mauer), sculptural decorations for city houses, a war memorial (1925) in the Zentralfriedhof, Vienna, and a monument to the Republic (1928) in the Schmerlingplatz, Vienna. In 1932 he was appointed professor of sculpture at the Akademie der Bildenden Künste in Vienna. In the same year, on the recommendation of Clemens Holzmeister, he was commissioned to make two monumental bronze statues, personifications of the *Old and New Turkey*, for the Emnyet monument in Ankara. This was his last major achievement, and was completed by his pupils after his death.

Hanak's art is close to that of Auguste Rodin. His more than life-size sculptures in marble, bronze, plaster and wood portray only the human form, often naked and massively solid. The figures appear liberated from gravity, in a condition of floating or metaphysical ecstasy. For his early public commissions he adopted a classical style, using carefully smoothed-down surfaces for the figures. In the sculptures executed for the social democratic city authorities in the 1920s and 1930s he worked in a more Expressionist style, particularly in his depictions of the 'new man', which reflected existential needs, torturing doubts and inner conflict in the raw, furrowed surface modelling. The most stirring example of this is the *Burning Man* (1922; Langenzersdorf, Anton Hanak-Freilichtmus.), a standing male figure with arms stretched up like a column of flame. His drawings have the same ecstatic character, with a nervous stroke that sometimes recalls Tintoretto. His pupils included the Austrian sculptor Josef Thorak (1889–1952) and Fritz Wotruba. In 1970 the Anton Hanak-Freilichtmuseum was opened in Langenzersdorf.

BIBLIOGRAPHY

M. Eisler: *Anton Hanak* (Vienna, 1921)

L. W. Rochowanski: *Der brennende Mensch: Aus den Tagebüchern Anton Hanaks* (Vienna, 1923)

M. Mrazek: *Anton Hanak, 1875–1934* (Vienna, 1969)

H. Steiner: *Anton Hanak: Werk, Mensch und Leben* (Munich, 1969)

G. Kapner: *Anton Hanak: Kunst und Künstlerkult: Ein Beispiel* (Vienna, 1984)

EDWIN LACHNIT

Hanamkonda and Warangal [Hanamkoṇḍa; Anmakoṇḍa and Warangal; Orguṅgallu; anc. Ānumakoṇḍa and Orukallu]. Cities, some 6 km apart, in Warangal District, Andhra Pradesh, India, that flourished *c.* AD 1100–1325. Both are temple sites and former capital cities of the KAKATIYA dynasty. Hanamkonda became the Kakatiya capital in the 11th century, when the rulers were given title to the Telingana region by the Chalukyas of Kalyana (*see* CHALUKYA, §2). The site rose to special prominence after the Kakatiyas asserted independence under Parola II (*reg c.* 1115–58) and Rudradeva (*reg c.* 1158–95).

The most important monument at Hanamkonda is the 'Thousand-pillared' temple dedicated by Rudradeva in 1163, according to an inscription. Set within a walled compound entered by a gateway on its east, the temple is of the triple-sanctum (Skt *trikūṭa*) type. It has a somewhat ambivalent orientation. As a whole it faces south, unusually, and its elevated platform (*upapīṭha*) extends into the vast, 300-pillared hall after which it is named. This hall is connected to the temple by a narrow platform, on which is an impressive image of the recumbent Nandi, the bull vehicle of Shiva, facing directly into the central sanctum, although this, surprisingly, is not the Shiva sanctum. The sanctums, dedicated to the gods Surya (on the east), Shiva (west) and Vishnu (central), are arranged on three sides of a hall of nine bays (*navaranga*). Each sanctum has a vestibule (*antarāla*) screened by finely carved lattices and with open-cut *makara toraṇa* arches (*see* TORANA).

The temple is built in the local Kakatiya variation of the contemporary Deccan style, characterized by compact structures densely covered with architectural detail and rendered in fine-grained stone. As in other contemporary Deccan temples, its wall is divided into a series of elaborate pilasters and niches. Each sanctum has a major exterior niche for sculpture, extended on each side. The relatively small amount of figural sculpture at the temple is notable for the metallic smoothness of the human forms set against the near-crystalline angularity of their jewellery and accoutrements. On the exterior the richly articulated sanctum walls are relieved by the airiness of the nine-bay hall; it is open for two-thirds of its elevation, silhouetting its slim pillars and elegant, extended eaves against the sky. The three superstructures (originally constructed in brick) do not survive, but their general form can be surmised from the temple models on the exterior niches and from the surviving form of the Ramappa temple at PALAMPET. In the interior the hall is surrounded by a parapet bench (*kakṣāsana*) and has intricately carved, finely polished pillars. The pillars are severely geometric, mixing prominent cubes and eight-sided panels with rings and discs.

The Kakatiya capital was shifted to the new fortress city of Warangal under Ganapati (*reg c.* 1198–1261). Most of the structures built within the mud and stone fortifications there were destroyed during or after the conquest of Muhammad ibn Tughluq (*reg* 1320–51) in 1323. The most impressive remains are the four giant grey granite arches (known as *haṁsa toraṇa*s) of the fort's main temple (the temple itself is in ruins) and the 16th-century Kush Mahal.

See also INDIAN SUBCONTINENT, §§III, 6(i)(f) and IV, 7(vi)(d).

BIBLIOGRAPHY
H. Cousens: *Chālukyan Architecture of the Kanarese Districts*, Archaeol. Surv. India, New Imp. Ser., xlii (Calcutta, 1926)
P. Sreenivasachar: *A Corpus of Inscriptions in the Telingāna Districts of H. E. H. Nizam's Dominions*, pt 2, Hyderabad Archaeol. Ser., xiii (Hyderabad, 1940)
K. R. Shrinavasam: *Temples of South India* (New Delhi, 1971)
M. R. Sarma: *Temples of Telingāna: The Architecture, Iconography and Sculpture of the Cālukya and Kākatīya* (Hyderabad, 1972)
S. Huntington and J. Huntington: *The Art of Ancient India: Buddhist, Hindu, Jaina* (New York, 1985), pp. 549–52

GARY MICHAEL TARTAKOV

Hanau Faience Factory. German ceramics manufactory. It was the first German faience factory and was established in Hanau, near Frankfurt am Main, in 1661 by the Dutch potters Daniel Behaghel (1625–98) and Jacobus van der Walle (*d* before 1693). The workers and the technical director Johannes Bally were also of Dutch origin. Mugs, pitchers, *Enghalskrugen* (narrow-necked jugs), writing utensils, vases, plates, trays, jars and other utilitarian objects were produced, mostly imitative of Dutch blue-and-white wares. East Asian figurative and floral decoration was used in addition to such European motifs as trade emblems, religious subjects and coats of arms (e.g. *Enghalskrug*, end of 17th century; Copenhagen, Kstindustmus.). During the period 1740 to 1786 the East Asian motifs were replaced with *Deutsche Blumen* (German flowers). Another typical ornament consisted of small sprays of flowers with birds on a pale-blue ground (e.g. gadrooned blue-and-white dish, *c.* 1750; Nuremberg, Gewmus.). Rococo table-services and stoves were also produced during this period. The competition, however, from English creamware (cream-coloured earthenware) and German porcelain at the end of the 18th century forced the factory to close in 1806. Attempts to produce creamware and porcelain failed.

BIBLIOGRAPHY
E. Zeh: *Hanauer Fayence* (Marburg, 1913/*R* Hanau, 1978)

WALTER SPIEGL

Hancarville, Pierre-François-Hugues, Baron d' (*b* Nancy, 1 Jan 1719; *d* Padua, 9 Oct 1805). French art historian and writer. He began as a captain in the service of Duke Christian Ludwig of Mecklenburg (*d* 1756). He mastered numerous languages and travelled in Germany, Spain, Portugal and Italy. Living the life of an adventurer, he was frequently in debt, for which he was imprisoned in 1750; it is not certain how he obtained his barony. He was the friend of Johann Joachim Winckelmann, who visited him in Naples in 1767. In 1764, when Sir William Hamilton (i), British Plenipotentiary in Naples, began to form his important collection of ancient vases, d'Hancarville was entrusted with the task of cataloguing them. The first volume of *The Collection of Etruscan, Greek and Roman Antiquities, from the Cabinet of the Honble Wm Hamilton etc* was published in Naples in 1766 and aroused Winckelmann's admiration; the second volume appeared in 1770, and the last two in 1776. The frontispiece and the vignettes, by Giuseppe Bracci (*fl c.* 1768), exerted some influence on contemporary design and taste; Josiah Wedgwood was among those who acquired a set of the plates.

In 1777 d'Hancarville travelled to London, where Charles Townley asked him to catalogue his collection of antiquities. In 1785, under the patronage of Townley and Richard Payne Knight, he published his *Recherches sur l'origine, l'esprit, et les progrès des arts de la Grèce*. In it he examined the religious and mythological origins of art, examining the significance of fertility symbols, and analysed themes of sexuality in Greek and Indian art. The interest of d'Hancarville's writings lies in his investigation of the irrational and exotic sources of creativity. His theories, which became associated with scholarly pornography, were taken up and developed by Payne Knight.

Although d'Hancarville welcomed the fall of the Bastille in Paris in 1789, he fled to Italy in the early days of the French Revolution. After his death his papers came into the possession of Wolstenholme Parr (*fl* 1791–1824), Fellow of Corpus Christi College, Oxford, who published a version of d'Hancarville's unpublished essay on Raphael.

WRITINGS
P. F. Hugues [P.-F.-H. d'Hancarville]: *The Collection of Etruscan, Greek and Roman Antiquities, from the Cabinet of the Honble Wm Hamilton etc*, 4 vols (Naples, 1766–76) [Eng. and Fr.]
Monumens de la vie privée des douze Césars d'après d'une suite de pierres gravées sous leur règne (Nancy, 1780)
Monumens du culte secret des dames romaines (Nancy, 1784)
Recherches sur l'origine, l'esprit, et les progrès des arts de la Grèce, 3 vols (London, 1785)
W. Parr, ed.: *Dissertation on the Helicon of Raphael* (Lausanne, 1824) [edn of an unpubd text]

BIBLIOGRAPHY
DBF
J.-C.-F. Hoefer, ed.: *Nouvelle biographie générale*, xxiii (Paris, 1858)
F. Haskell: *Past and Present in Art and Taste: Selected Essays* (New Haven and London, 1987), pp. 30–45, 230–32
M. Vickers: 'Value and Simplicity: 18th-century Taste and the Study of Greek Vases', *Past & Present*, cxvi (1987), pp. 98–137

AMAL ASFOUR

Hanch'ŏn. *See* YI CHAE.

Hancock, Robert (*b* Badsey, Hereford & Worcs, *bapt* 7 April 1731; *d* Brislington, Avon, 14 Oct 1817). English engraver and painter. He was apprenticed to George Anderton, an engraver, in Birmingham on 28 January 1745. In 1756 he joined the Worcester Porcelain Company of Dr John Wall (1708–76). He became a partner in the firm in March 1772. At Worcester, Hancock engraved copperplates for transfer-printing on porcelain. Many designs were adapted from contemporary engravings and paintings, particularly those of the French schools; such romantic scenes as *Amusements champêtres* and *Fêtes vénitiennes* were derived from compositions by Antoine Watteau. A series of children's games, including *Battledore and Shuttlecock*, *Blind Man's Buff* and *Marbles*, are based on a series of compositions engraved by Gravelot. Mugs with portraits of Frederick II, King of Prussia, dated 1757 (for illustration *see* WORCESTER), are based on an engraving by Richard Houston after a painting by Antoine Pesne and are among the best-known examples of Hancock's work. The English schools also provided subjects for Hancock's engravings. A half-length portrait of George III decorates Worcester mugs together with one of Queen Charlotte, both likenesses after engravings by James McArdell. Portraits of Admiral Edward Boscawen, General John Manners, the Marquess of Granby and William Pitt decorate mugs, and these likenesses are considered to be among the best of Hancock's work at Worcester. Hancock had two apprentices, Valentine Green and James Ross (1745–1821), both of whom later became well-known engravers.

After leaving Worcester on 31 October 1774 Hancock worked at the Salopian China Manufactory at Caughley, Salop, but his stay there was short, and he became a freelance artist living in south Staffordshire, first at Oldbury and by 1781 in Tividale. He provided plates for many book publishers, including the Birmingham firm of Pearson & Rollason, who commissioned a portrait of the *Rev. Mark Noble* for the 1784 edition of *Memoirs of the Protectoral House of Cromwell*. The same firm published a folio bible for which Hancock engraved a number of plates.

Shortly after he moved to Bristol *c.* 1795, Hancock made pencil, wash and watercolour portraits of *Robert Southey* and *Samuel Taylor Coleridge* (both 1796), *William Wordsworth* and *Charles Lamb* (both 1798; all London, N.P.G.). During this period he engraved many copperplates for mezzotint portraits, such as *Lady Chambers*, after a painting by Sir Joshua Reynolds, and a portrait of the musician and composer *Venanzio Rauzzini*, after a painting by Joseph Hutchisson (1747–1830). Two of his paintings, *Portrait of a Gentleman* and *Children and a Donkey* (both untraced), were exhibited at the Royal Academy, London, in 1805.

BIBLIOGRAPHY

A. R. Ballantyne: *Robert Hancock and his Works* (London, 1885)
C. Cook: *The Life and Work of Robert Hancock* (London, 1948); suppl. (London, 1955)

NORMAN STRETTON

Handler. Hungarian family of architects. They were active in the western Hungarian town of Sopron (Ger. Ödenburg). Jakab Handler (*b* Kismarton [now Eisenstadt, Austria], 20 Feb 1765; *d* ?Győr, Hungary) built residential blocks in an early Neo-classical style, though they show vestiges of the late Baroque as well. His own house (1815) at Sopron is an example. His son József Handler (*b* Lichtenwörth, Lower Austria, 1796; *d* Sopron, 12 Aug 1881) was an architect and building contractor whose works include a number of residential blocks in Sopron; these were built in the late Neo-classical style, with

occasional use of ornaments derived from medieval forms. From the mid-1850s József Handler worked in collaboration with his son Nándor (Ferdinánd) Handler (*b* Sopron, 27 Feb 1836; *d* Sopron, 12 Sept 1888), the most talented member of the family. Nándor visited Germany and Austria, probably the source of the medieval revival styles that permeate his work even in his later career, when he also adopted Renaissance and Baroque revival styles. The design of his residential block (1856) for Antal Horváth, Sopron, in late English Gothic style, was probably derived partly from a pattern book. The slender, single-spired church and adjacent convent and school of the Ursulines (1862), Sopron, blend German Romantic and late English Gothic features with elements derived from local Gothic churches. The houses built for Lajos Wanitschek (1868) and Károly Schreiner (1873), both in Sopron, are in the Renaissance and Baroque revival styles respectively, but the handling lacks any kind of academic rigour.

BIBLIOGRAPHY

E. Tompos: 'Handler Ferdinánd építész és családjának tagjai' [The architect Ferdinánd Handler and members of his family], *Soproni Szemle*, xvi (1962), pp. 17–32
G. Winkler: *Sopron építészete a 19. században* [The architecture of Sopron in the 19th century] (Budapest, 1988), pp. 35–9, 69–109

JÓZSEF SISA

Handley-Read. English collectors, writers and art historians. Charles Handley-Read (*b* 1916; *d* 15 Oct 1971) studied architecture at St Catherine's College, Cambridge, and also became associated with the circle around the philosopher Ludwig Wittgenstein. As a pacifist during World War II he was sent to Lingfield Epileptic Colony for children, where he introduced art therapy. He exhibited the results of this scheme in various places, including London and Paris, where the show particularly impressed Picasso. After the war he became a friend of Wyndham Lewis and wrote the first important study of the artist. In 1953 he married Lavinia Stainton (*d* 9 Dec 1971), who had studied at the Courtauld Institute of Art, University of London, specializing in 19th-century art. Both developed a keen interest in the art and design of the Victorian era, Charles favouring architecture, paintings and furniture and other decorative arts, while Lavinia specialized in Victorian sculpture. Their collection of paintings included works by Dante Gabriel Rossetti, Edward Burne-Jones, Lawrence Alma-Tadema, Frederic Leighton and Albert Moore. There were a few 20th-century paintings and sculptures, including works by Jacob Epstein, Wyndham Lewis and Henri Gaudier-Brzeska. The collection of Victorian sculpture included works by Alfred Gilbert, George Frampton, Alfred Drury, Frederick William Pomeroy and Charles Ricketts. It was especially strong in works by Gilbert, on whom Lavinia Handley-Read was an expert (e.g. *Victory*, *c.* 1887; London, V&A, and *Peace Leading St George to Victory*, *c.* 1906, see 1972 exh. cat., p. 109). Among the furniture and decorative objects were examples by William Burges, E. W. Godwin, Thomas Jeckyll, William De Morgan, Christopher Dresser, C. F. A. Voysey, C. R. Ashbee and Charles Rennie Mackintosh. On the deaths of the Handley-Reads some of the main items of the collection were bequeathed to the Victoria and Albert

Museum, London; other items were purchased by regional museums and the rest sold at auction.

WRITINGS
C. Handley-Read: *The Art of Wyndham Lewis* (London, 1951)

BIBLIOGRAPHY
H. Hayward: Obituary, *Burl. Mag.*, cxiv (1972), pp. 95–6
Victorian and Decorative Art: The Handley-Read Collection (exh. cat., ed. S. Jervis; London, RA, 1972)

Handmann, (Jakob) Emanuel (*b* Basle, 16 Aug 1718; *d* Berne, 3 Nov 1781). Swiss painter. He studied under Johann Ulrich Schnetzler (1704–63) in Schaffhausen from 1735 to 1739. He then went to Paris to work in the studio of Jean Restout II, who decisively influenced his work. In 1742 Handmann travelled through France, finding employment in a portrait partnership with Hörling in which Handmann painted the heads. He completed his studies in Italy, working principally in the studios of Marco Benefial and Pierre Subleyras in Rome, where he copied antique and Renaissance masterpieces. By June 1746 he was back in Switzerland and, apart from a trip to Germany in 1753, never again left his native land.

On his return from Italy, Handmann had painted mythological landscapes and religious paintings, but he is best known for his portraits in oil and pastel. His half-length of the mathematician and physicist *Leonhard Euler* (1753; Basle, Hist. Mus.), with its informal attitude and delicate handling, is typical of his French-derived style. In 1759 Handmann travelled through the Bernese Oberland with the artists Christian Georg Schutz and Johann Ludwig Aberli and stayed briefly in Basle before finally settling in Berne. He played a prominent role in the artistic life of this city with its fledgling academy (of which he was a member), and although most of his patrons were prominent Swiss citizens, his work entered collections as far afield as Estonia.

BIBLIOGRAPHY
Bénézit; *SKL*; Thieme–Becker

☐

Handschick, Brigitte (*b* Berlin, 14 July 1939; *d* Berlin, 26 Sept 1994). German painter. She studied at the Werkkunstschule (1957–61), Charlottenburg, Berlin. From an early stage she felt committed to a concept of art that is linked particularly with the tradition of painting in Berlin as promulgated, for example, by Werner Heldt. This tradition comprises a down-to-earth realism based mainly on observation, aiming to achieve clarity and simplicity and arising from a deep understanding of forms. She found her own way within the circle of her painter-friends in Berlin, adhering to the ethos of an attitude towards art formulated by Paul Cézanne. An important source of stimulus within this circle was Ernst Schroeder (1928–89).

Handschick used seemingly unchallenging subjects in her work: landscapes in her immediate vicinity, still-lifes, portraits. She used objectivity as a framework for arranging her pictures and applied a use of colour in her painting that was highly defined, allowing both spatial compactness and atmosphere to evolve. Forms were reduced to essentials. A number of her oil paintings were first conceived as watercolours. Among her most important paintings are *On the Teltow Canal in Altglienicke* (1978; Berlin, Alte N.G.) and a portrait of *Heinz* (watercolour, 1979).

BIBLIOGRAPHY
Deutsche bildende Künstlerinnen von der Goethezeit bis zur Gegenwart (exh. cat. by C. Keisch, E. Berlin, Staatl. Museen, 1975)
Brigitte Handschick (exh. cat., text by W. Sailer; E. Berlin, Gal. Torm, 1980)
Brigitte Handschick (exh. cat., text by A. Kühnel; Neubrandenburg, Zent. Bild. Kst, 1988) [pamphlet]
Brigitte Handschick: 24 Arbeiten auf Papier (exh. cat., text by A. Kühnel; Berlin, 1993)

ANITA KÜHNEL

Handwriting. *See* SCRIPT.

Han dynasty. Chinese dynasty dating to 206 BC–AD 220. Following the fall of the QIN DYNASTY in 221 BC, there was civil war until Liu Bang, posthumously known as Gaodi (*reg* 206–195 BC), became the first Han emperor. The Han was one of the golden ages in China's cultural history, during which the basic framework of Chinese civilization was established.

1. WESTERN HAN (206 BC–AD 9). The early period was one of consolidation of Qin laws and institutions in order to make China a unified and strong empire. The Western Han capital of Chang'an, a model of city planning with a grid street system, was sited south of the Wei River, a few kilometres north-west of modern Xi'an in Shaanxi Province (for illustration *see* XI'AN). The palace area occupied about two-thirds of the city area. Tomb models and textual evidence suggest the appearance of the various palaces built by Gaodi and later emperors. The imperial mausolea of Wendi (*reg* 180–157 BC) and Xuandi (*reg* 74–49 BC) are situated in the south-eastern suburbs, with nine other tombs north-west of the city. Tombs of statesmen and officials were furnished very lavishly in imitation of the houses of the living and to supply the dead with necessities for the afterlife. Generally, earlier tombs contained many real items and later ones more pottery items made in model form (*mingqi*). The MAWANGDUI tombs, Changsha, Hunan Province, dating to *c.* 186–168 BC, and the tomb complex of Wudi's brother at MANCHENG, Hebei Province, dating to *c.* 113 BC, were particularly rich in contents. Tomb chambers were often decorated with impressed motifs and painted bricks (*see also* CHINA, §II, 6(ii)(a)).

Under Wudi (*reg* 141–87 BC) there was a period of expansion: colonization and defence settlements extended into modern Guangdong, Yunnan and Sichuan provinces, and into Central Asia, Vietnam and Korea. Chinese trade was expanded via the SILK ROUTE through Central Asia and by sea to Burma and India; thus at least indirect contact was made with Iranian, Hellenistic and Roman cultures, all of which influenced and enriched Chinese art (*see also* CHINA, §I, 4(ii)(a)). Wudi created the imperial university, promoted Confucianism and encouraged new trends in music and poetry at his refined and luxurious court. Art was inspired not only by cosmopolitanism, but also by native motifs incorporating Daoist and Confucian elements (*see also* CHINA, §I, 6(i)). The government ran mines and craft workshops for silk and lacquer. It monopolized coinage, salt and iron production and sponsored astronomical, engineering and other projects. Western Han potters greatly improved kiln efficiency and increased production of both glazed and unglazed wares; they also introduced a lead glaze. Bronzes were plain, incised or inlaid (*see* CHINA, §VI, 3(v)). The 'spirit roads' (*shendao*) that lead to many tombs are lined with monumental stone sculptures of animals, such as the horse trampling a Xiongnu nomad in front of the tomb of Huo Qubing (*d* 117 BC) near Mao ling, Xingping County, Shaanxi Province (*see* CHINA, §III, 3).

2. EASTERN HAN (AD 25–220). The interloper Wang Mang, a member of one of the powerful consort families, usurped the throne in AD 9 and ruled as sole emperor of the Xin dynasty until his capture and death in AD 23. Then the Liu family reasserted itself, and Guangwudi (*reg* AD 25–57) proclaimed himself emperor, making Luoyang his capital. The remains of Eastern Han LUOYANG are about 100 km east of Chang'an and about 15 km east of modern Luoyang in Henan Province. The layout of the city was influenced by cosmological beliefs. As at Chang'an, the palaces occupied much of the city area, with northern and southern complexes connected by an arcade. Buddhism began to infiltrate China. Huandi (*reg* AD 147–67) made offerings to the Buddha and Laozi in his palace. Confucian, rather than Buddhist, influence is prevalent, however, in the Wu Family Shrine in Western Shandong (*see* SHRINE (i), §V), where reliefs illustrate historical, legendary and moral themes, such as those related to filial piety.

The contents of tombs demonstrate the wealth and power of the occupants, often officials and generals; sophisticated tomb models include bronze horses (*see* CHINA, fig. 168) from Leitai in Wuwei, Gansu Province. Palaces and other government offices were supplied with bronzes by the government. Silk continued to be exported, in exchange for pearls, rugs, woollens, grapes and other commodities. During this period, brown- and green-glazed pottery spread through the Yellow River valley and into the Yangzi valley. Tomb models of buildings provide an indication of contemporary architecture (*see* CHINA, figs 43 and 187). Pictorial bricks and engraved slabs in tombs were often mass-produced, and pictures showing scenes of harvesting, wine-making and banquets are indicative of contemporary painting techniques.

Paper was in general use by the end of the period (*see* CHINA, §XIII, 18). It was an exceptionally inventive time for calligraphy, with clerical script *lishu*, a modified form of small seal script (*xiao zhuanshu*), becoming formalized. Calligraphic achievements include monumental inscriptions on stone stelae, and calligraphic influence is evident in the decorative elements of many lacquers, embroideries, ceramics and bronzes (*see also* CHINA, §IV, 2(ii)(b)).

From about AD 88 the emperors were frequently young and influenced by powerful consort families and eunuchs; intrigues caused central government to lose much control to strong, local magnates. Huge peasant uprisings, some Daoist inspired and Messianic in character, such as the Yellow Turban rebellion, became a serious threat, and the last Han emperors were merely puppets. By AD 196 the Wei, Shu and Wu, known as the Three Kingdoms, had emerged, and in AD 220 the Han dynasty was finally overthrown.

BIBLIOGRAPHY
H. H. Dubs: *The History of the Former Han Dynasty*, 3 vols (Baltimore, 1938–55)

R. C. Rudolph and Wen Yu: *Han Tomb Art of West China: A Collection of First and Second Century Reliefs* (Berkeley, 1951)
H. Bielenstein: 'The Restoration of the Han Dynasty', *Bull. Mus. Far E. Ant.*, xxvi (1954), xxxi (1959), xxxix (1967) and li (1979) [whole issue]
B. Laufer: *Chinese Pottery of the Han Dynasty* (Leiden, 1909, rev. Tokyo and Rutland, VT, 1962/R 1970)
M. Loewe: *Everyday Life in Early Imperial China during the Han Period, 202 BC–AD 220* (London, 1968)
J. Fontein and Wu Tung: *Han and Tang Murals* (Boston, 1972)
H. Bielenstein: 'Loyang in Later Han Times', *Bull. Mus. Far E. Ant.*, xlii (1976), pp. 1–142
M. Loewe: *Chinese Ideas of Life and Death: Faith, Myth and Reason in the Han Period* (London, 1982)
M. Pirazzoli-t'Serstevens: *The Han Civilization of China* (Oxford, 1982)
Wang Zhongshu: *Han Civilization*, trans. K. C. Chang and others (New Haven, 1982)
D. Twitchett and M. Loewe, eds: *The Ch'in and Han Empires: 221 BC–AD 220* (1986), i of *The Cambridge History of China*, ed. J. K. Fairbank and D. Twitchett (Cambridge, 1978–)
W. Hung: *The Wu Lian Shrine: The Ideology of Early Chinese Pictorial Art* (Stanford, 1989)
M. J. Powers: *Art and Political Expression in Early China* (New Haven, 1991)

CAROL MICHAELSON

Hänel, Karl Moritz. *See* HAENEL, KARL MORITZ.

Hanequin de Bruselas [Hanequin de Egas] (*fl* 1448–70). Spanish architect. He was the brother of Egas Cueman (*see* EGAS, (1)) and is accordingly often incorrectly called Hanequin de Egas in bibliographies, although the documents refer to him as Hanequin de Bruselas. He introduced Flamboyant Gothic to Toledo and was the leader of a group of artists among whom were his brothers Egas Cueman and Antón Martínez de Bruselas (*fl* 1448–58), an architect's assistant. He is first documented in 1448 as Master of the Works of Toledo Cathedral, but he must have arrived in Toledo a little before 1440, probably to work on the funeral chapel of Alvaro de Luna in the cathedral, which had great influence on subsequent memorial chapels in Castile. About this time Hanequin probably also worked on the baptistery chapel for Archbishop Juan de Cerezuela who, in 1434, had come to Toledo from Seville where the new cathedral was being built. Around 1448 Hanequin probably began the second tier of the cathedral bell-tower. This seems to have been modelled on the famous spire of the Chapelle du Kreisker in Saint-Pol-de-Léon, Brittany, which was the native town of Pedro Guas, one of the team of masons and sculptors who accompanied Hanequin to Toledo. In February 1452 work began under Hanequin's direction on the magnificent Puerta de los Leones on the south transept, the richest and most beautiful of the cathedral portals, boldly Flamboyant in style. Hanequin probably also contributed to the residential quarters of Escalona Castle (Toledo) for Alvaro de Luna, the remains of which confirm the magnificence recorded by contemporary chroniclers.

At the beginning of 1454 Hanequin de Bruselas is documented as working with Egas Cueman in Cuenca Cathedral, where he directed work on the choir-stalls (now in the Colegiata, Belmonte) and probably contributed to the planned remodelling of the apse, which was based on the ambulatory of Toledo Cathedral (*see* CUENCA, §2). It must have been around this time that Hanequin undertook work at the fortified monastery of Calatrava, Ciudad Real, on the funeral chapel (destr.) of Pedro Girón, the Order's Grand Master. Hanequin is mentioned in connection with

3

5

the works of Toledo Cathedral up to 1470, but by 1475 the Master of the Works was Martín Sánchez Bonifacio. In addition to his brothers, there are references to Hanequin's brother-in-law Alfonso and to his sons Martín de Bruselas (*fl* 1461–75) and Hanequin, an official (*fl* 1465–70).

BIBLIOGRAPHY

J. M. Azcárate: 'El mestro Hanequin de Bruselas', *Archv Esp. A.*, xxi (1948), pp. 173–88
B. Gilman Proske: *Castilian Sculpture: Gothic to Renaissance* (New York, 1951), pp. 57, 109–13, 123, 170, 195, 479
J. M. Azcárate: *Le arquitectura gótica toledana del siglo XV* (Madrid, 1958), pp. 13–15
——: *Arte gótico en España* (Madrid, 1990), pp. 116, 122, 243

JOSÉ MARíA AZCÁRATE RISTORI

Hanfstaengl [Hanfstängl]**, Franz (Seraph)** (*b* Baiernrain bei Bad Tölz, 1 March 1804; *d* Munich, 18 April 1877). German lithographer and photographer. In 1816 he moved to Munich, where he studied drawing under the German sculptor Peter Schöpf (1757–1841) at the Polytechnische Schule and lithography under the German lithographer Hermann Josef Mitterer (1764–1829) at the Feiertagschule. From 1819 to 1825 he attended the Akademie der Künste in Munich. Acquiring a great mastery of lithography, he then worked as a portrait lithographer, producing works such as *Otto I, King of Greece* (1832; Vienna, Österreich. Nbib.). In 1833 he set up his own lithographic publishing house in Munich and the following year travelled to Paris to study under the lithographer Joseph Lemercier. In 1835 he was one of a number of artists commissioned by the government to provide lithographic reproductions of the paintings in the Königliche Gemäldegalerie in Dresden. Hanfstaengl in fact made the majority of these, 134 out of 195 being from his hand. The resulting prints were collected as *Dresdener Galeriewerk* and this project occupied him until 1852.

In 1848 he installed in his own firm the galvanographic reprographic method invented by the scientist Franz von Kobell (1803–75). After 1853 Hanfstaengl devoted his Munich business entirely to this new medium of photomechanical reproduction, which was increasingly successful. At the same time he turned again to portrait photography and from 1855 to 1860 published a series of photographs that formed the *Album der Zeitgenossen*. This contained portraits of famous contemporaries, such as *Hans Christian Andersen* (1860; see Gebhardt, p. 166); others in the series included *Ludwig I, King of Bavaria*, the chemist *Justus von Liebig* and the composer *Richard Wagner*. Continuing photography until the late 1860s, he also made a few photomontage group portrait works. He exhibited many photographs at the Deutsche Industrie-Ausstellung at the Glaspalast in Munich in 1854 and at the Exposition Universelle in Paris in 1855. At the latter he displayed several prints from retouched negatives, a process he pioneered. In 1868 he handed over his publishing business to his son Edgar Hanfstaengl (1842–1910).

BIBLIOGRAPHY

C. Diener and G. Fulton-Smith, eds: *Franz Hanfstaengl: Album der Zeitgenossen* (Munich, 1975)
H. Gebhardt: *Franz Hanfstaengl: Vom der Lithographie zur Photographie* (Munich, 1984)

Han Gan [Han Kan] (*b* Chang'an [now Xi'an, Shaanxi Province]; *fl c.* AD 742–83). Chinese painter. He was celebrated for his paintings of figures, goblins and spirits and, especially, for his depictions of saddled horses. He came from a poor family but as a young man was patronized by the great poet Wang Wei, who sponsored his painting studies under Cao Ba (*fl* 713–42), the pre-eminent horse painter of the day. Han Gan's achievement and influence eventually outstripped those of Cao.

In the *Lidai minghua ji* ('Record of famous painters of all periods'; 847), Zhang Yanyuan wrote that Emperor Xuanzong (*reg* AD 712–56) 'loved large horses and ordered Han to paint the most noble of his more than 400,000 steeds'. Han thus depicted imperial favourites such as Feihuang, Fouyun, Wuhua, Yuhuacong and Zhaoyebai, showing their extraordinary pelts, rounded bones and joints and thick hooves. Often they were seen in precarious situations, turning abruptly or toiling through deep swamps. Han also portrayed favoured steeds stabled among the imperial horses. Perhaps in reaction to the sinewy style established by such artists as Yan Liben and Zhan Ziqian, Han evidently liked to paint plump horses, a preference for which his contemporary, the poet Du Fu, had chided him, writing of the 'large, fat horses . . . pure flesh without bone, . . . allowing their spirit to dissipate'. The rebellion of An Lushan in 756 almost destroyed the large horses as a species, and Han was thus rendered idle. The story is told, however, that in response to a request, he painted a horse for a dead person and burnt the work in offering, to be rewarded later by a ghost riding forward to thank him.

Zhang Yanyuan also wrote of Han's 'marvellous' other works: a wall painting depicting three door guardians at Baoying si, wall paintings of *bodhisattva*s and the Pure Land in front of the Buddha Hall, and 24 sages at Zisheng si. Writing at about the same time as Zhang, Zhu Jingxuan ranked Han lowest (*xia*) of the three grades in the Divine Class (*shenpin*), noting that he excelled in 'saddled horses, high monks, Buddhist portraits, ghosts and divinities, human figures, flowers and bamboo'.

The great 11th-century poet and calligrapher Su Shi was a lover of Han Gan's horse paintings and left numerous long poems praising them. The *Xuanhe huapu* ('Xuanhe collection of painting'; preface 1120), the catalogue of the collection of the Song emperor Huizong (*reg* 1101–25), listed no fewer than 52 works by Han Gan, mostly horse paintings, although the now-famous portrait of the favourite mount of Emperor Xuanzong, *Zhaoyebai* (New York, Met.; see fig.), a title that reappeared in 16th-century texts, was not one of them. The extant version of *Zhaoyebai*, part of a handscroll executed in ink on paper, shows a spirited horse rearing its angry head in protest against being tethered to a post. The surface is defaced by collectors' seals and admirers' encomia, many belonging to the Qianlong emperor (*reg* 1736–96). The simple delineation and blocky formation of individual parts of the painting, as well as its spirited expression, indicate a Tang-period (AD 618–907) date. However, other features identify the work as an inaccurate copy of what may well have been an unfinished Tang-period sketch: the horse lacks a tail, the lower section of the left hind leg emerges erroneously from behind the right hind leg, with which it

Han Gan (attrib.): *Zhaoyebai* (detail), handscroll, ink on paper, 206×341 mm, *c.* AD 742–83 (New York, Metropolitan Museum of Art)

Mi Fu: *Hua shi* [History of painting] (preface 1103).*Xuanhe huapu* [Xuanhe collection of painting], 23 *juan* (preface 1120), *juan* 13; *R* in Huashi congshu (Taipei, 1974)

Deng Chun: *Hua ji* [Painting continued], 10 *juan* (preface 1167)

Zhou Mi: *Yunyan guoyan lu* [Clouds and objects passing by one's eyes: notes on objects seen by the author], 2 *juan* (late 13th century)

Yu Jianhua, ed.: *Zhongguo meishu jia renming cidian* [Dictionary of Chinese artists] (Shanghai, 1981)

JOAN STANLEY-BAKER

is mismatched, and the right front leg is shrivelled and lifeless.

Another postulated attribution to Han is an album leaf in slight colours and ink on silk entitled *Horses and Groom* (h. 270 mm; Taipei, N. Pal. Mus.), which shows a bearded Central Asian groom mounted on a white charger and leading a saddled chestnut stallion. The leaf bears an inscription dated 1107 in the style of Emperor Huizong reading 'Genuine autograph of Han Gan'. The painting is more modern in conception than *Zhaoyebai*, however, with mannerized rendition of drapery and neck folds and fine, effete brushwork. It is likely, therefore, that the artist had experience of Yuan-period (1279–1368) figurative painting.

Han Gan's most successful pupil was Kong Rong. Later admirers and followers of Han's style included the *baimiao* ('plain-line drawing') specialist Li Gonglin of the Northern Song (960–1127) period and the Yuan master Zhao Mengfu, who both copied the paintings of and admitted his deep indebtedness to Han Gan.

BIBLIOGRAPHY

Pei Xiaoyuan: *Zhenguan gongsi huashi* [Record of paintings in public and private collections in the Zhenguan era [AD 627–50]], 1 *juan* (preface AD 639); *R* in Huapin congshu

Zhu Jingxuan: *Tangchao minghua lu* [Record of famous painters of the Tang dynasty] (*c.*AD 840)

Zhang Yanyuan: *Lidai minghua ji* [Record of famous paintings of all periods], 10 *juan* (preface AD 847), *juan* 9

Guo Ruoxu: *Tuhua jianwen zhi* [Experiences in painting], 6 *juan* (preface 1075); *R* in Huashi congshu (Taipei, 1974); Eng. trans. in A. C. Soper: *Kuo Jo-hsü's 'Experiences in Painting' (T'u-hua chien-wen chih): An Eleventh Century History of Chinese Painting* (Washington, DC, 1951/*R* 1971)

Hangzhou [Hangchow, Hang-chou; formerly Lin'an]. Capital of Zhejiang Province, China. After Bianliang (modern Kaifeng), capital of the Northern Song dynasty (960–1127), fell to the Ruzhen (Jürchen) in 1126, Gaozong, a younger son of the Northern Song emperor Huizong, re-established the court as the Southern Song dynasty (1127–1279), at Lin'an, later known as Hangzhou. Its qualities of cultivated and natural beauty made Hangzhou, together with Suzhou, one of the most famous beauty spots in China. This is reflected in the popular saying '*Shang you Tian tang, xia you Su Hang*' ('Heaven above, Suzhou and Hangzhou on earth').

At Shuitianban, near Hangzhou, evidence of a local branch of the LONGSHAN culture has been unearthed, indicating that the area has been inhabited since the Neolithic period (*c.* 6500–*c.* 1600 BC). The region was settled more substantially at the beginning of the Qin period (221–206 BC), but it only became important during the Sui period (AD 581–618), when the Grand Canal was dug between 605 and 610 to link Xi'an with the southern provinces. Between AD 893 and 978, while Hangzhou served as the capital of the state of Wuyue, a lagoon off the Qiantang River was dammed to create the large freshwater lake known as Xi hu (West Lake). Its ideal natural setting and mild climate made it popular with scholars and intellectuals, and much of its scenery has been immortalized in the paintings and poems of the literati. Painters such as Gao Kegong created almost literal renderings of the lake region. Su Shi, who served as the governor of Hangzhou, described the beauty of the lake in many of his poems. In Europe and America the lake has been immortalized in the familiar willow pattern depicted on blue-and-white china.

The transfer of the Song capital from Bianliang to Lin'an confirmed the southward shift of focus of Chinese culture that had been going on for centuries. Lin'an was now the nucleus of the Chinese state rather than a place of exile, and it became the most sophisticated and wealthy city of its day, with collections of art treasures even finer than those of Bianliang. The emperors played an increasingly active role in the cultural life of the city as their political power declined. Both Gaozong and his grandson Ningzong (*reg* 1195–1224) supervised members of the imperial academy (*see* CHINA, §V, 4(i)(c)) in the decoration of the newly constructed palaces and pavilions.

The development of the visual arts in the Southern Song period under the leadership of the Academy was especially significant for Chinese painting. Gaozong reassembled the artists who had belonged to the Northern Song court and soon was able to reconstitute Huizong's painting academy. Li Tang was especially honoured among the old masters: his name was the first on the list of members; he was made *daizhao* ('painter in attendance') and received the traditional title *jindai* ('golden girdle'). Su Hanchen, Li Anzhong (*c.* 1117–1140), Li Di and Zhao Boju painted the traditional themes of birds, flowers, scholars at leisure and scenes of palace life in an attempt to recapture the glories of the past. Ma Yuan and Xia Gui, members of the Academy and also *daizhao*, pursued the approach seen in Li Tang's later landscapes and introduced significant compositional innovations. Their school, which became known as Ma-xia, was one of the most important and influential in the subsequent development of Chinese painting. Their use of conceptual space may reflect influences of Chan Buddhism (*see* CHINA, §V, 3(ii)). Ningzong conferred the *jindai* not only on members of the Academy such as Xia Gui but also on several members of the independent Chan Buddhist school in recognition of the artistic contribution made by the monasteries within the city and around the lake. It was here that Liang Kai and Muqi produced some of their most innovative work.

Hangzhou was also an important centre of ceramic production in the Southern Song period. Potters producing Guan ware (*see* CHINA, §VII, 3(iv)(b)) established themselves in the *judan* ('Altar of heaven quarter') and continued practices initiated in Bianliang. Some of the wares may have been for the court but some must also have been for more general use.

The life of culture and aristocratic leisure that developed under the Southern Song court continued even after the fall of the city to the Mongols in 1276. Marco Polo (*c.* 1254–1324), visiting Hangzhou in the 13th century, described it as one of the finest and most splendid cities in the world, marvelling at its material prosperity and luxury. He called the city Kinsai, which may be translated as 'Capital' but which has also been interpreted as Xingzaisuo, meaning the temporary residence of the emperor. The network of canals and bridges reminded him of Venice and he was awed by multi-storey buildings with shops on the ground level grouped around market squares. Brother Odoric of Pordenone (*c.* 1265–1331), a Franciscan friar, visited Hangzhou in the 1320s and, like Marco Polo, marvelled at the size of the city and likened it to Venice.

During the Ming (1368–1644) and Qing (1644–1911) periods the city was still immensely wealthy. Under the Ming, Hangzhou became a centre of book printing; large private libraries that spared no expense in the production of beautifully illustrated books were developed. During the Qing period the city was a favourite imperial summer resort, especially for the Qing emperors Kangxi (*reg* 1662–1722) and Qianlong. Tragically, much of the city was destroyed in the Taiping Rebellion (1850–64).

BIBLIOGRAPHY
C. P. Fitzgerald: *China: A Short Cultural History* (London, 1935, rev. 3/1961)
M. Loehr: 'A Landscape by Li Tang, Dated 1124', *Burl. Mag.*, lxxiv (1939), pp. 288–93
R. Grousset: *The Rise and Splendour of the Chinese Empire* (London, 1952)
A. Boyd: *Chinese Architecture and Town Planning (1500 BC–1911)* (London, 1962)
J. Cahill: *The Art of Southern Sung China* (New York, 1962)
K. Suzuki: 'Hsia Kuei and the Academic Style in Southern Song', *Proceedings of the International Symposium on Chinese Painting* (Taipei, 1970), pp. 417–43
MARY S. LAWTON

Han Ho [*cha* Kyŏnghong; *ho* Sŏkpong, Ch'ŏngsa] (*b* Kaesŏng, Hwanghae Province, 1547; *d* 1605). Korean calligrapher and scholar–official. He was one of three prominent calligraphers of the Chosŏn period (1392–1910), the others being Yi Yong and Kim Chŏng-hŭi. Han was awarded the *chinsa* degree in 1567 and served as district chief of Kap'yŏng, Kyŏnggi Province, and court official in charge of writing official documents. He excelled in regular, running and cursive scripts. During the Japanese invasions of Korea in 1592 and 1598 Han was in charge of writing most of the diplomatic documents that were sent to China and Japan (e.g. his letter of 1597; Seoul, Sunggun'gwan U. Mus.; see Kim, Choi and Im, fig. 124, p. 137). Consequently, his fame as calligrapher spread to China where he was praised by Wang Shizhen and Zhu Zhifan (*fl* early 17th century).

In the early Chosŏn period, the style of Zhao Mengfu was still dominant, as it had been since its introduction to Korea during the late Koryŏ period (918–1392), but calligraphers of the mid-Chosŏn period began to opt for the style of Wang Xizhi because they were tired of the restrictive nature of Zhao Mengfu's regular script (*see* KOREA, §V, 4 and 5). However, because no genuine specimen of Wang's writing was available for study, Han Ho apparently modelled his calligraphy on a spurious example. Nevertheless, he achieved a style that is both refined and robust. His special strength as a calligrapher lay in his ability to produce consistently good writing in enormous quantities. There are numerous extant examples of his works both in stelae and in albums (*see* KOREA, fig. 50). Among the most famous are the Tombstone of Kija in P'yŏngyang, the Stele at the Sŏnjuk Bridge in Kaesŏng and the album, *Sŏkpong ch'ŏnja mun* ('Thousand-characters essay'), written in 1583 at the request of King Sŏnjo (*reg* 1567–1608). Han Ho had a number of followers, including members of the royal family.

BIBLIOGRAPHY
Kim Yŏng-yun: *Han'guk sŏhwa inmyŏng sasŏ* [Biographical dictionary of Korean painters and calligraphers] (Seoul, 1959), pp. 152–4
Im Ch'ang-sun, ed.: *Sŏye* [Calligraphy] (1973), xi of *Han'guk misul chŏnjip* [The arts of Korea] (Seoul, 1973–5)
Kim ki-sŭng: *Han'guk sŏyesa* [History of Korean calligraphy] (Seoul, 1975)
Kim Won-yong [Kim Wŏn-yong], Choi Sun U [Ch'oe Sun-u] and Im Chang-soon [Im Ch'ang-sun], eds: *Paintings*, ii of *The Arts of Korea* (Seoul, 1979), p. 137
YI SŎNG-MI

Hanjirō Sakamoto. *See* SAKAMOTO, HANJIRŌ.

Hankar, Paul (*b* Frameries, 11 Dec 1859; *d* Brussels, 17 Jan 1901). Belgian architect and designer. A stonecutter's son from Hainaut, he served an apprenticeship as a decorative sculptor before entering the Brussels Académie in 1873, where he later met Victor Horta, whose career ran parallel to Hankar's for over a decade. Both were responsible for the introduction of ART NOUVEAU in Belgium in 1893.

From 1879 Hankar worked with the architect Henri Beyaert, eventually managing his practice. In 1893 he set up on his own and participated in the Symbolist movement Le Sillon, headed by his friends Xavier Mellery and Fernand Khnopff and sculptors such as Jef Lambeaux and Charles Van der Stappen. His first independent work was his own house in the Rue Defacqz, Brussels (1893), a sober structure in brick with blue stone dressings and horizontal bands, decorated with wrought-iron work and a monochrome mural by the painter Adolphe Crespin (1859–1944). Unlike the flowing, more flamboyant style of Horta's earliest private residences, Hankar's house is a model of formal restraint, showing a Japanese influence that had been disseminated by his friend the Belgian writer Jules Destrée's *Imagerie japonaise* (1888). He used the same style for the two Zegers–Regnard houses, Avenue Louise, Brussels (1894 and 1895, destr.), the Ciamberlani and Janssens houses, Rue Defacqz, Brussels (1897 and 1898), and the Renkin, Bartholomé and Kleyer houses, Brussels (1898, all destr.). These commissions established his reputation as one of Belgium's most outstanding domestic architects, particularly gifted at designing for narrow, cramped sites and using economical materials such as wood and brick. These inventive houses secured Hankar an international reputation.

Hankar's most lasting fame came through his shop-fronts. The first of these, Au Carnaval de Venise in the Rue de l'Ecuyer, Brussels (1896, destr.), was mentioned in *The Studio* in November, 1896. The second, Niguet's Shirt Shop, Rue Royale, Brussels (1897), with its astonishing decoration of Japanese-style window bars, curved mahogany tracery and chamfered lights, epitomized the flamboyant Art Nouveau shop front. It was so successful that Hankar gained the commission, in preference to Horta, to design the Exposition Congolaise at Tervuren, part of the Exposition Internationale of 1897 in Brussels. He commissioned a group of some 40 Symbolist sculptors, including Philippe Wolfers, together with Georges Hobé, Gustave Serrurier-Bovy and Henry Van de Velde, and the exhibition halls provided a spectacular expression of Belgian Art Nouveau at its peak.

From 1898 Hankar was obliged to curtail his activities owing to ill-health. At the same time he criticized excessive ornamentation and approached the treatment of space and materials more rigorously. His later work includes two cottages for the Wolfers brothers at La Hulpe (1899–1900, destr.). The interiors and the furniture that he also designed for them derived more from Chinese than from Japanese art and were strikingly modern. Despite his early death, Hankar's work was well received and influential, both nationally and internationally, as at Otto Wagner's Majolikahaus in Vienna (1898).

BIBLIOGRAPHY
C. Conrardy and R. Thibaut: 'Paul Hankar (1859–1901)', *La Cité*, iv (1923), no. 2, pp. 21–5; no. 3, pp. 37–42
C. De Maeyer: *Paul Hankar* (Brussels, 1963)
F. Borsi and H. Wieser: *Bruxelles: Capitale de l'Art Nouveau* (Brussels, 1971)
F. Russell, ed.: *Art Nouveau Architecture* (London, 1979)
F. Loyer: *Paul Hankar: La Naissance de l'Art Nouveau* (Brussels, 1986)
FRANÇOIS LOYER

Hankō. *See* OKADA, (2).

Hanly, Patrick (*b* Palmerston North, 2 Aug 1932). New Zealand painter. A year after leaving art school in 1956 he travelled widely in Europe and exhibited with some success in London, winning an Italian government scholarship in 1960. However, he became disillusioned with Europe and returned to New Zealand in 1962, settling in Auckland. His return was marked by paintings that tried to come to terms with the very different Pacific environment, but showed the influence of Picasso, Bacon and the British Pop art movement. A series of paintings, including *Figures in Light, 17* (1964; Auckland, C.A.G.), used sunbathers on a beach as the central theme.

In the late 1960s Hanly's technique changed dramatically after he experimented with painting in a darkened room. He began to introduce a 'drip' technique, similar to that of Jackson Pollock, into his paintings and prints. Later his work became more lyrical, with the early influences of Picasso still being assimilated. He also used his paintings to further campaigns for a nuclear-free Pacific by depicting such events as the arrival of nuclear submarines in the port of Auckland. He was a noted muralist, with major commissions in the Christchurch Town Hall (1972) and the Aotea Centre in Auckland (1990).

BIBLIOGRAPHY
G. H. Brown and H. Keith: *An Introduction to New Zealand Painting, 1839–1980* (Auckland, 1969, rev. 1982)
R. Haley: *Hanly: A New Zealand Artist* (Auckland, 1989)
JIM BARR, MARY BARR

Hann, Sebastian (*b* Lőcse, Upper Hungary [now Levoča, Slovak Republic], 1644; *d* Nagyszeben, Transylvania [now Sibiu, Romania], 1713). Romanian silversmith of Hungarian birth. He worked in Sibiu from 1675 and made *c.* 100 works. His first commissions came from Saxon patricians in Transylvania: cups and chalices donated or offered as official gifts to different evangelical churches, and luxury objects, such as jugs, goblets and items of jewellery. The majority of the pieces combine figurative with decorative composition, and Hann based his ornamental repertory on Renaissance and Baroque styles. His preference for using historical and heroic themes on cups and goblets had as its source the engravings of Matthäus Merian (i). Another source was the engravings of Dürer, which inspired his design for the cup of rhinoceros horn (1694; Sibiu, Brukenthal Mus.). Hann's virtuosity in the shaping of objects, together with his accomplished technique and his able use of the contrast of light and shadow, led to the creation of such remarkable objects as the chalice (1690–94) made for the evangelical church in Luna de Jos, the Frankenstein candlesticks (1691), the ciborium of Cisnadie (1692) and the relief work for the Saxon Valentin Franck (1697; all Sibiu, Brukenthal Mus.). He also received important commissions from the princes of Wallachia, including an oil lamp given to the Sărindar Monastery (1687) and two ornamentations of the Gospels, one donated by Constantine Brâncoveanu to the Metropolitan of Bucharest (1693) and the other to Hurezi Monastery (1709; all Bucharest, N. Mus. A.). The figurative decoration of these pieces follows the iconography of the Eastern Church, with details from the Western repertory.

BIBLIOGRAPHY
V. G. Marica: *Sebastian Hann* (Bucharest, 1972) [extensive bibliography]
V. Drăgut and D. Grigorescu: *History of Romanian Art* (Bucharest, 1990), p. 103
TEREZA-IRENE SINIGALIA

Hanna, Leonard C(olton), jr (*b* Cleveland, OH, 5 Nov 1889; *d* Kirtland Hills, OH, 5 Oct 1957). American businessman and patron. After graduation from Yale University he joined the family coal, iron ore and shipping business. His partnership and wise investments provided an income for his philanthropic interests. His mother's interest in collecting appears to have stimulated his own. Many pieces for his private collection were purchased from Jacques Seligmann & Co., Inc., New York, notably Edgar Degas's pastels *Race Horses* (1873–5) and *Dancers in Pink* (1883) and Pierre-Auguste Renoir's *The Apple Seller* (1890; all Cleveland, OH, Mus. A.). Through the trust fund he established in 1941, Hanna made donations to a number of Cleveland hospitals, to Yale University Art Gallery and to the Cleveland Museum of Art. From 1939 he purchased many individual works of East Asian art for the museum, which also received his private collection, consisting principally of French Impressionist and Post-Impressionist works, on his death. He bequeathed £500,000 to Yale University for the development of a Fine Arts department.

BIBLIOGRAPHY

In Memorial: Leonard C. Hanna, Jr (exh. cat., Cleveland, OH, Mus. A., 1958)

M. Gottlieb: 'Angel of the Art Museum', *N. OH Live* (5–18 Oct 1981), pp. 28–31

DARRYL PATRICK

Hanneman, Adriaen (*b* The Hague, *c.* 1604; *d* The Hague, *bur* 11 July 1671). Dutch painter. He came from a family of Catholic government officials. In 1619 he became a pupil of the portrait painter Anthonie van Ravesteyn (1580–1669), brother of Jan van Ravesteyn. Hanneman's only known early work is a *Portrait of a Woman* (1625; ex-St Lucas Gal., Vienna; see ter Kuile, no. 1), which is entirely in the style of the van Ravesteyn brothers. Around 1626 he settled in London, where he married Elizabeth Wilson in 1630. It is possible that Hanneman worked for some time as an assistant in the workshop of Anthony van Dyck, who settled in England in 1632. The few signed pieces that have been preserved from Hanneman's years in London, and his later paintings, show the strong influence of van Dyck's style of portraiture.

In or around 1638 Hanneman returned to The Hague, where he joined the painters' guild in 1640. In the same year he was married for a second time, this time to his master's niece, Maria van Ravesteyn. Soon after his return to The Hague he must have started his large portrait of *Constantijn Huygens and his Children* (1640; The Hague, Mauritshuis). The main design of the painting, with the placement of the figures in separate medallions, was probably worked out some years earlier by the architect and painter Jacob van Campen. Records indicate that Hanneman had already completed the painting in 1639, but the painting itself bears the date 1640. Although executed after his return to the northern Netherlands the influence of van Dyck still predominates. Hanneman's oeuvre after 1640 consists almost exclusively of portraits, most of which are deeply inspired by van Dyck. Yet Hanneman was more than a mere uncritical epigone of the Flemish master; he was a significant artist in his own right, who played a major role in disseminating van Dyck's influence throughout Holland.

Hanneman drew his clientele primarily from English citizens staying in the Netherlands, particularly from the many Royalist exiles who spent periods of time in The Hague from the late 1640s onward. English subjects painted by Hanneman include *Charles II when Prince of Wales* (1648–9; known only by a number of copies and reproductions, see ter Kuile, no. 14), his brother *Henry, Duke of Gloucester* (1653; Washington, DC, N.G.A.; see fig.) and *Sir Edward Nicholas* (1653; priv. col., see ter Kuile, no. 19). The portrait of the *Duke of Gloucester* is one of the artist's best works and is so close in style to Anthony van Dyck that it was attributed to him for many years. Hanneman's subjects in the 1650s also included the young *William of Orange*, later the Stadholder-King (1654; Amsterdam, Rijksmus.), and his mother *Mary Stuart* (1659 and 1660; a number of known variants, including Edinburgh, N.P.G., and Windsor Castle, Berks, Royal Col.), as well as various prominent Dutch government officials. Compared to portraits painted by other artists in The Hague at this time, his portraits are remarkable for their elegance and for the numerous borrowings of poses and gestures from the work of van Dyck.

Besides portraits Hanneman painted two allegories that were commissioned by government institutions. In 1644 he painted an *Allegory of Justice* (The Hague, Oude Stadhuis) for the town council of The Hague and in 1664 an *Allegory of Peace* (The Hague, Binnenhof) for the States of Holland.

Hanneman lived in an impressive house and for many years was taxed at a level indicating a growing fortune. In 1643 he became a member of the governing board of the painters' guild and in 1645 its dean. In 1656, when the painters and sculptors dissociated themselves from the guild and set up their own artists' organization, Pictura, Hanneman became its first dean (1656–9). After his

Adriaen Hanneman: *Henry, Duke of Gloucester*, oil on canvas, 1048×870 mm, 1653 (Washington, DC, National Gallery of Art)

retirement he was several times a member of the confraternity's governing board, and in the years 1663–6 he was once again its dean. Hanneman also apparently had a good name as a teacher; he trained many young artists, the best known of whom were Jan Jansz. Westerbaen the younger (1631–*c.* 1672) and Reinier de la Haye (*c.* ?1640–95).

In his last years Hanneman's fortunes began to decline. At the time of his third marriage with Alida Besemer in 1670, his capital had already dwindled considerably, and when he died in 1671 the estate proved to be of only minor value. The reasons for this reversal are not clear. Until 1668 the artist was still receiving many important commissions: for example, in 1664 he received the sum of 500 guilders for two copies of a portrait of *William of Orange* (London, St James's Pal. and Kensington Pal., Royal Col.) and 400 guilders for a posthumous portrait of the Prince's mother, *Mary Stuart* (The Hague, Mauritshuis). Hanneman was still popular among the foremost members of society in The Hague, as is evident from the surviving paintings of various members of court circles and of prominent citizens. No works dated after 1668 are known, possibly suggesting that the artist's career was broken off by illness. In addition to the many late portraits still completely in the style of van Dyck, there are a few portraits in the far more arid and sober traditional Dutch portrait style of the 17th century (e.g. the portrait of *Cornelia van Wouw*, 1662; The Hague, van Wouw almshouse, see ter Kuile, no. 72).

BIBLIOGRAPHY

A. Bredius and E. W. Moes: 'Adriaen Hanneman', *Oud-Holland*, xiv (1896), pp. 203–18

M. Toynbee: 'Adriaen Hanneman and the English Court in Exile', *Burl. Mag.*, xcii (1950), pp. 73–80; c (1958), pp. 249–50

The Age of Charles I: Painting in England, 1620–1649 (exh. cat. by O. Millar, London, Tate, 1972), p. 52

O. ter Kuile: *Adriaen Hanneman, 1604–1671: Een Haags portretschilder* (Alphen aan den Rijn, 1976) [with illustrated catalogue of works]

RUDOLF E. O. EKKART

Hanno, (Andreas Friedrich) Wilhelm von (*b* Hamburg, 15 Dec 1826; *d* Christiania [now Oslo], 12 Dec 1882). Norwegian architect, sculptor and painter of German birth. He studied at the Hamburgische Gesellschaft zur Beförderung der Künste und nützlichen Gewerben (1840–43), afterwards training, still in Hamburg, as an architect under Alexis de Chateauneuf and then as an architect and sculptor in Cologne (1849–50). In 1850 von Hanno followed de Chateauneuf to Christiania to assist him with the construction of Trinity Church (1850–58). De Chateauneuf returned to Hamburg in 1851 because of failing health; von Hanno completed the building, simplifying de Chateauneuf's design because of economic, as well as structural, problems. The church presents an unusual combination of a centralized, domed plan and a Gothic Revival style, much drier and heavier in detail than originally intended. Remaining in Norway for the rest of his life, von Hanno became one of Christiania's leading architects. In collaboration with Heinrich Ernst Schirmer (1814–87), with whom he was in partnership from 1853 to 1862, he built numerous office buildings, flats and houses in Christiania, as well as churches and railway stations in the rest of the country. Among their joint works, the Christiania Arsenal (1859–66) provides a particularly plain example of Norwegian 'romantic historicism', of which von Hanno and Schirmer were leading exponents and which is characterized by a simplified medievalism, and a use of unplastered red brick in keeping with a preference for 'natural' materials. However, although von Hanno always preferred medieval forms, he was nevertheless also competent in the classical style. His first independent work was possibly the five-storey building at 12 Karl Johans Gate (*c.* 1860) in Christiania. The façade is of the plastered brick that he preferred in his later works; its intricate, geometric ornament was unusual for Christiania. At the same time, attenuated piers intersect with sharply cut horizontal bands to give the building an oddly modern articulation. The Greenland fire station, school and church complex (1865–9) in Christiania is von Hanno's first documented independent work; each building is of red, unplastered brick in a decorative Romanesque Revival style. The principal later works, including Gjertsen's School (1868), the Military Society building (1876), the former Norway Geographical Survey building (1876–9) and the town houses on St Olavsgate (1870s), all in Oslo, were all of plastered brick. Von Hanno remained active as an ornamental sculptor, particularly of gravestones after his own designs, and he became an accomplished painter of architectural motifs, in both watercolours and oils, as well as a popular magazine and book illustrator. He also exercised considerable influence over his private students of architecture.

NKL

BIBLIOGRAPHY

C. Norberg-Schulz: 'Trefoldighetskirken' [The Trinity Church], *St Hallvard* (1958), pp. 241–61

T. Thiis-Evensen: *Steder i Oslo* [Places in Oslo] (Oslo, 1976)

CHRISTIAN NORBERG-SCHULZ

Hannover. German city, capital of Lower Saxony. Formerly the seat of the principality of Calenberg (1635), and subsequently of the Electorate (1692) and Kingdom (1815) of Hannover, it is an industrial city on the Mitteland canal in the valley of the River Leine. A settlement existed near a ford over the river in the first centuries AD; the existence of a town is mentioned in 1189 on the occasion of a fire. The three churches in the city were all built or rebuilt at the beginning of the 14th century, when Hannover had *c.* 4000 inhabitants: in the north is the Kreuzkirche (ded. 1333), comprising a single nave with four bays, and with an altarpiece by Lucas Cranach (i); in the south is St Aegidien (begun 1347; destr. 1943 and now a ruin), a Gothic hall church of three aisles, built on the site of an 11th-century chapel and a second church of *c.* 1160; and in the centre is the Marktkirche St Georg (begun 1335; vaulted *c.* 1353), a Gothic hall church with three aisles and five bays, which replaced an earlier church of *c.* 1125. It is the southernmost of the large brick churches in cities belonging to the Hanseatic League, of which Hannover became a member in 1386, and it contains important stained glass from the second half of the 14th century. The church was damaged in World War II and was rebuilt in 1946–52 with a simplified interior. Opposite the Marktkirche St Georg is the old town hall (begun *c.* 1230; later remodelled), built largely of brick, with elaborate stepped gables.

Hannover, aerial view from the south-east, showing the Calenberger Neustadt by Ernst Ebeling, left foreground, Waterlooplatz in the foreground and the river façade of the Leimeschloss behind it (both by Georg Ludwig Friedrich Laves), the Marktkirche St Georg and Laves's railway station beyond and his opera house to the right of it; from a steel engraving by Adolf Eltzner, 1851 (Hannover, Historisches Museum am Hohen Ufer)

The importance of Hannover increased with the arrival in 1636 of Duke Georg zu Braunschweig-Lüneburg-Calenberg, who built the Leineschloss (begun 1637). Now the seat of the Lower Saxony parliament, it was built on the site of a former Franciscan monastery and is a simple structure, partly half-timbered, built around two courtyards. Also of prime importance to the town's development was the foundation after 1660 of a new town, Calenberger Neustadt, on the left bank of the Leine opposite the Leineschloss, with the new Protestant church of St Johannis (1666–70; rebuilt 1956–8) at its centre. Of the early domestic architecture in Hannover, little has survived, an exception being the ornate façade of the Leibnizhaus (1652), which has since been rebuilt on a different site.

By 1675 the population of Hannover had risen to c. 8500 inhabitants. In the same period the embellishment of the Leineschloss was undertaken, partly as a result of a series of political successes around 1700, including the establishment of Hannover as an Electorate in 1692, the prospect by 1701 of Elector George Ludwig becoming George I, King of England, and the union of Hannover with the duchy of Lüneburg in 1705. The Leineschloss was redecorated internally, with stuccowork (destr.) by Dossa Grana (*fl* 1685–1702) and frescoes (destr.) by Tommaso Giusti (1644–1729), and with an opera house added as a new wing in 1688–9 (destr. 1853). Louis Rémy

de la Fosse (c. 1659–1725), court architect from 1706 to 1714, built two *maisons de plaisance* between Hannover and the electors' summer residence at Herrenhausen, and he also built the Ständehaus (1709–12; destr. 1881), a grand building in the form of a French *hôtel particulier* for the principality's estates. The Catholic church of St Clemens (1711–18; rebuilt), designed by Giusti, has a Greek cross plan, with a bay added for a vestibule. It is surmounted by a dome that was part of the original plan but not executed until 1957, when Giusti's design was simplified. Under Electress Sophie (1630–1714), the intellectual life of Hannover reached a peak, with Gottfried Wilhelm Leibniz (1646–1716) as court librarian, Andreas Scheits (c. 1655–1735) as court painter, and Tommaso Giusti and Johann Oswald Harms (1643–1708) providing designs for operas composed by Agostino Steffani (1654–1728). With the court's absence after the Elector George Ludwig's succession to the English throne in 1714, however, patronage of the arts in Hannover was severely curtailed.

Hannover underwent further changes after the appointment of GEORG LUDWIG FRIEDRICH LAVES as city architect in 1814 (see fig.). Laves gave the city a new appearance with his classical architecture, although his grand schemes for the city's expansion were only partly executed, as were the plans to rebuild the Leineschloss, the façade of which, modelled on Henry Holland's Carlton House (begun 1783; destr. 1827–8) in London, remained unfinished. His most important work in Hannover was the new opera house (1845–52), designed as part of a new suburb to the north of the city that also incorporated the railway station. Although Laves was able to provide Gothic Revival designs if required, most of his buildings are firmly classical. Other architects introduced historicism to Hannover: after becoming a Residenz again on the accession in 1837 of Ernst August as King of Hannover, an administration building was constructed, designed by Hermann Hunaeus (1812–93) in the new *Rundbogenstil*, which derived from Italian Renaissance architecture. In 1846–9 the house of the estates of Calenberg-Grubenhagen was built, designed by Ernst Ebeling (1804–51) in a castellated English Tudor style. In the second half of the 19th century, Conrad Wilhelm Hase developed a style of Gothic Revival brick architecture that was highly influential throughout northern Germany, partly because of Hase's teaching at the Technical University (*see* HASE, CONRAD WILHELM). An early example was the Christuskirche (1859–64; rebuilt with a modern interior), built at the expense of George V, King of Hannover (*reg* 1851–66). In 1877–82 he was involved in the thorough restoration of the old town hall.

The Kingdom of Hannover was annexed by Prussia in 1866, when the city was again without a court; nevertheless, considerable building activity took place in the 1870s and 1880s, reflected in the growth of population, which rose from *c.* 15,000 in 1821 to *c.* 122,000 in 1880. Work on a new railway station by Friedrich Hitzig began in 1870, but Hubert Stier (1838–1907) took over in 1875 as architect after protests against a 'Berlin-imported Renaissance' (*see* RAILWAY STATION, §1). Throughout the 1870s Hase's pupil Ferdinand Wallbrecht (1840–1905) tried to persuade the authorities to develop a new street across the old city, linking the suburb of Linden (where most of the industry was sited) and the railway station. This also necessitated the construction of new buildings for institutions that had to relinquish their old premises: a new Ständehaus was built by Wallbrecht in 1879–81; the Technical University (founded 1831) moved to the Welfenschloss (begun 1858), a palace designed by Heinrich Tramm (1819–61) for King George V; and a Gothic Revival wing was added to the old town hall by Hase in 1890. The last of the large historicist buildings to be constructed in Hannover was the new town hall (1903–13) by HERMANN EGGERT; it is set in a small park and prompted the development of a new area of the city, which included the Provinzialmuseum (now the Niedersächsisches Landesmuseum), a new museum (1897–1901) by Stier to house both a picture gallery and a department of natural history.

In the early 20th century there was a return to neoclassical principles, evident, for example, in the Stadthalle (1912–14) by Paul Bonatz, as well as in purpose-built industrial architecture by such architects as Peter Behrens, Hans Poelzig and Fritz Höger. Hannover was one of the most severely bombed cities in World War II, and the inner city was almost completely destroyed in October 1943. Nearly all the buildings mentioned above have been restored or rebuilt after the war, usually with modern interiors. Post-war urban planning, to designs by Rudolf Hillebrecht, was largely guided by the principle of wide streets and passages to accommodate the expected increase in traffic, so that the old street plan has been much altered. Hannover's arts collections are largely the result of municipal collecting and private foundations: apart from the Niedersächsisches Landesmuseum, there is the Kestner-Museum, containing Egyptian art and applied arts, and the more recent Sprengel Museum for modern art.

BIBLIOGRAPHY

T. Unger: *Hannover: Führer durch die Stadt und ihre Bauten* (Hannover, 1882/R 1978)
B. Dorries and H. Plath: *Alt-Hannover: Die Geschichte einer Stadt in zeitgenössischen Bildern, 1600–1900* (Hannover, 1960)
G. Schnath: *Das Leineschloss: Kloster, Fürstensitz, Landtagsgebäude* (Hannover, 1962)
H. Hammer-Schenk: *Bibliographie zur Baugeschichte der Stadt Hannover* (Hannover, 1978)
Hannover im 20. Jahrhundert: Aspekte der neueren Stadtgeschichte (exh. cat., ed. W. Röhrbein; Hannover, Hist. Mus., 1978)
C. Meckseper: *Das Leibnizhaus in Hannover* (Hannover, 1983)
W. Ness and others: *Stadt Hannover*, Denkmaltopographie der Bundesrepublik Deutschland, 2 vols (Brunswick, 1983–5)
Vom Schloss zum Bahnhof: Bauen in Hannover. Zum 200. Geburtstag des Hofarchitekten G. L. F. Laves, 1788–1864 (exh. cat. by H. Hammer-Schenk and G. Kokkelink, Hannover, Forum Landesmus., 1988)
K. Mlynek and W. Röhrbein: *Geschichte der Stadt Hannover* (Hannover, 1992) [contains extensive bibliog.]

JARL KREMEIER

Hannss von Gratz. *See* NIESENBERGER, HANS.

Hanover. *See* HANNOVER.

Hanover, House of. English dynasty of rulers, patrons and collectors, of German origin. With the death of Anne, Queen of Great Britain, in 1714, the Protestant line of the HOUSE OF STUART died out, and the throne of England and Scotland passed to George I, Elector of Hanover (who ruled as George I, King of Great Britain), a member of the WELF dynasty of Brunswick and great-grandson of James I, King of England. Consequently the Kings of England were also Electors (and Kings from 1814) of Hanover until 1837. Neither George I (*reg* 1714–27) nor his son George II (*reg* 1727–60) were distinguished patrons or collectors. George II's son and heir, (1) Frederick, Prince of Wales (who predeceased his father), however, promoted the dissemination of the Rococo style in England through his patronage of French (mainly Huguenot) and Italian painters and silversmiths. Frederick's younger brother, (2) William Augustus, Duke of Cumberland, a celebrated commander, commissioned paintings and sketches of military subjects.

There were numerous important political developments during the reign of George II's successor, (3) George III (*reg* 1760–1820), including the Declaration of Independence by the American colonies (1776) and the Act of Union with Ireland (1800). George III's most notable achievement as a patron was the establishment of the Royal Academy, London (1768). After George's health deteriorated, his son George, Prince of Wales, became Prince Regent in 1811 (succeeding to the throne as (4) George IV in 1820). The Prince was the most important British royal patron and collector since Charles I in the 17th century. The taste for French Neo-classicism, as well as extravagant and exotic Indian- and Islamic-inspired and chinoiserie decoration (as exemplified by the Royal Pavilion, Brighton), that he favoured characterizes the so-called

REGENCY STYLE. His extensive purchases of Dutch and Flemish, as well as British paintings greatly enriched the British royal collections.

As neither George IV nor his brother (5) William IV (*reg* 1830–37) had any surviving heirs, the throne passed to their niece, (6) Victoria (*reg* 1837–1901), who later also assumed the title Empress of India (1877). (The Kingdom of Hanover passed to her uncle, Ernest Augustus, Duke of Cumberland.) She married her first cousin (7) Prince Albert of Saxe-Coburg-Gotha. They employed such leading artists as Edwin Landseer and Franz Xaver Winterhalter. Prince Albert played a significant role in the design and refurbishment of both the royal palaces and, as Chairman of the Royal Commission, such public buildings as the Palace of Westminster, London; he also took a great interest in engineering and manufacture. One of his most important achievements was the organization of the Great Exhibition of Products of Industry of All Nations (1851) at the Crystal Palace, London. He also inspired the creation of a complex of museums and colleges of art, science and music and a concert hall (the Albert Hall) in South Kensington, London. Although for a brief period (1901–17) the British royal family took the name of the House of Saxe-Coburg-Gotha (from Prince Albert), the dynastic title of the House of Windsor was adopted in 1917 (*see also* CHARLES, Prince of Wales).

BIBLIOGRAPHY

O. Millar: *The Queen's Pictures* (London, 1977)

The Queen's Pictures: Royal Collectors through the Centuries (exh. cat. by C. Lloyd, London, N.G., 1991)

C. Lloyd: *The Royal Collection: A Thematic Exploration of the Paintings in the Collection of Her Majesty the Queen* (London, 1992)

(1) Frederick (Louis), Prince of Wales (*b* Hannover, 6 Jan 1707; *d* London, 20 March 1751). He was the eldest son of George II (*reg* 1727–60) and Caroline of Ansbach (1683–1737) and was educated in Hannover. On his father's accession to the British throne in 1727 he was created Duke of Cornwall and in 1729 became Prince of Wales. Unlike both his father and his grandfather, George I (*reg* 1714–27), Frederick was drawn to the arts and became one of the first significant royal patrons and collectors in Britain since Charles I, whom he consciously sought to emulate. He played the violoncello, gave lavish entertainments and cultivated the company of artists and writers. His Royal Barge (London, N. Mar. Mus.; *see* BARGE, STATE, fig. 1), designed for him in 1732 by William Kent as a 'floating coach', is a Baroque extravaganza richly decorated with carved and gilded figures of mermaids, dolphins, shells and garlands.

Frederick had begun to collect pictures while still an adolescent. His patronage helped to promote the reputations of French and Italian artists working in Britain, such as his Principal Painter, Philippe Mercier, and Jacopo Amigoni; both of them painted many portraits of the prince, such as Mercier's the *Music Party: Frederick, Prince of Wales, with his Three Eldest Sisters* (oil on canvas, *c*. 1733; versions Windsor Castle, Berks, Royal Col.; London, N.P.G.; Cliveden, Bucks, NT). He demonstrated a keen eye for paintings in his acquisition of works by Italian, French, Dutch and Flemish masters, mostly of the 17th century; they included Reni, Rubens, Claude, Poussin and Jan Breughel the elder (e.g. Breughel's *Flemish Fair*, oil on copper, 1600; Brit. Royal Col.).

In 1733 Frederick hired Joseph Goupy as drawing-master, painter, copyist and agent in the purchase of pictures, which led in 1737 to the ousting of Mercier. GEORGE WICKES, appointed Goldsmith to the Prince of Wales in 1735, supplied most of his plate for more than a decade; Frederick customarily gave to his friends presents of pieces made by Wickes (e.g. pair of silver soup tureens, 1744; Oxford, Christ Church). In April 1736 he married Augusta (1719–72), daughter of Frederick II, Duke of Saxe-Gotha, and was granted a wing of St James's Palace, London, and a modest country house at Kew, but the worsening relationship with his parents resulted in 1737 in his banishment from court. Although he and his family lived chiefly on credit, household ledgers reveal his continuing acquisition of silver plate, furniture and paintings. John Wootton painted many sporting pictures of him out hunting with friends, such as the *Shooting Party: Frederick, Prince of Wales, with John Spencer and Charles Douglas, 3rd Duke of Queensberry* (oil on canvas, 1740; Windsor Castle, Berks, Royal Col.).

From 1742 Frederick rented Leicester House in Leicester Fields (now Leicester Square), London, while Cliveden, Bucks, became his principal country residence. His admiration for French Rococo did much to ensure its popularity in early Georgian England. Paul de Lamerie, Nicholas Sprimont and George Wickes were among the artists who contributed pieces to a celebrated English Rococo silver-gilt dinner service (Brit. Royal Col.) on a marine theme that was made for the Prince between 1741 and 1745; Sprimont probably made the 'Neptune' centrepiece (1741), with its finely modelled figures of the sea-god, mermen, dolphins, sea-horses, seashells and garlands. Barred by his father from affairs of state, Frederick occupied himself with the royal collection; he supervised the restoration of works acquired by previous royal collectors and commissioned richly carved and gilded frames for his pictures. In 1747 he bought a pair of large landscapes by Rubens, *Winter* and *Summer* (*c*. 1620s; Brit. Royal Col.); they were praised by George Vertue who supplied in his *Notebooks* a description of the contents of Leicester House.

BIBLIOGRAPHY

'The Note-books of George Vertue', *Walpole Soc.* [indexed in xxx (1948–50)]

O. Millar: *The Tudor, Stuart and Early Georgian Pictures in the Collection of Her Majesty the Queen* (London, 1963)

E. Barr: *George Wickes, 1698–1761: Royal Goldsmith* (London, 1980)

(2) William Augustus, Duke of Cumberland (*b* London, 15 April 1721; *d* London, 31 Oct 1765). Brother of (1) Frederick. He became known as a formidable and ruthless military commander. He fought in Flanders and later, back in Britain, he defeated the Jacobites at the Battle of Culloden in 1746. He commissioned a series of pictures that combined his artistic and military interests. These were painted by such artists as David Morier (1705–70), whose *Grenadiers Regiments of Foot Guards* (Brit. Royal Col.) provides important documentary evidence for the uniforms worn by Cumberland's regiments. He also commissioned Morier to paint a series of equestrian portraits (*c*. 1745–50) and scenes depicting him in battle. In 1743

Cumberland appointed Thomas Sandby as his private secretary and draughtsman. Sandby accompanied him to Flanders and Scotland between 1743 and 1748 and made many sketches (Windsor Castle, Berks, Royal Lib.) of such battles as Culloden; he also produced panoramic views of their settings.

In 1746 Cumberland was appointed Ranger of Windsor Great Park, and Sandby became his assistant. Under Cumberland's supervision, Sandby enlarged the Great Lodge (Cumberland Lodge) and designed a new landscape garden. Cumberland's peace-time hobby of collecting racehorses led him to patronize Sawrey Gilpin who, with William Marlow, painted *The Duke Visiting His Stud* (Brit. Royal Col.). Cumberland also commissioned portraits from Reynolds (1758; Windsor Castle, Berks, Royal Col.) and others, and he owned one version of Richard Wilson's *Destruction of the Children of Niobe* (*c.* 1759–60; exh. London, Soc. Artists GB, 1760; New Haven, CT, Yale Cent. Brit. A.).

BIBLIOGRAPHY
A. E. Haswell Miller and N. P. Dawnay: *Military Drawings and Paintings in the Collection of Her Majesty the Queen*, ii (London, 1970), pp. 20–27

(3) George III, King of Great Britain [Elector and King of Hanover] (*b* London, 4 June 1738; *reg* 1760–1820; *d* London, 29 Jan 1820). Son of (1) Frederick. His artistic taste had been developed through youthful studies of architecture with William Chambers, perspective with John Joshua Kirby (1716–74) and drawing with Joseph Goupy and George Michael Moser. A capable draughtsman himself, the King imposed his taste on royal buildings by amending architectural plans. His interest in art was encouraged by John Stuart (ii), 3rd Earl of Bute, who introduced him to the work of Allan Ramsay and Johan Zoffany, among others.

In 1762 George III purchased Buckingham House, London, and hired Chambers to make alterations. He filled the house with his own choice of furniture, paintings and decorative arts, brought from other royal residences or purchased especially. In his search for suitable art, he relied on his librarian Richard Dalton, who acquired on his behalf miniatures, medals and furniture and Dutch and Italian paintings. In 1762 Dalton negotiated the purchase for £20,000 of Consul Joseph Smith's collection, which included contemporary Venetian paintings. George's acquisition of these works by Francesco Zuccarelli, Canaletto, Marco Ricci and Sebastiano Ricci helped increase the popularity of contemporary Venetian art in England. In the same year he augmented his Old Master collection by purchasing from Cardinal Alessandro Albani 300 volumes of Italian drawings by such artists as Domenichino and the Carracci family (Windsor Castle, Royal Lib.). He also encouraged contemporary painters working in England. In the 1760s he commissioned portraits and subject pictures from Francis Cotes, Angelica Kauffmann, Zoffany and Nathaniel Dance, among others. Dance's painting of *Timon of Athens* (1765; London, Hampton Court, Royal Col.) reveals the King's penchant for moralistic classicism, and Zoffany's portraits of *George, Prince of Wales, and Frederick, later Duke of York* and *Queen Charlotte with her Two Eldest Sons* (both *c.* 1765; Windsor

Castle, Berks, Royal Col.) indicate his appreciation of the informal conversation piece.

George III's most significant contribution to English art was his part in the foundation of the Royal Academy, London (*see* LONDON, §VI). The idea was first presented to him by a delegation that included his former teacher, Chambers. On 10 December 1768 the King signed the Instrument of Foundation, which stated that the Academy would be 'under our own immediate patronage and protection'. His literal interpretation of the charter induced him to provide premises for the Royal Academy in Old Somerset House, London, and to fund the institution through the Privy Purse until it became self-supporting in 1780. He also contributed drawings, books and antique casts from his collection to the Royal Academy Schools. Yet this generosity and support was balanced by his interference and favouritism. He appointed Chambers as the first Treasurer, and appointments to the posts of President, Keeper and Secretary had to be approved by him. In 1769 he personally made William Hoare and Zoffany Academicians, thus exempting them from the process of election. He also arranged for Dalton to have the honorary post of Antiquary. In 1799 George III approved the Academy's expulsion of James Barry on the grounds of his subversive lectures and criticisms of the institution, and in 1803 he vetoed the nomination of Robert Smirke as Keeper of the Schools.

George III showed strong personal and professional preferences in his relationships with the painters of the Academy. He disliked the President, Joshua Reynolds, and only reluctantly sat to him, even after Reynolds had been appointed Principal Painter to the King in 1784. George's taste inclined towards the courtly flourish of Ramsay, his first Principal Painter (from 1760), but, paradoxically, he also admired the crisp Neo-classicism of Benjamin West. He paid West a pension of £1000 in exchange for history paintings, for example the *Burghers of Calais* (1788; London, Kensington Pal., Royal Col.) and pictures with classical themes, believing that West's work in the manner of Nicolas Poussin would rival the history painting of the Académie Française. Both he and Queen Charlotte offered generous commissions to Zoffany, including the *Tribuna at the Uffizi* (1772–7; exh. RA 1780) and possibly the large group portrait of the *Royal Academicians* (exh. RA 1772; both Windsor Castle, Berks, Royal Col.). The King also admired the work of Thomas Gainsborough and commissioned from him 15 oval portraits of the royal family (1782; Windsor Castle, Berks, Royal Col.). He was not, however, pleased with Thomas Lawrence's portrait of *Queen Charlotte* (exh. RA 1789; London, N.G.), which he saw as disrespectfully naturalistic. The last portrait of the King to be exhibited at the Royal Academy in his lifetime was not by the prodigious Lawrence but was a tepid depiction by William Beechey.

In addition to his encouragement of painting, George III also set up a Royal Bindery at Buckingham House (1786–8), where he showed an interest in, and expressed opinions on, questions of type-face and style. He also commissioned 'Capability' Brown to remodel the gardens at Kew (*see* KEW, ROYAL BOTANIC GARDENS). His enthusiasm for collecting pictures was shared by Queen Charlotte, who owned drawings and paintings by Gainsborough and Giovanni Battista Cipriani; she also collected Sèvres and Wedgwood porcelain. Charlotte was also an avid patron of Mary Moser and commissioned from her decorative flower-pieces for Frogmore House, Windsor, Berks, which she had acquired in 1792. As the King's mental and physical health deteriorated, his relations with artists became stormy, and his patronage gradually ceased. Although Horace Walpole accused him of a 'general disposition to make purchases without judgment', his encouragement of the arts fostered competition among English artists, and his foundation of the Royal Academy provided a professional environment for the growth of a British school of art.

BIBLIOGRAPHY

M. Levey: *The Later Italian Pictures in the Collection of Her Majesty the Queen* (London, 1964), pp. 28–35
O. Millar: *The Later Georgian Pictures in the Collection of Her Majesty the Queen* (London, 1969)
George III: Collector and Patron (exh. cat., London, Queen's Gal., 1974–5)

SHEARER WEST

(4) George IV, King of Great Britain [George, Prince of Wales; Prince Regent; George IV, King of Hanover] (*b* 12 Aug 1762; *reg* 1820–30; *d* 26 June 1830). Son of (3) George III. As Prince of Wales, he was installed as Regent in 1811, following the prolonged illness of his father, George III. His activities as patron and collector were prodigious and directed mainly towards the enrichment of the royal residences and to the refinement of a court appropriate to the greatest of the great powers of post-Napoleonic Europe. He gave lavish patronage to painters, architects, designers, interior decorators, cabinetmakers, silversmiths and armourers, though all were likely to find him an unreliable paymaster, as his extravagances embroiled him in successive financial crises.

1. Architecture and the decorative arts. 2. Paintings.

1. ARCHITECTURE AND THE DECORATIVE ARTS. The Prince's first great achievement as a patron was the refurbishment of Carlton House (destr. 1827–8), given him as his official London residence in 1783. The transformation of this modest property on Pall Mall into 'the finest palace in the world' (Sauvran) began under William Chambers and continued, with the active involvement of the Prince himself, under HENRY HOLLAND, THOMAS HOPPER and JOHN NASH. The style of the building and its interiors evolved from a refined Francophile Neo-classicism, particularly in the work of Holland, to a heavier Roman Revival, while assimilating elements of both the Gothick style and the fantastic chinoiserie that was to reach its apogee in the Royal Pavilion at Brighton. Filled with treasures and endowed by a sybaritic luxury unprecedented in England or abroad, Carlton House was in the end spoilt by variety and proved inadequate to the needs of a monarch. Already bored with it, George had it demolished in 1827 when King, dispersing many fixtures and fittings to other buildings: the Corinthian capitals from the columned screen to the street, for example, were reused for William Wilkins's National Gallery, London (opened 1838).

The exoticism, self indulgence and caprice of the Prince Regent survives at its most full-blown, and largely intact, in the Royal Pavilion, Brighton (for illustration *see* BRIGHTON), the seaside 'pleasure dome' created for him, initially by Holland (in 1785), from a humble farmhouse. The Prince first occupied it in 1786 and for the next 35 years allowed successive enlargements. Between 1802 and 1804 the interior was luxuriously furnished and decorated by the firm of CRACE, with further elaborations in 1823. The stable building (now the Dome concert hall) was designed in 1803 in the Islamic style by William Porden, and by 1815 Nash had begun the redesigning of the main building in the 'Indian' style. By 1822, however, George had tired of it. As King, his final building projects were more sober and monarchical. In 1824 he ordered the substantial rebuilding (partly destr. 1992) of Windsor Castle (*see* WINDSOR CASTLE, §3) under Jeffry Wyatville (*see* WYATT, (3)), and in 1825 he commissioned Nash to remodel Buckingham Palace, although the work remained incomplete at the architect's death in 1835.

George constantly altered his residences, much to the distraction of his architects and designers and of his advisers who struggled to balance budgets continually overspent. Yet he had an unerringly acute sense of harmony in his transient and apparently wildly eclectic arrangements of pictures, furniture and objects of vertu. Fancying himself as an architect, he was in truth a consummate interior decorator. The REGENCY STYLE, a term used to describe the various forms of decorative arts produced from the 1790s to 1830, is often said to be characterized by a certain harmony, epitomized by the terraces of Nash or the furniture of Thomas Hope. It must be remembered, however, that the Prince Regent himself obeyed no such discipline. Yet throughout his building and collecting, certain themes are constant. In architecture and the decorative arts, his ruling passions were for things French and Neo-classical or for the outrageously exotic. His purpose was always to create a superb display (*see also* DISPLAY OF ART), whether of plate by the Crown Jewellers RUNDELL, BRIDGE & RUNDELL, of his unrivalled collection of 18th-century Sèvres porcelain, or of pictures, clocks, East Asian ceramics or French and English furniture. It was for Buckingham Palace and for Windsor Castle that his last and most spectacular purchases of French decorative arts were destined: these included Gobelins tapestries, furniture by André Charles Boulle, Martin Carlin and Jean-Henri Riesener, as well as candelabra by members of the Caffiéri family.

2. PAINTINGS. The Prince was not a leader of taste but, while neither wide-ranging nor original in itself, his acquisition of paintings did much to make an inherited collection more comprehensive in its scope. He paid high prices in a buoyant market to obtain what he wanted: superlative examples of major masters from important provenances. He was advised by various courtiers and by fellow collectors, including Francis Charles Seymour-Conway, 3rd Marquess of Hertford, Charles Long, 1st Baron Farnborough, by the dilettante writer, connoisseur and interior decorator Walsh Porter, by his medical and financial adviser Sir William Knighton and by the painters Thomas Lawrence, David Wilkie and Philippe Jacques de Loutherbourg. Even his confectioner, François Benois, was sent to Paris to buy works of art. His Surveyor of

Pictures was William Seguier, who had worked on the collection at Carlton House from at least 1818 and who was the first Keeper of the National Gallery and Superintendent of the British Institution. George took an active interest in both institutions, as he also did in the Royal Academy, and in 1826 and 1827 respectively lent 164 and 185 pictures to the British Institution. At Carlton House, the Prince lived among his pictures, as he did with his many other treasures. As monarch, his schemes became more formal, and his remodelling of Buckingham Palace included a picture gallery for the display of the royal collections.

(i) Flemish, Dutch and French. George's abiding love of the art of 17th-century Dutch and Flemish masters initially seems too sober to fit into his theatrical ensembles. It must be remembered, however, that these were the favourite Old Masters of the *ancien régime*; it was the dispersal of continental collections after the French Revolution that provided his most important opportunities for acquisition. Carlton House was adorned principally with Dutch and Flemish paintings. Some, including his greatest single purchase, Rembrandt's *Shipbuilder and his Wife* (1633; London, Buckingham Pal., Royal Col.), were bought in 1811 by private treaty from the dealer P. J. Lafontaine, having come from the collection of Smeth van Alphen sold in Amsterdam the previous year. Others, including Aelbert Cuyp's *Passage Boat* (Brit. Royal Col.)—one of seven works by Cuyp acquired by the Prince Regent and, for such contemporary painters as Turner and Augustus Wall Callcott, a paradigm of the fashionable style of tranquil marine scene—came from the collection of Sir Thomas Baring (1), bought outright in 1814. Many other works, including Rubens's *Portrait of a Woman* (Brit. Royal Col.), were acquired through John Smith, the London agent of the dealer C. J. Nieuenhuys in Brussels. The Prince Regent sold as well as bought. The 86 pictures bought in 1814 from Baring more than compensated for 40 sold in the same year from the 100 Dutch and Flemish works that the Prince had so far acquired. In that year he also made up most of the price of Rubens's *Landscape with St George and the Dragon* (1630; London, Buckingham Pal., Royal Col.), offered by the dealer William Harris, by the sale of pictures by Jan van Huysum, David Teniers (ii) and Adriaen van Ostade. Even though genre paintings were sold from the Prince's collection, many were still given special place: seven paintings by Jan Steen, among them *Woman at her Toilet* (1663; Brit. Royal Col.); Pieter de Hooch's *Card-players in a Sunlit Room* (1658; Brit. Royal Col.), of which the 'novelty', as Nieuenhuys observed in 1823, 'awakened the attention of collectors in both France and England' (see 1991 exh. cat., p. 146); and works by Gerrit Dou and Teniers (e.g. the latter's *Peasant Fair*, 1649; London Buckingham Pal., Royal Col.; *see* Teniers, (2), fig. 2). The Prince did not care for still-life, nor for the more 'primitive' periods of his favoured schools, turning down van Eyck's *Giovanni Arnolfini and Giovanna Cenami* (1434; London, N.G.) after it had been hanging in Carlton House on approval between 1816 and 1818. He largely ignored Italian painting but did, however, acquire superb 17th- and 18th-century French paintings,

his last important purchase being Claude's *Coast Scene with the Rape of Europa* (1667; Brit. Royal Col.).

(ii) British. In 1810 the Prince announced to Benjamin West, Surveyor to George III, that he intended to collect contemporary British art. He had already shown himself an enthusiastic supporter of Reynolds and compensated for his parents' relative neglect of their Principal Painter by sitting to him frequently and commissioning from him portraits of his family. He later acquired, through Reynolds's niece Lady Thomond, such important examples of Reynolds's history paintings as the *Death of Dido* (exh. RA 1781) and *Cimon and Iphigenia* (exh. RA 1789; both London, Buckingham Pal., Royal Col.). He not only commissioned portraits from Gainsborough but had also bought the artist's only surviving mythological painting, *Diana and Actaeon* (c. 1785; London, Buckingham Pal., Royal Col.), from the sale held in 1797 after the death of Gainsborough's nephew, Gainsborough Dupont. George acquired 18 paintings by George Stubbs (e.g. *William Anderson with Two Saddle-Horses*, 1793; Windsor Castle, Berks, Royal Col.), reflecting his love of animals and outdoor pursuits that also inspired commissions of horse and animal portraits from George Garrard, Sawrey Gilpin, Ben Marshall, Jacques-Laurent Agasse, Thomas Allwood (*fl* 1770) and his official Animal Painters, H. B. Chalon and Charles Henry Schwanfelder (1774–1837). James Ward (i) also produced paintings for the Prince but was denied the accolade of Royal Painter that was readily accorded to others. Among portrait painters of his own generation, the Prince Regent commissioned works from George Romney, William Beechey, John Hoppner, the miniature painter Richard Cosway and the pastellist John Russell, before finding in THOMAS LAWRENCE the truest interpreter of the age and the heir of van Dyck, whose paintings the Prince so treasured among his inherited pictures. Lawrence's theatrical glamour, poised assurance and superlative technique were perfectly attuned to the splendid settings of George's palaces, and these characteristics are inherent in his half-length portrait of *George IV as Prince Regent* (c. 1814; London, N.P.G.; see fig.). A commission for a group portrait of the Prince with Alexander I, Tsar of Russia (*reg* 1801–25), and Frederick William III, King of Prussia, the monarchs whose armies had defeated Napoleon, was never executed, but instead Lawrence painted a series of full-length portraits of the allied monarchs and their commanders, destined for Carlton House but eventually installed, after the King's death, in the Waterloo Chamber at Windsor Castle.

If Lawrence was the heir to van Dyck, DAVID WILKIE was at first considered by the Prince as the successor to Teniers and Ostade. He commissioned two masterpieces of Wilkie's early genre style, *Blind Man's Buff* (1812) and the *Penny Wedding* (1818; both London, Buckingham Pal., Royal Col.), and continued to support the artist's later development in the manner of the Old Masters, acquiring two paintings of Roman pilgrims and four subjects from the Spanish guerrilla campaigns during the Napoleonic War, including the heroic *Siege of Saragossa* (1828; London, Buckingham Pal., Royal Col.). Wilkie's *Entrance of George IV into Holyrood House* (Edinburgh, Pal. Holyroodhouse, Royal Col.), begun in 1822, the year of the King's accession

O. Millar: *The Later Georgian Pictures in the Collection of Her Majesty the Queen* (London, 1969)
G. de Bellaigue and P. Kirkham: 'George IV and the Furnishing of Windsor Castle', *J. Furn. Hist. Soc.*, viii (1972), pp. 1–34
H. M. Colvin, ed.: *The History of the King's Works*, vi (London, 1973)
J. M. Robinson: *The Wyatts: An Architectural Dynasty* (Oxford, 1979)
Sèvres Porcelain from the Royal Collection (exh. cat., London, Queen's Gal., 1979–80)
J. Summerson: *The Life and Works of John Nash, Architect* (London, 1980)
C. White: *The Dutch Pictures in the Collection of Her Majesty the Queen* (Cambridge, 1982)
R. Walker: *Regency Portraits*, London, N.P.G. cat. (London, 1985)
C. Wainwright: *The Romantic Interior* (London and New Haven, 1989)
The Royal Collection: Paintings from Windsor Castle (exh. cat. by M. Evans, Cardiff, N. Mus., 1990–91)
Carlton House: The Past Glories of George IV's Palace (exh. cat. by G. de Bellaigue, London, Queen's Gal., 1991–2)

DAVID BLAYNEY BROWN

(5) William IV, King of Great Britain (*b* London, 21 Aug 1765; *reg* 1830–37; *d* 20 June 1837). Third son of (3) George III and brother of (4) George IV. Not one of the most discerning of British royal patrons, he is known to have disapproved of Turner's *Battle of Trafalgar*, commissioned for St James's Palace, London, in 1824, on account of its inaccurate depiction of *HMS Victory*. As King his portrait (1832–3; London, Apsley House) was painted by Sir David Wilkie. He also ornamented his table with elaborate dinner services, including one created by the Worcester factory Flight, Barr & Barr.

□

(6) Victoria, Queen of Great Britain and Empress of India (*b* London, 19 May 1819; *reg* 1837–1901; *d* Osborne House, Isle of Wight, 22 Jan 1901). Niece of (4) George IV. Knowledge and appreciation of art did not feature prominently in her education, although she received regular drawing lessons from Richard Westall between 1827 and 1836. She disliked her earliest major commission, David Wilkie's the *First Council of Queen Victoria* (1838; Windsor Castle, Berks, Royal Col.), for its inaccurate costume. Factual correctness was always more important to her than artistic licence. Marriage to (6) Prince Albert of Saxe-Coburg-Gotha in 1840 encouraged her interest in art. She willingly submitted to his knowledge, confessing to Henry Cole her absence of taste. The Queen regularly purchased works of art as birthday and Christmas gifts for the Prince: although most were commissioned from contemporary artists, she also responded to the Prince's interest in Italian trecento and Early Renaissance art, purchasing works by Bernardo Daddi, the *Marriage of the Virgin* (*c.* 1340; London, Hampton Court, Royal Col.), and Cima, panels from an altarpiece depicting the *Annunciation, ?St Benedict, St George, St Theodore* and *St Stephen* (*c.* 1500; London, Hampton Court, Royal Col.). Her most important purchase of contemporary art was William Powell Frith's *Life at the Seaside* (or *Ramsgate Sands*, 1854; London, Buckingham Pal., Royal Col.; for illustration *see* FRITH, WILLIAM POWELL). She subsequently commissioned Frith's *Marriage of the Prince of Wales, 10 March 1863* (1863–5; Windsor Castle, Berks, Royal Col.). Besides this involvement with the fine arts, the Queen shared the Prince's enthusiasm for contemporary design, visiting the Great Exhibition in London (1851) 34 times.

George IV as Prince Regent by Thomas Lawrence, oil on canvas, 914×711 mm, *c.* 1814 (London, National Portrait Gallery)

visit to Scotland, and finished in 1830, confirmed the painter's transition from intimate genre to a national style, while endowing the portly monarch with something of the grandeur that Rubens had conferred on Marie de' Medici. In 1830 Wilkie succeeded Lawrence as the King's Principal Painter. George's fondness for narrative painting also prompted purchases from William Mulready (e.g. the *Wolf and the Lamb*, 1820; London, Buckingham Pal., Royal Col.), William Collins and Edward Bird. The last artist's attempts at history painting, while calculated to attract royal patronage, found little favour. Nor did the grander enterprises of Benjamin Robert Haydon, although the King was delighted with the painter's genre subject, the *Mock Election* (1827; London, Buckingham Pal., Royal Col.; for illustration *see* HAYDON, BENJAMIN ROBERT), purchased in 1828. To commemorate recent victories George commissioned paintings from George Jones and from Turner, whose immense *Battle of Trafalgar, 21 October 1805* (1823–4; London, N. Mar. Mus.) he later sent to the newly formed Picture Gallery at Greenwich Hospital.

BIBLIOGRAPHY
H. Clifford Smith: *Buckingham Palace* (London, 1931)
H. Aspinall: *The Letters of King George IV, 1812–1830*, 3 vols (London, 1938)
——: *The Correspondence of George, Prince of Wales, 1770–1812*, 8 vols (London, 1963–71)
S. Bury: 'The Lengthening Shadow of Rundell's', *Connoisseur*, clxi (1966), no. 648, pp. 79–85; no. 649, pp. 152–8; no. 650, pp. 218–22
D. Stroud: *Henry Holland: His Life and Architecture* (London, 1966)
George IV and the Arts of France (exh. cat., London, Queen's Gal., 1966)
J. Harris, G. de Bellaigue and O. Millar: *Buckingham Palace* (London, 1968)

After Prince Albert's death in 1861 most works commissioned by the Queen were intended to perpetuate his memory. These included the Royal Mausoleum (1864) at Frogmore, Windsor, Berks, by Dr Ludwig Grüner (1801–82) and Albert J. Humbert (1822–77) and sculptures of the Prince by William Theed III (e.g. of 1862; Windsor Castle, Berks, Royal Col.), Carlo Marochetti and Henri-Joseph-François Triqueti. Probably the best-known painting alluding to the Prince is Landseer's *Queen Victoria at Osborne, 1866* (1865–7; Osborne House, Isle of Wight, Royal Col.). Later portraits of herself and her family commissioned by the Queen were executed by Heinrich von Angeli and the sculptor Joseph Edgar Boehm. The latter, whose technical abilities were matched by convincing likenesses and meticulously rendered costumes, satisfied all that the Queen required from an artist. Following the purchase of *Ramsgate Sands*, the Queen occasionally bought paintings from successful Royal Academy exhibitors. The most important examples were Frank Holl (ii)'s *No Tidings from the Sea* (1870; London, Buckingham Pal., Royal Col.) and Lady Butler's *The Roll Call* (1874) and the *Defence of Rorke's Drift, January 22nd 1879* (1880; both London, St James's Pal., Royal Col.). Common to these works was a narrative and emotional appeal that touched the Queen as well as the public. One of her last major commissions was the Durbar Room, Osborne House, Isle of Wight (1890), by Bhai Rham Singh (*fl* 1885–1911) and John Lockwood Kipling (1837–1911). It was used for the display of her collection of Indian artefacts and reflected her commitment, as Empress of India, to the establishment of the British empire.

BIBLIOGRAPHY

F. Davis: *Victorian Patrons of the Arts* (London, 1963)
E. Longford: *Victoria R.I.* (London, 1964)
J. Steegman: *Victorian Taste* (London, 1970)
"This Brilliant Year": Queen Victoria's Jubilee, 1887 (exh. cat., ed. J. Maas; London, RA, 1977)
S. Weintraub: *Victoria: Biography of a Queen* (London, 1987)
O. Millar: *The Pictures in the Collection of Her Majesty the Queen: The Victorian Pictures*, 2 vols (Cambridge, 1992)

MARK STOCKER

(7) Prince **Albert (of Saxe-Coburg-Gotha)** [Prince Consort] (*b* Coburg, 19 Aug 1819; *d* Windsor, 14 Dec 1861). Husband of (6) Victoria. He was brought up in Coburg, educated at Bonn University and moved to England on his marriage to his cousin Victoria in 1840. Together with Queen Victoria, the Prince employed the leading artists of the day including Franz Xaver Winterhalter and Edwin Landseer. They also commissioned watercolours of their houses and estates, their excursions and the activities of their large family from Joseph Nash (1808–78), Eugène Lami, George H. Thomas (1824–68) and from the royal Drawing Master, William Leighton Leitch (1804–83). Sculptors employed included John Gibson (i), William Theed III and John Thomas. The royal couple were early patrons of photography and commissioned a number of works from Francis Bedford and other photographers.

Prince Albert collected works of the early Italian and early German schools, which was an unusual taste at that time. His purchases included a triptych portraying the *Crucifixion* by Duccio (Brit. Royal Col.), *Apollo and Diana* by Lucas Cranach (ii), both bought in 1846, and the *Death*

of Simon Magus by Benozzo Gozzoli (both Hampton Court, Brit. Royal Col.). In 1854 he purchased the entire collection of his relative Prince Ludwig von Oetingen-Wallerstein. The Prince also collected works by modern artists, including such leading British academicians of the day as William Powell Frith, Daniel Maclise and George Cruikshank, but he failed to purchase views of Coburg by J. M. W. Turner. He was advised in his purchases by leading art experts, including Dr Ludwig Gruner (1801–82) and HENRY COLE. Though his financial resources were limited, the pictures he acquired provide proof of his connoisseurship. Some have been retained in the British Royal Collection, others are in the National Gallery, London.

In 1841 the Prince was made Chairman of the Royal Commission set up to advise on the decoration of the new Houses of Parliament at the Palace of Westminster (*see* LONDON, §V, 3(iii)); he took a very personal part, insisting on a competition to find artists to paint frescoes and involving himself in the search for a technique that would be viable in 19th-century conditions. As part of this research he and the Queen commissioned a series of frescoes as decoration for a summer-house (destr.) in the grounds of Buckingham Palace. The themes were taken from Sir Walter Scott's *Waverley* novels and from Shakespeare and those for the central room from *Comus* by John Milton (1608–74). The artists employed included William Dyce, Charles Lock Eastlake, Maclise, William Charles Ross, Landseer and Thomas Uwins. This resulted in the heroic murals by Maclise and others throughout the building. Together with Henry Cole, the Prince, as President of the Society of Arts from 1843, attempted to improve the quality of British manufactures (*see* INDUSTRIAL DESIGN). The Prince's scholarly interest in art history is also strikingly illustrated by the Raphael research project, started in 1854 with his secretary, Dr Ernst Becker (1826–88), and completed by Dr Carl Ruland after his death. The study, which led to the publication of a catalogue raisonné of the artist's works (London, 1876), was based on the drawings in the royal collection, but the Prince later acquired prints and commissioned photographs of other works by Raphael. The resulting corpus of material is in the British Museum, London. The Prince also initiated the cataloguing of the collections of the British royal family, carried out by Richard Redgrave.

The Prince was an active architectural patron, involved in the building and extension of several royal homes. Buckingham Palace, remodelled by John Nash (i) for (4) George IV, was considerably extended between 1845 and 1856. The Prince's influence was significant; not only was he involved with the practical aspects of finance and engineering, he was also concerned with design, insisting that fireplaces and other fittings removed from the Royal Pavilion, Brighton (sold to pay for the new works), should be salvaged and installed in the main rooms, against the wishes of Edward Blore (1787–1879), the official architect. The Ballroom suite in the South Wing (1852–6), designed by James Pennethorne (1801–71), was decorated to the Prince's taste with Raphaelesque frescoes (destr.).

The Prince played an active role in the design of Osborne House, Isle of Wight (1845–51). He dispensed with an architect and employed the well-known London speculative builder, Thomas Cubitt, to carry out the plans. The resulting Italianate villa, with its formal gardens, has survived relatively unaltered. At Windsor Castle, Berks, the Prince was responsible for a number of new agricultural buildings, both practical and artistic, notably the Royal Dairy, designed by John Thomas. A local architect, William Smith (1817–91) of Aberdeen, was employed on the last royal palace, Balmoral Castle, Grampian (1853–6), built in the Scottish Baronial style.

Prince Albert was Chairman of the Royal Commission for the 1851 Great Exhibition of Products of Industry of All Nations at the Crystal Palace in London (*see* INTERNATIONAL EXHIBITION) and provided enormously important support at every stage. He was subsequently involved in the Dublin Exhibition of 1853 and the seminal Manchester Art-Treasures Exhibition of 1857, which brought together art objects from medieval armour and Old Masters to modern photographs on a scale never seen before, and never surpassed.

At Prince Albert's insistence the profit from the highly successful Great Exhibition was used to purchase land in South Kensington, familiarly known as 'Albertopolis'. He produced the outline scheme for the area, in which developed a series of national museums and university institutions: the South Kensington Museum, now the Victoria and Albert and Science Museums, the Imperial College of Science and Technology, the Royal Colleges of Art and of Music, and the Royal Albert Hall, designed by FRANCIS FOWKE and Maj-General H. Y. D. Scott. The Prince is commemorated not only in the Albert Memorial, but also in the lesser-known memorial to the Great Exhibition (on the south of the Royal Albert Hall) from which he surveys his creation. Funds from the foundation are still used for art and science scholarships. It is a fitting memorial to the Prince's artistic and educational interests.

WRITINGS
Principal Speeches and Addresses (London, 1862)
K. Jagow, ed.: *Letters of the Prince Consort* (London, 1938)

BIBLIOGRAPHY
T. Martin: *The Life of the Prince Consort*, 5 vols (London, 1875–80)
H. Bolitho: *Albert the Good* (London, 1932)
R. Fulford: *The Prince Consort* (London, 1949)
F. Davis: *Victorian Patrons of the Arts* (London, 1963)
W. Ames: *Prince Albert & Victorian Taste* (London, 1967)
E. Darby and N. Smith: *The Cult of the Prince Consort* (London, 1983)
H. Hobhouse: *Prince Albert: His Life and Work* (London, 1983)
R. Rhodes James: *Albert, Prince Consort* (London, 1983)

HERMIONE HOBHOUSE

Hans der Krumenauer. *See* KRUMENAUER, (1).

Hansen. Danish family of architects.

(1) (Hans) Christian Hansen (*b* Copenhagen, 20 April 1803; *d* Vienna, 2 May 1883). In 1816 he started his training at the Kongelige Danske Kunstakademi, Copenhagen, with G. F. Hetsch. In 1825–9 he went on to the School of Architecture, where C. F. Hansen was one of his teachers. In 1829 his design for an armoury and general staff headquarters won him a travel scholarship (1831–4). In Berlin he admired Schinkel's buildings, and in Dresden he visited Joseph Thürmer, who had published *Ansichten von Athen* (1823–5) with the Danish archaeologist

P. O. Brøndsted. In Nuremberg, Hansen met Carl Alexander von Heideloff, an expert on the Gothic style, continuing to Munich to see the works of Friedrich von Gärtner and Leo von Klenze. During six months in Rome he attempted to 'force his way into the spirit of the ancients' works'. He travelled to Naples, Segesta, Selinunte and Agrigento, and in August 1833 he reached Athens, where he was struck by the difference between Greek and Roman architecture and noted distinct traces of polychromy on friezes and ornaments.

In Greece, Hansen was immediately given several (unidentified) private architectural projects, and in 1834 he was appointed architect to Otto of Wittelsbach, King of Greece, in the new capital. He was subsequently responsible for numerous buildings in Athens, including the Mint, the Anglican church of St Paul (1836–41), the music conservatory (with Edouard Schaubert and S. Kleanthes) as well as the reconstruction (1835) of the Temple of Athena Nike on the Acropolis (with Ross and Schaubert). He also produced a town plan for Athens (again with Schaubert) and designed the civil hospital in Athens and the Roman Catholic church of St Paul in Peiraeus. Hansen's principal work, however, is the National Capodistrian University in Athens (begun 1837), which was later finished by his brother (2) Theophilus Hansen, working from Christian's drawings. It was always Hansen's aim to create, through thorough architectural study, a national architecture for the new Greek democratic state, growing naturally out of its Classical heritage, just as the Academy of Fine Arts in Copenhagen taught Danes to build in a national style. Modern Greece was to be reconstructed not only in the image of Classical antiquity, however, but also in the Byzantine style that represented Christian antiquity, and it was this style that Hansen later took back to Copenhagen.

In 1845 Hansen constructed buildings for the Austrian Lloyds Steamship Company in Kalamaki. In 1847 he built the Ophthalmological Clinic in Athens and in 1853–7 a naval arsenal for Lloyds in Trieste. Hansen also designed numerous buildings subsequently constructed by Greek architects, among them the chapel of St George (1849) in Athens. When he returned to Copenhagen in 1857 he succeeded his friend Gottlieb Bindesbøll as professor at the academy. His principal works there were the Copenhagen Municipal Hospital (1859–63), the Zoological Museum (1863–9) and the University Observatory (1859–61). He also restored numerous churches in Denmark and with his archaeological knowledge 'improved' C. F. Hansen's church of Our Lady with a polychrome interior. The style he adopted for his Danish buildings was determined by the location, the building-type and the Nordic climate.

BIBLIOGRAPHY
L. Ross, E. Schaubert and C. Hansen: *Die Akropolis von Athen*, i: *Tempel der Nike Apteros* (Berlin, 1839)
V. Villadsen: 'Universitetets bygninger', *Københavns Universitet*, ed. S. Ellehøj and L. Grane, iv (Copenhagen, 1980), pp. 240–51
I. Haugsted: 'The Architect Christian Hansen: Drawings, Letters and Articles Referring to the Excavations on the Acropolis, 1835–37', *Anlct. Romana Inst. Dan.*, x (1982), pp. 53–96
——: 'Universitetet i Athen', *Architectura: Arkithist. Aaskr.*, vii (1985), pp. 7–23
Arkitekten Christian Hansen i Grækenland, 1833–50 [The architect Christian Hansen in Greece, 1833–50] (exh. cat., ed. M. Bendtsen and I. Haugsted; Copenhagen, Bib. Kon. Dan. Kstakad., 1986)

'Neoclassical Architecture in Copenhagen and Athens', *Archit. Des.*, lvii/3–4 (1987)

M. Bendtsen: *Sketches and Measurings. Danish Architects in Greece, 1818–1862: Papers Published by the Royal Danish Academy of Fine Arts* (Copenhagen, 1993)

LISBET BALSLEV JORGENSEN

(2) Theophilus (Edvard) Hansen (*b* Copenhagen, 13 July 1813; *d* Vienna, 17 Feb 1891). Brother of (1) Christian Hansen. Although active for some time in Athens, much of his most important work was executed in Vienna, where, with FRIEDRICH VON SCHMIDT and HEINRICH VON FERSTEL, he was part of the triumvirate that dominated Viennese architecture in the 1860s and 1870s. During these years he created the *Wiener Stil*, a distinguished and elegant interpretation of High Renaissance art, and was one of the main protagonists in the making of the Ringstrasse (*see* VIENNA, §II, 3).

1. EARLY WORK, BEFORE *c.* 1859. He studied from 1829 at the Kongelige Danske Kunstakademi in Copenhagen, then an important centre of Neo-classicism. He was taught there by his brother, and he himself taught drawing at the academy until 1837. In 1838 Hansen won a scholarship and went first to Berlin, where he was deeply impressed by Schinkel's architecture, and then to Munich, where he was most interested by Leo von Klenze's Glyptothek (1816–30) and Walhalla. However, his stay in Munich was cut short when he accepted his brother's invitation to go to Athens, where he was able to study antique architecture and be involved in building activities. Hansen became especially interested in polychromatic Greek architecture, but he also admired Byzantine architecture and participated in the planning of the new Metropolitan church (1842–62). His other early important commission in Athens was the domed observatory (1843–6) on the slope of the Pnyx hill. After its completion he left Athens, when the constitutional monarchy dismissed all foreigners from public office.

Hansen moved to Vienna, where LUDWIG FÖRSTER offered him a partnership. For Hansen, the most important work produced by this partnership was the Waffenmuseum (1850–56) in the new Arsenal (1849–55; *see* VIENNA, §II, 3). In conception, the long brick block follows typical Neo-classical museum models, but in its architectural and decorative details Hansen applied his deep knowledge of Byzantine art. His Byzantine style helped enrich Viennese historicist architecture in the 1850s, creating such interesting works as the Greek Orthodox church (1857) on the Fleischmarkt and the Protestant cemetery chapel (1857–8) in Matzleinsdorf, brick buildings of great decorative richness, surmounted by lofty cupolas.

2. FROM *c.* 1859. Around 1859 Hansen's style changed completely as he abandoned his Byzantine-influenced Romanticism in favour of a new classical purity based on ancient and High Renaissance art. He thereby joined a movement that had been developing in France and Germany since the second quarter of the century. His new style enabled him to win a new clientele of wealthy bourgeois and aristocratic patrons, who were interested in owning a lucrative *Zinspalast* (block of flats) or a prestigious residence near the new Ringstrasse. Of Hansen's *Zinspalast*s, the Heinrichshof (1861–3; destr. 1945), opposite the Staatsoper (*see* VAN DER NÜLL & SICCARDSBURG) was the most famous example. The mighty 25-bay block with four roof pavilions and a central attic fronting the Ringstrasse, resembled a grand High Renaissance

Theophilus Hansen: Parlament, Vienna, 1873–83

palace. It rivalled Van der Nüll and Siccardsburg's Staatsoper, as did his Musikverein (1867–9) for the Music Society. The 'Greek Renaissance' exterior of the Musikverein displays a great purity of architectural and decorative forms, and its central projection, surmounted by a pediment, was a clear variation on the loggia motif of the Staatsoper. For the interior, Hansen designed an imposing concert hall. Its rich decoration is dominated by rows of caryatids that supported balconies and the magnificent, gilt-and-painted coffered ceiling.

In the 1860s Hansen's many private commissions included the palace (1864–8) for Archduke William of Austria (1827–94), the palace (1868–72) for the financier Epstein, both on the Ringstrasse, Vienna, and Hernstein Castle (1856–80) in Lower Austria for Archduke Leopold of Austria (1823–98). However, he had difficulty securing a public commission comparable to the Staatsoper. He repeatedly produced elaborate plans for important projects, including the layout of the Ringstrasse (1858), an imposing gateway to the Hofburg (1863), the Parlament (1865) and the new Imperial Museum (1867), but none was accepted. He was also appointed professor of architecture at the academy in Vienna (1868–83). Only in 1869, apparently at the emperor's wish, was Hansen commissioned to design the new Parlament (1873–83; see fig.), one of the four great public buildings that were to be erected on the former parade ground in Vienna. The Parlament became Hansen's most famous building. He chose a classical style to connote the political and artistic achievements of the Greeks. Corinthian porticos with richly sculpted pediments dominate the main façade on the Ringstrasse, and the great ramp leading up to the central portico makes the building a unique architectural monument in the context of the Ringstrasse. The heart of the building's interior is a great central hall, a Corinthian peristyle of 24 monolithic columns supporting a glass roof, forming an imposing entrance to the two semicircular chambers.

Other important Ringstrasse commissions then followed. In the Börse (1871–7) and the Akademie der Bildenden Künste (1872–7) Hansen used brick, with rich sculptural and painted exterior and interior decoration and with prestigious halls, such as the Doric Hall of the academy, which houses the museum of plaster casts. In these and other buildings of the 1870s and 1880s in Austria (such as Schloss Rappoltenstein in Lower Austria) Hansen's ideal of a contemporary equivalent to High Renaissance architecture was at its height, but the designs he continued to produce for buildings in Athens in this period, such as the academy (1859–87) and the National Library (1859–91) clearly show the enduring influence of antique architecture. In 1883 Hansen closed his architectural practice and left the academy, and none of the several great projects that occupied his last years was executed. After his death his architecture was remarkably never the object of the violent criticism levelled against historicism and the work of other Ringstrasse architects. This is probably due (see Wagner-Rieger) to the classical elements of his work.

BIBLIOGRAPHY

Thieme–Becker

G. Niemann and F. von Feldegg: *Theophilos Hansen und sein Werk* (Vienna, 1893)

H. Russack: *Deutsche Bauen in Athen* (Berlin, 1942)

H.-R. Hitchcock: *Architecture: Nineteenth and Twentieth Centuries*, Pelican Hist. A. (Harmondsworth, 1958, 4/1977/*R* 1978), pp. 212, 214–15

A. Strobl: *Das k. k. Waffenmuseum im Arsenal* (Graz and Cologne, 1961)

M. Fischer-Hölzl: *Theophil Hansens Leben und Frühwerk* (diss., Graz, Karl-Franzens-U., 1964)

J. Travlos: *Neo-classical Architecture in Greece* (Athens, 1967)

J. Ganz: 'Theophil Hansens hellenische Bauten in Athen und Wien', *Österreich. Z. Kst & Dkmlpf*, xxvi (Vienna, 1972)

R. Wagner-Rieger: *Theophil von Hansen*, Die Wiener Ringstrasse: Bild einer Epoche, viii/4 (Wiesbaden, 1980)

SUSANNE KRONBICHLER-SKACHA

Hansen, Carl Frederik. *See* SUNDT-HANSEN, CARL FREDERIK.

Hansen, C(hristian) F(rederik) (*b* Copenhagen, 29 Feb 1756; *d* Frederiksberg, 10 July 1845). Danish architect and teacher. In a career spanning half a century, Hansen achieved enormous professional authority in the highly centralized Danish kingdom through public and academic posts. His reputation as Scandinavia's greatest Neo-classical architect rests on a dramatic handling of volume and detail infused with a subtle sense of the picturesque.

1. TRAINING, EARLY WORK AND PRIVATE COMMISSIONS. The son of a shoemaker from Schleswig, Hansen entered the Kongelige Akademi for de Skønne Kunster in Copenhagen in 1766, advancing to the school of architecture in 1770. Like many architectural students at the time, he learnt bricklaying and carpentry there; Thiele's biography (see Langberg, 1963) refers to Hansen's lifelong belief in the equal importance of practical and 'artistic' studies. Studying under C. F. Harsdorff, Hansen shared the major gold medal in 1779, which entitled him to the academy's six-year travel stipend. This was not immediately available, however, and Hansen began working for Harsdorff. He was appointed Clerk of Works at the latter's Frederick V Chapel, Roskilde Cathedral in October 1781, before receiving funds for study abroad directly from the heir apparent, Prince Frederick (*d* 1805), the honorary president of the Akademi. He was also promised the post of Surveyor in Danish Holstein to be taken up on his return from Italy. A fragmentary travel diary (discovered 1969; Copenhagen, Rigsarkv) proves that Hansen did not follow Harsdorff's example and visit France but went instead to Italy. His stay was relatively short: a passport was issued in November 1782, and he presented his Roman drawings to the Academy in September 1784.

Most of Hansen's drawings are now in the Kongelige Danske Kunstakademi collection of architectural drawings. Only 41 show identifiably Roman subjects, and with the diary they constitute the only evidence of his visit. With the German architect Peter Joseph Krahe (1758–1840), Hansen made surveys of Early Christian basilicas, including S Crisogono in Trastevere, S Sabina, S Paolo fuori le Mura and S Pietro in Vincoli; he also made careful studies of the Pantheon and of the temple of Castor and Pollux. Again with Krahe, he also surveyed the Villa Giulia of Jacopo Vignola, having used a text with model orders based on those in Vignola's *Regola delli cinque ordini d'architettura* (Rome, 1562) as a student at the Academy.

In his drawing of the Palazzina of Pius IV on the Via Flaminia, however, Hansen added a frieze and removed what he apparently considered post-16th-century accretions in his attempt to restore what he thought was Vignola's work (actually by Pirro Ligorio) to its original purity; he thus revealed an aesthetic preference for clear architectonic volumes and bare walls, interrupted only by crisply defined door and window openings, that would continue to mark his style. In the same spirit he eradicated Baroque stucco in his sectional drawing of Baldassare Peruzzi's Palazzo Massimo delle Colonne (1532–6).

Hansen returned to Denmark in 1784 to take up the surveyorship he had been promised. In March 1785 he was admitted to the Akademi, by which time he was already established in Altona, the Danish city that served as a residential suburb of independent Hamburg. Hansen's official duties in Altona were light, and the only large public commission he completed in two decades there was the Altona Orphanage (1794; destr. 1944). In 1791 he petitioned for a titular professorship, admitting that this would impress potential clients, and in 1792 he married into a well-to-do Copenhagen family. Private commissions subsequently supplied the bulk of his income. Two houses that he built in crowded Hamburg were necessarily tall and narrow, but his houses on the Palmaille, Altona's most fashionable thoroughfare, as well as his mansions in the suburban villages along the north bank of the Elbe and country houses throughout Schleswig-Holstein showed his ability to respond to his patrons' explicit desire for English-style ease, elegance and reticence, although not on a lavish scale (most were of frame construction with sandstone dressing). The houses are now often described as neo-Palladian; contemporary admirers such as F. I. L. Meyer (1760–1844) characterized Hansen's houses and those of his colleagues Johann August Arens and Joseph Ramée as offering 'nobility of external form, convenience of internal arrangement and refinement of taste' in contrast to the retardataire vernacular (see Meyer: *Skizzen zu einem Gemälde von Hamburg* (Hamburg, 1801–2), i, pp. 339–46).

Hansen owned a wide range of English, French and Italian architectural books. Of these, Louis Ambroise Dubut's *Architecture civile* (1803), one of many publications responding to the turn-of-the-century vogue for the plain surfaces, abrupt juxtapositions of geometric forms and arcades of the Italianate vernacular, was a particular source of inspiration, reinforcing Hansen's memories of Italy. In his houses of this period, such as the villa for Georg

1. C. F. Hansen: Copenhagen Town Hall and Gaol, 1803–14; watercolour by Hansen, 415×507 mm, 1814 (Copenhagen, Kunstakademiets Bibliotek)

Friedrich Baur (completed 1805) at 49 Palmaille, Hansen never abandoned Palladian symmetry. The formality of the five-bay street elevation nevertheless contrasts with the livelier garden façade, with its varied window surrounds. There a first-floor loggia in the form of a triple arcade offered splendid views of the Elbe and of the ships that Baur owned. However, the trading barons were not Hansen's only patrons. In 1792 he designed two garden temples for Duke Peter Friedrich Ludwig of Oldenburg's English garden at Eutin Schloss, and he later became a protégé of Duke Friedrich Christian II of Augustenburg, the brother-in-law of Crown Prince Frederik.

2. MAJOR PUBLIC COMMISSIONS AND INFLUENCE. In 1800 Hansen offered to meet the commission planning the rebuilding of Copenhagen Town Hall, burnt down in the city fire of 1795. It had been proposed to house the town hall with its courtrooms and gaol in a wing of the Christiansborg Palace, itself burnt in a fire of 1794. Hansen argued for the separation of the penal and juridical facilities not only for practical reasons but also on the grounds of the 'character' theory, a legacy of Harsdorff's studies with Jacques-François Blondel: the town hall and gaol should have separate façades expressing the different characters of these building types. Hansen's plan for the Town Hall and Gaol on Nytorv was approved in March 1803, and the complex was finished 11 years later. His watercolour sketch (1814; Copenhagen, Kstakad. Bib.; see fig. 1.) shows a view on to the Slutterigade through the bridge arch. The elegant symmetry of the façade of the Town Hall (now the Law Courts), with its Ionic portico a monumentalized version of the Palladian villa-type, is belied by a free, asymmetrical plan. The latter was partly determined by the need to transfer prisoners quickly and discreetly via overhead walkways from the adjoining gaol into the courts. With its machicolations, heavy rustication and squat towers, the gaol represents a picturesque application of Blondel's tenets about the proper appearance of a prison, and Hansen designed abstract and menacing details, notably for the gaol's gates.

Hansen's plans for the rebuilding of Christiansborg Palace were also approved in 1803. His palace (destr. 1884) was severely constrained by the old foundations, but the application of a massive portico and the re-chiselling of capitals and other details ensured a result in keeping with the age. He had a freer hand with the Palace Chapel (consecrated 1826), a rectangular block relieved by little more than a strongly projecting tetrastyle Ionic portico and shallow dome raised on a high drum. Inside, the domed nave is abutted by barrel-vaulted bays. The attribution to Hansen (in the 1950s) of drawings of Vignola's S Andrea in the Via Flaminia confirmed a source of inspiration for the chapel that was already apparent.

The siege and bombardment of Copenhagen by the British navy in 1807 gave Hansen the last of his three great civic commissions, the rebuilding of Vor Frue Kirke (now Copenhagen Cathedral; see fig. 2). Arguing against a simple reconstruction of the Baroque church, he wrote in 1810 that he could build in a 'nobler and better' style than the previous Gothic, which he considered unsuitable in a new public building. Between 1811 and 1829, constrained though he was by the existing foundations, Hansen

2. C. F. Hansen: Vor Frue Kirke, Copenhagen (now Copenhagen Cathedral), 1811–29

transformed the ruins into a church whose severity still arouses hostility. The building has the appearance of an apsidal Early Christian basilica with an Italianate campanile (which he conceived as a *pharos* or lighthouse, the only tower form found in antiquity), erected behind a Greek Doric temple front showing his only use of fluted shafts. Inside, a coffered barrel vault rests on a gallery of Doric columns, which, although unfluted, have the projecting abacus and shallow echinus typical of the primitive Greek orders of Paestum. Hansen considered the combination of these varying elements to be justifiable as all were 'Greek', by which he meant 'pure', that is, antique in spirit if not necessarily in detail: he was not a Greek Revivalist in any strict sense.

When in 1808 the new post of Chief Superintendant of Building was created for him, Hansen's architectural supremacy was confirmed. He had ultimate authority over the design and regulation of all public construction in the kingdom and, in theory, over the maintenance of 'good taste' in private construction as well. Well into the 1830s, hapless local builders dreaded Hansen's scathing comments on their designs for the town halls that were the only public, secular building type then under construction. Town halls in Plön (designed 1816), Holstein and Åbenrå (completed 1830), South Jutland, stand as monuments to his anxiety that these provincial towns should present a modern face. Hansen enjoyed reworking a local design for a lunatic asylum in Schleswig (completed 1820). This hospital, carefully proportioned and detailed in the quasi-vernacular or rural manner approved by contemporary psychiatric theory, was the first purpose-built institution of its type in what is now Germany.

In 1808 Hansen was appointed Professor of Architecture at the Akademi, of which he was also the Director in 1811–18, 1821–7 and 1830–33. During this period not only was architectural instruction revitalized, but a new emphasis on perspective training encouraged the flowering of Danish architectural painting. In 1825, inspired by the publication from 1819 of Schinkel's *Entwurf*, Hansen became the first Danish architect to publish his own work. Small discrepancies between the engravings printed in his *Samling* and the buildings they represent (e.g. Christiansborg Palace Chapel) suggest that he took the opportunity to present an idealized version of his work, which had so often been hampered by practical considerations.

At the time of his death, Hansen's architecture had already begun to suffer attack for being too arid and cosmopolitan, incongruously Italianate for a northern land that had belatedly begun to interest itself in indigenous materials and forms. In 1909 Carl Jacobsens's offer to rebuild the spire of Vor Frue Kirke brought to a head a long-standing dispute among factions in the Danish architectural profession; only then was Hansen restored by such defenders and imitators as Aage Rafn and Carl Petersen to a position as one of Denmark's outstanding architects. The care with which Hansen composed his buildings and abstracted his forms prompted 20th-century architects to characterize him as a true classicist without the taint of historicism.

PRINTS
Samling af forskjellige offentlige og private bygninger tegnede og udførte under specielt opsyn af C. F. Hansen [Collection of various public and private buildings designed and executed under the particular direction of C. F. Hansen] (Copenhagen, 1825–*c.* 1840/*R* 1921)

BIBLIOGRAPHY
J. Rubow: *C. F. Hansens arkitektur* (Copenhagen, 1936) [excellent illustrations]
W. Jakstein: *Landesbaumeister Christian Friedrich Hansen der nordische Klassizist* (Neumünster, 1937) [excellent drgs of subsequently destroyed bldgs]
H. Langberg: *Omkring C. F. Hansen* [About C. F. Hansen] (Copenhagen, 1950)
——: *Arkitekturens oprindelse og andre perspektiver* [The origin of architecture and other perspectives] (Copenhagen, 1963) [transcription of MS. biog. by J. M. Thiele, 1830, written with Hansen's cooperation]
Arkitekt Christian Frederik Hansen, 1756–1845 (exh. cat., ed. H. Lund and C. L. Küster; Hamburg, Altonaer Mus., 1968)
H. Lund: 'Det andet Christiansborg' [The second Christiansborg], *Christiansborg Slot*, ed. K. Hvidt and others (Copenhagen, 1975) [with Eng. summary]
Claus M. Smidt: *Vor Frue Kirke: Historie og beskrivelse af Københavns domkirke* [The church of Our Lady: history and description of Copenhagen Cathedral] (Copenhagen, 1980)
——: 'Vor Frue Kirkes omgivelser: En studie i C. F. Hansens Byplanlaegning' [The surroundings of the church of Our Lady: a study in C. F. Hansen's town planning], *Architectura: Arkihist Aaskr.*, iii (1980), pp. 36–60
C. F. Hansen 1756–1845 und seine Bauten in Schleswig-Holstein (exh. cat., ed. G. Wietek; Schleswig, Schleswig-Holsteinisches Landesmus., 1982)
B. Bøggild Johannsen: *Christiansborg Slotskirke og kirkerne paa Københavns Slot* [The chapel of Christiansborg and its predecessors in Copenhagen Castle] (Copenhagen, 1985)
C. Stevenson: 'Architectural "Purity" in Early 19th-century Denmark', *AA Files*, ix (1985), pp. 16–30
A. L. Thygesen and H. Lund: *C. F. Hansen 1756–1845: Drawings Catalogue* (Copenhagen, 1986) [drgs in the Dan. Acad. of F. A.]
H. Lund and A. L. Thygesen: *C. F. Hansen*, 2 vols (Copenhagen, 1995)

CHRISTINE STEVENSON

Hansen, (Carl Christian) Constantin (*b* Rome, 3 Nov 1804; *d* Frederiksberg, 29 March 1880). Danish painter. In 1816 he entered the Kongelige Akademi for de Skønne Kunster, Copenhagen, intending to study architecture; however he later became attracted to painting and worked under C. W. Eckersberg from 1828 to 1833. Around the middle of the 1820s he started developing an individual style of portraiture, which had matured by 1830. He often used his sisters and friends as models; using simple costumes, poses and compositions, he managed to endow his pictures with the intimacy and warmth that mark the Danish Golden Age. The *Artist's Sisters Signe and Henriette Reading a Book* (1826; Copenhagen, Stat. Mus. Kst) is a fine example of his combination of natural observation with Neo-classical idealization. Under Eckersberg, who encouraged both, he strengthened his natural flair for painting serene architectural views of Copenhagen.

During the 1830s a concentration on specifically Danish subjects was officially promoted, and in 1834 Hansen won a competition for a view of a notable Danish monument with *Kronborg Castle* in Elsinore (Copenhagen, Stat. Mus. Kst). In 1835 he gained a two-year travelling scholarship to Italy; he stayed there until 1843. During his period in Rome he produced a series of sketchy *vedute* of well-known sites, such as the *Forum Romanum with the Capitol in the Background* (1837; Copenhagen, Ny Carlsberg Glyp.). In 1837 he painted his first serious Roman work, *Party of Danish Artists in Rome* (Copenhagen, Stat. Mus. Kst). The choice of subject is typical of both the time and the place. Beneath the apparent spontaneity of this scene of a group of friends enjoying a midday rest lies a paraphrase of Raphael's *School of Athens*. Another important work from Hansen's Italian period is *Scene from the Molo in Naples* (1839; Copenhagen, Stat. Mus. Kst). With the smoking Vesuvius as backdrop a large group gathers to hear an open-air recitation of Ariosto's *Orlando furioso*. A semicircle of figures, standing, sitting and lying, are arranged facing both the performer and the viewer; the various different responses of the mixed crowd are clearly displayed. The scene is crammed with everything a foreigner might regard as typically Italian: fruit and water vendors, housewives spinning, children playing, clerics and even a puppet-theatre. Yet even in this work, under the folksy clutter a classical sense of structure is discernible.

Hansen's studies from the sculptures and paintings in the Museo Borbonico in Naples gave him a first-hand familiarity with the Antique from which he benefited greatly when he began work on the embellishment of the entrance hall of the newly built University of Copenhagen. Returning to Denmark, he worked for almost ten years on this scheme, assisted by G. C. Hilker (1807–75). Depicting eight scenes from Greek mythology, this large-scale fresco is the most important Danish monument of the period; even in a European context it is an outstanding example of the Neo-classical style. After it was completed, Hansen's work declined in quality, although he did produce a few fine portraits such as *Michael Gottlieb Bindesbøll*, the architect of the Thorvaldsens Museum (1848–9; Copenhagen, Thorvaldsens Mus.), and a series of charming family scenes featuring his wife and children. His last major work, the *Constituent National Assembly* (1861–5; Hillerød, Frederiksborg Slot), depicts a crucial moment in

Danish political history; it also demonstrates his ability to arrange a large-scale group composition.

BIBLIOGRAPHY

E. Hannover: *Maleren Constantin Hansen: En studie i dansk kunsthistorie* [The painter Constantin Hansen: a study in Danish art history] (Copenhagen, 1901)

H. P. Rohde: *Danske kunstnere i Rom: Studier omkring et guldaldermaleri* [Danish artists in Rome: studies of a painting of the Golden Age] (Copenhagen, 1982)

Constantin Hansen 1804–1880 (exh. cat., ed. B. Jørnæs and S. Miss; Copenhagen, Thorvaldsens Mus.; Århus, Kstmus.; 1991)

JENS PETER MUNK

Hansen, Emil. *See* NOLDE, EMIL.

Hansen, Oskar (*b* Helsinki, 12 April 1922). Polish architect, urban planner, teacher and theorist of Finnish birth. He graduated from the Technical College in Vilna (now Vilnius, Lithuania) (1942), then studied in the Department of Architecture at the Technical University, Warsaw (1945–50), under Romuald Gutt. In the 1940s and the first half of the 1950s he also took up painting and sculpture, which he later dismissed as examples of 'Closed Form'. In 1948–50 he visited France, Italy and England and studied under Fernand Léger and Pierre Jeanneret; he also became acquainted with Le Corbusier, Henry Moore and Jerzy Sołtan. From 1950 to 1983 he lectured at the Academy of Fine Arts, Warsaw. He was also a member of the Groupe d'Etude d'Architecture Moderne and Team Ten. In 1959 he published his theory on 'Open Form', which allowed the user active participation in the creation of a work; it was a development of 'unlimited growth', an earlier concept of Le Corbusier and Sołtan. Hansen's theory had a fundamental influence on the Polish concepts of 'environment', '*dziela-procesu*' (works of process) and 'performance' in the 1960s. It was fully expressed in his competition plan (1957; with Jerzy Jarnuszkiewicz and Julian Pałka among others, unexecuted) for the international monument to the victims of Fascism at Auschwitz-Birkenau (now Oświęcim-Brzezinka); his proposal consisted of a path through the extermination camp, leaving most of its elements completely untouched. In the 1960s he developed the 'Open Form' theory into the 'linear continuous system' theory, which envisaged the extension of his principles to the arrangement of buildings and communications on a larger scale; projects included the housing estate (1963) at Przyczułek Grochowski, Warsaw, the district plan (1966–8) for Warsaw-Ursynów and proposals for town, regional and national plans. He also designed several international exhibition buildings during his career, as well as the Museum of Contemporary Art (1966), Skopje, and the Polish Embassy (1973), Washington, DC (both with others).

WRITINGS

with Z. Hansen: 'Open Form: The Art of the Great Number', *CIAM, 1959 in Otterlo*, ed. O. Newman (Stuttgart, 1961), pp. 190–96

BIBLIOGRAPHY

A. Moffet: 'Oskar Hansen', *Archit. Des.*, xxxviii/2 (1968), pp. 77–85

W kręgu Formy Otwartej [In the circle of the Open Form] (exh. cat., Warsaw, Mus. Acad. F.A., 1986)

WOJCIECH WŁODARCZYK

Hansen, Peter Marius (*b* Fåborg, 13 May 1868; *d* Fåborg, 6 Oct 1928). Danish painter. He studied at the Kunstnernes Studieskole in Copenhagen (1884–90). Hansen specialized in genre paintings with a great variety of motifs, drawn partly from the countryside and partly from provincial towns or cities in Denmark and Italy. He usually spent his summers at Fåborg on the island of Fyn, where he was strongly influenced by the activities in the town and by the surrounding countryside. Here he painted youths skating and bathing, as well as workmen (e.g. *Shipwrights at Fåborg Harbour*, *c.* 1922; Århus, Kstmus.), and landscapes showing the fields being sown or harvested. In the winters he lived mostly in Copenhagen, where his favourite motifs were city children and hooligans, including details such as the colour play on the house walls in the sunlight, or the shadow of a leaf reflected on a gable. As a contrast to his time on Fyn, Hansen made many visits to Italy, which had a decisive influence on his work. There are numerous paintings from Naples and Pompeii, depicting the sunburnt landscape of the Italian peasant in an unsentimental and realistic fashion, with both humour and a deep understanding; this sympathy for the people he portrayed was a major characteristic of his work, whether he was painting a child, a farmer, a beggar or an eccentric. Though Hansen's work is naturalistic, it is connected to Impressionism in its rhythmic forms and in the richness of its colouring.

BIBLIOGRAPHY

J. Zibrandtsen: *Moderne dansk kunst* (Copenhagen, 1969), pp. 32–7

G. Zahle: *Maleren Peter Hansen: Hans liv og arbejde* (Copenhagen, 1984)

RIGMOR LOVRING

Hansen, Svend Wiig. *See* WIIG HANSEN, SVEND.

Hansford, Sidney Howard (*b* London, 22 June 1899; *d* Limpsfield, Surrey, 1 April 1973). English art historian. He came into direct contact with Chinese art in the early 1920s through his involvement in the Chinese and Japanese import and export trade. In 1938 he received a scholarship from the Universities China Committee and visited Anyang, Henan Province, an important archaeological site of the Shang period (*c.* 1600–*c.* 1050 BC), where he became interested in the study of jade. During World War II he was employed by the British Foreign Office; between 1945 and 1947 he held a Chinese Government scholarship and completed his MA thesis, published in 1950 as *Chinese Jade Carving*. At the School of Oriental and African Studies, University of London, Hansford was lecturer in Chinese art and archaeology until 1955, when he became a professor and head of the Percival David Foundation of Chinese Art; he retired in 1966. His main publications are a *Glossary of Chinese Art and Archaeology* (1954), the catalogue he produced for part of the Seligman collection of Oriental art (1957; the collection itself was bequeathed to the Arts Council of Great Britain; examples now in London, BM and V&A) and *Chinese Carved Jades* (1968).

WRITINGS

'A Visit to Anyang', *Trans. Orient. Cer. Soc.*, xxiv (1948–9), pp. 11–22; xxvi (1950–51), p. 52

Chinese Jade Carving (London, 1950)

'Chinese Ivories', *Country Life*, cix (25 May 1951), pp. 1622–3

Glossary of Chinese Art and Archaeology (London, 1954, rev. 2/1961)

Chinese, Central Asian and Luristān Bronzes and Chinese Jades and Sculpture (London, 1957), i of *The Seligman Collection of Oriental Art* (1957–64)
Chinese Carved Jades (London, 1968)

MARGARET MEDLEY

Han Si-gak [*cha* Chayu; *ho* Solt'an] (*b* 1621; *d* after 1671). Korean painter of the Chosŏn period (1392–1910). He is best known for his Sŏn (Chin. Chan.; Jap. Zen) Buddhist figure painting and was by profession a court painter (*hwawŏn*), as were his father Han Sŏn-guk (*b* 1602) and his son-in-law Yi Myŏng-uk. Han Si-gak is also said to have been a teacher at the Bureau of Painting (Tohwasŏ). In 1655 he travelled with an embassy to Japan as an official painter. The Japanese mid-19th-century *Koga bikō* ('Handbook of classical painting'), in which he is referred to erroneously as Kim Solt'an, records that during his stay he painted two bamboo pictures; according to the third envoy of the same embassy (see Hong Sŏn-p'yo) he made sketches of Japanese landscapes (untraced). In Korea he is credited with a portrait of the Second Counsellor of State, Song Si-yŏl (1607–89). The last known point of reference for the painter's life is his contribution to a painting (untraced) documenting the wedding ceremony in 1671 of King Sukchong (*reg* 1674–1720). Typical of Han's work as a court painter is a scroll (ink and colours on silk, 6.741×0.579 m; Seoul, N. Mus.) showing various civil and military examinations held in the northern province of Hamyŏng. Competing horses and riders and observers of the events are all depicted with great exactness and liveliness. The surrounding landscape is painted in the Blue-and-green style (Chin. *qinglü*; see CHINA, §V, 3(iv)(a)), with stylistic elements of the early 16th century such as the use of short, quick strokes making a vivid rendering of the structure of the mountain. Entirely different from these illustrations, which were produced within the strict bounds of conservative models and intended to serve as historical documents, were Han's paintings of the Chinese monk Budai (e.g. hanging scroll, ink on paper, 1.18×0.29 m; Seoul, Cent. Stud. Kor. A., Kansong A. Mus.; *Kansong Munhwa* xviii (1980), pl. 9), some of which are in Korea, others in Japan. The preference for Sŏn Buddhist themes relates Han Si-gak's work closely to that of KIM MYŎNG-GUK, who also visited Japan in the 17th century. In contrast to the latter's forceful, deep black ink brushstrokes Han employs much softer strokes and lighter ink tones. The subjects and style of his pictures seem to indicate some influence from Japanese Zen Buddhist painting.

BIBLIOGRAPHY
Yi Tong-ju: *Ilbon sok-ŭi hanhwa* [Korean painting in Japan] (Seoul, 1973), pp. 59–60
Hong Sŏn-p'yo: '17–18 segi-ŭi han'ilgan hoehwa kyosŏp' [The relationship between Korean and Japanese paintings in the 17th and 18th centuries], *Kogo Misul*, cxliii/cxliv (1979), pp. 22–46
An Hwi-jun, ed.: *P'ungsokhwa* [Genre painting] (1985), xix of *Hanguk-ŭi mi* [Beauties of Korea] (Seoul, 1977–85), pp. 194, 207–8, pls 28–31

BURGLIND JUNGMANN

Hans Maler. *See* KNIEPER, HANS.

Hansom. English family of architects. Joseph Aloysius Hansom (*b* York, 26 Oct 1803; *d* London, 29 June 1882) began his career in a partnership with Edward Welch (1806–68) that broke up over the financially mismanaged Birmingham Town Hall (1834), a Roman Corinthian peripteral temple. He then took advantage of the growth in Catholic church work, but he did not follow A. W. N. Pugin's views on planning: his major church, St Walburga (1850–54; spire 1866), Preston, Lancs, is a massive hammerbeam-roofed hall of domestic inspiration, similar to contemporary Nonconformist churches. His mid-career partnership (1854–9) with his brother Charles Francis Hansom (*b* York, 1816; *d* Bristol, 30 Nov 1888) and then with E. W. Pugin (1862–3) produced less distinctive buildings. He was the inventor of the 'Patent Safety Cab' (the 'Hansom cab'), founding editor of the *Builder* (1842–3) and a radical socialist. He was joined (1869–82) by his son Joseph Stanislaus Hansom (*b* York, 1845; *d* 7 Nov 1931), who designed a series of spatially adventurous High Victorian churches: Our Lady Help of Christians (1867–9), Torquay, Devon; the Holy Name of Jesus (1869–72), Manchester; and St Philip Neri (now the cathedral; 1869–73), Arundel, W. Sussex.

Charles Francis Hansom, who trained with his brother, rivalled A. W. N. Pugin with his designs for All Saints' (1844–6), Hanley Swann, Hereford & Worcs; St Dominic (1846–9), Woodchester, Glos, and St Thomas of Canterbury (1849–51), Erdington, Birmingham. St John the Evangelist (1861–3), Bath, was his first major richly High Victorian church. Later he turned to Anglican and Nonconformist work in partnership with F. Bligh Bond (1864–1945). He also designed Clifton College (1860–80), Bristol, and Malvern College (1863), Hereford & Worcs. His son Edward Joseph Hansom (*b* 1842; *d* Newcastle upon Tyne, 17 May 1900) joined him (1867–71) before beginning a successful partnership (1871–93) with Archibald Matthew Dunn (*c.* 1833–1917) in Newcastle upon Tyne.

DNB
BIBLIOGRAPHY
Obituary notices, *The Architect*, xxviii (1882), p. 22; *Birmingham Daily Post* (1 July 1882), p. 5; *Builder*, xliii (1882), pp. 43–4; *Building News*, xliii (1882), pp. 8–9; *Cath. Times* (7 July 1882), p. 5; *Illust. London News*, lxxxi (1882), pp. 56–7; *Tablet*, lx (July 1882), p. 51; *Wkly Register*, lxvi (1882), pp. 50–59 [J. A. Hansom]
J. Gillow: *A Bibliographical Dictionary of English Catholics* (London, 1885–1902), vol. iii, pp. 115–19 [J. A. Hansom]
Obituary notices, *The Architect*, xl (1888), p. 323; *Builder*, lv (1888), p. 423; *Bldg News*, lv (1888), p. 763 [C. F. Hansom]
Directory of British Architects, 1834–1900, RIBA (London, 1993), pp. 405–6

RODERICK O'DONNELL

Hanson, Duane (*b* Alexandria, MN, 17 Jan 1925; *d* Boca Raton, FL, 6 Jan 1996). American sculptor. He entered Luther College in Decorah, IA, in 1943 but transferred in 1944 to the University of Washington in Seattle to major in art. In 1945 he moved to Macalaster College in St Paul, MN, working under Arnold Hauser. After graduating in 1946 he continued his studies at the University of Minnesota in Minneapolis and at Cranbrook Academy of Art, Bloomfield Hills, MI (MFA, 1951). He moved to West Gemany in 1953, teaching in Munich for four years, and then for three years in Bremerhaven, and working as a sculptor in a variety of media and styles.

On his return to the USA in 1960 Hanson came under the influence of Pop art, in particular in the sculpture of George Segal, and began to develop his mature style. His life-size figures in fibreglass and resin, cast from live models, and then painted and clothed, replicate real people with a deceptive illusionism. The extreme veristic technique of such works linked them to PHOTOREALISM, although their overt demonstration of social concern was uncharacteristic of the movement in general. In early works such as *War* (1969; Duisburg, Lehmbruck-Mus.), reflecting his concern over American involvement in Vietnam, he sometimes sought to embody movement, but he soon found this to be unsatisfactory. He then began to concentrate on static figures suggestive of the boredom and despair of everyday life, often presenting them as working class, as in *Woman with Laundry Basket* (1974; Adelaide, A.G. S. Australia). Later works such as *Football Player* (1981; Coral Gables, FL, U. Miami, Lowe A. Mus.) remained consistent in style with his earlier works but continued to expand their iconography of contemporary American life.

BIBLIOGRAPHY
M. H. Bush: *Duane Hanson* (Wichita, 1976)
K. Varnedoe: *Duane Hanson* (New York, 1985)

Hanson, Tomkin, Finkelstein. South African architectural partnership formed by Norman Leonard Hanson (*b* Johannesburg, 19 June 1909), S(amuel) N(orton) Tomkin (*b* London, 28 Aug 1908) and Nathan I. Finkelstein in 1932. Tomkin, initially ambivalent about modern architecture, soon developed understanding and facility in the new idiom. Finkelstein, primarily interested in the organizational and technological aspects of the building process, gave additional strength to the firm. Hanson, a friend and close associate of Rex Martienssen, was perhaps the dominant force in the partnership, as a motivated designer, versed and articulate in the modern movement's theories and philosophy. The approach and formal language of the partnership was that of the major architects of the 20th century: Le Corbusier, Gropius and Mies van der Rohe: the goal was a humanized technology and an aesthetic evocative of *l'esprit nouveau*. The firm's first significant project, House Saffer (1932), was in the Miesian manner; his influence remained apparent both in the plan of House Harris (1932–3), Johannesburg, and in the Brookstone swimming pool (1934), Johannesburg. A series of houses followed, together with three important blocks of flats in Johannesburg: Hotpoint House (1934), Reading Court (1937) and Denstone Court (1937). All showed continued allegiance to European sources, but with a growing originality, creative vigour and independence in their adaptations of the acknowledged international language. There was also a burgeoning sense of social responsibility, which led Hanson later to break openly with Le Corbusier. The last and perhaps finest work of the firm was the Twentieth Century Cinema and office block (1939–40; with Cowin & Ellis; destr. *c.* 1980; see Hanson, 1940, p. 295). The firm's reputation was based on the fact that they were the first practice in South Africa wholly committed to the modern movement.

WRITINGS
R. D. Martienssen, W. G. McIntosh and N. L. Hanson, eds: *Zerohour* (Johannesburg, 1933)
N. L. Hanson: 'Twentieth Century Cinema, Johannesburg', *S. Afr. Archit. Rec.*, xxv/8 (1940), pp. 282–97

BIBLIOGRAPHY
Contemp. Architects [entry on Hanson]
G. Herbert: *Martienssen and the International Style: The Modern Movement in South African Architecture* (Cape Town, 1975)

GILBERT HERBERT

Hans Saphoy von Salmansweiler. *See under* SAVOYE.

Hansson, Holger. *See under* MASTERS, ANONYMOUS, AND MONOGRAMMISTS, §I: MASTER OF BIELKE.

Hans von Böblingen. *See* BÖBLINGER, (1).

Hans [Hanns] **von Burghausen** [incorrectly Stehaimer] (*b* Burghausen, *c.* 1355–60; *d* Landshut, 10 Aug 1432). German architect. He was the most important architect of the German-speaking area in the late 14th century and the early 15th, and the founder of the tradition of Late Gothic hall churches in south Germany that lasted over a century and a half. Documentary sources are scarce: the earliest possible reference is in 1389, when 'Master Hans' is mentioned as master builder of the church of St Martin at Landshut, in a context indicating that he had already held this office for several years. On the assumption that he was then a mature man, he was probably trained in the builders' lodge of the large town church of St Jakob, Burghausen, which was built from 1360. Some features of his main work, St Martin at Landshut, suggest that he must have been familiar with the stylistic repertory of the cathedral lodge in Prague under Peter Parler (*see* PARLER, (3)), and that he may have known the *Backsteingotik* (brick) architecture of Lower Silesia and the north-east German coast. Although it should not be deduced from this that Hans spent time in all these areas during his travelling years, his works presuppose knowledge of international architecture of the highest standard. In their elegance, grace and abundance of light, his churches are unequalled.

The reference of 1389 can only apply to Hans von Burghausen. In 1406 Duke Henry IV (*reg* 1393–1450) gave him a house in Landshut, which was sold in 1415; on this occasion the architect was named as 'Master Hans of Burghausen, stone mason and master of works of St Martin at Landshut'. The most impressive testimony to his life and work is the epitaph that was placed in St Martin with a portrait bust shortly after his death. It establishes his date of death and lists the churches on which he worked as foreman and architect: St Martin and the Heilig-Geist-Spitalkirche in Landshut, and the parish churches of Salzburg (now the Franziskanerkirche, *see* SALZBURG, figs 1 and 2), Neuötting, Straubing and Wasserburg. The churches of Landshut provide the purest guide to Hans's artistic intentions, although neither was completed until long after his death. Both are hall churches: St Martin (*see* LANDSHUT, §2) owes much to large-scale mendicant churches, while the Heilig-Geist-Spitalkirche (1407–61) has an axial column in the ambulatory, so that the three aisles lead to what appears to be a centralized space, supported by a central pillar, reminiscent of English polygonal chapter houses. The chronology of the parish church of St Jakob in Straubing is too uncertain to determine Hans's exact contribution; furthermore the church was given new vaults and window arches in the

Baroque period. He probably constructed little more than the ground floor of the parish church of Salzburg (begun in 1408), which also underwent some Baroque modifications. The churches of St Nikolaus, Neuötting, and St Jakob, Wasserburg am Inn, were both begun in 1410; except for the chancel and the tower at Wasserburg, he was probably responsible for little more than the ground-plan in both cases. Despite the fragmentary quality of Hans von Burghausen's work as a whole, until well into the 16th century church architecture in south Germany can be seen as a continuation of or interaction with his ideas.

BIBLIOGRAPHY

J. W. Cook: 'A New Chronology of Hanns von Burghausen's Late Gothic Architecture', *Gesta*, xv/1–2 (1976), pp. 97–104

For further bibliography *see* LANDSHUT, §2.

PETER KURMANN

Hans von Esslingen. *See* BÖBLINGER, (1) and (2).

Hans von Geismar (*fl* Hannoversch-Münden, 1489; *d* Göttingen, 1502/3). German painter. His origin in the Göttingen area is suggested by recorded payments in Hannoversch-Münden (1489, 1490) and an entry in the municipal finance manuals of Göttingen (1493), as well as by the stylistic register of his painting. The panels of an altarpiece (1499; Göttingen, Albanikirche) are the only work by him for which documentary evidence exists. They show eight scenes from the *Life of the Virgin*, with the *Martyrdom of St Alban* and the *Last Judgement* on the outer sides of the outer pair of wings. Smoothly painted and with simply constructed compositions, this work competes with Hans Raphon's contemporary altarpiece of the *Passion* (ex-Paulinerkirche, Göttingen; Prague, N. Mus.).

By stylistic comparison, attribution of scenes from the *Childhood of Christ* (1494) on the outer sides of an altarpiece at Hevensen nr Uslar (Stadtkirche) is now considered as certain. This earlier work is characterized by free, somewhat unruly, broad brushstrokes and by landscape elements otherwise infrequent in the painting of Lower Saxony, for example the *Nativity* is set in a snow-scene. Hardly any Late Gothic panel paintings from Göttingen have survived, but a debt can be seen to paintings of *SS John and Lawrence* (*c.* 1490) on the altarpiece of the Stadtkirche at Uslar.

In 1497–8 Hans von Geismar acquired the house of the painter Clawe of Gotha and in 1499 was granted citizenship of Göttingen. He was not a member of a guild but in his final years probably ran a workshop, which produced for example panels of 1499 (Göttingen, Stadt. Mus.). His final work, of which attribution has only recently been established, comprises altarpiece panels showing *Martyrdoms* (1500; ex-Jakobikirche, Einbeck; Hannover, Niedersächs. Landesmus.).

BIBLIOGRAPHY

Kunst und Kultur im Weserraum, ii (exh. cat., Corvey, 1966), no. 106

A. Oberdiek: *Alte Göttinger Altäre* (Göttingen, 1984), pp. 11–54

HANS GEORG GMELIN

Hans von Judenburg (*fl* 1411–24). Austrian painter and wood-carver. He is named in 1411 and 1424 as a house-owner in Judenburg. He was head of an altarpiece workshop there and is mentioned as the maker of the former high altar retable of the town parish church of Bozen (now Bolzano), which was commissioned in 1421 and completed in 1424. Most of its figurative parts survive. In the shrine (centre panel) was a three-figure group of the *Coronation of the Virgin* (Nuremberg, German. Nmus.), together with *St John the Baptist* and *St Vigilius* (Cologne, Schnütgen-Mus.). The wing reliefs with scenes from the *Life of the Virgin* are scattered among various collections and the parish church of Deutschnofen (now Nova Ponente, Italy). The fragments indicate the style of at least two different wood-carvers. The composition of the *Coronation of the Virgin*, which goes back to Italian and South Tyrolean types, was the model in particular for the altarpieces of MICHAEL PACHER, whose contract for the Gries altarpiece specifically committed him to following the example at Bolzano.

Hans von Judenburg was often formerly identified as the MASTER OF GROSSLOBMING (*see* MASTERS, ANONYMOUS, AND MONOGRAMMISTS, §I), whose pupil he could have been. Several depictions of the Man of Sorrows (Vienna, Belvedere, Österreich. Gal; Graz, Steiermärk. Landesmus.; Veszprém, Eccles. Col.; and priv. col.) can be regarded as links between the styles of the two masters. A Crucifix in S Giorgio Maggiore, Venice, attributed to Hans (Rasmo) was formerly believed to be by Brunelleschi. Hans's translation of the over-refined 'beautiful' style into a more popular mode led to much imitation of his art, especially in South Tyrol, Carinthia and Slovenia, where a follower's workshop can probably be located. His early work was strongly influenced by his teacher: a *St Agnes* (Berlin, Skulpgal.) and the group of the *Virgin and St John* (Straubing, St Jakob) are variations of models from the Grosslobming workshop, and the facial type of the *Virgin Annunciate* in Grosslobming parish church was used by Hans as a sort of leitmotif. Fragments of a female saint (Linz, Oberösterreich. Landesmus.) and a *Virgin* (Bolzano, Mus. Civ.) are more independent. The Bolzano *Pietà* (Bolzano Cathedral) is closely related to that by the Master of Grosslobming in Lienz parish church. The ascription to Hans of all these works is uncertain. Only an *Annunciation* group in a private collection can be ascribed to him with any confidence. A *St John* (priv. col.) and an *Apostle* (Innsbruck, Tyrol. Landesmus.) from Parnegg, Styria, represent the style of the workshop as found in the parts of the Bolzano altar that remain at Deutschnofen. The central *Coronation* group of the Bolzano altar is anticipated by a similar group from Trofaiach (*c.* 1410–20; New York, Cloisters). If the *Virgin* in the parish church at Judenburg, which may be connected with foundation dates of 1415 or 1419, is also by an artist from Hans's workshop, which was evidently fairly large, some related works such as the *St Catherine* in the chapel of that name in Vienna Cathedral, or the *Virgin* in a street-chapel in Graz-Strassgang, would also emanate from there.

Contemporary with the Bolzano altarpiece is a mutilated *Virgin* (Trento, Mus. Dioc.). A *St John the Baptist* (Maribor, Reg. Mus.), a *St Oswald* in Ljubljana (N.G.) and a sainted king from Eisenerz (Berlin, destr. World War II) can be related to the saints in the central panel at Bolzano. A soldier saint (Munich, Bayer. Nmus.) and a *St Michael* (Berlin, Skulpgal.) represent the full range of the workshop style.

Certain features of Hans von Judenburg's style can be seen in works by followers of the Master of Grosslobming in Vienna, among them the *Passion* relief in the cathedral choir and the bosses in the Hofburgkapelle, which date from about the same time as the Bolzano altarpiece. To these may be added a shrine Madonna (a figure of the Virgin that opens to reveal a representation of the *Trinity*) from Schwarzau am Steinfeld, Lower Austria (Vienna, Dom- & Diözmus.). The last follows a French type, the angels bearing the Virgin's cushion suggesting Burgundian influence.

Because the contemporary paintings by the Master of the St Lambert Votive Altarpiece have assimilated similar influences, Hans von Judenburg has been identified with that master, but Schmidt has convincingly attributed the panels to another large workshop. An idea of Hans von Judenburg's painting style is given by a *sinopia* of *St John the Evangelist* in Bolzano parish church. Although it has close affinities with the St Lambert Votive Altarpiece workshop, it represents an independent tendency that is related to the group subsumed under the so called 'Murtal school'.

BIBLIOGRAPHY

K. Oettinger: *Hans von Tübingen und seine Schule* (Berlin, 1938)
N. Rasmo: 'Nuove acquisizioni alla conoscenza dell'arte medioevale dell'Alto Adige', *Cult. Atesina*, iv (1950), pp. 134–60
K. Garzarolli von Thurnlackh: 'Hans, Maler von Judenburg und sein Schmerzensmann vom Pfenningberg', *Kstjb. Stadt Linz* (1961), pp. 14–28
T. Müller: 'Die Marienkrönung aus Tschengels im Germanischen Nationalmuseum und andere Probleme der Geschichte der spätgotischen Skulptur in Tirol', *Anz. German. Nmus.* (1963), pp. 45–54
H. Stafski: *Die Bildwerke in Stein, Holz, Ton und Elfenbein bis 1450*, Nuremberg, German. Nmus. cat. (Nuremberg, 1965), pp. 192–7
G. Schmidt: 'Die österreichische Kreuztragungstafel in der Huntington Library', *Österreich. Z. Kst & Dkmlpf.*, xx/1 (1966), pp. 1–15
A. Schädler: 'Zur Rekonstruktion des Bozner Choraltars von Hans von Judenburg', *Anz. German. Nmus.* (1973), pp. 80–83
E. Kreuzer-Eccel: *Hans von Judenburg und die Plastik des weichen Stiles in Südtirol* (Calliano, 1976)
E. Cevc: 'Hans, Maler von Judenburg und seine Werkstätte', *Gotik in der Steiermark* (exh. cat., St Lambrecht, 1978), pp. 262–72
L. Schultes: 'Der Meister von Grosslobming und die Wiener Plastik des schönen Stils', *Wien, Jb. Kstgesch.*, xxxix (1986), pp. 1–40 (24–7, 33–7)
G. Bräutigam: 'Die Bozener Tafel: Schicksale und Rekonstruktion', *Ksthist. Jb. Graz*, xxiv (1990), pp. 221–32
E. Cevc: 'Die Marienkrönung aus dem Bozener Altar des Hans von Judenburg: Fragen zur Rekonstruktion, *Ksthist. Jb. Graz*, xxiv (1990), pp. 210-20
I. Flor: 'Die trinitarische Marienkrönung: 'Zur Entfaltung eines neuen ikonographischen Themas', *Ksthist. Jb. Graz*, xxiv (1990), pp. 233-52
L. Schultes: 'Der Meister von Grosslobming und Hans von Judenburg: Zeit- und Individualstil um 1400', *Ksthist. Jb. Graz*, xxiv (1990), pp. 253-67
Der Meister von Grosslobming (exh. cat. by A. Saliger, Vienna, 1994), cat. nos 7, 27, 29, 30, 48, 50-52

LOTHAR SCHULTES

Hans von Ulm. *See* ACKER, HANS.

Hans [Johannes] **von Worms** [?Hans Bilger] (*fl* 1475–96). German sculptor. He is documented as active in Frankfurt am Main, Höchst am Main and Aschaffenburg. His seal shows a crossed hammer and chisel with the inscription *hans bilhawer* [sculptor] *worms*. Five sculptured

altarpieces can be ascribed to him on documentary evidence (Frankfurt am Main, the Weissfrauenkirche, 1475–6, and the Bernhardskapelle, 1476–9; Kirchgarten, near Worms, Abbey Church, 1476; the high altar of the Justinuskirche, Höchst am Main, 1486; and the high altar of the monastery church of Aschaffenburg, 1489–96). Although none of these altars has survived, busts of four *Fathers of the Church* in Frankfurt (Frankfurt am Main, Liebieghaus), which are ascribed to Hans von Worms, may come from the Aschaffenburg altar, which was dismantled in 1770. Four half-figures are recorded from the predella, and the busts were described in 1606 by the painter Georg Rudolf Henneberger, who had been commissioned to renovate and remodel the altar.

The busts originally stood in front of a wall. They are of lime-wood and are deeply hollowed out at the back, their height varying between 455 and 595 mm. The Aschaffenburg busts can be compared to the busts of the *Church Fathers* by Hans Syfer from the altar (1498) of St Kilian's Church, Heilbronn. As Syfer is recorded in Worms (and may have been Hans's pupil), the comparison supports an artistic origin there. The idea of setting busts in a predella was taken from the Middle Rhenish successors to Nicolaus Gerhaert, and those by Hans von Worms and Syfer are the earliest known examples. The strongly differentiating treatment of the four male heads in the Liebieghaus (?Four Humours; ?Four Ages of Man) clearly reflects the prevalent late medieval tendency to create types out of ideal figures.

Two reliefs in wood, with compositions based on woodcuts by Albrecht Dürer, from 1503 and 1504 (the *Annunciation* and the *Visitation*; Worms, Mus. & Städt. Gemäldegal.) could also be from Hans von Worms's workshop and, if so, the treatment of drapery folds, reminiscent of the Danubian style, would be evidence that the workshop adopted this new stylistic trend.

Thieme–Becker   BIBLIOGRAPHY

A. Legner: *Spätgotische Bildwerke aus dem Liebieghaus* (Frankfurt am Main, 1961), cat. nos 18–21
W. Paatz: *Süddeutsche Schnitzaltäre der Spätgotik* (Heidelberg, 1963), p. 102
H. Beck: 'Bilder des Menschlichen vom Ende der Gotik', *Festschrift Kurt Rossacher* (Salzburg, 1983), pp. 3–8
M. Maek-Gérard: *Nachantike grossplastische Bildwerke*, iii: *Die deutschsprachigen Länder c. 1380–1530-40*, Frankfurt am Main, Liebieghaus cat. (Melsungen, 1985), pp. 189–95

VINCENT MAYR

Hantai [Hantaï]**, Simon** (*b* Bia, nr Budapest, 8 Dec 1922). Hungarian painter, active in France. He began his studies at the Hungarian Academy of Fine Arts, Budapest, in 1941 under Vilmos Aba-Novák (1894–1941) and Béla Kontuly (1904–83). At this time he started to experiment with various techniques, including washing out figures from a basic colour with a brush dipped in water, and scratching out outlines in thick, almost dry paint with a pointed instrument. This anticipated his later methods of production, influenced by Max Ernst. In 1947 he had an exhibition of selected works at the Budapest Forum Salon. His painting *On the Balcony* (1947–8; Pécs, Mod. Hung. Mus.) has a hallucinatory quality, which represents the transition to his Surrealist works of the 1950s. In 1948 Hantai visited Italy and in 1949 he settled permanently in Paris. At the end of 1952 he became acquainted with André Breton, who wrote the preface to the catalogue of Hantai's first French exhibition, held in 1953 at the Galerie l'Etoile Scellée, Paris. During this period he experimented with such techniques as *frottage*, collage, *découpage*, Tachism and *pliage*. In 1953–4 he became a member of the Surrealist group. His works typically evoked a nightmarish fantasy world in animated, forceful colours, filled with luxuriant organic forms, often arranged in vortices. The human figure, often with an animal head, took on a magical symbolic role.

Hantai's discovery of Georges Mathieu's gestural painting and Jackson Pollock's action painting persuaded him that the Surrealists' guiding principle, AUTOMATISM, could only be truly realized through abstract art. He broke with the Surrealist group in 1955 and began a close relationship with Mathieu, with whom, in 1957, he organized a commemoration of the Averroist Siger de Brabant, banned by the Inquisition in the 13th century. Under Mathieu's influence, Hantai turned to *Art informel*: his technique involved rubbing the canvas with paint, which he then spread with a spatula in forceful gestures. The spatula pushed away the surplus paint, allowing the irradiant ground to shine through the transparent layers, producing vibrant effects. In 1959 he organized an exhibition at the Galerie Kléber, Paris, which summarized the development of his work.

After this period, Hantai returned to a more restrained technique. He gave up gestural painting, and began to concentrate on a single technique, *pliage*, which he developed systematically in various series of works from 1960 (e.g. the *Mariales*, 1960; the *Catamurons*, 1963–4; the *Meuns*, 1967; and the *Tabulas*, 1975–81). Driven by a fear of the routine that was present in gestural painting, he sought to eliminate all vestiges of manual activity. His working process involved preparing the canvas with a black and then a white layer of varnish; subsequently, he rolled the canvas up, crumpled it and finally saturated it with thin transparent paints. On the canvas the painted and unpainted surfaces were separated by the folds, which appeared as accidental divisions after the canvas had been unfolded. The majority of his works contained two colours (black and white, or blue and white) but his later works became richer and more varied in colour. His activity with the SUPPORTS-SURFACES group was characteristic of his work, involving consciously repetitive methods, intended to protect the anonymous quality of his work. Hantai's ascetic disposition was influenced by East Asian philosophies. As participant of the exhibition *Dix ans d'art vivant: De 1955 à 1965* held in 1967 (Saint-Paul-de-Vence, Fond. Maeght), Hantai received an award. In 1976 he had a successful retrospective exhibition at the Musée National d'Art Moderne, Paris, which attracted much interest.

BIBLIOGRAPHY
A. Breton: 'Simon Hantai', *Le Surréalisme et la peinture* (Paris, 1965), p. 237 [preface of exh. cat. *Simon Hantai*, Paris, Gal. l'Etoile Scellée, 1953]
Hantai: Peintures, 1958–1968 (exh. cat. by F. Mathey, Saint-Paul-de-Vence, Fond. Maeght, 1968)
J. Clair: 'Simon Hantai', *Art en France: Une Nouvelle Génération* (Paris, 1972), pp. 93–6
Hantai (rétrospective) (exh. cat. by P. Hulten, F. Mathey, M. Pleynet and D. Fourcade, Paris, Mus. N. A. Mod., 1976)
Simon Hantai (exh. cat. by D. Bozo and Y. Michaud, Venice, Biennale, 1982)

FERENC TÓTH

Hanuš z Olomouce [Olmützer, Hans] (*b* Olomouc, *fl* 1473–1525). Moravian sculptor and painter. In 1473 he was training in Zurich with Peter Zeiner (after 1464–1510). In 1478 he was an independent master at St Gallen Abbey, though before 1478 and after 1479 he worked in Konstanz. In 1483 he became a citizen of Wrocław, Silesia (now Poland), where he worked with Jacob Beinhart (*fl* 1483; *d* 1525). Shortly before *c.* 1488–1503 he worked in Zgorzelec, Silesia, where he carved a winged altar of the *'Golden Virgin'* and in 1492 he sculpted a stone *Lamentation*; both works were for the former Franciscan church, now the Holy Trinity Church. The altars dedicated to the Virgin in Świdnica, Silesia (1492) and in the church of St Mary Magdalene in Wrocław were also made in his workshop or by his successors. From 1518 Hanuš worked in Prague on the reconstruction of Hradčany and in 1525 became a citizen of Prague. His work, which was close to that of Tilman Riemenschneider, influenced a number of sculpture workshops in Silesia, northern Moravia and Prague.

BIBLIOGRAPHY
Thieme–Becker
P. Toman: *Nový slovník československých výtvarných umělců* [New dictionary of Czechoslovak artists], i (Prague, 1947)
W. Biehl: 'Das Rätsel um Hans Olmützer', *Festschrift R. Jecht* (Leipzig, 1961)

IVO KOŘÁN

Hanwŏndang. *See* KIM KWANG-P'IL.

Haozous. *See* HOUSER, ALLAN.

Happenings. *See* PERFORMANCE ART and KAPROW, ALLAN.

Hapsburg. *See* HABSBURG.

Hara, Hiromu (*b* Nagano, 22 June 1903; *d* 26 March 1986). Japanese graphic designer. He graduated from the Tokyo Prefectural School of Technology in 1921 and taught there from 1922 to 1941. During this period he was exposed to the work of overseas avant-garde artists LÁSZLÓ MOHOLY-NAGY, HERBERT BAYER and EL LISSITZKY. He also established links with TOMOYOSHI MURAYAMA and other members of the Sankakai group of painters. These contacts had a great influence on his later designs and led to his emergence as the founder of Japanese modern design. In 1933 he participated in the founding of the Japan Studio (Nihon Kōbō). He designed the photography exhibitions in JUNZŌ SAKAKURA's Japan Pavilions for the Paris World Expositions of 1937 and the New York Exposition of 1939. These exhibits exemplified Hara's philosophy that the real work of the designer is the organization of graphic elements. His designs for the propaganda magazine *Front* (published by the Tōhōsha company) during the Pacific War (1941–5) set the standards for Japanese design. In 1951 Hara was a founder-member of the Japan Advertising Artists Club, which went on to play a leading role in post-war Japanese graphic design. In 1960 he took part in the setting up of the

Nippon Design Centre, Inc., whose aim was to develop the business potential of graphic design.

BIBLIOGRAPHY
Hara Hiromu (Tokyo, 1985)

HIROSHI KASHIWAGI

Hara, Hiroshi (*b* Kawasaki, Kanagawa Prefect., 9 Sept 1936). Japanese architect. He trained at Tokyo University (1955–9) under Kenzō Tange and Uchida. He was one of the oldest in a new generation of avant-garde New Wave architects, who were active from the late 1960s and early 1970s and who were sharply critical of the contemporary urban developments in Japan (*see* JAPAN, §III, 5). Yet, unlike many of his more radical contemporaries, such as Tadao Andō and Toyō Itō, Hara derived his design theories from his extensive studies of vernacular architecture and indigenous settlements in Asia and Africa, in an attempt to bridge the avant-garde and the ethnic. Thereafter he followed a unique anthropological approach to architecture somewhat similar in nature to the one put forward by the members of Team Ten in Europe. His early works (1970s), the so-called 'reflection houses', such as his own residence (1974) at Machida near Tokyo and the Niramu House (1978), Tokyo, display a negative attitude towards the chaotic and volatile conditions of the Japanese city and focus upon the internal order and other critical aspects of dwelling. They were all shaped along sequences of centrally and symmetrically arranged spaces and appeared as hollowed-out concavities. Many of them implemented scaled-down and metaphorical urban elements, including landmarks, intersections and plazas, and so could be regarded as attempts to create miniature and fantastic cities.

After the 1970s, in addition to his residential works, Hara received commissions for larger, public buildings such as the Sueda Art Gallery (1981) in Ōita and the Tsurukawa Nursery (1981) in Machida. At this time his architectural approach began to change, becoming more receptive to the natural and built landscape. Having internalized the metropolis by creating exterior-like interiors, he now seemed to turn this model inside out, making his new buildings metaphors of 'cities within the city'. In the Tasaki Museum of Art (1986), Karuizawa, and particularly in the Yamato International office building (1987) in Tokyo, the boundaries or transition between architecture and the surrounding environment are ambiguously defined. In his 'architecture of modality' extensively and intricately layered walls, imprinted translucent and transparent glass and polished aluminium surfaces, as well as fragmented elements and volumes, create an elusive atmosphere, which also reflects Oriental thought, especially Buddhism. These buildings, for example the Izu Stage of Dreams (1982), Nakatsuka House, Shizuoka, evoke images of fictive, vernacular villages while also alluding to such transitory natural phenomena as clouds, mist or mirage. Together they reveal Hara's long-standing resistance to Modernist and Constructivist architecture. His projects of the 1980s and 1990s (e.g. the Iida City Museum, 1988, and the new Kyoto Station) were increasingly large urban complexes in which the previous mode of design is complemented by the imaginative application of high technology, as in the spectacular Umeda Sky Building (1993) in Osaka. The exceptional quality of these works demonstrates Hara's significant role in contemporary Japanese architecture.

WRITINGS
'Modality—Central Concept of Contemporary Architecture', *Japan Architect*, 355–6 (Nov–Dec 1986), pp. 24–7

BIBLIOGRAPHY
C. Fawcett: 'Hiroshi Hara: An Introduction', *Archit. Assoc. Q.*, x/4 (1978), p. 4
——: *The New Japanese House: Ritual and Anti-ritual Patterns of Dwelling* (New York, 1980)
B. Bognar: *Contemporary Japanese Architecture: Its Development and Challenge* (New York, 1985)
K. Frampton: 'Twilight Gloom to Self-enclosed Modernity: Five Japanese Architects', *Tokyo: Form and Spirit* (exh. cat., Minneapolis, MN, Walker A. Cent., 1986), pp. 221–41
B. Bognar: *The New Japanese Architecture* (New York, 1990)
Y. Futagawa, ed.: *Hiroshi Hara: GA Architect 13* (Tokyo, 1993)
B. Bognar: *The Japan Guide* (New York, 1995)

BOTOND BOGNAR

Hara, Sankei [Aoki, Tomitarō] (*b* Gifu Prefect., 23 Aug 1868; *d* Yokohama, 16 Aug 1939). Japanese collector. He changed his name when he was adopted by his father-in-law, a silk merchant in Yokohama, who made him his heir. He began collecting after *c.* 1897, and his large collection contained a number of National Treasures. To exhibit it, he opened the Sankei'en in a new park in Yokohama. He encouraged and gave financial support to such artists as Yukihiko Yasuda and Gyoshū Hayami, prominent figures in the Japan Art Institute. He was a highly respected tea master in later life.

YOSHIKAZU IWASAKI

Harache, Pierre (*b* Rouen, *c.* 1630; *d* London, *c.* 1700). English goldsmith of French birth. On 21 July 1682 he became the first Huguenot goldsmith to be admitted to the Goldsmiths' Company in London. The change in taste from the Dutch to the French fashions during the 1680s and 1690s is illustrated by a set of four candlesticks (formerly at Althorp House, Northants) made by Harache in 1683. These are some of the first English candlesticks with faceted, cast baluster stems and are the earliest recorded pieces by him, with the exception of two other pieces hallmarked in the same year: a pair of candlesticks and a jug and cover (both untraced). His surviving pieces show a simplicity of form with the ornament largely applied or engraved (*see* SILVER, fig. 4). Much of the engraving on silver by Harache is attributed to either Blaise Gentot (1658–1700; e.g. toilet service, 1695; Burghley House, Cambs) or Simon Gribelin II. Harache's use of cut-card ornament can be seen on two silver-gilt ewers (1697; Leeds, Temple Newsam House) made for Charles Howard, 3rd Earl of Carlisle. Confusion often arises between the work of Pierre Harache and that of his son Pierre Harache (ii) (*b* 1653; *fl* 1698–1717), as their registered marks are similar.

BIBLIOGRAPHY
J. F. Hayward: *Huguenot Silver in England, 1688–1727* (London, 1959)
A. G. Grimwade: *London Goldsmiths, 1697–1837: Their Marks and Lives* (London, 1976, rev. 3/1990)

STEPHEN T. CLARKE

Haradum. *See under* HADITHA REGION.

Haranee. *See* QASR KHARANA.

Haranger, Pierre-Maurice, Abbé (*b* Paris, *c.* 1655; *d* Paris, 10 May 1735). French cleric and collector. In 1681 he was appointed sub-deacon in the diocese of Paris and canon at the abbey of St Germain-l'Auxerrois, close to the Louvre, the seat of the Académie Royale de Peinture et de Sculpture. The inventory taken after his death shows his enlightened taste and his love of precious furniture and of 'good paintings'; it also highlights his relationship with Antoine Watteau, confirming the painter's obituary in the *Mercure de France* (Aug 1721), which stated: 'He [Watteau] left his sketches to the abbé Haranchère [*sic*], his friend, canon of Saint Germain-l'Auxerrois.' Haranger, who un-doubtedly posed for Watteau and who also arranged for him his final home at Nogent, possessed at the time of his own death *c.* 1000 of the artist's drawings, almost half of his graphic work. Haranger's inventory, discovered by Jeannine Baticle in 1984, questioned the generally accepted theory that Watteau had divided his drawings among Haranger, Jean de Jullienne, Edmé-François Gersaint and Caylus. Haranger's legatees, his brother and sister, sold the collection: Gersaint, acting as dealer, deliberately undervalued the drawings, then bought a number of them for himself. This collection has now been dispersed.

BIBLIOGRAPHY

J. Baticle: 'Le Chanoine Haranger, ami de Watteau' and 'L'Inventaire après décès du chanoine Haranger, 17 mai 1735', *Rev. A.* [Paris], lxix (1985), pp. 55–68

NICOLE PARMANTIER-LALLEMENT

Harappa [Harappā]. Ancient city on the southern bank of the Ravi River, western Punjab, Pakistan, and the type site for the Indus civilization that flourished *c.* 2500–2000 BC (*see also* MOHENJO-DARO). Harappa is the name of the modern village adjacent to the mounds and is not thought to be of ancient derivation, although the place-name Hariyupiya does occur in the *Ṛg veda* and has been associated with the site by some scholars (see Wheeler, pp. 78–82). The archaeological site was first recognized in 1826 by Charles Masson, an early traveller in the region. The city as a whole was robbed for bricks in the mid-19th century and is not well preserved. Alexander Cunningham, the first Director–General of the Archaeological Survey of India, excavated part of the site in 1871–2 and published the first of a series of important stamp seals associated with the Harappan civilization. The results of excavations undertaken in 1922–3 by Rai Bahadur Daya Ram Sahni at Harappa and Rakhal Das Banerji at Mohenjo-daro led John Marshall to conclude that these ancient cities were part of a vast Bronze Age civilization of the Indus Valley. Subsequent discoveries have shown that sites associated with this culture extend across northern India, western Pakistan and Afghanistan. Excavations by Madho Sarup Vats were followed by some work (1934–40) that was never systematically published (see Nilakanta Sastri, pp. 39–40). In 1946 Mortimer Wheeler investigated the Cemetery R-37 and the AB Mound. The Pakistan Depart-ment of Archaeology excavated in Cemetery R-37 in 1966. A large-scale reinvestigation of the city begun by George Dales in 1986 continued in the 1990s under the direction of Richard Meadow.

Harappa contains material from three periods: the Early Harappan or Kot Diji period (*c.* 3200–2550 BC); the Urban or Mature-Phase Harappan city (*c.* 2550–2000 BC); and the Cemetery H Culture, a small, later settlement and cemetery (*c.* 2000–1500 BC). The site comprises several areas. The AB Mound is also called the 'High Mound' or 'Citadel'. Mound F to the north has the 'Granary', husking floors and other small, regular buildings and produced two very fine pieces of stone sculpture: a red jasper male torso in the round and a stone torso of a dancer (*see* INDIAN SUBCONTINENT, fig. 136). The southern mounds are poorly known but have been the focus of recent excavation (see Dales and Kenoyer). Excavations by the Pakistan Department of Archaeology of another settlement in the area between the AB Mound and Harappa village suggest that the original 100 ha estimate for the whole site may be too low. On the evidence available, Harappa appears to be similar in size to Mohenjo-daro, with an estimated population of 20,000–30,000. Harappa has produced the same range of artefacts as Mohenjo-daro and in a virtually identical style. Although poorly preserved, the site must have been comparable to Mohenjo-daro when inhabited.

See also INDIAN SUBCONTINENT, §§I, 2(i) and IV, 2.

BIBLIOGRAPHY

A. Cunningham: 'Harappa', *Archaeol. Surv. India Rep. 1872–73*, v (Calcutta, 1875), pp. 105–8
M. S. Vats: *Excavations at Harappa*, 2 vols (Delhi, 1940)
R. E. M. Wheeler: 'Harappa 1946: The Defences and Cemetery R-37', *Anc. India*, iii (1947), pp. 58–130
K. Nilakanta Sastri: *New Light on the Indus Civilization*, ii (Delhi, 1965)
M. Rafique Mughal: 'Excavations: Harappa, 1966 (Cemetery R-37)', *Pakistan Archaeol.*, v (1968), pp. 63–8
G. L. Possehl: 'Discovering Ancient India's Earliest Cities: The First Phase of Research', *Harappan Civilization: A Contemporary Perspective*, ed. G. L. Possehl (New Delhi, 1982), pp. 405–13
P. C. Rissman and Y. M. Chitalwala: *Harappan Civilization and Oriyo Timbo* (New Delhi, 1990), pp. ix and 155
R. H. Meadow, ed.: *Harappa Excavations, 1986–1990: A Multidisciplinary Approach to Third Millennium Urbanism*, Monographs in World Archaeology, iii (Madison, 1991)
G. F. Dales and J. M. Kenoyer: 'The Harappa Project, 1986–89: New Investigations at an Ancient Indus City', *Harappa Civilization: A Contemporary Perspective*, ed. G. L. Possehl (New Delhi, 1993), pp. 469–520

GREGORY L. POSSEHL

Harari, Ralph (Andrew) (*b* Cairo, 28 Oct 1892; *d* London, 26 May 1969). Merchant banker and collector. He was the elder son of Sir Victor Harari Pasha, a leading member of the Anglo-Jewish community in Egypt, and was educated at Lausanne and Pembroke College, Cam-bridge. On returning to Egypt, he became a junior officer in the Palestine campaign of Edmund Allenby and then finance officer to Ronalds Storrs, the military governor of Jerusalem. In 1920 he served under Herbert Samuel as director of the Department of Commerce and Trade in the British Mandate, but returned to Egypt in 1925 to help in the family business. With the outbreak of World War II, he became economic adviser to GHQ Middle East, and then served under Peter Ritchie-Calder, the director of plans in the Department of Political Warfare in London. After the war, he stayed in London as managing director of the merchant bank S. Japhet & Co., and when it was taken over he joined the board of the Charterhouse group. From the 1920s he was interested in Islamic metalwork, becoming an authority on the subject and contributing a chapter to the *Survey of Persian Art*. His collection of

Islamic metalwork, which was formed in Egypt, is now in the Museum of Islamic Art, Cairo. From the early 1930s he also collected drawings by AUBREY BEARDSLEY and other European artists of the late 19th century and early 20th. Rings and engraved gems of all periods were another passion. After World War II he turned his attention to Japanese paintings and drawings and amassed a fine collection, concentrating at first on KATSUSHIKA HOKUSAI and the *Ukiyoe* masters and later widening his scope to include other work, such as that of the *Nanga* and Shijō schools.

WRITINGS
'Metalwork after the Early Islamic Period', *Survey of Persian Art*, ed. A. U. Pope and P. Ackerman (London, 1939), pp. 2466–529

BIBLIOGRAPHY
DNB
J. R. Hillier: *The Harari Collection of Japanese Paintings and Drawings*, 3 vols (London, 1970–73)
M. Harari: *Memoirs, 1906–1969* (London, 1972)
J. Boardman and D. Scarisbrick: *The Ralph Harari Collection of Finger Rings* (London, 1977)

S. J. VERNOIT

Harat. *See* HERAT.

Haraŭski, Apalinary [Goravsky, Apollinary Gilyaryev-ich] (*b* Uborki, Minsk Province, 4 Feb 1833; *d* St Petersburg, 28 March 1900). Belarusian painter. In 1850 he entered the Academy of Arts in St Petersburg, where he was taught by Fyodor Bruni and Mikhail Vorob'yov (1787–1855). From 1855 to 1860 he worked in Düsseldorf with Andrey Achenbach (1815–1910) and then in Switzerland with Aleksandr Kalam (1810–64).

In works such as *Evening in Minsk Province* (*c*. 1870; Minsk, Belarus' A. Mus.) and *Italian Landscape* (1857; Irkutsk, A. Mus.) Goravsky revealed his mastery of technique, which helped to raise the standard of Belarusian art to the level of 19th-century Western European realistic landscape painting. A very prolific artist, in 1861 he was awarded the title of Academician for *View of the River Arve near Chamonix* (*c*. 1859), among other works. He also painted portraits, notably of the collector *Koz'ma Soldatenkov* (1857; Moscow, Tret'yakov Gal.) and the painters *Fyodor Bruni* (1871; Moscow, Tret'yakov Gal.) and *Lev Lagorio* (Minsk, Belarus' A. Mus.). In 1860 Goravsky returned to Belarus' where he lived and worked for 30 years, paying increased attention to effects and to producing variations of his successful devices, for example *In the Motherland* (1860s; Moscow, Tret'yakov Gal.). His style is close to the paintings of the French Salon artists; their influence led him away from the dry copying of nature of the Düsseldorf school towards broader, more generalized brushwork. During the winters he taught at the Society for the Encouragement of the Arts in St Petersburg (1862–6). His works were shown at art exhibitions in Paris (1867, 1878), London (1872), Vienna (1873) and Philadelphia (1876).

BIBLIOGRAPHY
L. Drobaŭ: 'Belaruskija pesažysty Haraŭskija' [The Belarusian landscapes of Goravsky], *Belaruskaje mastactva: zbornik artykulaŭ i materijalaŭ* [Belarusian art: a collection of articles and materials], iii (Minsk, 1962)
——: *Belaruskija mastaki XIX stahodždzia* [Belarusian artists of the 19th century] (Minsk, 1971)

SERGEY KUZNETSOV

Harcourt, Simon, 1st Earl Harcourt of Stanton Harcourt [2nd Earl Nuneham] (*b* 1714; *d* Nuneham, 16 Sept 1777). English patron and collector. He was the only son of the Hon. Simon Harcourt (1684–1720) of Stanton Harcourt, Oxon, and his wife Elizabeth, granddaughter of the diarist John Evelyn. When Harcourt was six years old, his father died; Harcourt succeeded to the family's estates and titles on the death of his grandfather, Simon Harcourt, 1st Viscount Harcourt (1661–1727). He was sent on an extensive Grand Tour of Europe in 1730, which lasted for four years. He married in 1735 and was created 1st Earl Harcourt in 1749 by George II, under whom he held posts in the royal household. He continued to serve in these posts under George III, whose tutor he briefly was, and whose future wife, Princess Charlotte, he conveyed to England from Mecklenburg-Strelitz. He reached the rank of general in the army and served as ambassador in Paris (1768–72) and as Lord Lieutenant of Ireland (1772–7).

Harcourt had a keen interest in architecture and antiquities and was one of the founders of the Dilettanti Society in 1732. He also built up a notable collection of pictures. Many of his purchases are recorded in a cashbook (1754–9; Oxford, Bodleian Lib.) and include commissions from George Knapton and Joshua Reynolds, whose portrait of *Simon, 1st Earl Harcourt*, remains in the family collection, as well as purchases of works then ascribed to Nicolas Poussin, Claude Lorrain, Giovanni Paolo Panini, Aert van der Neer and others. His collection included two paintings by Poussin—*Moses Purifying the Waters* (Baltimore, MD, Mus. A.), which he bought in 1755 for £50, and *Mars and Venus* (Boston, MA, Mus. F.A.), which he bought at the Furness Sale in 1758 for £105. His Dutch pictures included the magnificent *Yacht 'Mary' and other Vessels off Amsterdam* (1661; Stanton Harcourt Manor, Oxon) by Adriaen and Willem van de Velde II, probably bought in the late 1750s. Harcourt commissioned *Nuneham from the Lock Cottages—Morning* and its pendant (both 1760; Stanton Harcourt Manor, Oxon) from Paul Sandby, one of which was exhibited in London in 1760 at the first Society of Artists exhibition. Sandby, who remained a close friend, made sketches of the family, house and grounds, made aquatints of the flower garden (pub. in *The Virtuosi's Museum*, 1778), and took on Harcourt's eldest son George (1736–1809) as his pupil.

In 1756 Harcourt drew up plans for a Palladian villa to be built at Nuneham Courtenay near Oxford, on land overlooking the River Thames. The villa was designed and built by Stiff Leadbetter (*d* 1766) from 1756 to 1764; James Stuart, who had just returned from Greece, was responsible for much of its interior decoration. Harcourt became involved in plans for a new garden with William Mason (i), which was laid out from 1772; he also destroyed the village (1771) in the park to improve the view but built a replacement for the community on the main road to Oxford. Harcourt died by falling into a well at Nuneham, from which he had been trying to save a favourite dog. His eldest son, George Simon, 2nd Earl Harcourt, was a talented amateur artist who greatly enlarged the family's collection. He also participated in laying out Nuneham's flower garden and commissioned Lancelot 'Capability' Brown to remodel the house and park (1781–2). Shortly after World War II the Harcourt family sold the Nuneham estate to the University of Oxford and moved back to their refurbished ancestral home at Stanton Harcourt.

DNB
BIBLIOGRAPHY
E. W. Harcourt, ed.: *The Harcourt Papers*, 14 vols (Oxford, 1880–1905)
M. Batey: *Nuneham Courtenay, Oxfordshire* (Oxford, 1970, rev. 1979) [guidebk]

DAVID MOORE-GWYN

Hard-edge painting. Term applied to abstract paintings composed of simple geometric or organic forms executed in broad, flat colours and delineated by precise, sharp edges. The term was coined by the Californian art critic Jules Langsner in 1958 and intended by him merely as an alternative to the term 'geometric abstraction'. Generally, however, it is used in a more specific sense: whereas geometric abstraction can be used to describe works with large numbers of separate, possibly modelled, elements creating a spatial effect, hard-edge painting refers only to works comprised of a small number of large, flat forms, generally avoiding the use of pictorial depth. It is in relation to this type of painting, particularly as produced by artists such as Ellsworth Kelly, KENNETH NOLAND, Barnett Newman (*see* NEWMAN, BARNETT, fig. 2) and Ad Reinhardt from the mid-1950s to the end of the 1960s, that the term acquired general currency. Characteristic of this style are Newman's *The Gate* (1954; Amsterdam, Stedel.

Hard-edge painting by Ellsworth Kelly: *White Black*, oil on canvas, 3.05×2.29 m, 1961 (Chicago, IL, Art Institute of Chicago)

Mus.) and Kelly's *White Black* (1961; Chicago, IL, A. Inst.; see fig.).

BIBLIOGRAPHY
Systemic Painting (exh. cat. by L. Alloway, New York, Guggenheim, 1966)
I. Sandler: *American Art of the 1960s* (New York, 1988)

□

Hardegger, August (*b* St Gall, 1 Oct 1858; *d* Lucerne, 11 Jan 1927). Swiss architect. After studying architecture for two years (*c.* 1876–8) at the Hochschule, Stuttgart, under Adolf Gnauth and Christian Friedrich Leins (1814–92), he travelled in Italy and France. From 1879 he worked primarily in St Gall, but he also worked elsewhere in Switzerland. He won a gold medal at the Vatican Exhibition (1887–8), and in 1888 he was made a Knight of St Gregory the Great by Pope Leo XIII. Hardegger was an eclectic architect, using all the traditional historicist styles. His designs were often asymmetrical and irregular in both plan and elevation, as in the church of St Martin (1908–10), Olten; they also incorporated painting and sculpture, for example in the Haus zum Bürgli (before 1890), at St Gall, and they emphasized regional traditions, as at the parish church of Göschenen (1898–9). Following the construction of the parish church at Gossau (1890–91), the centralized interior became a hallmark of Hardegger's sacred buildings. In the Liebfrauenkirche (1893–4), Zurich, he created the most important evocation of an Early Christian basilica in Switzerland by merging several historical models in a single building. Hardegger's oeuvre includes restoration and conservation, such as the lengthening of the church of St Peter (1885–7) at Wil, and the historical investigation of indigenous art, seen in his work on the Stiftskirche, St Gall, which earned him a doctorate in 1917. He was a leading architect of his day and his importance lies particularly in his Roman Catholic churches, although his influence was not widespread.

BIBLIOGRAPHY
A. Meyer: 'August Hardegger: Architekt und Kunstschriftsteller', *Neujbl. Hist. Ver. Kant. St Gallen* (1970), pp. 1–30
——: *Neugotik und Neuromanik in der Schweiz: Die Kirchenarchitektur des 19. Jahrhunderts* (Zurich, 1973)

CORNELIA BAUER

Hardenbergh, Henry Janeway (*b* New Brunswick, NJ, 6 Feb 1847; *d* New York, 18 Mar 1918). American architect. He trained (1865–70) in the office of Detlef Lienau in New York. After setting up his own practice, Hardenbergh built (1871–3) a chapel, a library (destr.) and a geology building (destr.) at Rutgers College, New Brunswick, a commission obtained through family connections. Success came after 1879, when he built the Vancorlear, an early apartment block, on W. 55th Street, New York. This building brought him to the attention of Edward S. Clark, head of the Singer Sewing Machine Co., who had bought a plot of land between the present W. 72nd and 73rd Streets and Eighth and Ninth Avenues. Clark commissioned Hardenbergh to build a housing development (1880–86) for three different social classes, comprising row houses (some destr.), lower-middle-class apartments and, on the most valuable part of the plot fronting on to Eighth Avenue, a daring foray into the luxury apartment market, now known as the Dakota Apartments (1880–84). The façades are in an eclectic style that includes German

Renaissance and French château elements. For the Astor Estate in New York, Hardenbergh went on to build the lavish Waldorf Hotel (1893; destr. 1931) and Astoria Hotel (1896; destr. 1931), which established him as a leading architect for luxurious Edwardian hotels. Other such works in New York included the Martinique (1897) and the Plaza (1907; interior altered), and elsewhere the Windsor (1903) in Montreal, Canada, the Willard (1906) in Washington, DC, and the Copley Plaza (1912), in Boston, MA.

BIBLIOGRAPHY
M. Schuyler: 'The Works of Henry Janeway Hardenbergh', *Archit. Rec.*, vi (1897), pp. 335–75
R. F. Bach: 'Henry Janeway Hardenbergh', *Archit. Rec.*, xliv (1918), pp. 91–3
P. Goldberger: *The City Observed: New York: A Guide to the Architecture of Manhattan* (New York, 1979)

MOSETTE GLASER BRODERICK

Hardie, Martin (*b* London, 15 Dec 1875; *d* Tonbridge, 20 Jan 1952). English painter, printmaker, art historian and museum curator. Educated at St Paul's School, London, and Trinity College, Cambridge, he came from a family closely associated with the arts, one of his uncles being John Pettie. At Cambridge, Hardie studied etching under Frank Short (1857–1945), and he developed into an able etcher and watercolour painter (examples Oxford, Ashmolean); from 1908 he was a regular exhibitor in London at the Royal Academy, the Royal Society of Painter-Etchers and Engravers and the Royal Institute of Painters in Water-Colours. In 1898 Hardie was appointed to an assistant post at the Victoria and Albert Museum, London; in 1914 he was made Assistant Keeper, and from 1921 until his retirement in 1935 he served as Keeper in the Print Department. Under his direction the Department was extended to include the collection and study of posters and of various aspects of theatre arts. Hardie was a prolific writer, celebrating and recording all the arts with which he was for so long connected, and he produced books and pamphlets on numerous individuals, including Samuel Palmer, whose reputation had fallen into total neglect. He also wrote on posters and coloured books and produced an edition of *Miniatura*, a practical treatise on painting in miniature written in the 1640s by Edward Norgate. Hardie's principal achievement is his massive *Water-colour Painting in Britain*, which remains a corner-stone for study of the subject.

WRITINGS
English Coloured Books (London, 1904/*R* 1906/*R* Bath, 1973)
John Pettie RA (London, 1908)
Frederick Goulding: Master Printer of Copper Plates (Stirling, 1910)
ed.: E. Norgate: *Miniatura, or the Art of Limning* (London, 1919)
The Etched Work of W. Lee-Hankey R.E. from 1904 to 1920 (London, 1921)
Etchings and Dry Points from 1902 to 1924 by James McBey (London, 1925)
Samuel Palmer (London, 1928)
Charles Meryon and his Eaux-Fortes sur Paris (London, 1931)
Etchings, Dry Points, Lithographs by Sir Frank Short RA (London, 1940)
English Water Colours of the XVIII Century: A Preliminary Guide for the Collector (London, 1949)
D. Snelgrove, ed.: *Water-colour Painting in Britain*, 3 vols (London, 1966–8, rev. 1967–)

BIBLIOGRAPHY
DNB
Obituary, *The Times* (22 Jan 1952)

DAVID CAST

Hardin, Helen [Tsa-sah-wee-eh: 'Little Standing Spruce'] (*b* Albuquerque, NM, 28 May 1943; *d* 9 June 1984). Native American Pueblo painter of Santa Clara, NM. Her father was Herbert O. Hardin, an Anglo, and her mother was the Pueblo painter PABLITA VELARDE. She attended high school in Albuquerque, NM, and was awarded an Indian Art project scholarship in 1960, which influenced her decision to turn to art as a career. By the late 1960s she had developed a highly successful style. She worked in acrylics, casein, pen and ink, and just before her untimely death, of cancer, she had begun a series of etchings. After leaving Santa Clara Pueblo she lived most of her life in Española, NM. She had a brief marriage to Pat Terrazas, which ended in divorce, and later married Cradoc Bagshaw, a Santa Fe Anglo photographer. Greatly influenced by her mother, and even more so by Joe Hilario Herrera, a noted Cochití artist and son of TONITA PEÑA, Hardin became one of the most widely known Pueblo painters. Her early focus was the usual genre form, but in 1967 she developed a unique linear form, marked by pastel colours, abstract figures and quasi-symbolic motifs, which quickly gained favour. At the time of her death, her work was tremendously popular, a success that had created a rivalry between herself and her mother, adversely affecting the lives of both artists.

For general discussion of 20th-century developments in Native American paintings *see* NATIVE NORTH AMERICAN ART, §IV, 2.

BIBLIOGRAPHY
L. H. Culley: 'Helen Hardin: A Retrospective', *Amer. Ind. A.*, iv (Summer 1979), pp. 68–75
K. Shane: 'Helen Hardin: Casting her own Shadow', *SWA.* (June 1985), pp. 42–7
J. Scott: *Changing Woman: The Life and Art of Helen Hardin* (Flagstaff, 1989)

FREDERICK J. DOCKSTADER

Harding, Chester (*b* Conway, MA, 1 Sept 1792; *d* Boston, MA, 10 April 1866). American painter. This untrained, itinerant artist from rural New England became one of the most successful American portrait painters in the generation following Gilbert Stuart. A huge man with a hearty, genial personality, he combined a businesslike approach to painting with native talent and hard work. His colourful life epitomized the 19th-century American rags-to-riches success story. He painted the influential men and women of his time: American presidents, congressmen, Supreme Court justices, merchants and sea-captains of Boston and their wives, and members of the British aristocracy. In his memoir, *My Egotistography* (1866), he described his reaction to his first attempt at portraiture, a portrait of his wife, *Caroline Harding* (1816; Washington, DC, priv. col., see 1985 exh. cat., frontispiece): 'The moment I saw the likeness I became frantic with delight: it was like the discovery of a new sense.'

Harding's career began in the prosperous frontier towns of Kentucky, where between 1818 and 1820 he painted nearly 100 portraits at £25 each. After using this money for a brief study trip to Philadelphia, he went to St Louis, MO, where the Governor of the Territory, William Clark, became one of his first sitters. At Clark's request Harding painted the only portrait from life of the aged pioneer *Daniel Boone* (1818; Boston, MA, Hist. Soc.). In 1823 he enjoyed six months of overwhelming popularity in Boston, which he attributed to his being 'a backwoodsman newly caught'. Aware of his technical limitations, however, he left on 1 August for three years in England and Scotland.

Again Harding quickly found enthusiastic patrons, including the brother of George IV, Augustus Frederick, Duke of Sussex. He learnt through observation of other artists. In Kentucky he had absorbed the rudiments of portrait painting from the work of Matthew Jouett, and in Boston, Gilbert Stuart had temporarily influenced his style. Within days of his arrival in London, Harding's admiration for Thomas Lawrence manifested itself in the broad brushwork and dramatic pose of *Loammi Baldwin* (1823; Washington, DC, N.P.G.), and Lawrence's influence is also evident in such atmospheric Scottish portraits as *Alexander Hamilton Douglas, 10th Duke of Hamilton* (1825; priv. col., see 1985 exh. cat., p. 68) and *Mrs Thomas Graham* (exh. RA 1826; Glasgow, A.G. & Mus.). Once back in America, he quickly reverted to the factual immediacy that was his greatest strength. His deep admiration for the statesman Daniel Webster is manifested in more than 20 portraits (examples at Boston, MA, Athenaeum and Washington, DC, N.P.G.) based on two sittings and two daguerreotypes. At the Constitutional Convention in Richmond, VA (1829), he painted Presidents *James Monroe* (priv. col., see 1985 exh. cat., p. 51) and *James Madison* (e.g. Washington, DC, N.P.G.), along with other establishment figures of Virginian society. In 1830 he was commissioned to paint a portrait of *Chief Justice John Marshall* (Boston, MA, Athenaeum), one of his most polished works. He also painted *President John Quincy Adams* (e.g. Newport, RI, Redwood Lib.) and the ethereally aged *Charles Carroll of Carrollton* (1828; Washington, DC, N.G.A.), last living signatory of the Declaration of Independence. Harding made replicas of his well-known sitters' portraits for his own use and for reproduction as engravings. Charles Carroll's portrait was engraved by both John Sartain (1808–97) and Asher B. Durand.

With his family living in Springfield, MA, Harding maintained a studio and gallery at 22 School Street in Boston, where he rented rooms to other artists and provided exhibition space. In 1841 he was a founder of the Boston Artists' Association, a short-lived attempt to establish an art academy in Boston. After three annual exhibitions at Harding's Gallery, the group exhibited jointly with the Boston Athenaeum each year until disbanding in 1851. Harding continued to travel in search of clients. He made several trips to New Orleans between 1839 and 1849 and a second trip to England in 1847. He finished his last portrait, of *General William Tecumsah Sherman* (1866; New York, Un. League Club), only weeks before his death. Its tighter style reflects the new popularity of photography.

WRITINGS
My Egotistography (Boston, 1866)

BIBLIOGRAPHY
M. E. White, ed.: *A Sketch of Chester Harding, Artist, Drawn by his own Hand* (Boston, 1866/*R* New York, 1970) [incl. *My Egotistography* and Harding's Brit. diary]
L. Lipton: 'Chester Harding in Great Britain', *Antiques*, cxxvi (1984), pp. 1382–90
——: 'Chester Harding and the Life Portraits of Daniel Boone', *Amer. A. J.*, xvi (1984), pp. 4–19
A Truthful Likeness: Chester Harding and his Portraits (exh. cat. by L. Lipton, Washington, DC, N.P.G., 1985) [illus. checklist of *c.* 700 ptgs]
LEAH LIPTON

Harding, J(ames) D(uffield) (*b* Deptford, London, 1798; *d* London, 4 Dec 1863). English painter, engraver and writer. He received his first lessons in painting from his father, J. Harding (*d* 1846), who was a pupil of Paul Sandby. By 1807 the family had moved to Greenwich where Harding spent much of his time drawing and painting in Greenwich Park. In 1811 at the age of 14 he exhibited for the first time at the Royal Academy. He had lessons in watercolour painting from Samuel Prout and in 1816 he won the Society of Arts silver medal for landscape painting. He also learnt engraving from John Pye and subsequently became a skilled engraver and lithographer.

Harding travelled extensively throughout Britain and Europe painting topographical views, many of which were engraved and published in the landscape annuals which became popular in the middle of the 19th century. In 1836 he published *Sketches at Home and Abroad*, followed by a number of books on the teaching of drawing. John Ruskin was a pupil and a notable admirer of his teaching methods (particularly his theories on the drawing of trees, his speciality, and on direct observation from nature) and incorporated many of his lessons in the early volumes of *Modern Painters*. Harding's fame as a teacher has overshadowed his considerable gifts as an artist. He was equally at home painting architectural subjects as extensive landscape views, such as the fine panoramic watercolour *Berwick-upon-Tweed* (Newcastle upon Tyne, Laing A.G.). Good examples of his picturesque views of towns and villages in France and Italy are in the Victoria and Albert Museum, the Tate Gallery and the City of Birmingham Museum and Art Gallery.

Harding's best medium was watercolour. His accomplished technique, his flair for drawing trees and foliage and his ability to produce finely composed pictures on a small scale admirably suited the medium. His watercolours of British harbours and seaside towns are equal to the best of Clarkson Stanfield's work and are by no means overshadowed by Turner's more celebrated coastal views. His oil paintings are less successful. He failed to be elected ARA in 1846; however he exhibited 35 works at the Royal Academy between 1811 and 1858 and also showed at the British Institution, at Suffolk Street and at the Old Water-Colour Society.

The sale of his studio took place at Christie's, London, 19–20 May 1864.

WRITINGS
Elementary Art, or the Use of the Lead Pencil Advocated and Explained (London, 1834)
Sketches at Home and Abroad (London, 1839)
The Principles and Practice of Art (London, 1845)
Lessons on Art (London, 1849)
Lessons on Trees (London, 1850)
Drawing Models and their Uses (London, 1854)

BIBLIOGRAPHY
Obituary, *A. J.* [London], n. s., iii (1864), pp. 39–40
W. Walker: 'J. D. Harding', *Portfolio* [London], xi (1880), pp. 29–33
J. L. Roget: *A History of the Old Water-Colour Society* (London, 1891)
DAVID CORDINGLY

Hardman, John (*b* 1812; *d* 1867). English stained-glass maker and metalworker. Based in Birmingham, his company produced metalwork and stained glass for A. W. N. Pugin, whom Hardman first met in 1837. Together with other craftsmen, he exhibited examples of his work for Pugin, including a chalice (London, V&A), at the so-called Medieval Court in the Great Exhibition, London, in 1851. He also collaborated with Jean-Baptiste Charles François Bethune, who set up a stained-glass workshop in Bruges in 1845 with Hardman's assistance.

Hardouin-Mansart, Jules. *See* MANSART, (2).

Hardouin Mansart de Sagonne, Jacques. *See* MANSART, (3).

Hardstones. Mineral substances mostly non-transparent, compact, differently coloured and capable of being highly polished. Since prehistoric times they have been prized and have had a vast, uninterrupted popularity in the artistic culture of the West. Many factors have contributed to the popularity of these beautiful materials, which has endured through the history of art. First are the fascinating physical characteristics of these smooth, gleaming stones, the fabulous range and variety of colour of which are unrivalled in nature. Another reason for the great value of polished hardstones is that they are also less vulnerable to deterioration than many other materials. Patrons and collectors have been especially attracted to works of durable beauty, in which the intrinsic nature and rarity of the stones are enhanced by their sophisticated artistic treatment. Artists, in turn, have been inspired to experiment and perfect the difficult technique required to impose their inventive ideas on these resistant materials. The art of hardstone cutting and engraving had its greatest flowering in societies of extraordinary refinement and cultural development, such as the Greek and Roman civilizations and that of the Renaissance.

Some peripheral factors have also contributed to the high status of these minerals, especially the widespread belief in the magical qualities of stones, which dates from very ancient times and even survived in the late 20th century. There is a vast literature on this subject, written from the Classical age to the Renaissance. An important Renaissance example is the *Trattato delle pietre* (Florence, 1597) by Agostino del Riccio, composed in the climate of alchemical and naturalistic studies favoured by the court of Francesco I de' Medici. This treatise gives a careful definition of the different varieties of stone, as well as an account of their amazing magic virtues. These beliefs declined from the 17th century, with the increasingly naturalistic and scientific approach to minerals. At the same time, however, there was an increased interest in studying and using these fascinating natural materials, which was reflected in the field of art.

This article discusses the techniques and uses of hardstones for the production of items other than MOSAIC, intaglios and cameos (*see* GEM-ENGRAVING) and JEWELLERY.

See also JADE, JET, PIGMENT, ROCK CRYSTAL and the objects of vertu heading under country surveys.

1. Types. 2. Cutting and carving techniques. 3. History and uses.

1. TYPES. In Antiquity minerals were divided into three categories: very hard, hard and soft. The first group included those that cannot be scratched with a steel point (diamond, corundum, topaz, quartz etc), and the softest included talc, gypsum and graphite, which can be easily scratched. In 1812 the Austrian mineralogist Friedrich Mohs (1773–1839) proposed a scale of hardness, although its gradations are approximate, as they are based on the ability of one mineral to scratch another of similar or lower degree. The Mohs scale has ten degrees of hardness, each corresponding to a common mineral that can be found in nature in its pure state, and thus serves as a useful standard for comparison. The ten degrees are: 1. talc; 2. gypsum; 3. calcite; 4. fluorite; 5. apatite; 6. orthoclase; 7. quartz; 8. topaz; 9. corundum; 10. diamond. True hardstones are those in the 6th and 7th degrees on the Mohs scale, but in an artistic context a broader definition of hardstones can be used.

(i) True hardstones. The stones used most widely for cameos, intaglios and *commesso di pietre dure* (Florentine mosaic) can properly be called hard according to the Mohs scale, as they belong to the large group of quartzes. These include rock crystal, amethyst, chalcedony, agate, jasper and petrified wood. These minerals are based on silicon; they are subdivided into numerous varieties the nomenclature of which varies according to their colour or place of origin.

ROCK CRYSTAL (hyalite quartz) has been valued and worked since ancient times because of its glassy appearance and rainbow reflections, which produce a special effect when the stone is engraved. The largest deposits are in the Alps, despite extensive exploitation.

The fibrous variety of quartz known as chalcedony includes a wide range of stones, among which certain types are more widely used and valued for carving. The types that are light and generally uniform in colour are called 'common' chalcedony; these were used, for example, by the Grand Ducal Workshops in Florence for flesh tones in polychrome pietre dure sculpture. One of the best-known and most valued types is cornelian, a translucent stone that varies in colour from bright red to light yellow; it was widely used by the Romans, who obtained it in the Near East and India. Another type of chalcedony especially famous and valued in Antiquity is bloodstone, which is dark green with small blood-red flecks or veins. It comes mainly from India and was often used for goblets and vases in Roman times and in the Renaissance. Agates, known by different names according to the type of colouring and markings, are the semi-transparent or translucent varieties of chalcedony, of various colours, with a structure of parallel or concentric striations. Agate sardonyx, from India, Asia Minor and China, is a translucent type with zones of black or brown sard (a type of chalcedony). Onyx-chalcedony, with black zones alternating with bluish-grey or white ones, was often used for cameo work, using the light strata for the figure. Vast deposits of German agate, with regular zones of various colours, were widely exploited in the Middle Ages. In Renaissance Italy, Sienese agate was frequently used; this type has parallel striations in various shades from ochre to brown. Jaspers are similar to chalcedonies in hardness and composition but unlike the latter are completely opaque, although when polished they shine brightly. Blood jasper, with its vivid red colour, was known in Egypt from the most ancient times and was later quarried in the Alps, Germany and Sicily. Flowered jasper includes veins or flecks of semi-transparent agate and is prized for its variety of colours and alternating effects of opacity and transparency. Bohemian jasper, in delicate pastel tones enlivened by spots and speckles, was the material most favoured by the workshop established in 1588 in Prague by Ottavio Miseroni on the invitation of Rudolf II.

A geological curiosity much appreciated by artists is petrified wood (hardness 6.5–7). This is derived from tree trunks hardened by a process in which the organic matter is completely replaced by dissolved minerals that then crystallize. The structure of petrified wood is often so well preserved that the particular species of tree from which it came can be identified. It was obtained from the petrified forests of Germany and France and was used in European workshops mainly between the 16th and 19th centuries for mosaics and wall surfaces.

(ii) Other stones. In an artistic context the term hardstone extends to include some stones that are below the 6th degree on the Mohs scale. Lapis lazuli (hardness 4–5 degrees) has a distinctive intense ultramarine blue colour, with minute pyrite crystals, sometimes gold in colour, creating a beautiful golden shimmer (see colour pl. I, fig. 2 and PIGMENT, colour pl. IV, fig. 1). Some less pure varieties have white or grey spots owing to the presence of limestone. These have less commercial value but were widely and very successfully used by Florentine mosaicists, especially in the early 17th century, for example in the rendering of the sky with clouds or seascapes flecked with foam. During the Renaissance the type with the most intense and uniform colour came from the Badakhshan district in Afghanistan to the east of Iran. More mottled varieties were discovered in France, and at the end of the 18th century the discovery of vast, high-quality deposits in Siberia made Russia the main European centre for export.

Another stone widely used for decorative work is malachite (hardness 3.5–4 degrees), with its characteristic striations varying from brilliant green to dark black-green, arising from its chemical composition of copper carbonate. It was used in Ancient Greece and Rome and was popular again in the late 18th century and early 19th, when large deposits were found in the central Urals.

BIBLIOGRAPHY

L. Dolce: *Trattato delle gemme che produce la natura* (Venice, 1617)
F. Corsi: *Delle pietre dure antiche* (Rome, 1845)
M. Weinstein: *Precious and Semi-precious Stones* (London, 1944)
S. Cavenago-Biagnami Moneta: *Gemmologia* (Milan, 1965)
H. J. Schubnel: *Pietre preziose, gemme e pietre dure* (Novara, 1967)
A. Pampaloni Martelli: 'Le raccolte lapidee dell'Opificio delle Pietre Dure', *Splendori di pietre dure: L'arte di corte nella Firenze dei Granduchi* (exh. cat., ed. A. M. Giusti; Florence, Pitti, 1988–9), pp. 260–75

2. CUTTING AND CARVING TECHNIQUES. There are basically two techniques for working hardstones, depending on whether they are being fashioned into two- or three-dimensional objects. In both cases the resistance of the stones makes it necessary to use such abrasives as siliceous sands, metal powders or diamond chips, together with metal instruments for cutting or incising the surface.

Two-dimensional works in hardstone include a wide range of types, from simple geometrical slabs used for floors, wall cladding, table-tops etc to the complex ornamental or figurative images of the *commesso di pietre dure* (Florentine mosaic). The working of plain slabs involves two basic processes: cutting the block of stone, using metal saws lubricated with a dampened abrasive, and polishing the surface by repeated applications of an abrasive rubbed with lead blocks. A far more complex technique is required for the execution of *commesso di pietre dure*. A sketch, usually in watercolour or oil, is made and then traced in pen or pencil. On this 'cartoon' the different sections of the mosaic are laid out. Each of the sections is created using slices (small flat plates a few millimetres thick) cut from the block of hardstone, from which the artist chooses the appropriate colours for the desired effect. A paper pattern with the required outline is glued to each slice, which is then fixed in a vice and cut to shape using a saw made of a chestnut bow and a soft steel wire, with emery as an abrasive (see fig. 1). The craftsman works the saw with one hand in regular movements, and in the other he holds a spatula with which he continually deposits the wet abrasive on the wire to provide the cutting action. Once the stone sections are cut the edges are filed smooth so that the single pieces can be set together. To produce an inlay the sections are inserted in spaces carved (again with the abrasive wire) in the background stone, which remains in view. In the most traditional type of *commesso di pietre dure*, however, the entire composition is formed by fitting together the different stone sections; these are mounted on a support usually made of slate, which remains invisible. In both cases, the sections are bonded to the base and to each other with a glue made of hot beeswax and rosin or Colophony. The final phase is the polishing and buffing of the surface by repeated rubbing with abrasive powders applied with lead blocks

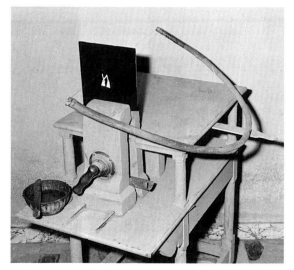

1. Bow-saw for cutting hardstones on a workbench (Florence, Museo dell'Opificio delle Pietre Dure)

or cloth-covered pads to produce a mirror-like smoothness.

Glyptics, the art of carving hardstones either by incising or in relief, is a term that is applied mainly to the production of cameos, gems, vases and small sculptures. To carve a hardstone vase, especially popular in the 16th and 17th centuries, large metal discs were fixed to a *castelletto* (vertical stand); their rotation with the abrasives (metal powders or diamond or ruby dust mixed to a paste with wax or petroleum jelly) modelled the forms of the vases. Any engraved sections were executed with finer-pointed instruments. Mosaic sculpture in the round or in high relief was practised almost exclusively in the Grand Ducal workshop in Florence and in Prague. This was built up of pieces of hardstone worked individually with the *castelletto*, using the same method as for engraving cameos. The hardstone is placed in the *castelletto*, which holds a transverse shaft into which the craftsman fixes the various drill points to suit the different requirements. The drill points are made to rotate by pulleys linked to a wheel that is turned by an assistant or worked by a pedal. The hardstones are then fixed together with small, invisible pins and glued.

UNPUBLISHED SOURCES

Florence, Bib. N. Cent., MS. Misc. Palagi 478 [G. A. Torricelli: *Trattato delle gioe e pietre dure e tenere, che s'adoperano nella Real Galleria e nella Cappella di San Lorenzo*]

BIBLIOGRAPHY

P. J. Mariette: *Traité des pierres gravées* (Paris, 1750)
A. P. Giulianelli: *Memorie degli intagliatori moderni in pietre dure, cammei e gioie* (Livorno, 1753)
K. T. Hecker: *Traité de la méthode antique de graver en pierres fines comparée à la méthode moderne* (London, 1754)
E. Kris: *Meister und Meisterwerke der Steinschneidenkunst in der italienischen Renaissance*, 2 vols (Vienna, 1929)
H. C. Dake: *The Art of Gem Cutting* (Portland, 1957)
F. Rossi: 'Le pietre dure, come si lavoravano, come si lavorano', *Scritti di storia dell'arte in onore di Ugo Procacci*, ii (Florence, 1977), pp. 637–51

3. HISTORY AND USES. There are many different types of artistic treatment of hardstones, but these reflect a certain continuity of tradition from ancient to modern times. Through all the changes in iconographies and styles, hardstones have always been carved in the form of cameos, gems, vases and small sculptures. In goldsmith's work they have been used in complex decorative schemes; they have also been used in monumental furnishings, mosaic floors and walls, such architectural structures as tabernacles, altars etc and such furniture as tables, cabinets, jewellery cases, clocks, reliquaries etc. In architectural work and furniture hardstones are often used in geometric, decorative or figurative mosaic compositions that exploit the natural colouring of the stones.

(i) Ancient world. (ii) Early Christian and medieval. (iii) Renaissance and after.

(i) Ancient world. The use of hardstones is documented from prehistoric times, when they were used for objects of personal or ritual use in their natural state; these were shaped, if at all, in a rudimentary way. The first evidence of such specific processes as cutting and polishing dates from *c.* 4000 BC in Mesopotamia, which seems to have developed more refined techniques of intaglio and engraving of hardstones, while the rest of the ancient world remained limited to the relatively primitive techniques of simple filing and drilling. In Mesopotamia the preferred stones were the more easily worked coloured marbles and limestones until, in the 3rd millennium BC, craftsmen were able to work the much harder stones chalcedony and agate. The favoured application for Near Eastern glyptics was in seals and signet rings, the iconographic repertory of which ranges from simple inscriptions and geometric incised designs to complex figurative compositions (*see* ANCIENT NEAR EAST, §II, 1). The oldest extant examples of polychrome stones combined in two-dimensional mosaic compositions come from Sumeria, one of the main centres of production. In the 'Royal Standard of Ur' (*c.* 2600 BC; London, BM; *see* UR, fig. 2), a wooden panel shows great expressiveness and technical achievement; the natural colours of the stones were used to create representations of war and victory incised into light-coloured limestone and set into a background of lapis lazuli. Mesopotamian influence extended in the 3rd millennium BC to Egypt, where an ornamental tradition developed, with carved stones set into gold objects. A particularly widespread object until the Greco-Roman period was the type of amulet-seal in the form of a scarab, sometimes incised in steatite or cornelian but more commonly made in such materials as soft limestone or vitreous paste.

In Ancient Greece glyptics reached extraordinary technical levels and formal qualities, and these had a decisive influence on Roman and later development. A predilection for vari-coloured stones culminated in the 6th century BC with the production of finely worked gems and cameos in which the representation of the human figure predominated (see colour pl. II, fig. 2). From the 4th century BC the splendour of the Hellenistic courts and the refined lifestyle brought an extraordinary increase in the use of hardstones in gold objects, furnishings, ornament and even architecture. Glyptics tended to enhance such stones as sard, cornelian and onyx, rather than the uniform brilliance of the quartz and chalcedony that were preferred in the 5th century BC.

Alexandria was an outstanding centre for hardstones, and most of the Ancient Greek pieces that survive originated there. An especially prestigious example is the Farnese Cup (see fig. 2), a large sard goblet, engraved on the outside with the Gorgon's head and on the inside with an allegorical scene of the Ptolemaic dynasty (323–30 BC), formerly in the collection of Lorenzo de' Medici.

In Rome and the Empire there was a widespread 'popular' glyptic production, serving a vast clientele of people of modest means who were content with smaller and less valuable stones than those used for the Emperors. These were engraved with symbols or images of Mercury, Fortune, Isis, Ceres etc and were 'mass produced' following standardized models. Small sculptures in the round using hardstones were a more sophisticated form of glyptics. This tradition began in Alexandria in Hellenic times and passed from there to Rome. These precious little stone statues were used in Alexandria to represent gods as well as royalty, while in Rome they were mostly reserved for portraits of the emperors and their families. An outstanding example is a head of *Augustus*, 60 mm high, carved in a brilliant turquoise (Florence, Pitti).

In Rome polychrome stones were not reserved exclusively for small glyptic works; their widest and most

2. Sard goblet known as the Farnese Cup, showing engraved interior allegorical scene, diam. 200 mm, from Alexandria, 2nd century BC (Naples, Museo Nazionale di San Martino)

significant application was in architecture. Only in rare cases, limited to the greatest Imperial residences, were real hardstones used for floors and wall cladding; these were extremely expensive and required an enormous amount of work. Instead the Romans generally used the polychrome marbles that came from the eastern provinces and from other parts of the Empire. It was therefore with marbles, which were softer and more workable than true hardstones, that the laborious technique of mosaic or *opus sectile* was developed and perfected. From the first and most simple geometrical floors, the designs of which were produced by combining different coloured slabs cut to the desired shape, in the 1st century AD the art developed to render complex ornamental and figurative themes, with polychrome marble slabs cut in complex designs and fitted perfectly together like a jigsaw puzzle to produce the overall composition. Among the most famous examples are the 4th-century AD inlaid panels (Rome, Mus. Conserv.) from the Basilica of Junius Bassus, Rome, which depict animals fighting and mythological themes.

(ii) Early Christian and medieval. During the last phase of the Roman Empire the general decline of the Roman civilization affected artistic techniques: the glyptic pieces that survive from the 4th and 5th centuries are generally quite modest and sometimes even primitive in execution. The technical tradition of Roman glyptics and for a certain time also its formal and iconographic traditions survived in Byzantium and the eastern territories of the Empire, but from the 9th century the art acquired a characteristic Byzantine style and iconography that remained almost unchanged for centuries. One application in Byzantium

was to the carving of hardstone vases, which were occasionally decorated with figures in relief but were more often designed to exploit the beauty of the stone and the well-turned form of the vase. These were mostly round or oval, sometimes faceted or finely ribbed. Examples are in the medieval treasuries of cathedrals (e.g. Paris, St-Denis; Venice, S Marco); during the Renaissance they were also acquired by such collectors as Lorenzo the Magnificent (*see* MEDICI, DE, (5)). Hardstone vases and useful objects were also greatly appreciated in the Islamic world. The treasures of the Umayyud (AD 650–750) and Fatimid (AD 910–1171) dynasties included collections of hardstone vases, which were extraordinary for their number, size and value. Among these the most esteemed were those made of rock crystal (*see* ISLAMIC ART, §VIII, 13). The purity of the material, the elegance of the forms and the technical excellence of the products of Islamic craftsmen can be seen in many examples (e.g. ewer inscribed with the name of the Fatimid caliph al-'Aziz; 975–96; Venice, Mus. S Marco; for illustration *see* FATIMID).

The classical inspiration of Carolingian art restored hardstone carving to a high level. Carolingian gems were carved mostly of rock crystal—prized throughout the Middle Ages for the symbolic value of divine light and purity suggested by its clarity and transparency—with sacred subjects but also with portraits of church dignitaries and emperors, who also used the gems as seals (*see* CAROLINGIAN ART, §VII). From at least the end of the 13th century Paris and Venice also specialized in the production of rock crystal vases inspired by Byzantine models, and by the end of the 14th century these were also produced in Germany. Venetian rock crystal was often carved and exported in flat slabs or geometrically shaped pieces to be mounted in precious gold crosses, monstrances, reliquaries etc.

(iii) Renaissance and after. The passion for the Antique that marked the Renaissance in Italy was decisive for the popularity and quality of glyptic products. Pier Maria Serbaldi da Pescia worked in the court of Lorenzo de' Medici and produced among other things some small sculptures in porphyry (e.g. *Polyhymnia*; *c.* 1500; Vienna,

3. Pietre dure casket, ebony carcase, after a design by Giovanni Battista Foggini, Grand Ducal Workshops, Florence, *c.* 1720 (The Vyne, Hants, NT)

Ksthist. Mus.), which initiated the Florentine vogue for that material. The art of carving porphyry was refined during the 16th century to such a degree that it could be used for monumental statues.

At the same time the cities of the Veneto became prestigious centres for glyptic work. Throughout the Middle Ages Venice had maintained an undisputed primacy in the carving of rock crystal. The Veronese Matteo dal Massaro (*d* 1547) moved in 1515 to the court of Francis I of France, of whom he made several portraits in cameo or intaglio (Paris, Bib. N., Cab. Médailles). He was also noted for his crowded scenes of hunts and battles carved on onyx. Valerio Belli from Vicenza gained international prestige for his extraordinary objects of carved and engraved rock crystal, which was the dominant material until the Baroque period. Belli's major work is a casket (1530–32; Florence, Pitti; *see* ITALY, fig. 93), made for Pope Clement VII, containing 25 deeply carved rock crystal plaques depicting scenes from the *Passion*. The Farnese Casket (1548–61; Naples, Capodimonte), commissioned by Alessandro Farnese, was based on drawings (Paris, Louvre; Chatsworth, Derbys) by Perino del Vaga and was executed by GIOVANNI BERNARDI in collaboration with the Florentine goldsmith Manno di Bastiano Sbarri (1536–76). Drawings by Vaga and by Michelangelo were also used by Belli; the collaboration between the designer and the craftsman guaranteed the excellence of these works.

In the first half of the 16th century the main centre of production in northern Italy was Milan. In addition to cameos Milan was noted for the carving of vases, especially in rock crystal (*see* MILAN, §III, 1). Hardstone vases, although they had antique precedents, took on such varied and often bizarre forms as ships, animals or grotesques, which pleased the Mannerist imagination. Rulers, popes, princes and cardinals all over Europe shared a passion for these unusual creations; ANNIBALE FONTANA carved especially luxurious and elaborate rock crystal pieces (e.g. chest; Madrid, Pal. Real), but the most productive workshop was that of the five SARACCHI brothers, who sold their creations to the major courts of Europe (*see* ROCK CRYSTAL, fig. 1).

In 1572 Grand Duke Francesco I, an important patron and collector, invited Ambrogio Caroni (*d* 1611), Stefano Caroni (*d* 1611) and Giorgio Gaffurri from Milan to Florence to found a glyptic tradition in that city, where it had lapsed after the period of Lorenzo the Magnificent. A lapis lazuli flask with a handle in the form of harpies and fittings of gold and enamel (Florence, Pitti) is an example of the extreme refinement of the new Florentine artistic workshops, which in 1588 were incorporated into the Grand Ducal workshop, the Galleria dei Lavori, which specialized in the working of hardstones. This establishment was active until the end of the 19th century in the service of the court. It continued to cultivate the art of intaglio, applying it to small polychrome sculptures, reliefs and, to a lesser extent, cameos; but above all it was outstanding for works in pietre dure mosaic. This used a technique developed from the *opus sectile* of ancient Rome, which attracted much attention in the early 16th century (e.g. table-top inlaid with hardstones, 1633–49; Florence, Mus. Opificio Pietre Dure; see colour pl. I, fig. 1).

Table-tops, cabinets, reliquaries, caskets (see fig. 3), pictures and various ecclesiastical and secular furnishings, in which the hardstones were often combined with ebony and gilded bronze, were created in Florence. These works were prized and sought after in the highest circles of Europe: Rudolf II in Prague (*see* PRAGUE, §III, 2), Louis XIV in Paris (1663; *see* GOBELINS, §3) and Charles VII, King of Naples (later Charles III of Spain), in Naples (1739; *see* NAPLES, §III, 2) and then in Madrid (1759; *see* MADRID, §III, 3) set up their own pietre dure workshops with artists taken from the Florence workshop. The splendours of the Baroque and the *ancien régime* offered the ideal social and cultural setting for hardstone pieces, which served admirably to express dynastic pomp but at the same time embodied a real wealth of invention and material and a highly cultivated technical ingenuity (see fig. 4).

The presence of such Italian craftsmen as GIOVANNI MARIA NOSSENI in German imperial courts and those of the Electors Palatinate prompted hardstone carving production, especially vases. Distinguished practitioners included Caspar Lehmann in Prague, gem and glass engraver, and his pupil Georg Schwanardt the elder (1610–67), who invented a system of polishing diamond-cut, rock crystal surfaces. The MISERONI moved their workshop from Milan to the court of Rudolf II in Prague in 1588,

4. Prasem bowl by Hans Vermeyen, gold, enamel, garnets, citrine, amethyst and hyacinth, h. 235 mm, *c.* 1600–05 (Vienna, Kunsthistorisches Museum)

continuing to carve vases and cameos there until 1684 (see colour pl. II, fig.1).

During the Neo-classical period, with its inspiration from the antique, glyptic craftsmanship was almost exclusively devoted to cameos and intaglios. In the 17th century, vast deposits of high-quality hardstones were discovered in the Urals and Siberia, and Catherine II established three imperial Russian workshops in the 18th. These deposits yielded enormous monolithic blocks, which were transformed according to designs by court architects into such accessories as vases, tripods and chandeliers, often of gigantic size. These were destined for the various imperial residences, and their transport and installation added a further laborious task to that of producing them (*see* RUSSIA, §X, 3). Smaller furnishings and domestic objects, mostly made of malachite, were avidly collected by a widespread clientele (see fig. 5); these were one of the great attractions of the international exhibitions of the second half of the 19th century, where the Florentine workshops also exhibited mosaics and floral reliefs. At the end of the 19th century and beginning of the 20th the St Petersburg-based workshop of CARL FABERGÉ exquisitely

5. Malachite urn with gilt-bronze mounts, Russian, *c.* 1810 (private collection)

carved hardstone miniatures for the Imperial family and the courtiers.

While widely used in goldsmith's work in the 20th century, hardstones have suffered a decline in other applications. This is due to changed economic and social conditions, which no longer favour such an élitist and sumptuous art form, and also to the development of industry and a consequent decline in manual skills.

BIBLIOGRAPHY

A. B. De Boodt: *Gemmarum et lapidum historia* (Hanau, 1609)
P. Mariette: *Traité des pierres gravées*, 2 vols (Paris, 1750)
A. P. Giulianelli: *Memorie degli intagliatori moderni in pietre dure, cammei e gioie dal secolo XV fino al secolo XVII* (Livorno, 1753)
A. F. Gori: *Historia gliptographica* (Florence, 1767)
E. Kris: *Meister und Meisterwerke der Steinschneidekunst in der italienischen Renaissance*, 2 vols (Vienna, 1929)
H. Wentzel: 'Mittelalterliche Gemmen in den Sammlungen Italiens', *Mitt. Ksthist. Inst. Florenz*, vii/3–4 (1956), pp. 239–78
H. Michel: *Cristal de roche et cristalliers* (Brussels, 1960)
M. L. Vollenweider: *Die Steinschneidekunst und ihre Künstler in spätrepublikanischer und augustinischer Zeit* (Baden Baden, 1966)
J. Boardman: *Greek Gems and Finger Rings, Early Bronze Age to Late Classical* (London, 1970)
Il tesoro di Lorenzo il Magnifico (exh. cat., Florence, 1972)
R. Diestelberger: 'Die Sarachi-Werkstatt und Annibale Fontana', *Jb. Ksthist. Samml. Wien*, lxxi (1975), pp. 95–164
A. M. Giusti, P. Mazzoni and A. Pampaloni Martelli: *Il Museo dell'Opificio delle Pietre Dure a Firenze* (Milan, 1978)
Prag um 1600: Kunst und Kultur am Hofe Kaiser Rudolfs II (exh. cat., Essen, Villa Hügel; Vienna, Ksthist. Mus.; 1988)
Splendori di pietre dure: L'arte di corte nella Firenze dei Granduchi (exh. cat., ed. A. M. Giusti; Florence, Pitti, 1988–9)
A. M. Giusti: *Hardstone in Furniture and Decoration* (London, 1992)

Hardwick. English family of architects.

(1) Thomas Hardwick (*b* London, 1752; *d* London, 16 Jan 1829). A pupil of William Chambers, he trained at the Royal Academy Schools, London, and won the first silver medal for architecture in 1769. From 1776 he spent three years in Rome preparing measured drawings of the most important buildings in the city, as well as making trips to Paestum, Pompeii and Venice. In 1791 he became a founder-member of the Architects' Club, whose membership was restricted to those who had visited Italy. Despite his travels on the Continent and his friendship with John Soane, whom he had met in Rome, Hardwick continued to work in an outmoded Neo-classical style that owed much to Chambers, his old mentor.

Unlike most successful 18th-century architects, Hardwick never had a large country-house practice but concentrated almost entirely on public buildings and churches. He earned his living from a number of salaried official appointments, including the surveyorship of St Bartholomew's Hospital (1809) and the post of Clerk of the Works at Hampton Court (1810) and Kew Palace (1815). He was the original architect of the Millbank Penitentiary in London (1812–13; destr. 1902; the site is now occupied by the Tate Gallery) but resigned because of the low remuneration. His completed work there included the boundary wall and gatehouse, but the foundations of the first pentagon were subsequently found too flimsy and had to be rebuilt by Robert Smirke (ii). Hardwick's best building is perhaps St John's (1822–3; tower added 1847), Workington, Cumbria. This is a handsome, if severe, classical building of stone with an impressive Tuscan portico copied from Inigo Jones's St Paul's, Covent

Garden, London, which Hardwick had carefully restored after a fire in 1795. His other churches include St Mary's (1787–90), Wanstead, Essex, and St Marylebone New Church (1813–17), London. The latter forms an element in Nash's layout for Regent's Park and has a grand Corinthian portico facing towards the park, framed by Nash's stucco terraces. Hardwick also designed St John's Chapel (1814) at the north-west corner of Regent's Park as part of the same programme of metropolitan improvements. This church has an Ionic portico, more suited to its smaller scale, and an elegant little cupola on top.

Hardwick was an excellent draughtsman and man of business. As well as practising as an architect he wrote a memoir of William Chambers that was published as an introduction to Gwilt's edition (1825) of Chambers's *Treatise on Civil Architecture*.

Colvin
BIBLIOGRAPHY
Obituary, *Gent. Mag.*, i (16 Jan 1829), p. 92
J. G. Dunbar: 'An English Architect at Naples', *Burl. Mag.*, cx (1968), pp. 265–6
RIBA Drawings Catalogue: G-K (Farnborough, 1973), pp. 89–95

(2) Philip Hardwick (*b* London, 1792; *d* Wimbledon, London, 28 Dec 1870). Son of (1) Thomas Hardwick. He was a pupil of his father, who brought him up to take over his architectural practice; he was enrolled at the Royal Academy Schools, London, in 1808. Like his father, Philip Hardwick travelled on the Continent for professional improvement, visiting Paris in 1815 and Italy in 1818–19. Also like his father, he held several official surveyorships from institutions in London, including those of architect to the Bridewell and Bethlehem hospitals (from 1816), St Katharine's Dock Company (from 1825), the Goldsmiths Company (from 1828) and the London and Birmingham Railway Company (from 1839). He succeeded Thomas Hardwick as surveyor to St Bartholomew's Hospital in 1826.

Philip Hardwick was notable for the scholarly quality of his work in a period of architectural eclecticism. His principal buildings vary in style from the severe Neoclassical of the warehouses at St Katharine's Dock (1827–9) to the Tudor Gothic of the new hall and library (1842–5) at Lincoln's Inn, London. Hardwick was associated with some of the greatest public engineering works of his age: St Katharine's Dock in London, the Dock Traffic Office at Albert Dock, Liverpool (designed in 1846, with a cast-iron portico inspired by St Paul's, Covent Garden), and Euston Station, the London terminus for the London and North Western Railway Company. Hardwick's great Doric propylaeum at the entrance to Euston (destr. 1962) had massive fluted columns and the name Euston proudly cut in letters of gold. His best surviving building is the Goldsmiths Hall (1829–35), which has a noble Corinthian façade of Portland stone and a richly appointed polychromatic interior. Its sources are derived from Wren and Webb's Royal Naval Hospital, Greenwich, rather than from Inigo Jones.

Philip Hardwick also played an active public role in contemporary architectural affairs. He was a founder-member of the Institute of British Architects in 1834 and became vice-president in 1839 and 1841, receiving the gold medal in 1854. He was much in demand as a referee in architectural competitions. In 1843 his health broke down, though he continued to run his practice and public affairs from his room with the assistance of his son Philip Charles Hardwick (1822–92), who took over much of his architectural work.

BIBLIOGRAPHY
Colvin
Obituary, *Builder*, xxix (1871), p. 24
Obituary, *Proc. Inst. Civ. Engin.*, xxxiii/1 (1871–2), pp. 215–16
J. Fawcett, ed.: *Seven Victorian Architects* (London, 1976)
JOHN MARTIN ROBINSON

Hardwick, Bess of, Countess of Shrewsbury. *See* TALBOT, (1).

Hardwicke, Earls of. *See under* GREY.

Hardy, Bert [Albert] (*b* London, 19 May 1913; *d* Oxted, Surrey, 3 July 1995). English photographer. He was from a working-class family and left school when he was 14. He learnt to take and develop photographs through his work at Central Photographic Services from 1927 to 1936 and William Davis Photographic Agency (1936–9). His first published photographs were for the cycling magazine, *The Bicycle* (*c.* 1930). After mastering the art of 35 mm 'candid' photography, he worked full time for *Picture Post*, edited by Tom Hopkinson (*b* 1905), from 1941 to 1957. Combining the imaginative use of difficult lighting with skill in the darkroom, Hardy produced successful human interest photo-essays during the Blitz, notably *Fire Fighters* (*Pict. Post*, 1 Feb 1941). Between 1942 and 1946 he often combined military assignments for the Army Film and Photography Unit with freelance work, documenting events such as the *Liberation of Paris* (*Pict. Post*, 2 Sept 1944).

In the 1940s and 1950s the photojournalistic essay was at its height and Hardy travelled extensively throughout Europe, Asia, Africa and North America covering political issues, war, sport and local customs (1946–57). In Britain topics included royalty, racism and rural and urban life; the last provided some of his most powerful images, such as the Glasgow Gorbals sequence (*Pict. Post*, 31 Jan 1948), revealing Hardy's sympathy with the injustices of urban deprivation. He extended photojournalistic practice by producing photo-essays using models and artificially dramatic lighting.

In 1950 Hardy and journalist James Cameron (1910–85) covered the Korean War. Their criticism of the United Nations' involvement led to an upheaval at *Picture Post* and Hopkinson's dismissal. The story was never published. Thereafter *Picture Post* lost its political edge, and Hardy was assigned to do many light-hearted studies of contemporary society. From 1951 *Picture Post*'s readership fell, and it eventually ceased publication in 1957. Hardy was successful in turning his photojournalistic talents to advertising, but in 1962 he became a farmer in Surrey. Having given up serious photography *c.* 1967, he maintained an interest only through the processing business Grove Hardy Ltd, which he had founded in 1960. His work was published as a collection in *Bert Hardy, photojournalist* (London, 1975) with an introduction by Tom Hopkinson.

WRITINGS
Bert Hardy: My Life (London, 1985)

BIBLIOGRAPHY
T. Hopkinson, ed.: *Picture Post 1938–50* (London, 1970, rev. 1984)

INGRID SWENSON

Hardy, Dudley (*b* Sheffield, Yorks, 15 Jan 1867; *d* London, 11 Aug 1922). English painter and illustrator. He studied with his father, T. B. Hardy (1842–97), and later at the Academy in Düsseldorf, in Antwerp and in Paris before returning to London. He was a prolific artist, exhibiting regularly at the Royal Academy from 1884 until 1922. His oils vary from oriental to Breton genre scenes. Other paintings bear a social message, such as *Sans Asile* (1888), depicting huddled figures sleeping in Trafalgar Square; this work was shown at the Royal Society of British Artists Galleries in London in 1893 (after exhibition in other European cities) and established his reputation. However, it was Hardy's graphic art that made his name. His talents coincided with the boom in illustrated magazines and the power of the poster at the turn of the century. The influence of French graphic style is seen in his fluent line and use of tone, and artists such as Jules Chéret influenced the *Gaiety Girl* series of posters of the 1890s. The most famous image is the *Yellow Girl*, which Hardy created to advertise the magazine *Today*. He designed many posters for the Savoy Theatre, including those for the D'Oyly Carte operas. There is a collection of his posters at the Victoria and Albert Museum, London.

BIBLIOGRAPHY
A. H. Lawrence: 'Mr Dudley Hardy RBA: Painter', *A. J.* [London] (Dec 1897), pp. 353–7
A. E. Johnson: *Dudley Hardy* (1909)
G. M. Waters: *Dictionary of British Artists Working 1900–50* (1975), p. 150
S. Houfe: *The Dictionary of British Book Illustrators and Caricaturists 1800–1914* (1978), p. 332

SARAH WIMBUSH

Hardy, Jean (*b* Nancy, 1653; *d* Versailles, 14 Jan 1737). French sculptor. Although a relatively minor artist in the team of sculptors employed in Louis XIV's ambitious schemes of embellishment at the royal palaces, he was in constant demand throughout his long career. His earliest known work was decorative stone sculpture for the Condé family at the château of Chantilly, including statues of *Acis*, *Galatea* and two *River Gods* (1682–4; *in situ*, heavily restored) on the great staircase of the terrace designed by André Le Nôtre. He became a member of the Académie Royale in 1688 on presentation of a marble bas-relief representing *Religion Crushing Idolatry* (Paris, Louvre), an allusion to the Revocation of the Edict of Nantes, executed in a strongly classical manner. All his ornamental and garden sculptures for the châteaux of Marly, Yvelines, and Meudon, Hauts-de-Seine, have been destroyed, with the exception of the lead fountain group of four *Naiads Sitting on Rocks* (in collaboration with Jean Thierry; 1706), which is now in the gardens of the Grand Trianon, Versailles, and the marble pedestal decorated with hunting trophies supporting Jean-Baptiste Poultier's *Companion of Diana* (1727; Bolbec, Seine-Maritime, Hôtel de Ville).

At Versailles, Hardy carved for the gardens two marble vases, one of them with a frieze representing the *Triumph of the Child Mars* (1684 and 1687; both *in situ*); he later executed two dragons in lead for a fountain at the Trianon (1702; *in situ*) and, also at Versailles, a lead fountain group of frolicking children for the *Isle of Children* (1710; *in situ*). He was part of the team that decorated the façades of the Trianon-sous-Bois (stone, 1705; *in situ*). From 1702 he received regular payments for repairs to the sculptures in the royal parks and for rocaille decorations for fountains.

BIBLIOGRAPHY
Lami; Souchal
J. Guiffrey: *Comptes des Bâtiments du Roi sous le règne de Louis XIV*, 5 vols (Paris, 1881–1901)

FRANÇOISE DE LA MOUREYRE

Hardy Holzman Pfeiffer Associates. American architectural firm formed in New York in 1968 by Hugh Gelston Hardy (*b* Mallorca, Spain, 26 July 1932), Malcolm Holzman (*b* Newark, NJ, 1940) and Norman Henry Pfeiffer (*b* Seattle, WA, 13 Nov 1940). Hardy received his architectural training at Princeton University, NJ, and opened his own office in New York in 1963. Holzman studied architecture at the Pratt Institute, New York, and became Hardy's partner in 1963. Pfeiffer studied architecture at the University of Washington, Seattle, and at Columbia University, New York, where he met Hardy and Holzman, and began to work in their office in 1965.

The firm achieved an international reputation for designing concert halls as well as in adaptive rehabilitation of older buildings. While creatively using inexpensive materials in unusual combinations, the firm won a number of awards for design excellence, particularly for their addition (1967) to the University of Toledo Performing Arts Center, Toledo, OH; the Columbus Occupational Health Center (1973), Columbus, IN; and their renovation of the Art Museum (1977), St Louis, MO, where they were working with Cass Gilbert's original building of 1904. Similarly they extended and renovated the celebrated Willard Hotel (1980–86), Washington, DC, originally designed by Henry Janeway Hardenbergh. The firm's facility in drawing out the best from unlikely source material is demonstrated in their adaptive reuse of a film theatre of 1928 and a Montgomery Ward shop of the 1940s to create the Madison Civic Center (1980), Madison, WI. Outside Buffalo, NY, they converted a chemical dump site into the ArtPark, a multi-purpose performing arts centre. The firm also renovated the imposing Andrew Carnegie Mansion, New York, designed by Babb, Cook & Willard in 1901, to house the Cooper-Hewitt Museum of 1976. Particularly successful have been their multi-purpose double-stage Hult Center for the Performing Arts (1978–82), Eugene, OR; a traditional rectangular concert hall (1975) in Minneapolis, MN; and the unusual Boettcher Concert Hall (1978–9), Denver, CO, in which the audience sits around the orchestra.

BIBLIOGRAPHY
Contemp. Architects
'Theaters and Auditoriums: Building Types Study No. 340', *Archit. Rec.*, cxxxvi/12 (1964), pp. 161–3
'Hardy Holzman and Pfeiffer', *A & U*, lxiii/3 (1976), pp. 27–60
B. Diamonstein, ed.: *American Architecture Now*, 2 vols (New York, 1980–85)
A. O. Dean: 'Profile: Hardy Holzman and Pfeiffer Associates', *Arena*, lxx/2 (1981), pp. 40–49
M. Sorkin: *Hardy Holzman Pfeiffer* (New York, 1981)

LELAND M. ROTH

Hare, David (*b* New York, 10 March 1917; *d* Dec 1991). American sculptor, painter and photographer. Throughout his career he was devoted to Surrealist ideas. He had no formal training, but at schools in New York, Colorado and California he graduated in biology and chemistry, which may have influenced his interest in primal origins and the biomorphic shapes in his sculptures and paintings. He worked briefly as a commercial photographer in New York around 1940, experimenting in 1941 with a thermographic technique invented by the Surrealists in which the negative was melted to distort the image. From 1941 to 1944 he was one of the Americans most closely associated with the European Surrealist emigrés, and he edited the Surrealist magazine *VVV* with assistance from Duchamp, Breton and Ernst. He became committed to the Surrealists' exploration of psychic automatism and to their use of mythological subjects (*see* UNITED STATES OF AMERICA, fig. 22).

Hare's first sculptures were plaster works produced in the mid-1940s and exhibited at Peggy Guggenheim's Art of This Century Gallery in New York in 1944 and 1946; a later example is *Man of Circles* (1948; untraced, see Sandler, pl. 12). Their dismissal of the traditional base, their openwork construction and bone-like protuberances suggest the influence of both Alexander Calder and Alberto Giacometti. In Hare's succeeding works in cast bronze and, from 1951, welded metal (e.g. *Figure Waiting in the Cold*, 1951; New York, Whitney), he continued to develop the expressive character of materials and symbolic vocabulary of forms that paralleled discoveries by such contemporary New York School sculptors as Herbert Ferber, Ibram Lassaw, Theodore Roszak and David Smith.

Hare worked in different media at different times during his career, turning to painting in the mid-1960s and resuming sculpture in the early 1970s. In the late 1960s and mid-1970s he created the *Cronus* series of paintings with collage, for example *Cronus Grown* (1968; New York, Whitney). He continued his emphasis on painting until the 1980s and subsequently focused on sculptural works. While many of Hare's contemporaries in the New York school evolved to large-scale and formally simplified sculptures, Hare continued using the mythological symbols and experimental, often disjunctive, materials that characterized his earlier creations and reveal his continued interest in Surrealism.

BIBLIOGRAPHY

R. Goldwater: 'David Hare', *A. America*, xliv (1956–7), pp. 18–20, 61

I. Sandler: *Three American Sculptors: Ferber, Hare and Lassaw* (New York, 1959)

H. Rosenberg: 'The Art World: An American Surrealist', *New Yorker*, li (1977), pp. 155–8

The Third Dimension: Sculpture of the New York School (exh. cat., ed. L. Phillips; New York, Whitney, 1984)

ROBERT SALTONSTALL MATTISON

Harff, Heinrich von. *See* ARFE, (1).

Hargesheimer, Carl-Heinz. *See* CHARGESHEIMER.

Haribans [Haribas] (*fl c.* 1580s–*c.* 1602). Indian miniature painter. His only known attributed work is in the *Jogbashisht* (1602; Dublin, Chester Beatty Lib., Ind. MS. 5), the Persian translation of a Sanskrit text on Vedanta philosophy. The manuscript has 41 illustrations produced at Allahabad under the patronage of Prince Salim (later the Mughal emperor Jahangir, *reg* 1605–27). However, Haribans began his career in the 1580s in the studio of Akbar (*reg* 1556–1605), for he is named 16th of the 17 painters listed in order of seniority in the *Āyīn-i Akbarī*, a contemporary account of Akbar's administration as it was *c.* 1590.

BIBLIOGRAPHY

The Imperial Image: Paintings for the Mughal Court (exh. cat. by M. C. Beach, Washington, DC, Freer, 1981)

The Art of the Book in India (exh. cat. by J. P. Losty, London, BL, 1982)

M. C. Beach: *Early Mughal Painting* (Cambridge, MA, 1987)

PHILIPPA VAUGHAN

Hariharālaya. *See* ROLUOS.

Häring, Hugo (*b* Biberach, nr Stuttgart, 22 May 1882; *d* Göppingen, 17 May 1958). German architect and writer. He was the son of a cabinetmaker and studied architecture in Stuttgart under Theodor Fischer, before working in Ulm and Hamburg. His early competition entries show not only a neo-classical influence but also a pioneering interest in exposed iron construction. During World War I he worked on the reconstruction programme for East Prussia, where he built a substantial country house. From 1916 to 1920 he worked on the Römer house in Neu-Ulm, for which he also designed all the fittings and furniture. Romantically medieval in appearance with its octagonal corner tower and Expressionist details, it was built around a former military blockhouse.

In 1921 Häring moved to Berlin, where he was invited by Mies van der Rohe to share an office. He exhibited work with the Novembergruppe and established a reputation for his competition designs. In 1924–5 he built his best-known work, the farm buildings at Garkau in Schleswig-Holstein; they are historically important both as examples of Häring's organic functionalism (*see* ORGANIC ARCHITECTURE) and for their bold use of expressed construction, which later influenced Brutalist architects (*see* BRUTALISM). He also designed a sausage factory in nearby Neustadt the following year.

In 1923–4 Häring and Mies founded the Zehnerring, later DER RING, established in support of Modernism, which actively opposed the neo-classicist approach of Ludwig Hoffmann, the city architect of Berlin. It included a number of notable German Modernists. In the same year Häring wrote the essay 'Wege zur form', which laid the foundations for his entire later theory. Its main themes were that function and expression should not be separated but made to coincide; that building forms need not be preconceived and imposed but should rather be allowed to grow from within. He believed that every place and task implies a form, and that it is the architect's job to discover it and to let it find its own expression. Häring's functionalism was, however, quite different from that of other German Modernists, for the real focus of his interest was not functional performance *per se* but the relation of use and meaning.

In 1926 Häring produced a design for an art gallery for the Berlin Secession (unexecuted; see fig.). An enormous sweeping staircase links ground-floor entrance and first-floor gallery, with a refreshments room and sculpture

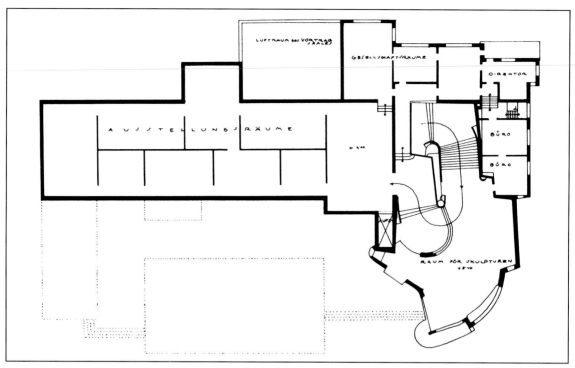

Hugo Häring: first-floor plan for an art gallery for the Berlin Secession (unexecuted), 1926

gallery on expanded stair landings. In many ways this flowing space anticipates post-war foyers in public buildings by Hans Scharoun and Alvar Aalto.

Two of the famous Berlin *Siedlungen* of the late 1920s included housing by Häring: Siemensstadt (1929–31) and Onkel Toms Hütte (1926–31). His blocks of flats at the former are remarkable for their vividly expressed concrete framing and colourful brick infill in dramatic contrast to the white render used by other architects. He was also actively involved in CIAM in this period, before resigning after a quarrel with Sigfried Giedion.

By 1933 Häring was working on three major projects. Modernism was, however, then suppressed by the Nazis, and during the Third Reich he was able to build only three private houses including the Haus Ziegler (1936), Berlin. In 1935, suffering financial difficulties, he accepted the directorship of the celebrated Reimann-Schule, founded by Albert Reimann, a sculptor, in 1902. Although Reimann had been forced to flee as a Jew, the Nazis kept the school open because of the vital foreign currency that its foreign students paid. Had the school actually been run by the Nazis, foreign students would have stayed away. However, with the 'degenerate' Modernist Häring as its director, such 'degenerate' artists as Oskar Schlemmer and Oskar Moll were allowed to be re-employed. The art school remained an island of liberal opinion in Nazi Berlin until it was bombed in 1943.

Häring returned to Biberach to work on his theory and an unfinished book to be entitled *Die ausbildung des geistes zur arbeit an der gestalt*. It marked a major shift from the functionalism of the the 1920s. He produced an elaborate reinterpretation of architectural history that redefined the traditional polarity between Classic and Gothic as 'geometry versus the organic'. Häring argued that architectural geometries had different meanings in different ages, reflecting the changing path of human cultural development; in the modern period geometry had lost its mystical significance, being reduced to a purely instrumental role, freeing artists to pursue instead the forms demanded by and representative of life.

In spite of a lack of genuine commissions, Häring produced numerous exploratory designs during the war years, mainly for houses and house types. In the post-war years he continued with this work, leaving an enormous number of drawings, but he built only two houses, for local friends, the Guido and Werner Schmitz houses (1949–52), Biberach. He published some substantial essays and gave celebrated lectures in the early 1950s, but his influence was probably more strongly felt through the work of Hans Scharoun, whom he advised on several projects. Häring was directly involved in the theoretical work for Scharoun's Mannheim theatre project, a forerunner of the Philharmonie in Berlin.

WRITINGS

The titles of Häring's writings are in lower case since he rejected on principle the capitalization of nouns usual in German.

'Funktionelles bauen: gut garkau/das viehhaus', *Die Form*, 1 (1925), pp. 16–17; also in Joedicke and Lauterbach, p. 17

'Wege zur form', *Die Form*, 1 (1925), pp. 3–5; Eng. trans. in *Form and Function*, ed. T. Benton and D. Sharp (Milton Keynes, 1975), pp. 103–5

M. Aschenbrenner, ed.: *Hugo Häring: die ausbildung des geistes zur arbeit an der gestalt fragmente* (Berlin, 1968) [posth. pubd work]

BIBLIOGRAPHY

J. Joedicke and L. Lauterbach, eds: *Hugo Häring: Schriften, Entwürfe, Bauten* (Stuttgart, 1964)

P. B. Jones: 'Hugo Häring', *Archit. Rev.* (London) (April 1982), pp. 41–7
——: 'Unknown Häring', *Archit. Rev.* (London) (June 1985), pp. 40–45
S. Kremer: *Hugo Häring (1882–1958): Wohnungsbau Theorie und Praxis* (Stuttgart, 1985)

PETER BLUNDELL JONES

Haring, Keith (*b* Reading, PA, 4 May 1958; *d* New York, 16 Feb 1990). American painter. He graduated from Kutztown Area Senior High School in 1976 and spent some time travelling across America before studying at the Art Centre in Pittsburgh. In 1978 he moved to New York to attend the School of Visual Arts, where his original approach was soon apparent in graffiti-inspired symbols expanded into large-scale designs of generative energy. At the height of the Punk Rock movement in the late 1970s he participated in the lively New York club scene, working with such street artists as 'Samo' (Jean-Michel Basquiat, *b* 1960). In the summer of 1980 he took up drawing, inventing intricate cartoon-style murals of mutant figures locked in hyper-physical engagement. He was a meteoric star in American art during the 1980s, exhibiting and working on projects throughout the USA, Europe and Asia, and his work became a symbol of the tribal undercurrents that permeate metropolitan life. His accessible imagery stems as much from Islamic and Japanese art as the sign language of contemporary culture. In 1986 the artist opened his own retail outlet, The Pop Shop, in New York and was continuously engaged in projects of an extraordinarily diverse nature, from murals on the Berlin Wall to paintings on hot air balloons, motor cars and decorative accessories. A giant 'spectacolour' billboard broadcast his famous *Radiant Child* image in Times Square, first in 1982. He fell victim to the AIDS epidemic in 1988 and died at the age of 31.

BIBLIOGRAPHY
L. Castelli: *Beyond the Canvas* (New York, 1985)
H. Fox: *Avant-garde in the Eighties* (Los Angeles, 1987)
J. Gruen: *Keith Haring* (London, 1991)

Harington, Lucy, Countess of Bedford. *See* RUSSELL, (1).

Hariri, Tell. *See* MARI.

Hårleman, Carl (*b* Stockholm, 1700; *d* Stockholm, 1753). Swedish architect. His father, Johan Hårleman (1662–1707), was a landscape gardener who collaborated with Nicodemus Tessin the younger at Steninge Manor and on the garden at Drottningholm, near Stockholm. Carl Hårleman first trained as a draughtsman and architect at the palace works in Stockholm under Tessin and G. J. Adelcrantz (1668–1739). On Tessin's recommendation he was sent to study in Paris and Italy (1721–6); he also visited Britain. In 1727 he was recalled to Stockholm to direct work on the Royal Palace as Tessin's successor, and in 1741 he was appointed Superintendent. He visited France in 1731–2 and 1744–5 to recruit artists and craftsmen to work on the interiors of the Royal Palace and Drottningholm in Stockholm. Such visits also enabled him to remain in touch with French stylistic developments.

There are close connections between Hårleman's designs for town and country houses and those of such French architects as Charles-Etienne Briseux and Jean-Baptiste Bullet. Svartsjö (1734), a royal hunting-lodge on a modest scale, is a typical early example: it is a simple, two-storey, rectangular building with a mansard roof and a projecting oval salon in the centre. The plaster façades, painted light yellow and grey to resemble French sandstone ashlar, are articulated with restrained rustication, while the window surrounds are decorated with festoons. The mansard roof has a tiled lower face and sheet iron on the upper. This simple layout became the prototype for Swedish country houses for several decades, and Hårleman himself developed it in several houses (e.g. Åkerö Manor, 1750). He applied it also to county governors' residences. Övedskloster in Scania is a manor house on a grander scale, having a *cour d'honneur* surrounded by pavilions. In his institutional and military buildings, such as the University Senate (1749) in Uppsala and the water-gate at Suomenlinna Fortress, near Helsinki, he again employed this austere Rococo vocabulary, emphasizing horizontal lines.

In his ecclesiastical designs Hårleman was influenced by Italian Baroque examples, particularly in the lanterned cupolas on the towers of Strängnäs Cathedral and Jakobskyrka in Stockholm (*c.* 1730), but the plan for the French Reformed Church (1748; later rebuilt) in Stockholm derives from the Herrnhut meeting-house with a rectangular room centred on the transverse axis. It was influential on subsequent Swedish and Finnish church architecture. As Superintendent, Hårleman exercised control over the plans of ecclesiastical buildings in Sweden and Finland: all churches had to be built on designs either made, or approved, by the Superintendent's office.

UNPUBLISHED SOURCES
Stockholm, Nmus. [Hårleman's collection of Italian and French architectural drawings]

BIBLIOGRAPHY
A. Stavenow: *Carl Hårleman: En studie i frihetstidens arkitekturhistoria* [Carl Hårleman: a study of architectural history in the era of freedom] (Uppsala, 1927)
H. O. Andersson and F. Bedoire: *Swedish Architecture: Drawings, 1640–1970* (Stockholm, 1986) [Eng. text]

□

Harley. English family of statesmen and collectors.

(1) Robert Harley, 1st Earl of Oxford (*b* London, 5 Dec 1661; *d* London, 21 May 1724). He was educated at a school in Oxfordshire and at Foubert's Academy near the Haymarket, London. He was elected MP for Tregony, Cornwall, in 1689, and his political career was built on his dogged independence and enormous knowledge of parliamentary procedure, rather than any brilliance of mind. He became Speaker of the House of Commons in 1701, Secretary of State three years later and Chancellor of the Exchequer in 1710.

Harley began to acquire manuscripts early in his career. In 1701 he was introduced to Humfrey Wanley, and two years later, on Harley's behalf, Wanley examined the library of Sir Simonds D'Ewes, which included prints, drawings, coins and pictures, as well as books and manuscripts. Harley bought D'Ewes's library for £450 in 1705 and continued to buy books and manuscripts, acquiring the collection of the antiquarian Randle Holme in 1710. In

1708 Wanley had begun to catalogue Harley's collection of manuscripts and in 1715, after Harley was impeached, Wanley recorded that the library consisted of 3000 books, 13,000 charters and 1000 rolls; the collection of papers was said to be 'much the best and most valuable and numerous of any now in England, excepting only that of Sir Robert Cotton'.

There is no evidence that Harley was particularly interested in painting or architecture. Unlike many of his contemporaries, he did not use the profits of his office to build a country house, preferring the pleasures of the study and the bowling-green. He befriended George Vertue, encouraged his research and supplied him with information. Vertue's *Note-books* indicate that Harley possessed works by Hans Holbein (ii) and Cornelis Jonson van Ceulen I, a copy of an inventory of Charles I's collection and a small pocket-book of drawings by Wenceslaus Hollar.

BIBLIOGRAPHY

E. Edwards: *Lives of the Founders of the British Museum*, 2 vols (London, 1870), i, pp. 203–46
E. S. Roscoe: *Robert Harley, Earl of Oxford, Prime Minister, 1710–1714: A Study of Politics and Letters in the Age of Anne* (London, 1902)
'The Note-books of George Vertue', *Walpole Soc.*, i–vi (1930–55)

(2) Edward Harley, 2nd Earl of Oxford (*b* 2 June 1689; *d* London, 16 June 1741). Son of (1) Robert Harley, 1st Earl of Oxford. He inherited the literary interests of his father but not the latter's political ambitions. He was educated at Westminster School and Christ Church, Oxford, and in 1711 became MP for Radnorshire. In 1713 he had begun to accumulate manuscripts and antiquities, as well as debts, and in the same year married Lady Henrietta Cavendish-Holles, who, on the death of her father John Holles, 1st Duke of Newcastle, in 1711, had inherited extensive wealth and property, including Welbeck Abbey, Notts, and Wimpole Hall, Cambs.

From *c.* 1713 Harley managed his father's great collections of manuscripts and printed books and began augmenting the collection under the direction of his father's librarian, Humfrey Wanley. In addition to books and manuscripts Harley also began to acquire coins and medals and a varied collection of antiquities, including Egyptian gems, a Roman inkpot, a Turkish general's truncheon and a cap of American feathers that had been presented to Elizabeth I. Many of these items were engraved by George Vertue from drawings by Giuseppe Grisoni (London, Soc. Antiqua.).

Harley knew and assisted a number of artists. He commissioned James Thornhill to paint the chapel at Wimpole in the early 1720s, which was built for Harley by James Gibbs from 1719, at a time when Charles Bridgeman was laying out landscaped grounds there. Michael Dahl painted portraits for him, for example *Mathew Prior* (1713; London, N.P.G.), and John Wootton provided hunting scenes and conversation pieces. He also helped the sculptor John Michael Rysbrack to obtain commissions. Bernard Lens (iii) bought and framed prints for Harley. Above all, Harley befriended George Vertue, who accompanied him several times on his travels throughout England, during which they recorded items of antiquarian interest. Yet there is no evidence that Harley was a particularly discriminating connoisseur or a patron who might be compared, for instance, with Richard Boyle, 3rd Earl of Burlington. Harley's interests were in portraits and memorials of his friends and in anything that was skilful, curious or had literary associations.

Towards the end of his life, Harley's debts forced him to sell Wimpole Hall to Philip Yorke, 1st Earl of Hardwicke, and he became an alcoholic. Following his premature death much of the collection was dispersed in a series of sales in March 1742. The Harleian Library was sold to the British Museum in 1753 by his daughter, Margaret Bentinck, 2nd Duchess of Portland.

BIBLIOGRAPHY

R. W. Goulding: 'The Welbeck Abbey Miniatures', *Walpole Soc.*, v (1914–15)
A. S. Turberville: *A History of Welbeck Abbey and its Owners*, i (London, 1938), pp. 291–387
J. Lees-Milne: *Earls of Creation: Five Great Patrons of Eighteenth-century Art* (London, 1962), pp. 155–200
C. E. Wright: 'Edward Harley, 2nd Earl of Oxford, 1689–1749', *Bk Colr*, xi (1962), pp. 158–74
J. Harris: 'Harley, the Patriot Collector', *Apollo*, cxxii (1985), pp. 198–203

CHARLES SAUMAREZ SMITH

Harlingen, Petrus Feddes van. *See* FEDDES VAN HARLINGEN, PETRUS.

Harlow, George Henry (*b* London, 10 June 1787; *d* London, 4 Feb 1819). English painter. After briefly attending Westminster School in London, he trained as a painter, first under Hendrik Frans de Cort, then under Samuel Drummond (1765–1844) and finally with Thomas Lawrence. Although Lawrence was paid a considerable sum to accept Harlow into his studio he did not formally teach him; instead he allowed the young man to copy and occasionally help with his work. After 18 months the two fell out and Harlow left to pursue his own career though the influence of Lawrence's style was lasting. Harlow made his début at the Royal Academy in 1804 with a portrait of *Dr Thornton* (untraced) and thereafter concentrated on this genre. There is a portrait of the painter *James Northcote* (*c.* 1815; London, N.P.G.) by him. He also attempted history painting, though with less success, partly due to his lack of a proper art education. He produced a number of portraits of actors and actresses (e.g. *Charles Mathews*, pencil, 1814; London, N.P.G.). In order to make up for his deficient education, in 1818 he travelled to Italy to study the Old Masters. There he became greatly admired for his technical facility and was befriended by Canova. He caused considerable amazement in Rome by painting a full-size copy of Raphael's the *Transfiguration* (1517–20; Rome, Pin. Vaticana) in only 18 days and was elected an Academician of Merit of the Accademia di S Luca in Rome, a rare honour for an English artist. He died from a throat infection soon after his return to England in 1819. An exhibition of his works was held after his death in Pall Mall, London.

DNB

BIBLIOGRAPHY

S. Redgrave: *A Dictionary of Artists of the English School* (London, 1878)
A. Graves: *The Royal Academy of Arts: A Complete Dictionary of Contributors and their Work, from its Foundation in 1769 to 1904*, iii (London, 1905/R 1970)

Harmal, Tell. *See under* DIYALA REGION.

Harmon, Arthur Loomis. *See under* SHREVE, LAMB & HARMON.

Harness and trappings.

1. Horse. 2. Elephant. 3. Camel.

1. HORSE. From an early stage, horses were used both as mounts and for pulling chariots in warfare or hunting. Most evidence for forms of harness in the ancient world comes from depictions in art, the earliest figural evidence dating from before 2000 BC in the Near East, although in a few contexts actual harness elements have survived. Even for later periods, secondary sources tend to provide the best evidence for the perishable leather and cloth parts of horse harness and trappings. More durable equipment, such as the horse armour used in medieval Europe, sometimes survives intact.

(i) Ancient world. (ii) Later history.

(i) Ancient world. Ancient chariot horses were attached to their yokes by means of neck or breast straps and backing straps or girths that ran under their bellies, just behind the forelegs. Mounts often wore saddle-cloths or, in later antiquity, primitive saddles held on by girths, breastbands and breechings or cruppers. Both chariot horses and mounts were controlled by bridles, consisting of headstalls and reins and, usually, bits. This equipment was often decorated in varying degrees.

(a) Late Bronze Age. In Egypt under the New Kingdom (*c.* 1540–*c.* 1075 BC), the preserved leather parts of royal parade harness were covered with gold foil in repoussé designs showing hunt and plant motifs. Royal chariot horses wore blinkers decorated in the same manner and carried crests of ostrich feathers with ribbons or tassels at either end. A 'cap'—often appearing to be of spotted hide—might cover the head from the occiput to the browband area. Royal horses are also shown wearing patterned, woven trappers, with tassels along the lower edges (see fig. 1). For Anatolia and the Levant there is little figured evidence beyond that appearing in Egyptian reliefs showing chariots from these areas; this indicates a great similarity to Egyptian practice. From the Aegean there is some secondary evidence (chiefly from wall paintings of the 13th century BC; Athens, N. Archaeol. Mus.) of discs as bridle ornaments and perhaps as strap distributors.

(b) Iron Age.

Assyria. Chariot horses represented on Assyrian palace reliefs of the 9th century BC (e.g. London, BM; Paris, Louvre; Berlin, Pergamonmus.) wear small, arched crests set with ostrich feathers. During the later 8th century BC these became stacked, round tassels, and during the 7th century BC they turned into something closely resembling the horsehair crests that run front-to-back on some human helmets. A substantial amount of ivory parade bridle equipment from the 9th–7th centuries BC was found at Nimrud (e.g. Baghdad, Iraq. Mus.; London, BM). Blinkers and frontlets of various shapes, carved with a variety of motifs, such as *wedjat*-eyes, scarabs, lions with prey, sphinxes and frontal, naked female figures often have

1. Ancient Egyptian horse harness and royal chariot, detail of a painted wooden garment box, 610×440×430 mm, from the tomb of Tutankhamun, Thebes, mid-14th century BC (Cairo, Egyptian Museum)

guilloche borders and volute endings. Reliefs illustrate frontlets, gorgets and discoid shoulder ornaments, certainly of bronze. Harness and bridle straps are often decorated with small metal plaques in rosette, discoid or 'banjo' form; bells and/or tassels may hang at the neck. Chariot horses may wear trappers covering the body; these may be of plain boiled leather or sewn with small, metal plaques. Only royal mounts in the 9th century BC are shown wearing saddle-cloths. These are fringed and secured by breastbands and breechings, also fringed. By the late 8th century BC mounted troops are shown riding on plain saddle-cloths and, under Sennacherib (*reg* 704–681 BC), in the early 7th century BC, on what are either trimmed fleeces or quilted saddle-cloths. Under Assurbanipal (*reg* 668–631 BC), these may be placed over oxhide trappers similar to those worn by military chariot horses. The royal mounts of both kings wear quilted saddle-cloths with small tassels along the bottom edge and larger ones at the corners, held on by wide, fringed breastbands (see fig. 2). (Actual harness elements from Assyria and Urartu are preserved at, for example, the Hermitage Museum, St Petersburg, and the Prähistorische Staatssammlung, Munich.)

Urartu. Urartian harness and bridling appear very similar to the contemporary Assyrian, but actual material found also includes large bronze (sometimes silver) spade-shaped blinkers, frontlets of various shapes and sizes, often with raised borders and engraved central designs, bossed strap distributors, large engraved and/or repoussé gorgets and breastplates.

Syria and Anatolia. The limited secondary evidence (reliefs e.g. in Ankara, Hittite Mus.) suggests that equipment in the Neo-Hittite states (9th–8th centuries BC) largely paralleled that in contemporary Assyria.

Cyprus. The evidence indicates that horse trappings here also closely paralleled the Assyrian, but with a certain time lag. At Salamis, decorated bronze blinkers, shoulder discs and frontlets (some of them with crest-holders) were

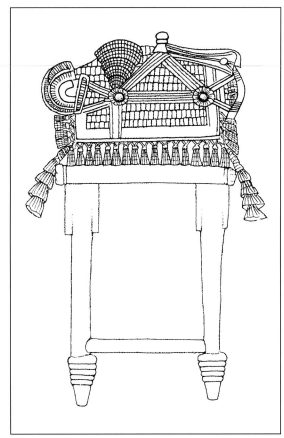

2. Assyrian bitted bridle with crest and frontlet lying on quilted saddle-cloth of royal mount; drawing of a detail of a stone relief from the palace of Assurbanipal, Nineveh, 668–631 BC (Berlin, Pergamon-museum, Vorderasiatisches Museum)

3. Scythian harness, showing horses with ceremonial saddles and bridles, from Pazyryk, 4th–3rd centuries BC; reconstruction drawing

found *in situ* on harness animals (8th–7th centuries BC; Nicosia, Cyprus Mus.).

Iran. While cheek-pieces of bits have been relatively simple in the cultures hitherto considered, they appear to constitute the main decorative elements of bridling in Luristan in western Iran during the earlier 1st millennium BC. Of cast bronze, they represent horses, moufflons and other hoofed animals—some of them winged—as well as griffins and composite creatures striding on base lines; 'Master of Animals' figures also occur, as well as V-shaped cheek-pieces crowned with heads of birds or animals. The headstall straps of Royal Achaemenid chariot horses had metal bead-like appliqués and strap distributors of boar's tusk inspiration; their forelocks were tied in tufts; bell-like tassels hung at the withers. The royal mounts depicted in reliefs at Persepolis display similar bridles, with the addition of browbands with little drop-like pendants. They may carry bells on beaded straps around their necks. When a saddle-cloth is shown, it is sometimes patterned and is often edged with tabs or 'crenellations' that suggest felt. It is secured by a girth and breastband.

Black Sea region. Actual bridle elements including gold, silver or bronze frontlets, headstall plaques, strap distributors and cheek-pieces of bits have been found in tombs of the 7th century BC to the 4th century AD (e.g. St Petersburg, Hermitage; Kiev, Hist. Mus.). These are often in relief, the most frequent motifs being horses, stags, griffins or raptor heads or protomes (often in Scythian ANIMAL STYLE) and vegetation.

Central Asia and southern Siberia. The steppe tribes spread many Animal-style motifs over a vast area. At Pazyryk, in the Altai mountains, frozen tombs (4th–3rd centuries BC) preserved organic elements of horse harness (St Petersburg, Hermitage). Elaborate designs in carved wood (stylized moufflons, stags, tigers, griffins, elk or human heads, vegetation), gilded or tinned, were sewn along bridle cheekstraps and nosebands, and formed the cheek-pieces of Scythian-type snaffle bits. Similar decorations often outlined the breastbands and cruppers. Pad saddles with low, wooden arches, front and back, were covered with coloured felt in Animal-style designs; long, felt shabracks, with felt appliqué decoration and often with a fringe, covered some saddles. Purely ceremonial harness included horse masks and headdresses supporting artificial antlers or models of real or fantastic animals, in a manner reminiscent of the crests of medieval European tournament helmets (see fig. 3).

Greek world. From East Greece, depictions in art of the 6th–5th centuries BC often show bridles with discoid decorations and harness straps with fringes of pendants or tassels. From mainland Greece painted decoration on numerous Black-figure and Red-figure vases (6th–5th centuries BC) shows headstall straps of both chariot horses and mounts sometimes decorated with small, discoid elements, usually widely spaced. Similar discs may appear on the reins. The breastbands of chariot horses may have surface decoration of wavy lines or circles; studs and small pendants or hanging loops are sometimes added. The criss-cross straps over the noses of horses being led up in several harnessing scenes are those of leather basket muzzles, to be removed once the horses are harnessed. Small, dotted rectangles or semicircles at the corners of the mouths of some horses represent bit burrs with their studs. Harness and bridle equipment from South Italy closely parallel those of contemporary mainland Greece. In addition, there are some bronze frontlets (6th–5th centuries BC) in the form of helmeted warriors' heads (e.g. Karlsruhe, Bad. Landesmus.).

Etruria. Horse harness of the Early Iron Age ('Villanovan') culture in northern Italy (9th–8th centuries BC; e.g. Bologna, Mus. Civ. Archeol.; Rome, Vatican, Mus. Gregoriano Etrusco) is primarily distinguished by the bits. Their cheek-pieces of openwork cast bronze are often in the form of stylized, Hallstatt-type horses, with stylized water-birds between their legs on the base-line and miniature horses on their croups. From small loops at either end of the base hang openwork jangles in a stylized vegetal form. There are also bronze cheek-pieces in the form of water-birds or little men, or in abstract design. Headstall strap distributors are sometimes shown as bossed. Reins occasionally appear to be laced at intervals with small verticals of uncertain material. Otherwise there seems to be little distinctive Etruscan harness (late 8th–3rd centuries BC).

Rome and the Empire. The bridles of racing chariot horses in figured documents are simple, with only a few metal bosses. Some teams carry leafy twigs upright on their heads. Single, crescent-shaped pendants (*lunulae*) may hang from the neck straps. Bridles of civilian and military mounts display discoid strap distributors. A large rectangular saddle-cloth lies beneath a rudimentary saddle, which is secured by a girth, crupper and breastband, the latter two usually adorned with large discs (*phalerae*) and sometimes with *lunulae* or a fringe. Horse armour used in Imperial period military games (stone reliefs are held in many museums in Italy and Germany) consists chiefly of elaborate triptych chamfrons of bronze, sometimes silvered, with mythological characters or attributes represented in repoussé (e.g. Vienna, Ksthist. Mus.; Pompeii, Antiqua.). The eyes are protected by hemispheric gratings or human faces pierced by many holes.

Celtic Europe. Rather plain bronze *phalerae* occur in Hallstatt culture contexts (*c.* 700–*c.* 400 BC) with other gear and are considered to have covered strap crossings or acted as frontlets. Much more elaborate ones of iron, bronze or silver, with engraved, repoussé or pierced designs, are associated particularly with chariot graves of the La Tène period (*c.* 400 BC–*c.* AD 100). Bronze or bronze-and-iron snaffle bits of the latter period often display typical stylized design in relief, occasionally inset with corals or enamel. Examples of two different types of chamfron with Celtic designs are known, one in bronze and the other in leather and bronze (e.g. Saint-Germain-en-Laye, Mus. Ant. N.; London, BM).

India. Adequate representations of chariot horses and mounts begin only in the 1st century AD, on reliefs of the great stupa at Sanchi. Chariot horses' headstalls are often decorated with discs or rosettes; they wear long, narrow frontlets. Head plumes, possibly of horsehair, are bushy, and horsehair tassels hang from just behind the ears, and

again at the withers. Bridling of mounts is similar. Riders sit on saddle-cloths that may be elaborately decorated and that are held in place by plain girths and wide breastbands and breechings decorated with rosettes.

China. Bridles of the earliest chariot horses in China found in the late Anyang phase (*c.* 1300–*c.* 1050 BC) of the Shang period have rectangular bronze bit cheek-pieces and both bossed and cruciform strap distributors, and small, pear-shaped frontlets. In Western Zhou times (*c.* 1050–771 BC), bronze bit cheek-pieces of chariot horses' bridles are commonly discoid but may be rectangular or irregular in shape; they are pierced and in the form of coiled animals or birds. Bridle elements include bronze frontlets in the form of fantastic animal masks in a variety of shapes and sizes. Elaborate basket muzzles of leather straps, outlined with cowrie shells, have also been found on buried horses. Traditional motifs continued to decorate bridles during the Spring and Autumn, Warring States, Qin and Western Han periods (722 BC–AD 9). Steppe influence is seen in horn cheek-pieces of some snaffle bits. The most significant change came with the introduction of cavalry (4th century BC), when Scythian S-shaped cheek-pieces appeared on the bits of riding horses. Chariot horses had more elaborate bridles, with frontlets, mask crests or plumes on the head and tassels at the throat. Harness straps were sometimes beaded. Actual harness elements are held in the Archaeology Institute of the Chinese Academy of Social Sciences, Beijing, and the Royal Ontario Museum, Toronto.

BIBLIOGRAPHY

J. Déchelette: *Manuel d'archéologie préhistorique, celtique et gallo-romaine*, ii (Paris, 1914), pp. 1190–1202

Å. Åkerström: *Architektonische Terrakottaplatten in Stockholm* (Lund, 1951)

S. I. Rudenko: *Kultura naseleniya govnogo altaya v skifskoye vremiya* (Moscow and St Petersburg, 1953); Eng. trans. as *Frozen Tombs of Siberia: The Pazyryk Burials of Iron Age Horsemen* (London, 1970)

E. F. Schmidt: *Persepolis*, i, Oriental Institute Publications, lxviii (Chicago, 1953)

H. Zimmer: *The Art of Indian Asia*, Bollingen Series, xxxix (Princeton, 1960)

M. von Dewall: *Pferde und Wagen im frühen China* (Bonn, 1964)

I. M. Stead: *The La Tène Cultures of Eastern Yorkshire* (York, 1965)

M. I. Artamonov: *Sokrovishche kifskikh kurganov* (St Petersburg, 1966); Eng. trans. as *Treasures from Scythian Tombs* (London, 1969)

J. A. H. Portratz: *Die Pferdetrensen des alten Orients* (Rome, 1966)

M. von Dewall: 'New Data on Early Chou Finds', *Symposium in Honour of Dr Li Chi on his Seventieth Birthday*, ii (Taiwan, 1967)

J. J. Orchardt: *Equestrian Bridle-harness Ornaments: Ivories from Nimrud, 1949–63* (Aberdeen, 1967)

F.-W. von Hase: *Die Trensen der Früheisenzeit in Italien*, Prähistorische Bronzefunde, XVI/i (Munich, 1969)

J. V. S. Megaw: *The Art of the European Iron Age* (Bath, 1970)

J. Garbsch: *Römische Paraderüstungen* (Munich, 1978)

A. E. Dien, trans.: 'Excavation of the Chi'n Dynasty Pit Containing Pottery Figures of Warriors and Horses at Ling T'ung, Shensi Province', *Chin. Stud. Archaeol.*, i/1 (1979), pp. 8–56

M. A. Littauer and J. H. Crouwel: *Wheeled Vehicles and Ridden Animals in the Ancient Near East* (Leiden and Cologne, 1979)

H. Donder: *Zaumzeug in Griechenland und Cypern*, Prähistorische Bronzefunde, XVI/iii (Munich, 1980)

J. H. Crouwel: *Chariots and Other Means of Land Transport in Bronze Age Greece*, Allard Pierson Series, iii (Amsterdam, 1981)

E. Berger, ed.: *Antike Kunst aus der Sammlung Ludwig II* (Mainz am Rhein, 1982), nos 218–19

E. Özgen: 'The Urartian Chariot Reconsidered', *Anatolica*, xi (1984), pp. 91–154

M. Schleiermacher: *Römische Reiter-Grabsteine* (Bonn, 1984)

M. A. Littauer and J. H. Crouwel: *Chariots and Related Equipment from the Tomb of Tut'ankhamūn*, Tut'ankhamūn's Tomb Series, viii (Oxford, 1985)

M. Sparreboom: *Chariots in the Veda* (Leiden, 1985)

Fu Tianchou, ed.: *The Underground Terracotta Army of the Emperor Qin Shi Huang* (Beijing, 1985)

J. H. CROUWEL, M. A. LITTAUER

(ii) Later history.

(a) Western Europe. (b) Eastern Europe. (c) Western Asia and Byzantine lands. (d) North Africa. (e) Indian subcontinent. (f) East Asia. (g) Americas.

(a) Western Europe. Following the collapse of the Roman Empire, evidence from grave goods, pictorial representations and written sources suggests that the horse did not occupy a prominent position among barbarian tribes for several centuries. Horse furniture found in graves probably belonged primarily to chieftains and their retinues. The tribes that migrated into Europe in the Dark Ages sometimes decorated their harness. In the 4th century AD, Goths used iron or copper-alloy fittings and covered their saddle arches with stamped copper-alloy plates. Germanic horsemen in the 7th century decorated bridles, breast and crupper straps with discs or plaques. Alemanni harness at this time consisted of decorated mounts, strap-ends and distributors on the headstall, and breastbands with ring-strap distributors, the ferrules sometimes bearing a spiral ornament. (*See also* PREHISTORIC EUROPE, §VI, 8.)

An early 9th-century bridle from Broa on Gotland (Oslo, U. Oldsaksaml.) is set with gilt copper-alloy mounts with geometric frameworks and animals, or the 'gripping-beast' motif. Other contemporary Norse mounts display interlaced animals or an abstract 'ring-chain' design terminating in animal masks. Stirrups had elaborate side-pieces that were sometimes decorated with silver and copper or copper-alloy. Several 10th-century horse collars are made of gilt copper-alloy over wood, with Jelling-style ribbon beasts and animal-head terminals (*see also* VIKING ART, §II, 1(v)). A 12th-century Norwegian wooden collar from Lom (Stockholm, Nordiska Mus.) is carved with gripping-beast designs.

Anglo-Saxon decorative plaques could be silver gilt, cast and decorated with animal and plant motifs in relief. Several early 11th-century stirrups combine such Scandinavian designs as Ringerike-style motifs with Saxon acanthus and birds. Some have copper and copper-alloy wire inlay.

Medieval decorative harness plaques were set along strapwork or hung from the breastband, crupper or browband of the headstall. Shield-shaped copper-alloy pendants decorated with enamel designs, often heraldic, were popular in the late 13th century and the 14th. Crupper straps often multiplied across the rump, and all straps were frequently coloured, pierced, set with plaques or enhanced by scalloped, vandyked, fringed or oak-leaf edging; occasionally fine gilded chain was substituted. Strap distributors and bit cheek-pieces could also be gilded or embossed. A 15th-century headstall (London, BM) is decorated with enamel arabesques in silver *cloisons* and gilt-wire floral scrolls on granular ground. Where double reins were used, one was frequently of wide decorated cloth or leather. Plumes or small revolving ornaments, occasionally with bird finials, were sometimes placed on the poll, as were fan crests and three-dimensional heraldic crests of cuir-bouilli. High pommel and cantle lent themselves to heraldic display, which was also seen on the long cloth trappers, popular from the 13th century, which often also enclosed the head and neck and might bear decorative edging. Silver and gilt thread, coloured silks, velvet and precious stones were sometimes employed on the harness, saddle and trapper. Tournament harness was lavishly decorated (see fig. 4); collars of bells were popular, while trappers often displayed humorous or allegorical scenes. Ear tassels were favoured in 16th-century Germany.

In war a mail trapper was worn occasionally from the later 12th century, but a leather or steel head defence (shaffron) was more common, sometimes painted to match the heraldic trapper. By the 15th century full horse armour of steel plates consisted of shaffron, neck defence (crinet), chest defence (peytral), back defence (crupper) and flank defence (flanchard). Largely during the 15th and 16th centuries, horse armour was painted, fluted, pierced, embossed, etched and gilded with floral, zoomorphic or heraldic motifs; only rarely was it silvered.

Several 15th-century saddles are overlaid with designs in coloured staghorn or bone, while padded saddles (examples of both, Leeds, Royal Armouries; London, Wallace) with embossed leather coverings later became more common. Steel-faced examples might be damascened with gold and silver. An iron muzzle was sometimes employed, especially in Germany, with openwork decoration that included animals and inscriptions. During the 17th century, saddles lost their high profile in favour of padding. One costly example (Paris, Mus. Armée) is

4. European horse trappings of the early 16th century showing knights preparing to joust, each horse wearing a padded bumper under a colourful trapper and hoods without eyeholes to prevent shying; woodcut by Hans Burgkmair I from *Maximilian's Triumphal Procession, c.* 1516–18 (London, British Library)

covered in red velvet, gallooned and embroidered with gold, the pommel and cantle studded with gilt round-headed nails, while the straps have multicoloured weave. Saddle-cloths, sometimes extremely large, occasionally employed embroidered silks and gold thread. Both cloth and harness were sometimes fringed with tassels or even bows. Stirrups might be chiselled, engraved, cast in relief, gilded or enamelled.

In the late 18th and 19th centuries, cavalry regiments decorated their equipment. The horse-cloth was sometimes ornamented; the housing comprised rectangles of cloth over the horse's back and fastened to the saddle, or continuing under or over the saddle to join the fur holster-covers at the front. A shabrack was laid over the saddle and holsters. Cloths might be covered with embroidery, gold or silver lace, regimental crests, devices, titles and battle honours, or coloured patterns of stripes. Hussar regiments began to employ sheepskin covers for the shabrack, with leopard or cheetah for officers.

(b) Eastern Europe. Oriental influences were absorbed into Slav culture; 9th-century Bulgar horsemen might have tassels hung at the horse's throat and from discoid plaques on breast and crupper strap. An 11th-century Polish saddle bore a copper-alloy mount around the edge of the pommel, with terminal heads and zoomorphic finials set along its length. Medieval harness occasionally had precious-metal pendants hung from plaques, while stirrups sometimes had geometric patterns in inlaid copper alloy. During the 16th and 17th centuries some Polish horses were painted with dyes. Their bridles and breastbands might have mounts of precious metal, sometimes with engraved or jewelled pendants, or with feathers or tassels. Some saddles were covered in velvet and decorated with precious stones, pearls, gold or silver. There were rich saddle-blankets with additional covers on the pistol holsters. Large wings of eagle or ostrich feathers adorned the horses of many East European peoples in the 16th century, sometimes attached to the back of the saddle. By the 17th century the Hungarian oriental-style saddle was often overlaid with a shabrack, the holster mouths by bearskin or wolf-skin, with a large horse-cloth beneath; the breastband was decorated in the centre with a leather ornament, also seen on the crosspieces on the forehead. Russian horses might be covered in decorated blankets and hanging tassels, the headstall with metal mounts and tassels. Tatars used high 'Yarchak' saddles, often with decorative horse-cloths, metal crescent pendants and neck collars with hanging horsehair tassels.

(c) Western Asia and Byzantine lands. From the 4th century to the 15th, Byzantine harness consisting of low saddle, horse-cloth, breast and crupper straps and bridle was sometimes decorated with metal discs or plaques. A 4th-century breastband (London, BM) has partly gilt pendants in the form of crescents and silver discs, the latter embossed with animal and bird motifs or openwork designs. Occasionally horsehair tassels hung from a neck collar.

The Sasanian Iranians (*c.* AD 224–651) favoured horse-hair plumes set on the poll, behind the ear, under the throat from a neck strap or hanging from the breast or crupper strap. The 7th-century *clibanarius* (armoured warrior riding on armoured horse) used iron or copper-alloy lamellae (thin plates) sometimes set with plumes. Saddle and harness bore embossed silver or gold discoid plaques and pendants. The bridle might be woven, while saddle-cloths were richly decorated, often with foliate motifs; deep, rounded versions were popular in 10th-century western Iran and the Caucasus. In 8th- and 9th-century Transoxiana a distinctive muzzle was used. Some Muslims in 7th-century Iran used the padded *tidjfāf* (felt) bard. Horse armour is rare in the pictorial art of the region until the 15th century, when plate shaffrons and quilted, scale or lamellar bards are more common, occasionally fringed and decorated in gold or silver. In the 16th century large plates were painted with gold and colours and tasselled, or metal was replaced by rich and sometimes studded fabric. After *c.* 1600 armour disappeared and large, embroidered shabracks and trappers were used.

Basic Islamic equestrian equipment did not change radically from the 11th century to the 19th. Saddles often bore rounded flaps, sometimes with scalloped edges, or hanging thongs ending in tassels. Saddle-cloths, some covering the rump, bore floral, geometric or abstract designs and might be fringed and tasselled. Metal mounts decorated the breast and crupper straps, the latter sometimes including a V-shaped flank strap terminating in a pendant or tassel. Headstalls were ornamented, while a decorated neck collar (perhaps edged with pendants), often of three straps, usually had a horsehair tassel below and sometimes a plume above. A little cap might also bear a plume, or tassels were worn behind the ear. If the mane was tied in short hanging plaits, these might end in metal finials. In Iran and Turkey saddles were painted in brilliant colours and decorated with precious metals and stones, the bridles embroidered with coloured silks with plates set with cornelians and turquoises.

(d) North Africa. In 18th-century Morocco and Tunisia, gold embroidered on velvet was used on saddle and cloth, breastband and gilt-metal neck amulets. An Egyptian saddle and harness (see fig. 5) are covered in cloth embroidered in gold and silk, with stirrups of copper gilt, leathers gallooned with gold and cotton, breastband decorated with silk and gilt-metal plaques, bridle and blinkers covered in cloth embroidered in gold, curb bit in polished steel and reins gallooned with gold and silk. The Muslims in northern Nigeria rode with a short stirrup and ring bits in the Arab style. The whole front of the horse was sometimes protected by a tasselled trapper, with metal strips over the neck ending in tassels and a tasselled fringe above the eyes. Some 19th-century Sudanese bridles and breastbands had embossed and inscribed gold plates. Steel, brass, copper-alloy or silver shaffrons and some horse armour of copper, leather or brilliantly coloured quilting were used. In Ethiopia brass shaffrons and quilted armour were used.

(e) Indian subcontinent. Iranian influence in India meant a similar taste in equipment. Harness was sometimes decorated with gilt crescentic pendants, embossed plaques and perhaps bells. Armour was made of lamellae linked by mail, or decorated mail, for example an 18th-century

5. Egyptian Mamluk saddle and harness, cloth embroidered in gold and silk, stirrups of copper gilt, breastband decorated with silk and gilt-metal plaques, curb bit of polished steel, late 18th century (Paris, Musée de l'Armée)

hood and crupper with patterns of copper-alloy links, the cloth below edged with velvet and a silk fringe (Leeds, Royal Armouries). Quilted, coloured trappers were also worn, occasionally powdered with a pattern of gilt nails. Saddles survive from the 18th century with bows of embossed silver or inlaid pearl shell (New York, Met.). In the Deccan, 18th- and 19th-century saddle-cloths used cotton, silk, satin, velvet, silver-gilt threads and gold embroidery.

(f) East Asia. On Chinese harness, yak-hair tassels were often suspended from breast, crupper and cheek straps. Many Tang period (AD 618–907) figures portray horse-cloths (London, BM), and mail or hide trappers were used. Scale and lamellar armour occur throughout the centuries. The breastband might have bells; lotus flowers on the crupper were augmented by metal pendants on the harness. Copper face masks appear in the Song period (AD 960–1279), and silver and gold saddles and bridle ornaments are mentioned. Mongols in the 13th century used lamellar, leather or scale trappers, crinet and shaffron. The use of a gilt bit, peytral, saddle and crupper is also mentioned at this time. A Ming period (1368–1644) scroll of the emperor's procession (Taipei, N. Pal. Mus.) shows a gilt dragon-mask shaffron with pheasant-feather 'horns' and a breastband with multicoloured fringes. Harness at this date bore gilt and pierced ornaments set with hardstones or cloisonné, with pendants and tassels in jewelled holders. A pair of thin tassels swung from the reins, and a pompom might be worn on the nose or rump. Saddles were occasionally covered with silk, or inlaid with bone, ivory or carved lacquer. Dragon decoration used on saddles was also seen on stirrup bows in China, Tibet and Korea. A padded silk trapper and shaffron (covering head and neck) sometimes had velvet borders. Basic horse trappings remained similar until the 20th century, when

saddles were covered with shagreen and edged with iron encrusted with silver wire in geometric or floral designs. A neck collar of copper-alloy bells might be added and stirrups damascened with silver, more rarely copper alloy.

Examples from 17th-century Tibet are faced with gilt steel, carved and pierced and set with precious stones (Leeds, Royal Armouries; London, V&A). Contemporary harness might be of silk braid and pierced and gilt iron with yak-hair tassels. Armour often consisted of leather with iron studs, or lamellae, with long fringes of silk and hair.

Decorated wooden saddles with inlaid shell were superseded in Japan in the 16th century by moulded lacquer—a fashion that lasted several centuries—and of matching saddle and stirrups. Designs of conch, decorative threads and tassels, cranes and waves were popular. Probably in the 16th century stirrups began to be decorated with copper alloy and silver inlay. The mail trapper of the 16th century was supplemented *c.* 1600 by decorated horse armour often consisting of small embossed leather scales, lacquered and gilded and sewn on to fabric, the whole held in place by silk cords ending in tassels. The shaffron was usually of papier mâché or leather, decorated in gilt lacquer and shaped like a dragon's head or caricature of a horse's head (see fig. 6). Iron muzzles bore openwork, stamped plant or zoomorphic designs. Long braid tassels were hung from the bridle. Breastbands and crupperbands might have a deep, decorative or (sometimes very long) tasselled edging. Large, ornamental saddle-cloths were embroidered with *mon* (heraldic badges) or made of skins. The bit cheek-pieces were occasionally circular with a punched or pierced (sometimes cruciform) design.

6. Japanese saddles and harnesses, with dragon's-head shaffrons, body coverings of lacquered and gilt-leather squares stitched on to cloth, and inlaid saddles and stirrups, 18th century (Florence, Museo Stibbert)

In Korea in the 17th and 18th centuries silver plates and enamels were used to decorate bridles, and saddles were covered in shagreen.

(g) Americas. Horses were reintroduced by 16th-century Spanish adventurers; in Mexico and latterly North America, the medieval war-saddle was adopted for use by cowboys. In the 19th century fancy examples of the Western stock-saddle were richly tooled and often inlaid with contrasting leathers and applied silver, sometimes with a matching breastband. Native American peoples used saddle-blankets, often decorated with coloured bead or quillwork or fringes, as were breast and crupper straps, stuffed pad-saddles and wooden saddles. Such peoples as the Cheyenne decorated the harness with German silverwork. Headstalls might be decked with coloured trade cloth. Some warriors painted their horses with designs. South American cowboys (gauchos) did not adapt the war-saddle, but instead used a wide, tough saddle made from two long cushions covered in sheepskin or leather. Bridles of plaited leather are fastened by leather rather than metal.

BIBLIOGRAPHY

H. Cogent: *Manuel du harnachement* (Paris, 1856)
O. M. Dalton: 'Notes on an Enamelled Head-stall in the British Museum', *Proc. Soc. Antiqua.*, 2nd ser., xxi (1906–7), pp. 376–80
B. Tozer: *The Horse in History* (London, 1908)
L. Mercier: *La Parure des cavaliers et l'insigne des preux* (Strasbourg, 1924)
C. Buttin: *Les Bardes articulées au temps de Maximilien 1er* (Strasbourg, 1929)
G. C. Stone: *A Glossary of the Construction, Decoration and Use of Arms and Armor in All Countries and in All Times* (New York, 1934)
C. G. Trew: *From Dawn to Eclipse: The Story of the Horse* (London, 1939)
L. Rousselot: *L'Armée française, ses uniformes, son armement, son équipement* (Paris, 1942)
C. G. Trew: *The Accoutrements of the Riding Horse* (London, 1951)
——: *The Horse through the Ages* (London, 1953)
E. Wagner, Z. Drobná and J. Durík: *Medieval Costume, Armour and Weapons* (London, 1958)
Z. Zygulski: *Ze studiów nad dawną sztuką siodlarską* [A contribution to the study of ancient saddlery] (Kraków, 1959)
R. Ettinghausen: *Arab Painting* (Geneva, 1962)
J. Mann: *European Arms and Armour*, London, Wallace cat., i (London, 1962, suppl. by R. V. B. Norman, 1986)
H. Lachouque: *Dix siècles de costume militaire* (Paris, 1963)
J. Marek and H. Knížková: *The Jenghiz Khan Miniatures from the Court of Akbar the Great* (London, 1963)
G. M. Meredith-Owens: *Turkish Illustrated Manuscripts* (London, 1963)
G. Tylden: *Horses and Saddlery* (London, 1965)
P. Paulsen: *Alamannische Adelsgräber von Niederstotzingen* (Stuttgart, 1967)
C. Chenevix-Trench: *A History of Horsemanship* (London, 1970)
N. Chih-Liang: *The Emperor's Procession: Two Scrolls from the Ming Dynasty* (Taipei, ?1970)
P. G. Foote and D. M. Wilson: *The Viking Achievement* (London, 1970)
K. Horedt and D. Protase: 'Das zweite Fürstengrab von Apahida (Siebenbürgen)', *Germania*, l (1972), pp. 174–220
G. M. Meredith-Owens: *Persian Illustrated Manuscripts* (London, 1973)
J. Eisler: 'Zu den Fragen der Beinsättel des Ungarischen Nationalmuseums', *Fol. Archaeol.*, xxviii (1977), pp. 189–209
B. W. Robinson: *Persian Paintings in the John Rylands Library* (London, 1980)
Man and the Horse (exh. cat. by A. Mackay-Smith, J. R. Druesedow and T. Ryder, New York, Met., 1984)
G. Sen: *Paintings from the Akbar Nama: A Visual Chronicle of Mughal India* (Varanasi, India, 1984)
M. D. MacCarthy: *La Cavalerie française et son harnachement* (Paris, 1985)
C. Bálint: *Die Archäologie der Steppe* (Cologne, 1989)
C. Spring: *African Arms and Armour* (London, 1993)

CHRISTOPHER GRAVETT

2. ELEPHANT. Elephants have a long history in the employ of man. From the 1st millennium BC until the 19th century, they have played a significant role in warfare, principally in South-east Asia and the Indian subcontinent, but at various times in areas as diverse as Western Asia, North Africa, Spain and Italy. They were valued for their immense strength and intelligence, and their ability to be trained in human service. Although they had uses for moving heavy loads, from forest timber to artillery pieces, their main role was as fighting animals; they could trample men and horses alike, pick up and throw a man and horse together, and wield swords attached to their tusks. In fact, their reputation was so fearful that it is difficult to discern from the primary sources their true value in war, for most of the Eastern accounts take their role for granted, while most of the Western accounts emphasize the occasions when these mighty creatures were defeated. In India, where elephants were most numerous, they also had a significant role to play in hunting, where they could provide a self-defended mobile tower for the hunting of tigers. Most of the elephants used in war were of the Indian species. Those used in Ptolemaic Egypt and Carthage were of the African forest species, which was once considered extinct, though a small number survive near Lake Chad.

(i) Armour. The relationship between elephant and driver, or *mahout*, was close and long-lasting. The *mahout* would sit astride the elephant's neck and direct the animal with his voice, feet, and with a hafted hook and spike called an *ankus*. The way in which these animals were employed in warfare meant that little equipment uniquely associated with the elephant was required. In addition to the *mahout*, crew would either sit astride the animal or stand in a *howdah*, a small tower, often shown with a crenellated top (lighter, unfortified *howdah*s, formed of wooden frames and seats with wicker sides, attached by chains to the elephant, were used for hunting).

*Howdah*s seem to have been used in limited quantities for war elephants since ancient times in India, but their crew are usually shown seated astride the animal, on carpets presumably thrown over padded seats and attached by ropes around the girth. In the west, that is to say the Carthaginian and Ptolemaic kingdoms of ancient Africa, and the Seleucid, Bactrian Greek and Sasanian kingdoms of Western Asia, elephants are almost always shown with towers. The crews of war elephants were usually armed with bows, sometimes with long spears or javelins, and occasionally with rockets, crossbows and, from the 15th century, firearms.

The most impressive artefact associated with the war elephant is the *bargustawan-i-pil* or elephant armour. These are recorded in India during the Delhi sultanate and Mughal empire, and in Iran under the Timurids. The only surviving example in a public collection is in the Royal Armouries Museum, Leeds, England (see fig. 7). It was probably made in one of the arsenals of the Mughals in north India, in the late 16th century or early 17th, and was acquired in India in 1801 by the second Lord Clive, Earl of Powis; the story that it was taken by the first Lord Clive at the the Battle of Plassey in 1757, and its consequent 18th-century dating, was pure supposition based on its preservation at Powis Castle. The armour is constructed

7. Elephant armour of mail and plate (shaffron, 2.4×1.9 m; throat defence, 2.50×0.75 m; front panel, 1.6×1.3 m; centre panels, 1.70×1.06 m; rear panel, 1.70×1.34 m), with a *mahout* holding an *ankus*, Indian, Mughal, *c.* 1600 (Leeds, Royal Armouries Museum)

BIBLIOGRAPHY
H. R. Robinson: *Oriental Armour* (London, 1967)
H. H. Scullard: *The Elephant in the Greek and Roman World* (London, 1974)

TOM RICHARDSON

(ii) Other accoutrements. Surviving elephant trappings from India date only from *c.* 1600. Representations in much earlier sculptures, as well as in miniature paintings from the 15th century onwards, provide a clear idea of the ways in which Indian elephants were ornamented and protected for processions, hunts and battles (*see also* §(i) above). Reliefs from Barhut and Bhaja (2nd–1st centuries BC) show elephants with metal headbands with hanging bells attached, and draped with richly embroidered cloths. Similar ornaments, along with harnesses and anklets, appear in reliefs from medieval temples, such as the Virupaksa at Belur (12th century). A folio from a 15th-century *Kalpasutra* manuscript (Hyderabad, Mittal Mus. Ind. A.) vividly depicts these various trappings. Even more elaborately decked is the elephant in a 17th-century painting from Bijapur (priv. col.), which, in addition to belled harnesses, tusk rings and a sumptuous saddle-cloth, wears garlands, whisks, and chains with bells hooked into its ears. Elaborate ceremonial elephant trappings were sent to Queen Victoria by the Nawab of Murshidabad in the mid-19th century. These included a magnificent towered *howdah*, brocaded hanging draperies, and garlands. Elephant drivers in miniatures usually hold a goad, or *ankus*, many of which survive in museum collections. The long handle terminates with two steel blades, one straight, the other hooked. In style they range from simple to ornate. A particularly elaborate example (17th century) from Tanjore or Mysore, now in the Musée Guimet, Paris, has a handle inlaid with gold filigree and blades faced with images of divinities, animals and scrollwork.

BIBLIOGRAPHY
S. Digby: *War-horse and Elephant in the Delhi Sultanate: A Study of Military Supplies* (Oxford, 1971)
S. K. Gupta: *Elephant in Indian Art and Mythology* (New Delhi, 1983)
Treasures from India: The Clive Collection at Powis Castle (London and New York, 1987)
J. Guy and D. Swallow, eds: *The Arts of India, 1550–1900* (London, 1991)

WALTER SMITH

of mail-and-plate, and in its present state weighs 118 kg; six of its original eight pieces survive (two of the three panels for the right side are missing), and it would originally have weighed 159 kg. (Such heavy protection was particularly useful when elephants were used as battering rams against castle doors, which were often fitted with sharp projecting spikes.) The side elements include square panels decorated with embossed trotting elephants, lotus flowers, birds and fish, but the armour is otherwise plain except for the scalloped edges of the small plates; it was probably covered with fabric except on the square panels, to judge by contemporary armours in Mughal miniatures, and was, for the comfort and protection of the elephant for which it was made, fitted with a padded lining. A pair of cast-iron tusk swords associated with this armour survives at Powis Castle, and other rather small and probably late examples of tusk swords from the now-dispersed Mysore Arsenal also survive.

3. CAMEL. Decorative trappings and harness are worn by men's riding camels and camels carrying women's litters or the tribal emblem. The Rwala is the only tribe with an extant emblem. There are two types of riding saddle, one similar to those bearing litters, and a halter. The basic saddle has a light wood framework with high pommels front and back fitting over the hump, and secured with breast and belly girths; saddles carrying litters have an additional tail girth (see Musil, pp. 351–2; Dickson, pp. 85–8). The alternative saddle, used in eastern Arabia and Oman for fast work, has miniature saddle arches in front of the hump with a breast girth; the rider sits on a pad joined to the saddle by ropes behind the hump (Dickson, p. 87). The saddle-frame is padded; the saddlebags go over the saddle, and above its straps is a blanket, plain over the saddle and decorated where it hangs over the camel's hips. Attached to the saddlebag straps are two streamers. The saddle itself is covered with a black goatskin or white sheepskin. Over the shoulderblades hangs another

cover, attached to the front of the saddle. All visible parts are patterned and decorated with tassels, fringes, plaiting and streamers (see fig. 8). Leather is an alternative to the more usual woven material. The halter has a woven band going round the back of the head and joined by a metal ring to a band over the nose; under the jaw is a loose chain, from which hangs another short chain where the single rein is attached. The cheek bands are decorated with tassels.

Women's litters had a basket framework, with variations across the peninsula. The basic litters were a boxy frame with a cushion, called *kenn* in northern Arabia and *maksar* in eastern Arabia; some tribeswomen had litters with huge extending wings, called *zitab* in the north (Musil, pp. 68–77) and *dhalla* or *chitab* in the east (Dickson, pp. 96–103). Eastern Arabian tribeswomen had *maksar*s and *dhalla*s, variations of the *kenn* and *zitab* (Dickson, pp. 96–103). Saddles were inlaid with shells and mirror, while litters were hung with streamers and covered with fringed and tasselled hangings; on the march they resembled swaying butterflies. The Rwala tribal emblem, the *markab*, is a litter whose frame is wrapped in ostrich feathers and plumes atop each upright (Musil, pp. 571–4; Lancaster, p. 90).

Men make saddles and women make litters from local wood, usually tamarisk. Metal nails, rings and decorative inlay are bought from traders or were made by travelling smiths. Women weave halters, cushions, blankets, bags and trappings for family members, or for sale; men make the plaited halter ropes. Tanning was women's work. The utilitarian harness and litter frames are enhanced by trappings carrying artistic and social content. The trappings, in which the women invest material, skill and time, demonstrate their esteem for the rider. Conversely, the decoration of the litters shows the affection men have for their women, since men buy the cloth, mirror, shells and beads used in addition to the woven streamers and hangings. Women find art in the skills of spinning, weaving, finishing and patterning (for techniques see Weir, pp. 31–49; Crocker and Glover, pp. 103–6). Men appreciate the enhancement of the camel's beauty, especially its grace and speed. Riding camels and litters are poetic motifs (e.g. Musil, pp. 249, 251–2, 272, 290, 624).

Camel harness and trappings date back to at least the late 2nd millennium BC. Available information from carvings shows little change in form from Assyrian reliefs (e.g. Barnett, pls 32–3; Bulliett, p. 81), Nabatean figurines (Parlasca, pp. 200–13), Palmyrene statuary (Michalowski, pl. 70) and Safaitic carvings (Macdonald, p. 25) to the recent past and present. The demise of camel-herding since the 1950s, largely through the introduction of modern transport, means harness and trappings are restricted to those who continue herding, together with racing stables in the Emirates and Oman and some military units, such as the Badia Corps in Jordan. Collections of camel harness and trappings are in the Museum of Mankind, London; the Folklore Museum, Amman; the Museum of Archaeology, Sharjah, Ra's al-Khayma Museum and Dubai Museum in the United Arab Emirates; and in the National Museum of Qatar.

BIBLIOGRAPHY

A. Musil: *Manners and Customs of the Rwala Bedouins*, American Geographical Society, Oriental Explorations and Studies, vi (New York, 1928/R 1978)

8. Camel with traditional harness and trappings

H. R. P. Dickson: *The Arab of the Desert* (London, 1949)
K. Michalowski: *Palmyra* (London, 1970)
R. Bulliett: *The Camel and the Wheel* (London, 1975)
R. D. Barnett: *Sculptures from the North Palace of Ashurbanipal at Nineveh (668–627 BC)* (London, 1976)
S. Weir: *The Bedouin* (London, 1976)
G. Crocker and B. Glover: 'An Omani Braiding Technique for Camel Reins', *J. Oman Stud.*, v (1979), pp. 103–6
W. Lancaster: *The Rwala Bedouin Today* (Cambridge, 1981)
I. Parlasca: 'Die nabataischen Kamelterrakotten: Antiquarische Aspekte und kulturgeschichtliche Bedeutung', *Petra: Neue Ausgrabungen und Entdeckungen*, ed. M. Lindner (Munich, 1986)
M. C. A. Macdonald: 'Camel Hunting or Camel Raiding', *Arab. Archaeol. & Epig.*, i (1990), pp. 24–8

WILLIAM LANCASTER, FIDELITY LANCASTER

Harnett, William Michael (*b* Clonakilty, Co. Cork, Ireland, 10 Aug 1848; *d* New York, 29 Oct 1892). American painter. He was brought up in a family of artisans in Philadelphia and was trained as an engraver of silverware. After studying at the Pennsylvania Academy, he moved to New York in 1869 and worked as an engraver while continuing his studies at the Cooper Union. In 1875 he exhibited at the National Academy of Design while supporting himself by painting small, precise still-lifes. He returned to Philadelphia in 1876 and by 1880 had saved enough for a European tour. He settled in Munich, working there and in Paris for six years and returning permanently to New York in 1886.

Although he had no pupils, Harnett was the most influential American still-life painter of the last quarter of the 19th century. Until about 1880 his works were simple table-top still-lifes in the *trompe l'oeil* tradition of Raphaelle Peale. Set against dark, shallow backgrounds they consisted of mugs, pipes, books, newspapers, currency, letters and writing materials, as in *Writing Table* (1877; Philadelphia, PA, Mus. A.). Carefully composed and balanced with realistic colour, precise detail and smooth brushwork, they reflect his training as an engraver. The *Artist's Letter Rack* (1879; New York, Met.) is a form of bulletin board with various flat objects— tickets, clippings, receipts, visiting-cards, stamps—haphazardly attached to a wooden board by a criss-crossing network of tapes. This format, widely copied in American painting, had its roots in Dutch 17th-century art. In Munich, Harnett's scale became almost miniature. He took as his subject-matter more precious objects: antique lamps, elaborate tankards and leather-bound books are arranged in pyramidal fashion against dark and undefined backgrounds. Harnett's most famous painting, *After the Hunt* (San Francisco, CA Pal. Legion of Honor), the last and largest version of four, was painted in Paris and exhibited there to considerable acclaim in the Salon of 1885. The following year he sold it to Theodore Stewart to display in his New York saloon, where it spawned hundreds of imitations. A large and minutely detailed *trompe l'oeil*, it is a trophy composed of dead birds, game and hunting accoutrements affixed to a battered wooden door. Harnett's late works include many paintings of single objects set against a green wooden door. The *Faithful Colt* (1890; Hartford, CT, Wadsworth Atheneum) consists of a single revolver hanging against the door, with a newspaper clipping below. *Plucked Clean* (1882; Chicago, IL, A. Inst.) features a scrawny chicken, plucked except for a few tufts of down; a rare glimmer of humour is implied in the title. The *Old Violin* (1886; priv. col., see Frankenstein, 1953, pl. 60) and *Old Cupboard Door* (1889; Sheffield, Graves A.G.), like most of his work, are infused with a gentle melancholy. Harnett, like his contemporary *trompe l'oeil* painters, received little official attention. The sale of his studio took place at Thomas Birch & Sons, Philadelphia, 23–4 February 1893. After his work was rediscovered by the Downtown Gallery, New York, in 1939, many forgeries of his paintings appeared, among them genuine compositions by John F. Peto to which Harnett's signature had been added. Frankenstein (1949) identified Harnett's genuine oeuvre.

BIBLIOGRAPHY

A. Frankenstein: 'Harnett: True and False', *A. Bull.*, xxxi (1949), pp. 38–56

——: *After the Hunt: William Michael Harnett and Other American Still-life Painters* (Berkeley, 1953, rev. 2/1969)

W. H. Gerdts and R. Burke: *American Still-life Painting* (New York, 1971), pp. 133–43, 248–50

William Michael Harnett (exh. cat., ed. D. Bolger, M. Simpson and J. Wilmerding; New York, Met.; Forth Worth, TX, Amon Carter Mus.; San Francisco, CA, F.A.Museums; 1992–3)

GERTRUDE GRACE SILL

Haro. French family of painters, colourmen, dealers, restorers and collectors. The father of Etienne-François Haro (*b* Paris, 13 April 1827; *d* Paris, 4 Feb 1897) was a painter but also a colourman and supplier of artists' materials in Paris, selling them from his shop the Palette d'Or (renamed Au Génie des Arts at Delacroix's suggestion). Two of the more important customers were Ingres, who patronized the shop from the late 18th century, and Delacroix, who from about 1826 bought his canvases and paints there. When Etienne-François's father died he left the business to his wife, from whose aunt they had inherited it.

Etienne-François Haro was the great-nephew of Hubert Robert and was a pupil of Ingres and Delacroix, maintaining a lifelong friendship with both. From the mid-1840s he took an active part in running the business with his mother, but by the first years of the Second Empire (1852–

70) he had taken over from her and had become one of the best-known dealers and art experts of his day. He bought contemporary paintings and works by Old Masters and visited England and Italy to buy stock and to increase his knowledge of art and the art market. Ingres generally showed an interest in Haro's collection, paid almost daily visits to his shop in Rue Bonaparte and on at least one occasion made a copy of a painting he saw there. Shortly before Ingres died he sold Haro 31 of his painted studies and over 40 drawings, which formed the nucleus of the sale of Ingres's works held by Haro at his premises on 6–7 May 1867. In that year Haro was appointed to the Ministry of Public Works and as a restorer to the Palais des Tuileries in Paris. He bought and sold a large number of works by Delacroix, purchasing them at public auctions but sometimes directly from the artist. He frequently acted as an intermediary between Ingres and his clients and did the same for Delacroix. One such commission was for a copy (1862; Paris, Louvre) of *Medea* (1838; Lille, Mus. B.-A.; *see* DELACROIX, EUGÈNE, fig. 4), ordered by Emile-Jacob Péreire from Delacroix through Haro. Haro's correspondence reveals that he was on friendly terms with several other artists, among them Manet, Courbet and Alfred Sisley, who valued his opinions and his expertise as a restorer. He built up a large private collection of works, including paintings by Delacroix, Ingres and 17th-century Dutch and Flemish masters; some of these were sold in 1892, and the remainder was auctioned after his death. His two sons Henri Haro (*b* Paris, 1855; *d* Paris, 7 May 1911) and Jules Haro (*b* Paris, 1855; *d* Paris, 1892) both studied painting under their father and under Carolus-Duran. They were also dealers, Henri becoming one only after the death of Jules.

UNPUBLISHED SOURCES

Paris, Bib. Doucet [letters from artists to the Haro family]

BIBLIOGRAPHY

A. Joubin: 'Monsieur Haro entre Ingres et Delacroix', *Amour A.* (March 1936), pp. 85–92

LINDA WHITELEY

Haro y Guzmán. *See* CARPIO, Marqueses del.

Harpignies, Henri-Joseph (*b* Valenciennes, 24 July 1819; *d* Saint-Privé, 28 Aug 1916). French painter and printmaker. He came from a prosperous, solidly bourgeois background. A precocious draughtsman, he received elementary art training at the municipal school and became a talented cellist who enjoyed playing the chamber music of Haydn and Beethoven in later life. His artistic career was delayed by employment in the family iron forges at Denain and at the Famars sugar refinery, although he drew caricatures under the influence of the great French satirical lithographers. In 1838 he was exposed to a wider variety of French landscape during a two-month tour with a family friend Dr Lachèze, who also introduced Harpignies to the landscape painter and etcher Jean-Alexis Achard (1807–84), with whom he studied in Paris in 1846. His first significant group of paintings and drawings in a marginally Realist style was made with his master at Crémieu in late 1847, but the Revolution of 1848 obliged him to return home. He then stayed with Achard in Brussels, producing his first sequence of etchings.

In May 1849 Harpignies travelled to southern Germany, visiting Lachèze in Baden and proceeding in November to Rome, where the austere forms of the Campagna under brilliant southern light formed a momentous and persistent influence. The Bay of Naples and, above all, Capri also entranced Harpignies who, by 1851, was producing his first serious watercolours. He was summoned home by March 1852 and settled in Paris. The second dominating influence on Harpignies was the landscapes of Corot, who encouraged him with purchases. Harpignies first exhibited at the Salon in 1853, showing a view of Capri and two landscapes near Valenciennes, and continued to do so regularly until 1912, to generally laudatory reviews and with consistent State acquisitions. He married, unrewardingly, Marguerite Ventillard in 1863, the year in which he commenced a visually stimulating return visit to Italy which lasted until April 1865.

In 1870 during the Franco-Prussian War, Harpignies served in the Garde Nationale at Hérisson, where he passed his summers for the rest of the decade, but otherwise his life appears to have been equable, uneventful and increasingly successful. His connection with the dealers Arnold & Tripp after 1883 ensured his prosperity. He was a Salon medallist in 1866, 1868 and 1869, winning a silver medal at the Exposition Universelle of 1878 with the *Colosseum in Rome* (Paris, Mus. d'Orsay; see fig.), the Grande Médaille d'honneur for *Banks of the Rhône* in 1897 (although he failed to be elected to the Institut) and the

Grand Prix at the Exposition Universelle of 1900. He became a member of the Société des Aquarellistes Français in 1881 and the Société des Artistes Français six years later. He rose through the ranks of the Légion d'honneur from Chevalier in 1875 to Grand Officier in 1911.

Although Harpignies painted occasional still-lifes, interiors and, early in his career, figure subjects, principally of children (e.g. *Sauve qui peut*, exh. Salon 1857; Valenciennes, Mus. B.-A.), he was primarily a painter of landscape and town, especially of Paris. He travelled widely but is associated above all with central France and the countryside around the River Loire and its tributaries, the Nièvre and the Allier. Fully assimilating the mannerisms of most of the Barbizon painters besides Corot, he carried their subjects, vision and stylistic assumptions into the 20th century, distilling an immediately recognizable personal style of limited range and sophisticated compositional variation. A blue luminosity is often the strongest colour note in a generally greyish-green palette of delicately nuanced tonal values, with a recurring disposition for overlapping planes in a frequently flattened perspective. Strength and concision also characterize his painting. He advocated linear clarity and distinct outline, but nevertheless fluctuated between a bland evenness of form and a diaphanous, feathery handling of separate touches. Within his overall naturalistic preoccupations, stylization is always apparent. A resolute conservative for over 60 years, adhering to a low-keyed conception of ordered nature, he

Henri-Joseph Harpignies: *Colosseum in Rome*, oil on canvas, 470×656 mm, exhibited 1878 (Paris, Musée d'Orsay)

showed hints of Art Nouveau and Japoniste taste and, for all his recorded antipathy, marginal traces of an Impressionist, even a Post-Impressionist, aesthetic. His range extended in scale from painted lampshades to decorative designs for public buildings in Paris (Opéra, Sénat, Hôtel de Ville).

From 1865 Harpignies increasingly took private pupils and after 1885 taught at his Paris school, becoming widely influential as a watercolourist; many of his drawings were dedicated to his bourgeois and aristocratic lady students. From 1879 he spent much of his time at his property La Trémellerie at Saint-Privé where motifs abounded, and along the coast, especially at Nice and Menton. In his last 15 years, with failing eyesight, he made many monochrome drawings for sale and presentation under the influence of Léon Lhermitte. Béraldi described 34 small and delicately wrought etchings (and one lithograph), but some fragile drypoints remained unpublished. His output during a long career was immense and his watercolours particularly have remained popular during the partial eclipse of his formidable reputation as a painter in oils.

BIBLIOGRAPHY

H. Béraldi: *Les Graveurs du XIXe siècle*, viii (Paris, 1889), pp. 61–3
L. Bénédite: 'Harpignies (1819–1916)', *Gaz. B.-A.*, n. s. 4, xiii (1917), pp. 207–53
Henri Harpignies (exh. cat., Valenciennes, Mus. B.-A., 1970)
P. Miquel: *Le Paysage français au XIXe siècle, 1824–1874*, iii (Maurs-la-Jolie, 1975)
P. Gosset: *Henri Harpignies (1819–1916)* (Valenciennes, 1982)

HARLEY PRESTON

Harrach. Austrian family of statesmen, diplomats, patrons and collectors. The Grafs von Harrach were among the most prominent families in the Habsburg empire. They played a decisive role in politics, particularly in the 17th and 18th centuries, but made a lasting name for themselves as collectors and patrons. The family arrived in Austria in the 12th century in the wake of Bavarian dukes. In 1524 Leonhard III von Harrach (1468–1527) bought the castle and sovereignty of Rohrau in Lower Austria, and his descendants were raised to the rank of Reichsfreiherr (1552) and Reichsgraf von Rohrau (1627). Subsequently three members of the family—Ferdinand Bonaventura, Graf von Harrach, (1) Aloys Thomas, Graf von Harrach, and Friedrich August, Graf von Harrach—played important roles in the history of Austria. Two became princes of the Church: Ernst Adalbert von Harrach (1598–1667), Cardinal-Archbishop of Prague, who effected the Catholic Counter-Reformation in Bohemia in 1625, and Franz Anton von Harrach (1665–1727), Prince-Archbishop of Salzburg and Primate in Germany. Unless stated otherwise, all works mentioned below are in the Graf Harrach'sche Familiensammlung, Schloss Rohrau, Rohrau.

Ferdinand Bonaventura, Graf von Harrach (*b* Prague, 14 July 1636; *d* Karlsbad, 15 June 1706), served as an imperial ambassador to Madrid (1673–6, 1697–8), making a comprehensive record of life at the Spanish court in his detailed diary (Vienna, Staatsarchv). He began to acquire pictures on a grand scale through personal contact with many collectors and painters, among them Juan Carreño de Miranda and Luca Giordano, as well as buying at numerous auctions. For example, on 14 September 1697 he bought at auction the *Three Women Playing Musical Instruments* (mid-16th century), the major work by the Master of the Female Half-Lengths. Among his most important acquisitions were the *Immaculate Conception* (1637) and *St Joseph with the Flowering Rod* (1644), both by Jusepe de Ribera, and portraits of *Charles II, King of Spain, in the Vestments of the Golden Fleece* and of *Queen Maria Anna of Spain*, both by Carreño de Miranda, *Isaac Blessing Jacob* (before 1654) by Giordano, and two still-lifes (both 1648), rare works by the painter Francisco de Palacios. In 1698 Graf Ferdinand Bonaventura had his portrait painted in Paris by Hyacinthe Rigaud and *c.* 1700 he built a palace in Vienna, probably from plans by Domenico Martinelli. His son (1) Aloys Thomas, Graf von Harrach, was one of the greatest statesmen of his time and also the most prestigious of the Harrach collectors.

Friedrich August, Graf von Harrach (*b* 18 June 1696; *d* 4 June 1749), the eldest son of (1) Aloys Thomas, Graf von Harrach, became Deputy-Governor of the Netherlands and in 1742 and 1745 a negotiator at the conferences that brought the First and Second Silesian Wars to an end. He is thought to have contributed 17th-century Dutch and Flemish paintings to the family collection, including the *Lamentation of Christ* and *Boy's Head* by van Dyck, *Portrait of a Woman* (*c.* 1626) by Cornelis de Vos and *SS Sebastian and Irene* (1624) by Jan van Bijlert. Like the following generations, his son Ernst Guido, Graf von Harrach (1723–83), played no decisive role on the political stage. He was the last to collect contemporary artists' work, preferring the Roman school. He acquired architectural scenes by Giovanni Paolo Pannini, landscapes by Adrien Manglard, Joseph Vernet and Carlo Bonavia, and works by Pompeo Girolamo Batoni, Sebastiano Conca, Placido Costanzi (including two paintings of 1750–51 on biblical subjects) and Anton Raphael Mengs. He made his purchases mainly through his dealer, Giuseppe Dioigio Crivelli; their correspondence (Vienna, Staatsarchv) is an important source of information about art and cultural life in Rome in the mid-18th century.

Franz Ernst, Graf von Harrach (1799–1884), built Schloss Hrádek (1841–54) near Königgratz (now Hradec Králové, Czech Republic) from plans by E. B. Lamb. Antiques were bought from all over Europe to furnish the interior, ceilings and wall panelling, as well as furniture of the 16th and 17th centuries, which was supplemented by reproductions. Schloss Hrádek, now Hradek u Nech at Nechanice and established as a museum, is a characteristic example of historicist architecture and interior decoration. Following the example of Holy Roman Emperor Joseph II (*reg* 1765–90), Graf Franz Ernst opened his collection to the public and created large exhibition spaces when the Stadtpalais in Vienna was rebuilt (1845–59). Acquisitions through dealers of works attributed to Old Masters adversely affected the character of the collection, and later some of the attributions were rejected. The historical value of the Harrach collection lies in the earlier counts' acquisition of contemporary paintings.

After World War II, Stephanie, Gräfin von Harrach, widow of Johann, Graf von Harrach, restored the Harrach-Palais in Vienna, which had been badly bombed, and the collection was reopened to the public in 1960. When the Viennese palace was sold, Gräfin Stephanie renovated

Harrach family collection displayed in Schloss Rohrau, showing 18th-century Roman paintings, including works by Sebastiano Conca and Pompeo Batoni (by the door), landscapes by Joseph Vernet, Adrien Manglard and Carlo Bonavia, and a portrait of *Aloys Thomas, Graf von Harrach* (right)

Schloss Rohrau, 40 km from Vienna, to which she brought the collection, reopening it to the public. In Schloss Rohrau, a 13th-century fortress rebuilt (1776–7) by Andreas Zach (1737–97), the collection is now presented for the first time in a series of rooms as it would have been at the time of the great Harrach collectors (see fig.). It includes over 200 paintings, notably of the 17th and 18th centuries, all of outstanding quality (for illustrations of two works in the collection *see* BIJLERT, JAN VAN, and CARREÑO DE MIRANDA, JUAN, fig. 2), with furniture and *objets d'art* of the same period. Some important paintings have, however, been sold in the late 20th century.

(1) Graf **Aloys Thomas von Harrach** (*b* Vienna, 7 March 1669; *d* Vienna, 1 Nov 1742). At the age of 27 he was ambassador to Madrid and from 1728 to 1733 he served as Viceroy of Naples and Sicily, restoring the kingdom's economy, revivifying the university and repairing the fortifications. He bought works of art on a much grander scale than his father, and above all he bought with a view to decorating palaces. His acquisition of contemporary Neapolitan Baroque paintings, unique north of the Alps, has determined the international importance of the

Harrach collection. These works included eight pictures by Francesco Solimena; seven by Luca Giordano; three by Bernardo Cavallino, among them the *Murder of Amnon*, a major work; the *Queen of Sheba before Solomon* by Mattia Preti; five animal paintings by Domenico Brandi (1683–1736); and three colossal paintings by Nicola Maria Rossi. The works by Rossi depict festive occasions in the Viceroy's life, and are extremely important both artistically and from an art-historical point of view. The history of southern Italian Baroque painting can be traced almost without a break through these and numerous other paintings.

Scarcely anything remains of the palaces and castles constructed by Graf Aloys Thomas's architect, Johann Lukas von Hildebrandt: only the Harrach summer palace in Vienna, with ceiling paintings by Rossi (Vienna, Ksthist. Mus.), and the chapel of S Januarius (1730–35; rest.) survive. Schloss Prugg in Bruck an der Leitha (begun 1707) was completely rebuilt in the 19th century. Although the hunting-lodge Halbthurn in Burgenland was burnt down in 1949, since 1971 the exterior has been restored. In 1714 Graf Aloys Thomas set up glassworks in Neuwelt (now Novy Svet, Czech Republic), which reached their peak during the Biedermeier period, particularly under Johann Pohl (1769–1850) and his son Franz Pohl III (1813–84), producing such collectors' items as Pasten covered with glass, black Hyalith glass, cut glass, Lithyalin glass, Chrysopras glass, yellow Isabellanglas, sea-green and tile-green glass as well as the lead-free Rubin glass and constantly new variations of Überfanglas. The Harrachov glassworks, sold under pressure during the Hitler regime, are now among the most important in the Czech Republic.

UNPUBLISHED SOURCES

Vienna, Staatsarchv [including inventories, correspondence and diaries of Ferdinand Bonaventura, Graf von Harrach]

BIBLIOGRAPHY

A. Gruss: *Verzeichnis der Gräflich Harrach'schen Gemälde-Gallerie zu Wien* (Vienna, 1856)

G. F. Waagen: *Die vornehmsten Kunstdenkmäler in Wien*, i (Vienna, 1866)

A. Gaedeke: 'Das Tagebuch des Grafen Ferdinand Bonaventura von Harrach während seines Aufenthaltes am Spanischen Hofe in den Jahren 1697 and 1698', *Archv Österreich. Gesch.*, xlviii (1872), pp. 163–302

E. Gerisch and K. Spaček: *Katalog der Erlaucht Graf Harrach'schen Bildergallerie* (Vienna, 1897)

Otto, Graf von Harrach: *Rohrau, 1288–1688* (Vienna, 1906)

G. Glück: *Die Harrach'sche Bildergalerie* (1923)

H. Ritschl: *Katalog der Erlaucht Gräflich Harrach'schen Gemälde-Galerie in Wien* (1926)

H. Benedikt: *Das Königreich Neapel unter Kaiser Karl VI* (Vienna, 1927)

G. Heinz: *Katalog der Graf Harrach'schen Gemäldegalerie* (Vienna, 1960)

R. Keyszelitz: 'The Counts of Harrach', *Great Family Collections* (London, 1965)

——: 'Die "Funzioni puppliche" des Vizekönigs von Neapel, Aloys Thomas Graf Harrach', *Du*, xxxi (1971), pp. 896–913

M. Konečný: 'Die beste Glashütte der Biedermeierzeit, zur böhmischen Glashütte Neuwelt, 1712–1987', *Die Weltkunst*, lviii/5 (1988), pp. 743–6

ROBERT KEYSZELITZ

Harran [anc. Carrhae]. Ancient city on the Anatolian plateau in Turkey, *c.* 30 km south of Urfa, where a trade route from the Euphrates crosses the modern Turco-Syrian frontier. The site was visited and described from the mid-19th century by such travellers as R. C. Chesney, C. Preusser, Gertrude Bell, K. A. C. Creswell and T. E. Lawrence. From 1950 onwards it was surveyed and excavated by S. Lloyd, W. Brice and D. S. Rice. The main mound, in the centre of the site, rises 20 m above the level of the plain, undoubtedly covering the ruins of an Assyrian temple to the moon-god Sin.

Harran was probably already a centre for the cult of the moon-god in the 2nd millennium BC. After the fall of Nineveh (*c.* 612 BC) the last Assyrian king, Assur-uballit II (*reg* 612–609 BC), transferred the remains of his court briefly to Harran. Three stelae bearing cuneiform inscriptions of the Babylonian king Nabonidus (*reg* 556–539 BC) have been found reused as paving stones in the mosque. The Islamic ruins cover an area, oval in shape, with a maximum dimension of 1250 m and are enclosed by a poorly preserved city wall, one gateway of which survives, bearing the date AH 588 (1192 AD).

On the north side of the mound are the remains of the Great Mosque (Jami' al-Firdaus), dating from the Umayyad period and probably built by the Caliph Marwan II (744–50), a patron of the city. Only the east façade and a square stone minaret remain standing. Near the east entrance an inscription dated 1192 mentions the Ayyubid ruler Salah al-Din (*reg* 1169–93). The castle (Qal'a), a powerful Islamic fortress, covers the remains of a temple of the Sabaeans, who preserved the elements of ancient Mesopotamian religion. Excavation of the east gate revealed a basalt archway with impost reliefs depicting leashed hunting dogs as well as a kufic inscription, including the founder's name, dated AH 451 (1059). The castle was rebuilt, for the fourth and final time, by the Crusaders.

Until recently a small modern village depended for drinking water on a well called Bi'r Ya'qub (Jacob's Well) outside the city's wall. This well corresponds in every detail to the description in the Bible (Genesis 24:45 and 29:2). In the area there are a number of beehive houses built without centering, a type of construction already recorded on Assyrian reliefs of the 8th century BC.

BIBLIOGRAPHY

Enc. Islam/2

S. Lloyd and W. Brice: 'Harran', *Anatol. Stud.*, i (1951), pp. 77–111

D. S. Rice: 'Studies in Medieval Harran', *Anatol. Stud.*, ii (1952), pp. 36–83

S. Lloyd: 'Harran and the Sabaean Sect', *Ill. London News* (19 Feb 1953)

D. S. Rice: 'Harran's Great Mosque', *Ill. London News* (21 Sept 1957)

K. M. Prag: 'Deep Sounding at Harran', *Levant*, ii (1970), p. 63

T. Allen: *A Classical Revival in Islamic Architecture* (Wiesbaden, 1986), pp. 41–6

SETON LLOYD

Harriet, Fulchran-Jean (*b* Paris, 1776; *d* Rome, 1805). French painter and draughtsman. He began his career in 1793 by winning second prize in the Prix de Rome with an entry that was praised by his teacher, David, and by Prud'hon. He exhibited portraits and subjects taken from ancient history in the Salons between 1796 and 1802. Harriet took part in the 'Pre-Romantic' movement made famous by his fellow disciples of David, Pierre Guérin and Anne-Louis Girodet. *Oedipus at Colonus* (1798–9; priv. col., see 1974 exh. cat., no. 97) is typical of this development in Neo-classicism. Harriet combined precise drawing of draperies, strong effects of light and symbolically divided landscape (the arid section on the left prefigured Caspar David Friedrich) with static, symmetrical composition. At the same time he won the 1798 Prix de Rome with the *Fight between the Horatii and the Curiatii* (Paris, Ecole N. Sup. B.-A.). He went to Rome, probably in 1802, where he undertook a vast heroic composition, *Horatius Cocles* (untraced), which, according to his contemporaries Landon and Wicar, was a masterpiece, although it was still unfinished when he died.

Harriet died very young and very few of his works are known. These include a charmingly naturalistic *Portrait of a Child* (1797; exh. Salon, ?1802; Orléans, Mus. B.-A.) and a *Portrait of Marat* (Versailles, Mus. Lambinet). Several of his designs were reproduced: for example *The Days of 9 Thermidor and of 31 May* (etched by J.-J. F. Tassaert; Paris, Carnavalet), in which he showed himself to be an impassioned witness of his times. Although always loyal to the example of David, Harriet had a rich and original talent, which is evident in his acerbic caricature from the Consulate period, *Parisian Tea, Supreme Style* (coloured etching by Adrien Godefroy (1777–1865); Paris, Carnavalet).

BIBLIOGRAPHY

J.-B. Wicar: 'Nouvelles littéraires', *Mag. Enc.*, vi (1805), pp. 375–8

C. P. Landon: *Annales du Musée et de l'école moderne des beaux-arts: Ecole française moderne*, i (Paris, 2/1832), pp. 375–8

De David à Delacroix (exh. cat., Paris, Grand Pal., 1974), pp. 478–81

P. Grunchec: *Le Grand Prix de peinture: Les Concours des Prix de Rome de 1797 à 1863* (Paris, 1983), p. 135

P. de la Vaissière: 'Un Adolescent malléable, durci par la Révolution: Le Peintre Fulcran-Jean Harriet', *Gaz. B.-A.*, ci (April 1983), pp. 141–4

PASCALE MÉKER

Harris. Canadian family of artists of British birth. The brothers (1) Robert Harris and (2) William Critchlow Harris moved with their family to Charlottetown, Prince Edward Island, in 1856. Robert pursued a career as a portrait painter, working in Europe and Canada. William Critchlow practised as an architect in Canada, mainly in Prince Edward Island and Nova Scotia. The careers of the two brothers rarely coincided, one exception being All Souls Chapel (1888) in Charlottetown, a characteristic Gothic Revival work designed by William Critchlow and decorated with 18 paintings by Robert.

ROBERT C. TUCK

(1) Robert Harris (*b* Tyn-y-groes, Gwynedd, 18 Sept 1849; *d* Montreal, 27 Feb 1919). Painter. He trained in Boston and in 1876 studied for one term at the Slade School of Art, London, under Alphonse Legros. In 1877–8 he studied in the studio of Léon Bonnat in Paris. He was attracted to Europe and spent several periods painting in England, France, Italy, Germany and Spain. He returned to Canada in 1879, settling in Montreal. In 1880 he was made an Academician of the newly formed Royal Canadian Academy of Arts, and he later served 13 years as its President.

Harris was the best portrait painter of his time in Canada and was in great demand. He painted at least 300 portraits (e.g. *Sir Hugh Allan*, 1885; Ottawa, N.G.). His most important commission was from the Canadian government to paint *The Fathers of Confederation* (*c.* 1885, destr.; oil sketch, 1883; Charlottetown, Confed. A.G. & Mus.) to commemorate the gathering of the delegates of British North America to discuss the confederation of the provinces of Canada. His portraits are painstakingly crafted, while in such genre scenes as *Harmony* (1886; Ottawa, N.G.) he experimented with a looser, Impressionist technique. Harris did much to promote Canadian art internationally, through his own efforts in showing at prestige exhibitions and through his influence on the many committees on which he served.

BIBLIOGRAPHY

M. Williamson: 'Robert Harris and *The Fathers of Confederation*', *Bull. N.G. Canada*, 12 (1968), pp. 8–21

——: *Robert Harris, 1849–1919: An Unconventional Biography* (Toronto, 1970)

——: *Robert Harris (1849–1919)* (Ottawa, 1973)

Robert Harris (1849–1919) (exh. cat. by Ll. D. Gruffydd, Cardiff, N. Mus., 1986)

LLYR D. GRUFFYDD

(2) William Critchlow Harris (*b* Bootle, Lancs, 30 April 1854; *d* Halifax, Nova Scotia, 16 July 1913). Architect, brother of (1) Robert Harris. In 1870–75 he was apprenticed to the architect David Stirling in Halifax. Harris specialized in the design of churches, but he also designed houses and commercial and civic buildings. His houses were influenced by contemporary architectural trends, first the Second Empire style and later Queen Anne Revival. These houses—for example The Cottage

(1895; now Caroma Lodge), Charlottetown, Prince Edward Island—display an eclectic inventiveness, with verandahs and balconies, oriel and bay windows, and gables with bargeboards. Until 1895 Harris's church designs were in the English Gothic style, as for example St James's, Mahone Bay, Nova Scotia. In 1895 he adapted the French Gothic style in St Paul's, Charlottetown, Prince Edward Island, setting a pattern for all his subsequent designs. The chancels, ending with an apse, are the same height and width as the naves, with shallow transepts and groined vaulting. Resonating panels and sounding-posts under the floors ensure excellent acoustics. Harris experienced great personal disappointment when he failed to win the commission to design the Anglican Cathedral in Halifax. Of 120 buildings constructed from his plans, 50 survive in Prince Edward Island, 40 in Nova Scotia and 1 in New Brunswick.

UNPUBLISHED SOURCES

Charlottetown, Confed. A.G. & Mus. [letters and memorabilia]

Charlottetown, K. Pickard priv. col. [folios of drawings]

BIBLIOGRAPHY

R. C. Tuck: *Gothic Dreams* (Toronto, 1978)

——: *The Island Family Harris* (Charlottetown, 1984)

ROBERT C. TUCK

Harris, E(mmanuel) Vincent (*b* Devonport, 1876; *d* Bath, 1 Aug 1971). English architect. He was articled to James Harvey in Plymouth, later studying at the Polytechnic of Central London and the Royal Academy evening school in London. From 1901 to 1908 he worked for the London County Council and his hand may be seen in a series of simple, monumental electricity sub-stations for tramways, the grandest being in Upper Street, Islington (1905). He established his own office when, in partnership with Thomas Anderson Moodie (1875–1948), he won the competition for Glamorgan County Hall (1908), Cardiff, with a design that was a fine example of the growing Beaux-Arts influence in English classicism. Harris and Moodie also designed a fine Lutyens-inspired fire station in Cardiff (1912; destr.; see Reilly). The same simple Italianate style was used for the brick front of 2–3 Duke Street, St James's, London (1910). In 1914 Harris won the competition for the Board of Trade building, Whitehall, which was only completed to his altered design in 1961.

Between World Wars I and II Harris was a conspicuous winner of competitions for municipal buildings. His circular Manchester Central Library (1925) and Sheffield City Hall (1926) are grandly classical; the former was linked to Alfred Waterhouse's Town Hall (1868) with Harris's contrasting Gothic-style extension of 1927–38. Leeds Civic Hall (1933), with twin Wren-like spires, in turn acknowledged Cuthbert Brodrick's Town Hall of 1858. Harris designed county offices at Kingston upon Thames (1925), Taunton (1932), Nottingham (1935) and Bristol Council House (1935–9). Braintree Town Hall (1928) is smaller but has a richly embellished interior. Other major works included a masterplan and several buildings at the University of Exeter (1931–58), including a chapel (1958) with a notable painted ceiling commissioned from Sir Thomas Monnington (1902–76). Harris also designed two buildings for the University of Durham (1945–52), and the Kensington Public Library (1946–60) in London. His style, closely modelled on Lutyens but with a characteristic aversion to emphasizing the centre of a composition, was by this time old-fashioned but Harris's work showed consistent quality of detail with good use of sculpture and murals. He was awarded the Royal Gold Medal for Architecture in 1951.

BIBLIOGRAPHY

C. H. Reilly: 'E. Vincent Harris', *Building*, iv (Sept 1929), pp. 393–9
'The Royal Gold Medallist 1951', *RIBA J.*, lviii/4 (1951), pp. 149–52
Obituary, *Building*, ccxxi/6690 (1971), p. 66

ALAN POWERS

Harris, Harwell Hamilton (*b* Redlands, CA, 2 July 1903; *d* 1990). American architect. He served a three-year apprenticeship with Richard Neutra (1928–32), and was one of the earliest American members of CIAM, joining in 1929. He began his architectural practice in Los Angeles in 1933 and soon distinguished himself as a designer by the completion of a home for himself on Fellowship Park Way, Los Angeles (1935). This tiny wooden pavilion with removable walls, which hovered dramatically over its steeply sloped site, established a restrained vocabulary of generous space, economical use of materials and simple but exact detailing, which became trademarks of his later work. He acknowledged influences as diverse as Louis Sullivan, Frank Lloyd Wright and Bernard Maybeck, but the strongest was probably his association with Neutra and Rudolf M. Schindler. Like Schindler he began from an unequivocally modernist point of view, but evolved a personal style based strongly on a pragmatic handling of local conditions and materials.

Harris's best-known work, the Havens House in Berkeley, CA (1941), employed a stack of three inverted triangular gables to support decks overlooking a dramatic view of San Francisco Bay. This was one of Harris's many designs that addressed the problems of the steep hillside sites so common in California. The truss structure of the Johnson House in Los Angeles (1947) is made up of many small components and shows his articulated but unaffected use of wood. Harris's academic career as director of the architecture programme at the University of Texas at Austin (1951–5) and as a faculty member at North Carolina State University in Raleigh (1962–73) took him away from California in his later years and expanded his practice, although it still consisted mainly of private houses.

WRITINGS

K. Smith, ed.: *Harwell Hamilton Harris: A Collection of his Writings and Buildings* (Raleigh, 1965)

BIBLIOGRAPHY

Contemp. Architects
S. Woodbridge, ed.: *Bay Area Houses* (New York, 1976)
E. McCoy: *The Second Generation* (Salt Lake City, 1984)
L. Germany: *Harwell Hamilton Harris* (Austin, 1985)

LAWRENCE W. SPECK

Harris, Lawren S(tewart) (*b* Brantford, Ont., 23 Oct 1885; *d* Vancouver, 29 Jan 1970). Canadian painter. He attended the University of Toronto in 1903 and then studied art in Berlin from 1904 to 1907. He returned to Toronto in 1908 and sketched in the 'Ward', a slum section of the city. Harris's early masterpiece, *Houses, Richmond Street* (1911; Toronto, A. & Lett. Club), with its flat perspective and bright colours, is characteristic of his

decorative treatment of urban scenes before 1920. In 1908 Harris was a founder-member of the influential Arts & Letters Club in Toronto and in 1911 he was elected to the Ontario Society of Artists.

Artistic taste in Toronto generally was provincial and conservative, dependent on British and European academic models; dissatisfied with this, Harris became a leading figure in creating and promoting a distinctly Canadian landscape art. Independently wealthy, he underwrote in 1913 the construction costs for the Toronto Studio Building, a home for the small group of painters who shared his vision of a vigorous national art rooted in the portrayal of the northern wilderness. In the same year Harris and J. E. H. MacDonald visited an exhibition of contemporary Scandinavian painting at the Albright–Knox Art Gallery in Buffalo, NY. Both were deeply impressed by examples of the northern Symbolist landscape tradition that evoked the experience of a wilderness setting similar to that of Canada. Harris's immediate response was a series of decorative compositions of snow-laden fir trees (1914–18), such as *Snow II* (1915; Ottawa, N.G.).

In early 1918 Harris suffered a nervous breakdown brought on by the recent deaths of his brother Howard and his friend and fellow artist Tom Thomson. On a recuperative train journey through northern Ontario, he was inspired by the rugged wilderness of the Algoma region and organized a sketching trip to the area with MacDonald and Frank Johnston (1888–1949) in the autumn of 1918. Similar trips with increased participation took place, and the collaborative spirit of the artists grouped around Harris led in May 1920 to the formation of the GROUP OF SEVEN.

During the early 1920s Harris replaced the decorative charm of his slum scenes with a stark geometry of forms that expressed an apocalyptic vision of human poverty. He became an active and dedicated follower of THEOSOPHY; his art and writings were deeply influenced by its esoteric religious doctrines. In the 1920s Harris painted the austere landscape of the north shore of Lake Superior, the Rocky Mountains and ultimately in 1930 the eastern Arctic; typically blue-toned compositions such as *North Shore, Lake Superior* (1926; Ottawa, N.G.; see fig.) are abstracted and hieratically composed to reveal his transcendental vision of cosmic and eternal order.

In the early 1930s Harris virtually stopped painting and in 1934 abruptly left for the USA. After divorcing his wife, he immediately married Toronto painter and fellow Theosophist Bess Housser (1890–1969). They settled in Hanover, NH, where Harris became unofficial painter-in-residence at Dartmouth College and experimented further with abstraction as a means of expressing his ideas. By 1936 he was wholly committed to a non-objective art in which complex and symbolically charged geometric arrangements were situated in ambiguous spatial contexts (e.g. *Equations in Space*, 1937; Ottawa, N.G.). In 1938 Harris moved to Santa Fe, NM, where he helped found the ten-member Transcendental Group of Painters. He used dynamic symmetry to organize his geometric abstractions. In 1940 Harris settled in Vancouver and continued to paint canvases such as *Composition No. 1* (1941; Vancouver, A.G.) in the style of his Santa Fe period. He again immersed himself in the cultural life of Canada,

Lawren S. Harris: *North Shore, Lake Superior*, oil on canvas, 1.00×1.25 m, 1926 (Ottawa, National Gallery of Canada)

encouraging local avant-garde artists. In the 1940s Harris was an active member of the Federation of Canadian Artists (National President, 1944–7) and the Council of the Vancouver Art Gallery (1941–57) and was the first artist-member of the Board of Trustees of the National Gallery of Canada (1950–61). In the 1950s his style became more colourful and lyrical under the influence of Abstract Expressionism, and he continued to paint large-sized abstractions until his health failed in 1968. Harris was posthumously awarded the Companion of the Order of Canada. His representational pictures of the 1910–30 period were well received, but his later works never found widespread acceptance; nonetheless, his energetic and intelligent espousal of non-objective art did much to promote the development of abstraction in Canada. Harris's son, Lawren P. Harris (1910–94), was also an artist.

WRITINGS
'Revelation of Art in Canada', *Can. Theosophist*, vii (1926)
A Disquisition on Abstract Painting (Toronto, 1954)
The Story of the Group of Seven (Toronto, 1964)

BIBLIOGRAPHY
B. Harris and R. G. P. Colgrove, eds: *Lawren Harris* (Toronto, 1969)
Lawren S. Harris: Urban Scenes and Wilderness Landscapes, 1906–1930 (exh. cat. by J. Adamson, Toronto, A.G. Ont., 1978)
D. Reid: *Atma Buddhi Manas: The Later Works of Lawren S. Harris* (Toronto, 1985)
P. Larisey: *Light for a Cold Land: Lawren Harris' Work and Life: An Interpretation* (Toronto, 1993)

JEREMY ELWELL ADAMSON

Harris, Tomás (*b* London, 10 April 1908; *d* Mallorca, 27 Jan 1964). English art dealer, collector and writer. The son of Lionel Harris (*d* 1943), a leading London dealer in Spanish art, and Enriqueta Rodriguez, he was educated at the Slade School of Fine Art (1923–6) and the British Academy in Rome. He was a talented artist but decided to become an art dealer and, after running his own establishment, joined his father in a partnership to run the gallery in Bruton Street, London. They encouraged a greater appreciation of Spanish art among collectors and historians and organized several notable exhibitions in London: of Spanish Old Master paintings (1931), Venetian art (1932) and early Flemish paintings (1935). After World War II, Tomás Harris gradually withdrew from business in order to spend more time in Spain and particularly Mallorca, where he designed and built his own house at Camp de Mar and concentrated on pursuing his own work as an artist and on developing his collection of graphic art. He had a particular interest in the art of Goya, whose prints he began to collect in the 1950s. His collection, which included the three albums of proofs, the *Disasters of War*, the *Caprichos* and the *Tauromaquia*, that the artist gave to his friend and adviser Juan Agustín Ceán Bermúdez, enabled him to make a close analysis of Goya's working methods and to write, with the assistance of Juliet Wilson, a book that quickly became the standard work on Goya as a graphic artist. He died in a motoring accident, and in 1979 his collection was presented to the British Museum in lieu of death duties.

WRITINGS

with J. Wilson: *Goya: Engravings and Lithographs*, 2 vols (Oxford, 1964)

BIBLIOGRAPHY

DNB

J. W. Bareau: *Goya's prints: The Tomás Harris Collection in the British Museum* (London, 1981)

JANET SOUTHORN

Harrison, Austen St Barbe (*b* Kent, *c.* 1891; *d* Athens, 11 Feb 1976). English architect. He studied at McGill University, Montreal (1909–13), and University College, London (1913–14). After World War I he returned to University College to complete his studies and to qualify for the Certificate in Town Planning. In 1919 he became an Associate and in 1927 a Fellow of the RIBA. Apart from a short period in London in 1922, including a few months in Edwin Lutyens's office working on the New Delhi project, his post-war years focused on Greece. In the Department of Reconstruction for Eastern Macedonia (1919–20) his work included plans for Nigrita and Gallipoli. He then studied Byzantine and early Islamic architecture at the British School, Athens. In 1923 he was appointed chief architect in the Department of Public Works, Palestine. Until his resignation in 1937 his department maintained a consistently high standard of public architecture. He was personally responsible for the design of several fine buildings, notably Government House (1926–31) and the Palestine Archaeological (Rockefeller) Museum (*c.* 1927–34), Jerusalem, and the Post Offices in Jaffa (1927–31) and Jerusalem (*c.* 1927–9).

Harrison's work was conservative in character, in marked contrast to the avant-garde Jewish architecture of the period; it was, however, characterized by its fine detail and its sensitivity to the physical and cultural context. In this sense he performed a notable service to the emerging architecture of Palestine. On leaving the country in 1937, he spent a short period in Britain, where he designed Nuffield College, Oxford (1938). On his return to the Mediterranean he settled in Lapithos, Cyprus, where his home became a point of pilgrimage for cultured British expatriates and travellers, including the writer Lawrence Durrell, who dedicated *Bitter Lemons* (1957) to him. Although based in Cyprus until he was displaced by the disturbances of 1958, when he moved to Athens, Harrison's buildings and projects were widely dispersed: in Aden and Iraq, Egypt and Malta (where he was commissioned to prepare a rehabilitation plan for war-ravaged Valletta in 1943). One of his important later works was the University of the Gold Coast, Ghana (1954).

WRITINGS

with P. Hubbard: *Valletta and the Three Cities: A Report to Accompany the Outline Plan for the Region of Valletta and the Three Cities* (Valletta, 1945)

BIBLIOGRAPHY

'The New Jerusalem Government House', *Archit. Rev.*, lxx (1931), pp. 106–7

'Palestine Archaeological Museum', *Architect & Bldg News*, clxii/308 (1935), pp. 279–82

'Palestine Archaeological Museum', *Amer. Architect*, cxlix/2650 (1936), pp. 54–63

A. Fuchs: *Austen St Barbe Harrison: A British Architect in the Holy Land*, DSc thesis, Haifa, Technion (1942) [text in Hebrew]

GILBERT HERBERT

Harrison [née Rossiter], **Mary P.** (*b* Liverpool, 1788; *d* Hampstead, London, 26 Nov 1875). English painter. She began painting watercolours while on honeymoon in France in 1814 and was the first Englishwoman to be given permission to copy paintings in the Louvre, Paris. From about 1830, when her husband's health and business failed, she turned to painting as a source of financial support for her large family. Of her twelve children, four became painters: William Frederick (1814–80), George Henry (1816–46), Maria (*fl* 1845–93) and Harriet. The family moved to London, where Harrison was a founder-member in 1832 of the New Society of Painters in Water-Colours and she exhibited there throughout her life. From 1833 to 1875 she exhibited at the Royal Academy, London, and elsewhere; her work was much sought after, and two of her paintings were purchased by Queen Victoria. Her subjects were usually fruit and flowers, sometimes birds' nests, and she became known as the 'rose and primrose painter'. Her pictures include such works as *Basket of Flowers* (1864), *Vase of Flowers* (both Liverpool, Walker A.G.) and the *History of a Primrose* (1862; untraced), the last of which is divided into three sections depicting 'infancy', 'second maturity' and 'decay'.

BIBLIOGRAPHY

Wood

Obituary, *A. J.* [London], xv (1876), p. 47

EMMA M. ROUTH

Harrison, Pakariki [Paki] (*b* Tairawhiti, NZ, 6 July 1928). Maori carver and craftsman. He was educated at Te Aute Maori Boys' College, Waipawa county, where he came under the direct influence of Pine Taiapa. He taught in rural schools for some years, and in 1958 resumed the craft of carving, practising it for 15 years and teaching it to adults in night classes. At the age of 45 he was offered his first major project, the Waiariki Meeting House, Otara, Auckland. He completed four more houses, the Otawhao House at Te Awamutu, Te Poho-o-Tipene (St Stephen's School) in South Auckland, the Tane-Nui-a-Rangi house at Auckland University, and the Harataunga community house at Kennedy's Bay. Each house represented five years of research, planning, architectural and design input, as well as the carving of wall panels and structural posts, and the co-ordination of all the other decorative arts used in Maori ceremonial houses. He became recognized as the leading *Tohunga Whakairo*, or Master Carver, of New Zealand: the title, an honorary one, is bestowed only on those who have conceived, designed and carved a number of complete *wharenui*, or traditional meeting houses. In Harrison's case such houses embraced tribal genealogies, myths and legends, and cosmologies. His work blended traditional Maori beliefs with an exciting use of contemporary materials, and his carvings were enhanced by the woven panels of his wife, Hinemoa Harrison, a fibre artist in her own right. In 1991 Harrison was awarded an honorary DLitt by the University of Auckland for his writings on Maori arts.

BIBLIOGRAPHY
K. Mataira: *Maori Artists of the South Pacific* (Raglan, 1984), pp. 26–33

JOHN HOVELL

Harrison, Peter (*b* York, 14 June 1716; *d* New Haven, CT, 30 April 1775). American architect of English birth. Born to Quaker parents, he probably trained in York with William Etty and his son John Etty. On the latter's death in 1739 he followed his seafaring elder brother Joseph and became first a mate and then a captain in the transatlantic trade until captured by a French privateer in 1744. He was imprisoned at Louisburg, Nova Scotia, where he secretly copied plans of the fortress and charts of the coastline. Released in early 1745, he passed the copies to William Shirley (1694–1771), Governor of Massachusetts, who then captured Louisburg in June that year. Harrison settled in Newport, RI, and in 1746 married Elizabeth Pelham (1721–84), a kinswoman of Shirley's wife, which secured his social position. Harrison had two advantages in the colonies: first-hand knowledge of English architecture and a unique library. His library was impressive for the American colonies and included works by Abraham Swan and Isaac Ware, James Gibbs's pattern books, several treatises on the art of building and drawings and books by Robert Morris (i), Sébastien Leclerc (i), Edward Hoppus and William Salmon covering ancient architecture, ornament, Palladio and contemporary English architecture. These resources, coupled with surveying, cartography, engineering and carpentry skills, established Harrison's reputation as a learned architect, an important consideration for colonial patrons who sought to keep up with their English cultural heritage, and many buildings have been attributed to him.

In 1746 Shirley commissioned Harrison to design his house, Shirley Place, Roxbury, near Boston; for this Harrison invented what George Washington later called 'rusticated boards', a method of making a timber house look as though built of stone. Shirley also provided him with a diplomatic passport that enabled him to visit France and the Veneto in 1748. Harrison's first building in Newport, the Redwood Library and Athenaeum (1749; see fig.), is Palladian in its detailing (*see* PALLADIANISM). He translated the more usual box-like form of colonial building into an American version of a Roman temple. The interior is essentially one grand hall flanked by two smaller reading rooms. He presented an imposing street façade with a pediment supported by four monumental Doric columns fronting a wooden façade emulating rusticated stone. Raised above a basement platform, the library is replete with a grand entry stair, triglyphs, guttae, brackets and a carved frieze above the massive entrance. The temple analogy is continued by the building's siting on an 'acropolis' overlooking the town, which slopes down to the waterfront. The Redwood Library was one of the few pre-Revolutionary buildings that symbolized the highest aesthetic attitudes of 18th-century America in being based on historical precedent, connected to English culture and erected to celebrate the high esteem placed by the upper classes on the world of knowledge.

Peter Harrison: Redwood Library and Athenaeum, Newport, Rhode Island, 1749

Almost immediately after his work on the Redwood Library, Harrison was invited to design a new Anglican church for Boston. King's Chapel (1749–58) was a larger commission, and it gave him the chance to work in stone on a more complex structure. The motif of paired columns that he used in the nave came from Nicolas Nicole's church of Ste Madeleine, Besançon, which Harrison must have seen under construction in 1748. He designed buildings for Cambridge, MA (Christ Church, 1760–61), and Charlestown, SC (St Michael's, 1751–61), but the bulk of his commissions were for Newport. Along with a number of prominent private houses, such as the elegant brick mansion on the waterfront for Francis Malbone (1760) or the John Banister House (1756) on the outskirts of the town, Harrison created two major public buildings for Newport: Touro Synagogue (1763) and the Brick Market (1761–72). For these, he once again used pattern books for the general layout and details. The Brick Market, erected to enlarge the storage space of the Long Wharf merchants and to create a new market on the ground level, was perhaps the most predictable of his designs in that it followed a scheme, popular in England at the time, of a grand order rising through two storeys set over an open arcaded basement. The design may be based either on Etty's Mansion House, York, or on Inigo Jones's Old Somerset House, as published in Colen Campbell's *Vitruvius Britannicus* (1715), although Harrison used bricks instead of stone and made other changes in dimensions and detailing while maintaining an orderly and monumental appearance. Harrison again showed himself to be sensitive to his given site as he designed the Brick Market facing the Colony House (1739–4), a governmental meeting-hall designed by Richard Munday, Newport's most prolific carpenter–builder of the previous generation; it symbolically balanced governmental and mercantile power across the square. For Touro Synagogue, Harrison blended knowledge of classical prototypes with the needs of the

Sephardic ritual. It remains a testimony to Harrison's sensitivity towards his patrons' needs and his ability to go beyond pattern books in designing the earliest synagogue building in the USA.

By the mid-1760s, when Harrison had lived in Newport for more than 20 years, several events altered the course of his life. Having pledged himself to such family and community pursuits as running his estate, enlarging Trinity Church and attending scientific lectures, he retreated from active public life after a serious illness in late 1765. His political sympathies as a loyalist supporter of the Crown were established through association with other prominent loyalist Newporters. It was further confirmed when he took the position of tax collector in New Haven, CT, that his brother Joseph had held since 1760 and from which he resigned in 1766 so that his brother might have the security of a government sinecure. By the time the Brick Market, Harrison's final building, was completed in late 1772, he was already in New Haven, and he probably did not see it completed. Harrison was elected to the American Philosophical Society in 1768, and he was consulted about the design of several other buildings (including one for Dartmouth College; unexecuted) but the last decade of his life was one of turmoil. He died during a period of increasing anti-English sentiment throughout the colonies, on the eve of the American Revolution. His library was ransacked, with books and drawings lost in raids by revolutionary groups in late 1775. Harrison received little more than a one-line obituary in the *Newport Mercury*, the newspaper for the town where he had left a most remarkable legacy of colonial building in America.

BIBLIOGRAPHY
Macmillan Enc. Architects
C. Bridenbaugh: *Peter Harrison: First American Architect* (Chapel Hill, NC, 1949)
A. F. Downing and V. J. Scully jr: *The Architectural Heritage of Newport, Rhode Island, 1640–1915* (Cambridge, MA, 1952)
P. Metcalf: 'Boston before Bulfinch: Harrison's King's Chapel', *J. Soc. Archit. Hist.*, xiii (1954), pp. 11–14
N. H. Schless: 'Peter Harrison: The Touro Synagogue and the Wren City Church', *J. Soc. Archit. Hist.*, xxx (1971), p. 242
Buildings on Paper: Rhode Island Architectural Drawings, 1825–1945 (exh. cat. by W. H. Jordy and C. P. Monkhouse, Providence, RI, Brown U., Bell Gal.; Providence, RI Hist. Soc.; Providence, RI Sch. Des., Mus. A.; New York, N. Acad. Des.; 1982)

RONALD J. ONORATO

Harrison, Thomas (*bapt* Richmond, N. Yorks, 7 Aug 1744; *d* Chester, 29 March 1829). English architect. His father was a carpenter. He was sent to Rome in 1769 with his friend George Cuitt (1743–1818), a landscape painter, by Sir Lawrence Dundas of Aske. There he studied Roman antiquities, and in 1770 he submitted to Pope Clement XIV a design for converting the Vatican Cortile del Belvedere into a museum for antique sculptures. In 1773 he entered the Concorso Balestra of the Accademia di San Luca, for which the theme was the replanning of the Piazza del Popolo. Harrison's design, the only one of his Roman projects to survive, was exhibited at the Royal Academy in 1777; it is more accomplished than those of his Italian competitors. His handling of the elements is closer to Roman Classicism and is characteristically Neo-classical in its marked independence of parts. When he found that he had been unsuccessful, he petitioned the

Pope, who presented him with gold and silver medals and made him *Accademico di Merito* in June 1773. The Pope later commissioned him to alter the sacristy of St Peter's, Rome, but died before work could begin. In 1776 Harrison visited the Roman temple at Pula (Pola) in Croatia, on his way back to England.

After a short stay in London, Harrison returned to Richmond, from where he sent exhibits to the Royal Academy: a National Monument (1779) and two elevations of a bridge across the Thames (1780). In 1782 he built the cupola of the town hall at Lancaster, a work of structural simplicity in the manner of Sir William Chambers. In 1783 he moved to Lancaster after winning the competition for the Skerton Bridge; from then on bridge building occupied him for the rest of his career, allowing him to combine his engineering and architectural skills; he had an excellent understanding of masonry construction and the handling of massive forms. The Skerton Bridge (completed 1788) had elliptical arches and a level road surface across the river, a device never before used in England on a large scale but pioneered in France by Jean-Rodolphe Perronet with his celebrated bridge at Neuilly-sur-Seine, Paris (1768–74; destr.). Probably because of its success Harrison was subsequently commissioned to rebuild St Mary's Bridge (1788–93), Derby, and the Stramongate Bridge (1791–7), Kendal; both were more modest interpretations of the same theme. In addition he held an unofficial appointment as bridge master of Lancashire (1792) and worked on several Cheshire bridges between 1800 and 1805; he was appointed county surveyor of Cheshire in 1815, having carried out the duties for 15 years. He also experimented with laminated timber constructions of his own devising at Warrington (1812; destr. 1837) and Cranage (1816; destr.). Although neither was a practical success these were daring works and the first of their type to be built in England; such structures were not developed until the civil engineer John Green (1787–1852) considered them for his Scotswood Bridge over the Tyne in 1827–8. Harrison's final and greatest engineering work was the Grosvenor Bridge (1827–33), Chester, then the largest single-span masonry arch in the world, measuring 60.96 m across. It appears almost too weak to bear its load, but the beautiful proportions are a merit rather than a defect. Harrison was consulted on several important commissions, including the Eden Bridge (1805), Carlisle, the Strand (later Waterloo) Bridge (1809), London, and the Ouse Bridge (1810), York. This made him known to engineers, including John Rennie, William Jessop (1745–1814), Jesse Hartley (1780–1860) and Thomas Telford, as well as to architects.

Harrison's most important public work, which he won in competition in February 1786, was the rebuilding (1788–1815) of Chester Castle in an innovative Greek Revival style. The work included felons' and debtors' gaols, the Shire Hall and offices, armoury, barracks and grand propylaeum, taking almost 30 years to build, during which he moved to Chester (1795). The polygonal plan of the felons' gaol, an outstanding solution to reformed prison design, was based on William Blackburn's Northleach Bridewell (1785), Glos; the Shire Hall portico was the first large-scale application in Britain of a baseless, unfluted primitivistic Greek Doric order, here modelled freely on the Tuscan order as described by Vitruvius and remarkable for its gigantic proportions. The interior hemicycle was inspired by the design of Jacques Gondoin for the Ecole de Chirurgie (1769–75), Paris, although Harrison introduced a simplified Ionic Ilyssus order. The exterior is notable for its sobriety, its long low silhouette and powerful masonry.

At about the same time (1786–99) Harrison was working on the reconstruction of Lancaster Castle in a Gothic Revival style to complement the existing buildings. The Shire Hall (c. 1791–2), Lancaster, is a Gothic rendering of the same building at Chester, and the male felons' prison (1792–3) is a hybrid of the polygonal and radial gaol plans used by Blackburn. Harrison's reputation as a public architect was made with these and other structures, including three early instances of Greek Revival buildings: the Liverpool Lyceum (1800–03) and the Portico Library (1802–6) and the Exchange (1806–9), both in Manchester.

Domestic architecture was a small but important part of Harrison's practice. His houses, apart from the triangular castellated Hawkstone Citadel (1824), Shropshire, are generally of two types: a plain fashionable type like those of Samuel Wyatt, characterized by finely cut masonry, minimal motifs, tripartite windows and domed bows, for example Kennet House (1793–4; destr. 1967), Central Region, and the idyllic stucco villa type with wide eaves, resembling the work of John Nash (i) and Henry Holland, for example St Martin's Lodge (1821–3), Chester, for himself. His plans developed from the villa type favoured by Robert Adam (i) and the Wyatts into more informal plans, with the principal rooms arranged asymmetrically. His only large house was Broomhall (1796–9), Fife, for Thomas Bruce, 7th Earl of Elgin; his suggestion that Elgin use his embassy in Constantinople to gather details of Greek architecture and sculpture resulted in the eventual acquisition of the Elgin Marbles (see BRUCE, THOMAS).

Harrison was the leading Greek Revivalist in the northwest, pioneering the baseless Doric and a simplified Ionic order with great assurance. His public works are characterized by a sense of construction, pure geometric shapes and a limited number of refined and simplified motifs. His domestic works are of great external simplicity. C. R. Cockerell noted, 'it is in the great intelligence of the masonry that Harrison's merit lies'. Blomfield later praised him as 'almost, if not quite, the first architectural genius in the kingdom, with a more clear apprehension of the principles of the art and a more accurate knowledge of the structural department of it than, perhaps, any man of his day'. Harrison was respected and admired by his contemporaries and achieved national recognition, but because of his retiring nature he remained in the north-west, where his major works ensure his reputation.

BIBLIOGRAPHY

Colvin
F. Milizia: Lettere al Conte Francesco di Sangiovanni (Paris, 1827), pp. 41–3
'Obituary of Thomas Harrison', Gent. Mag., i (1829), pp. 468–70
A. Blomfield: 'Biography of Thomas Harrison', Builder, xxi (1863), pp. 203–5
L. Pirotta: 'Thomas Harrison architetto inglese Accademico di San Luca per sovrano motu', Strenna Romanisti, xxi (1960), pp. 257–63
J. M. Crook: 'The Architecture of Thomas Harrison', Country Life, cxlix (15 April 1971), pp. 876–9; (22 April 1971), pp. 944–57; (6 May 1971), pp. 1088–91
D. Stillman: 'British Architects and Italian Architectural Competitions, 1758–1780', J. Soc. Archit. Hist., xxxii (1973), pp. 43–66
J. Farington: Diaries (1793–1821), ed. K. Garlick and A. Macintyre (i–vi) and K. Cave (vii–xvi) as The Diaries of Joseph Farington, 16 vols (London and New Haven, 1978–84)
M. A. Rudolf Ockrim: 'Thomas Harrison and the Rebuilding of Chester Castle: A History and Reassessment', Chester Archaeol. Soc. J., lxvi (1983), pp. 57–76
——: The Life and Work of Thomas Harrison of Chester, 1744–1829 (diss., U. London, Courtauld Inst., 1988)
M. Rudolf: 'Thomas Harrison and "the Structural Department of Art"', Georgian Group Journal (1992), pp. 68–78

MOIRA RUDOLF

Harrison and Abramovitz. American architectural partnership formed in New York in 1945 by Wallace K(irkman) Harrison (b Worcester, MA, 28 Sept 1895; d New York, 2 Dec 1981) and Max Abramovitz (b Chicago, 23 May 1908). After early office training in Worcester, Harrison worked intermittently with McKim, Mead and White in New York while studying with Harvey W. Corbett at Columbia University (1916–17) and after a year at the Ecole des Beaux-Arts, Paris (1919). He then won a travelling scholarship and visited Europe. Although he considered himself a modernist, his training had a lasting effect that included a deep interest in historic architecture. Back in New York, he worked for Bertram Goodhue before joining Corbett's firm and becoming a partner in Helmle, Corbett and Harrison (1927–9), then Corbett, Harrison and MacMurray (1929–35). This firm was one of three known as The Associated Architects that worked on Rockefeller Center (1931–40; for illustration see ROCKEFELLER), New York. Rockefeller Center was acclaimed as a pioneering concept of commercial, multilevel, superblock planning; its Art Deco skyscrapers, including the RCA Building, are grouped around a sunken plaza. Many are embellished with landscaped terraces. Here Harrison first displayed his characteristic support for a programme of modern art for the large complex. Here he also began a lifelong association with the Rockefeller family. Harrison and Abramovitz were later responsible for the more mundane towers (1959–74) on the Sixth Avenue side of the complex.

Max Abramovitz studied at the University of Illinois, Urbana–Champaign (BS 1929), Columbia University, New York (MS 1931), and at the Ecole des Beaux-Arts, Paris (1932–4). He joined Corbett, Harrison and MacMurray as a designer in 1934, then Harrison's new partnership in 1935 with J. André Fouilhoux (1879–1945), where he became a partner in 1941. Early buildings on which he worked with Harrison included the Rockefeller Apartments (1936) on West 54th Street, New York, and the highly original Trylon and Perisphere for the World's Fair (1939), New York. Both architects taught at the School of Architecture, Yale University, New Haven, CT (1939–42), transforming its programme from Beaux-Arts to modern. After Fouilhoux's death in 1945, the partnership of Harrison and Abramovitz was formed.

Harrison and Abramovitz were involved with some of New York's largest commissions: the United Nations headquarters (1947–53), Lincoln Center for the Performing Arts (1959–66) and the Nelson A. Rockefeller Empire

Harrison and Abramovitz: Lincoln Center for the Performing Arts, New York, 1959–66, showing (centre) the Metropolitan Opera House (1966) by Wallace K. Harrison and (lower right) the Philharmonic Hall (1962; now Avery Fisher Hall) by Max Abramovitz

State Mall, Albany (1967–71). For the United Nations complex (*see* GOVERNMENT BUILDINGS, fig. 2) Harrison became Director of Planning and Abramovitz Deputy Director, with a team of architects including Le Corbusier, who prepared the overall design with Oscar Niemeyer. The slender, 39-storey Secretariat block (1950) was one of New York's first glass curtain-wall skyscrapers. A further technical development made by the firm, seen first in Harrison's Alcoa Building (1953) in Pittsburgh, was the use of an external wall-cladding system of metal panels.

At Lincoln Center (see fig.) the partership undertook the master planning; Abramovitz also designed the Philharmonic Hall (1962; now Avery Fisher Hall) and Harrison the Metropolitan Opera House (1966). The complex included the New York State Theater (1964) by Philip Johnson, which together with Harrison and Abramovitz's buildings formed a central group around a plaza, as well as the Juilliard School of Music (1970) by Pietro Belluschi, two theatres (both 1958–64) by Eero Saarinen and the theatre museum library (1965) by Gordon Bunshaft. The three central buildings were in a monumental neo-classicist style that was criticized as retardataire. Harrison's work on the State Mall in Albany, which comprised several high-rise and other buildings grouped on a monumental platform, was also criticized for the heavy formalism of its buildings.

Throughout their partnership Harrison and Abramovitz undertook independent projects. Some of Harrison's smaller buildings allowed him more freedom to explore concerns of form: for example, the fish-shaped First Presbyterian church (1953–8), Stamford, CT, the various houses he designed for himself and for Nelson Rockefeller, and the Hall of Science (1963–4), Flushing, NY, all reveal a personal adaptation of modernism, some showing the influence of Alvar Aalto, others that of German Expressionism. Abramovitz built several important works for Brandeis University, Waltham, MA (1951–70), the University of Illinois, Urbana–Champaign (1963–9), and the University of Iowa, Iowa City (1969–72). His elliptical Phoenix Mutual Life Insurance building (1964), Hartford, CT, was one of the first buildings to use reflective glass cladding. He later designed some large commercial buildings in France. The increasing independence of the partners led to the dissolution of the partnership in 1976, when Abramovitz formed a new practice with Michael Harris (1907–82) and James Kingsland (*b* 1924). From 1976, Harrison, who received the Gold Medal of the American Institute of Architects in 1957, practised alone until his death.

WRITINGS

M. Abramovitz: *The Architecture of Max Abramovitz* (Urbana–Champaign, 1963)

BIBLIOGRAPHY

H. W. Wind: 'Architect', *New Yorker*, xxx (1954), no. 40, pp. 51–79; no. 41, pp. 51–85; no. 42, pp. 55–85

M. Tafuri and others: 'La città Americana dalla guerra civile al New Deal' (Bari, 1973; Eng. trans., Cambridge, MA, 1979), pp. 460–82

E. B. Young: *Lincoln Center: The Beginning of an Institution* (New York, 1980)

C. H. Krinsky: 'St Petersburg-on-the-Hudson: The Albany Mall', *Art the Ape of Nature* (New York, 1981), pp. 771–88

R. A. M. Stern, G. Gilmartin and T. Mellins: *New York 1930: Architecture and Urbanism between the Two World Wars* (New York, 1987), pp. 617–72, 727–55

V. Newhouse: *Wallace K. Harrison: Architect* (New York, 1989)

VICTORIA NEWHOUSE

Harsdorff, C(aspar) F(rederik) (*b* Copenhagen, 26 May 1735; *d* Copenhagen, 24 May 1799). Danish architect, interior designer and teacher. He was outstanding among the first group of architects trained at the Kongelige Danske Kunstakademi, Copenhagen, and won the gold medal in 1756. The ensuing travel scholarship allowed him to spend six years in Paris and Rome between 1757 and 1764. He was able to observe at first hand the radical change in architecture towards the strict and pure Neo-classicism to which he had been introduced by his teacher, Nicolas-Henri Jardin. On his return to Copenhagen, Harsdorff embarked on a successful career as a teacher, civil servant and practising architect; although economic and political upheavals restricted the number of his executed works, he was the leading figure in Danish architecture in the late 18th century. He was a member of the Academy by 1765 and was appointed professor in 1766 and court architect in 1770, playing a dominant role in the central building administration throughout his life.

Harsdorff's first major work was a sepulchral chapel (1766) at the medieval village church of Karise, Zealand, for the Lord Chamberlain, Count Adam Gottlob Moltke. With a few decisive alterations to the mediocre project already under construction, Harsdorff created a rich, solemn, centrally planned interior with a deeply coffered ceiling and a remarkably early use of Doric columns without base-mouldings. His masterpiece, the sepulchral chapel of Frederick V (begun 1774) at Roskilde Cathedral, was based on a project executed in 1763 while he was in Rome. A discreetly anonymous red-brick exterior, blending well with the Gothic body, houses a complex, monumental interior with a dark transverse vestibule, brilliantly lit side-spaces and a domed, barrel-vaulted Greek-cross chapel. The subtle but logical spacing of the Ionic order and the disciplined classical detailing in pale marble and plaster have the distinctly French air typical of all Harsdorff's work. As court architect, Harsdorff often created experimental ephemeral architecture in the many decorations required for festive public occasions. His love of the decorated façade was employed in several projects (some unexecuted), such as the giant Ionic screen (1774) to mask the front of Fredensborg Palace, Zealand, and the Doric temple-portico planned (1785) for his National Bank building next to the Copenhagen Exchange. Similar intentions are displayed in the Hercules Pavilion (1773) at the Rosenborg Gardens, where the crisply outlined front with a deep recess screened by columns is reminiscent of Claude-Nicolas Ledoux's pavilion (1770) at Louveciennes, and in the pedimented façade for his extension (1773–4) to the Royal Theatre, Copenhagen.

Harsdorff's unexecuted project (1780) for Amaliegade, Copenhagen, combining eight town houses in a palatial façade design, is unique in Danish architecture and recalls contemporary English solutions. His interest in the planning of town houses is also expressed at Kongens Nytorv

3–5 (1779–80), cleverly using a difficult site to demonstrate various façade configurations. His style became influential during the large-scale rebuilding necessary in Copenhagen after fires in 1795 and 1807. Examples include Peschier House (1796) with a pilaster façade and Erichsen House (1797–9) with a monumental, hexastyle Ionic portico unusual in Danish domestic architecture. Harsdorff adhered to the influences derived from his early travels while also keeping abreast of international developments. In the colonnade (1794) that connects two of the palaces in Amalienborg Square, Copenhagen, he demonstrated great sensitivity of proportion in the juxtaposition of his Neo-classical structure with the existing Rococo buildings, while displaying for the first time in Denmark full Greek Ionic capitals. His last and unexecuted project, the completion of the Frederikskirke, close to Amalienborg Palace, is a tribute by a devoted admirer to the Pantheon, Rome; the planned stern, cylindrical structure with low dome and pedimented portico survives in a fine model. Harsdorff was also active as an interior designer, especially in numerous remodellings for the royal family. His surviving interiors and furniture demonstrate architectural feeling and vigorous strength quite different from the more dainty and refined work of his contemporaries.

BIBLIOGRAPHY

N. L. Høyen: *Architektoniske værker af C. F. Harsdorff* [Architectural works by C. F. Harsdorff] (Copenhagen, 1859–71)

F. Weilbach: *Architekten C. F. Harsdorff* (Copenhagen, 1928)

C. Elling: 'Om Harsdorff kunst' [On Harsdorff's art], *Arkitekten* [Copenhagen], xlii/10 (1940), pp. 125–40

T. Clemmensen: *Møbler af N. H. Jardin, C. F. Harsdorff og J. C. Lillie* [Furniture by N. H. Jardin, C. F. Harsdorff and J. C. Lillie] (Copenhagen, 1973)

Arkitekten C. F. Harsdorff, 1735–1799 (exh. cat., ed. E. Hiort; Copenhagen, Kstindustmus., 1985)

HANNE RAABYEMAGLE

Hart, Abraham van der (*b* 27 May 1747; *d* Amsterdam, 1 Feb 1820). Dutch architect. He trained in the circle of the carpenters' guild in Amsterdam, of which both his father and grandfather were members. He must have been considered a good designer when he was still very young, for he was appointed city architect of Amsterdam in 1777, an influential post that he held until his death. Information about his work in Amsterdam is derived from numerous drawings that he prepared for the city, and particularly from his reports (1777–1820) for the public works department, which have been preserved. In his capacity as city architect, he designed, among other things, city decorations and institutions. He also designed some large houses, particularly in Haarlem, although little is known about his work outside Amsterdam. In its day his New Workhouse (1779), Amsterdam, enjoyed a degree of fame abroad as well as in the Netherlands. With this building he introduced in his own work the severe Neo-classicism of the second half of the 18th century. He used this style again for the Roman Catholic Girls' Home (1784), which has a harmonious façade with round-arched windows on the ground floor. The storeys above are linked by a giant order of pilasters. Apart from the pediment over the central projection, there are no other classicizing motifs.

Van der Hart achieved great fame not only with his up-to-date facilities in the field of hygiene, but also with the practical layouts of his buildings. This approach is apparent in his two designs for theatres, where he experimented with acoustics. His interior designs show a clear development as a result of his endeavours to apply new stylistic trends from abroad. His richest interiors date from the last decade of the 18th century and the first decade of the 19th; a fine example (1793) can be seen at the Rijksmuseum, Amsterdam. English influences are apparent, although he also drew from other sources. At the beginning of the 19th century an innovation may be noted in his omission of such classicizing details as pilasters and pediments, exemplified by the Van Brienen almshouses (1803) in Amsterdam. On the other hand, a marked classicist tendency returned, echoing to some extent the mature Dutch classicism of the 17th century; this trend is particularly evident in the house (1804) designed for Willem Philip Barnaart in Haarlem, with its stone central projection and Ionic pilasters, crowned with a pediment. The interior of this house is among the best to have been produced in the Empire style in the Netherlands.

Van der Hart's later designs, in a modest Neo-classical style, were clearly influenced by the French architect Jean Thomas Thibaut (1757–1826), who acted as court architect to Louis Bonaparte, King of Holland. Another later project was his design for a monument on Mont Cenis, near Lanslebourg, France, submitted to an international competition, which members of the Dutch Institute of Art and Science entered at the invitation of the French government. Among the few surviving drawings by van der Hart is a design (c. 1800) comprising a colossal pyramid with a temple at its base and a Gothic-style hall inside. This occupies a special place among Dutch architectural designs from the beginning of the 19th century, but it is unlikely that the idea for the pyramid was his.

BIBLIOGRAPHY
C. A. van Swighem: *Abraham van der Hart, 1747–1820: Architect-/Stadsbouwmeester van Amsterdam* (Amsterdam, 1965)

PAUL H. REM

Hart, James McDougal (*b* Kilmarnock, Strathclyde, 10 May 1828; *d* Brooklyn, NY, 24 Oct 1901). American painter of Scottish birth. He moved to America with his family in 1831. He grew up in Albany, NY, where he and his older brother, William Hart (1823–94), also a painter, were apprenticed to a coachmaker as decorators. He produced some amateur portraits during this time and cultivated his natural talent for landscape painting. In 1850 he went to study in Munich and Düsseldorf, where his principal teacher was Johann Wilhelm Schirmer; in 1853 he returned to Albany, exhibiting for the first time at the National Academy of Design, New York. By 1857 he had established himself in New York, and he lived there for the rest of his life.

Hart rose to prominence during the 1860s and 1870s, when there was a vogue for his landscapes and pastoral cattle scenes. His landscapes are invariably endowed with tranquillity and a romantically poetic sense of time and place, as in *On the Lake Shore* (1864; Boston, MA, Mus. F.A.) and *Pastoral Scene* (1876; New York, Met.). Such pastoral cattle scenes as *Threatening Weather* (1875; Boston, MA, priv. col.) attribute identifiable human emotions to the bovine creatures, frequently hinting at the moralistic themes that were then popular. In 1858 Hart was elected

an associate and in 1859 a full member of the National Academy of Design. He subsequently served for three years as its vice-president and, among other places, exhibited there regularly from 1853 to 1900. His sister, Julie Hart Beers Kempson (1835–1913), was a professional landscape painter.

BIBLIOGRAPHY
H. T. Tuckerman: *Book of the Artists: American Artist Life* (New York, 1867/*R* 1966)
G. W. Sheldon: *American Paintings* (New York, 1879)

JOHN DRISCOLL

Hart, Solomon Alexander (*b* Plymouth, April 1806; *d* London, 11 June 1881). English painter. His father, Samuel Hart, was a pupil of Abraham Daniel (*d* 1806), an engraver, miniature painter and jeweller. Hart moved to London *c*. 1820. His family could not afford to apprentice him to the line engraver Charles Warren, but in 1823 he entered the Royal Academy Schools. While studying there he painted miniatures and coloured theatrical prints for a living, exhibiting his first picture, a miniature, in 1826. In 1830 his *Interior of a Jewish Synagogue at the Time of the Reading of the Law* (1830; London, Tate) was purchased by the collector Robert Vernon. Not wishing to become a 'painter of merely religious ceremonies', Hart began to execute historical subjects, often taken from Shakespeare or, as with *Richard Coeur de Lion and the Soldan Saladin* (1835; Liverpool, Walker A.G.), from Walter Scott's novels. In 1835 he was elected ARA and in 1840 he became the first Jewish RA.

In 1841–2 Hart visited Italy and subsequently painted many scenes of Italian interiors, e.g. the *Interior of the Synagogue at Livorno (Simchat Torah)* (*see* JEWISH ART, fig. 20). He received several important portrait commissions from Jewish institutions, including that for *Sir Anthony de Rothschild* (exh. RA 1856) for the Jews' Hospital, London, and he also contributed drawings to Charles Knight's illustrated publications. Hart's historical and scriptural paintings show great technical skill and attention to detail, but although he continued to exhibit until his death, the quality of his work and reputation declined in later years. Between 1854 and 1863 Hart was professor of painting at the Royal Academy, and from 1865 until 1881 he was the librarian there.

WRITINGS
A. Brodie, ed.: *The Reminiscences of Solomon Alex. Hart, R.A.* (London, 1882)

BIBLIOGRAPHY
DNB; Foskett
Anglo-Jewish Exhibition, 1851–1951 (exh. cat., ed. J. Leftwich; London, Ben Uri A.G., 1951)
C. Roth: *Jewish Art: An Illustrated History* (London, 1971)

ALISON INGLIS

Hartford. North American city and capital of the state of Connecticut. It was founded in 1635 at a site on the west shore of the Connecticut River and is *c*. 50 km inland from New Haven. The city has a population of *c*. 136,000. Its broad range of architecture reflects the city's history. The Neo-classical Old State House (1792–6; now a museum) by Charles Bulfinch is in City Hall Square, laid out in 1637. Ithiel Town designed Christ Church Cathedral (1842–4; roof pinnacles, 1902; later additions), a notable Gothic Revival structure. Town also designed the Wadsworth

Atheneum (1842–4) with his partner A. J. Davis, which houses the American collection of DANIEL WADSWORTH; the paintings include works by John Trumbull and Thomas Cole. The museum also contains the J. Pierpont Morgan Collection of bronzes, Italian Renaissance objects, 17th-century silver and 18th-century porcelain, and the Wallace Nutting Collection of early American furniture, Central and South American art, and European paintings from the 14th to 20th century. Also in Gothic Revival is the Trinity College Group (1873–6) by William Burges; in the late 20th century the Mathematics, Computing and Engineering Center (1991) by Cesar Pelli completed the quadrangle proposed by Burges. The six-storey Cheney Building (1875–6) by H. H. Richardson is based on the arcaded English commercial style of the 1860s. The State Capitol (1878–82) by Richard Michell Upjohn is a classical model with motifs borrowed from contemporary Gothic Revival ecclesiastical architecture. Albert Kahn's inspired functionalism can be seen in the Test Laboratory of Pratt & Whitney Aircraft Company (1935). Works of the 1960s include Harrison and Abramowitz's Phoenix Mutual Insurance Company building, one of the first buildings to use reflective glass cladding, and I. M. Pei's Busnell Tower (1969). Other notable 20th-century buildings include several by Skidmore, Owings & Merrill: the Connecticut General Life Insurance Company building (1955–7), with interior court gardens containing *The Family* (1956–7), a massive sculptural group by Isamu Noguchi; the Aetna Building (1980), the state's tallest; and Goodwin Square (1988), a 30-storey office and hotel tower. The University of Hartford Library (1988) by Tai Soo Kim created a campus centre.

BIBLIOGRAPHY
'Hartford's Not-so-steady Habits', *Archit. Rec.*, clxxvi, pp. 100–02
J. Johnson: 'Presence of Stone', *Landscape Archit.*, lxxvi (1986), pp. 64–9
G. E. Andrews and D. F. Ransom: *Structures and Styles: Guided Tours of Hartford Architecture* (Hartford, 1988)

ANN McKEIGHAN LEE

Hartigan, Grace (*b* Newark, NJ, 28 March 1922). American painter. After studying briefly with local Newark painter Isaac Lane Muse (*b* 1905), Hartigan moved to New York in 1945. There she was profoundly influenced by Jackson Pollock's one-man exhibition held in 1948 at the Betty Parsons Gallery, and her earliest works (1948–52) were large-scale abstract canvases resembling those of Pollock and Willem de Kooning. These works were included in the important *New Talent* (1950; New York, Kootz Gal.) and *Ninth Street* (1951; New York, 60 E. Ninth Street) exhibitions. In 1952 Hartigan departed from non-representational art and made free variations upon Old Master paintings, as well as collaborating with the poet Frank O'Hara to produce 12 poem/paintings entitled *Oranges*. These experiments culminated in a series of imaginative portraits, shop window scenes, still-lifes and cityscapes created between 1953 and 1960; in works such as *City Life* (1956; Washington, DC, N. Trust Hist. Preserv.) Hartigan captured the excitement and complexity of modern urban life while embodying the gestural style of the Abstract Expressionists.

In 1959 Hartigan married and moved to Baltimore, which she made her permanent home, and continued to expand her range of subjects and styles. Her themes varied from movie stars to modern interpretations of historical figures, such as the foppish *Young Louis* (1983; New York, Met.). Her style alternated between lyrical and colourful stained canvases and deliberately complex and discordant brush-drawn works, while always exhibiting Abstract Expressionist tendencies toward projecting surface, overall design and discovery during the painting process and consistently exploring modern views of history, celebrity, urban existence and other concerns of our age. Generally associated with the second generation of Abstract Expressionists, Hartigan, in both her methods and her themes, took her art well beyond the limits that such a description would suggest.

BIBLIOGRAPHY
J. T. Soby: 'Interview with Grace Hartigan', *Sat. Rev.*, xl/8 (1957), pp. 26–7
R. S. Mattison: 'Grace Hartigan: Painting her own History', *A. Mag.*, lix (1985), pp. 66–72
A. Schoenfeld: 'Grace Hartigan in the Early 1950s: Some Sources, Influences, and the Avant-garde', *A. Mag.*, lx (1986), pp. 84–8

ROBERT SALTONSTALL MATTISON

Hartley, Marsden (*b* Lewiston, ME, 4 Jan 1877; *d* Ellsworth, ME, 2 Sept 1943). American painter and writer. He spent part of his youth in Cleveland, OH, where in 1896 he studied art with a local painter, John Semon. After study at the Cleveland School of Art (1898–9), he entered the Chase School in New York (1899) and the National Academy of Design (1900–04). From 1900 he regularly spent his summers in Maine, a state for which he maintained an enduring passion. At the end of autumn 1907 he moved from Maine to Boston, MA. By this stage his painting was progressing from an American form of Impressionism to a type of Neo-Impressionism. Partly inspired by illustrations in the German satirical magazine *Jugend*, he emulated the divisionist technique of Giovanni Segantini, for example in *Mountain Lake in the Autumn* (1908; Washington, DC, Phillips Col.).

In Boston, Hartley saw the Post-Impressionist work of Maurice Prendergast, who encouraged him and shared his enthusiasm for the art of Cézanne. Hartley moved in spring of 1909 to New York, where he mixed in avant-garde circles, and in May he had a one-man exhibition at the 291 gallery, run by Alfred Stieglitz. Stieglitz's support and tastes had a great impact on his development, but the immediate influence on sombre landscapes such as the *Dark Mountain* (1909; Chicago, IL, A. Inst.) was the art of Albert Pinkham Ryder.

Inspired by the introduction to European modernism that Stieglitz gave him in 1912, Hartley went to live in Paris, where he became friends with Gertrude Stein. The earliest of his paintings in Paris reveal his interest in Cézanne, Matisse and Picasso, whose work he had seen at Stein's home. The bright colours and decorative patterned fabrics employed in some of his still-lifes reflect the influence of Matisse's work. However, he soon became increasingly involved with his new discoveries: mysticism, the art of Vasily Kandinsky, and primitive objects illustrated in the almanac *Der Blaue Reiter*.

Hartley was very interested in the theories and work of Kandinsky, whom he met on travelling to Germany in 1913, along with Franz Marc and other avant-garde artists.

Although Hartley celebrated pre-war military pageantry in Berlin, he rejected the Futurists' admiration of military force in favour of pacifist Native American themes, which he depicted in *Indian Fantasy* (1914; Raleigh, NC, Mus. A.). He also enjoyed the city's homosexual subculture, falling in love with a Prussian officer, whose death he memorialized in 1914 in a series of emblematic abstractions influenced by Synthetic Cubism, including *Portrait of a German Officer* (New York, Met.; see fig.).

Forced by the war to return to the USA, Hartley lived a peripatetic existence. During summer 1916 he worked in Provincetown on Cape Cod, MA, where he produced geometric abstractions based on sailboat motifs, for example *Movement No. 9* (1916; Minneapolis, MN, Walker A. Cent.). In winter 1916–17 he stayed in Bermuda. From then until his return to Europe in 1921 he worked in Maine, New York, New Mexico and Gloucester, MA. During this period he abandoned abstraction and returned to landscape and still-life. He briefly experimented with painting on glass in 1917 and from 1918 produced a series of pastels and oil paintings of the New Mexico landscape, for example *Landscape, New Mexico* (1919–20; New York, Whitney). From 1925 to 1929 he painted in the south of France, basing himself at Vence and Aix-en-Provence,

Marsden Hartley: *Portrait of a German Officer*, oil on canvas, 1.74×1.06 m, 1914 (New York, Metropolitan Museum of Art)

where he emulated the work of Cézanne in studies such as *Trees and Rocks* (silverpoint on prepared paper, 1927; Ann Arbor, U. MI, Mus. A.).

In the 1930s Hartley painted in Mexico, Bavaria, Gloucester, Bermuda and Nova Scotia, before returning in 1937 to Maine, where, except for stays in New York, he lived and worked for the rest of his life. He began an important series of expressionist memory portraits in 1938, including *Adelard the Drowned, Master of the Phantom* (1938–9; Minneapolis, U. MN, A. Mus.) on the island of Vinalhaven, ME, and continued to develop his interest in the figure. His attachment to nature, and in particular to the Maine landscape and seascape, inspired many of his late works, such as *Mountain Katahdin* (1942; Washington, DC, N.G.).

WRITINGS
Adventures in the Arts: Informal Chapters on Painters, Vaudeville and Poets (New York, 1921/*R* 1972)
Twenty-five Poems (Paris, 1923)
Androscoggin (Portland, 1940)
Sea Burial (Portland, 1941)
H. W. Wells, ed.: *Marsden Hartley: Selected Poems* (New York, 1945)
W. I. Homer, ed.: *Heart's Gate: Letters between Marsden Hartley and Horace Traubel, 1906–1915* (Highlands, 1982)
G. R. Scott, ed.: *On Art by Marsden Hartley* (New York, 1982)
——: *The Collected Poems of Marsden Hartley, 1904–1943* (Santa Rosa, 1987)

BIBLIOGRAPHY
E. McCausland: *Marsden Hartley* (Minneapolis, 1952)
R. Burlingame: *Marsden Hartley: A Study of his Life and Creative Achievement* (diss., Providence, Brown U., 1953)
G. Levin: 'Marsden Hartley, Kandinsky and Der Blaue Reiter', *A. Mag.*, lii/3 (1977), pp. 156–60
——: 'Marsden Hartley and the European Avant-garde', *A. Mag.*, liv/1 (1979), pp. 158–63
——: 'Hidden Symbolism in Marsden Hartley's Military Pictures', *A. Mag.*, liv/2 (1979), pp. 154–8
B. Haskell: *Marsden Hartley* (New York, 1980)
G. Levin: 'Marsden Hartley and Mysticism', *A. Mag.*, lx/3 (1985), pp. 16–21
——: 'Photography's 'Appeal' to Marsden Hartley', *Yale U. Lib. Gaz.*; lxvii (1993), pp. 14–42

GAIL LEVIN

Hartman, Viktor (Aleksandrovich). See GARTMAN, VIKTOR.

Hartmann, Meister (*fl* 1417–28). German sculptor. He is mentioned in the workshop records of Ulm Minster between 1417 and 1421. The sculptures he was paid for in the records are identical with parts of the surviving figure programme in the west porch of Ulm Minster; the payments of 1418 and 1419 appear to involve the sculptures on the piers (the *Virgin*, SS *Martin, Anthony* and *John the Baptist*), those of 1420–21 the 19 figures on the front wall of the narthex (the *Virgin*, six female *Saints*, the *Twelve Apostles*; see ULM, fig. 3). However, the *Twelve Apostles* and the *Virgin* for which Hartmann was paid in 1420 are not—as assumed by Habicht—the archivolt figures on the west porch, which are now attributed to the Master of the Kreuzwinkel (*fl* 1387–91), but probably the lost *Apostle* cycle inside the minster, along the nave piers. Hartmann's name does not occur in the records after 1421, although in 1427 he was mentioned in the Ulm taxation list, and in 1428 he was granted the freedom of the city.

The works attributed to Hartmann show individuality and are characterized by decoratively arranged, limply hanging garments. The female heads have round faces framed by wavy strands of hair, with narrow mouths, high-arched eyebrows and strongly emphasized, often half-closed lids. Fluctuations in quality indicate the work of several assistants. Hartmann's style, which is unique to Ulm, has been traced to the central Rhineland, Cologne and even Prague, but its exact origins are unknown. Fine examples of related sculpture are found in other Swabian work: for example the wooden figures on the Dornstadt altarpiece (Stuttgart, Württemberg. Landesmus., Old Castle) repeat the types of Hartmann's figures at Ulm.

BIBLIOGRAPHY
C. Habicht: *Ulmer Münster-Plastik aus der Zeit 1391–1421* (Darmstadt, 1911)
J. Baum: 'Der bildnerische Schmuck des westlichen Münsterportales', *Ulm & Oberschwaben*, xxv (1927), pp. 33–42
G. Otto: *Die Ulmer Plastik des frühen 15. Jahrhunderts* (Tübingen, 1927)
G. Ringshausen: 'Die Archivoltfiguren des Ulmer Westportals', *600 Jahre Ulmer Münster. Festschrift*, ed. H. E. Specker and R. Wortmann, xix of *Forsch. Gesch. Stadt Ulm* (Ulm, 1977), pp. 209–41

CLAUDIA LICHTE

Hartmann, (Carl) Sadakichi (*b* Nagasaki, 8 Nov 1867; *d* St Petersburg, FL, 21 Nov 1944). American writer and lecturer of Japanese birth. He was born to a Japanese mother and German father and brought up by relatives in Hamburg and, from 1882, in Philadelphia, where he studied art. Under the influence of the poet Walt Whitman, he decided to become a writer. Later he worked as a journalist in Boston, where he launched a literary magazine. When publication ceased, he moved to New York and began his freelance career.

Hartmann's first article for *Camera Notes* was published in 1898 by Alfred Stieglitz, and he made regular contributions to *Camera Work* until 1904, but thereafter he published wherever he could and became a lecturer. He was one of the best-known spokesmen for photography in America, criticizing any work that did not make use of the fundamental qualities of the medium. A severe judge of early American painting, he singled out only Gilbert Stuart and John Vanderlyn for praise. Among later 19th-century American painters he preferred followers of the Barbizon school. His impact as a critic had lessened by the 1920s, although his views on the standards of 20th-century painting and photography attracted renewed attention in the 1970s.

WRITINGS
Shakespeare in Art (Boston, 1900)
Japanese Art (Boston, 1904)
A History of American Art, 2 vols (Boston, 1902, rev. 1932)
H. W. Lawton and G. Knox, eds: *The Valiant Knights of Daguerre* (Berkeley, 1978)

BIBLIOGRAPHY
DAB
G. Fowler: *Minutes of the Last Meeting* (New York, 1954)

ALAN M. FERN

Hart Nibbrig, F. *See* NIBBRIG, F. HART.

Hartung, Hans [Heinrich] **(Ernst)** (*b* Leipzig, 21 Sept 1904; *d* Antibes, 7 Dec 1989). French painter, draughtsman, printmaker and photographer of German birth. Early in his life he developed an interest in music, astronomy, philosophy and religion, but eventually above all in painting. His first enthusiasm was for the work of Rembrandt, then in 1921–2 for that of Lovis Corinth, Max Slevogt and the Expressionists, in particular Oskar Kokoschka and Emil Nolde. In 1922, before he knew anything about abstract art, he painted a series of completely abstract watercolours of a loose, non-formal kind, followed in 1923–4 by a number of abstract drawings in charcoal and chalk, for example *Scène goyesque III* (see exh. cat., no. 14). In 1924 he became a student of both philosophy and art history at Leipzig University and of painting at the Kunstakademie, and was present in 1925 at a lecture by Vasily Kandinsky, his first contact with the abstract movement. Although he was advised to study at the Bauhaus, he chose instead to go to the Kunstakademie in Dresden, where the teaching followed traditional lines. At the Internationale Kunstausstellung in Dresden in 1926 he saw for more or less the first time modern paintings from outside Germany, and in particular works by Henri Rousseau, Picasso, Georges Rouault, Henri Matisse and Georges Braque.

In 1926, after a summer visit to Italy, Hartung went to Paris to deepen his knowledge of contemporary art and, apart from a few journeys, remained in France until 1932. During these years he frequented museums and exhibitions and for a few weeks attended the painting academies of André Lhôte and Fernand Léger, but he had almost no contact with other artists. He made copies of works by Goya, El Greco, Frans Hals, Matisse and others, and produced paintings in the manner of Vincent van Gogh and Picasso. In 1927 he spent some time at Leucate, near Perpignan, where the southern landscape enhanced his interest in van Gogh and Paul Cézanne, but where he became especially preoccupied with Cubism and its treatment of space; he made landscapes of the beach, composed of stylized planes, lines and rhythms, and with proportions based on the golden section. He was obsessed with a search for harmony through the discovery of the fundamental laws of proportion, colour and movement, and spent the summer term of 1928 at the Kunstakademie in Munich studying painting techniques.

In 1929 Hartung married the artist Anna-Eva Bergman and visited Norway with her in 1932. Late in that year they went to live on Minorca, where in the next two years he started to break away from Cubism and develop a more instinctive style based on his abstract watercolours and drawings of 1922–4. In 1934 they were obliged to leave Minorca after their income was cut off by the Nazis, and they went first to Paris, then Stockholm, and in 1935 to Berlin, where they hoped to re-establish their financial position. Hartung, however, found himself under police surveillance, and in October they decided to leave Germany and settle permanently in Paris.

In the years approaching World War II, Hartung became a friend of Jean Hélion and Henri Goetz and met Kandinsky, Piet Mondrian, Alberto Magnelli, Joan Miró and Alexander Calder. He exhibited regularly at the Salon des Surindépendants but continued to be in a very precarious financial situation. In his drawings and paintings (the latter made only when he could afford canvas) he worked with free graphic forms and patches of black or colour to achieve spontaneous expression, for example in

Hans Hartung: *T. 1951-12*, oil on canvas, 965×1460 mm, 1951 (Basle, Kunstmuseum)

T. 1935-1 (oil on canvas, 1935; Paris, Pompidou). In 1938 the German Embassy confiscated his passport, and he and Anna-Eva Bergman divorced. Julio González invited him to work in his studio, where he made two welded iron sculptures under González's guidance; in 1939 he married González's daughter Roberta. After the outbreak of World War II he served in the Foreign Legion (1939–40) and with the Free French (1943–4), when he was wounded in action and had a leg amputated.

At the end of 1945 Hartung returned to Paris and resumed painting. In 1947 he had his first one-man exhibition. His post-war paintings and drawings were initially related to his works of the late 1930s but were less spontaneous and very complex and aggressive, with violent clashes of heavy black lines. Their gestural, graphic character, seen for example in *Painting 1948* (New York, MOMA) or *T. 1951-12* (Basle, Kstmus.; see fig.), made them forerunners of action painting, and he became associated with Gérard Schneider, Pierre Soulages and others who had similar interests. In 1952–4 his pictures began to be more static and serene, and the clarification of his work led in 1954–9 to a series of paintings with clusters of large sweeping rhythmical brushstrokes on more or less monochrome backgrounds, such as *T. 1956-14* (Paris, Pompidou). His works of 1957–61 also included a number of pastels. By this time he was one of the leading painters of the Ecole de Paris. In 1961 he started a new period of work, characterized by scratching rhythmical lines into dark paint that was still wet, as in *T. 1963–R6* (1963; London, Tate). This also led, from 1962 to 1967,

to a series of paintings, some fairly large, with blurred-edged expanses of black or dark blue paint sprayed over almost the entire surface and with few if any graphic elements. Among his pictures of *c.* 1971–3 are some with patches of brilliant colours over which lines were drawn that either followed the direction of the forms or cut across them. His later work tended to become more varied, drawing upon all his earlier abstract styles and combining them in different ways. He also made engravings and lithographs, and took photographs that often echo the same abstract and almost Tachist elements, for example *Watermark* (1977; see exh. cat., no. 248). From *c.* 1972 he and Anna-Eva Bergman, whom he re-married, divided their time between Paris and Antibes.

WRITINGS

Autoportrait (Paris, 1976)

BIBLIOGRAPHY

M. Rousseau, J. J. Sweeney and O. Domnick: *Hans Hartung* (Stuttgart, 1949)
P. Descargues: *Hartung* (Paris, 1977)
Hans Hartung: Malerei, Zeichnung, Photographie (exh. cat. by J. Merkert, Munich, Staatsgal. Mod. Kst, 1981)

RONALD ALLEY

Hartung, Karl (*b* Hamburg, 2 May 1908; *d* W. Berlin, 17 July 1967). German sculptor. After completing his apprenticeship as a wood-engraver and attending the Kunstgewerbeschule in Hamburg, he continued his studies in Paris (1929–32). At this time the artists who most influenced his approach to and expression of three-dimensional form were Charles Despiau, Emile-Antoine Bourdelle and Aristide Maillol. Maillol, in particular, and his view of sculpture as a work of art developing outwards from the inside, was to remain an important influence on Hartung's oeuvre. During his period in Florence (1932–3) Hartung explored the work of Donatello. He found especially fascinating the way that in the figurative sculptures the skeleton was apparent under the soft flesh. His encounter with Etruscan sculpture was also influential; its tendency to use representational forms derived from abstract symbols might have been a factor in Hartung's future development. Although he had been working in a mainly representational manner, after his return to Hamburg in 1935 he produced his first abstract forms. The way that Hartung created hollows and fissures in his sculptures—and their softness and smoothness—recall classical sculptors of the modern period, such as Brancusi, Arp and Henry Moore. Hartung would have encountered these sculptors' works during visits abroad. Abstract works such as *Hollowed-out Form* (1935; see Linfert, no. 1) fulfilled his objective of constructing a sculpture that, in his own words, 'was brimful of form from the inside outwards'. From 1936 he settled in Berlin.

Throughout his work Hartung treated the formal multiplicity of organic shapes as the germ of his creativity and as a continuous source of associations. Thus, parallel with his abstract patterns, he produced other works that unequivocally related to the human figure, while reducing it to its essential elements (e.g. *Large Standing Figure*, 1957; see Linfert, no. 9). An important aspect of Hartung's sculptures was his sensitive response to the material from which the form appeared to grow, whether bronze, iron, marble, granite or wood. Accordingly, his approach should be described as deductive rather than abstract. His patterns, which were reminiscent of branches, bark or fragments of stone, inextricably combined found and fashioned material. These works showed Hartung's concern not only with his material's inner structure but also with variations in surface structure; this became evident from the mid-1950s. Until then he divided up the sculptures' outer surfaces with smooth concavities, but thereafter he began to give them a slit-open, disintegrated and weather-beaten look, as if they had suffered long exposure to the elements. Hartung's drawings related to his sculptures; the coral-like drawings produced at this period illustrated this development, which, in a more controlled form, also characterized the artist's later oeuvre.

BIBLIOGRAPHY
Karl Hartung (exh. cat., W. Berlin, Haus Waldsee, 1952)
Karl Hartung (exh. cat., Hannover, Kestner-Ges., 1953)
C. Linfert: 'Karl Hartung', *Junge Kst*, lix–lx (1959), pp. 9–32
W. Hess: 'Karl Hartung', *Das Kstwk*, xiv/9 (1961), pp. 17–31
BEATRICE V. BISMARCK

Hartwell & Richardson. American architectural partnership established in 1881 by Henry Walker Hartwell (*b* Boston, MA, 4 Sept 1833; *d* Waltham, MA, 30 Dec 1919) and William Cummings Richardson (*b* Concord, NH, 12 March 1854; *d* Newton, MA, 17 Oct 1935). Hartwell began his architectural training in 1851 in the Boston office of Joseph E. Billings and Hammatt Billings (1818–75) and established his own practice in Boston in 1856.

Working alone until 1869 and then in partnership with other Boston architects, including Albert E. Swasey jr and George Tilden (1845–1919), until 1881, Hartwell produced a series of polychromatic Gothic Revival and Queen Anne style public buildings and churches south of Boston. In 1881 he received a commission to design a town hall for Belmont, MA, and formed a permanent partnership with William Richardson, a younger architect who had trained at the Massachusetts Institute of Technology. This partnership brought a new exuberance to their work and marked the beginning of the most productive period in both men's careers. Within the firm Hartwell was responsible for construction and management, and Richardson for design. The Queen Anne-style brick and terracotta Belmont Town Hall (1881–2) and Odd Fellows Hall (1884) in Cambridge, MA, are among their most original non-residential designs, while in Boston the First Spiritual Temple (1884) shows the increasing influence of H. H. Richardson on their work. Their best residential designs were graceful Shingle-style houses near Boston with elaborate interior woodwork, for example 37 Lancaster Street (1887–8), Cambridge. In the 1890s the firm designed some Colonial Revival houses, but specialized increasingly in classical-style public schools, most of which lacked the exuberance of their earlier buildings. In 1895 the English architect James Driver (1859–1923) joined the firm. After Hartwell's death in 1919 and Driver's departure in 1921 Richardson continued to practice as Hartwell & Richardson until his own death.

BIBLIOGRAPHY
S. Maycock Vogel: 'Hartwell and Richardson: An Introduction to their Work', *J. Soc. Archit. Historians*, xxxii/2 (1973), pp. 132–46
SUSAN E. MAYCOCK

Hartzer, Ferdinand (Carl Emmanuel) (*b* Celle, 22 June 1838; *d* Berlin, 27 Oct 1906). German sculptor. He first studied sculpture at Hannover (1854–9) and then at Munich under Max von Widnmann. In 1861 he continued his studies in Dresden where Ernst Friedrich August Rietschel, Ernst Julius Hähnel and Johannes Schilling were then training the next generation of sculptors. Hartzer left for Italy in 1866 and in 1869 he settled in Berlin. There he received his first important commissions through King William I of Prussia who had bought an early work *Amor with a Mask of Satyr* (plaster, *c.* 1870; Celle, Bomann-Mus.). He contributed eight large figures and some reliefs to the decorative programme of the Alte Nationalgalerie in Berlin (1872–5), though some of these were later removed. Over the following years he made numerous monuments of scholars, politicians and historical figures (e.g. the *St Bernward* monument, bronze, 1893; Hildesheim, nr Cathedral). He also sculpted such thematic monuments as *History* in Berlin and the two versions of *Victory* for sites in Silesia. As with his allegorical figures (e.g. the relief *Hope*, marble, *c.* 1880; Berlin, Dreifaltigkeits-Friedhof II, Mausoleum Schulze-Zitelmann), Hartzer modelled these monuments in a classical style, while his portraits and statues of contemporaries were executed in a realistic manner that sensitively expressed the mood of the sitter (e.g. *Georg Waitz*, marble, 1887; U. Göttingen, Aulagebäude). Indeed, portraiture was central to his work.

BIBLIOGRAPHY
M. Arndt and K. Arndt: *Der Bildhauer Ferdinand Hartzer, 1838–1906* (Berlin, 1986)
Ethos und Pathos: Die Berliner Bildhauerschule, 1786–1914, 2 vols (exh. cat., ed. P. Bloch, S. Einholz and J. von Simson; Berlin, Staatl. Museen Preuss. Kultbes., 1990), esp. *Ausstellungskatalog*, pp. 116–18

HANNELORE HÄGELE

Haruhiro. *See* ISODA KORYŪSAI.

Harunobu. *See* SUZUKI HARUNOBU.

Harushige. *See* SHIBA KŌKAN.

Harvey, Sir George (*b* St Ninian's, nr Stirling, 1 Feb 1806; *d* Edinburgh, 22 Jan 1876). Scottish painter. He studied at the Trustees' Academy in Edinburgh, first under Andrew Wilson and from 1826 under William Allan. He established his reputation with a series of paintings of scenes from the history of the Scottish Presbyterians, the Covenanters. The first of these, *Covenanters' Preaching* (Glasgow, A.G. & Mus.), was exhibited in 1830 and was followed by *Covenanters' Baptism* (1831; Aberdeen, A.G.), *Battle of Drumclog* (1836; Glasgow, A.G. & Mus.) and *Covenanters' Communion* (1840; Edinburgh, N.G.). These derive from David Wilkie's narrative history paintings, particularly the pioneering *Preaching of Knox before the Lords of Congregation, 10th June 1559* (1832; London, Tate), for which Wilkie had produced studies since at least 1822 and which was itself influenced by Walter Scott's novels. As in Wilkie's *Preaching of Knox*, the theme of Harvey's pictures also reflects the developing religious crisis in Scotland that culminated in the Disruption of the Church of Scotland in 1843. While his studies (Stirling, Smith A.G. & Mus.) are lucid and unsentimental, the paintings themselves are marred by an attempt to describe simple piety in the language of Wilkie's early, comic genre. Throughout the 1840s and 1850s Harvey continued to paint genre pictures in the manner of Wilkie (e.g. *School Skailin'*, 1846, and *The Bowlers*, 1850; both Edinburgh, N.G.), but in the latter part of his career he concentrated increasingly on landscapes, especially of the Highlands, for example *Sheep-shearing* (exh. RSA 1860; Stirling, Smith A.G. & Mus.). He was a founder-member of the Royal Scottish Academy and became its fourth president in 1864.

BIBLIOGRAPHY
J. Caw: *Scottish Painting Past and Present* (Edinburgh and London, 1908), pp. 112–14
D. Irwin and F. Irwin: *Scottish Painters at Home and Abroad, 1700–1900* (London, 1975)
Sir George Harvey PRSA (exh. cat. by A. Lindesay, Stirling, Smith A.G. & Mus. [1985])
D. Macmillan: *Scottish Art, 1460–1990* (Edinburgh, 1990), p. 192

DUNCAN MACMILLAN

Harvey, William (*b* Newcastle upon Tyne, 13 July 1798; *d* Richmond, London, 13 Jan 1866). English illustrator and engraver. He was the last pupil of Thomas Bewick, from whom he learnt the art of wood-engraving, assisting on the illustrations for the famous edition of the *Fables of Aesop* (Newcastle upon Tyne, 1818). In 1817 he moved to London, working in the studio of Benjamin Robert Haydon; his large woodcut of his master's history painting, the *Assassination of Dentatus* (1806–9; Marquess of Normanby priv. col.), completed in 1821, was much admired.

From 1824 he effectively abandoned wood-engraving and concentrated on designing illustrations on wood and cooper for various books ranging from editions of the Bible and Shakespeare to contemporary works, including such scientific publications as the *Gardens and Menagerie of the Zoological Society* (Chiswick, 1830–31). He was meticulous in the accuracy of his designs, and his early training gave him rare insight into the requirements of engravers, making him popular with publishers and printers alike. As the fashion for illustrated books developed, Harvey's career prospered. His masterpieces were *Northcote's Fables* (London, 1828–33) and Edward William Lane's edition of the *Arabian Nights* (London, 1839–41), both published by Charles Knight. The latter especially was praised for its grandeur and historical fidelity. A draughtsman of great facility, he completed over 3000 drawings on wood and copperplate, though later in life his designs became somewhat mannered. He played a major part in the progress of illustrated books in England.

BIBLIOGRAPHY
F. W. Fairholt: Obituary, *A. J.* [London], v (1866), pp. 88–90
A. Dobson: *Thomas Bewick and his Pupils* (London, 1884)

JUSTINE HOPKINS

Hasan. *See* MAMLUK, §II, 2(5).

Hasan [Pasha], **Nakkaş** (*fl c.* 1582–?1605; *d* ?1623). Ottoman statesman and painter. He was one of the last exponents of the Ottoman tradition of historical illustration (*see* ISLAMIC ART, §III, 4(vi)(e)), and his carefully composed depictions of events contain clearly drawn, recognizable figures in detailed settings. He is first recorded in 1581, when he left his post as a page in the imperial household to enter the corps of palace doorkeepers (*kapıcıs*). He rose steadily through the Ottoman administrative hierarchy, becoming a member of the Council of State (with the title of Pasha) in 1604. During this early part of his career he was also a prolific painter, from which he took his epithet Nakkaş ('the Painter'). He probably trained under Osman, the head of the imperial painting studio, for his style follows the tradition established by Osman in the 1570s. His earliest paintings are in the *Surname* ('Book of festivals'; Istanbul, Topkapı Pal. Lib., H. 1344), which records the circumcision festival held for the sons of Sultan Murad III in 1582. During the next two decades he contributed illustrations to over 20 manuscripts produced at court. For the six-volume copy of the *Siyer-i Nebi*, Darir's biography of the Prophet Muhammad (text completed 1594–5), for example, he painted all 139 illustrations in the first volume and 111 of the 125 illustrations in the sixth (Istanbul, Topkapı Pal. Lib., H. 1221, 1223).

In the 1590s Hasan began to supplant Osman as the leading illustrator at court, and he was the only painter to illustrate the works of Talikizade, the sultan's official court historian (*şehnameci*) from *c.* 1592–6 until his death in 1599. At the end of one of Talikizade's compositions, a description of Sultan Muhammad III's conquest of Eger in Hungary in 1596 (Istanbul, Topkapı Pal. Lib., H. 1609, fol. 74*r*), there is a portrait of the author, a calligrapher and the artist at work in the same room; Hasan is drawing a preparatory sketch for an illustration in the *Siyer-i Nebi*

(*Qaydar Hunting*; fol. 36*v*; see Tanındı, 1984, figs xiii and xv). Hasan's last illustrations are in the *Destan-i Ferruh u Hüma* ('Legend of Farrukh and Huma'; Istanbul, U. Lib., MS. T. 1975), dated 1601. Thereafter he seems to have devoted himself increasingly to affairs of state, producing only a few album paintings. His last known work is the illuminations on Sultan Ahmad I's huge imperial monogram (*tuğra*; paint and gold on paper, 1.48×2.51 m; Topkapı Pal. Lib., G. Y. 1394). This *tour de force* of Ottoman illumination is thought to have been made to celebrate a visit by the sultan to Bursa in 1605, when Hasan was serving as governor of the citadel of Bursa. His high rank in these years is reflected in the imposing mausoleum at Eyüp near Istanbul in which he is buried.

BIBLIOGRAPHY

Z. Tanındı: 'Nakkaş Hasan Paşa', *Sanat*, vi (June 1977), pp. 114–25
Z. Akalay: 'XVI. Yüzyıl Nakkaşlarından Hasan Paşa ve Eserleri' [The 16th-century painter Hasan Pasha and his works], *I. Milletlerarası Türkoloji Kongresi: İstanbul, 1979* [1st International Congress on Turcology], iii, pp. 607–26
Z. Tanındı: *Siyer-i Nebî: İslâm Tasvir Sanatında Hz. Muhammed'in Hayatı* [The *Siyer-i Nebî*: the life of the Prophet Muhammad in the Islamic art of portraiture] ([Istanbul], 1984)

ESIN ATIL

Hasan, Zaki Muhammad (*b* Cairo, July 1908; *d* Baghdad, March 1957). Egyptian historian. He was educated at the University of Cairo and in Paris, where he obtained his doctorate in 1934 with a thesis on the history and culture of Egypt in the 9th century AD. In Cairo he moved between the university—where he taught history—the Department of Antiquities and the Museum of Arab (later Islamic) Art, where he became director in 1951. After the 1952 revolution in Egypt, he went to Iraq, where he chaired the Department of Antiquities and Civilization at Baghdad University. His publications illustrate the multiple concerns of his generation, born in the 'Third World' and trained in the West to educate youth in the values of their cultural past through the medium of Western techniques and institutions. His scholarly work is exemplified by his study on the treasures of the Fatimid dynasty of Egypt (*reg* 969–1171). He also tried to meet the traditional opposition to the visual arts by writing on the specific theological issues involved and showing how the Islamic tradition never gave up representation. His third concern was pedagogical, and he wrote mostly in Arabic to reach a mass of people untouched by Western scholarship. His last major work was an atlas of Islamic painting and decorative arts, designed to make Islamic art known to those whose cultural heritage it is.

WRITINGS

Les Tulunides: Etude de l'Egypte musulmane à la fin du IXe siècle, 868–905 (Paris, 1933)
Al-fann al-islâmî fî miṣr [Islamic art in Egypt] (Cairo, 1935)
Kunūz al-fāṭimiyyn [Treasures of the Fatimids] (Cairo, 1937)
'The Attitude of Islam toward Painting', *Bull. Fac. A., Fouad I U.*, vii (1944), pp. 1–15
Funūn al-islām [The arts of Islam] (Cairo, 1948)
Moslem Art in the Fouad I University Museum (Cairo, 1950)
Aṭlas al-funūn al-zukhrufiyya wa'l-taṣāwīr al-islāmiyya [Atlas of Islamic decorative and pictorial arts] (Cairo, 1956)
'The Attitude of Islam toward Figurative Painting', *Islam. Rev.*, xliv/7 (1956), pp. 24–9

BIBLIOGRAPHY

E. Kühnel: Obituary, *Kst Orients*, iii (1959), pp. 95–6

OLEG GRABAR

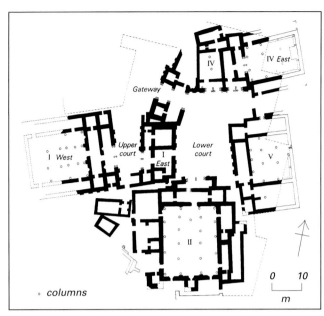

1. Hasanlu, level IVb, plan of Burned Buildings I West, I East, II, IV, IV East and V, *c.* 800 BC

Hasanlu [Pers. Ḥasanlŭ]. Site of a settlement in north-west Iran that flourished in the 1st millennium BC. It is situated in the Solduz Valley south of Lake Urmia (formerly Lake Riza'iyya) and consists of a stratified citadel mound with a settlement and cemetery area. A sequence of Iron Age buildings includes one almost complete structure from the earliest Iron Age I period. The site's most significant architectural feature is a complex of five large Burned Buildings of the Iron Age II period; the columned halls of these buildings probably influenced the later Persian apadana (*see* IRAN, ANCIENT, §II, 3). Hasanlu's chronological framework, with its tripartite Iron Age division, has since been applied elsewhere in Iran. Besides weapons and tools, the most important finds were luxury goods, including ivories and the famous Hasanlu gold 'bowl' (beaker). These artefacts (Philadelphia, U. PA, Mus.; Tehran, Archaeol. Mus.) have been an invaluable source of comparative material.

Twelve campaigns of excavation between 1956 and 1977 under the direction of Robert H. Dyson jr recovered evidence from the Neolithic to the Iron Age (6th millennium–1st millennium BC). The latter period provided by far the most significant remains, and these represent a different culture from that of the Bronze Age. The ancient name of the site (Hasanlu is the name of the modern local village) and the ethnic and linguistic background of its original inhabitants remain unknown, as no inscriptions were recovered.

1. ARCHITECTURE. Parts of six structures were recovered from the Iron Age I period (Hasanlu level V), which has been dated by radiocarbon analysis to about the 14th century BC. The one nearly complete building had at least three rooms: an anteroom, a large main room and a narrow side room. Against the walls on all sides of the main room were mud benches, and by the rear wall was a brick

platform. A raised hearth, enclosed by a kerb with a narrow opening, stood in the room's centre. At either side of the hearth was a flat plastered stone base on which a wooden column once stood. This and the other Hasanlu V structures have square or rectangular rooms with walls of mud-brick on foundations of free-standing, uncut stones; two other structures had benches along the walls, another had a raised platform, and one had a buttressed outer wall. There is no evidence for a second storey on any of these buildings. Two of the Hasanlu V structures preserve evidence of burning, but it is not known whether this indicates enemy destruction.

A number of the features mentioned recur in the succeeding structures from level IV. This recurrence, the continuation in level IV of monochrome wares, and the fact that the level V cemetery was still used, suggest continuity. The architectural remains from level IV are massive (see fig. 1). The five large buildings called Burned Building (BB) I, II, III, IV and V have been fully excavated, along with parts of several others. These buildings were destroyed, rebuilt, altered and added to over their long history, which may have begun as early as the 12th century BC (Iron Age II, level IVc) when BB II, IV East and V were built close together in the south-east part of the citadel, and BB III (not shown) was built to the north-west. Later all the buildings (except, apparently, BB III) were burnt and subsequently rebuilt (level IVb) with new walls placed directly over the earlier burnt ones. At the same time BB I West and BB I East, sharing a common court (the upper court), and BB IV were constructed. Columned porticos were added c. 1000 BC to some of the rebuilt structures, and the last structure to be built, BB I West, was erected with a portico as part of its original plan. A large central paved court with a gateway entrance was created, and an architectural complex or 'palace' area was thus formed, containing BB I West, I East, II, IV, IV East and V. All except the first building surrounded a north–south orientated paved lower court 28 m in length. This level IVb reorganization entailed a reorientation of BB V and BB IV East.

BB II was the largest and most impressive of the level IV buildings, but they all share certain characteristic features (many of which originated in the Iron Age I, Hasanlu level V, period). The walls are made of brick on free-standing uncut stone foundations. Each building had a columned hall at its centre surrounded by workrooms. The building was entered through a columned portico (added in IVb) and an anteroom with recessed door. The anteroom contained a stairway to a second storey. Benches lined the walls of the columned hall, in which there was also (in IVb) a raised hearth, a rear platform and a paved area. Each building faced a court, either its own or a shared one.

The central and side columns of the main halls indicate that a heavy superstructure was supported. The buildings were probably two storeys high, with the anterooms and the rooms surrounding the halls divided into two floors. The roof was probably flat, not gabled. No evidence exists for windows, and lighting and ventilation must have been a constant problem, although the paved areas suggest an opening in the roof.

The specific function of each of the buildings and whether they were public or private remain enigmatic. BB III, IV and IV East may have been residential, while BB II was probably the major palace or, perhaps, temple. The many artefacts recovered in BB II include weapons and domestic objects as well as luxury goods, but only a few objects that might be religious in nature. Three undecorated upright stelae were placed before the porticos of both BB II and IV, but whether they had a religious function remains unclear. Although each building had a prominent platform at the rear of the main hall, perhaps for the seating of a dignitary, only that of BB II had a small room associated with it.

T. Cuyler Young jr has noted that the megaron plan of the Mycenaean palaces, especially that at PYLOS in western Greece (destr. c. 1200 BC), parallels the columned hall plan of the Hasanlu buildings of level IVc (c. 12th century BC). One problem with this connection is the distance involved, but megara also occur in Anatolia in the Bronze Age (see TROY (i)) and again at GORDION in the 8th century BC (though they are not as complex, nor are they appointed as those at Hasanlu). Alternatively, the structure may have developed at Hasanlu itself, as all the characteristic features of the level IV halls existed in level V in simpler form. Since the state of Urartu had contact with, and eventually destroyed, Hasanlu, it seems probable that the 8th- and 7th-century BC columned halls recovered at some Urartian sites (e.g. ALTINTEPE) are related to, or perhaps derived from, those at Hasanlu. Similarly, the presence in Urartu of buttressed walls and recessed niches may have come from knowledge of their earlier use at Hasanlu. Within Iran itself the columned hall is dramatically represented in the south at two sites (probably Median) of the late 8th century BC, GODIN TEPE II and TEPE NUSH-I JAN. Later it attained its greatest development in the APADANA at the Achaemenid sites of Persepolis and Pasargadae. The Nush-i Jan hall has internal recessed niches, and that at Godin II has a bench along the walls and a platform at the rear wall. The problem still to be resolved is whether the architects at these later Iranian sites received their inspiration directly from Hasanlu, from another, unexcavated (and possibly later) site in Iran or from the Urartians. Alternatively, the similarity could have derived from a general socio-cultural tradition that, for functional reasons, was reflected in the architecture. In any event, there was a formal and chronological development within Iran from Hasanlu level IV to Nush-i Jan and Godin II and thence to the Achaemenid apadana.

About 800 BC Hasanlu (level IVb) was completely destroyed by invaders from Urartu and only briefly reoccupied by survivors (level IVa). In the late 8th century BC the site was resettled by people with a new culture, probably Urartians, who established a new settlement and built a monumental fortification wall (Hasanlu level IIIb, early Iron Age III).

2. ARTEFACTS. A large quantity and variety of artefacts were recovered from the debris of the Burned Buildings. Most were found in the fill, indicating that they fell from the second storeys, where they were used or stored. In addition to a large number of bronze and iron weapons, domestic tools and monochrome pottery and bronze

2. Hasanlu, scenes depicted around the outside of a gold vessel, probably late 2nd millennium BC (Tehran, Archaeological Museum); reconstruction drawing

vessels, there was a considerable number of exotic objects. These included a silver beaker decorated with a battle scene; gold, silver and bronze jewellery; gold, silver and iron plaques decorated with battle and hunt scenes; bronze animal-headed vessels; and bronze belts and horse trappings decorated in repoussé. The many fragmentary ivory and wood carvings, recovered primarily in BB II and in smaller quantity in BB IV East and V, are outstanding, including both locally made pieces and imported ivories from northern Syria and Assyria. The carvings include figures in the round representing deities and animals, plaques depicting religious, war and domestic scenes, and decorated boxes and bowls.

Perhaps the best-known object from Hasanlu is a decorated gold 'bowl' or beaker (Tehran, Archaeol. Mus.; see fig. 2) found in BB I West in the arms of a man killed in the destruction of *c.* 800 BC. The date of the bowl's manufacture is disputed but was probably the early 1st millennium BC. Framed at the top and bottom by a guilloche and arranged in three loosely defined registers are a series of scenes that seem to depict mythological events. At the top are three deities in chariots, one drawn by a bull, the others by equids; a figure (probably a priest) holds a vessel before them and is followed by attendants with sheep. At the base are various scenes, including a naked female deity standing on two rams, a male armed with a bow, two kneeling men harming a third, a female presenting a baby to a seated figure and a fantastic battle scene between a boxer and an apparent mountain deity placed above a recumbent lion. In the intervening register are placed the figures of an eagle carrying a female, a female deity seated on a lion, three isolated swords and a figure squatting before an empty throne. Interpretations of the scenes have occupied scholars for years. With no written identification or knowledge of the local religion and mythology, little more than tentative explanations based on comparison with scenes and myths known elsewhere in the Near East have been suggested, including a possible link with HURRIAN mythology.

BIBLIOGRAPHY

E. Porada: *The Art of Ancient Iran: Pre-Islamic Cultures* (New York, 1965), pp. 96–102, 108–20

T. C. Young jr: 'Thoughts on the Architecture of Hasanlu IV', *Iran. Antiq.*, vi (1969), pp. 48–71

R. H. Dyson jr: 'The Question of Balconies at Hasanlu', *From Athens to Gordion*, ed. K. De Vries (Philadelphia, 1975), pp. 149–57

——: 'Architecture of the Iron I Period at Hasanlu', *Le Plateau iranien et l'Asie centrale des origines à la conquête islamique*, ed. J. Deshayes (Paris, 1976), pp. 155–69

——: 'The Architecture of Hasanlu: Periods I to IV', *Amer. J. Archaeol.*, lxxxi (1977), pp. 548–52

O. W. Muscarella: *The Catalogue of Ivories from Hasanlu, Iran* (Philadelphia, 1980)

I. Winter: *A Decorated Breastplate from Hasanlu, Iran* (Philadelphia, 1980)

R. H. Dyson jr and O. W. Muscarella: 'Constructing the Chronology and Historical Implications of Hasanlu IV', *Iran*, xxvii (1989), pp. 1–27

Expedition, xxxi, 2/3 (1989) [whole issue]

OSCAR WHITE MUSCARELLA

Haschenperg, Stefan von [Mr Stephyn the devisor, Mr Stevins; Steven the Almayne, Steven Almain, the Alman] (*b* Moravia, *fl* 1535–43). German engineer and land surveyor, active in England. He offered his services to Henry VIII in 1535 'pro armamentario et architecto' and was granted a pension of £60 a year from October 1539, increased to £75 in July 1540. He designed the coastal artillery forts of Sandgate Castle (1539–40), Kent, Camber Castle (1539–40; remodelled 1541–3), E. Sussex, and four bulwarks in the Downs linked by earthwork lines between the forts of Sandown, Deal and Walmer (1539–40). He surveyed Cowbridge in the Welsh Marches in November 1540 and travelled north with the Duke of Norfolk in January 1541 to report on the fortifications intended for the Scottish Borders. By June 1541 he was active in Carlisle, and from 3 July he was in sole charge of 'setting forth of all the works there', which included the construction of a new citadel (now English Gate) at the south end of the walled area. He was suspended in May 1543 and deprived of his property and pension. By August 1544 he was in Antwerp, where Mary of Hungary, Regent of the Netherlands, wrote to Henry VIII on Haschenperg's behalf 'both for his virtues and because he is her subject as dowager of the kingdom of Bohemia'. The same month he tried unsuccessfully to enlist Sir Edward Carne (*d* 1561), the English Ambassador, in his cause. In August 1545 he wrote to Henry VIII from Lübeck to offer various services, most notably to improve the water supply to Nonsuch Palace, but his attempts were fruitless and he last appears, if it is he, as Hofmeister to Marcus Kuen, Bishop of Olmutz (now Olomouc) in 1553–65. Von Haschenperg was principally a land surveyor, in the practice of which the Privy Council thought him 'very expert'. The fortifications he devised on the south coast of England and at Carlisle were already old-fashioned and weak in comparison with the best contemporary work, for example at Deal, Portland, St Mawes and Pendennis (*see* MILITARY ARCHITECTURE AND FORTIFICATION, §III, 2(iv)), and his use of timber roofs, covered with canvas, pitch and tar, showed no appreciation of conditions under attack. The accusation that he cost the King several thousand pounds probably reflects the amount he was deemed to have wasted either at Carlisle or at Camber, where his fort had to be entirely remodelled a year or so later. A contemporary description of him as 'a man that will pretend more knowledge than he hath indeed' seems to have been a shrewd judgement.

BIBLIOGRAPHY

B. H. St. J. O'Neil: 'Stefan von Haschenperg, an Engineer to King Henry VIII, and his Work', *Archaeologia*, 2nd ser., xci (1945), pp. 137–55
H. M. Colvin, ed.: *The History of the King's Works*, iii (London, 1975), pp. 358n, 373–4, 401
M. Biddle and M. Merriman: *The History of the King's Works*, iv, ed. H. M. Colvin (London, 1982)

MARTIN BIDDLE

Hase, Conrad Wilhelm (*b* Einbeck, 2 Oct 1818; *d* Hannover, 28 March 1902). German architect. He studied architecture (1834–8) at the Höhere Gewerbeschule in Hannover, before starting a bricklaying apprenticeship there (1838–9), gaining his journeyman's certificate. In 1840 he travelled via Kassel, Marburg, Wiesbaden, Mainz, Worms, Speyer and Ulm to Munich, where he studied at the Kunstakademie under Friedrich Gärtner, and at the Polytechnikum. In spring 1842 he returned to Hannover via Regensburg, Nuremberg, Bamberg, Coburg and Eisenach and was employed in 1843 as a railway building supervisor by the Königlichen Hannoverschen Eisenbahn. The ideas he had absorbed in Munich and the impressions he had accumulated of medieval towns, churches and cathedrals on his two tours had a decisive impact on his later work. Between 1848 and 1854, Hase restored the monastery church in Loccum, and on its completion he was appointed to teach architecture at the Polytechnische Schule in HANNOVER; having been appointed a building inspector in 1851, he became a building consultant in 1858, a professor in 1878 (resigned 1894) and a privy counsellor in 1882. He also ran his own architectural practice, and acted as architect (1863–97) to the consistory for the Protestant church of the region. During his lifetime, he was responsible for 215 projects, including more than 100 churches.

Hase's work can be divided into three phases, the first ending *c.* 1852. The station buildings at Lehrte, Celle and Wunstorf were built in the *Rundbogenstil* while he was still under Gärtner's influence, while the designs for the

Museum für Kunst und Wissenschaft in Hannover used a repertory of forms with regional associations on which August Heinrich Andreae (1804–46), the city architect of Hannover, had already left his mark. In 1852 Hase's style altered abruptly under the influence of the teachings of the English architect A. W. N. Pugin, which had been brought to Germany by AUGUST VON REICHENSPERGER. For the tower of the Martinskirche and the Gropengiesser block of flats in Hannover and, amongst others, the churches at Hilter and Arpke, Hase adopted strictly Gothic Revival forms and, like Georg Gottlob Ungewitter, Vincenz Statz and Friedrich von Schmidt before him, became a disciple of von Reichensperger. He sought to create an individual style that could balance the dogmatic position of the Catholic von Reichensperger, and the requirements of Protestant Evangelical church building, and that would fit in with the North German landscape. This balance can be seen in the Christuskirche (1859–64) in Hannover, an entirely brick building, for which he drew inspiration from a variety of contemporary and medieval sources. Here Hase produced an individual and innovative building solution that answered the liturgical requirements of the Protestant service. The success of this building ushered in his last phase when he worked in a personal idiom marked by a passionate advocacy of Gothic Revival brick building and a purist approach to the use of natural materials, rejecting such substitutes as cast iron, plaster, stucco and paint. Including his own house in Hannover, he built more than 100 brick buildings after 1859 exemplifying this style. Hase's influence was widespread especially through his work as a teacher, and lasted until World War I. His ideas on architectural style were further disseminated in the architectural periodical *Bauhütte zum weissen Blatt*, which he founded with some of his pupils in 1880.

BIBLIOGRAPHY

NDB; Thieme–Becker
T. Unger: 'Die hannoversche Architekturschule', *Hannover: Führer durch die Stadt und ihre Bauten* (Hannover, 1882/*R* 1978), pp. 107–62
G. Schönermark, ed.: *Die Architektur der hannoverschen Schule*, 7 vols (Hannover, 1888–95)
Das geistige Deutschland am Ende des XIX. Jahrhunderts, i (Leipzig, 1898), pp. 270–71
G. Kokkelink: 'Die Neugotik Conrad Wilhelm Hases', *Hannover. Geschbl.*, n. s. 1, xxii (1968), pp. 1–211
Conrad Wilhelm Hase (exh. cat. by G. Kokkelink, Hannover, Hist. Mus. Hohen Ufer, 1968)

MICHAEL EISSENHAUER

Hasegawa, Itsuko (*b* Shizuoka, 1941). Japanese architect. She graduated from the School of Architecture at Kantō Gakuin University in Yokohama in 1963, and from 1963 to 1968 she worked with Kiyonori Kikutake. In 1969 she continued her studies with Kazuo Shinohara at the Tokyo Institute of Technology and in 1976 established her own studio in Tokyo. Initially she was strongly influenced by Shinohara and was also considered to be a member of the so-called 'Shinohara school', but the impact of his abstract Minimalism on her designs has always been complemented by the use of common elements. All her buildings are characterized by an extensive and straightforward application of industrial materials such as steel, aluminium, metallic paints, reinforced concrete and inorganic material.

The majority of Hasegawa's early works were small residences such as the house (1977) in Yaizu No. 2 or the house (1980) at Kuwahara in Matsuyama. In the 1980s she completed several larger public buildings, including the Aono building (1982) in Matsuyama and the Bizan Hall (1984) in Shizuoka. Projects such as the NC Housing (1984) and the house (1985) in Nerima in Tokyo are designed as composite entities of various formal and spatial elements and display a curious 'fragmentary' quality that she refers to as the 'architecturalization of nature'. Because of the wide use of metallic parts her buildings also appear as futuristic urban constructions incorporating technologically inspired images, for example the Shonandai Cultural Centre (1990) in Fujisawa and the Sumida Culture Factory (1994) in Tokyo.

BIBLIOGRAPHY
C. Fawcett: *The New Japanese House: Ritual and Anti-Ritual Patterns of Dwelling* (New York, 1980)
H. Yatsuka: 'Architecture in the Urban Desert: A Critical Introduction to Japanese Architecture after Modernism', *Oppositions*, xxiii (1981)
B. Bognar: *Contemporary Japanese Architecture: Its Development and Challenge* (New York, 1985)
H. Yatsuka: 'Itsuko Hasegawa', *Space Des.*, xxi/247 (1985) [special issue]
B. Bognar: *The New Japanese Architecture* (New York, 1990)
——: *The Japan Guide* (New York, 1995)

BOTOND BOGNAR

Hasegawa, Kiyoshi (*b* Yokohama, 9 Dec 1891; *d* Paris, 13 Dec 1980). Japanese printmaker and painter. He studied Western-style drawing under Seiki Kuroda at the Aoibashi Institute of the Hakuba-kai and Western-style oil painting under Saburōsuke Okada and Takeji Fujishima at the Hongō Institute. At the same time he became acquainted with examples of modern Western art, which was then being widely introduced into Japan; he was attracted to the work of William Blake and to Symbolist painters such as Edvard Munch and Odilon Redon. In 1913, while producing the cover picture for the magazine *Kamen* ('Mask'; 1913), Hasegawa taught himself woodblock printing. Shortly after this, he began to study etching and in 1916 helped found the Japanese Print Club. He played a leading part in the creative print movement in Japan, where the artist both cut the block and printed the work.

In 1919 Hasegawa went to France with the aim of making a further study of painting and printmaking and encountered a variety of techniques including drypoint and engraving. He was attracted by the neglected technique of mezzotint, which he revived with certain new methods of his own, producing works with beautiful gradations from black to white. His early Expressionist style, as seen in *Wind* (1915; Kyoto, N. Mus. Mod. A.), a woodblock print based on a poem by Yeats, gave way to a style full of dignity and tranquillity. He sometimes used the same motifs, for example *Female Nude* (engraving, 1936; Kyoto, N. Mus. Mod. A.) and, more often, landscapes of southern France, such as *Elm Tree* (drypoint, 1941; Kyoto, N. Mus. Mod. A.) or indoor still-lifes or flowers, such as *Time, Still-life* (mezzotint, 1969; Kyoto, N. Mus. Mod. A.).

Hasegawa's later work was characterized by a heightened symbolism, which conveyed a sense of the mysteriousness of nature and the cosmos. His work was highly regarded in France, where he was awarded the order of Chevalier de la Légion d'honneur in 1935 and the Ordre des Arts et Lettres in 1966. A collection of reminiscences, letters, essays and writings on art was published posthumously as *Hakuchū ni kami o miru* ('See the god in broad daylight'; Tokyo, 1982), edited by Hitoshi Hasegawa and Tadao Takemoto.

BIBLIOGRAPHY
Hasegawa Kiyoshi hanga sakuhin-shū [Collected prints of Kiyoshi Hasegawa] (Tokyo, 1981)

TORU ASANO

Hasegawa, Saburō (*b* Yamaguchi Prefect., 6 Sept 1906; *d* San Francisco, CA, 11 March 1957). Japanese painter and writer. In 1929 he graduated from Tokyo Imperial University, where he researched Tōyō Sesshū for his thesis. In 1930 he went to Paris where his work was selected for the Salon d'Automne; on returning two years later to Japan, he exhibited in the 19th *Nika Ten* (Second Division Society exhibition). In 1948 he exhibited *At the Lake* (1948; Kobe, Kōnan Senior High Sch.) in the 12th Jiyū Bijutsuka Kyōkai Ten (Society of Independent Artists exhibition) at the Tokyo Metropolitan Art Museum. In 1951 he corresponded with Franz Kline, exchanging views on Eastern and Western cultures. He exhibited *Rhapsody: At the Fishing Village* (frottage on paper mounted on four-fold screen, 1952; Tokyo, N. Mus. Mod. A.) at the Nihon Gendai Bijutsu Ten (Exhibition of Contemporary Japanese Art), organized by the Tokyo *Reader's Digest* in 1952. A year later he had a one-man exhibition at the New Gallery, New York and was a founder-member of the Nihon Abusutorakuto Āto Kurabu (Japanese Abstract Art Club). In 1954 he participated in the symposium *Abstract Art in the Contemporary World* (New York, MOMA). From 1955 he lectured in art history at the California College of Art and Crafts, Oakland, CA.

WRITINGS
Abusutorakuto āto [Abstract art] (Tokyo, 1936)

BIBLIOGRAPHY
Hasegawa Saburō (exh. cat., essay by K. Akane; Kobe, Hyōgo, Prefect. Mus. Mod. A., 1977)
Hasegawa Saburō To Sono Jidai [Saburō Hasegawa and his times] (exh. cat., essay by Y. Inui; Shimonoseki, Mun. Mus. A., 1988)

YASUYOSHI SAITO

Hasegawa Tōhaku [Nobuharu] (*b* Nanao, Noto Prov. [now Ishikawa Prefect.], 1539; *d* Edo [now Tokyo], 1610). Japanese painter and founder of the Hasegawa school of painters.

1. LIFE. He was one of the most important painters of the Momoyama period (1568–1600). Born into the Okumura family, retainers to the Hatakeyama clan who were overlords of the castle in Nanao, he was later adopted into the Hasegawa family, which ran a dyeing business. Tōhaku's early work was done under the name of Nobuharu (which can also be read Shinshun), and consisted primarily of ink paintings depicting Buddhist subjects. Several extant examples may be seen at Shōgakuin and Reisenji, temples in the area where he grew up, and at Daihōji, a temple in Takaoka in nearby Toyama Prefecture. One pair of *byōbu* (folding screens), *Rounding up Horses* (*c.* 1570; ink and colour on paper; Tokyo, N. Mus.), also demonstrates Tōhaku's early abilities within the *Yamatoe* tradition of painting subjects associated with the Japanese (*see* JAPAN, §VI, 3(iii) and 4(ii)).

In the early 1570s Tōhaku moved to Kyoto, where he is said to have studied formally with the leading painting school of the day, the KANŌ SCHOOL, possibly under Kanō Shōei or Kanō Eitoku (*see* KANŌ, (3) and (5)). It was in Kyoto that he also studied the works of *suiboku* (monochrome ink) painters of the Muromachi period (1333–1568) and Chinese works of the Song (AD 960–1279) and Yuan (1279–1368) periods that had been collected and admired in Japan since the 14th century. It was probably in the 1580s that he began using the name Tōhaku, out of regard for TŌYŌ SESSHŪ, the greatest of the Muromachi period ink painters: the first syllable of Tōhaku uses the same character as the first syllable in Tōyō. Tōhaku's *Flowers and Birds* (one of an original pair of painted screens (*byōbu*), ink and colour on paper; Myōkakuji, Okayama Prefect.) is closely based on Sesshū's treatment of similar themes.

Eventually, Tōhaku broke with the Kanō school and, like several of his contemporaries, including Kaihō Yūshō, Unkoku Tōgan and Soga Chokuan, chose independence. He lived at Honpōji, a temple in Kyoto, founded his own Hasegawa school there and competed vigorously for commissions to decorate temples and secular residences in the capital city and its environs. He made friends with the famed tea master SEN NO RIKYŪ (*see* JAPAN, fig. 204), who was well-connected both with the military rulers of the day and with priests at Daitokuji, the Kyoto Zen temple that was a repository for many of the Chinese paintings that Tōhaku so admired. Paintings by Tōhaku are to be seen in several of Daitokuji's subtemples (Jukōin, Sangen'in, Shinjuan), as well as at other Zen temples in Kyoto, such as Myōshinji, Shōkokuji and Nanzenji.

In 1592 Tōhaku's comments on painting, *Tōhaku gasetsu* ('Tōhaku's explanations of painting'), recorded by a follower, appeared. As his reputation grew, he was officially recognized with the Buddhist titles *hokkyō* (Bridge of the Law; 1604) and *hōgen* (Eye of the Law; 1605). He was patronized not only by Buddhist temples but also by members of the military élite, including the ruler Toyotomi Hideyoshi. It was Hideyoshi's successor, Tokugawa Ieyasu (1543–1616), who summoned Tōhaku to Edo (now Tokyo), where he remained until his death.

A key incident in his life was the attempt to settle whether Tōhaku or his rival UNKOKU TŌGAN had the better right to call himself the legitimate successor of Sesshū. Tōgan's claim was based on a lineage descending from Sesshū through one particular pupil, and was buttressed by his having been invited to occupy Sesshū's studio and to study and copy the latter's *Sansui chokan* ('Long Landscape handscroll'; ink on paper; 1485; Hōfu, Mōri Mus.), painted in his so-called 'hard' style. Tōhaku's claim to be the 'fifth generation after Sesshū' was based on lineage through a different pupil of Sesshū's, but seemed to derive largely from the need he felt for a more illustrious artistic ancestry than he had actually possessed. He may also have owned a shorter landscape scroll by Sesshū (handscroll, ink on paper; 1474; Yamaguchi, Prefect. Mus.) executed in the 'soft' manner.

The dispute is said to have led to a lawsuit that was decided in favour of Tōgan. Whatever the case, it is Tōhaku who is now generally regarded as the more brilliant and innovative of the two artists. Moreover, Sesshū's 'soft' style, with its emphasis on ink tonalities and wash, corresponds well with Tōhaku's mode of handling monochrome ink.

2. WORK. Perhaps Tōhaku's strongest work in the 'soft' tradition is the *byōbu* composition called *Pine Trees in Mist* (ink on paper; *c.* 1600; Tokyo, N. Mus.; see fig.), executed on a large scale appropriate to the prevailing taste for bold room decoration. Pine trees are the only forms; they cross the pair of screens with a dance-like rhythm, some emerging strongly from the mists with

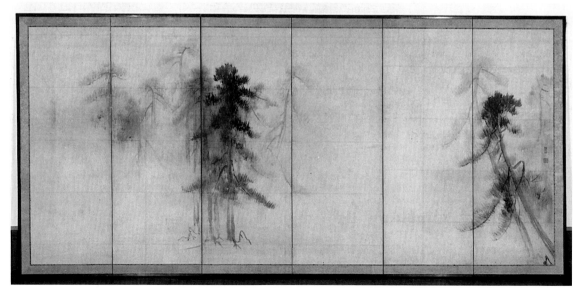

Hasegawa Tōhaku: *Pine Trees in Mist*, one of a pair of six-fold screens (*byōbu*), ink on paper, each 1557×3469 mm, *c.* 1600 (Tokyo, National Museum)

sharply brushed needles and exposed roots, others receding softly through the use of graded washes. Infused as it is with both lyricism and the expansiveness typical of the period, *Pine Trees in Mist* shows the potential of monochrome ink for vibrant boldness. It would not be mistaken for a work by Sesshū, but it shares his masterly control of formal arrangement and the tonal richness of his brushwork.

Monkeys and *Bamboo Grove* (pair of screens, ink with light gold wash on paper; Kyoto, Shōkokuji) make specific reference to the celebrated Chinese painter Muqi of the Southern Song period (1127–1279), whose *Gibbon and Child* and *Crane and Bamboo* (two-thirds of a triptych with *White-robed Guanyin* (Jap. Kannon, Skt Avalokiteshvara) in the centre; hanging scrolls, ink and light colour on paper; Kyoto, Daitokuji) were sources for both the theme and the brush style used by Tōhaku in this pair of screens.

Tōhaku's daring and lyrical monochrome ink works were balanced by his expressions of seasonal themes executed in *kinpeki* (gold-foil ground and bright opaque colour), with bold compositions using the *byōbu* or *fusuma* (sliding door) format. The outstanding examples of *fusuma* in this mode were created for Shōunji, a subtemple of Myōshinji built in 1591–2 by Hideyoshi in memory of his son who had just died in infancy. After Hideyoshi's own death in 1598 and the subsequent coming to power of Tokugawa Ieyasu, Shōunji was destroyed, and the *fusuma* were reinstalled at Chishakuin, a temple in Kyoto. The works depict seasonal trees, flowering plants and grasses. Tōhaku is generally credited with the *fusuma* depicting *Maple Tree and Autumn Plants*. The spring theme of *Flowering Cherry Tree* is variously attributed to Tōhaku and to his eldest son Hasegawa Kyūzō (1568–93), the leading painter in Tōhaku's studio, who also created the winter scene of *Pine Tree and Hibiscus*. Kyūzō would have succeeded his father had he not died soon after completing the work at Shōunji.

Tōhaku's painting of the maple tree has been somewhat cropped, but it is still remarkable for the contrast between the strength of shape of the tree spreading across the gold-foiled surface and the lavishly intricate surface detail. This strong sense of pattern may owe something to, or at any rate shares something with, the rich brocades used for *nō* costumes and other textile designs during the period. The work also shows evidence of a close observation of the forms of nature. The *Maple Tree* is an exemplar of taste in painting during the Momoyama period.

The fact that Hideyoshi gave the Shōunji commission to Tōhaku and his studio was significant also in that it broke the hold that the Kanō school had had on patronage at the highest official levels. The overturning of established hierarchies was indeed characteristic of the period in several ways, most obviously in the usurpation of power (*gekokujō*, 'those below overthrow those above') by Hideyoshi. Such mobility was short-lived, however, both politically and artistically; under the Tokugawa shoguns, successors to Hideyoshi, the Kanō school reclaimed its position as official painters to the shogunate (Edo period, 1600–1868) in a far more rigidly stratified society. More than any of his Kanō contemporaries, Tōhaku may be regarded as the paradigmatic painter of the Momoyama

period. Three of his other sons, Sōtaku, Sōya and Sakon, were active painters in the Hasegawa school, Sōtaku inheriting the studio after the death of his brother Kyūzō. Other names connected with the school are Tōin (*fl c.* 1620) and Sōen (*fl c.* 1620).

BIBLIOGRAPHY

T. Takeda: *Tōhaku, Yūshō*, Suiboku bijutsu taikei [Survey of ink-painting art], ix (Tokyo, 1973)
Momoyama: Japanese Art in the Age of Grandeur (exh. cat., ed. J. Meech; New York, Met., 1975)
T. Doi: *Hasegawa Tōhaku* (Tokyo, 1977)
T. Minamoto: *Muromachi*, Nihon bijutsu shiron [History of Japanese art], v (Kyoto, 1979)
J. Nakajima: *Hasegawa Tōhaku*, Nihon bijutsu kaiga zenshū [Complete collection of Japanese painting], x (Tokyo, 1979)
Of Water and Ink: Muromachi Period Paintings from Japan 1392–1568 (exh. cat., ed. A. Watanabe; Detroit, MI, Inst. A., 1986)

JOAN H. O'MARA

Haseltine, William Stanley (*b* Philadelphia, PA, 11 June 1835; *d* Rome, 3 Feb 1900). American painter. He was the son of a successful merchant and brother of the sculptor James H. Haseltine (1833–1907) and the art dealer Charles F. Haseltine (1840–1915). In 1850 Haseltine enrolled at the University of Pennsylvania in Philadelphia; after two years he transferred to Harvard College, Cambridge, MA, graduating in 1854. He first formally studied painting in that year on his return to Philadelphia, working with Paul Weber (1823–1916). Haseltine went abroad to Düsseldorf in 1855, where he became friends with his compatriots Albert Bierstadt, Emanuel Gottlieb Leutze and Worthington Whittredge. He painted throughout Europe for the next three years, returning from Italy to the United States late 1858. He was established in the Tenth Street Studio Building in New York by the winter of 1859 and played an active role in the city's art world, exhibiting at the Century and Salmagundi clubs and at the National Academy of Design, of which he was an associate by 1860 and an academician in 1861. During the years of the Civil War (from which he was exempt due to a chronic eye ailment), Haseltine journeyed repeatedly to the rocky Atlantic coastline of New England to sketch scenes of sea and shore that form the basis of his strongest work, for example *Indian Rock, Narragansett, Rhode Island* (1863; San Francisco, CA, de Young Mem. Mus.).

In 1866, following the death of his first wife and his remarriage, Haseltine and his family moved to Europe. They travelled throughout France, Switzerland and Italy; in 1874, after spending the previous winter in New York, Haseltine settled in the Villa Altieri in Rome. With the exception of extended trips, he lived there for the remainder of his life. He concentrated on picturesque depictions of European scenery that further explore his fascination with shoreline views, such as *Natural Arch at Capri* (1871; Washington, DC, N.G.A.). Haseltine, who was also a gifted draughtsman, worked in a closely detailed manner reflecting his German studies and his admiration of the Pre-Raphaelite Brotherhood. He tempered his concern with fact, however, with an appreciation of illusionistic light effects that added a progressive element to his traditionally plotted landscapes.

BIBLIOGRAPHY

H. Haseltine Plowden: *William Stanley Haseltine* (London, 1947)
M. Simpson, A. Henderson and S. Mills: *Expressions of Place: The Art of William Stanley Haseltine* (exh. cat., San Francisco, CA, F.A. Museums, 1992)

MARC SIMPSON

Hasenauer, Karl (*b* Vienna, 20 July 1833; *d* Vienna, 4 Jan 1894). Austrian architect. He studied (1850–55) under Eduard Van der Nüll and August Sicard von Siccardsburg at the Akademie der Bildenden Künste, Vienna. His earliest important designs were his entries in the two most prominent competitions in Vienna of the 1860s, for the Hofoper (1860–61) and the Hofmuseen (1867). His opera house proposal, distinguished by its boldness and richness of decoration, was placed third. Hasenauer's participation in the planning of the imperial museums, however, brought him the chance to become one of the leading architects of the Ringstrasse (*see* VIENNA, §II, 3). Of the four museum projects submitted by various architects, none was accepted, and early in 1869 Gottfried Semper, as the leading authority on historicist architecture in Germany, was asked to examine the plans. Semper suggested connecting the separate museum buildings (for the art and natural history collections) to a new, enlarged Hofburg, thus forming a spacious forum of imperial grandeur. His earliest design for this 'Kaiserforum' also included a new Hofburgtheater (*see* SEMPER, GOTTFRIED, fig. 2). When Semper's plan (1870; built 1871–89) was approved by Francis-Joseph, Emperor of Austria, Hasenauer, who was obviously most eager to be involved, succeeded in being appointed his assistant. Apparently because of Hasenauer's great ambition, the relationship between him and Semper was so unharmonious that a formal agreement had to be made (1876) in order to settle each architect's area of responsibility: Semper was entrusted with all artistic matters while Hasenauer supervised the construction and all technical and administrative works, a division that was maintained until Semper left Vienna (1877). Subsequently, Hasenauer slightly modified Semper's designs, especially for the exedra of the Hofburg. The interiors of the Kunsthistorisches Museum (vestibule and main dome) and of the Burgtheater, where the smaller vestibules contain the finest interior decoration of the 1880s in Vienna, are considered to be entirely Hasenauer's work. His last imperial commission (1881) was at Lainz, Emperor Francis-Joseph's favourite game park near Schönbrunn, where he built the Hermesvilla as a refuge for Empress Elisabeth. It was a prominent example of the refined Picturesque villa architecture of its date. Apart from his major projects Hasenauer built little, exceptions being the Austro-Hungarian pavilions for the world expositions in Paris (1867; destr.) and Vienna (1873; destr.) and a few private buildings in Vienna, for example the Azienda-Hof (1868–9) and the Palais Lützow in Giselastrasse.

BIBLIOGRAPHY

Ausschmückung des Interieurs des Kunsthistorischen Hofmuseums nach Entwürfen des Architekten Karl Frh. v. Hasenauer, k.k. Oberbaurat in Wien (Vienna, 1892)
A. Lhotsky: *Die Baugeschichte der Museen und der Neuen Burg* (Vienna, 1941)
K. Eggert: 'Die Hermesvilla im Lainzer Tiergarten bei Wien', *Alte & Mod. Kst.*, viii/66 (1963)
R. Wagner-Rieger: *Wiens Architektur im 19. Jahrhundert* (Vienna, 1970), pp. 152, 191–5, 254
——: *Vom Klassizismus bis zur Secession*, Gesch. Stadt Wien, vii/3 (Vienna, 1973), pp. 171, 182, 195, 207–9
U. Planner-Steiner and K. Eggert: 'Friedrich von Schmidt, Gottfried Semper, Carl von Hasenauer', *Die Wiener Ringstrasse: Bild einer Epoche*, ed. R. Wagner-Rieger, viii/2 (Wiesbaden, 1978)
Hermesvilla (exh. cat., Vienna, Hist. Mus., 1981)
J. Pemsel: *Die Wiener Weltausstellung von 1873 und ihre Bedeutung für die Entfaltung des Wiener Kulturlebens in der Franzisco-Josephinischen Epoche* (diss., U. Vienna, 1983)

SUSANNE KRONBICHLER-SKACHA

Hasenclever, Johann Peter (*b* Remscheid, 18 May 1810; *d* Düsseldorf, 16 Dec 1853). German painter. His artistic talent was recognized in 1827, while he was at school in Düsseldorf. The same year he embarked on a course in architecture at the Akademie in Düsseldorf. In 1828 he turned to the study of history painting. After a difference of opinion over the theory of art with the Director of the Akademie, Wilhelm von Schadow, Hasenclever went home to Remscheid. There he taught himself portrait painting. An example of his work from this period is the portrait of *Gertraude Scharff* (1832–3; Remscheid, Dt. Werkzeugmus. & Heimatmus.). From 1832 to 1838 Hasenclever again studied at the Akademie in Düsseldorf in a painting class taught by Ferdinand Theodor Hildebrandt (1804–74). In portraits and humorous genre paintings Hasenclever found a field suited to his gifts. Pithy commentaries on the everyday life of the lower middle classes are present in all of Hasenclever's work. He was best known for subjects such as wine-tastings and cellar scenes, and he also made a series of *Jobs* pictures, humorous, ironic interpretations of popular life based on the poem 'Jobsiade', a grotesque and comic heroic epic written by Carl Arnold Kortum in 1784. One of the last of the *Jobs* pictures was *Jobs as Schoolmaster* (1845; Düsseldorf, Kstmus.). The early works painted by Hasenclever in the 1830s already reveal the influence of the 17th-century Dutch 'petits maîtres'. He also found inspiration in the scenes and settings in the work of English painters such as William Hogarth or Thomas Rowlandson. In this respect *The Opening of the Will* by David Wilkie, which Hasenclever later saw in Vienna, was of special importance to him. Hasenclever was intrigued by the various types of heads with their exaggerated physiognomical features, the pronounced gestures, the theatrical quality of the scenery and the projection of light. In a similar manner, in *Scene in a Studio* (1836; Düsseldorf, Kstmus.), Hasenclever presented a satirical view of genre painters renouncing official art and the programme of the Düsseldorf Akademie.

In 1838 Hasenclever moved to Munich to continue his training with the still-life painter Johann Wilhelm Preyer and his brother Gustav Preyer (1801–39). In 1840 he travelled to Northern Italy, and he returned to live in Düsseldorf in 1842. In 1843 he married Caroline Trentini from Munich and made a second journey to Italy in her company. He became a member of the Berlin Akademie in 1843. From the early 1840s Hasenclever's painting became more fluid, with the transitions being more richly formed and the colours being applied boldly and with the freedom of a sketch. In addition to his activities in the realm of art Hasenclever was also active in the fields of social criticism and politics. He contributed satirical commentary to the *Düsseldorfer Monatshefte*, founded in 1847. Through his friendship with the poet Ferdinand Freiligrath

(1810–76) Hasenclever made contacts among the artistic opposition to the Akademie. In 1848 he was a co-founder of the Malkasten (Paintbox), an association that brought together artists sharing such views. In the autumn of the revolutionary year 1848 he produced one of his most important pictures, directly inspired by a demonstration of unemployed workers: *Workers before the City Authorities*. There are three versions of the picture (e.g. Düsseldorf, Kstmus.; Solingen, Bergisches Mus.; Münster, Westfäl. Kstver.), which shows a delegation of workers handing over a petition with a demand for work to the city authorities in the town hall. Hasenclever remained loyal to his progressive ideas until his death. As one of the most versatile representatives of genre painting in Düsseldorf in the first half of the 19th century, Hasenclever influenced those who came to study there, in particular American and Scandinavian artists.

BIBLIOGRAPHY
Thieme-Becker
W. Cohen: *Johann Peter Hasenclever* (Düsseldorf, 1925)
I. Markowitz: *Die Düsseldorfer Malerschule* (Düsseldorf, 1967)
Der Künstlerverein Malkasten: Die Anfänge (exh. cat., Düsseldorf, Kstlerver. Malkasten, 1973)
H. Bestvater-Hasenclever: *J. P. Hasenclever: Ein wacher Zeitgenosse des Biedermeier* (Recklinghausen, 1979)
Die Düsseldorfer Malerschule (exh. cat., Düsseldorf, Kstmus., 1979)
W. Hütt: *Johann Peter Hasenclever: Maler und Werk* (Dresden, 1983)

GUDRUN SCHMIDT

Hashem Muhammad al-Baghdadi [Hāshem al-Khaṭṭāṭ] (*b* Baghdad, 1917; *d* Baghdad, 1973). Iraqi calligrapher. He studied in Baghdad with Mulla 'Arif and then served an apprenticeship with Mulla Muhammad 'Ali al-Fadli (*d* 1948), who awarded him a calligraphy diploma in 1943. In 1944 he continued his studies in Cairo, where he was taught by Sayyid Ibrahim and Muhammad Husni at the Royal Institute of Calligraphy and received further awards. After returning to Baghdad, in 1946 he published a textbook on the *riqā'* style of calligraphy (*see* ISLAMIC ART, §III, 2(iii)(c)). He visited Turkey on several occasions and found favour with the Turkish calligrapher Hamid Aytaç of Istanbul, who awarded him diplomas in 1950 and 1952. In 1960 he was appointed lecturer in Arabic calligraphy at the Institute of Fine Arts in Baghdad and later became the head of the department of Arabic calligraphy and Islamic decoration. Hashem followed the classical Baghdad style of Yaqut al-Musta'simi and combined it with features from the Ottoman school of calligraphy. He was among the best calligraphers of the *thuluth* style. The other scripts he favoured were *naskh*, *nasta'līq*, *dīwānī*, *ijāza* and *muḥaqqaq*. He supervised the printing of a manuscript of the Koran by the Turkish calligrapher Muhammad Amin al-Rushdi, reilluminating missing letters, and adding other details. This Koran was published in Baghdad in 1951, and a second edition was published in Germany in 1966, for the supervision of which Hashem stayed in the country for three years. In 1961 he published an edition of his work ('The methods of Arab calligraphy') in Baghdad. His calligraphy adorns various buildings in Iraq, including al-Shahid Mosque, the mosque of Sheikh 'Abd al-Qadir al-Gilani, the Haydarkhana Mosque, the Muradiyya Mosque and the Bunia Mosque. He also designed Iraqi bank notes and coins for Morocco, Libya and Sudan. Although he planned to transcribe a copy of the Koran, he died before the project was completed. A statue of him was erected in his honour in al-Fadl quarter, Baghdad. He awarded only one diploma during his life, to his student Abdul Ghani al-Ani (*b* 1937).

BIBLIOGRAPHY
Hashem al-Khattat (exh. cat. by Y. H. Safadi, London, Iraqi Cult. Cent., 1978)
☐

Hashim [Hāshim] (*fl c.* 1598–1654). Indian miniature painter. It has been argued that Hashim joined the Mughal imperial atelier *c.* 1620 (rather than rising within its ranks) after serving at various courts of the Deccan, a position supported by the Deccani identities of the subjects of several of his early portraits. Though some critics date these paintings after the artist moved to the Mughal court, they cannot envision the paintings' apparently acute naturalistic description without direct observation, and thus assume that Hashim had prior personal contact with his subjects while he was in the Deccan. This argument is advanced particularly for portraits of two rulers, Malik 'Ambar of Ahmadnagar (London, V&A, IM.21-1925, and Paris, Mus. Guimet, n.7172) and Ibrahim 'Adil Shah II of Bijapur (New York, Met., 55.121.10.33*v*), both of whom refused to surrender in person to the conquering Mughal army. Accordingly, certain elements of Hashim's style, specifically the strong contours, Deccani costume details and palette, are considered to be vestiges of his Deccani

Hashim: *Shah Jahan*, opaque colour on paper, 251×158 mm, 1629 (Washington, DC, Freer Gallery of Art, 39.49)

origins, while his thoroughly Mughal rendering of facial features is attributed to the rapid stylistic changes made at Jahangir's direction.

The peculiar combination of artistic conservatism and radical change implicit in this theory is quite implausible. The absence of allegedly Deccani features from works that do not depict Deccani subjects underscores the optional nature of these Deccani elements and trappings, whose use was occasioned by the figure's identity. Moreover, the survival of the Deccani prototype (Boston, MA, Mus. F.A., 26.8) for Hashim's representation of the stocky Abyssinian figure makes it clear that Hashim drew solely on models of Deccani images for at least some of his portraits of Deccani personages.

Hashim's style remained consistent throughout his long career, from his earliest securely dated work, a majestic portrait of *Shah Jahan* (1629; Washington, DC, Freer, 39.49; see fig.), to his latest, a Mughal dynastic triumvirate (1653–4; Switzerland, priv. col.). The nature of Hashim's work, limited almost exclusively to profile views of isolated sovereigns and nobles, discourages an empathetic reaction to his figures. Hashim's style also contributes to this static, aloof quality; his predilection for crisply delineated forms and strong contours arrests any hint of movement, and the surface brilliance of his figures' garb often overwhelms their faces.

See also INDIAN SUBCONTINENT, §V, 5(i)(c) and (d).

BIBLIOGRAPHY
The Grand Mogul: Imperial Painting in India, 1600–1660 (exh. cat. by M. C. Beach, Williamstown, MA, Clark A. Inst.; Baltimore MD, Walters A.G.; Boston, MA, Mus. F.A.; New York, Asia House Gals; 1978–9)
S. C. Welch and others: *The Emperors' Album* (New York, 1987)
J. Seyller: 'Hashim', *Master Artists of the Imperial Mughal Court*, ed. P. Pal (Bombay, 1991), pp. 105–18

JOHN SEYLLER

Hashimoto, Heihachi (*b* Asakuma-mura, Mie Prefect., 17 Oct 1897; *d* Asakuma-mura, 1 Nov 1935). Japanese sculptor. He went to Tokyo in 1919 and the following year became a pupil of Chōzan Satō (1888–1963), a member of the Japan Art Institute; he lived with the Satō household for six years. In 1922 Hashimoto's sculpture *Cat* (wood, h. 350 mm, 1922; Tsu, Mie Prefect. A. Mus.) was accepted for the ninth In-ten exhibition. In 1923 he left Tokyo because of the Great Kantō earthquake and went to live in Nara. In 1926 he returned to his home town in Mie, settling there permanently. In 1927 he exhibited his statue of a *Naked Youth* (wood, h. 1.54 m, 1927; Tokyo U. A., A. Mus.) at the 14th In-ten exhibition, a work reminiscent of ancient Egyptian sculpture. In the same year he became a member of the Japan Art Institute. In 1930 he exhibited *Goddess Playing in a Flower Garden* (wood, h. 1.22 m, 1930; Tokyo U. A., A. Mus.) at the 17th In-ten exhibition, a characteristic work: the entire body of the goddess was carved so that the head, torso, arms and legs are like flower petals, and within this, the image of a butterfly can be seen; although representing a young female, the body seems genderless, and her facial expression is reminiscent of Buddhist sculptures. In his later years Hashimoto was deeply impressed by a 17th-century Buddhist statue that he saw in Takayama, Gifu Prefecture; this was done by the monk Enkū. Under Enkū's influence

he produced wooden sculptures with the sharp chisel marks still visible, such as that of the Buddhist monk *Ryōkan* (wood, h. 274 mm, 1934; Tokyo U. A., A. Mus.). His theory of sculpture was published in a book called *Junsui chōkoku ron* ('A theory of pure sculpture') in 1942.

BIBLIOGRAPHY
M. Honma: *Hashimoto Heihachi to Enkū* [Heihachi Hashimoto and Enkū] (Tokyo, 1973)
Hashimoto Heihachi to Enkū—Mokuchō.nata-bori no keifu [Heihachi Hashimoto and Enkū—the heritage of hatchet-carving and wood-carving] (exh. cat., essay by T. Kagesato; Tsu, Mie Prefect. A. Mus., 1985)

YASUYOSHI SAITO

Hashimoto Gahō [Hashimoto Masakuni; Gahō; Togansai] (*b* Edo [now Tokyo], 1835; *d* Tokyo, 1908). Japanese painter. One of the last masters of the KANŌ SCHOOL of painters (for family tree *see* KANŌ), he played an important role in the survival and modernization of traditional Japanese-style painting (*Nihonga*) in the late 19th century (*see* JAPAN, §VI, 5(iii)). He was the son of a minor professional painter supported by the Matsudaira family. In 1847 he entered the Kobikichō branch of the Kanō school in Edo where he studied under Kanō Shōsen'in Tadanobu (1823–80) and mastered the then waning Kanō ink painting traditions. In 1857 he succeeded Shōsen'in Tadanobu as head of the school. Three years later he established an independent studio in Edo. Following the Meiji Restoration of 1868, Western models were officially sanctioned and widely adopted, even in the arts, including art education and patronage. Painters of the Kanō school, having fallen from favour, were forced to seek other means of livelihood: from 1871 to 1886 Gahō made his living by teaching cartography and making maps for the Japanese navy.

Eventually traditional Japanese painting was rescued by a sympathetic group of state leaders. Further impetus to the movement was provided by Ernest Fenollosa, who had come to Tokyo from the United States in 1878 to teach at the newly established Imperial University, and his protégé Okakura Tenshin (1862–1913). Fenollosa and Okakura joined forces with the Ryūchikai (Dragon Pond Society), founded in 1879, to establish the Kangakai (Painting Appreciation Society) in 1884, which supported the practice of *Nihonga* and defended it against *Yōga* (Western-style painting; *see* JAPAN, §VI, 5(v)). Gahō and his fellow Kanō-school painter Kanō Hōgai (*see* KANŌ, (16)) were founder-members of the Kangakai and became the exemplary painters of the society. Gahō inspired Japanese artists of the next generation to preserve their artistic heritage, while at the same time adjusting their stylistic traditions to meet the challenge of Western art. He contributed to the evolution of a new style of Japanese painting by blending Kanō-school techniques with elements of Western naturalism, perspective and colour. This synthesis of Japanese and Western painting was less a revolution than a redefinition of Kanō-school eclecticism.

It was, however, as a teacher that Gahō made his most important contribution to the modernization of traditional Japanese painting. From 1888 to 1897 he taught painting at the Tōkyō Bijutsu Gakkō (Tokyo Art School) and from 1898 until his death, at the Nihon Bijutsuin (Japan Art Institute), also in Tokyo. Among his pupils were the leading *Nihonga* artists of the early 20th century, such as

Taikan Yokoyama, Kanzan Shimomura and Shunsō Hishida. Curiously, although Gahō lectured his pupils on the importance of 'feeling' (*kokoromochi*) in a painting, his own technically faultless works seem to lack that quality (e.g. the hanging scrolls *Bamboo and Cat*, 1896; Tokyo, N. Mus.; and *White Clouds and Autumn Leaves*, 1890; Tokyo, U. F.A. & Music); yet the works of Taikan, Kanzan and Shunsō, whose styles came out of Gahō's synthesis, have it in abundance. In 1890 Gahō was among the first artists appointed to the newly established Teishitsu Bijutsuin (Imperial Art Academy), and in 1907 he sat on the jury of the first national art exhibition, the Bunten, sponsored by the Monbushō (Ministry of Education).

BIBLIOGRAPHY
N. Uyeno: *Japanese Culture in the Meiji Era*, Centenary Cultural Council series, viii (Tokyo, 1958)

AYA LOUISA McDONALD

Hasior, Władysław (*b* Nowy Sącz, 14 May 1928). Polish sculptor. He studied at the State Secondary School for Arts and Crafts, Zakopane, from 1947 to 1952 under Antoni Kenar (*b* 1906), and at the Academy of Fine Arts, Warsaw, from 1952 to 1958, in the sculpture workshop of Marian Wnuk (*b* 1906); in 1959 he studied in Paris under Ossip Zadkine. He joined the international group of writers and artists Phases in 1961. He took part in many exhibitions at home and abroad (including the São Paulo Biennali of 1965 and 1971, the Venice Biennale of 1970 and one-man exhibitions at, among others, Moderna Museet, Stockholm, 1968 and the Louisiana Museum, Humlebœk, Denmark, 1972).

In 1957, while studying with Oskar Hansen, Hasior began to form assemblages by incorporating various objects into larger compositions (e.g. *The Widow*). In 1960 he made some concrete casts of a structure excavated from the ground (entitled *Sebastian*; see 1991 exh. cat., p. 51). His best-known and most characteristic compositions date from this period (e.g. *Niobe*; 1961; Łódź, Mus. A.; *The Guest*, 1960; see 1968 exh. cat.), as do his allusion-rich assemblages, which make use of objects in daily use, salvaged pieces and junk oddments to depict, metaphorically, themes deeply rooted in contemporary Polish affairs. At the same time these are encompassed in a form close to magic rituals of exorcism (burning candles, and totem- and altar-like compositional designs). In 1973 Hasior presented a procession of his new compositions, *Banners* (see 1991 exh. cat., pp. 90–93), whose form was associated with church banners, on the suburban hills of Łącko. From the late 1950s Hasior designed and executed monuments, for example that *To Those Who Lost their Lives in Consolidating the Authority of the People in the Podhale Region* (Czorsztyn, 1966; see 1991 exh. cat., p. 83), which was also known as the *Playing Organs* (when situated in a mountain pass in strong winds, this composition was supposed to give out an especially tuned sound). Hasior's work has often, rather rashly, been interpreted as a peculiar variation of Pop art or Nouveau Réalisme.

BIBLIOGRAPHY
Władysław Hasior (exh. cat., ed. C. Derkert; Stockholm, Mod. Mus., 1968)
A. Micińska: *Władysław Hasior* (Warsaw, 1983)
Władysław Hasior, Camiel van Breedam (exh. cat., Darmstadt, Ksthalle, 1991)

WOJCIECH WŁODARCZYK

Hasōhai. *See* CHŌDENSU MINCHŌ.

Hassam, (Frederick) Childe (*b* Dorchester, MA, 17 Oct 1859; *d* East Hampton, NY, 27 Aug 1935). American painter and printmaker. The son of Frederick F. Hassam, a prominent Boston merchant, and his wife, Rosa P. Hathorne, he was initially trained as an apprentice to a wood-engraver. From the late 1870s to the mid-1880s he executed drawings for the illustration of books, particularly children's stories. He had a long affiliation with the Boston firm of Daniel Lothrop & Co., for whom he illustrated E. S. Brooks's *In No-man's Land: A Wonder Story* (1885), Margaret Sidney's *A New Departure for Girls* (1886) and numerous other books.

Hassam's first significant body of non-graphic work was in watercolour. He executed a group of freely washed, light-filled drawings of local landscapes, which provided the basis for his first one-man show in 1882 at the Boston galleries of Williams & Everett. Hassam attended evening classes at the Boston Art Club and by 1883 had a studio on Tremont Street in Boston. His early career was established by his watercolours rather than by his few oils, which were thickly painted landscapes inspired by the Barbizon school. In 1883 he visited Europe for the first time, with fellow artist Edmund C. Garrett (1853–1929). Over 60 bright, illustrative watercolours from this trip were exhibited in Boston in 1884. During the mid-1880s Hassam established himself in Boston as a painter of urban street scenes, employing a tonalist style that emphasized atmospheric conditions, as in *Rainy Day in Boston* (1885; Toledo, OH, Mus. A.; see fig.).

Late in 1886 Hassam and his wife, Kathleen Maud (née Doane), departed for France and spent the next three years abroad. They settled in Paris, and Hassam began lessons in drawing at the Académie Julian with Gustave Boulanger and Jules Lefebvre. His work of these years reflects his growing awareness of the French Impressionists; he consistently used broken brushstrokes, and his palette rapidly became brighter (e.g. *Grand Prix Day, c.* 1887–8; New Britain, CT, Mus. Amer. A.). Hassam's Parisian oils and watercolours depict the more genteel and picturesque aspects of urban life: Montmartre shops, flower vendors, parks and private gardens. Although he adopted an Impressionist brushstroke, he retained a sense of solidity and form in his figures, creating a hybrid style that is characteristic of American Impressionism. Hassam preferred to consider himself a painter of 'light and air' in a general sense rather than be labelled an Impressionist, and he believed that the work of the French Impressionists was derived from earlier sources, particularly English art of the 18th century.

In 1889 Hassam settled in New York. He continued to depict the urban scene, a genre with which he became so closely identified that a monograph entitled *Three Cities* (New York, 1899) was devoted to reproductions of his imagery of Paris, London and New York. In the summer seasons he travelled to artistic resorts throughout New England. Around 1884 he visited Appledore Island, one of the Isles of Shoals off the Maine–New Hampshire coast, and he returned there repeatedly during the early 1890s to produce some of his finest and most sophisticated Impressionist watercolours and oils. His friendship with

Childe Hassam: *Rainy Day in Boston*, oil on canvas, 663×1220 mm, 1885 (Toledo, OH, Museum of Art)

Mrs Celia Thaxter, a poet and patron of the arts who owned a local hotel, inspired him to execute a series of extremely impressionistic pictures of her opulent flower gardens, including his splendid watercolour the *Island Garden* (1892; Washington, DC, N. Mus. Amer. A.).

By 1892 Hassam was exhibiting regularly at the annual exhibitions of most of the major art institutions on the East Coast, including the Boston Art Club, American Water Color Society, National Academy of Design, New York Water Color Club, Pennsylvania Academy of the Fine Arts and the Philadelphia Art Club. He achieved considerable success during this decade and was able to support himself by the sale of his pictures. In 1896–7 he and his wife spent 18 months in Europe, visiting Italy, France and England. His work from this trip indicates his continued adherence to an Impressionist style but reveals also a heightened palette and a new rigid, aggressive brushstroke. In addition to vivid colour, Hassam's pictures of 1897–8 show his awareness of Post-Impressionist and Symbolist art. As well as dazzling urban scenes (e.g. *Pont Royal, Paris*; Cincinnati, OH, A. Mus.), he executed numerous works in Normandy and Brittany, particularly in the village of Pont-Aven.

In 1898 he helped to organize the first exhibition, in New York, of the TEN AMERICAN PAINTERS, with whom he shared a desire to exhibit recent work in an environment both less constrictive and less aesthetically diverse than that of a major academy. Despite Hassam's avowed distrust of modern art, his own 20th-century work reflects his growing interest in the abstract and decorative qualities of paint on a surface. Around 1900 he explored symbolic and anti-naturalist subject-matter, producing many mythically titled nudes (e.g. *Pomona*, 1900; Washington, DC, N. Mus. Amer. A.). Although Hassam believed many of these pictures to be among his finest, they did not find as receptive an audience as his more naturalistic landscapes.

Between 1900 and 1910 Hassam continued to live and work in New York, during the warmer months visiting the artistic colonies at Cos Cob and Old Lyme, CT; his brand of Impressionism influenced not only students and amateur artists who gathered there, but also fellow American Impressionists such as Julian Alden Weir and Willard Leroy Metcalf. In the summers of 1904 and 1908 Hassam stayed in Oregon with his friend Colonel Charles E. S. Wood (1852–1944), a lawyer by profession but also an amateur painter, poet and patron of the arts. In addition to executing a mural for Wood's residence, Hassam produced over 40 bright impressionistic landscapes of the stark eastern Oregon desert, which were exhibited at Montross Galleries, New York, in 1909.

In 1910 and 1911 Hassam made his final trips to Europe, where he painted the Bastille Day celebration in Paris, *July Fourteenth, Rue Daunou* (1910; New York, Met.); this work prefigures his renowned series of flag paintings produced in New York between 1916 and 1918 depicting the patriotic parades along Fifth Avenue ('Avenue of the Allies') during World War I (e.g. *Allies Day, May 1917*, 1917; Washington, DC, N.G.A.).

At the age of 55 Hassam embarked on a career in printmaking, executing over 350 etchings and 40 lithographs. He depicted both the bustling activity of urban life, as in his etching *Fifth Avenue, Noon* (1915), and the charms of rural existence in his many landscapes, some including colonial cottages. His etchings were admired by contemporaries for their impressionistic technique. In 1919 he purchased an early 18th-century cottage in the Long Island community of East Hampton, NY, a gathering place for artists. He returned there and painted each summer for the next 15 years, depicting the lush farmlands and expansive beaches. Hassam persisted in producing such symbolic paintings as the overtly mythological *Young Apollo and the Flying Swan* (1921; East Hampton, NY, Guild Hall Mus.), perhaps with a nostalgic yearning not atypical of aging artists or the post-war period. Hassam left his entire artistic estate to the American Academy of Arts and Letters, New York, with instructions that the works be sold to establish a fund supporting young American and Canadian artists by purchasing their work for museum collections.

BIBLIOGRAPHY

N. Pousette-Dart, ed.: *Childe Hassam* (New York, 1922)
R. Cortissoz: *Introduction to the Etchings and Drypoints of Childe Hassam, N.A.* (New York, 1925)
P. Eliasoph: *Handbook of the Complete Set of Etchings and Drypoints of Childe Hassam, N.A.* (New York, 1933)
'Childe Hassam—Painter and Graver', *Index of Twentieth Century Artists*, iii (New York, 1935/R 1970), pp. 169–83
A. Adams: *Childe Hassam* (New York, 1938)
F. Griffith: *The Lithographs of Childe Hassam: A Catalogue* (Washington, DC, 1962)
Childe Hassam: A Retrospective Exhibition (exh. cat., Washington, DC, Corcoran Gal. A., 1965)
Childe Hassam, 1859–1935 (exh. cat., Tucson, U. AZ, Mus. A.; Santa Barbara, U. CA, A. Mus.; 1972)
D. Hoopes: *Childe Hassam* (New York, 1979)
Childe Hassam, 1859–1935 (exh. cat., East Hampton, NY, Guild Hall Mus., 1981)

KATHLEEN M. BURNSIDE

Hassan, Faik [Arab. Fā'iq Hasan] (*b* Baghdad, 1914; *d* 1992). Iraqi painter. He won a scholarship to the Ecole des Beaux-Arts, Paris, from which he graduated in 1938. On returning to Iraq he exhibited his work, and established and directed the department of painting and sculpture at the Institute of Fine Arts, Baghdad. He was influenced by a number of European movements, including Impressionism and Cubism, as well as by abstract art, but he also painted realistic scenes of life in Iraq. Between 1943 and 1946 he took part in the exhibitions of the Friends of the Arts Society in Baghdad, and in 1952 exhibited at the Ibn Sina Exhibition of Arab artists in Baghdad. In the 1950s he was president of the group of artists called The Pioneers (founded in 1950 as La Société Primitive), and was later succeeded in this position by his pupil Ismail Sheikhley (al-Chekhli; *b* 1924). This group held private exhibitions until 1962, the year in which Hassan withdrew from it. After the creation of the Iraqi republic in 1958 he worked on a mosaic mural with a nationalistic theme called the *Celebration of Victory*, located in Tiran Square, Baghdad. This mural reveals the influence on him of European works such as Picasso's *Demoiselles d'Avignon* (New York, MOMA). In the years 1962 and 1967 he held solo exhibitions, and in 1965 he showed with nine other Iraqi artists in Beirut. In 1967 he established a group called Al-Zawiya, with whom he exhibited; this group advocated the implementation of art to serve national causes. A retrospective exhibition of his work was organized by the Iraqi government in 1971. During the 1980s he reverted to an Impressionist technique.

BIBLIOGRAPHY

S. al-Rabi'i: *Al-fann al-tashkīlī al-mu'āsir fī'l-'Irāq* [Modern painting in Iraq] (Baghdad, 1972) [Arab. text]
S. Faris: *Al-manābi 'al-tārīkhiyya li'l-fann al-jidārī fī'l-'Irāq al-mu'āsir* [The historic origins of mural art in contemporary Iraq] (Baghdad, 1974) [Arab. text]
Iraqi Art of the 50s (exh. cat., London, Iraqi Cult. Cent., 1979)
A. A. Bogdanov: *Sovremennoe izobrazitel'noe iskusstvo Iraka (1900-e–1970-e godui)* [Contemporary art in Iraq] (Leningrad, 1982) [Rus. text]
W. Ali, ed.: *Contemporary Art from the Islamic World* (London, 1989), pp. 159–64

S. J. VERNOIT

Hasselberg, (Karl) Per [Petter; Peter] Åkesson (*b* Hasselstad, 1 Jan 1850; *d* Stockholm, 24 July 1894). Swedish sculptor. He trained as an ornamental sculptor and first practised in Stockholm. From 1876 he lived in Paris, where from 1877 to 1879 he studied at the Ecole des Beaux-Arts. In 1880 he exhibited at the Paris Salon and in 1881 got an honourable mention for *The Snow-clock* (Stockholm, N Mus.; replica, Göteborg, Kstmus.), a life-size sculpture in white marble of a young girl. The title refers to the snowdrop and to an awakening from innocence. Hasselberg's most original works were for the gallery of the private palace of the patron and art collector, Pontus Fürstenberg in Göteborg; he sculpted six allegorical groups of life-size figures in plaster (1884; Göteborg, Kstmus.) representing the technical exploitation of the forces of nature. Hasselberg was probably inspired by French models such as Emile Arthur Soldis's reliefs *Photography* and *Electricity* (1882) on the Hôtel de Ville in Paris, and by Michelangelo's Medici tombs in the New Sacristy in S Lorenzo, Florence, but the allegories are completely his own. In 1886 he sculpted the *Grandfather*, an aged sleeping philosopher with a naked slumbering boy on his knee. Considered indecent, it caused a lively press debate in 1895 when it was posthumously erected in Humlegården, Stockholm. *The Frog* (1890) and *Water Lily* (1892; both Göteborg, Kstmus.) are sensually modelled in white marble. They represent girls unaware of the power of their physical beauty. The latter was sculpted from Hasselberg's plaster model by Christian Eriksson (1858–1935). Hasselberg broke with the dry post-classical style of Swedish sculpture. His work shows the influence of Jean-Baptiste Carpeaux and French Salon sculptors of the 1880s, but also expresses a romantic natural lyricism.

BIBLIOGRAPHY

R. Bergh: *Per Hasselberg, 1850–1894: Minnesblad* [Memorial paper] (Stockholm, 1898)
A. Romdahl: *Per Hasselberg: Tre Studier* [Three studies] (Göteborg, 1909)
L. Wennberg: 'Natursymboliken hos Per Hasselberg' [The nature symbolism of Per Hasselberg], *Tidskr. Kstvet.*, xxix (1952), pp. 70–91
——: 'Ångan och magnetismen' [Steam and magnetism], *Tidskr. Kstvet.*, xxxii (1957), pp. 89–108
H.-O. Boström: 'Naketskilringar i Fürstenbergska galleriet' [Nude studies in the Fürstenberg gallery], *Konsthist. Tidskr.*, viii (1989), pp. 124–40

HANS-OLOF BOSTRÖM

Hassendō. *See* SAKAKI HYAKUSEN.

Hastie [Geste; Gesti], **William** [Vasily (Ivanovich)] (*b* ?Edinburgh, 1755; *d* Tsarskoye Selo [now Pushkin], 16 June 1832). Scottish architect, active in Russia. He arrived in Russia in 1784 as a mason, contracted, together with 72 other Scottish craftsmen, to assist Charles Cameron in constructing Catherine II's palace-and-park ensembles at Tsarskoye Selo. He was taken into Catherine's service on an independent basis in 1792. He then produced albums and sheets of architectural designs for country houses, pavilions and villas in the neo-Palladian and Gothic Revival styles (1794; St Petersburg, Hermitage). These resulted, in 1795, in his being appointed chief architect to Prince Platon Zubov (1767–1822), the new governor-general of the Yekaterinoslav and Crimean provinces. In this position he contributed to the restoration of the Khan's Palace (1798) at Bakhchisaray. Back in St Petersburg by the early 1800s Hastie designed the Admiralty's Izhora Ironworks at Kolpino (1801–8) and, having been appointed to Alexander I's new Ministry of Waterways, designed the first cast-iron transport bridges in Russia (e.g. the Police Bridge, St Petersburg, 1805–6). His success led to his being appointed chief architect of Tsarskoye Selo in 1808. There he planned and built a new town as regional centre. The plan was strictly geometrical, the buildings austerely Neo-classical. The suitability of Hastie's projects for standardization led to his appointment by Alexander I in 1811 as head of Russian urban planning. For over 20 years in this role he created a multitude of regularized plans and model projects (including façade types, on which he worked with Luigi Rosca) that were to transform the appearance of numerous Russian cities, from Krasnoyarsk to Onega.

WRITINGS
Razdeleniye gorodskikh kvartalov na uchastki [The division of city blocks into single lots] (St Petersburg, [1812])

BIBLIOGRAPHY
A. J. Schmidt: 'William Hastie, Scottish Planner of Russian Cities', *Proc. Amer. Philos. Soc.*, cxiv/3 (1970), pp. 226–43
M. Korshunova: 'William Hastie in Russia', *Archit. Hist.*, xvii (1974), pp. 14–21
D. Shvidkovsky: 'Classical Edinburgh and Russian Town-planning of the Late 18th and Early 19th Centuries: The Role of William Hastie (1755–1832)', *Archit. Her.*, ii (1991), pp. 69–78

JEREMY HOWARD

Hastinapura [Hastināpura]. Site of an ancient city, once capital of the Kauravas of *Mahābhārata* epic fame, on the right bank of the Ganga River in Meerut District, Uttar Pradesh, India. Excavation (1950–52) of the ancient mound yielded evidence of five cultural periods. Period I (pre-1200 BC), the earliest occupation, was characterized by Ochre Colour Ware and the absence of iron. Period II (c. 1100–800 BC) was distinguished by Painted Grey Ware (PGW), the first use of iron and evidence of the horse. Other objects included beads of cornelian, agate, jasper and bone, bangles of glass (the earliest so far in India) and terracotta figurines of animals. The PGW occupation was destroyed by heavy flooding of the Ganga River. Not only was there ample evidence of river erosion at the foot of the riverside face of the mound, but washed-away material was also encountered in borings in the riverbed, some 15 m below water-level. A late stage of PGW has also been found in the earliest levels at Kausambi. These two pieces of archaeological evidence provide circumstantial evidence for the Puranic statement that during the reign of Nichakshu, fifth king after the war related in the *Mahābhārata*, a flood destroyed Hastinapura and the capital was shifted to Kausambi. The site was subsequently reoccupied, and Period III (6th–3rd century BC) was noted for Northern Black Polished Ware (NBPW), use of kiln-fired bricks for house construction, terracotta ring-wells and the first evidence of coinage (punch-marked and uninscribed cast coins). Human and animal figurines and

beads of hardstone and glass were also found. Period IV (2nd century BC–3rd century AD) had exclusively red ware pottery and coins of the kings of Mathura, the Yaudheyas and Kushanas, while a terracotta figurine of the *bodhisattva* Maitreya has counterparts in Mathura sculpture. After a considerable hiatus, Period V (11th–15th century) evidences glazed ware, coins of Balban (*reg* 1266–87) and other artefacts indicative of Indo-Islamic occupation.

BIBLIOGRAPHY
K. D. Bajpai: *Hastināpur* (Lucknow, 1955)
B. B. Lal: 'Hastināpura, Hastinapur', *An Encyclopaedia of Indian Archaeology*, i (Leiden, 1990), pp. 164–6

B. B. LAL

Hastings, Hubert de Cronin (*b* London, 18 July 1902; *d* Bedham, Surrey, 20 Oct 1986). English architectural editor, publisher and writer. He studied architecture at the Bartlett School, University of London, and art at the Slade School, London, and in 1926 he joined the Architectural Press, of which his father was proprietor. In 1927–32 and 1935–7 he was editor of the *Architectural Review*, transforming it from a staid, academic magazine to one notable for its adventurous policies and original use of photographs and typography, which strongly influenced English magazine production. He was also editor of the *Architects' Journal* (1932–7) and a founder-member of the English modern architecture MARS Group (1933). In 1937 he left London for Sussex, where he farmed, but he remained chairman of the Architectural Press until his retirement in 1973 and retained a dominating influence over the conduct and policies of the company's publications. His special interests were planning and land use, about which he promoted influential features in the *Architectural Review*. Between 1942 and 1946, when its editor J. M. Richards was absent on war service, Hastings returned as co-editor with Nikolaus Pevsner, reinforcing the magazine's concern with the theory and practice of planning and initiating campaigns to further his belief in the applicability of the 18th-century theory of the picturesque to contemporary urban design. For his contribution to planning and his eminence as an editor, Hastings was awarded the Royal Gold Medal for Architecture in 1971. He wrote relatively little in the magazines he edited but published two books: *Italian Townscape* (1963), under the pseudonym Ivor de Wolfe, and *The Alternative Society* (1980) on economics.

WRITINGS
I. de Wolfe [H. de C. Hastings]: *Italian Townscape* (London, 1963)
The Alternative Society (North Pomfret, VT, 1980)

BIBLIOGRAPHY
Obituary, *Daily Telegraph* (8 Dec 1986)

J. M. RICHARDS

Hastings, Rafael (Eduardo Indacochea) (*b* Lima, 27 March 1945). Peruvian painter and sculptor. He studied at the Pontificia Universidad Católica de Lima, the Université Catholique de Louvain, the Université Libre in Brussels, the Royal College of Art in London and the Ecole du Louvre in Paris. Concerning himself primarily with the figure and with the destiny of the human race, he combined a firm and suggestive draughtsmanship with a balanced use of colour, later favouring intimate dreamlike atmospheres that are sometimes disquieting or suggestive of profound solitude.

LUIS ENRIQUE TORD

Hastings, T. *See under* CARRÈRE & HASTINGS.

Hatch, Stephen D(ecatur) (*b* Swanton, VT, 1839; *d* Plainfield, NJ, 1894). American architect. He trained in the New York office of the commercial architect John Butler Snook and set up in practice on his own in 1864. Hatch was adept at providing plain buildings, built sturdily and on time. His work was both commercial and domestic, using a free Second-Empire French style during the 1860s and 1870s and a looser late Victorian mode for his later commercial buildings. Much of his work has been destroyed. The commercial work included the iron-fronted Gilsey Hotel (1868), Windsor Hotel (1873; destr.), the Union Dime Savings Bank (1875–7; destr.) and the Murray Hill Hotel (1881; destr.), all in New York. Some of his commissions came from further afield, such as the Jubilee Hall (1876), at Fisk University, Nashville, TN, and the Liverpool and Globe Insurance building (1880; destr.) in London. His domestic work was usually in an Italianate manner and included some grand houses on Fifth Avenue bought by such rich clients as Jay Gould (1868; destr.) and William Rockefeller (1876–7; destr.). Although Hatch was well suited to fulfilling the straightforward requirements of clients following the American Civil War, by the 1880s he was losing ground to more fashionable architects who had trained abroad. When he died during the construction of the headquarters of the New York Life Insurance Company, he was succeeded by the Beaux-Arts firm of McKim, Mead & White.

BIBLIOGRAPHY
New York's Great Industries (New York, 1885)
Obituary, *Amer. Architect & Bldg News*, xvi (1894), p. 69; *Archit. & Bldg News* (21 Aug 1894)

MOSETTE GLASER BRODERICK

Hatching. Method of suggesting relief by shading in closely set parallel lines. It is used in linear styles of drawing, engraving and etching, and sometimes in painting. In egg tempera, the paint was sometimes applied in hatched single strokes so that it did not blend with the layer below. Crosshatching consists of two layers of parallel lines, crossing at an angle (*see* GOLTZIUS, HENDRICK, fig. 1).

RUPERT FEATHERSTONE

Hathaway, Rufus (*b* Freetown, MA, ?2 Feb 1770; *d* Duxbury, MA, 13 Oct 1822). American painter and physician. He may have been apprenticed to ship-carvers and decorators but he was not trained in fine art. His earliest known portrait, *Lady with her Pets* (1790; New York, Met.), demonstrates his unsophisticated, decorative style. Between 1790 and 1796 he seems to have worked as an itinerant artist; only portraits of relatives and friends survive. During his life he painted at least 25 portraits as well as miniatures, views and decorative overmantels. He also painted a genre subject, the *Welch Curate*, *c.* 1800 (see Valentine and Little, p. 641), which was freely adapted from an English mezzotint. He carved the frames for some of his paintings. From 1796 he studied medicine and established himself as a physician in Duxbury.

Hathaway communicated a sense of the sitter's individual character in his portraits. His style represented the culmination of the American limner tradition in which a simplified but recognizable facial likeness surmounts a conventionalized figure. He combined this method with an awareness of contemporary academic practice in portraiture, which he may have gained from prints or from works by John Smibert and John Singleton Copley seen in Boston. Since the 1930s his portraits have been admired for exemplifying the strength of design found in the work of many untrained American painters.

BIBLIOGRAPHY
N. F. Little: 'Rufus Hathaway', *American Folk Painters*, ed. J. Lipman and T. Armstrong (New York, 1980), pp. 35–40
L. Valentine and N. F. Little: 'Rufus Hathaway, Artist and Physician', *Antiques*, cxxxi (1987), pp. 628–41

DAVID TATHAM

Hatillo, El [Calderon Site]. Pre-Columbian site in Panama, near Parita, Herrera Province. It was first investigated by Matthew Stirling and Gordon Willey during the National Geographic Society/Smithsonian Institution Expedition in 1948, then by Russell Mitchell and John Acker in 1957–8 and by John Ladd and Thelma Bull in the early 1960s. Excavation focused on a series of mounds, some of which were burials accompanied by great quantities of grave goods, including ceramic vessels and bone, stone and gold objects. Analysis of these by Olga Linares interprets them as recognizably part of the long tradition of the COCLÉ culture, indicating occupation of the site in the Late Coclé and subsequent Herrera phases (*c.* AD 1200–*c.* 1500). Various reports describe from 10 to 13 mounds, possibly due to the fact that the site has been occupied and sufficiently disturbed in recent decades to change the nature of the plan. The basic layout consists of a series of small, low oval-shaped tumuli, 2–3 m high, in a nearly circular arrangement *c.* 100–150 m across. Excavations uncovered structural platforms and intentional burials. The human skeletons found had been buried in a flexed or seated position, or lying prone on top of small, four-legged *metates* (grinding stones). What appeared to be secondary burials had been placed inside Red Ware urns. All were associated with fire or charred materials, and some showed evidence of partial cremation. A few may have been sacrificial victims accompanying a high-status individual.

The pottery consists of a simple utilitarian Red Ware and elaborately decorated polychrome vessels referred to variously as El Hatillo ware, Parita ware and Herrera-phase pottery. Forms include jars and urns, bowls, plates and bird effigy vessels. Some rest on short tripod legs, while others are raised on cylindrical pedestals. Many have rounded bases and opposed loop or ribbon handles. Examples range in size from miniatures of 60 mm in diameter and 70 mm high to 330 mm in diameter and 280 mm high. Painted decoration consists mainly of black and red designs on a buff to white slip. The most common motifs are bands, chevrons and the YC or S scroll patterns so common in Coclé ceramics. Recognizable imagery includes highly stylized images of the Crocodile god, Bat god, snakes, sharks, frogs, vultures and felines. Others have fluted bodies or small effigy forms appended to the handles or vessel shoulders.

In addition to ceramics, the burials contained stone, shell, bone and metal objects. The stone implements were all celts ranging from 84 mm to 200 mm in length. The shell and bone objects, apparently intended for personal adornment, included pendants and beads. Stirling also reported excavating batons made from manatee ribs carved to represent stylized alligators or frogs, and a necklace made from several hundred human teeth. In contrast to the earlier dated Coclé site of SITIO CONTE, the only gold items recovered at El Hatillo were a small gold disc originally attached to a *tumbaga* (an alloy of gold and copper) pendant, and a larger, flattened, circular pectoral. Artefacts from the excavation of El Hatillo are now in the Museo Nacional de Panamá, Panama City, and in several small museums in Herrera Province.

For discussion of Pre-Columbian Panama *see also* SOUTH AMERICA, PRE-COLUMBIAN, §II.

BIBLIOGRAPHY
M. W. Stirling: 'Exploring the Past in Panama', *N. Geog.*, xcv (1949), pp. 373–99
R. H. Mitchell and J. Acker: 'A Pottery Collection from Parita', *Panama Archaeologist*, iv (1961), pp. 4–30
J. Ladd: 'Archaeological Investigations in the Parita and Santa Maria Zones of Panama', *Bureau Amer. Ethnol. Bull.*, cxciii (1964) [whole issue]
T. Bull: 'Report on Archaeological Investigations, Azuero Peninsula, Province of Herrera, Republic of Panamá', *Panama Archaeologist*, vi (1965), pp. 31–64
R. Mira: 'Los discubrimientos arqueológicos de Parita', *Rev. Lotería*, xi (1966), pp. 83–93
O. F. Linares: *Ecology and the Arts in Ancient Panamá: On the Development of Social Rank and Symbolism in the Central Provinces*, Studies in Pre-Columbian Art and Archaeology, xvii (Washington, DC, 1977)

JOAN K. LINGEN

Hatra [Arab. al-Ḥaḍr]. City in northern Iraq about 110 km south-west of the modern city of Mosul, in an area known as the Jazira. It flourished from the 2nd century BC to the 3rd century AD and was an important caravan city that played a significant role in the cultural and political development of the area. It was a great centre for Arab tribes since it had an abundance of fresh water from numerous springs and from the nearby Wadi Tharthar, and every house, temple or courtyard had at least one well. The site also had a strategic importance, for it controlled the military and trade routes across the desert and along the Tigris and Euphrates rivers. Consequently, wealth poured in, allowing its rulers to build new temples and public buildings and to strengthen the fortifications so that it became one of the wealthiest cities in Mesopotamia.

1. HISTORY. There are no literary sources concerning the foundation and development of the city, so that its early history is mainly dependent on archaeological and architectural evidence. It seems that the site was partially settled in the 2nd century BC. It lies on the route that connected Seleucia-on-the-Tigris with Antioch in Syria, passing through Dura Europos and Palmyra, and its settlement helped the Arab tribes to control the transport of Indian and Arabian goods from the various ports of the Gulf, mainly Chrax and Forat, to the Syrian ports and thence to Western markets, especially those of Rome, where they were in great demand. During the military

conflict between the Romans and Parthians, especially in the years between 69 and 36 BC, Hatra became strategically important.

Aramaic inscriptions mention Hatra as a chief centre in an area known as Arabaya, which was governed autonomously by an Arab dynasty, who called themselves kings of the Arabs; the city was probably fortified during this early period with a strong wall and a moat. Chieftains, known as 'mayors', chief-priests, priests and priestesses are also mentioned. Later the city was governed by 'lords' (*mry'*) who had both religious and administrative responsibilities. It seems that Nshryhb was the first *mry'* to reign in the city, and he is considered the founder of the ruling dynasty. He was responsible for the reconstruction of certain parts of the northern iwans (Arab: 'vaulted reception hall') of the Great Temple complex and was followed by Wrwd, who was involved in the building of the southern iwans. However, the best-known *mry'* was their successor Nsru (*reg c.* AD 114–38), who was responsible for the construction of the Temple of the Triad where two gods and a goddess were worshipped; his head is carved on two voussoirs. He also built Shrines V and X, completed the last stage of the great iwans and constructed the northern part of the wall of the Great Temple. He repaired the North Gate of the city, and the reclining statues that are carved on the lintel of the entrance there and in Shrine V probably represent him. He led the Hatrenes in their brave and successful defence against the invading Roman army under Trajan, probably in the spring of AD 117. This stand brought Hatra great fame and led the Arab tribes to donate generously to the city, establishing its pre-eminence.

Nsru's son Sanatruq I either built the Temple of Shamash or made additions to it in AD 177–8. He was responsible for the construction of many buildings, erecting numerous defensive towers and building a massive edifice inside the Great Temple, dedicated to the worship of Allat-Nemesis and adorned with reliefs and statues. Sanatruq was succeeded by his son and viceroy Abdsmy (*reg* ?AD 193–205). During this reign Hatra was again unsuccessfully besieged by a Roman army led by Septimius Severus. Abdsmy was followed by his son Sanatruq II, who probably reigned until AD 240–41. Like his predecessors, he constructed public buildings and strengthened the city walls. Around 226 the Sasanians overthrew the Parthian power at Ctesiphon and unsuccessfully attacked Hatra. With the resulting political instability, it received a Roman garrison in the time of Gordian III, as indicated by Latin inscriptions and Roman statues of Western divinities. However, the Hatrenes and the Arab tribes could not withstand the increasing power of Shapur I, the Sasanian who succeeded in capturing the city in 240–41. Though Hatra then disappeared from the political scene, an inscription indicates that it was not completely abandoned and remained a stronghold for the Arab tribes until finally destroyed by Shapur II (*reg* 309–79). In 363, when Ammianus Marcellinus passed by, it lay in ruins.

Hatra was visited in the 19th century by a number of travellers and pioneers such as A. H. Layard, J. Fergusson and C. Jacquerel, who described its ruins. At the beginning of the 20th century Walter Andrae surveyed the ruined city, excavated certain parts and published his work in two volumes. In 1951 the Directorate General of Antiquities of Iraq was entrusted with the excavation of the site. Iraqi archaeologists uncovered the most important buildings, such as the Great Temple, a group of tombs, some residential units, two main gates and thirteen shrines. The intensive excavations have yielded great amounts of sculpture of all kinds, some of which is housed in the restored iwans and in various museums in the country, especially the Iraq Museum in Baghdad.

2. ARCHITECTURE AND SCULPTURE. The excavations provide important data concerning the city's formidable fortifications. The main wall surrounding Hatra is almost circular; it is built of mud-brick on stone foundations and is 3 m thick. Archaeological evidence indicates that it was erected between the 1st century BC and the first half of the 1st century AD. This wall was strengthened with approximately 163 towers, some of which are decorated with reliefs of the kings of Hatra who were responsible for their construction. Around this wall is a moat 4–5 m deep and 8 m wide, of which the side closest to the wall was lined with hewn stones set in the bedrock and buttressed. A bridge 5 m wide leads across the moat to the North Gate. The city also has an outer earthen circumvallation located about 500 m from the main wall. Hatra's four gates, each 3.8 m wide and flanked by formidable towers, were built at the cardinal points and followed a broken axis arrangement for military purposes. Excavations have revealed that the main wall was double in most parts. The northern and eastern gates had open

areas containing two niches, one with an over-life-size statue of Herakles-Nergal and the other with a rectangular slab with a relief of an eagle and an inscription warning any person entering the city that theft was punishable by death.

Four main avenues lead from the gates to the Great Temple in the centre of the city. This is composed of separate buildings constructed of ashlar masonry and surrounded by a rectangular wall enclosing a space with maximum dimensions of 438×321.5 m. The wall has 11 entrances, in addition to the main eastern entrance, and numerous rectangular rooms open off it into the enclosed area. These rooms were offices for various transactions and an inn for visitors, so that the temple area had a similar function to that of a Greek agora. The temples in the Great Temple complex were dedicated to the main deities of the city. The great iwans (see fig. 1), orientated towards the east, are composed of three units, two of which consist of a central vaulted iwan flanked by smaller iwans, with rooms behind in two storeys, while the third unit is composed of two medium-sized iwans. The arches of the iwans are decorated with various types of mouldings and busts of gods and nobles; engaged columns with Corinthian capitals decorate the façade of the edifices. The triple iwan is a distinctive feature of the architecture of Hatra, as is the extensive use of the iwan, which may have originated in Iraq (*see* MESOPOTAMIA, §II, 6(iii)). The temples were dedicated to the Triad Mrn, Mrtn and Brmryn, to Shahiru, to Smy' and to the great Arab goddess Allat, who was identified with the Greek Nemesis. A

1. Hatra, iwans in the Great Temple complex, late 1st century AD–early 2nd

2. Hatra, Temple of Allat, relief with musical scene, second half of 2nd century AD

square temple was dedicated to Shamash, the head of the pantheon. The so-called Hellenistic temple occupies an area in the forecourt. It is heptastyle dipteral, the inner columns with Ionic capitals are erected on a podium 1.8 m high, while the outer peristyle has composite capitals.

Outside the Great Temple the excavators have uncovered 13 shrines of approximately the same layout; each includes a rectangular cella or broad room and a square cult niche at the back opposite the entrance, while some have two smaller rooms on each side for votive offerings. The plans resemble those of older Babylonian temples. Inscriptions show that the shrines were dedicated to certain gods: I and VIII to Nergal, X to Herakles-Nergal, III to Baalshamin, VI to Atargatis, V to Isharbel-Athena, VII to Herakles, XII to Nebo and XIII to Herakles-Genda. The city tombs, built of hewn stone, are situated in the eastern part of the city. They are of various types, the simplest form being two rooms connected by a corridor, while some have two storeys and their entrances were closed by heavy stone doors.

The statues and reliefs of Hatra (some *in situ*; others Baghdad, Iraq Mus.; and Mosul Mus.) are characterized by a frozen frontality, regardless of whether they are in Eastern or Western style, divinities or worshippers. There are a few exceptions, such as the relief with a musical scene (see fig. 2) that adorned the southern smaller iwan of the Temple of Allat and dates to the second half of the 2nd century AD (*in situ*). Technically the statues are well executed. Larger sculptures of limestone depict worshippers and deities, generally with one hand raised, and a wealth of detail is indicated. They provide much information on contemporary local fashions in dress and jewellery (*see also* ANCIENT NEAR EAST, §II, 7(iii)(c)) and on the Hatrene pantheon. Smaller figures, carved of alabaster, have squat proportions and over-large heads; they are not improved by staring eyes made of shell set in bitumen that emphasize their rigid frontality. The reliefs, such as that of the god of the netherworld Nergal, brandishing an axe, holding Cerberus on a leash and surrounded by symbols (Baghdad, Iraq Mus.), are generally more informative than aesthetic. Details on both the statues and reliefs are often picked out in paint or covered

in gold leaf. Some naturalistic reliefs on the walls of the buildings depict the camels that symbolized the wealth of this caravan city.

BIBLIOGRAPHY
S. Downey: 'Cult Banks from Hatra', *Berytus*, xvi (1966), pp. 97–109
M. Colledge: *The Parthians* (London, 1967)
S. Downey: 'The Jewelry of Hercules at Hatra', *Amer. J. Archeol.*, lxii (1968), pp. 211–17
W. al-Salihi: 'Hercules-Nergal at Hatra', *Iraq*, xxxiii (1971), pp. 113–15
——: 'Hatra: Excavations in [a] Group of Tombs', *Sumer*, xxviii (1972), pp. 17–20
J. T. Milik: *Dédicaces faites par des dieux* (Paris, 1972)
W. al-Salihi: 'Hercules-Nergal at Hatra (II)', *Iraq*, xxxv (1973), pp. 65–8
F. Safar and M. A. Mustafa: *Al-Ḥaḍr: Madīnat al-shams* [Hatra: the city of the sun god] (Baghdad, 1974)
W. al-Salihi: 'New Light on the Identity of the Triad at Hatra', *Sumer*, xxxi (1975), pp. 75–80
M. Colledge: *Parthian Art* (London, 1977)
W. al-Salihi: 'Ba'lshamīn, ilāh al-barq wa'l-maṭar fi'l-Ḥaḍr' [Baalshamin, god of lightning and thunder at Hatra], *Majallat Kullīyyat al-Ādāb Jāmi'at Baghdād*, xxv (1979), pp. 450–68
——: 'Al-Ḥaḍr: al-tanqīb fi'l-Bāb al-Shimālī' [Hatra: the excavations at the North Gate], *Sumer*, xxxvi (1980), pp. 158–89
H. al-Najafi: 'Mashhad mūsīqī min al-Ḥaḍr' [A musical scene from Hatra], *Sumer*, xxxiv (1981), pp. 131–42
W. al-Salihi: 'Palmyrene Sculptures Found at Hatra', *Iraq*, xlix (1987), pp. 53–61
                                                                    WATHIQ AL-SALIHI

Hatshepsut [Maatkare] (*reg c.* 1479–*c.* 1458 BC). Ancient Egyptian ruler of Egypt and patron. Daughter of Tuthmosis I and princess of the royal blood, Hatshepsut married her half-brother Tuthmosis II and, at the death of her father, became queen consort. Her considerable influence as queen and 'god's wife' of Amun continued unabated when her father died, and she acted for several years as regent for the young Tuthmosis III, her nephew and stepson. For reasons that remain conjectural, Hatshepsut assumed pharaonic titles, probably in year seven of Tuthmosis's reign, and insinuated herself as the senior partner of a co-regency.

Unlike previous women who had ruled Egypt, she was consistently portrayed in sculpture and relief as a male, creating a polite fiction that enabled her to legitimize her claim to the throne. Her sculpture generally conforms to the royal style of Tuthmosis III, although in certain instances the sculptor has attempted to soften the masculine conception of the vigorous and athletic youth that embodies the Tuthmosid ideal. Hatshepsut is occasionally depicted with slender elongated limbs that may well be an attempt to imbue the royal figure with a sense of femininity. She built extensively at Karnak (*see* THEBES (i), §II, 1), including a red quartzite sanctuary for the god Amun (the 'Chapelle Rouge') and a series of shrines for the deposition of portable divine barks, but her architectural masterpiece is her mortuary temple at Deir el-Bahri, a monument whose plan foreshadows the later funerary temples of the New Kingdom. The temple reliefs depict her commercial expedition to the land of Punt and romanticized accounts of her divine birth, her youth and her coronation by the gods. Perhaps because of the circumstances of her unorthodox accession Hatshepsut was the first to explore the uses of propaganda on public monuments; the earliest preserved accounts of oracles date from her reign. Hatshepsut's tomb in Thebes (KV 20: the earliest datable royal tomb in the Valley of the Kings) was intended to hold her remains and those of her father. Approximately

20 years after her death, her name and figure were hacked from her monuments and her statues broken into fragments by order of Tuthmosis III; the motive for her posthumous disgrace, however, remains as uncertain as the reason for her accession.

BIBLIOGRAPHY

LÄ: 'Deir el-Bahari III', 'Hatschepsut I'

K. Mysliwiec: *Le Portrait royal dans le bas-relief du Nouvel Empire* (Warsaw, 1976), pp. 46–9

R. Tefnin: *La Statuaire d'Hatshepsout: Portrait royal et politique sous la 18e dynastie* (Brussels, 1979)

PETER F. DORMAN

Hattusa. *See* BOĞAZKÖY.

Hatz, Elizabeth (*b* Lund, 20 June 1953). Swedish architect. She studied at the Architectural Association, London, from 1972 to 1977. She then worked in Paris for two years, and in 1979 she joined the firm Berg Architektkonter in Stockholm. As a leading member of the firm's design team, she was involved primarily with office buildings and research facilities. One of the most celebrated projects she worked on is the Stockholm Globe (1989), the world's largest spherical building. A sports arena seating 16,000, the facility also includes training arenas, offices, a hotel and restaurants. An adjoining building, The Triangle, which houses administrative offices, is a glass-encased structure raised on columns. This inventive use of form and space reflects Hatz's philosophy that architecture has to do with a sense of place and a sense of presence, as well as her interest in the creative use of light. In addition to her design work, Hatz taught at the Royal Technical High School of Architecture, Stockholm, from 1983 to 1986. She is a member of the National Swedish Board of Architects (SAR) and in 1987 was elected to the board of the Swedish Women Architects Association (ATHENA).

BIBLIOGRAPHY

C. Lorenz: *Women in Architecture: A Contemporary Perspective* (New York, 1990)

'Megastrutura para arena global', *Projeto*, 136 (1990), pp. 34–7

Hauberat, Guillaume de [d'] (*b* 1688; *d* Germany, 1749). French architect, active in Germany. He was the son of Jean Hauberat, an architect of the Bâtiments du Roi. He studied at the Académie de Peinture et Sculpture in Paris between 1704 and 1707 and served as an architect to Louis XIV before moving to Germany in 1716 as the director of works for Robert de Cotte. Hauberat's role was necessarily more than supervisory, but he always maintained close contact with de Cotte in Paris. By 1725 he had married in Bonn, and he subsequently settled in Germany. Hauberat's earliest work was on the residences of Joseph-Clement, Archbishop-Elector of Cologne, in Bonn and Poppelsdorf. At Bonn, of de Cotte's grandiose plan of 1715 only the modest Buenretiro wing and improvements to the existing palace (now part of the university) were executed. The palace at Poppelsdorf, a two-storey square plan with a circular arcaded courtyard, was contemporaneous with Bonn; work progressed extremely slowly and was abandoned in 1723 on the death of Joseph-Clement. His successor restored the extant fabric, and restarted the works only in 1744. Hauberat took over the works of the palace in Mannheim in 1726,

but resigned and appointed a supervisor when he was offered the Thurn und Taxis Palace (1731–41; destr. 1944), Frankfurt am Main, designed by de Cotte in 1727. This was Hauberat's most important work; it was, unusually for the Palatinate, resolutely French in style, comparable to de Cotte's Hôtel de Rohan (1728–42), Strasbourg, to which it was favourably compared. However, only the portal survives. Hauberat remained an influential figure in the development of French-inspired architecture in the Rhineland.

BIBLIOGRAPHY

P. du Colombier: *L'Architecture française en Allemagne*, 2 vols (Paris, 1956)

J. F. Oglevee: *Letters of the Archbishop-Elector Joseph Clemens of Cologne to Robert de Cotte (1712–1720), with Supplementary Letters from the Architect Guillaume d'Hauberat to de Cotte (1716–1721)* (Bowling Green, OH, 1956)

W. G. Kalnein and M. Levy: *Art and Architecture in France in the 18th Century*, Pelican Hist. A. (Harmondsworth, 1972)

Hauberisser, Georg (Joseph), Ritter von (*b* Graz, 19 March 1841; *d* Munich, 17 May 1922). German architect. He studied in Graz, in Munich from 1862 under Georg Friedrich Ziebland and Ludwig Lange (1808–68) and then in Berlin under Johann Heinrich Strack and Carl Boetticher. Continuing his studies in Vienna under Friedrich von Schmidt, he turned away from the Renaissance Revival style, which was then dominant in Munich, towards the Gothic Revival favoured by Schmidt. Hauberisser returned to Munich after winning the competition (1866) for the new Rathaus there at the age of 25. Thereafter he was one of the leading Gothic Revival architects in Germany. His audacious and highly controversial design was the first major Gothic Revival public building in Munich and Hauberisser played an influential part in establishing the style there. The first stage of the Rathaus showed his predilection for Flemish and French Gothic. Later extensions (1888–93 and 1899–1908) employed the same idiom, but the asymmetrical tower and the emphatic verticals marked a departure from the symmetry and the horizontality of the original building. These changes reflected the late 19th-century preference for picturesquely arranged façades and undogmatic historicism.

Town halls were Hauberisser's speciality. His Rathaus (1897–1900) at St Johann in Saarbrücken is strikingly similar to his work in Munich although it is simpler with even more vertical emphasis. That his virtuosity was not confined to the Gothic Revival is shown by the town halls in Kaufbeuren (1879–88) and Wiesbaden (1884–7), and by his competition entry (1894) for the Bayerisches Nationalmuseum in Munich, all of which were in the Flemish and French Renaissance styles. The same styles were almost always used for his private buildings, mainly in Munich, including houses for the painters Kaulbach and Franz von Defregger (Königinstr.27), and for himself (Theresienwiese).

Hauberisser was also a prominent Gothic Revival church architect, his principal work being St Paul's (1892–1906), Munich. He also designed its interior details, having a thoroughly medieval belief that craftsmanship was as important as architecture. He was a member of the jury of the Deutsche Gesellschaft für Christliche Kunst and thereby had considerable influence on Catholic church architecture in Germany.

Hauberisser was also a restorer of ancient buildings, most notably of town halls, including those in Landshut (1876–80), Landsberg (1876–9) and Ulm (1900). He also restored such churches as the Sebalduskirche (1888–1904) in Nuremberg, and castles, for example the castle of the Teutonic Knights (1895–1912) at Busau, Moravia (now Bouzov, Czech Republic), which contains his most outstanding interior decoration.

BIBLIOGRAPHY

Thieme–Becker

J. E. Huber: *Die St Paulskirche in München* (Munich, 1906)

München und seine Bauten (Munich, 1912)

H. Steffen: 'Georg von Hauberisser', *Christ. Kst*, xii (1915–16), pp. 200–10

O. Doering: 'Georg von Hauberisser', *Die Kunst dem Volke*, lii (1924)

H. Lehmbruch: *Georg Joseph Ritter von Hauberisser* (diss., Ludwig-Maximilians U., Munich, 1970)

J. Fekete: *Denkmalpflege und Neugotik im 19. Jahrhundert: Dargestellt am Beispiel des Alten Rathauses in München* (Munich, 1981)

JULIUS FEKETE

Haubert, Francisco de Leygonier y. *See* LEYGONIER Y HAUBERT, FRANCISCO DE.

Haudebourt-Lescot [née Lescot], **(Antoinette-Cécile-) Hortense** (*b* Paris, 14 Dec 1784; *d* Paris, 2 Jan 1845). French painter. At the age of seven Hortense Lescot became a pupil of Guillaume Lethière, a family friend and popular history painter who was appointed director of the Académie de France in Rome in 1807. She followed him to Rome in 1808 and remained there until 1816, depicting the customs and costumes of the Italian peasantry in veristic detail. This experience abroad, rare for a woman artist, was a decisive influence on her art which in its picturesque and anecdotal images of everyday Italian life prefigured the work of the genre specialists J.-V. Schnetz and Léopold Robert. She married the architect Louis-Pierre Haudebourt (1788–1849) in 1820.

Haudebourt-Lescot exhibited more than 100 easel paintings in the Salons from 1810 to 1840, winning second-class medals in 1810 and 1819 and a first-class medal in 1827. She received a number of government commissions. Even after her marriage, her production of sentimental genre scenes with domestic, moralizing, religious, amorous, humorous and literary themes did not slacken. Although she painted historical genre scenes, her reputation was based on exotic Italianate paintings and quaint domestic portrayals. These works were popularized by numerous prints made after them, and it is through reproductions that such works as the *Fair at Grottaferrata* (exh. Salon 1814), the *Notary Public* (exh. Salon 1817), the *Art Dealer* (exh. Salon 1824), the *First Step* (exh. Salon 1819) and the *Happy Family* (exh. Salon 1824) are still known (engravings in Paris, Bib. N.). Haudebourt-Lescot was also an accomplished portrait and watercolour painter; her *Self-portrait* (1825; Paris, Louvre) is particularly notable.

BIBLIOGRAPHY

A. Valabrègue: 'Mme Haudebourt-Lescot', *Lett. & A.* (1887), pp. 102–3

S. W. Robertson: *A. C. H. Haudebourt-Lescot, 1784–1845* (MS., New York U., Inst. F.A., 1973)

S. W. Robertson and I. Julia: 'A. C. H. Haudebourt-Lescot', *French Painting, 1774–1830: The Age of Revolution* (exh. cat., Paris, Grand Pal.; Detroit, MI, Inst. A.; New York, Met.; 1974–5), pp. 486–7

L. Nochlin: 'A.-C.-H. Haudebourt-Lescot', *Women Artists, 1550–1950* (exh. cat., Los Angeles, CA, Co. Mus. A., 1976–7), pp. 218–19

SARAH WELLS ROBERTSON

Haugen Sørensen, Jørgen (*b* Copenhagen, 3 Oct 1934). Danish sculptor. He began his training in 1949 as a potter and plasterer and also studied at the Kunsthåndværkerskole in Copenhagen. As a sculptor he was self-taught. Haugen Sørensen first exhibited in 1951 and began working with ceramics and bronze at an early stage. He produced realistic portrayals of animals and humans, often in scenes of life in Copenhagen (e.g. *Slaughter Group*, 1958; Copenhagen, Stat. Mus. Kst). Around 1960 he executed a series of non-figurative sculptures and reliefs in ceramic and bronze, including the *Stomping Animal* (1961; Humlebæk, Louisiana Mus.) and *Spiral Animal* (1964; Århus, Kstmus.).

In the 1960s Haugen Sørensen developed his own variety of abstraction based on organic forms. He continued to experiment with a range of materials from canvas to fibreglass, for example in *Material Sculpture in 8 Parts* (1964; Randers, A. Mus.). Between 1956 and 1975 he was a member of the artists' group Decembristerne (The Decembrists) and was influenced by the Danish artists Richard Winther (*b* 1926) and Hans Christian Rylander (*b* 1939) among others. In 1975 Haugen Sørensen became a member of Grønningen (The Greening).

After many visits to Italy Haugen Sørensen moved there, and during a stay in Pietrasanta in 1973 he began to work with Travertine marble, which later became his preferred material, used for example in *Green Post* (1977; Birkerød, Kommune) and *Landscape with Bridge* (1979; Humlebæk, Louisiana Mus.). If Sørensen's point of departure was a simple, expressionistic naturalism, his work with Italian marble directed him towards a weighty and plastic abstraction in which the luxuriance of the material constituted a vital part of the work. He executed a number of large decorative projects in Denmark, including those at Copenhagen University at Amager (1979) and at the Danish School of Journalism in Århus (1971–3). In 1969 he was awarded the Eckersberg Medal and in 1979 the Thorvaldsen Medal.

Haugen Sørensen's elder brother Arne Haugen Sørensen (*b* Copenhagen, 27 April 1932) became a painter and printmaker, producing images of biomorphic and grotesque disembodied forms based on human and animal figures (e.g. *Woman and Wild Animal*, 1973; Vejle, Kstmus.).

BIBLIOGRAPHY

B. Trotzig: *Jørgen Haugen Sørensen* (Copenhagen, 1978)

H. E. Nørregård Nielsen, ed.: *Dansk kunst*, 2 vols (Copenhagen, 1983)

MICHAEL FLINTHOLM

Haukeland, Arnold (Martin) (*b* Verdal, Nord-Trøndelag, 28 March 1920; *d* Baerum, 18 June 1983). Norwegian sculptor. He studied electrical engineering at the Norges Tekniske Høgskole, Trondheim, from 1940 and at the same time painted, drew and modelled in clay. In 1943–4 he broke off his studies and travelled to Oslo, where he received instruction at the 'illegal Academy' (the Kunstakademi was shut during the German occupation) from the sculptors Stinius Fredriksen (*b* 1902) and Per Palle Storm (*b* 1910). His first independent work was *Hope* (1945), a naturalistic and stately female figure, for the west portal of the reconstructed Nidaros Cathedral, Trondheim. The next year he studied Gothic art in England and France and was a pupil of Raymond Martin (*b* 1910) at the Académie Colarossi in Paris. He won a competition for a war memorial at the Baerum Town Hall in Sandvika with his distinctive bronze equestrian statue *Freedom* (1947–53). Its form is indebted to the Italian Renaissance, but its spiritual content salutes the fallen of Baerum; the powerful horse can be said to represent the nation's strength, and the proud, naked young rider symbolizes its longing for freedom.

Haukeland explored the relation between weightlessness and fixed mobility in the monument *Ball-playing Group* (1958; Sarpsborg Stadion). A large number of portrait busts, for example the bronze *Icelandic Woman* (1948; Oslo, Mus. Samtidskst), revealed his ability to capture, with a sense of immediacy, the characteristics of the model within a framework of near-classical austerity. Haukeland was long interested in modern and contemporary sculpture but regarded his encounter in the 1960s with the art of ancient Greece and with contemporary art at the Venice Biennale as the turning-point of his life. He accordingly began to give abstract and expressive form to his ideas and made his first non-figurative sculptures (exh. Oslo, Kstnernes Hus, 1961). His use of materials and his technique were regarded as revolutionary in Norway at that time, and many of the exhibited works were commissioned as open-air sculptures. The first, *Air II* (1961–2; U. Oslo), was the first non-figurative sculpture erected in a public place in Norway. It is an aggressive, smoothly polished steel construction. The sculpture's distinctiveness arises out of the play between sharp, drilled-through and rounded forms that dramatically shape the open area and variously lead the light up, allowing it to pass through the sculpture and reflect it. At this time a new open-air sculpture by Haukeland was erected nearly every year. These works were a natural continuation of his earlier sculptures; they communicate with their surroundings and portray the conflict between weight and motion. Their evocative, dominating and richly varied forms have delicately variegated surfaces exploiting rhythmic dissonance; they also display Constructivist and expressive tendencies, such as the focal point of his exhibition at the Venice Biennale in 1970, a copy of *Dynamic* (1966; orig. placed high on a natural concrete base on the Frognerstrand Promenade in central Oslo, with the sea behind and the motorway in front of it). At its centre is a collage-like polygonal core, which, with a vertically placed, powerful wedge, results in a sort of dislocated cross formation. It is a romantic synthesis that celebrates technology and energy along with untouched nature. Haukeland's unique sculpture, made for the blind, *Ode to Light* (1965–8; Skjeberg, Storedal Kultsent.), offers to those with a visual handicap the fundamental experiences of movement, touch and sound, visually bound in a tense contrast-filled construction. Like a human form with two outstretched arms, which celebrate life, light and nature, the black figure,

30 m high, is silhouetted against the open agricultural landscape, projecting from a glittering, undulating steel garland. Inside, concealed photographic and sound equipment coordinates the playing of Arne Nordheim's electronic music according to the level of light, thus transforming daily and seasonal rhythms.

As the qualities of both the form and the content of Haukeland's sculpture advanced, so did its technical execution. He worked his personal and social observations and reflections into sculptures made between 1970 and 1980, for example the kinetic work *Integration* (stainless steel, 1970; Oslo, Throne Holst Square) and *Red Wind* (1978, painted steel; Bergen, Municipal Park), a composition with thin red metal bands reminiscent of dried-out vegetation inspired by the artist's experience of the sirocco on Tenerife. Both works, like many of Haukeland's, were made in several editions. Inspiration for his sculpture includes the work of Futurism, Naum Gabo, Alexander Calder, Kenneth Armitage, Julio Gonzáles and Ramon Isern (*see* GRUPPE 5) as well as Picasso's formal language and John Rood's welding technique. Haukeland's determination, physical strength and technical mastery allowed him to execute his imposing monumental sculptures almost entirely on his own until the mid-1960s. His production ranged from traditional, intimate or humorous small sculptures to symbol-laden, expressive, abstract or non-figurative works. But it was his vital decorative and gigantic public works that significantly altered the Norwegian urban environment. His articles on the modernist understanding of form and his protests against artistic conventionalism also had an impact on the perception of art in Norway (see *Dagbladet*). In 1993 Haukeland's widow gave the Henie–Onstad Kunstsenter in Baerum, which had held several exhibitions of his work and owns, among other pieces, the famous *Sun Sculpture* of 1970, the responsibility of caring for *c.* 260 sculptures in the artist's possession at the time of his death.

WRITINGS

'Kunsten skal tale tidens språk' [Art shall speak the language of the times], *Dagbladet* (21 Oct 1959)

BIBLIOGRAPHY

P. Anker: 'Arnold Haukelands monumentalskulptur', *Kst Idag* [Art today], lxii (1962), pp. 4–29 [with Eng. summary]

P. Hougen: 'Arnold Haukeland', *Kst Idag*, xcii (1970), pp. 24–51 [with Eng. summary]

A. Haaland: *Arnold Haukeland: Runer i rommet* [Arnold Haukeland: runes in space] (Oslo, 1971) [Norw. and Eng. texts]

E. Dæhlin: *Arnold Haukeland* (Oslo, 1980)

S. Aamold: *Arnold Haukeland: Liv og werk* (diss., U. Oslo, 1992)

SUSANNE RAJKA

Haungooah. *See* SILVERHORN.

Haupt, (Karl) Albrecht (*b* Büdingen, 18 March 1852; *d* Hannover, 27 Oct 1932). German architectural historian and architect. He began studying architecture in Giessen in 1869. After serving in the Franco-Prussian War (1870–71) he entered architectural administration and continued his studies at Karlsruhe and Hannover. In 1876–8 he worked at the Schlossbauamt in Karlsruhe and in Büdingen. In 1878 he joined the architectural practice of Edwin Oppler in Hannover, opening his own office in 1880, when he also completed a dissertation qualifying him as a lecturer at the Technische Hochschule at Hannover.

Thereafter he pursued careers both as an academic and as an architect. As an architect he was much in demand in the 1880s and 1890s, designing many private villas and larger residences for an aristocratic clientele; these are mainly in a German Renaissance Revival style and include Schloss Basedow near Lauenburg, Villa Mummy at Wilhelmshöhe and Schloss Wiligrad near Schwerin. Haupt also became known as a restorer, both of churches, as at the Stadtkirche (1895) in Bückeburg and the Stiftskirche (1903–4) in Fischbeck, and of secular buildings, as at the Leibnizhaus (1890, destr. 1943), Hannover. He was a co-founder of the Bund Deutscher Architekten and its president from 1903 to 1908. However, his reputation depends chiefly on his work as a scholar. A DPhil at Leipzig University in 1893 and an honorary professorship at the Technische Hochschule in 1894 initiated his long and distinguished career as a teacher of architectural history. He wrote a large number of books, highly regarded at the time but now considered inaccurate; these include volumes on German architecture from the earliest periods up to the time of Charlemagne, several on Renaissance architecture in western Europe, brick construction and crematoria. In 1892 he was a co-founder of the Kunstgewerbemuseum (destr. 1943) in Hannover. His collection of prints and drawings on the history of architecture, known as the Sammlung Haupt, is kept at the Technische Hochschule, Hannover.

WRITINGS

Die älteste Kunst, insbesondere die Baukunst der Germanen von der Völkerwanderung bis zu Karl dem Grossen (Leipzig, 1909, Berlin, 3/1935)
Der deutsche Backsteinbau der Gegenwart und seine Lage (Leipzig, 1910)
Totenstädte der Zukunft: Eine Nekropole für eine Million (Leipzig, 1911)
Palastarchitektur von Oberitalien und in Toskana vom XIII.–XVIII. Jahrhundert, 6 vols (Berlin, 1911–22); Eng. trans., 3 vols (London, 1931)
Lissabon und Cintra (Leipzig, 1913)
Monumenta Germaniae architectonica, 2 vols (Leipzig, 1913)
Baukunst der Renaissance in Frankreich und Deutschland, 2 vols (Berlin, 1923)
Geschichte der Renaissance in Spanien und Portugal (Stuttgart, 1927)

BIBLIOGRAPHY

NDB; Thieme–Becker
Das geistige Deutschland am Ende des 19. Jahrhunderts (Leipzig, 1898), pp. 274–5
Reichshandbuch der deutschen Gesellschaft, i (Berlin, 1930–31), p. 676
P. Kanold: 'Albrecht Haupt', *Niedersächsische Lebensbilder*, ed. O. H. May, i (Hildesheim and Leipzig, 1939), pp. 205–19 [with portrait, list of works and bibliog.]

WERNER WILHELM SCHNABEL

Haupt, Georg (*b* Stockholm, 10 Aug 1741; *d* Stockholm, 18 Sept 1784). Swedish cabinetmaker. He was the son of the cabinetmaker Elias Haupt (*d* 1751) and in 1754 was apprenticed to the cabinetmaker Johan Conrad Eckstein (1722–85) a year earlier than guild regulations allowed, due to his family's connections. He completed his apprenticeship in October 1759 and *c.* 1762 departed with the cabinetmaker Christopher Fuhrlohg (1737–*c.* 1800) for Amsterdam. By 1764 they were in Paris, where Haupt may have trained under Simon Oeben (*c.* 1725–86), the brother of Jean-François Oeben. In 1766 Haupt, like Simon Oeben, worked for Etienne-François, Duc de Choiseul, at the château of Chanteloup, near Amboise; there he made and signed a plain, mahogany *bureau plat* (1767; Paris, Inst. Géog. N.). In 1766 he was joined in Paris by his nephew, the painter Elias Martin. In late 1767 or early 1768 they travelled to London, where they joined a Swedish colony that included Fuhrlohg, the furniture designer David Martin and (from 1769) Johan Christian Linning (1759–1801), another cabinetmaker. Fuhrlohg and Haupt almost certainly worked for John Linnell (i) in Berkeley Square, and Haupt was in contact with William Chambers. In 1769 he was promoted to Controller of the King's Works and made a neat table to a design by Chambers, decorated with nine specimen marbles and Neo-classical marquetry (1769; London, V&A; *see* ENGLAND, fig. 52).

Haupt returned to Sweden and on 17 July 1769 was appointed court cabinetmaker to Adolf Frederick of Sweden. He was commissioned to make a writing-desk for Queen Louisa Ulrica, the design of which was approved by the King at a guild meeting. The writing-desk (1770; Stockholm, Kun. Slottet) was completed in the middle of September and was shown to the guild on 14 December. It bears strong similarities to a medal-cabinet (*c.* 1769; Radier Manor, Jersey) made for Robert Child (1739–1782) of Osterley Park while Haupt was in England. In 1771 Haupt was given the freedom of Stockholm and took over the workshop of Anders Fogel (1732–71). In 1773–4 he made a monumental cabinet for a mineralogical collection (Chantilly, Mus. Condé), designed by Jean Eric Rehn, as a gift from Gustav III to Louis-Joseph, Prince de Condé (1736–1818); it was exhibited in Stockholm and further raised Haupt's reputation. After his death in 1784, his widow carried on the business with his former apprentice Gustaf Adolf Ditzinger (1760–1800), whom she married in 1789.

Haupt was a master of the advanced Neo-classical style of marquetry in which geometric parquetry is combined with such motifs as swags, husks, medallion heads, putti, vases, rosettes and ribbons and embellished with bold, gilt-bronze mounts. Haupt's luxurious commodes, *bureaux plats*, secrétaires, tables and desks remained true to this vigorous style, using Parisian forms of the 1760s (*see* SWEDEN, fig. 20). Such special commissions as a base made in 1776 for a cabinet (Vienna, Ksthist. Mus.) made during the reign of Rudolf II and brought to Sweden after the capture of Prague in 1648, or a ceremonial cradle (Stockholm, Kun. Husgerådskam.) made in 1778 for the Crown Prince Gustav Adolf (later Gustav IV) prompted some originality, but Haupt's work usually evinces a typically artisan combination of virtuosity in technique and conservatism in design.

BIBLIOGRAPHY

M. Lagerquist: *Georg Haupt: Ebéniste du roi* (Stockholm, 1979)
G. W. Beard and C. G. Gilbert, eds: *Dictionary of English Furniture Makers, 1660–1840* (Leeds, 1986)

SIMON JERVIS

Hausa. People living in north-west Nigeria beyond the confluence of the Niger and Benue rivers. The Hausa are one of the largest and most widespread of African peoples with a total population of some 15 million. Hausaland's approximate boundaries reach just north of Zinder, east of Hadejia, south of Zaria and west of Birnin Kebbi. The neighbours of the Hausa include the Tuareg to the north, the Kanuri to the east, the Gwari, Nupe, Yoruba and Igbo to the south and the Gurma to the west. Hausa expertise in trading and craftwork has also given rise to numerous small communities scattered throughout the towns and cities of West Africa, as well as larger, fluctuating communities in Niger, Cameroon and Ghana. Hausa are famous for their mostly non-figurative arts and crafts, representative collections of which are held by a number of museums (e.g. Edinburgh, Royal Mus. Scotland).

1. Introduction. 2. Textiles. 3. Ceramics. 4. Wall decoration. 5. Other arts.

1. INTRODUCTION. Hausaland is situated within the Sub-Saharan savanna region and contrasts strikingly with the hotter and more humid forest belt to the south. For the most part it is made up of open, gently undulating farmland, with a scatter of trees, compact villages and occasional large outcrops of rock. Most Hausa are farmers living in small villages surrounded by fields. There are, however, some large walled towns, such as KANO, Katsina and Zaria, which are important market and craft production centres.

The Hausa are the product of an ancient stock to which others have been added through migration, trade and slave raiding. These additions include nomadic Fulani who settled among the Hausa, usurping power in the 19th century. By contrast, the Gwari were brought to Hausaland as slaves, though they were soon integrated with the indigenous population. There are also Kanuri and Nupe immigrants who came as traders, craftsmen and Koranic teachers. The resulting heterogeneous population speaks a common language that, together with the increasing influence of Islam, has created an overall cultural unity.

Hausa art is dominated by utilitarian and decorative requirements. It combines African and Islamic characteristics with such elements derived from the West as lurex thread, brightly coloured, factory-made paint, and an enlarged range of imagery reflecting Western technology and the influence of the mass media. Ironworking, pottery, wood-carving and body decoration were already established before such West African Muslim traders as the Manding first introduced Islamic influences into Hausaland in the 15th century. The first people to be affected were the rulers and their immediate courtiers who adopted such commodities as tailored clothing as status symbols exclusive to themselves. Islamic influences were strengthened by the development of the Saharan trade routes from North Africa. Without a written language of their own, the Hausa gradually adopted the Arabic script. They used it in Koranic studies, for writing Hausa, and for making protective charms, such as the papers bearing Koranic phrases that are sewn into clothing or enclosed in small, decorated leather cases worn suspended from the neck. Imported copies of the Koran constituted one of the main sources of the interlacing motifs widely used by the Koranic teachers and other Hausa artists.

The process of Islamization among the Hausa has been one of diffusion rather than conquest. This, and the distance that separates Hausaland from the centres of strict Islamic practice, has allowed a degree of flexibility and unorthodoxy in such features of Hausa art as the asymmetrical arrangement of some embroidery and strikingly figurative motifs in mural decoration.

2. TEXTILES. In the 19th century huge quantities of Hausa cloth were traded within West Africa, but since then production of handwoven cloth, while continuing, has been drastically reduced. In traditional Hausa cloth, shades of indigo predominate (both thread and cloth are dyed). Indigo dye was obtained formerly from locally grown plants, while since the 1960s much dyestuff is imported. The dyeing is done in cement-lined pits several metres deep. There are thousands of these throughout Hausaland, the majority abandoned due to competition from mass-produced textiles.

Two types of loom are used, reflecting a common African division between men's and women's weaving. Hausa men use a double-heddle, treadle operated horizontal loom to make long, narrow strips of cloth. These are then sewn edge to edge to produce wider material for tailoring into such garments as wrappers, gowns, trousers and turbans. Women weave on a vertical loom, producing a broader cloth some 0.5 m wide and 2 to 3 m long. Women's cloths are sewn together to make women's and girls' turbans and wrappers.

The most elaborate woven decoration is done by the women. Decoration on men's cloths is restricted to slight variations of colour in the warp, resulting in bands of colour running the length of the cloth. The women, in addition to varying the colour of warp and weft, inlay designs during the weaving process. The range of motifs includes schematic representations of writing-boards, drums, mosques, aeroplanes, birds, horses and people.

Most Hausa embroidery is done by men on men's clothes, though since the 1960s women have been drawing

1. Hausa man wearing a hand-embroidered gown with 'eight-knives' motif, village near Zaria, Nigeria; from a photograph by David Heathcote, 1973

and sewing the decoration on men's caps as well as embroidering pillow-cases and bedcovers. Since the 1920s, the men have worked with treadle-powered sewing machines as well as by hand.

Some Hausa embroidery imitates the designs on such foreign products as those brought back by pilgrims returning from Mecca, but such established indigenous designs as the 'eight-knives' pattern (see fig. 1) are variations of types that have changed little since at least the 17th century. Older motifs include various sizes of the wedge shapes referred to as knives. These also occur in the decoration of leatherwork, baskets, calabashes and woven cloth and are combined with various other devices, including the interlacing motifs derived from Islamic sources.

Most motifs are named. One is referred to as the emir's drum, others have names of animals, trees, birds, buildings, household utensils, weapons, games or hairstyles. Some names are used by almost all embroiderers, others are exclusive to a particular locality. In spite of the Hausa fondness for naming individual motifs within embroidery patterns, there is no evidence that elaborate meanings are attached to designs as a whole. Embroidery can enhance a garment's worth considerably. Not only does its market value increase but it also reflects well on its wearer's social status.

3. CERAMICS. Most Hausa pottery comprises simple, functional cooking and water vessels. Enormous quantities of domestic pottery used to be made in Hausaland, but demand has been much reduced by plastics and enamelware. Pottery is largely a dry-season occupation. While some entire households are involved, the majority of potters are men.

Hausa potters work without a wheel using one of two principal methods. The first involves the use of a short pestle to beat the clay into shape while it is turned in a hollow in the ground. In the second method the clay is pressed around an upturned pot that functions as a mould for the new one. Firing, with temperatures rising to about 800°C, takes place in the open or more rarely within a low-walled enclosure. No kilns are used.

No true glazes are achieved and decoration is seldom elaborate. A pot may be burnished, textured or embellished with ridges and knobs; a marriage pot may have modelled birds added to it. Some pots are given incised decoration while impressions may be made with a finger or with a roulette made from the knobbly seed of the *dau'da* plant or twisted or plaited fibres. Some pots are coloured with white clay slip, laundry blue or golden-coloured mica schist powder.

While most Hausa pottery is utilitarian the Hausa women of Argungu make brightly painted, baked-clay toys. Some 100 mm or so high and rudimentary in form, they comprise miniature domestic furniture, and figures of animals and women. Some of the latter have a baby on their back, and each wears a distinctive hairstyle. Though the potters themselves refer to some of the human figures as soldiers, they are all female in form.

2. Hausa wall decoration, Hunkuyi village, Nigeria; the artist, Musa Yola, stands to the right, and the house owner's wife, Kattutu, stands in front of her portrait; from a photograph by David Heathcote, 1973

4. WALL DECORATION. Elaborate mud architecture has a long history in Hausaland, though few pre-20th-century buildings survive. The 20th-century Hausa exterior wall decoration developed from earlier interior work consisting of simple geometric motifs in mud plaster. Exterior decoration was first concentrated around door and window openings, a practice probably associated with the placing of written charms at entrances in order to ward off potential intruders and evil spirits. In the 1930s, several rooms in the Emir of Kano's palace were decorated with brightly painted moulded designs. These included schematic, but recognizable representations of sandals, spears, swords, rifles and other such royal regalia and weaponry. A rapid development of exterior decoration occurred in the 1940s, especially in Zaria and Kano. It coincided with increased affluence among the urban Hausa and the new availability of factory-made cement. The façades of wealthy traders' houses were adorned with repeating patterns of geometric and plant motifs incised into plaster, as well as with plaster-covered, moulded work incorporating a wide range of subject-matter. Clocks, bicycles, lorries and locomotives appeared alongside such religious symbols as the writing-board, inkpot and pen of the Koranic scholar. Since the 1960s painted decoration has become more common. The effects are sometimes garish, though one young painter, Musa Yola, of Fulani and Kanuri parentage, was very successful in the 1970s at portraying his Hausa patrons and their rapidly changing environment (see fig. 2).

See also AFRICA, fig. 69.

5. OTHER ARTS. Hausa practise a range of other arts and crafts, from calligraphy to basketry, leatherwork and metalwork. They are particularly skilled in calligraphy and the decoration of the Koran. The Hausa version of Arabic script, taught everywhere in the Koranic schools, is stylistically similar to North African *maghribī* (*see* ISLAMIC ART, §III, 2(iii)(b)). The writing materials are cornstalk pens and locally produced black and red inks, the latter made from the leaf-sheaths of a specially grown type of sorghum plant. The writing is practised on a wooden board, with a crescent-shaped handle, washed clean from time to time and reused. The board itself is a frequently recurring motif in such areas of Hausa art as wall decoration and women's weaving. The Koranic teachers are skilled calligraphers. As well as being pattern-makers, they create decorative motifs for the copies of the Koran they produce. They also decorate their pupil's writing-boards to celebrate the end of a set piece of learning.

The range of Hausa basketry includes coiled-basketry containers, food-bowl covers and woven circular trays, fans, and cases for cornstalk pens. Elephant grass and strips of palm fronds are used, some being dyed dull red or green. Decoration is angular and almost exclusively abstract.

Hausa use gourds to make food bowls, ladles, musical instruments and even simple rafts. Decoration is largely abstract, the gourds being scraped, carved, sawn, burnt, scorched, coloured with red dye or whitened with clay. Formerly, the best decorated gourds were prized by the women and assembled as showpieces. Since the 1950s

they have collected brightly coloured enamelware in large quantities instead.

The range of Hausa leatherwork is wide, comprising bags, wallets, boxes, charm coverings, satchels for carrying the Koran, sheaths and scabbards, cushions, gourd stands, horse trappings and several kinds of footwear. Leather is also often used in the making or decoration of straw hats, musical instruments, inkpots and Koranic writing-boards. The most common leather is goatskin, tanned and dyed locally, though cattle hide, sheep, lizard, snake and fish skin are also used. In the past Hausa supplied leatherwork to their neighbours, while some Hausa leatherwork, such as purses with a sliding cover and a cord for suspending it from the neck, are variations of Tuareg products. The main colours used are red and black, though yellow and a bright green are also used. Decoration is generally abstract, with the occasional use of a lizard or crocodile silhouette. A variety of decorative techniques is employed: staining, embroidery, incising, punching, knotting, plaiting, weaving, appliqué and stripping.

Leatherworkers have names for many of the motifs, some of which, for example 'bull's urine' and 'eye', suggesting that they have some functional, if not symbolic, significance: in this case to do with fertility, and protection against the evil eye. Since the 1940s the sale of semi-traditional leatherwork to visitors to Nigeria has become a sizeable industry.

Hausa blacksmiths have been working metals, including locally mined iron, for more than a thousand years, while since the 15th century Islamic influence has widened the formal and decorative range of Hausa utilitarian and ornamental metalwork. Hausa blacksmiths use forging, lost-wax, chasing, repoussé and counter-repoussé methods to produce a variety of decorated metalwork including musical instruments, bowls, baskets, ewers, rings, bracelets, anklets and earrings.

One of the most effective of the Hausa uses of metal is in horse trappings. These are often visually spectacular. Formerly, there were laws that restricted the use of certain items to the rulers. The most colourful trappings are brought out for parades in honour of visiting dignitaries and for such religious occasions as the Salla procession following the Ramadan fast (see AFRICA, fig. 17).

Wood-carving is carried out in rural areas. Stools and food bowls are decorated with carved or pokerwork linear patterns, while black stain and a little colour may be used.

BIBLIOGRAPHY
A. H. M. Kirk-Greene: 'Decorated Houses in Zaria', *Nigeria Mag.*, 68 (1961), pp. 52–78
D. Heathcote: 'Hausa Embroidered Dress', *Afr. A.*, v/2 (1972), pp. 12–19, 82, 84
——: 'Insight into a Creative Process: A Rare Collection of Embroidery Drawings from Kano', *Savanna*, i/2 (1972), pp. 165–74
——: 'Hausa Women's Dress in the Light of Two Recent Finds', *Savanna*, ii/2 (1973), pp. 201–17
——: 'The Princess's Apartments in Kano Old Treasury', *Savanna*, ii/1 (1973), pp. 61–5
——: 'The Art of Musa Yola', *Afr. A.*, vii/2 (1974), pp. 34–7
——: 'A Hausa Charm Gown', *Man*, n. s., ix/4 (1974), pp. 620–24 and pls 4a and 4b opp. p. 624
——: 'A Leatherworker of Zaria City', *Niger. Field*, xxxix/1 (1974), pp. 12–26; xxxix/3, pp. 99–117
The Arts of the Hausa (exh. cat. by D. Heathcote, London, World of Islam Festival Publishing Co. Ltd, 1977) [numerous illus.; extensive bibliog.]

D. Heathcote: *Hausa Art in Northern Nigeria* (London, 1977) [film, 16 mm]
——: *The Arts of the Hausa* (U. Chicago, 1977)
D. Leoni and J. Prichett: 'Traditional Hausa Pottery in Zaria City', *Savanna*, vii/1 (1978), pp. 3–17
D. Idiens: *The Hausa of Northern Nigeria: A Catalogue of the R. E. Miller Collection and Others in the Royal Scottish Museum*, Royal Scottish Museum Studies (Edinburgh, 1981)
J. C. Moughtin: *Hausa Architecture* (London, 1985)

DAVID HEATHCOTE

Hausenstein, Wilhelm (*b* Hornberg, Baden, 17 June 1882; *d* Munich, 3 June 1957). German art historian. He studied philosophy, classics and German philology at the university of Heidelberg (1900–02), art history at the university of Tübingen (1902) and art history, history and economics at the Ludwig-Maximilians-Universität in Munich (1903–5). He settled in Munich and travelled widely in Italy and France. Hausenstein's background in social history and economics informed his earliest writings on art history, which were devoted to the formal development of the nude in *Der nackte Mensch in der Kunst aller Zeiten* (1911) and to the sociology of art, as in *Die Soziologie der Kunst: Bild und Gemeinschaft* (1912). His study of the Baroque, *Vom Geist des Barock* (1919) was a landmark in the study of that period. At the same time Hausenstein was attracted to contemporary art, as evidenced by his influential study on Expressionism (1919), and he was acquainted with many leading artists, including Lovis Corinth, Max Beckmann and Paul Klee, whose work he introduced, through monographs, to a wider public. His commitment to modern art was reflected in two highly influential volumes in defence of non-Western art: *Exoten* (1921) and *Barbaren und Klassiker* (1922). He completed *c*. 80 books, including monographs on Breughel, Grünewald and Rembrandt, and edited a number of journals, including *Neue Merkur* and *Ganymed*, and such encyclopedias as *Die bildende Kunst der Gegenwart* (1914) and *Das Bild, Atlanten zur Kunst* (1922–4). He also edited the literary supplement of the *Frankfurter Zeitung* (1934–43). In 1950 he was invited to serve as Ambassador to France, a post he held until 1955.

WRITINGS
Der nackte Mensch in der Kunst aller Zeiten (Munich, 1911/*R* 1924)
Die Soziologie der Kunst: Bild und Gemeinschaft (Munich, 1912/*R* 1920)
Die bildende Kunst der Gegenwart (Stuttgart and Berlin, 1914/*R* 1923)
Über Expressionismus in der Malerei (Berlin, 1919/*R* 1973)
Vom Geist des Barock (Munich, 1919/*R* 1956)
Lovis Corinth (Munich, 1920)
Exoten (Munich, 1921)
Kairuan oder eine Geschichte vom Maler Klee (Munich, 1921)
Barbaren und Klassiker (Munich, 1922)
Max Beckmann (Munich, 1924)
Rembrandt (Stuttgart, 1926)
H. Melchers, ed.: *Die Kunst in diesem Augenblick: Aufsätze und Tagebuchblätter aus 50 Jahren* (Munich, 1960)

BIBLIOGRAPHY
W. E. Süskind, ed.: *Festgabe für Wilhelm Hausenstein zum 70. Geburtstag* (Munich, 1952)
T. Heuss: 'Wilhelm Hausenstein', *Würdigungen* (Tübingen, 1955), pp. 300–07
R. Minder: 'Wilhelm Hausenstein écrivain', *Allemagne aujourd'hui*, vi (1957), pp. 30–37
G. Hillard: 'Wilhelm Hausenstein', *Jahresring* (1958), pp. 296–307
G. Jedlicka: *Wege zum Kunstwerk* (Munich, 1960), pp. 272–86

RHYS W. WILLIAMS

Hauser, Arnold (*b* Timisoara, Romania, 8 May 1892; *d* Budapest, 29 Jan 1978). Hungarian art historian. He studied at the University of Budapest, where he obtained his doctorate in 1918. In 1921 he left Hungary for political reasons and continued his studies in Berlin, where he came under the influence of Adolf Goldschmidt and the sociologist E. Troeltsch. In 1938 he emigrated to England and after World War II was able to pursue his academic career, including a period at Leeds University (1951–7). In 1977 he received permission to live in Hungary, where he died. He is best known for the publications in which he, like his contemporary Frederick Antal, applied the principles of Marxism as a theory of history, not a political system, to the history of art.

During the 1940s Hauser wrote *The Social History of Art* (1951), his most widely read book, in which he reviewed the status of art in society from prehistoric times to the 20th century. His next major work, *Philosophie der Kunstgeschichte* (1958), was a more complex, methodological study in which Hauser expanded his theory of historical materialism, setting out his fundamental thinking on the sociology of art. *Der Manierismus* (1964) was the result of the application of his theory to a defined art-historical problem. In the preface to his last major work, *Soziologie der Kunst* (1974), Hauser summarized his development as an art historian.

WRITINGS
The Social History of Art (London and New York, 1951/*R* 1962)
Philosophie der Kunstgeschichte (Munich, 1958; Eng. trans., London, 1959)
Der Manierismus: Die Krise der Renaissance und der Ursprung der modernen Kunst (Munich, 1964; Eng. trans., London, 1965)
Soziologie der Kunst (Munich, 1974; Eng. trans., London and Chicago, 1982)

JANET SOUTHORN

Hauser, Erich (*b* Rietheim, Tuttlingen, 15 Dec 1930). German sculptor. Between 1945 and 1948 he trained as a steel engraver, while being taught drawing and etching by a Father Ansgar in the Kloster Beuron. He then attended the Freie Kunstschule, Stuttgart, until 1951. His early sculptures, fashioned from knotted and overlapping iron bars, were close in feeling to Tachism. From the 1960s on he remained constant to his abstract themes and the use of metal, which links his work with the sculpture of César, Berto Lardera and Picasso. Hauser employed prefabricated, stainless steel plates, assembled in geometric configurations. Their seams and pitted surfaces show clear traces of the working process, as in his *Steel 9/62* (1962; Hamburg, Ksthalle), but from the mid-1960s the surfaces were polished. His stelae and reliefs broke with sculptural traditions by not being volumetric, but by having rather braced hollow spaces with skinlike shells that merely imitate real weight despite their monumental appearance (e.g. *Room-column 24*, steel, 1969–70; Düsseldorf, Industhaus). The sculptural bodies, split in different ways, form a dialectical relationship between inner and outer spaces and between stasis and motion. He also created many public works from the 1960s, for example his *Column-Wall 32/68* at the Universität in Konstanz (steel, 3.0×2.2×1.0 m, 1968). With the Forum Kunst Rottweil seminars that he initiated in Rottweil, where he lived from 1970, he did much to encourage local interest in contemporary art. In his graphic work he dealt predominantly with spatial problems, employing fragmented surfaces and a network of linear structures—ideas developed in tandem with his three-dimensional pieces.

BIBLIOGRAPHY

Erich Hauser: Werkverzeichnis Plastik, 1962–69 (Nuremberg, 1970)
Erich Hauser (exh. cat., Rottweil, Forum Kst, 1978)
Erich Hauser: Werkverzeichnis Plastik, 1970–1980 (Nuremberg, 1981)

EVA MEYER-HERMANN

Haushofer, Max (*b* Nymphenburg, nr Munich, 12 Sept 1811; *d* Starnberg am Starnbergersee, nr Munich, 24 Aug 1866). German painter. In his early years he settled at Munich and, with his brother-in-law Christian Ruben, was among the founders of a summer colony of artists on Fraueninsel at Chiemsee. During 1835–7 he was in Italy. The ideally heroic landscapes of Carl Rottmann were a major influence on him, but he was also drawn to more naturalistic trends in the genre. Consequently, a part of his work consists of atmospheric but unsentimental small landscapes, together with *plein-air* studies of the changing effects of light on the atmosphere and landscape. He gradually turned to larger sizes (e.g. *On the Bank of Chiemsee, c.* 1858, Prague, N.G., Convent of St Agnes), depicting lakes and also mountain scenes. Haushofer made regular visits to Bavaria and the Tyrol, but he also painted the Bohemian Forest and other parts of Bohemia. From 1845 to 1866 he was professor of landscape painting at the Prague Academy of Fine Arts. He retained his connection with Munich painting and like his pupils responded to many other local and central European influences. Some of his students, such as Alois Bubák, followed in his footsteps; others—including Bedřich Havránek, Adolf Kosárek and Julius Mařák—went their own ways.

BIBLIOGRAPHY

Thieme–Becker
I. Obermayer: *Max Haushofer (1811–66): Ein Beitrag zur Münchener Landschaftsmalerei* (Munich, 1978) [bibliog., list of works]
H. Ludwig, ed.: *Münchner Maler im 19. Jahrhundert*, ii (Munich, 1982), pp. 106–9

ROMAN PRAHL

Hausmaler [Ger.: 'house painter']. Term used to describe painters of faience, porcelain and glass who bought blank factory wares to decorate at home or in their workshop. The practice developed in Germany during the 17th century and spread to other European countries, including Austria, France, the Netherlands and England. The most important *Hausmaler*s were German or Bohemian, who decorated whitewares supplied by such factories as those of Meissen and Vienna with enamels. At its best their work surpassed the finest decoration executed in the factories, contributing greatly to the prestige of early European porcelain. Much 18th-century porcelain decorated by *Hausmaler*s, however, was from cancelled, outmoded or imperfect stock, which explains why many *Hausmalerei* designs are often later in style than the ware itself. Another feature of *Hausmalerei* is that the decoration is frequently oversize.

Nuremberg became an important centre for *Hausmalerei* during the late 17th century and is particularly well known for its *Schwarzlot* (black decorated) ceramics and glass (*see* NUREMBERG, §III, 3). Outstanding artists using this method of decoration included Johann Schaper (1621–70). During the 18th century Augsburg became a major centre for *Hausmalerei*, where many goldsmiths who mounted faience and porcelain with gold and silver turned to decorative painting. Johann Auffenwerth (*d* 1728) was the first recorded Augsburg goldsmith and *Hausmaler*, who decorated porcelain from Meissen in polychrome and gold (e.g. cup and saucer, *c.* 1725; London, BM). His daughter Sabina Auffenwerth (*b* 1706) was also an accomplished porcelain *Hausmaler*. Pre-eminent among *Hausmaler*s was Ignaz Bottengruber (*fl* 1723–30), a miniature painter in Breslau (now Wrocław, Poland), who was known by 1723 as a painter of Meissen and Viennese porcelain. He favoured Bacchic, hunting and battle scenes, framed by bold *Laub und Bandelwerk* ornament (e.g. Meissen cup and saucer painted with a Bacchanalian scene, 1726; London, BM). The brothers Bartolomäus Seuter (1678–1754) and Abraham Seuter (1688–1747) ran a large workshop in Augsburg; they decorated faience from the factories in Bayreuth and Nuremberg and, by 1729, Meissen porcelain. Bartolomäus's work is characterized by his use of scrolls and C-scroll borders (e.g. teapot, *c.* 1730; New York, Met.). Other decoration used by the brothers included gilt silhouette chinoiseries, flowers, scenes after Watteau and *Schwarzlot* decoration.

Other celebrated *Hausmaler*s included the Preissler family from Bohemia (*see* PREISSLER (i)). Daniel Josef Norbert Preissler (1636–1733) worked in Friedrichswalde, Silesia, and decorated glass and East Asian porcelain; his son Ignaz Preissler (*bapt* 1676; *d* 1741) worked in Breslau and Kronstadt painting East Asian and European wares (e.g. Meissen teapot decorated in *Schwarzlot, c.* 1725; London, BM). Other notable *Hausmaler*s were Johann Friedrich Metzsch (*fl* 1731–66) of Bayreuth, who decorated wares with chinoiseries, landscapes and mythological subjects, and Franz Ferdinand Mayer (*fl* 1747–94) of Pressnitz, Bohemia, who decorated wares with pastoral or genre scenes.

As competition between independent decorators and the factories grew, several porcelain manufacturers allowed only defective wares to be purchased by *Hausmaler*s; Meissen ceased selling to workshops in Augsburg as early as 1728. Many *Hausmaler*s resorted to giving additional decoration to sparsely decorated wares. Dutch *Hausmaler*s were thought to have initiated such work on underglaze blue and white, and the German *Hausmaler* F. J. Ferner (*fl* 1745–50) was known to have redecorated imperfect blue-and-white Meissen. By the 1760s Meissen ceased supplying their porcelain to *Hausmaler*s altogether. With only poor quality porcelain and indifferent work the practice gradually fell into decline.

BIBLIOGRAPHY

G. Savage: *18th Century German Porcelain* (London, 1958)
E. Pauls-Eisenbeiss: *German Porcelain of the 18th Century* (London, 1972), i, pp. 540–67
H. Bosch: *Die Nürnberger Hausmaler* (Munich, 1984)

Hausmann, Raoul (*b* Vienna, 12 July 1886; *d* Limoges, 1 Feb 1971). Austrian photomontagist, painter, photographer, printmaker, writer and theorist. He trained in the academic artistic tradition under his father, Victor Hausmann (1859–1920). In 1900 he went to Berlin, where he later became a central figure in Dada. His important friendship with the eccentric architect and mystical artist Johannes Baader (1875–1956) began in 1905. In the first years of the next decade he was associated with such artists as Erich Heckel and Ludwig Meidner and produced numerous paintings, including *Blue Nude* (1916; Rochechouart, Mus. Dépt.), and woodcuts, several of which were published in his book *Material der Malerei Plastik Architektur* (Berlin, 1918). These works blended Expressionism with the influences of artists then exhibiting at Herwarth Walden's Sturm-Galerie: Fernand Léger, Alexander Archipenko, Robert Delaunay and Sonia Delaunay, Arthur Segal and others. Around 1915 his widening contacts with the writers Salomon Friedländer and Franz Jung led to innumerable theoretical and satirical writings that were published in *Der Sturm, Die Aktion, Die freie Strasse* and other magazines of the era. Hausmann's views reflected a diversity of influences ranging from biologist Ernst Haeckel and psychologist Otto Gross, to Nietzsche and Henri Bergson, to Eastern philosophers including Laozi, and to such anarchists as Max Stirner. In 1915 he also met Hans Richter and Hannah Höch; Höch became Hausmann's close companion until 1922. By 1917 he was associated with Richard Huelsenbeck, George Grosz, John Heartfield and Wieland Herzfelde, who together formed the nucleus of Dada in Berlin during 1918–22.

Hausmann abandoned oil painting and woodcuts and demanded the use of automatism in his 'Manifest von der Gesetzmässigkeit des Lautes' (1918), published in *Mécano*, 2 (1922), and the use of new materials in art in his Dada manifesto *Synthetisches Cino der Malerei* (1918; published Berlin, 1919). His innovative art forms were at once visual and auditory. They included 'poster-poems' and 'optophonetic' poetry that presented random sequences of letters as phonetic sounds (e.g. *OFFEAHBDC*, 1918, and *L'Inconnu*, 1919; both Paris, Pompidou); assemblages made of *objets trouvés* (e.g. *Mechanical Head: Spirit of Our Age*, 1919; Paris, Pompidou); and photocollages that combined fragments of photographs, typography, woodcuts and other materials (e.g. *The Art Critic*, 1920; London, Tate; see fig.). Although his works were often ironic celebrations of modern technology, mass media and the world of fashion, his message followed in the monist mystical tradition in which all matter is viewed as inextricably bound with spirit.

Seeking an alternative to the gallery and salon, the Berlin Dadaists staged riotous events that often surpassed those of the Futurists. In 1920 in Otto Burchard's gallery in Berlin they presented a *Dada-Messe*, which challenged German militarism, politics, the 'art for art's sake' stance and the social conventions associated with avant-garde enclaves. In *Der Dada* (three issues, 1918–20), Hausmann, referred to as the *Dadasoph*, used satire and irony in bold typographic layouts and woodcuts to identify and lampoon radical and conservative political positions, bourgeois and reactionary social values, and various artistic movements, above all Expressionism. The Expressionists' dream of the New Man was broadly revised by supplanting pathos and emotion with perception and sensation, by standardizing visual vocabulary, and by searching for the social conventions of behaviour and thought of the new society ('Lob des Konventionellen', *Die Pille*, iii/1–2, 1922). Hausmann's often architectonic compositions of repeated

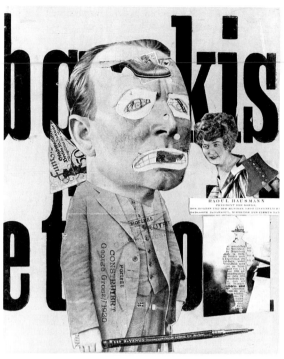

Raoul Hausmann: *The Art Critic*, collage of photographs, newsprint, stamp fragments, drawing and ink on paper, 318×254 mm, 1920 (London, Tate Gallery)

forms anticipated the functionalist aesthetic of Constructivism, simultaneously retaining the irregularities and co-incidences found in nature. Around 1920 he adopted the ambiguous spatial effects of de Chirico's metaphysical works and used precise and realistic technical drawing and watercolour to extol the engineer and technician, as seen in *Carrose's Stomach Where Dupont-Durand is Making Poems* (1920; Saint-Etienne, Mus. A. & Indust.); he meanwhile continued to make abstract drawings and gouaches such as *Abstract Image-Idea* (1921; Vienna, Mus. 20. Jhts).

During the 1920s Hausmann was influenced by the neo-Kantian philosopher Jacob Ernst Marcus to embrace physiology and the analysis of the senses. In a biologically directed course of development, he posed 'Presentism' in opposition to technologically inspired Constructivism. His associates at this time included Kurt Schwitters, László Moholy-Nagy, Viking Eggeling, Hans Richter, Theo van Doesburg, Lajos Kassák and Werner Graeff. After the photomontage *ABCD* (1923; Paris, Pompidou) he abandoned the process in favour of drawing, photography and stream-of-consciousness fiction, such as *Hyle* (1969). During the next 30 years he wrote numerous articles on photography in *A bis Z* (Cologne), *Camera* (Lucerne) and other journals. His principal photographic subjects were nudes, cityscapes, landscapes, still-lifes and *Ombres*, photographs in which shadows, shapes and the play of light were given a structural role. During the late 1920s Hausmann's preoccupation with a fundamental unity of the senses led to the optophone, a device intended to convert light into sound, a version of which was patented in 1935 as a 'calculating apparatus' (British patent no. 446,338).

In 1933 Hausmann fled to Ibiza, where he wrote ethnographic studies of indigenous architecture that were illustrated by his photographs and published in *Oeuvres* (1935), *L'Architecture d'aujourd'hui* (1935–6) and *Revue anthropologique* (1938). During a brief sojourn in Paris in 1934–5 he contributed photographs to Man Ray's book *Nus*. On the outbreak of the Spanish Civil War (1936), he fled to Zurich and then to Prague (1937). At this time he began experimenting with infra-red photography. While living in Paris in 1938 he contributed to the journal *Plastique* and made a living from photography. In 1939 he moved to Peyrat-le-Château in Haute-Vienne, where he earned a living as a language tutor. When he moved to Limoges in 1944, he resumed painting for the first time since the 1920s, producing colourful works in gouache. In the late 1940s he produced his first photograms and created gestural pictograms in drawings, gouaches and collages that developed gradually from geometric abstraction.

From the mid-1950s Hausmann's importance to Dadaism was increasingly recognized by contemporary artists and poets. He exhibited frequently, published prolifically and in 1959 resumed oil painting. His paintings became rich in pictographic imagery and revealed a renewed interest in colour, as seen in *The Sign* (1962; Limoges, priv. col., see 1980 exh. cat., p. 73). In the last 20 years of his life he produced numerous books, including retrospective accounts of his life, and recorded selections of sound poetry from throughout his career. In all its diversity, Hausmann's art was constantly directed towards the attainment of a new language of forms and signs appropriate to the modern psyche.

WRITINGS

Courier Dada (Paris, 1958)
'Manifesto on the Lawfulness of Sound', Eng. trans. R. Taylor in *Form*, 4 (1967), p. 32
Hyle: Ein Traumsein in Spanien (Frankfurt am Main, 1969)
K. Riha and G. Kämpf, eds: *Am Anfang war Dada* (Giessen, 1971, 2/1980) [incl. a comprehensive bibliog.]
M. Erlhoff, ed.: *Texte bis 1933*, 2 vols (Munich, 1982)

BIBLIOGRAPHY

R. Schacht: 'Raoul Hausmann tanzt', *Das blaue Heft*, iii (1921–2), pp. 887–8
Raoul Hausmann (exh. cat., Stockholm, Mod. Mus., 1967)
J.-F. Bory: *Prolégomènes à une monographie de Raoul Hausmann* (Paris, 1972)
Raoul Hausmann, autour de 'L'Esprit de notre temps': Assemblages, collages, photo-montages (exh. cat., Paris, Mus. N. A. Mod., Paris, 1974)
M. Giroud: *Raoul Hausmann: 'Je ne suis pas un photographe'* (Paris, 1975) [well illus.]
The Twenties in Berlin (exh. cat., London, Annely Juda F.A. Ltd, 1978)
A. Haus, ed.: *Raoul Hausmann: Kamerafotografien, 1927–1957* (Munich, 1979)
Raoul Hausmann (exh. cat., Malmö, Ksthall, 1980) [based on the artist's estate, Limoges]
Hausmann: Retrospektive (exh. cat., Hannover, Kestner-Ges., 1981)
M. Erlhoff: *Raoul Hausmann, Dadasoph: Versuch einer Politisierung der Ästhetik* (Hannover, 1982)
T. O. Benson: 'The Functional and the Conventional in the Dada Philosophy of Raoul Hausmann', *Dada/Dimensions*, ed. S. C. Foster (Ann Arbor, 1985), pp. 131–63
Gegen den kalten Blick der Welt: Raoul Hausmann—Fotografien, 1927–1933 (exh. cat., Vienna, Mus. 20. Jhts, 1986) [incl. newly discovered photographs by Hausmann]
Raoul Hausmann: 1886–1971 (exh. cat., Rochechouart, Mus. Dépt., 1986)
T. O. Benson: 'Mysticism, Materialism, and the Machine in Berlin Dada', *Coll. A. J.*, xlvi/1 (1987), pp. 46–55
——: *Raoul Hausmann and Berlin Dada* (Ann Arbor, 1987)

TIMOTHY O. BENSON

Hausner, Rudolf (*b* Vienna, 4 Dec 1914). Austrian painter. He studied at the Akademie der Bildenden Künste in Vienna from 1931 until 1936. During this period he also travelled to England, France, Italy, Greece, Turkey and Egypt. After he was designated a 'degenerate' artist in 1938 (*see* ENTARTETE KUNST), exhibition of his work was forbidden in Germany. From 1941 until 1945 he was a soldier. Before allying himself with the style of PHANTASTISCHER REALISMUS, based in Vienna, his works were mainly Expressionist-influenced images of suburbs, still-lifes and female models, most of which he destroyed.

In 1946 Hausner joined the Art-Club and had his first one-man exhibition in the Konzerthaus, Vienna. A key work of this period, *It's me!* (1948; Vienna, Hist. Mus.), shows his awareness of Pittura Metafisica and Surrealism in a psychoanalytical painting where the elongated being in the foreground penetrates what was apparently a real landscape, until it tears like a backdrop; another painting, *Forum of Inward-turned Optics* (1948; Vienna, Hist. Mus.), is evidence of his ability to depict the subject in a realist style while simultaneously overturning the laws of one-point perspective.

In 1962 Hausner met Paul Delvaux, René Magritte, Victor Brauner and Dorothea Tanning while travelling in Germany, the Netherlands, Belgium and France. The *Ark of Odysseus* (1948–51 and 1953–6; Vienna, Hist. Mus.) depicted the hero as a self-portrait and was a precursor to the series of *Adam* paintings in which Hausner painted his own features. From 1965 until 1980 he was a professor at the Hochschule für Bildende Künste in Hamburg, and he also taught in Vienna at the Kunstakademie.

BIBLIOGRAPHY

Die Wiener Schule des Phantastischen Realismus (exh. cat., Hannover, Kestner-Ges., 1965)
W. Schmied: *Rudolf Hausner* (Salzburg, 1970)
V. Huber, ed.: *Rudolf Hausner: Werkzeichnis der Druckgraphik von 1966 bis 1975* (Offenbach am Main, 1977)
H. Hollander: *Rudolf Hausner Werkmonographie* (Offenbach am Main, 1985)

INGEBORG KUHN-RÉGNIER

Haus-Rucker-Co. Austrian architectural partnership formed in Vienna in 1967 by Laurids Ortner (*b* Vienna, 26 May 1941), Günter Zamp Kelp (*b* Bistritz, 26 Aug 1941) and Klaus Pinter (*b* Schärding, ?1940). At the time of its formation the canon of Functionalism was beginning to disintegrate. Many of the early projects occupy a space between architectural design and *Aktionskunst*, for example *Balloon for Two*, (1967; see Feuerstein, p. 91), Vienna, and *Shell around Haus Lange Museum*, (1971; see Feuerstein, p. 93), Krefeld. Some schemes were utopian and remained unrealized such as *Pneumacosm* (1967; see Feuerstein, p. 92), an expansion plan for New York using pneumatic cells, or *Big Piano* (1972). In 1970 Haus-Rucker-Co. opened another studio in Düsseldorf and a third in New York in 1971. The group has been active in the propagation of a 'provisional', disposable concept of architecture that anticipates changes in the environment. This concept of a flexible architecture, which makes use of furniture as dividers of space and dismountable fittings, is expressed in their interior designs (e.g. BENE showrooms, Renngasse 6–8, Vienna, 1981). The group has been involved in many fair and exhibition projects, including *Oasis No. 7* at *Documenta 5* (1972; see Feuerstein, p. 94), Kassel, the temporary nature of which demands a versatile design approach. In 1987 Haus-Rucker-Co. won the competition for the Messepalast in Vienna, a large exhibition complex. Their highly individualistic design approach, which was equally at home displayed in architecture magazines as in galleries of modern art, earned them a place among the avant-garde of late 20th-century architecture. The most prominent member of the group, Laurids Ortner, is professor and director of the master class for structural design at the Academy of Design in Linz.

WRITINGS

Aktionen-Objekte (Vienna, 1970)
1967 bis 1983 (Brunswick, 1984)

BIBLIOGRAPHY

L. Ortner: *Provisorische Architektur—Medium zur Stadtgestaltung* (Düsseldorf, 1976)
G. Feuerstein: *Visionäre Architektur—Wien, 1958–1988* (West Berlin, 1988)

CLAUDIA BÖLLING

Häusser, Robert (*b* Stuttgart, 8 Nov 1924). German photographer and collector. He trained as a photographer and specifically as a photojournalist before he fought in World War II. From 1950 he studied at the Schule für Angewandte Kunst in Weimar. In 1952 he moved to Mannheim, where he set up a studio and organized numerous exhibitions of contemporary art. In the following years he produced many volumes of photographs, including portraits of cities. He also produced series of pictures that are narrative in intent but dramatic and heavy in tone. Between 1952 and 1954 his work became formally stricter but lighter in tone. The earlier poetic images progressed to critical and political messages on themes such as loneliness, desolation, doubt and death. Häusser's cryptic method of translating political content is particularly clear in *The 21 Doors of Benito Mussolini* (Cologne, Mus. Ludwig). Häusser was an active collector of works by German artists such as Gotthard Graubner, Karl–Otto Götz and Peter Brüning. A member of the jury of the Deutscher Künstlerbund, he was able to encourage the recognition of photography as an art form, and he organized the Künstlerbund's first photographic exhibition in 1987.

PHOTOGRAPHIC PUBLICATIONS

Ein Fotograf sieht Mannheim (Mannheim, 1957)
Welt am Oberrhein (Karlsruhe, 1961/*R* 1962/*R* 1963)
Gelsenkirchen (Düsseldorf, 1970)

BIBLIOGRAPHY

Robert Häusser: Fotografische Bilder (exh. cat. by H. Keller, Cologne, Josef-Haubrich-Ksthalle, 1972)
Robert Häusser: Magischer Realismus (exh. cat., Nuremberg, Inst. Mod. Kst, 1972)
Robert Häusser: Fotografische Bilder 1941–1984 (exh. cat., Mannheim, Städt. Ksthalle, 1984–5)
Robert Häusser: Fotographische Bilder 1941–1987 (exh. cat., Stuttgart, Württemberg. Kstver., 1988)

REINHOLD MISSELBECK

Haussmann, Georges Eugène, Baron (*b* Paris, 27 March 1809; *d* 11 Jan 1891). French administrator, urban planner and financier. Having graduated as a lawyer from the Université de Paris in 1831, he served as *sous-préfet* in various provincial towns and displayed excellent organizational abilities. The patronage of highly placed friends led him to be appointed to a series of administrative posts that involved the upkeep of public thoroughfares, school administration and the distribution of water. His work in Yonne and Bordeaux drew him to the attention of the Emperor Napoleon III (*reg* 1852–70), who was planning fundamental changes to the structure of Paris. The intention was to modernize the ancient fabric of the city and introduce new amenities, such as a sewage system and railway service. Other considerations were the encouragement of a growth in the population and the adaptation of the city to industrial life while facilitating methods of control against riots or warfare. Appointed *Préfet* of Paris in 1853, Haussmann was given exceptional powers to carry out the plan. Demolitions were carried out, new building lines were established, traffic routes were opened, and public gardens, influenced by English examples, were created. The main areas of his activity concerned the Louvre, the Tuileries, the approaches to the Hôtel de Ville, the Rue de Rivoli, the area around the Opéra, the avenues leading up to Place de l'Etoile (*see* PARIS, fig. 8), the Cité and the Grands Boulevards: in all *c.* 150 km of new roads (a meticulous photographic record was made at the time by Charles Marville). Planning regulations based on the classicism favoured by the Académie des Beaux-Arts determined the appearance of all new buildings, including urban furniture and monuments. At the same time, Haussmann encouraged the annexation of the suburbs and had the fortifications of Tiers demolished in 1840, hence modifying the boundaries of the city. Haussmann's collaborators included the engineer Adolphe Alphand, who worked on the Bois de Boulogne (1854); he also enlisted the services of the architects Jacques-Ignace Hittorff, Victor Baltard, Charles Garnier, Antoine Bailly and Louis Duc. Haussmann resigned his post in 1870, when the Third Republic was established, by which time a reaction had set in against his achievements. Haussman was an exceptional worker and clever financier and was successful in attracting private investment in public works.

See also PARIS, §II, 5.

WRITINGS

Mémoires du Baron Haussmann, 3 vols (Paris, 1890–93)

BIBLIOGRAPHY

J. des Cars and P. Pinon: *Paris Haussmann* (Paris, 1971)
H. Malet: *Le Baron Haussmann et la rénovation de Paris* (Paris, 1973)

MARC DILET

Hauswirth, Johann Jakob (*b* Saanen, Berne, 1809; *d* Château d'Oex, Vaud, 29 March 1871). Swiss *découpage* and silhouette artist. He is one of the few masters of Swiss popular folk art whose corpus of works have survived, although very little is actually known of his life. He was apparently a labourer who travelled widely in central Switzerland seeking itinerant employment and who, in his spare time, supplied rural communities with paper silhouettes and cut-outs that were used to decorate their homes. He sold his work door-to-door and used imagery that was easily comprehensible to his prospective buyers. Many of his works are extraordinarily complex in form and technique, often employing multiple layers of paper and various colour schemes. His subjects were frequently drawn from country life, depicting farm animals and traditional rituals, as seen in *Alpine Procession* (1867; Château d'Oex, Mus. Vieux-Pays d'Enhaut), which represents a large herd of cows going to summer mountain pastures. Some of his most intricate works are purely decorative patterns and blend more than a dozen colours in an equal number of layers of paper (e.g. *Flowers*, c. 1850; Château d'Oex, Mus. Vieux-Pays d'Enhaut). Few of his works are signed or dated. There are a number, however, that bear dates from the 1850s, indicating a particularly creative period in his life. His images are striking because they combine exquisite craftmanship with a fertile imagination.

BIBLIOGRAPHY

C. Bernoulli: 'Zu einem Scherenschnitt des Johann Jakob Hauswirth', *Z. Schweiz. Archäol. & Kstgesch.*, xxii (1962), pp. 136–8

F. Deuchler and others: *La Peinture suisse du moyen âge à l'aube du XXe siècle* (Geneva, 1975), p. 175

C. Apothéloz: *Deux imagiers du Pays-d'Enhaut* (Paudex, 1978)

WILLIAM HAUPTMAN

Hauszmann, Alajos (*b* Buda [now Budapest], 9 June 1847; *d* Velence, Fejér county, 31 July 1926). Hungarian architect. He studied at the Polytechnic at Buda and at the Bauakademie of Berlin. Later he travelled in Italy. From 1872 he was a professor at the Technical University of Budapest. In addition to his work in Szombathely (e.g. the Town Hall, 1876–91), his early works in Budapest, such as the two-storey pavilion (1873–4; destr.) in Elisabeth Square, the town house (1884) of Géza Batthyány (which is a scaled-down copy of the Palazzo Strozzi, Florence), and the brick-faced former Museum of Technological Industry (1889), are in an Italian Renaissance Revival style. Towards the end of the century his architectural office became a large and flourishing one, and he was one of the leading figures in Hungarian architecture around 1900, providing some highlights to its astonishing development in Budapest at this time. In his neo-Baroque buildings Hauszmann applied certain features of the Beaux-Arts style. The monumental Court of Justice (1891–6; Budapest, now the Museum of Ethnography), with its huge portico flanked by towers and its rich sculptural decoration, recalls Paul Wallot's Reichstag (1884–94) in Berlin. The so-called New York Palace (1892–4), Budapest, is more florid and individual. The central dome and the north wing of the Royal Palace (1891–1905; partly destr. 1945; rebuilt in simplified form), Budapest, an imposing neo-Baroque structure of jagged outline, were meant to enhance the city's status as a royal residence. Hauszmann was an honorary corresponding member of the RIBA, London, and, from 1924, an honorary member of the Hungarian Academy of Sciences.

BIBLIOGRAPHY

I. Czagány: 'Hauszmann Alajos müvészetének stílusváltozásai' [Changes in the style of Alajos Hauszmann's art], *Müvészettörténeti Értesítő*, xxvii (1978), pp. 225–55

JÓZSEF SISA

Hautecoeur, Louis(-Eugène-Georges) (*b* Paris, 11 June 1884; *d* Paris, 16 Nov 1973). French art historian. His family owned a bookshop selling prints and catalogues in the Rue de Rivoli, Paris. In 1908 he graduated brilliantly from the classical studies course at the Ecole Normale Supérieure, and was admitted to the Ecole de France in Rome, where he wrote his thesis on *Rome et la renaissance de l'antiquité à la fin du XVIIIe siècle* (1912). He was also for a time a student in St Petersburg and became, consequently, one of the few scholars to have known the Russia of the tsars. A result of the Russian visit was his work *L'Architecture classique à Saint-Pétersbourg à la fin du XVIIIe siècle* (1912). After the end of World War I Hautecoeur became a curator at the Louvre and then the Musée du Luxembourg, except for 1927–30, when he was in charge of the fine arts in Egypt. From then on he was a dominant figure in the history of art, but was also interested in contemporary art; each assignment brought from him an important work. From 1921 he taught on classical architecture in France at the Ecole Nationale Supérieure des Beaux-Arts, and from 1930 to 1939 at the Ecole du Louvre.

In July 1940 Hautecoeur helped to remove the French national collections to places of safety, before becoming Secrétaire d'Etat aux Beaux-Arts in the Vichy cabinet. After a postwar period in Geneva, where he had become a curator of the Musée des Beaux-Arts, he became in 1952 a member and from 1955–64 perpetual secretary of the Académie des Beaux-Arts, Paris. His monumental *Histoire de l'architecture classique en France* comprises seven volumes, of which he himself updated the first three, dealing with the Renaissance and the 17th century. Hautecoeur did not himself explore archival collections, except for those of the Louvre, but he brought old texts, scholarly studies and prints powerfully into play and was tireless in his researches. He was a nationalist, indifferent to the thought of art historians of the Vienna school, such as Emil Kaufmann (1891–1953) and Fiske Kimball, who approached the same periods in a different spirit. Erudite and analytical in his apprehension of facts, his general accounts of them were solidly constructed. All creative works were, according to him, explained by their placing in time. He has remained the greatest French art historian, of the same rank as Emile Mâle, Henri-Joseph Focillon and André Chastel.

WRITINGS

L'Architecture classique à Saint-Pétersbourg à la fin du XVIIIe siècle (Paris, 1912)

Rome et la renaissance de l'antiquité à la fin du XVIIIe siècle (Paris, 1912)

Histoire du Louvre, 1200–1908 (Paris, 1928)

L'Architecture en Bourgogne, 3 vols (Paris and Brussels, 1929)

Les Mosquées du Caire (Paris, 1932)

Littérature et peinture du XVIIIe au XXe siècle (Paris, 1942, rev. 1963)

Histoire de l'architecture classique en France, 7 vols (Paris, 1943–57)

Mystique et architecture: Symbolisme du cercle et de la coupole (Paris, 1954)

Histoire de l'art, 3 vols (Paris, 1959)

Les Jardins des dieux et hommes (Paris, 1959)

BIBLIOGRAPHY

DBF

'Bibliographie des travaux de M. Louis Hautecoeur', *Procès-verbaux de la Commission municipale du Vieux-Paris, Paris, 1968* [and suppl. for 1969–74]

J. Lavalleye: 'Louis Hautecoeur', *Bull. Cl. B.-A., Acad. Royale Sci., Lett. & B.-A. Belgique*, lvi (1974), pp. 22–6

DANIELLE GALLET

Hauteville, House of. Norman dynasty of rulers and patrons. The sons of Tancred of Hauteville served as mercenaries and acquired lands in southern Italy, notably Roger of Hauteville (*reg* 1072–1101), who conquered Sicily. The two most important patrons in the family were (1) Roger II and (2) William II, whose extensive building programmes at Cefalù, Palermo and Monreale reflected the cosmopolitan society over which they ruled.

(1) Roger II, King of Sicily (*b* 22 Dec 1095; *reg* 28 Sept 1105–54; *d* Palermo, 26 Feb 1154). The son of Roger de Hauteville and Adelaide of Savona, he succeeded his brother Simon (*reg* 1101–5), but his mother remained regent until 1112. His coronation as king of Sicily in 1130 was performed by the anti-pope Anacletus II (*reg* 1130–38) in return for his support in the papal schism. During the 1120s Roger fought military campaigns to unite the Norman territories in southern Italy with Sicily. In the 1130s he was forced to defend these gains against an alliance of Anacletus's rival Innocent II (*reg* 1130–43), the Holy Roman Emperor Lothar III and some of the mainland barons.

Under Roger, Sicily became a leading maritime power in the Mediterranean and one of the best-governed states in Europe. He ruled over a cosmopolitan society that was a medley of cultures, languages and religions: Normans, Greeks, Italians, Jews and Arabs all contributed to the richness of court culture that flourished in the capital (*see* PALERMO, §I). In many practical aspects of his rule, as well as in the language and imagery of his coins and documents, Roger sought to imitate the Byzantine emperors. The outstanding examples of his artistic patronage are the Byzantine mosaics of Cefalù Cathedral (*see* CEFALÙ, §2) and the Cappella Palatina in Palermo (*see* PALERMO, §II, 2(ii) and fig. 3), both of which he founded. In the church of the Martorana in Palermo, built by Roger's Syro-Greek minister George of Antioch, a mosaic panel shows the King in Byzantine robes being crowned by Christ.

(2) William II [the Good], King of Sicily (*b* 1154; *reg* May 1166–89; *d* Palermo, 18 Nov 1189). Grandson of (1) Roger II. He was the fourth member of the Norman Hauteville dynasty to rule Sicily, succeeding his father William I (*reg* 1154–66); his mother Margaret of Navarre acted as regent until 1171. In the mid-1170s he signed treaties with Venice and Genoa that granted them lucrative trading privileges and thereby pre-empted their potential support for the hostility of Frederick I, Holy Roman Emperor. In 1177 he married Joan (*d* 1199), daughter of Henry II, King of England.

William's most important piece of ecclesiastical and artistic patronage was the foundation of Monreale Cathedral (1174; *see* MONREALE CATHEDRAL, §1), which was designed to rival the rebuilding of Palermo Cathedral by Archbishop Gualtiero Offamilio (*reg* 1169–90), whose pretensions were strenuously opposed by William's chief adviser Matteo di Ajello (*d* 1193). Friendly relations with Rome ensured papal support for the project. The Byzantine mosaics and Romanesque cloister capitals of Monreale were executed during William's reign. In the cathedral, a mosaic panel above the royal throne shows William being crowned directly by Christ; another panel opposite shows the King offering the church to the enthroned Virgin Mary.

In the 1180s William launched a series of attacks on Byzantium and its territories, which came to nothing. He died in 1189, while planning to take part in the Third Crusade; he was buried in Monreale. His failure to produce an heir contributed to the instability that was to bring the period of Norman rule in Sicily to an end.

BIBLIOGRAPHY

F. Chalandon: *Histoire de la domination normande en Italie et en Sicile*, ii (Paris, 1907/*R* New York, 1969), pp. 305–418

E. Kitzinger: 'On the Portrait of Roger II in the Martorana in Palermo', *Proporzioni*, iii (1950), pp. 30–35; also in W. E. Kleinbauer, ed.: *The Art of Byzantium and the Medieval West: Selected Studies by Ernst Kitzinger* (Bloomington, 1976)

J. J. Norwich: *The Normans in the South, 1016–1130* (London, 1967, rev. 1981), pp. 280–331

——: *The Kingdom in the Sun, 1130–1194* (London, 1970, rev. 1981), pp. 3–163, 249–355

D. Matthew: *The Norman Kingdom of Sicily* (Cambridge, 1992), pp. 1–281

MARTIN KAUFFMANN

Haute-Volta. *See* BURKINA FASO.

Havana [La Habana]. Capital of Cuba. The city of San Cristóbal de La Habana was established three times between 1514 and 1519: first, on the south coast of Cuba at the mouth of the River Onicaxinal; second, on the north coast, on the banks of the River Casiguaguas (now the Almendares); and finally on the bay that sheltered the port of Carenas. It was founded in honour of the saint and the Indian chief Habaguanex. Its key position in the Caribbean made it the main city of the Spanish Antilles. In 1552 it became the capital, and in 1592 Philip II granted it the status of city. In 1610 its population rose to 10,000. Its grid plan was irregular, and its first streets, which ran parallel to the coast, were winding. In contrast to the monocentric urban development of cities in Latin American colonies, in Havana the activities of the community took place in different areas, giving rise to a polycentric plan that persisted throughout the city's history. Religious activities centred on the cathedral square; political, administrative and military activities on the Plaza de Armas; foreign commerce on the Plaza de S Francisco; and domestic trade on the Plaza Nueva (now Plaza Vieja). Government buildings and the mansions of the wealthiest families were situated around these squares. Until the 19th century the city was enclosed by walls and fortifications. It was protected by the latter until 1762, when the English fleet captured the castle of Los Tres Reyes del Morro. The population had been rising since the beginning of the plantation economy: in 1750 the city had 50,000 inhabitants; by 1827, 100,000. As the area within the walls proved to be too cramped, new settlements arose outside them; at the same time the Arsenal was constructed, the shipyard that produced some of the largest ships of the Spanish fleet. In 1837 the city was linked to the hinterland by rail.

Between 1834 and 1838 two basic axes of urban development were decided on, as well as the site for the future political, administrative and cultural centre: the Paseo del Prado and the Paseo de Isabel II (now Parque Central) and, perpendicularly, the Calzada de la Reina and the Paseo Militar (or Paseo Carlos III). Havana's compact growth was on the coastal plateau, with a system of roads dominated by parallel colonnaded avenues: Galiano, Belascoain and Infanta. The demolition of the city walls in 1863 released a central space, of which the upper middle class and the Government took advantage to build public edifices and Neo-classical mansions. In the second half of the 19th century the bourgeois suburbs of El Cerro and El Vedado arose, with their sumptuous mansions.

After the birth of the Republic (1902), Havana assumed a new dimension as a metropolis, expanding to incorporate the surrounding towns of Guanabacoa and Marianao. Social boundaries also appeared: to the west, along the coast, the upper middle class; to the south, the lower middle class; and at the back of the bay, the working class. In 1925 President Gerardo Machado invited the French landscape architect and urban planner J. C. N. Forestier (1861–1930) to draw up an overall plan of Havana, based on the type popularized by Baron Georges-Eugène Haussmann. Although it was never realized, it emphasized some public areas and attributed particular value to the sea-front esplanade, the Malecón (see fig.), as well as the Parque de la Fraternidad, Paseo del Prado, Avenida del Puerto and Avenida de los Presidentes. It also proposed a 'green' area via the Almendares River and culminating in the Gran Parque Metropolitano. In the 1950s the population of

Havana exceeded one million. Without strict urban planning, the city grew in disorderly fashion out towards the suburbs, leaving large open spaces as a result of land speculation. The introduction of several rapid-transit avenues (Vía Blanca, 41 and 51, Acosta and S Catalina) proved insufficient to recover the lost environmental cohesion. In 1956 the Town Planning Associates group (Paul Lester Wiener, Josep Lluís Sert and Paul Schulz) drew up a new plan for Havana in accord with the guidelines of the CIAM's Charte d'Athènes. In contrast to the 'office-city' of Forestier, they designed a 'leisure-city', planned to facilitate American tourism. New landmarks, hotels and luxury tower blocks arose. New emphasis was given to the symbolic significance of the civic square conceived by Forestier. The building of the bay tunnel made possible a new expansion zone, East Havana, near the new Presidential Palace, connected to the beaches frequented by the moneyed classes. Plans for the historic centre that would have permanently destroyed any continuity in the urban fabric were also envisaged but never realized.

The Cuban Revolution (1959) brought fundamental changes, including a social redistribution of urban space that transformed land use. Population movement was

Havana, view of the city with the Malecón in the foreground

reduced and growth restricted; only in 1990 did the city's population reach two million. Workers' housing developments were constructed at Habana del Este, Alamar, San Agustín and Atta Habana. The road system was enhanced by construction of ring-roads, and a large green area comprising the Parque Lenin, the Jardín Botánico and the Parque Zoológico Nacional was created. UNESCO's designation of Havana as a cultural heritage site in 1982 meant that the historic centre underwent an important rescue and restoration operation.

See also CUBA, §III.

BIBLIOGRAPHY
Directorio crítico de La Habana (Havana, 1883)
P. Martínez Inclán: *La Habana actual* (Havana, 1925)
I. A. Wright: *Historia documentada de San Cristóbal de la Habana en el siglo XVI*, 2 vols (Havana, 1927)
E. Roig de Leuchsenring: *La Habana, apuntes históricos*, 3 vols (Havana, 1963)
J.-P. Garnier: *Une Ville, une révolution: La Havane* (Paris, 1973)
R. Segre and others: *Transformación urbana en Cuba: La Habana* (Barcelona, 1974)
J. Rallo and R. Segre: *Introducción histórica a las estructuras territoriales y urbanas de Cuba, 1519–1959* (Havana, 1978)
G. Eguren: *La fidelísima Habana* (Havana, 1986)
A. Núñez Jiménez and C. Venegas Fornias: *La Habana* (Madrid, 1986)
E. Leal Spengler: *La Habana, ciudad antigua* (Havana, 1988)
Estrategia, Grupo de Desarrollo Integral de la Capital (Havana, 1988)
F. Chateloin: *La Habana de Tacón* (Havana, 1989)
G. Mosquera: *Contemporary Art from Havana* (London, 1989)
C. Venegas Fornias: *La urbanización de las murallas: Dependencia y modernidad* (Havana, 1990)

ROBERTO SEGRE

Havard, Henry (*b* Charolles, Saône-et-Loire, 1838; *d* Paris, 1921). French writer. His active role in Republican politics necessitated his absence from France under the Second Empire, a period that he spent working as a journalist and art critic. He was, successively, the foreign correspondent in Italy, Belgium and Holland for *Moniteur universel*, *Journal des débats*, *Monde illustré* and *L'Illustration*. After the Third Republic had been proclaimed (1871) he returned to France and was art critic for *Siècle* for 15 years. From 1875 he was sponsored by the French government to research the Dutch archives and subsequently wrote several books on the art and culture of Holland. Among these was *L'Art et les artistes hollandais* (Paris, 1879–81), in which, after a brief discussion of the beginnings of Dutch art, he surveyed the work of various artists, including Michiel van Miervelt, Govert Flinck, Pieter de Hooch, Carel Fabritius, Adrien van Ostade and Jan van de Velde. His interest in furniture and the applied arts resulted in a four-volume *Dictionnaire de l'ameublement et de la décoration depuis le XIIIe siècle jusqu'à nos jours* (Paris, 1887–9). His more general works included *Quatre derniers siècles: Etude artistique* (Haarlem, 1873), a brief survey of all the arts from 1400 to 1836 that, curiously, did not reproduce or cite specific works.

WRITINGS
Quatre derniers siècles: Etude artistique (Haarlem, 1873)
La Hollande pittoresque: Voyages aux villes mortes de Zuyderzée (Paris, 1874)
La Hollande pittoresque: Les Frontières menacées (Paris, 1876)
Histoire de la faïence de Delft (Paris, 1878)
L'Art et les artistes hollandais, 4 vols (Paris, 1879–81)
Dictionnaire de l'ameublement et de la décoration depuis le XIIIe siècle jusqu'à nos jours (Paris, 1887–9)
Van der Meer de Delft (Paris, 1888)

DBF
BIBLIOGRAPHY
G. Vapereau: *Dictionnaire des contemporains*, 2 vols (Paris, 1893)

Have, Theodore de. *See* HAVEUS, THEODORE.

Havell. English family of artists. Daniel Havell (*d* ?1826) was an engraver and publisher of topographical and architectural works distinguished by a delicacy of line. He worked in London and was for a time in partnership with Robert Havell I (1769–1832), a painter, engraver and publisher. The precise family relationship of Robert and Daniel is not certain: although some sources describe him as Daniel's son, there is evidence to suggest that he may have been his uncle. The family firm engraved work by (1) William Havell, a cousin of Daniel Havell, and a painter and traveller. Robert Havell I later became self-employed and set up in business for a time in Oxford Street with his son (2) Robert Havell jr. In 1839 Robert Havell jr went to the USA at the invitation of John James Audubon, for whom he had engraved many of the plates for *Birds of America*. (3) Ernest Binfield Havell, a great-nephew of (1) William Havell, seems to have inherited the family love of travel and painting and became a distinguished art teacher in India and a scholar of Indian art.

(1) William Havell (*b* Reading, 9 Feb 1782; *d* London, 16 Dec 1857). Painter. The son of a Reading drawing-master, he participated in several sketching societies in the early 19th century. In 1805 he contributed to the first exhibition held by the Society of Painters in Water-colours, of which he was a founder-member. At the same time he began to establish himself as an oil painter, in the manner of Richard Wilson and J. M. W. Turner, exhibiting at the Royal Academy and the British Institution. Initial success was followed by mounting criticism of his idealized treatment of brightly sunlit subjects. The disillusioned Havell accepted the post of official artist to the embassy of China led by William Pitt, Earl Amherst of Arracan (1773–1857), which set out in 1816; Havell was able to sketch the Chinese countryside as the embassy took the return route overland from Beijing to Guangzhou. From there he moved to India and Ceylon (now Sri Lanka), where he spent six years painting portraits and landscapes before returning to England in 1826. In 1828–9 he travelled in Italy. Subsequently he remained in England, exhibiting vivid landscapes that did not bring him the renown that he had once seemed likely to achieve.

In the late 1830s Havell experimented with 'photogeny' (together with his brother Frederick James) and incurred the hostile rivalry of Henry Fox Talbot. A number of his works were engraved, notably a *Series of Picturesque Views of the River Thames*, reproduced in coloured aquatint in 1811 by his uncle Robert I Havell; the latter also published a *Series of Picturesque Views of Noblemen's Seats* (1814–23), to which William contributed.

BIBLIOGRAPHY
A. Bury: 'William Havell', *Old Wtrcol. Soc. Club*, xxvi (1948), pp. 1–18
F. Owen: 'William Havell', *Connoisseur*, cxcvii (1978), pp. 96–103
William Havell, 1782–1857 (exh. cat. by F. Owen and E. Stanford, Reading, Mus. & A.G., 1981)

PATRICK CONNER

(2) Robert Havell, jr (*b* Reading, 25 Nov 1793; *d* Tarrytown, NY, 11 Nov 1878). Engraver and painter, cousin of (1) William Havell. He learnt the art of aquatint engraving from his father, Robert I Havell. He worked first in the family engraving business and then *c*. 1825–7 with Colnaghi's in London. In 1827 he undertook the execution in aquatint of the plates for John James Audubon's *Birds of America*, published in parts in London between 1827 and 1838. Havell engraved 425 of the plates and reworked the ten that had been engraved by William Home Lizars in Edinburgh. Havell's father printed and coloured some of the double elephant folio sheets in 1827–8 after which Havell took on those tasks himself, establishing himself as a master of aquatint. Among his other important works in the medium are the plates for Mrs E. Bury's *Selection of Hexandrian Plants* (London, 1831–4). In 1839, at Audubon's invitation, Havell moved with his family to New York and embarked on a new career as a landscape painter in the style of the Hudson River school, while also working as an engraver. He settled in the Hudson River villages of Ossining (1841) and Tarrytown (1857) but painted throughout north-eastern America. *View of Deerfield, Massachusetts* (1847; Hist. Deerfield, MA) is characteristic of his quietly romantic idealization of his subjects. *Niagara Falls from the Chinese Pagoda* (1845; New York, Pub. Lib.), engraved by Havell after one of his paintings, is among the best known of his American aquatints. Though his reputation rests largely on his work for Audubon, his original subjects gave him greater opportunities to display the full range of his aquatint technique.

BIBLIOGRAPHY

G. A. Williams: 'Robert Havell, Engraver of Audubon's *The Birds of America*', *Print Colr Q.*, vi (1916), pp. 227–57

H. Comstock: 'Complete Works of Robert Havell, jr', *Connoisseur*, cxxvi (1950), pp. 127–8

W. Fries: *The Double Elephant Folio* (Chicago, 1973)

DAVID TATHAM

(3) Ernest Binfield Havell (*b* 1861; *d* Oxford, 31 Dec 1934). Art teacher and historian, active in India, great-nephew of (1) William Havell. Havell came to prominence at the turn of the century as a champion of Indian art and aesthetics. He was trained at the Reading and South Kensington schools of art. He also studied art in Italy and Paris before going to India as a teacher. In 1884 he was appointed superintendent of the Madras School of Industrial Arts. Undertaking tours of various districts, Havell compiled a series of surveys of the art industries of the Madras Presidency, with a view to using the School of Industrial Arts as a forum for revival and preservation.

Havell became superintendent of the School of Art in Calcutta in 1896, emerging as a reformer and critic of colonial policy. His craft programmes reached a high point in his promotion of hand-loom weaving in Bengal in the face of British commercialism and in his circulation of choice examples of traditional Indian designs in glossy folios (the 'Technical Art Series') and cheaper pattern books for artisans. His scheme to reorganize the school's curriculum in order to make 'Indian art the basis of all teaching' was targeted at converting the school from an academy of drawing and painting into a school of Indian crafts and design. This scheme culminated in 1904 in Havell's controversial replacement of the gallery's collection of European painting and sculpture with Asian objects.

By then Havell had also developed an eye for Indian fine arts by collecting Mughal paintings for the gallery adjoining the school and discovering Abanindranath Tagore (*see* TAGORE, (3)), the pioneer of a new 'Indian style' of painting. Havell brought Tagore into the school as vice-principal in 1905, and in 1907 he promoted the establishment of the Indian Society of Oriental Art (*see* CALCUTTA, §3).

Havell's career as a writer began during his Calcutta years. After his return to England in 1905 he emerged as a scholar-ideologue of Indian art. Like ANANDA COOMARASWAMY, Havell sought to improve the position of Indian art in the eyes of Western scholars and to replace the 'archaeological' bias in British approaches to Indian art with an 'Indian' and 'artistic' point of view with roots in Hindu religion and philosophy. His *Indian Sculpture and Painting* (1908) and *The Ideals of Indian Art* (1911) became influential texts in the new Orientalist discourse. Havell's 1910 lecture 'Art Administration in India' and the debate it sparked off at the Royal Society of Arts, London, proved to be a dramatic turning point in the reception of Indian art in the West. However, unlike Coomaraswamy's work, Havell's writings never successfully made the transition from polemics to scholarship. His importance remains confined to a specific historical juncture when the new Orientalism first inspired nationalist art activities in India and turned the tide of international sympathy in favour of Indian art.

Havell was in Copenhagen between 1915 and 1921, working for the British legation. After that he took up residence in Oxford. Although he continued to write and lecture, he was never absorbed into the life of the university. In his last years he was sick, isolated and embittered by the lack of recognition for his efforts on behalf of Indian art and artists.

UNPUBLISHED SOURCES

London, India Office Lib. [col. of papers incl. correspondence, notes and unpublished writings]

WRITINGS

'Some Notes on Indian Pictorial Art', *The Studio*, xxvii/115 (Oct 1902), pp. 25–33

'British Philistinism and Indian Art', *19th C.*, [London] liii/312 (Feb 1903), pp. 198–209

A Handbook to Agra and the Taj, Sikandra, Fatehpur Sikri and the Neighbourhood (London, 1904)

Benaras, the Sacred City: Sketches of Hindu Life and Religion (London, 1905)

Handloom Weaving in India (Calcutta, 1905)

Monograph on Stone Carving in Bengal (Calcutta, 1906)

Indian Sculpture and Painting (London, 1908)

'Art Administration in India', *J. Royal Soc. A.*, lviii/2985 (4 Feb 1910), pp. 273–98

Essays on Indian Art, Industry and Education (Madras, 1910)

Indian Architecture: Its Psychology and Structure from Muhamaddan Times to the Present Day (London, 1911)

The Ideals of Indian Art (London, 1911)

The Basis for Artistic and Industrial Revival in India (Madras, 1912)

The Building of the New Delhi (Guildford, 1912)

The Ancient and Medieval Architecture of India: A Study of Indo-Aryan Civilisation (London, 1915)

The History of Aryan Rule in India from Earliest Times to the Death of Akbar (London, 1918)

A Handbook of Indian Art (London, 1920)

A Short History of India from the Earliest Times to the Present Day (London, 1924)
The Himalayas in Indian Art (London, 1924)

BIBLIOGRAPHY

P. Mitter: *Much Maligned Monsters: History of European Reactions to Indian Art* (Oxford, 1977)
M. Tarapor: *Art and Empire: The Discovery of India in Art and Literature* (diss., Harvard U., 1977)
——: 'Art Education in Imperial India: The Indian Schools of Art', in K. Ballhatchet, ed.: *City and Culture* (1984), iii of *Changing South Asia*, 5 vols (Hong Kong, 1984), pp. 91–8
T. Guha Thakurta: *The Making of a New 'Indian' Art: Artists, Aesthetics and Nationalism in Bengal, c. 1850–1920* (Cambridge, 1992)

TAPATI GUHA THAKURTA

Havemeyer [née Elder], **Louisine (Waldron)** (*b* New York, 28 July 1855; *d* New York, 6 Jan 1929). American collector and patron. At the age of 20, while attending school in Paris, she met Mary Cassatt, who became her cicerone to the arts and introduced her to the pleasures of collecting. Louisine pooled her own and her sisters' funds and bought her first modern French painting, Degas's *Ballet Rehearsal* (Kansas City, MO, Nelson–Atkins Mus. A.), in 1875. She went on to purchase works by Monet, Camille Pissarro and Cassatt. But, on her return to the USA, she discovered that the French artists she admired were either unknown or greeted with hostility.

In 1883 Louisine married Henry [Harry] Osborne Havemeyer (1848–1907), the ex-husband of her aunt. He was a collector in his own right and had assembled outstanding examples of Chinese porcelain, rugs, pottery and Japanese textiles with earnings from his sugar refining business. He bought in quantity and spared no expense. Although he showed a discerning eye in art objects, his judgement in painting tended toward the prosaic. Louisine persuaded him to buy a few paintings by the Impressionists, a passion he came to share by the late 1880s. In the coming years Louisine was the guiding force behind the accumulation of the finest collection of 19th-century French masters in the USA. It included works by Degas, Manet, Courbet, Alfred Sisley, Corot, Honoré Daumier, Jean-François Millet, Puvis de Chavannes and Renoir. In 1901 she bought her first Cézanne and eventually owned 11 of his canvases, including *Still Life, Flowers* (Munich, Franz Heinz col.) and *Flowers in a Glass Vase* (San Diego, CA, Timken A. G.).

The Havemeyer home at 1 East 66th Street, New York (1891–3; destr. *c.* 1948), designed by Charles C. Haight and decorated by the studios of Louis Comfort Tiffany and by Samuel Colman (ii), was built around the expanding collection. Paintings by French artists as well as such Old Masters as El Greco, whom the Havemeyers had come to admire on a tour of Europe in 1901, filled a two-storey gallery and an extension off the main hall. The master suite housed Corot's *Bacchante by the Sea* (1865) and *Bacchante in a Landscape* (1865–70; both New York, Met.), Manet's *Ball at the Opéra* (1873; Washington, DC, N.G.A.), and works by Courbet, Degas, Cassatt and Monet. Chinese porcelain and Cypriot glass overflowed the cabinets, while the Rembrandt Room contained numerous portraits by the Dutch master.

From the 1880s to 1907 the collection grew steadily. On 4 December 1907 Harry, whose firm had recently been accused of illegalities, died suddenly of kidney failure,

and thereafter Louisine's collecting slowed. On her death 1972 art objects were bequeathed by Louisine or donated by her children to the Metropolitan Museum of Art in New York. The National Gallery of Art in Washington, DC, received another portion of the collection, and still other items were sold at a private auction (10–19 April 1930) at the Anderson Gallery, New York. Louisine's youngest daughter, Electra Havemeyer Webb (1888–1960), also a collector, founded a museum in Shelburne, VT, in 1947 to exhibit the 125,000 objects she had collected in her lifetime. The bulk of the collection is made up of American folk and decorative arts, including early furniture, quilts and other crafts, pewter and glass.

WRITINGS

Sixteen to Sixty: Memoirs of a Collector (n.p., 1961) [privately printed]

BIBLIOGRAPHY

H. O. Havemeyer Collection: Catalogue of Paintings, Prints, Sculpture and Objects of Art (Portland, ME, 1931) [privately printed]
D. Sutton: 'The Discerning Eye of Louisine Havemeyer', *Apollo*, lxxxii (1965), pp. 231–5
L. B. Gillies: 'European Drawings in the Havemeyer Collection', *Connoisseur*, clxxii (1969), pp. 148–55
A. Faxon: 'Painter and Patron: Collaboration of Mary Cassatt and Louisine Havemeyer', *Woman's A. J.* (1982–3), pp. 15–20
F. Weitzenhoffer: *The Havemeyers: Impressionism comes to America* (New York, 1986)

KATHRYN BONOMI

Haven, van [von]. Norwegian family of artists, active in Denmark. The sons of the Bergen painter (1) Solomon van Haven—(2) Michael van Haven and (3) Lambert van Haven—were important artists at the Danish court in the mid-17th century. Lambert's son Nikolaj van Haven (*d* Copenhagen, before 5 Jan 1762) was a medallist.

(1) Solomon van Haven (*b* Stralsund, *c.* 1600; *d* ?Copenhagen, 17 March 1670). Painter, sculptor, designer and actor. From 1625 to 1636 he worked in Bergen as a clown, actor, scenery and dolls' costume designer and sculptor. During the visit of Christian IV, King of Denmark and Norway, to Bergen in 1641 the King invited van Haven to Copenhagen, but he declined. He executed commissions for the German colony in Bergen, and paintings in the town's Mariakirken are attributed to him, as well as portraits in west-coast churches. The *Four Eskimos from Greenland* (1654; Copenhagen, Nmus.) is generally attributed to him. He was a founder and teacher of the Bergen painting school during the 1630s and 1640s, teaching Elias Fiigenschoug (*b* early 17th century; *d* *c.* 1661) and his own sons Michael and Lambert. From 1666 he received a royal pension.

(2) Michael van Haven (*b* Bergen, before 1630; *bur* Hillerød, 24 Jan 1679). Painter, son of (1) Solomon van Haven. He was apprenticed to his father and probably to Elias Fiigenschoug. From 1644 he worked as Abraham Wuchters's assistant in Sorø, Denmark; by 1650 he was travelling abroad, funded by Frederick III, King of Denmark and Norway (*reg* 1648–70). Michael travelled with his brother, Lambert, and visited Italy, France and Germany. He returned to Denmark in 1657 and became a noted court painter. In 1664, at the peak of his career, he received a royal commission to teach at the Sorø academy. From 1675 onwards, he lived in Hillerød (nr Copenhagen) and worked on the decorations for Frederiksborg Castle in collaboration with his brother, who was in charge of the rebuilding. Michael died before completing the allegorical scene for the ceiling of the Audience Chamber in the castle. He executed a portrait of *Lambert van Haven* (1656; Hillerød, Frederiksborg Slot) and a *Portrait of a Woman* (1665; Göttingen, Kstsamml. U.).

(3) Lambert van Haven (*b* Bergen, 1630; *d* Copenhagen, 9 May 1695). Painter, sculptor and architect, son of (1) Solomon van Haven. Trained by his father and probably by Elias Fiigenschoug in Bergen, he was already a precocious artist when he was commissioned to paint his first portrait, *Priest Lammers's Family* (1648; Bergen, Mariakirken), which is very much in the style of Fiigenschoug. His father's connections enabled Lambert to become a court painter in Copenhagen during the 1650s. Under the patronage of Frederick III, he travelled to Italy with his brother from 1653 to 1657 and again, on his own, from 1660 to 1661. There is little evidence of his work in Denmark during the 1660s, but he is known to have been under the patronage of the court's most influential politician, Griffenfeld (Peder Schumacher; 1635–99).

From 1668 to 1670 Lambert was again travelling, this time to Germany, Italy, France and Flanders to study architecture and to purchase works of art for the King. On his return he was appointed master builder and 'inspector of painting and sculpture' by the new king, Christian V (*reg* 1670–99); this was an official position based on the French system. When Griffenfeld was disgraced in 1676, Lambert survived. He was highly regarded as a painter and sculptor, and he was influenced by contemporary sculptural work in the Netherlands and Flanders. His output was uneven, and few examples survive. His work as an architect is his finest, in particular the Vor Frelser, (1682–96), in Christianshavn, Copenhagen, an innovative cruciform design based on Netherlandish and Italian prototypes (*see* DENMARK, fig. 4), and the alterations to Frederiksborg Castle (1681–90), which indicate his knowledge of Charles Le Brun's work at Versailles. Lambert van Haven also worked on designs for the Royal Palace (1670–75), Copenhagen, for Rosenborg, Copenhagen (1672), and Griffenfeld's chapel in the Helligaandskirke, Copenhagen (1675). He had a considerable collection of engravings and architectural books as well as the study drawings he executed on his travels (Copenhagen, Stat. Mus. Kst.).

BIBLIOGRAPHY

NKL; Thieme-Becker

V. Lorenzen: *Lambert van Haven* (Copenhagen, 1936)

E. Lasson and others: *Billed Kunst og Skulptur, 1500–1750* [Painting and sculpture, 1500–1750], Dansk Kunst Historie, ii (Copenhagen, 1973), pp. 227–60

Aschehoug og Gyldenals Store Norske leksikon [Ashehoug and Gyldenals large Norwegian encyclopedia], v (Oslo, 1979), pp. 276, 537

J. H. Lexow and others: *Nedgangstid og ny reisning* [Decline and ascent], Norges Kunsthistorie, iii (Oslo, 1982), pp. 121–35

MARTA GALICKI

Haverman, Hendrik Johannes (*b* Amsterdam, 23 Oct 1857; *d* The Hague, 11 Aug 1928). Dutch painter and draughtsman. He was taught first by August Allebé at the Rijksacademie in Amsterdam and studied at the Antwerp and Brussels academies before returning to Allebé. Subsequently he travelled to Spain and North Africa. Impressions of this journey predominate in his earlier works, such as the colourful *Market outside the Walls at Tangier* (1889; The Hague, Gemeentemus.) and in light-filled etchings such as *Blind Beggar in Algiers* (1894). Nudes of this period such as *Spring* (1895; The Hague, Gemeentemus.) are rendered tonally: later work, for example *Mother and Child* (Amsterdam, Stedel. Mus.), makes a stronger use of line. This emphasis on shapes and contours is even more evident in the portraits that were his principal speciality, such as *Abraham Kuyper* (1908; The Hague, Gemeentemus.) and the drawing of *Lodewijk van Deyssel* (untraced; see de Boer, p. 364). From 1896 Haverman drew a series of portraits of well-known contemporaries for various periodicals; they are generally more aesthetic and less analytic than Jan Pieter Veth's similar works of 1891–8.

BIBLIOGRAPHY

H. de Boer: 'H. J. Haverman', *Elsevier's Geïllus. Mdschr.*, xxviii (1918), pp. 363–73

A. J. Vervoorn: 'De grafiek van H. J. Haverman', *Antiek*, 21 (1987), pp. 456–9

The Age of Van Gogh: Dutch Painting, 1880–1895 (exh. cat., ed. R. Bionda and others; Glasgow, Burrell Col.; Amsterdam, Rijksmus. Van Gogh; 1991), pp. 151–3

ANNEMIEKE HOOGENBOOM

Haveus, Theodore [Have, Theodor de] (*b* Duchy of Cleves; *fl* 1573–6). Sculptor and architect of German origin, active in England. He left northern Europe, perhaps as a Protestant refugee, and settled in Cambridge. He did carving on the monument to *Dr Caius* (1573–5) in the chapel of Gonville and Caius College, Cambridge, and was probably responsible for at least some of its singularly bold ornamental detail. In 1576 he presented to the College a remarkable sundial of his own devising composed of a stone with 60 dials raised on a column (destr.). He also carved and painted the arms of Queens' College over the entrance to its screens passage (1575).

In the annals of Gonville and Caius College, which has a portrait of him, he is described as an 'excellent artificer and distinguished architect' ('artifex egregius et insignis architecturae professor'), and he may well have been the person to whom Dr Caius gave the task of realizing his ideas for the Gate of Honour, erected in 1575. It is a small jewel of Renaissance architecture, comprising a triumphal arch at ground level and an upper stage with temple façades applied to the front and back surmounted by a domed hexagon. The source of the design is thought to have been an engraving published in 1550 of a temporary gateway made for a festival in Antwerp. Haveus has been identified with a Dutch merchant named de Have who fled to England in 1567, but this is unlikely.

BIBLIOGRAPHY

R. Willis: *The Architectural History of the University of Cambridge and the Colleges of Cambridge and Eton*, ed. and rev. J. W. Clark, 4 vols (Cambridge, 1886), i, pp. 177–82, 191–4; ii, p. 48

ADAM WHITE

Haviland. American family of ceramics decorators and manufacturers and collectors, active in France. They were of English Quaker origin, established in America since 1642. In 1838 David Haviland (1814–79), six of whose seven brothers were in the porcelain trade, formed an importation and retail business, D. G. & D. Haviland, with his brother Daniel (*b* 1799). In 1852 Robert Haviland joined the company, which became Haviland Brothers & Co. In 1840 David went to France, settling there in 1841, with the intention of improving the range of porcelain imported by the company by selecting it personally. In 1847 he opened a porcelain-decorating workshop, and in 1855 began porcelain production. He was helped in this by the French manufacturer Pillivuyt. In 1864 a new company, Haviland & Co. was founded by David together with his elder son Charles (*b* New York, 1839; *d* Limoges, 1921). His younger son Théodore (*b* Limoges, 12 Aug 1849; *d* 1919) was also involved with the new company. Charles settled in Paris in 1872 and the following year set up a decorating studio at Auteuil, a suburb of Paris, under the management of Félix Bracquemond (*see* BRACQUEMOND, (1)). In 1877 Charles married Madeleine Burty (*d* 1900), daugther of the critic and collector PHILIPPE BURTY. Burty's and Bracquemond's tastes were reflected in the character of the Auteuil studio's designs, in which the influence of Japanese art (*see* JAPONISME) and Impressionism is evident. A catalogue (Paris, Bib. A. Déc.) published in 1879 illustrates more than 250 designs, which were hand-painted in barbotine, mostly on vases. The firm continued to produce hand-painted designs until 1882, after which time it was forced to close this branch of its activities because of changes in taste. In 1865 Théodore had been sent to the USA to represent the Limoges firm. While there, he also encouraged an interest in the production of the Auteuil studio, particularly at the Centennial International Exhibition in Philadelphia in 1876. In 1880 he returned to Limoges. On 31 December 1891 the firm was dissolved. In 1892 Théodore set up an independent business, as did Charles with his son Georges Haviland. After 1925 the company split into two, one branch in Limoges for the manufacture of porcelain, and one in New York (the Haviland China Co.) for distribution of the product.

Charles Haviland built up an important collection of Japanese art, buying from Paris dealers, several of whom, such as S. Bing, were his friends. He bought works by Henri Fantin-Latour, Renoir, Manet and Monet. After his death, his collection was dispersed in 16 sales held in Paris between November 1922 and June 1925. Théodore Haviland also owned a fine collection of Impressionist paintings.

BIBLIOGRAPHY

J. d'Albis and L. d'Albis: 'Haviland et l'impressionnisme en céramique', *Paragone*, xxiii/273 (1972), pp. 66–71

J. d'Albis, L. d'Albis and J. P. Bouillon: *Catalogue de l'exposition: Céramique impressionniste: L'Atelier Haviland de Paris-Auteuil, 1873–1882* (sale cat., Paris, Hôtel Sens, Dec 1974–Feb 1975)

J. d'Albis: *Haviland* (Paris, 1988; Eng. trans. by L. d'Albis; bilingual text)

LINDA WHITELEY

Haviland, John (*b* Gudenham Manor, near Taunton, Somerset, 12 Dec 1792; *d* Philadelphia, PA, 29 March 1852). English architect and writer, active in the USA. He was apprenticed in 1811 to James Elmes (1782–1862), a successful London architect and writer on art and architecture. In 1815, after the minimal service of four years, Haviland set out for Russia where he hoped to gain an appointment in the Imperial Corps of Engineers. In St Petersburg he met the American ambassador and future president, John Quincy Adams (1735–1826), and his future brother-in-law, George von Sonntag, who encouraged him to emigrate to the USA. In 1816 John Haviland arrived in Philadelphia, where he hoped to set up an architectural practice like Benjamin Henry Latrobe before him. Philadelphia had changed, however, since the national capitol had moved to Washington, DC, and the economic centre had shifted to New York. Where Latrobe had pioneered the role of the professional architect in the USA, Haviland merely succeeded to his position of taste-maker, bringing fashionable English styles to anglophile Philadelphia. Like so many of his contemporaries, Haviland needed to use every opportunity to present his talents including teaching and publications. Shortly after his arrival he was conducting classes on architecture; simultaneously he wrote *The Builder's Assistant* (1818–21), a compendium of contemporary architectural practice.

Haviland showed his real abilities as a Greek Revival designer in Philadelphia, as characterized by the primitive Greek façade of the Pennsylvania Institute for the Deaf and Dumb (1823; now the Philadelphia College of Art), the abstract rectangularity of the Franklin Institute (1825; now the Atwater Kent Museum), derived from James Stuart and Nicholas Revett's rendering in *Antiquities of Athens* (1787) of the Choragic Monument of Thrasylus, and the Nash-like remodelling of the Walnut Street Theater (1827). He also designed churches, including St Andrew's Episcopal Church (now St George's Greek Orthodox Cathedral) at 256 South 8th Street. He was as adventurous in construction as he was in his designs, using iron as an external building skin in the Miners' Bank in Pottsville (1830; destr. 1926) and building on a hitherto unequalled scale in his great prisons. These were Haviland's most memorable commissions; he represented them as castellated Gothic fortresses (e.g. Eastern State Penitentiary, Philadelphia, Cherry Hill; begun 1821, completed 1823–5) and as Egyptian pylon temple-prisons as in Trenton, NJ (1832; altered), and in New York (1835; destr.); the latter, the Halls of Justice, entered popular terminology as 'The Tombs'. In Haviland's façades the influence of George Dance the younger's Newgate Prison, London (1770–85), could be seen, while the radiating plan incorporated features of the panopticon workhouse of Jeremy Bentham (1748–1832), with cells for solitary confinement. Fusing morality with economy, the scheme was widely imitated.

Haviland should have had greater success, for he was the logical successor to Latrobe after the latter's untimely death. However, real estate speculations raised the spectre of financial ruin, which Haviland attempted to resolve by applying funds from government work to his own account, with the result that most Federal work went to William Strickland and Robert Mills. Whereas Latrobe designed with a delicacy reminiscent of John Soane, Haviland introduced brutal proportions and a primitive force of character, which have been a great counterpoint in English design. This strong individuality found a natural home in Philadelphia and, although Haviland never had any particular following apart from his son, Edward Haviland (1823–

72), it remains a regional constant in Philadelphia architecture to this day.

WRITINGS

The Builder's Assistant, 3 vols (Philadelphia, 1818–21); rev. in 4 vols (Baltimore, 1830)
ed.: *Young Carpenter's Assistant* (rev. & enlarged, Philadelphia, 1830) by O. Biddle (1805)

BIBLIOGRAPHY

Obituary, *The Builder*, x/486 (1852), p. 381
N. B. Johnston: 'John Haviland: Jailor to the World', *J. Soc. Archit. Hist.*, xxiii/2 (1964), pp. 101–5
M. E. Baigell: *John Haviland* (diss., Philadelphia, U. PA, 1965)
S. Tatman and R. Moss: *Biographical Dictionary of Philadelphia Architects, 1700–1930* (Boston, 1985), pp. 343–7
J. Cohen: 'John Haviland', *Drawing towards Building: Philadelphia Architectural Graphics, 1732–1986* (exh. cat. by J. O'Gorman and others, Philadelphia, PA Acad. F.A., 1986), pp. 71–5

GEORGE E. THOMAS

Havlíček, Josef (*b* Prague, 5 May 1899; *d* Prague, 30 Dec 1961). Czech architect. He graduated in architecture (1924) from the Czech Technical University, Prague, and from 1923 to 1926 he studied at the Academy of Fine Arts under Josef Gočár. In 1920, on the basis of his Cubist-style painting, he was accepted as a member of Devětsil, the group of avant-garde artists, architects and writers centred on the figure of Karel Teige, and he took part in its first exhibition in 1922. In 1927–8 he worked in the design office of Jaroslav Polívka in Prague and during this period produced his office and residential block for the Habich company. The façade of the building was divided into horizontal sections reflecting its internal organization, with shops on the ground floor, three floors of offices with continuous horizontal strip windows, and three further floors of flats, stepped back and with balconies. It was one of the first Functionalist works of its kind to be built in Prague. In 1927 Havlíček designed a low-cost housing estate with seven alternative types of standardized, four-storey housing blocks and plans for minimalist flats. The whole design was based on the rationalist principles of linear urban planning, and one section was constructed in Brno in 1928 on the occasion of the Exhibition of Contemporary Culture there.

Havlíček became one of the key figures in Functionalism in Czechoslovakia, the pivotal period in his work being 1928–36 when he shared a studio and worked with Karel Honzík. In 1930 they presented a project for the 'koldom' (collective house) type of low-cost residential building, which was based on cellular flats with some functions shared in a central service area. Each cell of about 24 sq. m contained living space, a sleeping corner and cooking niche, sanitation facilities and an entrance hall, and the cells could be variously combined according to the needs of the tenants. The shared area contained a dining-room, bathrooms and swimming pool, and for every two or three blocks there was a common crèche, kindergarten and playground. The project was exhibited at CIAM III (1930) in Brussels but was never executed. The best-known work by Havlíček and Honzík is the elegant General Pensions Institute building (1929–34), Prague, which was won in competition. It was designed on a cruciform plan with slender blocks that had horizontal strip windows and a uniform, modular structural system, and it is one of the most important examples of Functionalist architecture in Czechoslovakia.

Like most leading Czech Functionalist architects, Havlíček joined the Left Front in 1929 and the Union of Socialist Architects in 1933. After ending his association with Honzík he built a sanatorium (1936–40), Poděbrady, and two blocks of flats (1937 and 1938) in Prague. He also entered a number of competitions and became more deeply involved in the design problems of high-rise buildings. He experimented with various forms based on geometric figures and arrived at a pyramidal design with a number of wings that was applied to skyscrapers in his project (1942; unexecuted) for the restructuring of Prague and to a later design (1958; unexecuted) for a new town hall in Toronto. In 1948 he became committed to the socialist organization of architecture and he was the first director of Stavoprojekt. From the mid-1950s he had his own studio at the State Institute for the Reconstruction of Historic Towns and Buildings. His last work included the design of residential tower blocks (1952–9) at Kladno.

WRITINGS

with K. Honzík: *Stavby a plány* [Buildings and plans] (Prague, 1931)
Návrhy a stavby [Designs and buildings] (Prague, 1964)

BIBLIOGRAPHY

Josef Havlíček: Přehled díla, 1925–1961 [Josef Havlíček: survey of works, 1925–1961] (exh. cat., Prague, Mánes Exh. Hall, 1963)
Tschechische Kunst der 20er und 30er Jahre: Avantgarde und Tradition (exh. cat., Darmstadt, Mathildenhöhe, 1988–9)
Devětsil: Czech Avant-garde Art, Architecture and Design of the 1920s and 1930s (exh. cat., ed. R. Švácha; Oxford, MOMA; London, Des. Mus.; 1990)
The Art of the Avant-garde in Czechoslovakia, 1918–1938 (exh. cat., ed. J. Anděl; Valencia, 1993)
Prague, 1891–1941: Architecture and Design (exh. cat., Edinburgh, City A. Cent., 1994)

RADOMÍRA SEDLÁKOVÁ

Havránek, Bedřich (*b* Prague, 4 Jan 1821; *d* Prague, 1 March 1899). Bohemian painter and draughtsman. He studied at the Prague Academy of Fine Arts under Antonín Mánes from 1836 to 1842, and between 1845 and 1847 under Max Haushofer. The idylls of Biedermeier painting seem to have given direction to his work throughout his life. By the end of the 1840s, however, he responded to the current fashion for landscape with grandiose, picturesque subjects (e.g. *Mountain Lake in the Bohemian Forest*, 1848; Prague, N.G., Convent of St Agnes). He was one of the first landscape painters to depict Bohemia and Moravia systematically, cultivating the tradition of townscape paintings and also documenting contemporary life, especially in Prague.

Minute precision of detail is characteristic of most of Havránek's work; he was also an outstanding draughtsman, as is apparent in his etchings (e.g. the *Old Jewish Cemetery in Prague*, 1858; Prague, Mus. City) and illustrations. He worked for illustrated journals and, after 1879, for topographical and travel publications (e.g. F. A. Šubert, ed.: *Čechy*, Prague, 1883, i). In his late period, his gouaches and watercolours, for the most part meticulously perfectionist (e.g. *Ruin of a Water-mill in the Punkva Valley*, *c.* 1892, Prague, N.G., Convent of St Agnes), bring him into contact with current trends towards Naturalism.

Thieme–Becker
BIBLIOGRAPHY

Bedřich Havránek (1821–1899) (exh. cat., ed. N. Blažíčková-Horová; Prague, N.G., 1985) [bibliog., list of works, summary in Ger.]

ROMAN PRAHL

Hawaii [Hawai'i]. Group of Polynesian islands and islets in the North Pacific Ocean *c.* 3500 km west of California. In 1959 it became a state of the USA. Of the eight large islands and *c.* fifty islets, only Kaua'i, Ni'ihau, O'ahu, Moloka'i, Lana'i, Maui and Hawai'i are inhabited, although three others, Kaho'olawe, Necker and Nihoa, were inhabited periodically in the past. Settlement of the Hawaiian Islands began *c.* AD 600 with the arrival by great double canoes of central-east Polynesians. By *c.* AD 1300 contact between Hawai'i and its homelands appears to have ceased, and the islands were isolated from significant cultural contact until 1778, when Capt. James Cook came on them during his voyage between Tahiti and the north-west coast of America. The artistic, social and cultural traditions described here have their roots in east Polynesia but have developed into a distinctive Hawaiian style. The Hawaiian language is closely related to south-east Marquesan and to Tahitian but is not mutually intelligible with either.

1. Introduction. 2. Featherwork. 3. Ornaments. 4. Bark cloth. 5. Tattoo. 6. Sculpture. 7. Modern developments.

1. INTRODUCTION. Art, in the Western sense, was not a category of traditional Hawaiian culture, but *no'eau* ('skilfulness' or 'cleverness') was a part of all activity. It can therefore be argued both that art did not exist and that art as *no'eau* was all-pervasive. The emphasis of *no'eau* seems to have been on the process. Some artefacts were passed on from generation to generation, and the occasions on which they were used became in a sense part of them. Such artefacts became chronicles of social relationships presented in visual form and were regarded both as products made with skill (i.e. works of art) and as information. Hence, an object's manufacture and later repair or refurbishing, in addition to its social significance and changing symbolism, were aspects of an aesthetic system concerned with continuing process and use.

A second concept, essential to an understanding of traditional Hawaiian art and aesthetics, is *kaona*, which can be translated as layered or veiled meaning. *Kaona* conveys the important Polynesian idea that a subject should not be approached directly but should be only alluded to. Moreover, especially in relation to words and their combinations, *kaona* was thought to have a power of its own that could harm as well as honour. Verbal and visual modes of expression were integrally associated, hence the visual arts must be understood in relation to chanted texts.

It is also important to understand the role of objects in the stratified social system in which gods, chiefs and people were mutually dependent on each other and on nature. Social prestige was derived from elevated genealogical descent, which could be traced to the gods and was associated with power and authority. Certain objects were inextricably linked with the socio-political system that honoured and validated rank-based distinctions. The overall system can be characterized as an aesthetic of inequality, and much Hawaiian material culture was socially distancing

art that separated the chiefs from their people. Possession of various cultural forms separated those with *mana* (sacred power) from those with lesser or no *mana*. Restrictions of various sorts (*kapu*, taboo) protected those with *mana*. Specialists (*kahuna*) produced specific cultural forms, and standards were set for critical evaluation based on *kaona*, skill and appropriateness for the occasion. Hawaiian visual arts included clothing, especially featherwork, bark cloth and ornaments; sculpture, including images of wood, stone and feathers; tattoo; rock-carvings or petroglyphs (*see* PACIFIC ISLANDS, §II, 5(ii)); plaited Ni'ihau mats; basketry; decorated gourd containers; and wooden bowls, drums and canoes. All of these were important for both genealogical and aesthetic reasons, helping to sustain social ranking and to enhance the position of the chiefs. Poetry with its attendant music and dance was also important.

2. FEATHERWORK. The most distinctive and visually spectacular Hawaiian works of art are featherwork cloaks and helmets, a sash associated with the right to rule and feathered standards (*kahili*). Feathered images, made on a wicker framework (*see* FEATHERWORK, fig. 2), and a unique feathered 'temple', collected by Cook (now Vienna, Mus. Vlkerknd.), served as repositories for the gods. Feathered cloaks and capes (*'ahu'ula*, 'red shoulder and back coverings') were visual objectifications of social inequality worn by male chiefs in dangerous or sacred situations. The *kaona* and social metaphor associated with these objects implied that one's genealogy provided protection. Such visual elements as the size of cape, kinds of feathers and the design were important genealogical indicators, although little detailed information on these aspects has been preserved. Feathers were part of the tax payment for the harvest festival (*makahiki*), and it is believed that major feather pieces were produced by people of rank working according to religious restrictions. The base was a knotted fibre structure (*nae*) made of *olonā* fibre (*Touchardia latifolia*). This backing was not necessarily uniform and was often made of small pieces sewn together to form the desired shape. Small bunches of feathers, which had previously been prepared and tied together, were attached to the *nae* in overlapping rows starting at the bottom. The feathers used were primarily red, the sacred colour, from the *'i'iwi* bird (*Vestiaria coccinea*), with designs incorporating yellow or occasionally black or green feathers from other honeycreepers or honeyeaters. Yellow feathers, associated with powerful chiefs, came from birds that were primarily black (the yellow tufts were removed and the bird released) making yellow feathers rarer and more valuable.

During the 18th century a variety of shapes and sizes of cape were made, ranging from small trapezoidal types to long cloaks with a straight neckline and curved hemline. During the 19th century a 'classic' form evolved with more shaped necklines and curved hemlines in a variety of widths, which resulted in shapes ranging from roughly triangular to semicircular. The differences can be seen by comparing the 30 pieces collected during the voyages of Capt. Cook with those acquired during the 19th century. Especially important examples are the cloaks of Chief

Kalani'ōpu'u (now Honolulu, HI, Bishop Mus.; Wellington, NZ, N. Mus.; see fig. 1). A unique medium-length cape collected during Cook's third voyage (1778–9) has the usual red-and-yellow feathered body but is completely overlaid with the tail feathers of red-and-white tropic-birds (*Phaethon*) and black cocks' feathers (Sydney, Austral. Mus.).

Feathered helmets (*mahiole*) were sometimes worn with the cloaks. Made of a basketry *'ie'ie* foundation (*Freycinetia arborea*), they were usually covered with red, black, green and yellow feathers. Two styles were made: the first, which may be attributed to the island of Kaua'i, has a wide low crest, and the whole helmet is covered with long, round, stiffened fibre strips to which feathers were attached; the second, more widespread, style has a high, narrow crest covered with a netting to which feathers are attached.

The most important feathered object was a sash, which, upon its investiture, gave a high chief the right to rule. The only existing complete example (3600×150 mm; Honolulu, HI, Bishop Mus.) is covered on both sides with red feathers, edged with yellow feathers and finished with rows of human and fish teeth. The statues of King Kamehameha I (*reg* 1810–19) in Honolulu (see Rose, 1988, p. 133) and Kona depict this charismatic leader wearing the sash and a cloak (Honolulu, HI, Bishop Mus.) said to consist of half a million yellow feathers taken from 80,000 *mamo* birds (*Drepanis pacifica*). Only a chief of Kamehameha's power could acquire such a vast amount of yellow feathers, setting him apart not only from commoners but also from his fellow chiefs.

3. ORNAMENTS. Feathered head and neck ornaments (*lei*) in a variety of colours and designs were made and worn by women. Other ornaments were made mostly of ivory and human hair. The most distinctive was the *lei niho palaoa*, consisting of an ivory hook-pendant hung from a necklace made from two multi-strand loops of finely braided human hair, which were attached to each other through a lateral hole in the ivory hook. Small hook ornaments made of rock oyster, calcite, wood, black coral, bone and whale ivory date from before AD 1000 to the 18th century. Most extant pieces are larger and made of walrus ivory; these date from the 19th century, after Europeans established trading relations between the Hawaiian islands and the north-west coast of America. A unique variation is a bone pendant carved in the shape of a human figure (New York, Met.). Bracelets were made of pieces of ivory carved in the shape of turtles strung on human hair, a series of carved pigs' tusks shaped and strung side by side, or links of carved dogs' teeth and turtle shell strung on fine coconut fibre. There were also necklaces of a variety of shells and seeds, and anklets of shells, seeds or dogs' teeth. These ornaments were worn primarily by female chiefs on ceremonial occasions.

4. BARK CLOTH. Hawaiian bark cloth (*kapa*) is among the finest in Polynesia both in texture and richness of design. As bedding, *kapa moe* were made in several layers sewn together along one edge, with the upper layer elaborately decorated. Women's wraparound skirts (*pā'ū*) were also made of sheets sewn together along one edge. Men's loincloths (*malo*) were long, narrow garments, often

1. Hawaiian cloak of Chief Kalani'ōpu'u, fibre with red and yellow feathers, l. 1.52 m, before 1779 (Wellington, NZ, National Museum)

with two separate designs divided along the centre line and folded lengthways to show both designs when tied. A shoulder garment (*kīhei*), was worn by both men and women for decoration and warmth.

Most extant bark cloth is made from the inner bark of *wauke* (*Broussonetia papyrifera*) and *māmaki* (*Pipturus albidus*), although other plants were also used. *Wauke* cloth was prepared in two stages. After a preliminary beating with a round beater, the strips were soaked in water, lightly beaten again, placed in layers between banana leaves and left for *c.* ten days to mature by retting. The partially rotted and layered strips were felted by beating into a finished rectangular piece. Designs were impressed into the cloth and applied to the upper surface. Examples from the 18th century are relatively thick, sometimes impressed by grooving; the designs are bold and angular, often composed of a series of straight or intersecting lines. Examples from the 19th century are thinner and finer in texture, and have an elaboration of impressed designs known as 'watermarks' that were impressed into the cloth during the second beating with intricately incised beaters, which are works of art in themselves. Designs are smaller, printed with narrow bamboo stamps, composed of tiny chevrons, triangles, diagonals, lines, diamonds, squares and circles. Notable *kapa* collections are in the British Museum, London, Royal Museum of Scotland, Edinburgh, Bernice Pauahi Bishop Museum, Honolulu, and the National Museum of Natural History, Smithsonian Institution, Washington, DC.

5. TATTOO. Hawaiian tattoo designs of the 18th century were similar to those used on bark cloth and were mostly linear, made up of rows of such motifs as triangles, chevrons, crescent arches and lizards. During the 19th century European-inspired designs were added, including goats, hunting horns and words. Extensive tattoo appears to have been associated with certain male chiefs, although some women were tattooed on the chest, arms, legs and back of the hands. Traditionally the designs were often placed asymmetrically on the body: on one half of the face or front of the body, on the inside or outside of one

arm or leg and on the outside of the hands. Such tattoos may have been magical and protective as well as of genealogical significance. During the 19th century tattoos became more symmetrical, and their function changed from one of protection to decoration.

6. SCULPTURE. Hawaiian sculpture was produced in a variety of materials. It was carved from wood, stone and sea-urchin spines, or constructed from basketry and feathers. It is primarily anthropomorphic, although there are also a few representations of animals and fish. In addition to free-standing sculpture, human and geometric forms were carved on drums, bowls, spear rests and carrying poles. Human figures are often androgynous rather than distinctly male or female, although such figures were also produced. As important remnants of the former religious system, Hawaiian images offer glimpses into a socioreligious complex that was irrevocably altered in 1819 when the state religious system was overthrown by the Hawaiians themselves, led by Kamehameha II (*reg* 1819–25), although it continued to exert an important influence on their lives for much of the 19th century. The sculptural tradition changed during the late 18th century and early 19th under the influence of a variety of ideas, visual images and changing world views. Also, imported metal tools made carving faster and easier. As a result 19th-century images are often larger and more elaborately carved. Wooden figures, known generically as *ki'i*, were of two main types. The *ki'i akua* were receptacles into which the high gods were called in the interest of the State, and the *ki'i 'aumākua* were repositories for the lesser gods, who were invoked for family or personal reasons or for the purposes of sorcery. It is possible that one image may have been used for several purposes, taking on different attributes depending on the occasion and the rank of the person using it. Hawaiian sculpture has been categorized into images used on temples, small images on pointed props and free-standing examples. This categorization has not, however, been universally accepted (1979 Honolulu exh. cat.). Nor is there agreement on what criteria should be used to decide whether images are traditional or authentic.

In studying the form, stance, exaggeration and stylization of specific aspects of these figures, and relating these visual features to the importance in Hawaiian culture of *kaona*, genealogy, respect and disrespect, certain images have been singled out as receptacles for Kūkā'ilimoku, the war god, while others have been identified as repositories for Lono, god of peace and agriculture (Kaeppler, 1982). Kūkā'ilimoku, according to this scheme, is a superior sorcery god characterized by the 'mouth of disrespect' in which the chin juts forward and the open mouth is distended backwards. The mouth has concentrically carved fluting, teeth and, sometimes, a protruding tongue, the eyes are often elongated and non-human, and flared nostrils are prominent (see fig. 2). Representations of Lono are superior household gods and genealogical representations characterized by backbones, elaborate headcoverings brought forward in an overhanging crest, a lower jaw carved to resemble a pig's mouth and human hair. All such ethnohistoric reconstructions, however, are derived from fewer than 200 surviving sculptures. The

2. Hawaiian wooden temple image of Kūkā'ilimoku, h. 2 m, late 18th century–early 19th (London, British Museum)

largest collections of wood and featherwork images are in the British Museum, London, and the Bernice Pauahi Bishop Museum, Honolulu.

7. MODERN DEVELOPMENTS. While such art forms as poetry, music and dance have survived in evolved forms, the making of sculpture virtually ceased in 1819 with the overthrow of the state religious system. Tattooing continued into the mid-19th century and the production of status-elevating dress continued in various forms for most of the 19th century. From the 1960s there was a recreation of many traditional forms of art, especially in featherwork and bark cloth. These have become associated

with Hawaiian ethnic identity, thus separating indigenous Hawaiians from other people rather than, as traditionally, chiefs from commoners. Rocky Ka'iouliokahihikolo'Ehu Jensen (*b* 1944; Rose, 1980, pl. 156) and Herb Kane ('The Isles of the Pacific', *N. Geog.*, 1974, pp. 756–68; L. Levatres, 1983, pp. 560–61, 568–9, 572, 576–7, 580–81) are two of the better-known modern Hawaiian artists. They have worked in a variety of media, carving wooden sculptures, painting in oils and watercolours and executing murals and wall hangings. Their work has been exhibited in museums and art galleries.

BIBLIOGRAPHY

W. T. Brigham: *Hawaiian Feather Work*, Mem. Bishop Mus., i/1 (Honolulu, 1899)

——: *Additional Notes on Hawaiian Feather Work*, Mem. Bishop Mus., i/5 (Honolulu, 1903)

——: *Mat and Basket Weaving of the Ancient Hawaiians*, Mem. Bishop Mus., ii/1 (Honolulu, 1906)

——: *Ka Hana Kapa: The Making of Bark-cloth in Hawaii*, Mem. Bishop Mus., iii (Honolulu, 1911)

——: *Additional Notes on Hawaiian Feather Work: Second Supplement*, Mem. Bishop Mus., vii/1 (Honolulu, 1918)

H. -M. Luquiens: *Hawaiian Art*, Bishop Mus. Special Pubn, xviii (Honolulu, 1931)

Te Rangi Hiroa [P. H. Buck]: 'The Local Evolution of Hawaiian Feather Capes and Cloaks', *J. Polynes. Soc.*, liii (1944), pp. 1–16

K. P. Emory: 'Hawaiian Tattooing', *Bishop Mus. Occas. Pap.*, xviii/17 (1946), pp. 235–70

Te Rangi Hiroa: *Arts and Crafts of Hawaii*, Bishop Mus. Special Pubn, xlv (Honolulu, 1957)

J. H. Cox and E. Stasack: *Hawaiian Petroglyphs*, Bishop Mus. Special Pubn, lx (Honolulu, 1970)

A. L. Kaeppler: 'Feather Cloaks, Ship Captains, and Lords', *Bishop Mus. Occas. Pap.*, xxiv/6 (1970), pp. 91–114

J. H. Cox with W. H. Davenport: *Hawaiian Sculpture* (Honolulu, 1974, rev. 1988)

'The Isles of the Pacific', *N. Geog.*, cxlvi (Dec 1974), pp. 756–68

A. L. Kaeppler: *The Fabrics of Hawaii (Bark Cloth)* (Leigh-on-Sea, 1975)

A. L. Kaeppler, ed.: *Cook Voyage Artifacts in Leningrad, Berne, and Florence Museums*, Bishop Mus. Special Pubn, lxvi (Honolulu, 1978)

'*Artificial Curiosities': Being an Exposition of Native Manufactures Collected on the Three Pacific Voyages of Captain James Cook, R.N.* (exh. cat. by A. L. Kaeppler, Honolulu, HI, Bishop Mus., 1978) [Bishop Mus. Special Pubn, lxv]

A. L. Kaeppler: 'A Survey of Polynesian Art', *Exploring the Visual Art of Oceania: Australia, Melanesia, Micronesia and Polynesia*, ed. S. M. Mead (Honolulu, 1979), pp. 180–91

Eleven Gods Assembled: An Exhibition of Hawaiian Wooden Images (exh. cat. by A. L. Kaeppler, Honolulu, HI, Bishop Mus., 1979)

The Art of the Pacific Islands (exh. cat. by D. Newton, A. L. Kaeppler and P. Gathercole, Washington, DC, N.G.A., 1979), pp. 81–5, 105–21

R. G. Rose: *Hawai'i: The Royal Isles*, Bishop Mus. Special Pubn, lxvii (Honolulu, 1980)

Pahu and Puniu: An Exhibition of Hawaiian Drums (exh. cat. by A. L. Kaeppler, Honolulu, HI, Bishop Mus., 1980)

A. L. Kaeppler: 'Genealogy and Disrespect: A Study of Symbolism in Hawaiian Images', *Res*, iii (1982), pp. 82–107

L. Levatres: 'Kamehameha—Hawaii's Warrior King', *N. Geog.*, clxiv (Nov 1983), pp. 558–99

A. L. Kaeppler: 'Hawaiian Art and Society: Traditions and Transformations', *Transformations of Polynesian Culture*, Memoirs of the Polynesian Society, xlv, ed. A. Hooper and J. Huntsman (Auckland, 1985), pp. 105–31

——: 'Hawaiian Tattoo: A Conjunction of Genealogy and Aesthetics', *Marks of Civilization: Artistic Transformations of the Human Body*, ed. A. G. Rubin (Los Angeles, 1988), pp. 157–70

R. G. Rose: 'Woodcarver F. N. Otremba and the Kamehameha Statue', *Hawai. J. Hist.*, xxii (1988), pp. 131–46

ADRIENNE L. KAEPPLER

Hawara. Egyptian site in the Faiyum, an oasis 80 km south-west of Cairo. Located at the site is the pyramid of AMMENEMES III (*reg c.* 1818–*c.* 1770 BC), a ruler of Egypt in the 12th Dynasty. Dieter Arnold's excavations (from 1976) have shown that Ammenemes III's first pyramid at Dahshur had become unsuitable for burial and that another pyramid was therefore erected in the Faiyum, an area in which the King took particular interest. Only the inner mud-brick structure of the pyramid remains, the outer stone casing having been removed over the centuries. Adjacent to the pyramid was a mortuary temple, the plan of which was so elaborate that the Classical writers referred to it as the Labyrinth. So little of this has survived that the building can be understood only through Classical descriptions. When the archaeologist Flinders Petrie discovered the entrance to the pyramid in 1889, he found an intricate system of galleries and hidden chambers designed to foil tomb robbers. This had been unsuccessful, however, as Petrie found that all the movable objects had been plundered and the coffin and mummy burnt. Although little remained on the site, fragments of funerary equipment, statues and architectural elements bearing the King's name assured the identification of Ammenemes III as the builder of the complex.

BIBLIOGRAPHY

LÄ: 'Hawara', 'Labyrinth'

I. E. S. Edwards: *The Pyramids of Egypt* (Harmondsworth, 1947, rev. 4/1991), pp. 220–27

D. Arnold: 'Das Labyrinth und seine Vorbilder', *Mitt. Dt. Archäol. Inst.: Abt. Kairo*, 35 (1979), pp. 1–9

R. J. LEPROHON

Hawarden, Clementina, Viscountess [née Elphinstone Fleeming] (*b* Cumbernauld, nr Glasgow, 1 June 1822; *d* London, 19 Jan 1865). Scottish photographer. She grew up in Scotland and England, but moved in 1857 with her husband Cornwallis Maude, 4th Viscount Hawarden, to his estate in Dundrum, Co. Tipperary, Ireland. She apparently took her first photographs, stereoscopic landscapes, in late 1857 or early 1858. In 1859 the Hawardens moved to London. In her drawing-room studio Lady Hawarden first made stereoscopic carte-de-visite-style portraits, but was soon using larger, single-image formats as well, and working in series. She posed her subjects in the windows and on the balcony of her home (see Ovenden, p. 45 and p. 80). From *c.* 1862 she concentrated on photographing her daughters in costume tableaux. She exhibited her work under the collective titles *Studies from Life* and *Photographic Studies* with the Photographic Society of London in 1863 and 1864, and was awarded the Society's silver medal in both years. Viscountess Hawarden produced *c.* 850 photographs, all albumen prints from wet collodion negatives. A large proportion of these are in the Victoria and Albert Museum, London. Sir Francis Seymour Haden, who etched at Dundrum, based some of his etchings on her photographs.

BIBLIOGRAPHY

G. Ovenden, ed.: *Clementina, Lady Hawarden* (London, 1974)

M. Haworth-Booth, ed.: *The Golden Age of British Photography, 1839–1900* (London, 1984), pp. 120, 122–5

V. Dodier: 'Haden, Photography and Salmon Fishing', *Print Q.*, iii/1 (1986), pp. 34–50

VIRGINIA DODIER

Hawes, John Cyril [Fra Jerome] (*b* Richmond [now in London], 7 Sept 1876; *d* Florida, 26 June 1956). Australian architect of English birth. He was articled to Edmerton and Gabriel, London, and he studied at the Architectural Association School, the Polytechnic and Central Arts and Crafts School, London (1892–6), under W. R. Lethaby and E. S. Prior. He began practice at Bognor Regis in 1897, and there built The White Tower (1898) in a style influenced by C. F. A. Voysey. Ordained an Anglican priest, he went as a curate-architect to rebuild churches after a hurricane in the Bahamas (1909–11), where he discovered Spanish Mission architecture. He then became a Franciscan priest and went as a missionary to Geraldton, Western Australia. Between 1915 and 1939 he designed a number of convents, presbyteries and churches in the region, using local materials and building much of the work with his own hands. Hawes was a romantic: based on Arts and Crafts principles and vernacular eclecticism, his work was distinguished by a powerful expressionism and interiors with mysterious lighting. The façade of his masterpiece, the Cathedral of St Francis Xavier (1916), Geraldton, was based on Californian Franciscan missions. Appointed Diocesan Architect in Perth, he also produced a design (unrealised) for Perth Cathedral in 1922. In 1937 he received the title of Monsignor and in 1939 left to become a hermit on Cat Island, Bahamas, where he was known as Fra Jerome and worked as a secular priest–architect.

BIBLIOGRAPHY

P. Anson: *The Hermit of Cat Island* (London, 1958)
A. G. Evans: *The Conscious Stone* (Melbourne, 1984)

IAN MOLYNEUX

Hawes, Josiah Johnson. *See under* SOUTHWORTH & HAWES.

Hawkes, T. G., & Co. American glass-cutting shop formed in 1880 by Thomas Gibbons Hawkes (*b* Surmount, Ireland, 1846; *d* Corning, NY, 1913). Hawkes was born into a glass-cutting family in Surmount. He arrived in the USA in 1863 and first worked at the Brooklyn Flint Glass Works, which moved to Corning, NY, in 1868; in 1871 he became supervisor of the Corning Glass Works. Hawkes's glass-cutting shop was founded in 1880, and he purchased blanks, which are plain, unadorned objects for cutting from the Corning Glass Works. After 1904 his craftsmen used blanks from the newly established Steuben Glass Works, which Hawkes had formed in partnership with members of his family and Frederick Carder. In addition to blanks Carder also provided designs for Hawkes's cutters. After Steuben became a subsidiary of the Corning Glass Works in 1918, Hawkes's blanks came from the Libbey Glass Co.

   T. G. Hawkes & Co. is perhaps best known for its 'Russian' pattern, a heavy, rich-cut design that decorated a service ordered for the White House, Washington, DC, by President Benjamin Harrison (1833–1901) in 1891 and enlarged by President Grover Cleveland (1837–1908) during his second term and by President Theodore Roosevelt (1858–1919). Along with other designs, the pattern was in continuous use in the White House until 1937, when President Franklin Roosevelt (1882–1945) ordered from Hawkes the 'Venetian' pattern, which remained in use during the administrations of Harry S. Truman (1884–1972) and Dwight D. Eisenhower (1890–1969) until 1958.

These commissions and others for important American families brought Hawkes's craftsmanship to international attention at the beginning of the 20th century. In 1889 the firm won the grand prize at the Exposition Universelle in Paris for the 'Grecian' and 'Chrysanthemum' patterns, and for many years it was considered to be one of the foremost glass-cutting establishments in the USA. The shop closed in 1962.

BIBLIOGRAPHY

A. C. Revi: *American Cut and Engraved Glass* (New York, 1965)
J. S. Spillman: *White House Glassware: Two Centuries of Presidential Entertaining* (Washington, DC, 1989)

ELLEN PAUL DENKER

Hawkins, John Heywood (*b* 1803; *d* Bignor Park, nr Petworth, 27 June 1877). English collector. He was the son of the author and traveller John Hawkins and was the Member of Parliament for Newport, Isle of Wight, from 1833 to 1841. Recognized as an important collector in his day, he augmented his father's collection of paintings and *objets d'art* with numerous prints and drawings. He owned a series of etchings by Rembrandt that were auctioned at P. & D. Colnaghi in London and eventually entered the collection of Walter Francis Scott, 5th Duke of Buccleuch. Hawkins also possessed an edition of Turner's *Liber studorium*. His collection was dispersed mainly through auction. Most drawings and prints were sold in an anonymous sale in 1850 (London, Sotheby's, 29 April). Drawings by Baccio Bandinelli, Guercino and Rembrandt were included, as well as prints by Mantegna, Dürer and Rubens. In a further sale on 9 May (London, Sotheby's), contemporary drawings were auctioned: these included works by Turner (e.g. *Fish Market, Rotterdam*), Gainsborough, Richard Parkes Bonington, David Wilkie, Watteau (e.g. *Four Heads*) and Jean-Honoré Fragonard. Hawkins also participated in the Mabery sale in 1851.

BIBLIOGRAPHY

F. Lugt: *Marques* (1921)

□

Hawksmoor, Nicholas (*b* ?East Drayton, Notts, 1661–2; *d* London, 25 March 1736). English architect. One of the most original architects of his generation, Hawksmoor used a rich, eclectic, scholarly and often unconventional vocabulary of detail to make real a feeling for the geometrical abstraction of solids and spaces. His unassuming personality probably lost him some preferment in his profession, but the boldness of his designs and his assiduity in promoting them show a different side of his character. Hawksmoor's work is distinct from, but nevertheless intricately connected with, that of Christopher Wren and John Vanbrugh, to each of whom he was at some time an assistant. Together these three architects were the greatest exponents of the Baroque in England.

1. Training, Easton Neston and other early works. 2. Collaboration with Vanbrugh. 3. Urban plans and Oxford buildings. 4. The Fifty New Churches. 5. Late works.

   1. TRAINING, EASTON NESTON AND OTHER EARLY WORKS. Hawksmoor came from a yeoman farming family. His style as a letter writer implies that he attended grammar school. Around 1679 the plasterer Edward Goudge took him to London and introduced him to Wren, who engaged

1. Nicholas Hawksmoor: east front of Easton Neston, Northamptonshire, built mostly 1695–1702

him as his personal clerk and subsequently taught him all he could about the theory and practice of architecture. A small sketchbook of the early 1680s (London, RIBA) contains drawings in Hawksmoor's hand of buildings and topographical views that show promise rather than achievement; but before the end of the decade he had not only learnt the techniques of draughtsmanship but had also developed a capacity for imagining sequences of rooms as a spatial experience, as his project for a 'Villa Chetwiniana' demonstrates (1688; Stafford, Salt Lib.).

In 1683–4 Hawksmoor represented Wren on site at Winchester Palace, then under construction; from 1687 he worked in the office concerned with the London City churches and from 1691 to 1712 in the drawing office of St Paul's Cathedral, London. Appointments of this kind were on a part-time or consultant basis, and his activity under Wren in these years is also documented at Chelsea Hospital and Hampton Court, and at Kensington House (later Kensington Palace), London, where he was Clerk of Works from 1689 to 1715. Late in life he referred to his nearly four decades' association with Wren, which lasted until the latter's dismissal as Surveyor of the King's Works in 1718. However, from *c.* 1688 Hawksmoor was also concerned with his own designs.

Hawksmoor's earliest commissions came to him through Wren. Of several references to Wren's 'man' or 'gentleman', the most important is in June 1692, when the formula of 'making the draughts' coupled with a payment

indicates that he was the designer of the new Writing School at Christ's Hospital (1692–5; destr. 1902), Newgate Street, London. Although constructed in a less impressive form than he first envisaged, it already shows his preference for large shapes, plain surfaces and simplified mouldings, in a style that seems to derive from a conception of architecture as a demonstration of solid geometry, on which his master Wren laid more emphasis in theory than in practice. By 1694 Hawksmoor was actively concerned with a country house at Easton Neston, Northants, whose owner, William Fermor, 1st Baron Leominster (*d* 1711), was related to Wren by marriage. The size of the house, built mostly between 1695 and 1702, was limited by the location of the two service wings, built about ten years earlier to an anonymous design; Hawksmoor later called the wings 'good for nothing' but claimed the main house as his own conception (see fig. 1).

Easton Neston was designed as much for show as for comfort, for its owner had bought the collection of Classical sculpture formed earlier in the 17th century by Thomas Howard, 2nd Earl of Arundel and Surrey. Hawksmoor managed to include, within one block, four big rooms on each of two floors, a two-storey hall, a grand and leisurely staircase and a gallery across the centre of the upper floor; the remaining spaces he filled with mezzanines to form a large number of private apartments at the ends of the house. Although around 1900 the hall was reduced to one storey and other changes were made, the interior retains much of its elegant plasterwork, panelling and ironwork and still offers the excitement of changes in scale and direction from one room to the next. Its ashlar exterior is distinguished by finely cut mouldings and by a giant Composite pilaster order whose close and subtly varied spacing gives the house an unusually tall and lively appearance among English classical houses. This character is the more remarkable because Hawksmoor never travelled abroad and his knowledge of European architecture came entirely from books and prints. In the end elevations of Easton Neston he used the mezzanine windows as the basis of a novel and surprising pattern of window shapes in which the giant order plays a subordinate part.

This pattern-making also appears in the brick and stone elevations of the King William block (1698–1707) at Greenwich Hospital, where Wren seems to have allowed Hawksmoor, as his assistant from 1696, a free hand in the remoter parts of the building; the ashlar-faced back (1700–03) of the Queen Anne block (whose front forms a pair to John Webb's original building of the 1660s) follows on from the monumental plainness of Hawksmoor's earlier Christ's Hospital design.

2. COLLABORATION WITH VANBRUGH. It was perhaps through William Vanbrugh, Secretary to the Greenwich Hospital Commissioners, that his cousin John Vanbrugh met Hawksmoor. By the summer of 1699 John Vanbrugh had not only decided to take up architecture but had also persuaded Charles Howard, 3rd Earl of Carlisle, to engage him to design Castle Howard. Hawksmoor's collaboration was an essential part of this enterprise, since he drew out Vanbrugh's designs, took charge of the detailing and negotiated prices with the contractors. In the first few years of the 18th century he must also have taught Vanbrugh much of what he himself had learnt from Wren 20 years earlier. Moreover the 'Vanbrugh–Hawksmoor style', as it is often called, was basically the Hawksmoor style: it was his invention and Vanbrugh found it sympathetic. Hawksmoor performed the same functions more officially at Blenheim Palace, which Vanbrugh was commissioned to build in 1705 and where Hawksmoor was Deputy Surveyor; he was probably responsible for the internal design of the hall and certainly for much of the detailing, including the various towers that contribute to Blenheim's unique skyline (see VANBRUGH, JOHN, §2(i)–(ii) and fig. 2).

Hawksmoor also made drawings for Vanbrugh's Kimbolton Castle, Cambs, in 1707–10, but they made no more joint designs. The discovery of a Treasury order to the Office of Works that the brick Orangery (1704–5) at Kensington Palace (for illustration see ORANGERY) should be built 'according to the alteration of the Draft proposed by Mr Vanbrugh' has been used to attribute that building to Vanbrugh. However, although Wren as Surveyor of Works was officially responsible for it, the design has the hallmarks of Hawksmoor's style: a complexity that included the patterning of windows and other features in three-bay groupings and an obsessive concern with the niceties of detailing in the external Doric and internal Corinthian orders. This is far removed from Vanbrugh's expressed belief in the supremacy of general rather than particular aspects of design.

3. URBAN PLANS AND OXFORD BUILDINGS. The fertility of Hawksmoor's imagination, irrespective of opportunities to realize it, is nowhere more evident than in his many projects for Oxford and Cambridge. Soon after 1710 various circumstances led him into the consideration of environmental plans: the new churchyard of St Paul's Cathedral, London; the completion of Greenwich Hospital with a detached chapel and a large forecourt; and projects for rebuilding the centres of the two university cities with vistas aligned on monuments and public buildings. Surviving sketches show the city plans to have embodied references both to antiquity and to Baroque Rome. None of these schemes was ever realized, and the completion of King's College, Cambridge, was carried out not according to his proposals but to the designs of James Gibbs and, in the 19th century, to those of William Wilkins. But at Oxford, where Hawksmoor continued until his last years to make designs for several colleges, he was entirely responsible for two completed projects: the University Printing House (1711–13; now the Old Clarendon Building; see OXFORD, fig. 4) and the north quadrangle of All Souls (1716–35).

The Old Clarendon Building was commissioned to house the two printing companies of Oxford University, one of which made money by producing the Authorized Version of the Bible, the other spending it in producing subsidized works of scholarship. His brief required two virtually separate sets of workrooms linked by a portico, which framed a central passage on the axis of the already standing quadrangle of the Bodleian Library. As both a utilitarian structure (though it no longer houses the presses) and an ornament to the University, Hawksmoor's building combined his understanding of the eloquence of plain monumentality with his sensitivity to the detailing of Classical architecture. He provided tetrastyle Doric porticos, prostyle towards the street and applied towards the Library; the rest of the exterior is astylar, except that the entablature of the giant order is carried all the way round. The wall surfaces are articulated and enlivened by changes in plane from bay to bay that also emphasize and exploit the massive thickness of the load-bearing walls. The windows have plain, raised architraves without any of the conventional mouldings, but all the windows in the raised basement and some on the top storey have exaggerated and dropped triple keystones, a motif usually associated with Italian Mannerism but one that Hawksmoor, by producing the boldest examples, made peculiarly his own.

By 1712 Hawksmoor had made several designs for the front quadrangle of the Queen's College and for All Souls. The Queen's College as built shows not his hand but his influence: the final design was probably by the Oxford amateur George Clarke (1661–1736) in collaboration with the mason William Townesend. However, in 1733 Hawksmoor did design the screen at the front of the college, with its elegant open circular temple above the gateway sheltering a statue of Queen Caroline. Hawksmoor's influence on the same designers can be seen in the library range of Worcester College, Oxford (begun 1720).

2. Nicholas Hawksmoor: north quadrangle, All Souls College, Oxford, 1716–35

At All Souls, Christopher Codrington's bequest of his books and a large sum of money to build a library for them was the first step towards the realization of Hawksmoor's design (see fig. 2). By building over the college garden he provided an almost entirely new quadrangle. On the south he retained the 15th-century chapel and added a hall on the same axis; the north side comprises the library, the east side has sets of lodgings and a common room and the west side a cloister with a gateway to Catte Street. Among a number of different projects, Hawksmoor offered the College the option of a complete rebuilding and also a choice between classical and 'Gothick' designs. The College chose to retain the existing buildings and to have the elevations of the new quadrangle in a pseudo-medieval style with classical interiors; the result is one of the earliest and also one of the best 18th-century 'Gothick' buildings. It is seen to best advantage on a sunny day, when the shadow pattern brings out the strength of relief modelling in the deep windows, the bold and simple mouldings and tall pinnacles recalling the general shapes rather than the particular details of Gothic architecture.

4. THE FIFTY NEW CHURCHES. In November 1710 a storm wrecked the old parish church at Greenwich; in response to a petition from the parishioners for help, in 1711 Parliament passed an act renewing the tax on London's coal supplies, which had previously paid for rebuilding St Paul's Cathedral and the City churches after the Great Fire of 1666. The tax was in future to be directed to the construction of churches in the new suburbs of London and Westminster that had developed in the preceding half century; with a combination of pragmatism and foresight, the writers of the act classified the village of Greenwich as a developing area and thus provided for the rebuilding of its church as the first of a proposed fifty buildings. The commission set up to carry out this programme appointed two surveyors or managing architects responsible for choosing and assessing sites, obtaining designs, inspecting the work of building and arranging for payment to the contractors.

Between 1711 and the closure of the commission in 1733 Hawksmoor, with a succession of partners, undertook this largely administrative task, but he also submitted numerous designs, of which six were carried out (the commission managed to build 12 churches). Two factors chiefly account for its failure to build even a quarter of the proposed total. First, most of the buildings were far more expensive than originally intended, and second, after the first four years the original commission was replaced by a new one more interested in economy than in architectural display: the project as originally conceived was not only a pious work but a monument to the Tory electoral success of 1710, to the High Church Anglicanism of the time and indeed to the person of Queen Anne as the figurehead, both political and religious. Hawksmoor himself is not known to have had any strong political allegiance, but the Whig victory in Parliament following Queen Anne's death in the summer of 1714 ensured that the new commission appointed by George I was Whig in sympathy and not disposed to lavish spending on a Tory monument.

Each of Hawksmoor's churches is an individual answer to the general brief. The extensive use of Portland stone for exteriors, the choice of open sites and the provision of impressive towers, steeples and porticos were part of this brief, which gave an opportunity unparalleled at the time to build churches that were not only practical and well ordered auditoriums but also eloquent architectural statements. In addition, most of Hawksmoor's churches show other characteristics: the provision of several entrances; a centralized plan; and a brooding solemnity, especially in the towers.

The first of these buildings was appropriately the rebuilt St Alfege at Greenwich (1712–14, consecrated 1718), which set the basic pattern of a rectangular interior with two axes intersecting at right angles; in this case there are no internal supports or divisions, the flat ceiling being carried entirely on the outer walls. The short axis, originally expressed internally by the seating pattern, is still marked by external projections on the long sides, which contain entrances as well as staircases to the side galleries that are a common feature of 18th-century Anglican churches. The small, half-oval chancel space at the east end is made to seem larger by the fictive coffering of its painted half-dome; its real size was limited by the need to provide an eastern portico facing the main street.

Hawksmoor was familiar with Inigo Jones's church of St Paul, Covent Garden, another single rectangular room with an eastern portico, but he brought to this formula the Doric grandeur and the layered wall surfaces he had devised a few months earlier for the Old Clarendon Building in Oxford. His intention of recasing the old tower was only partly realized, and the additional stages ending in a monumental open octagonal lantern were not carried out. The second commission registered its indifference to the provision of unnecessary steeples, and only in 1730–32, after persistent pressure from the inhabitants of Greenwich, did it agree to erect the present steeple to the design of John James. When he understood that the Greenwich tower would not be built, Hawksmoor transposed the octagonal lantern to St George-in-the-East (1714–22, consecrated 1729; see fig. 3). Original drawings show that, like many other features of the churches, the tower of this one evolved in a process of design that continued well after the commencement of building.

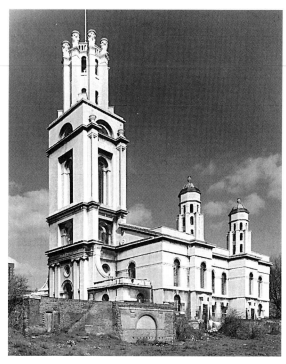

3. Nicholas Hawksmoor: St George-in-the-East, London, 1714–22

The plan of St George, like that of St Anne, Limehouse, built concurrently, is more obviously centralized. Essentially each is a Greek cross within a squat rectangle, the central space being defined by four columns. The provision of side galleries and one at the west end, and the emphasis on the west–east axis that followed from the commission's requirement of a small eastern chancel, result in an interior whose liturgical and formal aspects are at variance and ambiguously related; this can still be appreciated in the Limehouse church (reconstructed after a fire in 1850), whereas St George (gutted 1941) was rebuilt in a different form. Spatial ambiguity of this kind is consistently to be found in Hawksmoor's churches and those of Thomas Archer but in scarcely any others; it appears to be deliberate and to relate both to Hawksmoor's personal conception of his art and to the lack of a single liturgical focal point that distinguishes 18th-century Anglican churches from Roman Catholic ones. Other important visual features of these two churches in particular are less easy to explain in terms of function: the four turrets at St George that echo the belfry lantern; the steeple of St Anne that resembles English Late Gothic towers such as the famous 'Stump' at St Botolph, Boston, Lincs; and the domed circular western vestibule of St Anne that projects from the west front, forming at the same time half the substructure of the steeple.

Christ Church, Spitalfields (also begun 1714, consecrated 1729), appears at first sight to have a basilican plan but is in fact a centralized interior stretched along the west–east axis. The three central bays of the 'nave' are differentiated from those at the ends, and the cross axis is marked by side entrances. The design of Christ Church continued to develop during the 1720s: the Gothic broach spire, originally adorned with crockets, and the portico in the form of a giant, three-dimensional Venetian window were late additions.

St George, Bloomsbury, and St Mary Woolnoth in the City of London (both begun 1716) were designed for more restricted sites. That of St George was narrow from west to east, and Hawksmoor provided the principal approach through an impressive hexastyle portico on the south side, with another entrance through the west tower. Both axes were equally but differently emphasized, one by the large wooden niche that originally formed the altarpiece in the eastern apse, the other by the south portico. The ambiguity survives in the lines of the ceiling, although the altar has been moved to the north and the original north side gallery removed. The portico is one of several designed in London in the early 1720s, others being John James's St George, Hanover Square, and James Gibbs's St Martin-in-the-Fields. The steeple of Hawksmoor's church (designed 1723) consists of a stepped pyramid, a far from archaeological re-creation, which he took from Pliny's account of the Mausoleum of Halikarnassos. This serves to support a statue of King George I, which was originally accompanied by a heraldic lion and unicorn at the base of the pyramid. Hawksmoor's attitude to antiquity, as to medieval architecture, was erudite but romantically imaginative rather than academically correct.

St Mary Woolnoth, a rebuilding of a City church repaired after the Great Fire of 1666, is the smallest and most compact and powerful of the churches, being a perfect clerestoried square within a square. Because the site was open only on the north and west, architectural attention is concentrated on those sides: the windowless north wall is relieved by three huge rusticated niches, and the west front virtually consists of a single broad tower which ends in two separate balustraded turrets.

Hawksmoor and James jointly produced two further Commission churches: St John, Horselydown (1727–33; gutted 1940–41, destr.), and St Luke, Old Street (1727–33; destr. 1960). Their chief ornaments were their unusual spires, respectively a tapered Ionic column and a fluted obelisk; the latter is all that survives of these two churches, unhappy compromises between parsimony and fantasy.

5. LATE WORKS. The efficient promotion by Colen Campbell and James Leoni in 1715 of Palladianism as the way forward for architecture quickly made Hawksmoor's style and the English Baroque, of which it was a major component, old-fashioned. In response, Hawksmoor significantly changed his vocabulary of detail: the giant Venetian window that forms the Spitalfields portico is his most eccentrically personal use of a 'Palladian' motif, which he had introduced into the east window of this church as early as 1715. However, he did not change the principles of his art, which in 1724 he summarized as 'strong reason and good fancy [imagination], joined with experience and trials, so that we are assured of the good effect of it'.

Surviving preparatory drawings for some of his mature projects show the extent to which he used drawing as a means of research and experiment in design. Although he was one of the first in England, after Wren, to do this consistently, as a draughtsman he was skilled but old-fashioned. He had a talent for sharp lines, precise angles and succinctly stated profiles, but his drawings seem often closer to images than to diagrams, enlivened with grey wash freely applied to indicate the strong shadows and bold massing of his architecture, modulated with freehand decorative and perspectival details and annotated with remarks to himself or his client.

Hawksmoor still found patrons who were concerned with more than the latest fashion. His late contribution to the Queen's College, Oxford, has been mentioned; also in Oxford, at All Souls he built the classical hall and the adjoining stone-vaulted oval buttery (1730–33). At Blenheim, after Vanbrugh's resignation in 1716, Hawksmoor was indispensable to the Duchess of Marlborough from 1722 to 1725, not only for his sound practical advice but also for the fitting up of the south-east quarter of the house, the transformation by meticulously detailed plasterwork of a sequence of bare spaces into the magnificent Long Library, and the design of the triumphal arch at the Woodstock entrance to the park.

Hawksmoor continued to make medievalizing designs when that style seemed appropriate; he supervised a refurbishment of the Minster at Beverley, Humberside (c. 1716–20), and designed for the Fifty New Churches Commission the great tower of St Michael's, Cornhill (1718–24), at first sight a Late Gothic tower but actually containing not a single pointed arch. In 1723, on the death of Wren, he became architect to Westminster Abbey, the west gable (1735) and towers (1734–45) of which are his; they also are Gothic in texture and feeling rather than in detail. On this occasion the retiring side of his character extended to architecture, and few post-medieval completions have been so sympathetically successful.

His most constant patron was Charles Howard, 3rd Earl of Carlisle, who continued with the landscaping and outbuildings of Castle Howard until his death in 1738. Hawksmoor not only took charge of the temple of the Four Winds (1725–8) designed by Vanbrugh but also designed in those years the Pyramid, the castellated Carrmire Gate and several smaller structures. But most important of all is Lord Carlisle's own burial-place, the Mausoleum (1729–42; see fig. 4), a mile from the house. For a private commission of the time this building is exceptionally well documented by over fifty of the architect's letters, which give his reasons for many features of the design. The Mausoleum is a monumental variation on Bramante's Tempietto, a circular peripteral Doric temple with a domed cella rising above the peristyle. The unusually close spacing of the columns and the absence, in Hawksmoor's own design, of any obvious entrance reinforce the overpowering impression of the building as one into which the living are not welcome. Hawksmoor's feeling for the classical orders is impeccable but idiosyncratic. The lofty but claustrophobic interior has only one small door and is lit by windows beneath the dome. It is dominated by a ring of eight Corinthian columns, between which the wall seems to press inwards.

Hawksmoor's generation, born early in the Restoration, grew up familiar with the philosopher Thomas Hobbes's primitive theories of the subconscious imagination, and the emotive force of his architecture is not accidental.

4. Nicholas Hawksmoor: the Mausoleum, Castle Howard, North Yorkshire, 1729–42

Hawksmoor understood intuitively from illustrations and attempted to re-create the monumentality of Imperial Roman buildings. Henry Cheere's bust of him at All Souls, made in his last years, shows a well-built man with a sombre expression into which may be read not only suffering and disappointment but equally the pride of creation.

BIBLIOGRAPHY

H. S. Goodhart-Rendel: *Hawksmoor* (London, 1924)
G. Webb: 'The Letters and Drawings . . . Relating to the Building of the Mausoleum at Castle Howard', *Walpole Soc.*, xix (1931), pp. 111–64
D. Green: *Blenheim Palace* (London, 1951)
K. Downes: *Hawksmoor* (London, 1959, rev. 2/1979)
H. M. Colvin: *A Catalogue of Architectural Drawings of the 18th and 19th Centuries in the Library of Worcester College, Oxford* (Oxford, 1964)
K. Downes: *Hawksmoor* (London, 1969, rev. 3/1994) [a shorter study, with new material on work with Vanbrugh and on Hawksmoor's date of birth]
H. M. Colvin, ed.: *The History of the King's Works*, v (London, 1972)
D. J. Watkin, ed.: *Architects* (1972), iv of *Sale Catalogues of Eminent Persons* (London, 1971–), pp. 45–105
Hawksmoor (exh. cat., ed. K. Downes; London, Whitechapel A.G., 1977)
E. G. W. Bill: *The Queen Anne Churches: A Catalogue of the Papers in Lambeth Palace Library* (London, 1979)
K. Downes: 'Hawksmoor's House at Easton Neston', *Archit. Hist.*, xxx (1987), pp. 50–76
R. Hewlings: 'Hawksmoor's "Brave Designs for the Police"', *English Architecture, Public and Private: Essays for Kerry Downes*, ed. J. Bold and E. Chaney (London, 1993), pp. 215–29

KERRY DOWNES

Hawthorne, Nathaniel (*b* Salem, MA, 4 July 1804; *d* Plymouth, NH, 19 May 1864). American writer. He was born into an eminent Puritan family and educated at Bowdoin College, ME. Although his major novels, *The Scarlet Letter* (1850) and *The House of the Seven Gables* (1851), are on American themes, his term as consul in Liverpool (1853–7) resulted in *Passages from the English Notebooks* (1870), published posthumously and edited by his widow. While his main interest in the *Notebooks* was the literary and historical associations of England, he revealed a growing appreciation of European art and charted his progress from ignorant admiration to a recognition first of defects, then beauties, and finally the 'broader differences of style'. His taste was essentially conventional: he admired Bartolomé Esteban Murillo's sentiment, David Wilkie's attention to detail and the Dutch realists' suggestion of the spiritual within the domestic. He objected to Thomas Lawrence's meretriciousness and William Etty's 'diseased appetite for woman's flesh', but he was impressed by the Pre-Raphaelites' repudiation of visual beauty. He showed a gradual understanding of J. M. W. Turner's landscapes but preferred those of Claude Lorrain. His response to English architecture was less obviously subjective but was strongly influenced by the ideas of the Romantic revival in that he admired Gothic cathedrals for their 'secrecy' and 'twilight effect'.

Hawthorne's stay in Rome and Florence in 1858–9 resulted in *Passages from the French and Italian Notebooks* (1872). Again, his taste was conventional: he admired Michelangelo, Raphael, del Sarto, Giambologna, Rubens, Claude and Rosa but confessed that Giotto, Cimabue, Fra Angelico, Botticelli and Fra Filippo Lippi 'ought to interest me a great deal more than they do'. An element of parochialism is still apparent in his preference for George Loring Brown over Claude and in finding nudity in paintings tolerable if executed in a 'modest' and 'natural' fashion. His aesthetic judgements become gradually more sophisticated through the course of the *Notebooks*, however; he argued that an understanding of realistic art precedes a perception of the grand style and that artistic appreciation has no moral basis. Methods of hanging and mounting pictures in Italian galleries and churches also interested him, techniques that he felt the British had perfected. Hawthorne fictionalized his Italian observations in his novel *The Marble Faun* (1860), attempting to convert artistic judgements into metaphor. His characters' interactions uneasily represent New England moralism coming to terms with Italian aestheticism, the amorality of art and the dangerous lures of the Catholicism that fostered such art.

WRITINGS

The Marble Faun (Boston, MA, 1860)
S. Hawthorne, ed.: *Passages from the English Notebooks* (Boston, MA, 1870); repr. as *The English Notebooks* with additional essays, ed. R. Stewart (New York and London, 1941)
——: *Passages from the French and Italian Notebooks* (Boston, MA, 1872); repr. as *The French and Italian Notebooks* with additional essays, ed. T. Woodson (Columbus, OH, 1980)

BIBLIOGRAPHY

G. Clarke: 'To Transform and Transfigure: The Aesthetic Play of Hawthorne's *The Marble Faun*', *Nathaniel Hawthorne: New Critical Essays*, ed. A. R. Lee (London, 1982), pp. 131–47
T. Martin: *Nathaniel Hawthorne* (Boston, MA, 1983)
A. M. Donohue: *Hawthorne: Calvin's Ironic Stepchild* (Kent, OH, 1985)

EDWINA BURNESS

Haxhiu, Fatmir (*b* Tiranë, 28 Oct 1928). Albanian painter. He studied painting at the Higher Institute of Arts in Tiranë (1961–5). He specialized in monumental painting, in particular historical battle paintings, and also painted numerous large-scale figure compositions. Haxhiu's work is concentrated on three key moments in the history of Albania: the period of the Albanian–Ottoman wars and Skanderbeg in the 15th century (e.g. *Sword in Hand*, 4.5×5.5 m, 1978; Tiranë, Prime Minister's Office), the struggle for national independence from the Ottoman occupation (e.g. *Scorched Land*, 4×3 m, 1985; Tropojë, Hist. Mus.) and World War II (e.g. *Breaking through the Encirclement*, 2.2×2.0 m, 1978; Tiranë, A.G.). His work is noted for its historical truthfulness, the dramatic character of events and the compositional balance of his figures. The realistic outline of figures, their dynamic and eloquent movements, the penetrating psychology of the portraiture and the use of intense colour, as well as a wide range of gentle hues, all make his work effective. Besides battle paintings Haxhiu also painted subjects concerned with social development in socialist Albania, for example *Enver Hoxha at the Qemal Stafa School* (1970; Tiranë, Qemal Stafa School).

BIBLIOGRAPHY
Artet Figurative Shqiptare [Albanian figurative art] (Tiranë, 1978), pls 85–9
'Edhe tema parapërcakton gjininë që duhet trajtuar: Intervistë me piktorin e merituar Fatmir Haxhiu' [The subject determines the genre: interview with the Painter of Merit, Fatmir Haxhiu], *Drita* (11 Aug 1985), p. 7

GJERGJ FRASHËRI

Hay, Andrew (*b* Fife; *d* Oct 1754). Scottish dealer and painter. He trained as a portrait painter under Sir John Medina in Edinburgh before 1710. By the early 1720s he had given up painting for dealing, which involved frequent trips to France and Italy; he dealt in paintings, drawings, prints, marble busts, bas-reliefs, bronzes, manuscripts and books. Hay's earliest important clients were Thomas Coke and Edward Harley, later 2nd Earl of Oxford. He started working for them in 1715. His first important commission was to buy manuscripts and books for Edward Harley. While in Italy from 1720 to 1723 he began to deal in Old Master paintings and antique statues, which his brother and partner, George Hay (*fl c.* 1720–40), sold in England to individual patrons and at auction-rooms in London, including that of Christopher Cock between 1726 and 1739. Andrew Hay was a member of various London art clubs, including the Virtuosi of St Luke (1723–37) and the Rose and Crown; he was also a member in 1729 of the Academy of St Luke in Edinburgh. Having made himself rich, he had retired to his native Scotland by May 1745.

BIBLIOGRAPHY
The Diary of Humfrey Wanley, 1715–1726, ed. C. E. Wright and R. C. Wright, 2 vols (London, 1966)
I. Bignamini: 'George Vertue, Art Historian, and Art Institutions in London, 1689–1768', *Walpole Soc.*, liv (1988), pp. 1–148
I. Pears: *The Discovery of Painting* (New Haven and London, 1988), pp. 77–87

ILARIA BIGNAMINI

Hay, Jean. *See* HEY, JEAN.

Hay, Robert. *See under* JACQUES & HAY.

Hay, William (*b* Cruden, Aberdeenshire [now Grampian], 17 May 1818; *d* Joppa, Edinburgh, 30 May 1888). Scottish architect, active in Canada. He was trained in the architectural office of John Henderson (1804–62) in Edinburgh from 1844. He then became George Gilbert Scott I's Clerk of Works (1846–50) for the Anglican Cathedral (first phase) at St John's, Newfoundland. During his time there he worked on several churches in the province and designed one (1847–50; unexecuted) for St Francis Harbour, Labrador. He was back in Scotland in

1850, but by 1852 he had settled in Toronto where, over the next ten years, he became a leading architect. His experience with Scott instilled in Hay the ecclesiological principles of the Gothic Revival, which he used or adapted in his churches in Ontario and promoted in his writings. His Anglican churches at Brampton (1854), Orillia and Southampton (1861) were all rebuilt; those at Newcastle (1857) and Vienna (1860) survive. For the Roman Catholic Church he built St Basil's and the adjacent St Michael's College (both 1855–6; later remodelled), Toronto; and for the Presbyterian Church he built Gould Street Church (1855), Toronto, and St Andrew's (1857–8), Guelph. For his secular buildings Hay employed a variety of styles. His classical work included Toronto General Hospital (1853–6) and the House of Providence (1855–8), Toronto, both adaptations of the French Renaissance style, as well as the Commercial Bank (1853; now Empire Life), Kingston, and the Bank of Montreal, Hamilton, which were exercises in Renaissance classicism. He built several houses in Gothic Revival style, of which Thornton Cliff (1855), Brockville, and Oaklands (1860), Toronto, survive, albeit in remodelled form, and his Yorkville Town Hall (1859–60; destr.), Toronto, was designed in polychromatic High Victorian Gothic. Hay left Toronto in 1862 and subsequently spent two years in Halifax, Nova Scotia, in partnership with David Stirling, where he designed the mansion Keith Hall (1863). He then settled in Edinburgh, where he restored St Giles Cathedral (1872–83). In 1884, following a visit there, he designed the new Cathedral of the Most Holy Trinity in Hamilton, Bermuda, which was built after his death.

WRITINGS
'Architecture for the Meridian of Canada', *Anglo-Amer. Mag.*, ii (1853), pp. 253–5
'The Late Mr Pugin and the Revival of Christian Architecture', *Anglo-Amer. Mag.*, ii (1853), pp. 70–73

BIBLIOGRAPHY
DCB
E. Arthur: *Toronto: No Mean City* (Toronto, 1964, rev. 3/1986)
M. MacRae and A. Adamson: *Hallowed Walls* (Toronto, 1975)
W. Dendy: *Lost Toronto* (Toronto, 1978)

MALCOLM THURLBY

Hayakawa, Kunihiko (*b* Tokyo, 19 Nov 1941). Japanese architect. He graduated from Waseda University, Tokyo, in 1966 and received a Master of Environmental Design degree from Yale University, New Haven, CT, in 1971. Between 1966 and 1977 he was a member of the design department of Takenaka Komuten Co. Ltd, one of the largest construction companies in Japan. In 1978 he opened his own office in Tokyo. Hayakawa saw in the Tokyo cityscape a floating, fragmented quality that inspired his architectural approach. His designs resembled stage sets; he reduced buildings to compositions of lines and planes with the use of pastel colours. For example, his House at a Bus Stop (1982), Tokyo, addresses problems of urban living such as noise by 'layering' the street façade with a series of wall planes. The spaces between the layers let in light and create a gradual transition from the exterior to the interior world. Other works include House at a Crossroad (1983), Tokyo, Atrium (1985), a block of flats in Tokyo, and Angle (1988), a two-storey commercial and office complex in Himeji City.

WRITINGS
'Circuit of Expression', *Japan Architect*, 325 (1984), pp. 16–19

BIBLIOGRAPHY
Space Des., cclxxxiii (1988) [whole issue]

HIROSHI WATANABE

Hayami, Gyoshū (*b* Tokyo, 2 Aug 1894; *d* Tokyo, 20 March 1935). Japanese painter. He trained in 1908 at the Angadō Gajuku, the painting school of Fūko Matsumoto (1840–1923). He joined and studied with the innovative research group the Red Day Society (Sekiyōkai), which was co-founded by another student at Matsumoto's school, Shikō Imamura (1880–1916). In 1914 Hayami exhibited work in the revived Inten, the exhibition of the Japan Art Institute, and in 1917 he became a member of the institute. As a Japanese-style (*Nihonga*) painter (*see* JAPAN, §VI, 5(iii)), he was influenced by such painting as that of the Northern Renaissance and of the Chinese Song (960–1279) and Yuan (1279–1368) periods. His most typical and most respected works include the delicate and detailed *Kyoto Dancing Girl* (1920; Tokyo, N. Mus.), the illusionistic *Dance of the Flames* (1924) and the decorative *Camellia Surrounded by its Fallen Blossoms* (1929; both Tokyo, Yamatane Mus. A.).

BIBLIOGRAPHY
K. Yoshida: *Hayami Gyoshū* (Kyoto, 1975)
Hayami Gyoshū (Tokyo, 1977)

YOSHIKAZU IWASAKI

Hayanari. *See* TACHIBANA NO HAYANARI.

Hayasdan. *See* ARMENIA.

Hayatsor. *See* ÇAVUŞTEPE.

Hayberger [Hoyberger], **(Johann) Gotthard** (*b* Peuerbach, nr Grieskirchen, 28 April 1695; *d* Steyr, 7 March 1764). Austrian architect. He was probably taught by his father, who was a master mason; in 1720 he described himself as a qualified mason. Also in 1720 he moved to Steyr, becoming a citizen in the following year. He was subsequently entrusted with various municipal commissions there, including the renovation of the town wall (1731). In 1741 he succeeded Joseph Munggenast at Seitenstetten Abbey, where, even though the building was well under way, his designs for the staircase and entrance pavilion made his mark as an independent architect. His scheme for Kremsmünster Abbey, including plans for the observatory and library (before 1743), was not executed, nor were his huge plans for rebuilding ADMONT ABBEY (1742) carried out in their entirety for financial reasons; the library in the east wing is his main work there and is in the artistic tradition of the Hofbibliothek in Vienna. The interesting interior design was probably strongly influenced by Josef Hueber (1716–87), who completed the building in 1776. The influence of Jakob Prandtauer can be seen in the library wing at St Florian Abbey, where Hayberger completed Prandtauer's plan from 1744 with only very minor changes. Hayberger's late work included the façades of numerous town houses in Steyr. His design for the façade of Steyr Town Hall, which was carried out by Hueber in 1765–78, produced one of the most important Rococo buildings in Upper Austria: the narrow frontage is cleverly used for a building with five bays, four floors and a slender tower.

BIBLIOGRAPHY
E. Krobath: 'Die Bürgermeister der Stadt Steyr und ihre Zeit: Johann Gotthard Hoyberger, 1759–1764', *Veröff. Kultamt. Stadt Steyr* (1967), pp. 3–27
G. Brucher: *Barockarchitektur in Österreich* (Cologne, 1983), pp. 290–94, 311–12

A. GERHARDT

Haycock, Edward (*b* Shrewsbury, 29 July 1790; *d* Shrewsbury, 21 Dec 1870). English architect. He came from a family of builder-architects based at Shrewsbury. He had a professional training in London under Sir Jeffry Wyatville and exhibited at the Royal Academy between 1808 and 1810. Returning to Shrewsbury, he joined his father in the family building firm and continued to combine the business of a builder with the practice of an architect until about 1845, after which time he worked only as an architect. He was County Surveyor of Shropshire from 1834 to 1866 and achieved a position of importance in the social and political life of Shrewsbury. After his death his practice was continued by his son, also named Edward Haycock (*d* 1882).

Haycock built up a very extensive practice, not only in Shropshire and the adjacent counties, but also in Wales. In the second quarter of the 19th century his was the leading architectural practice in Wales, the only one to transcend the boundary between north and south. His churches and minor public buildings are routine products of their time; his churches in particular are mostly perfunctory essays in the Gothic 'Lancet Style'. However, as a Greek Revivalist he designed several buildings of distinction, including Lord Hill's Column at Shrewsbury (1814–16), in which he was assisted by Thomas Harrison of Chester, Clytha Court, Gwent (*c*. 1830), Millichope Park, Salop (1835–40), and the large mansion of Glynllifon, Gwynedd (*c*. 1836–40). Clytha is distinguished by detailing of great elegance, while at Millichope Haycock achieved unusual spatial effects.

BIBLIOGRAPHY
Colvin
J. L. Hobbs: 'The Haycocks', *Salop Mag.*, xi/8 (1960), pp. 17–18
J. Cornforth: 'Millichope Park, Shropshire', *Country Life*, clxi (10 Feb 1977), pp. 310–13; clxi (17 Feb 1977), pp. 370–73
R. Haslam: 'Clytha Park, Gwent', *Country Life*, clxii (8 Dec 1977), pp. 1718–21; clxii (15 Dec 1977), pp. 1826–9

HOWARD COLVIN

Haydar [Sayyid Ḥaydar ibn ʔAṣīl al-Din] (*d* 1325–6). Calligrapher. He was one of the six disciples of YAQUT AL-MUSTAʿSIMI and earned the nickname 'writer in large characters' (Pers. *kand-navīs*), presumably because of his masterful work designing architectural inscriptions in carved stucco. Two superb examples of his work in this medium survive in Iran: a band (1307–8) across the intrados of the north iwan of the mosque in the shrine complex at Natanz, and the mihrab (1310) in the winter prayer hall of the Friday Mosque at Isfahan (*see* STUCCO AND PLASTERWORK, fig. 6). He was a renowned teacher whose pupils included such famous calligraphers as ʿAB-DALLAH SAYRAFI, and the viziers Taj al-Din ʿAli Shah and Ghiyath al-Din, the son of RASHID AL-DIN. His son Muhammad was a calligrapher, too, and signed several calligraphic specimens (e.g. Istanbul, Topkapı Pal. Lib., H. 2160, fol. 29*v* and H. 2310, fol. 97*v*).

BIBLIOGRAPHY

Qāžī Aḥmad ibn Mīr Munshī: *Gulistān-i hunar* [Rose-garden of art] (*c.* 1606); Eng. trans. by V. Minorsky as *Calligraphers and Painters* (Washington, DC, 1959), pp. 61–2

S. S. Blair: *The Ilkhanid Shrine Complex at Natanz, Iran* (Cambridge, MA, 1986), pp. 13–14, 61

W. M. Thackston: *A Century of Princes: Sources on Timurid History and Art* (Cambridge, MA, 1989), pp. 339–40

SHEILA S. BLAIR

Haydar Ra'is [Haydār Ra'īs; Haydar Reis; Nigari; Reis Haydar] (*b* ?1492; *d* Istanbul, 1572). Ottoman painter, poet and naval captain. He is often known by the pseudonym Nigari (Ott. *nigārī*, 'the portraitist'), with which he signed several paintings of Ottoman sultans and court officials. His couplets are frequently included on his paintings. He seems to have painted portraits from life of the sultans Süleyman (*reg* 1520–66) and Selim II (*reg* 1566–74) and the grand admiral of the Ottoman fleet, Barbaros Hayreddin Pasha (*d* 1546). These single-leaf portraits were later incorporated into albums (e.g. Istanbul, Topkapı Pal. Lib., H 2134). The portraits reveal a realistic approach and depict the physical characteristics of the subjects, employing large figures painted in bold colours on a dark-green ground with minimal settings. In contrast to works by members of the imperial painting studio (*see* ISLAMIC ART, §III, 4(vi)(e)), Nigari's portraits are less refined and lack technical finesse: the sheets are not polished and the pigments are rapidly applied. Nevertheless, they display an individual style and a personal approach. His work helped to establish the genre of portraiture in Ottoman court circles that had been introduced in the 1480s. Although late 15th-century portraits show the impact of European art, Nigari's works are purely in the Ottoman tradition and his style remained untouched by outside influences, even though he copied prints of European rulers, including Francis I and Charles V (e.g. Cambridge, MA, Sackler Mus., 85.214a and b).

BIBLIOGRAPHY

A. S. Ünver: *Ressam Nigârî: Hayatı ve eserleri* [The painter Nigari: His life and works] (Ankara, 1946)

E. Binney, 3rd: *Turkish Treasures from the Collection of Edwin Binney, 3rd* (Portland, OR, 1979), nos 11–12 [*Cenap Paşa and his Staff* and Charles V, both *c.* 1570]

Arts of the Islamic Book: The Collection of Prince Sadruddin Aga Khan (exh. cat. by A. Welch and S. C. Welch, New York, Asia Soc. Gals; Fort Worth, TX, Kimbell A. Mus.; Kansas City, MO, Nelson–Atkins Mus. A.; 1982–3), no. 6 [*Selim II Holding a Cup, c.* 1570]

The Anatolian Civilisations (exh. cat., 18th Council of Europe exh.; Istanbul, 1983), iii, nos 67–9 and 107

E. Atıl: *The Age of Sultan Süleyman the Magnificent* (Washington and New York, 1987), figs 10–11 [*Süleyman with Two Attendants, c.* 1560; *Selim II, c.* 1570]

ESIN ATIL

Hayden, Henri (*b* Warsaw, 24 Dec 1883; *d* Paris, 12 May 1970). Polish painter, active in France. He began a course in engineering at Warsaw Polytechnic in 1902 but also enrolled as a student at the School of Fine Arts, and in 1905 he gave up engineering to devote himself entirely to painting. In 1907 he arrived in Paris, intending to stay for only a year, but lived in France until his death. He attended the Académie La Palette for several months and in 1909 visited Brittany, in particular Le Pouldu and Pont-Aven, where he went to work for a number of summers, and where he met and became friendly with the Polish painter Władysław Ślewiński, who had been a member of Paul Gauguin's circle.

By 1911 Hayden's work began to show the influence not only of Ślewiński and Gauguin but also of Paul Cézanne. His interest in formal simplification and pictorial construction in a manner indebted to Cézanne very gradually led him, from 1912, towards Cubism. In 1915 he met Juan Gris, who in turn introduced him to the dealer Léonce Rosenberg, but it was not until 1917 that he painted his first truly Cubist works, such as *Still-life with Bellows* (1917; see 1968 exh. cat., pl. 26). As a foreigner, he was able to continue painting throughout World War I and between 1915 and 1919 spent much time with Jean Metzinger, Gino Severini and Picasso. His Cubist paintings were mostly still-lifes, with such objects as bottles, pipes, guitars and newspapers, but he also painted several landscapes and figure studies, including pictures of figures playing musical instruments such as *Three Musicians* (1920; Paris, Pompidou). His friends included the composers of the group Les Six. Though influenced by the Synthetic Cubist styles of Picasso and Georges Braque, his works have a particularly sensuous quality of colour.

Hayden's Cubist period ended in 1922 when, feeling that he had exhausted its resources, he returned to the direct study of nature and went to the Midi, to Cassis and Sanary-sur-Mer, to paint landscapes. A long and difficult period followed when he tried, in solitude, with only limited success, to find his way again, working at times in a style similar to that of André Derain as in *Woman and Child* (1922; see 1968 exh. cat., pl. 53), and making visits to Honfleur in 1933, and to the Lot region, on the border of the Dordogne, between 1933 and 1937.

In June 1940 Hayden fled from Paris and took refuge first in the Auvergne, where he met up with Robert Delaunay, and then in the south of France, at Mougins and Roussillon-d'Apt, where he met and became very friendly with Samuel Beckett. When he returned to Paris in 1944, he found that his studio had been ransacked by the Germans.

After the war Hayden was able to work regularly again. In his old age he specialized in views of the Marne Valley, a gently undulating countryside where he first worked in 1954, and where he settled in 1962, in a house near La Ferté-sous-Jouarre. Working from studies made from nature or with still-life themes, for example *Chess in Ochre* (1961; London, Tate), he simplified forms into bold, rhythmical soft-edged designs, with rich, saturated colours that lent them a personal, increasingly visionary, air.

BIBLIOGRAPHY

Documents, 22 (1955) [issue ded. Hayden]

Hayden: Soixante ans de peinture, 1908–1968 (exh. cat. by J. Cassou and others, Paris, Mus. N. A. Mod., 1968)

Henri Hayden: Paysages de la Marne (exh. cat. by S. Beckett and J. Lassaigne, Paris, Mus. A. Mod. Ville Paris, 1977)

Henri Hayden, 1883–1970, rétrospective (exh. cat., ed. P. Ramade; Rennes, Mus. B.-A. & Archéol., 1979)

RONALD ALLEY

Haydon, Benjamin Robert (*b* Plymouth, 25 Jan 1786; *d* London, 22 June 1846). English painter, teacher and writer. The son of a printer and publisher, Haydon was educated at grammar schools in Plymouth and Plympton. Joshua Reynolds's *Discourses* fired his passion for history painting, while a Neapolitan employee of his father fostered his talent for drawing. After an unhappy apprenticeship to his father, he entered the Royal Academy, London, in 1805. He was an enthusiastic student who, like his friend David Wilkie, became interested in anatomy, attending lectures given by the anatomist and surgeon Charles Bell in 1806.

Haydon's first experiment in high art, *Joseph and Mary Resting on the Road to Egypt* (untraced), was exhibited at the Royal Academy in 1807. It was admired by the patrons George Beaumont and Henry Phipps, 1st Earl of Mulgrave, and bought the following year by Thomas Hope. Mulgrave commissioned Haydon's first major picture, the *Assassination of Dentatus* (1806–9; Marquess of Normanby priv. col.). Haydon despised the 'Low, Dutch taste' spread by Wilkie's genre paintings, and *Dentatus* was a heroic if inflated attempt to revive the historical tradition of Reynolds and Benjamin West. Chosen by Mulgrave because it had never been painted before, the subject of a hero cast down by a jealous establishment was prophetic of Haydon's life and artistic career, and its sublimity inspired him to a characteristically awkward combination of noble conception and cumbersome design. Typically also, the picture proved controversial. Haydon considered it 'an epoch in English art', while a *Quarterly* reviewer criticized its 'forced abortive grandeur'. Its removal to a rather less prominent position in the Academy in 1809 unleashed Haydon's lifelong mistrust of patrons and colleagues. Although the picture won a premium at the British Institution in 1810, Haydon almost always exhibited privately thereafter, with an admission charge.

While preparing *Dentatus* Haydon was greatly impressed by the Elgin Marbles from the Parthenon frieze (*see* BRUCE, THOMAS), of which he made drawings in 1808. He championed them vociferously against the disparaging opinions of such connoisseurs as Richard Payne Knight, and the poses of some of the *Dentatus* figures were based on the Parthenon metopes. Unfortunately the marbles encouraged Haydon's injudicious preference for working on a vast scale. A painting for Beaumont of a subject from *Macbeth* (1809; untraced) was the object of protracted disputes over its size before the patron reluctantly accepted a picture almost too large to fit into his house. Haydon pursued this tendency in the *Judgement of Solomon* (1812–14; J. B. Gold priv. col.) and *Christ's Entry into Jerusalem* (1814–20; Cincinnati, OH, St George's Semin.). These ventures into the traditions of Sebastiano del Piombo and Raphael drained time and resources: *Christ's Entry* took

Benjamin Robert Haydon: *Mock Election*, oil on canvas, 1.42×1.83 m, 1827 (London, Buckingham Palace, Royal Collection)

six years, during which Haydon refused other work and was effectively without income. Their lack of compositional integration was exacerbated by the long time span and by an eye defect that enabled Haydon to see only one part of a canvas at a time. Nevertheless both pictures show him at his best as a history painter; they were much admired by contemporaries and possess undeniable grandeur.

Haydon's exclusive concentration on these paintings put him heavily into debt, and in 1823 he suffered the first of a series of bankruptcies and imprisonments. His disputes with the Academy had alienated him from his colleagues and his journalistic activities had made him many enemies. The bite of his opinions, even when patently correct, gave considerable offence. His pamphlet of 1815, *On the Judgement of Connoisseurs Being Preferred to that of Professional Men: The Elgin Marbles etc.*, contained undeniable truths, informed as it was by a study of the marbles involving new techniques (including a comparison of the sculpture with dissected human specimens) and a deeper perception of the psychological relationships between the carved figures. But Haydon had also vilified Knight, whose disdain for the marbles sprang from the blander view of Antiquity nurtured by Johann Joachim Winckelmann and Anton Raphael Mengs. He had thus alienated the very class from whom a painter could hope for support in the absence of the State patronage he so earnestly desired. Disputes with patrons like Beaumont, which he paranoiacally exaggerated in his diary, isolated him further. But he refused to modify his historical ambitions, continuing to produce such uncompromising and enormous works as the *Raising of Lazarus* (1820–23; London, Tate) and *Marcus Curtius Leaping into the Gulf* (1836–42; Exeter, Royal Albert Mem. Mus.). He did not pursue the more lucrative avenues of portraiture or genre painting, although his highly Romantic *Wordsworth on Helvellyn* (1842; London, N.P.G.) and occasional humorous narrative scenes, such as the *Mock Election* (1827; London, Buckingham Pal., Royal Col.; see fig.) and *Punch or May Day* (1829; London, Tate), show considerable talent and express his passionate and impressionable temperament more clearly than the pictures on which he staked his reputation.

In 1812 Haydon had proposed decorating the Houses of Parliament with historical subjects. After the building's destruction by fire in 1834 he advocated frescoes for the decoration of its replacement. He studied fresco techniques and submitted *Adam and Eve* (untraced) to the competition for cartoon drawings held in 1843. But his rhetorical classical style involving vast figures and artificially dramatic gestures now seemed old-fashioned. His defeat by the rising generation of William Dyce and Daniel Maclise, the ignominious failure of an exhibition in 1845 of two huge pictures, *Nero* and *Aristides* (both Jengoult Smith priv. col., on loan to Melbourne, N.G. Victoria), and his crushing debts, all contributed to his decision to commit suicide. He shot himself before cutting his throat.

By opening discussion on the role of the State in artistic patronage and education, by setting new standards of aesthetic criticism in his defence of the Elgin Marbles and by his private activities between 1816 and 1823 as a teacher in his own school of design, guiding such pupils as William

Bewick and Edwin Landseer, Haydon contributed to English cultural life in a manner as innovative as his painting was outmoded. His diary and autobiography are major documents in English Romanticism, indispensable for the study of the period. The last major English painter in the historical grand style of Reynolds, he was as much the victim of his overweening ambition and combative personality as of changing tastes, and his sense of his own genius—a Romantic concept wholly in keeping with the period—was regrettably greater than his genius itself.

WRITINGS
On the Judgement of Connoisseurs Being Preferred to that of Professional Men: The Elgin Marbles etc. (London, 1815)
Lectures on Painting and Design (London, 1844–6)
T. Taylor, ed.: *The Life of Benjamin Robert Haydon, Historical Painter, from his Autobiography and Journals*, 3 vols (London, 1853, 2/1926)
F. W. Haydon, ed.: *Correspondence and Table-talk* (London, 1876)
W. B. Pope, ed.: *The Diary of Benjamin Robert Haydon*, 5 vols (Cambridge, MA, 1960–63)

BIBLIOGRAPHY
C. Olney: *Benjamin Robert Haydon: Historical Painter* (Athens, GA, 1952)
F. Cummings: 'Nature and the Antique in B. R. Haydon's *Assassination of Dentatus*', *J. Warb. & Court. Inst.*, xxvi (1962), pp. 145–57
——: 'B. R. Haydon and his School', *J. Warb. & Court. Inst.*, xxvi (1963), pp. 370–80
——: 'Phidias in Bloomsbury: B. R. Haydon's Drawings of the Elgin Marbles', *Burl. Mag.*, cvi (1964), pp. 323–8
E. George: *The Life and Death of Benjamin Robert Haydon* (Oxford, 1967)
J. Barrell: *The Political Theory of Painting from Reynolds to Hazlitt: The Body of the Public* (New Haven, CT, 1986), pp. 308–14

DAVID BLAYNEY BROWN

Hayes. Irish family of painters. Edward Hayes (*b* Co. Tipperary, 1797; *d* Dublin, 21 May 1864), a gifted portraitist and watercolourist, rarely worked on a large scale but specialized in detailed pencil studies, attracting the patronage of Dublin's literary and professional world, for example the poet *Thomas Moore* (Dublin, N.G.). He exhibited regularly at the Royal Hibernian Academy in Dublin but did not become a full member until 1861.

Edward's son Michael Angelo Hayes (*b* Waterford, 25 July 1820; *d* Dublin, 31 Dec 1877) was well known as a painter of military subjects and horses, being particularly interested in portraying animals in motion. He lectured and published on the subject and seems to have anticipated Eadweard Muybridge in his discoveries. Michael Angelo was especially vehement in his arguments against the motif of the 'flying gallop' as represented by earlier artists. Although he painted in both oils and watercolours, his most successful works are the large-scale drawings of cavalry charges that reflect the optimism of High Victorian imperialism, and his smaller drawings illustrating the uniforms of the British Army (examples in London, N. Army Mus.). Series of the latter were published in the 1840s, while a previous publishing venture, four drawings illustrating *Car-driving in the South of Ireland*, was a great success in the 1830s. He was made an Academician of the Royal Hibernian Academy at the age of 34 and was elected secretary on two occasions. An active member, he was deeply involved in a major schism within the institution that took place in 1856–7. In 1857 he published a pamphlet on the subject, suggesting major reforms of the Academy, a proposal that eventually resulted in a new constitution in 1859.

WRITINGS

M. A. Hayes: *The Royal Hibernian Academy: A Glance at its Former Management and Recent Proceedings* (Dublin, 1857)

BIBLIOGRAPHY

Strickland
A. J. [London] (1878), p. 108
Irish Art in the 19th Century (exh. cat., ed. C. Barrett; Cork, Crawford Mun. Sch. A., 1971)
Index to British Military Costume Prints, 1500–1914 (London, 1972)
C. Barrett: 'Michael Angelo Hayes RHA and the Galloping Horse', *A. Ireland*, i (1973), pp. 42–3
A. Crookshank and the Knight of Glin: *The Painters of Ireland, c. 1660–1920* (London, 1979), pp. 182–3, 193–5

FINTAN CULLEN

Hayet, Louis (*b* Pontoise, 29 Aug 1864; *d* Cormeilles-en-Parisis, 27 Dec 1940). French painter and writer. He was largely self-taught and initially earned his living as an itinerant painter-decorator. In 1881 he met Lucien and Camille Pissarro while painting landscapes near Pontoise and through them met Paul Signac in 1885 and Seurat in 1886. After a year's military service at Versailles, Hayet moved to Paris in the autumn of 1887. There he began to apply to his paintings Eugène Chevreul's theories of colour contrast with which he had become familiar by 1881. A gifted watercolour painter, he also experimented with the ancient technique of wax encaustic, painting on a prepared cotton that allowed light to filter through. The paint surface of works such as *The Grange* (Beauchamp, France, priv. col., see 1983 Pontoise exh. cat., no. 1) retains a vivid tonal freshness, while the subject of crowds of peasants gathered before the Paris agricultural market reveals a debt to Pissarro. During the second half of the 1880s he became obsessed with the notion of *passage*—the problem of the transitional areas between an object in space and the vibrating field that surrounds it. In an attempt to work out systematically all the tonal gradations possible when one colour is juxtaposed with another, he made at least eight chromatic circles and fifteen colour charts as a guide in his painting.

Hayet's overriding concern with detail and with optical effects led him to favour a small canvas format and a characteristic small brushstroke. He showed only once with the Neo-Impressionists at the Salon des Artistes Indépendants in 1889 and on the basis of a favourable reception was asked to exhibit at the Salon des Vingt in Brussels the following year. After a series of altercations with its members in the early 1890s, Hayet withdrew from the Neo-Impressionist group. From 1894 to 1897 he showed his work eight times in the exhibitions of Impressionist and Symbolist painters at Le Barc de Boutteville, and in 1895 he visited Lucien Pissarro in London. During this period he continued to favour the encaustic medium while painting in a more conventionally Impressionist manner. From 1902 to 1904 he attempted to revive his career by staging four one-man shows in various vacant shops and restaurants, but all were commercial failures. His poverty forced him to continue working as a decorator. He spent the remaining 35 years of his life painting stage sets for the Théâtre de l'Oeuvre, writing treatises on anarchism and colour and composing his memoirs.

UNPUBLISHED SOURCES
New Haven, CT, Yale U., Beinecke Lib. [papers of Jean Sutter]

WRITINGS
Autobiographie (Paris, 1924)
Essai sur l'art (Paris, 1935)

BIBLIOGRAPHY

[Paul Signac]: 'Catalogue de l'exposition des XX, Bruxelles', *A. & Crit.* (1 Feb 1890), p. 77
F. Fagus: 'Louis Hayet', *Rev. Blanche*, xxix (1903), p. 619
C. Saunier: 'Hayet, peintre inconnu', *Beaux-Arts*, liv (1934), p. 3
R. Herbert: 'Louis Hayet', *Neo-Impressionism* (exh. cat., New York, Guggenheim, 1968), p. 61
J. Sutter: 'Louis Hayet', *The Neo-Impressionists*, ed. J. Sutter (Greenwich, 1970), pp. 107–16
S. Monneret: *L'Impressionnisme et son époque*, i (Paris, 1978), p. 271
The Aura of Neo-Impressionism: The W. J. Holliday Collection (exh. cat. by E. W. Lee and T. E. Smith, Indianapolis, Mus. A., 1983), pp. 42–3
Louis Hayet, 1864–1940 (exh. cat., Pontoise, Mus. Pissarro, 1983)
G. Dulon: *Louis Hayet* (Valhermeil, 1991)

PETER J. FLAGG

Hayez, Francesco (*b* Venice, 11 Feb 1791; *d* Milan, 12 Dec 1882). Italian painter and printmaker. Italy's greatest exponent of historical Romantic painting, he was also greatly admired for his portraits. He played an important part in the cultural life of Italy during its emergence as a modern nation state.

1. Training and early work: Venice, Rome, Naples and Padua, to 1822. 2. Mature work: Milan, 1823–48. 3. Late work, after 1848.

1. TRAINING AND EARLY WORK: VENICE, ROME, NAPLES AND PADUA, TO 1822. The son of a fisherman originally from Valenciennes, Francesco was placed at a very early age in the Venetian studio of his uncle, the antiquarian Giovanni Binasco, who hoped to train him as a restorer of paintings. In 1798 he started to study painting under Francesco Maggiotto and gained his first experience of the Neo-classical style. His artistic education was completed, in the years 1800–03, by visits to the Galleria Farsetti, Venice, where he studied the plaster casts of antique sculptures and the reproductions of paintings by Giovanni da Udine Nanni from the Vatican. In 1803 he attended life drawing classes at the old Accademia di Pittura e Scultura in the Fonteghetto della Farina, and between 1802 and 1806 he studied the use of colour in classes run by the painter from Bergamo, Lattanzio Querena (1768–1853), a skilful portraitist and a copyist of 16th-century Venetian paintings. In 1807 Hayez produced a competent *Portrait of the Artist's Family* (Treviso, Mus. Civ. Bailo). In 1808 he was finally able to enter the Venice Accademia, recently modernized in its teaching methods by Conte Leopoldo Cicognara, who was to remain an important adviser and patron for Hayez. He then attended the painting school run by the Neo-classicist Teodoro Matteini (1754–1831).

In 1809 Hayez won a scholarship to study in Rome and left Venice in October, travelling south via Rovigo, Bologna, Florence (where he met the painters Pietro Benvenuti, Giuseppe Bezzuoli and Francesco Nenci, 1781–1850) and Siena. At Rome, as well as studying the Antique, he spent a great deal of time studying the works of Raphael in the Vatican Stanze and visiting the workshop of the sculptor Antonio Canova, who was to have an enormous influence on him. Hayez was also able to meet many Italian and foreign artists in Rome, for example Tommaso Minardi,

Jean Dominique Ingres and the Lukasbrüder, a group that would always hold a particular fascination for him. In 1811 he entered a competition set by the Accademia of Naples, to which he travelled in the company of his friend the sculptor Rinaldo Rinaldi (1793–1873). Despite his failure to be accepted for the competition, he remained in Naples in order to study its antiquities and to complete drawings of its Renaissance monuments for Leopoldo Cicognara's *Storia della scultura* (3 vols, Venice, 1813–18). Returning to Rome in 1812, he sent his painting *Laokoon* (Milan, Brera) to the competition run by the Accademia di Brera, where he tied for the first prize with Antonio De Antoni (*fl* 1812). Unwilling to keep to his undertaking to enter a second time, Hayez worked, instead, on an exceptional picture, *Rinaldo and Armida* (Venice, Ca' Pesaro; see fig. 1), which he sent to Venice: it was the greatest work of his Neo-classical period. Because of this erratic behaviour, however, Canova sent Hayez away from Rome. He returned in 1815, after spending time as a Murat scholar in Naples, where he began his large historical picture *Ulysses at the Court of Alcinous* (1814–16; Naples, Capodimonte). After his return, he won first prize in the competition established by Canova at the Accademia di S Luca, with his *Triumphant Athlete* (Rome, Accad. N. S Luca), beating the entries of such other artists as Ingres. Having provided excellent proof of his skills as a fresco artist while assisting Pelagio Palagi in the decoration of the Palazzo Torlonia in Rome in 1813, he was commissioned by Canova in 1816 to paint a number of fresco lunettes in the Chiaramonti corridor in the new wing of the Vatican Museums. Hayez disappointed Canova, however, because of his constant changes of mind and slowness in completing only three lunettes celebrating the artistic policies of Pope Pius VII: *Sculpture Restored to Honour*, the *Return to Rome of her Stolen Works of Art* and the *Founding of the School of Drawing* (all *in situ*); and Hayez was accordingly relieved of his commission.

In 1817 Hayez was able to devote himself to works better suited to his abilities, such as the portrait of the *Cicognara Family* (Venice, priv. col., see 1983 exh. cat., no. 2), which brought him back to Venice. Here, and in Padua, until 1821, he was involved in providing decoration for various palazzi: these included in Venice the Palazzo Ducale and the Palazzo Gritti, and in Padua the Palazzo Zabarella. Between 1818 and 1819, while engaged on a commission to restore the paintings by Tintoretto in the Ducal Palace, he was encouraged by Canova and Cicognara to study 15th-century Venetian masters such as Giovanni Bellini and Vittore Carpaccio. This new interest was soon reflected in Hayez's own work in the painting *Pietro Rossi* (Turin, priv. col., see 1983 exh. cat., no. 34), produced between 1818 and 1820. Having failed to find a buyer in Venice, Hayez sent the picture in 1820 to the Brera exhibition in Milan, where it was received with great acclaim and acquired by Marchese Giorgio Pallavicino Trivulzio. Because of its new style and its subject, taken from medieval history, the work soon came to be seen as a manifesto for the new Romantic painting, and Hayez thus won immediate fame in Milanese artistic and literary circles. Here he met the writer Alessandro Manzoni and

1. Francesco Hayez: *Rinaldo and Armida*, oil on canvas, 1.98×2.95 m, 1814 (Venice, Ca' Pesaro)

from the latter's historical tragedy, *Il conte di Carmagnola*, he derived inspiration for a picture of this name (untraced), documented by an engraving (Milan, Bib. N. Braidense) of Giuseppe Beretta (*b* 1804). When shown at the Brera in 1821, it was admired by Stendhal, who declared Hayez to be the greatest Italian painter of the day.

2. MATURE WORK: MILAN, 1823–48. After being appointed as a temporary replacement for Luigi Sabatelli as Professor of Painting at the Accademia di Brera, Hayez moved to Milan in 1823 and embarked on a highly successful career as a history painter and portraitist, showing his works almost every year at the annual exhibitions at the Brera. His work was invariably highly praised by the Romantics and disparaged by the Classicists. This was especially the case with such masterpieces of his early years in Milan as the splendid *Last Kiss of Romeo and Juliet* (1823; Tremezzo, Villa Carlotta) and the *Penitent Magdalene* (1825; Cernobbio, priv. col., see 1983 exh. cat., no. 29). He also painted some extremely fine portraits during this period, for example those of *Carlo Della Bianca* (1822; Milan, Brera) and *Carolina Zucchi* (1825; Turin, Gal. Civ. A. Mod.), and a *Self-portrait in a Group of Friends* (1824–7; Milan, priv. col., see 1983 exh. cat., no. 177). Among his most faithful patrons were men at the forefront of the fight for Italian independence, such as Conte Francesco Teodoro Arese, who had himself painted in chains by Hayez in one of the most outstanding portraits of the 19th

century (Milan, priv. col., see 1983 exh. cat., no. 45). Exhibitions of Hayez's history paintings, in which he often portrayed contemporary Milanese personalities in the guise of figures from the past, caused a great sensation, because of the novelty of their subject-matter and because of their style. One of the most significant aspects of his art, however, was his interest in events from Italian history, which he portrayed in paintings containing clear political allusions, such as the *Lampugnani Conspiracy* (1826–9; Milan, Brera). The two paintings with perhaps the strongest political content were *Peter the Hermit Preaching the First Crusade* (Milan, priv. col., see 1983 exh. cat., no. 50) and *Refugees of Parga* (Brescia, Pin. Civ. Tosio-Martinengo), shown at the Brera in 1829 and 1831 respectively. Because of the effectiveness of their patriotic message, the themes of the Crusades and the Greek struggle for independence were repeated in other works.

During this period Hayez also painted a number of individualistic and highly evocative portraits, such as the ones depicting the ballerina Carlotta Chabert as *Venus Playing with Two Doves* (Trent, Cassa di Risparmio) and the singer *Giovanni David in Theatrical Costume* (Milan, Brera), both of which caused a great stir at the Brera Exhibition of 1830. The following year he exhibited his beautiful portrait of *Cristina Belgiojoso* (Florence, priv. col., see 1983 exh. cat., no. 140), the princess who had been exiled by the Austrians. This sumptuous likeness was

2. Francesco Hayez: *Sicilian Vespers*, oil on canvas, 2.25×3.00 m, 1844–6 (Rome, Galleria Nazionale d'Arte Moderna)

painted on panel, a technique used by Hayez for his most demanding portraits and for works in which he wanted to achieve particular effects of transparency and chromatic nuance.

Throughout this period Hayez alternated painting with printmaking, achieving brilliant results with lithography, a new means of reproduction only recently introduced to Milan. Of particular importance are the two sets of prints *Lombards in the First Crusade*, illustrating the historical poem (1827–8) by Tommaso Grossi, and a series (Milan, Bib. N. Braidense) illustrating Walter Scott's novel *Ivanhoe* (1828–31). In 1833, when his fame was at its peak, he began work on a gigantic canvas intended to be his greatest work: *Thirst Suffered by the First Crusaders beneath the Walls of Jerusalem*, inspired by a variety of historical and literary sources. In 1838, having started work on the painting, he found a patron in the person of King Charles Albert of Sardinia, who was, however, never to see its completion when it was hung (1850) in the Hall of the Bodyguards in the Royal Palace, Turin. The painting (*in situ*), which still impresses today, partly through its echoes of Verdi's melodramatic opera *I Lombardi alla prima crociata*, marked a change of direction for Hayez: from that point on he appeared more influenced by memories of the Venetian Settecento (especially the work of Piazzetta and Giambattista Tiepolo) and also by aspects of contemporary German painting. A decisive factor in this change had been a trip to Munich to see recent German painting and to meet artists such as Peter Cornelius, Julius Schnorr von Carolsfeld, Heinrich Maria von Hess and Wilhelm Kaulbach. In 1838 the Austrian Emperor Ferdinand, in Milan for his coronation, unveiled the fresco by Hayez in the Royal Palace, representing the *Allegory of the Political Order of Ferdinand I of Austria* (destr. 1943; cartoon, Milan, Brera), and admired two new paintings by Hayez at the Brera exhibition. Hayez received a commission from the Emperor, who also acquired the beautiful *Two Foscari* (Milan, priv. col., see 1983 exh. cat., no. 91; replica, Florence, Pitti), a work that was to mark the start of a series of paintings of Venetian subjects that were to bring Hayez vast popularity. Recognition of the political commitment of his work, on the other hand, came from the politician Giuseppe Mazzini, who, in an article published in 1841, hailed Hayez as a great patriotic painter. In the meantime, Hayez's painting became increasingly sophisticated and refined, both in composition and in technique. This applied not only to more intimate works such as his *Self-portrait* (1848; Milan, Brera) but also to his great historical pictures, such as his new version of *Sicilian Vespers* (Rome, G.N.A. Mod.; see fig. 2), which was commissioned by the Neapolitan Prince Ruffo di Sant'Antimo, and which was begun in Sicily in 1844 (completed 1846). One of the significant features of these works is the way in which they relate to the contemporary melodramas of Verdi, a friend of the artist, whom Hayez often advised in the staging of his operas.

3. LATE WORK, AFTER 1848. After the unrest and violence of 1848, in which Hayez took an active part, his painting underwent a radical change. He almost entirely abandoned great historical subjects and devoted himself to painting allegories with strong political connotations,

such as two versions of *Meditation* (1850; Brescia, priv. col., see 1983 exh. cat., no. 117, and 1851; Verona, Gal. Civ. A. Mod. & Contemp.). He found great popularity with a Venetian trilogy, comprising *Secret Accusation* (1848; Pavia, Pin. Malaspina), *Plotting Revenge* (1851; Milan, priv. col., see Nicodemi, 1962, pl. 150) and *Women of Venice* (1853; Milan, priv. col., see Nicodemi, 1962, pl. 162). This was also a period of exceptional portraits, revealing great psychological insight and extraordinary skills in formal arrangement, as in the record of the singer *Matilde Juva Branca* (1851; Milan, Gal. A. Mod.). Hayez had little success with works sent to the Exposition Universelle in Paris in 1855, but he was well received on his second trip to Munich in 1858. He greeted the reunification of Italy with a small painting, *Kiss* (Milan, Brera, exh. 1859), symbolic of the new historical climate and now his best-known work. Despite his advancing years, he continued painting until the end of his life, devoting himself mainly to portraits, for example those of the author and statesman *Massimo d'Azeglio* (1864), of *Camillo Benso, Conte di Cavour* (1864) and of the composer *Gioacchino Rossini* (1870; all Milan, Brera). Most of these, however, were not painted from life, but taken from photographs of the sitters. His two most exacting late works were his large historical paintings, completed in 1867 and presented to the Accademie of Milan and Venice: *Marin Faliero Led to his Death* (Milan, Brera) and *Destruction of the Temple in Jerusalem* (Venice, Ca' Pesaro). The bleakly pessimistic message of these two canvases contrasts with the mood of his last work, shown at the Mostra Nazionale in Milan in 1881, a *Vase of Flowers at the Window of the Harem* (1881; Milan, Brera), a simple and joyful homage to the art of painting. In 1869 Hayez had begun dictating his memoirs, which provide the main source of information on his life. After the great success it had enjoyed during his lifetime, his historical work was not appreciated by later critics, who much preferred his portraits, until the positive reassessment of his oeuvre as a whole during the 1970s.

WRITINGS

Le mie memorie (Milan, 1890) [app. ed. G. Carotti] ed. F. Mazzocca (Vicenza, 1995)

BIBLIOGRAPHY

C. Boito: 'L'ultimo dei pittori romantici', *Nuova Antol.*, xxx/3 (1891), pp. 60–88, 281–307

R. Calzini: 'Ritratti di Francesco Hayez', *Dedalo*, iii (1922), pp. 44–66

Dipinti di Francesco Hayez (exh. cat., ed. G. Nicodemi; Milan, Castello Sforzesco, 1934)

G. Nicodemi: *Francesco Hayez*, 2 vols (Milan, 1962)

S. Coradeschi: *L'opera completa di Francesco Hayez* (Milan, 1971)

G. Pavanello: 'Hayez frescante neoclassico', *A. Veneta*, xxxi (1977), pp. 273–83

F. Mazzocca: *Invito a Francesco Hayez* (Milan, 1982)

Hayez (exh. cat., ed. M. C. Gozzoli and F. Mazzocca; Milan, Pal. Reale and Brera, 1983)

F. Mazzocca: *Francesco Hayez: Catalogo ragionato* (Milan, 1994)

FERNANDO MAZZOCCA

Hayllar. English family of artists. James Hayllar (1829–1920) was a successful painter. His early works were portraits, but from the mid-1860s he began to paint genre pictures of children (e.g. *Ready for the Party*; see Wood, April 1974, fig. 5) that proved extremely popular. All four of his daughters were painters and exhibited regularly at the Royal Academy. They used their house, its surroundings and contents as the setting for their work. Jessica

Hayllar (1858–1940) depicted quiet scenes (e.g. *A Coming Event*, 1886; London, Forbes Mag. Col.) that chart contemporary women's life, with an element of discreet iconoclasm in their oblique references to the debate then current over women and property rights. In 1900 she was crippled in an accident and thereafter painted flowerpieces. Edith Hayllar (1860–1948) specialized in such sporting subjects as lawn tennis, boating and fishing. Her work is close to that of Jessica, but there is an almost photographic realism in her depictions of the Victorian middle class at leisure (e.g. *Summer Shower*, 1883; London, Forbes Mag. Col.). In 1900 she married and ceased to paint. Mary Hayllar (Wells) (*fl* 1880–85) exhibited flower paintings, landscapes and figurative subjects. After marriage she limited her work to miniatures of children. Kate Hayllar (*fl* 1883–1900) painted flowers and still-lifes and showed twelve paintings at the Academy between 1885 and 1898, including six watercolours illustrating literary episodes. She became a nurse *c.* 1900 and ceased to paint.

BIBLIOGRAPHY

C. Wood: 'The Artistic Family Hayllar', *Connoisseur* (April 1974), pp. 166–73; (May 1974), pp. 2–9
J. Johnson and A. Greutzner: *The Dictionary of British Artists, 1880–1940* (Woodbridge, 1976), p. 238
A. Vincent: *A Companion to Victorian and Edwardian Artists* (Newton Abbot, 1991), p. 140

Haylmann [Heilmann; Heylman], **Jacob** [Frangk, Jacoff; Jacob von Schweinfurt] (*b* ?Schweinfurt; *fl c.* 1500; *d* Annaberg, Germany, before 30 Nov 1525). German architect. Around 1500 he was working in the chief Bohemian lodge at Prague Castle under Benedikt Ried, and he may have been the Master Jacob who worked on the courtroom there in 1503. He is not, however, to be confused with the foreman of the same name who worked at St Barbara's, Kutná Hora (Ger. Kuttenberg), Bohemia (now Czech Republic), in 1512. In 1515 Haylmann took over the construction of the Annenkirche, Annaberg, which he completed in 1521–2, with superb vaulting. At the same time he was involved in designing and advising on buildings elsewhere. In 1517 he presented a drawing for the new building of the church of the Assumption at Most (Ger. Brüx), Bohemia (now Czech Republic), and in the same year assisted in rebuilding St Wenzel, Naumburg, which had been destroyed by fire. In 1521 he advised on the construction of the Marienkirche and the new market hall at Zwickau and visited the unfinished castle at Meissen, where the north-east wing with the armorial hall was completed to his designs in the following year. In 1522–3 he made a design, which was not executed, for the vault of the Marienkirche, Zwickau.

Haylmann was one of the most important of Ried's pupils and introduced Ried's stylistic language, spatial organization and technical innovations to Upper Saxony. The Renaissance forms that appear for the first time in Saxony in the sacristy portal of the Annenkirche, Annaberg, follow the model of Ried's work at Prague and are certainly the result of his influence. Haylmann's curvilinear rib vaults at Annaberg and Most represent the culmination of Late Gothic architectural development. His position of pre-eminence is particularly evident in the central part he played in the dispute of 1518–22 at the Annaberg masons'

lodge, which eventually led to the formation of an independent Upper Saxon lodge.

UNPUBLISHED SOURCES

Annaberg, Stadtarchv; Naumburg, Stadtarchv; and Dresden, Sächs. Hauptstaatsarchv [doc.]

BIBLIOGRAPHY

NDB; Thieme–Becker
K. Oberdorffer: 'Jakob Haylmann aus Schweinfurt, ein fränkischer Baumeister der Dürerzeit', *700 Jahre Stadt Schweinfurt, 1254–1954* (Würzburg, 1954), pp. 113–26
G. Fehr: *Benedikt Ried* (Munich, 1961)
H.-J. Krause: 'Das erste Auftreten italienischer Renaissance-Motive in der Architektur Mitteldeutschlands', *Acta Hist. A. Acad. Sci. Hung.*, xiii (1967), pp. 99–114
H. Mannlová: *Kostel Nanebevzetí Panny Marie v Mostě v dějinách Československé pozdní gotiky* [The church of the Assumption, Most, in the history of the Czech-Saxon Late Gothic] (Most, 1970)
K. Kratzsch: *Bergstädte des Erzgebirges: Städtebau und Kunst zur Zeit der Reformation*, Münchn. Ksthist. Abh., iv (Munich, 1972)
H. Burkhardt: 'Jacob Haylmann: Leben und Werk des bedeutenden fränkischen Baumeisters (1475–1525)', *Heimatfreund Erzgebirge*, xviii (1973), pp. 37–41
H. Magirius: 'Neue Ergebnisse zur Baugeschichte der Annenkirche in Annenberg', *Sächs. Heimatbl.*, xxi (1975), pp. 149–57; also in *100 Jahre Kunstwissenschaft in Leipzig*, Wissenschaftliche Beiträge der Karl-Marx-Universität Leipzig (Leipzig, 1975), pp. 140–46
J. Homolka and others: *Pozdně gotické umění v Čechách, 1471–1526* [Late Gothic art in Bohemia, 1471–1526] (Prague, 1978)
N. Nussbaum: *Deutsche Kirchenbaukunst der Gotik: Entwicklung und Bauformen* (Cologne, 1985)
H. Magirius: *St Annen zu Annenberg* (Munich and Zurich, 1991)

HANS-JOACHIM KRAUSE

Hayls [Hales], **John** (*fl c.* 1645; *d* London, *bur* 27 Nov 1679). English painter. Either he or his wife, Katherine, was a cousin of the miniaturist Samuel Cooper. His name also appears in a notebook, mostly written in Rome in 1651–2, of Richard Symonds, who recorded a recipe given him by Hayls to 'Grynd Vermilion'. The recipe had supposedly been acquired from 'Mierevelt who livd in Holland in Prince Hen: time', but it is doubtful whether Hayls met Mierevelt or visited Italy.

Some portraits from the Civil War and Commonwealth periods can be attributed to Hayls on stylistic grounds, partly confirmed by inventories and inscriptions. Versions of his *Colonel John Russell* (Woburn Abbey, Beds, Marquess of Tavistock Col., and Warwick Castle, Warwicks), dating from *c.* 1645, distantly echo van Dyck's manner but are crudely handled. Somewhat later portraits of *c.* 1663–5, such as *Charles Bertie* and *Bridget Noel* (ex-Uffington House, Lincs), are more sensitive and individual, while a drawing of *Thomas Flatman* (Antony House, Cornwall, NT), engraved by William Faithorne, is reasonably accomplished.

Hayls is best known through the many references to him in Samuel Pepys's diary. Pepys commissioned his wife's portrait (as St Catherine) in February 1666 (presumed destr.; engraving by James Thomson, 1825, in Cambridge, Magdalene Coll.). Initially 'mighty pleased' with the result, he ordered his own portrait and described the sittings, commencing on 17 March 1666, in detail. The result (London, N.P.G.; *see* PORTRAITURE, fig. 11), which at £14 was, like its companion, relatively expensive, became an enduring image of the diarist in spite of the coarseness of Hayls's technique.

Pepys's entries suggested a figure of some affluence. In 1668 Hayls moved from Southampton Street to Long

Acre. He was one of three painters approached by the City Aldermen to paint the series of *Justices* for the Guildhall but lost the commission to John Michael Wright. His end was sudden as 'comeing from the necessary house, he dropt down dead in the Garden. being drest in a velvet suit to go to a Ld Mayors feast'.

UNPUBLISHED SOURCES

London, BM, MS. Egerton 1636, ff. 31, 39 [Richard Symonds's notebook]

BIBLIOGRAPHY

B. Buckeridge: 'An Essay towards an English School of Painters', *Abrégé de la vie des peintres, avec des réflexions sur leurs ouvrages*, by R. de Piles; Eng trans. by J. Savage as *The Art of Painting*, 3rd edn (London, 1750), pp. 382–3
G. Vertue: 'Note Books', iii, *Walpole Soc.*, xxii (1935), pp. 121–39
E. Croft-Murray and P. Hulton: *British Museum Catalogue of British Drawings*, i (London, 1960), pp. 343–5
S. Pepys: *Diary*, ed. R. C. Latham and W. Matthews (London, 1970–83)
E. K. Waterhouse: *Painting in Britain, 1530 to 1790* (Harmondsworth, 1953, 4/1978), pp. 100–01
M. Edmond: 'Limners and Picturemakers', *Walpole Soc.*, xlvii (1978–80), pp. 60–242

RICHARD JEFFREE

Hayman, Francis (*b* ?Exeter, ?1708; *d* London, 3 Feb 1776). English painter and illustrator. He was in London at the age of 10, and from 1718 until *c.* 1725 he was apprenticed to Robert Brown (*d* 1753), a decorative painter. From 1732 Hayman was employed as a scene painter at Goodman's Fields Theatre, where he painted allegorical works such as *The King Attended by Peace, with Liberty and Justice Trampling on Tyranny and Oppression* on the pit ceiling (destr.). He moved to Drury Lane Theatre in 1736, shortly before the Licensing Act closed Goodman's Fields. At Drury Lane he painted scenery for Thomas Arne's masque *The Fall of Phaeton* (1736) and was praised for his naturalistic landscapes. From the late 1730s he began accepting commissions for portraits and conversation pieces. His success in the field of portraiture rested on the dearth of good portrait painters in England at the time and his exploitation of a growing middle-class clientele. Hayman painted portraits of doctors, literary men and actors. These range from distinguished single figures such as *Dr Charles Chauncey* (1747; New Haven, CT, Yale Cent. Brit. A.) to informal groups such as *Samuel Richardson and his Family* (*c.* 1740–41; priv. col., see 1987 exh. cat., fig. 11), while *David Garrick and Mrs Pritchard in 'The Suspicious Husband'* (*c.* 1747; version, New Haven, CT, Yale Cent. Brit. A.) is one of the earliest examples of the theatrical conversation piece in England. For all his success, Hayman's portraits are often stolid and uninspired, relying on repetitious facial formulae and only occasionally exhibiting a refreshing informality.

Hayman's first major decorative commission came from his patron, the entrepreneur Jonathan Tyers (*d* 1767), and consisted of large paintings for the supper-boxes at Vauxhall Gardens (*see* LONDON, §V, 6). These paintings, executed *c.* 1741–2 and influenced by the French Rococo style, depict children's games such as *See-saw*, rural festivals such as *May Day, or the Milkmaid's Garland* (both London, V&A) and scenes from plays. Those from *King Lear*, *Hamlet*, *Henry V* and *The Tempest* were among the earliest representations in painting of incidents taken from Shakespeare.

Hayman's depictions from literary texts extended to book illustration as well, including designs for the works of William Congreve (*c.* 1752) and the sixth edition (1742) of Richardson's *Pamela*. He worked with Gravelot to produce designs for Thomas Hanmer's edition of Shakespeare (1743–4), for which he was advised by Garrick on appropriate gesture and expression. In 1770 he produced designs for Charles Jennens's unfinished edition of Shakespeare, in which he employed some of Garrick's earlier suggestions.

For most of his career, Hayman was involved in the promotion of British history painting, both through his own work and in his campaign for a public art academy (*see* LONDON, §VI). He was friendly with William Hogarth, who shared these views, and was a member of the St Martin's Lane Academy from *c.* 1745, acting as one of its directors from 1749. He accompanied Hogarth on a trip to France in 1748, and they collaborated on the decoration of the Foundling Hospital, London, with Hayman contributing the *Finding of Moses* (1746; *in situ*). His reputation as a history painter led to a number of decorative commissions. In 1743 he painted *Fame Crowning Science* on the domed ceiling of the stairwell at Dr Cox Macro's Little Haugh Hall at Norton, near Bury St Edmunds, Suffolk, and *c.* 1752 he completed an altarpiece depicting the *Good Samaritan* (New Haven, CT, Yale Cent. Brit. A.) for a private chapel near Doncaster, S. Yorks. His status diminished after 1755 with the arrival in England of Giovanni Battista Cipriani, a Neo-classical painter, but Hayman continued to receive commissions. Significant among these were the four large paintings of scenes from the recently ended Seven Years War (1761–4; all untraced), made for the Saloon at Vauxhall. Using allegory to augment the representation of contemporary events, they presaged Benjamin West's more radical *Death of General Wolfe* (1776; Ottawa, N.G.).

In 1755 Hayman was elected chairman of a 'Committee for Founding a Public Academy'. He was also instrumental in the foundation of the Society of Artists, the first formal exhibiting society in England; he was its chairman (1765–8) and exhibited there from 1760 to 1768. When the Royal Academy of Arts was established in 1768 he was one of the founder-members, and he exhibited religious and literary works there between 1769 and 1772. Increasing ill-health made painting more difficult, but, as compensation, in 1770 the Academy appointed him to the largely honorary post of librarian. Hayman's pupils included Thomas Gainsborough, although the exact nature of their relationship is uncertain. Hayman's collection of prints and drawings was sold at Langford's in London on 15 June 1776.

BIBLIOGRAPHY

L. Gowing: 'Hogarth, Hayman and the Vauxhall Decorations', *Burl. Mag.*, xcv (1953), pp. 4–19
Paintings, Drawings and Prints by Francis Hayman, RA (exh. cat., London, Kenwood House, 1960)
B. Allen: 'Jonathan Tyers's Other Garden', *J. Gdn Hist.*, i (1981), pp. 215–38
——: 'Joseph Wilton, Francis Hayman and the Chimneypieces from Northumberland House', *Burl. Mag.*, cxxv (1983), pp. 195–202
——: *Francis Hayman and the English Rococo* (diss., U. London, Courtauld Inst., 1984)

Francis Hayman (exh. cat. by B. Allen, New Haven, CT, Yale Cent. Brit. A.; London, Kenwood House; 1987) [full account of life and work]

SHEARER WEST

Hayq. *See* ARMENIA.

Hayreddin [Ḥayr al-Dīn; Hayrettin] (*d* Istanbul, 1512). Ottoman architect. His father, Ustad Murad, is said to have been an architect, and Hayreddin became royal architect at the Ottoman court. He designed complexes for Bayezid II (*reg* 1481–1512) in Amasya (1486) and EDIRNE (1488) and was probably responsible for Bayezid's complex in Istanbul (1506). He is also said to have founded the Mimar Hayreddin Mosque at Çarşıkapı in Istanbul (*c.* 1488; rest. 1898). Ottoman historical accounts credit Hayreddin with the construction of the mosque and *khānaqāh* of Emir Buhari in Bursu, a pair of mosques in Galata and stone bridges in Edirne, Osmancık, Geyve and Saruhan. He is credited with repairing the walls of Istanbul and the fortresses of Rumeli Hisar and Anadolu Hisar. Popularly considered the founder of the classical style of Ottoman architecture (*see* ISLAMIC ART, §II, 7(i)(b)), Hayreddin was an inventive and successful architect. He tried to give unity to the complex at Amasya through the plan, which includes two large domes in succession flanked by three smaller domes, and his plan for the complex at Edirne was so successful that it was repeated by his successor ALI ACEMI in the mosque for Selim I (1523) in Istanbul.

BIBLIOGRAPHY

Enc. Islam/2: 'Khayr al-Dīn'
L. A. Mayer: *Islamic Architects and their Works* (Geneva, 1956), pp. 81–2
R. M. Meric: 'Bayezid camii mimari' [The architect of the Bayezid mosque], *Ankara Ü. Ilahiyat Fak. Yıllık Araştırmalar Derg.*, ii (1958), pp. 4–77
——: 'L'Architecte de la mosquée Bayezit d'Istanbul', *Communications of the First International Congress of Turkish Art: Ankara, 1961*, pp. 262–5
G. Goodwin: *A History of Ottoman Architecture* (Baltimore, 1971), pp. 143–56

HOWARD CRANE

Hayter, Sir **George** (*b* St James's, London, 17 Dec 1792; *d* St Marylebone, London, 18 Jan 1871). English painter and printmaker. He was the son of Charles Hayter (1761–1835), miniature painter, author of manuals for art instruction and Professor of Perspective and Drawing to Princess Charlotte. In 1808 George entered the Royal Academy Schools, and in 1815 was appointed Painter of Miniatures and Portraits by Princess Charlotte. Hayter was awarded the British Institution's premium for history painting for the *Prophet Ezra* (1815; Downton Castle, Heref. & Worcs), purchased by Richard Payne Knight. Encouraged by his patron, John Russell, 6th Duke of Bedford, he travelled to Italy to study in 1816, gaining election as an honorary member of the Accademia di S Luca in Florence. Returning to London in 1818, Hayter practised as a portrait painter in oils and history painter and occasionally acted as an art dealer. Dubbed 'The Phoenix' by William Beckford, Hayter showed a pomposity that irritated his fellow artists, but he mixed freely with many aristocratic families. His unconventional domestic life (separated from his wife, he lived openly with his mistress) set him apart from official Academy circles: he was never elected to the Royal Academy.

Hayter was most productive and innovative during the 1820s. George Agar-Ellis (later Lord Dover) commissioned the *Trial of Queen Caroline in the House of Lords in 1820* (exh. 1823; London, N.P.G.); painted on a large scale (2.33×2.66 m), Hayter's first (and most successful) contemporary history painting revealed a taste for high drama effectively realized. In the *Trial of William, Lord Russell, in the Old Bailey in 1683* (1825; Woburn Abbey, Beds) Hayter celebrated John Russell's ancestry, in a work reminiscent of fashionable *tableaux vivants* of the country-house set.

In 1826 Hayter settled in Italy. The *Banditti of Kurdistan Assisting Georgians in Carrying off Circassian Women* (untraced), completed in Florence for John Proby, 1st Earl Carysfort, demonstrated Hayter's assimilation of the style and exotic subject-matter of contemporary French Romantic art. He was forced by the scandal of his mistress's accidental death in 1827 to move from Florence to Rome, and by late 1828 he was in Paris, where his portraits of English society members (some exhibited at the Salon in 1831) were stylistically akin to the work of recent French portrait painters such as François Gérard.

In 1831 Hayter returned to England. His grandiose plan to paint the first sitting after the passage of the Reform Bill resulted in *Moving the Address to the Crown on the Opening of the First Reformed Parliament in the Old House of Commons, 5 February 1833* (1833–43; London, N.P.G.), for which he executed nearly 400 portrait studies in oil. Having painted the young Princess Victoria (1832–3; destr.; oil sketch, Brit. Royal Col.), Hayter was not a surprising choice as the new Queen's Portrait and Historical Painter, but some Academicians were angered. In 1841 he became Principal Painter-in-Ordinary, and in 1842 he was knighted. Hayter painted several royal ceremonies, such as Queen Victoria's coronation of 1837 and marriage of 1840 (both Brit. Royal Col.), the latter being the only one actually commissioned by the Queen. He also painted royal portraits, but because Albert, the Prince Consort, preferred other painters such as F. X. Winterhalter, Hayter was eased out of royal circles.

By the 1840s Hayter's portrait style was considered old-fashioned. He adjusted his type of history painting to suit the more literal taste of the early Victorian era (e.g. *Wellington Viewing Napoleon's Effigy at Madame Tussaud's*; destr. 1925; engraving, 1854). He also produced fluent landscape watercolours (many of Italian views), etchings (he published a volume in 1833), decorative designs and sculpture. The contents of Hayter's studio were auctioned at Christie's, London, on 19 April 1871. His younger brother, John (1800–95), was also an artist, known chiefly as a portrait draughtsman in chalks and crayons.

BIBLIOGRAPHY

R. Ormond: *Early Victorian Portraits*, 2 vols, London N.P.G. cat. (London, 1973)
Drawings by Sir George and John Hayter (exh. cat. by B. Coffey [Bryant], London, Morton Morris, 1982) [incl. checklist of prints]
R. Walker: *Regency Portraits*, 2 vols, London N.P.G. cat. (London, 1986)
O. Millar: *The Victorian Pictures in the Collection of Her Majesty the Queen*, 2 vols (Cambridge, 1992)
B. Bryant: 'Sir George Hayter's Drawings at Duncombe Park: Family Ties and a "Melancholy Event"', *Apollo*, cxxxv (1992), pp. 240–50 [incl. newly pubd letter of 1827]

BARBARA BRYANT

Hayter, S(tanley) W(illiam) (*b* London, 27 Dec 1901; *d* Paris, 4 May 1988). English printmaker, draughtsman and painter, active in France and the USA. He came from a family of painters, including GEORGE HAYTER, but started his career by studying chemistry and geology at King's College, London (1917–21). After graduating he worked in the Persian Gulf for several years for the Anglo-Iranian Oil Company. In 1926 he settled in Paris, where he enrolled at the Académie Julian and studied burin engraving privately with the Polish artist Joseph Hecht (1891–1951), who also taught Anthony Gross. Hayter began to take his own pupils in 1927 and in 1933 named his workshop Atelier 17, after the street number of his studio in the Rue Campagne-Première. The hallmark of the workshop was its egalitarian structure, breaking sharply with the traditional French engraving studios by insisting on a cooperative approach to labour and technical discoveries. In 1929 Hayter was introduced to SURREALISM by Yves Tanguy and André Masson, who with other Surrealists worked with Hayter at Atelier 17. The often violent imagery of Hayter's Surrealist period was stimulated in part by his passionate response to the Spanish Civil War (e.g. *Combat*, 1936; New York, Brooklyn Mus.; *see* EN-GRAVING, fig. 9) and to the rise of Fascism. He organized portfolios of prints to raise funds for the Spanish cause, including *Solidarité* (Paris, 1938), a portfolio of seven prints, one of them by Picasso. Hayter exhibited frequently with the Surrealists during the 1930s, with works such as *Rape of Lucretia* (1934; see Black and Moorhead, no. 86), but left the movement when Paul Eluard was expelled. Eluard's poem *Facile Proie* (1939) was written in response to a set of Hayter's engravings. Other writers with whom Hayter collaborated in this way included Samuel Beckett and Georges Hugnet.

Hayter joined the exile of the Parisian avant-garde in 1939, moving with his second wife, the American sculptor Helen Phillips (*b* 1913), to New York. He ran a course entitled 'Atelier 17' at the New School for Social Research until 1945, when he opened the workshop independently in Greenwich Village, at 41 East 8th Street. Important figures in the emerging New York School associated with Hayter included Jackson Pollock, Robert Motherwell, Willem de Kooning, Mark Rothko, William Baziotes and David Smith. Critics considered Hayter himself to be a member of the new school. His theoretical writings on automatism and the expressive abstraction of his own work were a formative influence on Pollock and others. The touring exhibition *Hayter and Studio 17*, organized in 1944 by MOMA, New York, attracted more students to Atelier 17, including many artists who later ran printmaking departments in the expanded post-war American universities. Hayter's first book, *New Ways of Gravure* (1949), became an indispensable text for printmakers.

In the 1930s Hayter had concentrated his technical experimentation on adapting the traditional black-and-white techniques of etching and engraving to the aesthetic concerns of modern art, for example the collage potential of soft-ground etching. From the 1940s his primary technical preoccupation was with colour printing. In San Francisco, where he taught a summer course in 1940, he made his first screenprint, *Maternity* (1940; see Black and Moorhead, no. 132), and later used screens to apply inks

to the etching plate, enabling him to print in various colours simultaneously. *Cinq Personnages* (1946; see Black and Moorhead, no. 168) is credited as the first print in the history of the medium where this is achieved. In the 1950s, when he reopened the workshop in Paris at 278 Rue Vaugiraud, Hayter explored an entirely different method of colour etching, in which inks of contrasting viscosities were applied with rollers to a plate etched to different levels. This technique suited the increasingly Tachist look of his prints, in which he explored chance effects and his fascination with waves. From the 1970s Hayter reintroduced figurative elements in combination with a vibrant (often fluorescent) palette and lyrical freedom of brush-stroke or burin line in some of his most fluent and imaginative works.

WRITINGS

New Ways of Gravure (London and New York, 1949, 2/1966, rev. New York, 1981)
About Prints (London, 1962)

BIBLIOGRAPHY

'Hayter and Studio 17', *MOMA Bull.*, xii/1 (Aug 1944) [issue dedicated to Hayter]
G. Limbour: *Hayter* (Paris, 1962)
G. Reynolds: *The Engravings of S. W. Hayter* (London, 1967)
S. W. Hayter and Atelier 17 (exh. cat. by J. Moser, Madison, U. WI, Elvehjem A. Cent., 1977)
S. W. Hayter, Symphonic Poem of Lines (exh. cat., Kobe, Gallery Santica, 1985)
P. M. S. Hacker, ed.: *The Renaissance of Gravure: The Art of S. W. Hayter* (Oxford, 1988)
C. Esposito: *Hayter e l'atelier 17* (Rome, 1990)
P. Black and D. Moorhead: *The Prints of S. W. Hayter: A Complete Catalogue* (London, 1993)

DAVID COHEN

Haytley, Edward (*b* ?nr Preston, Lancs; *fl* 1740–61). English painter. He was first recorded working as a flower painter *c.* 1740. In London he began painting portraits in the manner of Arthur Devis and produced some life-size works; however, his skill proved to be for carefully observed topographical landscapes. In 1743 he began preparatory drawings for two outdoor conversation pieces for the Brockman family of Beachborough Manor, Kent, which resulted in the *Temple Pond Looking towards the Rotunda* and the *Temple Pond from the Rotunda* (both 1744–6; Melbourne, N.G. Victoria); these companion pieces show the Brockman family relaxing in their ornamental garden, whose design is enhanced by the landscape surroundings and more distant rolling hills. He was also employed by the family for miscellaneous tasks such as picture mending.

Haytley further developed his skill at the conversation piece in his portrait of the *Montagu Family* (1744; priv. col., see Devapriam, pl. III); beyond the family group is a georgic landscape of woods and fields in which a number of haymakers are unstrenuously employed. His portrait of *Sir Roger and Lady Bradshaigh* (1746; sold London, Sotheby's, Nov 1980, see Devapriam, fig. 1) shows the couple on the garden terrace of their Lancashire estate, Haigh Hall, with its house in the background. Here the figures are more prominent, but Haytley's rigid linear perspective—resulting in a distortion of the figures in relationship to the landscape background—created an unusual dissonance in his work. A small telescope next to his sitters appears in this and the above-mentioned conversation pieces; this device, possibly intended to direct interest towards the painted view, became something of a hallmark for Haytley. Around 1747 he contributed two topographical roundels to the Foundling Hospital: *Chelsea Hospital* and *Bethlem Hospital* (London, Foundling Hosp.); he exhibited at the Society of Artists in 1760 and 1761.

BIBLIOGRAPHY
The Montagu Family at Sandleford Priory by Edward Haytley (exh. cat., London, Leger Gals, 1978)
J. Harris: *The Artist and the Country House* (London, 1979), pp. 163, 165, 220–21
E. Devapriam: 'Two Conversation Pieces by Edward Haytley', *Apollo*, cxiv (1981), pp. 85–7
Manners and Morals: Hogarth and British Painting, 1700–1760 (exh. cat. by E. Einberg, London, Tate, 1987)

SHEARER WEST

Hayyim, Joseph ibn. *See* JOSEPH IBN HAYYIM.

Hayz el-. *See under* BAHARIYA OASIS.

Hazlitt, William (*b* Maidstone, Kent, 10 April 1778; *d* London, 18 Sept 1830). English critic and painter. He was the second son of William Hazlitt, a Unitarian minister; his elder brother, John Hazlitt (1767–1837), became a successful miniature painter. In 1793 he was sent to Hackney Theological College in London to study for the ministry, but, racked by doubt, he abandoned his studies and returned to his father's parish in Wem, Salop. There he met in 1798 the poet Samuel Taylor Coleridge, then a Unitarian preacher, and later that year stayed with him at Nether Stowey, Somerset. Being desperate for employment, he decided to become a painter like his brother, whom he joined in London in 1799 and from whom he probably received training. In the spring of 1799 Hazlitt saw an exhibition at the Lyceum of Italian Old Master paintings—from the collection of Philippe II, Duke of Orleans, sold by his great-grandson Louis Philippe II (1747–93), Duke of Orleans, in 1792—that were offered for sale by an English syndicate. This first exposure to great paintings was a revelation that inspired him to visit the great private collections in England. It was reinforced in the autumn of 1802, when he visited Paris to copy in the Louvre and was overwhelmed by the paintings and antiquities there, looted from Italy by Napoleon. In the same year he first exhibited at the Royal Academy with a portrait of his father, followed in 1805 by his only other exhibit, a *Portrait of a Gentleman* (both untraced).

On his return from Paris, Hazlitt practised as an itinerant portrait painter and in 1803 travelled to the Lake District to paint the families of his friends Coleridge and Wordsworth. The painting went badly; Hazlitt destroyed his portrait of *Wordsworth*, and those he completed were poor (extant pictures all Maidstone, Mus. & A.G.). In 1804, having completed his portrait of his friend *Charles Lamb* (London, N.P.G.), he abandoned painting and determined to become a writer.

After several false starts, Hazlitt found his métier as a journalist in 1812. He was a prolific writer and for the rest of his life contributed articles to most of the leading newspapers and journals; although he is best known for his writings on literature, he also wrote on drama, politics and art. His first art criticism, on Benjamin Robert Haydon's *Judgement of Solomon* (1812–14; J. B. Gold priv. col.), appeared in the *Morning Chronicle* in May 1814. The two men had an uneasy friendship, based on admiration for Napoleon and loathing for the Royal Academy, but undermined by the fecklessness, belligerence and arrogance of each; Hazlitt's criticism was, however, tempered by an awareness of Haydon's extreme sensitivity. His strength as a critic lay, primarily, in empathy; he evoked paintings that many of his readers would never see by description, literary analogy and, above all, by describing his own feelings. He also had an undoubted eye for quality. His choice of heroes, Titian, Raphael, Correggio and Rubens, was not particularly original, but he easily distinguished between great art and professional art, noting, for example, that the difference between van Dyck and later English portrait painters, from Lely to Reynolds, was not one of style, but of genius. The quality he most admired is 'gusto', used to describe the power and passion that great art should convey. This led him on the whole to prefer painterly to linear art and made him unresponsive to Neo-classicism in general and French Neo-classical painters in particular. He was largely dismissive of the English school, with the exception of Hogarth and Richard Wilson, and many painters considered him spiteful, including Haydon who wrote in his autobiography: 'mortified by his own failure, he resolved, as he had not succeeded no one else should'.

Hazlitt was a fierce critic of the Royal Academy, most notably in *The Catalogue Raisonné of the British Institution*, printed in *The Examiner* in 1816: 'The English are a shop keeping nation, and the Royal Academy are a society of hucksters in the Fine Arts'. Reynolds was a regular target; the theory on which Hazlitt purported to base his criticism was intended to rebut the concept of the Ideal, proposed by Reynolds in his *Discourses*. Hazlitt insisted that 'Art is (first and last) the imitation of Nature' and that 'The highest Art is the imitation of the highest Nature'. Naturalism is the sole foundation of his aesthetic theory, most completely expressed in his essay on 'The Fine Arts', contributed to the 7th edition (1824) of the *Encyclopaedia Britannica*. His personal reaction to paintings, however, seldom depended on his theoretical armature.

Some of Hazlitt's articles on art were collected in *Sketches of the Principal Picture-Galleries in England* (1824) and *Notes of a Journey through France and Italy* (1826), the latter being compiled from articles written for *The Chronicle* during a Continental tour in 1824. He published the first of his *Conversations of James Northcote* in 1826, in the *New Monthly* magazine; these are lively, diverting pieces, thought at the time to be extremely scurrilous. Northcote, a famed gossip, feigned disapproval after four issues, but a further eighteen articles appeared, and Northcote's *Life of Titian* (1830) was largely ghost-written by Hazlitt. Although his reputation rests on his literary criticism, Hazlitt was the first English art critic in a journalistic sense. He assumed a layman's point of view in a non-didactic manner for a wide audience.

WRITINGS
Sketches of the Principal Picture-Galleries in England (London, 1824)
Notes of a Journey through France and Italy (London, 1826)

Conversations of James Northcote esq. R.A. (London, 1830), rev. ed. F. Swinnerton (London, 1949)

H. M. Sikes, ed.: *The Letters of William Hazlitt* (London, 1979)

BIBLIOGRAPHY

W. C. Hazlitt: *Memoirs of William Hazlitt* (London, 1867)

E. Gosse: *Conversations with James Northcote R.A., with an Essay on Hazlitt as an Art Critic by Edmund Gosse* (London, 1894)

H. Baker: *William Hazlitt* (London, 1962)

William Hazlitt, 1778–1830 (exh. cat., London, BL, 1978)

S. Jones: *Hazlitt: A Life* (London, 1989)

DAVID RODGERS

Hazor [now Tell el-Qedeh; Tell Waqqas]. Major Canaanite and Israelite city of the 2nd and 1st millennia BC, situated *c.* 14 km north of the Sea of Galilee and *c.* 8 km south-west of Lake Huleh. The site comprises a mound (the Upper City), which rises about 40 m above plain level and covers an area of *c.* 6 ha at its summit, and, to the north, a large rectangular enclosure (the Lower City) *c.* 1000×700 m. This enclosure is protected to the west by a massive earthen rampart and a deep fosse, to the north by a similar rampart but without a fosse, and to the east by the steep slope reinforced by a glacis. The enclosure is separated from the mound on the south side by a deep ditch. The first trial soundings were conducted in 1928 by J. Garstang, but the results were not fully published. Extensive excavations were undertaken between 1955 and 1958 and in 1968 by Y. Yadin. Finds are in the Israel Museum in Jerusalem.

1. LOWER CITY. Excavations in areas C, D, E, '210', F, H, K and P produced a sequence of five occupation phases. The earliest, stratum 4, is of the Middle Bronze Age (18th century BC), and earthen ramparts enclosed the settlement. In area K a gateway flanked by two towers was built of mud-brick on stone foundations, and a number of rich tombs were excavated. In area F rock-hewn tombs, each consisting of a deep rectangular shaft giving access to a number of chambers, were connected by a network of tunnels.

In stratum 3 (17th–16th centuries BC) many infant jar burials were found beneath the floors of the houses in area C. In area F the remains of a large rectangular double temple were found, connected by a series of channels with the earlier tombs to form a drainage complex. Another temple in area H consisted of a wide room with a niche on the north side, and two columns in the centre to support the roof. The area in front of the temple was paved with a fine pebble floor. The gateway was three-piered with two large flanking towers, and in front of it a large, heavily revetted platform provided access for chariots. The city wall was of casemate construction. Stratum 3 was destroyed by fire.

Stratum 2 dates to the Late Bronze Age (16th–15th centuries BC). A gateway of almost identical design but built of large, well-dressed stones replaced the earlier one. The temple in area F was square and similar to that at Amman in Jordan. In area H the temple was identical to that of the previous stratum. A number of small platforms were found in the courtyard, including a rectangular altar (*bamah*), to the east of which, among a huge pile of cult objects and vessels, were fragments of a clay liver model used in divination.

Stratum 1B was contemporary with the Amarna age in Egypt (14th century BC). The earlier casemate wall was replaced by a solid brick wall some 3 m thick. The gateway was similar to that of the previous stratum, but the passageway was built of large cobblestones, and in the southern part there were workshops in which cult objects were discovered. Several important temples were constructed. A small temple (the Stelae Temple) in area C, on the inner slope of the rampart, was rectangular and contained small stelae, a lion orthostat and a statue (see fig.). The surrounding buildings were probably service workshops or stores. In area F a large altar built of ashlar blocks was associated with an important collection of cult vessels. The most impressive temple, found in area H, was of tripartite plan, on a long axis running north–south, and is similar to the description of Solomon's temple in

Hazor, sculpture from the Stelae Temple, basalt, max. h. 650 mm, 14th–13th centuries BC (Jerusalem, Israel Museum)

Jerusalem (I Kings 6). The lower parts of the walls of the holy of holies and the porch were lined with large, well-dressed basalt orthostats. A huge lion orthostat was probably one of a pair that originally flanked the entrance.

In stratum 1A (13th century BC) the buildings were generally constructed on the same plan as those of 1B but were not as well built or finished. The Stelae Temple in area C was reconstructed, and all its components were replaced in their original positions. Only a few additions and changes were made to the tripartite temple in area H: a rich find of cult vessels and objects in the holy of holies included a basalt incense altar engraved with a circle and cross, and a small basalt statue of a seated man. Stratum 1A was destroyed in the second half of the 13th century BC, probably by the Israelites, and the Lower City was abandoned.

2. UPPER CITY. Five areas were investigated on the tell itself (A, AB, B, G and C), with twenty-one occupation levels. The scant architectural remains in the lowest levels (strata XXI–XVIII) belong to the Early Bronze Age. Strata XVII–XVI correspond to strata 4 and 3 in the Lower City and belong to the Middle Bronze Age (18th–16th centuries BC); part of the city's fortification wall and a large rounded corner bastion were excavated in area G. A large building, possibly a palace, was discovered in area A and, adjacent to it, a rectangular temple with orthostat entrance. Both survived with modifications and rebuilding in strata XV and XIV (corresponding to strata 2 and 1B in the Lower City) but were extensively dismantled by the later settlers. The palace in stratum XIV had courtyards and squares paved with pebbles, and near by a large rain-fed reservoir was excavated. In stratum XIII, the final Late Bronze Age level, few new buildings were erected, those of the previous stratum being reconstructed and repaired. A small cult installation with stelae was, however, built to replace the now derelict orthostat temple in area A. Like stratum 1A in the Lower City, it was destroyed in the second half of the 13th century BC.

After a gap the site was again occupied, now by the Israelites. Strata XII and XI (12th–11th centuries BC) were marked by the absence of substantial architecture, though foundations for huts and tents, hearths and silos were found in both areas A and B. The settlement was unfortified. The remains of a ritual centre (high place) associated with cult vessels was found in stratum XI in area B. Among the finds was a statuette of a deity. During the 10th century BC (stratum X), Solomon established Hazor as a major Israelite city. Area A produced the remains of a casemate defensive wall together with a large gateway with six chambers, three on each side, and two towers flanking the passageway (see MILITARY ARCHITECTURE AND FORTIFICATION, fig. 3). Similar gates and walls at Gezer and Megiddo suggest the employment of a single 'royal' architect. Remains of the casemate wall were also encountered in area B where, on the west side, it had been expanded to form a citadel. Stratum IX (late 10th–early 9th centuries BC) shows a decline in the quality of building and appears to have been destroyed by fire.

Stratum VIII, assigned to the biblical dynasty of Omri (9th century BC), revealed evidence for extensive building activity. In area A a large storehouse was found with two rows of pillars along its centre. Area B produced what were probably the cellars of a massive rectangular citadel, with walls nearly 2 m thick, consisting of two halls running from west to east, surrounded by a series of rooms on three sides; the upper storeys, presumably brick-built, have not survived. Between the citadel and adjacent service buildings was found a monumental entrance way adorned with proto-Aeolic capitals and a monolithic lintel, both reused in later periods. The city wall, of which the citadel was an integral part, was otherwise the casemate wall of the previous strata rendered solid by a filling of stones and earth. The defences were extended to include area G on the northern edge of the eastern terrace of the mound, forming an outer citadel to protect the terrace and the approach to the south gate. A huge silo was dug into the centre of the terrace, and a postern gate gave access from the outer citadel to fields to the north. The underground water system discovered in area L, near the natural spring on the south edge of the mound, is also assigned to stratum VIII. This consisted of an entrance structure, a vertical shaft and a long sloping tunnel leading to a pool. The upper part of the shaft was cut through the mound, while the lower part was quarried out of the rock.

Stratum VII (9th century BC) represents a reconstruction of stratum VIII with a few changes and modifications, but it was destroyed. In stratum VI (8th century BC), while the citadel in area B continued in use, area A became a residential quarter with workshops and stores. Stratum VI was also destroyed, probably in the earthquake that struck Israel in the reign of Jeroboam II (reg c. 786–746 BC). Stratum V, also assigned to the 8th century BC, saw the reconstruction of the buildings of the previous phase in area A. In area B, however, the citadel was strengthened by an additional inset-offset wall on the west, north and south, and at the north-west corner a tower was built to command the northern approach to the city. Despite these measures, dense layers of ashes indicate that the city of stratum V was destroyed in a conflagration, which may be attributed to the conquests of Tiglath-Pileser III of Assyria in 732 BC. Stratum IV, a temporary unfortified settlement (late 8th century BC), is attributed to the return of Israelites following the destruction.

Stratum III consisted of the remains of a large citadel built by the Assyrians in the 7th century BC above the citadel of stratum V in area B, presumably as a fort to serve the military administration. It consisted of an inner courtyard surrounded by rooms on all four sides. On the east side there was another large courtyard enclosed by a wall. More extensive settlement returned in stratum II, which is ascribed to the Persian period (4th century BC). In area B the citadel continued in use but with considerable modifications. The excavated part of area G was covered with buildings: some of the larger examples used Bronze Age orthostats as bases for wooden columns. Most of area A appears to have been a cemetery. During the Hellenistic period (stratum I) Hazor again seems to have been no more than a military outpost with occupation confined to area B, where another citadel was built over the levelled remains of stratum II; it was not possible to distinguish the plan.

BIBLIOGRAPHY

J. Garstang: *Joshua–Judges* (London, 1931)
Y. Yadin and others: *Hazor*, 4 vols (Jerusalem, 1958–61)
Y. Yadin: *Hazor*, The Schweich Lectures of the British Academy, 1970 (London, 1972)
——: *Hazor: The Rediscovery of a Great Citadel of the Bible* (London, 1975)

JOHNATHAN N. TUBB

Hazzidakis, Joseph (*b* Melos; *d* 16 Feb 1936). Greek archaeologist. Hazzidakis was a doctor by training, but his enthusiasm for the archaeological heritage of Crete led to his foundation in 1878 of the Herakleion Society for the Promotion of Learning. He became President of the Society (or 'Syllogos') in 1883 and thereafter devoted his time to one of its particular aims, the preservation and study of the ancient monuments of Crete. Under the aegis of the Syllogos, Hazzidakis began a small museum in Herakleion where chance finds and gifts from private collectors were housed. This formed the basis for the now world-famous Archaeological Museum of Herakleion. After the liberation of Crete from Turkish rule in 1900, Hazzidakis and his colleague Stephanos Xanthoudides were recognized as the two first Ephors of Cretan Antiquities. Hazzidakis collaborated with foreign scholars (especially the Italian Frederico Halbherr) who excavated for the Syllogos and negotiated on Arthur Evans's behalf for the purchase of the site of Knossos. In 1915 and 1919 he conducted excavations in and around the Minoan palace of Mallia, before eventually handing the site over to French colleagues. The site with which he was most closely associated, however, was that of Tylissos, where he excavated in 1909 and 1912, revealing three fine Minoan villas, as well as buildings of later date.

WRITINGS

'Anaskaphai en Krete, para to chorion Malia' [Excavations in Crete in the area of Mallia], *Praktika Athen. Archaiol. Etaireias* (1915), pp. 108–30
'Anaskaphai en Maliois tes Kretes' [Excavations at Mallia, Crete], *Praktika Athen. Archaiol. Etaireias* (1919), pp. 50–62
Tylissos à l'époque minoenne (Paris, 1921)
Les Villas minoennes de Tylissos (Paris, 1934)

BIBLIOGRAPHY

G. Oikonomos: *Praktika Athen. Archaiol. Etaireias* (1936), pp. 1–26 (5)

J. LESLEY FITTON

H. B. *See* DOYLE, (1).

Head, Guy (*b* Carlisle, 4 June 1762; *d* London, 16 Dec 1800). English painter. Having entered the Royal Academy Schools, London, in 1778, he exhibited at the Free Society of Artists (1779), the Society of Artists (1780) and annually at the Royal Academy from 1779. In 1781 he exhibited *Landscape with the Story of Europa* (untraced), but a sketchbook (London, V&A) is all that survives to indicate his interest in landscape. That year he travelled to Europe, becoming a member of the Florence Accademia (1787) and of the Kassel Akademie (1788). By 1790 he had settled in Rome, where he was elected a member of the Accademia di S Luca in 1792. He presented a Neo-classical painting of *Iris* as his diploma piece, the design for which he derived from Guido Reni's *Fortuna* (*c.* 1623; both Rome, Accad. N. S Luca). A larger version of this work was exhibited at the Royal Academy in 1800 with its pendant, *Echo Flying from Narcissus* (Detroit, MI, Inst. A.). The allegorical subject-matter, idealized figure and crisp treatment of the drapery are derived from the contemporary Roman Neo-classical style. While in Italy he made a distinguished collection of ancient Greek vases. In 1799 he travelled through Sicily and then returned to England, where he painted several commissions for Augustus Frederick, Duke of Sussex, and William Frederick, 2nd Duke of Gloucester. He painted several portraits, the most forceful of which is *Lord Nelson at the Battle of the Nile* (1798; London, N.P.G.). After Head's death an auction of his work was held in April 1801, which included many of his paintings along with his collection of vases. In 1803 his widow, Jane Lewthwaite, a painter in watercolours of classical landscapes, returned from Rome with a further 50 of his works; these were sold in 1805 in Wigton and in London.

BIBLIOGRAPHY

Waterhouse: *18th C.*
N. L. Pressly: 'Guy Head and his "Echo Flying from Narcissus": A British Artist in Rome in the 1790s', *Bull. Detroit Inst. A.*, lx (1982), pp. 68–79

HUGH BELSEY

Head, Sir Edmund (Walker) (*b* Wiarton Place, nr Maidstone, 21 March 1805; *d* London, 28 Jan 1868). English historian, writer and governor. He was educated at Winchester and Oriel College, Oxford University (1823–7), where he obtained a first class degree in Classics. In 1830 he was elected a Fellow of Merton College, Oxford University, a position he retained until 1837. In 1846 he produced a translation of the second volume of Franz Kugler's *Handbuch der Geschichte der Malerei, von Constantin dem Grossen bis auf die neuere Zeit* (Berlin, 1837). He completely rewrote the part dealing with the Spanish and French schools, and this appeared as a separate volume, *A Handbook of the History of the Spanish and French Schools of Painting* (London, 1848). A translation of the whole of Kugler's work, edited by Head, appeared in 1854. In September 1854 he was appointed Governor-General of Canada, the highest office in the colonial service. He published several philological works, and a volume of ballads and poems (London, 1868) collected from *Fraser's Magazine* was published posthumously.

BIBLIOGRAPHY

DNB
Obituary, *The Times* (30 Jan 1868), p. 9
D. G. G. Kerr: *Sir Edmund Head: A Scholarly Governor* (Toronto, 1954)

JULIAN SHEATHER

Head, Tim (*b* London, 22 Oct 1946). English artist. He studied fine art at the University of Newcastle upon Tyne from 1965 to 1969 and has from his student days used photography. His belief in the medium's accessibility underpins his examination of the structures of the man-made environment and socio-political issues. Initially he constructed site-specific installations by superimposing projected 35 mm slide images of figures and objects over their real-life counterparts. In the early 1980s he turned his attention in photographs to diverse imagery from the domestic interior and the world of commerce in order to speculate on the roles of technology and corporate power and on how their functions become accepted as an inevitable part of daily existence. In *State of the Art* (1984; AC Eng), for example, the assumptions of advertising, film and the mass media are questioned. Head's work of the 1980s is distinguished by his innovative use of Ciba-chrome and Scanachrome processes on a mural-like scale, and by his new-found interest in painting.

BIBLIOGRAPHY
Tim Head: Recent Work (exh. cat., ed. F. Crichton; U. Cambridge, Kettle's Yard, 1978)
Tim Head (exh. cat. by N. Lynton, Venice Biennale, 1980)
Tim Head (exh. cat. by J. Fisher, Hasselt, Prov. Mus. Aktuele Kst, 1983)

PAUL BONAVENTURA

Heade [Heed], **Martin Johnson** (*b* Lumberville, PA, 11 Aug 1819; *d* St Augustine, FL, 4 Sept 1904). American painter. He began as a portrait painter, working in a primly selfconscious and laboured limner tradition; among his portraits are a small number of real distinction, such as the *Portrait of a Man holding a Cane* (1851; priv. col.). As with Fitz Hugh Lane, whose career suggests points of contact with Heade, his work was meticulous and restrained in handling and without painterly effects. Only in the early 1860s did Heade turn to a subject well suited to his artistic personality: the salt marshes of Newburyport, RI (e.g. *Sunrise on the Marshes*, 1863; Flint, MI, Inst. F.A.). He worked with a limited range of pictorial elements—haystacks, clouds, sky, water and a flatly receding earth—to create a precise spatial structure within which to explore the fleeting light effects of a coastal environment. Heade did not rely on rapid oil sketches or drawings carrying colour notations of the sort done by his friend Frederic Church; yet he remained responsive to atmospheric variations, transforming a relatively prosaic landscape into a visually heightened field of subtly shifting perceptions. The eerie 'luminist' precision of his landscapes and his independence from conventional composition contribute to the unsettling impression his work makes, as well as to its appeal to modern sensibilities.

Heade's work, in paintings such as *Lake George* (1862; Boston, MA, Mus. F.A.; see fig.), superficially resembles the detailed rendering and crystalline clarity of the American Pre-Raphaelites, such as William Trost Richards, whose practice was based on absolute fidelity to nature. Heade painted not according to a doctrine, but in order to reproduce the disquieting intensity of his own vision, evident in works such as *Approaching Storm: Beach near Newport* (*c.* 1865–70; Boston, MA, Mus. F.A.) or *Thunderstorm over Narragansett Bay* (1868; Fort Worth, TX, Amon Carter Mus.). These paintings exude a charged, ominously still atmosphere far removed from the reassuringly pastoral mood of the Hudson River school painters.

Heade worked primarily in a horizontal format, giving a planar organization to many of his landscapes. Such characteristics have earned him a place beside Fitz Hugh Lane and Sanford Gifford in retrospectively defining a luminist mode in American painting (*see* LUMINISM (i)). Heade preferred to paint objects at close range, or rendered familiar through repetition. Such preferences led him to paint a remarkable series of still-lifes of flowers from the 1860s, such as the *Magnolia Grandiflora* (1885–95; Boston, MA, Mus. F.A.). Inspired by a series of trips to South and Central America in 1863–4, 1866 and 1870, Heade began a series of paintings of orchids and humming-birds in a tropical setting that combined his interests in landscape and still-life and that occupied him intermittently until his death (e.g. *Orchids, Passion-flowers and Hummingbird*, 1875–85; New York, Whitney). Though, like Frederic Church, he produced panoramic landscapes of South America, such as the *View from Tree Fern Walk* (*c.* 1870–87; Mr and Mrs Patrick Doheny priv. col., on loan to Los Angeles, CA, Co. Mus. A.), he drew inspiration not from the exalting scope and breadth of nature, but from its exotic and sensuous forms, which assume a threatening vitality, defamiliarized by dislocations of scale and seductively rendered with characteristic visual intensity. Drawn to the lush profusion and strange mingling of life and

Martin Johnson Heade: *Lake George*, oil on canvas, 661×1264 mm, 1862 (Boston, MA, Museum of Fine Arts)

death in the tropics, Heade spent the last two decades of his life in Florida. There he also found a patron, Henry Morrison Flagler, who furnished him the nominal security and recognition he had hitherto lacked.

Scholarly interest in Heade has grown steadily since the 1940s, but he remains an elusive and poorly documented figure, known primarily through scattered correspondence, journalistic writings and an extensive oeuvre, much of which is unlocated; for example, the *Roman Newsboys* (*c.* 1848–9; Toledo, OH, Mus. A.) is a rare identified example of his genre paintings. While his art hints at broader stylistic developments in American landscape painting of the 1850s and 1860s, his genius resisted easy assimilation by popular and critical taste.

In an age of peripatetic artists, Heade was more widely travelled than most. His restless movement hints at a personality rarely at ease with the social environment of the post-Civil War years, in constant search of sympathetic subject-matter and exceptionally reticent. In a period when the growing cultural nationalism of the mid-19th century gave American artists a new legitimacy, Heade's own art retained a sardonic edge, distanced from the idealized, accessible vision of nature afforded by many of his contemporaries of the Hudson River school. Heade's nickname 'Didymus' may refer to St Thomas, the doubting apostle, a choice that suggests the artist's lifelong scepticism toward the facile pieties and progressive faith of America's 'age of expansion'.

BIBLIOGRAPHY
R. G. McIntyre: *Martin Johnson Heade* (New York, 1948)
B. Novak: *American Painting in the Nineteenth Century* (New York, 1969), pp. 125–37
Martin Johnson Heade (exh. cat. by T. Stebbins, New York, Whitney, 1969)
T. Stebbins: *The Life and Works of Martin Johnson Heade* (New Haven, 1975)
J. G. Sweeney: 'A Very Peculiar Picture: Martin J. Heade's *Thunderstorm over Narragansett Bay*', *Archvs Amer. A. J.*, xxviii/4 (1988), pp. 2–14
D. Miller: *Dark Eden: The Swamp in Nineteenth-century American Culture* (Cambridge, MA, 1989)
S. Cash: *'Ominous Hush': The Thunderstorm Paintings of Martin Johnson Heade* (Fort Worth, 1991)

ANGELA L. MILLER

Headpiece. Ornamental design at the top or head of a page of a manuscript or book.

Headstone. Stone slab set at the top of a grave, often inscribed with the name and dates of the deceased and carved with funerary imagery.

□

Heal, Sir Ambrose (*b* London, 3 Sept 1872; *d* Knotty Green, Bucks, 15 Nov 1959). English furniture designer and writer. He was educated at Marlborough College and the Slade School of Art, London, before following an apprenticeship as a cabinetmaker from 1890 to 1893, when he joined the family firm, Heal & Son, established in 1810 in London by John Harris Heal (*d* 1833). By 1897 furniture was produced to his designs; in 1898 he became a partner, and his first catalogue, *Plain Oak Furniture*, was issued, which, like *Simple Bedroom Furniture* (1899), contains designs in a simple Arts and Crafts style. Heal exhibited regularly at the Arts and Crafts Exhibition Society in London. His influence was evident in the catalogues and advertising of the firm (he had an enduring interest in typography), whose design policy he increasingly directed. In 1907 he was appointed Managing Director and in 1913 chairman. His inexpensive, stylish furniture was appropriate to the new garden-city developments, and in 1907 he furnished a cottage for the *Urban Cottages and Rural Homesteads Exhibition* in Letchworth. He was elected a member of the Art Workers' Guild in 1910 and was a founder-member of the Design and Industries Association in 1915 with, among others, his cousin, the architect Cecil Brewer (1871–1918), who at this time completed the rebuilding of the Heal & Son store, an important development in shop architecture. In the 1930s Heal experimented with new materials—steel tube, aluminium, wood laminates—for furniture. He was knighted in 1933. Alongside design and manufacturing, Heal was an active researcher and writer.

WRITINGS
London Tradesmen's Cards of the Eighteenth Century: An Account of their Origin and Use (London, 1925)
The English Writing-masters and their Copy-books, 1570–1800 . . . (London, 1931)
The London Goldsmiths, 1200–1800 . . . (London, 1935)
The Signboards of Old London Shops . . . (London, 1947)
London Furniture Makers from the Restoration to the Victorian Era, 1660–1840 . . . (London, 1953)

BIBLIOGRAPHY
G. Boumphrey: 'The Designers, 1: Sir Ambrose Heal', *Archit. Rev.* [London], lxxviii (Aug 1935), pp. 39–40
A Booklet to Commemorate the Centenary Exhibition of the Life and Work of Sir Ambrose Heal (London, 1972)
T. Benton: 'History of Taste, 6: Up and Down at Heal's, 1929–35', *Archit. Rev.* [London], clxiii (Feb 1978), pp. 109–16

MARGARET WAGSTAFF

Healy, George Peter Alexander (*b* Boston, MA, 15 July 1813; *d* Chicago, IL, 24 June 1894). American painter. At the age of 18 he set up a studio in Boston after receiving encouragement from Thomas Sully, who was painting portraits there. Despite his youth and lack of training, he presented himself to the society figure Mrs Harrison Gray Otis and asked if he might paint her portrait (untraced); she agreed and later sponsored Healy's first trip abroad. In 1834 he entered the studio of Antoine-Jean Gros; the French master's suicide the following year ended Healy's only sustained period of artistic study. In Gros's studio he first encountered Thomas Couture, but they did not meet again until the next decade, when Couture's friendship and example became important components of Healy's future success.

Healy opened a studio in Paris in 1835 but soon went to London. Four years later he returned to Paris, where his portrait of the American minister to France, *Gen. Lewis Cass* (1840; Detroit, MI, Hist. Mus.), brought him to the attention of Louis-Philippe. Winning the King's favour, he travelled back to London under royal patronage to copy portraits in Windsor Castle. Later he returned to America to paint US statesmen and presidents for the King's gallery at Versailles. During these years he created some of his most memorable portraits, including that of *Euphemia White Van Rensselaer* (1842; New York, Met.), painted in Paris and recalling the work of Ingres.

Healy was in America when Louis-Philippe was forced to abdicate in 1848, but the artist soon returned to France and completed two ambitious history paintings. One of them, *Franklin in the Court of Louis XVI* (*c.* 1855; destr. by fire, 1871; sketch, *c.* 1847–8, see Boime, p. 577), won him a gold medal at the Paris Exposition Universelle of 1855. The same year Healy accepted the invitation of a Chicago businessman to settle in his city. He became the leading artist in the American Midwest, painting hundreds of portraits (e.g. the *Bryan Family*, 1857; Richmond, VA, Mus. F.A.) and helping to organize expositions and artists' organizations. The US Civil War affected his schedule little as he was over-age for military service; between 1860 and 1865 he painted generals, statesmen and presidents. His portrait of a seated, reflective *Abraham Lincoln* (1864; Chicago, IL, Newberry Lib.) is among the most famous images of America's 16th president. He painted several versions and used it as the centrepiece of a historical composition, *The Peacemakers* (1868; Washington, DC, White House Col.).

Healy returned to Europe in 1867, strained by the hectic pace he had kept in America. (By some accounts he was painting nearly 100 portraits a year.) He lived in Rome from 1868 to 1872 and Paris from 1872 to 1892. He travelled ceaselessly, journeying through Italy and Spain and accepting commissions in America, Berlin and Romania. Throughout his career he made more than 30 Atlantic crossings. His last was in 1892, when he announced to his wife that '[Paris] is changing and we are not' and returned to Chicago to spend his final days.

Much of Healy's work was lost in the Chicago fire of 1871, and his remaining portraits include several that command little interest beyond the historical. As his career progressed his palette darkened to emphasize tonal contrasts, his touch became drier and his compositions more rigidly factual (e.g. *Emma Thursby*, 1879; New York, Hist. Soc.). Some of this change can be attributed to the influence of photography, although it also seems that Healy derived formulaic solutions to style and composition from Couture. Yet Healy remained a remarkably successful artist. His international fame was the result of natural facility, exceptional speed and great personal charm. His talents and character appealed to aristocrats, republicans and royalty alike; his sitters included Andrew Jackson, Charles Goodyear, Franz Liszt, Henry Wadsworth Longfellow, King Charles I and Queen Elizabeth of Romania, and Otto von Bismarck. Healy's reputation was unrivalled in his day, and his cosmopolitan career prefigured that of John Singer Sargent in the next generation.

WRITINGS
Reminiscences of a Portrait Painter (Chicago, 1894)

BIBLIOGRAPHY
M. de Mare: *G. P. A. Healy, American Artist: An Intimate Chronicle of the Nineteenth Century* (New York, 1954)
A. Boime: *Thomas Couture and the Eclectic Vision* (New Haven and London, 1980)
SALLY MILLS

Healy, Robert (*b* Dublin, *c.* 1743; *d* Dangan, Co. Meath, July 1771). Irish draughtsman and painter. Having trained at the Dublin Society Schools, he exhibited at the Dublin Society of Artists in 1766 and 1767. Principally remembered for his delicately drawn pastels in grey and white (which illustrate the high level of skill to be found in the Dublin Schools at that time), he excelled in both portraiture and animal painting. Only some 25 works have been firmly attributed to him. His portrait heads show that he had some knowledge of the tonal power of the mezzotints by Thomas Frye: two self-portraits (Dublin, N.G.) by Healy hint at a Frye-like interest in effects of light and texture. In 1768 or 1769 Healy received a commission from Tom Conolly, MP, for nine pastel drawings to be executed at Conolly's seat, Castletown, Co. Kildare. This commission, the most important of Healy's career, offers fascinating glimpses into the private pursuits of the Anglo-Irish ruling class; the drawings include scenes of horse-racing and other leisure activities, for example the *Castletown Hunt with Tom Conolly* and *Members of the Conolly Family Skating at Castletown* (both priv. col., see Crookshank and Glin, figs 59 and 60). One oil painting has been attributed to Healy: the *Death of the Hare* (*c.* 1770; New Haven, CT, Yale Cent. Brit. A.), in which the formal poses and relief-like arrangements of the figures are reminiscent of those in the Conolly drawings.

BIBLIOGRAPHY
Strickland
A. Crookshank and the Knight of Glin: *The Painters of Ireland, c. 1660–1920* (London, 1978), pp. 73–9
D. Guinness: 'Robert Healy: An Eighteenth Century Sporting Artist', *Apollo*, cxv (1982), pp. 80–85
FINTAN CULLEN

Heaphy. English family of painters.

(1) Thomas Heaphy (*b* London, 29 Dec 1775; *d* London, 23 Oct 1835). He trained at John Boyne's drawing school in Gloucester Street, Bloomsbury, London, and exhibited portraits at the Royal Academy from 1797. Following the success of a portrait of the Russian ambassador, Count Woronzow, he was appointed portrait painter to the Princess of Wales. Thomas Lawrence observed Heaphy's success and bought some of his pictures but had little cause to envy Heaphy's style, which owed much to the vocabulary of civic portraiture popularized by Joshua Reynolds (e.g. *Portrait of a Naval Officer*; London, V&A). Heaphy's largest project, *The Duke of Wellington in Consultation with his Officers Previous to a General Engagement* (Newcastle upon Tyne, Laing A.G.), was begun in Spain in 1813 during the Peninsular War and was finished in 1816. The engraving, which was intended to ensure Heaphy's fortune, was not released until 1822, by which time interest in the war had waned. Heaphy failed to finish his *Battle of Waterloo* (1816; untraced), another panoramic multiple portrait. Heaphy's other speciality, paintings of ports, markets, tradespeople and labourers, brought him great popularity between 1807 and 1811. Although censured by the Royal Academy for the 'expressive vulgarity' of such works as *Fish Market* (1808; untraced), Heaphy became a member of the Society of Painters in Water-Colours, and first president of the Society of British Artists in 1824.

BIBLIOGRAPHY
W. Whitley: *Thomas Heaphy* (London, 1933)

(2) Thomas Frank Heaphy (*b* London, 2 April 1813; *d* London, 7 Aug 1873). Son of (1) Thomas Heaphy. He visited Italy with his father in 1831, where he developed enthusiasms for Italian religious art and portraiture. In 1861 he published eight articles in the *Art Journal*, attempting to ascertain the origin of the likeness of Christ. Between 1859 and 1862 he exhibited a series of portraits of peasant women of various nationalities at the Royal Academy.

WRITINGS

The Likeness of Christ: Being an Inquiry into the Verisimilitude of the Received Likeness of Our Blessed Lord (London, 1880) [the *Art Journal* articles collected and more elaborately illustrated]

LEWIS JOHNSON

(3) Charles Heaphy (*b* London, 1820; *d* Brisbane, 3 Aug 1881). Son of (1) Thomas Heaphy. He studied at the Royal Academy Schools, London. In 1839 he was appointed artist and draughtsman for the New Zealand Company, in which capacity he travelled to the colony, where he made topographical views of settlements at Wellington, Wanganui and New Plymouth and painted landscape views in both the North and South Islands. Heaphy's watercolours are distinguished by his fresh, almost naive vision rendered with crisp outlining of forms and bright colour. In later years Heaphy settled in Auckland, where he was Provincial Surveyor and represented Parnell in the House of Representatives. Examples of his work are *Mt Egmont from the Southward* (watercolour, 1840; Wellington, NZ, Turnbull Lib.) and *Cape Brett, Bay of Islands* (watercolour, *c.* 1853; London, BL).

BIBLIOGRAPHY

A. Murray-Oliver: *A Folio of Watercolours by Charles Heaphy V.C.* (Christchurch, 1981)

B. Gordon and P. Stupples: *Charles Heaphy* (Wellington, 1987)

MICHAEL DUNN

Hearne, Thomas (*b* Marshfield, Avon, 22 Sept 1744; *d* London, 13 April 1817). English painter and engraver. From 1765 to 1771 Hearne studied printmaking as apprentice to the landscape engraver William Woollett, exhibiting watercolours meanwhile at the Free Society of Artists and the Society of Artists. In 1771 he abandoned engraving and accompanied Sir Ralph Payne to the Leeward Islands (where Payne had just been appointed Governor), returning in 1775; several of his fastidious watercolours of Antigua survive, for example the *Court House and Guard House in the Town of St John's in the Island of Antigua* (n.d.; London, V&A). From then on British topography was his main concern. He travelled widely in England, Scotland and Wales with Sir George Beaumont and from these excursions was able to provide 84 drawings which, engraved by William Byrne, were published as *The Antiquities of Great Britain* (1778–81). This series set new standards in the pictorial recording of medieval architecture. Hearne also provided drawings for etchings of landscapes and 'rural sports'. For Richard Payne Knight he executed a number of watercolours based on sketches taken on Knight's tour of Italy; later he recorded the newly landscaped grounds of Knight's estate at Downton, and illustrated the principles of landscape gardening put forward in Knight's didactic poem *The Landscape* (1794).

Hearne usually worked in wash or subdued watercolours over a fine but clear outline introduced in pencil, pen or brushpoint. He exhibited at the Royal Academy between 1785 and 1793, but subsequently relied on a few loyal collectors, notably Dr Thomas Monro, at whose house in Adelphi Terrace, London, works by (or after) Hearne were copied by younger artists such as Thomas Girtin and Turner. Unlike them, however, Hearne maintained his precise and judicious manner of tinted drawing until his death.

BIBLIOGRAPHY

Thomas Hearne, 1744–1817: Watercolours and Drawings (exh. cat., ed. D. Morris and B. Milner; Bolton, Mus. & A.G., 1985)

PATRICK CONNER

Hearst, William Randolph (*b* San Francisco, 29 April 1863; *d* Beverly Hills, 14 Aug 1951). American newspaper tycoon, politician and collector. Hearst was educated in art and antiquities in Europe by his mother, the philanthropist and architectural patron Phoebe Apperson Hearst (1842–1919); after Harvard he transformed a floundering San Francisco newspaper into a sensationally successful media empire and acquired wealth and political influence, becoming the subject of the renowned film *Citizen Kane* (1939) by Orson Welles. Before 1905 Hearst developed a passion for Navajo items. Unlike his indiscriminate collections of European antiquities, he rigorously sought out 'first-class examples' created in the Southwest between 1650 and 1920. Herman Schweizer, manager of the Fred Harvey Company Indian Department, helped him amass more than 200 superb examples of the striped and zigzagged blankets and serapes. Hearst was a promiscuous, uncontrollable, megalomaniacal collector of art, antiquities and architectural elements of very uneven quality. Usually purchased unseen from international agents or from sales catalogues, by 1926 they filled more than seven warehouses and the flamboyant castle that Julia Morgan built for him at San Simeon, CA (begun 1919), which was by then open to the public. He even purchased the entire 12th-century Cistercian monastery at Sacramenia, Spain. Although he had a particular interest in armour, tapestry, Hispano-Moresque pottery, Greek vases, English silver and more, a sense of spoils of war haunts the huge Hearst collection.

BIBLIOGRAPHY

W. A. Swanberg: *Citizen Hearst* (New York, 1961)

P. Failing: 'William Randolph Hearst's Enchanted Hill', *ARTnews*, lxxviii (January 1979), pp. 53–9

Hearst Collection Photographs and Acquisition Records (New York, 1987) [652 microfiches]

Navajo Textiles: The William Randolph Hearst Collection (exh. cat. by N. J. Blomberg, Los Angeles, CA, Nat. Hist. Mus., 1988)

DIANE TEPFER

Heartfield, John [Herzfelde; Helmuth] (*b* Berlin, 19 June 1891; *d* Berlin, 26 April 1968). German photomontagist, draughtsman, typographer and stage designer. After a difficult childhood owing to the persecution of his father for his political beliefs, he studied art at the Königliche Kunstgewerbeschule in Munich from 1907 to 1911, specializing in poster design. In 1912 he took his first job in a printing works in Mannheim, moving to Berlin in 1913, where he and his brother Wieland Herzfelde made contact with avant-garde circles. Heartfield's experiences in World War I led him to conclude that the only worthy art was that which took account of social realities. He destroyed all his early work.

From 1916 Heartfield shared a studio with George Grosz and, like Grosz, anglicized his name, although he did not adopt this form officially until after the war. His cynical criticism of bourgeois society found its expression in his commitment to the DADA group in Berlin, of which he was a founder-member in 1918. In the same year he became a member of the Communist Party. The magazine *Die Pleite*, established by Heartfield and his brother Wieland in early 1919, reflected their politicization; John Heartfield was responsible for all the design (e.g. cover, *Die Pleite*, 5; see März, p. 154). During the 1920s his art consisted of agitprop work for the Communist Party, including designs for books, book jackets and posters, collaboration with Erwin Piscator's *proletarisches Theater* and work for newspapers and magazines. He produced designs for *Der Knüppel* (1923–7), the satirical periodical of the Communist Party, and for *Rote Fahne*, whose front cover consisted of photomontages (see März, p. 160), and he designed advertising columns and demonstration banners. He also produced set designs such as that for Piscator's *Heimweh* (1928; see März, p. 165). Heartfield's photographic work helped him gain design experience, which he was able to draw on later in photomontages for the *Arbeiter-illustrierte-Zeitung* (*AIZ*), such as *Adolf the Superman Swallows Gold and Sports Junk* (17 July 1932; for illustration *see* PHOTOMONTAGE).

Heartfield was an innovator in the early 1920s in his use of photographs in the design of book jackets. His primary concern was still the connection between photography and typography; for example his book jacket for the German edition (1922) of John Reed's *10 Days that Shook the World*, a book that deals with the October Revolution, showed a photograph of an outstretched lower arm with a raised rifle bursting through the '0' of the number '10'. The remaining text occupied the clear area above the arm. Heartfield's use of photomontages began only when he started to work with *AIZ*, which was issued weekly from 1927, and for which he worked regularly from 1930 until his exile in London in 1938. For Heartfield montage was not only the medium best suited to rework political issues of the moment but also—through the use of photography, which became the key to understanding Heartfield's pictorial argumentation—the one that most closely approached most people's ways of receiving information.

Heartfield based many of his photomontages on material from so-called working people's photographs. One of his best-known works was the photomontage *I've Got Millions behind me*, which appeared as a front cover of *AIZ* in 1932, illustrating Hitler's dependence on certain sections of big business by merging two originally independent photographs into one entity. The exaggerated physiognomic contrasts were a purely pictorial means of emphasizing the figures' mutual dependence. Furthermore he created a sense of pictorial reality through photography's own special impact. In 1933 Heartfield emigrated to Prague, and in 1938 he fled to exile in London, where he worked at the publishing house of Drummond. In 1950 he returned to East Germany, working mainly as a stage designer.

BIBLIOGRAPHY

E. Siepmann: *Montage: John Heartfield* (Berlin, 1977)
R. März, ed.: *John Heartfield: Der Schnitt entlang der Zeit* (Dresden, 1981)
D. Kahn: *John Heartfield: Art and Mass Media* (New York, 1985)
K. Thomas, ed.: *John Heartfield* (Cologne, 1991)

BARBARA LANGE

Heath. English family of artists. James Heath (*b* London, 9 April 1757; *d* London, 15 Nov 1834) was an engraver in line and stipple. He studied under Joseph Collyer (1748–1827) and established his reputation engraving small plates for such publishers as G. & J. Robinson. He also engraved the delicate designs by his friend Thomas Stothard for Harrison's *Novelist's Magazine* (22 vols, 1780–86). His first major plate was the *Riot on Broad Street* (1790) after the painting (destr.) by Francis Wheatley, the first of ten done for John Boydell. In 1785 Heath began the *Death of Major Peirson* after John Singleton Copley (painting 1782–4; London, Tate; *see* COPLEY, JOHN SINGLETON, fig. 2). As a result of pressure of work for the book trade, illness and a quarrel with Boydell that lasted from 1792 to 1794, it took Heath over 11 years to complete it. *Peirson* was, however, well received and described as 'perhaps the finest historical engraving that ever was executed by a British artist' (*Monthly Mirror*, May 1796).

In 1790 Heath became an Associate Engraver of the Royal Academy, to the disappointment of his peers, and in 1794 Historical Engraver to King George III. In 1797 he published the *Dead Soldier* after the painting (exh. London, RA 1789; USA, James Ricau priv. col.) by Joseph Wright; despite the help of assistants the project took him nearly eight years. The Napoleonic Wars discouraged ambitious undertakings, and an illustrated edition of Shakespeare projected by Heath and G. & J. Robinson in 1792 did not appear until 1802–4; their bankruptcy in 1804 cost Heath £4000. In 1805, as a joint venture he and Benjamin West embarked on a print of West's painting of the *Death of Lord Nelson* (1806; Liverpool, Walker A.G.); this finally appeared in 1811. His last major print was a *Drowned Fisherman* (1821) from a picture (untraced) painted in 1815 for Heath by Richard Westall as a companion to the *Dead Soldier*. He also reworked Hogarth's plates for J. Nichols's edition of 1822.

Heath had two sons: Charles Heath (i) (*b* 1785; *d* London, 18 Nov 1848) and William Heath (*b* London, 1795; *d* London, 7 April 1840). Charles Heath (i) was taught by his father and was one of the first members of the Society of British Artists. He engraved many plates after paintings by such artists as van Dyck, West and Reynolds. One of his best-known prints is *Lady Peel*, after the painting (1826–7; New York, Frick) by Thomas Lawrence. He published many illustrations in such periodicals as *The Keepsake* and *The Amulet*. His brother William Heath was a prolific etcher, engraver and designer of book illustrations as well as a draughtsman and painter of portraits and battle scenes. Under his pseudonym Paul Pry, he became best known for his singly issued caricatures of such leading political figures as General von Blücher (1821). A series of his watercolours of Shakespeare's *Henry IV* are in the Victoria and Albert Museum, London. Charles Heath's son Charles Heath (ii) (*fl* 1825) was a painter and engraver who exhibited portraits and scenes from Milton and Torquato Tasso at the Royal Academy and the Society of British Artists.

BIBLIOGRAPHY
DNB; O'Donoghue; Thieme–Becker
Obituary, *Gent. Mag.*, iii (Feb 1835), p. 213 [James Heath]
A. Graves: *The Royal Academy of Arts: A Complete Dictionary of Contributors and their Works from its Foundation in 1769 to 1904*, 8 vols (London, 1905–6)
K. Garlick, A. MacIntyre and K. Cave, eds: *The Diaries of Joseph Farington*, 16 vols (New Haven, 1978–84)
J. Heath: *The Heath Family Engravers 1779–1878*, 2 vols (Aldershot, 1993)

DAVID ALEXANDER

Heaton, Butler & Bayne. English firm of stained-glass manufacturers. In 1855 Clement Heaton (*b* Bradford on Avon, 1824; *d* 1882), a glass painter, went into partnership with James Butler (*b* Warwick, 1830; *d* 1913), a lead glazier, to make stained glass. They initially shared premises in London with the newly established firm of Clayton & Bell, providing the technical expertise for the latter's designing skills. The firm was known as Heaton, Butler & Bayne from 1862, when Robert Turnill Bayne (*b* nr Warwick, 1837; *d* 1915), a Pre-Raphaelite artist, became partner and chief designer. Bayne's striking and linear designs were carried out in an exceptionally wide range of coloured glass, developed by Heaton as a result of his researches into medieval techniques. Typical windows produced at this time are at St Nicholas (south chancel, 1863), East Dereham, Norfolk, and Peterborough Cathedral (north transept, 1864). By the late 1860s the firm was seen as more advanced in design than Clayton & Bell, whose dependence on the Gothic Revival style made them less fashionable. The distinctive, classicizing style of Henry Holiday, employed as a freelance designer between 1864 and 1878, can be seen in work executed in 1876 for St Luke's, Camden, London. Heaton's son, CLEMENT J. HEATON, worked for the firm and became a partner in 1882. By the last years of the century the vibrancy of the earlier windows had been replaced by muted tones and the detailed drawing and painting of the period. The firm closed in 1953.

BIBLIOGRAPHY
F. Skeat: 'Heaton, Butler and Bayne: A Famous Victorian Firm', *Fam. Hist.*, x (1979), pp. 231–50
M. Harrison: *Victorian Stained Glass* (London, 1980)
S. B. M. Bayne: *Heaton, Butler & Bayne: A Hundred Years of the Art of Stained Glass* (Montreux, 1986)
M. Galicki: *Victorian and Edwardian Stained Glass* (London, 1987)

CAROLA HICKS

Heaton, Clement J(ohn) (*b* Watford, Herts, 21 April 1861; *d* New York, 27 Jan 1940). English designer and maker of stained glass, metalwork and enamel. In the mid-1870s he was apprenticed to the London firm of Burlison & Grylls, makers of stained glass in the Gothic Revival style. He later joined Heaton, Butler & Bayne, the firm of stained-glass manufacturers and painters founded by his father, Clement Heaton (1824–82), whom he succeeded as a partner in 1882. In 1884 he left London for Neuchâtel, Switzerland, where he collaborated with Paul Robert on the decoration of the monumental staircase (*in situ*) of the Musée d'Art et d'Histoire, experimenting with cloisonné enamel as an enrichment for the pilasters, mouldings and cornices. On his return to England in 1885 Heaton executed enamel designs for A. H. Mackmurdo and provided designs for metalwork and lamps for the Century

Guild of Artists. Following a dispute in 1885, Heaton left Heaton, Butler & Bayne and established Heaton's Cloisonné Mosaics Ltd, which produced plaques, book covers and lamps. After 1887 he lived principally in Neuchâtel, where his studio produced Gothic-inspired stained glass, cloisonné mosaics and embossed wallpapers by a process that he patented. His major commissions in Switzerland included glass mosaics for the Historisches Museum, Berne, and decorations for the Lausanne Law Courts and Cathedral, as well as for various churches in Strasbourg, Neuchâtel and Chaux-les-Fonds. He won a gold medal at the Exposition Universelle, Paris (1900). In 1914 he moved to New York, where he made stained-glass windows for the Church of the Blessed Sacrament and, in collaboration with his son Maurice Heaton (*b* 1900), windows for the Rockefeller Center. His other works in the USA include windows for the Trinity Chapel and the Museum of Art, Cleveland, and for the court rooms of the Bay County Building in Bay City, New York.

WRITINGS
'Design, Craftsmanship and the Imitation of Nature in Ancient Art', *Brooklyn: Inst. A. & Sci. (Mus.) Q.*, vi (1919), p. 135

BIBLIOGRAPHY
C. H. Walker: 'Notes on Stained Glass and the Art of Clement Heaton', *Amer. Architect* (Sept 1929)
S. B. M. Bayne: *Heaton, Butler & Bayne: A Hundred Years of the Art of Stained Glass* (Montreux, 1986)

LISA ZEIGER

Hebel [Hebbel], **Markus** (*fl* Holstein, 1639; *d* Stockholm, 1664). German sculptor and wood-carver, active in Sweden. He worked in Sweden from *c.* 1640 and was one of the sculptors employed (1641) in decorating the 'Peerless' palace (destr. 1825) of the De la Gardie family in Stockholm. Assisted by Hans Jerling (*fl* 1654; *d* 1695), he executed the monument (1660/61) to *Johan Pontusson De la Gardie* (1583–1652) in the parish church of Veckholm, Uppland. Notable among his works in wood are fireplace encasements (1650s, completed after his death) in Skokloster Castle and a trophy ornament on the segment gable (1657; all *in situ*) terminating the entrance front of the same building. Hebel's fireplace encasements are mostly directly copied from a set of prints by J. Barbet (*Livre d'architecture*, Paris, 1633) but with slightly altered proportions. To their classical French ornaments Hebel added German scrollwork; their themes are martial, with heavy clusters of trophies mingling with figures from Classical mythology and coats of arms. Three altarpieces, formerly attributed to Hebel and his workshop, in the German Church (1659), Stockholm, in St Nicholas's Church (1661), Örebro, Närke, and in the parish church (1656) of Vadsbro, Södermanland (all *in situ*), may have been executed by others–the two former ones perhaps by Hans Jerling, the third by Johan Wendelstam. The compositions of the fireplace encasements by Hebel seem more modern than those of the three altarpieces. The altarpieces in the German Church, Stockholm, and in St Nicholas's Church, Örebro, resemble each other: they are both triangular, three-storey compositions with columns and entablatures, figures of evangelists, apostles, angels and angels' heads combined with scrollwork. The one in Vadsbro, on the other hand, is late medieval in character, with a central corpus and flanking side-doors; its columns, figures and scrollwork, however, are of the same modern design as that of the other two altarpieces.

BIBLIOGRAPHY

SVKL

H. Rabén: *Träskulptur och snickarkonst i Uppsverige under renässans och barock* [Woodcarving and the carpenter's art in northern Sweden during the Renaissance and the Baroque period] (Stockholm, 1934)

E. Andrén: *Skokloster* (Stockholm, 1948)

G. Axel-Nilsson: *Dekorativ stenhuggarkonst i yngre Vasastil* [Ornamental sculpture in the later Vasa style] (Stockholm, 1950)

——: *Makalös: Fältherren greve Jakob De La Gardies hus i Stockholm* [The Peerless Palace: the Stockholm house of the field marshal count Jakob De La Gardie] (Stockholm, 1984)

L. Angström: *Altartavlor i Sverige under renässans och barock* [Altarpieces in Sweden from the Renaissance and Baroque] (Stockholm, 1992)

TORBJÖRN FULTON

Hébert (i). French family of sculptors. Pierre Hébert (*b* Villabé, Seine-et-Oise, 1804; *d* 1869) studied at the Ecole des Beaux-Arts in Paris, exhibiting at the Paris Salon from 1836 to 1869. He provided monuments for Toulouse, Orange, La Rochelle, Carcassonne and elsewhere. His statues of *Louis de Rouvroy, Duc de Saint-Simon* and of *Jules, Cardinal Mazarin* (both stone) are on the Palais du Louvre, Paris. He trained his daughter Héléna Hébert (*b* Paris, 4 July 1825; *d* Saint-Michel-de-Chavaignes, Sarthe, 20 April 1909) and son (Pierre-Eugène-)Emile Hébert (*b* Paris, 12 Oct 1828; *d* Paris, 20 Oct 1893) as sculptors.

Héléna Hébert was a regular Salon exhibitor and a participant in architectural decorative schemes including the Paris Opéra and the rebuilt Hôtel de Ville, Paris, where she provided a statue of *Jean-Siméon Chardin* (stone, 1881). She was in the forefront of the campaign for the rights of women artists: in 1881 she founded the Union des Femmes Peintres-Sculpteurs-Graveurs, Décorateurs, becoming its first president; she also sought the admission of women to the Ecole des Beaux-Arts, Paris, and to the Prix de Rome competition. Having exhibited under the pseudonym Allélit in 1849, as the wife of the painter Léon Bertaux (*b* 1827) she exhibited under the name Mme Léon Bertaux from 1857.

Emile Hébert studied not only with his father but with Jean-Jacques Feuchère. He was competent in the field of official sculpture for public buildings and executed a successful commemorative monument to *François Rabelais* (bronze, 1880; Chinon, Place de l'Hôtel de Ville). His main achievement, however, was in his treatment of imaginary subjects, most notably *Mephistopheles* (plaster, exh. Salon 1853; bronze; 1855; Barnard Castle, Bowes Mus.), *Bellerophon* (bronze, exh. Salon 1874; CA, priv. col.; see Stump, p. 46) and above all *And Always! And Never!* (plaster, exh. Salon 1859; bronze, *c.* 1863; Lawrence, U. KS, Spencer Mus. A.). This group of a maiden swooning in the arms of a skeletal lover elicited an enthusiastic response from Charles Baudelaire in his review of the Salon of 1859. Its macabre eroticism, hinting at a folklore source, parallels the treatment of similar subjects in second generation Romantic poetry.

BIBLIOGRAPHY

Lami

Catalogue of the 95th Salon of the Union des Femmes Peintres-Sculpteurs-Graveurs, Décorateurs (Paris, Pal. Luxembourg, 1979)

The Romantics to Rodin: French Nineteenth-century Sculpture from North American Collections (exh. cat., ed. P. Fusco and H. W. Jansen; Los Angeles, CA, Co. Mus. A.; Minneapolis, MN, Inst. A.; Detroit, MI, Inst. A.; Indianapolis, IN, Mus. A.; 1980–81)

J. Stump: 'The Sculpture of Emile Hébert: Themes and Variations', *Register* [Lawrence, U. KS, Spencer Mus. A.], v/10 (1982), pp. 28–61

PHILIP WARD-JACKSON

Hébert (ii). Canadian family of artists.

(1) Louis-Philippe Hébert (*b* Sainte-Sophie-de-Mégantic, Que., 27 Jan 1850; *d* Montreal, 13 June 1917). Sculptor. In 1869 he enlisted in the papal guard and went to Rome, where the many works of art were a revelation to him. When he returned to Canada, he was taken on in 1873 as a pupil and assistant by Napoléon Bourassa, a Montreal architect and painter. During his six-year training as a sculptor Hébert took part in decorating the chapel of Notre-Dame de Lourdes (1875–8) in Montreal. In the 1880s he devoted himself to wooden religious sculpture, working mainly at Notre-Dame Cathedral in Ottawa (1879–87) and the church of Notre-Dame in Montreal (1883–6). At the same time he turned gradually to producing monumental bronze statuary. Following an important commission for the Assemblée Nationale in Quebec, consisting of six historical figures, two allegorical groups and a fountain depicting the *Rest in the Forest* and *Indian Fisherman with a Spear* (all *in situ*), he was able to go to Paris from 1888 to 1894 to finish his training in monumental sculpture. He spent three further periods in Paris, 1898–1902, 1906–7 and 1911–14.

Hébert became the foremost Canadian monumental sculptor and benefited from the vogue for commemorative monuments in Canada in the late 19th century and early 20th. The monumental sculptures that brought him fame and fortune include *Michel de Salaberry* (1881; Chambly), *George-Etienne Cartier* (1885; Ottawa, Parliament Hill), *Paul de Chomedy, Sieur de Maisonneuve* (1895; Montreal, Place d'Armes), *Monseigneur François de Laval* (1908; Quebec) and *Madeleine de Verchères* (1913; Verchères). Hébert also produced a series of statuettes, busts and reliefs of famous people, public figures and friends. He was respected by his contemporaries as the first great Canadian sculptor. His work, characterized by stiff poses and heavy masses, belongs to the realm of academic art but is tinged with classicism, Romanticism and Naturalism.

BIBLIOGRAPHY

B. Hébert: *Philippe Hébert, sculpteur* (Montreal, 1973) [with list of works]

MARIO BÉLAND

(2) Adrien Hébert (*b* Paris, 12 April 1890; *d* Montreal, 20 June 1967). Painter, son of (1) Louis-Philippe Hébert. He studied painting at the Monument National, Montreal, from 1904 to 1906 and then under William Brymner at the Art Association of Montreal from 1906 to 1911. Uncertain that he wanted to pursue a career as an artist, he was enrolled by his father in 1912 in Fernand Cormon's studio in Paris; while there he was inspired by the work of the Impressionists, particularly Monet and Alfred Sisley. After returning to Montreal in 1914 he was appointed to teach drawing at the Monument National, which he continued to do for 35 years. Hébert's mature style had developed by 1923, and he had evolved the few themes that persisted throughout his career. He was fascinated by mechanization and the urban landscape, as reflected in his series of the Montreal port. In *Elevator No. 1* (*c.* 1929; Hamilton, Ont., A.G.) the figure is dwarfed by the surrounding buildings, creating an austere atmosphere. His compositions emphasize the solidity of objects, without defining them sharply. The snowy scene *Hyman's Tobacco Store, St Catherine and Bleury Streets, Montreal* (1937; Montreal, Mus. F.A.), although crowded with figures, evokes a stillness comparable to that found in the paintings of Edward Hopper. Hébert worked, especially after 1950, in a limited palette, with the paint thickly applied. He also created interior scenes (e.g. *Inside my Studio*, c. 1938; priv. col., see 1971 exh. cat., p. 53) and landscapes of the Quebec countryside (e.g. *Percé*, charcoal, c. 1927; Quebec, Mus. Qué.). He was a member of L'Arche, the Montreal group of radical artists and writers. His brother Henri Hébert (1884–1950) was a sculptor.

BIBLIOGRAPHY

Adrien Hébert: Trente ans de son oeuvre/Thirty Years of his Art, 1923–1953 (exh. cat. by J.-R. Ostiguy, Ottawa, N.G., 1971)
J.-R. Ostiguy: *Adrien Hébert: Premier interprète de la modernité québecoise* (Saint Laurent, Quebec, 1986)

ALEXANDRA PEL

Hébert, (Antoine-Auguste-)Ernest (*b* Grenoble, 3 Nov 1817; *d* La Tronche, Isère, 4 Nov 1908). French painter. He took drawing lessons from the painter Benjamin Rolland (1777–1855) in Grenoble from the age of ten, but his father wished him to become a lawyer and in 1834 Hébert moved to Paris to study law. While there he also studied painting and drawing, first under Pierre-Jean David d'Angers and later under Paul Delaroche, and in 1836 he entered the Ecole des Beaux-Arts. His early paintings were portraits and landscapes of his native Dauphiné. In 1839, the year he passed his law exams, he won the Prix de Rome with the *Cup of Joseph Found in the Sack of Benjamin* (1839; Paris, Ecole N. Sup. B.-A.). Following this success his father allowed him to become an artist, and in 1839 he made his début at the Salon with *Le Tasse in Prison Visited by Expilly* (1839; Grenoble, Mus. Peint. & Sculp., on loan to La Tronche, Mus. Hébert). He arrived in Rome in January 1840 to study at the Académie de France. On his way to Italy he met the Comte de Nieuwerkerke. While there Hébert was in regular contact with his cousin, the novelist Stendhal, then consul at Civitavecchia, and became a friend of the composer Charles Gounod. The Director of the Académie on Hébert's arrival was Ingres, who exerted a great influence on him, but Ingres was replaced later in the year by the less distinguished Victor Schnetz.

Hébert remained in Italy until 1847, working in Florence and Ischia, and he made several copies of the works of Michelangelo. Following a period of convalescence in Marseille after a fall, he returned to Paris in 1848. His entries for the Salon of 1848 and 1849 passed largely unnoticed, but his exhibit of 1850, *Malaria* (1850; Paris, Louvre, on loan to Paris, Mus. Hébert), won him a first-class medal and established his reputation. The work depicts an Italian family fleeing in a boat from a malaria epidemic and includes several doleful young females of the type that appear in many of his subsequent works. In 1853 he exhibited the *Kiss of Judas* (1853; Paris, Louvre, on loan to Paris, Mus. Hébert), a dramatic work using strong light effects.

Late in 1853 Hébert travelled to Italy again, living in Cervara, 60 km from Rome, where he painted the everyday life and landscape of the area, as in *Girls of Alvito* (1855; Paris, Mus. Hébert). He returned to Paris in 1858 and soon acquired great popularity painting portraits of society women, producing such works as *Mme d'Attainville* (1860; Paris, Louvre). Through the influence of Nieuwerkerke he was appointed Director of the Académie de France in Rome in December 1866. While in Rome he painted a number of works that, like *Girl in the Rushes* (1871; Paris, Louvre), depict erotic female figures. During the Franco-Prussian War, to protect his house in La Tronche, he made a vow that in 1872 he fulfilled by painting the *Virgin of the Deliverance* for the church. This is considered one of his major works. He was elected a member of the Académie des Beaux-Arts in 1871 and was President from 1878 to 1879. In 1884 he completed a commission for a mosaic for the apse of the Panthéon in Paris, *Christ Revealing to the Angel of France the Destiny of her Country*. During this period he continued to produce such portraits as *Eléanore d'Uckermann* (1884; Paris, Mus. Hébert) and from the 1880s also painted works on the theme of music, among them *Music* (Paris, Petit Pal.).

In 1885 Hébert was appointed Director of the Académie de France in Rome for a second term. In contrast to his successful earlier period there, he had difficulties in his dealings with the younger artists. Nevertheless, he retained the post until 1890 and remained in Rome until 1896. From this later period date such works as *Sleep of the Infant Jesus* (1886; Paris, Louvre), the dark, mysterious spirituality of which has affinities with Symbolism. He continued to paint on his return to Paris, producing such portraits as the *Marchese da Modena* (1897; Paris, Mus. d'Orsay). The Musée Hébert was inaugurated in 1977 at 85 Rue du Cherche-Midi in Paris, and in 1979 his property at La Tronche was given to the State and became the Fondation Hébert–d'Uckermann.

BIBLIOGRAPHY

G. Lafenestre: *La Tradition dans la peinture française* (Paris, 1898), pp. 293–348
A. Soubies: *Les Directeurs de l'Académie de France à la Villa Médicis* (Paris, 1903), pp. 89–102
——: *Les Membres de l'Académie des beaux-arts depuis la fondation de l'Institut* (Paris, 1904–17), iii, pp. 237–45
H. Roujon: *Notice sur la vie et les travaux d'Ernest Hébert* (Paris, 1909)
Peladan: *Ernest Hébert: Son oeuvre et son temps d'après sa correspondance intime et des documents inédits* (Paris, 1910)
R. P. d'Uckermann: *Ernest Hébert, 1817–1908* (Paris, 1982)

Hebert [Martínez de Hebert], **Pedro** (*fl* Madrid, 1865). Spanish photographer. He was considered the finest of the early portrait photographers in Madrid, and he had his most prosperous studio in the heart of Madrid's photographic district (Calle del Prado, 10). At the time when cartes-de-visite began to flourish, Hebert became portrait photographer to the Spanish Royal House; in keeping with this station, he applied an academic style to his work. In his earliest years as portrait photographer he was also a painter of canvases and miniatures; this skill carried over into his photographic portraits, which were sometimes illuminated painstakingly by hand (Madrid, Pal. Real). His album of views of Salamanca (Montreal, Cent. Can.

Archit.) is his highest achievement; although uncharacteristic of his day-to-day work, it is technically innovative and is probably the most accomplished and aesthetically appealing treatment of Salamanca found in 19th-century photography.

BIBLIOGRAPHY

L. Fontanella: *La historia de la fotografía en España desde sus orígenes hasta 1900* (Madrid, 1981)
Photography in Spain in the Nineteenth Century (exh. cat. by L. Fontanella, Dallas, Delahunty Gal.; San Francisco, Fraenkel Gal.; 1983)

LEE FONTANELLA

Hebrew art. *See under* JEWISH ART.

Heckel, Erich (*b* Döbeln, nr Dresden, 31 July 1883; *d* Radolfzell, nr Konstanz, 27 Jan 1970). German painter, printmaker and sculptor. He was one of the founders of the group DIE BRÜCKE and one of its most influential and active members. His work was central to German EXPRESSIONISM.

Heckel began painting and drawing as a schoolboy in Chemnitz, where he became a friend of Karl Schmidt (later Schmidt-Rottluff). In 1904 Heckel went to Dresden to study architecture under Fritz Schumacher at the Technische Hochschule, where he met Ernst Ludwig Kirchner and the artist Fritz Bleyl (1880–1966). In 1905 the four artists, united by common artistic desires and aims, formed Die Brücke. Heckel abandoned his architectural studies in order to pursue his creative work and to organize the group, although he continued to work as a draughtsman and site manager for the architect Wilhelm Kreis until 1907. In common with other members of the group, Heckel drew and painted life models, either in the studio or *en plein air*, and he furnished his studio with furniture and sculpture he had carved himself and with painted wall hangings. Heckel took part in the group's summer holidays on the Moritzburg lakes near Dresden in 1909–11. He took on the role of 'business manager' for the group and, with his studio acting as the group's 'business centre', he made contacts and negotiated exhibition possibilities. Heckel kept the group together, always staying on good terms with the members despite the occasional disagreements among them. He and Kirchner

were the most active members in terms of their aesthetic input as well as organizational ability.

For all the artists of Die Brücke, prints, especially woodcuts, were of central importance, and Heckel was particularly extreme in emphasizing flatness and simplification of form. His coloured woodcuts from the Brücke years, for example *Reclining Woman* (1909; Essen, Mus. Flkwang), are among the most important prints of the 20th century. He also made woodcuts for the group's invitation and membership cards (for illustration *see* BRÜCKE, DIE). Individual artists began moving away from the communal Brücke style only after 1911, when the group gradually moved from Dresden to Berlin. At the same time there was a general stylistic development within the group from the bright colours of the Dresden Brücke style to a milder palette, and the harsh contrasts of complementary colours were eliminated. Instead, the graphic element in their painting took on increased importance, and this change can be seen in Heckel's style also (e.g. *Canal in Berlin*, 1912; Cologne, Wallraf-Richartz-Mus.).

In the period between his move to Berlin and the outbreak of World War I, Heckel carried out some of his most original works, for example the painting *Two Men at Table* (1912; Hamburg, Ksthalle), a scene inspired by Fyodor Dostoyevsky's *The Idiot*; the powerful triptych *Convalescence of a Woman* (1912–13; Cambridge, MA, Busch-Reisinger Mus., see fig.), with its combination of sophisticated and primitive motifs; and the painting *Glassy Day* (1913; Munich, Staatsgal. Mod. Kst), where the zigzag form of the landscape is balanced by the warm-coloured sculptural form of the woman and rocks in the foreground. Whereas models and landscapes predominated among the works of the Brücke period, Heckel at this point used more symbolic figural representations.

Heckel volunteered for military service at the outbreak of World War I. He spent the war in a medical unit in Belgium run by the art historian Walter Kaesbach (1879–1961), in which many other artists served, including Max Beckmann. A major work from this period is the *Madonna of Ostend* (1915; destr., see Vogt, p. 161). In Berlin after the end of the war, Heckel became a co-founder of the

Erich Heckel: *Convalescence of a Woman*, triptych, oil on canvas, each part 813×708 mm, 1912–13 (Cambridge, MA, Busch-Reisinger Museum)

Arbeitsrat für Kunst and for a short time was also a member of the Novembergruppe. From 1922 to 1923 he worked on the mural cycle *Stages of Existence* for the Angermuseum in Erfurt (*in situ*), commissioned by Kaesbach, then the Director of the museum.

With the start of Nazi rule in Germany, Heckel suffered restrictions and persecution. His work was declared 'degenerate' (*see* ENTARTETE KUNST) in 1937, and in 1941 he left Berlin for Carinthia. In 1944, the year in which he returned, his studio and its contents were destroyed by bombing, and he moved to Hemmenhofen on Lake Constance. From 1949 to 1955 he taught at the Kunstakademie in Karlsruhe, otherwise living in semi-retirement in Hemmenhofen, where he continued to paint. His later work was much calmer and characterized by his efforts to integrate the achievements of Die Brücke with more traditional treatments. Among the more successful later works were his watercolour landscapes (examples in Berlin, Brücke-Mus.).

BIBLIOGRAPHY

A. Dube and W.-D. Dube: *Erich Heckel: Das graphische Werk*, 3 vols (New York, 1964–74)

P. Vogt: *Erich Heckel* (Recklinghausen, 1965)

K. Badt: *Erich Heckel: Handzeichnungen* (New York, 1973)

Erich Heckel: Gemälde, Aquarelle, Zeichnungen (exh. cat. by M. Sauerlandt and others, Schleswig, Schloss Gottorf, 1980)

Expressionism: A German Intuition, 1905–1920 (exh. cat., ed. P. Vogt; New York, Guggenheim; San Francisco, CA, MOMA; 1980), pp. 25, 93–4, 102–23

Z. Felix, ed.: *Erich Heckel, 1883–1970* (Munich, 1983) [with bibliog.]

A. Henze: *Erich Heckel: Leben und Werk* (Stuttgart, 1983)

Erich Heckel, 1883–1970: Der frühe Holzschnitt: Zum Gedenken an den 100. Geburtstag des Künstlers (exh. cat., ed. L. Reidemeister; Berlin, Brücke-Mus., 1983)

Erich Heckel: Zeichnungen, Aquarelle, Dokumente (exh. cat. by K. Gabler, Karlsruhe, Städt. Gal. Prinz-Max-Pal.; Aschaffenburg, Schloss Johannisburg, Staatsgal.; Regensburg, Städt. Gal.; Höchst, Jhthalle; 1983–4)

LUCIUS GRISEBACH

Hecker, Christian Friedrich (*b* Saxony, *c.* 1754; *d* Rome, 15 April 1795). German gem-engraver, active in Italy. He is first mentioned in church records in Rome in 1784. His friendship with the sculptor Alexander Trippel was close, and they both belonged to the Freemasons' Lodge founded in Rome in 1785 by Friedrich Münter (1761–1830), a Danish theologian, classical scholar and writer. Entries in Münter's diary indicate that Hecker was working as an independent gem-engraver in 1785 and that Münter posed for a portrait in wax by him (untraced).

Like many of his contemporaries, Hecker mainly copied antique sculpture, basing his designs on such popular works of Classical sculpture as the *Apollo Belvedere* (Rome, Vatican, Mus. Pio-Clementino), the *Venus de' Medici* (Florence, Uffizi) and the Capitoline *Venus* (Rome, Mus. Capitolino). When working from such models, he confined himself to profiles. It is not possible to establish whether he based his work on copper-engravings and drawings by others or whether he made his own drawings from the original.

The 40 works by Hecker that have been found all seem to have been commissions and so did not allow him to give his imagination free rein. His surviving works nonetheless demonstrate his efforts to give a three-dimensional effect to the figures and heads; by cutting deeply into the onyx and skilful modelling of the individual parts he managed to create an effect of light and shade. He was influenced by the gem-engraver Giovanni Pichler and adopted his style of conveying hair, a mouth with barely closed lips, an expressive form of the eye, as well as his skill in catching the individual character in a face, in spite of some idealization resulting from a simplification of the features. In his full-figure representations there is a certain stiffness and lack of sureness, although he attempted to correct this in such works as *Terpsichore* (cut in sardonyx), only an impression of which has survived (Rome, Dt. Archäol. Inst., Cades col. 67B, 476). Heinrich Meyer, in his article 'Entwurf einer Kunstgeschichte des Achtzehnten Jahrhunderts' published in Johann Wolfgang von Goethe's *Winckelmann und sein Jahrhundert* (Weimar, 1805), assessed Hecker as one of the finest gem-engravers after Pichler. Hecker carved Goethe's portrait for him in sardonyx (intaglio; Weimar, Goethe-Nmus. Frauenplan), which was based on a bust (Arolsen) by Trippel and was in the possession of Goethe's mother by 1789. He also produced portraits of such other personalities as *Clement XIV* (1784; ex-Piatti Collalto priv. col., Vienna), *Pius VI* (New York, Met.), *George III* (Kraków, N. Mus.), *Prince Bishop Clemens Wenzel of Trier* (1789; ex-Rollett priv. col., Vienna) and *Jean-Jacques Rousseau* (?after 1790; Italy, priv. col.).

According to the scholar and poet Giovanni Gherardo de Rossi (1754–1827), in 1793 Hecker was a skilled draughtsman and engraver specializing in the production of cameos. The landscape painter Philipp Hackert commissioned Hecker to make cameos with the profiles of Maecenas and Antinous-Bacchus and an intaglio with the profile of *Frederick II* (untraced; sulphur impression, 1810, in Weimar, Goethe-Nmus. Frauenplan). He also received commissions (1784–5) from Heinrich von Offenburg, marshal at the court of Charles, Duke of Kurland, and may have been commissioned by Jean-Baptiste Mallia of Vienna to make six cameos (St Petersburg, Hermitage), although Mallia possibly acquired these through intermediaries. His works were also in the possession of the art historian Hermann Rollett (1819–1904) and the collector Tobias Biehler. Shortly before his death Hecker carved a large three-figure intaglio in chalcedony of *Eros between Nemesis and Elpis* (Germany, priv. col.) for Augustus, Duke of Sussex (1773–1843). The motif is taken from a Neo-Attic marble krater dating from the time of Hadrian in the Chigi collection (Ariccia, Pal. Chigi). The Duke had also commissioned a large cameo with a depiction of St George, although this was never executed.

Hecker's works are marked HECKER or C. F. HECKER FEC. and in two cases with the Greek 'ΕΚΕΡ. The collections of Tommase Cades (1772–1840) and Pietro Paoletti both include impressions and glass-paste copies of Hecker's work (respective collections in Rome, Dt. Archäol. Inst. and Pal. Braschi).

BIBLIOGRAPHY

Thieme-Becker

G. Lippold: *Gemmen und Kameen des Altertums und der Neuzeit* (Stuttgart, 1923)

I. Sattel Bernardini: 'Christian Friedrich Hecker: Ein Gemmenschneider der Goethezeit', *Xenia*, xv (1988), pp. 73–98 [incl. source mat. and bibliog.]

INGRID SATTEL BERNARDINI

Willem Heda: *Still-life with a Gilt Goblet*, oil on panel, 1.13×0.88 m, 1635 (Amsterdam, Rijksmuseum)

Heda, Willem (Claesz.) (*b* Haarlem, 1594; *d* Haarlem, 1680). Dutch painter. He was a still-life painter, who, like Pieter Claesz., is noted for his monochrome breakfast-pieces, which are, however, more opulent than those of Claesz. Heda's earliest dated work is a *Vanitas* (1621; The Hague, Mus. Bredius), which shows a still-life from a high viewpoint, composed of various objects bearing *vanitas* associations (e.g. a bowl of glowing embers, smoker's requisites, an overturned glass and a skull); the colouring is in brownish-grey tones and represents one of the earliest examples of a Dutch monochrome still-life ('monochrome' refers to the range of tones, rather than of colours). Even in this early work Heda's skill at painting textures is evident. A more balanced composition is achieved in another *Still-life* (1629; The Hague, Mauritshuis) and in the *Breakfast Table* (1631; Dresden, Gemäldegal. Alte Meister), in both of which the objects, set against a neutral background, are linked by a strong diagonal. The Mauritshuis still-life also gives an early indication of Heda's interest in painting the effects of light. In 1631 he became a member of the Haarlem Guild of St Luke (of which he served as deacon on several occasions after 1637).

By the mid-1630s Heda's work had matured, and his compositions were now built up by means of a larger number of objects, mostly in the foreground, whereas elements of his earlier works had been disposed more towards the background. In paintings such as the *Still-life with a Gilt Goblet* (1635; Amsterdam, Rijksmus.; see fig.), a fallen tazza or a vase often links the horizontal and vertical accents of the composition. This work also demonstrates Heda's skill in accurately depicting reflections: not only can a cross-bar window outside the picture be seen in the glass and the salt-cellar, but within the picture the goblet is reflected in the pewter jug, and the knife picks up light on its decorated handle.

Despite his limited subject-matter and the inevitable repetition of themes, Heda managed to create individual pictures on each occasion, and he experimented with a vertical format as well as the more conventional horizontal format for his still-lifes. In his *Still-life with Plates and Dishes* (1638; Hamburg, Ksthalle) the accumulation of tall objects is emphasized by the vertical draped folds of the white tablecloth. In later years, perhaps under the influence of Willem Kalf, Heda chose to paint more sumptuous objects: Venetian fluted glasses, brightly ornamented silverware and costly porcelain are arranged on the tables in an apparently disciplined disorder. The placement of each object, however, was carefully considered, and a plate balanced on the edge of a table conveys both a sense of dynamism and depth for the composition. Even though the objects of his later pictures were richer, Heda's work does not have the sense of exuberance found in similar work by Abraham van Beyeren and Willem de Heem, and his last known paintings of 1664 and 1665 lack the perfection and subtlety he achieved in the 1630s. Heda painted on panel and canvas, but panel paintings predominate. His colours are mainly greys, browns and greens with the addition of silvery tones. His brushwork is assured and controlled, and his paint solid and rich, but not too heavy. Two of his still-life paintings have landscape backgrounds (1634; Ghent, Mus. S. Kst.; and 1654; sold Amsterdam, Sotheby Mak van Waay, Oct 1979), but it seems likely that the landscapes are later additions. Some portraits and other figure studies have also been ascribed to the artist.

Heda seems to have been reasonably affluent, and his work was much in demand during his lifetime; Rubens owned two paintings by him, and copies after Heda appear in other Antwerp inventories. Jan de Bray painted his portrait in 1678 (untraced). Heda's son and pupil Gerrit Willemsz. Heda (b Haarlem, c. 1620; d Haarlem, before 1702) became a member of the Haarlem Guild of St Luke in 1642 and painted still-lifes so like those of his father that their work has often been confused. Other pupils included Maerten Boelema (c. 1620–?after 1664), Arnold van Beresteyn (c. 1620–54) and Hendrick Heerschoop (1620/21–after 1672).

BIBLIOGRAPHY

A. P. A. Vorenkamp: *Bijdrage tot de geschiedenis van het Hollandsche stilleven in de 17de eeuw* (Leiden, 1933)

H. E. van Gelder: *W. C. Heda, A. van Beyeren, W. Kalf* (Amsterdam, [1941])

I. Bergström: *Dutch Still-life Painting in the Seventeenth Century* (London, 1956), pp. 123–34, 139–43

L. J. Bol: *Holländische Maler des 17. Jahrhunderts nahe den grossen Meistern* (Brunswick, 1969), pp. 67–70

W. Bernt: *The Netherlandish Painters of the Seventeenth Century* (London, 1970), i, p. 51

N. R. A. Vroom: *A Modest Message as Intimated by the Painters of the 'Monochrome banketje'*, 2 vols (Schiedam, 1980) [incl. chronological cat. of works]

B. Haak: *The Golden Age: Dutch Painting in the 17th Century* (New York and Amsterdam, 1984), pp. 247–9

H. G. DIJK-KOEKOEK

Hedin, Sven (Anders) (b Stockholm, 19 Feb 1865; d Stockholm, 26 Nov 1952). Swedish explorer, scientist and artist. His travels started in 1885 when he took up a position as a tutor in Baku (Azerbaijan). His proficiency in languages allowed him to act as an interpreter in 1890 with the Swedish–Norwegian mission to the Qajar ruler of Iran, Nasir al-Din (reg 1848–96). When the mission was completed he travelled from Tehran via Mashhad (Iran), Merv (Turkmenistan), Bukhara and Samarkand (both in Uzbekistan) to Kashgar (now Kashi in the Xinjiang Autonomous Region of China). From 1893 to 1896 he undertook his first long expedition from Orenburg in Bashkiria through the Kirghiz steppe, the Pamir region, East Turkestan (now the Xinjiang Autonomous Region), Tibet, Mongolia and northern China to Beijing. His second expedition was to East Turkestan and Tibet (1899–1902) and included the discovery of the ancient town of LOULAN and the exploration of the Gobi Desert. His third expedition (1905–8) involved an exploration of the Himalayan

mountain range of Tibet and he made a detailed map of the country.

Items collected by him at Khotan and Loulan on the Silk Route in 1900 were displayed at an exhibition of Chinese art in Stockholm in 1914. His collection is now housed in the Östasiatiska Museet, Stockholm. His pro-German sympathies during World War I lost him the trust of the British, Russian and Chinese governments; and in 1916 he redirected his travels to West Asia. In 1920 an exhibition of his drawings and watercolours, arranged for the benefit of a School for War Children in Stockholm, resulted in a book, *En levnads teckning*, or *Sketches of a Life-Time*, in which he related his work with a sketchbook in Asia. In 1923 he travelled around the world, including a visit to the United States. From 1927 to 1933 he initiated and conducted an important Sino-Swedish expedition in Central Asia with scientific specialists, which established the location of 327 archaeological sites in an area now largely covered by the Inner Mongolia Autonomous Region of China. The expedition also revealed the presence of an extensive Stone Age culture in present desert and steppe areas, including artefacts from Neolithic periods. Finds from the expedition were deposited in the Etnografiska Museet, Stockholm.

WRITINGS

Through Asia: Illustrations from Sketches and Photographs by the Author, 2 vols (London, 1898)

Southern Tibet: Discoveries in Former Times Compared with My Own Researches in 1906–08, 13 vols (Stockholm, 1917–23)

My Life as an Explorer, trans. by A. Huebsch (New York, 1925)

The Silk Road, trans. by F. H. Lyon (London and New York, 1938)

BIBLIOGRAPHY

SBL

P. Hopkirk: *Foreign Devils on the Silk Road* (London, 1980/R Oxford, 1984)

Hedlinger, Johann Karl (b Schwyz, 28 March 1691; d Schwyz, 14 March 1771). Swiss medallist. Son of the painter Johann Baptist Hedlinger (1653–1711), he trained as a goldsmith and in 1713 engraved dies for the Lucerne Mint. While in Lucerne he worked with the goldsmith Wilhelm Krauer (1661–1718), as did his brother Johann Anton Hedlinger (1689–1755). In 1716 he travelled to France, where he worked for Ferdinand de Saint-Urbain and, the following year, at the Paris Mint. In 1718 he became Chief Engraver at the Stockholm Mint, where he produced medals, coins and seals, including medals commemorating events in the reigns of Charles XII, Queen Ulrica Eleonora and King Frederik, as well as a series of medals depicting Swedish rulers from the 9th century onwards (silver and bronze, c. 1728–45). He remained in Sweden until 1745, apart from visits to Italy (1726), St Petersburg (1735–7) and Fribourg (1741–3). In 1745 he returned to Schwyz, where he continued to execute medals until his death.

BIBLIOGRAPHY

Forrer; Thieme–Becker

C. de Mechel: *Oeuvre du chevalier Hedlinger* (Basle, 1776)

P. Felder: *Médailleur Johann Carl Hedlinger, 1691–1771* (Frankfurt am Main, 1978)

T. Talvio: 'Hedlinger's Medals of Swedish Universities', *Medal*, xi (1987), pp. 37–8

PHILIP ATTWOOD

Hédouin, (Pierre-)Edmond(-Alexandre) (*b* Boulogne-sur-Mer, 16 July 1820; *d* Paris, 12 Jan 1889). French painter, printmaker and illustrator. He studied engraving and lithography under Célestin Nanteuil (1813–73) from 1835 and in 1838 entered the Ecole des Beaux-Arts in Paris, where he studied under Paul Delaroche. He made his Salon début with a peasant genre scene in 1842 and at the Salon of 1846 was singled out for praise by Baudelaire for his powerful handling of colour.

Hédouin's Orientalist work dates from a visit made to Algeria in the company of Adolphe Leleux in 1847. Sketches executed during this trip provided the themes of finished paintings throughout his subsequent career (*Café at Constantine*, 1868; Narbonne, Mus. A. & Hist.). Hédouin's pleasing, realistic scenes of French, Spanish and Arab peasant life were much to the taste of Second Empire officialdom, and a number of the artist's works were acquired by the State during his own lifetime: for example, *The Gleaners* (1857; Paris, Mus. d'Orsay) and the *Sheep Market at St Jean de Luz* (1863; Valenciennes, Mus. B.-A.). In 1861 he painted decorative panels and medallions on the theme of the Liberal Arts for the Galeries des Fêtes in the Palais Royal in Paris (*in situ*) and later executed schemes in the style of Watteau for the foyer of the Théâtre Français (*in situ*) and for the old Hôtel de Ville (destr. 1871).

Hédouin's interest in printmaking dates from the early 1840s, when he provided lithographs for *L'Artiste*.

1. Jan Davidsz. de Heem: *Sumptuous Still-life with a Great Tit*, oil on canvas, 1.40×1.16 m, *c.* 1650 (The Hague, Rijksdienst Beeldende Kunst, on loan to Utrecht, Centraal Museum)

Around 1845 he abandoned lithography for etching and became one of the founder-members of the Société des Aquafortistes in 1863. His later years were devoted principally to engraving copies of Old Master paintings (Boucher, David Teniers II and Henry Raeburn), and to illustrating the literary works of Sterne (*Le Voyage Sentimental*, 1875), Rousseau (*Confessions*, 1881), Janin and Molière (1888).

Hédouin was awarded medals for painting at the Salons of 1848, 1855 and 1857, and for engraving in 1868 and 1872, when he was also made Officier of the Légion d'honneur.

BIBLIOGRAPHY

T. Gautier: *Les Beaux-arts en Europe* (Paris, 1856)
H. Béraldi: *Les Graveurs du XIXe siècle*, viii (Paris, 1889), pp. 68–74
J. Adhémar, J. Lethève and F. Gardey: *Bibliothèque nationale: Inventaire du fonds français*, x (Paris, 1958), pp. 163–76

JANE MUNRO

Hedvig Eleonora, Dowager Queen of Sweden (*b* Gottorp, Schleswig-Holstein, 23 Oct 1639; *d* Stockholm, 24 Nov 1715). Swedish patron and collector. She was married to Karl X Gustav of Sweden (*reg* 1654–60) in 1654 and became a widow in 1660. Her surviving accounts bear witness to the large sums she spent on building projects and acquisitions of works of art. Her main architectural commission was Drottningholm Slott (*see* STOCKHOLM, §4(ii)), built outside Stockholm from 1662 by Nicodemus Tessin (i), and after his death in 1681 by Nicodemus Tessin (ii). Hedvig had the palace's state apartments furnished and decorated in magnificent contemporary Baroque taste. Work was commissioned from various artists, including Burchardt Precht, Nicolaas Millich, Carlo Carove and Johan Georg Breuer, who carved her state bed (*see* SWEDEN, fig. 19). Hedvig also employed such painters as David Klöcker Ehrenstrahl: the decoration is still partly preserved. The court painter Ehrenstrahl also executed many portraits (Mariefred, Gripsholm Slott and Stockholm, Drottningholm Slott) of Hedvig Eleonora, her children, grandchildren and dogs and horses. Indeed Hedvig Eleonora surrounded herself principally with portraits of her numerous German relatives (now Mariefred, Gripsholm Slott). The Treasure Vault in the Kungliga Slott in Stockholm owes to Hedvig the majority of its collection: jewels, bowls, wine-cooling vessels and jugs, made in gold and silver with agate, jasper, crystal, amber and ivory, and acquired from the Netherlands and Italy, together with ceramics, particularly from the Netherlands and China.

BIBLIOGRAPHY

B. von Malmborg, ed.: 'Drottningholm', *Åb. Svensk. Stat. Kstsaml.*, xiii (Stockholm, 1966)
S. Fogelmarck: 'Den svenska skattkammarsamlingen' [The Swedish treasury collection], *En värld i miniatyr* [A world in miniature], Skrifter från Kungl Husgerådskammarsamlingen [Publications from the Royal Household], ii (Stockholm, 1983)

PONTUS GRATE

Heem, de. Dutch family of painters. (1) Jan Davidsz. de Heem is considered one of the most eminent STILL-LIFE painters of the 17th century. He had many followers, including two of his sons, (2) Cornelis de Heem and (3) Jan Jansz. de Heem, and a grandson, (4) David de Heem. Jan Davidsz.'s influence continued until the 19th century.

(1) Jan Davidsz. de Heem (*b* Utrecht, April 1606; *d* Antwerp, 1683–4). Born as Johannes van Antwerpen, the painter called himself Johannes de Heem but has always been mentioned as Jan Davidsz. de Heem in the literature. His father, a musician, died in 1612. His mother, two sisters and stepfather moved to Leiden in 1625. The following year Jan married Aletta van Weede (*d* 1643), who bore him three children, including (2) Cornelis de Heem. During the early 1630s Jan moved to Antwerp, where he spent most of the rest of his life. He married Anna Ruckers in 1644, the year after his first wife died. Six children were born of this second marriage, including (3) Jan Jansz. de Heem. Jan the elder went to Utrecht quite often and lived there from 1667 until 1672, when he returned to Antwerp. He had a workshop in Utrecht with collaborators and pupils, the most famous being Abraham Mignon.

1. WORK. Jan Davidsz.'s early works, produced in Leiden in the late 1620s, show the influence of interiors by Rembrandt and Jan Lievens, both active locally, as well as of tonal fruit-pieces by Balthasar van der Ast from Utrecht and 'monochrome' banquet-pieces by Pieter Claesz. from Haarlem. During the 1630s de Heem integrated elements of the local Antwerp painters of monumental kitchen-pieces and still-lifes Frans Snyders and Adriaen van Utrecht and later of the flower garlands and cartouches of Daniel Seghers.

De Heem's paintings include fruit-pieces, *vanitas* still-lifes and flower-pieces, but he became most famous for his ornate or sumptuous still-lifes (*pronkstilleven*). Like the book still-life, a special type of *vanitas* painting produced in Leiden, the sumptuous still-life, which de Heem started in his Antwerp period, was one of his own inventions. Several other subjects painted by him, even if only occasionally, constitute new iconographic forms, for instance a stable-piece (1631; Leiden, Stedel. Mus. Lakenhal) and herb-pieces (i.e. paintings with flowers or fruit in the open air, a ruin or a grotto). Characteristic of Jan Davidsz.'s work, however, are combinations of several types into one complex composition, such as a flower bouquet with fruit and *vanitas* objects. The sumptuous still-lifes are, in fact, examples of such combinations. They include precious objects, such as gold- and silversmith's work, Venetian glass and exotic shells, beside fruit and other food. The meaning of several of the paintings is made explicit by inscribed texts, usually referring to *vanitas* and Christian symbolism. Proverbs about moderation (e.g. 'Not how much, but how noble') are contrasted with the abundance of the sumptuous still-lifes.

De Heem's innovations are not limited by theme and combination only. Already in his earliest paintings he experimented with composition, brushstroke, light and colour. The compositions are given depth by means of architectural features in the background and foreground and through the effects of highlights and shadows. This can be seen, for example, in the *Sumptuous Still-life with a Great Tit* (The Hague, Rijksdienst Beeld. Kst, on loan to Utrecht, Cent. Mus.; see fig. 1), which shows a chair and a small table with objects on a terrace; depth is suggested by the sky in the vista and the curtain-covered wall and pillars behind the table. This picture also features de

2. Jan Davidsz. de Heem: *Prince William III*, *c.* 1670 (Lyon, Musée des Beaux-Arts)

Heem's subtly refined repetitions of basic shapes, such as triangles and ovals (e.g. the striped lute and melon). As far as technique is concerned, he sometimes painted broadly but also used delicate glazes, often in the same painting. The skimming light is concentrated on essential objects. Harmonious colour pattern with subtle transitional shades is the result of a development from 'monochrome' and 'tonal' approaches using shades of grey and brown. De Heem integrated the large and colourful Flemish style, with its strong contrasts, with the relatively small, simple, sober and intimate paintings more typical of the northern Netherlands.

2. CRITICAL RECEPTION AND POSTHUMOUS REPUTATION. No painter had such an influence on the development of Netherlandish still-life painting during the 17th century as Jan Davidsz. de Heem. His large sumptuous still-lifes of the 1640s made a particularly profound impression. Nearly all the still-life painters since, including great figures such as Willem Kalf and Abraham van Beyeren, were affected by him, and many tried to imitate his work. The impact of his art was strongest in three centres: Antwerp, Utrecht and Leiden. Only a small number of pupils are documented, among them Alexander Coosemans (1627–89) in Antwerp. Joris van Son (1623–67) was one of the most successful followers there. Important followers in Utrecht were Jacob Marrell (1614–81) and, especially, Abraham Mignon, who collaborated on several of de Heem's paintings. Local substitutes in Leiden included Pieter de Ring (1615–60) and a circle around him. Foremost among de Heem's collaborators, however, were his sons Cornelis and Jan Jansz. de Heem. A *Flower-piece with a Crucifix and Vanitas Objects* (Munich,

Jan Jansz. de Heem (attrib.): *Still-life with a Monkey*, oil on canvas, 1.18×1.69 m, *c.* 1680 (London, Wallace Collection)

Alte Pin.) is signed by Jan Davidsz. de Heem, Jan Jansz. de Heem and the Antwerp still-life painter Nicolaes van Veerendael. Jan Davidsz. de Heem's influence was still apparent throughout the 18th century, for instance in works by the still-life painters Rachel Ruysch and Jan van Huysum.

Jan Davidsz. de Heem was also considered one of the greatest painters by his contemporaries. He was well paid for his work: a portrait of *Prince William III* surrounded by a cartouche of flowers and fruit (Lyon, Mus. B.-A.; see fig. 2) was sold for 2000 guilders, one of the highest prices ever paid for a painting during the Golden Age. His works have been appreciated ever since, both in the literature and on the art market. They are among the most expensive Dutch paintings.

See also FLOWER PAINTING, fig. 2; STILL-LIFE, fig. 3; VANITAS, fig. 2.

(2) Cornelis (Jansz.) de Heem (*bapt* Leiden, April 1631; *d* Antwerp, 16 May 1695). Son of (1) Jan Davidsz. de Heem. He spent a great deal of his life in Antwerp, where he was taught by his father. Cornelis also worked in Utrecht in 1667, in nearby IJsselstein in 1676 and in The Hague from 1676 for more than ten years. His best works approach the quality of his father's, particularly in works executed during the decade starting in 1655. Cornelis's still-lifes can be distinguished by daring colour harmonies, sometimes with a strong blue. His compositions are often simpler: fruit-pieces, floral bouquets, festoons and garlands and sumptuous still-lifes, only

occasionally in large formats. His technique changed from a more painterly to a more graphic style.

(3) Jan [Johannes] Jansz. de Heem (*bapt* Antwerp, 2 July 1650; *d* after 1695). Son of (1) Jan Davidsz. de Heem. He also taught by his father and was in Utrecht with his father's family from 1667 until 1672. Little is known about Jan Jansz. de Heem, but it is now thought that a considerable portion of the paintings signed *J. de Heem*, which were previously attributed to Jan Davidsz. de Heem, are works by his son Jan Jansz. (e.g. New York, Met.; London, Wallace, see fig.; The Hague, Mauritshuis). The dimensions are sometimes larger than those of his father, and the brushstroke and detailing are usually simpler, with less elaborate glazing.

(4) David (Cornelisz.) de Heem (*bapt* Antwerp, 27 Feb 1663; *d* The Hague, before 1714). Son of (2) Cornelis de Heem. There has been considerable confusion about the identification of one or more painters called David de Heem. In fact, there is only one, the son of Cornelis, who most probably taught him. David left Antwerp for The Hague after 1693 and is mentioned for the last time in a document of his widow in 1714. His work shows many similarities with his father's, particularly during his early period. His later paintings are executed in a less painterly or a more graphic, somewhat harsh style, a development similar to that of his father.

BIBLIOGRAPHY

I. Bergström: *Dutch Still-life Painting in the Seventeenth Century* (London, 1956)

Jan Davidsz. de Heem en zijn kring (exh. cat. by S. Segal; Utrecht, Cent. Mus.; Brunswick, Herzog Anton Ulrich-Mus.; 1991)

SAM SEGAL

Heemskerck, Egbert (Jaspersz.) van, I (*b* Haarlem, 1634–5; *d* London, 1704). Dutch painter and draughtsman, active also in England. He is said to have been a pupil of Pieter de Grebber. In 1653 and 1655 he was living in Haarlem, and on 24 May 1655 he was on the point of leaving for Italy. Thereafter he lived mostly in Amsterdam (1661, 1665 and 1669); in between he also spent periods near The Hague (1663) and in Weesp (1667). On 26 June 1674 he was still in Holland. He then moved to England, where he lived in London as well as Oxford. His work consists primarily of painted scenes of the Temptation of St Anthony, witchcraft, drinking bouts, satirical subjects and Quaker meetings, the latter theme (e.g. London, Hampton Court, Royal Col.) being his most original contribution, for which he established the iconography. Although of a lower quality, his work resembles that of Adriaen Brouwer (whose name often appears on van Heemskerck's unsigned drawings), David Teniers (ii) and Adriaen van Ostade. A painting of King Charles II surrounded by his favourite ladies-in-waiting (untraced) is said almost to have cost van Heemskerck his head. One of King Charles's most licentious courtiers, John Wilmot, 2nd Earl of Rochester (1645–80), is thought to have been the artist's patron. Van Heemskerck apparently left behind a son of the same name (*d* 1744), who was also a painter but later became an actor. Attempts to distinguish the work of father and son have not yet been successful.

BIBLIOGRAPHY

Hollstein: *Dut. & Flem.*; Thieme–Becker; Waterhouse: *16th & 17th C.*; Wurzbach

A. Bredius: 'Bijdragen tot de biographie van Egbert van Heemskerck', *Oud-Holland*, xlii (1925), pp. 111–14

F. Saxl: 'The Quakers' Meeting', *J. Warb. & Court. Inst.*, vi (1943), pp. 214–16

W. Bernt: *The Netherlandish Painters of the 17th Century* (London, 1970), p. 53

INGEBORG WORM

Heemskerck, Maarten [Maerten; Martinus] **van** (*b* Heemskerck, 1498; *d* Haarlem, 1 Oct 1574). Dutch painter, draughtsman and print designer. He was among the second generation of Netherlandish artists to travel to Italy, where he was profoundly affected by the work of contemporary artists in Rome and by the examples of Classical sculpture to be seen in the city (*see* ROMANISM). On his return to the north, van Heemskerck had a long and successful career. His extensive oeuvre (over 100 paintings) comprises large altarpieces, portraits and smaller works (with both religious and mythological subjects). He also produced a vast number of drawings for prints. He helped spread the influence of Michelangelo and Giulio Romano in the northern Netherlands, through his strong, monumental style, with much emphasis on anatomical detail. He was thus an important figure in the dissemination of late Mannerism in northern Europe, particularly through the hundreds of prints executed after his drawings.

1. Apprenticeship and early work in Haarlem, before 1532. 2. Visit to Italy, 1532–6/7. 3. Later career in Haarlem, 1537–74.

1. APPRENTICESHIP AND EARLY WORK IN HAARLEM, BEFORE 1532. The most important source for his life is van Mander, who worked on his *Schilder-boeck* in Haarlem and Heemskerk from 1583, where he interviewed relatives and friends of the artist. Van Heemskerck was first apprenticed to Cornelis Willemsz. (*fl* 1481–?1552) in Haarlem, who had also been master to Jan van Scorel, and then trained with Jan Lucasz. (*fl* 1515–20), of whom little is known, in Delft. When van Heemskerck heard that van Scorel had returned from Italy and had established himself temporarily in Haarlem (1527–30), he moved back to the city. There he joined van Scorel's workshop and copied his master's Italian style; this was completely new to the Netherlands and was greatly admired by van Heemskerck, whose work from this period closely reflects that of van Scorel, as can be seen from his *Virgin and Child* (Washington, DC, N.G.A.). Van Heemskerck's style, however, is stronger and more three-dimensional than van Scorel's and shows more attention to the rendering of materials. His portraits from this period, in particular, are characterized by a strong sense of plasticity and powerful modelling, as in, for example, the portraits of *Anna Codde* and *Pieter Bicker* (both 1529; Amsterdam, Rijksmus.). When van Scorel left Haarlem, van Heemskerck moved to the house of Pieter Jan Foppesz., a sheriff and a member of Haarlem's city corporation. Van Heemskerck portrayed him with his family in what is known as the *Family Portrait* (*c.* 1530; Kassel, Schloss Wilhelmshöhe; *see* NETHERLANDS, THE, fig. 14). Van Heemskerck soon moved to the house of the goldsmith Joos Cornelisz. During this period he painted a portrait of his own father, *Jacob Willemsz. van Veen* (1532; New York, Met.), three years before the latter's death. On 23 May 1532 van Heemskerck completed *St Luke Painting the Virgin* (Haarlem, Frans Halsmus.), which he presented as a farewell gift to his colleagues in the Guild of St Luke on his departure to Italy. From the monumentality and the strong sense of plasticity of this work, it is clear that van Heemskerck was, in fact, already a fully formed artist before his visit to Italy and that he had by then already been influenced indirectly by the Italian Renaissance.

2. VISIT TO ITALY, 1532–6/7. In the early summer of 1532 van Heemskerck arrived in Rome, where he probably stayed with Cardinal Willem van Enckenvoirt from Utrecht and where he met Vasari. In Rome, van Heemskerck concentrated on drawing from nature, making sketches of Classical ruins, statues, views of the city, landscapes and architectural fragments. He also sketched sculptures by contemporaries and frescoes by Raphael, Michelangelo and others. The enormous influence of contemporary Italian painting on van Heemskerck's later work suggests that he must have made many more drawings than have survived. He devoted much attention to human anatomy under the influence of antique sculpture, and his studies of ruins provided background material for many of his later paintings and prints. Some of his drawings were made in a small sketchbook that was subsequently dismembered (the leaves are now kept, together with other drawings of Rome, in two albums in

1. Maarten van Heemskerck: *View of the Forum Boarium, Rome*, pen and brown ink, 214×286 mm, 1532–6 (Berlin, Kupferstichkabinett)

Berlin, Kupferstichkab.; see fig. 1). Only a few of the paintings van Heemskerck executed in Rome survive; these are all on canvas and dated 1536. Among them are a *Venus and Cupid in Vulcan's Forge* (Prague, N.G., Šternberk Pal.) and a *Landscape with the Abduction of Helen* (Baltimore, MD, Walters A.G.). The latter is an enormous, imaginary, panoramic landscape with Classical ruins and statues, showing Paris and Helen embarking for Troy. While in Rome, van Heemskerck also contributed to the decoration of a triumphal arch made for the occasion of Charles V's Joyous Entry into Rome on 5 April 1536. Towards the end of 1536, or early in 1537, van Heemskerck left Italy to return to Haarlem. On his way home he may have stopped in Mantua, which would explain the influence of Giulio Romano in his work. (For other examples from this period see ROME, figs. 12 and 33 and ITALY, fig. 107.)

3. LATER CAREER IN HAARLEM, 1537–74. It is clear that on his return to Haarlem, van Heemskerck was a very productive, devout, inventive and erudite artist, much appreciated in his own time. On a social level he also achieved high rank. Shortly before or after 1540–41 the artist married Marie Jacobs Coninghsdr, who died in childbirth 18 months later. His second wife, Marytgen Gerritsdr, whom he married *c.* 1559, came from a wealthy

background. From 1550 until 1552 he was an assay master and in 1553–4 he was dean of the Guild of St Luke in Haarlem. From 1552 to 1574, moreover, he was church warden of St Bavo in Haarlem, and from 1568 to 1571 he was elected one of the city fathers of Haarlem. He was a member of one of the chambers of rhetoricians, probably the 'Chamber of the Vineyard Tendrils' which was a relatively new one. He maintained friendships with Dirck Volkertsz. Coornhert, the engraver, writer and philosopher, the humanist Hadrianus Junius, and various families of magistrates in Haarlem, such as the van Zurens and the van Beresteyns. He was also on close terms with Cornelis Musius, prior of the monastery of St Aagten in Delft, something that may account for his many commissions for that city. Van Heemskerck's name also appears in various financial transactions involving the purchase of land. In 1558 he decreed that after his death the annual proceeds of one of these pieces of land were to be paid into the dowry of two orphan girls. In 1570 he erected a monument in the form of an obelisk on his father's grave in Heemskerck. During the siege of Haarlem, he sought refuge in Amsterdam, where he was put up by Jacob Rauwaert (*d* 1597), a former pupil who had become an art dealer. During 1573 he returned to Haarlem. The same year, together with a number of other wealthy citizens, he lent a large sum of money to the city of Haarlem, which was needed to redeem the goods plundered from the city by the Spaniards. A year later, he died at the age of 76. He was buried in St Bavo's, in accordance with instructions made in his will on 31 May 1572.

(i) Paintings and related drawings. After returning to the Netherlands, van Heemskerck received important commissions from both Haarlem and other Dutch cities. The contract for the wings intended to complement Jan van Scorel's *Crucifixion* (destr.) in the Oude Kerk in Amsterdam dates from November 1537; van Heemskerck completed these wings in 1541, but they were destroyed by iconoclasts in 1566. From 1538 to 1542 he worked on the enormous triptych of the *Passion* with predella and scenes from the life of *St Lawrence* on the wings for the St Laurentiskerk in Alkmaar (Linköping Cathedral). In 1543 he painted a large *Crucifixion* (Ghent, Mus. S. Kst.), in 1544 a triptych with an *Ecce homo* (Warsaw, N. Mus.) for the Drenckwaert family in Dordrecht and in 1546 the wings for the Clothmakers' Altarpiece for St Bavo's Church, Haarlem (Haarlem, Frans Halsmus.). Two triptychs, an *Ecce homo* (Haarlem, Frans Halsmus.) and an *Entombment* (Brussels, Mus. A. Anc.), were both executed for churches in Delft in 1559–60. Another version of *St Luke Painting the Virgin* (Rennes, Mus. B.-A. & Archéol.; see fig. 2) dates from the early 1550s and may have been intended for the Guild of St Luke in Delft. In the

2. Maarten van Heemskerck: *St Luke Painting the Virgin*, oil on panel, 2.06×1.44 m, *c.* 1550–53 (Rennes, Musée des Beaux-Arts et Archéologie)

background of the painting is the courtyard of the Casa Sassi in Rome, which was famous for its Classical sculptures. Van Heemskerck added to this a sculptor at work and surrounded the evangelist–doctor with medical attributes.

Van Heemskerck also received commissions from private individuals, for portraits and paintings mainly with biblical and mythological themes. The paintings belonging to this latter category clearly show the influence of Italian masters both in style and the choice of subject-matter. They include a *Venus and Cupid* (1545; Cologne, Wallraf-Richartz-Mus.), *Momus Criticizing the Works of the Gods* (1561; Berlin, Gemäldegal.) and *Parnassus* (1565; Norfolk, VA, Chrysler Mus.). His portraits feature prominent citizens, such as *Johannes Colmannus* (1538; Amsterdam, Rijksmus.), prior of the monastery of St Aagten, Delft, and *Andries Willemsz. van Sonnevelt* and his wife *Wilhelmina Paling* (both Alkmaar, Stedel. Mus.). In 1553 van Heemskerck painted a *Self-portrait* (Cambridge, Fitzwilliam), with the Colosseum in the background, another reference to the strong influence of Rome on his work.

The *Lamentation* (1566; Delft, Stedel. Mus. Prinsenhof) was completed in the year of the Iconoclastic Riots and is one of van Heemskerck's last paintings with a traditional religious subject. The political and religious turmoil of 1566–7 almost ended the flow of commissions from churches he had been receiving. His last two dated paintings are a *Christ at the Sea of Tiberius* (1567; Barnard Castle, Bowes Mus.) and an *Allegory of Nature* (1567; Pasadena, CA, Norton Simon Mus.). There is only one known preparatory study for a painting, a drawing of the *Crucifixion* (1554; Berlin, Kupferstichkab.). The remaining drawings after his return from Rome were practically all designs for prints (*see* §(ii) below), though he seems also to have executed designs for stained-glass windows, as payment was made to him in 1544 for the windows of the Carmelite church in Haarlem.

Although van Heemskerck is likely to have had various assistants, little is known about his three pupils: Jacob Rauwaert, Cornelis van Gouda (1510–*c.* 1550) and Symon Jansz. Kies (*d* 1620). The fact that the quality of van Heemskerck's work is variable suggests that the contribution of his assistants may have been substantial. In his best work, however, van Heemskerck shows himself to be a fine painter, using a wide range of colours made with pigments rarely employed by his contemporaries.

(ii) Drawings for prints. Van Heemskerck made drawings for nearly 600 prints, which were transferred on to copper by professional engravers. Even after he had abandoned painting, he continued his activities as a print designer and in 1570 was exempted from the municipal tax because of his services to the printmaking industry. Vasari listed the prints after van Heemskerck, and Hadrianus Junius (1588) described how engravers such as Dirck Volkertsz. Coornhert and Philip Galle transferred these designs on to copper. He was the first Dutch artist to use the medium professionally and by leaving the execution to others achieved his considerable output. The first print based on a design by van Heemskerck, *Prudence and Justice* (1537), was engraved by Cornelis Bos; however, van Heemskerck's production of prints really began properly in 1547,

when Coornhert became his partner as etcher, engraver and probably also wood-engraver. Numerous series of prints executed by Coornhert (e.g. the histories of Abraham, Isaac, Jacob and Joseph) were published until 1559. Shortly before or after that time some of the engraving work was taken over by Philip Galle. Other engravers who executed substantial numbers of van Heemskerck's prints were Herman Jansz. Muller and Cornelis Cort. From 1553 onwards many of the prints were published and sold in Antwerp by Hieronymus Cock. After Cock's death in 1570, Philip Galle took over the business of publishing the prints.

Van Heemskerck's designs depict a wide range of subjects: biblical stories (primarily those from the Old Testament and the Parables), edifying religious themes, moral lessons, cosmic allegories and mythological and historical subjects. In accordance with humanist ideals of the 16th century, the prints are mostly of a didactic and moral nature, but at the same time the subjects show van Heemskerck's ability to invent original compositions and add unusual details. He was nonetheless inspired by printed Bibles and individual German prints. Most of van Heemskerck's prints form parts of series and have captions in verse, sometimes in Dutch (probably by Coornhert) but usually in Latin. The Latin verses were composed by Hadrianus Junius, the humanist who supplied material for van Heemskerck's mythological and historical images. His drawings are usually signed and dated and many have been preserved. (There is a particularly large group in Copenhagen, Stat. Mus. Kst.) The early designs are somewhat sketchy and show little use of crosshatching, but in the course of the 1550s they became more elaborate and detailed while more room was reserved for subsidiary scenes and the background. The plates were printed in large editions and continued to be reprinted until the 18th century. Rembrandt had a collection of prints after van Heemskerck and several times used them as a source of inspiration. Until well into the 18th century van Heemskerck's images were also reproduced on painted glass panels or roundels, furniture, tapestry, reliefs and pottery.

BIBLIOGRAPHY

Hollstein: *Dut. & Flem.*; Thieme–Becker
G. Vasari: *Vite* (1550, rev. 2/1568); ed. G. Milanesi (1878–85), v, pp. 436–8
H. Junius: *Batavia* (Leiden, 1588), pp. 238–9
K. van Mander: *Schilder-boeck* ([1603]–1604), fols 244*v*–74*r*
T. Kerrich: *A Catalogue of the Prints Which Have Been Engraved after Martin Heemskerck* (Cambridge, 1829)
L. Preibisz: *Martin van Heemskerck: Ein Beitrag zur Geschichte des Romanismus in der neiderländischen Malerei des XVI. Jahrhunderts* (Leipzig, 1911)
C. Hülsen and H. Egger: *Die römischen Skizzenbücher von Marten van Heemskerck im Königlichen Kupferstichkabinett zu Berlin*, 2 vols (Berlin, 1913–16)
M. J. Friedländer: *Die altniederländische Malerei*, xiii (Berlin, 1936), pp. 71–83; Eng. trans. as *Early Netherlandish Painting*, xiii (Leiden, 1975), pp. 40–45
G. J. Hoogewerff: *De Noord-Nederlandse schilderkunst*, iv (The Hague, 1941–2), pp. 290–386
B. Cnattingius and A. L. Romdahl: *Maerten Heemskercks Laurentiusaltare i Linköpings Domkyrka* (Stockholm, 1953)
J. Bruyn: 'Vroege portretten van Maerten van Heemskerck', *Bull. Rijksmus.*, iii (1955), pp. 27–35
Tegninger af Maerten van Heemskerck (exh. cat. by J. Garff, Copenhagen, Stat. Mus. Kst, 1971)
B. Cnattingius: *Maerten van Heemskerck's 'St Lawrence' Altarpiece in Linköping Cathedral* (Stockholm, 1973)
I. M. Veldman: *Maarten van Heemskerck and Dutch Humanism in the Sixteenth Century* (Maarssen, 1977)
E. A. Saunders: 'A Commentary on Iconoclasm in Several Print Series by Maarten van Heemskerck', *Simiolus*, x (1978–9), pp. 59–83
J. C. Harrison: 'Maerten van Heemskerck and Alkmaar: A Painting Reattributed and a Relationship Clarified between the Painter and his Patrons', *Kennemer Contouren*, iii (1979), pp. 87–107
R. Grosshans: *Maerten van Heemskerck: Die Gemälde* (Berlin, 1980)
I. M. Veldman: 'Seasons, Planets and Temperaments in the Work of Maarten van Heemskerck: Cosmo-astrological Allegory in Sixteenth-century Netherlandish Prints', *Simiolus*, xi (1980), pp. 149–76
J. Bruyn and M. Thierry de Bye Dolleman: 'Maerten van Heemskercks *Familiegroep* te Kassel: Pieter Jan Foppesz. en zijn gezin', *Oud-Holland*, xcvii (1983), pp. 13–24
I. M. Veldman: 'The *Concert of the Muses* in the Work of Maarten van Heemskerck', *Hoogsteder-Naumann Mercury*, i (1985), pp. 35–41
J. C. Harrison: 'The Detroit *Christ on Calvary* and the Cologne *Lamentation of Christ*: Two Early Haarlem Paintings by Maerten van Heemskerck', *Ned. Ksthist. Jb.*, xxxvii (1986), pp. 175–94
I. M. Veldman: 'De Boekillustratie als inspiratiebron voor de Nederlandse prentkunst van de zestiende eeuw', *Eer is het lof des deuchts: Opstellen over renaissance en classicisme aangeboden aan dr. Fokke Feenstra* [Honour is the glory of virtue: essays presented to Dr Fokke Feenstra] (Amsterdam, 1986), pp. 261–77
——: 'Leerzame dwaasheid: De invloed van het *Sotten schip* (1548) op zottenvoostellingen van Maarten van Heemskerck en Willem Thibaut' [Instructive folly: the influence of the *Ship of Fools* (1548) on images of folly by Maarten van Heemskerck and Willem Thibaut], *Ned. Ksthist. Jb.*, xxxvii (1986), pp. 195–224
Kunst voor de beeldenstorm: Noordnederlandse kunst, 1525–1580 [Art before the iconoclasm: North Netherlandish art, 1525–1580] (exh. cat., ed. J. P. Filedt Kok, W. Halsema-Kubes and W. T. Kloek; Amsterdam, Rijksmus., 1986)
Leerrijke reeksen van Maarten van Heemskerck [Instructional series by Maarten van Heemskerck] (exh. cat. by I. M. Veldman, Haarlem, Frans Halsmus., 1986)
J. C. Harrison jr: *The Paintings of Maerten van Heemskerck: A Catalogue Raisonné*, 2 vols (Ann Arbor, 1987)
E. Filippi: *Maarten van Heemskerck: Inventio urbis* (Milan, 1990)
I. M. Veldman: 'Maarten van Heemskerck en Italie', *Ned. Ksthist. Jb.*, xliv (1993), pp. 125–42
——: *The New Hollstein: Dutch and Flemish Etchings, Engravings and Woodcuts, 1450–1700*, ed. G. Luijten, 2 vols (Amsterdam, 1993–4)

ILJA M. VELDMAN

Heemskerck van Beest, Jacoba (Berendina) van (*b* The Hague, 1 April 1876; *d* Domburg, 3 Aug 1923). Dutch painter and draughtsman. She was the daughter of the Dutch painter J. E. van Heemskerck van Beest (1828–94). She studied at the Koninklijke Academie van Beeldende Kunsten in The Hague and in 1901 moved to the Gooiland area, north of Utrecht, where she was taught printmaking by Ferdinand Hart Nibbrig. In 1904–5 she lived in Paris, working in the studio of Eugène Carrière. From 1906 she spent her summers at the country house of the collector and patron Marie Tak van Poortvliet (1871–1936), near Domburg, where a studio was set up for her in the garden. From 1908 van Heemskerck painted landscapes in a luministic style (drawings, Rotterdam, Boymans–van Beuningen) under the influence of Jan Toorop and Piet Mondrian, who also spent the summers in Domburg during that time and by whom she was taught. Around 1911 she was influenced by Cubism, but shortly afterwards her work showed the influence of German Expressionism and of Kandinsky's abstract art (*Painting 1914*, 1914; The Hague, Gemeentemus.). This stage in her development owed much to Herwarth Walden, who in 1912 organized exhibitions in the Netherlands of the work of the Italian Futurists and of Kandinsky, and in 1913 of Franz Marc. Marie Tak van Poortvliet's collection of contemporary paintings was also an important point of contact with the European avant-garde for van Heemskerck; it included works by Mondrian, Picasso, Fernand Léger, Georges Braque, Lyonel Feininger, Marc and Kandinsky.

In 1910 and 1911 van Heemskerck exhibited in Domburg with the artists' colony and in Amsterdam with the St Luke's Society, also exhibiting in 1911 at the Moderne Kunstkring in Amsterdam and at the Salon des Indépendants in Paris. She also contributed to the Erste Deutscher Herbstsalon in Berlin in 1913, the year in which she met Walden on a trip to Berlin with Marie Tak. Following Walden's stay as a guest of Marie Tak in Domburg during the summer of 1914, a lively correspondence ensued between him and van Heemskerck. Through his efforts she was promoted in Germany as one of the most important of contemporary artists, alongside Kandinsky, Marc and Klee. From 1915 to 1917 she exhibited in the Sturm-Galerie in Berlin. In addition to paintings and drawings she also produced illustrations, woodcuts and mosaics (woodcuts, see 1982–4 exh. cat., pp. 81–7). In 1918 she exhibited designs for stained-glass windows, which she subsequently executed and placed in houses in and around Domburg. From 1918 she carried out some experiments with the Dutch artist F. W. Zeylmans van Emmichhoven (1883–1961) on the emotional effect of colour. In 1919 some of her stained-glass window designs were executed by the Heinersdorff studio in Berlin. These designs were exhibited at the Haagse Kunstkring in 1920, the year in which she was commissioned to design some stained-glass windows for the Wulffraat house in Wassenaar, near The Hague, which was built by Jan Buijs (some designs, The Hague, Gemeentemus.). In 1921 she received a similar commission for the Navy Barracks in Amsterdam (designs, The Hague, Rijksdienst Beeld. Kst.) and in 1922 for the staircase of the G. G. & G. D. (local health authority) in Amsterdam (some *in situ*). A large selection of her work is in the Gemeentemuseum in The Hague.

BIBLIOGRAPHY
M. Tak van Poortvliet and others: *Jacoba van Heemskerck* (Berlin, 1924)
R. Oxenaar: 'Jacoba van Heemskerck (1876–1923)', *Meded. Dienst Kst. & Wet. Gemeente 's-Gravenhage*, ix (1953), pp. 72–9
P. Citroen: 'Jacoba van Heemskerck', *Museumjournaal*, v (1960), pp. 142–4
Kunstenaren der idee: Symbolistische tendenzen in Nederland, ca 1880–1930 (exh. cat., The Hague, Gemeentemus., 1978)
Jacoba van Heemskerck, 1876–1923: Kunstenares van het expressionisme (exh. cat., text by A. H. Huussen and H. Henkels; The Hague, Gemeentemus.; rev. W. Berlin, Haus Waldsee; Stuttgart, Württemberg. Kstver.; Bonn, Rhein. Landesmus., and elsewhere; 1982–4)

JOHN STEEN

Heemstede. Dutch house and garden at Houten in the province of Utrecht. In 1680 Diderick van Velthuysen (1651–1716) bought the manor of Heemstede. The house had been built in 1645 and was surrounded by a rectangular garden with a symmetrical plan traversed by paths and canals. Van Velthuysen planned his garden as a visible demonstration of his loyalty to the house of Orange Nassau, and it is among the finest examples of Dutch classicizing gardens (*see* GARDEN, §VIII, 4(v)). The plan may be French-inspired (and has been attributed to Daniel Marot I), but the 'introspection' of the individual gardens, each with its own views and decorations, is typically Dutch. The main axis runs east–west the full length of the

garden, through wooded areas, avenues and formal gardens. All the paths are narrow, to disguise the narrowness of the estate itself. Behind the house are *parterres de broderie* decorated with statues and fountains, with William III symbolized by the statue of *Hercules*. A triumphal arch leads from the parterres to the orangery garden, which is closed at the western end by the semicircular orangery with a central pavilion giving a view back to the house, a design similar to that at Zorgvliet. In the southern vegetable garden is an Italian-style shell grotto, completed in 1699 and based on that at Dieren (owned by William III). Van Velthuysen's house also has been attributed to Marot, and the red and grisaille marble panels of the great hall are similar to those for De Voorst. A number of watercolours and a bird's-eye view by Isaac de Moucheron (Haarlem, Teylers Mus.) record the estate's appearance *c.* 1700. The house was largely destroyed by fire in 1987, with only the great hall remaining intact. The original garden design, despite later changes, is still recognizable.

BIBLIOGRAPHY
H. W. M. Van der Wijck: *De Nederlandse buitenplaats* [Dutch garden plans] (Alphen aan de Rijn, 1982), pp. 157–76
The Anglo-Dutch Garden in the Age of William and Mary (exh. cat., ed. J. Dixon Hunt and E. de Jong; Apeldoorn, Pal. Het Loo; London, Christie's; 1988–9), pp. 193–8 [special double issue of *J. Gdn Hist.*, vii/2–3 (1988)]
L. B. Wevers: *Heemstede: Architectonisch onderzoek van een zeventiende-eeuwse buitenplaats in te provincie Utrecht* (Delft, 1991)

□

Heep, (Adolf) Franz (*b* Fechbach, Silesia, 24 July 1902; *d* Paris, 4 March 1978). Brazilian architect of Silesian birth. He studied architecture in Germany at the Kunstschule, Frankfurt am Main, where he met Adolf Meyer and became his assistant in Frankfurt until Meyer's death in 1929. He then moved to Paris and worked for Le Corbusier. In 1932 he set up an office with Jean Ginsberg, designing blocks of flats that successfully adapted the design principles of Le Corbusier's villas to the typology of the infill building, and he became well known in the Paris region. He left Paris in World War II and moved to Brazil where he settled in São Paulo, at first working in engineering and construction offices and then establishing his own architectural office in 1950. He became a naturalized citizen in 1952 and obtained official recognition as an architect in 1959. Since 1870 the city of São Paulo had shown a marked preference for foreign architects; Heep therefore found himself in a favourable environment and was able to make a considerable mark on the city centre with his buildings. His work was characterized by rigorous technical design in construction, specifications and finishes, and by careful planning; it was strongly influenced by Le Corbusier but also by German design of the 1920s and by innovative design in Brazil. Important examples in São Paulo include the Itália building (1956–9), an office building designed as a triangular tower with curved corners, covered with *brise-soleil*, that was the tallest structure in Brazil; the Lausanne (1953–8) and Lugano-Locarno (1962) buildings, blocks of flats; and the church of S Domingos, designed in 1952, attached to the Dominican convent and parish headquarters at Perdizes, on which he worked for 14 years and which he considered to be his finest work. He taught at the Mackenzie School of

Architecture, São Paulo, and also worked for the United Nations (1965–8) as a member of the Architecture Council for Latin American countries.

BIBLIOGRAPHY
C. A. C. Lemos: *Arquitetura brasileira* (São Paulo, 1979)
Y. Bruand: *Arquitetura contemporânea no Brasil* (São Paulo, 1981)
W. Zanini, ed.: *Historia geral da arte no Brasil* (São Paulo, 1983)
C. Gati: 'Perfil de Arquiteto: Franz Heep', *Projeto*, 97 (1987), pp. 97–104

JULIO ROBERTO KATINSKY

Heeramaneck, Nasli M. (*b* Bombay, 1902; *d* New York, 1971). American dealer of Indian birth. Following the decline of the family textile business, his father, Munchersa Heeramaneck, became an antiquities dealer and shrewdly developed a speciality in Chinese ceramics. As a youth, Nasli was assigned to the New Delhi office, but in 1922 he was sent to Paris to study and open a branch. He soon moved to New York, which became the final location for Heeramaneck Galleries. In 1939 Heeramaneck married Alice Arvine, an American portrait painter from New Haven, and she became an active partner in the business. They were responsible for the acquisition of many great works of Indian, Tibetan and Nepali sculpture, Mughal and Rajput painting, Ancient Near Eastern and Islamic art, and Central Asian (including nomadic) art by major American museums. They also formed a comprehensive private collection of South Asian art, including superlative paintings and sculptures from the Himalayan regions, and a smaller collection of ancient Near Eastern and Islamic art, both purchased by the Los Angeles County Museum of Art. A smaller group of important South Asian works was acquired by the Virginia Museum in Richmond. The Heeramanecks also gave a collection of Pre-Columbian art to the National Museum of India, New Delhi.

BIBLIOGRAPHY
The Arts of India and Nepal: The Nasli and Alice Heeramaneck Collection (exh. cat., Boston, MA, Mus. F.A., 1966)
P. Pal, ed.: *Islamic Art: The Nasli M. Heeramaneck Collection* (Los Angeles, 1974)
A. Heeramaneck: *Masterpieces of Indian Painting Formerly in the Nasli M. Heeramaneck Collections* (Verona, 1979)
——: *Masterpieces of Indian Sculpture from the Nasli M. Heeramaneck Collections* (Verona, 1979)

MILO CLEVELAND BEACH

Heere, de. South Netherlandish family of artists. Jan de Heere the elder (*b* 1502/5; *d* 1576/8) worked in Ghent from 1526 or earlier, probably following his apprenticeship in Mechelen, where he was born. He worked in the studio of the sculptor Jan de Smijtere (*d* 1528) and married his daughter Anna, a painter of miniatures. Little survives of his work, although he was the leading architect and sculptor in Ghent for several decades. He collaborated with Jan Gossart in 1529 on the mausoleum of Isabella of Austria (1501–26) and with Frans Floris in 1562 on the altar to St Luke in St Bavo's Cathedral, Ghent. His work spans the transition from Gothic to Renaissance styles in the southern Netherlands. In 1559 he designed the rood screen for St Bavo's, commissioned to celebrate the 23rd Chapter of the Order of the Golden Fleece. Two sons from his marriage, Jan de Heere the younger and (1) Lucas de Heere, both became painters. The latter remains the best-known member of the family through his activities in the fields of painting, literature and politics. Jan de Heere the younger is documented as having assisted his brother with the civic decorations for the official Entry of William the Silent into Antwerp in 1577.

BIBLIOGRAPHY
NBW; Thieme–Becker

(1) Lucas de Heere (*b* Ghent, *c.* 1534; *d* ?Ghent, *c.* 29 Aug 1584). Painter, tapestry designer, draughtsman and poet. He was probably trained by his parents. The suggestion that he became a member of the Ghent Guild of St Luke before 1540 was derived from an incorrect interpretation of the Guild records for 1574–5. Van Mander recorded that, as a boy, de Heere accompanied his father on his trips to the stone-quarries of the Meuse region, where he made topographical drawings. Lucas was sent to Frans Floris's studio *c.* 1555 or shortly before to complete his training, and he may have collaborated with his master on tapestry cartoons and stained-glass designs, although no cartoons or preparatory drawings survive. During this period de Heere also became noted as a poet in the local rhetoricians' chambers. His father's influence helped him to gain commissions in Ghent from 1555, and, according to Marcus van Vaernewijck (1568), he worked on new stained-glass windows for the St Janskerk in Ghent in the same year. In 1559 de Heere also worked on the rood screen built to his father's designs in St Bavo's and painted *Solomon and the Queen of Sheba* (Ghent, St Bavo Cathedral), in which the composition and the figures were strongly influenced by Floris; the quality of the execution, however, is poor.

Between 1559 and 1561 de Heere was in Paris and at Fontainebleau, where, according to his own testimony, he was in the service of Catherine de' Medici as a tapestry designer. This visit gave him the opportunity to study the work of the Italians Niccolò dell' Abate, Rosso Fiorentino and Primaticcio as well as the local Mannerist artists of the Fontainebleau school.

De Heere's most productive period was from *c.* 1561 to 1567, when he was back in Ghent, at which time van Mander was one of his pupils. Several paintings are known from the period, including a *Crucifixion* for the village church of Sint-Pauwels near Sint-Niklaas, between Ghent and Antwerp (*in situ*), a *View of the Estate of St Bavo, near Ghent* (Ghent, Rijksuniv.), both of 1564, and *The Liberal Arts Awakened by Mercury after the War* (Turin, Gal. Sabauda). He also provided drawings to illustrate the *Emblemata* of Johannes Sambucus (1531–84), published by Christoph Plantin (Antwerp, 1564). De Heere was also active as a writer: his most important poems appeared in these years, and he is believed to have begun a series of artists' biographies in verse.

De Heere's marriage to Eleonora Carboniers, daughter of the mayor of Veere in Zeeland, may have influenced his decision to join the Calvinists. His religious and political sympathies made him suspect to the Spanish authorities, and this is probably the reason for his departure for London in April 1567. His exile in England enabled him to compile several treatises on the history and culture of the British Isles and to collect source material for a costume book, the *Théâtre de tous les peuples et nations de la terre* (Ghent, Rijksuniv., MS. 2466), which was probably produced for Edward Fiennes de Clinton, 1st Earl of Lincoln.

Most of de Heere's commissioned work, however, was for portraits of the English aristocracy (although a number of the works formerly attributed to him and bearing the signature HE are now attributed to Hans Eworth). John de Critz and Marcus Gheeraerts (ii) worked as de Heere's pupils in London.

After the Pacification of Ghent (8 Nov 1576) de Heere returned to the city and devoted himself to the cause of William the Silent. He organized the entries of William (1577) and François, Duc d'Anjou (1587), into the city, while the designs for the Valois Tapestries (1582–5; Florence, Uffizi) have been shown to be by de Heere (see Yates). These eight tapestries were commissioned by Prince William and intended as a gift to Henry III, King of France, in an attempt to win his support for the Dutch cause. De Heere drew his inspiration from drawings of court festivities by Antoine Caron (Paris, Louvre); the resulting tapestries are among the finest of their kind.

WRITINGS
Den hof en boomgaerd der poësien [The garden and orchard of poetry] (Ghent, 1565) [incl. an ode to Hubert and Jan van Eyck's Ghent Altarpiece]
Beschrijving der Britische Eilanden [Description of the British Isles] (*c.* 1573–5; London, BL, Add. MS. 28, 330); ed. T. M. Chotzen and A. M. E. Draak (Antwerp, 1937)
Beschriyving van het . . . incomste van d'excellentie des Princen van Oraengien (Ghent, 1578)
L'Entrée manifique de Monsieur Francoys (Ghent, 1582; Berlin, Kupfer-stichkab., MS. 78 D6)

NBW   BIBLIOGRAPHY
F. Yates: *The Valois Tapestries* (London, 1959)
A. Piron: 'Lucas d'Heere, peintre et poète gantois', *An. Ver. Gesch. Belg. Protestantisme*, iv (1965), pp. 361–78; v (1966), pp. 403–20
C. Van de Velde: 'Enkele gegevens over Gentse schilderijen, I: Het stadsgezicht van Lucas de Heere' [Rare information about Ghent's painters, I: the city views of Lucas de Heere], *Gent. Bijdr. Kstgesch. & Oudhdknd.*, xx (1967), pp. 193–217
J. Becker: 'Zur niederländischen Kunstliteratur des 16. Jahrhunderts: Lucas de Heere', *Simiolus*, vi (1972–3), pp. 113–27
A. Derolez: 'Aantekeningen omtrent structuur, datering en betekenis van het Kostuumboek van Lucas de Heere' [Notes concerning the structure, dating and significance of Lucas de Heere's costume book], *Handelingen van het XXIXe Vlaams Filologencongres: Antwerp, 1973*, pp. 261–71
W. Waterschoot: 'Leven en betekenis van Lucas d'Heere' [The life and importance of Lucas de Heere], *Versl. & Meded. Kon. Acad. Ned. Taal- & Lettknd.* (1974)
——: *Ter liefde der const: Uit het 'Schilder-boeck' (1604) van Karel van Mander* [For the love of art: from the *Schilder-boeck* (1604) of Karel van Mander] (Leiden, 1983)

                    CARL VAN DE VELDE

Heerup, Henry (*b* Copenhagen, 4 Nov 1907; *d* Copenhagen, 30 May 1993). Danish sculptor, painter, designer and printmaker. He studied painting at the Konelige Danske Kunstakademi, Copenhagen, under Aksel Jørgensen and Ejnar Nielsen, and he briefly studied sculpture until informed he lacked talent. From 1942 he exhibited at the *Cornerudstilling* and *Høstudstilling*, and from 1949 he was a member of the group Decembristerne (the Decembrists). He had close connections with the avant-garde periodicals *Linien*, *Helhesten* and *Cobra*, and he participated in the great international Cobra exhibitions. Heerup's work, however, was always individual. His popular pieces have timeless and universal subjects depicted in bright colours and a narrative, naively simplified, formal language. He often used the Trinity of the family: man, woman and child and such symbols as the wheel of life,

the heart, the cross and the bell, and he often incorporated a portrait of himself, with a bicycle and a goblin's cap. Over the years he became something of a myth, as the happy 'foreman of the Goblins' Union', as he styled himself. He also tackled darker subject-matter such as death, pain and separation, however.

Many of Heerup's most important paintings derive directly from his everyday life, for example the *Vanlose Madonna* (1934; see Wilmann, pl. 15), the *Suckling Babe* (1934; see Wilmann, pl. 16), *Night and Day* (1944; see Wilmann, p. 212) and *Frieze of Life* (1952; see Wilmann, pl. 39). Over the course of many years he created paintings, debris sculptures and stone sculptures in his allotment garden in Rodøvre, a suburb of Copenhagen, from which he borrowed many of his subjects, for example the cats. The debris sculptures include the *Gramophone Man* (1935; see Wilmann, pl. 36), the *Ironing-board Madonna* (1937), a *Soldier* (1940) and *Death Coughs* (1943; see Wilmann, pl. 31). Typically Heerup's first study trip was a bicycle tour to see the medieval stone at Jelling, with its Viking ornament. The granite and limestone sculptures he himself chiselled are in his own garden, and at the Sculpture Garden at the Louisiana Museum, Humlebæk, where they seem to grow out of the earth. He also undertook a large number of decorative commissions, including the Tivoli Gardens Play Park, Copenhagen (1958), the Children's Park at Vesterbro (1963) and Køge Bugt Beach Park (1982). He also illustrated a number of books and designed chemists' envelopes, book covers, wine labels and posters, among other things. On his 80th birthday he was honoured with a torchlight procession.

WRITINGS
Fløjte Huggas Billedbog [Whistling Hugga's picture book] (1953) [Hugga was Heerup's pet name]
Nis og Nutte (1965) [children's bk]
Min arbejdsbog [My workbook] (1966)

BIBLIOGRAPHY
C. Dotremont: *Henry Heerup*, Cobra Biblioteket, i/12 (Copenhagen, 1950)
P. Wilmann: *Henry Heerup* (Copenhagen, 1962) [Dan. and Eng. text]
Henry Heerup: Linoleumssnit og litografier [Henry Heerup: linocuts and lithographs] (Copenhagen, 1962)
P. Vad: *Henry Heerup* (Copenhagen, 1971)
H. Moestrup: *Henry Heerups grafiske værk, 1930–80* [Henry Heerup's graphic work] (Charlottenlund, 1981)
Blomster fra Heerups have [Flowers from Heerup's garden] (exh. cat. by R. Dahlmann Olsen, Copenhagen, Kstforen., 1987)
Henry Heerup (exh. cat., Århus, Kstmus., 1988) [Dan. and Eng. text]

VIDEO AND FILM RECORDINGS
J. J. Thorsen: *Et år med Henry* [A year with Henry], Denmark, Statens Filmcentral (1968) [film, 16 mm]

                    BIRGIT HESSELLUND

Hees, Willem van. *See* HESIUS, WILLEM.

Hefele, Melchior (*b* Kaltenbrunn, Tyrol, 11 Jan 1716; *d* Steinamanger [now Szombathely, Hungary], 17 April 1794). Austrian architect. From 1734 he helped with the drawings for the famous ornamental railings (destr. 1821) erected by Johann Georg Oegg (1703–80) in front of the Residenz at Würzburg. He then studied at the Akademie der Bildenden Künste, Vienna, and later taught architecture in the city. In 1756 he was commissioned to erect an altarpiece and pulpit in the pilgrimage church at Sonntagberg, the design for which secured him election to the

Akademie in 1757. In 1763 he began the reconstruction of the archbishop's palace at Passau (completed 1771) in the Rococo style. His duties as drawing master to the Life Guard of Hungarian Nobles probably brought him into contact with the Captain General of the Guards, Prince Miklós Esterházy, who commissioned him in 1764 to carry out huge extensions to the family palace at Esterháza (now FERTŐD) in Hungary. Only the central block, however, was completed to Hefele's designs, the wings being added by the estate architect E. Mödlhammer, and when in 1784 Miklós Jacoby published a description and plans of the building and claimed authorship for the whole palace, Hefele renounced all claims to the design in protest. The Rococo exuberance of his work at Sonntagberg and Passau reappears in the high altar and St Stephen's altar (1771–3) in Győr Cathedral. Hefele's first foray into Neo-classicism was his redecoration of the chapel of St Peregrinus in the Servite church in Vienna, using black Lilienfeld marble picked out in gold, but the Palace of the Primates that he built (1777–81) at Pressburg (now Bratislava, Slovakia) for the Cardinal Archbishop Joseph Batthyány was designed in a mature Neo-classical style (*see* BRATISLAVA, fig. 2). He did not abandon his past style completely, however, and the cathedral and bishop's palace (begun 1791) built for Bishop János Szily at Steinamanger retain Baroque rather than Neo-classical proportions.

UNPUBLISHED SOURCES

Budapest, N. Széchényi Lib., MS. Hung. 2151 [essay on the palace at Esterháza by J. Hárich, 1944]

BIBLIOGRAPHY

L. Kemény: *Melchior Hefele* (Pozsony, 1915)
P. Voit: 'Schloss Esterházy', *Paläste, Schlösser, Residenzen* (Brunswick, 1971), pp. 222–32

PÁL VOIT

Hegedušić, Krsto (*b* Petrinja, 26 Nov 1901; *d* Zagreb, 7 April 1975). Croatian painter and illustrator. He graduated from the Zagreb Academy in 1926. He spent the following two years studying painting in Paris. On his return he lived in Zagreb and Hlebine, where he helped to develop the HLEBINE SCHOOL of naive painters. He was one of the co-founders of the left-wing group Zemlja in 1929 (*see* LAND GROUP), acting as its secretary until 1935, when it was banned by the police. He began to teach at the Zagreb Academy of Fine Arts in 1937 and was appointed Professor of the Academy after World War II. After 1950 he led a master workshop for postgraduate students of painting.

Hegedušić's early career coincided with a revival of realism in its many forms, including Surrealism, Neue Sachlichkeit and socially critical art. He was sympathetic to the ideologies of these movements, for the Zemlja group, too, consisted of artists who were committed fighters for social justice. There was a clear reference to Pieter Bruegel I in the iconography and style of peasant scenes, which provided a suitable subject-matter for them and for Hegedušić in paintings such as *Iustitia* (1936; Skopje, A. G.).

After World War II Hegedušić remained faithful to his style of painting, the horrors of past experience having heightened his awareness of the individual's helplessness in the face of social and ideological repression. His realism was characterized by the exclusion of superfluous descriptive details, a flat depiction of the scene, schematized,

puppet-like figures, and a specific, monotonous atmosphere that was often heightened by a simple choice of colours. Such paintings as the *Dead Waters* (1956; Belgrade, Mus. Contemp. A.) and *Finale 1945* (1957; Dubrovnik, A.G.) contain poignant reminiscences of the war's horrors, portraying them without pathos, thirst for revenge or Socialist propaganda. The painter's mastery lies in his way of rendering the mood and macabre atmosphere purely through the use of the most rudimentary figurative vocabulary and by sticking fragments of unorthodox material such as printed paper, fabric, soil or metal on to the canvas.

Hegedušić was preoccupied with thoughts of man, man's existence, fate and transitoriness. In his last 20 years he put an even greater emphasis on the tragedy of man's loneliness, especially in an urban setting (e.g. *Liqueur Foxy*, 1958; Zagreb, priv. col., see 1980 exh. cat.).

BIBLIOGRAPHY

M. Krleža: *Krsto Hegedušić: Podravski motivi* [Krsto Hegedušić: scenes from Podravina] (Zagreb, 1933)
Krsto Hegedušić (exh. cat., text M. Šolman; Zagreb, Gal. Mod. A., 1973)
M. Krleža, V. Milenković and D. Schneider: *Krsto Hegedušić* (Zagreb, 1974)
M. Matković: 'Krsto Hegedušić', *Forum*, iv–v (1975)
Jugoslovensko slikarstvo seste decenije [Yugoslav painting of the 1950s] (exh. cat., Belgrade, Mus. Contemp. A., 1980)

JURE MIKUŽ

Hegel, Georg Wilhelm Friedrich (*b* Stuttgart, 27 Aug 1770; *d* Berlin, 14 Nov 1831). German philosopher. From 1788 until 1793 he was a student at the university at Tübingen where he read philosophy and theology. He held academic posts at Jena between 1801 and 1806, but his career there was cut short by the Napoleonic occupation of the city. After a period as a newspaper editor and then as rector of a gymnasium at Nuremberg, he returned to university teaching, holding a chair of philosophy at Heidelberg in 1816 and one at Berlin two years later. The works he published during his lifetime fell mainly within the spheres of metaphysics, epistemology and political theory; while at Berlin, however, he also gave extensive lecture courses on other branches of philosophy, including aesthetics. The lectures on aesthetics, which Hegel delivered on various occasions during the 1820s, were edited and published posthumously in 1835.

In developing his philosophical system, which was formidable in its scope and daunting in its complexity, Hegel assigned to aesthetics a position of great importance. He considered art, along with religion and philosophy, one of the fundamental modes of consciousness whereby human beings acquired a profound comprehension both of themselves and of the world they inhabited. Thus he felt obliged to undertake a careful investigation of its nature and significance. But the close attention he paid to it also had a more personal source: Hegel was deeply responsive to, and knowledgeable about, certain forms of artistic achievement.

1. ART AND NATURE. Hegel's treatment of art was copiously illustrated with examples, therein contrasting markedly with that of his major predecessor in aesthetics, Immanuel Kant. This was connected with a further divergence over the relative importance of natural and

artistic beauty. In his *Kritik der Urteilskraft* (Berlin, 1790) Kant had argued that, to count as a proper object of aesthetic appreciation, a thing had to exhibit a satisfying but purely formal coherence or design, the distinctive pleasure it occasioned not being determined by any possible cognitive or practical interest on the part of the viewer. In choosing candidates for such appreciation he tended to give priority to products of nature rather than to human artefacts; and, although in the sections he specifically devoted to the fine arts he introduced significant modifications to his position, the overall impression left by his book is that—at least in terms of what he called 'free beauty'—it was nature, not art, that ultimately had the superior claim to aesthetic attention and admiration.

The emphasis in Hegel's *Vorlesungen über Ästhetik* is altogether different; he stressed at the outset that the essential concern of aesthetics was with art rather than nature. It was not enough merely to affirm that the beauty of art ranked 'higher' than that of nature, although Hegel began by asserting just this. The very suggestion, implicit in much of what Kant wrote, that the two domains could be judged according to some common scale of aesthetic comparison itself betrayed a basic misunderstanding. Hegel had no desire to deny that human beings commonly ascribed beauty to natural objects. Nevertheless, the context in which this was done was wholly distinct from that to which works of art belonged, and the Kantian implication that a fundamental continuity existed between natural and artistic beauty had therefore to be rejected. The creations of art, by contrast with those of nature, were 'born of the mind' and could be properly appreciated only in the light of that crucial difference. To perceive an object as being an uncontrived product of natural conditions was one thing; to recognize it as an expression of human thought and intention was quite another, bringing into play a range of responses and considerations that had no counterpart in the passive enjoyment of nature. Only mind, Hegel affirmed, was 'capable of truth', and it was as 'partaking in this higher element' that the superiority of the artistic standpoint asserted itself. Art had a cognitive dimension: it was 'a specific way of expressing and representing the true'.

In formulating his ideas concerning how art expressed and represented the true, Hegel was at pains to dissociate his own position from two cardinal misconceptions. According to the first of these, art was simply a means of conveying a determinate meaning or message that could be communicated without substantial loss in some alternative manner—for example, through an abstract proposition that expressed exactly the same sense, albeit in a less attractive or palatable form. According to the second, which had a long and variegated history, art amounted to no more than the reproduction of sensuous appearances in another, artificial, medium; its truth consisted in the faithful imitation of nature. Each of these views distorted—in opposite but equally trivializing ways—what was essentially at issue. Although art did involve both sensuous and intellectual elements, neither could be treated in abstraction from the other: the work of art stood 'in the *middle* between immediate sensuousness and ideal thought' and in a fashion that entailed an indissoluble fusion of the two. Fine art, Hegel claimed, 'embodies thought', and by this he meant that the intellectual or 'spiritual' content of an artistic work permeated the individual form in which it was sensuously revealed, the latter constituting its uniquely adequate expression; such a work might be compared to 'a thousand-eyed Argus, so that the inner soul and spirituality can be seen at every point'. So understood, art could be said concretely to display or 'show forth' its cognitive insights into, and presentiments about, reality at the level of the purely intuitive, i.e. non-discursive, consciousness: in Hegel's phrase, it was 'the sensuous appearance [*Scheinen*] of the Idea'.

2. THE HISTORICITY OF ART. In the light of the above conception of art's distinctive character Hegel embarked upon the detailed examination of its various manifestations that occupied the main body of his lectures. In his eyes this conception typically functioned as an ideal of beauty, which was by no means completely exemplified in all the recognizable modes of artistic achievement. It is arguable, indeed, that there was only one phase of art's development in which he saw this ideal as fully actualized. This was connected with the fact that he elaborated his aesthetic theory against the background of a teleological interpretation of history that ultimately derived from his Idealist metaphysics. Thus the human mind or spirit was assumed to change and progress over time, realizing itself in different types of life and culture and ascending thereby to higher stages of self-knowledge and understanding. According to Hegel, these successive stages were reflected at the level of artistic expression in the emergence of three corresponding 'art-forms', broadly divided into the 'symbolic', the 'classical' and the 'romantic'.

Such a historically orientated viewpoint had two significant consequences. First, no given work of art could be truly understood and appreciated without taking into account its social and cultural context; and here Hegel's approach proved to be hugely influential on subsequent generations of German critics and art historians. Secondly, it led Hegel himself to suggest that each of the various artistic media was especially well adapted to manifesting the kind of outlook or vision implicit in one particular art form. This idea had some curious implications, and in his own practice Hegel did not always apply it with systematic rigour. Even so, it played a prominent role in the account he provided of the visual arts, where architecture was specifically aligned with symbolic art, sculpture with classical art and painting with romantic art. His manner of portraying these affinities, in which conceptual and religious themes were confusingly interwoven with his characteristically historical preoccupations, is often elusive and raises notorious difficulties of interpretation.

3. VARIETIES OF VISUAL ART. For Hegel, symbolic art exemplified a mode of consciousness in which the mind had only an inadequate intimation of its own nature and of its relation to the material world. This found essential expression in architecture, a non-representational type of art where matter was manipulated in a fashion that afforded no more than a hint of the 'spiritual inner life' towards which it enigmatically pointed. One example adduced by Hegel was that of the Egyptian pyramid, which was related in a purely external way to the inner entity it

housed, and he also referred to the allegedly symbolic significance of such constructions as obelisks and Indian pagodas.

By contrast, classical art exhibited an outlook wherein external matter and interior spirit were seen as wholly integrated, one being the complete expression of the other. Here the perception of an underlying unity of mind and body was pre-eminently captured by the sculpted human forms of ancient Greece. In these works 'no expression is left to the sensuous which is not an expression of spirit itself', the two appearing 'in their eternal peace and essential self-sufficiency'. In Hegel's opinion, which here as elsewhere was strongly influenced by the writings of Johann Joachim Winckelmann, such art constituted the 'pinnacle' of artistic beauty—'nothing', he wrote, 'can be or become more beautiful'. Finally, Hegel regarded romantic art, which was broadly speaking associated with the history of Christian Europe and whose most profound products lay in the fields of painting, music and literature, as manifesting a deeper insight into the subjective determinations of the human spirit, an insight that could no longer be satisfied by the expressive forms that endowed classical works with their poignant and unrepeatable aesthetic quality. In the case of painting, this emphasis on subjective inwardness was reflected in the reduction of three-dimensional reality to the limits of a surface plane, thus 'curtailing' its externality; at the same time, a painting (unlike a statue) presented its content from one particular viewpoint with which the spectator necessarily identified, his own consciousness being thereby inextricably involved in that content. Hegel connected such features, somewhat obliquely, with the spiritual significance of Christianity. But, while he considered pictorial art to be ideally suited to the presentation of Christian themes, he never implied that it should confine itself to these. Both portraiture, as revealing the individual soul of the sitter, and landscape painting, as expressive of a deeply felt inner accord with the eloquent forms of nature, were fully accepted as being among its proper concerns.

Set out in bare and abstract terms, the framework within which Hegel approached the visual arts may appear theoretically constrictive and in many ways historically unbalanced or implausible. The enduring interest of what he wrote on the subject, however, lies less in its overall structure than in the imaginative and subtle fashion in which he deployed some of his leading ideas to throw light on particular works and styles: here his detailed observations, especially about painting, were often acute and at times apparently prescient. One may cite, for example, his celebration of the incisive brilliance with which 17th-century Dutch painting illuminates the seemingly trivial preoccupations of everyday life and his further claim that a time had come when the artist 'stands above specific consecrated forms and configurations' and can range freely 'in an inexhaustible self-abandon of imagination', his powers engaged in an unconstrained 'innocent play', an 'infinite plasticity' (*unendliche Herumbildung*). Certainly no major philosopher, either before Hegel wrote or since, has shown a more comprehensive appreciation of art's contribution to the development of the human mind or has displayed greater daring in attempting to identify and explain what that contribution involved.

WRITINGS
Vorlesungen über Ästhetik (Berlin, 1835, rev. 1842); Eng. trans. by T. M. Knox as *Hegel's Aesthetics: Lectures on Fine Art*, 2 vols (Oxford, 1975)

BIBLIOGRAPHY
J. Kaminsky: *Hegel on Art* (New York, 1962)
E. H. Gombrich: *In Search of Cultural History* (Oxford, 1969)
C. Taylor: *Hegel* (Cambridge, 1975), chap. 17
C. Karelis: 'Hegel's Concept of Art: An Interpretative Essay', *Hegel's Introduction to 'Aesthetics'*, Eng. trans. by T. M. Knox (Oxford, 1979), pp. xi–lxxvi
M. Moran: 'On the Continuing Significance of Hegel's *Aesthetics*', *Brit. J. Aesth.*, xxi (1981), pp. 214–39
M. Podro: *Critical Historians of Art* (London, 1982)
S. Bungay: *Beauty and Truth: A Study of Hegel's Aesthetics* (Oxford, 1984)
P. Gardiner: 'Kant and Hegel on Aesthetics', *Hegel's Critique of Kant*, ed. S. Priest (Oxford, 1987), pp. 161–71

PATRICK GARDINER

Hegemann, Werner (Manfred Maria Ellis) (*b* Mannheim, 15 June 1881; *d* New York, 12 Apr 1936). German urban planner, writer and editor. He studied urban planning, art history and economics in Berlin, Munich, Paris and Strasbourg, and at the University of Pennsylvania, Philadelphia. He took a doctorate in political science at Munich in 1908. His travels made him aware from an early date of the importance of social issues in urban planning. He organized planning exhibitions in Boston (1909), Berlin (1910) and elsewhere, and he published his conclusions in an influential two-volume work, *Der Städtebau* (1911–13), which led directly to the formation of Berlin's municipal structure, the Zweckverband Gross-Berlin, in 1912; in 1920 this became the Einheitsgemeinde Gross-Berlin, an organization that survived until the division of the city in 1948. From 1913 to the end of World War I, Hegemann was in the USA, working both as a teacher and as a planner. Back in Germany, from 1924 to 1933 he edited the architectural monthly *Wasmuths Monatshefte für Baukunst*, which amalgamated with another periodical, *Der Städtebau*, in 1930. His principal critical work as a writer was *Das steinerne Berlin* (1930). This was not only a polemical account of the growth and architecture of Berlin but also a vigorous demand for action. Hegemann called for the abandonment of the capitalist system of land ownership and use, proposing instead a rationalization of the metropolitan structure and a transport policy based on social priorities, including an efficient high-speed rail network. He also published numerous works of literature and criticism, mainly under pseudonyms, including studies of Frederick II, King of Prussia, Napoleon and other historical figures, whose critical stance earned him the hatred of the conservatives and right-wing radicals. Deprived of his citizenship when the Nazis came to power in 1933, he went to the USA and taught urban planning at Columbia University, New York.

WRITINGS
Der Städtebau nach den Ergebnissen der Allgemeinen Städtebau-Ausstellung in Berlin, 2 vols (Berlin, 1911–13)
The American Vitruvius (New York, 1922/*R* 1972)
Das steinerne Berlin (Berlin, 1930, rev. 1963)

BIBLIOGRAPHY
D. Calabi: 'Werner Hegemann: O dell'ambiguità borghese dell' urbanistica', *Casabella*, xli/428 (1977), pp. 54–60
C. Crasemann Collins: 'A Visionary Discipline: Werner Hegemann and the Quest for the Pragmatic Ideal', *Center: J. Archit. America*, v (1989), pp. 74–85

GÜNTHER KÜHNE

Hegewald, Zacharias (*b* Chemnitz, Saxony, 1596; *d* Dresden, 30 March 1639). German sculptor. He was the son of a sculptor, Michael Hegewald (*fl* 1595–1626). He trained with Sebastian Walther, whose daughter he married in 1626. He was first influenced by Giovanni Maria Nosseni, on whose tomb in the Sophienkirche in Dresden (now Dresden, Mus. Gesch. and Dresden, Frauenkirche; for illustration *see* WALTHER, (4)) he worked with Walther until 1616. As well as producing small-scale sculptures for the court of the Elector John-George I of Saxony, which later earned him the title of court sculptor, he was employed from 1626 in the workshop for the Lusthaus (destr. 1746) in Dresden. His wax model for a bronze statue of *Electress Sophie* was lost in a casting accident in 1627–8. He made for the Elector the life-size statues of *Adam* and *Eve* (1630–31; Dresden, Skulpsamml.; destr. 1945), which were the first pure nudes of monumental format to be produced in Saxony. In them the influence of Michelangelo is evident, as well as that of the Flemish Mannerism of Adriaen de Vries. Hegewald's smaller sculptures include the sandstone *Ecce homo* on the monument to *David Peifer* (Dresden, Kreuzkirche). In the altar of the church at Kötzschenbroda near Dresden, completed in 1638, a figurative relief is incorporated into a very lively and elaborate scrollwork frame. Hegewald's early Baroque oeuvre is completed by figurative tomb carvings, such as the epitaph for *Wolf E. von Ponickau* (1617; Kamenz, Stadtkirche) and the funerary monuments of *Michael Schulze* and *Elisabeth von Haugwitz* (1631; Dresden, Sophienkirche), all of which were destroyed in 1945.

BIBLIOGRAPHY
Thieme–Becker
W. von Seidlitz: *Kunst in Dresden*, i (Dresden, 1921), pp. 386, 395, 424
W. Hentschel: *Dresdener Bildhauer des 16. und 17. Jahrhunderts* (Weimar, 1966), pp. 88–92, figs 100–05
Barockplastik in Norddeutschland (exh. cat., ed. J. Rasmussen; Hamburg, Mus. Kst & Gew., 1977), pp. 294–303

CHRISTIAN DITTRICH

Hegias [Hegesias; Hagesias] (*fl* early 5th century BC). Greek sculptor. In the absence of original statues or attributed copies, almost nothing can be said of his works or style; what little is known comes primarily from literary sources. Pausanias (*Guide to Greece* VIII.xlii.10) recorded that Hegias was an Athenian, a contemporary of Onatas of Aigina and of Ageladas, the reputed teacher of Myron and Polykleitos; Dio Chrysostomos (*Orationes* LV.1) referred to him as the teacher of Pheidias. Pliny cited him as a contemporary of Kritios and Nesiotes, and mentioned several statues by him (*Natural History* XXXIV.xix.49, 78): the *Dioscouroi* in front of the Temple of Jupiter Tonans in Rome; a group of boys riding racehorses; an *Athena*; *King Pyrrhus*, undoubtedly the son of Achilles rather than the Hellenistic king; and a *Herakles*. His signature survives on an inscribed statue base from the Athenian Acropolis (*Inscr. Gr./2*, i, 526) dated to before 480 BC, though confusion exists as to the spelling of the name in literary sources. Quintilian (*Institutio oratoria* XII.x.7) and Lucian (*Rhetorum praeceptor* IX) both referred to Hegesias as having a hard and sinewy style, which Lucian linked to that of Kritios and Nesiotes. Pliny (XXXIV.xix.78) cited Hagesias; both names are accepted as a corruption of Hegias.

BIBLIOGRAPHY
Pauly–Wissowa
J. Overbeck: *Die antiken Schriftquellen zur Geschichte der bildenden Künste bei den Griechen* (Leipzig, 1868), nos 452–6
G. M. A. Richter: *The Sculpture and Sculptors of the Greeks* (New Haven, 1929, rev. 4/1970), p. 156
A. E. Raubitschek: *Dedications from the Athenian Acropolis* (Cambridge, MA, 1949), no. 94

NANCY SERWINT

Hehl, Christoph (Carl Adolf) (*b* Kassel, 11 Oct 1847; *d* Berlin, 18 June 1911). German architect. He was a pupil (1862–6) at the Höhere Gewerbeschule in Kassel where one of his teachers was GEORG GOTTLOB UNGEWITTER who had a considerable influence on him. Hehl then went to England where he stayed until 1869, working for a time in the office of George Gilbert Scott I. From 1869 to 1872 he worked with Edwin Oppler in Hannover where he came into contact with Conrad Wilhelm Hase. In 1872 Hehl started his own office which he ran until 1894. Within a few years his practice had become one of the largest and most important in Hannover. It was at that period that most of the projects attributed to him (estimated at *c.* 170) were executed; of these *c.* 60 buildings are known to survive. His many churches, such as the Dreifaltigkeitskirche (1880–83) in Hannover, were especially admired. However, his secular buildings were more numerous; like the churches, they were generally designed as brick buildings using the Gothic Revival repertory of the Hannover school, as promoted by Hase. These included blocks of flats (the Poppe block in Hannover, 1873), large manor houses and villas (e.g. Villa Leonhardi, Minden, 1879–80), imposing detached houses (e.g. Haus Möller, near Bielefeld, 1881) and hospitals and innumerable parsonages. Hehl repeatedly entered architectural competitions, with great success: his design (1893) for the garrison church in Dresden attracted particular attention. Although it was excluded from the assessment for formal reasons, the design nonetheless led to Hehl's appointment in 1894 to the chair of medieval architecture at Charlottenburg, Berlin. Despite his new commitments Hehl managed to run his own practice in Berlin too, but from then on he limited his building and design work mainly to churches, including the Herz Jesu-Kirche (1897–8) in Berlin.

BIBLIOGRAPHY
Thieme–Becker
T. Unger: 'Die Hannoversche Architekturschule', *Hannover: Führer durch die Stadt und ihre Bauten* (Hannover, 1882/*R* 1978), pp. 107–62
G. Schönermark, ed.: *Die Architektur der Hannoverschen Schule*, 7 vols (Hannover, 1888–95)
H. Reuther: 'Die Sakralbauten von Christoph Hehl', *Niederdt. Beitr. Kstgesch.*, viii (1969), pp. 211–64
H. Behrens: *Die Profanbauten von Christoph Hehl* (diss., Berlin, Tech. U., 1978)

MICHAEL EISSENHAUER

Heian period. Period in Japanese history, AD 794–1185, the beginning of which coincides with the establishment of the imperial capital in Heian (modern Kyoto; *see* KYOTO, §I) and during which the first flowerings of a truly native cultural expression appeared (*see* JAPAN, §I, 2). The imperial capital was transferred to Heian from Nara (*see* NARA, §I) by Emperor Kanmu (*reg* 781–806) in

794, with a view to distancing the throne from the political threats posed by ambitious members of the Buddhist clergy and a growing struggle for power among competing noble families. The plan of Heian was similar to that of Nara but on a larger scale. The new city was on a plain surrounded on three sides by mountains; the rapid currents of the Kamo River gave access to the Inland Sea and the major port of Naniwa (*see* OSAKA, §I, 2) and provided a plentiful water source for the gardens within the aristocratic homes, not available earlier in land-locked Nara.

The Heian period is generally divided into two parts (sometimes extended to three, with a middle period). Early Heian culture of the 9th century continued to reflect close ties with the Asian continent. Two Buddhist clerics KŪKAI (Kobo Daishi) and Saichō (767–822) introduced into the Heian court from China the Shingon ('True Word') and Tendai (Lotus) Buddhist sects respectively (*see* BUDDHISM, §III, 10). Both sects relied heavily on strict religious discipline and complex rituals performed before altars richly adorned with paintings, sculpture and other symbolic objects. Kūkai taught that art was indispensable to the proper understanding of the scriptures, and the deep mysteries of these new teachings, combined with intense visual appeal of the ceremonies, won the generous patronage of the Heian court.

In 894, the Japanese government ceased to send formal missions to China, and the strong Chinese influence that had been so significant for the cultural life of the preceding two centuries began to wane. During the next three centuries the imperial court was dominated by one family, the Fujiwara, who had risen steadily to political eminence since the 7th century and whose name has become synonymous with the late Heian period and the development of a Japanese culture out of the earlier borrowings from the Chinese. Nowhere are the mores and customs of the Heian aristocracy more brilliantly presented than in the *Genji monogatari* ('Tale of Genji'), written in the early 11th century by Murasaki Shikibu, a Fujiwara court lady. The tale of the amorous life of Genji became popular at court, where it was read with relish. A century later, illustrations of key moments in the novel were commissioned through the Edokoro (Imperial Painting Bureau). These illustrations (*c.* 1120–40) represent the earliest extant example of *Yamatoe* ('Japanese-style' painting; *see* JAPAN, §VI, 3(iii)), incorporating the lyrical and decorative elements, love of nature and close attention to the world of human feelings that have traditionally been basic Japanese aesthetic values. Neither Buddhism nor religious art escaped the transforming influence of Fujiwara wealth and patronage. The BYŌDŌIN, a temple complex dedicated to the worship of the Amida Buddha by Fujiwara no Yorimichi (990–1074) in 1053 is the epitome of refinement in architecture, sculpture, painting and garden design, with religion and art uniting to re-create on earth the Buddha's heavenly Western Paradise.

BIBLIOGRAPHY

Murasaki Shikibu: *Genji monogatari* (11th century); Eng. trans. as *The Tale of Genji*, by A. Waley (Boston, 1925–33); by E. Seidensticker (New York, 1976)
T. Fukuyama: *Byōdōin to Chūsonji*, Nihon no bijutsu [Arts of Japan], ix (Tokyo, 1964); *Heian Temples: Byodo-in and Chuson-ji*, Heibonsha Surv. Jap. A., ix (New York and Tokyo, 1976)
I. Morris: *The World of the Shining Prince: Court Life in Ancient Japan* (New York, 1964)
T. Akiyama: *Japanese Painting* (New York, 1977)
H. Ishida: *Esoteric Buddhist Painting* (Tokyo, 1987)

BONNIE ABIKO

Heiberg, Jean (Hjalmar Dahl) (*b* Kristiania [now Oslo], 19 Dec 1884; *d* Oslo, 27 May 1976). Norwegian painter. He was a student at the Håndverks- og Kunstindustriskole, Kristiania, in 1903–4 and the year after with Heinrich Knirr (1862–1944) in Munich. In 1905 he studied briefly with Jules Renard at the Académie Colarossi in Paris, and in 1908 he was the first Norwegian artist to apply to Henri Matisse's newly opened academy. While his earlier paintings can be characterized as naturalistic in their colour values, he later learnt to build up his compositions with the help of complementary colour pairs derived from the principle of the colour triad, as in *Nude* (1912; Bergen, Meyers Saml.). Heiberg stayed in Paris until 1912 and pursued his interest in Paul Cézanne's art and theory, an influence reflected in the landscape *Heath, Ula* (1911; Oslo, N.G.). He again lived in Paris, apart from holidays in Norway, from 1919 to 1929.

Heiberg was strongly influenced by Neo-classicism. In 1921 he came into contact with Pedro Araujo, who preached the importance of the 'eternal laws', with emphasis on the study of the Golden Section. The preparatory studies for *The Family* (1925; Oslo, N.G.) show how Heiberg constructed his compositions according to this principle. Contact with Georg Jacobsen (1887–1976), the Danish theorist of painting, reinforced his interest in geometric systems. Heiberg was prominent as a figure painter, but he also painted portraits and landscapes, such as *Blue Sea* (1913; Stockholm, Mod. Mus.). Heiberg was influential as a professor at the Kunstakademi in Oslo (1935–55) and was its director from 1946 to 1955. His instruction emphasized the importance of form and draughtsmanship.

NKL

BIBLIOGRAPHY

H. Sørensen: 'Jean Heiberg', *Kst & Kult.* [Oslo], xix (1933), pp. 65–78
H. Stenstadvold: *Idékamp og stilskifte i norsk malerkunst 1900–1919* [Battle of ideas and stylistic change in Norwegian painting, 1900–1919] (Trondheim, 1946)
R. Revold: *Norges billedkunst i det 19. og 20. århundre* [Norway's pictorial art in the 19th and 20th centuries], ii (Oslo, 1953), pp. 31, 91, 96, 97–111, 139, 159, 267
B. Rise: *Jean Heiberg* (Oslo, 1955)
K. Berg and others, eds: *Nasjonal vekst* [National growth] (1981), v of *Norges kunsthistorie* (Oslo, 1981–3), pp. 295–8
——: *Mellomkrigstid* [The interwar period] (1983), vi of *Norges kunsthistorie* (Oslo, 1981–3), pp. 114–17
——: *Inn i en ny tid* [Into a new era] (1983), vii of *Norges kunsthistorie* (Oslo, 1981–3)
M. Werenskiold: *The Concept of Expressionism: Origin and Metamorphoses* (Oslo, 1984)
——: 'Matisse og Skandinavia', *Louisiana Revy*, xxv/2 (1985), pp. 42–5
Scandinavian Modernism: Painting in Denmark, Finland, Iceland, Norway and Sweden, 1910–1920 (exh. cat., ed. C. T. Edam, N.-G. Hökby and B. Schreiber; Göteborg, Kstmus.; Oslo, N.G.; Stockholm, Mod. Mus. and elsewhere; 1989–90)
M. Lange and T. Skedsmo: *Nasjonalgalleriet: Katalog: Norske malerier* (Oslo, 1992)

INGEBORG WIKBORG

Heide [Heyde], **Henning von der** (*d* Lübeck, 1521). German sculptor. His career as an independent master in Lübeck probably began in 1485, the year of his marriage, or two years later, when he purchased a house. His early works are stylistically very similar to those of BERNT NOTKE, indicating that he was trained in Notke's Lübeck workshop; scholars disagree on the delineation between the oeuvres of the two masters. The debated works include the *St Jerome* in Vadstena Abbey; the altarpiece of the *Mass of St Gregory* in Rytterne church; the Crucifix from the St Nicolai Chapel in Stockholm (now in Stockholm Cathedral); and the *Pietà* from the Heilig-Geist-Spital, Lübeck (Lübeck, St Annen-Mus.). Although there is no consensus on the body of works for which von der Heide was responsible, it is generally agreed that he tempered the abrupt anatomical exaggerations and facial severity of Notke's striking figures, imbuing his own images with subtle modulations that lent a new individuality to the human figure.

Von der Heide must have been highly regarded among his fellow artists, for in 1513 he presided over the Lübeck painters' and glaziers' guild, to which sculptors also belonged. Although the substantial fortune that he bequeathed shows that he must have headed a highly successful workshop, only two monuments are documented. The Corpus Christi Altarpiece (Lübeck, St Annen-Mus.), commissioned in 1496–7 for the Burgkirche by a Lübeck confraternity, is composed of polychrome reliefs and painted panels. Only the central representation of the *Mass of St Gregory* is considered to be the work of von der Heide himself. His best-known work, the free-standing *St George Killing the Dragon*, carved in 1504–5 for the chapel of St George, Lübeck (Lübeck, St Annen-Mus.), is incomplete, lacking its original dragon, polychrome and socle.

A large number of figures has been attributed to von der Heide and his workshop. They include a *St Stephen* (Skara, Västergötlandsmus.); a *Calvary* (Breningen; Copenhagen, Kstindustmus.); the Crucifix in St Mary's church, Bal Segeberg, the *Head of St John the Baptist* from Norrby church (Stockholm, Nmus.); a standing *Apostle* (Wellesley Coll., MA, Mus.); the *St John the Evangelist* in St Mary's, Lübeck, and the misericords on a choir-stall also in St Mary's. It has been suggested that von der Heide provided the model for the bronze epitaph of Duchess Sophia of Mecklenburg (*d* 1504) in St Mary's, Wismar. Von der Heide came closer to the style of the Italian Renaissance than any other north German sculptor of the Late Gothic period.

BIBLIOGRAPHY

NDB; Thieme–Becker

F. Bruns: 'Die St. Jürgen-Gruppe des Lübecker Museums und ihr Meister', *Z. Ver. Lübeck. Gesch. & Altertknd.*, xv (1913), pp. 213–27 [incl. written sources]

J. Roosval: 'Henning von der Heyde', *Ksthist. Tidskr.*, v (1936), pp. 2–22 [Eng. summary]

T. Demmler: *Skulpturen im Deutschen Museum* (Berlin, 1937), p. 84

W. Paatz: *Bernt Notke und sein Kreis*, i (Berlin, 1939), pp. 147–68

W. Pinder: *Die deutsche Kunst der Dürerzeit* (Leipzig, 1940), pp. 231–2

C. af Ugglas: 'Ett mästerverk', *Fornvännen*, xxxviii (1943), pp. 201–12 [Ger. summary]

S. Karling: *Medeltida träskulptur i Estland* (Göteborg, 1946), pp. 193–216, 277–8 [Eng. summary]

C. af Ugglas: *Efterlämnade konsthistoriska studier av Carl R. af Ugglas* (Stockholm, 1951), pp. 149–58, 300–01 [Fr. summary]

R. Norberg: 'Johannesfatet från Norrby', *Fornvännen*, xlviii (1953), pp. 84–110 [Ger. summary]

W. Meyne: *Lüneburger Plastik des XV. Jahrhunderts* (Lüneburg, 1959), pp. 118–24

M. Hasse: *Lübeck Sankt Annen-Museum: Die sakralen Werke des Mittelalters*, Lübecker Museumsführer i (1964), pp. 32–5, 116–24

——: 'Lübecker Maler und Bildschnitzer um 1500', *Niederdt. Beitr. Kstgesch.*, iii (1964), pp. 285–318

G. von der Osten and H. Vey: *Painting and Sculpture in Germany and the Netherlands, 1500 to 1600*, Pelican Hist. A. (Harmondsworth, 1969), p. 51

P. Tångeberg: 'Madonnan från Tyresö kyrka i Södermanland: Ett rhenländskt arbete?', *Fornvännen*, lxxii (1977), pp. 171–80 [Ger. summary]

D. Gillerman: 'Gothic Sculpture in American Collections. The Checklist: i. The New England Museums (Part 2)', *Gesta*, xx (1981), p. 358

M. Hasse: *Die Marienkirche zu Lübeck* (Munich, 1983), p. 141

CORINE SCHLEIF

Heideck [Heydeck], **Carl Wilhelm**, Freiherr von (*b* Saaralben, Lorraine, 6 Dec 1788; *d* Munich, 21 Feb 1861). German soldier, painter and printmaker of Swiss descent. He took drawing lessons in Zurich from Johann Heinrich Meyer (1755–1829), Johann Caspar Huber (1752–1827) and Konrad Gessner. In 1801 he studied briefly in Munich under Domenico Quaglio II. Towards the end of 1815 or shortly afterwards he returned to Munich, where Johann Christian von Mannlich instructed him in landscape painting. Hitherto Heideck had worked exclusively in watercolours and gouache but from 1816 onwards he also began to paint in oils. He first exhibited in 1823, showing a painting entitled *Bavarian Woodcutters* at the Munich Akademie, of which he was elected an honorary member in 1824. In 1829, on his return to Munich from Greece, he paid a lengthy visit to Rome, returning there again in 1842. Having concurrently pursued a distinguished military career, he began to paint full-time in 1835. His campaigns in the Tyrol, the Iberian Peninsula and Greece provided him with valuable material for his paintings and he became a frequent exhibitor both in Munich and in Berlin. His output was varied and included not only battle-pieces and other military subjects, such as *Philhellene Camp during the Greek War of Independence* (1835; Karlsruhe, Staatl. Ksthalle), but also genre paintings and topographical landscapes recording views and architectural sites, especially in Greece (e.g. *View of the Acropolis*, 1835; Munich, Neue Pin.) and Spain. He is also known to have produced a few etchings and lithographs.

BIBLIOGRAPHY

Thieme–Becker

COLIN J. BAILEY

Heidegger, Martin (*b* Messkirch, 26 Sept 1889; *d* Messkirch, 26 May 1976). German philosopher. He studied theology then philosophy and science at the University of Freiburg, where he taught until his death. The main influence on his thought was the PHENOMENOLOGY of Edmund Husserl, which he turned against its founder, first criticizing Husserl's Cartesian assumption that intentional consciousness mediates between the mind and things in the world, and then criticizing any ahistorical attempt to understand human beings and being in general.

Heidegger spoke of art only occasionally, but he dedicated one important essay to the subject: 'Der Ursprung des Kunstwerkes' (1950, written in 1935). Here Heidegger holds that a work of art is an object with a special function: it is 'a being in the Open . . . in which the openness takes its stand and attains its constancy'. The Open for Heidegger is the world of a culture. It is a space opened up by a particular understanding of what it is to be a thing, a person, an institution and so on, in which something can show up *as* something. This shared understanding of the meaning of being is present in the practices of a people and need not, indeed cannot, be captured as a set of beliefs. It can, however, be manifest in an object such as a temple, an epic or a painting. When a work of art functions in this way—when an art work 'works', Heidegger would say—it transforms the practices it manifests: 'It gives to things their look and to men their outlook on themselves'. What Heidegger has in mind here can best be understood by comparing the function of a work of art with the role in science of what Thomas Kuhn (in *The Structure of Scientific Revolutions*, Chicago, 1962) called a 'paradigm'. A paradigm, according to Kuhn, is a perspicuous example of what all members of a scientific community agree is a good way of posing and solving problems. By being socialized into the community by training, scientists learn how to act in accord with one another and to come to share agreements in judgements without being able to make explicit, or 'rationalize', what is essential about the paradigm. Heidegger's work of art might best be regarded as a cultural paradigm, and the fact that the paradigm can never be rationalized but only imitated gives rise to what Heidegger calls the struggle between earth and world. For Heidegger a 'working' art work tends to make all relevant practices explicit and coherent—this is its world aspect. But at the same time it exhibits a resistance to paraphrase and rationalization: this Heidegger calls 'showing forth the earth'. The work of art shows what is at stake in the culture but also shows that it cannot be made explicit, thus setting up a conflict of interpretations that is itself a fruitful struggle that generates the culture's history.

It should be clear from the above that works of art can cease to 'work', and thus become mere cultural objects that can be visited by tourists or hung in museums. When things no longer function as cultural paradigms they become the objects of aesthetic experience. Heidegger is opposed to treating works of art as objects to be studied in aesthetics, since the root meaning of aesthetics suggests that art has to do with feeling, and he considers 'experience the element in which art dies'.

Heidegger also opposes a representational view of art, since thinking of art as a copy of something or even as a symbol does not capture the way the art work activity modifies the practices of those for whom it is 'working'. What Heidegger means by a work of art, therefore, only partially overlaps with what is usually picked out by the concept, although Heidegger is indifferent to this disparity. He is solely interested in pointing out that there are entities that have as their special function 'the fixing in place of truth in figure' and that without such entities historical cultures would not be possible.

In his later work Heidegger returned to the 'saving power' of art works. At the end of his essay *Die Technik und die Kehre* (1954) he states that in Greece 'the arts brought the presence of the gods' and asks whether the arts can 'found anew' our understanding of being. He may well have been thinking again of an art work when in his last interview he remarked: 'Only a god can save us now'.

See also HERMENEUTICS.

WRITINGS

'Der Ursprung des Kunstwerkes', *Holzwege* (Frankfurt, 1950), pp. 7–68; Eng. trans. in *Poetry, Language, Thought* (New York, 1971), pp. 15–88
'Die Technik und die Kehre', *Vorträge und Aufsätze* (Pfullingen, 1954), pp. 13–44; Eng. trans. in *The Question Concerning Technology and Other Essays* (New York, 1977), pp. 3–35
Gesamtausgabe (Frankfurt, 1975–)

BIBLIOGRAPHY

O. Pöggeler: *Der Denkweg Martin Heideggers* (Pfullingen, 1963)
W. B. Macomber: *The Anatomy of Disillusion: Martin Heidegger's Notion of Truth* (Evanston, 1967)
M. Haar: *Le Chant de la terre: Heidegger et les assises de l'histoire de l'être* (Paris, 1987)
F. Olafson: *Heidegger and the Philosophy of Mind* (New Haven, 1987)
P. Lacoue-Labarthe: *La Fiction du politique: Heidegger, l'art et la politique* (Paris, 1988)

HUBERT L. DREYFUS

Heidel, Hermann Rudolf (*b* Bonn, 20 Feb 1810; *d* Stuttgart, 29 Sept 1865). German sculptor, medallist and designer. He studied medicine until 1835, after which he was a pupil of Ludwig von Schwanthaler at the Akademie der Bildenden Künste in Munich. In 1839, at the Kunstverein in Cologne, he exhibited a drawing for a frieze, the *Life of Minerva*, and also showed a bust of *Beethoven*. From 1839 to 1842 he lived in Italy—mostly in Rome—and became a close friend of the Viennese painter Karl Rahl (1812–65). After 1843 he resided in Berlin and in 1848, at the Kurfürstliche Akademie der Künste, he exhibited four medallions and plaster models of mythological subjects. He also executed a set of eight drawings based on Goethe's *Iphigenie auf Tauris*; these were engraved in 1850 by Hermann Sagert (1822–89) of Berlin. By 1852 he had settled in Bonn and had begun his most productive period. Commissions from this time include a set of portrait medallions and busts of scientists (1855–7; Kiel, Christian-Albrechts U., Ksthalle) for the University of Kiel, a bronze monument to *George Frideric Handel* (1859; Halle, Marktplatz), a marble bust of the historian and statesman *Barthold Georg Niebuhr* (Berlin, Humboldt-U.) and a monument and a bust of the philosopher and psychologist *Johann Friedrich Herbart* for the city of Oldenburg. Heidel was particularly interested in Greek mythology, and he created numerous reliefs and marble statues with Classical themes. For the monument to the writer *Philipp Joseph von Rehfues* (*c*. 1843; Bonn, Old Cemetery) he carved a portrait and a relief of *Psyche and Persephone*. In 1852 Frederick William IV, King of Prussia, bought *Iphigenia in Tauris* (Potsdam, Orangerie), an under life-size marble statue. His competition sketch for the monument to the poet *Ernst Moritz Arndt* in Bonn was rejected, which made him bitter and less inclined to sculpt. Heidel also designed such functional objects as vases, cups and lampshades.

BIBLIOGRAPHY

ADB; Thieme–Becker
I. Zacher: 'Friedhofsanlagen und Grabmäler der kommunalen rheinischen Friedhöfe', *Kunst des 19. Jahrhunderts im Rheinland*, ed. E. Trier and W. Weyres, iv (Düsseldorf, 1980), pp. 385–442

HANNELORE HÄGELE

Heidelberg. City of *c*. 130,000 inhabitants in Baden-Württemberg, Germany, at the entrance to the valley of the River Neckar where it flows into the Rhenish Plain. Heidelberg was the seat of the Electors Palatine from 1329, and its university, dating from 1386, was the second

Heidelberg, view looking south-east towards the castle; from a photograph of 1935

to be founded in the Holy Roman Empire after Prague. The castle, whose ruined buildings in the early 19th century were an important source of inspiration for the German Romantic movement, reflects Heidelberg's greatest period of prosperity in the 16th century and the early 17th; in its present form, however, the town essentially dates from the 18th century. Heidelberg was incorporated into the Grand Duchy of Baden in 1803.

It was a Celtic site, and a Roman military base existed there from the mid-1st century AD, with a civil settlement from the 2nd century; there was a temple of Mithras at what is now Heidelberg-Neuenheim. St Vitus's parish church in Heidelberg-Handschuhsheim is mentioned as the chapel of St Nazarius in 774, and the ruined Benedictine abbey of St Michael on the Heiligenberg north of the river was founded around 870, but the medieval town in the valley is first documented only in 1196. The town, the castle (Obere Burg) and the market were held by Count Palatine Ludwig I of Bavaria (reg 1214–27) from 1225, the first town walls being built ten years later. The city flourished in the 14th century, being extended westwards in 1392. The present Heiliggeistkirche, built 1399–1441, is a three-naved hall church with galleries (which once housed the Bibliotheca Palatina of the university, incorporated into the Biblioteca Apostolica Vaticana in 1623). The tower was finished in 1544 and surmounted by a bulbous cupola in 1709. The Peterskirche, begun 1485 to replace an earlier building, was remodelled in the 19th and 20th centuries.

Survivals from the city's 16th-century heyday include an entrance gate of the Wormser Hof, an early 17th-century garden pavilion, and the Haus zum Ritter, built in 1592 for the Huguenot merchant Charles Bélier, with a richly decorated Renaissance façade. The group of former stables and arsenal on the left bank of the Neckar, mostly dating from this period, is now used by the university: a building on the south side, erected in the early 19th century by Friedrich Weinbrenner to replace a late 16th-century ornamental structure, was demolished in 1966 to make way for a new seminar building.

The period is, however, fully reflected in the castle complex, which dominates the town from Königstuhl (see fig.) and was extended to its present dimensions in the 16th century. The only medieval remains are the Ruprechtsbau, built by Rupert III (reg 1398–1410), and some towers. Ludwig V (reg 1436–49) added the Ludwigsbau and made other alterations and additions, but the most important building phase was that of the German Renaissance from the mid-16th century. The ruined Ottheinrichsbau (see GERMANY, fig. 5), built by Elector Otto Henry (reg 1556–9; see WITTELSBACH, §II(1)), combines an idiosyncratic display of north Italian architectural detail with a wealth of sculpture by masters including ALEXANDER COLIN, although the underlying theory of Renaissance design was not fully understood. A similar vocabulary was employed for the Friedrichsbau (1601–4), built for Frederick IV (reg 1583–1610) by Johann Schoch; the castle chapel and sculptures were restored 1895–1903 by Carl Schäfer. Frederick V (reg 1610–23) added the Englischer Bau, with a giant order of columns facing the valley, a relatively early example of Palladian architecture north of the Alps (perhaps influenced by Inigo Jones) and the Elizabeth Gate (1615). From 1613 until work abruptly ceased in 1618, SALOMON DE CAUS created the Hortus Palatinus, a garden in Italian late-Renaissance style, which was highly significant in the development of European landscape gardens (traces remain).

Heidelberg was laid waste in the Thirty Years War (1618–48) and again during the War of the League of Augsburg in 1689 and 1693. In the reconstruction of the town after 1697 the medieval plan was largely preserved. The elector's residence was moved to Mannheim, and the castle was not rebuilt. The Lutheran Providenzkirche (1659–61) survived the destructions, but 18th-century churches include the Hospitalkirche St Anna (1714) by J. J. Rischer (1662–1755) and the Jesuit church and college, completed by 1759 by Franz Wilhelm Rabaliatti (1716–82) after plans by Johann Adam Breunig (d 1727). The church tower was added in 1868–70. The town hall (rest. 1960–61) was built in 1701–5 and the old university in 1712–13 to plans by Breunig. Other civic and university buildings and aristocratic residences also survive, including the former Palais Morass (1712), which houses the enlarged Kurpfälzisches Museum. In the late 18th century two gates were built, the Karlstor (1775–81; by Nicolas de Pigage) and the Brückentor (1768–88), as were the stone bridge across the Neckar, fountains and statues.

The university library (1901–5) was built by Josef Durm and the new university (1930–35) by Karl Gruber (b 1885). Since the 1960s the university has expanded considerably over the Neuenheimer Feld. The Max-Planck Institute for Astronomy was built at Königstuhl in 1976 by Carlfried Mutschler (b 1926).

BIBLIOGRAPHY
A. Haupt: *Zur Baugeschichte des Heidelberger Schlosses* (Frankfurt am Main, 1902)
A. von Oechelhaeuser: *Die Kunstdenkmäler des Amtsbezirks Heidelberg* (Tübingen, 1913)
R. Sillib and K. Lohmeyer: *Heidelberg* (Leipzig, 1925)
F. Piel: *Baden Württemberg*, i of *Dehio-Handbuch* (Munich and Berlin, 1964), pp. 188–203
Veröff. Heidelberg. Altstadt (1969–)
R. Patterson: 'The Hortus Palatinus at Heidelberg and the Reformation of the World', *J. Gdn Hist.*, i (1981), pp. 67–104, 179–202
P. A. Riedl, ed.: *Die Gebäude der Universität Heidelberg*, i and ii (Berlin, 1987)

JÜRGEN ZIMMER

Heidelberger, Ernst Johann [Arnošt Jan] (d Prague, before 1668). German sculptor, active in Bohemia. He worked principally in wood. Before 1618 he participated in the decoration of the Spanish Hall of Prague Castle; in 1630–32 he was employed by Albrecht, Graf von Wallenstein, both at his estate at Jičín and at his enormous palace in the Lesser Quarter of Prague. For the latter he carved an altar in the chapel. Its figures of angels and of *St Wenceslas* are elongated in proportion and have contrived, graceful gestures; these marionette-like carvings, the draperies of which are cut in sharp, protruding folds, probably represent the most extreme expression of sculptural Mannerism in Bohemia. A number of figures of Franciscan saints on the walls of St Mary of the Snows, Prague, were probably made in Heidelberger's workshop, after 1620 for the church's original high altar, and the best wood-carving made in Prague around 1630, the statue of *St Francis of Paola* in the Týn church, also originated in his circle. It is a spiritually austere but deeply expressive work.

It is possible that Heidelberger took part in the decoration of Wallenstein's Carthusian monastery at Valdice, near Jičín, where the stone statues have a more robust construction and more dynamic draperies than the sculptures associated with the earlier phase of his career. If this were the case, then Heidelberger would also be the author around 1650 of the largest early Baroque high altar in Prague, the new high altar at St Mary of the Snows. As late as 1654 he decorated the temporary *castrum doloris* in St Vitus's Cathedral, Prague, for the obsequies of Ferdinand IV, King of Bohemia. Although the outlines of Heidelberger's career are far from clear, he would seem to have been the sculptor responsible for the stylistic transition in Prague from the sculpture of late Mannerism to that of the early Baroque.

BIBLIOGRAPHY
Thieme–Becker
P. Toman: *Nový slovník československých výtvarných umělců* [New dictionary of Czechoslovak artists] (Prague, 1947)
O. J. Blažíček: *Sochařství baroku v Čechách* [Baroque sculpture in Bohemia] (Prague, 1958), pp. 60–61 [with Fr. and Ger. summary]
I. Kořán: *Sochařství in Praha na úsvitu nových dějin* [Sculpture in Prague at the dawn of modern history] (Prague, 1988), pp. 442–5

IVO KOŘÁN

Heidelberger, Thomas (b before 1541; d before 1597). German cabinetmaker and wood-carver. Although in the high quality of his craftsmanship he was an important representative of South German cabinetmaking and is thought to have produced an extensive oeuvre in Upper Swabia and Switzerland, little evidence of it has survived. Probably in collaboration with the Augsburg cabinetmaker Hans Kels (fl 1537–65/6) and commissioned by the monastery of Ottobeuren, he produced an organ case and choir-stalls with rich inlaid ornamentation; their remains were later incorporated into a sacristy cupboard. Again collaborating with Kels, in 1583–5 he produced five portals (four *in situ*; one, Stuttgart, Württemberg. Landesmus.), the architectural structure of which was accentuated by lavish figural and ornamental carving and supplemented by inlays and reliefs, together with a coffered ceiling, for the Benedictine abbey at Ochsenhausen. Through his extensive use of contemporary pattern books while designing, Heidelberger combined delicate decorative elements from the early Renaissance with the more robust forms of the later 16th century.

BIBLIOGRAPHY
Thieme–Becker
R. Stratmann-Döhler: 'Möbel', *Die Renaissance im deutschen Südwesten*, ii (exh. cat., Heidelberg, Schloss, 1986), p. 761

ELISABETH GUROCK

Heidelberg Painter. *See* VASE PAINTERS, §II.

Heidelberg school. Group of artists active in the late 19th century in Heidelberg, a suburb of Melbourne, who introduced *plein-air* Impressionism to Australia. The most important members were Tom Roberts, Frederick McCubbin, Arthur Streeton and Charles Conder.

Most of the group began their careers at the National Gallery of Victoria's School of Art in Melbourne; several later studied overseas. Roberts, Streeton and Conder painted in each other's company both at their various outer suburban *plein air* camps (Box Hill, mainly 1885–6;

Mentone, Port Phillip Bay, 1887–8; for illustration *see* CONDER, CHARLES; the 'Eaglemont' estate at Heidelberg 14 km from Melbourne, 1888–90; for illustration *see* STREETON, ARTHUR; and in Sydney) and in Melbourne where they often shared or occupied adjoining studios. McCubbin often worked with them. When apart they corresponded regularly, recalling their artistic camaraderie with great nostalgia. Davies and many lesser-known figures, such as Jane Sutherland, Clara Southern, John Mather (1848–1916), Tom Humphrey (1858–1922), Aby Altson (1866–1949), Charles Douglas Richardson (1853–1932) and Artur Loureiro (1853–1932), also painted the Yarra valley landscape around Heidelberg and Templestowe. They generally exhibited with the Australian Artists' Association from 1886 to 1888 (as opposed to the more conservative Victorian Academy of Arts) and the Victorian Artists' Society from 1889. Roberts initiated the deliberately controversial but ultimately most successful *9 by 5 Impression Exhibition* (Aug 1889): seven artists presented 182 small oil sketches in the style of Whistler (mostly on cigar-box lids measuring 228×127 mm) and called themselves 'impressionists' for the first time. Meanwhile they painted ambitious large-scale canvases intended for public galleries (then purchasing chiefly academic European art), for example Streeton's brilliant and broadly painted *Golden Summer, Eaglemont* (1889; Perth, W. J. Hughes priv. col.) or '*Fire's On*' (1891; Sydney, A.G. NSW; *see* AUSTRALIA, fig. 9), Roberts's heroic *Shearing the Rams* (1890; Melbourne, N.G. Victoria; for illustration *see* ROBERTS, TOM), Davies's crepuscules and McCubbin's poignant pioneering narratives (for illustration *see* MCCUBBIN, FREDERICK). These monumental landscapes and naturalist figure subjects have become extremely popular 'national images'.

By the mid-1890s, however, the optimistic collective momentum of the Heidelberg school artists was on the wane. In 1890 Conder returned to Europe; Streeton (1890) and Roberts (1891) went to Sydney. The Heidelberg district remained a focus of artistic activity led by Walter Withers and Emanuel Phillips Fox, although in the 20th century the dynamic vision of the original artists became hackneyed in the hands of numerous conventional imitators.

The Heidelberg school was formed from the first important group of Australian artists who did not emigrate from Europe fully trained. They supplanted traditions established by such colonial precursors as John Glover, Abram-Louis Buvelot and Eugene von Guérard and transformed local landscape painting with new informality of composition, breadth of handling and an emphasis on characteristically Australian effects of light and colour. Although they were influenced by aspects of European Impressionism and Aestheticism, their consciously 'national' sentiments and subject-matter were encouraged by contemporary intellectuals and the local press. Roberts, McCubbin and Streeton were first grouped as 'the trio of the "Box Hill School" [with] the same feeling, a common thought, and a similar mannerism, while they hunt on the same Box Hill camping ground' (*Daily Telegraph*, Melbourne, 1 May 1888). The term 'Heidelberg School' was coined by a visiting American critic Sidney Dickinson (1851–1919) in 1891, describing Streeton and Withers 'for the purposes of distinction' as members of 'the "Heidelberg School"', for their work has been done chiefly in this attractive suburb, where, with others of like inclination, they have established a summer congregation for out-of-door painting'. William Moore used the term in 1934, and most writers since Bernard Smith (1945) have accepted it as a useful art-historical label.

BIBLIOGRAPHY
F. J. Broomfield: 'Art and Artists in Victoria', *Centennial Mag.*, i (1889), pp. 882–9
S. Dickinson: 'Two Exhibitions of Paintings', *Australasian Critic* (1 July 1891), p. 240
W. Moore: *The Story of Australian Art: From the Earliest Known Art of the Continent to the Art of Today*, i (Sydney, 1934/R 1980), pp. 70–84
B. Smith: *Place, Taste and Tradition: A Survey of Australian Art since 1788* (Sydney, 1945, rev. 2/1979), pp. 78, 120–46
U. Hoff: 'Reflections on the Heidelberg School', *Meanjin*, x (1951), pp. 125–33
D. Thomas: 'Roberts, Conder and Streeton in Sydney', *A.G. NSW Q.*, ii/4 (1961), pp. 71–4
A. McCulloch: *The Golden Age of Australian Painting: Impressionism and the Heidelberg School* (Melbourne, 1969)
C. B. Christensen, ed.: *The Gallery on Eastern Hill: The Victorian Artists' Society Centenary* (Melbourne, 1970)
P. McCaughey and J. Manton: *Australian Painters of the Heidelberg School: The Jack Manton Collection* (Melbourne, 1979)
H. Topliss: *The Artists' Camps: Plein Air Painting in Melbourne 1885–1898* (exh. cat., Melbourne, Monash U., A.G., 1984)
L. Astbury: *City Bushmen: The Heidelberg School and the Rural Mythology* (Melbourne, 1985)
J. Clark and B. Whitelaw: *Golden Summers: Heidelberg and Beyond* (exh. cat., Melbourne, N.G. Victoria, 1985, rev. 1986)
W. Splatt and D. McLellan: *The Heidelberg School: The Golden Summer of Australian Painting* (Melbourne, 1986)

JANE CLARK

Heideloff, Carl [Karl] **Alexander von** (*b* Stuttgart, 2 Feb 1789; *d* Hassfurt, 28 Sept 1865). German architect, painter, sculptor, printmaker and writer. He belonged to a large family of artists descended from Franz Joseph (Ignatz Anton) Heideloff (1676–1772), who was a sculptor and possibly also a painter. He was trained by the architect Nikolaus Friedrich von Thouret, the sculptor Johann Heinrich von Dannecker and the painter Johann Baptist Seele. He also studied mural painting as assistant to his father, Victor (Wilhelm Peter) Heideloff (1757–1817). As a young man he became interested in Gothic and Romanesque architecture, and while he was in Mainz in 1814 he made the acquaintance of Ernest I, Duke of Saxe-Coburg and Gotha (*reg* 1826–44), who employed him as his architect until 1821. In 1822, having settled in Nuremberg, he was appointed curator of the city's historical monuments; he used this position to encourage widespread interest in early German art and to rescue many examples from destruction. He also taught at the local Polytechnische Schule from its foundation in 1823 until 1854. In 1824–6 he made the first of many tours in Germany and France in pursuit of his study of medieval architecture.

Active in his early years as a history painter, Heideloff subsequently turned his energies towards sculpture, the design and restoration of buildings, and writing on art and architecture. His own buildings included Schloss Lichtenstein (1839–42) in Württemberg and churches in Güstrow, Ingolstadt, Leipzig (S Trinitatis, 1845–76) and Sonneberg (St Peter, 1843–4). Among his restorations were many buildings in Nuremberg, including Dürer's house, the cathedral of Bamberg (restored 1831–4) and numerous churches, notably the Stiftskirche (1840–41), Stuttgart. His zeal to conserve and restore earlier German architecture and sculpture blinded him to the merits of almost everything that was Baroque or Rococo in style and he unhesitatingly demolished any post-Renaissance work.

WRITINGS

Nürnbergs Baudenkmale der Vorzeit, oder Musterbuch der altdeutschen Baukunst, 2 vols (Nuremberg, 1838–43)
Die Ornamentik des Mittelalters, 3 vols (Nuremberg, 1838–55)
Die Bauhütte des Mittelalters in Deutschland (Nuremberg, 1844)
Die Kunst des Mittelalters in Schwaben (Stuttgart, 1855)

BIBLIOGRAPHY

Macmillan Enc. Architects; Thieme–Becker
W. Hoppe: 'Karl Alexander von Heideloff', *Mailande,* xvi (1965), pp. 65–88
W. Müller: 'Friedrich Hoffstadts und Carl Alexander Heideloffs Turmkonstruktionen vor dem Hintergrund der oberdeutschen Steinmetzlehre des 16. bis 18. Jahrhunderts', *Z. Kst.,* xli/1 (1978), pp. 41–56

COLIN J. BAILEY

Heidenreich [Haidenreich; Haydenreich; Heydenreich]. German family of architects and sculptors.

(1) Erhard Heidenreich (*d* Regensburg, 1524). He probably came from Franconia and worked as an apprentice on Regensburg Cathedral under Wolfgang Roriczer. From 1514 he was a citizen of Regensburg and was appointed cathedral architect after the execution of Roriczer in that year. The six large windows in the cathedral cloister (*c.* 1520), which contain some of the earliest Renaissance decoration in Germany, are generally attributed to him: candelabrum colonnettes, acanthus leaf and antique-style sections of entablature instead of Gothic archivolts are squeezed together to fill the window arches. Earlier he had worked on the tower (begun 1509) of the parish church of St Martin at Amberg. From 1509 to 1524 he was engaged as architect on the parish church of Unsere Liebe Frau in Ingolstadt. Around 1520, with his son (2) Ulrich Heidenreich, he built the chapels between the interior buttresses north and south of the west end of the nave. The vault is covered with a net-like pattern of curved, intersecting ribs, from which project gnarled, thorny, branch-like ribs, as if hovering in mid-air, on which are set pendant boss-rosettes. The transformation of the free ribs into delicate plant branch motifs shows great skill: the chapels are a high point in the Late Gothic art of south Germany. He also worked at Eichstätt. As a sculptor he made a miraculous statue of the 'Schöne Maria von Regensburg' (before 1519; destr.), which may have been the model used by Albrecht Altdorfer for his woodcuts of the Schöne Maria. In 1519 Erhard Heidenreich had a violent quarrel with Hans Hieber, the architect of the pilgrimage church 'Zur Schönen Maria' at Regensburg.

(2) Ulrich Heidenreich (*fl* 1520s). Son of (1) Erhard Heidenreich. He moved with his father from Amberg to Regensburg, where they occasionally collaborated. From *c.* 1520 he worked with his father on the western buttress chapels in the parish church of Unsere Liebe Frau at Ingolstadt, with their elaborate vaults. It is impossible to distinguish their contributions with certainty. After his father's death Ulrich was appointed to his positions at Regensburg Cathedral and Ingolstadt, but by then most of the work on these buildings had ceased.

BIBLIOGRAPHY

H. von Walderdorff: *Regensburg in seiner Vergangenheit und Gegenwart* (Regensburg, 4/1896), pp. 167, 441
B. Riehl: *Bayerns Donautal* (Munich and Leipzig, 1912)
H. Bock: 'Architektur: Niederlande, Deutschland, Frankreich, England, Skandinavien', *Spätmittelalter und beginnende Neuzeit,* Propyläen Kstgesch., vii (Berlin, 1972), pp. 339–70 (352–3)
E. Ullmann: *Deutsche Architektur und Plastik, 1470–1550* (Gütersloh, 1984)
N. Nussbaum: *Deutsche Kirchenbaukunst der Gotik* (Cologne, 1985), pp. 282, 301

VERENA BEAUCAMP

Heightening. Term for the addition of white or a pale tone on top of a darker tone or background colour to complete the depiction of form in a painting or drawing (*see* DRAWING, figs 1–3 and 5). During the Renaissance an application of lead white in an aqueous medium was used, for instance, to heighten drawings in metalpoint on tinted paper; this lead white often oxidizes, negating the original function of the heightening, but the process is reversible through conservation.

RUPERT FEATHERSTONE

Heihachirō Fukuda. *See* FUKUDA, HEIHACHIRŌ.

Heijō. *See* NARA.

Heiligenkreuz Abbey. Cistercian abbey in the Vienna Woods, Lower Austria. Heiligenkreuz, the oldest Cistercian abbey in the region once ruled by the house of Babenberg, was founded in 1135 by Margrave Leopold III of Austria (*reg* 1096–1136). It was settled with monks from Morimond Abbey in France, and a temporary building was consecrated in 1136. From the time of Leopold IV (*reg* 1136–41) Heiligenkreuz was the preferred burial place of the Babenbergs.

The nave of the church, begun before 1147 and consecrated in 1187, is an ashlar building, which at first had a flat ceiling. Excavations have shown that the original east end consisted of three apses without a transept. In 1147 Henry II (*reg* 1141–77) donated the village of Münchendorf and its revenues to the abbey, making it possible to vault the church, and a further endowment in 1156 enabled the monastic buildings to be rebuilt in stone. The five-bay aisled nave, the proportions of which are based on a module derived from the crossing square, has alternating supports. The aisles are groin-vaulted, but the main vessel has domical vaults with ribs of a plain, rectangular profile, the transverse arches resting on short pilasters corbelled above the arcade (see fig.). These are thought to be the earliest such vaults in Austria; unpersuasive attempts have been made to trace their source to northern Italy, Burgundy or Alsace.

Around 1200 the east end of the abbey church was transformed. A transept the same height as the nave (19.9 m) was added, and the east end was reshaped with radiating chapels following the scheme of CLAIRVAUX ABBEY ('Clairvaux III'). The monastery seems to have used some of its own lay brothers as masons (*Veronius conversus lapicida,* 1206; see Watzl, p. 6, no. 48). According to Gaumannmüller, this building campaign dates from after 1209, when the monastery had recovered from a crisis and received further support from the Babenbergs. During a restoration *c.* 1260, following damage to the

Heiligenkreuz Abbey, interior of the nave looking west, begun before 1147

abbey during the Kuman raid of 1252, two new portals were added to the west front, probably commissioned by Ottokar II, King of Bohemia, whose wife Margarethe was a Babenberg. Ottokar probably also erected the monumental tomb of *Frederick II* (*d* 1246), the last Babenberg Duke, in the chapter house, the earliest tomb with a recumbent effigy to survive in Austria.

Towards the end of the 13th century the choir was remodelled: a three-bay aisled hall with a straight east end was built on to the early 13th-century transept. The main vessel, 21.1 m high, has quadripartite rib vaulting, while the aisle vaults have five ribs and the corner bays six. The main vessel has a single, broad traceried east window, emphasizing the axiality of the hall plan. The hall choir of Heiligenkreuz, consecrated in 1295 before Albert I (*reg* 1298–1308), is regarded as a masterpiece of early Habsburg architecture. Its form seems to be related to the Dominican nuns' church of Tulln (Lower Austria; destr.), founded in 1289 by Rudolf I, and it anticipates later Habsburg foundations in Vienna (e.g. Albert I's choir in the Stephansdom from 1304) and Neuberg (from 1327) in Styria. The planning and construction of Heiligenkreuz, however, may have begun under Ottokar II. This may also be true of the nonogonal lavatorium, in the middle of the south range of the cloister, which has window tracery related to the choir. Around the interior of the lavatorium at socle level is a series of gables with blind tracery, which

has been interpreted as an allusion to the Heavenly Jerusalem. The cycle of stained-glass windows surviving in the lavatorium has been dated to the 1290s. It depicts Babenberg princes prominent as founders of monasteries; this pointed reference to the traditions of Heiligenkreuz can be explained in terms of the Habsburgs' political aims.

For unknown reasons, after 1227 the monastic buildings were demolished and rebuilt, their completion being marked by a consecration of the whole monastery. They were situated south of the church. The east cloister range, with the chapter house (a three-aisled, rib-vaulted hall of three bays separated by piers), the day room (a three-aisled, groin-vaulted hall with round columns) and the dormitory on the upper floor (a three-aisled, rib-vaulted hall with piers and a night stair) have survived. There are only scanty remains of the medieval warming room and refectory in the south range. Except for the lavatorium, the cloister itself was built between 1227 and 1240. It has domical vaults, with pear-shaped profiles to the ribs, supported on corbels; the arches into the cloister garth are subdivided into three or four smaller arches and richly decorated with slender red marble colonnettes, with crocket and foliate capitals. The stylistic development of the forms indicates that building progressed from the north, through the east and south, to the west. At the same time the north range was given ornamental grisaille stained-glass windows, the largest group of their type to survive in a Cistercian building. Like the church, the monastic buildings were built of sandstone.

The cloister of Heiligenkreuz is the third in a series of related cloisters in Austria, coming after Zwettl (from 1204) and Lilienfeld (before 1230). The cloisters of St Emmeram, Regensburg, and Maulbronn Abbey in Germany are comparable with the Austrian group; in the Czech Republic the somewhat earlier Louka provides a comparison, while Tišnov is regarded as a copy of the Austrian models. The richness of colour provided by the red marble colonnettes at Heiligenkreuz is reminiscent of the windows in the Broletto (1215) in Como.

The Baroque enlargement of the monastic complex in the 17th century by Angelo Canevale left the medieval work largely untouched. Johann Michael Rottmayr and Martino Altomonte contributed to the painted decoration. Many works by the sculptor GIOVANNI GIULIANI are preserved, among them the Trinity Column of 1739 in the Baroque courtyard of the Quadratur in front of the façade of the church, as well as a collection of 179 clay models. In 1887 Dominik Avanzo (1845–1910) erected a Gothic Revival high altar ciborium in the church.

BIBLIOGRAPHY

F. Watzl: *Die Cisterzienser von Heiligenkreuz* (Graz, 1898)

R. K. Donin: 'Romanische Portale in Niederösterreich', *Jb. Ksthist. Inst. K.-K. Zent.-Komm. Dkmlpf.*, ix (Vienna, 1915), pp. 35–6, 39–44

D. Frey: *Die Denkmale des Stiftes Heiligenkreuz*, Österreichische Kunsttopographie, xix (Vienna, 1926)

A. Schmeller: *Die Klosterkirche Heiligenkreuz und die süddeutsche Baukunst des 12. Jahrhunderts* (diss., U. Vienna, 1946)

F. Gaumannmüller: 'Die mittelalterliche Klosteranlage der Abtei Heiligenkreuz', *Festschrift zum 800: Jahrgedächtnis des Todes Bernhards von Clairvaux* (Vienna, 1953), pp. 167–227

R. Wagner-Rieger: 'Architektur', *Gotik in Österreich* (exh. cat., Krems, Hist. Mus., 1967), pp. 338–9, 378–9, no. 350

E. Frodl-Kraft: *Die mittelalterlichen Glasgemälde in Niederösterreich*, Corp. Vitrearum Med. Aevi, Österreich, ii (Vienna, 1972), pp. 104–25

R. Wagner-Rieger: 'Architektur', *1000 Jahre Babenberger in Österreich* (exh. cat., Lilienfeld Abbey, 1976), pp. 148–9

——: 'Bildende Kunst: Architektur', *Die Zeit der frühen Habsburger: Dome und Klöster, 1279–1379* (exh. cat., ed. F. Röhrig; Wiener Neustadt, Stadtmus., 1979), pp. 107–9

M. Schwarz: *Studien zur Klosterbaukunst in Österreich unter den letzten Babenbergern* (diss., U. Vienna, 1981), pp. 130–33

S. Hauser-Seutter: 'Ein Triskeles und ein Lockenköpfchen im Brunnenhaus von Heiligenkreuz', *Pro arte antiqua: Festschrift für Hedwig Kenner*, i (Vienna, 1982), pp. 150–69

MARIO SCHWARZ

Heiliger, Bernhard (*b* Stettin [now Szczecin, Poland], 11 Nov 1915). German sculptor, painter, printmaker and collagist. He studied sculpture from 1933 to 1936 at the Werkkunstschule für Gestaltende Arbeit in Stettin, and from 1938 to 1941 at the Vereinigten Staatsschulen für Freie und Angewandte Kunst in Charlottenburg, Berlin, under Richard Scheibe. During his stay in Paris in 1939 Heiliger saw sculptures by Aristide Maillol, Brancusi and Arp, which were the inspiration for his first important creative phase from 1945 to 1962. He began by modelling the female body, under the influence of Henry Moore, and made heads in plaster, stucco, cement or bronze. He also painted portraits of such well-known personalities as *Karl Hofer* (1951; Berlin, Staatl. Museen, Neue N.G.). His interest in the reduction of form led to his concentration on torsos and abstract configurations such as *Unknown Political Prisoner* (stone, metal and bronze, 594×901× 901 mm, 1952; London, Tate). The themes of dream, death, metamorphosis and vegetative state marked the end of this first phase of the 1950s, in which Heiliger's figurative organic sculptures represented a dynamic, upward striving gesture in space. The winged *Flame* (bronze, 6.0×5.5×4.5 m, 1962; Berlin, Ernst-Reuter-Platz) was the prelude to his second creative phase from 1962 to 1970, in which he used themes such as the flight of birds and vegetable forms. He made mass and free forms, smooth polished, sometimes with traces of damage, symbolizing the static and dynamic, as well as weight and weightlessness (e.g. *Miracle I*, aluminium, polyester and perspex, 810×520×220 mm, 1968; see Salzmann and Romain, p. 85). This phase came to an end with *Kosmos 70* (aluminium, 9×18×4 m, 1970; Berlin, Reichstagsgebäude). Space flight, the cosmos and planets now became his themes, and to depict these he used industrially processed materials such as aluminium, rods, sheet metal and polyester, or wood, rather than traditional bronze casts. Colour also assumed a bigger role. After 1980 Heiliger produced objects in relief such as sculptures on ground level made out of iron and steel. Individual elements, such as spheres, circle surfaces and linear wires balance playfully and monumentally in contrapositional arrangement, as in *Alberto between 2 Worlds* (steel, 1.6×3.3×7.0 m, 1982; Schleswig, Schloss Gottorf). As fields of energy and fields of force they aspire to break through space and overcome gravity, symbolically converting nature and technique into central themes. From 1951 to 1986 Heiliger was a professor at the Hochschule für Bildenden Künste in West Berlin.

WRITINGS
Skizzen-Figuren-Entwürfe (Berlin, 1957)
'Bronze voll innerer Kraft (Brancusi)', *ZEIT-Mag.*, 5 (1988)

BIBLIOGRAPHY
S. Salzmann and L. Romain: *Bernhard Heiliger* (Frankfurt am Main, 1989)
Bernhard Heiliger (exh. cat. by H. J. Papies, Berlin, Staatl. Museen, 1991)
ULRIKE LEHMANN

Heilmann, Jacob. *See* HAYLMANN, JACOB.

Heim, François-Joseph (*b* Belfort, 16 Jan 1787; *d* Paris, 30 Sept 1865). French painter. His father, Joseph Heim (*fl* 1781–after 1788), a decorative painter and drawing-master in Alsace, intended Heim for a career in mathematics but, recognizing his skill in drawing, sent him instead to the studio of François-André Vincent in 1803. He won second prize in the competition for the Prix de Rome in 1806 with *Return of the Prodigal Son* (untraced) and took the prize with *Theseus, Conqueror of the Minotaur* (Paris, Ecole N. Sup. B.-A.) in 1807. *Theseus* is characterized by the elongated forms, simple outlines and theatrical light effects that recur in extreme form in the audaciously mannered *Arrival of Jacob in Mesopotamia* (Bordeaux, Mus. B.-A.), painted in Rome and exhibited in the Salon of 1812; in the *Robe of Joseph Shown to Jacob* (exh. 1817; Paris, Louvre); and in the two works on the theme of Titus (exh. 1819; both Paris, Louvre), painted as overdoors for the château of Versailles. The imperial government rewarded him by commissioning a picture very different from his academic work, the *Defence of Burgos* (1813; Versailles, Château), which he painted in the panoramic manner of L. F. Lejeune (1775–1848), but with a better sense of atmosphere and composition. The empire fell too soon to allow Heim to build on his successful beginning as a battle painter. The Restoration government gave him a less promising theme from recent history, the *Recovery of the Royal Bones from Saint-Denis in 1817* (1822; Saint-Denis, Abbey), which Heim painted with a memorable range of light effects, culminating in the eerie silhouette of Saint-Denis against a moonlit cloud.

The mannerism of Heim's early work gave way to a greater naturalism and energy in drawing and painting the human figure, evident in the *Destruction of Jerusalem by the Romans* (exh. Salon, 1824; Paris, Louvre) and in the *Victory of Judas Maccabaeus* (*c.* 1824; Dijon, Mus. Magnin), for which there is a brilliant, typically explosive sketch in the Musée Bonnat, Bayonne. There was, however, little demand for violent pictures of ancient history; the State, Heim's chief patron, had more use for religious, decorative and commemorative works. Heim was drawn into all three fields and became a master in each. His early works on Old Testament themes, encouraged perhaps by his interest in Jewish history, prepared him for the commissions that the Prefect of the Seine handed out to artists in the Restoration. Heim painted at least ten major works for churches in Paris and elsewhere in this period, beginning with the *Martyrdom of SS Cyr and Juliette* of 1819 for the transept of SS Gervais et Protais, Paris (*in situ*), a rhythmic composition of big, clear, well-drawn figures, and ending with two large grisailles in 1828, the *Adoration of the Magi* and the *Presentation in the Temple* in the apse of St Germain-des-Prés, in which the energy and expression of the earlier work gave way to a quieter, frieze-like elegance. Heim rarely showed at Salons after this. His major religious works in the churches of Notre-Dame-de-Lorette (1836),

François-Joseph Heim: *Charles X Distributing Prizes after the Salon of 1824*, oil on canvas, 1.73×2.56 m, 1825 (Paris, Musée du Louvre)

St Sulpice (1845) and St Séverin (1849) were not framed pictures but large decorative murals in the manner of the work in St Germain. His secular decorative work began with a commission to paint the ceiling of the eighth room in the Musée Charles X with *Vesuvius Receiving Fire from Jupiter to Destroy the Towns of Herculaneum, Pompeii and Stabiae*, with six scenes of desolation in the frieze. The allegorical ceiling *Renaissance of French Art*, which he painted on commission in the Louvre in 1833, is less energetic and more elegant than the other, in keeping with the subject but also with the general tendency in Heim's art away from the dynamism he admired in Michelangelo. In 1844 he decorated the conference room in the Chamber of Deputies with four compositions, twelve allegorical figures and twelve medallions.

Heim developed a speciality in painting large group portraits, following the success of *Charles X Distributing Prizes after the Salon of 1824* (1825; Paris, Louvre; see fig.), exhibited in 1827, skilfully composed with 108 recognizable celebrities. He followed this with *Richelieu Receiving the First Academicians* (1833), the *Duc d'Orléans Receiving Deputies in 1830* (1834), *Andrieux Reading in the Comédie Française* (1847; all Versailles, Château) and others. The success of these compositions relied on a vast output of preparatory portrait drawings, of which he exhibited 64 at his last Salon in 1859 (e.g. *Comte de Nieuwerkerke*, 1859; Paris, Louvre). Like Abel de Pujol, whose career followed a similar course, Heim spent his whole life working for the Church and State. He rarely worked for private patrons. In 1855 he received a special *grande médaille* as his reward. Apart from Ingres, he was the only surviving artist of his generation who was still respected in the Second Empire.

BIBLIOGRAPHY
M. de Saint-Santin [P. de Chennevières]: 'M. Heim', *Gaz. B.-A.*, xxii (Jan 1867), pp. 40–62
P. Lafond: 'François-Joseph Heim', *Gaz. B.-A.*, n. s. xvi (Dec 1896), pp. 441–5; xvii (Jan 1897), pp. 27–36
De David à Delacroix: La Peinture française de 1774 à 1830 (exh. cat., Paris, Grand Pal., 1974), pp. 483–6
L'Art en France sous le Second Empire (exh. cat., Paris, Grand Pal., 1979), pp. 447–8
B. Foucart: *Le Renouveau de la peinture religieuse en France (1800–1860)* (Paris, 1987), pp. 179–82

JON WHITELEY

Heimatstil [Ger.: 'regional style']. Name of a 20th-century movement in architecture, interior decoration and the decorative arts, aimed at protecting and promoting regional and native characteristics. It developed in individual ways in a number of European countries, for example Germany, Switzerland, Poland and Finland, and flourished with varying intensity until the end of the 1940s. *Heimatkunst* (Ger.: 'regional art') was, similarly, linked to local and regional traditions without being folk art as such. *Heimatstil* was at its height in Switzerland in the years leading up to, and during, World War II, advocating a nationalist culture based on the traditional rural society, as opposed to the grandeur and modern functionalism of cosmopolitan urban culture. It was believed that architecture and the decorative arts should reflect such typically Swiss values as modesty, honesty and being at one with nature. These national characteristics, turned into material form, should make an impact on a new, more natural way of life that was inherently tied to the notion of country. *Heimatstil* saw as beautiful only that which was in accordance with the essence of the inhabitants of a particular region.

Heimatstil was characterized by an emphasis on the fitness for purpose and durability of buildings and objects and the use of natural materials of Swiss origin, primarily wood: furniture was not generally painted or stained and was given a matt finish in order to bring out the simple graining of the native wood. The revival of traditional craft methods, for example frame construction in architecture and solid construction in furniture, was an important element in the movement. An emphasis on basic functional form and clear construction was also important: such visible methods of construction as dovetail joints, arrises or frame construction emphasized craft traditions while at the same time making it easier to dispense with superfluous decoration. A formal language was developed that was intended to express the relationship between form and function and to encompass and appeal to reason and to emotion. This language was linked to Biedermeier and craft traditions, but the idea was not merely to imitate historical traditions but to adapt them in a manner appropriate to the time. Such organizations as Heimatschutz (founded 1905), Heimatwerk (founded 1930) and the Verein zur Förderung des Kunsthandwerks in der Schweiz (founded 1936) all made a success of publicizing *Heimatstil*. This was achieved through such campaigns as 'Mehr Holz in unsere Bauten' (1937–42), influential journals, for example *Raum und Handwerk* and *Das ideale Heim*, and exhibitions aimed at educating taste, for example *Das massive Möbel aus einheimischem Holz* (1937), *Das Haus aus unserem Holz* (1938) and *Die Aussteuer* (1939), all held in the Kunstgewerbemuseum, Zurich. Advisory centres were established, as were further education institutions. There was also a perceptible influence on architecture from advocates of the Modern Movement, but it was mainly those circles hostile to modernism that were active in the promotion of traditional forms in architecture and objects for everyday use. To this end, they pursued political and ideological interests, for example the identification and regeneration of rural culture, or the legalization of economic and political measures that protected farmers and craftsmen or, as in the case of Heimatwerk, promoted job creation in the economically deprived mountain areas. In 1938 traditional rural values were adopted as official cultural policy in the programme of 'Geistige Landesverteidigung'. An eloquent expression of this was provided by examples of everyday objects used in rural societies and rural architecture in the Landesausstellung held in Zurich in 1939.

The Swiss *Heimatstil* of the 1930s and 1940s should be seen as a reaction to an internal political crisis and to the external political threats of the time. Switzerland was searching for a new national identity, which it discovered in a combination of an ideology of growth and a cultural conservatism. *Heimatstil*, advocating modernity modified by traditionalism, reflected this basic national consensus. From 1936 its influence led to a wide return to rural architecture and lifestyle in the urban environment. Refinement of craft was, nonetheless, still the prerogative of the upper middle classes. The majority of objects loosely classified as part of *Heimatstil* did not actually reflect the traditional crafts or skills. Goods with only an outward appearance of craft traditions were mass produced, while aspects of regional architectural traditions were used only as decoration and not in construction.

BIBLIOGRAPHY

P. Artaria: *Schweizer Holzhäuser* (Basle, 1936)
E. Laur jr: 'Neue Schweizerstuben', *Heimatwerk*, ii/1 (1937), pp. 2–7
'Das massive Möbel aus einheimischem Holz: Ausstellung im Kunstgewerbemuseum Zürich', *Raum & Handwk*, ii/10 (1937), pp. 7–17
'Warum lieben wir Bauernmöbel?', *Raum & Handwk*, ii/1 (1937), p. 10
Das Haus aus unserem Holz (exh. cat., Zurich, Kstgewmus., 1938), Wegleitungen des Kunstgewm. Zürich, cxxxvii
Die Aussteuer (exh. cat., Zurich, Kstgewmus., 1939), Wegleitungen des Kunstgewm. Zürich, cxlii
'Unsere Wohnungen: Landesausstellung: Ein Bilderbuch schweizerischer Wohnkultur', *Ideale Heim* (Winterthur, 1939)
J. Leuthard: *Der Massivmöbelbau im schweizerischen Handwerksschaffen* (Chur, 1946)
A. Roth: 'Zum Problem des Wohnmöbels', *Das Werk*, xxxiii/12 (1946), pp. 407–20
R. Hamann and J. Hermand: *Stilkunst um 1900* (Berlin, 1967)
C. Cattaneo: 'Der Bauernhof zwischen Funktionalismus und Heimatideologie', *Dreissiger Jahre Schweiz* (exh. cat., Zurich, Ksthaus, 1982), pp. 210–17
——: 'Wohnungsbau zwischen Neuem Bauen und Heimatstil', *Dreissiger Jahre Schweiz* (exh. cat., Zurich, Ksthaus, 1982), pp. 172–81
G. Frey: *Schweizer Möbeldesign 1927–1984* (Berne, 1986), pp. 39–40
J. Gisler: 'Tradition und Fortschritt im Schweizer Heim: Möbel und Design als Ausdruck des schweizerischen Selbstverständnisses vor und nach dem zweiten Weltkrieg', *Sonderfall?: Die Schweiz zwischen Réduit und Europa* (exh. cat., Zurich, Schweiz. Landesmus., 1992), pp. 197–206

JOHANNA GISLER

Heimbach, Wolfgang (*b* Ovelgönne, nr Oldenburg, *c*. 1615; *d* after 1678). German painter. The son of a bookkeeper at the corn exchange, he was known because of a disability as 'the Ovelgönne mute'. An aristocratic sponsor, probably Graf Anton Günther (1603–67) of Oldenburg, sent him to train in the Netherlands: stylistic considerations would suggest that this was in the 1630s. The *Evening Scene* (1637; ex-art market, Berlin; Göttsche, no. 8) shows him adapting the style of Caravaggio as practised in Utrecht to the kind of social gathering depicted by Dirck Hals or Anthonie Palamedesz. He uses an artificial light source to exaggerate the modelling of the figures and the space. This characteristic of his art also shows in the *Evening Banquet* of 1640 (Vienna, Ksthist. Mus.), which might represent a stop on a southward journey to Italy: works from this time suggest contact with southern Germany and Austria. It is only after his arrival in Italy, working under the influence of Gerrit van Honthorst, that Heimbach's painting achieves a dramatic impact. His 1645 portrait of *Innocent X* (Copenhagen, Stat. Mus. Kst) indicates his presence in Rome that year, and a letter of 1646 mentions Ferdinando II, Grand Duke of Tuscany, as his patron.

One year later Heimbach was back in the north, painting portraits of *Prince Christian of Denmark* and *Prince Frederick of Denmark* (both Copenhagen, Rosenborg Slot). He was at Náchod Castle in Bohemia in 1651. In May 1652 he entered into a contract with Graf Anton in Oldenburg for a six-month trial appointment. Although he was 'graciously' released in November, he had already completed nine paintings. From 1654 Heimbach worked at the court of Frederick III of Denmark, where he was made court painter. The *Portrait of a Young Man* (1662; London, N.G.) is the last work stated as having been painted in Copenhagen. From 1665 he was back in Oldenburg, where he painted the *Sick Man* (1669; Hamburg, Ksthalle) and *Festival in Venice* (Drensteinfurt, nr Hamm). His last known work, a *Portrait of a Man* (Schloss Blankenburg), dates from 1678.

In spite of the fresh, colourful quality of Heimbach's paintings, which derived from the influence of the Haarlem group centred on Dirck Hals, the clumsiness of his technique can hardly be overlooked. As well as portraits and nocturnal pictures he created religious works, often modelled on the Caravaggist paintings of Carlo Saraceni and often using a considerable iconographical superstructure, as in the *Holy Family in front of the Inn* (Budapest, Mus. F.A.). In scenes depicting social gatherings, there is a predominance of archaically austere, symmetrically arranged, rigid figures shown full-face or in profile, set against a rich and lively background. The narrative elaboration of detail, reminiscent of still-life painting, emphasizes the genre-like character of these candle-lit scenes with their overtones of Utrecht. Heimbach achieved an atmospheric merging of space and figure only occasionally, as in the *Evening Gathering* (Gotha, Schloss-Friedenstein). Often he did little more than comment on what he had encountered elsewhere. His use of a variety of models—Giovanni Biliverti (1576–1644), Giusto Suttermans, Bartolomeo Manfredi, Domenico Fetti, Georges de La Tour and Pieter Codde—resulted in a lack of stylistic homogeneity. Reflecting this was the constant changing of his monogram in a search for an immutable personal style.

BIBLIOGRAPHY

G. Göttsche: *Wolfgang Heimbach: Ein norddeutscher Maler des 17. Jahrhunderts* (Berlin, 1935)

S. J. Gudlaugsson: 'Twee jeugdwerken van Wolfgang Heimbach', *Ksthist. Meded. Rijksbureau Ksthist. Doc.*, iii (1948), pp. 4–5

R. Fritz: 'Wolfgang Heimbach, Hofmaler Christoph Bernhards von Galen', *Westfalen*, xl (1962), pp. 315f

HANNES ETZLSTORFER

Heince [Haentz; Hainsse; Heins; Heintze; Hinse; Hintz], **Zacharie** (*b* ?Paris, 1611; *d* Paris, 22 June 1669). French painter, draughtsman and engraver. He is principally known for his collections of portraits, for which he furnished the drawings; they were engraved by François Bignon (*b c*. 1620) and published jointly with him. They included *Voicy les portraicts au naturel . . . de messieurs les plénipotentiaires assemblez à Munster et Onasburg pour faire la paix générale* (Paris, 1648), which has 33 plates, and *Les Portraits des hommes illustres françois qui sont peints dans la galerie du Palais Cardinal de Richelieu* (Paris, 1650), which has 26 plates and a frontispiece. Although he was not received (*reçu*) by the Académie Royale until 1663, Heince was described as early as 1648 as Peintre Ordinaire du Roy. The goldsmiths' corporation of Paris commissioned him on two occasions, in 1654 and 1665, to paint the Mays intended for the chapter of the cathedral of Notre-Dame: the *Conversion of St Lydia Purpuraria* and *Simon Magus Offering Money to St Peter* (both untraced). As an engraver, Heince left three prints after Francesco Primaticcio: the *Mater dolorosa*, the *Children's Bacchanalia* (1631) and the *Handsome Haberdasher*. Also attributed to him are the designs for twelve ornamental engravings by Bignon

and Michel Dorigny, in the form of friezes representing tritons and naiads: these were dedicated to Chancelier Séguier.

BIBLIOGRAPHY

A.-P.-F. Robert-Dumesnil: *Le Peintre-graveur français*, iv (1839), p. 19; v (1841), pp. 131–4; xi (1871), pp. 1, 110

ALEXANDRA SKLIAR-PIGUET

Heindl, Wolfgang Andreas [Andre] (*b* Linz, 1693; *d* Wels, 1757). Austrian painter. He was the son of a master cooper in Linz and may have served an apprenticeship with the Wels painter Johann Cyprian Wimberger (1671–1719). In 1717–18 he completed his first work, frescoes for the collegiate church of St Nikola in Passau. Following these he developed a popular and highly distinctive style of fresco painting, typical of the Bavarian school, in frescoes in the abbey church of St Mauritius (1719–22) Niederaltaich; the abbey church of St Michael (1722–4), Metten; the Kalvarienbergkirche (1724) Lambach; the sacristy in Kremsmünster Abbey (1725); St Johannes Baptist (1728), Rinchnach; and Maria Himmelfahrt (1734), Spital am Pyhrn.

In 1735 Heindl established himself as a painter and innkeeper in Wels, painting frescoes for the Kalvarienbergkirche (1737–8), Kremsmünster; the Rathaus (1739) in Wels; the Benedictine abbey (1740) at Lambach; and the parish churches at Viechtwang (1742); Bad Hall (1748); Hartkirchen (1751–2); and Hofkirchen an der Trattnach (1754). He also painted 11 cycles of the *Passion* between 1733 and 1754 for churches in the Wels area. Heindl belonged to the Bavarian school of painting, which concentrated on expressive, popular values and considered indigenous traditions more important than Italian ones. Distortion and caricature underlie his paintings, enhancing them with many narrative and entertaining details. His sons Franz Xaver Heindl (1722–72) and Ignaz Heindl (1727–91) were also painters, and his grandson Franz Anton Heindl died as a painter in Vienna in 1785.

BIBLIOGRAPHY

E. Guldan: *Wolfgang Andreas Heindl* (Vienna and Munich, 1970)

BRIGITTE HEINZL

Heine, Thomas Theodor (*b* Leipzig, 28 Feb 1867; *d* Stockholm, 26 Jan 1948). German painter, printmaker and illustrator. Having established a reputation as a caricaturist while still a schoolboy through drawings contributed to his school magazine (a satirical weekly), he entered the Kunstakademie in Düsseldorf in 1885. Expelled a year later because of his irreverent treatment of the image of the Laocoön, he studied briefly at the Akademie der Bildenden Künste in Munich before being allowed to return. He then studied under Peter Janssen until 1889. He moved again to Munich and in the nearby artists' colony of Dachau produced around 30 impressionist landscape paintings, for example *The Angler* (1892; Munich, Lenbachhaus). In 1892 he worked on the bourgeois family magazine *Fliegende Blätter*. He began to work with the publisher Albert Langen in 1895, designing covers for brochures and books. Drawings by Heine appeared in the art magazine *Pan*, and he rose to sudden fame in 1896 with the first issue of the magazine *Simplizissimus*, produced with Langen and Ludwig Thoma.

Unlike other artists working for the magazine, Heine provided the captions for his own pictures. He also had a large variety of styles at his command and used these to different ends. He was particularly influenced by the graphic work of Henri de Toulouse-Lautrec and Aubrey Beardsley and by Japanese woodcuts. In images where contrasting areas of colour are connected by the curving lines of *Jugendstil*, Heine parodied the German petit-bourgeoisie, the double standards of the Wilhelmine period and the sheep-like subservience to authority. He also made ink-drawings, which avoid ornamental and decorative elements; these deal critically with unsatisfactory social conditions. Heine's favourite targets were the law, the military and the nobility. In 1898 he was sentenced to six months in prison on an accusation of insulting the monarchy. Even in 1914, when *Simplizissimus* entered a nationalist and chauvinistic phase, Heine remained true to his principles.

Heine also made important contributions to book illustration, for example in Hebbel's *Judith* (1908), Thomas Mann's *Wälsungenblut* (1921) and to poster art (for the new *Simplizissimus*, 1896; and the *Red Bulldog* for the third exhibition of the Berlin Secession, 1902). The *Devil*, a recurrent theme, was also produced as a bronze sculpture in 1902 (Munich, Lenbachhaus). After leaving Germany in 1933 Heine lived successively in Prague (until 1938), Oslo (until 1942) and Stockholm. He gained great popularity, especially in Sweden. In 1945 he published an autobiographical novel.

NDB   BIBLIOGRAPHY
E. Hölscher: 'Th. Th. Heine und das Buch', *Imprimatur*, n. s., v (1965–7), pp. 56ff
L. Lang, ed.: *Th. Th. Heine*, Klassiker der Karikatur, 1 (Munich, 1970)
E. Stüwe: *Der "Simplizissimus"-Karikaturist Thomas Theodor Heine als Maler: Aspekte seiner Malerei* (Frankfurt am Main, 1978)
                                              SEPP KERN

Heinecken [Heineken], **Karl Heinrich von** (*b* Lübeck, 24 Dec 1707; *d* Alt-Döbern [Niederlausitz], nr Dresden, 23 Jan 1791). German art scholar and collector. At school in Lübeck he became acquainted with the ideas of Leibniz and Christian Wolff; from 1724 he studied law and literature in Leipzig. There he developed an interest in the Enlightenment thinking of Johann Christoph Gottsched and in art, particularly the many private collections. In 1730 he became a private tutor in the Dresden house of the elector's court poet Johann Ulrich König. Two years later he published a treatise on morality, *Die wahren Absichten des Menschen*. Heinecken then became steward at the house of the minister, Graf Sulkowsky. After Sulkowsky's fall Graf Heinrich von Brühl, the most powerful man at the Saxon court, took on Heinecken as librarian and private secretary. In 1737 he translated Longinus' *On the Sublime* from the Greek. In this work Heinecken pointed to the importance of ancient art theory long before Winckelmann, attracting much attention and the enmity of Gottsched. Under Brühl's protection Heinecken, who was without wealth, was knighted, awarded the Alt-Döbern estate and managed Brühl's estates, factories and finances. He was promoted to Oberamtsrat at the Saxon court; his unusual expertise in art and his clear judgement caused the king, Frederick Augustus II, to appoint him director of the Kupferstichkabinett (1746). During his 17 years in this post Heinecken increased the royal collection by some 50,000 engravings. On his advice the collection bought early German engravings, e.g. by Dürer; this was a neglected period at that time. One of Heinecken's major achievements was the method he devised to systematize the collection, which is expounded in his *Idée générale d'une collection complète d'estampes, avec un dissertation sur l'origine de la gravure et sur les premiers livres d'images* (1771). His own extensive library contained rare first editions and illuminated manuscripts from the 15th and 16th centuries. As Brühl's intendant he also influenced the purchases for the royal picture gallery, and its cataloguing and method of display. He travelled on diplomatic missions to Holland in 1750 and 1768, buying works by Rembrandt and van Dyck there, and to France in 1754 and 1761. He directed the purchases of paintings through middlemen such as Francesco Algarotti in Italy.

As the stock of paintings increased—in 1746 the Modena Collection came to Dresden, in 1754 Raphael's Sistine *Madonna*—Heinecken published a magnificent volume containing 106 engravings of works in the picture gallery. As an author, Heinecken described contemporary events and personalities in his *Nachrichten von Künstlern und Kunstsachen* (2 vols, Vienna and Leipzig, 1768/71) and his *Dictionnaire des artistes* (from 1778). The latter, making use of old material and documents, conveys all the essential information on artists and still serves as useful source material today. Laid out in 30 volumes, it shows Heinecken's encyclopaedic concerns and his scholarly meticulousness, rooted in the ideas of the Enlightenment. With the end of the Seven Years' War and the return of the Saxon court from Warsaw, Heinecken was accused before a court of misappropriating works of art and money. Although his innocence was proved, he was relieved of his duties and obliged to leave Dresden. At his estate at Alt-Döbern he devoted himself to agricultural projects and remained until his death a writer and an enthusiastic art collector.

                    BIBLIOGRAPHY
C. Dittrich: 'Heinrich von Heineckens kunsthistorische Schriften', *Jb. Staatl. Kstsamml. Dresden* (1965/6), pp. 79–85
M. Santifaller: 'Carl Heinrich von Heinecken e le acqueforti di Giambattista Tiepolo a Dresda', *A. Ven.*, xxvi (1972), pp. 145–53
                              PETRA SCHNIEWIND-MICHEL

Heinecken, Robert (*b* Denver, CO, 29 Oct 1931). American photographer and printmaker. His training as a painter and printmaker led him to produce eclectic photographic works that appropriate pre-existing mass-media imagery. Considering himself a 'paraphotographer', he seldom took his own photographs, instead selecting visual elements from pornographic magazines, advertisements and television and combining them to make ideological statements about contemporary culture. He made manifest the subliminal suggestions of advertising so as to reveal the ulterior hypocrisy and sexual provocation in the media. His finished pieces are notable for their inventive combinations of media and techniques such as photosensitized fabrics, high-contrast transparencies, acrylics, pastel, collage elements, offset lithography, transfer rubbings and Polaroid prints. He began teaching at the University of California, Los Angeles, in 1961.

PHOTOGRAPHIC PUBLICATIONS
Are You Rea (Los Angeles, 1968)
Mansmag (Los Angeles, 1969)
Just Good Eats For U Diner (Los Angeles, 1971)
He:/She: (Chicago, 1980)

BIBLIOGRAPHY
J. Enyeart, ed.: *Heinecken* (Carmel, 1980)
L. Katzman: *Photography in California, 1945–1980* (New York, 1984)
RICHARD LORENZ

Heine-Geldern, Robert, Freiherr von (*b* Grub, 16 July 1885; *d* Vienna, 26 May 1968). Austrian art historian, archaeologist and anthropologist. In 1923 he pioneered South-east Asian anthropology with the chapter 'Südostasien' in Georg Buschan's *Illustrierte Völkerkunde*. He had also become interested by this time in South-east Asian art history and archaeology. During World War II he sought refuge at the American Museum of Natural History, New York. He was co-founder of the East Indies Institute of America (later known as the South-east Asia Institute) and a member of the Austrian Academy of Sciences, the Royal Asiatic Society and the Royal Anthropological Institute, as well as the Ecole Française d'Extrême-Orient. His research embraced such themes as the conceptions of state and kingship in South-east Asia, and cultural contacts and cultural change, including prehistoric migration and contacts across trade routes. As an art historian Heine-Geldern provided valuable information on old Javanese bronzes, South-east Asian sword handles and the archaeology and art of Sumatra and Nias. His writings showed an ability to handle both grand themes and minutiae.

WRITINGS
'Südostasien', *Illustrierte Völkerkunde*, ed. G. Buschan (Stuttgart, 1923), ii, pp. 689–968
Altjavanische Bronzen (Vienna, 1925)
'The Archaeology and Art of Sumatra', *Sumatra: Its History and People*, ed. E. M. Loeb (Vienna, 1935), pp. 305–31, 339–42
'L'Art prébouddhique de la Chine et de l'Asie du sud-est et son influence en Océanie', *Rev. A. Asiat.*, xi (1937), pp. 117–206
'Sculptured Sword-hilts, Showing Scenes from Buddhist Legends', *J. Ind. Soc. Orient. A.*, v (1937), pp. 147–58
'Conceptions of State and Kingship in Southeast Asia', *Far Eastern Quarterly*, ii (1942), pp. 15–30
'Survivance de motifs de l'ancien art bouddhique de l'Inde dans l'île de Nias', *Artibus Asiae*, xxiv (1961), pp. 299–306
'Some Tribal Art Styles of Southeast Asia: An Experiment in Art History', *The Many Faces of Primitive Art*, ed. D. Fraser (Englewood Cliffs, 1966), pp. 165–221

BIBLIOGRAPHY
C. Holt: Obituary, *Indonesia*, vi (1968), pp. 188–92 [with selected bibliog.]
P. Kirchoff: Obituary, *Z. Ethnol.*, xciv (1969), pp. 163–8
H. Manndorff: Obituary, *Archv Vlkerknd.*, xxiii (1969), pp. 1–2
E. Kaneko: Obituary, *Asian Persp.*, xiii (1970), pp. 1–10 [with bibliog.]
S. J. VERNOIT

Heinouchi Masanobu (*d* 1645). Japanese master builder. He was the head of a family of hereditary carpenters who had flourished in the Kyoto region under the patronage of the Toyotomi family in the Momoyama period (1568–1600). They specialized in the *Wayō* style, a continuation of the rectilinear temple style that had first flourished in the 7th and 8th centuries in Japan. Masanobu's father, Yoshimasu (*fl c.* 1585–99), was in charge of the construction of the Great Buddha Hall (Daibutsuden) at the temple of Hōkōji for TOYOTOMI HIDEYOSHI; it was one of the largest and most spectacular buildings constructed in Japan. The young Masanobu received his early training on this project. After 1600, with the military defeat of the Toyotomi, the family suffered a drastic fall from its preeminence, although under Masanobu they eventually regained a position of importance as one of the families of official master builders to the Tokugawa shoguns who ruled Japan throughout the Edo period (1600–1868). Masanobu and members of his family participated in the construction of the Taitokuin mausoleum dedicated to the second Tokugawa shogun Hidetada (1579–1632) in 1632, but the worship hall (*haiden*) they built was less favourably received than the main hall (*honden*) constructed by their rivals, the Kōra (*see* KŌRA MUNEHIRO BUNGO). Heinouchi Masanobu's extant work consists of a few scattered subsidiary buildings. The most important is the Tenmangū, a shrine dedicated to the scholar–statesman Sugawara no Michizane, in Wakayama, completed in 1606 after Masanobu had left Toyotomi service. Masanobu's most enduring memorial is the architectural treatise he compiled in 1608 detailing the secret traditions of his family practice. Entitled *Shōmei* ('The elucidation of architectural design'), it was divided into five volumes: gateways, shrines, pagodas, temple halls and residential buildings.

BIBLIOGRAPHY
W. H. Coaldrake: *Architecture and Authority in Japan* (in preparation)
W. H. COALDRAKE

Heinrich, Duke of Saxony. *See* WETTIN, (4).

Heinrich, Ede (*b* Pest [now Budapest], 1819; *d* Milan, 26 Jan 1885). Hungarian painter and teacher. He studied from 1841 in the Akademie der Bildenden Künste in Vienna under Leopold Kupelwieser, and later in Italy. In 1840 his landscapes and in 1841 his portraits and genre paintings were shown in the exhibitions of the ARTISTS ASSOCIATION OF PEST. In Pest he was one of many academy-trained artists who painted shop signs. He published a lithograph of his historical picture of János Hunyadi in the Artists Association paper of 1847, but it was badly reviewed in the national press. From the early 1840s until 1863 he worked in Italy, for a time under Károly Markó (i). From Italy he sent to the Pest exhibitions such paintings as *The Antiquarian* (1846; Budapest, N.G.). In 1854 he showed his painting *Four Seasons* in Vienna, and subsequently the Habsburg Archduke Maximilian (later Emperor of Mexico) commissioned him to paint pictures for Miramare Castle, near Trieste. After his return home he ran a painting school for a few months in Pest, where he conducted classes in life drawing, landscape, decorative and flower drawing. In 1863 he executed the frescoes for the Festetich Palace in Budapest and made two sketches for the new dining hall at the Vigado Concert Hall (*Attila the Great's Banquet* and *King Matyas's Wedding*), although the commission went to Károly Lotz and Mór Than. In 1866 Heinrich painted a *St Cecilia* altarpiece for the organ loft of the cathedral at Szekesfehérvár and an *Annunciation* for its south chapel. In 1867 his picture of *Francis-Joseph's Coronation* (Budapest, N.G.) was bought by the Emperor. At the end of the 1860s he became a successful portrait painter in Vienna, and in the early 1870s he was commissioned by Miklos Ybl to paint portraits of Titian and Veronese for the medallions on the garden wall of Buda Castle. At the end of his life he eked out a living by painting portraits.

BIBLIOGRAPHY

T. Szana: *Száz év a magyar művészet történetében* [A century of Hungarian art] (Budapest, 1901), pp. 53, 56, 76, 87

K. Divald: *A Magyar Tudományos Akadémia palotája és gyűjteménye* [The palace and collection of the Hungarian Academy of Sciences] (Budapest, 1917), p. 75

B. Biró: *Mihály Kovács* (Budapest, 1930), pp. 25–6

——: *Magyar művészek Olaszországban a 19. sz. első felében* [Hungarian artists in Italy in the first half of the 19th century] (Budapest, 1954), pp. 531–45

JÚLIA PAPP

Heinrich von Gmünd [Heinrich von Freiburg]. *See* PARLER, (7).

Heinrik, Gerard [Heinrich, Gerhard] (*b* ?Amsterdam, *fl c.* 1587; *d* before Feb 1616). Netherlandish sculptor, active in Silesia and Bohemia. He was the son of Gerrit Hendricksz. (*d* 1585), a Netherlandish sculptor. Before 1587 he travelled in France, Italy and Germany, becoming a citizen of Breslau (now Wrocław, Poland) in 1587. He is said to have been in Danzig (now Gdańsk, Poland) in November 1589. His chief works were the chancel (1605; destr.) of the Schlosskirche in Oels (now Oleśnica, Poland) and the elaborate marble funerary monument to the Austrian *Feldmarschall Melchior von Redern* on an altar in the Dekanatskirche in Friedland (modern Frýdlant, Czech Republic). The monument, commissioned by von Redern's widow, the Gräfin Schlick, was completed in 1610 but was severely damaged in the Thirty Years War. Its original appearance can be reconstructed from the sculptor's description in a book that he published in the same year—*Kurtze Beschreibung des herrlichen Monumenti und Begräbnuess* (Breslau, 1610). The monument was made of green, white and red marble and originally had gilt-bronze ornamentation. The three colonnaded levels bore life-size statues of von Redern, the Gräfin Schlick and their son Christoph von Redern in the dress of their time, as well as reliefs depicting three of the Feldmarschall's most famous military engagements.

Thieme–Becker

BIBLIOGRAPHY

A. Schultz: *Gerhard Heinrich von Amsterdam: Bildhauer in Breslau* (Breslau, 1888)

G. Cuny: *Danzig und seine Bauten im 16. und 17. Jahrhundert* (Frankfurt am Main, 1910), p. 74

JANE CAMPBELL HUTCHISON

Heins, John Theodore [Dietrich] (*b* ?Germany, *c.* 1697; *d* Norwich, 1756). Painter and engraver, probably of German birth, but active in Great Britain. He settled in Norwich and by 1720 was working on a series of portraits of members of prominent local families. In 1732 he was commissioned to execute portraits of local civic dignitaries (Norwich, St Andrew's Hall). While most of his portraits of adults are stolid and bourgeois, those of children are more engaging. Many of his finer works were commissioned by the Astley family of Melton Constable; they include *Musical Party* (1734; Astley priv. col.) and the children *Edward and Blanche Astley* (1732; sold London, Christie's, 10 Dec 1985; lot 100). Heins also depicted allegorical and historical subjects and candle-light scenes, and he produced genre pieces such as two *Scenes from the Life of Thomas Guy* (London, Sotheby's, 18 Nov 1981;

lot 59). He engraved a few inferior mezzotints. His son John Theodore Heins the younger (1732/3–71) was also a portrait painter but had more success as a miniaturist and, particularly, as a topographical etcher.

UNPUBLISHED SOURCES

C. H. Collins Baker: MS notes (London, N.P.G. Lib.)

BIBLIOGRAPHY

Waterhouse: *18th C.*

F. Dunleep Singh: *Portraits in Norfolk Houses*, i, ii (Norwich, n.d.)

T. Fawcett: 'Eighteenth-century Art in Norwich', *Walpole Soc.*, xlvi (1978), pp. 73–5

Manners and Morals (exh. cat., ed E. Einberg; London, Tate, 1988), pp. 92, 243

RICHARD JEFFREE

Heinse, (Johann Jakob) Wilhelm (*b* Langewiesen, 15 Feb 1746; *d* Aschaffenburg, 22 June 1803). German poet, novelist and art historian. He initially studied law at Jena, then moved to the University of Erfurt (1768–71), where study with Christoph Martin Wieland (1733–1813) and Ludwig Gleim (1719–1803) developed his commitment to literature and art and helped him gain familiarity with aesthetic writings. In 1773 he began his literary career while serving as tutor to the von Massow family in Halberstadt. He moved to Düsseldorf in 1774, where he met Friedrich Heinrich Jacobi (1743–1819) and Johann Georg Jacobi (1740–1814) and their circle. He met Johann Wolfgang von Goethe and contributed to the early Sturm und Drang movement, for example with the publication of his reactions to the paintings in the Gemäldegalerie in Düsseldorf in a series of letters printed in Wieland's *Der Teutscher Merkur* (1776–7). In the letters he described paintings with the same passion that Johann Joachim Winckelmann had brought to sculpture and Goethe had directed to architecture. Although primarily descriptive, the letters also had theoretical impact, advocating the primacy of colour over drawing within painting, exploring the link between art and society, and promoting nature over learning in the creation and experience of art. Genius, nature and imagination were the qualities admired by Heinse, and he discovered them particularly in Rubens's work, whose paintings he described in highly sensual prose.

In June 1780 Heinse set off on a three-year Italian journey, subsidized by Gleim and Friedrich Heinrich Jacobi. He travelled via St Gotthard, Geneva and Genoa to Venice, where he studied from November 1780 to June 1781. After a month in Florence he moved to Rome (1781–3), where he was closely associated with Ferdinand Kobell and Friedrich Müller. Heinse's experience in Rome deepened his commitment to nature and confirmed his suspicions of 'phantasticists', those, particularly classicists, whose enthusiasm for the symbolic or literary resonance of works of art blinded them to the sensuous reality of those works. On a trip to Naples in July and August 1782 he met Jacob Philipp Hackert and Angelica Kauffman, and his enthusiasm for landscape increased. Heinse's Italian journals (published 1909) contain numerous analyses of a wide range of antique and Renaissance works of art. On his return to Düsseldorf he developed some of his Italian experiences in the essay 'Drei Fragmente' in the *Deutsches Museum* (1785–6). Those fragments were incorporated in his novel *Ardinghello und die glückseligen Inseln*

(Lemgo, 1787), the first German novel devoted to an artist-hero, in which the author advocated a spirited individualism and utopianism within a sensual vision of Greece and 16th-century Italy. The book described Renaissance and antique works of art with exuberant subjectivity, and it influenced numerous artists, including Peter Cornelius.

From 1786 until his death Heinse was lecturer and librarian to Friedrich Karl von Erthal, the Archbishop of Mainz, and his successor, Karl Theodor von Dalberg, while remaining active in literary circles.

WRITINGS
'Über einige Gemälde der Düsseldorfer Galerie', *Teutscher Merkur* (1776–7)
Ardinghello und die glückseligen Inseln: Eine italiänische Geschichte aus dem sechszehnten Jahrhundert, 2 vols (Lemgo, 1787/*R* Stuttgart, 1980, rev. 2/1794)
Sämtliche Werke, ed. C. Schüddekopf, 10 vols (Leipzig, 1904–25)

BIBLIOGRAPHY
NDB
K. D. Jessen: *Heinses Stellung zur bildenden Kunst und ihrer Ästhetik* (Berlin, 1901)
F. Noack: *Das Deutschtum in Rom seit dem Ausgang des Mittelalters*, 2 vols (Berlin, 1927/*R* 1974), ii, p. 250
E. H. Lehmann: *Die Anfänge der Kunstzeitschrift in Deutschland* (Leipzig, 1932), pp. 101–20
K. Harnisch: *Deutsche Malererzählungen: Die Art des Sehen bei Heinse, Tieck, Hoffmann, Stifter und Keller* (Berlin, 1938)
H. Koch: 'Zu Wilhelm Heinses Antikebeschreibungen', *Deutschland-Italien Festschrift für Wilhelm Waetzoldt* (Berlin, 1941), pp. 244–85
H. C. Hatfield: *Aesthetic Paganism in German Literature: From Winckelmann to the Death of Goethe* (Cambridge, 1964), pp. 73–84
H. W. Kruft: 'Heinses italienische Reise', *Dt. Vjschr. Litwiss. & Geistesgesch.*, xli (1967), pp. 82–98

ROBERT E MCVAUGH

Heinsius [Heintz; Heinze], **Johann Ernst** (*b* Ilmenau, Thuringia, 21 May 1731; *d* Erfurt, 18 Oct 1794). German painter. He received his training from his father, Johann Christian Heintze, who was originally a gunsmith before becoming court painter in the tiny principality of Saxony-Hildburghausen. In 1772 Heinsius was appointed court painter in Weimar, which became one of the centres of intellectual life in Germany at this period. There he painted portraits, for example of *Charles Augustus, Duke of Saxe-Weimar* and of poets of the 'Musenhof' such as *Johann Wilhelm Gleim* and *Johann Karl Musäus*. However, he did not receive particular recognition with these works. A period of leave in Hamburg (1781–4) was more successful and artistically fruitful. He returned to Weimar and produced a number of portraits, for example *Anna Amalia, Duchess of Saxe-Weimar*, of great maturity.

Heinsius' awkward, choleric temperament and his lack of education did not help to make him popular at a time when the artist–scholar was in demand. His financial position was somewhat improved by an appointment as artist at the Freie Zeichen Schule at Weimar. He was a simple craftsman who had turned his hand to portraits; these had an unvarnished truthfulness that did not flatter the sitter. His conception of art owed much to the ideals of the Baroque, his portraits lacking pathos and sentimentality and showing no trace of classical idealization. However, due to their naturalism, his portraits are of great documentary value. His brother, Johann Julius Heinsius (1740–1812), was also a painter, whose work has been confused with his own (e.g. by Oulmont and Thieme–Becker).

BIBLIOGRAPHY
Thieme–Becker
C. Oulmont: *J.-E. Heinsius, peintre des mesdames de France* (Paris, 1913)
B. Rein: 'Die Ilmenauer Familie Heinsius', *Die Henne, Ilmenauer Nachrichtenblatt*, 88 (1931)
H. Dauch-Schroeder: *Johann Ernst Heinsius* (diss., Jena, Friedrich Schiller U., 1937)

VOLKER HELAS

Heins & La Farge. American architectural partnership formed in 1886 by George Lewis Heins (*b* Philadelphia, PA, 24 May 1860; *d* Mohegan Lake, NY, 25 Sept 1907) and C(hristopher) Grant La Farge (*b* Newport, RI, 5 Jan 1862; *d* Saunderstown, RI, 11 Oct 1938), son of JOHN LA FARGE. Grant La Farge trained with his father before enrolling at the Massachusetts Institute of Technology, where he met George Heins. La Farge joined the practice of Henry Hobson Richardson and Heins worked for Leroy S. Buffington in Minneapolis. Later they were both employed as draughtsmen for Cass Gilbert, and in 1884 they became assistants to John La Farge in Manhattan. Their formal partnership began in 1886, La Farge specializing in design, Heins in technical and administrative affairs.

In 1891 Heins & La Farge won the competition for the Episcopal cathedral of St John the Divine in New York. Aged 31 and 29 respectively, and professionally unproven, they were chosen from over 70 firms to become architects of the grandest ecclesiastical project in America. Their design was a Byzanto-medieval hybrid and reflected the influence of Richardson; however, this style fell from favour as the Gothic Revival style rose in popularity. Burdened by the enormous stylistic and structural problems of the cathedral and by concurrent responsibilities as New York State Architect, Heins died prematurely. When the choir and crossing were consecrated in 1911, Ralph Adams Crams replaced La Farge with the intention of remodelling and completing the cathedral in the Gothic style (it remains unfinished).

The initial success of Heins & La Farge brought them numerous church commissions, most notably the Roman Catholic cathedrals of St Matthew in Washington, DC (1893), and St James in Seattle (1906), both in Renaissance style. They also designed the original buildings for the New York Zoological Park (1899–1911) and the handsomely tiled IRT subway stations in Manhattan, as well as private residences.

BIBLIOGRAPHY
Macmillan Enc. Architects
J. La Farge: *The Manner is Ordinary* (New York, 1954)
Buildings on Paper: Rhode Island Architectural Drawings, 1825–1945 (exh. cat., ed. W. H. Jordy and C. P. Monkhouse; Providence, RI, Brown U., Bell Gal., 1982), p. 221
J. Adams: *The Cathedral of Saint John the Divine in New York: Design Competitions in the Shadow of H. H. Richardson, 1888–1891* (diss., Providence, RI, Brown U., 1989)

JANET ADAMS

Heintsch [Hainsch; Heimsch; Heinrich; Heinsch], **Johann Georg** (*b* Kladsko, 1647; *d* Prague, 1712). German painter, active in Bohemia. In 1678 he settled in Prague, where he set up a large studio and found his most important clients among the Jesuits. His first extant pictures date from the 1680s. Influenced above all by the realism of Karel Škréta (*d* 1674), he became the foremost representative of this trend in the late 17th century. Although his painting, unlike Škréta's, is always purely descriptive, lacking Baroque imagination and compositional sense, he was a close observer of contemporary life and an impressive portrayer of human misery. Miraculous and legendary events are given everyday settings, notably in his lives of the saints, for example *St Francis Borgia in a Humble Tavern* (after 1680), *St John* (1690), *St Luke Painting St Mary* and *St John Nepomuk* (both 1705; all Prague, N.G., Convent of St George), and a painting of 1710 (Prague, Clementinum). With their strong impact, these paintings constituted an effective Counter-Reformation weapon for the Jesuits. In the 1690s Heintsch attempted to accommodate new stylistic trends, and his work lost its former tension. In 1702 he became a lay brother of the Augustinian Order.

BIBLIOGRAPHY

J. Neumann: *Malířství XVII. století v Čechách: Barokní realismus* [Czech painting in the 17th century: Baroque realism] (Prague, 1951), pp. 96–111, 120–24

K. M. Swoboda, ed.: *Barock in Böhmen* (Munich, 1964), pp. 148, 205, 325, no. 126

CAROLA WENZEL

Heintz. Swiss family of artists of Italian descent. The stone mason, sculptor and architect (1) Daniel Heintz (i) worked as foreman and master builder on the minsters of Basle and Berne. His son (2) Joseph Heintz (i), the most important representative of the family, worked mainly as a painter, executing religious works and portraits, but in the last years of his life undertook architectural commissions. His brother (3) Daniel Heintz (ii) succeeded their father as municipal master builder in Berne and also designed and directed work on buildings throughout Calvinist Switzerland. In contrast, (4) Joseph Heintz (ii), son of Joseph Heintz (i), used his talents as a painter in the service of the Counter-Reformation, though he is best known for his depictions of Venetian festivities and ceremonies. His son Daniel Heintz (iii) (1640–1709) also worked in Venice, as did his daughter Regina Heintz (ii) (*c.* 1646–before 1709), to whom no works have been definitely attributed.

(1) Daniel Heintz (i) (*b* Alagna Valsesia, *c.* 1530–35; *d* Berne, before 1 Dec 1596). Mason, sculptor, architect and engineer. Although originally from northern Italy, he was active in Switzerland, and he was granted citizenship in Basle on 27 November 1559. A year later he and his wife Katharina took a house in the Rittergasse, a select quarter, which points to a degree of prosperity. As a master builder, architect and sculptor he was much in demand by both the civic authorities and the wealthier citizens. He worked for a number of private clients in Basle, but many of his commissions came from the city council, for which he constructed, in the interior of the Rathaus, a stone spiral staircase with a stairwell in a rich, Late Gothic style and a figure of *Justice* (completed 1581). He was probably also responsible for the design and execution of the Geltenzunfthaus (Winetraders' Guildhall; completed 1578) and may have been involved in other municipal buildings in Basle. In 1580 he worked on a stone altar-table for Basle Minster.

Daniel Heintz (i): *Justice* (1575), sandstone figure on the central pillar of the west portal of Berne Minster; angels by Erhart Küng, *c.* 1495

In 1571 the city council of Berne approached Heintz, wishing to make use of his skill in Gothic vaulting. He was commissioned to build the vaulting over the main aisle of Berne Minster and to design and construct a rood screen for the church. By September 1573 he had closed the vault, and the rood screen was completed at the beginning of 1574 (destr. 1864). In 1581 the council of Berne again approached Heintz to ask him to move to Berne to continue the construction of the Minster. He declined at first because of his obligations to Basle, but it is not certain whether he had a permanent contract with the city or was merely thinking of his duties as a citizen. In 1585 he built a well at the old Basle hospital. However, in April 1588 he moved with his family to Berne, probably because the Berne council's offer seemed to promise more permanent work than was available in Basle. In Berne he evidently had to act as both master builder to the Minster and Municipal Building Director. From 1592 Heintz was in charge of building the tower of Berne Minster, and he was also commissioned to plan and execute the Gesellschaftshaus zu Pfistern (new Bakers' Guildhall; from 1593) and the Grosses Zeughaus (from 1595). The Gesellschaftshaus zu Pfistern is a Late Gothic structure with superimposed Renaissance and classical ornamentation. He died while these were being built, in the summer of 1596, and the buildings were continued by his son, (3) Daniel Heintz (ii).

Heintz was repeatedly called on to supply technical reports (e.g. by Basle, in the winter of 1589–90, to assess an arch of the stone bridge over the Rhine that was damaged by ice, and to advise on another question to do with waterways). Until he attained civic rights in Berne in 1591 Heintz was merely on leave from Basle, which tried to win him back in 1590 with the offer of an appointment as city mason; he decided in favour of Berne. In spring 1596 the Berne council, citing the competence of the master builder at its minster, attempted to win back from Zurich its old position as the foremost stoneworking town in the Confederation. It applied for the privilege to Emperor Rudolf II, but Heintz died before a decision was reached, and the outcome of the application is unknown.

Daniel Heintz was undoubtedly one of the most able master builders of his time north of the Alps. He had a wide technical knowledge, as well as proven artistic competence. He could work both in the Gothic style (e.g. staircase in the Basle Rathaus and the vaulting and tower of Berne Minster) and in a judicious, 'modern', Renaissance style (e.g. the rood screen in Berne Minster, the altar-table at Basle and the façades of the Geltenzunfthaus and the Spiesshof, Basle); thus the Geltenzunfthaus façade seems to take up a structure used by Jacopo Vignola in his work at Bologna (Portico dei Banchi). Heintz's work frequently shows hybrid forms using very Late Gothic and Renaissance elements (e.g. the façade and vaulting of the Spiesshof in Basle). At the same time, Heintz was one of the most important Swiss sculptors of his time. Two figures of *Justice*—one on the west portal of Berne Minster (1575; see fig.) and one in the Basle Rathaus (1581)—demonstrate his considerable skill. If, as some experts believe, the so-called *Berne Tell* (c. ?1585; Berne, Hist. Mus.) was carved by Heintz, it would show that he had maintained contacts with his north-Italian homeland, where saint figures were produced that have a realistic character very close to that of the Berne sculpture.

Thieme–Becker

BIBLIOGRAPHY

C. H. Baer: *Die Kunstdenkmäler des Kantons Basel-Stadt, i: Vorgeschichtliche, römische und fränkische Zeit; Geschichte und Stadtbild; Befestigungen, Areal und Rheinbrücke; Rathaus und Staatsarchiv*, Kstdkml. Schweiz (Basle, 1932), pp. 352, 364, 441–5

L. Mojon: *Die Kunstdenkmäler des Kantons Bern, iv: Das Berner Münster*, Kstdkml. Schweiz (Basle, 1960)

C. Debiaggi: 'Daniel Heintz architetto di Pietre Gemelle', *Boll. Soc. Piemont. Archeol. & B.A.*, n. s., xix (1965), pp. 101–4

F. Maurer: *Die Kunstdenkmäler des Kantons Basel-Stadt, v: Kirchen, Klöster und Kapellen, 3: St Peter bis Ulrichskirche*, Kstdkml. Schweiz (Basle, 1966), pp. 186, 407–8

C. Debiaggi: *Dizionario degli artisti valsesiani, dal secolo XVI al XX* (Varallo, 1968), pp. 82ff

R. Heyer: *Die Kunstdenkmäler des Kantons Basel-Landschaft, i: Der Bezirk Arlesheim*, Kstdkml. Schweiz (Basle, 1969), p. 241

J. Strübin: 'Das Zunfthaus zu Weinleuten in Basel (Geltenzunft)', *Basl. Z. Gesch. & Altertknd.*, lxxvii (1977), pp. 170–75

E. Landolt: 'Daniel Heintz, Balthasar Irmi und der Spiesshof in Basel', *Z. Schweiz. Archäol. & Kstgesch.*, xxxv (1978), pp. 32–42

——: 'Künstler und Auftraggeber im späten 16. Jahrhundert in Basel', *Unsere Kstdkml.*, xxix (1978), pp. 315–22

F. Maurer: 'Entwurf einer Baugeschichte des Spiesshofes in Basel', *Z. Schweiz. Archäol. & Kstgesch.*, xxxv (1978), pp. 43–51

J. Strübin: 'Das ehemalige Gesellschaftshaus zu Pfistern in Bern: Ein Werk von Daniel Heintz dem Älteren', *Z. Schweiz. Archäol. & Kstgesch.*, xliv (1987), pp. 171–86

(2) Joseph Heintz (i) (*bapt* Basle, 11 June 1564; *d* Prague, 15 Oct 1609). Painter, draughtsman, architect and artistic adviser, son of (1) Daniel Heintz (i).

1. LIFE AND PAINTED WORK. He began his training as a painter *c.* 1579 with Hans Bock I (*c.* 1550–*c.* 1623) in Basle. His first surviving drawings (1580) show something akin to Holbein's manner in his stained-glass window designs. After completing his apprenticeship he went *c.* 1584 to Rome, where he studied the works of antiquity, and those of Raphael, Michelangelo, Polidoro da Caravaggio and others. In 1587 he went via Florence to Venice, absorbing the works of Tintoretto, Titian and Veronese. In autumn 1591 the Holy Roman Emperor Rudolf II summoned him as 'portraitist and court painter' to Prague but soon sent him back to Italy, where he drew ancient statues in addition to producing his own work and acting as art agent for the Emperor. In 1592–5 he stayed mainly in Rome, then returned to Prague. In the following years he worked indefatigably as a draughtsman, painter, architect and artistic adviser, moving between Augsburg and Prague.

Heintz was a virtuoso draughtsman, working in pen and red and black chalk; he applied washes in various colours to his drawings and gave them a richly coloured effect by the use of white heightening and tinted paper. He painted religious histories on canvas as altarpieces (e.g. the *Pietà with Angels*, 1607; Augsburg, St Michael, and *Sacra conversazione*, *c.* 1600; Prague, St Thomas, chapel of St Barbara), on panel as epitaphs (e.g. *Elijah Ascending to Heaven*, 1607; Augsburg, St Anna), and also on copper (e.g. *St Martin and the Beggar*, 1600; Augsburg, St Anna). However, following the taste of the Emperor, he gave preference to 'Ovidian histories' and mythological *poesie*, which he painted on copper panels, usually in small format, as in *Diana and Actaeon* (1590s; Vienna, Ksthist. Mus.), *Satyrs and Nymphs* (1599; Munich, Alte Pin.; see fig.) and the *Rape of Proserpina* (*c.* 1600; Dresden, Gemäldegal. Alte Meister). His most important portrait commission, from the Emperor, was for a series of full-length portraits of the Styrian Habsburgs (1603–4; Vienna, Ksthist. Mus.). Half-figure and group portraits of his own family done in the most 'modern' style include a *Self-portrait with Brother and Sister* (1596; Berne, Kstmus.). He used no assistants and had no apprentices, but Matthäus Gundelach and Anton Gasser (*fl* 1610–22) made an intensive study of his style. In 1598 he married Regina, daughter of an Augsburg goldsmith, Salomon Gretzinger, and became a citizen of Augsburg. After 1600 he travelled to Graz, Innsbruck, Stuttgart and Neuburg an der Donau, working for the Counts Palatine of Neuburg, the Fuggers and other

Joseph Heintz (i): *Satyrs and Nymphs*, oil on copper, 240×325 mm, 1599 (Munich, Alte Pinakothek)

Augsburg patricians, and for the council of Augsburg. In 1602 he was ennobled, with his brother (3) Daniel Heintz (ii), by Rudolf II.

Heintz's development can be traced in more than 85 original drawings (e.g. Augsburg, Städt. Kstsammlungen; Basle, Öff. Kstsamml.; Berlin, Kupferstichkab.; Budapest, Mus. F.A.; Göttingen, Kstsamml. U.; Vienna, Albertina), among which studies after other works predominate in the early period. Although the most important influences on him were those of Rome, Bologna, Florence, Cremona, Parma, Milan and Venice, only very seldom did he quote from the works of others in his inventions, which seem to have been heavily governed by fashion. His copies are easily recognized as such. Within the art at Rudolf II's court, his painting was the most 'Italian', but its originality derived from an underlying old-German, Upper-Rhenish element. His main models were the Zuccaro family, the Carracci, the Sienese Salimbeni and Vanni, Correggio and perhaps the Campi circle in Cremona. By contrast, his later work shows comparatively few traces of a study of the great Venetians. He developed a very personal, highly painterly style, distinguished by violently agitated figures acting on a shallow stage, and by a powerful use of colour, with a complex interplay of mainly cool tones.

2. ARCHITECTURAL WORK. In the last seven years of his life Heintz worked primarily on architectural commissions. His designs for the Augsburg council included the east façade of the new Zeughaus (1602–7), the Weinsiegelhaus (1604–c. 1606; destr. 1809), a centralized Heilig-Grab-Kapelle (1604; unexecuted) and a council loggia (1607–9; unexecuted). For Neuburg an der Donau he developed a plan (1603–6) for a town centre with a church, chancery, town hall and other buildings that was only partly realized, or in modified form. For his patron Zacharias Geizkofler (d 1617) he designed a new parish church at Haunsheim (1609), painted an altarpiece for the castle chapel, now known only through an engraving (1606; Zimmer, 1971, no. 92) by Lucas Kilian, and designed such decorative pieces as a fireplace in Geizkofler's Schloss Haunsheim and a stone epitaph (1607–9) for him in the new church. He probably also worked on projects for the Emperor and the Protestant communities in Prague. In Augsburg he collaborated with the master builder Elias Holl (i) (*see* HOLL (i), (2)), in Neuburg an der Donau with the court master builder Siegmund Doctor (*fl* 1605–c. 1617) and in Prague with the north Italian architect Giovanni Maria Filippi. The architectural forms he developed were based on his father's ideas and on contemporary architecture in Rome, Venice and, above

all, Lombardy. The adaptation of these ideas to the milieu north of the Alps gave an important stimulus to their further development.

Heintz's works have survived through their reproduction by Aegidius Sadeler II and Lucas Kilian in engravings, which were in turn imitated, copied and translated into other media countless times.

BIBLIOGRAPHY

NDB; Thieme–Becker
K. van Mander: *Schilder-boeck* ([1603]–1604), fol. 291*r*
V. Löwe von Adorf: *Eine kurtze evangelische Trost-Predigt gehalten zu Prag . . . bei dem volckreichen Begräbnis Herrn Joseph Heintzens, Röm: Kay: Majest: Gewesenen Cammermahlers etc.* (Leipzig, 1610)
J. von Sandrart: *Teutsche Academie* (1675–9); ed. A. R. Peltzer (1925), pp. 149–50
K. H. von Heinecken: *Nachrichten von Künstlern und Kunst-Sachen* (Leipzig, 1768), pp. iv–vi
C. W. Hardmeyer: 'Der Maler Joseph Heinz aus Bern', *Neujbl. Kstges. Zürich*, n. s., ii (1842), pp. 1–2
B. Haendcke: *Die schweizerische Malerei im 16. Jahrhundert diesseits der Alpen* (Aarau, 1893), pp. 237–53
——: 'Joseph Heintz, Hofmaler Kaiser Rudolfs II', *Jb. Ksthist. Samml. Wien*, xv (1894), pp. 45–59
J. Zimmer: *Joseph Heintz d.Ä. als Maler* (Weissenhorn, 1971)
T. Gerszi: 'A Newly Identified Drawing by Joseph Heintz the Elder', *Essays in Northern European Art Presented to Egbert Haverkamp-Begemann on his Sixtieth Birthday*, ed. A. M. Logan (Doornspijk, 1983), pp. 94–6
T. DaCosta Kaufmann: *L'Ecole de Prague* (Paris, 1985), pp. 226–43
J. Zimmer: 'Joseph Heintz als Architekt', *Elias Holl und das Augsburger Rathaus*, ed. W. Baer and others (Regensburg, 1985), pp. 98–118
——: *Joseph Heintz der Ältere: Zeichnungen und Dokumente* (Munich, 1988)

(3) Daniel Heintz (ii) (*b* Berne, 20 Aug 1575; *d* Berne, before 24 April 1633). Mason, architect and engineer, son of (1) Daniel Heintz (i). He succeeded his father as Municipal Building Director in Berne in 1596 and was subsequently put in charge of erecting the new Gesellschaftshaus zu Pfistern (Bakers' Guildhall, 1595–8) and the Grosses Zeughaus (1597–1602), both begun by his father. His first original work was the municipal staple house (1599–1608) in Berne, although he had worked on private buildings in the city at an earlier date. As Building Director, he was responsible for official building work in and around Berne, and in particular for buildings erected to accommodate provincial governors (Münchenbuchsee, 1600–03; Büren an der Aare, 1620–25; ?Landshut, 1626) and officials (Aarberg, 1608–10). He was also involved in castle building in and beyond Berne (Rougemont and Fribourg, 1608; Burgdorf, 1616; Nidau, 1626–33; Lenzburg and Aargau, 1620). For the most part these were not new schemes but extensions and alterations to existing complexes. From 1609 to 1613 he also directed the alterations to the Bürgerbibliothek in Berne. In 1602 Heintz replaced Hans Thüring (or Düring, *fl* 1596–1612) as Master of the Works at Berne Minster, while Thüring became Municipal Building Director; from 1612 Heintz held both offices. In the former capacity he designed the armorial bearings (before 1611) for the great bell of the Minster, by which time he had built its tower to the level of the first belfry.

Heintz's (mainly technical) expertise had won him commissions from outside the area of Berne at an early stage in his career. In 1608 he was engaged to extend the church tower at Yverdon (Vaud) and later, in the second half of the 1620s, he worked frequently in French-speaking Switzerland. In 1627 he was invited to submit plans for the choir and sacristies of Fribourg Cathedral, but the Protestant authorities in Berne were opposed to his participation, declaring that he should 'tear down papist churches rather than build them'. Heintz did, however, design the pulpit of Lausanne Cathedral in 1632. In the early 1620s he was asked to modernize the fortifications in Berne, after he had replaced the old moat bridge by a more modern three-arched structure (1613). He redesigned the most important town gates (Untertorbrücke, Schanzentore and Obertor) and adapted them to the latest concepts in fortification. In 1622–3 he directed the building of a new rifle clubhouse. Heintz was later involved in building Calvinist churches and rectories, acting either as the designer or building director, for example at Schangau (1618), Habkern (1621), Renan (1627–31), Wynigen (1630), Eggiwil (1630–32) and Därstetten (possibly as early as 1610).

Although Heintz seems to have been a gifted architect and engineer, the extent of his artistic ability has not been established. Even in his ornamental stone escutcheons (Willading relief, *c.* 1600; relief on the Berne staple house, 1603–4; relief on Schloss Rougemont, 1608, untraced) and in the pulpit at Lausanne Cathedral (his last work), the artistry is inferior to his father's sculptures. Heintz's architectural works seem comparatively unambitious, but this may be due to the nature of his commissions; like his father, he used a mixture of Gothic and Renaissance styles in his oeuvre, albeit on a more modest scale.

BIBLIOGRAPHY

Thieme–Becker
R. Riggenbach: *Ulrich Ruffiner von Prismell und die Bauten der Schinerzeit im Wallis* (Brig, 1934)
P. Hofer: *Kanton Bern, iii: Die Staatsbauten der Stadt Bern*, Kstdkml. Schweiz (Basle, 1947)
——: *Kanton Bern, i: Die Stadt Bern*, Kstdkml. Schweiz (Basle, 1952)
M. Strub: *Canton de Fribourg, ii: La Ville de Fribourg*, Kstdkml. Schweiz (Basle, 1956)
P. Hofer: *Kanton Bern, ii: Die Stadt Bern: Gesellschaftshäuser und Wohnbauten*, Kstdkml. Schweiz (Basle, 1959)
L. Mojon: *Kanton Bern, iv: Das Münster*, Kstdkml. Schweiz (Basle, 1960)
C. Debiaggi: *Dizionario degli artisti valsesiani, dal secolo XVI al XX* (Varallo, 1968), p. 93
J. Schweizer: *Bern Land, i: Burgdorf*, Kstdkml. Schweiz (Basle, 1985)
M. Fontannaz: 'La Chaire de la Cathédrale de Lausanne et sa postérité en pays de Vaud', *Unsere Kstdkml.*, xxxviii (1987), pp. 533–9

(4) Joseph [Giuseppe] **Heintz** [Heintz; Ens; Enzo; Heintz di Augusta] **(ii)** (*b* Augsburg, *c.* 1600; *d* Venice, 24 Sept 1678). Painter and etcher, son of (2) Joseph Heintz (i). He served his apprenticeship (1617–21) as a painter with his stepfather, Matthäus Gundelach, in Augsburg. His artistic beginnings are traceable in drawings produced in Augsburg (e.g. the *Painter at his Easel*, 1621; Gdańsk, N. Mus.), and Venice (e.g. *Genius of Painting*, 1625; Vienna, Albertina). His great panel painting *Christ in Limbo* (late 1620s or early 1630s; sold London, Sotheby's, 6 July 1994, lot 4391) bears witness to his conversion to Catholicism, without which he could hardly have established himself in Venice. He probably spent long periods in Rome in the 1630s or 1640s, and before 1644 Urban VIII made him a Knight of the Golden Spur. Many of his paintings on religious themes, including works supporting the Counter-Reformation, were predominantly for churches in Venice and its dominions. However, his special importance for Venetian painting lies not in the field of religious art but in his depictions (mostly Venice, Bib.

Correr) of the city's festivities and state ceremonies, featuring large numbers of figures, in which he was a direct precursor of Luca Carlevaris and Canaletto, as revealed especially in his *Piazza S Marco* (after 1640; Rome, Gal. Doria-Pamphili). Presumably he knew of the similar endeavours of his cousin Joseph Plepp (1595–1642) in Berne. He also produced genre paintings, such as the *Fishmonger* (1650s; Italy, priv. col., see 1959 exh. cat., p. 123) votive pictures, including the *Adoration of the Magi* (?1669) and *Sacra conversazione* (1669; both Breguzzo, S Andrea); allegories, for example the *Allegory of Venice* (1674; Vienna, Ksthist. Mus.); pictures showing the activities of the months and mythological scenes of which there is so far only a literary record.

Heintz's whole oeuvre was regarded as extraordinary and bizarre by his contemporaries, his profane pictures being peopled not only with a multitude of small figures in sometimes grotesque attitudes, as might be demanded by the depiction of festivities, but including, in the allegories in particular, fabulous hybrid creatures or monsters drawn from the repertory of Hieronymus Bosch and his successors or partly invented by himself, as in the *Allegory of Venice* (Vienna, Ksthist. Mus.) and *Vanitas* (Milan, Brera). Even in old age (1674) he quoted from the works of his father. He also worked on occasion as an etcher; for example his painting *Loreto* (1650; Italy, priv. col., see Longo, 1983) is accompanied by an etching in two states by his hand (Hamburg, Ksthalle). Marco Boschini praised the style of his old age for its naturalness, bravura and vivacity. In his early seventies he taught Francesco Trevisani in his workshop in the Sestiere S Polo.

Thieme–Becker
BIBLIOGRAPHY

M. Boschini: *La carta del navegar pitoresco* (Venice, 1660); ed. A. Pallucchini (Rome, 1966), pp. xxvii, lxvii–lxix, 83–4, 547, 572–3, 591, 594, 600, 607, 628

T. Frimmel: 'Bemerkungen über den jüngeren Joseph Heintz', *Neue Bl. Gemäldeknd.*, i (1922), pp. 203–14

Z. Kalista: 'Humprecht Jan Černín jako mecenáš a podporovatel výtvarných umění v době své benátské ambasady (1660–1663)' [Humprecht Jan Černín as patron and supporter of the arts during his Venetian legation (1660–1663)], *Památky Archeol.*, xxxvi (1928–30), pp. 53–78

Le feste e le maschere veneziane (exh. cat. by G. Lorenzetti, Venice, Ca' Rezzonico, 1937), pp. 31, 33–4

M. Levey: *Painting in 18th-century Venice* (London, 1959), pp. 73–4

La pittura del seicento a Venezia (exh. cat., Venice, Ca' Pesaro, 1959)

I vedutisti veneziani del settecento (exh. cat. by P. Zampetti, Venice, Doge's Pal., 1967), pp. 2–7

C. Donzelli and G. M. Pilo: *I pittori del seicento veneto* (Florence, 1967), pp. 208–9

R. Pallucchini: *La pittura veneziana del seicento*, 2 vols (Venice, 1981), i, pp. 152–5; ii, pp. 623–9

L. Longo: 'La "translatio" Lauretana di Joseph Heintz il Giovane ritrovata', *A. Ven.*, xxxvii (1983), pp. 101–8

P. L. Fantelli: 'Aggiunte al catalogo di Joseph Heintz il Giovane', *Stud. Trentini Sci. Stor.*, n.s, lxi (1984), pp. 201–2

L. Longo: 'Joseph Heintz der Jüngere und Pietro Vecchia in der Kirche S Antonino in Venedig', *Jb. Zentinst. Kstgesch.*, 2 (1986), pp. 317–27

JÜRGEN ZIMMER

Heinzelman. *See* HAINZELMANN.

Heinzelmann, Konrad [Chunrad] (*b* ?Dettwang, nr Rothenburg ob der Tauber, ?before 1400; *d* Nuremberg, between 6 April and 23 April 1454). German architect. He is first mentioned in 1429 as deputy to the head foremen Hans Kun and Hans Felber on the reconstruction of the Georgskirche, Nördlingen. He had moved to work for the town of Rothenburg ob der Tauber by 1438 and was probably also briefly involved in building the Jakobskirche. In a letter of 6 April 1439 to the Council of Esslingen he is already mentioned as a candidate for the new position of Warden (foreman) on the building of the Frauenkirche there, but in a letter to Rothenburg dated 18 May 1439 the Council of Nuremberg enquired about Heinzelmann's abilities, as they were planning to offer him a contract to build the parish church of St Lorenz. The rebuilding of St Lorenz began on 28 October 1439, and Heinzelmann was in charge until his death, although in 1446 he briefly advised on building the town church at Amberg. From 1445/6 to 1448/9 'Maister Chunrad' received a quarterly salary in Nuremberg of 20 gulden, and from 1445 until at least 1449 he was also Master Gunsmith to the town. The hall choir of St Lorenz (for illustration *see* LATE GOTHIC), with details modelled on the choir of the church of the Holy Cross, Schwäbisch Gmünd, is his most important and individual achievement, although it was completed by his successors.

NDB
BIBLIOGRAPHY

A. Gümbel: 'Rechnungen und Aktenstücke zur Geschichte des Chorbaus von St Lorenz in Nürnberg unter der Leitung Konrad Heinzelmanns', *Repert. Kstwiss.*, xxxii (1909), pp. 1–30

——: 'Der Baumeister und Stückegiesser Hans Felber von Ulm, dessen Beziehungen zu Nürnberg und Todesjahr: Nachträgliches zur Biographie Konrad Heinzelmanns', *Repert. Kstwiss.*, xxxiv (1911), pp. 232–54

O. Schulz: 'Der Chorbau von St Lorenz zu Nürnberg und seine Baumeister', *Z. Dt. Ver. Kstwiss.*, x (1943), pp. 55–80

A. Ress: *Stadt Rothenburg o. d. Tauber: Kirchliche Bauten*, v/8 of *Die Kunstdenkmäler von Bayern* (Munich, 1959)

W. Bernhardt: 'Die Quellen zur Geschichte der Esslinger Frauenkirche und ihrer Meister', *Essling. Stud.*, xix (1980), p. 51

FRANZ BISCHOFF

Heinzmann, Carl Friedrich (*b* Stuttgart, 2 Dec 1795; *d* Munich, 9 July 1846). German painter and printmaker. He was a pupil in Stuttgart of Johann Baptist Seele, whose stiff drawing style he at first adopted. After taking part in the Napoleonic Wars he moved to Munich in December 1815 to study landscape painting at the Akademie der Bildenden Künste under Wilhelm Alexander Wolfgang von Kobell. His first oil paintings were copies of hunting scenes after Franz Joachim Beich, whose works were in the royal collection at Schloss Schleissheim. He also copied pen drawings by Kobell and Johann Georg von Dillis. His first original oil paintings (e.g. *Militia Picket at Schlettstadt*, 1816; Stuttgart, Staatsgal.) depicted scenes from his own life as a soldier. Between 1818 and 1822 he painted many landscapes replete with genre-like details of the area around Munich and the Bayerisches Oberland, and these were widely disseminated as lithographs (e.g. *Excursion on the Tegernsee*, 1818; e.g. Munich, Staatl. Graph. Samml.). The composition tends to draw attention first to the active figures in the foreground and then to an open view of the countryside, a device recalling the works of Kobell. These early naturalistic scenes are characterized by an affinity for nature and by the depiction of people at work.

In 1822 Heinzmann was given a permanent position as a porcelain painter at the Nymphenburg Porcelain Factory. Although he was employed to paint landscapes, he began by decorating plates with designs copied from the 17th-century Netherlandish works in the royal collection. In 1823 the factory sent him on a tour of Bavaria to draw picturesque views of towns and to copy outstanding folk costumes; in 1824 he also visited Switzerland to produce additional preliminary drawings for topographical lithographs. In 1827 he painted plates with scenes after such artists as Claude, Poussin and Francisque Millet. He continued to paint in oils, however, and his finest works—*Landscape near Murnau* (1828) and the *Fortress at Kufstein* (1834; both Leipzig, Mus. Bild. Kst.)—are in this medium. From 1832 the Kunstverein in Munich increasingly employed him to produce lithographs of paintings by contemporary artists, for example *Ave Maria, nach einem Gemälde von H. Kaufmann* (1832; e.g. Munich, Staatl. Graph. Samml.). The porcelain dishes (Munich, Neue Pin.) with *vedute* of Munich, presented in 1833 to Otto of Greece (*reg* 1832–62) by his native city, were designed by Heinzmann but executed by other artists. Because of the success of his paintings on porcelain, he was given the commission for the Nymphenburg Factory's presentation vase, ordered in 1835 as a State gift for Mahmud II, Sultan of Turkey (*reg* 1808–39); it depicts a scene of a Bavarian military camp with a border of various weapons. Heinzmann's delicate brushwork can also be seen on vases with scenes of the *Chapel at Fiesole in Lamplight* (1834; Munich, Bayer. Nmus.) and the *Villa at Terracina by Moonlight* (1834; priv. col., see F. H. Hofmann: *Die Geschichte der bayeischen Porzellan: Manufaktur Nymphenburg*, iv (Leipzig, 1923), p. 641). An eye condition forced him to abandon porcelain painting in 1840. The humorous etching *Apple Thief at the Christmas Fair* (1843; e.g. Munich, Stadtmus.) is one of his last works.

BIBLIOGRAPHY

Thieme–Becker

H. Thoma: *Staatliche Porzellan-Manufaktur Nymphenburg, 1747–1947* (Munich, 1947)

M. Roethlisberger: 'Claude Lorrain: Some New Perspectives', *Stud. Hist. A.*, xiv (1984), pp. 47–65

A. ZIFFER

Heise, Jacob (*fl* ?Königsberg [now Kaliningrad], 1654–63). German amber-carver. He is known through three signed and dated works: two amber nautilus cups (1654, ex-Königsberg, Kstsamml. Stadt, untraced; 1659, Dresden, Grünes Gewölbe) and a bowl (1663; Budapest, Mus. F.A.). All three pieces are rich in figurative carving and evince a sculptural use of the material. The cup of 1659 and the bowl are signed *Jacob Heise ... Königsberg...*, although it is not known whether he belonged to the guild of amber-carvers in Königsberg, as no records of members between 1643 and 1710 are extant. Other works in amber have been attributed to him on the basis of style or been linked to his circle, for example the figure-group of Frederick William, Elector of Brandenburg, and his consort Luise Henriette (Kassel, Hess. Landesmus.) and a two-handled bowl (London, V&A).

BIBLIOGRAPHY

A. Rohde: *Bernstein: Ein deutscher Werkstoff* (Berlin, 1937), pp. 40–43

M. Trusted: *Catalogue of Ambers in the Victoria and Albert Museum* (London, 1985), p. 43

MARJORIE TRUSTED

Heisei period. Period in Japanese history, beginning 7 January 1989 and concurrent with the reign of Emperor Akihito (*b* 1933). The name Heisei means 'establishing or attaining peace'. Japan is the only country still to adhere to a system of era names (*gengō* or *nengō*). The practice began in the Taika period (AD 645–50), was abandoned for a time after World War II and was re-established by the Gengōhō (New Era Name Law) of 1979. Japanese artists in this period continue to challenge convention, as movements such as New Painting (*see* JAPAN, §VI, 5(v)) and New Sculpture (*see* JAPAN, §V, 6) testify, and they increasingly make an active contribution to the development of international art.

BIBLIOGRAPHY

Kodansha Enc. Japan

Heishirō. *See* KANŌ, (10).

Heisig, Bernhard (*b* Breslau [now Wrocław, Poland], 31 March 1925). German painter, printmaker and teacher. His father, Walter Heisig (*b* 1909), a painter and printmaker, inspired him towards painting. He attended the Kunstgewerbeschule in Breslau (1941–2). After his military service, completed in 1945, he worked as a graphic artist in the office of information and propaganda in Wrocław until 1947. Heisig studied at the Kunstgewerbeschule in Leipzig (1948–9) under Walter Münze (1895–1978) and at the Akademie für Graphische Künste in Leipzig (1949–51) under Max Schwimmer (*d* 1960). In his early years he was indebted to the 19th-century Realists such as Gustave Courbet, Il'ya Repin, Adolph Menzel and Wilhelm Leibl, but he increasingly looked to the art of 20th-century German painters, for example Lovis Corinth, Oskar Kokoschka and Max Beckmann. Early in his career Heisig showed his commitment to socially concerned painting that dealt with contemporary problems. The 19th-century hierarchical ranking of paintings was anchored in his consciousness: the figurative painting carrying a thematic message had greater merit than the portrait, the landscape and the still-life. Questions relating to the past, present and future of human development were always linked in Heisig's mind with the quest for truth. They were closely associated with a search to establish the relationship in the struggle for freedom between the desire for power on the one hand and tolerance on the other, between social aspiration and illusion, between intrepid courage and fear. He has looked for pictorial means of expressing these concerns in large-scale pictures. Where the message made it appropriate he often used the triptych as a form. He quoted historical subjects as parables.

Heisig taught at the Hochschule für Grafik und Buchkunst, Leipzig (1954–68), and was its Principal (1961–4). From 1965 to 1968 he ran the college's department of painting and graphics. Between 1956 and 1972 he painted numerous pictures on the theme of the Paris Commune and the fighting on the barricades. Early versions still lean heavily on the illustrative historical paintings of the 19th century. In later versions there is a clear attempt at reduction, at condensation, and a search for figures that carry many layers of expression thus elucidating the ambivalence of his questioning. This condensation relied upon the experience gained from the portraits that Heisig drew and painted in the same period, for example *Portrait of the Mother* (oil, 1970; Berlin, Alte N.G.) and portrait of *Vaclav Neumann* (1973; Leipzig, Mus. Bild. Kst.). In *Brigadier II* (oil, 1969–70; Leipzig, Mus. Bild. Kst.) he attempted in an individual physiognomy of a slightly heroicized construction worker to express his concept of a picture that applies generally to a whole class. After working for some time on a freelance basis, in 1976 he was recalled as Principal of the Hochschule für Grafik und Buchkunst, retaining the post until 1986.

Heisig used the subject of Icarus as an image of the search for truth, producing variants on this theme between 1966 and 1979 (e.g. *Icarus—Difficulty in the Search for Truth*, 1973; Leipzig, Mus. Bild. Kst., and *Death of Icarus*, oil, 1979; priv. col., see 1985 exh. cat., p. 127). In the 1960s his works were permeated by a vital and painterly fluency of touch that went hand in hand with his attempts to achieve a unified total form. His predilection for a meaningful overall form, generally axially arranged, was particularly noticeable from the 1970s, and it evolved mainly from the Icarus pictures. The composition, which includes several figures, is resolved fragmentarily. Symbolic conglomerates are placed centrally: on the one hand they are difficult to work out, while on the other they lead to banal line-ups that can only be read verbally. Often strips of writing are inserted. Figure-types are deprived of their portrait-like individuality and give the impression of being labelled. Heisig uses comparisons from the Bible and quotations from 20th-century art (Dix and Beckman) alongside quotations from the Classics. Wind instruments (trumpets and horns) frequently appear as symbols of warning and seeing, of prophecy, while the motif of the loudspeaker is used to denote demagogy.

Works dealing with Fascism including the *Fascist Nightmare* (1967–8; Leipzig, Mus. Bild. Kst.), a series of 30 lithographs, and the *Persistence of Forgetfulness* (oil, 1977; Berlin, Alte N.G.) form another important group in Heisig's work. The combination of vital painterly power and intellectual symbolic overloading has had an impact on many younger artists (e.g. Johannes Heisig and Hubertus Giebe), but in some pictures it detracts from the total form that Heisig attempted to achieve. Even his still-lifes and landscapes often show a lack of unity and discipline in the composition of the picture. His thematic pictures are generally made less approachable by their intellectual overloading and their simultaneous loss of sensuality.

BIBLIOGRAPHY

Bernhard Heisig (exh. cat., Leipzig, Staatl. Hochsch. Graph. & Buchkst, 1963)
Bernhard Heisig (exh. cat., Dresden, Gemäldegal. Neue Meister; Leipzig, Mus. Bild. Kst.; 1973)
R. Hartleb: *Bernhard Heisig* (Dresden, 1975)
H. Schumann: *Ateliergespräche* (Leipzig, 1976), pp. 107–27
Bernhard Heisig (exh. cat., Bremen, Gal. Holz, 1980)
K. M. Kober: *Bernhard Heisig* (Dresden, 1981)
Bernhard Heisig (exh. cat., Leipzig, Mus. Bild. Kst., 1985)
Bernhard Heisig: Retrospektive (exh. cat., ed. J. Merkert and P. Pachnicke; W. Berlin, Berlin. Gal.; Bonn, Rhein. Landesmus.; Munich, Bayer. Staatsgemäldesammlungen; 1988–90)
Bernhard Heisig: Retrospektive: Graphik und Illustration (exh. cat., Hannover, Sprengel Mus.; Oberhausen, Städt. Gal.; 1990)
Zeit zu Leben: Max Beckmann, Minna Beckmann-Tube, Bernard Heisig (exh. cat., Berlin, Berlin. Gal., 1991)

ANITA KÜHNEL

Heiss, Johann (*b* Memmingen, 1640; *d* Augsburg, 1704). German painter and draughtsman. He was apprenticed first to Johann Friedrich Sichelbein (*c.* 1625–90), then in Augsburg to Johann Heinrich Schönfeld, whose style fundamentally determined his own. He was also influenced by Joseph Werner and French Baroque painters, and the knowledge of Italian landscape and architecture evident in his pictures suggests an Italian journey or the influence of an artist recently returned from Italy.

Heiss, a Protestant, began his career *c.* 1663–4 in the service of Eberhard VIII, Duke of Württemberg (*reg* 1628–74), then returned to Memmingen, where he undertook numerous commissions for altar paintings in monasteries and cathedrals in Upper Swabia. In the 1670s he settled in Augsburg, and his fondness for learned subject-matter and painstaking treatment of realistic detail suggest a connection with the city's Kunstakademie, as does his frequent use of the Akademie as subject-matter, for example in the *Sculptor's Atelier with two Female Models* (*c.* 1690; Augsburg, Schaezlerpal.) and *Hall of the Academy with Young Sculpture Students* (*c.* 1690; Dessau, Staatl. Gal.). However, his two paintings entitled *Room at the Academy . . .*, one with a male model, the other a female (*c.* 1690; Brunswick, Herzog Anton Ulrich-Mus.), are evidently to be taken as allegories. In all Heiss's extensive oeuvre, Schönfeld's influence is notable, above all in *Venus and Mars in Vulcan's Forge* (1675; Sibiu, Brukenthal Mus.), with its elegant figures and gentle lights. Heiss's allegories, mythological scenes and historical paintings were very much prized by contemporary collectors.

BIBLIOGRAPHY

Augsburger Barock (exh. cat., Augsburg, Rathaus and Holbeinhaus, 1968), pp. 113–18, 198
B. Bushart: 'Die Barockisierung des Augsburger Domes', *Jb. Ver. Augsburg. Bistumsgesch.*, iii (1969), pp. 109–29

CAROLA WENZEL

Heisterkamp, Peter. *See* PALERMO, BLINKY.

Heizaburō. *See* TORII, (4).

Heizer, Michael (*b* Berkeley, CA, 4 Nov 1944). American sculptor, painter and printmaker. He studied painting at the San Francisco Art Institute from 1963 to 1964 and moved to New York in 1966. His early imagery showed an awareness of Minimalist ideals. In 1967, however, he temporarily renounced painting and pursued what became a lasting interest in LAND ART. His 'excavations' in the desert of the American Southwest were prefigured by childhood travels to Pre-Columbian and Egyptian archaeological sites with his father, anthropologist Robert Heizer. The earthworks of the late 1960s and early 1970s consisted of moving vast, yet precise quantities of soil in regions of virtual inaccessibility, a strategy he shared with other artists such as Walter de Maria, Robert Smithson and James Turrell. *Double Negative* (1969–70; Los Angeles, CA, Mus. Contemp. A.) exemplifies his concern for juxtaposing the monumental with the ephemeral. The work displaced *c.* 250,000 tonnes of desert rock, while cutting a horizontal shaft across the lip of an eroding precipice, thus poising the artist's heroic gesture against the imminent forces of nature. Works produced for museum and gallery exhibitions, for example *Windows/Matchdrop* (1969; Düsseldorf, Städt. Ksthalle), where a sidewalk is incised according to the dictate of several fallen matchsticks, demonstrate also his debt to earlier modernist questionings of the creative context and authority of the artist. Heizer incorporated the role of chance in his work's design.

When Heizer returned to painting in 1972, his production was marked by its renewed concern for formal problems, and in this respect his large, often shaped canvases such as *Untitled 7* (1974; see Bell, p. 57) continued the dialogue between positive and negative spatial relationships that began in his land art. Subsequently, his sculptural idiom broadened to include free-standing geometric constructions in stone, wood and metal, and he extended his pictorial repertoire to pursue experiments in various print media including monotype (*Monotype VII-2*, 1983; see *ARTnews*, lxxxii/8, 1983, p. 87). At the same time, his public commissions sparked open controversy over the nature and value of public arts in the USA.

PUBLISHED WRITINGS
'The Art of Michael Heizer', *Artforum*, viii/4 (1969), pp. 32–9

BIBLIOGRAPHY
D. Waldman: 'Holes without History', *ARTnews*, lxx/3 (1971), pp. 44–8, 66–8
J. Bell: 'Positive and Negative: New Paintings by Michael Heizer', *A. Mag.*, xlix/3 (1974), p. 57
Michael Heizer (exh. cat., ed. Z. Felix; Essen, Mus. Flkwang; Otterlo, Kröller-Müller; 1979)
F. Colpitt: 'Heizer's Extracts', *A. America*, lxxii/10 (1984), pp. 132–7
Michael Heizer (exh. cat., ed. J. Brown; Los Angeles, CA, Mus. Contemp. A., 1984)

DERRICK R. CARTWRIGHT

Hejduk, John (*b* New York, 19 July 1929). American architect, conceptual artist, teacher and writer. He studied at the Cooper Union, New York (1947–50), University of Cincinnati, OH (1950–52), Harvard University, Cambridge, MA (1952–3), and the University of Rome (Fulbright scholar, 1954). Hejduk began teaching architecture in 1954, and in 1964 he joined Cooper Union, becoming Dean of the School of Architecture there in 1975. He also worked in various architectural offices in New York, including that of I. M. Pei (1956–8), and in 1965 he established his own office in New York. From 1954 to 1963 he worked in a purposefully dry, reductive style strongly influenced by Le Corbusier, Mies van der Rohe and De Stijl. This is illustrated in the Nine Square Problem (*c.* 1954), a linear grid concerned with such concepts as frame, post, centre, periphery, extension and compression, which was developed as a pedagogical tool for first-year students. It became the basis for his Texas Houses project (1954–63; unexecuted): seven designs ranging from classicizing simplicity to complex architectural renderings of Cubist principles. The Diamond Projects (1963–7; unexecuted) comprised a series of house designs that addressed the formal ramifications of Mondrian's tipping of the square canvas by 45° while retaining the internal arrangements of pure horizontals and verticals. Hejduk participated in the NEW YORK FIVE exhibition at MOMA, New York, in 1969, and his work continued to be widely exhibited throughout his career. In 1975 he completed the renovation of the Cooper Union Foundation Building, New York, the one major project actually built up to that time. Around 1975 narrative and 'anthropomorphization' began to appear in his projects, with structures taking part in disquieting, personal allegories. Here precise architectural drawings, models and loose renderings placing the monuments in landscapes reminiscent of de Chirico, together with accompanying notes, constitute the total work (e.g. the allegorical trilogy *Cemetery for the Ashes of Thought*, 1975; *Silent Witnesses*, 1976; and *Thirteen Watchtowers of Cannaregio*, 1979). The aspect of the architectural project as narrative setting took full form in the *Masques* (1979–83) and subsequent renderings of urban landscapes (e.g. *Vladivostok* and *Bovisa*, *c.* 1987–9). During the 1980s Hejduk built a number of structures, for example the House of the Painter and House of the Musician (1983) in the Great Hall, Gropiusbau, Berlin; House of the Suicide (1986–90) at the Georgia Institute of Technology, Atlanta; and buildings for social housing (1988)—three in Friedrichstadt, Berlin, and one at Tegel Harbour, Berlin—which were 'characters' or parts of the settings in the urban scenes. He also completed a series of lithographs illustrating Thomas Mann's *The Black Swan* (New York, 1990); some recall Suprematist compositions, others show architectural forms in stark silhouette. Hejduk was often characterized as a 'paper architect', but in the 1980s more of his structures were being built at a time when his projects were increasingly conceptual, which supported assertions of the fundamentally architectural concerns of his work.

WRITINGS
Mask of Medusa: Works, 1947–83 (New York, 1985)
Vladivostok (New York, 1989)

BIBLIOGRAPHY
Contemp. Architects
7 Houses (exh. cat., ed. K. Frampton; New York, Inst. Archit. & Urb. Stud., 1980)
Bovisa (exh. cat., ed. J. R. Moneo; Cambridge, MA, Harvard U., Grad. Sch. Des., 1987)

WALTER SMITH

Hejia cun [Ho-chia ts'un]. Site in the southern suburbs of Xi'an, Shaanxi Province, China. A hoard of precious objects from the Tang period (AD 618–907) was discovered in the village in 1970. Two large pottery jars contained about 1000 objects of both Chinese and foreign origin, including jades, precious stones, medicinal minerals such as cinnabar, stalactite, amethyst and litharge, coins and more than 270 silver and gold items. The hoard was buried within the area of the Tang capital, Chang'an, at the site of the mansion of Li Shouli, Prince of Bin, who died in AD 741. Some Chinese coins and silver discs date to the Kaiyuan reign period (713–41; the latest inscribed date on a silver disc corresponds to AD 731). There were also five coins from Japan, minted between 708 and 715. Thus, the treasure was possibly hidden in AD 756, when the Prince's son fled from the capital with Emperor Xuanzong (*reg* 712–56) to Sichuan Province during the rebellion of General An Lushan.

Some items in the hoard were imported from West Asia, including a glass bowl, an onyx rhyton (*see* CHINA, fig. 307), Persian coins of Chosroes II (*reg* AD 591–628), Byzantine coins of Heraklio I and silver and gold vessels.

The shape and decoration of other items were clearly Western-inspired: some silver and gold vessels display the influence of Sasanian Persia. Most of the silver and gold objects were utensils; others were either ornaments, such as dragon figures, bells, hairpins and bracelets, or ingots and coins. There were 117 eating utensils, mainly bowls and plates, decorated in repoussé, embossed and chased designs. Many were shaped in lotus-petal or peach forms, or were six-lobed. There were 27 drinking vessels, including round stem cups and round or octagonal cups with handles, with hammered, cast, chased, embossed and filigree decoration. Of 51 medicinal vessels, some were used for preparation, such as small griddles on three legs, while round and square boxes, lidded jars and ewers were used as containers; there were also incense burners in openwork, either cast or hammered, with chased or embossed design, or plain. There were 14 washing bowls and basins with handles, most without decoration. Objects for daily use include 17 cast and gold-plated silver locks.

Decorations, usually set against a ring-matted ground, consist of floral sprays and scrolls, acanthus, human figures, hunting scenes and various animal motifs, including representations of lions, foxes, horses, birds, fish and tortoises. The most famous vessel in the find is a silver ewer with an embossed and gilded depiction of a horse holding a wine cup in its mouth. This lends support to the much doubted account that at the court of Xuanzong 400 horses were trained to dance, and that in a drinking dance some of the horses picked up a wine cup. On the octagonal cups with handles (a Persian shape), each face displays a musician or a dancer in high relief. On one cup the figures have Hellenistic and Persian features, indicating the significance of a foreign influence, whereas on two other cups they have a Chinese appearance and are clad in Chinese clothes.

BIBLIOGRAPHY

J. Fontein and Tung Wu, eds: *Unearthing China's Past* (Boston, 1973), pp. 176–85
Lu Jiugao and Han Wei, eds: *Tang dai jinyinqi* [Gold and silver of the Tang period] (Beijing, 1985), pls 2–4, 7, 30–109

BENT L. PEDERSEN

Held, Al (*b* New York, 12 Oct 1928). American painter. He was in Paris from 1950 to 1952, along with Ellsworth Kelly, George Sugarman, Jack Youngerman (*b* 1926) and Sam Francis. On his return to New York he made contact with Abstract Expressionist painters, painting in a subdued, impressionistic manner. The hard-edge paintings that developed from these works were partly a reaction to painterly rhetoric, but were remarkable for their forceful presence, the effect of robust simplicity and mammoth scale, with alphabet forms seeming to expand beyond the limits of the canvas. In 1967 he rejected the flatness, symmetry and strictures against illusionism that at the time dominated American painting and embarked on the diagrammatic reinterpretation of Cubism that over the next 20 years was to be refined into a sophisticated abstract style. By 1974 he had established a linear vocabulary that contrasted inscribed circles with the thicker bars of cubes or prisms, initially in black and white and later in colour. These geometric solids, appearing by turns opaque, transparent, or as impossible fictions, presented a peculiarly abstract space, the world of planetary motions or equally of molecular structure. Despite their clean-cut look, the paintings originated in loose painterly improvisation, with all the re-working erased by an electric sander. In his distrust of theory and his insistence that order must be won from chaos, Held thus maintained in his own style the ethic of Abstract Expressionism.

BIBLIOGRAPHY

Al Held (exh. cat. by M. Tucker, New York, Whitney, 1974)
I. Sandler: *Al Held* (New York, 1984)

JAMES FAURE WALKER

Helderberg [Helderbergh; Helderenberg; van Helderberghe], **Jan Baptiste** (*b* Antwerp, *c.* 1651; *bur* Ghent, 19 July 1734). Flemish sculptor. He served as town sculptor in Ghent from 1684 to 1693. Among his works for Ghent churches are statues of *Apostles* and *Church Fathers* (in collaboration with Jan Baptist Gillis, 1717–52) for St Peter's, the altarpiece of the *Trinity* (1691–3) for St Jacob's, a wooden pulpit (1696) and two marble reliefs of the *Holy Family* for St Michael's, and a tabernacle (1696) for St Martin's. He also executed a number of secular works, the most important of which was his colossal statue of *Neptune* (1690; destr. 1872 and since replaced) for the portico of the Ghent Fish Market. He is best known, however, for the effigy and sarcophagus he contributed to the monument of *Bishop Philippe Erardus van der Noot* (1730; Ghent, St Bavo, Chapel of the Blessed Sacrament). The magnificent black-and-white marble wall tomb, designed by Louis Cnudde (*c.* 1719–20), also includes a group showing the *Flagellation* by his pupil Jan Boeksent (1660–1727) and an *Angel* by his relation Pieter de Sutter (*d* 1723). A number of Helderberg's later works, including the oak statues (1731) for the pulpit of the Klein Begijnhof (Begijnhof Onze-Lieve-Vrouw ter Hoye) in Ghent, were done in collaboration with his son and pupil Lieven Jan Helderberg (*b* 1686). He may also have taught Laurent Delvaux.

BIBLIOGRAPHY

Thieme–Becker

H. Rousseau: *La Sculpture aux XVIIe et XVIIIe siècles* (Brussels, 1911), p. 74
P. Wengraf: 'Jan-Baptist van Helderberghe as a Maker of Bronzes', *Burl. Mag.*, cxxx (1988), pp. 913–15

CYNTHIA LAWRENCE

Heldt, Werner (*b* Berlin, 17 Nov 1904; *d* Ischia, Italy, 3 Oct 1954). German painter and draughtsman. Although most of his ancestors were craftsmen specializing in metalwork, his father was pastor at the parish church and he was given a Protestant, humanist education. He was brought up in the old centre of Berlin, which he was later to make his primary subject-matter, and began painting around the time that he left school in 1922; he also wrote poetry and prose, followed later by studies in art theory. After producing small oil sketches with religious subjects or burlesque scenes from Berlin night-life, such as *Ackerstrasse* (*c.* 1920) and *Ball Scene* (*c.* 1922; both Berlin, Tiergarten, N.G.), he persuaded his parents to allow him to train as a painter. He left the Kunstgewerbeschule in Berlin after one term in 1924 and in 1925 enrolled at the Hochschule für Bildende Künste in the Charlottenburg district, finishing his studies in March 1930; he spent two prolonged intervals in these studies teaching himself.

During his student years Heldt befriended the German painter Hans Kuhn (*b* 1905), and in 1924 he got to know Heinrich Zille, whose depictions of the Berlin milieu, like the street scenes of the German painter Lesser Ury (1861–1931), influenced his work. His paintings continued to be dominated by night scenes in dark tones, with rustic tavern scenes and subjects drawn from the environs of the Klosterstrasse, where he lived, as in *Evening Street Scene* (*c.* 1926–7; Berlin, Tiergarten, N.G.). In the same period he was interested in contemporary French art, German Expressionism and Neue Sachlichkeit, although none of these directly affected his own painting. In 1929 he began writing an essay, 'Von Baudelaire bis Picasso' (unpubd), which he revised several times and which can be taken as his artistic profession of faith; another essay, 'Einige Beobachtungen über die Masse', which he wrote from 1927 to 1936 (first published in full in 1976 in Schmied's monograph), was even more revealing in its pessimistic reflections on the spirit of the age.

In 1929 and 1930 Heldt experienced recurrent bouts of depression, which he tried to overcome through psychoanalysis, while moving towards modernism in his painting after travelling to Paris, where he met Maurice Utrillo. In paintings such as *Street* (*c.* 1930; Berlin, Tiergarten, N.G.) and *Pink Wall I* (1930; Hamburg, Ksthalle) he applied brighter colours in flat areas and adopted simpler compositional formats. He began to treat walls as autonomous elements, discarding their descriptive function, and to use views through windows, which he later presented as metaphors for the inner loneliness of the city-dweller. The influence of Pittura Metafisica is also discernible in paintings such as *View of Berlin* (1930; Berlin, Tiergarten,

N.G.) and *The Panke Flows through Berlin* (1930; Berlin, priv. col., see 1987 exh. cat., p. 35).

Heldt left Germany for Mallorca in 1933, after Hitler's seizure of power, but he returned to Berlin in 1936. He produced only a few oil paintings in Mallorca, such as *Street in Andraitx* (*c.* 1934; Hannover, Sprengel Mus.), all showing the same street in Andraitx. He also made charcoal drawings of similar subjects and dream-like scenes of Berlin, in which current events such as mass marches are linked to historical ones such as the Revolution of 1848. On his return to Berlin he lived in the artists' community at 75 Klosterstrasse, where Käthe Kollwitz, the sculptors Hermann Blumenthal and Ludwig Kasper and the painters Hermann Teuber (*b* 1894), Herbert Tucholski (*b* 1896) and Werner Gilles also worked; he formed a lifelong friendship with Gilles in particular. Although this was the first time that he had his own studio, he was so depressed that he produced only about 12 works during these years. He held his first solo exhibition in 1937 at the Galerie Gurlitt in Berlin, showing works from the 1920s.

In 1940 Heldt was called up for war service. He served in anti-aircraft units in France, Belgium and the Netherlands, and in 1945 he became a British prisoner of war; he produced drawings while in detention, which were included in a one-man show at the Galerie Gerd Rosen in West Berlin. From 1946 to 1949 Heldt lived in East Berlin. In 1947 he held another exhibition, this time at the Galerie Anja Bremer in West Berlin, for which he wrote an introductory text, 'Berlin am Meer'. Its subject was the triumph of nature over human creations, a theme that preoccupied him in almost all his later pictures, especially

Werner Heldt: *Ice Saints' Day*, oil and tempera on canvas, 510×800 mm, 1950 (Berlin, Neue Nationalgalerie)

in drawings dating from 1947–50, such as *Berlin by the Sea* (1949; Berlin, Tiergarten, N.G.), in which the city appears as a sea of rubble. He introduced similar imagery in lithographs such as *City Picture* (1949; see 1987 exh. cat., p. 49) from his portfolio *Berlin*. Heldt's painting *Window View with Dead Bird* (1945; Hannover, Sprengel Mus.) marks the beginning of his most important period, which reached a climax in 1947. This painting, long thought to be one of the prison pictures interpreted by Erhart Kästner as representing the fate of a whole generation, shows a view through a window with a dead crow and jug on the sill against a crumbling and deserted urban landscape.

In later years Heldt's work was dominated by still-lifes in windows with the empty city as a backdrop. In works such as *Dark Day* (1953; Hannover, Sprengel Mus.) he subjected the individual objects, such as jugs, mandolins and skulls, to a process of abstraction that made them increasingly difficult to identify; the walls, huddled together and punctuated by black rectangles representing windows, seem like cardboard scenery for an absent life. Although these works are formally indebted to Cubism, in particular to the still-lifes of Juan Gris, the stylistic debt has been decisively transmuted. The cheerful colourfulness of pictures such as *Whit Sunday* (1952; Berlin, Tiergarten, N.G.), composed of pastel hues and dotted and patterned areas, is coupled to a curious death-wish immanent in the emptiness of the townscape, suggesting a link with the work of Gilles.

In 1950, after he moved to West Berlin, Heldt experienced certain successes, and his spirits temporarily rose: he won the Berliner Kunstpreis and turned down an offer of a professorship, and Eberhard Seel, Director of the Deutscher Künstlerbund, took over the selling of his work. Before turning more decisively to abstraction in his last two years, Heldt once again took up earlier motifs, as in *Ice Saints' Day* (1950; Berlin, Neue N.G.; see fig.). The windows again have crossbars, there are trees between the façades and rooms are visible. The city is still deserted, but not dead. In the last paintings such as *Composition (Berlin Houses with Stovepipe)* (1954; Berlin, Tiergarten, N.G.), the walls again fold together like pages; the city, inaccessible and unrecognizable, has dissolved.

BIBLIOGRAPHY
Hermann Blumenthal–Werner Heldt (exh. cat., Hannover, Kestner-Ges., 1949)
Werner Heldt: Gedächtnisausstellung (exh. cat., W. Berlin, Haus Waldsee, 1954)
Werner Heldt (exh. cat., Hannover, Kestner-Ges., 1957)
Werner Heldt (exh. cat., Hannover, Kestner-Ges.; Mannheim, Kstver.; W. Berlin, Neue Ges. Bild. Kst; Düsseldorf, Städt. Ksthalle; 1968)
W. Schmied: *Werner Heldt, mit einem Werkkatalog von Eberhard Seel* (Cologne, 1976) [with texts by artist and bibliog.]
Werner Heldt: 'Berlin am Meer': Bilder und Graphik von 1927–1954 (exh. cat., W. Berlin, Gal. Brusberg, 1987)
Werner Heldt (exh. cat., Nuremberg, Ksthalle; W. Berlin, Berlin. Gal.; Bremen, Ksthalle; 1989) [with texts by artist and bibliog.]
ANGELA SCHNEIDER

Helgadóttir, Gerður (*b* Neskaupstaður, 11 April 1928; *d* Reykjavík, 17 May 1975). Icelandic sculptor and stained-glass artist. She studied at the Myndlista-og handíðaskóli Islands (Icelandic School of Arts and Crafts, Reykjavík, 1945–7), the Accademia in Florence (1948–9) and in 1950–51 with Ossip Zadkine in Paris. She lived and worked in

France and the Netherlands from 1950 onwards. Helgadóttir's earliest sculptures, made of terracotta, show the influence of her mentor, Zadkine. In 1952, partly inspired by an exhibition of the work of Julio González at the Musée National d'Art Moderne in Paris, as well as by her friendship with Robert Jacobsen, she began a series of iron constructions, black-painted and severe in form, the first non-objective sculptures made by an Icelandic artist. During the late 1950s, Helgadóttir abandoned iron constructions for steel wires and an increasingly symmetrical composition. This was partly a response to the work of Richard Lippold, whose work she saw in Paris in 1955, but also an attempt to find a pictorial equivalent for theosophical ideas she had begun to study at that period. In the 1960s Helgadóttir began to incorporate different textures and semi-precious stones into her openwork, often symmetrical, sculptures, giving them the appearance of large-scale ornaments.

Helgadóttir's first stained-glass windows date from 1957. During her brief career she executed stained-glass windows for 14 religious institutions in Iceland and Germany, as well as religious artefacts out of precious metals for a number of churches in France and Germany. Public sculptures and mosaics by her can be found in Paris, Herchen and Linnich in Germany, Bamaco in the Republic of Mali, and in Iceland. The Art Museum of Gerður Helgadóttir, devoted to Helgadóttir's work, opened in 1994 in her home town of Kópavogur, Iceland.

BIBLIOGRAPHY
Knaurs Lexikon der modernen Plastik (Munich and Zurich, 1961), p. 114
E. Palmadóttir: *Gerður, Ævisaga myndhöggvara* [Gerður; biography of a sculptor] (Reykjavík, 1985)
AÐALSTEINN INGÓLFSSON

Helin and Siitonen. Finnish architectural practice established by Pekka Helin (*b* Tampere, 1945) and Tuomo Siitonen (*b* Helsinki, 1946) with other architects in 1973. Both Helin and Siitonen studied at the Technological University in Helsinki, Helin graduating in 1971 and Siitonen in 1972. They opened a joint office in Helsinki in 1980.

In their work Helin and Siitonen's primary concerns are materials, sites and the buildings' users; the basic form of the architecture and its details are defined by the environmental factors and the specific requirements of each project. In the Metalworkers' Union Training Centre (1977), Murikka, Tampere, the building's large volume is divided into smaller masses that sensitively follow the bouldered shoreline. The main building, sports centre and accommodation building, which is divided into four units that wind round a glass-walled side corridor, all face on to a sheltered inner courtyard. The centre is constructed mainly of concrete elements, but the trade of its users is reflected in the use of steel constructions, pillars and open grids and Finnish raw materials such as copper in the cladding, in a style that hints at traditional log building. The housing project Ylätuvanpolku (1981) in Helsinki comprises eight semi-detached houses in which the partners attempted to develop compact urban family dwellings by combining traditional aspects of Finnish town building with modern mass-production techniques. They made a study of the possibilities of changing interior spaces on various levels into exterior spaces through glass porches and balconies. The simplified basic form is articulated with fences, bay windows and projections and the use of different surface materials and finishing techniques in a concrete façade: the finishes include skim plastering, tile hanging and painted wood. The UKK Institute (1984) in Tampere is situated on the charming northern shores of Lake Näsijärvi and comprises a laboratory wing, gymnasium, exhibition space, auditorium and a café-restaurant with terraces opening out over the lake. The different buildings are linked by a blue-tiled wall that dominates the entrance, through which a door leads to the heart of the building via a tall hall roofed with glass prisms. The interiors are white and pastel, the concrete façades blue and white. Helin and Siitonen derived the architectonic and functional nature of the Hollola swimming baths (1986) from the idea of a spa. The interior is composed of simple geometrical three-dimensional shapes with a dimpled concrete roof, tiled in white; the hall receives light from windows both in the roof and in the walls, which open on to a forest landscape. Rows of pillars surround the pools, which are articulated with tiled islets.

Among the practice's most ambitious office buildings is that for Oy Nokia Ab in Keilalahti, Espoo, near Helsinki (unexecuted). The plan attempts to solve the problem of dealing with 1200 identical rooms by dividing the building into small geometrical units, which bear interesting relationships to each other and form a varied whole. Helin and Siitonen also undertook restoration work, such as the refurbishment of a 19th-century barracks at Suomenlinna, an island in Helsinki Harbour, into the Nordic Arts Centre (1985).

MARJA-RIITTA NORRI

Heliogravure. See under PHOTOGRAPHY, §I.

Hélion, Jean (b Couterne, Orne, 21 April 1904; d Paris, 27 Oct 1987). French painter and writer. His family background was modest and unconnected with the arts: his father worked as a taxi-driver. At school he was attracted to poetry and later began to study chemistry until 1921, when he moved to Paris to further his ambitions as a poet. There he financed his studies at the Ecole des Arts Décoratifs by working as an architectural draughtsman; while copying decorative details at the Louvre he encountered for the first time the work of Poussin and Philippe de Champaigne, which redirected his interests towards painting. Living in Montmartre, he remained largely self-taught in art, and in 1925 he gave up his architectural employment to concentrate exclusively on painting. His early work consisted typically of still-lifes and figures, somewhat in the manner of Chaïm Soutine, until he met Joachím Torres García, who introduced him to Cubist and abstract art.

In 1929 Hélion produced his first abstract painting and, together with Theo Van Doesburg, Otto G. Carlsund and the Armenian painter Leon Tutundjian (1905–68), created the Art Concret group. He supervised the first (and only) issue of the journal *Art Concret*, in which he called for 'pure painting, controlled by logic', which describes the kind of orthogonally structured abstraction, related to Mondrian, that he was painting at this time. This rather fundamentalist group later expanded into the Abstraction–Création movement, which included Arp, Albert Gleizes, Auguste Herbin and Robert Delaunay. Hélion contributed a number of articles to the journal *Abstraction–Création: Art non-figuratif*, as well as to *Cahiers d'art*, *Axis* and *Partisan Review*, and during the 1930s acted as a persuasive proponent of abstract art to an international readership. In the same period he met the British artists Ben Nicholson, Barbara Hepworth and John Piper and visited the USA, where he worked in Rockbridge Baths, VA, for long periods between 1935 and 1939. His first solo exhibition was at the Galerie Pierre, Paris, in 1932, and his work was included in A. E. Gallatin's Gallery of Living Art at New York University in 1933. In America he was important for the generation of Gorky and de Kooning and especially the American Abstract Artists group, through both his painting and his intellectually rigorous attitudes to art.

By 1933, through the *Equilibres* series, more curved and freely floating elements developed in Hélion's painting, and a study of Poussin and Seurat led to large-scale compositions using complex rhythmic structures, as well as subtle arrangements of hue and tone, incorporating volumetric modelling, as in *Ile-de-France* (1935, London, Tate; for illustration see ABSTRACTION-CRÉATION). Progressively these forms took on allusions to the human figure, and in *Fallen Figure* (1939; Paris, Pompidou) both the form and the title indicate the final position in his programme of abstraction. This was confirmed in a series of synthetic, hatted heads (1939), the 'Emile', 'Edouard' and 'Charles' types. In 1940 Hélion left America for war service in France. He was captured by the Germans but escaped from a prisoner-of-war camp and found his way back to the USA in 1942. His book *They Shall Not Have Me* (1943), based on these experiences, became a popular success. An exhibition of his abstract painting in 1943 at the Art of This Century gallery in New York achieved a high level of critical acclaim. He moved from Virginia to New York in 1944, and the city's streets provided a range of motifs, such as shop-window mannequins and men smoking; but these works that appeared to reject abstraction so definitely were not well received at a time of budding interest in Abstract Expressionism and Tachism.

In 1946 Hélion returned to Paris and remained in France for the rest of his career. *A rebours* (see fig.) served as a manifesto painting, declaring his position within the abstraction/figuration debate. The painter (a self-portrait) stands between a schematic version of his earlier abstract painting, which is placed between the negative sign, 'Ne', and an equally schematic representation of a female nude. The implication is that, despite superficial appearances, there is in essence no distinction between the two strategies of painting. However, this apparent disavowal of radical abstraction proved as controversial in Paris as it had in New York, and he suffered considerable adverse criticism on this account. Between 1947 and 1952 he evolved a series of archetype figures, 'the newspaper reader', 'the nude model', 'the poet/outsider as passive witness', which seem to reflect the mood of existentialism then prevailing in Paris, and Hélion's work at this time can be compared

Jean Hélion: *A rebours*, oil on canvas, 1.13×1.45 m, 1947 (Paris, Pompidou, Musée National d'Art Moderne)

with that of Balthus and Giacometti; *Grande Journalerie* (1950), for example, with its rigid symmetry, its aggressive drawing and acid colour, is determinedly anti-sentimental. Hélion's motifs from this period included a range of objects that were precisely scrutinized in plastic terms but that remained largely metaphorical in meaning, with hats, loaves, umbrellas and sliced pumpkins taking on surrogate sexual roles. During the 1950s these themes were presented in a more realistic but still carefully organized manner, as in *Nude with Loaves* (1952; London, Tate). The life of the Parisian streets and markets provided the subject-matter for a number of works, for example *Things Seen in May* (Paris, Pompidou), which was based on the student demonstrations of 1968. The celebration of the quotidian and its power to signify acquires a mural scale and an allegorical force in the *Dragon Triptych* (1967; Brittany, Fond Régional d'Art Contemporain) or the *Market Triptych* (1973–4; Normandy, Caen, Fond Régional d'Art Contemporain).

During his last period of working, from 1982 to 1983, aware of impending loss of sight, Hélion undertook a series of works that he called *Remakes*. They were painted in a purposefully direct, even crude manner of colour and drawing, as if to expose the deceptive pleasures of aesthetic painting, in what might be considered a Post-modernist gesture. These paintings take up again the major themes of his previous work, as in the *Painter Trampled by his Model*, where a tone of irony, or *parodie grave*, is used to allegorize the act of painting and the pretensions of the artist. The 1970s and 1980s saw a revival of appreciation from a younger generation of artists and critics that was reflected by his inclusion in *A New Spirit in Painting* (London, RA, 1981), *Panorama de l'art français, 1960–80* (Vienna, 1982) and *Peinture en France* (Venice, Biennale, 1984).

WRITINGS

They Shall Not Have Me (New York, 1943)
Journal d'un peintre: vi, *Carnets, 1929-1962*; vii, *Carnets, 1963-1984* (Montronge, 1992)

BIBLIOGRAPHY

D. Abadie: *Hélion, ou la force des choses* (Brussels, 1975)
R. Micha: *Hélion* (Paris, 1979)
Hélion: Les Années 50 (exh. cat. by K. Flinker and F. Ponge, Paris, Gal. Karl Flinker, 1980)
Jean Hélion: Painting and Drawing from the Years 1939–60 (exh. cat. by L. Alloway, New York, Robert Miller Gal., 1981)
Jean Hélion: Abstraktion und Mythen des Alltags (exh. cat. by A. Zweite, M. Schipper and P. Bruguière, Munich, Lenbachhaus; Paris, Mus. A. Mod. Ville Paris; 1984)
Hélion: Peintures et dessins, 1925–1983 (exh. cat. by A. Moeglin-Délcroix and P. Bruguière, Paris, Gal. Karl Flinker, 1984)
Hélion: Peintures de 1929 à 1983 (exh. cat. by L. Lang, Paris, Louis Carré, 1987)

Jean Hélion (exh. cat., intro. H. -C. Cousseau; Valencia, IVAM Cent. Julio
Gonzalez; Liverpool, Tate; 1990)
H. -C. Cousseau: *Hélion* (Paris, 1992)

ROBERT RADFORD

Heliopolis (i) [anc. Egyp. Iunu; Bibl. On; now Tell
Hisn]. Site near Cairo, Egypt. It was the capital of the 13th
Lower Egyptian *nome* (administrative province) and a cult
centre of the sun-god in its various guises (Re, Atum,
Khephri). The symbol of Heliopolis was the *benben*, the
precursor of the pyramid and obelisk, which represented
the primeval hill on which the sun first rose. The oldest
monolithic *benben* found at Heliopolis dates to the 6th
Dynasty (*c.* 2325–*c.* 2150 BC). An obelisk of Sesostris I (*reg
c.* 1918–*c.* 1875 BC) still stands on the site; two other
obelisks of Heliopolitan origin—'Cleopatra's needles'—are
now in London and New York. Remains of a *temenos* wall
and chapel reliefs testify to the city's importance as a
religious centre as early as the Early Dynastic period
(*c.* 2925–*c.* 2575 BC). IMHOTEP, who bore the title 'Greatest
of seers' and served in Heliopolis under the 3rd Dynasty
(*c.* 2650–*c.* 2575 BC), was instrumental in the creation of
the Step Pyramid at Saqqara.

Excavations at Heliopolis have produced evidence of
various New Kingdom (*c.* 1540–*c.* 1075 BC) temples dating
to the reigns of Amenophis III, Sethos I, Ramesses II,
Ramesses IX and Merenptah. There are also remains of
tombs of 6th Dynasty high priests (south-east of the
Sesostris I obelisk), a necropolis of the Ramesside (*c.* 1190–
c. 1075 BC) and Late (*c.* 750–332 BC) periods (at the nearby
site of Ard el-Na'am) and a series of tombs of Mnevis-
bulls (north-east of the obelisk). The city itself maintained
a reputation as a scientific centre until the rise of
Alexandria.

BIBLIOGRAPHY
W. M. F. Petrie and E. Mackay: *Heliopolis, Kafr Ammar and Shurafa*
(London, 1915)
L. Habachi: *The Obelisks of Egypt* (New York, 1977)
A. A. Saleh: *Excavations at Heliopolis*, 2 vols (Cairo, 1981–2)

NABIL SWELIM

Heliopolis (ii). Greco-Roman site in Lebanon; *see*
BAALBEK.

Helladic. Culture that flourished during the Greek Bronze
Age (*c.* 3600–*c.* 1050 BC) in central and southern mainland
Greece, excluding most of Thessaly (see fig. 1); only
during the late Middle Helladic and the Late Helladic
periods did coastal Thessaly become an integral part of
the Helladic world. During the Bronze Age period this
region, which had been inhabited probably since the
Middle Palaeolithic period, developed styles of art and
architecture influenced by those of the Aegean islands of
Crete (*see* MINOAN) and the Cyclades (*see* CYCLADIC). By
the Late Helladic II–III period the mainland Mycenaeans
dominated the whole of the Aegean. Throughout the area
they created a community of cult, customs, language, art
forms and techniques. In the process they assimilated
several diverse tribes, races and regional cultures and
merged them into a homogeneous civilization. This first
Greek culture contained in embryo all the elements on
which Hellenic and, later, Western thought were nurtured
and grew to maturity.

For the later history of the mainland *see* ANCIENT GREECE and the
modern Hellenic Republic of GREECE.

BIBLIOGRAPHY
F. Matz: *Die Ägäis*, Handbuch der Altertumswissenschaft, ii/1 (Munich,
1950)
F. Schachermeyr: *Die ältesten Kulturen Griechenlands* (Stuttgart, 1955)
Archaeology, xiii (1960), pp. 2–75 [special issue]
E. T. Vermeule: *Greece in the Bronze Age* (Chicago, 1964, rev. 1973)
S. Marinatos and M. Hirmer: *Kreta, Thera und das mykenische Hellas*
(Munich, 1973)
S. E. Iakovidis and others: *Prehistory and Protohistory*, i of *History of the
Hellenic World* (Athens, 1974)
S. Hood: *The Arts in Prehistoric Greece*, Pelican Hist. A. (Harmondsworth,
1978)
O. T. P. K. Dickinson: *The Aegean Bronze Age*, Cambridge World Ar-
chaeology (Cambridge, 1994)

I. Introduction. II. Architecture. III. Pottery. IV. Wall painting. V.
Sculpture. VI. Ivory and bone. VII. Metalwork. VIII. Jewellery. IX.
Faience. X. Seals. XI. Forgeries. XII. Museums and collections.

I. Introduction.

1. Geography and climate. 2. Trade. 3. Religion and iconography. 4.
Chronological overview.

1. GEOGRAPHY AND CLIMATE. Mainland Greece is
the southern tip of a mountain range that runs into the
Mediterranean and is continued eastwards by the peaks
forming the Aegean islands and Crete. Only one-fifth of
the region is flat arable land. The small fertile plains and
grazing grounds are situated along the coast, separated by
mountain chains or peninsulas and connected by valleys
and narrow passes, while the rugged interior offers only a
few cultivable plateaux. In ancient times overland travel
was difficult, but no area is more than 100 km from the
sea, and the numerous gulfs, coves and inlets that indent
the coastline provide a multitude of safe anchorages,
making communications often easier by sea. Indeed, while
indigenous cultural developments in prehistoric Greece
tended to begin as purely regional phenomena, unifying
influences generally came from overseas. The region's
limited natural resources also made it dependent on
overseas trade for anything other than mere subsistence.
Its climate is temperate, with northern winds and adequate
winter rainfalls. The soil, although rich in potter's clay, is
poor in minerals but nevertheless of sufficient quality to
produce staple crops such as wheat, olives, grapes and
various vegetables and fruit. Since the vegetation dries up
in summer, it is better suited to feeding small livestock
such as sheep, goats and pigs than larger grazing animals.

BIBLIOGRAPHY
A. Philippson and E. Kirsten: *Die griechischen Landschaften*, 4 vols (Frank-
furt, 1950–59)
O. Rackham: 'Land Use and the Native Vegetation of Greece', *Archaeo-
logical Aspects of Woodland Ecology*, ed. M. Bell and S. Limbrey (Oxford,
1982), pp. 177–98
T. H. van Andel, C. N. Runnels and K. O. Pope: 'Five Thousand Years of
Land Use and Abuse in the Southern Argolid, Greece', *Hesperia*, lv
(1986), pp. 103–28
T. H. van Andel and C. N. Runnels: *Beyond the Acropolis: A Greek Rural
Past* (Stanford, 1987)   □

2. TRADE. The main evidence for trade is the finding
of objects from one country in another, most commonly
pottery, which is highly durable. However, this type of
evidence, although it shows that the two lands were linked
by some kind of trading route, cannot indicate who was

1. Map of the Helladic region; those sites with separate entries in this dictionary are distinguished by CROSS-REFERENCE TYPE

involved in the trading mechanisms nor if the two lands were in direct contact or if the goods were carried by middlemen. Moreover, large quantities of perishable goods may be traded, leaving no trace whatsoever in the archaeological record.

Even in the Early Bronze Age there must have been a lively Aegean trade in certain commodities, for example in obsidian from the island of MELOS. This very hard volcanic material, useful for making tools and weapons, would probably have been acquired initially by sailing to the island in small boats and bringing quanitites of it back to the Greek mainland. The introduction of metalworking was a great stimulus to trade, as Greece had only limited supplies of copper and no sources of tin, which was alloyed with copper to make bronze; small quantities of lead were also in circulation in the Early Bronze Age. Luxury metals such as gold and silver began to be imported towards the end of the Early Bronze Age, in addition to other precious materials such as hardstones and ivory. Early Bronze Age importation of such items must have been on a small scale, and there is no information on the mechanisms of the trade.

There is increased evidence for trade in the Middle Bronze Age. Although mainland Greek settlements were mostly still fairly small, general demand in the Aegean as a whole must have greatly increased during this phase, with the flourishing palace culture on Crete drawing in luxury goods and raw materials from the eastern Mediterranean and Egypt (*see* MINOAN, §I, 4(ii)). There is some evidence, largely from pottery, that the mainland Greeks were to some extent participating in this trade: Middle Helladic Grey Minyan Ware was exported; it has been found not only in the nearby Cycladic islands but also as far as Troy (*see* §III, 3 below). Small quantities of luxury raw materials were still circulating on the Greek mainland, as in the Early Bronze Age.

The Mycenaeans had access to very wide trading routes in the Late Bronze Age, as is clear from objects buried with the first Mycenaean rulers in the early tholos tombs of Messenia and the royal shaft graves at Mycenae. The growing size of settlements and the institution of palace culture on the mainland in the Late Bronze Age must have greatly intensified the demand for luxuries and the need for necessities such as metals. The large quantities of bronze tools, weapons and vessels from the shaft graves (*see* §VII, 2 below) show that mainland Greece in the Late Bronze Age must, for instance, have been importing large quantities of tin. It was once thought that Cyprus supplied Greece with copper, but it now appears that the Greeks were in fact exploiting local resources of this metal. Materials such as ivory, faience and ostrich eggs were apparently reaching the Mycenaeans in the early years of the Late Bronze Age through trade routes established by the Minoans (*see* MINOAN, §I, 2). Amber beads from the shaft graves show that the Mycenaeans had access to amber from the Baltic, which must have reached them over long and complicated trade routes by land and sea. As Mycenaean economic power grew, so also did their access to routes and their direct involvement in trade. Their apparent control of Knossos on Crete from the Late Helladic II period saw an intensification of exchange, with the Mycenaeans moving into formerly Minoan spheres of influence.

The nature and intensity of Mycenaean trade with other lands varied considerably from region to region, and a highly complex network of trading routes linked the east and west Mediterranean. Minoan and Mycenaean clay vessels that once probably contained perfumes and oils have been found on Cyprus, the Levantine coast and at various sites in Egypt. Likewise, faience amulets, scarabs and alabaster vessels from both the Near East and Egypt have been found in the Aegean. Studies of ancient shipwrecks in the Mediterranean area have shed some light on these trading links, most notably in respect to the Cape Gelidonya shipwreck near Finike, Turkey, and another off the Anatolian coast at Ulu Burun. Both of these Late Bronze Age wrecks contained an extraordinary variety of goods from all over the Mediterranean. There is also evidence for trading links between the Mycenaeans and the western Mediterranean from the 16th century BC, at least with the Aeolian island of Lipari, off the north coast of Sicily. Mycenaean pottery dating from the 14th century BC onwards has been found on the other Aeolian islands, on the Italian mainland and in Sicily. These small amounts of pottery were not necessarily traded for their own sake but may represent incidental activity around more important trading patterns. It seems likely that the Mycenaeans were trading with Etruria and Sardinia for copper and tin, in exchange for which they must have provided mostly perishable goods, as so little has been preserved in the archaeological record.

BIBLIOGRAPHY

O. T. P. K. Dickinson: *The Origins of Mycenaean Civilisation*, Stud. Medit. Archaeol., xlix (Göteborg, 1977)
A. E. Harding: *The Mycenaeans and Europe* (London, 1984)
N. H. Gale, ed.: *Bronze Age Trade in the Mediterranean*, Stud. Medit. Archaeol., xc (Göteborg, 1991)
R. Laffineur and L. Basch, eds: *Thalassa: L'Egée préhistorique et la mer* (Liege, 1991)

LOUISE SCHOFIELD

3. RELIGION AND ICONOGRAPHY. The study of Mycenaean religion is based on depictions of cult scenes and other themes in wall paintings and on larnakes (clay coffins), cult objects, decorative items etc—the same sources that on Crete provide information for Minoan religious practices—but in addition on the evidence of the Linear B tablets found mainly at Pylos and at Knossos following its Late Helladic (LH) II apparent occupation by Mycenaeans. The tablets indicate that by LH III the Mycenaeans worshipped a pantheon of gods, many recognizable in Classical Greek religion (Zeus, Hera, Athena, Poseidon, Hermes and others). In the early Mycenaean period (LH I–II), however, there appears to have been an eagerness to adopt Minoan religious symbols and practices. Mycenaean iconography was largely taken from the Minoans, including a goddess figure and priestesses, sacred plants and animals; the Minoan snake cult was apparently adopted, and other similarities include the use of painted plaster offering tables, the practice of animal sacrifice and the appearance of horns of consecration and double axes in religious contexts.

Mycenaean decorative work in such media as ivory, faience, gold and silver often included Minoan cult motifs such as dolphins, figure-of-eight shields and lilies (*see* §§IV, 2(iv) and IX below), though by the end of the Bronze Age any original religious associations may well have been lost. An ivory plaque from Mycenae (see fig. 17 below) depicts a griffin seated beaneath a papyrus plant, employing an animal and plant motif firmly associated with Minoan/Cycladic cult (*see* MINOAN, §I, 3, and CYCLADIC, §I, 3), but again, it cannot be assumed to have the same meanings. The ivory statuette of two women in Minoan-style dress and a child, also from Mycenae (see fig. 16 below), may well depict deities. Mycenae has also yielded a large plaster head of a sphinx or perhaps a deity (see fig. 14 below), its features indicated by paint. A number of smaller heads are known from various sites (*see* §V, 2(i) below). Many terracotta statuettes either served as idols in shrines or as votive figurines and are found on virtually all Mycenaean sites; they are mostly female, with upraised arms or with arms crossed over the chest (see fig. 15 below).

Final Neolithic	c.4500-c.3600/3000 BC	
Early Helladic (EH)	c.3600/3000-c.2050 BC	
	EH I	c.3600/3000-c.2900/2600 BC
	EH II	c.2900/2600-c.2400 BC
	EH III	c.2400-c.2050 BC
Middle Helladic (MH)	c.2050-c.1600 BC	
Late Helladic (LH)	c.1600-c.1050 BC	
(a)	LH I	c.1600-c.1500 BC
	LH IIA	c.1500-c.1440 BC
	LH IIB	c.1440-c.1390 BC
	LH IIIA:1	c.1390-c.1360 BC
	LH IIIA:2	c.1360-c.1335 BC
	LH IIIB:1	c.1335-c.1240 BC
	LH IIIB:2	c.1240-c.1180 BC
	LH IIIC	c.1180-c.1050 BC
(b)	LH I	c.1700-c.1610 BC
	LH IIA	c.1610-c.1475 BC
	LH IIB	c.1475-c.1440 BC
	LH IIIA:1	c.1440-c.1375 BC
	LH IIIA:2	c.1375-c.1325 BC
	LH IIIB	c.1325-c.1180 BC
	LH IIIC	c.1180-c.1050 BC
Sub-Mycenaean	c.1050-c.1000 BC	

2. Chronological chart showing the major Helladic periods with their subdivisions: (a) chronology used in this dictionary; (b) alternative chronology of the Late Helladic period

Surviving wall paintings suggest that the Minoan nature cult died out with Minoan cultural hegemony in the Late Bronze Age. Though animals continued to appear in Mycenaean art, by the LH III period they were always shown heraldically disposed, flanking a throne for example (for illustration see PYLOS), rather than in a natural setting (see also MYCENAE, fig. 2, for the relief carving of rampant lions flanking an altar topped with a column above the Lion Gate).

The favourite Mycenaean artistic themes (not just in wall paintings but in other media as well) were scenes or symbols of aggression—hunting and warfare—and colourful, though regimented, scenes of processions. In many cases these processions were depicted bringing offerings to a deity, to a goddess in two cases from Mycenae where the recipient is preserved (Athens, N. Archaeol. Mus.). Paintings from Thebes (LH II-IIIA) and Tiryns (LH IIIB) include women bringing offerings, wearing the typical Minoan flounced skirt and open bodice, and similar figures occur on fragments recovered from Pylos. Male figures were also depicted. The goddess often appears in association with symbols of warfare (see §IV, 2(iv) below), and scenes of combat were evidently popular in the palaces, as, for example, the *Battle Scene* fresco from Pylos (see §IV, 2(v) and fig. 13 below) and scenes of horses and chariots and armed warriors at Mycenae.

Helladic sites have not produced as many shrines and sacred places as Minoan sites, though some well-preserved examples of cult centres do exist. The best documented is the shrine complex or Cult Centre (LH IIIB) on the south-west slope of the acropolis at Mycenae, near the building known as Tsountas's House. To the east, the so-called 'temple' consisted of two rooms and a vestibule, the innermost room containing male and female terracotta idols, pots of jewellery (possibly to adorn the statues), terracotta snakes, offering tables, lamps and braziers. Access to this room was via another shrine room with columns and raised platforms, on one of which stood a female statuette with offerings before her; an alcove held more figurines and terracotta snakes. The structure immediately to the west of this building constituted a separate cult area (perhaps dedicated to a different deity?) that contained a female statue with painted jewellery and a long robe; offerings of jewellery were in front of her. Both complexes were painted with frescoes depicting processions: the walls of the western shrine had women in Minoan-style flounced skirts bringing offerings (see fig. 11 below), while the 'temple' contained a procession of daemons along with sacred symbols, including a palm tree, a goddess with a small griffin, and a shrine (see fig. 12 below). Fragments of wall paintings showing female figures (goddesses or priestesses) and an altar bearing horns of consecration were found in association with the Citadel House, to the north-west of the Cult Centre, confirming the sacred nature of the place.

For detailed discussion of Mycenaean wall painting see §IV below, especially §IV, 2(iii) for discussion of depictions of cult ritual and religious figures.

BIBLIOGRAPHY

M. P. Nilsson: *The Minoan–Mycenaean Religion and its Survival in Greek Religion* (Lund, 1927, rev. 1950)
A. W. Persson: *The Religion of Greece in Prehistoric Times* (Berkeley, 1942)
W. D. Taylour: *The Mycenaeans* (London, 1964, rev. 1983)
——: 'New Light on Mycenaean Religion', *Antiquity*, xliv (1970), pp. 270–80
P. Warren: *The Aegean Civilizations: From Ancient Crete to Mycenae* (Oxford, 1975, 2/1989)
Sanctuaries and Cults in the Aegean Bronze Age. Proceedings of the First International Symposium at the Swedish Institute at Athens: Athens, 1980
G. Mylonas: 'The Cult Centre at Mycenae', *Proc. Brit. Acad.*, lxvii (1981), pp. 307–20
B. Rutkowski: *The Cult Places in the Aegean* (New Haven and London, 1986)
Early Greek Cult Practice. Proceedings of the Fifth International Symposium at the Swedish Institute at Athens: Athens, 1986
Celebrations of Death and Divinity in the Bronze Age. Proceedings of the Sixth International Symposium at the Swedish Institute at Athens: Athens, 1988
O. Dickinson: *The Aegean Bronze Age*, Cambridge World Archaeology (Cambridge, 1994)

For further bibliography see MINOAN, §I, 3.

4. CHRONOLOGICAL OVERVIEW. Archaeologists divide the Helladic Bronze Age into three periods: Early, Middle and Late Helladic (EH, MH, LH). These are themselves subdivided on the basis of pottery styles (see fig. 2). Considerable precision is possible in the late phase, which is also known as the Mycenaean period. There was extensive contact between Helladic centres and the Bronze Age cultures of Crete and the Cyclades, and the chronological divisions established for the Helladic culture

broadly parallel those applied to the other two (*see* MI-NOAN, §I, 4 and CYCLADIC, §I, 4). Approximate absolute dates for these chronological periods are derived from radiocarbon analysis and from links with Crete, Egypt and the Near East; in the latter two regions, relatively secure dates are based on historical dynastic sequences (*see* EGYPT, ANCIENT, fig. 2, and ANCIENT NEAR EAST, fig. 2). Nevertheless, the field of Aegean Bronze Age chronology has been the subject of considerable scholarly controversy since the late 1980s. Many archaeologists believe that some dates should be higher by a century. This last argument is based largely on new radiocarbon dates suggesting that the eruption of the volcanic island of THERA took place *c.* 1625 BC instead of *c.* 1525 BC, making the beginning of the Late Bronze Age approximately 100 years earlier (see fig. 2b). However, not all archaeologists are convinced of the efficacy of the new scientific dating methods for the periods in question, not least because the higher chronology tends to weaken proven links with ancient Egypt. The traditional chronology (see fig. 2a) is accepted by most archaeologists, although individual scholars may vary the details.

Although the chronological periods in this system are separated into discrete units, there was some overlap from one phase to the next: the inhabitants of one site might retain older pottery types for many years while another site changed to new styles. This 'regionalism' was particularly common during the Neolithic and EH periods, and at the end of the LH period.

BIBLIOGRAPHY

Pauly–Wissowa: 'Frühhelladikum', 'Mittelhelladikum', 'Übergang zum Späthelladikum', cols 1427–47, 1452–74

A. Evans: *Essai de classification des époques de la civilisation minoenne* (London, 1906)

A. J. B. Wace and C. W. Blegen: 'The Pre-Mycenaean Pottery of the Mainland', *Annu. Brit. Sch. Athens*, xxii (1916–18), pp. 179–89

J. B. Haley and C. W. Blegen: 'The Coming of the Greeks', *Amer. J. Archaeol.*, xxxii (1928), pp. 141–54

E. Vermeule: *Greece in the Bronze Age* (Chicago, 1964)

S. Hiller: 'Die Ethnogenese der Griechen aus der Sicht der Vor- und Frühgeschichte', *Ethnogenese europäischer Völker*, ed. W. Bernhard and A. Kandler-Pálsson (Salzburg, 1986), pp. 21–37

P. Warren and V. Hankey: *Aegean Bronze Age Chronology* (Bristol, 1989)

D. A. Hardy and A. C. Renfrew, eds: *Chronology*, iii of *Thera and the Aegean World III* (London, 1990)

P. M. Warren: 'The Minoan Civilisation of Crete and the Volcano of Thera', *J. Anc. Chron. Forum*, iv (1990–91), pp. 29–39 [n. 22 with previous bibliog.]

C. D. FORTENBERRY

(i) Early Helladic. (ii) Middle Helladic. (iii) Late Helladic.

(i) Early Helladic.

(a) General. The proto-urban way of life based on metallurgy and classes of artisans and merchants that had originated in Mesopotamia reached Greece at the beginning of the Bronze Age, in the south via the Aegean islands and in the north (Thrace and east Macedonia) by way of Troy and the adjacent islands, and it resulted in a marked increase in wealth and population. But the persistence of many distinctive features of the indigenous culture, particularly its pottery, argues against any significant demographic movements. This cultural continuity is even more noticeable in the Axios Valley, in west Macedonia and especially in Thessaly, where the transition from Final Neolithic to Early Bronze Age seems to have been smooth

and independent. Further south the influence of the Cycladic civilization is manifest, but again, it does not supplant the basic local cultural traits.

Information about EH I is scanty. Metals were introduced and gradually came into general use, while settlements, built on low hills, indicate a growth of population; of these, only the stone-built foundations survive. Pottery, enriched with a new class of polished bowls, was still hand-moulded in the Neolithic tradition; with which there is no evidence of a clean break; it was a period of slow transition.

The EH II phase is better documented. It was a peaceful and prosperous period of change and rapid progress during which Cycladic trading posts were established along the mainland coast, introducing new goods (e.g. obsidian) and skills and fostering profitable contacts abroad. New mineral resources were discovered, including lead and silver mines at Thorikos, while bronze foundries and forges were established at Raphina and Askitario. Trade links, attested by sealings and pottery, reached as far as Troy, and the increase in wealth and the growth of population led to the founding of new settlements, some of which were fortified. Besides farmers, livestock breeders and sailors, the inhabitants of these sites included specialist craftsmen producing metalwork, jewellery, incised or painted pots in new imaginative shapes and seals engraved with curvilinear motifs. Figural works of the period encompass crude human and animal figurines and occasionally animals incised on pottery. The dead were buried in cist graves, underground chambers or clefts in the rocks.

During the EH III period several waves of destruction swept the mainland. Not all sites suffered, but settlements were abandoned, overseas contacts were forsaken, and the culture regressed to a purely agrarian economy. Changes in pottery coincided with the introduction of the potter's wheel, and a new apsidal type of house prevailed. Both the upheaval and the new cultural elements are often attributed to the invasion of proto-Greek-speaking peoples.

By the end of EH III there were radical changes in the ethnic structure and the cultural and political balance in the East Mediterranean. Egypt was invaded by Asiatic tribes, the Levant was conquered by the Amorites, Asia Minor was overrun by Indo-European tribes, and the Greek mainland had been entered by warlike farmers and cattlebreeders who spoke a proto-Greek language, used a new type of pottery, introduced the horse and the chariot and had different burial customs. They occupied the whole of Greece and absorbed the earlier population, blotting out completely the preceding pan-Aegean EH culture.

☐

(b) Artistic developments. The artefacts produced during EH I and EH II are generally plain but neatly made. Pottery, although not spectacular, excels in its simple basic shapes: superfluous elaboration and decoration is avoided. Simple incised patterns and moulded bands are occasionally found, but most vessels are evenly coated in thin, sometimes metallic glaze or merely left plain. Consistently sound workmanship is an outstanding feature, and among the most elegant Early Helladic shapes is the 'sauceboat' (see fig. 6b below), with its cuplike body and upturned

flared spout. The refinement of Early Helladic pottery (*see* §III, 2 below) may reflect the development of an urban culture during EH II.

Although no settlements have been completely excavated, some provide evidence of systematic planning in EH I and EH II, with well-organized layouts in which roads and architectural units are rationally juxtaposed. The best houses, which were often grouped in blocks, are efficiently designed, with those consisting of more than one room sometimes organized around a single axis. The so-called 'corridor houses', with their complex arrangements of rooms, attest the EH builders' ability to organize space. Their high standards of construction are combined with monumentality and functionalism, and in their scale (up to 25 m long and 15 m wide) they are comparable with the great megara of Early Bronze Age Troy, though their plans are more complicated. The eponymous 'corridors', which flank the long sides of the houses, ascend to an upper floor, and in the most elaborate examples, such as the House of the Tiles at Lerna (for illustration *see* LERNA) and the White House on Aigina, the ground floor has an approximately symmetrical layout: two anterooms (or porches) lead into a pair of halls that open on to a smaller room in the middle of the house, possibly a common light well. A high level of technical achievement is indicated by finely plastered walls, baked roof tiles and built-in circular hearths. Together with the use of sealings, these features may reflect the development of an elaborate economic system. Such architectural sophistication was, in any case, not attained again before the building of the Mycenaean palaces (*see* §II, 3 below). It is possible that some Classical Greek architectural terms, including *plinthos* (brick), *aidossa* (portico) and megaron (hall), date from this pre-Greek era.

The ornamental patterns on some 70 extant clay sealings (*see* §X below) also evince sophisticated workmanship. These come mainly from two deposits associated with Lerna phase III (EH II). They were impressed by circular seals (now lost) that were probably made of wood, and they display a remarkable variety of intricate designs combining central motifs, such as loops, interrupted spirals, swastikas and trefoil motifs, with frames of entwined lines. A concern with order and balance is again apparent, and like the well-organized 'corridor houses', these patterned seals have no recognizable precursors. The characteristics of EH II culture may derive from foreign influence, which may have encouraged the development of small urban settlements; these settlements are considerably more sophisticated than those elsewhere in Europe at that time and compare more easily with Near Eastern cities of the 3rd millennium BC. Towards the close of EH II, Anatolian influence is evident in such developments as black-polished one-handled tankards or apsidal houses, anticipating the next cultural era.

In pottery the break between EH II and EH III is apparent mainly in changes that coincided with the introduction of the potter's wheel. A new aesthetic tradition began to be evident in both shapes and decoration. New decorative motifs, such as triangle groups, are found, and besides the one-handled tankards, other new shapes appeared, such as plates and bowls (see fig. 6d–f below).

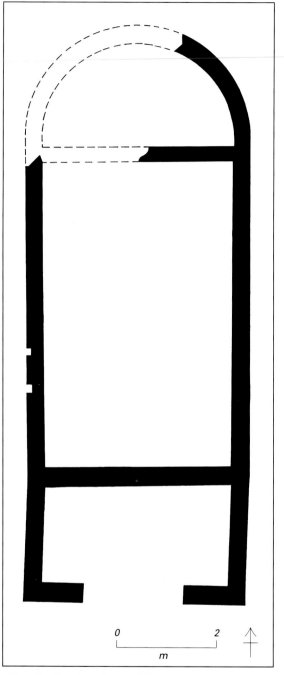

0   2

m

3. Plan of an Early Helladic III apsidal house

The architecture of EH III is distinguished by the prevalence of the new apsidal type of house (see fig. 3). Like rectangular-plan houses, these comprised an open porch, a hall and a rear room that may have been for storage. With the exception of Aigina, where regular rows of houses have been discovered, all known settlements were essentially villages, and dwellings dating from EH III (and MH) are more rustic than those of EH II and are grouped irregularly rather than in blocks (*see also* §II, 1 below).

BIBLIOGRAPHY

J. L. Caskey: 'The Early Helladic Period in the Argolid', *Hesperia*, xxix (1960), pp. 285–303

——: *Greece, Crete and the Aegean Islands in the Early Bronze Age*, Cambridge Anc. Hist., i/2 (Cambridge, 1972), pp. 771–807

G. Cadogan, ed.: *The End of the Early Bronze Age in the Aegean*, Cincinnati Classical Studies, n. s., vi (Leiden, 1986)

STEFAN HILLER

(ii) Middle Helladic.

(a) General. The chronological subdivisions proposed for the Middle Helladic (MH) period by Wace and Blegen are no longer fully accepted. EH III and MH are increasingly regarded as a single coherent period, notwithstanding minor changes in the pottery sequence. Most of the MH era seems to have progressed slowly. It was only in the final phase that the pace of development accelerated, under Cycladic and especially Minoan influence, forming the basis for the Mycenaean civilization.

Grave gifts from the royal tombs at Messenia and Mycenae, and evidence from Thera, suggest that by the end of the MH period the inhabitants of the mainland had the ships and the seamanship to establish close contacts with the Cyclades, Crete, Egypt and the Levant. The development of a trade-based economy led inevitably to the re-emergence of merchants and specialist craftsmen, and the upper levels of mainland society appear to have been reorganized on the model of Minoan Crete. Initially, Minoan influence also pervaded mainland art, and only the subject-matter was distinctively Helladic. Once they had mastered Minoan techniques, however, mainland artists began to improve on them and to discard Minoan elements. Helladic goods were exported further afield than Minoan ones had ever been, and Helladic culture began to shape and influence neighbouring civilizations. ☐

(b) Artistic developments. Two common MH pottery types, known as Minyan and Matt-painted, both of them from the central Helladic region, show a continuity of development from EH III wares (*see also* §III, 2 below). Minyan vases (see fig. 7a–b below), usually wheelmade, have angular outlines and are undecorated. Matt-painted vessels (see fig. 7c–d below) are handmade and ornamented with rectangular panels and zones that are filled in with linear or geometric motifs. Though the level of artistic accomplishment is modest and the repertory of designs restricted, the compositions are well balanced and may relate to architectural frame structures. A few rare figural vases, mostly from Aigina, are painted in a highly stylized fashion that anticipates later Geometric (*c.* 900–*c.* 720 BC) works (*see* GREECE, ANCIENT, §V, 3). Like the houses of EH III, those of MH are haphazardly grouped, though some later MH villages are surrounded by fortifications.

BIBLIOGRAPHY

A. J. B. Wace and C. W. Blegen: 'The Pre-Mycenaean Pottery of the Mainland', *Annu. Brit. Sch. Athens*, xxii (1916–18), pp. 179–89

J. L. Caskey: *Greece and the Aegean Islands in the Middle Bronze Age*, Cambridge Anc. Hist., ii/1 (Cambridge, 1973), pp. 117–40

P. Warren: 'Problems of Chronology in Crete and the Aegean in the Third and Earlier Second Millennium BC', *Amer. J. Archaeol.*, lxxxiv (1980), pp. 487–99

STEFAN HILLER

(iii) Late Helladic.

The Late Helladic (LH) period is also known as the Mycenaean period.

(a) General. In the LH II period the Mycenaean inhabitants of the mainland appear to have conquered Knossos on Crete and came to dominate the Aegean. By LH IIB they had developed a complex system of state organization based on advanced production methods and written records kept by palace accountants in the Linear B script adopted from Crete, and they had extensive trading contacts with the Levant and the western Mediterranean. During LH IIIA and B these trade links were substantially expanded. Trading posts were set up in both the east and the west (e.g. at Ugarit, Miletos and Taranto), and Mycenaean products may have been exported as far as central Europe and Britain. The main imported goods were metals and precious stones, the main exports pottery, jewellery, textiles, olive oil and perfumes. Politically Greece appears to have been organized into four or five large and several small independent states that generally coexisted peacefully. Each was ruled by a king (wanax) based in a palace or citadel and assisted by civil and military officials.

The demise of the Helladic civilization was again connected with its reliance on the sea. Towards the end of LH IIIB the states of the Near East were ravaged by a loose alliance of marauding bands known as the Sea Peoples, and the great eastern trading ports ceased to exist. Deprived of their trading partners the centralized palace bureaucracies in Greece no longer had any function, and Mycenaean society disintegrated. Large-scale emigration to Cyprus, the Dodecanese and Asia Minor left the mainland depopulated and led to the gradual abandonment of the palaces. Taking advantage of this, primitive Greek tribes from the mountain fringes of the region gradually began to resettle it, mingling with the remnants of its earlier inhabitants and creating the tradition of a 'Dorian invasion'. During the ensuing Dark Age, vague memories of the great Mycenaean civilization survived for the most part only in epic poetry. ☐

(b) Artistic developments. Among the earliest artefacts assigned to the LH period are the many exquisitely crafted and precious objects dating from MH III–LH IIA found in the shaft graves at MYCENAE and in other contemporary tombs. These include, from Mycenae, a silver rhyton depicting a siege and various daggers with scenes of hunting, inlaid in niello technique (*see* MYCENAE, fig. 3); golden cups from Vapheio, depicting the capture of wild cattle (*see* MINOAN, fig. 25); and golden signet rings with scenes of combat (all Athens, N. Archaeol. Mus.). There is continuing controversy over the origins of these splendid works: by and large they must either have been based on Minoan models or, perhaps more likely, have been imported from Crete or produced by Cretan craftsmen working on the mainland. The predilection in the decoration for scenes of fighting and hunting is undoubtedly Mycenaean, but this need not imply Mycenaean workmanship. Thus the development of native Mycenaean styles is probably better attested by painted pottery.

The development of Mycenaean pottery begins with glaze-painted vessels introduced along with several new pottery shapes and decorative motifs, all of which were largely inspired by Minoan ceramics. During the LH II period, Mycenaean and Minoan ceramics resembled each other so closely as often to be virtually indistinguishable, and it is assumed that Minoan craftsmen and artists were probably employed by Mycenaean kings. Before long, however, Mycenaean pottery began to exhibit a typically Helladic tendency towards formalism, first apparent in the development of a specific class of goblets, called 'Ephyraean', which have a single floral or marine motif at the centre of each side (see fig. 8e below). At the same time, the decorative motifs themselves became increasingly stiff and schematic. During the next phase, motifs derived from natural forms became wholly linear and abstract, and geometrical patterns were frequently used. The culmination of this process was reached with the introduction in early LH IIIB of the 'deep bowl' (see figs 9b and 10a below), decorated in the so-called 'Metope' style, with friezes of vertical rectangular motifs alternating with rounded elements (corresponding to the metopes and triglyphs of Doric architecture, hence the name). These characteristics recall Middle Helladic Matt-painted pottery before the onset of Minoan influence; the revival of indigenous traditions continued in the LH IIIB period. At the end of the Late Mycenaean period, the only shapes in production seem to have been local Hellenic ones, such as amphorae, jugs and bowls, and these were decorated either with simple linear designs or with a monochrome wash. These vases anticipate Protogeometric (c. 1000–c. 900 BC) pottery (see GREECE, ANCIENT, §V, 2), which also shows affinities with the 'Metope' style of LH IIIB.

In most of the figurative arts, such as wall painting (see §IV below) and seals (see §X below), Mycenaean artists followed Minoan models. Their own tradition appears to have been confined to the choice of subject-matter and to the increasing tendency towards stylization of individual motifs. It is only in artefacts that have no Minoan parallel, such as the relief stele erected over the Mycenae shaft graves and the gold face masks on the bodies inside them (Athens, N. Archaeol. Mus.), that a native Mycenaean tradition establishes itself.

Some important Mycenaean architectural forms are also indigenous: for instance, the strong axial arrangement of the main elements (propylon, court and megaron) in Mycenaean palaces (see fig. 4 below) is alien to Minoan planning, and though some subsidiary details, such as the form of the columns, reveal Minoan influence, the plan of the megaron itself represents a mainland type that dates back at least to MH times. Similarly, the colonnaded porch and hall with central hearth formed an integral part of the MH house, while the vestibule was a Mycenaean innovation. Whether the tholos tomb with its corbelled vault developed independently on the mainland or was introduced from Crete is disputed (see THOLOS TOMB). Its most advanced form, however, is clearly Mycenaean. Thus, although a façade door flanked by two half-columns occurred in the New Palace at Phaistos (Middle Minoan III), the same scheme in the Treasury of Atreus at Mycenae (see fig. 5 below) has a new and typically Mycenaean monumentality. The tholos tombs also reveal the progress made by the Mycenaeans in engineering, as do their well-built roads, elegant bridges and huge dykes.

BIBLIOGRAPHY

C. Tsountas and J. J. Mannatt: *The Mycenaean Age* (Boston and New York, 1897)
G. E. Mylonas: *Mycenae and the Mycenaean Age* (Princeton, 1966)
F. H. Stubbings: *The Rise of Mycenaean Civilization*, Cambridge Anc. Hist., ii/1 (Cambridge, 1973), pp. 627–58
V. R. d'A. Desborough: *The End of Mycenaean Civilization and the Dark Ages*, Cambridge Anc. Hist., ii/2 (Cambridge, 1975), pp. 658–77
F. H. Stubbings: *The Expansion of Mycenaean Civilization*, Cambridge Anc. Hist., ii/2 (Cambridge, 1975), pp. 338–58
O. T. P. K. Dickinson: *The Origins of Mycenaean Civilisation*, Stud. Medit. Archaeol., xlix (Göteborg, 1977)
S. Hiller: 'Die Ethnogenese der Griechen aus der Sicht der Vor- und Frühgeschichte', *Ethnogenese europäischer Völker*, ed. W. Bernhard and A. Kandler-Pálsson (Salzburg, 1986), pp. 21–37

STEFAN HILLER

II. Architecture.

Constructions throughout the Helladic Bronze Age were predominantly of mud-brick. After the Early Helladic 'corridor houses' no further monumental architecture is evident on the Greek mainland until the Late Helladic period, when the architectural genius of the era was most completely realized in royal palaces and royal tombs.

1. EARLY HELLADIC. Early Helladic (EH) settlements were usually built on low hills, preferably near or on the coast and not far from freshwater springs. The houses were often grouped around a large building positioned near the periphery of the settlement rather than in the centre. After the middle of the EH II period coastal sites were surrounded by defensive walls, repeatedly extended and remodelled. The walls, 2.0–2.5 m thick, were single (e.g. Raphina, Askitario, Aigina) or double, connected by cross-walls creating casemates between them (e.g. LERNA). Square or horseshoe-shaped towers provided fighting platforms and flanked the bending narrow entrance gates.

EH I houses, built of perishable materials, left no traces other than low stone foundations, but after mid-EH II constructions were durable, reaching at times monumental proportions. Except for one or two osier or reed huts, as at Lerna, the typical EH habitation is small, rectangular and single-storey. Individual houses had two or three rooms, some with small fixed hearths and an occasional support for the roof. Built in blocks of two or three with party walls, they were separated by gravelled or cobbled streets and courtyards. After the cultural changes in EH III (see §I, 4(i) above), the apsidal house-plan prevailed (e.g. Lerna, Aigina; see fig. 3 above), but rectilinear houses were still erected, including an irregular, oblong, three-room structure at Eutresis, regarded by some as a primitive form of megaron. Some settlements were arranged haphazardly rather than in blocks.

'Corridor houses', the buildings that constituted the focal points of many EH II settlements, seem to have had no predecessors, unless they evolved from a simpler, free-standing type of house having a vestibule, as existed at Eutresis, Ayios Kosmas and Askitario, for example, and possibly an upper storey. Fully developed, they were stately, two-storey structures with large rooms, tiled roofs and corridors containing stairways (e.g. Lerna, Aigina, Akovitika, Thebes; see THEBES (ii), §1). The House of the Tiles at Lerna is the most imposing (for illustration see LERNA). It was entered from all four sides and had two large square halls alternating with two oblong rooms, of which the middle one may have been a light well. The south end of this room formed a small square compartment equipped with shelves. Corridors running along the north and south walls accommodated stairways leading to an upper floor; clay benches were attached to these walls on the outside. Named after the roof tiles found in its ruins, the house seems to have been a communal storage and trade centre.

Another form of EH communal building is the circular granary, known from ASINE, ORCHOMENOS and TIRYNS. The example at Tiryns, 27.6 m across, is the largest and most complex. Built on a stone platform, it consists of four concentric walls around a circular inner room. The outer two were connected with elliptic insets to form a strong outer shell, topped by a solid mud-brick wall. The inner rings are divided by radial cross-walls into compartments floored with clay or stone and accessible only from above. The Orchomenos granaries also had thick walls built around a single circular space 6 m in diameter.

These substantial EH constructions, including granaries and fortifications, had mud-brick walls built on stone herringbone socles twice as thick and plastered with clay or lime. Floors were of packed earth with pebbles. Wood was used for stairs resting on bottom steps of solid clay and for doors pivoting on flat stones. Terracotta and schist tiles laid in clay show that roofs were sloped.

The dead were interred in Cycladic-type cist graves (e.g. Attica), underground chambers accessible by vertical shafts (Corinth, Chalkis) and circular stone platforms with inset cists or pithoi.

2. MIDDLE HELLADIC. In the Middle Helladic (MH) period, as in EH III, blocks of houses were uncommon (exceptions have been uncovered in Eutresis). The newcomers settled in small, unplanned villages of free-standing long houses, first apsidal, then rectilinear, having two or three rooms, open porches or closed vestibules and small hearths. Ovens, kilns or foundries were sometimes attached to them. Houses had mud-brick walls built on socles of rubble faced with rounded stones, while thresholds were often stone built, sometimes monolithic. Beaten earth or clay was used on floors. Roofs, probably thatched, seem to have been ridged. At first villages were unwalled, but later some of them, including Brauron, Aigina, ARGOS, Dorion, Geraki, then Peristeria, Midea and the Dymaean Wall, were surrounded with 1–5 m-thick fortification walls built of undressed blocks with a core of rubble. Narrow openings, straight or bent, sometimes flanked by wing walls, served as gates or sally ports. At Dorion the rocky slope was dressed to form a glacis at the foot of the wall.

Graves were slab-lined cists, sometimes built within low tumuli. Later they became elongated with walls lined with slabs or rubble, entered from above or from the side. Towards the end of the period tholos tombs (circular chambers with a stone-built parabolic corbelled vault) began to appear.

3. LATE HELLADIC. The surviving Late Helladic (LH) houses, palaces and fortifications date from LH IIIA:2 onwards. Most date to LH IIIB and some examples to LH IIIC. They have the same basic features as their MH

4. Late Helladic palace complex at Pylos; main building from the south-east

predecessors but show strong Minoan influences in technique and decoration. Settlements consisted of separate groups of usually free-standing one- or two-room houses. At the larger sites habitations were more crowded and more complex, having basements and upper storeys; they were separated by lanes or were built along roads. The main room, which was rectangular with a hearth and supports for the roof, often had a vestibule and a courtyard in front and was divided by corridors from the rest of the house. Sometimes this apartment had the form or at least the basic features of a MEGARON. Basements were used for storage.

Palaces were vast complexes covering from 1.5 acres (as at PYLOS; see fig. 4) to 2 acres (as at MYCENAE). They were divided by corridors into wings, each having several rooms linked by doors and passages and serving a specific purpose (residence, administration, workshops, storerooms). The main complex was surrounded by apartments, the exterior walls of which formed a continuous enclosure. Each palace had one or two lesser courts and a main one situated in front of the state apartment, which had the form of a tripartite megaron. The main halls (*domoi*) of the megara (11.8×9.7 m at Tiryns; 12.9×11.2 m at Pylos; 12.9×11.5 m at Mycenae) had four central columns around a large circular hearth fronting a throne at the middle of the right-hand wall. There were also bathrooms, guest-rooms and lesser megara. At Mycenae the middle wing seems to have been occupied by a terrace in front of the residential quarters overlooking the state apartment.

Walls of LH buildings had socles of undressed stones, sometimes as high as the top of the basements. The upper part was built of mud-brick, bonded, as in Crete, by a framework of timbers inserted into both faces and held together by cross-ties. Wall surfaces in the humbler houses and in basements were coated with clay. Elsewhere they were plastered with white clay or lime, usually painted.

5. Late Helladic IIIB tholos tomb, dromos of the Treasury of Atreus, Mycenae

Exterior walls were emphasized at Mycenae and Pylos by the use of ashlar masonry. Thresholds were of clay, wood or stone, the latter mostly monolithic with sockets for the revolving wooden doors, the pivot poles for which were sheathed in bronze. Door frames were wooden, the jambs resting on stone bases. Windows had wooden frames and shutters. Interior stairways were also wooden, some with first flights of dressed soft stone. Exterior stairs were of stone slabs or flat blocks. Columns had the flat capitals of their Minoan prototypes and the same downward tapering wooden shafts resting on stone bases. In the palaces they were fluted (Pylos) or sheathed in bronze (Mycenae). Roofs are assumed by most scholars to have been flat, but the discovery of terracotta roof tiles in all major and many lesser sites indicates that they continued to be sloped. Practically all Mycenaean buildings, including granaries (as at GLA), were decorated with wall paintings, for which the technique and stylistic conventions had been borrowed from Crete (*see* §IV below). A dado, sculptural (as at Tiryns) or painted, ran along the bottom of the wall, above which the main themes were painted.

The most characteristic achievement of LH architecture is the citadel, built on a hill, fortified by a massive circuit wall broken by gates and sally ports and enclosing the palace, its dependencies and smaller houses. The wall, founded on bedrock, followed the curves of the summit plateau, the size of which determined the extent of the fortified area. The walls, 7.5 m thick at Tiryns and 5 m at Mycenae, were over 7–8 m high. The fortifications of Athens (*see* ATHENS, §II, 1(i)), Gla, Midea and all the lesser sites were left unmodified, but at Tiryns and Mycenae they were repeatedly extended to enclose more space, and finally (in LH IIIB:2) the gates were flanked by bastions restricting the approach area and exposing attackers to cross-fire from above (for illustrations *see* TIRYNS and MYCENAE, fig. 1). Walls were built in the Cyclopean manner, out of rough boulders bonding with a core of smaller blocks. More uniform materials were employed around the gates, changing at Mycenae from rough limestone to conglomerate pseudo-ashlar. At Mycenae and Tiryns the gates were framed with gigantic, smoothly dressed monolithic slabs. The weight of the lintel over the main gate at Mycenae, the so-called Lion Gate, was relieved by an empty triangle above it, bordered on either side by corbelled walls and masked by a relief depicting two lions (*see* MYCENAE, fig. 2). The same corbel system was used to span passages left in the wall or galleries built inside it.

Late Helladic tombs were of three types: shaft graves, given up in LH IIA; underground chambers accessible through a narrow open trench (dromos); and their royal versions, THOLOS TOMBS, which were 3.5–14.5 m in diameter and erected below or above ground. Doorways had built jambs and monolithic lintels occasionally relieved by gaps in the courses above them or by triangles. Dromoi, cut at first as simple trenches, were later lined with masonry. Lintels, initially rectilinear, were then cut to follow the inner curve of the vault. Some vaults were built of rubble, others of roughly squared blocks. After each interment doorways were walled up.

The last three tholoi at Mycenae were constructed in LH IIIB of regular conglomerate ashlar blocks. The magnificent Treasury of Atreus is the best preserved. The sides of its dromos are lined with large pseudo-ashlar blocks (see fig. 5). The door, 5.4 m high, was flanked by two half columns of green marble (London, BM). The façade above it was ornamented with two more spiral-decorated half columns and with slabs of sculpted coloured stone masking the relieving triangle. The vault, 14.5 m across and 13.2 m high, was built of 33 ashlar conglomerate courses and had a square side chamber, now stripped of its decoration, as had the similar tholos at Orchomenos, famous for its sculpted ceiling (*see* §V, 2(ii) below). The Treasury of Atreus, with its well-balanced proportions, its majestic façade, the smooth, effortless curve of its soaring vault and the superb workmanship of its flowing surfaces, is one of the great funerary monuments of all time.

Pauly–Wissowa

BIBLIOGRAPHY

S. Marinatos: 'Greniers de l'Helladique ancien', *Bull. Corr. Hell.*, lxx (1946), pp. 338–451

S. Sinos: *Die vorklassischen Hausformen in der Ägäis* (Mainz, 1971)

S. E. Iakovidis: 'Building and Architecture', *Prehistory and Protohistory*, i of *History of the Hellenic World* (Athens, 1974), pp. 310–21

—: *Vormykenische und mykenische Wehrbauten*, Archaeologia Homerica, E:1 (Göttingen, 1977), pp. 161–210

R. Hägg and D. Konsola, eds: 'Early Helladic Architecture and Urbanization', *Proceedings of a Seminar Held at the Swedish Institute at Athens: Athens 1985*

I. Mylonas Shear: *The Panaghia Houses at Mycenae* (Philadelphia, 1987)

J. W. Shaw: 'The Early Helladic II Corridor House: Development and Form', *Amer. J. Archaeol.*, xci (1987), pp. 59–79

III. Pottery.

Pottery is found in great quantities on Helladic sites in all Bronze Age phases, but kilns have been identified only rarely and deposits of wasters, which would indicate the range of a kiln's production, only once or twice. Conclusions about the organization and processes of manufacture must therefore be deduced almost entirely from the pottery itself; little analysis bearing on these questions has yet been undertaken, however. Traditionally, the main wares have been identified in visual terms, with a concentration on the finer material; only the shapes and motifs of the Mycenaean style have received intensive study, resulting in a sophisticated classification (*see* §4 below). Scientific studies have been concerned mainly with methods of decoration, and fabric study has concentrated on establishing provenance. A promising development in this field, which suggests that fabrics and the traditional 'wares' do not necessarily coincide, is still in its early stages.

Within the Helladic region the provinces of the Argolid, Corinthia, Attica and Boiotia frequently played a leading role in pottery production as in other fields, and they will be referred to collectively below as the 'central Helladic region'.

1. Materials and techniques. 2. Historial survey.

1. MATERIALS AND TECHNIQUES. Pottery had been made for several millennia in mainland Greece before the Bronze Age, and the Helladic potters inherited considerable technical knowledge from their Neolithic predecessors. They knew how to choose clays, tempering them, if necessary, with fragments of stone or other materials (inclusions), and they knew how to fire them to achieve a special appearance or quality. However, their technical equipment and level of organization do not appear to have

been complex. Although some pottery may have been produced within the household, particularly in the earlier stages of the Bronze Age, most was doubtless produced by specialists, though these are likely to have been part-timers who also farmed land, unless they were directly supported by a palace or similar establishment. The evidence suggests a wide spread of potters established in separate workshops. These may have specialized in particular fabrics, as the study of fabrics is beginning to suggest, and in some cases their products may have been widely distributed from a single centre, but mostly they seem to have served small neighbourhoods.

For most of the Early Helladic (EH) period all pottery was handmade, and some of the finer ware, at least, must have been kiln-fired. It is widely believed that late in the period a form of potter's wheel, probably a simple turntable on a pivot, was introduced, but there is continuing disagreement over what proportion of the pottery was wheel-thrown before the Late Helladic (LH) period, though much was evidently kiln-fired. In the LH period, use of the wheel has often been assumed to have been almost universal, and even cooking pots are reported to have been wheel-thrown at Mycenae and other central sites. LH decorated pottery is so homogeneous for most of the period and so well adapted to mass production that it seems likely that Mycenae gave the stylistic lead, and it is quite possible that the pottery was produced to a standard by provincial centres serving wide regions. There is, however, evidence for local variation to a limited extent at several major southern Peloponnesian sites, and certain household wares, perhaps even a large proportion of total production in remote regions such as Thessaly, may have continued to be handmade, as did a class of miniature decorated pots even in the Argolid. But in all probability most if not all pottery was kiln-fired by this time, if in rather small and, to judge from their rarity, often impermanent structures.

In all Helladic phases several qualities of pottery were produced; in LH times this reflects the choice of different clays, and the same is likely earlier. The finest wares, often only a few millimetres thick, were generally fired a light colour, although dark wares fired under reducing conditions were sometimes favoured. The most popular shades were light buff, yellow or near-white, and where local clays did not produce these naturally a slip of such a colour might be applied. Polishing or burnishing was normally used to give fine wares a lustrous surface and to improve the glossiness of paint. Other wares of good quality can have even surfaces but feel rough to the touch even when decorated, and when thick may contain large inclusions. These are different, however, from true coarse ware, which is generally of a distinctive red or brown fabric (containing much tempering matter) and which tends to have an uneven surface that is variegated in colour, whether from the original firing or from constant use on the hearth, for this is the ware of cooking pots. (Late Helladic cooking ware, however, though of similar fabric, is of much higher quality.) Finally, large storage jars (pithoi) were produced throughout the period; their fabric, normally several centimetres thick, contains many stone inclusions and other tempering matter but is generally light-surfaced and often smooth. They may even be slipped and painted, although decoration with applied bands of clay is more common.

2. HISTORICAL SURVEY.

(i) Early Helladic. (ii) Middle Helladic. (iii) Late Helladic.

(i) Early Helladic. The earliest EH wares had likely antecedents in the latest Neolithic phases. These include not only the red-slipped and burnished ware characteristic of Attica and central Greece that has traditionally been termed EH I, which has a range of simple rounded shapes, principally bowls, jars and jugs, but also a newly defined group, 'Talioti ware', which is particularly well represented in the Argolid. The finer pieces in this group have a slightly glossy red or brown-red coating and are decorated with incision, while the coarser storage vessels often have finger-impressed bands; there is a wider range of shapes than in central Greek EH I wares, including fruit-stands. How these relate to each other and how the far more sophisticated style of EH II developed from them are questions that need investigation.

'Classic' EH II wares were of a remarkable quality and homogeneity throughout the Helladic region. The finest are light in colour, hard-fired and often extremely thin, almost certainly the product of specialized workshops (one of which may be represented by pottery deposits, identified as wasters, at Vouliagmeni, near Corinth). They might be coated partly or wholly with dark paint that is often lustrous, probably as a result of burnishing ('Urfirnis'), or have a burnished slip, which could be deliberately mottled; the evidence from Lerna suggests a trend from painted to plain surfaces during the period. The most characteristic shapes are the ring-based small bowl or saucer and the 'sauceboat', the hallmark of EH II (see fig. 6a–b); the popularity and relative quantities of both

might suggest their use in ceremonial drinking parties as drinking and pouring vessels respectively. The 'sauceboat' developed over the period from a shallow to a deep open-spouted vessel, the purpose of which is unclear; the taut curves of its profile can be matched in other shapes such as the askos (fig. 6c), and there is no compelling reason to relate its shape to metalwork (the extant gold examples are of the mature form, so can hardly represent the original inspiration). These two shapes constituted the great bulk of pottery exports, which were popular in the Cyclades and reached as far as Crete, Macedonia and Troy.

Another class of pottery of particular interest consists of the large pithoi of the Argolid, also clearly produced by a specialist workshop. These were decorated with running patterns in relief on raised bands, produced by some form of roller; one of the most elaborate patterns, two rows of running spirals with doglike creatures neatly fitted between, is found on examples from Lerna, TIRYNS and ZYGOURIES, which must therefore have been distributed from a single centre or made by an itinerant group (as pithoi have been in modern times).

The relative chronology of the late EH period, when the preceding homogeneity broke up, is controversial. On the view preferred here, a new pottery tradition, often known as 'Lefkandi I' from the Euboian site where it was first identified, appeared before the end of EH II in Euboia, central Greece, Aigina and some north Cycladic islands, most often mixed with EH II or Early Cycladic II types (*see* CYCLADIC, §III, 1). It has good parallels in the Troad and neighbouring regions, and there are other grounds for suspecting some movement of population from that area into the Aegean at the time, but the nature of this movement is still unclear. The most characteristic shapes are plates (fig. 6d) and bowls, two-handled drinking vessels and beaked jugs, all in black-, brown- or red-burnished wares; traces of a potter's wheel have been recognized on this material.

The characteristic fine shapes of EH III probably represent a fusion of Lefkandi I and EH II forms, first developed in central Greece and spread, perhaps by local migration, to the northern Peloponnese. This provides the best evidence for a link between the two phases, although it does not explain all the new features of the pottery attributed to EH III, a phase of notable heterogeneity in which at least two distinct traditions can be detected in the central Helladic region alone. These have in common most shapes and many motifs but differ in a preference for white decoration on a dark coat (Ayia Marina ware) in central Greece, and dark decoration on a light ground (Lerna IV Patterned ware) in the northern Peloponnese. The patterns are mainly variations on large upright triangle groups on the shoulders of the bigger shapes and arrangements of horizontal line groups on the smaller ones, such as the characteristic tankard (fig. 6e); the style may draw on rare earlier classes of decorated pottery in the Helladic and Cycladic regions and on basketry patterns. Wholly or partly coated and plain burnished wares are also common, the two-handled bowl being an especially popular shape (fig. 6f). A rare grey ware seems particularly associated with use of the potter's wheel and is clearly the direct ancestor of Middle Helladic Grey Minyan ware.

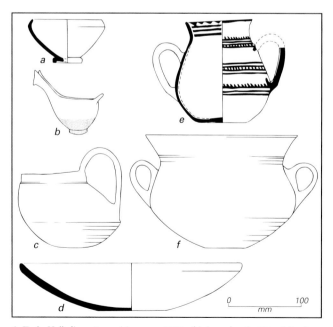

6. Early Helladic pottery: (a) saucer, EH II; (b) 'sauceboat', EH II; (c) askos, EH II; (d) plate, Lefkandi I; (e) tankard, Lerna IV Patterned ware, EH III; (f) two-handled bowl, EH III

(ii) Middle Helladic. The obscurity surrounding the final EH stages extends to the process whereby the MH pottery tradition spread, since a relatively full sequence has been discovered at only a few sites. It has become clear, however, that the traditional description of MH pottery, which laid much stress on Grey Minyan and Matt-painted wares, gives the wrong impression. The only truly universal MH ware was the domestic coarse ware; Grey Minyan and Matt-painted were characteristic only of the central Helladic region, and the classic Matt-painted ware is now believed, on the basis of its fabric, to be Aiginetan in origin. However, the basic pattern of complementary fine wares, plain burnished or polished and dark-painted, was widespread, and it is possible to detect a family resemblance between the local fine pottery traditions of all the mainland regions south of Thessaly. Both groups had clear EH III antecedents in shapes and techniques, but the use of manganese-based matt paints, rather than potentially lustrous iron-oxide-based paints, was a new phenomenon, with Cycladic affinities. These are particularly clear in the Aigina-derived ware, whose shapes, like the popular barrel jar (see fig. 7c), often have Cycladic parallels (*see* CYCLADIC, fig. 5).

The burnished group consists almost entirely of open vessels, especially two-handled bowls and kantharoi. Its best-known manifestation is Grey Minyan, the finest ware produced for most of the MH period. This was of well-levigated clay, polished (rather than burnished) on all surfaces, evenly fired in a reducing kiln; somewhat inferior grey and dark burnished varieties with a very similar range of shapes were produced in slightly different fabrics, and comparable plain wares occur throughout the mainland. At first the shapes were round-bodied like their EH III ancestors, but by the mature stage the well-known angular shapes were standard (fig. 7a–b). These often have elaborately modelled rims, sharply carinated bodies and horizontal faceting or rilling on the shoulder, all features that, like the ringed stem on the most elaborate shape, the goblet (fig. 7a), seem to require use of a wheel; any traces of the wheel's use have generally been removed by polishing or burnishing. The frequent suggestion that these features reflect metallic originals is implausible, both because the MH culture was scarcely rich enough to support the production of metal vessels and because far from being naturally suitable for metal, such features will place a strain on plate. However, these shapes, particularly the goblet, were undoubtedly very popular, being imported and imitated in the Cyclades and Macedonia, and at Troy.

The painted wares are largely closed vessels, jars and jugs, with simple ovoid or near-globular shapes, though bowls and kantharoi are also found; in general, they seem to be handmade. The decoration is simple, consisting generally of hatched or nested triangles set on bands or a coated area on the upper body (fig. 7d); slightly more adventurous patterns can be found on the Aiginetan Matt-painted shapes, especially the barrel jars. A ware well known in the eastern Peloponnese, particularly the Argolid, is decorated with semi-lustrous dark paint but has very similar shapes and motifs; nevertheless, it seems from its fabric and technique of manufacture to be a product of the 'Minoanizing' workshop that is likely to have been based at either Lerna or Ayios Stephanos in Lakonia, since

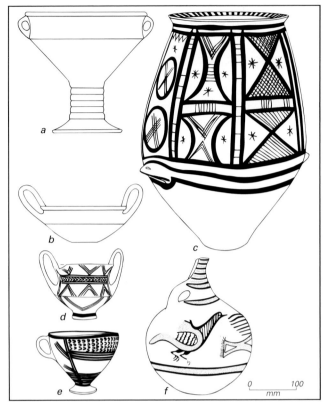

7. Middle Helladic pottery: (a) ring-stemmed goblet, Grey Minyan ware; (b) kantharos, Grey Minyan ware; (c) barrel jar, Aiginetan Matt-painted ware; (d) kantharos, Matt-painted ware; (e) Matt-painted cup, with 'panelled' style of decoration; (f) jug, Mainland Polychrome style

most of the products have been identified at these two sites. This 'Minoanizing' pottery is the only Helladic class to show marked foreign influence for most of the period; it has particularly close links with the local Minoan style of Kythera (*see* KYTHERA, §1), presumably the source of the workshop's founders. It includes both fine and coarse wares, in which cups, bowls, jugs and larger closed vessels were produced; they were decorated in white and other colours, principally red, on a dark coat in a manner similar to the simpler Middle Minoan styles of Crete (*see* MINOAN, §III, 4).

In the latest stages of the MH period light-coloured fine wares were increasingly favoured. In some parts of the central Helladic region Grey Minyan was largely supplanted by Yellow Minyan, a similar ware fired in oxidizing conditions, in which low-stemmed goblets were produced; closed vessels with burnished exteriors are of similar fabric. But unburnished plain wares were also common, and the graves of the period, which supply much of the available evidence, contain a wide range of plain and painted small vessels as Cycladic origins, as do motifs used on them, such as spiral-based forms, plants and birds. Yet these wares do not imitate any Aegean ware closely and seem rather to be local developments, particularly in parts of the central Helladic region. Especially notable are the

Matt-painted burnished ware and its characteristic 'panelled' style of decoration, which seems to have been a product of the northern Peloponnese (fig. 7e), and the Mainland Polychrome style, which may have been based in central Greece (fig. 7f). These and other wares overlap substantially with the earliest Mycenaean pottery. Their relative chronology has not yet been fully worked out, but their earliest forms probably preceded the development of LH I pottery, and their diversity reflects the atmosphere of experiment in which the first Mycenaean pottery was produced.

(iii) Late Helladic. The terms 'Late Helladic' and 'Mycenaean' have become almost interchangeable, but the adoption of a new pottery style was in fact one of the latest developments in the evolution of the Mycenaean culture; nevertheless, it was to become the most widespread and characteristic of all Mycenaean features. Analysis of Lerna fabrics strongly suggests that the new style was created in the well-established 'Minoanizing' workshop, and there is good reason to suppose that at first it was produced in only a few Peloponnesian centres.

The first stage of the style, LH I, is characterized by a fine decorated ware with a restricted range of shapes and motifs, both of which had most often a Minoan origin. But there is a non-Minoan, presumably local, element that includes one of the most popular shapes, the squat jug (see fig. 8b), and while the style is close to that of Late Minoan IA (*see* MINOAN, §III, 5), particularly the variant produced in Kythera, it has a distinctive character. Ideally, the ware is thin and hard-fired, having a light polished surface decorated with lustrous paint that normally fired red or near-black; dots and lines in dull white paint were frequently superimposed on painted areas, particularly exterior rim-bands. Decoration is normally confined to a single zone on the upper body, bounded by bands or coated areas and subdivided by the handles if there are more than one; usually the same motif occurs in each subdivision. All accessory parts of the body were normally coated (cup-handles might be obliquely barred), and a band runs round the inside of the rim. The motifs are a mixture of geometric and stylized natural forms; variants of running spiral and linked circle motifs and plant forms, particularly foliate bands, dominate (fig. 8a–b). The shapes are mostly small cups, jugs and jars with rounded profiles, the major exception being the Vapheio cup (fig. 8a), which is essentially a flaring cylinder, most often divided by a

a, b, d, e

0 ——————————— 100
mm

0 ——————————— 200
mm

8. Late Helladic pottery, LH I–II: (a) Vapheio cup, LH I; (b) squat jug, LH I; (c) pithoid jar, Palatial style, LH IIA; (d) alabastron, LH IIB; (e) 'Ephyraean' goblet, LH IIB

midrib (a common feature on metal examples of the shape); a liking for piriform profiles, sometimes extremely compressed, is apparent in the closed shapes.

There are indications of primitive technique in the shaping and finishing of many vases, though there are clear signs of the use of the wheel, and interiors of open shapes were commonly left unslipped and unpolished; encircling bands were often unevenly painted, and some motifs could be inexpertly handled (e.g. spirals can have a 'squashed' look). In such features LH I pottery compares poorly with the best examples of the late wares in the MH style, which still commonly appeared in northern Peloponnesian contexts and continued to dominate in central Greece. (After the LH I period the Mycenaean style became wholly dominant, and only a few simple forms of Matt-painted decoration survived on large vessels.) However, the plain and domestic wares found with LH I pottery essentially continued MH traditions, though improving in quality. The commonest shapes are low-stemmed goblets and other open vessels that are clearly in the Minyan tradition, although more often rounded than angular in

profile; in some regions these could still be produced in grey and dark wares, but light wares were to become the norm. The only Minoan introductions so far identified in this class are the tripod cooking pot, conical cup and lamp, none of which was common by Cretan standards.

The preferences in shape and the decorative principles established in LH I remain characteristic of the Mycenaean style for the rest of its history, although the range of motifs and shapes was greatly extended. The deployment of the motifs was standardized, seeming to obey quite strict rules, so that identical vases are commonly found; this mass-producible quality may have been a factor in the style's success. At first Minoan influences continued to be strongly felt, particularly in the 'Palatial' class of LH IIA, which consists of elaborately shaped and decorated closed vases that have many parallels in contemporary Late Minoan IB pottery. But even here there are distinctive Mycenaean features, such as the fondness for pithoid jars decorated with plant patterns (fig. 8c), which may be attributed to local stylistic development.

9. Late Helladic pottery, LH IIIA–IIIB:1: (a) kylix, LH IIIB:1; (b) deep bowl, LH IIIB; (c) pyxis, LH IIIA:2; (d) piriform jar, LH IIIB:1; (e) stirrup jar, LH IIIB:1; (f) krater, Pictorial style, LH IIIB:1

The ability to reproduce elaborate Minoan shapes and motifs argues for considerable increases in the skills of mainland potters, some of whom may have been immigrants from Crete or the 'Minoanized' Cycladic islands; there is also a detectable improvement in the quality of the ordinary decorated ware. This remained essentially separate from the 'Palatial' class, although it adopted some of the motifs in a simplified form, and the typical LH I shapes continued to be popular, joined by the characteristically Helladic alabastron (fig. 8d), a low three-handled shape that was made increasingly so squat that it must have been quite difficult to throw on the wheel, and the goblet (fig. 8e), which became more popular as a drinking vessel at the expense of the cup shapes. These two shapes appear in the Late Minoan II pottery style, providing plausible evidence for Helladic influence on Minoan pottery at a subsequent stage.

By LH IIIA:1 the Mycenaean style was fully formed, and the plain ware had become as standardized as the decorated, at least in the central Helladic region. The best is of comparable quality to the decorated, with a finely polished surface, but the majority is only smoothed. The decorated and plain wares continued to have largely distinct ranges of shapes, coinciding particularly in the open shapes, not least the kylikes, which now largely replaced the goblets and which, with their tall stems and shallow, gracefully curved bowls, are among the most attractive Mycenaean shapes (see fig. 9a). Other common decorated types are the two-handled deep bowl (see figs 9b and 10a below), which is one of the hallmarks of LH IIIB; a variety of containers, including the alabastron, pyxis, piriform jar and stirrup jar (fig. 9c–e); and a range of jugs. The cooking wares are dominated by tripod pots and broad-mouthed jug/jar types; specialized forms of the kind found in earlier Minoan pottery are rare, but this class remains poorly researched. Ceremonial or ritual forms are rare in any ware.

The same range of motifs was now used on large and small bases; the 'Palatial' class had effectively disappeared at the end of LH II, and the only distinctive class is the Pictorial, which consists largely of kraters. These deep, broad-mouthed vessels are rare and probably prestigious, perhaps used as mixing bowls for drink, like their Classical successors; their decoration, perhaps inspired by frescoes, most often centres on bulls or chariot processions (fig. 9f). Clay analysis supports the view that, although popular in Cyprus, the majority of the standard examples were made in the Argolid, perhaps principally at Berbati, where wasters from a potters' establishment include Pictorial pieces; at a late stage, local versions (the so-called Pastoral, or Rude, style) began to be produced in Cyprus (see CYPRUS, §II, 4(iii)). They may well have been produced largely as an 'export' ware, and the same workshop(s) may be the source of Cypriot and Levantine shapes decorated in Mycenaean style.

Such sophistication in production was not to be found everywhere, but the LH IIIA:1, IIIA:2 and IIIB:1 phases represent a peak of quality and homogeneity in Mycenaean pottery, in which the standard set by the Argolid was followed without significant variation elsewhere. The ideal was a neatly balanced arrangement of one or at most two decorative zones and groups of bands, painted with great

dexterity, which covered most of the vase on small closed shapes but was confined mainly to the upper body on others. On some classes of vessel, chiefly open shapes, the mannerism of isolating a motif in the centre of the vase with little or no accessory decoration was used to great effect (fig. 9a), but such classes always remained isolated developments.

Motifs could run through a zone, be spaced along it or be arranged in it to flank a more elaborate central motif; they include such geometric forms as the ever-popular spiral and groupings of bars, such zone-fillers as scale and net patterns, and increasingly stylized versions of flowers, octopuses, argonauts and shells. There are many parallels with contemporary Late Minoan III styles, but Mycenaean and Minoan are readily distinguishable; any influences went from the former to the latter.

The Mycenaean pottery of these phases was widely exported in the east and central Mediterranean, and imitation wares were produced in many areas, a striking testimony to its popularity. Small containers such as the stirrup jar were particularly popular, no doubt primarily for their contents (probably perfumed oil), and were imitated in faience and stone in Egypt and Palestine. Open vessels and ceremonial types were also exported in smaller quantities. After LH IIIB:1 there was a marked falling off in identifiable exports, which may have prompted increasing production of a local Mycenaean style on Cyprus.

In fact, there are signs of general decline in pottery of the LH IIIB:2 phase. The 'filled' or 'Metope' style (see fig. 10a) was influential over a much more restricted area, outside which there was little independent development but rather stagnation. Some shapes ceased to be produced, or like the kylix are found only in their plain form, and there was a narrowing of the range of motifs and more common use of simple banding and coating. These features represent the prelude to the collapse of homogeneity in the final, LH IIIC phase, when increasingly the different parts of the Mycenaean world developed divergently. The bulk of the pottery produced in LH IIIC continued to be of fair quality, but the range of shapes was progressively limited, until by the end only about ten were common and such standards as the kylix and stirrup jar had disappeared from many areas. Decoration was increasingly simplified; the wavy line was one of the commonest motifs (fig. 10e), and much use was made of banding and coating (the plain ware was ultimately absorbed into this minimally decorated class).

Side by side with this limited and monotonous material small classes of extremely elaborate vases were produced in a number of related but distinctive local styles. The impetus for this development seems to have come from the Dodecanese and Cyprus, which were linked with each other and Crete in a pattern of cross-influences from the beginning of the phase, but important centres of the mainland and Cyclades also produced well-known styles (see CYCLADIC, §III, 3). Common to all is the use of narrow zones filled with linear motifs, which might be arranged between band-groups to cover the bulk of the vase, as in the Argive Close style (fig. 10b), or might be used as bordering or dividing motifs for broader zones of pictorial decoration, in which octopuses (fig. 10c) and other animals, especially birds, marching warriors (fig. 10d) or more complex scenes are displayed. Only a few shapes,

10. Late Helladic pottery, LH IIIB:2–IIIC: (a) deep bowl, 'filled' or Metope style, LH IIIB:2; (b) stirrup jar, Argive Close style, LH IIIC; (c) stirrup jar, Octopus style, LH IIIC; (d) krater, Pictorial style, LH IIIC; (e) deep bowl, LH IIIC

principally the stirrup jar and krater, were decorated in these styles. (For an illustration of a LH IIIC octopus stirrup jar from Ialysos *see* RHODES, fig. 2.) They may have been a response to the disappearance of higher forms of art, but they did not last long. In the final stages of LH IIIC, production was reduced to a narrow range of functional shapes, still wheel-thrown and technically good but showing little trace of creativity in the decoration. Yet this reduced remnant was the direct ancestor of Protogeometric (*c.* 1000–*c.* 900 BC), the first true Greek style of vase painting (*see* GREECE, ANCIENT, §V, 2).

BIBLIOGRAPHY

GENERAL

A. J. B. Wace and C. W. Blegen: 'The Pre-Mycenaean Pottery of the Mainland', *Annu. Brit. Sch. Athens*, xxii (1916–18), pp. 175–89

R. E. Jones: *Greek and Cypriot Pottery: A review of Scientific Studies* (Athens, 1986)

O. T. P. K. Dickinson: 'Pottery', *The Aegean Bronze Age*, Cambridge World Archaeology (Cambridge, 1994)

EARLY HELLADIC

J. L. Caskey: 'The Early Helladic Period in the Argolid', *Hesperia*, xxix (1960), pp. 285–303

J. B. Rutter: *Ceramic Change in the Aegean Early Bronze Age. The Kastri Group, Lefkandi I, and Lerna IV: A Theory Concerning the Origins of*

Early Helladic III Ceramics, Occasional Paper 5, Institute of Archae-
ology, U. CA (Los Angeles, 1979)
——: 'Fine Gray-burnished Pottery of the Early Helladic III Period: The
Ancestry of Gray Minyan', *Hesperia*, li (1983), pp. 327–53
H.-J. Weisshaar: 'Die Keramik von Talioti', *Tiryns Forschungen und
Berichte*, xi (1990), pp. 1–34
J. B. Rutter: 'Early Helladic Pottery: Inferences about Exchange and
Production from Style and Clay Composition', *Proceedings of the
International Conference 'Wace and Blegen: Pottery as Evidence for Trade
in the Aegean Bronze Age, 1939–1989': Amsterdam, 1993*, pp. 19–37

MIDDLE HELLADIC

R. J. Buck: 'Middle Helladic Matt-painted Pottery', *Hesperia*, xxiii (1964),
pp. 231–313
J. B. Rutter and S. H. Rutter: *The Transition to Mycenaean*, Monumenta
Archaeologica, iv (Los Angeles, 1976)
J. L. Davis: 'The Mainland Panelled Cup and Panelled Style', *Amer. J.
Archaeol.*, lxxxii (1978), pp. 216–22
H. B. Siedentopf: *Mattbemalte Keramik der mittleren Bronzezeit*, Alt-Agina,
iv/2 (Mainz, 1991)
C. W. Zerner: 'New Perspectives on Trade in the Middle and Early Late
Helladic Periods on the Mainland', *Proceedings of the International
Conference 'Wace and Blegen: Pottery as Evidence for Trade in the Aegean
Bronze Age, 1939–1989': Amsterdam, 1993*, pp. 39–56

LATE HELLADIC

A. Furumark: *Mycenaean Pottery: Analysis and Classification*, Skrifta ut-
givna av Svenska Institutet i Athen, xx (Stockholm, 1941/*R* 1972)
E. S. Sherratt: 'Patterns of Contact: Manufacture and Distribution of
Mycenaean Pottery, 1400–1100 B.C.', *Interaction and Acculturation in
the Mediterranean*, ed. J. G. P. Best and N. M. W. de Vries (Amsterdam,
1980)
——: 'Regional Variation in the Pottery of Late Helladic IIIB', *Annu.
Brit. Sch. Athens*, lxxv (1980), pp. 175–202
E. Vermeule and V. Karageorgis: *Mycenaean Pictorial Vase-painting* (Cam-
bridge, MA, 1982)
P. A. Mountjoy: *Mycenaean Decorated Pottery*, Stud. Medit. Archaeol., lxxiii
(Göteborg, 1986) [contains citations of almost all significant stud. of
Mycenaean pott. since Furumark]
Å. Åkerström: *Berbati, II: The Pictorial Pottery*, Skrifta utgivna av Svenska
Institutet i Athen, xxxvi/2 (Stockholm, 1987)

O. T. P. K. DICKINSON

IV. Wall painting.

Little is known of the earliest paintings on the Greek
mainland. All that survives is from the late Helladic (LH),
or Mycenaean, period.

1. Introduction. 2. Subject-matter.

1. INTRODUCTION. Mycenaean painting was rooted
in the traditions and techniques of wall painting in Minoan
Crete (*see* MINOAN, §IV). Unfortunately, architectural
remains for the LH II period, the time of greatest Minoan
influence on the mainland, are largely missing; yet a few
fragments—from Mycenae, Tiryns, Argos and Kokla—
show that painting did exist in LH II. The majority of
surviving paintings, however, date to LH IIIA and especially
LH IIIB. With the collapse of the Mycenaean palaces at the
end of the Bronze Age, wall painting as an art came to an
end in mainland Greece, not to be revived for centuries.

Wall painting was essentially a palatial art. Most extant
works come from the major palaces—at MYCENAE, TI-
RYNS, PYLOS, Thebes (*see* THEBES (ii), §1) and ORCHO-
MENOS—with some fragments from centres such as GLA,
ARGOS and ASINE. Some private houses (perhaps of
palace officials) at Mycenae and Tiryns were painted, as
were sanctuary buildings at Mycenae and a few tombs. As
on Crete, most Helladic wall paintings were found in small
fragments fallen to the ground. The relationship of scenes
to one another is thus frequently lost, leaving vignettes

whose place in the architectural space is unclear. Many
paintings were recovered from dumps, having been
stripped from the walls when the artists redecorated.
Those paintings that were still on the walls at the time of
the final destruction of the palaces are invariably burnt
and difficult to read. The best indications of painting
programmes are the remains from the cult centre at
Mycenae and the final phase at Pylos.

Mycenaean painting of the LH IIIB period is characterized by a tendency towards schematization and a concentration on the human figure. The rich expression of the
natural world found in Minoan art is absent. The few
indications of landscape are reduced to stylized trees and
conventionalized rocks. Animals do not appear in their
natural surroundings but are hieratically and solemnly
arranged, for example guarding a throne or in rows. Close
relationships in theme and execution suggest that artists
travelled between the palaces. Themes were repeated, and
in some cases, the similarities of execution suggest the
same hand.

2. SUBJECT-MATTER. Spirals, rosettes, griffins and
bull-sports continue the Minoan iconographic tradition,
but the procession (*see* §(iii) below), a theme that began at
Knossos (*see* MINOAN, §IV), was transformed into something quintessentially Mycenaean. Divergence from Minoan ideals is also particularly evident in the secular themes
of Mycenaean painting: here the male domain of warfare
and the hunt predominate (*see* §(v) below), reflecting a
heroic society of aristocratic palace lords such as is
described in the later Homeric epics.

(i) Abstraction from the natural world. (ii) Bull-sports. (iii) Processions
and religious programmes. (iv) Sheilds. (v) Hunting and warfare.

(i) Abstraction from the natural world. In Mycenaean
painting nature takes second place to the human figure.
Vestiges of Minoan themes (e.g. the *Bluebird*, *Nautilus*
and *Women and Deer* friezes at Pylos) repeat their motifs
but with little variation and minimal context. Floor decoration, such as the squares of dolphins and octopus from
Tiryns, take the tendency to abstraction still further. The
Deer frieze from Tiryns has more variety of pose, but the
hides of the animals are schematized with rows of crosses,
and the background is an empty blue. At Pylos, griffins
and lions take an emblematic stance, flanking the throne
or arranged in a frieze (for illustration *see* PYLOS).

(ii) Bull-sports. Of the three known Mycenaean examples
of bull-leaping, a theme clearly inspired by Minoan prototypes, two are early. The fragments of toreadors and
bulls from Mycenae came from a deposit below the Ramp
House (LH II/IIIA). The figures are smaller than those in
the Minoan *Toreador* paintings at KNOSSOS, also arranged
in panels with both male and female participants. Associated with toreadors and bulls at Mycenae were representations of architectural features, including one fragment
with women watching from windows, from which hang
festoons attached to double axes. These are on a miniature
scale (comparable to the *Shrine* frieze from Knossos) and
suggest a relationship between sport and audience. A
single fragment of a bull-leaper (LH IIIA) was found at
Pylos. At Tiryns, in the only later example from the
mainland (LH IIIB), the artist has depicted, with an unsure

hand, a dappled bull with a vaulting figure. Like the scenes from nature and the miniature frieze, bull-sports died out as a theme and gave way to the religious and secular subjects of Mycenaean palace art.

(iii) Processions and religious programmes. The procession is the most frequently repeated theme of Mycenaean painting and is known for all the main palaces. Stately figures are shown carrying offerings, and though the recipient is rarely preserved, a goddess or her representative may have been intended; two female recipients appear in the Mycenae Cult Centre processions (see below). Earlier, Cretan processions differ substantially from those of the Mycenaean palaces, not least in that they are composed of male figures, whereas the large-scale Mycenaean processions are, except at Pylos, of female figures. The theme may also have derived inspiration from Egyptian painting, though it is much transformed.

The procession represented in the palace at Thebes may be the earliest on the mainland (LH II–IIIA). From nine to twelve life-size figures wearing Minoan-style flounced skirts with open bodices are set against a background of undulating horizontal colour zones. Most face right. They hold offerings of either flowers, (ivory) boxes or a stone jar. The earliest processional theme at Mycenae, from the Ramp House, is similar to that from Thebes and may be contemporary. Other depictions of the theme at Mycenae, most of them fragmentary, include two from the Pithos area (female, life-size and half life-size); one from the House of the Oil Merchant (man carrying a (?)palanquin, with women and a charging bull); and a single male figure from the area of the megaron. The Tiryns procession had at least eight life-size women moving in both directions. The background is blue, and the figures walk on simulated wood. The stylization and exaggeration of their profile pose suggest a date late in LH IIIB. Fragments of an earlier frieze of smaller women were also found.

Both male and female processional figures occurred at Pylos in several different paintings found in the North-west Slope Dump, including a '*Cup-bearer*' and the '*White Goddess*', thought to be a recipient of offerings. The life-size women may be compared with those from the other palaces. These paintings have lost their context, unlike those found within the palace itself. There the figures are shown entering the palace, moving towards the Throne Room. A single fragment suggests a life-size procession in the Outer Propylon. (The wall-fill of the Inner Propylon revealed a miniature male procession.) Part of a processional male figure was preserved *in situ* in Corridor 13 adjacent to the Vestibule, which leads from the Propylia and Court to the Throne Room. In the Vestibule itself, male processional figures accompany a large sacrificial bull, all moving left towards the door to the Throne Room. Some dressed in kilts carry portable furniture. Others in robes bring offerings in boxes or shallow bowls and walk in pairs (man and boy or priest and acolyte). A single woman dressed in a flounced skirt is perhaps a priestess or member of the ruling family. The background changes colour vertically along wavy lines. The figures must have been in two registers, perhaps either side of the massive bull. On the south-east wall of the Throne Room (i.e. the other side of the Vestibule procession wall) was a male

11. Fragment of a processional wall painting depicting *Mykenaika*, from the Cult Centre, Mycenae, LH IIIB (Athens, National Archaeological Museum)

procession moving towards the throne situated on the east wall. A central hearth in the Throne Room, facing the throne, suggests the resting place for the bull. These paintings must be visual echoes of actual religious processions that took place in the palaces.

The large megaron-style Throne Room was the goal of the processional figures. Entering the door from the Vestibule, the figures led to the major composition on the wall behind the throne, which depicted large-scale protective griffins and lions, a theme that echoes that of the Throne Room at Knossos (*see* MINOAN, §IV, 2(v)). (These creatures were repeated in a frieze from Hall 46, the only other room in the palace to have a central hearth.) To the right (south-east) of the throne came the scene known as the '*Bard at the Banquet*'. A small-scale, robed figure sits high up on a multicoloured rock and plays a lyre, as a large crested bird flies in front of him. Below him, to the left, are two small pairs of robed men seated on stools at tables. Further to the left, towards the throne, is a large-scale bull, presumably the sacrificial animal brought through the Vestibule by the men. Next come the griffins and lions, and on the opposite wall is a painting of deer with papyrus, an animal that is iconographically the prey of the protector-predators.

At Mycenae, the processional theme is central to the iconographic programme of the Cult Centre. From Area B came numerous fragments of a procession of women wearing Minoan-style flounced skirts. The best preserved, the *Mykenaika*, holds an offering of a necklace (see fig. 11). Two fragments belong to a scene in which a statuette is offered to a seated figure. The *Mykenaika* and the recipient of the statuette appear to be the focal-points of two processions on neighbouring walls. In another (apparently later) painting from near by a woman holds an offering of a lily. Area A and the adjacent Tsountas's House yielded fragments of a procession of ass-headed daemons holding a rope (see fig. 12), a palm tree, a shrine and a female warrior carrying a miniature griffin. The themes suggest a programme concerned with life-giving protection: the daemon nurtures (in glyptic scenes he waters leaves); the warrior goddess and the emblematic griffin protect.

12. Wall painting depicting a procession of ass-headed daemons, from Tsountas's House, Mycenae, LH IIIB (Athens, National Archaeological Museum)

A series of cult images was found along the east wall of the Citadel House, to the north-west of the Cult Centre. On the lower level is a priestess or goddess holding sheaves of (life-giving) grain, and a small animal (?griffin). They face towards an altar platform, on which are painted horns of consecration and 'beam-ends', images that denote a holy area. Above the altar are two (?)goddesses, one with the warrior attribute of a sword, the other with a staff or spear. Between them hover two tiny figures, schematically rendered, one red, one black, their arms outstretched. These may well be unique renderings of souls.

(iv) Shields. Large-scale figure-of-eight shields with oxhide markings appeared on the walls of most palaces. By the time of the palace wall paintings this previously functional shield type had become purely emblematic. A frieze of

13. *Battle Scene*, wall painting from Hall 64, Pylos, LH IIIB (Chora, Archaeological Museum); reconstruction

shields at Knossos (Late Minoan II) is the ancestor of the mainland shield friezes for which there is evidence at Tiryns, Thebes (single fragment) and Mycenae (two friezes). Those from Mycenae came from the Cult Centre in association with the female processions. This religious context for the motif is not unique. A painted plaque found near by shows two female figures flanking a figure-of-eight shield with a (?)small head above, which has been identified as emblematic of a warrior goddess. The association between a female figure and warfare is repeated in the paintings from the Citadel House—goddess with a sword—and in a miniature fragment from Thebes that shows a female warrior wearing a helmet and carrying a small griffin.

(v) Hunting and warfare. The walls of the megaron at Mycenae were painted with friezes relating to warfare. The figures appeared at different levels, associated with horses, chariots and buildings. The fragments (of LH IIIB date) were badly burnt. On the (?)entrance wall was a scene of preparation for battle: horses led by grooms wearing greaves, an unyoked chariot and horse-drawn chariots. (Chariots in Mycenaean society seem to have been used only to convey men to the battle or the hunt.) A fragmentary battle scene on two levels shows a horse galloping above (reconstructed with a chariot) and a warrior falling below, hurtling past a building with a woman at a window. Other fragments show women standing before a palace façade and more warriors, some in hand-to-hand combat.

The theme was evidently popular at Mycenae. Another, slightly earlier (LH IIIA–IIIB:1) preparation scene came from the entrance to the palace (western portal). Grooms with their horses stand on a single plane, and an indication of setting is provided by descending rockwork in the upper zone. Fragments of architectural constructions, women and horses (unpublished) were also found in the House of the Oil Merchant, and a scene with men and a chariot was found in the vestibule leading into the cult area. Fragments comparable to the Mycenae megaron frieze were also found at Orchomenos, with buildings, a horse and chariot, and men wearing greaves. Two men often interpreted as bull-leapers probably belong instead to this scene.

Warfare was also important at Pylos. Its scenes are unlike those at any other centre and include a *Battle Scene* from Hall 64 depicting Mycenaean warriors in protective kilts, greaves and boar's-tusk helmets fighting sheepskin-clad barbarians (see fig. 13). (This 'barbarian' theme also occurred in an earlier painting, found in the North-west Slope Dump, in which there are two men wearing animal skins and one (in a (?)tunic) holding up an animal.) The men in the *Battle Scene* fight in pairs, as in the Homeric duel, with daggers and spears, limbs flailing and bodies tumbling to the ground. Below this painting was a frieze of some 20 life-size, overlapping, seated dogs, a hunting adjunct to the theme of warfare.

The hunt was as popular a theme as the battle. Examples are known from Tiryns, Pylos and Orchomenos. The elements of the scenes are often similar to those of warfare—men, horses and chariots—and the themes are closely linked. Two hunt scenes are known from Tiryns: an earlier (LH IIIA–IIIB) version with horses and charioteers and men carrying spears, and a later, better preserved version (LH IIIB) with aristocratic ladies (?spectators or participants) riding in chariots while men, accompanied by hunting dogs, attack wild boar in a setting with stylized plants and trees. The Mycenaeans hunted boar for its tusks, which were sliced and mounted on a leather cap to make the prized boar's-tusk helmets; clearly a prestige item, the helmet symbolized the strength of man. Pieces with a small stag and a hare may have belonged to the scene. Also found with these pieces (in the West Slope Dump) were fragments of a *Deer* frieze, probably part of the same programme. Fragments of a very similar boar hunt were found at Orchomenos, with hunters carrying spears, some wearing boar's-tusk helmets; dogs attacking a boar; and ladies of the palace watching from their chariots.

The *Hunt Scene* from Pylos is more closely related to the Pylos *Battle Scene* than to the hunts of the other palaces. From a large room above Hall 46, it has the same background as the *Battle Scene* (with undulating colour changes) and shows men in tunics and greaves carrying spears, a stag speared by a man and large hunting dogs. The *Hunt* frieze ran on one side of the room, and on the opposite was the *Return from the Hunt*, with men carrying tripods for a feast. Pieces of an earlier hunt scene were found in wall-fill in Room 27.

BIBLIOGRAPHY

H. Bulle: *Orchomenos*, i (Munich, 1907)

G. Rodenwaldt: 'Fragmente mykenischer Wandgemälde', *Mitt. Dt. Archäol. Inst.: Athen. Abt.*, xxxvi (1911), pp. 221–50

G. Rodenwaldt, ed.: *Die Fresken des Palastes* (1912), ii of *Tiryns* (Athens, 1912); see especially N. Heaton: 'Report on the Nature and Method of Specimens of Painted Plaster from the Palace of Tiryns', pp. 211–12

W. Lamb: 'Excavations at Mycenae: Frescoes from the Ramp House', *Annu. Brit. Sch. Athens*, xxiv (1919–21), pp. 189–99

G. Rodenwaldt: *Der Fries des Megarons von Mykenai* (Halle, 1921)

W. Lamb: 'Excavations at Mycenae: Palace Frescoes', *Annu. Brit. Sch. Athens*, xxv (1921–3), pp. 249–55

H. Reusch: 'Ein Schildfresco aus Theban', *Archäol. Anz.*, lxviii (1953), pp. 16–25

——: 'Vorschlag zur Ordnung der Fragmente vom Frauenfries aus Mykenai', *Archäol. Anz.*, lxviii (1953), pp. 26–56

——: *Die zeichnerische Rekonstruktion des Frauenfrieses im böotischen Theben* (Berlin, 1956)

E. Vermeule: *Greece in the Bronze Age* (Chicago, 1964, rev. 1973), pp. 184–202

W. H. Smith: *Interconnections in the Ancient Near East* (New Haven and London, 1965)

M. L. Lang: *The Frescoes* (1969), ii of *The Palace of Nestor at Pylos in Western Messenia* (Princeton, 1966–73)

W. D. Taylour: 'Mycenae 1968', *Antiquity*, xliii (1969), pp. 91–7

——: 'New Light on Mycenaean Religion', *Antiquity*, xliv (1970), pp. 270–80

G. E. Mylonas: *Ton kentron thriskeutikou ton Mykinon* [The Cult Centre of Mycenae] (Athens, 1972)

E. S. Hirsch: *Painted Decoration of the Floors of Bronze Age Structures on Crete and the Greek Mainland*, Stud. Medit. Archael., liii (Göteborg, 1977)

M. A. S. Cameron: 'Theoretical Interrelations among Theran, Cretan and Mainland Frescoes', i of *Thera and the Aegean World I*, ed. C. Doumas (London, 1978), pp. 579–92

S. Hood: *The Arts in Prehistoric Greece*, Pelican Hist. A. (Harmondsworth, 1978)

C. Boulotis: 'Zur Deutung des Freskofragmentes Nr. 103 aus der Tirynther Frauenprozession', *Archäol. Korrbl.*, ix (1979), pp. 59–67

E. S. Hirsch: 'Another Look at Minoan Mycenaean Interrelationships in Floor Decoration', *Amer. J. Archaeol.*, lxxxiv (1980), pp. 453–62

M. Shaw: 'Painted "Ikria" at Mycenae?', *Amer. J. Archaeol.*, lxxxiv (1980), pp. 167–79

N. Marinatos: 'The Fresco from Room 31 at Mycenae', *The Excavations* (1981), i of *Well-built Mycenae, the Helleno-British Excavations within the Citadel at Mycenae, 1959–69*, ed. W. D. Taylor, E. B. French and K. A. Wardle (Warminster, 1981–92)

S. Peterson: *Wall Paintings in the Aegean Bronze Age: The Procession Frescoes* (Ph. D. diss., Minneapolis, U. MN, 1981)

I. Kritseli-Providi: *Toichographies tou thriskeutikou kentrou ton Mykinon* [The wall painting from the Cult Centre at Mycenae] (Athens, 1982) [Eng. review by L. Morgan: *Amer. J. Archaeol.*, lxxxviii (1984), pp. 77–8]

C. Boulotis: 'Mycenaean Wall Painting', *The Mycenaean World: Five Centuries of Early Greek Culture, 1600–1100 BC*, Ministry of Culture, The National Hellenic Committee, ICOM (Athens, 1988), pp. 35–7

N. Marinatos: 'The Fresco from Room 31 at Mycenae: Problems of Method and Interpretation', *Problems in Greek Prehistory: Centenary Conference of the British School of Archaeology at Athens: Manchester, 1986*, pp. 245–52

S. A. Immerwahr: *Aegean Painting in the Bronze Age* (University Park, PA, and London, 1990)

L. Morgan, ed.: *Aegean Painting: A Tribute to Mark Cameron* (in preparation)

LYVIA MORGAN

V. Sculpture.

1. EARLY AND MIDDLE HELLADIC. The only known Early Helladic (EH) sculptural works are an ithyphallic terracotta figurine from Zerelia in Thessaly (Volos, Athanassakeion Archaeol. Mus.); another highly stylized human figurine from Zygouries (EH II; Corinth, Archaeol. Mus.); some abstract zoomorphic vessels and figurines from Eutresis (Thebes Mus.), Zygouries, Palaiopyrgi, Tiryns (Navplion, Archaeol. Mus.) and Corinth (Corinth, Archaeol. Mus.); and a series of carefully modelled, almost naturalistic bovine figurines from Lithares in Boiotia (EH III; Thebes Mus.). Middle Helladic (MH) works are even rarer, being confined to two terracotta bull rhyta from Eleusis (Eleusis Mus.). They too are stylized, but their muscular bodies, hunched shoulders and lifelike heads are clearly and forcefully portrayed.

2. LATE HELLADIC. Examples of Late Helladic (LH), or Mycenaean, sculpture are better known; they were produced in stone, clay and plaster, in the round and in relief. The tools available to Mycenaean artists for stonework were stone hammers, chisels, drills, saws and abrasives such as emery, pumice or sand. Drills were reeds or bronze tubes turned back and forth by a rope or bow, which thus bored rings, rather than complete holes; to create holes the stone core within the drilled ring was broken out. Saws were straight or curved toothless bronze blades, or pieces of wire. Both were used as grinding implements in conjunction with sand or emery powder, probably applied wet. When carving reliefs, the sculptor outlined the composition by drilling a series of closely packed rings and then hammering out their cores and the thin walls between them. Then he cut the surface back to the level of the background with stone hammers or emery chisels and effaced tool marks and sharp edges using an abrasive. A compass was sometimes employed for cutting circles, and borers and small stone or bronze chisels were used for detailed work.

(i) Sculpture in the round. About two dozen examples have survived, all belonging to LH IIIB–C and thus representing the final phase of LH sculpture. They comprise the plaster head of a goddess or sphinx and the small head of a statuette, both from MYCENAE (Athens, N. Archaeol.

14. Late Helladic head of a goddess (or sphinx), painted plaster, h. 168 mm, from Mycenae, LH IIIB (Athens, National Archaeological Museum)

Mus.), a small fragmentary clay head from Athens (Athens, Acropolis Mus.) and another from Asine (Navplion, Archaeol. Mus.), all probably originally attached to wooden bodies. The large head from Mycenae (see fig. 14) is two-thirds life-size and is made of white plaster, with the features (eyes, mouth, ears, facial tattoos, headband and cap) indicated or enhanced by paint. It is more expertly fashioned than the small head from the same site, which

is closer to the examples from Athens and Asine; these are also painted white and embellished with added colour. The modelling of the Mycenae and the Athens heads is stylized but fairly regular, and their proportions are roughly correct: the Asine head, known as the Lord (or Lady) of Asine, is much cruder, with protruding eyes, a triangular nose, beardlike chin and flat ears. However, all four share one basic trait: unlike the smoothly rounded contemporary Cretan and Cycladic statues (see MINOAN, §V and CYCLADIC, §IV, 1) they are modelled in four distinct planes (face, sides and back) that meet rather than merge.

There are also 19 wheelmade female terracotta idols from the Cult Centre at Mycenae (LH IIIB; Navplion, Archaeol. Mus.). These are even more rudimentary and conventional than the heads. Their tubelike bodies with small, pointed breasts support spherical heads with long noses and incised mouths, while their short, stunted arms are raised up on either side, stretched forwards or folded across the chest. Their eyes, mouths and hair are either moulded or painted, while perishable accessories such as plaits or jewellery were inserted into small holes made before firing.

In addition to the large-scale sculptures, there are a few anthropomorphic or zoomorphic vessels and thousands of small, stylized terracotta figurines of women (or goddesses), animals and birds, discovered on practically all LH sites. The terracotta figurines (see fig. 15), cylindrical from the waist down and with flattened torsos and arms, are so abstracted that the general shape of the human body is barely recognizable. Their only moulded details are a flat-topped hat, a pinched-out nose, pellets for breasts and occasionally a tress at the back. All other features (eyes, clothes, jewellery) are simply painted on. Most are female figures with upraised or crossed arms, but some represent women kneading dough (Athens, priv. col.), holding a child or seated on either a throne (Navplion, Archaeol. Mus.) or a pack animal (Athens, N. Archaeol. Mus.). Other figurines depict chariots, with or without charioteers (Navplion, Archaeol. Mus.), and horsemen (Navplion, Archaeol Mus.). The animal figurines (mostly bovines) are even more schematic, so that when they have no obvious distinguishing features such as horns or manes it is often impossible to identify them. The features on the plastic vessels, mainly rhyta, are equally sketchy and stereotyped but are painted rather than modelled. Some represent humans, but there are also birds (Patras, Archaeol. Mus.), a pack animal with wine skins (Rhodes, Archaeol. Mus.), an oxhead (Rhodes, Archaeol. Mus.), a fish (Navplion, Archaeol. Mus.) and two high boots with upturned toes (Athens, N. Archaeol. Mus.).

(ii) Reliefs. Again, about two dozen have been preserved, of which the 14 or so soft limestone tomb markers from the royal graves at Mycenae are the earliest (LH I; Athens, N. Archaeol. Mus.). They were decorated with spiral, meander or rosette patterns or with crudely designed and inexpertly incised or carved scenes involving chariots, such as hunting, racing or warfare scenes. The flat, single-plane designs were outlined to a uniformly shallow depth using a wood-carving technique: only on one slab is there a rudimentary attempt at modelling.

15. Late Helladic terracotta figurines, LH III: (a) Phi type, h. 80 mm, probably from Melos; (b) Tau type, h. 95 mm, from Athens; (c) Psi type, h. 115 mm, probably from Athens (London, British Museum)

The next extant works are a few scraps of well-modelled architectural reliefs from Mycenae, Thebes and Tiryns, produced three centuries later. These were carved in coloured stone or alabaster and ornamented respectively with spirals, a net pattern and bisected rosettes. Similar but more sophisticated are the spiral and floral designs sculpted on the ceiling of the side chamber of the Treasury of Minyas (LH IIIB), a tholos tomb at Orchomenos, and the bead-framed zigzag bands of spirals on the half columns of the Treasury of Atreus at Mycenae (LH IIIB; parts now at London, BM; Munich, Staatl. Antikensamml.; Athens, N. Archaeol. Mus.; Navplion, Archaeol. Mus.); from this tomb also a few frieze fragments depicting the feet and head of a bull standing next to a tree survive.

The most significant LH relief is that on a limestone slab concealing the relieving triangle over the lintel of the Lion Gate at Mycenae (LH IIIB; *in situ*; *see* MYCENAE, fig. 2). It represents two confronted rampant lions who rest their front paws on a double altar surmounted by a column supporting a length of entablature. The lions' heads, now missing, were probably of softer stone, perhaps steatite. Their musculature is modelled in fairly low relief with a few bold planes. There is little anatomical detail, and the proportions are stylized, but overall the work creates a naturalistic impression of raw power.

Another relief occurs on the menhir-like stone slab from Soufli Magoula in Thessaly (late LH IIIB; Larisa, Archaeol. Mus.), though its style is unusual and its date uncertain. It represents a barely recognizable life-size human figure wearing a pointed helmet, five necklaces, a dagger and a belt, flanked by wriggling snakes. Its right hand hangs down by its hip, while its left is held across its chest. The design and execution are so crude that only its find spot and the shapes of the helmet and dagger link the piece to other Mycenaean works.

BIBLIOGRAPHY
W. A. Heurtley: 'Mycenae: The Grave Stelai', *Annu. Brit. Sch. Athens*, xxv (1921–3), pp. 126–46
G. E. Mylonas: 'The Figured Mycenaean Stelae', *Amer. J. Archaeol.*, lv (1951), pp. 134–47
H.-G. Buchholz and V. Karageorghis: *Altägäis und Altkypros* (Tübingen, 1971); Eng. trans. by F. Garvie as *Prehistoric Greece and Cyprus* (London, 1973)
E. French: 'The Development of Mycenaean Terracotta Figurines', *Annu. Brit. Sch. Athens*, lxvi (1971), pp. 101–87
S. Hood: *The Arts in Prehistoric Greece*, Pelican Hist. A. (Harmondsworth, 1978), pp. 94, 96–112

VI. Ivory and bone.

Articles made from bone or antler are sometimes mistaken for ivory, although in both texture and colour ivory is a superior material. Few work areas for ivory-carving have been identified, although they may have been situated in a settlement's artisan quarter, as well as in its palace. Storerooms or assembly areas may have existed: this would explain the large number of articles found in the House of Shields at Mycenae, for example. The tools used were probably similar to those employed by wood-carvers, and lathes may have been introduced before the end of the Bronze Age. Evidence of tinting with colours has survived: red stains on some ivory discs (LH IIA) from Kakovatos and blue on an ivory duck's head (LH IIIA) from Asine. Unless stated otherwise, specific examples

referred to in this subsection can be found in the National Archaeological Museum, Athens.

1. EARLY AND MIDDLE HELLADIC. In the Early Helladic (EH) period, bone was used mainly for tools, but by the Middle Helladic (MH) era fine pins had appeared as well as some bone inlay and appliqué, for example on a dagger sheath from Asine decorated with spiral designs (Navplion, Archaeol. Mus.): whether or not this was a local development is unclear. But even in the late MH shaft graves at MYCENAE bone objects were not common; nor were articles in ivory, but it was at this time that ivory production became more plentiful, and excavators have recovered ivory knife-handles, pommels, combs, pyxides and a mirror-handle from the shaft graves. Ivory has always signified status, but there is nothing overtly ritual about these or other finds.

2. LATE HELLADIC. Late Helladic (LH) II was a formative phase during which some technically and aesthetically sensitive work in ivory was produced, including a pyxis from Routsi near Pylos decorated with dolphins and a cover from Tiryns. But the period was short and the output limited. In LH IIIA, the repertory of motifs grew repetitive. Even so, Mycenaean concepts began to influence Near Eastern work (Syria–Palestine, Cyprus): a degree of cross-fertilization resulted, making some pieces stylistically difficult to assign. However, after LH IIIB:2–IIIC ivory production progressively collapsed, and heirlooms may account for certain items, such as some discs from Perati (LH IIIC). Cyprus and the Near East took over

16. Ivory statuette of two women and a child, h. 78 mm, from Mycenae, LH II–IIIA (Athens, National Archaeological Museum)

as centres of production, patterns persisting there into the 9th and 8th centuries BC (*see* CYPRUS, §II, 5(iii)).

On the mainland, as in Crete, ivory was often used instead of wood for combs and mirror-handles. Initially, combs had 'horned' handles: one LH II example from Routsi, illustrating an attack on birds by catlike creatures, recalls a similar scene on an inlaid dagger from the Mycenae shaft graves; another 'horned' handle was found at Analipsis. Later (LH II–IIIC) the canonical ribbed form developed, frequently plain, sometimes carved with rosettes and animals in relief (including pieces from Argos, Mycenae, Pylos, Spata and Thebes). Mirror-handles too changed in spirit, from the style typified by a shaft grave specimen depicting lions and one from Routsi with carved rosettes (LH II) to the fine LH III series from Mycenae with pairs of women in flounced skirts on each side. Items of jewellery were uncommon, apart from pins from Mycenae.

Ivory pyxides, ultimately inspired by Cretan workmanship (*see* MINOAN, §VI), were normally circular, though some LH IIIA examples from Asine and Mycenae are duck-shaped or perhaps represent duck-headed boats. Relief decoration became standard, though some early pyxides were incised (e.g. specimens from the shaft graves and from Routsi). Motifs were sometimes geometric, such as the spirals on LH II examples from Thorikos and Routsi, but more often they made use of animals, either as patterns—see the design of argonauts on the LH IIIA pyxis from a tomb in the area of the later agora at Athens (Athens, Agora Mus.)—or in scenes, perhaps the most remarkable of which, from the same tomb, shows griffins attacking a herd of deer (LH IIIA; Athens, Agora Mus.); others portray sheep (from Menidi, LH IIIB) or sphinxes (from Thebes in Boiotia; Thebes Mus.).

Objects carved in the round are not often found. Apparently Minoan in inspiration if not in origin are the fine LH II or IIIA statuette of two women and a child cut

from a single piece of ivory, which was found on the acropolis at Mycenae (see fig. 16), and a leg and an arm evidently from figurines made in several pieces, also from Mycenae; other human figurines were more obviously locally made, such as an unfinished female, also from the Mycenae acropolis. From the same source and dating from the same period, LH IIIB, come the head of a young man wearing a diadem, and a crouching lion (both Navplion, Archaeol. Mus.). No less remarkable, though it might have been imported, is a carved tusk segment depicting a man in a 'natural' setting with goats, trees and an Egyptian bird, found in a tomb at Mycenae (LH III).

Many ivory inlays and appliqués were destined for the decoration of wooden furniture—a set of clay tablets from Pylos bears Linear B inscriptions that are taken to refer to such inlays. Arguably the craft's finest achievements are relief plaques with animal scenes, including wild goats from Thebes (LH IIIA; Thebes Mus.), a griffin from Mycenae (LH II–IIIA; see fig. 17) and sphinxes, also from Mycenae (LH IIIB). Other notable plaques feature a lion attacking a bull (LH IIIB–C from Spata in Attica) and a female figure (LH from Mycenae; Paris, Louvre). Footstools in particular were often decorated with reliefwork, an LH IIIA:2 example from Thebes deploying shields (Thebes Mus.), as did another from Mycenae, and LH II examples from Midea and Mycenae using spirals. Several plaques in the shape of helmeted heads have been found on the mainland, as have columns and half columns from Mycenae and Delos. Chair legs have been recovered at Thebes (Thebes Mus.), and what seem to be finials at Pylos.

Generally, inlay was effected by the massing of small pieces of ivory with a minimum of incised details: rosettes and lilies were very common—hundreds have been found in the House of Shields at Mycenae—dolphins and argonauts only slightly less so. Prestige items include an LH IIIB carved lyre from Menidi and another with reliefwork from Mycenae, probably dating from LH II. Also prestigious were scabbard mounts and sword pommels. Although pommels were usually plain—see the LH I–II examples from Mycenae—some decorated ones have survived, with such features as lions or, from Mycenae, spirals (LH I).

BIBLIOGRAPHY

O. T. P. K. Dickinson: *The Origins of Mycenaean Civilisation*, Stud. Medit. Archaeol., xlix (Göteborg, 1977)
J.-C. Poursat: *Catalogue des ivoires mycéniens du Musée National d'Athènes* (Athens, 1977)
——: *Les Ivoires mycéniens: Essai sur la formation d'un art mycénien* (Paris, 1977)
I. A. Sakellarakis: *To elephantodonto kai i katergasia tou sta mykinaika chronia* [Ivory and its working in Mycenaean times] (Athens, 1979)
O. H. Krzyszkowska: *Ivory and Related Materials: An Illustrated Guide* (London, 1990)
——: *Well-built Mycenae: The Ivories* (in preparation)

D. EVELY

VII. Metalwork.

1. GOLD AND SILVER. A gold sauceboat (Early Helladic II; Paris, Louvre; for shape see fig. 6b above), reportedly from Heraia in Arcadia, indicates that mainland Greeks were making vessels of precious metal from an early period, and Middle Helladic (MH) Minyan ware, with its sharply angled profiles (for shape see fig. 7a–b above),

17. Ivory low-relief plaque with a griffin seated under papyrus, h. 70 mm, from Mycenae, LH II–IIIA (Athens, National Archaeological Museum)

appears to be imitating metalwork; nevertheless, what little gold and silver survives comes almost exclusively from unrobbed, high-status tombs of the Late Helladic (LH) period. The shaft graves of Grave Circle A at MYCENAE (MH III–LH IIA) contained a staggering wealth of gold and silver items, and smaller quantities have been found in graves elsewhere in the Mycenaean world. Despite grave robbing, enough has survived to demonstrate that the Mycenaeans achieved very high standards of artistry in the working of precious metals. (Unless indicated, all objects are in Athens, N. Archaeol. Mus.)

Large amounts of sheet gold were worn by those buried in Grave Circle A. Five wore death masks of thin sheet gold, each one with individual features (see fig. 18). An electrum mask, made of a natural alloy of gold and silver, was found in Grave Gamma of Grave Circle B (MH III–LH I). Gold breast-plates, either plain or decorated with spirals, were also found on some of the skeletons; these were of thin sheet gold and were probably purely for funerary use. The women wore large gold diadems and had thin gold cut-outs sewn on to their funerary clothing. A complete suit made of pieces of sheet-gold was found in Grave III of Grave Circle A; it once adorned a child.

Many gold and silver vessels were also found in Grave Circle A and Circle B at Mycenae, and some very fine examples have survived in Mycenaean tombs elsewhere in the country. These vessels fall into three broad categories: plain, decorated with repoussé technique and inlaid. They appear to have been made from the mid-LH I period to LH IIIB. The plain vessels include various forms of cups, such as the kantharos (a two-handled cup); a shallow, one-handled cup; the so-called Vapheio cup (tall and straight-sided); and the stemmed goblet. Perhaps the finest of these is the stemmed goblet from Grave Circle A known as Nestor's Cup, with a bird perched on each of two double handles. Vessels with repoussé decoration include an exceptionally beautiful, one-handled, shallow cup from the tholos tomb at DENDRA in the Argolid. Made of sheet gold, it was decorated using repoussé and incision with octopuses and dolphins (LH IIB). Two gold cups from a tholos tomb at Vapheio near Sparta (LH IIA; see Sparta, §I) gave the name to the straight-sided cup already mentioned. These cups have a plain inner lining and a spool-handle, and their outer casings are exquisitely decorated in repoussé with scenes of bull-hunting, one a very turbulent scene, the other more peaceful. One of the finest of the silver vessels from the Mycenae shaft graves is the fragmentary rhyton from Grave IV of Grave Circle A. Its surviving pieces are decorated with battle scenes and the siege of a city. Two other exceptionally fine rhyta from the same grave are a silver bull-head rhyton with gilded horns and a gold rhyton in the form of a lion's head. Sheets of gold were also used to plate non-precious materials: from Grave V of Circle A, for example, came 12 plaques of sheet gold embossed with scenes of animals hunting.

An early example of an inlaid vessel is an electrum stemmed goblet from Grave IV of Circle A, which has a row of gold and glossy black inlaid plants around the rim. Two very similar cups, from Dendra and Enkomi on Cyprus (LH IIB; Nicosia, Cyprus Mus.), are hemispherical silver cups with one wishbone handle, decorated with

18. Gold mask, the so-called Mask of Agamemnon, 260×265 mm, from Shaft Grave V, Mycenae, LH I (Athens, National Archaeological Museum)

bulls' heads and floral motifs in gold and a black material that may be a form of niello (an alloy of copper, silver and sulphur). A shallow cup with a ribbon handle from a chamber tomb at Mycenae (LH IIIB) is decorated with inlaid bearded profile heads. Detached heads of a very similar type (also LH IIIB) from the Palace of Nestor at Pylos must be from the same type of inlaid cup.

An inlay technique was also used to decorate the blades of what were probably ceremonial daggers (LH I–II); they are some of the finest products of the age. Several examples dating to the second half of LH I were found in Grave Circle A at Mycenae and a fragmentary blade of the same date on the island of Thera (Copenhagen, Nmus.); LH II examples have been found at the Argive Heraion, at Vapheio and in a tholos tomb at Routsi, near Pylos. The blade of these daggers is of bronze, with a strip of oxidized silver or, less commonly, gold slotted into it. This strip was then inlaid with detailed scenes using gold, silver, copper and black niello. The Mycenae daggers are decorated with such scenes as leopards hunting birds in a Nilotic landscape, running lions and a particularly intricate scene of warriors hunting lions (see MYCENAE, fig. 3). One of the inlaid daggers from Routsi has a preserved gold hilt and is decorated with leopards hunting in a forest; the other Routsi dagger depicts argonauts in a marine landscape. Sometimes a single motif was enough: on the example from the Argive Heraion there is a dolphin on one side and a flying fish on the other.

For discussion of Helladic gold and silver jewellery see §VIII, 1 below.

BIBLIOGRAPHY
R. Higgins: *Minoan and Mycenaean Art* (London, 1967, rev. 1981)
E. N. Davis: *The Vapheio Cups and Aegean Gold and Silver Ware* (New York, 1977)
A. Xenaki-Sakellariou and C. Chatziliou: *'Peinture en métal' à l'époque mycénienne* (Athens, 1989)

2. BRONZE. The basic functional metal of the Greek Bronze Age was, naturally, bronze. Though bronze daggers are known from Early and Middle Helladic times, most surviving remains are from the Late Helladic period. Mycenaean Greeks used bronze for making tools, weapons and armour, for vessels and for dress and cosmetic items.

Bronze weapons included swords, daggers, spearheads and arrowheads. Two types of long sword are known from the Mycenae shaft graves. The first, known as Type A, could reach almost a metre in length, with a triangular blade strengthened by a midrib. The shoulder of the blade was rounded, and a short tang affixed it to a perishable handle, sometimes made of gold or ivory. The Type B sword, marginally shorter than Type A, had a similar triangular blade with a midrib, but it had a broad, squared shoulder with flanged edges and a longer tang, to fix the blade more securely to the handle.

Much shorter swords were also part of the Mycenaean warrior's repertory, and beginning in the Late Helladic II period sturdier swords with higher midribs and thicker blades began to appear, with tangs that eventually broadened to form a true hilt cast in one piece with the blade. Bronze weapons were sometimes decorated: a beautiful butterfly with outstretched wings was engraved on a long sword (Athens, N. Archaeol. Mus.) from Grave Circle B at Mycenae, for example, and ceremonial bronze daggers were often inlaid with scenes in gold, silver and niello (see §1 above).

The earliest bronze spearheads appeared during the MH period and at the very beginning of the LH period; these were made in a bi-valve mould and comprised a bronze blade with a shoe-socket on each side, into which a split wooden shaft was inserted. An alternative form of spear that appeared in the Mycenae Shaft Graves and lasted throughout the LH period was one with a leaf-shaped blade, a medial rib and a socket for a wooden shaft. Archery was also practised: the arrows, which in the MH period were mostly made of flint and obsidian, began to be made of bronze in appreciable numbers in the MH III–LH I period.

Just as bronze was used for offensive weapons, so it was sometimes used for defensive armour. A unique set of Mycenaean armour, including a corselet with shoulder guards, skirt and greaves, was found in chamber tomb 12 at Dendra (LH IIB; Navplion, Archaeol. Mus.); pieces from similar sets of armour were found in Dendra tomb 8 and at Thebes (Thebes Mus.). In addition to those at Dendra, bronze greaves have also been found on Cyprus (Nicosia, Cyprus Mus.), in Athens (Athens, N. Archaeol. Mus.) and near Patras (Patras, Archaeol. Mus.).

Metal vessels were manufactured throughout the Mycenaean period, made of sheets of hammered bronze riveted together. Many of the surviving examples come from graves, e.g. the Mycenae shaft graves and Dendra (Athens, N. Archaeol. Mus., and Navplion, Archaeol. Mus.). Some smaller vessels have been found in excavations of settlements, such as that of Mycenae. Small bronze vessels include phiale (shallow, one-handled cups) and Vapheio cups, as well as bowls and basins; larger bronze containers include amphorae, jugs (see fig. 19) and cauldrons. As well as vessels themselves, cast tripod stands in openwork also survive. Items of personal adornment and for cosmetic

19. Bronze piriform jug, h. 170 mm, max. diam. 120 mm, from Asine, chamber tomb I:5, LH IIIA (Athens, National Archaeological Museum)

use include fibulae for fastening clothing and pins, sometimes with rock-crystal heads, such as those found in Grave Omikron of Grave Circle B at Mycenae. Round bronze mirrors, originally affixed to what was probably a wooden handle, were polished until they shone. Other items of bronze for personal and domestic use include needles, tweezers and, at the very end of the Bronze Age, spatulas.

BIBLIOGRAPHY
A. M. Snodgrass: *Early Greek Armour and Weapons* (Edinburgh, 1964)
J. D. Muhly: *Copper and Tin* (New Haven, 1973)
K. Branigan: *Aegean Metalwork of the Early and Middle Bronze Age* (Oxford, 1974)
H. Catling: *Cypriot Bronzework in the Mycenaean World* (Oxford, 1974)
LOUISE SCHOFIELD

VIII. Jewellery.

1. EARLY AND MIDDLE HELLADIC. The principal source for Early Helladic jewellery is a rich collection alleged to come from the Thyreatis in the Peloponnese, south of Lerna on the Argolic Gulf (now in Berlin, Antikenmuseum). A secondary source is from a tomb on the Ampheion Hill near Thebes (now in Corinth, Archaeol. Mus.). Both sources date to the Early Helladic (EH) II–III period.

The Thyreatis Treasure, which shows strong influence from Troadic jewellery, consists of beads, pendants and a pin, all of gold or electrum. A number of the beads are composed of concentric hoops of wire, from some of which are suspended chains supporting wedge-shaped pendants (see fig. 20). There is one bead in the shape of an axehead, and another consists of a pair of tight wire spirals on either side of a thin bar. The pin has a head in the form of a bull's head. From the tomb near Thebes come three identical, elaborate pendants; they incorporate a barrel-shaped bead, a vertical rod, a double (or spectacle) spiral and two floral clusters respectively.

Jewellery was extremely rare in the Middle Helladic (MH) period. The range was generally restricted to beads of bronze, rock crystal, cornelian, steatite and faience, and to pins of bronze and bone. There are a few gold hoop earrings, and a diadem and bracelets of silver were found at Corinth, dating to the later MH period.

2. LATE HELLADIC. The Late Helladic (LH) period was very rich in jewellery. Trade and cultural contacts with Crete had been resumed at the end of the MH period and were rapidly intensified (see §I, 2 above). The results of this contact are reflected particularly in the fabulously wealthy royal shaft graves at MYCENAE in the Argolid and in a few graves elsewhere in Greece. Jewellery was less common in the Mycenae shaft graves than plate of precious metals or weapons (see §VII, 1 above), but what did survive (Athens, N. Archaeol. Mus.) is almost all of gold and is of high quality. Some items were imported from Crete, others show Minoan and Balkan influences.

Oval, crown-like diadems found in the shaft graves were worn by both sexes. They were decorated with embossed circles and other simple patterns, some having leaves or rosettes along their upper edge. A pair of elaborate hoop earrings with granulated decoration is perhaps a Minoan import; they are closely paralleled in a LH wall painting from Thera (LH I; Athens, N. Archaeol. Mus.; see CYCLADIC, §VI). Other earrings from the shaft graves, believed to be imports from the Balkans, are hoops of faceted wire, with subsidiary spirals within the hoops. A woman's burial held a necklace of pomegranate-shaped beads, forerunners of the relief-beads of the next phase. Bracelets are rare, but two pairs, of sheet-gold decorated with rosettes, were found in the Mycenae shaft graves. Of higher quality are two magnificent signet rings, believed to come from women's burials; the subjects depicted are known as the *Battle in the Glen* and the *Stag Hunt*. Such scenes of war and the chase are typically Mycenaean: they are rare in Minoan art, but the superb design and craftsmanship of these rings is surely Minoan. They were perhaps made by a Cretan goldsmith to the orders of a Mycenaean master.

Many clothing ornaments were also found in the Mycenae shaft graves. These were hammered flat into stars and other shapes and sewn on to garments. They exhibit an eclectic style, with Anatolian, Syrian and Minoan elements. Dress pins are also common among the shaft grave finds from Mycenae. The finest, of silver, has a gold pendant depicting a Minoan goddess. A gold pin has a head in the form of an ibex, and there are bronze pins with rock-crystal heads.

The developed phase of Mycenaean jewellery, which succeeded the age of the shaft graves, spanned the rest of Late Bronze Age. The new style is much more homogeneous and is really a development of the Minoan. Indeed, much of the best jewellery may well have been made by

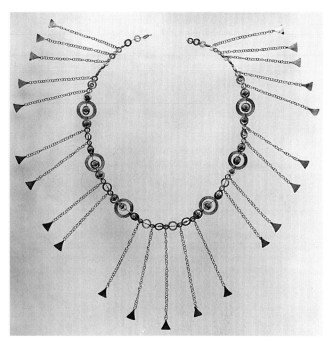

20. Gold pendant, l. 640 mm, from the Thyreatis Treasure, EH II (Berlin, Antikenmuseum)

Cretan goldsmiths for Mycenaean customers. The techniques employed are repoussé, stamping sheet-gold or working it into moulds, filigree, granulation, inlaying with stones or glass and (for the first time in the Aegean) enamelling. The repertory is virtually limited to plain and relief-beads, finger-rings and clothing ornaments.

Relief-beads (see fig. 21) were made in large numbers, but in only a few forms, which continued to be used until the end of LH IIIB and occasionally later. The subjects are nearly all three-dimensional versions of the paintings on Minoan vases, marine life and plants being especially

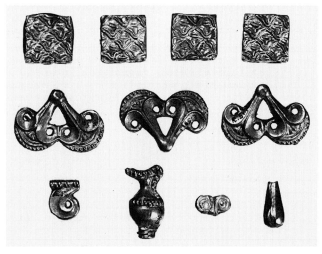

21. Gold relief-beads, h. (largest) 18 mm, from a tomb at Mycenae, LH IIIA:1 (Oxford, Ashmolean Museum)

popular. The designs were stamped out in relief on sheet-gold. Between LH II and LH IIIA the decoration often included added granulation and occasionally blobs of blue enamel (examples in Athens, N. Archaeol. Mus.). After LH IIIB the technique deteriorated. Thereafter the beads were made of glass and covered with gold foil. Finger-rings were also popular, particularly the Minoan type with a plain oval bezel at right angles to the hoop. Sometimes the bezel was engraved for use as a signet, as for example on the Danicourt Ring (LH IIA; Péronne, Mus. Danicourt); on other examples the bezel was decorated with inlay or enamel. By LH IIIC Mycenaean jewellery was becoming scarce, and by the end of the Bronze Age production had ceased altogether.

See also §IX below.

BIBLIOGRAPHY

R. Higgins: *Greek and Roman Jewellery* (London, 1961, rev. 1980), pp. 47–87

C. W. Blegen, H. Palmer and R. S. Young: *The North Cemetery* (1964), xiii of *Corinth: Results of Excavation Conducted by The American School of Classical Studies at Athens* (Princeton, 1929–)

S. Hood: *The Arts in Prehistoric Greece*, Pelican Hist. A. (Harmondsworth, 1978), pp. 192–207

REYNOLD HIGGINS

IX. Faience.

Other than incidental finds in Macedonia and the Chalcidice of beads dating to the Early Helladic (EH) and, especially in the north-east Peloponnese, the Middle Helladic (MH) periods, mainland Greece provides little evidence for production of faience articles before the late Bronze Age. By the beginning of the Late Helladic (LH) period, however, Minoan-influenced faience pieces, including vases, jewellery and inlays for composite objects, became plentiful. The larger amount of faience recovered from the late MH and LH I phases reflects the extravagant burial customs of that era, but the element of ritual, apparent for example in Minoan figurines (*see* MINOAN, §VII), seems lacking. The relative scarcity of faience objects in the second half of the 2nd millennium BC probably mirrors changing social customs: production was limited to appliqué figurines, beads and small jewellery pieces. Most of the LH I material may have been Minoan, imported from Crete, and the break in manufacture in Crete in the Late Minoan IB period may have been reflected on the mainland. However, faience production continued and was maintained throughout LH IIIA–B on the mainland (for example at Thebes); there are vases and items of jewellery from this time that are of clear Mycenaean inspiration. The disturbances afflicting the palatial centres at the end of the Bronze Age probably led to the decline of faience production.

Many faience vases have been found at MYCENAE, as well as Kakovatos and Ktimeni. (All artefacts are located at the National Archaeology Museum in Athens.) From the MH and LH I phases come many vessels, including jugs, cups, an alabastron, ewers, a triton shell and a chalice. Many are closely paralleled by Cretan examples found in the Temple Repositories at Knossos and ultimately reflect vessels in stone, metal and ceramics; the chalice, however, a tall, cylindrical vessel with flaring rim, is simpler than those from Crete, which have moulded rims and feet and leafy sprays down their sides.

A lid from Chamber Tomb 529 at Mycenae (LH II–III) may be Minoan. Also Minoan in concept and execution are three or four rhyta, each based on an ostrich egg, from Shaft Graves IV and V at Mycenae; in these, faience elements are combined with gold, a sheet of another metal (probably bronze) and wood. By LH IIIB, however, polychrome faience was also being made: at the House of the Shields, Mycenae, a polychrome jar handle and sherds were found, together with monochrome stemmed bowls (see fig. 22) and rhyta. The Mycenaean polychrome faience used the primary colours of red, yellow and blue, although Minoan imports often made use of a wider range of colours. The forms of these vases are based on ceramic shapes (*see* §III, 4 above), while their iconography, and the technique of moulding the vases in segments, with 'inlay' polychrome effects, reflects a tradition quite different from the earlier Minoan-inspired one.

Personal ornaments represent the main and widest thread of continuity in the production of faience. The shaft graves at Mycenae (MH III–LH IIIA) yielded moulded and plain necklace elements, some of glass; moulded examples include geometric shapes and an ivy leaf. The plain items were spherical.

From the start there was a tendency to mix faience with metals and stones. This was continued until LH II–III, when moulded glass beads were more widespread and were produced with an extensive range of motifs, taken from both faience and gold items (*see also* §VIII, 2 above). From graves and settlements such as Prosymna, Asine, Dendra, Mycenae and Goumenitsa many faience articles have been recovered: plain spheres and discs; segmented, grooved and fluted geometric shapes; and naturalistic shapes, including cockles, a rosette, wheat grains and a bull's head.

Faience cylinder seals were not common and were probably imported from the eastern Mediterranean coastal region (*see also* §X below). Examples were found at

22. Faience kylix or stemmed bowl, decorated with black paint, h. *c.* 130 mm, from the House of the Shields, Mycenae, LH IIIB (Athens, National Archaeological Museum)

Mycenae in Chamber Tomb 517 (LH I–II) and the North Terrace (LH III), and at Prosymna in Chamber Tombs 24 and 38 (LH II).

Faience plaques and inlays were much rarer on the mainland than in Crete, but there are exact parallels in Minoan artefacts, in a variety of substances, for faience examples found in shaft-grave contexts, such as the five dolphins on an ostrich-egg rhyton, sacral knots and parts of a gaming-board. Later, mould-made pieces included necklace elements in the shape of female figures from Chamber Tomb 9 at Dendra and from the acropolis at Mycenae (LH II–III) and inlays such as the 'figure-of-eight' shields from Mycenae (LH IIIB:2). Larger faience inlays for sword or dagger hilts and pommels were found at Mycenae on the acropolis and in Chamber Tombs 102 and 529. These all date to LH II–III and echo others in stone and ivory.

Despite the rich Minoan inheritance, the Mycenaeans failed to develop a strongly original style of faience work; they were more successful with glass. Nonetheless, faience was produced by the Mycenaeans on a greater scale and to a later date than by the Minoans. Evidence for this Mycenaean predominance includes the LH IIIA–B work areas at Thebes, the scattered moulds of the LH period found at Mycenae and Thebes and the presence of *ku-wa-no-ko-i* (glass-paste workers) documented by Linear B tablets found in the Citadel House at Mycenae (LH IIIB). Helladic faience contributed to the Late Bronze Age development of faience production in such eastern Mediterranean areas as Cyprus (*see* CYPRUS, §II, 5(ii)).

BIBLIOGRAPHY

C. Tsountas: 'Archaiotetes ek Mykenon' [Ancient finds from Mycenae], *Archaiol. Ephemeris*, iii (1887), pp. 155–72

R. C. Bosanquet: 'Some "Late Minoan" Vases Found in Greece', *J. Hell. Stud.*, xxiv (1904), pp. 342, no. 4908

K. Müller: 'Alt-Pylos II: Die Funde aus den Kuppelgräbern von Kakovatos', *Mitt. Dt. Archäol. Inst.: Athen. Abt.*, xxxiv (1909), pp. 269–328

W. A. Heurtley and C. A. R. Radford: 'The Prehistoric Sites in Chalchidice, I', *Pap. Brit. Sch. Athens*, xxix (1928), pp. 149–50

E. Porada and A. J. B. Wace: 'A Faience Cylinder', *Pap. Brit. Sch. Athens*, lii (1957), pp. 200–04

R. A. Higgins: *Greek and Roman Jewellery* (London, 1961, rev. 1980), p. 54

G. E. Mylonas: *Grave Circle B of Mycenae*, Stud. Medit. Archaeol., vii (Göteborg, 1964)

E. Vermeule: 'A Mycenaean Jeweller's Mould', *Bull. Mus. F.A. Boston*, lxv (1967), pp. 19–31

E. J. Peltenberg: 'The Glazed Vases', *Excavations at Kition I: The Tombs*, by V. Karageorghis (Nicosia, 1971), pp. 105–44

S. Symeonoglou: *Kadmeia I: Mycenaean Finds from Thebes, Greece: Excavations at 14 Oedipus St*, Stud. Medit. Archaeol., xxxv (Göteborg, 1973)

O. T. P. K. Dickinson: *The Origins of Mycenaean Civilisation*, Stud. Medit. Archaeol., xlix (Göteborg, 1977), p. 36

S. Hood: *The Arts in Prehistoric Greece*, Pelican Hist. A. (Harmondsworth, 1978), pp. 132–3

K. P. Foster: *Aegean Faience of the Bronze Age* (New Haven, 1979) [best general account; well illustrated]

M. S. Tite: 'Characterisation of Early Vitreous Materials', *Archaeometry*, xxix/1 (1987), pp. 21–34

D. EVELY

X. Seals.

On the Greek mainland seal use and production was spasmodic. Though their prime function seems to have been for printing patterns on cloth or hide, large Neolithic clay stamps with deeply incised geometric designs may also have been used as seals. The hatched quadrant

23. Clay sealing with spider motif, diam. 22 mm, from Lerna, EH II (Argos, Archaeological Museum)

common on seals throughout the eastern Mediterranean was already in evidence at this time and continued to be used in the Early Helladic (EH) period on clay and softstone stamp seals. A fine school of seal-carving flourished in the Argolid at Lerna in the Early Helladic (EH) II period. The actual seals (probably of wood) have not survived, but impressions of their circular faces on clay nodules used to seal storage jars and wooden chests (Argos, Archaeol. Mus.) bear witness to a sophisticated sense of design. Their compositions tend to be orientated around a central point, filling the entire field while respecting its circular confines. They exhibit a keen awareness of symmetry, even to the extent of introducing the occasional subtly balanced asymmetrical element. Designs are geometric, based on meanders, interlocking loops, trefoils, swastikas and spirals, the latter betraying Cycladic influence (*see* CYCLADIC, §III, 1); rare representational motifs, such as a spider or beaked jug, appear only as minor elements in a composition (see fig. 23). At Lerna and elsewhere seal impressions also occur on pottery: cylinders probably of wood were used by itinerant potters to decorate earthenware pithoi and hearths, producing continuous bands of geometric patterns based on zigzags, herringbones, wavy lines, spirals and concentric circles. Sometimes the field was divided vertically into panels, or disparate elements were juxtaposed but balanced so that repeat rolling created a unity of design.

The Lerna school had no direct successor: Middle Helladic (MH) communities seem to have had little use for glyptic art. Such seals as are securely dated to this period are few and poor, mostly clay or softstone stamps with simple linear patterns. However, the beginning of the Late Helladic (LH) period saw a new blossoming of glyptic art on the mainland under the influence of Crete. Minoan seals were imported, and hardstone seals and gold signet rings, which were inspired by Cretan models (*see* MINOAN, fig. 23) but suited to the mainland taste for more formal and monumental compositions, were made by both Minoan and Mycenaean craftsmen. So interrelated are the styles of the finest work that they are often grouped together as 'Minoan/Mycenaean', though Mycenaean seals tend to be more rigid and heraldic in concept, preferring stylized detail to naturalism and with increasing emphasis on the raw tool marks undisguised by secondary modelling. Subjects include cult scenes and symbols, scenes of combat and hunt, animals (particularly lions) and mythical beasts such as griffins.

Of mainland origin also are a series of mould-made glass lentoids with animal motifs and a cheap 'Popular' group. The latter evolved in LH IIIA following the decline in hardstone engraving and is characterized by lentoids of black steatite crudely gouged in a linear style with a limited repertory of ornamental motifs and quadrupeds—bulls, goats and deer—often so schematized as to be unidentifiable. Although existing seals continued to be used officially until the destruction of the palace at Pylos and were worn as jewellery or amulets and dedicated as votive offerings at shrines, seal manufacture in Greece ceased in the final phases of the Late Bronze Age and was not resumed until the Geometric period.

BIBLIOGRAPHY

A. Sakellariou: *Die minoischen und mykenischen Siegel des Nationalmuseums in Athen*, Corpus der minoischen und mykenischen Siegel, i (Berlin, 1964)

J. Boardman: *Greek Gems and Finger Rings* (London, 1970)

I. Pini and others: *Kleinere griechische Sammlungen*, Corpus der minoischen und mykenischen Siegel, v (Berlin, 1975)

S. Hood: *The Arts in Prehistoric Greece*, Pelican Hist. A. (Harmondsworth, 1978), pp. 209–32

J. G. Younger: *A Bibliography for Aegean Glyptic in the Bronze Age*, Corpus der minoischen und mykenischen Siegel, suppl. iv (Berlin, 1991)

MARGARET A. V. GILL

XI. Forgeries.

The group of suspect Helladic items is small and heterogeneous. This is partly because, unlike Cycladic stone figurines (*see* CYCLADIC, §IV, 2), the most admired Helladic pieces are in precious materials, especially gold, and partly because they are frequently highly individual, so that items that resemble them closely automatically attract suspicion. Since a too exact resemblance to a famous object or, conversely, peculiarities of style and subject-matter are the main criteria for suspecting forgery, judgement is largely subjective, and items can rarely be proved to have been forged. There is general agreement that the 'Thisbe Treasure' gems (Oxford, Ashmolean) are so unusual that they must be fakes, but it would be rash to use such grounds to reject items whose archaeological context seems secure, such as the larger Tiryns Treasure ring (Athens, N. Archaeol. Mus.), particularly in the absence of financial motives.

All pre-Mycenaean precious vessels are supposedly Early Helladic (see Davis, pp. 59–66), and all are problematic except for a gold sauceboat in the Louvre, whose acquisition in 1887, before the shape became familiar, guarantees its authenticity. Its virtual duplicate in Jerusalem (Israel Mus.) is more doubtful. Despite circumstantial

details given by Calligas (1984), the provenance, if not the genuineness, of the group of bowls supposedly from Euboia (Athens, Benaki Mus.; New York, Met.) must be questioned. Nothing similar has been found at the major Early Helladic Euboian site, Manika, and their parallels are Anatolian and Cycladic.

Of supposedly Mycenaean items, two gold goblets in Athens and Brussels (Athens, Benaki Mus.; Brussels, Musées Royaux A. & Hist.) are remarkably close in their decorative themes to the otherwise unique specimen 656 from Shaft Grave V at Mycenae (Athens, N. Archaeol. Mus.; see Laffineur, nos 114–15). Such similarities are almost unparalleled among figure-decorated vessels, and although the Benaki goblet was reputedly found with rings and jewellery that seem genuine, both it and the poorer quality Brussels goblet are hard to accept. The authenticity of the 'Ring of Nestor' (Oxford, Ashmolean), purchased by Evans (1925), has been defended, but Tomb A at Kakovatos, from which it supposedly came, had been heavily robbed, while its figure-crammed composition is not found on other rings, Minoan or Mycenaean, and its general style is too 'Minoan' for a mainland piece. Like the Thisbe gems, it was probably made in the early 1900s, when any distinction between the Minoan and Mycenaean civilizations was discounted. Other rings and seals with claimed mainland provenances have occasionally been doubted (e.g. one in Athens, Stathatos priv. col., see Younger, p. 243, n. 66), though far fewer than comparable Minoan pieces. Finally, at least two inlaid daggers that have appeared on the international art market (e.g. Tenri, Nara Prefect., Sankōkan Mus.) cannot be accepted unreservedly, though reproducing their technical features would be a considerable challenge to any forger.

BIBLIOGRAPHY

A. J. Evans: '"The Ring of Nestor": A Glimpse into the Minoan Afterworld', *J. Hell. Stud.*, xlv (1925), pp. 1–75

J. A. Sakellarakis: 'Über die Echtheit des sogenannten Nestorringes', *Pepragmena tou 3 diethnous Kretologikou Synedriou; Rethymnou, 1971* [Proceedings of 3rd International Cretan Conference: Rethymnon, 1971], i, pp. 301–18

E. N. Davis: *The Vapheio Cups and Aegean Gold and Silver Ware* (New York, 1977)

R. Laffineur: *Les Vases en métal précieux à l'époque mycénienne*, Stud. Medit. Archaeol. (Göteborg, 1977)

J. G. Younger: *Towards the Chronology of Aegean Glyptic in the Late Bronze Age* (Ann Arbor, 1978)

P. G. Calligas: 'Euboea and the Cyclades', *Cycladica: Studies in Memory of N. P. Goulandris*, ed. J. L. Fitton (London, 1984), pp. 88–98

T. J. Papadopoulos; 'A Mycenaean Inlaid Dagger from Messenia(?) in Japan', *Philia epe eis G. E. Mylonan* [Friendly messages for G. E. Mylonas], i (Athens, 1986), pp. 127–35

R. Hägg: 'Bemerkungen zum Nestorring', *Kolloquium zur ägäischen Vorgeschichte: Mannheim, 1986*, Schriften des deutschen Archäologen-Verbandes, ix, p. 57

O. T. P. K. DICKINSON

XII. Museums and collections.

The most comprehensive and extensive collections of Helladic archaeological material are found in Greece itself. The National Archaeological Museum in Athens contains, in addition to Early and Middle Helladic (EH to MH) pottery and other artefacts from Attica, Boiotia and Thessaly, the spectacular finds from the two shaft grave circles at Mycenae and a wide range of other Late Helladic (LH) objects, including gold-, bronze- and ivorywork, weaponry, jewellery, glyptic and pottery from tombs and settlements in the Argolid, Lakonia, Messenia, Attica, Boiotia and elsewhere, several of them excavated before the end of the last century. Also in Athens, the Agora Museum houses a great number of EH to LH finds from prehistoric excavations within the area of the Classical city. Examples of MH and LH pottery and terracottas can be found in the N. P. Goulandris Collection in the Goulandris Museum of Cycladic and Ancient Greek Art, while the Paul and Alexandra Canellopoulos Museum, which houses a collection presented to the state in the 1960s, includes some LH pottery, bronzes and terracotta figurines among its exhibits. Some fine examples of Helladic goldwork and pottery can also be seen among the collections displayed in the Benaki Museum. The Stathatos Collection also includes some Helladic material.

Elsewhere in Greece a large number of provincial or local archaeological museums contain material from sites in their vicinities. Particularly noteworthy are the museums at Patras (where material from various sites in Achaea is stored), Navplion (containing material from Mycenae, Tiryns, Dendra and Asine in the Argolid—though a new museum at Mycenae was built to house material from more recent excavations at that site), Corinth (material from Helladic sites in Corinthia) and Thebes (material from Thebes itself and surrounding sites, including a series of LH painted clay coffins from Tanagra (see TANAGRA, §1)). A small museum at Chora near Pylos in Messenia houses material (mainly pottery) from the Palace of Nestor at Ano Englianos, though the more spectacular finds from this LH site, including the inscribed clay tablets, are to be found in the National Archaeological Museum in Athens. Material from Lerna, perhaps the best-known EH and MH site in southern Greece, can be found in the museum at Argos. Museums at Sparta in Lakonia, Volos in southern Thessaly, Argostolian Kephallenia and new museums at Tripolis in Arcadia, Chalkis in Euboia, Chaironea in Boiotia and Olympia in Elis also display good collections of Helladic finds from their respective regions. Outside the Greek mainland, museums on a number of Cycladic islands, which became part of the Mycenaean cultural world during the Late Bronze Age, preserve LH material. Further east in the Dodecanese, the Rhodes Museum has a particularly large collection from excavations of the numerous LH cemeteries on the island. In addition, LH pottery exported from Greece to Cyprus during the 14th and 13th centuries BC and discovered in Cypriot tombs is well represented in public and private collections both in Cyprus and elsewhere (see CYPRUS, §II, 4(iii)).

In the rest of western Europe and in North America, Helladic material is preserved in many of the major museums and in various other public and private collections. While much of the material included in these is unfortunately of unknown or uncertain provenance, having been acquired through the art market, other objects derive from excavations carried out in the last century or in the earlier part of this century.

Two particularly impressive exhibitions consisting largely of Helladic material drawn mainly from Greek museums have been held in recent years: one, *Das mykenische Hellas, Heimat der Helden Homers,* was held in Berlin in 1988 to mark Berlin's year as European City of Culture. Later in the same year it was exhibited in Athens. This exhibition consisted of a wide range of the finest LH objects (well over 300 in all) from the National Archaeological Museum in Athens and many other Greek and Cypriot museums, as well as a few other objects of the same date from Troy and northern Europe. The second exhibition, *Troy, Mycenae, Tiryns, Orchomenos,* was held in Athens, then Berlin, between June 1990 and January 1991 to mark the centenary of the death of Heinrich Schliemann. It included EH, MH and LH objects and later material uncovered by Schliemann at the three important sites of Mycenae, Tiryns and Orchomenos, as well as material from his excavations at Troy—almost 400 exhibits in all.

BIBLIOGRAPHY

A. Sakellariou and G. A. Papathanasopoulos: *Prehistoric Collections,* National Archaeological Museum: A Brief Guide, vol. A, trans. by H. Wace, E. Wace-French and S. Sandford (Athens, 1964)

J. A. Sakellarakis: *The Mycenaean Collection of the National Archaeological Museum of Athens* (Athens, 1971)

M. Andronicos, M. Chatzidakis and V. Karageorghis: *The Greek Museums* (Athens, 1975)

The Mycenaean World: Five Centuries of Early Greek Culture, 1600–1100 BC (exh. cat., ed. K. Demakopoulou; Berlin, Freie U.; Athens, N. Archaeol. Mus.; 1988)

Troy, Mycenae, Tiryns, Orchomenos. Heinrich Schliemann: The 100th Anniversary of his Death (exh. cat., Athens, N. Archaeol. Mus.; Berlin, Altes Mus.; 1990–91)

SUSAN SHERRATT

Hellbrunn, Schloss. Castle in Salzburg, Austria. To the south of Salzburg, Archbishop Marcus Sitticus von Hohenems (*reg* 1612–19) commissioned SANTINO SOLARI to build a small castle to be used as a summer palace. Schloss Hellbrunn (1613–19) is a most perfect realization of the Italian villa suburbana and the earliest of its kind north of the Alps. Situated at the end of a long avenue, the building is a cube of classic simplicity, with a bifurcate staircase opening on to a *cour d'honneur*. The most remarkable interior features are the Festsaal (banqueting hall), set asymmetrically on the west side, and its projecting octagon, with frescoes by Arsenio Mascagni (1579–1636). Hellbrunn's main attraction, however, is its gardens. The Lustgarten or Pleasure Garden was laid out north of the castle and furnished with an unusual variety of grottoes, fountains, ponds and other features including the Roman Theatre, a miniature exedra dominated by a statue of *Roma*. Here, the famous Stone Table with seats, supplied with ingenious hydro-mechanism that still works, was erected to entertain the Archbishop's guests. A later addition (*c.* 1750) was the Mechanical Theatre by Lorenz Rosenegger and others, in which various scenes from court life were performed by automata. South of the castle the vast Ziergarten or Flower Garden was laid out; this was altered *c.* 1730 from an Italian to a French garden. Towards the end of the 18th century an English garden was added. On the slope of the hill at Hellbrunn the Stone Theatre (*c.* 1617), the first open-air theatre north of the Alps, was constructed. With its artificial stone stage, it blends perfectly into the natural surroundings of the castle.

BIBLIOGRAPHY

Reclams Kstführer

P. Buberl: 'Die Denkmale des Gerichtsbezirkes Salzburg', *Österreich. Ksttop.,* xi (1916), pp. 163–262

G. Stenzel: *Von Schloss zu Schloss in Österreich* (Vienna, 1974), pp. 138–9

G. Dehio: *Dehio-Handbuch: Die Kunstdenkmäler Österreichs* (Vienna, 1986), pp. 676–81

SUSANNE KRONBICHLER-SKACHA

Hellenraedt, Edmond [Emond] (*b* Düren, Westphalia; *fl c.* 1600–50). German architect, active in the Netherlands. He settled in Zutphen, where he was appointed city architect in 1620. His first known work is the tower of the municipal wine store (1618). The tower has a square brick shaft articulated by broad Tuscan pilasters, above which rises an octagonal feature with slender, free-standing Tuscan columns. The brick is alternated with sandstone for the pilasters and decorative bands. Construction was interrupted halfway through, resumed in 1637 and completed in 1641 (destr. 1920; rebuilt 1924). Although the composition is imperfect, the tower has a pleasing decorative quality. In 1639 Hellenraedt built the former cavalry guard-house (now a garage) in Zutphen, but very little of the original building survives. A notable feature is the high-rising central section, which has stone scrolls and is crowned with a broken pediment containing a ball pinnacle. The town hall at Lochem was also built to his design. In 1644 he was appointed municipal master mason of Zutphen. Hellenraedt's decision to work as an architect in the Netherlands is proof of the attraction exerted by the rich culture of the period, centred in Amsterdam. His style was undoubtedly influenced by the Amsterdam city architect Hendrik de Keyser I.

Thieme–Becker   BIBLIOGRAPHY
E. H. ter Kuile: *De Nederlandse monumenten van geschiednis en kunst* [Dutch monuments of history and art], ii (The Hague, 1958)

PAUL H. REM

Helleputte, Joris [Georges] (*b* Ghent, 31 Aug 1852; *d* Leuven, 22 Feb 1925). Belgian architect and politician. In 1873 he obtained his diploma in civil engineering at the Ecole Spéciale de Génie Civil of the State University of Ghent. In 1874 he was appointed assistant professor and from 1878 to 1907 was full professor at the Catholic University of Leuven (Ecoles Spéciales de Génie Civil, des Arts et des Manufactures et des Mines), where he developed a training programme in architectural engineering. While a student he met Louis Cloquet and was influenced by the Belgian Gothic Revival movement, which was founded by Jean-Baptiste Bethune, also the founder (in 1862) of the St Luke School, Ghent. Helleputte's architecture is similar to that of the first generation of St Luke architects in its almost undecorated and rather stern style. Its formal characteristics, modelled on the local Late Gothic style and traditional brick and limestone architecture, are strictly determined by constructional and functional needs. His most important works were built in Leuven for the Catholic University: the Anatomy Theatre (1877), the Philosophy Institute and Leo XIII Seminar (1893–4), and the Justus Lipsius College (1878–9). For this last building he brought together individual craftsmen who were then trained and organized along the lines of medieval guilds. Helleputte saw this as an experiment for the corporate reorganization of contemporary society. In his later work he abandoned strict Gothic Revival formulae by introducing new constructional techniques, such as the steel rib vaults of St Francis of Sales in Liège (1890–94,

destr. 1988). In the early 1890s Helleputte progressively devolved his activities as architect to his younger colleagues, having been elected a member of the Belgian Parliament for the Catholic Right in 1889; this launched a successful political career that he used to further his artistic and social ideals.

                    BIBLIOGRAPHY
BNB; *NBW*
R. Ernotte: *Les Aléas d'un idéal corporatif: Georges Helleputte et la Gilde des Métiers de Louvain, 1878–1914* (Leuven, 1963)

LUC VERPOEST

Hellerau. German town and suburb of Dresden. It was created by Karl Schmidt (1873–1948), a carpenter by profession and founder in 1898 of the Deutsche Werkstätten für Handwerkskunst GmbH Dresden und München, and it was built between 1909 and 1914 as the first German GARDEN CITY. Around 1890, while travelling as a working craftsman, Schmidt was inspired by the workshops of the Arts and Crafts Movement in Britain. In 1898, with the help of two assistants, he founded the Werkstätte, and by 1908 the firm employed over 500 workers. Through an unusual copyright, collaboration and compensation policy, Schmidt aimed to bring artists, workers and craftsmen together to learn from each other and to produce practical, yet aesthetically inspired, furniture and decorative arts. Between 1905 and 1907, influenced by the German translation (1907) of Ebenezer Howard's *Garden Cities of Tomorrow* (London, 1902), Schmidt developed his ideas for Hellerau. He needed a larger factory and saw an opportunity to provide sensible workers' housing and to demonstrate by practical example that all levels of German society would improve through higher quality in design and architecture. The formation of Hellerau was closely intertwined temporally and ideologically with the founding (1907) of the DEUTSCHER WERKBUND, an association that he actively supported.

Schmidt purchased 140 ha of woods and farmland just outside the city limits of Dresden in the area where the villages of Klotzsche and Rähnitz met. In 1906 more than 100 workers at the Werkstätte had filled out questionnaires and had submitted designs for homes that would strongly influence the designs that were realized. Schmidt's brother-in-law, architect and designer RICHARD RIEMERSCHMID, drew up the overall plans, and an architectural commission coordinated the designs. Streets followed the natural topography, and the area was divided into five zones: workers' houses, villas, a business and shopping area, a factory area and open land. Community organization was somewhat hierarchical, with small workers' houses near the factory and larger homes set on the crest of a hill, but equality in community was also emphasized. Gartenstadt Hellerau GmbH and Baugenossenschaft Hellerau GmbH were responsible for its administration. Riemerschmid designed the factory, market-place and numerous homes, and HERMANN MUTHESIUS, HEINRICH TESSENOW, THEODOR FISCHER, M. H. Baillie Scott, Karl Bertsch (1873–1933), BRUNO PAUL and Le Corbusier also contributed designs. In 1909 Hellerau had only 79 residents, but by 1912 the population had increased to 2000.

Around 1911 Wolf Dohrn (1878–1914), a leading member of the Deutscher Werkbund, became a virtual working partner of Schmidt's, resulting in a partial but significant change in the community's direction. Dohrn sought to develop the community's potential as an artistic utopia and brought Emile Jaques-Dalcroze (1865–1950) to Hellerau to establish a school of eurhythmic dance. Tensions mounted over conflicting goals, and several members of the commission, including Schmidt and Riemerschmid, protested against Tessenow's Neo-classical designs for Jaques-Dalcroze's school. Hellerau began to gain international attention as a literary and artistic centre and was called the 'Bayreuth of Dresden'. Christoph Willibald Gluck's *Orfeo* (1762) was performed there in 1912, and such literary figures as Peter de Mendelssohn, Jakob Hegner and Paul Claudel were residents. In 1914 Dohrn's death and the outbreak of World War I terminated the community's initial and most significant phase. From 1922 to 1934 further building took place, involving the construction of prefabricated log homes, or *Holzhäuser*. In 1945–6, the Werkstätte was finally dismantled, and in 1955 Hellerau was given a preservation order.

See also DEUTSCHE GARTENSTADTGESELLSCHAFT.

BIBLIOGRAPHY
W. Dohrn: *Die Gartenstadt Hellerau: Ein Bericht* (Jena, 1908)
H. Thiersch, ed.: *Wir fingen einfach an: Arbeiten und Aufsätze von Freunden und Schülern um Richard Riemerschmid* (Munich, 1953)
K. Hartmann: *Deutsche Gartenstadtbewegung: Kulturpolitik und Gesellschaftsreform* (Munich, 1976)
H. Wichmann: *Aufbruch zum neuen Wohnen: Deutsche Werkstätten und WK-Verband, 1898–1970* (Basle and Stuttgart, 1978)
K.-P. Arnold: 'Zur Geschichte der deutschen Werkstätten Hellerau, 1898–1930', *Jb. Staatl. Kstsamml. Dresden* (1978–9), pp. 41–70

LAURIE A. STEIN

Helleu, Paul-César(-François) (*b* Vannes, 17 Dec 1859; *d* Paris, 23 March 1927). French painter and printmaker. In 1870 he entered the Ecole des Beaux-Arts, Paris, where he studied under Jean-Léon Gérôme, a pupil of Ingres. He proudly described himself as 'the grandson of Ingres' and advocated that artists should 'always be classical'. He quickly formed a group of close friends including Sargent, Degas, Whistler, Alfred Stevens and Giovanni Boldini. As a student he was very poor and to earn a living spent 10 years decorating plates for the potter Joseph-Théodore Deck. In 1885 he visited London with Gérôme to paint a panorama (untraced). This was the start of a lifelong affection for England, where he returned almost every year.

Helleu established his reputation with the exhibition of several large pastels at the Salons of 1885 and 1886, including *Woman with a Fan* (exh. Salon 1886; Minneapolis, MN, Inst. A.); Blanche claimed that never before had an unknown artist received such a rapturous reception. Degas invited Helleu to contribute to the Impressionist exhibition of 1886, but he refused because of his dislike of Gauguin's work, a decision that later harmed his reputation. Helleu was a *plein-air* painter; his subjects and style are in the Impressionist mood, though his colours are cooler. In 1886 he married Alice Guérin, then aged 16, who became his favourite model (see fig.). Helleu's many sketches and drypoints of his wife and children are among his most charming works (see Helleu).

In 1887 Helleu met Comte Robert de Montesquiou, who bought several of the artist's works and commissioned a series of pastels of hydrangeas for his house at Versailles

Paul-César Helleu: *The Artist's Wife, Alice*, 720×530 mm, *c*. 1895 (London, Bury Street Gallery)

(untraced). He introduced Helleu into French society and became his greatest admirer and patron. Helleu painted several portraits of Montesquiou's cousin, Mme de Greffulhe (e.g. 1897; France, priv. col.), on whom Marcel Proust based the Duchesse de Guermantes in *A la recherche du temps perdu*, while the painter Elstir is principally based on Helleu himself. Montesquiou's book on Helleu remains the standard work on his oils, pastels and drypoints (a quarrel between them arose, however, over the book's design).

In 1886 James Tissot gave Helleu the diamond he used to draw drypoints on copper, for he regarded Helleu as his natural successor. Helleu proved to be a great master of this difficult medium. He exhibited 59 works in 1895 at the Robert Dunthorne Gallery, London, with a catalogue prefaced by Edmond de Goncourt. Princess Alexandra visited the show and commissioned a drypoint portrait of herself. Helleu soon became renowned for these drypoints of fashionable beauties, which he could produce in an hour and a half and for which he charged 1200 francs. Although sometimes unique, they could be produced in editions as large as 150 (examples in Paris, Bib. N.). His sitters were drawn from the aristocracy (e.g. *Duchess of Marlborough*, 1900), the demi-monde (e.g. *Liane de Pougy*, *c*. 1910) and from literary circles (e.g. *Anna de Noailles*, *c*. 1905). The precise draughtsmanship of his drypoints contrasts strongly with the flowing brushwork of his paintings; Helleu's work in both media, however, shows the influence of Japanese prints in his choice of compositional perspective.

The last exhibition of Helleu's oils, including seascapes, pictures of cathedrals and views of the park at Versailles, was held at the Salon du Champs de Mars, Paris, in 1897. He had just met Proust, whose admiration for *Autumn at Versailles* (*c.* 1897; Paris, Mus. d'Orsay) led to a lifelong friendship. Proust visited the artist on his yacht and in his elegant flat, which was entirely decorated in white, his favourite colour.

Helleu visited America in 1902, 1912 and 1920. He admired the beauty and chic of American women and portrayed many of them, including *Helena Rubinstein* (drypoint) and the Director of the Pierpont Morgan Library *Belle de Costa Greene* (drawing in coloured chalks, 1912; New York, Pierpont Morgan Lib.). He also painted the ceiling of Grand Central Station (1912; rest. 1990s) with the signs of the zodiac. Despite the encouragement of his artist friends, Helleu doubted the worth of his oil paintings, which, as Blanche observed, were 'carefully hidden from the public'. The popularity of his drypoint portraits of society beauties has prevented a general recognition of his considerable talents as a painter and pastellist.

WRITINGS

Nos bébés (Paris, *c.* 1912)

BIBLIOGRAPHY

R. de Montesquiou: *Paul Helleu: Peintre et graveur* (Paris, 1913)
J. E. Blanche: *Propos de peintre*, iii: *De Gauguin à la Revue nègre* (Paris, 1928), pp. 115–49
E. de Goncourt and J. de Goncourt: *Journal des Goncourts*, ix (Paris, 1895; Eng. trans., 1937)
P. Howard-Johnston: '"Bonjour M. Elstir"', *Gaz. B.-A.*, n. s. 6, lxix (1967), pp. 247–50
Exposition Paul Helleu (exh. cat., ed. A.-M. Bergeret-Gourbin and M.-L. Imhoff; Honfleur, Mus. Boudin, 1993)

JANE ABDY

Hellich, Josef Vojtěch (*b* Choltice, 17 April 1807; *d* Prague, 23 Jan 1880). Bohemian painter. He studied at the Prague Academy of Fine Arts between 1824 and 1836 under Josef Bergler and František Waldherr (1748–1835). He then travelled abroad, living in Germany, Italy, Paris and London until 1840, when he returned to Prague. Hellich represents the academic trend in Czech patriotic art. One of the leaders of the movement among Bohemia's artists for their rights in disputes with the Academy and other art institutions, he became president in 1848 of the shortlived but important Bohemian Association of Fine Artists opposing political and national oppression. Twenty years earlier, Hellich and Josef von Führich were two of the most prominent members in the circle of students that reacted against the eclectic classicism of the Prague Academy and sought a new religious and national art. One of the late expressions of this trend in Prague is the neo-Gothic reconstruction of the old *St Luke's Altar* (*c.* 1850; Prague, Týn Church) in which Hellich was the leading artist. He also played an important part in encouraging Czech art through his outstanding portraits, for example of the writer Božena Němcová (1845; Prague, Hradčany Castle) and of the historian *František Palacký* (1846; Prague, N. Mus.). Later in his career he concentrated on painting altarpieces. He excelled as a draughtsman—a discipline with its own tradition in Prague. Hellich helped to create a linear-plastic style of figural types that was considered a national one. Thus in the 1840s and 1850s he assisted in the stylistic development from František Tkadlík to Josef Mánes.

BIBLIOGRAPHY

Thieme–Becker
K. Sklenář: 'Archeologická činnost J. V. Hellicha v Národním Muzeu (1842–7)' [The archaeological work of J. V. Hellich in the National Museum (1842–7)], *Sborn. N. Muz. Praze*, section A, xxxiv (1980), pp. 109–235 [summary in Eng.]

ROMAN PRAHL

Hellmer, Edmund (von) (*b* Vienna, 12 or 17 Nov 1850; *d* Vienna, 9 March 1935). Austrian sculptor. After an initial interest in architecture he devoted himself to sculpture and assisted his uncle Josef Schönfeld. Since the Vienna Akademie offered only elementary instruction he joined the studio of Hans Gasser. On Gasser's death in 1868, Hellmer began to establish himself as an independent sculptor. His first works showed a touch of noble and academic Neo-classicism, but soon he was influenced by the increasing fashion for French neo-Baroque. The *Apollo* group of the Komische Oper, Vienna (1874; destr. in fire of 1881), was Parisian in type but with more elegance and an avoidance of overly dynamic effects. A tendency towards a synthesis of Neo-classical and neo-Baroque features is also to be found in other works by Hellmer, which were mainly created for buildings of the new Viennese Ringstrasse. Notable among these are the *Austria* for the Justizpalast (started in 1875) and several figures for the Rathaus (from 1877), the University (from *c.* 1877) and the Kunsthistorisches Museum (*c.* 1877–8). Also in 1877–8 Hellmer designed and executed the main pediment of the new Parlament: *Emperor Francis Joseph, Surrounded by the Crown Lands, Bestows the Constitution*, a commission that involved serious quarrels with the architect, Theophilus Hansen. Hellmer shared with many contemporaries the view that sculpture and architecture should play equally important parts in a fully developed *Gesamtkunstwerk*, whereas Hansen demanded the sculptor's absolute accommodation to architectural style.

In 1879 Hellmer was appointed professor at the Vienna Akademie. Amid increasing popular enthusiasm for the Baroque style he designed the *Monument to the Defeat of the Turks* for St Stephen's (1882–94; partly destr. 1945) in the form of a Baroque altar; but rather than compose an agitated whirl of form he characteristically allowed the individual groups to stand out within the work as a whole. Hellmer's work during the following years revealed more and more his preference for such Baroque traits as light-and-shadow modelling, open form and unorthodox compositions, and yet showed a continuing resistance to a wholesale adoption of Baroque style. His manner gradually moved towards an unbiased and dense realism although with rather economic use of details. His concentration on the human figure and the portrait benefited his work for monumental and tomb sculpture, but in the field of architectural sculpture there was a certain uneasiness, as in his group, *Austria's Power on Land* (1897; Vienna, Hofburg, Michaelertrakt). Though not highly mobile, Hellmer's figures excel in concentrated psychological persuasive power while notably avoiding merely anecdotal appeal. In this respect his work seems in many instances an obvious parallel to Secessionist portrait painting.

Hellmer created his best and most popular works towards the turn of the century, notably the monument to the painter *Emil Jacob Schindler* (1895; Vienna, Stadtpark) and the monument to *Goethe* (1890–1900; Vienna, Ringstrasse), the latter marking a significant triumph ´over Hellmer's lifelong enemy V. O. Tilgner and the historicizing neo-Baroque style. Also important were several imperial (for Emperor Francis Joseph) and public commissions, such as the monument to *Empress Elizabeth* (1901) for Salzburg, the Kastalia Fountain (1904, erected 1910) for the University's great courtyard and the statue of *Empress Maria-Theresa* (*c.* 1902; Vienna, Haus-, Hof- & Staatsarchv). More flowingly modelled is the monument to *Johann Strauss the younger* (begun 1906; Vienna, Stadtpark), which ingeniously reinterprets the motif of the triumphal arch in surrounding the bronze figure with a swirling stone circle of Danube maidens. Because of World War I the monument was unveiled only in 1921. Among Hellmer's numerous tomb sculptures are the memorials to *Nicolaus Dumba* (*c.* 1903) and the composer *Hugo Wolf* (1904; both Vienna, Cent. Cemetery); the latter comes close to the stylized figure painting of Gustav Klimt and Franz Matsch (1861–1942). Hellmer was also influenced by the sculptor Adolf von Hildebrand: Hellmer's text on sculpture, *Lehrjahre der Plastik* (1900), reflects some of Hildebrand's major principles; and several of Hellmer's portrait busts, for example that of *Jean de Bourgoing* (1907; Vienna, Belvedere), recall Hildebrand's approach. More striking, however, are Hellmer's portrait busts in a lively, almost impressionistic style, for example his bust of *E. J. Schindler* (*c.* 1890–92; Vienna, Hist. Mus.). Hellmer was knighted in 1912: by this time he was esteemed as an artist far beyond Vienna and renowned as a teacher to whom many younger artists, among them Anton Hanak, were indebted.

BIBLIOGRAPHY
Thieme–Becker
R. Feuchtmüller and W. Mrazek: *Kunst in Österreich, 1860–1918* (Vienna, 1964)
R. Wagner-Rieger, ed.: *Die Wiener Ringstrasse*, i: *Das Kunstwerk im Bild* (Vienna 1969); ix, 1, G. Kapner and others: *Ringstrassendenkmäler* (Wiesbaden, 1973); ix, 2, W. Krause: *Die Plastik der Ringstrasse, 1890–1918* (Wiesbaden, 1976); ix, 3, M. Potzl-Malikova: *Die Plastik der Wiener Ringstrasse von der Spätromantik bis zur Wende um 1900* (Wiesbaden, 1980)
W. Kitlitschka: *Grabkult und Grabskulptur in Wien und Niederösterreich* (St Pölten, 1987)
Edmund Hellmer, 1850–1935: Leben und Werk eines Wiener Bildhauers (exh. cat. by E. Hellmer, Vienna, 1990)

WALTER KRAUSE

Hellyar, Christine (*b* New Plymouth, 2 Oct 1947). New Zealand sculptor. She studied at the School of Fine Arts, Auckland (1966–9). During 1974 and 1979 she lived and worked in Britain. In 1982 she became a lecturer in sculpture at the School of Art, Auckland. Hellyar's sculpture makes extensive use of found objects and recycling. In her early works, many of which show the influence of Pop art and the women's movement, she used latex as a material and chose to avoid the solid, monumental qualities of bronze and stone. She also used stone tool forms and craft techniques, reflecting her interest in ethnography. Much of her work is presented in pieces arranged on trays, on the floor or in cupboards and boxes. Examples of her sculpture are *Country Clothesline* (1972; New Plymouth, NZ, Govett-Brewster A.G.) and *Tool Trays* (1982; Auckland, C.A.G.).

BIBLIOGRAPHY
P. Cape: *Please Touch: A Survey of the 3-dimensional Arts in New Zealand* (Auckland, 1980)
P. Pitts: *Christine Hellyar* (diss., U. Auckland, 1983)

MICHAEL DUNN

Helm, Willem (Leendertsz.) van der (*b* Leiden, ?1625; *d* Leiden, 1675). Dutch architect. From 1662 until his death he was town architect of Leiden, for which he designed a number of buildings. It is remarkable that he did not restrict himself to one particular architectural style throughout his career. In 1658 he designed the Wittevrouwen-Tor, an entrance gateway through the medieval fortifications of the town; for this he employed a Gothicizing style with pointed arches, while the crowning feature is crenellated. In 1663 he designed the Waardkerk (not completed; destr.), where the long sides of the nave each featured two apses, in the manner of the Nieuwe Kerk at The Hague (begun 1649) by Pieter Noorwittius and Bartholomeus van Bassen. In Helm's design for the Morschpoort (1669), the influence of Hendrik de Keyser I is evident, characterized by the use of a segmental open pediment and an octagonal domed tower. The alternation of stone and brick and the ball pinnacles on the corners of the gate create a picturesque effect. Helm also produced some designs in the Dutch classicist style prevailing at the time, in which he followed such leading architects as Pieter Post and Philips Vingboons. One example of this style is the court-house in Leiden (1671), which was not situated in the town hall but formed a part of the Gravensteen, the prison of the Dutch courts: here a high podium supports an order of Corinthian pilasters, and the central bays are surmounted by a pediment filled with sculpture. The court-house was built during the transitional period from the pilaster style to the severe style, the final phase of Dutch classicism. It is one of the last buildings in the Netherlands to display a complete order of pilasters.

BIBLIOGRAPHY
E. H. ter Kuile: *De monumenten van geschiedenis en kunst* [Monuments of history and art], vii (The Hague, 1944)
W. Kuyper: *Dutch Classicist Architecture* (Delft, 1980)

PAUL H. REM

Helman, Isidore-Stanislas-Henri (*b* Lille, 1743; *d* Paris, ?1806–9). French engraver and printseller. One of the first pupils at the free school of drawing in Lille, he studied under Louis-Jean Guéret (*fl* 1767–77) and Louis-Joseph Watteau. He completed his training in the Paris studio of Jacques-Philippe Lebas and is considered one of his best pupils. By 1777 his reputation as an engraver of genre scenes was well established. Among his most successful works are those he engraved after Jean-Michel Moreau for the second *Suite d'estampes pour servir à l'histoire des modes et du costume en France*, which illustrates the life of a fashionable young mother (e.g. *N'ayez pas peur, ma bonne amie*, 1776; Paris, Bib. N. cat. no. 29; *Les Délices de la maternité*, 1777; Bib. N. cat. no. 30; *L'Accord parfait*, 1777; Bib. N. cat. no. 31), and those for the third suite, on the theme of a man about town (e.g. *Le Souper fin*, 1781; Bib. N. cat. no. 53). (Both suites were republished with a text by Restif de La Bretonne in 1789 as the *Monument du* *costume*, a title often used for the first edition.) Helman also engraved genre subjects after Pierre-Antoine Baudouin, Jean Duplessis-Bertaux (1747–1819), Nicolas Lavreince, or Niclas Lafrensen (1737–1807), and Jean-Baptiste Le Prince.

Helman was not only a talented engraver but also an astute businessman. One of his profitable commercial ventures was the *Conquêtes de l'empereur de la Chine* (1783; Bib. N. cat. nos 54–77), a suite of folio reductions of drawings made by French missionaries, including Jean-Denis Attiret (1702–68), for Qianlong, emperor of China from 1736 to 1796. These were engraved under the direction of Charles-Nicolas Cochin (ii), but as the emperor had stipulated that all the proofs should be returned to China only a very few copies remained in France, in the hands of the royal family. Taking advantage of their rarity, and of the general interest in Chinese subjects, Helman produced his suite and was so encouraged by its success that he undertook two more Chinese suites, the *Abrégé historique des principaux traits de la vie de Confucius* (Bib. N. cat. nos 83–106) and the *Faits mémorables des empereurs de la Chine* (Bib. N. cat. nos 111–34).

Helman is best known, however, for his *Principales journées de la révolution* after Charles Monnet (1732–1808) (Bib. N. cat. nos 142–56). Published between 1790 and 1802, these represent in grisly detail the 15 most important days of the French Revolution, including the decapitation of Louis XVI. (For illustration of a further engraving after Monnet *see* PÀRIS, PIERRE-ADRIEN.)

Throughout his life Helman engraved book illustrations, contributing one or more plates to twenty different publications, including three for Jean-Benjamin de La Borde's *Tableaux . . . de la Suisse* (1780–86; Bib. N. cat. nos 38–40) and four after Jean-Baptiste Hilair for the Comte de Choiseul-Gouffier's *Voyage pittoresque de la Grèce* (1782; Bib. N. cat. nos 49–52). In 1775 he became engraver to Louis-Philippe-Joseph, Duc de Chartres, later Duc d'Orléans (Philippe-Égalité). In 1784 he became a member of the Académie des Arts, Lille.

BIBLIOGRAPHY

Inventaire du fonds français: Graveurs du XVIIIe siècle, Paris, Bib. N., Dépt. Est. cat., xi (Paris, 1970), pp. 267–302

L'Image de la révolution française (exh. cat., ed. C. Hould; Québec, Musée du Québec, 1989) [incl. reprs of seven of the *Principales journées de la révolution*]

M.-E. HELLYER

Helmarshausen, Roger of. *See* ROGER OF HELMARSHAUSEN.

Helmarshausen Abbey. Former Benedictine abbey in the Weser Valley *c.* 30 km north of Kassel, Germany. It was founded in 999, and the abbey church of St Peter (mostly destr.) was consecrated in 1011; additions to the church were made in the 12th century, when it was also dedicated to St Modoaldus. The goldsmith ROGER OF HELMARSHAUSEN was a monk at the abbey during the first half of the 12th century, and Helmarshausen was also a major centre of illuminated manuscript production throughout the 12th century. The earliest manuscripts, three Gospel books (*c.* 1100–20; Trier, Domschatz, Cods 137–9), have Evangelist portraits in an Ottonian manner deriving from Corvey manuscripts of the late 10th century and from the Echternach school of the 11th century. In MS. 139, the latest of the group, the influence of the work of Roger of Helmarshausen is evident in some head types and fold forms. A fourth Gospel book (*c.* 1130; Malibu, CA, Getty Mus., MS. Ludwig II.3) shows much greater influence from Roger's work and establishes the Helmarshausen style, which continued for 50 years. In this period the abbey made Gospel books and Psalters for other religious houses (e.g. Corvey, Lund) and at the order of secular patrons. Its most elaborate product, one of the most richly decorated of all 12th-century manuscripts, is the Gospel book (Wolfenbüttel, Herzog August Bib., Cod. Guelf. 105 Noviss. 2°; Munich, Bayer. Staatsbib., Clm. 30055; for illustrations *see* CHRYSOGRAPHY and WOLFENBÜTTEL) made by the scribe and painter Herimann for Henry the Lion, Duke of Saxony and Bavaria, as a gift to Brunswick Cathedral. In this book, perhaps as a result of Henry's close political links with England, influence from English 12th-century illumination is evident. The manuscript is dated to *c.* 1185–8 and contains 41 full-page miniatures of scenes of the *Life of Christ* and many elaborate ornamental pages and initials. The final work of the school, a Gospel book (Wolfenbüttel, Herzog August Bib., Cod. Guelf. 65 Helmst.), is dated 1194 and shows strong Byzantine influence from painting in the late Komnenian style. In monumental painting, work of the Helmarshausen style is found in the wall painting (1121–40) of Idensen church.

LM

BIBLIOGRAPHY

F. Jansen: *Die Helmarshausener Buchmalerei zur Zeit Heinrichs des Löwen* (Leipzig, 1933/*R* Bad Karlshafen, 1985)

A. Goldschmidt: 'A German Psalter of the Twelfth Century Written in Helmarshausen', *J. Walters A.G.*, i (1938), pp. 19–23

Kunst und Kultur in Weserraum, 800–1600 (exh. cat., ed. B. Korzus; Münster, Westfäl. Landesmus., 1966), nos 64, 178–95, 248–58, 449, 545

E. Krüger: *Die Schreib- und Malerwerkstatt der Abtei Helmarshausen bis in die Zeit Heinrichs des Löwen* (Darmstadt, 1972)

R. Haussherr: 'Zur Datierung des Helmarshausener Evangeliars Heinrichs des Löwen', *Z. Kstwiss.*, xxxiv (1980), pp. 3–15

E. Freise: 'Roger von Helmarshausen in seiner monastischen Umwelt', *Frühmittelalt. Stud.*, xv (1981), pp. 181–293

——: 'Roger von Helmarshausen', *Monastisches Westfalen* (exh. cat. by G. Jászai and H. L. K. Schulze, Münster, Westfäl. Landesmus., 1982), pp. 287–307

A. von Euw: 'Zur Problematik stilverwandter Phänomene: Vom Evangeliar Ludwig MS. II 3 in Malibu zum Evangeliar Herzog Heinrichs des Löwen (1139–1195)', *Jb. Berlin. Mus.*, xxix–xxx (1987–8), pp. 37–46

D. Kötzsche and others: *Das Evangeliar Heinrichs des Löwen* (Frankfurt am Main, 1988) [facs. and commentary]

F. J. Ronig: *Das Helmarshausener Evangeliar im Trierer Domschatz* (Paderborn, 1992)

NIGEL J. MORGAN

Helmbreker [Elembrech; Helmbreecker]**, Dirck** [Teodoro; Theodoor; Theodor] (*b* Haarlem, 1633; *d* Rome, early summer 1696). Dutch painter and draughtsman, active in Italy. He studied with the figure painter Pieter de Grebber in Haarlem in the late 1640s. He enrolled in the Guild of St Luke there in 1652, but the following year he left the Netherlands for Italy in the company of Cornelis Bega, Guillam Dubois (*c.* 1610–80) and Vincent Laurentsz. van der Vinne. He travelled by way of Venice and by 1654 was in Rome, where in 1659 he settled. Filippo Baldinucci wrote a comprehensive biography of Helmbreker in 1694, based on information from the cleric and collector Francesco Marucelli, who owned 21 works by Helmbreker.

Through Marucelli it is known that the Dutch painter was greatly esteemed in Italy and that the most famous collectors in Florence and Rome (Marucelli, Folco Rinuccini, Pierantonio Gerini (1650–1707), Cardinal Flavio Chigi, Count Angiolosa and the Colonna family) fought over his works, which were sold at that time for large sums of money.

Helmbreker is associated with the third generation of Dutch Italianates in Rome. He was one of the last exponents of the *bambocciate* (paintings of low-life subjects) made popular by Pieter van Laer and his circle. Most of his genre compositions, for example the *Distribution of Soup to the Poor* (London, priv. col., see Laureati, fig. 16.4) and *Banqueting Scene* (ex-art market, Rome, see Laureati, fig. 16.3) are in private collections. Such works as *The Charlatan* (Kassel, Schloss Wilhelmshöhe) feature numerous figures depicted in complex compositions with many different anecdotal scenes. His landscape backgrounds with ruins anticipate the idealized landscapes of such 18th-century artists as Andrea Locatelli, and his emphasis on light-hearted themes links his work more with the later tradition of the capriccio than with the intensely observed reality of the low-life scenes depicted by the Bamboccianti. Yet his success was due in part to being the only late 17th-century Dutch painter to continue the popular style and subject-matter of the Bamboccianti, even if in a slightly diluted form.

Helmbreker also painted many religious subjects for private individuals, religious confraternities and churches in Rome (e.g. the *Death of St Francis Xavier* for the oratory of the Caravita). His drawings are rare and consist mainly of portraits and studies of heads. A presumed *Self-portrait* (Washington, DC, N.G.A.), drawn in red chalk, shows a remarkable stylistic affinity with the chalk drawings of his native townsmen.

BIBLIOGRAPHY
F. Baldinucci: *Notizie* (1681–1728); ed. F. Ranalli (1845–7)
G. J. Hoogewerff: 'Theodor Helmbreker: Schilder van Haarlem', *Oud-Holland*, xxxi (1913), pp. 27–64
A. Busiri Vici: 'Dirk Helmbreker en zijn voorstellingen van Romeins volksleven' [Dirk Helmbreker and his representations of Roman popular life], *Oud-Holland* (1959), pp. 59–79
L. Salerno: *Pittori di paesaggio del seicento a Roma* (Rome, 1977–80), ii, pp. 866–871, iii, p. 1038
L. Laureati: 'Theodor Helmbreker', *I Bamboccianti: Pittori della vita quotidiana a Roma nel seicento*, by G. Briganti, L. Trezzani and L. Laureati (Rome, 1983; Eng. trans., Rome, 1983), pp. 341–9
——: 'Theodor Helmbreker', *I Bamboccianti: Niederländische Malerrebellen im Rom des Barock* (exh. cat., ed. D. A. Levine and E. Mai; Cologne, Wallraf-Richartz-Mus., 1991; Utrecht, Cent. Mus., 1992), pp. 178–9
LAURA LAUREATI

Helmer, Herman (*b* Harburg, 13 July 1849; *d* 2 Feb 1919). German architect. In 1873 he formed a highly successful partnership with FERDINAND FELLNER, with whom he designed many theatres in central and eastern Europe, as well as the observatory (1874–80) in Vienna. Their eclectic style, which drew in particular on Renaissance and Baroque styles, is exemplified by the Opera and Ballet Theatre (1884–7), Odessa, and the National Theatre (1906), Sofia; the latter building also contains Art Nouveau elements, which appear in the architects' later buildings. □

Helsby (Hazel), Alfredo (*b* 1862; *d* 1933). Chilean painter. He studied painting under Alfredo Valenzuela Puelma (1856–1909), *c.* 1885, and Juan Francisco González before travelling in 1907 on a government grant to Europe, where he exhibited at the Salon de la Société des Artistes Français in Paris and at the Royal Academy of Arts in London. While in Europe he became acquainted with contemporary artistic tendencies and also with the work of earlier artists, notably Turner, whose physical representation of light-filled, wet atmosphere he emulated. Helsby, who was attracted from an early age to landscape painting, superimposed the most delicate hallucinations on visions of reality; in paintings such as *Rainbow over the Canals of Chiloé* (Santiago, Mus. N. B.A.) he pulverized the plasticity of his forms with a puzzling technique that transformed them into a diaphanous surface of air, light and reflections. Such interests affected also his outdoor figure scenes, such as *Paseo Atkinson* (Valparaíso, Mus. Mun. B.A.), which were essentially naturalistic in approach.

One constant factor in Helsby's mature painting was his handling of the material properties of his paints. He used a palette knife to work on dense multi-coloured paint, creating suggestive textural effects. Through a skilful use of smudging and the density of his surfaces he represented plants and earth in harmony with translucent shadows and the vibrant transparency of distant elements and skies. His colour schemes often consist of a single dominant hue together with shades of the same colour. He also painted portraits, for example of *Juan Mochi* (see Galaz and Ivelič, p. 144). The artist signed himself either as Alfredo Helsby or Helsby Hazel; however, writers refer to him as Alfredo Helsby Hazel.

BIBLIOGRAPHY
G. Galaz and M. Ivelič: *La pintura en Chile desde la colonia hasta 1981* (Santiago, 1981), pp. 125–6, 128–9, 144–53, 179, 187
Alfredo Helsby (exh. cat. by F. de la Lastra, Santiago, 1983)
Alfredo Helsby (exh. cat. by C. Lastarria, Valparaíso, 1984)
CARLOS LASTARRIA HERMOSILLA

Helsingborg [Hälsingborg]. Town in north-west Skåne, Sweden (Denmark until 1658), at the entrance to Öresund, the narrow channel between Sweden and Denmark. It takes its name from the castle sited on the hill above the town, of which only the tower, known as the Core (Kärnan), survives. The town, first documented in 1085, quickly developed into a strategic and commercial centre and has remained an important seaport, although it declined after Malmö became the administrative centre of the region after the Swedish Conquest.

1. CASTLE. The foundations of a round tower (diam. *c.* 14 m), probably built in the 12th century, are marked by stones west of the Core. The tower was set within an oval (*c.* 180×150 m) surrounded by high encircling walls, which extended westward along the steep shore. There was a deep moat outside these walls, which were completed by at least the 13th century with projecting, semicircular flanking towers of the same type as at the Danish castles of Vordingborg and Nyborg on the Great Belt. In the west part stood a 12th-century round church in which the chapel of St Michael was incorporated.

The present tower, the Core (see fig.), one of the most interesting secular medieval buildings in Sweden, is close

Helsingborg Castle, view looking north, begun 1312

in character to western German tower forts, and dates from 1312. The tower, which was both defensive and residential, originally had a chemise probably half its height. Only the foundations survive. In front of the chemise was a stair-turret, and the castle well lay between the Core and the chemise wall. There were supplementary buildings within the castle area. The castle lost its military significance from the 16th century, and everything except the medieval tower was demolished c. 1680. The walls of the tower (c. 15 m square) are c. 4.5 m thick at the base, narrowing towards the top. They are clad in brick with an inner kernel of rubble, but sandstone ashlars are used on the interior. The present height of the tower is 34.5 m, with a stair-turret projecting another 4 m higher in the north corner. As the tower is situated 33 m above sea-level it commands a wide-ranging view over the Öresund and the surrounding country.

Defence was concentrated in the upper part, where the battlements may have had a projecting wooden balcony. The present upper parts, dating from the restoration of 1893–4, give no idea of the original appearance and function. In addition to the cellar, the tower originally had six floors. Each floor comprised a single square room; small side-rooms were built into the thickness of the walls on some floors. During the late Middle Ages the four upper floors were joined together to make two. The rooms are characterized by deep window embrasures with very narrow openings to the exterior. The floors are connected

by the spiral staircase in the turret, which is accessible only from the ground floor c. 6 m above ground level.

The ground floor, which was presumably the guard's or garrison room, has a stove and parlour, and the cellar is reached through a trap-door. The main entrance to the tower is on this floor, probably connected to the chemise by a wooden bridge. The second floor served as the kitchen, with an oven, hearth and drain. This floor also has a chamber linked to a projecting garderobe. Of the two floors making up what is now the third floor, the lower was the lord's living-quarters. These also appear to have been accessible from the chemise via the wooden stairs and bridge. There was a stove as well as a parlour and privy. The brick rib vaults with figured limestone consoles date from the late medieval conversion of the room to a chapel when a rectangular, rib-vaulted choir was carved out of the wall. The altar, which has now been hacked out, is marked by a pointed niche, with on one side a round window and traces of a piscina. The present fourth floor, presumably the arsenal and storeroom, was also covered with a late medieval brick rib-vault; the present barrel vault was erected in the 1650s. A photogrammetric survey by the Helsingborg Museum from 1987, together with a dendrochronological analysis of surviving wooden material, should give a more secure date for the tower's building phases.

BIBLIOGRAPHY

L.-G. Kindström: *Kärnan*, Helsingborgs Museum, Småskrift i (Helsingborg, n.d.)
T. Mårtensson: *Hälsingborgs slott under medeltiden* [Helsingborg Castle during the Middle Ages] (Hälsingborg, 1934)
A. Roussell: *Danmarks middelalderborge* [Denmark's medieval castles] (Copenhagen, 1942)
A. Tuulse: *Kärnan i Hälsingborg: Ett rekonstruktionsförsök* [The Core at Helsingborg: a reconstruction] (Stockholm, 1949) [Ger. summary]
——: *Borgar i Västerlandet: Ursprung och typutveckling under medeltiden* [Castles in Västerland: origins and stylistic development during the Middle Ages] (Stockholm, 1952)

MARIAN ULLÉN

Helsingør [Elsinore]. Danish town on the north-east tip of Zealand, at the narrowest point of the Öresund, opposite the Swedish town of Helsingborg.

1. HISTORY AND URBAN DEVELOPMENT. The history of Helsingør is traceable to the 13th century, but its significance stems from the decision by King Erik VII of Pomerania (*reg* 1412–39) to exact a toll from the foreign ships plying the Baltic trade. To enforce this demand he had a castle, Krogen, the future Kronborg (*see* §2 below), built on a spit north of the town, while the town itself received new privileges in 1426 that encouraged the construction of masonry buildings. He also founded monasteries for the Franciscan (1420), Dominican (1425) and Carmelite orders. New prosperity followed the construction of Kronborg (1574–85) by Frederick II, and by 1625 Helsingør was the country's largest market-town, with a cosmopolitan flavour derived from its many foreign merchants and craftsmen. After Denmark lost the Skåne provinces in 1660, Helsingør, now a border town, stagnated until after 1750, when trade increased again, although the reduction and later the abolition of the toll in the 19th century hit the town hard; more recently, it has established

a new economic base as a ferry terminus with border trade.

Old Helsingør, which retains the rectangular plan established under Erik of Pomerania, has more historic houses than any other Danish provincial town. Best represented is the 18th century, but fine medieval and Renaissance examples are preserved, and medieval cores lie behind more recent façades. Most important among the ecclesiastical buildings are two large brick churches, St Olai and St Marie. The first is an aisled basilica with remnants of the town's 13th-century parish church. Its present form reflects building from the end of the 15th century to the mid-16th. St Marie, an aisled hall with fine gable façades treated with tightly composed vertical recesses in varying shapes, constitutes the south wing of the Carmelite abbey, mainly built in the second half of the 15th century and now Denmark's best preserved conventual complex. The net vault in the chapter house is attributed to Adam van Düren. After the Reformation the abbey was converted to a hospital, and the church was used by the town's German-Netherlandish congregation. On the site of the Franciscan monastery Frederick II built, in 1587, an Italianate pleasure palace, Lundehave, which was rebuilt between 1759 and 1763 by the architect Nicolas-Henri Jardin and renamed Marienlyst.

BIBLIOGRAPHY

L. Pedersen, ed.: *Helsingør i sundtoldtiden, 1426–1857* [Elsinore in the time of the sound toll, 1426–1857], 2 vols (Copenhagen, 1926–9)
E. Moltke and E. Møller: *Frederiksborg amt* [Frederiksborg county] (1964), ii/1 of *Danmarks kirker* (Copenhagen, 1933–), pp. 37–561
P. Eller: 'Borgerne og billedkunsten på Christian den Fjerdes tid' [Townspeople and pictorial art in the time of Christian IV], *Fra Frederiksborg amt* (Hillerød, 1975), pp. 1–185 [local yearbook]
R. Egevang: *Old Elsinore* (Copenhagen, 1976)
J. Svanberg: 'Adam van Düren: A German Stonemason in Scandinavia in the Early Sixteenth Century', *Hafnia: Copenhagen Papers in the History of Art, 1976* (Copenhagen, 1977), pp. 125–39
H. H. Engqvist: 'Syv senmiddelalderlige gårde i Helsingør' [Seven late medieval houses in Elsinore], *Hikuin*, xiii (1987), pp. 155–202 [with Eng. summary]
J. Faye and H. Stephensen, eds: *Marienlyst slot* (Copenhagen, 1988)

2. KRONBORG CASTLE. In spite of later alterations the castle is essentially the creation of Frederick II and the outstanding symbol of his royal power. The original Krogen or 'Ørekrog' was laid out in the 1420s by Erik of Pomerania. A high curtain wall with wall-walks and a gatehouse enclosed three stone buildings: the royal residence at the north-east, the palace and ceremonial hall at the south-west and, to the south-east, a building that probably contained the chapel. By the mid-16th century the fortifications were obsolete, and new plans were ordered, in 1558–9, from Hans von Diskow (*d* 1563) but only partially realized. From 1574 Frederick started afresh and rebuilt Krogen, adding projecting bastions and curtain walls, under the direction of Hans van Paeschen. The name was changed to 'Kronborg' in 1577, the year that Antonis van Obberghen replaced van Paeschen. By 1585 the castle had become a magnificent royal residence and one of the strongest fortresses in northern Europe: a symbol of Danish royal power, erected with funds from foreign merchant ships.

Kronborg was repaired by Christian IV after fire damage in 1629 and sacked and occupied by the Swedes in 1658–60. It was strengthened on the land side with the so-called

'Kronværk' (1688–90), designed by Jobst Scholten and Domenico Pelli. In the 18th century the fortress was extended and the castle restored, serving as a garrison from 1785 to 1924; the palace chapel was restored from 1838 to 1843. Other restorations were carried out from 1866 to 1897 and from 1925 to 1937. In 1915 the Trade and Shipping Museum was installed in the north wing.

The plan of Kronborg was determined by its predecessor, which it effectively encapsulated, its outer surround corresponding to the medieval curtain. Frederick II's rebuilding began with the great cannon tower over the southern part of the palace, while the old royal residence was extended to the west for the castellan's apartments and the administrative offices. The castle chapel was installed in the south wing. By 1579 a third storey had been added to the south wing to accommodate the great ceremonial hall, and the octagonal stair-tower heightened and equipped with a balcony for trumpeters ('Trumpeters' Tower'). The other wings were then raised to match. The fourth wing to the east, facing the Öresund, was built as a narrow, three-storey connecting corridor, with closed galleries in the upper two storeys, leading directly from the queen's apartments to the chapel and the ballroom. The castle was originally built with red brick walls and sandstone details; from 1580, beginning with the south wing, it was faced in sandstone. The roof tiles were replaced with copper.

The finished building (see fig.) was a four-wing complex, crowned by the wall-walks between the towers with their pointed spires. Its medieval core is apparent in the uneven depth of the wings and the irregularity of the window axes. Renaissance ideas are confined to the architectural details, of which the finest are the rusticated ground floor on the courtyard side of the east wing and the classically composed display gable façade of the south wing with the corner tower 'Kakkelborg'. In addition to the architectural ornament, these parts display figural sculptures (Classical gods, Old Testament kings and Christian Virtues) celebrating the might of the king. The king's status as the ruler of the seas provided the theme of the bronze Neptune fountain, supplied by Georg Labenwolf (*see* LABENWOLF, (2)) in 1583 (remains in Stockholm, Nmus.).

The only major room to survive is the palace chapel (consecrated 1582), an aisled hall whose vault is supported by Tuscan columns with pronounced entasis. The ballroom above lost its carved wooden ceiling, wall paintings and two alabaster and marble fireplaces in the fire of 1629, but it has been reconstructed in all its imposing dimensions. The tapestry workshop (*see* DENMARK, §XI, 1), established at Kronborg by Frederick II in 1577, produced a series of 43 tapestries, of which 15 are preserved at Kronborg and at the Nationalmuseum in Copenhagen; they show Danish kings from the mythical Dan to Frederick II, who ordered them in 1581 from HANS KNIEPER, together with a magnificent canopy (Stockholm, Nmus.).

Christian IV's rebuilding of 1631–7 under Hans van Steenwinckel (ii) (*see* STEENWINCKEL, VAN, (3)) included alterations to the spires and dormers, and in the royal apartments new doorframes, fireplaces and ceiling paintings by Hans's brother Morten Steenwinckel (1595–1646) as well as ceiling paintings (1635) by Gerrit van Honthorst.

Helsingør, Kronborg Castle, east front of the Renaissance castle, rebuilt 1574–85

For the ballroom, the largest project, the King (in 1639) ordered ceiling paintings to supplement Knieper's tapestries, showing heroic episodes from Denmark's history, from the 'best Netherlandish artists' (among them Honthorst, Abraham Bloemaert, Claes Cornelisz. Moeyaert and Adriaen van Nieulandt). The 84 preparatory drawings (planned 1637), from which it was also intended to make engravings, are partly preserved (Copenhagen, Stat. Mus. Kst), but only 15 of the paintings, which hung at Kronborg from the early 1640s until their removal by the Swedes (1658–60), are known: two at Kronborg, one at Frederiksborg (Hillerød, Frederiksborg Slot) and twelve in Sweden (four at Skoklosters Slott, four at Vittskövle Slott, one each at Maltesholm Slott, Drottningholm Slott and Östra Ryd church, and one in a private collection).

Kronborg is a masterpiece of the Netherlandish Renaissance, designed by Netherlandish architects and including Netherlandish decorative influences. During the 1570s and 1580s it provided work for numerous Netherlanders, especially after the fall of Antwerp in 1576. Kronborg was thus the main port of entry for Netherlandish influence on Renaissance architecture and painting in Denmark. Through the illustrations in Braun and Hogenberg's *Civitatis orbis terrarum* (Cologne, 1574) the castle became known throughout Europe, as may be seen in William Shakespeare's setting of *Hamlet* there.

BIBLIOGRAPHY

F. Beckett: 'Hans von Dieskau og Danmark', *Aab. Nord. Oldknd. & Hist.* (1930), pp. 65–82
M. Mackeprang: 'En skjoldefrise fra Erik af Pommerns tid paa Krogen Slot' [An escutcheon frieze at Krogen Castle from the time of Erik of Pomerania], *Fra Nmus. Arbejdsmk.* (1932), pp. 78–80
F. Beckett: *Kristian IV og malerkunsten* [Christian IV and the art of painting] (Copenhagen, 1937)
V. Wanscher: *Kronborgs historie* (Copenhagen, 1939)
C. Christensen: *Kronborg: Frederik II.s Renæssanceslot og dets senere skæbne* [Frederick II's Renaissance castle and its later fortunes] (Copenhagen, 1950) [with Eng. summary]
M. Mackeprang and S. F. Christensen: *Kronborgtapeterne* [The Kronborg tapestries] (Copenhagen, 1950) [with Fr. summary]
O. Norn: *Kronborgs bastioner* (Copenhagen, 1954)
E. Moltke and E. Møller: *Frederiksborg amt* [Frederiksborg county] (1964), ii/1 of *Danmarks kirker* (Copenhagen, 1933–), pp. 562–636
E. Gasiorowski: 'Antonius van Obbergen', *Hafnia: Copenhagen Papers in the History of Art, 1976* (Copenhagen, 1977), pp. 71–90
H. Langberg: *Kronborg Castle* (Copenhagen, 1979)
H. H. de Lichtenberg: 'Some Netherlandish Artists Employed by Frederik II', *Hafnia*, viii (1981), pp. 51–71
H. Langberg: *Dansesalen på Kronborg* [The ballroom at Kronborg] (Copenhagen, 1985) [appendix]
——: 'The Castle of Elsinore, Castel S Angelo in Rome and St Birgitta of Sweden', *Saggi in onore di Guglielmo De Angelis d'Ossat* (Rome, 1987), pp. 129–34
H. D. Schepelern and U. Houkjær: *The Kronborg Series: King Christian IV and his Pictures of Early Danish History* (Copenhagen, 1988)
O. Kongsted: *Kronborg-Brunnen und Kronborg-Motetten* (Copenhagen, Flensburg and Kiel, 1991)
H. Langberg: *Kronborgs Kronværk: Glimt af en europæisk fæstnings historie* [The Kronværk of Kronborg: a glimpse of the history of a European fortress] (Copenhagen, 1991)
H. H. de Lichtenberg: *Johan Gregor van der Schardt: Bildhauer bei Kaiser Maximilian II, am dänischen Hof und bei Tycho Brahe* (Copenhagen, 1991)

HUGO JOHANNSEN

Helsinki [Swed. Helsingfors]. Capital of Finland since 1812, in the district of Uusimaa on a peninsula of the north shore of the Gulf of Finland, an arm of the Baltic Sea. The largest city in the country, it is the principal financial, educational and cultural centre, with a population of *c.* 500,000.

1. HISTORY AND URBAN DEVELOPMENT. The town was commissioned in 1550 by the Swedish King Gustav I (*reg* 1523–60) to compete with the Hanseatic towns for trade with Russia. It was to be built on the estuary of the River Vantaa and to be populated from other towns in the area. The initial efforts were unsuccessful, as the coastal waters were too shallow for shipping, and in 1640 the development was relocated at Vironniemi (now Kruunuhaka). Largely owing to the rocky nature of the topography, for many years the original project remained nothing more than a small, arbitrarily developed town. Helsinki revived when SUOMENLINNA FORTRESS was built at the harbour entrance from 1748, but the town was taken over by the Russians with the rest of Finland in 1808; and in the same year it was destroyed by fire.

In 1812, when Tsar Alexander I (*reg* 1801–25) guaranteed the autonomy of Finland, he declared that Helsinki should replace Turku (Swed. Åbo) as the capital city. A new city plan, prepared to the instructions of the statesman Johan Albrecht Ehrenström (1762–1847), was approved in 1817. The concept of a Neo-classical city was typical of the period, and its successful implementation was largely due to one architect, the German CARL LUDWIG ENGEL. Having studied Russian Neo-classicism in St Petersburg, Engel introduced the style to Helsinki. His proposals consisted mainly of three-storey buildings in the central area with large single-storey timber houses in large gardens in the peripheral districts. The heart of the plan was dominated by the Lutheran cathedral (see fig. 1), which still stands higher than most other buildings in the city. Engel was also responsible for many other monumental buildings, including two other existing churches (both 1826 and both temporary: one, the Old Church, was for Lutherans; the other, the Holy Trinity, was for the Russian Orthodox faithful), three hospitals, the University (*see* ENGEL, CARL LUDWIG, fig. 2), several barracks and houses. Today, the original Neo-classical city has completely disappeared, together with all the elegant wooden houses in the Empire style. When Engel died in 1840, the population had reached 18,000. An inactive period followed his death. Railways were built in the 1860s, opening up the hinterland, and there was the inevitable growth of industrialization. In 1868 the Uspenski Cathedral, by Aleksander Gornostajev, was built to satisfy the growing demands of an increasing population of Orthodox believers. Many new five-storey buildings were constructed, replacing the old wooden houses. Frans Anatolius Sjöström (1840–85) and Theodor Höijer were responsible for many of the buildings in the central area, and Höijer's best work, the Hotel Kämp (1887; now extended), and the adjoining Grönqvist House (1883), survive in Pohjois-Esplanadi. GUSTAF NYSTRÖM also contributed to this distinctive Neo-classical period (e.g. Union Bank of Finland, 1896–8).

Towards the end of the 19th century, the emerging interest in Finland's national heritage gave rise to the NATIONAL ROMANTICISM movement, manifested in architecture by the utilization of such natural building materials as wood and granite. GESELLIUS, LINDGREN &

1. Helsinki, Lutheran cathedral, by Carl Ludwig Engel, 1830–40; lithograph by F. Tengström from *Vuer af Helsingfors*, 1837–8 (Helsinki, National Museum of Finland)

SAARINEN designed the the National Museum of Finland (1902–11) and the offices of the Pohjola Insurance Company (1899–1901). Lars Sonck designed offices for the Telephone Company (1905), and Valter Thomé and Karl Lindahl built the Poli (the former Student Club House for the Institute of Technology) in 1903. National Romanticism soon gave way to the more dominant Art Nouveau influences from central Europe as a reaction to imitative solutions to contemporary architectural and planning problems. Important architects at this time were Selim Lindqvist, Sigurd Frosterus and Eliel Saarinen, the latter designing the Helsinki Railway Station (1904–14; for illustration *see* SAARINEN, (1)). There were also new attitudes to urban planning, central to which was the concept of considering towns as works of art and not as mundane exercises in the manipulation of land development, transportation and public services. By 1914 the population had reached 320,000. In 1915 Saarinen produced a great master-plan for the Munkkiniemi/Haaga district, which was never realized. In 1918 he also prepared a general plan for Greater Helsinki, which anticipated the decentralization of the late 20th century.

In the 1920s Pauli Blomstedt's writings on functionalism convinced many Finnish architects of the need to be in harmony with the new era that had emerged after World War I and the gaining of independence from Russia in 1917. Romanticism briefly reappeared, manifest in the form of a historicist Italianate style, the principal example of which is the granite Parliament Building (1927–31) by J. S. SIRÉN. A more comprehensive general city plan was essential following the war. The small garden-city neighbourhood developments proposed in the Saarinen plan of 1918 were never realized, but from 1920 to 1925 the workers' housing suburb Puu-Käpylä was built by MARTTI VÄLIKANGAS, using traditional timber construction in a typical garden-city context, reflecting modern trends. The post-war planning proposals for Greater Helsinki followed the principles established by Saarinen's plan, yet there was much piecemeal planning, and little attention was given to public transport. An outstanding exception is Tapiola Garden City, built to a master plan by Aarne Ervi (1954),

2. Helsinki Municipal Theatre, by Timo Penttilä, 1967

the result of a competition sponsored by a housing foundation and with contributions from such architects as Ervi, Viljo Revell, Aulis Blomstedt, Heikki & Kaija Sirén, Reima Pietilä and many others. It aimed to achieve a high standard of architectural quality and to include a variety of services with segregated traffic systems. Adjoining Tapiola is Otaniemi, an even more successfully cohesive cultural centre, with buildings by ALVAR AALTO, Heikki & Kaija Sirén and Reima Pietilä.

In the 1960s prefabrication was used for the first time on a massive scale, as at Pihlajamäki, a small district of Helsinki. Such technology enabled construction to be more independent of the harsh winter climate, fostering greater accuracy and improved development economics. There were few sites remaining for development in the city centre; consequently, taxpayers migrated to surrounding municipalities, generating extreme land exploitation. This trend, together with the growth of prefabricated systems and a minimal contribution from architects, led to many unsatisfactory results. With the increase in road traffic, many parks and open public spaces became choked with vehicles. Small shops and cafés in the city were forced to close due to the competition from vast suburban supermarkets, and many older blocks of flats were converted for commercial use. The unchecked 'destructive renewal' of the old city eventually became a matter of public concern, when the block opposite Saarinen's railway station was redeveloped in a very unsympathetic manner.

In the early 1970s Aalto prepared a plan for the Töölönlahti area of Helsinki that included the compact continuous development of Hesperia Park. The City Council called for modifications, which led to a looser plan incorporating Aalto's Finlandiatalo (1967–75), as well as Timo Penttilä's Municipal Theatre (1967; see fig. 2). The first stages in the development of Vantaa and Espoo, the two new cities adjoining Helsinki, also took place in the 1970s. Together with Helsinki they constitute a large metropolitan region consisting of the three administrative city centres. Of the many schemes completed in the 1970s, two of the more successful, Olari and Kivenlahti, can be found at Espoo. Elsewhere, the construction of dreary developments provoked lively discussion about quality and techniques. In the 1980s a new residential development was successfully completed in a former dockside

area in the Katajanokka district of Helsinki, and to the east, at Itäkeskus, a new local centre was built to high standards of functionalism and aesthetic balance. The city's first underground railway was also begun in the 1980s. More attention was paid than in the 1970s to the preservation of the townscape, with many public buildings undergoing extensive repair and refurbishment.

BIBLIOGRAPHY
N. E. Wikberg: *Finnish Architecture* (Helsinki, 1959)
O. Meurman: *Helsinki Architectural Guide* (Helsinki, 1963)
J. M. Richards: *A Guide to Finnish Architecture* (London, 1966)
S. Saarikivi, K. Niilonen and H. Ekelund: *Art in Finland/Les Beaux-arts finlandais/Die bildende Kunst in Finnland* (Helsinki, 1967) [trilingual text]
J. B. Smith: *The Golden Age of Finnish Art: Art Nouveau and the National Spirit* (London, 1970)
K. Fleig, ed.: *Alvar Aalto: Das Gesamtwerk/L'Oeuvre complète/The Complete Work*, 3 vols (Zurich, 1970–78) [trilingual text]
H. von Hertzen and P. D. Spreiregen: *Building a New Town: Finland's New Garden City Tapiola* (Cambridge, MA, and London, 1971)
E. E. Suolahti: *Helsinki: A City in a Classic Style* (Helsinki, 1973)
N. E.Wikberg: *Carl Ludwig Engel: Builder of Helsinki* (Helsinki, 1973)
G. Nicol: *Finland* (London and Sydney, 1975), pp. 187–98
Helsinki/Helsingfors: Arkkitehtuuriopas/Arkitektur Guide/Architectural Guide, Museum of Finnish Architecture [Suomen Rakennustaiteen Museo] (Helsinki, 1976) [trilingual text]
A. Ilonen: *Helsinki: An Architectural Guide* (Helsinki,1990)

COLIN-JOHN COLLINS

2. ART LIFE AND ORGANIZATION. Helsinki is the most important centre for the visual arts in Finland. The first public collections were opened in the 19th century. Those of the Atheneum Art Museum (Ateneumin Taidemuseo) originated in the collections of the Finnish Art Association (Suomen Taideyhdistys), founded in 1846 at the time of the national awakening. In 1887 a new building (see fig. 3) was constructed to house the collections. It also contained an art school and a crafts school run by the Finnish Society for Applied Arts (Suomen Taideteollisuusyhdistys). The collection and the art school were subsequently handed over to the Fine Arts Academy of Finland (Suomen Taideakatemia), founded in 1940. The collection was then donated to the Finnish National Gallery (Valtion Taidemuseo), founded in 1990. The art school of the Academy of Fine Art (Suomen Taideakatemian Koulu) became the government-funded Academy of the Visual Arts (Kuvataideakatemia).

Other art museums in Helsinki include the City Art Museum (Helsingin Kaupungin Taidemuseo), founded in 1911; the Amos Anderson Museum of Art (Amos Anderson Taidemuseo) opened in 1965; Juhani Kirpilä's House; the Didrichsen Art Museum (Didrichsenin Taidemuseo), founded in 1965; the Lauri and Lasse Rietz Collection, founded in 1971; and the Villa Gyllenberg, opened in 1980. These last four are administered by private foundations. The City Art Museum also has a separate subsidized space in the city centre, the Kluuvi Gallery, where it exhibits mainly avant-garde art and the work of emerging artists.

The Helsinki Art Exhibition Hall (Helsingin Taidehalli), founded in 1928, is run by an artists' association and receives considerable public funding. Although originally a stronghold of modernist and radical thought, its programme now consists of annual exhibitions, young artists' exhibitions and displays of the work of various artists' societies. It also hosts the annual 'Artist of the Year' show

3. Helsinki, Athenaeum Art Museum, by Theodor Hoijer, 1887

for the Helsinki Festival, as well as numerous international shows. The acquisition schemes for public art in Helsinki are centred on the City Art Museum, which owns all public works of art, however acquired, and is responsible for their upkeep. The Museum directs the expenditure of the funds for public art: large-scale works are usually commissioned by competition or invitation. Thus, the Museum publicizes the work of professional artists.

In Finland artists' organizations have had great significance in shaping the field of art, and the central ones are based in Helsinki. The original purpose of the Finnish Society of Artists, founded in 1864, was to defend the rights of artists working in all media, but as the sculptors, graphic artists and painters now have their own societies it acts as an umbrella organization. The interaction of artists' associations with the central government and local authorities is typical of Finland. Since the 1960s, when the current system of arts administration was created, these artists' associations have had a particularly strong role. The artists' associations also run galleries that function as private spaces but benefit from public funding channelled through them. There are also about 30 or 40 private galleries in Helsinki, of which approximately 10 can be said to be of international standard, for example Galeri Hörhammer, Artegrafica and Galeri Hagelstam.

BIBLIOGRAPHY
Catalogue of the Art Gallery in the Ateneum (Helsinki, 1937)
Guide to the National Museum [Suomen Kansallismuseo] (Helsinki, 1952)
Suomen Taideakatemian pieni taidesarja (Helsinki, 1960)
S. Sarajas-Korte and A. Lindström: Ateneum taidetta (Helsinki, 1971)
A. O. Arponen, ed.: Museot/Museer/Museums: Helsinki, Espoo, Vantaa (Helsinki, 1979) [trilingual text]
MARJA-LIISA BELL

Helst, Bartholomeus van der (*b* Haarlem, *c.* 1613; *d* Amsterdam, *bur* 16 Dec 1670). Dutch painter. He was the son of a Haarlem inn-keeper and presumably undertook part or all of his training in Amsterdam. His earliest works suggest that the painter Nicolaes Eliasz. Pickenoy was his master. Although van der Helst had probably already established himself as an independent master by the time he married Anna du Pire in Amsterdam in 1636, his earliest known work, a portrait of *The Regents of the Walloon Orphanage, Amsterdam* (Amsterdam, Maison Descartes), dates from 1637. Stylistically it is close to the work of

Pickenoy. His portrait of a *Protestant Minister* of 1638 (Rotterdam, Boymans–van Beuningen) reveals the influence of Rembrandt. The young artist must have risen rapidly to fame in Amsterdam, for as early as 1639 he received the prestigious commission for a large painting for the Kloveniersdoelen (Arquebusiers' or Musketeers' Hall): *The Civic Guard Company of Capt. Roelof Bicker and Lt Jan Michielsz. Blaeuw* (Amsterdam, Rijksmus.), which formed part of the same series as Rembrandt's '*Night Watch*' (Amsterdam, Rijksmus.). Van der Helst may not have completed this commission until 1642 or 1643. The ingenious arrangement of the figures in a broad composition shows the artist's special talent for composing large groups. Pickenoy's influence is less noticeable here than in the portrait of 1637; the self-assured poses of the individual figures were to become a characteristic feature of van der Helst's work. The successful execution of this portrait established van der Helst's reputation: from 1642, when he began to receive an increasing number of commissions for individual portraits, until 1670 he was the leading portrait painter of the ruling class in Amsterdam. From 1642 his technique in portrait painting gradually became more fluent and the rendering of costume materials more detailed. Some typical portraits of his earlier period are those of *Andries Bicker* (Amsterdam, Rijksmus.), his wife *Catharina Gansneb Tengnagel* (Dresden, Gemäldegal. Alte Meister) and their son *Gerard Bicker* (Amsterdam, Rijksmus.), all of 1642, and the *Portrait of a Young Girl* (1645; London, N.G.). In 1648 van der Helst painted a second civic guard portrait, *The Celebration of the Peace of Münster at the Crossbowmen's Headquarters, Amsterdam* (Amsterdam, Rijksmus.), a superbly composed and well painted portrait that, until the late 19th century, was considered one of the masterpieces of the Golden Age but later lost popularity because of its smooth and modish execution. It can nevertheless still be regarded as one of the most important group portraits of the 17th century. Its technical perfection, characterized by a well-modelled rendering of the figures and a smooth handling of the brush, dominated the rest of van der Helst's oeuvre.

Van der Helst's considerable reputation led to commissions from prominent people outside Amsterdam, a rare phenomenon in the history of 17th-century Dutch portraiture. In 1652 he was even commissioned—it is not known by whom—to paint the official portrait of *Mary Henrietta Stuart* (Amsterdam, Rijksmus.), widow of William II of Orange Nassau. This was a rare case of the court commissioning a portrait from an artist who worked primarily for the ruling class in Amsterdam—a class ill-disposed towards the court.

In 1650 van der Helst painted the portrait of *Two Governors and Two Governesses of the Spinning House* (a house of correction for women) (Amsterdam, Hist. Mus.), and between 1653 and 1656 he produced three more group portraits of high-ranking officers of Amsterdam's civic guard (Amsterdam, Hist. Mus. and Rijksmus.), the last contributions to an impressive series of Amsterdam militia pieces completed in 1656. All four group portraits are outstandingly well composed and technically well-executed representations of important sitters, in which the liveliness of the composition is enhanced by the addition of a few genre-like details. Among van der Helst's best works is the double portrait of *Abraham del Court and his Wife, Maria Keerssegieter* (1654; Rotterdam, Boymans–van Beuningen; see fig.), in which the artist casually included a number of emblematic motifs and achieved an unrivalled rendering of surface textures (e.g. satin).

Van der Helst's individual portraits, of which there are over a hundred, many of them pendants, can be seen in many museums both in Europe and the USA; they consist of shoulder-length portraits, half-length figures and monumental three-quarter-length pieces. He also painted some life-size family portraits, such as the *Portrait of a Couple with their Daughter* (1654; London, Wallace) and *Anthonie Reepmaker and his Family* (1669; Paris, Louvre). The latter

was painted towards the end of van der Helst's life. Also from his final period are a number of single portraits, such as that of *Vice-Admiral Aert van Nes* and his wife, *Geertruida den Dubbelde*, and *Vice-Admiral Johan de Liefde* (all 1668; Amsterdam, Rijksmus.). In each of these portraits the background was executed by Ludolf Bakhuizen.

Besides portraits, van der Helst painted a few genre pictures, for example *Woman Selling Vegetables on the Nieuwmarkt in Amsterdam* (1666; St Petersburg, Hermitage), and a few biblical scenes and mythological subjects. In all these paintings, however, the portrait element is dominant.

Documents mention hardly any pupils of van der Helst. His son Lodewijk van der Helst (1642–after 1684) trained with him; the father's influence can be clearly recognized in the son's work. Little is known about van der Helst as a master, but it is clear that he strongly influenced his contemporaries both in Amsterdam and elsewhere—artists such as Abraham van den Tempel, Nicolaas de Helt Stocade (1614–69) and Paulus Hennekyn (1611/14–72). In the past works by his followers have been wrongly attributed to van der Helst, resulting in a distorted view of his oeuvre.

BIBLIOGRAPHY
J. J. de Gelder: *Bartholomeus van der Helst* (Rotterdam, 1921)
W. Martin: *De Hollandsche schilderkunst in de zeventiende eeuw*, 2 vols (Amsterdam, 1935–6)
E. Plietzsch: *Holländische und flämische Maler des XVII. Jahrhunderts* (Leipzig, 1960)
C. J. de Bruyn Kops: 'Vergeten zelfportretten van Govert Flinck en Bartholomeus van der Helst', *Bull. Rijksmus.*, xiii (1965), pp. 20–29
B. Haak: *The Golden Age: Dutch Painters of the Seventeenth Century* (New York, 1984), pp. 290–91, 371

RUDOLF E. O. EKKART

Bartholomeus van der Helst: *Abraham del Court and his Wife, Maria Keerssegieter*, oil on canvas, 1.72×1.47 m, 1654 (Rotterdam, Museum Boymans–van Beuningen)

Helsted, Axel (Theophilus) (*b* Copenhagen, 11 April 1847; *d* Copenhagen, 17 Feb 1907). Danish painter. He trained at the Kunstakademi in Copenhagen and then travelled to Paris, where he probably studied with Léon Bonnat. He then went to Italy, where he lived from 1870 to 1879. Most of his early works are portraits, although in Italy he produced many humorous folk scenes. He adhered to an old-fashioned conception of art well into the 1880s, but his genre scenes from these years do show his interest in depicting individual, idiosyncratic types as part of an objective presentation of reality. He also achieved a fair degree of psychological penetration in works such as *Father and Son* (1882; Copenhagen, Stat. Mus. Kst), the real subject of which is the anxiety of Helsted's inner struggle; he was awarded an exhibition medal (1882) for this work.

Helsted was an academic painter, and he was not innovative as a stylist. Other popular paintings, such as *The Town Council* (1885; Hamburg, Ksthalle), are more satirical, and the tension, drama and conflict in such scenes are conveyed through the types and individuals carefully set against each other. In his later years, after the death of his wife, Helsted became deeply religious. In 1890 he travelled to Palestine in search of inspiration for large biblical compositions such as *The Epileptic* (1891) and *'Woe unto you yourselves, ye scribes'* (1894–6; both Copenhagen, Stat. Mus. Kst). In spite of their pious seriousness, these ingenious and pointed presentations of New Testament subjects did not have the powerful impact Helsted intended.

BIBLIOGRAPHY

K. Zahrtmann: *En mindebog* [A memoir], ed. F. Hendriksen (Copenhagen, 1919)
S. Schultz: *Dansk genremaleri* [Danish genre painting] (Copenhagen, 1928)

GITTE VALENTINER

Hem, Laurens van der (*b* Amsterdam, 1621; *d* Amsterdam, 1678). Dutch lawyer, collector and patron. He came from the Hem family from Broek in den Hem, a family of ruling-class Catholics, who because they remained loyal to their faith were not allowed to hold office in the government. Laurens's father was Ysbrand Harmensz. Hem, an Amsterdam merchant; his mother was Geertrui Spiegel, daughter of the poet Hendrick Laurensz. Spiegel (1549–1612). Ysbrand acquired the right to call himself van der Hem through his brother Arend who was twice ennobled, first by the German emperor (1586) and later by the king of Sweden (1618).

As a young man Laurens seems to have travelled extensively and apparently lived in Italy for a while. Eventually he became a lawyer, like his elder brother Hendrik, and established himself in his native city. His extreme wealth (an assessment of 1674 estimated the total value of his property at 211,000 guilders) enabled him to build an important library and art collection, which included works by the great Dutch masters, among them Rembrandt. A catalogue of his valuable collection of books, *Bibliotheca Hemmiana . . .*, survives (London, BL, SC 564 SCH 10695). Prominent visitors from all over the world—among them Cosimo III de' Medici—came to admire his collection whenever they visited Amsterdam.

The highlight of Laurens's collection must have been the Atlas van der Hem (Vienna, Österreich. Nbib.), sometimes also known as the Atlas of Prince Eugene of Savoy, after one of its later owners. It consists of 46 bound volumes, 4 supplements and a portfolio of drawings. The main body of the work is formed by the Latin edition of Johannes Blaeu's *Atlas Maior*, published in 11 volumes in 1662. To this Laurens added numerous maps and topographical prints and drawings, bringing the total to over 2000 works on paper, including drawings by Lambert Doomer, Jan Hackaert, Adriaen Matham, Roelandt Savery, Reinier Nooms, his own brother Herman van der Hem and Willem Schellinks, by whom there are no less than 120 drawings. The nature and abundance of this material suggest that Schellinks must have worked directly for van der Hem, who presumably paid for at least some of the topographical study trips made by Schellinks and others.

BIBLIOGRAPHY

K. Ausserer: 'Der Atlas Blaeu der Wiener National-bibliothek', *Beiträge zur historischen Geographie, Kulturgeographie, Ethnographie und Kartographie, vornehmlich des Orients* (Leipzig and Vienna, 1929)
H. de la Fontaine Verwey: 'De Atlas van Mr Laurens van der Hem', *Amstelodamum*, xxxviii (1951), pp. 85–9
P. H. Hulton: 'Drawings of England in the Seventeenth Century by William Schellinks, Jacob Esselens and Lambert Doomer, from the Van der Hem Atlas of the National Library, Vienna', *Walpole Soc.*, 2 vols, xxxv (1954–6)
R. Wagner: *Die überseeischen Gebiete in Atlas Blaeu-van der Hem der österreichischen Nationalbibliothek: Eine Dokumentation* (diss., U. Vienna, 1976)

H. de la Fontaine Verwey: 'De glorie van de Blaeu-atlas en de Meester afsetter' [The glory of the Blaeu Atlas and the master swindler], *Uit de wereld van het boek*, iii: *In en om de vergulde sonnewyser* [From the world of books, iii: in and around the gilded sundial] (Amsterdam, 1979), pp. 195–225
B. Aikema and others: *W. Schellinkx Ft, viaggio al sud, 1664–1665* (Rome, 1983)

PIERRE F. M. MENS

Hemavati [Hēmāvati; anc. Henjeru]. Site in Anantapur District, Andhra Pradesh, India, capital of the NOLAMBA dynasty during the 9th–10th centuries. Although Hemavati is a main centre for architectural, sculptural and inscriptional remains from the Nolamba period, none of the monuments have irrefutable patronage identifications. The late 9th- or early 10th-century Siddeshvara temple, with renovated exterior, enshrines in the inner sanctum an imposing seated Bhairava (over 1.5 m high) that epitomizes the Nolamba/Hemavati style. Comparable is a large-scale goddess image (Madras, Govt Mus. & N.A.G.). In an adjacent compound, the granite Doddeshvara temple (*c.* 920–30) is distinctive with its refined relief sculptures embellishing the entrance and pillars, and fine figural images in the perforated windows. Other monuments include the Virupaksha, Malleshvara, Akka and Tangi shrines.

See also INDIAN SUBCONTINENT, §§III, 5(i)(h) and IV, 7(vi)(c).

BIBLIOGRAPHY

D. Barrett: *Nolamba Temples at Hemavati* (Bombay, 1958)
C. Sivaramamurti: *Nolamba Sculptures in the Madras Government Museum* (Madras, 1964)
A. L. Cohen: *Temple Architecture and Sculpture in Noḷambavāḍi* (diss., U. Chicago, 1989)

ANDREW L. COHEN

Hemba. Bantu-speaking farming and hunting people of eastern Zaïre. The Hemba are especially famous for their wood statuary, though they also produce a variety of other types of sculptured objects and masks (for extensive illustrations, see Neyt). Hemba art is closely related to the widespread LUBA culture of south-eastern Zaïre. Outside Hembaland, Hemba art is dispersed in a variety of private and public collections (e.g. Kinshasa, Inst. Musées N.; Tervuren, Kon. Mus. Mid.-Afrika).

1. Introduction 2. Ancestor figures. 3. Other arts.

1. INTRODUCTION. The Hemba, numbering some 200,000 people, live between the River Zaïre in the west and the River Lukuga, the outlet of Lake Tanganyika, in the south. Their territory is divided into two distinct regions: northern Shaba and the Maniema plain. The southern Hemba live in Shaba between the Portes d'Enfer rapids on the River Zaïre, in the area surrounding Kongolo, and the River Luika. The northern Hemba occupy the Maniema to the north of the Luika. The whole area is about 100 km by 100 km. The terrain south of the Luika consists of grasslands and wooded plains, the land being rich and fertile, and undulating with valleys, hills and small mountains. In the north are the wide expanses of the Maniema.

The geographical characteristics of the country, in conjunction with its drainage system, have influenced the history of its inhabitants. In general, the population density varies between 10 and 19 persons per sq. km, and it is even higher in the Kongolo–Sola–Katele triangle, at between 20 and 49 per sq. km. The density of population has favoured the birth of diverse and impressive art forms. The population is made up of a local populace and immigrants from the east. The Luba gave the name 'Hemba' to the people who came from the east to live in the region lying between the River Zaïre and Lake Tanganyika. The Luba–Hemba region to the south of the Lukuga (*see* LUBA) is to be distinguished from that dealt with here, to the north of the Lukuga, as the populations, languages and cultures of the two areas are different.

The name 'Hemba' refers to a complex social reality. The Hemba of the northern Shaba region are made up of a group of lineages, clans and chiefdoms all of which recognize the Hundu mountains, between the Luama and the Lulindi, as their place of origin. They appear to come from a common stock. These people include the Niembo, who have patrilineal clans (the Baga Mbele) and matrilineal clans (the Samba), as well as the Honga, Mambwe, Kahela, Nkuvu, Kayungu, Muhona and Yambula. In the Maniema, to the north of the Luika, Hemba have mixed in a more complex way with Zula, Nonda, Bangubangu, Boyo and other local groups. The Hemba of the Maniema region are divided into six principal groupings: the Mogasa, Katego, northern Muhona, Kagulu, Kagulu Kamalungu and Hombo. To the north and the south of the Luika, every territorial boundary is marked by running water, a spring, a distinctive rock, a hill or a swamp. Migrations, movements in search of land for cultivation and conflicts resulting, for example, from the struggle to defend hunting-grounds resulted in the gradual demarcation of the area of each group. These groups definitively consolidated their territories during the colonial period.

Certain aspects of Hemba social organization, as well as some of their cultural practices such as their food taboos, link them with the traditions of the Kundu in the south and of the Boyo in the north. In fact, the Baka Kinga of the Boyo have produced ancestor statues of a similar style to those of the Hemba. The Hemba have cultural and social links with the patrilineal societies of the north-east, especially the Bangubangu. Moreover, Hemba dialects are closely related to Bangubangu; and as these two tonal languages are linked to Tetela, Songya and Holoholo, they are also connected to the Luba language group. Overall, then, Hemba society is linked especially to that of the Bangubangu and shows the imprint of Luba culture on a range of its social institutions.

The ancestor cult is a fundamental aspect of Hemba life. The large number of ancestor figures (*see* §2 below) bears witness to this. Also, the Hemba plant a large tree, *muvula* (*Chlorophora exclesa*), in the middle of their villages. This is honoured by the head of the family and evokes the presence of the ancestors. Moreover, it is from the wood of the *muvula* tree that the master sculptors carve the ancestor figures.

There are, however, other important facets to Hemba religious life. For example, sacrifices are offered to the spirits of nature. These are implacably opposed to agriculture and are found in such characteristic places as rocks, copses, mountains, hot springs and even in the Portes d'Enfer rapids on the Lualaba, a geological phenomenon whose spirits are venerated on both banks of the river.

Thus, natural surroundings and movements of population come together in the form of a spirit cult.

2. ANCESTOR FIGURES. The Hemba produce a range of figure sculptures, the most important of which are the ancestor figures, which lie in the semi-darkness of funeral huts. These are marvellous effigies of dead chiefs with half-closed eyes looking into the next world. The ancestor effigies belong to a cult based both on the idea of an afterlife and on the Hemba kinship system. While there are references to ethical, religious and metaphysical values within the cult, the social meaning and function of the sculptures should not be neglected. Every ancestor is included in it, assigned to a particular place in the sequence. He bestows on his keeper a link with the exact genealogy that records the history of his lineage and, above all, the lineage's authority over the lands it occupies. Some large lineages among the southern Niembo own numerous ancestor statues, sometimes as many as 20, distributed between the different houses of their members.

In carving ancestor figures a sculptor follows a precise sequence. He carves out the main volumes—head, hairstyle, neck, trunk etc—according to a system of recurring equal measurements. Through this system, based on a cube alternating with an intermediate component, the Hemba carving technique creates a steady rhythm, which in turn gives a strong impression of equilibrium. This can be seen as expressing the stability of the ancestor watching over his lineage through successive generations. The finished figure, varying in height between 500 mm and 1 m, stands in a symmetrical position with hands on stomach, on either side of the navel.

Morphological classifications of Hemba ancestor figures have been made (e.g. Neyt). In the first instance, the relevant criteria are the shape of the head, the face, eyes, nose, mouth, ears, neck, the plane of the shoulders, the torso, back, upper limbs, hands, buttocks, lower limbs, feet and the stand or base. Examination of such secondary characteristics as hairstyle, ornament, scarification patterns and prestige emblems can be added to the analysis.

Hairstyles are an extremely important indicator of ethnic origin and social status among the Hemba. As well as the most famous cross-shaped hairstyle, observed by the earliest explorers in the area, there were also horn-shaped hairstyles in the north, plaited, pigtail and twisted styles, and also, in the Maniema, male styles of cones and sheets. The systematic study of hairstyles provides useful information for classifying the sculptures. To this may be added the study of the whole range of accessories that contribute to the elegance of the hairstyle: various kinds of pins, raffia squares holding up the plaits and tiaras made of wire, ivory or iron nails, cloth or a double row of cowries.

Some of the figures also show Newgate frills (i.e. narrow beards along the jawline), ringed necks covered with pearl necklaces, scarification marks and prestige objects. Among the latter are ceremonial adzes (*mutolo*), carried over the shoulder; long staffs (*langa*); ceremonial spears (*gambasa*); large display knives (*ulembo* or *kahilu*); highly prized loincloths made from bark cloth in the Maniema; and animal skins including those of humming-birds, young leopards and lynxes. Loincloths were held on by a large belt, sometimes decorated with shells, a precious, symbolic object, evoking the unity of the family group that the chief represented, and passed on to his successor as a sign of authority.

Morphological analysis of ancestor statues by volumes and anatomical detail, matched with signs of ethnic identity and social status and information gathered in the field, from archives and from the literature, allows the art historian to place each figure in a particular sculptor's workshop and within a particular style. It is also possible to fix some art forms as earlier or later than others. In fact, by comparing forms and their evolution, it is possible to recognize not only 11 distinct styles of Hemba statues but also, within these, a prototype, a major work, an antique replica of this same work, pieces from the same workshop, works in a series—whether antique, recent copies or forgeries. Consequently, even within a morphological analysis that is by definition structural, a historical dimension to the study of the sculptures can also be given. Every ancestor figure contributes in its own way to the study of the history of a social group and its territory.

Among the eleven Hemba styles recognized by scholarship, three seem to predominate: that of the southern Niembo around Mbulula, that of the Luika Niembo and that of the northern Hemba. In works from southern Niembo, the carved head is egg-shaped, while the sculptures of the Luika Niembo and the northern Hemba have more elongated heads, with the plane of the cheeks following parallel contours. (In the variant Muhona and Nkuvu styles, the face is more oval or even more triangular.) The two Niembo styles have half-closed or slightly open eyes; the northern Hemba have large almond-shaped eyes, in rare instances with cowries inlaid in carved eye sockets. Among other relevant details that distinguish the three major styles is the shape of the hairstyle. The basic principle is similar in all cases: the hair is gathered into four sections by plaits coming from the four quarters of the head. This is the famous cross-shaped hairstyle observed among the Luba-Hemba south of the Lukuga by early explorers. Among the southern Niembo, the hair is gathered on to the nape in four plaits that lie behind the head, supported in the nape area by a raffia square, which is sometimes decorated. Most of these are major works of high quality. In figures from the Luika Niembo workshops the cross-shaped hairstyle is at an angle of 45° on the head (e.g. Kinshasa, Inst. Musées N., no. 72.746.70). Among the northern Hemba, the cross-shaped hairstyle is particularly bulbous and sometimes has an openwork effect. It is placed on top of the skull. More generally, the figures carved by the southern Niembo exhibit a harmonious treatment of contours, while works made by the northern Hemba have more vigorously accentuated volumes. Sculptures of the Luika Niembo often hold a prestige object and have sacrifications. These three major styles are distributed geographically along a south-west to northeast axis, from the southern Niembo through the Luika Niembo to the northern Hemba. This axis has a clear connection with the history of the migrations of the groups in question.

The other styles are variants of these major styles, or else show clearly the effects of neighbouring cultures. They include the Honga style, which has neckrings, the Sayi style, the Yambula style, the Muhona and Nkuvu styles, the Buli style, the Kusu style and the style with the domed hairstyle, as well as the Kahela, Mambwe and Hombo styles. There are also a number of atypical Hemba works that cannot be fitted into this list of main styles.

1. Hemba ancestor figure (Buli style), wood, h. 835 mm, from Zaïre, before 1903 (Berlin, Museum für Völkerkunde)

The discovery of two ancestor figures in the Buli style, one in Berlin (Berlin, Mus. Vlkerknd.; see fig. 1), the other observed *in situ*, has added to our knowledge of this style. The latter figure was observed in the village of Kankunde, to the north of Sola, in the Nkuvu chiefdom. The names of twelve of the keepers of the statue, and even that of the sculptor Ngongo ya Chintu, have been preserved. The Buli style is an original creation that combines elements of Luba, Hemba and Kusu modelling styles.

It seems that the great statues were carved during a period of cultural, social and economic expansion; in any case, at a date before slavery, which flourished in a situation of internal conflict between different social groups. The great tradition of ancestor statues dates, in all probability, from the first half of the 19th century. In other respects, however, records of the widespread incidence of the standing male statue with hands on stomach, and of its appearance in a wide variety of representations and usages—from SONGYE cult effigies, west of the River Zaïre, to TABWA statues along the shores of Lake Tanganyika as far as Zambia—make it seem more appropriate to look back to the 17th century, and probably even earlier, for the prototype of these sculptural traditions.

3. OTHER ARTS. The range of other Hemba art forms includes sculptured stakes, fetish figures and caryatid stools, wooden and ivory figurines (often set on calabashes), and such other anthropomorphic objects as chiefs' staffs, dance rattles and masks. The stakes (*lagalla*), with their tips carved in the form of a head or addorsed double head, are placed at the edges of the village to watch over it, like gates marking the borderline between the hostile forces of nature and the forces of culture. Several of these *lagalla*, guardians of the lineage, may be found in the same village. Among the Mambwe, the *lagalla* always has an addorsed double head, as it frequently does in the villages of the Niembo, the Nkuvu and the Muhona. Offerings of food are made to the *lagalla*, and children are not forbidden from coming into contact with it.

The most important of the ritual objects peculiar to the Hemba is the *kabeja*, a wooden fetish with an addorsed double head. It is a highly fearsome object, kept away from women and children, that only the head of the family may touch. It presides over all sacrifices and offerings, of whatever kind. The figure, about 300 mm high, has a single torso with four arms and four legs, as well as its addorsed heads. It alludes to the myth of a man, Makua, and a woman, Abeja, who gave birth to a deformed child. (It is difficult to interpret this myth, but it is known that the Hemba used to sacrifice deformed infants.) On his investiture, a new clan chief inherits the *kabeja* fetish along with the statues of the ancestors, the *lagalla* gates, the village guardians and other sacrificial sites and places of offering.

Other spirits are represented in a variety of ways. For example some, such as the *muyombwe*, are modelled from clay or else represented in the form of hunting fetishes. The caryatid stool (*kihona*) is a symbol of authority, representing political power. The geographical area over which these seats are found exceeds considerably the region in which the great Hemba statues are found. It includes the Luba area of the Kamina region in southern

Shaba, where the stools are as common among the Luba-Hema to the east of the river as they are among the Luba-Shankadi to the west, and stretches towards the shores of Lake Tanganyika in the east, to the territory of the Songye in the west, and beyond Hemba territory in the north as far as the Zula and the Zimba, at the edge of the forest belt. Below the River Lukuga, the caryatid almost always takes the form of a woman in a kneeling or squatting position. The volumes of the body are full and rounded, and the lower limbs are folded under the body (see fig. 2).

Hemba sculptors also carve pretty wooden and ivory figurines with hands resting on breasts or stomach. Some of these objects have religious uses or are fixed on to diviners' baskets and calabashes.

There are only a few Hemba anthropomorphic face masks. Their stylistic features connect them with sculptures peculiar to the southern Niembo in the Mbulula region. Little is known about their use. In contrast, in the Mambwe and Hombo regions are found simian masks (*sokomutu*), with a variety of astonishing stylistic expressions (see Blakely and Blakely). Some masks are worn over the face, while others are fixed to the belt. The masks are kept inside the huts and are related to the ancestor cult. They protect lineage members, assuring them of life

2. Hemba caryatid stool, wood, h. 485 mm, from Shaba, Zaïre, probably 19th century (Tervuren, Koninklijk Museum voor Midden-Afrika)

and happiness. They sometimes have a judicial function. The maskers also wear full bark cloth costume.

BIBLIOGRAPHY

J. Thomson: 'Journey of the Society's East African Expedition', *Proc. Royal Geog. Soc.*, ii/2 (1880), pp. 721–40 and map between pp. 784 and 785
E. C. Hore: 'On the Twelve Tribes of Tanganyika', *J. Anthropol. Inst. GB & Ireland*, xii (1882), pp. 2–21 and pl. I
V. Jacques and E. Storms: 'Notes sur l'ethnographie de la partie orientale de l'Afrique équatoriale', *Bull. Soc. Anthropol. Bruxelles*, v (1886–7), pp. 91–202 and pls 3–14
F. M. Olbrechts: *Plastiek van Kongo* (Antwerp, 1946)
L. Zangrie: 'Les Institutions, la religion et l'art des Ba Euye: Groupes Ba Sumba, Du Ma Nyéma (Congo belge)', *Ethnographie*, n. s., xxxxv (1947–50), pp. 54–80
F. Neyt and L. de Strycker: *Approche des arts Hemba*, Col. A. Afrique Noire (xi (1974) suppl.) (Villiers-le-Bel, 1975)
F. Neyt: *La Grande Statuaire Hemba du Zaïre*, Publications d'Histoire de l'Art et d'Archéologie de l'Université Catholique de Louvain, xii (Leuven, 1977)
D. P. Biebuyck: *Statuary from the Pre-Bembe Hunters: Issues in the Interpretation of Ancestral Figurines Ascribed to the Basikasingo–Bembe–Boyo—Statuary in the Collections of the Royal Museum of Central Africa, Tervuren, Belgium* (Tervuren, [1981])
——: *The Arts of Central Africa: An Annotated Bibliography*, Ref. Pubns A. Hist. (Boston, MA, 1987)
T. D. Blakely and P. A. R. Blakely: 'So'o Masks and Hemba Funerary Festival', *Afr. A.*, xxi/1 (1987), pp. 30–37, 84–6

FRANÇOIS NEYT

Hemerken, Thomas. *See* KEMPIS, THOMAS À.

Hemessen. South Netherlandish family of painters.

(1) Jan Sanders van Hemessen (*b* Hemessen, nr Antwerp; *fl* Antwerp, 1519–56). He was the most original artist working in Antwerp between the death of Quinten Metsys in 1530 and the 1550s, when Pieter Bruegel the elder began his career. Hemessen's moralizing genre and biblical scenes reveal his firm grasp of the human form and an earthy approach to narrative. His muscular and vigorously three-dimensional figures fill the foregrounds of his densely packed, sometimes confusing compositions and create a flamboyant sense of movement.

1. Life and work. 2. Subject-matter. 3. Working methods and collaborators. 4. Influence and critical reception.

1. LIFE AND WORK. Originally from the village of Hemessen (Hemishem) outside Antwerp, Jan Sanders was apprenticed in 1519–20 to Hendrik van Cleve I (before 1489–after 1520), a master in the Antwerp Guild of St Luke. Stylistic evidence suggests that he may then have worked with the Master of the Magdalen Legend at the royal court at Mechelen, where Hemessen could have come into contact with the court painters Jan Cornelisz. Vermeyen and Jan Gossart. Hemessen made an extensive trip to Italy during the 1520s, confirmed by his painted copy (untraced) of Andrea del Sarto's fresco of *Charity* (Florence, Chiostro Scalzo), as well as the influence of Italian Renaissance art evident in his work. By 1524 Jan had become a master in the Guild of St Luke in Antwerp, where he established a workshop that flourished for over 30 years. Aided by a felicitous marriage, before 1535, to Barbara de Fevere, the daughter of a successful Antwerp cloth merchant, Hemessen evidently became a wealthy man. During the late 1530s and early 1540s his paintings no doubt commanded high prices, since in 1539 he was

able to purchase a house on the Lombaardevest, where the Lombard pawnbrokers were located, and, just two years later, a second house on the fashionable Hochstetterstraat.

Hemessen was dean of the Antwerp Guild of St Luke in 1548. In 1551 he applied for permission to send his sons, Gillis and Hans (both presumably artists), on a trip to Italy. He is known to have been in Antwerp in 1555, when a servant, Betteken, gave birth to his bastard son, Peter. Jan's last dated painting is of 1556. Van Mander's mention of Hemessen as a painter from Haarlem led to the suggestion that he settled there late in life, but this has never been documented. Archival records and 20 signed and dated panels provide a firm basis for the reconstruction of his life and work.

Hemessen shared the fascination of his south Netherlandish contemporaries with Italian art, but his assimilation of influences from Classical antiquity and the Renaissance was both more eclectic and more idiosyncratic than Italianate northerners such as Bernard van Orley or Lambert Lombard. Hemessen's *Penitent St Jerome* (1.10×1.49 m; 1531; Lisbon, Mus. N. A. Ant.) draws both on Michelangelo's heroic nudes and on the *Laokoon* rediscovered in 1506. Hemessen painted a forceful frieze of fleshy nudes in his impressive triptych of the *Last Judgement*, executed for the family chapel of the prominent Antwerp burgomaster Adriaen Rockox in the St Jacobskerk, Antwerp (*c.* 1536–7; *in situ*). The central panel is indebted to Luca Signorelli's frescoes at Orvieto Cathedral, to which Hemessen added dramatic chiaroscuro and

1. Jan Sanders van Hemessen: *Judith with the Head of Holofernes*, oil on panel, 997×773 mm, *c.* 1549 (Chicago, IL, Art Institute of Chicago)

expressive features modelled on Raphael's *Transfiguration* (Rome, Vatican, Pin.), and a tightly intermeshed Mannerist relief composition emulating Rosso Fiorentino's paintings for the Gallery of Francis I at the château of Fontainebleau. Hemessen's *Virgin and Child* (*c.* 1535–6; Bruges, Groeningemus.), a copy after Raphael's *Holy Family of Francis I*, then at Fontainebleau (Paris, Louvre), confirms that he visited Fontainebleau in the mid-1530s.

Hemessen's adaptation of the Classical ideals of the Renaissance was counterbalanced by a fundamental strain of northern realism influenced by Quinten Metsys, Joos van Cleve, Marinus van Reymerswaele and perhaps also Lucas van Leyden and Hans Holbein the younger. During the 1530s he developed progressive illusionistic compositions of bulky half-length figures, placed in the immediate foreground in realistic settings. His expressive physiognomies and gestures reveal intense observation, sensitivity to narrative drama and a feeling for psychological ambiguity. His realistic concerns are demonstrated by a series of paintings of St Jerome in his study, which reflect Albrecht Dürer's treatment of the subject (1521; Lisbon, Mus. N. A. Ant.), painted on a visit to Antwerp.

Hemessen's figures became increasingly monumental and sculptural during the 1540s. A stark three-quarter-length *Man of Sorrows Holding the Cross* (1540; Linz, Oberösterreich. Landesmus.) harked back to Michelangelo's marble *Risen Christ* (Rome, S Maria sopra Minerva). The emphatically modelled *Penitent St Jerome* (1543; St Petersburg, Hermitage) was based on the antique Belvedere *Torso*. Hemessen's impressive *Nursing Virgin* (1543; Stockholm, Nmus.) and *Isaac Blessing Jacob* (*c.* 1544–5; Munich, Alte Pin.) combined energetic Italianate contrapposto with breathtaking passages of Netherlandish naturalism. In late works Hemessen frequently drew on the refined *maniera* in the work of such artists as Bronzino and Cellini. His three-quarter-length nude *Judith with the Head of Holofernes* (*c.* 1549; Chicago, IL, A. Inst.; see fig. 1) adopted the fashionable *figura serpentinata*. Stylistic evidence from this period indicates contact with the young painter Frans Floris, recently returned from working with Tintoretto in Venice. After 1550 his style became harsh and uneven, marked by brutal realism, angularity and jarring stylistic deformations, as in *Isaac Blessing Jacob* (1551) in the parish church at Österby, Sweden.

2. SUBJECT-MATTER. Hemessen can be credited with originating innovative moralizing genre and biblical painting in Antwerp in the 1530s. The *Double Portrait of a*

2. Jan Sanders van Hemessen: *Calling of St Matthew*, oil on panel, 1.14×1.37 m, *c.* 1548–9 (Vienna, Kunsthistorisches Museum)

Husband and Wife Playing Tables (1532; Balcarres, Fife), showing a burgher couple playing an early form of backgammon, is based on prototypes of courtly love and refers to both the traditional allegorical combat between virtues and vices and the Renaissance emblematic paradox of *discordia concors*. His *Parable of the Prodigal Son* (1536; Brussels, Mus. A. Anc.) focuses on the prodigal son's seduction in a tavern brothel, incorporating low-life characters from popular morality drama and late medieval iconography of the deadly sins.

In another panel from 1536 (Munich, Alte Pin.) Hemessen depicted a wealthy, middle-aged money-broker interrupted at the counting table by an unseen visitor. During the 17th century a figure of Christ was added at the right making the subject the Calling of St Matthew, but the original composition, preserved in an early copy (Marquis of Lothian priv. col.), was intentionally ambiguous, suggesting alternatives of death or salvation for the miser/Matthew, who teeters on the brink of penitential reform. In Hemessen's polished version of the *Calling of St Matthew* (*c.* 1539; Vienna, Ksthist. Mus., inv. no. 985), St Matthew is a concealed portrait of Emperor Charles V.

Thematic aspects of Hemessen's work of this time indicate close ties with the *Violieren*, the Antwerp Chamber of Rhetoric, whose members also belonged to the Guild of St Luke. In two tavern scenes entitled *Wayfarer in a Brothel* (*c.* 1539; Karlsruhe, Staatl. Ksthalle; and 1543; Hartford, CT, Wadsworth Atheneum) Hemessen represented an elderly wayfarer, the generic *Elckerlijk* (Everyman), a popular figure in Netherlandish Renaissance morality drama.

During the Reformation, a time of intense religious ferment and rapid economic expansion in the southern Netherlands, Hemessen responded to the crisis with lyrical, pious Christian images, for example the *Descent from the Cross* (*c.* 1526; Brussels, Mus. A. Anc.) and *Man of Sorrows* (1540; Linz, Oberösterreich. Landesmus.). In the later 1540s, in emotional religious subjects such as *Christ Carrying the Cross* (1549; Toledo, Mus. Santa Cruz), Hemessen adopted a sombre and moody, non-Mannerist approach. His painting became increasingly involved with the preoccupations of the Counter-Reformation. Numerous 16th-century copies of Hemessen's impassioned third version of the *Calling of St Matthew* (*c.* 1548–9; Vienna, Ksthist. Mus., inv. no. 961; see fig. 2) indicate that it was widely admired in the Counter-Reformation period. His late works such as the extraordinary *Stone Operation* or *Cure of Folly* (*c.* 1556; Madrid, Prado), *Tobias Cures his Father's Blindness* (1555; Paris, Louvre), the *Parable of the Unmerciful Servant* (Ann Arbor, U. MI, Mus. A) and his last dated panel, the *Expulsion of Merchants and Money-lenders from the Temple* (1556; Nancy, Mus. B.-A.), may suggest criticism of the repressive religious and political climate.

3. WORKING METHODS AND COLLABORATORS. Hemessen practised the traditional early 15th-century Netherlandish method of painting in oil on wooden panels and, like his Netherlandish forebears, he was highly skilled at depicting textures and fabrics, still-life and naturalistic portraits. He preferred a warm palette with rich brown, orange and ruddy tones, and modelled his figures with strong contrasts of light and shade.

Hemessen registered several apprentices in the Antwerp Guild of St Luke, indicating a sizeable workshop, and workshop copies of a number of original and lost paintings have survived. Hemessen's work has sometimes been confused with paintings by a close follower known as the Master of the Augsburg *Ecce homo* from a panel now on deposit at the Alte Pinakothek in Munich. The Augsburg Master, who was familiar with Hemessen's late style, painted a caricatural *Christ Carrying the Cross* (Soestdijk, Kon. Pal.) derived from Hemessen's version of 1553 (Esztergom, Dioc. Mus.), and *St Jerome in Prayer* (Antwerp, Rockoxhuis) copied from a lost work by Hemessen of the 1530s (Schubert).

During the 1530s Hemessen collaborated with a talented artist who painted background scenes of energetic small figures for several of his panels, including the *Parable of the Prodigal Son*, the *Last Judgement* and *Wayfarer in a Brothel*. For some time scholars regarded this collaborator as the so-called Brunswick Monogrammist, author of the *Parable of the Great Feast* (Brunswick, Herzog Anton Ulrich-Mus.). In the late 19th century the monogram on the Brunswick panel, *I S A (?) V H (?) M*, was identified with the initials of Jan Sanders van Hemessen. Friedländer subsequently suggested that the Monogrammist's oeuvre was done by the young Jan Sanders. Diez noted as early as 1909, however, that Hemessen always signed his name *de Hemessen* rather than *van Hemessen*. There is now a general consensus that Hemessen and the Brunswick Monogrammist were different artists and the Monogrammist is most often identified with Jan van Amstel.

Controversy continues over the author of the background scenes with small figures that appear in Hemessen's work. Schubert retains the view that they were the work of the Brunswick Monogrammist. Bergmans has argued for Hemessen's daughter Catharina, notwithstanding the marked chronological disparity. Wallen has suggested that the collaborator was JAN SWART, a painter and printmaker at Antwerp *c.* 1525, whose drawings demonstrate stylistic and iconographic correlations with the Hemessen backgrounds from the 1530s. Genaille regards the small figures as Hemessen's own work.

4. INFLUENCE AND CRITICAL RECEPTION. Hemessen had considerable influence at Antwerp on Pieter Aertsen and Joachim Beuckelaer, who developed his compositional innovations and investigations of moralized genre. His numerous iconographic references to contemporary religious and political issues anticipate Pieter Bruegel the elder. Hemessen was mentioned by Vasari, Guicciardini and van Mander, but they gave little information about him and van Mander failed to appreciate the avant-garde aspects of his work, characterizing him as an archaizing painter. While Hemessen had slipped into obscurity by the end of the 16th century, his paintings were owned by important collectors, including the Emperor Rudolf II, Queen Christina of Sweden, the Elector Maximilian I of Bavaria and the Archduke Leopold William of Austria.

BIBLIOGRAPHY

BNB; Thieme–Becker

G. Vasari: *Vite* (1550, rev. 2/1568); ed. G. Milanesi (1878–85), vii, p. 583

L. Guicciardini: *Description de tout le Pais Bas* (Antwerp, 1567), p. 142

C. van Mander: *Schilder-boeck* ([1603]–1604/*R* 1969), p. 205

E. Diez: 'Der Braunschweiger Monogrammist', *Sber. Kstgesch. Ges.*, vii 1909), pp. 7–11

F. Graefe: *Jan Sanders van Hemessen und seine Identifikation mit dem Braunschweiger Monogrammisten* (Leipzig, 1909)

L van Puyvelde: 'Nouvelles oeuvres de Jean van Hemessen', *Rev. Belge Archéol. & Hist. A.*, xx (1951), pp. 57–71

G. Marlier: *Erasme et la peinture flamande de son temps* (Damme, 1954)

S. Bergmans: 'Le Problème Jan van Hemessen, monogrammiste de Brunswick', *Rev. Belge Archéol. & Hist. A.*, xxiv (1955), pp. 133–57

L. van Puyvelde: *La Peinture flamande au siècle de Bosch et Breughel* (Paris, 1962), pp. 182–94

Le Siècle de Bruegel (exh. cat., Brussels, Mus. A. Anc., 1963), pp. 110–13

M. J. Friedländer: *Early Netherlandish Painting* (1967–76), xii, pp. 44–9

G. T. Faggin: *La pittura ad Anversa nel cinquecento* (Florence, 1968)

G. von der Osten and H. Vey: *Painting and Sculpture in Germany and the Netherlands, 1500–1600*, Pelican Hist. A. (Harmondsworth, 1969), pp. 197–9

D. Schubert: *Die Gemälde des Braunschweiger Monogrammisten* (Cologne, 1970)

P. Philippot: *Pittura fiamminga e rinascimento italiano* (Turin, 1970), pp. 170–77

K. Renger: *Lockere Gesellschaft* (Berlin, 1970)

B. Wallen: 'The Portraits of Jan Sanders van Hemessen', *Oud-Holland*, lxxxvi (1971), pp. 70–87

D. Schubert: 'Eine zweite "Sintflut" vom "Meister des Augsburger Ecce Homo"', *Wallraf-Richartz-Jb.*, xxxiii (1971), pp. 321–8

B. Wallen: *Jan van Hemessen: An Antwerp Painter between Reform and Counter-Reform* (Ann Arbor, 1983)

R. Genaille: 'Qui a peint *La Tentation (Lockere Gesellschaft)* du Musée de Karlsruhe?', *Rev. Belge Archéol. & Hist. A.*, liii (1984), pp. 67–90

(2) Catharina van Hemessen (*b* Antwerp, 1528; *d* ?Antwerp, after 1587). Daughter of (1) Jan Sanders van Hemessen. Both Vasari and Guicciardini mention her, along with the illuminators Levina Teerlinc, Susanna Horenbout and others, as a prominent Netherlandish woman painter. According to van Beverwyck, she studied painting under her father. She acknowledged filial respect by signing an aristocratic *Portrait of a Man* (London, N.G.): *Catharina filia Ioannes de Hemessen Pingebat 1552*. The suggestion that Catharina painted background scenes for some of her father's pictures (Bergmans) is unacceptable on both stylistic and chronological grounds.

Catharina was 20 years old when she executed her *Self-portrait* (1548; Basle, Kstmus.), which shows her painting at an easel, dressed in primly elegant attire. In a contemporary portrait of a *Young Woman Playing the Virginal* (Cologne, Wallraf-Richartz-Mus.), she painted a young woman of similar appearance to herself (perhaps her elder sister Christina). In 1554 Catharina married Chrétien de Morien (or Marin), an organist at Antwerp Cathedral. The talented couple were admired by Mary of Hungary, sister of Emperor Charles V, and in September 1556 they left for Spain in Mary of Hungary's entourage. According to Guicciardini, on her death in 1558 Mary of Hungary 'left them provision for their entire lives'. Jan van Hemessen's late painting *A Musician and his Muse* (The Hague, Mauritshuis) may refer to his daughter's marriage. No paintings by Catharina have survived dated after 1552, and her artistic career was apparently eclipsed by her husband's. Eight small portraits and two religious pictures bearing her signature have survived, dating between 1548 and 1552. In contrast to her father's monumental, highly mannered style, Catharina van Hemessen painted fairly small panels in a restrained, tasteful idiom. In several of her portraits she adopted the severe two-thirds-length

format preferred by Anthonis Mor, free master at Antwerp in 1547. While noticeably flat and attenuated, Catharina's delicate figures possess a graceful charm. She had a sensitive feeling for stylish costumes and accessories. Her religious work, for example *Christ Carrying the Cross* (Mons, priv. col., see Tufts, 1974, fig. 23), was less successful. Her *Infant Christ and St John the Baptist Playing with a Lamb* (sold Vienna, 1937, see Wallen, 1983, fig. 130) is probably a partial copy of a lost *Holy Family* by Jan Sanders van Hemessen of 1547.

BIBLIOGRAPHY

Thieme–Becker

G. Vasari: *Vite* (1550, rev. 2/1568); ed. G. Milanesi (1878–85), vii, p. 588

L. Guicciardini: *Description de tout le Pais Bas* (Antwerp, 1567), p. 134

J. van Beverwyck: *Uitnementheyt des vrouvelicken geslachts* [Excellence of the female gender] (Dordrecht, 1639)

F. J. Van den Branden: *Geschiedenis der Antwerpsche schilderschool* (Antwerp, 1883), pp. 99–100

S. Bergmans: 'Le Problème Jan van Hemessen, monogrammiste de Brunswick', *Rev. Belge Archéol. & Hist. A.*, xxiv (1955), pp. 133–57

Le Siècle de Bruegel (exh. cat., Brussels, Mus. A. Anc., 1963), p. 110

E. Tufts: *Our Hidden Heritage: Five Centuries of Women Artists* (London, 1974), pp. 50–57

Women Artists: 1550–1950 (exh. cat. by A. S. Harris and L. Nochlin, Los Angeles, CA, Co. Mus. A., 1976), p. 105

B. Wallen: *Jan van Hemessen: An Antwerp Painter between Reform and Counter-Reform* (Ann Arbor, 1983), pp. 23–5, 123–4

BURR WALLEN

Heming, Thomas (*b* Ludlow, Salop, 1722–3; *d* 1801). English goldsmith. In 1738 he was apprenticed to the Huguenot goldsmith Peter Archambo. He first entered a mark at Goldsmiths' Hall, London, in 1745, when he gave his address as Piccadilly, London, and became a freeman of the Goldsmiths' Company in 1746. Some of Heming's work is distinctly French in character, and this may be due to the influence of Archambo, seen for example in a pair of Neo-classical candlesticks (1769; New York, Met.). Nevertheless, Heming used an eclectic range of sources, from the designs for silver in *Eléments d'orfèvrerie* (1748) by Pierre Germain (Heming's trade card depicts a ewer designed by Germain) to *A New Book of Ornaments* (1752) by Matthias Lock and Henry Copland (*c.* 1706–53). The curving table-feet depicted in the latter appear on Heming's épergnes.

Heming was an influential and highly regarded goldsmith. In 1760 he was appointed Principal Goldsmith to George III, a position that he held until 1782. The size of Heming's business, based by 1773 in New Bond Street, London, can be gauged by the fact that in 1775 Georg Christoph Lichtenberg recorded that Heming had received an order to make a silver service valued at £30,000. This was probably the service ordered by the Governors of Tula, Russia, which included 38 candlesticks, 31 meat-dishes and 9 salvers, made by Heming in 1766–7. Some of his most important pieces include the wine-cistern (1770; Belton House, Lincs, NT) of the Speaker of the House of Commons, which was made as part of the official plate issued by the Jewel House, and two toilet services, one made in 1766 for Caroline Matilda, posthumous daughter of Frederick, Prince of Wales (Copenhagen, Kstindustmus.), and the other in 1768 for the marriage of Sir Watkin Williams-Wynn and Lady Henrietta Somerset (Cardiff, N. Mus.).

BIBLIOGRAPHY

A. Grimwade: *Rococo Silver, 1727–1765* (London, 1974)

——: *London Goldsmiths, 1697–1837: Their Marks and Lives* (London, 1976, rev. 3/1990)

P. Glanville: *Silver in England* (London, 1987)

EMMA PACKER

Hemis. Buddhist monastery *c.* 45 km south-east of Leh in Ladakh, India. Founded by King Senge Namgyel in the 17th century, Hemis became the leading monastery in the region of the Tibetan Drukpa sect. Its buildings comprise chortens (stupas), *mani* walls, monastic dwellings and a large rectangular courtyard used for the annual monastic dance ceremony. This court is surrounded by a balcony with a throne used by the head lama on such occasions; small paintings of saintly figures appear on the rear wall of the balcony. Within the court are four tall poles decked with prayer flags and yak tails. On the right-hand side are two large temples, the Dukhang and the Chökhang; each is two storeys high and preceded by a wooden verandah containing Tibetan-style paintings of protector deities.

In the Dukhang are numerous modern paintings of Buddha figures and Tantric deities executed in the traditional Tibetan style; enormous red-painted pillars support a cupola that illuminates the interior of the hall. The Chökhang contains a fine image of the historical Buddha, Shakyamuni, a large, early 18th-century chorten and many other chortens ornamented with silver, gilt and hardstones. Images and paintings of Buddhas, great lamas and Tantric teachers abound. The Lhakhang Nyingpa Temple, at the rear of the monastery, contains the finest wall paintings at Hemis. The paintings of great abbots and Tantric masters are in an Indian style but show Chinese influence; adjoining paintings illustrating scenes from the Buddha's life and furiously energetic Tantric deities also have a strong Chinese character. One of the most beautiful paintings depicts the 18th-century monk Shambunath delicately painted in a Kashmiri–Central Asian style.

See also TIBET, §II.

BIBLIOGRAPHY

D. L. Snellgrove and T. Skorupski: *The Cultural Heritage of Ladakh*, i (New Delhi, 1977)

J. Rizvi: *Ladakh: Crossroads of High Asia* (Delhi, 1983)

W. A. P. MARR

Hemispeos. *See under* SPEOS.

Hemmel von Andlau, Peter (*b* Andlau, Alsace; *fl* 1447; *d c.* 1501). German glass painter. His commissions and influence extended from the area around Strasbourg into southern Germany and Austria. Hemmel became a citizen of Strasbourg through marriage in 1447 with the widow of a local glass painter named Heinz. His work shows figure types similar to contemporary engravings, in particular those of Martin Schongauer; Hemmel's *Adoration of the Magi* in the Nonnbergkirche, Salzburg, is derived from a Schongauer print of the same subject. Distinctive among his many commissions are the Kramer window (1479–80) in Ulm Minster and the axial choir window of *St Anne and the Virgin* (*c.* 1478–9) in the Stiftskirche, Tübingen. The balance of the intense purple, scarlet and deep blue against extensive silver-stain yellow and white glass creates a

tension between spatial planes. Hemmel's draughtsmanship in his *Virgin and Child with Lily* from the Nonnbergkirche, Salzburg (*c.* 1470–80; Darmstadt, Hess. Landesmus.; *see* STAINED GLASS, colour pl. IV), shows a sculptural treatment of drapery and form that dominates the composition. The extraordinarily lush treatment of the architectural frame, often developed through sprouting and intertwining branches, seen especially in large-scale work, is one of Hemmel's most distinctive contributions.

Wentzel attributed numerous panels in Strasbourg, Ulm, Colmar, Nuremberg and elsewhere to Hemmel. Becksmann and others have, however, proposed that a number of major independent workshops, possibly as many as eight, were operating at this time in Strasbourg, and that Hemmel's achievement should be assessed in the context of these competing masters.

For further discussion *see* STAINED GLASS, §II, 1.

BIBLIOGRAPHY

H. Wentzel: *Meisterwerke der Glasmalerei* (Berlin, 1954), pp. 63–71

P. Frankl: *Peter Hemmel, Glasmaler von Andlau* (Berlin, 1956)

R. Becksmann: *Die mittelalterlichen Glasmalereien in Schwaben von 1350 bis 1530 ohne Ulm*, Corp. Vitrearum Medii Aevi: Deutschland, I/ii (Berlin, 1986) [esp. Tübingen, pp. 257–316]

VIRGINIA CHIEFFO RAGUIN

Hempel, Eberhard (*b* Dresden, 30 July 1886; *d* Dresden, 16 Sept 1967). German art historian. He studied art history in Vienna and Munich, where he gained a PhD under Heinrich Wölfflin. From 1921 to 1923 Hempel worked at the Albertina in Vienna, and then he qualified as a university lecturer in Graz in 1924. From 1933 until 1955 he was professor of art history and Director of the Institute for Architectural History at the Technische Hochschule in Dresden. As a member of the historic monuments council after World War II Hempel was involved in the restoration of historical monuments in Dresden. An early interest in the work of Carlo Rainaldi and Roman Baroque architecture led to a broader study of 17th- and 18th-century architecture and of the work of Michael Pacher. Hempel's research was positivist in style, combining a thorough analysis of form and content with a concern for real historical context. However, he also studied the works of recent and even contemporary artists, as shown by his works on Bonaventura Genelli, Rudolf Schuster (1848–1902), Reinhold Langner (*b* 1905) and Georg Nerlich. Hempel also wrote reviews of important art historical studies, and he acknowledged the influence of such art historians as Hermann Egger (1873–1949), Karl Woermann (1844–1933), Richard Hamann and Otto Schubert. In his most significant work, *Baroque Art and Architecture in Central Europe*, he transcends the traditional geographical boundaries of his subject by looking not only at western Europe but also at central and eastern Europe. Hempel seldom wrote about the methodology of art history: his only critical essay about this appeared in 1934. His works reflect more the art historical methodology of the first quarter of the 20th century, but stand out because of his independent, practical and realistic approach, attempting to trace the process of artistic creation in Baroque architecture through a study of architectural drawings and other sources.

WRITINGS

Carlo Rainaldi: Ein Beitrag zur Geschichte des römischen Barocks (diss., U. Munich, ?1916)

Francesco Borromini, Römische Forschungen des Kunsthistorischen Instituts Graz (Vienna, 1924)

Michael Pacher (Vienna, 1931)

'Ist eine "strenge Kunstwissenschaft" möglich?', *Z. Kstgesch.*, iii (1934), pp. 155–63)

Geschichte der deutschen Baukunst (Munich, 1949)

'Buonaventura Genellis Umrisse zu Dantes *Göttlicher Komödie*', *Dt. Dante-Jb.*, xxxiii (1954), pp. 62–86

with W. Krönert: *Gaetano Chiaveri, der Architekt der katholischen Hofkirche in Dresden*, Dresdner Beiträge zur Kunstgeschichte (Dresden, 1955)

Baroque Art and Architecture in Central Europe, Pelican Hist. A. (Harmondsworth, 1956)

Die Kunstdenkmäler Österreichs (Vienna, 1956)

BIBLIOGRAPHY

H. Sedlmayer: *Die Entstehung der Kathedrale* (Freiburg, 1950); review by E. Hempel in *Dt. Litztg*, 73 (1952), pp. 603–6

L. Bruhns: *Die Kunst der Stadt Rom, ihre Geschichte von den frühesten Anfängen bis in die Zeit der Romantik* (Vienna, 1951)

'Festschrift: Eberhard Hempel zum 70. Geburtstag', *Wiss. Z. Tech. Hochsch. Dresden*, vi (1956/7)

E. Lehmann: 'Eberhard Hempel zum 80. Geburtstag', *Forsch. & Fortschr.*, xl (1966), pp. 220–22

H. G. Franz: 'Eberhard Hempel', *Kunstchronik*, xx (1967), pp. 386–8

JÜRGEN ZIMMER

Hemudu [Ho-mu-tu]. Site of a Neolithic village in Yuyao County, Zhejiang Province, China. It was excavated in 1973–4 and 1977–8. Of the four cultural layers identified, the upper two layers (1 and 2), radiocarbon dated to *c.* 3700 BC, correspond to the neighbouring Songze culture. The lower two layers (3 and 4), radiocarbon dated to the late 6th millennium BC and early 5th, are particularly rich in cultural material and best represent the early phase of the Neolithic Hemudu culture (*c.* 5200–*c.*3300 BC) located south of Hangzhou Bay. Vast quantities of discarded faunal and floral remains include the earliest known evidence of rice cultivation in China, dating from *c.* 5000 BC. The extensive and well-preserved remains of wooden pile dwellings show carefully constructed mortice-and-tenon joinery. Numerous bone utensils were found, particularly hoes carved and polished from mammal scapulae, paddles, spindle whorls, handles and weaving shuttles; some of these were engraved with horizontal and diagonal lines and figures of birds. A red lacquered wooden bowl from layer 3 is the earliest known lacquerware from China (*see* CHINA, §IX). Hemudu pottery is thick and grey-black; it was handmade and fired at an estimated temperature of 800–850° C. The surface is often burnished, cord-impressed or incised with animal and plant designs. Vessel types include cooking pots with an external waist-ring, plates, basins and shallow *ding* tripods. Other artefacts include crude clay figurines of pigs, sheep and humans, and incised ivory and wood, with bird motifs, particularly the double bird, being the most notable.

BIBLIOGRAPHY

K. C. Chang: *The Archaeology of Ancient China* (New Haven, 1963, rev. New Haven and London, 4/1986)

'Hemudu yizhi di yi qi fajue baogao' [Report on the first excavation of the Hemudu site], *Kaogu Xuebao* (1978), no. 1, pp. 39–94

'Zhejiang, Hemudu yizhi di er qi fajue de zhuyao shouhuo' [Important results of the second excavation of the Hemudu site, Zhejiang], *Wenwu* (1980), no. 5, pp. 1–15

ROBERT E. MUROWCHICK

Hemy, Charles Napier (*b* Newcastle upon Tyne, 24 May 1841; *d* Falmouth, Cornwall, 30 Sept 1917). English painter. He was born into a musical family. An early artistic influence was the teaching of William Bell Scott, Head-master of the Government School of Design in Newcastle. But in the 1850s Hemy's painting had to compete with his Catholicism and the call of the sea. By the mid-1860s he had settled down and had adopted a Pre-Raphaelite style, exemplified in his early masterpiece *Among the Shingle at Clovelly* (1864; Newcastle upon Tyne, Laing A.G.). He was inspired by contact with the circles of William Morris and George Pinwell, but criticism of his draughtsmanship led him to study under Baron Henry Leys at Antwerp from 1867 to 1869. This resulted in several religious subjects (e.g. *At the Foot of the Cross*; exh. RA 1870; untraced).

On his return to London in the 1870s, his maritime subjects were influenced by Whistler and James Tissot, and he became associated with the Grosvenor Gallery, where *Saved* (Glasgow, A.G. & Mus.) was the sensation of the exhibition of 1880. This was apparently his first work not painted directly from life. In 1881 Hemy moved to Falmouth, where he worked, with a broadening technique, from floating studios. *Pilchards* (1897; London, Tate) is the masterpiece of his maturity, but much of the work of this period, though scrupulously and sensitively observed and confidently executed, is repetitive in subject: fishing boats and yachts predominate.

Puritanical and chauvinistic, he was unsympathetic to the artistic developments of the late 19th century. He was elected ARA in 1898 and RA in 1910. Two brothers, Thomas Madawaska Hemy (1852–1937) and Bernard Benedict Hemy (1845–1913), were also painters, though of lesser talent.

BIBLIOGRAPHY

A. Fish: 'The Work of C. Napier Hemy A.R.A.', *Mag. A.* (Nov 1899), pp. 1–8

Charles Napier Hemy R.A., 1841–1917 (exh. cat., ed. A. Greg; Newcastle upon Tyne, Laing A.G., 1984)

ANDREW GREG

Hénard, Eugène Alfred (*b* Paris, 1849; *d* Paris, 1923). French architect, engineer and writer. He studied in the studio of his father Antoine-Julien Hénard (1812–87), a professor at the Ecole des Beaux-Arts, Paris. Graduating in 1880, he secured a position with the municipal architectural offices of the city of Paris and continued to work there throughout much of his career, specializing in school construction. Hénard's most original contributions were in the planning and construction of the Expositions Universelles, Paris, of 1889 and 1900. In 1887 he proposed a 'train continu', actually a travolator, to transport visitors around the Exposition of 1889. The idea was rejected at the time but was realized by others in the later international expositions in Chicago (1893) and Paris (1900). At the Exposition of 1889 Hénard supervised the building of the Galerie des Machines (destr. 1909) by Charles-Louis-Ferdinand Dutert and Victor Contamin (1840–98) and later published an extraordinarily detailed account of its construction. He was among three finalists in the competition for a comprehensive plan for the Paris Exposition of 1900. No single plan for the exposition was adopted, but it was Hénard who furnished the idea of linking the

Esplanade des Invalides with the right bank of the Seine, ultimately realized in the construction of the Pont Alexandre III (1896–1900). Hénard also designed the Palais de l'Electricité and the Palais des Illusions and was awarded a Grand Prix for his contributions to the planning of the Exposition of 1900.

Hénard's most important publication was *Etudes sur les transformations de Paris*, published in eight instalments (1903–9). These included analyses of pedestrian and vehicular circulation, plans for increasing park spaces and suggestions for changing or extending the routes of several major boulevards. The fourth instalment of the *Etudes* was a highly imaginative plan to transform the Champ de Mars in central Paris into a sports park and central dirigible port for the city. Hénard campaigned untiringly to save the Galerie des Machines, which in his plan would have been used as the dirigible hangar. During the first decade of the 20th century Hénard became a leading international authority on urban planning, and he was recognized particularly for his studies on park spaces and traffic circulation problems. In 1913 he became the first president of the Société Française des Architectes Urbanistes.

WRITINGS
Le Palais des Machines: Notice sur l'édifice et sur la marche des travaux (Paris, 1891)
Etudes sur les transformations de Paris (Paris, 1903–9)

BIBLIOGRAPHY
P. M. Wolf: *Eugène Hénard and the Beginning of Urbanism in Paris, 1900–1917* (The Hague, 1969)

ROBERT JAY

Henderson, Alexander (*b* Edinburgh, 9 July 1831; *d* Montreal, 4 April 1913). Canadian photographer of Scottish birth. He emigrated to Canada shortly after his marriage to Agnes Elder Robertson in October 1855. They settled in Montreal, where he worked in accountancy for several years. About 1857 he took up photography as a hobby, and in 1866 he went into it as a profession. In the early period of his business he made portraits, but his international reputation was based on his landscape photography. He received medals for work shown in London, Dublin, Paris and New York. He documented the major cities and resort areas of Quebec and Ontario and many of the villages in Quebec. He was especially fond of the wilderness and made many trips by birch bark canoe to the Blanche, the Rouge and other noted eastern rivers for the purpose of taking pictures for later sale, for example *Ready for the Portage* (albumen print, 1863–5; Montreal, McGill U., McCord Mus.; Notman Photographic Archvs).

In 1872 Henderson began a series of photographs on the construction of the Intercolonial Railway. This led to a contract from that railway company in 1875 and to further commissions from other railway and bridge construction companies. In 1885 he was sent west by the Canadian Pacific Railway Company, and, although his journey was cut short by sickness, he returned with some superlative views. In 1892 he was employed by the Canadian Pacific Railway Company to set up and manage a new photographic department. His duties required him to spend four months in the field each year. That summer he made his second trip to the west, and he may have made others as well. He kept his position until 1897, when he retired from the company and apparently gave up photography. On his death he left his collection of thousands of glass negatives in the basement of his home. In 1964 his only surviving descendant discarded them.

BIBLIOGRAPHY
S. G. Triggs: 'Alexander Henderson: Nineteenth Century Landscape Photographer', *Archivaria*, 5 (1977–8), pp. 45–59
——: *Alexander Henderson: Landscape Photographer* (in preparation)

STANLEY G. TRIGGS

Henderson, Nigel (*b* London, 1 April 1917; *d* Thorpe-le-Soken, Essex, 15 May 1985). English photographer and collagist. He studied biology at Chelsea Polytechnic in London (1935–6) and then worked as an assistant to Helmuth Ruhemann (1936–9). In the later 1930s he produced paintings influenced by Yves Tanguy, as well as collages. After serving as a pilot for coastal command in World War II, he studied at the Slade School of Fine Art in London (1945–9). There he befriended Eduardo Paolozzi, with whom he visited Paris, meeting Brancusi, Léger, Giacometti, Braque and Arp. After leaving the Slade he began to experiment with photography, and between 1949 and 1952 he took numerous documentary photographs of Bethnal Green in east London, where he was then living. In other photographs of the period he achieved unusual effects by altering negatives or by placing objects directly on light-sensitive paper to create photograms. He was associated with the INDEPENDENT GROUP on its foundation in 1952, and with Paolozzi and others he participated in the *Parallel of Life and Art* exhibition at the ICA in London in 1953 and also in the pioneering Pop art exhibition *This Is Tomorrow* at the Whitechapel Art Gallery in London in 1956. At the latter he showed the large and disturbing altered photograph *Head of a Man* (1.59×1.21 m, 1956; London, Tate). After his first major one-man show at the ICA in 1961, Henderson began colouring some of his photographs with paint, as in *Plant Tantrums* (1961; London, Tate). From 1965 to 1968 and from 1972 to 1982 he ran the photography department at the Norwich School of Art while continuing his own photographic work. He often produced works in series that were connected by a particular striking image, as in the *Face at the Window* series (e.g. see 1983 exh. cat., p. 2), which he worked on from 1977 into the 1980s. This centred on the image of a bandaged face, which Henderson had found on a cigarette card. It was followed in the 1980s by the two series *Heads in Blocks* and *Single Heads*, in which he made different versions of a self-portrait image (e.g. *Letting it All Hang Out*; 1980–82; see 1982 exh. cat., p. 16).

BIBLIOGRAPHY
Nigel Henderson: Photographs, Collages, Paintings (exh. cat. by F. Whitford, U. Cambridge, Kettle's Yard, 1977)
Nigel Henderson (exh. cat. by C. Mullen, Norwich, Sch. A. Mus., 1982)
Nigel Henderson: Headlands: Self Portraits and Imagined Landscapes, 1960–83 (exh. cat. by C. Mullen, London, Serpentine Gal., 1983)

□

Hendricksz. (Centen), Dirck [Teodoro d'Errico] (*bur* Amsterdam, 20 Nov 1618). Flemish painter, active in Italy. He trained in the Netherlands in the circle of Anthonie Blocklandt and arrived in Italy in 1567, where he absorbed the late Mannerist style practised in Rome by Bartholomäus Spranger and Jan Speeckaert. From 1574 he was active in Naples and southern Italy, where he developed into a leading exponent of a delicate and decorative painting style, derived from the elegance of international Mannerism and from the principal Roman workshops, notably those led by Teodoro Zuccaro, Federico Zuccaro, Jacopo Bertoia and Raffaellino da Reggio at the Villa Farnese, Caprarola. His status in Naples is indicated by the scale of the commission to decorate the gilded and painted wooden ceiling (*c.* 1582) of S Gregorio Armenio, directing a workshop of Italian and Flemish artists. He also worked on the impressive carved and painted ceiling (1587–90) of S Maria Donnaromita, Naples. In the city and its surrounding region he executed a series of altar-pieces of the *Virgin of the Rosary* (e.g. 1585, Santa Maria a Vico, S Maria Assunta; 1586, Saviano, S Giacomo Maggiore). These are more devout and Italianate in style, and demonstrate the influence of Counter-Reformation devotional fervour on his decorative style. His last works, the *Birth of John the Baptist* (1604; Airola, Annunziata) and the *Virgin and Child with St Catherine and a Bishop* (1608; Arienzo, Annunziata), in which he was assisted by his son Giovan Luca, display a more moving idiom. He left Naples for Amsterdam in 1610. The drawings ascribed to the Master of the Egmont Albums have recently been attributed to him.

BIBLIOGRAPHY

C. Vargas: *Teodoro d'Errico: La maniera fiamminga nel Viceregno* (Naples, 1988)

N. Dacos: 'Le Maître des Albums Egmont: Dirck Hendricksz. Centen', *Oud Holland*, civ/2 (1990), pp. 49–68

CARMELA VARGAS

Hendrickx, Ernest (*b* Brussels, 11 April 1844; *d* Brussels, 30 Aug 1892). Belgian architect. The son of the architect Henri Hendrickx (1810–94), he trained in Paris (1866–8) in the office of Viollet-le-Duc, then under the latter's disciple Anatole de Baudot. Returning to Brussels (1868) he designed a 'model farm' and investigated solutions to the problems of modernization and rationalization of methods in crop farming. He also taught design and architecture at the Université libre de Bruxelles and other institutions in Brussels and was involved in the debate on town planning and the teaching of social politics initiated by CHARLES BULS, later burgomaster of Brussels. In 1872 Hendrickx was commissioned by Buls to design a 'model school', specifically to respond to the needs of a new method of teaching. It opened in 1875 on the Boulevard du Hainaut. From 1884 until his death, Hendrickx was principally engaged in enlarging the Université de Bruxelles. His work as a designer of industrial workshops and private houses is now forgotten but his importance lies in his introduction to Belgium of the new French ideas about rational architecture propagated by Viollet-le-Duc and Henri Labrouste. His published functional schemes demonstrate clearly his main architectural interests.

WRITINGS

'Ecole modèle, construite pour 400 élèves, boulevard du Hainaut 80 à Bruxelles', *L'Emulation*, v (1879), cols 82–4, pls 40–43

'Université de Bruxelles', *L'Emulation*, xvi (1891), col. 190, pls 29–43; xvii (1892), col. 172, pls 18–23; xviii (1893), col. 188, pls 18–19

BIBLIOGRAPHY

Obituary, 'Ernest Hendrickx, architecte, professeur à l'Université libre de Bruxelles, à l'Ecole normale des arts du dessin de Saint-Josse-ten-Noode, et à l'Ecole industrielle de la ville de Bruxelles', *L'Emulation*, xvii (1892), col. 157–9

ANNETTE NEVE

Hendrickx, Frans [Henriques, Francisco]. *See under* MASTERS, ANONYMOUS, AND MONOGRAMMISTS, §I: MASTER OF SAN LORENZO DELLA COSTA.

Hendrik III, Count of Nassau. *See under* NASSAU.

Hendriks, Wybrand (*bapt* Amsterdam, 21 June 1744; *d* Haarlem, 23 Jan 1831). Dutch painter, draughtsman, curator and collector. He was the son of a sculptor of modest means, and presumably he, together with his brothers, first trained in his father's workshop. In 1765 Wybrand became an active member of the Amsterdam Drawing Academy, where from 1772 to 1774 he won top prizes. Until 1772 he worked as a landscape painter in the Amsterdam wallpaper factory of Johannes Remmers. The staffage in Hendriks's landscapes was added by Willem Joseph Laquy (1738–98). In 1772 Hendriks bought his own small wallpaper factory in Amsterdam, which he ran until 1776. Around 1775 he made a short trip to England with Hendrik Meijer (1737–93), a Haarlem painter, etcher and wallpaper manufacturer, and in 1776 moved to Haarlem, where he painted still-lifes and made watercolour copies after 17th-century masters for collectors. From 1782 to 1785 Hendriks was in Ede, where he drew and painted mostly landscapes. He returned to Haarlem in 1785 and until 1819 was curator of the art collections of the Teylers Foundation, the earliest Dutch public museum for the arts and sciences. He took great care in extending the museum's drawings collection. He also painted and drew various subjects connected with the museum, such as the famous little panel of the *Oval Room of the Teylers Foundation* (1810; Haarlem, Teylers Mus.).

Hendriks became Haarlem's most sought after portrait painter and depicted many prominent citizens, including the *Governors of the Teylers Hofje* (1786; Haarlem, Teylers Hofje) and the artists' biographer *Adriaan van der Willigen* (1807; Haarlem, Frans Halsmus.). In other works Hendriks showed himself a sharp observer of the political, social and cultural climate of Haarlem at the time, as in a drawing of the *Swearing In of the Patriotic Civic Guard* (1787; Haarlem, Gemeentearchf) and the painting of a *Festival in the Grote Markt* (1825; Haarlem, Frans Halsmus.). Hendriks's drawings and paintings are characterized by a realism at times close to caricature, a somewhat clumsy handling of figures and space and, occasionally, a completely idiosyncratic composition. His considerable art collection was sold in February 1832.

BIBLIOGRAPHY

Scheen

J. Knoef: 'Een portretgroep van Wybrand Hendriks', *Oud-Holland*, lv (1938), pp. 175–8

——: 'Het voorbeeld voor een portretgroep van W. Hendriks?', *Ksthist. Meded. Rijksbureau Ksthist. Doc.*, ii (1967), pp. 11–13

Dutch Masterpieces from the Eighteenth Century: Paintings and Drawings, 1700–1800 (exh. cat. by E. R. Mandle, Minneapolis, MN, Inst. A.; Toledo, OH, Mus. A.; Philadelphia, PA, Mus. A.; 1971–2), pp. 50–52

S. A. C. Dudok van Heel: 'Wybrand Hendriks en de behangselmaker Remmers', *Mdbl. Amstelodamum*, lix (1972), pp. 102–9

FRANS GRIJZENHOUT

Henegouwe, Jan [Iennin; Janin; Jennyn] **van.** *See* GOSSART, JAN.

Henen-nesut. *See* HERAKLEOPOLIS MAGNA.

Henge. Type of prehistoric monument widely distributed throughout Britain, Ireland and Europe. The term derives from the name of STONEHENGE ('hanging stone') in Wiltshire, England: the 'hanging' element in this case consists of stone lintels that rest on pairs of upright stones (*see also* MEGALITHIC ARCHITECTURE, §1). Following the excavation of a nearby timber version of this structure, which became known as Woodhenge, the 'henge' part of these site names was adopted for all monuments of the same class. Henges are generally circular, comprising a bank with an internal ditch (in contrast to fortifications, where the ditch is outside the bank); an exception is Stonehenge itself, which has an external ditch. There may be one, two or four entrances. Henges vary in size: Stonehenge measures 105–10 m in diameter, while Durrington Walls, also in Wiltshire, is 520 m across. When excavated, henges have revealed internal structures: some of these may have been domestic, although many are thought to have been connected with the activities—possibly ritual—taking place at the site. The internal structures often take the form of several concentric rings of posts (there is disagreement as to whether these were roofed), and the remains at Woodhenge closely resemble similar structures found within larger henges. The purpose of these monuments is unclear: they are associated with a form of pottery found at certain sites from the Orkney Islands in the north of Scotland to southern England, and they date to the Late Neolithic period and Early Bronze Age, *c.* 2500–1500 BC.

See also PREHISTORIC EUROPE, §§IV, 2(iv)(a) and V, 3(ii).

BIBLIOGRAPHY
G. Wainwright: *The Henge Monuments* (London, 1989)

SARA CHAMPION

Henle, Fritz (*b* Dortmund, 9 June 1909). American photographer of German birth. He began taking photographs at the age of 15, before studying physics. He first published a photograph, of a Dortmund blast-furnace, as early as 1929. He studied photography in 1930–31 at the Bayrische Staatslehranstalt für Lichtbildwesen, Munich. After this he stayed in Italy, where he was commissioned to photograph Renaissance works of art, and he travelled extensively in Italy for Lloyd Tours. After travelling in China and Japan he made contacts with *Life* magazine and emigrated to the USA, where he worked as a freelance press photographer for such magazines as *Fortune*, *Life* and *Harper's Bazaar*. He consistently used a Rolleiflex camera and photographed American subjects. He gave up his studio in New York in 1958 and moved to St Croix, Virgin Islands. He continually emphasized the positive side of life in his work; in the Virgin Islands he found that original beauty whose portrayal he saw as his particular task. His archive is largely at the University of Texas, Austin.

WRITINGS
with G. B. Wright: *Fritz Henle's Guide to Rollei Photography* (New York, 1956)

PHOTOGRAPHIC PUBLICATIONS
This Is Japan (Munich, 1937)
The Virgin Islands (New York, 1949)
Fritz Henle's Figure Studies (New York, 1954/R London, 1957)
Casals (New York, 1975)

BIBLIOGRAPHY
N. Hall and B. Burton, eds: *Fritz Henle: Great Photographs 2* (London, 1954)
F. Kempe and others, eds: *Fotografie 1919–1979, Made in Germany: Die GDL Fotografen* (Frankfurt, 1979)
Paris 1938 (exh. cat., Dortmund, Mus. Kst & Kultgesch., 1989)

REINHOLD MISSELBECK

Henne, Joachim (*b* ?1630–40; *d* after 1707). German ivory- and wood-carver, wax modeller and miniaturist. He was the foremost master of small-scale sculpture active in northern Germany and Denmark in the Baroque period, basing his work on pictorial and sculptural models from the earlier 17th century. The strong influence on his sculpture of the work of Artus Quellinus (i) and other sculptors in the circle of Rubens, and of Georg Petel and his followers, suggests that Henne made a study journey through the Netherlands and southern Germany. From 1663 to 1665 he worked in Hamburg, where he made oval ivory portrait reliefs of the local patricians. These works, such as the *Portrait of a Man* (Hamburg, Mus. Kst & Gew.), represent the sitters half-length, turned at an angle to the viewer, and with the features, hair and draperies treated with meticulous realism. Henne also executed portrait medallions and small-scale single figures and groups with mythological or religious subjects. His ivory figure of the *Mourning St John* (Hamburg, Mus. Kst & Gew.), with its clumsy draperies and unconvincing depiction of emotion, is representative.

Henne left Hamburg in 1665 and worked for the court at Gottorf, travelling to Copenhagen in 1671, where until 1676 he was Royal Ivory Carver. Although he received prestigious commissions for royal portrait busts, his realism of presentation was still noticeable (e.g. *Queen Sophia Amalia*; London, V&A). The ivory relief the *Adoration of the Shepherds* (1675; London, V&A) is one of his few signed and dated works and provides a point of reference for stylistic attributions. On the basis of its distinctive sad-faced, long-bodied putti, the Løvenøns cup (Lejre, Ledreborg), one of the finest surviving Baroque ivory drinking vessels, has been attributed to Henne. Further works by him are the boxwood pair of mythological lovers (Cologne, Kstgewmus.), with a highly realistic treatment of details such as veins and axillary hair, and the ivory group *Veritas filia temporis* (Copenhagen, Nmus.). The latter is one of numerous small works made by Henne for the Danish royal collection that demonstrate his virtuoso abilities as an ivory-carver.

It is possible that most of Henne's sculptural works date from the decade after his arrival in Copenhagen, since in 1691 and 1696 he is recorded only as a seal-cutter and miniaturist in Copenhagen. In 1702 he went to Berlin to work for Frederick I, who had admired his miniature portrait of *Crown Prince Frederick William of Prussia* (untraced). In 1707 he was recorded as 'Court Painter of Miniature Portraits'.

BIBLIOGRAPHY
A. Rohde: 'Der Elfenbeinschnitzer Joachim Henne', *Der Cicerone*, xvii (1925), pp. 489–97, 555–61

Barockplastik in Norddeutschland (exh. cat., ed. J. Rasmussen; Hamburg, Mus. Kst & Gew., 1977), pp. 373–404

J. Rasmussen: 'Joachim Henne, ein höfischer Kleinmeister des Barock', *Jb. Hamburg. Kstsamml.*, xxiii (1978), pp. 25–64

A. GERHARDT

Henne [Hennen, Henner], **Jost** [Joest] (*b* Westphalia; *fl* 1629–44; *d* 1644). German sculptor and master builder active in Sweden. He is known to have decorated the memorial chapel (1632–3) of Gustav II Adolf, King of Sweden (*reg* 1611–32), in Riddarholm Church, Stockholm, and to have executed the south portal (1643) of the German Church in that city. Between 1637 and 1644 he worked on the black marble and white alabaster monument to Magnus Brahe (1564–1633) in Västerås Cathedral and between 1642 and 1644 on the portal of Queen Christina's summerhouse in Stockholm (since the 1680s the house of the Landtmäteristyrelsen (office of land surveyors)).

BIBLIOGRAPHY

SVKL

W. Nisser: 'Brahegraven i Västerås domkyrka' [The Brahe grave in Västerås Cathedral], *Tidskr. Kstvet.*, xxii (1939), pp. 33–60

G. Axel-Nilsson: *Dekorativ stenhuggarkonst i yngre vasastil* [Decorative sculpture in the early Vasa style] (Stockholm, 1950)

——: *Makalös: Fältherren greve Jakob De la Gardies hus i Stockholm* [The peerless palace: the Stockholm house of the Field Marshall Jacob De la Gardie] (Stockholm, 1984)

TORBJÖRN FULTON

Henneberg, Hugo (*b* Vienna, 27 July 1863; *d* Vienna, 11 July 1918). Austrian photographer. From 1882 to 1887 he studied physics, chemistry, astronomy and mathematics in Vienna and Jena, obtaining his doctorate in 1888. He began photography in 1887 and first exhibited his work in Salzburg in 1893. In 1894 he became a member of the LINKED RING. Through the Wiener Camera-Klub he met Hans Watzek in 1891 and Heinrich Kühn in 1894, the three forming a group that exhibited under the names of Das Kleeblatt and Trifolium from 1897 to 1903 and toured Germany, Italy and the Netherlands. On seeing Robert Demachy's gum prints, he experimented in the medium, partly in collaboration with Watzek and Kühn. Landscape remained his preferred subject. He exhibited three-coloured gum prints with the Vienna Secession in 1902 and joined the new Wiener Photo-Klub in 1904. He made regular contributions to the *Wiener photographische Blätter* from 1895 to 1898. By 1910 he had given up photography and turned to wood-engraving and etching.

BIBLIOGRAPHY

M. Matthies-Masuren: 'Hugo Henneberg', *Phot. Centbl.* (Sept 1899), pp. 357–60

O. Hochreiter and T. Starl, eds: *Geschichte der Photographie in Österreich*, 2 vols (Bad Ischl, 1983)

HANS CHRISTIAN ADAM

Hennebique, François (*b* Neuville Saint-Vaast, Pas de Calais, 25 April 1842; *d* Paris, 7 March 1921). French engineer. Born into a peasant family, he began his career as a stone-dresser, rising rapidly to site supervisor. He formed his own company in 1867 and became interested in reinforced concrete, which he studied for 12 years, during which time he carried out systematic experiments on combining iron and concrete. Unlike most inventors of systems of reinforced concrete, Hennebique aimed at a rigorous understanding of the behaviour of iron and concrete in a load-bearing beam. He observed that, under compression, concrete is preferable to iron, that it does not impede expansion and that its use offers a means to avoid shearing. Accurate deductions based on considerable practical knowledge of and experiments with the material enabled him to devise a system to calculate the correct position for the reinforcement within the concrete, first patented in 1892 when the scientific equipment for the study of concrete was extremely rudimentary.

Hennebique made his first slabs reinforced with iron rods in 1879 and took out his first patents in 1888. In 1892 and 1894 he patented girders reinforced with iron stirrups, which bound together lower and upper layers of iron rods. In 1894 he also built the first railway bridge in reinforced concrete at Viggen, Switzerland, with a span of 2.4 m. He also built various industrial buildings, for example the Charles VI spinning-mills (1895) at Tourcoing and the Barois mills (1896) at Fives-Lille. In the latter, where the gaps in the reinforced-concrete structure were glazed, Hennebique created a building method that was later adopted in residential buildings by avant-garde architects of the 1920s. At the mill (1896) at Nort sur Erdre he created a system of infilling, which was later used by Auguste Perret: the voids of the structure were filled with two prefabricated panels, or glazing, framed by prefabricated posts. Hennebique's method allowed a considerable reduction of fire risk and made large spans possible, while remaining reliable and cheap. Its success was immense. His perfection of an aggressive commercial policy based on the direct exploitation of his own patents enabled him to build up a business empire. Between 1894 and 1909 he opened 42 agencies throughout the world, notably in Brussels, New York, St Petersburg and Turin. His slogan was: 'Concrete enables you to do great things with modest means.' By 1902 his firm and its agencies had already built 7025 structures and by 1909 the total had risen to 20,324, of which 1300 were worked on by his own office. Through the connections he made with architects and his activity as a propagandist for reinforced concrete, particularly through the publication of the review *Le Béton armé, organe des concessionaires et des agents du système Hennebique* (1898–1921), he played a pre-eminent role in architectural circles. Architects as important as Tony Garnier, Michel Roux-Spitz, Henri Sauvage and Perret made use of his system.

One of the most significant works built to Hennebique's specifications is the Risorgimento bridge (1908–10) in Rome, the 100-m span of which was then a world record. Hennebique was also a pioneer in his use of reinforced concrete for residential blocks, including those at 9 Rue Claude-Chahu (1902; designed by C. Klein), Paris, and his own house (1904) at Bourg-la-Reine, with its 4-m overhang and turret staircase giving access to the terrace garden. His own office building (1898) at 1 Rue Danton, Paris, designed by Edouard Arnaud, was probably the first large building to be made entirely of reinforced concrete. It is sumptuously designed and stylistically eclectic, but the building's structure is hidden beneath a facing of cement imitating stone.

BIBLIOGRAPHY

R. Flament-Hennebique: *Le Centenaire de F. Hennebique* (Paris, 1943)

N. Pevsner: *The Sources of Modern Architecture and Design* (London, 1968)

M. Emery: *Un Siècle d'architecture moderne en France* (Paris, 1971)
L'Architecture et les ingénieurs (exh. cat. by S. Deswartes and B. Lemoine, Paris, Pompidou, 1980)

JEAN-FRANÇOIS PINCHON

Hennecart [Hennequart], **Jean** (*fl* 1454–70). South Netherlandish illuminator. His name appears several times in the account books of the Burgundian court, and he was among the artists employed to produce decorations for the famous 'banquet du faisan' organized by Philip the Good, Duke of Burgundy, in Lille in 1454. Hennecart also worked for Charles the Bold, Duke of Burgundy, while the latter was still Comte de Charolais, painting coats of arms and producing banners for him, among other things. In 1457, on the occasion of the birth of Mary, Duchess of Burgundy, he illuminated a rotulus with a motet (untraced). One documented work by the artist survives: according to a bill of 1470 Hennecart was paid for the illumination of two copies of the *Instruction d'un jeune prince*, a didactic text formerly attributed to Georges Chastellain and now regarded as the work of Guillebert de Lannoy. One of these copies (Paris, Bib. Arsenal, MS. 5104), containing three miniatures, bears the initials of Charles the Bold and Margaret of York (fol. 66*r*) and must therefore have been produced after their marriage in 1468; this accords with the dating given by the document of 1470.

Stylistically, Hennecart's illuminations show the influence of the MASTER OF THE GIRART DE ROUSSILLON (*see* MASTERS, ANONYMOUS, AND MONOGRAMMISTS, §I), but he must also have known the frontispiece of the *Chroniques de Hainault* (Brussels, Bib. Royale Albert 1er, MS. 9242, fol. 1*r*), attributed to Rogier van der Weyden (*see* WEYDEN, VAN DER, (1)); from it he borrowed an interior and a figure-group almost exactly (see fig.). Like van der Weyden he depicted a detailed interior with a bed, curtain, baldacchino, tiled floor, beamed ceiling and windows; yet his foreshortening is considerably less skilful, and he also encountered some problems in the arrangement of the figures in the picture space. (This is equally true of his landscape scenes.) However, his lively figure-types are convincing. Their costumes are comparable with those depicted by the MASTER OF ANTOINE OF BURGUNDY (*see* MASTERS, ANONYMOUS, AND MONOGRAMMISTS, §I): prominent among other features are the tall, blunt, cone-shaped headdresses. Another characteristic of Hennecart's work is the very thin application of colour, so that the surface is often not fully covered. His flesh tints are frequently yellowish and pale, with a blotchy appearance, and it is possible that the pigment was not durable. His predilection for medallions with coats of arms, mottoes or other marks of ownership in the borders is also notable, as are the high-quality branchwork initials. Little can be said about Hennecart's development and historical position, as this manuscript is his only authenticated work, but further works by him may be identified among the numerous and stylistically diverse illuminations attributed to the Master of Antoine of Burgundy.

BIBLIOGRAPHY

H. Martin: 'Jean Hennecart, peintre de Charles le Téméraire', *Gaz. B.-A.*, xiii (1917), pp. 155–72
P. Durrieu: *La Miniature flamande au temps de la cour de Bourgogne (1415–1530)* (Brussels and Paris, 1921)
F. Winkler: *Die flämische Buchmalerei* (Leipzig, 1925, *R* Amsterdam, 1978)

Jean Hennecart: *Deathbed of a King*, with the coat of arms of Charles the Bold, from Guillebert de Lannoy: *Instruction d'un jeune prince*, *c.* 1470 (Paris, Bibliothèque de l'Arsenal, MS. 5104, fol. 5*r*)

Le Siècle d'or de la miniature flamande (exh. cat. by L. M. J. Delaissé, Brussels, Pal. B.-A.; Amsterdam, Rijksmus.; Paris, Bib. N.; 1959), p. 149
G. Dogaer: *Flemish Miniature Painting in the 15th and 16th Centuries* (Amsterdam, 1987), pp. 84–6

BODO BRINKMANN

Hennequin, Philippe-Auguste (*b* Lyon, 1762; *d* Leuze, nr Tournai, 12 May 1833). French painter. He was precociously talented and by the age of 15 had been Donat Nonnotte's pupil at the Académie des Beaux-Arts at Lyon and had arrived in Paris. There he worked for a time in Jacques-Louis David's studio, from which he was expelled after being accused of theft. He completed his studies at the Académie Royale de Peinture in 1784 and visited Rome at the expense of an English patron named Mills. Because of masonic connections he was forced to flee in 1789, returning to Lyon. His politics tended towards Jacobinism, and during the Revolution he was appointed to a commission entrusted with saving works of art. After the fall of Robespierre in 1794 he fled to Paris, where he suffered imprisonment and narrowly avoided the guillotine.

In 1798 Hennequin exhibited *Paris Tearing himself from Helen's Arms* and in 1799 was commissioned to paint the

Triumph of the French People, 10th August 1792 (fragment, Rouen, Mus. B.-A.). In 1800 he painted a ceiling for the Salle des Antonins in the Louvre with the *French Hercules* (*in situ*) and also won first prize for the *Remorse of Orestes* (damaged; Paris, Louvre). Vivant Denon commissioned him to paint for Napoleon the *Battle of Quiberon* (exh. Salon 1804; Toulouse, Mus. Augustins), *Distribution of the Crosses of the Légion d'Honneur* (Versailles, Château) and *Battle of the Pyramids* (exh. Salon 1806; Versailles, Château). Exiled from France by the restoration of the Bourbon monarchy, he went to live in the southern Netherlands, first in Brussels, then in Liège, where he became director of the new Athénée des Arts, and finally (1819) in Tournai, where he taught at the Académie. In 1831 his post was abolished; he died in poverty. His *Mémoires*, not published until 1933, reveal a genuine talent for writing.

Hennequin was a Neo-classical painter of the generation of François Gérard, Anne-Louis Girodet and Antoine-Jean Gros. His pictures have frieze-like compositions and figures derived from Classical sculpture. Their subjects are taken from the great deeds of ancient or contemporary history, from heroic mythology, or are allegories representing the virtues or alluding to contemporary personalities. However, his sharp, incisive drawing celebrates the human frame of bone and muscle; the folds of the draperies are stiff and the movements awkward; everything vibrates with tension.

Hennequin occasionally painted landscapes; his *Ancient Dance* (Tournai, Mus. B.-A.) shows groups of people in a space organized in receding parallel planes, punctuated by the verticals of medieval towers and ovoid trees, the whole enveloped in a vague, misty atmosphere. His religious paintings, from the Belgian period, are passionately expressive. In his *St John on Patmos* (1814; Liège, St Jean Evangéliste) the saint, whose disproportionately large hands and feet are characteristic of Hennequin, raises his face to the sky in a violently contrasted chiaroscuro. Hennequin's bust-length portraits, such as the *Conseiller de Saint-Martin* (between 1811 and 1819; Liège, Mus. B.-A.), are intensely expressive of character and mood, in spite of a neutral background. The full-length portrait of *Dominique-Catherine de Pérignon, Maréchal de France* (1804; Versailles, Château), against a background of mountains and sky, is Neo-classical in composition but animated by a wholly Romantic passion.

WRITINGS

J. Hennequin, ed.: *Mémoires* (Paris, 1933)

BIBLIOGRAPHY

A.-M. Benso: *Hennequin, la vie et l'oeuvre* (diss., U. Lille III, 1975)

J. Benoit: *Philippe-Auguste Hennequin, 1762–1833* (Paris, 1994)

CELIA ALEGRET

Hennequin de Liège. *See* JEAN DE LIÈGE (i).

Hennequin de Marville [Hannequin]. *See* JEAN DE MARVILLE.

Henner, Jean-Jacques (*b* Bernwiller, Alsace, 5 March 1829; *d* Paris, 23 July 1905). French painter. He was born into a peasant family in the Sundgau and received his first artistic training at Altkirch with Charles Goutzwiller (1810–1900) and later in Strasbourg in the studio of Gabriel-Christophe Guérin (1790–1846). In 1846 he enrolled at the Ecole des Beaux-Arts in Paris as a pupil of Michel-Martin Drolling and, from 1851, of François-Edouard Picot. While a student he was particularly drawn to portraiture, and during his frequent visits to Alsace he made portraits of his family as well as of the notables of the region. He also painted scenes of Alsatian peasant life (e.g. *Marie-Ann Henner Churning Butter*, 1856; Paris, Mus. Henner).

In 1858 Henner won the Prix de Rome with *Adam and Eve Finding the Body of Abel* (Paris, Ecole N. Sup. B.-A.). He then spent five years at the French Academy in Rome, where he discovered Caravaggio, Titian and Correggio, and was inspired by the landscapes of Rome and its surroundings (visited in 1859), of Florence, Venice and Milan (1860), and of Naples and Capri (1862).

Paintings he produced in Italy include the *Repentant Magdalene* (1860; Colmar, Mus. Unterlinden) and the *Chaste Suzanne* (1864; exh. Salon 1865; Paris, Mus. d'Orsay), both of which show the influence of Titian on his treatment of the nude, and of Corot on his landscape. Henner employed strong chiaroscuro effects, setting his pale figures against a dark background. Their contours were softened by the use of *sfumato*, for which he was indebted to Correggio, and wide, heavy brushstrokes.

In 1864 he returned to France and exhibited with enormous success at the Paris Salon between 1865 and 1903. After working for a time on quasi-mythological subjects, notably nymphs and naiads (e.g. *Byblis*, exh. Salon 1867; Dijon, Mus. B.-A.), he turned towards 'idyllic' painting and, after 1870, to Symbolism, occasionally with explicit political overtones. *Alsace* (1871; Paris, Mus. Henner), which shows a young Alsatian woman in mourning, is a political comment on the German annexation of the province after the Franco-Prussian War. The image achieved a wide circulation in the engraving (1871) by Léopold Flameng (1831–1911).

After 1870 Henner's entire oeuvre became a meditation on the theme of death in various guises, notably in the *Magdalene* series (e.g. *Magdalene in the Desert*, exh. Salon 1874; Toulouse, Mus. Augustins; *Magdalene Weeping*, 1885, untraced), the *Dead Christ* series (e.g. *Jesus in the Tomb*, exh. Salon 1879; Paris, Mus. d'Orsay; *Dead Christ*, exh. Salon 1884; Lille, Mus. B.-A.), *Andromeda* (1879, untraced) and the *Levite of Ephraim* (exh. Salon 1898; Ottawa, Tannenbaum priv. col.). The Italian landscape featured in his early work was gradually replaced by the typically Alsatian Sundgau, expressing the artist's nostalgia for his homeland.

Through the contacts he made in Rome, Henner obtained many portrait commissions, for example *Félix Ravaisson-Mollier* (exh. Salon 1886; Paris, Petit Pal.) and *Laura Leroux* (exh. Salon 1898; Angers, Mus. B.-A.), and these continued to be an important part of his output throughout his life. In 1923 his heirs founded a museum dedicated to him in Paris, in which most of his studio collection was housed.

BIBLIOGRAPHY

G. Cheyssial: *Musée National Jean-Jacques Henner*, Petits Guides des Grands Musées, 54 (Paris, n.d.)

L. Loviot: *J. J. Henner et son oeuvre* (Paris, 1912)

E. Durand-Greville: *Entretiens de J. J. Henner* (Paris, 1925)

P.-A. Meunier: *La Vie et l'oeuvre de Jean-Jacques Henner* (Washington, DC, 1927)

Jean-Jacques Henner, Henri Zuber (exh. cat., Strasbourg, Mus. B.-A., 1973)

G. de Lorenzi: *J. J. Henner e lo spiritualismo* (Florence, 1982)

I. de Lannoy: *Jean-Jacques Henner (1829–1905): Essai de catalogue*, 5 vols (diss., Paris, Ecole Louvre, 1986)

ISABELLE DE LANNOY

Henning. Scottish family of sculptors. The most prominent members were (1) John Henning (i) and his son (2) John Henning (ii); another son, Samuel Henning (*d* 1832), worked with his father but died of cholera at an early age.

(1) John Henning (i) [the elder] (*b* Paisley, 2 May 1771; *d* London, 8 April 1851). After local schooling he worked with his father, Samuel Henning (*fl* 1760–80), as a carpenter. Turning to sculpture, he modelled profile portraits in wax from life and later worked from life-size sketches, completing medallions in his workshop. From wax originals he produced copies in plaster, bronze or vitreous enamel. In 1801 he moved to Glasgow. Henning's medallion portrait subjects included *James Watt* (enamel, exh. 1810; Edinburgh, N.P.G.); *Sir Walter Scott* (plaster, 1808; Edinburgh, N.P.G.); *Princess Charlotte*, daughter of George IV (wax, copper mould, 1812; Paisley, Mus. & A. Gals); and *Arthur Wellesley, 1st Duke of Wellington* (copper, exh. London, RA, 1812; Paisley, Mus. & A. Gals; plaster, Edinburgh, N.P.G.). Josiah Wedgwood produced six of Henning's medallions as pottery cameos.

In July 1811 Henning moved to London. After seeing the Elgin Marbles (now London, BM), he obtained permission to draw them, in spite of strong opposition from Benjamin West, PRA, and spent over 12 years drawing the Parthenon friezes and those from the Temple of Apollo at Bassai (London, BM); and also copying Raphael's tapestry cartoons for the *Acts of the Apostles* (now London, V&A). Princess Charlotte (1796–1817) requested Henning to prepare a miniature of the Parthenon in ivory; at the suggestion of his son (2) John Henning (ii), he carved moulds of the friezes in slate (h. 76.2 mm) and produced plaster replicas at £31.50 a set. These were pirated; one dealer in Paris claimed in 1835 to have sold 12,000 copies. A larger version of the Parthenon frieze was used to decorate buildings, for example the exterior of the Athenaeum Club (London, Pall Mall), where the younger John Henning did the work, with his father's help, and the interior of the Royal College of Surgeons (London, Lincoln's Inn Fields).

Henning executed memorials to *John Heaton* (1818; Havering-atte-Bower, Essex, St John the Evangelist) and to *John Ellis* (1836; Wyddial, Herts, St Giles). He occasionally did metalwork, producing the seal matrix for the Independent Gas Light and Coke Company (1829) and medals of the *Duke of Wellington* and the *Duke of Clarence* (later William IV, 1765–1837). Henning was a founder-member of the British Society of Artists and a member of the Royal Scottish Academy (1827) and of the Glasgow Dilettanti Society (1832); in 1846 he became a freeman of Paisley. Despite all his success, he died in poverty.

(2) John Henning (ii) [the younger] (*b* Glasgow, 1802; *d* London, 1857). Son of (1) John Henning (i). He began work at an early age; at 13 he made a drawing of the *Duke of Wellington on Horseback*, which was later (1827) used for the reverse of his father's copper medallion of the same subject. In 1816 he was awarded the Silver Isis medal by the Society of Arts, for a relief of the *Good Samaritan* (untraced). He worked with his father on producing copies of the Parthenon and Bassai friezes, giving him considerable help in his later years. In 1828 Henning provided classical reliefs for Decimus Burton's triple screen at Hyde Park Corner, London, and in 1836 he carved the reliefs *Architecture, Painting, Sculpture, Wisdom, Astronomy* and *Mathematics* for the front of Manchester Art Gallery. He exhibited in 1844 a statue of *Lord Bacon* and a group, *Boadicea*, in Westminster Hall, London (both untraced). In 1845 he executed the reliefs for the column erected to the memory of *George Townshend, 1st Earl of Leicester* (1755–1811) at Holkham Hall, Norfolk; and also the reliefs around the Colosseum (destr. 1875) in Regent's Park, London. In 1850 he executed reliefs based on Hogarth's engravings of the *Industrious Apprentice* and the *Idle Apprentice* at the Freemen's Orphan School in Brixton, London, and in 1852 reliefs of *The Vintage* and *Music and Painting* for the Mansion House, London.

Henning produced and exhibited a number of busts, including those of his father, *John Henning* (exh. RA 1848; destr.), *George Rigby* (exh. RA 1849), *Ann, Duchess of Bedford* (Woburn Abbey, Beds) and *John Churchill, 1st Duke of Marlborough* (Windsor Castle, Berks, Royal Col.). He died shortly after completing a memorial to *Charles Heaton Ellis* (1857) at St Giles, Wyddial, Herts, where his father had erected a memorial to *John Ellis*.

Gunnis

BIBLIOGRAPHY

R. J. Malden: *John Henning: A Very Ingenious Modeller* (Paisley, 1979)

JOHN MALDEN

Henning, Gerhard (*b* Stockholm, 27 May 1880; *d* Hellerup, 16 Sept 1967). Danish sculptor of Swedish birth. He trained in the painting trade in Sweden, later spending 1903–4 in Italy and France. As a young man he drew adventure series. In 1909 he settled in Denmark, becoming a Danish citizen in 1931. He was employed by the Kongelige Porcelainsfabrik (1904–14 and 1920–25), where he produced painterly refined small groups with embellished overglazing decoration influenced by French Rococo. He was awarded a medal for porcelain in the Paris Salon in 1912.

Henning's main career was in sculpture. Inspired by Rodin and Maillol he created large female figures, freely employing a lyrical imagination and a strong sense of eroticism. He shared common ideals with his friend Kai Nielsen, who inspired him to adopt a more monumental format. Henning's breakthrough as a sculptor came at the Kunstnernes Efteraarsudstilling (The Artists' Autumn Exhibition), Copenhagen, in 1924, and he exhibited at Den Frie Udstilling (The Free Exhibition), Copenhagen, from 1932. Through beautifully modelled small works, often with titles from Classical mythology, he came to life-size statues such as *Danaë* (plaster and later bronze, 1927; Copenhagen, Stat. Mus. Kst) and a series of Junoesque, harmonious, over-life-size female figures. *Standing Girl* (1928–9; Copenhagen, Stat. Mus. Kst) and *Sitting Girl* (1937–8; Copenhagen, Ny Carlsberg Glyp.) are both sandstone works with precise modelling. Apparently classical, they nevertheless lack the usual gravity of Neoclassicism. Henning can be said to have continued, sensitively and authoritatively, the innovation in Danish sculpture created by Kai Nielsen.

BIBLIOGRAPHY

P. Hentz: *Billedhuggeren Gerhard Henning* [The sculptor Gerhard Henning] (Copenhagen, 1931)
H. Rostrup: *Gerhard Hennings Tegninger* [Gerhard Henning's drawings] (Copenhagen, 1959)
H. Bramsen: 'Gerhard Henning', *Dan. Ksthist.*, v (1975)
H. Rostrup: *Gerhard Henning: En mindebog* [Gerhard Henning: a book of reminiscences] (Copenhagen, 1980)

GRETHE KUSK

Henningsen, Poul (*b* Ordrup, 9 Sept 1894; *d* Hillerød, 31 Jan 1967). Danish designer, architect and critic. He gained international fame with his development of the 'PH' lamp (1925–6), a 'classic' of Danish industrial design, which has remained in continuous production. Henningsen's education was unorthodox but practical: he boarded with a carpenter, then studied mechanical engineering and architecture in Copenhagen, although he never formally qualified in either profession. He painted in a late Impressionist style, but championed Danish Cubism and Expressionism when he became an art critic in 1918.

During the 1920s he was a strong critic of architecture and urban planning, and in 1926 he founded the influential journal *Kritisk Revy* ('Critical Review'), which ran for two years and had contributors from other Nordic countries including Uno Åhrén and Alvar Aalto. It became the journal for emerging Danish Functionalism and aligned itself with international movements, but its divergence from the technologically inspired Modernist aesthetic (such as that of the Bauhaus) was typical of Henningsen's independent approach. He advocated, among other things, that the terraced house should be the democratic residential form of the future and challenged manufacturers and craftsmen with his demand for 'honest industrial design' that would reflect modern life.

In 1919 he began his lighting experiments and at the *Exposition des Arts Décoratifs* (Paris, 1925) he won a gold medal with a prototype of the 'PH' lamp. Its simple standard elements in metal and moulded glass were cheap to mass-produce. It had three lightweight, nested shades, all with mathematically determined curvatures that dispersed dazzle-free reflected light, yet had a wide spectral range. Developing these criteria, Henningsen created a system that eventually consisted of several hundred variations of more than 40 types of lamp, such as 'Artichoke' and 'PH5' (both 1958). His ideas about lighting were particularly developed during his editorship, from 1941, of Louis Poulsen's company journal *LP-Nyt*. Functional aesthetics also marked Henningsen's other industrial designs. In a range of steel furniture of the 1930s, the chairs linked new materials with traditional forms such as the 'Thonet' chair and were intended to be more comfortable than the standard types available. In the same decade he produced metallic pianettes and grand pianos, with transparent celluloid and chromed wavy legs, designed to accentuate their character as modern jazz instruments. Henningsen had an aversion to teak and the supposed 'good taste' of Danish design; he expressed this, from 1960, in the international design journal *Mobilia*.

Henningsen's few single-family dwellings and larger architectural projects were of limited influence. In 1919 he began a short-lived partnership with Kay Fisker; the neo-classical apartment block Hornbækhus, Copenhagen (1923), was characteristic of their work. Of Henningsen's independent work, the rhythmically divided block of flats at St Kjeldsgade 2–12, Copenhagen (1924), represented a departure from the monotonous façades typical of contemporary Danish architecture, while the architectural expression of his desire for functional honesty was the unpretentious Dehn's steam laundry, Copenhagen (1936), where the firm's name dominated the pediment field.

During the 1930s Henningsen revived the popular musical revue tradition with the PH Revues, where jazz and Cubist decorations were combined with his idiosyncratic satirical lyrics. His controversial documentary *Danmarksfilm* ('Film of Denmark', 1935) was a landmark in Danish film history. He was also prominent among the anti-fascist artists. In his search for a consciously didactic politic of culture, he spent the last decade of his life writing and lecturing primarily on consumerism and the entertainment industry. He founded the consumer journal *Tænk* ('Think') in 1964 and gained public recognition for his liberal views on education, women in society and sexuality. Always controversial, Henningsen became the most influential critic of his generation in Denmark.

WRITINGS

'A Classical Novelty', *Mobilia*, xxiv (1958), pp. 21–38 [on the 'PH5' and 'Artichoke' lamps]
'Concerning a Shoehorn...', *Mobilia*, xxvi (1960), pp. 27–8
C. E. Bay and O. Harsløf, eds: *Poul Henningsen: Kulturkritik*, 4 vols (Copenhagen, 1973)
E. Christensen and others, eds: *Om lys* [About light] (Copenhagen, 1974)

BIBLIOGRAPHY

DBL
S. Frandsen: *PH's eksempel* [PH's example] (Copenhagen, 1978)
Scandinavian Modern Design, 1880–1980 (exh. cat., ed. D. R. McFadden; New York, Cooper-Hewitt Mus., 1982)
L. Dybdahl: '"Ansigtet imod den lykkeligere fremtid": Tidsskriftet *Kritisk Revy* (1926–8)' ['Facing the happier future': the journal *Kritisk Revy* (1926–8)], *Nordisk funktionalisme, 1925–1950: Nordisk Forum for Formgivningshistorie: København, 1985*, pp. 31–7
P. Hammerich: *Lysmageren: En krønike om Poul Henningsen* [The lightmaker: a chronicle about Poul Henningsen] (Copenhagen, 1986)

LARS DYBDAHL

Henrard, Robert Arnold (*b* Dinant, 1615/17; *d* ?Liège, 18 Sept 1676). Flemish sculptor of French birth. He trained in Liège before leaving for Rome, where he worked in the circle of François Du Quesnoy. Although Du Quesnoy's classicism made a deep impression on him, Henard's style retained a significant personal element. By 1664 Henrard had returned to Liège, where he joined the Carthusian Order and decorated the cloister (destr.) of the Carthusian monastery. He restored the rood screen (destr.) of Liège Cathedral and executed a new marble high altar (destr.) donated by Maximilian-Hendrick of Bavaria, Prince Bishop of Liège. A white marble figure of the *Virgin and Child* (Liège, St Paul), which recalls Du Quesnoy's *St Susanna* (Rome, S Maria di Loreto), has been attributed to him. Henrard also designed figures that were later executed by the foremost silversmith of Liège, Henri de Flémalle (*fl c.* 1672; *d* ?1686). These include a reliquary with *St John the Baptist* (Liège, St Paul), which is based on Du Quesnoy's figure of *St Andrew* (Rome, St Peter's), and a figure of *St Catherine of Alexandria* (*c.* 1675; Maaseik, St Kathelijn), which is a reworking of Bernini's *St Bibiana* (Rome, St Bibiana). Henrard is a little-known figure, frequently confused with Jean Arnold de Honthoir. He was perhaps the teacher of Jean Delcour.

BIBLIOGRAPHY

P. Colman: 'Robert Henrard', *De beeldhouwkunst in de eeuw van Rubens* [Sculpture in the century of Rubens] (Brussels, 1977), pp. 126–8

CYNTHIA LAWRENCE

Henri, Florence (*b* New York, 28 June 1893; *d* Compiègne, Oise, July 1982). Swiss photographer and painter. Born of a French father and German mother, she spent her childhood in Paris, Vienna and the Isle of Wight. When she was 16 she went to Rome, where she came into contact with the Futurists. In Berlin she studied the piano with Egon Petri and Ferruccio Busoni in 1911–14 and painting with Kurt Schwitters at the Staatliche Hochschule für bildenden Künste in 1914. From 1915 to 1919 she attended the Hofmann Schule für Moderne Kunst in Munich. She continued her painting studies in Paris, at the Académie André Lhote in 1922–3 and under Léger and Amédée Ozenfant at the Académie Moderne in 1924–5. Her paintings of this period show the influence of Cubism and Geometric Abstraction, as shown by the brightly coloured *Composition* (1922; Montrouge, priv. col., see 1979 exh. cat., no. 86). The most significant element of Henri's artistic training was, however, at the Bauhaus in Dessau, where she was taught by Josef Albers and László Moholy-Nagy in 1927. Under Moholy-Nagy's influence she became interested in photography and continued his investigations into the possibilities of this medium. To this end she began to use mirrors and panes of glass to alter and multiply the object image, leading to highly complex works such as the still-life *Abstract Composition* (1929; Genoa, priv. col., see 1979 exh. cat., no. 129) and such portraits as that of *Fernand Léger* (1934; Genoa, priv. col., see 1979 exh. cat., no. 257). She worked freelance in Paris from 1929 to 1963 as a portrait, advertising and fashion photographer. From 1928 to 1947 she also taught photography and in the 1930s became associated with the CERCLE ET CARRÉ group. From 1963 she lived in Compiègne, where she concentrated on painting.

BIBLIOGRAPHY

E. de Miro: *Florence Henri* (Genoa, 1974)

S. Pagé and H. Molderings: *Florence Henri* (Paris, 1978)

Florence Henri: Aspetti di un percorso 1910–1940 (exh. cat. by G. Marcenaro and others, Genoa, Banco di Chiavarie, 1979)

☐

Henri, Robert [Cozad, Robert Henry] (*b* Cincinnati, OH, 24 June 1865; *d* 12 July 1929). American painter and teacher. He changed his name in 1883 after his father killed someone; in honour of his French ancestry, Henri adopted his own middle name as a surname, taking the French spelling but insisting all his life that it be pronounced in the American vernacular. After living with his family in Denver, CO, and New York, in 1886 he entered the Pennsylvania Academy of Fine Arts, Philadelphia, where he studied with Thomas Anshutz and Thomas Hovenden. In 1888 he attended the Académie Julian in Paris, where he received criticism from the French painters William-Adolphe Bouguereau and Tony Robert-Fleury. He returned to Philadelphia in 1891 and painted in an Impressionist manner, for example *Girl Seated by the Sea* (1893; Mr and Mrs Raymond J. Horowitz priv. col., see Homer, pl. 1).

In 1895 Henri returned to Europe and adopted a dark-toned, broadly brushed style influenced by Velázquez, Frans Hals and the early paintings of Manet. His portrait studies in this style were accepted in the Paris Salons of 1896 and 1897. Through a one-man exhibition in Philadelphia in 1897, he came to the attention of William Merritt Chase, who introduced Henri into the New York art world. In 1900 he established himself in New York and began teaching at the New York School of Art, founded by Chase, until 1908 when he established his own school.

At this early stage Henri was helping younger artists in their struggle for independence against the New York art establishment. By 1906 when he was elected to the National Academy of Design, he had begun to undermine its authority. Angered by the restrictive exhibition policies of the Academy, Henri helped organize an independent exhibition in 1908 at the Macbeth Galleries, New York, of a group of artists who came to be known as THE EIGHT (i). Henri also helped organize the Exhibition of Independent Artists in 1910. Henri's chief followers were a group of artist newspaper illustrators whom he had encouraged to become painters: John Sloan, William J. Glackens, George Luks and Everett Shinn. They formed the core of the group later dubbed the ASHCAN SCHOOL, who painted with bold, bravura brushwork that imparted a certain spontaneity to their works. For subject-matter they turned to the vitality of everyday urban life in New York, for example *West 57th Street* (1902; New Haven, CT, Yale U., A.G.) by Henri.

Henri painted mainly portraits and landscapes, using impasto brushwork and strong chiaroscuro, as in *Laughing Child* (1907; New York, Whitney) and *The Masquerade Dress: Portrait of Mrs Robert Henri* (1911; New York, Met.). After 1909 his paintings became progressively more colourful as he experimented with the techniques of painter and colour theorist Hardesty Maratta (*b* 1864). Henri's reputation was, however, based on his ability as a teacher and leader of the Ashcan school. His ideas were disseminated further in *The Art Spirit* (1923), a collection of his lectures, precepts and attitudes towards art.

See also ARMORY SHOW and NEW YORK, fig. 7.

WRITINGS

M. Ryerson, ed.: *The Art Spirit* (Philadelphia, 1923, rev. New York, 1960)

BIBLIOGRAPHY

N. Pousette-Dart: *Robert Henri* (New York, 1922)

G. P. du Bois: 'Robert Henri', *Amer. Mag. A.*, xxii (June 1931), pp. 435–55

J. J. Kwiat: 'Robert Henri and the Emerson-Whitman Tradition', *Pubns Mod. Lang. Assocs*, lxxi/1 (1956), pp. 617–36

M. Sandoz: *Son of the Gamblin' Man: The Youth of an Artist* (New York, 1960)

W. I. Homer: *Robert Henri and his Circle* (Ithaca, 1969)

John Sloan/Robert Henri: Their Philadelphia Years, 1886–1904 (exh. cat., Philadelphia, PA, Moore Coll. A. & Des., Goldie Paley Gal., 1976)

B. B. Perlman: *Robert Henri: His Life and Art* (New York, 1991)

M. SUE KENDALL

Henricus. *See* JANSEN, HENDRICUS.

Henricus Malinis [van Mechelen] [Hennequin de Meecle]. *See* BROECK, VAN DEN, (3).

Henriet, (Charles-)Frédéric (*b* Château-Thierry, Aisne, 6 Sept 1826; *d* Château-Thierry, 24 April 1918). French painter, writer and engraver. He began his career in Paris as a law student and while completing his degree published short pieces on art and the theatre in satirical journals under a pseudonym. In 1851 the Comte de Nieuwerkerke hired him to assist in the organization of the Salons and then to be his personal secretary (1854–9).

Henriet published Salon reviews in 1852 and 1853. In 1851 he had met the landscape painters Corot and Charles-François Daubigny in the studio of the glass painter and restorer Nicolas Coffetier (1821–84). His friendship with these artists led him to write about their work and finally, having returned to Château-Thierry after his retirement from government service in 1859, to become a painter. Following the acceptance of his landscape *At Corbiers, near Jouarre* (untraced) in the Salon of 1865, he exhibited at the Salon regularly until 1880, albeit without medals. One painting, the *Marne at Tancrou*, was bought by the State in 1868 for the Musée Municipal Hôtel Dieu in Vire.

Henriet's paintings, engravings and watercolours (e.g. the *Farm of Gléret*, exh. Salon 1874; untraced) record his beloved homeland: the Marne River, the Ourcq canal, the village of Jouarre and that of Mézy on the Seine. In pastoral mood, tonal palette and deeply receding horizontal format they echo the plains and valleys, wide, slow waterways and rutted village roads of the Marne Valley, an area painted by his more illustrious colleagues Daubigny and Léon Lhermitte. Throughout his life, Henriet remained a Barbizon painter of the Marne. In Château-Thierry between 1898 and 1912 he helped administer and publish the *Annales* of the town's Société Historique et Archéologique, as well as being the curator of the town's art museum, the Musée Jean de La Fontaine, where three of his works now hang (the *Village of Montgoins*, the *Banks of the Meuse at Revin* and the *Keep of Vic-en-Aisne*).

WRITINGS

Coup d'oeil sur le Salon de 1853 (Paris, 1853)
Daubigny: Esquisse biographique (Montdidier, 1857)
Chintreuil: Esquisse biographique (Paris, 1858)
Le Paysagiste aux champs (Paris, 1866, 2/1876)
Daubigny et son oeuvre (Paris, 1875)
Les Campagnes d'un paysagiste (Paris, 1891)
Les Eaux-fortes de Léon Lhermitte (Paris, 1905)
Etienne Moreau-Nélaton: Notes intimes (Paris, 1907)

BIBLIOGRAPHY

Bénézit
Eaux-fortes par F. Henriet (Paris, n.d.)
H. Beraldi: *Les Graveurs du XIXe siècle*, viii (Paris, 1889), pp. 76–7
E. Moreau-Nélaton: *Mon bon ami Henriet* (Paris, 1914)

NANCY DAVENPORT

Henriet, Israël (*b* Nancy, *c.* 1590; *bur* Paris, 25 April 1661). French painter, etcher, draughtsman and print-publisher. He was the son of Claude Henriet II (*c.* 1540–1603/4), court painter to Charles III, Duke of Lorraine. Henriet, like his compatriot and friend Jacques Callot, travelled to Italy, where he studied engraving (1618–21) in Rome, in the studio of Antonio Tempesta. However, he did very little printmaking and only some 20 etchings inspired by Callot are, with reservations, attributed to him;

he nevertheless distinguished himself through the quality of his pen-and-ink drawings, and Louis XIII himself is said to have asked him to teach him drawing. However, once Henriet had settled in Paris (1622), his chief activity became the publication of prints.

The success of Henriet's business 'in the Rue de l'Arbre Sec, near the Croix du Trahoir, at the abode of Monsieur le Mercier, the Queen's goldsmith', was principally due to Jacques Callot, whose sole publisher he was. Henriet also commissioned work from François Collignon (who in 1640 was godfather to one of his daughters), Stefano della Bella, Claude Goyrand (*fl* 1627–49), Jean Marot I and Gabriel Pérelle, as well as from his nephew and godson Israël Silvestre, who subsequently inherited his stock of plates.

BIBLIOGRAPHY

Thieme-Becker
R.-A. Weigert: *Inventaire du fonds français: Graveurs du dix-septième siècle*, Paris, Bib. N., Cab. Est. cat., v (Paris, 1968), pp. 212–17
M. Grivel: *Le Commerce de l'estampe à Paris au XVIIe siècle* (Paris, 1986)
M. Préaud and others: *Dictionnaire des éditeurs d'estampes à Paris sous l'Ancien Régime* (Paris, 1987)

MAXIME PRÉAUD

Henrietta Maria, Queen of England and Scotland. *See* STUART, House of, (7).

Henri-Eugène-Philippe-Louis d'Orléans, Duc d'Aumale. *See* ORLÉANS, (10).

Henrion, Adrien-Joseph. *See* ANRION, ADRIEN-JOSEPH.

Henrique, King of Portugal. *See* AVIZ, (11).

Henriquel-Dupont [Henriquel, Louis-Pierre] (*b* Paris, 13 June 1797; *d* Paris, 20 Jan 1892). French draughtsman and engraver. From 1812 to 1815 he studied painting at the Ecole des Beaux-Arts, Paris, and in the studio of Pierre Guérin, after which, with a view to commercial prospects, he devoted himself to the graphic arts and studied under Charles-Clément Bervic, who made him copy the masterpieces of engraving from the 16th and 17th centuries. He competed unsuccessfully for the Prix de Rome for graphic art in 1816 and 1818 and in the latter year established his own studio, where he produced engravings from works by Alexandre Desenne (1785–1827) and Achille Déveria for such books as La Fontaine's *Fables* (Paris, 1819) and Voltaire's *La Pucelle d'Orléans* (Paris, 1820). His style, formed by his training in the classic works of the past, gradually grew less severe, influenced by such English engravers as William Woollett. His friendship with Ingres, which began in the late 1820s, and his engraving of the *Abdication of Gustav Vasa* (1831; Paris, Bib. N.) were instrumental in winning him critical acclaim. In the 1840s and early 1850s he made engravings after, among other works, Paul Delaroche's (*see* DELAROCHE (2)) *Hémicycle* for the Ecole des Beaux-Arts (1853; Paris, Bib. N.), for which he was awarded the medal of honour at the 1853 Salon. He subsequently devoted himself increasingly to religious work and portraits, producing, for example, the *Deposition* (1855; Paris, Bib. N.) after Delaroche and *Jean-Baptiste Dumas* (1884; Paris, Bib. N.). In 1863 he was appointed Professor of Graphic Arts at the Ecole Nationale des Beaux-Arts and in 1871 was elected President of the Académie des Beaux-Arts, of which he had been a member since 1849.

DBF   BIBLIOGRAPHY
G. Vapereau: *Dictionnaire universel des contemporains* (Paris, 1858, rev. 6/1893)
Inventaire du fonds français après 1800 (Paris, Bib. N., Dépt. Est. cat., x (Paris, 1958), pp. 281–92

☐

Henriques, Francisco (*fl* 1502; *d* Lisbon, 1518). Painter probably of south Netherlandish origin, active in Portugal. His art shows both south and north Netherlandish influences. He would have known the great series of Netherlandish panels depicting the *Life of the Virgin* (1500) painted for the high altar of Évora Cathedral (Évora, Mus. Évora), on which he may have collaborated. From about 1502 to 1508 he painted the high altar of the church of S Francisco, Évora, an impressive work comprising sixteen panels in four thematically unrelated series: the Eucharist (the *Fall of Manna*, *Abraham and Melchisedech*, *Mass of St Gregory*, *Last Supper*), Franciscan Saints (*Martyrs of Morocco*, *SS Bernardino of Siena and Francis*, *SS Bonaventura and Louis* (all Lisbon, Mus. N. A. Ant.) and a fourth panel (untraced)), the Life of the Virgin (*Annunciation*, *Nativity*, *Adoration of the Magi*, *Presentation of Christ in the Temple* (All Alpiarça, Casa Mus. Relvas)) and the Passion of Christ (*Garden of Gethsemene*, *Road to Calvary*, *Descent from the Cross*, *Deposition* (all Lisbon, Mus. N. A. Ant.)). There is marked Netherlandish influence in the work, and in the *Last Supper* the use of engravings by the Master IAM of Zwolle is apparent.

In 1508 Henriques was contracted to paint the stained-glass windows for Santa Cruz, Coimbra, which were never executed. He worked at this date on the stained glass for the Convent of the Pena, Sintra. In Évora he worked on the stained glass at S Francisco, and between 1509 and 1511 he painted the altarpieces for the side chapels of the same church, of which six exist: the *Virgin Enthroned between SS Julita and Querito*, *Daniel Freeing Susanna*, *Noli me tangere*, *Pentecost*, the *Virgin of the Snow* and *St Thomas with SS Cosmas and Damian* (all Lisbon, Mus. N. A. Ant.). Henriques's style is well represented by the last panel, with its monumental figures of the saints standing in a room with a vivid tile floor that leads the eye back to an arched doorway and through it to a typical Netherlandish square. The saints are dressed in richly coloured costumes, and there is the same interest in detail, such as the glass and pottery vessels, as there is in the earlier *Adoration of the Magi* (1502–8), now at Alpiarça, where silver and gold objects are prominent. In 1510 Henriques also painted a statue of *St Francis* intended for the high altar of S Francisco, Évora (untraced).

Between 1512 and 1514 Henriques was in Flanders, where he went to engage assistants and where he renewed contact with the work of Quinten Metsys and Gerard David, of which there were already traces in the earlier series of the *Life of the Virgin* (1502–8) at Évora. After 1514 he painted the glass for a window of the chapter house at the monastery of Batalha. He was commissioned by Manuel I in 1518 to paint banners for the celebrations of his third marriage, to the Infanta Eleanor. In the same year Henriques began the decoration of the Tribunal da Relação, Lisbon (destr. 1755), where he worked in collaboration with Cristóvão de Figueiredo, Garcia Fernandes and seven unknown Netherlandish painters. Henriques and his Netherlandish assistants died in the plague of 1518, leaving the work unfinished.

BIBLIOGRAPHY
R. dos Santos: 'O pintor Francisco Henriques: Identificação da sua obra e esboço crítico da sua personalidade', *Belas A.*, iv (1938), pp. 5–38
C. V. Barros: *O vitral em Portugal: Séculos XV–XVI* (Lisbon, 1983)
DAGOBERTO L. MARKL

Henry, Duke of Saxony. *See* WETTIN, (4).

Henry, King of Portugal. *See* AVIZ, (11).

Henry, Prince of Wales. *See* STUART, House of, (4).

Henry [Heinrich] **II**, Holy Roman Emperor. *See* SAXONY, (4).

Henry II, King of England. *See* PLANTAGENET, (1).

Henry II, King of France. *See* VALOIS, (15).

Henry [Henri] **II**, Prince of Condé. *See* CONDÉ, (1).

Henry [Heinrich] **III**, Holy Roman Emperor. *See* SALIAN, (1).

Henry III, King of England. *See* PLANTAGENET, (2).

Henry III, King of France. *See* VALOIS, (17).

Henry [Heinrich] **IV**, Holy Roman Emperor. *See* SALIAN, (2).

Henry [Henri] **IV**, King of France. *See* BOURBON, §I(5).

Henry VI, King of England. *See* LANCASTER, (3).

Henry VII, Holy Roman Emperor. *See* LUXEMBOURG, (1).

Henry VII, King of England. *See* TUDOR, (1).

Henry VIII, King of England. *See* TUDOR, (2).

Henry XII, Duke of Bavaria. *See* WELF, (1).

Henry, Bon-Thomas (*b* Cherbourg, 2 March 1766; *d* Paris, 7 Jan 1836). French dealer, collector, museum official and painter. He studied under Charles Landon and Jean-Baptiste Regnault. In 1793 he began to deal in pictures and until 1812 spent part of his time travelling abroad (mainly in Italy) to increase his knowledge of art. In October 1816 he was appointed Commissaire-expert des Musées Royaux, a post he held until his death. Between 1810 and 1830 he assembled an eclectic collection, purchasing either privately or at sales, among them the posthumous sales (1826 and 1827) of Vivant Denon. His tastes in Italian art ranged from the work of Fra Angelico to that of the 17th-century Bolognese masters, and he also bought several works by such 17th-century French artists as Poussin (*Life Spent in the Environs of Rome*), Philippe de Champaigne (*Assumption of the Virgin*, 1660), Charles Le Brun and Eustache Le Sueur. He owned paintings by the 18th-century French artists Jean-François de Troy (portrait of *François Dorban*) and Hubert Robert (*Ruins of an Antique Temple*), but the most distinctive aspect of his collection was the large number of late 18th-century and early 19th-century Flemish and French paintings, including works by David (*Philoctète Abandoned on the Island of Lemnos*), Anne-Louis Girodet, Pierre-Paul Prud'hon and the genre painters Marguerite Gérard, Charles-Marie Bouton (1781–1853) and Jean-Baptiste Mallet. He also owned several paintings by Troubadour artists (*see* TROUBADOUR STYLE) and by such landscape artists as Jean-Louis Demarne (*Haymakers' Lunch*; all Cherbourg, Mus. Thomas-Henry), who was influenced by the 17th-century Dutch masters. In 1834 Henry offered a large part of his collection to the town of Cherbourg, and on 29 July 1835 a museum to house his works was opened on the second floor of the Hôtel de Ville; it was later named the Musée Thomas-Henry. The first catalogue of the collections, which he himself wrote, listed 62 French paintings, 51 Flemish, 32 Italian, 7 Spanish and 1 English. After his death the residue of his collection was sold in Paris (23–5 May 1836).

BIBLIOGRAPHY
Miel: 'Notice', *An. Soc. Libre B.-A.*, vi (1836), pp. 29–34
Clement de Ris: 'Le Musée Henry à Cherbourg', *Rev. Univl. A.*, xxi (1865), pp. 197–208

LINDA WHITELEY

Henry, Charles (*b* Bollweiler, Alsace-Lorraine, 16 May 1859; *d* Coyes, nr Versailles, Nov 1926). French scientist and philosopher. He studied science under the physiologist Claude Bernard in the 1870s in Paris, where he also learnt Greek, Latin, Sanskrit and German. In 1881 he became a librarian at the Sorbonne. He was in close contact with such writers as Jules Laforgue, Gustave Kahn, Félix Fénéon and Paul Valéry as well as the painters Georges Seurat (whom he met in 1886) and Paul Signac. He wrote many articles on aesthetics for Symbolist magazines such as *La Vogue* and *La Revue blanche* and on mathematics, psychology and chemistry for specialist scientific journals. In 1910 he wrote his doctoral thesis in two parts (*Sensation et énergie* and *Mémoire et habitude*) and was appointed director of the Laboratory of the Physiology of Sensations at the Sorbonne. His abstruse magnum opus, *Essai de généralisation de la théorie du rayonnement* (Paris, 1924), was an attempt to synthesize his extraordinary polymathic knowledge into a complete mathematically based system.

Henry's project, following on the work of Hermann von Helmholtz, Gustav Fechner and others, was to develop a body of theory called psychophysics, which would, among other things, unite science and aesthetics. In a series of books and articles he described an evolutionist vision of man's attainment of harmony through enhanced aesthetic pleasure. All colour, form and line that increases pleasure will, in Henry's scheme, expand and transform consciousness. These forms and colours Henry termed 'dynamogenous'; their opposites were 'inhibitory'. These ideas can be found in the writings of many Symbolist poets and in the art and theory of Seurat (*see* SEURAT, GEORGES, §2), Signac and other Post-Impressionists and Symbolists, who were all indebted to Henry's theories. The spiralling movement and contrasting colours in the background to Signac's *Portrait of Félix Fénéon* (1890;

New York, priv. col., see *Post-Impressionism: Cross-Currents in European Painting*, exh. cat., London, RA, 1979–80, p. 138) are a particularly vivid illustration.

WRITINGS
Introduction à une esthétique scientifique (Paris, 1885)
Cercle chromatique et rapporteur esthétique (Paris, 1888)

BIBLIOGRAPHY
Cah. Etoile, 13 (Jan–Feb 1930) [special issue devoted to Henry]
J. A. Argüelles: *Charles Henry and the Formation of a Psychophysical Aesthetic* (Chicago and London, 1972) [full bibliog.]

RICHARD HUMPHREYS

Henry, E(dward) L(amson) (*b* Charleston, SC, 12 Jan 1841; *d* Cragsmoor, NY, 11 May 1919). American painter. He received his first art instruction in New York from Walter M. Oddie (1808–65), followed by two years at the Pennsylvania Academy of the Fine Arts, Philadelphia (1858–60). After this he left for a two-year stay abroad, studying with Paul Weber (1823–1916), Charles Gleyre and Courbet. In 1864 he served as a captain's clerk on a boat taking supplies to the Union army. Two notable pictures that emerged from this experience were *City Point, Virginia, Headquarters of General Grant* (1865–72; Andover, MA, Phillips Acad., Addison Gal. A.) and *Westover Mansion* (1869; Washington, DC, Corcoran Gal. A.). He soon won recognition and was elected to the National Academy by 1869. Many of his paintings were sold before exhibition, and he had the reputation of always selling his work on varnishing day.

Henry's earliest paintings were of genre scenes and buildings around Philadelphia and later in New York. He made numerous sketches with details of early buildings and old woodwork, which he was intensely interested in preserving. His paintings of old buildings include the *North Dutch Church* (1869) and *Saint George's Church* (1875; both New York, Met.). In addition to collecting furniture, he kept his own museum of old carriages and costumes, in order to be accurate in his historical paintings.

Henry's interest in all forms of transportation is seen in *Station on the Morris and Essex Railroad* (1864; New York, Chase Manhattan Bank A. Col.) and the *9:45 Accommodation at Stratford, Connecticut* (1867; New York, Met.). The latter was commissioned by John Taylor Johnston, President of the New Jersey Central Railroad and first president of the Metropolitan Museum of Art, New York. Henry's widely reproduced watercolour *Before the Days of Rapid Transit* (1890; Albany, NY, Inst. Hist. & A.) portrays a packet-boat on the Erie Canal in the 1830s. The D & H Canal, connecting the Delaware and Hudson rivers, was a popular theme for Henry and other artists.

Henry had a wry but gentle sense of humour. Peter Brown, the town drunk of Ellenville, NY, was one favourite subject, and Henry also sought out other local characters to pose for his genre scenes. One of his most important paintings, the *Opening of the First Railroad in New York State, August, 1831, between Albany and Schenectady* (1892–3; Albany, NY, Inst. Hist. & A.), won a special prize at the World's Columbian Exposition in Chicago in 1893. His minutely detailed style of painting, so popular when he achieved his early fame, remained unchanged throughout his life.

Henry participated in and helped to develop the artists' colony at Cragsmoor, NY. He was a member of the Century Association, the American Watercolor Society and the Salmagundi Club. By the time of his death, his reputation was waning, but subsequently his work was valued for its warm, accurate and friendly look at the past. Many of Henry's paintings were reproduced and copyrighted by Christian Klackner in platinotypes, etchings and photogravures, while others appeared on calendars and elsewhere.

BIBLIOGRAPHY

E. McCausland: *The Life and Work of Edward Lamson Henry, NA, 1841–1919* (New York, 1945)
E. L. Henry's Country Life: An Exhibition (exh. cat. by M. Radl and J. P. Christman, Cragsmoor, NY, Free Lib., 1981)
M. Mann: Monograph and catalogue raisonné (in preparation)

MAYBELLE MANN

Henry, George (*b* Ayrshire, 1858; *d* London, 23 Dec 1943). Scottish painter. He trained at the Glasgow School of Art and painted in the early 1880s in W. Y. Macgregor's life studio and outdoors with James Guthrie, Joseph Crawhall and E. A. Walton. This resulted in his first major exhibit, *Head of the Holy Loch* (1882; Glasgow, A.G. & Mus.). Study in Paris at the Académie Julian in 1883 and 1886 confirmed his realist style deriving from Jules Bastien-Lepage and seen, for instance, in *Cottar's Garden* (1885; Broughton House, Dumfries & Galloway). In his *Galloway Landscape* (1889; Glasgow, A.G. & Mus.), however, he abandoned this for his mature decorative style of heightened impasto colour and vigorous arabesque design. This was further developed in collaboration with E. A. HORNEL in two symbolic paintings, *The Druids* (1890) and *Star in the East* (1891; both Glasgow, A.G. & Mus.), and in mural paintings for Glasgow buildings, such as *Granting the First Charter to Glasgow* in the City Chambers (1899–1901). Part of the Celtic Revival, *The Druids* anticipates the search for primitive national origins that took Henry and Hornel to Japan in 1893–4. In his Japanese watercolours and oils, such as *At Home in Japan* (1894; Glasgow, A.G. & Mus.), Henry explored new features of simplified geometric design. After settling in London in the early 20th century he became popular as a portrait painter, but heavy reliance on Whistler and Velázquez replaced the originality of earlier work.

BIBLIOGRAPHY

P. Bate: 'The Work of George Henry, R.S.A.: A Review and an Appreciation', *The Studio*, xxxi (1904), pp. 3–12
J. Taylor: 'Some Watercolour Drawings by George Henry, A.R.A.', *The Studio*, lxviii (1916), pp. 73–9
G. Buchanan: 'A Galloway Landscape', *Scot. A. Rev.*, vii/4 (1960), pp. 13–17
D. Irwin and F. Irwin: *Scottish Painters at Home and Abroad, 1700–1900* (London, 1975), pp. 386–8
W. Hardie: *Scottish Painting 1837 to the Present* (London, 1976)
Mr Henry and Mr Hornel Visit Japan (exh. cat., ed. W. Buchanan; Glasgow, A.G. & Mus., 1979)

For further bibliography *see* GLASGOW BOYS.

CLARE A. P. WILLSDON

Henry, Lucien (Felix) (*b* Sisteron, Provence, 1850; *d* Le Pave, St Léonard-de-Noblat, Haute Vienne, 10 March 1896). French painter, sculptor, designer and teacher, active in Australia. He trained under the architect Viollet-le-Duc and at the Ecole des Beaux-Arts, Paris, under Jean-Léon Gérôme. In 1871 he was sentenced to death for his political activities in the Paris Commune; this was commuted to transportation to New Caledonia. He arrived in Sydney in 1879 after the granting of political amnesty. He was appointed instructor in modelling at the Sydney Mechanics' School of Arts and in 1883 became the first lecturer in art at the Sydney Technical College. He also taught privately. His influence on a generation of students that included Lucien Dechaineux (1870–1957), later director of the Hobart Technical College, A. G. Reid, the sculptor, B. E. Minns (1864–1937) and Sydney Cathels, was profound. A founder-member of the Art Society of New South Wales, his frequent contributions to their exhibitions included portraits and busts. Henry sought to establish a national style in the applied arts through the use of distinctive colours and motifs based on native flora and fauna. His delight in the Australian shrub waratah is seen in the design for two large stained-glass windows in the Sydney Town Hall and in the curious designs for a folio of 50 graphic works to be entitled *Australian Decorative Arts*. The folio was never published, but the designs, including *Kookaburra* and *Electric Lamp for Bedroom*, are held at the Museum of Applied Arts and Sciences, Sydney.

WRITINGS

'Australian Decorative Arts', *Austral. A.* (Feb 1888), pp. 9–12; also in *Documents on Art and Taste in Australia*, ed. B. Smith (Melbourne, 1975), pp. 238–44

AUDB
BIBLIOGRAPHY

R. T. Baker: *The Australian Flora in Applied Art* (Sydney, 1915)
T. Lane and J. Serle: *Australians at Home* (Melbourne, 1990)

BARBARA B. KANE

Henry, Paul (*b* Belfast, 11 April 1876; *d* Co. Wicklow, 24 Aug 1958). Irish painter. He had his first lessons in drawing in Belfast when he was 15, from an English artist, Thomas Bond Walker. On leaving school, he was apprenticed at the Broadway Damask Company, and about a year later he attended the Belfast School of Art. From 1898 to *c*. 1900 he was in Paris, where he attended the Académie Julian and studied poster design under Alphonse Mucha before moving to London, where he shared lodgings with the writer Robert Lynd. During this period he made many charcoal drawings reminiscent in mood of Whistler's work and worked as an illustrator. After his first visit to the island of Achill in 1912, he adopted a strong vigorous outline and thick impasto, as in the *Potato Diggers* (1912; Dublin, N.G.), in which monumental figures are boldly silhouetted against a cloudy sky.

Henry worked for some years in the Erris peninsula, exhibiting in Belfast; in 1917 he and his wife Grace Henry (1868–1953) held the first of a series of exhibitions at the Mills Hall, Dublin. In 1920 he moved to Dublin, where he founded the Dublin Painters. The simplification of his late painting style was affected by his experience of designing posters for the London, Midland and Scottish Railway in the mid-1920s. *Connemara Cottages* (*c*. 1929; Dublin, N.G.) is a fine example of what was later regarded unfairly as a stereotyped composition, with low-lying cottages, turf stacks and no figures, beneath huge grey and white cumuli. Henry became blind in 1945 and spent his last years living in Wicklow, writing his autobiography.

WRITINGS
An Irish Portrait (London, 1951)
Further Reminiscences (Belfast, 1973)

BIBLIOGRAPHY
S. O'Faolain: 'The Loveliest Thing I Have Seen', *Bell*, i/1 (1940), pp. 40–43
Paul Henry, 1876–1958 (exh. cat., intro. G. Dawson; Dublin, Trinity Coll., Hyde Gal., 1973)
J. Hewitt: *Art in Ulster 1* (Belfast, 1977), pp. 79–82

Henry de Gower (*b* Gower, south Wales, *c.* 1278; *d* St David's, 25 April 1347). Welsh bishop, scholar and patron. He was of aristocratic descent. He matriculated in the University of Oxford *c.* 1295 and was educated at Merton College, graduating as doctor of civil law in 1320 and doctor of canon law in 1322. He was Chancellor of Oxford from 1322 to 1325. Gower became Canon of St David's, Pembrokeshire (now Dyfed), *c.* 1314, Archdeacon in 1319 or 1323 and was elected Bishop on 21 April 1328; he was consecrated at Canterbury on 12 June. He was on good terms with the popes John XXII and Benedict XII as well as Edward III. Three sets of his statutes, regularizing worship and canonical life in his cathedral, survive.

Gower is best remembered as a patron of architecture often being known as the 'Welsh Wykeham'. He repaired a number of episcopal residences, including his palace (destr.) at Llanddewi, Gower. In addition to his extensive works at St David's, he founded the large hospital of the Blessed David, Swansea, in 1332. He reconstructed Swansea Castle and added to the episcopal palace at Lamphey, incorporating in both the arcaded parapet that was virtually his trademark. In conceiving, organizing and financing ecclesiastical building projects, he stood supreme in medieval Wales. He is buried in St David's Cathedral in the magnificent tomb he himself designed.

DNB   BIBLIOGRAPHY
G. G. Francis: 'A Brief Memoir of Henry de Gower', *Archaeol. Camb.*, vii (1876), pp. 1–19
C. A. Ralegh Radford: 'The Palace of the Bishops of St David's at Lamphey, Pembrokeshire', *Archaeol. Camb.*, xciii (1938), pp. 1–14
A. B. Emden: *A Biographical Register of the University of Oxford*, ii (Oxford, 1958)
W. Greenway: 'Henry de Gower: Bishop of St David's, 1328–47', *Gower*, xi (1958), pp. 13–17
G. Williams: 'Henry de Gower (?1278–1347): Bishop and Builder', *Archaeol. Camb.*, cxxx (1981), pp. 1–18

GLANMOR WILLIAMS

Henry [Heinrich] **Julius**, Duke of Brunswick-Wolfenbüttel. *See* WELF, (2).

Henry of Blois (*b* 1099; *d* 8 Aug 1171). Anglo-Norman bishop and patron. The grandson of WILLIAM I, King of England, he was educated at Cluny Abbey and held, among other offices, the abbacy of Glastonbury (1126–71) and the bishopric of Winchester (1129–71). He greatly extended his power and influence as papal legate (1139–43) and, during the reign of his brother Stephen (*reg* 1135–54), was a central figure in affairs of state and an active participant in the civil war. He was a man of taste and a leading patron of architecture and the arts in 12th-century England.

Of Henry's six castles and three palaces, only Wolvesey (ruined), the bishop's palace at Winchester, remains as testimony. From the extensive suite of monastic buildings that he erected at Glastonbury only a few capitals (*c.* 1150) in blue lias have survived; the choice of material was without precedent and may reflect the search for local substitutes for imported marbles. Both black Tournai marble and grey-green Purbeck 'marble' had been used in the refurbishment (1141–54) of Wolvesey Palace. The use of Purbeck at Hyde Abbey, the Cluniac priories of Faversham and Lewes, and in the works of Henry's kinsmen and protégés may be attributed to his influence. Although there is little material evidence of his building activity at Winchester, the cathedral 'treasury' (*c.* 1160) and the church of the hospital of St Cross (founded *c.* 1136) are works of some pretension, both in their use of architectural motifs derived from Classical and early French Gothic architecture, and in their rich sculptural detailing.

Henry's gifts and benefactions indicate a discerning and assiduous collector: for Wolvesey he bought antique marble statuary in Rome in 1151, and may have given further antiquities (including a large cameo) to Winchester Cathedral; to Glastonbury Abbey he gave precious 'Saracen' carpets; to Cluny Abbey a bowl of Byzantine work and a silver statue of *Constantine the Great* (all destr.). For each he commissioned a great gold or silver-gilt crucifix, decorated with pearls and numerous precious stones and gems. Other artefacts, including vestments, ornaments and furnishings of breathtaking costliness, fill the gift lists. Among the few that survive, the Mosan enamel plaques (London, BM; *see* ROMANESQUE, §VII) attest to the quality of his patronage. Henry also commissioned the making and transcription of books, some of which were decorated and illuminated. Works made at Winchester in his time but not certainly associated with him include the Winchester Psalter (*c.* 1150; London, BL, Cotton MS. Nero C. IV) and two Bibles (Oxford, Bodleian Lib., MS. Auct. E. inf. 1-2; Winchester Cathedral Lib.; *see* WINCHESTER BIBLE), which rank among the finest manuscripts to have survived from the Romanesque period.

BIBLIOGRAPHY
L. Voss: *Heinrich von Blois, Bischof von Winchester, 1129–1171* (Berlin, 1932)
D. Knowles: *The Episcopal Colleagues of Archbishop Thomas Becket* (Cambridge, 1951)
——: *Saints and Scholars: Twenty-five Medieval Portraits* (Cambridge, 1962)
English Romanesque Art, 1066–1200 (exh. cat., ed. G. Zarnecki, J. Holt and T. Holland; London, Hayward Gal., 1984), nos 147–9, 151, 277
M. Biddle: *Wolvesey: The Old Bishop's Palace, Winchester* (London, 1986)
G. Zarnecki: 'Henry of Blois as a Patron of Sculpture', *Art and Patronage in the English Romanesque*, Society of Antiquaries of London, Occasional Papers, n. s., viii (London, 1986), pp. 159–72
E. Salter: *English and International: Studies in the Literature, Art and Patronage of Medieval England* (Cambridge, 1988), pp. 4–28

JEFFREY WEST

Henry of Prussia, Prince. *See* HOHENZOLLERN, (8).

Henry the Lion, Duke of Saxony. *See* WELF, (1).

Hensel, Wilhelm (*b* Trebbin, Potsdam, 6 July 1794; *d* Berlin, 26 Nov 1861). German painter and draughtsman. From 1811 he studied painting at the Kunstakademie, Berlin. From 1818 to 1820 he worked on the decoration of Schinkel's Schauspielhaus, Berlin, painting scenes from tragedies, and in 1821 he was commissioned to execute 12 pictures of *tableaux vivants* from Thomas Moore's *Lalla Rookh* (1817), a poem with an Indo-Persian setting. These were to be presented to guests attending a festival in honour of the visiting heir to the Russian throne, Crown Prince Nicholas (later Nicholas I), and his wife, Princess Charlotte of Prussia. He also produced 53 portraits (Berlin, Kupferstichkab.) of members of the nobility who were attending the festival in Oriental costume. In 1823 he was awarded a royal grant to study in Italy, where he remained until 1828. While there he painted a copy (Potsdam, Orangerie) of Raphael's *Transfiguration* (Rome, Pin. Vaticana) for the Prussian court and *Christ and the Woman of Samaria* (1828; Potsdam, Orangerie). He returned to Berlin and became a member of the Akademie der Künste and court painter in 1829, the year of his marriage to Fanny Mendelssohn-Bartholdy, sister of the composer Felix Mendelssohn-Bartholdy. He became Professor of History Painting at the Akademie in 1831.

Hensel visited Rome three times and also made trips to Paris, Belgium (1835) and London (1838 and 1843). He painted biblical subjects (e.g. *Christ before Pilate*, 1835, destr.; oil sketch, Heidelberg, priv. col., see *Mendelssohn-Studien*, iii, p. 33), as well as historical themes (e.g. *Duke of Brunswick on the Eve of the Battle of Waterloo*, 1842, sold London, Christie's, 1976; and *Emperor Wenceslas*, 1844, Frankfurt am Main, Römer). Hensel left a significant collection of over 1000 pencil drawings of members of the high society of the time, among them *Edward, Prince of Wales*, *Heinrich Heine* and the Swedish singer *Jenny Lind* (Berlin, Kupferstichkab.). Earlier works from this series were done with classical precision, while later drawings display mannerist tendencies.

BIBLIOGRAPHY

NDB

T. Fontane: 'Wanderungen durch die Mark Brandenburg', *Spreeland: Kapitel an der Nuthe, Trebbin* (1872) [biog.]

P. O. Rave: 'Die Bildnis-Sammlung Wilhelm Hensels', *Berlin. Mus.*, n. s., vi (1957), pp. 37–44

C. Lowenthal-Hensel and R. Elvers, eds: *Mendelssohn-Studien: Beiträge zur neueren deutschen Kultur- und Wirtschaftsgeschichte*, iii (1972), pp. 163–99

Preussische Bildnisse des 19. Jahrhunderts: Zeichnungen von Wilhelm Hensel (exh. cat. by C. Lowenthal-Hensel, W. Berlin, N.G.; Nuremberg, Ger. Nmus.; Bonn, Stift. Preuss. Kultbes., Wisszent.; Düsseldorf, Stadtmus.; 1981–3)

19th Century Society Portraits: Drawings by Wilhelm Hensel (exh. cat. by C. Lowenthal-Hensel, London, Goethe-Inst., 1986)

VERA LEUSCHNER

Henselmann, Hermann (*b* Rossla, nr Nordhausen, 3 Feb 1905). German architect and writer. After training as a carpenter he studied at the Kunstgewerbeschule, Berlin (1922–5). He then worked with Leo Nachtlicht and Werner Issel. He also worked independently and built several houses, including the Burier house on Lake Geneva near Montreux (1930). In 1945 he took over direction of the Hochschule für Baukunst und Bildende Künste in Weimar until 1950. From 1951 until 1972 he directed various planning authorities in Berlin and played a major role in the construction of the Stalinallee. His Punkthaus by the Weberwiese (1951) marked the beginning of this broad 'national reconstruction work' and was also the first

example of the historicist 'national tradition' style demanded by the government. He designed the dominant multi-storey buildings on the Straussberger Platz (1952–3) and the Frankfurter Tor (1955–6).

Between 1953 and 1959 Henselmann worked on fundamental land-use and traffic plans for the reconstruction of East Berlin and on design concepts for the city centre; he suggested building the television tower in the centre as a new symbol of the city. In his capacity as chief architect of the Institut für Städtebau und Architektur he devoted himself from 1966 until 1972 to the re-creation of the destroyed centres of a number of towns. He proposed giving dominating buildings 'personalities' by fashioning them in the shape of such iconic signs as sails, books, crystals and telescopes. The 34-storey tower at Leipzig University (1969–74) and the multi-storey research building in Jena (1969–75) are examples. By using such popular figurative references, which did not, however, symbolize any real social values, he attempted to create concise, traditional 'town crowns' to provide urban focal points, in contrast to the anonymity of capitalist towns.

WRITINGS

Wir bauen an der neuen Stadt (Berlin, 1960)

Gedanken, Ideen, Bauten Projekte (Berlin, 1978) [contributions by W. Heise and B. Flierl]

Drei Reisen nach Berlin (Berlin, 1986)

BIBLIOGRAPHY

Hermann Henselmann: In Würdigung seines Schaffens (Berlin, 1975) [incl. lists of his writings and works]

KARL-HEINZ HÜTER

Hentrich, Helmut (*b* Krefeld, 17 June 1905). German architect. He studied architecture from 1924 to 1928 at the universities in Freiburg and Vienna (Dr. Ing. 1929) and also at the Technische Hochschule, Charlottenburg, Berlin, under Hans Poelzig. He then became director of restoration work in the local government offices in Düsseldorf. Between 1930 and 1932 he worked with Ernö Goldfinger in Paris and Norman Bel Geddes in New York. He became a government architect in 1933 and then an independent architect, founding an office with Hans Heuser in 1935. In 1936 he was appointed a member of the Deutsche Akademie für Städtebau und Landesplanung in Düsseldorf. His work concentrated on office and administration buildings; early examples include the Bankhaus Trinkaus (1949–50) and Drahthaus (1951–2), Düsseldorf, and the BASF-Hochhaus (1953), Ludwigshafen. After the death of Heuser in 1953, Hentrich entered into partnership with HUBERT PETSCHNIGG. Their work included the well-known Thyssen-Hochhaus (1957–60; now the Phoenix-Rheinrohr building), Düsseldorf, Unilever-Haus (1961–4) and Finnlandhaus (1961–6), both in Hamburg. Orientated towards functional requirements, these buildings were strongly influenced by Mies van der Rohe and American high-rise curtain-wall architecture. The clear, simple appearance of Hentrich's buildings characterizes him as a member of the second generation of modern architects. In 1960 he became a professor and in 1969 his firm expanded to become Hentrich-Petschnigg & Partner (HPP). Later works included the Europa Centre (1963–5), Berlin, a 22-storey retail and leisure complex; the Standard Bank Centre (1965–70), Johannesburg; main administration offices for Rank Xerox (1966–71), Düsseldorf; a diamond sorting building (1970–74) for De Beers in Kimberley; and the conversion (1975–7) of the partially destroyed Tonhalle by Wilhelm Kreis into the Rheinhalle, Düsseldorf. In 1976 Hentrich was awarded the Bundes-Verdienstkreuz.

BIBLIOGRAPHY
H.-R. Hitchcock: *Hentrich-Petschnigg & Partner: Bauten und Entwürfe* (Düsseldorf, 1973)
H. Klotz: *Architektur in der Bundesrepublik* (Frankfurt am Main, 1977)
H. Bofinger and others: *Architektur in Deutschland* (Stuttgart, 1981)
BRIGITTE JACOB, WOLFGANG SCHÄCHE

Hephaistion (*fl* 1st half of the 2nd century BC). Greek mosaicist working in Pergamon (now in Turkey). The inscription *Ephaistion epoiei* (Gr.: 'Hephaistion made') appears in two lines on a cartellino in an emblema in the middle of a tessellated floor (Berlin, Pergamonmus; *see* GREECE, ANCIENT, fig. 137) from a peristyle building (Palace V) at Pergamon associated with Eumenes II (*reg* 197–159 BC). The emblema was divided horizontally by a strip of marble; nothing remains of either part except traces of a myrtle garland at the top of the lower part and at the bottom centre a blue-grey area with the off-white piece of parchment on which the letters are in black. The cartellino is shown as held at the corners by blobs of scarlet wax, but that on the bottom right has broken, and the corner curls up, casting a shadow. This charming touch of untidiness recalls the account by Pliny (*Natural History* XXXVI.clxxxiv) of a famous floor, also at Pergamon, called the 'Unswept Floor', by SOSOS, the only mosaicist mentioned in the literary record. Hephaistion's emblema was on a white floor within a series of concentric squares of pattern border. One, near the centre, has a floral scroll full of insects and erotes (*see* GREECE, ANCIENT, fig. 138). A broader one further out was completely removed, with care, in antiquity, perhaps to take to Rome, and was surely figured. We cannot be sure whether Hephaistion was claiming responsibility for the whole floor or only for the emblema, but the former, at least as far as design goes, seems more probable.

See also ANCIENT GREECE §VI, 1(iii).

BIBLIOGRAPHY
G. Kawerau and T. Wiegand: *Die Paläste von Hochburg* (1930), V/i of *Altertümer von Pergamon* (Berlin, 1885–), pp. 63–90
MARTIN ROBERTSON

Hepplewhite, George (*d* London, ?June 1786). English furniture designer. Though a household name in the context of late 18th-century furniture, he remains a shadowy figure. *Lowndes's London Directory* of 1786 records his business at Redcross Street, Cripplegate, London, and after his death the administration was granted to his widow, Alice, on 27 June 1786. The *Public Ledger* of 10 October 1786 announced an auction of his stock-in-trade and household furniture. In 1788 his widow published the *Cabinet-maker and Upholsterer's Guide*. Its aim was 'to follow the latest and most prevailing fashion' and to adhere 'to such articles only as are of general use'. The intended public included both the cabinetmaker or upholsterer and the client (the 'mechanic and gentleman', as Alice Hepplewhite put it). There followed a slightly revised edition in 1789 and an 'improved' one in 1794, with an extra plate and revised chair designs. Six engravings bearing Hepplewhite's name appeared in Thomas Shearer's *Cabinet-makers' London Book of Prices* (1788).

Hepplewhite's *Guide* was the first major pattern book of furniture to be published since the third edition of Chippendale's *Gentleman and Cabinet-maker's Director* (1762), excluding those designs in the first two volumes of *Works in Architecture* (1773–9) by Robert and James Adam (i). Hepplewhite's designs most closely compare with Adam's drawings of the late 1780s, sharing their fashionably attenuated quality of design. The furniture is slender, and most of the decoration inlaid or painted rather than carved. Pier-glasses, for example, have narrow rectangular frames, and the decoration tends to be confined to the crests. Common motifs are sunbursts, paterae, husk chains and fronded scrolls. Hepplewhite favoured shield-shaped and square chair backs, often with the 'Prince of Wales's feathers' motif, but he died before he could assimilate the styles developed at Carlton House (destr.), London, the new residence of the Prince of Wales (later George IV). Hepplewhite was aware of the possibilities offered by gadgetry, a trend that was to grow in the early years of the 19th century, but a more conservative element in his work can be seen in his use of window-stools with curving arms but no backs that were first designed by Robert Adam as early as the 1760s. Decorative figures (humans, nymphs and putti) occasionally feature on chair backs and the crests of pier-glasses. His *Guide* reflected rather than originated a domestic version of the Adam style that was current during the 1780s, and it was highly influential in North America and northern Europe. It was reprinted in 1897 by Batsford, at a time when 18th-century furniture styles were enjoying a revival. No documented or labelled item of furniture from Hepplewhite's workshop is known.

WRITINGS
The Cabinet-maker and Upholsterer's Guide (London, 1788, rev. 2/1789, rev. 3/1794/*R* 1897/*R* New York, 1969)

BIBLIOGRAPHY
C. Musgrave: *Adam and Hepplewhite and Other Neo-classical Furniture* (London, 1966)
G. Beard and C. Gilbert, eds: *Dictionary of English Furniture Makers, 1660–1840* (Leeds, 1986)
JAMES YORKE

Heptastyle. Term applied to a building with a portico of seven columns.   □

Hepworth, Dame **Barbara** (*b* Wakefield, 10 Jan 1903; *d* St Ives, 20 May 1975). English sculptor and draughtswoman. She trained as a sculptor at Leeds School of Art in 1919 and at the Royal College of Art, London, from 1920 to 1923, where she was associated with other artists from Leeds, including Henry Moore. Though she lost the 1924 Rome Scholarship to the English sculptor John Skeaping (1901–80), she was able to accompany him to Italy on a West Riding Scholarship, and they were married in 1925. They lived in the British School in Rome, where Skeaping consolidated his interest in carving in stone. His superior knowledge of direct carving must have been influential for Hepworth, for this practice had not been on the syllabus at art school.

Hepworth and Skeaping moved to Parkhill Road in Hampstead, north London, in 1928. They exhibited together in London at the Beaux Arts Gallery in 1928 and at Arthur Tooth & Sons in 1930. Hepworth made an isolated venture into piercing the form in 1931 with a carving in alabaster, *Abstraction* (destr., see Hepworth, 1978, p. 22), a line of enquiry developed by Moore before Hepworth was to return to it. Hepworth's carvings up to the mid-1930s, such as *Figure of a Woman* (Corsehill stone, h. 555 mm, 1929–30; London, Tate), are chunky, resolutely solid and basically figurative, displaying much less interest in the 'savage' side of non-Western carving than those of Moore; unlike Moore, moreover, she was unaffected by Surrealism. Her development of piercing and of a progressive opening of form to light and space ran parallel to a process of refinement in her work through the 1940s epitomized in *Pelagos* (1946; London, Tate; see fig.). During this period she rid her work of references to the human body, venturing as early as 1936 from biomorphic to crystalline forms while never abandoning her liking for curves. Like Moore, she experimented from the late 1930s with tautly stretched strings and their effect on the opened-up sculpture, as in *Sculpture with Colour, Deep Blue and Red* (1940; St Ives, Barbara Hepworth Mus.), and continued to play with the formal effects of incised line on the surfaces of more closed forms.

Hepworth again exhibited at Arthur Tooth & Sons' Gallery in 1932, this time with Ben Nicholson, whom she had met in 1931 and married in 1932 after her divorce from Skeaping. Together with Moore and other English modernists, they were enthusiastically promoted by Herbert Read and other critics, notably Adrian Stokes and J. D. Bernal (1901–71). During the 1930s Nicholson and Hepworth visited a number of artists in France, including Pablo Picasso, Georges Braque, Hans Arp and Constantin Brancusi, becoming especially close to those practising geometric abstraction. In 1933 they joined Abstraction-Création and were founder-members of Unit One, a group of architects, painters and sculptors committed to Constructivism or Surrealism. From 1935 she exhibited with the 7 & 5 Society, and in 1936 she took part in a seminal exhibition, *Abstract & Concrete*, held at 41 St Giles in Oxford. Together with a group of eminent European exiles who arrived in London in the mid-1930s, including Piet Mondrian, Naum Gabo, László Moholy-Nagy, Marcel Breuer and Erich Mendelsohn, she and other English artists based in Hampstead became the centre of an informal but intellectually cohesive group committed to avant-garde ideas.

Just before the outbreak of World War II Hepworth and Nicholson went to stay with Stokes in Carbis Bay, near ST IVES, where they were joined by Gabo. St Ives, which Hepworth made her permanent home, was then developing into an artistic community in which she was able to flourish, although she was able to resume work only in 1942, when the family moved to larger premises. Her first retrospective, combined with an exhibition of paintings by Paul Nash, was held at Temple Newsam House in Leeds in 1943. Drawings continued to play a constant, if minor, role in her art, and in 1948–9 she made

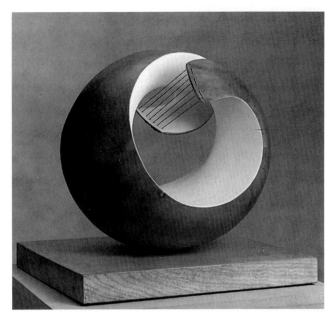

Barbara Hepworth: *Pelagos*, wood with painted interior and strings, h. 368 mm, 1946 (London, Tate Gallery)

a series of drawings depicting doctors and nurses at work in a hospital operating theatre, such as *Fenestration of the Ear (The Hammer)* (1948; London, Tate); these were among the most delicate and subtle of all her works on paper. In 1949 she bought Trewyn Studio in St Ives, where she lived permanently after the dissolution of her marriage to Nicholson in 1951.

Hepworth's work underwent further changes after her participation in the Venice Biennale in 1950; her observations there of the proportions and postures of people in relation to the architectural spaces were of lasting influence on her growing interest in the relationship between man and the landscape, expressed in her tendency to play off two or more forms against each other, as in *Group I (Concourse) February 4 1951* (Serravezza marble, h. 247 mm, 1951; London, Tate). The commissions she received for the Festival of Britain in 1951, for example *Contrapuntal Forms* (blue limestone, h. 3.05 m; see Hepworth, 1978, p. 54), were followed by other large outdoor public commissions. Through the 1940s her sculpture had become more upright in emphasis, monolithic but for the piercings, as in *Bicentric Form* (blue limestone, h. 1.59 m, 1949; London, Tate). On her return from Greece in 1954 she produced a series of large carvings in African hardwood, which renewed the interest in the relationship between internal and external forms expressed in her work of the 1930s, for example *Corinthos* (h. 1.04 m, 1954–5; London, Tate). These led to a number of ovoid and strung forms, on a larger scale than before. This return to techniques used in her earlier carvings made it all the more surprising that in 1956 she began to work in metal; by the end of the year she was producing bronzes from forms modelled in plaster, such as *Stringed Figure (Curlew) Version II* (1956; London, Tate). Some judged this development a betrayal of her early commitment to direct carving and truth to material, although she continued to use and carve stone and wood; others saw it as a sign of her increased confidence and knowledge of materials and of a desire to create on a larger scale. During the 1950s she also extended her work into other areas, such as stage design, notably with the 1954 production of Michael Tippett's opera *The Midsummer Marriage*.

From the late 1950s Hepworth was awarded many honorary degrees and prizes and had her work shown widely internationally; she was also the subject of several films. In 1958 she was created CBE, and in 1959 she won the major award at the São Paulo Biennale. During this period her work became more geometric, harder and less human in its appeal, as in works of the mid-1960s such as *Marble with Colour (Crete)* (Rotterdam, Boymans–van Beuningen). Partly because of the increased pressure of public commissions, she worked increasingly in bronze. In the 1960s she acquired a much more spacious studio in St Ives, which made it easier for her to produce work on a larger scale, for example a tribute to Dag Hammarskjöld, *Single Form*, unveiled in 1964 at the United Nations Secretariat in New York. She was created DBE in 1965 and in the same year became a Trustee of the Tate Gallery, serving until 1972. Hepworth died in a fire at her home in 1975. In compliance with the wishes expressed before her death, her old studio became the Barbara Hepworth Museum and was opened in 1980 as an outpost of the Tate Gallery.

WRITINGS

'The Sculptor Carves because he Must', *The Studio*, 104 (Dec 1932), p. 332
'Sculpture', *Circle: International Survey of Constructive Art*, eds N. Gabo, J. L. Martin and B. Nicholson (London, 1937), pp. 113–15
'Approach to Sculpture', *The Studio*, 132 (Oct 1946), pp. 97–101
A. Adams, ed.: *A Pictorial Autobiography* (Bradford-on-Avon, 1970, rev. 1978)

BIBLIOGRAPHY

A. Stokes: 'Miss Hepworth's Carving', *The Spectator* (3 Nov 1933), p. 621
H. Read, ed.: *Unit One* (Kassel, 1934) [with a statement by Hepworth]
H. Frankfort: 'New Works by Barbara Hepworth', *Axis*, 3 (July 1935), p. 54
W. Gibson: *Barbara Hepworth* (London, 1946)
Barbara Hepworth: Sculptures and Drawings (exh. cat., Wakefield A.G., 1951)
H. Read, ed.: *Barbara Hepworth: Carvings and Drawings* (London, 1952)
Barbara Hepworth: Retrospective Exhibition, 1927–1954 (exh. cat., intro. D. Baxandall; London, Whitechapel A.G., 1954)
J. P. Hodin: *Barbara Hepworth: Life and Work* (London, 1961)
M. Shepherd: *Barbara Hepworth* (London, 1963)
Barbara Hepworth (exh. cat., intro. R. Alley; London, Tate, 1968)
A. M. Hammacher: *Barbara Hepworth* (London, 1968)
A. Bowness, ed.: *The Complete Sculpture of Barbara Hepworth, 1960–69* (London, 1971)
M. Gardiner: *Barbara Hepworth* (Edinburgh, 1982)
Barbara Hepworth: A Retrospective (exh. cat. by P. Curtis and A. Wilkinson, Liverpool, Tate, 1994)

PENELOPE CURTIS

Heraeus, Karl Gustav (*b* Güstrow or Stockholm, 1671; *d* Vienna, 6 Nov 1725). German numismatist and poet. After study trips throughout Europe, he was appointed curator of the extensive coin collection at the Schwarzburg–Sondershausen court in Thuringia *c*. 1701. He also composed occasional verse and planned programmes of ephemeral architecture, in particular funerary settings. In 1709 he went to Vienna, where he converted to Catholicism. In 1710 he was appointed Inspector of Medals and Antiquities by Emperor Joseph I, a post he retained under Charles VI. In Vienna he organized the Habsburgs' coins and medals into a collection that was opened in 1717; designed a series of medals, *Historia metallica seu numismatica* (Vienna, Ksthist. Mus.; designs published 1721 in *Inscriptiones et symbola*), glorifying Charles VI's achievements; and from 1711 until the 1720s conceived the programmes for all court funerary architecture, as well as countless schemes of festive decoration for Viennese palace façades. These were then executed by the court architects Johann Bernhard Fischer von Erlach, Johann Lukas von Hildebrandt and Ferdinando Galli-Bibiena. He published his programmes in Latin and German on several occasions. Heraeus composed much occasional verse, chiefly panegyrics on the Emperor and court nobles. In 1713 he wrote the preface to Joseph Emanuel Fischer von Erlach's *Prospecte und Abrisse einiger Gebäude von Wien*, and Johann Bernhard Fischer von Erlach drew on his expertise in reconstructing ancient buildings in his *Entwurff einer historischen Architektur* (Vienna and Leipzig, 1721).

WRITINGS

Vermischte Neben–Arbeiten (Vienna, 1715)
Bedeutungen und Innschriften einiger wienerischen redenden Erleuchtungen (Vienna, 1716)
Gedichte und lateinische Inschriften (Nuremberg, 1721)
Inscriptiones et symbola (Nuremberg, 1721)

BIBLIOGRAPHY

J. Bergmann: 'Über Kaiser Carl VI: Rath und Hof-Antiquarius Carl Gustav Heraeus, dessen Stammbuch und Correspondenz: Ein Beitrag zur Geschichte des k.k. Münz- und Antiken-Cabinets', *Sber. Philos.-Hist. Cl. Ksr. Akad. Wiss. Wien*, xiii (1854), pp. 40–61, 539–625
——: 'Über die Historia metallica seu numismatica Austriaca und Heraeus' zehn Briefe an Leibniz', *Sber. Philos.-Hist. Cl. Ksr. Akad. Wiss. Wien*, xvi (1855), pp. 132–68
C. von Wurzbach: *Biographisches Lexikon des Kaiserthums Österreich*, vii (Vienna, 1861), pp. 320–23
F. Matsche: *Die Kunst im Dienst der Staatsidee Kaiser Karls VI.: Ikonographie, Ikonologie und Programmatik des 'Kaiserstils'* (Berlin and New York, 1981), pp. 75–88

FRANZ MATSCHE

Herakleia Lynkestis. *See* BITOLJ.

Herakleia under Latmos. Ancient site in Caria (southwest Turkey) that flourished from *c*. the 5th century BC to the 2nd century AD. It lies on the lower slopes of Mt Latmos (Beş Parmak), some 35 km from Miletos. It was once accessible from the sea but is now situated on the shore of Lake Bafa, which was created by the silting of the River Maeander. The original settlement, Latmos, which lay east of the Hellenistic fortification wall of Herakleia, was a member of the Delian League in the 5th century BC. By the late 4th century BC the city had moved to Herakleia, Latmos becoming a necropolis; the site remains unexcavated. Its most outstanding feature is its system of Hellenistic fortifications, a 6.5-km circuit with 65 towers, well-preserved sections of curtain wall, gates and posterns of isodomic, trapezoidal and Cyclopean masonry; foundation cuttings are visible in the bedrock where the walls themselves do not survive. The layout of the town is orthogonal, perhaps influenced by that at Miletos. The most important buildings are the Temple of Athena, a Doric temple *in antis* built of local limestone with a marble façade, identified and dated by inscriptions to *c*. 200 BC; a 2nd-century BC bouleuterion (council chamber) with Doric architectural features similar to that at Priene; and the Hellenistic agora (130×60 m) with its two-storey market-building; this building supports the southern end of the agora terrace; its lower storey was entered from outside the agora, while its upper storey enclosed the south side of the square. Roman-period remains, to the north-west of the agora, include baths, a theatre, a nymphaeum and possibly a gymnasium. South of the agora is a small hexastyle prostyle temple with a rock-cut, apsidal cella; it was dedicated to Endymion, the mythical founder of the city. Remains of early Christian basilicas dating from the 4th to the 6th century AD represent the last phase of settlement before Herakleia was abandoned, and the old site of Latmos was resettled.

BIBLIOGRAPHY

F. Krischen: *Die Befestigung von Herakleia am Latmos* (1922), ii of *Milet III* (Berlin, 1906)

G. E. Bean and J. M. Cook: 'The Carian Coast, III', *Annu. Brit. Sch. Athens*, lii (1957), pp. 138–40

G. E. Bean: *Aegean Turkey* (London and New York, 1966), pp. 252–8

F. E. Winter: *Greek Fortifications* (Toronto, 1971)

A. Peschlow-Bindokat: 'Herakleia am Latmos', *Archäol. Anz.* (1977), pp. 90–104

A. W. Lawrence: *Greek Aims in Fortification* (Oxford, 1979)

SARAH CORMACK

Herakleopolis Magna [anc. Egyp. Henen-nesut; Copt. Ahnas; Arab. Ihnasya el-Medina]. Egyptian site *c.* 15 km west of Beni Suef. The city of Henen-nesut was known in the Greco-Roman period (332 BC–AD 395) as Herakleopolis Magna because of the identification of the local ram-headed god Harsaphes with the Greek Herakles. However, it first rose to prominence as the national capital during the First Intermediate Period (*c.* 2150–*c.* 2008 BC), when the Herakleopolitan 9th and 10th dynasties ruled Egypt. The city also flourished during the Third Intermediate Period (*c.* 1075–*c.* 750 BC), when it became an independent princedom. The site was excavated by Edouard Naville (1890–91), Flinders Petrie (1904) and the Spanish Archaeological Mission under the direction of J. López from 1966.

The earliest remains, in a necropolis of the First Intermediate Period, consist of an important group of tombs belonging to prominent officials. These are decorated with polychrome reliefs depicting offering-bearers and scenes of rural life, as well as stelae of the false-door type (*see* STELE, §2), all representing Old Kingdom themes. The quality of the reliefs shows clearly that the high level of artistry at Herakleopolis Magna continued throughout the First Intermediate Period.

The principal temple was consecrated to Harsaphes and dates at least as far back as the Early Dynastic period (*c.* 2925–*c.* 2575 BC); however, little is known of it until the early Middle Kingdom (*c.* 2008–*c.* 1630 BC), when it was destroyed by the Theban 11th Dynasty and had to be rebuilt. The surviving parts of the temple date mainly from the reign of Ramesses II (*reg c.* 1279–*c.* 1213 BC). Its layout consists of a courtyard flanked by colossi of Ramesses II and dominated by two huge statues of divine triads (Cairo, Egyp. Mus.); a portico decorated with reliefs of Ramesses II; a hypostyle chamber in which was found a 23rd Dynasty golden statuette of Harsaphes (Boston, MA, Mus. F.A.; see fig.); a pronaos or vestibule; and the sanctuary proper. The other important Middle Kingdom monument

Herakleopolis Magna, statuette of the god Harsaphes from the temple, gold, h. 60 mm, Third Intermediate Period, 23rd Dynasty, *c.* 823–*c.* 732 BC (Boston, MA, Museum of Fine Arts)

at Herakleopolis is the temple of Kom el-Aqarib, which includes blocks and columns bearing 12th Dynasty inscriptions, as well as two colossi attributed to the Middle Kingdom. Other remains at Herakleopolis include a necropolis of several tombs belonging to Libyan notables of the Third Intermediate Period, and the monuments of Kom el-Dinar from the Roman period. The city's principal necropolis, at the neighbouring site of Sedment, *c.* 7 km to the south-west, comprised tombs dating from the Old Kingdom and First Intermediate Period to the Greco-Roman period. It was excavated by Petrie in 1920–21.

In the Coptic period (4th–7th century AD) Herakleopolis was known as Ahnas, and the site was dominated by the basilica of el-Kanisa. The importance of the Coptic sculpture discovered at Ahnas—particularly the 4th-century pieces decorated with pagan motifs—gave rise to the term 'school of Ahnas' (*see* COPTIC ART, §III). Most of the sculpture, principally comprising fragments of architraves and friezes, is now in the Coptic Museum, Cairo.

BIBLIOGRAPHY

LÄ

E. Naville: *Ahnas el Medineh (Heracleopolis Magna)* (London, 1894)

W. M. F. Petrie and C. T. Currelly: *Ehnasya, 1904* (London, 1904)

U. Monneret de Villard: *La scultura ad Ahnâs: Note sull'origine dell'arte copta* (Milan, 1923)

Arte faraónico (exh. cat., ed. M. Almagro Basch, M. J. Almagro Gorbea and M. C. Pérez Die; Ministry of Education and Science, Madrid, Zaragoza, Barcelona, 1975–6), pp. 67–86

M. G. E. Mokhtar: *Ihnasya el-Medina (Herakleopolis Magna)* (Cairo, 1983)

JOSEP PADRÓ

Heraklios I (*b c.* AD 575; *reg* 610–41; *d* Constantinople [now Istanbul], 11 Feb 641). Byzantine emperor and patron. Although it is sometimes claimed that Heraklios was of Armenian descent, contemporary sources record his family origins in Cappadocia. His father was the exarch of Carthage. In 610 Heraklios usurped the imperial throne from the tyrant Phokas (*reg* 602–10) and thus initiated the rule of the Heraklian dynasty which lasted until 711. He and his first wife Eudoxia (*d* 612) had two children, Epiphania and Heraklios, the latter of whom later became Constantine III (*reg* 641). After the death of Eudoxia, Heraklios married his niece Martina, who bore him ten children.

A competent military leader, Heraklios defeated the Persians at Nineveh in 627. He is often credited with the reorganization of the provinces into administrative units called themes, but whether or not this institution originated under Heraklios is debatable. References in contemporary sources to scientific treatises on chemistry and astrology by Heraklios suggest that he was well educated.

In 627 Heraklios enlarged a portico linking two triclinia in the palace of Blachernai (*c.* AD 500; destr.) in the north-west corner of Constantinople and in the same area constructed a new fortification wall that ran from the prisons of Anema to the Xyloporta (wooden gate) on the Golden Horn. This wall, known as the Monoteichos or Kastellion of Blachernai, was 3.70 m thick and defended by towers. It has been suggested that the nine silver plates with scenes from the *Life of David* (610–29; Nicosia, Cyprus Mus., and New York, Met.) from Lapithos (*see* CYPRUS, §III, 4) were made for Heraklios.

BIBLIOGRAPHY

R. Janin: *Constantinople byzantine: Développement urbain et répertoire topographique* (Paris, 1950), pp. 248, 266

M. van Grunsven-Eygenraam: 'Heraclius and the David Plates', *Bull. Ant. Besch.*, xlviii (1973), pp. 159–174

E. Coche de La Ferté: *L'Art de Byzance* (Paris, 1981)

THOMAS E. RUSSO

1. The Achievement of Arms of the Duke of Norfolk, Earl Marshal of England, annotated to show component parts: (a) crests; (b) Peer's helm; (c) mantling; (d) Duke's coronet; (e) supporters; (f) shield; (g) two gold batons in saltire: the insignia of the Earl Marshal; (h) motto

Heraldic manuscripts. *See under* GENEALOGICAL AND HERALDIC MANUSCRIPTS.

Heraldry. Science that comprises all the duties of a herald: the marshalling of ceremonies, supervision of tournaments, ambassadorial functions and, in some countries and periods, the recording and granting of armorial bearings, the study of which can also be called armory. This article will concentrate on the latter, especially as an art and as an essential tool for the historian of European art of the Middle Ages and the Renaissance.

I. Introduction. II. Western. III. Islamic lands. IV. Japan.

I. Introduction.

Armory is all that pertains to armorial bearings (hereditary personal devices borne on shields for the identification of the user in battle or elsewhere) and of their adjuncts (see fig. 1). The basic shield device may also be displayed on banners, flags (*see* FLAGS AND STANDARDS), surcoats (hence the term 'coat of arms', usually abbreviated to 'arms') or horse trappers (*see* §IV below). The shield (f) may be combined with a crest ((a); a device set on the helm and mantling worn by the medieval knight), a crown, a coronet (d) or such other indications of rank as orders of knighthood, mitres, crosiers or swords. Supporters ((e); two figures or beasts upholding the shield) or a single supporter holding the shield (*Schildwächter*) may also be found. Badges, used primarily for the identification of the lord's retinue and for his standards, or the impresa (a personal device often bearing a motto; *see* IMPRESA) could also form part of heraldic display in the later Middle Ages and Renaissance. The arms may be combined with those of the bearer's wife or of an office such as a bishopric or abbey held by him. Over the centuries other coats of arms representing fiefs derived from ancestors, grant or conquest, could be marshalled with the paternal coat. In German practice, but rarely elsewhere, such quarterings were accompanied by the related crest. The multiplicity of quarterings in the modern period sometimes led, as in Sweden, to the adoption of a simplified version for ordinary use, or even just the ruler's monogram. Viewed in this way, heraldry is a European development; the relatively short-lived devices used particularly in the Mamluk period in the Levant were apparently borne for offices (*see* §VI below). Closer parallels may be found in the Japanese *mon*, hereditary military devices used, but not borne on shields, by the daimyo and samurai (*see* §VII below), and in the Mongolian *tamgha*s ('signs of property').

Arms may be depicted in a wide variety of media or blazoned, that is, described in precise technical terms that enable an artist to reproduce the original design in whatever style is desired. The language of blazon started to develop in France in the 12th century and had become well established by the end of the 13th. Many rolls of arms in both France and England were blazoned rather than painted, although both blazon and depictions were sometimes used so that one illustrates the other. Elsewhere, particularly in the Holy Roman Empire, Italy, Spain and Portugal, the armorials were painted rather than blazoned. In Germany the more precise French system was not adopted until the late 19th century, but elsewhere its obvious convenience led to its general adoption, save in Poland where each design used by the noble clans had its own name.

The language of blazon is essential for understanding and using the descriptions in reference books. The description (London, Coll. Arms, MS. R.22 fol.99) of a simple coat granted to Hans Kentz of Nuremberg by Emperor Charles V in 1544, as presented in a literal translation (London, Coll. Arms, MS. W2 fol.139), demonstrates its advantages very clearly:

> A Shield parted from the undermost formost part belowe, to the Corner of the hindermost part above, the uppermost yellowe or gould couler and the nethermost part blacke: In the whole Shield a Unicorne with a horn crooked forwardes thrusting out a redd tongue upright redy to leape and parted according to the couler of the Shield, upon the Shield a Tilt helmett with yellow (or gold couler) Unicorne with a Crooked horne putting forth his twoe formost feete & a red tongue.

In normal blazon this can be written: 'Per bend sinister Sable and Gold, a unicorn salient counter-coloured; the Crest, on a wreath of the colours, a demi-unicorn salient Gold.' Some descriptions made by those unversed in the technical language may resort to similar circumlocutions or to invented phrases not found in textbooks and dictionaries.

The rules of heraldic syntax are quite simple. The description starts with the field, or background of the shield. This may be of one colour, divided by the axial lines or other linear divisions into two or more colours, or strewn with (semy of) small charges (or objects). The principal charge is then described, stating whether it is between other charges, or has charges on or over it, or both. Finally any borders, labels and other marks of difference or cadency are described. The term dexter refers to the viewer's left, sinister to the right.

The varied sources for the study of heraldry can be grouped in two main categories: those that identify the bearers of the designs, including armorials, seals and monuments; and those in which the arms or other devices, when identified, may provide information about the date, history or identification of the work of art in which they appear. The latter includes architectural decoration, paintings and manuscript illuminations, stained glass, plate and jewellery (see §IV below).

See also GENEALOGICAL AND HERALDIC MANUSCRIPTS.

BIBLIOGRAPHY

P. Palliot: *La Vraye et Parfaite Science des armoiries, ou l'indice armorial du feu maistre Louvan Geliot* (Paris, 1660/R 1895)

J. Burke and J. B. Burke: *A General Armory of England, Scotland, and Ireland* (London, 1842, rev. J. B. Burke, 1878/R 1884 and 1961)

J. B. Rietstap: *Armorial général, contenant la description des armoiries des familles nobles et patriciennes de l'Europe* (Gouda, 1861, rev., 2 vols, 1884–7)

J. W. Papworth and A. W. Morant: *An Alphabetical Dictionary of Coats of Arms . . . Forming an Extensive Ordinary of British Armorials* (London, 1874)

T. de Renesse: *Dictionnaire des figures héraldiques*, 7 vols (Brussels, 1892–1903)

J. Parker: *A Glossary of Terms Used in Heraldry* (Oxford, 1894/R 1970)

J. Foster: *Some Feudal Coats of Arms and Others* (Oxford, 1902)

W. H. St J. Hope: *A Grammar of English Heraldry* (Cambridge, 1913); rev. A. R. Wagner (Cambridge, 1953)

A. R. Wagner: *Heralds and Heraldry in the Middle Ages* (Oxford, 1939/R 1956)

D. L. Galbreath: *Manuel du blason* (Lausanne, 1942); rev. L. Jéquier (Paris, 1977)

G. Stalins: *Vocabulaire-atlas héraldique en six langues: Français-English-Deutsch-español-italiano-nederlandsch* (Paris, 1952)

H. Jäger-Sunstenau: *General-Index zu den Siebmacher'schen Wappenbüchern, 1605–1961* (Graz, 1964)

O. Neubecker: *Heraldry: Sources, Symbols and Meaning* (London, 1976) [good illustrations]

C. R. Humphery-Smith: *Anglo-Norman Armory Two: An Ordinary of Thirteenth-century Armorials* (Canterbury, 1984)

T. Woodcock and J. M. Robinson: *The Oxford Guide to Heraldry* (Oxford, 1988)

II. Western.

1. Art of Heraldry. 2. Secular. 3. Ecclesiastical. 4. Heraldry in art.

1. ART OF HERALDRY. The art of heraldry consists in the correct rendering of armorial bearings in the chosen style and in accordance with the prescriptions of the blazon. Arms are composed of tinctures (colours) and charges (elements of design). Certain aspects of the subject are important for appreciating the results as works of art, while others, such as the shape of the shield and the style of drawing, can be helpful in dating or localizing a depiction.

(i) The shield. The shape of the shield changed over the centuries, at first in response to modifications in the knight's armour, but later to follow changes in the styles of the decorative arts. Romanesque shields as depicted in books and on the BAYEUX TAPESTRY were kite-shaped and reached from the shoulder to the feet. By the mid-12th century the length had been reduced, and some were deeply curved at the sides, while from *c.* 1180 the rounded top became flatter (e.g. Zurich, Schweizer. Landesmus.). In Italy the almond-shaped shields of the Late Romanesque type were revived in the 14th century, perhaps because of the extra space they offered for the chiefs (ordinaries; see §3 below) added to the paternal coat to indicate political allegiance. Some early 13th-century shields were triangular, with straight sides, but more commonly the sides were curved. This Gothic, or heater-shaped, shield became the classic type (e.g. Marburg, Umus. Kultgesch.). With the increase of quartered coats in the later Middle Ages, the sides were drawn with the upper part straight, or the squarer type of shield with the lance notch, developed for tournament use, was adopted (e.g. Munich, Bayer. Nmus.). In Spain and Portugal shields often had straight, sometimes slightly tapering, sides with a rounded base; while in Italy the *testa di cavallo* shield, based on the shaffron (the plate down the front of the horse's nose), became popular in the late 15th century.

The shape of the shield had a marked influence on the way in which the charges were disposed within it. In the roughly triangular Gothic shield the small charges would normally be placed two above and one below, an exception being made for some animals, such as the leopards of England, which were placed one above the other so as to fill the available space more easily. Five charges could be placed in cross or in saltire (St Andrew's cross), but in Iberian heraldry, owing to the use of round-based shields, six charges were common and were most often placed in pairs.

(ii) Tinctures. The tinctures used in heraldry were limited and in the Middle Ages could be classified in several ways. For practical purposes they were regarded as comprising (a) the metals: Or (gold) and Argent (silver); (b) the colours: Gules (red), Azure (blue), Sable (black), Vert (green) and Purpure (purple), the last two being rare; and (c) the furs: Ermine and Vair (squirrel) with their variants. Natural colours for beasts and plants were avoided in the shield. To ensure maximum legibility the rule was early established that a metal, colour or fur should not be placed on another of the same group. There are rare exceptions, as in the arms of the Latin kings of Jerusalem: Silver a cross potent between four crosslets potent Gold. The field could be divided, usually along one or more of the axial lines, and these segments could be of metals, colours or furs, without infringement of the rule.

Medieval heraldic textbooks contain elaborate systems for ranking the tinctures, derived from contemporary theories about light and colours and the association of certain colours with the four elements. Such authors as the Italian jurist Bartolo di Sasso Ferrato (1313–59), John de Bado Aureo (*fl c.* 1395) and Nicholas Upton (*c.* 1400–57) attempted to prove that certain colours or combinations were more noble than others. On the few occasions when the colour symbolism is referred to in 15th- and 16th-century grants of arms, they do not often correspond, and the popularity of colour combinations seems to owe more to the example of those borne by the local rulers. During the 16th century fewer armorials were painted, and abbreviations were devised to indicate the colours. This tricking of arms was followed in early printed armorials, most systematically in the plates of the *Grosses und allgemeines Wappenbuch* (Nuremberg, 1605) by JOHANN SIBMACHER. About the same time experimental schemes were introduced to indicate the tinctures in engravings by means of different hatchings. By the 18th century this system, perfected by Father Sylvester Petra Sancta in his *Tesserae gentilitiae* (Rome, 1638), had been widely adopted, although some artists preferred to omit them.

(iii) Charges. Partitions and ordinaries are among the most common elements in heraldic design, the simple partition lines following the axial lines of the shield and most of the ordinaries being bands of colour in the same directions. Some of these could be multiplied, a field divided into six vertical divisions being called paly; if more or fewer than six were found the number was to be given (e.g. three pales or paly of eight). Their width depended originally on the proportions suggested by the whole design and by the optical effects of the colours involved. During the 16th century fixed proportions were laid down for each ordinary in the textbooks, such as those by Gerard Legh (*d* 1563) and John Guillim (1565–1621); although these are still often repeated, they have no basis in earlier practice and have generally been ignored by the better artists. Medieval painters usually made the ordinaries more slender, perhaps one-ninth of the shield height if uncharged. When other charges were placed on the ordinaries the latter were drawn wider to accommodate them. The overall design of the quarterings had to be clearly visible at a distance; some

of the small charges were occasionally omitted in Italian work, a practice that can mislead the unwary.

Simple geometric forms were supplemented from the outset by a wide range of beasts, birds, fishes, plants and almost any object or part thereof. While some animals were familiar domestic creatures, others, even more popular, were drawn from the imagined dragons, unicorns and other creatures found in Bestiaries and similar collections of natural history. The choice could be due to caprice, although in the later Middle Ages the need to make simple but distinctive patterns led to some new introductions; but others could be chosen as a pun on the bearer's name (e.g. two trumpets for the arms of Trumpington) or in allusion to the arms of his overlord. As with the colours, there are regional patterns for certain common beasts evidently based on those of the rulers.

Bartolo di Sasso Ferrato's *Tractatus de insigniis et armis* (*c.* 1347) gives clear guidelines for the ways in which animals should be depicted:

> The said animals ought to be depicted according to their noblest act, and also where their strength is displayed.... Draw, therefore, the lion erect stretching out, biting with its mouth, tearing with its teeth; and the same with other animals.... Certain animals are not ferocious, and likewise ought to be depicted according to their diverse noblest acts.

This is very similar to the descriptions in such Bestiaries as that in verse (early 12th century; London, BL, Cotton MS. Nero A. V, fols 41*v*–82*v*) by the Anglo-Norman Philippe de Thaon (*fl* 1100–35), who described the lion in heraldic terms:

> He has a frightful face, the neck hairy and great,
> Square his breast before, bold and pugnacious;
> Slender his shape behind, a tail of large fashion,
> And the legs, straight right to the agile feet;
> The feet large and cleft, the claws long and curved.

This description is also perfectly fitted to the drawing of a lion 'after the life' in the portfolio (*c.* 1220–40; Paris, Bib. N., MS. fr. 19093) of Villard de Honnecourt.

The *Tractatus de armis* (*c.* 1395) by John de Bado Aureo lists some 20 creatures with brief notes on each; later editions include a well-illustrated English translation (late 15th century; Oxford, Bodleian Lib., MS. Laud. misc. 733). A much longer list was given by Nicholas Upton in his *De studio militari* (*c.* 1446–7). Both authors drew on the Bestiary for information but changed the theological or moral applications to a suitable symbolism for their new role in armory. Despite the use in medieval arms of a variety of plants that are not always easy to identify, little attention was paid to them by such writers as John and Nicholas, perhaps because herbals were concerned more with the medical and culinary uses of plants than their possible symbolic meanings in the Bible.

(iv) Aesthetics. Although there are no medieval texts on aesthetics, philosophers did speculate in other contexts on the nature of beauty. From these statements, and from allusions in other writings, a fairly clear idea of the qualities thought to make an object beautiful may be derived. These seem equally to have been applied in armory. Villard de Honnecourt began his notes on drawing: 'here begins the art of drawing as the discipline of geometry teaches it, so

explained as to make the work easy.' The drawings themselves show many creatures fitted to geometrical frames to determine their proportions. The herald to Sir John Chandos (*d* 1369/70), in his life of Edward the Black Prince, written *c.* 1386, described how: 'Then might you see banners and pennons unfurled to the wind, whereon fine Gold and Azure shone, Purple, Gules, and Ermine . . . there was many a precious banner of silk and sendal also' (1910 ed., pp. 143, 157). Beauty was found in a well-drawn representation, with bright and clear colours, while the proportions should be harmonious and based on geometry and the relation of the parts to the whole.

Indifferent or bad work can be found from all periods, even on such prestigious works as Westminster Abbey, London, where the 13th-century carved shields in the aisle arcading vary greatly in quality. The rules ensured that the colours of the arms were easy to identify, the proportions of the charges, particularly the ordinaries, to the shield being important. Further simple rules were followed in regard to other charges. For example, if three were to be placed in the shield, the one in base would be drawn slightly larger; the leopards of England were arranged so that limbs, heads and tails filled the shape of the shield and the spaces between each beast to the best advantage. The fashion in much post-medieval heraldic art for the charges to be drawn of equal size was not favoured. A further refinement, preferred in Germanic heraldry more than elsewhere, was the custom of turning charges to face towards the centre of the shield, all the quarterings and crests of the dexter (left) side being turned in this way (e.g. the arms of auf Homberg, 1754). Finally, the colours could be enhanced by the skilful use of diaper, finely drawn scrolling patterns burnished into gold and silver or painted in a darker hue on the colours. *Paillé*, a special form of diaper based on textile patterns with small beasts in linked circles, was used in Normandy.

BIBLIOGRAPHY

Chandos Herald: *Le Prince noir* (*c.* 1386; U. London, Lib., ULI MS. I); ed. and Eng. trans. M. K. Pope and E. C. Lodge (Oxford, 1910)
G. Legh: *The Accedens of Armory* (London, 1562/*R* 1612)
J. Sibmacher: *Grosses und allgemeines Wappenbuch* (Nuremberg, 1605); augmented as *Neues Wapenbuch* (Nuremberg, 1609); ed. and rev. O. Titan von Hefner (Nuremberg, 1854–1961/*R* Neustadt, 1970–76)
J. Guillim: *A Display of Heraldrie* (London, 1610, 6/1724)
G. W. Eve: *Heraldry as Art* (London, 1907)
W. H. St J. Hope: *Heraldry for Craftsmen and Designers* (London, 1913)
E. J. Jones: *Medieval Heraldry* (Cardiff, 1943) [texts of Bartolo di Sasso Ferrato, John de Bado Aureo and Nicholas Upton]
H. Child: *Heraldic Design: A Handbook for Students* (London, 1965)
C.-A. von Volborth: *The Art of Heraldry* (Poole, 1987)

2. SECULAR. A clear distinction may be drawn between heraldic and other military or personal devices used in early periods or coevally with European heraldry in other cultures. As some of these are still discussed in books on heraldry, they will be examined briefly below.

(i) Pre-heraldic devices. (ii) Armory. (iii) Attributed arms.

(i) Pre-heraldic devices. The earliest known examples of territorial devices appear in the form of plastic standards depicted on ancient Egyptian artefacts, such as a palette of NARMER (*c.* 3100 BC; Cairo, Egyp. Mus.; *see* FLAGS AND STANDARDS, fig. 4). On another palette, conquered towns are portrayed with the local device set inside a wall, with a hawk or other device perched above it (*c.* 2750 BC;

2. Pre-heraldic devices of emblems and towns on the Town Palette, slate, 2nd Dynasty, *c.* 2750 BC (Cairo, Egyptian Museum)

Cairo, Egyp. Mus.; see fig. 2). These standards were ancestral to the later nome standards depicted in the temples. Each device used the beast associated with the local deity; this system, at first limited to Upper Egypt, was extended to the rest of the country in the Greco-Roman period. Although found on some early labels, including an ivory plaque from the tomb of Queen Neithhotpe at Naqada (*c.* 2920 BC; Cairo, Egyp. Mus.; for illustration *see* NAQADA), these standards do not appear to have acquired a personal character.

Although attempts have been made to find a system in the shield devices that appear on Greek vase paintings of the 6th to 4th centuries BC, the wide variety attributed to the same deity or hero shows that, whatever their significance may have been, it was not heraldry as now understood. That civic devices (*parasima*) were used on shields is clear from references in Herodotus' *Hellenica* (*c.* 430 BC), although it is curious that most of those described do not occur on the coins of the cities named (*see* GREECE, ANCIENT, §X, 2(i) and (ii)). Coins examined for the consistent use of devices by Archaic and Classical Greek mints show that a quarter have no recognizable device and that of the remainder only some used the same device for several centuries. Several bear variations on the theme of the local deity and associations with the cult. The Macedonian royal house may have used the device of a star, since this occurs prominently on their gold funerary caskets, jewellery and, more rarely, coins (all Thessaloniki, Archaeol. Mus.).

Roman legionary devices (*see* FLAGS AND STANDARDS, fig. 5) were not personal, and most of the evidence for the late Roman period is derived from the *Notitia dignitatum*, a work of uncertain reliability initially compiled *c.* AD 395. Scattered allusions in early chronicles suggest that some memories of the Roman military insignia lingered on in Western Europe. The conversion of Constantine the Great in AD 313 led to the adoption of the chi-rho monogram as a shield device for the imperial bodyguard, as depicted in the mosaic of Justinian (*c.* 546–7; *see* MOSAIC, fig. 6) in S Vitale, Ravenna, and to its being updated to a cross in Carolingian miniatures, such as those in the Lothair Gospels (849–51; Paris, Bib. N., MS. lat. 266). The only suggestion of a possible personal device appears on the shields carried by some Byzantine emperors, including Justinian, on coins issued between 395 and 602. Only the upper part of the shield is depicted, and it is not clear whether the horseman shown on it was the old iconography of the ruler triumphing over the barbarian or St George. It may be significant that the Great Princes of Moscow, and after them the Tsars, used an escutcheon of St George in their arms.

In his *De excidio Britanniae*, Gildas, writing *c.* 540, addressed Maelgwn Hir, Prince of Gwynedd (*reg c.* 517–47), as 'dragon of the island'; three centuries later, Nennius, in his *Historia britonum*, could regard the red dragon as the emblem of the British and the white dragon that of the Saxons. All these images were presumably derived from the Roman *draco* (cohort standard). Like the triangular banners with a form of triskele found on the coins (London, BM) of the 10th-century Danish kings at York, however, these were state or tribal, not personal, devices, although they do seem to have had a role in the development of true heraldry.

One of the earliest references to the use of a banner as a sign of investiture is to one sent by Pope LEO III to Charlemagne as a token of his investiture as 'Patrician and Duke of the Romans', and the office of Gonfalonier (standard-bearer) of the Roman See can be traced back to the 11th century. When in 1004 Emperor Henry II enfeoffed his brother-in-law as Henry V, Duke of Bavaria

3. Seal of Hugues Candavène, Count of St Pol, showing five garbs in a cross, 1223; from G. Demay: *Inventaire des sceaux de l'Artois et de la Picardie*, ii (Paris, 1877)

(*reg* 1004–26), it is said that he 'gave the duchy with an ensign on a spear' (Ganshof, p. 112), an act that would have been meaningless unless this was already known to be connected with the territory.

(ii) Armory. Although the use of banners and pennons in early medieval warfare is well attested, as is the custom of enfeoffment with the banner, only a few fiefs were hereditary as a matter of right before the 11th century. About the same time the knightly class evolved under the kings and magnates, and the tournament as an occasion for the exercise of martial skills was created. The earliest evidence for the use of arms is found on 12th-century seals as part of the equestrian effigies of great magnates, such as that (*c.* 1145; London, PRO) of Gilbert, Earl of Hertford (*d* 1152). The appearance of identical devices on seals in subsequent generations demonstrates that they are true heraldic devices. That the decades around 1100 were of crucial importance to the development of heraldry can be seen in the use of the same, or closely related, coats of arms in some family groups who shared a common ancestor in the 11th century. Although the material evidence for the use of arms by lesser families is almost non-existent before the 13th century, some knights used arms based on those of their overlords, and some of these must have been created in the 12th century. No formal grants survive from this period, but William Camden recorded later medieval grants from lords to tenants or retainers. During the 12th and 13th centuries the system was less rigid than it later became, and arms could be changed from the paternal coat to one belonging to a mother's family if a more important fief was inherited from her.

Some of the earliest coats of arms can be traced to devices used on coins and seals, some of the former dating from the 11th century. The Counts of St Pol (Artois) issued coins with an ear, later a sheaf, of oats (med. Fr. *avène*; mod. Fr. *avoine*), punning on their family name; the garb (sheaf) appears on the seal of Enguerrand *c.* 1141–50, and another seal for Hugues Candavène in 1223 had five garbs in cross (Demay, 1875–7; see fig. 3). This is a good example of the way in which the earliest arms took a few generations to settle down in their familiar forms (*see* COINS, §II).

The French romances of the 12th and 13th centuries are a valuable literary source of the earliest examples of blazons and contain vivid descriptions of the use of the new devices in tournament and war (*see* ROMANCE, MANUSCRIPT). They also testify to the spread of arms to the lesser nobility and knights at this period.

While heraldry originated from military needs it was soon recognized as a means of identification for other purposes, and its use disseminated rapidly in the social order. Already in the 12th century, arms were used on the seals of some ladies: Joan (1165–99), the daughter of Henry II, King of England, for example, is depicted on the reverse of her silver seal (1196–9; London, BL) seated holding a Toulouse cross in reference to one of the fiefs of her second husband, Raymond VI, Count of Toulouse (*reg* 1194–1222). Seals for Rohaise de Clare (*d* 1156), wife of Gilbert de Gand, Earl of Lincoln, are covered with the chevrons of her paternal coat (e.g. London, BL), and another kite-shaped seal used in 1189 by Mathilde of Portugal, Countess of Flanders (*d* 1218), bore an early version of the Portuguese royal arms (Demay, 1873).

During the 13th century the use of arms spread to almost all sections of society, including institutions. Cities, often bound to contribute to the feudal army, began to use arms: the earliest evidence comes from the towns of northern Italy, which were gaining considerable autonomy from the imperial authorities. In early 13th-century London the civic militia under the aldermen of the wards had their banners, and by the middle of the century some aldermen had armorial seals (London, Guildhall, Corp. London Rec. Office). The guilds also acquired coats of arms in the later Middle Ages, the first grant by an English king of arms being made to the Drapers of London in 1440. There is also evidence for the use of corporate arms, based on those of the partners, by some of the Italian trading and banking houses, such as the Bardi of Florence (before 1346; London, PRO, E 43/141). The higher clergy soon adopted arms for their dioceses, and, before the end of the 13th century, bishops and leading abbots were using their own personal arms (*see* §V below).

(a) Regional variations. (b) Marshalling and differencing. (c) Crests, crowns and other insignia.

(a) Regional variations. Evidence for the development of regional variations in European heraldry exists from the 13th century, not only among different countries but sometimes within them as well. This is most clearly seen in the differences between Central Europe, France and the British Isles, the Iberian Peninsula, Italy, Poland, Hungary and the Balkans. From the outset the differences are important, being reflected not only in the choice of charges and preferred shield shapes but also in the adoption of the crest (*see* §5 below) and the exterior ornaments of the shield. These are especially noticeable in ecclesiastical heraldry, both in the Middle Ages and later. Such variations can be helpful in the identification of arms, since many charges and combinations of tinctures occur in several countries: the precise way in which they are depicted and the ornaments chosen to accompany the shield can often aid in deciding between possible alternatives. Unfortunately it is still not possible to give precise details for every region, as the published source material is very uneven.

France. The borders of medieval France varied greatly from century to century, as many of the duchies became virtually independent despite technically being fiefs of the French crown. In the south-west, the Basque- and Catalan-speaking areas used the same types of armorial design as their fellow countrymen in Spain (*see* §(iv) below). By the end of the 13th century the kings of Aragon had extended their rule to several places in France, as later did the kings of Navarre. Elsewhere the great fiefs defined areas of variation. In the north-west, the Bretons and Normans used distinct styles, while, in the east, Alsace adopted types of charges and styles of art similar to those of the Rhineland. French influence also extended beyond the present frontiers, to the south Netherlands and to parts of Switzerland and Italy. In many respects France was the most important area for the development of heraldry in medieval Europe. It was here that the language of blazon arose, and the pattern for both ecclesiastical and secular insignia of rank was largely a French creation that spread with variations to other countries during the later Middle Ages.

British Isles. While the origins of heraldry in Britain were closely connected with France, as was the nobility, there are marked differences in its development in various areas. To some extent this reflected the degree of royal control, external relations and the nature of the local society. In Ireland little evidence remains for either the Anglo-Norman nobility or the Irish chieftains. Medieval heraldry in Wales fell into two categories: the Anglo-Norman families in the south and the Welsh princes in the north and centre. The latter claimed descent from nobles who migrated from Strathclyde in Scotland after the end of Roman rule and established dynasties, the pedigrees of which were memorized by the bards. By the end of the Middle Ages arms had been attributed to these early princes and were borne by all their descendants.

The earliest evidence for the use of arms in Scotland comes from the Lowlands, where both English and French influence was strong: for example, the arms on seals of Scottish prelates used such symbols as the crosier in the French style long before they were used in England. As Orkney and Shetland were under Norwegian suzerainty until the 15th century, the use of composed coats (those combining elements from the arms of a husband and wife to make a new design) may have been due to Norse influence. The loss at sea of the Lyon Office records, while being returned from London in 1661, led to a new Statute (1672) governing the use of arms in Scotland. Under this all members of a family were required to matriculate differenced versions of the arms, and an elaborate system using borders and other charges was developed to meet this need.

Germany and Scandinavia. With the death of Emperor Frederick II in 1250 the Electors and other magnates became in effect independent rulers, although the emperors continued to make grants of arms and noble titles. Each of the fiefs making up the Holy Roman Empire regarded itself as a separate entity, and arms identical with those borne in another fief could therefore be used freely. German heraldry also employed a greater variety of charges than elsewhere. As in most other countries, the heralds exercised no control over the use of arms by burghers. In such major cities as Nuremberg and Augsburg the more important burgher families were recognized as patricians and associated with the lower ranks of the nobility, using the barred helmet and other indicia of their rank.

A marked feature of German heraldry was its strong territorial basis, reflected in the use of quarterings for each fief held, each with its own crest; an example appears on the Garter stall plate of Albert, Prince of Saxe-Coburg, in St George's Chapel, Windsor (Hope, 1901). In the achievements of prelates, the mitre would be placed on a helm flanked to the dexter by the crests of their fiefs, both lay and ecclesiastical, and to the sinister by those of their family. During the 18th century this system caused great problems, for example when Prussia conquered other states, each with its own armorial identity. The great arms so ensuing were quite impractical for everyday use, and so the cypher was often preferred. Scandinavian heraldry presents several features in common with German practices, but the lack of hereditary surnames, the small number of surviving seals and no rolls of arms makes it difficult to say much about its formative period. It does, however, seem that there was a common pattern to much of the heraldry in the countries bordering the Baltic.

Iberia. Both Spanish and Portuguese heraldry present marked differences to the styles found elsewhere in medieval Europe. It is also one of the few areas where there is any evidence for the use of the true arms by Muslims and Jews during the Middle Ages (*see* §VI below). As is seen in the seals and armorials that have been published, a round-based shield was the preferred form in both Spain and Portugal, and this influenced the way in which charges were placed in it. Spanish heraldry also uses some charges seldom found in other countries, a typical example being a bend with the ends issuing from the mouth of a lion or dragon. Cauldrons and, in the Basque region, trees, often with a wolf standing in front, are also common. In later coats much use is made of charged borders and inscriptions, frequently of a religious nature, such as the AVE MARIA, GRACIA PLENA that appears on the Mendoza arms. As well as the round-based, shield-shaped seals, which continued in use in Spain long after they had fallen into desuetude elsewhere, other unusual types include spiked quatrefoils with small shields or charges set in the lobes.

Italy. As in Germany, heraldry in Italy was complicated by the number of states into which the peninsula was divided before the 19th century. Three main areas can be identified: the northern region, where the cities became independent of the imperial authorities in the 12th century; the Papal States in the centre; and Naples and Sicily in the south. Local pride and the importance of the northern city states in the Renaissance means that much more is known about their heraldic history than that of either of the other major regions. Some cities, such as Florence, acquired different coats of arms as the balance of political power changed from Guelph to Ghibelline or from the major to lesser families. Arms were also adopted by the quarters within many of the cities, those at Siena still being used in the annual Palio. In the 15th century such ruling families as the Medici, Este and Gonzaga acquired augmentations from either the emperor or the French king. During the 16th century the Venetian ambassadors to the English court were normally granted an augmentation to their arms before leaving London.

Little control over personal arms seems to have been exercised, save for a brief period in Genoa when an attempt was made to group all the patrician families under the 28 'Alberghi' and to make them drop their old arms. It failed. More significant was the polarization into supporters of the Angevins in Naples or of the Hohenstaufen during the mid-13th century, when, as a sign of their political allegiance, families added a chief of either Anjou or the Empire to their paternal coat. Other chiefs were later added to the list, and the idea was adopted by the Knights Hospitaller as a means of distinguishing the arms of the Bailiffs Grand Cross from those of the ordinary knights. In the north there was considerable French influence in Piedmont and Savoy, with German heraldic ideas dominant in the South Tyrol and Ticino. In Naples the French influence stemming from the Angevins was

4. Counterseal of Leszek III, Prince of Małopolska (Lesser Poland) and Kraków (*reg* 1279–88); from F. A. Vossberg: *Siegel des Mittelalters von Polen, Lithauen, Schlesien, Pommern und Preussen* (Berlin, 1854)

overlaid by Spanish as the Aragonese acquired first Sicily (1282) and then Naples itself (1435).

Poland. The one armorial system in Europe that evolved quite separately was that of Poland. The nobility belonged to clans of voivodes, all theoretically equal, and ennoblement could be attained only by adoption into one of these clans. There were 126 named designs (*herb*) for the arms borne by the clans. Some of the designs appear to have been based on runic devices and may be of great antiquity, while others use the horseshoe; the cross features prominently in many of the coats. Very few Polish arms were known to heralds in western Europe during the Middle Ages, apart from those borne by the kings and other rulers (see fig. 4). During the later Middle Ages Polish nobles travelling abroad often received grants of titles from the emperor and, after the late 18th-century partitions, the granting of titles of rank from the new rulers became common.

Hungary and the Balkans. Although Hungarian coinage provides some of the earliest examples of the use of heraldry in European coin design, the sources for the study of medieval heraldry are scarce. After 1308 the crown passed to the Angevin house of Naples, but it is not clear how far French heraldry influenced contemporary Hungarian practice. Certainly the designs found in the patents that have been collected and published seem to be quite distinctive and to have had some influence in the Balkans.

In the south Slav states coins show the use of a number of devices, including crested helms in 14th-century Serbia, but only one roll is known. There are a few copies of this, ascribed to Stanislav Rubčić, 'king of arms' to Tsar Stephen Uroš IV Dušan (*reg* 1331–55). Apart from the improbability of this office in a court based on Byzantine officers, the alleged original on Mt Athos is untraced. It was probably created in the 16th century, drawing on partly understood evidence. A small number of seals has been published, together with some monuments, mainly of the late 15th century or the 16th, with the arms of the deceased. In the voivodates of Transylvania, Moldavia and Wallachia, graveslabs and books from the 15th century onwards provide some evidence for the arms borne by the rulers and some of the lesser voivodes. Certainly there seems to be a much wider variation between different versions of the same coat than normally applies in other countries.

Although in some medieval rolls the arms 'Gules a cross between 4 letters B gold', are given for Constantinople (perhaps deriving from the old Byzantine coin reverse or a port flag, since they also appear in the portulans), there is relatively little evidence for the use of arms by medieval Greeks. After the fall of Constantinople in 1453, the descendants of the Palaiologi used an eagle coat both in Italy and England. On Chios, for long a Genoese colony, the local families adopted arms, although the evidence for their detailed history is not always clearly established. In Cyprus, apart from the use of panels with an eagle and lion motif under the canopies of the iconostasis in some of the old churches (e.g. *c.* 1500; Morphou, Hagios Mamas) during the period of Venetian rule (1489–1571), there is little evidence for the regular use of arms by the Greeks.

Russia. The use of arms in Russia seems to have begun with the adoption of European titles of rank under Peter the Great (*reg* 1682–1725). Little use seems to have been made of them in the arts.

Americas. Although shield devices were common among the Aztecs and the Inca in Pre-Columbian America, true heraldry was introduced only with the Europeans. In the Spanish and the later English or French colonies the leading families frequently came from noble or armigerous stock and continued to use their family arms. In Peru some arms based on older Inca devices were created for noble Inca families, members of which had intermarried with Spaniards; with this exception, the arms in the New World, as in the other colonies scattered across the globe, stemmed from the mother countries and were used in identical ways to those in Europe.

(b) Marshalling and differencing. The need to combine different coats of arms in one shield for particular purposes (to indicate marriage, the fiefs held or the offices of the bearer) was solved in various ways. Some were used only at an early period, while others were more favoured or used exclusively in one area. By the beginning of the 13th century the practice of dimidiation had begun, that is taking the dexter and sinister halves of the two coats and combining them, as appears on the arms of Emperor Otto IV (*reg* 1198–1218) as given by Matthew Paris (London, BL, Royal MS. 14 C.VII, fol. 84*r*). Obviously this could present problems: chevrons would become bends, and it was seldom suitable when animals were involved (see fig. 4 above). While the practice continued into the 14th century, it was gradually dropped in favour of impalement, where the two coats were placed whole in the shield or simply side by side. At first used for marriages, impalement was also used for combining arms of office, a bishopric or abbey for example, with those of the holder. It was also used for certain royal arms, the earliest being the impalement of the arms of Jerusalem and Lusignan by the kings of Cyprus from the 13th century, and those of Anjou and Hungary modern by Charles Robert of Anjou, King of Hungary (*reg* 1308–42; e.g. London, BM). His successors quartered impaled coats for Jerusalem, Anjou and Hungary as a triple impalement.

In the 12th and 13th centuries arms were sometimes adopted when important fiefs were inherited and the older coat abandoned. Later the preferred method was to quarter the arms in one shield. Normally the paternal, or pronominal, coat was placed first but might occasionally come second, as with the English royal arms between 1340 and 1707. In the Holy Roman Empire quartering was often the preferred method for marshalling arms of office. The Grand Master and Bailiffs of the Teutonic Order quartered their personal arms with those of the Magistracy or the Order respectively. Prelates also used the method: when holding several benefices and fiefs the arms for each would be quartered, and their personal coat placed on an escutcheon over all, a practice more often used for the arms of an heiress wife. Secular lords similarly quartered the arms of their fiefs, however acquired, and added a plain red quarter if possessed of royal rights. Each fief had its own

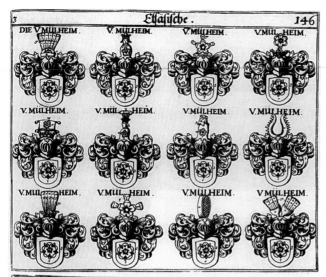

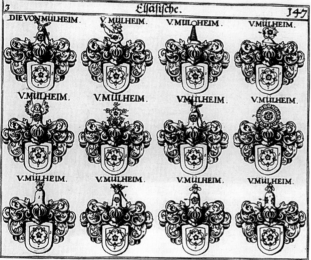

5. Arms and crests of the Mülheim family; from Johann Sibmacher: *Grosses und allgemeines Wappenbuch* (Nuremberg, 1605)

crest, and these were marshalled, in the case of prelates with a central barred helmet bearing the mitre. In this case the crests of the benefices and fiefs annexed to them would be ranged on the dexter side, and those of his family fiefs on the sinister. The six Electors also added to their quarterings the arms of their hereditary offices in the Empire on escutcheons. There is some evidence that during the 19th century quartered arms with a single crest were being granted to newly ennobled persons, perhaps to distinguish them from the established nobility.

Occasionally in Spain, and in Sicily after its acquisition by the crown of Aragon, coats could be marshalled per saltire (as the segments of a saltire cross) instead of quarterly. When this was done the segments in chief and base were regarded as the principal ones. Another occasional medieval practice was to place a coat to be marshalled on a quarter, as in the arms of Brittany under the Dreux family, but this was seldom resorted to.

Dimidiated quarterings can be confusing. They were occasionally employed between the 15th and 18th centuries, especially in England, as an expedient to fit quarterly coats with impalements more easily into the Gothic shield. If either half of the shield has a simple coat it is easy to identify; but where two quarterly coats are so combined it can be more difficult to disentangle them.

In Italy a pale with the *ombrellino*, or pavilion, and crossed keys, denoting the office of Gonfalonier of the Church, was often placed between the quarterings of the family arms. A pale with the tiara and keys could be marshalled by those families of whom a member had been elected to the Papal See. Cardinals and other officials of the Roman Curia could also impale the pontiff's arms with their own as a token of respect to their patron.

In most countries the need to distinguish the different members of a family was clearly felt, and as there were no fixed rules various solutions were tried. One German family in the 13th century decided to adopt different crests for each branch (see fig. 5). A label could mark the arms of the eldest son during his father's lifetime, and a bendlet or border could be added to the arms of younger sons. Other methods were more drastic and could change the appearance of the coat quite substantially: tinctures could be reversed or changed, small charges added to an ordinary, or this could be changed for another.

In early 15th-century England a system of cadency marks (the label, crescent, molet, martlet, annulet and fleur-de-lis) was invented for the first six sons in a family. Its first systematic use seems to have been by the English heralds at their Visitations (county surveys made from the 1530s onwards), but the method could lead to absurdities when it became necessary to add one on top of another, and it was later criticized; probably no single system can cover all eventualities, and, apart from Scotland (*see* §4(ii) above), most such systems have largely been ignored.

(c) Crests, crowns and other insignia. The idea of having a device set on top of the helmet may have been a northern invention. In the Anglo-Saxon poem *Beowulf* there is mention of the helmets worn by the Geats in Scandinavia: 'Above the cheek-guards shone the boar images, covered with gold, gleaming and tempered. The fierce-hearted boar held guard over the warlike men'. Boars or boars' heads appear on surviving Anglo-Saxon helmets, such as those from Sutton Hoo (London, BM) and Benty Grange, Derbys (mid-7th century; Sheffield, City Mus.). Contemporary bronze plates from Vendel and Valsgärde, Sweden, depict warriors wearing helmets with a stylized bird of prey on the end of the crest ridge (Stockholm, Stat. Hist. Mus.).

As the 12th-century helmet, resting on the mail coif, would not have provided a very solid base for a crest, the use of such a crest on the helm, perhaps combined with the pagan associations of the types mentioned above, was slow in becoming established. An intervening phase seems to be represented by helmets painted on the sides with the arms of the bearer, or some part of them. This may be seen in the depiction of *Geoffrey V Plantagenet, Count of Anjou* (*reg* 1129–51), on the enamel plaque (Le Mans, Mus. Tessé) from his tomb. Several such crests can also be seen in Peter of Eboli's *Carmen de bello siculo: Liber ad*

6. Heraldic display on helmet and shield; miniature from Peter of Eboli: *Carmen de bello siculo: Liber ad honorem Augusti*, 330×200 mm, 1195–6 (Berne, Burgerbibliothek Bern, Cod. 120 Bongarsiana Coll., fol. 130*r*)

triangular shield and the circumference of the seal with wyverns or other small beasts, for example on the seal (1329) of Jean de Prez (Vaud). In southern France a little later the Evangelists' symbols, such as appear on the seal (1356) of Pierre de Cajetan, Sénechal of Beaucaire and Nîmes, were often chosen for the purpose. Although sometimes found as the crest, for example on that (1616; London, Coll. Arms, MS. E 16, fol. 25*v*) of Philip Herbert, 4th Earl of Pembroke and 1st Earl of Montgomery, and repeated on the horse's armour, the wyverns were mostly decorative. During the 14th and 15th centuries, as the use of the crested helm became more common, two beasts were often placed, climbing up the canted shield, to support the former. In Italy and northern Europe, for example on the coinage of Louis II, Count of Flanders (*reg* 1346–84; see fig. 7), a single beast could be depicted wearing the helm and crest, perhaps with a second holding the shield or, as in some of Jean, Duc de Berry's books and seals (e.g. the Great Seal; *c.* 1370; Paris, Archvs N.), slung from the neck of his swan device. Occasionally a single figure was used: an attractive design found in France and Germany shows a seated maiden clasping the shield. By the 16th century the use of supporters was being restricted to the nobility and certain patrician families.

By the end of the 13th century the use of arms had spread far beyond the nobles and knights and had been adopted by many classes in society. It is perhaps natural to find that new elements were gradually introduced to indicate the rank of the user. As early as 1291–7 the French royal arms appear crowned on a seal for Bordeaux, and this example was followed in 1315 by the Dukes of Brittany and in 1344 by Peter IV, King of Aragon (*reg* 1336–87). About the same time the papal tiara and the cardinal's hat were associated with personal arms, at first being placed on a shield by the side. The crosier was often placed within, later behind, the shield by bishops and

honorem Augusti (1195–6; Berne, Burgerbib., Cod. 120 Bongarsiana Coll., fol. 130*r*; see fig. 6) and on the Helmet deniers of Antioch struck earlier in the 12th century. The addition of a fan or vane on top of the helm, painted with all or part of the arms, is found before the end of the 12th century on seals from both England and France and in the *Carmen de bello siculo*. In the Holy Roman Empire the use of the crest developed so rapidly from these tentative beginnings that the crested helm could be used alone, for example on the seal (1282) of Günter of Kevernburg from Thuringia; although it is possible that most of these examples were used as counterseals, with the obverse bearing the shield, few publications make this clear. Elsewhere the use of the crest spread more slowly: in England many of the armigerous families in the 16th- and 17th-century Heralds' Visitations entered arms but no crest. It would seem likely that the crest was regarded as something mainly used in tournaments and, judging by some of the later medieval depictions of battles, by the commanders rather than all the knights taking part in the engagement.

Towards the end of the 13th century the custom grew up of filling the spaces between the sides of the roughly

7. Crest and supporters of Louis II, Count of Flanders, on a gold heaume, *c.* 1370; from J. Porteous: *Coins in History* (London, 1969), pl. 137

abbots, and this could be combined with their mitre and, when they possessed the right of high justice, a sword.

The military orders active in the Levant during the 12th century (*see* KNIGHTS HOSPITALLER; KNIGHTS TEMPLAR; and TEUTONIC ORDER) were followed in the 14th and 15th centuries by the secular orders of knighthood, tournament and other knightly societies (*see* CHIVALRY, ORDERS OF). These all possessed insignia that could be collated variously with family arms to proclaim membership of these select groups. So popular were these that some 15th-century knights, such as Jorg von Ehingen, travelled around the courts of Europe collecting Orders, Liveries and other devices from rulers, and these would be depicted on their tombs and achievements of arms (*see* §IV, 3 and 6 below).

The later 14th century and the 15th were also the heyday of the badge, primarily a device worn by retainers of the great lords, and these could be incorporated into displays of arms and other devices. In the 16th century these tended to be replaced by imprese, which were more often used as an alternative to the older arms in tilts as a form of disguise. After most of the medieval badges had ceased to be used, some families substituted their crest on the silver badges worn by their servants. A few examples of these have survived, along with the larger badges worn by certain royal servants (*see* §IV, 1(ii) below).

BIBLIOGRAPHY

W. Camden: *Remaines of a Greater Worke, Concerning Britaine* (London, 1605)
G. Demay: *Inventaire des sceaux de la Flandre*, 2 vols (Paris, 1873)
——: *Inventaire des sceaux de l'Artois et de la Picardie*, 2 vols (Paris, 1875–7)
W. H. St J. Hope: *The Stall Plates of the Knights of the Order of the Garter, 1348–1485* (London, 1901)
F. L. Ganshof: *Feudalism* (London, 1952)
L. Lacroix: 'Les "Blasons" des villes grecques', *Etud. Archéol. Class.*, i (1955–6), pp. 91–114
J. A. Goodall: 'Heraldry in Italy during the Middle Ages and Renaissance', *Coat of Arms*, v (1958–9), pp.148–55
——: 'The Use of Armorial Bearings by London Aldermen in the Middle Ages', *Trans. London & Middx Archaeol. Soc.*, xx (1958–9), pp. 17–21

8. Arms attributed to the Nine Worthies; miniature from Thomas of Salazzo's *Chevalier errant, c.* 1394–5 (Paris, Bibliothèque Nationale, MS. fr. 12599, fol. 125*r*)

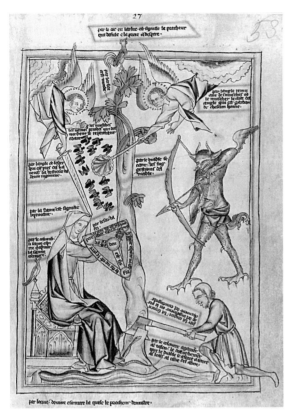

9. Arms of the Trinity; miniature from the Lambeth Apocalypse, *c.* 1260–67 (London, Lambeth Palace Library, MS. 209, fol. 53)

W. B. Emery: *Archaic Egypt* (Harmondsworth, 1961/*R* 1984)
C. M. Kraay: *Archaic and Classical Greek Coins* (London, 1966)
D. J. A. Ross: *Illustrated Medieval Alexander-books in Germany and the Netherlands* (Cambridge, 1971)
R. Grigg: 'Inconsistency and Lassitude: The Shield Emblems of the *Notitia Dignitatum*', *J. Roman Stud.*, lxxiii (1983), pp. 132–42
M. Pastoreau: *Armorial des chevaliers de la Table Ronde* (Paris, 1983)
J. A. Goodall: 'Shield Devices in Greek Vase Paintings and the Earlier Coin "Signs" of Cities: A Review of the Evidence for a Proto-heraldic System',*Coat of Arms*, n.s., vii (1988), pp. 62–70
——: 'Civic Devices and Pre-Hellenistic Greek Coin Types: A Survey', *Seabys Coin & Medal Bull.*, 844 (1989), pp. 231–5; 849 (1990), pp. 67–72; 850 (1990), pp. 102–7

For further bibliography *see* §I above.

(iii) Attributed arms. As most medieval writers and artists saw the past in strictly contemporary terms, heroes of the Trojan War and Theban history were described as using contemporary methods of warfare and fashions in dress, from which it followed that they were assigned arms. Apart from a few major characters, these could vary a great deal from text to text, and some left much to the discretion of the illustrators. Charlemagne, Arthur and others, grouped together from the early 14th century as the Nine Worthies, had their attributed arms fixed thereafter, as seen in Thomas of Salazzo's *Chevalier errant* (*c.* 1394–5; Paris, Bib. N., MS. fr. 12599, fol. 125*r*; see fig. 8). The military saints were depicted as medieval knights, with devices added to their shields. Those with a widespread cult following had many designs attributed to them: more than 30 different coats of arms appear in the

depictions of St Maurice between the 12th and 15th centuries. It is possible to discern certain regional styles: in Cologne works, such as the Hyghalmen Roll (mid-15th century; London, Coll. Arms, 1st MS. 5), a cross potent fitched at the foot (with a spike in the foot) seems to have been used invariably in the 15th and 16th centuries. Other charges derived from an established emblem, for example the keys of St Peter, while a few seem to have been derived from families who numbered other saints among their ancestors. The latter case is well illustrated by the arms attributed by later Roman families to the early popes, such as Leo IX (*reg* 1049–55).

The 12th-century illustrations of the Virtues in the *Psychomachia* of Prudentius were given contemporary shields, and at the end of the century those set in the west portal of Notre-Dame, Paris, were given distinctive devices based on a range of patristic authorities, placed on either roundels or Gothic heater-shaped shields. They were echoed later in the Painted Chamber (1290s; destr. 1834) of the Palace of Westminster, London, and the Arena Chapel (1304–5), Padua. In the 14th century another set was devised in southern Germany for the Theological and Cardinal Virtues and the Seven Deadly Sins. The contemporary Latin text gave an array of authorities for the choice of each charge used for shield, crest, banner, surcoat and the beast on which they were mounted.

About the mid-13th century the verbal emblem of the Trinity appeared, at first on an aptly shaped triangular shield (e.g. London, Lambeth Pal. Lib., MS. 209, fol. 53; see fig. 9), and this continued in popularity down to the 16th century. The cult of the *Arma Christi* was inaugurated in 1246 by Pope Innocent IV (*reg* 1243–54); by the mid-14th century a shield using the Instruments of the Passion had been created, for example on a seal for the Greyfriars of Cambridge (London, BM). From this simple device,

10. Arms of the Cardinal-camerlengo; from A. C. Fox-Davies: *The Art of Heraldry* (London, 1904), plate CXI, fig. 2

described in a 14th-century English verse as 'A schelde of red/a crosse of grene', stem the later series of shields, each bearing one of the Instruments of the Passion.

A number of 14th- and 15th-century books and rolls contains pedigrees and histories of the ruling houses with coats of arms assigned to those who lived— if at all—long before the rise of heraldry (*see* GENEALOGICAL AND HERALDIC MANUSCRIPTS). The English rolls begin with the Trojan Brutus, who was said by Geoffrey of Monmouth (*d* 1155) in his *History of the Kings of Britain* to have come to England after the siege of Troy. In some cases the arms of the medieval family were projected back into the remote past, but many were invented and, like the arms of saints, can be found in many forms.

JOHN A. GOODALL

3. ECCLESIASTICAL. As armorial bearings were first employed by knights in tournaments and war, the clergy initially had no use for them, but they soon adopted heraldic insignia for their seals and tombs. In the Zurich Roll of Arms (*c.* 1340; Zurich, Schweizer. Landesmus.) 27 standards of bishoprics and abbeys show heraldic charges that later became their arms, having earlier appeared on the flags of territories of which the prelates were temporal lords. Armorial bearings became customary in the Church through their use on seals, and the higher clergy and chapters used them increasingly as marks of identity, authority and authentication. The earliest surviving example in England is the seal of Fulk Basset, Bishop of London (1244–59; London, BM; de Gray Birch, no. 1909); another early instance is the seal of William de Luda, Bishop of Ely (1290–98; London, BM; de Gray Birch, no. 1500). In continental Europe the slightly later seal (1297) of Bishop Landolf of Brixen (now Bressanone) shows the arms of the diocese, the paschal lamb, above the Bishop's portrait. His successor, Alberto de Egna, used in 1327 a portrait seal (the bishop with mitre and crosier) with, on the dexter, a shield with the paschal lamb and, on the sinister, the Egna family arms.

Pope Boniface VIII (*reg* 1294–1303) is the first pope of whose arms there are contemporary examples (for the attributed arms of early popes *see* §III, 3 above). The earliest papal emblems were the keys, which appeared with representations of St Peter as early as the 5th century AD (e.g. Rome, S Costanza). The most exalted emblem of the popes as temporal sovereigns is the tiara, at first with only one crown; the second was added by Boniface VIII, and the third appeared soon after, between 1303 and 1314. Unlike the mitre the tiara is not liturgical, but together with the keys it became the heraldic sign of papal dignity. The pavilion (It. *ombrellino*), a large pointed umbrella with vertical stripes Or and Gules, appears in the 12th-century frescoes of SS Quattro Coronati in Rome, in the frescoes (1502–9) by Pinturicchio in the Libreria Piccolomini attached to Siena Cathedral, and on the sculpted frieze of Bramante's Tempietto (1535) in S Pietro in Montorio, Rome. The pavilion emblem is used by all papal basilicas and, with the keys, on the arms of the Cardinal-camerlengo (see fig. 10), who is in charge of the Vatican State during an interregnum.

The first emblems to mark episcopal and abbatial arms were the mitre and the crosier, soon to be joined by the

pilgrim hat, all of which were substitutes for the knightly helm. The hat first appeared above a cardinal's shield on the tomb of *Riccardo Petroni* (*d* 1314) by Tino da Camaino in Siena Cathedral and on a tomb in Avignon in 1328. Hats differ in colour and the number of tassels: it was at the Council of Lyon in 1246 that Innocent IV (*reg* 1243–54) decreed that the cardinal's hat should be red. Cardinals have 15 tassels pendent on each side; patriarchs, archbishops and bishops have green hats with 15, 10 (see fig. 11) or 6 tassels and a double or single cross behind the shield. Their arms are also succinctly marked by a double or single cross. Anglican bishops and dioceses most often display the mitre by itself; Scotland and the Eastern churches have their own forms.

Ecclesiastical heraldry is best served by Gothic styles, which also conform to modern taste by avoiding pomposity and needless scrolls. There are, however, masterly heraldic achievements by Renaissance and Baroque artists, for example the arms of Leo X on one of Raphael's tapestries (Rome, Pin. Vaticana) for the Sistine Chapel, and, also in Rome, those of Paul III (*reg* 1534–49) on the ceiling attributed to Luzio Luzzi (*fl* 1548–73) in the Sala dell'Apollo of the Castel S Angelo and of Pius IV in S Giovanni Laterano. The last were also sculpted by Michelangelo on the Porta Pia (1561–5), with two angels holding swords as supporters (not usual in official church heraldry). The arms of Urban VIII are carved twice on each support of Bernini's baldacchino in St Peter's, with

ALES DIEI NUNTIUS

11. Arms of Maurice Couve de Murville, Archbishop of Birmingham

differences in the Baroque ornaments of the eight shields; they discreetly represent a woman giving birth. The arms of Alexander VII (*reg* 1655–67) in S Maria del Popolo are supported by an angel and a putto.

Less ambitious heraldic works are still made for churches and tombs, yet arms are most frequently used on engraved letterheadings, seals and die-stamps, which after a period of decline are re-emerging as objects of sensitive design. In Europe and the USA most dioceses have their own arms. Newly appointed bishops often have to adopt or obtain arms, granted by the legal heraldic jurisdiction of the country concerned, or, if that does not exist, based on competent advice. The rich world of heraldic symbols and colours offers all that is needed to create artistic achievements capable of identifying a place or a person in a fashion appropriate, distinctive, unique and aesthetic.

BIBLIOGRAPHY
W. K. Riland Bedford: *The Blazon of Episcopacy* (London, 1858, rev. 2/1897)
A. H. Warren: *Arms of the Episcopates of Great Britain and Ireland* (London, 1868)
W. de Gray Birch: *Catalogue of Seals in the Department of Manuscripts in the British Museum*, 6 vols (London, 1887–1900)
J. Woodward: *A Treatise on Ecclesiastical Heraldry* (Edinburgh and London, 1894)
H. G. Ströhl: *Heraldischer Atlas* (Stuttgart, 1899)
F. Pasini-Frassoni: *I cappelli prelatizi* (Rome, 1908)
M. Prinet: *Les Caractéristiques des saints dans les armoiries familiales* (Paris, 1908)
H. G. Ströhl: *Die Wappenrolle der Päpste* (Mönchen-Gladbach, 1909) [Ger. and Fr. text]
E. du Fornel du Roure de Paulin: *L'Héraldique ecclésiastique* (Paris, 1910)
M. Prinet: *Les Insignes des dignités ecclésiastiques dans le blason français du XVe siècle* (Paris, 1911)
D. L. Galbreath: *Papal Heraldry* (1930), i of *A Treatise on Ecclesiastical Heraldry* (Cambridge, 1930–; rev. G. Briggs, London, 2/1972)
L. de Laszloczky: *Gli stemmi e sigilli dei Principi Vescovi di Bressanone* (Bolzano, 1953)
S. T. Achen: *Symboler* (Copenhagen, 1975)
B. B. Heim: *Heraldry in the Catholic Church: Its Origin, Customs and Laws* (Gerrards Cross, 1978, rev. 1981)
J. Martin: *Heraldry in the Vatican* (Gerrards Cross, 1987)

BRUNO BERNARD HEIM

4. HERALDRY IN ART. The use of heraldry in art was coeval with its birth, although the 12th-century evidence is scanty and less well preserved than that for later periods. Arms could be used in art for three principal objectives: to denote ownership or the identity of donor and recipient; to set forth one's ancestry, fiefs and relationships; and as pure decoration, sometimes using shields invented for the purpose. The earliest craftsmen involved were goldsmiths and other metalworkers, closely followed by masons, painters and illuminators, embroiderers, weavers, glaziers and others. References in inventories and accounts help to expand knowledge of lost works, especially those in precious metals, and sometimes reflections of their lost splendours may be glimpsed in base-metal objects.

Between the 12th and 18th centuries heraldic design followed the changes in artistic styles. The later phases, Baroque, Rococo and Neo-classical, while sometimes producing charming and even imaginative creations, were, on the whole, less successful, since the qualities that had given medieval and Renaissance heraldic art its vitality had been lost. During the 19th century the approach was eclectic, and efforts were made to revive the art by looking back for inspiration. While English artists tended to turn to medieval or, occasionally, Italian Renaissance models, their German contemporaries looked to engravings by Albrecht Dürer and the Little Masters of the 15th and 16th centuries. Attempts in the 20th century to create heraldic works of art in a contemporary idiom have seldom been successful, as the artists have been ignorant of or chosen to ignore the rules governing the art.

(i) Metalwork. (ii) Architecture. (iii) Tomb sculpture. (iv) Wall coverings. (v) Stained glass. (vi) Panel painting. (vii) Manuscripts, printed books and bookplates. (viii) Ceramics and glass. (ix) Embroidery and other arts.

(i) Metalwork. This category covers seals, which provide some of the earliest evidence for arms, jewellery, including brooches, clasps and rings, engraved and enamelled plate, and coins and medals.

(a) Seals. Seals, especially those ordered by kings and magnates, were made by the leading goldsmiths of the day. While few of the silver or latten dies survive, the large numbers of impressions in archives and libraries provide the largest, and mainly unedited, corpus of heraldic art. The older seals have a peculiar importance before the production of rolls of arms (*see* GENEALOGICAL AND HERALDIC MANUSCRIPTS), but the greatest pieces date from the 14th and 15th centuries. Royal and aristocratic seals, such as that (*c.* 1380; Paris, Bib. N., Cab. Médailles) of Louis II, Duke of Bourbon (*reg* 1356–1410), echoed the ways in which arms and devices were being displayed. Some of the best examples, particularly from the Empire,

12. Arms of Alice, Countess of Northampton, on a gold brooch, 40×21 mm, from Folkingham Castle, Lincolnshire, *c.* 1180 (London, British Museum)

13. Hanap cover, silver gilt and enamel, c. 1297 (Oxford, All Souls College)

such as the seal (Ljubljana, Archv Repub. Slovenia) of Rudolf IV, Duke of Austria (reg 1358–65), display the ways in which the arms of subsidiary fiefs were worked into the design. In the later Middle Ages signet rings (e.g. London, V&A) appeared, often without the owner's name, bearing either shield or achievement, crest, badge or device. In the 16th century these were sometimes engraved in rock crystal and painted on the back, to give the impression when worn of a fully tinctured armorial ring, albeit in reverse. The signet was replaced in the 18th century by the fob seal, only to return in the 19th century (e.g. London, V&A). During the Italian Renaissance many seals were designed by leading artists, who appear to have provided their clients with lost-wax bronze casts of the proposed design.

(b) Jewellery and plate. The earliest known example of the use of arms in jewellery design dates from c. 1180: a small, gold, kite-shaped shield brooch with a lion rampant (London, BM; see fig. 12), made for Alice, Countess of Northampton (d 1185). The loss of most of the finest medieval jewellery means that knowledge of belts worked with shields, armorial mantle clasps and the like is dependent on depictions in other arts, notably tombs. Among the surviving pieces are some clasps (c. 1371–81) with the arms and crest of the Angevin kings of Hungary. Other brooches and clasps were designed incorporating part of the arms of the ruling families, the earliest being a 12th-century eagle brooch (Darmstadt, Hess. Landesmus.) from the Rhineland and a fleur-de-lis clasp (c. 1365–7; Paris, Louvre) traditionally said to have belonged to Louis IX. Small base-metal shields for horse-bridles and a few brooches survive from the 13th century onwards (e.g. London, BM).

Although armorial plate was made in large quantities, little survives. One of the earliest pieces is the hanap cover (Oxford, All Souls Coll.; see fig. 13), almost certainly made for Philip IV, King of France, as a wedding present for Raoul de Nesle, Constable of France (d 1302), on his marriage c. 1297 to Isabel of Hainault. By the 14th century engraved or enamelled heraldic designs had become commonplace in goldsmiths' work. Perhaps most were single coats, but more elaborate schemes are described in inventories: the Wardrobe accounts for 1317–18 state that plate with the arms of the Pope, the King and others was purchased for Edward II (reg 1307–27). Despite losses during the Reformation and the Civil War, the Oxford and Cambridge colleges have notable collections of medieval and later plate, much of it with armorial decoration. Most pieces are English, but a few came from abroad. A series of large, late 15th-century cups survives: most of the known examples are German (e.g. London, V&A), but to judge from inventories they were in general use. They were made for display with the knop of the lid cast with a small figure holding a shield of the owner's arms enamelled and gilt. These include the Foundress's Cup, given to Christ's College, Cambridge, in 1507 by Margaret Beaufort, Countess of Richmond. From the late 16th century onwards English silversmiths often cast the knop for the lid or cover of a vessel in the form of a crest, the arms being engraved on the body, for example on the Bacon Cup (1574; London, BM). Arms from this period are, however, an inaccurate guide to ownership, as plate was often re-engraved when sold, and ambassadors and officers of state were given plate adorned with the royal coat of arms. Enamelling continued to be used for arms on some pieces of plate until the late 16th century, when it seems to have gone out of favour. In the 19th century, enamel was reintroduced under the influence of the Gothic Revival. The style of engraving on plate from the 16th century onwards follows the changing styles found in bookplates (*see* §7(ii) below). In London, at least, much of

14. Engraving for a plate, by Benjamin Rhodes, from his workbook, 1694–8 (London, C. Hoare & Co., Archive)

PLATE I   Hardstones

1. Black marble table-top inlaid with pietre dure, including lapis lazuli, chalcedonies, agates and jaspers, diam. 1.25 m, made by Jacopo Ligozzi and Bernadino Poccetti at the Opificio delle Pietre Dure, Florence, 1633–49 (Florence, Museo dell' Opificio delle Pietre Dure)

2. Lapis lazuli piece carved with figures in a mountain landscape, h. 240 mm, from China, Qing dynasty, 18th century (San Francisco, CA, Asian Art Museum of San Francisco)

1. Moss-agate bowl with gold enamel setting by Ottavio Miseroni, h. 171 mm, made in Prague, *c.* 1600 (Vienna, Kunsthistorisches Museum)

2. Five-layered onyx cameo with gold rim, known as the *Gemma Claudia*, depicting (*left*) Emperor Claudius and Agrippina the younger and (*right*) Germanicus and Agrippina the elder, h. 120 mm, from Rome, AD ?49 (Vienna, Kunsthistorisches Museum)

PLATE III   Heraldry

Vlrich kepel für Auf dem waſſer
Auß dem widerland Zum hey-
ligen Grab 1 4 6 2 Jar

1. Memorial plaque to *Ulrich Ketzel* with his coat of arms and badges of orders of knighthood, oil on panel, 680×600 mm, 1462 (Nuremberg, Germanisches Nationalmuseum)

2. Coat of arms of Charles the Bold, Duke of Burgundy, detail from the centre of a *millefleurs* tapestry, wool, silk, gold and silver thread, 3.06(originally *c.* 4.46)×7.05 m, made by Jan de Haze, Brussels, 1466 (Berne, Historisches Museum)

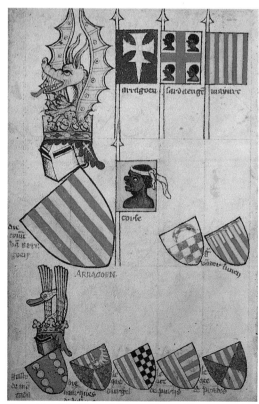

Armorials of the kings of Aragon, France, Hungary and Scotland showing shields, helms and crests; illustrations from the *Armorial Gelre*, 1370–86 (Brussels, Bibliothèque Royale Albert 1er, B.R.MS. 15.652–6, fols 46*r*, 52*v*, 62*v*, 64*r*)

it was done by such specialist craftsmen as Benjamin Rhodes (*fl* 1694–1723), whose workbook for 1694–8 has been preserved (London, Hoare & Co., Archv; see fig. 14). Some work can be ascribed to better-known artists, such as William Hogarth and Simon Gribelin II, who were employed during their apprenticeships on engraving for their masters: Gribelin, for example, probably engraved the arms of Sir William Courtenay of Powderham on a hexagonal waiter by Benjamin Pyne (1698; London, V&A; *see* ENGLAND, fig. 76).

During the second half of the 13th century large numbers of heraldic enamels were produced at Limoges and exported to most of Europe. Some items, particularly candlesticks, seem to have been specially commissioned, as the arms on them are usually easily identified and the connections between the different coats can be explained by the pedigrees of the families concerned. Many shields that cannot be traced in the contemporary rolls of arms, apart from a large central shield often with the arms of Old France, are to be found on pyxides and even gemellions (shallow bowls; e.g. London, BM). Some enamels were made elsewhere, such as the Valence Casket (London, V&A), which was probably made in a London workshop between 1305 and 1312, and the distinctive Spanish harness-mounts. Morses or cope clasps were frequently adorned with the arms of the prelate for whom they were made, or of the see or abbey, such as those of Warden Abbey (15th century; London, V&A).

The most common examples of heraldic motifs in 14th- and 15th-century jewellery were the devices or badges worn by lordly retainers. Most were of base metal, but some, such as the Percy crescent (15th century; Alnwick Castle, Northumb.) and a pair of crest badges for the Cholmondeley family (late 16th century; e.g. London, BM; see fig. 15), were made of silver. During the 16th century, imprese were also used as designs for jewels (*see* IMPRESA); other small pieces of the 17th and 18th centuries with heraldic elements may represent short-lived court decorations.

(c) Coins and medals. Although heraldic elements can be found on some coins from the 12th and even the 11th centuries (*see* §III, 2 above), it was not until the 14th century that the use of arms on coins became widespread in Europe, coinciding with the reintroduction of gold coins, first in such Italian city-states as Florence and Venice, and then in France, England and elsewhere. The designs of the silver and copper coins were fixed by long tradition and changed very slowly, to make their recognition easy. In England gold coins were struck in 1344 but never circulated: a florin with Edward III seated under an architectural canopy with a background of fleurs-de-lis, a cloth of estate declaring his claim to France; a half-florin, the 'leopard', with a crowned leopard wearing a mantle with the arms of Old France quartering England; and a quarter-florin or 'helm' with his crested helm (all London, BM; see fig. 16). Although these designs were not followed in later issues, the coinages of Europe from the 14th century present a fine collection of heraldic art, the coins made for the French and Burgundian courts being especially fine examples of the diemakers' art. In the Holy Roman Empire there were many mints with a wide range

15. Crest badges of the Cholmondeley family, silver, late 16th century (London, British Museum)

of coin types. The mints of the Electors, especially those of Cologne, Mainz and Trier, produced fine series with armorial reverses of great beauty. These are particularly useful since, apart from the changing personal arms of the bishops, they provide a constant type that can be traced through the varying styles from the Gothic to Rococo.

At the end of the 14th century the casting of large medals, at first imitating Late Antique prototypes, began in either France or Italy. The most important of the early medallists was Pisanello, several of whose medals had armorial or imprese reverse designs. Before the end of the 15th century medals were being made in many places in northern Europe, and heraldic reverses were especially popular, designed by mint officials or sometimes by such major artists as Dürer.

(ii) Architecture. Apart from the attributed arms mentioned above (*see* §III, 3 above), the earliest reference to the use of arms in decorating a building appears in Matthew Paris's *Chronica maiora*, which mentions a hall in the Temple, Paris, decorated with shields before 1254. This example was followed in the 13th-century work at Westminster Abbey (*see* LONDON, §V, 2(ii)(a)), where the arcading spandrels of the monks' choir aisles were filled with carved shields of St Edward the Confessor (*reg* 1042–66), the Emperor, the kings of England and France and English nobles. Between 1299 and 1307 the hall and chamber (destr. 1553) at Hesdin, Artois, were painted with the shield and motto of the Counts of Artois. Perhaps the largest surviving scheme of armorial decoration is found

16. Half- and quarter-florins of Edward III, gold, 1344 (London, British Museum)

17. Gate-house of Butley Priory, Suffolk, c. 1320s

at York Minster (c. 1310), which has carved shields in the nave and others painted in the clerestory windows, providing a large 'roll' of English nobles, which may commemorate some of those taking part in Edward I's wars in Scotland. A ceiling in the Haus zum Loch, Zurich (now Zurich, Schweizer. Landesmus.), was decorated c. 1306 with an extensive collection of arms related to those recorded in the Zurich Roll of Arms (c. 1340; Zurich, Schweizer. Landesmus.).

Gate-houses provided an obvious focus for heraldic display: two fine early examples survive at Kirkham Priory (N. Yorks; 1290s) and Butley Priory (Suffolk; c. 1320s; see fig. 17). Later in the 14th century the Old Town Bridge Tower in Prague was adorned with the arms connected with the fiefs of Emperor Charles IV (reg 1346–78); others were painted on the vault. The choice of arms can be paralleled on Charles's great seal. In the early 16th century Abbot Kirkton's gate at Peterborough Cathedral was decorated with Tudor and ecclesiastical arms and badges. Oxford and Cambridge college gate-houses, such as that of St John's College (1511–20), Cambridge, often made great use of the founder's arms and badges in their design. Officials of medieval Italian cities placed carvings of their arms, with their name and date of office, on civic buildings as a record of their service to the State, for example on the Palazzo dei Priori (1208–57), Volterra. This custom was followed by such Venetian officials as the Donato family on the entrance of the former Palazzo Pubblico (destr. early 20th century) in Nicosia, Cyprus, and by the Knights Hospitaller on many of their buildings in Rhodes and, most prolifically, at the castle of St Peter, Bodrum, Turkey.

Many of the arms set up in the Inns of Court in London in the 16th and 17th centuries similarly commemorate building works by the officials of the Inn. A most elaborate

display appears on the façade of the Colegio de S Gregorio (completed 1496) at Valladolid (for illustration see HISPANO-FLEMISH STYLE). The façade of the Georgskapelle (1449–60) at Wiener Neustadt, Austria, designed by Peter von Pusica, bears 107 carved arms detailing Emperor Frederick III's lands, while the armorial tower (destr. 1766), Innsbruck, was similarly painted in 1497 with the arms of Maximilian I's domains.

During the 16th century, changes in domestic architecture led to new forms of heraldic display. The elaborate plaster ceilings could incorporate the arms of the owner as the centrepiece, or else arms or devices of relations could be set in the compartments. The chimney-breast was also often chosen for the display of a large achievement of arms. Elements of the arms and other devices could be worked into the design of façades, as on the William III apartments (1688–94) by Christopher Wren at Hampton Court Palace, near London.

In the 18th century, with the growing use of more purely classical designs, heraldic ornament was less frequently employed, being largely limited to crests or supporters and shields on gate-posts, arms worked into the design of wrought-iron gates and the occasional achievement in a pediment. Buildings that included much heraldic interior decoration, such as Schloss Augustusburg, Brühl, near Bonn, built for Elector-Archbishop Clemens August of Cologne, were exceptional.

With the Gothic Revival in the 19th century the use of heraldry once more became general, one of the most extensive series ever executed being the arms and badges, royal and otherwise, for the new Palace of Westminster (1840–60), London. Other notable schemes can be seen in London on the Law Courts (1874–82, by G. E. Street) in The Strand and on the offices in High Holborn built from 1877 by Alfred Waterhouse for the Prudential Assurance Co. The rebuilding in the City of London after World War II included some imaginative examples of heraldic motifs being incorporated in the designs of new buildings.

(iii) Tomb sculpture. From the 12th century arms were used as part of the depiction of the deceased, one of the earliest and most important examples being the enamel plaque (Le Mans, Mus. Tessé) of Geoffrey V Plantagenet, Count of Anjou (reg 1129–51). By the end of the 13th century more extensive arrays of arms commemorated the deceased and his relations, some including the arms of friends, tenants and comrades-in-arms. Two of the most extensive such series (destr.) were recorded c. 1610 by Nicholas Charles (d 1613) on the tombs in Westminster Abbey of William de Valence, Earl of Pembroke and Edmund Crouchback, Earl of Lancaster (both d 1296). Pembroke's tomb had 27 small shields and Lancaster's 62 (Armytage). In the later Middle Ages and the Renaissance the choice of additional shields was governed by a desire to proclaim the illustrious ancestry of the deceased by including those of the maternal ancestors. The tombs of Mary, Duchess of Burgundy (c. 1495–1502; see fig. 18) and Charles the Bold, Duke of Burgundy (erected c. 1559–62) in Onze Lieve Vrouwe, Bruges, had complete pedigrees set out by the shields, those on the sides of the latter giving his Seize Quartiers.

18. Tomb of *Mary, Duchess of Burgundy*, c. 1495–1502, Onze Lieve Vrouwe, Bruges

In Germany the use of the 'death shield', often in gilded and painted wood, with an inscription and a smaller shield for the wife's arms, became common in the later 14th century and the 15th, for example that of Ulrich Haller the elder (c. 1456; Nuremberg, Ger. Nmus.). Effigial tombs continued to be made, some including all the insignia of knightly orders, liveries and other devices that the deceased had acquired when travelling from court to court. It was not until the 14th century that the use of near life-size equestrian statues as part of memorials was revived in north Italy, probably inspired by the destroyed Roman equestrian statue at Ravenna. The oldest series seems to be those erected between 1329 and 1375 at S Maria Antica, Verona, to members of the ruling della Scala family (*see* VERONA, §3(iii)). Another example comes from the tomb of *Bernabò Visconti* (1363; ex-S Giovanni in Conca, Milan; now Milan, Castello Sforzesco) by Bonino da Campione. Although inspired by Classical prototypes, all of these were dressed in contemporary armour with surcoats and crested helms.

(iv) Wall coverings.

(a) Wall painting. In the later Middle Ages armorial decoration went far beyond the simple use of shields. The Painted Chamber in the Palace of Westminster included *Virtues* with shields (probably painted 1260s), one of the latter being based on the king's coat. Much use was made of heraldic motifs in the general decoration. In St Stephen's Chapel in the same palace, Edward III and his sons were depicted on the altar wall wearing their coats of arms (c. 1350–60; both buildings destr. 1834; *see* LONDON, §V, 3(i)(b)). Schemes in continental Europe are better preserved, with some notable examples dating from the 14th century and the early 15th in Italy. One of the earliest is the fresco of *Guidoriccio da Fogliano before Montemassi* (c. 1330; Siena, Pal. Pub.; *see* SIENA, fig. 11) attributed to Simone Martini. A fine series of the Nine Worthies and Nine Heroines of Antiquity, standing in a landscape with their shields hung from the trees, was painted c. 1416 at

the Castello della Manta, near Saluzzo in Piedmont. These have been attributed variously to Giacomo Jaquerio or Aimone Dux of Padua (*fl* 1416–61) and show strong French influence, the choice of the Nine Heroines stemming from *Le Chevalier errant* (1403–4; Paris, Bib. N., MS. fr. 12559, fol. 125) by Thomas III, Margrave of Saluzzo (*reg* 1396–1416). Other series are known from Germany, both in painting and statuary.

(b) Tapestry. In northern Europe tapestries were particularly favoured for interior decoration, and although few survive the titles recorded in inventories suggest that they often included heraldry, as part of the picture or for its own sake. Some of the earliest secular tapestries, with scenes from the Arthurian cycle, are German; at least one 14th-century set was commissioned by a wealthy citizen of Freiburg im Breisgau. Commissioned series include the *Life of St Peter* (Beauvais, Cathedral; Boston, MA, Mus. F.A.; Paris, Mus. Cluny; Washington, DC, N.G.A.) for Guillaume de Hellande, Bishop of Beauvais (1444–62). The allegorical *Lady with the Unicorn* tapestries (Paris, Mus. Cluny; *see* TAPESTRY, colour pl. I, fig. 1) bear the arms of Jean le Visite, President of the Court of Aids (*d* 1500). By the 16th century sets of tapestries made to order from existing cartoons had the purchaser's arms woven into them. When the tapestries changed hands these would be covered by the painted or embroidered arms of the new owner, as with a set (Hardwick Hall, Derbys, NT) acquired in London by Elizabeth Talbot, Countess of Shrewsbury.

19. Shields presenting the arms, pedigree and connections of Gilbert de Clare, Earl of Gloucester, stained glass, early 14th century, St Mary, Selling, Kent

In the 15th and 16th centuries arms were incorporated into tapestry designs in different ways: set in a *millefleurs* background (e.g. the armorial of Charles the Bold, Duke of Burgundy, 1466; Berne, Hist. Mus.; see colour pl. III, fig. 2); with the arms surrounded by large leaves in line with the larger verdure tapestries of the period (e.g. the imperial armorial of Charles V, *c.* 1540; Vienna, Ksthist. Mus.); and with arms and devices combined in Renaissance compositions of panels separated by pilasters and friezes, such as appear on a set of room hangings (1488–1515; Boston, MA, Mus. F.A.) bearing the arms and devices of Louise of Savoy (1476–1531) and Charles, Comte d'Angoulême (1459–96). During the 17th century elaborate armorial tapestries were woven in Flanders and elsewhere for the nobility, such as one decorated with the arms of a knight of St James of Compostela (Boston, MA, Mus. F.A.). In the 18th century the arms were more usually confined to a central position in the upper border, as in the series the *Noble Pastorale* (1756; various collections) designed by François Boucher and woven at Beauvais.

(v) Stained glass. Glaziers first used arms as part of the iconography in windows commemorating the military saints, but by the mid-13th century Henry III of England (*reg* 1216–72) ordered shields of his own arms and those of his father-in-law, Raymond-Berengar IV, Count of Provence (*reg* 1209–45), for his palaces, including Havering Palace (destr.) in Essex, where both the chapel and the Queen's Chamber (1268) were glazed with shields. Other important heraldic glazing schemes (both destr.) were created at Westminster Abbey and in Salisbury Cathedral before the end of the century. During the 14th century the Bishop's Palace at Lincoln was glazed with a series of shields for European and 'Oriental' kings (destr.), a scheme clearly derived from a general roll of arms. Donor figures would be shown in their surcoats, while large standing figures in the choir clerestory (1340–44) of Tewkesbury Abbey, Glos, depict the patron's pedigree. More modestly, the illustrious connections of Gilbert de Clare, Earl of Gloucester (*d* 1307), were set out in shields, arranged in a chevron in allusion to his arms, across the east window of St Mary, Selling, Kent (see fig. 19). Later in the 14th century a series of seated figures in the Stephansdom, Vienna, gave a long pedigree. Other glazing schemes commemorated campaigns or the relations and comrades-in-arms of the donor. In the absence of an inscription these larger schemes can be identified only by careful analysis of all the arms depicted. Interpretation can thus be difficult, if not impossible, unless the whole can be reconstructed from old church notes.

Remains of medieval domestic glazing are very rare, but records of the halls of the City Livery Companies of London show that they were adorned with the arms of the craft and of former members of the court of the company (all destr.). The larger windows of late medieval houses gave greater opportunities for the use of stained glass: a rare survival in the hall at Ockwells Manor (1446–56), Berks, depicts the arms of the Nine Worthies, and the windows (16th-century and later) in the halls of the Inns of Court in London show how a rich collection of armorial glass could enhance the interior.

(vi) Panel painting. As with the other arts, arms could appear in panel paintings as part of the iconography and could also be used to identify the donors or, when placed on the back, the ownership of the picture. Works in the last category vary from such finely finished paintings on a gold ground as the achievement and badge of Richard II (*reg* 1377–99) on the back of the Wilton Diptych (probably 1390s; London, N.G.) to more summary renderings added later. The donors' arms could be depicted on surcoats, gowns or mantles, painted on the kneeling-desks or simply placed near the figures. Early portraits sometimes showed the sitter wearing a tabard, such as a 15th-century representation of an Earl of Shrewsbury (London, Coll. Arms), or else devices could be worked into the design (e.g. London, Soc. Antiqua.), but it was not until the 16th century that northern painters systematically added the arms, or more rarely a device, of the sitter in one corner to identify him.

In Germany and the Netherlands a category of 'epitaph painting' became popular in the 15th century, although few south Netherlandish examples survive. In Germany the deceased might be depicted kneeling with his arms and insignia of orders (e.g. *Ulrich Ketzel*, 1462; Nuremberg, Ger. Nmus., Gm 581; see colour pl. III, fig. 1). The designs suggest that some of the later south Netherlandish brasses, such as that to *Margaret de Scornay, Abbess of Nivelles* (engraved *c.* 1460; Nivelles, Ste Gertrude), derived from these paintings.

(vii) Manuscripts, printed books and bookplates. This section is concerned with the ways in which heraldry was used in the decoration and illustration of books, whether manuscript or printed (for armorials and other manuscripts wholly concerned with heraldry *see* GENEALOGICAL AND HERALDIC MANUSCRIPTS; see also colour pl. IV).

(a) Manuscripts. The earliest surviving manuscripts to depict warriors in contemporary armour with the long, kite-shaped shield painted with devices date from the later 12th century, such as the Winchester Bible (*c.* 1170; Winchester, Cathedral Lib., fol. 69*v*), and most retained the Late Antique prototypes for the Old Testament scenes at least until that time. Even as late as the 13th century many of these shields were clearly not intended to be identifiable. Apart from the Anglo-Norman Apocalypses, the illustrations of Henry I's dream in copies of Florence of Worcester's Chronicle (*c.* 1130–40; Oxford, Corpus Christi Coll., MS. 157) and Henry of Huntingdon's Chronicle (early 13th century; Baltimore, MD, Walters A.G., MS. 793) both have knights with shields not found in any early roll of arms. Before the end of the 12th century, however, two German books display identifiable heraldic illustrations: a copy of Heinrich von Veldeke's *Eneide* (*c.* 1186–8; Berlin, Staatsbib. Preuss. Kultbes., cod. germ. fol. 282) and Peter of Eboli's *Carmen de bello siculo* (1195–6; see fig. 6 above). The former is the first heraldically illustrated copy of a romance with arms and crests attributed to the heroes of the Trojan War, the latter a record of a 12th-century campaign. Together with the illustrations in the works of Matthew Paris, for example the *Liber additamentorum* (London, BL, MS. Cotton Nero D.I, fols 171*r* and 171*v*) and the *Chronica maiora* (*c.* 1250;

Cambridge, Corpus Christi Coll., MSS 16 and 26), they provide the oldest illustrated rolls of arms.

An English Psalter of *c.* 1230–40 (Stockholm, Nmus., MS. B. 2010) has a large collection of shields in the borders, antedating by a century such similar schemes as that in the fragmentary Book of Hours of *c.* 1320–30 (London, BL, Harley MS. 6563). The inclusion of a whole roll of arms, with or without names, in this fashion must always have been rare. More customary was the inclusion of arms to indicate ownership. Perhaps the earliest example of this is in the Alphonso Psalter (*c.* 1284; London, BL, Add. MS. 24686, fol. 11*r*; see fig. 20), in which are depicted the shield of Alphonso (*d* 1284), son of Edward I, King of England, and that of Holland, representing Alphonso's intended bride, Margaret, daughter of Floris V, Count of Holland (*reg* 1256–96). The so-called 'East Anglian' manuscripts of the first decades of the 14th century made considerable use of heraldic ornament, as did Walter of Milemete (*fl* 1326–73), the Oxford illuminator, in his treatise *De secretis secretorum* (*c.* 1326–7; Oxford, Christ Church Lib., MS. 92), which he compiled for the future King Edward III. In addition to the use of the whole shield, charges from the arms were used as line-fillers, rather like the borders of some contemporary windows and tile floors.

Later in the 14th century there is evidence that individual patrons commissioned many books decorated with their arms, crests, badges and devices, as in the series made in England for several members of the BOHUN family and those made for Jean, Duc de Berry (*see* VALOIS, (3)). The purchaser's arms could be added to the otherwise finished page, as in the Hours of Isabella Stuart, Duchess of Brittany (*c.* 1417; Cambridge, Fitzwilliam, MS. 62, fol. 199*r*). In an extension of this practice, most of the arms of Jean II le Meingre de Boucicaut in the Hours of Maréchal de Boucicaut (begun after 1401; Paris, Mus. Jacquemart-André, MS. 2) were replaced after 1490 by those of Aymar de Poitiers.

Sumptuous copies of Arthurian and other romances and translations of world histories continued to provide a wealth of imaginary heraldic illustration until the 15th century. Since full blazons were not always provided by the text, traditions of attributions developed and, for the Arthurian cycle, culminated in books, both manuscript and printed, giving the arms of the Knights of the Round Table. An interesting group of vernacular Alexander romances in north Netherlandish and German manuscripts gives Alexander a coat with three bells (e.g. New York, Pierpont Morgan Lib., MS. PM 782, fol. 187*v*), quite different from that attributed to him (lion sitting in a chair) as one of the Nine Worthies in the same area (Ross).

Spanish royal charters included a *signo rodado*, a depiction of the royal arms in a circle, as part of their authentication, a practice introduced into Neapolitan chancery by the Aragonese kings in the 15th century. Elsewhere some charters were also prepared with illuminated borders, which could include armorial decoration, such as the Eton College foundation charter (1440; London, PRO, Pat. 19 Hen. VI, pt. ii, n. 20). Monastic or family cartularies, with the arms painted in initials or elsewhere in the books, are generally reckoned among the rolls of arms. A very few, such as the Great Coucher Book of the Duchy of Lancaster

20. Shields of Alphonso, son of Edward I, and of Holland; marginal illustration from the Alphonso Psalter, *c.* 1284 (London, British Library, Add. MS. 24686, fol. 11*r*)

(*c.* 1410; London, PRO, MS. D of L/42), have some of the finest heraldic paintings of the period. In Italy civic officials often had their arms painted on the covers or in the account-books and other records produced under their administration, such as the Sienese BICCHERNA. A notable English example of such work is the indenture for Henry VII's chapel at Westminster Abbey decorated with his arms and beasts and a silver gilt skippet for the great seal (both London, Westminster Abbey, Muniment Room & Lib.). Other heraldic paintings, sometimes by professional illuminators rather than heralds, can be seen on the grants of arms and patents of nobility.

(b) Printed books and bookplates. The armorial decoration of early printed books followed the patterns familiar from manuscripts, often being added by the same craftsmen. Italian books often included a panel of decoration at the foot of the first text-page with a blank shield or roundel for the owner's arms to be painted in after purchase. A few books have impressive collections of arms. The *Conciliumsbuch* (Augsburg, 1485), the chronicle of the Council of Konstanz by Ulrich von Richental (*d* 1436–7), includes 1156 coats of arms, reprinted without acknowledgement by Virgil Solis in 1555. The successive editions of Johann Stumpf's chronicle of 1548 include increasingly larger collections of arms for the families mentioned in the text. For many of these the woodcuts used multiple blocks, the shield and helm with mantling being cut on one block, with the crest on a separate one. Misregistration on several of the pages reveals this clearly.

In eastern Europe printed books are often important sources for early heraldic art, but the quality of the block-cutting can vary greatly. Little is easily accessible, except for those in Romanian books published between 1508 and 1830, which were illustrated in the national bibliography. The earliest Romanian example consists of a version of the state arms in a Missal printed at Tîrgovişte in 1508, but other books have the arms of voivodes and even one bishop before the end of the 17th century.

Towards the end of the 15th century the custom began of having small armorial prints made to paste in books as a mark of ownership, which proved a very popular and long-lasting form of heraldic art. During the 16th century such bookplates, or ex-libris, became more general and could be designed by leading artists, the armorial plates by Dürer being well-known examples (*see* BOOKPLATE). From a simple shield or achievement, crest or monogram, to elaborate designs with many coats of arms setting out the user's claims to ancestry, the bookplate is without doubt the most prolific form of post-medieval heraldic art. While many were produced by trade engravers of small artistic attainment, others have been commissioned by discriminating owners from leading artists and engravers. An alternative to the bookplate was the library stamp. A few early 16th-century London blindstamped bindings include the Tudor royal arms and badges, but before the end of the century many bindings were being made incorporating the arms of the owner, for example a volume (1576; Edinburgh, N. Lib.) bound for James Beaton, Archbishop of Glasgow (1517–1603). The same stamps can also be found on leather furniture.

(viii) Ceramics and glass. During the 13th century arms were introduced into tiles and other ceramic wares. The tile floor of the chapter house (1250s; *in situ*) at Westminster Abbey incorporated large shields with the arms of England. Another series of tiles (1250–70; London, BM) found near Chertsey Abbey, Surrey, included depictions

of the Romance of Tristram showing him with the lion shield assigned to him in the texts. By the end of the 13th century more modest tiles were being produced by itinerant tilers, and examples of their work survive in many churches. As evidence they need to be used with discrimination, since certain well-known coats continued to be made, for example Clare chevrons and the checky coat of Warenne (e.g. London, BM), long after those families became extinct in the male line.

A group of painted wares, often with a shield under the spout, was exported from France to many places in Europe in the later 13th century (e.g. London, BM). The arms depicted on them cannot be identified and are comparable to those found on the contemporary Limoges enamels (*see* §1(ii) above). A group of jugs (Oxford, Ashmolean) made in England early in the 14th century has small relief shields on the shoulder, including the Clare coat, but the combinations do not seem to be explicable genealogically.

In Spain the Moorish tradition of lustrewares led to a thriving export trade, and already in the late 14th century Francesco di Marco Datini (*d* 1410), a Prato merchant, ordered a service (untraced) to be painted with his arms, a copy of which was sent to his factor. Many examples of 15th-century Spanish lustrewares with Italian coats of arms survive, including dishes (e.g. 1404–30; London, Wallace), and some, using shield shapes then known only in Italy, must also have been made from drawings sent from Florence (e.g. London, V&A). Since the colours were limited to blue and gold their identification can sometimes present a problem.

Armorial decoration, not always identifiable, played an important role in the design of Italian tin-glazed wares from their beginnings in the 14th century. With the limited range of colours available before the 16th century, the correct tinctures of the arms could seldom be reproduced, but some conventions seem to have been followed generally, or at least among the wares of a locality. Manganese-brown was used for Gules on wares made at Orvieto, Faenza and near Florence, and cobalt blue served for Sable, the latter still being used in the early 16th century. After 1500 a wider range of choices appeared. A brown hue for Gules was used at Faenza, Cafogglio and Deruta; ruby lustre at Gubbio and Deruta; and yellow or orange at Faenza, Deruta, Casteldurante and in the work of Nicola da Urbino. Italian maiolica had a wide export market, with services being ordered by patrician families in south Germany early in the 16th century, by Anne de Montmorency, Constable of France, in 1535 (e.g. London, BM) and, before the end of the century, by the Spanish court and grandees.

During the 17th and 18th centuries armorial wares were made at many places throughout Europe, often in blue-and-white imitations of Delftware. The finest wares, however, were those imported from Guangzhou (Canton) by the Dutch, English and French East India Companies; the designs were sent to China, often in the form of the owner's bookplate, and could be misinterpreted by the Chinese craftsmen (e.g. London, V&A).

A few examples of early 14th-century glass vessels with enamelled armorial decoration are known, and fragments of others have been found in excavations in Italy, Germany and London (e.g. London, BM and Mus. London). Almost all have German coats of arms, and several pieces are signed: one of the names is known from the Venetian archives to be that of a glass painter. A speciality for the German market in the 16th and 17th centuries were large beakers (Ger. *Reichsadlerhumpen*; *see* GLASS, colour pl. VI, fig. 1) decorated with the *Quaternionenadler*, the imperial double eagle with the wings painted with sets of four shields for the different ranks in the Empire, also found in coeval armorials. Designs were formerly enamelled (e.g. 1492; Bologna, Mus. Civ. Med.; *see* VENICE, fig. 10), but from the second half of the 16th century most armorial glass was engraved (*see* POLAND, fig. 20), and the placement of the arms and their style follow those found on contemporary silver and ceramics.

(ix) Embroidery and other arts. Between the 13th and 17th centuries many items, including church vestments, secular garments, horse trappers, purses and cushions, were embroidered with heraldry. Much *opus anglicanum* made for the English market included armorial decoration and must have been specially commissioned. Inventories show that in the second half of the 13th century several English bishops had copes worked with their personal arms, and several examples of armorial vestments survive from the early 14th century. The most remarkable are a stole and maniple, and another stole now serving as the border to the Syon Cope (all London, V&A). Together the stole and maniple have 64 small shields of English lords and appear to be unique in presenting such a roll of (unnamed) arms. More common were the larger apparels for albs mounted on the Syon Cope.

Most vestments displayed the arms only of the donor, sometimes with those of his wife or other close relatives. Some seal-bags embroidered with coats of arms associated with the City of London (e.g. 1319; London, Guildhall, Corp. London Rec. Office) and St Edward the Confessor were made about this time and are precious survivals of the secular embroidery of the age. An earlier fragment, worked on linen before 1270, has the cross from the arms of the Counts of Aumale (London, BM). The most splendid surviving examples of armorial embroidery are the panels (*c.* 1338; Paris, Mus. Cluny; see fig. 21) from horse trappers subsequently made into a chasuble, with the arms of England worked in raised silver and silver-gilt thread and the whole background richly diapered. Kept at the Premonstratensian Convent at Altenberg, near Solms, Hesse, until 1802, they were presumably given by Edward III either when he visited the Emperor at Koblenz in 1338 or when he acted as Imperial Vicar.

Arms were also embroidered on flags and furnishings. Among the latter the canopies and cloths of estate were the most important, being limited to the kings and higher nobility. The backcloth or canopy of the bed could also be worked with the family arms, as occurred in 1342, when the arms of England and France were worked into the bed-hangings of Lionel of Antwerp, second son of Edward III, on the occasion of his betrothal. Even more common were the cushions so frequently mentioned in wills and inventories between the 15th and 17th centuries. In the later 16th century embroidered armorial table-carpets were also made (e.g. Ipswich, Christchurch Mansion).

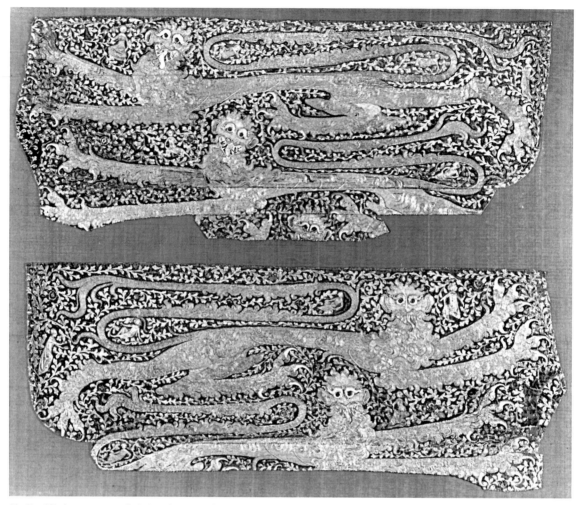

21. Heraldic horse trapper depicting the arms of England, silver and silver-gilt thread, silks, pearls and cabochon crystals on velvet, 595×1300 mm, *c.* 1338 (Paris, Musée de Cluny)

Medieval and Renaissance furniture was often decorated with arms. Some heraldic table-tops are known from German collections or of German origin, such as a folding table (*c.* 1400; Paris, Mus. Cluny) that may have come from Wienhausen Abbey, but most numerous are the Italian cassoni with the arms or imprese of the husband and wife for whose marriage they were made (*see* CASSONE, §1). Smaller caskets and cases for personal effects would also be adorned with the arms of the owner, often in cuir-bouilli; these can be very fine (e.g. the Aldobrandini crosier case, 14th century; London, V&A), but coats incised on scabbards (London, Mus. London) found in excavations in London are crudely done and seldom identifiable.

BIBLIOGRAPHY

GENERAL AND EXHIBITION CATALOGUES

Memorial Catalogue: Heraldic Exhibition (exh. cat., ed. F. J. Grant; Edinburgh, 1891)
The Illustrated Catalogue of the Heraldic Exhibition (exh. cat., London, Soc. Antiqua., 1894)
G. W. Eve: *Decorative Heraldry* (London, 1897)
P. Ganz: *Geschichte der heraldischen Kunst in der Schweiz im XII. und XIII. Jahrhundert* (Frauenfeld, 1899)
Catalogue of a Collection of Objects of British Heraldic Art to the End of the Tudor Period (exh. cat., ed. E. E. Dorling; London, Burlington F.A. Club, 1916)
Heralds' Commemorative Exhibition, 1484–1934 (exh. cat., London, Coll. Arms, 1934; rev. 1936/R 1970)
L'Art et la vie au moyen âge à travers les blasons et les sceaux (exh. cat., Paris, Archvs N., 1950)
British Heraldry from its Origins to c. 1800 (exh. cat., ed. R. Marks and A. Payne; London, BM, 1978)
Die Parler und der schöne Stil, 1350–1400: Europäische Kunst unter den Luxemburgern, 5 vols (exh. cat., ed. A. Legner; Cologne, Schnütgen-Mus., 1978)
Les Fastes du gothique: Le Siècle de Charles V (exh. cat., Paris, Grand Pal., 1981)
English Romanesque Art, 1066–1200 (exh. cat., ed. G. Zarnecki, J. Holt and T. Holland; London, Hayward Gal., 1984)
Gothic and Renaissance Art in Nuremberg, 1300–1550 (exh. cat., New York, Met.; Nuremberg, Ger. Nmus.; 1986)
C.-A. von Volborth: *The Art of Heraldry* (Poole, 1987) [excellent plates of 19th- and 20th-century usage]
Age of Chivalry: Art in Plantagenet England, 1200–1400 (exh. cat., ed. J. Alexander and P. Binski; London, RA, 1987)
J. Cherry: 'Heraldry as Decoration in the Thirteenth Century', *Harlaxton Medieval Studies*, ed. W. M. Ormrod, i (Stamford, 1991), pp. 123–34
J. Stratford: *The Bedford Inventories: The Wordly Goods of John, Duke of Bedford, Regent of France (1389–1435)* (London, 1993)

ARCHITECTURE

A. Marquand: *Robbia Heraldry* (Princeton, 1919)

N. Rodolico and G. Marchese: *I palazzi del popolo nei comuni toscani del medio evo* (Milan, 1962)

E. Bachmann, ed.: *Gothic Art in Bohemia: Architecture, Sculpture and Painting* (Oxford, 1977)

J. Bony: *The English Decorated Style* (London, 1979)

J. A. Goodall: 'Rolls of Arms of Kings: Some Recent Discoveries in the British Library', *Antiqua. J.*, lxx (1990), p. 82

TOMB SCULPTURE

G. Ferrari: *La tomba nell'arte italiana dal preromano periodo all'odierno* (Milan, n.d.)

V. Carderera y Solano: *Iconografía española: Colección de retratos, estatuas, mausoleos . . . desde el siglo XI hasta el XVII*, 2 vols (Madrid, 1855–64) [Sp. and Fr. text]

G. J. Armytage, ed.: *Charles' Roll of the Reigns of Henry III and Edward I* (London, 1869)

M. Gerlach and H. Bösch: *Todtenschilder und Grabsteine* (Vienna, 1892)

K. Lind: *Sammlung von Abbildungen mittelalterlicher Grabdenkmale aus den Ländern der österreichisch-ungarischen Monarchie*, 2 vols (Vienna and Leipzig, 1892–4)

A. Durán Sanpere and J. Ainaud de Lasarte: *Escultura gótica*, A. Hisp., viii (Madrid, 1956)

M. Norris: *Monumental Brasses*, 3 vols (London, 1978)

J. Garms, R. Juffiner and B. Ward-Perkins, eds: *Die Grabplatten und Tafeln* (1981), i of *Die mittelalterlichen Grabmäler in Rom und Latium vom 13. bis zum 15. Jahrhundert* (Rome and Vienna, 1981–)

WALL COVERINGS

P. d'Ancona: 'Gli affreschi de castello della Manta nel Saluzzese', *L'Arte*, viii (1905), pp. 94–106

B. Kurth: *Der deutsche Bildteppich des Mittelalters*, 3 vols (Vienna, 1928)

C. van Mander: *Dutch and Flemish Painters* (New York, 1936)

M. Davies: *Paintings and Drawings on the Backs of National Gallery Pictures* (London, 1946)

Masterpieces of French Tapestry (exh. cat., London, V&A, 1947)

P. Binski: *The Painted Chamber at Westminster* (London, 1986)

'La sala baronale del Castello della Manta', *Quad. Rest.*, ed. G. Romano, 9 (Milan, 1992)

MANUSCRIPTS AND PRINTED BOOKS

J. Stumpf: *Gemeiner loblicher Eydgnoschafft Stetten, Landen und Völckeren Chronickwirdiger*, 2 vols (Zurich, 1548); rev. as *Schweytzer Chronick* (Zurich, 1606)

Virgil Solis: *Wappenbüchlein zu Ehren der Römischen Kay. und Ku. Mt., auch Bäbstlicher Heyligkeit . . . durch Virgilz Solis Maler und Burger zu Nürnberg, mit sonderm fleys gemacht* (Frankfurt am Main, 1555/R Munich, 1886)

I. Bianu and N. Hodoș: *Bibliografia romanéscă, veche 1508–1830*, 4 vols (Bucharest, 1903–44)

G. Gerola: 'L'elemento araldico nel portolano di Angelino Dall'Orte', *Atti Reale Ist. Ven. Sci., Lett. & A.*, xciii (1933–4), pp. 407–43

M. R. James and E. G. Millar: *The Bohun Manuscripts: A Group of Five Manuscripts Executed in England about 1370 for Members of the Bohun Family* (Oxford, 1936)

A. Boeckler: *Heinrich von Veldeke: 'Eneide': Die Bilder der Berliner Handschrift* (Leipzig, 1939)

F.-J. Heyen, ed.: *Kaiser Heinrichs Romfahrt: Die Bilderchronik von Kaiser Heinrich VII und Kurfürst Balduin von Luxemburg, 1308–1313* (Boppard am Rhein, 1965)

M. Meiss: *French Painting in the Time of Jean de Berry: The Late Fourteenth Century and the Patronage of the Duke*, 2 vols (London, 1967)

D. J. A. Ross: *Illustrated Medieval Alexander-books in Germany and the Netherlands* (Cambridge, 1971)

M. C. Diaz y Diaz and others: *Los tumbos de Compostela* (Madrid, 1985)

BOOKPLATES AND STAMPS

F. Warnecke: *Die deutschen Bücherzeichen (ex-libris) von ihrem Ursprunge bis zur Gegenwart* (Berlin, 1890)

W. Hamilton: *French Book-plates* (London, 1892)

E. Castle: *English Book-plates Ancient and Modern* (London, 1894)

C. D. Allen: *American Book-plates* (London, 1895)

O. von Heinemann: *The Ex-libris Collection of the Ducal Library at Wolfenbüttel: One Hundred and Sixty Selected Bookplates from the XVth to the XIXth Century* (London, 1895)

A. Bertarelli and D. H. Prior: *Gli ex-libris italiani* (Milan, 1902)

E. Olivier, G. Hermal and R. de Roton: *Manuel de l'amateur de reliures armoriées françaises*, 30 vols (Paris, 1924–38)

L. Borgia and others, eds: *Le Biccherne: Tavole dipinte delle magistrature senesi, secoli XIII–XVIII* (Rome, 1984)

JOHN A. GOODALL

III. Islamic lands.

The devices used in the Islamic world differed from those used in Europe and the Frankish states of the Levant because they were related only to the court office held by the bearer and were not personal and hereditary. The earliest known description of emblems refers to the court of the Khwarazmshah Muhammad ibn Takish (*reg* 1200–20) in western Central Asia. Members of his personal entourage were identified by black emblems on their banners: an inkwell for the secretary, a bow for the arms-bearer, a basin for the bearer of the washbasin, a square of cloth for the wardrobe-master, a horseshoe for the marshal and a parasol for the guard. The use of these devices flourished, however, under the Mamluks (1260–1517), the sultans of Turkish origin who ruled Egypt and Syria. In Mamluk usage the sword seems to have been more common than the bow, while other charges, such as the polo-sticks of the polo master, can be identified. While devices are known to have been given to an amir when the sultan elevated him to this rank, this may not always have been the case. The Arabic terms for these devices were *rank* ('colour') and *shi'ār* ('emblem'); the custom of using 'blazon' for them is misleading since this implies a written description of a coat of arms and not its depiction. Such devices as the lion used by Baybars I (*reg* 1260–77) or the bicephalic eagle are often considered heraldic devices, but they are more properly understood as signs of sovereignty and not emblems of office held.

The devices are worked into the decoration of an object or carved beside an inscription on buildings. Most often they are seen on metalwork (see fig. 22), glass lamps and ceramics and are often identified with a particular user by

22. Islamic device on the base of a candlestick, made for the amir and cupbearer Zayn al-Din Kitbugha, brass inlaid with silver, gold and copper, h. 260 mm, Mamluk period, probably made in Damascus, *c.* 1295–7 (Baltimore, MD, Walters Art Gallery)

the accompanying inscription. They also appear on some issues of copper coins in the 13th and 14th centuries, but none can be shown to have been used by the sultans in whose names they were issued. Several of the forms of display, on boats for example, have not survived, and those on textiles, such as a wool fragment embroidered with a circular shield enclosing six charges (New York, Met., 1972.120.3), are very rare. The charges could be displayed on roundels, but occasionally a pointed or almond-shaped shield is found. The field could be plain, or it could be divided into three parts either horizontally or, more rarely, vertically. The central zone is usually much wider than the other two, although in some of the composite devices the divisions could be approximately one third of the height, depending on the relative size of the charges. The cup, inkwell and lozenge-shaped napkin are the most common charges drawn from official insignia. Rosettes and fleurs-de-lis also appear, especially on coins. A small group of emblems, such as the key-like device on the basin known as the 'Baptistère de St Louis' (*c.* 1290–1310; Paris, Louvre; *see* ISLAMIC ART, fig. 153), seem to be related to Mongol emblems known as *tamgha*s ('signs of property'; e.g. Leiden, Bib. Rijksuniv., MS. Or. 419w), but the reason for their adoption under the Mamluks is unknown. The Mongol khans used their *tamgha*s on their coins in the 14th century (e.g. London, BM).

From the mid-14th century there appear composite devices, in which several different charges were combined in one frame. The earliest examples, such as the eagle above the cup used by the amir Tuquztimur (*d* 1345) on an inlaid bronze basin (Cairo, Mus. Islam. A.), were fairly simple. Sometimes a single charge could be multiplied or placed on another, for example an inkwell on a cup. Under the later Mamluks a single shield increasingly contained several charges relating to different offices. The precise significance of these combinations is unknown, although the idea that they represented a string of honours appears to be baseless.

In addition to pictorial devices, epigraphic devices were common. Those of the Mamluk sultan al-Nasir Muhammad (*reg* 1294–1340 with interruptions) were inscribed in the central band of the roundel, while those of Qa'itbay (*reg* 1468–96) fill all three registers. In Islamic Spain acquaintance with European heraldry led to unusual combinations. The Nasrid rulers of Granada (1230–1492) used a Gothic shield with a bend inscribed with their motto, as seen for example on some tiles at the Alhambra, and some Muslim families in Spain used seals with such armorial charges as the fleur-de-lis or roundels and their names inscribed in Arabic. The Ottoman sultans (1281–1924) developed the use of the TUGHRA, the elaborated formal writing of the sultan's names. It was used on all official documents, seals and coins, in much the same ways as the arms of European sovereigns. European writers of the 18th century recorded that the Ottoman Janissary troops had devices that identified their tents when on campaign.

BIBLIOGRAPHY

Enc. Islam/2: 'Rank' [colour, dye]
L. A. Mayer: *Saracenic Heraldry* (Oxford, 1933)
D. S. Rice: 'The Blazons of the "Baptistère de Saint Louis"', *Bull. SOAS*, xxiii (1950), pp. 367–80
J. A. Allan: 'Mamluk Heraldry and the Numismatic Evidence', *J. Royal Asiat. Soc. GB & Ireland* (1970), pp. 99–112
Renaissance of Islam: Art of the Mamluks (exh. cat. by E. Atil, Washington, DC, Smithsonian Inst., 1981)
E. Whelan: 'Representations of the *Khāssakīyah* and the Origins of Mamluk Emblems', *Content and Context of Visual Arts in the Islamic World*, ed. P. Soucek (University Park, PA, and London, 1988), pp. 219–54

IV. Japan.

The Japanese *mon*, originally textile 'patterns' and often mistranslated as 'crests', are hereditary badges used in much the same way as European arms. There are, however, certain important differences between the two systems. *Mon* were used by all members of an élite family, without any marks to distinguish them from each other, and they were not borne on shields. As clan devices they bear a certain superficial resemblance to the arms borne by Polish noble clans in the Middle Ages (*see* §III, 4(vi) above). The precise date when they came into use is not wholly certain, but it is likely to have been before or during the Taira–Minamoto War (1180–85), which led to the establishment of the Kamakura shogunate. *Mon* were an indigenous creation, reflecting the needs of a military feudal society, and nothing resembling them has been found in either China or Korea, which were frequent routes for foreign influences on the Japanese.

Although some references exist to grants of badges to samurai, and of imperial or shogunal devices to the higher-ranking daimyo, there was no heraldic authority controlling and recording their use. Inevitably there often seems to have been uncertainty about the precise nature of the designs borne by a particular family. The oldest known book of heraldry (*bukan*), ascribed to the Muromachi period (1333–1568) by its transcriber, Arai Hakuseki (1657–1725), contains about 255 designs, some of which differ markedly from those usually found in the later printed editions of *bukan*. The collections were arranged under the name of the family or by design, the latter arranged under the *iroha* order (a writing system in which the entries were arranged by sound). The former often gave additional information about the daimyo, their rice income and other insignia to which they were entitled during their obligatory progresses under the alternate-residence system (*sankin kōtai*) to the shogunal capital Edo (now Tokyo). The *Irohabiki moncho* ('Iroha mon collections') are of small use, except to artisans looking for a particular design, since they omit the names of the bearers.

About 160 basic designs were used in the Edo period (1600–1868), more than in Islamic heraldry but markedly fewer than in Europe, apart from the 126 Polish *herb*, or devices of the noble clans. Some of the simple geometric patterns resemble European charges, but most are floral. Water-plantain, hollyhock or mallow leaves, paulownia, wisteria and wood-sorrel flowers are among the most common, while the best-known is the chrysanthemum badge of the imperial house. Animals, birds (apart from the crane) and fish are extremely rare in the Edo period, although butterflies, singly or in groups of two or three, were fairly common. Such artefacts as well-heads and different kinds of fan, the latter often charged with other devices, were also used. As calligraphy was the foremost art form in East Asia, it was inevitable that single characters

23. *Mon* of the Mori family, Saiki, Bungo province, on a laquered *tsuba* box, decorated with arrow-flight and paulownia, 119×109 mm, 1601 (London, British Museum)

that formed part of the family name were written in stylized ways and incorporated into *mon*.

During the Edo period rudimentary methods existed of differentiating the badges used by junior branches of a family. Sometimes a secondary badge of the main line could be adopted as the primary device of a junior line, or else a frame could be added. No rules governing the use of these can be ascertained. In some families each branch used a different design for its badges; in others, the same design was used by all. The badges probably originated in textile patterns, hence their normal circular form. A fragment of Heian-period (AD 794–1184) embroidery (Seattle, WA, A. Mus.) depicts two confronted beasts, perhaps bears, in a circular pattern of a type that could have given rise to the *mon*. Such confronted beasts were also used in Chinese self-patterned silk textiles from at least the Tang period (AD 618–907).

Apart from their use on clothing and armour, including the small flags worn on the back (*hata*), *mon* were used in very similar ways to European heraldry in the decorative arts. *Mon* were sometimes worked into the design of sword-guards (*tsuba*), and lacquerers frequently made use of them for decorating writing and other boxes (see fig. 23). Some temple furniture (e.g. 19th-century; London, V&A) had the *mon* of the donor placed on it. During the Edo period special *mon* were adopted by kabuki actors and courtesans, who sported the *mon* of the house for which they worked; these are often seen in *ukiyoe* prints (*see* JAPAN, §VI, 4(iv)(b)). Townspeople also made use of them for curtains in shop-doors and windows.

BIBLIOGRAPHY
Arai Hakuseki, ed.: *Kemmon shoka-mon* (*c.* 1700/*R* 2 vols, Tokyo, 1976)
H. G. Ströhl: *Japanisches Wappenbuch 'Nihon Moncho'* (Vienna, 1906)
J. W. Dower: *The Elements of Japanese Design: A Handbook of Family Crests, Heraldry & Symbolism* (New York and Tokyo, 1971)

JOHN A. GOODALL

Herat [Harat; Harāt]. City in western Afghanistan that served as capital of the Timurid dynasty from 1405 to 1507.

1. History and urban development. 2. Centre of production.

1. HISTORY AND URBAN DEVELOPMENT. Located on the trade routes from the Levant to India and China and commanding a rich hinterland, Herat has a long history as a trading centre. Several ancient cities were located at or near this site, including one built by Alexander the Great. In AD 660 Herat was captured by Arab forces and an Arab governor appointed. The 10th-century geographers mention its four gates, strong inner citadel and extensive suburbs. The city prospered under the Ghurid dynasty (*reg c.* 1000–1215). The congregational mosque, which had been founded in the late 11th century and destroyed several times, was rebuilt on the same site by the Ghurid ruler Ghiyath al-Din Muhammad ibn Sam (*reg* 1163–1203) at the beginning of the 13th century. Constructed of baked brick, it had four iwans disposed around a court, a domed sanctuary and a tomb for the founder (destr. 1940s). Remains such as the portal on the south-east and plaster decoration near the qibla iwan suggest that the dimensions and general configuration of the Ghurid mosque have been preserved. Some of the city walls may also date from the Ghurid period.

Herat was twice sacked by the Mongols in the 1220s, but revived under the Kart dynasty (*reg* 1245–1389). As local rulers, they were closely identified with the city and its landmarks. Herat at this time had strong walls and an inner citadel, with two major streets dividing the city neatly into four quarters. To the north lay an extensive suburb, watered by canals. This plan, despite later developments, remained relatively unchanged until the late 19th century (*see* ISLAMIC ART, §II, 10(ii)). The Karts, who took up residence in the citadel, reconstructed the royal bazaar and added mosques and other buildings.

In 1380 Herat was besieged by Timur (*reg* 1370–1405) and incorporated into Timurid domains. It was the major city in Khurasan, but Timur's capital was at Samarkand. Following his death in 1405, however, his son Shahrukh (*reg* 1405–47), then governor of Herat, made the city capital of the Timurid empire. In 1409–10 the walls and citadel were repaired and the bazaars reconstructed. The Sultan ordered a madrasa and hospice for Sufis to the east of the citadel, and his wife Gawharshad embarked on an even more ambitious project to the north of the city. Her large complex (1417–38) included a four-iwan congregational mosque (63.5×116 m; inner court 50 m to a side) and a large madrasa with a tomb for the founder (*see* ISLAMIC ART, §II, 6(i)(b)). Most of it was destroyed in 1885, but the intricate vaulting in the domed mausoleum, designed by QAVAM AL-DIN SHIRAZI, and the two surviving minarets attest to the high level of work she was able to command. The Sultan also ordered a shrine for the mystical poet Ansari (*d* 1089) in the village of Gazurgah 5 km north-east of Herat. The complex (1425–9), called a *ḥaẓīra*, consists of a large rectangle with an inner court (ext. 51×84 m) in which the cenotaph of the Sufi master lies in the open air in front of a monumental iwan. The transverse vaulting in some of the rooms and the spectacular tile revetments are some of the finest surviving examples of Timurid work. Shahrukh and his court were equally interested in the patronage of secular buildings, and texts mention three imperial gardens and a half-dozen estates with orchards and plantations.

Herat reached its apogee in the second half of the 15th century and was the most refined city in Asia and a centre of Persian and Turkish culture. The sultan Abu Sa'id (*reg* 1459–69) ordered the new Royal Canal (Pers. *jū-yi sulṭānī*), which allowed more land to be cultivated and developed to the north of the city. Sultan Husayn Bayqara (*reg* 1470–1506) and his boon companion and informal minister of culture, 'ALISHIR NAVA'I, conducted a wholesale renewal of Herat's shrines and mosques, and at least 60 buildings are known to have been erected during the Sultan's reign. The shrine at Gazurgah was envisaged as a royal burial ground, and a platform with marble revetment for the cenotaphs of the Sultan's ancestors was erected in the court in 1477. A line of funerary enclosures with domed mausolea was built along Royal Avenue (Pers. *khiyabān-i sulṭānī*) leading from the city to the shrine. 'Alishir had the congregational mosque in town substantially repaired (1498–1500) and the dome chamber rebuilt as an extended iwan. Sultan Husayn built a large ensemble (1492–3) with madrasa and *khānaqāh* to the north of Gawharshad's complex; the remaining minarets are decorated with complex patterns of tile mosaic. Just beyond it on the other side of the Injil Canal, 'Alishir ordered a large (5 ha.) complex called the Ikhlasiyya, which included a residence, madrasa, mosque, school for Koran recitation and hospice for Sufis. The Sultan's own residence was a huge (70 ha) estate called the World-adorning Garden (Pers. *bāgh-i jahānārā*) on the slopes near Gazurgah.

This brilliant period in Herat's history ended soon after Husayn Bayqara's death in 1506. In the following year the city was taken by the Uzbek chief Muhammad Shaybani (*reg* 1500–10), and three years later it passed to the Safavids (*reg* 1501–1732), who held it, with minor interruptions, for the next two centuries. In 1716 the city was captured by the Afghans, who have maintained control, except during the rule of Nadir Shah Afshar (*reg* 1736–47) and brief Persian occupations. In the 19th century the British fear of Russian expansion into Afghanistan led to two British–Afghan wars during which many of Herat's finest monuments, such as the complexes of Gawharshad and Husayn Bayqara, were destroyed. It revived in the 20th century: a new city (Pers. *shahr-i naw*) with European-style boulevards, parks, hotels, houses and museum was built, and several of the monuments, most notably the congregational mosque (1940s), restored.

BIBLIOGRAPHY

Enc. Islam/2: 'Harāt'

V. V. Bartol'd: 'Mir 'Ali Shir', *Mīr 'Alī Shīr: Shornik k pyatisotletiyu so dnya rozhdeniya* [Collection of articles on the quincentenary of his birth], ed. V. V. Bartol'd (Leningrad, 1928), pp. 100–64; Eng. trans. by V. Minorsky and T. Minorsky as iii of *Four Studies on the History of Central Asia* (Leiden, 1962), pp. 1–72

K. Afghan: *Āthār-i harāt* [Monuments of Herat], 3 vols (Herat, 1930–31)

L. Golombek: *The Timurid Shrine at Gazur Gah* (Toronto, 1969)

D. Brandenburg: *Herat: Eine timuridische Hauptstadt* (Graz, 1977)

H. Gaube: *Iranian Cities* (New York, 1979)

T. Allen: *A Catalogue of Toponyms and Monuments of Timurid Herat* (Cambridge, MA, 1981)

——: *Timurid Herat* (Wiesbaden, 1983)

L. Golombek: 'The Resilience of the Friday Mosque: The Case of Herat', *Muqarnas*, i (1983), pp. 95–103

L. Golombek and D. Wilber: *The Timurid Architecture of Iran and Turan* (Princeton, 1988), pp. 301–21

2. CENTRE OF PRODUCTION. Throughout the Islamic period Herat was renowned for the production of fine metalwares and textiles, and under Timurid patronage it became the centre for the finest books produced in the Islamic world.

(i) Metalwares and textiles. In the period before 1100 Khurasan was a major centre for cast bronzes, and a group of white or high-tin bronzes decorated with geometric patterns have been attributed to the early Islamic period there. In the 12th and 13th centuries cast bronzes were replaced by superb inlaid wares, which are distinguished by their innovative techniques, unusual shapes and elaborate motifs. Herat is named as the site of production on one of the most famous pieces of Islamic metalwork, the Bobrinsky Bucket (1163; St Petersburg, Hermitage; *see* ISLAMIC ART, fig. 140). A craftsman with the epithet al-Haravi (from Herat) signed an inlaid ewer made in 1181–2 (Tbilisi, Mus. A. Georg.), and a group of inlaid ewers and candlesticks that are stylistically similar were probably manufactured there as well. The extraordinary technical sophistication of work in Herat is illustrated by these pieces, which are hammered from a single sheet of bronze and decorated in high relief.

In the 13th and 14th centuries, the centres of metalworking creativity shifted westward, but smiths in Herat maintained their technical ability to cast bronze, for a huge basin (diam. 1.75 m) made in 1374–5 for the Kart ruler

Ghiyath al-Din Muhammad stands in the court of the congregational mosque there. This was the prototype for the enormous basin (diam. 2.43 m) ordered by Timur in 1399 for the shrine of Ahmad Yasavi in Yasi (now Turkestan, Kazakhstan). Herat was the most important metalworking centre under the Timurids, and both inlaid and engraved and tinned wares were made there. They are often decorated with crosshatching and inscribed with Persian verses by contemporary poets from Herat. Some of the pieces are signed by artists with epithets referring to villages near Herat. Inlaid wares were still produced in Herat during the first two decades of the 16th century, and engraved and tinned wares may have been produced there in later centuries, as they are decorated with such traditional Khurasani designs and motifs as crosshatching and poetry and bear owners' names referring to places in Khurasan. (For further details and bibliography, *see* IS-LAMIC ART, §IV.)

Textual sources from the 8th century already mention precious robes and striped materials from Herat, but the kind of textile most often associated with the city is the carpet. Herat was known for its fine carpets in the 15th century and carpets are frequently depicted in book paintings executed there, but few, if any, examples are known to have survived from the Timurid period. The most famous rugs attributed to Herat are the pair of Emperor Carpets (Vienna, Österreich. Mus. Angewandte Kst, T8334, and New York, Met., 43.121.1), said to have been presented to Leopold I of Austria by Peter the Great of Russia in 1698. Each carpet has a dark greenish–blue border and a ruby-red field covered with a symmetrical system of spiralling vines decorated with palmettes, cloud bands and animal heads. Many of the motifs are known from Timurid book painting. The combination of red field and blue border, the overall scroll design and individual motifs such as serrated leaves and cloud bands are found in a related group of several dozen carpets in the Herat style. The finest examples have silk foundations, others have mixed foundations of wool, silk and cotton, and some are enriched with gold and silver. In the 17th century this style of carpet was produced on a commercial scale with a simplified design, cotton foundations and wool pile. The several hundred examples in this Indo-Persian style have been attributed to Khurasan, Isfahan and India, but Khurasan seems likely, especially for those with a distinctive asymmetrical knot that is tied over four, rather than the usual two, warps. Carpets woven in Khurasan in the late 18th and 19th centuries continue the distinctive colour scheme and design and distinctive knot. (For further discussion and bibliography, *see* ISLAMIC ART, §VI, 4.)

(ii) Arts of the book. Herat's rise to prominence as a centre for the production of luxury books was due to Timurid patronage, and the two major phases of manuscript production in the 15th century coincide with the reigns of Shahrukh (*reg* 1405–47) and Husayn Bayqara (*reg* 1470–1506). Despite frequent clashes between the Safavids and Uzbeks, illustrated manuscripts continued to be produced in the 16th and 17th centuries. The most fruitful periods coincide with the dominance of a family of Shamlu Turkomans who governed for the Safavids in 1515–34,

1575–87 and 1598–1641. The persistence of certain elements during this 250-year period testifies to some artistic continuity despite shifts in the political situation.

Documentary and pictorial evidence shows that artists working at Herat followed traditions established under the Jalayirids in western Iran or under the Timurid prince Iskandar Sultan in Shiraz. Noted painters and calligraphers associated with these courts, such as JA'FAR, joined the Timurid court at Herat. Despite their different origins, the manuscripts they produced at Herat are remarkably homogeneous, and it is possible to speak of a Herat school of book painting. Typically, these early manuscripts, such as a copy (Dublin, Chester Beatty Lib., MS. P. 119) dated 1426 of the *Gulistan* ('Rose garden') of Sa'di, have only a few, full-page illustrations done in exquisite, carefully modulated colours. Compositions are built on several levels, with strong diagonal elements used to create balance, and individual figures are minutely executed and highly finished. Compositions were repeated by using patterns or models, a technique borrowed from inlaid metalwork. The consistency of painting, calligraphy and illumination suggests the work of a cohesive group with a strong leader.

Some manuscripts produced at the end of the 15th century contain only a few highly accomplished paintings, and some compositions, such as those in a copy (London, BL, MS. Or. 6810) of Nizami's *Khamsa* ('Five poems') dated to 1494–5, are virtually identical with ones used earlier in the century. Other manuscripts, such as a copy (Baltimore, MD, Johns Hopkins U., Garrett Lib.) of Sharaf al-Din Yazdi's *Zafarnama* ('Book of victory') dated 1467–8 or a copy (Cairo, N. Lib., Adab Farsi 908) of Sa'di's *Bustan* ('Orchard') dated 1494–5, display new features. Compositions have a greater richness of personal and anecdotal detail as well as more elaborate architectural and spatial structures. Scenes depicted include new topics such as grave diggers, shepherds and panoramic landscapes with sailing boats and hunters. These innovations are usually credited to BIHZAD, described by literary sources as the outstanding painter of this epoch. Many of the new themes and techniques were important ingredients in the development of painting in Tabriz under the Safavids in the early 16th century.

Manuscripts produced in Herat under the Safavids show a strong continuity with the style practised by Bihzad (*see* MANUSCRIPT, colour pl. VI) and his contemporaries. During the first decades of the 16th century, painters such as SHAYKHZADA executed paintings with elaborately patterned architectural settings, such as the one in *Episode in a Mosque* from a *Divan* ('Collected poems'; *c.* 1526–7; Cambridge, MA, Sackler Mus.; New York, Met.) of Hafiz, but these works often lack the spirit and animation of Bihzad's style. This variant of the Herat style spread to Bukhara. Herat painting from the third quarter of the 16th century is also strongly indebted to Bihzad. Such artists as MUHAMMADI drew on the pictorial canons of the late 15th century, producing lightly tinted drawings reminiscent of the preparatory sketches used by 15th-century painters in Herat. Other artists active in Herat during the late 16th century and the early 17th also favoured scenes with a few large figures in a simplified setting.

BIBLIOGRAPHY

M. G. Lukens: 'The Historical Background and Illustrative Character of the Metropolitan Museum's *Mantiq al-Tayr* of 1483', *Islamic Art in the Metropolitan Museum of Art*, ed. R. Ettinghausen (New York, 1972), pp. 39–72

E. J. Grube: 'The School of Herat from 1400 to 1450', *The Arts of the Book in Central Asia, 14th–16th Centuries*, ed. B. Gray (London, 1979), pp. 147–78

M. Lukens-Swietochowski: 'The School of Herat from 1450 to 1506', *The Arts of the Book in Central Asia, 14th–16th Centuries*, ed. B. Gray (London, 1979), pp. 179–214

B. Schmitz: *Miniature Painting in Harat, 1570–1640* (diss., New York U., 1981)

PRISCILLA SOUCEK

Herbal. Book, usually illustrated, comprising descriptions of herbs and their medicinal properties; it provides information on their appearance, when they should be gathered and in what form they are effective as medicines. In the West, such texts originated in the 4th century BC in ancient Greece, culminating in the *Enquiry into Plants* and *Aetiology of Plants* of Theophrastus (*c.* 372–288 BC). After this, the two most important herbals were those of Dioskurides (1st century AD), known in Latin translation as *De materia medica*, and the Latin *Herbarium* of the pseudo-Apuleius (late 4th century AD). These two works influenced the writers of herbal compilations both in the West and in the Islamic world during the Middle Ages: for example Albertus Magnus (*c.* 1190–1280), Serapion the younger and various compilations emanating from the scholars of the medical faculty of the University of Salerno. Also influential was a work by the 11th-century physician Ibn Butlan (Lat. Albukasem de Baldac), which in its Latin version was known as the *Tacuinum sanitatis*.

1. MANUSCRIPT. As originally the usefulness of such texts for practical medicine depended on the correct identification of the herbs, many herbals were illustrated. The earliest surviving copies are Late Antique: some exist only as fragments of papyrus, but others are complete manuscripts, for example the luxury herbal drawn from Dioskurides' *De materia medica*, made in Constantinople and given to the Princess Juliana Anicia *c.* 512 (Vienna, Österreich. Nbib., Cod. med. gr. 1; *see* EARLY CHRISTIAN AND BYZANTINE ART, §V, 2(vi)). In addition to the 183 images of herbs, there is a series of prefatory miniatures: two of these show the seated figures of famous Greek physicians; these are followed by two portraits of the author, the first with a personification of Discovery, the second writing his book in the presence of Thought while a painter works on one of the illustrations; the dedication miniature shows Juliana Anicia flanked by personifications. Each plant is accompanied by a full-page, fully painted illustration, many of which are remarkably accurate. Such early manuscripts were copied in later centuries, for instance a copy possibly made for the Emperor Constantine VII Porphyrogenitus (10th century; New York, Pierpont Morgan Lib., MS. M. 652). Arabic translations were also produced (e.g. Paris, Bib. N., MS. arab. 4947; *see also* ISLAMIC ART, §III, 4(ii)(a)). In some of the later Greek manuscripts of Dioskurides (e.g. Mt Athos, Great Lavra Monastery Lib., MS. Ω 75) figures are introduced into the plant pictures, and such additions were also made in Islamic manuscripts. The inclusion of figures is developed

1. Herbal with illustration of *Pimpernels*, Salerno, early 14th century (London, British Library, Egerton MS. 747, fol. 107)

in 13th- and 14th-century herbals, and later in the associated medical handbooks, the *Tacuinum sanitatis*, perhaps partly influenced by the Islamic versions.

In the medieval West, the Latin herbal of the pseudo-Apuleius was the most frequently copied. The pictorial tradition from Late Antiquity to the early printed editions is one of the most enduring in the history of book illustration. As a result of copying, however, the plant illustrations in later herbals became far removed from their natural appearance, as recorded faithfully in the Late Antique manuscripts. A Late Antique herbal of the second half of the 6th century is the earliest extant copy of this text and has quite accurate, naturalistic portrayals of the plants (Leiden, Bib. Rijksuniv., MS. Voss. lat. Q. 9). Early medieval examples include two south Italian products of the 9th century (Lucca, Bib. Stat., MS. 296; Montecassino Abbey, Archv Badia, MS. 97) and a much damaged Carolingian copy of the late 9th century (Kassel, Landesbib., 2° phys. & hist. nat. MS. 10). The Italian examples are illustrated with small, unframed drawings of the plants, the Carolingian copy with paintings. The same tradition continues in an Anglo-Saxon copy of the early 11th century (London, BL, Cotton MS. Vitell. C. III), possibly from Christ Church, Canterbury, and two of the late 11th century from Canterbury and probably Bury St Edmunds (Oxford, Bodleian Lib., MS. Ashmole 1431 and MS. Bodley 130, respectively). Manuscripts of the late 12th century from the Mosan region, northern France and

England continue the same format (e.g. London, BL, Harley MS. 1585), but in some, frames are introduced around the plants, and they are painted in brighter colours with extensive use of gold (e.g. London, BL, Sloane MS. 1975; Oxford, Bodleian Lib., MS. Ashmole 1462). In these manuscripts, although the painting is of high quality, the plants have become stylized into often unrecognizable forms. A return to representations showing some observation of nature occurs in manuscripts of the *Tractatus de herbis* (also known as the *Compendium salernitatum*), produced in Italy between the late 13th century and early 15th (e.g. London, BL, Egerton MS. 747; see fig. 1). Remarkably naturalistic images illustrate several north Italian herbals of *c.* 1400, for example a manuscript made for Francesco II, Lord of Padua (*reg* 1390–1405), and its copy (London, BL, Egerton MS. 2020; Venice, Bib. N. Marciana, MS. lat. VI. 59, respectively).

At about the same time, also in northern Italy, a series of manuscripts of the *Tacuinum sanitatis* was produced, also containing recognizable plants. While not strictly herbals, these health handbooks place figures, animals and birds beside sometimes magnified, tree-like forms of the plants, as if in a landscape. Some have more than 200 illustrations, covering certain foodstuffs as well as herbs, with accompanying texts on their nutritional value. These books seem to have been made for courtly patrons, probably in Lombardy, and the figures are often shown as lovers in elegant dress, as in contemporary tapestries. Other figures include peasants or servants picking or gathering the herbs. They may have been influenced by scenes of the months of the year, which existed in such monumental wall paintings as those of *c.* 1400–07 in the Torre Aquila of Trent Castle, where both courtly activities and peasant labours are shown in the same landscape setting (for illustration *see* BUONCONSIGLIO CASTLE). The earliest of the *Tacuinum sanitatis* manuscripts were produced in the circle of the Lombard illuminator Giovannino dei Grassi (U. Liège, Bib. Gén., MS. 1041; Paris, Bib. N., MS. nouv. acq. lat. 1673), probably dated *c.* 1370–90. The later Paris manuscript has figures of more courtly elegance. Early in the 15th century another manuscript of the same series of pictures (*c.* 1400; Vienna, Österreich. Nbib., Cod. s.n. 2644) was in the possession of Georg von Lichtenstein, Bishop of Trent (*reg* 1390–1416), who commissioned the Trent wall paintings. In all these manuscripts, fully painted full-page miniatures accompany the text passages describing the plants and their medicinal properties. They are luxury products usually ascribed to Lombardy, although Verona has been suggested for a copy made later in the 15th century (in two parts, Rouen, Bib. Mun., MS. 3054 and sold London, Sotheby's, 17 Dec 1991, lot 50).

In the early 16th century there was a renewed interest in the illustrated herbal, and many copies with more naturalistic illustrations were produced, for example the early 16th-century French translation of the *Tractatus*, the *Livre des simples médicines*, attributed to Platearius (Paris, Bib. N., MS. lat. 12322), and from the same period, an English manuscript combining paintings of flowers and herbs (Oxford, Bodleian Lib., MS. Ashmole 1504). At the time when these illuminated manuscripts were made, printed herbals were already being produced in large numbers, taking over directly from the manuscript tradition.

2. PRINTED. From their earliest days, printed illustrated herbals were popular. The *Herbarium* of the pseudo-Apuleius was printed in Rome around 1481–3 with 131 woodcut illustrations, and a herbal of Macer Floridus was published in Milan in 1482. Numerous editions of herbal texts printed in Germany, France and the Netherlands appeared in the last two decades of the 15th century and, particularly, in the first quarter of the 16th. A German version of the pseudo-Apuleius by Johann Wonnecken von Cube, published by Peter Schoeffer (*fl* 1457–*c.* 1495) as *Herbarius zu teutsch* (Mainz, 1485), and Otto Brunfel's *Herbarium vivae eicones* (Strasbourg, 1530–36), both contain woodcuts that demonstrate increasingly close observation of the plants. This trend continued in later publications, such as Leonhard Fuchs's *De historia stirpium* (Basle, 1542), which has more than 500 woodcuts. In Italy, Pierandrea Mattioli (1501–77) published a Latin commentary on Dioskurides (Venice, 1554), which contained 562 woodcuts. In Flanders, Rembert Dodens's *Stirpium historiae* was published by the Plantin press

2. Illustrated frontispiece, woodcut, from *The Herball or Generall Historie of Plantes* by John Gerard, London, 1597 (Oxford, Bodleian Library)

(Antwerp, 1583), with over 1300 woodcuts, and in England, John Gerard's *Herball* appeared in 1597 (see fig. 2).

BIBLIOGRAPHY
Dict. Middle Ages
E. S. Rohde: *The Old English Herbals* (London, 1922)
R. T. Gunther: *The Herbal of Apuleius Barbarus* (London, 1925)
C. Singer: 'The Herbal in Antiquity', *J. Hell. Stud.*, xlvii (1927), pp. 1–52
F. W. T. Hunger: *The Herbal of Pseudo-Apuleius from the Ninth-century Manuscript in the Abbey of Montecassino* (Leiden, 1935)
K. Weitzmann: *Illustrations in Roll and Codex* (Princeton, 1947, rev. 1970)
O. Pächt: 'Early Italian Nature Studies', *J. Warb. & Court. Inst.*, xiii (1950), pp. 13–47
K. Nissen: *Die botanische Buchillustration*, 2 vols and suppl. (Stuttgart, 1951–66)
——: *Kräuterbücher aus fünf Jahrhunderten* (Munich, 1956)
Dioscurides, Codex Vindobonensis Med. Gr. 1 der Österreichischen Nationalbibliothek, Codices Selecti, xii (Graz, 1965–70) [facs. and commentary vol.]
K. Weitzmann: 'The Greek Sources of Islamic Scientific Illustration', *Studies in Classical and Byzantine Manuscript Illumination*, ed. H. L. Kessler (Chicago, 1971), pp. 20–44
L. Donati: *Bibliografia della miniatura* (Florence, 1972), pp. 445–8
C. H. Talbot and F. Unterkircher, eds: *Medicina antiqua, libri quattuor medicinae*, Codices Selecti, xxvii (Vienna, 1972)
H. Kunze: *Geschichte der Buchillustration in Deutschland: Das 15. Jahrhundert* (Leipzig, 1975), pp. 319–31
L. Cogliati Arano: *The Medieval Health Handbook: 'Tacuinum sanitatis'* (London and New York, 1976)
L. E. Voigts: 'A New Look at a Manuscript Containing the Old English Translation of the *Herbarium Apulei*', *Manuscripta*, xx (1976), pp. 40–60
——: 'One Anglo-Saxon View of the Classical Gods', *Stud. Iconog.*, iii (1977), pp. 3–16
H. Grape-Albers: *Spätantike Bilder aus der Welt des Arztes* (Wiesbaden, 1977)
B. Witthaft: 'The *Tacuinum sanitatis*: A Lombard Panorama', *Gesta*, xvii/1 (1978), pp. 49–60
W. Blunt and S. Raphael: *The Illustrated Herbal* (London, 1979)
F. Unterkircher: *Das Hausbuch der Cerruti* (Dortmund, 1979)
A. Pazzini and E. Pirani, eds: *Herbarium (Codex 4182 Biblioteca Casanatense)* (Milan, 1980) [facs.]
J. Spencer: *The Four Seasons of the House of Cerruti* (New York, 1984)

NIGEL J. MORGAN

Herbart, Johann Friedrich (*b* Oldenburg, Niedersachsen, 4 May 1776; *d* Göttingen, Niedersachsen, 14 Aug 1841). German philosopher and psychologist. His philosophy was based on a development and criticism of that of IMMANUEL KANT. At its centre was a psychological theory about the satisfaction and dissatisfaction felt by the mind in bringing coherence to its perceptions. This was both an aesthetic theory of mental development and a theory of aesthetics. His theory was fundamental to subsequent formalist aesthetic theories of the 19th century. The most general objective of his theory was to construct an account of mental development that avoided the extreme positions of John Locke and Gottfried Wilhelm von Liebniz. He opposed the former's notion that the mind was a structureless *tabula rasa* that developed ideas from the sensory data received from outside. He also rejected Leibniz's view that the mind develops from within itself and sought to unite these two theories without resorting to Kant's faculty psychology. Herbart conceived of mental life as the emergence and interaction of experiences, which he thought of as initially being sensory presentations (*Vorstellungen*). It was in the nature of these presentations that they should strive to remain in consciousness, and each presentation is thus seen as having a quantum of force or energy. Once the mind is exposed to other stimuli there is, potentially, a conflict between the new and the old presentations to occupy the mind's attention. Such conflicts provide the dynamics of mental life and the mode of its development.

Central to these dynamics is the notion that presentations fuse with and reinforce each other in being similar and compete to keep each other out of consciousness in being dissimilar. Consonance and dissonance being the result of similarity and dissimilarity, the paradigm of this process is found in the harmonic relation of musical notes, which he first analysed in *Psychologische Bemerkungen zur Toulehre* (1811). Dissonant notes inhibit the entry of each other into consciousness so that neither could be clearly heard, while consonant notes mutually facilitate entry and enable each other to remain in consciousness. According to the degree of consonance or dissonance, they enhance or inhibit consciousness of each other. The relationship is not stable, however, for a second order effect may be the progressive ascendency of reinforcement over inhibition or vice versa. Herbart described such relations of inhibition and enhancement as 'aesthetic relations'. For these to take place the presentations must be of the same modality: colours can only inhibit or reinforce other colours, sounds can do likewise with other sounds, and so on. The problem in using musical notes as the paradigm is that it obscures the distinctions between (i) a relation between two qualities of the same object; (ii) a relation between two objects of which we are conscious; and (iii) a relation between two experiences or perceptions. The least confusing way of understanding Herbart's theory is to assume it applies to configurations presented by objects within the visual, aural, tactile or other perceptual fields. The pattern of reciprocal inhibition and fusion of representations underlies the way we assimilate new experiences. Past presentations leave a deposit in the mind, and the more often such a pattern of representation is repeated, the more it dominates how we respond to new presentations, tending to make the new experience conform to the old pattern.

Herbart sought scientific rigour for his account of the interaction of presentations by defining them through differential equations, but the initial quantities lacked any strict criteria of individuation or measurement. Nevertheless, his attempt to organize his work mathematically presaged modern perceptual psychology, even though his theories were speculative rather than experimental. Herbart applied his theories to vision and the visual arts only in the most limited way. He opposed the conception that the interest of art lay in some undefined emotional state that a work precipitated and looked rather at the way we resolve the relation between different features or configurations in perception. He saw the experience of art as exemplary of the underlying principles of mental functioning. His aesthetics are not presented in any one work but pervade his philosophical, psychological and educational writings. His ideas were developed by Robert Zimmermann (1824–98), in the architectural theory of Adolf Goeller (*d* 1902) and subsequently by Heinrich Wölfflin. Goeller brought together two aspects of Herbart's philosophy in his architectural theory, which makes it important in the historiography of art. His discussion of the use of past architectural forms in new conjunctions is based on an analogy with Herbart's notion that old patterns of presentations are sustained and interact in new configurations.

WRITINGS

K. Kehrbach and others, eds: *Sämtliche Werke*, 19 vols (Langensalza, 1887–1912)

BIBLIOGRAPHY

R. Zimmermann: *Leibnitz und Herbart: Eine Vergleichung ihrer Monado-logien* (Vienna, 1849)
——: *Geschichte der Aesthetik als philosophischer Wissenschaft* (Vienna, 1858), pp. 754–805
H. Lotze: *Geschichte der Aesthetik in Deutschland* (Munich, 1868), pp. 225–56
R. Zimmermann: 'Perioden in Herbarts Geistesgang', *Sber. Wien. Akad.* (1876), pp. 179–234
G. S. Brett: *History of Psychology*, 3 vols (London, 1912–21), ed. and abridged by R. S. Peters (London and New York, 1962), pp. 545–63
E. Boring: *A History of Experimental Psychology* (New York, 1929, rev. 1950), pp. 250–61
M. Podro: *Manifold in Perception: Theories of Art from Kant to Hildebrand*, Oxford Warburg Series (Oxford, 1972), pp. 61–79

MICHAEL PODRO

Herbert. English family of patrons, collectors and an architect. The family seat, Wilton House, near Salisbury, Wilts, is a former abbey; following the Dissolution of the Monasteries it was granted in 1544 to the Welshman William Herbert, later 1st Earl of Pembroke (1551). Wilton House was reconstructed in the Palladian style from 1636 for (1) Philip Herbert, 4th Earl of Pembroke, a keen collector of Venetian art and an important patron of Anthony van Dyck and other court painters. His grandson (2) Thomas Herbert, 8th Earl of Pembroke, enlarged the family's collection through his extensive purchases of Old Master paintings, coins and statues. (3) Henry Herbert, 9th Earl of Pembroke, established himself as a leading Palladian architect in the second quarter of the 18th century. Those works of art still in family ownership are at Wilton House.

BIBLIOGRAPHY

R. Cowdry: *A Description of the Pictures, Bustos, Basso-relievos and Other Curiosities at the Earl of Pembroke's House at Wilton* (London, 1751)
J. Kennedy: *A Description of the Antiquities and Curiosities in Wilton House* (Salisbury and London, 1769)
Sidney, 16th Earl of Pembroke: *A Catalogue of the Paintings and Drawings in the Collection at Wilton House* (London, 1968)

(1) Philip Herbert, 4th Earl of Pembroke and 1st Earl of Montgomery (*b* Wilton House, Wilts, 10 Oct 1584; *d* Westminster, London, 23 Jan 1649–50). He rose to power under James I (*reg* 1603–25) and in 1626 was made Lord Chamberlain of the Royal Household. He retained this post, which included responsibility for the King's collection of paintings, under Charles I until dismissal in 1641, when he joined the Parliamentarian cause in the English Civil War. Philip and his brother William, 3rd Earl of Pembroke (1580–1630), whose title he inherited, established an important picture collection, housed at Wilton House and Durham House (destr.) in the Strand, London. Although a salaried agent, Tovars (or Towers), the Keeper at Durham House, purchased paintings on their behalf, the 4th Earl acted as negotiator for certain works acquired from the royal collection. He exchanged Raphael's *St George* (Washington, DC, N.G.A.), for example, for a volume of drawings (Windsor Castle, Berks, Royal Lib.) by Hans Holbein (ii), then in Charles I's possession.

Pembroke's collection also included a number of 16th-century Venetian works by Titian, Giorgione, Correggio and Domenico Tintoretto.

Pembroke was an enthusiastic patron of court painters: Daniel Mijtens I painted his portrait (Wilton House, Wilts) *c.* 1625. Pembroke particularly favoured Anthony van Dyck, the leading painter in England at the time. One of Pembroke's earliest commissions was a half-length portrait of himself bearing the Lord Chamberlain's wand (*c.* 1628; Melbourne, N. G. Victoria). A subsequent picture, *Philip Herbert, 4th Earl of Pembroke, and his Family* (*c.* 1633–4; Wilton House), is one of van Dyck's largest and most impressive works; it was probably commissioned in part to celebrate Pembroke's marriage in 1630 to Lady Anne Clifford. It was first hung at Durham House but was transferred after 1652 to the Double Cube Room at Wilton, for which it may have originally been intended. Other artists who received commissions included Peter Lely (e.g. *Lady Anne Clifford*, *c.* 1650; priv. col., see *Sir Peter Lely*, exh. cat. by O. Millar, London, N.P.G., 1978, fig. 4).

Pembroke was also responsible for the rebuilding of the south range of Wilton House in the Palladian style, as well as its magnificent new gardens (destr.), both of which were undertaken in the 1630s by Isaac de Caus (*see* WILTON, §1). Inigo Jones may have advised de Caus on the design. When the new part of the house was destroyed by fire in 1647, Pembroke commissioned John Webb to rebuild the south range with its six staterooms, including the Double and Single Cube Rooms. After Pembroke's death his executors disposed of part of the collection displayed there and at Durham House; the remainder passed to his son Philip Herbert, 5th Earl of Pembroke (1619–69), who sold further works to defray building costs.

DNB

BIBLIOGRAPHY

O. Millar, ed.: 'Abraham van der Doort's Catalogue of the Collections of Charles I', *Walpole Soc.*, xxxvii (1960) [whole issue]
C. Brown: *Van Dyck* (Oxford, 1982)
A. McGregor, ed.: *The Late King's Goods: Collections, Possessions and Patronage of Charles I in the Light of the Commonwealth Sale Inventories* (Oxford, 1990)

SUSAN JENKINS

(2) Thomas Herbert, 8th Earl of Pembroke (*b* 1656; *d* 22 Jan 1733). Grandson of (1) Philip Herbert. He was educated at Christ Church, Oxford, and on the Continent; in Montpellier he met the philosopher John Locke, who later dedicated the *Essay Concerning Human Understanding* (1690) to him. In 1678 Herbert acquired works from the collection assembled in the early 17th century by Thomas Howard, 2nd (14th) Earl of Arundel. Herbert inherited the title from his brother Philip Herbert, 7th Earl of Pembroke (*d* 1683), and in 1689–90 was President of the Royal Society. Under William III and Queen Anne he held important offices of state.

Pembroke collected coins (which Sir Andrew Fountaine used in 1705 for his *Numismata anglo-saxonica & anglo-danica*), antique marbles (which included acquisitions from the Mazarin, Giustiniani and Valetta collections), and pictures, the last with the advice of Sir Andrew Fountaine and Hugh Howard. He bought few English or French works (only one by Nicolas Poussin and one by Claude

Lorrain), nor did he patronize contemporary artists, but the Italian Old Master paintings he purchased included Lorenzo Lotto's *St Anthony in the Wilderness* and Tintoretto's *Christ Washing the Feet of his Disciples*; among the Dutch and Netherlandish pictures he acquired were Rembrandt van Rijn's *Portrait of his Mother* and Lucas van Leyden's *Card Players* (all Wilton House, Wilts). Following the death of Roger Palmer, Earl of Castlemaine (1634–1705), Pembroke was able to add the Wilton Diptych (London, N.G.), a small, late 14th-century panel depicting Richard II and saints at prayer, to his collection, which was kept at Wilton House. The collection was catalogued by Count Carlo Gambarini in 1731, and the sculptures were engraved by Cary Creed. Pembroke was also responsible for setting up the Wilton Royal Carpet Factory by settling a group of French weavers in the nearby town (*see* WILTON, §2).

BIBLIOGRAPHY

A. Michaelis: *Ancient Marbles in Great Britain* (London, 1882)
J. Cornforth: 'Conversations with Old Heroes: The Collections of Thomas, 8th Earl of Pembroke', *Country Life*, cxliv (26 Sept 1968), pp. 748–51
——: 'A Virtuoso's Gallery: The 8th Earl of Pembroke's Collection of Pictures', *Country Life* (3 Oct 1968), pp. 834–41

(3) Henry Herbert, 9th Earl of Pembroke (*b* 29 Jan 1693; *d* London, 9 June 1751). Architect, son of (2) Thomas Herbert. He studied at Christ Church, Oxford, and, after a tour in Italy in 1712, held a series of court offices for which he was temperamentally unsuited, preferring the company of such antiquarians as William Stukeley, with whom he visited Stonehenge. In 1722 Herbert joined the Society of Roman Knights and in 1743 was made a Fellow of the Royal Society. Many of his contemporaries described him as mad; he is known to have been violent and intemperate but also a vegetarian. He was an enthusiastic amateur architect and, like Richard Boyle, 3rd Earl of Burlington, strongly promoted Palladianism. In 1717 he acquired leasehold land at Whitehall, London; Pembroke House was built on it (completed 1724; destr.), probably by Colen Campbell, although Lord Herbert was almost certainly involved. During the 1720s he established a close partnership with Roger Morris. Together they probably designed Marble Hill House (1724; *see* VILLA, fig. 8), Twickenham, London, a Thames-side villa for Henrietta Howard, Countess of Suffolk; in 1727 Morris and Lord Herbert began White Lodge in Richmond Park, London, for George I and in 1729 Castle Hill, Devon (with Lord Burlington).

Herbert succeeded to the earldom of Pembroke in 1733 and during the 1730s continued his involvement in architectural schemes, including the Column of Victory (1731), erected in the park at Blenheim Palace, Oxon, and Wimbledon House (1732–3; destr.), London, for Sarah Churchill, 1st Duchess of Marlborough. His major work is, however, the Palladian Bridge (1736–7) built to his designs, with the advice of Morris, in the grounds of the family seat, Wilton House, Wilts; this was the prototype for garden bridges built by others at Stowe, Bucks, Prior Park, Avon, Hagley Park, Hereford & Worcs, and elsewhere. He was also an influential supporter of the Swiss engineer Charles Labelye (1705–81), who built Westminster Bridge (destr.), London, between 1739 and 1747.

Pembroke was less interested in collecting works of art than his father, although he commissioned a set of views of Westcombe House (built *c*. 1730 by Pembroke and Morris; destr.), Blackheath, London, from George Lambert (i) and views of Lincoln's Inn Fields and Covent Garden in London from Samuel Scott. In addition he is thought to have purchased Rubens's *Landscape with a Shepherd* (Wilton House). In 1747 he paid Louis-François Roubiliac £30 for a portrait bust of *Sir Andrew Fountaine*; two years later he purchased one of *Martin Folkes* (both Wilton House).

BIBLIOGRAPHY

Colvin
J. Lees-Milne: *Earls of Creation: Five Great Patrons of Eighteenth-century Art* (London, 1962), pp. 41–82
M. P. G. Draper: *Marble Hill House and its Owners* (London, 1970)
R. J. B. Walker: *Old Westminster Bridge* (Newton Abbot, 1979)

CHARLES SAUMAREZ SMITH

Herbert, J(ohn) R(ogers) (*b* Maldon, Essex, 23 Jan 1810; *d* Kilburn, London, 17 March 1890). English painter. In 1826 he entered the Royal Academy Schools, London. He began exhibiting portraits at the Royal Academy in 1830 and until 1836 made his living chiefly through portraiture and book illustration. In 1836 Herbert visited Italy, and for the next few years his work consisted chiefly of Italian historical genre paintings such as the *Appointed Hour* (exh. London, Brit. Inst., 1835; untraced). Herbert greatly admired the architect A. W. N. Pugin and probably in 1840, through Pugin's influence, was converted to Roman Catholicism. Subsequently, Herbert's religious beliefs dictated the subjects of his work, for example *Sir Thomas More and his Daughter* (1844; London, Tate). Herbert was employed by William Dyce at the Schools of Design by 1842, at which time the two artists collaborated on a book of nursery rhymes, tales and jingles. Herbert's style, like that of Dyce, was influenced by the Nazarenes, and he shared their concern with historical authenticity and their use of bright colours and hard outlines.

In 1841 Herbert was elected ARA and, in 1846, RA. His diploma picture, *Pope Gregory Teaching the Boys to Sing* (London, RA), reflected his desire to promote Roman Catholicism through his art and reveals his view (shaped by Pugin) of the medieval past as a morally superior age. The same year he was among the artists who were commissioned to decorate the interior of the New Palace of Westminster. His work there included a series of nine Old Testament scenes on the theme of Human Justice (1858–64) for the Peers' Robing Room and *King Lear Disinheriting Cordelia* (1852) for the Upper Waiting Room. In 1847 Herbert exhibited the *Youth of Our Lord* (London, Guildhall A.G.) at the Royal Academy, a work which in style and subject anticipated John Everett Millais's *Christ in the Carpenter's Shop* (1850; London, Tate). Many of Herbert's religious paintings were reproduced as chromolithographs, their didactic tone making them popular in Sunday schools. Queen Victoria was an admirer of Herbert's work, and in 1860 he painted the *Virgin Mary* (Brit. Royal Col.) for her.

Herbert was a man of strong convictions: he was a great conversationalist and became increasingly outspoken about the importance of religion to his art. Besides promoting religious asceticism through his work, he adopted what he believed to be the appearance of a medieval artist: he grew a long beard and long hair and habitually wore a dressing-gown. Critics often saw him as an easy target for abuse, and his views on the immorality of contemporary French art brought him ridicule from a number of younger artists; Whistler saw his art and interests as old-fashioned and classified him with such artists as William Etty as one of 'the excellent army of mediocrity' (*The Gentle Art of Making Enemies*, London, 1890; p. 166). Herbert's later works were criticized for their poor quality, and his standing as an RA was questioned by a number of artists who were antagonistic towards him. In 1881 Herbert opened the Herbert Gallery in New Bond Street to show his own works. *The Saturday Review* later described the exhibition as 'acres of. . . pallid purple canvases with wizened saints and virgins in attitudinizing groups' (7 Aug 1886, p. 192). This judgement, typical of critical disdain for Herbert at the time, was fuelled as much by a dislike of his religious views as his paintings. In 1886 he retired as an academician although he continued to exhibit at the Academy until 1889. He had three sons who were artists: Arthur John Herbert (1834–56), Cyril Wiseman Herbert (1847–82) and Wilfred Vincent Herbert (*fl* 1863–91).

DNB

BIBLIOGRAPHY

S. C. Hall: *The Acquittal of the Seven Bishops* (London, 1846)
L. Errington: *Social and Religious Themes in English Art, 1840–1860* (London, 1984)

MARTIN POSTLE

Herbin, Auguste (*b* Quiévy, Nord, 29 April 1882; *d* Paris, 30–31 Jan 1960). French painter. He studied drawing at the Ecole des Beaux-Arts, Lille, from 1898 to 1901, when he settled in Paris. The initial influence of Impressionism and Post-Impressionism visible in paintings that he sent to the Salon des Indépendants in 1906 gradually gave way to an involvement with Cubism after his move in 1909 to the Bateau-Lavoir studios, where he met Pablo Picasso, Georges Braque and Juan Gris; he was also encouraged by his friendship with Wilhelm Uhde. His work was exhibited in the same room as that of Jean Metzinger, Albert Gleizes and Fernand Léger in the Salon des Indépendants of 1910, and in 1912 he participated in the influential Section d'Or exhibition (*see* SECTION D'OR (ii)). After producing his first abstract paintings in 1917, Herbin came to the attention of Léonce Rosenberg who, after World War I, made him part of the group centred on his Gallerie de l'Effort Moderne and exhibited his work there on several occasions in 1918 and 1921. Herbin's radical reliefs of simple geometric forms in painted wood, such as *Coloured Wood Relief* (1921; Paris, Pompidou), challenged not only the status of the easel painting but also traditional figure–ground relationships. The incomprehension that greeted these reliefs and related furniture designs, even from those critics most favourably disposed towards Cubism, was such that until 1926 or 1927 he followed Rosenberg's advice to return to a representational style. Herbin himself later disowned landscapes, still-lifes and genre scenes of this period, such as *Bowls Players* (1923; Paris, Pompidou), in which the objects were depicted as schematized volumes.

As a member of the Communist party, Herbin found himself under pressure to practise an illustrative, moralizing art, but his resolute belief in abstraction culminated in 1931 in the creation with Georges Vantongerloo of the ABSTRACTION-CRÉATION group. Within this association Herbin's sympathies were more with the artists who had been associated with CERCLE ET CARRÉ, who advocated metaphorical use of geometric forms and continued contact with nature, than with Theo van Doesburg's concept of concrete art as an enclosed and independent system of forms. Herbin's interest in colour theory, which dated back to 1924, led to his publication of *L'art non-figuratif non-objectif* (Paris, 1949), in which he established a system of correspondences between colours, forms, notes of music and letters of the alphabet which he later employed in paintings such as *Friday I* (1951; Paris, Pompidou). In the 1950s he initiated the Salon des Réalités Nouvelles, of which he remained a member until 1955, and exerted a strong influence on a younger generation of abstract painters. During his last years he also applied his theories of abstraction to tapestry designs.

WRITINGS
L'art non-figuratif non-objectif (Paris, 1949)

BIBLIOGRAPHY
A. Jakovski: *Auguste Herbin* (Paris, 1933)
Auguste Herbin, 1882–1960 (exh. cat., Amsterdam, Stedel. Mus., 1963)
Auguste Herbin (exh. cat., Hannover, Kestner-Ges., 1967)
Herbin: Alphabet plastique (exh. cat., intro. J. Lassaigne; Paris, Gal. Denise René, 1972)
Auguste Herbin (exh. cat., Céret, Mus. A. Mod., 1994) [major retrospective]

VANINA COSTA

Herboso, José Grajera y. *See* GRAJERA Y HERBOSO, JOSÉ.

Herbst [Herbster], **Hans** (*b* Strasbourg, 1470; *d* Basle, 1552). German painter, active in Switzerland. He left Strasbourg when young, and was probably apprenticed among Swabian masters. In 1492 he was made a citizen of Basle. His best work was done in the three decades after 1500. In 1512 and 1515 Swiss campaigns took him to northern Italy. But after opposing the reformed faith in Basle, he was imprisoned and forced to recant under the threat of the sword. His negative attitude to the Reformation is understandable in that it largely destroyed his livelihood as a religious painter. After 1530 he was awarded only minor commissions by the city, and it must be assumed that his church paintings were almost all lost in the iconoclasm in Basle. Some work can be traced in archives; for example the main altar in the Klosterkirche of St Maria Magdalena.

Herbst's art is primarily known from his one surviving painting, a table-top (1515; Zurich, Schweizer. Landesmus.; see fig.) commissioned by the Basle patron Hans Baer the younger, who died in the Battle of Marignano (14 Sept 1515). This was long thought to be an early work of Hans Holbein the younger. Ambrosius Holbein was a guest at Herbst's house in 1516; but Hans Holbein only arrived in Basle at the very end of 1515, whereas Herbst's name is twice inscribed on the table-top in concealed places, so that there can be no doubt as to his authorship.

The table-top exhibits wit and intelligence, and is artistically a masterpiece. The wooden panel has a black painted ground that makes it look like slate. Its middle

Hans Herbst's painted table-top (oil on wood, 1.09×1.39 m, 1515; Zurich, Schweizerisches Landesmuseum) as drawn by Georg Subic, pen, black ink and wash, 1.19×1.53 m, 1875 (Zurich, Schweizerisches Landesmuseum)

section shows 'Saint Nobody' and the grocer—stock comic figures in Late Gothic art—being robbed by monkeys, surrounded by innumerable everyday objects, some treated in *trompe-l'oeil*. Around the edges pastimes are shown: hunting, fishing, hawking, jousting. Bird-catching is combined with girl-catching—an iconographically unique feature. Of the few surviving painted table-tops—a form fashionable *c.* 1500—Herbst's has the most interesting content. Stylistically closest to it are the marginal drawings in the manuscript of Erasmus's *Praise of Folly* (Basle, Kstmus.) from the beginning of 1515. This close similarity has led to the attribution of some of the marginal drawings to Herbst. Other works hitherto ascribed to Hans Holbein also show features of Herbst's art, for example the schoolmaster's sign (1516; the side with the children being taught, Basle, Kstmus.) and the five canvases of the *Passion* (1515–16; Basle, Kstmus.) which has recently been attributed to Hans Dig. Various murals, drawings, book illustrations and even paintings from Basle soon after 1500 or from the circle of the Holbein brothers might be linked to Herbst and his studio. A portrait by him in the Basle Kunstmuseum has been interpreted as a self-portrait. Sixteenth-century biographical texts refer to Herbst as a famous painter. His son was the Basle book-printer Johannes Oporin (1507–68).

BIBLIOGRAPHY

NDB; Thieme–Becker

Die Malerfamilie Holbein in Basel (exh. cat., Basle, Kstmus., 1960), pp. 20, 168–172, 217, 287

L. Wüthrich: 'Quellen zur Biographie des Malers Hans Herbst', *Z. Schweiz. Archäol. & Kstgesch.*, xxxv (1978), pp. 170–89

Oberrheinische Buchillustration 2, Basler Buchillustration, 1500–1545 (exh. cat. by F. Hieronymus, Basle, Öff. Bib. U., 1984)

J. Rowlands: *Holbein: The Paintings of Hans Holbein the Younger* (Oxford, 1985), pp. 17–22, 230

L. Wüthrich: 'Der sogenannte "Holbein-Tisch": Geschichte und Inhalt der bemalten Tischplatte des Basler Malers Hans Herbst: Ein frühes Geschenk an die Burger-Bibliothek Zürich 1663', *Mitt. Antiqua. Ges. Zürich*, lvii (1990)

LUCAS WÜTHRICH

Hercolani. *See* ERCOLANI.

Herculaneum [now Ercolano; formerly Resina]. Roman site in Italy. It lies about 10 km to the east of Naples and was described by ancient authors (Sisenna: frag. 53; Dionysos of Halikarnassos: I.xliv; Strabo: V.iv.8) as a small fortified town built at the foot of Mt Vesuvius on a spur of land facing the sea, and as a healthy and pleasant place to live because of the south-west winds. It was destroyed with Pompeii in AD 79, but its architecture, art and furniture was preserved in mud for over 1600 years. All the finds are in Naples, Museo Archeologico Nazionale, unless otherwise indicated.

I. Introduction. II. Architecture. III. Sculpture. IV. Painting. V. Mosaics. VI. Rediscovery.

I. Introduction.

The town was founded, according to legend, by Hercules on his way back from Spain; its history is somewhat obscure in the early period. Until the 4th century BC the population was probably Oscan and Samnite but was open to Greek influences from Parthenope (Naples). After the second Samnite War the Romans took control of the town, together with Nocera and Pompeii, and brought it into the Roman confederacy (*c.* 307 BC). Herculaneum joined the rebels in the Social War but fell in 89 BC to Titus Didius, the legate of Cornelius Sulla, who was himself to take Pompeii a few years later. Now a Roman *municipium*, Herculaneum was settled by a colony of veterans and, at the same time, by the wealthy from the capital who built their suburban villas on the Campanian coast. The earthquake of AD 62 destroyed a large part of the town. The reconstruction work, left unfinished in AD 79, was aided by the emperor Vespasian, who rebuilt the Temple of the Magna Mater, and by such wealthy inhabitants as M. Nonius Balbus, who rebuilt the basilica, the town gates and the walls at his own expense. Herculaneum met its tragic end on 24–25 August AD 79 during the eruption of Vesuvius. While the more distant towns of Pompeii and Stabiae were covered with ashes and pumice, Herculaneum was engulfed by torrents of boiling mud bearing ashes and volcanic substances. This oozing mass filled the streets, the houses and the buildings. Once it had solidified it formed a layer of tufa 12–20 m thick that encased the whole town, preserving the buildings and some beautiful pieces of furniture in carbonized wood, often *in situ*, due to its impermeability.

Immediately after the catastrophe the emperor Titus appointed a commission of ex-consuls to examine the possible ways of saving the ruined towns, but, faced with a disaster of such magnitude, he was forced to abandon all plans to rebuild them. The debris of several centuries and the lava from later eruptions of Vesuvius, particularly those of 1631, altered the appearance of the site, made the sea recede by over 600 m and wiped the memory of Herculaneum from the minds of the people. At the time of its discovery in 1709 (*see* §VI below) the site was called Resina, and nobody knew exactly where the lost town lay. It was only in 1969 that the name of Resina was changed to Ercolano in memory of the town of antiquity.

The early excavations of the 18th century used the tunnelling technique. Since 1927 open excavations have revealed only about a third of the ancient town, which must have covered an area of 12 ha. Archaeological work carried out in the area of the ancient shoreline has contradicted the generally accepted theory that the inhabitants of Herculaneum had time to escape during the eruption of Vesuvius. The discoveries of over 100 skeletons in fishermen's shelters and on the beach, and of a boat lying overturned a few metres below the level of the suburban baths, have given a glimpse of a more tragic end. It seems likely that, when people heard the rumbling of the volcano and found themselves in the path of the flow of hot mud, they fled towards the sea, hoping to find boats to take them to safety, but the boiling sea and the violent tidal waves trapped them on the shore where they died of suffocation, like Pliny at Pompeii (Pliny the Younger: *Letters* VI. xvi), and were buried in the torrents of mud.

II. Architecture.

1. URBAN PLANNING. The town was built according to a regular plan (see fig. 1), divided into squares by the *decumani*, large streets running east–west, and the *cardines*,

1. Herculaneum, 1st century AD, plan: (a) *decumanus maximus*; (b) palaestra; (c) cryptoporticus; (d) meeting-room; (e) city baths; (f) suburban baths; (g) sacred enclosure; (h) Samnite House; (i) House of the Black Hall; (j) House of the Bicentenary; (k) House of the Relief of Telephus; (l) House of the Mosaic Atrium; (m) House of the Stags; (n) House of the Wooden Partition; (o) House of Neptune and Amphitrite

streets running downhill from north to south. These streets thus ran at right angles, marking out the *insulae* or rectangular blocks (each 80–85×40–45 m) that contained dwellings and shops with entrances from the street. Most of the streets consisted of a roadway 2.5–3.6 m wide, paved with volcanic stone or limestone, and raised pavements *c.* 1 m wide. Only the *decumanus maximus* (1a) was unusually wide, measuring 12.3 m with a roadway of 6.3 m. This area was closed to traffic and was perhaps used as a forum or market-place. Some of the pavements were shaded by balconies supported by colonnades. In the area uncovered by the modern excavations one can see the remains of the southern walls and of two vaulted gates through which pedestrians could reach the shore.

The public services were highly developed: from the time of Augustus (*reg* 27 BC–AD 14), Herculaneum benefited from a water supply from an aqueduct, and a drainage system. Drinking water was brought by the aqueduct to a central water-tower (not yet discovered), from where it was distributed by a network of lead pipes and local reservoirs to the public fountains, which were generally

installed at crossroads, and to certain houses. These fountains are in travertine, their mouths decorated with such mythological figures as Venus, Neptune, Hercules and Medusa. The used water was collected, in part of the town at least, in conduits running beneath the centre of the streets out to the sea.

2. PUBLIC BUILDINGS. It was on the site of the theatre that Maurice, Prince d'Elboeuf, made the first discoveries in 1709 while sinking the shaft for a well. The theatre was then explored by the Bourbons, who stripped it of its statues, decorations and marble revetments. It still remains in the buried north-west part of the ancient town, 26 m beneath the modern town. It is a semicircular building (diam. 53 m) built on 19 brick arches; it was donated by the magistrate L. Annius Mammianus Rufus and built by the architect P. Numisius in the first half of the 1st century AD. Its plan, typical of Roman theatre design, is composed of a *cavea*, an *orchestra*, two side galleries and a raised stage. The *cavea* held 23 rows of seats, 16 in the central section, and seated between 2000 and 2500 spectators. The front

wall of the stage is decorated with niches that held small statues, while the architectonic *scaenae frons* (façade of the stage-building), made up of two storeys of niches and columns and with three openings for doors, was richly decorated with coloured marbles and sculptures. Near the entrances to the *orchestra* the spectators could admire the statues set up in honour of the consul Claudius Pulcher and of M. Nonius Balbus, the great patron of the town.

The palaestra (1b) is on the other side of the town, in the north-east *insula*. Built in the last phase of the town's urban development, the whole complex covers an area over 120 m long and 80 m wide. The north wing, spread out on three levels, includes a cryptoporticus (1c), upper loggias communicating with spacious halls and a large meeting-room (1d; 26.60×11.25 m), entered by a vestibule that lies on the axis of the *decumanus maximus*. The palaestra proper is a large rectangular area (78×57 m) surrounded on three sides by colonnades and on the north side by the cryptoporticus, which is lit by windows and leads to a large vaulted hall. In the centre of the open area is a cruciform swimming-pool 5.5 m wide with axes 55 m long. At its centre stands a fine bronze fountain 2.42 m high in the form of a five-headed hydra entwined round a tree. The shallowness of this pool (1.1 m) would suggest that it was not intended for adults to swim in; for this purpose there was a small pool (30×5 m) opposite the cryptoporticus.

Two sets of public baths have been found in Herculaneum. That in the centre of the town (1e) was built in the first quarter of the 1st century BC and occupied the greater part of one *insula*. In the women's section a beautiful mosaic representing a Triton among dolphins and fish decorates the floor of the *apodyterium*. The men's section adjoins a small palaestra surrounded by porticos and comprises an *apodyterium*, a *frigidarium*, a *tepidarium* with a hollow floor and walls made of hollow bricks, and a *caldarium*. The suburban baths (1f), housed in an almost square building outside the city walls and facing the sea, were probably built after the earthquake of AD 62. They are of more modest dimensions but more modern in their design. The entrance is lit by a square light well, the opening of which is supported by four pillars linked by arches, under which stands a fountain in the shape of a herm and a basin. Its floor is paved with coloured marble in *opus sectile* (cut shapes), and its walls are decorated with relief motifs in stucco.

Opposite the suburban baths, and also standing against the town wall, are two small shrines, perhaps dedicated to Venus and Bacchus, built in a rectangular enclosure (1g). In a small rectangular space between the sacred enclosure and the baths stands a funerary altar and a base bearing a marble statue in honour of M. Nonius Balbus. All these monuments were built 3 m above the beach, on a terrace supported by arcades that were used as shelters by fishermen.

In addition, Herculaneum had a Temple of the Magna Mater, which was restored by Vespasian after the earthquake of AD 62; the only trace of this basilica is a record of its restoration by M. Nonius Balbus, a macellum built by M. Spurius Rufus and decorated with the help of a contribution by L. Mammius Maximus Rufus, and an office of weights and measures run by M. Remmius Rufus

and his son. Some scholars identify as the basilica a building situated to the north of the *decumanus maximus*, at the edge of the area uncovered by the excavations. This building, which is still buried, was explored and stripped of its decorations in the 18th century. The finds include bronze and marble statues representing several emperors and empresses including Augustus, Tiberius, Claudius, Livia, Agrippina and Domitilla, and marble equestrian statues. The back walls of this building displayed some remarkable paintings (*see* §IV below).

Opposite this building, and separated from it by a monumental four-sided arch of brick covered with stucco, which must have been crowned by the bronze chariot-team discovered by the Bourbons in the 18th century, was the seat of the College of Augustales, the association of officers of the imperial cult. The 18th-century explorers seem to have found some temples linking the 'basilica' to the theatre in this still-buried part of the town.

3. PRIVATE BUILDINGS. Herculaneum offers some valuable evidence for the study of the development of Roman domestic architecture. There is a wide range of houses, some built on the old plan of the Italic atrium house (*see* ROME, ANCIENT, §II, 1(i)(c)), while others followed a composite plan combining traditional forms with Hellenistic porticos, and others were developing towards a type of building divided into several apartments on two or three floors.

2. Herculaneum, Samnite House, view of the atrium, 2nd century BC

The Samnite House, the oldest house to survive (2nd century BC; see figs 1h and 2), is an example of the typical Italic house. The entrance corridor, decorated with First Style paintings in imitation of plaques of coloured marble, leads into a large atrium also decorated with architectonic structures in stucco; the floor is in *opus signinum* (concrete with crushed tiles) embellished with geometric designs in white marble tesserae. The houses of the Black Hall (1i), of the Bicentenary (1j) and of the Relief of Telephus (1k) represent the composite type with atrium and peristyle. The fashion for building villas facing the Gulf of Naples must have influenced the erection of houses on the south façade of the town, above the ancient fortification walls, notably the 1st-century AD House of the Mosaic Atrium (see fig. 1l) and the House of the Stags (1m), in which the peristyle was replaced by a cryptoporticus and which had panoramic terraces with *diaetae* (summer-houses).

In contrast to the houses inhabited by a single family, we also find buildings of a new type, in which the atrium with *impluvium* (rainwater tank) was replaced by a courtyard into which separate rooms or apartments opened, sometimes on two or three storeys. The House of the Wooden Partition (1n) and the buildings in the neighbourhood of the palaestra are examples of this modern type of dwelling, which answered the needs of the new urban working class; rich and poor did not live in separate parts of the town but seem to have been well integrated.

The degrees of wealth are apparent not only from the size of the houses but also from their floor and wall decoration and furnishings. In modest houses the floor was in *opus signinum*, the walls were usually painted according to the taste of the time, and the furniture was wooden. In wealthy houses the floor was paved with mosaics or, after the earthquake of AD 62, with *opus sectile*; walls were always painted, except in some panoramic rooms in the House of the Relief of Telephus, where the walls were covered with coloured marble, a rare luxury at this period, and several houses contained attractive pieces of wooden or marble furniture and bronze sculptures. Indeed, the quantity and variety of artefacts found at Herculaneum suggest that its inhabitants followed the tastes of the Roman aristocracy closely, and that they had the means to acquire masterpieces.

The most splendid and the most representative collection of artistic treasures in these patrician houses was found in the Villa of the Papyri (mid-1st century BC). The excavations carried out by means of underground tunnels from 1750 to 1765 uncovered about 100 sculptures in marble and bronze and 600 papyrus rolls (the latter in Naples, Bib. N.). Scholars have been working on the papyri for two centuries but have been able to unroll only a small proportion of them, which have proved mainly to be copies of the works of the Epicurean philosopher Philodemus. The owner of the villa was perhaps L. Calpurnius Piso, a friend and patron of Philodemus and the father-in-law of Julius Caesar and enemy of Cicero; he must at least have been a cultivated man and a follower of Epicureanism. The villa itself stretched over a length of 250 m on a promontory facing the sea, 100 m to the west of the town. It included spacious bedrooms with windows looking out over the splendid countryside, peristyles for walking in, panoramic terraces and two pools amid gardens skilfully shaded with trees, bushes and flowers. The atrium, paved with black-and-white mosaics, was enlivened by fountains in the form of statues (a Silenus, a cupid pouring water) placed around the *compluvium* (open space to collect rainwater), and with statues and busts in niches. In the centre of the first, square peristyle with ten columns on each side there was a small pool, at the corners of which stood fountains with bronze herms. The large peristyle held a sort of sculpture gallery with statues and busts in bronze and marble displayed between the columns or on either side of the pool in the garden (*see also* §III below).

BIBLIOGRAPHY

Enc. A. Ant.: 'Ercolano'
C. Waldstein and L. Shoobridge: *Herculaneum: Past, Present and Future* (London, 1908)
A. Maiuri: *Ercolano: I nuovi scavi*, 2 vols (Rome, 1958)
M. Brion: *Pompeii and Herculaneum: The Glory and the Grief*, trans. J. Rosenberg (London, 1960), pp. 174–92
A. Maiuri: *Herculaneum and the Villa of the Papyri* (Novara, 1963)
Tran tam Tinh: *La casa dei Cervi a Herculaneum* (Rome, 1988)
T. Ganschow: *Untersuchungen zur Baugeschichte in Herculaneum* (Bonn, 1989)
A. Wallace-Hadrill: *Houses and Society in Pompeii and Herculaneum* (Princeton, 1994)

TRAN TAM TINH

III. Sculpture.

At their initiation in 1738 the excavations at Herculaneum were regarded as new sources of potential wealth for the local rulers rather than as valuable cultural documents. Among the earliest discoveries were two marble replicas after lost Greek bronzes, the so-called *Grande Erculanèse* and *Petite Erculanèse* (Dresden, Skulpsamml.). The figures depict draped women, one mature, the other younger, their arms wrapped in mantles and composed according to the Classical type of four-square and frontal structure. They were highly prized throughout the classical revivals of the 18th and 19th centuries and spurred further explorations at the site; their fame and archaeological significance, however, have been eclipsed by finer versions of the types since discovered.

Two marble equestrian statues of M. Nonius Balbus, one as a youth and the other as a mature man, were discovered near the 'basilica'. The *Younger Balbus* was actually excavated in 1746, although since the 1740s the date of its discovery has wrongly been given as 1739. By 1748 the statue was placed under military guard and enclosed within iron barriers in the courtyard at the entrance to the royal palace of Portici, some 2 km from the site. Soon after its discovery another equestrian statue, the *Elder Balbus*, then claimed to be the father, was found; in 1751 it too was installed at the palace entrance. Because they were relatively accessible to the public, the two equestrian statues of Balbus remained better known than any other sculptures associated with Herculaneum.

One of the last celebrated discoveries of the 18th century, a marble statue described as 'un filosofo', was found in 1779. In the early 19th century it was known as *Aristides*; by the end of the century it was properly identified as a copy of a bronze original from the 4th century BC portraying the orator *Aeschines*. Like most other works discovered at Herculaneum, the statue never achieved the fame accorded to antiquities exhibited in Rome, largely owing to its poor display at Portici.

A bronze statuette of *Alexander the Great* on horseback, his right arm holding aloft a sword to fend off an enemy, may be a diminutive copy after the Granikos monument. The celebrated original consisted of at least 25 bronze equestrian figures, including a portrait of Alexander, and also some figures of infantrymen. Set up at Dion in Macedonia by Lysippos *c.* 330 BC, the Granikos monument was transported to Rome by Q. Metellus Macedonicus in 146 BC, and few other traces of it survive than this statuette.

On 3 August 1758 the most celebrated work of art from Herculaneum was discovered in the peristyle of the Villa of the Papyri: the *Seated Mercury*, a 1st-century BC bronze copy of an original dating from the late 4th century BC or early 3rd in the tradition of Lysippos (see fig. 3). It was ranked with other famous sculptures found at the villa, the *Drunken Faun* (which is in the tradition of the more famous Barberini *Faun*) and *Wrestlers* (now identified as runners at the start of a race), whose reputations fared less well. Winckelmann considered the *Seated Mercury* the most perfect of bronzes at Portici; since its caduceus could not be found at the site, he concluded that the piece had been transported from Greece. The Comte de Caylus also identified most of the sculptures from Herculaneum as Greek originals because the site had once been a Greek colony.

The sculpture recovered from the Villa of the Papyri epitomizes the eclectic character of Roman collections. In addition to those pieces noted above, a bronze bust of the

3. Herculaneum, *Seated Mercury*, bronze, h. 1.05 m, 1st-century BC copy of late 4th- or early 3rd-century BC original (Naples, Museo Archeologico Nazionale)

Doryphoros of Polykleitos, a copy of one of the famous Classical Amazon types, a Praxitelean *Artemis* and a bust of the Praxitelean *Dionysos* known as the Sardanapalos type were recovered, along with a vast array of portraits of various types and styles representing Hellenistic political leaders (e.g. a *Ptolemy*, *Philetairos*, *Demetrios Poliorketes* and *Seleukos I Nikator*; for an illustration of the last *see* SELEUCIDS), philosophers (such as *Zeno* and *Epicurus*) and literary figures (including the blind Homer type and the bronze *Pseudo-Seneca*, which may actually represent Hesiod). Works in the archaistic and Neo-classical styles display the retrospective attitude found throughout the late Hellenistic period. The rich findings demonstrate that before AD 79 Rome and its milieu had become a centre for historicism in art, where copies of 'Old Masters' were displayed with the revivals of earlier styles applied to new creations and caprices (*see also* ROME, ANCIENT, §IV, 2(i) and (ii)).

BIBLIOGRAPHY
E. Pozzi, ed.: *Le collezioni del Museo Nazionale di Napoli* (Rome, 1989)

PETER J. HOLLIDAY

IV. Painting.

Wall paintings in various states of preservation have been found in the 'basilica', the palaestra and other public buildings, as well as in about 40 houses, some of them richly decorated mansions along the coast. In the 18th century trophies for the museum at Portici were sought in the excavations, although only the finest parts of the often partially collapsed walls were removed; in the 20th century, however, care was taken not only to leave the paintings *in situ* but to restore fallen fragments to their places on walls and ceilings. Unfortunately, only a small proportion of the restored paintings can be regarded as published, although progress has been made in establishing the provenance of fragments cut out previously. They can hardly be distinguished from those found in Pompeii (on the techniques, dating, types of wall articulation, image types, workshop problems and iconology, *see* POMPEII, §IV). The solidified muddy volcanic mass that covered Herculaneum caused considerably greater destruction, through its weight and heat, than the *lapilli* (pumice) that engulfed Pompeii, so that colour changes, for example, through the effect of heat (e.g. from yellow to red) are more frequent than in Pompeii.

The four Pompeian styles are represented in the same sequence in Herculaneum, the First and Second in only a few examples, the Third more fully and the Fourth by far the most often. A series of figural paintings on stucco from the late Second or early Third Style (i.e. the time of the Emperor Augustus; *reg* 30 BC–AD 14) were found removed from their original decorative context and leaning against the wall in a room of the palaestra. They were probably intended for reuse in the new decoration of the palaestra after the earthquake of AD 62. From about the same date are a number of classicizing mythological images painted on marble; some of them bear artists' signatures. The paintings from the large apses of the 'basilica', which were valued by the excavators more highly than those of Raphael, include *Theseus and the Minotaur*, *Hercules and Telephus* (see fig. 4), *Chiron and Achilles* and *Marsyas and*

4. Herculaneum, wall painting from the 'basilica' depicting *Hercules and Telephus*, 1st century AD (Naples, Museo Archeologico Nazionale)

Olympus, as well as a small-figure cycle of the *Labours of Hercules*. Probably dating from the reign of Claudius (*reg* AD 41–54), their very high quality reflects their official function in decorating the rear part of this public building in which the town's imperial cult ceremonies took place before the statues located there. The depiction of Hercules alludes not only to the town's foundation legend but also to the Romans' mythical origins in Arcadia and Troy; the picture of the liberator Theseus can be seen as a flattering allegory of the reigning emperor; and Chiron and Achilles represent restraint, in contrast to the immoderate Marsyas. Greek paintings from the Late Classical or Hellenistic periods seem to have served as models for these works. The College of Augustales contains two important Fourth Style paintings of Hercules, one either side of a lost statue. In *Hercules, Deianeira and Achelous* the hero is about to attack Achelous, who is carrying off Deianeira; in the *Apotheosis of Hercules* he is received into Olympus by Minerva and Juno. Mythological subjects are less frequent than at Pompeii. This is in part due to poorer conditions for preservation at Herculaneum, where pictures on upper wall areas have survived more often than the main compostitions in the centre of the lower zones—although those in the tablinum of the House of the Bicentenary, which depict *Mars and Venus* as an example of positive love, and *Pasiphaë with Daedalus and the Minotaur* as its antithesis, are well preserved. The long cryptoporticus of the House of the Stags contained more than 60 small pictures (pinakes) of erotic scenes, landscapes and still-lifes (12 *in situ*; 18 in Naples, Mus. Archeol. N.; the rest untraced or destr.). The architectural fantasies of the

Fourth Style, which often use the curtain motif, are extremely rich. Against their largely monochrome, often dark, backgrounds the attenuated architectures, highlighted in white, create a filigree effect that is flat rather than three-dimensional (examples in the House of the Mosaic Atrium and the House of the Stags), though the bombastic fantasies from the palaestra (Naples, Mus. Archeol. N.; only a few examples *in situ*) are an exception to this. Painted ceilings have survived only in rare cases, for example an early Fourth Style ceiling in the House of the Black Hall. The few surviving fragments of wall paintings in the House of the Papyri include significant remains of Second Style landscapes or still-lifes as well as of Fourth Style pictures. Workshops active in Herculaneum have not so far been shown to have worked in Pompeii as well.

BIBLIOGRAPHY

G. Cerulli Irelli: *Le pitture della Casa dell'Atrio a mosaico* (1971), III/i of *Monumenti della pittura antica scoperti in Italia* (Rome, 1936–)

M. Manni: *Le pitture della Casa del Colonnato Tuscanico* (1974), III/ii of *Monumenti della pittura antica scoperti in Italia* (Rome, 1936–)

H. Mielsch: 'Zur Deutung und Datierung der *Knöchelspielerinnen* des Alexandros', *Mitt. Dt. Archäol. Inst.: Röm. Abt.*, lxxxvi (1979), pp. 233–48

A. Allroggen-Bedel: 'Dokumente des 18. Jhs. zur Topographie von Herculaneum', *Cron. Ercolanesi*, xiii (1983), pp. 139–58

V. von Graeve: 'Marmorbilder aus Herculaneum und Pompeji', *Dialoghi Archeol.*, n.s. 2, iii/2 (1984), pp. 89–113

E. M. Moormann: 'Le pitture della Villa dei Papiri ad Ercolano', *Atti del XVII Congresso internazionale di papirologia: Napoli, 1984*, pp. 637–74

——: 'Die Wandmalereien in der Casa del Mobilio Carbonizzato in Herculaneum', *Cah. Archéol. Romande*, xliii (1987), pp. 127–34

Tran tam Tinh: *La Casa dei Cervi a Herculaneum* (Rome, 1988)

M. Manni: 'Per la storia della pittura ercolanese', *Cron. Ercolanesi*, xx (1990), pp. 129–43

A. Allroggen-Bedel: 'Lokalstile in der campanischen Wandmalerei', *Köln. Jb. Vor- & Frühgesch.*, xxiv (1991), pp. 35–41

W. Wohlmayr: 'Der hellenische Meister in Herculaneum', *Köln. Jb. Vor- & Frühgesch.*, xxiv (1991), pp. 43–9

G. Cerulli Irelli and others, eds: *La Peinture de Pompéi* (Paris, 1993), ii, pp. 209–36, figs 376–453

VOLKER MICHAEL STROCKA

V. Mosaics.

Mosaics and pavements at Herculaneum followed the same general development as at Pompeii (*see* POMPEII, §V) but have been less well studied. All the mosaics mentioned here are *in situ*. From the pre-Roman period decorated floors of *opus signinum* survive, such as the fine example in the Samnite House, with dolphins and palmettes in white tesserae around a circle of lozenges, as well as pavements of *crustae* (irregular pieces of coloured limestone in a cement setting) and irregular white chips. Pictorial mosaics in the Hellenistic tradition and polychrome geometric mosaics appear to have been lacking, though it is possible that some of the figured panels now in the Museo Archeologico Nazionale in Naples may come from Herculaneum.

The majority of the excavated houses have floors typical of the late 1st century BC and the 1st century AD. Most have black-and-white geometric designs, some are in *opus sectile* and some have fragments of marble in a setting of plain tesserae (often called *lithostroton*). The House of the Mosaic Atrium gives a good example of the range of types in use. Very rich *opus sectile* is found in the House of the Relief of Telephus, on both floors and walls, and in the

House of the Stags. In the city baths, beside several rooms with black-and-white all-over geometric designs, are two with black-and-white silhouette-style figured mosaics depicting a Triton surrounded by sea creatures. Interior details and highlights are marked by patches of white, recalling contemporary painting.

A few fountains and nymphaea with wall mosaics also survive. The most important is that in the House of Neptune and Amphitrite, dating from the last years of the city. The fountain niches are decorated with pumice, Egyptian blue frit and seashells; the wall surface of the fountain has mosaics of floral motifs, hunting scenes and scrolls on backgrounds of blue and green glass tesserae. Another wall of the same courtyard has a mosaic panel with Neptune and Amphitrite standing within a complex semi-architectural, semi-ornamental frame. Garden paintings adjoined it on either side. In the House of the Stags the pediment overlooking the garden is decorated with a mosaic depicting a frieze of erotes on seahorses, and a scroll with a head at the centre; the background is of blue glass, and shells border the frieze.

BIBLIOGRAPHY

A. Maiuri: *Ercolano: I nuovi scavi, 1927–58*, i (Rome, 1958)
G. Cerulli Irelli: *Le pitture della Casa dell'Atrio a mosaico* (1971), III/i of *Monumenti della pittura antica scoperta in Italia* (Rome, 1936–)
F. Sear: *Roman Wall and Vault Mosaics* (Heidelberg, 1977)

KATHERINE M. D. DUNBABIN

VI. Rediscovery.

Although Pompeii had been systematically plundered by survivors who returned after the eruption of Mt Vesuvius, the treasures at Herculaneum remained securely buried. The heavy rains accompanying the eruption resulted in a torrential flow of muddy lava that completely submerged the city. The plastic mass of mud created a matrix of the objects it enveloped, preserving them in almost perfect condition: bronze received a delicate patina, and marble was not calcined.

Herculaneum was accidentally discovered in 1709 by labourers deepening a well; little was done to exhume the city until 1738, when regular excavations were made. The first finds, several marble architectural members from the amphitheatre, were brought to the attention of Maurice, Prince d'ELBOEUF. Additional tunnelling produced several statues in excellent state. The extravagance of the Prince's way of life precluded him from keeping his finds. While he sent many works of art openly as presents to various countries, he secretly exported three marble statues of maidens, then known as the *Vestal Virgins*, to Vienna as a diplomatic gift for his brother Eugene, Prince of Savoy (from whose niece they were purchased in 1736 for Dresden by the Elector of Saxony, Frederick-Augustus II); two of them are still known by their traditional names, the *Grande Erculanèse* and *Petite Erculanèse* (*see* §III above). In 1738 Charles VII, King of Naples (*reg* 1734–59; *see* BOURBON, §II(4)), decided to build a new royal residence at Portici and commanded that the excavations at Herculaneum be resumed systematically under court control. Excavation at the amphitheatre—using a system of underground tunnels—not only yielded further architectural marbles but also bronze and marble sculptures; work continued there until 4 March 1780.

On 12 September 1739 the 'basilica' was discovered with some of the finest paintings yet recovered from antiquity (*see* §IV above); later two marble equestrian statues of M. Nonius Balbus were discovered in the same area. Across the western gully from Herculaneum the suburban Villa of the Papyri was discovered in June 1750; excavation continued there until February 1761, when noxious fumes in the tunnels forced the suspension of work. An important collection of bronze and marble sculptures of every size was recovered, including numerous busts of philosophers, poets and orators (many of them with inscriptions aiding the identification of objects in other collections), copies of famous Greek works and some excellent Roman portraits, as well as many graceful decorative pieces and fountain figures. The discovery of the *Seated Mercury* (see fig. 3 above), *Drunken Faun* and *Wrestlers* added to the growing renown of the finds.

Unlike the Prince d'Elboeuf, neither King Charles nor his son Ferdinand IV (*reg* 1759–1825) permitted any sales, and the Bourbons never sought to encourage wide popular knowledge of the sculpture collection. The security measures at Portici were extreme, and numerous visitors, from Charles de Brosses in 1739 onwards, described their difficulties in obtaining permission to see the antiquities; sketching and the taking of notes were prohibited. As a consequence the illustrations provided by Cochin II and Bellicard for their book on the antiquities of Herculaneum were made from memory, as were those in the *Recueil d'antiquités* (1752–67) of the Comte de CAYLUS. In 1752 Bayardi, the court antiquary, disappointed the learned world with his notoriously inept *Prodromo* and catalogue of the royal collection at Portici. Charles reacted by establishing the Accademia Ercolanese in 1755 under the direction of the Marchese Tanucci. Beginning in 1757 the Accademia issued a series of eight volumes entitled *Le antichità di Ercolano esposte*. At first the volumes were for presentation only, but after the failure to suppress Martyn and Lettice's partial translation the first five volumes were made available for sale. After 1789 Piroli issued cheap volumes with copies after the official plates, and the antique paintings became widely reproduced and adapted. Although the sculpture found at Herculaneum was more widely admired than the paintings, the inability to make good copies kept it from being as influential as the paintings.

Acting on the advice of Philipp Hackert (*see* HACKERT, (1)) in 1787, Ferdinand planned to combine his collections from Portici, Caserta and Capodimonte in a new museum at Naples in the Palazzo dei Vecchi Studi, originally designed as the viceregal stables, later altered and extended to serve the university and further transformed to fulfil its new function. With the approach of the French armies in 1805, Emma Hamilton directed the removal, through a subterranean passage to the shore, of the treasures still at Portici, which, with the court, were taken to Palermo under the protection of the British navy. On their return to Naples the Bourbons renamed the new museum the Museo Borbonico (22 February 1816). By 1822 the transfer of antiquities from Portici and Palermo was completed. Only after 1860, when the Museo Borbonico became the Museo Nazionale, did the most admired statues from Herculaneum and Pompeii begin to be reproduced and appreciated as extensively as those at Rome and Florence.

Explorations took place at Herculaneum in 1828–35, when the open method of excavation was adopted, and again in 1869–75, but they uncovered only a small part of the town. Excavations resumed on a greater and more systematic scale in 1927 and still continue.

BIBLIOGRAPHY

O. A. Bayardi: *Prodromo delle antichità di Ercolano* (Naples, 1752)

Comte de Caylus: *Recueil d'antiquités égyptiennes, étrusques, grecques, romaines et gauloises*, 7 vols (Paris, 1752–67)

C. N. Cochin and J. C. Bellicard: *Observations sur les antiquités de la ville d'Herculaneum* (Paris, 1754)

Le antichità di Ercolano esposte, Accademia Ercolanese, 8 vols (Naples, 1757–92)

J. J. Winckelmann: *Recueil de lettres . . . sur les découvertes faites à Herculanum, à Pompeii, à Stabia, à Casert, et à Rome* (Paris, 1784)

A. W. van Buren: *A Companion to the Study of Pompeii and Herculaneum* (Rome, 1938)

F. Haskell and N. Penny: *Taste and the Antique* (New Haven and London, 1981)

F. Bologna: 'The Rediscovery of Herculaneum and Pompeii in the Artistic Culture of Europe in the Eighteenth Century', *Rediscovering Pompeii* (exh. cat., New York, IBM Gal. Sci. & A., 1990), pp. 78–91

PETER J. HOLLIDAY

Herculia. *See* SZÉKESFEHÉRVÁR.

Herder, Johann Gottfried (*b* Mohrungen, 25 Aug 1744; *d* Weimar, 18 Dec 1803). German theorist. He was the most consistent and influential critic of German Enlightenment philosophy and aesthetic theory. His impeccable Enlightenment pedigree as a student of Kant at the University of Königsberg in the early 1760s and his acquaintance with Diderot and Jean le Rond d'Alembert during his visit to Paris in 1769 were combined with a friendship and sympathy for the person and works of Johann Georg Hamann and other professed opponents of the Enlightenment. His insight into the strengths and weaknesses of the Enlightenment enabled him to offer an alternative theoretical basis for the work of the younger *Sturm und Drang* writers of the 1770s, headed by Goethe. In 1776 he was appointed at Goethe's behest to the post of General Superintendent of the Lutheran Church in Weimar, where he remained until his death.

Although Herder published in several fields, ranging from the philosophy of language and epistemology to aesthetics and theology, all he wrote revolved around a critique of the ahistorical character of the German Enlightenment. His thought combines two main elements: the recognition that reason is grounded in sentiment, a position later described as 'metacritical'; and the perception that the grounding of reason is the product of a specific history, and cannot be understood apart from it.

Herder took from Alexander Gottlieb Baumgarten's *Aesthetica* (1750–58), a crucial early influence, the notion of the progressive development of the lower faculty of knowledge, and extended it into a full-scale philosophy of history. From Baumgarten's thought he derived the radical conclusion that the rational faculties not only developed out of the sensible, but that they represent a partial and imbalanced expression of them. This position underlies his prize essay 'Abhandlung über den Ursprung der Sprache' (1778), and the later *Metakritik* (1799) discussing Kant's *Kritik der reinen Vernunft* (1781), and *Kalligone*

(1800) discussing his *Kritik der Urteilskraft* (1790). Herder's *Metakritiken* proposed to 'go beyond' Kant's critiques, by tracing the history of the emergence of reason from the sensibility. This idea also characterizes his remarks on Enlightenment aesthetics. He questioned the ahistorical character of Moses Mendelssohn and Johann Georg Sulzer's theories of art, among others. The historicist view of art that Herder elaborated in a series of essays, mainly concerned with literature and painting, had several important implications. It extended the category of art to include folk art and non-European art, so including genres and artefacts not previously recognized as art. It also insisted on the importance of the social and political context for the creation and understanding of art.

These and other characteristics are apparent in Herder's most sustained work in the philosophy of the visual arts, *Plastik*, a tract on sculpture written in 1768–70 and published in 1778. A thinly veiled critique of Gotthold Ephraim Lessing's *Laokoön*, it relates the ahistoricism of Enlightenment theory to its privileging of visual representation over embodiment. (He subsequently related this dominance of the gaze to the dominance of the State over civil society; cf. Michel Foucault.) For example, the distinction in the *Laokoön* between poetry and painting assumes that the creation and enjoyment of art is contemplative: painting represents an object viewed in space, poetry an action viewed over time. Against this Herder insists that painting, as representation, must be distinguished from sculpture, as embodiment; that a work of sculpture—especially Greek sculpture—was not produced to be viewed from a single viewpoint, and is present in a way that exceeds vision. The work ends with some pointed comments directed against Lessing's reliance on reproductions of sculpture. Herder claims that a Greek statue cannot be appreciated through engravings or representations, but must be experienced as a three-dimensional object, and that this experience must also take into account the original cultic and political setting of the work.

Herder's comprehensive historicist critique of the Enlightenment was subsequently developed by Hegel and the Schlegel brothers. His distinction between sculpture and painting contributed to Hegel's formulation in the *Vorlesungen über die Aesthetik* (1832–40) of the distinction between classical and romantic art. Herder's metacritique brings into purview the primitive and folk art excluded by the classical, rational tradition, and shows the ways in which this tradition emerges from sources which it suppresses, suggesting further that this suppression be furthermore set within a historical and political framework.

WRITINGS

Kalligone (Leipzig, 1800; *R* Weimar, 1959, ed. H. Begenau)

B. Suphan, ed.: *Sämtliche Werke*, 33 vols (Berlin, 1877–1913)

U. Gaier, ed.: *Herder, fruehe Schriften* (1986)

BIBLIOGRAPHY

M. Wedel: *Herder als Kritiker* (Berlin, 1928)

W. Nufer: *Herders Ideen zur Verbindung von Poesie, Musik und Tanz* (Berlin, 1929)

A. Gillies: *Herder* (Oxford, 1945)

R. T. Clark: *Herder: His Life and Thought* (Berkeley and Los Angeles, 1955)

J. K. Fugate: *The Psychological Basis of Herder's Aesthetics* (The Hague, 1966)

F. Ostermann: *Die Idee des Schoepferischen in Herders Kalligone* (Berne and Munich, 1968)

G. Guenther and others: *Herder Bibliographie* (Weimar, 1978)

HOWARD CAYGILL

Herdman, Robert (*b* Rattray, Perthshire, 17 Sept 1829; *d* Edinburgh, 10 Jan 1888). Scottish painter. He attended the University of St Andrews before moving to Edinburgh in 1847 to study painting under Robert Scott Lauder at the Trustees' Academy. He travelled in Italy in 1855–6 but remained in Edinburgh after his return, rather than moving to London as did many of his colleagues. Like John Pettie and William Quiller Orchardson, he specialized in costume genre and between 1863 and 1878 produced a number of compositions based on Walter Scott's Waverley novels for the Royal Society for the Promotion of the Fine Arts in Edinburgh. Pettie and Orchardson tended to focus on the small dramas of ordinary life, even when set in the past, but Herdman generally sought to render the high drama of major historical events (e.g. *Execution of Mary Queen of Scots*, 1867; Glasgow, A.G. & Mus.). This brought him closer to the academic tradition of history painting, and he was much influenced by John Everett Millais's later work. He was, however, capable of psychological subtlety, as shown by *Interview between Effie Deans and her Sister in Prison* (1872; priv. col., see Errington, 1988, p. 22) and such portraits as *Sir Theodore Martin* (1876; London, N.P.G.). In later life he became interested in the Celtic Revival, as is evident from such paintings as *St Columba Rescuing a Captive* (1883; Perth, Tayside, Mus. & A.G.).

BIBLIOGRAPHY

J. Caw: *Scottish Painting Past and Present* (Edinburgh and London, 1908), pp. 174–6

D. Irwin and F. Irwin: *Scottish Painters at Home and Abroad, 1700–1900* (London, 1975)

Master Class: Robert Scott Lauder and his Pupils (exh. cat. by L. Errington, Edinburgh, N.G.; Aberdeen, A.G.; 1983)

L. Errington: *Robert Herdman, 1829–88*, Scottish Masters (Edinburgh, 1988)

DUNCAN MACMILLAN

Héré [de Corny], Emmanuel (*b* Nancy, 12 Oct 1705; *d* Lunéville, 2 Feb 1763). French architect. He was the son of Paul Héré (*d* 1733), a mason from the Tyrol who became Clerk of Works to Leopold, Duke of Lorraine (*reg* 1697–1729). He probably trained under his father and under the Court Architect Jean-Nicolas Jennesson (1686–1755) on the numerous royal and aristocratic building projects in Nancy, Lunéville and other places in Lorraine. Leopold's first architect was then Germain Boffrand, and Boffrand's style was to be the decisive influence on Héré. In 1736 Stanislav Leszczyński, the former king of Poland, became Lorraine's new head of state; two years later he named Héré his first architect, in preference to Jennesson. There was a successful marriage of minds between Stanislav and Héré, with Stanislav fully involving himself in decisions on architectural design. Héré's career was spent almost entirely in his service, and his works can be divided into three groups: the new buildings, alterations and reconstructions carried out at the châteaux near Nancy (which Stanislav had inherited from Leopold) between 1737 and 1750, including their gardens and *fabriques*; various designs and building works for churches, monasteries and hospitals in the 1740s; and the replanning of

the centre of Nancy in the 1750s. Héré was ennobled by Louis XV in 1752.

Héré's first new building for Stanislav was the kiosk (1737; destr.) in the gardens of the château at Lunéville (for illustration *see* LUNÉVILLE), followed by his first major commission, Notre-Dame de Bonsecours (1738–41) in Nancy, a funerary and thanksgiving church for Stanislav and his family. This church has a tall west front with a single tower and an applied portico of four giant columns, the latter salvaged from Boffrand's château of Malgrange, which had never been completed. Notre-Dame's richly stuccoed interior recalls southern German Baroque churches rather than French models. Héré made only minor alterations to the château at Lunéville built by Boffrand from 1708, but at Malgrange he destroyed Boffrand's old and incomplete château of 1712–15, building a new complex to replace it (1739–40; destr.). This new pleasure palace was a loosely composed ensemble, having a principal building faced with faience tiles and flanked by colonnades and covered walkways. At Commercy after 1747 Héré added a kiosk (destr.) to the gardens and related them more closely to the palace. He also designed three small pavilions (destr.) as annexes to Lunéville, as well as the *galerie* (summer dining-room) at the hunting-lodge of Einville (destr.) and the *ménagerie* (small country estate) at Jolivet (destr.).

Héré's garden buildings at Lunéville and Commercy have an oriental appearance owing to their curving roofs. At least as unusual were the salon at Chanteheux (a twice recessed cube; destr.), the Pavillon de la Cascade at Lunéville (destr.) and the Pavillon Royal at Commercy (destr.). These buildings were characterized by groupings of round and segmentally arched openings. In the mixture of materials their interior decoration far exceeded in richness and colour the established norm in France. In addition, there were many mirrors and lights, as well as the play of water from fountains, cascades and jets—most notably from the Colonnade Hydraulique on a bridge at Commercy (destr.), where water spilt down columns, and the kiosk, the windows of which were veiled by fine streams. Stanislav had at his disposal a number of excellent hydraulic engineers responsible for the creation of these marvels, among them François Richard; the largest undertaking of this kind was the Théâtre d'Automates du Rocher (1742; destr.) below the garden terrace at Lunéville. This was a complete miniature landscape and village inhabited by water-powered automata in the forms of people and animals. It is difficult to assess how far Héré was involved in planning the waterworks at these places, for the ideas came largely from Stanislav himself. This also applies to the religious motifs to be found in the gardens (hermitages at Lunéville; the mission cross with the Procession to Calvary and miniature monastery at Malgrange; all destr.) and to the division of gardens into small units, for example at Lunéville in the grounds lying between the ducal apartments and the kiosk. *Singularité, surprendre, enchanter, beaux rêves* were the words used by contemporary critics for these light and perishable structures.

Héré's replanning of the centre of Nancy from 1752 came about in response to a long-held wish to unite the old and new towns, which were separated by fortifications (*see* NANCY, §1). At the south-east end of the main axis,

Emmanuel Héré: Hôtel de Ville, Place Stanislas, Nancy, 1752–6

which links the two parts of the city, on the broad side of the Place Royale (now Place Stanislas) stands the Hôtel de Ville (see fig.). Two side streets cut through the centres of the narrow sides of the square on the axis of the statue of *Louis XV*. The curved corners are defined with triumphal arches in wrought iron by Jean Lamour (1698–1771; *see* NANCY, fig. 2). Opposite the Hôtel de Ville are low, arcaded blocks, flanking the Arc de Triomphe, which leads to the Place de la Carrière with long, uniformly treated façades and a central tree-lined avenue. This widens into the Hemicycle where the Intendance acts as a counterpoint to the Hôtel de Ville. The formal arrangement at Nancy and the concentration of public buildings—which includes the Hôtel de Ville, law courts, theatre, academy and stock exchange—were inspired by submissions to the competition in Paris in 1748 for a Place Royale (now Place de la Concorde) in Nancy. Dedicated to Louis XV, the Place Royale determined the further urbanization of the city and influenced other royal squares built soon after (e.g. Reims, 1758, and Antoine-Mathieu Le Carpentier's unexecuted designs of 1756 for Rouen). The pleasing effect is due to the alternation of open and closed vistas and of high and low components, the uniform façades of the square, the triumphal arches and colonnades, decorative fountains and ironwork and the balustrades and statues.

Boffrand's compositional modes provided Héré with the basis for his own monumental designs. Héré's use of colonnades connecting or fronting buildings, as at Malgrange, derives from Boffrand's projects for Lunéville and Malgrange, and the cubic pavilion with a central hall (1740; destr.) at Chantheux from Boffrand's Croismare. Héré, however, achieved lighter and more decorative effects by means of large openings, which break up the solidity of the wall with sculptural embellishments. Héré's less monumental pleasure palaces owe something to Boffrand's Pavillon Rohan at Saint-Ouen and to models from the engraved designs by Charles-Etienne Briseux and Jacques-François Blondel; and he took ideas from smaller buildings in and around Versailles, such as the Grand Trianon, and

from Marly. In addition to the essentially French repertory of forms, Héré had an affinity with, and was probably influenced by, the Baroque of southern Germany, Austria and Saxony. One can find many points of reference in his architecture with the ensemble of the Zwinger in Dresden, and there is the obvious pleasure taken in exuberant decoration and colour—the interiors of the pleasure palaces and Notre-Dame de Bonsecours, for example—as well as a taste for playfulness, illusionism and the theatrical. Examples of this are the spires and organ case at St Jacques (1743–7; for illustration of the interior *see* HALL CHURCH, fig. 2), Lunéville, the high altar of the Carmelite church (1739; destr.) at Lunéville and the staircase (altered in 1862) of the Hôtel de Ville at Nancy. Héré was not an inventor of forms. He had little sensibility for mass and plasticity; he loosely assembled similarly shaped elements into light, decorated surfaces, although his collaboration with others, such as the ironworker Lamour, was always a decisive factor. Héré possessed a limited but fortuitous genius for transforming available forms into new compositions.

WRITINGS

Recueil des plans, élévations et coupes . . . des châteaux, jardins et dépendances que le roy de Pologne occupe en Lorraine, i (Paris, 1752), ii (Lunéville, 1762)
Plans et élévations de la Place Royale de Nancy (Paris, 1753)

BIBLIOGRAPHY

P. Boyé: *Les Châteaux du roi Stanislas en Lorraine* (Nancy, 1910)
A. E. Brinckmann: *Die Baukunst des 17. und 18. Jahrhunderts: I. Romanische Länder* (Berlin, 1919, rev. 4/1922)
L. Hautecoeur: *Architecture classique*, iii (1950)
H. Lavedan: 'La Place Royale de Nancy et son influence', *Vie Urb.* (1952), pp. 250–62
P. Marot: *Emmanuel Héré (1705–1763): Biographie du premier architecte du roi Stanislas d'après les notes de Pierre Boyé* (Nancy, 1954)
——: *La Place Royale de Nancy: Image de la réunion de la Lorraine à la France* (Nancy, 1966)
W. Graf Kalnein and M. Levey: *Art and Architecture of the Eighteenth Century in France*, Pelican Hist. A. (Harmondsworth, 1972), pp. 276–8
J. Ostrowski: 'Le Rocher: Théâtre d'automates du roi Stanislas à Lunéville', *Pays Lorrain*, liii (1972), pp. 175–84
——: 'Nurt egzotyczny w architekturze Stanislawa Leszczyńskiego w Lotaryng' [The exotic trend in the architecture of Stanislav Lezczyński in Lorraine], *Kwart. Arkhit. & Urb.*, xvii (1972), pp. 161–76

J. Rau, Gräfin von der Schulenburg: *Emmanuel Héré: Premier architecte von Stanislav Leszczyński in Lotharingen (1705–1763)* (Berlin, 1973)

J. Ostrowski: 'Temple de plaisir: Niezwykły Pałac Stanisława Leszczyńskiego w Chanteheux' [Temple de plaisir: the extraordinary palace of Stanislas Lezczyński in Chanteheux], *Kwart. Arkhit. & Urb.*, xix (1974), pp. 293–316

——: 'L'Eglise Notre-Dame de Bonsecours à Nancy', *Pays Lorrain*, lvi (1975), pp. 26–37

I. Dennerlein: *Die Gartenkunst des Régence und des Rokoko in Frankreich* (Worms, 1981)

A. France-Lanord: *Emmanuel Héré: Architecte du roi Stanislas* (Nancy, 1984)

JÖRG GARMS

Hereford, Walter of. *See* WALTER OF HEREFORD.

Herend Ceramics Factory. Hungarian ceramics factory. It was established by Vince Stingl as a stoneware workshop before 1825, but by 1826 it was producing porcelain. In 1840 the porcelain painter Móric Farkasházi-Fischer (1799/1800–1880) bought the workshop and developed it into a factory. The early wares included goods for everyday use and clearly showed the influence of the Vienna and Meissen porcelain factories. The considerable competition from mass-produced Czechoslovak wares forced the factory to produce fine merchandise. Herend became most famous for reproducing 18th-century East Asian and European porcelain. The factory was particularly successful at the international exhibitions, and, at the Great Exhibition of 1851 in London, Queen Victoria ordered a dinner service decorated with butterflies and flowers, which became known as the 'Victoria' design. Under the management of Farkasházi-Fischer's sons the factory declined, and in 1884 it became a public company. Farkasházi-Fischer's grandson Jenö Farkasházi-Fischer, who became the managing director in 1896, introduced the Art Nouveau style and *pâte-sur-pâte* decoration. He also produced wares inspired by Hungarian folk art. Between 1918 and 1939 the factory also produced figures. The factory continued to produce wares throughout the 20th century using traditional techniques.

BIBLIOGRAPHY

C. Boncz and K. Gink: *Herend China* (Budapest, 1962)

G. Sikota: *Herendi porcelán* (Budapest, 1977)

FERENC BATÁRI

Herigoyen, Emanuel Joseph von (*b* Belas, nr Lisbon, 4 Nov 1746; *d* Munich, 27 July 1817). Portuguese architect, active in Germany. After five years' service in the Portuguese Navy, Herigoyen went in 1767 to Paris, where he studied architecture and mathematics for two years. From 1769 to 1772 he held various posts in Vienna, and in 1778 he obtained an engineer's commission in the army of the Electorate of Mainz. For the Elector Friedrich Carl Joseph von Erthal (*reg* 1774–1802) he laid out the grounds at Schönbusch, near Aschaffenburg, in the English landscape manner and set a cubic pavilion (1778–9), designed in an early Neo-classical style with some Baroque elements, between the lake and the canal. In Aschaffenburg itself, the second Residenz town, Herigoyen worked on the interior of the Renaissance castle, endowing the east wing with a central portal and a fine staircase. He was also responsible for churches at Esselbach (1779) and Sulzbach am Main (1786).

In 1789 Herigoyen went on a study tour to Belgium, the Netherlands and England. He continued his army career in garrison at Mainz and was promoted to Lieutenant-Colonel in 1803. The following year Carl Theodor von Dalberg (*reg* 1802–3), von Erthal's successor, moved to Regensburg and took Herigoyen with him. In Regensburg, Herigoyen built the Civic Theatre (1804; destr. by fire 1849 and rebuilt differently), an assembly hall, the French Embassy and the Kepler Memorial (1808) in the shape of a circular temple. In 1810 Regensburg became Bavarian, and Herigoyen was made Chief Surveyor of Buildings at Munich by King Maximilian I Joseph (*reg* 1806–25). As such, he was mostly concerned with administration and planning policy. His most important architectural works in Munich were the Volkstheater (destr. 1953) on the Isartorplatz and the Greek Revival entrance gate to the Old Botanical Gardens (1812). Here, a square opening between blocks of rusticated masonry is flanked on each façade by a pair of Doric columns without responds, carrying an architrave surmounted by an attic bearing a dedicatory inscription. Another Neo-classical façade is displayed by the Palais Montgelas (1810–11) on the Promenadenplatz, now refitted internally as a hotel. Two superimposed orders of Corinthian pilasters articulate the elevation above a rusticated base in a manner characteristic of the Louis XVI Classic Revival style in France, as popularized in François de Neufforge's *Recueil élémentaire d'architecture* (1757–68), a volume of designs that Herigoyen consulted, together with the neo-Palladian *Lectures on Architecture* (1734) by Robert Morris. The different classicist trends presented in these writings influenced Herigoyen deeply, although not to the exclusion of occasional Baroque manifestations.

BIBLIOGRAPHY

H. Reidel: *Emanuel Joseph von Herigoyen* (Munich and Zurich, 1982)

HERMANN REIDEL

Hering, Loy (*b* Kaufbeuren, *c.* 1485; *d* Eichstätt, after 1 June 1554). German sculptor. The son of Michael Hering (*fl* 1460–90), a goldsmith from Kaufbeuren, he was one of Germany's most productive sculptors in the earlier 16th century. On 15 April 1499 Loy was registered as a pupil of Augsburg sculptor Hans Beierlein and is next mentioned in 1511 and 1512 as paying taxes in Augsburg and living in the house of sculptor Jacob Murmann. Hering moved to Eichstätt probably in 1512 and definitely by 1515, when he was documented as working on an altar in the Willibald choir of the cathedral. Except for brief trips to Augsburg, Neuburg and other nearby towns, Hering remained in Eichstätt. He served on the inner and outer city councils (1519, 1522), in the tax office, and in 1523 and 1533 was one of the town's four mayors.

Hering was an unusually prolific sculptor. Reindl (1977) attributes 133 projects to Loy and his workshop. Most were made for churches in Eichstätt or its diocese; however, his carvings were also created for clients in Augsburg, Boppard am Rhein, Heilsbronn Monastery, the cathedrals of Bamberg, Speyer and Würzburg, and the Austrian cities of Schwaz and Vienna, among others. The majority of these are monuments and altars carved in fine-grain Solnhofen limestone. The quality varies depending on the importance of the commission and the level of workshop involvement. Hering frequently followed a basic formula: the central relief of a biblical scene, sometimes with free-standing kneeling patrons, surrounded by a Renaissance-style architectural frame with an inscription tablet at the bottom and, in many examples, a coat of arms in the pediment. As with other contemporaries, Loy often borrowed the compositions for his reliefs from prints. An extreme example is the Wolfstein Altar (1519–20; Eichstätt Cathedral), which copied Dürer's woodcut of the *Death and Coronation of the Virgin* (1511; Bartsch 94) for the shrine carving and Martin Schongauer's engraving of *St John on Patmos* (*c.* 1475; B. 55) for the relief in the rounded pediment. Nevertheless, the altar is a highly original creation. Two polychromed wooden angels sit on top of the detached composite columns. The sculptor has augmented the whitish limestone with colour highlights for the figures and painted red-veined marble patterns for the background of the two reliefs and the flanking pilasters.

Of the four projects attributed to Loy while he was still living in Augsburg, the most significant is the Hörwarth Altar (1511–12) for the Hörwarth family's chapel in the newly built Georgskirche. Although only the central statue survives (a stone *Christ the Saviour*, h. 2 m, in a shallow niche), the overall composition was copied, with minor alterations, in Hieronymus Höpfer's 1521 etching (B. 22). It shows an elaborate frame with Christ in the centre, putti standing atop flanking composite columns, four half-length figures of saints set within scalloped niches and Italianate decorative motifs seemingly inspired by Venetian models. If the dating is correct then the Hörwarth Altar was among the earliest Renaissance sculptural projects in Germany. The semi-nude body and general pose of Christ may have been influenced by an antique Roman *Mercury* relief (Augsburg, Röm. Mus.) that was discovered and displayed in the cloister of SS Ulrich and Afra, Augsburg, *c.* 1500. The elongated face and body of Christ as well as the linearity of the heavy cloak still retain the Late Gothic influence of Beierlein.

With at least eight major sculptors already active in Augsburg, Hering moved to Eichstätt perhaps as early as 1512. Beierlein, who had worked there previously for Bishop Gabriel von Eyb (1496–1535), may have provided the necessary introductions for his pupil. The Bishop put Hering to work *c.* 1514 on a coat of arms for the episcopal residence, and by 1520 on an elaborate monument for the Bishop in Eichstätt Cathedral. The life-size statue of *Gabriel von Eyb*, which stands within a shell niche and a Renaissance frame, clearly recalls the Hörwarth Altar. Hering later carved the Bishop's tombstone. However, he may have been called to Eichstätt originally to make the monument to *St Willibald*. In 1512 von Eyb initiated the project to honour the first bishop of Eichstätt with a huge shrine set at the entrance to the Willibald or western choir. The over life-size seated statue of *St Willibald* (see fig.), a symbol of the bishopric's age and prestige, is one of the finest sculptures in 16th-century Germany. According to an account of 1515, Hering carved two statues for the altar that was behind the monument. Although Schädler (1975) attributes the figure of *St Willibald* and a *Crucifixion* group that once stood on top of the monument to Gregor Erhart and his workshop, the style of the saint seems closer to Hering's sculpture. The fleshy face of St Willibald

Loy Hering: *St Willibald*, limestone, over life-size, *c.* 1512–15 (Eichstätt Cathedral); frame is an 18th-century replacement

with its wrinkles and benign expression has a strongly realistic quality, analogous to the slightly less modelled and detailed portraits of *Gabriel von Eyb* and of *Bishop Georg III of Bamberg* (1518–20; Bamberg Cathedral). In addition, the drapery of *Bishop Georg* is similar to that of the *St Willibald* monument. It may be inferred that Hering's exceptional efforts for this important commission and the success of subsequent projects caused his prestige to soar in the following years as public offices and an ever-increasing number of commissions were bestowed upon him. Erhart, on the other hand, had no documented ties with Eichstätt before, during or after the erection of the *St Willibald* monument.

Hering's most inventive and technically demanding sculptures were made before the mid-1520s. The monument to *Bernhard Arzt* (*c.* 1517; Eichstätt Cathedral) includes a *sacra conversazione* with almost fully rounded figures; the *Wetzhausen-Seckendorf* monument (1519/20; Eichstätt Cathedral), by contrast, includes an illusionistically convincing low relief of the *Agony in the Garden*. Like Hans Daucher and other contemporary Augsburg sculptors, Hering also made small-scale reliefs intended for sophisticated collectors. His limestone *Garden of Love* (*c.* 1525; Berlin, Gemäldegal.), one of his rare secular scenes, includes a cartellino with his initials and a picture of a herring. His *Rhea Silvia* (1532–5; London, V&A; numerous replicas and bronze copies exist) is particularly attractive, with a fine rendering of the nude.

Loy Hering and his workshop continued to be active, though working increasingly to formula, into the early 1550s. His sons, Thomas (Doman) Hering (*c.* ?1510–49) and Martin Hering (1515–60), were accomplished sculptors. Thomas was active in Munich and Landshut where he was court sculptor to Ludwig X, Duke of Bavaria, from 1540. His finest carvings include the *Hercules* roundels and chimney reliefs (1541) in the Italian Hall of Ludwig's Stadtresidenz in Landshut, as well as the limestone monogrammed relief of the *Judgement of Paris* (*c.* 1535) and the limestone relief portrait of *Emperor Charles V* (1532; both Berlin, Gemäldegal.). Thomas was more adept than his father in his representations of nudes and of figures in action. Martin worked for Ottheinrich, Count Palatine, in Neuburg (*c.* 1535–42). He lived briefly in Munich in 1543 before returning permanently to Eichstätt. His finest sculptures are the red marble hunting scene (1535–40) on the building inscription plaque of Ottheinrich's hunting-lodge at Grünau and the *Crucifixion* altar (1540–42) in the palace chapel at Neuburg. Back in Eichstätt, Martin collaborated with his father on such work as the monument to *Johannes von Stain* (1543; Eichstätt Cathedral) and after 1554 inherited the family shop.

BIBLIOGRAPHY

F. Mader: *Loy Hering: Ein Beitrag zur Geschichte der deutschen Plastik des XVI. Jahrhunderts* (Munich, 1905)

P. Cannon-Brookes: 'Loy Hering and the Monogrammist DH', *Apollo*, xciv (1971), pp. 46–9

P. Reindl: 'Loy Herings Epitaph in Hänn: Munden als Typus eines süddeutschen Renaissance-Epitaphs', *Niederdt. Beitr. Kstgesch.*, x (1971), pp. 143–87

V. Liedke: 'Zwei unbekannte Werke des Eichstätter Bildhauers Loy Hering', *A. Bavar.*, i (1973), pp. 84–9

W. A. Bulst: 'Der "Italienische Saal" der Landshuter Stadtresidenz und sein Darstellungsprogramm', *Münch. Jb. Bild. Kst.*, xxvi (1975), pp. 123–76

A. Schädler: 'Das Eichstätter Willibalddenkmal und Gregor Erhart', *Münch. Jb. Bild. Kst.*, xxvi (1975), pp. 65–88 [a highly original article questioning the attrib. of the *Willibald* monument to Hering]

P. Reindl: *Loy Hering: Zur Rezeption der Renaissance in Süddeutschland* (Basle, 1977) [superb monograph with critical commentary on Schädler's article]

Der Mensch um 1500 (exh. cat., Berlin, Staatl. Museen Preuss. Kultbes., 1977), pp. 68–71, 126–7, 138–42

J. C. Hutchison: *Early German Artists*, 8 [VI/i] of *The Illustrated Bartsch*, ed. W. L. Strauss (New York, 1978–)

W. L. Strauss: *Sixteenth-century German Artists*, 10 [VII/ii] of *The Illustrated Bartsch*, ed. W. L. Strauss (New York, 1978–)

Die Renaissance im deutschen Südwesten, 2 vols (exh. cat., Heidelberg, Schloss, 1986), ii, pp. 550–52

J. C. Smith: *German Sculpture of the Later Renaissance, c. 1520–1580: Art in an Age of Uncertainty* (Princeton, 1994), pp. 51–2, 54, 57–9, 61, 128–9, 139–42, 247–51, 340–41, 375–7

JEFFREY CHIPPS SMITH

Heriot, George (*b* Haddington, Lothian, 1759; *d* London, 22 July 1839). Scottish painter, active in Canada. His artistic training began in Edinburgh and continued under Paul Sandby at the Royal Military Academy, Woolwich, London. In 1792 Heriot was posted to the garrison at Quebec as an ordnance clerk. A career in the colonial service afforded him the opportunity to travel and paint widely in Upper and Lower Canada, especially after he was appointed Deputy Postmaster General of British North America in 1800.

Heriot's sketchbooks (Montreal, McGill U., McCord Mus.) reveal a keen topographical sense balanced by a poetic use of idealization. His large 'finished' watercolours, such as *Lake St Charles near Quebec* (*c.* 1801; Ottawa, N.G.), are often masterpieces of the genre. This example of the picturesque landscape style is generalized to the extent that it looks like a European view. Many of Heriot's less formal sketches, on the other hand, reflect the specificity of the Canadian landscape and culture and are valued as both aesthetic and historical artefacts.

Heriot is a central artist in the history of pre-Confederation Canada. An amateur watercolourist of considerable skill, he applied the picturesque landscape theory and technique that he had learnt in England to the scenery of the Canadas from 1792 until 1816, when he returned to Britain. Heriot is also remembered for his *History of Canada from its First Discovery* (London, 1804) and for one of the earliest picturesque travel books executed in North America, *Travels through the Canadas* (2 vols; London, 1807).

BIBLIOGRAPHY

G. Finley: *George Heriot: Postmaster-painter of the Canadas* (Toronto, 1983)

MARK A. CHEETHAM

Heritage. Term applied broadly to whatever of the past is considered to hold cultural significance; closer definition has become contentious in the late 20th century. Architecture, the fine and applied arts, and objects of archaeological interest are frequently the physical objects of heritage (literature, academic learning, music etc being other aspects), although by no means is every building or work of art regarded as significant. Exactly what is deemed part of heritage and thus worthy of preservation depends on prevailing attitudes to art and the art market, as well as notions of statehood and cultural history, and other issues regarding ownership, such as the public right of access to a particular work. The role of museums and the problems of looting form part of these issues.

Since the mid-20th century the European use of the word 'heritage' has taken on greater overtones of 'nationhood' than before: heritage is not an issue merely of preserving works, but of keeping them within the borders of the country of origin and acknowledging them as part of the nation's culture. This concept does not appear to have been so strongly formed in the past in Europe, although the basic sentiment in heritage—that artefacts can have a historic, cultural value—can be traced back over millennia. The acquisition of art as a device of power and empire-building exemplifies the sentiment. Victorious Roman armies took booty as a kind of status symbol: the Emperor Titus, for example, returned from Jerusalem with the treasures of the Second Temple. From the Renaissance onwards, the acquisitiveness of collectors and patrons, particularly for Italian works of art, started to clash with emerging feelings of nationalism and cultural identification. Italians' attitudes to their own heritage varied. Pope Pius V announced in 1566 that he would dispose of the Holy See's collection of antique sculpture—such pagan works were felt to be inappropriate for the Roman Catholic Church. The reaction was a mixed one of alarm and excitement. Minor pieces were disposed of to the Holy Roman Emperor, the Medici and the king of Spain. The European nobility were always eager to buy, and from the 16th century those on the Grand Tour (particularly Englishmen) removed large numbers of works from Italy, although they did not succeed in gaining any of the most highly esteemed Classical marbles. Napoleon's looting of Italy in the early 19th century was done under the cloak of treaties, and certain rules were observed: private collections were not touched and churches were treated carefully.

A new factor emerged in the late 19th century, the effects of which were to help shape modern notions of heritage. The Americans had little art and lots of money; the Europeans had plenty of art and wanted money. In California, Hearst Castle and its contents stand as testimony to the thriving trade that resulted. But the trade aroused resentment in Europe. During World War II the Nazis plundered the art of the occupied countries, although there was comparatively little outcry compared to that against US trade. After World War II, however, increasing attention was paid to issues of heritage in the Western world. Italy banned exports of works of art, and many other countries imposed tight controls.

In the late 20th century attitudes to heritage vary around the world. Countries in which it is treated as a serious issue include Japan and China. The Japanese have taken an interest in their heritage since the late 19th century, but the interest quickened after World War II, perhaps because of the huge losses that the country suffered from atomic bombs. Legal protection for cultural objects includes a system of controls on exports; it is almost impossible to export legally certain significant objects. There is also a special category of Living National Treasures to honour great cultural achievements. These treasures include such practising artists as Osamu Suzuki, a ceramic artist working in the tradition of Shino ceramics, and Kako Moriguchi, a textile artist using the Yuzen tradition of dyeing. Many objects of Japanese origin are bought back from the countries to which they were exported, the reverse of the flow of art from Europe to the USA. The Japanese traditionally revere age and thus until the late 20th century they honoured only the earlier periods of their art history. Art traditions such as *netsuke* (toggles) and *inrō* (small containers) were admired more in the West than in Japan up to this time.

China's ancient heritage suffered heavily due to factors ranging from the acquisition of objects by Western nations in the 19th century to the widespread destruction of art during the Cultural Revolution of the 1960s. Unsupervised and unscientific excavations after the 1960s also resulted in the loss of works to the nation. The pre-Ming ceramics, jade and archaic bronzes from these excavations are of interest to international specialists rather than lay collectors. In the late 20th century the Chinese government felt strongly enough about the country's heritage to ban exports of works of art and impose the death penalty for smugglers.

Countries such as Turkey, Israel and Mexico have come to attach great importance to the past because it is closely linked to strongly formed sentiments of nationalism. Artefacts can prove a continuing link between the land and the people: the Dead Sea Scrolls (Jerusalem, Israel Mus.) are held in reverence by Israel, and a significant Jewish site is the fortress of Masada, where Jewish rebels made their last stand against the Roman army in AD 73. Nationalistic sentiments in Turkey are in direct conflict with the ongoing pillaging of its archaeological wealth.

By contrast, the USA has no laws controlling the export of works of art. The word 'heritage' does, however, have special overtones, concerned not so much with preserving physical objects from the past as with celebrating political and historic events of special importance to the nation: thus the 'Heritage Foundation' is an organization with a conservative political agenda. Local history societies and preservation groups abound, and *ad hoc* groups spring up to preserve individual building works, such as a covered bridge. American preservation of heritage is distinctive in two ways. First there is the system of 'landmarking', the legal declaration that a building is a landmark and should be preserved; this system often clashes with the interests of the owners, as when a downtown church with a small congregation, of the greatest interest to the real-estate developer, is declared a landmark. The other feature is the work of the National Park Services, which is federally run. The NPS is responsible for such heritage features as Stanford White's Vanderbilt Mansion at the town of Hyde Park, NY, as well as the natural Yellowstone and Yosemite national parks.

The difficulty of the issue of heritage was discussed in the first annual report of Britain's National Heritage Memorial Fund, established in 1980 by the government. The report starts by explaining that the trustees had asked themselves how they might define 'the national heritage', but they had concluded this was not possible: 'We could no more define the national heritage than we could define, say, beauty or art'. However, the trustees went on to say that certain works of art, created by such British artists as Turner, Constable, Henry Moore and Barbara Hepworth, were clearly part of British heritage, as were such buildings as Chatsworth House and Edinburgh Castle. 'But beyond that, there was less assurance. So we decided to let the national heritage define itself. We awaited requests for assistance from those who believed they had a part of the national heritage worth saving.' As a result of this approach the National Heritage Memorial Fund had the opportunity to assess individual works ranging from portraits by Reynolds to the peal of bells at Durham Cathedral and seaside theatres, and to conclude that the national heritage of Britain is remarkably rich. The report states that Britain's 'potential for enjoyment must be maintained, and its economic value in attracting tourists . . . must be appreciated and developed'. A breakdown of the National Heritage Memorial Fund's financial aid for different categories of heritage in its first nine years reveals that the highest percentage of the budget was devoted to works of art and other museum objects, followed closely by money spent on buildings. Other needs—such as land of scenic or scientific interest, industrial, transport and maritime history, and manuscripts and archives—took a lower priority.

Any nation's heritage, in its physical and tangible senses, is under threat from many angles. Intensive farming and tax regimes that force the break-up of collections are some of the more unusual factors blamed for the loss of heritage. The illegal excavation of archaeological sites and the smuggling of objects pose a greater threat, because these things are closely connected with and dependent on the market-place. Generally, the price of antiquities, antiques and works of art goes up steadily, or sometimes dramatically. This increase in value encourages the looting of archaeological sites. Museums demonstrate excellent preservation facilities and represent the best public access to art, but their international collections sometimes contain looted objects, whether purchased unwittingly or otherwise. Museums have been criticized from all angles; the Egyptologist Flinders Petrie described them as charnelhouses of murdered evidence, and in the early 20th century Henry James was referring to the Metropolitan Museum of Art when he suggested that 'Acquisition—acquisition if need be on the highest terms—may, during the years to come, bask here as in a climate it has never before enjoyed'. There was money in the air, he wrote, 'for all the most exquisite things, except creation, which was to be off the scene altogether' (see Mayer).

The concern of individual countries over the loss of objects not by destruction but by their export to other countries is well illustrated by two contrasting pressure groups working in Britain in the 1990s. 'Save Britain's Heritage' is concerned with buildings of architectural merit and campaigns against the developer's bulldozer, the 'philistine' owner's indifference, and everyone's negligence. 'Heritage in Danger' is mostly concerned with paintings and other objects that are 'of museum quality' and in danger of being exported. However, the concentrated attention on the 'dangers' of export brought about a counter-reaction during the late 1980s in Britain. The National Heritage Memorial Fund summed up its thoughts on the matter, suggesting that it may be better to save 'land and buildings that are at risk of development or demolition and their heritage value being lost for ever' than to keep 'a £10 million painting that will be cherished and protected wherever it goes'.

The late 20th-century preoccupation with heritage can be seen in the commercialization of nostalgia. The more blatant forms of this have been deplored by many, even if commercial success runs alongside purposes of education and raising awareness. In Britain, reconstructions of old villages or settlements, such as the Jorvik Centre in York, which is on the site of a Viking settlement, attract adverse comment as well as praise. In addition, Hewison suggested that a fondness for nostalgia has blinded people to the unpleasant aspects of the past.

BIBLIOGRAPHY
K. E. Mayer: *The Plundered Past: The Traffic in Art Treasures* (London, 1977)
First Annual Report of the National Heritage Memorial Fund (London, 1980–81)
F. Haskell and N. Penny: *Taste and the Antique* (New Haven and London, 1981)
R. Hewison: *The Heritage Industry* (London, 1987)
Ninth Annual Report of the National Heritage Memorial Fund (London, 1988–9)
G. Darley: 'History as Bunk', *Financial Times* (2 Dec 1989)

DONALD WINTERSGILL

Herkomer, Sir **Hubert von** (*b* Waal, Bavaria, 26 May 1849; *d* Budleigh Salterton, Devon, 31 March 1914). English painter, illustrator, printmaker, stage designer, film maker, writer and teacher of German birth. He was the only child of Lorenz Herkomer (*d* 1887), a wood-carver, and Josephine (née Niggl), an accomplished pianist and music teacher. They left Bavaria for the USA in 1851 and lived briefly in Cleveland, OH, before settling in Southampton, England, in 1857.

Herkomer received his first art instruction from his father and from 1864 to 1865 he attended the Southampton School of Art. Later he often criticized the crippling academic methods to which he was exposed as a student. In 1865 he briefly attended the Munich Academy and spent the summer terms of 1866 and 1867 at the South Kensington Art School in London, where he found the teaching 'aimless and undirected'. With the encouragement of his fellow student Luke Fildes, Herkomer took up black-and-white illustration; his first wood-engraving appeared in *Good Words* in November 1869, and in 1870 his illustrations, which often depicted poverty and distress, began to appear regularly in the *Graphic*. These animated and expressive engravings profoundly influenced the art of van Gogh, who collected them and frequently mentioned Herkomer's work in his letters.

Herkomer exhibited annually at the Royal Academy, London, from 1869. The *Last Muster: Sunday at the Royal Hospital, Chelsea* (exh. RA 1875; Port Sunlight, Lady Lever A.G.) is based on his wood-engraving which had appeared in the *Graphic* (18 Feb 1871) as *Sunday at Chelsea Hospital*. Its depiction of a group of Chelsea pensioners seated at a service in the Chelsea Hospital chapel was admired for its touching motif and boldly realistic style. The painting was phenomenally successful and assured the artist a lasting fame.

Herkomer painted a number of pictures that revealed his sympathy for the poor and disadvantaged, a characteristic fostered in part by his own humble origins. Among them are *Eventide: A Scene in the Westminster Union* (exh. RA 1878; Liverpool, Walker A.G.), which depicted elderly women in a workhouse; *Hard Times* (exh. RA 1885; Manchester, C.A.G.), which showed an unemployed worker and his family; and his diploma picture *On Strike* (exh. RA 1891; London, RA). The impact of these images is heightened by looming foreground figures and an exaggerated perspective. A stylistically inconsistent painter, Herkomer oscillated between the delicate idealism of Frederick Walker (whom he greatly admired) and his own more vigorous and idiosyncratic style influenced by contemporary German realism.

Herkomer also exhibited landscapes and Bavarian peasant scenes. From 1871 he spent several months of almost every year in Germany, living there after 1885 in his own house, the Mutterturm (Landsberg-am-Lech, Bavaria), built in memory of his mother. His reputation in Germany was assured by frequent exhibitions of his work there and by numerous portrait commissions from prominent academics, businessmen and members of the nobility, for example *HRH Prince Luitpold Regent of Bavaria* (1895; Munich, Neue Pin.). He also painted two huge group portraits of town council members for the Landsberg Rathaus (1891, 1905). In 1899 William II awarded Herkomer the Order of Merit, which entitled him to add the prefix 'von' to his name.

Although Herkomer continued to exhibit genre subjects throughout his career, the principal focus of his painting after 1880 was portraiture. His sitters consistently comprised the most distinguished figures of his day, his most notable portraits including those of *John Ruskin* (1879; London, N.P.G.), *Archibald Forbes* (exh. RA 1882; Hamburg, Ksthalle) and *Thomas Hawksley* (1887; London, N.P.G.). Herkomer was elected ARA in 1879 and RA in 1890. The financial rewards of portrait painting enabled him to build a castle residence, Lululaund (1894; destr. 1939), in Bushey, Herts, named in memory of his second wife, Lulu. Its Romanesque exterior was designed by the American architect H. H. Richardson, one of his friends.

A controversial figure because of his outspoken enthusiasm and no-nonsense personality, Herkomer was often in the public eye through his lecturing, writing and other interests. He continually experimented with engraving techniques, publishing two books on the subject, as well as working with enamel and ivory. He wrote plays and musical diversions, performing in them at the Herkomer Theatre in Bushey. His innovative set designs and stage-lighting concepts influenced the stage-craft of Edwin Gordon Craig, who acknowledged his debt to Herkomer's theatre experiments. A pioneer of the British film industry, he made and appeared in several films from 1912 to 1914. His art school at Bushey, which flourished from 1883 to 1904, drew students from Sweden, South Africa, America and Australia, most notably William Nicholson. His gifts as a teacher were further acknowledged when he succeeded Ruskin as Slade Professor of Fine Arts (1885–94) at Oxford University. Herkomer received many public honours, among them a knighthood in 1907.

WRITINGS
Etching and Engraving: Lectures Delivered at Oxford (London, 1892)
My School and my Gospel (London, 1908)
A Certain Phase of Lithography (London, 1910)
The Herkomers, 2 vols (London, 1910–11)

BIBLIOGRAPHY
W. Meynell: 'Hubert Herkomer, ARA', *Mag. A.*, iii (1880), pp. 259–63
A. L. Baldry: *Hubert von Herkomer, CVO, RA: A Study and a Biography* (London, 1901)
L. Pietsch: *Herkomer* (London, 1901)
J. Saxon Mills: *The Life and Letters of Sir Hubert von Herkomer C.V.O, R.A.: A Study in Struggle and Success* (London, 1923)
R. Pickvance: *English Influences on Vincent van Gogh* (exh. cat. by R. Pickvance, U. Nottingham, A.G., 1974)
G. Longman: *The Beginning of the Herkomer Art School* (Bushey, Herts, 1983)
L. M. Edwards: *Hubert von Herkomer and the Modern Life Subject* (diss., New York, Columbia U., 1984)
——: ' "Sympathy for the Old and for Suffering Mankind": Hubert von Herkomer and his Paintings of Social Conscience', *Hard Times* (exh. cat. by J. Treuherz, Manchester, C.A.G., 1987–8), pp. 90–103
LEE M. EDWARDS

Herland, Hugh (*fl c.*1360; *d* ?Kingston-on-Thames, Surrey, before 1412). English carpenter. He was chief carpenter to Richard II (*reg* 1377–99), designing and building the open-timber roof of Westminster Hall, London, the largest medieval hall in England. He may have been the first carpenter to employ the angel hammerbeam motif in a large-scale structure.

Herland was probably the son of William Herland (*d* 1375), master carpenter to Edward III, with whom he worked *c.* 1360 at Westminster, the Tower of London and at Windsor, where he met such master masons as William Wynford, employed by William of Wykeham, Bishop of Winchester, Herland's future patron. At Windsor, Herland possibly helped to build the arch-brace roof for Edward III's new hall (destr.; engraving by Wenceslaus Hollar, *St George's Hall*, 1663).

In 1375 Herland became 'Disposer of the King's Works of Carpentry' and with a brief hiatus (1378) continued in this post until 1405. Of all his documented royal works, only the Westminster Hall roof survives, with the possible exception of the testers above the tombs of *Philippa of Hainault* and *Edward III* in Westminster Abbey. His other major works were built with Wynford for Wykeham's collegiate foundations, of which the timber vault of Winchester College Chapel (1393–4), an elegant proto-fan (conoidal) vault, survives. Despite their limited number, Herland's extant works clearly establish him as a master builder of the first rank, who made an important contribution to the general flourishing of monumental carpentry in 14th-century England.

BIBLIOGRAPHY
Harvey
J. Harvey: 'The King's Chief Carpenters', *J. Brit. Archaeol. Assoc.*, 3rd ser., xi (1948), pp. 13–24
H. M. Colvin, ed.: *The History of the King's Works*, i, ii (London, 1963)
L. T. Courtenay: 'The Westminster Hall Roof and its 14th-century Sources', *J. Soc. Archit. Hist.*, xliii/4 (1984), pp. 295–309
L. T. Courtenay and R. Mark: 'The Westminster Hall Roof: A Historiographic and Structural Study', *J. Soc. Archit. Hist.*, xlvi/4 (1987), pp. 374–93
LYNN T. COURTENAY

Herle, Wilhelm von. *See under* WILHELM OF COLOGNE, MASTER.

Herlin, Friedrich (*b c.* 1425/30; *d* Nördlingen, 1500). German painter and altarpiece contractor. His earliest surviving work, two wings from an altarpiece with scenes from the *Life of the Virgin* (Munich, Bayer. Nmus.; Nördlingen, Stadtmus.), is dated 1459. Although a signature on an altarpiece (1462; Nördlingen, Stadtmus.) and Nördlingen citizenship documents (1467) identified him as Friedrich Herlin from Rothenburg, he may have lived there only temporarily and was possibly born in Ulm, where a painter named Hans Herlin was active from 1449 to 1468. Friedrich Herlin's borrowings from Rogier van der Weyden, particularly from the Columba Altarpiece (*c.* 1455; Munich, Alte Pin.), already explicit in the panels for the Nördlingen altarpiece of 1462, suggest he had visited Cologne and the Netherlands during his formative years. Since the rediscovery (1971) of the date 1462 on that altarpiece (ex-St Georg, Nördlingen; wings, Nördlingen, Stadtmus.; sculpture *in situ* but in Baroque setting from 1683), its sculpture has been attributed to Nicolaus Gerhaert, suggesting that Herlin's contacts reached to the

Friedrich Herlin: *Presentation in the Temple*, oil on panel, inner wing panel from the high altarpiece, 1466 (Rothenburg ob der Tauber, Jakobskirche)

Rhineland and to one of the foremost sculptors of his time.

As seen in the altarpiece (1466; *in situ*) of the Jakobskirche, Rothenburg ob der Tauber (for illustration *see* ROTHENBURG OB DER TAUBER), Herlin's paintings provide telling examples of the adaptation of Netherlandish pictorial ideas in German art in the third quarter of the 15th century, and of the way in which paintings on the wings of a sculptural shrine were designed in relation to the sculptural interior. In the eight scenes on the exterior of the wings, depicting the *Life and Legend of St James*, the illusionistic portrayal of figures in space is ultimately terminated by a gold ground behind the scenes so as to emphasize the covering function of the wing over the shrine. In the scenes from the *Life of the Virgin* on the inside panels, the figures are set in the immediate foreground, which heightens their corporeality and presents

them in alignment with the carved figures of the shrine. The exceptions to this are the *Annunciation* and *Presentation in the Temple* (see fig.), compositions with architectural settings borrowed from van der Weyden's Columba Altarpiece that reach much further into depth than the others. Thus this altarpiece illustrates both the progressive trend of illusionism from the Netherlands and the traditional restriction of pictorial space in a triptych in which the wings answer to the exigencies of a sculptural shrine.

Herlin's tax exemptions in Nördlingen in 1467 and his controlling hand in the production of large and complex altarpieces indicate that he was a highly valued artist. His signature alone appears on altarpieces for which he delivered the paintings, even when important sections were carved by someone else. Once his design for an altarpiece was approved, he would subcontract the construction of the housing and architectural ornament as well as the carved figures that were to be placed in the shrine. His signature on an altarpiece, dated 1472, in the parish church at Bopfingen, near Nördlingen, indicates that he was considered the author of an altarpiece even when an anonymous assistant executed the paintings and an unnamed carver made the sculpture. His contract with the Nuremberg sculptor Simon Lainberger to deliver carved figures for an unspecified altarpiece commissioned in 1477 cannot pertain, as once believed, to those in the 1462 Nördlingen altarpiece but perhaps to the *St Peter* altarpiece (before 1478; Nuremberg, St Sebaldus). Although Herlin died in 1500, no works by him are known to be later than the altarpiece (Nördlingen, Stadtmus.) dated 1488 in which he and his wife appear as donors with their children.

BIBLIOGRAPHY

Thieme–Becker

F. Haack: *Friedrich Herlin: Sein Leben und seine Werke*, xxvi of *Studien zur deutschen Kunstgeschichte* (Strasbourg, 1900)

F. Thöne: 'Friedrich Herlin', *Pantheon*, xxv (1940), pp. 49–55

K. Martin: 'Ein unbekannter Altar von Friedrich Herlin und seine Herkunft', *Münchn. Jb. Bild. Kst*, n. s. 2, ii (1951), pp. 89–104

H. Ramisch: 'Der rechte Flügel eines Kreuzaltars von Friedrich Herlin in der ehemaligen Stiftskirche Herrieden', *Jb. Bayer. Dkmlpf.*, xxviii (1970–71), pp. 152–66

H. Baumhauer: *Der Herlin-Altar zu Bopfingen und seine Stadtkirche* (Stuttgart and Aalen, 1972)

J. Taubert: *Farbige Skulpturen* (Munich, 1978), pp. 150–94

V. Liedke: 'Zwei Rechnungsbelege zur Ausführung des Hochaltars in der Jakobskirche zu Rothenburg ob der Tauber, ein Werk des Nördlinger Malers Friedrich Herlin vom Jahr 1466', *A. Bavar.*, xiii (1979), pp. 43–52

H. Ramisch: 'Der Petersaltar von St. Sebald in Nürnberg und das Herlin-Lainberger-Problem', *A. Bavar.*, xiii (1979), pp. 65–88

CHARLES TALBOT

Herm. Statue type consisting of a plain shaft surmounted by a head, shoulder bust or sometimes a head and torso. It originated in ancient Greece and has been used since in a variety of settings, often architectural or open-air. Herms also occur, especially in classicizing contexts, as decorative motifs.

Ancient Greek herms usually featured a head of the god Hermes, from which the type derives its name, and the front of the shaft was carved with male genitals. They are known from surviving examples, the earliest of which date from the Archaic period (*c.* 600–480 BC; e.g. a herm from Siphnos, *c.* 520 BC; Athens, N. Archaeol. Mus., 3728), as well as inscriptions and other literary sources, and from depictions in vase paintings. There is evidence, even at an early stage, of numerous variations: in addition to Hermes, other gods including Dionysos, Ares, Artemis and Aphrodite were shown, and portrait herms include the statue of *Pericles* by Kresilas (original *c.* 425 BC, copy in London, BM).

Herms were characteristically located out of doors, often in streets and highways, borders and open countryside, as well as in sporting complexes such as gymnasia and palaestras. Herms in ancient Athens served as wayside shrines, marked sacred places or were set up as memorials (Kimon donated three to Athens in commemoration of his victory at Eurymedon in 468 BC). The range of locations variously reflects Hermes' nature as a phallic fertility deity, as a mediator (the Homeric messenger of the gods) and bringer of good luck; he was later adopted as the tutelary deity of the arts and sciences, of heralds, markets and roads.

Herms continued to be made in Roman times (*see* ROME, ANCIENT, §IV, 1(iv)(a)) and later, often with heads of other deities or portraits of individuals (*see also* BUST). Similar statues displaying the head of Terminus, Roman god of boundaries and landmarks, are known as terms. The Romans created herm galleries, and herms also occur as motifs in Roman wall paintings. Despite Hermes' pagan nature, Christianized herm statues are also known.

The herm was revived in European sculpture of the Renaissance and the Neo-classical art of the 18th century, always retaining its strong associations with Greek and Roman art. In common with other Classical forms and subject-matter, it became part of the European iconographic repertory, being used—like sphinxes or erotes—simply as a vaguely classicizing reference, wholly divorced from the genuinely numinous qualities it possessed for the ancient Greeks. Parallels to the herm can be found in other cultural contexts, for example the significance and location of sculptures of trickster figures in Africa (*see* AFRICA, §IV, 8).

BIBLIOGRAPHY

H. Wrede: *Die antike Herme* (Mainz, 1985)

Herman, Josef (*b* Warsaw, 3 Jan 1911). Polish painter and collector, active in Britain. He attended the Warsaw Academy from 1930 to 1931 and later exhibited with the Phrygian Cap, a group of left-wing idealist artists, opposed to the art of Bonnard. In 1938, fleeing from Poland's growing anti-semitism, he chose exile in Brussels (where he met Constant Permeke, a lasting influence) and then in Glasgow, where he and Jankel Adler joined the circle around the poet Hugh MacDiarmid (1892–1978). Herman's lively pen-and-wash drawings, such as *Jewish Peasant Milking a Goat* (1940–43; see 1985 exh. cat., p. 2), were reminiscences of a lost central European Jewry, owing much to Chagall.

In 1944 Herman moved to the Welsh village of Ystradgynlais, whose miners became the vehicle for his 'modern humanism'. As a Jew he was close to David Bomberg, and to Jacob Epstein, who guided him in establishing an unrivalled collection of miniature African tribal figures. His own paintings, such as *Peasants Digging for Roots*

(1949–50; York, C.A.G.), created a kind of tribal vernacular from a fusion of the primitive with the block forms of Mario Sironi and Frans Masereel.

In 1950 Herman was impressed by the murals in Mexico City, and in 1951, for the Festival of Britain, he completed his only public commission, the frieze *Miners* (6.3 m; Swansea, Vivian A.G. & Mus.), which he considered his masterpiece. The dark tonality and glowing, glazed colour reappeared in many subsequent easel paintings, whose subject was 'the pride of human labour and the calm force which promises to guard its dignity' (Herman, 1975, p. 102). These paintings retained a mural-like simplicity and monumentality. Presenting timeless situations—mother and child, man and donkey, birds, trees, lovers—his work stood consciously against the era of Pop Art. Only in the artists' debates that marked the end of the 1970s and through his autobiography *Related Twilights* did Herman re-emerge to become a significant presence to a new generation.

WRITINGS

Related Twilights: Notes from an Artist's Diary (London, 1975)

BIBLIOGRAPHY

B. Taylor: *Josef Herman Drawings* (London, 1956)
J. Berger: *Permanent Red: Essays in Seeing* (London, 1960), pp. 90–94
E. Mullins: *Josef Herman* (London, 1967)
W. Fagg: *Miniature Woodcarvings of Africa from the Herman Collection* (London, 1970)
T. Hyman: 'Josef Herman', *Artscribe*, 22 (1980), pp. 38–41
Josef Herman (exh. cat., foreword J. Tysoe, intro. P. Overy; London, Camden A. Cent., 1980)
Josef Herman, 'Memory of Memories'—the Glasgow Drawings (exh. cat., Glasgow, Third Eye Cent., 1985)

Herman de Limbourg. *See under* LIMBOURG, DE.

Herman d'Italie [Monsieur Herman]. *See* SWANEVELT, HERMAN VAN.

Hermann [Hörmann]. German family of painters. Members of the family, which came from Kempten in the Allgäu, were active from the mid-17th century to the early 19th. Franz Georg Hermann (i) (*b* Kempten, 1640; *d* Kempten, 1689) worked as a court painter in Kempten, tending to adopt a clear, Italian Renaissance approach to composition in such altarpieces as the *Guardian Angel* (1664) in SS Peter and Paul, Petersthal, and the *Marriage of the Virgin* (1673) at Roveredo, South Tyrol. He depicts detail with a naive narrative power, but his crudely typified figures seem stiff. His son, Franz Benedikt Hermann (1664–1735), gave initial training to his grandson, Franz Georg Hermann (ii) (*b* Kempten, 29 Dec 1692; *d* Kempten, 25 Nov 1768). Franz Georg Hermann (ii) then went to the Accademia di S Luca in Rome. He won a first prize in 1713 for a drawing of the *Miracle of St Andrea Avellino* (Rome, Accad. N. S. Luca); his main influences were Maratti, Sebastiano Conca and Francesco Trevisani. Working on frescoes (1720–23) for St Mang monastery, Füssen, he met Giovanni Pellegrini, and accompanied him back to Venice. He adopted the contemporary Venetians' soft contours, atmospheric treatment of light and detailed substantiality. Even when strongly influenced by the work of others, his strength lay in epic narrative power and a liking for complicated allegorical connections. Hermann's chief works are the ceiling and wall paintings in the Residenz at Kempten (1730–45), those at the Wallfahrtskirche of Maria Steinbach, including the ceiling fresco of the *Story of the Salvation of Mankind* (1752–63), and the ceiling fresco of the *Apotheosis of Divine Wisdom* (1755–7) in the library at Schussenried.

BIBLIOGRAPHY

C. Bohm: *Franz Georg Hermann: Der Deckermaler des Allgäu im 18. Jahrhunderts* (Munich, 1968)

G. Hojer: 'Der Concorso Clementino von 1713: Der Fund barocker Aquarelle in der Accademia di San Luca', *Die Weltkunst*, 1 (1980), pp. 114–18, 214–18

MICHAELA FEULNER

Hermann-Paul [Paul, Georges Hermann René] (*b* Paris, 27 Dec 1864; *d* Les Saintes-Maries-de-la-Mer, Bouches-du-Rhône, 23 June 1940). French illustrator, printmaker and painter. After briefly studying sciences to please his father, he entered the Ecole des Arts Décoratifs in Paris and then studied painting under Henry Lerolle and Gustave Colin. He soon made a reputation through his lithographs and drawings for a number of journals. He worked in 1894 on the *Courrier français* and on *Le Rire*, in 1897 on *Cri de Paris*, in 1898 on the anarchist periodical *La Feuille*, in 1901 on *Assiette au beurre*, in 1904 on *Temps nouveaux* and in 1906 on *La Guerre sociale*. During the Dreyfus affair in 1899 he acquired some notoriety through his pro-Dreyfus drawings for *Le Figaro*.

From 1894 to 1931 Hermann-Paul illustrated a number of books, such as Laurent Tailhade's *Au pays du mufle* (1894), Emile Zola's *L'Assommoir* (1920), François Rabelais's *Gargantua* (1921), Colette's *Mitsou* and Henri de Montherlant's *Les Bestiaires* (1926), and he was a frequent collaborator with the editor Léon Pinchon. Though it was through his lithographs and drawings that he established his reputation, he also executed a number of watercolours and oil paintings. His portrait of *Cézanne* (1904) was shown in Paris at the Salon d'Automne where it received much acclaim. From 1926 he exhibited at the Salon des Indépendants. He had a great love for Spain, especially bullfighting, and so felt attracted to the Camargue in France. In 1937 he founded the Association Libre des Amis de la Camargue and in 1938 established the Musée Camarguais at Saintes-Maries-de-la-Mer.

BIBLIOGRAPHY

Edouard-Joseph

R. Geiger: *Hermann-Paul* (Paris, 1929)

M. Varille: *Hermann-Paul: Peintre-graveur* (Lyon, 1941)

Hermannstadt. *See* SIBIU.

Hermans, Charles (*b* Brussels, 17 Aug 1839; *d* Menton, 7 Dec 1924). Belgian painter. He came from a bourgeois family who encouraged him in his artistic ambitions. He studied with Louis Gallait in Brussels before attending Atelier Saint-Luc, a free studio in Brussels for artists who opposed traditional academic teaching. Between 1858 and 1861 he was in Paris where he studied with Charles Gleyre and also at the Ecole Centrale des Beaux-Arts. He spent 1862–6 in Italy where he developed a particular interest in the lives of monks: they provided subjects for several paintings, such as *Monks Playing Bowls*, and his treatment of them reveals him as a shrewd observer.

Hermans had considerable success with these works on his return to Brussels in 1866, but he wished to take on more elevated subjects and thus in 1872 painted *Job Visited by his Friends*, which he treated in a realistic style devoid of authentic religious feeling. Hermans then turned to contemporary scenes, particularly of working-class life, such as the *Sunday Visit to the Children's Clinic at the Hôpital Saint-Pierre* (1873; Dendermonde, Stedel. Oudhdknd. Mus. Vleeshuis). With *Dawn* (1875; Brussels, Mus. A. Mod.) he painted a genre scene that took on the dimensions of history painting. In the early morning a group of revellers, men in tailcoats and young women in disordered clothes, find themselves face to face with some labourers setting off for work. The painting could not be dismissed as anecdotal because of its large dimensions and life-size figures; and the contrast between the two groups was variously interpreted. It shocked those who saw in it an element of social criticism, but aroused enthusiasm in others. In its wilful realism and modernity, it was close to the work of the painters associated with the Société Libre des Beaux-Arts, and it became the centre of a debate between the advocates of Romantic historicizing painting and those who supported the modernist painters whose ideas found expression in the contemporary Belgian journals *L'Art libre* and *L'Art universel*. *Dawn* also showed the results of Hermans's continuing study of light effects. These fascinated him throughout his career, and he explored them in landscapes such as *The Beach at Ostend* (Brussels, Mus. A. Mod.), scenes with figures such as the *Woman Carrying Beerglasses* (untraced) and, later on, in many female nudes, such as *Rest* (1881; Namur, Mus. Hôtel de Croix).

Hermans's social concerns reappeared in several later works: in *Circe* (1881) a prostitute like the sorceress who turned Ulysses's companions into pigs contemplates a drunken young debauchee. Such later paintings as the skilfully composed *Ball at the Opera* (1880; Philadelphia, PA Mus. F.A.) are largely free of social comment. The exceptional success of *Dawn* proved short-lived and subsequently Hermans suffered a period of discouragement which affected his work. In later years he spent much time travelling in Italy and Spain, bringing back studies, portraits, scenes of popular life and many watercolour and gouache landscapes, such as *Countryside near Rome* (Liège, Mus. B.-A.).

BNB

BIBLIOGRAPHY

C. Lemonnier: *L'Ecole belge de peinture, 1830–1905* (Brussels, 1906), pp. 135–6

H. Hymans: *L'Art au XVIIe et au XIXe siècle dans les Pays-Bas* (Brussels, 1921), pp. 283–5

L. Solvay: 'Notice sur Charles Hermans', *Annu. Acad. Royale Sci., Lett. & B.-A., Belgique* (1926), pp. 43–78

De Ingres à Paul Delvaux (exh. cat., Brussels, Pal. Acad., 1973), pp. 10–11

RICHARD KERREMANS

Hermant. French family of architects.

(1) Pierre-Antoine-Achille Hermant (*b* Paris, 6 Dec 1823; *d* Paris, May 1903). He studied at the Ecole des Beaux-Arts, Paris, under Guillaume-Abel Blouet from 1842. He took part in many public competitions, winning first prize for the reformatory (*c.* 1874; chapel, 1881) in Nanterre, Hauts de Seine, which became a model among

French penitential establishments of the 19th century. In Paris he built the Mairie (completed 1876) for the VIIIe arrondissement, and in 1880 he was appointed architect to the city of Paris. In this capacity he built the barracks (completed 1887) for the Garde Républicaine in the Place Monge. He was made a Chevalier of the Légion d'honneur in 1889.

(2) Jacques Hermant (*b* Paris, 7 May 1855; *d* Paris, 1930). Son of (1) Pierre-Antoine-Achille Hermant. He studied under Joseph-Auguste-Emile Vaudremer and Gustave-Laurent Raulin (1837–1910) at the Ecole des Beaux-Arts, Paris, and in 1880 won second place in the competition for the Prix de Rome with a project for a hospice on the Mediterranean coast. He was an eclectic architect, at one time attracted to the Art Nouveau style, and he perpetuated eclecticism well after World War I, although he incorporated modern details into some of his buildings. His career began when he collaborated with his father on the barracks in the Place Monge, and in 1890 he won the competition to build further barracks (completed 1896) in the Boulevard Henri IV. Here, Louis XIII-style stone façades, with eclectic French and Italian Renaissance details, conceal large metal roof trusses, in the manner used by Victor Baltard to conceal his structural ironwork at the church of St Augustin, Paris. Hermant designed the French pavilions for the World's Columbian Exhibition in Chicago in 1893 and the Exposition Internationale, Brussels, in 1897. The façades of the Palais du Génie at the Exposition Universelle, Paris, of 1900 were treated in a Spanish Revival style, while he turned to the Louis XVI style for the Salle Gaveau (1907) in the Rue St Honoré. This was the first concert hall in Paris to be built of reinforced concrete.

Hermant's most important work was the registered office of a bank, the Société Générale, in the Boulevard Haussmann, Paris. He retained the façades of three residential buildings, which had been built in compliance with the criteria laid down for façades near the Opéra, and produced a vast and magnificent office complex around a central dealing hall with a glass roof and a mosaic floor. Both features are exceptional for the quality of their Art Nouveau decoration, surprising in the context of an otherwise classical building. Other buildings by Hermant included Le Magasin des Classes Laborieuses (1898), Rue St Martin, and a block of flats (1901) at 10 Rue Legendre, both in Paris; a private house (1904) at 25 Rue Malzeville, Nancy, a classical building with some Art Nouveau details; a château at Voisénin, Seine et Marne; a garage (1908) for Paris Automobiles in the Rue d'Anjou, Paris; and schools and offices. Hermant's various official appointments included chief architect to the Bâtiments Civils et des Palais Nationaux, architect to the city of Paris and member of the Conseil Supérieur des Habitations à Bon Marché. In the latter capacity he built 150 low-cost housing developments after World War I.

BIBLIOGRAPHY

'La Salle Gaveau à Paris', *Architecte* (1909), pp. 95–7

E. A. Delaire: *1893–1914: Les Architectes élèves de l'Ecole des Beaux-Arts* (Paris, 1914)

M. Emery: *Un Siècle d'architecture moderne, 1850–1950* (Paris, 1971)

P. Chemetov and B. Marrey: *Architecture Paris, 1848–1914* (Paris, 1976)

Nancy: Architecture 1900 (exh. cat., Nancy, Mus. Ecole Nancy, 1976)

B. Marrey: *Les Grands Magasins des origines à 1939* (Paris, 1979)

T. Kozak: *Le Siège social de la Société Générale du Boulevard Haussmann par Jacques Hermant* (MA thesis, Paris IV, 1987)

JEAN-FRANÇOIS PINCHON

Hermeneutics. Term applied, in the most general sense, to the practice and theory of interpretation. The word is derived from the name of the Greek god Hermes, the divine messenger. The objects of hermeneutics are primarily spoken utterances and written texts, especially those that appear obscure or are presumed to convey a hidden message, but the term is very broadly used. Every human product, from individual works of visual art to whole social and cultural systems, can be subject to interpretation. According to MARTIN HEIDEGGER and Hans-Georg Gadamer (*b* 1900), the activity of interpretation constitutes the essence of human life.

1. USE AND MEANING OF THE TERM. Modern hermeneutics began as the theory and practice of the interpretation of the text of the Bible. The emergence of Protestantism placed great emphasis on the proper understanding of the biblical text, since it denied the authority of the Church's accepted readings. By the mid-18th century in Germany, study of the Bible aimed at discovering the abiding moral truths hidden in the apparently naive and mythological stories of the text. This 'historical–critical' approach to the Bible made heavy use of the methods then being developed by classical philology, particularly grammatical analysis and research into the historical context of the text's composition.

FRIEDRICH SCHLEIERMACHER first conceived of hermeneutics as a unified approach to all understanding, in asking what is involved in the act of understanding another's utterance. He believed that understanding involves re-experiencing the mental processes of a text's author, and he emphasized the importance of the interpreter's reconstructing the author's psychological state. WILHELM DILTHEY generalized the notion of hermeneutics even further. Dilthey identified philosophy with the study of life and claimed that this study must be based upon the broadest possible knowledge of all of life's manifestations. These manifestations are the objects of the human sciences (*Geisteswissenschaften*) as opposed to the natural sciences (*Naturwissenschaften*). The human sciences include psychology, history, economics, philology, literary and art criticism, jurisprudence, comparative religion and finally philosophy itself, which is to supply the others with a method. This method is hermeneutics, whose aim is 'understanding' (*Verstehen*) in contrast to the objective explanation (*Erklärung*) characteristic of the natural sciences. *Verstehen* refers to the understanding of a mental content, a meaning, manifested or expressed in words, pictures, gestures, books or even whole institutions. It involves a sympathetic identification with the mind of another, and it requires some familiarity with fundamental human mental processes (a condition always partially fulfilled), knowledge of the concrete context of the original manifestation and an understanding of the social and cultural systems that always determine the nature of such manifestations. These conditions, which Dilthey considered essential and peculiar to the human sciences, give rise to the hermeneutic circle.

2. THE HERMENEUTIC CIRCLE. The circle arises because the meaning expressed by a cultural artefact does not depend simply on its creator's intention; it also depends on the whole system of which the artefact is a part, much as the meaning of a sentence depends on the language to which it belongs or the meaning of a part of a painting depends on the whole work of art of which it is a part. To understand each part, therefore, implies an understanding of the whole. Yet there is no way of understanding the whole independently of its parts.

For Schleiermacher and Dilthey this was a problem peculiar to the sympathetic understanding sought by the human sciences. For the 'phenomenological hermeneutics' of Heidegger, who saw hermeneutics as essential to all human existence (*Dasein*), the circle is absolutely all-encompassing. According to Heidegger all our interactions in the world are hermeneutical, because the world as it confronts us consists not merely of objects but of objects that are significant *for us* and are therefore interpreted as such in the very process of our coming to be aware of them and of ourselves among them. The hermeneutic circle is therefore characteristic of all existence. A hammer (to use Heidegger's own example) is what it is, not by itself but only in relation to nails, walls, other tools and the whole practice of carpentry. To recognize anything for what it is, we must already understand the system to which it belongs, and to understand that system we must already be familiar with its parts.

In Heidegger's view, as well as in *Wahrheit und Methode* (1960), the influential work by his pupil Gadamer, all knowledge is subject to this circle, including the knowledge allegedly characteristic of the natural sciences. Accordingly, both deny the traditional idea that there is, or can be, such a thing as absolutely objective knowledge of the world. All understanding begins *in medias res*, with some 'pre-understanding' or 'prejudice' already in place. For Gadamer, too, hermeneutics provided the principles of all our interactions with the world. He used as his paradigm the understanding of a work of art by a later audience. Unlike Schleiermacher and Dilthey (and also Erwin Panofsky, who expressed the same view in 1940), Gadamer insisted that temporal distance cannot be overcome; the exact recreation of an original artist's meaning can never be attained. Both the original artist and the contemporary interpreter are bound by their different social, cultural and intellectual horizons. He described the interpretation of a work of art as a 'dialogue', as an effort to alter one's current horizon so as to encompass the horizon of the work. The resulting effect is that both horizons are changed in the process, and that neither the meaning of the work nor the nature of the interpreter remains the same after interpretation.

Again unlike his predecessors, Gadamer thought of interpretation not as a sympathetic psychological leap into another's mind but as a linguistic event. Past and present, text and interpreter are connected through a common language, which is the product of previous interpretations and to which each new interpretation makes its own contribution. The importance of tradition for Gadamer led Jürgen Habermas (*b* 1929) to claim that Gadamer's hermeneutics is essentially conservative. But the language in which a work of the past is understood is always the language of the interpreter. This, in turn, gave rise to the claim that Gadamer's view is relativist and does not permit us to prefer any interpretation to any other.

3. INTERPRETATION OF THE WORK OF ART. The claim outlined above was advanced as a criticism by E. D. Hirsch (*b* 1928), who argued that, if the 'horizon' of a work of art is constantly changing as a result of the different interpretations to which the work is subjected in the course of history, and if, in addition, new interpreters come to the work with their own 'pre-understandings', then every age and every interpreter is condemned to understand a work differently. There is no such thing as the correct interpretation of a work of art. Every view of a work is as good as any other, and this undermines the legitimacy of any form of teaching (which Hirsch takes for granted).

Hirsch's answer was to distinguish the meaning of a text or a work of art more generally, which he considered objective and unchanging, from its significance, which is what the work has meant at different times to different people and which is naturally variable. Hirsch identified the meaning of the work of art with its creator's intention. The aim of interpretation, Hirsch claimed, is the establishment of meaning, while literary and art history are concerned with significance, and criticism addresses value. It is a controversial matter whether Hirsch's view does restore objectivity, since it raises the question how the intention of an artist can be accurately captured ('in its own terms', as Hirsch insisted), especially if all understanding is linguistic and the terms in which an original intention is couched are themselves in need of interpretation. This, it might seem, simply pushes the problem one stage further back.

Intentionalism persists in one form or another, however, and in *Painting as an Art* (1988) Richard Wollheim (*b* 1923) gave forceful expression to the view that the meaning of a work of art is fixed by the fulfilled intention of the artist. Wollheim's view made serious use of the findings of psychoanalysis, itself one of the major contributions to the development of hermeneutics in our century. In fact, Sigmund Freud, along with Karl Marx (1818–83) and Friedrich Nietzsche, was taken by Paul Ricoeur (*b* 1913) to represent a deeply sceptical tradition, which he called 'the hermeneutics of suspicion'. This tradition challenges not only the objectivity of hermeneutics but the power of hermeneutics to recover the meaning human expressions reveal. According to Ricoeur, Nietzsche, Marx and Freud showed that the interpretation of signs always reveals only the presence of further signs and interpretations. POST-STRUCTURALISM and DECONSTRUCTION in particular are the heirs of this approach to hermeneutics, and their implications for the interpretation of art are important and far-ranging.

BIBLIOGRAPHY

F. D. E. Schleiermacher: *Sämtliche Werke* (Berlin, 1835–64)
W. Dilthey: *Gesammelte Schriften* (Leipzig and Berlin, 1914–36, rev. 3/Stuttgart and Göttingen, 1957–60)

M. Heidegger: *Sein und Zeit* (Halle, 1927); Eng. trans. as *Being and Time* (New York, 1962)

E. Betti: *Teoria generale della interpretazione*, 2 vols (Milan, 1955)

E. Panofsky: 'The History of Art as a Humanistic Discipline', *Meaning in the Visual Arts* (New York, 1955), pp. 1–25

H.-G. Gadamer: *Wahrheit und Methode* (Tübingen, 1960); Eng. trans. as *Truth and Method* (London, 1975)

P. Ricoeur: *De l'interprétation: Essai sur Freud* (Paris, 1965); Eng. trans. as *Freud and Philosophy: An Essay on Interpretation* (New Haven, 1970)

E. D. Hirsch: *Validity in Interpretation* (New Haven, 1967)

J. Habermas: *Erkenntnis und Interesse* (Frankfurt am Main, 1968); Eng. trans. as *Knowledge and Human Interests* (Boston, 1971)

R. E. Palmer: *Hermeneutics* (Chicago, 1969)

E. H. Gombrich: 'The Evidence of Images', *Interpretation: Theory and Practice*, ed. C. S. Singleton (Baltimore, 1969), pp. 35–104

J. Wolff: *Hermeneutic Philosophy and the Sociology of Art* (London, 1975)

F. D. E. Schleiermacher: *Hermeneutics: The Handwritten Manuscripts* (Missoula, 1977)

K. Mueller-Vollmer: *The Hermeneutics Reader* (Oxford, 1986)

R. Wollheim: *Painting as an Art* (Princeton, 1988)

ALEXANDER NEHAMAS

Hermitage. Place of retreat. The term refers to a building or group of buildings designed to allow a solitary form of existence. The outward forms of hermitages are extraordinarily diverse, reflecting in architectural terms the difference between the religious solitude of hermits and monks (*see also* MONASTERY) and the profane, worldly solitude of, for example, a ruler withdrawing from his official residence. While 'hermitage' refers literally to the religious aspect it conceals, the profane tradition lacks a special term; the most apt is 'retreat', although *trianon* (Fr.) and *casino* (It.) have been used occasionally (*see also* GROTTO), and these should be distinguished from religious hermitages.

The architectural prototype of the worldly retreat in the Western tradition is the Island Villa of Hadrian's Villa (AD 118–34), near Tivoli (*see* TIVOLI, §2(i)). Its small size and centralized structure express its close relation to the Emperor's individual life, while its isolation within the enormous villa complex and the circular moat around it indicate its function as a place of withdrawal. The centralized configuration influenced the Baroque profane hermitage through Andrea Palladio's Villa Rotonda (begun 1550s), which was built on a hilltop site chosen for its suitability as a place for withdrawal (*see* VICENZA, §2). While a court retreat can be lavishly furnished and pompous of form, the religious hermitage tends to negate architecture as such, being located, on the model of early Christian anchorites, in caves or ruins. The hermitage of Bretzenheim (nr Bad Kreuznach), first mentioned in 1043, contains a three-nave Romanesque church carved in the rock face; a chapel was added in 1723 (destr. 1796). The *Klause* of Kastel (nr Trier) consists of a dwelling and chapel (both *c.* 1600) carved in rock above the River Saar; restored in 1835 by Karl Friedrich Schinkel, it now contains the tomb of King John the Blind of Bohemia (*d* 1346). The religious and the court ideas were combined in the court hermitages of the 16th to 18th centuries, as in that built by William Kent for Queen Caroline (1683–1737) at Richmond, Surrey (see fig.); here an atmosphere of religious solitude was added to the retreat, in reference to the medieval literary motif of the meeting of the knight with a hermit in a lonely place in a wood. Spatially and conceptually the lonely place (Lat. *locus desertus*) defines the opposite pole to the residence.

The combination of retreat and hermitage appeared at Gaillon (*c.* 1560), possibly by Jacques Androuet Du Cerceau (i), where a small hermit's dwelling in the middle of a pond with a Gothic chapel (destr. 1798) on the bank were located opposite a contemporary casino. The hermitage ensemble appears as a theatrical property of the casino, illustrating the idea of solitude. Earlier examples of this type include the 15th-century hermitage of the Dukes of Burgundy at Vieil-Hesdin (destr. 1553), which consisted of a retreat and chapel for a hermit with a garden and garden house for the ruler near by. In the park of the Palacio del Buen Retiro (from 1631; destr.), built by Philip IV of Spain in Madrid, were scattered at least eight hermitage villas serving as dwellings for favoured courtiers; with chapels and luxurious furnishings, they combined the retreat and hermitage in a single building. Louis XIV's château (1676; destr. early 19th century) and garden of MARLY-LE-ROI included a central casino in the tradition of Hadrian's Villa as well as 12 smaller pavilions alluding to the idea of the hermit's cell. A variation on this structure is found in the Hermitage at BAYREUTH (1715–18; altered 1743–54), which comprised a four-winged main building with an illusionistic imitation of a rock outer wall and several small hermitages scattered about the park.

Within a landscape garden the hermitage could maintain the tradition of the court retreat in its interior furnishings, but it often became merely an attribute of the melancholy scene of the garden, its illusionist, visual character becoming preponderant. Simple, low buildings with the aspect of ruins or grottoes, or covered in bark, are typical of this type (*see* FOLLY).

Hermitage designed by William Kent for Queen Caroline, Royal Gardens, Richmond, Surrey, 1733 (destr.); wash drawing attributed to Bernard Lens (iii) (London, Museum of London)

BIBLIOGRAPHY
RDK: 'Eremitage'

D. Watkin: *The English Vision: The Picturesque in Architecture, Landscape and Garden Design* (London, 1982)

C. M. Sicca: 'Like a Shallow Cave by Nature Made: William Kent's "Natural" Architecture at Richmond', *Architectura* [Munich], xvi/1 (1986), pp. 68–82

REINHARD ZIMMERMANN

Hermogenes (*fl* ?late 3rd century BC–early 2nd). Greek architect. He may have been the Prienian and son of Harpalos who is referred to in an inscription from Priene as having dedicated the plan of a building (?temple) constructed by him (see Hiller von Gaertringen, pp. 143–4, no. 207). Like his predecessor PYTHEOS and his probable contemporary Arkesios, Hermogenes considered the Doric order inappropriate for temples (Vitruvius IV.iii.1), and he changed to Ionic the Doric design proposed for a temple of Dionysos, possibly the one at TEOS. He wrote descriptive and theoretical treatises, frequently cited by Vitruvius, to whom his later reputation is largely due, on two of his most important works: the Temple of Artemis at MAGNESIA ON THE MAEANDER (begun late 3rd century BC; Vitruvius III.ii.6; VII.Pref.12) and the Temple of Dionysos at Teos (*c.* 200 BC). The former was pseudodipteral, a type of temple plan probably systematized, rather than invented, by Hermogenes; the latter employed the eustyle scheme for Ionic peristyles, which he developed (Vitruvius III.iii.6–9). He may also have designed the entire Sanctuary of Artemis at Magnesia, as well as the agora, and perhaps the early 2nd-century BC Temple of Zeus Sosipolis. His authority of the latter is disputed (see M. Uz in Hoepfner and Schwandner, p. 61, n. 47).

Hermogenes was the most famous Hellenistic architectural theorist, and he influenced not only later Hellenistic designs and designers (e.g. the Hekataion at Lagina and, possibly, the architect Hermodoros of Salamis) but also Roman architectural practice. Vitruvius discussed the Ionic order largely in Hermogenean terms and effectively transmitted Hermogenes' ideas to the architects of the Renaissance.

BIBLIOGRAPHY
Pauly–Wissowa; Thieme–Becker
Vitruvius: *On Architecture*
F. Hiller von Gaertringen: *Die Inschriften von Priene* (Berlin, 1906)
W. Hahland: 'Der Fries des Dionysostempels in Teos', *Jhft. Österreich. Archäol. Inst. Wien*, xxxviii (1950), pp. 66–109
W. Hoepfner: 'Zum ionischen Kapitell bei Hermogenes und Vitruv', *Mitt. Dt. Archäol. Inst.: Athen. Abt.*, lxxxiii (1968), pp. 213–34
P. Gros: 'Le Dossier vitruvien d'Hermogénès', *Mél. Archéol. & Hist.: Ecole Fr. Rome*, xc (1978), pp. 687–703
B. Wesenberg: *Beiträge zur Rekonstruktion griechischer Architektur nach literarischen Quellen* (Berlin, 1983)
W. Hoepfner and E. L. Schwandner, eds: *Hermogenes und die hochhellenistische Architektur* (Mainz, 1990)

F. E. WINTER

Hermonthis. *See* ARMANT.

Hermopolis Magna [anc. Egyp. Khmun; Arab. el-Ashmunein]. Ancient Egyptian site on the east bank of the Nile, *c.* 30 km south of el-Minya. A Greco-Roman redevelopment of the pharaonic town of Khmun, it is now marked by a mound of ruins *c.* 1.5 km in diameter, adjacent to the modern settlement of el-Ashmunein. The town was occupied from the Old Kingdom (*c.* 2575–*c.* 2150 BC) to the Coptic period (4th–7th century AD). In pharaonic times it was a nome capital and the chief cult centre of Thoth, god of writing and wisdom. Thoth was later identified with Hermes, hence the Greco-Roman name of the city; its earlier name of Khmun means 'City of the Eight' and refers to the eight gods who figured in the local creation myths.

In the centre of the town was a large Temple of Thoth, constructed in the New Kingdom (*c.* 1540–*c.* 1075 BC), principally in the reigns of Amenophis III (*reg c.* 1390–

Hermopolis Magna, Temple of Thoth, 4th century BC (destr. 19th century); engraving from V. Denon: *Travels in Upper and Lower Egypt*, i (London, 1803), pl. XIV

c. 1353 BC), Horemheb (*reg c.* 1319–*c.* 1292 BC) and Ramesses II (*reg c.* 1279–*c.* 1213 BC). The first pylon of this building, excavated by the German archaeologist Günther Roeder, who worked at Hermopolis between 1929 and 1939, contained more than 1500 blocks brought from structures at el-Amarna. Little is now visible of the main temple, but a subsidiary shrine built by Ramesses II and decorated under Merneptah (*reg c.* 1213–*c.* 1204 BC) and Sethos II (*reg c.* 1204–*c.* 1198 BC) still stands on the site. A separate small temple, also constructed by Ramesses II, at the south end of the site was excavated by the Egyptian archaeologist Abdel Moneim Abu Bakr in 1946.

Of earlier remains only a limestone gateway survives, built by Ammenemes II (*reg c.* 1876–*c.* 1842 BC). In 370 BC a much larger Temple of Thoth (destr. 19th century; see fig.) was constructed within a vast mud-brick enclosure in the northern part of the town. The decoration of this building dates chiefly from the reign of Philip Arrhidaeus (*reg* 323–316 BC). From the foundations came portions of four colossal quartzite statues of baboons, one of the sacred animals of Thoth, inscribed for Amenophis III. Two of these have been reconstructed; they are among the largest monolithic animal sculptures from ancient Egypt. The later temple was approached by a processional street named the Dromos of Hermes, which was maintained throughout the Greco-Roman period (332 BC–AD 395) as a principal thoroughfare of the city. The Dromos crosses another route (Antinoë Street) at a monumental tetrastyle portico in the heart of the Hellenistic city. Greek papyri found at the site mention the names of numerous Roman public buildings, including a komasterion (priests' meeting-place), a nymphaion, an agora and temples to Aphrodite and Athena.

In the desert, 7 km west of el-Ashmunein, is a cemetery (Tuna el-Gebel) used by the later population of Hermopolis Magna. The necropolis is centred on another temple of Thoth, attached to a series of catacombs that contain ibis and baboon burials of the Persian (525–404 BC and 343–332 BC) and Greco-Roman periods (*see* EGYPT, ANCIENT, §VIII, 2(iii)). The rest of the site is occupied by an extensive area of funerary houses, tomb chapels and accommodation for pilgrims dating from Ramessid to Roman times, in which the wall paintings often combine elements of both Egyptian and Greek subject-matter. The unusual tomb chapel of Petosiris (*c.* 300 BC; *see* PETOSIRIS, TOMB OF) also includes painted relief carvings in a mixture of Greek and Egyptian styles. (For a discussion of the Coptic cathedral at el-Ashmunein *see* COPTIC ART, §II, 3.)

BIBLIOGRAPHY

LÄ

B. Porter and R. Moss: *Topographical Bibliography of Ancient Egyptian Hieroglyphical Texts, Reliefs and Paintings*, iv (Oxford, 1934), pp. 165–75

A. J. B. Wace, A. H. S. Megaw and T. C. Skeat: *Hermopolis Magna, Ashmunein: The Ptolemaic Sanctuary and the Basilica* (Alexandria, 1959)

G. Roeder: *Hermopolis, 1929–1939* (Hildesheim, 1959)

G. Grimm: 'Tuna el-Gebel, 1913–1973', *Mitt. Dt. Archäol. Inst.: Abt. Kairo*, xxxi (1975), pp. 224–34

A. J. Spencer: *The Topography of the Site* (1983), *The Temple Area* (1989), *The Town* (1993), i–iii of *Excavations at el-Ashmunein* (London, 1983–)

D. M. Bailey: *Buildings of the Roman Period* (1991), iv of *Excavations at el-Ashmunein* (London, 1983–)

A. J. SPENCER

Hernández (Navarro), Agustín (*b* Mexico City, 29 Feb 1924). Mexican architect. He graduated in architecture from the Universidad Nacional Autónoma de México and was admitted to the profession in 1954. His early work, mostly in the area of housing, consisted of simple, functional buildings in which he gradually espoused a more innovative sculptural expression based on a rigorous but varied geometric style. The Escuela de Ballet Folklórico (1968), Mexico City, was the first of a series of richly plastic works inspired by Mexico's Pre-Columbian heritage, in which autochthonous features are treated in a wholly contemporary manner. There followed a series of houses in Mexico City in which Hernández experimented with various geometrical modules: the hexagon was the basis for the Casa Silva (1969), the circle for the Casa Alvárez (1971), and the triangle for the Casa Amalia Hernández (also 1971). In 1971 Hernández was also commissioned to design the Heroico Colegio Militar at Tlalpan, a monumental complex of buildings to the south of Mexico City (completed 1976; in collaboration with Manuel González Rul). The school's design recalls Pre-Columbian ceremonial sites and forms, with some of the individual units having sloping walls that accentuate the reclamation of cultural roots. Similar forms appear in a contemporary hospital (1974–6) for the Instituto Mexicano del Seguro Social, Mexico City (1974–6), which again demonstrates the architect's sculptural and formal interests.

Among Hernández's most imaginative works, however, is his own highly innovative studio (1976) at Bosques de las Lomas, Mexico City, which is notable both for its construction techniques and for its formal and functional approach. Analogous to a fir tree, the studio's slender central unit or 'trunk' rises from a steeply wooded hillside and is crowned by four interlocking pyramidal forms, two under tension and two under compression. Hernández returned to curvilinear geometries for the Casa Neckelmann (1979) and Casa Betech (1981): the design of the former, partially subterranean, is of distinctive mollusc-shell form, a spiriform volumetric progression derived from the golden section. A more abstruse form, producing a remarkable array of interior spaces on two main levels and an even more remarkable external shape, was used in the next non-residential building, the Centro de Meditación (1984–6) at Cuernavaca, Morelos. The principal forms here are derived from the mandala of Hinduism and comprise an imaginative interplay of open cylindrical spaces interposed within essentially rectangular units.

Later works by Hernández use complex solid geometries and display structural virtuosity, as in one of the most remarkable of late 20th-century houses, the Casa en el aire (1988–91), in Bosques de las Lomas, Mexico City. Here two closely spaced rectilinear concrete pylons, both pierced by huge circular voids, rise from a steep slope. A rhombic-section steel-framed element, comprising the living accommodation, rests on the hilltop at one end and penetrates the two circular voids of the pylons to different depths at the other. Hernández's main building material was concrete, and all his constructions are notable for the high quality of their finish and their imaginative functional solutions. His work also always had an element of innovation, however, since he regarded creativity as being inextricably linked to the originality and uniqueness of each project. Moreover, his deep understanding of structural geometry, which allowed him to create surprising shapes and spaces, was always complemented by consultation with specialist engineers, and this enabled him to construct some of the most controversial buildings in modern Mexican architecture.

WRITINGS

Gravedad, geometría y simbolismo (Mexico City, 1989)

BIBLIOGRAPHY

'Análisis de la actividad arquitectónica de Agustín Hernández', *Constr. Mex.*, 9 (1978), pp. 6–16

L. Noelle: *Agustín Hernández: Arquitectura y pensamiento* (Mexico City, 1982)

C. Bürkle: 'An Architect for Mexico', *Conn. A.*, 27 (1982), pp. 62–7

J. Glusberg: 'Agustín Hernández', *Seis arquitectos mexicanos* (Buenos Aires, 1984)

L. Noelle: 'Agustín Hernández', *Arquitectos contemporáneos de México* (Mexico City, 1988)

——: *Agustín Hernandez* (Barcelona and Mexico City, 1995)

LOUISE NOELLE

Hernández [Morrillo], Daniel (*b* ?Hurpay, Huancavelica, 1 Aug 1856; *d* Lima, 23 Oct 1932). Peruvian painter and draughtsman. In 1860 he was brought to Lima and at an early age displayed considerable artistic talent. In 1870 he started studying with the Italian painter Leonardo Barbieri, and in 1875 he went to Europe, having won a scholarship from the Peruvian government. In Paris he met Ignacio Merino who recommended that he study in Rome. He spent ten years in Italy absorbing the aesthetics of Classical art and returned to Paris where he met Mariano Fortuny y Marsal, Francisco Pradilla, Armando Villegas and others. He took part in numerous exhibitions, winning several prizes, including the gold medal at the Exposition Universelle in 1900. From 1912 he spent some time in Montevideo and Buenos Aires, returning to Europe *c.* 1914. In 1917 he returned to Lima and in 1919 set up the Escuela Nacional de Bellas Artes, at the invitation of President José Pardo, and remained as its Director until his death. His works include watercolours, drawings and murals, and his themes range from seascapes, landscapes, still-lifes and historical paintings to portraits. He is perhaps best known for his *Reclining Women* series, typical of which is *Reclining Woman* (1902; priv. col.). His portraits included *D. Nicolás de Piérola* (1889; Lima, Mus. N. Hist.) and *Sra Mesones* (1883; Lima, Pin. Mun.). His work has been criticized for portraying a slightly idealized, superficial world; he was concerned 'with the strength of the lines, sincerity of vision' and with 'avoiding frivolous preoccupation with superfluous details' (Villacorta Paredes).

BIBLIOGRAPHY

J. Villacorta Paredes: *Pintores peruanos de la República* (Lima, 1971), pp. 34–5

J. A. de Lavalle and W. Lang: *Pintura contemporánea: Primera parte, 1820–1920*, Arte y tesoros del Perú (Lima, 1975), pp. 116–27

W. IAIN MACKAY

Hernández, Julio Antonio Rodríguez. *See* JULIO ANTONIO.

Hernández, Julio L(ópez) (*b* Madrid, 1 Feb 1930). Spanish sculptor. He studied at the Escuela de Bellas Artes de San Fernando in Madrid from 1949 to 1954. His overtly figurative work was initially met with critical incomprehension, given the vogue for abstraction at that time, but it was later promoted as part of a realist movement in Spanish painting and sculpture. He specialized in human figures in a variety of materials, including marble, stone, brick dust, polyester and shale agglomerate, often presenting them as if eroded by time to emphasize their perishable nature as well as a longing for immortality; their fidelity to appearances and to anatomical accuracy is notable even in works conceived under life-size, as in *Young Woman Walking* (bronze, h. 1 m, 1958; Alicante, Col. A. Siglo XX).

Among Hernández's other works are those in which the figure is shown in fragmented form, as in *Manuscript* (bronze, h. 430 mm, 1971; see 1973 exh. cat.), a tabletop on which a right forearm is shown writing on the pages of a notebook being held up by a left forearm. Hernández also made works, such as *Bedroom* (wood and bronze, h. 1.04 m, 1972; see 1973 exh. cat.), in which he recreated genre scenes or entire rooms on a small scale.

BIBLIOGRAPHY

Julio L. Hernández: Escultura, obra reciente, 1968–1973 (exh. cat. by A. Bonet Correa, Madrid, Gal. Juana Mordó, 1973)

Lo real imaginario en la escultura de Julio López Hernández (exh. cat. by A. Bonet Correa, Madrid, Min. Cult., 1980)

JOSÉ CORREDOR-MATHEOS

Hernández, Mateo (*b* Béjar, Salamanca, 21 May 1884; *d* Meudon, nr Paris, 26 Nov 1949). Spanish sculptor, active in France. He was the son and brother of stonemasons and mastered the technique of carving in stone while a boy. He studied from 1902 to 1905 at the Escuela de Artes y Oficios in Béjar and later for a short time in Madrid but was otherwise self-taught. In 1913 he settled in Paris and never returned to Spain, although he always remained on the margin of various artistic circles and avant-garde movements. His first years were marked by great economic hardship; he was obliged to make his sculptures from paving stones or from the remains of tombstones. In 1920, however, he exhibited in the Salon d'Automne, after which his success increased, culminating in a one-man exhibition in Paris at the Pavillon de Marsan (1927), when he was awarded the Légion d'honneur. He was shy and retiring by nature and spent most of his life working tirelessly in his villa in Meudon, where he had installed a private zoo whose animals served as models. The sculptures he created from this readily accessible subject-matter were remarkable for their simplified forms and volumes, showing clearly the influence of Sumerian and Egyptian sculpture. His preferred materials were the hardest stones, such as porphyry, schist, diorite and granite, and he paid particular attention to the final polishing of his sculptures. Hernández died almost blinded by stone splinters, his lungs damaged by silicosis caused by his carving.

Most of his work is in the Museo Municipal in Béjar, and his sculpture of the gypsy dancer, *Portrait of Maria Albaiciu* (black granite, h. 280 mm, 1923), is in the Centro de la Reina Sofía in Madrid; one of his finest pieces, *Black Panther* (1925), life-size in diorite, belongs to the Metropolitan Museum of Art in New York, and there are others in the Musée Nationale d'Art Moderne in Paris.

BIBLIOGRAPHY

J. L. Majada Neila: *Mateo Hernández, 1884–1949* (Madrid, 1979)

J. Alix Trueba: *Escultura española, 1900–1936* (Madrid, 1985), pp. 80–82, 257–60

JOSEFINA ALIX TRUEBA

Hernández, Santiago (*b* Mexico City, 1833; *d* Mexico City, 1908). Mexican illustrator and lithographer. He studied at the Escuela Militar de Ingenieros, Mexico City. When the school was reorganized following the American invasion of 1847, he was commissioned to execute portraits of the *Child Heroes*. During the French intervention he founded a number of political newspapers, including *El espectro*, *El perico* and *Palo de ciego*, for which he executed caricatures and lithographs. Persecution forced him into hiding, but he re-emerged in 1865 as interpreter and chief draughtsman to the Comisión Científica del Imperio. Following the death in 1868 of Constantino Escalante, Hernández became the caricaturist for the periodical *La orquesta*; he also produced lithographs for *El artista* (e.g. *The Rattle*; see Fernández, fig. 227). He collaborated with Hesiquio Iriarte on, among other things, illustrations for *El libro rojo* (1870), a novel by Vicente Riva Palacio, director of *La orquesta*. At the time of his death Hernández was producing caricatures for *El hijo del ahuizote*.

BIBLIOGRAPHY

J. Fernández: *Arte moderno y contemporáneo de México* (Mexico City, 1952, R/1983)

R. Alvárez: *Enciclopedia de México* (Mexico City, 1966)

C. Díaz y de Ovando: 'El grabado comercial en la segunda mitad del siglo XIX', *Hist. A. Mex.*, 85–6 (1982)

ELOÍSA URIBE

Hernández Cruz, Luis (*b* San Juan, 1936). Puerto Rican painter, printmaker, sculptor and draughtsman. He studied painting at the University of Puerto Rico, receiving his BA in 1958, and completed his MA at the American University in Washington, DC, in 1959. From the 1960s he was one of the most consistent advocates of abstract painting in Puerto Rico, and in 1977 he co-founded Frente with artists Lope Max Díaz, Antonio Navia and Paul Camacho with the aim of bringing together abstract and experimental painters and of renewing artistic institutions in Puerto Rico. Hernández Cruz was also a founder-member and President of the Congress of Abstract Artists that took place in Puerto Rico in 1984.

In his paintings Hernández Cruz used landscape and figures as points of reference for a symbolic language of abstract and organic forms. The lyrical, evocative qualities of colour and the material, rhythmic qualities of textual surfaces were fundamental in the evolution of his abstract vocabulary. During the 1960s he explored intense colour under the influence of Fernando de Szyszlo and Rufino Tamayo before turning to more structural concerns that he explored also in constructions and totem-like sculptures. In the 1970s he was concerned primarily with the organization of forms in space, but he later returned to the human figure in a dynamic neo-expressionist style of heavy impasto and vibrant colours.

BIBLIOGRAPHY

Luis Hernández Cruz: Pinturas y grabados (exh. cat. by M. Traba, San Juan, Inst. Cult. Puertorriqueña, 1972)

Luis Hernández Cruz: Obra reciente: Pinturas (exh. cat. by M. de Tolentino, Ponce, Mus. A., 1984)

Luis Hernández Cruz: Pinturas y dibujos (exh. cat. by M. Benítez, San Juan, Inst. Cult. Puertorriqueña, Arsenal Puntilla, 1985)

MARI CARMEN RAMÍREZ

Hernández Estrada, Jerónimo (*b* Avila, 1540; *d* Seville, 27 July 1586). Spanish sculptor and architect. In 1553 he was apprenticed in the studio in Avila of Juan Bautista Vázquez, whom he accompanied to Seville in 1561. There, before 1568, he married the daughter of the architect Hernán Ruiz II. In 1573 he was examined in the art of the sculptor and architect ('*arte de escultor y entallador al romano y arquitecto*'). In 1578, having completed his years of apprenticeship, he left Vázquez's studio.

Hernández Estrada carved the fine Herculean figure of *St Jerome* (1565–6) for the retable of the Visitation in Seville Cathedral. His design for the retable (1570–79) in the church of S Mateo, Lucena, shows a knowledge of Sebastiano Serlio. The *Virgin of la O* (Nuestra Señora de la O, Ubrique, Cadiz), holding the standing Child, is from his retable of Our Lady (1575) in the church of El Salvador, Carmona, a figure that is repeated in the *Virgin of Granada* in the sanctuary of the same name at Guillena. Hernández Estrada's retable dedicated to *St John the Evangelist* (1580–81; Seville, Convent of Madre de Dios) is designed in the form of a double triumphal arch. The seated image of his *Virgin of the Rosary* (1571–2; fragment, Seville, Convent of Madre de Dios) has a majestic pose similar to that of his *Virgin of la Paz* (Seville, Church of Santa Cruz). The statue of the *Immaculate Conception* (1580–85; Seville, Church of S Andres) belongs to another of his lost altarpieces. The standing *Christ Child* (1581–2) and the *Resurrection* (1582–3; both Seville, Church of La Magdalena), both carved in wood, show a highly effective use of contrapposto. His façade (1582; destr.) for the convent of Regina Angelorum, Seville, is known only from photographs. Hernández Estrada was a designer and draughtsman who showed much innovation and originality in the iconography of his subjects and who introduced Mannerist forms to Seville through his sculpture and the frames of his altarpieces.

BIBLIOGRAPHY

Ceán Bermúdez

F. Pacheco: *Arte* (1649); ed. F. Sánchez Cantón (1956), I, pp. xxxiv, xlvii, 51, 248–9, 424, 439; II, pp. 3, 7

A. A. Palomino de Castro y Velasco: *Museo pictórico* (1715–24)

J. Gestoso Perez: *Ensayo de un diccionario de los artífices que florecieron en Sevilla desde el siglo XIII al XVIII inclusive*, 3 vols (Seville, 1899–1908)

C. Lopez Martinez: *Desde Jerónimo Hernández hasta Martinez Montañes* (Seville, 1928)

J. Hernández Diaz: *Imaginería hispalense del bajo renacimiento* (Seville, 1951), pp. 50–64

J. A. Moralez Martinez and J. M. Serrera Contreras: 'Aportaciones a la obra de Jerónimo Hernández', *Archv Esp. A.*, 54 (1981), pp. 405–26

J. M. Palomero Paramo: 'El contrato de aprendizaje de Gerónimo Hernández con Juan Bautista Vázquez el Viejo', *Archv Hisp.*, 64 (1981), pp. 139–42

——: *Gerónimo Hernández* (Seville, 1981)

——: *El retablo sevillano del renacimiento: Análisis y evolución (1560–1629)* (Seville, 1983), pp. 258–92

MARGARITA ESTELLA

Herodes Atticus [Lucius Vibullius Tiberius Claudius Atticus Herodes] (*b* Athens, AD 103; *d* Athens, AD 177). Teacher, writer, politician and patron. He was born into a family long distinguished for its services to Athens. A sophist, Herodes also followed a Roman career, serving in

AD 134–5 as financial officer for the province of Asia. He overspent the budget for a new aqueduct for the city of Alexandria Troas, displeasing the Emperor Hadrian (*reg* AD 117–38). In AD 139–40 Herodes directed the Pan-athenaic festival in Athens. He commissioned a mechanical ship to carry Athena's robe to the Acropolis; the ship was later conserved above the stadium at Ardettos, rebuilt by Herodes to seat 50,000 spectators. The stadium at Delphi was replated with marble, and Herodes gave an aqueduct and fountain decorated with family and imperial portraits to the Panhellenic sanctuary at Olympia (*see* OLYMPIA, §1). He also gave fine statues at Isthmia and Corinth, where he is said to have rebuilt the theatre. Implicated in his wife's death in *c.*AD 160, he built a large ODEION to her memory south of the Athenian Acropolis. He also rebuilt the centre of Orikon (Epiros) after an earthquake and gave a spa to Thermopylai in Thessaly. Herodes was buried at Athens in a mausoleum facing the Temple of Tyche that he had endowed above the stadium at Ardettos. Herodes' buildings provided grand locations for the fashionable pursuit of traditional Greek culture. With baths, aqueducts and fountains, he gave visitors to old Greece the benefits of Roman Imperial civilization.

BIBLIOGRAPHY

Philostratos: *Lives of the Sophists* II/i

W. Ameling: *Herodes Atticus*, 2 vols (Hildesheim, 1983)

R. Bol: *Das Statuenprogramm des Herodes-Atticus-Nymphäums* (Berlin, 1984)

SUSAN WALKER

Herodotus (*b* Halikarnassos [now Bodrum, Turkey], *c.* 484 BC; *d* ?Thurii [nr Sibari, Calabria], *c.* 425 BC). Greek historian. His life is poorly documented, but after early political exile from Halikarnassos he seems to have spent time on Samos and in the Athenian colony of Thurii in southern Italy, as well as in Athens itself. His travels included voyages to Egypt and to the Black Sea region (*see* SCYTHIAN AND SARMATIAN ART, §1). Herodotus is known as the 'father of history', since he was the first to approach the writing of history in a systematic manner with an attempt to authenticate evidence and present it cogently. He left one work, the *Histories*, which centres on the Greco-Persian wars of 499–479 BC; these ended with the defeat of the Achaemenid forces by Athens around the time of Herodotus' birth. The first half of the *Histories* explores the background to the might of the Achaemenid empire, while the second follows the course of the wars with Greece. Herodotus' narrative, later divided into nine books ('Muses'), embraces a wealth of geographical, historical and political commentary, as well as a repertory of fantastical travellers' tales. These last have earned him the alternative sobriquet 'father of lies', although many of his other observations have been endorsed by modern scholarship and archaeology. Herodotus is not only an important source for Greek history in the period *c.* 550–479 BC, but his accounts of Egypt and the Near East often provide crucial literary evidence for comparison with the archaeological record (for example, his descriptions of the ethnology and customs of the inhabitants of the Black Sea region).

WRITINGS

Histories (MS.; *c.* 430 BC); ed. and Eng. trans. by A. D. Godley, Loeb Class. Lib., 4 vols (London and New York, 1920–24)

BIBLIOGRAPHY

Pauly–Wissowa

J. L. Myres: *Herodotus: Father of History* (Oxford, 1953/R1971)

MICHAEL BIRD

Herod the Great (*b c.* 79 BC; *reg* 37–4 BC; *d* 4 BC). King of Judaea and patron. By a series of successful intrigues and pro-Roman policy, he established himself as the heir of the Maccabean kings and considerably extended their territory. He more or less re-established the ancient kingdom of Judah and achieved virtual independence. With the arrival in the East of the Roman general Pompey (66 BC), the balance of power changed and Rome began to absorb this territory. Herod, by skilful diplomacy and intrigue, maintained himself as king of Judaea, with independence in local affairs. He was a great admirer of Rome and Greco-Roman culture; he set out to make his towns and cities similar to the Hellenistic towns of the Roman Empire. The historian Josephus recorded that Herod erected a vast number of buildings both in his own kingdom and as far afield as the Dodekanese, Tyre and Beirut. He refounded the city of SAMARIA as Sebaste, in which he built a temple to Rome and Augustus. In his own kingdom he founded a new town and port at Caesarea. He is also credited (Josephus: *Jewish War* I.422) with paving a street at Syrian Antioch and lining it with a colonnade. In Jerusalem he rebuilt the Temple of Solomon, enlarging it and embellishing the surrounding area, and built a palace for himself, which incorporated a Kaisareion hall and an Agrippaion hall named after Augustus and Agrippa respectively (*see* JERUSALEM, §I, 1).

BIBLIOGRAPHY

A. H. M. Jones: *The Herods of Judaea* (Oxford, 1938)

J. B. Ward-Perkins: *Roman Imperial Architecture*, Pelican Hist. A. (Harmondsworth, 1981), pp. 309–14

D. Braund: *Rome and the Friendly King* (London and New York, 1984)

MARGARET LYTTELTON

Herold[t], Johann Gregorius. *See* HÖROLDT, JOHANN GREGORIUS.

Heron, Patrick (*b* Leeds, 30 Jan 1920). English painter and critic. In the 1950s he became identified with the ST IVES group of painters, although the roots of his aesthetic date back to earlier experiences, which included working as a designer for his father's firm, Cresta Silks (1935–9, 1944–50), and assisting at Bernard Leach's pottery (1944–5). Insights gained through friendships with Herbert Read, T. S. Eliot, Henry Moore, Ben Nicholson and Ivon Hitchens were also important. Influenced by Braque and Matisse, he evolved a flat, linear style in a series of still-lifes and interiors such as the ambitious *Christmas Eve* (1951; artist's col., see 1985 exh. cat., p. 29), in which the lightly filled-in colours create an airy, luminous effect. In his writings as a critic for the *New English Weekly*, *New Statesman and Nation* and *Arts* (New York) between 1945 and 1958, Heron was unconvinced of the necessity for pure abstraction. His early paintings are in an ART INFORMEL style, but he then began to produce paintings composed of horizontal bands of colour, such as *Horizontal Stripe Painting* (1957–8; London, Tate). These simple bars of thinned oil paint, softly brushed on in one movement so the colours intermingle, still seem to refer to coastal landscape in their form and colour, bringing them as close to Hitchens's abstractions from nature as to the Post-painterly Abstraction of Morris Louis, whose work Heron claimed to have foreshadowed. From the 1960s he concentrated on simple forms such as rectangles and a repertory of distinctive shapes that emphasized decorative values and contrasts of saturated colour. In the 1970s he favoured large surfaces of colour painted with small Japanese brushes (e.g. *Long Cadmium with Ceruleum in Violet (Boycott)*, 1977; London, Waddington Gals), relaxing these self-imposed restrictions in the 1980s in more informal abstractions that hinted once again at landscape associations (e.g. *Pale Garden Painting*, 1984; artist's col., see 1985 exh. cat., p. 45).

As a critic in the 1950s Heron exerted considerable influence through his measured assessments of post-war English artists, his response to Abstract Expressionism and his support of Picasso and Matisse in the face of English prejudice against modern art. After a period when he renounced critical writing he became a vigorous critic of the English Establishment's capitulation to American influence and an effective champion of the autonomy of art schools. He has been at his most articulate in numerous articles, lectures and television interviews, notably those describing how colour sensations govern his aesthetic.

WRITINGS
Regular contributions to *New English Weekly* (1945–7), *New Statesman and Nation* (1947–50), *Arts* [New York] (1955–8)
The Changing Forms of Art (London, 1955) [collected essays]
Ivon Hitchens, Penguin Mod. Masters (Harmondsworth, 1955)
Braque (London, 1958)
'The Shape of Colour', *Studio Int.*, clxxxvii (1974), pp. 65–75; also in *Concerning Contemporary Art: The Power Lectures, 1968–1973*, ed. B. Smith (Oxford, 1975)
'The British Influence on New York', *The Guardian* (10, 11, 12 Oct 1974)
'The Colour of Colour', *E. William Doty Lectures in Fine Arts 1968* (Austin, TX, 1979)

BIBLIOGRAPHY
A. Gouk: 'Patrick Heron', *Artscribe* (1982), 34, pp. 40–54; 35, pp. 32–43
Patrick Heron (exh. cat. by V. Knight, J. F. Walker and A. Gouk, London, Barbican A.G., 1985)
V. Knight: *Patrick Heron* (London, 1988)
M. Gooding: *Patrick Heron* (London, 1994)

JAMES FAURE WALKER

Heroon [pl. heroa]. Monument or sanctuary, of any form or size, used in the ancient Greek world for celebrating hero cults. Heroa abounded in the countryside and in town centres, in agoras, on acropoleis and in large sanctuaries. They were centres of extremely popular cults, usually local, which were one of the most lively aspects of Greek religion. Heroes were considered to be intermediary spirits between the gods and man, and there were innumerable different cults, each city having its own. For Athens alone, at the end of the 6th century BC, Kleisthenes had proposed to the oracle at Delphi a list of 100 names. From among these the Pythian priestess picked out at random those of ten 'eponymous heroes', who bore the names of the new Attic tribes. Some heroes, however, did not have proper names and were known only by the efficacy of their interventions: for example the 'doctor hero' (Iatros) at Rhamnous, the 'guardian hero' (Phylakos) at Delphi and the 'saviour hero' (Sosipolis) at Olympia. Most often the hero was an actual or presumed historical figure, having a recognized place in society and endowed with superhuman powers through the brilliance of his

gifts: he might be an athlete (Theogenes of Thasos), poet (Archilochos of Paros), founder of the city (Theseus at Athens, Anios at Delos), legislator (Lykourgos at Sparta) or soldier (Brasidas at Amphipolis). Each city hoped, through an appropriate cult, to capture after the hero's death the beneficial, semi-divine influence he had exercised while alive, and sometimes to dispel the evil influence of a vengeful hero by funerary honours. For example, at Temesa in southern Italy a drunken sailor who had raped a virgin was stoned to death and left unburied by the furious population, and at Delphi the inhabitants killed Neoptolemos in the Sanctuary of Apollo after a sordid quarrel: both these impieties unleashed plagues that ceased only when the two victims, though hardly 'heroic', were honoured by a heroon.

Many heroa were located in the agora of a city, where the protection they conferred appears to have been particularly desirable. Such heroa include the tombs of founders (e.g. Battos at Cyrene) or benefactors (Themistokles at Magnesia on the Maeander); the statues of the ten 'eponymous heroes' (see above) and of Harmodios and Aristogeiton (at Athens); the cenotaph of Glaukos, Leptines' son, who died in combat; and the altar and receptacle for dedications to Theogenes on Thasos. Sometimes the hero was even interred in the city's bouleuterion, where important political decisions were taken (for example the hero Aisymnos at Megara, and the anonymous hero whose monumental tomb was next to the bouleuterion of Miletos). In this way, the close link between the cult of the hero and the life of the city was evident.

Heroa of different dates have been found throughout the Greek world: an early example is the Dark Age heroon at LEFKANDI (early 10th century BC). A later example exists at KALYDON. A heroon often took the form of a *sekos* (sanctuary enclosed by a wall) near the entrance to the city. This area might contain the hero's tomb (e.g. Eretria), a sacred grove, and an *eschara* (low altar) for the sacrifices associated with chthonic rites. At Temesa, in the sailor's heroon, there was a shrine surrounded by wild olive trees. At Delphi, Neoptolemos' *sekos* contained a sacred grove, an altar of ashes and the hero's tomb, on which the Delphians celebrated important rites and sacrifices. At Olympia the Pelopion, the heroon of the legendary founder, Pelops, contained a raised mound marking the hero's tomb, an altar, trees and statues, within a hexagonal enclosure with a Doric porch. At Athens, between the Agora and the Acropolis was the heroon of Theseus, a place of lawful asylum and the setting for stately ceremonies, adorned on its *sekos* with paintings by Mikon, which were probably protected by a peristyle. The best-preserved heroon of this type, the 'Archegeseion', was excavated on Delos. This was the sanctuary of the *archegetes* (founder) hero, Anios, and only admitted inhabitants of Delos. An open porch in the *sekos* led to a flagged courtyard surrounded by a peristyle with the *eschara* in the middle. Statues, various offerings and a series of rooms (possibly for funerary banquets) completed the heroon. It is further worth recalling that at Athens Plato and Aristotle installed the Academy and the Lyceum in their school in the sacred groves of the heroes Akademos and Lykos. A heroon could also form part of a building dedicated to another divinity. Thus at Olympia the temple of Eileithyia contained the heroon of Sosipolis in its adyton, while at Athens the Erechtheion held the heroa of Erechtheus, Boutes, Kekrops and Pandrosos.

When a hero was deified, his worshippers faithfully remembered the time when he had been mortal. Besides his temple at Thasos, where he was honoured as a god, Herakles was given a heroon in the form of an *eschara*, where the rites proper to a hero were perpetuated. The same was true of the cult of Asklepios at Epidauros: the temple contained his cult statue (i.e. of the god), while the sumptuous tholos was his tomb or heroon. The latter prefigured such types of Christian shrine as the 'holy sepulchre' and martyria.

BIBLIOGRAPHY

L. R. Farnell: *Greek Hero Cults, and Ideas of Immortality* (Oxford, 1921)
E. Dyggve: *Das Heroon von Kalydon* (Copenhagen, 1934)
M. Delcourt: *Légendes et cultes des héros en Grèce* (Paris, 1942)
J. Schäfer: *Pergamonische Forschungen* (Berlin, 1968), ii
H. A. Thompson and R. E. Wycherley: *The Athenian Agora XIV, the Agora of Athens: The History, Shape and Uses of an Ancient City Center* (Princeton, 1972), pp. 124–6

GEORGES ROUX

Heroöpolis. See MASKHUTA, TELL EL-.

Herp, Willem [Guillaume] **van, I** (*b* Antwerp, ?1614; *bur* Antwerp, 23 June 1677). Flemish painter. He trained from 1625 to 1629 with Damiaan Wortelmans (*b* 1588/9) and Hans Biermans, both minor painters, and eventually, perhaps after spending some time abroad, became a master in the Antwerp Guild of St Luke in 1637–8. From at least 1651 he worked for Matthijs Musson, the Antwerp art dealer. From the considerable quantity of surviving works, it appears that he must have worked on a semi-industrial basis to supply the art market (*see* CABINET PICTURE, fig. 1). The majority of his paintings are religious scenes, fairly small in size, often painted on copper and existing in more than one version (e.g. *St Anthony of Padua Distributing Bread*, London, N.G.). Often they are copies or pastiches of compositions by Peter Paul Rubens, Anthony van Dyck or by history painters of the second rank, such as Gerard Seghers and Jan Boeckhorst. From Musson's business correspondence and from the great number of works by van Herp discovered in Spain in the 1970s, we know that many of these paintings were intended for Spanish buyers.

Van Herp also made a few genre pictures, mostly peasant scenes in the manner of David Teniers (ii), which may have been intended primarily for the Antwerp market (e.g. *Merry Company*, 1654; Mertoun, St Boswells, Borders). No stylistic development within van Herp's oeuvre has been distinguished, since only a few of his works are dated. But his personal style can easily be recognized, especially in the slightly mannered way of drawing and in the expressiveness of his figures. Both his sons were also painters.

BIBLIOGRAPHY

L. van Puyvelde: 'Guillaume van Herp, bon peintre et copiste de Rubens', *Z. Kstgesch.*, xxii (1959), pp. 46–8
F. C. Legrand: *Les Peintres flamands de genre au XVIIe siècle* (Brussels, 1963), pp. 167–75
M. D. Padron: 'Obras de Guillaume van Herp en España', *Archv Esp. A.*, l (1977), pp. 361–2; li (1978), pp. 1–27

HANS VLIEGHE

Herr, Michael (*b* Metzingen, Württemberg, 1591; *d* Nuremberg, 1661). German painter and draughtsman. He completed his apprenticeship, no doubt in Stuttgart, before 1611, when he is recorded as a journeyman working in Nuremberg. He was in Venice and Rome in 1614: a book of travel sketches is filled with copies after Veronese, Taddeo Zuccaro and others (pages, Brunswick, Herzog Anton Ulrich-Mus.; Coburg, Veste Coburg). He was already using a secret script containing Cyrillic letters in inscriptions on drawings at that time. Contact with Italian art drew him away from Mannerism, a move expressed in the sturdy, thickset 'non-artistic' figures in his drawings. He travelled in Swabia (1617–20) before returning to Nuremberg, where he obtained his master's certificate in 1622.

Herr's work seems extraordinarily varied in terms of both style and content. It includes religious allegories (with a Protestant slant) and secular stories, *vedute*, genre paintings and many portraits, for example *Andreas Imhoff III* (1635; Nuremberg, Ger. Nmus.). The numerous drawings, often monogrammed, reveal him as a fresh and enthralling narrator, almost in the folklore tradition, with an early Baroque realism. As a Protestant, he showed an early preference for genre themes inspired from the Netherlands. His scenes of contemporary life include *Nuremberg under Siege during the Thirty Years War* (1631; Germany, priv. col.) and *Swedish Soldiers Encamped before Nuremberg* (*c.* 1631–2; Berlin, Kupferstichkab.). In his large-scale, occasionally crudely simplified designs he incorporated subject-matter of the most varied kind and origin, including stories relating to his time and emblematic symbols. *The Four Seasons* (?1640s; Berlin, Kupferstichkab.) exemplifies this approach.

Much of Herr's work is known through etchings by Peter Isselburg, Peter Troschel and others. Herr did assured preliminary drawings for engravings for illustrations and title pages in Protestant religious tracts, for instance *Sacra emblemata* (Nuremberg, 1624), and other printed works, as well as for flysheets for the Merian house in Frankfurt am Main. It seems that Herr, coming from Swabia, had some influence on the local development of Baroque art in Nuremberg. His influence can be detected in the work of such artists as Conrad Strauch.

BIBLIOGRAPHY

Thieme–Becker
Barock in Nürnberg, 1600–1750 (exh. cat., Nuremberg, Ger. Nmus., 1962), pp. 541–5
Zeichnung in Deutschland: Deutsche Zeichner, 1540–1640, i (exh. cat. by H. Geissler, Stuttgart, Staatsgal., 1979–80), pp. 220–23
Michael Herr, 1591–1661: Ein Künstler zwischen Manierismus und Barock (exh. cat. by S. Gatenbröcker, Metzingen, Rathaus, 1991)

HEINRICH GEISSLER

Herrad von Landsberg [von Hohenbourg] (*fl* 1160–70; *d* Hohenbourg, Alsace, 25 July 1195). German writer and ?illuminator. She was Abbess (1167–95) of the convent of Ste Odile in Hohenbourg. She is best known for writing (*c.* 1175–95) a complex pictorial encyclopedia in Latin called the HORTUS DELICIARUM ('Garden of delights'), a compendium of medieval learning intended for the women in her convent. This encyclopedic work covered biblical, moral and theological material. It was accompanied by several hundred miniatures that depicted biblical scenes, allegorical figures (*see* ALLEGORY, fig. 2) and gardening hints, as well as a portrait of Herrad with the nuns of Hohenbourg. Referring to herself metaphorically as a bee, she described the book in the following way: 'I drew from many flowers of sacred and philosophic writing this book...and have put it together to the praise of Christ and the Church, and to your enjoyment'. The original manuscript was destroyed by fire at the municipal library of Strasbourg during the city's bombardment in 1870, but there survive notes and line drawing copies of the illustrations made by scholars in the 19th century before its destruction. Since there is a close relationship between text and image, it has been suggested that Herrad participated directly in the illustration; however, this is by no means certain. Manuscripts that emphasized the illustrations were unusual at the time, and the *Hortus deliciarum*, along with Hildegard of Bingen's *Scivias* (1140s), was considered innovative in the 12th century. Herrad was an active teacher and was a model figure in her community of women. The *Hortus deliciarum* is considered to have influenced the Alsace school of painting.

BIBLIOGRAPHY

K. Petersen and J. J. Wilson: *Women Artists* (New York and London, 1976)

D. G. Bachman and S. Piland: *Women Artists: An Historical, Contemporary and Feminist Bibliography* (Metuchen, NJ, and London, 1978), p. 50

R. Green and others: *The Hortus deliciarum of Herrad of Hohenbourg*, 2 vols (London, 1979) [facs. of copy of *Hortus*]

A. Sutherland Harris and L. Nochlin: *Women Artists, 1550–1950* (New York, 1989)

W. Chadwick: *Women, Art and Society* (London and New York, 1990), pp. 46–8

For further bibliography *see* HORTUS DELICIARUM.

Herrán, Saturnino (*b* Aguascalientes, 9 July 1887; *d* Mexico City, 8 Oct 1918). Mexican painter. After moving to Mexico City he entered the Escuela Nacional de Bellas Artes in 1904, studying drawing under Antonio Fabrés and painting under Germán Gedovius; he in turn taught there from 1910 until his premature death. His first paintings took as their subjects allegories of nature (e.g. *Flora*, 1910; Mexico City, Sergio Zaldívar priv. col., see Ramírez, 1989, pl. 3), local mythology (e.g. *The Legend of the Volcanoes*, 1910; Saltillo, Ateneo Fuente) and scenes of work that were either optimistic in tone (e.g. *Labour*, 1908; Aguascalientes, Mus. Aguascalientes), conceived as allegories (e.g. two decorative panels for the Escuela de Artes y Oficios, 1910–11; Mexico City, Inst. Poli. N.) or imbued with social criticism through an emphasis on the oppression and misery of the workers, as in *Glass Grinder*, *Pot Sellers* (both 1909; Aguascalientes, Mus. Aguascalientes).

Herrán used very free brushwork to capture the vibration of light and to create a blurred effect for his backgrounds, but he outlined his figures with clearly marked contours. Among the diverse influences on his early paintings were the work of Frank Brangwyn, Joaquín Sorolla y Bastida and Ignacio Zuloaga. In 1912 he began to stress local colour in his decadent, *fin-de-siècle* subject-matter by setting his scenes against colonial Mexican architecture: in *Blind Men* (1914; Aguascalientes, Mus. Aguascalientes), for instance, the despairing figures seem crushed beneath the weight of the cupola of the church of Loreto, while the tragic agony of the old man in *The Last Song* (1914; Aguascalientes, Mus. Aguascalientes) is given shelter by the façade of the Sagrario Metropolitano. The refinement of Herrán's draughtsmanship and use of colour balances the naturalistic imagery in these works combining drawing with watercolour, a technique adapted from Spanish painters such as Néstor de la Torre.

From *c.* 1913 Herrán transcended the late 19th-century zeal for recording picturesque local customs by charging his representations with symbolic significance, and in so doing he became one of the principal exponents of the nationalist modernism that came to dominate Mexican art until the mid-1920s. In one of his most representative paintings, *The Offering* (1913; Mexico City, Mus. N. A.), he treated the theme of the three ages of man, while in paintings such as *El jarabe* and *La tehuana* (both 1914; Aguascalientes, Mus. Aguascalientes) the *fin-de-siècle* motif of the femme fatale was tinged with surprising vernacular suggestions.

From *c.* 1915 Herrán made a significant contribution to the iconic expression of the 'nation's soul', a task that was considered fundamental by the members of his generation. Herrán felt that Mexican identity was singled out and defined by the fact that it was of mixed race, and he devoted his most important late works to expressing this sense of national identity, exalting the spiritual beauty of the native people of Mexico in exquisite drawings of Indians whose languid silhouettes stand out against freely-interpreted backgrounds of Pre-Columbian sculpture. He celebrated Mexico's Spanish roots in the series *Las criollas*, culminating in two allegorical oil paintings, *The Shawl* (1916) and *Criolla with Mantilla* (1917–18; both Aguascalientes, Mus. Aguascalientes), which depict a number of female nudes half-covered by the typical garments indicated by the titles and surrounded by emblematic fruits, with the Baroque profiles of the Sagrario and Mexico City Cathedral rising up in the background.

From late 1914 until his sudden death from a gastric infection in 1918, Herrán worked on *Our Gods* (see exh. cat., pp. 40–41), a mural frieze in triptych form for the Teatro Nacional (now the Teatro de Bellas Artes), which was then under construction in Mexico City. Although he completed only one of the lateral panels, representing the native worshippers (Mexico City, Alicia G. de Herrán priv. col.), the project survives in three watercolour drawings (Aguascalientes, Mus. Aguascalientes). The lateral wings were to represent a double procession of Indians and Spaniards coming to pay tribute to the syncretic deity of the central panel in which the images of Christ and Coatlicue coalesce in a vivid expression of his theme concerning the mixture of the two races.

BIBLIOGRAPHY

M. Toussaint: *Saturnino Herrán y su obra* (Mexico City, 1920)

L. Garrido: *Saturnino Herrán* (Mexico City, 1971)

F. Ramírez: *Saturnino Herrán* (Mexico City, 1976)

Saturnino Herrán, 1887–1987 (exh. cat., essay F. Ramírez; Mexico City, Inst. N. B.A., 1987)

F. Ramírez and others: *Jornadas de homenaje a Saturnino Herrán* (Mexico City, 1989)

FAUSTO RAMÍREZ

Herrenhausen. Palace and garden on the outskirts of Hannover, Germany. After Duke Georg of Calenberg (*d* 1641) had elevated Hannover to the status of *Residenzstadt*, his summer residence was developed from an existing palace to the north-west of the town (from 1638). The modest palace, which was altered several times, was almost completely destroyed in 1943, but its Baroque gallery-building (1694–6) survives. The banqueting hall and residential wings are richly decorated: the frescoes (including an *Aeneas* cycle) were painted by the Venetian Tommaso Giusti (1644–1729), while the stucco decoration was executed by Dossa Grana, Pietro Rosso (*fl* 1695–1706) and others. To the south of the Residenz lies the park, the Grosser Garten, for which Herrenhausen is famed. The first pleasure garden, inspired by Venetian villa design, was created in 1666 by the landscape gardener Michael Grosse and developed (from 1674) by Henry Perronet (*d* 1690) with the collaboration of the French fountain specialist Cadart and the Augsburg grotto specialist Michel Riggus. However, the true creators of the Grosser Garten are considered to be Electress Sophie (1630–1714), wife of Ernest-August, Duke of Brunswick-Lüneburg, later Elector of Hanover, and the French landscape gardener Martin Charbonnier (*d* 1720), a pupil of André Le Nôtre, whom she appointed in 1682. Together they produced the finest formal garden in Germany, combining Italian, French and Dutch elements. The parterre, consisting of flower borders to the north and four hedged squares with fountains at their centres to the south, is supplemented by numerous painted sandstone figures on mythological and allegorical themes. The garden theatre (1689–93), the earliest hedged theatre of the Baroque period, was conceived as part of the garden layout: hornbeam hedges behind the stage are set off by gilded lead sculptures (1678–82) by Pieter von Empthusen. Work on the Great Fountain (h. 36 m) was begun only in 1720, although the philosopher and scientist Gottfried Wilhelm Leibniz (1646–1716) had advised on the hydraulic arrangements in 1690.

BIBLIOGRAPHY

U. v. Alvensleben and H. Reuther: *Herrenhausen: Die Sommerresidenz der Welfen* (Hannover, 1966)

Sophie Kurfürstin von Hannover (1630–1714) (exh. cat., Hannover, Hist. Mus. Hohen Ufer, 1980)

W. Ness and others, eds: *Stadt Hannover*, X/i of *Denkmaltopographie Bundesrepublik Deutschland: Baudenkmale in Niedersachsen* (Brunswick, 1983), pp. 201–7

W. Fiedler and M. Heinzburger: 'Der Pflanzenbestand des Barockgartens zu Herrenhausen in frühen 18. Jahrhundert und heute', *Ber. Dkmlpf. Niedersachsen*, iv/3 (1984), pp. 82–93

W. Hübner: 'Das Galerie-Gebäude im grossen Garten in Hannover-Herrenhausen', *Niederdt. Beitr. Kstgesch.*, xxx (1991), pp. 119–66

JOHANNES ZAHLTEN

Herrera. Spanish family of artists. The illuminator and engraver Juan de Herrera Aguilar worked in Seville in the second half of the 16th century, although documentation on his life and career is scarce. His son (1) Francisco de Herrera (i) was active primarily in Seville. The latter's son (2) Francisco de Herrera (ii) also worked in Seville and Madrid, becoming one of the most important Spanish Baroque artists.

BIBLIOGRAPHY

A. A. Palomino de Castro y Velasco: *Museo pictórico* (1715–24/*R* 1947)

D. Angulo Iñíguez: *Pintura del siglo XVII*, A. Hisp., xvi (Madrid, 1971)

(1) Francisco de Herrera (i) [*el viejo*] (*b* Seville, *c.* 1590; *d* Madrid, ?29 Dec 1654). Painter and engraver. He studied under his father, Juan de Herrera Aguilar, who trained him in the Mannerist style common in Seville in the late 16th century, but the influence of Francesco Pacheco is also evident in his early works. His first recorded works as an engraver date from 1609, when he executed the frontispiece for the *Constituciones del Arzobispado de Sevilla* (Seville, 1609), after a design by Diego López. This and the frontispiece for the *Relación de la fiesta de beatificación de S Ignacio* (Seville, 1610) show, in the garlands of fruit and flowers, a development from Mannerism towards naturalism, possibly derived from the work of Juan de Roelas. Around 1610 Herrera may have been Velázquez's first teacher, although Palomino (p. 128) emphasizes that his difficult character made him unsuitable for the profession of teaching. His subsequent uneasy relationship with the rigid guild system in Seville, which led to continuous litigation, seems to confirm this aspect of his personality. Between 1614 and 1616 Herrera received his first documented commissions as a painter: for a series of 12 canvases for the Fraternity of Vera Cruz in the monastery of S Francisco in Seville. Two survive: the *Vision of Constantine* (Seville, Hosp. Caridad) and the *Virgin with Franciscan Nuns* (Seville, Pal. Arzobisp.). Other paintings from this period include the *Immaculate Conception* (1616; Seville Cathedral) and the *Arrival of the Holy Ghost* (1617; Toledo, Casa & Mus. El Greco).

One of the first works to anticipate Herrera's mature style, most evident from 1620 onwards, is the *Triumph of St Hermengild* (*c.* 1618; Seville, Mus. B.A.), painted for the Jesuits of the Colegio de S Hermenegildo, Seville. It is a balanced and clearly structured work, but with a significantly complex iconography that draws on the early history of Catholicism in Spain and the first Spanish martyrs. *St Francis Xavier in Ecstasy* (*c.* 1622–5; U. Seville) was also commissioned by the Jesuits for the Casa Profesa de la Compañía, Seville. In 1626–8 Herrera is recorded as working for the Franciscan Order at the Colegio de S Buenaventura, Seville, designing the plasterwork decoration and executing wall paintings as well as four canvases in a series of eight dedicated to the *Life of St Bonaventure* (the others were by Zurbarán). Of these, the *Vow of St Bonaventure* (Madrid, Prado) is painted somewhat severely, Herrera's Mannerist technique having given way to broad, vigorous brushstrokes, expressions of vital naturalism in the faces and a simple colour scheme rich in shadow. The closing work of this period, the *Last Judgement* (1628; Seville, S Bernardo), is a balanced and archaizing composition yet with a vigorous treatment of the figures reminiscent of the *Triumph of St Hermengild*. Here the light acquires a symbolic value, condemning the sinners to the shadows of Hell.

Herrera's gentle modelling of the nude figure acquires a more poignant character in *Job Tempted by the Demon* (1636; Rouen, Mus. B.-A.; see fig.). The dramatic nature of this painting contrasts, however, with the softness and general serenity of such other works of the 1630s as the *Presentation of the Virgin* (*c.* 1636–7; Madrid, Real Acad. S Fernando, Mus.) or *The Epiphany* (*c.* 1636–8; Barcelona, Mus. A. Catalunya). The same qualities can also be found in two small series, one of *St Paula* (*c.* 1637–8; Seville,

Francisco de Herrera (i): *Job Tempted by the Demon*, oil on canvas, 2.15×1.51 m, 1636 (Rouen, Musée des Beaux-Arts)

Convent of S Paula) and one painted in 1638–9 for the altarpiece of the Colegio de S Basilio, Seville (parts now dispersed in the Louvre, Paris, and in the Museo de Bellas Artes, Seville). The compositions of the paintings in the series become progressively more complex and rich; this is also true of the *Vision of St Basil* (*c.* 1638; Seville, Mus. B.A.), with its typically Baroque gradations from light to dark. In the 1640s Herrera painted some of the most beautiful and intimate works of his career. In the *Miracle of the Loaves and Fishes* (*c.* 1640–45; Madrid, Pal. Arzobisp.), painted for the refectory of the Colegio de S Hermenegildo in Seville, the depiction of the subjects within the landscape contrasts the proximity of Christ and the Apostles with the remoteness of the dispersed multitudes. *St Joseph with the Christ Child* (1648; Madrid, Mus. Lázaro Galdiano) is a monumental yet intimate work in which the Child, in a gesture foretelling his coming Passion, offers the Crown of Thorns to St Joseph. A painting of the same subject in the Museum of Fine Arts in Budapest, although dated 1645, is now thought to have a false signature and to be a work from the end of the 17th century, as the faces are too much influenced by Murillo.

Herrera was also a painter of *costumbrista* and other popular subjects, as in *Blind Musician with his Guide* (*c.* 1645–8; Vienna, Ksthist. Mus.). Although not unanimously accepted as authentic, this work nevertheless reveals the popularity of this type of subject-matter in Seville, evident also in the paintings of such artists as Murillo and Pedro Núñez de Villavicencio. About 1650,

shortly after the Plague had decimated Seville, Herrera moved to Madrid, possibly with the intention of seeking an appointment as Pintor del Rey to Philip IV, a position already held by Velázquez and Zurbarán. However, no paintings executed while in Madrid are accounted for.

BIBLIOGRAPHY
A. Martínez Ripoll: *Francisco de Herrera 'El Viejo'* (Seville, 1978)
E. Valdivieso and J. M. Serrera: *Historia de la pintura española: Pintura sevillana del primer tercio del siglo XVII* (Madrid, 1985)

ISMAEL GUTIÉRREZ PASTOR

(2) Francisco de Herrera (y Aguilar) (ii) [*el mozo*] (*b* Seville, *bapt* 28 June 1627; *bur* Madrid, 25 Aug 1685). Painter, architect and stage designer, son of (1) Francisco de Herrera (i). His study of the work of Titian and Rubens led him to develop a High Baroque style, in accordance with the tastes of the court of Philip IV in Madrid. All of his extant paintings are religious, but inventories record that he painted portraits, still-lifes and other secular subjects. In addition to his work in Madrid he was also active in Seville, and his career can be divided into four phases.

1. BEFORE 1650. On 9 September 1647 Herrera married in Seville, but the marriage failed. He did not remarry and no children are recorded. He is next documented on 7 February 1650 in Madrid. According to Palomino, Herrera also travelled to Rome, where his study of art and architecture resulted in his mature style, but no documentary or stylistic evidence verifies Palomino's account. The earliest painting attributed to Herrera is *St Catherine of Siena Preaching before Pope Urban VI* (*c.* 1647; Bormujos, Seville, Convent of S María el Real). The influence of the elder Herrera is present in the crowded space and the unpleasant features of the individual figures, but the areas of strong, bright colour and the passages of light and animated brushwork are quite unlike the father's art. A *St Thomas Aquinas* (Seville, Mus. B.A.) is only a little later in date.

2. MADRID, 1650–54. On 7 November 1650 Herrera was documented as a master painter in Madrid; he signed his first contract on 17 July 1654. The agreement stipulated that Herrera should paint 14 pictures for the high altarpiece of the convent church of the Discalced Carmelites in Madrid. The only surviving work is the *Triumph of St Hermengild* (Madrid, Prado; see SPAIN, fig. 15), a painting in the High Baroque style: it is brightly coloured, the surface is animated by free brushwork, the figures are shown in movement and with strong emotions and the composition is open. Herrera may have visited Italy sometime between 1648 and 1650, or 1651 and 1654, and may have learnt his new High Baroque style there, but it is more probable that he created it in Madrid. The two primary influences on his new manner were Rubens and Titian, both of whose work was abundantly available for study in Madrid. The artistic taste of the court there was largely determined by the king, Philip IV, who particularly admired these two artists. Their work was thus emulated by Spanish painters who wished to be successful at Court. Herrera, for example, adapted the idea for the *St Hermengild* from the *Assumption of the Virgin* by Rubens (1611–15; The Hague, Mauritshuis), which he would have known

from the contemporary print by Schelte Bolswert. The outlining of the music-playing angels and putti was derived from Rubens's sketches for the Torre de la Parada series (1636–8; Madrid, Prado), and the pure blue highlights on the armour also have sources in Rubens. The coloured shadows and the impasto technique, however, are derived from Francisco Rizi, whose own style was also based on the art of Rubens and Titian. The use of solidly modelled foreground figures strongly lit from behind is characteristic of Herrera's work from 1654 to 1657 and here emphasizes the soaring movement of the central figure. It was the activity of his compositions that distinguished Herrera most from his Spanish contemporaries.

3. SEVILLE, 1655–60. Herrera the elder died intestate in Madrid in 1654, and his son soon left the capital for Seville in order to collect his inheritance. He arrived there by the spring of 1655 at the latest. The process of claiming his inheritance proved lengthy, and in the interim Herrera re-established himself both socially and artistically. He joined the influential Brotherhood of the Most Holy Sacrament of the Cathedral on 19 December 1655 and painted for them the first of his Sevillian masterpieces, the *Allegory of the Holy Sacrament Adored by the Virgin of the Immaculate Conception* (Seville Cathedral). The picture was begun late in 1655 and completed by the first week of

Francisco de Herrera (ii): *St Francis in Ecstasy*, oil on canvas, 5.70×3.63 m, 1656–7 (Seville Cathedral, Chapel of St Francis)

1656; it is signed and dated. There is a notable decrease in the impasto working of the paint surface, and an increase in scumbling in the central area results in an astonishingly vaporous effect. The bright colour, compositional energy and free brushwork all contrast strongly with the style of Murillo and Zurbarán.

In 1655 Murillo had been praised as the best painter in Seville, and in 1656 he painted the largest and most expensive altarpiece produced up to that time in Seville; despite these successes, it was Herrera who received the next important altarpiece commission. His *St Francis in Ecstasy* in Seville Cathedral (see fig.) was begun late in 1656 and was in place by June 1657. The *St Francis* was the first public work in the High Baroque style in Seville, and it established the new manner to such an extent that Murillo did not receive another commission in Seville while Herrera remained in the city. The *St Francis* is simply an adaptation of the idea of the *St Hermengild*. It is characteristic of Herrera that he was more concerned with the visual impression of his art than with iconographic subtlety. Herrera remained in Seville for three years, but no other contracts are recorded, and he may have painted relatively little during this period. In 1660 he was elected the first co-President, with Murillo, of the Academy. Herrera was last recorded in Seville on 3 August 1660, when the Inquisition requested a picture of the *auto da fé* of 13 April 1660. They praised Herrera as the finest painter in the city, but he demanded too much money and lost the commission. His name is absent from the Academy lists beginning in November 1660, and by then he had probably left Seville for Madrid, possibly motivated by a desire to become a court artist.

4. FROM 1661. Herrera is documented in Madrid on 3 April 1663. A number of paintings may be dated by their style to between 1661 and 1663. The earliest works are in a lateral altar in the Ermita del Cubilo near Aldeavieja in Soria: *St Louis of France*, *St Anthony of Padua*, the *Flight into Egypt* and, possibly by Herrera, a ruined *Annunciation*. The *Flight* includes a splendid landscape that again emphasizes the importance of Titian for Herrera. A group of small pictures still *in situ* in a lateral altar in the Madrid convent of Corpus Christi were painted only a little later. These are: *St Martin Sharing his Cloak with the Beggar*, *St Joseph Holding the Christ Child*, *St Augustine and the Child Emptying the Ocean with a Shell*, *Christ as the Good Shepherd* and *St Anne Teaching the Virgin to Read*. The *Dream of St Joseph* (Madrid, priv. col.) is also from this period. The style of these paintings is similar to that of Herrera's middle period in Seville.

The most important new development in Madrid during Herrera's absence in Seville had been the arrival in 1658 of the Bolognese *quadratura* specialists Agostino Mitelli and Angelo Michele Colonna. Together these two artists had established a tradition of illusionistic frescoes in Madrid. Herrera probably learnt the fresco technique in Madrid in the early 1660s, although his father also painted in fresco. The assumption that the younger Herrera's use of the medium was indebted to Pietro Berrettini da Cortona is hypothetical. According to Palomino, Herrera had first worked in fresco in the monastic church of S Felipe el Real in Madrid, and his success there led to a contract, signed on 3 April 1663 and in partnership with the Bolognese *quadratura* specialist Dionisio Mantuano, for frescoes in the convent church of Nuestra Señora de Atocha in Madrid. On 1 April 1664 the contract was remade, and Herrera stated that the Italian had done no work, and that he himself would complete the programme. All of the frescoes by Herrera have been destroyed, but they were probably figural rather than architectural. Palomino stated that the Atocha frescoes earned Herrera a position as painter to the king, and although this is undocumented elsewhere, Herrera identified himself thus in the remade contract of 1664.

In 1671 Herrera undertook several projects for the celebration of the canonization of Ferdinand III of Castile, held in Seville. Among these projects was the design of the silver-gilt reliquary urn for the body of the saint, one of the great pieces of Spanish Baroque metalwork. In addition, Herrera's memorial of 30 October 1671 concerning the urn and its placement is the first reference to his interest in architecture, and he also provided an etching for the book commemorating the celebration. During 1672–3 he received several payments for painting sets for a play performed at Court on 22 December 1672. He recorded these in drawings (Vienna, Österreich. Nbib.). In November 1672 he was appointed to a salaried post as painter to Charles II. On 10 October 1674 the contract was signed for the architecture for the high altarpiece (destr.) of the church of the Royal Hospital of Aragon in Madrid. The designs were by Herrera, and because they were executed by the founders of the Churriguera dynasty of architects, it has been contended that Herrera was in part responsible for the Churrigueresque style. However, the retable architecture was entirely Sevillian. Probably also dating from 1674 was the painting *St Vincent Ferrer Preaching* (untraced) on one of the side altars of the church. This was renowned for its satirical details, which included a dog gnawing the jawbone of an ass, a rat tearing at the paper with the painter's signature and a boy making the derisive gesture of the 'fig'. These unusual inclusions were Herrera's commentary on those who did not accept his genius; he had a reputation for both his wit and his temper.

During the 1670s Herrera's style changed. Extant works from this period include an *Ecce homo* and a *Christ Bearing the Cross* (Madrid, Mus. Cerralbo), and the paintings on canvas from the cupola of the monastic church of the Reformed Augustinians of *Pope Leo the Great*, *St Anne Teaching the Virgin to Read*, *St Nicholas of Tolentino*, *St Teresa of Avila* and an unidentified *Augustinian Nun* (all Madrid, Prado). The mood of these scenes is more sombre, with dark violets and umbers dominating. Herrera also began to use workshop assistance around this time. On 29 July 1677 he was appointed to the court post of Assistant Keeper of the Palace Keys, and on 31 July 1677 he was appointed Royal Architect. In 1679 he designed the new cathedral of Nuestra Señora del Pilar in Saragossa, his only independent architectural commission. By October 1680 he was in Saragossa, where he remained until 1682. Work on the cathedral began in 1681, but Herrera's plans were not fully accepted by the cathedral chapter, largely due to reasons of cost, and the cathedral was remodelled in the following century. Herrera's idea for the rectangular church with four corner towers and a central dome was derived from Juan de Herrera, and the colonnaded porticos were adapted from Michelangelo. Neoclassical critics condemned Herrera for bringing the style of Borromini to Spain, but only the scale of the undertaking can be considered Baroque in the plan for the Pilar. On 28 July 1680 a delegation of Spanish painters petitioned for a Spanish Academy to be established in Rome, designating Herrera as head of the Academy in Madrid. His response to the petition (Madrid, Bib. N.) is remarkable for showing his preference for an academy of architecture rather than one of painting. His remaining activities as Royal Architect were to oversee and evaluate work done by craftsmen.

BIBLIOGRAPHY

Ceán Bermúdez
El manuscrito de la Academia de Murillo (Seville, 1660–74); ed. A. de la Banda y Vargas (Seville, 1982)
A. Ponz: *Viaje* (1772–94); ed. C. M. de Rivero (1947)
E. Llaguno y Amirola: *Noticias* (1829)
Conde de la Viñaza: *Adiciones al diccionario* (1889–94)
T. Ríos: 'Algunos datos para la historia de las obras del actual santo templo metropolitano de Nuestra Señora del Pilar de Zaragoza', *Bol. Mus. Prov. B.A. Zaragoza*, ix (1925), pp. 1–79
J. López Navio: 'Testamento de Francisco de Herrera, el joven', *Archv Hispal.*, xxviii (1961), pp. 261–74
J. Brown: 'Herrera the Younger: Baroque Artist and Personality', *Apollo*, lxxxv (1966), pp. 34–43
J. Vélez de Guevara: *Los celos hacen estrellas*, ed. J. E. Varey and N. D. Shergold (London, 1970)
H. Sancho Corbacho: 'Historia de la construcción de la urna de plata que contiene los restos de San Fernando', *Estudio de arte sevillano* (1973), pp. 93–139
J. Brown: 'Pen Drawings by Herrera the Younger', *Hortus imaginum* (Lawrence, KS, 1974), pp. 129–38
V. Tovar Martín: *Arquitectos madrileños de la segunda mitad del siglo XVII* (Madrid, 1975)
J. Brown: 'Drawings by Herrera the Younger and a Follower', *Master Drgs*, xiii (1975), pp. 235–40
A. Martínez Ripoll: *Francisco de Herrera 'El Viejo'* (Seville, 1978)
M. L. Caturla: 'La verdadera fecha del retablo madrileño de San Hermengildo', *Actas del XXIII Congreso Internacional de Historia del Arte: Granada, 1978*, iii, pp. 49–55
A. Domínguez Ortiz: *Autos de la Inquisición de Sevilla (siglo XVII)*, Biblioteca de temas sevillanos (Seville, 1981)
D. Kinkead: 'Francisco de Herrera and the Development of the High Baroque Style in Seville', *Rec. A. Mus., Princeton U.*, xli (1982), pp. 12–23
S. Orso: 'Francisco de Herrera the Younger: New Documentation', *Source*, i (1982), pp. 29–32
Carreño, Rizi, Herrera y la pintura madrileña de su tiempo, 1650–1700 (exh. cat. by A. E. Pérez Sánchez, Madrid, Prado, 1986)
A. E. Pérez Sánchez: *Historia del dibujo en España de la edad media a Goya* (Madrid, 1986)
A. E. Pérez Sánchez: *Pintura madrileña del último tercio del siglo XVII*, Historia de la pintura española (Madrid, in preparation)
E. Valdivieso: 'Una propuesta a Francisco Herrera el joven', *Bol. Semin. Estud. A. & Arqueol.* (in preparation)

DUNCAN KINKEAD

Herrera, de Pimentel y. *See* BENAVENTE, Condes de.

Herrera, Juan de (*b* Mobellán, Santander, *c.* 1530; *d* Madrid, 15 Jan 1597). Spanish architect, theorist and inventor. He was the principal architect to Philip II, King of Spain, from the early 1570s until he retired from official duties *c.* 1587. He is often credited with replacing the chaotic diversity of Late Gothic and classicizing regional styles of the 1540s and 1550s with a new authoritative classicism that remained a model for Spanish architects until the 18th century. Although his contribution to this process was shared by many other classicizing architects active in Spain towards the end of the 16th century, he was the first Spaniard fully to embody the Renaissance conception of a great architect, as defined by Leon Battista Alberti.

1. Royal patronage and the Escorial. 2. Civic commissions. 3. Churches. 4. Engineering works and urban planning. 5. Influence and reputation.

1. ROYAL PATRONAGE AND THE ESCORIAL. Herrera was born into a hidalgo family of modest means. He studied Latin and philosophy at Valladolid University until 1548 and then joined the retinue of the crown prince Philip on his progress through Italy and Germany to meet Charles V, Holy Roman Emperor, in Brussels in 1549. Herrera enlisted in the army in 1553 and left for the Italian campaigns, eventually making his way to Flanders in 1555 and arriving back in Spain the next year. In the 1560s he was still referred to as 'the soldier from the German guard'. It was unprecedented in 16th-century Spain for someone of Herrera's background to become an architect, although he may have gained experience of fortification design, calligraphy and engineering while in the army (he was later considered an expert in these fields). He invented various instruments and machines for navigation, industry and building, and served Philip II as an unofficial adviser on scientific matters. In 1562 he prepared scientific illustrations for an astronomical treatise to be used by the tutor of Philip's son (Ruiz de Arcaute, 1936; exh. cat., 1986).

Herrera's architectural apprenticeship probably began in 1563, when the King appointed him assistant to his architect Juan Bautista de Toledo. It was in this capacity that Herrera became involved with the plans for the monastery of S Lorenzo el Real del Escorial (1563–84; *see* ESCORIAL, §2), although he could have done very little actual designing before de Toledo's death in 1567. While Juan Bautista de Toledo should be credited with the general plan and overall conception of the complex, by 1570 Herrera had emerged as an independent designer, a favourite of the King and the architect in charge of designing the Escorial. He redesigned the main staircase as an open-well imperial stair in 1573 (*see* ESCORIAL, fig. 4) and prepared the working drawings of the basilica in 1574–5, using the earlier project of Juan Bautista de Toledo and that drawn up in 1562 by Francesco Paciotto (Simancas, Archv Gen., Obras & Bosques, leg. 2–274; Kubler). The façades of the basilica (see fig. 1) and the library on the Patio de los Reyes are considered to be Herrera's work. When the completion of the Escorial's stonework was celebrated in 1584, he proudly took the credit: more than two-thirds of the complex was built during his tenure. He also designed the service buildings, the Casas de los Oficios, along the north side of the Plaza Promenade. The first was built in 1581 and the second in 1587–8 under the direction of Herrera's former pupil and assistant Francisco de Mora (i). While de Toledo seems to have worked in a simplified version of contemporary Roman High Renaissance architecture that maintained the sculptural value of classical ornamentation, Herrera used this as a basis for a new, radically abstract style, the ESTILO DESORNAMENTADO, which has always been associated with Herrera and the Escorial. The contrast between the styles is particularly evident at the eastern corner of the Sun Corridors. In de Toledo's lower storey, simple Doric columns are set boldly

1. Juan de Herrera: monastery church of S Lorenzo el Real del Escorial, 1575

free from the wall, whereas in Herrera's upper storey (completed after 1574), a series of thin Ionic pilasters is integrated into a web of abstract geometrical panels and mouldings that merge with the wall surface and deprive the order of any sculptural effect.

After 1567 Herrera inherited responsibility for other royal building projects, the largest of which was at the ARANJUEZ PALACE. Juan Bautista de Toledo had prepared a design for the Jardín de la Isla and for the palace itself, but he completed only the first level of the chapel. Plans after old drawings (*trazas antiguas*), copied by Juan Gómez de Mora (i) in 1626, are thought to reflect de Toledo's design (Íñiguez Almech, 1952). The west wing of the palace was begun under Herrera's direction and continued slowly throughout the 1580s. He was probably responsible for closing in the open arcades of the main façade and adding a high frontispiece in the manner of French châteaux; these changes are visible in a 16th-century idealized view of the palace (Madrid, Escorial). He also designed the Casas de Oficios (begun 1585; extended later by others) and continued to develop the site's main feature, the gardens. A plan (1581) attributed to Herrera shows the area north of the palace, the Picotajo, as a loosely arranged diagonal pattern of tree-lined avenues combined with a grid of fields and garden plots. While the layout was modelled on French and Flemish parks, which Philip preferred to the rigid symmetricality of contemporary Italian gardens, the extent of Herrera's landscaping was completely original.

The Alcázar in Toledo had been under reconstruction by royal masters of the works since 1538. Herrera was responsible for the design of the high, rusticated south façade (1573–8; destr. 1936; reconstructed), executed in brick and stone, which echoed the rich surface texture of Alonso de Covarrubias's plateresque north façade. Between 1574 and 1576 Herrera also remodelled the main staircase, originally designed by Covarrubias before 1550 and subsequently reworked by Francisco de Villalpando into a symmetrical open-well design. Herrera used this plan to create a scenographic space with a decorated stairwell, the south façade of which is articulated in ten bays of pilastered openings in two storeys above a rusticated basement, and capped by a mirador.

The Palace of Charles V in the Alhambra, Granada (*see* GRANADA, fig. 2), designed by Pedro Machuda in 1527 in a Roman High Renaissance style, was still under construction in 1572 and 1580, when Herrera revised the designs of Juan de Orea (*d* 1583), Machuda's successor (Rosenthal). He imposed his own abstract style on the building through Juan de Minjares (*d* 1599), who was appointed to head the works in 1583. The results may be seen in the courtyard and surrounding gallery and in the modifications to the chapel.

Herrera accompanied the King to Portugal in 1580, where he may have revised Filippo Terzi's proposed additions to the old royal palace, the Paço da Ribera (destr. 1755), Lisbon. The tall pavilion, articulated with pilasters and crowned by a domical wooden roof, seems to have been influenced by north European models, including French châteaux. As Palace Quartermaster (Aposentador de Palacio) he was responsible for royal lodgings, and as official Architect to His Majesty (Arquitecto de Su Magestad) from 1579 he was concerned with all the royal buildings, notably the palace at El Pardo (remodelled 1772) and the Alcázar in Madrid (destr. 1734). From 1574 he had revised the designs of Juan de Salamanca (*d* 1576) for remodelling the castle at Simancas, where work continued into the 1590s under Francisco de Mora (i).

2. CIVIC COMMISSIONS. The second major sphere of Herrera's activity was urban planning and the design of civic buildings. In 1574 city officials in Toledo requested designs for their town hall. He provided a set of 12 drawings (lost) and brief instructions, noting that 'one has only to follow the design, because if this is done, nothing will be lacking' (Cervera Vera, 1981). Since the production of drawings had become the major function of the architect, they were priced accordingly: in this case 1500 ducats for the set, or five times the annual salary of a supervising architect in the royal works. The design, which employs a series of bays framed by attached columns above a rusticated base, is a modification of a scheme shown in Sebastiano Serlio's *Il settimo libro d'architettura* (Frankfurt am Main, 1575). Herrera supervised construction of only the two low corner towers, which were altered in the 17th century, leaving the rest to local architects working to his designs.

About 1585 Herrera may have advised on the design of the town hall (destr.) at Valladolid, which had been begun in 1561 by Francisco de Salamanca (*d* 1573). Herrera's ideas may be reflected in a surviving wooden model (Valladolid, Mus. Arqueol.), which is similar to the Toledo design except that, instead of a rusticated base, the ground floor is plain with large windows. During this period he also seems to have provided designs for the city meat market and bakery at Valladolid.

Herrera's designs for the Lonja de los Mercaderes (Merchants' Exchange) in Seville (see fig. 2) may have been devised as early as 1573, but final plans were not delivered until 1582. They were executed by Juan de Minjares between 1585 and 1598. Its layout, a series of large halls around a courtyard, diverges from the usual hall-church scheme. The soberly ornamented design, in which vault bays are marked externally with single pilasters and load-bearing walls with paired ones, is Herrera's, but the vaults were executed later in a different style, and the decoration on the monumental staircase is also of a later date.

3. CHURCHES. Many Spanish churches, especially in Castile, have been traditionally attributed to Herrera, either because they resembled the Escorial or merely because their architecture was classicizing. In fact, Herrera was involved in the design of very few ecclesiastical buildings, only one of which had similarities with the Escorial. The church depicted in a design for an unidentified monastery, originally attributed to Herrera as a design for Uclés (Ruiz de Arcaute) but later attributed to Juan Bautista de Toledo and identified (Rivera Blanco) as the Franciscan monastery of Nuestra Señora la Real de la Esperanza (1560s), near Ocaña, closely resembles the centralized two-towered plan of the Escorial basilica.

Herrera's involvement is documented in the designs for S Domingo el Antiguo, Toledo, commissioned by Luís de Castilla from Nicolas Vergara (ii) in 1576 but revised that same year by Herrera. He did not radically alter the Latin-cross plan but replaced the dome by a timber and slate-roofed octagonal lantern, subsequently altered by Vergara in the execution (completed 1579). Another domeless Latin-cross church to be revised by Herrera was S Maria (1580; originally designed by Juan de Orea) in the Alhambra, Granada, although this was apparently rehandled by Francisco de Mora (i) in the 1590s.

2. Juan de Herrera: Lonja de la Mercaderes (now Archivo General de Indias), Seville, west façade, 1585–98

3. Juan de Herrera: Valladolid Cathedral; wooden model to designs of 1578–86 (Valladolid, Museo Diocesano y Catedrálicio)

Herrera has been attributed with the plan for the monastery church of S Vicente de Fora (begun 1582), Lisbon, although his involvement in the design is not documented. The ornamentation and façade, however, are undoubtedly the work of Filippo Terzi, who was in charge of Philip II's works in Portugal throughout the 1580s. The plans of the churches at Granada and Toledo, with their shallow nave chapels, resemble those in Italy sponsored by Counter-Reformation movements, such as Jacopo Vignola's Il Gesù in Rome, although the plan had long been used in Spanish medieval architecture. At S Vicente there are references to Leon Battista Alberti's S Andrea in Mantua, but the deep choir and squared east end are traditional Spanish features.

Between 1578 and 1586 Herrera prepared a complete set of designs for rebuilding the collegiate church (later cathedral) at Valladolid (see fig. 3). This was one of the largest projects of its time, comparable to the Escorial and to the great earlier 16th-century cathedrals at Seville, Segovia and Salamanca. Rodrigo Gil de Hontañón had already prepared plans in 1527 for a vast new church in the Gothic style. Herrera replaced this with a classicizing design, double-square in plan, with a square-ended nave and chancel, each in four bays, with the aisles marked off by massive rectangular piers, symmetrically disposed about a domed central transept, and with four corner towers.

Some of Herrera's drawings, carefully annotated with measurements and signatures, are preserved in the cathedral archives, together with copies by later architects. The drawings show the building with mathematical precision in unshaded lines: it is abstract and entirely unsculptural. The design was respected by successive masters of the works until construction came to a halt in 1668, leaving the building only half-finished. None of Herrera's designs for the vaulting survive, and the present vaults were designed by others. The upper part of the main façade (1730–33) was designed by Alberto Churriguera. In 1589 Herrera advised on designs for continuing the Gothic cathedral of Salamanca but did not present any designs of his own.

4. ENGINEERING WORKS AND URBAN PLANNING. Herrera's radical abstraction created a bond with engineering and utilitarian building, which he approached with the same care as the more traditional forms of monumental architecture. After 1576 he was probably involved with Francisco de Montalbán (*fl* c. 1576–95) in the construction of the elaborate water-supply system for the Escorial: some of the buildings connected with this remain in the hills above the complex. In the 1570s he was also mentioned in connection with similar schemes at Aranjuez,

Colmenar de Oreja and Ontígola. In 1578 he was successfully involved in a dispute with Giovanni Battista Sittoni over designs for the canal on the Jarama River. The water-system designed in the early 1570s for Ocaña has been attributed to Herrera: there the fountain frames one side of a great sunken plaza, and the utilitarian forms of plain walls, washing pools and drainage channels are raised to the status of monumental architecture. In the 1580s he was called in after Francisco de Montalbán to design the municipal water-system for Valladolid, for which he was paid 1000 ducats.

Herrera was active as a bridge designer. The monumental Puente de Segovia, at the south-east entrance to Madrid, was designed in the late 1570s and built by Juan de Nates (*fl* 1572–1613) by 1588; its magnificent esplanade was later built over. Herrera also designed two bridges over the Guadarrama River: a small one (1582–3) near Galapagar, on a route from Madrid to the Escorial, and a larger structure (*c.* 1590) near Brunete. These served as models for others near the Escorial (some, perhaps, also to his design) and at Segovia, possibly designed by Francisco de Mora (i). Herrera may also have influenced the rebuilding of the Puente Mayor (destr.) at Valladolid, which was undertaken by Juan de Nates in 1584.

These projects all belonged to a vast programme of public works, notably for urban renewal in Spain and the American colonies, initiated by Philip II in the 1560s and pursued by Herrera over the next two decades. He was probably responsible for the general scheme for New World towns described in Philip's *Ordenanzas de descubrimiento, nueva población y pacificación de las Indias* (1573), in which colonists were ordered to build their towns around the nucleus of a porticoed main square, laid out as a rectangle in the proportion 2:3 with a broad porticoed street running out from the centre of each side, and with two small streets at each corner. Herrera applied the ideal of the *Ordenanzas* to his projects for the Plaza Mayor in Madrid (*see* MADRID, §I, 1). He may already have been involved in plans for Madrid during the 1560s, since in 1586 he mentioned designs he had made for the city 'ever since the court was in residence'. Little progress was made until the 1580s, however, when the King established an urban planning board (Junta de Urbanismo) with Herrera as the architect member. Herrera introduced the idea of regular open space in which a uniform architecture mirrored the regularity of the plan and extended along the axes of broad porticoed streets. These ideas are reflected in two plans (Madrid, Escorial) that contrast the existing square with his proposal for a rectangular, porticoed main plaza with a secondary triangular plaza separated by an open portico from the main square (Iñiguez Almech, 1952). The urban renewal of Madrid continued after Herrera retired from the Junta in 1590. The two plazas of his scheme were merged into one in the early 17th-century designs of Juan Gomez de Mora (i), but the present Plaza Mayor is the work of Juan de Villanueva, who rebuilt it after a fire in 1791.

Herrera also prepared designs for a new Plaza de Zocodover (rebuilt) in Toledo, after a fire in 1585. An 18th-century plan and several elevation drawings (Madrid, Archv Hist. N.) copied from his designs show how the urban space was regularized to create a clear triangular form, while the main arteries from Madrid and to the Alcázar were given monumental porticos, three columns deep, and there was a massive gateway on the west side of the square. While a porticoed central market-square was a traditional feature of Spanish towns, Herrera's treatment of civic space had an authority and a regal dimension that markedly influenced urban design in the Hispanic world.

5. INFLUENCE AND REPUTATION. Herrera and Philip II were closely associated for most of their lives. Without the King, Herrera could not have become an architect, since he lacked the training and qualifications of a traditional master of the works. Philip deliberately reorganized his building bureaucracy to accommodate their shared ideal of practice, as propounded by Alberti. After the King returned from the conquest of Portugal in 1583, he founded an Academy of Mathematics in Madrid, based on a similar institution in Portugal, where mathematics, architecture and civil and military engineering were taught in public lectures (Moreira). Herrera became its unofficial mentor and sponsored Cristóbal de Rojas's *Teórica y prática de fortificación* (Madrid, 1598) and translations of Euclid and Archimedes.

Herrera became a renowned intellectual: a mathematician, scientist and follower of the philosopher Ramón Lull (1235–1316). The inventory of his library (Cervera Vera, 1977) reveals that he owned every major published text on mathematics and mechanics and an impressive collection of scientific books and architectural treatises, prints and drawings. He made notes in his copy (Madrid, Real Acad. S Fernando) of Guillaume Philander's commentary on Vitruvius, *Annotationes* (Strasbourg, 1550). His writings included a short explanation of the principles of mechanics for Philip II and a primer in which the fundamental ideas of Lull's philosophy were expounded in terms of the geometry of a cube. The only example of his writing published in his lifetime was the *Sumario . . .* (Madrid, 1589), a brief explanatory text accompanying 12 magnificent plans, elevations and sections of the Escorial (*see* ESCORIAL, fig. 1), which were prepared from drawings by Herrera and engraved by Pedro Perret.

Herrera's style was highly influential but difficult to imitate, owing to its eccentricity. For a great Renaissance classicist, he used the orders sparingly and eliminated decorative sculpture in almost every context except explicitly sculptural programmes, such as the main retable in the Escorial basilica (*see* ESCORIAL, §3) or the central fountain in the Patio de los Evangelistas. The capital, moulding and base type of his orders, derived from canonical modern examples, were uniform to the point of monotony. More than any other architect, he made mathematics a powerful component of his architecture. He vastly increased the visual importance of abstract geometrical form, emphasizing modular rhythms and stonework patterns in a style where classical decoration serves to provide purely abstract panels and bands, and he virtually reduced the orders to plain strips and half cylinders. With their delicate contrasts and combinations of geometric shapes, however, his compositions are neither rigid nor dull.

Herrera enlisted two pupils in 1579, of whom Francisco de Mora (i) took over as the King's designer when ill-health forced Herrera to curtail his activities in the late

1580s. Mora subsequently trained his cousin Juan Gómez de Mora (i) to succeed him as Master of the King's Works, and thus Herrera's model of the architect survived into the reign of Philip IV. Herrera's style remained strongly associated with Philip II and was revived whenever architects and their patrons wished to evoke the memory of the golden age of Spanish power.

WRITINGS

Tratado del cuerpo cúbico, conforme a los principios y opiniones del 'Arte' de Raimundo Lulio (Madrid, Escorial, MS. d. III 25; 1563, 1584; Madrid, 1935)

Tratado de arquitectura y máquinas (1575; Simancas, Archv Gen., MS. leg. 258, fol. 488); ed. A. Ruiz de Arcaute in *Juan de Herrera, arquitecto de Felipe II* (Madrid, 1936), pp. 36–8

Sumario y breve declaración de los diseños y estampas de la fábrica de San Lorenço el Real del Escurial (Madrid, 1589); ed. L. Cervera Vera in *Las estampas y el sumario de El Escorial por Juan de Herrera* (Madrid, 1954)

BIBLIOGRAPHY

Macmillan Enc. Architects
K. Justi: 'Philip II als Kunstfreund', *Miscellaneen aus drei Jahrhunderten spanischen Kunstlebens* (Berlin, 1908), ii, pp. 1–36
A. Ruiz de Arcaute: *Juan de Herrera, arquitecto de Felipe II* (Madrid, 1936)
M. López Serrano: *Trazas de Juan de Herrera y sus seguidores para el monasterio del Escorial: Estudio preliminar* (Madrid, 1944)
F. Chueca Goitia: *La catedral de Valladolid* (Madrid, 1947)
A. Portables Pichel: *Los verdaderos artífices de El Escorial y el estilo indebidamente llamado Herreriano* (Madrid, 1947)
F. Iñiguez Almech: *Casas reales y jardines de Felipe II* (Madrid, 1952)
A. Portables Pichel: *Maestros mayores, arquitectos y aparejadores de El Escorial* (Madrid, 1952)
F. Chueca Goitia: *Arquitectura del siglo XVI*, A. Hisp., xi (Madrid, 1953)
J. J. Martín González: 'El Palacio de Aranjuez en el siglo XVI', *Archv Esp. A.*, xxxv (1962), pp. 237–52
L. Cervera Vera: 'Semblanza de Juan de Herrera', *El Escorial, 1563–1963: IV. centenario: Madrid, 1963*, ii, pp. 7–103
F. Iñiguez Almech: *Las trazas del Monasterio de S. Lorenzo de El Escorial* (Madrid, 1965)
L. Cervera Vera: *Inventario de los bienes de Juan de Herrera* (Valencia, 1977)
——: *Documentos biograficos de Juan de Herrera, 1572–1581*, Colección de documentos para la historia del arte en España, i (Zaragoza and Madrid, 1981)
G. Kubler: *Building the Escorial* (Princeton, 1982)
A. Bustamante Garcia: *La arquitectura clasicista del foco vallisoletano* (Valladolid, 1983)
F. Marías: *La arquitectura del renacimiento en Toledo, 1541–1631*, 4 vols (Toledo, 1983–5)
J. J. Rivera Blanco: *Juan Bautista de Toledo y Felipe II: La implementación del clasicismo en España* (Valladolid, 1984)
E. Rosenthal: *The Palace of Charles V in Granada* (Princeton, 1985)
J. Miguel Moran Turina and F. Checa Cremades: *Las casas del rey* (Madrid, 1986)
Herrera y el clasicismo (exh. cat., ed. J. I. Linazasoro; Valladolid, Colegio Santa Cruz, 1986) [esp. article by A. Rodríguez Gutiérrez de Ceballos and A. Casaseca]
R. Moreira: *A escola de arquitectura do Paço da Ribeira e a academia de matemáticas de Madrid* (Madrid, 1987)
C. Wilkinson-Zerner: *Juan de Herrera: Architect to Philip II of Spain* (New Haven, 1994)

For further bibliography *see* ESCORIAL.

CATHERINE WILKINSON-ZERNER

Herrera, Velino [Ma-Pe-Wi] (*b* Zia Pueblo, NM, 22 Oct 1902; *d* Santa Fe, NM, 18 Jan 1973). Native American Pueblo painter. He was a student at the Santa Fe Indian School (*see* NATIVE NORTH AMERICAN ART, §IV, 2) in 1918 when Elizabeth DeHuff (1887–1983), wife of the school superintendent, invited him and several other students, including FRED KABOTIE and Otis Polelonema (1902–1981), to spend afternoons painting in her living room. After a showing at the Museum of New Mexico, the work was exhibited at the Annual Exhibition of the Society of Independent Artists in New York in 1920. Extensive press coverage stimulated so much interest that, in effect, the early Santa Fe Native American art movement was thus launched. Thereafter, Herrera's paintings were widely exhibited throughout the US and Europe. He illustrated several books, including educational material for the Bureau of Indian Affairs. In 1939 he painted murals in the Department of Interior Building in Washington, DC, and in 1954 he was awarded the French government's Palmes d'Académiques for his contribution to Native American art. Herrera constantly developed and

Velino Herrera: *Ceremonial Buffalo Dance* (detail), tempera on paper, 570×730 mm, *c.* 1948 (Tulsa, OK, Philbrook Art Center)

added to his skills. He came to excel in realistic compositions displaying a command of perspective and modelling, fine detail and sensitive portraiture. His inventive abstract compositions, based on traditional Pueblo symbolism, were emulated by many other artists. Nevertheless, through most of his life he was estranged from his native Pueblo because its elders objected to his paintings of ceremonial dances (see fig.). In 1955, a crippling automobile accident cut short his career.

BIBLIOGRAPHY

C. L. Tanner: *Southwest Indian Painting: A Changing Art* (Tucson, 1957, rev. 1973)
D. Dunn: *American Indian Art of the Southwest and Plains Areas* (Albuquerque, 1968)

ARTHUR SILBERMAN

Herrera Barnuevo. Spanish family of artists.

(1) Antonio de Herrera Barnuevo (*fl* 1621; *d* 1646). Sculptor. He was active at court in Madrid, where he executed sculptures for stage settings for plays performed at the Royal Palace. In 1622 he was appointed Escultor de Cámara. He also carved religious sculpture in polychromed wood. In 1638 he carved the sculptures of *Venus and Adonis* and a group of the *Three Magi* for the Hermitage of S Jerónimo in the grounds of the Madrid Palace, El Buen Retiro. These hermitages had their own chapels and combined works of religious and profane art.

Royal devotion to the dogma of the Immaculate Conception is expressed in Philip III's commission to Herrera Barnuevo for the impressive *Immaculate Conception* (1621) destined for the Madrid convent of the Descalzas Reales (*in situ*). In 1621 the sculptor carved another image of the *Immaculate Conception* for Segovia Cathedral in honour of the celebrations in that city devoted to the Immaculate Conception. In 1623 Herrera Barnuevo was commissioned to execute a retable for the convent of S Francisco in Madrid, signing himself as 'Escultor de su Majestad'. His statue of *St Bruno* for the Cartuja de Miraflores, Burgos, is untraced but was praised by the painter Vicente Carducho (1633).

BIBLIOGRAPHY

V. Carducho: *Diálogos de la pintura* (Madrid, 1633); also in F. J. Sánchez Cantón, ed.: *Fuentes literarias* (Madrid, 1933)
Marqués de Saltillo: 'Efemérides artísticas madrileñas', *Bol. Soc. Esp. Excurs.*, lii (1948), pp. 5–41
——: 'Artistas madrileños, 1592–1850', *Bol. Soc. Esp. Excurs.*, lvii (1953), pp. 137–243
J. J. Martín González: 'Arte y artistas del siglo XVII en la corte', *Archv Esp. A.*, xxxi (1958), pp. 125–42
M. Agulló: *Documentos sobre escultores, entalladores y ensambladores de los siglos XVI al XVIII* (Valladolid, 1978), pp. 87–90

J. J. MARTÍN GONZÁLEZ

(2) Sebastián de Herrera Barnuevo (*b* Madrid, 1619; *d* Madrid, 1671). Painter, draughtsman, sculptor and architect, son of (1) Antonio de Herrera Barnuevo. His father was probably his first teacher, but Sebastián later studied with Alonso Cano, who had moved from Seville to Madrid in 1638. He was probably Cano's chief assistant in Madrid during the 1640s; statements in Cano's will of 1667 indicate that they remained friends. In 1649 Herrera Barnuevo received his first important royal commission, a design for the ephemeral decorations erected in Madrid for the state entry of Mary Anne of Austria, celebrating her marriage to Philip IV. As a result he was rewarded in 1649 with the royal appointment of *ayuda de cámara* (chamberlain).

Like Cano, Herrera Barnuevo was active as painter, sculptor and architect. There is little existing evidence of the work that he completed as a designer of shrines, altars and reliquaries except in the drawings for them, which reveal him to be one of the most brilliant of 17th-century Spanish draughtsmen. His exuberant late Baroque study for an altar of *St Isidro* (1653–5; Madrid, Bib. N.) exemplifies his style as architect, sculptor and draughtsman. This pen-and-wash drawing is touched with watercolour in a way that intensifies the colouristic vibrance. These effects are seen in the green base and pilasters, in the tabernacle with its blue columns and rose cupola, while the drapery of the baldacchino is worked with purple, and the terrestrial globe crowns the whole with pale blue. The royal escutcheon included in a *Project for an Altar* (Madrid, Bib. N.) may refer to Herrera Barnuevo's appointment to the important post of Chief Architect to Charles II in 1662.

Herrera Barnuevo's skill as architect and painter is evident in his altar of the *Holy Family*, commissioned by the Jesuits for S Isidro Cathedral, Madrid. He designed the architectural framework and painted the large canvas representing the *Two Trinities* (*c*. 1653–5), the heavenly Trinity above with the Holy Family in the earthly realm below. The frame of the altarpiece (*c*. 1650–55) is characterized by classical restraint, but the style of the painting typifies the more exuberant tendencies of late Baroque artists in Madrid. It is a style that reflects a fresh study of 16th-century Venetian paintings as well as of the Flemish Baroque paintings by Peter Paul Rubens and Anthony van Dyck, all of which were well represented in the Spanish royal collections. These influences are aptly reflected in the *Two Trinities*, with its richly coloured and lively draperies, the substantial figures shown in movement before a deep landscape and the lively putti tumbling through the open sky above.

In 1653 Herrera Barnuevo decorated the small chapel of Nuestra Señora de Guadalupe in the convent of the Descalzas Reales, Madrid. He designed the sculptured Habsburg eagles that surmount the entrance and painted the mirrors that decorate the altar and walls of the chapel. The sculptured *Virgin of Guadalupe* done for the altar, like all the other sculptures by Herrera Barnuevo, has disappeared. The Marian programme of the chapel, with specific reference to the doctrine of the Immaculate Conception, includes images of Old Testament heroines (prefigurations of the Virgin) and scenes from the *Life of the Virgin*. On the altar frontal is an image of the *Virgin of the Immaculate Conception*, a vision of light and colour soaring triumphantly over the serpent of Original Sin. The individual pictures reflect in miniature Herrera Barnuevo's painting style. The chapel is important evidence of the multifaceted nature of his talent. The combination of gilt wood sculptures, mirrors and paintings results in a brilliantly conceived decorative whole. An evaluation of his career must remain based on the promise inherent in his drawings and in his continued success at court. In 1662 he was appointed First Painter (*pintor de cámara*) of Charles II, a position he held until his death.

BIBLIOGRAPHY

H. E. Wethey: 'Herrera Barnuevo's Work for the Jesuits of Madrid', *A. Q.* [Detroit], 17 (1954), pp. 335–44

——: 'Decorative Projects by Sebastián de Herrera Barnuevo', *Burl. Mag.*, 98 (1956), pp. 40–46

H. E. Wethey and A. S. Wethey: 'Herrera Barnuevo and his Chapel in the Descalzas Reales', *A. Bull.*, 48 (1966), pp. 15–34

SUZANNE STRATTON

Herrerabarría, Adriano (*b* Santiago, Veraguas, 28 Dec 1928). Panamanian painter. He completed his studies in art and education in 1955 in Mexico City at the Academia San Carlos and at the Escuela Normal Superior. In Panama, Herrerabarría was for many years a teacher and, later, Director of the Escuela Nacional de Artes Plásticas (former Academia, then Escuela, Nacional de Pintura). His early paintings reflect the influence of social realism and of the Mexican muralists. In later works, such as *Earth of Races* (1981, Panama City, artist's col., see E. Wolf-schoon: *Las manifestaciones artísticas en Panamá*, Panama City, 1983, p. 264), a dramatic image of faces trapped in a web of biomorphic shapes, political, social and racial issues are intertwined with mystical and Existentialist themes and organic forms derived from Surrealism.

BIBLIOGRAPHY

R. Miró: 'Cuatro artistas panameños contemporáneos', *Ocho expresiones artísticas* (exh. cat., Panama City, Cent. Convenciones Atlapa, 1981)

MONICA E. KUPFER

Herreran style. *See* ESTILO DESORNAMENTADO.

Herrera Toro, Antonio (*b* Valencia, 16 Jan 1857; *d* Caracas, 26 June 1914). Venezuelan painter and writer. He studied in Caracas under Martín Tovar y Tovar, José Manuel Maucó and Miguel Navarro y Cañizares. In 1875 the government awarded him a fellowship to study in Europe. He went to Paris and two years later to Rome, where he was taught by Modesto Faustini (1839–91), Cesare Maccari and Francesco Santoro (*b* 1844). He returned to Venezuela in 1880. From 1882 he taught at the Academia de Bellas Artes in Caracas and distinguished himself as a portrait painter and as a painter of historical scenes in an academic style: among his best-known works are *Fire Started by Ricaurte in San Mateo* (1883) and *Self-portrait, Standing* (1895; both Caracas, Gal. A. N.). He also completed the decoration of Caracas Cathedral in 1883 and of the soffit of the Municipal Theatre of Valencia in 1892. That year he also founded the humorous publication *El Granuja*, and from 1909 to 1912 he was Director of the Academia de Bellas Artes.

WRITINGS

Manchas artísticas y literarias (1898)

BIBLIOGRAPHY

J. Calzadilla: *Antonio Herrera Toro* (Madrid, n.d.)

A. Boulton: *Historia de la pintura en Venezuela*, ii (Caracas, 1972)

MARÍA ANTONIA GONZÁLEZ-ARNAL

Herrería, Julián de la [Cervera, Andrés Campos] (*b* Asunción, 1888; *d* Valencia, Spain, 1937). Paraguayan painter, engraver and ceramicist. He studied at the Real Academia de Bellas Artes de San Fernando, Madrid, and spent six years studying in Paris in private studios. His first exhibition, in Asunción in 1920, marked a turning-point in the history of Paraguayan art. He showed oil paintings inspired principally by Cézanne and the Fauvists, and the arbitrary colours and heavy impasto of his stylized landscapes introduced local artists to the innovations of Impressionism and Post-Impressionism previously unknown in Paraguay; as a result other painters began to use them in their work. In his engraving Herrería used a simplified line based on flat contrasts of colour. From 1922 he began to work in ceramics, developing themes derived from Pre-Columbian Latin-American traditions and scenes of daily rural life in Paraguay. His plates and small sculptures had designs influenced by Art Deco. The series of motifs used in his ceramics show a deep understanding of Paraguayan humour and popular art and give a vivid portrait of everyday life that transcends the merely picturesque.

BIBLIOGRAPHY

M. A. Fernández: *Art in Latin America Today: Paraguay* (Washington, DC, 1969)

J. Plá: *El espíritu del fuego: Biografía de Julián de la Herrería* (Asunción, 1977)

T. Escobar: *Una interpretación de las artes visuales en el Paraguay* (Asunción, 1984)

TICIO ESCOBAR

Herreyns, Guillaume-Jacques (*b* Antwerp, ?May 1743; *d* Antwerp, 10 Aug 1827). Flemish painter and teacher. Because his work continued the tradition of 17th-century Flemish painting, he has long been considered as the last of the school of Rubens and opposed to innovative trends. However, although it is true that most of his religious works remained faithful to the traditionalist mainstream, his friendship with Andries Cornelis Lens and Jan Cardon, his teaching and his political ideas all show open-mindedness towards new ideas.

He was apprenticed to his father Jacques Herreyns (*fl* 1743–59), also a painter, and to his uncle, Guillaume Herreyns (*d* 1772), a sculptor. Guillaume-Jacques entered the Academy of Antwerp as a student of drawing and architecture, where he was taught by Balthazar Beschey. He finished his studies in 1764, and a year later took over the teaching duties of Cornelis d'Heur (1707–62), who had just died, and replaced Lens as Director of the Academy. In 1767 Herreyns left the Academy and visited Germany. In the same year the President of the Brabant States commissioned him to paint the principal historical events of the country. Herreyns also painted a portrait of *Lens in his Studio* (*c.* 1769–75; Antwerp, Kon. Mus. S. Kst.). This work, despite its closeness to the court portraiture of the period in pose and use of fabrics, is also a sympathetic and penetrating study of the artist. In 1771 Herreyns settled in Mechelen, where he founded a free school of drawing, which became a royal academy in 1776, with pupils such as Jan Frans van Geel, Pierre-François De Noter, Jean-Jacques de Raedt (1759–1838) and Pierre-Antoine Verhulst (1751–1809). He received a large number of church commissions at this time and also did occasional decorative work.

In 1775 Herreyns co-ordinated the celebrations for the thousandth anniversary of St Rombaut; he designed a series of floats inspired by those of Rubens in 1635 and collaborated with Lens on four paintings illustrating the saint's life. Herreyns became Premier Peintre to the Brabant States and was then Painter to the King of Sweden.

In 1783 he refused an invitation to become Director of the Brussels Academy. During the same year he painted a portrait of *Emperor Joseph II* (Brussels, Hôtel de Ville). During the French occupation of the Netherlands he was a teacher at the Antwerp Academy and became its Director in 1804. His pupils included Antoine Wiertz, Petrus Kremer (1801–88), Jan Joseph Verellen (1788–1815), Joseph François and Gustaf Wappers.

Herreyns's works are highly coloured and show a certain mastery, but they lack originality, and technical defects in the pigments have tended to turn the paint in many of his works a reddish colour over the years. In his religious works (e.g. the *Crucifixion*, Antwerp, Kon. Mus. S. Kst., and the *Assumption*, Ghysagem, St Martin) Herreyns remained faithful to the 17th-century tradition. However, in his portraits of politicians and churchmen, which number about 30, his receptiveness to new ideas, especially from France, is apparent—as, for example, in the portrait of *Bollandist Ghesquière* (Antwerp, Kon. Mus. S. Kst.) and the portraits of *L. Solvijns* and his wife (ex-art market, Paris, 1933, see Bautier, p. 19)—with their simple modelling, straightforward poses and attempts to capture profound psychological expression. Herreyns painted almost nothing after 1814. His last painting, exhibited in the Antwerp Salon of 1816, was *David Accompanying himself on the Harp* (untraced). He devoted himself mainly to his administrative and honorific duties but dominated the artistic life of Antwerp until his death.

BIBLIOGRAPHY

P. Bautier: *La Peinture en Belgique au XVIIIe siècle* (Brussels, 1945)

C.-H. Nyens: 'Guillaume-Jacques Herreyns', *1710–1830, Autour du Néoclassicisme en Belgique* (exh. cat., Brussels, Mus. Ixelles, 1985–6), pp. 94–5, 401

DOMINIQUE VAUTIER

Herri. *See* ERRI.

Herri met de Bles. *See* BLES, HERRI MET DE.

Herring. English family of painters, of Dutch descent. J(ohn) F(rederick) Herring (i) (*b* Surrey, 1795; *d* Meopham, Kent, 23 Sept 1863) was the most prolific and financially successful member of the family. His brother, Benjamin Herring (i) (*b* Surrey, 1806; *d* 1830), had a brief career largely devoted to producing passable imitations of the work of several early 19th-century sporting painters. Having eloped with Anne Harris to Doncaster at the age of 18, John Frederick (i) began a seven-year career as a coach driver on regular routes to London and then Halifax, meanwhile practising as a painter in his spare time. Work with horses and constant travel through the countryside may have stimulated his interest in animal and rural subject-matter—the areas in which he specialized after becoming a full-time professional artist *c.* 1820, having exhibited his first painting at the Royal Academy in 1818. Regular employment was provided by the *Doncaster Gazette* for which, since 1815, he had been painting designs for engraved portraits of the annual winner of the St Leger. Later, in a similar series, he painted the winners of the Derby between 1827 and 1847. Prominent among his early private patrons were Charles Spencer-Stanhope and Frank Hawkesworth. He moved to Newmarket in 1830 and to Camberwell in 1833, where he fell into debt and was rescued by the industrialist W. T. Copeland. He lived for some years on the latter's estate in Essex and there produced, among many paintings, designs for hunting scenes to be used on Copeland Spode porcelain. Introductions to and commissions from Ferdinand, Duc d'Orléans, Victoria of Saxe-Coburg-Saalfeld, Duchess of Kent (1786–1861; to whom he was appointed Official Painter in 1845), and her daughter Queen Victoria helped to secure his reputation among the nobility. He was able to retire to a substantial (if leased) country estate in Meopham Park, Kent, in the early 1850s. His non-sporting works of the late 1850s are perhaps among the most successful of his total output, notably *The Harvest* of 1857 (New Haven, CT, Yale Cent. Brit. A.), which reveals his certain competence as a landscape and figure painter. His *Memoir* was published in Sheffield in 1848. All three of his sons, J(ohn) F(rederick) (ii), Charles and Benjamin (ii), occasionally contributed to his canvases as well as painting their own.

J(ohn) F(rederick) Herring (ii) (*b* Doncaster, *c.* 1820; *d* Cambs, March 1907) was the most able son of John Frederick (i) and financially less dependent on his ultimately wealthy father than his brothers. Stylistically, the works of John Frederick (ii) and his father are confusingly close (mutual accusations of plagiarism reportedly led to the early severance of their artistic and social relationship). However, the younger man's noticeably unambitious approach to composition and tentative handling of paint distinguishes his work from that of his father.

Charles Herring (*b* Doncaster, 1828; *d* Meopham, 1 June 1856) was a more respectful imitator of John Frederick (i) than his brothers, but he died before being able to establish his career properly.

Benjamin Herring (ii) (*b* Doncaster, 1830; *d* 1871) was the youngest son of John Frederick (i). He reputedly lacked the inclination to work seriously, but his work was evidently no less competent than that of his brothers, and it was widely engraved. Many aquatints were made after his paintings; among the better known are *Silks and Satins of the Turf* and *Silks and Satins of the Field*, published by J. McQueen in 1867 and 1868, shortly before the sporting art trade began to contract due to the emerging commercial possibilities of photography—a circumstance which apparently dissuaded the next Herring generation from any concerted attempt to perpetuate the family tradition.

Only one other painter of the same family is known: the 'Mrs J. F. Herring' who exhibited at the Royal Academy between 1852 and 1866. It is unclear whether she was the wife of John Frederick (i) or (ii).

BIBLIOGRAPHY

O. Beckett: *J. F. Herring and Sons* (London, 1981)

STEPHEN DEUCHAR

Herrmann [Hermann; Herman]**, Hans** [Johannes] **(Emil Rudolf)** (*b* Berlin, 8 March 1858; *d* Berlin, 1942). German painter. From 1874 to 1879 he studied at the Königlich-akademische Hochschule für Bildende Künste in Berlin. In 1880 he moved to Düsseldorf, where until 1883 he attended the landscape class of Eugen Dücker (1841–1916). From Düsseldorf he made study tours to the Netherlands, which he then continued every year after his return to Berlin in 1886. *Meat Market in Middelburg* (1887; Berlin, Tiergarten, N.G.) clearly reveals how at this time he was trying to break away from an illusionistic construction of space for a structure based on the immediate visual impression. In *Messberg in the Evening* (1890; Hamburg, Ksthalle) the immediacy of the optical impression is already more firmly in the foreground. The apparently arbitrary detail shown in the painting is particularly striking. The figures in the foreground, typical for this market, also testify, however, that Herrmann could not entirely abandon anecdotal details, and that his initial attempts at presenting visual impressions through painterly means did not consistently go any further. In 1892, with Walter Leistikow, Max Liebermann and others, he formed the Gruppe der XI, a forerunner of the Berlin Secession, although he played only a very minor role in its history.

BIBLIOGRAPHY

R. Hamann and J. Hermand: *Naturalismus*, Epochen deutscher Kultur von 1870 bis zur Gegenwart, ii (Berlin, 1959)
——: *Impressionismus*, Epochen deutscher Kultur von 1870 bis zur Gegenwart, iii (Berlin, 1960)

BARBARA LANGE

Herrnhuters. *See* MORAVIAN BRETHREN.

Herschel, Sir John (Frederick William) (*b* Slough, 7 March 1792; *d* Collingwood, Kent, 11 May 1871). English artist, photographer, scientist and writer. The only son of the astronomer Sir William Herschel (1738–1822), John Herschel emerged as a commanding figure in 19th-century British science, making significant contributions to mathematics while still at school. Herschel's scientific viewpoint came from the 18th-century 'natural philosopher's' desire to pursue an eclectic exploration of the physical world. At the same time he was equally conversant with the implications of the explosive technological growth and change of the 19th century, when the term 'natural philosopher' gave way to 'scientist'.

Within a week of learning of the public announcement of the concept of photography early in 1839, Herschel had independently perfected his own working process. Much of his previous research in light, optics and chemistry was immediately applicable to the new invention, and the involvement of a scientist of Herschel's stature did much to lend credence to early British efforts. His friendship and working alliance with William Henry Fox Talbot, the British inventor of photography, forestalled total French domination of the emerging art. In the first years of photography, Herschel made many significant technical contributions. His 'hypo' (sodium thiosulphate) fixer is still universally employed by photographers today, and his 1842 cyanotype (or blueprint) process is the oldest photographic process surviving in continuous regular use (*see* PHOTOGRAPHY, §I). ANNA ATKINS pioneered the application of the cyanotype in *British Algae, Cyanotype Impressions* (1843–53).

Equally important were Herschel's contributions to the nomenclature of the emerging art; the terms 'positive' and 'negative', 'snap-shot' and the word 'photography' itself can all be traced to his writings. Herschel soon returned from the production of images to his main interest: the analysis of the effects of light. His thousands of experiments were the first systematic exploration of the field that would become photo-chemistry and laid a solid theoretical groundwork for a disordered and rapidly emerging art. Throughout his life he was a valued source of technical and aesthetic counsel for photographers, most importantly for Julia Margaret Cameron.

Herschel was also a highly accomplished camera lucida artist. Unlike Talbot, whose confessed that his failure to master the camera lucida motivated him to invent photography, Herschel's desire to practise photography was minimized by his proficiency with the drawing instrument. His corpus of camera lucida drawings (Malibu, CA, Getty Mus.), produced over a span of some 60 years, is impressive. Frequently annotated with scientific observations, they form the only fully documented group of camera lucida images known.

Herschel's major scientific contributions were in mathematics, astronomy, chemistry, physics and optics. He was active in scientific societies and in educational and monetary reform and was created a baronet in 1838. Troubled throughout his life by poor health, he nevertheless sustained considerable personal interests in addition to science, including music, horticulture and poetry. His marriage to Margaret Brodie Stewart in 1829 produced three sons and nine daughters, who carefully preserved the Herschel family archives (priv. col.).

BIBLIOGRAPHY

R. S. Schultze: 'Re-discovery and Description of Original Material on the Photographic Researches of Sir John F. W. Herschel, 1839–1844', *J. Phot. Sci.*, xiii (1965), pp. 57–68
G. Buttmann: *John Herschel: Lebensbild eines Naturforschers* (Stuttgart, 1965); Eng. trans. by B. E. J. Pagel, ed. D. S. Evans as *The Shadow of the Telescope: A Biography of John Herschel* (New York, 1970)
E. Ostroff: 'Herschel and Talbot: Photographic Research', *J. Phot. Sci.*, xxvii (1979), pp. 73–80
L. J. Schaaf: 'Sir John Herschel's 1839 Royal Society Paper on Photography', *Hist. Phot.*, iii (1979), pp. 47–60
——: 'Herschel, Talbot and Photography: Spring 1831 and Spring 1839', *Hist. Phot.*, iv (1980), pp. 181–204
——: 'L'Amour de la lumière: Herschel, Talbot, et la photographie', *Les Multiples Inventions de la photographie*, Association française pour la diffusion du patrimoine photographique (Paris, 1989), pp. 115–24
——: *Tracings of Light: Sir John Herschel & the Camera Lucida* (New York, 1989)
——: *Out of the Shadows: Hershel, Talbot and the Invention of Photography* (New Haven and London, 1992)

L. J. SCHAAF

Hersent, Louis (*b* Paris, 10 March 1777; *d* Paris, 2 Oct 1860). French painter and printmaker. His parents sent him to Baron Jean-Baptiste Regnault's studio where he made rapid progress. In 1797 he won second place in the Prix de Rome with the *Death of Cato* (untraced) behind the joint winners, Pierre Bouillon (1776–1831), Pierre Guérin and Louis André Gabriel Bouchet (*fl* 1797–1819). In 1798, seriously ill, he withdrew from the competition and left the studio. His parents put him into commerce where he lasted 18 months, painting on Sundays, until his kinsman, M. Crouzet, director of the military academy at St Cyr, gave him a post as drawing-master to the students. He made his Salon début in 1802 with *Narcissus* (Arras, Mus. B.-A.). He sent *Achilles Receiving Briseis* (untraced) to the Salon of 1804 and then extended his range with the *Aerial Tomb* and *Atala in the Arms of Chactas* (1806; untraced), derived like Anne-Louis Girodet's famous version (but two years before Girodet) from Chateaubriand's story *Atala* (1801). *Atala* won Hersent a gold medal in the Salon of 1806. To an academic figure painter like Hersent, American Indians were as good a subject as ancient Greeks and had the advantage of being more interesting. Many of his mature pictures were painted with an academic sense of light and shade and composition, but using modern heroes in place of Greeks and Romans, and sentiment and anecdote in place of history. This mixed genre, neither history nor daily life, was popular with the new aristocracy of the First Empire. The Empress Josephine bought *Fénelon Returning a Cow to a Family of Peasants* (exh. 1810; Malmaison, Château N.), and the government commissioned him to paint the *Crossing of the Bridge of Landshut* (Versailles, Château) at the request of the Prince d'Eckmuth. Hersent returned to the Indian theme in 1814 with *Las Casas Rent by Savages* (untraced).

Collectors at the Restoration court were even more enthusiastic about Hersent's paintings, encouraged, in part, by a royalist tendency in his choice of subjects. *Louis XVI Distributing Charity to the Poor in the Winter of 1788* (exh. Salon, 1817; Versailles, Château), an apocryphal episode, composed in the manner of Antoine-Jean Gros's *Bonaparte Visiting the Victims of the Plague at Jaffa, 11 March 1799* (1804; Paris, Louvre), was commissioned in 1816 for the Tuileries and awarded the prize given by Louis XVIII in 1817 for the best genre painting at the Salon. In the *Death of Dr Bichat* (exh. 1819; U. Paris V, Mus. Hist. Médec.), he translated the heroic deathbed scenes of Poussin and David into a touching anecdote from modern life. In 1819 the Duc d'Orléans (the future King Louis-Philippe) commissioned eight pictures from young artists through the intermediation of François Gérard. The *Abdication of Gustav Vasa* (destr. 1848), commissioned from Hersent, was a sensational success at the Salon of 1819, a forerunner of many similar historical pictures painted in the 19th century in Düsseldorf, Antwerp, Paris and elsewhere. Hersent painted several other pictures for the Duc d'Orléans, which were hung in the Galerie du Palais-Royal, a prototype of the Musée Historique at Versailles; illustrating the history of the palace, these paintings were destroyed in the sack of 1848. Louis XVIII, who was more attracted by the anecdotal side of Hersent's art, commissioned *Ruth Requesting Boaz to take her in Protection* as a gift for the miniature painter Lizynka Rue, later Mme de Mirbel (1796–1849), with a punning reference to her name, but gave it instead to Mme de Cayla, who had taken her place in the King's favour by the time the picture was completed. *Monks on St Gothard Taking Care of a Family Attacked by Brigands* (exh. 1824; Mortagne, Mairie) was commissioned for the King by the Comte d'Artois (later Charles X), who thought the subject would appeal to the King's piety and to his interest in attractive young women. Considering his close links with the Duc d'Orléans, it is surprising that Hersent was not much involved in the Musée Historique at Versailles. But he continued to paint many portraits during the July Monarchy, especially of the Orléans family.

Hersent also practised lithography, illustrating Auguste, Comte de Forbin's *Voyages dans le Levant* (1819) and the *Fables de La Fontaine* and reproducing a handful of his own pictures. His best-known works were reproduced by other artists in large, popular editions. In 1822 he was elected to the Institut. He succeeded Girodet as a professor at the Ecole des Beaux-Arts in 1825 and opened his own teaching studio. Charles Gleyre, Paul Chenavard and Jacques-Raymond Brascassat were among his pupils. In 1821 he married Louise-Marie-Jeanne Mauduit (1784–1862), a successful painter who had her own teaching studio for women artists.

BIBLIOGRAPHY

G. Hédiard: *Louis Hersent: Les Maîtres de la lithographie* (Paris, 1901)
De David à Delacroix: La Peinture française de 1774 à 1830 (exh. cat., Paris, Grand Pal., 1975), pp. 486–8

JON WHITELEY

Herter, Christian (*b* Stuttgart, 8 Jan 1839; *d* New York, 2 Nov 1883). American cabinetmaker and designer of German birth. He studied at the Ecole des Beaux-Arts in Paris and arrived in New York *c.* 1860 to join his half-brother, Gustave Herter (1830–98), who ran a decorating business. After several years he went back to Paris to study with Pierre Victor Galland, returning to New York *c.* 1870, when he bought Herter Bros from Gustave. In 1870 he toured England where he saw the work of the most prominent design reformers, including the architect E. W. Godwin, who promoted an enthusiasm for things Japanese. Although Herter's best Eastlake-style furniture reflects many of the reform ideas, he also used earlier Renaissance Revival and Néo-Grec designs. Much of his work shows a strong Japanese flavour, with angular, ebonized cherry cases enlivened with wild flower, insect and bird marquetry. On the blonde bedroom furniture (*in situ*) purchased around 1880 for Lyndhurst in Tarrytown, NY, home of the wealthy financier Jay Gould (now owned by the National Trust for Historic Preservation), Herter made use of imported Japanese tiles, and he designed one of the finest Japanese-inspired interiors in the USA for William H. Vanderbilt's house (*c.* 1882; destr. 1927) on Fifth Avenue, New York. Typical of his best furniture is the exquisite ebonized wardrobe (1870s; New York, Met.) in his Anglo-Japanese style. The cornice features inlaid, flowering branches from which blossoms shower down the long doors to accumulate on the two drawers below. Although Herter retired in 1879, the firm continued in existence until *c.* 1907.

BIBLIOGRAPHY

M. J. Bordes: 'Christian Herter and the Cult of Japan', *Rec. A. Mus., Princeton U.*, xxxiv (1975), pp. 20–27
D. Hanks: *Christian Herter and the Aesthetic Movement in America* (New York, 1980)
Herter Brothers: Furniture and Interiors for a Gilded Age (exh. cat.; Houston, TX, Mus. F. A.; New York., Met.; 1995

OSCAR P. FITZGERALD

Herter, Ernst (*b* Berlin, 14 May 1846; *d* Berlin, 21 Dec 1917). German sculptor. He trained from 1863 at the Künstakademie, Berlin, under August Fischer (1805–66), and he was also an assistant in Gustav Blaeser's studio. In 1866 Herter was awarded the Akademie prize as a student in the composition class, allowing him to travel to Copenhagen to study works in the Thorvaldsen Museum. Between 1867 and 1869 Herter was a student of Albert Wolff, whom he assisted with work for the equestrian monument to *Emperor Frederick William III* for the Lustgarten in Berlin, providing the figure of a smith for the pedestal (destr.).

Herter established himself as an independent artist in 1869, when he produced the design for an *Antigone*. He showed the work (marble; Homburg von der Höhe, Bib.) at an Akademie exhibition in 1872. At the same exhibition Herter showed a *Kneeling Angel*, conceived as a funerary ornament. This was often reused, for example for Herter's own grave in a smaller, cast zinc version of about 1900 (Berlin, Schöneberg, Zwölf Apostel Friedhof).

After a journey to Rome in 1875, Herter produced the *Reclining Alexander* (bronze, 1876; Berlin, Alte N.G.). He exhibited a related figure, the *Dying Achilles*, at the Akademie exhibition in Berlin in 1879, and in 1883 the Empress Elisabeth of Austria (1837–98) commissioned a marble version (Corfu, Achilleíon; marble copy, 1886; Berlin, Alte N.G.). Herter carried out commissions for the district courts in Potsdam and Flensburg as well as for the criminal court in Berlin. As a counterpart to the figures of Alexander he designed an *Aspasia* (see Malkowsky, p. 55) in 1885, which first appeared in cast zinc and was later made also in marble (1886). In 1885 Elisabeth of Austria commissioned him to make a marble *Hermes* for Schloss Lainz (1888; now Villa Hermes) near Vienna. In 1886 Herter made the relief, *Battle of the Amazons*, an independent work, which he integrated into the vestibule of his Berlin house in 1900 (*in situ*).

In 1887, through the Empress Elisabeth, Herter was awarded the commission for a monument to *Heinrich Heine* for Düsseldorf. For political and ideological reasons, however, work on the monument was halted in 1893. Herter's design, with an altered iconographical scheme, was then used for the *Loreley Fountain*, installed in the Franz Gigel Park in the Bronx, New York City, in 1899 (*in situ*); Heine appears as a relief figure on the pedestal of the main figure. In 1890 Emperor William II visited Herter in his studio and saw the figure group *Rare Catch* (many copies; e.g. of 1900; Berlin, Viktoriapark), showing a fisherman holding a struggling mermaid. In 1891 Herter was awarded the commission for an extensive programme for the Lange Brücke in Potsdam, including eight individual figures and an equestrian statue of *Emperor William I* (destr.; see Malkowsky, pp. 134–5). Herter produced figures of nymphs and tritons for the Von-der-Heydt-Brücke (1895–6; destr.) in Berlin. He won a further state contract for the Dreikaiser Halle in Kiel-Holtenau with the medallion reliefs of Kaisers *William I, Frederick III* and *William II* (1894; *in situ*). Between 1897 and 1900 Herter made a monument to *Emperor William I* (destr.) for the city.

BIBLIOGRAPHY

G. Malkowsky: *Ernst Herter: Beitrag zur Geschichte der Berliner Bildhauerschule* (Berlin, 1906)
P. Bloch and W. Grzimek: *Das klassische Berlin: Die Berliner Bildhauerschule im 19. Jahrhundert* (Vienna, 1978)
B. Hüfler: *Ernst Herter, 1846–1917: Werk und Porträt eines Berliner Bildhauers* (diss., Berlin, Freie U., 1978)
Berlin und die Antike (exh. cat., W. Berlin, Charlottenburg, Grosse Orangerie, 1979)
Rheinland-Westfalen und die Berliner Bildhauerschule des 19. Jahrhunderts (exh. cat., Bottrop, Mod. Gal.; Cappenberg-Salm, Schloss Cappenberg; 1984)
Von Begas bis Barlach: Bildhauerei im wilhelminischen Berlin (exh. cat., W. Berlin, Kolbe Mus., 1984)
'O ewich is so lanck': Die historischen Friedhöfe in Berlin-Kreuzberg (exh. cat., W. Berlin, Landesarchv, 1987)

BRIGITTE HÜFLER

Hertervig [Hertervik]**, Lars** (*b* Borgøya, nr Haugesund, 16 Feb 1830; *d* Stavanger, 6 Jan 1902). Norwegian painter. He was born into a poor Quaker family. After completing his apprenticeship as a painter with the Aanensen brothers *c.* 1849, he received funding from wealthy merchants in Stavanger, which enabled him to study first at the Royal School of Drawing under Johannes Flintoe (1786–1870) and Joachim Frich (1810–58) from 1850 to 1852, and later in Düsseldorf (1852–6), where he spent a year as a private pupil of Hans Gude. In Düsseldorf, Hertervig soon won acclaim for his Rhine landscapes (e.g. *Landscape near Düsseldorf*, 1853; Oslo priv. col., see Koefoed, no. 2), but from the summer of 1853 and for the rest of his time in Germany he took his themes from the dramatic and varied coastal scenery of Western Norway. He painted dark and threatening storm studies, for example *Rullestadjuvet* (*c.* 1855; Stavanger, Rogaland Kstmús.), *Summer Landscape in a Thunderstorm* (1856; Oslo, N.G.) and *By the Forge* (1856; Bergen, Billedgal.).

Hertervig's studies in Düsseldorf were interrupted by a mental illness and, after a period in Gaustad Asylum in Christiania (now Oslo) from 1856 to 1858, he was declared incurable and for the rest of his life was supported by public funds. Hertervig continued to paint right up to the last year of his life. A few paintings from 1865 to 1867 demonstrate the later development of his technique and style. They show his approach to nature growing more serene and harmonious, while light is rendered with greater intensity in fjord pictures such as *Seascape, Ryfylke, near Haugesund* (1867; Stavanger, Rogaland Kstmús.) and *View from Tysvær* and *Borgøya* (both 1867; Oslo, N.G.). In his later works, mostly gouache on paper, Hertervig focused on light and on the sun, as in such works as *View towards Pyntesundet, Stavanger* (*c.* 1870; Oslo priv. col., see Koefoed, no. 291). Hertervig died forgotten by his contemporaries, but, since his rediscovery in 1914, his work has been reassessed in the context of Norwegian Romantic painting.

BIBLIOGRAPHY
NKL
A. Kielland: 'En efterglemt' [One forgotten], *Dagbl.* (7 June 1893)
H. Ødegaard: *Norske malere Mathias Stoltenberg og Lars Hertervig* [The Norwegian painters Mathias Stoltenberg and Lars Hertervig] (Christiania, 1914)
A. Blytt: *Lars Hertervig* (Oslo, 1939)
H. Koefoed: *Lars Hertervig: Lysets maler* [Lars Hertervig: painter of light] (Oslo, 1984/*R* 1992)

HOLGER KOEFOED

Hertford, 1st Earl of. *See* SEYMOUR, EDWARD.

Hertford, Marquesses of. *See* SEYMOUR-CONWAY.

Hertzberger, Herman (*b* Amsterdam, 6 July 1932). Dutch architect and teacher. He graduated from the Technische Hogeschool, Delft, in 1958 and immediately established his own professional practice, having won the competition for the Students' Residence in Weeperstraat, Amsterdam, which he completed in 1966. His next commissions were the Montessori Primary School (1960–66) at Jacoba van Beierenlaarn, Delft, which he extended in 1968–70 and 1977–81, and the Lin Mij factory extension. It was with these buildings that Hertzberger first used the structuralist principle for which his work is best known, which ordered the plan using a matrix of repeated modules.

His aim was to create in his buildings a series of cellular spaces that the individual inhabitants could occupy and make their own. These spaces were linked by common areas where individuals could meet, and a spatial hierarchy was thus developed between private, semi-public and public areas. To assist in this personalizing process, Hertzberger's buildings were deliberately 'unfinished' in order to encourage individual occupants to install their own possessions and impose their personal identity on the spaces. This philosophy was developed at Die Drie Hoven (1964–74), an elderly and disabled people's housing development at Slotervaart, Amsterdam, which is modelled around the analogy of the traditional village with its streets and square; different 'zones' are defined with the help of such architectural devices as seating areas, stable doors and interior windows.

In 1968 Hertzberger was commissioned to design the Centraal Beheer insurance headquarters building at Apeldoorn, completed in 1972 (with Lucas & Niemeijer), which was his most important work in the structuralist tradition. Hertzberger's intention at Centraal Beheer was to provide not simply an office but a building that would encourage a new approach to the working life—an aim probably influenced by Frank Lloyd Wright's Larkin Building (1904) Buffalo, NY. The design of Centraal Beheer (see fig.) is based entirely on a repeated structural tartan grid that provides an overall structural clarity and creates modules that can themselves be individually planned and assembled in many different ways. The

Herman Hertzberger: interior of the Centraal Beheer building, Apeldoorn, completed 1972

planning freedom that the spatial units of the grid allows within the imposed modular system expresses, more than any other of his buildings, Hertzberger's essential philosophy of providing for the individual within a democracy. Using the standard dimensional module, he created a typology of office planning, a lexicon of spatial arrangements and elemental details related to the structural grid, including metal lamps, concrete parapets, tables and benches. The interior concrete blockwork was left exposed to encourage the office workers to decorate and 'finish' their own spaces. The building reflects the analogy of the city with its network of streets and private enclosures, and the individual workplace modules in the building relate to common naturally lit atrium and gallery spaces. Hertzberger's architecture is essentially anti-monumental and non-authoritarian, and the exterior of Centraal Beheer is a rambling, loosely assembled cubic composition projected from the grid plan, with a highly understated entrance.

At the Muziekcentrum Vredenburg, Utrecht, a 1700-seat concert hall built in 1973–8, Hertzberger aimed to integrate music-making into the daily life of the community by making performances in the hall easily accessible to the general public. The auditorium itself has a centralized arena plan influenced by Hans Scharoun's Philharmonie, Berlin, and it was designed to give even the furthermost members of the audience a sense of involvement in the performance. The hall lies at the core of the building and is adjoined by foyers that are themselves surrounded by small-scale enclosed shopping galleries, like the medieval alleys of the old town outside. The street life of the city was thus extended to the inside of the building. To diminish any sense of exclusivity in the concert hall, the structure and the concrete blockwork were left exposed throughout the building, but this unfortunately gives a rather bleak and impoverished appearance. The transient occupancy of the concert hall meant that the spaces could not be personalized by individual users, as at Centraal Beheer, and Hertzberger built in many individual features.

Hertzberger's early housing projects included eight experimental Diagoon houses (1969–71) in Gebbenlaan, Delft, where the finishes were intended to be completed by the occupants, and 40 houses (1978–80) at Westbroek, near Utrecht. His later housing projects were considerably more refined in terms of scale and composition, even with a hint of classicism. These include two in Germany, at Heinrich Schutzallee (1979–82), Kassel, and Lindenstrasse/Markgrafenstrasse (1982–6), Kreuzberg, West Berlin, and an elderly people's housing development, De Overloop (1980–84), at Boogstraat, Almere Haven. During the 1980s Hertzberger also built three schools in Amsterdam, the Montessori School on Witenstraat/Apollolaan, Willemsparkschool (both 1980–83) and De Evenaar kindergarten and elementary school (1984–6) at Ambonplein, all of which were more formally planned than the earlier school at Delft. The two former schools owe particular acknowledgement to Dutch constructivist designs before World War II, especially Johannes Duiker's Open-Air School (1929–30), Amsterdam. Hertzberger's buildings are twin schools set diagonally to each other and having a simple orthogonal layout with four classrooms per floor. Each block is split along its east–west axis, and the two halves are linked by free-standing staircases.

Hertzberger worked within the Dutch tradition of expressing the logic of construction, and his roots can be found in the work of H. P. Berlage (who was himself influenced by H. H. Richardson and Frank Lloyd Wright) and in pre-war Dutch constructivism, in particular the work of Duiker. His frequent use of filtered top lighting and side lighting with glass blocks, as well as of Constructivist metal stairways, includes reference also to the Maison de Verre (1932), Paris, by Pierre Chareau and Duiker's partner Bernard Bijvoet. In his creation of 'place' Hertzberger was influenced by his teacher, ALDO VAN EYCK, as he also was in developing hierarchies of public and private space that encourage what van Eyck called the harmony of 'the individual and the collective'. Hertzberger's work is, however, less formalistic than that of other pupils of van Eyck, for example Piet Blom. Hertzberger in particular rejected the principle of architecture as the creation of sculptural form, and he viewed his buildings as significant only when they were filled with people. It is this interplay between structure and human action that distinguishes his work from the functionalist tradition of the Modern Movement. From 1959 to 1963, with Aldo van Eyck, Jacob Bakema and others, Hertzberger was co-editor of the important architectural journal *Forum* in Amsterdam. He also taught at the Academie van Bouwkunst, Amsterdam, from 1965 to 1970, and after 1970 he was Professor of Architecture at the Technische Hogeschool, Delft; he was also a visiting professor at several universities in North America.

WRITINGS
'Homework for More Hospitable Form', *Forum*, xxiv/3 (1973) [special issue]
Lessons for Students in Architecture (Rotterdam, 1991)

BIBLIOGRAPHY
'Focus Herman Hertzberger: Dutch Architect', *A & U*, 75 (1977), pp. 45–6, 67–146 [special feature]
J.-M. Hoyet and A. Pelissier: 'Entretien avec Herman Hertzberger', *Tech. & Archit.*, 362 (1985), pp. 72–85
O. Selvafolta: *Herman Hertzberger: Six architectures photographiées par Johan van der Keuken* (Milan, 1985)
'Herman Hertzberger: Recent Work', *Archis*, 12 (1986), pp. 7–53
A. Lüchinger, ed.: *Herman Hertzberger: Buildings and Projects, 1959–86* (The Hague, 1987)
R. Continenza: *Architettura di Herman Hertzberger* (Rome, 1988)
A. W. Reinink: *Herman Hertzberger: Architect* (Rotterdam, 1990)

MICHAEL FORSYTH

Hervey. British family of patrons and collectors. John Hervey I, Baron Hervey of Ickworth and 1st Earl of Bristol (*b* Bury St Edmunds, 27 Aug 1665; *d* ?Ickworth, 20 Jan 1751), was a Whig politician whose portrait (1742; Ickworth, Suffolk, NT) was painted by Jean-Baptiste van Loo. He also commissioned a pair of silver wine-coolers (*c*. 1710–15; Ickworth, Suffolk, NT) from the Huguenot goldsmith Philip Rollos. His younger son, John Hervey II, Baron Hervey of Ickworth (*b* London, 15 Oct 1696; *d* London, 5 Aug 1743), was a memoir writer, pamphleteer and MP for Bury St Edmunds, Suffolk, and a rather more active patron. He commissioned plans, which date from 1718, for a new or re-styled house at Ickworth from John Vanbrugh and had a portrait bust carved (1729; Ickworth, Suffolk, NT) by the French sculptor Edme Bouchardon. John Hervey II's third son, (1) Frederick Augustus Hervey, was the most important patron and collector of the family.

(1) Frederick Augustus Hervey, 4th Earl of Bristol [5th Baron Howard de Walden] (*b* 1 Aug 1730; *d* Albano, Italy, 8 July 1803). He originally intended to practise law but was appointed Bishop of Cloyne (1767) and Bishop of Derry (1768) through the influence of his brother George Hervey (1721–75), who was Lord-Lieutenant of Ireland. The latter bishopric was richly endowed and helped finance Frederick Augustus Hervey's passions for architecture and art collecting. He became Earl of Bristol on the death of his elder brother Augustus John Hervey, 3rd Earl of Bristol (1724–79). Although he spent long periods of time away from his diocese travelling in Europe, his Irish nationalist sympathies and his opposition to discrimination against Roman Catholicism were sincere and courageous. This stance, as well as his intractable eccentricity, capriciousness and Deist proclivities, isolated him politically.

Hervey played a significant role in the promotion of the Early Gothic Revival in the architecture of north-west Ulster. He funded construction of the spire (1776–8; destr. 1802) of St Columb's Cathedral, Londonderry, and several churches in Co. Londonderry, including St Moresius, Banagher (1780–84), Tamlaght Finlagan parish church, Ballykelly (1795; attributed to Michael Shanahan (*fl* 1770–1803)), and St Guarie, Aghadowey (rebuilt 1797). He is best-known, however, for building country houses. In 1780 he invited John Soane (his travelling companion in Naples the previous year) to submit designs for Downhill Castle, Co. Londonderry. These were rejected, as were those by Robert Adam; the designs attributed to James Wyatt possibly influenced the form of the eventual building (1784–5; destr. 1851; rest. 1876), the construction of which was supervised by Shanahan. Ballyscullion (1787–9; destr. 1813), Co. Londonderry, also by Shanahan, was intended to house Hervey's art collection. Its oval rotunda and quadrant corridors were a prototype for Hervey's largest country house, Ickworth (begun 1796), Suffolk, by Mario Asprucci (1764–1804) and Francis Sandys (*fl* 1788–1814), which was also intended as a museum.

The destruction of Hervey's papers, together with the confiscation and dispersal of his works of art, has resulted in tantalizingly sparse documentation of his collection. What distinguished Hervey was his art-historical consciousness. His aim of hanging his collection according to various schools and periods was highly advanced for its time, and his choice of artists was both eclectic and original. As well as the then unfashionable paintings by Cimabue and Giotto, he owned works attributed to Michael Wolgemut, Dürer, Raphael, Titian, Tintoretto, Guercino and Rembrandt. In 1776 he bought three frescoed Roman interiors to be installed at Downhill Castle (destr.). His collection also included a Roman mosaic pavement (Downhill Castle, Co. Londonderry, NT) and Classical statues. However, his interest in antiquity was less scholarly than that of his lifelong friend Sir William Hamilton (i).

Hervey's patronage of contemporary art was equally enthusiastic. His best-known commission is John Flaxman's marble group of the *Fury of Athamas* (1790–93; Ickworth, Suffolk, NT). He also commissioned items from Canova, Thomas Banks and Joseph Wright of Derby but rejected them either because of cost or of personal whim.

Other acquisitions included portraits by Pompeo Batoni, Angelica Kauffman, Elisabeth-Louise Vigée Le Brun, Anton von Maron and William Hoare (ii); landscapes by Jacob More, Thomas Jones and Philipp Hackert; and sculpture by Christopher Hewetson and John Deare. He assisted artists whose careers were jeopardized by the impending Napoleonic Wars (1803–15), among them Simon Denis (1755–1813) and Nicolas-Didier Boguet. In 1798 much of Hervey's collection, then stored in Rome, was confiscated by the French army. Two petitions, each signed by over 300 artists, requested restitution. Despite this tribute to Hervey's patronage, the petitions were ignored, and the collection was dispersed. After nine months' imprisonment in Milan (1798–9), Hervey resumed his patronage but was only able to send several minor works to Britain before his death.

BIBLIOGRAPHY

W. S. Childe-Pemberton: *The Earl Bishop* (London, 1924)
P. Rankin: *Irish Building Ventures of the Earl Bishop of Derry* (Belfast, 1972)
B. Ford: 'The Earl Bishop: An Eccentric and Capricious Patron of the Arts', *Apollo*, xcix (1974), pp. 426–34
B. Fothergill: *The Mitred Earl: An Eighteenth-century Eccentric* (London, 1974)
G. Jackson-Stops, ed.: *Ickworth* (London, 1992)

MARK STOCKER

Hervey Islands. *See* COOK ISLANDS.

Hervier, (Louis-Henri-Victor-Jules-François) Adolphe (*b* Paris, 1818; *d* Paris, 18 June 1879). French painter, draughtsman and printmaker. He was first taught by his father, Marie-Antoine Hervier (*fl c.* 1810–20), a successful miniature painter and former pupil of David, and he later studied under Léon Cogniet and Eugène Isabey. From the start his work had an individual style. His work first appeared at the Salon in 1849 but, according to Philippe Burty (sale catalogue, Paris, Hôtel Drouot, 26 Feb 1876), was exhibited there only eight more times, with 23 rejections. Gautier, the Goncourt brothers, Champfleury, Corot and Rodolphe Bresdin praised his work, but their admiration brought him little money, and he was forced to paint backgrounds for other artists, such as the military painter Edouard Armand-Dumaresq (1826–95).

A skilled draughtsman with a lively style, Hervier learnt to etch about 1840 and became a gifted printmaker. His etchings, which are frequently small, resemble sketchbook pages with their innovative use of various printmaking techniques and their fresh ideas. He published several different editions of his prints in his lifetime, and in 1888 the editor and bookseller L. Joly compiled a posthumous *Album Hervier*, containing 43 plates drawn and etched by the artist between 1840 and 1860. His figure style, which, like Daumier's, has elements of caricature, gives expressive life to the peasants and workers he frequently portrayed, for example in *Market at Caen* (*c.* 1860; Dijon, Mus. B.-A.). His paintings are solidly constructed, with considerable sensitivity to effects of light, perhaps a reflection of the time he spent working around Barbizon with artists such as Charles Jacque. In the last two decades of his life Hervier sacrificed some of his early vigour for a broader, more facile approach, notably in his watercolours. Several sales of Hervier's work were held during his lifetime, though none was very successful.

BIBLIOGRAPHY

T. Gautier: *Les Beaux-arts en Europe*, ii (Paris, 1857), pp. 158–9
P. Hamerton: 'Modern Etching in France', *F.A. Q.*, ii (1864), pp. 83–4, 102
H. Beraldi: *Les Graveurs du XIXème siècle*, viii (Paris, 1889), pp. 110–16
E. de Goncourt and J. de Goncourt: 'Le Salon de 1852', *Etud. A.* (1893), pp. 89–90
R. Bouyer: 'Petits maîtres oubliés, I: Adolphe Hervier', *Gaz. B.-A.*, xvi (1896), pp. 61–72
R. Marx: 'Cartons d'artistes, maîtres et petits maîtres du XIXème siècle: Adolphe Hervier, 1819–1879', *Image* (1896–7), pp. 18–23
A. Baudin: *Recherches sur la vie et l'oeuvre du peintre français, Adolphe Hervier (1819–1879), avec le catalogue des oeuvres peintes et dessinées* (MA thesis, U. Lille, 1972)
J. van der Noort: *Catalogue Raisonné* of Hervier's Prints and Watercolours (in preparation)

JAMES P. W. THOMPSON

Hervieu, Louise (*b* Alençon, Orne, 26 Oct 1878; *d* Versailles, 11 Sept 1954). French draughtswoman, painter and writer. She studied drawing in Paris and then worked with Lucien Simon, René Menard and André Dauchez (1870–1948). She began to paint around 1905 and exhibited at the Salon des Indépendants in Paris. She had a one-woman show in 1910 at the Galerie Eugène Blot in Paris and was then persuaded by her parents to give up her artistic activities. She stopped painting but around 1915 began to concentrate on pastels, charcoal drawing and other graphic arts. Though never participating in the most avant-garde movements of her time, she became associated with Bonnard, Vuillard and Félix Vallotton. In her pastels and charcoal drawings Hervieu most frequently depicted still-lifes and interiors, which she endowed with a sense of mystery. She achieved great dramatic effect by the use of strong chiaroscuro drawing, as in *Woman at a Console* (1922; Paris, Pompidou). She also devoted much time to book illustration, providing plates for editions of Charles Baudelaire's *Les Fleurs du mal* (Paris, 1920) and *Le Spleen de Paris* (Paris, 1922), among others. Since childhood Hervieu had suffered from inherited chronic meningitis, which caused her eyesight to deteriorate. Around 1927 she was forced to abandon the visual arts and she turned her attention to writing. In 1925 a group of artists that included Bonnard, Maurice Denis, Picasso, Rouault and André Lhote illustrated her book *L'Ame du cirque* (1925). Her novel *Sangs* won the Prix Femina in 1935.

DBF

BIBLIOGRAPHY

R. Huyghe and G. Bazin: *Histoire de l'art contemporain* (Paris, 1935/R New York, 1968), pp. 206–7

□

Herwijck, Steven van (*b* Utrecht, *c.* 1530; *d* London, *c.* 1565). Dutch medallist. Although he was a skilled artist, his identity was not discovered until 1921. For many years the initials with which he signed his works were thought to stand for 'Stephen of Holland', a misconception that arose from speculation by George Vertue. His earliest medals, such as those depicting *George van Egmond* and *Engelken Tols*, date from 1558, when he was working in his native town. In 1559 he was working in Antwerp, where he produced several medals including the fine portrait of *Jacobus Fabius*, and in 1561 he portrayed *King*

Sigismund II of Poland and other members of the Polish royal family. In 1562 he travelled to England and produced the first medals of private individuals to be made there. These portray *William, Marquess of Northampton*; *Elizabeth, Marchioness of Northampton*; *William, Earl of Pembroke*; *Anne Heneage*; *Thomas Stanley*, *Richard Martin and Dorcas Eglestone*; *Edmund Withipoll* (two different medals); *Maria Dimock*; and *Michel de Castlenau* (all 1562). All are cast and chased, and each is a masterpiece of portraiture. The reverse of the *Stanley* medal consists of a coat of arms in the Netherlandish tradition, but the delicately modelled allegorical reverses of others, such as the *Pembroke* and *Dimock* medals, and the elegant lettering clearly show the influence of 16th-century Italian medals. Van Herwijck's *Bacchus* and *Ceres* medals furnish additional evidence of the importance to him of Classical subject-matter. He must also have known the work of Jacques Jonghelinck. He had returned to Utrecht by 1564, as is demonstrated by the homely medal of *Hillegoent van Alendorp*, but by the time of his death he was again living in London with his family.

BIBLIOGRAPHY

Forrer; Thieme–Becker
E. Hawkins, A. W. Franks and H. A. Grueber: *Medallic Illustrations of the History of Great Britain and Ireland* (London, 1885)
V. Tourneur: 'Le Médailleur anversois Steven van Herwijck', *Rev. Belge Numi.* (1921), pp. 27–55

PHILIP ATTWOOD

Herzfeld, Ernst (Emil) (*b* Celle, 23 July 1879; *d* Basle, 21 Jan 1948). German architect, archaeologist, historian and philologist. He was educated at the universities of Munich and Berlin and at the Technische Hochschule, Charlottenburg, where he trained as an architect. In 1903 he visited the Middle East by participating as field architect in the excavation of ASSUR by the Deutsche Orient-Gesellschaft. The expedition was led by Friedrich Delitzsch, Herzfeld's instructor in Assyrian and Arabic, and it enabled him to learn the techniques of excavation and to develop his interest in early Islamic culture. After returning to Germany, he made a journey through Luristan to visit PASARGADAE and PERSEPOLIS, and following the acceptance of his doctoral thesis on Pasargadae by the University of Berlin in 1907, he travelled with FRIEDRICH SARRE, his lifelong colleague and friend whom he had met in 1905, from Istanbul via Aleppo and Baghdad to the Gulf to find an Islamic site suitable for excavation. The choice fell upon SAMARRA', the capital of the Abbasid dynasty in the 9th century AD, and their travels were published in *Archäologische Reise im Euphrat- und Tigris-Gebiet*.

Herzfeld's academic career began in 1908 with his involvement with the Prussian State Museums, and in 1909 he was appointed Privatdozent for Historical Geography at the University of Berlin. In 1910 he conclusively argued that the façade of the palace at MSHATTA, brought earlier in the decade to Berlin, was datable to AD 744 during the reign of the Umayyad caliph al-Walid II, and he and Sarre also published *Iranische Felsreliefs*, an important contribution to Sasanian achaeology. The Samarra' excavations (1911–13) resulted in extremely important discoveries for understanding early Abbasid art. In 1920 he was made a full professor at Berlin, a post he retained

until 1935. After gaining concessions from the Iranian government, he directed excavations at Persepolis (1931–4) under the sponsorship of the Oriental Institute of the University of Chicago. His discoveries were reported in his own periodical, *Archäologische Mitteilungen aus Iran*. Not wishing to return to Germany, he moved to London in 1934, where he gave the Schweich Lectures at the British Academy and continued to write. Two years later he left for the USA, where he gave the Lowell Lectures in Boston (1936) and became professor at the Institute for Advanced Study, Princeton. He also taught at the Institute of Fine Arts at New York University. His interests ranging from pre-Islamic to Islamic civilization are attested by almost 200 books, articles and reviews in such periodicals as *Der Islam* and *Ars Islamica*. In 1944 he again travelled to the Middle East, but fell ill at Cairo. In 1946, aware that his health was failing, he presented all his scholarly materials to the Smithsonian Institution, Washington, DC, to be kept in the Freer Gallery of Art.

WRITINGS

'Die Genesis der islamischen Kunst und das Mshatta-Problem', *Der Islam*, i (1910), pp. 27–63
with F. Sarre: *Iranische Felsreliefs* (Berlin, 1910)
with F. Sarre: *Archäologische Reise im Euphrat- und Tigris-Gebiet*, 4 vols (Berlin, 1911–20)
Erster vorläufiger Bericht über die Ausgrabungen von Samarra (Berlin, 1912)
Der Wandschmuck der Bauten von Samarra und seine Ornamentik (Berlin, 1923), i of *Die Ausgrabungen von Samarra* (1923–48)
Die Malereien von Samarra (Berlin, 1927), ii of *Die Ausgrabungen von Samarra* (1923–48)
Archaeological History of Iran (London, 1935) [Schweich Lectures of 1934]
Iran in the Ancient East (London and New York, 1941)
'Damascus: Studies in Architecture, I–IV', *A. Islam.*, ix (1942), pp. 1–53; x (1943), pp. 13–70; xi–xii (1946), pp. 1–71; and xiii–xiv (1948), pp. 118–38
Zoroaster and his World, 2 vols (Princeton, 1947)
Geschichte der Stadt Samarra (1948), vi of *Die Ausgrabungen von Samarra* (Berlin and Hamburg, 1923–48)
Matériaux pour un corpus inscriptionum arabicarum: Deuxième partie: Syrie du Nord: Inscriptions et monuments d'Alep, 2 vols (Cairo, 1954–6)
The Persian Empire, ed. G. Walser (Wiesbaden, 1968) [posth. ed. from Herzfeld's writings]

NDB

BIBLIOGRAPHY

G. C. Miles: 'The Writings of Ernst Herzfeld', *A. Islam.*, vii (1940), pp. 82–92; suppl. *A. Islam.*, xv–xvi (1951), pp. 266–7
R. Ettinghausen: 'Ernst Herzfeld, 1879–1948', *A. Islam.*, xv–xvi (1951), pp. 261–6
G. C. Miles, ed.: *Archaeologica Orientalia in Memoriam Ernst Herzfeld* (Locust Valley, 1952)

S. J. VERNOIT

Herzfelde, Helmuth. *See* HEARTFIELD, JOHN.

Herzog, Fülöp. *See under* SCHICKEDANZ, ALBERT.

Hesar, Tappeh. *See* HISSAR, TEPE.

Heschler, David (*b* Memmingen, *bapt* 24 Sept 1611; *d* Ulm, 22 June 1667). German ivory- and wood-carver. A member of a large family of sculptors active in southern Germany and Switzerland, he studied with his father, Sigmund Heschler (*b* 1584; *d* after 1658). They collaborated on figures (1631; rest. 1955–8) on the high altar of the former Klosterkirche at Buxheim, near Memmingen, which exemplify the influence of 16th-century Italian sculpture—and that of Georg Petel—on German sculpture in wood in the early Baroque period. Heschler became best known for his small-scale figures. His carvings reflect subjects taken from late 16th-century Dutch and Italian originals, though stylistically they resemble the works of Georg Petel, influenced by Rubens, as can be seen in his *Henchman* (pearwood, *c.* 1630; Cologne, Kstgewmus.), *St Sebastian* (ivory, *c.* 1640–50; Leipzig, Mus. Ksthandwks) and *Deposition* (ivory, *c.* 1650; Stockholm, Nmus.).

BIBLIOGRAPHY
A. Schädler: 'Der Ulmer Bildhauer und Elfenbeinschnitzer David Heschler (1611–1667)', *Studien zur Geschichte der europäischen Plastik: Festschrift Theodor Müller* (Munich, 1965), pp. 293–303
C. Theuerkauff: 'Fragen zur Ulmer Kleinplastik im 17./18. Jahrhundert, I. David Heschler und sein Kreis', *Alte & Mod. Kst.*, cxc–cxci (1983), pp. 23–34
F. Fischer: *Der Meister des Buxheimer Hochaltars* (Berlin, 1988)

FRITZ FISCHER

Hesdin, Jacquemart de. *See* JACQUEMART DE HESDIN.

Hesius [van Hees]**, Willem** (*b* Antwerp, June 1601; *d* Brussels, 4 March 1690). Flemish architect. He joined the Jesuits in 1617 and went to school in Antwerp from 1619 to 1621, at which time the church of St Carolus Borromeus was being built after the design of Franciscus Aguilonius and Peter Huyssens. Initially, Hesius came to prominence as a preacher and an important figure in religious politics, and he did not become active as an architect until he was nearly 50. During the third quarter of the 17th century he was his order's most important architectural adviser. The plans for St Michielskerk, Leuven, one of the most important examples of Flemish Baroque architecture, have been attributed to him and date from 1650. They show the influence of Vitruvius (known in the Netherlands through the translations of Pieter Coecke van Aelst and Sebastiano Serlio), as well as the influence of illustrations by Jean Maggius. The design is characterized principally by a high lantern tower with a dome above the junction of transept and nave. The church, completed in 1666, was not built under the supervision of Hesius alone, but was the work of several Jesuit artists and craftsmen. In 1660 cracks were discovered in the capital of one of the pillars intended to support the dome, which had not yet been built. Lucas Faydherbe was commissioned to lead the repair work, but construction difficulties prevented the execution of the majestic dome. The Gothic gable, completed by the Jesuit Jan van der Steen, is incongruous in relation to the initial design.

BIBLIOGRAPHY
BNB; Thieme–Becker
J. Braun: *Die belgischen Jesuitenkirchen* (Freiburg im Breisgau, 1907)
J. H. Plantegna: *L'Architecture religieuse dans l'ancien duché de Brabant depuis le règne des archiducs jusqu'au gouvernement autrichien, 1598–1713* (The Hague, 1926)
J. Gilissen: 'Le Père Guillaume Hesius, architecte du XVIIe siècle', *An. Soc. Royale Archéol. Bruxelles*, xlii (1938), pp. 216–55
J. van Ackere: *Barok en classicisme in België* (Brussels, 1974)

J.-P. ESTHER

Hess, Heinrich Maria von (*b* Düsseldorf, 19 April 1798; *d* Munich, 29 March 1863). German painter. After training (1813–17) under Peter von Langer (1756–1824) at the Akademie der bildenden Künste in Munich, he painted religious subjects under the influence of Peter Cornelius. In 1821 he joined the Lukasbrüder, and the circle around Crown Prince Ludwig I of Bavaria, in Rome. *Apollo among the Muses* (1824; Munich, Neue Pin.), painted for Maximilian I, shows Hess to be among the most gifted of the German artists working in Rome. The influence of Raphael, glowing but carefully harmonized colours, gliding figures and drapery animate this early masterpiece. Among other important works from this time are exquisitely detailed and colouristically sophisticated, intimate character portraits with early Renaissance settings, such as that of *Marchesa Marianna Florenzi* (1824; Munich, Neue Pin.), as well as fresh and lively Naturalist landscapes from the environs of Rome, for example *Campagna Landscape near Ponte Nomentano* (1821–6; Hamburg, Ksthalle).

After returning to Munich in 1826, Hess's many royal commissions sapped his creative strength. Numerous fresco cycles designed in an unpopular archaic style, for example that in St Bonifaz (destr.) in Munich, were rushed to completion by untalented assistants and thus contributed little to his reputation. Preparatory drawings for these large-scale works, for example the *Adoration of the Shepherds* and the *Adoration of the Magi* for the Royal Chapel (1830–31; now Karlsruhe, Staatl. Ksthalle), affirm his former strength in drawing and composition.

BIBLIOGRAPHY
W. Lessing: 'Heinrich Hess—Bildnisse', *Die Kunst*, xxxxv (1922), pp. 227–32
R. Oldenbourg: *Die Münchner Malerei im neunzehnten Jahrhundert* (Munich, 1922, rev. 1983)
E. Ruhmer: *Schack-Galerie*, cat., ii (Munich, 1969)

RUDOLF M. BISANZ

Hess, Hieronymus (*b* Basle, 1799; *d* Basle, 8 June 1850). Swiss painter and draughtsman. He first trained in Basle with Maximilian Neustück (1756–1834). In 1819 he went to Naples and then Rome, where he lived until 1823. While in Rome he met Joseph Anton Koch and the Nazarene artists, whose work was to have a lasting influence on his religious and historical paintings (e.g. *Murder of King Albert*, 1829; Basle, Kstmus.). While studying in Nuremberg on the recommendation of Bertel Thorvaldsen, he became familiar with popular contemporary drawings. As a talented draughtsman, and to a lesser extent as a successful colourist, he subsequently established his reputation as one of the most important social caricaturists in Switzerland. In his caricatures, which are full of coarse humour, he attached particular value to the subject's physiognomy, which he used to reveal individual character (e.g. *Prof. Dr Med. Johann Jakob Stöckelberger und Frau Ochs geb. Bauler, auf der Mittleren Brücke zu Basel*, 1826; priv. col., see Pfister-Burkhatter (1964–6), p. 152). His fame, however, rests primarily on his copies after the fragments (Basle, Kstmus.) of Hans Holbein the younger's lost frescoes (1521–2) in the Rathaus: *Death of Charondas*, *Blinding of Zaleukos* and *Curius Dentatus* (all 1817; Basle, Kstmus.). In spite of their craftsmanlike quality, these drawings are important to research and represent historical documents of great interest.

BIBLIOGRAPHY
SKL; Thieme–Becker
M. Pfister-Burkhatter: *Hieronymus Hess, 1799–1850* (Basle, 1952)
——: 'Zeichnungen von Hieronymus Hess (1799–1850)', *Öff. Kstsamml. Basel, Jber* [(1964–6)], pp. 145–54

SEPP KERN

Hess, Ludwig (*b* Zurich, 16 Oct 1760; *d* Zurich, 13 April 1800). Swiss painter and engraver. The son of a butcher, he learnt his father's trade, and as a livestock-dealer made several journeys across the Alps, where he determined to be a painter. Around 1778 he became Johann Heinrich Wüest's pupil, and he later grew friendly with the poet Salomon Gessner, who encouraged him. He undertook numerous study trips into the Glarus, Grisons and Ticino Alps. In summer 1792 he travelled via the Bernese Oberland to Chamonix, and in autumn 1794 he visited Rome. In his *plein-air* work Hess developed a technique of dry gouache applied to dark-dyed paper, and his landscape painting opened up many previously unexplored alpine areas. From 1798 onwards he began producing some 80 different engravings after his own pictures. In 1799 he took part in the first local exhibition of the Zürcher Künstlergesellschaft. Together with Caspar Wolf, Hess was the leading pre-Romantic pioneer of realistic alpine painting in Switzerland. Unlike Wolf, his landscapes, such as the *Rhône Falls in the Valais* (1798; Zurich, Ksthaus), were imbued with a melancholy atmosphere rather than drama.

SKL

BIBLIOGRAPHY

J. H. Meyer: *Ludwig Hess, Landschaftsmaler* (Zurich, 1800)
F. M. Brandenberger: *Ludwig Hess, 1760–1800: Zur zürcherischen Landschaftsmalerei des 18. Jahrhunderts* (Zurich, 1941)
L. Fromer-Im Obersteg: *Die Entwicklung der schweizerischen Landschaftsmalerei im 18. und frühen 19. Jahrhundert* (Basle, 1945), pp. 52–3, 79–87

MATTHIAS FREHNER

Hess, Thomas B. (*b* Rye, NY, 14 July 1920; *d* New York, 13 July 1978). American writer and art critic. After graduating from Yale University, New Haven, CT, and starting a career as a writer, he worked as an associate editor of *ARTnews* (1946–50). He also acted as a managing editor from 1950 to 1965 and as an executive editor from 1965 to 1972. From 1972 until his death he was art critic of the newly founded *New York Magazine*, also writing freelance for other magazines and journals, including *Saturday Review, Encounter, New York Times* and *Museum Journal*.

Hess served as a major critic and tastemaker, with particular interest in and impact on the acceptance of Abstract Expressionism; he wrote books and catalogues for MOMA, New York. He was a major supporter of Willem de Kooning, the subject of his first monograph and of a major exhibition organized by Hess at MOMA in 1968. Hess was also active in several arts organizations and was president of the Longview Foundation in Longview, Texas.

WRITINGS

Abstract Painting: Background and American Phase (New York, 1951)
Willem de Kooning (New York, 1959, rev. 1967)
Barnett Newman (exh. cat., New York, MOMA, 1969)
Woman as Sex Object (New York, 1972)
Aaron Siskind (New York, 1976)

DAVID M. SOKOL

Hesse. French family of artists.

(1) Nicolas-Auguste Hesse (*b* Paris, 28 Aug 1795; *d* Paris, 14 June 1869). Painter and lithographer. He initially studied under his brother, the painter Henri-Joseph Hesse (1781–1849), and then, in 1810, under Antoine-Jean Gros.

In 1811 he entered the Ecole des Beaux-Arts in Paris, winning the Prix de Rome in 1818 with *Philemon and Baucis Receiving Jupiter and Mercury* (1818; Paris, Ecole N. Sup. B.-A.). He then went to Rome, where ill-health prevented him from fully devoting himself to painting. Nevertheless he produced a number of works on Classical and mythological subjects while in Italy and exhibited at the Salon for the first time in 1824. He rapidly established himself as an important official painter, receiving numerous State commissions. In 1827 he exhibited the *Foundation of the Sorbonne College around the Year 1256*, which now decorates the chapel of the Sorbonne. The Duchesse Caroline de Berry employed Hesse in 1829 to decorate the chapel at the château at Rosny, near Paris. The same year, he painted the allegorical figures *Theology* and *History* for the Ancienne Salle du Conseil d'Etat in the Louvre. He won a first-class medal at the Salon of 1838 for *Christ at the Sepulchre* (1838; Périgueux Cathedral; reduced variant version, 1845; Paris, Louvre) and *General Meeting of the Etats-Généraux on 23 June 1789* (1838; Amiens, Mus. Picardie). The latter was installed in the Chamber of Deputies. He worked for King Louis-Philippe in 1846, decorating his château at Corbeil in Brittany, and in 1848 he won the competition to provide a symbolic representation of the Republic for the Galerie des Fêtes in the Hôtel de Ville in Paris (destr. 1871).

A large portion of Hesse's output was devoted to decorating churches, and in 1835 he provided an *Adoration of the Shepherds* for the nave of Notre-Dame de Lorette in Paris. Among his other commissions in Paris were decorations for the chapel of the Virgin at Notre-Dame de Bonne-Nouvelle (1840), for the choir of St-Pierre-de-Chaillot (1843) and for Ste-Elisabeth-du-Temple (1852). He also designed stained-glass windows (1849) for the chapel of the Virgin at St-Eustache, Paris, and for Ste-Clotilde (also in Paris) in 1853. On account of these numerous commissions for churches and public monuments, Hesse exhibited at the Salon comparatively infrequently, though he continued to send works until 1868. His subjects were invariably historical or religious, executed in an academic style characteristic of the official art of the Second Empire. He also turned his hand to lithography, producing works of a similar tone and style to his paintings; a typical example is *Annibale Carracci after a Self-portrait* (1825; Paris, Bib. N.). In 1840 Hesse was awarded the Légion d'honneur, and in 1863 he succeeded Delacroix as a member of the Académie des Beaux-Arts.

DBF; Hoefer

BIBLIOGRAPHY

A. Soubies: *Les Membres de l'Académie des Beaux-Arts*, 4 vols (Paris, 1905–17), iii, pp. 32–4
Inventaire du fonds français après 1800, Paris, Bib. N., Cab. Est. cat., x (Paris, 1930), p. 381

(2) Alexandre-Jean-Baptiste Hesse (*b* Paris, 30 Sept 1806; *d* Paris, 7 Aug 1879). Painter, nephew of (1) Nicolas-Auguste Hesse. He was the son of Henri-Joseph Hesse. He entered the studio of Jean-Victor Bertin in 1820, enrolling at the Ecole des Beaux-Arts the following year. He then travelled in France, visiting the Midi in 1825. In 1830 he visited first Rome, where he met Horace Vernet, Director of the Académie Française, and then Venice. In 1833 he exhibited *Funeral Honours Rendered to Titian after* *his Death at Venice during the Plague of 1576* (Paris, Louvre) at the Salon, where he won a first-class medal. The same year he returned to Italy, where he made copies of Renaissance masterpieces in Florence and Venice. In 1836 he received a State commission to paint *Henry IV Brought back to the Louvre after his Assassination* (1836; Versailles, Château), which was destined for the Galerie d'Apollon in the Louvre.

In 1842 Hesse exhibited the large work *Adoption of Godefroy de Bouillon in 1097 by the Emperor Alexius Comnenus* (1842; Versailles, Château), which had been commissioned by the State two years previously and for which he was made a Chevalier de la Légion d'honneur that year. Like his uncle, he took part in the 1848 competition to provide an allegorical figure of the Republic. Apart from his Salon paintings he worked on a number of church decorations in Paris, including the chapel at St Séverin (1852) and the church of St Gervais–St Protais (1864–7). He continued to exhibit at the Salon until 1861. His painting was most notable for its intense colours, earning him the name 'the last Venetian'. He travelled regularly and was in Rome again from 1845 to 1857 and in Belgium in 1870. He was elected a member of the Académie des Beaux-Arts in 1867, succeeding Ingres, and in 1869 was made Officier de la Légion d'honneur.

DBF

BIBLIOGRAPHY
E. Bellier and L. Auvray: *Dictionnaire général des artistes de l'école française*, 3 vols (Paris, 1868–85)
P. Nicard: *Alexandre Hesse: Sa vie et ses ouvrages* (Paris, 1883)

Hesse, Eva (*b* Hamburg, 11 Jan 1936; *d* New York, 29 May 1970). American sculptor and painter of German birth. She arrived in New York in 1939. From 1954 to 1957 she studied at Cooper Union in New York and in 1959 at Yale University School of Art in New Haven, CT, under Josef Albers. Her individual style first appeared in drawings shown in the early 1960s, for example at her first one-woman exhibition at Allan Stone Gallery in New York (1963). Hesse considered herself a painter until 1965, when, during a year in Germany, she constructed and exhibited 14 papier-mâché reliefs, with cord-wrapped wires embedded, projecting or dangling from them, at the Kunsthalle, Düsseldorf; among these exhibited works was *Tomorrow's Apples (5 in White)* (1965; London, Tate). Hesse's friends included Sol LeWitt, Robert Smithson, Nancy Holt (*b* 1938), Mel Bochner (*b* 1940) and Dan Graham.

In the years before her early death Hesse's sculpture grew in scale and daring from easel-sized reliefs to *Expanded Expansion* (1969; New York, Guggenheim), whose latex-covered cheesecloth 'curtains', draped between 16 plexiglass poles (h. 3.1 m), are extendable laterally, and *Right After* (1969; Milwaukee, WI, A. Mus.), whose light-filled fibreglass strands are suspended irregularly in space, usually up to *c*. 5 m wide. Her mature sculpture abounds in contradictions: chaos and order, organic and geometric, absurd and tragic. Hesse was one of the first and most influential artists to question the austere, immobile exactitude of serial Minimalism and imbue it with a capacity to move, change and vary from the norm like a living being.

For illustrations *see* UNITED STATES OF AMERICA, fig. 24, and SOFT ART.

UNPUBLISHED SOURCES
Oberlin Coll., OH, Allen Mem. A. Mus., Eva Hesse Archv [diaries, notebooks, sketches, correspondence]

BIBLIOGRAPHY
L. Lippard: *Eva Hesse* (New York, 1976) [extensive bibliog.]
Eva Hesse: A Retrospective of the Drawings (exh. cat. by E. H. Johnson, Oberlin Coll., OH, Allen Mem. A. Mus., 1982)
B. Barrette: *Eva Hesse Sculpture: A Catalogue Raisonné* (New York, 1989)

ELLEN H. JOHNSON

Hesse, Ludwig Ferdinand (*b* Belgard, 23 Jan 1795; *d* Berlin, 8 May 1876). German architect and painter. After training at the Berlin Bauakademie (1819–25), he travelled to southern Germany and Austria in 1826–7 to study vaulting to aid his completion of Schinkel's Friedrich-Werdersche-Kirche (1824–30; *see* SCHINKEL, KARL FRIEDRICH, fig. 2) in Berlin. In 1831 he became Inspektor of the Ministerialbaukommission (bridges and canal construction), and the following year he was made Hofbauinspektor. In 1838 he designed an innovative cable bridge at the Tiergarten in Berlin, and in 1839–40 he designed the Neoclassical Tierarzneischule, also in Berlin.

Although his early works show a clear, simple and effective classical approach, they were not as successful as the works of his contemporaries Friedrich August Stüler and Ludwig Persius. From 1840 he worked in Potsdam, completing plans by Stüler and Frederick William IV for the Pfingstenbergschloss and Orangerie, and Persius's Friedenskirche. His Weinberghaus (1847) and similar Potsdam villas were built in a 16th-century Italian villa style. He was also active at Schloss Charlottenburg, Berlin, extending Queen Luise's mausoleum in 1841. In 1865 Hesse succeeded Stüler as Direktor of the Schlossbaukommission, undertaking restoration and extension of Prussian palaces (e.g. Schloss Charlottenburg, Berlin). Hesse also painted architectural views, landscapes and portraits, which he exhibited at the academy in Berlin. His sons Carl Hesse (1827–95) and Rudolf Hesse (1829–86) collaborated with him on his projects in Potsdam.

WRITINGS
'Die Tierarzneischule in Berlin', *Allg. Bauztg Abbild.: Österreich. Vjschr. Öff. Baudienst*, viii (1843), pp. 21–6
Ländliche Wohngebäude in der Umgegend von Sanssouci und Potsdam, i, ii (Berlin, 1854), iii (Berlin, 1857)
Sanssouci in seinen Architekturen unter der Regierung . . . Friedrich Wilhelms IV (Berlin 1854–6)

BIBLIOGRAPHY
Macmillan Enc. Architects; Thieme–Becker
A. Kopisch: *Die königlichen Schlösser und Gärten zu Potsdam* (Berlin, 1854)
O. N.: 'Ludwig Ferdinand Hesse: Skizze zum 50jährigen Dienstjubiläum', *Dt. Bauztg*, iii (1869), p. 218
Obituary, *Dt. Bauztg*, x (1876), p. 200
E. Börsch-Supan: *Berliner Baukunst nach Schinkel, 1840–1870* (Munich, 1977)

EVA BÖRSCH-SUPAN

Hesse-Kassel, House of. German family of rulers, collectors and patrons. In 1567 Philip the Generous, Landgrave of Hesse (*reg* 1509–67), divided Hesse among his four sons; by 1604 only Hesse-Darmstadt and the more important Hesse-Kassel remained. Philip's eldest son, William IV, Landgrave of Hesse-Kassel (1532–92; *reg* 1567–92), developed KASSEL as the main residence of the House of Hesse-Kassel. The town was heavily fortified and the construction of its Schloss (destr. 1811) completed. In its 'Güldener Saal' William installed a portrait gallery of all Christian princes reigning between 1530 and 1583, following the model of the collection of Archduke Ferdinand of Austria in Schloss Ambras, Innsbruck. William IV also built the first permanent observatory in Europe (1560; destr. 1811) and brought the astronomer Tycho Brahe to his court. He was succeeded by his son Maurice 'the Learned', Landgrave of Hesse-Kassel (b Kassel, 25 May 1572; reg 1592–1627; d Eschwege, 15 March 1632), who was so politically inept that he was obliged to abdicate, but during his reign Kassel became an important cultural centre in Germany. His interests included alchemy, astronomy and architecture, although his particular inclination was music and the theatre, and he was a composer and writer. Possibly his most significant enterprise was the construction of the first permanent theatre in Germany, the Ottoneum (1604–5), radically altered in 1696 for use as an art gallery. Its original appearance is uncertain, but the design was probably similar to that of Palladio's Teatro Olimpico in Vicenza.

Hesse-Kassel suffered during the Thirty Years War (1618–48), only recovering under Maurice's great-grandson (1) Charles, Landgrave of Hesse-Kassel (reg 1670–1730), whose reign marked the beginning of a century of cultural prosperity. His son (2) William VIII, Landgrave of Hesse-Kassel (reg 1751–60), enriched the cultural life of Kassel with his art gallery. William VIII's son (3) Frederick II, Landgrave of Hesse-Kassel (reg 1760–85), one of the foremost German princes of the age of the Enlightenment, built the Museum Fridericianum (1769–79; closed 1913), the first known purpose-built museum in Europe. Frederick II's son William IX, Landgrave of Hesse-Kassel (reg 1785–1803), who later reigned as William I, Elector of Hesse (reg 1803–21), was a patron of architecture, constructing Schloss Wilhelmshöhe (1786–98; see KASSEL, §3) and other buildings in the Habichtswald, notably the English-inspired Löwenburg (1793–1801). During French dominion (1806–13) the collections were depleted, and subsequently the rulers of Hesse-Kassel ceased to play an important role in the arts, though William II, Elector of Hesse (reg 1821–31), had the Classicist 'Rotes Palais' built (1821–6). The Electorate of Hesse was annexed by the Kingdom of Prussia in 1866.

BIBLIOGRAPHY

C. von Rommel: Geschichte von Hessen, 10 vols (Marburg and Kassel, 1820–58)
A. Holtmeyer: Die Bau- und Kunstdenkmäler im Regierungsbezirk Cassel, iv (Marburg, 1910); vi (Marburg, 1923)
K. Knetsch: Das Haus Brabant (Darmstadt, 1931)
W. Leist, ed.: Schrifttum zur Geschichte und geschichtlichen Landeskunde von Hessen, 7 vols (1965–84)
G. Schweickhart: 'Kunst und Kultur in Kassel unter Landgraf Moritz dem Gelehrten', Heinrich Schütz (Kassel, 1985), pp. 13–34

B. SCHNACKENBURG, H. SCHNACKENBURG-PRAÉL

(1) Charles [Karl], Landgrave of Hesse-Kassel (b Kassel, 3 Aug 1654; reg 1670–1730; d Kassel, 23 March 1730). He led his country out of the aftermath of the Thirty Years War both politically and culturally. In 1688 he employed the architect Paul Du Ry (see DU RY, (2)), one of the group of French Huguenots that had settled in Kassel after 1685, to plan the Oberneustadt district of Kassel, with the Karlskirche (1698–1710) for his coreligionists. The largest Huguenot settlement in Hesse-Kassel, at Karlshafen an der Weser, was built from 1699 to the Landgrave's own design. From the 1680s he also developed two large complexes of parks and castles, the Karlsaue, on the left bank of the Fulda, and the Wilhelmshöhe (see KASSEL, §3) on the east slope of the Habichtswald. The former, in the Franco-Dutch style, was embellished with the Orangerieschloss (1703–30; destr. 1944); the Marmorbad (1722–30), which was decorated with sculpture by PIERRE-ETIENNE MONNOT, was added later (1717–28).

In 1699–1700 the Landgrave visited Italy, where gardens and water displays inspired his own waterfall projects in the Habichtswald. In 1701 Giovanni Francesco Guerniero (1665–1745) took charge of the costly installations at Wilhelmshöhe, planning a series of cascades descending in 600 stepped levels from a pool below the Riesenschloss, an octagonal pavilion (for illustration see KASSEL); between 1713 and 1717 this was transformed into a monument, with the addition of a steep-sided pyramid with a statue of Hercules (1713–17), modelled on the Farnese Hercules. Only the top third of the scheme of cascades was executed (1701–18). Eight painted ideal views (Kassel, Schloss Wilhelmshöhe) by Jan van Nikkelen (1656–1721) show a project that had been extended still further.

Under the Landgrave's patronage Christoph Labhardt (c. 1641–95) and Franz Gondelach made Kassel a centre of gem-cutting and glass-engraving, and the sculptor JACOB DOBBERMANN worked on a small scale in ivory and amber. The Landgrave also founded a faience factory in 1680 (see KASSEL, §2). The Landgrave's extensive collection of coins and gems was complemented by the striking of numerous commemorative and display coins of his own. The major part of the diverse collections was housed in the Ottoneum, which was converted into an art gallery by Paul Du Ry in 1696.

BIBLIOGRAPHY

G. Gronau: 'Landgraf Carl: Fürstliche Repräsentation des Hochbarock', Die Gemäldegalerie der Staatlichen Kunstsammlungen Kassel, ed. E. Herzog (Hanau, 1969), pp. 12–15
H. Philippi: Landgraf Karl von Hessen-Kassel: Ein deutscher Fürst der Barockzeit (Marburg, 1976)

H. SCHNACKENBURG-PRAÉL

(2) William [Wilhelm] **VIII**, Landgrave of Hesse-Kassel (b Kassel, 10 March 1682; reg 1751–60; d Rinteln, 1 Feb 1760). Son of (1) Charles, Landgrave of Hesse-Kassel. He embarked on a military career in the Netherlands in 1701, distinguishing himself in battles and becoming military governor of Breda (1713) and Maastricht (1723). He returned to Kassel in 1727. A connoisseur of Dutch art and culture, he is recorded as having his own collection of pictures from 1716. His collecting activities reached their peak, however, between 1748 and 1752 and were brought to an end in 1756 by the Seven Years War. In 1750 he acquired the 64 pictures in the collection of Valerius Röver in Delft, including eight works by Rembrandt. The Landgrave had the largest collection of Rembrandts of his day and the first important collection of Frans Hals's work. Among leading Flemish painters, Jacob Jordaens was particularly well represented. William's collection, which also featured delicately painted cabinet pieces (Kassel, Schloss Wilhelmshöhe), including 22 works by Philips Wouwerman, forms a large part of the collection of Old Masters in the Schloss Wilhelmshöhe, Kassel. The first building for William VIII's gallery was constructed from 1749 to 1751 in Oberneustadt. It was designed by François de Cuvilliés I, who also produced the plans for Schloss Wilhelmsthal (*c.* 1745–65). The most important artists involved there were Johann Heinrich Tischbein I, court painter from 1753, and JOHANN AUGUST NAHL der Ältere, court sculptor from 1755.

BIBLIOGRAPHY

W. von Both and H. Vogel: *Landgraf Wilhelm VIII von Hessen-Kassel: Ein Fürst der Rokokozeit* (Munich and Berlin, 1964)
G. Gronau: 'Landgraf Wilhelm VIII: Der grosse Sammler und Begründer der Galerie', *Die Gemäldegalerie der Staatlichen Kunstsammlungen Kassel*, ed. E. Herzog (Hanau, 1969), pp. 15–40

(3) Frederick [Friedrich] **II**, Landgrave of Hesse-Kassel (*b* Kassel, 14 Aug 1720; *reg* 1760–85; *d* Kassel, 31 Oct 1785). Son of (2) William VIII. After a military career he reformed his country in the spirit of enlightened absolutism. The porcelain factory (1766–88) that he established was used to serve artistic and commercial interests. From 1763 the Friedrichsplatz, one of the largest squares in Europe, was laid out by Simon Louis Du Ry, who constructed there the Museum Fridericianum (1769–79; for illustration *see* DU RY, (4)), one of the first purpose-built museums in Europe. The collections (now in Kassel, Schloss Wilhelmshöhe) previously housed in the Otto-neum were moved there and were grouped round a library and a collection of antiquities. The Landgrave expanded his father's painting collection, but his main interest was in antiquities. In 1776–7 in Rome he made his most important purchases, including the Kassel *Apollo* (2nd century AD; Kassel, Schloss Wilhelmshöhe), an unusually well-preserved marble copy after Pheidias. In 1777 Frederick II founded an academy of art, with Du Ry, Johann Heinrich Tischbein I and Johann August Nahl der Ältere as its directors. He promoted site archaeology and in 1780 issued the first German decree relating to the preservation of monuments.

BIBLIOGRAPHY

W. von Both and H. Vogel: *Landgraf Friedrich II. von Hessen-Kassel: Ein Fürst der Zopfzeit* (Munich and Berlin, 1973)
Aufklärung und Klassizismus in Hessen-Kassel unter Landgraf Friedrich II, 1760–1785 (exh. cat., Kassel, Staatl. Kstsammlungen, 1979)

B. SCHNACKENBURG

Hesselin, Louis (Cauchon), Seigneur de Condé (*b* ?1600; *d* Paris, 8 Aug 1662). French official, patron and collector. He held positions in the royal household and *c.* 1655 was appointed Intendant of the Menus Plaisirs du Roi, with responsibility for organizing royal festivities. His portrait was twice engraved by Robert Nanteuil.

In *c.* 1641–4 the Hôtel Hesselin, 24 Quai de Béthune, Ile Saint-Louis, Paris (destr. 1935; engraved by Jean Marot), was built by LOUIS LE VAU. Jacques Sarazin supervised the sculptural decorations by Gilles Guérin and Gerard van Obstal, and painted decorations were undertaken by Michel Dorigny (working under the supervision of Simon Vouet), Jean Blanchard and Rémy Vuibert. Charles Le Brun and Eustache Le Sueur may also have worked in the hôtel. Hesselin's château de Chantemesle (destr.), near Essonnes, was famous for the ballets he

organized there. It contained a ceiling painted by Le Brun and work by Sébastien Bourdon and Jean Blanchard; the interior and garden sculpture were executed by Guérin to Sarazin's designs. The English diarist John Evelyn commented in 1644 on its fountains and cascade.

The inventory of Hesselin's collection made after his death describes *c.* 230 paintings, including works by or attributed to Andrea del Sarto, Titian, Giorgione, Tintoretto, Veronese, Bassano, Vouet, Le Brun, Poussin and Claude Lorrain. Hesselin also owned silverware designed by Sarazin, a collection of sculpture and Stefano della Bella's *Book of Ballets* (Paris, Bib. N.), which passed to the French royal collection together with some of his furniture.

BIBLIOGRAPHY

H. Sauval: *Histoire et recherches des antiquités de la ville de Paris*, iii (Paris, 1724), p. 14
E. Bonnaffé: *Dictionnaire des amateurs français du XVIIe siècle* (Paris, 1884)
R. de Crèvecoeur: 'Louis Hesselin', *Mém. Soc. Hist. Paris & Ile-de-France*, xxii (1895), pp. 225–48
G. Wildenstein: 'L'Inventaire après décès de Louis Hesselin (1662)', *Gaz. B.-A.*, n.s. 6, xlix (1957), pp. 57–63, 111

R. BERESFORD

Hesselius. American family of painters, of Swedish origin.

(1) Gustavus Hesselius (*b* Falun, Sweden, 1682; *d* Philadelphia, PA, 23 May 1755). He was trained in Sweden as a wood-engraver, gilder and painter. In 1712 he accompanied his brother, a Lutheran pastor, to America, where he settled in Philadelphia, PA. About 1720 he moved to the Annapolis, Maryland, area, returning before 1730 to Philadelphia, where he lived until his death. He was one of the first European-trained painters to settle permanently in America and introduced a greater technical skill and increased realism into Colonial painting. His painterly, atmospheric style, which derived from European Baroque, contrasted with the more linear technique of American-born painters. During most of his career he was the leading painter of the Middle Colonies. In addition to mythological scenes, altarpieces and portraits of prominent individuals, Hesselius undertook utilitarian work that included painting the country seat at Springettsbury of Thomas Penn (1702–75) and the interior of the Pennsylvania State House, as well as flower-boxes, chairs, gates and altar-rails. He was also paid, probably as contractor and supervisor, for the construction and installation of an organ for the Moravian church in Bethlehem, PA.

Probably dating from quite early in Hesselius's career are two Classical subjects, *Bacchanalian Revel* (Philadelphia, PA Acad. F.A.) and *Bacchus and Ariadne* (Detroit, MI, Inst. A.), perhaps the first examples of mythological themes painted in America. The portrait of *Thomas Bordley* (Baltimore, MD Hist. Soc. Mus.)—which, before it was cut to bust-length, depicted the prominent jurisprudent standing full-length in legal robes—was painted during his stay in Maryland. Probably his finest extant works are two portraits of chiefs of the Delaware Indians, *Tishcohan* and *Lapowinsa* (Philadelphia, PA, Hist. Soc.), painted in 1735 for John and Thomas Penn on the occasion of a meeting between representatives of the Penns and the Indians to settle a land dispute. These sensitive portraits are the first likenesses produced in America that realistically depict the facial characteristics of the North American Indian. His

Self-portrait and his portrait of his wife *Lydia Hesselius* (both *c.* 1740; Philadelphia, PA, Hist. Soc.) reveal his ability to infuse his subjects with a strong sense of character. *Faithful Richardson* (priv. col.) dates from shortly before his death and reflects the growing taste in the Colonies for brighter colours and increased elegance in portraiture during the quarter century before the Revolution. Although Hesselius is known to have produced two altarpieces in the Colonies, neither seems to have survived. Records indicate that James Claypoole was his apprentice.

BIBLIOGRAPHY

Gustavus Hesselius (exh. cat. by C. Brinton, Philadelphia, PA, Mus. A., 1938) [several unsound attributions]
H. E. Keyes: 'Doubts Regarding Hesselius', *Antiques*, xxxiv (1938), pp. 144–5
E. P. Richardson: 'Gustavus Hesselius', *A. Q.* [Detroit], xii (1952), pp. 56–63
R. E. Fleischer: *Gustavus Hesselius* (diss., Baltimore, MD, Johns Hopkins U., 1964)
Philadelphia Painting and Printing to 1776 (exh. cat., ed. S. Whitin; Philadelphia, PA Acad. F.A., 1971), pp. 18–22
R. E. Fleischer: 'Gustavus Hesselius: A Study of his Style', *American Painting to 1776: A Reappraisal: Winterthur Conference Report, 1971*, pp. 127–58
Gustavus Hesselius: Face Painter to the Middle Colonies (exh. cat. by R. E. Fleischer, Trenton, NJ State Mus., 1988)

ROLAND E. FLEISCHER

(2) John Hesselius (*b* ?Philadelphia, PA, 1728; *d* Anne Arundel Co., MD, 9 April 1778). Son of (1) Gustavus Hesselius. Records suggest that he was trained by his father, but there is little evidence of Gustavus's influence in his work. He was one of the leading portrait painters in the Middle Colonies in the third quarter of the 18th century. His lack of European training was possibly responsible for his unaffected attitude towards painting, which allowed him, unlike his contemporaries, to carry his interpretation of the Rococo portrait style to a middle-class, rather than powerful and wealthy, clientele. More eclectic than creative throughout most of his career, Hesselius is important for his reflection and improvement on the imported styles of others. He relied on the European mezzotint prints then popular in the Colonies for the composition and fashion detail in his works; his earliest known works are virtually coloured copies of these prints. He expressed himself primarily through line and colour, but in this too he was often influenced by others.

With his apparent early knowledge of the work of the New England artist Robert Feke, Hesselius developed a use of clear, strong colour that became an identifying feature of his portraits. In the late 1750s he adopted elements of the style of the more prominent itinerant English portrait painter John Wollaston, in particular the puffy, almond-eyed features of most of his American portraits. However, he surpassed Wollaston in such works as *Elizabeth Calvert* (1761; Baltimore, MD, Mus. A.) in his clarity of colour and lightness of line. Although he is generally credited as the first art teacher of Charles Willson Peale *c.* 1764, there is little in Peale's work to suggest a strong influence, but it is noteworthy that the portrait of *John Paca* (*c.* 1765; Peabody Inst., on dep. Baltimore, MD Hist. Soc. Mus.), long published as by Peale, bears the signature of John Hesselius. Virtually all traces of the Feke and Wollaston influences disappeared in Hesselius's later

works, for example *Mrs Thomas Gough* (1777; Hagerstown, MD, Washington Co. Hist. Soc. Mus.), which shows an increased emphasis on the physical likeness and character of the sitter.

BIBLIOGRAPHY

T. Bolton and G. C. Groce: 'John Hesselius: An Account of his Life and the First Catalogue of his Portraits', *A. Q.* [Detroit], ii/1 (1939), pp. 77–91
R. K. Doud: *John Hesselius: His Life and Work* (diss., Newark, U. DE, 1963)
—: 'The Fitzhugh Portraits by John Hesselius', *VA Mag. Hist. & Biog.*, lxxv/2 (1967), pp. 159–73
—: 'John Hesselius: Maryland Limner', *Winterthur Port.*, v (1969), pp. 129–53
R. E. Fleischer: 'Three Recently Discovered Portraits by John Hesselius', *Antiques*, cix (1981), pp. 666–8

RICHARD K. DOUD

Hester, Joy (*b* Melbourne, 20 Aug 1920; *d* Melbourne, 4 Dec 1960). Australian draughtsman. She studied at the National Gallery School, Melbourne, from 1937 to 1938, and early in her career decided to draw rather than to paint; this suited her rapid method of working and her predilection for the dramatic effects of black and white. Hester's portraits reveal her desire to capture fleeting expressions on the human face, but they also probe psychological depths. By the mid-1940s they had taken on an intense, often anguished mood underscored by a vivid expressionistic style, influenced both by Picasso's work from this period and by the forms of Expressionism adopted by her circle of painters (which included Albert Tucker, her first husband; Sidney Nolan; and Danila Vassilieff). She also extended her subject-matter to include imagery from newsreel footage of Nazi concentration camps, while continuing to draw friends whom she sketched while she sat on the floor, a favourite method of working.

Hester's work was often produced in series: in *Faces* (1947–8; e.g. in Melbourne, priv. col., see Reid, p. 50), one of the most powerful, the subjects are abstracted to resemble masks, while enlarged, distorted eyes register extreme states of mind. In her next major series, *The Lovers* (1956; e.g. in Melbourne, priv. col., see Reid, p. 47), the intimacy of the embrace becomes a metaphor for the tragic struggle between man and woman for possession and liberty. In her lifetime Hester's work was badly received and little valued. In 1947 she contracted Hodgkin's disease, to which she succumbed in 1960.

BIBLIOGRAPHY

B. Reid: 'Joy Hester: Draughtsman of Identity', *A. & Australia*, iv/1 (1966), pp. 45–53
J. Burke: *Joy Hester* (Melbourne, 1983)

JANINE BURKE

Hesyre [Hesy; Hezire]**, tomb of.** Ancient Egyptian burial site at SAQQARA. Hesyre (*fl c.* 2620 BC) lived at the time of Djoser, holding the offices of Overseer of Royal Scribes and 'greatest of physicians and dentists'. His tomb, to the north of Djoser's pyramid, was excavated by James Quibell (1911–12); it was an imposing structure of mud brick, the superstructure of which was 43 m long. The substructure was immensely deep, descending 21 m, with rooms on three levels, including storerooms in which pottery, stone vases and a clay sealing of Djoser were found. The offering chamber, a long interior passage, stretched across the whole eastern face of the mastaba, according to the custom of the time. The inside of the chamber was decorated with wall paintings, including matting designs, scenes of cattle, human figures (*in situ*) and a crocodile (Cairo, Egyp. Mus.). This inner corridor also contained paintings of stone vases and of storerooms stocked with oils, weights and measures, furniture and cult-stands of pottery and

Tomb of Hesyre, wooden relief panel from the offering chamber, h. 1.14 m (whole stele), 3rd Dynasty, *c.* 2620 BC (Cairo, Egyptian Museum)

alabaster. The unique representations of furniture, such as beds, parallel actual objects found in tombs of the 1st Dynasty (*c.* 2925–*c.* 2775 BC).

There was a row of eleven offering niches along the east wall of the offering chamber. Originally all of these contained wooden stelae or panels, but only six have survived (all Cairo, Egyp. Mus.): five from the southern niches (see fig.) and one from the northernmost. These stelae, bearing raised relief decoration, are the most important discovery from the tomb. Their average height is 1.11 m, and the thickness varies from 90 to 200 mm. They show Hesyre in various poses, such as holding a ritual vase, seated before an offering table with his scribal equipment or standing with a staff.

BIBLIOGRAPHY
J. E. Quibell: *The Tomb of Hesy: Excavations at Saqqara, 1911–12* (Cairo, 1913)
L. Borchardt: *Denkmäler des alten Reiches* (Cairo, 1937), i, pp. 108–10

E. P. UPHILL

Hetepheres I, tomb of. Tomb at Giza (see GIZA, §1) lying south of the causeway of the Great Pyramid and containing the secondary burial of Queen Hetepheres I, the wife of Sneferu (*reg c.* 2575–*c.* 2551 BC) and mother of Cheops (*reg c.* 2551–*c.* 2528 BC). Her original burial, probably in the funerary complex of Sneferu at DAHSHUR, had been plundered, and the remainder of her funerary furniture was moved to this well-concealed tomb comprising a small, undecorated chamber at the bottom of a shaft over 30 m deep. When the tomb was excavated by George Reisner in 1925, the Queen's alabaster sarcophagus was empty—presumably her body had been destroyed by tomb robbers searching for jewellery—although the quartzite canopic box containing her mummified viscera was found. The tomb contents were in chaos, with objects piled upon each other in the narrow chamber, and the numerous wooden artefacts had decayed and shrunk; it was only through Reisner's painstaking excavation that the deposit was saved.

The tomb yielded a rich array of objects (all Cairo, Egyp. Mus.) that give a good impression of what an unplundered Old Kingdom royal burial might have contained. These include several pieces of gold-sheathed wooden furniture with sophisticated decoration (*see* EGYPT, ANCIENT, §XVI, 6); in particular the chairs, the palanquin and the bed with its portable canopy display great technical assurance and economy of line. The design of the canopy, with its slender papyriform columns, clearly derives from more ephemeral prototypes of reeds and matting, while the inner faces of its doorframes have hieroglyphs composing her husband's titles worked in repoussé on the gold sheathing (see fig.). The palanquin's wooden carrying poles also had papyriform terminals, and the back of its seat was ornamented with Hetepheres' own name and titles in gold on ebony, showing immense sensitivity to the decorative qualities of the hieroglyphs. Whether this furniture was made exclusively for the Queen's burial or had been used during her lifetime is debatable; Reisner believed that some of the items showed signs of use.

Among the smaller objects found were numerous alabaster and hardstone vessels, probably manufactured

Tomb of Hetepheres I, detail of gold sheathing on bed-canopy, 4th Dynasty, *c.* 2575–2465 BC (Cairo, Egyptian Museum)

for the burial, and four metal ewers, one of copper and three of gold. Cosmetic equipment included gold and copper razors and manicure instruments, and a compart-mented toilet-box containing eight small alabaster vases originally filled with kohl and ointment. In a badly decayed chest, its lid ornamented with faience inlays, were twenty silver bracelets arranged on two tapered poles approxi-mating to the shape of human arms (*see* EGYPT, ANCIENT, fig. 90). Made by shaping thin shells of silver over wooden cores—a technique reflecting the relative scarcity of the metal in the Old Kingdom—they were decorated with a butterfly motif that did not appear again in Egypt and may have been influenced by Near Eastern art.

BIBLIOGRAPHY
G. A. Reisner and W. S. Smith: *A History of the Giza Necropolis*, ii (Cambridge, MA, 1955)
W. Stevenson Smith: *The Art and Architecture of Ancient Egypt*, Pelican Hist. A. (Harmondsworth, 1958, rev. 1981), pp. 87–95
DOMINIC MONTSERRAT

Hetet, Rangimarie (*b* Oparure, NZ, 1892). Maori weaver. Her tribal affiliation was Ngati Maniapoto/Ngati Kinohaku. Hetet was taught the traditional skills of weaving by her mother and other local women elders in the late 19th century, when weaving was still a part of daily life, rather than a craft. During the 1950s she intensified her activity as a weaver, regularly producing cloaks and other items with the encouragement of the Maori Women's Welfare League, an organization set up in 1951 to enable Maori women to play an effective part in the cultural, social and economic development of their community, and one of whose concerns was to ensure the survival of the ancient art of weaving. Hetet was a traditionalist, well-versed in all aspects of weaving, from the preparation of traditional materials and dyes, to the methods and techniques involved in producing the fin-ished article. She was widely acknowledged as the leading authority in the arts of *whatu, taaniko* and *raranga*, and as an expert in *kakahu* (cloak weaving), the most prestigious form of Maori weaving. She was also largely responsible for the revival of *harakeke* (flax fibre). She passed on her skills not only to her family, notably her daughter, Digger-ess Te Kanawa, also a well-known weaver, but also to many other women throughout New Zealand.

BIBLIOGRAPHY
K. Mataira: *Maori Artists of the South Pacific* (Raglan, 1984), p. 20
M. Penfold and E. Eastmond: *Women and the Arts in New Zealand: Forty Works, 1936–86* (Auckland, 1986), pl. 15 [incl. biog.]
E. Puketapu-Hetet: *Maori Weaving* (Wellington, 1989), p. 52
MEGAN TAMATI-QUENNELL

Het Loo. Royal palace at Apeldoorn, the Netherlands. In 1684 William, Prince of Orange and stadholder of the Netherlands, purchased the Oude Loo property and commissioned designs for a new hunting-lodge from the Académie d'Architecture in Paris. In the following year, work began on Het Loo; designed by van Swieten and Jacob Roman, it remains unknown to what extent they actually used the plans that had been prepared in Paris in 1685. The hunting-lodge (1685–6) initially consisted of a square main building, which was connected to the wings on the forecourt by arched colonnades. At this time the gardens probably extended no further than what are now the Lower Gardens on the rear side. After the Glorious Revolution (1688–9) Het Loo became too small for the extensive household of William and Mary, who had by that time been proclaimed King and Queen of England (*reg* 1689–1702). After 1690 the stadholder's hunting-lodge was enlarged and embellished to become the royal summer residence. The colonnades between the main building and the flanking wings were replaced by square pavilions that provided quarters for members of the household as well as room for a chapel and a new dining-room. The architect who played a key role during this operation was the Frenchman Daniel Marot I. In 1692 he designed the dining-room in one of the new pavilions as well as the decorations for the main staircase, the hall on the first floor and the royal apartments in the main building (for illustration of Queen Mary's bedroom *see* MAROT I, (2)), which were redecorated at the same time. Marot may also have been responsible for the new layout of the gardens (*see* GARDEN, fig. 53): in 1690 various springs in the surrounding Veluwe region had been purchased by the King, enabling 50 different types of waterworks to be constructed in the Upper Gardens (*see* FOUNTAIN). The arched colonnades that had previously linked the main building with the forecourt were re-erected to separate the Upper Gardens from the Lower Gardens. The two gardens were linked by the main avenue that ran through the centre. It seems likely that Marot also designed the elegantly ornamented parterres, since these form a unity with the stylistically related interior decorations.

The structure of the main building is strictly symmetrical. The interior of the palace evokes a gradually increasing sense of space, an effect that had been developed in French palaces during the 17th century. The central hall is dominated by cool tones: a marble floor and wooden panelling painted to simulate white marble. The rear wall of the hall has three open arches: the one in the middle leads directly to the steps at the rear of the palace, which overlooks the garden; the two side arches lead to the grand staircase that ascends with double flights to a halfway landing, from where the stairs turn through 180° and lead straight up to the first floor. The upper hall on the first floor is decorated in a wide range of colours. The panelling is painted to resemble various types of coloured marble, while the spaces between the pilasters are decorated with landscapes. The hall looks out over the forecourt and opens on to the royal apartments: on the west side were those of King William and on the east side were those of Queen Mary. Both these apartments have—following French fashion—an antechamber, a *chambre* (the most important room, with the royal bed), a cabinet and a dressing-room. The antechambers are both at the front of the building, the windows of the *chambres* look out from the sides, while the cabinets are situated on the corners at the back and offer the best view of the gardens.

The outer walls have hardly any decoration; only the entrance is embellished, with Ionic pilasters. The building's monumental nature is achieved by the rhythm of the massive blocks. From the forecourt, the pavilions, which were erected in 1692 between the main building and the wings on the front, seem somewhat cramped; what is particularly unfortunate here is that the arched pediments of the outer pavilions are partly hidden from view by the roofs of the wings on the front. The building is thus most impressive when seen from the gardens: the main building projects forward from the flanking wings, which form a regimented group of closed brick structures of geometric simplicity. In this respect, the architecture of Het Loo follows the general development of the grand country houses of the nobility in the last quarter of the 17th century, recalling the estates of Amerongen and Zeist (both near Utrecht), which had been built ten years earlier, and anticipating Middachten, which was to follow ten years later.

BIBLIOGRAPHY

W. Harris: *A Description of the King's Royal Palace and Gardens at Loo* (London, 1699/R The Hague, 1985)

M. D. Ozinga: *Daniel Marot: De schepper van den Hollandschen Lodewijk XIV-stijl* (Amsterdam, 1938)

H. W. M. van der Wyck: 'Het Loo: De geschiedenis van een koninklijk domein', *Bull. Kon. Ned. Oudhdkd. Bond*, lxxv (1976), pp. 183–248

The Anglo-Dutch Garden in the Age of William and Mary: De gouden eeuw van de Hollandse tuinkunst (exh. cat., ed. J. D. Hunt and E. de Jong; Apeldoorn, Pal. Het Loo; London, Christie's; 1988–9); also in *J. Gdn Hist.*, viii/2–3 (1988) [whole issue]

K. A. OTTENHEYM

Hetsch. German and Danish family of painters and architects.

(1) Philipp Friedrich von Hetsch (*b* Stuttgart, 10 Sept 1758; *d* Stuttgart, 31 Dec 1838). Painter. At the age of 13, against the wishes of his parents who intended him to become a court musician like his father Christian Heinrich, Hetsch entered the Ducal Military Academy (Herzogliche Militärakademie or 'Karlsakademie') to train as an artist. The Militärakademie incorporated the Académie des Arts, founded by the court painter Nicolas Guibal in 1761 on the model of the French Académie Royale de Peinture et de Sculpture. Its training was wide-ranging, and, in response to the literary requirements then demanded of history painters, included such subjects as French, Italian and Latin, the history of art, mythology and the natural sciences. Hetsch's practical training, under Guibal, a history painter, and to a lesser extent the landscapist Friedrich Harper, was marked by the eclecticism of the transition between late Baroque and Rococo, and the more up-to-date Neo-classical style. This informed, and in part hindered, his entire career as a painter.

In 1780 Hetsch left the Academy with the title of court painter and undertook the customary journey to Paris, where he studied under the then eminent Joseph-Marie Vien. In 1782 he returned to Stuttgart, but spent the following year again in Paris, where he concentrated on portrait painting, absorbing French examples from Charles Le Brun to Jean-Baptiste Greuze and Adélaïde Labille-Guiard. Around the end of 1783 Hetsch met Jacques-Louis David, who began to exert the strongest influence on him, in particular during Hetsch's stay in Rome (1785–7), where he became especially interested in history painting. Two paintings dating from 1784–6 demonstrate David's impact on Hetsch. In *Generosity Rewarding Genius* (Stuttgart, Altes Schloss, Württemberg. Landesmus.), sent to Stuttgart from Paris in 1784, a general Rococo composition and soft colouring are tempered by the influence of Vien's decorative classicism in the academic nude figure of Genius. In contrast, *Tullia Driving over the Corpse of her Father* (1786; Stuttgart, Altes Schloss, Württemberg. Landesmus.) presents sharply designed figures, high-keyed, unharmonized local colours, and an architectural background close in spirit to David's *Oath of the Horatii* (see DAVID, JACQUES-LOUIS, fig. 1). Hetsch's most Davidian history painting, *Death of the Consul Papirius* (1786; Nuremberg, Ger. NMus.) was also produced in Rome and reveals his limitations in that style in its somewhat artificially calm and lifeless quality. In 1787 Hetsch became an honorary member of the Accademia delle Belle Arti of Bologna.

Away from David's direct influence, Hetsch returned to a softer, more lyrical classicism that seems to have better suited his artistic temperament, in a painting such as *Cornelia, Mother of the Gracchi* (1794; Stuttgart, Altes Schloss, Württemberg. Landesmus.), painted during a second stay in Rome (1794–6). In the same year he also painted the life-size, elegant yet informal and affectionate *Self-portrait with Family* (Stuttgart, priv. col.; see Fleischhauer). On his return to Stuttgart in 1787, he developed an extensive practice as a portraitist, painting the local minor nobility and upper bourgeoisie, and moving in the pietistic and literary–artistic circles of his patrons. In 1787 Hetsch was appointed professor at the Karlsakademie, a post he held until 1794, when the academy was closed by

Duke Charles-Eugene of Württemberg's successor, Ludwig-Eugene. In 1795, under the new duke, Frederick-Eugene of Württemberg, Harper retired as director of the ducal painting gallery in the Ludwigsburger Schloss, and Hetsch was appointed his successor, although he did not receive an income for this position until 1797.

After the death of his first wife in 1800 and the divorce from his second wife in 1801, Hetsch began to suffer from the depressions that overshadowed the rest of his life. He became a member of the Prussian Academy in Arts in 1801. During a third artistically and socially isolated period in Rome in 1802–3, Hetsch produced the large painting *Oedipus and his Daughters* (untraced; oil sketch in Stuttgart, priv. col.) and *St Cecilia* (Stuttgart, Altes Schloss, Württemberg. Landesmus.), which were received favourably by the public though disparaged in critical circles. During a visit to Hetsch's studio in 1797, Goethe had praised his portraits and his technical abilities, but criticized his choice of subjects in history painting as often too literary and insufficiently active. Hetsch's reputation in Stuttgart was heightened with the painting the *Departure of Regulus* (1803–4; Stuttgart, Altes Schloss, Württemberg. Landesmus.), but otherwise he worked less, reduced his output as a portraitist and in the years 1803–7 painted only smaller pictures, remarkable mainly for their subjects from Nordic legends (e.g. the *Knight Albonak with his Daughters before King Alfred*, 1807; *Odin and the Prophetess*, 1807, ex-Stuttgart, Altes Schloss, untraced). During a last journey to Paris in 1808–9 Hetsch executed two of the history paintings most acclaimed by his contemporaries, the *Ascension of Christ* altarpiece for the Schlosskirche in Stuttgart (1808; Stuttgart, Altes Schloss, Württemberg. Landesmus.) and *Brutus and Portia* (1808; Stuttgart, Altes Schloss, Württemberg. Landesmus.) as well as the beautiful, large yet intimate portrait of the Württemberg Ambassador to Paris, *Graf von Zeppelin and his Family* (Biberach, priv. col.). Subsequently, while he continued to paint successful portraits, his inventive qualities in history painting sharply declined. Though ennobled in 1808, Hetsch indignantly retired from his position as court painter and largely from artistic activity when Johann Heinrich von Dannecker was given the leadership of the projected Academy of Arts and was appointed director of the royal painting gallery in 1816.

BIBLIOGRAPHY

Thieme–Becker

W. Fleischhauer: *Philipp Friedlich Hetsch: Ein Beitrag zur Kunstgeschichte Württembergs* (Stuttgart, 1929)

ANNE PUETZ

(2) G(ustav) F(riedrich) Hetsch (*b* Stuttgart, 28 Sept 1788; *d* Copenhagen, 7 Sept 1864). Architect and teacher, son of (1) Philipp Friedrich von Hetsch. After a preliminary architectural education in Tübingen he went in 1808 with his father to Paris, where he studied and worked under Charles Percier and Jean-Baptiste Rondelet until 1812. That year he went to Württemberg and then Rome, where he was introduced to Bertel Thorvaldsen's circle of friends, and the Danish architect Peder Malling (1781–1865) persuaded him to go to Denmark. By the time of his arrival in Copenhagen in 1815, Hetsch was well versed in the architectural language of Romantic Classicism and the Empire style but was also interested in medieval architecture. He began his architectural career by helping C. F. Hansen, who later twice became his father-in-law, with the interior decoration (1815–32) of Christiansborg Palace. Hetsch's interiors of the 1820s were influenced by the French Empire style, but in the 1830s a less heavy late classical and Pompeian style emerged, and in the late 1830s and the 1840s he also created some Gothic Revival interiors.

Hetsch's first important building was the synagogue (1829–33) in Copenhagen. This was a strong, simple, classical structure with Egyptian elements and a few stylistic debts to Schinkel. In 1836–8 he restored the small Svanninge Church on Funen, converting the partly Romanesque, partly Gothic structure to produce a uniformly Gothic Revival interior and exterior, the first such work of this type in Denmark. In 1840–42 he built the Roman Catholic church of St Ansgar in Copenhagen in the mixture of Early Christian, Romanesque and Renaissance styles sometimes known as *Rundbogenstil*, and he was to some extent influenced by four churches built in Berlin by Schinkel in the 1830s. Using patterns of red and yellow brick, he reintroduced exposed brickwork into Copenhagen. Hetsch's other projects were few, but he is important as the first architect in Denmark to make significant use of diverse historical styles. Influenced by his early, rationalistic French education, he stressed common sense and truth of structure and material, and he was fascinated by technical innovations, as well as being deeply interested with polychromy.

Hetsch also contributed to Danish architecture through his progressive teaching at the Kongelige Danske Kunstacademi in Copenhagen. His pupils included Gottlieb Bindesbøll, Christian Hansen, Theophilus Hansen, Harald Conrad Stilling, Johan Daniel Herholdt and Ferdinand Meldahl. Hetsch was also the artistic director of the Royal Porcelain Manufacture and indefatigably supported all the most important craftsmen of the period, although here his tastes were strictly Neo-classical (*see* DENMARK, §IX, 1).

WRITINGS

Fortegninger for Haandvaerkere (Copenhagen, 1839–43)

Bemaerkninger angaaende kunst, industri og haandvaerk (Copenhagen, 1863)

BIBLIOGRAPHY

K. von Folsach: *Fra Nyklassicisme til Historicisme: Arkitekten G. F. Hetsch* (Copenhagen, 1988)

KJELD VON FOLSACH

Hetzendorf von Hohenberg, Johann Ferdinand. *See* HOHENBERG, JOHANN FERDINAND VON.

Heuneburg. Site of a fortified hilltop settlement at Sigmaringen in Baden-Württemberg, Germany. Set on a natural hill overlooking the River Danube, the Heuneburg comprises a roughly triangular area measuring *c.* 300× 150 m. This area was first enclosed by defences erected between the 15th and 14th centuries BC, during the Late Bronze Age. The site was subsequently occupied for over 2600 years, and at least 22 subsequent settlement horizons, associated with 10 rebuildings or restructurings of the walls, have been recognized. The final defences were built in the 11th century AD. Archaeological investigation of the site began with the cutting of the first trial trenches in 1921. This was followed in 1950 by a major excavation campaign under the direction of Kurt Bittel, Wolfgang Kimmig and Egon Gersbach, which was to last, with a break of three years, until 1979. Until 1959 the investigation concentrated on the defences, but from 1963 the focus of attention shifted to the settlement of the interior. The material recovered during excavation is held by the Württembergisches Landesmuseum in Stuttgart, and the Institut für Vor- und Frühgeschichte, Universität Tübingen.

The original timber-framed Bronze Age rampart may have been rebuilt three times during its century of existence. The area it enclosed was greatly disturbed by later settlement, but rectangular post-built structures associated with pottery and a little metalwork were identified. However, the Heuneburg's main period of architectural and artistic importance came during the Iron Age (*c.* 750– *c.* 50 BC), especially between *c.* 600 and *c.* 400 BC (*see* PRE- HISTORIC EUROPE, §VI), when it achieved major European significance as a political and economic centre. The first Iron Age wall was constructed of timber and stone; excavations in the south-eastern corner of the enclosed area revealed groups of structures built on long, horizontal sleeper beams. Organized, though not uniform, in plan and internal arrangement, the buildings were loosely grouped within palisades and drainage gullies.

In the first half of the 6th century BC, the timber-framed wall sequence was abruptly broken by the construction of a wall of sun-dried bricks built on a 3 m-wide stone foundation. If the building material, exotic and unsuitable for the damp central European climate, was probably copied from Mediterranean models, so probably were the close-set towers that ran along the exterior of the north and west walls. The interior of the enclosure, at least in the south-eastern quarter, was rigidly laid out with close-set houses of regular shape and size clearly arranged in narrow streets according to a strict plan (see fig.). The mechanisms that brought such new building techniques,

architectural concepts and urban planning styles from the Mediterranean to this and similar sites are disputed. However, most scholars would agree that either a southern builder or a local architect who had trained in, or at least visited, the Mediterranean, must have been involved in the design of the Heuneburg brick wall.

Evidence for links between the Heuneburg and the Mediterranean during this period is reinforced by numerous finds of Greek Black-figure wares, Massiliote wine amphorae and red coral. Such imported wares also occur in the rich burial mounds associated with the site, signifying an élite class with considerable control over the acquisition of both local labour and foreign goods. The strictly organized settlement of the south-eastern quarter during this phase may have been a metalworking centre: finds from the area include debris from bronze- and ironworking, including a mould for a bronze handle of Etruscan type, and furnaces and tools. The Heuneburg is also thought to have been the production centre for the fine painted pottery found there and at other contemporary central European settlements.

During the second half of the 6th century BC the brick wall was partially demolished and replaced by a new style of timber-framed rampart, which was periodically rebuilt until the abandonment of the site at some time after 400 BC. House styles of the period changed to a three-aisled pattern foreshadowing much later European types, and were again grouped within enclosures, suggesting a less rigid organization of space.

BIBLIOGRAPHY

W. Kimmig and E. Gersbach: 'Die neuen Ausgrabungen auf der Heune-burg', *Germania*, xlvi (1966), pp. 163–92

W. Kimmig: *Die Heuneburg an der oberen Donau*, Führer zu archäologischen Denkmälern in Baden-Württemberg (Stuttgart, 1968, rev. 1983)

SARA CHAMPION

Heurich, Jan, the younger (*b* Warsaw, 16 July 1873; *d* Warsaw, 11 Dec 1925). Polish architect. Son of the Warsaw architect Jan Kacper Heurich (1834–87), he studied at the Academy of Arts in St Petersburg (1890–96) then travelled in Western Europe and North Africa on a Grand Prix de Rome fellowship (1897–9) before returning to Warsaw. Until about 1905 he worked mostly on commissions from various Polish aristocratic families, designing palaces, villas and manors in the Kingdom of Poland, Lithuania, Volhynia and Podole. His work here was marked by eclectic arrangements of forms, mainly Baroque and Neo-classical: his palace chapel (1903–4) at Kozłówka near Lublin, designed for Count Zamoyski, is a copy of the chapel at Versailles.

It is, however, to work of a far more radical style, executed in Warsaw after 1905, that Heurich owes his reputation. The large town house at 2 Małachowski Square (1907–10; destr. 1939–44, rebuilt 1948–9), the 'Under the Eagles House' Bank of Co-operative Societies at 1 Jasna Street (1912–17; partly destr. 1939–44, rebuilt 1948–50), the building of the Hygiene Society at 31 Karowa Street and the Public Library at 26 Koszykowa Street (1912–14) are key works in the early phase of Polish architectural Modernism. They are notable both for their supremely logical construction and for their moderation in the use of decorative detail.

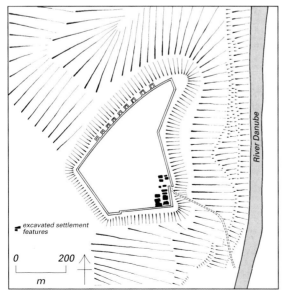

excavated settlement features

0   200

m

Heuneburg, plan of the site in the early 6th century BC

Heurich played a leading role in the organization of architectural training in Warsaw in the years up to 1914; from 1900 he lectured frequently on architecture at the Wawelberg and Rotwand School of Technology, and in 1904 he was among the founders of the Warsaw School of Fine Arts. In 1915 he established the Architecture Department of Warsaw Technical University. From 1917 he held a number of important official posts in institutions concerned with the reconstruction of cultural life in the newly independent Poland.

BIBLIOGRAPHY
S. Łoza: *Architékci i budowniczowie w Polsce* [Architects and builders in Poland] (Warsaw, 1954), pp. 116–17
A. Olszewski: *Nowa forma w architekturze polskiej 1900–1925* [A new form in Polish architecture, 1900–25] (Wrocław, 1967)
ANDRZEJ ROTTERMUND

Heusch, Willem de (*b* Utrecht, 1625; *bur* Utrecht, 9 March 1692). Dutch painter and etcher. He was probably a pupil of Jan Both; at any rate he painted entirely in Both's style. In about 1640 he may have gone to Italy, returning by 1649, when his presence is recorded at a lottery of paintings, for which he served as one of the experts. In the same document (Obreen, p. 72) he is referred to as Dean of the Utrecht College of Painters alongside, among others, Jan Both, who at that time was an *overman* (governor) of the Utrecht guild. In 1655–6, 1660–64 and 1669 de Heusch himself was a governor of the guild.

De Heusch painted primarily landscapes in the style of the DUTCH ITALIANATES, sometimes with figures added by Johannes Lingelbach. His motifs and technique, as for example in the *Italianate Landscape at Sunset* (Amsterdam, Rijksmus.), clearly reveal the influence of Jan Both, although his manner of painting was smoother and less varied. His cousin Jacob de Heusch (1657–1701), another Dutch Italianate artist, became his pupil. As both artists used the initial G ('Guillaume' for Willem, 'Giacomo' for Jacob), the attribution of their work is often a confusing matter. After 1670 Willem seems to have been reduced to poverty, for at his death he was buried at the town council's expense.

BIBLIOGRAPHY
F. D. O. Obreen: *Archief voor Nederlandsche kunstgeschiedenis*, 7 vols (Rotterdam, 1877–90), ii, pp. 72, 77
B. N.: 'Exhibition at the Alfred Brod Gallery', *Burl. Mag.*, cviii (1966), p. 155
W. Stechow: *Dutch Landscape Painting of the Seventeenth Century* (London, 1968), p. 165
I. de Groot: *Landscape Etchings by the Dutch Masters of the Seventeenth Century* (London, 1979), pp. 188–91
B. Haak: *The Golden Age: Dutch Painters in the Seventeenth Century* (London, 1984), pp. 34, 321, 402
TRUDY VAN ZADELHOFF

Heuvel, Antoon van den (*b* Ghent, *c.* 1600; *d* Ghent, 5 Aug 1677). Flemish painter. In 1628, the year he became a master in the Ghent guild of painters, he declared that he had spent the previous ten years in Antwerp and Rome. He thereafter remained in Ghent, painting altarpieces for churches in the city and its surroundings. It is difficult to give an accurate definition of van den Heuvel's style: he is erroneously considered to be one of the international Caravaggisti. His earlier work displays a preference for contrasting colours and strong lighting, with few transitional tones. But compared with his contemporary Jan Janssens, who is correctly called one of the Ghent Caravaggisti, van den Heuvel rarely displayed genuine Caravaggesque features in his work. In only one instance, the *Instigation of the Rosary* (1634; Nazareth, parish church), did he adopt one of Caravaggio's motifs: from the *Madonna of the Serpent* (Rome, Gal. Borghese). Generally van den Heuvel's linear compositions and bright treatment of light appear classical, closer to the works of the Carracci and their followers, which he must have encountered while in Rome. Van den Heuvel also borrowed motifs and compositions from such painters as Rubens and Gaspar de Crayer. His later work, painted between *c.* 1640 and 1650, is duller in colour and consequently seems less expressive.

BIBLIOGRAPHY
D. Roggen, H. Pauwels and A. De Schrijver: 'Het Caravaggisme te Gent', *Gent. Bijdr. Kstgesch. & Oudhdknd.*, xii (1949–50), pp. 286–322
J. S. Held: 'A Supplement to "Het Caravaggisme te Gent"', *Gent. Bijdr. Kstgesch. & Oudhdknd.*, xiii (1951), pp. 7–12
D. Roggen and H. Pauwels: 'Nog bij "Het Caravaggisme te Gent"', *Gent. Bijdr. Kstgesch. & Oudhdknd.*, xiv (1953), pp. 201–5
B. Nicolson: *The International Caravaggesque Movement* (Oxford, 1979), p. 57
HANS VLIEGHE

Heward, (Efa) Prudence (*b* Montreal, 2 July 1896; *d* Los Angeles, 19 March 1947). Canadian painter. She enrolled at the Art Association of Montreal under William Brymner and Randolph Hewton (1888–1960) in 1918. She went to Paris, studying briefly with Charles Guérin at the Académie Colarossi and with Bernard Naudin (1876–1946) at the Ecole des Beaux-Arts in 1925, as well as at the Scandinavian Academy in 1929.

Recognition came slowly. Two of Heward's portraits were selected for the British Empire Exhibition (1925; London) and the Exposition d'Art Canadien (1927; Paris, Mus. Jeu de Paume). She exhibited portraits and landscapes with the Group of Seven (1928) and was awarded the Willingdon Prize in 1929 for *Girl on the Hill* (1928; Ottawa, N.G.), a monumental figure in a landscape. She had her only solo exhibition in Montreal in 1932 (William Scott & Sons Gals).

Heward achieved international acclaim for *Rollande* (1929; Ottawa, N.G.), a modern nationalist image celebrating the strength women derive from the land. Heward challenged contemporary conventions of representing women by stressing isolation, vulnerability and solemnity, using an increasingly brilliant palette. Key examples of this include: *Sisters of Rural Quebec*; *Femme au bord de la mer* (both 1930; Windsor, Ont., A.G.); *Dark Girl* (1935; U. Toronto, Hart House); and *Hester* (1937; Kingston, Ont., Queen's U., Agnes Etherington A. Cent.).

Heward was a charter member and vice-president (1933–9) of the Canadian Group of Painters, a founder-member of the Contemporary Arts Society (1939) and became a member of the Federation of Canadian Artists in 1941. The National Gallery of Canada mounted a memorial exhibition of her work in 1948.

BIBLIOGRAPHY
Memorial Exhibition: Prudence Heward, 1896–1947 (exh. cat., intro. A. Y. Jackson; Ottawa, N.G., 1948)

Canadian Painting in the Thirties (exh. cat., ed. C. Hill; Ottawa, N.G., 1975)

From Women's Eyes: Women Painters in Canada (exh. cat., ed. D. Farr and N. Luckyj; Kingston, Ont., Queen's U., Agnes Etherington A. Cent., 1975)

Visions and Victories: 10 Canadian Women Artists, 1914–1945 (exh. cat., ed. N. Luckyj; London, Ont., Reg. A.G., 1983)

Expressions of Will: The Art of Prudence Heward (exh. cat., ed. N. Luckyj; Kingston, Ont., Queen's U., Agnes Etherington A. Cent., 1986)

NATALIE LUCKYJ

Hewetson, Christopher (*b* Thomastown, Co. Kilkenny, *c.* 1736; *d* Rome, 1798). Irish sculptor. He went to school at Kilkenny College, after which he may have studied briefly in Dublin. By 1765 he was in Rome, where he remained for the rest of his career. He established himself as one of the finest of Neo-classical portrait sculptors of the period, and he became a leading member of the Anglo-Roman community. Occasionally he signed his work *Christophorus Hewetson Hibernus Fecit*, in an assertion of his Irish origins.

Among his early commissions in Rome are several portrait busts of British aristocrats: that of *Sir Watkin Williams Wynn* (terracotta, 1769; Dublin, N.G.), that of the antiquary *Charles Towneley* (marble, 1769; priv. col.), and one of *William Henry, Duke of Gloucester* (1772; Windsor Castle, Berks, Royal Col.). In 1771 he was commissioned to execute two identical marble busts of the pope, *Clement XIV*; later he produced at least two further versions (Beningborough Hall, N. Yorks, NT; New Haven, CT, Yale Cent. Brit. A.). Together these works, especially the papal busts, reveal Hewetson's rapid

Christopher Hewetson: monument to *Dr Richard Baldwin* (detail), marble, granite and gilt-bronze, 1781–4 (Dublin, University of Dublin, Trinity College)

advance to technical mastery, his controlled carving enabling him to convey the intricate embroidery of Clement's garment, including the gentle tug of its front tassel. His sitter's face is lively and convincingly authoritative, although Hewetson appears to have made little attempt to capture any sense of psychological depth. This diminution by Hewetson of the personality of each of his sitters is also found in the portrait busts of artists, writers and others that he carved over the years: *Anton Raphael Mengs* (1781; Rome, Pin. Capitolina), *Gavin Hamilton* (1784; U. Glasgow, Hunterian A.G.), and *Gottfried Wilhelm von Leibniz* (late 1780s; Hannover, Wilhelm-Busch-Mus.), the last of which is a colossal marble depicting the philosopher in a suitably self-absorbed mood.

Although Hewetson's livelihood lay in bust portraiture, on at least two occasions he executed large marble funerary monuments. Such commissions gave greater scope for his skills as a carver and for his aptitude for Neo-classical design. The first of these funerary monuments was to *Dr Richard Baldwin* (*d* 1758), the former provost of Trinity College, Dublin (see fig.). Carved by Hewetson in Rome in the early 1780s, it was set up in 1784 against the west wall of the College's Examination Hall (which had been designed by Sir William Chambers) under the supervision of the carver Edward Smyth, who was later to work on the façade of James Gandon's Custom House in Dublin. A recumbent Baldwin is shown enfolded in classical drapery and held in the arms of Science, while a greeting angel proffers him eternal fame. The three figures form an elegant triangle, one that is greatly strengthened by the massive pyramid behind, made in what Hewetson described as 'Red Oriental Granit'. In a document discovered around 1906 he wrote of how he was 'the first who applied Granit[e] to this use'. Baldwin's memorial was the first truly Neo-classical sculptural ensemble ever seen in Dublin. Hewetson's second monument, to *Cardinal Giambattista Rezzonico*, nephew to Clement XIII, was commissioned shortly after Rezzonico's death in 1783. Consisting of a sarcophagus and a portrait bust flanked by putti, together with an epitaph in Latin, it is located against the south wall of the south transept of S Nicola in Carcere, Rome. The bust of the cardinal is one of Hewetson's least distinguished works, but the two putti—one mourning (head bowed, torch extinguished), the other triumphant and brandishing a scroll—are brilliantly executed.

BIBLIOGRAPHY

W. Strickland: *A Dictionary of Irish Artists*, i (Dublin, 1913), pp. 479–80

K. A. Esdaile: 'Christopher Hewetson and his Monument to Dr Baldwin in Trinity College, Dublin', *J. Royal Soc. Antiqua. Ireland*, lxxvii (1947), pp. 134–5

T. Hodgkinson: 'Christopher Hewetson: An Irish Sculptor in Rome', *Walpole Soc.*, xxxiv (1954), pp. 42–54

The Age of Neo-classicism (exh. cat., London, RA and V&A, 1972), pp. 244–5

B. de Breffny: 'Christopher Hewetson: Biographical Notice and Preliminary Catalogue Raisonné', *Irish A. Rev.*, iii (1986), no. 3, pp. 52–75

FINTAN CULLEN

Hexastyle. Term applied to a building with a portico of six columns (*see* ATHENS, fig. 10, GREECE, ANCIENT, fig. 8c, e and g).

Hexham Abbey. Former Augustinian priory church in Northumberland, England, noted for its Anglo-Saxon crypt and Early Gothic transept. Founded *c.* AD 675 by St Wilfrid (*d* 709), Hexham was an important Anglo-Saxon building, and a cathedral from 681. Richard of Hexham (12th century) described the early church as 'larger than any other house this side of the Alps', while William of Malmesbury (*c.* 1124) said that Hexham displayed the 'glories of Rome' and that Wilfrid had brought Roman masons to build it. The church, dedicated to St Andrew, was a basilica with square piers supporting galleries over the aisles, perhaps extending around the west, and a clerestory. Access to the upper floor was by spiral stairs. The crypt 'of wonderfully dressed stone' (Eddius) survives beneath the present church. Other potentially early features suggest a bema-like eastern termination. A 7th-century English basilican church with both crypt and galleries is exceptional and recalls S Agnese fuori le Mura (*c.* 630), Rome. Wilfrid constructed three churches at Hexham: St Andrew's itself; St Peter's, perhaps the small apsed structure beneath the present choir; and an unidentified centralized building dedicated to the Virgin. This arrangement of an axial string of churches recalls St Augustine's (*c.* 600), Canterbury.

The crypt (see fig.) resembles that at Wilfrid's church (*c.* 670) at Ripon, N. Yorks. It has a rectangular, barrel-vaulted relic chamber with a southern clergy entrance passage and stair, and a central western door from a cross-axial vestibule. This operated the public one-way system: a straight entry stair from the nave, and a side exit north, via another small chamber, to a dog-leg passage and stair. The masonry is 'broached' with diagonal gashes, as at St John the Evangelist, Escomb, and Jarrow Abbey. Among

much reused Roman material are blocks with imperfect inscriptions. The arched doorheads are shaped, not turned.

Hexham was abandoned after Viking attacks *c.* 875 but rebuilt as an Augustinian priory *c.* 1180. The diocese was not revived. The 12th-century cruciform church had an aisled, six-bay choir longer than the nave. The transept (*c.* 1200) extends four bays each side of the crossing tower and has an eastern aisle. The nave is modern on earlier foundations. The present east façade dates from *c.* 1860, but the choir originally ended in a low ambulatory aisle containing five altars, recalling Abbey Dore (Hereford & Worcs; 1180–*c.* 1280). The monochrome, unvaulted three-storey choir interior is typical of many northern Transitional buildings, especially Ripon Minster. The arcades have thick, deeply moulded arches on clustered piers with keeled shafts, moulded capitals and strong abaci. Tripled shafts resting on foliate corbels unite the middle storey and clerestory, their simple moulded capitals supporting the later wooden roof. The dominant middle storey has twin pointed arches within a round-arched frame rising from densely packed colonnettes and vertical strips of dogtooth. The sub-arch spandrels have pierced quatrefoils. The clerestory recalls Ripon's transept, with a deep wall passage and triple-arched elevation, the arches notably stilted and passage ceilings characteristically flat. The main wall oversails above the arcade and reaches a depth of 1.86 m. The clerestory exterior has blind lancets flanking the windows, typical of contemporary northern Cistercian buildings.

The transept is the most celebrated interior at Hexham. The trefoil dado arcade takes no account of the divisions above, while the exceptionally tall lancets above have ridiculously stilted arches above a wall passage. The clerestory has elongated arches of quite disproportionate height, their dark interiors flanking the clerestory lancets. The aisled eastern elevations are variants of the choir, with thinner, oversailing walls. The southern arm preserves the monks' night stair raised above the claustral slype. The wooden roofs are later.

The medieval nave was destroyed by the Scots in 1296; its replacement, completed in 1908 by Temple Moore, stands on undated medieval footings. It has a single north aisle, the medieval wall against the cloister surviving to a greater extent. Surviving fittings include loose Roman and Anglo-Saxon sculpture and extensive late medieval woodwork. The Frith stool, a throne of *c.* 680, has Anglo-Saxon interlace, while part of an elaborate cross came from the grave of St Acca (*d* 740). The wooden rood screen (1491–1523) is perhaps the best major English example. The priory possessed a complete range of claustral buildings south of the nave, of which parts of the cellarer's range, chapter house and dormitory survive.

BIBLIOGRAPHY

Eddius: *The Life of Bishop Wilfrid* (8th century); ed. B. Colgrave (Cambridge, 1927)

William of Malmesbury: *De gestis pontificum* (*c.* 1124); ed. N. Hamilton, Rolls Series (London, 1870), p. 225

J. Raine: *The Priory of Hexham* (1864)

W. T. Taylor: *Hexham Abbey* (Hexham, 1969)

R. N. Bailey and D. O'Sullivan: 'Excavations over St Wilfrid's Crypt at Hexham, 1978', *Archaeol. Aeliana*, n. s. 4, vii (1979), pp. 145–58

E. Cambridge: 'C. C. Hodges and the Nave of Hexham Abbey', *Archaeol. Aeliana*, n. s. 4, vii (1979), pp. 159–68

Hexham Abbey, crypt, 7th century

R. Morris: *Cathedrals and Abbeys of England and Wales* (London, 1979)
E. Fernie: *The Architecture of the Anglo-Saxons* (London, 1983)

FRANCIS WOODMAN

Hey [Hay], Jean (*fl* 1494–1504). Netherlandish painter, active in France. An *Ecce homo* (1494; Brussels, Mus. A. Anc.) bears a signed and dated inscription with his name and that of the patron, Jean Cueillette, an official of Charles VIII. The style of the painting, his surname and the epithet *teutonicus* suggest that he was of Netherlandish origin. Jean Hey was included in Jean Lemaire de Belges's list of the greatest living painters (1504), and he has been identified as the Master of Moulins.

For further discussion and bibliography *see* MASTERS, ANONYMOUS, AND MONOGRAMMISTS, §I: MASTER OF MOULINS.

CATHERINE REYNOLDS

Heyboer, Anton (*b* Sabang, Dutch East Indies [now Indonesia], 9 Feb 1924). Dutch printmaker and painter. His experience in a Nazi concentration camp in 1943, where he nearly died, marked his work. In 1951, after a voluntary stay in a mental hospital, he decided to devote himself to a life as an artist. After 1961 Heyboer lived in an isolated community in a barn at Den Ilp, north of Amsterdam, which he shared with three women. His images from the early 1950s, almost exclusively etchings, show ships in Ijmuiden port and his shabby living dwellings. The first etchings reflecting his mental condition also date from this period. In *Awareness of the Wound* (1954; The Hague, Gemeentemus.) he depicted himself as a simplified Man of Sorrows, wearing a crown of thorns and displaying his stigma, a bleeding heart. In the same year Heyboer recorded crucial moments of his life in works such as *Defence of Immature Things*, which consists of a large number of sheets of paper bearing definitions of 'being', 'conscience', 'suffering', 'innocence' and related concepts. Heyboer's source of reference was Christian symbolism. To express the relationship with his fellow men he used the cross as the symbol of suffering. In 1957 he introduced this motif to his etchings, in such works as *The System with Two Figures* (1957; The Hague, Gemeentemus.). The highly stylized, mummy-like figures of early works were incorporated in a network of lines; where these lines intersected a number was added to refer to a particular emotion or experience. Apart from these coded line patterns, the visual elements of the Heyboer system include text fragments and colour, which the artist added by hand. His ritualistic system altered only when something new happened to Heyboer, such as the arrival of a third woman in his community (1974), which led him to take up painting. The complex system that Heyboer developed through his etchings was continued in the paintings, with the additional variations of the larger scale and greater freedom of technique available in paint. The deliberately esoteric nature of his images prevents them from being easily intelligible (e.g. *The Creative Man*, gouache, 1984; priv. col., see Slegers, p. 96), but his concerns with sexuality, creativity and mortality address universal themes. He regarded the trinity symbolized by his three women (referred to as his 'brides' by the media) as his most important creation.

BIBLIOGRAPHY
Anton Heyboer (exh. cat., ed. J. L. Locher; The Hague, Gemeentemus., 1967)
J. L. Locher: *Anton Heyboer* (Amsterdam, 1976)
M. Slegers: *Anton Heyboer: Signalen en symbolen* (Eindhoven, 1988) [Dut., Eng. and Fr. text]

HANS EBBINK

Heyde, Henning von der. *See* HEIDE, HENNING VON DER.

Heydeck, Carl Wilhelm. *See* HEIDECK, CARL WILHELM.

Heyden, Jacob van der (*b* Strasbourg, 1573; *d* Brussels, 1645). Flemish engraver, print publisher, sculptor and painter. His father, Jan van der Heyden (*fl* 1590; *d* before 1645), was a painter from Mechelen who left to settle in Strasbourg because of religious turmoil. Jacob trained in Brussels with Raphael Coxie (1540–1616), who was also from Mechelen; it seems probable, however, that Jacob continued to make his home in Strasbourg until 1635, subsequently moving to Brussels, where he worked until his death.

Van der Heyden's extensive artistic activity extended over several genres. Among his documented paintings and sculptures were a painting of the *Adoration of the Magi*, listed in a Strasbourg catalogue of 1668, a *Portrait of a Man with the Neck-chain of an Order* (ex-Hollandt Col., Brunswick), and a gilt-bronze sculpture of *Venus* (all untraced). His principal work, however, lay in the domain of engraving and publishing. At the time when he founded his own publishing house, Strasbourg was a flourishing centre of graphic production. He published prints by numerous artists, including Matthäus Merian the elder, and he himself worked as an engraver for other publishers, such as Henning Gross (1553–1621) in Leipzig and Eberhard Kieser (*fl* 1609–25) in Frankfurt am Main.

Van der Heyden's own numerous engravings cover almost the whole range of pictorial subject-matter; they include scenes from the Old and the New Testament and landscapes and allegorical series, as well as small-format sheets with genre subjects. Portraits, mainly of ecclesiastical and secular rulers, predominate, although he also portrayed *Galileo Galilei, Johannes Kepler, Sebastian Brant* (see fig.), *Martin Luther* and other eminent writers, scholars and theologians. Van der Heyden's outstanding artistry was much valued by his contemporaries and secured him aristocratic patrons, such as those at the courts of Hesse and Baden-Durlach. In 1607, with his brother Johannes van der Heyden, he produced a portrait engraving of *George-Frederick, Margrave of Baden-Durlach*, showing him within a rich architectural frame; he also designed a series of 15 engravings with a title-page tracing the genealogy of the House of Habsburg (Nuremberg, 1660), the portraits being likewise surrounded by frames and text. Van der Heyden's large equestrian portraits of famous generals of the Thirty Years War, depicted against a background showing glorious deeds, should be seen in the context of the vogue for such contemporary subjects.

However, it was the illustrated broadsheet that primarily reflected the period's political unrest and wars of religion. Strasbourg was a centre of Protestant broadsheet production, in which van der Heyden was actively involved. As well as glorifying military leaders and their battles, he

Jacob van der Heyden: *Sebastian Brant*, engraving, 84×69 mm (design image), 183×89 mm (plate), 1631 (Amsterdam, Rijksmuseum)

showed the cruel and inhuman aspect of the war. A broadsheet of *c.* 1622 impressively depicts the horrors of battle and the suffering of the peasants, seen against the background of their destroyed village. In 1617, to commemorate the centenary of Luther nailing up his 95 theses to the door of the Schlosskirche, Wittenberg, van der Heyden published a broadsheet containing Luther's portrait and biography and an extensive account of his significance. Jacob's brother Isaac van der Heyden (*fl* 1633–44) was a painter and engraver active in Strasbourg.

BIBLIOGRAPHY
Hollstein: *Ger.*; Thieme–Becker
H. Rott: *Kunst und Künstler am Baden-Durlacher Hof bis zur Gründung Karlsruhe* (Karlsruhe, 1917)
Die Renaissance im deutschen Südwesten, 2 vols (exh. cat., Heidelberg, Schloss, 1986)
ELISABETH GUROCK

Heyden, Jan van der (*b* Gorinchem, 5 March 1637; *d* Amsterdam, 28 March 1712). Dutch painter, draughtsman, printmaker and inventor. In 1650 he moved to Amsterdam with his family; his father, a Mennonite, who had pursued various occupations rather unsuccessfully, died that year.

Jan's artistic training may have begun with drawing lessons in the studio of a relative, perhaps his eldest brother, Goris van der Heyden, who made and sold mirrors; Jan may also have studied the reverse technique of glass painting with an artist in Gorinchem. Painting occupied relatively little of his time, however, although he continued to pursue it throughout his long life. His prosperity was mainly due to his work as an inventor, engineer and municipal official. He designed and implemented a comprehensive street-lighting scheme for Amsterdam, which lasted from 1669 until 1840 and was adopted as a model by many other towns in the Netherlands and abroad. In 1672, with his brother Nicolaes van der Heyden, he invented a fire engine fitted with pump-driven hoses, which transformed the efficiency of fire-fighting.

As an artist, van der Heyden is best known as one of the first Dutch painters to specialize in the TOWNSCAPE; architectural motifs certainly dominate his compositions, though he also painted village streets, country houses and some forty landscapes, at least two of which are painted on glass (e.g. *View of the Woods*; Amsterdam, Rijksmus.). His later works are mainly still-lifes (e.g. *Corner of a Room with Rarities on Display*; Budapest, Mus. F.A.). Unlike the Haarlem-based brothers Job and Gerrit Berckheyde, whose townscapes were influenced by traditions of genre, *bambocciate* and architectural painting, van der Heyden's approach was closer to 'pure' landscape. His main subjects were Amsterdam and the region near the Dutch–German border, which he visited for business and recreation. A group of 14 paintings is connected with the village of Maarssen, some probably made for Joan Huydecoper II, the Amsterdam burgomaster who developed real estate around that village. In 1674 he commissioned van der Heyden to execute paintings of his house and estate at Goudstein (version, London, Apsley House).

Van der Heyden's townscapes are only loosely based on actual views, topographical accuracy being the least of his concerns. He seems to have attempted instead to distil into a single concentrated image the distinctive character of a town, in such a way that the experience of visiting it would be enhanced. A notable exception is his architectural 'portrait' of the *Westerkerk, Amsterdam* (London, Wallace). All other townscapes show the buildings only partially depicted, with much attention paid to surrounding structures and open spaces. He delighted in picturesque contrasts between modern (mostly imaginary) buildings and historical settings, between buildings and trees, as in *Architectural Fantasy with the Old Stadhuis, Amsterdam* (*c.* 1667–72; London, Apsley House; see fig.) and between large structures and open spaces, as in *View of the Heerengracht, Amsterdam* (Paris, Louvre) and *View of the Huis ten Bosch* (London, N.G.; for illustration of the latter see POST, (1)). Despite his naturalistic style, these are all idealized views, deliberately lacking up-to-date items from the real world, such as the street lamps and fire engines he himself invented. It is impossible, moreover, to distinguish between townscapes with identifiable elements and those that are completely imaginary.

The great clarity of incidental detail in van der Heyden's paintings, such as the rendering of brickwork, is impressive and must have been achieved with the aid of a magnifying glass. Yet it is so skilfully handled that it does not distract

Jan van der Heyden: *Architectural Fantasy with the Old Stadhuis, Amsterdam*, oil on panel, 477×590 mm, *c.* 1667–72 (London, Apsley House)

attention from the impact of the whole scene. He may have made use also of a camera obscura, lenses and mirrors, but this is unlikely since he was rarely recording actual views. Only one preparatory drawing connected with a painting is known. Adriaen van de Velde and Johannes Lingelbach sometimes provided the figures in his painted works (for a collaborative work with van de Velde *see* TOWNSCAPE, fig. 1).

In the drawings van der Heyden made as designs for etchings, all of which advertise his inventions, he took unusual care, as is clear from surviving preliminary studies (e.g. Amsterdam, Rijksmus.) for illustrations to his book on the new fire engine, *Beschryving der nieuvlyks uitgevonden en geoctrojeerde slang-brand-spuiten en hare wyze van brand-blussen* ('Description of the newly discovered and patented hose fire engine and her way of putting out fires'; Amsterdam, 1690). His first sketches are rather awkward; each subsequent step in the creative process added detail, refinement and quality, which he seems to have conquered painstakingly, without any trace of spontaneity or virtuosity. He made extensive use of counterproofs of his drawings so that the images, once transferred to the etching plate, would be depicted correctly in the final print. For instance, after working up his original drawing of a burnt-out house with brush and wash to establish the light and shade effects, he introduced small figures separately on to a counterproof. The final prints also provide rare historical documentation of poor and industrial areas of Amsterdam not seen in townscapes of the period. In the production of these and other publications, van der Heyden collaborated with other artists, including the printmaker Jan van Vianen (1660–after 1726) and his own son Jan van der Heyden the younger. Van Vianen, for example, drew the figures in van der Heyden's largest print (1699) illustrating a technical development in fire-fighting equipment.

Van der Heyden died a wealthy man, with over 70 paintings in his possession. Although no pupils or immediate followers are recorded for him, he was an important

influence on the development of townscape painting in the mid-18th century.

BIBLIOGRAPHY
H. Wagner: 'Jan van der Heyden als Zeichner', *Jb. Berlin. Mus.*, xii (1970), pp. 111–50
——: *Jan van der Heyden, 1637–1712* (Amsterdam and Haarlem, 1971)
I. H. van Eeghen: 'Archivalia betreffende Jan van der Heyden', *Amstelodamum*, lx (1973), pp. 29–36, 54–61, 73–9, 99–106, 128–34
L. de Vries: 'Post voor Jan van der Heyden', *Oud-Holland*, xc (1976), pp. 267–75
Opkomst en bloei van het Noordnederlandse stadsgezicht in de 17de eeuw/The Dutch Cityscape in the 17th Century and its Sources (exh. cat. by B. Bakker and others, Amsterdam, Hist. Mus.; Toronto, A.G. Ont.; 1977)
Dutch Figure Drawing from the Seventeenth Century (exh. cat. by P. Schatborn, Amsterdam, Rijksmus.; Washington, DC, N.G.A.; 1981–2), pp. 124–6
G. Schwartz: 'Jan van der Heyden and the Huydecopers of Maarsseveen', *Getty Mus. J.*, xi (1983), pp. 197–220
L. de Vries: *Jan van der Heyden* (Amsterdam, 1984)
LYCKLE DE VRIES

Heyden, J(acques) C(ornelis) J(ohan) van der (*b* 's Hertogenbosch, 23 June 1928). Dutch painter, conceptual artist and writer. He trained as a painter at the Academie voor Beeldende Kunsten in 's Hertogenbosch and at the Jan van Eyck Academie in Maastricht. In 1956 he settled in 's Hertogenbosch as a painter. During that same year he was given an exhibition at Galerie Swart in Amsterdam. He stopped painting in 1967 when he was given a grant for research into the perception of light, time and space. He made a study of electro-acoustics, images and sound, and produced work for television, including *Art is Only for Beginners* (1969–70). During 1970 he worked on geographic space-relations (e.g. drilling a hole in his living room 'to New Zealand' and interchanging the soil with some from the other side of the earth). In 1972 he built an open-air studio. From 1973 to 1974 he experimented with time and investigated the energy used in breathing, feeding and recycling, and in 1975 he reworked pre-1967 paintings. From 1976 his work mainly consisted of aerial landscapes. His journeys to India in 1977 and the Himalayas in 1979 inspired him to make simplified paintings derived from photographic aerial landscapes, which he exhibited regularly from 1980 (e.g. *Network, with Velasquez, van Gogh, Mondrian, Breughel and Emperor Zhu Gaozhi*, mixed medium, 1990; Utrecht, Cent. Mus.). He also published several texts.

WRITINGS
'Himalaya', *J. C. J. van der Heyden* (exh. cat., Utrecht, Cent. Mus., 1981)
BIBLIOGRAPHY
J. C. J. van der Heyden (exh. cat., The Hague, Gemeentemus.; Eindhoven, Stedel. Van Abbemus.; 1977)
J. C. J. van der Heyden (exh. cat., Eindhoven, Stedel. Van Abbemus., 1983)
J. C. J. van der Heyden (exh. cat., Rotterdam, Boymans–van Beuningen, 1990)
JOHN STEEN

Heyden, Pieter van der [a Merice [a Merige, Ameringus, Merecinus, Merecynus, Miricenis, Miricenys, Miricinus, Miriginus, Mirycinis, Myricenis, Myricinus, Myriginus], Petrus; Verheyden, Peter [Pieter]] (*b* Antwerp, ?*c.* 1530; *d* Berchem, nr Antwerp, after March 1572). Flemish engraver. In 1557 he became a master in the Antwerp Guild of St Luke. In the early part of his career, from 1551, but mainly between 1556 and 1559, he worked with the publisher Hieronymus Cock, a collaboration that lasted until the latter's death in 1570. Hundreds of van der Heyden's reproductive prints were issued through Cock's publishing house, Aux Quatre Vents, and he also had contacts with the publisher Christoph Plantin. In 1571 van der Heyden moved to a country house at Berchem (nr Antwerp) rented by Plantin, who paid him for engravings for the last time in March 1572. It is assumed that van der Heyden died there during the Spanish Fury of 1576.

Van der Heyden's printed oeuvre is very diverse and includes religious, mythological, allegorical, satirical and genre scenes as well as portraits and ornaments. The prints are notable for their faithful replication of the original artist's style and thus lack individuality. During the early years of his collaboration with Cock (from 1551 to c. 1556), he engraved mainly reproductive prints after the work of Andrea del Sarto, Frans Floris (e.g. the ornamental designs *Compertimenta pictoriis flosculis manubiisque bellicis variegata*, Hollstein, nos 70–104), Lambert Lombard and Pieter de Vos. From 1556 his prints were almost exclusively after the work of Pieter Bruegel I (e.g. the *Seven Virtues*, Hollstein, nos 30–36, and the *Seven Vices*, Hollstein, nos 37–43), Hans Bol (e.g. the *Parable of the Blind Men*, Hollstein, no. 19, and *Autumn* and *Winter*, Hollstein, nos 65–6) and Hieronymous Bosch (e.g. the *Last Judgement*, Hollstein no. 17, and *Big Fishes Eat the Smaller Fishes*, Hollstein no. 46). In a series of engravings of portraits of royalty 20 of the prints (Hollstein, nos 140–58) were by van der Heyden. For Plantin he engraved three allegorical frontispieces (Hollstein, nos 137–9) for the Polyglot Bible (1569) after drawings by Luis Manrique. His engraved *View of Antwerp* (Hollstein, no. 69), after a drawing by Lambert van Noort, was published by Hans Leifrinck.

Van der Heyden usually signed his prints with his monogram. His Latinized name 'Petrus a Merica' or 'Mirycinis', in full or in monogram, also occurs; the name 'Verheyden' is rarely encountered. Various interpretations have been made of the Latinized form of his name. Renouvier and others claimed that 'a Merica' was a Latin translation of 'van der Heyden' ('of the heath'). Nagler, on the other hand, maintained that 'Merica' indicated the artist's birthplace, perhaps Meereyck; according to him, the Latin word for 'heath' is 'erica' not 'merica'. Wurzbach believed that 'myrica', which can also mean 'tamarisk', referred to the fantastic prints by van der Heyden after Bruegel and Bosch. De Pauw de Veen, who corroborated the meaning of 'myricia' in the sense of 'heath', supported Renouvier's explanation.

BIBLIOGRAPHY

BNB; Hollstein: *Dut. & Flem.*; *NBW*; Thieme-Becker; Wurzbach

G. K. Nagler: *Neues allgemeines Künstler-Lexikon*, vii (Munich, 1839), p. 369; ix (Munich, 1840), p. 312

P. Renouvier: 'Des Types et des manières des maîtres graveurs', *Mém. Acad. Montpellier*, iii (1855), pp. 120, 148

G. K. Nagler: *Monogrammisten* (1858–1920), i, p. 959; ii, pp. 1689, 2287; iv, pp. 1557, 1771

M. Rooses: *Christophe Plantin: Imprimeur anversois* (Antwerp, 1882), pp. 124–6, 287

——: *Plantin et l'imprimerie plantinienne* (Antwerp, 1886), pp. 286ff

C. Le Blanc: *Manuel de l'amateur d'estampes*, iii (Paris, 1888), pp. 30–31

A. J. J. Delen: 'Les Artistes collaborateurs de Christophe Plantin', *Sept études publiées à l'occasion du quatrième centenaire du célèbre imprimeur anversois, Christophe Plantin* (Brussels and Antwerp, 1920), pp. 119–20

——: *Histoire de la gravure dans les anciens Pays-Bas et dans les provinces belges des origines jusqu'à la fin du XVIIIe siècle, II: Le XVIe siècle: Les Graveurs illustrateurs* (Paris, 1934), pp. 163–4

——: *Les graveurs d'estampes* (Paris, 1935)

L. Lebeer: 'Les Estampes de Pierre Bruegel l'Ancien', *An. Soc. Royale Archéol. Bruxelles*, xlv (1941), pp. 163, 168, 170–71, 178–9

A. J. J. Delen: *De grafische kunsten door de eeuwen heen* (Antwerp and Amsterdam, 1956), pp. 102, 112, 118

L. Lebeer: 'De Zuidnederlandse prentkunst in de zestiende eeuw', *Kunstgeschiedenes der Nederlanden, IV: Renaissance* (Zeist and Antwerp, 1963), pp. 658, 668, 670

E. Scheyer: '*The Wedding Dance* by Pieter Bruegel the Elder in the Detroit Institute of Arts: Its Relations and Derivations', *A. Q.* [Detroit], xxvii/3 (1965), pp. 167–93

Vijftien jaar aanvinsten sedert de eerste steenlegging tot de plechtige invijding van de Bibliotheek [Fifteen years of acquisitions since the ceremonial laying of the foundation-stone of the library] (exh. cat., Brussels, Bib. Royale Albert Ier, 1969), pp. 230, 232–3, nos 235–6

CHRISTINE VAN MULDERS

Heydenreich, Ludwig Heinrich (*b* 23 March 1903; *d* 14 Sept 1978). German art historian. He obtained his doctorate (pubd Munich, 1971) at the Universität Hamburg in 1929. In company with other German art historians, among them Heinrich Bodmer (1885–1950), Friedrich Kriegbaum and Ulrich Middeldorf (1901–83), he was then closely associated with the work of the Kunsthistorisches Institut in Florence, and he was also one of the founders of the Zentralinstitut für Kunstgeschichte in Munich. His two principal areas of scholarly research were the architecture of the Italian Renaissance and the art of Leonardo da Vinci. His various studies of Leonardo, several devoted to the artist as architectural designer, represent a major enquiry into the genius of Leonardo. No less significant were Heydenreich's studies of Italian Renaissance architecture in general, including his contributions to Ulrich Thieme and Felix Becker's *Allgemeines Lexikon der bildenden Künstler von der Antike bis zur Gegenwart*, 37 vols (Leipzig, 1907–50) and to O. Schmidt and K.-A. Wirth's *Reallexikon zur deutschen Kunstgeschichte* as well as his many articles for the scholarly journals *Zeitschrift für Kunstgeschichte* and *Kunstchronik*. As far as the English-speaking world was concerned, Heydenreich's most accessible and therefore influential work was *Architecture in Italy, 1400–1600*, written in collaboration with Wolfgang Lotz (Heydenreich contributed the section on 15th-century architecture), which was published (1974) in the Pelican History of Art series.

WRITINGS

Die Sakralbau-Studien Leonardo da Vinci's Untersuchungen zum Thema: Leonardo da Vinci als Architekt (diss., U. Hamburg, 1929; Munich 1971)

Leonardo (Berlin, 1943)

Arte e scienza in Leonardo (Milan, 1945)

Leonardo da Vinci, 2 vols (London, New York and Basle, 1954)

'Die Capella Rucellai von San Pancrazio in Florenz', *De Artibus Opuscula XL: Essays in Honor of Erwin Panofsky* (New York, 1961), pp. 219–29

Leonardo architetto (Florence, 1963)

with W. Lotz: *Architecture in Italy, 1400–1600*, Pelican Hist. A. (Harmondsworth, 1974)

Regular contributions to *Kunstchronik* and *Z. Kstgesch.*

BIBLIOGRAPHY

W. Lotz and L. L. Möller, eds: *Studien zur toskanischen Kunst: Festschrift für Ludwig Heinrich Heydenreich zum 23 März 1963* (Munich, 1964) [with full writings list]

W. B. Sauerländer, ed.: *Studien zur Architektur der Renaissance* (Munich, 1981)

JANET SOUTHORN

Heydt, August, Freiherr **von der** (*b* Elberfeld, 1851; *d* Bonn, 1929). German banker and collector. He became a partner in his family's banking firm in Elberfeld in 1878. He was married to Selma (née) Haarhaus, with whom he had two sons, August von der Heydt (*b* 1881) and Eduard von der Heydt (*b* 1882). He was a founder-member of the Elberfeld Museumsverein, and, after its campaigning led to the establishment of a permanent municipal art gallery (the Städtisches Museum, Elberfeld) in 1902, he and his wife lent and donated numerous works of art to it. They also funded various public monuments in the town, including the imposing Fountain of Justice by Bernhard Hoetger (1910). In 1918 their collection consisted of over 250 works. It combined modern French art from Courbet onwards with contemporary German art, including 'expressionist' works by Ernst Ludwig Kirchner, Emil Nolde and Franz Marc, and 27 paintings by Paula Modersohn-Becker. This choice reflected the belief that a new, vital, German art, commensurate with the country's economic and political importance, was emerging through free interaction with other currents in European culture, notably the French. The von der Heydts' fortune was badly affected after 1919 by the economic instability of the Weimar Republic, and they stopped buying art on a large scale at this time. They had intended to leave the collection to the Elberfeld museum (which in 1929 became the Städtisches Museum, Wuppertal). However, much of the collection was destroyed in an air raid in 1943. Of the surviving works, 67 were given by their son to the Wuppertal museum (renamed the Von der Heydt-Museum in 1961) between 1949 and 1961.

BIBLIOGRAPHY

C. G. Heise: *Die Sammlung des Freiherrn August von der Heydt, Elberfeld* (Leipzig, 1918)

G. Aust: 'Sammlungen und Ausstellungen in Elberfeld und Barmen', *Der westdeutsche Impuls* (exh. cat., Wuppertal, Von der Heydt-Mus., 1984), pp. 105–20

A. Birthalmer: 'August und Eduard von der Heydt: Zwei Mäzene und ihr Lebenswerk', *Avantgarde und Publikum*, ed. H. Junge (Cologne, Weimar and Vienna, 1992), pp. 157–64

MALCOLM GEE

Heyerdahl, Hans (Olaf Halvor) (*b* Smedjebakken, Dalarne, 8 July 1857; *d* Christiania [now Oslo], 10 Oct 1913). Norwegian painter. He was born into an enlightened but conservative family, his father being an engineer, occasional architect and writer of Nordic saga poetry, and he spent his childhood and youth in the rapidly expanding town of Drammen, 40 km from the capital Christiania. In 1873 he was admitted to the Kongelige Tegneskole in Christiania, where he studied under Peder C. Thurmann, a landscape artist trained in Düsseldorf. For more advanced training, Heyerdahl was obliged to go abroad, and in 1874 he enrolled at the Munich Akademie. He was encouraged by Professor Ludwig von Löfftz (1845–1910) to give up landscape in favour of history painting and portraits (e.g. the artists *Christian Skredsvig*, 1876, and *Eilif Peterssen*, 1877; both Oslo, N.G.). In 1877, under the guidance of Professor Wilhelm Lindenschmit (1829–95), Heyerdahl finished his most inventive and brilliant composition, the *Expulsion from the Garden* (Oslo, N.G.). Using over life-size figures, set in a barren tempestuous landscape, Heyerdahl skilfully contrasted the youthful rage

of Adam with the resigned despair of Eve. This sombre work won him a third prize medal at the Exposition Universelle in Paris in 1878.

In the same year Heyerdahl moved to Paris and studied briefly in the studio of Léon Bonnat. He gradually adapted his palette to that of the French plein-air painters in such works as *At the Window* (1881; Oslo, N.G.). In 1879 he made his debut at the Paris Salon with an austere portrait of the Norwegian composer *Johan Svendsen* (Oslo, N.G.). The year after he participated with *Nymph Speaking to a Starling* (untraced), and in 1881 he showed what he considered to be a 'modern painting', *Dying Child* (Riom, Mus. Mandet), a domestic tragedy rendered in cool light and with the pathos of a staged drama. For this he was awarded the Grand Prix de Florence, which allowed him two years in Italy and a grant of 5000 francs. Meeting Arnold Böcklin in Florence rekindled an old ambition of Heyerdahl to paint mythological subjects, particularly those from the Nordic sagas. However, his attempts in this field were largely a failure, the only lasting result being his development of a palette of more saturated colours.

Returning to Norway in 1884, Heyerdahl settled in Christiania but spent most of the following summers in the small coastal town of Aasgaardstrand. Here he produced the works that established him as one of Norway's finest colourists, such as *A Rest* (1885; priv. col.), *Bathing Resort* (1886; Bergen, Billedgal.), *The Sisters* (1887; Oslo, N.G.) and the *Strawberry Girl* (1888; Lillehammer, Bys Malsaml.). These all show people, in particular children, at ease with themselves and their surroundings. However, Heyerdahl also painted less serene subjects, such as the sensual nude *Black Anna* (*c.* 1887; Oslo, N.G.; see fig.), the Pietà-like *Deathbed of a Worker* (1889; Trondheim,

Hans Heyerdahl: *Black Anna*, oil on canvas, 540×440 mm, *c.* 1887 (Oslo, Nasjonalgalleri)

Kstforen.) and the vigorous *Girl with a Cat* (?1895; Bergen, Meyers Saml.). In 1890 Heyerdahl set up as a painter of fashionable portraits, at first attempting a rather grand style, but soon striving for intimacy and a decorative, pastel-like quality. Around 1895, influenced by English Symbolism and contemporary Norwegian Romantic Nationalism, Heyerdahl again tried to paint subjects from the sagas, but he had little success with such works (e.g. the *Hell-journey of Brynhild*, 1897; priv. col.). During a second stay in Paris, from 1900 to 1907, Heyerdahl took Montmartre as his main subject. Back in Norway, he ended his career with a steady output of landscapes of his beloved Aasgaardstrand.

Heyerdahl was perhaps the most promising Norwegian painter of his generation, but for all his restless experimentation he seems not to have understood the true nature of his own talent, which was for naturalistic representation combined with sumptuous use of colour. Heyerdahl lacked Christian Krohg's or Erik Werenskiold's dedication to social and nationalist themes, tending to favour Art for Art's Sake. The impact of Heyerdahl's work was slight; the young Edvard Munch seems to have been the only major artist who responded to his themes and technique.

BIBLIOGRAPHY

NKL

G. Cederström: *Gammalt och nytt: Hans Heyerdahl* [Old and new: Hans Heyerdahl] (Eskilstuna, 1929)

L. Östby: 'Hans Heyerdahl', *Kst & Kult.*, ii (1935), pp. 77–96

E. Werenskiold: 'Den unge Heyerdahl', *Kst & Kult.*, ii (1935), pp. 73–6

Hans Heyerdahl (exh. cat. by T. Aslaksby, Åmot, Modums Blaafarvevaerk, 1981) [extensively illus.]

T. Aslaksby: 'Hans Heyerdahl i Paris', *Kunst og Kommentar*, ed. S. O. Hoff (Oslo, 1992), pp. 48–67

TROND ASLAKSBY

Heylan. Flemish family of engravers, active in Spain. Francisco Heylan (*b* Antwerp, 1584; *d* Granada, 1650) was trained in the tradition of Flemish engraving and was influenced by the three Wierix brothers, Hans Collaert and Hans Strasser. He arrived in Seville *c.* 1606 and late in 1611 moved to Granada, where he enjoyed considerable success as an engraver–typographer, founding a school where from 1616 he directed the Imprenta de la Real Cancillería. The high quality of his work is evident in the plates of *Plataforma de Granada*, containing fine views of the city, and *Sección de la Capilla Mayor* of Granada Cathedral (both after 1616). Bernardo Heylan (*b* Antwerp, 1588; *d* Granada, 1661), Francisco's brother and pupil, accompanied him to Spain. A series of engravings of the *Immaculate Conception* are his best works. Bernardo's son José Heylan (*d* ?Granada, 1676) was also an engraver. Francisco's sister or daughter Ana Heylan (*b* Antwerp; *d* Granada, 29 April 1655) was active from 1637, specializing in engravings of the Virgin and Child for religious books. She probably collaborated with Francisco.

BIBLIOGRAPHY

Bénézit; Hollstein: *Dut. & Flem.*

M. Gómez Moreno: 'El arte de grabar en Granada', *Rev. Archvs, Bib. & Mus.*, iv (1900), pp. 463–83

J. Ainaud de Lasarte: *Grabado*, A. Hisp., xviii (Madrid, 1962)

A. Moreno Garrido: 'El grabado en Granada durante el siglo XVII', *Cuad. A. U. Granada*, xiii (1976), nos 26–8, pp. 56–63; cat. nos 19–195, pp. 79–142

A. Gallego: *Historia del grabado en España* (Madrid, 1979), p. 219

E. Páez Ríos: *Repertorio* (1981–3), ii, pp. 18–23

B. García Vega: *El grabado del libro español: Siglos XV–XVI–XVII*

(Valladolid, 1984)

N. Sánchez Esteban and others: 'El Escorial y la cultura arquitectónica de su tiempo', *El Escorial en la Biblioteca Nacional de Madrid* (exh. cat., Madrid, Bib. N., 1985–6), pp. 149–221 [176]

BLANCA GARCÍA VEGA

Heylman, Jacob. *See* HAYLMANN, JACOB.

Heymans, Adrien [Adriaan] **Joseph** [Josef, Jozef] (*b* Antwerp, 11 June 1839; *d* Brussels, Dec 1921). Belgian painter. He studied at the Koninklijke Academie voor Schone Kunsten in Antwerp from 1854 to 1856, and in Paris from 1856 to 1858. In Paris he met Charles-François Daubigny, Jean-François Millet, Théodore Rousseau and Jean-Baptiste-Camille Corot, whose ideas he absorbed; under their influence he overcame the rigid training he had received in Antwerp. After returning to Belgium he worked with a group of young artists that included Franz Courtens, Jacob Rosseels (1828–1912) and Isidore Meyers (1836–1917) at Kalmthout, north-east of Antwerp, and at Termonde on the River Escaut. The artists' colony at Kalmthout was visited by the painter Théodore Baron (1840–99), with whom Heymans soon became friends. Heymans moved to Brussels in 1869, and the two artists worked together in a studio there, although Heymans also worked at Wechel-ter-Zande in the Campine region. He became associated with the Société Libre des Beaux-Arts in Brussels. His works of this period show the influence of the Barbizon school, as in *Sunset* (1875; Ghent, Mus. S. Kst.).

Heymans was one of the first members of Les XX when it was founded in 1884 and after exhibiting with this group joined its successor, the Association de la Libre Esthétique. He was a co-founder, with Emile Claus, of the Société de l'Art Contemporain and of the Vie et Lumière group. By *c.* 1890 his painting showed the influence of Impressionism, which lightened his brushstroke and brightened his palette, for example *Spring* (*c.* 1895; Brussels, Mus. A. Mod.). At the turn of the century Heymans experimented with Neo-Impressionism in such works as *Moonlit Sky* (1907; Brussels, Mus. A. Mod.). After this, however, he returned to his earlier, more direct style of painting. Many of Heymans's paintings depict the landscapes he visited in the Campine area, and he was particularly interested in incorporating in his work the effects of light caused by fog, moonlight and starlight.

BIBLIOGRAPHY

G. Vanzype: *Nos Peintres*, iii (Brussels, 1905), pp. 66–82

C. Lemonnier: *L'Ecole belge de peinture, 1830–1905* (Brussels, 1906)

P. Colin: *La Peinture belge depuis 1830* (Brussels, 1930)

E. de Seyn: *Dictionnaire biographique des sciences, des lettres et des arts en Belgique* (Brussels, 1935)

S. Monneret: *Impressionnisme et son époque* (Paris, 1978)

Heysen, Sir (Ernst) Hans (Franz) (*b* Hamburg, 8 Oct 1877; *d* Hahndorf, nr Adelaide, 2 July 1968). Australian painter and printmaker of German birth. His family settled in South Australia in 1884. Having attended the Norwood Art School under James Ashton (1859–1935), he studied in Paris at the Académie Julian, Colarossi's academy and the Ecole des Beaux-Arts and travelled in Europe. He was particularly influenced by Constable, the Barbizon school,

George Clausen, Ernest Atkinson Hornel and Frank Brangwyn. In 1904, after returning to Adelaide, he sold major oils to the National Gallery of New South Wales, Sydney (*Coming Home*), and the National Gallery of South Australia, Adelaide (*Mystic Morn*). In 1908 he moved to Hahndorf in the Adelaide Hills. Heysen recorded the labours of the German farmers who had settled in the area, in oils, watercolours, drawings and (occasionally) etchings: for Heysen the rural labourers of Hahndorf were the equivalent of Millet's Fontainebleau peasants. This aspect of his work reached its peak in *Red Gold* (1913; Adelaide, A.G. S. Australia; *see* AUSTRALIA, fig. 10); his later paintings were somewhat repetitive.

Anti-German prejudice during World War I and a succession of family misfortunes encouraged Heysen to move to the Flinders Range of South Australia (1926–33). The contrast between Heysen's nostalgic studies of rural labour in the enclosed, quasi-European landscape of the Adelaide Hills and the vast, unpeopled spaces of the Flinders Range as depicted in *Foothills of the Flinders* (1929; Adelaide, A.G. S. Australia) was marked. The Flinders Range, especially under the drought conditions the artist favoured, correlated with both the modern Post-Impressionist style he was adopting and, perhaps, his bleak state of mind. He also painted still-lifes and landscapes of the south coast of South Australia.

One of Australia's most famous landscape artists, Heysen turned the gum tree into one of the clichés of Australian art. He married a Barbizon style to an Australian location with considerable expressive authority and opened up the outback as a subject for art. He was knighted in 1959. There is a comprehensive collection of his work in the Art Gallery of South Australia, Adelaide.

BIBLIOGRAPHY
C. Thiele: *Heysen of Hahndorf* (Adelaide, 1968)
Hans Heysen Centennial Retrospective (exh. cat., ed. I. North; Adelaide, A.G. S. Australia, 1977); rev. as *Heysen* (Melbourne, 1979)
IAN NORTH

Hezelo [Etselo; Hézelon] (*fl c.* 1100). Monk of Cluny. A short passage in a letter written between 1139 and 1145 by Peter the Venerable, Abbot of Cluny (*reg* 1122–56), in which Hezelo is designated *magister* and formerly a canon of an unspecified chapter at Liège, has led several authors to claim him as the architect of the huge third abbey church at Cluny (begun 1088; *see* CLUNIAC ORDER, §III, 1). Peter praised him as a learned man who 'more than all other men except the Spanish and English kings constructed the corporal fabric of the new church'. Various charters may or may not refer to the same Hezelo and give him an aristocratic Burgundian pedigree, but it is certain that before 1120 he wrote the earliest recorded biography (lost) of St Hugh, Abbot of Cluny (*reg* 1049–1109).

The allegation that Hezelo was in a modern sense the architect of Cluny III is highly speculative. As Peter the Venerable associates him as constructor of the church with Alfonso VI of Léon-Castile (*reg* 1066–1109) and Henry I of England (*reg* 1100–35), both known from other sources to have given large sums towards the building of the church, he is less likely to have been the 'architect' of Cluny III than an 'appeal secretary' (Evans).

See also GUNZO.

BIBLIOGRAPHY
Peter the Venerable: *Letters* (1139–45); ed. G. Constable, 2 vols (Cambridge, MA, 1967), i, p. 229; ii, pp. 157–8
J. Evans: *The Romanesque Architecture of the Order of Cluny* (Cambridge, 1938), pp. 10–11
J. Stiennon: 'Hézelon de Liège, architecte de Cluny III', *Mélanges offerts à René Crozet* (Poitiers, 1966), pp. 345–58
NEIL STRATFORD

Hezire. *See under* HESYRE, TOMB OF.

Hiba, Tell al-. *See* LAGASH.

Hiberno-Saxon art. *See* INSULAR ART.

Hickel. Austrian family of painters of Bohemian birth. The portrait painters (1) Joseph Hickel and (2) Anton Hickel were the sons and pupils of the painter Johann Hickel (*c.* 1705–78) from Prague.

(1) Joseph Hickel (*b* Český Krumlov, Bohemia [now in Czech Republic], 19 March 1736; *d* Vienna, 28 March 1807). In 1756 he was accepted as a student at the Akademie der Bildenden Künste in Vienna, where he studied for about ten years. In 1768 he was commissioned by Empress Maria-Theresa to go to Italy to paint portraits of the nobility in Milan, Parma and Florence; he became a member of the Accademia di Belle Arti in Florence in 1769. In 1772 he was appointed deputy head of the Vienna Gemäldegalerie and in 1776 became painter to the imperial court. He was granted full membership of the Akademie in Vienna that same year, submitting the *Portrait of a Man Aged 104 from Bohemia* (Vienna, Akad. Bild. Kst.) on his admission.

In the 1780s Hickel was one of the most sought-after portrait painters in Vienna. He is believed to have painted more than 3000 portraits, including those of the Austrian imperial family, *Pope Pius VI* (1782) and *Ferdinand IV and Maria Carolina*, rulers of Naples, and members of the nobility, middle classes and actors at the Hofburg theatre. Engravings after these untraced portraits, for example by Johann Peter Pichler (1766–1807), reveal that his paintings follow the late Baroque tradition of Martin van Meytens (1695–1770).

(2) Anton Hickel (*b* Český Krumlov, Bohemia [now in Czech Republic], 1745; *d* Hamburg, 30 Oct 1798). Brother of (1) Joseph Hickel. In 1758 he enrolled at the Akademie der Bildenden Künste in Vienna, where he was still mentioned as a pupil in 1761. He then painted under the tutelage of his brother until 1777. In 1779 he began a career as a travelling portrait painter. He stayed in Munich, where he painted public figures, for example *Elector Karl Theodor* (replica versions, Munich, Residenzmus. and Schloss Nymphenburg). After visiting southern Germany and Switzerland, he went to Mannheim and Mainz to execute portrait commissions. He then spent a longer period in Switzerland from 1785, where he learnt of his appointment as court painter to Josef II, Holy Roman Emperor. In 1786 he travelled to Paris, where Marie

Antoinette, Queen of France, and her friend Marie Thérèse Louise of Savoyen-Carignan, Princess of Lamballe, were his patrons; he painted a full-length portrait of the latter (Vaduz, Samml. Liechtenstein).

The revolution in France in 1789 forced Hickel to leave France; he went to London, where he started to exhibit regularly and soon established a considerable reputation. His masterpiece from this period is considered to be a representation of Parliament in session, a huge painting with 96 life-size portrait figures, *William Pitt Addressing the House of Commons on the French Declaration of War, 1793* (1793–5). It was commissioned by Joseph II and given to the National Portrait Gallery in London by Francis Joseph, Emperor of Austria, in 1885. Hickel also painted such MPs as the Whig statesman *Charles James Fox* (*c.* 1793) and *Ellis Welbore, Baron Mendip* (1793; both London, N.P.G.).

In 1797 Hickel finally settled in Hamburg and painted several distinguished members of the city's cultural circles, for example an expressive portrait of the poet *Friedrich Gottlieb Klopstock* as an old man (1798; Hamburg, Staats- & Ubib.). His outstanding qualities as a portrait painter are his great technical skill and ability to render likenesses, although his pictures often suffered from hasty execution. At times he worked together with his brother, for example in preparing portraits of actors at the Hofburg theatre in Vienna (Vienna, Bundestheaterverband).

NDB

BIBLIOGRAPHY

A. Feulner: *Katalog der Gemälde im Residenz-Museum München und in Schloss Nymphenburg* (Munich, 1924)

J. Neuwirth: *Zur Geschichte der Kammermaler Josef und Anton Hickel aus Böhmisch-Leipa* (Vienna, 1927)

Runge in seiner Zeit (exh. cat., Hamburg, Ksthalle, 1977–8)

Maria Theresia und ihre Zeit (exh. cat. by W. Koschatzky, Vienna, Schloss Schönbrunn, 1980)

INGRID SATTEL BERNARDINI

Hickey, Dale (*b* Melbourne, 31 July 1937). Australian painter. He studied graphic design from 1954 to 1957 at the Swinburne Technical College in Melbourne, where Robert Rooney was a fellow student. For the next two years he worked as a graphic artist for ABC Television in Melbourne and in 1964 had his first one-man show at the Toorak Galleries there. His early work of the mid- to late 1960s was based on a reduction of mundane objects into a geometrical pattern. *Untitled* (1967–8; Melbourne, N.G. Victoria), for example, is derived from an eiderdown and like many works of this period creates an ambiguity between flatness and depth through *trompe l'oeil* modelling. This process of reduction was carried to extremes from 1967 to 1970 with, for example, an exhibition of fences in 1969.

Hickey's interest in mass-produced objects and patterns led to a pictorial search for the essence or archetypes of objects in the 1970s. The *Cup Series* (1972–3; Melbourne, Pin., see 1973 exh. cat., pl. 22), in which nine naturalistically rendered cups are painted on nine uniform canvases, is an attempt to capture the archetype of a cup. Hickey then began to devote himself to still-lifes and landscapes, again in a naturalistic style. His later works were landscapes executed on a large scale and in bright colours, as in *Cottlesbridge Landscape* (1980; Melbourne, N.G. Victoria). Here the dominant colours are strong blues and reds and the decorative effect and linear style show the influence of Japanese art and of Matisse.

BIBLIOGRAPHY

Recent Australian Art (exh. cat. by F. McCarthy and D. Thomas, Sydney, A.G. NSW, 1973), pp. 40–41

Project 15: Dale Hickey (exh. cat. by R. Lindsay, Sydney, A.G. NSW, 1976)

Australian Perspecta, 1981 (exh. cat. by B. Murphy, Sydney, A.G. NSW, 1981), pp. 90–91

□

Hickey, John (*b* Dublin, 7 Nov 1751; *d* London, 12 Jan 1795). Irish sculptor, also active in England. He worked under a local carver before coming to England in 1776 and entering the Royal Academy Schools. From 1777 he exhibited regularly at the Academy. In 1778 he won the Academy's Gold Medal with a relief representing the *Massacre of the Innocents* (sold London, Christie's, 15 March 1798). His portrait of *Sarah Siddons as 'Cassandra'* (exh. RA 1786; ex-Cyril Humphries col.; sold New York, Sotheby's, 11 Jan 1995, lot 163) is a finely carved marble statuette, unusual at the time in England for its small scale (h. 730 mm). Hickey's marble portrait busts include his champion *Edmund Burke* (1785; Wentworth Woodhouse, S. Yorks; replica, London, BM) and *George Thicknesse* (1791; London, St Paul's Sch.). Appointed Sculptor to the Prince of Wales (later George IV) in 1786, he produced for the Grand Staircase at Carlton House (destr.), London, a pair of plaster figures of Atlas and Time supporting a clock, the model for which (untraced) he exhibited at the Royal Academy in 1788. Hickey's finest work is the monument to *David La Touche* (red and white marble, h. *c.* 7.6 m, 1790; Delgany, Co. Wicklow), a five-figure group comprising three heroic mourning figures bound by swathes of drapery supporting a sarcophagus surmounted by a draped urn. Above, a pediment supports a statue of the deceased in contemporary dress, flanked by a giant cornucopia and reclining female figure representing Commerce. His most ambitious work in England, the marble monument to *Elizabeth Hawkins and her Family* (1782; Abingdon, Oxon, St Helen), is more obviously derivative (particularly recalling John Bacon), as are his smaller relief memorials. Edmund Burke was enthusiastic in promoting Hickey and secured for him the commission for the monument to *David Garrick* in Westminster Abbey, London; his second choice was Thomas Banks. Hickey died before work could begin, and the monument was executed by Henry Webber (1754–1826). Thomas Hickey (*fl* 1753–1816), his brother, worked as a portrait painter in Dublin, London and India.

Gunnis

BIBLIOGRAPHY

W. G. Strickland: *A Dictionary of Irish Artists* (London and Dublin, 1913), i, pp. 480–82

JULIUS BRYANT

Hickox, Elizabeth (*b* Karuk territory, CA, 26 July 1875; *d* Somesbar, CA, 19 July 1947). Native American basket-weaver. She was born of a Wiyot mother and Euro-American father. She achieved a secure life with her second marriage, in 1895, to Luther Hickox, a half-blood miner and mill-owner who later became Justice of the Peace. She directed her weaving to the élite market, specializing in a lidded 'gift basket' with undulating profile and a high knob. On these she delineated main designs with supreme attention to the relationship of positive and negative elements and embellished them with a complex scheme of bordering designs and shifts in weaving technique. Her second daughter, Louise Hickox (*b* 29 April 1896; *d* 18 Sept 1962), also a basket-weaver, achieved almost equal results. Both were interviewed extensively by anthropologist Lila O'Neale in 1928 and provided most of the technical information for O'Neale's 1932 publication of Yurok–Karok basketwork. Their baskets were featured in a 1990 exhibition at the Southwest Museum in Los Angeles. In 1908 Elizabeth Hickox met Grace Nicholson, the premier basketwork dealer, who operated her business in Pasadena, CA, but who travelled through the far west each summer to collect basketwork and ceremonial objects. Nicholson began purchasing Hickox's work, and by 1910–11 had acquired exclusive rights to the weaving of both mother and daughter. Nicholson recorded over 90 Hickox baskets in her ledger, identified by number, dimensions and sketches. Nearly half of these are also documented in photographs. Almost no records exist for Hickox baskets woven after 1922, when Nicholson appears to have suspended these ledger entries, perhaps because of her growing interest in Oriental arts. In the late 1920s Elizabeth Hickox produced primarily miniatures, due to the disintegration of the élite market for fine art curios. By 1934 Nicholson ceased collecting from the Hickoxes, who then gave up weaving. The Nicholson materials, which provide most of the information on the Hickoxes' careers, are divided between the Phoebe Apperson Hearst Museum of Anthropology at the University of California at Berkeley and the Huntington Library in San Marino, CA.

See also NATIVE NORTH AMERICAN ART, §XIV, 4.

BIBLIOGRAPHY

L. O'Neale: 'Yurok-Karok Basket Weavers', *U. CA Pubns Amer. Archaeol. & Ethnol.*, xxxii/1 (1932), pp. 1–184

M. Cohodas: *High on the Rivers: Basketry Art of Elizabeth Hickox* (in preparation)

MARVIN COHODAS

Hicks. American family of painters.

(1) Edward Hicks. (*b* Attleborough [now Langhorne], PA, 4 April 1780; *d* Newtown, PA, 23 Aug 1849). He was raised by a devout Quaker family following his mother's death. At thirteen he was apprenticed for seven years to a coachmaker, where he developed the techniques of painting and lettering. By 1801 he had gone into business as a coach-, house- and sign-painter, later expanding his trade to include such items as milk-buckets, clockfaces and elaborate fireboards. Profoundly affected by his Quaker upbringing, he began to disapprove of painting as trifling and insubstantial, and in 1812 he became a Quaker minister. Hicks received no formal artistic training, and it was not until *c.* 1820 that he began to paint creatively. His paintings are infused with his intense religious conviction, and he reconciled his two vocations by keeping the former 'within the bounds of innocence and usefulness' and by creating images of morality. Most of his pictures were variations on Isaiah's biblical prophecy (Isaiah 11:6–9). Hicks's *Peaceable Kingdom* pictures were 'painted sermons', executed from about 1820 to the time of his death.

Allegorical in nature, they depict the fulfilment of Isaiah's prophecy: benign animals and trusting infants co-exist with equanimity, while, in the background, William Penn can invariably be seen effecting his famous treaty with the Indians. The *Peaceable Kingdoms* are imaginative in composition and serene and sincere in mood, although technically unsophisticated. They were generally produced as gifts or commissioned works for relatives and friends. Occasionally Hicks indulged in homily when he lettered rhymed scriptural texts around the border of a picture.

Hicks worked exclusively in oils, and his stylized forms, simple figures, strong sense of design, flat decorative colours and careful lettering were all derived from sign-painting. Indeed, he persisted in seeing himself as a craftsman rather than an artist, continuing throughout his life to paint wagons, signs, farm equipment and other such utilitarian objects. The *Peaceable Kingdom of the Branch* (*c.* 1825–30; New Haven, CT, Yale U. A.G.), painted in oil on a wooden fireboard, neatly combines both Hicks's art and practical craftsmanship. His most accomplished pictures are farm scenes, such as the *Cornell Farm* (1848; Washington, DC, N.G.A.), a large canvas brilliant in colour and full of detail. Most of his compositions were based on popular prints and engravings, often of historical scenes— George Washington at the Delaware; the Declaration of Independence—after the likes of Thomas Sully, John Trumbull and Benjamin West. These were then translated into Hicks's own naive decorative style. His effective use of colour and design provide an intrinsic charm that makes his work appear much more original than it is. Hicks was not widely known outside Pennsylvania until the 1920s and 1930s, when his *Peaceable Kingdoms* began to be included in American folk art exhibitions.

UNPUBLISHED SOURCES

New York, Frick ['Miscellaneous Extracts about Edward Hicks, Author of the "Peaceable Kingdom", Compiled by the Newton Library Corporation', 1935]

WRITINGS

Memoirs of the Life and Religious Labours of Edward Hicks (Philadelphia, 1851)

BIBLIOGRAPHY

A. E. Bye: 'Edward Hicks, Painter-preacher', *Antiques*, xxix (1936), pp. 13–16

J. Lipman and A. Winchester, eds: *Primitive Painters in America, 1750–1950: An Anthology* (New York, 1950)

J. Held: 'Edward Hicks and the Tradition', *A. Q.* [Detroit], xiv (1951), pp. 121–36

A. Ford: *Edward Hicks: Painter of the Peaceable Kingdom* (Philadelphia, 1952)

J. T. Flexner: *American Painting: The Light of Distant Skies* (New York, 1954)

E. P. Mather: *Edward Hicks: His Peaceable Kingdoms and other Paintings* (Newark and New York, 1983)

A. Ford: *Edward Hicks: His Life and Work* (New York, 1985)

STEPHEN F. THORPE

(2) Thomas Hicks (*b* Newtown, PA, 18 Oct 1823; *d* Trenton Falls, NY, 8 Oct 1890). Cousin of (1) Edward Hicks. After being apprenticed (*c.* 1835–9) in the sign-painting shop of his cousin, he studied at the Pennsylvania Academy of the Fine Arts in Philadelphia (1839–40) and at the National Academy of Design in New York (1840–44). He then sketched and painted in England, Italy and France before becoming a student of Thomas Couture in Paris (1848–9). On his return to the USA in 1849, he established a studio in New York and quickly became a popular portrait painter, although his portrayals only rarely have enough psychological depth to make them of more than documentary interest. *Hamilton Fish* (1852; New York, City Hall) is among his stronger works. Hicks also painted genre subjects, such as *Musicale: Barber Shop, Trenton Falls* (1866; Raleigh, NC Mus. A.), and landscapes, the latter chiefly near Thornwood, his summer residence at Trenton Falls, NY. His early landscape style, which was in the manner of the Hudson River school, gave way to an Impressionist technique in the 1870s.

BIBLIOGRAPHY

G. W. Sheldon: *American Painters* (New York, 1879), pp. 35–9

D. Tatham: 'Thomas Hicks at Trenton Falls', *Amer. A. J.*, xv (1983), pp. 4–20

DAVID TATHAM

Hicks, David (Nightingale) (*b* London, 25 March 1929). English designer. He was educated at Charterhouse School, Surrey, and studied painting, illustration, typography and stage design at the Central School of Arts and Crafts, London. He served in the British Army Educational Corps (1949–51), then travelled in Europe for a year, pursuing a keen interest in architecture and interiors. In 1953 he redecorated his mother's London house, a photograph of which was published and led to several similar commissions, and established his own design studio in London. In 1955 he formed a partnership with an English antiques dealer, Tom Parr (*b* 1930), and together they ran Hicks & Parr, a small decorating and antiques shop in Chelsea. Among their early successful projects were the redecoration of the residences of Sir Rex and Lady Benson, Frederick and Mary Ponsonby, 10th Earl and Countess of Bessborough, and President Kwame Nkrumah in Ghana. In 1959 Hicks set up independently as David Hicks Ltd, then as David Hicks Associates and later David Hicks International Marketing, with branch offices in France, Belgium, Switzerland, Germany, Pakistan and Australia. During the 1960s Hicks became one of the most fashionable decorators in Britain, noted for his eclectic tastes, use of strong colours and designs for geometric-patterned carpets and textiles, inspired by the work of Matisse and Edouard Vuillard. His employment of wall-to-wall carpeting in geometric-repeat motifs, together with his mix-and-match furnishing fabrics, became widely popular. He supplied designs to some 500 furnishing fabric and carpet manufacturers in North America and Britain during the 1960s and 1970s. He decorated the private apartments (1965) at Windsor Castle, Berks, for Charles, Prince of Wales, and Princess Anne and designed the interiors of the ocean liner *Queen Elizabeth II*, Raffles nightclub, London, and yachts for the Saudi Arabian royal family, as well as offices for the government of New South Wales, the British Steel Corporation and the British Embassy, Washington, DC. He worked for such film stars as Douglas Fairbanks jr and the film directors Richard Lester and Joseph Losey. He sought to give character to modern rooms by the introduction of antiques and enlivened period rooms with large, abstract paintings and perspex or steel coffee tables or Louis XVI style chairs reupholstered with his fabrics. Hicks's ideas gained general currency throughout the 1970s and early 1980s, notably his use of Classical statuary and eclectic, table-top groups of massed

objects. From 1977–8 he designed men's shoes and ties and women's accessories, as well as textiles, tableware, silver and tiles. He wrote books on taste in interior decorating.

WRITINGS

with N. Jenkins: *Living with Design* (London, 1979)

Style and Design (London, 1988)

BIBLIOGRAPHY

H.-J. Bonellie: *The Status Merchants: The Trade of Interior Decoration* (South Brunswick, NY, and London, 1972), pp. 45–6

Hicks, George Elgar (*b* Lymington, Hants, 13 March 1824; *d* Odiham, Hants, 4 July 1914). English painter. Son of a prosperous Hampshire magistrate, he trained in London at Henry Sass's Academy and entered the Royal Academy Schools in 1844. He regularly exhibited picturesque landscapes and small genre scenes from 1848, but his first major painting was *Dividend Day: Bank of England* (1859; London, Bank of England). This was a large 'modern life' canvas, showing in great detail a crowd of investors queueing for their quarterly dividends, and was almost certainly painted to emulate Frith's success with *Ramsgate Sands* (1854; British Royal Col.) and *Derby Day* (1858; London, Tate). Despite mixed reviews, *Dividend Day* was one of the most popular paintings at the Academy exhibition of 1859 and Hicks was immediately commissioned by the dealer Henry Wallis to paint another panoramic scene, *The General Post Office: One Minute to Six* (exh. RA 1860; London, Mus. London). This shows a romanticized view of the rush to catch the last post at London's main office. Although critics found the work meretricious and theatrical, and attacked Hicks for ignoring the dingy realities of London life, the public flocked to see it. In this choice of subject, as with some of his other paintings depicting contemporary life, Hicks was probably inspired by the writings of the journalist G. A. Sala (1828–96).

Hicks turned to the more earthy setting of *Billingsgate Fish Market* (exh. RA 1861; London, Fishmongers' Co.) for his next large painting. It received good reviews, although one commentator felt that 'the general result is by no means equal to the beauty of the details, and this through defective composition and unimpressive colour. . . . We sincerely wish we could make Mr Hicks understand this matter, for he is one of the very best among our young artists' (*A. J.* [London], 1 July 1861, p. 196). The following year Hicks was commissioned by the dealer L. V. Flatow to paint *Changing Homes* (London, Geffrye Mus.), which shows a wedding party in a bourgeois drawing-room after the church ceremony. This was widely seen as an eminently suitable subject for the artist, who was described when the work was exhibited in 1863 as 'a disciple in the Frith style. He glides smoothly over the surface of society; he depicts character with a point seasoned often by satire; and for execution no man is more brilliant' (*A. J.* [London], 1 June 1863, p. 111).

In 1863 Hicks also exhibited a triptych entitled *Woman's Mission*, representing Victorian woman in 'three phases of her duties as ministering angel' (*The Times*, 27 May 1863, p. 6). The central section, *Companion of Manhood* (London, Tate), shows a faithful wife consoling her grief-stricken husband. This was flanked by *Guide of Childhood* and *Comfort of Old Age* (untraced; studies Dunedin, NZ, Pub. A.G.).

Hicks's last painting of London life was *An Infant Orphan Election at the London Tavern: 'Polling'* (1865; priv. col., see 1982 exh. cat., pl. ix), which records the election of 'deserving' children to an orphanage at Wanstead. He depicted the event with uncritical detail, using the names of real orphans on placards in the painting. *Before the Magistrates* (1866; priv. col., see 1982 exh. cat., pl. x) was his final scene in this genre. The market for such works was falling, and critics felt that it was no advance on *Dividend Day* or *The General Post Office*.

During the next few years Hicks painted a mixture of historical, biblical and small genre scenes, and from the mid-1870s to the end of the century was an extremely successful society portrait painter (e.g. *Lady Iveagh*, 1892; ex-Forbes Mag. Col., London; sold London, Sotheby's, 9 June 1994, lot 191), often working in a broad 18th-century manner. He exhibited at the Royal Academy until 1903 and continued painting until 1911.

WRITINGS
A Guide to Figure Drawing (London, 1853)

BIBLIOGRAPHY
J. Dafforne: 'British Artists', civ: 'George Elgar Hicks', *A. J.* [London] (1 April 1872), pp. 97–9
George Elgar Hicks: Painter of Victorian Life (exh. cat., ed. R. Allwood; London, Geffrye Mus., 1982) [transcribes his notebooks, 1852–1911]

ROSAMOND ALLWOOD

Hicks, Sheila (*b* Hastings, NE, 24 July 1934). American fibre artist. She studied at Yale University, New Haven, CT, under Josef Albers and Rico Lebrun (1954–9). She moved to Paris in 1963 but continued to travel and exhibit internationally. Hicks's first interest was in Pre-Columbian Peruvian textiles and traditional techniques of Mexican hand-weaving. These inspired her miniature woven pieces of the early 1960s. Towards the mid-1960s she studied a variety of industrial methods to enlarge the scale of her productions. Heavy, woven fabrics were embedded with cotton to add sculptural density, and works included linen and silk wall pieces, such as those held at the Ford Foundation, New York, or the floor piece *L'Epouse préférée occupe ses nuits* (diam. 4.06 m, 1972; for illustration *see* FIBRE ART). Hicks's technical expertise and versatility allowed her to manipulate fabrics in 'free-fall' structures of chords, discs and tubes, in brilliant colour harmonies that present textile art as a provocative experience, situated between sculpture and performance.

BIBLIOGRAPHY
R. Kauffmann: *The New American Tapestry* (New York, 1968)
M. Levi-Strauss: *Sheila Hicks* (Paris, 1973)
Sheila Hicks (exh. cat., Amsterdam, Stedel. Mus., 1974)

Hidalga (y Musitu), Lorenzo de la (*b* Alava, Spain, 1810; *d* Mexico City, 1872). Spanish architect, painter and teacher, active in Mexico. He graduated as an architect from the Real Academia de Bellas Artes de S Fernando, Madrid, but also worked in painting, sculpture and pastel miniatures. In 1836 he worked in Paris under Henri Labrouste, and in 1838 he went to Mexico City, where he opened a school of drawing. As one of the outstanding

architects in Mexico at the time, he was made an *académico de mérito* of the Academia de S Carlos and its director of architecture. His chief work was the Teatro de Santa Anna (1842–4; later Teatro Nacional; destr. 1901), Mexico City, a Neo-classical building that was for a long time the most costly in the city. The principal façade had a portico with four large Corinthian columns rising through two storeys. He also rebuilt the dome (1845–8) of the side chapel of the church of S Teresa la Antigua, Mexico City. His solution was a Neo-classical dome supported by a double drum, producing interesting light effects in the interior. The windows of the upper drum, concealed by an incomplete vault rising from the lower one, illuminate paintings around the bottom of the dome. Few of his other works have survived.

BIBLIOGRAPHY
E. García Barragán: 'Lorenzo de la Hidalga', *Del Arte: Homenaje a Justino Fernández* (Mexico City, 1977)
J. Urquiaga and V. Jiménez: 'Antecedentes: El antiguo teatro nacional', *La construcción del Palacio de Bellas Artes* (Mexico City, 1984)

MÓNICA MARTÍ COTARELO

Hidalgo, José García. *See* GARCÍA HIDALGO, JOSÉ.

Hidcote Manor Garden. English garden in Gloucestershire, 5 km north-east of Chipping Campden. It was laid out from 1907 by Lawrence Johnston (1871–1958), the owner of Hidcote Manor, who presented the property to the National Trust in 1948. The garden is arranged along an axis independent of the house and consists of a series of compartments connected by walks and steps, with areas of woodland gardens beyond their boundaries. Each compartment is a separate garden with individual planting; they are enclosed by hedges, many of them featuring copper-beech or a variety of foliage types for polychrome effect. Further uses of topiary range from the forms of peacocks and doves through to columns and a 'stilt garden'—a rectangular enclosure bounded by an aerial hornbeam hedge. Numerous compartments, such as the White Garden or the Fuchsia Garden, are profusely planted with flowering shrubs and herbaceous plants, arranged in a deliberately unsystematic manner to contrast with the formal effects created by such features as the lines of hedge, the twin brick summer-houses, steps and gates.

At first little known except to Johnston's coterie of gardening acquaintances, Hidcote became famous in 1948 as the first 'garden of outstanding merit' to be presented to the National Trust. By praising its 'haphazard luxuriance' and describing it as 'a cottage garden on the most glorified scale', Vita Sackville-West, the owner and designer of the gardens at Sissinghurst Castle, Kent, and a popular newspaper columnist on gardening, established Hidcote as an influential model for later gardens in Britain.

BIBLIOGRAPHY
Hidcote, NT Guidebk (London, 1979)
J. Brown: *The English Garden in our Time* (London, 1986)
D. Ottewill: *The Edwardian Garden* (London, 1989), p. 132

BRENT ELLIOTT

Hideo Sugita. *See* EI, KYŪ.

Hideyori. *See* KANŌ, (4).

Hideyoshi. *See* Toyotomi hideyoshi.

Hieber, Hans (*b* ?Augsburg, *c.* 1480; *d* Regensburg, 1521–2). German architect. A Hans Hieber, the son of a brewer, appears in the Augsburg tax records from 1505 onwards, but he gave up his Augsburg citizenship in 1514 and obtained temporary citizenship in Regensburg for four years in 1515; that this Hans Hieber is the same as Hieber the master mason who was active in Regensburg in 1519 is only speculation. Hans Hieber certainly learnt his mason's craft at Augsburg, among other places. There he was one of the highly qualified foremen in the service of Burkhard Engelberg. He may have organized on Engelberg's behalf the building of the Fugger chapel founded in 1506 at St Anna, Augsburg.

After Engelberg's death (1512), Hieber quickly established himself as an independent master. He and his workshop were possibly involved from *c.* 1512 in the alterations and rebuilding of the Fugger houses in the Weinmarkt. His collaboration as a mason on the Dominican nuns' new church of St Katharina (1515/16) is recorded in later sources. In 1515/16 he was also a consultant or planner for the parish church of St Martin at Lauingen an der Donau. In 1519 Hieber was once again working on a design for Augsburg, receiving 12 florins for preparing a wooden model (Augsburg, Maximilianmus.) of the proposed Perlach tower.

At Regensburg Hieber was probably in the service of the very wealthy Trainer family of custom-house officials. Büchner-Suchland's plausible theory that he worked on the building of the Bischofshof at Regensburg *c.* 1520 and on the bishop's castle at Wörth an der Donau is based only on stylistic evidence. Hieber's most important achievement was the design for the Neupfarrkirche, the later pilgrimage church dedicated to Schöne Maria at Regensburg. Until his apparently sudden death Hieber was in charge of the building work at the church, being a respected master. It was not completed in its proposed form, but a wooden model (Regensburg, Stadtmus.; *see* Germany, fig. 4), unique among architectural models of the early 16th century, shows the original design: a hexagonal centralized building with a long chancel and decorated twin towers, which is clear evidence of Hieber's training at Augsburg. The church, like Hieber's proposed design for the Perlach tower, would have combined in a new way the Late Gothic stonework traditions of Engelberg's circle with the decorative forms of northern Italian Renaissance architecture. This 'mixed style' had no direct following, however, perhaps because of Hieber's early death.

BIBLIOGRAPHY

I. Büchner-Suchland: *Hans Hieber: Ein Augsburger Baumeister der Renaissance* (Munich, 1962)

R. H. Seitz: 'Der Augsburger Baumeister Hans Hieber und die Lauinger Stadtpfarrkirche', *Jb. Hist. Ver. Dillingen*, lxxvii (1975), pp. 106–12

Welt im Umbruch: Augsburg zwischen Renaissance und Barock, i (exh. cat., foreword by B. Bushart; Augsburg, Rathaus & Zeughaus, 1980), pp. 126–8

F. Bischoff: *Burkhard Engelberg und die süddeutsche Architektur um 1500: Anmerkungen zur sozialen Stellung und Arbeitsweise spätgotischer Steinmetzen und Werkmeister* (diss., U. Bamberg, 1987)

——: '"Hans Engelberg": Der angebliche Sohn des Burkhard: Ein Beitrag zur Plannungsgeschichte der Augsburger Dominikanerinnenkirche St Katharina und zu Hans Hieber', *Z. Hist. Ver.*, lxxxiii (1990), pp. 9–29

FRANZ BISCHOFF

Hieizanji (Hieizan Enryakukji). *See* Enryakuji.

Hiepes [Yepes], Tomás (*b* ?1610; *d* Valencia, 16 June 1674). Spanish painter. He is recorded as living and working in Valencia from 1643, achieving local fame in his lifetime for his still-life and flower paintings. In a comparatively early pair of small still-lifes with figs and grapes, signed and dated 1649 (both Madrid, Prado), the fruits are delicately painted and depicted with an almost botanical exactitude reminiscent of still-lifes from northern Europe. Hiepes's last known work, *Still-life with Basket of Bread* (1668; Madrid, Prado), typifies the style he used for large and elaborate pictures. It is characterized by studied effects of strong, direct lighting and pronounced shadows. Although the painting recalls contemporary Neapolitan still-lifes in subject-matter and composition, Hiepes's careful depiction of the details of objects and his meticulous technique contrast with the broad brushwork of Neapolitan artists and his Valencian contemporary Miguel March. Hiepes's curious flower paintings are among his most beautiful works. The *Vase of Carnations* (1664; Madrid, priv. col., see 1983 exh. cat., p. 135) illustrates his highly personal interest in the simplified and symmetrical presentation of his subject-matter, in sharp contrast to the flower-pieces of his contemporaries in Madrid. This work also shows the artist's refined sense of colour, his subtle arrangement of the bouquet and concentration on details of the blooms.

BIBLIOGRAPHY

Pintura española de bodegones y floreros de 1600 a Goya (exh. cat. by A. E. Pérez Sánchez, Madrid, Prado, 1983), pp. 134–7 [good plates]

Spanish Still Life from Velázquez to Goya (exh. cat. by W. B. Jordan and P. Cherry, London, N.G., 1995), pp. 118–28

PETER CHERRY

Hierakonpolis [anc. Egyp. Nekhen; now Kawm al-Ahmar]. Ancient Egyptian site, midway between Luxor and Aswan, on the west bank of the Nile, opposite el-kab. Hierakonpolis is the source of many of the most important monuments and artefacts of the Predynastic and Early Dynastic periods (*c.* 6000–2575 BC). Extensive remains of Predynastic settlement and a number of Predynastic cemeteries are scattered along the edge of the low desert to the west of Kawm al-Ahmar, covering an area of about 3 sq. km. The site as a whole has been excavated by a number of different expeditions, including those of J. E. Quibell and F. W. Green (1896–7), John Garstang (1907), J. De Morgan and A. Lansing (1935). The most important monument of the Predynastic period, Tomb 100 or the 'decorated tomb' (dating to the Naqada II period; *c.* 3200 BC), was found by Quibell's expedition. The exact location of the tomb is now lost, but it was a mud-brick lined underground chamber (*c.* 4.5×2.0 m) preserved to a depth of 1.5 m. The tomb was divided by a low half-crosswall in mud-brick in the northern half. The decoration was applied on a mud-plaster ground covered with a yellow ochre wash, and the paintings were executed in yellow, white, red, green, blue

Hierakonpolis, detail of painting in Tomb 100, *c.* 3200 BC; drawing from J. E. Quibell and F. W. Green: *Hierakonpolis*, ii (London, 1902), pl. LXXVA

and black pigments. Below the field of decoration was a blue–black dado capped by a line of red pigment. The painting combines many motifs known from Predynastic pottery decoration, including scenes of hunting and combat, boats and desert animals (see fig.). As is the case with the painted ceramics of the period, the scenes are not structured in any narrative sense, and in all probability the entire composition is symbolic rather than a depiction of actual historical events. One of the most interesting features is a painting of a man holding back two lions. This scene, clearly inspired by the Mesopotamian 'Divine Hero' motif, illustrates the extent to which Egyptian art and society were affected by foreign contacts at this period.

To the west of Tomb 100 was a large mud-brick model funerary palace (60.5×52.5 m), mistaken by early excavators for a fort. It has been dated to the reign of King Khasekhemwy of the 2nd Dynasty (*c.* 2775–*c.* 2650 BC) and is similar to buildings of the first two dynasties known from ABYDOS. To the north of the palace, in the present area of cultivation, lies Kawm al-Ahmar itself, a low mound that consists of the remains of a settlement and a temple dating back to the 3rd Dynasty (*c.* 2650–*c.* 2575 BC). This area was excavated by Quibell and Green in 1897–9. The original temple appears to have consisted of a mound (*c.* 56 m in diameter) revetted with a rough stone wall and possibly built of reed or other perishable materials. The temple was enlarged in brick and stone over the succeeding dynasties. The excavations in the temple precinct uncovered several pits in which various sacred objects and temple furniture were buried. The most important of these caches was known as the 'Main Deposit' and contained a number of important historic and artistic monuments, including the NARMER Palette (Cairo, Egyp. Mus.), the

King Scorpion macehead (Oxford, Ashmolean), life-size copper statues of Pepy I and his son (*see* EGYPT, ANCIENT, §XV, 1) and a statue of a falcon with gold head and crown (both Cairo, Egyp. Mus.). Additional deposits included ivory figurines, stone vases and other maceheads, faience objects and ceramics dating from the Predynastic period to the New Kingdom.

Tombs of various dates, from the Predynastic to the New Kingdom, are situated in the desert around the wadi containing the Early Dynastic funerary palace. The most important of these is the tomb of Horemkawef, a provincial official of the First Intermediate Period (*c.* 2150–2008 BC).

BIBLIOGRAPHY
J. E. Quibell and F. W. Green: *Hierakonpolis*, 2 vols (London, 1900–02)
A. Lansing: 'The Egyptian Expedition, 1934–35', *Bull. Met.* (Nov 1935), pp. 37–45
W. A. Fairservis jr and others: 'Preliminary Report on the First Two Seasons at Hierakonpolis', *J. Amer. Res. Cent. Egypt*, ix (1971–2), pp. 7–68
B. Adams: *Ancient Hierakonpolis* (Warminster, 1974) [with suppl.]
PETER LACOVARA

Hierapolis [now Pamukkale]. Site in south-west Anatolia, Turkey. The town was built on a travertine terrace formed by sediments of hot mineral-rich springs, overlooking the Meander (Turk. Menderes) Valley. It was founded in the 2nd century BC by the Pergamene kings at an important strategic position; it became part of the Roman province of Asia in 133 BC, and during the Empire it was a prosperous trading centre. In the 4th and 5th centuries AD it was the seat of a bishop, and from the 6th century AD of a metropolitan. It gradually fell into decay and was probably abandoned with the coming of the Saljuqs (12th century). The city was first researched in 1898 by a German mission; since 1957 excavations have been directed by the Italians.

1. ARCHITECTURE. The city follows the Hellenistic tradition of main roads crossed at right angles, dividing the urban area into rectangular blocks of 100×250 Attic feet (29.6×70.0 m), each block supposedly containing ten houses. In AD 60 it was destroyed by an earthquake, but in the following years it was rebuilt and enlarged. The main north–south street was extended with stretches ending with monumental gates consisting, as often in Asia Minor, of a triple arch flanked by towers. The north gate, dedicated to the Emperor Domitian (reg AD 81–96), is particularly well preserved.

The Hellenistic theatre, built against the hill, was replaced (2nd century AD) by a new one, four blocks large, in the urban centre. Its cavea is slightly more than semicircular; the stage-building (h. 3.7 m) is richly decorative (see §2 below); its scaenae frons was rebuilt in the early 3rd century AD to include three orders of architecture. In front of the theatre is the Temple of Apollo (3rd century AD on Hellenistic foundations), built over a cave—the Plutonium mentioned by ancient sources—from which noxious gases still exude. Two substantial thermal baths (2nd and 3rd centuries AD) are typical of Asia Minor, with barrel-vaulted halls placed side by side along an east–west axis. Also of interest is an elaborately ornamented nymphaeum (4th century AD). The necropoleis surrounding the city on three sides include several kinds of tomb: the tumulus with round tomb chamber, the temple-tomb, the house-shaped tomb and sarcophagi, some resting on bases. Numerous inscriptions provide important social and historical documentation. At the end of the 4th century AD the city was surrounded with walls, of which towers, gates and posterns are still preserved.

During the Christian period several churches were built, but the most important monument is the martyrium of St Philip the Apostle (late 4th century AD) built on the hill to the north-east of the city on an original plan, perhaps derived from the church of the Holy Apostles in Constantinople (see ISTANBUL, §III, 9(i)). Its vaulted octagonal central space is enclosed by a square (20×20 m), with rooms on the outer and inner faces. The 6th-century AD basilica provided the city's cathedral, which has three naves with matronei, apse, narthex and atrium.

DARIA DE BERNARDI FERRERO

2. SCULPTURE. Since the beginning of the Italian excavations in 1957 an increasing number of statues and architectural reliefs have been discovered in the theatre, the Sanctuary of Apollo and in various other parts of ancient Hierapolis (Pamukkale, Archaeol. Mus. and in situ). Of outstanding significance is the large sculptural complex found in the theatre. Dedicatory and explanatory inscriptions, a series of friezes and more than 20 statues of various sizes make up a sophisticated pictorial programme that, in its relatively complete state of preservation, is comparable to only a few other theatres in Asia Minor. Much of the architectural and sculptural remains date from c. AD 205–11, when the theatre was extensively restored. Subjects include deities of local importance,

personifications of moral and social concepts, local dignitaries, victors of contests in sports and performing arts, and members of the imperial family. Among the statues representing the major cults of Hierapolis are Sarapis-Hades, Apollo, Artemis and Leto. The main friezes above the stage refer to Apollo and Artemis, showing scenes from their lives and from their cults. Further reliefs represent some of the local agonistic events, giving them increased importance by including the emperor Septimius Severus and his family. Fighting gladiators, the hunting of wild animals (venationes), Dionysos among his followers, and medallions (imagines clipeatae) of Eumenes II (reg 197–160 BC) and Attalos II (reg 160–139 BC), the founders of Hierapolis, show themes more commonly used in theatre decoration. The north necropolis, which contains some 1650 sarcophagi, represents the largest existing cemetery of the Classical world. Most sarcophagi are simple stone coffins, but others, many of them belonging to the regionally produced columnar type, are richly decorated.

KALINKA HUBER

BIBLIOGRAPHY
C. Humann and others: Altertümer von Hierapolis, Jb. Dt. Archäol. Inst., suppl. iv (Berlin, 1898)
E. Schneider-Equini: La necropoli di Hierapolis di Frigia: Contributi allo studio dell'architettura funeraria di età romana in Asia Minore, Monumenti Antichi, xlviii, Serie miscellanea, I/ii (Rome, 1972)
P. Verzone: 'Hierapolis di Frigia nei lavori della missione archeologica italiana', Quad. Ric. Sci., c (1978), pp. 391–473
J. Inan and E. Alföldi-Rosenbaum: Römische und frühbyzantinische Porträtplastik aus der Türkei: Neue Funde (Mainz, 1979), nos 44, 223
F. D'Andria and T. Ritti: Le sculture del teatro (1985), ii of Hierapolis: Scavi e ricerche (Rome, 1985–)
T. Ritti: Fonti letterarie ed epigrafiche (1985), i of Hierapolis: Scavi e ricerche (Rome, 1985–)
Hierapolis di Frigia, 1957–1987 (exh. cat., Izmir, Archaeol. Mus.; Ankara; Milan, and elsewhere; 1987)
G. Bejor: Le statue (1991), iii of Hierapolis: Scavi e ricerche (Rome, 1985–)

DARIA DE BERNARDI FERRERO, KALINKA HUBER

Hiernle [Hiernlein; Hirnl; Hirnle], **Karl** [Karel] **Josef** (b c. 1693; bur Prague, 7 Feb 1748). Bohemian sculptor of German origin. His family were active as sculptors in Landshut and later in Mainz. He probably trained in Prague with Matej Václav Jäckel and perhaps in the Brokof family workshop. His earliest work seems to be a stone group of St John Nepomuk between Angels (Žebrák, Town Square) made in 1727 for Wenceslas Square, Prague. His first certain works date from 1728–30, when he decorated Kilian Ignaz Dientzenhofer's church of St Hedwig at Wahlstatt, Silesia (now Legnickie Pole, Poland), supplying stone statues for the façade and wooden statues for the interior. In this commission he employed two kinds of figure types, often used thereafter in his work: one type is ponderous, with softly modelled draperies reminiscent of Classical Roman sculpture; the other has a small head and draperies arranged in numerous sharp folds. Hiernle used the first type in his carved wood decoration of the north altar in the Barnabite convent on the Hradčany, Prague. The features of the second figural type became even more pronounced in the signed stone groups made in 1730 for the Benedictine abbey at Broumov, Bohemia. These include an Annunciation and an Agony in the Garden as well as wood and stone statues of saints. In 1740 Hiernle worked at Břevnov Abbey, near Prague, with Dientzenhofer, carrying out decorations for the gateway, the church and the chapter house. The stone group of *St John Nepomuk between Angels* at Břevnov is also by Hiernle, whose sculptures are in a transitional style between late Baroque and the grace of early Rococo.

BIBLIOGRAPHY
Thieme-Becker
P. Toman: *Nový slovník československých výtvarných umělců* [New dictionary of Czechoslovak graphic and plastic artists] (Prague, 1947)
O. J. Blažíček: *Sochařství baroku v Čechách* [Baroque sculpture in Bohemia] (Prague, 1958), pp. 173–5 [with Fr. and Ger. summaries]

IVO KOŘÁN

Hieronymites [Jeronimites]. Monastic order formed in Spain and Italy in the 14th century. It received papal confirmation in 1373.

1. INTRODUCTION. The original intention of the Spanish founders of the order, Fray Fernando Yáñez de Figueroa and members of the noble Pecha family, was to pursue an ascetic, eremitic life while following the so-called rule of St Augustine. The order swiftly developed a monastic existence, however, based on communal life, and its religious and political importance subsequently came to be reflected in the magnificence of such houses as those of Belém Abbey (*see* BELEM (i) and PORTUGAL, fig. 3), the ESCORIAL, YUSTE MONASTERY or the monastery of

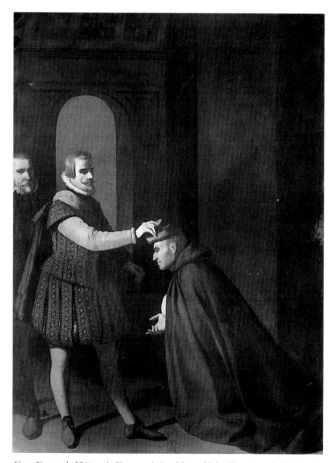

Fray Fernando Yáñez de Figueroa before Henry III by Francisco de Zurbarán, oil on canvas, 2.90×2.22 m, 1639 (Guadalupe, Hieronymite monastery)

GUADALUPE. The eventual privileged position of the order under Philip II of Spain (*reg* 1556–98) was reflected in the King's attempts to use its members to reform houses of other religious orders. In Italy, however, the origins of the Hieronymites lay among the more zealous branches of the Franciscans, and especially members of the Third Order of St Francis, who were inspired by a veneration of St Augustine as well as a concern for St Jerome. They came to believe that Jerome's own eremitic existence had taken the form of a fully professed monasticism. The Italian followers of this tradition initially formed a number of distinct congregations, associated originally with north and central Italy, and also the Gesuati, who were later suppressed but whose name is still recorded by one of the churches of Venice. Individual zealots carried this pristine ideal from Italy to Spain, while in both Italy and Spain nuns' convents associated with the movement also developed.

As Hieronymite houses were established in the Iberian peninsula during the 14th and 15th centuries, their presence was eventually extended to the Spanish empire overseas. While not all the Italian groups inspired by the cult of St Jerome survived beyond the 17th century, Spanish influence also reinforced the Italian movement. The indisputable patristic authority of St Jerome attracted the devotion of ascetics, who would have risked censure within the radical elements of Franciscan reform, and enabled them to avoid the more dangerous disputes over the ideal of poverty in the late medieval and Renaissance Church. The original detachment of the Hieronymites from conspicuous scholarship was seriously modified, however, most notably in the fame of the Escorial with its library as a seat of learning from the end of the 16th century. The example of St Jerome also inspired a prominent Marian cult, and Guadalupe remains known as a centre of Marian pilgrimage.

2. PATRONAGE. In Spain, 45 Hieronymite houses were founded between 1373 and 1516, while in Italy there were over 100 houses by the end of the 16th century. Through endowments some of the Spanish foundations became wealthy landlords (although royal patronage was not without its complications for the order). The community at the Escorial, for example, was especially endowed with extensive properties and feudal rights over arable and other agricultural land throughout Spain. Another lucrative right of the Escorial community was the issuing of liturgical books and the printing of Crusade indulgence bulls, for sale in Spain and subsequently in other Spanish-ruled territories. Many Italian artists were employed in the decoration of the Escorial, especially those working in a Mannerist style. Pellegrino Tibaldi, for example, painted frescoes of *Allegories of the Liberal Arts* in the library (1590–92; *in situ*); by contrast an altarpiece by El Greco depicting the *Martyrdom of St Maurice* (1580–83; Madrid, Escorial, Nuevos Mus.), originally intended for the basilica, was relegated to another part of the building and replaced by a retable on the same subject by Diego de Romulo Cincinnato.

Elsewhere the wealth of some of the Hieronymite houses, while inspiring a movement for stricter observance in some communities, also allowed the commissioning of work from major artists. At Guadalupe, for example, in 1638–9 Francisco de Zurbarán (*see* ZURBARÁN, (1)) provided the sacristy with eight large paintings showing scenes from the lives of Hieronymite monks (e.g. *Fray Fernando Yáñez de Figueroa before Henry III*, 1639; see fig.), as well as three scenes from the *Life of St Jerome* in the adjoining chapel. For the monastery of Buenavista (destr.), near Seville, Juan de Valdés Leal (*see* VALDÉS LEAL, (1)) provided a series of paintings of scenes from the *Life of St Jerome* (1657–8; some in Seville, Mus. B.A.) as well as portraits of Hieronymite nuns and monks, such as *St Paula* (Le Mans, Mus. Tessé) or *Fray Alonso de Ocaña* (Grenoble, Mus. Peint. & Sculp.).

3. ICONOGRAPHY. Depictions of St Jerome were not peculiar to Hieronymite foundations but were naturally found there. Existing medieval traditions were further developed in the Renaissance to show the saint in eremitic penance in the desert (as in the series painted by Valdés Leal for Buenavista and Giovanni Toscani's *The Penitent St Jerome*, 1426–30; Princeton U., NJ, A. Mus), as a monk (as in Zurbarán's series for Guadalupe) or a scholar defending Marian and Trinitarian doctrine by his writings (e.g. Ghirlandaio's *St Jerome in his Study*, 1480; Florence, Mus. Ognissanti). Often he appears accompanied by a lion, according to legend (e.g. Benozzo Gozzoli's *St Jerome Extracts a Thorn from the Lion's Paw*, 1452; fresco, Montefalco, S Francesco), and even when shown as a hermit or monk he was in the later Middle Ages and Renaissance commonly identified by a cardinal's dress, or at least a red hat, adjacent to him, by a retrospective elevation to that Roman dignity. In Counter-Reformation iconography Jerome also appears in visionary response to the call to the Last Judgement (e.g. Zurbarán's *St Jerome*, *c.* 1640; San Diego, CA, Mus. A.), as well as in inspired translation of scripture (e.g. Federico Zuccaro's *St Jerome*, 1586–8, Madrid, Escorial); the authority of the saint, who was responsible for the Vulgate, a translation of the Bible into Latin, was thus reasserted in opposition to Protestant attempts to deploy him as a critic of clerical vice as well as of textual error. His image as a monk was also a counter to Protestant criticism of celibacy and religious vows. A traditional representation also showed his famous dream of the dangers of attachment to Ciceronian Classical learning, and it has been argued that even Piero della Francesca's much-debated *Flagellation* (1458–66; Urbino, Pal. Ducale) refers to this episode (*see* PIERO DELLA FRANCESCA, §I). In the Baroque period the Last Communion of St Jerome was a particularly popular subject, treated for example by Domenichino in a painting of 1614 for S Girolamo della Carità, Rome (*see* DOMENICHINO, fig. 1). Here the iconography was a counter to Protestant attack on the sacramental doctrine of transubstantiation.

Another figure associated with Hieronymite iconography was St Augustine (e.g. Alonso Sánchez Coello's *SS Jerome and Augustine*, 1580; Madrid, Escorial), while at the Escorial the imagery of St Lawrence, to whom the foundation is dedicated, is naturally emphasized, not least in the building's plan (*see* ESCORIAL). Other, supposedly more occult, symbolism in the dimensions or details of the Escorial, in the work there of Juan Bautista de Toledo and Juan de Herrera, has been much disputed. An image particularly associated with Hieronymite nuns' convents is that of St Jerome instructing noble nuns in the scriptures, for example in Zurbarán's *St Jerome Explains the Bible to Paula and Eustochium* (*c.* 1638–40; Washington, DC, N.G.A.), painted for the Hieronymite convent of St Paula, Seville.

BIBLIOGRAPHY

J. de Sigüenza: *Historia de la orden de San Jerónimo*, ed. J. Catalina García, 2 vols (Madrid, 1907–9)

A. Sicroff: 'The Jeronymite Monastery of Guadalupe in 14th and 15th Century Spain', *Collected Studies in Honour of Américo Castro's Eightieth Year*, ed. M. Hornik (Oxford, 1965), pp. 397–422

Studia hieronymiana: VI centenario de la orden de San Jerónimo, 2 vols (Madrid, 1973)

H. Pecha: *Historia de Guadalaxara y como la religión de Sn. Gerónymo en España fue fundada, y restaurada por sus ciudadanos* (Guadalajara, 1977)

G. Kubler: *Building the Escorial* (Princeton, 1982); review by J. Bury in *Burl. Mag.*, cxxiv (1982), pp. 768–9

J. Revuelta: *Los Jerónimos: Fundación y primera expansión, 1373–1414* (Guadalajara, 1982)

J. R. L. Highfield: 'The Jeronimites in Spain: Their Patrons and Success, 1373–1516', *J. Eccles. Hist.*, xxxiv (1983), pp. 513–33

——: 'How Much Did it Cost to Found a Jeronimite Monastery in Late Medieval Spain?' *Studies in Medieval History Presented to R. H. C. Davis*, ed. H. Mayr-Harting and R. J. Moore (London, 1985), pp. 271–81

E. F. Rice jr: *Saint Jerome in the Renaissance* (Baltimore, 1985)

G. Sánchez Meco: *El Escorial y la orden Jerónima* (Madrid, 1985)

R. Mulcahy: 'Federico Zuccaro and Philip II: The Reliquary Altars for the Basilica of San Lorenzo de el Escorial', *Burl. Mag.*, cxxix (1987), pp. 502–9

A. D. WRIGHT

Higashiyama, Kaii (*b* Yokohama, 8 July 1908). Japanese painter. He graduated from the *Nihonga* (Japanese-style painting) Department of Tokyo School of Fine Arts. He studied in Germany in 1933, and he was chosen as one of the first German-Japanese cultural exchange students in the following year, studying art history at Berlin University. After returning to Japan in 1935, he exhibited mainly at the New Bunten and Nitten exhibitions and won recognition with his pure clear landscapes such as *Road* (Tokyo, N. Mus. Mod. A.), *Autumn Canopy* and *Blue Echo* (Tokyo, N. Mus. Mod. A.). He travelled in northern Europe in 1962 and in 1963 exhibited a series of paintings of the spartan scenery of that region; in 1967 he showed the landscape series the *Four Seasons of Kyoto*. He thus captured the landscapes of both Japan and Europe in simple forms and warm elegant colours. He also painted large-scale works including murals for the new Imperial Palace (1965–8) and screen painting for Tōshōdai Temple (1971–81). In 1965 he became a member of the Japan Art Academy and in 1969 he received the Order of Cultural Merit. He exhibited in Europe, China and Japan.

BIBLIOGRAPHY

Higashiyama Kaii zenshū [Complete works of Kaii Higashiyama], 10 vols (Tokyo, 1979–80)

YOSHIKAZU IWASAKI

Higginson, Augustus Barker (*b* Stockbridge, MA, 1866; *d* Santa Barbara, CA, 17 June 1915). American architect. After graduating from Harvard University he studied (1889–91) with the Boston firm of Andrews & Jacques and at the Ecole des Beaux-Arts (1892–4), Paris. On returning to the USA he began his practice in Chicago, where he received various commissions for residential buildings. A representative example is the house (*c.* 1900) of Edwin S. Fechheimer, Winnetka, IL. This wood-shingled house exhibits flowing interior spaces and an interest in the natural colours and textures of building materials. The subtle contrasts of lightly stained pine beams and panels of coarse beige canvas placed between them provide a sophisticated backdrop for the handmade furniture, pottery and brass decorations, the total ensemble being a collaboration between architect and client. The interior and its contents reflect Higginson's involvement in the Arts and Crafts Movement. In 1905 he moved to Montecito, CA, and worked in the Santa Barbara area until his death. He built several houses there in the Arts and Crafts style, including the Higginson House (1905–10) at 1000 Channel Drive, Montecito, and the Coe House (1909), Santa Barbara.

BIBLIOGRAPHY

Macmillan Enc. Archit.; Withey

V. Robie: 'A Bachelor's Cottage in the Country', *House Beautiful*, xvii/5 (1905), pp. 30–31

High Gothic. Stylistic term applied to what is widely considered to be the 'classic' period in Gothic architecture (*see* GOTHIC, §II, 1), which encompassed the series of cathedrals built in northern France between *c.* 1195 and *c.* 1230. In English the term has an added connotation of literal height. As a term in English, High Gothic gained currency only after World War II, although the concept of a classic phase of Gothic architecture is a mid-19th-century idea that developed in the scholarship of several countries, including England and Germany, as well as France. It was Viollet-le-Duc who gave the idea its most thorough-going expression in French studies. Most of the older ideas about the style of the early 13th century and the labels applied to it are conveniently summarized and analysed by Frankl (1960), although both Pevsner and Watkin added significant British scholarship.

The term High Gothic has been applied to exclude as well as to include. At its narrowest it includes the cathedrals of Chartres (*see* CHARTRES, §I, 1), Reims (*see* REIMS, §IV, 1(i)) and Amiens, with the occasional addition of Soissons and the grudging acceptance by some of Bourges (*see* BOURGES, §II, 1(i)). In the broadest sense, as used by Frankl (1962), it includes all Gothic architecture from 1195 to 1300 (see fig.). This usage follows German scholarship, which defines all architecture between the Early Gothic and the LATE GOTHIC, that is, between *c.* 1195 and *c.* 1350, as *Hochgotik*.

The concept of High Gothic, as the peak achievement of Gothic architecture, is based on a value judgement grounded in the scholarship of Italian Renaissance art. Its usage devalues both the architecture that precedes it and that which succeeds it. It gives the concept of the classic a privileged position over both the experiments of Early Gothic and the emphasis on decorative complexity and ingenuity of the RAYONNANT STYLE. In this reading High Gothic is the inevitable product of Early Gothic experiments. The problem is not whether the number of buildings included in it is restricted but whether scholars should continue to endorse a deterministic view based on an organic model and conception of style.

Bony and Grodecki define the term High Gothic, and the limits of its applicability, before they accept its usage,

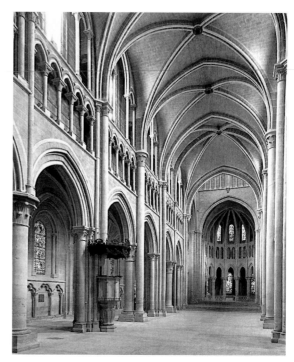

Lausanne Cathedral, interior of the choir, 1190–1232

Bony arguing that it constitutes a 'convenient shorthand term. . .as an element of strict stylistic definition' (p. 246), but not implying any sense of superiority. Equally important is Wilson's argument that continued use of the term tends to stigmatize the Rayonnant by seeing the latter's greater homogeneity as repetitive, over-refined and a symptom of decline. Chartres and the other cathedrals of the early 13th century present coherent and comprehensive images of the Gothic church carried out more or less as they were initially planned, and the exceptionally clear and satisfying linear sequence of development of Chartres and its immediate followers at Reims and Amiens reinforces the organic, deterministic model, ensuring the success of the term High Gothic.

Study of the buildings included in High Gothic, as well as those excluded from it, suggests that the term should be abandoned altogether. By general agreement 'High Gothic' begins with the reconstruction of Chartres following the fire of 1194 and, adhering to traditional datings, continues (occasionally) with Bourges (begun 1195), more often with Soissons (now thought to predate Chartres; *see* SOISSONS, §1), then Reims (begun 1208) and the nave of Amiens (begun 1218–20). It can, however, be argued with equal validity that Chartres, Bourges and Soissons represent the final flowering and full variety of possible solutions available to builders after a half-century of extraordinary architectural experiment. Bony has characterized Chartres as a radical simplification of ideas from a variety of earlier sources. The design of Soissons is another sort of simplification, but one still firmly rooted in previous experiments. Continuing this line of reasoning, Bourges represents the ultimate complexity arising from these same experiments. This leaves Reims Cathedral alone as 'the most complete expression of the classic phase of Gothic architecture' (Branner, 1961), because the design of the nave of Amiens already represents a decided shift in the direction of more complex design and decoration that announces the Rayonnant. Under 'High Gothic' the importance of Chartres is exaggerated; its stylistic impact is largely confined to Reims. The latter's importance as the source for the simplified three-storey elevation incorporating bar tracery windows and double tiers of flying buttresses topped by pinnacles is incontestable, but as a solution the design of Reims is less radical than those adopted at Chartres, Soissons or Bourges. If it is recognized that the elements at Reims constituted refinements to existing techniques and designs, it, too, becomes the product of builders with full knowledge of previous experiments.

Thus it is time to question the whole concept of 'High Gothic' and discard both the deterministic models and concepts of stylistic development based on the organic models, as well as value judgements that enhance one aspect of a style above another. The continued use of the concept of 'High Gothic' prejudices the understanding of the Rayonnant as a distinct and independent architectural development based on different values.

If the notion of the classic moment of the Gothic style, the so-called Chartrain scheme, is discarded in favour of an acceptance that early 13th-century buildings continued the rich tradition of experimentation, all those structures previously relegated to the sidelines and excluded from the 'High Gothic' assume their rightful places as other, more varied accomplishments. A much richer, multi-faceted picture of the architecture of the early 13th century emerges, and recognition of the continued interest in experiment becomes possible.

The only 'dislocation' concerns the cathedrals of Amiens (see AMIENS, fig. 2) and Beauvais (see BEAUVAIS, fig. 3), both of which, but especially the former, are usually included in the High Gothic canon. If it is recognized, however, that both designs exhibit significant shifts in interest from those of Chartres and Reims, then the realization that both herald the new decorative complexity of the Rayonnant becomes possible. Such a reorganization does not give them pre-eminence over later Rayonnant solutions any more than over such precedents as Reims; rather it restores to them a measure of originality.

BIBLIOGRAPHY

P. Frankl: *The Gothic: Literary Sources and Interpretations through Eight Centuries* (Princeton, 1960)

R. Branner: *Gothic Architecture* (New York, 1961)

P. Frankl: *Gothic Architecture*, Pelican Hist. A. (Harmondsworth, 1962)

H. Jantzen: *High Gothic* (London, 1962)

R. Branner: 'High Gothic Architecture', *A Background Survey*, ed. F. Deuchler (1970), ii of *The Year 1200* (New York, 1970–75), pp. 7–32

N. Pevsner: *Some Architectural Writers of the Nineteenth Century* (Oxford, 1972)

W. Dynes: 'Gothic, Concept of', *Dictionary of the History of Ideas*, ed. P. P. Weiner, ii (New York, 1973), pp. 366–74

L. Grodecki: *L'Architecture gothique* (Paris, 1976; Eng. trans., New York, 1977)

D. Watkin: *The Rise of Architectural History* (London, 1980)

J. Bony: *French Gothic Architecture of the Twelfth and Thirteenth Centuries* (Berkeley, 1983)

D. Kimpel and R. Suckale: *Die gotische Architektur in Frankreich, 1130–1270* (Munich, 1985)

C. Wilson: *The Gothic Cathedral: The Architecture of the Great Church, 1130–1530* (London, 1990)

C. Radding and W. Clark: *Medieval Architecture, Medieval Learning: Builders and Masters in the Age of Romanesque and Gothic* (New Haven, 1992)

WILLIAM W. CLARK

Highmore, Joseph (*b* London, 13 June 1692; *d* Canterbury, 3 March 1780). English painter and writer. The son of a coal merchant and the nephew of Thomas Highmore (1660–1720), Serjeant-Painter to the King, he was articled to an attorney on 18 July 1707. Bored with his duties, he attended Kneller's Academy from 1713 and in 1715 abandoned law, setting up as a portrait painter in the City of London. From 1720 he attended the St Martin's Lane Academy, where he was able to study contemporary French styles in art and design, particularly that of Gravelot. He read widely and mastered Brook Taylor's system of perspective (1715). He also attended William Cheselden's anatomy lectures and contributed designs to that author's *Anatomy of the Human Body* (1722). In 1723 Highmore moved to Lincoln's Inn Fields, which lay to the west of the City—a more convenient location for those who needed to find a market for their art. In 1725 he was employed by John Pine (1690–1756) to make 20 drawings for engravings of the recently revived order of the Knights of Bath; among these was his portrait of the *Duke of Richmond* (Goodwood House, W. Sussex). In 1732 he travelled to the Low Countries to study works by Rubens and van Dyck, and two years later he went to Paris, where he saw the art collections at Versailles and in the Palais du Luxembourg and the Louvre, as well as several important private ones. In the following years he secured commissions from the royal family, such as *Queen Caroline of Ansbach* (*c.* 1735; London, Hampton Court, Royal Col.); however, his patrons were more often middle-class sitters.

In 1739 Highmore presented his earlier portrait of *Thomas Emerson* (1731; London, Foundling Hosp.) to the Foundling Hospital upon Emerson's assumption of its Governorship in that year. He also painted for the same institution a rare historical work, *Hagar and Ishmael* (1739; London, Foundling Hosp.), that suggests some uneasiness on his part with problems of space and depth.

In the 1740s Highmore's work was increasingly aimed at a middle-class clientele, his popularity with whom was in part due to his ability to capture a likeness in one sitting and to create an informal composition. This can be seen in his conversation pieces, such as that of *Mr Oldham and his Guests* (1740s; London, Tate), an unpretentious and unflattering depiction of a group of men seated around a table drinking and smoking. His portraits of *An Unknown Man with a Musket* (1745; Cambridge, Fitzwilliam) and *Samuel Richardson* (1747; replica London, N.P.G.) are further examples of the faithful likeness and unpretentious format sought by such sitters. Highmore's series of 12 paintings from *Pamela* (1744; Cambridge, Fitzwilliam; Melbourne, N.G. Victoria; London, Tate) were designed especially to be engraved and to capitalize on the success of Richardson's eponymous novel (1740–41). Although following the serial tradition of Hogarth's *Harlot's Progress* (?destr. 1755) and *Marriage à la mode* (London, N. G.), Highmore's *Pamela* was illustrative rather than inventive, and compositionally simple, not crowded and complex. The depicted narrative was intended to be read at a glance rather than interpreted and considered in the way that

Joseph Highmore: *Pamela and Mr B. in the Summer House*, oil on canvas, 629×756 mm, 1744 (Cambridge, Fitzwilliam Museum)

Hogarth's narratives were. *Pamela and Mr B. in the Summer House* (Cambridge, Fitzwilliam; see fig.) is a typical example of how Highmore used an uncluttered interior setting and the minimum number of figures to make events in the novel immediately identifiable. The engravings of this series, by Antoine Benoist (1721–70) and L. Truchy (1731–64), published on 1 July 1745, enjoyed widespread and immediate popularity.

Highmore exhibited at the Society of Artists and Free Society in 1760 and 1761. He sold the contents of his studio in 1762 and retired to Canterbury with his daughter and son-in-law. In retirement he pursued a second career, that of a writer, which he had begun in 1754 with a critical examination of Rubens's ceiling decorations in the Banqueting Hall, London. In articles written for the *Gentleman's Magazine* Highmore further defended Rubens (1766) and examined colour theory (1778), postulating the idea that pure, unmixed colours would, from a distance, appear to blend. He also wrote a book on Brook Taylor's theory of perspective (1763), and his collection of moral essays (1766) included a consideration of why artists were not the only proper judges of art. His son Anthony Highmore (*d* after 1780) was a landscape painter, whose works were occasionally engraved.

WRITINGS

A Critical Examination of those Two Paintings [by Rubens] on the Ceiling of the Banqueting House at Whitehall (London, 1754)
The Practice of Perspective, on the Principals of Dr Brook Taylor (London, 1763)
Essays, Moral, Religious and Miscellaneous (London, 1766) [incl. some writings on art]
'Remarks on Some Passages in Mr Webb's "Enquiry into the Beauties of Painting"', *Gent. Mag.*, xxxvi (1766), pp. 353–6 [incl. disc. of Rubens]
'A Poetical Epistle to an Eminent Painter', *Gent. Mag.*, xlviii (1778), pp. 525–8 [on colour theory]
E. Johnston, ed.: 'Joseph Highmore's Paris Journal, 1743', *Walpole Soc.*, xlii (1970), pp. 61–104

BIBLIOGRAPHY

Obituary, *Gent. Mag.*, l (1780), pp. 176–9
J. Scobell Armstrong: 'Joseph Highmore: Painter and Author', *Connoisseur*, lxxxvi/350 (1930), pp. 209–19
'Note-books of George Vertue', *Walpole Soc.*, xxii (1933–4)
F. Antal: '*Mr Oldham and his Guests* by Highmore', *Burl. Mag.*, xci (1949), pp. 128–32
Joseph Highmore (exh. cat., London, Kenwood House, 1963)
A. S. Lewis: *Joseph Highmore, 1692–1780* (diss., Cambridge, MA, Harvard U., 1975)
J. W. Goodison: 'Two Portraits by Joseph Highmore', *Burl. Mag.*, lxxii (1983), pp. 125–6

SHEARER WEST

High Tech. Stylistic term applied to the expressive use of modern technology, industrial components, equipment or materials in the design of architecture, interiors and furnishings. It was first employed in print by Joan Kron and Susan Slesin in magazine articles of 1977. High Tech described the then-fashionable style of decoration using out-of-context, brightly coloured elements of industrial design (e.g. factory lamps, warehouse shelving, office chairs, work-benches, duct-work, glass bricks etc) in domestic interiors and shops. In their book *High-Tech: The Industrial Style and Source-book for the Home* (1978), however, Kron and Slesin cited a number of buildings, most notably the Centre Georges Pompidou (1971–7), Paris, by Richard Rogers and Renzo Piano, to add weight to their argument that 'the industrial aesthetic in design . . . is one of the most important design trends today'. By 1980 this building (*see* PARIS, fig. 14) had become the standard exemplar of High Tech architectural design and remained a monument of definition thereafter. The bright colours of its exposed ducts, its transparent escalator tubes hung on the exterior of its boldly exhibited structural system and its general air of technological optimism made it a convincing large-scale demonstration of the Kron and Slesin aesthetic.

In an architectural context, the words 'high technology' had already acquired a different and highly charged polemical meaning—as the opposite of 'low tech' or even of 'appropriate technology'. In the late 1960s and early 1970s so-called 'levels of technology' had become an issue, as environmental awareness, concern for the under-developed areas of the world, fuel crises and cultural pessimism had led many architectural thinkers to abandon the faith in technological progress that had sustained modern architecture since the 19th century and to foresee a more modest and less energy-intensive future. The *Architectural Review* (May 1977) declared a doubt that the world could afford any more buildings like the Centre Pompidou. Six years later, however, the *Architectural Review* devoted an entire issue (July 1983) to High Tech and appeared to have forgotten its doubts and concerns. High Tech had become a respected—if still controversial—tendency in contemporary architecture. Its established leaders were Richard Rogers and Norman Foster; they had been partners briefly (as Team 4) in the mid-1960s, and the outstanding product of that partnership, the prize-winning Reliance Controls Factory (1967) at Swindon, Wilts, was seen as the beginning of a supposed High Tech movement. A respectable ancestry of outstanding buildings was soon traced and included Pierre Chareau's and Bernard Bijvoet's Maison de Verre (1929–32; *see* GLASS, fig. 7), Paris, and the house that the Eames designed for themselves (1948–9) in Pacific Palisades, Los Angeles, as well as major works of engineering back to and including the Eiffel Tower, Paris, and the Crystal Palace (destr.), London. It could also be linked (especially by Foster) to the prestige of recent advanced engineering, as represented by space-vehicles for example.

The controversy surrounding High Tech had three main causes. The first was the jealousy caused by its egregious success, as it fell to Rogers and Foster to design two of the most notable financial buildings of the 1980s: the Hongkong & Shanghai Bank (1985), Hong Kong (Foster Associates; for illustration *see* FOSTER, NORMAN), and the Lloyds of London headquarters (1986; Richard Rogers +

Architects; for illustration *see* ROGERS, RICHARD). The second cause of controversy was that, with this conspicuous success, High Tech seemed to prevail over other movements such as Post-modernism, which had been expected to be the dominant successors to an exhausted Modernism, and the wrath of anti-Modernists was extreme. The third cause of controversy—and one that provoked even those who still maintained faith in Modernism—was that in laying obvious claim to be the true heir to the former Modernist tradition, High Tech as practised seemed to discount the work of the revered masters of the Modern Movement, Gropius, Le Corbusier and Mies van der Rohe, and to establish a lineage that descended from the less celebrated visionaries of the Futurist, Expressionist and Constructivist movements. In its emphasis on precision engineering, transparency and light weight, in what the engineer Frank Newby called its 'structural exhibitionism', in its bright colours and high finishes, in its often intricate and elaborate 'machine' detailing, High Tech departs decisively from Gropius's aesthetic of 'large, compact forms' or Le Corbusier's 'play of volumes assembled in light'.

Although some of the buildings commonly described as High Tech may differ from the International Style in materials and finishes, they do adhere more or less to its compositional preferences for compact rectangular forms in simple abstract relationships, even if they range from the suave, brushed-metal and black-glass headquarters building for Porsche of Great Britain (1964) near Reading, Berks, by the Dewhurst Haslam Partnership, to the startling red-and-yellow, corrugated-metal Provincial Center (1986), Flin-Flon, Manitoba, by IKOY Partnership. Indeed, one of the problems of High Tech as a stylistic label is to identify some central and essential qualities within the wide range of extreme designs that it is currently made to embrace. Other examples of the diversity of High Tech include the remarkable tented structure for the Schlumberger Laboratories (1984), Cambridge, England, by Michael Hopkins and Partners (with the engineer Tony Hunt); the Sainsbury Centre for Visual Arts (1977) at the University of East Anglia, Norwich, a vast airy corrugated metal shed designed by Foster Associates (also with Tony Hunt; for illustration *see* SPACE-FRAME); and the Renault Distribution Centre (1984; see fig.), Swindon, Wilts, also by Foster (with Ove Arup & Partners), which has bright yellow steel supports. At yet another extreme are the galleries of the Menil Collection in Houston, TX, which are filled with natural light controlled by a system of overhead sunshades, fixed and non-mechanical but precisely calculated for the architect, Renzo Piano, by the engineers Peter Rice and Tom Barker, with whom he had worked following the Centre Pompidou.

If there is a theme that unites all these diverse works, it is the 'attitude that assumes that architecture has no further task than to perfect its own technologies', which Alan Colquhoun supposed to be the design philosophy behind the Centre Pompidou. A notable and striking feature of High Tech is the dominance within it of British talent, even outside the British Isles. Although the designer of what is regarded by many as the true successor to the Centre Pompidou, the Cité des Sciences et de l'Industrie (1986) in the Parc de la Villette, Paris, is the French

Norman Foster (with Ove Arup & Partners): Renault Distribution Centre, Swindon, Wiltshire, 1984

architect Adrien Fainsilber, the coloured duct-work, which is the dominant feature of its interior, is the work of a largely British team, and the two gigantic skylights over its central lobby were designed by the London-based partnership of Peter Rice and Ian Ritchie. Examples of the High Tech aesthetic in furniture—also by British designers—include the Omkstack chair (1971) and Graffiti shelving (1983) by Rodney Kinsman (*b* 1943) and Foster's Nomos office furniture (1986) in chromium-plated steel, glass and plastic.

See also TENSION STRUCTURE.

BIBLIOGRAPHY

R. Banham: 'Centre Pompidou, Paris', *Archit. Rev.* [London], clxi/693 (1977), pp. 270–94
J. Kron and S. Slesin: *High-Tech: The Industrial Style and Source-book for the Home* (New York, 1978)
Archit. Rev. [London], clxix/1037 (1983) [issue on High Tech]
G. Bylinsky: *High Tech: Window to the Future* (Hong Kong, 1985)
Space Des., 1 (1985) [issue on High Tech]
C. Davies: *High-Tech Architecture* (New York, 1988)

REYNER BANHAM

High Wycombe. English centre of furniture production. The town is situated in Buckinghamshire near the Chiltern Hills, where there is a plentiful supply of timber, particularly beech. The 'Windsor' chair, with which High Wycombe is particularly associated, was available in the London market *c.* 1720, and London chairmakers drew from the High Wycombe area billets of beech and probably such turned components as legs and stretchers. Turners,

known as 'bodgers', would fell timber and directly convert it on simple pole lathes. Complete chairs were probably being manufactured in the High Wycombe area by the mid-18th century. Furniture workshops first appeared in the town after 1750, using turned components produced by the 'bodgers', making other parts such as the seat and assembling complete chairs for wholesale or retail sale. Four makers were listed in a directory of 1784, three being members of the Treacher family, and in the 1790s William Treacher was offering 'Windsor, dyed and fancy chairs'. Another early maker was Thomas Widgington (*b c.* 1776), and one factory owned by James Gomme was producing cabinet work as early as 1790. A militia return of 1798 lists 58 chairmakers in the borough and parish of High Wycombe and the adjoining village of West Wycombe.

In the 19th century production expanded, and large quantities of chairs were sold in London and the Midlands. Mechanization was introduced to keep pace with demand, and by 1864 one maker was using steam-power. Extensive orders were executed for basic turned chairs: for example, an order for 19,200 chairs was completed in connection with Moody and Sankey revivalist meetings, while in 1874 4000 chairs were ordered from the firm of Walter Skull for St Paul's Cathedral, London. Some firms moved away from simple chairs to items of greater value and prestige and extended their ranges accordingly. One of the leading Victorian manufacturers was Edwin Skull, who by the 1860s was offering 140 different chair designs, which he published in trade catalogues (also produced by other firms from *c.* 1860). In 1884 the firm produced presentation chairs for the Prince and Princess of Wales (later Edward VII and Queen Alexandra), and in 1891 chairs were produced for the wedding of the Duke of York (later George V) and Princess (later Queen) Mary. The firm of William Birch began making chairs in 1840, but by the end of the century they were noted for their range of furniture in the Art Nouveau style, which was exported to Europe and the USA. The firm also had a London factory where semi-finished goods manufactured at High Wycombe could be completed to customer requirements. In 1851 Benjamin North & Sons was established, and by the 1880s it was producing Japanese-style seat-furniture and furniture in a 'new and modified Chippendale' style.

In the 20th century High Wycombe retained its importance. Parker Knoll Ltd started production in 1898, and in 1901 it was commissioned for some 80 'Chippendale' chairs for the liner *Ophir.* In 1928 the German Willy Knoll licensed the firm to use horizontal-coil tension springs, which enabled the production of lighter, fireside chairs, marketed under the name Parker-Knoll. G Plan Ltd developed from a chairmaking firm established by Ebenezer Gomme in the late-19th century. In the 1930s they introduced ranges of furniture using laminated bentwood construction and after World War II were one of the first British manufacturers to market room-dividers and unit furniture. Ercol Furniture Ltd was founded by an Italian immigrant, Lucian R. Ercolani. Using traditional materials and forms popular in the Wycombe trade, Ercolani redesigned them for mass production. In the 1950s and 1960s Gomme, Ercol and Parker-Knoll were the leading companies in mass-producing ranges that reflected the taste of the period and were retailed by high street independents and such chain stores as Times Furnishing. The Wycombe Chair Museum, High Wycombe, has a representative collection of locally made chairs.

BIBLIOGRAPHY

L. Weaver: *High Wycombe Furniture* (London, 1929)
L. J. Mayes: *History of Chairmaking in High Wycombe* (London, 1960)
B. D. Cotton: *The English Regional Chair* (Woodbridge, 1990)

BRIAN AUSTEN

Hijikata, Teiichi (*b* Gifu Prefecture, 25 Dec 1904; *d* Kanagawa Prefecture, 23 Dec 1980). Japanese critic and museum official. In 1930 he graduated in art history from the University of Tokyo. He worked from 1942 in Beijing for the Kohoku Sōgō Chosa Kenkyūjo (Research centre for the study of synthesis in Northern China) but in 1949 became a professor at Chiba Technical College, Narashino. In 1951 Hijikata became Associate Director of the Kanagawa Prefectural Museum of Modern Art in Kamakura, and in 1965 Director. He also became Director of the Zenkoku Bijutsukan Kaigi (Congress of Japanese museums) in 1969. He was involved in the planning and judging of the Kōtarō Takamura and Teijirō Nakahara prizes awarded for the promotion of modern sculpture in Japan, and in curating the biennial *Gendai chōkoku ten* (Exhibition of modern sculpture), held first in Ube in 1965 and in Kobe in 1968. In 1966 he became a specialist member of the Bunka Zai Hogo Shingikai (Society for the protection of cultural treasures). He wrote numerous works including a monograph on the Japanese painter *Kishida Ryūsei*

(1941), as well as studies of Bruegel (1963) and modern Japanese art (1966). He received medals from Norway, Belgium, France, Italy and Poland for his service to the international art world.

WRITINGS

Kishida Ryūsei (Tokyo, 1941)
Buryugeru [Bruegel] (Tokyo, 1963)
Nihon no kindai bijutsu [Modern Japanese art] (Tokyo, 1966)
Hijikata Teiichi chosakushū [Collection of writings by Teiichi Hijikata] 12 vols (Tokyo, 1976–8)

BIBLIOGRAPHY

Kaikan 40 shūnen kinen 40nen no ayumiten [Commemoration of the 40th anniversary of the opening of the museum—exhibition of 40 years' progress] (exh. cat., essay by S. Sasaki; Kamakura, Kanagawa Prefect. Mus. Mod. A., 1991), pp. 21–4, 25–8

YASUYOSHI SAITO

Hikisch, Rezső (*b* Budapest, 3 Sept 1876; *d* Budapest, 28 June 1934). Hungarian architect. After graduating from the Architectural High School, Budapest, he studied (1896–9) under Paul Wallot at the Akademie der Bildenden Künste in Dresden and worked for a year in Munich with Theodor Fischer. After a study trip to Paris and Italy he returned to Budapest in 1902, where he was employed in the office of Rezső Ray (1874–1938) until he opened his own office in 1905. His first significant work was the multi-purpose town hall (*c.* 1906; with Henrik Kotál), Kiskunhalas, which reflects the influence of Hungarian Secessionism in its characteristic broken cornice and gable, embroidery-pattern plasterwork and arrow loops. A high sturdy tower dominates the picturesque grouping of the building's masses. In contrast his elementary school (1909) on Szentendrei Street, Budapest, two-storey with gables and a high roof, is influenced by the objectivity and simplicity of Fischer's designs such as the school building (1902–4), Elisabethplatz, Munich. The Hotel Astoria (1913), Budapest, reveals a classicizing, monumental conception of form. On the ground floor Hikisch placed an elegant marble-columned foyer, and there is a horizontal 'girdle' of windows on the first floor. The balustraded window balconies on the second, third and fourth floors are separated by huge pilasters, above which is a massive cornice. The moderate use of neo-classical ornament, such as ionic columns and key-pattern string courses, characterizes his later work, including the block of small flats (1927; with Ferenc Paulheim), Bécsi Street, Budapest, and the Fenyő Villa (*c.* 1930), Városmajor Street, Budapest. His tomb designs and monuments express a love of celebratory, grand forms, with subtle classical details, as in his several designs (1903–32; unexecuted) for a monument to *Queen Elizabeth, Empress of Austria and Queen of Hungary.*

BIBLIOGRAPHY

F. Vadas: 'Hikisch Rezső, 1876–1934', *Magyar Építőmüveszet*, vi (1984), pp. 54–9
N. Pámer: *Magyar építészet a két világháboru között* [Hungarian architecture between the two World Wars] (Budapest, 1986)

ÁKOS MORAVÁNSZKY,
KATALIN MORAVÁNSZKY-GYÖNGY

Hilberseimer, Ludwig (Karl) (*b* Karlsruhe, 14 Sept 1885; *d* Chicago, IL, 6 May 1967). American urban planner, architect, critic and teacher of German birth. After studying at the Technische Hochschule, Karlsruhe, with Friedrich Ostendorf and Hermann Billing (1906–11), he moved to Berlin. His early projects, for example for an opera house in Berlin (1911), followed Ostendorf's neo-classical lines. During World War I he was first an assistant and later in control of a government department that laid the plans for aircraft workshops and hangars in Staaken and for a flying school and flight research institute in Müritzsee.

Hilberseimer's style changed after 1918 from neo-classical to Elementarism in which, with the abandonment of classical details, buildings are combined in blocks, are given an uncluttered structure and are organized uniformly and, in the preference for natural materials such as brick over the use of colour, can often create a somewhat barren impression. In 1919 he joined the Novembergruppe and Arbeitsrat für Kunst and in 1924 Der Ring, and he embarked on a series of critical writings on the fine arts, arts and crafts, and architecture, primarily for the *Sozialistischen Monatshefte*, *Bauwelt* and *Die Form*. From 1923 the problems associated with large cities became his general area of concern and the subject of his book *Grossstadtbauten* (1925). His designs for suburbs and studies of the problems of the city were exhibited at the Grossen Berliner Kunstausstellung in 1924 and 1928; he built a detached family house for the Werkbundausstellung, Weissenhofseidlung, Stuttgart (1927), the Rheinlandhaus, a shop building on the Mehringdamm, Berlin (1927), and an experimental block of flats at 118–122 Anna Seghers Strasse, Aldershof (1929–30).

Hilberseimer's contribution to the debate on modern city planning was influential. His plans for a Berlin suburb consisted of an open block development made up of residential housing on the two long sides, connected by a short low section at one end that was designated for shops. With the aim of reducing rush-hour congestion he also designed a vertical, high-rise metropolis in which the residential area was housed in a 15-storey building, provided with its own pedestrian spaces and thoroughfares, and built directly above the five-storey commercial area comprising whole blocks and served by its own vehicular access. In *c.* 1930 he undertook a critical examination of his own suburb and metropolis system of mixed development, in which ten-storey 'arbour houses' for single people and married couples, distributed singly or in pairs, were placed within a spread of low buildings in the form of corner houses or terraces designed for families with children. By dovetailing such mixed developments into industrial zones he succeeded in forming metropolitan units. Further such units, separated by open spaces, made up the city. In 1932, under the direction of Ludwig Mies van der Rohe, he took over the Department of House Building and Urban Development at the Bauhaus, Dessau, where he had taught design since 1928. With students from the Bauhaus he carried out a climatic, social and economic analysis of Dessau and drew up a planning model for the city (1932).

Hilberseimer emigrated to the USA in 1938, where he was given a professorship in city and regional planning at the Illinois Institute of Technology, Chicago, again under Mies van der Rohe; in 1955 he assumed direction of the newly founded Department of City and Regional Planning

there. In the USA he continued his theoretical work on urban planning, using Chicago as his chief example. He also worked as a planner on specific commissions with practising architects, such as Alfred Caldwell (Evergreen I and II City Redevelopment Plans, Chicago, 1938–50) and Mies van der Rohe (Hyde Park, Chicago, 1956).

WRITINGS

Grossstadtbauten (Hannover, 1925)
The New City (Chicago, 1944)
The Nature of Cities (Chicago, 1955)
Contemporary Architecture: Its Roots and Trends (Chicago, 1963)

BIBLIOGRAPHY

R. F. Malcolmson: 'Elementos de la nueva ciudad: La obra de Ludwig Hilberseimer', *Hogay & Archit.* (May–June 1968)
D. Spaeth: *Ludwig Karl Hilberseimer: An Annotated Bibliography and Chronology* (New York and London, 1981)

KARL-HEINZ HÜTER

Hild, József (*b* Pest [now Budapest], 8 Dec 1789; *d* Pest, 6 March 1867). Hungarian architect. The son of the architect János Hild (*b* Bohemia; *d* Pest, 22 March 1811), he is thought to have attended the Akademie der Bildenden Künste, Vienna. He worked for a few months in Karl Moreau's office in Vienna and in 1816 made a study tour of Italy. On his return he established his practice in Pest. From the 1820s, operating a large office, he built a great number of Neo-classical residential blocks in Pest, thereby transforming the appearance of substantial parts of the city with what was virtually a new building type in Hungary. Typically Hild's blocks are built close together in a row and comprise several storeys, sometimes as many as four, with open galleries on each floor overlooking a central courtyard. They often contain spacious and ornate entrance passages and wide staircases. Those with pedimented fronts appear more stately than those with simple façades.

During the 1830s Hild became the foremost designer of churches in Hungary. Eger Cathedral (1831–7), an axial building, on an imposing hill-top site, has a Corinthian colonnade on its west façade, a dome, and two campanile-like towers on either side of the chancel. Other ecclesiastical buildings he designed include the small parish church (1832–4) at Lovasberény, the centrally planned Calvinist church (from 1835) at Cegléd and perhaps also the domed cathedral (1830–37) of Szatmárnémeti (now Satu Mare, Romania). In 1840, after János Packh's death, Hild was put in charge of the construction of the Archiepiscopal Cathedral of St Adalbert (1822–69) at Esztergom, half completed by that time (*see* ESZTERGOM, fig. 2). His chief contribution is the dome, which has a colonnade surrounding its tall drum. The Neo-classical St Stephen's Basilica (designed 1845–7) in Pest was to have been a centrally planned structure of a grandeur similar to Esztergom. Work began in 1851 but in 1868, in the course of construction, its dome collapsed. (It was completed later, to designs by Miklos Ybl and József Kauzer, in a different style.) The Hermina Chapel (1842–56) in Pest, a small, compact building, is an early example of the Gothic Revival style in Hungary.

Hild's secular buildings include the county hall (1838–42), Eszék (now Osijek, Croatia), which is remarkable for its projecting central pavilion decorated with engaged columns. The so-called Lloyd Palace by Hild (1827–30;

destr. 1945), built in Pest for the corporation of the merchants of the city, was adorned with an elegant Ionic portico and was considered his finest building in the city. His other large buildings in Pest include the palatial A. Valero silk factory (1839; now the Ministry of Defence), the Császár Baths (extended 1841–5), which had rows of Doric columns on its courtyard wings (destr. *c*.1990), and the Maria-Theresa barracks (1845–8; now Council offices), which originally had crenellated parapets on its projections. He also designed inns and small porticoed villas, situated mainly in the hills west of Budapest, and country houses. The country house (1835–41) of Count Sándor Teleky at Gyömrő is an oblong block with an Ionic portico. Hild was among the most prolific Hungarian architects of the first half of the 19th century and, with Mihály Pollack, one of the most accomplished.

BIBLIOGRAPHY

A. Zádor and J. Rados: *A klasszicizmus építészete Magyarországon* [The architecture of Neo-classicism in Hungary] (Budapest, 1943)

J. Rados: *Hild József: Pest nagy építőjének életműve* [József Hild: the work of the great architect of Pest] (Budapest, 1958)

A. Zádor: 'La fortuna del Palladio in Ungheria', *Boll. Cent. Int. Stud. Archit. Andrea Palladio*, xxii/1 (1986), pp. 289–96

JÓZSEF SISA

Hildburgh, Walter Leo (*b* New York, 1876; *d* London, 25 Nov 1955). American collector and art historian. He was a man of private means who travelled widely before settling in London in 1912. Initially trained as a scientist, he turned to the arts and from the beginning of the 20th century was an avid collector with wide-ranging interests and was one of the greatest benefactors of the Victoria and Albert Museum, London, especially in the fields of sculpture and metalwork. Perhaps his most significant and conspicuous gift to the museum was his entire collection of over 260 English medieval alabaster carvings, which he donated on his 70th birthday in 1946. Hildburgh's collections formed the starting-point for his numerous publications and for his many lectures presented to the Society of Antiquaries of London, of which he became a Fellow in 1915. He added greatly to the research of St John Hope and Philip Nelson on English alabasters, publishing his findings almost every year from 1916 until his death. His only book, on Spanish medieval enamels, made a less profound contribution to scholarship. Although his writings on English medieval alabasters and medieval metalwork were his most important, he had an unusually broad knowledge: his writings on Italian art included articles on Donatello, Cellini, Francesco Bertos, Pietro da Barga and—more esoterically—Italian wafer-irons of the 15th and 16th centuries. He also wrote on Chinese art, the carving of various hardstones and amber, and more general subjects, such as 'The Evil Eye in Art'. He also had a deep knowledge of folklore, about which he published many papers, especially in connection with amulets. Among his other accomplishments, he was a figure-skater of international standard.

WRITINGS

Medieval Spanish Enamels (London, 1936)

BIBLIOGRAPHY

Obituary, *The Times* (28 Nov 1955), p. 13

J. Pope-Hennessy: Obituary, *Burl. Mag.*, xcviii (1956), p. 56

F. Cheetham: *English Medieval Alabasters: With a Catalogue of the Collection in the Victoria and Albert Museum* (Oxford, 1984) [esp. pp. 342–3 for writings list]

PAUL WILLIAMSON

Hildebrand, Adolf von (*b* Marburg, 6 Oct 1847; *d* Munich, 18 Jan 1921). German sculptor, theorist and writer. As a boy he developed an interest in drawing and, after spending two years at the Kunstgewerbeschule in Nuremberg, he went to Munich in 1866 to study under the sculptor Kaspar Clemens Zumbusch. In 1867 he accompanied Zumbusch on a trip to Verona, Florence and Rome. In Rome he made the acquaintance of the philosopher and art theorist Konrad Fiedler and the painter Hans Reinhard von Marées, both of whose 'ideal-formalist' theories of art were to be of great importance to him. At the end of 1869 the three friends met again in Berlin and in 1872 Hildebrand moved to Italy, which became his second home. In 1873 he assisted Marées in the decoration of the Stazione Zoologica in Naples, devising the designs for the frieze and pilasters, collaborating with him on the decorative paintings and producing the portrait busts of the scientists *Charles Darwin* and *Carl Ernst von Baer* (both *in situ*). In 1873, at the Weltausstellung in Vienna, he exhibited successfully for the first time, showing a portrait bust of *Theodor Heyse* (marble; Berlin, Alte N.G.). As a result, in 1874 he was able to buy the former monastery of S Francesco di Paola near Florence and to install a studio for Marées and himself, though in 1875 Marées returned to Rome.

It was in the Renaissance sculpture of Florence, with its references to antique guidelines, that Hildebrand found a point of reference for fashioning his image of man. The marble portrait of *Julia Brewster* (1881; Cologne, Wallraf-Richartz-Mus.) quite clearly alludes to Verrocchio's *Woman Holding Flowers* (*c*.1480; Florence, Bargello). However, the fact that arms and hands are included in Hildebrand's composition is exceptional. It is repeated on only one other occasion, in the portrait of *Frau Fiedler* (1882; Hamburg, Ksthalle). As a rule his busts end at the neck or in a curtailed breastplate with no arms. From 1878 to 1883 he worked on a *Bacchus* group that he eventually abandoned, though it gave rise to *The Net Carrier* (marble, 1886; Munich, Neue Pin.; see fig.). The impact that Marées's powerful personality had made on him is seen in this sculpture: the naked figure of a fisherman would be inconceivable had Hildebrand not studied the model of Marées's fishermen in the fresco on the north wall of the Stazione Zoologica. In its sketchlike quality, so different from his later work, *The Net Carrier* reflects another Florentine influence, that of the sculptures of Michelangelo, particularly his *Brutus* (1537–8; Florence, Bargello). Hildebrand became known to a wider public in Germany when an exhibition of his works was held in Berlin in 1884. In 1887 he visited Greece with Fiedler and soon afterwards saw Marées's triptychs in Rome (e.g. *The Hesperides*, 1884–7; Munich, Neue Pin.). These two events inspired him to create such works as the three-part relief *Archers and Amazons* (1887–8; cement version; Cologne, Wallraf-Richartz-Mus.). He won first prize in 1889 for a national monument to *Emperor William I*, but the project was never realized owing to the opposition of William II.

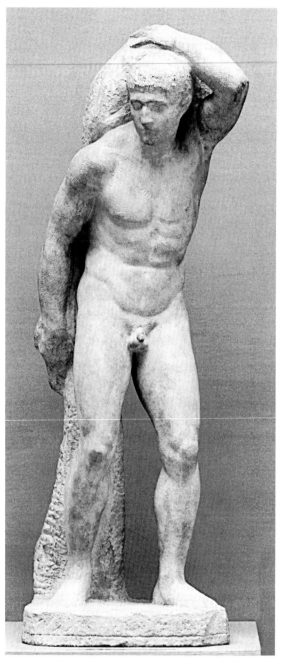

Adolf von Hildebrand: *The Net Carrier*, marble, h. 1.45 m, 1886 (Munich, Neue Pinakothek)

From 1891 until the beginning of World War I he lived alternately in Florence and Munich, where by 1897 he had built a house to his own design.

In 1891 he received his first large commission, for the Wittelsbach Fountain (Lenbachplatz, Munich; partly destr.). He had begun the designs for this complex in 1889, and it was completed in 1895. It depicts two allegorical equestrian groups representing the destructive and beneficent power of water and shows his heavy debt to Bernini's designs for Roman fountains. It is, however, less important for its iconography than for its concept of town planning. The fountain is a harmonious and successful integration of sculpture and architecture with their surroundings. With this work he finally achieved general recognition as an artist, and this was reflected in numerous commissions for other fountains such as the Reinhard Fountain (1903) in Strasbourg (removed 1919) and *Father Rhine and his Daughters* (1921–2) in Cologne. He also executed numerous monuments (e.g. *Johannes Brahms*, bronze, 1898; Meiningen, Schlosspark) and portrait busts (e.g. *Otto Back*, 1904; Strasbourg, Mus. B.-A.).

Hildebrand, along with Max Klinger, was the most important sculptor in Germany during the reign (1888–1918) of William II. In the final decades of the 19th century and at the beginning of the 20th he exerted a considerable influence on the art world and particularly on a number of art scholars such as Wölfflin, both through his extensive oeuvre and his essay *Das Problem der Form in der bildenden Kunst*. First published in Strasbourg in 1893 and reprinted many times, this essay represents the theoretical basis of his work. His insights into the process of artistic creation were imbued with the philosophy of German idealism. Central to his thinking was the concept of form, which starts from reality but simplifies it. Like Fiedler and the literary critic Francesco De Sanctis (1817–83), he assumed that chaos preceded form, which explains his rejection of Impressionism as 'apparent chaos'. The term 'art' he understood to mean the completed form that has its ultimate expression in relief or outline. As his guiding principle of artistic achievement he followed the tradition derived from Greek antiquity. A precondition of artistic creativity was the combining of perception with the inner idea of the artist. Thus, the 'correct' copying of nature is contrasted with the 'true' picture given by art. Ideally, truth is revealed as absolute form, independent of content. In practice, Hildebrand was not fully able to meet the demands he placed on himself though in art history his ideas led to a formalist attitude to art that culminated in the writings of Wölfflin. For a long time Hildebrand was seen as representing the antithesis of Rodin, who managed to make an enduring impression on a younger generation of artists, even in Germany. With the advent of modernism in the early 20th century Hildebrand's reputation went into a sharp decline. The declared aim was again to create sculpture in the round that could be viewed from many angles, and this was at odds with his call for the elaboration of a surface image with a requisite fixed viewing point for the observer. Finally, the art ideologists of National Socialism adopted him as one of the forefathers of their pseudo-classical monumental sculpture. Even so, no-one today would concur with the annihilating assessment of the sculptor Rudolf Belling, two generations younger than Hildebrand, who stigmatized his work and his writing as 'an all-time low in sculpture' (W. Nerdinger: *Rudolf Belling und die Kunstströmungen in Berlin, 1918–1923* (Berlin, 1981), p. 217).

WRITINGS

Das Problem der Form in der bildenden Kunst (Strasbourg, 1893, rev. 5/1905; Eng. trans. New York, 1907)

B. Sattler, ed.: *Adolf von Hildebrand und seine Welt: Briefe und Erinnerungen* (Munich, 1962)

H. Bock, ed.: *Adolf von Hildebrand: Gesammelte Schriften zur Kunst* (Cologne and Opladen, 1969)

BIBLIOGRAPHY

H. Wölfflin: 'Adolf von Hildebrand zu seinem 70. Geburtstag', *Kst & Kstler*, xvi (1918), pp. 6–20; also in *Kleine Schriften* (Basle, 1946), pp. 89–99

J. Wittstock: 'Der Wittelsbacher Brunnen in München', *Oberbayer. Archv*, ci (1976), pp. 7–67

A. Haas: *Adolf von Hildebrand: Das plastische Porträt* (Munich, 1984) [list of works]

SEPP KERN

Hildebrandt, Eduard (*b* Danzig, Pomerania [now Gdańsk, Poland], 9 Sept 1818; *d* Berlin, 25 Oct 1869). German painter. He first studied painting in Danzig as his father had done and in 1838 he went to Berlin, where he was refused admission at the Akademie der Künste by Johann Gottfried Schadow because of insufficient artistic talent. He then became a pupil of the marine painter Wilhelm Krause (1803–64). In 1840 he undertook study trips to Scandinavia, England and Scotland, and the following year he went to Paris. He spent six months in the studio of Eugène Isabey, learning his technique of painting in watercolour. This was a formative period for his artistic development, and Isabey's influence would persist in his later oils and watercolours. While in Paris he painted mainly landscapes but also harbour scenes and seascapes. In 1843 he returned to Berlin, where he met Alexander von Humboldt (1769–1859), with whom he enjoyed a close friendship. Through Humboldt, he received a commission from Frederick William IV to paint a view of Rio de Janeiro (the *Bay of Rio de Janeiro*, 1844; Berlin, Alte N.G.), and he arrived there in 1844, using the city as a base for further explorations of Brazil. He returned to Germany by way of Boston, Philadelphia, New York, Buffalo and Niagara Falls, bringing with him a portfolio of *plein-air* studies in watercolour, and pencil and chalk (e.g. *Landscape with River and Mountains*, 1844; Berlin, Alte N.G.). These consist of panoramas of towns; views of colonial buildings, harbours and native settlements; landscapes and genre scenes; and studies of the inhabitants as well as a few of plants and fish. From sketches done in South America he executed a number of paintings (e.g. *Sunset at Rio de Janeiro*, 1851; Hamburg, Ibero Amerika Ver., on loan to Hamburg, Ksthalle), paying utmost attention to the effects of light in nature.

The light effects he encountered in Brazil inspired him to study them in other parts of the world as well. In 1847 he travelled to England, visited Scotland and then journeyed to Madeira, the Canary Islands, Spain and Portugal, returning to Berlin in 1849. In 1851–2 he was in Italy, Egypt, Syria, Palestine, Turkey and Greece. Four years later he made an expedition to the North Cape to observe the midnight sun and other light phenomena in the Arctic, where he painted several watercolours, including *Glacier Landscape near Tromsoe* (1856; Berlin, Alte N.G.). In 1862 he embarked on a voyage round the world, visiting India, Ceylon, China and Japan and staying for a short time in Mexico and Panama. After his return to Berlin in 1864 he held an exhibition of 300 watercolour studies from his trip. A selection of these was chromolithographed and published in three volumes as *Reise um die Erde* (Berlin, 1867). On the advice of Humboldt, William I bought a large number of Hildebrandt's travel studies. He also

commissioned paintings from him and awarded him the order of the Roter Adler.

Hildebrandt was principally concerned with the rendering of memorable light effects, and it is this that distinguishes him from other German painters of coastal and marine scenes. He also had a strong tendency to cultivate contrasts and to dissolve forms with his brushstrokes. His major artistic achievement, however, was as a painter of such distant lands as South America and northern Scandinavia. His work was highly regarded by his contemporaries, and soon after his death in 1869, Fanny Arndt published an extensive study of his life and work. Many of his watercolours and drawings are in the collections of the Staatliche Museen, Nationalgalerie, Berlin. His brother, Fritz Hildebrandt (1819–55), was a marine painter.

BIBLIOGRAPHY

F. Arndt: *Eduard Hildebrandt, der Maler des Kosmos* (Berlin, 1869)

Eduard Hildebrandt: Aquarelle, Zeichnungen aus Beständen der National-Galerie von der Sowjetunion 1958 übergeben (exh. cat. by K.-H. Janola, Berlin, Alte N.G., 1959)

R. Löschner: *Lateinamerikanischen Landschaftsdarstellungen der Maler aus dem Umkreis von Alexander von Humboldt* (diss., Berlin, Tech. U., 1976)

S. TRÄGER

Hildebrandt, Johann Lukas [Lucas; Jean Luca] **von** (*b* Genoa, 14 Nov 1668; *d* Vienna, 16 Nov 1745). Austrian architect. With his rival, Johann Bernhard Fischer von Erlach, Hildebrandt was a leading innovator of independent Baroque architecture within the German-speaking lands. His works quickly reached and then surpassed contemporary international standards. Unable to make his mark at court in competition with Fischer, he became the architect of the aristocracy, developing an attractive, decorative style that was moving away from Roman High Baroque and anticipating French Rococo. Unlike his rival he had no ambitions as an architectural theorist; he made practical architecture his sphere, and his patrons valued his adaptability. At the same time his field of action was larger than Fischer's: he received commissions not only from the nobility, clerics and occasionally the imperial family, but also from the wealthy middle classes. During his many journeys of inspection he maintained contact with the architecture of areas with differing artistic heritages; the architecture of Bohemia and Lower Franconia as well as that of Austria was significantly influenced by him.

1. Early work, before 1713. 2. Mature work, from 1713.

1. EARLY WORK, BEFORE 1713. He was the son of a German officer in the Genoese army, and he trained with Carlo Fontana (iv) and Colonel Cerutti of the Engineering Corps in Rome as a military and civil architect. During 1695–6 he took part in three of Prince Eugene of Savoy's campaigns in Piedmont as a volunteer engineer, and there is documentary evidence that by the end of 1696 he was in Vienna. He worked for noble patrons there from 1697 and two years later applied unsuccessfully for the post of Court Architect. In 1700 he was, however, appointed Imperial Court Engineer. From 1704 Hildebrandt collaborated on drawing up a map of Vienna and the surrounding area. In 1711 he took charge of the Imperial Office of Works (Hofbauamt), but in 1713 he was obliged to

relinquish this position to his rival, Fischer von Erlach. Ennobled in 1720, he was promoted three years later to Chief Court Architect on the death of Fischer von Erlach, but the equally influential post of Senior Court Engineer went to Fischer's son, Joseph Emanuel. Hildebrandt was employed mainly by Prince Eugene, the Harrach family and Prince Bishop Friedrich Karl von Schönborn, and, by the time Maria-Theresa came to the throne in 1740, his title of Chief Court Architect no longer accurately reflected his waning participation in building projects at court.

In his capacity as building inspector for the Austrian estates of the Schönborn family, Hildebrandt was usually involved in several projects simultaneously, some of them at considerable distances from one another. He thus travelled a great deal from 1699, making journeys to Franconia, Bohemia, Moravia and Hungary. Troubled by epilepsy and later in life by poor eyesight, he also had family problems and intermittent financial difficulties. In his rivalry with Fischer von Erlach he revealed an extremely quarrelsome personality; after he was ennobled and so raised above the normal social standing of an architect, he in turn was arrogant in his dealings with Balthasar Neumann.

Hildebrandt's first design drawings predate his work as a military engineer; they show a *Convent Building for S Maria di Carignano in Genoa* (from *c.* 1690–95; see Grimschitz, 1959, pls 1–6). It is possible to see in them the influence of Fontana, and such details as the gables (in the style of Francesco Borromini) on the windows of the east façade (rev. design) are generally reminiscent of the architecture of Roman High Baroque. The first large commission he carried out in Vienna, the Gartenpalais Mansfeld-Fondi (begun 1697; now Palais Schwarzenberg; see fig. 1), is also the first documented project by him and the main work from his early period as a creative architect. The drawings of it that survive show the direction he was to follow in later projects. Faced in this instance with a site directly outside the city walls, Hildebrandt experimented with 'thinking in wide open spaces' (Grimschitz), an exercise already familiar to him from his military experience. The palace and its ancillary buildings occupy the entire width of the deep site; the curving *cour d'honneur* near the entrance faces towards the town, and the gardens lie behind the palace on rising ground. The *cour d'honneur* elevation of the main building has two slightly inflected end wings in four bays flanking a seven-bay central tract, from the middle of which juts an arcaded portico approached by two ramps. The main storey and a mezzanine floor of the *corps de logis* are articulated by a giant order of Ionic pilasters standing on plinths, which frame the fenestration of a podium floor. A second mezzanine is lit by windows inserted in the frieze of the entablature, and above this is an attic. In the centre a circular crown rises above the attic storey indicating the Festsaal; this convex element of the composition acts as a counterpoise to the concave shape of the ramps running up to the entrance portico in front, and softens the horizontality of the façade. On the garden side a central convex projection indicates the position of the Festsaal. When the Gartenpalais Mansfeld-Fondi passed into the hands of Prince Schwarzenberg in 1716, Fischer von Erlach made certain alterations to it, inserting two rows each of three arched windows between the double pilasters of the curved projection and allowing the heads of the top row to protrude into the entablature. The effect of contrast on the exterior of the building was further heightened by this addition, and more light entered the interior. The concept of a curvilinear feature framed between rectangular blocks

1. Johann Lukas von Hildebrandt: Gartenpalais Mansfeld-Fondi (now Palais Schwarzenberg), Vienna, begun 1697

may derive from Guarino Guarini's Palazzo Carignani, Turin, which Hildebrandt had had the opportunity of studying. Fischer von Erlach, too, had used it, with an articulation closer to Guarini's, at the University Church (1694–1707), Salzburg.

Guarini's influence on Hildebrandt can be seen particularly clearly in the Dominican church of St Laurenz (begun 1699) at Jablonné v Podještědí (formerly Deutsch-Gabel), Bohemia. The nave, a convex-sided octagon inscribed in a square, seems to be a variant on the plan of Guarini's church of S Lorenzo in Turin. Adjoining it are the oval spaces of the choir and nave and the narrow transeptal side chapels, all of which intrude into the central space with their convex protruberances rising from canted piers with niche chapels. The undulating rhythm this creates is continued vertically, through the arches and pendentives, to the soffit of the dome. Three-dimensional ribs mark the junctions where spaces interpenetrate at high level, an innovation in Bohemia. The façade mirrors the dynamism of the interior; two towers stand on either side of the tripartite middle area, which is convex in shape but with the central bay dished inwards, revealing the thickness of the wall. Hildebrandt's original intention to emphasize this feature by a straight cut with a pilaster placed in front of it was not realized: the area was in fact obliterated by a moulding. Nor is the present appearance of the dome as Hildebrandt intended. Despite a lack of documentary proof that the Piarists' church of Maria Treu (1716–31) in Vienna is also by Hildebrandt, it is stylistically very close to St Laurenz: he probably worked on plans for both buildings at around the same time; the Maria Treu has, however, also been attributed to FRANZ JÄNGGL.

2. MATURE WORK, FROM 1713. The Stadtpalais Daun-Kinsky in Vienna (1713–16; see fig. 2) is especially significant in the development of Hildebrandt's architectural style. Owing to an unfavourable building plot, the façade area had to be narrow; Hildebrandt set it out in seven bays, with a high podium floor surmounted by two storeys articulated by a giant order, and finally, a mezzanine floor on top. The central projection in three bays with herm pilasters makes a special contribution to the grand effect. These vertical elements were becoming characteristic in Hildebrandt's work and are part of his subtle treatment of walls, in which the decorative, rather than the structural, function prevails. In this, Hildebrandt's approach to architecture differed fundamentally from that of Fischer von Erlach, and in the Stadtpalais Daun-Kinsky he designed what amounts to a counter-scheme to his rival's Palais Batthyány (now Schönborn). It signalled the start of the decorative approach that became an increasingly important element in Hildebrandt's treatment of wall surfaces. The horizontal structuring, so dominant in his early works, is here brought into harmonious balance with the vertical (the giant order of pilasters, the windows ranged above one another). The staircase of the Daun-Kinsky runs up one wall of a narrow range flanking a courtyard, but still creates a dramatic effect of light and space from the second floor upwards, culminating in a view of a mysterious top storey, apparently inaccessible and with a hidden light source.

2. Johann Lukas von Hildebrandt: Stadtpalais Daun-Kinsky, Vienna, 1713–16

The designs for the palace at POMMERSFELDEN (1711–18) date from the same period as those for the staircase at the Stadtpalais Daun-Kinsky. Prince Bishop Friedrich Karl Schönborn, for whom Hildebrandt had already worked on several occasions, commissioned Johann Dientzenhofer to design the palace itself and Hildebrandt to design the central area of the palace, its monumental inner staircase (see PALACE, fig. 2) and the Kaisersaal. The idea for a staircase ascending in two arms came from the owner Lothar Franz Schönborn, the Prince Bishop's uncle and owner of Pommersfelden. Hildebrandt inserted the staircase into a gallery three storeys high, along which the corridors gave access to the adjacent areas and at the same time provided a gala background as backlit tiers to the ascent to the Kaisersaal. The importance accorded to staircases in the Baroque period and the close relationship between theatre and court ceremonial are both evident here.

Hildebrandt's masterpieces are the Lower Belvedere (1714–16) and Upper Belvedere (1721–4; see VIENNA, fig. 17), a group of two interrelated castle complexes commissioned by Prince Eugene of Savoy (for whom he had already worked as architect on several occasions) and extensive gardens outside the gates of Vienna (see VIENNA, §V, 6). In the original plan only the Lower Belvedere was shown, facing the town and with terraced gardens rising behind it in an arrangement similar to that at the Gartenpalais Mansfeld-Fondi. When the Upper Belvedere was built, with its garden front facing the former main building and the town, its main entrance area faced away from the direction of Vienna. The Lower Belvedere, Eugene's summer residence, is an extensive building consisting of five linked rectangular pavilions without much architectural incident: only the three central bays have an upper floor. On the courtyard side, wings reach back towards a gate-house building. After the complex had been extended, the garden front assumed the appearance of a 'surface that acts as an optical boundary to the falling movement of space from the more elevated Oberes [Upper] Belvedere' (Grimschitz). The site, which Hildebrandt developed into a harmonious continuum by means of ramps and flights of steps, is punctuated by flower-beds, pools with fountains and sculptures.

Poised above the gardens is the Upper Belvedere, designed to be both a prestige building and a monument. Its walls are reduced to a delicate framework by the large number of windows. It has no wings and is stopped at the ends by elongated octagonal pavilions. In the centre of the north or garden façade a five-bay polygonal pavilion juts out, with the *sala terrena* at its rear. In the centre of the south façade, overlooking the *cour d'honneur*, is a portico with ramps. The staircase hall (*Treppenhaus*) lies immediately behind it: the middle flight of stairs leads down into the *sala terrena*, while the flights on either side lead up to the Festsaal on the first floor. Externally, the staggered height of the roofing reflects the subdivision of the building into a raised polygonal pavilion in the centre, flanked by a pair of five-bay blocks of almost equivalent height, which are joined by low-rise ranges to the corner pavilions. The protruding parts of the façade are articulated on the upper storeys by delicate double pilasters, and these and the other sculptural decoration leave just enough room for the windows: the wall thus 'disappears', and the building is relieved of its heaviness. Hildebrandt's treatment of the façades shows his mastery of imaginatively elaborate building ornament. Such dominant motifs as the 'Hildebrandt gable', used here to top the three-arched portico in the centre of the *cour d'honneur* façade with an outline that corresponds with the roof, are also characteristic of his style. It is recorded that Prince Eugene took a great interest in the progress of the design of the Upper Belvedere, and many ideas may have originated from him. The concept of the staircase must have been prompted by Genoese models.

In the Deutschordenskirche (1717–25; now Seminarkirche) in Linz, Hildebrandt made use once more of the longitudinal ellipse in his design, which shows him at last a master of Baroque fluency. The façade projects forward and recedes in the centre. His designs for Göttweig Monastery (begun 1719) and the Hofburg (1724–5) in Vienna turned away from the 'extreme use of sculptural illusion in interpreting the façade surfaces' (Grimschitz), but the architect continued to employ the devices that had become characteristic of his work: herm pilasters, ornamental discs and variations on the 'Hildebrandt gable'. He was unable, however, to implement his ambitious projects for rebuilding the Hofburg (see VIENNA, §V, 5(i)). The total complex designed for Göttweig involved a huge symmetrical plan with a domed church on a central axis between public and private courts, the whole set amidst bastioned fortifications on a site above the River Danube. Of the completed building, with its many alterations, only the airy staircase (1739) can be directly attributed to Hildebrandt. When Hildebrandt remodelled Schloss Mirabell (originally Altenau) in Salzburg (1721–7) he was hampered by having to take account of the original fenestration, but his replacement of the extant staircase provided the opportunity for a scheme in which sculptural decoration could appear to full advantage. The flights climb the walls of the central well, supported by slant-faced piers: lavish scrollwork in stone with putti and wall recesses containing figures give the staircase its ceremonial aspect (see SALZBURG, fig. 3). Georg Raphael Donner executed the sculpture (1726–7). Following a fire the whole building was considerably altered in the 19th century.

Of the many commissions Hildebrandt received to renovate buildings that no longer satisfied the stylistic demands of the day, the most important came from Prince Eugene c. 1730 to enlarge Schloss Schlosshof im Marchfeld. The castle, which originally consisted of four ranges, was extended by the addition of a court flanked by two wings, each with nine bays, and an enormous park layout. Its appearance after Hildebrandt's alterations (and before later rebuilding) is recorded in paintings by Bernardo Bellotto (Vienna, Ksthist. Mus.). The substantial treatment of the walls and the clearly divided terraces in the garden are reminiscent of the Upper Belvedere, where Hildebrandt played down the concept of mass and moved harmoniously from one garden level to another. It is, however, difficult to make a direct comparison between the garden façade of the Upper Belvedere and that of the Würzburg Residenz (see WÜRZBURG, §2). When Friedrich Karl Schönborn became Prince Bishop of Würzburg in 1729, Hildebrandt was assigned an important role alongside Balthasar Neumann in work on the Residenz building. After an initial meeting in Vienna (1730) Hildebrandt made several journeys to Würzburg, but it is hard to reconstruct the individual design processes. His influence is most evident in the *cour d'honneur* and garden façades. It is uncertain whether Neumann was allowed or obliged to adapt designs drawn up by his rival, or whether he had been influenced by Hildebrandt's buildings in Vienna and, with his patron's consent, drew up plans of his own (see NEUMANN, BALTHASAR, §1(i)). When the vaulting of the church at Würzburg was being constructed to Neumann's designs, an intervention by Hildebrandt led to the insertion of an intermediate zone, to ensure that the Prince's box could occupy a prominent position. The splendid design of the railings of the *cour d'honneur* (1739–44; destr. 1820), which had been an important focal point when the complex was viewed from the town, is now known to us only from an engraving.

Karl Friedrich's summer residence, Schloss Werneck, is a similar example of involuntary cooperation yielding positive architectural results: Neumann had to submit his designs for altering and extending the building to Hildebrandt in Vienna. Hildebrandt's last large-scale enterprise was the Monastery of Louka (Klosterbruck) near Znojmo. The idea of a layout forming a square goes back to his plans for Göttweig. Building work did not start until after his death, and only about half of the planned project was built.

BIBLIOGRAPHY

Macmillan Enc. Archit.; Thieme-Becker

B. Grimschitz: *Johann Lukas von Hildebrandts Kirchenbauten* (Vienna, 1929)

——: *Wiener Barockpaläste* (Vienna, 1944)

E. Hainisch: 'Zum Baugedanken des Oberen Belvedere-Schlosses in Wien', *Wien. Jb. Kstgesch.*, xvi (1954), pp. 205–11

R. Wagner-Rieger: 'Die Piaristenkirche in Wien', *Wien. Jb. Kstgesch.*, xvii (1956), pp. 49–62

B. Grimschitz: *Johann Lukas von Hildebrandt*, 2 vols (Vienna and Munich, 1959) [good illustrations and ground-plans]; review by G. Passavant in *Kstchronik*, xiii (1960), pp. 197–203

H. G. Franz: *Bauten und Baumeister der Barockzeit in Böhmen* (Leipzig, 1962)

W. J. Hofmann: *Schloss Pommersfelden: Geschichte seiner Entstehung* (Nuremberg, 1968)

W. G. Rizzi: 'Die Kuppelkirchenbauten Johann Lukas von Hildebrandts', *Wien. Jb. Kstgesch.*, n. s., xxix (1976), pp. 121–56

——: 'Zu Johann Lukas von Hildebrandts Tätigkeit auf den niederösterreichischen Schlössern des Reichsvizekanzlers Schönborn', *Alte & Mod. Kst*, xxi [148–9] (1976)

——: 'Die Barockisierung der ehemaligen Augustinereremitenkirche in Bruck/Leitha und einige neue Beiträge zu den Landkirchen Johann Lukas von Hildebrandts', *Österreich. Z. Kst & Dkmlpf.*, xxxiv (1980), pp. 35–47

ANDREW JOHN MARTIN

Hilder, J(essie) J(ewhurst) [Hood, Anthony] (*b* Toowoomba, Queensland, 23 July 1881; *d* Sydney, 10 April 1916). Australian painter. He arrived in Sydney in 1904, where he worked for the Bank of New South Wales and painted in his spare time. Early paintings by Hilder were signed 'Anthony Hood' so as not to attract the attention of his employers. In 1906 he was introduced to Julian Ashton by fellow painter Fred Leist (1878–1945) and enrolled in Ashton's evening classes at the 'Academy Julien' (later the Sydney Art School). Here Hilder was influenced and encouraged by Ashton's partner, Sydney Long, who was also president of the local Society of Artists. He sent watercolours to the Society's spring exhibition (1907), and these were highly praised. His paintings are small and decorative—ethereal, gemlike visions of the Australian landscape such as *Coogee* (1907; Sydney, A.G. NSW).

In 1909 Hilder resigned from the Bank of New South Wales in order to paint full-time, exhibiting with both the Society of Artists and its rival, the Royal Art Society. His work became increasingly muted in colour and more concerned with the representation of rural activity, as in *Ploughing* (1910; Sydney, A.G. NSW). In 1914 Hilder had a one-man show in Melbourne, which gave him the opportunity to study Corot's *The Bent Tree* (Melbourne, N.G. Victoria). Corot's work had fascinated Hilder for some years, but he had known it hitherto only through magazine reproductions. *The Bent Tree* influenced much of Hilder's later work, in particular his paintings of Dora Creek: for example *Morning at Dora Creek* (1915; Sydney, A.G. NSW). At this time Hilder's tubercular condition worsened and led to his death the following year at the age of 34.

BIBLIOGRAPHY

J. Ashton and others: *J. J. Hilder, Watercolourist* (Sydney, 1916)

S. U. Smith and B. Stevens: *The Art of J. J. Hilder* (Sydney, 1918)

B. Hilder: *The Heritage of J. J. Hilder* (Sydney, 1966)

J. J. Hilder and Contemporaries (exh. cat. by U. Prunster, Sydney, A.G. NSW, 1981)

JONATHAN WATKINS

Hildesheim. German city in Lower Saxony on the River Innerste, *c.* 40 km south-east of Hamburg, with a population of *c.* 103,000 (1987). A bishopric was founded on the site by Louis the Pious (*reg* 781–840) in 815 to complement those founded by Charlemagne in Münster, Osnabrück, Paderborn and Halberstadt. A cathedral, presumably a modest wooden structure that had replaced an earlier circular chapel, existed at the time of Bishop Gunthar (*reg* 814–34), and the settlement expanded to the north of the hill on which it stood. During the late Ottonian period under Bishop BERNWARD (*reg* 993–1022) the arts flourished and the monastery of St Michael was founded (*see* §2(i) below). Shortly afterwards Bishop Hezilo (*reg* 1054–79) founded the Heiligkreuzkirche and the Mauritiuskirche (1058–68), and in 1133 the St Godehardikirche was founded by Bishop Bernhard I (*reg* 1130–53). From the 11th century Hildesheim had a market, and *c.* 1220 the Neustadt was established to the east by the burghers; on the Marktplatz there the original Rathaus was erected during the 13th century (rebuilt 1443). A rivalry developed between the secular Neustadt and the Altstadt under episcopal control. The demands of the burghers for self-government later resulted in a feud (1519–23), after which they were granted civil privileges. In the late Middle Ages the Andreaskirche (1389–1504) and the Lambertikirche (1473–88) were built. The medieval city was largely destroyed during World War II (1945), but the cathedral, St Michael and other buildings were faithfully restored.

1. Cathedral. 2. St Michael.

1. CATHEDRAL.

(i) Architecture. Bishop Altfried (*reg* 851–74) laid the foundation stone of the first stone cathedral, which he dedicated (872) to the Virgin and other saints. In 963 the relics of St Epiphanius were interred in the confessio. Altfried's building was destroyed by two fires in 1013 and 1046. Bishop Azelin (*reg* 1044–54) started a new building to the west, on the same axis, with the intention of incorporating the west end of the old building as the new east choir. Unstable foundations, however, led to its collapse. A new cathedral was constructed by Bishop Hezilo over the foundations of Altfried's building and dedicated in 1061. Bishop Berthold (*reg* 1119–30) extended the straight east end by adding an apse. There was a tower over the crossing (replaced by a Baroque cap after it collapsed in 1718). Chapels were added to the side aisles betwen 1318 and 1330. The upper storey of the paradise (1412) adjoining the north transept houses the Godehard choir, which opens on to the cathedral. The Annenkapelle in the cloisters and the Laurentiuskapelle on the south side of the cathedral, now the sacristy, are also Gothic. Baroque alterations were carried out *c.* 1720, but very few have been preserved. In 1840 the westwork was replaced by a twin-towered elevation. During World War II the apse, crossing, transept, north aisle, central nave and west end of the building were virtually destroyed (1945). The cathedral was reconstructed (1950–60), and the west end rebuilt in its pre-1840 form with a narthex, a transverse transom and a raised bell house.

The aisled, flat-ceilinged basilica with its alternating system of piers, apse, transept and isolated crossing corresponds to the cathedral built under Hezilo. Gothic chapels with tracery windows and lucarnes adjoin the side aisles. Parts of the east end have been preserved from Altfried's cathedral, the oldest part being the crypt beneath the choir, which was extended eastwards by three bays in 1061 and by an apse in 1120.

(ii) Furnishings. Of the furnishings, the items dating from the late Ottonian period are especially outstanding. The two 'bronze' (actually brass) doors on the inside of the main west portal (*see* DOOR, fig. 3), which according to the inscription were cast in 1015, had been donated to St Michael's by Bernward. Their relief sequences are marked by profound theological thought, and the figures have remarkable sculptural power (for further discussion *see* OTTONIAN ART, §V, 2). Two large lions' heads with rings cast into the doors serve as handles. The Column of Christ (*see* CLASSICISM, fig. 1) in the south transept was also donated by Bernward to St Michael's (transferred to cathedral 1893). Modelled on Trajan's Column (ded. AD 113) or the Column of Marcus Aurelius (*c.* AD 176–93) in Rome, it has a rising band of reliefs depicting the *Life of Christ* in 24 scenes, from the *Baptism* to the *Entry into Jerusalem*. Since the Passion is not included it is conceivable that the column, which was cast *c.* 1020, held the Bernward Cross (silver-gilt, *c.* 1007–8; Hildesheim, Diözmus. & Domschatzkam.; *see* CROSS, fig. 4) containing a relic of the True Cross and was used for the rite of the raising of the Cross, known from Byzantium. Two wheel-shaped Romanesque candelabra survive in the cathedral (*see also* ROMANESQUE, §VI, 4); the one in the choir (1055–65; diam. 6 m; holds 72 candles) was donated by Bishop Hezilo and is of chased, partly gilded copper. It represents the *Heavenly Jerusalem* (Revelation, 21:10–27) with 12 gateways and 12 towers bearing the names of the prophets and apostles, and a city wall, formerly ornamented with small silver angels (untraced).

The bronze baptismal font (*c.* 1225) is evidence of the enduring tradition of bronze casting in Hildesheim. Four kneeling figures representing the paradisiacal rivers of *Geon, Tigris, Euphrates* and *Phison* support the bowl of the font. Allegories of *Moderation, Bravery, Rectitude* and *Wisdom* appear above them as small half-length figures, surrounded by bands. On the bowl are four relief panels that depict the *Crossing of the Red Sea*, the *Baptism*, the *Crossing of the Jordan* and, as a dedicatory image, the *Virgin and Child*, and four medallions show half-length figures of *Jeremiah, Daniel, Ezekiel* and *Isaiah*. Above them are the four Evangelists' symbols. The font cover is decorated with four reliefs depicting the *Massacre of the Innocents* (baptism by blood), *Mary Magdalene Anointing the Feet of Christ* (repentance), *Charitable Works* (atonement) and *Aaron's Rod* (symbolizing the virginity of Mary). Above are depictions of *Jeremiah, David, Isaiah* and *Solomon*. The cathedral also houses two golden reliquaries, of St Epiphanius (*c.* 1140) and St Godehard (mid-12th century), which have rich figural decoration, as well as figures of the Virgin, tombs and the works of art in the treasury.

BIBLIOGRAPHY

A. Zeller, ed.: *Die Kunstdenkmäler der Provinz Hannover*, ii/4 (Hannover, 1911)
V. H. Elbern, H. Engfer and H. Reuther: *Der Hildesheimer Dom: Architektur, Ausstattung, Patrozinien* (Hildesheim, 1974)
G. Dehio and E. Gall: *Bremen, Niedersachsen*, ed. G. Kiesow and others, Hb. Dt. Kstdkml. (Munich and Berlin, 1977)
V. H. Elbern: *Der Domschatz zu Hildesheim* (Hildesheim, 1977)

BETTINA GEORGI, ERNST ULLMANN

(iii) Treasury. The Diözesanmuseum mit Domschatzkammer houses the collection of liturgical objects that has grown up since the cathedral's dedication. It includes numerous reliquary shrines, the oldest being a 10th-century silver capsule with a relic of the Virgin; many manuscripts, including the 'Small' Bernward Gospels (10th century; Cod. 13) and the Guntbald Gospels (1011; Cod. 18), both with a Byzantine ivory cover, the Bernward Bible (early 11th century; Cod. 61; *see* OTTONIAN ART, §IV, 2) and the Ratmann Sacramentary (1159; Cod. 37); and head reliquaries such as that of St Oswald, King of Northumbria (*reg* 633–41). This last consists of a wooden core covered in thin silver-gilt sheet and has a dome-shaped architectural base (dome *c.* 1170–80; head *c.* 1300, from England or Brunswick). The crown is embellished with gemstones and cameos. Other head reliquaries are those of St Cecilia (14th century) and St Bernward (13th century; donated *c.* 1500). There are also several shrines, for example that (*c.* 1132) of St Godehard (Bishop, 1022–38; *see* SHRINE (i), §I, 2); a number of box altars (11th and 12th centuries; *see* STONE, colour pl. IX, fig. 1); the crosiers of bishops Erkanbald of Fulda (*reg* 996/7–1011), Bernward and Otto I (*reg* 1260–79); Gothic monstrances (15th century); chalices (14th–18th centuries); crosses, notably the silver-gilt Bernward Cross (*c.* 1007–8; *see* CROSS, fig. 4) and the 'Jerusalem' processional cross (12th century; from the Byzantine–Russian cultural sphere); bronze candlesticks from Hildesheim and Liège; and three splendid bronze disc-backed crosses (11th–12th centuries; *see* OTTONIAN ART, §V, 2, and ROGER OF HELMARSHAUSEN). In the 18th century some large Baroque silver candelabra and a large embossed silver antependium were acquired. Among other items is a wooden enthroned *Virgin and Child* (early 11th century). The chasuble of Bernward (11th century) probably came from an Islamic workshop, whereas the works in precious metals and bronze and the medieval manuscripts were produced largely in Hildesheim workshops.

BIBLIOGRAPHY

J. M. Kratz: *Der Dom zu Hildesheim, seine Kostbarkeiten, Kunstschätze und sonstigen Merkwürdigkeiten* (Hildesheim, 1840)
S. Beissel: *Der Heilige Bernward von Hildesheim als Künstler und Förderer der deutschen Kunst* (Hildesheim, 1895)
A. Bertram: *Geschichte des Bistums Hildesheim*, 3 vols (Hildesheim, 1899–1925)
R. Herzig: *Der Dom zu Hildesheim und seine Kunstschätze* (Hildesheim, 1911, rev. 1/1921)
V. H. Elbern and H. Reuther: *Der Hildesheimer Domschatz* (Hildesheim, 1969)

G. REINHECKEL

2. ST MICHAEL. The Protestant parish church, originally part of a Benedictine monastic foundation, stands on a hill outside the original city walls. Following the devastation caused by bombing during World War II, the church was rebuilt in its late Ottonian/early Romanesque form (completed by 1960). Excavations, archaeological studies, drawings dating from 1622 and an old wooden model provided the information on which the reconstruction was based. The Late Romanesque ceiling painting (*see* §(iii) below) had been put in store during the war and survived unscathed.

(i) Architecture. (ii) Sculpture. (iii) Painting.

(i) Architecture. In 993 Bernward began the construction of a chapel (ded. 996) to house the fragment of the True Cross given to him by the emperor on his recent consecration as Bishop of Hildesheim. In his first will of 1010

he expressed his intention of establishing monks there and specified the furnishing of the monastery. The same year Bernward issued an endowment document and laid the foundation stone—presumably the stone discovered in 1908 bearing the inscription s[anctus] BENIAMIN/ S[anctus] MATHEUS A[postolus]/B[ernwardus] EP[iscopus] MX; the name BENRWARD was also found stamped on a brick. Between 1011 and 1013 Provost Goderamus (*d* 1030) of St Pantaleon in Cologne was summoned to Hildesheim to serve as abbot. Bernward's second will (1019) refers to 'founding a new church whereby I have both fulfilled my promise to further the praise and glory of the name of the Lord, and cared for holy Christendom'.

From the very beginning work was based on a unified plan. The crypt was consecrated by 1015, and the dedication of the church to the Archangel Michael followed in 1022, the same year that Bernward was laid to rest in the crypt. Building work continued until 1033. Immediately after the consecration a fire necessitated repairs. After a second fire in 1162 the nave supports and their capitals were replaced, under Bishop Adelog (*reg* 1171–90), and the church was rededicated in 1186. Following Bernward's canonization in 1193 it became necessary to extend the west choir and the crypt into the crossing. Choir screens

and a rood screen were erected, and the Marienaltar in the crypt was rededicated in 1197. At the beginning of the 13th century the west transept and the choir bay were vaulted over, and the west apse was rebuilt with two rows of windows (the second of which was eliminated when the church was rebuilt). The nave ceiling was painted with a *Tree of Jesse* (*see* §(iii) below). In the Gothic period large windows and two doorways were inserted into the south aisle. In 1543 St Michael became a Protestant parish church. The rood screen collapsed in 1566. In 1650 the east choir and the side apses were dismantled, and part of the east crossing tower collapsed, but it was rebuilt in 1667–9 and was given a cap in 1679. The west crossing tower and the south arm of the west transept were dismantled from 1662 (rebuilt 1907–10). The crypt vaulting in the crossing was broken up and the south choir screen destroyed. In 1882 the external wall of the north aisle was dismantled. A first restoration was undertaken in 1855–67. The reconstruction of Bernward's original building after World War II took place between 1945 and 1960.

The church has two choirs, creating a balance between east and west, with the nave stretching between them. Each transept has a square tower over the crossing and a stair turret, octagonal in section at the bottom and round

1. Hildesheim, St Michael, exterior view from the south-west, restored 1945–60

at the top, on each gable end. These give the church a compact appearance (see fig. 1). In the east the short presbytery terminates in an apse, and tall side apses project from the transept arms. In the west, beyond the west transept, is a cubic west choir with an apse and a low ambulatory encompassing the crypt. In the main axis of the ambulatory at the westernmost end is an imposing doorway: two columns support a large round arch, which is separated from the cornice above by a frieze of round arches. The fenestration of the apse exhibits forms from the period c. 1200. The building appears to be constructed of fine ashlars, but they are in fact a facing for rubble masonry, which is visible in the clerestory and upper levels of the towers. There were pilaster strips with blind arches on the walls of the side aisles; buttresses reinforce the crypt ambulatory. In the south aisle the large Gothic window openings have been preserved.

The interior of the aisled, flat-ceilinged vessel of the church has an alternating system of columns and piers (ABBABBABBA; for discussion and illustration *see* AL-TERNATING SYSTEM) with the balanced harmony of a centrally planned space based on two centres. A simple cornice divides the arcading from the clerestory, the ten windows of which are not axial to the nine arches. The nave and transepts intersect at the same height, and the crossings are both isolated by four round arches. The side aisles, which are two-thirds of the width of the nave, are separated from the transepts at both ends by pairs of arches. The columns rest on clearly modelled Attic bases with no corner spurs. At the east end of the north arcade and in the transepts the cushion capitals of the original building have been preserved, while other columns have richly ornamented capitals (reminiscent of those at SS Peter and Paul, Königslutter), dating from the time of Adelog. The piers and arches at the crossings and also the arcading are accentuated by the use of alternating light and dark stone (see fig. 2).

At the ends of the transept arms are arcaded galleries with two arches at ground-floor level, four in the first storey and six in the second (fig. 2). In the east transept the apses occupy the wall between the presbytery and the galleries. The shallow east presbytery has a much smaller apse than that of the square west choir. The north choir screen of the choir extension still stands in the west crossing. The crypt beneath the west choir consists of three aisles of equal height; the tomb of *Bishop Bernward* is at the foot of the Marienaltar. The crypt ambulatory is richly structured with recesses (but *see also* AMBULATORY). Above, in the roof area of the ambulatory, is the Michaels-kapelle; its altar recess has been hollowed out of the wall of the west apse, and there is a small round window opening on to the body of the church. Near the west choir above the ambulatory were the scriptorium and the sacristy.

The importance of measurement and numbers in the design of Bernward's church suggests a microcosmic significance. The square formed by the west crossing was the module for the west choir and was repeated three times in the nave and in the east crossing, while the *Gebundenes System* of Romanesque architecture was applied, albeit somewhat inconsistently, in the vessel. The nave is twice as high as the crossing square is wide. The

2. Hildesheim, St Michael, interior of north transept

transept galleries (see above) are another example of a numerical series. The cushion capitals, being the intersection of a sphere and a cube, provide a geometrically exact transition from the circular section of the column to the square of the springer (*see also* ROMANESQUE, §II, 2(i) and figs 2 and 3).

At St Michael the architectural developments of the Carolingian–Ottonian period are integrated in a unique way, and at the same time the early Romanesque style is manifested. The church has direct links with the original Ottonian structure of Magdeburg Cathedral (*see* MAGDE-BURG, §1) and with the abbey churches of St Cyriakus, Gernrode (*see* ROMANESQUE, §II, 2), and especially Memleben. It relates closely to St Pantaleon, Cologne (*see* COLOGNE, §IV, 6(i)), from which the first abbot and monks came, and to the cathedral of Bishop Willigis (*reg* 975–1011) in Mainz (*see* MAINZ, §2(i)(a)), which Bernward knew from his time as secretary to Willigis; both churches are very similar to St Michael in their transepts, each with one central and two side towers. The crypt and ambulatory are reminiscent of the choir and ambulatory at St Martin, Tours (*see* TOURS, §3), which was visited by Bernward while under construction. Bernward may also have seen the arcaded galleries in Old St Peter's, Rome, which was perhaps the precedent for the location of his tomb.

It has also been suggested that the layout of the church (the location of the tomb; the central plan of the crypt with ambulatory; the nave, which when viewed from the transepts appears to have five aisles; and the east crossing with the altar of the Cross and the Column of Christ; *see* §1(i) above) may relate to the Church of the Holy Sepulchre in Jerusalem (*see* JERUSALEM, §II, 2(i) and fig. 7), with the Holy Sepulchre, the crypt of St Helena and Calvary. In his second will Bernward stated that divine grace was to be won through 'architectura meritorum' (architecture of merit). His church, with its numerical order, may be seen as an emulation of the Temple of Solomon (*see* BERNWARD) but also, standing on a hill protected by towers, as a symbol of the Heavenly Jerusalem, richly furnished with bronze doors, the Column of Christ, candelabra and crosses, and a relic of the True Cross. As well as being a magnificent temple of God, both architecturally and symbolically, Bernward's church is also a monument to its builder.

BIBLIOGRAPHY

D. Andersen and W. Marzahn: *St Michael zu Hildesheim* (Hildesheim, n.d.)

H. Beseler and H. Roggenkamp: *Die Michaeliskirche in Hildesheim* (Berlin, 1954)

O. Karpa: *Die Kirche St Michaelis in Hildesheim* (Hildesheim, 1965)

J. Sommer: *St Michael zu Hildesheim* (Königstein, 1978)

U. Faust: *Die Benediktinerklöster in Niedersachsen, Schleswig-Holstein und Bremen* (Munich, 1979), pp. 218–51

G. Binding: *Bischof Bernward als Architekt der Michaeliskirche in Hildesheim* (Cologne, 1987)

BETTINA GEORGI, ERNST ULLMANN

(ii) Sculpture. The masterpieces of Ottonian metalwork commissioned for St Michael by Bernward—the cast bronze doors at the west end and the great bronze column in the east end—were subsequently installed in the cathedral (the doors by Bernward's successor Godehard; the column at the end of the 19th century; *see* §1(ii) above). Still remaining in the church, however, is the carved stone sarcophagus (*c.* 1020) that Bernward planned for his own burial. Based on Early Christian sarcophagi, it is a rectangular container 2 m long, made out of a single block of sandstone with a separate gabled lid. The casket body is plain with an inscription around the upper edge. The lid is carved on all four faces, the head end with the *Lamb of God* in a medallion flanked by stylized clouds or flames, the foot end with a plain cross. On each of the long sides a biblical quotation (Job 19: 25–7) in Roman majuscule letters frames a row of angel busts (four on one side, five on the other) symbolizing the nine choirs of angels; these alternate with the same cloud-like shapes as on the end, which parallel similar forms on the bronze doors. The sarcophagus was originally sunk deeply into the ground and covered with a sandstone slab bearing an inscription and carved with a large cross set with medallions of the *Lamb of God* and the *Evangelists' Symbols*, which resemble those of contemporary manuscripts. It was raised to a higher level during restoration in the 1950s, and the slab placed above it, on columns. The symbolism of the tomb and its links with other media are further evidence of the artistic patronage of Bernward.

For illustration of later work *see* STUCCO AND PLASTERWORK, fig. 4.

BIBLIOGRAPHY

F. J. Tschan: *Saint Bernward of Hildesheim*, 3 vols (Notre Dame, 1942–52)

P. Lasko: 'The Tomb of St Bernward of Hildeshiem', *Romanesque and Gothic: Essays for George Zarnecki*, ed. N. Stratford (Woodbridge, 1987), pp. 147-52

CAROLA HICKS

(iii) Painting. The painted wooden ceiling of the church is one of very few surviving examples of its kind. It covers the whole of the nave and represents an elaborate version of the *Tree of Jesse*, the genealogy of Christ. It was painted not as a series of separate panels before the ceiling was assembled but *in situ*. Various dates have been suggested. The dating *c.* 1193–7 (under Abbot Theodoric) seems much too early for the style, and a *c.* 1240–50 dating in the time of Abbot Godescalc, when letters of indulgence were still being granted for donations for work at the abbey, seems more likely.

The main figures of the genealogy are in the centre panels, beginning with Adam and Eve, before Jesse, and ending with the Virgin and Christ. These are flanked by the Evangelists, the rivers of Paradise and standing figures of the prophets. The outer borders contain circular medallions of the lesser ancestors of Christ. The style is of the middle phase of the *Zackenstil*, represented in the same region by two illustrated manuscripts—the Wolfenbüttel Model Book (*c.* 1230; Wolfenbüttel, Herzog August Bib., Cod. Guelf. 61.2 Aug. 8°) and the Goslar Gospels (Goslar, Rathaus)—and by the wall paintings (*c.* 1240–50) of the choir of Brunswick Cathedral. The Wolfenbüttel Model Book, which derives from Byzantine sources, gives a clear indication of how the early *Zackenstil* was modified by new Byzantine influences. In this phase the folds become more numerous, and the jagged contours are somewhat modified, better to convey the impression of the pose and physical form of the figures.

See also GOTHIC, §IV, 5(iii).

BIBLIOGRAPHY

J. Sommer: *Das Deckenbild der Michaeliskirche zu Hildesheim* (Hildesheim, 1966)

O. Demus: *Romanesque Mural Painting* (London, 1970), pp. 143, 145, 614–15, pls 271–2

NIGEL J. MORGAN

Hilgers, Carl [Karl] (*b* Düsseldorf, 14 April 1818; *d* Düsseldorf, 3 Dec 1890). German painter. From 1833 to 1844 he attended the Staatliche Kunstakademie in Düsseldorf as a master pupil of Johann Wilhelm Schirmer. Apart from a four-year residency in Berlin, he lived almost continuously in Düsseldorf, though he made several study trips to other parts of Germany and to Belgium, the Netherlands and France. He was one of the best-known painters of the Düsseldorf school, as is indicated by the full-length portrait (1850; Düsseldorf, Stadtmus.) of him by Johann Peter Hasenclever. He was praised by his contemporaries for his free brushwork and his sure mastery of technique, which may be compared to the work of his fellow Düsseldorf painter Caspar Scheuren (1810–87). As subject-matter Hilgers favoured atmospheric, mist-shrouded winter landscapes based in part on localities in and around Düsseldorf (e.g. the *Wasserburg in Winter*, 1845, and the *Conradsheim in Winter*, 1890; both Düsseldorf, Gal. Paffrath), the romantic character of which is heightened by the incidental figures. After his death, the popularity of his paintings rapidly declined, and he was quickly forgotten.

Thieme–Becker

BIBLIOGRAPHY

Carl Hilgers (exh. cat., Düsseldorf, Gal. Paffrath, 1979); review by
K. Vogler in *Die Weltkunst*, xlix (1979), p. 1100

S. TRÄGER

Hill. American family of artists.

(1) John Hill (*b* London, 9 Sept 1770; *d* Clarksville,
NY, 6 Nov 1850). Engraver of English birth. He was one
of the most important graphic artists working in America
in the first half of the 19th century. He learnt his craft in
London and worked for publishers of prints and illustrated
books, including Rudolph Ackermann. Hill achieved considerable success as an aquatinter of works by J. M. W.
Turner, Thomas Rowlandson, Philippe de Loutherbourg
and others, but concern about his ability to support his
growing family in a highly competitive market encouraged
him to leave England. Settling in Philadelphia, PA, in
1816, he quickly became the leading printmaker in the
area.

Hill was closely associated with two projects important
to the history of American printmaking: Joshua Shaw's
Picturesque Views of American Scenery and William Guy
Wall's *Hudson River Portfolio* (issued serially between 1821
and 1825). Begun in 1819, *Picturesque Views* was the first
major series of landscape scenes, often of a romantic
nature, to be printed in America. Since the 17th century
American views had been published generally in England
or on the Continent. With Hill's arrival quality aquatints
were produced in America. Wall's *Hudson River Portfolio*
is a cornerstone in the development of American printing
and landscape painting. The 20 views trace for 320 km the
course of the Hudson River from Luzerne to Governor's
Island, near Manhattan. The undertaking required Hill to
move to New York in 1822. Throughout the 1830s he
worked on further editions of this enormously popular
series, an American variation on similar projects dealing
with British and European rivers. Hill also engraved
numerous single prints and pairs of views, compiled two
artists' manuals and contributed plates to Fielding Lucas's
Progressive Drawing Book (1827–8). Around 1840 Hill
retired to Clarksville, Rockland Co., not far from New
York.

BIBLIOGRAPHY

R. J. Koke: 'John Hill, Master of Aquatint', *NY Hist. Soc. Q.*, xliii/1
(1959), pp. 51–117
——: *A Checklist of the American Engravings of John Hill, 1770–1850*
(New York, 1961)

EDWARD J. NYGREN

(2) John William Hill (*b* London, 13 Jan 1812; *d* West
Nyack, NY, 24 Sept 1879). Painter and illustrator, son of
(1) John Hill. At the age of seven he moved to Philadelphia,
PA, with his family. In 1822 he moved to New York
where he was apprenticed to his father for seven years.
During this time, he worked on the aquatint plates for
William Guy Wall's *Hudson River Portfolio* (1820–25),
which influenced his early paintings.

By 1828 Hill was submitting his landscapes to the
National Academy of Design, New York, and he continued
to do so until 1873. He was elected an Associate Academician in 1833, and in the same year he visited London to
study Old Master paintings. From 1836 to 1841 Hill served
as a topographical artist for the New York State Geological

Survey and from 1842 provided illustrations for James E.
De Kay's *Natural History of New York, Part 1: Zoology*.
After joining the Smith Brothers publishing firm in the
late 1840s, he travelled extensively to sketch views of
major North American cities. In 1850 he was a founder-
member of the short-lived New York Water Color Society,
precursor of the American Water Color Society.

About 1855 Hill read the first two volumes of John
Ruskin's *Modern Painters* (London, 1843–6), which significantly changed the direction and style of his art. From
then on he devoted himself to painting directly from
nature, depicting flowers, plants, fruit and birds in natural
backgrounds (e.g. *Bird's Nest and Dogroses*, 1867; New
York, NY Hist. Soc.). By adopting the stipple technique—
pin-point dabs of pigment applied to a white ground—he
was able to achieve brilliant colour and a high degree of
exactitude.

In 1863 Hill became President of the American Pre-
Raphaelite organization, the Society for the Advancement
of Truth in Art. Hill exhibited almost yearly at the Brooklyn
Art Association, which held a memorial retrospective of
his work soon after his death. Such late landscapes as
View on Catskill Creek (1867; New York, Met.) focus on
the area around his home in West Nyack. One of his sons,
John Henry Hill (1839–1922), was a watercolourist; he
perpetuated his father's memory by publishing an illustrated biography and by promoting his work at major
museums.

BIBLIOGRAPHY

J. H. Hill: *An Artist's Memorial* (New York, 1888)
R. Koke, ed.: *American Landscape and Genre Painting in the New York
Historical Society* (Boston, 1982)

ANNETTE BLAUGRUND

Hill, Anthony (*b* London, 23 April 1930). English painter
and sculptor. He studied at St Martin's School of Art
(1947–9) and at the Central School of Art (1949–51),
where he came into contact with the Constructivist tradition of abstraction. At this time he was friends with Victor
Pasmore, Adrian Heath (*b* 1920) and Kenneth and Mary
Martin, and soon after he began corresponding with
Charles Biederman, Max Bill and Marcel Duchamp.

Hill incorporated relief elements into his paintings of
the early 1950s, such as *Progression of Rectangles* (plastic on
board, 1954; Adrian Flowers priv. col, see 1983 exh. cat.,
p. 19), and from 1954 made reliefs that were asymmetrical
and orthogonal in form, such as *Relief Construction* (plastic
and aluminium on enamelled stove back, 1959; priv. col.,
see 1983 exh. cat., p. 37), composed of parallel planes of
plastic or metal sheet with elements of L-shaped aluminium. His concern with such materials and with mathematical systems and shallow physical depth led him to abandon
painting in 1957.

In 1960 Hill organized the exhibition *Construction:
England, 1950–60* at the Drian Galleries, London. In his
reliefs he began using short lengths of extruded aluminium
in systemic arrangements. In his later work he continued
to explore industrial and synthetic materials including
white-faced laminated plastic sheets, while in sculptures
such as *Co-structure, Version 1, No. 3* (plastic tubing,

1970; see 1983 exh. cat., p. 60) he assembled geometric configurations from lengths of tube.

WRITINGS

'Constructivism—the European Phenomenon', *Studio Int.*, clxxi/876 (1966), pp. 140–47
ed.: *Data: Directions in Art, Theory and Aesthetics* (London, 1968) [includes his own essay, 'Programme. Paragram. Structure', pp. 251–69]

BIBLIOGRAPHY

'Anthony Hill Interviewed by Kenneth Frampton', *Studio Int.*, clxxii/882 (1966), pp. 200–01
Anthony Hill (exh. cat. by A. Grieve, London, Hayward Gal., 1983)

ADRIAN LEWIS

Hill, Carl Fredrik (*b* Lund, 31 May 1849; *d* Lund, 22 Feb 1911). Swedish painter and draughtsman. He grew up in the university city of Lund, where his father was a mathematics professor. Despite severe opposition from his father, he studied landscape painting at the Konstakademi in Stockholm (1871–2), under Johan Edvard Bergh and Per Daniel Holm (1835–1903). He also frequently copied Dutch Old Masters, particularly Jacob van Ruisdael. After seeing the work that Alfred Wahlberg had sent home from Paris, Hill began to abandon his initial approach to form and colour, and he left for Paris in November 1873. His most important experience there was his encounter with the painting of Jean-Baptiste-Camille Corot: 'Corot has discovered a new world, because he has discovered a new way of looking at the old', he wrote in a letter. Other contemporary French painters Hill admired were Alexandre-Gabriel Decamps, Charles-François Daubigny, Jean-François Millet and Théodore Rousseau. From Courbet he learnt how to use colour to suggest the surface texture of stone quarries and gravel hills. In Barbizon in 1874 and 1875 Hill met the Hungarian painters Laszlo Paál and Mihaly von Muncacsy. His paintings of this time, for example *Autumn Landscape, Evening: Fontainebleau* (1875; Malmö, Kstmus.), are characterized by their dark 'luminarism' and their debt to Corot's later works.

Under the influence of Impressionism, the dark bitumen colours disappeared from Hill's painting in 1876. Hill called this approach 'the most realistic' and considered that he had discovered the true painting. However, he never adopted a typical Impressionist style, even though he used a broad, painterly technique and often employed a palette knife. His development was rapid, and he worked at a feverish pitch. In 1875 he was represented at the Paris Salon, but he was forced to exhibit his more radical paintings of 1876 in the Salon des Refusés that year. He was also represented at the Exposition Universelle in 1878. He had few contacts with other Swedes in Paris because of his reclusive character. He preferred to live and work in the countryside, moving in 1876, after his time in Barbizon, to the towns of Champagne sur l'Oise, Montigny (nr Fontainebleau) and Luc-sur-Mer, and in 1877 to Bois-le-Roi on the Seine.

The period from 1876 until he succumbed to mental illness in January 1878 marked the pinnacle of Hill's production and is characterized by continuous activity and artistic struggle. His landscapes are often intensely expressive with thick impasto, suggesting a mood of fatalism. In his landscapes from Bois-le-Roi, for example *Blossoming Apple Tree* (1877; Stockholm, Nmus.), a softer, more harmonious mood predominates. He also painted an extensive series of river views whose classically serene character is reminiscent of Claude Lorrain, for example *The Tree and the River Bend III* (1877; Stockholm, Nmus.). His works reached full maturity at this time, and he would undoubtedly have achieved a prominent international reputation if illness had not intervened; for example *Villa on the Seine* (Malmö, Kstmus.), probably painted in Bois-le-Roi in 1877 and characterized by synthetic simplification of forms, foreshadows the later development of Edvard Munch.

After the onset of his illness, Hill was cared for in his parents' home in Lund from 1883. There he spent nearly 30 years and executed thousands of drawings in coloured chalks, charcoal or India ink, often on brown wrapping paper. (Over 2500 of these are in Malmö Museum and the Nationalmuseum, Stockholm.) In the works produced during his illness, Hill, like his friend Ernst Josephson, created a highly personal imaginary world. He used figures taken from literature or illustrated magazines, which he often set against a background of fantastic architecture, for example *Oriental Interior* (Malmö, Kstmus.).

BIBLIOGRAPHY

A. Anderberg: *Carl Fredrik Hill: Hans liv och verk* [Carl Fredrik Hill: His life and work] (Malmö, 1926)
G. Ekelöf: *C. F. Hill* (Göteborg, 1946)
E. Blomberg: *Carl Fredrik Hill: Hans friska och sjuka konst* [Carl Fredrik Hill: His art during sickness and health] (Stockholm, 1949)
C. F. Hill: Drawings, intro. E. Blomberg (Paris, 1950, rev. Stockholm, 1960)
A. Anderberg: *Carl Hill: Hans liv och hans konst, med en essay om Hills produktion under sjukdomsåren av L. Hagerf* [Carl Hill: His life and his work, with an essay on Hill's output during his years of illness by L. Hagerf] (Malmö, 1951)
N. Lindhagen: *Carl Fredrik Hill: Sjukdomårens konst* [Carl Fredrik Hill: His art during the years of illness] (Malmö, 1976)
Carl Fredrik Hill (exh. cat., Malmö, Ksthall, 1976) [with Eng. summary]
S. Å. Nilsson: *Hillefanten: Konstvetenskapliga studier i C. F. Hill's värld* [Hill's moment: Research studies of C. F. Hill's art world] (Lund, 1977)
N. Lindhagen: *Hill skaldar: C. F. Hill i dikter och bilder* [Hill makes poetry: C. F. Hill in poems and pictures] (Stockholm, 1980)
S. Å. Nilsson: *Carl Fredrik Hill, 1876* (Stockholm, 1992)

TORSTEN GUNNARSSON

Hill, Sir George Francis (*b* Berhampore, Bengal, 22 Dec 1867; *d* London, 18 Oct 1948). English archaeologist and art historian. He was born at a mission station, the youngest of five children, and later had a brilliant career as a student of Classics, first at University College, London, then at Merton College, Oxford. In 1893 he was appointed as an assistant in the Department of Coins and Medals at the British Museum, and he helped on a series of museum catalogues of Greek coins; over the years 1897 to 1922 he wrote six of the volumes in the series. He also wrote numismatic handbooks, a manual of Greek inscriptions and a volume of sources for Greek history. His activities as an art historian included founding the Vasari Society. He wrote a long series of articles and notes (1896–1941) on medals, and published a biography of Pisanello in 1905. He was appointed Keeper of the Department of Coins and Medals in 1912. In 1915 he gave the Rhind lectures at Edinburgh, and these were published as *Medals of the Renaissance* (1920). In 1930 his work on the Italian medal culminated in the monumental *Corpus of Italian Medals of the Renaissance before Cellini*, and in 1931 he was appointed Director of the British Museum.

WRITINGS

Pisanello (London, 1905)

'Notes on Italian Medals', *Burl. Mag.*, ix (1906)–xlii (1923) [27 articles]

Portrait Medals of Italian Artists of the Renaissance (London, 1912)

The Medallic Portraits of Christ (Oxford, 1920)

Medals of the Renaissance (Oxford, 1920, rev. G. Pollard, 1978) [contains a complete list of Hill's writings on medals]

Drawings by Pisanello (Paris and Brussels, 1929/*R* New York, n.d.)

A Corpus of Italian Medals of the Renaissance before Cellini (London, 1930/*R* Florence, 1984)

'An Autobiographical Fragment', *The Medal*, xii (1988), pp. 37–48

BIBLIOGRAPHY

Who's Who

Obituary, *The Times* (20 Oct 1948)

A Tribute to Sir George Hill on his Eightieth Birthday, 1867–1947 (Oxford, 1948) [privately printed; contains full list of writings]

E. S. G. Robinson: 'George Francis Hill, 1867–1948', *Proc. Brit. Acad.*, xxxvi (1950), pp. 241–50

J. G. POLLARD

Hill, Joan [Cheah Sequah: 'Red Bird'] (*b* Muskogee, OK, 19 Dec 1930). Native American Creek–Cherokee painter and sculptor. Her father, William McKinley Hill, and mother, Winnie Dixie Harris, were both Creek–Cherokee. She attended elementary and high school, then Muskogee College for an AA degree, and Northeastern College for a BA (1952). She studied under various artists, including RICHARD WEST at Bacone College, Frederic Taubes (1900–82), Millard Sheets (1907–89) and Dong Kingman (*b* 1911). Much of her later painting reflects this training. Her family included George Washington Hill, Chief of the Creek Nation, 1925–8, a background giving her work unusual fidelity. She taught briefly, but retired to paint full-time in Muskogee. She is one of the few Native American women artists to achieve success and has been a strong influence on younger women. She has been the recipient of many awards and prizes for works in almost every medium, including sculpture and collage. As a teacher she has provided a strong influence for her students and devotes considerable time to younger artists. For a decade, 1980–90, the illness of both parents forced her to abandon painting, but in the 1990s she returned to the studio. International recognition includes the Gold Commemorative Medal, Great Britain; the Oscar d'Italia Award, Accademia Italia, Cremona (1984); 'People of the Century', Smithsonian Institution, Washington, DC; she was the first woman to be named a FCTM Master Artist, 1972, and was one of the recipients of the New York Fashion Industry '10 Outstanding Indians' Award, 1972.

For general discussion of 20th-century developments in Native American art *see* NATIVE NORTH AMERICAN ART, §XV.

BIBLIOGRAPHY

J. O. Snodgrass: *American Indian Painters*, Contributions from the Museum of the American Indian, Heye Foundation, xxi/1 (New York, 1968), pp. 75–6

FREDERICK J. DOCKSTADER

Hill, Oliver (*b* London, 15 June 1887; *d* Sapperton, Glos, 28 May 1968). English architect. On the advice of Sir Edwin Lutyens, a family friend, he first worked for a builder in London and was then articled to the architect William Flockhart (1854–1913). From 1909 to 1911 he also attended the Architectural Association evening school in London where he designed elaborate, finely draughted classical schemes. His principal early work involved garden design and house additions at Moor Close (1910–13),

Binfield, Berks, a rich, eclectic baroque ensemble. After serving in World War I, he returned to his practice and designed Cour (1922), Kintyre, Argyll, a stone country house, low-lying and picturesque. During the 1920s he became a fashionable architect who used neo-vernacular and Neo-Georgian styles, with simple interiors exploiting colour and texture, for example at Woodhouse Copse (1926), Holmbury St Mary, Surrey.

After 1930 Hill showed an increasing interest in modern architecture; this resulted in the white-walled, flat-roofed design of Joldwynds (1933), Holmbury St Mary, Surrey, the Midland Hotel (1933), Morecambe, Lancs, and a modernist sea-side suburb (1934) at Frinton Park, Essex, which was only partly realized. In 1933 and 1934 he designed and organized exhibitions at Dorland Hall, London, to promote Modernism in architecture and industrial design, and he also designed the British Pavilion at the Exposition Internationale des Arts et Techniques dans la Vie Moderne in Paris in 1937. In 1939 he built a primary school of a completely modern character at Whitwood Mere, Castleford, W. Yorks. From 1945 to the end of his career Hill used both modern and traditional styles according to his clients' demands; he found considerable common ground between them, particularly in his love of curved and circular plans. Thus the bus station (1949) at Newbury Park, Essex, incorporated a concrete arched canopy, while the war memorial and library (1949) at Uppingham School, Leics, were in Lutyens style and the Pavilion (1961), Kingston upon Thames, and the Priory (1966) at Long Newnton, Glos, were both classical houses. In retirement he lived at Daneway House, Sapperton, a famous medieval stone manor house, which he decorated in a bizarre but imaginative fashion.

WRITINGS

Fair Horizon, Buildings of To-day (London, 1950)

with J. Cornforth: *English Country Houses: Caroline, 1625–1685* (London, 1966)

BIBLIOGRAPHY

R. Gradidge: 'The Architecture of Oliver Hill', *Archit. Des.*, xlix/10–11 (1979) [pt of 'Profile 24: Britain in the Thirties', ed. G. Stamp, pp. 30–41]

A. Powers: *Oliver Hill, Architect & Lover of Life, 1887–1968* (London, 1989)

ALAN POWERS

Hill, Thomas (*b* ?1661; *d* Mitcham, Surrey, 1734). English painter. According to his friend George Vertue, he was trained by William Faithorne and by Dirk Freres (1643–93), a Dutch history and decorative painter. Stylistically, he appears to have been strongly influenced by Michael Dahl. He was in independent practice by 1694. Several of his portraits were engraved. He painted some formal episcopal portraits, including *Philip Bisse, Bishop of Hereford* (Oxford, New Coll.; engraved by Vertue 1719); *George Hooper, Bishop of Bath and Wells*, signed and dated 1723 (Wells Cathedral); and *William Wake, Archbishop of Canterbury* (?*c*. 1730; London, N.P.G.).

Hill was patronized by two generations of the Strangways family at Melbury House, Dorset, where he was 'received perfectly friendly ... as one of the family'. In about 1698 he painted a vast mural above the staircase there, portraying the entire family, and also executed individual portraits, such as the signed *Susanna Strangways* (all Melbury, Dorset, Lady Teresa Agnew priv. col.). He was associated with the circle of Robert Harley, 1st Earl of Oxford, and became a close friend of his great librarian Humfrey Wanley, whom he painted several times between 1711 and 1722 (e.g. Oxford, Bodleian Lib.; London, N.P.G.). He probably retired in about 1725, when his collections were sold. A gentleman and an intellectual, Hill was a refreshing painter, displaying a refinement and sensibility absent from the work of most contemporary rivals in England.

BIBLIOGRAPHY

Thieme–Becker; Waterhouse: *18 C.*

'The Note-books of George Vertue', *Walpole Soc.*, xviii (1930), pp. 24, 55, 68, 70–72, 137; xx (1932), p. 8; xxii (1934), pp. 3, 72; xxvi (1938), p. 17; xxx (1955), p. 121

RICHARD JEFFREE

Hill, Thomas Noel, 2nd Baron Berwick (*b* Shrewsbury, 21 Oct 1770; *d* Naples, 3 Nov 1832). English patron and collector. In 1789 he inherited Attingham Park, Salop, designed for his father, Noel Hill, 1st Baron Berwick, by George Steuart (*c.* 1730–1806). In 1792 he set out on the Grand Tour in the company of Edward Daniel Clarke. In Rome he sat to Angelica Kauffman for a full-length portrait (1793) and commissioned from the same artist *Cupid's Wound* (1793) and *Bacchus and Ariadne* (1794; all Attingham Park, Salop, NT). Payment for the paintings was made through the agency of Thomas Jenkins. Both Hill and his brother, William Noel-Hill (who succeeded him as 3rd Baron Berwick), patronized Philip Hackert, by whom there are nine paintings at Attingham, including the *Ruins of Pompeii* (1799). In 1805 he employed John Nash to design a picture gallery to accommodate his large collection, which included many copies of famous pictures and antique sculptures; this is one of the earliest examples in England of a top-lit gallery and is further distinguished by the use of curved cast-iron ribs. Nash also designed the main gate (1807), on a site proposed by Humphry Repton in his Red Book of 1797–8. The expense of his building and collecting activities, and of electioneering on his brother's behalf, eventually overtook him and his collection was largely dispersed through a series of sales (London, Phillips, 6–7 June 1825; Attingham Park, George Robins, 30 July–14 Aug 1827; London, Christie's, 17, 30 Nov and 1 Dec 1827). Some of the paintings, including the works by Kauffman, were bought back by his brother.

BIBLIOGRAPHY

Attingham Park, Shropshire, National Trust cat. (London, 1979, rev. 1985)

M. F. Forbes Adam and M. Mauchline: 'Attingham Park, Shropshire', *Country Life*, clxxxvi (2 July 1992), pp. 88–91

J. M. MARSDEN

Hill and Adamson. Scottish photographic partnership formed in 1843 by David Octavius Hill (*b* Perth, 1802; *d* Edinburgh, 17 May 1870) and Robert Adamson (*b* St Andrews, 26 April 1821; *d* St Andrews, 18 Jan 1848). The partnership lasted little more than four years from June 1843 but is one of the most remarkable associations in photographic history. Their complementary skills achieved results with the primitive calotype process that have served as a standard and challenge to later photographers.

Robert Adamson had apparently trained as an engineer but found his health unequal to the work. Sir David Brewster (1781–1868), an associate of William Henry Fox Talbot, prompted him to take up photography instead. He set up a photographic studio in Rock House on Calton Hill, Edinburgh, in May 1843, having learnt Talbot's calotype process from his brother, Dr John Adamson.

Robert Adamson's arrival in Edinburgh coincided with an extraordinary upheaval in the Presbyterian Church of Scotland. The disruption of the Church and the forming of the Free Church of Scotland had an impact on such bystanders as the painter David Octavius Hill. He proposed a great historical painting and had begun the sketches for his picture during the Free Church meetings, when he encountered Brewster, who suggested using photography as an aid and introduced him to Adamson. They took photographs of many of the 474 people to be included in Hill's group painting, the *Signing of the Deed of Demission* (1843–65; Edinburgh, Free Ch. Assembl. Hall). Within a month Hill and Adamson became so fascinated with the possibilities of the calotype process that they entered into a formal partnership to explore it effectively. At the beginning of July their first calotypes were on public view alongside Hill's preliminary studies for the painting; and Hill and Adamson's work had prompted its first aesthetic review, written by Hugh Miller (1802–56) for *The Witness.*

In the next six months Hill and Adamson, besides taking portraits of Free Church ministers in Edinburgh and Glasgow, began work on calotypes of Newhaven fishermen and women (see fig.) and Greyfriars' churchyard. The Scottish Academicians took a particularly close interest in the studio from the beginning. In 1843 Sir

David Octavius Hill and Robert Adamson: *Mrs Elizabeth Johnstone Hall (Newhaven 14)*, calotype, 1843–4 (Edinburgh, National Portrait Gallery)

William Allan posed for photographs in Rock House and Sir George Harvey commissioned calotypes of Greyfriars to use as studies. At least 26 members of the Royal Academy and Royal Scottish Academy were sufficiently interested to appear in Hill and Adamson's photographs.

In 1844 Hill moved into Rock House to work more closely with Adamson. They advertised six volumes of photographs: the fishermen and women of the Firth of Forth, Highlanders, the architecture of Edinburgh and of Glasgow, the old abbeys and castles of Scotland and distinguished Scots. Photographs (Edinburgh, N.P.G.) exist for all of these subjects but Glasgow, although the volumes were never published. Of these, the most interesting and radical project was their photographs of the fishermen and women, taken principally in the village of Newhaven to the north of Edinburgh. They took about 150 photographs, which combine great beauty with a powerful insight into an admirable working community. With these photographs, they effectively invented the fine art of social documentary.

Hill commissioned a new camera, probably the largest in use at the time, from the Edinburgh optician Thomas Davidson (1798–1878). He wanted to increase the size of the calotypes from the standard 8×6 ins (208×157 mm) to a size comparable with the best contemporary engravings. The new camera took photographs up to 16×13 ins (430×325 mm) and the results were among their finest work, for example the calotypes of *Durham* (Edinburgh, N.P.G.), *York Minster* (Edinburgh, Royal Scot. Mus.) and *Linlithgow* (Edinburgh, N.P.G.) and the portraits of *Alexander Campbell* and *Thomas Chalmers's Family Group* (both Edinburgh, N.P.G.). Regrettably, the inadequacies of the paper and the lens resulted in too many failures so that the smaller-scale photographs were far more practicable.

Groups of work that appeared from 1844 onwards came from specific photographic sessions, the most productive of which were at Merchiston Castle School and Bonaly Towers (both in Edinburgh). In October 1844 they obtained Talbot's permission to photograph the meeting in York of the British Association for the Advancement of Science. Their photography was not at its best in York, probably because Adamson prepared the paper in advance (it was more sensitive when freshly impregnated) but also because the discussions of photography at the meeting displayed hostility to Talbot's patent and by extension to his process. Hill was depressed by the York meeting and by the end of the year considered abandoning photography. His enthusiasm revived when David Roberts reported from London that the Graphic Society and Spencer Compton, 2nd Marquis of Northampton (1790–1851), had received the calotypes well. Hill and Adamson immediately drew up a proposal to enter the English art market and planned a series of great English portraits to parallel those of the distinguished Scots. Talbot never replied to this proposal, presumably because Antoine Claudet held the licence for calotype portraits in England.

Hill also attempted to market a volume of 100 calotypes which he regarded as 'a sort of *Liber Studorium*' on the model of J. M. W. Turner's landscape studies. Hill saw the photographs he and Adamson had taken as an aesthetic exploration of the calotype process, extending Turner's idea rather than imitating it, as most of their successful calotypes were portraits not landscapes. The expense of these volumes at £50, and the doubt incurred by the fading of Talbot's published prints, prevented their sale. In 1846 the calotype work was much reduced, although Hill was using such photographs as those from the group of the 92nd Gordon Highlanders as studies for his painting. Adamson's health was deteriorating and at the end of 1847 he returned to St Andrews.

In three years Hill and Adamson took over 3000 photographs. With a few brilliantly constructed exceptions, such as the *Tree and Fence in Colinton Wood* (Edinburgh, N.P.G.), they concentrated on portrait and group photography. Much of the strength of their work comes from Adamson's technical mastery of an unstable process; he was able to maintain consistently rich printing. Both Hill and Adamson were interested in the use of light to exploit and exaggerate the character of the calotype, bouncing the sun's light and even photographing across it. Hill used his knowledge of art not to imitate painting but to compose pictures appropriate to the new medium. His compositions were made through the camera and have an active structural power within the frame of the photograph. Their joint work is distinguished as solid and rich in appearance and capable of expressing strength and scale.

BIBLIOGRAPHY

H. Miller: 'The Calotype', *The Witness* (12 July 1843)
J. M. Gray: *Calotypes by D. O. Hill and R. Adamson . . . Selected from His Collection by Andrew Elliot* (Edinburgh, 1928)
H. Schwartz: *David Octavius Hill: Der Meister der Photographie* (Leipzig, 1931; Eng trans., London, 1932)
A Centenary Exhibition of the Work of David Octavius Hill, 1802–1870, and Robert Adamson, 1821–1848 (exh. cat., ed. K. Michaelson; Edinburgh, Scot. A.C., 1970)
D. Bruce: *Sun Pictures: The Hill–Adamson Calotypes* (London, 1973)
C. Ford and R. Strong: *An Early Victorian Album: The Photographic Masterpieces (1843–1847) of David Octavius Hill and Robert Adamson* (London, 1974)
S. Stevenson: *David Octavius Hill and Robert Adamson: Catalogue of their Calotypes Taken between 1843 and 1847 in the Collection of the Scottish National Portrait Gallery* (Edinburgh, 1981)
J. Ward and S. Stevenson: *Printed Light: The Scientific Art of William Henry Fox Talbot and David Octavius Hill with Robert Adamson* (Edinburgh, 1986)
The Photographs of David Octavius Hill and Robert Adamson (exh. cat., ed. K. Bell; Saskatoon, Mendel A.G., 1987)
S. Stevenson: *Hill and Adamson's 'Fishermen and Women of the Firth of Forth'* (Edinburgh, 1991)

SARA STEVENSON

Hillebrandt, Franz Anton (*b* Vienna, 2 April 1719; *d* Vienna, 25 Jan 1791). Austrian architect. He studied at the Kaiserliche Freye Hof-Academie der Mahlerey/Bildhauerey und Baukunst in Vienna from 1734. His journeyman years were spent in the Netherlands and Germany, three of them in Balthasar Neumann's studio in Würzburg. After 1741 Hillebrandt worked in Vienna, Hungary, Moravia and Slovakia. His first executed work was the Palais Ulfeld-Dietrichstein (1753) in Vienna. In 1750 he submitted plans for the cathedral in Oradea (Romania), where he was also responsible for the Bishop's Palace (from 1762). In 1757 Hillebrandt was appointed First Architect to the Hungarian Exchequer in Bratislava (Slovakia), where he erected a large number of palaces. He also rebuilt the cathedral tower there (1764; later alterations) and after

1767 carried out alterations to the castle. In Buda (Hungary) he was in charge of renovating the castle (from 1765), and in Esztergom (Hungary) he was commissioned to rebuild the church of St Adalbert (from 1767; destr.). In 1772 Hillebrandt became Chief Architect to the Imperial Board of Works in Vienna; he was responsible for developments in the city centre, where he erected the war ministry (1773; destr.), among other buildings. In collaboration with his son Joseph Hillebrandt he converted the Jesuit monastery building in Buda into new administrative centres (1783–5). He was commissioned by the imperial court to carry out alterations and decorations at the castles at Halbturn and Schlosshof (both Austria) and Holič (Slovakia). As official architect Hillebrandt was also responsible for drawing up and approving all the building and engineering projects of the Treasury. His restrained designs were made up of simple building-blocks with animated roof and attic profiles. The shallow relief of his façades, which incorporated stuccoed areas without three-dimensional articulation, reveals Hillebrandt's preference for classical forms of French and south German provenance. A strong revival of 17th-century architectural forms is also visible in his works.

BIBLIOGRAPHY

Thieme–Becker
A. R. Franz: 'Wiener Baukünstler im theresianischen Zeitalter', *Jb. Ksthist. Inst. Wien*, xiii (1919), pp. 20–62 [insert]
J. Kapossy: *Franz Anton Hillebrandt* (Budapest, 1924)
G. Kelenyi: *Franz Anton Hillebrandt* (Budapest, 1976)
G. W. Rizzi: 'G. Kelenyi: Franz Anton Hillebrandt', *Österreich. Z. Kst & Dkmlpf.*, xxxi/3–4 (1977), pp. 146–7
P. Fidler: 'Der Turmbau der Domkirche St Martin in Pressburg: Ein Beitrag zum Oeuvre Franz Anton Hillebrandts', *Wien. Jb. Kstgesch.*, xxxv (1982), pp. 185–90

PETER FIDLER

Hiller, Karol (*b* Łódź, 24 Nov 1891; *d* Łódź, 7 Dec 1939). Polish painter, printmaker and designer. He studied at the Artistic Craft School, Łódź (1907–10), the Higher Technical School, Darmstadt (1910–12), and Warsaw Technical University (1912–15). He was evacuated during World War I to Russia; after the revolution of 1917 he studied at the Academy of Fine Arts in Kiev (1918–21). On his return to Łódź in 1921 he produced a cycle of religious paintings influenced by Byzantine Orthodox painting. An important feature of these is the technical skill of their execution, which is seen as a miracle of action on matter. A singular naturalism and alchemical mysticism are evident in all his works.

The experience of Hiller's Russian period drew him towards the political left and rendered him susceptible to the influence of Cubo-Futurism and Constructivism, especially in Vladimir Tatlin's 'romantic-engineering' version. Hiller's linocuts of industrial landscapes in Łódź of the 1920s do show an affinity with the machine aesthetic, and in 1923 he began designing sets for the amateur political theatre Scena Robotnicza (Workers' Stage) and covers for cheap popular novels, his aim being to seek out areas of life upon which art could exert a direct influence and to establish contact with proletarian clients. His first abstract paintings, geometric compositions from 1928, bring to mind the works of Victor Servranckx and Willi Baumeister. Hiller produced his most Constructivist compositions during a brief period at the end of the decade.

In 1928 he initiated a technique he termed heliography (Pol. *heliografia*); this involved covering transparent celluloid negative plates with compositions in white distemper, which then underwent complex processing including *grattage* and *frottage* and were finally printed on light-sensitive paper in sunlight (a form of *cliché-verre*). Hiller's paintings and graphic works after 1930 contain biomorphic forms and cosmic visions of matter subjected to constant transformation. At the end of the 1930s the composition and differentiation of treatment became less noticeable, and there was an apparent synthesis of organic and constructional tendencies.

BIBLIOGRAPHY

Karol Hiller, 1891–1939 (exh. cat., ed. R. Stanisławski; Łódź, Mus. A., 1967)
Constructivism in Poland, 1923–1936, Blok., Praesens, a. r. (exh. cat., ed. R. Stanisławski and others; Essen, Mus. Flkwang, 1973)
A. Turowski: *Konstruktywizm polski: Próba rekonstrukcji nurtu 1921–1934* [Polish constructivism: an attempt to reconstruct the current of 1921–34] (Wrocław, 1981)

EWA MIKINA

Hiller, Susan (*b* New York, 7 March 1942). British installation artist of American birth. She studied Mesoamerican archaeology and anthropology, tribal art and linguistics, and conducted anthropological fieldwork in Central America before moving to London and taking British residency in 1967. From the early 1970s Hiller included social, anthropological and feminist concerns within her persistent questioning of traditional artistic notions of authorship, subject-matter and methodology, which she articulated using painting, sculpture, sound, printed texts, video, photography and drawing in numerous large-scale installations. *Dedicated to the Unknown Artists* (1972–6; exh. Brighton, U. Sussex, Gardner A. Cent., 1976) consisted of 305 'rough sea' postcards collected by the artist from England, Scotland and Wales, with accompanying charts and notes exploring the relationship between the linguistic description and visual depiction of 'rough seas'. Photographed anonymously, the uncredited postcards were seen by Hiller as cultural artefacts, and her role as that of a collaborator who relocates them in an (installational) art context with her detailed document recording the entire process. Later works include the installation *Monument* (41 colour photographs arranged on a wall, sound tape, park bench for viewers' use, 3.05×6.10 m, 1980–81; three versions, e.g. Leeds, C.A.G.), based on memorial plaques, and *Belshazzar's Feast, the Writing on your Wall* (1983–4; London, Tate), consisting of low band U-matic colour videotape and 12 C-type photographs on Agfa-lustre paper heat-sealed under Perspex, each *c.* 508×406 mm, with ink or pencil scripts.

WRITINGS

Rough Sea (Brighton, 1976)

BIBLIOGRAPHY

The Revenants of Time (exh. cat., London, Matt's Gal.; Sheffield, Mappin A.G.; Glasgow, Third Eye Cent.; 1990)

CECILE JOHNSON

Hillerød, Frederiksborg Castle. Former royal castle in north Zealand, Denmark. The medieval village of Hillerød can be deduced from the first mention, in 1275, of a manor house, Hillerødsholm, built on an islet in a marshy area surrounded by forests. In 1560 King Frederick II acquired Hillerødsholm and converted it into a royal residence, renaming it Frederiksborg. The plan of the existing castle is still based on Frederick's hunting-lodge, with the buildings disposed on three islets in an artificial lake (dammed in the 1560s). The servants' buildings on the first islet have been preserved, with heavy corner towers at the north bearing the King's motto and the date 1562 in iron ties. Other surviving buildings include the pantry wing (1580s), on the west bank in front of the third islet, and the baths, built by Hans Floris (d 1600) in the park north-west of the lake. The buildings are of red brick, with some stepped gables and details in light sandstone, following Netherlandish building traditions, which are most pronounced in the baths. Records, excavations and two views by Hans Knieper—one on a tapestry, which originally hung in the ballroom at Kronborg Castle, Helsingør (Copenhagen, Nmus.), and the other on a panel painting, originally at Frederiksborg Castle (Mariefred, Gripsholm Slott)—show that the royal residence was on the third islet; it was a double house, probably already in existence and altered in 1575 by the King. On the middle islet there was a large half-timbered kitchen building with, facing west, a chapel embellished with Italianate Renaissance gables.

Christian IV, who was born at Frederiksborg, probably planned to convert the manor into a princely residence in the European manner soon after his accession. In 1599 work began on a pleasure palace known as Sparepenge ('Savings'; destr. 1720), which served as a temporary residence on the north bank of the lake from 1602 to 1611 while the main castle was being built on the third islet.

The quadrangular castle was built in phases to 1623: first the royal residence to the north, then the west wing with the chapel (interior arranged 1608–17) beneath the ballroom, as in Kronborg Castle (see HELSINGØR, §2), and finally the princesses' wing and the low terrace wing to the south. At the outbreak of the Kalmar War (1611–13) the main exterior was completed, and there followed three new buildings on the middle islet: the house of the lord of the manor, the chancellery and a huge gate-tower by the bridge to the first islet, where the buildings from Frederick II's reign were allowed to remain standing, contrary to the original intentions.

The first architect of Christian IV's castle is unknown. Hans van Steenwinckel I, whose son Hans II was attached to the building programme from 1614, has been suggested, but only the names of the leading craftsmen, including Jørgen Friborg (fl 1588–1625) and Caspar Boegaert (d 1612), are mentioned in the records. The apparent lack of a chief architect until after the Kalmar War may explain the inconsistencies of planning. The French-inspired plan of the castle's main building with its cour d'honneur opening axially on to the basse-cour of the middle islet, above the low terrace wing, was only partially achieved because neither Sparepenge nor the old buildings on the first islet are on the north–south main axis. In the main castle building the symmetrical requirements of the Renaissance style are broken by the large clock-tower on the chapel wing, while the three wings are effectively independent houses superficially merged to form a whole. There are numerous instances of improvisations and changes during building.

The castle thus combines old and new. The exterior, like its predecessor, is in Netherlandish Renaissance style, red brick buildings with sandstone details, embellished by sweeping gables and imaginative spires. The resulting picturesque quality was evidently more important than the rigorous requirements of symmetry. Moreover, of greatest importance for the builder was the lavish sculptural decoration, which glorifies Christian IV as the leading Protestant prince through themes from astrology and ancient mythology (the Mint gate-house, the terrace wing and marble gallery, and the Neptune Fountain of 1615–24 by Adriaen de Vries; original now Stockholm, Drottningholms Slott) and ancient Roman and Danish history (e.g. pedestal statues of Alexander the Great and Julius Caesar, and emperors and legendary kings in the window gables). This triumphal process culminates in the chapel (see fig.), the entire decoration of which can be seen as a demonstration of the King's theocratic princely ideal. The chapel, with its gallery system, represents a further development of the architectural traditions from the Protestant princely chapel of the 16th century (e.g. in Germany at Schloss Hartenfels, Torgau and Schloss Wilhelmsburg, Schmalkalden) and is closely related to the recently built chapel at Koldinghus Castle, Jutland. It is the only stateroom to be almost entirely preserved from the time of the castle's original building. The ballroom, with its tapestries by Karel van Mander II (c. 1579–1623) depicting Christian IV's coronation and victories in the Kalmar War (now only partially known through copy drawings of 1858 by Heinrich Hansen (1821–90) and Frederick Christian Lund (1826–1901)), and the King's private oratory, installed and

Hillerød, Frederiksborg Castle, interior view of the chapel, 1608–17

decorated from 1615 to 1620 in the north end of the chapel, with paintings by Pieter Lastman, Adriaen van Nieulandt and others, were destroyed by fire in 1859 and can be reconstructed only from early descriptions and representations prior to that date.

In 1659 Frederiksborg was occupied by the Swedes, who removed several art treasures, including the Neptune Fountain (replaced in 1888 by a copy). The interior of the Mint gate-house and the secret passage, added to the west side of the main palace building from 1612, were redecorated as an audience chamber in 1681–8 in glorification of the absolute monarch Christian V (*reg* 1670–99) by his chief architect, Lambert van Haven. In 1720 a formal garden in the French style was laid out north of the lake (where Sparepenge was formerly situated) by Johan Cornelius Krieger. The kings now resided at Frederiksborg rarely, and it was only with the onset of 19th-century Romanticism that the building became a commemorative castle to the glorious past of Denmark–Norway, a favourite subject for such artists as Christen Købke (e.g. Copenhagen, Stat. Mus. Kst.) and P. C. Skovgaard (e.g. Hillerød, Frederiksborg Slott), and a royal residence once again under Frederick VII (*reg* 1848–63). The fire in the main castle in 1859, however, spared only the chapel and the gate-house. This was felt to be a national catastrophe, and a rebuilding programme was soon started under the direction of Ferdinand Meldahl. In 1875 the exterior of the main palace was essentially completed, and in 1877 the Nationalhistoriske Museum på Frederiksborg was established at the initiative of the brewer Jacob Christian Jacobsen, under whose direction the interior was reconstructed with funding from his newly established Carlsberg Foundation.

The town of Hillerød was always dependent on the castle, since it was difficult to persuade people to settle in that remote, wooded region. It became a place of residence for building-workers, courtiers and foreign guests, and the castle chapel was its parish church from 1631. Owing to the fires of 1692, 1733 and 1834 no significant historic buildings have been preserved from before the Neoclassical period of the early 19th century, the most important example of which is the former grammar school (1834) by Jørgen Hansen Koch (1787–1860). Among more characteristic buildings from the second half of the 19th century, the most important are by Vilhelm Holck (1856–1936) in a historicist style inspired by Christian IV's Renaissance castle (e.g. the town hall, built 1887–8, and the 'Sparekassen' bank, built 1898–1900).

BIBLIOGRAPHY

J. A. Berg: *Kurtze und eigentliche Beschreibung des fürtrefflichen und weitberühmten königlichen Hauses Friederichsburg* (Copenhagen, 1646)

F. Beckett: *Frederiksborg*, 2 vols (Copenhagen, 1914–18) [with Fr. summary]

A. Uhrskov, ed.: *Hillerødbogen* [The Hillerød book] (Hillerød, 1948)

J. Steenberg: *Christian IVs Frederiksborg* (Hillerød, 1950)

E. Moltke and E. Møller: *Frederiksborg amt* [Frederiksborg county] (1964–70), ii of *Danmarks kirker* (Copenhagen, 1933–), ii/1, pp. 637–49; ii/3, pp. 1673–1934

M. Stein: 'The Iconography of the Marble Gallery at Frederiksborg Palace', *J. Warb. & Court. Inst.*, xxxv (1972), pp. 284–93; also in *Christian den Fjerdes billedverden* [The imagery of Christian IV] (Copenhagen, 1987)

H. Johannsen: 'Regina firmat pietas: Eine Deutung der Baudekoration der Schlosskirche Christians IV. zu Frederiksborg', *Hafnia: Copenhagen Papers in the History of Art, 1974* (Copenhagen, 1976), pp. 67–140

'Art in Denmark, 1600–1650', *Leids Ksthist. Jb.*, ii (1983), pp. 37–84 [articles by M. Bligaard, H. Honnens de Lichtenberg and L. O. Larsson]

H. Johannsen: 'Den ydmyge konge: Omkring et tabt maleri i Christian IVs bedekammer i Frederiksborg slotskirke' [The humble king: a lost painting in Christian IV's oratory in Frederiksborg Chapel], *Kirkens bygning og brug* [The church, its building and uses]: *Studies Dedicated to Elna Møller* (Copenhagen, 1983), pp. 127–54 [with Eng. summary]

M. Bligaard: *Hillerød gamle Rådhus og dets arkitekt Vilhelm Holck* [Hillerød Old Town Hall and its architect Vilhelm Holck] (Hillerød, 1988)

H. Lund: 'Frederiksborg Slotshave: J. C. Kriegers mestervaerk gennem tiderne' [Frederiksborg Palace gardens: J. C. Krieger's masterpiece through the ages], *Architectura: Arkithist. Aaskr.*, xii (1990), pp. 7–35

HUGO JOHANNSEN

Hilleström, Pehr (*b* Väddö, nr Stockholm, 18 Nov 1732; *d* Stockholm, 13 Aug 1816). Swedish painter and tapestry-weaver. In 1743–4 he was apprenticed to the tapestry designer and decorative painter Johan Filip Korn (1728–96) in Stockholm and at the same time was a pupil at the Kungliga Akademi för de Fria Konsterna, where he took drawing lessons. In 1744 Christian Fehner, a German fan painter living in Sweden, took him as his apprentice. In 1747 CARL HÅRLEMAN apprenticed him to the French high-warp weaver Pierre-Louis Duru (*d* 1753), and for the next ten years he served as Royal Weaver to the Swedish Court. His first large commission was the throne canopy (1746–53) for the Audience Chamber in the Kungliga Slott in Stockholm. In 1757–8 he went to Paris to study weaving at the Savonnerie factory but instead he took classes in pastel and oil painting from Boucher and Chardin. After his return to Sweden he wove parade carpets and did tapestry portraits of Hårleman (Mariefred, Gripsholm Slott), and of Gustav III and his sister Princess Sofia Albertina (Mariefred, Gripsholm Slott) after originals by Boucher, Jean-Baptiste Oudry, and Lars Bolander (*fl* 1774–95). After 1773 he became more interested in painting than in tapestry-weaving and he executed more than 1000 paintings between 1773 and 1810. He was appointed Painter to the Royal Court in 1776 and became a professor at the Akademi the following year. He was a pioneer in the depiction of Swedish folk life. Lovisa Ulrica, Queen of Sweden, commissioned him to paint *Haymakers' Feast at Svartsjö Slott* (1782; priv. col.), while for Gustav III he executed a series of studies of farmers dressed in different regional costumes and gathered together for celebrations. He also portrayed court life at the royal palaces in Stockholm and Drottningholm (e.g. *Conversation at Drottningholm*, 1779; *in situ*) in a series of somewhat naive paintings and for Gustav III he painted 21 scenes based on operas and plays. Hilleström was Sweden's first painter of historical subjects. He did a series of paintings based on the early legends of Ingjald Illråde. In addition, he depicted more recent Swedish history in such portraits as *Gustav I* (*reg* 1523–60) and *Adolf Frederick* (*reg* 1751–71). In his later years he was Principal of the Modellskola of the Akademi and was the Director of the Akademi from 1810 until his death. His son Carl Peter Hilleström (1760–1812) was a landscape painter.

BIBLIOGRAPHY

SVKL

O. Sirén: *Pehr Hilleström d.ä., väfvaren och målaren: Hans lif och hans verk* [Pehr Hilleström the elder, weaver and painter: his life and work] (Stockholm, 1900)

Pehr Hilleström (exh. cat. by M. Winqvist and H. Kruse, Stockholm, Nmus., 1979)

A.-G. WAHLBERG

Hill-figure of the Long Man of Wilmington, East Sussex, cut into chalk, h. *c.* 75 m

Hill-figure. Type of landscape art. It is apparently unique to Britain, and the earliest hill-figures probably pre-date the Roman conquest of the 1st century BC. Hill-figures are produced by removing turf to expose the underlying rock or soil. In the majority of cases—most figures are found in southern England—this is chalk, and thus almost all the figures appear white on a green background. One notable exception was the no longer extant Red Horse of Tysoe in Warwickshire, England, where reddish clay was exposed. Two figures at Strichen in Aberdeenshire, Scotland, were filled with quartz and limestone to give a white appearance, and a small horse-figure at Woolbury Camp, Hampshire, England, was made of flint that has been whitewashed in the past. Most hill-figures feature large cut areas, with details left as uncut patches of turf. A number of the earliest figures, however, were drawn as outlines, with the edges and details marked by cutting, leaving the main body of the figure dark; the same technique was used for some 20th-century signs and badges. For some of the earlier examples, records exist of elaborate cleaning and scouring rituals, for which the participants were paid; seven years seems to have been a regular interval for the cleaning of many figures. Some English figures, such as the UFFINGTON HORSE in Oxfordshire and the Cerne Abbas Giant in Dorset, have traditionally been attributed with powers to confer good luck or fertility—possibly an indication of the monuments' considerable antiquity.

The earliest extant figure is likely to be the Uffington Horse; probably pre-Roman in date, it was the source of inspiration for a number of horse figures cut in the 18th and 19th centuries AD. The Red Horse of Tysoe was mentioned by the antiquarian WILLIAM CAMDEN in 1605; there have been attempts to link it with Saxon settlement in the area, and a date of AD 600 has been suggested. Geophysical and other work attempting to date this now invisible figure has not yet yielded useful results, but its existence by 1605 places it earlier than most of such figures.

Two other extant English figures generally believed to be early are the Cerne Abbas Giant (*see* EROTIC ART, fig. 3) and the Long Man of Wilmington, East Sussex. The Cerne Abbas figure is of a nude male, drawn in outline but with facial details, nipples, ribs and genitalia clearly shown. Measuring *c.* 60 m high, with the eyes 1 m in diameter, in the right hand the figure holds a knobbed club measuring 40 m long, while the left arm is outstretched. Suggestions of an iconographic connection to depictions of Hercules carrying an animal-skin over the left arm have been strengthened in recent years by aerial photographs indicating the original presence of something similar in an area now grassed over. While there is no record of the giant before the 18th century, the style of the figure has been classed as Romano-British. Its association with fertility rites, together with its proximity to the Trendle earthwork immediately above it, may suggest an early date, although some scholars firmly believe it to belong to the 18th century AD. The Long Man of Wilmington (see fig.) is also undated, with a first record dating to the 18th century. This is again an outline figure, but without body details; it measures *c.* 75 m high and has been claimed as the largest representation of a human figure in the world. The figure holds a long staff in either hand, and has been compared with similar figures on Saxon artefacts and on late Roman coins. Early references, however, describe the staffs as a scythe and a rake, so the stylistic links may not be so close. Documentary evidence records other English giant figures no longer visible: on Plymouth Hoe in Devon, payment of 8d. was made in 1529–30 for cleansing the 'Gogmagog' (Gog and Magog were the names given to the last two survivors of a mythical race of British giants), while a reference of 1605 mentions the Gogmagog giants at Wandlebury, near Cambridge. There is no subsequent reference to the cutting of human figures, so the two extant giants may well pre-date the 18th century.

A small group of crosses and an obelisk-shaped mark are also difficult to date. The Whiteleaf Cross in Buckinghamshire was mentioned by the antiquarian WILLIAM STUKELEY in 1757, while the nearby Bledlow Cross was not, and thus may not have been cut by that date. A few miles from the latter, in Oxfordshire, the Watlington obelisk mark is thought to have been cut in 1764. The geographical proximity of these three figures may imply a connection in their cutting dates. The other cross is at Ditchling in East Sussex, where local history connects it with the Battle of Lewes of 1264, although there are no satisfactory records to confirm this.

A large group of figures, almost all horses, belongs to the 18th and 19th centuries. Eight of these are in Wiltshire, and seven were cut between 1780 and 1864. The exception is the Westbury Horse, which was first recorded in 1742; the original figure was destroyed by remodelling in 1778, but sketches of it have led some scholars to see stylistic similarities to Celtic coins, suggesting an antiquity parallel to that of the Uffington Horse. The remaining horses in this group are at Inkpen in Berkshire (cut 1868), Litlington in Sussex (cut 1838), Kilburn in Yorkshire (cut 1857) and Osmington in Dorset. The only known representation of a horse with rider, the Osmington figure is said to portray King George III and to have been cut between 1789 and 1807. Strichen has figures of a horse (probably not cut before 1773) and a stag, cut in 1870.

English 20th-century hill-figures include second horses at Litlington, cut in 1924, and at Pewsey in Wiltshire, cut in 1937 under the supervision of George Marples, an authority on hill-figures. Among other animal figures are a lion cut into the Dunstable Downs in Bedfordshire in 1935 to advertise Whipsnade Zoo and a panda at Laverstock, Wiltshire, cut by students in 1969. An outline crown at Wye in Kent was cut in 1902 and illuminated in celebration of the coronation of Edward VII. The remaining signs comprise regimental badges at Canterbury in Kent (cut in 1922 but no longer extant) and in Wiltshire, where many badges were cut between World War I and the 1950s; some of these, including the figure of a kiwi cut by New Zealand troops, remain visible.

BIBLIOGRAPHY
M. Marples: *White Horses and Other Hill Figures* (London, 1949)
P. Newman: *Gods and Graven Images: The Chalk Hill-figures of Britain* (London, 1987)

SARA CHAMPION

Hilliard [Hillyarde]. English family of miniature painters. (1) Nicholas Hilliard was the eldest son of Richard Hilliard (*c*. 1518–94), a goldsmith working in Exeter. Nicholas practised as a goldsmith all his life and trained a number of apprentices in the craft, but he is primarily known for his outstanding portrait miniatures and for his treatise *The Arte of Limning*. (2) Laurence Hilliard, the third son of Nicholas Hilliard by his first wife, was the only one to pursue the art of painting; he also worked as a medallist.

(1) Nicholas Hilliard (*b* Exeter, ?1547; *bur* London, 7 Jan 1619).

1. Life and work. 2. *The Arte of Limning*. 3. Critical reputation.

1. LIFE AND WORK.

(i) Early years. His father was a strong supporter of the Reformed religion and sent his son abroad to escape the Marian persecution. In 1559 Nicholas was listed in Geneva in the household of John Bodley, an Exeter merchant and staunch adherent of the Protestant faith who became the publisher and part-translator of the Geneva Bible. Here Hilliard learnt the French language and presumably acquired the foundations of a humanist education and some knowledge of contemporary French art, as practised by Huguenot emigrants from France. He is believed to have accompanied Bodley to London on his return in 1559. In the following year, aged 13, Nicholas made his first known miniatures: a posthumous portrait of the Protector *Edward Seymour, Duke of Somerset* (Duke of Buccleuch priv. col.), after an unknown original in the manner of Holbein, and a *Self-portrait Aged 13* (two versions, Duke of Buccleuch priv. col., and ?replica, Welbeck Abbey, Notts). Although immature, these juvenilia show that he had a precocious talent for portrait miniature painting and was already acquainted with its basic techniques.

In 1562 Hilliard was apprenticed to the eminent London goldsmith Robert Brandon (*fl c.* 1547–91) and became a freeman of the Goldsmiths' Company in 1569. The source of his instruction in limning, the art of miniature painting, is unknown. There were many illuminators of documents who could have taught him the use of the materials. The leading portrait limner of the time appears to have been Levina Teerlinc, in royal service 1546–76, but attempts to identify her work have not so far been convincing, and it is not possible to say if she influenced Hilliard's early style. In his treatise *The Arte of Limning* Hilliard is reticent about his origins. He states: 'Holbein's manner of limning I have ever imitated, and hold it for the best', and also advocates the exact copying of engravings by Albrecht Dürer for mastery in hatching; this suggests that he was mainly self-taught.

(ii) First achievements. The earliest dated miniature of Hilliard's maturity is the *Man Aged 35 in 1571* (Welbeck Abbey, Notts). Possibly assisted by the wealth and prestige of the Goldsmiths' Company, he was soon under the patronage of Robert Dudley, Earl of Leicester, and his standing at court is attested by his miniature of *Elizabeth I*, dated 1572 (London, N.P.G.). It is clearly a portrait from life and is his earliest known use of the oval format. Hilliard records in *The Arte of Limning* a conversation when the Queen first sat for him. She expressed her dislike of pronounced shadows in portraits and chose to sit 'in the open alley of a goodly garden' to avoid this defect. Hilliard always maintained that there should be no emphatic chiaroscuro in miniatures.

The restrained modelling and breadth of drawing that are characteristic of Hilliard's fully developed style are demonstrated by another miniature of 1572, the *Unknown Man Aged 24* (London, V&A; see fig. 1), a sympathetic rendering of a flamboyant character. The design shows

1. Nicholas Hilliard: *Unknown Man Aged 24*, vellum laid on playing card, 60×48 mm, 1572 (London, Victoria and Albert Museum)

the influence of French and Flemish portraiture interpreted in a wholly personal way. During the 1570s Hilliard, who shared the Elizabethan love of mercantile adventure, was involved with the painters and lapidaries Cornelius Devosse (*fl* 1566; *d* ?1586) and Arthur Bronckorst (*fl* 1573–83) in an unsuccessful search for gold in Scotland. Such speculations, combined with the Queen's notorious dilatoriness over payment, plagued him with financial worries and forced him to look for patrons outside the royal circle. He told Sir Robert Cecil, later 1st Earl of Salisbury, in 1601 that he could not have continued in the royal service 'if the common works for other persons had not been more profitable unto me'.

In 1576 Hilliard married Alice Brandon, a daughter of his former master. Shortly afterwards he took his bride to France to increase his knowledge and 'upon hope to get a piece of money of the lords and ladies [there] for his better maintenance in England at his return' (Auerbach, p. 16). He became Valet de Chambre to François, Duc d'Alençon, and may have been expected to supply portraits to revive Alençon's flagging courtship of Elizabeth I. Hilliard stayed in France for two years, exceeding his leave of absence and apparently disappointed in his financial expectations. The few miniatures painted at this time include the masterly *Self-portrait Aged 30*, *Richard Hilliard Aged 58* and *Alice Hilliard Aged 22* (all London, V&A). Among his friends were the poet Pierre de Ronsard and the painter Jacques Gaultier (*fl* 1577–93). The writer Blaise de Vigenère arranged for him to engrave two small wood blocks with portraits of the Duc and Duchesse de Nevers for the covenant of a charity. This was an unusual extension of his skills, though in 1574 he had designed a title border for a woodcut by another artist, probably Christopher Tressell (*fl c.* 1570–83). Soon after his return to England in the autumn of 1578, Hilliard painted a miniature of *Mary, Queen of Scots* (versions Windsor Castle, Berks, Royal Col. and London, V&A), which became the source for many posthumous oil paintings.

(iii) Elizabethan works. Hilliard's best works date from the 1580s. Isaac Oliver is believed to have become his pupil at the beginning of the decade. In 1581 Hilliard painted two miniatures of *Sir Francis Drake* (Vienna, Ksthist. Mus.; smaller version, London, N.P.G.). In 1584 he was commissioned to make the design for the Queen's second Great Seal with Derick Anthony (*fl* 1550; *d* 1599), graver to the Mint, and in the same year a draft patent reserved for him the monopoly of limned portraits of Elizabeth I, which he produced in increasing numbers until the end of her reign. His portraits of *Charles Blount*, later Earl of Devonshire (1587; priv. col., see Auerbach, pl. 73), and of the unidentified *Man Clasping a Hand from a Cloud* (London, V&A), dated 1588, are among many important works of the period.

It was probably in 1588 that Hilliard painted a miniature long recognized as a representative masterpiece of Elizabethan art, the *Young Man Leaning against a Tree among Roses* (London, V&A; *see* MINIATURE, fig. 3). Here his emphasis on linear design is blended with a personal interpretation of his Mannerist models and an evident delight in the natural setting that sets the tone for later British landscape painting. Hilliard inscribed many of his

portraits of the 1580s with mottoes conveying an intimate and private message. The inscription on this miniature, *Dat poenas laudata fides*, is a quotation from Lucan's *De bello civili*. Like all mottoes for IMPRESA, this held a private meaning for the subject's friends that may no longer be accessible. The young man appears to be a disconsolate lover encouraged by the roses but suffering from the thorns of love. Yet in Lucan, the phrase (trans. Ben Jonson) 'a praised faith is her own scourge' is qualified by the clause 'when it sustains their states whom fortune hath depressed' in a speech urging the assassination of Pompey: the reference would therefore be, not to amorous suffering, but to the political danger of loyalty to those in disfavour. It has been proposed that the sitter is Robert Devereux, 2nd Earl of Essex, but it is difficult to believe that he could have made such sentiments public in 1588.

This courtly image is one of a series of ambitious full-length portraits that Hilliard produced almost to the end of the century, among them those of *Sir Robert Dudley* (Stockholm, Nmus.), *Sir Anthony Mildmay* (Cleveland, OH, Mus. A.) and *Henry Percy, 9th Earl of Northumberland* (Amsterdam, Rijksmus.), who is represented lying in a secluded garden with the emblem of a pen outbalancing the globe. A notably allusive full-length miniature of *George Clifford, 3rd Earl of Cumberland* (*c.* 1590; London, N. Mar. Mus.; see fig. 2) shows him dressed as Queen's Champion at an Accession Day tilt. On a tree hangs a

2. Nicholas Hilliard: *George Clifford, 3rd Earl of Cumberland*, watercolour, 165×245 mm, *c.* 1590 (London, National Maritime Museum)

shield bearing an impresa of the sun and moon circling the earth with the motto *Hasta Quan[do]*, implying that Cumberland's loyalty is as enduring as the planetary motions.

In the last decade of Elizabeth I's reign, Hilliard was called on to portray her in idealized youth as the mythical Virgin Queen. When the Goldsmiths' Company renewed the lease of his house in Gutter Lane, London, in 1600, they stipulated that he should present them with a 'fair picture in great of Her Majesty', evidence that he also did panel paintings in oils, though no certain example is known. The earlier 'Pelican' and 'Phoenix' portraits of the Queen (Liverpool, Walker A.G. and London, N.P.G.) are close to his style, but their attribution to him is conjectural. In the complaints about ill-health, finances and competition from pupils that he made to Sir Robert Cecil, who had replaced the Earl of Leicester as his chief friend at court, Hilliard emphasized that he was a goldsmith as well as limner to the Queen. Yet apart from the second Great Seal little is known about his goldsmith's work. A jewelled case on which he enamelled the Battle of Bosworth Field is lost, though the four miniatures of Elizabeth I's forebears that it contained are still in the Royal Collection at Windsor Castle. Presumably he designed some of the gold and silver presentation medals of Elizabeth I, and he may have been responsible for the richly jewelled and enamelled settings for some of his own miniatures, such as the 'Armada Jewel' (London, V&A), which contains a portrait of the Queen by him.

(iv) Jacobean works. Hilliard's miniature of an unknown *Young Man* of 1599 (Holkham Hall, Norfolk) marked the beginning of a more restrained approach to his subjects. Uniquely, it is signed in full in gold on the back *N. Hillyarde. fecit 1599*; yet it is an unassuming work, lacking the bravura of his earlier portraiture. Following his accession in 1603, James I continued to employ Hilliard as royal limner. He was given many commissions for routine miniatures and medals in which he probably had the help of pupils, in particular his son Laurence. He also painted a few miniatures of the Queen, *Anne of Denmark*, and her children, *Prince Charles* (later Charles I) and *Princess Elizabeth* (all London, V&A), but it is evident that they preferred the more up-to-date idiom of Isaac Oliver. Sometimes, however, Hilliard was able to recapture his former interpretative power in miniatures such as *Lady Elizabeth Stanley* (ex-Viscount Bearsted priv. col., see Auerbach, pl. 147), inscribed with references to constancy in love, and the *Unknown Man Aged 20* of 1616 (Welbeck Abbey, Notts). In 1617 James I granted him a monopoly over the engraving of royal portraits. This appears to have renewed an existing arrangement by which Hilliard tried to prevent unauthorized repetition of his images: a posthumous engraving (*c.* 1617–19) of Elizabeth I by Francis Delaram acknowledges Hilliard as its source in accordance with this proclamation. Hilliard was paid for a portrait of the King as late as Michaelmas 1618, three months before his death.

2. THE 'ARTE OF LIMNING'. When Richard Haydocke published his translation of the first five books of Giovanni Paolo Lomazzo's *Trattato dell'arte della pittura, scoltura ed architettura* in 1598, he announced that he had persuaded Hilliard to write about the art of limning, of which he was the perfect exponent. Hilliard's text, known as *The Arte of Limning*, survives in a scribe's copy of an unrevised draft (Edinburgh, U. Lib.) and was first published in 1912. In it he combines technical advice with a rare degree of personal reminiscence and self-revelation. He endorses the Renaissance view that painting is an art for gentlemen and considers that miniature painting is especially so because it can be pursued in secret and its products are for private enjoyment. He is fastidious in requiring absolute cleanliness and a calm atmosphere: 'Let your apparel be silk, such as sheddeth least dust or hairs . . . Take heed of the dandruff of the head shredding from the hair and of speaking over your work for sparkling'; 'Discreet talk or reading, quiet mirth or music offend not . . . in any wise avoid anger, shut out questioners or busy fingers'. He considers that the perfection of painting 'is to imitate the face of mankind' and that portraiture should not be attempted until the painter is proficient in history painting. Above all, he is an enthusiast for the English countenance: 'Rare beauties are, even as the diamonds are found among the savage Indians, more commonly found in this isle of England than elsewhere'. This is another reason why the limner should be gentle, since he can hardly watch 'those lovely graces, witty smilings, and those stolen glances . . . without blasting his young and simple heart'. His experience as a goldsmith is evident in the analogy he draws between the five principal colours and the five most precious stones. In other more autobiographical passages he laments the penury and ill reward of the conscientious artist, busy about one work while 'the botcher dispatches six or seven'.

The Arte of Limning is the first known writing by an English Renaissance artist and is of great value as a description of the atmosphere and methods of a studio *c.* 1600. It also reveals the personality of an artist whose delight in his work and his materials was undimmed by the worries that beset him. Six autograph letters to Sir Robert Cecil are the only other writings by Hilliard known to survive (Marquess of Salisbury, on dep. to London, PRO).

3. CRITICAL REPUTATION. When any Elizabethan, such as Sir John Harington, Richard Haydocke, Francis Meres or later Henry Peacham, wished to extol the artistic achievements of his countrymen, Hilliard's name was the first to come to mind. Henry Constable and John Donne praised him in their poetry, and he enjoyed a high repute abroad. However, when Horace Walpole wrote his *Anecdotes of Painting in England* in 1760 he considered that 'the greatest obligation we have to Hilliard is his having contributed to form Isaac Oliver'. Since then his standing has been linked with that of Oliver; some commentators have taken a partisan view, extolling one at the expense of the other, and until recently the works of the two artists were often confused. But all such comparisons are misguided since they are dealing with two wholly dissimilar artists. Oliver was Hilliard's pupil, but he emerged half a generation later into a changed artistic climate and with a different artistic character. Hilliard came to maturity in the 1570s, when Philip Sidney and Edmund Spenser were

laying the foundations for the revival of English poetry. Hilliard established a distinctively English type of vision, dependent on clear lighting and elegant line, and in his work embodied the creative urge and lyricism of the Elizabethan period.

WRITINGS

The Arte of Limning, ed. R. K. R. Thornton and T. G. S. Cain (Manchester, 1981) [transcription of original MS. alongside modernized version]

BIBLIOGRAPHY

C. Winter: *Elizabethan Miniatures* (London, 1943) [pioneering in the scholarly reassessment of Hilliard and Oliver]
Nicholas Hilliard and Isaac Oliver (exh. cat. by G. Reynolds, London, V&A, 1947, 2/1971) [fully illus.]
G. Reynolds: *English Portrait Miniatures* (London, 1952, rev. Cambridge, 1987)
E. Auerbach: *Nicholas Hilliard* (London, 1961) [standard monograph, listing most of Hilliard's known work and copiously illus.]
M. Edmond: *Hilliard and Oliver* (London, 1983) [additions and emendations to Auerbach]
V. J. Murrell: *The Way Howe to Lymne* (London, 1983) [description of Hilliard's technical methods]
Artists of the Tudor Court (exh. cat. by R. Strong and V. J. Murrell, London, V&A, 1983)
R. Strong: *The English Renaissance Miniature* (London, 1983)
J. Murdoch: *Catalogue of the 17th Century Portrait Miniatures in the Victoria and Albert Museum* (in preparation)

(2) Laurence Hilliard (*b* London, 1582; *d* London, 1648). Son of (1) Nicholas Hilliard. He was trained by his father and was made a freeman of the Goldsmiths' Company by patrimony in 1605. Nicholas Hilliard, writing to his patron Robert Cecil, 1st Earl of Salisbury, in 1606, said that Laurence 'doth His Majesty good service, both in limned pictures, and in the medal[ling] of gold'. In 1608 a royal patent granted Laurence the reversion of his father's salaried post of King's Limner. He duly succeeded to that office on the death of Nicholas Hilliard in 1619.

Laurence Hilliard's portraits of James I have not so far been distinguished from those of his father. Some half-dozen miniatures signed with the initials LH and bearing dates between 1621 and 1644 are known, and a few additions can be made to this group because they are signed or on stylistic grounds. These show him to have practised a weaker version of his father's manner. His signed portrait of an *Unknown Man* (1640; Cambridge, Fitzwilliam) is inscribed in a hand akin but inferior to Nicholas Hilliard's calligraphy and the style of portraiture is rigorously conservative, showing no recognition of the change in taste brought about by Daniel Mijtens and Anthony van Dyck. The small amount of surviving work by Laurence suggests that in spite of his official standing he was passed over in favour of the more up-to-date John Hoskins and Peter Oliver.

BIBLIOGRAPHY

H. Farquhar: *Portraiture of our Stuart Monarchs on their Coins and Medals* (London, 1909)
G. Reynolds: 'Portraits by Nicholas Hilliard and his Assistants of King James I and his Family', *Walpole Soc.*, xxxix (1952–4), pp. 14–26
E. Auerbach: *Nicholas Hilliard* (London, 1961)
M. Edmond: *Hilliard and Oliver* (London, 1983)

GRAHAM REYNOLDS

Hilliard, John (*b* Lancaster, 29 March 1945). English artist working with photography. He studied sculpture at St Martin's School of Art, London, from 1964 to 1967, but began working with photography when he recognized that his earlier three-dimensional projects were better known in the form of illustrations than as physical objects in their own right. His subsequent self-reflexive works, exemplified by *Camera Recording its own Condition (7 Apertures, 10 Speeds, 2 Mirrors)* (1971; London, Tate), illustrate the ambiguities and constraints specific to the medium and demonstrate the degree to which manipulation of the photographic image can affect an understanding of the visual world.

From the mid-1970s Hilliard confronted a wider range of issues in his work, especially those associated with age, race and gender. Stimulated by developments in linguistics, semiotics and semiology, he was inspired by imagery reminiscent of billboard advertising and the cinema, adapting his earlier formalist approach to the requirements of narrative composition. His Cibachrome double images of a variety of subjects are concerned with the notion of reciprocity and illustrate the consequences of simple editorial decisions. By dwelling on the ways by which appearances are mediated through photography, he questioned both representation and the role of the artist in the presentation of an image or an event. Hilliard continued to elaborate on his approach to the medium by expanding into Scanachrome reproduction.

BIBLIOGRAPHY

The New Art (exh. cat., ed. A. Seymour; London, Hayward Gal., 1972)
John Hilliard (exh. cat., ed. J. Fisher and W. Herzogenrath; Cologne, Kstver., 1983)
John Hilliard (exh. cat. by M. Newman, London, ICA, 1984)

PAUL BONAVENTURA

Hills, Robert (*b* Islington [now in London], 26 June 1769; *d* London, 14 May 1844). English painter and etcher. After taking drawing-lessons from John Alexander Gresse (1740–94), he enrolled at the Royal Academy Schools, London, in 1788. Village and rural scenes, and in particular studies of animals, occupied him throughout his working life; his favourite subjects were cattle, sheep, donkeys, pigs and above all deer, which he stalked for the purpose of sketching. As well as making *plein-air* drawings, Hills carried out careful anatomical studies of animal bones and joints. Between 1798 and 1815 he issued an extensive series of *Etchings of Quadrupeds*; the British Museum holds the artist's collection of his own etchings, which number over a thousand. He worked mostly in watercolour but also occasionally in oils.

In 1804 Hills was closely involved in the foundation of the Society of Painters in Water-Colours and was elected its first secretary. In 1823 he was re-elected to the reconstituted Society, becoming treasurer in 1827 and secretary from 1831 until his death. His first venture abroad was to Paris in 1814. The next year he visited Waterloo shortly after the battle, a journey that gave rise to his *Sketches of Flanders and Holland*, with both text and etchings by Hills. In 1817 he modelled a red deer in terracotta, which was subsequently reproduced in bronze and displayed at the International Exhibition of 1862 in London.

Hills often collaborated with other artists—such as George Fennel Robson (with whom he travelled), George Barret the younger (1767–1842) and William Andrews Nesfield (1793–1881)—supplying foreground animals to their landscapes. In the 1830s his drawing became less sharp and his reputation declined, although his etchings were still widely used as models by other artists. One of his last commissions, in 1839, was to record the first giraffe (albeit short-lived) to be born in England.

UNPUBLISHED SOURCES

London, BM [etchings]

PRINTS

Sketches of Flanders and Holland (London, 1816)

BIBLIOGRAPHY

B. Long: 'Robert Hills, Water-colour Painter and Etcher', *Walker's Q.*, xii (1923), pp. 1–48

L. Herrmann: 'Robert Hills at Waterloo', *Connoisseur*, cl (1962), pp. 174–7

PATRICK CONNER

Hilo. *See* HADDA.

Hilton, Roger (*b* Northwood, Greater London, 23 March 1911; *d* Botallack, Cornwall, 23 Feb 1975). English painter. He studied at the Slade School of Fine Art from 1929 to 1931 and during the 1930s alternated between London, where he showed annually with the London Group (1935–8) and had his first exhibition at the Bloomsbury Gallery (1936), and Paris, where he studied periodically at the Académie Ranson under Roger Bissière. During World War II he served with the commandos (1940–42), was captured during the raid on Dieppe and spent three years as a prisoner of war. After the war he taught at Bryanston School (1946–7) and resumed his visits to Paris.

From 1950 to 1952 Hilton turned from his early figurative painting to a form of abstraction indebted to *Art informel* and particularly to *Tachism*, in which ragged brushstrokes were played against patches of colour that evoked natural phenomena. He showed these works in the company of younger British abstract artists at the A.I.A. Gallery and Adrian Heath's studio. Following his first post-war one-man exhibition at Gimpel Fils in 1952, he began, in works such as *June 1953 (Deep Cadmium)* (1953; Edinburgh, N.G. Mod. A.), to simplify his means, constructing bold designs of irregular shapes in strong colours. His friendship with the Dutch artist Constant, whose paintings were similar in form, seems to have been a factor in this change. Hilton accompanied Constant to the Netherlands in 1953. That he studied Mondrian's work there is evident in the colour schemes of white, black and red that he briefly adopted in paintings such as *February–March 1954* (1954; London, AC Eng), although his insistent individualism precluded him from following Mondrian's idealism to its logical conclusion. Around 1956 Hilton began to be compared with the Abstract Expressionists. Although he mocked the idea of action painting as implying 'more action in one type of work rather than another', he did consider that in painting 'the act makes the meaning' (exh. cat., London, ICA, 1958).

In many of the paintings from this period, for example *Grey Figure* (1957; Southampton, C.A.G.), Hilton's initial inspiration was derived from the rhythms and colours of

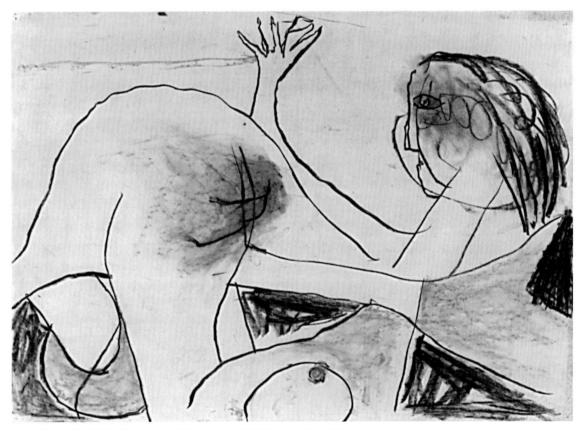

Roger Hilton: *Two Nude Women*, pastel, 559×762 mm, *c*. 1965 (London, Tate Gallery)

the natural world. This has generally been interpreted as a mark of his association with the St Ives artists, corroborated by his frequent visits to that town from the late 1950s culminating in his move to St Just, Cornwall, in 1965. Parallels, however, can be drawn with the work of those American and French painters who, in the same period, were also evoking landscape associations through their gestural abstractions.

By the late 1950s Hilton was speaking of his wish to 'reinvent figuration', demonstrating not only his frustration with the limitations of abstract painting but also his discovery that images could be generated out of the process of painting itself. The imagery that had consistently featured in his drawing-books emerged sporadically in his works of the 1960s, for example in the female nudes of *Oi Yoi Yoi* (1963) and *Two Nude Women* (*c*. 1965; both London, Tate; see fig.), and finally in the works on paper that Hilton began to produce in 1970, when he was bedridden with a muscular disease.

Using cheap poster paints and children's brushes, which required exceptional inventiveness of handling, Hilton returned to the childlike subjects that had characterized his early work: animals, boats, a horse and cart and nudes. These now provided metaphors for adult concerns. Dreams of sensual (often sexual) pleasure co-exist with worries concerning impotence, ill-health and approaching death. Images of stasis and spiritual voyaging abound. Memory, observation and the simple joy of making marks constitute a complex variety of impulses behind these late works, in which Hilton retrieved a childlike freshness of vision, but one marked by a lifetime's experience.

WRITINGS
Letter to Peter Townsend, *Studio Int.*, clxxxvii/964 (1974)
Night Letters and Selected Drawings, intro. M. Canney (Penzance, 1980)

BIBLIOGRAPHY
Roger Hilton: Paintings and Drawings, 1931–1973 (exh. cat. by N. Lynton and R. Hilton, London, Serpentine Gal., 1974)
Roger Hilton: The Early Years, 1911–55 (exh. cat. by A. Lewis, Leicester, Poly., Exh. Hall., 1984)
Roger Hilton (exh. cat., ed. M. Caiger-Smith; London, Hayward Gal., 1993–4)

ADRIAN LEWIS

Hilton, William (*b* Lincoln, 3 June 1786; *d* London, 30 Dec 1839). English painter. The son of the japanner, theatrical scenery and portrait painter, William Hilton sr (1752–1822), William jr first studied with John Raphael Smith, the mezzotint engraver. He entered the Royal Academy Schools, London, in 1806, and he was elected ARA in 1813 and RA in 1819. His diploma piece the *Rape of Ganymede* (1819; London, RA) was the first of a long sequence of mythological subjects. Hilton was also renowned for his biblical paintings, such as the *Raising of Lazarus* (exh. RA 1816) presented to Newark Church, Notts. In 1827 he became Keeper of the Royal Academy.

Hilton enjoyed the patronage of some of the keenest collectors of contemporary art. The *Rape of Europa* (Petworth House, W. Sussex, NT) was painted for Sir John Fleming Leicester in 1818. *Marc Antony Reading Caesar's Will* (London, Soane Mus.) was commissioned by Sir John Soane in 1834 for 100 guineas. *Jacob Separating from Benjamin* (exh. London, Brit. Inst., 1832; untraced) belonged to William Wells, while its companion, *Rebecca*

at the Well (exh. RA 1833; London, Tate), was in the collection of Robert Vernon. Discussing Vernon's collection, Gustav Waagen described Hilton as: 'an artist of unusual talent for historical painting, being intellectual in invention, careful in drawing and execution, and warm though not always true in colouring' (*Treasures of Art in Great Britain*, i, London, 1854, p. 372). Despite these commissions, Hilton suffered hardship; the interest of individual patrons did not compensate for the lack of large-scale state patronage.

Hilton also painted portraits. In 1819 he executed a sketch of John Keats, although his subsequent portrait (n.d.; London, N.P.G.) follows Joseph Severn's miniature of the poet (exh. RA 1819; London, N.P.G.). In 1820 Hilton painted a portrait of the poet John Clare (London, N.P.G.).

Hilton travelled to Rome via Milan and Venice in the company of Thomas Phillips in 1825. His journal and his letters home reveal a predictable admiration for Raphael and Michelangelo, a carefully cultivated disposition to compare originals with the engraved copies with which he had long been familiar and a capacity to enjoy Gothic architecture. The drawings that Hilton produced during this journey and throughout his life possess a lively and sharply focused quality, which seems at odds with the heavily worked eclecticism of his canvases. Many of the latter are large; for example, *Una and the Satyrs* (exh. RA 1832; Lincoln, Usher Gal.) measures 2.40 m×1.55 m. Hilton's confident use of bitumen has left many of his most celebrated paintings in a virtually ruined condition, for instance *Edith Finding the Body of Harold* (1834; London, Tate). His choice of subjects from English history, English literature (e.g. Edmund Spenser) and the Bible is typical of the period, but he brought to his work a grasp of composition and a delight in handling paint that merit attention. Many of Hilton's paintings were engraved by, among others, Charles Heath (i) and Peter Lightfoot (1805–85).

Hilton's sister Harriet married his close friend Peter De Wint in 1810. Both men had studied under J. R. Smith and had shared a house. Hilton and De Wint are commemorated jointly in a monument in Lincoln Cathedral.

UNPUBLISHED SOURCES
Lincoln, Usher Gal. [Hilton's journal and letters and Harriet De Wint's press cuttings book, relating to De Wint and Hilton]

BIBLIOGRAPHY
'William Hilton', *Art-Union*, ix (1847), p. 50
M. Pointon: 'The Italian Tour of William Hilton RA in 1825', *J. Warb. & Court. Inst.*, xxxv (1972), pp. 339–58
——: 'Keats, Joseph Severn and William Hilton: Notes on a Dispute', *Notes & Queries*, ccxviii (1973), pp. 49–54

MARCIA POINTON

Hiltz, Jean. *See* HÜLTZ, JOHANN.

Himeji. Japanese city in Hyōgo Prefecture, west of Osaka on the Ichi River, at the junction of the main roads linking the coastal districts along the Inland Sea and the Japan Sea coast.

1. URBAN DEVELOPMENT AND ART LIFE. Himeji was the site of the capital of Harima Province in the Nara

(AD 710–94) and Heian (794–1185) periods but the modern city dates back to the establishment of a castle and castle town in 1577 by TOYOTOMI HIDEYOSHI (see §2 below). A succession of rulers expanded the urban area and by the 18th century it had 78 wards and a population of about 23,000. The population stabilized at about this level until the 20th century. It now stands at about 450,000. After the abolition of Himeji domain in 1871 in the reforms of the Meiji period (1868–1912), Himeji Castle became an army base. The Japanese self-defence forces still maintain a base in the city. Industrialization began in 1878, when a cotton mill was established to provide employment for impoverished former samurai, and Himeji proceeded to develop a substantial industry in textiles. By 1903, the commercial centre of the city had already begun to move away from the highway that meandered through the old part of the city. Although the urban area was razed by bombing in World War II, Himeji recovered rapidly to become a centre for chemical and heavy industry and is now part of Harima Industrial Zone. Post-war reconstruction of the city was such that the original layout and buildings of the castle town were virtually lost. The magnificent castle and a few notable attractions remain, such as the temple Enkyōji on the edge of the city.

As a castle town and major trade centre, Himeji must have had its own flourishing regional culture in art, literature and the performing arts. The Sakai family, daimyo of Himeji from 1749 until 1871, had a tradition of patronage of the arts and of creative personal accomplishment in poetry, although one of the best known, SAKAI HŌITSU, spent his creative life in Edo. Hōitsu was responsible for reviving and reinterpreting the painting style of the famous Rinpa artist Ogata Kōrin (see OGATA, (1), and JAPAN, §VI, 4(v)), whom his family had earlier patronized.

2. HIMEJI CASTLE [Shirasagijō]. Castle in Himeji City. Himeji is an example of a *hirayamajiro* ('castle on a low-lying plateau on a plain'). Its inner defences are the best, both aesthetically and militarily, to have survived in a Momoyama-period (1568–1600) castle (see JAPAN, §III, 4(ii)(c)). The nine buildings of the DONJON complex are National Treasures; the remaining 74 structures (27 turrets, 15 gates, 32 breastworks) are all designated Important Cultural Properties. The remains of the inner and middle castle are a protected historical site.

A castle, initially owned by the Akamatsu family, has existed on the site since *c.* 1333 to control traffic between western Honshu and Kyoto. The general TOYOTOMI HIDEYOSHI expanded the old castle in 1580. Ikeda Terumasa (1564–1613), who supported Tokugawa Ieyasu (1543–1616) at the Battle of Sekigahara, was given the castle and domain in 1600; he rebuilt the castle between 1601 and 1609. Honda Tadamasa (1575–1631) added four turrets and connecting galleries forming a corridor (l. 300 m) on the outer wall of the western enceinte and probably remodelled the enceinte itself in 1618, completing the expansion of the castle. Himeji thus became one of the most heavily fortified castles of its time.

Terumasa's castle consisted of three enceintes: Sannomaru (Third), Ninomaru (Second) and Honmaru (Main). They were divided by moats and walls, which enclosed the inner section in a spiral pattern winding towards the

north-eastern corner, where the donjon complex stood. The outer moat (5232×14 m) enclosed most of the castle town (*jōkamachi*) of Himeji. The middle moat (4323× 20 m) separated the footsoldiers', townsmens' and temple quarters from the samurai quarters in the middle castle. Inside the extant inner moat was the inner castle, which housed the domain administrative offices and the living quarters of the daimyo and his family. The major gates of the three main fortress walls were constructed to form a rectangular courtyard or double barbican (*masugata*). Urban development after 1871 destroyed the outer defences and the eastern and western sides of the middle and therefore only the inner castle retains its original outlines.

The inner castle has more than seven enceintes, subdivided by gates and stone walls, rising in a spiral arrangement to the main donjon complex. The site covers some 23 ha and is dominated by the four-towered donjon (*tenshukaku*) on a hill (h. 45 m) in the north-eastern corner. The spacious Third Enceinte is entered through the stone walls of what was a triple-barbicaned gate. This was the administrative and residential centre until it became an army base in 1872 and all original buildings were demolished. Owing to the later destruction of sections of the castle, it is now possible to proceed almost straight to the Water Chestnut Gate (Hishimon) between the Sannomaru and Kami-no-Yamasoto, which gives on to the heart of the castle. The Water Chestnut Gate leads into a square yard enclosed on all sides by walls. From this point the donjons are visible over a series of imposing stone walls (see fig.). Two spiralling paths lead from the yard to the donjons. The 'high road' to the left twists and turns up through either the Western (Nishinomaru) or the Lower Second Enceinte (Shimono Ninomaru) towards the main donjon. An intruder would thus have been repeatedly led into the line of fire from the many geometrically shaped loopholes (*hazama* or *sama*) and funnelled into progressively narrower spaces. The effectiveness of the defences on this side depended largely on the complex layout: the gates, for example, are small and narrow. The 'low road' follows a simpler and more direct route to the right through the Kami-no-Yamasoto Enceinte but is guarded by high stone walls and heavily fortified gates. The climb is steep, and the different layers of walls, breastworks and turrets towering above combine to create a powerful sense of movement.

The stone base of the donjon complex rises 15 m from the Main Enceinte and follows the natural contours of the foundation, producing an irregular shape, particularly in the north-eastern corner. The complex consists of a major donjon (*daitenshu*) and three minor donjons (*shōtenshu*), linked by covered fortified corridors. The main donjon, which stands in the south-eastern corner of the complex, rises 31.5 m from its stone walls to a level almost 100 m above the plain. It has five exterior levels; the interior contains seven storeys and a basement. It is built in the earlier *Bōrō* (Watch-tower) style, as three structures piled one on top of each other. It consists of a two-storey base, a middle third storey that is structurally unconnected to the base or to the superstructure and a three-storey tower on top. Characteristics of the *Bōrō* style include an irregular

Himeji Castle, donjon complex seen from inside the Water Chestnut Gate, early 17th century; the lower fortifications are (in descending order) the covered gallery of the Kami-no-Yamasato Enceinte and the breastworks of the Lower Second Enceinte (Shimono Ninomaru)

base-line and a resultant irregular roof line, which necessitates the use of many gables (15 in this case); and a discrepancy between the outer roof layers and the internal floor levels. An architectural advance, however, is seen in the two central pillars that rise from the foundation to the floor of the sixth storey to join the structure together. The three minor donjons each stand three storeys above their base: the connecting covered galleries rise to two. The complex is built as a fortress and lacks permanent residential quarters.

The donjons are designed to present a different roof line from each direction, having various styles, including Chinese, dormer and hip-and-gable. Decorative bell-shaped windows are used on the southern and western walls of the complex facing the main gate and the residential areas; heavily latticed square windows are used elsewhere. The roof-tiles are held down with white plaster, which emphasizes the curvature of the roofs. The outer wooden walls of the donjon complex are covered with white plaster up to the eaves, making the decorative exposed pillar on the sixth storey invisible from a distance. Most of the breastworks and turrets are also white, giving the castle the appearance of a white heron spreading its wings for flight, whence its alternative name, Shirasagijō (White Heron Castle).

The maintenance of the castle was discontinued in 1871, and in 1877 the dilapidated buildings were offered for auction. They were saved by Colonel Nakamura of the Army Ministry, and repairs in 1889, 1909 and 1910–11 saved the buildings from collapse. Full-scale restorations were carried out in 1925–8 and 1950–56.

BIBLIOGRAPHY
K. Hirai: *Shiro to shoin* [Castles and palaces], Nihon no bijutsu [Arts of Japan] (Tokyo, 1965); Eng. trans. by H. Sato and J. Ciliotta as *Feudal Architecture of Japan*, Heibonsha Surv. Jap. A., xiii (New York and Tokyo, 1973)
——: *Jōkaku I* [Castles I], Nihon kenchikushi kiso shiryō shūsei [Collection of the basic materials in Japanese architectural history], xiv (Tokyo, 1978)
T. Katō: *Himeji jō no kenchiku to kōzō* [The architecture and structure of Himeji Castle], Nihon jōkakushi kenkyū sōsho [The library of studies of Japanese castles], ix (Tokyo, 1981)
K. Nishi: *Himejijō to Nijōjō* [Himeji Castle and Nijō Castle], Meihō Nihon no bijutsu [Famous treasures of Japanese art], xv (Tokyo, 1981)
T. Katō, ed.: *Himejijō* [Himeji Castle], Nihon mei jō shūsei [Collection of famous castles in Japan], i (Tokyo, 1984)

J. F. MORRIS

Himera [Imera]. Site of an ancient Greek city in Sicily. Himera was founded *c.* 649 BC on a ridge overlooking the central north coast of Sicily and flourished until its destruction by Carthaginians in 409 BC. In 407 BC a second settlement was made 12 km to the east, at Thermai Himeraiai (Termini Imerese). Himera was celebrated in antiquity as the site of a major Greek victory over Carthaginians in 480 BC. Excavations of the upper city have uncovered four non-peripteral temples (temples A, B, C and D) and areas of habitation notable for the early use (*c.* 500 BC) of a strict orthogonal plan. The earliest of the temples dates from the late 7th century BC, and all were probably dedicated to female deities. A stretch of the Archaic city wall is also preserved. The monumental 'Temple of Victory' was built near the shore *c.* 470–*c.* 460 BC, presumably in commemoration of the great battle. Built in the Doric order of local limestone, on a platform measuring 22.9×55.8 m, the temple had a peristyle of 6×14 columns, a pronaos, an opisthodomos and a cella with a pair of internal stone staircases leading to the attic. The platform, most of the lower column drums, part of the inner stairs and the lower walls are preserved *in situ*, and blocks from the superstructure remain on the site. Much of the lion's head sima (gutter) and pieces of pedimental sculpture are in the Museo Regionale di Palermo.

BIBLIOGRAPHY

P. Marconi: *Himera: Lo scavo del tempio della Vittoria e del temenos* (Rome, 1931)
A. Adriani and others: *Himera*, i (Rome, 1970)
N. Allegro and others: *Quaderno imerese* (Rome, 1972)
——: *Himera*, ii (Rome, 1976)
——: *Secondo quaderno imerese* (Rome, 1982)
B. Barletta: *Ionic Influence in Archaic Sicily* (Göteborg, 1983)
V. Alliata and others: *Himera*, iii (Rome, 1988)
Lo stile severo in Sicilia (exh. cat., Palermo, Mus. Reg., 1990)

M. M. MILES

Himid, Lubaina (*b* Zanzibar, 25 July 1954). British painter. She studied theatre design at Wimbledon School of Art and cultural history at the Royal College of Art, London. She was particularly interested in discussing and tackling her position as a black woman through the practice of painting, and held the view that painting is the common form and tool for dialogue about art, illusion and prophecy. Conscious too that painting has a history of use in the adornment of architecture, homes, bodies and fabrics, and involves cultures and artists that are marginalized, she worked at a point of intersection between these two areas. She was best known for her sensuous, painterly rewritings of history: depictions of moments where women are within history and are active in determining and changing its course. In *Five* (acrylic on canvas, 1.5×1.2 m, 1991; Griselda Pollock priv. col.), for example, two black women discard maps of a white, imperialist, patriarchal world. In other works Himid used patterns that allude to modernist abstraction as well as to the patterns in fabrics made by women in Africa and other parts of the world (e.g. *Invasion*, acrylic on canvas, 2.1×1.5 m, 1991). All her work, however, addresses issues of painting and history, mourning such historical injustices as slavery while celebrating the pleasures of her own life and friendships and the sensuality of paint.

BIBLIOGRAPHY

New Robes for MaShulan: Lubaina Himid: Work Past and Present: A Room for MaShulan (exh. cat., Rochdale, A.G., 1987)
Lubaina Himid: Revenge (exh. cat. by J. Morgan and M. Sulter, Rochdale, A.G., 1992)

□

Himyar. *See under* ARABIA, PRE-ISLAMIC, §§I, III and IV, 1–2.

Hincz, Gyula (*b* Budapest, 17 April 1904; *d* Budapest, 26 Jan 1986). Hungarian painter, illustrator, mosaicist, tapestry designer, stage designer, poster designer, printmaker, sculptor, teacher and administrator. From 1922 to 1929 he studied at the Hungarian Academy of Fine Arts (Magyar Kepzőművészeti Főiskolá) in Budapest under Gyula Rudnay (1878–1957) and János Vaszary (1867–1939). In the mid-1920s he became acquainted with Béla Uitz's *General Ludd* series (1923; Budapest, N.G.) and in Venice he saw the work of such Russian avant-garde artists as Rodchenko and El Lissitzky and such Italian Futurists as Severini. In 1926 in Paris he studied the works of Léger, Braque, Picasso and others in the collection of Léonce Rosenberg. He was also influenced by the art of Brancusi and Joseph Csáky, as well as André Breton's *Manifeste du surréalisme* (Paris, 1924). From the outset, Hincz's work revealed a number of different objectives. Although he experimented with abstraction, the reference to the figure is always present in one form or another. His profound interest in humanity and its social interaction was based on, and motivated by, this interest in the figure. His early paintings are expressionist in mood and are composed of flattened forms in a shallow space in a manner reminiscent of Cubo-Futurist art. Elements of Purism and Surrealism are also present. After World War II he became increasingly preoccupied with realism, political agitprop art and the problems inherent in creating new symbols; a study trip to Korea, China and Vietnam in 1947–8 provided him with new ideas. His history paintings, genre studies and portraits were inspired by the realistic art of the 1950s. He worked in a wide variety of media in the 1960s, producing large decorative works in the form of murals, paintings on glass and mosaics (e.g. *Technology and Science*, glass mosaic, 1970; Budapest, Tech. U. Bldg). His large tapestries (e.g. *Science*, 1967; Debrecen, Agric. Coll.) often combine symbolic forms and natural and illustrative details. As a stage designer, he was a Hungarian pioneer of the dynamic, emblematic theatre initiated by Russian artists. He was also a gifted poster designer, printmaker and sculptor and was one of the most important book illustrators in Hungary, executing drawings for the writings of such authors as François Villon and Anatole France. He taught (1946–9) at the Hungarian Academy of Crafts and Design (Magyar Iparművészeti Főiskolá) in Budapest and was its director from 1958 to 1963. He also taught (1949–63) at the Academy of Fine Arts in Budapest.

BIBLIOGRAPHY

Hincz Gyula állandó gyüjteménye, Vác [Gyula Hincz's permanent collection, Vác] (exh. cat., ed. M. Losonci; n.d.) [Rus., Ger. and Eng. summaries and bibliog.]
Hincz Gyula, intro. by S. Láncz (Budapest, 1972) [trilingual text; album of his prints]
J. Bauer: *Hincz Gyula*, Mai magyar művészet sorozat [Contemporary Hungarian art series] (Budapest, 1975)
Művészet [Art], xx/3 (1979), pp. 2–31 [issue dedicated partly to Hincz; Eng. and Rus. summaries]

S. KONTHA

Hind, Arthur Mayger (*b* Horninglow, Burton-on-Trent, 26 Aug 1880; *d* Henley-on-Thames, 22 May 1957). English art historian, museum administrator, writer and lecturer. He entered the Department of Prints and Drawings at the British Museum in 1903, following a period of study with

Max Lehrs at Dresden. He assisted the keeper, Sidney Colvin (1845–1927), on a catalogue (1905) of British and foreign engravers working in England in the 16th and 17th centuries. His first major work was on the *Catalogue of Early Italian Engravings in the British Museum* (1910), edited by Colvin, which he later expanded into four volumes (1938) and yet later three more. He was Slade Professor of Fine Art at Oxford (1921–7), a professor at Harvard and a Leverhulme research fellow. In 1933 he succeeded Laurence Binyon as keeper of the department of Prints and Drawings at the British Museum, retiring in 1945.

WRITINGS
A Short History of Engraving and Etching (London, 1908; rev. 3 as *A History of Engraving and Etching from the 15th Century to the Year 1914*, London, 1923/*R* 1963)
Catalogue of Early Italian Engravings Preserved in the Department of Prints and Drawings in the British Museum, 2 vols (London, 1909–10); rev., 4 vols (1938); rev. 2, 7 vols (1948)
Rembrandt's Etchings: An Essay and a Catalogue with Some Notes on the Drawings, 2 vols (London, 1912)
Catalogue of Drawings of Claude Lorrain Preserved in the Department of Prints and Drawings (London, 1926)
Rembrandt: Being the Substance of the Charles Eliot Norton Lectures Delivered before Harvard University 1930–31 (London, 1932)
An Introduction to a History of Woodcut, with a Detailed Survey of Work Done in the Fifteenth Century, 2 vols (London 1935/*R* New York, 1963)
Engraving in England in the 16th and 17th Centuries, 3 vols (Cambridge, 1952–64)

BIBLIOGRAPHY
DNB
Obituary, *The Times* (23 May 1957)
A. E. Popham: Obituary, *Burl. Mag.*, xcix (1957), p. 242
LAURA SUFFIELD

Hind, William G(eorge) R(ichardson) (*b* Nottingham, 12 June 1833; *d* Sussex, NB, 1888). Canadian painter of English birth. He settled in Canada in 1861 and travelled in Labrador with his brother, the scientist and explorer Henry Youll Hind (1823–1908). In 1862 he accompanied the gold-seeking Overlanders to British Columbia as expedition artist. He travelled extensively in Canada, making oils, watercolours and pencil studies that display a meticulous attention to detail. They are generally small in size, done directly in front of the subject, and rather dry and impersonal. In the mid-19th century most artists recorded the Canadian landscape in a romantic spirit, often theatrically and panoramically. Hind's vision, however, was more circumscribed. His paintings are filled with minutiae, as in *Wood Interior with Tree Stump* (*c.* 1880; Hamilton, Dr Duncan Hind priv. col.), in which a decaying tree trunk partially covered with moss is shown in close-up.

The claustrophobic sense of space in his pictures may have been due to his familiarity with the works of the Pre-Raphaelite Brotherhood. Such works as *Bar in a Mining Camp* (1865; Montreal, McGill U., McCord Mus.) display a stilted objectivity and miniature-like quality similar to paintings by Ford Madox Brown and John Brett. Hind's 'truthfulness to nature' is also evident in his few portraits and self-portraits (e.g. *Self-portrait, c.* 1865; Montreal, McGill U., McCord Mus.). There is a notable awkwardness and naivety in his drawing, colour and proportion that may indicate little or no previous training in art.

BIBLIOGRAPHY
A Collection of Drawings and Watercolours by the Canadian Artist William George Richardson Hind (exh. cat., London, Sotheby's, 1967)
William G. R. Hind (1833–1888), a Confederation Painter in Canada (exh. cat. by J. R. Harper, Windsor, Ont., Willistead A.G., 1967)
J. R. Harper: *William G. R. Hind*, Canadian Artists Series, 2 (Ottawa, 1976)
Through Canadian Eyes: Trends and Influences in Canadian Art, 1815–1965 (exh. cat. by M. Williamson, Calgary, Glenbow-Alta Inst., 1976)
KIRK MARLOW

Hindoo style. *See* MOORISH STYLE.

Hinduism. A term that may be defined as referring to the religion of the Hindus. It should be used with care owing to the protean nature of Hindu doctrine and the fact that Hinduism represents a way of life rather than a creed. A Hindu may be defined as a person of Indian origin who does not claim to be non-Hindu or as a person of non-Indian origin who claims to be Hindu.

GENERAL BIBLIOGRAPHY
K. Morgan, ed.: *The Religion of the Hindus* (New York, 1953)
L. Renou, ed.: *Hinduism* (New York, 1961)
R. C. Zaehner: *Hinduism* (London, 1962)
T. Mahadevan: *Outlines of Hinduism* (Bombay, 1971)
A. Embree, ed.: *The Hindu Tradition* (New York, 1972)
J. Hinnells and E. Sharpe: *Hinduism* (Newcastle upon Tyne, 1972)
W. D. O'Flaherty: *Hindu Myths* (Harmondsworth, 1975)

I. India. II. South-east Asia.

I. India.

The term 'Hindu' gained international currency in the 18th century as an omnibus term to describe an adherent of the major religious tradition of India. Today it is used to indicate an Indian citizen or person of Indian origin who is not Muslim, Christian, Zoroastrian, Jewish, Jaina, Buddhist or Sikh. The fact that, at least initially, one identifies a Hindu as an Indian who is not a non-Hindu serves to indicate the close bond between the Hindu religion and India. Over 90% of the world's Hindus reside in the Republic of India, and over 80% of India's citizens are Hindus. However, apart from in South-east Asia (*see* §II below), there are also significant Hindu communities in Sri Lanka, Bangladesh, south-east Africa, the Caribbean and Oceania, all as the result of migration rather than conversion. The Hindus do not seek converts as such, although they accept them.

1. History. 2. Scriptures. 3. Basic teachings. 4. Religious practices.

1. HISTORY. The history of Hinduism is best summarized in relation to the four major turning-points in its long existence: the Aryan immigration of 1500 BC, the rise of Buddhist–Jaina heterodoxy in the 6th century BC, the Islamic incursions of *c.* AD 1200 and the encounter with Christianity from 1800.

The earliest information about Hinduism derives from two radically different sources, the relationship between which is not entirely clear. These sources are the archaeological remains of the Indus civilization of the 3rd millennium BC and the literary evidence of the Vedas, especially the *Ṛg veda*, usually placed in the 2nd millennium BC (*see* §2 below). The general assumption is that the Aryans, as the people of the *Ṛg veda* called themselves, conquered the Indus Valley with the help of their military innovation—the horse-drawn war chariot—and in so doing absorbed many religious elements that are not directly traceable to the Vedas but that appear in later Hinduism. It seems that the people of the Indus Valley venerated a prototype of the god Shiva, as well as the mother goddess, the *pīpal* tree (a member of the *ficus* family) and the *linga*, the phallic symbol of Shiva (*see* INDIAN SUBCONTINENT, figs 150 and 174). The ample provisions for bathing at Indus Valley sites suggests a concern with ritual purification (for example, *see* MOHENJO-DARO). These elements are found in present-day Hinduism as well. Another indication of the longevity of early ideas is the fact that from the 8th century BC, if not before, the Upanishads gave rise to forms of intellectual Hinduism the influence of which persisted down the centuries.

The next great challenge in the history of Hinduism was posed by the rise of the heterodox movements of the 6th century BC, especially by Buddhism (*see* BUDDHISM, §III, 1). It was during this period of interaction that the various philosophical schools of Hinduism were systematized and their basic texts composed. These schools, all of which accepted the authority of the Vedas, were Nyaya (the school of logical realism), Vaishesika (the school of atomistic pluralism), Samkhya (the school of matter–spirit dualism), Yoga (the school concerned with meditational techniques), Purva-Mimamsa (the school of Vedic ritualism) and Uttara-Mimamsa (the school based on Vedic philosophical speculation). At the social level, this was the period when encompassing sociological doctrines were formulated and synthesized through the various *Dharma sūtra*s, collections of legal aphorisms. Owing to the proliferation of such aphoristic works, the immediately post-Vedic phase is called the Sutra period of Hinduism.

In the period following the Sutra phase, sociological doctrines were fully formulated in law-books, or *smṛti*s (*see* §2 below). In addition to salvation (*mokṣa*), emphasized in Buddhism, Hinduism recognized three valid goals of life: the leading of a normative life in the world (*dharma*), the pursuit of wealth (*artha*) and the pursuit of sensual pleasures (*kāma*)—both of the latter to be pursued in a manner consistent with morality. The Hindus also developed the doctrine of the four stages of life: that of the celibate student (*brahmacarya*), that of the householder (*gṛhastha*), that of the hermit (*vānaprastha*) and that of the renunciant (*saṃnyāsī*). Each phase was supposed to cover a quarter of the idealized lifespan of 100 years. Hindus came to see society as hierarchically organized into four classes (*varṇa*s): those of priests and scholars (*brāhmaṇa*s or Brahmans), warriors (*kṣatriya*s), merchants (*vaiśya*s) and labourers or servants (*śūdra*s). Some sections of society, especially those engaged in polluting work, fell outside the pale of the fourfold system. The Hindus incorporated theism into their lives with the rise of the devotional (*bhakti*) movement, which developed in the south. Also during this period the *Rāmāyaṇa*, *Mahābhārata* and Puranas were composed, and temples were built on a massive scale, notwithstanding the aniconic nature of the Vedic tradition. The latter was also supplemented by works of the Agamic (Tantric) tradition, whose adepts sought the power gained by worshipping the union of male and female energies. By *c.* 1200 the Hindu response

to Buddhism had proved overwhelming, and the latter died out as a separate religion in India.

Hinduism then had to come to terms with Islam (*see* ISLAM, §§I and II). While the beliefs of earlier invaders had either been embroidered on to the fabric of Hinduism or woven successfully into it, this was not possible with Islam. Although it never penetrated some parts of India, where it did it was accepted by many. By 1800 one in every four Indians was a Muslim. The mass of Hindus rejected Islam, however, presenting a kind of cellular defence by tightening the rules of caste. There was also increased emphasis on *bhakti* as represented by the flowering of devotional literature, including the *Rāmāyaṇa*, in the regional languages. The best-known instance is the 17th-century *Rāmacaritamānasa* ('Deeds of Rama') of Tulsidasa, which became the religious text par excellence in Hindu homes in north India during this period (*see* INDIAN SUBCONTINENT, §II, 4). Some innovators, however, attempted synthesis. Prominent among them were Kabir, a 15th-century philosopher who rejected the formalism of both Hinduism and Islam, and Nanak (1469–1538), whose followers, combining the Hindu world-view with an Islamic rejection of image-worship and emphasis on the revealed book, ultimately evolved into a distinct group (*see* SIKHISM).

Two decisions were important in the process by which the British gained power in India beginning in the mid-18th century. One was the decision to allow Christian missionaries to operate freely in British territories from 1813. The other was the decision to introduce English as virtually the official language in 1835, partly to facilitate conversion to Christianity. With the spread of British rule, the whole of India became the theatre in which the encounter between Hinduism and Christianity/Western influence was played out. Hinduism failed to absorb Christianity just as it had failed to absorb Islam. Initially, Christian evangelization seemed to meet with considerable success, but gradually the rate of conversion slowed. By 1947, when British rule ended, only about 2% of Indians had been converted. The rejection of Christianity is best typified by the Arya Samaj, a society established in 1875 by Swami Dayananda, who criticized both Christianity and Islam and attacked Hindu practices he regarded as un-Vedic. Swami Dayananda started the Suddhi movement, which was directed towards reconverting to Hinduism those who had converted to other religions. But acceptance and rejection of Christianity were two extreme reactions. The more typical Hindu response was one of synthesis and assimilation. For example Swami Vivekananda, the 19th-century founder of the RamaKrishna Mission, defended Hinduism with vigour while at the same time emulating Christian missionary techniques.

2. SCRIPTURES. Sacred scriptures are classified in Hinduism as 'that which is heard' (Skt *śruti*) and 'that which is remembered' (*smṛti*). The former represents revelation, the latter, by contrast, tradition. The revealed literature is represented by the Vedas, of which there are four: *Ṛg*, *Sāma*, *Yajur* and *Atharva*. Of these the *Ṛg veda* is the earliest and primary one, supplying much of the material for the rest. Each of the Vedas possesses a fourfold division, which seems to correspond roughly to

1. *Krishna Stealing the Clothes of the Cowherds*, gouache on paper, 225×310 mm; from a Kangra-style *Bhāgavata purāṇa*, *c.* 1770 (New Delhi, National Museum)

the evolution of Vedic religion as it passed through different phases of growth. These are the *samhitā* division (marked by simple hymnal prayers addressed to the various gods), *brāhmaṇa* division (describing the details of the complex rituals that came to accompany these hymns), the *āraṇyaka* division (marking the beginnings of investigations into the meaning of ritual that initiated a trend towards philological speculation) and the Upanishads (marking the climax of this trend). As the Upanishads constitute the last section of the Vedas, they are also known as *vedānta*, or the end of the Vedas. This process of evolution appears to have occurred between 1500 BC and 300 BC, although these dates are speculative (*see* INDIAN SUBCONTINENT, §I, 2).

The *smṛti* literature of Hinduism is less clearly organized and is vaster than the *śruti*. As a category of literature *smṛti* has two distinct senses. In its narrower sense it means a law-book that lays down the rules of right living for Hindus. In its wider sense it also includes the two great national epics, the *Rāmāyaṇa* and the *Mahābhārata*, the 18 Puranas, the Agamas (devoted to the deities Vishnu, Shiva and Shakti), the Darshana literature (philosophical treatises) and even Buddhist and Jaina works, apart from works in regional languages. Of the two great epics, *Rāmāyaṇa* deals with the life and adventures of Rama, the hero who is recognized as an incarnation of the god Vishnu. The story of the birth of Rama, his marriage to Sita, his exile, the abduction of Sita by Ravana, the demon–king of Sri Lanka, and Sita's recovery by an army of monkeys led by Hanuman is known in every Hindu home. Similarly, the story of the fratricidal struggle for the throne of what is now the region around Delhi that forms the nucleus of the *Mahābhārata*, perhaps the longest epic in the world, is also known to every Hindu. (For the place of the *Rāmāyaṇa* and *Mahābhārata* in Indian art, *see* INDIAN SUBCONTINENT, §II, 4. For scenes from the *Rāmāyaṇa*, *see* INDIAN SUBCONTINENT, figs 12, 274 and 277.) The popular *Bhagavadgītā* ('Song of God'), a minuscule part of the *Mahābhārata*, has acquired a status of its own. This text of about 700 verses, couched in the form of a dialogue between Krishna, another incarnation of Vishnu (*see* INDIAN SUBCONTINENT, fig. 292), and the hero Arjuna on the eve of a major battle, is now looked upon as a revealed text in which Hinduism comes closest to possessing a universal scripture. The Puranas are also known to virtually every Hindu. These works deal with the main gods of the Hindu pantheon. The best known is the *Bhāgavata purāṇa*, which describes the early life of Krishna in the bucolic region around Mathura (see fig. 1). The Vedas, by comparison, are known only to a few.

3. BASIC TEACHINGS. The basic teachings of Hinduism centre around the nature of ultimate reality, of the

universe, of humanity in the universe and of the interrelationship between God, the universe and humanity. In Hinduism the ultimate reality is designated by the term *brahman* or *brahma*, a word of neuter gender derived from a root meaning 'to spread'. This reality is both immanent and transcendent. The universe is part of it, yet it stands 'ten digits beyond'. Ultimate reality contains the universe within it just as the mind entertains a thought or dream. The second important point about *brahman* is that it is regarded, paradoxically, as both devoid of and possessing attributes or qualities, as both without and with distinguishing features, as both without and with form. Featureless (*nirguna*) *brahma* may be compared to water and *brahman* with features (*saguna brahma*) to the same water acquiring distinctiveness in the form of cubes of ice. *Brahman* without form or features cannot be described except negatively, but ultimate reality possessing form can be visualized as either female or male. In its female version ultimate reality can be worshipped as the Goddess (Devi). In its male version it is called God or Ishvara. God can be looked on as the originator or creator, as the preserver or sustainer, or as the destroyer or terminator of the universe.

These cosmic roles provide the Hindu pantheon with its three chief gods, Brahma, Vishnu and Shiva, respectively. For various reasons the worship of Brahma (*see* INDIAN SUBCONTINENT, fig. 219) is no longer a prominent feature of Hinduism; Vishnu and Shiva are the two gods to whom Hindus pay their reverence. In his role as preserver, Vishnu intervenes from time to time to save the cosmos from untimely dissolution by incarnating himself in the universe. Hindus recall with special devotion two such interventions—as Rama and as Krishna—and Vishnu is often worshipped in these forms. (For representations of Vishnu in various guises, *see* INDIAN SUBCONTINENT, figs 3, 135, 185, 191 and 201.) As the third member of the Hindu threefold form of God (*trimūrti*), Shiva presides over the destruction of the universe and can be an awesome figure. But his destructive function can also have a creative aspect; he can destroy illness, enemies, bad luck and even the very process of an individual's involvement in the universe (*samsāra*). (For representations of Shiva *see* INDIAN SUBCONTINENT, figs 2, 169, 171, 184, 194, 195, 207, 296 and 301.)

This functional trifurcation of God-with-form is the basis not only of Hindu theism but also of Hindu sectarianism. When sectarian developments became divisive in the past, attempts were made to synthesize the two chief gods, Vishnu and Shiva, into one. Similarly, Hindu theology does not always accord a totally independent status to the female aspects of the gods, known as *śaktis*. One of these is often shown as the spouse of Shiva, frequently as the dominant partner. Sometimes Hindu

2. *Shiva, Parvati and Skanda*, bronze, 480×605 mm, from Tamil Nadu, *c.* 1100 (London, British Museum)

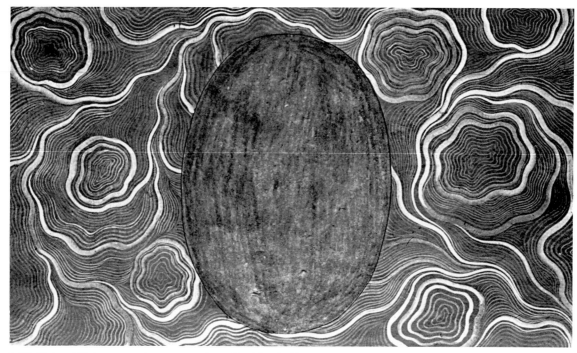

3. *The Universal Embryo*; watercolour on paper, from a Basohli-style *Bhāgavata purāṇa, c.* 1730 (Varanasi, Banaras Hindu University, Bharat Kala Bhavan)

syncretism combines the male and female aspects, as in depictions of Shiva Ardhanarishvara (Shiva as half-male and half-female; *see* INDIAN SUBCONTINENT, figs 6, 181 and 202).

The chief Hindu gods have families (see fig. 2) as well as animals they use as mounts (*vāhana*s), and these are also regarded as objects of worship. The depiction of Vishnu is favoured in art, especially as reclining on the cosmic serpent, Ananta or Shesha (*see* INDIAN SUBCONTINENT, fig. 177). So are his various incarnations, either individually—as in the temples of Krishna at Brindaban and Mathura or of Rama at Rameswaram—or collectively as at the Dashavatara Temple at Bhitargaon. The Nataraja images of Shiva as the performer of the cosmic dance (*see* INDIAN SUBCONTINENT, figs 2 and 211), found mainly in south India, are famous (*see also* INDIAN SUBCONTINENT, §IV, 7(vi)(a)). The use of images in worship is considered to have merit because—in the words of the 13th-century Vaishnava theologian Pillai Lokacarya—'the image is like the still pool from which anyone any time could slake his thirst'.

The universe (*brahmāṇḍa*) or 'egg of Brahma', as it is frequently described (see fig. 3), cannot exist apart from *brahman*, though again the exact nature of the relationship is a matter of philosophical debate. The universe, without beginning or end, undergoes phases of manifestation and dissolution that are calculated in figures of mind-boggling magnitude. In this universe the itinerant individual soul (*jīva*) moves from one life to another. This process of the soul's involvement in the cosmos through a process of rebirths is called *saṃsāra*. The guiding principle that governs the soul's movement in these various rebirths,

including those as animals or celestial beings, is called *karma*. The word refers to both actions and the results of those actions, whether good or bad. According to the Hindu doctrine of the three bodies the physical body is only one of the three bodies that humans ultimately possess. The second one consists of the psyche. The third body, the causal body, is said to consist of primal ignorance, which prevents us from perceiving ultimate reality. Thus the pure radiance of the soul (*ātman*) becomes caught in the process of *saṃsāra*. The ultimate truth about human beings is that they are the *ātman*, the quintessential soul, but erroneously identify themselves with the three bodies. Since human existence is impermanent, perfect and permanent happiness can never be obtained in the shifting sands of *saṃsāra* but must be sought outside it. This is salvation (*mokṣa*). This salvation follows from union with *brahman* and the process by which one achieves such union is called *yoga*.

The word *yoga* is etymologically related to the English word 'yoke', which can mean both union and discipline. Thus it stands for a system of discipline that leads to union with *brahman*. While numerous *yoga*s are recognized within Hinduism, three are emphasized. The *yoga* of knowledge (*jñāna yoga*) emphasizes experiential realization of featureless *brahma* as the means of release from *saṃsāra*. The *yoga* of devotion (*bhakti yoga*) emphasizes devotion to any of the various gods of Hinduism, but especially to Vishnu and Shiva, as the means of salvation. The yoga of works (*karma yoga*) is the third major *yoga*. The word *karma* in this context can mean ritual action or action in general, especially in relation to one's allotted station in life. Implicit in the doctrine of *yoga*s is the belief that different beings possess different temperaments and that *jñāna*, *bhakti* or *karma yoga* may be suited to individuals of varying personalities.

4. RELIGIOUS PRACTICES. Hindus are generally most concerned with living their lives in ways that might be conducive to better lives in future incarnations. In order to achieve this end and to express the religious dimension of the human personality, Hindus engage in certain characteristic practices.

Hinduism is very much a religion of the household. In most Hindu homes there is a shrine, or *pūjā* room, for the performance of ritual or prayer (see fig. 4). Most Hindus follow the devotional (*bhakti*) path. The chosen household deity is worshipped with offerings of flowers, rice etc and with hymns of praise and gestures of supplication.

Temples are usually dedicated to Vishnu (or one of his incarnations) and to Shiva. The ritual followed basically conforms to or combines two models: those of royalty and of hospitality. According to the royalty model, the enshrined deity is treated like a king or queen and is served by priests as his or her servants. The deity is awakened in the morning with hymns, is bathed and fed and holds court, and in the evening is fed again and put to sleep with due ceremony. According to the hospitality ritual the deity is treated as a welcome guest. His or her presence is requested, words of praise are sung, and the deity is offered sweetmeats. Camphor is burnt and an arc of light waved around him or her. The two models can, of course, be combined, the deity being treated as a royal guest. It is interesting to note that though these models of worship can be traced back to Vedic times, the main form of

4. *A Devotee Performing Pūja*, gouache on paper, possibly Mewar style, 212×164 mm, *c.* 1520–40 (London, Victoria and Albert Museum)

worship then current—sacrifices offered in fire—is now the preserve of only a few ritualistic priestly families. Apart from worship at home and in temples, objects of nature are often worshipped, such as the sacred *pīpal* tree or stones sacred to Shiva or Vishnu. Among these objects of worship the sun is of interest as representing the divine in its effulgent aspect.

The importance attached to individual communion with God in Hinduism has led to belief that congregational worship plays a minor role. This does not seem to be true. Congregational worship is not merely recognized but even emphasized in the assembling of devotees (*satsang*). This can take place in a home or at a temple and consists of religious discourse and/or the singing of hymns (*bhajan*s). An associated institution is that of *katha*, or reading from the great epics, usually the *Rāmāyaṇa*, accompanied by musical recitation and homiletic exegesis, which can also take place in a temple or at home. It is considered an act of religious merit to fund or organize such an event.

Individual or congregational worship can of course be performed at any time, but is frequently associated with the observance of festivals or holy days. These are often connected with stories relating to Vishnu or his incarnations, or to Shiva or his female aspect. Prominent festivals include Holi and Divali (for representations of Holi *see* INDIAN SUBCONTINENT, figs 275 and 312). Pilgrimage to holy places such as Allahabad and Varanasi is also an important Hindu religious practice. On these occasions many Hindus don traditional dress. Hindu women are usually clad in colourful *sārī*s while celebrating festivals but dress more soberly when observing fasts or vigils. In most parts of India it is customary to serve vegetarian food at these feasts and festivals. Eating meat and drinking wine are looked upon as spiritually deleterious.

Just as the passage of the year has certain points marked out for special attention, so does the individual's passage through life. The orthodox list of these rites includes about 16, the two universal ones being rites associated with marriage and death. Already outlined in the Vedas, they are believed by historians to have originated before the Indo-Europeans moved out of their original homeland. The rite of marriage essentially consists of the bride and bridegroom circumambulating the sacred fire seven times. Although at one time marriage was considered indissoluble, it no longer is.

Obsequies consist of cremation, ideally performed by the eldest son. On the death of a Hindu, after due interval, the *śrāddha* rites follow. These are offerings of food and drink to the dead that are actually consumed by invited members of the priestly caste. This ceremony is performed annually, sometimes at places considered particularly auspicious.

An important ceremony for the three higher castes has been the *upanayana*, during which a child was initiated into Vedic studies and given a sacred thread to wear. Duly invested with the thread and then married, a full-fledged Hindu householder of the three upper castes was expected to perform five sacrifices (*pañca mahāyajñā*s) daily. These consisted of making offerings to the gods, studying the Vedas, offering libations to ancestors, feeding animals and birds, and extending hospitality and charity to fellow humans. While these rites are rarely observed to the letter, they are indicative of the spirit underlying Hindu domestic rites and attitudes. Astrology also plays an important role in Hindu life. In most Hindu households horoscopes are cast at the time of a birth, and astrologers are consulted frequently.

For an overview of world religions in India, *see* INDIAN SUBCONTINENT, §I, 7(i); on the concept of art in India and its relation to specific philosophical and religious ideas, *see* INDIAN SUBCONTINENT, §I, 8; and for surveys of Hindu iconography and subject-matter, including a full discussion of the various deities and their attributes, *see* INDIAN SUBCONTINENT, §II, 1 and 4–8.

BIBLIOGRAPHY

S. Stevenson: *The Rites of the Twice-born* (London, 1920/*R* Delhi, 1971)
H. Whitehead: *The Village Gods of South India* (London, 1921)
S. Radhakrishnan: *The Hindu View of Life* (London, 1927)
P. Kane: *History of Dharmaśāstra*, 5 vols (Poona, 1941)
D. S. Sarma: *Studies in the Renaissance of Hinduism in the Nineteenth and Twentieth Centuries* (Banaras, 1944)
S. Radhakrishnan, ed.: *The Principal Upaniṣads* (London, 1953)
A. L. Basham: *The Wonder That Was India* (London, 1954; rev. 1957)
P.-N. Prabhu: *Hindu Social Organization* (Bombay, 1954)
M. Marriott, ed.: *Village India* (Chicago, 1955)
W. T. de Bary, ed.: *Sources of Indian Tradition*, 2 vols (New York, 1958)
S. Radhakrishnan: *The Brahma Sūtra* (London, 1960)
A. Bharati: *The Tantric Tradition* (London, 1965)
O. Lewis: *Village Life in Northern India* (New York, 1965)
A. K. Majumdar: *Bhakti Renaissance* (Bombay, 1965)
M. Singer, ed.: *Krishna: Myths, Rites and Attitudes* (Honolulu, 1966)
L. Dumont: *Homo hierachicus: Essai sur le système de caste* (Paris, 1967); Eng. trans. *Homo hierarchicus: The Caste System and its Implications* (London and Chicago, 1970/*R* 1972)
L. I. Rudolph and S. H. Rudolph: *The Modernity of Tradition* (Chicago, 1967)
D. S. Sarma: *Hinduism through the Ages* (Bombay, 1967)
S. Chatterjee and D. Datta: *An Introduction to Indian Philosophy* (Calcutta, 1968)
J. Gonda: *Viṣṇuism and Śivaism: A Comparison* (London, 1970)
P. J. Marshall, ed.: *The British Discovery of Hinduism in the Eighteenth Century* (Cambridge, 1970)
U. M. Sharma: 'The Problem of Village Hinduism: "Fragmentation" and "Integration" ', *Contrib. Ind. Sociol.*, iv (1970), pp. 1–21
T. Hopkins: *The Hindu Religious Tradition* (Belmont, 1971)
W. H. Wiser and C. V. Wiser: *Behind Mud Walls, 1930–1960* (Berkeley, 1971)
F. Edgerton: *The Bhagavad Gītā* (Cambridge, 1972)
J. Kirk: *Stories of the Hindus* (New York, 1972)
M. Singer: *When a Great Tradition Modernizes* (London, 1972)
L. Babb: *The Divine Hierarchy* (New York, 1975)
J. Santucci: *An Outline of Vedic Literature* (Missoula, 1976)
M. Hiriyanna: *The Essentials of Indian Philosophy* (London, 1978)
A. Sharma: *The Puruṣārthas: A Study in Hindu Axiology* (East Lansing, 1982)
——: *Studies in Alberuni's India* (Wiesbaden, 1983)
——: *The Hindu Gītā* (London, 1986)

ARVIND SHARMA

II. South-east Asia.

There is still much scholarly argument about how Hinduism and Buddhism were first introduced into South-east Asia in the early centuries of the 1st millennium AD and about the nature and extent of the subsequent social, political and cultural process to which the somewhat misleading term 'Indianization' has been generally applied. One likely explanation is that local rulers, anxious to establish their legitimacy and consolidate their power, invited Brahmans and scholars to come from India to instruct them and to place their magic powers at their disposal. It is now widely accepted that, although commercial relations between South-east Asia and the Indian subcontinent existed long before the arrival of Indian religions in the region, the dissemination of those religions was not directly due to the activities of Indian traders, still less to any extension of Indian power either by conquest or by peaceful political intervention.

Both Hinduism and Mahayana Buddhism in South-east Asia were transmitted through the medium of the sacred language of Sanskrit and so probably remained, at least at first, largely confined to the royal courts and the ruling classes. The earliest recorded example of this type of Indianized state in South-east Asia is Funan in the Mekong delta; according to Chinese annals (the *Liang shu*) it was founded by a Brahman named Kaundinya in the 1st century AD. Chinese sources also mention the existence of Hindu states in Peninsular Malaysia and in central Vietnam at the end of the 2nd century AD. However, no material evidence of Indianization has survived from before the 4th and 5th centuries, when there already existed a Hindu kingdom ruled by the Chandra dynasty in Arakan, the Pyu kingdom of Shrikshetra in Upper Burma, the Mon kingdom of Dvaravati in the Chao Phraya basin in Thailand, the kingdom of Champa in central Vietnam and, in Indonesia, the kingdoms of Taruma in western Java and Kutei in eastern Borneo.

Even where the process of Indianization was most pervasive and left the most conspicuous mark on the art and architecture, the autochthonous beliefs of the mass of the population seem to have remained largely intact and to have blended syncretically with the new religion. Very few Hindu or Buddhist monuments and images made in South-east Asia have an exact equivalent in Indian art, suggesting that Indian elements were absorbed into an existing, highly evolved indigenous culture. In eastern Java, for example, towards the end of the Hindu period in the 14th century these ancient autochthonous beliefs reasserted themselves and found new expression in the iconography of the Hindu relief sculptures on the monuments of the Singhasari and Majapahit kingdoms.

This merging of Hindu with indigenous pre-Hindu beliefs is particularly well illustrated in the religion of the Balinese, the only people in South-east Asia, apart from the Badui of West Java, the Tengger of East Java and some Cham groups, who in the late 20th century still adhere to the Hindu religion, albeit in a highly idiosyncratic form. Balinese society and culture are deeply imbued with Hinduism, and Balinese of all classes devote much of their time and their remarkable and versatile artistic talents to honouring and making offerings to the Hindu gods. The rulers of Bali, although they no longer have political power, are still invested with spiritual authority as intermediaries and interpreters of the will of the gods and consequently as guardians of the social order. Yet the three superior castes (Balinese *triwangsa*)—Brahmans (who bear the title Ida), *kṣatriya*s (Cokorde or Deva) and *vaiśya*s (Gusti)—constitute only 7% of the population of the island, and the rest, including the indigenous population, are deemed to belong to the fourth caste (*śūdra*) and so are in effect casteless.

In the Indianized kingdoms of South-east Asia, Buddhist and Hindu rulers alike generally marked the establishment of their power and asserted its sacral nature by building a royal capital with a state temple at its centre. This was conceived both as the heart of the realm from which royal power radiated and as a microcosm of Mt

Meru, abode of the gods and centre of the Hindu universe. The temple itself was therefore often built at the summit of a mountain or an artificial mountain, and a cult was established there of an Indian deity associated with the person of the ruler and symbolizing the unity of the kingdom. In this way Indian concepts of kingship were combined with ancient indigenous beliefs in the sacredness of high places. Some scholars define such a temple and the state, or polity, of which it was the ritual centre as a *maṇḍala*, a Sanskrit term that, in a strictly religious context, means a magical diagram. However, it is also used to denote a political entity with a ritual centre where the ruler dwells and whence his power emanates, but which has no fixed frontiers or clearly defined authority at the fringes. A notable example of a Javanese Hindu temple in the form of a *maṇḍala* is the temple complex of Loro Jonggrang at Prambanan in Central Java (*see* INDONESIA, §I, 2 and 3), built by a ruler of the Hindu Sanjaya dynasty in the early 9th century.

In the western Javanese kingdom of Taruma the evidence of inscriptions on a site near Bogor suggests that, as early as the 5th century, the link between royal authority and divine sanction had been established. The carved footprints of Vishnu found on this site suggest that King Purnavarman, whose victories are celebrated in the inscriptions, was identified, even if only after his death, with the god Vishnu. Much later, in East Java, this tendency to identify the ruler with a specific deity is apparent in such sculptures as the late 13th-century image of Shiva that is believed to come from Candi Kidal, near Malang, East Java, and to be a funerary statue of King Anusapati (*reg* 1227–48), second ruler of Singhasari (see fig. 5).

In Cambodia, the Khmer rulers of Angkor developed the cult of the *devarāja* (Skt: 'the god who is king'), in other words of the god as a tutelary deity protecting the kingdom through the intermediary of the king. In this cult the worship of Shiva played a predominant part, and the majority of the Hindu temples built by Khmer rulers were dedicated to Shiva, principally in the form of a *liṅga*, Shiva's phallic emblem. In the Hindu sculpture of Cambodia and elsewhere in South-east Asia the *liṅga* is sometimes represented simply as a stylized phallus, but sometimes as the axis of the universe and so as Mt Meru, the cosmic mountain. The belief that Mt Meru had five peaks accounts not only for the quincuncial arrangement of the towers in many Khmer temples, but also for the frequent presence of four balls round the central column of the *liṅga* image. Representations of the *liṅga* rising out of its female counterpart, the *yoni*, symbolizing male–female dualism, are also widespread throughout Indianized South-east Asia. Other manifestations of Shiva—Rudra, Bhairava, Sharva, Isha, Bhima, Ugra and Mahadeva—were also objects of worship, as were his consorts (*sakti*s) Parvati, Uma and Durga, his sons Ganesha, the elephant-headed god of wisdom, Skanda, the war god, Indra, commander of the thunder and rains, and Surya, the sun god, and his mount, the bull Nandi. A remarkable feature of early Hinduism in South-east Asia, particularly among the Khmers, was the cult of Harihara, who combines the names and features of Vishnu (Hari) on the left side and of Shiva (Hara) on the right side and has the attributes of both (*see* CAMBODIA, fig. 16).

5. *Shiva*, andesite, h. 1.23 m, perhaps from Candi Kidal, East Java, late 13th century (Amsterdam, Tropenmuseum)

In Javanese and Balinese Hinduism Shiva was also adopted as supreme god, and the status of other deities tended to be reduced to the level of manifestations of Shiva. Balinese Hinduism has always shown a tendency to blend Shaivite and Buddhist cults, and both Buddhist priests (Balinese *pedanda boda*) and Shaivite priests (*pedanda siva*) play an essential part in religious ceremonies, although the latter greatly outnumber the former. Balinese Hinduism also attaches importance to the precepts of the Shaiva Siddhanta sect, in which study and meditation enable the soul to free itself from the delusions of existence and achieve a mystical union with Shiva in his aspect of

Paramashiva, the third of three manifestations of which Maheshvara, known in Bali as Batara Guru or Batara Siva, is the first. Seats (Skt *padmāsana*; 'lotus seat') are erected at the back of many Balinese temple compounds at the point closest to the mountains where the gods dwell, for the gods to use when they come down to visit temple ceremonies. These seats usually include one specifically designated for Shiva in his aspect of Surya (Shivaditya or Shivasurya). Sometimes triple seats are erected for the three members of the Hindu trinity (*āgama tīrtha Trimurti*, Balinese *tiga sakti*) of Shiva, Vishnu and Brahma. The trinity is also represented in various triadic forms in the *navasanga* (Skt *nava*, 'nine'; Balinese *sanga*, 'nine'), a system of classification in which the eight cardinal directions represented by Vishnu, Sambu, Ishvara, Maheshvara, Brahma, Rudra, Mahadeva and Sankara are grouped round Shiva in the centre. The *nagasari* tree, a symbol of Shiva and Uma, is considered especially sacred. Another deity who figures prominently in South-east Asian Hinduism is Shri, Vishnu's consort, whose name is synonymous with prosperity and fertility, and who plays an important part in ceremonies in connection with rice cultivation, marriage and childbearing.

Even in those South-east Asian kingdoms where Theravada Buddhism was adopted as the religion of the ruler and of the majority of his subjects, Hindu deities were accorded an important place. A striking example of this is afforded by the Thai kingdom of Sukhothai, where in the 14th century large and imposing images of Shiva, Vishnu and Harihara, richly adorned in royal attire, were made for use in court rituals conducted by Brahman priests (*see* THAILAND, §IV, 4). These rituals are still performed by Brahman priests at the court ceremonies of Bangkok and Phnom Penh.

Indian elements persist in the drama and dance of all South-east Asian countries, not least in Malaysia and Indonesia, where the majority of the population is now Muslim. Indian literature, notably the two great Hindu epics, the *Mahābhārata* and *Rāmāyaṇa* (*see* §I, 2 above), has provided the themes for these dramas and dances since the time of the first Indianized rulers, and Arjuna, Krishna and Rama are still popular heroes. At first the dramas were performed in Sanskrit, but already by the 9th century they had evidently been translated into the local languages. Local variants, for example the *Ramakien* and the *Reamkear*, respectively the Thai and Cambodian versions of the *Rāmāyaṇa*, became national epics in which the hero is identified with the ideal ruler; it is for this reason that all nine rulers of the Chakri dynasty in Thailand have been called Rama. In the Indonesian shadow play (*wayang kulit*; *see* INDONESIA, §VI, 1(i)), the mountain (*gunungan*)—the leather figure used to separate the different parts of the drama—may be seen as a highly stylized representation both of Mt Meru and of the Tree of Life.

BIBLIOGRAPHY
R. Goris: *Bali: Cults and Customs/Bali: Atlas Kebudajaan/Bali: Cultuur geschiedenis in beeld* (Jakarta, n.d.) [trilingual text]
W. F. Stutterheim: *Indian Influences in Old Balinese Art* (London, 1935)
L. P. Briggs: 'The Ancient Khmer Empire', *Trans. Amer. Philos. Soc.*, xli/1 (1951) [whole issue]
R. Le May: *The Culture of South-East Asia* (London, 1954/R 1956)
F. D. K. Bosch: 'The Problem of the Hindu Colonisation of Indonesia', *Selected Studies in Indonesian Archaeology* (The Hague, 1961), pp. 1–22
C. Hooykas: 'Five Studies in Hindu Balinese Religion', *Meded. Kon. Ned. Acad. Wet.*, lxx (1964) [whole issue]
J. Gonda: 'Siva in Indonesien', *Wien. Z. Knd. Südasiens & Archv Ind. Philos.*, xiv (1970), pp. 1–72
S. J. O'Connor: 'Hindu Gods of Peninsular Siam', *Artibus Asiae*, suppl. xxviii (1972)
C. Hooykas: *Religion in Bali* (Leiden, 1973)
A. J. Bernet Kempers: *Monumental Bali: Introduction to Balinese Archaeology and Guide to the Monuments* (The Hague, 1977, rev. Berkeley and Singapore, 1991)
I. W. Mabbett: 'Kingship at Angkor', *J. Siam Soc.*, lxvi/2 (1978), pp. 1–58
M. C. Subhadradis Diskul: *Hindu Gods at Sukhodaya* (Bangkok, 1990)
Court Arts of Indonesia (exh. cat. by H. I. Jessup, New York, Asia Soc. Gals, 1990)

JOHN VILLIERS

Hine, Lewis W(ickes) (*b* Oshkosh, WI, 26 Sept 1874; *d* Hastings-on-Hudson, NY, 4 Nov 1940). American photographer. Following several years as a factory worker in Oshkosh, and a short period at the University of Chicago, where he studied sociology and pedagogy (1900–01), he went to New York to teach at the Ethical Culture School (1901–8). There he acquired a camera as a teaching tool and soon set up a club and ran classes at the school, while improving his own skills as a self-taught photographer. In 1904 Hine's interest in social issues led him to document newly arrived immigrants at Ellis Island as a way of demonstrating their common humanity, for example *Young Russian Jewess at Ellis Island* (1905; see Rosenblum, Rosenblum and Trachtenberg, p. 43). Thereafter he sought to demonstrate the efficacy of the photograph as a truthful witness, accepting commissions from social-work agencies. Towards the end of the first decade he became official photographer on the Pittsburgh Survey, a seminal investigation of America's archetypal industrial city, producing such images as *Tenement House and Yard* (1907–8; Rosenblum, Rosenblum and Trachtenberg, p. 56).

This experience, coupled with the fact that half-tone process printing had made photographic reproduction more accessible to popular and specialized periodicals, impelled Hine to leave teaching to devote himself entirely to the documentation of social conditions. During almost a decade as staff photographer for the National Child Labor Committee (NCLC), he travelled throughout the USA photographing child workers in mills, mines, on the streets and in fields and canneries. These images, for example *Breaker Boys in Coal Shute, South Pittston, Pennsylvania, January, 1911* (see Rosenblum, Rosenblum and Trachtenberg, p. 59), were used by the NCLC in periodicals, pamphlets, exhibitions (for a time designed by Hine), and as lantern slides for public lectures in an effort to bring about legislation regulating child labour. Hine's photographs, however, transcend basic documentation in that he sought out poses, facial expressions and gestures that not only would be perceived as truthful but would also stir the viewer's sympathy and spur them to action.

By 1918 the aftermath of American involvement in World War I had dampened enthusiasm for reform programmes. Hine joined an American Red Cross expedition to the Balkans, where he documented devastation and dislocation unlike anything he had seen in his native land. On his return he felt moved to portray the American worker with dignity, in what he felt was a positive light. While he was able to support himself for a period by supplying images to the *Survey* and a number of industrial magazines, his emphasis on the human element was not in tune with the era's interest in the machine, and he suffered financially.

At the beginning of the 1930s, however, Hine won a commission to document the construction of the Empire State Building in New York. He portrayed the workers and the structure that grew from their labour with a sense of the drama involved in erecting the world's tallest building (see Rosenblum, Rosenblum and Trachtenberg, pp. 107–16). This was the last major project of documentation that Hine was called upon to do. Despite the renewed interest in social imagery in the USA during the remainder of the 1930s, and attempts by Berenice Abbott and writer Elizabeth McCausland to arouse interest in Hine and his work, the photographer was largely ignored from then until his death in 1940.

PHOTOGRAPHIC PUBLICATIONS

Men at Work (New York, 1932)
Through the Threads of the Shelton Looms (New York, 1933)

BIBLIOGRAPHY

J. M. Gutman: *Lewis W. Hine and the American Social Conscience* (New York, 1967)
N. Rosenblum, W. Rosenblum and A. Trachtenberg: *America and Lewis Hine* (New York, 1977)
D. Kaplan: *Lewis Hine in Europe: The Lost Photographs* (New York, 1988)
——: *Photo Story: Selected Letters and Photographs of Lewis W. Hine* (Washington and London, 1992)

NAOMI ROSENBLUM

Hinglajgarh [Hinglājgaḍh]. Fort near Bhanpura in Mandasor District, Madhya Pradesh, India. It is in the territory of Malwa, a region that achieved prominence under the rule of the PARAMARA dynasty, who seem to have established the fort during the apogee of their power in the 10th and 11th centuries. After their demise the fort fell into disuse and ruin. With the ascendancy of Holkar rule in the 19th century the fort was restored; some palace buildings, temples and gateways remain from this era. The most important structure in the fort is the still active shrine of the goddess Hinglaj Mata, which may date from the 9th century or earlier. Both sculptural and inscriptional evidence suggests that goddess worship in this area has an ancient and extensive history.

Hinglajgarh is best known for the large number of sculptures recovered from the site; most of them are now in the Birla Museum and the State Archaeological Museum in Bhopal, the Central Museum, Indore, and the site museum at the fort, and all are of a pale grey sandstone. In addition, the remains of numerous temples and shrines are scattered around the base of the fort and embedded in its walls. The surviving sculptures include some extraordinarily detailed and refined images of a variety of deities. The majority date from the 10th and 11th centuries, but there are at least two images from the 8th century, one of Shiva with Parvati (Uma-Maheshvara), the other representing Shiva as a mendicant (Bhikshatana; both Indore, Cent. Mus.). The most celebrated sculptures of the Paramara era are the Tantric (*śākta*) manifestations of goddesses, including some especially sophisticated images of Chamunda, whose horrific attributes have been rendered with unparalleled sensitivity (Indore, Cent. Mus.; Bhopal, Birla Mus.). Other sects are also represented; works include sculptures of Vishnu and Surya as well as syncretic images such as Harihara (a composite of Vishnu and Shiva) and Jaina *tīrthaṅkaras* and goddesses. Like the majority of the Paramara-era sculptures from Hinglajgarh, these are distinguished by exquisite craftsmanship, minutely detailed iconographic attributes and tremendous sensitivity of expression.

BIBLIOGRAPHY

R. N. Mishra: '"Paramara" Art: An Alternative Framework', *Art of the Paramaras of Malwa*, ed. R. K. Sharma (Delhi, 1979), pp. 29–34
R. S. Garg: *Śākta-pratimāyē* [Goddess sculptures] (Bhopal, 1980)
N. P. Joshi: 'Regional Trends in Some of the Medieval Brahmanical Sculptures of Malwa', *Malwa Through the Ages*, ed. M. D. Khare (Bhopal, 1981), pp. 106–17
R. S. Garg: *Śiva Pratimāyē* [Shiva sculptures] (Bhopal, 1982)

CYNTHIA PACKERT ATHERTON

Hinloopen, Michiel (Thijmensz.) (*b* Amsterdam, 1619; *bur* Amsterdam, 19 March 1708). Dutch collector. He was from a wealthy merchant family, part of the ruling élite of Amsterdam. He studied law at the university at Orléans, France (1644–6), and then travelled in France and Italy on a Grand Tour. In 1647 he was in Rome, where he received a collection of prints from Andrea Giustiniani illustrating the latter's inherited collection of antique sculpture. He returned to Amsterdam in 1648 or 1649 and in 1671 is recorded as regent of the Amsterdam orphanage (Burgerweeshuis) and in 1684 as captain of the city militia company of the 13th quarter of Amsterdam. He owned books, Greek and Roman coins, and Dutch and Flemish paintings but is best known for his large print collection consisting of 7034 prints in 52 albums (now Amsterdam, Rijksmus.). He bequeathed the latter to the art gallery established in the Amsterdam Stadhuis (*see* AMSTERDAM, §III, 2), and it became the first print collection to be open to the public for a small fee. It was organized in three sections. The first was historical and included French topographical prints, portraits of contemporary Dutch people and 26 volumes of prints that formed an atlas of ancient and contemporary Rome. The nucleus of the Roman atlas were the prints published by ANTOINE LAFRÉRY under the title *Speculum Romanum magnificentiae*, a popular work that was much augmented and reprinted since its first publication in the 16th century. The second section of Hinloopen's print collection comprised reproductive prints of Italian, French and German paintings arranged by school, including reproductions of some well-known collections of paintings, such as those of Jan Reynst, Louis XIV of France and Archduke Leopold William, whose excellent collection of Italian paintings had been engraved by, among others, Wenceslaus Hollar. There was also an album devoted exclusively to the prints of Hercules Segers and another to prints of interest from a technical point of view. The third part of the collection contained prints illustrating themes from Ovid and from the Bible, engraved, for example, by Antonio Tempesta, Hendrick Goltzius and Crispijn de Passe (i). The whole collection was indexed and annotated by Hinloopen, who recorded the names of the engravers and original artists and made cross-references to related images in the collection.

BIBLIOGRAPHY

De prentschat van Michiel Hinloopen, 1619–1708 (exh. cat. by J. van der Waals, Amsterdam, Rijksmus., 1988)

Hinse [Hintz], **Zacharie.** *See* HEINCE, ZACHARIE.

Hiolle, Ernest-Eugène (*b* Paris, 5 May 1834; *d* Bois-le-Roi, 5 Oct 1886). French sculptor. He studied at the Ecole Académique in Valenciennes before entering the studio of François Jouffroy at the Ecole des Beaux-Arts in Paris. In 1862 he won the Prix de Rome. His first Salon exhibit, the statue *Orion Sitting on a Dolphin* (marble, 1866–70; Paris, Mus. d'Orsay), was executed during his time at the Académie de France in Rome. After several years during which he devoted himself mainly to portrait busts because of a lack of state commissions, he participated in the great public building projects of the Third Republic (after 1870), contributing decorative sculpture to the Paris Opéra and the Hôtel de Ville, among other buildings. Such works as his statues *Narcissus* (marble, 1869; Valenciennes, Mus. B.-A.) and *Eve* (marble, 1883; Troyes, Mus. B.-A. & Archéol.) demonstrate the influence of his years in Italy. He was occasionally assisted by his brother Maximilien-Louis Hiolle (1843–1938).

Lami
BIBLIOGRAPHY
LAURE DE MARGERIE

Hippodamos (*fl* 5th century BC). Greek city planner. He designed the plan of the new port of Athens at PEIRAEUS immediately after the end of the Persian wars (480/479 BC). More than thirty years later (444/443 BC) he took a leading part, together with philosophers and other experts, in the foundation of the ideal city of Thourion. Although he is attributed with the rebuilding of his home town of MILETOS, which was begun immediately after 479 BC, this is doubtful.

The 'division' of Peiraeus mentioned by Aristotle (*Politics*, 1267b) apparently referred not only to a grid system of streets and to the 'Hippodamian Agora' that was connected with it, but also to a sophisticated overall plan, in which the functional uniform dwellings were an important constituent; the practical private houses of the city are expressly mentioned in connection with the 'Hippodamian principle' (*Politics*, 1330b). Moreover, a scholion to Aristophanes (*Knights*, 327) mentioned that Hippodamos himself lived in Peiraeus and had a house there that was *demosia* ('public'). Presumably this was a show house erected by Hippodamos in connection with the plan for the overall layout of the city, in order to demonstrate to the Athenians his ideas for standardized dwellings. Excavations at Thourion have revealed scarcely any details of the town, except for its rectangular street system. RHODES, on the other hand, is much better known. The city was laid out in 408/407 BC, presumably not by Hippodamos, but by one of his followers. By 424 BC, when the *Knights* was performed, Hippodamos seems already to have been dead; Aristophanes has his son appear in his stead as the model of an important and good citizen.

The Hippodamian city, characterized by individual districts and a large-scale road network, represented a considerable advance on the older strip cities such as were built in Magna Graecia, where houses were continuously added to form long rows, the remaining space being left for public buildings. The introduction of standard houses corresponded to the largely homogeneous nature of the city populations, and is undoubtedly connected with the new political order of *isonomia*, later to be called 'democracy' (rule by the people). The wide-ranging concerns of Hippodamos, who was one of the first state theorists and an agitator for reform of the still new judicial system (*Politics*, 1267b) suggests that he was a leading representative of the new democratic age after the reforms of Kleisthenes (*c.* 508 BC) and the Persian wars.

Thieme–Becker
BIBLIOGRAPHY
F. Castagnoli: *Ippodamo di Mileto e l'urbanistica a pianta ortogonale* (Rome, 1956)
J. Szidat: 'Hippodamos von Milet', *Bonn. Jb. Rhein. Landesmus. Bonn & Ver. Altertfreund. Rheinlande*, clxxx (1980), pp. 31–42
W. Hoepfner and E. L. Schwander: *Haus und Stadt im klassischen Griechenland* (Munich, 1986, 2/1993), pp. 301–30
WOLFRAM HOEPFNER

Hippodrome. *See* CIRCUS, ROMAN.

Hippolite, Hector. *See* HYPPOLITE, HECTOR.

Hippo Regius [now Annaba, Arab. al-'Annāba; formerly Bône]. Site in Algeria that flourished from *c.* 200 BC to AD 430. It lies close to the Mediterranean coast on flat ground, nearly at sea-level, between two low hills. The town once possessed an excellent harbour as well as a fertile hinterland. It probably began as a Phoenician settlement, but the site has yielded few finds earlier than *c.* 200 BC and virtually no structures earlier than a great sea-wall of *c.* 40 BC. Hippo was a Numidian royal centre before being annexed by Rome in 46 BC. It developed in an unplanned way; having received municipal status under Augustus (*reg* 27 BC–AD 14), it was promoted to colonial status only in the 2nd century AD.

Evidence of the town's great affluence includes the impressive remains of the forum, built in the reign of Vespasian (AD 69–79); it is among the largest in Africa, its paved square measuring 76×43 m. It is notable for a huge inscription on the paving-stones to the proconsul of Africa, C. Paccius Africanus, and is surrounded by fluted Composite columns. Other major monuments include: a market (1st century AD; renovated and extended AD 364–7) with a circular temple in the middle; a huge theatre; a temple to the Dii Consentes; imposing public baths of Severan date (AD 193–235); and a magnificent multi-storey residence set into the side of a hill. There was also a rich and thriving Christian community, which had a huge basilican church with three naves and a nearby baptistery, both embellished with fine mosaics. Built towards the end of the 4th century AD, the basilica is contemporary with Hippo's most famous citizen, St Augustine, who died there during the Vandal siege of AD 430. In medieval times large parts of the town were used as an Arab cemetery.

BIBLIOGRAPHY
J.-P. Morel: 'Recherches stratigraphiques à Hippone', *Bull. Archéol. Alg.*, iii (1968), pp. 35–84
S. Dahmani: *Hippo Regius* (Algiers, 1973)
T. W. POTTER

Hiraga Gennai [Shiroishi; Kyūkei; Fūrai Sanjin] (*b* Shido, Sanuki Prov. [now Kagawa Prefect.], 1728; *d* Edo [now Tokyo], 1780). Japanese writer, naturalist, scholar and painter. He was born into a low-ranking samurai family in the Takamatsu Domain (now in Kagawa Prefect.) on Shikoku. His interest in the natural sciences developed while working in the medicinal herb garden of his lord, Matsudaira Yoritaka. In 1752–4 he was sent to study in Nagasaki, where he encountered Western and Chinese scientific ideas and methods. After studying in Osaka with the herbalist Toda Kyokuzan (1696–1769), Gennai travelled *c.* 1757 to Edo, where he became a student of the government physician and naturalist Tamura Genyū (1718–76). Through Tamura he met the physician and scholar of Western learning Sugita Genpaku (1733–1817) and others interested in empirical science. This group conducted symposia, investigating the properties of a wide range of materials. Drawing on these studies, Gennai wrote his most important book, *Butsurui hinshitsu* ('Classification of various materials'; 1763), which contained descriptions of some 360 specimens. It was illustrated mainly by the Nagasaki school painter SŌ SHISEKI, whose work displays the close observation of nature consistent with Gennai's methodology (*see also* JAPAN, §VI, 4(vi)(c)).

In 1770–72 Gennai stayed a second time in Nagasaki, where he familiarized himself with a number of useful European devices, industrial techniques and fine arts. He experimented with oil painting and developed an appreciation for the representational capabilities of Western art. In 1773 he was invited to the Akita Domain (now Akita Prefect.) to apply his knowledge of mineralogy. While his efforts to revive the copper industry there failed, the instruction in Western painting techniques that he provided for the domain lord, SATAKE SHOZAN, and one of his retainers, ODANO NAOTAKE, led to the formation of the Akita school of painting. Gennai later found a talented disciple in the Edo artist SHIBA KŌKAN. Gennai himself was neither artistically gifted nor prolific; his one extant oil painting, *Portrait of a Western Lady* (*Seiyo fujin zu*; Kobe, City Mus.), is awkward and derivative. Rather, it is in his intellectual espousal of Western realism and empirical scientific inquiry that his importance lies.

BIBLIOGRAPHY

T. Haga: *Sugita Gempaku, Hiraga Gennai, Shiba Kōkan* (Tokyo, 1971)
C. French: *Shiba Kōkan: Artist, Innovator and Pioneer in the Westernization of Japan* (New York and Tokyo, 1974)
M. Kawakita: *Modern Currents in Japanese Art* (New York and Tokyo, 1974)
I. Jōfuku: *Hiraga Gennai no kenkyū* [Hiraga Gennai studies] (Tokyo, 1976)

MARK H. SANDLER

Hiraizumi. Japanese city in the Nishi Iwai District, southern Iwate Prefecture, in the region of Tōhoku (formerly Ōshū, comprising the ancient provinces of Mutsu and Dewa), northern Honshu.

1. Introduction. 2. Buildings.

1. INTRODUCTION. Hiraizumi is first mentioned in records of the 8th century AD, when the central government established a military base near the Koromo River in an effort to subdue the native inhabitants, the Ezo (Ainu). In the mid-11th century AD the area was occupied by the Abe family. The city is perhaps best known as the capital of the Fujiwara family of Ōshū (also called Mutsu) from the late 11th century AD to the late 12th. The first of the Ōshū Fujiwara rulers was Fujiwara no Kiyohira (1056–

1128), who came to power *c.* 1090 as a result of a series of bloody territorial wars, displacing a line of local chieftains who for centuries had ruled the Kitakami Basin of Ōshū. To mark his victory and his status, Kiyohira chose to establish his headquarters and administrative centre at Hiraizumi, which was strategically located at a riverine and overland crossroads at the southern tip of the Kitakami Basin. The family derived its subsequent wealth partly from gold mines in the region. Over the next hundred years, under Kiyohira's rule and that of his son Motohira (*c.* 1105–57), grandson Hidehira (?1122–87) and great-grandson Yasuhira (1155–89), Hiraizumi evolved into an almost completely autonomous political entity. The four generations of the Ōshū Fujiwara created a cultural centre that rivalled aspects of the imperial capital in Kyoto and of the ancient capital of Nara. Hiraizumi was important as the first provincial city to develop a political consciousness representing the interests of north-eastern Japan.

Kiyohira actively introduced the aristocratic culture of Kyoto to Hiraizumi, and, as part of his building programme, he sponsored the construction of the temple of Chūsonji (*see* §2(i) below), which is a splendid example of late Heian-period (AD 794–1185) provincial architecture. His descendants continued a tradition of architectural and artistic patronage. Motohira built the temple Mōtsuji (*see* §2(ii) below) and spent lavishly on the city's cultural life. Only the Konjikidō (Golden Hall) of Chūsonji and the garden at Mōtsuji remain from this era. Historical and archaeological evidence indicates that Motohira's wife sponsored the erection of the temple of Kanjizaiōin to the east of Mōtsuji. Hidehira constructed the temple of Muryōkōin, supposedly in imitation of the BYŌDŌIN in Uji, near Kyoto; like Mōtsuji and Chūsonji, it was ornately decorated with gold and silver.

Chūsonji and Mōtsuji were located in the mountains to the north-west and west, respectively, of the city centre. In this area too were the homes of the aristocracy, including the palatial residences of the Fujiwara such as the Karagosho (Chinese Palace) of Hidehira, near Muryōkōin, and such government buildings as the judicial Takakan (also known as the Hangankan). The south-eastern section of the city was inhabited by commoners. A main road ran north to south through the city. Hiraizumi declined during the political turmoil that occurred during the rule of Yasuhira. In 1189 the city was destroyed by fire, and Yasuhira was assassinated during a punitive expedition against the Ōshū Fujiwara by Minamoto Yoritomo (1147–99). This effectively marked the end of a Ōshū Fujiwara rule.

In the late 20th century the city had a population of approximately 10,000. Museums include the Hiraizumi Art Museum, the Hiraizumi Museum (Hiraizumi Hakubutsukan) and the Chūsonji Treasure House. On the outskirts of the city is the Takkoku no Iwaya, a temple (reconstructed in 1961) that contains a statue of *Dainichi Nyorai Buddha* (Skt Mahavairocana Tathagata) carved into the surface of a cliff. Only the head and shoulders of the figure, which are sculpted in a style characteristic of the Heian period, have survived.

BIBLIOGRAPHY

Kodansha Enc. Japan
T. Takahashi: *Ōshū Fujiwara shi yondai* [The history of the four generations of the Ōshū Fujiwara], Jinbutsu sosho [A library of personalities], xii (Tokyo, 1958)

G. Fujishima, ed.: *Hiraizumi: Mōtsuji to Kanjizaiōin no kenkyū* [Hiraizumi: Research on Mōtsuji and Kanjizaiōin] (Tokyo, 1961/*R* Ichinoseki, 1980)

G. Itabashi: *Ōshū Hiraizumi*, Nihon rekishi shinsho [New writings on Japanese history], lxx (Tokyo, 1961/*R* 1973)

Ōshū Fujiwara shiryō [Historical material on the Ōshū Fujiwara] (1969), ii of *Tōhoku shi shiryōshū* [Collection of historical materials on Tōhoku history], Tōhoku Daigaku Tōhoku Bunka Kenkyūkai (Tokyo)

AMY REIGLE STEPHENS

2. BUILDINGS.

(i) Chūsonji. (ii) Mōtsuji.

(i) Chūsonji [Kanzan Chūsonji]. The Buddhist temple of Chūsonji occupies *c.* 6 ha of hilly, forested terrain on the slopes of Kanzan, which lies at the confluence of the Kitakami and Koromo rivers. It is the head temple of the Tendai sect in the Tōhoku (formerly Ōshū) region (northern Honshu). Its principal tutelary shrines are Hakusan Shrine (Hakusan Jinja) and Hie Shrine (Hie Jinja).

(a) History. Temple tradition holds that Chūsonji was founded in AD 850 by the Tendai patriarch Ennin (Jikaku Daishi; AD 794–864) and was originally called Kōdaijuin. It was named Chūsonji in 859. Its development into a significant site began *c.* 1090 with the arrival in Hiraizumi of the first of the Ōshū Fujiwara family of rulers, Fujiwara no Kiyohira (1056–1128; *see* §1 above), after his victory over local chieftains. Kiyohira had Chūsonji constructed on the foundations of Kōdaijuin, to commemorate the war dead and, perhaps more importantly, to symbolize a religious mandate for his own lineage. It was consecrated in 1126 in a ceremony marking the renewal of the temple and attended by scores of monks from ENRYAKUJI. By the end of the 12th century there were at least 40 halls at Chūsonji.

Kiyohira's son Motohira (*c.* 1105–57) and grandson Hidehira (?1122–87) continued the rule of the Ōshū Fujiwara family during the end of the Heian period (AD 794–1185) and commissioned further temples in Hiraizumi, notably Mōtsuji (*c.* 1138; *see* §(ii) below) and Muryōkōin (*c.* 1170). After the fall of Hiraizumi to Minamoto forces in 1189 and the subsequent annihilation of the Ōshū Fujiwara house, Chūsonji was maintained by Minamoto no Yoritomo (1147–99), founder of the Kamakura shogunate. The temple continued to flourish in the 13th century but declined under the Ashikaga regime that followed during the Muromachi period (1333–1568). In 1337 a fire consumed virtually the entire complex, sparing only one *kyōzō* (*sūtra* repository) and the Konjikidō (Golden Hall), a small *Amidadō* or hall for the worship of Amida (Skt Amitabha; the Buddha of the Western Paradise). Chūsonji's fortunes continued to decline until the war-lord and ruler of Sendai and Ōshū, Date Masamune (1567–1636), granted it renewed patronage. The temple began to thrive again in the Meiji period (1868–1912) and by the late 20th century had regained much of its earlier prestige. Although most of its buildings are reconstructions dating from the 16th century or later, the original flavour of the temple has been well preserved. A series of archeological investigations and architectural studies were undertaken between 1959 and 1968.

(b) Architecture and interior decoration. Construction began about 1105, and the complex evolved over several decades in at least two stages. The first buildings to be completed were the Tahōji, which enshrined figures of the historical Buddha, Shaka (Skt Shakyamuni) and Tahō (Skt Prabhutaratna), and the pagoda. By 1107 the Daichōjujin, a two-storey *Amidadō*, had been constructed. It enshrined at least nine monumental gilt-wood sculptures of Amida and seems to have been an adaptation of the *kutaidō* or *kutai Amidadō* ('nine-image Amida hall') format. The *Shakadō*, a hall for the worship of Shaka, had been built by 1108. It enshrined 100 golden images of Shaka and was modelled on the *Shakadō* (completed 1027) at Hōjōji, the palatial temple complex commissioned in 1020 by Fujiwara no Michinaga (966–1028). The Ryōkaidō was also completed *c.* 1108: this was a hall for the worship of Taizōkai (Womb Realm; Skt Garbhadhatu), a realm symbolizing one of two aspects of Dainichi Nyorai (Skt Mahavairocana), the central Buddha in Esoteric Buddhism. The other realm was Kongōkai (Diamond Realm; Skt Vajradhatu). The Ryōkaidō was said to contain all the deities of the Taizōkai and Kongōkai *mandala*s, the pictorial representations of these realms.

The two *kyōzō* and the Konjikidō were constructed in the second stage of the Chūsonji project, which was initiated *c.* 1117. One *kyōzō*, a two-storey, three-bay-square structure, was built on the southern perimeter of the complex as part of a precinct that was never completed. This 'greater' *kyōzō* was completed by 1126 and is believed by Fujishima Gaijirō and others to have enshrined gilt-wood sculptures of the *bodhisattva* of supreme wisdom, Monju (Skt Manjushri), and attendants, and to have housed a sumptuous votive transcription of the *Issaikyō* ('all the *sūtra*s', the canon of Mahayana or 'greater vehicle' Buddhism). The lesser *kyōzō* was a one-storey building, three bays square, constructed at the same time as the Konjikidō (i.e. 1121–4) and only metres away. It enshrined votive transcriptions of the Lotus *sūtra* and, like the Konjikidō, seems to have been more personally significant to Kiyohira than Chūsonji's larger, more public structures.

The Konjikidō is the most famous building of the temple and the only structure dating from the time of the Ōshū Fujiwara. According to an inscription on its memorial ridge-pole placard, the Konjikidō was completed in 1124. The plan is characteristic of many Amida halls of the period. It is a one-storey, three-bay-square building in the *hōgyō zukuri* ('pyramidal roof construction') format, with cypress-bark shingle roofing. The entire structure is about 8 m sq., with a height also of 8 m from foundation to roof finial; its *moya* (central architectural space) measures approximately 5 m sq. With the exception of the roof, the exterior of the building is covered in gold leaf over a black-lacquer ground. The hall is encased completely within a modern, concrete *sayadō* ('pod hall'; protective structure), although until the Muromachi period it stood in the open, earning the sobriquet Hikaridō ('The Hall that Shines').

Much of the interior is also covered in gold leaf and is dominated by a tripartite altar with three daises, elaborately decorated with mother-of-pearl. Each dais enshrines small gilt-wood sculptures of an *Amida Triad*, consisting of the Niten (Two Guardian Kings) and the Roku Jizō (Six Forms of Jizō; Skt Kshitigarbha, the *bodhisattva* of deliverance). This alone made the Konjikidō unique; also unprecedented was the use of the tripartite altar as a tomb for the mummies of Kiyohira, Motohira and Hidehira. The central altar, which entombs the mummy of Kiyohira, occupies the *moya* beneath a coffered, latticed and gilded ceiling. Temple historians maintain that the north-west and south-west daises contain the remains of Motohira and Hidehira respectively. Stylistic and technical analysis suggests that the central dais was completed in 1124 and that the subsidiary daises were added *c.* 1160 by Hidehira as tombs for his father and himself. The ornamentation of the altar, *moya* and *moya* pillars is an ornate blend of the techniques of *sukashibori* (openwork) in bronze and of mother-of-pearl (*raden*) inlay in lacquer (*see* LACQUER, fig. 177). The *sukashibori* work includes engraved (*senbori*) and gilt-bronze plates attached to lacquered surfaces, some over a blue coloured-glass ground. Each mother-of-pearl shell is inlaid with clear glass over a painted cavity (*fusezaishiki*) and is set into a lacquer ground often flecked with gold (*ikakeji*). The decorative motifs are floral and consist largely of *hōsōge* ('Buddha-visage flowers'; peony-like flowers) and *karakusa* ('Chinese grasses'; vine-like leaves and tendrils). The Konjikidō is a fully articulated example of the aesthetics of the Heian period aristocracy. It is, however, also representative of an idiosyncratic regional interpretation of mainstream Japanese Buddhist culture, as the use of the altar as a mausoleum eloquently testifies.

Both the Konjikidō and the 'lesser' *kyōzō* were extensively restored in modern times. The Konjikidō in particular has attracted scholarly interest, and between 1962 and 1968 it was dismantled, studied and reconstructed in its original form, so that its appearance was entirely consistent with the historical record.

BIBLIOGRAPHY

Kodansha Enc. Japan: 'Chūsonji'
Azuma kagami [Mirror of the East] (late 13th century), xxxii and xxxiii of *Shintei zō ho kokushi taikei* (Tokyo, 1932); ed. R. Abe (Tokyo, 1976)
S. Hosaka: *Chūsonji* (Tokyo, 1962)
T. Fukuyama: 'Byōdōin to Chūsonji', *Nihon no Bijutsu*, ix (Tokyo, 1964); Eng. trans. by R. K. Jones as *Heian Temples: Byodo-in and Chuson-ji* (1976), Heibonsha Surv. Jap. A., ix (New York and Tokyo, 1972–7)
G. Fujishima: *Chūsonji* (Tokyo, 1971)
H. Sudo and M. Iwasa: *Chūsonji to Mōtsuji* (Tokyo, 1989)

MIMI HALL YIENGPRUKSAWAN

(ii) Mōtsuji. The Buddhist temple of Mōtsuji survives only as foundation-stones and a pond garden. It was constructed west of Hiraizumi. Around 1126 Fujiwara no Kiyohira (1056–1128) had dedicated the temple of Chūsonji (*see* §(i) above) on Kanzan, and his son Fujiwara no Motohira (*c.* 1105–57) built the elaborate temple complex of Mōtsuji at the base of the hill. Despite Hiraizumi's location in the remote mountains of northern Honshu, archaeological and documentary evidence indicates that the buildings and grounds of Mōtsuji were expanded versions of, and equal in splendour to, the famous temples constructed during the Heian period (AD 794–1185) in the imperial capital of Heian (now Kyoto). The two chapels at Mōtsuji, called Enryūji and Kashōji, contained main images of Yakushi (Skt Bhaishajyaguru, the Buddha of healing), but the building compounds were typical of the chapels in and near Kyoto (e.g. BYŌDŌIN) dedicated to Amida (Skt Amitabha, the Buddha of the Western Paradise). Each of the compounds consisted of a central hall with flanking pavilions and interconnecting corridors set around a rectangular courtyard used for ritual ceremonies. Kashōji was completed by Motohira's son Fujiwara no Hidehira (?1122–87) some time after 1157.

The chapel of Enryūji had a large central hall facing south, with L-shaped corridors extending forward on each side, connecting with a drum-tower and belfry near the water's edge. On the same axis as the chapel was a short bridge leading to a small island and a longer bridge from the island to the south shore, where a two-storey gate-house served as the formal entrance to the Mōtsuji complex. Behind Enryūji, to the north-west, was a lecture hall, and to the east were two small buildings, the Hokedō (Lotus *Sūtra* Hall) and Jōgyōdō (Meditation Hall), joined together by a porch. The Kashōji compound was built to the west of Enryūji and duplicated its U-shaped layout of central hall and flanking wings. After these structures burnt down in the 13th century, the foundation stones were left essentially undisturbed until the second half of the 20th century, when extensive excavations were conducted.

To the south of the two chapels at Mōtsuji is a single large pond garden with rock arrangements considered to be the finest example of their kind from the Heian period. Like the chapels, the pond garden was intended to suggest the Pure Land realm of the afterlife. The shallow pond is about 180 m east–west and 90 m north–south, with an irregular shoreline, which includes some rounded earthen banks, a short peninsula and curving shore of smooth beach stones, a craggy point with an islet of jutting rocks and an artificial hill with various boulders. The rockwork copies natural formations, but the placement of some of the rock groupings is highly picturesque, resembling those described in the Heian period garden manual *Sakuteiki* ('Records of making gardens'; *see* GARDEN, §VI, 3), and the small stream that feeds into the pond from north-east of the Enryūji chapel is typical of such waterways in Kyoto gardens. The plantings of beautiful flowers around the Mōtsuji pond garden have not been restored to 12th-century styles, but the large iris swamp at the western end of the pond has long been famous. Pine-clad hillsides provide a dramatic backdrop to the pond area in the north and west.

East of the Mōtsuji complex is the Kanjizaiōin, another Buddhist temple with a large pond garden, founded at an unknown date by Motohira's wife. This complex had two chapels dedicated to Amida on the north shore, but they had no corridors or flanking pavilions. East of the Kanjizaiōin pond was a belfry and a three-storey Fugendō (a hall dedicated to the worship of the *bodhisattva* Fugen; Skt Samanthabadra), usually depicted in Japan as one of the two attendants of the historical Buddha, Shaka (Skt Shakyamuni), who represent his teaching and practice. On the western shore was an artificial hill and cascade. An island near the south shore was probably reached by a bridge from the south gate. Mōtsuji and Kanjizaiōin together are thought to have housed about 500 monks in nearby dormitories.

BIBLIOGRAPHY

Kodansha Enc. Japan: 'Mōtsuji'
T. Fukuyama: 'Byōdōin to Chūsonji', *Nihon no Bijutsu*, ix (Tokyo, 1964); Eng. trans. by R. K. Jones as *Heian Temples: Byodo-in and Chuson-ji* (1976), Heibonsha Surv. Jap. A., ix (New York and Tokyo, 1972–7)

G. Fujishima: *Hiraizumi, Chūsonji, Mōtsuji no zenyō* [A complete look at Hiraizumi, Chūsonji and Mōtsuji] (Ichinoseki, 1986)

BRUCE A. COATS

Hirayama, Ikuo (*b* Hiroshima, 5 June 1930). Japanese painter. He graduated from the *Nihonga* (Japanese-style painting) department of Tokyo School of Fine Arts in 1952. He became a pupil of Seison Maeda, and his first submission to the Inten exhibition in 1953, *Homeward Bound* (Hiroshima, Prefect. A. Mus.), was accepted. Until 1959 his activities were centred on the Inten exhibitions, but after this date he became known for his series of paintings on the story of Buddha. In the later 1960s his main subjects were of China and its western regions, India and the Middle and Near East, thus reversing the route along which Buddhism had been introduced into Japan. In 1964 he became a member of the Japan Art Institute. He continued to make annual sketching trips to China, India and countries of the Middle East and produced a series of superb landscapes and portraits depicting the Silk Road, the route of culture and trade, its historical remains and the people who live along it. In 1969 he became Assistant Professor at Tokyo University of Arts, and Professor in 1973, later becoming President.

WRITINGS
Hirayama Ikuo gashū [Collected paintings of Ikuo Hirayama] (Tokyo, 1990)
[Complete works], 7 vols (Tokyo, 1990–91)
[Long journey: Biographical works and writings] (Tokyo, 1991)
[Cultural remains of the world] (Tokyo, 1994)
with S. Takashina: [Japanese paintings from a global perspective] (Tokyo, 1994)
[Straight and narrow road] (Tokyo, 1994)

YOSHIKAZU IWASAKI

Hi-Red Center [Haireddo Senta]. Japanese group of installation artists founded in 1963 and active until 1964. The group's name comprised a translation of the first part of each founder's surname: 'Taka' from JIRŌ TAKAMATSU, 'Aka' from Genpei Akasegawa (*b* 1937) and 'Naka' from Natsuyuki Nakanishi (*b* 1935). The group attempted to draw attention to their neo-Dadaist ideas through the staging of public installations and performances. In the *Dairoku ji mikisa keikaku* ('The sixth blender plan') exhibition at the Miyata Clinic, Shinbashi, Tokyo (1963), for example, Nakanishi covered himself in metal clothes-pegs. The *Shieruta puran* ('Shelter plan') event in the Teikoku Hotel, Tokyo (1964), involved the creation of personalized nuclear fall-out shelters by the group's members. Hi-Red Center also produced a number of pamphlets in addition to their other activities.

WRITINGS
Tokuhō! Tsūshin eisei wa nanimono ni tsukawareteiru ka! [News flash! Can anyone use the information satellite!] (Tokyo, 1964)
G. Akasegawa: *Tokyo mikisa-keikaku—Haireddo senta chokusetsu kōdō no kiroku* [Tokyo blender plan—Hi-Red Center record of direct action] (Tokyo, 1984)

BIBLIOGRAPHY
Reconstructions: Avant-garde Art in Japan, 1945–1965 (exh. cat. by D. Elliot and K. Kaido, Oxford, MOMA, 1985), pp. 66–90

YASUYOSHI SAITO

Hirnl [Hirnle], **Karl** [Karel] **Josef.** *See* HIERNLE, KARL JOSEF.

Hiromichi. *See* SUMIYOSHI, (1).

Hiromi Tsuchida. *See* TSUCHIDA, HIROMI.

Hiroshige. *See* ANDŌ HIROSHIGE.

Hiroshi Hamaya. *See* HAMAYA, HIROSHI.

Hiroshi Izue. *See* IZUE, YUTAKA.

Hiroshima. Japanese city, the seventh largest in Japan (area 740 sq. km, population in 1986 *c.* 1 million), and capital of Hiroshima Prefecture. It is a bustling port and industrial city on the Inland Sea coast of Honshu, west of Osaka and Kobe. Hiroshima was created in 1589 by Mōri Terumoto (1553–1625), the local daimyo, after he had seen the new urban and commercial centre of OSAKA built around its huge castle. The original city was laid out on the low-lying alluvial plain and delta islands of the Ōta River, in imitation of the orderly grid pattern of KYOTO (*see also* JAPAN, §IV). Hiroshima grew to have some 70 commercial wards in addition to its samurai wards. These were divided by 109 (later 75) large wooden gates, locked for security every evening at about eight o'clock. Houses within the samurai wards around the castle were spacious, averaging 2874 sq. m in Hakushima Ward and 1392 sq. m in Sarugaku Ward. Townsmen's houses, however, had to cram their various buildings (shops and storehouses) into much smaller sites and were allotted little space for gardens. While the arts and scholarship flourished in both the samurai and townsmen sections of the city, no major works were produced. Hiroshima was subject to regular heavy flooding because of its location, and its density of population, particularly in the commercial district, also made it prone to major fires, so that the urban area was periodically devastated.

The domain of Hiroshima was abolished in 1871, and the city became the administrative centre for Hiroshima Prefecture. Having good rail and port facilities, Hiroshima was a temporary capital during the Sino-Japanese War of 1894–5 and was chosen as the site of the imperial military headquarters during the Russo-Japanese War of 1904–5. After World War I, Hiroshima continued to grow into the largest military base and industrial supply centre in Japan, with military establishments occupying 40% of the urban area. In the atomic bomb attack of 6 April 1945, 92% of the urban area was damaged or destroyed, including the castle. Hiroshima's reconstruction was remarkably rapid. Its pre-war industries revived to make the city a major centre, although they ceased to produce for military purposes, and Hiroshima became the spearhead for Japan's peace and nuclear disarmament movement. The donjon of Hiroshima Castle and the garden of the villa of the daimyo, Shukkei'en, both destroyed by the bomb, were restored, and the Peace Park—with its memorial and Peace Memorial Museum designed by KENZŌ TANGE and Peace Bridge designed by ISAMU NOGUCHI—and various sculptures and other civic architecture in the centre of the city symbolize the city's rebirth and transformation.

BIBLIOGRAPHY
Heibonsha Surv. Jap. A.

J. F. MORRIS

Hiroshi Oe. *See* OE, HIROSHI.

Hirozumi. *See* SUMIYOSHI, (2).

Hirsau Congregation. Federation of monasteries reformed from the abbey of Hirsau, near Calw, Baden-Württemberg, Germany. The abbey was originally dedicated to St Aurelius and developed at the foot of the Nazariusberg around a church that housed the saint's relics from AD 830. Benedictine monks from Fulda settled there in 838. It was refounded in 1049 by Count Adalbert II of Calw, the nephew of Pope Leo IX (*reg* 1049–55), and the church was rebuilt (1059–71). Monks from Einsiedeln were introduced in 1065. The most important influence on the abbey's development was Abbot William (*reg* 1068–91), who supported the papacy during the Investiture crisis and made Hirsau a centre of ecclesiastical reform in south-west Germany, Thuringia, Austria and Alsace. He rejected lay investiture and tried to weaken dependence on secular patronage. Pope Gregory VII (*reg* 1073–85) granted the abbey immunity in 1075.

Further reforms were introduced after 1079, when Cluniac customs were adopted (*see* CLUNIAC ORDER, §III, 1 (i)), although the abbey did not become a Cluniac dependency. The house's observance was codified in the three volumes of the Hirsau Customary (1082–4), which was compiled for William by Ulrich, prior of Zell, after a visit to Cluny. Many other monasteries were reformed, and despite episcopal opposition a loose confederation or Congregation developed that at its peak numbered up to 100 houses.

Hirsau Congregation, former abbey church at Alpirsbach, begun *c.* 1100, interior looking west

The new abbey church of SS Peter und Paul (1082–91; ruined 1692) was strongly influenced by Cluny II (*see* CLUNY ABBEY, §III, 1(i)). It had a basilican plan with apses at both ends and a flat wooden ceiling. The western atrium was reworked between 1095 and 1120 to create a narthex with twin towers, of which the northern Eulenturm survives. This design, which was characterized by substantial masonry and heavy mouldings, is best illustrated by the former abbey church (now Protestant parish church) at Alpirsbach (begun *c.* 1100; see fig.; *see also* ROMANESQUE, §II, 2). About 1120 the St-Aurelius-Kirche at Hirsau was similarly rebuilt more closely to reflect the liturgical requirements of the customary. Owing to the widespread adoption of the design at many of the Congregation's houses, such as Paulinzella (1112–24) in Thuringia, literature from the 19th century commonly referred to a 'Hirsau school' of architecture. Hoffmann, however, argued that there was no school as such, but that Hirsau's architectural influence simply spread in piecemeal fashion to the houses that it reformed.

Hirsau retained its importance for much of the 12th century. Manuscripts produced by its scriptorium included the Hirsau Passional (first half of the 12th century; Stuttgart, Württemberg. Landesbib.). The abbey, however, was unable to remain independent: many of its possessions were ceded to Frederick II in 1215, and it finally succumbed to imperial rule in 1225. It joined the Congregation of Bursfeld in 1458 and was secularized in 1535.

BIBLIOGRAPHY
S. *Willelmi constitutiones Hirsaugienses seu Gengenbacenses* (1082–4); ed. in *PL*, cl (1844)
W. Hoffmann: *Hirsau und die 'Hirsauer Bauschule'* (Munich, [1950])
H. Jakobs: *Die Hirsauer* (Cologne and Graz, 1969)
                            ANNE FRANCES DAWTRY

Hirsch, Robert von (*b* Frankfurt am Main, 1883; *d* 1 Nov 1977). German connoisseur and collector. As a young man he entered his uncle's leather firm, Offenbach, and proved to be a very good businessman. He brought the firm international fame; the Tsarina and her brother, Ernest-Ludwig, Grand Duke of Hesse and the Rhine, visited the factory in 1913. At first Hirsch and his brother collected French and German first editions of books in fine bindings. In 1905 Hirsch met Georg Swarzenski (1876–1957), director of the Städelsches Kunstinstitut, Frankfurt, who raised his interest in art. Through their extensive travels together Hirsch gained considerable knowledge about art. Under the guidance of Swarzenski and later also Edmund Schilling (1888–1974), head of the prints department, he acquired works of art ranging from paintings, drawings and sculpture to furniture and porcelain. In 1907 he bought his first painting, the *Redhead in a White Blouse* (now Boston, MA, Mus. F.A.), by Toulouse-Lautrec. The second was Picasso's *Street Scene*. On their visit in 1913, the Grand Duke and the Tsarina admired the growing art collection and granted Hirsch the prefix 'von'. Hirsch assembled his collection of Medieval and Renaissance works of art mainly during the 1920s and 1930s through the Hermitage sales and the dispersal of the Guelph Treasure and Hohenzollern–Sigmaringen collections. In 1925 he lent 12 paintings to an Old Master exhibition in Frankfurt. In 1930 he became administrator for the Städelsches Kunstinstitut.

By 1933, however, owing to the threat of war, Hirsch had transferred his business interests to Basle and emigrated to that city. In order to be able to export his art collection, he had to leave the *Judgement of Paris* by Lucas Cranach (i) to the German State (the painting was returned to him after 1945). In Basle he made new friends. His collection became world-famous and was visited by many international museum directors and specialists. Soon after his arrival in Basle he became a member of the Board of the Kunstmuseum. After the war he married the sculptress Martha Dreyfus–Koch (*d* 1965), whose taste became apparent in his art collection; she also created a beautiful botanical garden around their house in the Engelgasse, Basle. The couple entertained frequently, and Hirsch was known for his hospitality, which continued after his wife's death. He had built up an excellent art library and acquired his knowledge of art through extensive travel, reading and study; Bernard Berenson referred to him with respect as one of the very few collectors with a great deal of knowledge. His collection was extremely diverse and contained Ottonian ivories, medieval enamels, Italian and German paintings, Renaissance bronzes, Dutch, German and Italian Old Master drawings, paintings and furniture of the 18th century, and Impressionist and contemporary paintings. After his death, part of his collection was sold at auction by Sotheby's, London, in 1978, but part was given to friends, relatives and museums, such as the *Blinding of St Victor* by 'Ugolino-Lorenzetti' (tempera on panel, 1340) and a drawing by Rembrandt, the *Prodigal Son Feasting with Harlots* (*c.* 1635–40), both in the Städelsches Kunstinstitut und Städtische Galerie, Frankfurt am Main.

BIBLIOGRAPHY
The Robert von Hirsch Collection (sale cat., London, Sotheby's, June 1978), i

☐

Hirsch, Walter (*b* Leningrad [now St Petersburg], 12 April 1935). Swedish photographer and teacher. He moved to Sweden before World War II. He studied photography in 1956 at the Kursverksamheten School of Photography, Stockholm. From 1964 to 1970 he taught at the Stockholms Fotografiska Skola. He came to nationwide attention when his collection *Midsummer Feast* was published in *Aktuell Fotografi* (1967), and when his exhibition *London April 13th, 1968, between hrs 0900–2300* was held the same year at the Moderna Museet in Stockholm, the first one-man show there by a Swedish photographer. During the 1960s and 1970s Hirsch worked as a stills photographer at film recordings and as a commercial and fashion photographer. In 1970 he had a one-man show at the International Museum of Photography at George Eastman House in Rochester, NY, and the Fotografiska Museet in Stockholm later included his work in the exhibitions *Thailand* (1975) and *Hjärtats Journal* (1980).

PHOTOGRAPHIC PUBLICATIONS
Bilder, 1960–80 (Helsingborg, 1982)
Dobbers bok (Stockholm, 1984) [illustrations of Hirsch's work as a commercial photographer]
Sara och Sam (Stockholm, 1984)

BIBLIOGRAPHY
T. I. Odulf: 'Man bland vänner: Walter Hirsch intervjuad', *Populär Fotografi*, 2 (1967), pp. 22–34, 70
LEIF WIGH

Hirschfeld, Christian Cay Laurenz (*b* Nüchel, Holstein, 16 Feb 1742; *d* Kiel, 20 Feb 1792). German writer. From 1770 he was Professor of Philosophy and Fine Arts at Kiel (and also the first Professor of Art History there). His lectures were particularly concerned with the history of philosophy and the arts, and with rhetoric. He became more widely known when he published two small works on gardens, *Anmerkungen über die Landhäuser und die Gartenkunst* and *Theorie der Gartenkunst*, and followed these with a more comprehensive *Theorie der Gartenkunst* in five volumes. He also edited the journal *Der Gartenkalender* (1782–9), which was continued by Wilhelm Gottlieb Becker as *Taschenbuch für Garten Freunde* (1795–9). These publications served to propagate the concept of landscape gardening in the English manner; they also provided a critique of the Baroque garden style typified by Versailles, which Hirschfeld associated with the political system of despotic absolutism. The larger *Theorie der Gartenkunst* contains, as well as theory, many descriptions, mostly by other authors, of exemplary gardens. Hirschfeld's principal sources were the English theories of William Chambers, Thomas Whately and Henry Home, Lord Kames; he recognized the importance of association and subjective feeling in garden aesthetics, and he categorized gardens and their individual 'scenes'. He knew the English gardens only from a random selection of engravings; he had botanical knowledge and skill, but never worked as a practising landscape gardener. Nevertheless, he was a major influence in mediating English ideas and stimulating new forms of landscape gardening in Germany.

WRITINGS
Anmerkungen über die Landhäuser und die Gartenkunst (Leipzig, 1773)
Theorie der Gartenkunst (Leipzig, 1775)
Theorie der Gartenkunst, 5 vols (Leipzig, 1779–85)

BIBLIOGRAPHY
W. Schepers: *Hirschfelds 'Theorie der Gartenkunst', 1779–1785* (Worms, 1980)
W. Kehn: *Christian Cay Lorenz Hirschfeld 1742–1792: Eine Biographie* (Worms, 1993)
REINHARD ZIMMERMANN

Hirschfeld-Mack, Ludwig (*b* Frankfurt am Main, 11 July 1893; *d* Sydney, 7 Jan 1965). German painter, printmaker and teacher, active in England and Australia. From 1912 to 1914 he attended the progressive school run by Wilhelm von Debschitz in Munich and studied art history at Munich University. His training was then interrupted for four and a half years by military service. In 1919 he enrolled at Adolf Hölzel's pioneering academy in Stuttgart. Hölzel communicated to his pupils, who also included Johannes Itten and Oskar Schlemmer, his interest in abstract formal relationships and colour contrasts. At this time Hirschfeld-Mack is known to have been working in the style of the German Expressionists.

In October 1919, attracted by Walter Gropius's Bauhaus Manifesto, Hirschfeld-Mack enrolled at the Weimar Bauhaus. After taking the *Vorkurs* devised by Itten, he enrolled in the printing workshop, where he soon emerged as one of the most important apprentices. He worked closely with the Form Master, Lyonel Feininger, helping to prepare *Zwölf Holzschnitte von Lyonel Feininger*, published in 1921, and the *Neue europäische Grafik* portfolios of 1923–4. In 1922 he was the first Bauhaus student to pass the journeyman's examination. His works from these years include *League of Nations* (1920; Mrs L. Hirschfeld priv. col., see exh. cat. no. 40), a powerful black-and-white woodcut incorporating the circular form that recurs in his work. Other woodcuts are boldly coloured and bear strong traces of Cubism in their approach to form.

Hirschfeld-Mack also worked in watercolour. Some of his watercolours of this period, in which he analysed tableware in terms of the basic geometric forms of the cylinder, cone and circle, show the influence of Fernand Léger, whom he met in Paris in 1923, and of the Purists. *The Accordion Player* (1922; Mrs L. Hirschfeld priv. col., see exh. cat., no. 45) is an attempt to analyse the complexities of his accordion (which he played in the Bauhaus band) in strictly cylindrical and corrugated forms. His palette of strong yellows and oranges is much brighter than that of either the Cubists or the Purists. Other watercolours treat exotic subjects in a more fluid style. The work of Schlemmer, a friend, encouraged an interest in the fantastic and the theatrical throughout the Weimar Bauhaus period. Paul Klee, too, was greatly attracted by fantastic subject-matter. There are, moreover, strong stylistic parallels between his work and Hirschfeld-Mack's, evident in one of the latter's finest works from the Bauhaus period, *Reaching the Stars* (colour lithograph, 1922; Sydney, A.G. NSW; see fig.). The delicate use of line and texture, the fine gradations of colour and even the title are reminiscent of Klee's work. In 1921 both Klee and Hirschfeld-Mack began to use a drawing technique, which they called *Durchdrückzeichnung*, as a means of creating delicate graphic effects. It could be used in conjunction with lithography to produce multiple impressions.

Hirschfeld-Mack had a strong interest in colour theory and attended Klee's courses in 1922–3 with great interest. He himself gave a colour seminar as part of Itten's *Vorkurs*, and a number of his colour charts survive (Berlin, Bauhaus-Archv). His contribution to the range of Bauhaus educational toys was a spinning top, or optical colour mixer, which demonstrated the laws of colour combination and the colour theories of Johann Wolfgang von Goethe and Arthur Schopenhauer. In 1922 he began work on his *Lichtspiele* or reflected light compositions. These arose from his need to express the rhythmic and dynamic qualities of colour through movement and music. He designed a complex apparatus to project coloured forms, frequently overlapped in progressive tonal gradations, on to a screen. The effect was of an abstract film, although each show was a unique performance. Hirschfeld-Mack and his team performed his *Lichtspiele* in several European cities during 1923–5, and he himself provided the musical accompaniment. In 1964 three of his compositions were reconstructed on film at the Bauhaus-Archiv in West Berlin.

Rather than following the Bauhaus to Dessau in 1925, Hirschfeld-Mack joined the Freie Schulgemeinde at Wickersdorf in Thuringia, where he taught art and craft. In late 1928 or 1929 he returned to Weimar to give a preliminary course in the use of materials for architects at Otto

Ludwig Hirschfeld-Mack: *Reaching the Stars*, colour lithograph, 442×316 mm, 1922 (Sydney, Art Gallery of New South Wales)

Bartning's Staatliche Hochschule für Handwerk und Baukunst. In 1930 he became the first Professor of Art and Craft at the newly founded Pädagogische Hochschule in Frankfurt an der Oder, where he was able to implement Bauhaus principles. Following the closure of the school in 1932, he lectured for a year at the older and less radical Pädagogische Hochschule in Kiel.

By 1936, with his commitment to modern art, progressive education and Jewish descent, Hirschfeld-Mack was forced to flee Germany. He moved to London, where he re-established contact with another émigré, Gropius. Hirschfeld-Mack had a wide range of employment in England, which included working for the Subsistence Production Society, supervising building projects and teaching at the Pontypool Settlement in South Wales. In London he adapted the principles of the *Lichtspiele* for use in stage lighting and investigated the use of light in advertising design. In conjunction with Abbatt Toys he designed musical instruments for children and taught children at the pioneer Health Centre at Peckham and at Dulwich Preparatory School, both in London.

In the late 1930s Hirschfeld-Mack resisted appeals from Josef and Anni Albers and Gropius to go to the USA, and in 1940 he was interned as a German alien. In May he was deported to Australia. He made several moving woodcuts of the internment camps at Tatura and Orange in 1941, including the bleakly expressive *Desolation* (Sydney, A.G.

NSW). In 1942 he was appointed art master at Geelong Grammar School where he remained until retirement in 1957. During his last years he was active as an artist and teacher and was responsible for introducing Bauhaus ideas to Australia.

WRITINGS

The Bauhaus: An Introductory Survey (London, 1963)

BIBLIOGRAPHY

H. M. Wingler: *Das Bauhaus* (Bramsche and Cologne, 1969; Eng. trans. Cambridge, MA, and London, 1969, rev. 1976)

Two Masters of the Weimar Bauhaus: Lyonel Feininger and Ludwig Hirschfeld Mack (exh. cat. by N. Draffin, Sydney, A.G. NSW; Melbourne, N.G. Victoria; 1974)

A. Rowland: *The Bauhaus Source Book* (Oxford, 1990)

ANNA ROWLAND

Hirschfeld Painter. *See* VASE PAINTERS, §II.

Hirschsprung, Heinrich (*b* Copenhagen, 7 Feb 1836; *d* 8 Nov 1908). Danish collector and industrialist. The owner of a tobacco factory, he bought his first work of art in 1866, and his collection of 19th-century Danish art grew rapidly thereafter. With his interest in contemporary art Hirschsprung created a collection that was unique in its time. The artists include P. S. Krøyer and others of the naturalistic painters working at Skagen, Theodor Philipsen, Kristian Zahrtmann, Laurits Andersen Ring, Vilhelm Hammershøi, Joakim Skovgaard and other Danish Symbolists, and the Fynboerne (Fyn painters). At the same time he assembled a comprehensive collection of art from the Golden Age in Denmark, with masterpieces by C. W. Eckersberg, C. A. Jensen, Christen Købke, Wilhelm Marstrand, Johan Thomas Lundbye, P. C. Skovgaard,

Dankvart Dreyer, Christen Dalsgaard and Hans Ludvig Smidth among others. Hirschsprung, unusually for the period, understood the significance of drawings as independent works of art and collected representative examples by a wide range of artists. In 1888 the collection was exhibited for the first time, in Copenhagen, and in 1902 it was offered to the nation on the condition that a museum with its own building be founded under independent direction. The Danish government accepted the gift in 1907. The museum was built in the Park Østre Anlæg in Copenhagen to the design of the architect H. B. Storck (1839–1922); the collection was arranged by the art historian Emil Hannover (1864–1923), who had acted as Hirschsprung's adviser since the beginning of the century. The Hirschsprungske Samling opened to the public in 1911 and comprises about 2900 Danish works of art from the 19th century, of which a quarter are paintings and the rest drawings, cartoons and sketches for sculptures. There is also an important collection of 19th-century artists' furniture (*see* DENMARK, §VI).

BIBLIOGRAPHY

Katalog over Den Hirschsprungske Samling af danske kunstneres arbejder/Catalogue of The Hirschsprung Collection of Works by Danish Artists (Copenhagen, 1989) [with Eng. summary]

E. H. Brünniche: *Imkring Hirschsprungs Museum* (Copenhagen, 1994)

MARIANNE SAABYE

Hirschvogel [Hirsfogel; Hirsvogel]. German family of artists. They were Nuremberg's leading stained-glass painters during the late 15th century and the 16th. (1) Veit Hirschvogel the elder, the son of a glazier named Heinz (*d* 1485), established the family workshop and became the city's official glazier. His son Veit Hirschvogel the younger (1485–1553) succeeded him as official glazier, being succeeded in his turn by his son Sebald Hirschvogel (1517–89), who remained in the post for 33 years. The brothers of Veit the younger, Hans Hirschvogel (*d* 1516) and (2) Augustin Hirschvogel, also joined the glass-painting workshop, but Augustin, the most talented of the family, left it in 1525 to pursue a varied career outside Nuremberg, producing many etchings and also innovations in cartography. It is supposed that the Viennese goldsmith Veit Hirschvogel (1543–74) was Augustin's son.

BIBLIOGRAPHY

Hollstein: *Ger.*; *NDB*; Thieme–Becker

(1) Veit Hirschvogel the elder (*b* Nuremberg, 1461; *d* Nuremberg, 24 Dec 1525). Glass painter. He directed his workshop during the last great flowering of stained glass production in Nuremberg (*c.* 1485–1526). Around 1500 the workshop shifted from an old-fashioned style, based on the stained glass of the Strasbourg master Peter Hemmel von Andlau, to one based on the art of Albrecht Dürer. Dürer, along with his students Hans von Kulmbach, Hans Baldung, Hans Schäufelein and Sebald Beham, provided the workshop with numerous designs, and his drawing and graphic styles became its trademark. Due to Dürer's influence, many of the advances made in panel painting were applied to stained glass. He replaced the compartmentalized and decorative approach with a more monumental conception where a composition with imposing figures in an illusionistic setting unifies all the panels of a window. In the Pfinzing window (*c.* 1515;

Veit Hirschvogel the elder: *Death on Horseback Taking Aim*, painted stained glass, after a design from the circle of Albrecht Dürer, 400×370 mm, *c.* 1502 (Nuremberg, Germanisches Nationalmuseum)

Nuremberg, Sebalduskirche), for instance, a monumental Renaissance-style triumphal arch spans the entire window and unites 17 figures spatially and compositionally. The workshop's technical mastery of the application of washes and particularly of silver stain to create effects from yellow to red also endowed its stained glass with increased spatial illusion and translucency.

Even though the individual drawing style of a designer from the Dürer school is often identifiable from the glass itself, the degree of dependency of the glass painters on these outside designs is debated. Frenzel (1961) maintained that the glass painters were not limited to the mere mechanical transposition of other artists' designs; between the initial sketch from an outside designer to the finished full-scale cartoon, ample opportunity existed for creative input. At least some of the workshop members were sufficiently creative and adept in the styles of the Dürer school to work up cartoons, designs or variations either from sketches supplied from the Dürer circle, from the large workshop reserve of stained-glass designs, or even from contemporary woodcuts. By comparing the techniques and designs of several signed and unsigned stained-glass panels, Frenzel (1960) also attempted to identify the work of individual members of the Hirschvogel workshop and distinguished the more conservative (Veit the elder and Veit the younger) from the more progressive and experimental (Hans and Augustin).

The Hirschvogel workshop production includes windows in the Sebalduskirche (Bamberg window, 1501–2; Margrave's window, 1515; Emperor's window, 1514; Pfinzing window, 1515), in the Lorenzkirche (Löffelholz window, 1506; Schmidmayer window, 1509; windows in the Annenkapelle, 1510; see NUREMBERG, §IV, 1(ii) and 2), in the Landauerbruderkapelle of the Zwölfbruderhaus (1508), the Rochuskapelle (1520–21), and several windows (1505–13) formerly in the Carmelite cloister, Nuremberg, now in the parish churches at Grossgründlach and Wöhrd. The workshop also created numerous *Kabinettscheiben* ('glass panes for a small room'; i.e. rectangular, round or trefoil-shaped stained-glass panels to be set in bull's-eye glazing and viewed up close), popular in this period for windows in chapels, cloisters or private houses. They depict religious or profane subjects, for example the panel of *Death on Horseback Taking Aim* (*c.* 1502; Nuremberg, Ger. Nmus.; see fig.) from the house of the humanist Dr Sixtus Tucher (1459–1507), which matches another panel of Dr Tucher standing before his open grave. They often display some of the workshop's most creative and progressive work.

BIBLIOGRAPHY
G. Frenzel: 'Veit Hirschvogel: Eine Nürnberger Glasmalereiwerkstatt der Dürerzeit', *Z. Kstgesch.*, xxiii (1960), pp. 193–210
——: 'Entwurf und Ausführung in der Nürnberger Glasmalerei der Dürerzeit', *Z. Kstwiss.*, xv (1961), pp. 31–59
K. A. Knappe: *Albrecht Dürer und das Bamberger Fenster in St Sebald in Nürnberg* (Nuremberg, 1961)
Gothic and Renaissance Art in Nuremberg, 1300–1550 (exh. cat., New York, Met., 1986), pp. 87–92, cat. 157–9, 172–4

(2) Augustin Hirschvogel (*b* Nuremberg, 1503; *d* Vienna, 1553). Glass painter, etcher, cartographer and mathematician, son of (1) Veit Hirschvogel the elder. He trained as a stained-glass painter in his father's workshop and remained there until his father's death in 1525. In that year Nuremberg accepted the Reformation, spelling the end of monumental stained-glass commissions. This must have profoundly reduced the production of the workshop, now run by his elder brother Veit, and may have forced Augustin to become more versatile. By 1530 he had established his own workshop but in 1531 formed a partnership with the Nuremberg potters Hanns Nickel (*fl c.* 1530) and Oswald Reinhart (*fl c.* 1530), presumably to share their kiln. This partnership, coupled with Johann Neudörfer's confusing comments about Hirschvogel in his *Nachrichten* (1547), formerly led to speculation about his having made a ceramic stove and pots in a classicizing Italianate style. It is more likely that the vessels made by Augustin and described in documents as in a Venetian style were glass, not earthenware.

Over 60 pen-and-ink drawings and several stained-glass panels by Hirschvogel survive from his early Nuremberg period (until 1536). The 53 hunting scenes in the Museum of Fine Arts, Budapest, for an extensive series of stained-glass roundels, demonstrate that he was an able and independent draughtsman, well-schooled in Dürer's drawing style. His drawings most closely resemble those of his contemporaries, the Nuremberg Little Masters such as Sebald Beham and Georg Pencz. Several stained-glass panels, including two roundels from the hunt series and a group of three rectangular panels of angels holding coats of arms from the parsonage of the Sebalduskirche (1520s), show Augustin's modification of his father's linear style of glass painting to achieve more tonal, painterly effects. No evidence remains of his documented simultaneous activity of carving armorials.

In 1536 Augustin left Nuremberg for Ljubljana (Laibach) and did not return until 1543. The original purpose for his journey is unknown. His maps of Turkish borders (1539) and of Austria (1542, for Ferdinand I), however, document his earliest known activities as cartographer. He also made etchings during this period, to which he referred in his preface to *Geometria* (pubd Nuremberg, 1543), a book containing 37 etchings of geometric and perspectival constructions. Commissions for armorials for Franz Igelshofer and Christoph Khevenhüller (1503–57) indicate that by 1543 he had already established contacts with members of the imperial court in Vienna.

In 1544 Hirschvogel moved to Vienna, where he was engaged as a cartographer, mathematician, etcher and stained-glass painter by an expanded patronage of the city, court and private citizens. The motto 'Spero fortunae regressum' (I hope for a return of fortune), found on two self-portrait etchings from 1548, suggests hard times and his aspirations for greater success in the imperial capital. In 1547 the city employed him to make a design for new bastions as well as two etched views and a plan of Vienna (Vienna, Hist. Mus.). His views of Vienna were the first ever done according to scale, and the circular plan was the first ever made by triangulation, a trigonometric system of surveying which Hirschvogel himself developed. The city council sent him to King Ferdinand I in Prague and to Charles V in Augsburg to explain the fortification plans and his triangulation system. For this achievement, the King granted him an annual pension of 100 gulden.

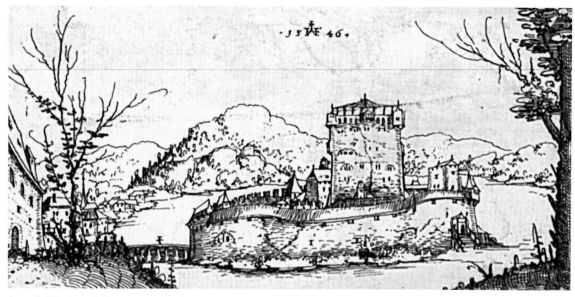

Augustin Hirschvogel: *Fortress on an Island*, etching, 78×154 mm, 1546 (Vienna, Graphische Sammlung Albertina)

During this last decade of his life in Vienna, Hirschvogel produced most of his 300 etchings. He was one of the first etchers to make regular use of copper (rather than iron) plates and to experiment with multiple bites. He provided 23 etchings for the 1549 edition of the *Rerum Moscoviticarum commentarii* by Sigmund Freiherr von Herberstein (1486–1566). He completed at least 113 Old and New Testament scenes, containing awkward, mannered figures, to illustrate the verses that the Hungarian reformer Peter Perényi (1502–48) composed for the *Konkordanz*, published only in 1550 in incomplete form. His other single sheets include 17 fanciful designs for vessels, 19 ornamental designs, 6 geometrical and column constructions, 23 coats of arms, 17 portraits, 4 self-portraits, 12 religious, mythological and historical subjects, 6 genre and animal subjects and 35 landscapes. These reveal that Hirschvogel had a much greater natural aptitude for ornament than for figural design; many of his figure studies and compositions seem derivative in character, reflecting the influence of Dürer, Sebald Beham, Hans Burgkmair, Agostino del Musi and the school of Raphael.

Hirschvogel's reputation as a major creative graphic artist lies with his 35 landscape etchings (1545–9) in the manner of the Danube school. His interest in landscape, already evident in his earlier hunt drawings, may have been further stimulated by his map-making work and travels along the Danube. These later pure landscapes, often in a narrow horizontal format as for example *Fortress on an Island* (see fig.), reflect the influence of Albrecht Altdorfer and Wolfgang Huber. The absence of strong shadows or atmospheric effects endows his delicate, idyllic little scenes with a sunlit transparency and tranquil mood. His achievement lies in creating a picturesque scene where calligraphic effects take precedence over a rendering true to nature. Hirschvogel took advantage of the freedom allowed by the etching needle to create wiry lines, knots and curlicues,

a style encouraged by his analogous activity of etching lines through the paint layers of his stained glass.

BIBLIOGRAPHY

K. Schwarz: *Augustin Hirschvogel*, 2 vols (Berlin, 1917, 2/1971) [standard monograph, with cat. rais. of graphic work]
E. Baumeister: 'Zeichnungen Augustin Hirschvogels aus seiner Frühzeit', *Münchn. Jb. Bild. Kst.*, n. s., xiii (1938–9), pp. 203–11
Prints and Drawings of the Danube School (exh. cat., ed. C. Talbot and A. Shestack; New Haven, CT, Yale U. A.G., 1969), pp. 88–93
M. Forster: *Die Landschaftsradierungen des Augustin Hirschvogel* (diss., U. Vienna, 1973)
J. S. Peters: 'Early Drawings by Augustin Hirschvogel', *Master Drgs*, xvii (1979), pp. 359–92 [with cat. of early drgs]
——: 'Frühe Glasgemälde von Augustin Hirschvogel', *Anz. Ger. Nmus.* (1980), pp. 79–89
——: *German Masters, 1550–1600*, 18 [IX/i] of *The Illustrated Bartsch*, ed. W. L. Strauss (New York, 1982), pp. 95–363

JANE S. PETERS

Hirshfield, Morris (*b* Russian Poland, 10 April 1872; *d* New York, 26 July 1946). American painter of Russian–Polish origin. He claimed to have carved wooden ceremonial objects as a young boy, but ceased to create until he retired from his clothing manufacturing concern and began to paint. When Sidney Janis was arranging an exhibition of American folk art for MOMA in 1939, he saw Hirshfield's naive works in a gallery in New York. He exhibited two in the show and organized a one-man show for the artist in 1943; he also purchased two works, including *Beach Girl* (1937; New York, MOMA). In such paintings Hirshfield based large areas of the overall design on the fabrics with which he worked during his years in business, and his outlined forms on the art of patternmaking. In this and slightly later works, such as *Inseparable Friends* (1941; New York, MOMA), an ambiguous treatment of young female sexuality is played off against the patterns and the repetition of forms.

Hirshfield also made reference to his Jewish origins, incorporating the blue and white of the Zionist flag, patterns of six-pointed stars and stylized candleholders.

He painted by leaning his canvases against a chest of drawers in his bedroom, or flat on his bed, and avoided live models, saying to Sidney Janis: 'If I paint a tiger, can I have a tiger pose for me? And I couldn't very well bring a nude woman in and paint her. It wouldn't look right.'

BIBLIOGRAPHY

S. Janis: *They Taught Themselves: American Primitive Painters of the 20th Century* (New York, 1942), pp. 14–39
——: 'The Paintings of Morris Hirshfield', *Bull. MOMA, NY*, xi (1943)
W. Saroyan: *Morris Hirshfield* (Parma, 1975)

DAVID M. SOKOL

Hirshhorn, Joseph H(erman) (*b* Mitvau, Latvia, 11 Aug 1899; *d* Washington, DC, 31 Aug 1981). American financier, collector and museum founder of Latvian birth. One of 13 children supported by a widowed mother, he left school at the age of 12 to work in Wall Street, New York, and was a millionaire in stocks-and-bonds by the age of 25, withdrawing from the market just before the stock market collapse in 1929. Despite the risks, he invested in and successfully operated gold and then uranium mines in Canada during the 1930s, 1940s and early 1950s, by which time he was not only vastly wealthy but also avidly committed as an art collector. He bought voraciously on trips abroad as well as in the USA. By the mid-1960s his large Connecticut house and garden, his New York offices and warehouse space overflowed with his collection.

Although guided in later years by a personal curator, Abram Lerner (also founding director of the Hirshhorn Museum), and fuelled by the enthusiasm of his fourth wife, Olga Zatorsky Cunningham, Hirshhorn's collecting instinct was decidedly his own. Born out of a fascination as a child with wall-calendar art reproductions, it grew from an attraction to 19th-century Salon painting and Impressionism (which constituted one of his first collections, auctioned in the 1940s) to a consuming passion in three areas: new works by living artists, including Francis Bacon, Balthus, Arshile Gorky, Willem de Kooning, Jean Dubuffet, Edward Hopper and Mark Rothko; late 19th- and early 20th-century American painting, in which he helped to spark a revival of interest, particularly in the work of Thomas Eakins, the Ashcan school and such early modernists as Marsden Hartley; and modern sculpture, where his purchases excelled, most notably much of Henri Matisse's important work in the medium, a broad selection of work by Henry Moore, Alberto Giacometti and David Smith, and a cast of Rodin's *Burghers of Calais* (1886).

Although Hirshhorn was courted widely, it was the Smithsonian Institution, seeking to fill a long-unrealized governmental mandate for a national museum of modern art, that won his collection in 1966. In 1974 the Hirshhorn Museum and Sculpture Garden, situated on the National Mall, Washington, DC, opened its collection of 6000 pieces to the public. Hirshhorn continued, however, to collect and eventually bequeathed another 5500 works to the museum, stipulating that curators and trustees could dispose of, recraft and add to his legacy in any way they saw fit.

BIBLIOGRAPHY

E. Hughes: 'Joe Hirshhorn, the Brooklyn Uranium King', *Fortune Mag.*, lv (Nov 1956), pp. 154–8, 160, 164, 166, 171–2
A. Saarinen: 'Little Man in a Big Hurry', *The Proud Possessors* (New York, 1958), pp. 269–86
Modern Sculpture from the Joseph H. Hirshhorn Collection (exh. cat., New York, Guggenheim, 1962)
J. Jacobs: 'Collector: Joseph H. Hirshhorn', *A. America.*, lvii/4 (1969), pp. 56–71
A. Lerner, ed.: *The Hirshhorn Museum and Sculpture Garden* (New York, 1974)
H. Rosenberg: 'The Art World: The Hirshhorn', *New Yorker*, l/37 (4 Nov 1974), pp. 156–61
B. Hyams: *Hirshhorn: Medici from Brooklyn* (New York, 1979)
J. A. Lewis: ' "Every Day is Sunday" for Joe Hirshhorn', *ARTnews*, lxxviii/6 (1979), pp. 56–61
J. Russell: 'Joseph Hirshhorn Dies: Financier, Art Patron', *New York Times* (2 Sept 1981), section A, p. 17
K. Taylor: 'Three Men and their Museums: Solomon Guggenheim, Joseph Hirshhorn, Roy Neuberger and the Art they Collected', *Museum* [New York], ii/6 (1982), pp. 80–86
J. Demetrion: *An Introduction to the Hirshhorn Museum and Sculpture Garden* (Washington, DC, 1987)
J. Zilczer: 'Artist and Patron: An Exchange of Letters', *Willem de Kooning in the Hirshhorn Museum Collection* (exh. cat., Washington, DC, Hirshhorn, 1993)

SIDNEY S. LAWRENCE

Hirt, Aloys (*b* Bella, nr Donaueschingen, 27 June 1759; *d* Berlin, 29 June 1836). German art historian, writer and teacher. Born into a peasant family living close to the Swiss border, he was educated by the Benedictine monks of Donaueschingen. After attending the Gymnasium there, he went to Nancy in France to study philosophy, where he was impressed by the writings of Jean-Jacques Rousseau and Voltaire (1694–1778). After a short period reading law at Freiburg University, Hirt studied in Vienna (1779–82) and then went to Italy, where he stayed for 14 years. He travelled extensively to Venice, Florence, Rome, Naples, and in Sicily. Influenced by Johann Joachim Winckelmann's theories on aesthetics, Hirt began to concentrate on studying art theory and history. He was particularly interested in the techniques, rather than just the aesthetics, of Classical architecture, and he supported and elaborated Winckelmann's theory that Greek masonry architecture was derived from wooden construction. While in Rome, Hirt mixed with many German travellers and expatriates, including Goethe, and he caused much controversy with his views.

When Hirt returned to Germany in 1796 he became a member of the Akademie der Wissenschaft und Künste, Berlin, where one of his most famous pupils was Karl Friedrich Schinkel. In 1809 *Die Baukunst nach den Grundsätzen der Alten*, a work that made him the dominant theorist of Franco–Prussian Neo-classicism in the first half of the 19th century, was published. In 1810 the university of Berlin was founded and Hirt became its professor for art history. His theories on Classical architecture influenced a generation of German architects from Schinkel to Heinrich Gentz and Friedrich Weinbrenner. Weinbrenner, who had prepared the plates for Hirt's book, spread his ideas through his own architecture school in Karlsruhe. Hirt's position was vigorously challenged in the 1820s by Weinbrenner's pupil Heinrich Hübsch, in particular in his book *In welchem Style sollen wir bauen?* (1828), from which the *Rundbogenstil* developed.

Hirt was equally influential in the field of art education. The foundation of the first public museum in Berlin, the Altes Museum, built by Schinkel in 1823–30, was largely due to his efforts. He outlined as early as 1797 his proposals for the building of a public museum, complete with detailed suggestions on siting, architectural requirements and the internal arrangements and hanging of the collection. He promoted the arrangement of works of art according to schools, and he was convinced that the foremost role of art was didactic. When the scheme for the museum was finally realized after the Napoleonic Wars, Hirt participated in the commission charged with selecting the collection. In 1828 Gustav Waagen, the future director of the painting gallery, published a pamphlet that placed enjoyment ahead of learning as the proper role of the museum, a view incompatible with the views of Hirt, who resigned from the commission in 1829.

WRITINGS
Osservazioni istorico-architettoniche sopra il Panteon (Rome, 1791)
Die Baukunst nach den Grundsätzen der Alten (Berlin, 1809)
Über die Bildung der aegyptischen Gottheiten (Berlin, 1820)
Die Geschichte der Baukunst bei den Alten (Berlin, 1821–7)
Kunstbemerkungen auf einer Reise über Wittenberg und Meissen nach Dresden und Prag (Berlin, 1830)
Herr Dr Waagen und Herr V. Rumohr als Kunstkenner dargestellt von A. Hirt. In Antwort auf die Schrift des Herrn Dr Waagen gegen Hirt (Berlin, 1832)
Die Geschichte der bildenden Künste bei den Alten (Berlin, 1833)

BIBLIOGRAPHY
NDB; Thieme–Becker
H. Hübsch: *Über griechische Architektur: Zweite mit einer Vertheidigung gegen A. Hirt vermehrte Ausgabe* (Heidelberg, 1824)
——: *In welchem Style sollen wir bauen?* (Karlsruhe, 1828/*R* 1984) [postscript by W. Schirmer]
F. Denk: 'A. Hirt', *Neue Jb.*, iv (1928), pp. 672–7
R. Petras: *Die Bauten der Berliner Museumsinsel* (Berlin, 1987)
D. Watkin and T. Mellinghoff: *German Architecture and the Classical Ideal 1740–1840* (London, 1987)

Hirth, Georg (*b* Gräfentonna, Thuringia, 13 July 1841; *d* Tegernsee, Bavaria, 28 March 1916). German writer, publisher and editor. In 1875 he co-founded the publishing company Knorr & Hirth based in Munich. *Werke unserer Väter*, an exhibition of German Renaissance arts and crafts held in Munich in 1876, stimulated his interest in art, and in that year he began to edit and publish a series of handsomely produced art books and prints in affordable editions. In 1881 he took over the printing of the *Münchner neuesten Nachrichten*, developing it into one of Germany's leading daily newspapers. He himself wrote on a wide range of issues. In *Ideen über Zeichenunterricht und künstlerische Berufsbildung* (1887), for example, he advocated a democratizing reform of the teaching of art; in *Das plastische Sehen als Rindenzwang* (1892) he took issue with the optical theories of Hermann von Helmholtz by propagating the idea that the optical function was physiologically inborn. Although he initially favoured German Gothic and early Renaissance art, by the 1890s he had become interested in contemporary art. In 1892 he was active in the founding of the Munich Secession (*see* SECESSION, §1) and was supposed to have given the group its name. In 1895 he founded the weekly illustrated art journal *Jugend*, the first issue of which appeared on 1 January 1896. The journal's stated aim was 'to give liberal support to the young striving literary and artistic forces' and it became one of the major mouthpieces for Symbolist and Art Nouveau ideas of the *fin-de-siècle*. *Jugendstil*, the German branch of Art Nouveau, derived its name from the magazine.

WRITINGS
ed.: *Das deutsche Zimmer der Gotik und Renaissance, des Barock-, Rococo- und Zopfstils* (3/1885, 4/1899), i of *Das deutsche Zimmer vom Mittelalter bis zur Gegenwart*, 2 vols, ed. G. Hirth (Munich and Leipzig, 1899)
Ideen über Zeichenunterricht und künstlerische Berufsbildung (Munich and Leipzig, 1887, 3/*c.* 1892)
Das plastische Sehen als Rindenzwang (Munich and Leipzig, 1892)
ed.: *Der Stil in den bildenden Künsten aller Zeiten*, 3 vols (Munich and Leipzig, 1898–1902, 2/1912–22)

BIBLIOGRAPHY
NDB
E. Müller and A. Aschenbrenner, eds: *Georg Hirth zur Erinnerung gewidmet* (Munich, 1917)
F. C. Endres: *Georg Hirth, ein deutscher Publizist* (Munich, 1921)

Hirtz [Hirtze], **Hans** (*b* ?Strasbourg, *c.* 1400; *d* before 4 Aug 1463). German painter. Judging by the evaluation of later critics, he must have been one of the most highly regarded artists of his time. In his outline of German history, the *Epithoma rerum Germanorum* (1505), Jakob Wimpfeling wrote that 'extremely famous and exquisite pictures in Strasbourg, his birthplace' bore witness to Hirtz's skill. In his German interpretation of the Gospels (*Evangelia mit usslegung*, 1517), the popular preacher Johann Geiler of Kaysersberg refers to Hirtz, whose 'delightful panels' stand on the altars and can be immediately recognized by anyone. Hirtz's work was supposed to be in a coarse, vernacular style that would have corresponded to Geiler's preferences. Because of these references, the MASTER OF THE KARLSRUHE PASSION (*see* MASTERS, ANONYMOUS, AND MONOGRAMMISTS, §1), who worked in the Upper Rhine area, has sometimes been identified with Hirtz, but there is as yet no certain proof to connect Hirtz's name with any extant painting.

In 1421 'Hirtze, der moler' (Hirtze, the painter) acquired a house in the Lange Strasse in Strasbourg. In 1438 he was one of the accused in a trial between the goldsmiths and some painters who wanted to be members of both guilds, clearly because of the greater earnings to be made from free trade. In 1451 he restored a *Crucifixion* in the cathedral (the only documentary evidence of his work as a painter). In 1453 the church of St Thomas was determined as his place of burial, and in 1455 he made a will in favour of the civic hospital, among other beneficiaries. He may have died as a hostage of Captain Alwig von Sulz, who took five wealthy citizens of Strasbourg captive during a conflict with Count Palatine Friedrich I.

BIBLIOGRAPHY
H. Rott: *Der Oberrhein, Quellen I* (1936), iii *Text* (1938) of *Quellen und Forschungen zur südwestdeutschen und schweizerischen Kunstgeschichte im XV. und XVI. Jahrhundert* (Stuttgart, 1933–38)
L. Fischel: *Die Karlsruher Passion und ihr Meister* (Karlsruhe, 1952), pp. 16–19
F. Blasius: *Bildprogramm und Realität: Untersuchungen zur oberrheinischen Malerei um die Mitte des 15. Jahrhunderts am Beispiel der 'Karlsruher Passion'* (Frankfurt am Main and New York, 1986), pp. 100–05

DETLEF ZINKE

Hisarlık. *See* TROY.

His de la Salle, (Aimé-Charles-)Horace (*b* Paris, 11 Feb 1795; *d* Neuilly-sur-Seine, 28 April 1878). French collector. He was the son of the writer Charles-Antoine-Hyacinthe His, and grew up in the sophisticated Parisian society of his mother, Hélène de Nervo, a talented musician. He attended military school and in 1815 served Louis XVIII at Ghent. He left the military in 1826 to accompany his ailing mother to Italy, where she died. His de la Salle began collecting prints and lithographs, especially military subjects by Nicolas-Toussaint Charlet and Théodore Gericault, while he was still in the army. His knowledge and taste grew more sophisticated through his travels and informal study in Italy, Germany, Holland and France, and his frequent visits to auction rooms and art dealers in Paris. After his return to Paris, he was closely associated with the collectors Louis Lacaze and Frédéric Reiset, the conservator at the Musée du Louvre. Like them, he emphasized quality over quantity in collecting. The strength of his collection lay in drawings by early Italian masters, including Fra Angelico and Botticelli, and 17th-century Dutch and Flemish masters such as Rembrandt, Rubens and van Dyck. He also owned important German and French works and collected medals and bronzes. In 1851 His de la Salle donated to the Louvre nine drawings by Pierre-Paul Prud'hon, Anne-Louis Girodet, Antoine-Jean Gros and Gericault, followed in 1866 by a set of ten drawings for the *Seven Sacraments* by Nicolas Poussin. Just before his death he gave approximately 300 additional drawings to the Louvre. He also made important donations to the musées des Beaux-Arts in Dijon (1862), Lyon and Alençon, as well as to the Ecole des Beaux-Arts and to the Bibliothèque Nationale in Paris. In addition to two sales in Paris (1856 and 1877) prior to his death, there were five posthumous sales in London and Paris.

DBF

BIBLIOGRAPHY

L. Both de Tauzia: *Notice des dessins de la collection His de la Salle exposés au Louvre* (Paris, 1881)

C. Ephrussi: 'Les Dessins de la collection His de la Salle', *Gaz. B.-A.*, n. s. 2, xxv (1882), pp. 297–309; xxvi (1882), pp. 225–45, 486–96

F. Lugt: *Marques* (1921), p. 238

Dessins de la collection His de la Salle, Dijon, Mus. B.-A. cat. (Dijon, 1974)

AMY WALSH

Hishida, Shunsō (*b* Nagano Prefect., 21 Sept 1874; *d* Tokyo, 16 Sept 1911). Japanese painter. In 1895 he graduated from the painting department of the Tokyo School of Fine Arts, where he then worked as a lecturer. In 1898 he participated in the establishment of the Japan Art Institute, Tokyo, and he received theoretical instruction from Tenshin Okakura. With Taikan Yokoyama he actively continued to experiment in an effort to create a modern form of Japanese-style painting (*Nihonga*; see JAPAN, §VI, 5(iii)). He visited India (1903), where he met Abanindranath Tagore, and travelled in the USA and Europe (1904–5). After his return to Japan, Hishida's painting style became deeply lyrical, while being based on intellectual composition and keen observation. His major works include *Patriarch Xiangxiang* (1907; Tokyo, N. Mus.) and *Fallen Leaves* (1909; Tokyo, Eisei Bunko).

BIBLIOGRAPHY

Hishida Shunsō: Dai Nihon kaiga [Great Japanese painting] 5 vols (1976)

YOSHIKAZU IWASAKI

Hishikawa Moronobu (*b* Hota, Chiba Prefect., *c.* 1620; *d* 1694). Japanese print designer and painter. He is popularly known as the father of *ukiyo-e* ('pictures of the floating world'; *see* JAPAN, §§VI, 4(iv)(b) and IX, 2(iii)(a)), a position he shares with IWASA MATABEI, whose genre paintings predate Moronobu's. He was the son of Hishikawa Kichizaemon (*d* 1662), an embroiderer and textile designer from Hota. Moronobu initially followed his father's trade, but moved to Edo (now Tokyo) upon Kichizaemon's death. He studied the painting style of the KANŌ and TOSA schools, but soon turned to depictions—often sexually explicit—of the *demi-monde* of the Edo *kabuki* and Yoshiwara pleasure quarter. In the 1660s Moronobu first attracted attention because of the quality of his paintings and drawings. Looking for greater freedom as a draughtsman, Moronobu turned to illustrating picture books (*ehon*). By 1673 his success with book illustrations led him to seek and obtain a wider circulation and public by designing single-sheet prints (*ichimaie*), which included *yakushae* ('pictures of actors') and *bijinga* ('pictures of beautiful women').

Moronobu, who did not produce *ukiyo-e* paintings before 1662, must have known about the work of Iwasa Matabei, who had died in 1650, yet he claimed to be the originator of *ukiyo-e*. According to Ficke, Matabei and Moronobu were both founders of *ukiyo-e*, but with the qualification that Matabei's activities were confined to painting, while Moronobu extended to picture books and single-sheet prints. He describes Moronobu as the first of the great print designers. His production of print designs was primarily in black and white (*sumizurie*), although copies of his prints were hand-coloured by other artists. Yellow and green were common, but vermilion prints (*tan'e*) were particularly popular. Because Moronobu signed few, if any, of his prints, many late 17th-century black-and-white prints are attributed to him.

Moronobu took several students, including members of his family, and a school was formed that bore his family name, Hishikawa. His most successful pupil was Sugimura Jihei (*fl c.* 1681–1703), who specialized in book illustration and *shunga* ('spring pictures'; erotic prints). Another outstanding student was Furuyama Moroshige (*fl* 1678–98), who produced high-quality *bijinga* and was allowed to sign his work with his master's name. Moronobu's eldest son and pupil Hishikawa Morofusa (*fl* 1685–1703) gave up printmaking and returned to the family's traditional textile business. This contributed to the decline of the Hishikawa school, which also suffered from competition with other emerging *ukiyo-e* studios, such as the TORII. Torii Kiyonobu I, the founder of the Torii school in Edo, had been a pupil of Moronobu, under whom he studied book illustration and single-sheet printmaking.

BIBLIOGRAPHY

L. Binyon: *Painting in the Far East* (London, 1908), pp. 228–31

A. D. Ficke: *Chats on Japanese Prints* (London and New York, 1915/*R* 1966), pp. 69–79

M. Narazaki: *The Japanese Print: Its Evolution and Essence* (Tokyo and Palo Alto, 1966)

The Floating World: Japanese Popular Prints, 1700–1900 (exh. cat. by R. A. Crighton, London, V&A, 1973)

R. Neuer and H. Libertson: *Ukiyo: 250 Years of Japanese Art* (Milan, 1978), pp. 55–61

A. Newland and C. Uhlenbeck, eds: *Ukiyo-e to Shin Hanga* (Leicester, 1990)

JAMES GLENDINNING

Hisht-Tepe. Site of a small Buddhist temple complex in southern Tajikistan that flourished from the late 7th century AD to the 8th. It is situated in the Obimazar Valley, 12 km from Khovaling (anc. Khuttal', in the region of Tokharistan). The site was excavated by Mullokandov between 1985 and 1988. The complex (c. 30×30 m) is built of clay and mud-brick and had a domed hall (room 1, 7×7 m) and a temple sanctuary (room 12) in the centre, surrounded by corridors (rooms 7–10), another sanctuary (room 20) containing a small clay stupa (3.2×3.1 m) and residential and storage rooms. In the main sanctuary (room 12) was a pedestal with a niche in the centre, flanked by columns of the *kuzagi* type (i.e. with a bulbous lower section). The pedestal was originally covered by an awning supported on poles. The remains of wall paintings with vegetal and geometric designs and some traces of gold leaf have been found in the corridors. The only figural painting to survive is a fragmentary scene depicting a procession of birds, possibly from a later period. The stupa in room 20 is cruciform but is much more poorly preserved than analogous stupas at Adzhina Tepe. At Hisht-Tepe over sixty miniature model stupas of two types were found, which precisely convey many details of the architectural decoration of such structures. Clay tablets of three types with a ritual text proclaiming the Buddhist teachings (*dharma-paryaya*) written in the Brahmi script were found inside more than thirty model stupas. The finds are housed in the Tajikistan Academy of Sciences, Donish Institute of History, Archaeology and Ethnography in Dushanbe

BIBLIOGRAPHY

M. Mullokandov: 'Rannesrednevekovyy buddiyskiy monastyr' Khisht-tepa v Khovalingskom rayone Tadzhikistana' [The early medieval Buddhist monastery of Hisht-Tepe in the Khovaling region of Tajikistan], *Inf. Byull. Mezhdun. Assot. Izucheniyu Kul't. Tsent. Azii*, xvii (1990), pp. 21–5

V. Vertogradova: 'Glinyanyye tabletki s indiyskimi tekstami iz Khisht-tepa' [Clay tablets with Indian texts from Hisht-Tepe], *Inf. Byull. Mezhdun. Assot. Izucheniyu Kul't. Tsent. Azii*, xvii (1990), pp. 12–18

YE. V. ZEYMAL'

Hispaniola. Caribbean island lying between Puerto Rico and Cuba. Christopher Columbus arrived on the island in 1492 and named it the Isla Española. It is divided into two countries: HAITI in the west and the DOMINICAN REPUBLIC in the east.

Hispano-American artists. *See* LATIN AMERICAN ARTISTS OF THE USA.

Hispano-Flemish style. Style of Spanish architecture and decoration associated with the reign of Isabella I of Castile (1474–1504), when Netherlandish forms were introduced to Castile and fused with those of the *Mudéjar* style, which had dominated Castilian art in the first half of the 15th century. Although it has also been called the Isabelline style, a term coined by Emile Bertaux, the name Hispano-Flemish is now more generally used because this refers to the style's origins and is less likely to be confused with the so-called Isabelline style, referred to in Spanish historiography, which corresponds to the reign of Isabella II (1833–68).

The Hispano-Flemish style is particularly associated with two great creative centres: Toledo, the more important, and Burgos. To these, in its final stages, should be added Palencia and Valladolid, where began the transition towards Renaissance forms, influenced from Italy. Apart from Isabella herself, patron of the most important buildings of the period, three great patrons were responsible for introducing the style: Don Alvaro de Luna, Master of Santiago, in Toledo; Archbishop Alonso de Cartagena in Burgos; and the Dominican Bishop of Palencia, Fray Alonso de Burgos.

The style began in Toledo around the middle of the 15th century during the reign of John II of Castile, when *Mudéjar* had reached the height of its decorative and formal development. This was a time of strong Netherlandish influence in many aspects of life. The work of Hanequin de Bruselas, who arrived in Toledo *c.* 1440, was fundamental because, although his art contains no trace of Islamic influence, Netherlandish richness of decoration coincided to some degree with the Islamic aesthetic as practised by Castilian *Mudéjar* artists in the final phase of the style. The Hispano-Flemish style was actually created by Hanequin's disciple, Juan Guas, Queen Isabella's official architect, and was crystallized in his most representative works, the monastery of S Juan de los Reyes in Toledo (begun 1476; *see* TOLEDO, fig. 3) and the Palacio del Infantado, Guadalajara (begun 1480; for illustrations *see* GUADALAJARA, PALACIO DEL INFANTADO, and GUAS, JUAN). Guas's influence appears in many Castilian buildings and, at the very end of the 15th century, was to be taken on by the brothers Antón Egas and Enrique Egas, who continued to work in the style during the first decades of the 16th century.

In Burgos the style began with the arrival of Juan de Colonia, who was probably brought to the city by Archbishop Alonso de Cartagena *c.* 1440, but it was Juan's son, Simón de Colonia, who was responsible for the most characteristic Hispano-Flemish buildings, such as the Capilla del Condestable (begun 1482) in Burgos Cathedral and the lantern of the Cathedral. Here, and in his many other works, his style was distinctively different from the Toledan school, influenced by his German origins and the different character of the *Mudéjar* style in Old Castile.

The Hispano-Flemish style also developed in Valladolid and Palencia, again in a slightly different way. The traditions of both Toledo and Burgos were blended in work at Palencia Cathedral, the Colegio de S Gregorio in Valladolid, begun in 1487 by Juan Guas, and the nearby monastery of S Pablo (by Simón de Colonia; see fig.), buildings promoted by the same patron, Fray Alonso de Burgos; and the interpretation of the style by a new generation of artists from Cantabria, such as Juan Gil de Hontañón (i), the brothers Bartolomé Solórzano (*d* ?1510) and Martín de Solórzano and Juan de Ruesga (*d* 1514), among others, established a link with the new Renaissance forms without breaking with Gothic tradition. This tendency was to be encouraged by the building of the Colegio de Santa Cruz in Valladolid before 1491. The connections of its patron, Cardinal Mendoza, with Isabella's court were intrinsic to the creation of the Plateresque style, the first stage in the development of the Spanish Renaissance, the most representative buildings of which are found in Salamanca.

Owing to the close connections between the two kingdoms, the initial stages of the Hispano-Flemish style

Hispano-Flemish style façade of the monastery of S Pablo, Valladolid, by Simón de Colonia, 1497

were closely connected to the Portuguese Manueline style developed during the reign of Manuel I (1495–1521). The style epitomized Castilian culture during Isabella's reign, combining the two main artistic trends of medieval Castile, neither of which had parallels elsewhere in Europe. Moreover, the characteristics of the style persisted into the Spanish Renaissance, and the transition from medieval to modern art occurred without any sudden stylistic break. The three main factors of early 16th-century Castilian culture—Gothic, Islamic and Italian—became integrated, as, for example, in the staircase of the Colegio de S Gregorio in Valladolid, which has a *Mudéjar* ceiling and both Plateresque and Netherlandish Gothic decoration.

BIBLIOGRAPHY
E. Tormo: 'Las conferencias de M. Bertaux', *A. Esp.*, i/3 (1912–13), pp. 107–28
Marqués de Lozoya: *Historia del arte hispánico* (Barcelona, 1931–49), ii, iii
L. Torres Balbás: *Arquitectura gótica*, A. Hisp., vii (Madrid, 1952)

JOSÉ MARIA AZCÁRATE RISTORI

Hissar, Tepe [Hesar, Tappeh]. Site consisting of several separate mounds 12 ha in area, located 2 km south of DAMGHAN in northern Iran. The extensive excavations in 1931–2 (see Schmidt) concentrated on prehistoric levels but also examined a Sasanian palace. Approximately 1000 prehistoric burials and their grave goods were the primary focus. A re-study project in 1976 (see Dyson jr and Howard) concentrated on clarifying the prehistoric cultural sequence and investigating the ancient economy, including environment, architecture and a wide range of specialist crafts (copper metallurgy, pottery production and working of flint and such hardstones as lapis lazuli). Finds are in the Archaeological Museum, Tehran.

Hissar I (mid-5th millennium BC to mid-4th) is characterized by thin-walled buff pottery painted with geometric plant and animal motifs. Typical vessels include deep bowls and pedestal-based bowls and jars. In Hissar II (mid-4th millennium BC to early 3rd) grey wares ranging from relatively coarse to fine, burnished pottery became dominant. Characteristic vessel forms include tall, pedestal-based bowls, goblets and chalices. Pattern burnishing replaced painted decoration. The making of lapis lazuli beads and the large-scale production of copper smelting were also important. Hissar III (early/mid-3rd millennium BC to early 2nd) continued the grey ware ceramic tradition, with characteristic pear-shaped bottles, spouted jars and canteens. A wide range of alabaster artefacts (discs with handles, common pottery forms and pedestals) occurs in late Hissar III. Architectural details and artefacts such as compartmented bronze seals, beads and alabaster discs provide cultural links with Altyn Tepe in Central Asia.

BIBLIOGRAPHY
E. F. Schmidt: 'Tepe Hissar Excavations 1931', *Mus. J.*, xxiii/4 (1933) [whole issue]
——: *Excavations at Tepe Hissar, Damghan* (Philadelphia, 1937)
R. H. Dyson jr and S. M. Howard, eds: *Tappeh Hesar: Reports of the Restudy Program, 1976* (Florence, 1989)

ROBERT C. HENRICKSON

Hissar Fortress. Site in Tajikistan, 25 km west of Dushanbe above the confluence of the Khanaka River and the Kafirnigan River. The pisé walls of the fortress, arched gateways and flanking towers of fired brick, two madrasas and the nearby mosque date from the 16th–19th century, when the fortress was the residence of the Hissar bek. Excavations (1980–82) by Ye. V. Zeymal' revealed that the fortress was erected on an artificial hill comprising occupation layers dating at least from the 3rd–2nd century BC onwards. The large Tup-khona burial ground containing Yueh-chih and Kushana burials (1st century BC–3rd century AD) was clearly associated with the inhabitants of the Hissar site. Another burial ground near Hissar appears to be earlier than the 7th century AD in date. The tentative identification of the Hissar Fortress with the town of Shuman, mentioned in written sources of the 10th–12th century, has not yet been substantiated by reliable evidence. The site is now a historical and archaeological museum reserve, and the finds are housed in the Tajikistan Academy of Sciences, Donish Institute of History, Archaeology and Ethnography in Dushanbe.

BIBLIOGRAPHY
M. M. D'yakonov: 'Raboty Kafirniganskogo otryada' [The works of the Kafirnigan detachment], *Trudy Sogdiysko-Tadzhikskoy Arkheol. Eksped.* [Papers of the Sogdian-Tajik Archaeological Expedition], i (1946–7), *Mat. & Issledovaniya Arkheol., SSSR*, xv (Moscow, 1950), pp. 151–3, 182
Ye. V. Zeymal': 'Arkheologicheskiye raboty v Gissarskoy doline v 1980 g.' [Archaeological work in the Hissar Valley in 1980], *Arkheol. Raboty Tadzhikistane*, xx (1980), pp. 148–56

YE. V. ZEYMAL'

Historia. *See* ISTORIA.

Historia scholastica. *See* BIBLE, §I, 3(iii).

Historiated initial. *See under* INITIAL, MANUSCRIPT.

Historicism. Term used to describe a tendency in the work of some artists and architects to see their work as part of a general process of cultural development capable of historical analysis. The term was first used in this sense by the German art historian Hermann Beenken to describe German Romantic architecture and in particular to distinguish the Romantic approach to the past from the eclecticism and revivalist movements that dominated Western architecture in the later 19th century. The term has also been used more loosely, however, to characterize the general interest in historical context evident in much 19th-century art and architecture, including eclectic and revivalist movements.

There were many reasons for this interest. By the second quarter of the 19th century many artists were questioning the almost tyrannical reign of Neo-classicism, with its implicit timelessness. Moreover, artists, and particularly architects, were increasingly equipped with a broad knowledge of examples from different periods and different cultures and with new technological possibilities. They were also in some cases faced with the requirement to design new building types (such as administrative buildings or factories) for which no obvious stylistic model existed, or to build on a new scale (for example in housing developments). However, while some architects in the first half of the 19th century, such as Léon Vaudoyer (*see* VAUDOYER, (2)), were motivated by historical creeds implicit in their political beliefs and sought to emphasize the inexorable logic of progress, in other cases (e.g. in Germany, Austria, Hungary and Finland in the second half of the century) many architects were more simply seeking to redefine their country's artistic identity, often after periods of imperial rule. This artistic ambition was particularly evident in major building schemes, such as museums and government and legislative buildings in capital cities, for example Imre Steindl's Parliament Building in Pest (1884–1904; *see* HUNGARY, fig. 4). While this artistic purpose obviously involved a reappraisal of their artistic heritage, it also led some architects and designers either simply to espouse in an unmodified form artistic styles associated with a previous era (often a period of national greatness, as with the Celtic Revival in Ireland) or to adopt and combine individual elements from one or more previous architectural styles. The simple reiteration of earlier styles (e.g Gothic Revival, Byzantine Revival, Renaissance Revival or Baroque Revival) subsequently became known as revivalism, while the stylistically more heterogeneous approach became known as ECLECTICISM. While there are many individual buildings that can be said to incorporate diverse styles in this eclectic manner, the Ringstrasse in Vienna constitutes an unusual example of what might be called eclectic urban planning, with edifices built and decorated in different revival styles being deliberately placed side by side in order to emphasize the historical dimension (*see* VIENNA, §II, 3).

Among many European painters and sculptors, too, the choice of style, technique and subject-matter in the 19th century also reflected a concern for historical and nationalist identity. For example, at the beginning of the century the Austrian artists Friedrich Overbeck, Franz Pforr and other members of the NAZARENES sought to emulate the working conditions, style and fresco technique of the medieval period, while in mid-19th-century England such artists as William Dyce and the members of the Pre-Raphaelite Brotherhood sought to match the purity, piety and naturalism of 15th-century Netherlandish art (*see* PRE-RAPHAELITISM). Such paintings as Dante Gabriel Rossetti's *Girlhood of Mary Virgin* (1849; London, Tate) recall the detail and hidden symbolism used by Robert Campin and Jan van Eyck. Sometimes historical subject-matter was used as a way of addressing contemporary issues. In Hungary, for example, Gyula Benczúr's *Capture of Prince Ferenc II Rákóczi* (1869; Budapest, N. Mus.) recalled an episode in an 18th-century Hungarian rebellion against the Habsburgs in order to express discontent about the union of Austria and Hungary under the Dual Monarchy (1867). Elsewhere in Europe many other artists took subject-matter derived from their nation's past as a means of emphasizing national identity (*see* HISTORY PAINTING, §II), without necessarily returning to earlier styles or techniques. Similar concerns were apparent in the 20th century. In Germany, for example, the group Die Brücke (formed 1905) hoped to achieve a social regeneration through their revival of the German woodcut, an approach echoing that of William Morris in the 1860s.

Since the mid-20th century, historicism has often been taken to refer to these attempts to forge a historical consciousness and to emphasize the relationship between the present and past, whether this be one of continuity or disjuncture. Initially, however, discussions of historicism centred on the question of the artist's, and especially the architect's, stylistic attitude to the past. Beenken, like many of his contemporaries, saw eclecticism and revivalism as in fact deeply unhistorical, since both tendencies undervalued the intrinsic connection between an artistic style and its broader cultural context. In contrast, he sought to confer a renewed respectability on works that referred creatively to the past but that acknowledged the present. In seeking to re-evaluate Romantic architecture in this way, he stimulated a discussion of the way in which the modern architect or artist can articulate his or her understanding of the historical context in which he or she works. This historiographical discussion was confused, however, by a lack of terminological agreement. For example, Beenken's contemporary Nikolaus Pevsner (1943) was critical of a historicist approach to architecture; this was because for Pevsner historicism was 'the meticulous imitation of past styles' rather than a true expression of, or response to, the artist's cultural context as part of a continuum. In speaking thus pejoratively of historicism, Pevsner was in fact equating it with revivalism.

Pevsner's scorn for tradition has been criticized by such critics as David Watkin, but more importantly, perhaps, the differences of interpretation offered by Beenken and Pevsner instigated a terminological confusion that persisted and was propagated to the point where historicism took on three distinct meanings. Following Beenken, the term was used to describe the work of those artists and architects who sought to respond creatively to the present, but it was also used more loosely to describe any use in art of past styles. For this reason the word is now often qualified, with terms such as 'Romantic historicism' being used in contrast to the infelicitously named 'strict historicism' of the revivalists. The third use of the term referred to the appropriation of historical subject-matter, usually to evoke particular associations and in order to serve particular nationalist or other purposes. Although this tendency was at its height in the late 19th century, examples of historicism in this sense can be traced back to the art of Classical Rome.

The issue of historicism took on a particular importance in the late 20th century among architects and their critics. With the revivalism of the 19th century being seen as itself the product of a previous era, architects were forced once again to consider the nature of their relation to the past. Transcending a simple opposition between traditionalists and Modernists, attempts to respond to the historical context can be traced in the works of architects who have embraced widely varying styles. While some architects associated with extremely conservative tendencies in the 1920s and 1930s (such as Marcello Piacentini) have been cited as historicists, the same label has also been applied to much more Utopian architects, such as Bruno Taut. In the mid-20th century in the developing world the influence of the search for national identity can be said to have inspired historicist works by such figures as Luis Barragán, while in Europe in the second half of the century the rational architecture of Aldo Rossi could be seen as a historicist attempt to re-create the ambience of urban typologies. Among Post-modernist architects such as Philip Johnson, the tendency to incorporate historical elements ironically into modern designs can also be seen as a manifestation of the historicist spirit.

See also GRÜNDERZEIT.

BIBLIOGRAPHY

F. Meinecke: *Die Entstehung des Historismus* (Munich, 1936)
N. Pevsner: 'The Romantic Movement, Historicism, and the Beginning of the Modern Movement, 1760–1914', *An Outline of European Architecture* (Harmondsworth, 1943)
H. Beenken: *Schöpferische Bauideen der Romantik* (Mainz, 1952)
D. E. Lee: 'The Meaning of "Historicism"', *Amer. Hist. Rev.*, lix (1954), pp. 568–77
N. Pevsner: 'The Return of Historicism', *Studies in Art, Architecture and Design*, ii (London, 1968)
P. Reill: *The German Enlightenment and the Rise of Historicism* (London, 1975)
Essays on Historicism, supp. *Hist. & Theor.*, xiv/4 (1975)
D. Watkin: *Architecture and Morality* (Oxford, 1977)
P. Paret: *Art as History: Episodes in the Culture and Politics of Nineteenth-century Germany* (Princeton, 1988)
H. Aram Veeser: *The New Historicism* (London, 1989)
R. J. Van Pelt and C. W. Westfall: *Architectural Principles in the Age of Historicism* (New Haven and London, 1991)

History painting. The depiction of several persons engaged in an important or memorable action, usually taken from a written source: a sense that stems from Leon Battista Alberti's use of the word *historia* (Lat.: 'story') in 1435 to describe a narrative picture with many figures. The way in which understandings of this term developed in 15th- and 16th-century Italy is discussed in ISTORIA. As the term was understood in the academic doctrines of the

17th and 18th centuries, the action depicted might equally be one of factual record or of fable. Thus defined, history painting could include religious themes, or depictions of momentous recent events, but the term was most frequently associated with Classical subject-matter. This type of work was seen as the most demanding and exalted type of painting, the form most conducive to public edification. As such it was claimed to be subject to various requirements of decorum (*see* GRAND MANNER)—notably the use of a generalizing uniform of Classical dress, distinguishing it from GENRE painting, the depiction of the particularities of everyday life. These standards, formulated by theorists such as Joshua Reynolds, gave way in the late 18th century as the aims of history painters started to include many aspects of genre. Much of the 19th-century history painting following this convergence deals with 'history' in the modern sense, that is, with the exploration of the past for its own particular qualities. Thus the later history of the form concerns a substantially altered concept.

I. Before *c.* 1760. II. After *c.* 1760.

I. Before c. 1760.

1. Origins. 2. 16th century. 3. 17th century. 4. 1700–*c.* 1760.

1. ORIGINS. The emergence of the concept of history painting was closely related to the new ways that Renaissance artists saw themselves and their role in society. With the Renaissance the artist gradually sought means to free himself from his role as an anonymous craftsman within the medieval guild structure, and to work on an equal footing with free men. Naturally, he sought to invoke the authority of the Ancients in this quest, but seeing that few ancient paintings survived and that few ancient writers discussed the visual arts, it was necessary to relate painting to the activities honoured as the 'seven liberal arts'—in particular Grammar and Rhetoric. In *De pictura* (1435), the foundation of all thinking on the visual arts in the Renaissance, LEON BATTISTA ALBERTI attempted to summon Italian painting up to a standard of narrative relevance, decorum and economy through an extended analogy with the component parts of Classical rhetoric as propounded by Cicero and Quintilian. Thus, while the elements within a painting were to be arranged according to an elaborate grammatical theory of *compositio*, the painting as a whole should represent and interpret human emotions: it should move the viewer by showing 'men painted in the picture [who] outwardly demonstrate their own feelings as clearly as possible' (*De pictura*, 41). Within the painting, 'there should be every abundance and beauty of things', not only human figures, but landscape, still-life and animals, for without 'variety and abundance' no painting would merit praise (*De pictura*, 60). The artist should work out the *historia* thus constituted by means of small sketches, of the whole and of its parts, which should be so thorough that the painter had in his imagination a complete idea of the painting before he executed it. The human figures themselves should be as near life-size as possible, and should be studied individually from the model. The resulting painting should 'reveal itself to be so charming and attractive as to hold the eye of the learned

1. Sandro Botticelli: *Calumny of Apelles*, tempera on panel, 2.03×3.14 m, 1490s (Florence, Galleria degli Uffizi)

and the unlearned spectator for a long while with a certain sense of pleasure and emotion'.

Most of Alberti's illustrations of his theory were drawn from literary descriptions (such as Pliny's in *Natural History*, Book XXIV) of ancient paintings: the only post-Classical painter he mentioned was Giotto (*De pictura*, 42), whose *Navicella* (fragments, Boville Ernica, S Pietro Ispano; Rome, Grotte Vaticane) he praised for showing the 11 disciples with clearly differentiated expressions as Jesus walked on the water. Indeed, it is not clear whether Alberti's theories had much immediate influence on artists. However, around the turn of the 16th century, Mantegna increasingly illustrated texts or worked to the recipe of scholars: Pietro Bembo, for example, may have devised the *Introduction of the Cult of Cybele* (1505–6; London, N.G.); and the patronage of Isabella d'Este, who commissioned paintings of subjects from Greek literature and novel allegories devised for her by scholars, especially Paride Ceresara (1466–1532), resulted in a succession of history paintings. Mantegna even illustrated some of the specific subjects proposed by Alberti, whom he may have met in Mantua in 1463 or 1470; for instance the *Calumny of Apelles* appears in a late drawing (*c.* 1504–6; London, BM). Otherwise, only Botticelli came near to Mantegna in his interpretation of literature and fable (see fig. 1).

2. 16TH CENTURY. The last book in Alberti's *De pictura*, touching on the relationship between painting and other arts, was the first in a long series of learned examinations that developed over the next four centuries, culminating in the sophisticated literary form of the PARAGONE. It was, however, only when Aristotle's *Poetics* and Horace's *Ars poetica* became widely available in the 1490s that the relationship between painting and literature was explored fully. Aristotle had written that 'human nature in action is the proper sphere of both painters and poets' (*Poetics* II.1), further arguing that just as plot was the most essential element in tragedy, so a figure in outline was more pleasing than formless colours, however beautiful (*Poetics* VI.19–21). Horace, on the other hand, had placed his celebrated simile UT PICTURA POESIS (Lat.: 'as is painting so is poetry') in a very specific context, arguing that a sensible critic will look not only at the details of a work of literature or of art but also at the broad impression, which must be seen at a distance to be pleasing (*Ars poetica* 361–5). Renaissance theorists from Leonardo on used these texts to justify the status of painting as a noble art and to propose that painters should depict only superior beings, gods and heroes. In practice, this aim could be achieved by painting a generalized and ideal type of human, rather than a specific one. These principles are demonstrated most clearly in Raphael's more important altarpieces, for example the *Entombment* (completed 1507; Rome, Gal. Borghese) and the *Road to Calvary*, also known as the *Spasimo di Sicilia* (completed 1517; Madrid, Prado); in the frescoes (1509–17) in the *stanze* of the Papal Apartments in the Vatican Palace (*see* RAPHAEL, fig. 4); and in the cartoons (*c.* 1515–16; British Royal Col., on loan to London, V&A; *see* RAPHAEL, fig. 5) for

tapestries. In their ideal types, number and scale of figures, clarity of gesture, ordered composition and decorous colouring, these works provided later artists and writers with models of perfection in history painting.

During the 16th century, the majority of Italian paintings, whether of religious, mythological, literary or historical subject-matter could at some level be classed as history painting. Unfortunately, many of the most celebrated examples of public, secular historical subjects have been destroyed, such as Leonardo's *Battle of Anghiari* (1504–5; fragment and cartoon destr.) and Michelangelo's *Battle of Cascina* (unexecuted; cartoon of 1505 destr.) for the Sala del Maggior Consiglio of the Palazzo della Signoria (now Palazzo Vecchio), Florence, or Titian's *Battle of Spoleto*, also known as the *Battle of Cadore* (1538; destr. 1577) for the Sala del Maggior Consiglio in the Doge's Palace, Venice—although some are known through copies or preparatory drawings. However, a renewed impetus was given to religious subjects by the Council of Trent (1545–63), as it endeavoured to curb the increasingly eccentric fantasies of Mannerist artists.

3. 17TH CENTURY. In a sense, the gradual shift from the religious Middle Ages to secular modernity was reflected in the gradual confinement of history painting to a genre competing with other genres, but it also coincided with the rise of naturalism. This began in Northern Europe, but during the 16th century it began to be felt in Rome. It is ironic that the CARRACCI, the principal proponents in Rome of the academic and of history painting itself, should have contributed so much to the emergence of history painting's principal rivals: still-life, landscape and genre painting. Around 1600 these began to evolve into separate and collectible genres in themselves. Annibale Carracci himself made a number of superbly atmospheric landscapes, while his huge *Butcher's Shop* (*c*. 1583; Oxford, Christ Church Pict. Gal.), arguably a genre scene, has, with its life-size figures and variety of pose and gesture, all the hallmarks of a history painting save the essential reference to a literary text. As the genres diverged, elements from history painting might be retained: in Claude Lorrain's landscapes of the mid-17th century diminutive figures act out stories from mythology or history, but the paintings were never intended to compete with history painting. History painting itself, however, was by no means moribund; in Rome, Paris and elsewhere it still constituted the principal commissions, and the major aesthetic debates still centred around the significance of the genre. In Paris, one of the most important commissions of the first half of the century was a series of 48 large paintings by Rubens depicting scenes from the life of Henry IV (*reg* 1589–1610) and his consort Marie de' Medici, of which only those of the Queen were executed (1622–5; Paris, Louvre; see fig. 2). By including allegorical figures with contemporary (and near-contemporary) ones, Rubens created a type of political history painting that at the same time glorified the protagonists and placed them in a grander, timeless realm. This Baroque glorification contrasts with the more naturalistic approach of Velázquez in his historical scenes for the Salón de Reinos in the Buen Retiro Palace, Madrid. The *Surrender of Breda* (1635; Madrid, Prado; *see* VELÁZQUEZ, DIEGO, fig. 4), for example, depicts an event of

recent history in a relatively straightforward way, all the while maintaining the grand dignity and sweep befitting a royal context.

During the same period in Rome, the celebrated quarrel, which may be apocryphal, between Andrea Sacchi and Pietro da Cortona over the latter's decoration of the ceiling in the Palazzo Barberini illustrates the vitality of the genre. In 1636, Sacchi complained in the public forum of the Accademia di S Luca that in Cortona's vast and complex *Triumph of Divine Providence and the Accomplishment of its Ends through the Pontificate of Urban VIII Barberini* (1632–9; *in situ*; *see* ROME, fig. 61) the impression was created by sheer numbers, and that the painting did not conform to the acceptable definition of history painting, in which each of the few figures should contribute, by gesture, expression and movement, to the main story, thereby maintaining Aristotle's principle of unity. Cortona argued that such a painting should be structured like an epic poem, with a main plot and subsidiary incidents. Although neither side or its followers in the camps of the High Baroque and the classicizers can be said to have won the debate in 1636, the high ground moved to the latter, and to one of Sacchi's closest allies in Rome, Nicolas Poussin; from him it would move to Paris.

In terms of his subsequent influence on the course of French painting, Poussin was the most important painter in the 17th century, but he left little written evidence of his aesthetic views, which must mostly be deduced from his painting. His last letter to Fréart de Chambray (1 March 1665) defines the aim of painting as 'la délectation'

2. Peter Paul Rubens: *Felicity of the Regency*, oil on canvas, 3.94×2.95 m, *c*. 1625 (Paris, Musée du Louvre)

(enjoyment). The subject must be noble, and 'in order to give the painter an opportunity to show his intelligence and his hard work, it must be capable of being represented by ideal human figures'. The increasing severity of Poussin's compositions and their reliance on antique models and exaggerated gestures and expressions were praised by his contemporaries as Poussin sent his paintings from Rome to Paris, and were commended to young French painters as models of the nobility of history painting. It was in Paris that history painting was codified, in the teaching and practice of the Académie Royale de Peinture et de Sculpture, as expounded by Charles Le Brun and André Félibien. Like earlier academies in Italy, the Académie's function was to ensure that painters were no longer treated as craftsmen belonging to the old guilds, but were equal in status to writers and other intellectuals. The Académie established a rigid hierarchy of genres, with history painting at the top, followed by landscape, portraiture and still-life. The great programme of decoration of the château of Versailles marks the high point of history painting in the service of the state and the last manifestation of the GRAND MANNER before its promoters were obliged to sustain it artificially (see VERSAILLES, §1).

The dominance of history painting can be seen even in the 17th-century art of the Netherlands, where—notwithstanding its prevalent image as a 'realistic' art—history painting was in fact held in the highest esteem both in theory and in practice. At the beginning of the century, Karel van Mander I, in his *Schilder-boeck* (1604), argued that artists must strive to excel in 'beelden en Historien', although he magnanimously encouraged lesser artists in lesser genres (see MANDER, (1)). Towards the end of the century, Rembrandt's pupil SAMUEL VAN HOOGSTRATEN expressed much the same opinion in his *Inleyding* (1678). Van Hoogstraten's sophisticated discussion even proposed a hierarchy in figure subjects, topped by 'illustrious histories'—paintings 'depicting the most noble movements and desires of the thoughtful man'. This was followed by religious painting—not simple scenes from the *Life of Christ*, but depictions of enlightening episodes from the Old and New Testaments which reflect the human soul. A similar emphasis is seen in the *Lof der schilder-konst* of Philips Angel, which recommends that artists should burrow in ancient and musty volumes to find unusual histories, thereby reinforcing the Renaissance ideal of the learned painter. Significantly, Angel lavished great praise on Rembrandt's *Wedding of Samson* (1638; Dresden, Gemäldegal. Alte Meister), the only painting he discussed at length (see ANGEL, PHILIPS (ii)). Nor was the history painter without props: van Mander helpfully supplied chapters on the interpretation of Ovid's *Metamorphoses* and on 'How to render figures, what they mean and what they represent'. Indeed, the use of illustrated emblem books, manuals of mythology and prints of pagan gods became so widespread that by 1707 Gérard de Lairesse complained in *Het groot schilder-boek* (Amsterdam) that artists had rather defeated the purpose of being learned since they never read the original texts.

Although most history paintings in 17th-century Holland were of religious subjects, the most celebrated painting in Amsterdam was Ferdinand Bol's *Pyrrhus and Fabritius* (1656; Amsterdam, Sticht. Kon. Pal.; see BOL,

FERDINAND, fig. 1), which served as a lesson to the burgomasters on incorruptibility and virtue. Municipal buildings continued to be decorated with moral exemplars, on such themes as the *Judgement of Cambyses* or the *Wisdom of Solomon*, but these were gradually replaced by group portraits, and although van Hoogstraten appeared to consider Rembrandt's group portrait the '*Night Watch*' (1642; Amsterdam, Rijksmus.; see AMSTERDAM, fig. 4) as fully the equal of a history painting, it could not be said to be a history painting as such. However, the grandest decorative scheme of the century was pure history painting: the Great Hall (now the Oranjezaal) in the Huis ten Bosch, The Hague, was decorated with scenes glorifying the reign of the stadholder Frederick Henry, by Jacob Jordaens I, Pieter de Grebber and Cesar van Everdingen (all *in situ*), to a programme devised by the architect Jacob van Campen and the writer Constantijn Huygens (i) for Frederick's widow Amalia van Solms (for further discussion see ORANGE NASSAU, (4)). Contemporary commentators argued that the history painter was seduced by the more lucrative fields of portraiture and the genre scene. Thus, Vermeer began as history painter (e.g. *Christ in the House of Mary and Martha*, c. 1655; Edinburgh, N.G.) before turning to the interior scenes on which his fame rests. The complaint was to be echoed throughout Europe in the next century, as patrons came to prefer erotic mythologies or reflections of their own surroundings to moralizing histories.

4. 1700–c. 1760s. In France taste moved in the early century towards decoration generally in the 'small manner'—not so much heroic incidents from history as brightly coloured mythologies, suitable for the hôtels built by courtiers as the court moved back from Versailles to Paris in 1715. The exceptions were the two great decorative schemes of Antoine Coypel—the scenes from the *Aeneid* for the Galerie d'Enée in the Palais Royal, Paris (1702–15; Paris, Louvre; Arras, Mus. B.-A.; Montpellier, Mus. Fabre)—and of François Lemoyne in the Salon d'Hercule at Versailles (1736; *in situ*). In general, however, history painting in the earlier 18th century was transformed by Rococo taste into the prettiness relayed by the peripatetic Venetians Giovanni Antonio Pellegrini (see fig. 3) and the Ricci and Tiepolo families, as well as Lemoyne and his pupil François Boucher. The challenges from other genres grew during the century. In 1717 Antoine Watteau was received (*reçu*) into the Académie Royale on presentation not of a history painting but of a newly defined genre, the *fête galante*; while Chardin's genius in still-life and genre was recognized by contemporaries as being at least equal with that of his fellows in history painting. Seeking for moral inculcation in painting, Denis Diderot was obliged to turn in his criticism to the modern subjects of Jean-Baptiste Greuze.

Official circles, and critics such as ETIENNE LA FONT DE SAINT-YENNE, recognized that without their intervention history painting, and with it the future dignity of French painting, was at risk. Successive Directeurs-Généraux des Bâtiments repeatedly took steps to encourage history painting. In 1727 the Duc D'ANTIN organized a *concours* to stimulate history painting, and his successor Charles Le Normand de Tournehem held another in 1747.

3. Giovanni Antonio Pellegrini: *Head of Pompey Presented to Caesar*, oil on canvas, 1.62×1.50 m, before 1708 (Caen, Musée des Beaux-Arts)

In both, one history painting was commissioned from each of the officers of the Académie Royale; in 1747 each was to be rewarded with a portfolio of blue morocco and 1500 francs. Financial incentives accompanied other innovations: for instance, portraits were paid at a lesser rate than history paintings. A new class of Academician, the *associé libre*, was created to encourage interest in history painting among wealthy patrons. The schools of the Académie were reorganized, with a renewed emphasis on drawing after the Antique and a vastly expanded library of historical and classical works (for further discussion *see* PARIS, §VI, 1). In 1764 Le Normand's successor, the Marquis de Marigny, promoted a further project to stimulate history painting, which illustrates the extreme difficulty of influencing official taste. In 1764 he commissioned Noël Hallé, Carle Vanloo and Joseph-Marie Vien to paint a series of scenes illustrating the lives of the Roman emperors (Amiens, Mus. Picardie; Marseille, Mus. B.-A.) to decorate the royal château of Choisy. Unfortunately, but understandably, Louis XV found them distasteful and inappropriate, and they were replaced by a set of nudities by Boucher.

In England, meanwhile, where there was no native tradition of history painting before the end of the 17th century, it was the artists themselves who were attempting to promote it. William Hogarth, for example, began his career painting serious religious subjects, such as the large *Pool of Bethesda* (1736; London, St Bartholomew's Hospital), and as late as 1756, when his success as a painter of modern moral subjects was assured, his acceptance of the commission for an altarpiece (Bristol, Mus. & A.G.) for St Mary Redcliffe at Bristol suggests his striving after this type of seriousness; although in some unpublished passages for his *Analysis of Beauty* he could be bitterly scathing

of the pretensions of history painters. The most enthusiastic advocate of history painting in 18th-century England was Joshua Reynolds, first President of the Royal Academy. In the *Discourses*, delivered to the members and students of the Royal Academy, he continually advocated the study of the Old Masters of the Roman and Bolognese schools, and of the Antique, and the use of subjects from Greek, Roman and scriptural history which were not 'degraded by the vulgarism of ordinary life in any country', as means of achieving the Grand Manner. Ironically, he himself produced very few examples of history painting. Instead, he used the genre, already developed in France and the Netherlands, of the 'composite portrait', in which a sitter was portrayed with the attributes of a mythological or historical character, to elevate his pictures to the level of historical generalities.

BIBLIOGRAPHY

L. B. Alberti: *On Painting and Sculpture: The Latin Texts of* De Pictura *and* De Sculptura (Florence, 1435); ed. and trans. C. Grayson (London, 1972)
A. Félibien: *Entretiens* (1666–8, rev. 1725)
W. Hogarth: *'The Analysis of Beauty', with the Rejected Passages from the Manuscript Drafts and Autobiographical Notes* (London, 1753/*R* Oxford, 1955)
J. Reynolds: *Discourses on Art* (London, 1778); ed. and intro. K. Fry (London, 1905); ed. R. R. Wark (San Marino, 1959/*R* New Haven and London, 1975)
A. Fontaine: *Les Doctrines d'art en France: Peintres, amateurs et critiques de Poussin à Diderot* (Paris, 1909/*R* Geneva, 1970)
J. Locquin: *La Peinture d'histoire en France de 1747 à 1785* (Paris, 1912/*R* 1978)
A. Blunt: *Artistic Theory in Italy, 1450–1600* (Oxford, 1940)
R. W. Lee: *'Ut pictura poesis*: The Humanistic Theory of Painting', *A. Bull.*, xxii (1940), pp. 197–269; as booklet (New York, 1967)
J. R. Spencer: *'Ut rhetorica pictura*: A Study in Quattrocento Theory of Painting', *J. Warb. & Court. Inst.*, xx (1957), pp. 26–44
M. Baxandall: *Giotto and the Orators: Humanist Observers of Painting in Italy and the Discovery of Pictorial Composition, 1350–1450* (Oxford, 1971) [esp. pp. 51–139]
P. Rosenberg: 'Le Concours de peinture de 1727', *Rev. A.* (1977), pp. 29–42
Gods, Saints and Heroes: Dutch Painting in the Age of Rembrandt (exh. cat. by A. Blankert and others, Washington, DC, N.G.A.; Detroit, MI, Inst. A.; Amsterdam, Rijksmus.; 1980)
M. Sandoz: 'La Peinture d'histoire comme trait marquant du siècle des lumières finissant', *Stud. Voltaire & 18th C.*, cxcix (1981), pp. 263–85
Reynolds (exh. cat., ed. N. Penny; Paris, Grand Pal.; London, RA; 1986)
B. Jobert: 'The "Travaux d'encouragement": An Aspect of Official Arts Policy in France under Louis XVI', *Oxford A.J.*, x/1 (1987), pp. 3–14
La Grande Manière: Historical and Religious Painting in France, 1700–1800 (exh. cat., ed. D. Rosenthal; U. Rochester, NY, Mem. A.G., 1987)
The Loves of the Gods: Mythological Painting from Watteau to David (exh. cat. by C. B. Bailey, Paris, Grand Pal.; Philadelphia, PA, Mus. A.; Fort Worth, TX, Kimbell A. Mus.; 1991–2) [important essays]

II. After c. 1760.

1. Neo-classical history painting. 2. Romanticism and historical genre. 3. Later 19th century. 4. 20th century.

1. NEO-CLASSICAL HISTORY PAINTING. It was in Rome, where Poussin's works of the mid-17th century had set the standard for history painting, that the tradition was being effectively revived a century later. Stimulated by the teachings of Johann Joachim Winckelmann (*see* NEO-CLASSICISM), painters in Rome starting with Joseph-Marie Vien in the 1750s, followed by Nathaniel Dance-Holland, Gavin Hamilton, Angelica Kauffman, Benjamin West and James Barry, set to work on primly restrained

and dignified treatments of themes from antiquity. Hamilton's *Oath of Brutus* (1763–4; London, Drury Lane Theat.) prompted a painting on the same theme (Nevers, Mus. Mun.) by Jacques-Antoine Beaufort that helped introduce the new style to the Paris Salon in 1771. The greatest exponent of Neo-classicism, Jacques-Louis David, came to the style with *Belisarius Receiving Alms* (exh. Salon 1781; Lille, Mus. B.-A.), a painting that finally satisfied Diderot's long-standing critical demand for serious edification in French painting. In the *Oath of the Horatii* (exh. Salon 1784; Paris, Louvre; *see* DAVID, JACQUES-LOUIS, fig. 1), the painting that established his reputation, David adapted the composition of Beaufort's *Oath* to create a vast, rigorously designed, intensely dramatic affirmation of patriotism. This and the *Death of Socrates* (exh. Salon 1787; New York, Met.) were exactly the kind of inspiring history painting projected in the policies of the Comte d'Angiviller, the last Directeur-Général des Bâtiments du Roi.

Benjamin West, an American by birth, took the Neo-classical manner from Rome to London, where he became history painter to George III. In this position he made an innovation that was to prove crucial to the genre when in 1770 he depicted a historic moment from 11 years earlier, the *Death of General Wolfe* (Ottawa, N.G.). While the figure grouping, the gestures and sentiments of this painting belong thoroughly with the tradition of history painting, the costume and details—including a grieving American Indian chief—are entirely contemporary. Reynolds, among others, objected that this broke decorum; but on being told that 'it was very ridiculous to exhibit heroes in coats, breeches and cock'd hats', West appealed to a higher ideal: Classical costume was unknown in 18th-century Canada, and 'the same truth that guides the pen of the historian should govern the pencil of the artist'. The ensuing vast public success of the picture led Reynolds to concede that 'it would occasion a revolution in the art'. It led other painters to turn news into myth: thus the American John Trumbull initiated a national school of history painting with pictures such as the *Death of General Montgomery* (1786; New Haven, CT, Yale U. A.G.), to be followed at the turn of the century by John Vanderlyn.

More than this, West's work marked a growing redefinition of the whole genre. *Wolfe* was followed, at the King's request, by two side-pieces, the *Death of Bayard* (1772) and the *Death of Epaminondas* (1773; Windsor Castle, Berks, Royal Col.): history now extended to medieval as well as Classical subjects. The Society of Arts had in fact been funding since 1759 a prize for subjects from British history, won by artists such as John Hamilton Mortimer, to cater for a growing fascination with the quality of the past. A vogue for the medieval, with its opportunities for fancy dress and ornamental charm, also emerged in France in paintings such as Jean-Simon Berthélemy's *Recapture of Paris from the English* (1787; Versailles, Château). The modern sense of 'history' was being overlaid on Alberti's sense of *historia*. All these strands were present in the exhibitions organized from 1789 in London by John Boydell, who invited all the leading British painters to depict scenes from the national classics of Shakespeare and Milton in a private initiative to stimulate the growth in Britain of 'the noblest art,

Historical Painting'. The results of his highly successful venture included Reynolds's *Death of Cardinal Beaufort* (1787; Petworth House, W. Sussex, NT).

The French Revolution of 1789 led to an extraordinary imposition of Neo-classical décor on everyday Paris life: caught up in this project as a major participant, David had not the time ever to complete the painting that celebrated this fusion of antiquity and actuality, the *Oath of the Tennis Court* (1791; Versailles, Château). After a return to the use of Classical themes allegorically with the *Intervention of the Sabine Women* (1799; Paris, Louvre) he became for many years a propagandist for Napoleon. In this he was joined by younger talents such as Antoine-Jean Gros with his *Bonaparte Visiting the Victims of the Plague at Jaffa* (1804; Paris, Louvre; *see* GROS, ANTOINE-JEAN, fig. 1). David's *Coronation of Napoleon* (1805–7; Versailles, Château; for detail *see* DAVID, JACQUES-LOUIS, fig. 4) shows in gigantic form the inherent problem of painting contemporary history: the hoped-for delivery of symbolic impact collapses under the banal accumulation of factual detail. Nevertheless Napoleon and his wars inevitably commanded the Europe-wide attention of history painters: in Italy he found enthusiasts in Andrea Appiani and Pietro Benvenuti, while in England West countered with the *Death of Nelson* (1807; London, Buckingham Pal., Royal Col.). After his defeat his exploits stimulated the expansion through the earlier 19th century of the adjacent genre of BATTLE PICTURES AND MILITARY SCENES. French nationalism was met with alternative nationalisms. Thus in Germany, where a generation of painters in the 1790s—Christian Gottlieb Schick, Eberhard Wächter, Philipp Friedrich von Hetsch—had done history paintings in a Neo-classical manner, Franz Pforr's *Entry of Rudolf von Habsburg into Basle in 1273* (1810; Frankfurt am Main, Städel. Kstinst. & Städt. Gal.; for illustration *see* PFORR, FRANZ) led off a new, consciously archaistic style, harking back to German Gothic painting. Pforr's colleague from the Lukasbrüder, Peter Cornelius, went on to design energetically linear treatments of national history for Ludwig I of Bavaria in Munich from the 1820s. A tamer version of national sentiment was seen in Vienna in paintings of the deeds of the Austrian Emperor Francis by Peter Krafft, a pupil of David's. In the southern Netherlands Mathieu Ignace Van Brée helped form the sense of a national tradition with scenes from Flemish history; Antonín Machek performed a comparable function in Bohemia in the 1820s. A nationalistic version of Italian history was offered by Giuseppe Bezzuoli, while in Portugal the Neo-classicist Domingos António de Sequeira made a solitary effort to set up a national school. In a sense Goya's *Third of May 1808* (1814; Madrid, Prado; *see* GOYA, FRANCISCO DE, fig. 4), showing a massacre of Spanish civilians by Napoleon's troops, belongs with this nationalistic consciousness-raising, but the rawness and newness of its brutal reportage, excluding any hope of edification, make it a tradition-breaking work.

2. ROMANTICISM AND HISTORICAL GENRE. A comparable sense of desperate personal witness entered the Paris Salon in 1819 with Gericault's *Raft of the Medusa* (Paris, Louvre; *see* GERICAULT, THÉODORE, fig. 3). Gericault, a painter trained on copying Poussin, saw how the

elements of the history painting tradition could be adopted to make something that was at once an aggressive indictment of the French government (which had been involved in a cover-up of the shipping disaster depicted) and a visionary image of human suffering. Delacroix followed Gericault in an imaginative and passionate reading of the tradition, though his *Massacres at Chios* (1824; Paris, Louvre) is less of a political deposition, more contemporary reportage as a pretext for liberated colour and energy; however, he produced in *Liberty Leading the People* (1830; Paris, Louvre), which fuses allegory and reportage in celebrating the 1830 July Revolution, one of the most potent French national images (*see* ALLEGORY, fig. 10).

Against Delacroix's Romanticism stood Ingres, the principal pupil of David and the apostle of the Classical tradition, dismissing the modern mixture of genre and history painting from his eminence within the State's artistic institutions. Curiously, he produced relatively few history paintings that fell within his own definitions, but instead diverted himself with anecdotes from history, showing its great men caught off-duty: for instance *Henry IV Playing with his Children* (1817; Paris, Petit Pal.). Like the practitioners of the contemporary TROUBADOUR STYLE, Ingres was approaching the past in these pictures not so much as a regulatory ideal, but more as a zone of nostalgic fascination; instead of edificatory import, it offered charm.

Between Delacroix and Ingres, *le juste milieu* was—according to contemporary critics—achieved in the 1820s by Paul Delaroche. Delaroche, as seen in such Salon successes as the *Princes in the Tower* (1831; Paris, Louvre), combined a taste for the sensationally dramatic and for fulsome colour with an illusionistically polished finish and closely researched detail, attending to the idea of 'history' through factual verisimilitude; he was everything contemporary taste desired, everything modernist taste was to loathe. His theatrical renditions of scenes from English and French history were greatly influential across Europe in the 1830s and 1840s, inspiring the Russian Karl Bryullov and the English Edward Armitage as well as French colleagues and successors such as Eugène Devéria, Paul Chenavard and the slightly later Joseph-Nicolas Robert-Fleury. Delaroche's vision of history painting—'historical genre' as it was dubbed—was paralleled by the contemporary Belgian school of history painters, Gustaf Wappers, Louis Gallait and Henri Leys, though some of these leant on national precedents in giving their scenes a look of Rubens. Likewise in Italy Francesco Hayez gave stirring renditions of the national past in a manner flavoured by the High Renaissance. Eduardo Rosales Martínez's *Testament of Isabela la Católica* (1863; Madrid, Prado; *see* ROSALES MARTÍNEZ, EDUARDO, fig. 1) is an outstanding Spanish example of the stylistic wave. Delaroche's most fertile influence, however, was probably in Germany, in the work of the DÜSSELDORF SCHOOL.

History painting in Germany was, in the wake of the Lukasbrüder, linear and idealistic in manner; Cornelius's schemes in Munich (*see* §1 above) were followed by the work of Wilhelm von Kaulbach, between 1828 and 1840, on a series depicting 'the history of world culture and ideas' (Berlin, Altes Mus.)—this from the land that nurtured the philosophy of history. The Düsseldorf school,

founded in 1827 by Wilhelm Schadow, learnt from Delaroche the appeal that could be made by closely factual rendering within a theatrical presentation. The most famous painting of the school, Carl Friedrich Lessing's *Hussite Sermon* (1836; Dusseldorf, Kstmus., on loan to Berlin, Altes Mus.) gave the immediacy of reportage to a medieval scene of protest against the Church, thus giving voice to contemporary radical sentiments in the Rhineland. A similarly democratic agenda inspired Emanuel Leutze, who took the group's style to America, with considerable impact, in *Washington Crossing the Delaware* (1851; New York, Met.). Another alumnus, Alfred Rethel, was by contrast an apologist for authority: his monumental series on the life of Charlemagne in the Rathaus at Aachen (1847–52; damaged World War II) gave a consciously German vision of imperial power. The influence of the German painters spread to Britain, where history painting, never a very successful cause in the hands of David Wilkie (who turned from it to portraiture), William Etty (who turned to nudes) and Benjamin Robert Haydon (who would commit suicide, feeling his art rejected, in 1846), was again revived in the scheme set up in 1842 to decorate the Palace of Westminster, London; this was dominated by the Munich-trained William Dyce and Daniel Maclise. Of the murals, which proved to be a technical disaster, the most interesting and ambitious remnant is Maclise's *Death of Nelson* (1863–5; study, Liverpool, Walker A.G.).

3. LATER 19TH CENTURY. In Paris, meanwhile, where the parameters of 19th-century history painting had been

4. Ernest Meissonier: *The Barricade, Rue de la Mortellerie, June 1848*, oil on canvas, 290×220 mm, 1848 (Paris, Musée du Louvre)

set, the style began to be edged out of artistic pre-eminence. The year after Thomas Couture exhibited his vast and blowzy extravaganza *Romans of the Decadence* (1847; Paris, Louvre), another revolution stained the streets, to be recorded by Ernest Meissonier (*The Barricade, Rue de la Mortellerie, June 1848*, 1848; Paris, Louvre; see fig. 4), another artist working at the opposite extreme of the tradition stemming from Gericault; shortly afterwards, Courbet began exhibiting canvases in the format of history painting that defiantly refused to take up its subject-matter (*Burial at Ornans*, 1849–50; Paris, Mus. d'Orsay; *see* COURBET, GUSTAVE, fig. 1). Following the 1848 Revolution French history painting gradually began to retreat from its potential for grand public statement in the hands of such academic painters as Jean-Léon Gérôme, Alexandre Cabanel and William Bouguereau, whose works were principally devoted to antique themes that permitted displays of both archaeological exactitude and of sumptuous quantities of naked women. (A similar development was echoed in Britain from the 1860s, in the work of Frederic Leighton, Edward Poynter and Lawrence Alma-Tadema.) Flaubert, writing in 1854, nailed the sense of diminished values: 'The leading characteristic of our century is its historical sense. This is why we love to confine ourselves to relating the facts.' The French avant-garde movements of the later 19th-century—Impressionism, Symbolism etc—turned decisively away from both the factual detail and the lofty delivery of academic history painting: Manet's *Execution of Emperor Maximilian* (1867; Mannheim, Städt. Ksthalle) is uncharacteristic in this regard, a history painting by an avant-garde artist; but its cool, affectless relation of an episode that reflected dishonour on the French government sets it at odds with its forebear, Goya's *Third of May 1808*. A comparably laconic tone cools much reportage of warfare in the later 19th century: the work of Silvestro Lega or Giovanni Fattori on the Italian Risorgimento or, in the USA, Winslow Homer's *Prisoners from the Front* (1866; New York, Met.).

Historical themes remained enormously popular in France and England in the later part of the century, whether done academically or anecdotally (as for instance by Jean-Paul Laurens or William Frederick Yeames), and were exported from Paris to new domains: by Viktor Madarász, who rallied Hungarian nationalist sentiment with *László Hunyadi on the Bier* (1859; Budapest, N.G.; for illustration *see* MADARÁSZ, VIKTOR), and by Theodor Aman, who from the late 1850s created historical imagery for the new Romanian state. In Germany historical themes were by no means played out: they found a highly individual interpreter in Adolph Menzel, who painted scenes from the life of Frederick the Great (begun 1849; Berlin, Alte N.G.; *see* MENZEL, ADOLPH, fig. 2), and a highly populist, dramatic one in Karl Theodor von Piloty (*Seni before the Body of Wallenstein*, 1859; Munich, Neue Pin.). Piloty, Wilhelm von Kaulbach's successor at the Munich Akademie der Bildenden Künste, was an important teacher for the generation of artists who brought history painting to the fore in central and eastern Europe during the 1870s and 1880s, such as the Austrian Hans Makart, the Hungarians Gyula Benczúr and Mihály Munkácsy and the Pole Jan Matejko. Matejko's opulent dramatic canvases (e.g. *The Homage of Prussia*, 1880–82; Kraków, N. Mus.; for illustration *see* MATEJKO, JAN) exemplify the power of the historical form to give voice to otherwise inarticulated national feelings; hence their great importance in a politically suppressed culture. In Russia history painting was also charged with political significance; whether promoting Slavophil sentiments, as in the work of Vasily Surikov, or liberal ones, as in that of Il'ya Repin.

4. 20TH CENTURY. History painting thus moved out, as the 19th century ended, from the centres of European artistic sophistication to contexts where collective edification was still in demand. In western Europe, while official commissions for decorative schemes continued to

5. Pablo Picasso: *Guernica*, oil on canvas, 3.51×7.82 m, 1937 (Madrid, Centro de la Reina Sofía)

lean on history, the most challenging work in the 20th century came when sophisticated artists, working from a position of individualism, attempted to reach back to the multi-figure composition and the memorable action as a way of invoking communality—for instance Giuseppe Pellizza da Volpedo's *Fourth Estate* (1898–1901; Milan, Gal. A. Mod.; *see* PELLIZZA DA VOLPEDO, GIUSEPPE, fig. 2) or Pablo Picasso's *Guernica* (1937; Madrid, Cent. Reina Sofía; see fig. 5). In the Soviet Union communality, in the form of SOCIALIST REALISM, was imposed from above from the late 1920s; hence the fossilized perpetuation of a history style, epitomized by Aleksandr Deyneka's *Defence of Petrograd* (1928; Moscow, Tret'yakov Gal.), into the 1960s, a style also imposed on other countries within the Communist bloc. Against these State-programmed types of banality must be set the State-sponsored inspiration of the Mexican muralists—Diego Rivera, José Clemente Orozco and David Alfaro Siqueiros—who worked with the revolutionary regime of their country during the 1920s and 1930s to forge a new historical style out of a cultural situation quite unlike any in Europe (*see* MURAL, §2). Their example was also inspiring for American painters working for the Federal Arts Program during the 1930s (*see* MURAL, §3, and UNITED STATES OF AMERICA, §III, 3).

Individual artists in the late 20th century could use the terms of history painting to reach for a communal conscience, as in the work of the American Leon Golub or the German Jörg Immendorf; they could alternately adapt those terms to serve Post-modernist ironies; they could contemplate the idea of history without resorting to figure composition, as in the work of Anselm Kiefer. The continuity of the form is bound up with the vitality of ideas of nation and community.

BIBLIOGRAPHY

D. Rivera: 'The Revolution in Painting', *Creative A.*, iv (1929), p. 28
P. Brieger: *Die deutsche Geschichtsmalerei des 19. Jahrhunderts* (Berlin, 1930)
E. Wind: 'The Revolution of History Painting', *J. Warb. Inst.*, ii (1938), pp. 116–27; also in *Hume and the Heroic Portrait: Studies in Eighteenth-century Imagery*, ed. J. Anderson (Oxford, 1986), pp. 88–99
C. Mitchell: 'Benjamin West's *Death of General Wolfe* and the Popular History Piece', *J. Warb. & Court. Inst.*, vii (1944), pp. 20–33
J. B. Sloane: 'Manet and History', *A.Q.*, xiv (1951), p. 103
G. Busch: *Eugène Delacroix: Die Freiheit auf den Barrikaden* (Stuttgart, 1960)
P. G. Thielen: 'Zur Historienmalerei der Bismarck-Zeit', *Festschrift M. Braubach* (Munich, 1964)
F. Zelger: *Heldenstreit und Heldentod: Schweizerische Historienmalerei im 19. Jahrhundert* (Zurich, 1973)
A. Boime: 'New Light on Manet's *Execution of Maximilian*', *A.Q.* [Detroit], xxxvi/3 (1973), pp. 172–208
W. Hofmann: *Das irdische Paradies* (Munich, 1974)
R. Schoch: *Das Herrscherbild in der Malerei des 19. Jahrhunderts* (Munich, 1975)
E. Vancsa: 'Überlegungen zur politischen Rolle der Historienmalerei des 19. Jahrhunderts', *Wien. Jb. Kstgesch.*, n. s., xxviii (1975), pp. 145–58
D. Chapeaurouge: 'Die deutsche Geschichtsmalerei von 1800 und ihre politische Significanz', *Z. Dt. Ver. Kstwiss.*, xxxi/1–4 (Berlin, 1977), pp. 115–42
R. Strong: *Recreating the Past: British History and the Victorian Painter* (London, 1978)
R. Scholz: *Volk, Nation, Geschichte: Deutsche historische Kunst im 19. Jahrhundert* (Rosenheim, 1980)
P. Barz: *Motiv Geschichte: Berühmte Gemälde, berühmte Ereignisse* (Brunswick, 1981)
A. Hilton: 'Scenes from Life and Contemporary History: Russian Realism of the 1870s–1880s', *The European Realist Tradition*, ed. G. P. Weisberg (Bloomington, 1982)
G. Tapley Vincent: *The American Artist and the Changing Perceptions of American History, 1770–1940* (diss., Newark, U. DE, 1982)
J. Ziesener-Eigel: *Das Historienbild des 18. und frühen 19. Jahrhunderts in Frankreich* (diss., U. Cologne, 1982)
H. T. Wappenschmidt: *Allegorie, Symbol und Historienbild im späten 19. Jahrhundert* (Munich, 1984)
A. U. Abrams: *The Valiant Hero: Benjamin West and Grand-style History Painting* (Washington, 1985)
F. Pupil: *Le Style troubadour ou la nostalgie du bon vieux temps* (Nancy, 1985)
D. S. Russcol: *English Historical Themes in French Painting c. 1815–1848* (diss., U. New York, 1985)
M. Schäfer: *Historienmalerei und Nationalbewusstsein in Russland, 1860–1890* (diss., U. Cologne, 1985)
H. W. Schmidt: *Die Förderung des vaterländischen Geschichtsbildes durch die 'Verbindung für historische Kunst', 1854–1933* (Marburg, 1985)
E. Mai and A. Repp-Eckert, eds: *Triumph und Tod des Helden: Europäische Historienmalerei von Rubens bis Manet* (exh. cat., Cologne, Wallraf-Richartz-Mus., 1987)
W. H. Gerdts and M. Thistlethwaite: *Grand Illusions: History Painting in America* (Fort Worth, 1988)
K. Lankheit: *Von der napoleonischen Epoche zum Risorgimento: Studien zur italienischen Kunst des 19. Jahrhunderts* (Munich, 1988)
R. Rosenblum: 'Notes on Benjamin West and the Death of Nelson', *Kunst um 1800 und die Folgen* (Munich, 1988), pp. 81–6
J. Szabó: *Die Malerei des 19. Jahrhunderts in Ungarn* (Budapest, 1988)
M. Christadler: 'Geschichte in der amerikanischen Malerei zwischen Revolution und Bürgerkrieg, 1770–1870', *Bilder aus der Neuen Welt* (exh. cat., ed. T. W. Gaehtgens; Berlin, Staatl. Museen Preuss. Kultbes., 1988), pp. 36–42
J. K. Ostrowski: *Die polnische Malerei vom Ende des 18. Jahrhunderts bis zum Beginn der Moderne* (Munich, 1989)
H. Wine: 'The End of History? Painting in France c. 1700–1800', *Tradition and Revolution in French Art, 1700–1880: Paintings and Drawings from Lille* (exh. cat. by H. Wine and others, London, N.G., 1993), pp. 13–30

□

Hitchcock, George (*b* Providence, RI, 29 Sept 1850; *d* Marken, 2 Aug 1913). American painter, active in the Netherlands. A descendant of Roger Williams (the founder of Rhode Island), he practised law for several years in New York before deciding in 1879 to become an artist. He studied in Paris with Gustave Boulanger and Jules Lefebvre, in Düsseldorf, and in The Hague with H. W. Mesdag. He settled in Egmond-aan-Zee, near Alkmaar, in 1883, and was soon widely known for his paintings of religious subjects in contemporary settings and of sunlit views of tulip fields. He returned to the USA only occasionally in later years. Hitchcock's style, similar to Impressionism, has been appreciated more in Europe than in the USA. A good example of his style is the *Blessed Mother* (1892; Cleveland, OH, Mus. A.). He received some recognition in the USA, such as election to associate membership in the National Academy of Design, New York, and he was the first American to be made a member of the Akademie der Bildenden Künste, Vienna, and the first to become an officer of the Order of Franz Josef. He was also a chevalier of the Légion d'honneur.

BIBLIOGRAPHY

George Hitchcock (exh. cat., ed. C. Brinton; U. Rochester, NY, Mem. A.G., 1915)
P. Boswell: 'The George Hitchcock Memorial Exhibition to be Held at a New York Gallery', *A. & Dec.*, xiv (1921), p. 297

MARK W. SULLIVAN

Hitchcock, Henry-Russell (*b* Boston, MA, 3 June 1903; *d* New York, 19 Feb 1987). American architectural historian. He studied architecture briefly (1923–4) at Harvard University, Cambridge, MA, before taking his master's degree in art history in 1927. He taught at Vassar College,

Poughkeepsie, NY (1927–8), and Wesleyan University, Middletown, CT (1929–41), before moving in 1941 to Smith College, Northampton, MA, where he remained a member of the faculty until 1968. His other teaching assignments included the Institute of Fine Arts of New York University (1940), Massachusetts Institute of Technology, Cambridge, MA (1946–8), Yale University, New Haven, CT (1952–3, 1959–60), Cambridge University, England (1962), and Harvard (1965).

Hitchcock's immense reputation derived, however, from his research and publications, many of which were devoted to the modern period. His first major book, *Frank Lloyd Wright* (1928), was followed rapidly by *Modern Architecture* (1929) and *J. J. P. Oud* (1931). With Philip Johnson, the first director of the department of architecture at the newly formed MOMA in New York, Hitchcock toured Europe in 1930 and helped Johnson to organize the memorable *Modern Architecture: International Exhibition* (1932) at MOMA, which brought the foremost European avant-garde architects such as Gropius, Le Corbusier, Oud and Mies van der Rohe to the notice of Americans for the first time. In the same year Hitchcock collaborated with Johnson in the publication of *The International Style*, the newly named style often applied indiscriminately to virtually all modernist architecture from the 1920s to the 1970s. Hitchcock's knowledge was encyclopedic, and he was renowned for stylistic nuance. His other principal scholarly studies, which cover a wide range of topics, include the modern architecture of Latin America, and one of his best works, *Architecture: Nineteenth and Twentieth Centuries* (1958).

WRITINGS
Frank Lloyd Wright (New York, 1928)
Modern Architecture (New York, 1929)
J. J. P. Oud (Paris, 1931)
with P. Johnson: *The International Style: Architecture since 1922* (New York, 1932)
In the Nature of Materials, 1887–1941: The Buildings of Frank Lloyd Wright (New York, 1942)
Early Victorian Architecture in Britain (New Haven, 1954)
Latin American Architecture since 1945 (New York, 1955)
Architecture: Nineteenth and Twentieth Centuries (Baltimore and Harmondsworth, 1958)

BIBLIOGRAPHY
H. Searing, ed.: *In Search of Modern Architecture: A Tribute to Henry-Russell Hitchcock* (New York, 1983)

FRANZ SCHULZE

Hitchcock, Lambert (*b* Cheshire, CT, 28 May 1795; *d* Unionville, CT, 3 April 1852). American cabinetmaker and furniture manufacturer. He came from a land-owning Connecticut family and in 1826 established a factory near Barkhamsted, CT, in an area renamed Hitchcocksville (now Riverton) after him. His chief product was an American adaptation of a late Sheraton-style, open-backed side chair, painted black with stencilled decoration, known as the 'Hitchcock' chair. In 1832 he entered into a partnership with his brother-in-law Arba Alford (1808–81), and the firm was called Hitchcock, Alford & Co. Hitchcock's use of stencilled decoration on his painted chairs emulated the gilt and lacquered furniture being imported from Europe. The factory turned out hundreds of these 'fancy' chairs, made from hickory, maple, birch and poplar with rush or cane seats. They have a 'bolster' or flat-fronted top rail, with round, splayed, ring-turned front legs, sometimes tapered with ball feet, and round front, back and side stretchers, also ring-turned. Back uprights and back legs are all-in-one. Decoration consists of large floral and fruit designs, banded patterns or Greek anthemia, mostly in gold or bronze. From *c.* 1835 chair backs were flat and steam-bent backwards for comfort. The 'Hitchcock' chair was well-made and much copied, but few had the jaunty, inimitable air of the originals. In 1848 Hitchcock severed his relationship with the company, which continued to make furniture until 1853 as the A. & A. Alford Co., and until 1864 as the Phoenix Co. In 1946 the factory, unused since the 1930s, was taken over by the Hitchcock Chair Co., newly formed to restore and expand the premises and produce reproductions of Hitchcock's furniture. The John Tarrant Kenney Hitchcock Museum was established in Riverton in 1972.

BIBLIOGRAPHY
'Lambert Hitchcock of Hitchcock-ville, Connecticut', *Bull. Antiqua. & Landmarks Soc. CT*, xviii (1965)
19th-century America: Furniture and Other Decorative Arts (exh. cat., New York, Met., 1970)
E. Kenney Glennon: 'The John Tarrant Kenney Hitchcock Museum, Riverton, Connecticut', *Antiques*, cxxv (1984), pp. 1140–47

□

Hitchens, Ivon (*b* London, 3 March 1893; *d* Lavington Common, nr Petworth, 29 Aug 1979). English painter. He studied at St John's Wood School of Art and at the Royal Academy Schools intermittently between 1912 and 1919. He exhibited with the 7 & 5 SOCIETY in 1921 and continued to do so throughout the 1920s. He soon became part of the circle of artists known as the LONDON GROUP and exhibited with Ben Nicholson, Barbara Hepworth, Henry Moore and others during the 1930s. Hints of his mature style can be found in the delicate green-grey shades of a still-life such as *Spring Mood No. 2* (1933; artist's estate), which was influenced by Braque, but he also experimented with pure abstraction, as in *Coronation* (1937; London, Tate). After his house was bombed in 1940 he moved to a patch of woodland near Petworth, W. Sussex, living at first in a caravan which later acquired numerous outbuildings. He worked there for the next 40 years, distanced from the predominantly literary currents of British modern art. In his commitment to colour and open brushwork he was closer to the modern French masters, especially in his Fauvist orange nudes set in sunlit interiors. He painted mostly outdoors, however, and his technique developed from a tonal treatment that recalled the informality of Constable's sketches, as in *Damp Autumn* (1941; London, Tate), where the motif is clearly legible, to brushmarks that became wider, quickening in pace as they deflected vertical and horizontal movement, as in *Arno No. 4* (1965; London, Tate).

Hitchens's landscape paintings are better understood as being not pictures of woodland scenery but experiences, memories of having been in a specific landscape; of the noise and the vibration of light when hearing birdsong; feeling what is above, below, behind; sensing the moisture, the presence of ferns, oaks, the passing moods of rustling trees and rippling water. To include all of these sensations and to translate the totality into the illusion of mobile colour, Hitchens used a long, horizontal format, heavily framed to give a panoramic vista. He registered the sensations of the weather and woods around him as frontal planes, with oil paint often damp and earthy in colour and laid on to the canvas with forthright sweeps and stabs of broad brushes. His characteristic manner was the deftly placed blocks of brushed pigment set on a bare white ground, sometimes with a few straggling lines scratched in with a palette knife. In *Firwood Ride No. 4* (1957; London, Tate), these blocks of mingling colour suggest transience and are placed at rhythmic intervals to articulate plasticity, contrast and the play of light and dark. Hitchens referred to effects of light as the Japanese principle *notan* (literally, 'light and shade'), which he learnt as a student from the painters' manual by Arthur Wesley Dow (1857–1922) entitled *Composition* (New York, 1899).

Hitchens neither painted landscape as a detached observer, nor did he abstract forms from nature, and he valued the disciplines of Cézanne too highly to allow structure to be controlled by subjective response alone. His output was prodigious, but of uneven quality, and included large-scale commissions such as the mural in Cecil Sharp House, Regent's Park Road, London (1954). The freshness of colour in the paintings of his last years could either burst open in glorious flourishes, or lie dormant in secretive greys. He was an isolated figure but his art was never eccentric, and as a colourist his legacy is best found in the painting of Patrick Heron.

BIBLIOGRAPHY
P. Heron: *Ivon Hitchens*, Penguin Mod. Masters (Harmondsworth, 1955)
A. Bowness, ed.: *Ivon Hitchens* (London, 1973)
Ivon Hitchens: A Retrospective Exhibition (exh. cat. by A. Causey, London, RA, 1979)

JAMES FAURE WALKER

Hitofushi no Chitsui. *See* KUBO SHUNMAN.

Hitoshi Watanabe. *See* WATANABE, HITOSHI.

Hittite. Name given to the people of the central Anatolian plateau of the 2nd millennium BC, speakers of Hittite, the oldest attested member of the Indo-European language group. The Hittites are known largely from excavations, principally of their capital city Hattusa (modern BOĞAZ-KÖY) and also the sites of their vassal kingdoms in Syria, especially UGARIT (modern Ras Shamra) and Emar (*see* MASKANA, §1); archives of cuneiform tablets were found at all three sites and the Hittites also appear in Egyptian records. The term Hittite comes, through the Old Testament, from the land of Hatti, within the bend of the River Halys, where Hattusa was located, and it is also applied to a people of south-east Anatolia and north Syria, otherwise designated Late or Neo-Hittites, who survived the fall of the Hittite empire *c*.1200 BC in small city-states of the early 1st millennium BC. In contrast to the Hittites of Hattusa, these wrote, and presumably spoke, not Hittite but the closely related Luwian.

The Hittites' place of origin was presumably north of the Caucasus and the Black Sea, and they entered Anatolia at an uncertain date before 2000 BC, along with their kinsmen, the speakers of Luwian and Palaic. Already in the Assyrian Colony period (*c*.1920–1740 BC; *see* ANATOLIA, §I, 2(ii)(a)), the Hittites formed a substantial proportion of the population, being recognized from their names in the tablets from KÜLTEPE (Kanesh, Nesa). Their own naming of their language as Nesite implies that this city was an important centre for them. This period ended with the violent destruction of Kanesh and other leading Anatolian cities. The Hittites must have been involved, but details are lacking.

The Old Kingdom (*c*. 1650–1500 BC) begins when the Hittite capital was established at Hattusa by Hattusili I. In his reign and that of his grandson and successor Mursili I, the Hittites secured their domination of central Anatolia and expanded dramatically into Syria, conquering Aleppo and raiding as far as Babylon *c*.1595 BC. Thereafter, however, dissension in the royal family sapped the power of the state. The Old Kingdom terminated in a dark age, sometimes inappropriately referred to as the Middle Kingdom (*c*. 1500–1400 BC).

A revival *c*. 1400 BC was followed by renewed crisis, in which Hattusa was beset by enemies from every side. Suppiluliuma I (*reg c*. 1380–1346 BC) not only re-established control in Anatolia, but also conquered Syria *c*. 1360 BC, driving out the Egyptians and destroying the Hurrian kingdom of Mitanni (*see* MITANNIAN). His heirs maintained this empire for four generations. A powerful federation of Luwian states in western Anatolia, the kingdom of Arzawa, was dissolved by Suppiluliuma's son Mursili II (*reg c*. 1345–1320 BC). His son Muwatalli (*reg c*. 1320–1294 BC) checked the revived power of Egypt under the 19th dynasty at Qadesh in Syria, *c*. 1300 BC, an event depicted in Egyptian reliefs, notably from Thebes, and Egypt and Hatti recognized each other's spheres of interest in Palestine and Syria respectively.

The Hittites built in a style combining stone, timber and mud brick. Their palaces and temples made use of courtyards and porticos, often with basement storerooms. Typically the wall-footings were faced with stone orthostats often carved with religious and secular scenes (e.g. at ALACA HÖYÜK). Gates and doorways were flanked by guardian figures of lions and sphinxes, and fortifications had monumental gates. Rock faces, often associated with springs, and rock-cut shrines (see fig. and *see* YAZILIKAYA (i)) were carved with reliefs, and commemorative inscriptions were placed on orthostats, rock faces, seals and dedicated objects. Hittite pre-eminence in the art of metalwork can be inferred from the rather meagre remains recovered by archaeology. (For further details *see* ANATOLIA, especially §§I, 2 and 3, II–VI; and BOĞAZKÖY.)

The end of the Late Bronze Age was marked by population movements of which the destructive progress of the Sea Peoples along the coast of the Levant was only one. Written records abruptly cease *c*. 1200 BC, and archaeology reveals fierce destruction of the Hittite cities, especially Hattusa, and a marked discontinuity of settlement. A new dark age (*c*. 1200–1000 BC) intervened, and the political geography of the Ancient Near East was drastically altered. The Hittites disappeared from the central Anatolian land of Hatti, but in the former Hittite provinces of south-east Anatolia and north Syria Hittite peoples maintained themselves in independent city-states, which flourished *c*. 1000–700 BC. The Hattusa tradition of writing on cuneiform clay tablets was abandoned, but the use of the Hittite hieroglyphic script for monumental stone inscriptions, and on lead and perishable materials

Hittite relief, King Tudhaliya IV in the embrace of the god Sarruma, on the east wall of Chamber B, Yazılıkaya, *c.* 1230 BC

such as wood, was continued and expanded. Although the language of the inscriptions is Luwian, these city-states continued to be referred to by their neighbours, the Assyrians and the Hebrews, as Hatti, hence the terms Late or Neo-Hittites. All the salient features of this civilization reflect continuity from the traditions of the Hittite empire, in particular the architecture and art.

While the Late Hittites held north Syria, newcomers established themselves in the south, namely the Semitic ARAMAEANS, and there emerged a general fusion of cultures. Recognizably Hittite states included Tabal and Tuwana in Anatolia, Que and Hilakku in Cilicia (*see* KARATEPE), Melid (*see* ARSLANTEPE), Kummuh and Gurgum between the Upper Euphrates and the Taurus mountains, and Unqi in the plain of Antioch (*see* TAYINAT, TELL). The most distinctively Hittite of all remained the great city of CARCHEMISH on the Euphrates, the former seat of the Hittite empire in Syria. In Hamath (*see* HAMA, §1) on the River Orontes a 9th-century BC Hittite dynasty was replaced in the 8th century BC by an Aramaean one, while the small state of Sam'al (*see* ZINCIRLI) at the eastern foot of the Amanus mountains had a mixed Aramaean-Hittite dynasty.

Assyrian pressure became acute in the later 9th century BC but was replaced by Urartian in the early 8th century BC. Finally in the second half of the 8th century BC the Assyrians systematically subjected and broke up the Hittite and Aramaean states, as well as the Hebrew kingdom of Israel. This was the end for the Hittites. Their language and civilization disappeared, and they became merged with the other subject peoples of Mesopotamia.

BIBLIOGRAPHY
O. R. Gurney: *The Hittites* (Harmondsworth, 1952, rev. 1990)
E. Akurgal: *The Art of the Hittites* (London, 1962)
S. Lloyd: *Early Highland Peoples of Anatolia* (London, 1967)
O. R. Gurney: 'Anatolia *c.* 1750–1600 BC'; 'Anatolia *c.* 1600–1380 BC', Cambridge Anc. Hist., ii/1 (rev. Cambridge, 1973), pp. 228–55, 659–84
A. Goetze: 'The Struggle for the Domination of Syria'; 'Anatolia from Shuppiluliumash to the Egyptian Wars of Muwatallish'; 'The Hittites and Syria', Cambridge Anc. Hist., ii/2 (rev. Cambridge, 1975), pp. 1–20; 117–29; 252–73
J. C. Macqueen: *The Hittites and Their Contemporaries in Asia Minor* (London, 1975)
K. Bittel: *Die Hethiter* (Munich, 1976)
J. D. Hawkins: *The Neo-Hittite States in Syria and Anatolia*, Cambridge Anc. Hist., iii/1 (rev. Cambridge, 1982), pp. 372–441

J. D. HAWKINS

Hittorff, Jacques-Ignace [Jakob-Ignaz] (*b* Cologne, 20 Aug 1792; *d* Paris, 25 March 1867). French architect, architectural historian, urban planner and writer. He was the only son of a family of prosperous craftsmen from the Rhineland who acquired French nationality after Cologne was annexed by France in 1794. Hittorff was apprenticed as a mason and studied mathematics and drawing with an architectural career in prospect. As a French citizen he was then able to study in Paris, where he moved in 1810; he entered the Ecole des Beaux-Arts in 1811 and joined the atelier of Charles Percier. In the same year he assisted on the first important metal structure erected in France, the iron dome of the Halle au Blé (1808–13), under the direction of François-Joseph Bélanger. Following the return of the Rhineland provinces to Prussia in 1814, Hittorff was unable to continue with his French education and could not enter for the Prix de Rome. However, he and another young architect, Joseph Lecointe (1783–1858), were taken on by Bélanger, who had been reappointed Architecte des Fêtes et Cérémonies Royales upon the restoration of the Bourbons. Working at first under Bélanger's guidance and then, after his death (1818), taking over his position themselves, Hittorff and Lecointe designed the settings and decorations for many important court ceremonies, including the removal of the remains of Louis XVI to Saint-Denis (1815), the baptism of the Duc de Bordeaux (1821), the funeral of Louis XVIII (1824) and the coronation of Charles X at Reims (1825)—the last coronation held in Reims Cathedral.

Hittorff's early educational travels took him first to England (1820), then to Germany (1821) and to Berlin, where he met Karl Friedrich Schinkel. He passionately wanted to visit Italy to undertake archaeological excavations and produce reconstructions, which he considered essential to the advancement of his career, and in 1822 he set off at his own expense on a tour that took him first to Rome. From September 1822 to June 1824, accompanied by LUDWIG VON ZANTH, he carried out extensive studies and surveys, in particular of the ancient architecture of Sicily. On his return to Paris he presented to the Académie des Beaux-Arts the results of his research, together with his theory on the polychromy of ancient buildings, which he had developed from investigations on site. This theory, which aimed to prove that ancient Greek architecture had been entirely covered with intense colour, broke with the aesthetic principles of the Neo-classical ideal, attracted the attention of learned circles throughout Europe and unleashed a long-lasting dispute among scholars (*see* POLYCHROMY, §1(ii), and GREECE, ANCIENT, §II, 1(iii)(c)).

In 1824 Hittorff married the daughter of the architect Jean-Baptiste Lepère and took up permanent residence in

Paris, where he embarked on a dazzling career that began in theatre design. Working with Lecointe, he restored the Salle Favart (1825) and rebuilt the Théâtre de l'Ambigu-Comique (1828). The achievements that brought him fame, however, date from the 1830s when he was appointed architect for the church of St Vincent-de-Paul (1832–44), Paris, initially commissioned from his father-in-law. Hittorff designed this as a model building and published a programme for it: all the arts, from sculpture and monumental painting to cabinet making and stained glass, were represented in the building and coordinated by Hittorff. St Vincent-de-Paul should be seen as the link between ideas derived from antiquity and more recent European art, which it combined in an eclectic manner. The western façade (see fig.) has a projecting Ionic portico reached by a wide flight of steps, and a pediment full of sculpture, but this is set between a pair of slender towers that echo the traditional medieval format, although they have classical details. The church has a rectangular plan and its interior recalls Early Christian work, with a wide apse encompassing the aisles as well as the nave; the nave itself has a powerful Doric colonnade, with friezes painted by Hippolyte Flandrin (see FLANDRIN (2)) and a Corinthian colonnade above. Hittorff intended to apply polychromatic decoration to the exterior of the building as well, with enamelled panels, friezes and murals, but this proposal was rejected.

Hittorff was also a talented urban planner, as seen in his numerous designs for the layout of the Place de la Concorde, Paris, and its realization (1829–54). The adjacent Promenade des Champs-Elysées was also altered in

accordance with Hittorff's plans, and he produced two notable buildings for the avenue, which was transformed into an elegant boulevard under Louis-Philippe: the Cirque National (1839–41), which was the prototype for many buildings of its kind erected in the second half of the 19th century, and the Rotonde des Panoramas (1838–9; destr. 1857), the roof frame of which was worked out in accordance with the principle of suspended structures. Hittorff revealed his skills as a daring builder in other works, for example the Cirque Napoléon (Cirque d'Hiver; 1851–2) on the Boulevard des Filles du Calvaire, a polychrome structure covered with an iron roof. This was the first building erected in Paris during the reign of Napoleon III, who commissioned Hittorff in 1853 to design the façades of the town houses around the Place de l'Etoile, the Maison d'Education Eugénie-Napoléon (1857) and the Mairie of the 1st arrondissement (1860), as well as a large number of other projects, such as the layout of the Bois de Boulogne and a Palais de l'Industrie, which were rejected by the prefect GEORGES-EUGÈNE HAUSSMANN, a declared enemy of Hittorff. Hittorff's last work was the Gare du Nord (1861–4; see PARIS, fig. 9), an iron-framed train shed with a façade incorporating Greek columns and pediments together with wide arches; on this project he worked in close collaboration with company architects. Hittorff was an innovator, like the rationalists Henri Labrouste, Louis Duc and Félix-Jacques Duban. He was a member of the Académie des Beaux-Arts and numerous learned societies and became famous in his own day. He was, however, largely forgotten after the Franco-German hostilities of 1870.

See also GREEK REVIVAL.

WRITINGS

with J. Lecointe: *Description des cérémonies et des fêtes qui ont eu lieu pour le baptême de son altesse royale . . . duc de Bordeaux* (Paris, 1827)
with L. von Zanth: *L'Architecture antique de la Sicile* (Paris, 1827)
——: *L'Architecture moderne de la Sicile* (Paris, 1835)
'Le Programme décoratif de St Vincent-de-Paul', *L'Artiste* (1842)
Restitution du temple d'Empédocle à Selinonte ou l'Architecture polychrome chez les Grecs (Paris, 1851)
'Mémoire sur Pompéi et Pétra', *Mém. Acad. Inscr. & B.-Lett.*, xxv (1866), pp. 377–416

BIBLIOGRAPHY

K. Hammer: *Jakob-Ignaz Hittorff: Ein Pariser Baumeister, 1792–1867* (Stuttgart, 1968)
D. D. Schneider: *The Works and Doctrine of Jacques-Ignace Hittorff, 1792–1867*, 2 vols (New York and London, 1977)
Hittorff: Un architecte du XIXème siècle (exh. cat., Paris, Carnavalet, 1986–7)
Jakob Ignaz Hittorff: Ein Architekt aus Köln im Paris des 19. Jahrhunderts (exh. cat., Cologne, Wallraf-Richartz-Mus., 1987)

THOMAS VON JOEST

Hitzig, (Georg Heinrich) Friedrich (*b* Berlin, 8 April 1811; *d* Berlin, 11 Oct 1881). German architect. After passing the land surveyor examination in 1829, he did practical work on the Oderbrücke at Stettin (now Szezecin, Poland) and, in 1830, on Schinkel's Sternwarte Observatory in Berlin. He then studied at the Bauakademie (1830–37) in Berlin with a break for a journey to Paris in 1835. His activities as a private architect increased with the city's expansion and the proliferation of villa building in the residential areas. As the monthly competitions of the Architekten-Verein in 1832 show, Hitzig, having been one of the youngest pupils of Schinkel, was in a position to

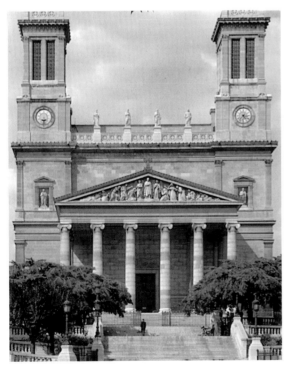

Jacques-Ignace Hittorff: façade of St Vincent-de-Paul, Paris, 1832–44

produce, ready-made, the perfected Italianate villa style developed by Schinkel and Ludwig Persius. He combined it with influences from Charles Percier and Pierre-François-Léonard Fontaine and with elements taken from the Italian Renaissance, which he had studied on a trip to Italy in 1845, thereby creating an elegant and rich style that owed its clarity to the predominance of classical content. With this he created for Berlin a stylistic vocabulary for the houses of the wealthy, which, depending on the chosen site, were built either as urban villas (e.g. Lennéstrasse 8, 1838), or as exclusive blocks of flats, like the buildings on the Königsplatz (1845–7) and in the Viktoria Strasse (1856–8). The façades were animated with rustication at the lower levels and with balustrades and decorated window groups; the structures were articulated with loggias, gables, pediments and belvederes. The house of the sculptor Friedrich Drake, a narrow three-storey building with pitched roof (1841–2), resembled a high temple with caryatids and pedimental relief sculpture (similar to a contemporary house by Friedrich August Stüler, Leipziger Strasse 111, and to Johann Heinrich Strack's Galerie Raczynski of 1843). Later work, such as the two cube-shaped Villas Hansemann of 1864 (Tiergartenstrasse 30–31, incorporating the Villa Mölter by Friedrich Gilly), and the Palazzo Revoltella at Trieste (1857 and 1863) showed more leanings towards the Renaissance. This may have been due to the influence of Gottfried Semper, whose Palais Oppenheim (1848) in Dresden was closely emulated by Hitzig in his design for the Palais Pourtalès on the Königsplatz (1852), Berlin. Occasionally, for instance in the Palais Kronenberg (1866–70; destr.) in Warsaw, Hitzig used the mansard roof, which followers of Schinkel rejected. Examples of his villa types can be found in the plans for the Albrechtshof (1863) and Neu-Tempelhof estates, Berlin. In his designs for plain country houses he developed a less than totally convincing variant of his villa style: with striped brickwork, segmental-arch openings and highly ornamented roof edges. His mainly Gothic Revival country palaces in Mecklenburg and Pomerania, such as Schloss Kittendorf and Schloss Neetzow, and Schloss Graf Schwerin in Göhren of 1851, are on the other hand full of life. Interesting in form and construction, the Ottosche Zirkus (completed by 1860) was an octagon with a tent roof, decorated inside with classical ornament and a figurative frieze. Almost all Hitzig's monumental buildings in Berlin resulted from municipal or private commissions. He won the competition for the Börse in 1855 with a bold design: giant orders between projecting pavilions along the Spree River, similar to the east façade of the Palais du Louvre. The Börse (1859–63; destr. 1945) was the first sandstone structure of the 19th century in Berlin, whose buildings were traditionally of brick and stucco. The exchange floor (l. 69 m, w. 26.7 m and h. 20 m) was vaulted with an iron structure of segmental arches. Hitzig built the first market hall in Berlin in the form of a six-aisled basilica at the Schiffbauerdamm (1865–8; largely rebuilt as the former Friedrichstadtpalast; destr. 1985). The Deutsche Reichsbank (1869–76; destr. 1945) in Jäger Strasse was a blocklike brick structure with surface patterning, built in the Rundbogenstil with some Italian features. Its basically plain form was raised to monumentality by means of a central projection with

giant orders—similar to the portico of the royal palace—and with richly decorated window niches on the *piano nobile*. In his work to complete the Technische Hochschule (begun 1878) in Charlottenburg, Hitzig achieved a similar effect by tightening up the design by Richard Lucae (omitting the domes and using round-arch motifs throughout). Apart from a few country houses, the rear elevations and inner courts of the Technische Hochschule (now Technische Universität) are the only surviving Hitzig buildings. Hitzig gained high offices (from 1850 member of the Technische Bau-Deputation; given the title Baurat in 1851; member of the Akademie der Künste from 1855 and President from 1876). His notable foreign travels included trips to Egypt, Turkey and Greece (1856–7). Together with Georg Erbkam (1811–76) he founded the periodical *Zeitschrift für Bauwesen* in 1851.

WRITINGS

Regular contributions to *Z. Bauwsn* (1851–80)
Ausgeführte Bauwerke von Friedrich Hitzig, 2 vols (Berlin, 1855–66)
with J. H. Strack: *Der innere Ausbau von Wohngebäuden* (Berlin, 1855–63)
Wohngebäude der Viktoriastrasse in Berlin (Berlin, 1859, 2/1864)

BIBLIOGRAPHY

Thieme–Becker
[K. E. O. Fritsch]: 'Die neue Börse zu Berlin', *Z. Prakt. Baukst*, xxiii (1863), pp. 291–300; xxiv (1864), pp. 189–92; xxv (1865), pp. 11–14
Berlin und seine Bauten, Architekten- und Ingenieurverein Berlin (Berlin, 1877, 2/1896 as 2 vols, *R* 1984)
K. E. O. Fritsch: 'Friedrich Hitzig und sein Jubiläum', *Dt. Bauztg*, xiii (1879), pp. 137–9
Obituary, *Zentl. Bauverwalt.*, i (1881), p. 252
K. E. O. Fritsch: 'Der Umbau des Zeughauses zu Berlin', *Dt. Bauztg*, xv (1881)
——: 'Das Haus der Technischen Hochschule zu Berlin in Charlottenburg', *Dt. Bauztg*, xviii (1884)
I. Wirth: *Die Bau- und Kunstdenkmäler Berlins: Bezirk Tiergarten* (Berlin, 1955)
——: *Die Bau- und Kunstdenkmäler Berlins: Bezirk Charlottenburg* (Berlin, 1961)
E. Börsch-Supan: *Berliner Baukunst nach Schinkel, 1840–1870*, Studien zur Kunst des neunzehnten Jahrhunderts, xxv (Munich, 1977)
H. Schmidt: *Das Tiergartenviertel*, i (Berlin, 1983) [suppl. 4 of *Die Bau- und Kunstdenkmäler Berlins*]
G. Baier and others: *Die Bau- und Kunstdenkmale in der DDR: Bezirk Neubrandenburg* (Berlin, 1986)

EVA BÖRSCH-SUPAN

Hiw. *See* DIOSPOLIS PARVA.

Hjertén, Sigrid (Maria) (*b* Sundsvall, 27 Oct 1885; *d* Stockholm, 24 March 1948). Swedish painter. From 1905 to 1908 she studied at the Konstindustriellaskola in Stockholm. She specialized in weaving and worked with the weaver Selma Giöbel (1843–1925). Having decided to become a painter, Hjertén studied at Matisse's academy in Paris (1909–11). There she met the Swedish painter ISAAC GRÜNEWALD; they married in 1911. The same year Hjertén wrote the first article to present the art of Cézanne to Sweden (in *Svenska Dagbladet*, 24 Sept 1911). Along with Grünewald and other painters who had studied at Matisse's academy, she introduced French modernist art to the country. In 1915 Hjertén and Grünewald exhibited at Herwarth Walden's Sturm-Galerie, Berlin. Besides Matisse, both Futurism and German Expressionism influenced Hjertén's work.

Hjertén's paintings from 1914 to 1919 are of particular importance. In *Interior of a Studio* and *The Red Blind* (both 1916; Stockholm, Mod. Mus.) she expressed her conscious and unconscious response to her life as a woman, a painter and a mother. The hostility and harsh criticism that Hjertén and Grünewald met when they exhibited modernist work during the 1910s, however, made Hjertén retire from the official art scene (until a big retrospective exhibition in 1936). In 1920–30 they lived in Paris. During the 1930s Hjertén experimented with colour and made strong colouristic compositions inspired, for example, by her observations of the harbour in Stockholm and by her travels to the south of Europe. She suffered from severe depressions and in 1937 entered a psychiatric hospital, where she died some years later.

BIBLIOGRAPHY
B. Berg: *Sigrid Hjertén, en svensk Matisseelev* [Sigrid Hjertén, a Swedish pupil of Matisse] (BA thesis, U. Uppsala, 1983)
E. Haglund: *Sigrid Hjertén* (Stockholm, 1985)

ELISABET HAGLUND

Hjorth, Bror (*b* Marma, Gävleborg, 22 April 1894; *d* Uppsala, 21 May 1968). Swedish sculptor and painter. In 1915 he studied under Althins Hallström and Gunnar August Hallström (1875–1943) in Stockholm and in 1919 moved to Copenhagen where he attended the Kongelige Danske Kunstakademi. He travelled to Paris in 1921 where he studied under Emile-Antoine Bourdelle until 1924. In Paris he was influenced by Cubism and produced such sculptures as *Cubist Girl* (bronze, 1921; Stockholm, Mod. Mus.). The influence of vernacular art is evident in such works as the expressive *Girl's Head* (wood, 1922; see 1967–8 exh. cat., p. 26). He participated in various group exhibitions in Paris, Stockholm and elsewhere in the late 1920s. During this time his painting began to show the influence of the Swedish folk art tradition, as in the naively executed *At the Kitchen Table* (1923; Göteborg, Kstmus.). This tradition supplanted the influence of Cubism in his sculpture, leading to more realistic works such as *Girl with Violin* (bronze, 1929; Stockholm, Mod. Mus.). In 1932 he was a co-founder of FÄRG OCH FORM, under whose sponsorship he received his first one-man show in 1935 in Stockholm; he exhibited with the group regularly. He worked in Copenhagen in 1938 and in 1939 produced reliefs for Skogskyrkogårdens Crematorium in Stockholm. The solid, bulky figures of *Rodin and his Muse* (bronze, 1936; Stockholm, Mod. Mus.) were typical of the works of this period. In 1944 he produced sculpture and relief work for the chapel at Borås Crematorium. His painted wood reliefs, such as *Bernadette of Lourdes* (1943; Stockholm, Mod. Mus.), are roughly carved and are in the same expressive style as his paintings. From 1949 to 1959 Hjorth was professor of drawing at the Konsthögskola in Stockholm, and from 1951 to 1953 he visited Paris, Italy and Greece. Religious themes recur in his painting, as in *Jesus and Mary Magdalene* (1958; see 1973 exh. cat., p. 6), which has the firm outlines and uniform colouring characteristic of the works of the later 1950s. The same spirit is evident in his sculpture, for example *Dance Group* (papier-mâché, 1959; Stockholm, Mod. Mus.). In 1963 Hjorth painted the *Entry into Jerusalem* for Salabacke Church in Uppsala. His sculpture *Water Sprite Polka* (bronze, 1960) was installed in front of the railway station in Uppsala in 1967. Reducing the forms to a minimum, it

consists of a column with a figure and waterlilies surmounted by a dancing couple. With Sven Erixson, Hjorth was influential in revitalizing the folk art tradition in Sweden.

BIBLIOGRAPHY
Bror Hjorth (exh. cat. by U. Linde, Stockholm, Mod. Mus., 1967–8)
Sven Erixson, Bror Hjorth (exh. cat. by U. Linde, Oslo, Kstnernes Hus, 1973)
Bror Hjorth (exh. cat. by S. Carlén, Göteborg, Kstmus., 1979)

Hjorth, Lauritz Adolph (*b* Rønne, Bornholm, 27 Dec 1834; *d* Rønne, 9 Dec 1912). Danish potter and ceramic manufacturer. He served his apprenticeship as a potter in the workshop of Edvard Christian Sonne (1810–76) and then travelled for three years through northern France, Switzerland and Germany, where he worked in various ceramic factories in the Rheinland stoneware region. In 1859 he founded the L. Hjorth's Terracotta factory in Rønne, where he produced simple, utilitarian wares. In 1862 he began to produce more artistic transfer-printed wares decorated with idyllic landscapes and flower motifs. In 1872 he set up a painter's studio at the factory and also sent fired wares to artists in Copenhagen, such as the painter and writer Holger Drachmann (1846–1908), for decoration. About 1870 Hjorth began to produce terracotta copies of Greek vases. His inspiration came from the painter Kristian Zahrtmann, who provided drawings and photographs of Greek vases to be used as models. In the 1890s the factory began to manufacture black pottery in Art Nouveau and old Nordic styles.

In 1902 Hjorth's son Hans Hjorth (1878–1966) began to experiment with stoneware clays from Bornholm and won a gold medal for his wares at the Exposition Universelle of 1910 in Brussels. This matt, greyish-brown stoneware, decorated with birds, flowers and fruit, dominated the factory's production. After Hjorth's death, the business was continued by his sons Peter Hjorth (1873–1959) and Hans Hjorth. One of the factory's specialities was cylindrical gallipots (drug jars), which were originally made for the pharmacy in Rønne (*c.* 1929) but continued to be made in the late 20th century for other purposes.

BIBLIOGRAPHY
P. Hjorth, M. Ertberg and H. Vensild: *L. Hjorth: En keramisk virksomhed i Rønne* [L. Hjorth: A pottery works in Rønne] (Rønne, 1977)

LENE OLESEN

HKPA. *See* HOWELL KILLICK PARTRIDGE & AMIS.

Hlebine school [Hlebinska slikarska škola; Hlebine Primitives]. Croatian group of painters who worked in Hlebine and the neighbouring village of Podravina, near Zagreb, from *c.* 1932. Its principal members included KRSTO HEGEDUŠIĆ, IVAN GENERALIĆ, Franjo Mraz (1910–81) and Mirko Virius (1889–1943). The first mention of the group was in 1932, when Hegedušić began to encourage peasants from the area to paint. The Croatian authorities at that time favoured an art programme based on a folk style and aimed at an authentic national artistic expression, and Hegedušić's idea corresponded with prevailing populist support for ruralism and its manifestation in various artistic media. An art independent of western European ideas was also preferred. Hegedušić exerted a strong influence on his collaborators (among the first of whom were Generalić and Mraz) through his use of rural motifs and his technique of painting on glass. He also organized several exhibitions in which the work of the Hlebine school was shown with that of the LAND GROUP (Zemlja). After World War II Generalić was the most important artist of the group to work in the region. The painters Franjo Filipović (*b* 1930), Dragan Gaži (1930–83), Mijo Kovačić (*b* 1935), Ivan Večenaj (*b* 1920), Martin Mehkek (*b* 1936), Ivan Lacković-Croata (*b* 1932) and Josip Generalić (*b* 1936) gathered round him and formed the 'second Hlebine school'. Unlike the first generation, who had been preoccupied with themes of social criticism, the second generation nostalgically evoked idyllic peasant life and labour and celebrated their beauty. The Hlebine Primitives became well known internationally, exhibiting at the Biennale in São Paulo in 1955 and at the Exposition Universelle et Internationale in Brussels in 1958. This frequent international exposure created the impression that their primitivist work was representative of modern Yugoslav art. Their most important works are in the Gallery of Primitive Art in Zagreb.

BIBLIOGRAPHY

Hlebinski krug-petdeset godina naivnog slikarstva [The Hlebine school of painting: fifty years of naive painting] (exh. cat. by M. Špoljar and T. Šola, Zagreb, Gal. Primitive A., 1981)

JURE MIKUŽ

Hlito, Alfredo (*b* Buenos Aires, 4 May 1923). Argentine painter. He studied at the Escuela Nacional de Bellas Artes in Buenos Aires from 1938 to 1942 and in 1945 was a founder-member of the ASOCIACIÓN ARTE CONCRETO INVENCIÓN. He played a leading role in the development of abstract art in Argentina during the 1940s and 1950s. From 1945 he worked in a Constructivist style that took as its starting-point the notion of a line fracturing the plane in the work of Joaquín Torres García; by the early 1950s this was elaborated into compositions of pure geometrical forms. From 1954 to 1962 he explored effects of vibrating colour, first using discernible forms conveyed in a pointillist technique and then by juxtaposing lightly applied flat brushstrokes in diluted colours to create a shimmering veil-like surface.

While living in Mexico from 1963 to 1973 Hlito developed a vocabulary of rhythmic, fundamentally organic forms using curved lines; these led to acrylic paintings in a vertical format in which vibrant atmospheres, interpenetrated by dynamic planes, generated monumental spaces of glittering colour. In 1976 he returned to earlier experiments but with a greater expressive force. In 1985 he was awarded the Premio Di Tella. He exhibited at the Salon des Réalités Nouvelles in Paris (1948), at the São Paulo Biennale (1954, 1975), at the Venice Biennale (1956) and at the second Exposition de l'Art Concret (Zurich, Ksthalle, 1960).

BIBLIOGRAPHY

R. Brill: *Hlito* (Buenos Aires, 1981)
Alfredo Hlito: Obra pictórica, 1945–1985 (exh. cat. by M. Nanni, Buenos Aires, Mus. N. B.A., 1987)

HORACIO SAFONS

Hlungwani [Hlungwane], **Jackson (Mbhazima)** (*b* Nkanyani, northern Transvaal, *c.* 1923). South African sculptor. He was taught by his father to use hand tools and extended his skills from the making of practical objects to representational carvings, which were first documented in the 1960s. But his period of intense activity as a sculptor was inaugurated by a religious vision around 1978, when he was planning suicide to find relief from ulcerous sores. As spiritual leader of his own sect, Hlungwani built a monumental stone shrine, his New Jerusalem, on a hilltop near Mbhokota in the northern Transvaal, and populated it with great carved images, which bear witness to his experience.

Hlungwani's sculpture brings together traditional Tsonga concepts and Christian theology, fusing time-honoured symbols from two cultures, a dichotomy that makes the works very personal. His many images of *Fish*, for example, may refer to biblical iconography, but are also private metaphors of the spirit, suggested by the free movement of fish in water. The representational carvings in raw indigenous woods combine bold form with delicately carved detail. His great skill as a visionary carver brought him recognition as an artist, and his works, although undoubtedly created as part of a personal belief system, became prized as art objects. Even the great altarpiece from New Jerusalem has been transposed into a museum setting at the University of the Witwatersrand Art Galleries, Johannesburg. While the dispersal of Hlungwani's works was problematic, their display in galleries and in a major exhibition in 1989 made them accessible to a wide and appreciative audience.

BIBLIOGRAPHY

Jekiseni Hlungwani Xagani (exh. cat., ed. R. Burnett; Johannesburg, Communic. Dept., BMW South Africa, 1989)

ELIZABETH RANKIN

Ho, Tao (*b* Shanghai, 17 July 1936). Hong Kong architect, designer, teacher and writer of Chinese birth. After leaving China for Hong Kong in 1949 he received his further education in the USA, where he studied art history at Williams College, Williamstown, MA (1956–60), and subsequently architecture at the Graduate School of Design, Harvard University, Cambridge, MA, under Sigfried Giedion and Josep Lluís Sert. After receiving his diploma in 1964 he briefly joined various American offices, among them Walter Gropius's TAC (The Architects Collaborative). After returning to Hong Kong, Ho worked for local architects before setting up his own practice, TAOHO Design, in 1968.

Ho worked in many fields of design, such as interior and graphic design, as well as architecture. His exhibition buildings, which formed the major part of his early career, include the Olivetti Pavilion for the C.M.A. exhibition, Hong Kong, in 1968 and the Hong Kong Government Pavilion for the C.M.A. exhibition, Hong Kong, in 1969. His first major commission was the extension (1975) to the International School, Repulse Bay, Hong Kong. The seven-storey building is notable for its roof-terrace playground and curved shape, which follows the contours of the site. The translation of traditional design elements into a modern idiom, an important element in his design philosophy and later work, was first introduced in the hexagonal 22-storey Hua Hsia Building (1975–7), Hong Kong, where the windows in particular were derived from

Chinese traditional forms. His reference to traditional architecture is dramatically applied in the Hong Kong Arts Centre (1974–7), a 19-storey complex housing two theatres, a concert hall and exhibition spaces. Built on a narrow site, its functions are expressed in its exterior form, a fact accentuated by the use of brightly coloured service ducts and vents. The parallel with traditional Chinese architecture lies explicitly in the use of structural features such as beams and spandrels to form decorative surface patterns, as in the Chinese pagoda. The Arts Centre, the first of its kind in the highly commercial environment of Hong Kong, reflects at a symbolic level Ho's view of the interrelatedness of architecture to the visual, dramatic and musical arts. This is a theme he has expounded in his writings.

Ho also designed a number of commercial buildings in Hong Kong, Toronto and Djakarta, and had an extensive practice designing interiors for corporate offices in Hong Kong. He participated in the International Design Competition for the Urban Environment of Developing Countries, organized in conjunction with the United Nations Habitat Conference (1979). Here, for the impoverished squatters of Manila, he developed the Basic Open Shell (BOS) system, consisting of standardized components that contain the necessary services and define the physical boundaries of the dwelling. From there each occupant can complete his or her own house according to individual preferences and financial constraints. As chairman of the Visual Arts Committee at the Hong Kong Arts Centre, Ho designed and organized c. 20 exhibitions. He also lectured widely, organized exhibitions in the USA and wrote several art historical publications.

WRITINGS
'Chinese Architecture and Town Planning, 1500 BC to AD 1911', *Landscape Archit.*, liv/4 (1963), p. 308
The Colour of Monet, The Sound of Debussy and the Spiritual Realm of Huang Pin-Hung (Hong Kong, 1978)

BIBLIOGRAPHY
M. Seelig: *The Architecture of Self-help Communities* (New York, 1978)
S. Cantacuzino: 'Tao Ho Tower', *Archit. Rev.* [London], clxvi/994 (1979), pp. 360–63
U. Kultermann: *Architekten der dritten Welt* (Cologne, 1980)
□

Hoadley, David (*b* Naugatuck, CT, 1774; *d* Waterbury, CT, 1839–40). American builder. He was brought up near Litchfield, CT, where the Scottish builder William Sprats (*c.* 1758–1810) had introduced a rich new ornamental vocabulary into the local vernacular, and he later moved to New Haven, CT, where he also came into contact with the technical innovations and more sophisticated Adamesque style of the English builder Peter Banner. Hoadley's work is associated with the architectural flowering that came in the wake of Sprats and Banner and distinguishes Federal architecture in central Connecticut. Whether Hoadley was a designer, or simply a builder and joiner is unclear. Undocumented attributions have been widely repeated, but with the exception of Yale's Philosophical building for which he made a plan in 1819, most are questionable. The most important is the United Church in New Haven (1813–15), which has often been cited as Hoadley's masterpiece but was, in fact, designed by Peter

Banner, Ithiel Town, and Ebenezer Johnson, although Hoadley was the contractor.

Hoadley's reputation rests securely on his skill in handling the constructional innovations of his time and his artistry as a joiner. Examples of his restrained ornamental style are Christ Church (1810), Bethany, CT, and the Congregational churches of North Milford [Orange], CT (1810), Norfolk, CT (1813), and Avon, CT (1818). Other notable works in which he is known to have had a part are the Nathan Smith (*c.* 1815) and DeForest (*c.* 1819) houses, New Haven (both destr. *c.* 1908), the Eli Whitney house (*c.* 1825; destr.) designed by Ithiel Town, New Haven, the Tontine Hotel (1827; destr.) also by Ithiel Town, New Haven, and the Samuel Russell house (1829) by Town and Davis, Middletown, CT.

BIBLIOGRAPHY
MEA
H. Bronson: *The History of Waterbury, Connecticut* (Waterbury, 1858)
E. E. Atwater, ed.: *History of the City of New Haven* (New York, 1887)
J. F. Kelly: *Early Connecticut Meetinghouses* (New York, 1948)
E. M. Brown: *The United Church on the Green, New Haven, Connecticut: An Architectural History* (New Haven, 1965)
W. H. Watkins: *David Hoadley, Connecticut Builder* (diss., Oneonta, State U. New York Coll., 1974)
ELIZABETH MILLS BROWN

Hoare (i). English family of bankers, patrons and collectors. The foundations of the family fortune were laid by Richard Hoare (1648–1718), a goldsmith who set up a banking business in 1672 at the sign of the Golden Bottle, 37 Fleet Street, London. He was knighted in 1702 and elected Lord Mayor of London in 1712. Of his 17 children, his son Henry Hoare the elder (1677–1724) continued the banking business and in 1717 bought property at Stourton, Wilts, thus initiating the family's connection with the STOURHEAD estate; he commissioned Colen Campbell to replace the existing building with a Palladian villa (1721–4). This was duly bequeathed to his son (1) Henry Hoare the younger, called the Magnificent, who was responsible for laying out the garden at Stourhead and for building up a notable collection of paintings; he also inherited a partnership in the bank. Henry's son died while on a Grand Tour in Naples in 1752, so that the estate passed to (2) Colt Hoare, son of his second daughter Anne and her cousin Richard Hoare (1734/5–87; created baronet in 1786). Among those who executed portraits of the family were the pastellist Francis Cotes (e.g. *Sir Richard Hoare*, 1757), William Hoare (*see* HOARE (ii), (1)) and Henry Edridge (*Colt Hoare in his Library*, 1820). The marriage of William's daughter Mary to Henry Hoare (1744–85), one of (1) Henry Hoare's nephews and active in the family bank, forged another link between the two families.

Although Sir Henry Ainslie Hoare (1824–94) sold some of the family heirlooms in 1883, many remain at Stourhead (all those mentioned in this article are there unless otherwise stated). On the death of Sir Henry Hugh Arthur Hoare (1865–1947) the house and garden were donated to the National Trust.

(1) Henry Hoare the younger (*b* ?London, 7 July 1705; *d* London, 8 Sept 1785). He began buying paintings for Stourhead around 1724. Among the English painters he patronized was John Wootton (e.g. *Hunting Group*, 1729). He also bought portraits and Italian views painted by

Arthur Pond, a dealer who further supplied him with engraved prints. Most of Hoare's collection was built up while he was in Italy *c.* 1738–41, during which time he collected paintings, sculptures and other items that were shipped home from Livorno and Venice.

Hoare continued to expand his collection after his return to England. In 1747 he purchased Nicolas Poussin's *Hercules at the Crossroads* at the sale following the death of James Brydges, 1st Duke of Chandos; later he was to acquire Poussin's *Rape of the Sabines* (New York, Met.). In 1758 he acquired Gaspard Dughet's *Landscape with Eurydice* through Sir Horace Mann in Florence. The following year, through the dealer Thomas Jenkins, he commissioned the *Meeting of Octavian and Cleopatra* from Anton Raphael Mengs. About this time Carlo Maratti's *Marchese Pallavicini Conducted by Apollo to the Temple of Fame* entered his collection, and during the 1760s he bought several paintings by Joseph Vernet. Horace Walpole visited Stourhead in 1762 and mentioned seeing paintings by Canaletto, Claude Lorrain and Rembrandt, among others ('Horace Walpole's Journals of Visits to Country Seats', *Walpole Soc.*, xvi (1928), pp. 41–3). Hoare also had several copies made after such Old Masters as Guido Reni and Guercino; the copy at Stourhead of Reni's *Salome with the Head of John the Baptist* (1639–40; Chicago, IL, A. Inst.) is attributed to Pompeo Batoni.

The extensive improvements to the gardens at Stourhead were mostly undertaken for Hoare between the 1740s and the 1770s. The architect Henry Flitcroft was responsible for the Temple of Flora (1744–6) and the Pantheon (1753–4). Hoare also commissioned several sculptures from Michael Rysbrack, most notably the marble *Hercules* (1756).

(2) Sir (Richard) Colt Hoare (*b* ?Barn Elms, London, 9 Dec 1758; *d* Stourton, 19 May 1838). Grandson of (1) Henry Hoare. Following his wife's death in 1785, and that of his grandfather a few months later, he was driven by deep unhappiness and a surplus of leisure to travel abroad. His prolonged Grand Tour lasted from 1785 until 1791, apart from one brief interlude at Stourhead. The artists he patronized included Carlo Labruzzi, Louis Ducros (e.g. *The Falls of Tivoli*, 1787), John 'Warwick' Smith and John Robert Cozens, from whom he was to buy several views of Italy, including *Lake Nemi*. Hoare's tour extended to Sicily, Malta, Switzerland, Spain and the Low Countries, but during the latter part of it, with Labruzzi, he became particularly interested in Etruscan remains in Italy and the course of the Appian Way. This awoke in him an enthusiasm for archaeology.

Following his return to Stourhead in 1791, Hoare began reorganizing its interiors. In 1793 building began on two new wings for the villa, in order to provide space for a picture gallery and a library. He also bought a substantial amount of furniture from Thomas Chippendale (ii). Although he had bought some Old Masters in Italy, his interest in painting was not particularly keen. He was, however, an early (if limited) patron of J. M. W. Turner, from whom he commissioned *Aeneas and the Sibyl, Lake Avernus* (*c.* 1798; London, Tate, Clore Gal.); he seems not to have responded to the work of John Constable, who visited Stourhead in 1811, and appears to have been

content to patronize minor artists, such as Samuel Woodforde (1763–1817) and Francis Nicholson.

The real heart of Stourhead during Colt Hoare's ownership was its library (completed 1802), in which he kept his ever-growing collection of books on British history, topography and travel. As the Napoleonic Wars made foreign travel virtually impossible, he spent much of his time thereafter travelling through Britain, particularly in Wales. He became a fellow of the Society of Antiquaries, and in 1806 he brought out an edition of Gerald of Wales's *Itinerary of Archbishop Baldwin through Wales, AD 1188*. He also began organizing digs in Wiltshire, in the course of which many barrows and mounds were opened up. His detailed research, undertaken with other antiquaries, led to the publication of his major works, *The Ancient History of South Wiltshire* (1812) and *The Ancient History of North Wiltshire* (1819). His other undertaking, *The History of Modern Wiltshire* (1822–43), which was to set new standards of scholarship for county histories, was completed after his death.

WRITINGS

A Description of the House and Gardens at Stourhead (Salisbury, 1800)
The Ancient History of South Wiltshire (London, 1812)
The Ancient History of North Wiltshire (London, 1819)
A Classical Tour through Italy and Sicily, 2 vols (London, 1819)
The History of Modern Wiltshire, 7 vols (London, 1822–43)

BIBLIOGRAPHY

DNB
K. Woodbridge: *Landscape and Antiquity: Aspects of English Culture at Stourhead, 1718 to 1838* (Oxford, 1970)
J. Gage: 'Turner and Stourhead: The Making of a Classicist?', *A. Q.* [Detroit], xxxvii (1974), pp. 59–87

Hoare (ii). English family of artists. The precise relationship between earlier generations of this family and the Hoare family of bankers (*see* HOARE (i)) is difficult to establish. In 1765, however, (1) William Hoare, who had established a fashionable portrait practice in Bath, was commissioned by his friend Henry Hoare the younger to decorate one of the temples at Stourhead, Wilts, although this work was not executed. William's eldest daughter, Mary Hoare (*c.* 1753–1820), was also an artist, and there are examples of her work, mostly in crayon, at Stourhead, which also has the most substantial holdings of paintings and sculpture by other members of the family. William's brother (2) Prince Hoare I was a sculptor, and his second son (3) Prince Hoare II was a painter who had considerable success as a playwright.

BIBLIOGRAPHY

DNB; Waterhouse: *18th C.*
E. Newby: 'The Hoares of Bath', *Bath Hist.*, i (1986), pp. 90–127

(1) William Hoare [of Bath] (*b* nr Eye, Suffolk, *c.* 1707; *d* Bath, 12 Dec 1792). Painter and printmaker. He received a gentleman's education in Faringdon, Berks. Showing a marked aptitude for drawing, he was sent to London to study under Giuseppe Grisoni, who had left Florence for London in 1715. When Grisoni returned to Italy in 1728, Hoare went with him, travelling to Rome and continuing his studies under the direction of Francesco Imperiali. He remained in Rome for nine years, returning to London in 1737. He failed to establish himself there and settled in Bath, an expanding spa town with a constant influx of visitors eager for portraits, whose needs he met by producing pastels influenced by Rosalba Carriera. He was closely involved with the running of the Royal Mineral Water Hospital in Bath from 1742 and became acquainted with its notable visitors and the neighbouring landed families. He obtained numerous commissions for oil portraits, the most important being for official portraits of political men (e.g. *William Pitt the Elder*, *c.* 1754; London, N.P.G.); there are several versions of most of these, suggesting that he had a studio, and they were further publicized by the production of mezzotints by leading engravers of the day. Hoare himself was a delicate etcher and published a number of private plates, mostly of family and friends, including *Miss Hoare* (probably Mary), *Henry Somerset, 3rd Duke of Beaufort* and *Christopher Anstey* (all London, BM).

In 1752, after a tour of France and the Netherlands cut short by his sister's death, Hoare made another attempt to settle in London, encouraged by important commissions from the Pelham family. There he became a member of the Society for the Encouragement of Arts, Manufacture and Commerce (Society of Arts), but, unable to compete with Francis Cotes and Allan Ramsay, he soon returned to Bath, where his position was assured. The city was now beginning its second major period of expansion, and potential sitters remained numerous, a situation that attracted painters of the calibre of Thomas Gainsborough to live there. Hoare, however, was returning to his early aspirations to be a history painter. In 1766 he was commissioned to paint a large altarpiece of the *Pool of Bethesda* (Bath, Mason. Hall) for the newly built Octagon Chapel in Bath, and he had already begun to produce mildly erotic and very popular pastels with Classical themes, such as two works entitled *A Nymph* and a third entitled *Sleeping Nymph* (all Stourhead, Wilts, NT). These were based on recollections of antique statues studied in Rome or admired in the great houses to which he had access.

Hoare exhibited fairly regularly in London, in 1761 and 1762 at the Society of Artists, where he showed such works as *Dr Oliver and Mr Peirce Examining Patients* (Bath, Royal N. Hosp. Rheumatic Diseases), and from 1770 at the Royal Academy, of which he became a founder-member in 1768 at the special request of George III. Because of his continued residence away from London, however, he played little part in the activities of the Academy. He last exhibited there in 1779 and painted little after that date. He founded no school: indeed, during his long career he occasionally reflected the styles of his younger contemporaries. He remained the respected and sympathetic doyen of Bath artists and gave encouragement to such figures as Alexander Cozens, Ozias Humphry and Thomas Lawrence, for whose studies in Italy he offered to pay.

BIBLIOGRAPHY

'The Note-books of George Vertue', *Walpole Soc.*, xxii (1934) [indexed in xxix (1940–42)]

M. Holbrook: 'Painters in Bath in the Eighteenth Century', *Apollo*, xcviii (1973), pp. 375–84

William Hoare of Bath RA, 1707–92 (exh. cat. by E. Newby, Bath, Victoria A.G., 1990)

(2) Prince Hoare I (*b* ?nr Eye, Suffolk, *c.* 1711; *d* Bath, 5 Nov 1769). Sculptor, brother of (1) William Hoare. He trained under Peter Scheemakers (ii) in London, after which he followed his brother to Bath. There he received a number of commissions, both for monuments and for busts—for example the marble bust of *Philip Dormer Stanhope, 4th Earl of Chesterfield* (1741; London, Ranger's House). Hoare was in Italy for much of the 1740s, returning to Bath in 1749; two years later he married a wealthy heiress, although he continued his career as a sculptor. In 1759 he made a number of statues for Henry Hoare (i) the younger at Stourhead, Wilts, and in 1760–62 he carved chimney-pieces for Corsham Court, Wilts. He remained active principally as a sculptor of busts and monuments: in 1761, for example, he made a bust of *Richard 'Beau' Nash* (Bath, Guildhall) and a church monument to the poet *Alexander Pope* (Twickenham, London, St Mary).

BIBLIOGRAPHY

Gunnis

M. Whinney: *Sculpture in Britain, 1530–1830*, Pelican Hist. A. (Harmondsworth, 1964, rev. J. Physick, 1988), p. 457, n. 20

(3) Prince Hoare II (*bapt* Bath, 9 Oct 1755; *d* Brighton, 22 Dec 1834). Painter and writer, son of (1) William Hoare. He showed an early aptitude for drawing, closely fostered by his father. He won a prize for a drawing of outlines from the Society of Arts in 1772 and in 1773 entered the Royal Academy Schools. He was greatly infuenced by a trip to Italy in 1776, first to Florence, then to Rome. In Rome he became a valued member of Henry Fuseli's circle, which included such artists as Johan Tobias Sergel, Henry Tresham and James Northcote, all of whom were intent on expressing an emotionally charged version of Neo-classicism. The effects of this can be seen in Hoare's *Roman Sketchbook* (London, V&A). He also visited Naples and travelled home through northern Italy and Venice, where he contributed to the series of artists' self-portraits collected at the Uffizi in Florence (*c.* 1779–80; *in situ*). This Italian period was the most fruitful of his career. Soon after Hoare's return to England, in 1780, Thomas Macklin approached him for subjects for his projected Poets' Gallery, but although Hoare exhibited both portraits and history paintings at the Royal Academy until 1785, increasing ill-health forced him to abandon painting. After a recuperative visit to Portugal in 1788 he returned to London and began to write light comedies. These were often set to music by Stephen Storace (1763–96), and such works as *No Song, No Supper* (1789) and *The Prize* (1792) met with considerable success. Hoare maintained not only the friendships he had made in Rome, notably with Fuseli and Northcote, but also his interest in the art world, collecting biographical material on British artists. A gifted linguist, he became in 1799 the Secretary for Foreign Correspondence at the Royal Academy and discussed with Joseph Farington the propriety of publishing that body's transactions, which Hoare collected and arranged as *Academic Annals of Painting* (London, 1805–9). He also published several books of criticism, including *Epochs of the Arts* (London, 1813). In his later years he lived mainly in Brighton for his health and died there from the delayed effects of a carriage accident.

BIBLIOGRAPHY

J. Farington: *Diaries* (1793–1821); ed. K. Garlick and A. Mackintyre (i–vi) and K. Cave (vii–xvi) as *The Diaries of Joseph Farington*, 16 vols (New Haven and London, 1978–84; index in preparation)

The Fuseli Circle in Rome: Early Romantic Art of the 1770s (exh. cat., ed. N. L. Pressley; New Haven, CT, Yale Cent. Brit. A., 1979)

EVELYN NEWBY

Hoban, James (*b* Kilkenny, Ireland, *c*. 1758; *d* Washington, DC, 8 Dec 1831). American architect of Irish birth. He studied architecture under the guidance of Thomas Ivory at the Dublin Society's School of Architectural Drawing *c*. 1779. Faced with limited professional prospects in Ireland, Hoban emigrated to the USA in 1785, settling first in Philadelphia. Two years later he moved to Charleston, SC, where private residences and public buildings such as the former State House (1789; now a court-house) are attributed to him. In 1787 he met George Washington, who was then on a tour through the southern states; this meeting led to Hoban's participation in the competition of 1792 for the design of the President's House (now the White House; *see also* WASHINGTON, DC, fig. 6). He won with a design for a three-storey rectangular stone building, with a projecting central section of engaged columns above a heavy base. The central section and the floor plan resembled Leinster House, Dublin, the residence of the Dukes of Leinster, built in 1745. After the competition, Washington altered the design to provide additional stone embellishments and an extension of the outer dimensions of the house.

Following his success in the competition, Hoban left Charleston and settled in Washington, DC, where he supervised the construction of the President's House and other public works projects in the city, including the US Capitol building. Among his private commissions was Blodgett's Hotel (1793–4; destr.). After the President's House was burnt by the British in 1814, Hoban was invited to design and supervise the rebuilding of the house, a process that was completed in 1820. He also oversaw the rebuilding of the State and War Department structures (1818–20; destr.), which flanked the President's House to the east and the west respectively. Hoban remained in Washington until his death, serving on its city council and designing and building many of its modest Federal style private buildings.

DAB

BIBLIOGRAPHY

F. D. Owen: 'The First Government Architect: James Hoban of Charleston, SC', *Archit. Rec.*, xi (1901), pp. 581–9
D. D. Reiff: *Washington Architecture, 1791–1861: Problems in Development* (Washington, DC, 1971–7)
W. Seale: *The President's House*, 2 vols (Washington, DC, 1986)

ANTOINETTE J. LEE

Hobbema, Meindert [Meyndert] (*b* Amsterdam, *bapt* 31 Oct 1638; *d* Amsterdam, 7 Dec 1709). Dutch painter. Although limited in subject-matter and working from a remarkably narrow repertory of motifs and compositional devices, he nonetheless managed to imbue his area of specialization—the wooded landscape—with memorable vitality.

1. Life and work. 2. Critical reception and posthumous reputation

1. LIFE AND WORK.

(i) Early career, before 1663. The son of Lubbert Meyndertsz., a carpenter, Meindert adopted the surname 'Hobbema' at an early age, although it appears to have had no family precedent. In 1653, together with his younger brother and sister, he was taken into the care of the Amsterdam orphanage. Two years later he had left this institution, and it was then, or shortly after, that he entered the studio of the Haarlem landscape painter Jacob van Ruisdael, who had recently moved to Amsterdam. On 8 July 1660 Ruisdael testified that Hobbema had 'served and learned with him for some years'. In spite of his period of apprenticeship with Ruisdael, Hobbema's paintings from the 1650s are river scenes that show the impact of Cornelis Vroom and Salomon van Ruysdael. His earliest dated work is a *View of a River* (1658; Detroit, MI, Inst. A.). This modest painting, executed when the artist was only 20, reveals a tranquil setting with a diagonally slanting riverbank along which slender, insubstantial trees, cottages and several figures are placed at gentle intervals. It is broadly painted with muted greens, browns and greys. The general composition of the painting, in particular the silhouetting of the somewhat awkward trees against a light sky, is reminiscent of Salomon van Ruysdael's works of the mid-1650s.

Around 1662 the influence of his famous master Jacob van Ruisdael became markedly visible in Hobbema's work. In particular, a number of landscapes with water-mills from this year take their central motif and other elements from Ruisdael's *Water-mill* (1661; Amsterdam, Rijksmus.). A typical example of Hobbema's dependence is *Landscape with Water-mill* (Toledo, OH, Mus. A.), undated but evidently painted during 1662, which is an almost exact copy of Ruisdael's painting. Hobbema's touch, however, is broader and his tones brighter, especially in the light-filled middle distance; the melancholic, more brooding quality that infuses Ruisdael's work with so much mystery is absent.

(ii) Middle period, 1663–8. The period of close alignment with Ruisdael was short-lived. Hobbema's later paintings from the 1660s, which are on a larger, more ambitious scale, show a greater spatial clarity and expansiveness, a more fluid touch and a heightened sense of colour. The years between 1663 and 1668 were the most productive in his career. In his *Wooded Landscape: The Path on the Dyck* (1663; see fig. 1), the strong vertical accent of the central cluster of spindly trees with their lacy foliage is relieved by the two pathways, which plunge in diverging directions and on plateaux of varying levels into the distance. This double vanishing-point is frequently repeated in Hobbema's work and gives his compositions a feeling of freshness they would otherwise lack. By reducing the horizon line, greater emphasis is given to the sky with its huge billowing clouds, which echo the sprawling mass of trees and shrubbery below. His palette is full of subtle variations of bright green, yellow, grey and brown, which produce an overall silvery tonality. Also characteristic of Hobbema is the shaded foreground, with occasional flickers of half-light that lengthen the cast shadows of figures and cows and contrast with an area of intense light in the background. As with much of Hobbema's work, this painting gives the impression that although he has taken his original inspiration from nature, his final conception is formed by a desire to present landscape as an idyllic environment, ordered and regulated by man. The staffage

1. Meindert Hobbema and Adriaen van de Velde: *Wooded Landscape: The Path on the Dyck*, oil on canvas, 1.1×1.3 m, 1663 (Dublin, National Gallery of Ireland)

was painted by Adriaen van de Velde, who often collaborated with Hobbema.

In a number of paintings from *c.* 1665, among them *The Water-mill* (London, Wallace), Hobbema returned to a theme with which he is closely associated. The subject of the water-mill was a particular favourite of Hobbema and he painted it on over 30 occasions. Variously interpreted as a symbol of the transience of human life and as a wonder of modern industry, it is difficult to determine with certainty what associations the water-mill evoked for a contemporary audience. A number of Hobbema's landscapes have also been shown to be representations of actual mills found on the estate of Singraven near Denekamp in the province of Overijssel, and he may have accompanied Ruisdael on a sketching trip to this area. The specific mill in the above-mentioned painting and that in a close variant (Chicago, IL, A. Inst.) have not been identified. Unlike his earlier paintings of this subject, which were closely based on Ruisdael, the water-mill is placed less conspicuously in the middle distance and flooded by a brilliant light that spreads to the distant prospect glimpsed through the slender tree-trunks and feathery leafage.

With the *Wooded Landscape* (1667; Malibu, CA, Getty Mus.) the beginning of a new period of restraint and stillness can be detected. A greater freedom of brushstroke is apparent also, and foliage that was previously more precisely delineated is now summarily indicated. The juxtaposition of a darkened foreground, where shadows shimmer on the glassy surface of the water, with the sunlit fields beyond, greatly accentuates the sense of distance. The lively figures punctuating the banks of the pool, together with the billowing clouds and soaring birds, successfully create the impression of a wild and blustery day. In his *Forest Pond* (1668; Oberlin Coll., OH, Allen Mem. A. Mus.), Hobbema created an even more simplified composition with less elaborate trees carefully placed around a gently rippling brook. Also noticeable is the sketchy manner in which the grass and vegetation in the right foreground is painted. The mood here is again one of calm, achieved through a harmonious distribution of the pictorial elements.

Townscape is a rarity in Hobbema's oeuvre and the *View of the Haarlem Lock and the Herring-packers' Tower, Amsterdam* (London, N.G.) is his only widely accepted work in this genre. This marvellously vivid glimpse of Amsterdam canal life is an accurate portrayal of one of the city's principal sluice-gates and surrounding architecture. Although it has been dated to before 1662 (since it is known from later topographical sources that alterations were made to some of the buildings in that year), it is much more likely on stylistic grounds to have been executed in the latter half of the decade.

2. Meindert Hobbema: *Avenue of Trees at Middelharnis*, oil on canvas, 1.03×1.41 m, 1689 (London, National Gallery)

(iii) Late works, 1668–1709. In October 1668, Hobbema married Eeltje Pieters Vinck, four years his elder and kitchen-maid to the Amsterdam burgomaster Lambert Reynst. Hobbema must have maintained his links with his teacher during these years, as Ruisdael acted as a witness to the marriage. At this time also, Hobbema became a wine-gauger to the Amsterdam customs; this was a minor salaried post (which he held until his death), involving the supervision of the weighing and measuring of imported wines. It was long thought that Hobbema all but ceased to paint after his marriage and his subsequent municipal appointment. However, a revised reading of previously accepted dates on a number of established paintings and the discovery of new works has resulted in the reassessment of a small body of late landscapes. Nevertheless, it is apparent that Hobbema's activity as a painter greatly declined after 1668, and there are no certain paintings from the last two decades of his long life.

A decline in his artistic powers is also discernible in some of these late works. His painting of the *Ruins of Brederode Castle* (1671; London, N.G.), a picturesque structure near Haarlem that had suffered great damage in the Eighty Years War, lacks the inventiveness of earlier designs and is contrived in appearance. The trees that frame the ruined castle on a hill in the middle distance are thin and lifeless, their outlines brittle against a pale sky. There is a lack of modulation in the painting of the ruins and the general effete approach is emphasized by the awkward variations in tone and harsh colouring. The ducks, placed prominently in the foreground, are by a different hand, probably that of Dirck Wijntrack (before 1625–78). However, Hobbema still had one last ace to play, and his best-known work from these later years is the *Avenue of Trees at Middelharnis* (1689; see fig. 2). Hobbema's conception of a tree-lined avenue with a view of a distant town beyond receding perpendicularly from the picture plane is markedly in contrast to similar landscape compositions by Aelbert Cuyp and Jan van Kessel, a fellow pupil of Ruisdael with whom Hobbema is known to have remained in contact. Greater spaciousness is achieved by minimizing the number of trees to two slender rows that define both the depth and the height of the composition. The painting differs from other 17th-century Dutch landscapes not only in its highly organized and symmetrical design but also in the inclusion of a gardener actively engaged in tending saplings. Indeed, attention has been drawn to the contrast between the more rugged view of nature on the left and the nurtured plantation in the right foreground. Hobbema's final years must have been difficult, not only financially but also because he had to endure the deaths of his two children and that of his wife in 1704. He was buried in a pauper's grave.

Hobbema was also apparently active as a draughtsman, although no signed drawings by him are known. Giltay has attributed a group of seven drawings to him, including five of water-mills. Given the paucity of surviving work by Hobbema in this medium compared to other 17th-century Dutch landscape artists, preparatory drawings may only have played a minor part in his working method.

2. CRITICAL RECEPTION AND POSTHUMOUS REPUTATION. To judge from the few followers he attracted and from his failure to receive even a brief mention by Arnold Houbraken, Hobbema's achievements as painter must have been overlooked by his contemporaries. His name seldom appears in 17th- or 18th-century auction catalogues and his work often realized quite low prices. Indeed, it was well into the 19th century before he was rescued from obscurity; as late as 1859 the French art historian Théophile Thoré [pseud. Willem Bürger], who did much to rekindle interest in overlooked Dutch masters, bemoaned the lack of appreciation of Hobbema. However, it was in England in the second half of the century that the taste for Hobbema, and for his master Ruisdael, reached new heights, stimulated in part by the praise heaped on naturalistic Dutch landscape painting by artists such as Turner and Constable. Earlier, Hobbema had also been held in great affection by the Norwich school of landscape painters, especially by John Crome, whose *Poringland Oak* (London, Tate) recalls the work of the Dutch master in its treatment of a gnarled oak against a glowing sky with vistas into the distance. The collecting of Hobbema's work also grew apace during these years, and in 1850 at The Hague, Richard Seymour-Conway, 4th Marquess of Hertford, paid what was then a record price for a landscape when he bought *The Water-mill* (London, Wallace) for 27,000 guilders.

BIBLIOGRAPHY
W. Stechow: 'The Early Years of Hobbema', *A. Q.* [Detroit], xxii (1959), pp. 3–18
——: *Dutch Landscape Painting of the Seventeenth Century* (London, 1966)
J. Giltay: 'De tekeningen van Jacob van Ruisdael', *Oud-Holland*, xciv (1980), pp. 141–208 [with Eng. summary]
Masters of 17th-century Dutch Landscape Painting (exh. cat., ed. P. C. Sutton; Amsterdam, Rijksmus.; Boston, MA, Mus. F.A.; Philadelphia, PA, Mus. A.; 1987–8)

JOHN LOUGHMAN

Hobbs, Brockunier, & Co. American glass manufactory. In 1845 the firm of Barnes, Hobbs & Co. was established in Wheeling, WV, by John L. Hobbs (1804–81) and James B. Barnes (*d* 1849), who had both worked for the New England Glass Co. In 1863 the firm became Hobbs, Brockunier & Co., and comprised Hobbs, his son John H. Hobbs, company bookkeeper Charles W. Brockunier and a silent partner, William Leighton sr (1808–91), son of Thomas H. Leighton (1786–1849) of the New England Glass Co. William Leighton was a scientist and superintendent of the firm, and his son William Leighton jr (1833–1911) succeeded him on his retirement in 1867.

By 1879 Hobbs, Brockunier & Co. was one of the largest glass factories in the USA and was making fine cut and engraved lead crystal, as well as an extensive range of pressed glass using the soda-lime formula developed by Leighton sr. This formula revolutionized pressed-glass making after 1865. The firm's great success during the Aesthetic period in America can be traced to the expertise of the company's members, whose previous associations had prepared them for producing exquisite art glass in a wide range of colours, patterns and textures. But it was the fancy glass in the Aesthetic taste that secured the firm's reputation. 'Craquelle', a crackled glass, was the first of a long line of these art wares. In addition to types using opal and shaded effects, the firm also made spangled glass with flecks of gold or silver foil in clear glass overlaid with tinted glass. Its most famous line was 'Peachblow', begun in 1886, to imitate a transmutational glaze used on Chinese porcelain known as peach-bloom.

The firm's success was brought to an end by the retirement of Brockunier and Leighton jr in 1887. Although Hobbs continued the works, the poor economic climate of the era adversely affected the business, which was taken over by the United State Glass Co. in 1891.

BIBLIOGRAPHY
D. B. Burke and others: *In Pursuit of Beauty: Americans and the Aesthetic Movement* (New York, 1986), pp. 440–41

ELLEN PAUL DENKER

Hobbs, Sir Joseph John Talbot (*b* London, 24 Aug 1864; *d* at sea, 21 April 1938). Australian architect of English birth. He was educated in London and worked as draughtsman for a builder, John Hurst. In 1886 he emigrated to Western Australia and established an architectural practice in Perth in 1887. From 1905 he was in partnership with E. H. Dean Smith (1860/1–1906) and W. J. Waldie Forbes. In 1891 Hobbs won a competition for the Weld Club, corner of Esplanade and Barrack Street, Perth, a red-brick, Queen Anne style building with a square tower completed in 1892. Hobbs was particularly adept in the classical style, many variations of which pervade his commercial work. Examples include the grandiose Italian Renaissance Revival Western Australian Bank (1891) and the Baroque Revival Victoria Hall (1896), both in High Street, Fremantle, and the rich Italianate façade of Samson's Offices (1899), Cliff Street, Fremantle; his buildings were some of the most popularly admired in Perth and Fremantle 50 years after his death. His church and university college buildings employed Gothic and Tudor elements (e.g. Scots Presbyterian Church, 1890, Fremantle), and his residential work included interpretations in the Arts and Crafts manner of the vernacular Australian homestead (e.g. 56 The Esplanade, 1896, Peppermint Grove). He was awarded the Street Architecture Medal for Newspaper House (1935; destr.), Perth, and was President of the Western Australian Institute of Architects. Hobbs also had a distinguished military career; he attained the rank of Lt-General and was created KCB (1918) and KCMG (1919). He died en route to the unveiling of a war memorial built to his design at Villers-Bretonneux, a French town recaptured under his command in World War I.

UNPUBLISHED SOURCES
Perth, Battye Lib. [copy of O. F. Watts: *Lieut. Gen. Sir John Joseph Talbot Hobbs* (1961); with extensive bibliog.]
BIBLIOGRAPHY
J. S. Battye: *The Cyclopedia of Western Australia* (Perth, 1912/*R* 1985)
I. Molyneux: *Looking Around Perth* (Perth, 1981)

IAN MOLYNEUX

Hobé, Georges (*b* Brussels, 7 Jan 1854; *d* Brussels, 6 March 1936). Belgian architect and designer. He was the son of a joiner and cabinetmaker and began his career as an interior and furniture designer. His lack of academic training allowed him to join up quickly with the precursors of the Art Nouveau style. In 1895 he exhibited several chairs at the second Salon de la Libre Esthétique; this work followed by the design of a shop in Rue Montagne de la Cour, placed him among the main protagonists of the new style in Brussels. Together with Paul Hankar, Henry Van de Velde and Gustave Serrurier-Bovy, Hobé was commissioned to design the Exposition Congolaise at Tervuren, part of the Exposition Internationale (1897), which became an expression of Belgian Art Nouveau at its peak. During this period, he also undertook a trip abroad and studied traditional cottages in southern England. Their architecture and interiors became his chief source of inspiration, and he built numerous houses in this style in the main holiday resorts of Belgium. The interiors he showed at the Esposizione Internazionale d'Arte Decorativa in Turin (1902) and the Esposizione Internazionale del Sempione in Milan (1906), which combined the lines of Art Nouveau with the sobriety of English furniture, received international attention. Between 1906 and 1913 he completed several projects for the Casino and the outskirts of the citadel of Namur, which showed a progressive integration of motifs from the classical tradition. He also worked on various projects for King Léopold II on the coast and at Tervuren. Hobé played an important role in spreading the popularity of English domestic architecture and furniture, which were considered to be models of comfort and sobriety. His studio contributed to the training of many outstanding architectural figures, including Antoine Pompe, Fernand Bodson and P. L. Kramer.

BIBLIOGRAPHY

Antoine Pompe et l'effort moderne en Belgique, 1890–1940 (exh. cat., eds M. Culot and F. Terlinden; Brussels, Mus. Ixelles, 1969)

ERIC HENNAUT

Hobson, Robert Lockhart (*b* 26 July 1872; *d* Horsham, Sussex, 5 June 1941). English art historian. In 1897 he joined the staff of the British Museum, London, to assist in the preparation of catalogues of English pottery and porcelain. This subject remained of interest even after his move to the study of Chinese ceramics in 1909, when he compiled a catalogue on this subject for an exhibition held in 1910 by the Burlington Fine Arts Club. His *Chinese Pottery and Porcelain*, a comprehensive history in which he made extensive use of original Chinese texts, remains an essential reference source. In 1921 he became Keeper of Oriental Antiquities at the British Museum, retiring in 1933. He was a founder-member of the Oriental Ceramic Society, the leading society for the study of Asian art in Britain, and he worked with other members of the society's council in the organization of the International Exhibition of Chinese Art (London, RA, 1935–6), the first exhibition in Europe to show objects from the Chinese imperial collections. His other major works examine Chinese ceramics of the Ming (1368–1644) and Qing (1644–1911) periods. He also compiled valuable catalogues of the Chinese ceramic collections of Sir Percival David and Leonard Gow, and of the George Eumorfopoulos collection of Chinese, Korean and Persian pottery and porcelain.

WRITINGS

Handbook of Marks on Pottery and Porcelain (London, 1909, rev. 1912)
Exhibition of Early Chinese Pottery and Porcelain (exh. cat., London, Burlington F.A. Club, 1910)
Chinese Pottery and Porcelain, 2 vols (London, 1915/*R* in 1 vol., New York, 1976)
with A. L. Hetherington: *The Art of the Chinese Potter from the Han Dynasty to the End of the Ming* (London, 1923/ *R* New York, 1982)
The Wares of the Ming Dynasty (London, 1923)
Handbook of the Pottery and Porcelain of the Far East in the Department of Oriental Antiquities, London, BM cat. (London, 1924)
The Later Ceramic Wares of China (London, 1925)
The George Eumorfopoulos Collection: Catalogue of the Chinese, Corean and Persian Pottery and Porcelain, 6 vols (London, 1925–8)
Catalogue of the Leonard Gow Collection of Chinese Porcelain (London, 1931)
with others: *Chinese Ceramics in Private Collections* (London, 1931)
A Guide to the Islamic Pottery of the Near East, London, BM cat. (London, 1932)
A Catalogue of Chinese Pottery and Porcelain in the Collection of Sir Percival David (London, 1934)

MARGARET MEDLEY

Höch, Hannah (Johanne) (*b* Gotha, 1 Nov 1889; *d* Berlin, 31 May 1978). German painter and photomontagist. She moved to Berlin in 1912 to study at the Städtischen Kunstgewerbe- und Handwerksschule Charlottenburg. Her course was interrupted by the outbreak of World War I, and she then enrolled at the Lehranstalt des Kunstgewerbemuseums in Berlin, where she studied under Emil Orlik until 1920. She had a relationship with RAOUL HAUSMANN from 1915 to 1922, and through him came into contact with the literary and artistic circle that formed the Club Dada (*see* DADA) in 1918. The collective activities of this avant-garde movement came to a climax between 1918 and 1922 in exhibitions, demonstrations and multimedia events. PHOTOMONTAGE, which was its own expressive art form, was created by Höch and Hausmann in 1918, partly as a response to the instability of the war years, and partly as an anti-academic alternative to German Expressionism.

Höch's best-known photomontage, *Cut with the Dada Kitchen Knife through the Last Era of the Weimar Beer-belly Culture* (1140×900 mm, 1919–20; Berlin, Alte N.G.), was exhibited at the First International Dada Fair in 1920. It represented post-war confusion and misery, political upheaval and the consolidation of a young republic; Höch laid out the contemporary images rhythmically, in order to convey the pace and heterogeneity of this revolution. Her other early photomontages show isolated, exposed objects in abstract spatial constructions. She put them together in three thematic cycles entitled *From an Ethnographic Museum* (1925–9), *Love* (*c.* 1926; see Adriani, p. 164) and *Portraits* (1924–30), which included *The Melancholic* (1925; see Adriani, p. 148). She was particularly interested in the ironic banter concerning the 'new' type of woman, which was propagated at that time.

Höch's paintings of the 1920s show a similar tension between abstract–constructivist creative tendencies and objective–surreal compositions. A few of them, for example *Rome* (900×1060 mm, 1925; Berlin, Berlin. Gal.), simulate the constituent elements of photomontage and demonstrate a lively interaction between the different areas of her work. Asta Nielsen and Benito Mussolini appear among silhouetted architectural quotes, and the actress sends Mussolini out of the square. Other works from this period come close to Magic Realism in the striking way the objects are depicted. In the 1920s Höch also began to design patterns for materials and wallpaper (some are now in the V&A, London), and produced linowork, fashion drawings, illustrations for book covers, as well as costume and theatre designs for the planned *Anti-Revue* of KURT SCHWITTERS. In 1922 and 1923 she installed two 'grottoes' in Schwitters's *Merzbau* (destr. 1943).

In 1926 Höch met the Dutch author Til Brugman (1888–1956), living with her until 1929 in The Hague and then until 1935 in Berlin. The move to Germany was the first step towards an inner exile. Despite the threat of persecution she worked on. Numerous photomontages and paintings were created in response to contemporary political events. *Trainer* (collage, *c.* 1930; Zurich, Ksthaus; see fig.) and the *Strong Men* (collage, 245×135 mm, 1931; Stuttgart, Inst. Auslandsbeziehungen) play on the body-building muscle-men image of the Nazi Brownshirts. In combining the impressive masculine pose with fragments of female bodies Höch introduced the theme of the struggle of the sexes into her work. At the same time the expressive aspect of her painting became increasingly important. The composition became more dynamic by applying the colour smoothly or splashing it on and by increasingly purifying the figurative images. Höch had been classed as a 'cultural Bolshevist' by the Nazis, and she completed her process of withdrawal in 1939 when she moved to the protective isolation of Heiligensee, a rural suburb of Berlin.

Höch's *Pictures of Times of Misery* all sprang from impressions of contemporary events. In *Wild Uprising* (oil on canvas, 940×820 mm, 1933) and *1945 (The End)* (oil on canvas, 940×810 mm, 1945; both Berlin, Berlin. Sparkasse) she used visionary codes to depict epochal events. In the first example a figure springs out of a huge boorish body, looking resolutely out of the picture, but in the second picture it sways like a lifeless shell. This forced expressiveness could be interpreted as a protest against Fascist art legislation. Compared to the dramatizing of the content and form of pictures, many photomontages kept their subtle, cutting irony. The persecutor of the *Flight* (collage, 230×184 mm, 1931; Stuttgart, Inst. Auslandsbeziehungen) was thus transformed into a chicken with wasted limbs. The *Seven Mile Boots* (collage, 229×322 mm, 1937; Hamburg, Ksthalle) illustrates a promising means of locomotion, to escape from a national, petty-bourgeois landscape. After World War II the points of emphasis in the photomontages and pictures shifted. Höch anchored concrete symbols of sentimental personal value, which were associative and related to reality, in geometric spatial constructions; in place of mocking ironic details, the collages were more like surreal abstractions and the titles were a guide to their interpretation.

The many sides of reality, which were previously expressed by the stylistic heterogeneity of Höch's work, were transposed in her later work by exposing the inner crystalline structures. She turned to the secret world of forms, in order to deprive tangible reality of its true terms of existence and so to disclose the way in which these terms worked. In such photomontages as *Fata Morgana* (212×282 mm, 1957; Düsseldorf, Gal. Remmert & Barth)

Hannah Höch: *Trainer*, collage, 355×260 mm, *c.* 1930 (Zurich, Kunsthaus Zürich); the original is completed by a brown leather frame

Höch was successful in creating complete coherence between motif and image. The aesthetic transformation is totally in accord with the hidden meaning of the object. However, the late works all express the secret poetry of an unseen cosmic order. Here her artistic intentions were close to those of Max Ernst, Paul Klee or Meret Oppenheim. Like Höch, they were all searching for an aesthetic analogy to the universal regular laws of nature. Appreciation of Höch's work grew particularly after the 1970s.

BIBLIOGRAPHY
G. Adriani, ed.: *Hannah Höch: Fotomontagen-Gemälde-Aquarelle* (Cologne, 1980)
J. Dech: *Hannah Höch: Schnitt mit dem Kuchenmesser Dada-Spiegel einer Bierbauchkultur* (Frankfurt am Main, 1989)
Hannah Höch: Eine Lebens-Collage: Archiv-Edition (Berlin, 1989)
Hannah Höch, 1889–1978: Ihr Werk, ihr Leben, ihre Freunde (exh. cat., Berlin, Berlin. Gal., 1989)
J. Dech and E. Maurer, eds: *Da-dazwischen Reden zu Hannah Höch: Dokumentation des internationalen Hannah-Höch-Symposium* (Berlin, 1991)
M. Lavin: *Hannah Höch, Photomontage and the Representation of the New Woman in Weimar Germany, 1918–1933* (New York, 1991)
E. Maurer: *Das malerische Werk von Hannah Höch bis 1945* (diss., U. Munich, 1991)
ELLEN MAURER

Hocheder, Karl (*b* Weiherhammer, 7 March 1854; *d* Munich, 21 Jan 1917). German architect. He was one of the most important exponents of late historicist architecture in southern Germany. He studied architecture (1874–8) at the Technische Hochschule, Munich, where in 1881 he became assistant to Friedrich von Thiersch. After serving as building assessor in Amberg (1883) and Munich (1886), he became building officer of Munich (1889) and professor of building studies at the Technische Hochschule (1899–1917). Apart from residential and religious buildings he produced a number of public buildings for the city in a style based on the contemporary south German Renaissance and Baroque Revival idioms using a picturesque ensemble of forms. His Müllersches Volksbad (1899–1901), Munich, one of the most successful examples of a large public bath, of which many were being built at this period, was of national importance. Its individual functional parts (large and small bath-halls, a Turkish bath, water-tower and heating building) are clearly identifiable from outside. The spatial conception owes something to Roman baths and the details show sparing *Jugendstil* ornamentation. His last and most extensive work was the large Baroque Revival complex of the Bavarian Ministry of Transport (1905–13; largely destr. 1945) in Munich. Its large, ribbed dome, 32 m in diameter, was regarded as a pioneering work of reinforced concrete construction. Outside Munich he designed mansions and country houses in Bavaria (e.g. at Murnau and Weilheim), and in the South Tyrol (e.g. at Levico [now in Italy]), as well as the Baroque Revival Rathaus (1907) in Bozen (also South Tyrol, now Bolzano, Italy), a bath in Hermannstadt (now Sibiu, Romania), and a health-resort garden at Banki, near Sofia (Bulgaria).

BIBLIOGRAPHY

Thieme–Becker; Wasmuth

München und seine Bauten, Bayerischer Architekten und Ingenieur-Verein (Munich, 1912)

B. Hartmann: *Das Müller'sche Volksbad in München* (Munich, 1987)

DIETRICH NEUMANN

Ho-chia ts'un. *See* HEJIA CUN.

Höchst Ceramics Factory. German ceramics manufactory. Although Höchst was founded in 1746 by Adam Friedrich von Löwenfinck as a porcelain factory, at first it was only possible to produce high-quality faience painted with enamels. A wide range of wares was produced, including such tablewares as tureens in the shape of animals, fruit and vegetables (e.g. boar's head tureen and dish, *c.* 1750; Frankfurt am Main, Mus. Ksthandwk) and figures. After Löwenfink resigned in 1749, Johann Kilian Benckgraff (1708–53) and Joseph Jakob Ringler (1730–1804) took over the technical direction of the factory and immediately began to produce porcelain. At first they used the old faience forms and models, but from 1758 they became increasingly influenced by wares from Meissen and Frankenthal. Höchst became famous for its variety of figures by such modellers as Simon Feilner (1726–98), Johann Hermann Meyer (*fl* 1746–9), Carl Gottlieb Lück (*c.* 1730–75), his brother Johann Friedrich Lück (1727–97) and Johann Peter Melchior (1742–1825).

Among the early figures are two groups of characters from the *commedia dell'arte* in the style of the engraver François Joullain and engravings from Augsburg. Johann Friedrich Lück's figure of a dancer with a black mask is considered his most brilliant achievement. Melchior modelled busts and portraits, as well as sentimental figures of children and young couples situated on grassy, rockwork bases (e.g. *Grapethief*, 1770–75; Frankfurt am Main, Mus. Ksthandwk). Most of the figures, however, which are reminiscent of the work of Etienne-Maurice Falconet, cannot be attributed to a particular modeller (e.g. *Venus and Cupid*, 1771; Cologne, Kstgewmus.).

The production of tableware included dinner-services, tea- and coffeepots, cruet-stands, basketwares with trellis decoration, fruit and sweetmeat dishes and garnitures. Particularly outstanding painted decoration included landscapes, chinoiseries, harbour and battle scenes, putti, flowers, ribbons, scrolling foliage and portrait silhouettes. After the factory closed in 1796, the designs were sold to other firms: in 1840 they were sold to Ernst Müller of the Damm Pottery in Aschaffenburg and in 1909 to the porcelain factory of Dressel, Kistler and Co. in Passau, which used them until 1942. The Höchst factory reopened in 1966, and some of the models by Melchior were remoulded.

BIBLIOGRAPHY

H. Jedding: 'Höchster Porzellan-Geschirr aus Fayence-Formen', *Keramos*, 7 (1960), pp. 3–12

K. H. Esser: *Höchster Porzellan* (Königstein, 1962)

K. H. Esser and H. Reber: *Höchster Fayencen und Porzellan* (Mainz, 1964)

E. Kramer: 'Höchster Porzellangruppen von Johann Peter Melchior', *Keramos*, 56 (1972), pp. 3–68

WALTER SPIEGL

Höckelmann, Antonius (*b* Oelde, Westphalia, 26 March 1937). German sculptor, painter and draughtsman. He served an apprenticeship in Oelde as a sculptor in wood (1951–7) and subsequently studied at the Hochschule für Bildende Künste, Berlin (1957–61), where the formal approach of his teacher Karl Hartung was evident in his work. His activities in drawing and sculpture began with a four-month stay in Naples, where he researched 16th-century Mannerism, and studied the drawings of Georg Baselitz. In 1970 Höckelmann settled in Cologne and until 1979 earned a living as a post-office worker, while continuing to make art. He saw drawing as 'more sculptural than sculpture', and his paintings evoke wildly proliferating organic structures, reminiscent of whirlwinds or magnetic fields in dialogue with the picture plane, as in *Untitled* (1979; Bonn, Städt. Kstmus.). Echoes of female forms in his work took on a more unambiguous iconographic status in the 1970s and 1980s. He also dealt repeatedly with biblical themes, as in *Judith and Holofernes IV* (1981; Wuppertal, von der Heydt-Mus.). His sculptures are assembled from such diverse materials as polystyrene, aluminium foil, cardboard and gauze crumpled and painted to give an impression of structure (e.g. *Face with Bow*, 1984; Mannheim, Stadt. Ksthalle). In the 1980s he added painted wood and bronze casts to the materials employed. He was also known for his masks.

BIBLIOGRAPHY

Michael Werner: 'Interview mit Antonius Höckelmann', *Kstforum Int.*, x (1974), pp. 143ff

Antonius Höckelmann (exh. cat., Leverkusen, Schloss Morsbroich, 1975)

Antonius Höckelmann: Skulpturen, Handzeichnungen (exh. cat. by W. Kahicke and S. Gohr, Cologne, Josef-Haubrich-Ksthalle, 1980)

Antonius Höckelmann (exh. cat., ed. K.-E. Vester; Hamburg, Ksthalle, 1986)

EVA MEYER-HERMANN

Höckert, Johan Fredrik (*b* Jönköping, 26 Aug 1826; *d* Göteborg, 16 Sept 1866). Swedish painter. He grew up in a wealthy home and started his art education early. He was briefly a pupil at the art academy in Stockholm (1844–5) before he set off with his friend J. C. Boklund (1817–80), the history painter, for Munich, where he studied until 1849 at the Akademie and with the Danish painter, F. L. Storch (1805–83). It was during this period that Höckert first became interested in historical subjects, which, together with pictures of the life of the common people and to a lesser extent portraits, were the dominant themes of his paintings. His fascination with rural genre subjects was inspired by the Nordic Exhibition at the art academy in Stockholm in 1850, which introduced to Sweden the Düsseldorf school of painting, mainly through the work of the Norwegian painters, Adolph Tidemand and Hans Fredrik Gude. The same year Höckert toured Lapland, visiting the lake at Hornavan in a region that had hitherto not been explored by artists. His studies of landscapes and of different types of people, which he collected during his travels, formed the basis of some of his most important paintings.

The decisive period in Höckert's artistic development was between 1851 and 1857 when he was living in Paris. From sketches made in Munich he completed the large historical painting *Queen Christina Commands her Bodyguards to Kill Monaldeschi in the Palace of Fontainebleau, 1657* (exh. Paris Salon 1857; Göteborg, Kstmus.). The influence of Delacroix's rich palette and Paul Delaroche's historical canvases, which dominated Höckert's mature style, was already apparent in this painting.

After a short trip to Sweden, Höckert began work on *Service in the Chapel of Lövmokk in Lapland* (1855; Norrköping, Kstmus.), which depicts, on a considerable scale (over 4 m wide), numerous figures in a small chapel in Lapland. It proved his greatest success. At the Exposition Universelle in Paris it received an enormous amount of attention and was awarded the highest distinction. Napoleon III bought it and donated it to the Musée des Beaux-Arts, Lille. (It was returned to Sweden in 1952.) Encouraged by his success, Höckert continued to paint motifs from Lapland while in Paris, some in silvery tones inspired by Thomas Couture. He also painted scenes from everyday life in contemporary Paris with an extremely refined sense of colour (e.g. *The Poster*; Stockholm, Nmus.).

In 1857 Höckert returned to Stockholm. The following summer he undertook a study tour in Dalecarlia where he found inspiration for another series of images of the lives of the Swedish common people, for example *Woman from Rättvik at the Stove* (1860) and *Godmother's Visit, Motif from Orsa* (1866; both Göteborg, Kstmus.). He also painted portraits such as *Carl XV in Freemason's Costume* (1861; Stockholm, Ulriksdalsslott). In the autumn of 1861 Höckert made a long journey to Italy, Spain, North Africa and London. During this trip he was commissioned by Carl XV to paint a portrait of *The Bey of Tunis* (1862; Stockholm, Nmus.), which is regarded as one of his greatest paintings.

On his return, Höckert was appointed professor at the art academy in Stockholm in 1864. The following year, working from an earlier sketch, he began his last and finest picture, the *Fire at the Palace in Stockholm, 7 May 1697* (Stockholm, Nmus.). In this painting, which was left unfinished at his early death in 1866, Höckert proved himself one of the greatest colourists in Swedish 19th-century painting. By his painterly manipulation of colour and animated compositions, he revived the genre of history painting in Sweden. However, the novel style of the painting proved too much for contemporary critics and it was coolly received. (It only entered the Nationalmuseum 15 years after his death.) More so than any other Swedish painter during the 1840s to 1860s, Höckert was concerned with colour and painterly qualities. His principal achievement was to pave the way for a much more free and lively style of painting modelled on French examples, which emerged in Sweden in the 1870s.

BIBLIOGRAPHY
A. Borelius: *Johan Fredrik Höckert, 1826–1866* (Stockholm, 1927)
G. Nordensvan: *Svensk konst och svenska konstnärer i det 19 århundradet* [Swedish art and Swedish artists in the 19th century], ii (Stockholm, 1928), pp. 61–77
A. Gauffin: 'Kring Höckerts Lappkapell: Ett återfunnet dokument' [Thoughts on Höckert's chapel in Lapland: A retrieved document], *N. Mus. Årsbok* (1929), pp. 105–14

TORSTEN GUNNARSSON

Hockney, David (*b* Bradford, 9 July 1937). English painter, printmaker, photographer and stage designer. Perhaps the most popular and versatile British artist of the 20th century, Hockney made apparent his facility as a draughtsman while studying at Bradford School of Art between 1953 and 1957, producing portraits and observations of his surroundings under the influence of the Euston Road School and of Stanley Spencer. From 1957 to 1959 he worked in hospitals as a conscientious objector to fulfil the requirements of national service. On beginning a three-year postgraduate course at the Royal College of Art, London, in 1959, he turned first to the discipline of drawing from life in two elaborate studies of a skeleton before working briefly in an abstract idiom inspired by the paintings of Alan Davie.

Encouraged by a fellow student, R. B. Kitaj, Hockney soon sought ways of reintegrating a personal subject-matter into his art while remaining faithful to his newly acquired modernism. He began tentatively by copying fragments of poems on to his paintings, encouraging a close scrutiny of the surface and creating a specific identity for the painted marks through the alliance of word and image. These cryptic messages soon gave way to open declarations in a series of paintings produced in 1960–61 on the theme of homosexual love, for example *We Two Boys Together Clinging* (1961; London, ACE), which took its title and some of its written passages from a poem by Walt Whitman. The audacity of the subject-matter was matched by the sophisticated but impetuous mixture of elevated emotions with low life, of crudely drawn figures reminiscent of child art with the scrawled appearance of graffiti, and a rough textural handling of paint. These pictures owed much to the *faux-naïf* idiom of Jean Dubuffet and to the example of Picasso, whose retrospective at the Tate Gallery in the summer of 1960 had a decisive impact on Hockney's free-ranging attitude to style. Early in 1962 he exhibited a group of paintings under the generic title *Demonstrations of Versatility* (priv. col.;

see Livingstone, pls 24–5, 36), each proposing a different style chosen at will: flat, illusionistic, scenic. The force of Hockney's personality and humour, together with his commanding draughtsmanship and with subjects drawn from his own experience and literary interests, enabled him to transcend his influences and to establish a clear artistic identity at an early age. He was awarded the Royal College of Art gold medal for his year in 1962.

Hockney's subsequent development was a continuation of his student work, which was initially regarded by critics as part of the wave of Pop art that emanated from the Royal College of Art, although a significant change in his approach occurred after his move to California at the end of 1963. Even before moving there he had painted *Domestic Scene, Los Angeles* (1963; priv. col., see Livingstone, pl. 33), an image of two men in a shower based partly on photographs found in a homosexual magazine. It is clear that when he moved to that city it was, at least in part, in search of the fantasy that he had formed of a sensual and uninhibited life of athletic young men, swimming pools, palm trees and perpetual sunshine. Undoubtedly Hockney's popularity can be attributed not simply to his visual wit and panache but also to this appeal to our own escapist instincts.

On his arrival in California, Hockney changed from oil to acrylic paints, applying them as a smooth surface of flat and brilliant colour that helped to emphasize the pre-eminence of the image. The anonymous, uninflected surface of works such as *Peter Getting Out of Nick's Pool* (1966; Liverpool, Walker A.G.; *see* GAY AND LESBIAN ART, fig. 4) also suggests the snapshot photographs on which they were partly based. The border of bare canvas surrounding the image reinforces this association, allowing Hockney to return to a more traditional conception of space while maintaining a modernist stance in the suggestion of a picture of a picture. By the end of the decade Hockney's anxieties about appearing modern had abated to the extent that he was able to pare away the devices and to allow his naturalistic rendering of the world to speak for itself. He was particularly successful in a series of double portraits of friends, for example *Mr and Mrs Clark and Percy* (1970–71; London, Tate), later voted the most popular modern painting in the Tate Gallery. While some of the paintings of this period appear stilted and lifeless in their reliance on photographic sources, Hockney excelled in his drawings from life, particularly in the pen-and-ink portraits executed in a restrained and elegant line, for example *Nick and Henry on Board, Nice to Calvi* (1972; London, BM). It is as a draughtsman and graphic artist that Hockney's reputation is most secure.

Hockney's originality as a printmaker was apparent by the time he produced *A Rake's Progress* (1961–3; see 1979 exh. cat., nos 17–32), a series of 16 etchings conceived as a contemporary and autobiographical version of William Hogarth's visual narrative. Hockney's large body of graphic work, concentrating on etching and lithography, in itself assured him an important place in modern British art, and in series inspired by literary sources such as *Illustrations for Fourteen Poems from C. P. Cavafy* (1967; see fig.), *Illustrations for Six Fairy Tales from the Brothers Grimm* (1969; see 1979 exh. cat., nos 70–108) and *The Blue Guitar*

David Hockney: *In the Dull Village*, etching and aquatint, 360×230 mm, 1966; from *Illustrations for Fourteen Poems from C. P. Cavafy* (London, 1967)

(1977; see 1979 exh. cat., nos 199–218), he did much to revive the tradition of the *livre d'artiste*.

Hockney's work for the stage since 1975 brought out his essential inventiveness and helped free him of the ultimately stultifying constraints of his naturalistic mode. His most notable designs included productions at the Glyndebourne Opera Festival of Stravinsky's *The Rake's Progress* in 1975 (*see* THEATRE, fig. 23) and of Mozart's *Die Zauberflöte* in 1978, and at the Metropolitan Opera, New York, of Ravel's *L'Enfant et les sortilèges*, as well as other French works in 1980 and a Stravinsky triple-bill in 1981. These were followed by other ambitious designs, for example for Wagner's *Tristan und Isolde* at the Los Angeles Music Center Opera in 1987, for Puccini's *Turandot* at the Lyric Opera of Chicago in 1992, and for Strauss's *Die Frau ohne Schatten* at the Royal Opera House, Covent Garden, in 1992. The example of Picasso, especially after his death in 1973, was also an important factor in Hockney's return to the stylistic gamesmanship that distinguished him as a student. His obsessiveness, energy and curiosity resulted in large bodies of work in different media, including the *Paper Pools* and other pulped paper works of 1978, as well as experiments with polaroid and 35 mm photography: several hundred composite images in which he applied the multiple viewpoints of Cubist painting to a mechanical medium. These experiments were part of a continuing fascination with technology that led him to produce 'home made prints' on photocopiers in 1986 and later images conveyed by fax machine or devised on a computer. The photographs also directed his attention to theories on perspective in large panoramic paintings that combine direct observation with memory as a means of suggesting movement through space, for example *A Visit with Christopher and Don, Santa Monica Canyon* (1984; artist's col., see Livingstone, 2/1987, pp. 230–31), a painting on two canvases measuring 1.83×6.1 m overall. His restless desire for innovation was vividly manifested in the series of *Very New Paintings* (see 1994 exh. cat., pp. 140–43) initiated in 1992, in which he gave almost abstract form to his experience of the Pacific coastline and the Santa Monica mountains as an intoxicating succession of plunging perspectives, dazzling views, brilliant light and intense colour. Hockney's identification with Picasso, Matisse and other modern masters has been viewed with suspicion by those who think his motives cynical and self-promoting. Such an interpretation, however, seems foreign to an artist whose ambition was consistently to claim for his work a range and openness rare for his generation.

WRITINGS

N. Stangos, ed.: *David Hockney by David Hockney* (London, 1976) [essential first-hand account]
——, ed.: *Paper Pools* (London, 1980) [paper pulp works of 1978]
——, ed: *That's the Way I See it* (London, 1993) [substantial account of work in all media after the mid-1970s]

BIBLIOGRAPHY

David Hockney: Paintings, Prints and Drawings, 1960–70 (exh. cat., ed. M. Glazebrook; London, Whitechapel A.G., 1970)
Travels with Pen, Pencil and Ink (exh. cat., intro. E. Pillsbury; London, 1978) [excellent standard of repr.]
David Hockney Prints, 1954–77 (exh. cat., intro. A. Brighton; ACGB, 1979) [fully illus. cat. rais.]
M. Livingstone: *David Hockney* (London, 1981, rev. 2/1987) [survey of Hockney's work in all media]
M. Friedman, ed.: *Hockney Paints the Stage* (New York, 1983; add. insert pubd 1985) [substantial survey of Hockney's work for the theatre]
L. Weschler: *David Hockney Cameraworks* (New York, 1983) [thorough account and excellent illus. of composite photos of 1982–3]
David Hockney: A Retrospective (exh. cat., ed. M. Tuchman and S. Barron; Los Angeles, CA, Co. Mus. A., 1988)
Hockney in California (exh. cat., ed. M. Livingstone; Tokyo, Takashimaya Gal., 1994)
David Hockney: A Drawing Retrospective (exh. cat. by U. Luckhard and P. Melia, London, RA, 1995–6)

For further bibliography *see* POP ART.

MARCO LIVINGSTONE

Hodart, Filipe [Philippe] (*b* France, *c.* 1490; *d* ?after 1536). French sculptor active in Spain and Portugal. He was an important figure of the Iberian Renaissance, though his work knew neither precedent nor followers. Details of his education are not known, but he must have had a knowledge of early 16th-century Italian sculpture and, more specifically, of sculpture made in Rome. The few known documents referring to him are dated between 1522 and 1535. One of these, a contract signed in Coimbra, states his French origin. Between 1522 and 1523 he worked on the choir-stalls at Santo Domingo de la Calzada Cathedral, near Burgos. This work had been commissioned in 1521 from Andrés de Nájera, whom Guillén de Holanda sometimes replaced as head of a team of wood-carvers and sculptors that included Hodart, Lucas de Burgos, Francisco de San Gil and Juan de Castro el Borgoñón.

Hodart's work between 1523 and 1525 is documented at the Cathedral of Toledo. The *Domine Quo Vadis* group above the door of the treasury tower; the powerful image of Christ at the column adjacent to the clerks' door; and two, or perhaps three, of the carved panels on the pillars of the transept can all be attributed to him. By 1530 he was in Portugal at Coimbra, where he was commissioned to make a monumental terracotta *Last Supper* for the new refectory at the Monastery of Santa Cruz. The *Last Supper* (incomplete, Coimbra, Mus. N. Machado de Castro) shows a group of large seated figures at the moment when Christ reveals that one of them has betrayed him. The attitudes of the Apostles express bewilderment and astonishment, except for Judas, who finds himself revealed. The gestures of the figures are carefully studied and executed with a remarkable realism, and the group has little of the theatrical tone of similar works by Italian artists such as Niccolò dell'Arca. Rather than depicting broad, commonplace gestures Hodart gives his Apostles a refinement and dignity absent from the works of his contemporaries. The sculptor reveals a psychological insight and knowledge of human anatomy rare among contemporary artists.

Hodart was still in Coimbra in 1534, when he was witness to a contract signed at the Monastery of Santa Cruz. His sculptures for the halls of the colleges of the Augustinian Canons, Coimbra, have disappeared. The limestone statues depicting the praying figures of *Dom Luís da Silveira* (1530–35), at the church at Góis, and of *Dom Duarte de Lemos* (1535), at the church of Trofa do Vouga, have been attributed to him on stylistic grounds and because of their distinct personalities and studied realism. In them Hodart initiated the practice of representing praying figures on Portuguese funerary monuments. These works also display an exuberance and agitation which herald a new phase in Portuguese Renaissance taste and come closer to the dramatic emotional style of Juan de Juni and Alonso Berruguete working in the central region of the Iberian peninsula.

Also attributed to Hodart on stylistic grounds are the porch sculptures and those on the tower of the chapel annexed to the Casa dos Coimbras in the northern city of Braga (works of unknown date). This is further corroborated by the material used, Ança limestone from Coimbra, and the church was designed by Diogo de Castilho and contained an altarpiece by João de Ruão, two masters with whom Hodart had previously worked in Trofa and Góis as well as at Coimbra.

BIBLIOGRAPHY

V. Correia: 'Hodart', *Terra Port.*, 38 (1924), pp. 3–17
R. dos Santos: *A escultura em Portugal*, 2 vols (Lisbon, 1950–51)
J. J. Martín González: *La huella española en la escultura portuguesa* (Valladolid, 1966)
P. Dias: 'A presença de artistas franceses no Portugal de Quinhentos', *Mundo A.*, 15 (1983), pp. 3–20

PEDRO DIAS

Hodges, Charles Howard (*b* London, 23 July 1764; *d* Amsterdam, 24 July 1837). English painter and printmaker active in the Netherlands. He was the son of a miniature painter and grew up in artistic circles. In 1782 he enrolled at the Royal Academy Schools in London. After a visit to the Netherlands with the art dealer William Humphrey (?1740–?1810), Hodges, decided to settle there. In 1792 he moved to The Hague, where in 1793 he joined the artists' confraternity Pictura. Initially Hodges concentrated on mezzotint engravings, mostly after the work of English masters (Reynolds, Romney, Hoppner and others), but he soon achieved fame with his portraits in oils and pastel.

After moving to Amsterdam in 1797, Hodges's reputation continued to grow. There he painted vast numbers of bankers, merchants, shipowners and members of the aristocracy. He received many commissions from the van Wickevoort Crommelin-van Lennep family and their circle. Among Hodges's sitters were such eminent political figures as *R. J. Schimmelpenninck* (1806; priv. col.), *Louis Napoleon* (1809; Haarlem, Frans Halsmus.) and *William I* (1816; Amsterdam, Rijksmus.). Hodges's portraits generally give a flattering impression of his sitters whose elegance derives more from the richness of their clothing or surroundings and from the artist's remarkable rendering of different materials than from a convincing characterization. In 1815 he was a member of the committee in charge of recovering Willem V's art collection which had been looted by the French in 1795 (now in The Hague, Mauritshuis).

BIBLIOGRAPHY

A. van der Feltz: *Charles Howard Hodges, 1764–1837* (Assen, 1982)

FRANS GRIJZENHOUT

Hodges, William (*b* London, 28 Oct 1744; *d* Brixham, Devon, 6 March 1797). English painter. He first attended classes at William Shipley's Academy in the Strand, London, and from 1758 to 1765 was apprenticed to Richard Wilson (about whom he published a short biographical essay in 1790). Hodges followed Wilson's classical landscape style periodically throughout his career, but, particularly during his travels, he also occasionally abandoned it in favour of freer handling, bolder juxtapositions of colour and a more empirical response to the natural world.

In 1765 Hodges joined the Incorporated Society of Artists and became a regular exhibitor. *The Pantheon, Oxford Street, London* (Leeds, C.A.G.), an important early example of his interest in architecture and effects of natural light, was exhibited in 1772, as were some views of Switzerland and Germany made from a trip across the Alps the previous year. In 1772 he travelled as the official artist on Capt. James Cook's second voyage to the South Pacific. As the *Resolution* rounded the Cape of Good Hope, Hodges made oil pictures and rapid wash drawings of the shore; some of these (examples in London, N. Mar. Mus.) were sent to London for exhibition in 1774 with the Free Society of Artists. Cook's expedition continued towards the South Pole, and Hodges attempted to capture the region's unusual optical and meteorological effects (examples in Sydney, Mitchell Lib.). The remainder of this three-year voyage was spent in the South Pacific. The lush and spectacular scenery of New Zealand and the Pacific islands was in marked contrast to the harsh landscape of

William Hodges: *A Storm and Waterspouts off Cape Stephens, New Zealand*, oil on canvas, 1.36×1.93 m, 1776 (London, National Maritime Museum)

the Antarctic, and sketches by Hodges of dramatic water-falls, cliffs and awesome weather conditions were clearly inspired by the current early Romantic sensibility for the Sublime. One painting, finished after his return to London, *A Storm and Waterspouts off Cape Stephens, New Zealand* (1776; London, N. Mar. Mus.; see fig.), reveals Hodges's attempts to organize the visual material gathered on this trip into a more classical form of composition, with idealized figures used as staffage and placed in the fore-ground, in a manner reminiscent of Wilson's *Ceyx and Alcyone* (Cardiff, N. Mus.). While in New Zealand, Hodges also drew ethnographic portraits of the Maori population.

On his return to England in 1775 Hodges was employed by the Admiralty to paint large-scale works based on his sketches and to supervise engravings based on his illustra-tions; the latter were published in Cook's *A Voyage towards the South Pole* (1777). He began exhibiting at the Royal Academy and radically altered the realistic approach he had adopted in his sketches in order to conform with academic taste for 'correct' composition and elevated presentation. In his *View Taken in the Bay of Otaheite Peha* (Anglesey Abbey, Cambs, NT) and *Tahitian War Galleys in Matavai Bay, Tahiti* (New Haven, CT, Yale Cent. Brit. A.), both exhibited in 1776, Hodges hoped to transcend his reputation as a painter of 'curiosities'. Many contemporary critics considered his more innovative paint-ings of his travels to appear unfinished or bizarre; as with the work of Thomas Jones (also a pupil of Wilson's), they are remarkable in their anticipation of 19th-century natu-ralism and *plein-air* aesthetics.

In 1779 Hodges travelled to India. He remained there until 1783, during which time he was patronized by Warren Hastings, the Governor-General of Bengal. India inspired some of Hodges's most Romantic landscapes, such as the *View of the Jungle Ferry, Bengal – Moonlight* (exh. RA 1786; priv. col., see Stuebe, no. 371) and *Mrs Hastings near the Rocks of Colgong* (1790; New Haven, CT, Yale Cent. Brit. A.). His drawings made on this trip (examples at New Haven, CT, Yale Cent. Brit. A.) range from freely executed sketches of atmospheric conditions to detailed records of the scenery along the River Ganges; 48 of them were published as aquatints in *Select Views in India* (1785–8). Hodges subsequently published his *Travels in India* (1793), which describes places of historical or architectural interest as well as the subcontinent's climate. He returned to England with substantial wealth, and in 1786 he was elected to the Royal Academy. He continued to travel, touring in England and across the Continent, going as far as Russia in 1792. Pursuing a direction suggested in Joshua Reynolds's *Discourses* (1769–90), Hodges developed an increasing interest in ennobling his landscape paintings with historical subject-matter. He became involved in John Boydell's project for a Shakespeare Gallery, and in 1795 he privately exhibited two huge moralizing landscapes, the *Effects of Peace* and the *Consequences of War* (both un-traced). The volatile political climate of the time was such that Prince George (later George IV) objected to the democratic implications that lay behind these landscapes. The Prince's censorship effectively put an end to Hodges's career, and in July of that year he retired to Devon.

See also SOCIETY ISLANDS, fig. 2.

WRITINGS

Dissertation on the Prototypes of Architecture: Hindoo, Moorish, Gothic (London, 1787)
'An Account of Richard Wilson, Esquire, Landscape Painter, F.R.A.', *Eur. Mag. & London Rev.*, xvii (June 1790), pp. 402–5
Travels in India during the Years 1780, 1781, 1782, 1783 (London, 1793) [with prints after Hodges's drgs]

BIBLIOGRAPHY

I. C. Stuebe: *The Life and Works of William Hodges*, 2 vols (New York, 1979)
R. Joppien and B. Smith: *The Art of Captain Cook's Voyages*, 2 vols (New Haven, 1985)

NADIA TSCHERNY

Hodgkin, Howard (*b* London, 6 Aug 1932). English painter, printmaker and collector. He studied at the Camberwell School of Art (1949) and at the Bath Academy of Art, Corsham (1950–54). He did not seriously exhibit until he was 30. His preference was for emotionally charged figurative groupings in which the figures appeared embed-ded in the matrix of the picture, as if growing out of their surroundings, such as the *Interior of a Museum* (1956–9; London, Tate). The often manic humour helped place Hodgkin in the climate of Pop art, although he was not directly associated with the movement; early subjects included Joe Tilson in *The Tilsons* (1965–7; ex-Stuyvesant priv. col., London), whose goggle eyes stare out from his own gaudy carpentered constructions. Hodgkin was always concerned to make the picture an object, and from 1970 he worked not on canvas but on assertive wooden supports, such as drawing boards or door frames.

Hodgkin's paintings are generally small in scale, con-sciously conceived within the tradition of European easel painting. They refer to memories of specific moments, but as Hodgkin insisted, 'the most complete expression of such a subject would not necessarily involve description' (Reichardt, p. 140). He painted extremely slowly, some-times taking up to four years or more on one work. During this process the clarity of the original imagery was often obscured, and the spectator was invited to decipher the finished image as a kind of riddle.

A white line representing a table divides the composition of *Dinner at West Hill* (1966; London, Tate), the egg-like heads of the guests rising on the right and, from the red areas opposite, establishing the spectator's presence. The sense is of the social event having generated another level, evident in the painted flecks which dance like thoughts above the heads of the guests. Hodgkin's repeated dots or blobs stand for the vibrations of feeling, almost as meta-physical substance.

In the 1970s Hodgkin's work shifted from a collaged geometric flatness to a more complex fluid patterning, from the exemplar of Matisse's *Moroccans* (1916; New York, MOMA) to Vuillard's intimist interiors. The deco-rative patterning, gorgeous colour and framing devices of paintings such as *Dinner at Smith Square* (1975–9; London, Tate; see fig.), as well as the eclectic mix of styles, owe much also to Pahari miniature paintings, of which Hodgkin was an avid collector, visiting India almost every year. He applied a restricted range of simple shapes and marks to a variety of moods: lyrical and poetic, as in *The Moon* (1978–80; Kitaj priv. col., see 1984 exh. cat., p. 55), painted on a bread board and marvellously evoking a lunar romance;

Howard Hodgkin: *Dinner at Smith Square*, oil on hardboard with integral wood surround, 946×1251 mm, 1975–9 (London, Tate Gallery)

humorous, as in *A Small Henry Moore at the Bottom of the Garden* (1975–7; priv. col., see 1984 exh. cat., p. 31), where the frame overpowers the subject; or openly erotic, as in *Goodbye to the Bay of Naples* (1980–82; priv. col., see 1984 exh. cat., p. 67), with a belly and penis in the foreground set into a frame representing repeated eruptions from Mount Vesuvius.

Hodgkin's prints followed a similar development. In the late 1960s and early 1970s the artist favoured screen printing and lithography as suitable media for effects of flat printed colour, as in the series of 12 screen prints, *Indian Views A–L* (1971; London, Tate). The emphasis from the mid-1970s on the physical substance of layers of paint had a corresponding effect on his decision to change to intaglio methods such as etching and aquatint, emphasizing the textures and marks in prints such as *Interior (Day)* and *Interior (Night)* (both 1974; London, Tate). In later works, such as *Bleeding* (lithograph, 1982; see 1983 exh. cat., p. 45), he hand-coloured the image after printing.

Hodgkin consistently stressed the self-sufficiency of the marks and formal structure of his work. The oblique and even mystificatory imagery, however, also entailed a defence of intimate values in expressing the most fugitive, human and vulnerable sensations.

WRITINGS
'How to Be an Artist', *Burl. Mag.*, cxxiv/954 (1982), pp. 552–4

BIBLIOGRAPHY
J. Reichardt, ed.: 'On Figuration and the Narrative in Art', *Studio Int.*, 172 (1966), pp. 140–44
Howard Hodgkin: Forty-five Paintings, 1949–1975 (exh. cat. by R. Morphet, ACGB, 1976)
T. Hyman: 'Howard Hodgkin Interviewed by Timothy Hyman', *Artscribe*, 15 (1978), pp. 25–8
P. Gilmour: 'Howard Hodgkin', *Prt Colr Newslett.* (March–April 1981), pp. 2–5
Howard Hodgkin, Prints, 1977 to 1983 (exh. cat., intro. R. Morphet; London, Tate, 1983)
Howard Hodgkin: Forty Paintings, 1973–84 (exh. cat. by J. McEwen and D. Sylvester, London, Whitechapel A.G., 1984)
A. Graham-Dixon: *Howard Hodgkin* (New York, 1994)
Howard Hodgkin: Paintings, 1975–1995 (exh. cat., Fort Worth, TX, Mod. A. Mus.)

□

Hodgkins, Frances (Mary) (*b* Dunedin, 28 April 1869; *d* Herrison, 13 May 1947). New Zealand painter. Widely considered New Zealand's most significant expatriate artist of the early 20th century, she spent her formative years in Otago. She was encouraged to take up watercolour painting by her father, William Mathew Hodgkins (1833–98), who was himself adept at landscape watercolours in the English manner. In 1893 she attended classes given in Dunedin by Girolamo Nerli, who inspired her to embark on figure subjects and use a bolder technique. By 1896 she received local recognition for her portraits and intimate genre themes. To realize an ambition to travel abroad, she took up art teaching and left for London in 1901. Outside the restricting confines of colonial society, Hodgkins acquired an appetite for sketching excursions in Europe (Italy, France, the Netherlands), and she also sought picturesque motifs in Morocco. One of her Moroccan figure paintings, showing a robust technique similar to that of Frank Brangwyn, was accepted by the Royal Academy exhibition in 1903. Family ties prompted several return visits to New Zealand, but by the end of 1908 she had settled in Paris, which remained her base until 1914. Hodgkins exhibited at the Paris Salon and elsewhere, commanding attention for her skill as a watercolour painter. She established classes in watercolour at the Académie Colarossi, becoming its first woman instructor. By 1912 she was employing an increasingly vivid palette, producing landscapes and images based on the figure with large decisive sweeps of the brush.

During World War I Hodgkins sought refuge in England, choosing to live at St Ives. With the curtailment of exhibiting and teaching commitments and a restriction to her peripatetic lifestyle, she adopted larger formats and started working in oils. The artist spoke of this period as her 'experimental days'. No longer content to sum up natural appearances in an attractive semi-Impressionist manner, she became more uncompromising in her approach. Myfanwy Evans, in an early account of the artist (1948), linked her work at this point with Paul Gauguin and Henri Matisse, stating that like them she 'had a simplicity that was not innocence'. In November 1926 Hodgkins held a comprehensive solo exhibition in Manchester, but by then she had resolved to seek recognition among progressive artists in London. Through the painter Cedric Morris, Hodgkins gained access to the London Group and was elected a member of the 7 & 5 Society in 1929, exhibiting alongside Ben Nicholson, Barbara Hepworth, John Piper, David Jones and Ivon Hitchens. Watercolours, pencil studies and oils combining landscape and still-life elements became her hallmark for several years, as in the watercolour *Two Plates* (1931; Wellington, Mus. NZ, Te Papa Tongarewa) and the oil *Wings over Water* (1932; Leeds, C.A.G.). In order to fulfil exhibition obligations, Hodgkins painted widely in England and Wales, Spain and the Balearic Islands. The calligraphy of her brushwork became paramount, with objects and inventive patterns of colour merging into one another. From 1935 she took up gouache, a medium that ideally suited her spontaneous, intuitive style.

Although Hodgkins was known in the 1930s as a member of the English avant-garde, it was only towards the end of her life that she won wide critical recognition. Her exhibition in April 1940 at the Lefevre Gallery, London, prompted Eric Newton (1893–1965) in the *Sunday Times* to describe her as 'a painter of genius'. In the spring of that year she was chosen to represent Britain at the Venice Biennale. One of the most commanding images of this time was the oil *Self-portrait: Still-life* (1941; Auckland, C.A.G.), a composition made up of personal possessions — her beret, scarf, shoes and bag. Together these components form a gay jigsaw of decorative fragments. A major retrospective was staged by her dealer in London in November 1946, and after her death memorial

shows followed in Manchester (1947), and in London at St George's Gallery (1949) and the Tate Gallery (1952). New Zealand honoured her with a centenary exhibition in 1969–70, which after a national tour went to Melbourne and London.

BIBLIOGRAPHY
M. Evans: *Frances Hodgkins*, Penguin Mod. Painters (London, 1948)
J. Rothenstein: *Modern English Painters*, i (London, 1952), pp. 114–20
E. H. McCormick: *Portrait of Frances Hodgkins* (Auckland, 1981)
A. Kirker: *New Zealand Women Artists: A Survey of 150 Years* (Auckland, 1986, Sydney, 2/1993), pp. 42–53
A. McKinnon: *Francis Hodgkins, 1869–1947* (London, 1990)

ANNE KIRKER

Hodgkinson, Patrick (*b* London, 8 March 1930). English architect and teacher. He played an important role in English architecture from the late 1950s, first as a pioneer in housing design and subsequently as a teacher. He studied (1950–56) at the Architectural Association School, London, spending a year of this studentship in the office of Alvar Aalto. Subsequently he worked for the engineers F. J. Samuely and Partners in London, before joining the office of Sir Leslie Martin in Cambridge in 1957–63. Here he developed ideas for low-rise, high-density housing that became instrumental over the following decade in shifting housing policy away from point block solutions based, often inaccurately, on the thinking of Le Corbusier, and towards a more humane, user-oriented form. In 1958–62, within the Martin studio, he designed the renowned Harvey Court student accommodation block for Gonville and Caius College, Cambridge, and in 1960–62 he was responsible for the basis of the St Cross Library buildings at Oxford. Hodgkinson's best-known work, however, is the Brunswick Centre (1959–72) for part of the old Foundling Hospital Estate in Bloomsbury, London. Here he developed a partially inverted stepped section, incorporating shops and commercial usage at ground level, with well-oriented flats above, all of which have balcony space. The scheme was generally acclaimed as a breakthrough in post-war English housing. Hodgkinson remained in independent practice with projects and buildings in Cambridge, Oxford and Bath, before becoming Professor of Architecture and Urbanism at the University of Bath in 1990.

BIBLIOGRAPHY
'The Battle of Brunswick', *Architects' J.*, cxcvi/3 (1992), p. 7

MICHAEL SPENS

Hödicke, K(arl) H(orst) (*b* Nuremberg, 21 Feb 1938). German painter, film maker and teacher. In 1959 he studied under Fred Thieler at the Staatliche Hochschule für Bildende Künste, Berlin, but turned away from his mentor's abstraction to a more figurative Expressionist style of painting. In 1961 he joined a group called 'Vision' and in 1964 co-founded Grossgörschen 35, an artists' co-operative that exhibited a range of figurative work by artists who rejected abstraction. *Passage V* (1964; Düsseldorf, priv. col., see 1986 exh. cat., p. 32) is typical of Hödicke's interest at the time in light and reflections: a car speeds past a department store at night and the instant is caught as rapid streaks of light; lights from the car collide with the artificial lights of the glass façade.

In 1966 the Grossgörschen group dissolved and Hödicke temporarily abandoned painting for a more conceptual approach. He moved to New York where he made a number of experimental films, such as *Victory* (1967), and then spent a year at the Villa Massimo in Rome on a scholarship (1967–8). Returning to Berlin in 1968 he focused his attention on the immediate environment of the city and created a series of works on sections of sky seen between tenement walls, as in the photomontage *Sky over Schöneberg* (1974; see 1986 exh. cat., p. 54). These were followed by monumental depictions of cityscapes in which the buildings of Berlin, such as the *Ministry of War* (1977; Berlin, Berlin. Gal.), were cast in twilight shadows like theatrical stage sets. In 1974, Hödicke was made a professor at the Staatliche Hochschule für Bildende Künste in Berlin, where he exerted a significant influence on the next generation of artists, including Wolfgang Cilarz (*b* 1954) and Helmut Middendorf (*b* 1953).

BIBLIOGRAPHY

K. H. Hödicke (exh. cat. by U. Schneede, Hamburg, Kstver., 1984)
K. H. Hödicke: Gemälde, Skulpturen, Objekte, Filme (exh. cat. by E. Billeter and others, Düsseldorf, Kstsamml. Nordrhein–Westfalen, 1986)

DEBORAH NASH

Hodin, Jacquemart de. *See* JACQUEMART DE HESDIN.

Hodler, Ferdinand (*b* Berne, 14 March 1853; *d* Geneva, 19 May 1918). Swiss painter. He came from a poor family and lost both of his parents at an early age. He received his first training from Ferdinand Sommer (1822–1901), a painter from Thun who produced lake and mountain landscape views for tourists. In 1871 or 1872 Hodler moved to Geneva to attend lectures in natural science at the Collège de Genève and to copy paintings by Alexandre Calame and François Diday in the museum there. In 1873 he became a pupil of Barthélemy Menn at the Ecole des Beaux-Arts in Geneva and while there undertook an intensive study of Dürer's writings on proportions. In 1878 he travelled to Madrid, spending almost a year there, and was strongly influenced by the Spanish landscape and by the works of such masters as Titian, Poussin, Claude, Velázquez and Goya in the Museo del Prado. He returned to Switzerland in 1879, having learnt to lighten his colour.

Hodler's central works of the period from 1875 to 1890 are the idealized representations of artisans, as in *Joiner at his Drawing Stool* (*c.* 1876; Winterthur, Stift. Oskar Reinhart). *Gazing into Eternity* (1885; Berne, Kstmus.) demonstrates his close links with the artisan class from which he himself had come. In the same period he also painted landscapes flooded with light (e.g. *Langenthal, c.* 1882; Zurich, Ksthaus), portraits (e.g. *Girl with a Poppy*, 1880; Berne, Kstmus.), interiors (e.g. *At the Sick-bed*, 1885), large-scale representations of figures (e.g. *Ahasuerus*, 1886; both Winterthur, Stift. Oskar Reinhart) and the occasional still-life. Such early works as *Dialogue with Nature* (1884; Berne, Kstmus.) show his liking for expressive poses, which he carefully studied from the model, and this aspect of his art became more fully developed later on. His declared aim was to place truth above beauty. His efforts to achieve architectonic strictness and rhythmic articulation, which are characteristics of all his later works, can sometimes be seen even in early work, as in the cartoon (destroyed by Hodler himself) for the *Gymnasts' Meeting* (1877–8; Zurich, Ksthaus). In his works up to

1890 Hodler tried to perfect his composition, stylize the gestures, emphasize form and concentrate on the expressive potential of a lighter, more differentiated colouring. In order to support himself financially he entered several competitions. In 1886 he submitted *Surprised by the Storm* (Winterthur, Stift. Oskar Reinhart) to the Concours Diday, a biennial art exhibition in Geneva. This multi-figured composition has an unnatural lighting that creates a theatrical and dramatic effect.

By 1890 Hodler had reached a point where he was no longer concerned with simple genre paintings or with the reproduction of nature; he came to care about meaning in the idealist sense and the representation of primordial mental states. He achieved his first real success with *Night* (1890; Berne, Kstmus.), a multi-figured visionary composition dealing with the themes of sleep, dream and death. This painting, regarded as his principal work, was initially not exhibited in Geneva because of Hodler's moral misgivings, although it was successfully shown in 1892 at the first Salon de la Rose + Croix exhibition, from which time the idealist and Symbolist tendencies in his work increased. Its companion piece *Day* (Berne, Kstmus.) was not painted until 1900. In *Disillusioned Souls* (1892; Munich, Neue Pin.), depicting five people sitting in a slumped pose, and *Eurhythmy* (1894–5; Berne, Kstmus.), showing five people striding one behind the other, the artist again considered the theme of death. In many of his paintings there is an unmistakable erotic element: it can be seen in the *Chosen One* (1893; Berne, Kstmus.), where a naked boy sits in front of a small newly planted tree while angels hover around him, and in *A Youth Admired by a Woman* (versions, 1903 and *c.* 1915; both Zurich, Ksthaus). *Spring* (1901; Essen, Mus. Flkwang; see fig.), a picture symmetrically arranged in horizontal layers, depicts a naked young male sitting in a flowering landscape and being gazed upon by a young girl in Greco-Roman dress. Hodler regarded these allegoric and symbolic large-scale paintings, done without any commission, as his most important creative achievements.

Hodler saw symmetry and rhythm as the constructive principles of human society, embodying them in his compositional system of 'parallelism', which he also applied to landscape. While his earlier landscape paintings are characterized by a viewpoint looking upwards out of a valley, necessitating a foreground enlivened with vegetation, his later paintings have a higher viewpoint. The tops of the Swiss mountains now rise massively from banks of cloud or mist. 'Parallelism' is most clearly expressed in his pictures of Lake Geneva and Lake Thun: the horizontally layered landscape in *Lake Geneva* (?1911; Aarau, Aargau. Ksthaus) is almost abstract in effect. In it, the bands formed by the shoreline, the mountains and their reflection on the surface of the water, together with the three-part rhythmic frieze of clouds, have been composed to form a cosmological whole.

Among his contemporaries Hodler was especially esteemed for his large-scale historical paintings, which satisfied the demand for idealized, patriotic art. In 1896, for the Schweizerische Landesausstellung in Geneva, he painted 26 over life-size male figures (e.g. *Wilhelm Tell*, Solothurn, Kstmus.) and in 1897 he was commissioned to decorate the Weapons Room of the Schweizerisches

Ferdinand Hodler: *Spring*, oil on canvas, 0.99×1.29 m, 1901 (Essen, Museum Folkwang)

Landesmuseum in Zurich with large frescoes, executed in 1900. These depict such historical scenes as the *Retreat of the Swiss Troops near Marignano (1515)* (*in situ*), and the project was the subject of great controversy. Wall paintings for the Rathaus in Berne, planned in 1898, were never executed. By the first decade of the 20th century, Hodler was beginning to gain international recognition, resulting in a greater demand for his work. In 1907–8 he painted the *Departure of the Jena Students for the Napoleonic Wars (1813)* for the Universität Jena (*in situ*). In 1909 he prepared designs for banknotes for the Schweizer National-albank, and a further public commission was offered to him in 1911, when he worked for two years on the murals (e.g. *Unanimity: The Reformation Oath by the Citizens of Hannover, 1533*; *in situ*) in the Assembly Rooms of the Rathaus in Hannover. In these paintings, as well as in the ones at Jena, the colours are subdued compared to his earlier works. He did a cartoon (1915–17; Geneva, Mus. A. & Hist.) for the *Battle of Murten*, a fresco intended for the Schweizerisches Landesmuseum in Zurich but never executed. His pictures of single figures, often women dancers and warriors (e.g. *Jena Student (Officer)*, 1908; Solothurn, Kstmus.), were mostly produced in connection with his allegories and historical pictures or cycles. He also

painted more than 50 self-portraits, particularly in his early and late periods (e.g. *Self-portrait*, 1914; Solothurn, Kstmus.), and after 1910 he increasingly painted portraits. These are characterized by coloured shadows, strong contours and a central alignment in front of a neutral background. He used several women, as well as his son Hector Hodler (1887–1920), as models and in his later years produced a series of intimate yet powerful paintings and drawings depicting the suffering and death of his companion, Valentine Godé-Darel (1873–1915) (e.g. the *Dead Valentine Godé-Darel*, 1915; Solothurn, Kstmus.). In 1914 he signed a protest against the bombardment of Reims Cathedral and was debarred from all German artists' associations. His final years were marked by illness and depression. He helped revitalize the art of monumental wall painting, and his work is regarded as embodying the Swiss federal identity. Furthermore his Symbolist painting represents a considerable contribution to the art of *fin-de-siècle* Europe.

BIBLIOGRAPHY

C. A. Loosli: *Ferdinand Hodler: Leben, Werk und Nachlass*, 4 vols (Berne, 1921–4)

E. Bender and W. Y. Müller: *Die Kunst Ferdinand Hodlers*, 2 vols (Zurich, 1923–41)

H. Mühlestein and G. Schmidt: *Ferdinand Hodler, 1853–1918: Sein Leben und sein Werk* (Zurich, 1942)

Ferdinand Hodler (exh. cat. by P. Selz, Berkeley, U. CA, A. Mus.; New York, Guggenheim; Cambridge, MA, Busch-Reisinger Mus.; 1973)

Ein Maler vor Liebe und Tod: Ferdinand Hodler und Valentine Godé-Darel: Ein Werkzyklus, 1908–1915 (exh. cat. by J. Brüschweiler, Zurich, Ksthaus; St Gall, Kstver.; Munich, Villa Stuck; Berne, Kstmus.; 1976–7)

Der frühe Hodler: Das Werk, 1870–1890 (exh. cat. by F. Zeiger and L. Gloor, Zurich, Schweizer. Inst. Kstwiss., 1981)

S. L. Hirsh: *Ferdinand Hodler* (London, 1982)

Ferdinand Hodler (exh. cat., ed. J. Brüschweiler and G. Magnaguagno; Berlin, Neue N.G.; Paris, Petit Pal.; Zurich, Ksthaus; 1983)

Ferdinand Hodler: Landscapes (exh. cat., Schweiz. Inst. Kstwiss., Zurich; Los Angeles, UCLA, Wight A. G.; Chicago, IL, A. Inst.; New York, N. Acad. Des.; 1987)

SEPP KERN

Hódmezővásárhely. *See* GREAT PLAINS PAINTING.

Hoe, Robert (*b* New York, 10 March 1839; *d* London, 22 Sept 1909). American collector. He was the grandson of Robert Hoe, the manufacturer of printing machines and presses, who had made a fortune after emigrating to America. Hoe entered the family firm in 1856 and became its director in 1886. His thorough understanding of the printing business was allied to a love of books and an expert knowledge of the history of printing, on which he wrote and published various works.

Hoe's collection included illuminated manuscripts, among them a 13th-century Book of Hours, and a large number of early printed books, including a first edition of the *Works* of Ben Jonson (1616) and of the *Comedies and Tragedies of Francis Beaumont* (1647) and a folio first edition of the works of John Donne, which had belonged to Samuel Johnson. He was also a collector of fine bindings and owned a Procopius of 1509 from the library of Thomas Maioli, 11 examples of bindings from the library of Jean Grolier and works from the libraries of Diane de Poitiers and Louis XIII. Other works included examples from the Plantin and Aldine Presses, a copy of Albrecht Dürer's *Treatise on Proportion* printed by Formscheyder of Nuremberg (1528) and an edition of the *Cosmographie Universelle* (1556) bound for Henry III, King of France.

Hoe's firm was instrumental in the development of high speed and fine-art colour lithography printing, producing some of the largest and most innovative printing machines then in existence. Hoe himself was also one of the founders of the Metropolitan Museum of Art and a founder-member of the Grolier Club in New York. His collection of almost 21,000 titles was valued at over £1 million and after his death was sold by the Anderson Auction Company in New York on 1 May 1911.

WRITINGS

A Lecture on Book-binding as a Fine Art (New York, 1866)

A Short History of the Printing Press (?New York, 1902)

BIBLIOGRAPHY

DAB

O. A. Bierstadt: *The Library of Robert Hoe* (New York, 1895)

——: *Catalogue of the Library of Robert Hoe*, 8 vols in 4 (New York, 1911–12)

JACQUELINE COLLISS HARVEY

Hoecke, Jan van den (*b* Antwerp, *bapt* 4 Aug 1611; *d* Antwerp, 1651). Flemish painter and draughtsman, active also in Italy and Austria. He may have received his first training with his father, the Antwerp painter Caspar van den Hoecke (*fl* 1595–1648), who also taught his half-brother Robert van den Hoecke (1622–68); he then became a pupil of Rubens. Together with his father, Jan contributed to the decorations for the Joyous Entry of Ferdinand into Antwerp in 1635: the monumental figures of the King of Hungary and the Cardinal-Infante on the Arch of Ferdinand were by Jan. The draughtsman-like precision of the details is characteristic of his manner of working, while he hardly bothered to paint in the inner forms once they had been established. Other early works from this Antwerp period include the oil sketch of the *Triumph of David* (Fort Worth, TX, Kimbell A. Mus.).

Soon afterwards van den Hoecke left Antwerp for Rome, where he was present from at least 1637 until 1644. His familiarity with the paintings of Guido Reni is clearly recognizable in such early works as the *Virgin and Child in a Floral Wreath* and *Hero Lamenting the Death of Leander* (both *c.* 1637; Vienna, Ksthist. Mus.). Besides the influence of Reni, van den Hoecke was clearly inspired by antique sources, from which, for instance, the idealized figure of Leander is derived. He left Italy a staunch advocate of classicizing trends.

Van den Hoecke next entered the service of Archduke Leopold William, first at the imperial court at Vienna and later in Brussels. The paintings van den Hoecke created in Vienna clearly reflect his Roman experience. Reni's idealized figure types are present in the *Allegory of Chastity*, while the styles of Domenichino and Poussin had a decisive influence on its pendant, *Virtue Overcoming Avarice*. Familiarity with the works of Andrea Sacchi is suggested in the portraits of *Emperor Ferdinand III* and *Archduke Leopold William*. Although van den Hoecke painted copies after Titian and Veronese while in Italy (untraced; mentioned in the inventory of the Archduke's collection), the influence of Venetian painting is not apparent in his own compositions. However, after leaving Italy, he gradually modified his own reticent style, adopting more closely Rubens's approach of *c.* 1610–20 rather than the master's picturesque virtuoso late style, as can be seen in the *Massacre of the Innocents* (ex-Samml. Liechtenstein, Vaduz) and the figure of Cupid that van den Hoecke contributed to Paul de Vos's *Amor vincit omnia* (1640s; Vienna, Ksthist. Mus.). In both works the movement of the bodies is characteristic of High Baroque painting, and in the former van den Hoecke did not shrink from the distressing subject-matter. Aspects of his reticent temperament remained, however. This is evident in the large, official portrait of *Archduke Leopold William on Horseback*, which must have been painted in Vienna shortly before 1647, when his patron became Governor of the Southern Netherlands and they both moved to Antwerp; its static composition differs markedly from comparable subjects by Rubens and Anthony van Dyck.

Van den Hoecke's largest commission for Archduke Leopold William was a series of designs (*c.* 1650) for *Vanitas* allegories originally comprising twelve separate images: *Day* and *Night*, six pictures of *The Months*, the *Four Seasons*, the *Four Elements* and the *Triumph of Time*. Ten preparatory oil sketches for the series have survived (four in Vienna, Ksthist. Mus.), as have eight tapestries based on the designs for *Day* and *Night* and *The Months*: a first series (Stockholm, Kun. Slott) manufactured by

Jan van den Hoecke: *March and April*, oil on canvas, 3.18×4.25 m, *c.* 1650 (Vienna, Kunsthistorisches Museum)

Redams, Leyniers, van der Strecken and Leefdael and a second series (Vienna, Ksthist. Mus.) from the workshops of Leyniers and Aegidius Habbecke. The same eight designs were also executed as large collaborative canvases (seven, Vienna, Ksthist. Mus.). Of the remaining designs, only the *Triumph of Time* was used, in a huge canvas by Cornelis Schut, after van den Hoecke's early death. The inspiration for this project derived from Rubens's two series of tapestry cartoons for the *Triumph of the Eucharist* (1625–7) and the *Life of Achilles* (*c.* 1630). Typically, van den Hoecke did not frame the compositions with a uniform border but surrounded each with still-life motifs based on the month in question. This link between framing motifs and central composition is also found in the pictures of *Day* and *Night*, in each of which the twelve putti of the hours hover around the central figures of Apollo (Day) and the Virgin and Child (Night). The combination of the brilliantly realistic still-life elements in the borders and the single figures stylistically derived from Classical statuary gives the latter great impact. These figures were clearly based on his Roman studies after the Antique, but their greater immediacy suggests that van den Hoecke also incorporated studies from life. In the figures the influence of Rubens's works of *c.* 1610–20 is again apparent. The oil sketches indicate that, while van den Hoecke was responsible for the overall design of the series, several other painters collaborated in the execution of this large commission. In the large painted canvases, Thomas Willeboirts (1614–54) and Pieter Thijs painted some of the figures, and Adriaen van Utrecht and Jan Breughel the younger carried out most of the still-lifes, while van den Hoecke himself may have painted part of the border decorations, as in *March and April* (see fig.).

Late works by van den Hoecke, such as the *Crucifixion* (Bruges Cathedral) and *St Francis Adoring the Virgin and Child* (Antwerp, Kon. Mus. S. Kst.), show that towards the end of his career his style was influenced by van Dyck. Overall, his importance rests in his ability to adapt, in a highly individual way, the classicizing trends of Italian Seicento painting to the style he had learnt in the Antwerp studio of Rubens.

For further illustration *see* BRUSSELS, fig. 8.

BIBLIOGRAPHY

Thieme–Becker; Wurzbach

M. Rooses: *Geschiedenis der Antwerpsche schilderschool* (Antwerp, 1879)

F. J. Van den Branden: *Geschiedenis der Antwerpsche schilderschool* (Antwerp, 1883)

R. Oldenbourg: *Die flämische Malerei des 17. Jahrhunderts* (Berlin, 1918)

H. Gerson and E. H. ter Kuile: *Art and Architecture in Belgium, 1600–1800*, Pelican Hist. A. (Harmondsworth, 1960)

G. Ollinger-Zinque: *Etude sur le peintre van Hoecke* (Brussels, 1961)

G. Heinz: 'Studien über Jan van den Hoecke und die Malerei der Niederländer in Wien', *Jb. Ksthist. Samml. Wien*, lxiii (1967), pp. 109ff

H. Vlieghe: 'Nicht Jan Boeckhorst, sondern Jan van den Hoecke', *Westfalen: Hft. Gesch., Kst & Vlksknd.*, lxviii (1990), pp. 166–83
                                                GÜNTHER HEINZ

Hoeckgeest, Gerrit. *See* HOUCKGEEST, GERRIT.

Hoefnagel, Joris [Georg] (*b* Antwerp, 1542; *d* Vienna, 1601). Flemish illuminator and draughtsman. He was the last of the great Flemish manuscript illuminators and the foremost topographical draughtsman of his age. His work forms a critical link between earlier manuscript illumination and ornamental design and the genre of floral still-life painting, which emerged in northern Europe at the end of the 16th century.

1. ANTWERP, 1542–76. He was the son of Elisabeth Veselaer and Jacques Hoefnagel, a wealthy jewel and tapestry merchant. According to van Mander, Hoefnagel drew secretly as a youth but was compelled by his father to pursue a career in business. Although van Mander reports that he probably received some instruction from Hans Bol, this was probably informal training since he described himself as an autodidact on a drawing (1578; Berlin, Kupferstichkab., KdZ 3991). He travelled extensively during his youth, visiting France (1560–62), Spain (1563–7) and England (1568–9). He returned to Antwerp in 1569–70 and married Susanna van Onssen in 1571.

Among Hoefnagel's earliest works is a group of topographical drawings recording his travels, including views of Nonsuch Palace, Surrey (London, BM), Granada (see fig. 1) and Poitiers (both in Vienna, Albertina, which houses a large collection of his topographical drawings). These drawings are perspective renderings of cities and monuments seen from the surrounding countryside, with the foregrounds animated by figures showing local customs and costumes. The views were used as models for engravings in Georg Braun and Franz Hogenberg's *Civitates orbis terrarum* (Cologne, 1572–1618), whose six volumes constitute the most extensive atlas of the period. Hoefnagel worked on the *Civitates* throughout his life and apparently acted as an agent for the project, commissioning views from other artists as well as completing more than 60 illustrations himself, among them views of Bavaria, Italy and Bohemia. Often working from earlier sketches from life, Hoefnagel conveyed in his finished drawings for the engravings a Mannerist sense of fantasy and wit through the use of dramatic perspectives and ornamental cartouches. At the same time he preserved a high degree of topographical accuracy that foreshadows the realist trend in 17th-century Dutch landscape art.

Probably dating to the early years of his career is the Hours of Philippe of Cleves (Brussels, Bib. Royale Albert 1er, MS. IV.40), a 15th-century illuminated manuscript to which Hoefnagel added floral marginalia, demonstrating his selfconscious continuation of the earlier tradition of Flemish manuscript painting.

2. MUNICH, 1577–91. In November 1576 Antwerp was ravaged by Spanish troops in the so-called Spanish Fury. Prompted by this politically and economically unsettling event, Hoefnagel travelled south with the cartographer Abraham Ortelius in autumn 1577. During a visit to Munich they met Albert IV Wittelsbach, Duke of Bavaria, who, after inspecting some of his miniatures, hired Hoefnagel as a court artist, probably the first appointment of Hoefnagel's professional artistic career. After going to Italy, where he visited Venice, Naples and Rome, Hoefnagel returned to Munich in spring 1578 to serve Albert IV and his son William V Wittelsbach, Duke of Bavaria, receiving a yearly salary from 1579 to 1591.

During this period Hoefnagel completed the major work of his early career, a four-volume manuscript of natural history miniatures (various folios dated 1575 to 1582; ex-Rosenwald priv. col.; Washington, DC, N.G.A.; single leaves in Berlin, Kupferstichkab.; Paris, Louvre;

1. Joris Hoefnagel: *View of the Alhambra, Granada*, pen, brown ink and watercolour wash, 254×513 mm, 1564 (Vienna, Graphische Sammlung Albertina)

SIMIARVM PVLCHRR: DEFORMIS EST.

XXIX.

AVT CVCVRBITAM, AVT CVCVRBITAE FLORĒ.

2. Joris Hoefnagel: *Animalia quadrupedia et reptilia (terra)*, watercolour and gouache with gold, on vellum; from *The Four Elements* (1575–82), ii, fol. 29 (Washington, DC, National Gallery of Art)

Prague, N.G. Lib.; Weimar, Graph. Samml.; and several private collections). Entitled *Animalia rationalia et insecta (ignis)*; *Animalia quadrupedia et reptilia (terra)* (see fig. 2); *Animalia aquatilia et conchiliata (aqua)*; and *Animalia volatilia et amphibia (aier)*, it contains thousands of exquisitely painted creatures divided according to the four elements. Inscribed throughout with Latin mottoes, epigrams and Bible verses, it resembles an emblem-book. Despite the frequent assumption that Hoefnagel worked from life, he copied many of his specimens from other works including the woodcuts in Konrad Gessner's *Historia animalium* (Zurich, 1551–87) and a series of drawings by the Antwerp animal painter Hans Verhagen der Stomme (Berlin, Kupferstichkab., and Vienna, Österreich. Nbib., Cod. min. 42). The four-volume manuscript seems to have been conceived as a natural history compendium of the entire known animal world and as such is an important monument of 16th-century science. Although there are no existing documents for its commission, it once belonged to Rudolf II, Holy Roman Emperor, in Prague, who, according to van Mander, bought it from Hoefnagel for 1000 gold crowns.

While in Munich, Hoefnagel was employed by Archduke Ferdinand of Austria, Count of the Tyrol (*reg* 1564–95; *see* HABSBURG, §I(9)) between 1581 and 1590 to illuminate a copy of the Tridentine version of the Roman Missal (Vienna, Österreich. Nbib., Cod. 1784). Comprising 658 vellum folios with illuminations throughout, its decoration includes nature imagery and grotesque borders. Particularly beautiful are the calendar pages, embellished with minuscule gaming-boards, instruments, animals and other seasonal attributes linked by strapwork. Much of the imagery is imbued with emblematic content, usually in reference to the particular religious text it accompanies or to the patron. Hoefnagel signed the manuscript *exornator hieroglyphicus* ('one who embellishes with emblems'), thereby making explicit the learned content of his imagery. He seems to have visited Archduke Ferdinand at Innsbruck intermittently throughout the project.

3. IMPERIAL SERVICE, 1591–1601. Hoefnagel entered the service of Rudolf II in 1591 and settled in Frankfurt am Main from 1591 to 1594. There he illuminated for the Emperor a modelbook of calligraphy (Vienna, Ksthist. Mus., 975; for illustration *see* HABSBURG, §I(10)) that had been written in 1571–3 for Rudolf's father, Maximilian II, Holy Roman Emperor, by the virtuoso calligrapher and imperial scribe Georg Bocskay. One of the crowning achievements of Rudolfine art, its diverse imagery includes flora and fauna, imperial imprese, mythology, portraiture,

city vistas and battle scenes, all glorifying the Emperor as the supreme terrestrial power and the protector of the Catholic faith. Stylistically, it is one of the most visually striking of Hoefnagel's manuscripts, with its decorations ingeniously woven around Bocskay's flamboyant script. In 1594 Hoefnagel moved from Frankfurt to Vienna, where he died in 1601.

Probably shortly after his arrival in Vienna, Hoefnagel began illuminating a second calligraphy codex for Rudolf II (Malibu, CA, Getty Mus., MS. 20, Inv. 86.MV.527), which had been written by Bocskay in 1561–2 during the reign of Rudolf's grandfather Ferdinand I, Holy Roman Emperor. The manuscript, the only major one by Hoefnagel devoted to botanical specimens, is decorated primarily with colourful flowers, then considered exotic, such as anemones, tulips and lilies, as well as fruits and insects. Many folios present individual still-life compositions with the various natural elements placed together in a single unified space. At the end of the manuscript is a constructed Roman alphabet with grotesque borders containing Rudolfine imprese, with the last folio signed by Hoefnagel and dated 1596.

During his final decade Hoefnagel also made independent floral still-lifes on vellum, such as that in the Ashmolean Museum, Oxford (dated 1594), and the diptych in the museum at Sibiu, Romania (dated 1597). Painted *trompe l'oeil*, with the flowers arranged in stylized, radial compositions around a large central blossom, these works were among the earliest independent floral still-lifes by a Netherlandish artist and were a great influence on Roelandt Savery and Jacques de Gheyn II.

Hoefnagel was a highly cultured man who also acted as a drawings dealer, corresponded with other humanists and wrote distinguished Latin poetry, as preserved in the *Album amicorum* of Abraham Ortelius (Cambridge, Pembroke Coll.). He also made a number of works of art dedicated to friends, such as the *Allegory for Johannes Radermacher* (oil on panel, signed and dated 1590; Rotterdam, Boymans–van Beuningen). Hoefnagel's son Jacob Hoefnagel (1575–*c*. 1630), also an artist at the Rudolfine court, perpetuated his father's style in such works as *Archetypa studiaque patris Georgii Hoefnagelii* (Frankfurt am Main, 1592), a series of engravings of insects and flowers after his father's work.

UNPUBLISHED SOURCES

G. Bocskay and J. Hoefnagel: *Mira calligraphiae monumenta* (late 1590s); ed. L. Hendrix and T. Vignau-Wilberg (London, 1992)

PRINTS

G. Braun and F. Hogenberg: *Civitates orbis terrarum*, 6 vols (Cologne, 1572–1618), facs. ed. R. A. Skelton and A. O. Vietor, 3 vols (Cleveland, 1966)

BIBLIOGRAPHY

BNB; Thieme–Becker
K. van Mander: *Schilder-boeck* ([1603]–1604), ii, fols 78–9
J. von Sandrart: *Teutsche Academie* (1675–9); ed. A. R. Peltzer (1925), p. 169
E. Chmelarz: 'Georg und Jacob Hoefnagel', *Jb. Ksthist. Samml. Allhöch. Ksrhaus.*, xvii (1896), pp. 275–90
E. Kris: 'Georg Hoefnagel und der wissenschaftliche Naturalismus', *Festschrift für Julius Schlosser* (Vienna, 1927), pp. 243–53
O. Benesch: *Die Zeichnungen der niederländischen Schulen des XV. und XVI. Jahrhunderts* (1928), ii of *Beschreibender Katalog der Handzeichnungen in der graphischen Sammlung Albertina* (Vienna, 1928–33)
R. van Roosbroeck: *Patientia: 24 politieke emblemata door Joris Hoefnagel, 1569* (Antwerp, 1935)

A. E. Popham: 'Georg Hoefnagel and the *Civitates orbis terrarum*', *Maso Finiguerra*, i (1936), pp. 182–201
——: 'On a Letter by Joris Hoefnagel', *Oud-Holland*, liii (1936), pp. 145–51
I. Bergström: *Dutch Still-life Painting in the Seventeenth Century* (London, 1956)
E. Schilling: 'Zwei Landschaftszeichnungen des Georg Hoefnagel', *Kunstgeschichtliche Studien für Hans Kaufmann* (Berlin, 1956), pp. 233–9
I. Bergström: 'Georg Hoefnagel, le dernier des grands miniaturistes flamands', *L'Oeil*, xcvii–cii (1963), pp. 2–9
T. A. Wilberg Vignau-Schuurman: *Die emblematischen Elemente im Werke Joris Hoefnagels*, 2 vols (Leiden, 1969)
——: 'Joris Hoefnagel's groteskenserie en de *Amorum emblemata* van Otto van Veen', *Opstellen voor H. van de Waal* (Leiden, 1970), pp. 214–32
I. Bergström: 'Flower Pieces of Radial Composition in European 16th- and 17th-century Art', *Album amicorum J. G. van Gelder* (The Hague, 1973), pp. 22–6
J. Spicer-Durham: *The Drawings of Roelant Savery*, 2 vols (diss., New Haven, CT, Yale U., 1979)
Drawings from the Holy Roman Empire (exh. cat., ed. T. DaCosta Kaufmann; Princeton U., NJ, A. Mus., 1982)
M. L. Hendrix: *Joris Hoefnagel and the 'Four Elements': A Study in Sixteenth-century Nature Painting* (diss., Princeton U., NJ, 1984; microfilm, Ann Arbor, 1986)
L. Nuti: 'Alle origini del Grand Tour: Immagini e cultura della città italiana negli atlanti e nelle cosmografie del secolo XVI', *Stor. Urb.*, xxvii (1984), pp. 3–35
M. L. Hendrix: 'Elementa depicta', *F. M. R. Mag.*, ix (March 1985), pp. 78–85 [excellent pls]
T. DaCosta Kaufmann: *L'Ecole de Prague* (Paris, 1985; rev. Eng. trans., Chicago, 1988) [excellent pls]
T. Vignau-Wilberg: 'Joris Hoefnagels Tätigkeit in München', *Jb. Ksthist. Samml. Wien*, lxxxi (1985), pp. 103–67
Albrecht Dürer und die Tier- und Pflanzenstudien der Renaissance (exh. cat., ed. F. Koreny; Vienna, Albertina, 1985; rev. Eng. trans., Boston, 1988) [excellent pls]
T. DaCosta Kaufmann: 'The Nature of Imitation: Reflections on Dürer and Nature Painting towards 1600', *Jb. Ksthist. Samml. Wien*, lxxxii–lxxxiii (1986), pp. 116–44
P. Dreyer: 'Zeichnungen von Hans Verhagen dem Stummen von Antwerpen: Ein Beitrag zu den Vorlagen der Tierminiaturen Hans Bols und Georg Hoefnagels', *Jb. Ksthist. Samml. Wien*, lxxxii (1986)
T. Vignau-Wilberg: '*Qualche deseigni d'importancia*: Joris Hoefnagel als Zeichnungssammler', *Münchn. Jb. Bild. Kst*, n. s. 3, xxxviii (1987), pp. 185–214
M. L. Hendrix: 'An Introduction to Hoefnagel and Bocskay's *Model Book of Calligraphy* in the J. Paul Getty Museum', *Prag um 1600: Beiträge zur Kunst und Kultur am Hofe Rudolfs II* (Freren, 1988), pp. 110–17
L. Hendrix and T. Vignau-Wilberg, eds: '*Mira calligraphiae monumenta*': A Sixteenth-century Calligraphic Manuscript Inscribed by Georg Bocskay and Illuminated by Joris Hoefnagel (Malibu, CA, 1992; London, 1993)
S. Androssov: 'Two Drawings by Hoefnagel', *Burl. Mag.*, cxxxvi/1095 (1994), pp. 369–72

LEE HENDRIX

Hoehme, Gerhard (*b* Greppin bei Dessau, 5 Feb 1920; *d* Neuss, 29 June 1989). German painter, printmaker and sculptor. He studied calligraphy in Halle in 1951 under Herbert Post (*b* 1903). In the same year he moved from East to West Germany, and after 1952 lived in Düsseldorf, where he studied for three terms at the Kunstakademie, Hochschule für Bildende Künste, under Otto Coester (*b* 1902). He also met his sponsor and subsequently the owner of the gallery where he exhibited, Jean-Pierre Wilhelm, who encouraged his artistic inclination to Tachism and who introduced him to Jean Fautrier and Jean Dubuffet in Paris. In the rhythmic-gestural, impasto application of colour Hoehme discovered both dynamic principle and a source of power and energy. He thought of painting primarily as idea. In 1954 he took over the chairmanship of Gruppe 53. From 1955 to 1957 he worked on his series of *Black Pictures* (e.g. *Black Spring*, 1956;

Düsseldorf, Kstsamml. Nordrhein–Westfalen). By damaging the surface and integrating string he gave the painting the appearance of spatial depth. In 1957 he produced the first 'shaped canvases' (e.g. *Entropy*, 1957; Bonn, Rhein. Landesmus.), 'colour posts' and 'colour objects', and in 1958 the *Bark Paintings* (e.g. *The Junk Painting*, 1958; Saarbrücken, Landesmus. Vor- & Frühgesch.), in which the colour of old paintings was smoothed and then worked in relief. The range of colour became ever richer, and scraps of newspapers were incorporated into the painting. In 1959 he painted jumbled characters, which from 1960 turned into 'letter-paintings', as syntheses of information and association (e.g. *Roman Letter*, 1960; Stuttgart, Staatsgal.). Hoehme started on linear structures in 1963–4, subsequently painting on sewing patterns, which in 1965 were frontally extended by foregrounds of linear strings and nylon threads to form painting-boxes. Using coloured polythene string he succeeded in connecting up the material picture canon and picture-space with real space to create a 'space-painting'. After 1967 string was used for free-standing sculptured pictures (e.g. *Radiating Fall*, nylon string and perspex, 1967; artist's estate, see Argan and Thurn, p. 170). Hoehme developed relationships between the individual parts and the work itself (imaginary space) and the observer (real space). In 1968 Hoehme wrote his manifesto *Relationen* and gave his works titles accordingly. In the 1970s he extended the use of string and cable in conjunction with pictures that acquired political content and became 'thought-spaces'. After 1980 he developed his *Etna Cycle* on Sicily, in which volcanic rock, perspex and PVC cord are combined with painted colour, to form textures that allude playfully to myth. Hoehme's intention was to play on myth and to illustrate volcanic movement through light, colour and painting gestures.

WRITINGS
Relationen (Berlin, 1968)

BIBLIOGRAPHY
Gerhard Hoehme: Wenn man nichts sieht, schaut man länger hin (exh. cat., ed. J. Partenheimer; Düsseldorf, Städt. Ksthalle; Heidelberg, Kstver.; Heidelberg, Schloss; 1979) [incl. text of *Relationen* and other writings]
G. C. Argan and H. P. Thurn: *Gerhard Hoehme: Werk und Zeit, 1948–1983* (Stuttgart, 1983)
L'Etna: Mythos und Wirklichkeit (exh. cat., ed. E.-G. Güse; Saarbrücken, Saarland-Mus., 1990)

ULRIKE LEHMANN

Hoeimaker [Hoeymaecker], **Hendrik** (*b* Tournai, 22 Dec 1559; *d* Ghent, 11 Nov 1626). Flemish architect and Jesuit brother. The son of a master bricklayer, he followed his father's trade. When he was 26 he joined the Jesuit order and lived in various towns in the southern Netherlands, where from 1587 he built numerous colleges and churches for his order. He both drew up the plans and participated in the construction, as did his confrère Pieter Huyssens. His buildings, conceived within the Late Gothic tradition, were erected before the advent of early Baroque in the Netherlands. His preference was for vaulted three-aisled churches whose finishing details often betray a Renaissance influence. From his sketchbook (Ghent, Stadsbib.) it appears that he knew the work of Philibert de L'Orme. His most important works were the college church at Tournai (1601–4), the only work of his still intact, and the flamboyant Gothic college church at Ghent

(1605–19; destr.). Set into the gable of the church at Tournai is a Renaissance portal of 1603. In May 1606 work started on the Jesuit church in Brussels, for which Hoeimaker had produced the initial plans. After the intercession of Franciscus Aguilonius, Rector Johannes van Wintershoven allowed the court architect Jacob Francart to complete the church in 1616. Francart's intervention led to the rejection of Gothic in favour of Baroque, a significant turning-point in the history of southern Netherlandish architecture.

BIBLIOGRAPHY
Thieme–Becker
J. Braun: *Die belgischen Jesuitenkirchen* (Freiburg im Breisgau, 1907)
P. Parent: *L'Architecture des Pays-Bas méridionaux (Belgique et Nord de la France) aux XVIe, XVIIe et XVIIIe siècles* (Paris, 1926)
J. H. Plantenga: *L'Architecture religieuse dans l'ancien duché de Brabant* (The Hague, 1926)
J. van Ackere: *Barok en classicisme in België* (Brussels, 1974)
L. Brouwers: *De Jezuïeten te Brussel, 1586–1773–1833* (Mechelen, 1979)

J.-P. ESTHER

Hoelzel, Adolf. *See* HÖLZEL, ADOLF.

Hoet. Dutch family of artists and writers. (1) Gerard Hoet (i), the son of Moses Hoet (*d* after 1665), a glass painter, was principally a history painter in the Dutch Italianate style of Cornelis van Poelenburch but was also active in other artistic forms, including drawing, on which he wrote a textbook. His elder son, (2) Gerard Hoet (ii), painted in his father's manner, before becoming an art dealer; he is chiefly remembered for the controversies in which he engaged concerning the art trade. Hendrick Jacob Hoet (1693–1733), the younger son of Gerard Hoet (i), was a genre and still-life painter.

(1) Gerard Hoet (i) (*b* Zaltbommel, Gelderland, 22 Aug 1648; *d* The Hague, 2 Dec 1733). Painter, draughtsman and writer. He trained with his father and with Warnard van Ryssen (*b c.* 1625; *fl c.* 1664), a pupil of Cornelis van Poelenburch. In 1672 Hoet moved to The Hague, then to Paris; after a year he returned to the northern Netherlands via Brussels. He settled in Utrecht, where he founded a drawing academy in 1697 with Hendrick Schoock (*fl* 1669–96). From 1714 Hoet resided in The Hague. He depicted mainly religous, mythological or Classical subjects set in landscapes, which were painted on a small scale in the style of van Poelenburch, but he also produced larger works, often with many figures, in an elegant, classicizing style. Examples of this decorative painting are his ceiling and wall paintings at the castle of De Slangenburg at Doetinchem. Hoet also painted portraits and some genre pieces. His book on drawing, with 103 prints by Pieter Bodart (*fl* early 18th century), was published in 1712. Hoet also designed many illustrations for bibles.

WRITINGS
Ontslote deure der tekenkunst [Opened doors in the art of drawing] (Leiden, 1712)

BIBLIOGRAPHY
Bénézit; *NKL*; Thieme–Becker
A. Houbraken: *De groote schouburgh* (1718–), iii, pp. 239–42
J. Campo Weyerman: *De levenbeschrijvingen der Nederlandse konstschilders en konstschilderessen*, iii (The Hague, 1729), pp. 90–94
J. van Gool: *Die nieuwe schouburg* (1750–51), ii, pp. 415–22

(2) Gerard Hoet (ii) (*b* Utrecht, *bapt* 6 March 1698; *d* The Hague, 1760). Painter, art dealer and writer, son of (1) Gerard Hoet (i). He was his father's pupil and copied his work but also painted portraits and decorative works of his own. In 1751 he wrote a pamphlet entitled *Brief aan een' vrient* ('Letter to a friend'), in response to the publication in 1750 of the first volume of *De nieuwe schouburg der Nederlantsche kunstschilders en schilderessen* ('The new theatre of Dutch painters'), a collection of artists' lives by the painter JAN VAN GOOL, in which the art trade, as promoter of 17th-century painting, was held responsible for the decline of Dutch painting in the 18th century. In his pamphlet Hoet, writing as a dealer, attributed the decline to the mediocre standards achieved by contemporary artists. Following the publication of the second volume of van Gool's book in 1751, Hoet concluded the dispute in 1753 with his *Aanmerkingen* ('Commentary') on both volumes, in which he included a list of 130 painters who, according to him, had unjustly been omitted from *De nieuwe schouburg*. Hoet's most important work is the first two volumes of *Catalogus of naamlyst van schilderijen, met derzelven pryzen* ('Catalogue or list of titles of paintings with their prices'), an index of old Dutch auction catalogues that, for the first time, attempted to document the prices of paintings. This work also included catalogues of important contemporary picture collections; the third and final volume was compiled in 1770 by Pieter Terwesten (1714–98).

WRITINGS

Brief aan een' vrient [Letter to a friend] (The Hague, 1751)
Catalogus of naamlyst van schilderijen, met derzelven pryzen, zedert een langen reeks van jaaren zoo in Holland als op andere plaatzen in het openbaar verkogt: Benevens een verzameling van lysten van verscheyden nog in wezen zynde cabinetten [Catalogue or list of titles of paintings with their prices, sold publicly over many years in Holland as well as elsewhere: plus a selection of lists of various collections currently in existence], 2 vols (The Hague, 1752/*R* Soest, 1976)
Aanmerkingen op het eerste en tweede deel des 'Nieuwen schouburgs der Nederlantsche kunstschilders en schilderessen', door Johan van Gool [Commentary on the first and second volumes of the *New Theatre of Dutch Painters* by Jan van Gool ([The Hague], [?1753])

BIBLIOGRAPHY

NKL; Thieme–Becker
L. de Vries: 'De kunsthandel is zoo edel als eenigen, vermits "er geen bedrog in is": De Pamflettenstrijd tussen Gerard Hoet en Johan van Gool' [Dealing in art is as noble as anything, provided 'there is no deception in it': the war of pamphlets between Gerard Hoet and Jan van Gool], *Leids Ksthist. Jb.*, iv (1985), pp. 1–16
——: *Diamante gedenkzuilen en leerzaeme voorbeelden: Een bespreking van Johan van Gools Nieuwe Schouburg* [Diamond commemorative columns and instructive examples: A discussion of Johan van Gool's New Theatre] (Groningen , 1990), pp. 217–65

C. J. A. WANSINK

Hoetger, Bernhard (*b* Hörde, 4 May 1874; *d* Interlaken, 1949). German architect and sculptor. As a youth he worked as a stonecutter. In 1897 he enrolled as a sculpture student in the Kunstakademie, Düsseldorf. In 1900 he went to Paris and stayed there for seven years. He was initially influenced by the work of Rodin but later looked to archaic Greek sculpture. In 1905 he participated in the first Salon d'Automne and in 1907 he returned to Germany. He became a member of the artists' colony in Darmstadt in 1911. The colony transformed the Mathildenhöhe, a ducal estate, into a display of Art Nouveau architecture and design. His contribution was a set of sculptures (1912–14) in the grove of plane trees planted in the park's main terrace, which stood in front of the Wedding Tower and Exhibition Hall, built by Joseph Maria Olbrich in 1908. The sculptures include a fountain decorated with four reliefs entitled Sleep, Resurrection, Life and Spring. At the end of the terrace his sculpture of a dying mother and her child, a classically inspired grouping, looks back at the tower. Elsewhere in the grove, friezes of standing and crouching nude youths hint at the beginning of his appreciation of German Expressionism, the movement with which most of his architecture is associated. Their self-consciously awkward forms suit their folkloric themes.

Hoetger's first building was Brunnenhof, a villa built for himself in Worpswede in 1915. Never trained as an architect, he sculpted models of his buildings in clay. The Bahlsen company in Hannover asked him to design a company town for them: built in the shape of the firm's Egyptianizing trademark, the project was published in Hannover in 1917. In 1921 he built a second house for himself in Worpswede, Weyerberg (now the Hoetger Hotel). In it he combined the traditional hunting lodge with villas in the Arts and Crafts style to form an Expressionist work. Spirits are painted on the walls and ceiling of the bedroom. The furniture and half-timbering are carved into evocations of Nordic folk art. Vernacular architectural forms are caricatured in richly textured elevations of brick walls braced with timbering and wrapped in low-pitched tile roofs. Patterned bricks are laid in reliefs that project from the plane of the wall.

Hoetger repeated the patterned brick motif in the Böttcherstrasse development (1923–31) in Bremen, built for Ludwig Roselius, a local coffee importer, industrialist and banker. Nine buildings frame a crooked pedestrian street. Roselius shared Hoetger's nationalist ideology, which celebrated Germanic medieval and folk art. Hoetger's revival of Hanseatic architecture in the Böttcherstrasse was also begun in the same year as Fritz Höger's Chilehaus in nearby Hamburg was completed. The climax of Hoetger's half-medieval, half-idiosyncratic complex is the building he designed to house Roselius's collection of paintings by Paula Modersohn-Becker (now the Paula-Modersohn-Becker-Haus). Its last building, Atlantis Haus, has his characteristically theatrical reworkings of the International style's mechanical imagery. Economical depression and political change ended Hoetger's career. His attempts to collaborate with the Nazis ceased when Hitler himself criticized Böttcherstrasse. His last building was a house for himself in Berlin-Frohnau (1939–40). In 1933 he moved to Switzerland.

BIBLIOGRAPHY

C. Uphoff: *Bernhard Hoetger* (Leipzig, 1919)
S. Gallwitz: *Dreissig Jahre Worpswede* (Bremen, 1922)
L. Roselius: *Reden und Schriften zur Böttcherstrasse* (Bremen, 1922)
W. Pehnt: *Expressionist Architecture* (London, 1973), pp. 129–36
Kunstkolonie Mathildenhöhe Darmstadt, 1899–1914 (exh. cat., Darmstadt, Ausstellhallen Mathildenhöhe, 1976), pp. 100–65
Bernhard Hoetger, 1874–1949: Plastiken aus den Pariser Jahren, 1900–1910 (exh. cat., Bremen, Graph. Kab. Ksthandel Wolfgang Werner, 1977)

KATHLEEN JAMES

Hofer, Karl [Carl] (**Johannes Christian**) (*b* Karlsruhe, 11 Oct 1878; *d* Berlin, 3 April 1955). German painter, draughtsman and printmaker. He was brought up by two great-aunts and later in an orphanage because his father died when he was still an infant, and after leaving primary school he became apprenticed to a bookselling business in Karlsruhe. He began to draw at this time, visiting the Staatliche Kunsthalle in Karlsruhe and (with the help of the mother of his friend Leopold Ziegler, who later became a philosopher) obtaining a scholarship at the Grossherzogliche Badische Akademie der Künste in Karlsruhe in 1897. He learnt little from the painters who taught him, Robert Poetzelberger (1856–1930), Leopold Kalckreuth and Hans Thoma, and instead was influenced by the paintings of Arnold Böcklin. Hofer made the first of his prints in 1899, eventually producing 17 woodcuts, 69 etchings and 190 lithographs closely related in style and subject-matter to his paintings. On travelling to Paris in 1900 on a scholarship he came into contact with Impressionism and the work of Paul Cézanne, but he was little affected by them. On returning to Germany he became a postgraduate pupil of Hans Thoma, following him to Stuttgart in 1902. One of the few paintings of this period not destroyed by Hofer is *Children at Prayer* (1901), a genre picture in the style of Thoma; its arrangement of people as in a still-life in an indeterminate space anticipates features of his later work.

In summer 1901 Hofer painted a portrait of the poet Hans Reinhart (1880–1963) and through him met the Reinhart family in Winterthur; their financial support enabled him to study in Rome from 1903 to 1908. Few of his paintings of this period, mainly of nude girls and boys based on Classical models, have survived. One of the best examples is *Three Bathing Youths* (1907; Winterthur, Kstmus.). Travelling through Italy with Hermann Haller and the Italian sculptor and painter Ernesto de Fiori (1884–1945), he was particularly impressed by Pieter Bruegel I's *Parable of the Blind* (1568) in Naples, which left its mark especially on his work of the 1940s and 1950s, and by frescoes (1873) showing views around Naples by Hans von Marées at the Stazione Zoologica research institute in Naples.

In 1908 Hofer left Rome for Paris on the advice of his friend Julius Meier-Graefe, in order to develop his sense of colour by familiarizing himself with the paintings of Delacroix and Cézanne. At the invitation of the Reinharts he made two journeys to India in 1910 and 1911, producing mainly drawings. He settled in Berlin in 1913, but during World War I he was interned in France; Theodor Reinhart (1849–1919) helped obtain his release in 1917, upon which he moved to Switzerland. There he discovered the scenery of Ticino, which became a constant motif in his paintings, as in *Ticino Landscape* (1925; Cologne, Mus. Ludwig); he regularly spent the summer months there until the late 1930s, painting landscapes of this seemingly Arcadian world, which appears hospitable in spite of being devoid of human figures. These pictures, generally simple and balanced in their compositional structure, contain echoes of Cubism and Pittura Metafisica.

Some of Hofer's finest works, on generalized humanitarian themes, date from the 1920s. In the early 1920s he concentrated on unpretentious figure groups: couples, girls with their arms around one another, young men playing cards and pictures such as *Circus People* (*c.* 1921;

Essen, Mus. Flkwang) and *Masquerade Painting* (1922; Cologne, Mus. Ludwig). *Company at Table* (1924; Winterthur, Kstmus.) is typical of these works in its use of an indeterminate space within which to portray people in relaxed contact with one another, suggesting human solidarity. In the second half of the 1920s Hofer became more concerned with conveying symbolic meaning, concealing dark prognoses of approaching disaster within scenes such as *Harlequin, Dummy and Skeleton, Yellow Dog Blues* (1928; Switzerland, priv. col., see Rigby, fig. 29) and *The Black Rooms* (1928, second version, 1943; Berlin, Tiergarten, N.G.; see fig.). It was during this period that Hofer gained official recognition, becoming a professor at the Vereinigte Staatsschulen für Freie und Angewandte Kunst in Charlottenburg, Berlin, in 1920 and a member of the Preussische Akademie der Künste in 1923. In 1928 retrospective exhibitions of his work were held in Berlin and Mannheim to mark his 50th birthday. He visited the USA as a German representative on the jury of the Carnegie International Exhibition in Pittsburgh in 1927 and found the urban life of New York particularly fascinating. He was awarded the second prize of the Carnegie Institute in Pittsburgh for *Pastoral* (1933; Frankfurt am Main, Elisabeth Furler priv. col., see Rigby, fig. 33) in 1934 and their first prize for *In the Wind* in 1938.

Hofer briefly adopted an abstract style in 1930–31 but quickly returned to symbolic pictures of fate. In late June 1934 he was dismissed from his teaching post and subsequently forbidden to paint or exhibit his work. Some of

Karl Hofer: *The Black Rooms*, oil on canvas, 1.49×1.1 m, 1943 (Berlin, Tiergarten, Nationalgalerie)

the 311 works by him confiscated from German institutions were displayed in Munich in 1937 at an exhibition of 'degenerate art' (*see* ENTARTETE KUNST). In 1943 a bomb destroyed about 150 paintings and 1000 drawings in his studio; he produced new versions of a few of the most important of these, such as *The Black Rooms*, working from photographs. In *Black Moonlit Night* (1944) he summarized the destiny of his generation, which was to wander round as homeless sacrifices beneath a gloomy starlit sky.

Hofer's reputation was rehabilitated at the close of World War II with his appointment as Director of the Hochschule für Bildende Künste in Berlin-Charlottenburg, and he held a one-man exhibition in 1946. He painted several theatrical pictures of ruins and tried to come to terms with the fact of the war and the inseparably linked questions of guilt and responsibility. With the exception of *Atom Serenade* (1947; Berlin, Elisabeth Hofer priv. col., see Rigby, fig. 54), his pictures of this period, such as *Cain and Abel* (1946; Ettlingen, Schloss) and *Death Watch* (1949; Berlin, Elisabeth Hofer priv. col., see Rigby, fig. 57), all relate to the tradition of the *memento mori*, but are directed specifically towards those who escaped accepting blame for their actions.

Hofer's decisive role in the cultural life of Berlin after World War II was reflected in many honours bestowed on him. In 1948 he received an honorary doctorate from Humboldt University, in 1950 he became President of the Deutscher Künstlerbund, in 1952 he was made a member of the Order 'Pour le Mérite' in the peace class, and in 1953 he was awarded the prize for art of the city of Berlin. The Berlin 'Festwochen' festival organized a large exhibition in honour of his 75th birthday. Despite this recognition Hofer felt misunderstood, as his art was relegated to the background by the visible dominance of abstract painting. His polemical attack on abstraction, published first in the periodical *Der Monat* and then in the Berlin daily newspaper *Der Tagesspiegel*, led to a break with his colleagues and provoked an equally polemical reply from Will Grohmann. Ernst Wilhelm Nay, Fritz Winter and Willi Baumeister resigned from the Deutscher Künstlerbund in protest against Hofer, with whom they never became reconciled. He died in the middle of this debate about the meaning and value of abstract art.

WRITINGS
Erinnerungen eines Malers (Berlin, 1953)

BIBLIOGRAPHY
B. Reifenberg: *Karl Hofer: Mit einer Selbstbiographie des Künstlers* (Leipzig, 1924)
A. Jannasch: *Carl Hofer* (Potsdam, 1946)
G. Strauss and A. Behne: *Festgabe an Carl Hofer zum siebzigsten Geburtstag, Berlin, 11 Oktober 1948* (Potsdam, 1948)
E. Rathenau, ed.: *Karl Hofer: Das graphische Werk*, intro. K. Martin (New York, 1969)
I. K. Rigby: *Karl Hofer* (New York and London, 1976) [extensive bibliog.]
E. Furler: *Karl Hofer: Leben und Werk in Daten und Bildern* (Frankfurt am Main, 1978)
Karl Hofer, 1878–1955 (exh. cat., W. Berlin, Staatl. Ksthalle; Karlsruhe, Bad. Kstver.; 1978)
E. Hofer-Richold, U. Feist and G. Feist: *Karl Hofer: Bilder im Schlossmuseum Ettlingen* (Berlin, 1983)

ANGELA SCHNEIDER

Hofer, Philip (*b* Cincinnati, OH, 14 March 1898; *d* Cambridge, MA, 9 Nov 1984). American museum curator, collector and writer. He graduated from Harvard University, Cambridge, MA, in 1921. After some years in business he returned to study for a Master's degree in the history of art, which he obtained in 1929. He was Curator of the Spencer Collection of the New York Public Library from 1930 to 1934, when he became the first Assistant Director of the Pierpont Morgan Library, New York. In 1938 he returned to Harvard, where he founded the Department of Printing and Graphic Arts, and was its Curator up to 1968. He was also Secretary of the Fogg Art Museum at Harvard University from 1952 to 1964. He began collecting rare books while still at school and developed a specialist interest in the art of the book: its decoration, layout and illustration, and the link between drawings and prints. He amassed a remarkable private collection of German, Iberian and particularly Italian illustrated books of the 18th century. Both the Houghton Library at Harvard and the Fogg Art Museum benefited from Hofer's acquisitions. These reflect the breadth of his interests and include medieval manuscripts, Ethiopian, Persian, Indian, Chinese and Japanese books and manuscripts, fine printed and illustrated books of the 16th century (in particular early Florentine woodcut books), and modern private press editions. A similarly wide range is covered in his major publications, including works on Baroque illustration, two important catalogues of French and Italian illustrated books in the Harvard College Library, and a study of Edward Lear as a landscape draughtsman.

WRITINGS
Baroque Book Illustration: A Short Survey from the Collection in the Department of Graphic Arts, Harvard College Library (Cambridge, MA, 1951)
Eighteenth Century Book Illustrations (Los Angeles, 1956)
Edward Lear as a Landscape Draughtsman (Cambridge, MA, 1967)
Catalogue of Italian Illustrated Books in the Recollection of the Department of Graphic Arts, Harvard College Library (Cambridge, MA, 1974)

BIBLIOGRAPHY
Drawings for Book Illustration: The Hofer Collection (exh. cat., by D. P. Becker, Cambridge, MA, Harvard U., Houghton Lib., 1980)
Obituary, *The Times* (22 Nov 1984)

□

Hoff, Povl Ernst (*b* Copenhagen, 24 Aug 1903). Danish architect. He was in partnership with architect Bennet Windinge (1905–86) from 1942. Blocks of flats with communal facilities and institutions had a central place in their production. The block of flats Høje Søborg, Copenhagen (1949–51), was a pioneering work in Denmark. Similarly innovative were the high-rise blocks for the handicapped in Copenhagen (Hans Knudsens Plads, 1960) and Ålborg (Grønlands Torv, 1963), the students' residence at Sorø Akademi (1963), and Værebro Park (1966), a large block of flats with integrated communal facilities. They also supervised the construction of the Montebello neurological hospitals in Gentofte and Helsingør (1963) and formed part of the team of architects that designed the high-rise housing complex Høje Gladsaxe (1962–8), including the shopping centre, schools and other facilities. These large buildings, based on prefabrication and industrial assembly techniques, were designed with a sense for the possibilities for this kind of project within a Modernist framework, but the architects' abilities to create gently shaped and attractive surroundings came to the fore in smaller, institutional projects. A high point in their work, and in modern Danish domestic architecture in general, was, however, Søndergårdparken (1950), Gladsaxe, a modest, traditional arrangement of terraced houses in park-like surroundings.

BIBLIOGRAPHY

'Kollektivhuset Høje Søborg', *Arkitekten*, liv (1952), pp. 173–84

'Søndergård Park', *Arkitekten*, lv (1953), pp. 174–81

P. E. Skriver: 'Montebellos Dag og Nathospital', *Arkitektur DK*, vii/4 (1963), pp. 121–31

——: 'Nye alumnatsbygninger ved Sorøakademi' [New students' building at Sorø Academy], *Arkitektur DK*, vii/4 (1963), pp. 132–7

JØRGEN SESTOFT

Hoff, (George) Rayner (*b* Isle of Man, 27 Nov 1894; *d* Sydney, 19 Nov 1937). Australian sculptor of British birth. He studied at Nottingham School of Art from 1910 to 1915 and again, after active service in World War I, in 1919. He then transferred to the Royal College of Art, London, and was awarded a diploma in sculpture in 1921. In 1922 he received a British School in Rome scholarship for study in Italy but cut this short and emigrated to Australia in May 1923 to become head teacher of the sculpture department at East Sydney Technical College.

Hoff's work belongs to an inter-war classical revival and his sculptures attest to his absorption of the Paganist–Vitalist theories promoted in Australia in the 1920s and 1930s by his close associate Norman Lindsay. Hoff's work was generally life-affirming and sexually adventurous for its period. His major paganist sculpture is the relief *Deluge: Stampede of the Lower Gods* (4.5 m wide; 1925–7; Canberra, N.G.), which depicts crowds of mermaids, dryads, tritons, satyrs and Australian Aborigines. The life-size *Australian Venus* (*c.* 1927; Sydney, A.G. NSW) is Hoff's attempt to transpose the perfection of classical proportions on to an Australian subject.

Hoff was responsible for several of the most significant Australian memorials to World War I: the South Australian war memorial (1927–9)—the largest Australian sculpture at that date—and the Anzac memorial (1930–34), the culminating work of his career now standing in Hyde Park, Sydney, which was executed in conjunction with the architect Bruce Dellit. The latter is a particularly successful union of architecture and sculpture, combining classical traditions and Art Deco. Hoff worked to create an adequate training programme for young Australian sculptors, and he encouraged the rise of an unusually coherent school of sculpture in Australia during the 1920s and 1930s.

BIBLIOGRAPHY

Art in Australia, n. s. 3, 46 (1932) [Rayner Hoff number]

S. Napier: *The Book of the Anzac Memorial, NSW* (Sydney, 1934)

W. Lygon: *The Sculpture of Rayner Hoff* (Sydney, 1934)

D. Edwards: 'This Vital Flesh: The 1920s Sculpture of Rayner Hoff', *A. & Australia*, xxiv/1 (1986)

DEBORAH EDWARDS

Hoff, Robert van 't (*b* Rotterdam, 5 Nov 1887; *d* New Milton, Hants, 25 April 1979). Dutch architect and designer. He studied from 1906 to 1911 at the Birmingham School of Art, where he was influenced by the Arts and Crafts Movement, the Glasgow school and the theories of W. R. Lethaby. He then studied (1911–14) at the Architectural Association in London, where he met David Bomberg and became acquainted with the Futurist and Vorticist

avant-garde. His first executed designs—Løvdalla (1911), Huis ter Heide, near Utrecht, and Augustus John's house (1913–14), Chelsea, London—show a predilection for varied façades and simple floor-plans; details are executed with great care. In 1914 he went to the USA to study the architecture and theories of Frank Lloyd Wright. The summer-house for J. N. Verloop (1914) and the country villa for A. B. Henny (1915–19), both at Huis ter Heide, reflect his admiration for Wright, and the latter, nicknamed the 'Concrete villa' for its inventive use of concrete-frame construction, established van 't Hoff's reputation. The house was adopted, first by the architects associated with De Stijl and later by architects of Het Nieuwe Bouwen, as a model of 'abstract' architecture. In 1917 van 't Hoff came into direct contact with De Stijl, providing financial support for the movement and publishing articles in its periodical. The movement's influence is evident in his design for a house-boat (*Woonschip De Stijl*, 1917–18) and his interior and furniture designs (1918–20). Van 't Hoff became a member of the Communist Party in 1918–19; he initiated an exchange programme with Soviet artists and worked on designs for blocks of flats and mass construction, but none of these projects was realized. For van 't Hoff the relation between the artistic avant-garde and the proletarian revolution was self-evident, but in 1919, when the international revolution failed to materialize, he withdrew from De Stijl and eventually from artistic life altogether. He built himself a small cottage, devoid of aesthetic pretence, and in 1933 he moved to England to join an anarchic experimental commune, calling himself Robert Van ('t Hoff), ex-architect.

WRITINGS

'Architecture and its Development', *De Stijl*, i/5 (1918), pp. 57–9; ii/4 (1919), pp. 40–42; ii/5 (1919), pp. 54–5

'Annotations to Appendix xx', *De Stijl*, ii/10 (1919), pp. 114–16

'Letters from Robt van 't Hoff', *De Stijl*, ii/79–84 (1927), p. 24

BIBLIOGRAPHY

T. van Doesburg: 'Annotations to Appendix xi: Spatial-plastic Interior Architecture', *De Stijl*, i/6 (1918), pp. 71–2

——: 'Some Thought about Modern Architecture in Relation to the Summer Cottage at Huis ter Heide, Architect Robt van 't Hoff', *De Stijl*, ii/3 (1919), pp. 31–2

Robert van 't Hoff (exh. cat., Eindhoven, Stedel. Van Abbemus.; Delft, Tech. U., Fac. Archit.; 1967)

J. Leering: 'Rob van 't Hoff, de ex-architect', *Wonen TA-BK*, xi (1979), pp. 2–3

E. Vermeulen: 'Robert van 't Hoff', *De beginjaren van De Stijl, 1917–1933*, ed. C. Blotkamp (Utrecht, 1982; Eng. trans., Cambridge, MA, 1986)

For further bibliography *see* DE STIJL.

EVELINE VERMEULEN

Hoffman, Friedrich Gottlob (*b* Belgern, nr Leipzig, 1741; *d c.* 1806). German cabinetmaker. By 1770 he was established as a master cabinetmaker in Leipzig. An important early patron was the art dealer Karl Christian Heinrich Rost (1742–98), who commissioned furniture closely based on French and English models. In 1788 Hoffman obtained a loan to extend his business in Leipzig and a subsidiary workshop at Eilenburg; his total workforce was 16 tradesmen. In 1789, after a dispute with the local guild of cabinetmakers, he published his first pattern book, *Abbildungen der vornehmsten Tischlerarbeiten, welche verfertiget und zu haben sind bey Friedrich Gottlob Hoffmann,* *wohnhaft auf dem alten Neumarkt in Leipzig*, an anthology of designs for household furniture, mostly inspired by the Louis XVI Neo-classical style. In 1795 he produced a second catalogue, *Neues Verzeichnis und Muster-Charte des Meubles-Magazin*, in which English design types are dominant. A number of pieces corresponding to plates in these two pattern books have been identified (e.g. sofa, *c.* 1789, and cylinder secrétaire, *c.* 1795; both Dresden, Schloss Pillnitz; table, *c.* 1789; Weimar, Kirms-Krockow-Haus & Herder-Mus.). From 1788 to 1795 Hoffman supplied furniture to the German courts in Gotha, Weimar, Dresden, Brunswick and Dessau and to Berlin, Hamburg, Vienna, Constantinople and St Petersburg. By 1797 he had repaid his loan and was employing 42 workmen. His name appears in Leipzig directories until 1806.

BIBLIOGRAPHY

K. Krull: 'Friedrich Gottlob Hoffman: A Late Eighteenth Century Leipzig Cabinetmaker', *Furn. Hist.*, xxv (1989), pp. 120–23

CHRISTOPHER GILBERT

Hoffmann, Hans (*b* ?Nuremberg, *c.* 1545–50; *d* Prague, between 14 Oct 1591 and 12 June 1592). German painter and draughtsman. He was first mentioned in 1576 in the Nuremberg *Ratsverlässe* as a painter and a citizen of the town. (It is uncertain whether he is the Hans Hoffmann who, with his wife Eva, baptized a son in the church of St Sebald in December 1572.) He lived in Nuremberg until 1584, when he was called by Duke William V of Bavaria to the court in Munich. From 1585 he was court painter to Emperor Rudolf II in Prague, where he received an annual salary of 100 thalers until his death.

The artistic achievement of Hoffmann's Nuremberg period is much better documented than his later career: most of his known paintings and drawings date from the years between 1573 and 1585. The Nuremberg collector Paulus Praun owned more than 100 works by the artist. Because the collection remained together until the beginning of the 19th century, many of these drawings and paintings can still be identified. Over 50 drawings, once

Hans Hoffmann: *Peony, Irises and Beetles*, watercolour and gouache on vellum, 308×383 mm, 1582 (Malibu, CA, J. Paul Getty Museum)

part of the contents of a portfolio in the Praun collection, are preserved in Budapest (Mus. F.A.). Hoffmann's first signed work, a painted portrait of woman *Barbara Möringer* (1573; Munich, Bayer. Nmus.), was strongly influenced by Nicolas Neufchatel. The stiffness of the figure suggests the work of a young artist. His development as a portrait artist can be traced through a painting of 1580 depicting a *Nuremberger Goldsmith* (Nuremberg, Ger. Nmus.), two drawings portraying *Willibald Imhoff* (1580; Budapest, Mus. F.A.) and the head of *Paulus Pfinzing* in black and white chalk (1591; Nuremberg, Ger. Nmus.). Portraits of the sculptor *J. G. van der Schardt*, of *Claus Narr* and others are now lost, but they are recorded as having been in the Praun collection.

Hoffmann is perhaps best known for his numerous copies after drawings by Albrecht Dürer which he would have seen in the Nuremberg collection of Willibald Imhoff. He was among the most gifted of the many artists working at the end of the 16th century in a stylistic trend that has come to be known as the DÜRER RENAISSANCE. He made not only exact or slightly changed copies but also free variations of Dürer's originals. He often made several copies and also different versions of one and the same drawing, signing perhaps one with his own monogram, another with that of Dürer. One of his free variations of Dürer's *Hare* (Vienna, Albertina), in this case a panel painting in oils (priv. col., see 1985 exh. cat., no. 47), is recorded as having been bought by Emperor Rudolf II in October 1585 for 200 guilders. Another oil painting by him, *The Expulsion* (Vienna, Ksthist. Mus.), once probably also belonged to the Emperor. Many of Hoffmann's numerous nature studies, dating mostly from his Nuremberg period (e.g. *Peony, Irises and Beetles*, 1582; Malibu, CA, Getty Mus.; see fig.), are copied after Dürer or other artists; some, however, are apparently drawn from life. Two entries in the inventory of Rudolf II's collection—a book with animal and plant drawings by Hoffmann and another with animals, partly by him—suggest that he drew nature studies in Prague as well. One of these entries possibly refers to a manscript (Vienna, Österreich. Nbib., Cod. min. 42) that includes some depictions of animals by Hoffmann. Besides the portraits, one further signed painting by Hoffmann is known: a copy of Dürer's portrait of woman *Hieronymus Holzschuher* (1578; Nuremberg, Ger. Nmus.). Two paintings of *Christ among the Doctors* (Brunswick, Herzog Anton Ulrich-Mus.; Warsaw, N. Mus.) are attributed to him on the basis of a similar signed drawing (Budapest, Mus. F.A.). The attribution to Hoffmann of several *Ecce homo* paintings (some with an AD monogram) is doubtful, since none of them is signed, and their painterly technique and manner differ from those of the signed paintings.

BIBLIOGRAPHY

Thieme–Becker

F. Winkler: 'Dürerstudien III: Verschollene Meisterzeichnungen Dürers', *Jb. Preuss. Kstsamml.*, liii (1932), pp. 68–89

P. Strieder: 'Zur Nürnberger Bildniskunst des 16. Jahrhunderts', *Münchn. Jb. Bild. Kst*, n. s., 2, vii (1956), pp. 134–7

K. Pilz: 'Hans Hoffman: Ein Nürnberger Dürer-Nachahmer aus der 2. Hälfte des 16. Jahrhunderts', *Mitt. Ver. Gesch. Stadt Nürnberg*, li (1962), pp. 236–72

F. Koreny: *Albrecht Dürer und die Tier- und Pflanzenstudien der Renaissance* (Munich, 1985)

K. Achilles: 'Naturstudien von Hans Hoffmann in der Kunstsammlung des Nürnberger Kaufmanns Paulus II Praun', *Jb. Ksthist. Samml. Wien*, lxxxii–lxxxiii (1986–7), pp. 243–59

Prag um 1600: Kunst und Kultur am Hofe Rudolfs II. (exh. cat. ed. J.F. Koreny and S. Segal: 'Hans Hoffman–Entdeckungen und Zuschreibungen', *Jb. Ksthist. Samml. Wien*, lxxxv–lxxxvi (1989–1990), pp. 57–65

K. Achilles-Syndram: *Die Zeichnungssammlung des Nürnberger Kaufmanns Paulus II. Praun (1548–1616): Versuch einer Rekonstruktion* (diss., Berlin, Tech. U., 1990)

Kunst des Sammelns: Das Praunsche Kabinett; Meisterwerke von Dürer bis Carracci (exh. cat. by K. Achilles-Syndram, Nuremburg, Ger. Nmus., 1994)

SZILVIA BODNÁR

Hoffmann, Hans Ruprecht (*b* Worms, 1543; *d* Trier, June 1616). German sculptor and medallist. He was the most important German sculptor working west of the Rhine during the late 16th century and early 17th. He was apprenticed to Dietrich Schro (*c.* 1515–94) in Mainz from 1554 and may have worked for Johann von Trarbach (*fl* 1568–1610) in Simmern (Rheinland-Pfalz). By 1568 'Ruprecht the sculptor' was in Trier, and soon afterwards he began to receive important commissions. Hoffmann and his large workshop produced at least 100 altars, religious reliefs, pulpits, epitaphs and other stone-carvings, mainly for towns in the archbishopric of Trier. Most of his finest works are in Trier Cathedral and the adjacent Liebfrauenkirche. Between 1570 and 1572 he carved the elaborate sandstone cathedral pulpit. The seven reliefs on the pulpit and stair are modelled on prints by Maarten van Heemskerck. In the *Last Judgement* scene Hoffmann ably reproduced Heemskerck's emphatic, twisting nude forms and emotional drama. Although Hoffmann borrowed motifs from both Heemskerck and Cornelis Floris, including strapwork, pilasters and console masks, he combined these elements in an attractive and clearly legible ensemble, in which the architecture and sculpture are balanced. From the late 1590s Hoffman's workshop, in which his son Heinrich Hoffmann (1576–1623) also worked, produced an increasingly large amount of stone-carving, with a resulting unevenness of quality.

By contrast with his earlier works, the heavy architectural frame of Hoffmann's late masterpiece, the sandstone All Saints' altarpiece (1614; Trier Cathedral), threatens to be engulfed by the abundance of relief carvings and statuettes. Here, he experimented with contrasts of light and shade and recession. The free-standing statuette of the *Virgin* appears to step forward from the surrounding group of saints and apostles, who are carved in varying degrees of high relief. Closer to the viewer are the near life-size statues of *St Michael* and the kneeling donor, the *Archbishop-Elector Lothar von Metternich*. His later designs became increasingly complex, but he continued to stress the stylistic unity of his compositions.

Hoffmann also made portrait and religious medals. Habich identified eight medals dating from between 1560 and 1583, including three of the archbishop of Trier and four with the artist's monogram *HRH* (e.g. Vienna, Ksthist. Mus.; Nuremberg, Ger. Nmus.). He held several important civic positions, including that of representative of the Stonemasons' Guild on the city council in 1581 and church-master of St Gangolf in Trier in 1614.

NDB

BIBLIOGRAPHY

F. Balke: *Über die Werke des kurtrierischen Bildhauers Hans Ruprecht Hoffmann* (Trier, 1916)

G. Habich: *Die deutschen Schaumünzen des XVI. Jahrhunderts* (Munich, 1931), I/ii, pp. 245–6

A.-M. Zander: 'Über Geburtsort und Lehrmeister des kurtrierischen Bildhauers Hans Ruprecht Hoffmann', *Kurtrier. Jb.*, xvi (1976), pp. 38–9

F. J. Ronig, ed.: *Der Trierer Dom* (Neuss, 1980), pp. 252–73

J. C. Smith: *German Sculpture of the Later Renaissance, c. 1520–1580: Art in an Age of Uncertainty* (Princeton, 1994), pp. 116–20, 217, 226, 333, 359–60, 377–8, 464

JEFFREY CHIPPS SMITH

Hoffmann, Josef (Franz Maria) (*b* Pirnitz, Moravia [now Brtnice, Czech Republic], 15 Dec 1870; *d* Vienna, 15 May 1956). Austrian architect, designer and draughtsman. He had a natural gift for creating beautiful forms, and he proceeded to make the most of it during a career that spanned more than 50 years. In this half century the conditions and nature of architectural practice changed profoundly, but Hoffmann's fundamental approach remained the same. He relied on his intuition to produce works that were unmistakably his own in their formal and compositional treatment, yet mirrored all stylistic changes in the European architectural scene.

1. Life and work. 2. Working methods and technique. 3. Character and personality. 4. Critical reception and posthumous reputation.

1. LIFE AND WORK. He grew up as the mayor's son in a small market town in rural surroundings and throughout his life remained emotionally attached to his birthplace and to the arts and crafts of the Moravian peasantry. After hesitations about his career choice, he enrolled in the department of building of the Staatsgewerbeschule at Brünn (now Brno, Czech Republic). After a year of practice in Würzburg, Germany, in October 1892 he gained admission to Karl Hasenauer's class at the Akademie der Bildenden Künste, Vienna. It was, however, Hasenauer's successor Otto Wagner who exerted the strongest influence on Hoffmann. Wagner in July 1895 admiringly described Hoffmann's final school project, *Forum orbis insula pacis*, as a 'masterwork'. This project consisted of an international congress palace, *c.* 1.5 km long, on an island connected to the mainland by a bridge. Its forms recalled the historicism of Hasenauer's work and of Wagner's early projects.

The project won the State Travelling Fellowship (the Rome Prize), which enabled Hoffmann to travel and sketch in Italy. He seems to have been most strongly impressed by the Greek temples he saw in southern Italy and by the vernacular architecture, particularly that of Capri. He later published an article ('Architektonisches von der Insel Capri: Ein Beitrag für malerische Architekturempfindungen', *Architekt* [Vienna], iii (1897), pp. 13–14), illustrated by his own handsome sketches, in praise of the folk architecture of Capri, at the same time commending 'England's interest in the Arts and Crafts'. The Mediterranean region with its classicism, and the British Arts and Crafts tradition with its ethical standards, social concerns and picturesque solutions, were to remain guiding lights throughout his career, and he admired C. R. Ashbee and Charles Rennie Mackintosh.

After Hoffmann's return from Italy he worked in Wagner's office (1896–7), participated in architectural competitions and joined the newly founded Vienna Secession group (*see* SECESSION, §3). Several successful exhibition installations for the Secession, various interiors and the Apollo Candle shop (1899; destr., see Sekler, 1982, pp. 32, 258) in the centre of Vienna, all under the stylistic influence of Art Nouveau, quickly established his reputation, and in 1899 he was appointed Professor at the Kunstgewerbeschule, Vienna. His teaching reflected the wide scope of his practice; in addition to architecture he also designed furniture, utensils and objects of many kinds, jewellery, dresses, book bindings, posters, and surface patterns that could be used for textiles or wallpapers. Between 1903 and 1932 many of his designs were produced for the WIENER WERKSTÄTTE, an enterprise he had founded with Kolo Moser, with financial backing by the industrialist and collector Fritz Wärndorfer (*b* 1868). Hoffmann and Moser were among Werkstätte members who designed for Lötz Witwe and J. & L. Lobmeyr (for illustration *see* LOBMEYR, J. & L.); Hoffmann produced many designs for the latter firm.

In 1900 Hoffmann's style changed dramatically from the exuberant curvilinearity of his Secessionist work to a much more restrained and sober mode, characterized by the prevalence of rectilinearity and simple shapes, chief among them the square. At the same time white and black became the favoured colours, though by no means the only ones to be employed. Several interiors, including those in his early houses (1900–02) on the Hohe Warte in Vienna, were treated in this manner, but the most impressive examples were the 14th exhibition of the Secession (1902; destr.; see Sekler, 1982, pp. 32, 258) and the sanatorium (1903–5; remodelled) at Wienerstrasse, Purkersdorf, near Vienna. The exhibition was conceived around Max Klinger's sculpture of *Beethoven* (1902; Leipzig, Mus. Bild. Kst.) and was meant to express the Secession group's highest aspirations. Hoffmann created a setting that evoked associations with sacred architecture and included two stucco reliefs from his own hand. They were made up of overlapping planes and in their degree of pure abstraction were as revolutionary for the period as the simple cubic forms of the Purkersdorf sanatorium.

The sanatorium (see fig. 1), destined for a well-to-do clientele, was a flat-roofed, three-storey building that had all the discipline of classicism in its symmetry and proportioning but made no allusions to any historical models. Decoration was used very sparingly, and the architectural

vocabulary was pared down to very few, essential elements: planes, cubic and slablike elements, piers, and beam-and-slab ceilings of reinforced concrete. The result was an architectural statement so powerful in its clarity and restraint that it invites comparison with the most advanced work of such contemporaneous masters as Charles Rennie Mackintosh and Frank Lloyd Wright.

Hoffmann's next major commission, the Palais Stoclet (1905–11; see fig. 2), Avenue de Tervueren, Brussels, continued and elaborated the architectural language of the Purkersdorf sanatorium. Here, however, he was called upon to provide the palatial accommodation for Adolphe Stoclet, a highly sophisticated art collector of practically unlimited means. The architect on this occasion enriched his abstract language by an effectively used decoration that at times anticipated the devices of Art-Deco, and he combined the compositional discipline of classicism, though not its explicit formal language, with the freedom of spatial handling that came from the architecture of the Arts and Crafts Movement.

The plan of the main building's upper floors is roughly symmetrical around an axis that runs through the galleried great hall and the recessed entrance from the garden. On the ground-floor the plan is asymmetrical because a service wing and courtyard adjoin the main building. The great hall is the centre of an elaborate sequence of spatially and colour-coordinated magnificent function-rooms that include a large dining-room (*see* BELGIUM, fig. 29). Gustav Klimt's mosaics for this room contributed to making it one of the greatest interiors in the entire history of secular architecture. Works by many other artists were also incorporated in the Stoclet interiors, while the furniture and all appointments, including carpets, fittings, lamps, tableware and linen, came from the Wiener Werkstätte.

On the outside the most striking feature, other than the staircase tower with its monumental sculptures, is the use of gilt bronze mouldings that frame all surfaces and openings. They contribute to the atectonic quality of the façades since they negate the classical tectonic relationship between load and support by appearing to hold the slabs of marble cladding in place on all four edges. The framing of surfaces or their component parts remained one of Hoffmann's favourite devices, and it often gave his interiors a strong sense of measured order.

During the years before World War I, in keeping with the general trend of European architectural development, Hoffmann turned increasingly towards classicism and the vernacular in his formal language, although he never directly copied classical or neo-classical forms; rather he modified them in various ways, often by denying their tectonic significance. Examples of this were the highly acclaimed Austrian exhibition pavilions (1911; destr., see Sekler, 1982, pp. 144–6, 339–40) at Rome and at the Werkbund exhibition (1914; destr., see Sekler, 1982, pp. 159–61, 363–5) in Cologne, as well as a number of private residences such as the sumptuous Ast house (1909–11) at the Hohe Warte, the Bernatzik house (1912–13), the Kaasgraben estate (1912–13) and the large Skywa/Primavesi house (1913–15), Gloriettegasse, Vienna. Set in ample grounds, enriched with sculptures by Anton Hanak and extremely generous in its dimensions and appointments, the Skywa/Primavesi house was the last of

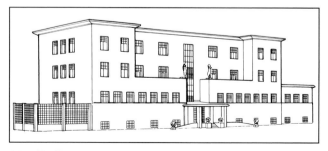

1. Josef Hoffmann: Purkersdorf sanatorium, near Vienna, 1903–5; upper storey added by Leopold Bauer, 1926

2. Josef Hoffmann: Palais Stoclet, Brussels, 1905–11

its kind; after the dissolution of the Austro-Hungarian monarchy the social stratum from which the clients for such houses came ceased to exist. Only the Knips house (1919–24) remotely recalls the style of life embodied in the pre-war houses. Hoffmann's most striking experiment with folkloristic forms was the Primavesi country house (1913–14; destr. 1922, see Sekler, 1982, pp. 128–31, 361–2) at Winkelsdorf (now Kouty, Czech Republic), where he designed a large loghouse with thatched roof in deference to local building traditions.

After World War I, when economic conditions in the Austrian Republic were bad, Hoffmann designed a few houses outside the country, in Czechoslovakia, Hungary and Romania. In Austria he did the Ast summer-house (1923–4; remodelled 1934) at Aue near Velden on the Wörthersee, Carinthia, that had the striking appearance of a cube with horizontally striated sides. At this phase in his artistic development Hoffmann was fond of horizontal articulations, and he used them in the shape of enlarged and attenuated horizontal double S mouldings to enliven in a most unusual manner the façades of his Austrian pavilion (1925; destr., see Sekler, 1982, pp. 182–4, 403) at the Exposition Internationale des Arts Décoratifs et Industriels Modernes, Paris. He still used narrowly spaced horizontal striations at the Austrian pavilion for the Venice Biennale (1934), the last exhibition pavilion to be built from his designs.

Hoffmann had always been acutely aware of changes in the artistic and architectural climate around him, and consequently the leading art movements of the post-war period are also reflected in his designs, from the Expressionist peaked battlements of his project for the town hall (1916–18; unexecuted, see Sekler, 1982, pp. 163, 378) in Ortelsburg (now Szczytno, Poland) to echoes from Cubism in the use of transparency in his interiors. De Stijl and the early works of Le Corbusier also did not fail to make their impact, especially after Oswald Haerdtl had joined him, first as an assistant and later, until 1939, as a partner. Hoffmann designed several public housing schemes for the city of Vienna and four terraced houses for the Vienna Werkbund estate (1930–32). He also participated, with a large project, in an invited international competition for the new palace of the great national assembly of Turkey at Ankara (1936; see Sekler, 1982, pp. 215–18, 434–5). His most congenial commissions, however, were those that permitted him to give free reign to his fertile imagination in exhibitions and expensive interiors; he was happiest when he was able to secure the cooperation of artists while at the same time relying on his own facility of formal invention and knowledge of materials and techniques. In Austria such opportunities were not frequent in the troubled period between the two world wars, and Hoffmann went through some very trying years when financial hardship was coupled with ill-health. He also was the butt of attacks against the outdated Arts and Crafts mentality, and he experienced the liquidation of the Wiener Werkstätte. A great retrospective exhibition and a richly illustrated Festschrift on the occasion of his 60th birthday, and his arrangement of and contribution to the Vienna Werkbund exhibition of the same year (see Sekler, 1982, pp. 201, 421), still were convincing testimony of his stature in the world of architecture, but in the following years little work of importance was built from his designs.

After Germany's annexation of Austria, Hoffmann, who had good relations with the new regime (although he was not politically active himself), at first received some commissions: to remodel a historic palace into a House of Fashion (1938; destr., see Sekler, 1982, pp. 221, 439) and to adapt the former German embassy as an officers' club, the Haus der Wehrmacht (1940; destr., see Sekler, 1982, pp. 222, 442). World War II soon put an end to his architectural activity. After the war his practice as an architect remained very limited, although he was involved with some public housing schemes. He was active, however, in the reorganization of the Secession group and as the Austrian commissioner for the Venice Biennale. He never stopped drawing and, even in his old age, created graphic works of considerable charm. While in these he recapitulated decorative topics from his long, fruitful life, he, at the same time, was interested in the future. He wrote essays with utopian visions about the future of Vienna ('Gedanken zum Wiederaufbau Wiens', *Wiener Ztg* (23 Dec 1945; 21 April 1946)), and one year before his death he made a preliminary design of a town hall for Addis Ababa (see Sekler, 1982, pp. 449), conceived entirely with glass façades.

2. WORKING METHODS AND TECHNIQUE. In his work as a designer Hoffmann above all relied on intuition, as he once made clear in the following statement:

> There are two kinds of artists, the ones who build up a matter rationally and develop it systematically, and the others who have a sudden inspiration—I am more for those with inspiration. One should not obstruct the intuition . . . . I for myself always have to close my eyes and imagine the matter before I begin it.

Surviving small holograph sketches that show perspective views of buildings corroborate his written testimony and in addition prove that he had been trained at the Akademie to form a conception mentally and to put it on paper immediately at the inception of a project. He also had received a sound training in building construction, but later he showed no great interest in the practical questions of building technology. He preferred to leave this to a specialist in his office, allowing himself to concentrate purely on design and questions of visual treatment.

For his drawings Hoffmann almost invariably employed sheets or double sheets of opaque graph paper. He often drew directly in ink and frequently used colour (crayons or watercolour). As a rule he did not correct drawings by erasing but preferred to start anew. When he arrived in his office at the usual hour, he would hand to an assistant a design that was almost completely worked out in plan, section and elevation, all drawn freehand, without the use of a T-square. Difficult details were clarified by small sketches in the margin, and at times materials were indicated in writing. These sheets often possessed considerable graphic attractiveness, since Hoffmann would include human figures (usually women) and vegetation in

his renderings. His pattern designs and his graphic works, from early travel sketches to late abstract decorative compositions, display a strong sense of form, rhythm and, where applicable, colour. In order to stress the character of a shape, for example that of a vase, he at times cut it out from coloured paper, which he then pasted on white sheets. He insisted on high quality in execution, a habit apt to have serious financial consequences, and his budget overruns were responsible for a good deal of trouble with clients.

3. CHARACTER AND PERSONALITY. From the recollections of those who knew him well (though not intimately because a certain shyness and reserve on his part precluded intimacy), and from the evidence of his writings, Hoffmann emerges as a difficult man. He valued his privacy highly and would rather hide than meet people he disliked. He was easily offended and in his later years protected his vulnerability by restricting his contacts to comparatively few trusted friends and by limiting his utterances to a few non-committal statements. He shunned theoretical arguments, considering art as something one should practise if one were capable of doing so, but not discuss. Accordingly his written statements are few and, on the whole, disappointing, although now and then an idea stands out by its originality, or a sentence reveals an unusual, even idiosyncratic, way of seeing things and conditions. Hoffmann never abandoned the ideals that had inspired him when he was young, and John Ruskin, William Morris and Otto Wagner remained his guides even at a time when the precepts of the Arts and Crafts Movement were no longer tenable in an economy and society that had drastically changed from the days of his youth.

Although he said little to his students, Hoffmann was a highly esteemed and admired teacher. He tried to bring out the best in each member of his class by means of challenging assignments, which were occasionally work on real commissions. Where he detected talent among young artists he was willing or eager to promote it; Oskar Kokoschka, Egon Schiele and Le Corbusier were the most prominent beneficiaries of his benevolence towards a promising next generation. Le Corbusier was offered a job in his office, Schiele was helped financially and Kokoschka was given work in the Wiener Werkstätte. As a member of the international jury for the competition to design a palace for the League of Nations at Geneva in 1927, he belonged to the minority who voted for Le Corbusier's project, and the latter always spoke with admiration of his Viennese colleague. From his first wife he had a son Wolfgang (1900–69) who became an interior designer and photographer in the USA.

4. CRITICAL RECEPTION AND POSTHUMOUS REPUTATION. The critical reception of Hoffmann's oeuvre has faithfully mirrored the changing tastes and ideologies in the history of 20th-century architecture. He received favourable attention from the critics early in his career; in 1901 *The Studio* brought him to the attention of the English-speaking world through an illustrated article written by Fernand Khnopff. He was also given extensive coverage in the special volume *The Art Revival in Austria* that was published by *The Studio* in 1906. In France, *Art*

et décoration published favourable reviews of his early and his mature work. Naturally his most extensive and detailed reviews are found in German-language periodicals, in particular *Deutsche Kunst und Dekoration* where many well-illustrated articles were devoted to his designs. His international exhibition work also helped to make his name widely known, and many distinguished contributors to the Festschrift on his 60th birthday acclaimed him as a master. Honours bestowed on him included the cross of a commander of the Légion d'honneur and the Honorary Fellowship of the American Institute of Architects. The critic Henry-Russell Hitchcock in 1929 wrote, 'In Germany as well as in Austria, Hoffmann's manner has profoundly influenced the New Tradition'. Only three years later, however, when together with Philip Johnson Hitchcock he published *The International Style*, he no longer even mentioned Hoffmann's name. Siegfried Giedion in his influential *Space, Time and Architecture* did not do justice to Hoffmann's oeuvre because it would not fit easily into his polemically simplified version of architectural history. Despite honours and praise on the occasions of Hoffmann's 80th and 85th birthdays, he was virtually forgotten by the time of his death. Although his true stature and contribution were acknowledged by such masters as Alvar Aalto, Le Corbusier, Gio Ponti and Carlo Scarpa, the younger generation of architects and historians ignored him.

The process of rediscovery and reappraisal began in 1956 with a small book by Giulia Veronesi and during the 1970s gained momentum with a number of exhibitions and smaller publications. In the 1980s several monographs were published and major exhibitions held. Imitations of his style also began to occur, and replicas of his furniture, fabrics, and of some objects he had designed became commercial successes, while original pieces and drawings from his hand fetched record prices in the auction-rooms.

For an example of the applied arts of Josef Hoffmann *see* VIENNA, fig. 12.

BIBLIOGRAPHY

F. Khnopff: 'Josef Hoffmann: Architect and Decorator', *The Studio*, xxii (1901), pp. 261–6
L. Kleiner: *Josef Hoffmann* (Vienna and Berlin, 1927)
A. Weiser: *Josef Hoffmann* (Geneva, 1930)
Josef Hoffmann zum 60. Geburtstag (Vienna, 1930)
L. W. Rochowanski: *Josef Hoffmann* (Vienna, 1950)
G. Veronesi: *Josef Hoffmann* (Milan, 1956)
H. Ankwicz-Kleehoven: 'Josef Hoffmann (1870–1956)', *Grosse Österreicher: Neue österreichische Biographie ab 1815*, x (Vienna, 1957), pp. 171–9
D. Baroni and A. d'Auria: *Josef Hoffmann e la Wiener Werkstätte* (Milan, 1981)
G. Fanelli and E. Godoli: *La Vienna di Hoffmann architetto della qualità* (Bari, 1981)
F. Borsi and A. Perizzi: *Josef Hoffmann: Tempo e geometria* (Rome, 1982)
W. J. Schweiger: *Wiener Werkstaette: Kunst und Handwerk, 1903–1932* (Vienna, 1982; Eng. trans., 1984)
E. F. Sekler: *Josef Hoffmann: Das architektonische Werk* (Salzburg, 1982; Eng. trans., 1985; rev. Salzburg, 2/1986; Fr. trans., 1986; It. trans., 1991)
Josef Hoffmann: Design Classics (exh. cat. by D. Gebhard, Fort Worth, TX, A. Mus., 1982)
E. F. Sekler: 'Josef Hoffmann, Adolf Loos und die Vereinigten Staaten', *Akten des XXV. internationalen Kongresses für Kunstgeschichte: Wien, 1983*, viii, pp. 125–35
P. Vergo: 'Fritz Waerndorfer and Josef Hoffmann', *Burl. Mag.*, cxxv/964 (1983), pp. 402–10
Josef Hoffmann: Ornament zwischen Hoffnung und Verbrechen (exh. cat. by P. Noever and O. Oberhuber, Vienna, Mus. Angewandte Kst, 1987)
Josef Hoffmann: Variationen (exh. cat. by H. Amanshauser, Vienna, Mus. 20. Jhts, 1987)
Josef Hoffmann: Drawings and Objects from Conception to Design (exh. cat. by E. Longhauser, Philadelphia, PA, Moore Coll. A. & Des., Goldie Paley Gal., 1991)
E. F. Sekler: 'Ein neu entdeckter Entwurf aus dem Atelier Josef Hoffmann...', *Hülle und Fülle, Feschrift für Tilmann Buddensieg* (Alfter, 1993)

EDUARD F. SEKLER

Hoffmann, Karl (*b* Wiesbaden, 23 March 1815; *d* Frascati, nr Rome, 8 July 1886). German sculptor. From 1833 to 1837 he studied in Munich under Ludwig von Schwanthaler and then lived in Paris until 1839. That year he returned to Wiesbaden and in 1842 went to Rome. There he met Friedrich Overbeck and was influenced by his designs for sculptures. Hoffmann lived in Cologne from 1845 to 1850, executing a few secular sculptures (e.g. the monument to *Maximilian Weyhe*, 1848–50; Düsseldorf, Hofgarten), which had a quality of narrative introversion despite their classical contours, gestures and glances. Religious works became his main subject-matter and were often treated with sentimental pathos, such as the stone *Crucifixion* (1850; Cologne, Melaten Cemetery). After being unsuccessful in his bid for the sculptural decoration of the cathedral, in 1850 Hoffmann returned to Rome, where from 1853 he shared a studio with Overbeck. He was influenced by late medieval and Quattrocento art as early as the 1840s, and the classically generous structure, accentuated gestural language and idealized facial expressions of his sculpture are in keeping with the piety and formal simplicity of Nazarene painting, particularly the work of Overbeck. Such sculptures as the marble *St Joseph* (1865; Rome, S Maria della Pietà) reflect this Nazarene spirit. His portrait and sepulchral sculpture is classical in mood yet with realistic detail, e.g. the marble portrait bust of *Friedrich Overbeck* (before 1869; Lübeck, Mus. Behnhaus) and the wall-mounted tomb of *Overbeck* (*c.* 1870; Rome, S Bernardo alle Terme), which creates unity between the Renaissance tradition of the recumbent figure in high relief and an exactly rendered portrait of old age. After Overbeck's death, Hoffmann returned to Wiesbaden and remained there until 1880. He spent his last years once more in Italy. His son Karl Hoffmann (1838–after 1900) was a painter.

BIBLIOGRAPHY

P. Bloch: 'Das Grab Friedrich Overbecks und sein Meister', *Festschrift Gert von der Osten* (Cologne, 1970), pp. 221–8
——: *Skulpturen des 19. Jahrhunderts im Rheinland* (Düsseldorf, 1975), pp. 26–9
E. Trier: 'Bildwerke für Kultus und Andacht', *Kunst des 19. Jahrhunderts im Rheinland*, ed. E. Trier and W. Weyres, iv (Düsseldorf, 1980), pp. 87, 93, 95

M. PULS

Hoffmann, Ludwig (Ernst Emil) (*b* Darmstadt, 30 July 1852; *d* Berlin, 11 Nov 1932). German architect and writer. He attended the Kunstakademie, Kassel (1873), and the Bauakademie, Berlin (1874–9), where his teachers included Johann Heinrich Strack and Richard Lucae, and he won the Schinkel prize. In 1879 he took the government examination in architecture and became a government architect (1884). In 1885 he won a competition, with Peter Dybwad (1859–1921), for the Reichsgericht in Leipzig and a subsequent commission to revise the design; work was carried out on this monumental, neo-classicist law court between 1887 and 1895. In early April 1896 Hoffmann was elected city architect of Berlin, a post he retained until 1924 (*see* BERLIN, §I, 4). As city architect he was responsible for all types of public buildings in Berlin: swimming baths, bridges, fountains, monuments, fire stations, hospitals, arts and festival buildings, residential buildings, schools, social facilities, municipal and administration buildings. Notable examples include the swimming baths (1896–1901), Kreuzberg; the Märkisches Museum (1896–1908); a complex of nursing homes (1899–1929; now the Städtisches Klinikum), Buch; the fairy-tale fountain (1901–13) in the public park in Friedrichshain, with sculptures by Josef Rauch, Ignatius Taschner and Georg Wrba; and the execution of the Pergamonmuseum (1909–30), designed by Alfred Messel. Hoffmann worked in a neoclassical style influenced by Karl Friedrich Schinkel, and in the 1920s he became a target for attack by German modernists, particularly the radical group Der Ring; a member of Der Ring, Martin Wagner, followed Hoffmann as city architect in 1926. Hoffmann received several honours during his career, including membership of the Königliche Akademie der Künste in Berlin (1906).

WRITINGS
Neubauten der Stadt Berlin, 11 vols (Berlin, 1902–12)

BIBLIOGRAPHY
W. Hegemann: 'Berliner Neubauten und Ludwig Hoffmann', *Wasmuths Mhft. Baukst*, xi (1927)
J. Posener: *Berlin auf dem Wege zu einer neuen Architektur, Das Zeitalter Wilhelms II* (Munich, 1979)
H. J. Reichhardt and W. Schäche: *Ludwig Hoffmann in Berlin: Die Wiederentdeckung eines Architekten* (Berlin, 1986)

BRIGITTE JACOB, WOLFGANG SCHÄCHE

Hoflehner, Rudolf (*b* Linz, 8 Aug 1916). Austrian sculptor and painter. He attended the Staatsgewerbeschule für Maschinenbau (1932–6) in Linz and studied architecture at the Technische Hochschule (1936–8) in Graz, before entering the Akademie der Bildenden Künste in Vienna. After serving in World War II he taught at the Kunstgewerbeschule (1949–51) in Linz. In 1951 he moved to Vienna and until 1954 worked in Fritz Wotruba's studio. Under his influence Hoflehner developed a style of simplification, reducing a work to its geometric foundations, which were only meaningful as a composite entity when in the context of their space. Like Wotruba's, his sculptures grew from the human figure. However, instead of solidity, he gave the individual components great lightness and fragility, so that they appear more buoyant and mobile as they penetrate space.

Hoflehner's early works were in wood. From 1951 he turned to iron, and initially he structured this as if it were a linear element. Only gradually did he attempt a new kind of design, using massive cubes, discs and square surfaces, creating connections between ponderously heavy components, and small-scale linear elements that hold the whole structure together (e.g. *Figuration, Turning Movement*, both iron, h. 820 mm, 1953; Vienna, Belvedere). In 1953 Hoflehner received a prize in connection with the competition for a monument to the *Unknown Political Prisoner* in London. In 1954, through a UNESCO scholarship, he spent six months in Greece, which had a profound influence on his sense of form. From 1954 he worked in his studio in Vienna. In 1962 he took up an appointment at the Staatliche Akademie der Bildenden Künste in Stuttgart. During this time he acquired an international reputation, and showed his work at numerous one-man exhibitions and many important group exhibitions throughout Europe.

In 1965 Hoflehner visited New York. Around 1970 he stopped working on sculpture and turned to drawing and painting, experimenting with combinations of person and space, of body, sculpture and image. At the centre of his pictorial creativity stood the human figure, its development and transformation, its natural growth and movement (e.g. *Deux Silhouettes*, watercolour; Vienna, Albertina). At the heart of this creativity lay his exploration of psychic experiences. Emotional tensions between the individual and the external world determined his formal language.

BIBLIOGRAPHY
W. Hofmann: *Hoflehner* (Stuttgart, 1965)
Rudolf Hoflehner: Gemälde und Zeichnungen (exh. cat., Stuttgart, Württemberg. Kstver., 1982)

ULRIKE GAISBAUER

Hofman, Vlastislav (*b* Jičin, 6 Feb 1884; *d* 1964). Czech designer. He was involved in developing the Cubist-influenced design and architectural style known as Czech Cubism, created in Prague shortly before World War I. He was a member of the GROUP OF PLASTIC ARTISTS (founded 1911), who created modern furniture, Cubist ceramics and such objects as candlesticks and ashtrays in non-ferrous metals.   □

Hofmann, Hans [Johann] (**Georg Albert**) (*b* Weissenberg, Bavaria, 21 March 1880; *d* New York, 17 Feb 1966). American painter, teacher and theorist of German birth. He moved with his family to Munich in 1886 and in 1896 left home to become assistant to the director of public works of the State of Bavaria; he distinguished himself with a number of inventions, including an electromagnetic comptometer, a radar device for ships, a sensitized light bulb and a portable freezer unit for military purposes. In spite of his parents' strong objection and their hopes for his career as a scientist, in 1898 he enrolled in the art school run by Moritz Heymann (*b* 1870) in Munich. Hofmann subsequently studied with a succession of teachers and was particularly influenced by Willi Schwarz (*b* 1889), who familiarized him with French Impressionism, a style that affected his earliest known paintings, such as *Self-portrait* (1902; New York, Emmerich Gal., see Goodman, 1986, p. 14).

In 1903 Hofmann was introduced by Schwarz to Phillip Freudenberg, an art collector and the son of a wealthy owner of a department-store from Berlin. Freudenberg's patronage enabled Hofmann to live in Paris from 1904 to 1914, accompanied by Miz (Maria) Wolfgegg, whom he had met in 1900 and whom he married in 1929. Hofmann continued his art studies in Paris at the Académie Colarossi and at the Académie de la Grande Chaumière, and he met major artists such as Picasso, Matisse, Braque, Léger and Robert Delaunay; he also came to know the influential German art dealers Richard Goetz and Wilhelm Uhde and the American collector Leo Stein. He also maintained his contacts in Germany, which he visited each summer, participating in the Neue Sezession exhibitions in Berlin in 1908 and 1909 and holding his first one-man exhibition in 1910 at Paul Cassirer's gallery in Berlin.

Almost all the work produced by Hofmann in Paris was destroyed in World War I. He was visiting Germany when war was declared and was unable to return to France, but for health reasons he was pronounced unfit for service. To support himself he opened his own art school in 1915, the Hofmann Schule für Moderne Kunst, in Schwabing, the artists' district of Munich. He had relatively few pupils during the war, but as his fame spread after 1918 he attracted students from all over the world; among them were a number of artists who later achieved international prominence, including Alfred Jensen, Louise Nevelson and Wolfgang Paalen. Hofmann taught in Munich until the early 1930s and during these years drew copiously but had little time to paint. Only one painting of this time is known to have survived, a Cubist-derived still-life, *Green Bottle* (1921; Boston, MA, Mus. F.A.).

Hofmann visited the USA in the summers of 1930 and 1931 to teach at the University of California at Berkeley at the invitation of a former student, Worth Ryder. In 1932 he settled in New York, where he taught at the Art Students League and where thanks to his first-hand experience of Europe he came to personify the Ecole de Paris for those students eager to learn the fundamentals of modern art. In autumn 1933 he left the Art Students League to open his own school, the Hans Hofmann School of Fine Arts, which after several moves was based at 52 W. 8th Street in the Greenwich Village area of New York. In 1935 he opened a summer school in Provincetown, MA, which became the focus of the large art community on Cape Cod. It was during this period that Hofmann began painting regularly again, initially favouring portraits and figure studies, landscapes, interiors and still-lifes; the strongest influence on his works of this period, such as *Japanese Girl* (1935) and *Table with Fruit and Coffee-pot* (1936; both Berkeley, U. CA, A. Mus.), was that of Matisse.

In the 1930s and 1940s Hofmann played an increasingly prominent role in American art, particularly in transmitting modernist theories and new artistic developments. He taught many younger artists who later became established figures, including Lee Krasner, Helen Frankenthaler and Larry Rivers, and he continued teaching throughout the year until 1958, when he finally closed his schools and devoted all his time to painting. The importance of his own art was for a long time overshadowed by his immense influence as a teacher and theorist, but by the late 1950s he was beginning to be recognized as one of the major figures of ABSTRACT EXPRESSIONISM. Like other artists of his generation in the USA, in the early 1940s he became interested in procedures of automatism derived from Surrealism, in his case less as a way of using the subconscious than as a technique for creating new forms. In works such as *The Wind* (oil, duco, gouache and India ink on poster board, ?1942; Berkeley, U. CA, A. Mus.) he produced some of the earliest examples of drip painting; although the dating of these works is open to question, they may have preceded the exploitation of similar techniques by Jackson Pollock, to whom Hofmann was introduced by Lee Krasner in 1942.

Hans Hofmann: *Fantasia in Blue*, oil on canvas, 1.52×1.32 m, 1954 (New York, Whitney Museum of American Art)

In spite of an initial hostility between Hofmann and Pollock, a close friendship evolved between them, which affected them both as artists. The imagery and techniques of Pollock's mythological paintings such as *Moon-Woman Cuts the Circle* (1942; Venice, Guggenheim), for example, were directly reflected in paintings by Hofmann such as *Idolatress I* (1944; Berkeley, U. CA, A. Mus.). Within a few years, however, Hofmann had developed a highly distinctive form of abstraction based on patches of vivid colour, vigorous gestures and textural contrasts, as in *The Third Hand* (1947; Berkeley, U. CA, A. Mus.). Although the dense surfaces and impulsive application of paint in his works of the 1950s, such as *Le Gilotin* (1953; Berkeley, U. CA, A. Mus.) and *Fantasia in Blue* (1954; New York, Whitney; see fig.), can be associated with action painting, it soon became apparent that his work was distinguished by a rigorous concern with pictorial structure, spatial illusion and colour relationships. He is most admired for his late paintings such as *Magnum Opus* (1962; Berkeley, U. CA, A. Mus.), in which he placed rectangles of single colours against more loosely painted backgrounds to establish dynamic pictorial relationships as well as a strong surface design. His influence among younger abstract artists, such as Helen Frankenthaler and the English painter John Hoyland, remained undiminished long after his death.

BIBLIOGRAPHY
F. S. Wight: *Hans Hofmann* (Berkeley, 1957)
C. Greenberg: *Hofmann* (Paris, 1961)

H. Rosenberg: 'Hans Hofmann's "Life" Class', *Port. & ARTnews Annu.*, vi (1962), pp. 16–31, 110–15

F. Bultman: 'The Achievement of Hans Hofmann', *ARTnews*, lxii (Sept 1963), pp. 43–5, 54–5

S. Hunter: *Hans Hofmann* (New York, 1963) [incl. five essays by Hofmann]

H. Rosenberg: 'Hans Hofmann and the Stability of the New', *New Yorker*, xxxix (2 Nov 1963), pp. 100, 103–5, 108–10

Hans Hofmann (exh. cat. by W. Seitz, New York, MOMA, 1963)

T. Hess: 'The Mystery of Hans Hofmann', *ARTnews*, lxiii (Feb 1965), pp. 39, 54–5

I. Sandler: 'Hans Hofmann: The Pedagogical Master', *A. America*, lxi (May 1973), pp. 48–57

Hans Hofmann (exh. cat. by W. D. Bannard, Houston, Mus. F.A., 1976)

C. Goodman: 'Hans Hofmann as Teacher', *A. Mag.*, liii (April 1979), pp. 22–8

——: *Hans Hofmann* (New York, 1986) [incl. bibliog. and list of Hofmann's writings]

Hans Hofmann: The Late Paintings (exh. cat., intro. J. Hoyland; London, Tate, 1988)

CYNTHIA GOODMAN

Hofmann [Hoffmann], **Samuel** (*b* Sax, St Gall, 1595; *d* Frankfurt am Main, 24 January 1649). Swiss painter, active also in the northern Netherlands and Germany. He was descended on his father's side from an old farming family from the Zurich Oberland; his father was a Protestant pastor. From 1608 to 1611 he trained as a painter with the Zurich painter Gotthard Ringgli (1575–1635). In 1613 he did some restoration work at the monastery of Töss in Winterthur before setting off to travel. By 1615 he was in Amsterdam, where he worked for the next seven and a half years. On 22 May 1622 he married, and the couple lived on the Oude Zijds-Achterburgval. According to Sandrart, he served an apprenticeship with Peter Paul Rubens; this remains unproven. In 1622 he returned to Zurich with his wife and soon became the most popular portrait painter in the town; between 1622 and 1643 he painted most of its dignitaries and numerous citizens (e.g. the burgomaster *Hans Heinrich Holzhalb*, 1635; Zurich, Ksthaus; *Portrait of a Man Aged 60*, 1624; Zurich, Schweizer. Landesmus.). Portrait commissions took him in 1628 to Heiligenberg on Lake Constance, where he painted members of the Fürstenberg family (e.g. *Leopold Ludwig Egon, Grafen von Fürstenberg-Heiligenberg*, Heiligenberg, Schloss Heiligenberg), and in 1630 to the court of the Margrave of Baden-Baden; Sandrart reported that he painted portraits of generals active in the Thirty Years War. Even after leaving Amsterdam he remained in touch with artistic developments in Antwerp and the Netherlands. Some of his full-length court portraits follow the latest trends, and by 1629 he had become one of the first to adopt the style of Anthony van Dyck. In the equestrian portrait of *P. F. König* (1631; Fribourg, Mus. A. & Hist.), he adopted a type from Rubens. His still-lifes, which include small-format fruit pieces (e.g. *Still-life with Fruit and Wineglass*, 1636; Zurich, Ksthaus) as well as large-format kitchen studies with several figures (e.g. *Kitchen Still-life with Figures*, 1640; Zurich, Zunfthaus Meisen), reveal the influence of works by Frans Snyders and Adriaen van Utrecht. In some still-lifes he broke away from his Flemish models and achieved an expressive style of his own, a unique achievement that enriched Swiss painting.

In 1643 Hofmann moved to Basle. He already had good contacts there, having painted a portrait of the burgomaster *J. R. Wettstein* (Basle, Kstmus.) in 1636; he also met Margrave Friedrich V of Baden Durlach there. At the instigation of a number of merchants, Hofmann then moved with his family to Frankfurt am Main in July 1644. To obtain permission to settle there he painted the *Discovery of Ericthonius* (1645; Frankfurt am Main, Hist. Mus.) for the town hall. His application for residence reveals that he was also painting portraits of the Herzogin of Lothringen (Lorraine) and her daughters at the time. Complaints by Frankfurt painters to the town council objecting to Hofmann's admission specify that he operated a workshop, employing his daughter, a journeyman and apprentices. Hofmann planned to return to the Netherlands from Frankfurt but fell ill and died; his widow and children moved to Amsterdam. Hofmann's work underlines the great influence of Flemish and Dutch painting of the 'Golden Age'; he was its most prominent exponent in Switzerland and was one of the most important 17th-century Swiss painters.

BIBLIOGRAPHY

J. von Sandrart: *Teutsche Academie* (1675–9); ed. A. R. Pelzer (1925), p. 343

A. Houbraken: *De groote schouburgh* (1718–21), i, pp. 77–8

H. Helmerking: *Samuel Hofmann* (Uster, 1928)

I. Schlégl: *Samuel Hofmann (um 1595–1649)* (Munich, 1980)

ISTVÁN SCHLÉGL

Hofstätter & Domány. Hungarian architectural partnership formed *c*. 1936 by Béla Hofstätter [Hofstädter] (*b* Budapest, 1891; *d* Budapest, Dec 1944) and Ferenc Domány (*b* Gyöngyös, 30 April 1899; *d* Folkestone, 9 Sept 1939). Hofstätter graduated from the Technical University, Budapest, in 1913. His first Modernist blocks of flats were designed at the beginning of the 1930s and are characterized by sharp, hard contours and vertical divisions of alternating balconies and bay windows. Domány studied in Budapest under Dezső Hültl and then in Berlin, where he worked until 1933. On returning to Budapest he designed cinemas and other buildings. In the late 1930s Hofstätter and Domány established a reputation through their designs for blocks of flats in Budapest. Popular with the middle class, these were characterized by modernist construction methods and appearance, their restrained elegance and the use of high-quality materials, particularly in the decoration of stairwells and vestibules. Their first work in partnership was the six-storey riverbank block (1937) near St István Park, Budapest, one of the biggest of the period. The original design consisted of a modernist terraced structure but was not approved by the conservative-minded city authorities. The existing building, with a combination of balconies and bay windows dividing up its huge mass, represents a compromise. Much attention was paid to the interior decoration with each of the three stairwells receiving a different treatment and their curved forms contrasting with the angularity of the façade. The block of flats (1938), Margit Boulevard, Budapest, built in a U-shape on a hillside corner site is formed of two blocks of unequal height connected only by a common stairwell. The shapes of the building are soft and rounded reflecting the contemporary fashion for streamlining. Its most original feature is its oval stairwell, which together with the glassed-in cylindrical lift, reflects the architects' Modernist spirit. In 1939 Domány moved to London, where he won a prize in a competition for a Post Office building.

BIBLIOGRAPHY

'Hofstätter Béla bérházépitkezései' [The lodging-houses of Béla Hofstätter], *Magyar Épitőmüvészet*, xxxv/1–3 (1936), pp. 2–16
Tér és Forma, x (1937), pp. 115–42
Tér és Forma, xi (1938), pp. 180–94
G. Preisich and A. Benkhard: 'Budapest épitészete a két világháboru között' [The architecture of Budapest between the two World Wars], *Épités- & Közlekedéstudományi Közlemények*, xi (1967), pp. 461–524 [with list of works and bibliog.]

FERENC VADAS

Hofstede de Groot, Cornelis (*b* Dwingeloo, nr Assen, 9 Nov 1863; *d* The Hague, 14 April 1930). Dutch art historian and collector. He was, with his older contemporaries, Wilhelm van Bode and Abraham Bredius, one of the founders of the study of 17th-century Dutch art. Hofstede de Groot studied art history at Leipzig under Anton Springer and took his degree there in 1891. From 1891 to 1896 he was the assistant director of the Mauritshuis in The Hague under Bredius, and from 1896 to 1898 he was the director of the Rijksprentenkabinet in Amsterdam. Following a dispute, he resigned and established himself in The Hague as a freelance art historian. From his student days, Hofstede de Groot had assembled extensive photographic documentation as well as excerpts from catalogues concerned with Dutch paintings, which subsequently proved very useful to him. He produced various books and numerous articles and contributed to Thieme and Becker's dictionary. However, his magnum opus was the complete reworking of the Dutch section of John Smith's *Catalogue Raisonné of the Works of the most Eminent Dutch, Flemish and French Painters* (1829–37), which Hofstede de Groot published in 10 volumes, covering 40 artists. He was assisted in his work by younger art historians, most of them Germans, including W. R. Valentiner, Kurt Bauch, Wolfgang Stechow and Horst Gerson. Hofstede de Groot bequeathed his complete collection of documents to the Netherlands State, and it forms the core of the Rijksbureau voor Kunsthistorische Documentatie in The Hague. He also owned an important collection of drawings and a small collection of paintings, many of which he left to the Rijksprentenkabinet and the Groninger Museum.

WRITINGS

Beschreibendes und kritisches Verzeichnis der Werke der hervorragendsten holländischen Maler des 17. Jahrhunderts, 10 vols (Esslingen and Paris, 1907–28); Eng. trans. by E. G. Hawke, 8 vols (London, 1908–27)
Contributions to Thieme–Becker; regular contributions to *Jb. Kön.-Preuss. Kstsamml.* and *Oud-Holland*

BIBLIOGRAPHY

BWN
H. E. van Gelder: *Levensbericht van Dr C. Hofstede de Groot, met bibliografie samengesteld door H. Gerson* [The life of Dr C. Hofstede de Groot, with bibliography compiled by H. Gerson] (Leiden, 1931); Eng. trans. in J. Bolten: *Dutch Drawings from the Collection of Dr C. Hofstede de Groot* (Utrecht, 1967), pp. 17–36

RUDOLF E. O. EKKART

Hofwijck. Country house at Voorburg, The Hague. In 1639 Constantijn Huygens (i), poet, scholar and secretary to Frederick Henry, Stadholder of the Netherlands, purchased a plot just outside Voorburg with the intention of building a secluded country house. He named the house Hofwijck, which means 'far from the court'. Huygens

probably designed both the house and its gardens (destr.) himself in 1639–42, in collaboration with the architects Pieter Post and Jacob van Campen. The house is built of brick; its cubic form and pyramidal roof typify the simplicity of Post's oeuvre. The façades have no explicitly classical features; they are decorated only with *trompe-l'oeil* paintings of statues between the windows, which are arranged in three rows, one above the other. Huygens's poem about the house, *Vitauliam: Hofwijck*, provides the most complete description of the house and an explanation of its symbolism. The overall plan of the house and gardens was intended to symbolize the human form, with the house itself representing the head and the gardens the body.

BIBLIOGRAPHY

C. Huygens: *Vitaulium: Hofwijck* (The Hague, 1653)
R. J. van Pelt: 'Man and Cosmos in Huygens' Hofwijck', *A. Hist.*, iv/2 (1981), pp. 150–74

K. A. OTTENHEYM

Hōgai. *See* KANŌ, (16).

Hogan, João (Manuel Navarro) (*b* Lisbon, 4 Feb 1914; *d* Lisbon, 17 June 1988). Portuguese painter and printmaker. He was known primarily as a landscape painter, although the imagery of his graphic work is often fantastic and dream-like. The expressionism of his early paintings gave way in the 1940s and 1950s to a more sober style emphasizing the density and plasticity of the landscape in broad planes of earthy colours. At around the time of his first solo exhibition (1951; Lisbon, Soc. N.B.A.) Hogan experimented briefly with figure paintings and interiors reminiscent of Vuillard. From 1957 he taught graphics at the Cooperative Society of Portuguese Engravers, specializing in black and white techniques. He spent some time in Paris, Belgium and the Netherlands on a fellowship in 1958. In 1971 his work was included among those selected for the redecoration of the Lisbon café A Brasileira. While there is great stylistic consistency in the uninhabited landscapes that he painted throughout his career, from the early 1970s his work became more stylized, for example *Landscape* (1983; Lisbon, Casa Mus. Gonçalves).

BIBLIOGRAPHY

M. T. Chicó and others, eds: *Dicionário da pintura universal* [Complete dictionary of painting], iii (Lisbon, 1973)
M. Martins da Silva: *Obra gravada de João Hogan* [Engraved work of João Hogan] (Lisbon, 1984)

RUTH ROSENGARTEN

Hogan, John (*b* Tallow, Co. Waterford, 14 Oct 1800; *d* Dublin, 27 March 1858). Irish sculptor. He began his career making decorative carvings for the architect Thomas Deane. He studied the collection of casts of the Vatican marbles, which arrived in Cork in 1818, having been assembled by Antonio Canova for presentation to the Prince Regent (later George IV). Hogan's talent was noticed by William Paulet Carey, a visiting dealer, who raised a public subscription on his behalf, enabling Hogan to travel to Rome in 1824. While there he studied at the English Academy and was in contact with John Gibson, Vincenzo Camuccini and Bertel Thorvaldsen, who influenced his style. He remained in Rome until the Revolution of 1849 when he returned to Ireland permanently.

Hogan worked exclusively in marble. Initially he sought to excel in Neo-classical subjects, as seen in *Shepherd Boy* (1824; ex-Powerscourt, Co. Wicklow), which blends realism and idealization. He subsequently concentrated on religious works, such as *Dead Christ* (1829; Dublin, St Teresa), which reflects the demands of resurgent Irish Catholicism after Catholic Emancipation of 1829. In 1840 he won the competition for a memorial to *Bishop James Doyle* (1840; Carlow Cathedral). This inaugurated the main phase of his career as a sculptor of public memorials, for example *Daniel O'Connell* (1846; Dublin, City Hall) and *Hibernia with a Bust of Lord Cloncurry* (1846; Lyons House, Co. Kildare), which is a combination of allegory and portraiture. Hogan also did many portrait busts and created a large number of church memorials, such as *Jeanette Farrell* (*c.* 1843; Dublin, St Andrews, Westland Row), which shows the influence of Flaxman, and *William Beamish* (1844; Cork, St Michael), which has a strong neo-Baroque quality.

Hogan's work could be realistic, but in general he aimed at idealized portrayals; his imaginative range was limited and bounded by the conservatism of late Neo-classicism in Rome. He was conscious of his Irish and Catholic identity, but he accepted commissions from both Nationalist and Unionist patrons in Ireland.

BIBLIOGRAPHY

DNB; Gunnis; Strickland

[S. Atkinson]: 'John Hogan', *Irish Q. Rev.*, viii (1858), pp. 493–588

J. Turpin: *John Hogan: Irish Neoclassical Sculptor in Rome, 1800–1858* (Dublin, 1982)

——: 'John Hogan, Irish Sculptor, 1800–1858', *Apollo*, n. s., cxv (1982), pp. 98–103

JOHN TURPIN

Hogarth, William (*b* London, 10 Nov 1697; *d* London, 25–26 Oct 1764). English painter and engraver. He played a crucial part in establishing an English school of painting, both through the quality of his painting and through campaigns to improve the status of the artist in England. He also demonstrated that artists could become independent of wealthy patrons by publishing engravings after their own paintings. He is best remembered for the satirical engravings that gave the name 'Hogarthian' to low-life scenes of the period.

1. Life and work. 2. Stylistic development and technique. 3. Writings.

1. LIFE AND WORK.

(i) Training and early work, to 1730. (ii) Mature work, 1731–58. (iii) Last years, 1759–64.

(i) Training and early work, to 1730. William Hogarth was born in St Bartholomew's Close, London. His father, Richard Hogarth, was a Latin scholar and schoolmaster,

1. William Hogarth: *The Beggar's Opera, Act III*, oil on canvas, 575×762 mm, version, 1729–31 (London, Tate Gallery)

who also became the proprietor of a coffee-house that failed; as a consequence, he was confined for four years (1708–12) as a debtor in the Fleet Prison. His misfortunes powerfully impressed Hogarth with the importance of maintaining financial independence. Having shown a talent for drawing, on 2 February 1713 he was apprenticed to Ellis Gamble, a silver-plate engraver of Blue Cross Street, Leicester Fields (now Leicester Square), London, and by 23 April 1720 (the date on his shop card, see Paulson, 1965, rev. 3/1989, no. 3) he was in business on his own account as an engraver, both of metalwork and prints (*see* SILVER, fig. 2 and EPHEMERA, PRINTED, fig. 2). His earliest prints would have been such hack-work as trade cards, funeral tickets and small book illustrations.

In October 1720 Hogarth enrolled as one of the initial subscribers (at two guineas) to the academy (in St Martin's Lane) founded by John Vanderbank and Louis Chéron. There he first studied life drawing. In 1721 he engraved the first-known of his satires, the *South Sea Scheme* (P 43), one of a spate of satirical engravings engendered by the financial scandals of the period; he followed it in 1724 with *The Lottery* (P 53). These emblematic treatments of current events, based on Dutch models, were to prove the beginning of the rich tradition of British graphic satire. Although early states of both satires carry the publication line 'Sold by Mrs Chilcot in Westminster Hall R. Caldwell Print-seller in Newgate Street', Hogarth had already started publishing and selling his own prints by February 1724, when the publication of a piracy led him to announce in the *Daily Courant* that his satirical engraving the *Bad Taste of the Town* (or *Masquerades and Operas*, P 44) was available only from himself or certain named print-sellers. He was determined to avoid the 'cruel treatment' his father had suffered from booksellers and printers in attempting to publish a Latin dictionary.

On 4 March 1724 Charles Gildon's satirical book *New Metamorphosis* was advertised in the *Daily Courant* as having 'cuts engraved by Mr Hogarth' (P 45–51), suggesting that the artist's name must already have been known to the public. By then Vanderbank and Chéron's academy had closed; in November 1724 Hogarth joined James Thornhill's free academy in the Great Piazza, Covent Garden.

The *Bad Taste of the Town* provides the earliest evidence of Hogarth's much proclaimed xenophobia, since it attacked the Italian opera and the masquerades arranged by the Swiss John James Heidegger (1659–1749), as well as the Palladian taste in architecture being propagated by Richard Boyle, 3rd Earl of Burlington, and by William Kent. In September 1725 Hogarth attacked Kent again with a burlesque of his altarpiece for St Clement Danes, London, hinting that its Italianate style carried overtones of popery and Jacobitism. In February 1726, perhaps because Hogarth was as yet reluctant to undertake the financial risk of a major project, his 12 large illustrations (P 82–93) to Samuel Butler's satirical poem *Hudibras* were published by Philip Overton (*fl* 1707; *d* 1745). This series, issued with verses from the poem as explanatory captions, foreshadowed the 'moral progresses' for which Hogarth is best remembered. It was published by subscription, a method that since the end of the 17th century had been used for volumes of poetry and some major series of reproductive prints, notably those after Thornhill's decorations for St Paul's Cathedral. Hogarth adopted this method of guaranteeing his income in advance when he began to publish in his own right. On 23 March 1729 he became a member of Thornhill's family by marrying their daughter Jane Thornhill (*c.* 1709–89).

George Vertue recorded that it was after the publication of the *Hudibras* series that Hogarth took up painting. His first major success as a painter was in 1728, when he was commissioned to paint several versions of a scene from John Gay's enormously popular satirical ballad opera *The Beggar's Opera* (version, 1729–31; London, Tate; see fig. 1). Throughout his career the conventions of the theatre provided Hogarth with a model for satirical narrative.

(ii) Mature work, 1731–58. In the early 1730s Hogarth was in demand as a painter of conversation pieces of noblemen's and gentlemen's families. Among these are the *Assembly at Wanstead House* (*c.* 1731; Philadelphia, PA, Mus. A.), which depicts the family of Richard Child, 1st Viscount Castlemaine; the *Wollaston Family* (1730; on loan to Leicester, Mus. & A.G.); the *Wedding of Stephen Beckingham and Mary Cox* (1729–30; New York, Met.); and the *Family Party* (*c.* 1730–35; New Haven, CT, Yale Cent. Brit. A.; *see* CONVERSATION PIECE, fig. 1). In the same period Hogarth began work on a genre painting of low life, showing a prostitute in her room about to be apprehended by a magistrate. He then formed the idea of painting companion pictures, showing earlier and subsequent stages of her history, from her arrival as a country girl in London and her corruption by a bawd, to her wretched death and funeral. This commonplace story was enlarged into a generalized satire on society and was lent immediacy by the introduction of a number of identifiable persons and locations. The resulting six paintings (recorded as destr. 1755; the attribution of pictures on the art market in recent years is disputed), entitled *A Harlot's Progress* and known from the engravings (P 121–6) that Hogarth published in April 1732, were the first of his moral progresses, moral stories narrated in series of pictures. *A Harlot's Progress*, while strongly satirical, tells its story with a wealth of detail that is both realistic and emblematic. The series was an enormous success. Vertue stated that at least 1240 sets, priced at one guinea, were printed for subscribers. Hogarth experienced deep satisfaction at not only discovering a new form of art but also finding a way to earn his living as an artist without having to rely on patronage. Piracies of *A Harlot's Progress* appeared immediately, which led Hogarth to authorize a cheaper version engraved by Giles King (*d* 1746) and, with more lasting effect, to undertake a campaign for an Act of Parliament granting copyright to engravers. The success of *A Harlot's Progress* prompted him to start work on another moral history, *A Rake's Progress* (London, Soane Mus.); in eight pictures it narrates the decline of a spendthrift, debauched young man about town, from riches to death in a madhouse. This satire on the fashionable life vividly portrays many contemporary social types.

Hogarth had, however, ambitions to work at the highest levels of society. Also in the early 1730s he painted *A Performance of 'The Indian Emperor or the Conquest of*

2. William Hogarth: *George Arnold*, oil on canvas, 908×705 mm, *c.* 1740 (Cambridge, Fitzwilliam Museum)

Mexico by the Spaniards' (1732–5; priv. col., see 1987–8 exh. cat., no. 68). In this portrayal of private theatricals he used, as in the scene from *The Beggar's Opera*, the device of a theatrical performance for a group portrait of the actors and audience; his sitters included younger members of the royal family and their friends. At about the same time Hogarth was commissioned to paint a portrait of George II with Queen Caroline and their children; two preliminary sketches of the whole composition survive (the *Family of George II, c.* 1732–3; Windsor Castle, Berks, Royal Col.; Dublin, N.G.), as well as a study of the son of George II, *William Augustus, Duke of Cumberland* (*c.* 1732; New Haven, CT, Yale Cent. Brit. A.). However, according to Vertue, William Kent, no doubt in order to revenge Hogarth's earlier slurs on his work, intervened at court to have the commission cancelled. Permission was also withdrawn for a painting of the wedding in 1733 of Anne, the Princess Royal, to William IV, Prince of Orange Nassau.

In the same year Hogarth essayed the traditional genre of portraits of famous criminals with his portrait of a notorious murderess, *Sarah Malcolm in Prison* (Edinburgh, N.G.), of which he also made a print (P 129). Hogarth's ambitions went further, however, towards seeking recognition as a history painter, a genre new to him. His first attempts, for which he charged no fee, were painted for St Bartholomew's Hospital, London; they are the *Pool of Bethesda* (1736), with over life-size figures whose ailments are identifiably portrayed, and a less complex composition, the *Good Samaritan* (1737; both *in situ*).

On 5 February 1735 Hogarth, together with Vertue, George Lambert, Isaac Ware, John Pine (1690–1756), Gerard Vandergucht and Joseph Goupy, signed a petition to Parliament that resulted in the Engravers' Copyright Act, prohibiting unauthorized copies of engravings for 14 years after their first publication. The Act, which gave engravers a guaranteed income from their work and was followed by an enormous development in printmaking in Britain, came into force on 24 June 1735; the following day Hogarth published his engravings of *A Rake's Progress* (P 132–9). The price to subscribers of one and a half guineas included an engraving (P 131) after his *Southwark Fair* (1733; priv. col., see Paulson, 1971, i, pl. 116).

In the years that followed, Hogarth's concern with the position of British artists showed itself in other ways. In 1735 he set up a drawing academy organized on a basis of equality in St Martin's Lane, London. The annual subscription was two guineas. The members included Francis Hayman and others who frequented Old Slaughter's Coffee House in St Martin's Lane, and their work tended to be influenced by the elegant style of Gravelot. They gained a much-needed opportunity to display their work to the public by undertaking the decoration of Vauxhall Gardens, *c.* 1740. These pleasure gardens on the south bank of the Thames had from 1728 been under the management of Hogarth's friend Jonathan Tyers (*d* 1767), and according to Nichols (1781) the idea of embellishing them with pictures had originated with Hogarth *c.* 1730. The paintings at Vauxhall included versions by Hayman of Hogarth's *Four Times of Day* of *c.* 1736 (*Morning* and *Night*, Upton House, Warwicks, NT; *Noon* and *Evening*,

3. William Hogarth: *Self-portrait with a Pug*, oil on canvas, 900×699 mm, 1745 (London, Tate Gallery)

4. William Hogarth: *The Countess's Morning Levée*, scene iv from the series *Marriage à la Mode*, oil on canvas, 705×908 mm, 1743 (London, National Gallery)

Grimsthorpe Castle, Lincs). A rare example of Hogarth's involvement in a current political issue occurred with the publication in May 1738 of *Strolling Actresses Dressing in a Barn* (P 150; issued with the *Four Times of Day*, P 146–9) as a protest against the censorship imposed on the theatre by Robert Walpole's Licensing Act of 1737. At the same time Hogarth used a tawdry back-stage setting to subvert conventional pompous representations of Classical deities.

The arrival in England in December 1737 of the fashionable portrait painter Jean-Baptiste van Loo had been seen by Hogarth as a threat and led him to develop a larger-scale portrait style that owed much to Baroque precedents. In the 1740s he painted a number of portraits of contemporary worthies, such as *George Arnold* (Cambridge, Fitzwilliam; see fig. 2), *Benjamin Hoadly, Bishop of Winchester* (London, Tate) and *Mary Edwards* (New York, Frick); the finest example is *Captain Thomas Coram* (1740; London, Foundling Hosp.). There is further evidence of Hogarth's respect for 17th-century continental models in his *Self-portrait with a Pug* (1745; London, Tate; see fig. 3), in which he depicted himself in the manner of Murillo's *Self-portrait* (London, N.G.). In the same period he once again embarked on the moral progress form in the eight paintings of *Marriage à la Mode* (1743; London, N.G.), in which he satirized the mores of high society by portraying

the sordid course and tragic end of an arranged marriage between a young nobleman and the daughter of a wealthy merchant. A particularly vivid episode in this is *The Countess's Morning Levée*, in which the wife, surrounded by foppish hangers-on, plans a tryst with her lover (see fig. 4).

Hogarth's undoubted talent for the lively portrayal of both adults and children did not bring him financial success. Wealthy sitters probably preferred the flatteringly bland portraits of Thomas Hudson, but Hogarth blamed jealous rivals. On 28 February 1745 he held an auction of a number of his paintings, issuing as a ticket of admission an etching of the *Battle of the Pictures* (P 157) in which his own work is shown under attack from ranks of Old Masters drawn up by the auctioneer Christopher Cock. The prices at the auction must have been disappointing: *Sarah Malcolm* (Edinburgh, N.G.) went to Horace Walpole for 5 guineas; *A Harlot's Progress* fetched 84 guineas; *A Rake's Progress*, 176 guineas; *Strolling Actresses Dressing in a Barn* (destr.), 26 guineas; the *Four Times of Day*, 121 guineas; and *Danaë* (untraced), 60 guineas.

On 8 July 1745 Hogarth published engravings (P 158–63) after his paintings of *Marriage à la Mode* (for illustration of the engraving of *Shortly After the Marriage* see SATIRE, fig. 1). In the subscription ticket (P 156) he illustrated the distinction between 'characters' and 'caricaturas' that the novelist Henry Fielding had drawn in discussing Hogarth's work in the preface to *Joseph Andrews* (1742). It was always Hogarth's contention that his moral subjects were not caricatures, but showed the true nature of the characters depicted. The high-quality engravings, for which Hogarth had employed French masters, sold less well than the earlier moral progresses and were still being advertised in January 1746. A projected parallel series, the *Happy Marriage*, was abandoned after oil sketches had been made *c.* 1745; they include the *Wedding Banquet* (Truro, Co. Mus. & A.G.) and *The Dance* (London, Tate). In 1746 Hogarth made a deliberate move towards the French market, asking André Rouquet to write an explanation in French of his work; it appeared as *Lettres de Monsieur [Rouquet] à un de ses amis à Paris pour lui expliquer les estampes de Monsieur Hogarth*. These letters on *A Harlot's Progress*, *A Rake's Progress* and *Marriage à la Mode*, with notes on nine others, provide the only full commentary on Hogarth's prints known to have been approved by him. From 1746 artists from the St Martin's Lane group found another chance to exhibit their work to the public by making gifts of paintings to the Foundling Hospital; those from Hogarth included, beside the above-mentioned portrait of Coram, a history painting, *Moses Brought before Pharaoh's Daughter* (1746), and the *March to Finchley* (1749–50; both *in situ*). Around 1750 Rouquet published a commentary on the print after the latter painting (P 184).

On 25 August 1746 Hogarth published a popular print of *Simon Fraser, Lord Lovat* (P 166), who was executed for his part in the 1745 rebellion. The print, which was a return to the genre of cheap portraits of famous criminals, sold, at one shilling, in its thousands. Hogarth turned again to the popular market in 1747, publishing *Industry and Idleness* (P 168–79) on 30 September. In February 1751 he issued *Beer Street* and *Gin Lane* (P 185–6) and the *Four Stages of Cruelty* (P 187–90). Unlike his earlier series, these were not conceived as paintings and subsequently published as engravings; they were engraved and published as cheaply as possible, with the avowed reforming purpose of castigating the vices of the poorest class of people. Around the same time Hogarth was occupied with his first commissioned history painting, *Paul before Felix* (1748; London, Lincoln's Inn), painted for the Benchers of Lincoln's Inn, who paid Hogarth £200 for it. In 1751 he made considerable alterations and in the following year published engravings (P 192, 192/1) of both states of the picture. He employed Luke Sullivan (1705–71) at a fee of £100 to make the second plate.

In August 1748 Hogarth travelled to France with Henry Cheere, Francis Hayman, Thomas Hudson and Joseph van Aken. While sketching in Calais he was arrested as a spy and on his return he immediately began the painting *O the Roast Beef of Old England* (or *Calais Gate*; London, Tate), which satirizes the French with such familiar stereotypes as the ragged soldier feeding on thin soup and the already overfed monk receiving a fine sirloin of British beef.

On 6 June 1751 Hogarth auctioned the *Marriage à la Mode* pictures and sold them to the sole bidder. His pique at the lack of interest in this sale was such that he tore down the gilded head of *Anthony van Dyck*, which was

the sign of his business, outside his house in Leicester Fields. In November 1753 Hogarth published his most sustained theoretical work, *The Analysis of Beauty*. His fellow artists then subjected him to criticism that he interpreted as abuse. There was an immediate spate of satirical prints, most notably those by Paul Sandby (London, BM, Satires, nos 3238–49). In March 1755 Allan Ramsay renewed the criticism in his *Dialogue on Taste*; and Joshua Reynolds developed it further in three letters to 'The Idler', published in the *Universal Chronicle* in the autumn of 1759. Much of this harshness may be explained by the fact that the publication of *The Analysis of Beauty* coincided with Hogarth's estrangement from the St Martin's Lane artists, caused by the project, discussed at a meeting held by Hayman in November 1753, to set up a public academy under royal patronage.

Hogarth's next important project was another series of satirical genre paintings, *An Election* (London, Soane Mus.), probably begun in 1753; Hogarth opened the subscription (ticket, P 197) for the engravings (P 198–201) after the paintings on 28 March 1754. The immediate inspiration of the series was probably the notorious Oxford election of 1754, the campaign for which had already begun in 1752. Although Hogarth introduced a number of identifiable persons, the satire appears to have been aimed at the corrupt and their dupes of all parties. He delivered the first plate on 24 February 1755 but continued to make alterations, and the completion of the series was not announced until March 1758. According to Joseph Farington (diary entry, 7 March 1802) Hogarth considered selling the four paintings (*An Election Entertainment*, *Canvassing for Votes*, *The Polling* and *Chairing the Member*) by lottery, but in the event they were bought by David Garrick in 1762 for 200 guineas.

The church of St Mary Redcliffe, Bristol, commissioned Hogarth in May 1755 to paint an altarpiece. The huge triptych (5.18×15.55 m in all; now Bristol, Mus. & A.G.) depicts the *Sealing of the Sepulchre*, *The Ascension* and the *Three Marys at the Sepulchre* and must have been completed by 14 August 1756, when Hogarth received his fee of £525. In the *London Evening Post* of 24–26 February 1757 Hogarth, apologizing for the delay in delivering the *Election* engravings, announced that he intended 'to employ the rest of his time in portrait painting chiefly'. In that year he painted a delightful double portrait of *David Garrick and his Wife* (Windsor Castle, Berks, Royal Col.). According to Ireland (1794–9), about this time Hogarth conceived the notion of saving sitters' time by painting portraits in only four sittings of a quarter of an hour each. His portrait of *Saunders Welch* (*c.* 1760; Houfe priv. col., see Paulson, 1971, ii, pl. 263), which shows only the sitter's face, is said to have been painted by this method.

On 6 June 1757 Hogarth was appointed Sergeant-Painter to the King and from then on earned several hundred pounds a year from fees for supervising decorative works. He inscribed his new title under the print after his self-portrait, *Hogarth Painting the Comic Muse* (*c.* 1757; London, N.P.G.; for illustration *see* EASEL), which he published on 29 March 1758; no doubt he took pride in having succeeded to an office previously held by Sir James Thornhill, his father-in-law. Around 1758 Hogarth received a commission from James Caulfield, 1st Earl of

Charlemont, for a painting of his own choice of subject. The result was the *Lady's Last Stake* (1758–9; Buffalo, NY, Albright–Knox A.G.), depicting, in Hogarth's own words, a 'virtuous married lady that had lost all at cards to a young officer wavering at his suit whether she should part with her honour or no to regain the loss which was offered to her'. Charlemont paid £100 for this elegant combination of Rococo style with titillating subject-matter, in which Hogarth's sensibility may be compared to that of François Boucher. It was the last of a type of picture that Hogarth from time to time produced for patrons of rakish taste. He had earlier painted the two versions of *Before* and *After*, showing a man and a girl before and after an sexual intercourse (*c.* 1730–31; Cambridge, Fitzwilliam; Malibu, CA, Getty Mus.); *A Night Encounter* (*c.* 1738; New Haven, CT, Yale Cent. Brit. A.); *Charity in the Cellar* (*c.* 1739; priv. col., see Paulson, 1971, ii, pl. 268); *Sir Francis Dashwood at his Devotions* (*c.* 1742–6; priv. col., see Paulson, 1971, ii, pl. 269); and *Frank Matthew Schutz Vomiting* (*c.* 1755–60; Norwich, Castle Mus.).

(iii) Last years, 1759–64. Sir Richard Grosvenor (later 1st Earl Grosvenor), having seen the *Lady's Last Stake* before its completion, also commissioned from Hogarth a painting on a subject of the artist's own choice. He seems to have been hoping for another amorous subject and on being presented in June 1759 with a subject from Boccaccio, *Sigismunda Mourning over the Heart of Guiscardo* (London, Tate), for which Hogarth was asking 400 guineas, he refused the picture. Hogarth was deeply hurt by the rejection, which delighted his enemies, and the ensuing anxiety brought on a year's illness. At the same time further moves were taking place towards the establishment of a public academy. The first of a series of annual exhibitions opened on 21 April 1760 under the auspices of the Society for the Encouragement of Arts, Manufactures and Commerce. Hogarth did not become involved until 1761 in what had by then become the Society of Artists of Great Britain. He contributed a frontispiece and a tailpiece to the exhibition catalogue (9–30 May 1761) and showed *Sigismunda*, *Calais Gate*, the *Lady's Last Stake*, three portraits and *An Election Entertainment*; the first was withdrawn after some 12 days, presumably because of adverse criticism, and replaced by *Chairing the Member*.

On 15 December 1761 Hogarth was elected to the committee of the Society of Artists, but he did not exhibit again. In April 1762 he did his best to antagonize some of his fellow artists by organizing a burlesque 'Grand Exhibition of the Society of Sign Painters' immediately before the third annual Society of Artists' exhibition. On 7 September 1762 he published an engraving, entitled *The Times: Plate I* (P 211), supporting the attempts of the Prime Minister, John Stuart, 3rd Earl of Bute, to end the war with France and portraying his opponents, such as William Pitt the elder, as pandering to City interests. This entry into party politics provoked the final and most painful attacks on Hogarth. He was subjected to a further series of satirical prints by Sandby (London, BM, Satires, nos 3890, 3910, 3955 and 3971) and others (London, BM, Satires, nos 3916 and 3973–8); an essay by the politician John Wilkes in the *North Briton* (no. 17, 25 Sept 1762); and in June 1763 Charles Churchill's *Epistle to William*

Hogarth. He responded with an engraving of *John Wilkes* (16 May 1763, P 214), treated as a pair to his popular print of the traitor Lord Lovat; and with an engraving of Churchill, *The Bruiser* (1 Aug 1763; P 215), shown as a bear with a pot of beer and a club, poignantly taking the place of Hogarth's own head in the plate of *Self-portrait with a Pug* (P 181). Hogarth was said to have sold 4000 impressions of the Wilkes engraving at one shilling each.

Hogarth spent his final year of life working on his *Autobiographical Notes* and strengthening and reworking plates. On 3 March 1764 he published an engraving with the title *The Bathos* (or the *Art of Sinking in Sublime Paintings*), to be bound at the end of each volume of his prints. He died of an aneurysm at his house in Leicester Fields and was buried at St Nicholas, Chiswick (now London), where a monument with an epitaph by Garrick was erected in 1771. Mrs Hogarth continued to sell her husband's prints and issued a number of catalogues. Her posthumous sale on 24 April 1790 consisted chiefly of work by Hogarth: his prints, many framed and glazed; 16 pictures (portraits of family and friends and sketches for larger works); and a number of drawings.

2. STYLISTIC DEVELOPMENT AND TECHNIQUE. Hogarth's formal training was as an engraver, and although he studied drawing with Vanderbank and Chéron and with Thornhill he appears to have been largely self-taught as a painter. He developed rapidly from the early, rather stiff single figures and group portraits (e.g. *Sir Robert Pye*, 1730; London, Marble Hill House) on a small scale. Satirical leanings and an interest in subjects from everyday life meant that he naturally turned for inspiration to Dutch drolls, as in *The Denunciation* (*c.* 1729; Dublin, N.G.), but a French Rococo influence was also apparent at an early stage. He was indebted to the *commedia dell'arte* compositions of Claude Gillot and Antoine Watteau in introducing theatrical subjects to British art, as in his *Falstaff Examining his Recruits* (1728; priv. col., see Bindman, p. 33) and the scene from *The Beggar's Opera*.

After 1737 Hogarth turned to larger-scale portraits and developed a bravura technique derived from the masters of the French Baroque. His new style was exemplified in the portrait of *Captain Thomas Coram* and in numerous half-length portraits, such as *Lavinia Fenton, Duchess of Bolton* (*c.* 1740; London, Tate), *Frederick Frankland* (1740; San Marino, CA, Huntington A.G.) and *Mary Blackwood, Mrs Desaguliers* (1741; priv. col., see 1987–8 exh. cat., no. 119), as well as a large full-length of *David Garrick as Richard III* (*c.* 1745; Liverpool, Walker A.G.). Three group portraits of children that Hogarth painted in this period were enhanced by poignant emblematic references: *The Grey Children* (1740; St Louis, MO, Washington U., Gal. A.); *The Graham Children* (1742; London, N.G.); and *The Mackinnon Children* (*c.* 1742; Dublin, N.G.). In these pictures Hogarth combined the tradition of van Dyck (especially the *Five Eldest Children of Charles I*, Windsor Castle, Berks, Royal Col.), which for him represented the best in British painting, with Gravelot's informal treatment of childhood themes.

Hogarth's first commissioned history painting, *Paul before Felix*, included in the composition anecdotal elements that appear to have met with criticism. In 1751 he made considerable alterations to achieve a more monumental, Raphaelesque effect (see Paulson, 1975, pp. 51–4). In *Paul before Felix Burlesqued* (P 191), the subscription ticket for the engraving after the reworked painting, Hogarth responded to accusations of having followed the current 'Dutch taste' in the original version; his burlesque set out to satirize the 'imitation of Rembrandt' and to demonstrate that he himself had not succumbed to it. His huge altarpiece (1755–6; Bristol, Mus. & A.G.) for St Mary Redcliffe, Bristol, also drew on Italianate prototypes, but the composition was less coherent than that of his smaller-scale pictures. Hogarth had few models for the organization of large religious subjects, and the fact that no engraving after the altarpiece was published in his lifetime suggests that he was not satisfied with it.

The rapidly executed portrait of *Saunders Welch* and the somewhat similar head of *James Caulfield, 1st Earl of Charlemont* (c. 1759; Northampton, MA, Smith Coll. Mus. A.) may be compared with the virtuoso group portrait of six of *Hogarth's Servants* (c. 1750–55; London, Tate). These portraits demonstrate Hogarth's ability to convey a sense of the sitter's character without any of the usual narrative props or scene setting.

Hogarth's success as an engraver was in large part due to his skill at creating compositions that are clear and easily read, even when many levels of meaning are being conveyed. As early as 1726 he showed his ability to tell a story without words in the large *Hudibras* series; and by 1732, in *A Harlot's Progress*, he was able to combine narrative with a graceful style influenced by contemporary developments in France. He did not, however, pretend to the technical virtuosity of the best French engravers. As early as 1735 he employed Louis-Gérard Scotin (b 1690) to help with the engraving of *A Rake's Progress* and thereafter he appears to have used French engravers whenever he wanted to appeal to a more sophisticated audience. The *Marriage à la Mode* plates were engraved by Scotin, Bernard Baron and Simon Francis Ravenet, and Hogarth advertised (*Daily Post*, 2 April 1743; *Daily Advertizer*, 8 Sept 1744) that he had gone to Paris especially to find 'the best masters'.

A simple, broad etching technique was used for such single sheets as *Sarah Malcolm*, *Simon Fraser*, *Lord Lovat* and *John Wilkes*, which were intended to be sold widely and cheaply. Hogarth also exploited the genre of the popular print with the *Industry and Idleness* series, and with *Beer Street*, *Gin Lane* and the *Four Stages of Cruelty*, all of which were conceived from the outset as engravings and made directly from preliminary drawings; the moral message aimed at a mass public was best conveyed by a simple style. Hogarth went further with the *Four Stages of Cruelty* by employing J. Bell (fl 1721–64) to make woodcuts after his engravings; woodcuts could be printed in far larger editions than engravings but were more expensive to make, and the project was abandoned after Bell had cut blocks of the last two pictures in the series.

Hogarth used drawings sparingly. Only about a hundred survive, and a large proportion of these are connected with the engravings that were not based on paintings. The most illuminating are those that demonstrate the development of major series: *Hudibras* (Windsor Castle, Berks, Royal Col., see Oppé, nos 5–11), *Industry and Idleness*

(London, BM, o 40–63), *Beer Street* and *Gin Lane* (New York, Pierpont Morgan Lib., o 76–7) and the *Four Stages of Cruelty* (New Haven, CT, Yale Cent. Brit. A., o 70; New York, Pierpont Morgan Lib., o 71–3, 75; Windsor Castle, Berks, Royal Col., o 74). Studies used for the more ambitious works can be identified, such as those of the soldier in the Bristol altarpiece (New York, Pierpont Morgan Lib., o 84) and the woman in the *Pool of Bethesda* (Windsor Castle, Berks, Royal Col., o 25), probably made at St Martin's Lane and preserved by the artist for reference. For the most part, Hogarth appears to have created directly on to the canvas; pentiments can be detected in many works. Preliminary oil sketches were used for some complex compositions (e.g. the study for the *Pool of Bethesda*, Manchester, C.A.G.).

3. WRITINGS. Hogarth's writing was for the most part theoretical or polemical. He provided no keys to his own, often complex, narrative paintings and engravings, leaving them, apart from Rouquet's authorized explanation, open to the viewer's interpretation. The earliest written publication with which Hogarth can be associated is a pamphlet, *The Case of Designers, Engravers, Etchers, etc. Stated in a Letter to a Member of Parliament* (c. 1733), arguing for copyright protection for printmakers; this was part of the campaign leading to the Engravers' Copyright Act of 1735. Hogarth's first attack on the connoisseurs and dealers in foreign pictures whom he saw as acting against British artists was a letter signed 'Britophil', published in the *St. James's Evening Post* in June 1737.

Hogarth's major written work, *The Analysis of Beauty*, provides a manifesto of his view of art in opposition to that of the connoisseurs, as exemplified by Jonathan Richardson (*Theory of Painting*, 1715); his prime objection was to their ideal notion of art improving on nature and the corresponding use of the Old Masters as authorities for artists. His own art was based, he insisted, on analysis of 'whatever pleases and entertains the eye' and on 'the fundamental principles, which are generally allowed to give elegance and beauty, when duly blended together, to compositions of all kinds whatever…fitness, variety, uniformity, simplicity, intricacy, and quantity'. The taste expressed is Rococo, but the notion of the primacy of nature anticipated later theories of the Picturesque and Romantic. While rejecting a simple-minded adherence to the work of earlier painters, Hogarth was ready to quote theories that reinforced his own, referring to Giovanni Paolo Lomazzo's use of the flame form to express motion as a prefiguration of his serpentine 'line of beauty'. He benefited from the collaboration of scholarly friends in composing the treatise, and, however rudely his fellow-artists abused him for venturing into the field of theory, the work was favourably received in learned circles; two German editions appeared in 1754 and one in Italian in 1761.

In 1760 or 1761 Hogarth made notes for *An Apology for Painters*, reiterating his lifelong concerns with the state of the arts in Britain. His *Autobiographical Notes*, on which he worked towards the end of his life, are not only a personal valediction, but a final, bitter view of his career in the context of the 18th-century art world.

For further illustrations *see* HUGUENOTS; *see also* LONDON, fig. 18.

WRITINGS

Letter, signed 'Britophil': *St. James's Eve. Post* (7–9 June 1737) [repr. in Paulson, 1971, ii, pp. 491–3]

The Analysis of Beauty (London, 1753); ed. J. Burke (Oxford, 1955)

An Apology for Painters (*c.* 1760–61; London, BL, Add. MS. 27993); ed. M. Kitson in *Walpole Soc.*, xli (1966–8), pp. 46–111

Autobiographical Notes (*c.* 1764; London, BL, Add. MS. 27991); ed. J. Burke in *The Analysis of Beauty* (Oxford, 1955), pp. 201–36

BIBLIOGRAPHY

'The Note-books of George Vertue', *Walpole Soc.*, xviii (1930), xx (1932), xxii (1934), xxiv (1936), xxvi (1938), xxix (1942) [index], xxx (1952)

J. A. Rouquet: *Lettres de Monsieur [Rouquet] à un de ses amis à Paris pour lui expliquer les estampes de Monsieur Hogarth* (London, 1746, 2/1748)

A. Ramsay: *A Dialogue on Taste* (London, 1755)

J. Reynolds: Letters 76, 79 and 82 to 'The Idler', *Univl Chron.* (29 Sept, 20 Oct, 10 Nov 1759); repr. in *The Discourses of Sir Joshua Reynolds* (Oxford, 1907), pp. 249–60

J. Wilkes: Essay in the *North Briton*, 17 (25 Sept 1762)

C. Churchill: *An Epistle to William Hogarth* (London, 1763)

J. Trusler: *Hogarth Moralized* (London, 1768)

J. Nichols: *Biographical Anecdotes of William Hogarth* (London, 1781)

J. Ireland: *Hogarth Illustrated*, 3 vols (London, 1791–8)

S. Ireland: *Graphic Illustrations of Hogarth*, 2 vols (London, 1794–9)

G. C. Lichtenberg: *Ausführliche Erklärung der Hogarthischen Kupferstiche*, 14 vols (Göttingen, 1794–1834); Eng. trans. as *Lichtenberg's Commentaries on Hogarth's Engravings* (London, 1966)

J. Nichols, G. Steevens and I. Reed: *The Genuine Works of William Hogarth*, 3 vols (London, 1808–17)

A. Dobson: *William Hogarth* (London, 1891, 4/1907)

S. E. Read: 'Some Observations on William Hogarth's *Analysis of Beauty*: A Bibliographical Study', *Huntington Lib. Q.*, v (1941–2), pp. 360–73

A. P. Oppé: *The Drawings of William Hogarth* (London, 1948) [O]

R. B. Beckett: *Hogarth* (London, 1949)

R. Paulson: *Hogarth's Graphic Works*, 2 vols (New Haven and London, 1965, rev. 3/1989) [P]

——: *Hogarth: His Life, Art and Times*, 2 vols (New Haven and London, 1971)

Hogarth (exh. cat. by L. Gowing, London, Tate, 1971–2)

B. Nicolson and J. Kerslake: *The Treasures of the Foundling Hospital* (London, 1972)

R. Paulson: *The Art of Hogarth* (London, 1975)

D. Bindman: *Hogarth* (London, 1981)

Manners and Morals: Hogarth and British Painting, 1700–1760 (exh. cat. by E. Einberg, London, Tate, 1987–8)

E. Einberg and J. Egerton: *The Age of Hogarth: British Painters Born 1675–1709*, Tate Gallery Collections, ii (London, 1988), pp. 74–148

R. Paulson: *Hogarth*, 3 vols (New Brunswick and Cambridge, 1992–3)

SHEILA O'CONNELL

Hogenberg [Hogenbergh; Hohenberg; Hoogenberg]. Netherlandish family of artists, active in northern Europe. (1) Nicolas Hogenberg worked in Mechelen for most of his career, producing prints with religious and historical subjects. His son Remigius Hogenberg (*b* Mechelen, *c.* 1536; *d* ?England, *c.* 1588) worked as an engraver. In 1570 Remigius executed a *View of Münster* (Hollstein, no. 20), which suggests a visit to that city, but by 1573 he was in the service of the Archbishop of Canterbury, Matthew Parker, whose portrait he engraved in the same year (H 16). He worked on the *Genealogy of English and French Kings* (1574; H 19) for Parker and produced a number of maps of English counties for Christopher Saxton's *Atlas of England and Wales* (1579). The existence of several portraits of Huguenot nobles (e.g. *Charles, Duc de Lorraine*, H 6) indicates a possible visit to France. (2) Franz Hogenberg, also Nicolas's son, worked mainly in England and Germany and is noted for his *Civitates orbis terrarum*, an atlas containing maps of Europe. Franz Hogenberg's two sons, Johann [Hans] Hogenberg (*b* ?Munich, *c.* 1550; *fl* 1594–1614) and Abraham Hogenberg (*fl* 1608–after 1653), were both engravers. Johann worked

in Mechelen and Cologne, mainly as a portrait engraver, but he produced a few religious subjects and a series of 12 plates depicting birds and animals (H 43–54). Abraham Hogenberg assisted his father with the plates for Abraham Ortelius's *Theatrum orbis terrarum* (Antwerp, 1570) and designed and engraved frontispieces for booksellers, possibly also working in Cologne.

BIBLIOGRAPHY

BNB; *DNB*; Hollstein: *Dut. & Flem.* [H]; Thieme–Becker; Wurzbach

A. M. Hind: *Engraving in England* (London, 1952), pp. 64–72

(1) Nicolas [Nikolaus; Hans; Johann] **Hogenberg** (*b* ?Munich, *c.* 1500; *d* Mechelen, before 23 Sept 1539). Engraver, etcher and woodcutter. It is thought that he worked in Augsburg in the early years of the century, but he is recorded in Mechelen by 1527. Hogenberg has been identified by Friedländer as the Monogrammist NH, an artist who executed a number of fine woodcuts and etchings dated 1522–4, including a pair depicting *The Patriarchs* and a *Group of Saints with SS Peter and Christopher* (1524; H 17, 20), and *Jeremiah Dropped into the Pit* (1525; H 2), in all of which the artist depicts monumental figures in a classicizing and Italian style, with strong chiaroscuro effects and frequent use of foreshortening; the architectural backgrounds have pronounced verticals and horizontals. Hogenberg etched a frieze consisting of 40 plates representing the *Entry of the Emperor Charles V into Bologna* (1530; H 31–70), suggesting a possible visit to Italy. Four etchings of the *Life and Death of Margaret of Austria* (1530; H 27–30) are also attributed to the artist. Van Mander stated that Hogenberg worked as a painter and produced a series of scenes from the *History of Caleb and Joshua* for a chapel in Mechelen Cathedral. After Hogenberg's death, Frans Crabbe took over his workshop and issued a number of his prints.

BIBLIOGRAPHY

K. van Mander: *Schilder-boeck* ([1603]–1604), fol. 228

M. J. Friedländer: 'Nicolas Hogenberg und Frans Crabbe, die Maler von Mechelen', *Jb. Preuss. Kstsamml.*, xlii (1921), pp. 161–8

The Prints of Lucas van Leyden and his Contemporaries (exh. cat. by E. L. Jacobowitz and S. Loeb Stepanek, Washington, DC, N.G.A.; Boston, MA, Mus. F.A.; 1983), pp. 295–301 [with bibliog.]

(2) Franz [Frans] **Hogenberg** (*b* Mechelen, *c.* 1540; *d* Cologne, *c.* 1590). Painter, engraver, etcher and publisher, son of (1) Nicolas Hogenberg. He was probably a pupil of the cartographer H. Terbruggen in Mechelen but later worked in Antwerp, producing such engravings as the *Allegory with Fortune* (1561; Hollstein, no. 39), the *Battle between Lent and Carnival* (etching, 1558; published by Hieronymus Cock, H 40), the *Fools' Dance* (H 41), and a portrait of *Mary I, Queen of England* (1554; H 54). It was probably in Antwerp that he executed several maps for the *Theatrum orbis terrarum* of Abraham Ortelius, which was published in 1570 (H 131). It is also possible that he travelled to Poitiers in 1560, as his name and that date appear on an engraving by Joris Hoefnagel of the 'Celtic Stone' at Poitiers. A visit to England is suggested by the 1568 engraved portrait of *William Cecil, Lord Burghley* (1568; H 43). Also from the period are the portraits of *Robert Dudley, Earl of Leicester* (H 45) and *Elizabeth, Queen of England* (H 46); all three portraits were published in the 'Bishop's Bible' of Matthew Parker (1568). Hogenberg also engraved two *Views of the Royal Exchange in London* (H 58, 59).

Religious troubles probably account for his return to the Netherlands, and from 1570 he is recorded in Cologne, where he engraved various topographical illustrations including maps for the *De Leone Belgico . . .* of M. Aitsinger (1583; H 127), a frontispiece and map for Aitsinger's *Terra promissionis topographice* (1582; H 128) and maps for the *Civitates orbis terrarum* (1572–94), which he produced with Georg Braun. Hogenberg also engraved portraits in Cologne including those of *Archbishop Ernest of Cologne* (1583, 1584; H 49 and 48), *Gerard Mercator* (1574; H 55) and *Archbishop Gebhard Truchsess of Cologne* (1583; H 57), as well as such historical series as the *Scenes of the Religious and Civil Wars from the History of the Netherlands, France and England from 1559* (to 1597; H 51) and the *Funeral Procession of John William, Count of Jülich* (1593; H 115–26). Among his best work is the series of the *Story of Psyche and Cupid* (1575; after Raphael). In 1585, 1588 and again in 1588 he was working in Hamburg, Denmark and again in Hamburg.

PRINTS

A. Ortelius: *Theatrum orbis terrarum* (Antwerp, 1560/R Amsterdam, 1965) [facs. edn, intro. by R. A. Skelton]
with G. Braun: *Civitates orbis terrarum*, 6 vols (Cologne, 1572–1617/R 3 vols, Cleveland and New York, 1967) [facs. edn, intro. by R. A. Skelton]

BIBLIOGRAPHY

G. K. Nagler: *Monogrammisten* (1858–1920), ii, pp. 2150, 2169
J. J. Merlo: *Kölnische Künstler in alter und neuer Zeit* (Düsseldorf, 1895), pp. 358–79
J. Denucé: *Oud-Nederlandsche kaartmakers* (Antwerp and The Hague, 1912–13)
L. Lebeer: 'Het hooi en de hooiwagen in de beeldende kunsten: De monogrammist FB, FHB en zijn verwanted RB, FHB' [The hay and the haywain in the plastic arts: the monogrammist FB, FHB and the related RB, FHB], *Gent. Bijdr. Kstgesch.*, v (1938), pp. 141–8
——: 'De blauwe huyck' [The blue cloak], *Gent. Bijd. Kstgesch.*, vi (1939), pp. 161–229
——: 'La Kermesse d'Hoboken', *Miscellanea Léo van Puyvelde* (Brussels, 1949), pp. 99–103
R. György: *Alte Veduten aus G. Braun's und F. Hogenberg's 'Civitates orbis terrarum'* (Budapest, 1959)
J. Keuning: 'The *Civitates* of Braun and Hogenberg', *Imago Mundi: Rev. Early Cartography*, xvii (1963), pp. 41–4
J. Kozak: 'Civitates orbis terrarum: "Pana Francise kniha mest"', *Uměni*, xxxi (1983), pp. 381–91
A. Monballieu: 'Nog eens Hoboken bij Bruegel en tijdgenoten', *Jb.: Kon. Mus. S. Kst.* (1987), pp. 185–206
I. M. Veldman: 'Keulen als toevluchtsoord voor Nederlandse kunstenaars (1567–1612)', *Oud-Holland*, 107 (1993), pp. 34–57

CHRISTINE VAN MULDERS

Höger, (Johann Friedrich) Fritz (*b* Bekenreihe, Holstein, 12 June 1877; *d* Bad Segeberg, 21 June 1949). German architect. He was the son of a carpenter and himself served an apprenticeship as a carpenter (1895–6) before attending the Baugewerkschule, Hamburg (1897–9). From 1901 to 1905 he worked in the architectural practice of Lund & Kallmorgen in Hamburg, and from *c.* 1905 to *c.* 1907 he worked for the building firm of his father-in-law Fritz Oldenburg. Höger absorbed the North German building traditions, particularly of brickwork, which had been characteristic of the area since the Middle Ages. He also felt an affinity with the Gothic, which he expressed by trying to create a 20th-century Gothic architecture, without actually imitating Gothic forms.

Having established an independent practice in Hamburg (1907), Höger's first buildings exemplified the prevailing style of late historicism, particularly the brick-built office blocks in Mönckebergstrasse, Hamburg, such as the Klöppnerhaus (1913), which was decorated with August Gaul's bronze *Mercury* (Hamburg, Ksthalle). Closer to the Baroque is the very conservative, palace-like administrative building (1919–20) of the Schleswig-Holsteinische Strom Company, Hamburg. With the Chilehaus (1921–3; *see* EXPRESSIONSM, fig. 1), Hamburg, one of the most famous Expressionist buildings in Germany, Höger gave an unforgettably dramatic shape to a tall brick-built mass. An 11-storey office block, with the top three storeys set back, it is built around several inner courtyards. The façade (l. 200 m) is partly curved to follow the street and tapers to a point at one end. Equally important to the effect is the columniated wall, which gives the building a vertical emphasis. Höger described the Chilehaus as 'the opposite of eclecticism and the opposite of classicism, but above all a victory over NEUE SACHLICHKEIT' (Kamphausen, p. 85). He also claimed that the work owed its spiritual value to its 'Gothic dynamic'. The eight-storey Sprinkenhof office block (1927–43), Hamburg, is similar to the Chilehaus in its setback top storeys, its concrete core with brick cladding attached in a diamond pattern and its partly curved ground-plan. The nine-storey Hannoverscher Anzeiger building (1927–8), Hannover, is also comparable to the Chilehaus for its gothicizing expressiveness. The dominating elements are prominent triangular lesenes emphasizing the verticality of the building and the copper-clad dome. Also with echoes of Expressionism are the head office (1928) of the Konsumverein Leipzig, Leipzig, and the Reemtsma cigarette factory (1926–9), Hamburg-Wandsbeck. By contrast, the Rathaus (1928–9), Wilhelmshaven-Rüstringen, is very close to Neue Sachlichkeit. In his dynamic, monumental articulation of the masses Höger approached a declamatory neo-classicism.

Höger's Evangelical church (1930–33), Hohenzollernplatz, Berlin, is one of the more important Protestant churches of the inter-war period. Its exterior is notable for the way its reinforced concrete frame is hidden behind colourful brick cladding and a copper roof. The internal supports, by contrast, are reminiscent of pointed Gothic arches, imparting a note of solemnity. Höger's domestic architecture is, without exception, more traditional, as in his last major work, the Siebertsburg estate (1935–8), Wilhelmshaven.

He received, however, no other large commissions under the Nazis, who tolerated neither Expressionism nor his individual style.

WRITINGS

with P. Broecker: *Die Architektur des Hamburger Geschäftshauses* (Hamburg, 1910)
Bauwerke und Entwürfe (Hamburg, 1923)

BIBLIOGRAPHY

C. I. H. Westfal: *Fritz Hoeger: Der niederdeutsche Backsteinbaumeister* (Wolfshagen-Scharbeutz, 1938)
J. Gebhard: *Fritz Höger, Baumeister in Hamburg: Ein Beitrag zum Wiederaufbau* (Hamburg, 1952)
A. Kamphausen: *Der Baumeister Fritz Höger* (Neumünster, 1972)
Fritz Höger: Baumeister-Zeichnungen (exh. cat., ed. E. Berckenhagen; W. Berlin, Kstbib. & Mus., 1977)

VOLKER HELAS

Hohen, Alexander von. *See* GOGEN, ALEKSANDR.

Hohenberg. *See* HOGENBERG.

Hohenberg, Johann Ferdinand (Hetzendorf) von (*b* Vienna, 7 Feb 1732; *d* Vienna, 14 Dec 1816). Austrian architect and teacher. After training as a painter of architecture, he studied architecture itself at the Akademie der Bildenden Künste in Vienna. He seems to have established contact with the Viennese court early in his career, since his first commission was to redesign the court theatre (from 1766) at the imperial Schloss Schönbrunn in Vienna. In the same year he was ennobled. With the assistance of Prince Wenzel Anton Kaunitz-Rietberg (patron of the Akademie and artistic adviser to Maria-Theresa, Queen of Hungary and Empress of Austria) Hohenberg was appointed in 1770 to teach architecture at the Akademie. He worked in this capacity until his final years, influencing successive generations of students. In 1772 he redesigned the gardens at Schönbrunn (*see* VIENNA, §V, 7(ii)). His imaginative plan, based on the Antique, was only partially realized in subsequent years, in particular with the Gloriette (1773–5), a triumphal arch flanked by colonnaded screens that closes the view on the height above the parterre, and the Roman Ruin (1778), inspired by Giovanni Battista Piranesi. In both structures he used components from buildings that had been part of the original 'Neugebäude', a pleasure palace built (from 1564) outside the gates of Vienna for Maximilian II, Holy Roman Emperor. In 1776 Hohenberg was appointed Court Architect, with responsibility for the direction of official building beyond the Linienwall, or outer ramparts of Vienna, but he also continued to work for various noble clients. In the large gardens and grounds that he designed for Graf Christian Johann von Fries (1719–85) at Vöslau (from 1774) and for Freiherr Peter Friedrich von Braun (1758–1819) at Schönau (from 1796), the grottoes are an outstanding feature among the other unusual and evocative buildings he created there. The Haus der Laune or 'Maison de Caprice' in the park of the imperial country seat at Laxenburg (model dated 1799) is his masterpiece in this genre. A painted tower in a variety of styles (including Gothic and Egyptian Revival), its interiors eloquently convey their functions (music room, devil's kitchen, etc) by means of appropriate decoration. Hohenberg also designed an unexecuted extension (1816) in the Gothic style for Laxenburg.

Hohenberg's works cover an extraordinarily wide range of styles. In 1784 he renovated two Gothic churches in Vienna (the Augustinerkirche and the Minoritenkirche), using severe, rigid forms that were closely linked to the Gothic originals, thereby creating a unified whole. From 1786 he built the large parish church at Austerlitz (now Slavkov u Brna) in Moravia for Prince Kaunitz-Rietberg. A monumental work in an early Neo-classical style, it may be regarded as characteristic of the reforms in church building that Joseph II (co-regent with Maria-Theresa from 1765; *d* 1790) strove to implement (*see* AUSTRIA, §II, 4). In 1783–4 Hohenberg had erected a large town house for Graf von Fries on the Josefsplatz in Vienna, opposite the Baroque imperial library designed by Johann Bernhard Fischer von Erlach. A simple, austerely articulated block, the building (now the Palais Fries-Pallavicini) attracted controversy and vehement criticism because of its lack of ornamentation. In 1786 Hohenberg was compelled to add a rich framing for the doorway (caryatids by Franz Anton Zauner) as a concession to traditional ideas of grandeur in palace architecture. Towards the end of his career he demonstrated a similarly severe, unadorned classicism in his plans (1807–9) for extending the Hofburg in Vienna as an imperial residence for the newly created Austrian Empire. The versatility of style apparent in Hohenberg's work was unmatched during his lifetime. He simultaneously represented (in strongly individual interpretations) the Gothic Revival and strictly classical schools of thought: in this way he was in many respects already anticipating the historicist solutions of the later 19th century.

BIBLIOGRAPHY

E. Hainisch: *Der Architekt Johann Ferdinand Hetzendorf von Hohenberg* (Vienna, 1949)

R. Wagner-Rieger: *Wiens Architektur im 19. Jahrhundert* (Vienna, 1970)

Klassizismus in Wien: Architektur und Plastik (exh. cat., Vienna, Hist. Mus., 1978)

HELLMUT LORENZ

Hohenberg, Johann Martin. *See* ALTOMONTE, (1).

Hohenbourg, Herrad von. *See* HERRAD VON LANDSBERG.

Hohenems. *See* ALTEMPS.

Hohenems, Marcus Sitticus von, Prince-Archbishop of Salzburg (*b* Hohenems, 24 June 1574; *d* Salzburg, 9 Oct 1619). Austrian churchman and patron. He prepared for a career in the Church by studying in Milan and Rome, where he enjoyed the special support of his uncle, Cardinal Marcus Sitticus ALTEMPS. In 1598 he was appointed canon in Salzburg, through the endeavours of his cousin Wolf Dietrich von Raitenau, Prince-Archbishop of Salzburg, whom he succeeded as Prince-Archbishop in 1612. His continuation of the neutral political stance adopted by his predecessors saved the city from devastation in the Thirty Years War (1618–48). From his foundation of a Benedictine school in 1617, Salzburg University emerged a decade later.

Despite his comparatively short reign, Marcus Sitticus von Hohenems made a decisive impact on the appearance of Salzburg (*see* SALZBURG, §1(ii)). This was due largely to his introduction of such Italian artists as Donato Arsenio Mascagni (1579–1636) and SANTINO SOLARI. His portrait (1618; Salzburg, Schloss Hellbrunn) by Mascagni depicts him showing his two most important projects: the building of Salzburg Cathedral (*see* AUSTRIA, §II, 3(i) (a) and fig. 5) and Schloss Hellbrunn (*see* HELLBRUNN). He laid the cathedral's foundation stone in 1614, abandoning a design (1611) by Vincenzo Scamozzi and using the west-east alignment of the Romanesque cathedral (destr. 1598). The building had reached roof height at the time of his death. The neighbouring Residenz (1612–19) in Salzburg was designed by Solari and decorated with secco paintings by Mascagni. At Schloss Hellbrunn (1613–15), the Archbishop's retreat, a Roman Theatre and a Stone Theatre were erected in the extensive park, and in the numerous grottoes he placed sculptures by Gerolamo Preosto (*fl* 1614–19), Bernardo Zanini (*fl* 1614–17) and Hans Leonhard Waldburger (*c.* 1543–1622). The Monatsschlossl, on the Hellbrunnerberg, which the Archbishop commissioned for the visit of Archduke Maximilian of Austria, was built extremely swiftly (1612–13) by calling on all available builders in the neighbourhood of Salzburg.

BIBLIOGRAPHY

F. Martin: *Salzburgs Fürsten der Barockzeit* (Salzburg, 1952), pp. 66–84
E. Stahl: *Marcus Sitticus von Hohenems: Leben und Spiele eines geistlichen Fürsten* (Vienna, 1988)

JOHANNES RAMHARTER

Hohenfurth Abbey. *See* VYŠŠÍ BROD ABBEY.

Hohenstaufen. German dynasty of rulers and patrons. They rose to prominence in the late 11th century in imperial service, and in 1138 Conrad of Hohenstaufen was elected Emperor. At Conrad's death in 1152 the title passed to his nephew, (1) Frederick I. (2) Frederick II was the grandson of Frederick I. The line died out with the murder of Frederick II's grandson, Conradin, in 1268 (*see* ANJOU).

BIBLIOGRAPHY

Die Zeit der Staufer, 5 vols (exh. cat., Stuttgart, Württemberg. Landesmuseums, 1977)

(1) Frederick I [Barbarossa], King of Germany and Holy Roman Emperor (*b c.* 1122–4; *reg* 1152–90; *d* Self [Turkey], 10 June 1190). His reign marked a return to conflict with the Papacy, the result of his attempt to restore the complete imperial power attained by CHARLEMAGNE. He had Aachen Cathedral decorated (*c.* 1165–70) with a great wheel candelabrum (*see* AACHEN, §2(ii)(c)), symbolizing the Heavenly Jerusalem. It came from the same Aachen workshop that produced the Emperor's *Christening Cup* (*c.* 1160; Berlin, Schloss Köpernick), with an engraving of his baptism, a gift to his godfather Otto, Graf von Cappenberg (*d* 1171), in whose will it is mentioned, as is a gilt bronze bust of the Emperor (1150–71; Cappenberg, St Johannes). In 1164 Frederick removed the relics of the Magi from Milan and presented them to Cologne Cathedral, where they were later enshrined (*see* NICHOLAS OF VERDUN, §2(i)). In 1165 Frederick had Charlemagne canonized, raised his mortal remains, and had a reliquary (Paris, Louvre) made for the arm bones, on which Frederick I and members of his family are depicted (see (2) below). A pair of bracelets (*c.* 1170) from the Rhine–Meuse region, which have pictures of the *Crucifixion* (Nuremberg, Ger. Nmus.) and *Resurrection* (Paris, Louvre), was made for the Emperor's vestments. The *Welfenchronik* (1185–90/91; Fulda, Hess. Landesbib. Fulda, Schloss Fasanerie, Cod. D. 11), produced in Weingarten, shows the Emperor enthroned between his sons. The dedication picture in *Historia Hierosolymitana* (*c.* 1189; Rome, Vatican, Bib. Apostolica, Vat. Lat. 2001) by Robert of St Remi (*c.* 1055–1122) depicts him standing, as a crusader.

BIBLIOGRAPHY

P. E. Schramm: *Die deutschen Kaiser und Könige in Bildern ihrer Zeit 751–1190* (Berlin, 1928, rev. Munich, 1983), pp. 261–70
P. E. Schramm and F. Mütherich: *Denkmale der deutschen Könige und Kaiser* (Munich, 1962, rev. Munich, 1981), pp. 179–82, 487

R. Kahsnitz: 'Armillae aus dem Umkreis Friedrich Barbarossas', *Anz. Ger. Nmus.* (1979), pp. 7–46

ULRICH KUDER

(2) Frederick II, King of Sicily and Holy Roman Emperor (*b* Jesi, nr Ancona, 26 Dec 1194; *d* Castel Fiorentino, 13 Dec 1250; *bur* Palermo Cathedral). Patron, architect, scientist and writer. Orphaned at the age of three, he was the son of Emperor Henry VI (*reg* 1191–7) and Constance, daughter of Roger II of Sicily, and the grandson of (1) Frederick I [Barbarossa]. Frederick consolidated his inheritance of the Holy Roman Empire and the Norman kingdom of southern Italy and Sicily. He extended his influence in Italy and the Holy Land and sought to revive the ancient Roman Empire, an aspiration that is expressed in his patronage of art.

In 1196 he was chosen as German king and in May 1198 crowned King of Sicily. Pope Innocent III served as his guardian and Regent of Sicily. At 15 Frederick married the widowed Constance of Aragon (*d* 1223). He acknowledged papal supremacy in Sicily and various rights in Germany, and he vowed to crusade and suppress heresy. The *puer apuliae* was crowned King of the Romans at Aachen on 25 July 1215, and reinterred Charlemagne's remains in the reliquary commissioned by his grandfather (*see* (1) above and AACHEN, §2(ii)(c)). On 22 November 1220 Pope Honorius III crowned him Holy Roman Emperor at St Peter's, Rome. Frederick postponed his crusade to quell political disorder and to institute a centralized government in Sicily. In 1225 he married Isabella (Yolande) of Jerusalem (*d* 1227). His crusade of 1228–9 culminated in the repossession of Bethlehem and Nazareth, and the division of Jerusalem's holy sites between Muslims and Christians as negotiated with the Egyptian sultan al-Kamil (*reg* 1218–38). Frederick had himself crowned King of Jerusalem in March 1229.

During much of his rule Frederick exerted diplomatic and military pressures on opposing Guelph factions in Germany, the Lombard League cities of northern Italy and the papal forces of Gregory IX (*reg* 1227–41). His impressive military victories in Lombardy and growing influence in papal territories, despoliation of the Sicilian Church and heretical toleration of Muslims and Jews led in 1239 to his excommunication by Gregory IX. Between 1228 and 1250 these conflicts were enhanced by propaganda campaigns borne out in letters, edicts, accounts of contemporary writers and the commission of works of art. Denounced as a heretic and Antichrist for his political ambitions, which challenged the supreme authority of the papacy, Frederick nevertheless presented himself as World Ruler, a Roman Emperor of Peace like Augustus, and a new David, consistent with the Messianic prophecies propounded by Peter of Eboli at the court of his father, Henry VI.

Frederick maintained a highly cultured court life that centred on his personal interests: philosophy, medicine, mathematics, poetry, rhetoric, astrology and religion. He corresponded with Arab scholars and princes on matters of science and mathematics. He established the University of Naples in 1224 for the study of law and rhetoric and was a patron of the medical college of Salerno. In collaboration with Petrus di Vinea he promulgated the

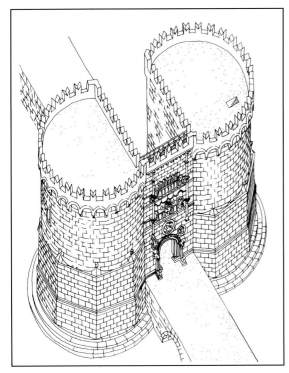

Capua Gate, built and possibly designed by Frederick II, 1234–40; reconstruction drawing

Sicilian law compilation the *Liber Augustalis* or Constitutions of Melfi of 1231. His passion for falconry resulted in his illustrated scientific treatise, *De arte venandi cum avibus* (Rome, Vatican, Bib. Apostolica, MS. Pal. Lat. 1071) with the intent 'to show those things that are, as they are'. For similar reasons he collected exotic animals, which travelled with the court. He also collected antiquities. His palace at Lucera (Puglia) housed Roman sculptures from Naples and oriental ceramics, as well as his notorious Saracen bodyguard, harem and menagerie.

Frederick's patronage helped to promote his political revival of the Roman Empire. His novel gold coin issue, the *augustales* of 1231 (e.g. London, BM), was an allusion to Augustus, Emperor of Peace: it bore his laureate imperial portrait and the caption IMPERATOR ROMANORUM CAESAR AUGUSTUS, with the imperial eagle and his name FRIDERICUS on the reverse. Antiquities inspired the classicizing art of Frederick's workshops, including imperial portrait busts (Barletta, Mus.-Pin. Com.), cameos (e.g. Paris, Bib. N; *see* GEM-ENGRAVING, §I, 9) and architectural sculpture (Capua, Mus. Prov. Campano). The classicizing design of the Capua Gate (1234-40; *see* CAPUA), attributed to Frederick himself, similarly conveyed these themes (see fig.). Its life-size enthroned togate statue of Frederick (Capua, Mus. Prov. Campano), unprecedented in the Middle Ages, emphasized his supreme authority and, with accompanying figures, enunciated the imperial law and justice that would produce order and peace. Frederick's other notable architectural monuments, built between 1233 and 1240, include the castles and hunting lodges at

Catania (*see* CATANIA, §2), Lucera, Castel Maniace, Lagopesole, Bari, Prato (Tuscany) and CASTEL DEL MONTE, which combine architectural and decorative features based on local tradition, Cistercian building methods and Roman and Islamic elements. Most have unusual polygonal plans, polychrome masonry, rib-vaulted interiors and sculptured decoration with corbel-busts, eagles and figural reliefs.

Frederick was unique among medieval rulers in his statecraft, lifestyle and patronage. He eclectically combined elements from his Sicilian and German heritage, the Roman imperial past and contemporary Arab princes. Although his political achievements ended with the death of his son Manfred in 1266, his artistic enterprises provided a source of the so-called proto-Renaissance in late 13th-century Tuscany.

BIBLIOGRAPHY

E. Kantorowicz: *Kaiser Friedrich der Zweite* (Berlin, 1927; Eng. trans., London, 1931)

C. A. Willemsen and D. Odenthal: *Apulia: Imperial Splendour in Southern Italy* (London, 1959)

T. C. van Cleve: *The Emperor Frederick II of Hohenstaufen: Immutator Mundi* (Oxford, 1972)

C. A. Willemsen: *Kaiser Friedrich II. und sein Dichterkreis* (Wiesbaden, 1977)

Atti del III settimana di studi di storia dell'arte medievale dell'Università di Roma. Federico II e l'arte del duecento italiano: Rome, 1978, 2 vols

C. A. Willemsen: *Bibliografia federiciana: Fonti e letteratura storica su Federico II e gli ultimi svevi* (Bari, 1982)

D. Abulafia: *Frederick II: A Medieval Emperor* (London, 1988)

JILL MEREDITH

Hohenstein, Thun-. *See* THUN-HOHENSTEIN.

Hohenzollern, House of. German dynasty of rulers, patrons and collectors (see fig.). Members of the family ruled as electors of Brandenburg (1415–1806), kings of Prussia (1701–1918) and emperors of Germany (1871–1918). Minor branches of the dynasty ruled small territories in southern Germany and members of the Sigmarigen line became kings of Romania (*see* CAROL I). In 1415 Frederick VI, Burgrave of Nuremberg, was invested as Frederick I, Elector of Brandenburg (*reg* 1415–40). Thereafter the House of Hohenzollern was largely responsible for guiding the difficult development of art and culture in that area, as neither the nobility nor the bourgeoisie proved desirous or capable of doing so until the late 18th century. The first member of the family to emerge clearly as a patron was (1) Albert of Brandenburg, who employed Albrecht Dürer, Matthias Grünewald and Lucas Cranach the elder. His patronage affected Brandenburg only indirectly, in that his nephew, (2) Joachim II, Elector of Brandenburg, aspired to emulate it. Subsequent electors were constrained by the poverty of the country, and the Thirty Years War (1618–48) almost totally annihilated what modest artistic activity there was.

(3) Frederick William, Elector of Brandenburg, was the first ruler to forge artistic links with western Europe, Holland in particular; but it was not until the reign of his successor, (4) Frederick I, King of Prussia, that achievements that could rank alongside the best in Europe were attained in the fields of architecture and sculpture, mainly in the work of Andreas Schlüter. At Schloss Monbijou Sophia Dorothea of Hannover (1687–1757), wife of (5) Frederick William I, King of Prussia, maintained the artistic culture of her court at a fitting level, but the King himself

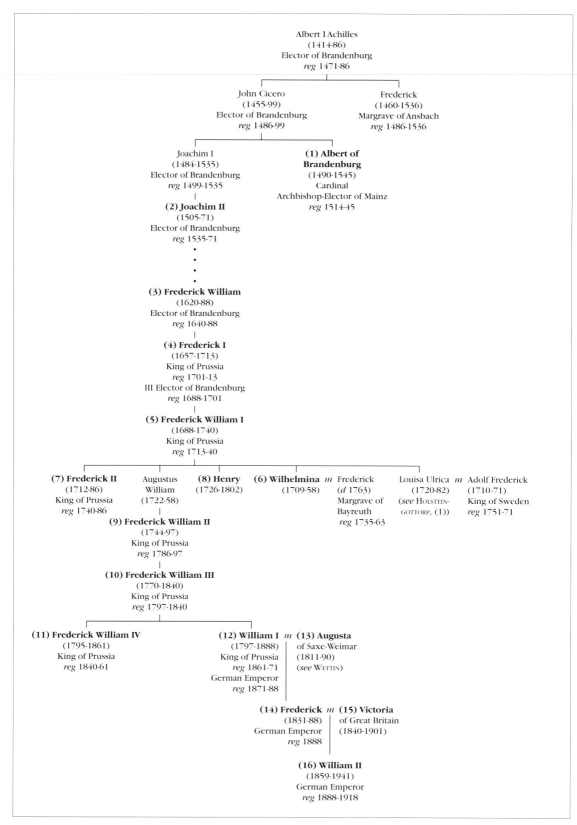

Family tree of the Hohenzollern dynasty

abjured all court splendour because of the need for economy, leaving the arts to atrophy until *c.* 1730. However, their daughter (6) Wilhelmina, Margräfin of Bayreuth, presided over one of the most cultured minor courts in Germany, and in the reign of their son (7) Frederick II, King of Prussia, known as Frederick the Great, there was a second blossoming of the arts, inspired mainly by French culture, in the style known as Frederician Rococo, indicating its close association with its instigator. The King's brothers, notably (8) Henry of Prussia, tastefully furnished their residences in Berlin, Oranienburg, Rheinsberg and Friedrichsfelde, though a relatively small group of artists fulfilled their requirements.

The reign of (9) Frederick William II, King of Prussia, coincided with the emergence of bourgeois art alongside court art and barely distinguishable from it: both used mainly classical forms. (10) Frederick William III, King of Prussia, ardently supported indigenous artists and emphasized middle-class simplicity. In Karl Friedrich Schinkel he found a publicist of the principle that art had the primary function of educating the people; thus the Königliches Museum was opened in Berlin in 1830. His successor, (11) Frederick William IV, King of Prussia, known as the 'architect king', was himself a talented artist and took a romantic view out of step with his time, seeing artistic enterprises as interpreting his religiously based concept of monarchy. His brother, (12) William I, King of Prussia and proclaimed Emperor of the newly united Germany on 18 January 1871, was by contrast a modest patron, whose own acquisitions reflected the bourgeois taste and milieu that he preferred; his wife (13) Augusta, however, had more luxurious and refined taste, favouring English landscape gardening and French art and culture. Their son (14) Frederick, German Emperor, had liberal political convictions and, as Protector of the Royal Museums, took a personal interest in the humanizing role of these institutions; his wife (15) Victoria, daughter of Queen Victoria of Great Britain and Prince Albert, shared his concerns. Their son (16) William II looked back to the beliefs of his great uncle Frederick William IV and tried to emulate the latter's ambitious architectural patronage, showing only a limited appreciation of contemporary artistic trends in painting. He was forced to flee when the Liberal Democrats came to power in 1918, and his abdication in November 1918 marked the end of the rule of the Hohenzollern dynasty.

See also GERMANY, §XIII.

BIBLIOGRAPHY

P. Seidel: *Gemälde alter Meister im Besitze seiner Majestät des deutschen Kaisers und Konigs von Preussen* (Berlin, 1906)
M. Kühn: *Der Gemäldebesitz der brandenburgisch-preussischen Schlösser: Gedankschrift Ernst Gall* (Berlin and Munich, 1965)
H. Börsch-Supan: *Die Kunst in Brandenburg-Preussen* (Berlin, 1980)

HELMUT BÖRSCH-SUPAN

(1) Cardinal **Albert of Brandenburg**, Archbishop-Elector of Mainz (*b* Cöllner Schloss, 28 June 1490; *d* Martinsburg zu Mainz, 24 Sept 1545). The youngest son of John Cicero, Elector of Brandenburg (1455–99; *reg* 1486–99), he was elected Archbishop of Magdeburg and administrator of Halberstadt in 1513, and Archbishop-Elector of Mainz (*ex officio*, chancellor of the Empire) in

1514. He became a cardinal in 1518. His political importance was as a Catholic force against Protestantism and he was also a lavish patron of religious art. He commissioned works from Lucas Cranach the elder, Albrecht Dürer and Matthias Grünewald, the last being his court painter at Mainz (1516–26). After the dedication of the Stiftskirche at Halle in 1523 he refurbished the interior, commissioning five altarpieces from Cranach, of which Cranach executed *Man of Sorrows* (1524; Freiburg im Breisgau, Augustinmus.), the rest being executed from his designs by his assistants. He also commissioned sculpture by Dietrich Schro (*fl* 1550) and his funeral monument from Hans Vischer and Peter Vischer (ii). When Halle became Protestant in 1541, he moved most of his treasures to Aschaffenburg, where the present arrangement of his monument in the collegiate church of SS Peter and Alexander is not original. It consists of the Cardinal's epitaph (1525; Aschaffenburg, SS Peter and Alexander), a bronze slab with his portrait by Peter Vischer (ii) and, in the centre, and a second slab depicting the *Virgin* (1530) and a rectangular bronze baldacchino (1536), both by Hans Vischer. The Cardinal also brought together the Hallesches Heiltum, a collection of relics, which he gave new settings, mostly commissioned at Nuremberg. It is now dispersed but is well documented in the *Hallesches Heiltumsbuch* (Aschaffenburg, Schloss Johannisburg, Hof- & Stiftsbib., MS. 14), an inventory with coloured drawings and a prime source for goldsmith work of that period, showing its transitional style between Late Gothic and early Renaissance.

Albert was one of the last patrons to commission illuminated manuscripts in great numbers. Of particular importance is his Book of Hours (2 vols, before 1523; Amsterdam, Bib. Philos. Hermetica) by Simon Bening and the Hallense Missal (1534; Aschaffenburg, Schloss Johannisburg, Hof- & Stiftsbib., MS. 10) by Nikolaus Glockendon (*fl* 1509; *d* 1534) from Nuremberg. The Cardinal is depicted as a saint in some initials of the Missal and as St Erasmus in Grünewald's *Meeting of SS Erasmus and Maurice* (*c.* 1520–25; Munich, Alte Pin.; *see* GRÜNEWALD, MATTHIAS, fig. 3) and was portrayed by Dürer in engravings of 1519 (B. 102) and the *Great Cardinal* (1523; B. 103; preparatory drawing, ?1518; Vienna, Albertina).

BIBLIOGRAPHY

A. von Bartsch: *Le Peintre-graveur*, vii (Vienna, 1808) [B.]
A. Biermann: 'Die Miniaturhandschriften des Kardinals Albrecht von Brandenburg', *Aachen. Ksthl.*, xlvi (1975), pp. 15–310
J. Rasmussen: 'Untersuchungen zum Halleschen Heiltum des Kardinals Albrecht von Brandenburg', *Münchn. Jb. Bild. Kst*, xxvii (1976), pp. 59–118, xxviii (1977), pp. 91-132
Albrecht von Brandenburg, Kurfürst, Erzkanzler, Kardinal (exh. cat. by B. Roland, Mainz, Landesmus., 1990)

JARL KREMEIER

(2) **Joachim II**, Elector of Brandenburg (*b* Berlin, 9 Jan 1505; *reg* 1535–71; *d* Köpenick, 3 Jan 1571). Nephew of (1) Albert of Brandenberg. In his reign there was an unprecedented blossoming of art in Brandenburg, since he wanted to live in the style of a Renaissance prince and loved display. He had no great artistic discernment, however, and was inclined to be spendthrift, and the forced pace of artistic development could be achieved only by bringing in outside talent. His most ambitious building project was the replacement of the medieval fortified castle at Berlin-Cölln by a modern castle modelled

on the châteaux of Blois, Chambord and on Schloss Hartenfels, near Torgau in Saxony; from 1537 CASPAR THEISS implemented the plans of Konrad Krebs (*see* BERLIN, §IV). Various hunting lodges were built in the Berlin area, but the only one to survive is Jagdschloss Grunewald (1542–3) by Theiss. The former Dominican church in Berlin was given cathedral status in 1536 and lavishly decorated with paintings and gold treasures along the lines of Halle Cathedral. The principal sculptor was Hans Schenck, who was summoned from Saxony in 1536. Some of his lively, touching reliefs, mainly stone epitaphs, have been preserved. Of the many works by Lucas Cranach the elder originally in the Königliches Schloss and Cathedral, a few are still extant. From the mid-16th century an Italian influence was prevalent along with that of Saxony, notably through the work of Francesco Chiaramella (*fl* 1552–78), who from 1562 was in charge of building work at the fortress of Spandau, the most important project of the Elector's later years. Although several goldsmiths were active in Berlin during Joachim's reign, it is not possible to gain any precise idea of the style of their work.

BIBLIOGRAPHY

F. Nicolai: *Nachricht von den Baumeistern, Bildhauern, Kupferstechern, Malern, Stukkaturern und anderen Künstlern, welche vom dreyzehnten Jahrhunderte bis jetzt in und um Berlin sich aufgehalten haben* . . . (Berlin and Stettin, 1786)

A. Geyer: *Geschichte des Schlosses zu Berlin* (Berlin, 1936)

E. Berckenhagen: *Die Malerei in Berlin vom 13. bis zum ausgehenden 18. Jahrhundert* (Berlin, 1964)

(3) Frederick William [Friedrich Wilhelm], Elector of Brandenburg (*b* Berlin, 16 Feb 1620; *reg* 1640–88; *d* Potsdam, 9 May 1688). Descendant of (2) Joachim II. He came to be known as 'The Great Elector' for the political achievements that marked his long reign. He rebuilt his country, which had suffered severe damage in the Thirty Years War (1618–48), and drew the scattered territories of Brandenburg into a firmly established state with an absolutist government. He cultivated the arts as far as his limited means and his involvement in wars prior to 1679 allowed and followed almost exclusively Dutch taste (*see* BERLIN, §II, 1); his marriage (1646) to Princess Louise Henrietta of Orange Nassau (1627–67) also created cultural links with the Netherlands. Dutch architects, engineers, sculptors, painters and craftsmen were summoned to Brandenburg and the court often resided at Cleve.

The first pressing necessity to which Frederick William attended was for a type of architecture that satisfied practical requirements. From 1657 the city of Berlin was encircled by star-shaped fortifications built to plans by Johann Gregor Memhardt (*fl* 1640–78), who had built Schloss Oranienburg (1651–5), near Berlin, for the Electress and was commissioned in 1662 to redesign the castle (1664–70) in Potsdam, in the Dutch Baroque style. The Elector was able to turn his attention to extending the Königliches Schloss only as his reign neared its end. Ecclesiastic buildings were given low priority, but Frederick William very much enjoyed gardens and the pleasure garden at the Königliches Schloss was laid out in 1646 with ornamental statues (*see* BERLIN, §I, 1).

The glorification of the electoral family was a major function of sculpture at this time, and for the same reason the art of medal-making flourished. Statues of the Elector

in marble included a full figure (1651) by François Dieussart. From 1667 the leading sculptor in Berlin was Michael Döbel, court sculptor and court architect from 1702, who executed a life-size sandstone bust of Frederick William, Elector of Brandenburg (Berlin, Jagdschloss Grunewald). In 1668 the sculptor and metal-caster Gottfried Christian Leygebe was summoned from Nuremberg; he also produced superb small sculptures, as did Leonhard Kern, court sculptor from 1648. BARTHOLOMEUS EGGERS executed numerous sculptures for Frederick William, including life-size marble depictions of the *Electors of Brandenburg* (*c.* 1685; 14, Potsdam, Schloss Sanssouci) and Artus Quellinus (i) executed work in Amsterdam for Frederick William.

The Dutch influence is clearly perceptible in the collection of paintings formed by the Elector. His endeavour to assemble a collection that could stand comparison with those of other rulers met with only limited success, owing to his restricted means, his shortcomings as a connoisseur and his lack of good advice. He admired the work of Gerrit von Honthorst and Anthony van Dyck and owned at least four paintings by Rembrandt. Among the painters employed at his court were Michael Willmann (in 1657–8) and Jan Lievens from 1653 to 1654. The Elector's commission of the *Birth (Death) of Prince William Hendrik III of Nassau* (1650; Potsdam, Neues Pal.) was a milestone in the career of Govaert Flinck. Of the Dutch artists who worked for a long period in Berlin, the most outstanding were Nicolas van Wieling (1640–78), Abraham Begeyn, Willem van Honthorst (1594–1666) and Willem Frederik van Royen (1645–1723). The court painter Hendrik de Fromantiou (1633/4–1694 or 1700) also acted as one of the Elector's art agents. Towards the end of the Elector's reign the Dutch influence yielded somewhat to the French, due to the welcome accorded to immigrant Huguenots after the Revocation of the Edict of Nantes (1685). The painters Abraham Romandon and his son Gedeon Romandon, for example, came to Berlin in 1686, when Abraham was appointed court painter; he was succeeded after his death by Gedeon, who remained in the employ of Frederick III (*see* (4) below). Frederick William was also an energetic patron of such applied arts as textiles and glass (*see* GERMANY, §VIII, 2 and BRANDENBURG GLASSWORKS). A posthumous equestrian monument of *Frederick William the Great Elector* (1696–1700; Berlin, Schloss Charlottenburg; for illustration *see* BERLIN, fig. 6) was executed by Andreas Schlüter.

BIBLIOGRAPHY

G. Galland: *Der Grosse Kurfürst und Moritz von Nassau* (Frankfurt am Main, 1893)

Der Grosse Kurfürst, Sammler, Bauherr, Mäzen (exh. cat., Potsdam, Neues Pal. and Schloss Sanssouci, 1988)

(4) Frederick [Friedrich] **I**, King of Prussia [Frederick III, Elector of Brandenburg] (*b* Königsberg [now Kaliningrad], 11 July 1657; *reg* 1701–13; *d* Berlin, 25 Feb 1713). Son of (3) Frederick William, Elector of Brandenburg. From 1688 he continued the extension of Hohenzollern domains by purchasing neighbouring lands. Through his financial contributions to the Holy Roman Emperor Leopold I in the War of the Spanish Succession (1701–13), he was created King of Prussia in 1701. His interest in the arts was limited to their capacity to add to the prestige and splendour of his palace and court. To this end he summoned artists from various European countries; the result was stylistic disunity and divergence of quality but also an open attitude towards the diversity of European movements in art. From 1694 he employed ANDREAS SCHLÜTER, to whom he entrusted the alterations and extensions required to transform the Königliches Schloss, Berlin, into a modern palace (*see* BERLIN, §IV, 1 and fig. 10 and SCHLÜTER, ANDREAS, fig. 2). The expansion of Berlin into a brilliant capital and centre of the arts at Frederick's instigation (*see* BERLIN, §I, 2) spurred Schlüter to such extraordinary feats as the sculptures (*c.* 1696; *see* SCHLÜTER, ANDREAS and fig. 1) in the courtyard of the Zeughaus, Berlin (now Museum für Deutsche Geschichte), the first large-scale High Baroque building in the city, begun by Johann Arnold Nering in 1695 and finished by Jean de Bodt in 1707. Schlüter also produced the equestrian statue of *Frederick William the Great Elector* (1696–1700; Berlin, Schloss Charlottenburg; *see* BERLIN, fig. 6) on the Lange Brücke, the marble pulpit (1702–3) in the Marienkirche and a series of superb buildings, but he failed to use his authority to plan an ordered development of the arts. The then Elector admitted the need for this when in 1697 he created the Akademie der Künste, modelled on the Académie in Paris, but it failed to have much impact (*see* BERLIN, §II, 2).

Initially there was a predominantly Dutch element in the number of painters who came to Berlin: Augustin Terwesten I and his brother Matthäus Terwesten (1670–1757) went there in 1692 and 1698 respectively. The need to decorate the interiors of the Königliches Schloss with ceiling paintings inevitably led to a greater Italian influence and a demand for historical painting. Such local painters as Johann Friedrich Wentzel (1670–1729) and Samuel Theodor Gericke (1665–1730) were, thus, sent to train in Rome. The purchase of antiquities was important in relation to the official use of all art forms, which led to the publishing of an unusually lavish three-volume catalogue (1696–1701) by Lorenz Beger of all the antiquities in the Elector's possession, which had been considerably increased by the purchase in 1698 of parts of Giovanni Pietro Bellori's collection of sculptures and other antiquities. The collection of paintings begun by the previous elector was not expanded, but the art of medal-engraving was refined by Raimund Faltz, who entered Frederick's service in 1690 and produced a large number of medals for the Prussian court (e.g. *Queen Sophia Charlotta of Brandenburg*; 1693). The luxurious nature of court life led to a general flourishing of the decorative arts.

From 1699 the Swedish architect JOHANN FRIEDRICH EOSANDER was court architect and succeeded Schlüter on the Königliches Schloss, though he was far less talented. By his introduction of the French Régence style in Berlin, the use of the decorative style involving emotionally powerful sculptures that had reached a peak in Schlüter's interiors for the Königliches Schloss declined (*see* BERLIN, §IV, 1). The foremost sculptor besides Schlüter was Guillaume Hulot (*fl* 1685–1720). In 1711 Frederick appointed Antoine Pesne as court painter. He incorporated Dutch and Italian elements into his lively painting and, with his many pupils, founded a painting tradition that lasted into the 19th century in Berlin.

BIBLIOGRAPHY
J.-B. Broebes: *Vues des palais et maisons de plaisance de sa majesté le Roy de Prusse* (Augsburg, 1733)
P. Seidel: 'Die bildenden Künste unter Friedrich I.: Kunst und Künstler am Hofe', *Hohenzoll.-Jb.*, iv (1900), pp. 247–68
Berlin und die Antike (exh. cat., ed. W. Arenhövel and C. Schreiber; Berlin, Schloss Charlottenburg, 1979)

(5) Frederick William [Friedrich Wilhelm] **I**, King of Prussia (*b* Cölln am Spree, 14 Aug 1688; *reg* 1713–40; *d* Potsdam, 31 May 1740). Son of (4) Frederick I. When he succeeded his father in 1713 state finances were in a catastrophic condition; consequently there was a drastic reduction in building activities and in expenditure on works of art, and many artists emigrated. When the state finances had been consolidated by the end of the 1720s, however, a distinct artistic style developed, particularly in Berlin and Potsdam. In both cities Frederick William I continued the building work of his father. The most notable features were the many terraces, which were intended to give the cities a uniform appearance. This was especially true in the town of Potsdam, which was rapidly enlarged and where a characteristic surviving area, the 'Dutch Quarter' (1734–42), was designed by the Dutch architect JOHANN BOUMANN, which had 134 red-brick and mostly Dutch-gabled houses. In Friedrichstadt in Berlin, in particular, a simple, uniform style of building was introduced, which anticipated 20th-century terraced housing and was intended to enable the less affluent to become house-owners. Distinguished work was also executed by the architect Philipp Gerlach (1679–1748). Outstanding works of sculpture were produced, especially by Johann Georg Glume (1711–78), who continued the tradition founded by Andreas Schlüter. In painting the King was satisfied with modest works in the field of portraiture, although he continued to employ Antoine Pesne. He spent significant amounts, however, on silver made in Augsburg (e.g. silver buffet by Johannes Ludwig Biller, 1731–3; Berlin, Schloss Köpenick), but the few paintings he acquired were mainly from Dutch masters. His collection of drawings forms the basis of the collections of the Kupferstichkabinett, Berlin. The paintings by his own hand (e.g. *Young Man with Peaked Cap*, 1735; Berlin, Schloss Charlottenburg), mainly copies, that are documented from 1733 are somewhat crude.

BIBLIOGRAPHY
F. Nicolai: *Nachricht von den Baumeistern, Bildhauern, Kupferstechern, Malern, Stukkaturern und anderen Künstlern, welche vom dreyzehnten Jahrhunderte bis jetzt in und um Berlin sich aufgehalten haben . . .* (Berlin and Stettin, 1786)
C. Hinrichs: *Friedrich Wilhelm I, König in Preussen* (Hamburg, 1941)
E. Berckenhagen: *Die Malerei in Berlin vom 13. bis zum ausgehenden 18. Jahrhundert* (Berlin, 1964)
H. Börsch-Supan: *Die Kunst in Brandenburg-Preussen* (Berlin, 1980)
Friedrich Wilhelm I: Der Soldatenkönig als Maler (exh. cat., Potsdam, Orangerie, 1990)

(6) (Frederica Sophia) Wilhelmina, Margravine of Bayreuth (*b* Berlin, 3 July 1709; *d* Bayreuth, 14 Oct 1758). Daughter of (5) Frederick William I. Although her marriage in 1731 to Crown Prince Frederick of Bayreuth (*reg* 1735–63) did not give her much scope for creating an artistically rich setting, there is evidence of her personal taste, with its Prussian overtones, in Bayreuth (*see* BAYREUTH, §1). From 1735 she extended the Hermitage (1715–18), adding two wings with idiosyncratic interior decoration featuring chinoiserie. In its park, the ruined theatre and the hermits' cells in particular exemplify the predilection for setting court life in the context of Nature charged with philosophical references. The Bayreuth opera house (1745–8), one of the great 18th-century theatres, was designed by JOSEPH SAINT-PIERRE, with interior decoration by Giuseppe Galli-Bibiena and Carlo Galli-Bibiena. After a fire at the Altes Schloss in Bayreuth the Neues Schloss (1753–4) was created, in which Saint-Pierre skilfully linked separate existing buildings to create a total complex in which there is a surprising variety of interiors with a wide use of natural motifs; in 1757–64 an Italianische Bau was added by Karl Philipp Christian Gontard. With its similarities to Schloss Sanssouci and the rock garden at SANSPAREIL (from 1744), it is another illustration of the desire to set court life in the context of Nature. Wilhelmina (herself an amateur painter) had a strong predilection for antiquity that was reflected in her collection of paintings (dispersed); this predilection was heightened by a journey to Italy in 1755, in the course of which she met Anton Raphael Mengs and Pompeo Girolamo Batoni.

WRITINGS

Lebensbeschreibung . . . (Brunswick, 1811); Eng. trans., ed. N. Rosenthal, as *The Misfortunate Margravine* (London, 1970)

BIBLIOGRAPHY

Markgräfin Wilhelmine von Bayreuth und ihre Welt (exh. cat., Bayreuth, Staatsgal. Neuen Schloss, 1959)
L. Seelig: *Friedrich und Wilhelmine von Bayreuth: Die Kunst am Bayreuther Hof, 1732–1763* (Munich, 1982)
A. M. Kluxen: 'Die Ruinen—"Theater" der Wilhelmine von Bayreuth', *Arch. Gesch. Oberfranken*, lxvii (1987), pp. 187–255

(7) Frederick [Friedrich] **II** [Frederick the Great], King of Prussia (*b* Berlin, 24 Jan 1712; *reg* 1740–86; *d* Potsdam, 17 Aug 1786). Son of (5) Frederick William I. Although he was undoubtedly the most cultivated and talented of the Hohenzollern rulers, he esteemed literature, science and music more highly than architecture and the fine arts. Rather than serving as an expression of royal power, during his reign the fine arts were related to pleasure and belonged in the private realm of his palaces, in which construction and decoration were subject to his personal taste. Lacking the education of an art connoisseur, as he had little opportunity for travel, he followed his own inclinations when buying works of art. French culture was his main interest, but as a philosopher he also admired the Classical world. This is reflected in his purchase in 1742 of the collection of classical sculpture of MELCHIOR DE POLIGNAC and in his acquisition in 1764 of Philipp, Baron von Stosch's collection of prints and coins, for which he commissioned Karl Philipp Christian von Gontard to build the Temple of Antiquity (Antikentempel, 1768–70) in the park of the Neues Palais, Potsdam. He also drew inspiration, particularly in architecture, from England and Italy.

As Crown Prince, Frederick lived in Schloss Rheinsberg, which, modernized and extended by his favourite architect, GEORG WENCESLAUS VON KNOBELSDORFF, was the cradle of Frederician Rococo. He acquired works by Antoine Watteau and Nicolas Lancret, painters whom he admired because of their affirmation of the joy of living. The important collection of paintings by Watteau in Berlin includes 12 from his collection, among them *L'Enseigne de Gersaint* (1721; Berlin, Schloss Charlottenburg; *see* DRESS, fig. 43) and the second version of the *Pilgrimage to the Isle of Cythera* (1718–19; Berlin, Schloss Charlottenburg).

In the first ten years of his reign Frederick II built new palaces and had apartments decorated for his own use in those already existing. Several of the works (mainly French) that he bought to furnish those apartments were purchased with a specific position in mind. Painters and sculptors—who were employed mainly to decorate the interiors and furniture—as well as architects worked closely with each other and with the King. Knobelsdorff was the dominant architect; the outstanding decorative sculptors were Johann August Nahl (i) and Johann Michael Hoppenhaupt the elder and his brother Johann Christian Hoppenhaupt (*see* HOPPENHAUPT); the leading painter was Antoine Pesne who, although primarily a portrait painter, was also charged with executing pictorial compositions, sometimes in the form of ceiling paintings. Thus, immediately after his accession Frederick commissioned the opera house in Berlin, began the new wing at Schloss Charlottenburg (*see* BERLIN, §IV, 2), had the Potsdam Stadtschloss altered between 1744 and 1752 and in 1745 had apartments modernized at the Königliches Schloss. From 1745 to 1747 his most famous palace Schloss Sanssouci was built (*see* POTSDAM, §2 and fig. 2) but it marked the end of the finest flowering of Frederician Rococo. From *c.* 1750 his attitude towards art changed: he took a greater interest in historical works and preferred to buy paintings by such renowned Dutch and Italian artists as Rubens, Anthony van Dyck, Rembrandt, Adriaen van der Werff and Guido Reni, which filled the picture gallery at Schloss Sanssouci, opened in 1764 after the end of the Seven Years War. The Neues Palais in the park of Schloss Sanssouci, built to impress and outmodedly Baroque in its dimensions, was designed by Jean-Laurent Legeay, Johann Gottfried Büring, KARL PHILIPP CHRISTIAN VON GONTARD and Heinrich Ludwig Manger (1728–89); construction work began in 1763. Here the forms of Frederician Rococo were coarsened and the sophisticated juxtapositions with a personal note that are a feature of the earlier palace interiors are missing. The King filled the Neues Palais with furniture and Italian, Dutch and French paintings from the 17th and 18th centuries. Overburdened with administrative duties, in the late 18th century he took little further part in the artistic development of the period; nor did he do much to encourage native artists through the Akademie der Künste in Berlin. The expansion of the porcelain works bought from the merchant and financier Johann Ernst Gotzkowski (1710–75) in 1763 was a favourite project (*see* BERLIN, §III, 3), the other being his collection of snuff-boxes, which he is said to have considered as valuable as his paintings (*see* GERMANY, §X, 3(ii) and fig. 77). A number of magnificent, dramatic buildings were constructed in Berlin at the end of his reign, for example the two cathedrals on the Gensd'armenmarkt, the Royal Library (1774–80) and the Königskolonnaden (1777–80); however, the project he had devised with von Knobelsdorff for a 'Forum Fridericianum' was only partly realized (*see* BERLIN, §I, 2).

BIBLIOGRAPHY

M. Oesterreich: *Beschreibung aller Gemälde, Antiquitäten . . . so in den beiden Schlössern von Sans-Souci, wie auch in dem Schlosse zu Potsdam und Charlottenburg enthalten sind* (Berlin, 1773)
P. Seidel: *Friedrich und die französische Malerei seiner Zeit* (Berlin, 1892)
——: *Französische Kunstwerke des 18. Jahrhunderts im Besitz seiner Majestät des deutschen Kaisers* (Berlin and Leipzig, 1900)
——: *Friedrich der Grosse und die bildende Kunst* (Leipzig and Berlin, 1922)
T. Eggeling: *Studien zum friderizianischen Rokoko* (Berlin, 1980)
H.-J. Giersberg: *Friedrich als Bauherr: Studien zur Architektur des 18. Jahrhunderts in Berlin und Potsdam* (Berlin, 1986)
Friedrich II und die Kunst (exh. cat., Potsdam, Neues Pal., 1986)
Z. Dt. Ver. Kstwiss., xlii/1 (1988) [whole issue]

(8) Prince **Henry of Prussia** (*b* Berlin, 18 Jan 1726; *d* Rheinsberg, 3 Aug 1802). Son of (5) Frederick William I. He was influenced by his brother, Frederick II, in his artistic taste, showing a preference for French art; he nevertheless had ideas of his own and from the 1770s kept in touch with modern trends. He owned, for example, seven pieces of sculpture by Jean-Antoine Houdon, including two of himself (1784, Weimar, Ksthalle; 1789, Potsdam, Schloss Sanssouci). He liked large-scale paintings and tapestries and bought a tapestry series of the *Loves of the Gods* based on cartoons by François Boucher and also owned a painting by him. At Schloss Rheinsberg near Berlin, given to him by Frederick II after the latter's accession in 1744, he made substantial alterations (1762–9; *in situ*) in the *Zopfstil* and also altered the garden, adding a neo-Gothic lighthouse (1771) on the Grienericksee. The last of the many buildings erected in the park was a truncated pyramid that became his tomb. His castle-like townhouse, the Palace of Prince Heinrich (1748–64; after 1809 the Friedrich-Wilhelm University; after 1949 Humboldt University), was designed by JOHANN BOUMANN. Built in Berlin and laid out in three wings, it housed an important collection of paintings, including works by Rubens, Anthony van Dyck, Murillo, Antoine Watteau and Nicolas de Largillierre. The Prince also owned a copy of *The Draughtsman* and the *Woman Sealing a Letter* (1733) by Jean-Siméon Chardin. Among the German painters who worked for him was Anton Graff, the leading contemporary portrait painter.

BIBLIOGRAPHY

P. Seidel: 'Die Kunstsammlungen des Prinzen Heinrich, Bruders Friedrich des Grossen', *Jb. Preuss. Kstsamml.*, xiii (1892), pp. 55–95
——: *Französische Kunstwerke des 18. Jahrhunderts im Besitz seiner Majestät des deutschen Kaisers* (Berlin and Leipzig, 1900)

(9) **Frederick William** [Friedrich Wilhelm] **II**, King of Prussia (*b* Berlin, 25 Sept 1744; *reg* 1786–97; *d* Potsdam, 16 Nov 1797). Nephew of (7) Frederick II. During his reign Neo-classicism finally became established in Prussia, relatively late, and English rather than French influence predominated. The King was more interested in music than fine art but loved luxury. In Potsdam he was responsible for laying out the Neuer Garten with the Marble Palace (1786–9) and park buildings, designed by KARL PHILIPP CHRISTIAN GONTARD and Carl Gotthard Langhans, and the landscaping of the Pfaueninsel in the River Havel, on which a small castle was built (*see* POTSDAM, §1). In Berlin, great suites of rooms in the Königliches Schloss, Schloss Charlottenburg and Schloss Monbijou were entirely refurbished, notably by Friedrich Wilhelm Erdmannsdorff, who was entrusted with the decoration of seven rooms in the Königliches Schloss and

two at Schloss Sanssouci. Painting generally played a purely decorative role in these interiors; the King himself bought few paintings by contemporary artists and none by earlier ones. There were more important developments in sculpture, in particular the work of Johann Gottfried Schadow, the leading contemporary Neo-classical sculptor, from whom Frederick William commissioned the monumental marble tomb of his illegitimate son *Alexander, Graf von der Mark* (1788–90; on loan to Berlin, Alte N.G.) and a double statue of *Princesses Luise and Friederike* (full-size plaster model, 1795; Berlin, Schinkelmus.; marble version, 1796–7; Berlin, Alte N.G.; *see* SCHADOW, (1) and fig. 1). The renovation of the Berlin Akademie in 1786 and the exhibitions held there regularly served mainly to encourage native artists and craftsmen.

BIBLIOGRAPHY

H. Schmitz: *Berliner Baumeister vom Ausgang des 18. Jahrhunderts* (Berlin, 1925)
G. Peschken and H. W. Klünner: *Das Berliner Schloss* (Berlin, 1982)

HELMUT BÖRSCH-SUPAN

(10) **Frederick William** [Friedrich Wilhelm] **III**, King of Prussia (*b* Potsdam, 3 Aug 1770; *reg* 1797–1840; *d* Berlin, 7 June 1840). Son of (9) Frederick William II. His modesty and good intentions and his revered first wife, Louise, Duchess of Mecklenburg-Strelitz (1776–1810), ensured him lifelong popularity. The defeat and occupation of Prussia by armies of Emperor Napoleon I in 1806 provoked a moral regeneration, and the patriotic fervour that began with Johann Gottlieb Fichte's *Reden an die deutsche Nation* in 1807 prompted Frederick William to issue the proclamation 'An mein Volk' from Breslau (now Wrocław, Poland) in 1813 and, allied with Russia, to declare the Freiheitskriege against Napoleon. After victory in 1815, Prussia extended from Aachen in the Rhineland to Königsberg (now Kaliningrad) in East Prussia. The population of Berlin doubled in size and the presence of artists of exceptional ability, such as Johann Gottfried Schadow, Freidrich Tieck, Christian Daniel Rauch, Carl Begas (i) and Carl Daniel Freydanck (1811-87), ensured its position as a great cultural centre. KARL FRIEDRICH SCHINKEL rose through the ranks of the Prussian civil service to gain almost total control over royal and public buildings. He designed the Museum (1823–30; partially restored 1960s; now the Altes Museum), one of the earliest buildings designed specifically for the display of works of art arranged according to medium, period and place of origin (*see* GERMANY, §XIV). Frederick William's acquisition in 1812 of 73 paintings from the collection of Vincenzo, Marchese Giustiniani (including four rare Caravaggios; *see* GIUSTINIANI (i), (2)), followed in 1821 by 3000 paintings from EDWARD SOLLY, an English merchant resident in Berlin, shifted the emphasis from the French paintings of Frederick II (see (7) above) to the Italian school. Ancient sculpture and vases, as well as coins and other smaller objects, were acquired from various other sources to augment the museum's collections.

The revolutionary activity of 1830 confirmed the King's distaste for royal display, and he concentrated on projects that contributed to economic prosperity. A network of paved roads and bridges, the beginnings of a railway system and an optical telegraph using church towers, as well as new station houses, facilitated commerce and administration. Schinkel designed houses for those who guarded and maintained the highways and, in Berlin, new and larger customs depots. Frederick William is buried alongside Queen Louise in the Mausoleum der Königin Luise, designed by Schinkel with Heinrich Gentz, in the park of Schloss Charlottenburg.

NDB

BIBLIOGRAPHY

F. R. Paulig: *Friedrich Wilhelm III* (Berlin, 1906)

(11) Frederick William [Friedrich Wilhelm] **IV**, King of Prussia (*b* Berlin, 15 Oct 1795; *reg* 1840–61; *d* Potsdam, 2 Jan 1861). Son of (10) Frederick William III. He was known as the 'architect king', and his reign coincided with the high tide of German Romanticism and a period of political turmoil that he could only partially comprehend. Convinced that the Hohenzollern dynasty ruled by divine right, he refused to use force during the uprising of 1848 and even paraded the streets wearing the black and gold colours of Germany. The following year he declined the crown of a united Germany that was offered him on the basis of his apparent liberalism and spent the remainder of his life in a private realm of romantic idealism.

His first tutor, Friedrich Delbrück, was a member of a German philosophical movement known as Philanthropismus, much indebted to Jean-Jacques Rousseau, and strongly encouraged his artistic interests; the Hofbauinspektor Karl Ludwig Krüger taught him perspective and architectural drawing. As King, he amused himself during state dinners and council meetings by covering the back of menu cards and agendas with architectural sketches. Karl Friedrich Schinkel was a frequent guest during the 1820s at the famous 'tea evenings' in the apartments that he had designed (1824) for the Crown Prince in the Königliches Schloss, and in many of his commissions Schinkel was obliged to clarify ideas supplied by the Crown Prince. For the Tornow peninsula, south-west of Potsdam, Frederick William designed in 1823 a palatial residence, Belriguardo (unexecuted), in the Classical manner, which would have contrasted dramatically with Frederick II's 18th-century maison de plaisance at Schloss Sanssouci, with which it was axially linked across the River Havel. This Olympian scheme provided the basis for two projects conceived by Frederick William, a royal palace (1834) on the Athenian Acropolis for his nephew, King Otto of Greece (*reg* 1832–62), and a summer palace for the Crown Prince's sister Alexandra Fyodorovna (1798–1860), Empress of Russia, at Orianda, near Yalta, in the Crimea (1838). Both projects remained unexecuted but were published in Schinkel's *Werke der Löheren Baukunst* (Potsdam, 1840–48).

Frederick William's dream of transforming the town- and riverscape around Potsdam into a conceptually unified chain of parks adorned with picturesquely sited buildings came close to fulfilment. He collaborated with Schinkel and the landscape architect Peter-Joseph Lenné in the design of summer retreats for himself and his brothers Charles and William at Schloss Charlottenhof, Klein Glienicke and Schloss Babelsberg respectively (*see* SCHINKEL, KARL FRIEDRICH, §4). When Schinkel died shortly after Frederick William's accession, LUDWIG PERSIUS, court architect from 1841, continued work on this romantic idyll. Persius's lofty dome on Schinkel's Nikolaikirche

(dome added 1843–9; restored 1949) satisfied the wishes of Frederick William while both his Friedenskirche (from 1843) in the Marlygarten at Schloss Sanssouci and the Heilandskirche (1841–4) in Sacrow, near Potsdam, across the Havel from the park at Klein Glienicke, were inspired by the King's projects to rebuild the Berliner Dom in the form of an Early Christian basilica with campanile.

Other buildings conceived by the King for Potsdam include the Orangerie (designed by Persius and completed between 1851 and 1860 by Friedrich August Stüler) at Sanssouci and the large Belvedere (1849–52; executed by Stüler) for the Pfingstberg, both in Renaissance style. The vision of a Greek temple on the Mühlenberg as a monument to Frederick the Great was superseded by a bronze equestrian statue of *Frederick II the Great* (*c*. 1835–51; Potsdam, Park Sanssouci; *see* RAUCH, CHRISTIAN DANIEL and fig.), unveiled in Unter den Linden in Berlin in 1851. Stüler's Neues Museum (1843–50; rebuilt) in Berlin was the first result of the King's 1841 decree declaring the entire Spreeinsel behind Schinkel's Altes Museum a 'sanctuary for art and science'.

In 1858 mental instability forced the childless Frederick William to cede his royal duties to his brother William, who acted as Regent until his elder brother's death. Frederick William is buried alongside his wife, Elisabeth of Bavaria, in the crypt of the Friedenskirche.

BIBLIOGRAPHY

G. Poensgen: *Die Bauten Friedrich Wilhelms IV in Potsdam* (Berlin, 1930)

L. Dehio: *Friedrich Wilhelm IV von Preussen: Ein Baukünstler der Romantik* (Berlin, 1961)

R. Carter: 'Ludwig Persius and the Romantic Landscape of Potsdam', *Arquitectonica*, iv (1989), pp. 115–60

(12) William [Wilhelm] **I**, King of Prussia and Emperor of Germany (*b* Berlin, 22 March 1797; *reg* Prussia 1861–71, Germany 1871–88; *d* Berlin, 9 March 1888). Son of (10) Frederick William III. His mother was Louise, Duchess of Mecklenburg–Strelitz (1776–1810). He succeeded his childless elder brother Frederick William IV (*see* (11) above) to the Prussian throne in 1861, becoming Emperor of the newly united Germany in 1871. Prevented for dynastic reasons from marrying Elisa von Radziwill (a great-niece of Frederick the Great), in 1829 he married (13) Augusta, Duchess of Saxe–Weimar, younger sister of Mary, Duchess of Saxe–Weimar, wife of his brother Charles. William's simple, manly virtues maintained the best traditions of the Hohenzollern dynasty. Although inclined towards the military, he shared Frederick William's talent for drawing, Charles's enthusiasm for collecting and the feeling for the romance of old castles of his cousin 'Fritz Louis', Prince Frederick of Prussia (1794–1863). In 1822 he visited several excavations near Naples, and this may have inspired the design of the Pompeiian Room in the Palais Kaiser Wilhelms I. He commissioned Karl Friedrich Schinkel to remodel the Generalkommando Unter den Linden as a temporary residence for himself in 1828 and had Schinkel prepare several projects for a new palace in Berlin, although the Palais Kaiser Wilhelms I, the construction of which was completed in 1837, was designed by Karl Ferdinand Langhans and involved the demolition of the Generalkommando. However, in 1833, Schinkel did begin the construction of Schloss Babelsberg, a summer house in the style of a picturesque English

Tudor manor overlooking the River Havel and the town of Potsdam. The building was completed after Schinkel's death in 1841 by Ludwig Persius and Johann Heinrich Strack as a romantic castle. Its park, designed by Peter Joseph Lenné, was considerably altered by Hermann Ludwig Pückler-Muskau. Although William admired the opulence of the Russian court at St Petersburg where his sister Charlotte Alexandra was Tsarina, his own preferences for collecting were more modest and practical. Many of the objects made of silver, malachite and lapis lazuli in his collection were gifts from his sister and her husband, Tsar Nicholas I (*reg* 1825–55), but his own acquisitions, mostly of old armoury and family portraits, reflected the bourgeois taste and milieu that he preferred. Despite a cordial and respectful relationship with Schinkel in the 1820s and 1830s, William appeared uncritical when confronted with the obvious decline in the standard of design after 1871, when he became Emperor. Yet Wilhelm von Bode, in his memoirs *Mein Leben* (Berlin, 1930), speaks of a visit in 1880 to the Berlin museums by the elderly Emperor and his wife, Augusta, during which he surprised Bode by pausing before the works of better quality in the collection. In 1888, at the age of 90, he died in the Kronprinzenpalais and was buried with his parents in the Mausoleum der Königin Luise (1810–12), designed by Schinkel with Heinrich Gentz, in the park of Schloss Charlottenburg.

BIBLIOGRAPHY

E. Marcks: *Kaiser Wilhelm I* (Leipzig, 1897, rev. 1943)

E. Berner, ed.: *Briefe, Reden, Schriften Kaiser Wilhelms I*, 2 vols (Berlin, 1906)

F. Delbrück: *Die Jugend des Königs Friedrich Wilhelm IV von Preussen und des Kaisers und Königs Wilhelm I: Tagebuchblätter* (Berlin, 1907)

K. Jagow: *Wilhelm und Elisa* (Berlin, 1930)

J. Sievers: *Bauten für die Prinzen August, Friedrich und Albrecht von Preussen: Ein Beitrag zur Geschichte der Wilhelmstrasse in Berlin* (1954), viii of *Karl Friedrich Schinkel: Lebenswerk*, ed. P. O. Rave (Berlin, 1950-)

——: *Die Arbeiten von Karl Friedrich Schinkel für Prinz Wilhelm, späteren König von Preussen* (1955), ix of *Karl Friedrich Schinkel: Lebenswerk*, ed. P. O. Rave (Berlin, 1950-)

R. Carter: 'Ludwig Persius and the Romantic Landscape of Potsdam', *Arquitectonica*, iv (1989), pp. 115–60

(13) Augusta, Queen of Prussia and Empress of Germany (*b* Weimar, 30 Sept 1811; *reg* Prussia, 1861–71, Germany 1871–88; *d* Berlin, 7 Jan 1890). Wife of (12) William I. She grew up in the enlightened atmosphere of Weimar in the first decades of the 19th century and studied art with Louise Seidler and with the Director of the Freies Zeichen-Institut, Heinrich Meyer. Her music teacher was the Kapellmeister Johann Nepomuk Hummel (1778–1837). In 1829 she married the then Prince William of Prussia. In Berlin she was associated with artists active in the royal household, among them Karl Friedrich Schinkel and Christian Daniel Rauch, and in later years her circle included the archaeologist Ernst Robert Curtius (1814–96) and the Egyptologist Karl Richard Lepsius (1810–84). During the 1830s she took an active role in the design of the summer residence at Schloss Babelsberg, providing its architect Schinkel with drawings based on her study of the publications of such English landscape designers as Humphry Repton (e.g. *Sketches and Hints on Landscape Gardening*, London, 1795) and John Buonarotti Papworth (e.g. *Hints on Ornamental Gardening*, London, 1823), both

of whose works she admired. As queen, and later as empress, in contrast to the enduring bourgeois milieu of her husband, she favoured French art and culture and strove for a more luxurious and refined atmosphere in her surroundings. Her private apartments were decorated with paintings depicting guardian angels, nuns, cloisters and ruined churches, and her bedroom in the Palais Kaiser Wilhelms I in Berlin contained a prie-dieu, an unusual article of furniture in a Protestant household.

BIBLIOGRAPHY

G. Schuster and P. Bailleu, eds: *Aus den literarischen Nachlass der Kaiserin Augusta* (Berlin, 1912)

M. von Bunsen: *Kaiserin Augusta* (Berlin, 1940)

(14) Frederick [Friedrich], Emperor of Germany [Frederick III, King of Prussia] (*b* Potsdam, 18 Oct 1831; *reg* 1888; *d* Potsdam, 15 June 1888). Son of (12) William I and (13) Augusta. He studied at the Rheinische Friedrich-Wilhelms-Universität, Bonn, in 1849–50, and in 1858 he married (15) Victoria, Princess Royal of Great Britain and eldest daughter of Queen Victoria. The influence of his mother and that of his father-in-law Albert, Prince of Saxe-Coburg, confirmed his liberal political convictions. As a loyal Prussian he distinguished himself in the army, even when not in total agreement with his country's foreign policy. As Crown Prince, his crucial role in the unification of Germany has not been fully credited by those historians more interested in the political machinations of Otto von Bismarck, Prime Minister of Prussia and later Chancellor of Germany. Frederick became emperor in March 1888 but by then was in the advanced stages of the throat cancer that would claim his life 99 days later. In the years prior to his reign he had become the hope of German progressives, but his death so soon after his accession prevented the realization of the reforms to which he and his wife had so long been committed. Nevertheless, his short reign was marred by the unscrupulous attacks of reactionaries. He was a strong supporter of the excavations begun in 1871 at Pergamon by the archaeologist Carl Humann (1839–96) and in 1875 at Olympia by his former tutor Ernst Robert Curtius (1814–96). Appointed Protector of Royal Museums in 1871, he took a personal interest in the humanizing mission of those institutions established by his grandfather Frederick William III (*see* (10) above) and expanded under his uncle Frederick William IV (*see* (11) above). In contrast to the practice of museums elsewhere, the collections in Berlin were organized on scholarly principles by such professionals as Wilhelm von Bode, who joined the staff of the Königlich Preussischen Museen in 1872. Planning began in 1882 for the gallery of painting and sculpture, which opened in 1905 as the Kaiser-Friedrich-Museum (now the Bodemuseum). In 1897 the Kaiser-Friedrich-Museums-Verein, an organization of its supporters, was founded in honour of Frederick. He and his wife are buried in the mausoleum built in 1889 by Julius Raschdorff, located next to the Friedenskirche (1843–54) in Potsdam.

BIBLIOGRAPHY

R. Rodd: *Frederick, Crown Prince and Emperor* (London, 1888)

M. von Poschinger: *Kaiser Friedrich*, 3 vols (Berlin, 1898–1900; Eng. trans., London and New York, 1901)

M. Philippson: *Das Leben Kaiser Friedrichs* (Wiesbaden, 1900)

(15) Victoria, Queen of Prussia and Empress of Germany (*b* London, 21 Nov 1840; *d* Schloss Friedrichshof, nr Frankfurt am Main, 5 Aug 1901). She was the eldest daughter of Victoria, Queen of Great Britain, and Albert, Prince of Saxe-Coburg-Gotha. In 1858 she married the then Prince Frederick of Prussia, whose reign as King of Prussia and Emperor of Germany lasted for only 99 days in 1888. The liberal political views acquired from her father were shared by her mother-in-law Augusta (*see* (13) above) but not by her eldest son William II (*see* (16) below). Her desire to transform Prussian politics according to the English model was seen as a challenge to Otto von Bismarck, Prime Minister of Prussia and Chancellor of Germany, who referred to her as 'the Englishwoman'. Her own impetuousness and sharp tongue were a further hindrance to her popularity. She was, however, interested in the fine arts and brought Heinrich von Angeli to Potsdam in 1874 to paint the first (Potsdam, Neues Pal.) of several portraits of her and to supervise her efforts as an amateur artist. An avid draughtsman, in 1861 she illustrated Tennyson's *Idylls of the King* (London, 1859). She was also an advocate of higher education for women and founded both the Victoria-Schule and the Victoria-Lyceum in Berlin. She can be credited with introducing modern plumbing at the old Berlin Stadtschloss on the Spreeinsel, where she resided as a newlywed, and for carrying out similar improvements at the Kronprinzenpalais. As Crown Princess she resided at the Neues Palais in Potsdam and as Queen and Empress at Schloss Charlottenburg, in Berlin. She was responsible for the remodelling of Schloss Friedrichshof (1889–94; by Ernst Eberhard Ihne), near Frankfurt am Main, for her use after Frederick's death, devoting her final years to its extensive gardens and to the library commemorating her late husband.

BIBLIOGRAPHY

F. Ponsonby, ed.: *The Letters of the Empress Frederick* (London, 1929)
E. C. Conte Corti: *Wenn... Sendung und Schicksal einer Kaiserin* (Graz, 1954); Eng. trans. as *The English Empress: A Study in Conflicting Loyalties* (London, 1957)
R. Barkeley: *The Empress Frederick* (London, 1956)
A. Sinclair: *The Other Victoria: The Princess Royal and the Great Game of Europe* (London, 1981)

(16) William [Wilhelm] **II**, King of Prussia and Emperor of Germany (*b* Berlin, 27 Jan 1859; *reg* 1888–1918; *d* Doorn, nr Utrecht, 4 June 1941). Son of (14) Frederick and (15) Victoria. His left arm was rendered useless owing to an injury at birth, and he was further scarred by the Spartan cruelty of his Calvinist tutor, Dr Hinzpeter. After studying at the Gymnasium in Kassel and at the Rheinische Friedrich-Wilhelms-Universität, Bonn, he was for several years occupied with military duties. In 1881 he married Augusta Victoria, Duchess of Schleswig-Holstein-Sonderberg-Augustenburg (1858–1921), and became King of Prussia and Emperor of Germany in 1888. By means of his personal charm he sought to improve relations with his European neighbours and to extend Germany's influence abroad. He travelled frequently and thus came to be known as the 'Reise-Kaiser'. He was convinced that Germany had a civilizing mission in the world, and in 1906 initiated a policy whereby professors would be exchanged between German and American universities. A devout Christian, he supported the building of 25 Protestant churches commanding vistas along streets in Berlin (e.g. the Kaiser-Wilhelm-Gedächtniskirche, 1891–5, by Franz Schwechten), as well as nine Catholic churches (e.g. St Bonifatius, 1903–07). He also commissioned from Julius Raschdorff the Cathedral (1888–1905) in the Lustgarten (now part of Marx-Engels Platz) in Berlin. He commissioned the Siegesallee, in Berlin, an enormous sculptural ensemble (1895–1901; dismantled after World War II) that stretched from the Königsplatz to the Kemperplatz. It consisted of 32 monuments to German rulers and included work by leading contemporary German sculptors (*see* GERMANY §IV, 4). William II maintained a belief in his divine right to rule, taking an active role in excess of constitutional limitations. Although he was well-intentioned, he was a victim of bad advice and was overwhelmed by the catastrophe of World War I. The revolution of November 1918 swept the Social Democrats into power and forced him to flee to the Netherlands, where he abdicated on 28 November, the last ruler of the Hohenzollern line. In 1922, after his first wife's death, he married Hermine of Schönaich-Carolath (1887–1947) and lived in exile in the Netherlands until his death in 1941.

BIBLIOGRAPHY

J. von Kürenberg: *The Kaiser: A Life of William II, Last Emperor of Germany* (New York, 1955)
V. Cowles: *The Kaiser* (New York, 1963)
M. Balfour: *The Kaiser and his Times* (Boston, 1964)
R. Taylor: *Hohenzollern Berlin: Construction and Reconstruction* (Port Credit, Ont., 1985)

RAND CARTER

Hohenzollern-Sigmaringen, Karl of, Prince of Romania. *See* CAROL I, King of Romania.

Höijer, (Carl) Theodor (*b* Helsinki, 20 Feb 1843; *d* Helsinki, 31 Oct 1910). Finnish architect. He was trained at the Kungliga Akademi för de Fria Konsterna in Stockholm and set up his practice *c*. 1870. His career coincided with changes in Finnish building practices and architecture, including an increased use of masonry rather than timbering. His large production was concentrated mainly in Helsinki, where his buildings formed part of the new high-rise cityscape. He achieved initial recognition with a timbered exhibition building (1876), a library, the People's Library and Reading Room (1881; now a branch of the City Library of Helsinki), and a vast block of flats and commercial premises (1882–3) at Pohjoisesplanadi 25–27. Traditional masonry construction was the basis of Höijer's architectural compositions, although in his early industrial buildings he combined iron constructions with vaulting. He used cast-iron or steel and wrought-iron in the building for the Voluntary Fire Brigade (destr.; see Viljo, pp. 90–91, 94) in Helsinki and in the Atheneum Art Museum (1887; rebuilt; *see* HELSINKI, fig. 3), Kaivokata 2–4, built to house the schools of art and collections of the Finnish Art Society and the Society for Applied Art. Until the 1890s Höijer sought to assimilate medieval and Renaissance architectural elements in his works. He used such façade details as string courses, pilasters and quoins for decorative effects, which, particularly in the buildings of the 1880s, were heightened with lavish stucco ornaments. In the former main fire station of Helsinki (1891) at

Korkeavuorenkatu 26, the brick is used to create a lively surface. His simpler late style emphasizes building volumes with plain brick surfaces and ornament in low relief.

BIBLIOGRAPHY
E. M. Viljo: *Theodor Höijer. En arkitekt under den moderna storstadsarkitekturens genombrottstid i Finland fran 1870 till sekelskiftet*, Suomen Muinaismuistoyhdistyksen aikakauskirja—Finska Fornminnesföreningens tidskrift, 88 (Vammala, 1985) [incl. summary in Eng.]

EEVA MAIJA VILJO

Hōin. *See* SOGA, (1).

Hoin, Claude(-Jean-Baptiste) (*b* Dijon, 25 June 1750; *d* Dijon, 16 July 1817). French painter, teacher and museum administrator. The son of a prominent doctor in Dijon, he began his career there under the architect Claude-François Devosge II (1697–1777). He received a sound training in the principles of allegory and composition, which he put to good use in his earliest known work, the wash drawing of a filial *Allegory in Honour of Jean-Jacques-Louis Hoin* (1769; Dijon, Mus. B.-A.). Although he remained in lifelong contact with his first teacher and with the provincial bourgeois milieu of his youth, Hoin went to Paris in 1772 or 1773. There, under Jean-Baptiste Greuze, he immediately began copying portraits of young girls 'to improve the delicacy of his touch' (Portalis). In 1776 he was made a corresponding member of the Dijon Académie, and, although he was not a member of the Académie Royale in Paris, two years later he joined the académies of Lyon, Rouen and Toulouse. The fine pastel *Portrait of a Young Girl* (Toulouse, Mus. Augustins) was his *morceau de réception* for Toulouse. In 1779 he first exhibited at the Salon de la Correspondance in Paris; in 1782 he exhibited a gouache of his parents' tomb (Dijon, Mus. B.-A.), and the following year he followed up with a series of pastel portraits and various miniatures. His official career had progressed in the meantime: in 1779 he was made professor of drawing at the Ecole Royale Militaire, and late in 1785 he was named official painter to the Comte de Provence (later Louis XVIII). He continued to paint simple genre scenes, allegories and actresses in costume. These gouaches, which he produced throughout the 1780s, were straightforward in composition, though occasionally he executed works of greater complexity, such as *La Danse champêtre* and *La Conversation galante* (both 1784; Vienna, Albertina). Miniatures he executed around this time include the *Duchesse de La Trémoille and her Son* (1788; priv. col., see 1963 exh. cat., pl. ix)—two tiny profile busts in a landscape setting—and *Madame Elisabeth and the Dauphin* (1793; Paris, Louvre).

Following the outbreak of the French Revolution Hoin moved back to Dijon, joining the local Société Populaire des Arts in 1794. Although he stayed in Paris for a short period, exhibiting at the open salons of 1800 and 1801, he returned to Dijon in 1804 with his new wife, Amélie, to take up the position of professor of drawing at the Lycée. He made a modest living in this post, while waiting for the directorship he had been promised of the recently created Musée des Beaux-Arts to fall vacant. This finally happened early in 1811, and he took up the post immediately. Soon afterwards Hoin suffered the deaths of his wife and his old friend and teacher Devosge, and he devoted the last six years of his life to the museum's administration and expansion. He bequeathed to it several fine works of his own, including some of the most attractive examples: large chalk portrait studies on blue paper of which the best, *Head of a Child* (1791) and *Young Girl in a Black Hat* (n.d.; both Dijon, Mus. B.-A.), have a vivacity that makes a refreshing change from the studied quality of many of the more formal works he produced during his career, for example the *Allegory in Honoured Memory of Legouz de Gerland* (1776, Dijon, Mus. B.-A.).

BIBLIOGRAPHY
R. de Portalis: 'Claude Hoin', *Gaz. B.-A.*, n.s. 2, xxii (1899), pp. 441–61; xxiii (1900), pp. 10–24, 203–16, 293–309
Claude Hoin (exh. cat., intro. P. Quarré; Dijon, Mus. B.-A., 1963)

JOSHUA DRAPKIN

Hōitsu. *See* SAKAI HŌITSU.

Hŏju. *See* YI (ii), (3).

Hokkei. *See* TOYOTA HOKKEI.

Hokusai. *See* KATSUSHIKA HOKUSAI.

Hokusōō. *See* HANABUSA ITCHŌ.

Holabird & Roche. American architectural partnership formed after 1881 by William Holabird (*b* American Union, NY, 11 Sept 1854; *d* Evanston, IL, 19 July 1923) and Martin Roche (*b* Cleveland, OH, 1 Aug 1853; *d* Chicago, IL, 6 June 1927). Holabird was the son of an army general. He became a cadet at the US Military Academy, West Point, but left in 1873 after two years. With this brief introduction to engineering he moved to Chicago and entered the office of architect William Le Baron Jenney. There he met Martin Roche, who had moved as a boy to Chicago, where he attended the Art Institute, which he left in 1867 to begin an apprenticeship as a cabinetmaker. In 1872 Roche entered Jenney's office, where the approach to architectural design was highly functional, with concern for economy of means, the opening up of interior space and the maximum use of natural light. Both Holabird and Roche probably served as draughtsmen on Jenney's First Leiter Building (1879; destr.), Chicago, which exemplified Jenney's functionalist approach.

In 1880 Holabird left Jenney to form a partnership with Ossian C. Simonds (1857–1931); Roche joined them as a partner in 1881. In 1883 Simonds withdrew to pursue a career as a landscape architect, and the firm became Holabird & Roche. Due to the recession of the mid-1880s, building commissions in those first years were rare, and Roche returned to designing furniture. In 1886, however, Holabird & Roche won the commission for a 12-storey office block, the Tacoma Building (1888–9; with the engineer Carl Seiffert; destr.), which propelled the firm to the forefront of the profession in Chicago and represented their first contribution to the development of the SKYSCRAPER. In collaboration with Seiffert the architects employed a complete riveted metal frame, using all the available forms of iron, wrought iron and steel. The street elevations were true curtain walls of glass and brick, but the rear walls were load-bearing.

Although the Tacoma Building had rudimentary diagonal bracing to resist lateral wind forces, Holabird &

Roche employed extensive portal wind bracing in the 17-storey Old Colony Building (1893–4; with the engineer Corydon T. Purdy), Dearborn and Van Buren Streets, Chicago. In the Marquette Building (1894–5; with Purdy), Dearborn and Adams Streets, Chicago, the firm arrived at a straightforward expression of the office-building metal frame that they continued to employ with great success for another 30 years. These buildings typically comprised a lower section incorporating entrance, shops and lobby with lift; above this was a transitional mezzanine and the tall mid-section, where the bulk of the office cells were arranged in a U around an internal light court. In this mid-section the vertical lines were strongly emphasized, with slender, projected piers and recessed spandrel panels, and the wall was opened up with broad windows. At the top was a two- or three-storey crown set off by strong horizontals and a prominent terminating cornice. Other notable examples included the Cable Building (1898–9; destr.); the McClurg Building (1899–1900), 218 S. Wabash Street, Chicago; the Champlain Building (1903), State and Madison Streets, Chicago; and the Republic Building (1904–5; destr.). After 1910 the firm adopted more eclectic and historic forms, particularly in a series of large hotels and most especially in their classical City-County Building (1910–11), Chicago. They also designed a number of well-proportioned Georgian colonial town houses and residences, but virtually all have been demolished. Shortly before Holabird's death the founders' final office building was begun, 333 North Michigan Avenue (1927–8), with setbacks inspired by Eliel Saarinen's Tribune Tower competition entry (1922). This office tower introduced the Art Deco skyscraper style to Chicago. The firm's successor Holabird & Root was formed in 1927.

BIBLIOGRAPHY
DAB; Macmillan Enc. Archit.
J. C. Webster: 'The Skyscraper: Logical and Historical Considerations', *J. Soc. Archit. Hist.*, xviii (1959), pp. 126–39
C. W. Condit: *The Chicago School of Architecture: A History of Commercial and Public Building in the Chicago Area, 1875–1925* (Chicago, 1964)
——: *Chicago, 1910–29: Building, Planning and Urban Technology* (Chicago, 1973)
J. Zukowsky, ed.: *Chicago Architecture, 1872–1922: Birth of a Metropolis* (Munich, 1987)

LELAND M. ROTH

Holanda, de [Hollanda, de; Ollanda, d']. Portuguese family of artists. (1) António de Holanda was born in the Netherlands but in 1500 moved to Portugal, where he worked for the court as an illuminator and as an officer of arms. His son (2) Francisco de Holanda trained as an illuminator and travelled (1538–40) in Italy, spending most of the time in Rome, where he met Michelangelo. He returned to Portugal with numerous drawings and later wrote a number of theoretical works. The most important is *Da pintura antigua* (MS., 1548), which sets out his Neo-Platonist theory of art followed by four dialogues with Michelangelo. Having also met Sebastiano Serlio in Venice on his travels, he helped to generate a new interest in architectural theory in Portugal and proposed various urban plans for Lisbon. In addition, like his father, he worked as a court artist, producing illuminations, miniature portraits and drawings as well as being engaged on a few architectural projects.

(1) António de Holanda (*b* South Netherlands, ?1480; *d* Lisbon, 1557). Illuminator, miniaturist and officer of arms. He learnt the art of Ghent–Bruges illumination, probably alongside Simon Bening, in the workshop of Sanders Bening, where numerous prayerbooks were illuminated for the Portuguese royal family. His decision to move to Portugal was in part due to the enormous demand for illuminators there. According to Markl, he arrived in Portugal *c.* 1500 with a painter of Flemish origin, Francisco Henriques, who belonged to the workshop of the Master of the Polyptych of Évora Cathedral, which Holanda himself may have worked in. According to other historians, he arrived on the occasion of the marriage of Manuel I and Dona Maria of Castile, on 30 October 1500, bringing the polyphonic missal (Vienna, Österreich. Nbib., Cod. 1783) sent by the future Hapsburg king of Spain Philip I (*reg* 1504–6), which is sometimes attributed to him. He married a member of the Homem family of cartographers.

Holanda's work is well known above all through the writings of his son (2) Francisco de Holanda, who credits him with, among other things, the invention of a stippled technique of great delicacy. He worked in the illumination workshop of the Royal Archives, alongside Alvaro Pires (*fl* 1504–39), on the *Leitura Nova* (after 1504; Lisbon, Arquiv. N.; e.g. frontispiece of the *Mistico 2*, 1511) and on the *Chronicles of the Kings of Portugal* (e.g. the frontispiece with a view of Lisbon in the *Crónica de Dom Afonso Henriques* by Duarte Galvão; Cascais, Mus.-Bib. Conde de Castro Guimarães). He may also have collaborated with Pires on the other great work of illumination in the reign of Manuel I, the antiphonaries of the royal monastery of Belém. As Francisco noted in his *Da ciência do desenho* (1571), his father illuminated such prayerbooks of the royal family as the *Book of Hours of King Manuel*, begun in 1517 and continued under John III (Lisbon, Mus. N.A. Ant.), and the *Breviary of Queen Dona Leonor* (untraced).

In 1518 Holanda became a herald, with the rank of pursuivant at arms, a position that fell vacant with the death that year of Henriques. He received his herald's training from António Rodrigues, Rei de Armas Portugal e Principal (from 1512 to *c.* 1560). In his position, he was now more closely associated with the court and attended all the ceremonies. Apart from his work as heraldic illuminator, he carried out various tasks as court artist, such as designing (*c.* 1521) the royal sceptre for John III and painting miniature portraits of the royal family. In 1529 he was invited by Emperor Charles V and Empress Isabel to Toledo to paint their portraits (untraced), with Prince Philip (*b* 1527) in the arms of his mother. Among the works he illuminated for the Infante Dom Fernando is his masterpiece, the *Genealogy of the Infante Dom Fernando* (vellum, 13 detached leaves, 559×394 mm; London, BL, Add. MS. 12531). Executed in collaboration with Simon Bening, who coloured Holanda's drawings at Bruges under the supervision of the humanist Damião de Góis (1502–74), it was never completed owing to the death of the Infante in 1534. In collaboration with the pursuivant at arms, João Menelau, he illuminated the *Genealogy of Dom Manuel Pereira, 3rd Conde de Feira* (signed and dated 22 Feb 1534; sold London, Sotheby's,

5 Dec 1989, lot 103), which shows his skill in miniature portraiture in a style close to that of Lucas Horenbout.

From 1535 to 1537 Holanda is documented as being at court at Évora. He illuminated (1533–7) the choir books (untraced) of the convent of Christ in Tomar and perhaps also those (1536–9; Lisbon, Bib. N., L.C. 136–9) of the monastery of S Maria do Paraíso, Évora. Assisted by Francisco, at this time he returned to the illumination of the *Book of Hours of King Manuel*, executing in black and white the *Presentation in the Temple*. Later, Francisco claimed his father was the best illuminator in black and white in Europe. Though he had signed royal documents for coats of arms since 1533, Holanda did not officially become Escrívão da Nobreza and Rei de Armas Algarve until 1538, and after 1542 he attained the rank of Rei de Armas India. After the return of Francisco from his Italian journey in 1540, António often collaborated with him, for example on the creation of new coins for the kingdom and on the design (1556) of the coat of arms of Dom António, son of the Infante Dom Luis. António's work for Queen Catherine is attested by payments in 1541 and 1555, and included the valuation (1544) of a Book of Hours illuminated by Simon Bening (untraced), which Damião de Góis had given to the Queen.

BIBLIOGRAPHY
Ceán Bermúdez; Thieme–Becker

A. de Aguiar: 'Acerca de António de Holanda, um dos autores da Genealogia de D. Manuel Pereira, 3º Conde da Feira', *Arquiv. Distr. Aveiro*, xxv (1959), pp. 5–36

——: *A genealogia iluminada do Infante Dom Fernando por António de Holanda e Simão Bening: Estudo histórico e crítico* (Lisbon, 1962)

J. Stichini Vilela: 'Hollanda, António', *Diccionário da pintura portuguesa* (Lisbon, 1973), pp. 179–80

S. Deswarte: *Les Enluminures de la Leitura Nova, 1504–1552* (Paris, 1977)

D. Markl: *Livro de Horas de D. Manuel* (Lisbon, 1983)

T. Kren: 'Flemish Manuscript Illumination, 1475–1550', *Renaissance Painting in Manuscripts: Treasures from the British Library* (exh. cat., ed. T. Kren; Malibu, CA, Getty Mus.; New York, Pierpont Morgan Lib.; London, BL; 1983–4), pp. 69–78

M. de Albuquerque and J. P. de Abreu e Lima: *A genealogia do Infante Dom Fernando de Portugal* (Oporto and Lisbon, 1984)

C. Radulet and A. de Vasconcelos Saldanha: *Instituição de capela e morgado do cronista Rui de Pina: Códice quinhentista iluminado atribuído a António de Holanda* (Lisbon, 1988)

(2) Francisco de Holanda (*b* Lisbon, 1517; *d* Lisbon, 19 June 1584). Illuminator, writer, theorist, miniaturist, painter, draughtsman and architect, son of (1) António de Holanda.

1. To 1540. 2. 1540–57. 3. From 1557.

1. TO 1540. As a boy he was a page in the houses of Infante Dom Fernando and Cardinal-Infante Dom Afonso. He was educated principally at Évora, then the seat of the court and the centre of humanism in Portugal. Trained by his father as an illuminator, Francisco produced two illuminations in black and white for the *Book of Hours of King Manuel* (begun 1517; Lisbon, Mus. N.A. Ant.) at Évora: the *Annunciation* and *Pentecost*. Through his mother's family, he acquired the skill of cartographic illumination, making a map of Africa (untraced) for Dom Martinho de Portugal, Primate of India (*d* 1547). Aside from the Flemish training from his father, Holanda was in contact with artists influenced by Renaissance Italy, such as the sculptor Nicolau Chanterene, who was in Évora from

1533. At Évora, in the palace of the Cardinal-Infante, he received a sound humanist education from the tutors of the royal siblings, the Infantes Dom Duarte and Dom Henrique. Two humanists had a decisive influence on him: André de Resende, the humanist scholar appointed to the household of Dom Afonso, who instilled in him an interest in antiquity and epigraphy, and a conviction that the life of the artist was superior to that of the courtier, and Dom (later Cardinal) Miguel da Silva, former ambassador to the Holy See, a close friend of popes Clement VII and Paul III, who awakened Holanda's desire to go to Rome.

On 5 January 1538 Holanda left Lisbon for Rome in the suite of the ambassador to the Holy See, Dom Pedro Mascarenhas. At Barcelona, where he spent three months (Feb–April), the visiting Portuguese Infante Dom Luis, Duque de Beja, asked him to draw all the fortifications and military installations he saw on his way. This led to the book of 112 drawings, *As antigualhas* (Madrid, Escorial, Bib. Monasterio S Lorenzo, Inv. 28.I.20; see fig. 1). The fortifications constitute one of the principal themes of the book, alongside antiquities and contemporary works of art in Italy. Holanda must subsequently have presented the book to the Infante since in 1571 it belonged to his son, Dom António, Prior of Crato, before passing (1581–3) into the possession of Philip II of Spain.

1. Francisco de Holanda: *Roma*; drawing from *As antigualhas*, 1538–40 (Madrid, Escorial, Biblioteca del Monasterio de San Lorenzo, Inv. 28.I.20, fol. 4*r*)

Holanda arrived at Rome in the late summer of 1538. Through Lattanzio Tolomei and Blosio Palladio, friends of da Silva, he soon made the acquaintance of Michelangelo and Vittoria Colonna. In the *Diálogo da pintura em a cidade de Roma*, which constitutes Book II of *Da pintura antigua* (1548), he wrote four dialogues that purportedly occurred at the end of 1538 and involved, among others, himself, Colonna, Michelangelo, Tolomei, the Dominican Fra Ambrogio Caterino, the illuminator Giulio Clovio and Valerio Belli. The first three dialogues take place at S Silvestro al Quirinale and the fourth in Clovio's workshop. Together with the *Antigualhas*, *Da pintura antigua* is the principal source of information for his Italian journey. After being discussed by Raczynski in 1846, in the 20th century it became the subject of endless debate over its authenticity and value as a primary source on Michelangelo and his ideas. The truth of the friendship between Holanda and Michelangelo is, however, confirmed by a letter (15 Aug 1553; Florence, Casa Buonarroti) that Holanda sent to Michelangelo from Lisbon, asking him to send a drawing by his own hand. Holanda did in fact receive one (Darmstadt, Hess. Landesmus., Inv. A. E. 1280), on which he inscribed the words OPUS MICAELIS ANGELI. Even if the 'Diálogo de Roma' is partly fictional, it does provide the most penetrating of all the contemporary intellectual portraits of Michelangelo.

Apart from those already mentioned, Holanda also associated with many of the other distinguished artists then in Rome, such as Baccio Bandinelli, Sebastiano del Piombo, Perino del Vaga and Antonio da Sangallo the younger. He took particular interest in drawing after the Antique, the prime subject of his *Antigualhas*, and in studying the paintings of Raphael, Baldassare Peruzzi, Polidoro da Caravaggio, Michelangelo and others. He started his collection of drawings and engravings at this time, and in Rome and Venice he purchased the books that were to serve as the foundation for his treatise on painting. From Rome Holanda made several journeys in Italy, including a visit to Venice, perhaps in January 1539, shortly after the election (19 Jan) of Doge Pietro Lando, whose portrait he painted for the *Antigualhas* (it also has portraits of Michelangelo and Pope Paul III). At Venice he was also received by Sebastiano Serlio who presented him with *Regole generali* (Venice, 1537), which deals with the Classical orders and constitutes Book IV of his architectural treatise.

2. 1540–57. Holanda arrived back in Lisbon in June 1540, after the death (21 April 1540) of Cardinal-Infante Dom Afonso. He consequently moved into the household of King John III and during the 1540s made two or three journeys to Spain. As court artist he moved with the court to Almeirim, Santarém, Lisbon, Sintra and Évora. By 1556 he was receiving the considerable annuity of 100,715 *reais*. Among Portuguese humanists he was celebrated both as a painter and a theorist. On his return from Italy he began his great theoretical work, *Da pintura antigua*, the first treatise on painting in the Iberian Peninsula (untraced; 1790 copy, Lisbon, Acad. Ciênc., MS. 650 Azul). Book I, the first theoretical part without dialogues, and Book II, the *Diálogo da pintura em a cidade de Roma*, were completed in Lisbon in 1548. The supplement, *Do tirar polo natural*

(untraced; 1790 copy, Lisbon, Acad. Ciênc., MS. 650 Azul), is the first known treatise on portraiture since antiquity. Written in the form of a dialogue with his childhood friend, Brás Pereira Brandão, at Oporto, it was completed at Santarém in 1549. The philosophical approach found in *Da pintura antigua* differs profoundly from that of contemporary Italian treatises, which define painting as the imitation of nature. Inspired by Michelangelo and the Florentine Neo-Platonists, Marsilio Ficino and Cristoforo Landino, Holanda sees the 'true' painter as possessing an inner gift, which, linked with tireless devotion to his art, permits him to transcend the physical world in a state of 'divine fury' and to contemplate, on a supercelestial level, ideas that he can immediately transcribe through drawing. Through his use of the Platonic notion of the 'Idea', Holanda developed for the first time a coherent theory of the painter as 'an original creator, guided by inspiration', which, two centuries later, was to become the central idea of Romanticism. Existing only in manuscript form until the 19th century, *Da pintura antigua* was translated into Spanish by Manuel Denis in 1563 (Madrid, Real Acad. S Fernando, MS. 361/13; pubd Madrid, 1921) and exerted a direct influence on Felipe de Guevara as well as on Federico Zuccaro during his stay in Spain (1585–8). Holanda's treatise also had repercussions on the dialogue genre in Portugal.

While still engaged on his treatise, in 1545 Holanda began work at Évora on his depiction of the seven days of the *Creation of the World* in his book of drawings, *De aetatibus mundi imagines* (154 drawings, including 15 coloured; Madrid, Bib. N.), continuing them at Santarém and Almeirim in 1547 and 1551, up to the depiction of Noah and the Flood. *The First Day* (see fig. 2) is a rare work in Christian iconography in that God is not represented anthropomorphically. It depicts the creation of the world according to Genesis ('Let there be light') and the Gospel of St John (the circle with three triangles representing the unity of the Trinity), but also according to Plato: creation as being based on the play of circles and triangles, the material world as an imperfect copy of the supercelestial world and the crater in the earth where the 'third essence' is fused. Other images in the *Creation* reveal a considerable knowledge of astronomy acquired from Portuguese navigators and cosmographers.

With his knowledge of Italian art and architectural theory, Holanda was influential at court as artistic counsellor to John III and the Infante Dom Luis, Duque de Beja. It was no doubt at his instigation that the royal family commissioned from Michelangelo in 1545 a *Madonna of Mercy* (unexecuted) and in 1550 obtained through Cardinal Gaddi at Rome a plan (Lisbon, Arquiv N.; unexecuted and by an unidentified architect) for the royal palace at Xabregas. Having returned from Italy with Serlio's Book IV, Holanda was largely responsible for the growing interest in architectural theory in Portugal, as shown, for example, by the translation of Vitruvius by Pedro Nunes in 1541 and that of Alberti's *De re aedificatoria* by Resende in 1553. Well acquainted with the latest innovations in military architecture, Holanda can also be connected with the introduction into Portugal of the new style of fortification with bastions and Italian work methods (team work and use of models). He provided the model for this style

2. Francisco de Holanda: *The First Day*; drawing from *De aetatibus mundi imagines*, 1545–73 (Madrid, Biblioteca Nacional)

in the fortress of Mazagão (now El Jadida) in Morocco, the result of meetings between architects and engineers in Lisbon in April 1541, and largely completed by the end of the same year, no doubt modified *in situ* by Benedetto da Ravenna, the Italian engineer of Charles V. Holanda also proposed to the King and the Infante Dom Luis a complete urban programme for Lisbon: fortification, the Aguas Livres aqueduct, bridges and road paving, though economic problems prevented their realization. He has been credited with the small chapel (1542) of the Quinta da Penha Verde of Dom João de Castro (1500–48) at Sintra, dedicated to the Infante Dom Luis, and also the beautiful loggia of the Açougues (converted into the church of the Misericordia in 1550; rest. 1944) erected by the Infante Dom Luis at Beja on the model of the Pescherie (1535) of Giulio Romano at Mantua and Serlio's illustrations.

In addition Holanda carried out his duties as court artist, enumerating them in *Da ciência do desenho* (1571). He designed costumes and décor for royal fêtes, for example for royal marriages in 1543 and 1552. He designed liturgical vestments, paraments and accessories for the royal monastery of Belém, and the figure of Christ for the mould of the host used in all the churches of Portugal. In collaboration with his father he illuminated the new coats of arms, for example that of Dom António (1556), the son of the Infante Dom Luis, and designed new coins, which marked a revival in numismatic art in Portugal.

Painting the portraits of the royal family was also one of Holanda's main responsibilities. He had learnt the art of portraiture in miniature from his father and probably under Giulio Clovio in Rome. It was the growing importance of the portrait in his activity that inspired him to write *Do tirar polo natural*. To some extent he prepared the way for Anthonis Mor (in Lisbon in 1552) and the vogue (1552–7) for the portrait at the Portuguese court. Among others he painted the portrait of *John III* (*c.* 1543) and that of the *Infanta Dona Maria*, the half-sister of the King (both untraced). A series of miniature portraits of members of the royal family (Parma, G.N.), formerly at the Palazzo Farnese in Rome, have been attributed to him (Bertini). In 1553 he included a group portrait of the royal family in his *Veneration of St Maria of Belém*, with the *Descent into Limbo* on the reverse side, a small ex-voto painting on panel (Lisbon, Mus. N.A. Ant.), presented to the Belém monastery probably by Queen Catherine. Holanda also specialized in small paintings, such as the *Baptism of St Augustine by St Ambrose* (untraced).

3. FROM 1557. After the death of John III (1557) and his brother, the Infante Dom Luis (1555), Holanda enjoyed a further felicitous period under the regency (1557–62) of Queen Catherine, becoming a knight of the Order of Christ in 1560 and marrying a lady-in-waiting of the Queen, Luisa da Cunha de Sequeira. The regency (1562–8) of the Cardinal-Infante Henrique was a difficult period for Holanda. Unable to exercise his art and feeling himself a 'useless man', he found consolation in composing two large-scale, illuminated poetic works (both untraced). Throughout these years Queen Catherine remained his sole support, commissioning from him illuminations for her religious foundations (payment for six parchments, 1564) and possibly also the design of the royal mausoleums with supporting elephants in the chancel, rebuilt (1571–2) by Jerónimo de Ruão for the Queen in the church of the Belém monastery. In this period he also illuminated the *Compromisso das Almas de S. Julião* (1568; Setúbal, Bib. Mun.).

After King Sebastian of Portugal reached his majority (1568), Holanda sought a position at the Spanish court at a time when Queen Catherine, his protectress, was threatening to return to her native Spain. Through his friend Don Juan de Borja, the Spanish ambassador, he offered his services to Philip II in 1570, subsequently (1572) writing him a letter with which he sent two black-and-white illuminations (untraced), doubtless hoping to participate in the illumination of the antiphonaries of S Lorenzo, El Escorial. Although unsuccessful, in 1573 he received a commission—perhaps for the *Virgin and Child with St Anne* (completed 1575; untraced)—from the King's secretary, Gabriel de Zayas. In the same year Holanda returned to the *De aetatibus mundi imagines*, adding more than a hundred drawings to produce a figurative chronicle of the world in six ages, perhaps with a view to offering them to Philip II.

Holanda also sought to gain favour with King Sebastian. He offered him the 'medal of the perfect king painted with the features of Alexander', for which he was rewarded (1568) with a pension of 16,000 *reais* for three years. He also sent him two memoirs, *Da fábrica que falece à cidade de Lisboa*, followed by *Da ciência do desenho* (1571), the manuscript of these being one of the few by Holanda preserved in Portugal (Lisbon, Bib. Ajuda, MS. 51-III-9). In the former he encouraged the King to recommence the urban programme planned for Lisbon under John III, adding further suggestions, including the construction of a royal funerary chapel dedicated to the Holy Sacrament in the Paço da Ribeira (unexecuted; palace destr. 1755). *Da fábrica* led the King to order detailed studies for the construction of the Aguas Livres aqueduct (from 1573, by Nicolau de Frias; finally built in the 18th century). It also inspired the fortifications (1580, by Filippo Terzi) at the mouth of the Tagus on the eve of the Battle of Lisbon. In *Da ciência do desenho* Holanda demonstrated to the King the value of the art of design both in war and peace. He recapitulated his theory of artistic creation and the 'Idea', his impenitent Neo-Platonism incurring the censure of the Inquisitor, Bartolomeu Ferreira, in 1576. Together with *Da pintura antigua* (1548), the work prepared the theoretical ground for the persistent social claims of Portuguese painters from 1577 onwards. With the accession of Philip II of Spain to the throne of Portugal in 1581, Holanda had to validate his good intentions towards the Spanish crown, recalling his earlier offers of service and presenting to the King, probably in 1582 at Lisbon, his *De aetatibus mundi imagines*. In 1583 his pension was confirmed, with the assurance that his wife would continue to receive it after his death.

For further illustration *see* MILITARY ARCHITECTURE AND FORTIFICATION, fig. 11.

WRITINGS

Da pintura antigua (MS., Books I and II, 1548); ed. A. González García (Lisbon, 1984); ed. J. F. Alves, 2 vols (Lisbon, 1984)
Diálogo da pintura em a cidade de Roma (MS., 1548); pubd (Lisbon, 1984) [Book II of *Da pintura antigua*]
Do tirar polo natural (MS., 1549); pubd (Lisbon, 1984) [supplement to *Da pintura antigua*]
Da ciência do desenho (MS., 1571; Lisbon, Bib. Ajuda); pubd (Lisbon, 1985)
Da fábrica que falece à cidade de Lisboa (MS., 1571; Lisbon, Bib. Ajuda); pubd (Lisbon, 1984)

BIBLIOGRAPHY

A. Raczynski: *Les Arts en Portugal* (Paris, 1846), pp. 5–80
J. de Vasconcelos: *Francisco de Holanda: Vier Gespräche über die Malerei geführt zu Rom 1538* (Vienna, 1899)
E. Tormo: *Os desenhos das antigualhas que vio Francisco d'Ollanda pintor português (1539–1540)* (Madrid, 1940)
R. J. Clements: 'The Authenticity of Francisco de Holanda', *Pubns Mod. Lang. Assoc.*, lxi (1946), pp. 1018–28
Fr. Cordeiro Blanco: 'Identificación de una obra desconocida de Francisco de Holanda', *Archv Esp. A.*, xxviii (1955), pp. 1–37
J. Segurado: *Francisco d'Ollanda* (Lisbon, 1970) [includes facs. ed. of *Da fábrica que falece à cidade de Lisboa* and *Da ciência do desenho*]
J. B. Bury: *Two Notes on Francisco de Holanda: I. The Authenticity of the Roman Dialogues; II. Catalogue of Francisco de Holanda's Writings, Drawings, Paintings and Architectural Designs*, Warb. Inst. Surv., vii (London, 1981)
R. Moreira: 'Novos dados sobre Francisco de Holanda', *Sintria* [Sintra], i–ii (1982–3), pp. 619–92
S. Deswarte: 'Francisco de Holanda', *Os descobrimentos portugueses e a Europa do renascimento* (exh. cat., 17th Council of Europe exh.; Lisbon, 1983), ii, pp. 57–119
——: 'Les "De aetibus mundi imagines" de Francisco de Holanda', *Mnmts Piot*, lxvi (1983), pp. 67–190; rev. as *As imagens das idades do mundo de Francisco de Holanda* (Lisbon, 1989)
J. Segurado: *Francisco d'Ollanda: De aetatibus mundi imagines: Livro das idades* (Lisbon, 1983) [bilingual text]
S. Deswarte: 'Francisco de Holanda collectionneur', *Rev. Louvre*, iii (1984), pp. 169–75
A. González García: *Francisco de Holanda: Da pintura antigua* (Lisbon, 1984)
S. Deswarte: 'Antiquités et nouveaux mondes: A propos de Francisco de Holanda', *Rev. A.* [Paris], lxviii (1985), pp. 55–72
——: 'Francisco de Holanda, teórico entre renascimento e o maneirismo', *O maneirismo*, ed. V. Serrão, vii of *História da arte em Portugal* (Lisbon, 1986–9), pp. 11–29
——: 'OPUS MICAELIS ANGELI: Le Dessin de Michel-Ange de la collection de Francisco de Holanda', *Prospettiva* [Florence], lii–liv (1988–9), pp. 388–98
G. Bertini: 'La Miniature farnésiane', *F.M.R. Mag.*, xv/74 (1989), pp. 81–91
S. Deswarte: *Rome déchue*: Décomposition d'une image de Francisco de Holanda', *Mnmts Piot*, lxvi (1990), pp. 97–181
A. M. Jordan Gschwend: 'Images de majesté: Le Portrait de cour au Portugal (1552–71)', *Portugal et Flandre: Visions de l'Europe (1550–1680)* (exh. cat., Brussels, Europalia, 1991), pp. 118–25
S. Deswarte: *Ideias e imagens em Portugal na época dos descobrimentos: Francisco de Holanda e a teoria da arte* (Lisbon, 1992)

SYLVIE DESWARTE

Holanda, Cornielis (de) (*b* Flanders, *c.* 1495; *d* ?Santiago de Compostela, after 1547). South Netherlandish sculptor active in Spain. He lived in Orense, where in 1521 he is documented as '*Maestre Corniellis flamenco imaginario*', and where he is thought to have lived from 1516 until 1524, when he moved to Santiago. His name appears on important works in Galicia until 1547. The retable (1516–20) of the cathedral at Orense has traditionally been attributed to him because of its similarity to his documented work. It has a Gothic structure in a style characteristic of the late 15th century and was built under the auspices of the Precentor (Chantre) Alonso de Piña. It has four storeys and five vertical sections, and among the finest of the central scenes are the *Pietà*, *St Martin of Tours* and the *Coronation of the Virgin*. In 1524 de Holanda was commissioned to make a retable '*de obra romana*', for the Hospital Real, Santiago; from this work only the predella, with busts of the Apostles, is *in situ*. In 1526 he carved the retable (untraced) and the sepulchre, with its recumbent funerary statue of *Antonio Rodriguez Agustín*, canon of the cathedral (*in situ*), for the Capilla de Prima, Santiago Cathedral; it is surmounted by a segmental arch and decorated with Renaissance ornament. De Holanda also carved the retable (1531–4) of the cathedral at Lugo (dismantled; only the panels in the crossing *in situ*). In 1541 he carved the façade of the church of S María, Pontevedra, with Juan Noble (*fl* 1541–8). It is designed in the form of an altarpiece and is one of the finest examples of Galician Plateresque art.

The information on de Holanda shows that he introduced Renaissance forms to Galicia. He had close links with Flemish art, and his work developed slowly towards an abandonment of Gothic structures. His expressive figures were designed with increasing naturalism, and the compositions of his vivid reliefs became increasingly structured.

Ceán Bermúdez

BIBLIOGRAPHY

J. Villaamil y Castro: 'Reseña histórica de la erección del gran Hospital Real de Santiago', *Galicia Hist.: Col. Dip.*, ii/8 (1903), pp. 519–21
M. Martinez Sueiro: 'Cornielis de Holanda y su retablo de Orense', *Bol. Com. Prov. Mnmts Orense*, iv/124 (1919), pp. 73–84
J. Filgueira Valverde: 'El escultor Cornielis de Holanda en Pontevedra', *Mus. Pontevedra*, i (1942), pp. 20–31
M. Gomez Moreno: 'Sobre Cornielis de Holanda', *Mus. Pontevedra*, i (1942), pp. 76–8

M. Chamoso Lamas: 'El escultor Cornielis de Holanda: Introducción del arte del renacimiento en Galicia', *Abrente*, 5 (1973), pp. 7–30

J. Gonzalez Paz and G. Calvo Moralejo: 'El escultor Cornielis de Holanda en Orense: Nuevas aportaciones para su estudio', *Abrente*, 9 (1977), pp. 35–42

MARGARITA ESTELLA

Holanda, Juan de. *See* JOEST, JAN.

Holbein. German family of artists. (1) Hans Holbein (i), who became one of the leading painters in south Germany, was the son of Michael Holbein, a tanner, who may have settled in Augsburg from Basle, and of Anna Mair, through whom he was related to important artists working in and near Augsburg. These included his uncles Hans Mair (probably identical with the painter Mair von Landshut) and Michel Erhart, and his cousins Gregor Erhart, Paulus Erhart and Hans Daucher, all of whom were sculptors. Apparently included in Hans Holbein (i)'s workshop was his brother Sigmund Holbein (*d* Berne, 1540), whom Hans portrayed in a drawing (1512; London, BM). In 1501 they were together at Frankfurt am Main and in 1516–17 Sigmund took proceedings against his brother, who had already left Augsburg. No documented work by Sigmund Holbein survives. Hans Holbein (i) married *c.* 1494, but the identity of his wife is unknown; their two sons, (2) Ambrosius Holbein and (3) Hans Holbein (ii), also became artists, the latter being among the most important portrait painters in northern Europe during the Reformation.

BIBLIOGRAPHY

P. Ganz and E. Major: *Die Entstehung des Amerbach'schen Kunstkabinets und die Amerbach'schen Inventare* (Basle, 1907)

E. Schilling: *Zeichnungen der Künstlerfamilie Holbein* (Basle, 1954; Eng. trans., New York, 1955)

Die Malerfamilie Holbein in Basle (exh. cat. by B. Busholt and others, Basle, Kstmus., 1960) [extensive bibliog.]

(1) Hans Holbein (i) (*b* Augsburg, ?1460–65; *d* 1534). Painter and draughtsman.

1. LIFE AND WORK. The date of his birth has been estimated from his earliest signed painting, the *Death of the Virgin* (Budapest, Mus. F.A.), which is dated 148(?). His earliest surviving dated altarpiece is the St Afra Altarpiece, produced for the church of SS Ulrich and Afra, Augsburg (1490; Eichstätt, Bischöf. Pal.; Basle, Kstmus.). In 1493 he was recorded, buying a house in Augsburg, as 'Hans Holbein the painter, citizen of Ulm'; he was then working in Ulm with the sculptor Michel Erhart on the Weingartner Altarpiece, depicting scenes from the *Life of the Virgin*, for the chapel of the Virgin in the Benedictine monastery at Weingarten (1493; panels, Augsburg Cathedral; carvings untraced); here the style of the paintings reveals the influence of the Netherlandish style of Rogier van der Weyden. By this date, however, Holbein had already developed stylistic traits of his own: the ability to depict individual facial characteristics, the clear and symmetrical organization of his figures within the available space (here placing them within various architectural structures, which serve both to delineate the subsidiary scenes and to unify the separate panels of the altarpiece) and the use of warm, glowing colour.

Holbein set up a large workshop in Augsburg, taking his first apprentices in 1496–8. In 1499–1500 he painted the *Passion* in grisaille (?ex-SS Ulrich and Afra, Augsburg;

Donaueschingen, Fürstenberg-Samml.), in which Netherlandish influence is again noticeable. The mostly frieze-like scenes are carefully linked by compositional echoes, while the figures are less static than in earlier work, and facial expressions are used to evoke a mood of pathos rather than to emphasize the brutality of the scenes.

In 1501 Holbein travelled to Frankfurt am Main, where he and his workshop painted an altarpiece for the Dominikanerkirche. The only complete surviving parts of the inner panels represent the *Death of the Virgin* (Basle, Kstmus.) and the *Presentation in the Temple* (Hamburg, Ksthalle); a carved statue and two wings are untraced. On the outside of the outer wings was the *Tree of Jesse* (Frankfurt am Main, Städel. Kstinst. & Städt. Gal.); the outside of the inner wings consisted of scenes from the *Passion* (seven, Frankfurt am Main, Städel. Kstinst. & Städt. Gal.; one, priv. col.). The *Death of the Virgin* shows an increased feeling for depth and spatial unity in the way in which the composition employs a recessed architectural background. Moreover, although Netherlandish influence is still evident, notably in the depiction of the kneeling saint, the heads are especially strongly characterized, and the use of colour (notably greens and reds) as well as the inclusion of striking, variegated marble columns give a particularly rich and luminous effect. Another major commission undertaken by Holbein and his workshop in this period was for an altarpiece for the Dominican Klosterkirche at Kaisheim, with panels of the *Passion* and the *Life of the Virgin* (1502; Munich, Alte Pin.). Holbein collaborated on this commission with sculptors from Augsburg, including Gregor Erhart and Adolf Daucher, whose work is untraced; only Holbein's panels, with their rhythmically interlocking figures and flowing drapery, survive. Three panels, of the *Crucifixion*, the *Deposition* and the *Entombment* (Augsburg, Schaezlerpal.), may be connected with this altarpiece, or they may have formed a separate altarpiece in the same church.

Between 1499 and 1504 Holbein and other Augsburg painters, including Hans Burgkmair I and the Monogrammist LF, were commissioned to paint a series of scenes representing the seven main churches of Rome for the Katharinenkloster in Augsburg, in celebration of the Papal Jubilee of 1500. Holbein painted the *Basilica of S Maria Maggiore* (1499) and the *Basilica of S Paolo fuori le Mura* (1504; both Augsburg, Schaezlerpal.; see fig.). The earlier painting shows the *Coronation of the Virgin* within Gothic tracery (above), with the basilica and the *Nativity* (below, left) and the *Martyrdom of St Dorothy* with the donor Dorothea Rehlinger (right). Most notable in the colourful and powerfully depicted scenes of the *Basilica of S Paolo* is the opening out of the space: in the central scene of martyrdom attention is directed to a considerable recession of space beyond the martyrdom itself by the careful placing, just off centre, of a female figure, her back elegantly turned to the viewer, thus leading the eye inwards. The left-hand scene contains a self-portrait of the artist with his two young sons.

In 1509–10 Holbein interrupted work for Augsburg Cathedral to travel to Alsace, probably to undertake a commission for an altarpiece for the Hohenburg Klosterkirche on the Odilienberg, near Strasbourg. The powerful yet still graceful figures of the grisaille wings show the

Hans Holbein (i): *Basilica of S Paolo fuori le Mura*, oil on panel, 2.17×3.08 m, 1504 (Augsburg, Schaezlerpalais)

Legend of St Ottilie (Prague, N. Mus); for the first time the figures in the main scenes are set within a Renaissance-style border of foliage. A further change of style is evident in the wings of the altarpiece of *SS Katherine and Peter* (1512; Augsburg, Schaezlerpal.), in which the martyrdom of each saint is vigorously depicted. In all the scenes the figures are more solidly drawn, and some are more grotesque, than the earlier figures in the Netherlandish style. In addition, a Renaissance-style border and architecture emphasize a particularly strong sense of decorative surface pattern: the figures themselves are carefully placed to form mirror-image patterns of each other, and there is little sense of recession. Holbein's last important work at Augsburg was an altarpiece of *St Sebastian* (1515–16; Munich, Alte Pin.), probably painted for the Dominican Katharinenkloster. In this work the saints in the wings are placed in a Renaissance framework, and the figure of St Sebastian himself adopts a contorted Italianate contrapposto; the sense of space is again shallow.

In the winter of 1516–17, after Holbein had left Augsburg, his brother Sigmund Holbein lodged a complaint against him. Hans the elder is reported to have gone to 'Eyssnen' (Isenheim), where he may have worked for the monastery of St Anthony. In 1517 he was in Lucerne, working with his son (3) Hans Holbein (ii) on the decoration of the house (destr.) of Jacob von Hertenstein. In the *Fountain of Life* (1519; Lisbon, Mus. N. A. Ant.) the Virgin and saints are depicted in a dramatically receding perspective background dominated by a classical triumphal arch of a pattern already used in Augsburg sculpture, which suggests that it was painted at Augsburg, although it also reveals a knowledge of the work of Martin Schongauer, with which Holbein had probably renewed acquaintance in Alsace. In 1520–21 father and son again collaborated on the Oberried Altarpiece (Freiburg im Breisgau Cathedral), for which the elder Hans probably painted the donor figures.

Holbein appears to have painted few independent portraits, although some of his religious commissions, for example the *Schwarz Family* votive picture (?1508; Augsburg, Schaezlerpal.), included donor portraits, here showing his skill in the characterization of individuals as well as the increasing solidity of his figures. The independent *Portrait of a Woman Aged 34* (c. 1512; Basle, Kstmus.), shows the vivacity that he could impart to his portraits, making the sitter glance out of the portrait, her head tilted and her body slightly turned.

2. WORKING METHODS AND TECHNIQUE. Holbein ran a workshop that must have been fairly large to cope with the commissions for traditional large-scale altarpieces that he undertook, and he collaborated with sculptors as well as goldsmiths and stained-glass painters. In 1496 he took on as an apprentice Sebastian Kriechbaum, who was probably the brother of an apprentice in Gregor Erhart's

workshop; the following year Holbein had two pupils, probably Leonhard Beck and his own brother Sigmund.

Holbein shared with most German and Netherlandish artists of the 15th century the practice of making preliminary drawings for commissions, usually in metalpoint on prepared paper or in pen and ink. An exceptionally large number of his drawings survive, around 200 probably by his own hand and further drawings that were probably produced in his workshop. The inventory (1586) of the Amerbach collection in Basle records 56 drawings by Holbein (now Basle, Kstmus.); and a particularly large collection of portrait drawings is preserved at the Kupferstichkabinett in Berlin (for illustration *see* RORICZER, (3)). The surviving drawings can be loosely divided into two groups according to their technique: sketches and more finished compositional studies in pen and wash; and studies of details of figures, especially heads, which are mostly in metalpoint. Large numbers of copies of drawings have also been preserved, but since it is not known exactly how Holbein's workshop functioned, the precise use of many of these drawings remains unknown. A pattern book (Schloss Wolfegg, Fürst. Kstsamml.) contains many motifs taken from works by Holbein and his workshop, but it cannot be established with certainty whether this book was used by the workshop or was made for use in another. A few drawings in which Holbein used a chiaroscuro technique may have been made for glass painting or prints, but others can be connected with specific paintings.

It is possible, though the evidence is not straightforward, that Holbein used preparatory metalpoint drawings for his painted portraits: for example, there is a clear relationship between a drawing of an *Unknown Woman* (London, BM) and the painted *Portrait of a Woman Aged 34* (Basle, Kstmus.), but the drawing appears to copy the painting rather than being a study for it, and it may be a workshop record. In the case of the portrait of an *Unknown Man* (?1517; Norfolk, VA, Chrysler Mus.), the drawing of the same man (Berlin, Kupferstichkab.) faces in the opposite direction and cannot have been used directly as the basis for the portrait. Most of the portrait drawings, however, which include some of Holbein's most beautiful and vigorous work (often depicting Augsburg citizens), appear to have been executed independently. Many were probably executed for their own sake rather than for particular commissions, but some were certainly used in paintings, for example the *Basilica of S Paolo fuori le Mura* (see fig. above), while others remained as independent studies, for example his drawing of *Ambrosius and Hans Holbein the Younger* (1511; Berlin, Kupferstichkab.).

BIBLIOGRAPHY

H. Reinhardt: 'Bemerkungen zum Spätwerk Hans Holbein des Älteren', *Z. Schweiz. Archäol. & Kstgesch.*, xv (1954–5), pp. 11–19

C. Beutler and G. Thiem: *Hans Holbein der Ältere: Die spätgotische Altar- und Glasmalerei* (Augsburg, 1960)

N. Lieb and A. Stange: *Hans Holbein der Ältere* (Munich, 1960)

Hans Holbein der Ältere und die Kunst der Spätgotik (exh. cat. by G. Schmidt and H. Reinhaurdt, Augsburg, Rathaus, 1965)

W. Pfeiffer: 'Das Patrizierporträt der Sammlung Chrysler von Hans Holbein der Ältere', *Pantheon*, xxiv (1966), pp. 140–46

B. Bushart: 'Der "Lebensbrunnen" von Hans Holbein dem Älteren', *Festschrift Wolfgang Braunfels* (Tübingen, 1977), pp. 45–70

T. Falk: *Katalog der Zeichnungen des 15. und 16. Jahrhunderts im Kupferstichkabinett Basel* (Basle and Stuttgart, 1979)

B. Bushart: *Hans Holbein der Ältere* (Augsburg, 1987) [colour pls of details from ptgs]

Das Amerbach-Kabinett: Zeichnungen Alter Meister (exh. cat. by C. Müller, Basle, 1991)

J. Rowlands and G. Bartum: *Drawings by German Artists in the Department of Prints and Drawings in the British Museum. The Fifteenth Century and the Sixteenth Century by Artists born before 1530*, 2 vols (London, 1993)

(2) Ambrosius Holbein (*b* Augsburg, ?1494; *d* after 1519). Painter, draughtsman and designer of woodcuts, son of (1) Hans Holbein (i). In the drawing of *Ambrosius and Hans Holbein the Younger* (1511; Berlin, Kupferstichkab.) by their father, Hans's age is given as 14, and although that of Ambrosius cannot be read clearly, he appears to have been the elder brother. In 1514 he was probably working near the Bodensee, and a *Virgin and Child* (Basle, Kstmus.), with the coat of arms of Johann von Botzheim, Canon of Konstanz Cathedral (*c.* 1480–1535), appears to be his work. In 1515 he was working as a journeyman to the painter Thomas Schmid (*c.* 1480–*c.* 1550–60) on the decoration of the abbot's Festsaal in the Benedictine St Georgkloster at Stein-am-Rhein, which included allegorical figures of women, one of which, *Death with a Female Lute-player* (*in situ*), is signed AH. Also in 1515 he joined his brother Hans in Basle, where together they decorated with marginal drawings (1515–16) the copy of Erasmus's *Praise of Folly* (Basle, Kstmus.) belonging to the schoolmaster Myconius (Oswald Geisshüsler; *d* 1552); the distinction between the hands of the two brothers can be made only on stylistic grounds. They also painted a school sign for Myconius, each apparently working on a

Ambrosius Holbein: *Portrait of a Man Aged 20*, oil on panel, 440×325 mm, 1518 (St Petersburg, Hermitage)

different side. On 25 July 1516 Ambrosius was recorded staying in the house of the painter Hans Herbst, in whose workshop he may have been employed. On 14 February 1517 he was enrolled in the Basle painters' guild, and on 5 June 1518 he became a citizen of the city. Numerous woodcut designs executed for Basle printers from 1517 onwards and signed with Ambrosius Holbein's initials survive, most of which are set in architectural frameworks inspired by the Italian Renaissance, although there is no evidence that he ever visited Italy. His designs include that for the Basle edition (1518) of Thomas More's *Utopia*, incorporating a landscape map of the island. References to Ambrosius cease after 1519.

Only a small group of paintings by Ambrosius Holbein survive, in addition to the woodcuts after his designs. His religious paintings include the *Praying Christ* (c. 1515; Basle, Kstmus.), which is documented as his work in the Amerbach inventory (1586). The inventory also records two paintings entitled *Portrait of a Young Boy* (c. 1516; Basle, Kstmus.), each in a Renaissance-style arch; they were probably originally intended to hang as a diptych in joined frames, and two sensitive metalpoint preparator, drawings survive (Basle, Kstmus.; Vienna, Albertina). A *Portrait of a Man Aged 20* (1518; St Petersburg, Hermitage; see fig.) signed AHB (Ambrosius Holbein of Basle), also includes a Renaissance-style arch, reminiscent of many of his woodcut designs and of the contemporary work of his brother. The main stylistic differences between the brothers are perhaps most evident in their graphic work: Ambrosius's touch was more tentative and delicate and less fluently linear, and his sense of overall design was less developed, but his figures show a lively and often humorous animation and the small compositions reveal a vivid mastery of incidental detail.

BIBLIOGRAPHY

H. A. Schmid: *Die Wandgemälde im Festsaal des Klosters St Georgen in Stein-am-Rhein aus den Jahren 1515/16* (Frauenfeld, 1936)

(3) Hans Holbein (ii) (*b* Augsburg, 1497–8; *d* London, 1543). Painter, draughtsman and designer, active in Switzerland and England, son of (1) Hans Holbein (i). He is best known as the most important portrait painter in England during the Reformation, although he began his career in Basle, where he worked mainly as a painter of altarpieces and designer of woodcuts. Dissatisfaction with patronage in Switzerland led him to visit England in 1526–8, where, through Erasmus, he met Sir Thomas More and his circle. On returning to Basle, he completed projects that he had begun before his trip to England, undertook commissions for the city authorities and produced designs for stained glass and goldsmiths' work. In 1532 he returned to England, where he worked almost exclusively as a portrait painter, mainly under the patronage of King Henry VIII and his courtiers.

I. Life and work. II. Working methods and technique.

I. Life and work.

1. Switzerland, 1516–26. 2. England, 1526–8. 3. Switzerland, 1528–32. 4. England, 1532–43.

1. SWITZERLAND, 1516–26. The earliest surviving works by Hans Holbein (ii) are the confidently designed and painted portraits of the Basle Burgomaster *Jacob Meyer*

and his wife *Dorothea Kannengiesser* (both 1516; Basle, Kstmus.), which were almost certainly intended to be hung as a diptych in joined frames, since the compositions of the portraits are united by the use of a Renaissance-style arch shown in perspective. Two careful preparatory metalpoint studies (both Basle, Kstmus.) have perhaps a slightly more vivacious air than the finished portraits, which lack the sense of movement implicit in the portraits of Hans Holbein (i). In 1517 the younger Hans seems to have been working in Lucerne, where he collaborated with his father on the decoration of the house of Jacob von Hertenstein (destr.) and was probably responsible for the elaborate illusionistic scheme for the façade. He carried out at least one similar scheme at Basle, on the Haus zum Tanz (1520–25; destr.; designs, Berlin, Kupferstichkab.), owned by the goldsmith Balthasar Angelrot (c. 1480–1544), which incorporated, among Italianate architectural motifs, a line of dancing peasants and a vertiginously balanced rider, whose horse seemed about to leap forward into the street. Holbein was clearly familiar with Renaissance decorative vocabulary, which he used to great effect in other works of this period, notably in his designs for woodcuts, but there is no evidence that he went to Italy, and he may well have gained his knowledge by studying engravings after Mantegna and other northern Italian artists.

In 1519 Holbein became a master in the Basle guild of painters, and in the same year he painted the portrait of *Bonifacius Amerbach* (Basle, Kstmus.). It is clear from this work that his approach to portrait painting had already matured: this head-and-shoulders portrait, which includes a Latin inscription commenting on the fidelity of the likeness, exemplifies his mastery of depth coupled with an extreme economy of design. Of several portraits commissioned by the humanist Erasmus, one type shows him in profile, writing (1523, Basle, Kstmus.; 1523–4, Paris, Louvre), while a more elaborate half-length, three-quarter-profile version (1523; Longford Castle, Wilts; on loan to London, NG) depicts him in his study, hands resting on a book inscribed in Greek 'The Labours of Herakles'. In 1521 Holbein was commissioned by the authorities in Basle to paint the recently completed Council Chamber at the Rathaus with scenes from Classical antiquity and the Old Testament, representing Justice and other Virtues, all set within an architectural framework, which resembled that used by Holbein in his painted house façades but which was here much less exuberant. Only a few fragments of the scheme survive (Basle, Kstmus.), and the drawings (Basle, Kstmus.) do not give a clear idea of the whole; yet his clear organization of groups of figures in a limited space is apparent. Work on the scheme began in June 1521 and continued the following year, but the project was not completed until 1530, after he returned from his first visit to England.

During the early 1520s Holbein's commissions for religious works included designs for stained glass as well as altarpieces and smaller paintings. The Oberried Altarpiece (1521; Freiburg im Breisgau Cathedral), with its strikingly lit depiction of the *Nativity* by night, was painted in collaboration with Hans Holbein (i) who, on stylistic grounds, was probably responsible for the donor figures.

A dramatic altarpiece of the *Passion* (1525–6; Basle, Kstmus.), comprising two wings, that almost certainly stood alone, demonstrates Holbein the younger's mastery of subtle and fluent arrangements of figures in action. Perhaps his most remarkable religious work of this period, however, is the *Dead Christ* (1521–2; Basle, Kstmus.), which is listed in the Amerbach inventory (1586) merely as the image of a dead man. X-radiographs have show that alterations were made during the course of painting, one of which appears to have been a change from a tomb with an arched top. It is one of Holbein's most forceful paintings, graphically showing the decaying corpse in a manner unusually expressionistic for the artist: the characteristically elongated side view of Christ's face is here further distorted by exaggerated foreshortening, starkly emphasizing the stiffness of the corpse's face and the rigidity of the eye sockets.

The Meyer Altarpiece, depicting the *Virgin and Child with Burgomaster Jakob Meyer zum Hasen and his Family* (Darmstadt, Hess. Landesmus.; see fig. 1), was commissioned by Jakob Meyer *c.* 1526, but it too was not completed until *c.* 1530, after Holbein returned to Basle from England; owing to the deaths of Meyer's two sons, Holbein was required during the second phase of the painting to insert the portrait of Meyer's deceased first wife, turning the whole into a memorial picture. The groupings of figures, particularly the heads, which are painted with great clarity and delicacy, show Holbein's

1. Hans Holbein (ii): *Virgin and Child with Burgomaster Jakob Meyer zum Hasen and his Family*, oil on panel, 1.46×1.02 m, *c.* 1526–*c.* 1530 (Darmstadt, Hessisches Landesmuseum)

careful attention to and rhythmic arrangement of the figures in space; here the shallow space typical of his compositions of this period is broken only by the strikingly foreshortened arm of the Christ Child. Among Holbein's last works at Basle during this period were the *Lais Corinthiaca* and *Venus and Cupid* (both 1526; Basle, Kstmus.), in which the dryness and flatness of his earlier paintings give way to much richer effects: striking colouring (contrasting deep reds, oranges and greens, enhanced by the effects of light and shade on the deep folds of silks and velvets) combined with the use of gesturing hands and tilted, shaded faces with Leonardesque expressions hinting at a smile.

In addition to his religious paintings of this period, Holbein produced drawings and designs for woodcuts. He had already demonstrated his facility with line in the marginal drawings (1515–16) in a copy of Erasmus's *Praise of Folly* (Basle, Kstmus.), which he executed with his brother Ambrosius for the schoolmaster Myconius, as well as in numerous title-page designs, which combine fluency of line with a fine sense of balance and economy. In two single woodcuts on the theme of the abuses of the Church, *Christ, the True Light* and the *Traffic in Indulgences* (both 1524), Erasmian ideas have been translated into appealingly rhythmic groupings, effectively expressing the need for simplicity in religious belief. The famous *Dance of Death* series of 49 woodcuts and the *Old Testament* series of 91 woodcuts (both before 1526; pubd as *Historiarum veteris testamenti icones*, Lyon, 1538) demonstrate Holbein's mastery of economy and variety of expressive effect and gesture. In the small *Dance of Death* series, in particular, a remarkable sense of depth is conveyed by Holbein's uninsistent use of perspective in both buildings and landscape, while the range of dramatic emotion conveyed in both gesture and facial expression, beautifully rendered by the woodcutter Hans Lützelburger, is exceptional for the medium (*see also* PROPAGANDA). The *Old Testament* scenes are even more economical in their use of line and place less emphasis on depth, in keeping with the development of Holbein's style in the mid- to late 1520s. The *Dance of Death* series contains references to French architecture, derived from his visit to France in 1524, when he may have been seeking a position at the French court.

2. ENGLAND, 1526–8. In August 1526 Holbein left Basle to travel to England via Antwerp, where, through Erasmus, he met the painter Quinten Metsys. In England a further introduction from Erasmus resulted in Holbein painting a head-and-shoulders portrait of *Sir Thomas More* (1527; New York, Frick; *see* PORTRAITURE, fig. 6), which shows him as a statesman, not a scholar. Its colouring (the green curtain, the rich red velvet of More's sleeve) and the attention to textures (e.g. the way the stubble on More's chin glints in the light) continue the direction of Holbein's interests pursued in the last works he painted at Basle. The sense of depth in the portrait, far more abruptly conveyed in earlier works, is here controlled and softened by the angle of More's pose and the inclusion of the curtain and parapet, as well as by the subtle use of lighting and cast shadows. Holbein also painted a group portrait of *Sir Thomas More and his Family* (1526–7; destr. 1752),

for which there survive his studies for seven of the heads (Windsor Castle, Royal Lib.) and his sketch of the whole group (Basle, Kstmus.; *see* DRESS, fig. 34) with annotations for alterations, notably that Lady More should sit rather than kneel; this was the only indication that he intended to change the context of the portrait to a secular one. A later 16th-century copy of the group portrait (Nostell Priory, W. Yorks) by Rowland Lockey not only followed the alterations but also changed other figures, as well as removing rosaries present in the group drawing and giving the sitters Classical texts to hold; it may thus not be a completely accurate representation of the finished picture. What is certain is that Holbein's final composition was carefully built up from individual sittings, as the drawings show; the picture was not a direct record of the More family together, although it may well reflect particular occasions on which they prayed or read together. As a composition, it differs from earlier, stiffer, northern European groupings in family portraits and representations of the Holy Family. Holbein's mastery of the effective and rhythmic grouping of a series of figures in an interior, evident in his *Dance of Death* woodcut designs, is here employed to give a sense of depth, which must have been startling when the work was hung against a wall, as well as a feeling of animated and serious communication between the family members.

Holbein painted further portraits of Erasmus's friends in 1527, including one of *William Warham, Archbishop of Canterbury* (Paris, Louvre) as a gift for Erasmus in return for the latter's portrait by Holbein sent to Warham in 1524. Two versions were painted, the only surviving one of which shows the Archbishop in a pose that directly echoes that of Erasmus in the earlier portrait: Warhams's crozier and mitre stand in place of the background of the scholar's study in the earlier portrait, and instead of the sitter's hands resting on a book, they rest, perhaps slightly incongruously, on a cushion. The portrait of *Nicholas Kratzer* (1528; Paris, Louvre), the German-born Astronomer Royal and tutor to More's children, showing him half-length, making an instrument, employs a similar compositional pattern. Also in 1527 Holbein painted the Comptroller of the Royal Household *Sir Henry Guildford* (Windsor Castle, Berks, Royal Col.) and his wife *Lady Guildford* (St Louis, MO, A. Mus.), both three-quarter-length portraits designed to be hung together, with a curtain rail connecting the two compositions and the smaller figure of Lady Guildford carefully balanced to match the bulk of her husband by the inclusion of a Renaissance-style pilaster. It may have been through Kratzer or Guildford that in 1527 Holbein ('Master Hans') was employed on the decorations of a temporary festival building at Greenwich. His large-scale paintings (untraced) included a depiction of the *Battle of Thérouanne* and a ceiling painting, devised with Kratzer, showing *The Heavens*. Holbein does not appear to have been offered a permanent position at court, however, and by August 1528 he had returned to Basle, having expended the two years' absence permitted to Basle citizens without loss of citizenship.

3. SWITZERLAND, 1528–32. Holbein's return to Basle was marked by his purchase of a house there in August 1528 and by the completion of two projects he had begun before his first visit to England: the alterations to the Meyer Altarpiece and the completion (1530) of the wall paintings in the Council Chamber at the Rathaus (*see* §1 above). Preparatory drawings for two scenes painted in this period, *Samuel and Saul* and *King Rehoboam*, as well as a fragment of the latter painting (all Basle, Kstmus.), show Holbein moving towards a new, more linear style, setting figures closely together and slightly flattened against the picture plane. Also from this period is Holbein's moving portrait of the *Artist's Wife and Two Elder Children* (1528; Basle, Kstmus.): painted on paper and using an unusual and effective grouping, it reveals his ability to depict emotion as well as his highly fluent and accurate use of line.

In 1529 iconoclastic riots broke out in Basle, and a strict Protestant regime was established. Holbein said that he needed a better explanation of the new Protestant service before he would attend it, but only months later he was recorded among the congregation. He continued to receive commissions from the town council (in 1531 he was paid for painting a clock), but it seems the work offered was insufficiently demanding or lucrative, and by 1532 he had returned to England, where he remained despite the council's strenuous attempts to make him return to Basle.

4. ENGLAND, 1532–43. Holbein returned to England in the summer of 1532 to find that most of his former patrons were dead or in political disgrace, but he evidently quickly found new powerful and influential patrons, through whom he might attract the King's notice. Between 1532 and 1534 he painted the portrait of *Thomas Cromwell* (New York, Frick), shortly before the latter became Henry VIII's secretary, and Holbein was probably the 'Hans' recorded in 1533 as painting figures of *Adam* and *Eve* made by the goldsmith Cornelis Hays. Much of Holbein's surviving work of the early 1530s, however, consists of portraits of the German Hanseatic merchants then residing in London. Nearly all are dated, and some contain inscriptions of a type otherwise seen only in royal portraits in England at this time, such as the Latin verses on the portrait of *Derich Born* (1533; Windsor Castle, Berks, Royal Col.) that allude to the skill of the artist in confusing the distinction between illusion and reality. Holbein had pursued this theme in the complex portrait of *Georg Gisze* (1532; Berlin, Gemäldegal.): the establishment of illusion by such means as the virtuoso treatment of Gisze's sleeve shown through the curved surface of a glass vase of flowers is contradicted by such details as the unexpectedly cutaway corner of the table and by the inclusion of a cartellino, which might be attached to the wall or to the painting's surface. A series of inscriptions and other, probably symbolic, details invoke the idea of the instability of life.

Holbein is attributed with two large-scale commissions for the Hanseatic merchants. A drawing of *Parnassus* (1533; Berlin, Kupferstichkab.) accords with the description of the Hanseatic merchants' contribution to the pageantry in the City of London to celebrate the coronation of Anne Boleyn in 1533. Evidence of two large paintings on linen representing the *Triumphs of Riches* and the *Triumphs of Poverty* (both destr.) survives in a drawing for the *Triumph of Riches* (*c.* 1532–3; Paris, Louvre) and in copies of both—by Matthäus Merian (ii) (1640) and Jan de Bisschop (*c.* 1670; both London, BM)—indicating that the paintings were executed in grisaille; the slightly flattened yet graceful forms echo the stylistic traits seen in the completed designs for the Council Chamber at the Rathaus in Basle of 1530.

In 1533 Holbein painted '*The Ambassadors*' (London, N.G.; see fig. 2), a full-length double portrait of the French ambassador Jean de Dinteville (1504–57) and his compatriot the Bishop Georges de Selve (1509–42). Its most unusual feature, an anamorphic representation of a skull, centrally placed between the two sitters and fully recognizable only from an acute angle, turns the portrait into a *memento mori*; still-life objects such as a broken-stringed lute and a globe marked with de Dinteville's château have

both personal and more general significance, probably of worldly disharmony, but a final sign of hope and a spiritual dimension are embodied in the carefully angled, semi-concealed crucifix. Once again, the subtlety of Holbein's skills in manipulating rationally ordered space to purposeful effect is evident: as the viewer's perceptions of the space depicted in the picture are altered, so the meanings come into focus.

The English Reformation produced few paintings or woodcuts in its cause, but those by Holbein are outstanding examples of his art. An *Allegory of the Old and New Testaments* (Edinburgh, N.G.) is undated but belongs stylistically and ideologically to the early 1530s; iconographically it develops a theme established in the late 1520s in the circle around Martin Luther and Lucas Cranach (i), although its original patron is unknown.

2. Hans Holbein (ii): '*The Ambassadors*', oil on panel, 2.07×2.09 m, 1533 (London, National Gallery)

Details of its composition look back to Holbein's own *Old Testament* woodcuts, but the vivid, yet subtle colouring, the dramatic lighting and the clarity of organization and compositional detail on a small scale make it a striking reminder of his abilities as a subject painter at a period when he was painting almost exclusively portraits.

The Coverdale Bible title-page, designed for the first complete English translation of the Bible (1535), is one of Holbein's most accomplished woodcut designs and one of the most important title-page designs of the period. He again used the opposition of the Old and New Testaments, but with the emphasis on the propagation of the word of God. Each scene is set out with marvellous economy of space, displaying great variety of facial expression and suggesting depth without overcrowding. Henry VIII is portrayed in the lower part of the design, with the Hebrew letters for God placed directly above, symbolizing the King's break with the intermediary of the Church; he distributes the Bible to a group that may include a portrayal of Thomas Cromwell in his role as Vice-Regent. It was probably through Cromwell that Holbein received this commission, which may originally have been one of a group of title-pages, only one of which was published in its intended context. Another small group of woodcuts, satirizing monks, was not published until the firmly Protestant reign of King Edward VI (*reg* 1547–53).

Holbein was first recorded as the King's Painter in 1536 and he was recorded as salaried in the royal accounts in 1538 (the sequence from 1531 to 1538 being untraced). He was paid slightly less than another King's Painter, Lucas Horenbout, although their roles seem to have differed: Holbein was apparently less closely attached to the court (he lived in the parish of St Andrew Undershaft in the City of London) and had a large private clientele. Even if the commissions Henry VIII gave Holbein were relatively few, they were all highly important. The most splendid was for the dynastic wall painting of *Henry VII, Elizabeth of York, Henry VIII and Jane Seymour* at Whitehall Palace (1537; destr. 1698), London, known from two copies (1667, Windsor Castle, Berks, Royal Col.; 1669, Petworth House, W. Sussex, NT) by Remi van Leemput and from part of Holbein's own cartoon (London, N.P.G.; *see* ENGLAND, fig. 15) showing the figures of Henry VII and Henry VIII. In the original painting the four full-length figures were arranged around a plaque inscribed with Latin verses celebrating the Tudor dynasty (invisible in the surviving fragment of the cartoon, but its presence in the original is confirmed by a 16th-century transcription). The figures were set against a background with a richly ornamental Renaissance-style frieze. Although the details of the original setting are unknown the painting would clearly have made its greatest impact if the architectural decoration and perspectives of the background reflected exactly the room in which it was painted. It was painted for a room described in the following century as the privy chamber, not necessarily identical with Henry VIII's room of that name. Although Henry VIII is shown in three-quarter profile in the cartoon, he appears in the copies and in other images deriving from Holbein's portrait as a full-face, entirely frontal and overwhelmingly imposing image. A small, exquisitely painted head-and-shoulders portrait of *Henry VIII* (1536; Madrid, Mus.

3. Hans Holbein (ii): *Henry VIII*, oil on panel, 280×200 mm, 1536 (Madrid, Museo Thyssen-Bornemisza)

Thyssen-Bornemisza; see fig. 3) uses the three-quarter-profile image but was evidently derived from the same sitting as the wall painting. The portrait of *Henry VIII with the Barber-Surgeons' Company* (1541; London, Barber-Surgeons' Hall) uses the frontal depiction of the face in an almost hieratic image of the King, who appears on a slightly larger scale than the other figures.

Among the relatively few other commissions for Henry VIII is a deceptively simple three-quarter-length portrait of *Jane Seymour* (1536–7; Vienna, Ksthist. Mus.), based on the pattern of the wall painting but with a change of costume; it is painted with tightly controlled virtuosity and was presumably intended for the King. A head-and-shoulders portrait of *Edward, Prince of Wales* (Washington, DC, N.G.A.), which includes a Latin poem by the humanist Richard Morison, was probably the portrait presented by Holbein to Henry VIII as a New Year's gift in 1539. Holbein's period of greatest activity for Henry VIII, however, was in 1538–9, when he was sent on several journeys abroad in order to portray prospective candidates for the royal marriage. Three such works survive: from 1538 there is a full-length painted portrait of *Christina of Denmark, Duchess of Milan* (London, N.G.), in which Christina's face is highlighted against a restrained blue background and the black of her dress (the placing of her figure, together with the lighting employed, giving an impression of depth and even of slow movement towards the viewer); from the following year is a head-and-shoulders miniature of *Anne of Cleves* (1539; London, V&A) and a three-quarter-length frontal portrait of her on parchment (Paris, Louvre). All three were probably worked up at home, a supposition supported by the presence of pouncing in the large painted portrait of *Anne*, indicating that it was made from a cartoon. Holbein also collaborated with goldsmiths on several pieces, such as a gold cup for Jane Seymour (drawings, London, BM; Oxford, Ashmolean), some of which were probably royal commissions and some commissioned by others for the King, for example Sir Anthony Denny's New Year's gift of a clock (drawing, London, BM), on which Holbein collaborated with Nicholas Kratzer.

Holbein's patrons outside royal circles included nearly a quarter of the peerage and many of the most important political figures of the day. Although religious painting was certainly not outlawed in England at this early stage of the Reformation, the lack of competent portrait painters in England evidently encouraged the commissioning of such work from Holbein, to the virtual exclusion of other genres. Some of the portraits are recorded only in preparatory drawings, including exquisite studies in a mixture of coloured chalks and ink, or in copies. During this period Holbein also produced several portrait miniatures, outstanding examples being that of *Henry Brandon, 2nd Duke of Suffolk* (see fig. 4) and that of a *Mrs Pemberton* (c. 1540; London, V&A; see MINIATURE, fig. 2) in which Holbein's decorative and balanced placing of his sitter, with her hands, arms and dress arranged in his usual unemphatic way within the roundel, is such that the figure could be enlarged without any loss of effect; this is typical of his ability to work successfully at different scales. The surviving full-scale portraits are usually half-lengths and evenly lit, the sitters rarely calling attention to themselves through

gesture. They have the simplest of blue–green backgrounds, frequently with gold lettering indicating the date and the age of the sitter and cancelling the impression of background space, as in the portrait of *Richard Southwell* (1536; Florence, Uffizi). Comparison of two portraits from the beginning and end of Holbein's second visit to England—for example the *Portrait of a Member of the Wedigh Family* (1532; New York, Met.) and the *Portrait of an Unknown Man* (1541; Vienna, Ksthist. Mus.)—shows many stylistic as well as compositional similarities: the method of rendering glossy black satin, the depiction of the eyes and face, the frontal poses and the inclusion of a desk with objects carefully depicted on it. Such similarities refute the notion that Holbein's style in the 1530s underwent a radical change towards a much flatter, more stylized mode of depiction; the only significant difference is in the simplification of backgrounds and, in this example, the increasing restriction of the space around the sitter, both serving to avoid any sharp background recessions and to limit the impression of depth in order to emphasize the illusion of the painted portrait, an illusion to which inscriptions or objects more often call attention in earlier works.

Although Holbein visited Basle briefly in 1538 (when his splendid clothes and relative wealth were noted), there is no evidence that he subsequently returned to the city, despite his promise to go back.

II. Working methods and technique.

Hans Holbein (ii) is not known to have had a workshop, and the quality of his surviving work indicates singlehanded execution, apart from those examples in which the collaborative hand of his father or brother may be detected. The problem of whether Holbein himself organized the replication of some of his English portraits is unresolved. Both stylistically and in his approach to the organization of his work, the younger Holbein can thus be seen to belong to a different artistic world from that of his father. Nevertheless, links with Hans the elder's working methods are apparent: for example, the first surviving portraits by Hans the younger, of *Jacob Meyer* and his wife *Dorothea Kannengiesser* (*see* §I, 1 above), were based on careful preparatory drawings (Basle, Kstmus.) using metalpoint and coloured chalks. He also used portrait drawings as a basis for religious paintings: a drawn *Portrait of a Young Woman* (c. 1522; Paris, Louvre) was the basis for the head of the *Virgin* (1522; Solothurn, Kstmus.). Like his father, he also occasionally employed a chiaroscuro technique, for example in a drawing of *Christ* (1519; Berlin, Kupferstichkab.), although this technique seems to have been used for drawings that were finished works in themselves, or for paintings, rather than for preparatory drawings. The surviving drawings for glass paintings, for example the *Passion* series (c. 1525–6; Basle, Kstmus.), are in a bold, monochrome wash.

Drawings connected with large-scale works at Basle, particularly for the Council Chamber at the Rathaus, take the form of careful sketches, but they are freer than the compositional sketches of his father. Only in connection with the large-scale English works, however, is it possible to understand how Holbein proceeded from drawing to finished painting, for two cartoons survive for such works,

4. Hans Holbein (ii): *Henry Brandon, 2nd Duke of Suffolk*, watercolour on parchment, laid on to card, diam. 57 mm, 1535 (British Royal Collection)

for the dynastic portrait of *Henry VII, Elizabeth of York, Henry VIII and Jane Seymour* and the portrait of *Henry VIII with the Barber-Surgeons' Company.* Both are made up of several sheets of paper joined together; the Barber-Surgeons' cartoon (London, Royal Coll. Surgeons England) is completely overpainted, but the fragment of the other cartoons, depicting the two kings, is boldly drawn in a mixture of chalk and wash, monochrome in effect, although the finished painting (destr. 1698), to judge from the 17th-century copies, was coloured normally. Both cartoons are pricked along the outlines with small holes, through which charcoal dust would have been pounced to transfer the outlines of the drawings to the surface that was to be painted. Only one portrait drawing survives that is similarly pricked, that of *Sir Thomas More* (1526; Windsor Castle, Royal Lib.), which suggests that this was not the method Holbein normally used for portraits, although over 80 portrait drawings by him survive (most at Windsor). In contrast with the earlier drawings, which made greater use of metalpoint as the drawing instrument, these are mostly in a mixture of coloured chalks and ink on pink-primed paper (see fig. 5), with a few in chalks alone on unprimed paper. In many cases these beautiful, careful studies, often annotated with details of colours and textures, can be linked to surviving painted portraits; those on unprimed paper using coloured chalks alone (a French technique) can be associated with painted portraits dating from Holbein's first visit to England (1526–8), while those

using pink priming are linked to paintings of the second visit (1532–43).

A single reference survives to a portrait sitting given to Holbein, although the circumstances were so particular that the details may not be applicable to the majority of his portrait commissions. When, in 1538, Holbein was sent by Henry VIII to make the portrait of *Christina of Denmark, Duchess of Milan* at Brussels, the sitting lasted three hours; on his return, the King was delighted with the result. No drawing survives, but the full-length painted portrait (1538; London, N.G.) was presumably worked up after Holbein's return from Brussels, as it seems unlikely that he would have taken such a large panel abroad with him. In the allotted time, however, he may have made several drawings: studies of dress and hands, for example, as well as of the face, similar to his studies of the *Hands of Erasmus* (*c.* 1523; Paris, Louvre) and of the costume for his *Portrait of an English Woman* (*c.* 1532; Oxford, Ashmolean; Basle, Kstmus.). Drawings from his English visits comprise mostly head-and-shoulders studies, although an exception is the three-quarter-length drawn portrait of *Queen Jane Seymour* (1536–7; Windsor Castle, Royal Lib.), which must have been used both for the dynastic wall painting, in which she was depicted full length, and for the surviving painted portrait (Vienna, Ksthist. Mus.). In both paintings her dress and jewellery differ from those shown in the drawing, although the pose is the same, and it would have been easy for different accessories to have been supplied to Holbein when he was working up his paintings from the drawings, once the basic pose and likeness had been established: the latter seem to have been considerably more important.

The portrait of *Queen Jane Seymour* also provides some insight into the methods that Holbein may have used to work from his drawing to the painted panel. The preparatory drawing for the Vienna portrait corresponds precisely in its dimensions to the painting, suggesting that he must have used a mechanical means of transferring it to the panel. Since only one of his surviving portrait drawings is pricked for use as a cartoon, it seems that the method he is most likely to have used involved laying a piece of chalk-coated paper between his drawing and the panel, and tracing the outlines of the drawing with a stylus, a technique that requires only slight pressure and leaves the outlines of the drawing more or less intact. Indeed, the outlines of several of the drawings have been indented with a stylus, including the study for *Queen Jane Seymour* and the drawing of *Lady Butts* (1532–45; Windsor Castle, Royal Lib.), where the dimensions again correspond with the painted portrait (1543; Boston, MA, Isabella Stewart Gardner Mus.). Infra-red photographs and reflectograms provide further evidence of the way in which Holbein then worked up his portrait. These reveal, for instance, that Holbein began to work on his panel of *Lady Butts* using a mixture of chalk and brushwork; only the outlines of the drawing were carefully copied, and the details of the features were more freely rendered using the drawing as a reference; this can be seen clearly by comparing the numbers of wrinkles around Lady Butts's eyes, which are fewer in the painting than in the drawing. A painted portrait for which no drawing survives, of *Nicholas Kratzer*, can be seen with

5. Hans Holbein (ii): *Portrait of an Unidentified Man*, black and coloured chalks, and ink applied with pen and brush, on pink-primed paper, 272×210 mm, *c.* 1534 (Windsor, Windsor Castle, Royal Library)

the aid of infra-red reflectography to be based on exquisitely fluid, yet controlled brush drawing. Another technique that Holbein is said by van Mander to have mastered in England is that of illumination, and several portrait miniatures are attributable to him, as well as initial letters in the *Canones Horoptri* (Oxford, Bodleian Lib.), a book presented to Henry VIII as a New Year's gift in 1529.

BIBLIOGRAPHY

K. van Mander: *Schilder-boeck* ([1603]–1604), fols 220*v*–224*r*

A. Woltmann: *Holbein und seine Zeit*, 2 vols (Leipzig, 1865; Eng. trans., London, 1872)

R. N. Wornum: *Some Aspects of the Life and Works of Hans Holbein, Painter, of Augsburg* (London, 1867)

E. His: 'Holbeins Verhältnisse zur Basler Reformation', *Repert. Kstwiss.*, ii (1879), pp. 156–9

M. F. S. Hervey: *Holbein's 'Ambassadors', the Picture and the Men: An Historical Study* (London, 1900)

L. Cust: 'John of Antwerp, Goldsmith, and Hans Holbein', *Burl. Mag.*, xxxi (1906), pp. 356–60

P. Ganz: *Hans Holbein der Jüngere des Meisters Gemälde*, Klass. Kst Gesamtausgaben, xx (Stuttgart, 1912)

A. B. Chamberlain: *Hans Holbein the Younger*, 2 vols (London, 1913) [also discusses careers of other members of the Holbein family]

H. Koegler: 'Holbeins Triumphzüge des Reichtums und der Armut', *Öff. Kstsamml. Basel, Jber.*, n. s., xxviii–xxix (1931–2), pp. 57–95

P. Ganz: *Die Handzeichnungen Hans Holbein der Jüngere: Kritischer Katalog* (Berlin, 1937)

C. Dodgson: 'Woodcuts Designed by Holbein for English Printers', *Walpole Soc.*, xxvii (1938), pp. 1–11

O. Kurz: 'Holbein and Others in a Seventeenth-century Collection', *Burl. Mag.*, lxxxiii (1943), pp. 279–82

O. Pächt: 'Holbein and Kratzer as Collaborators', *Burl. Mag.*, lxxxiv (1944), pp. 134–9

K. T. Parker: *The Drawings of Hans Holbein in the Collection of His Majesty the King at Windsor Castle* (London, 1945/*R* 1983)

H. A. Schmid: *Hans Holbein der Jüngere: Sein Aufstieg zur Meisterschaft und sein englischer Stil*, 3 vols (Basle, 1945–8)

P. Ganz: *The Paintings of Hans Holbein* (London, 1950)

F. Grossmann: 'Holbein, Torrigiano and Some Portraits of Dean Colet', *J. Warb. & Court. Inst.*, xiii (1950), pp. 203–26

——: 'Holbein Studies, I' *Burl. Mag.*, xciii (1951), pp. 39–44, 111–14

H. Rheinhardt: 'Die *Madonna* des Bürgermeisters Meyer von Hans Holbein dem Jüngeren: Nachforschungen zur Entstehungsgeschichte und Aufstellung des Gemäldes', *Z. Schweiz. Archäol. & Kstgesch.*, xv (1954–5), pp. 244–54

H. von Einem: 'Holbeins *Christus im Grabe*', *Öff. Kstsamml. Basel, Jber.* (1961), pp. 51–8

F. Grossmann: 'A Religious Allegory by Holbein the Younger', *Burl. Mag.*, ciii (1961), pp. 491–4

H. Krummacher: 'Zu Holbeins Bildnisse rheinischer Stahlhofkaufleute', *Wallraf-Richartz-Jb.*, xxv (1963), pp. 181–92

R. Strong: 'Holbein's Cartoon for the Barber-Surgeons Group Rediscovered: A Preliminary Report', *Burl. Mag.*, lv (1963), pp. 4–14

——: *Holbein and Henry VIII* (London, 1967)

——: *Tudor and Jacobean Portraits*, London, N.P.G. cat., 2 vols (London, 1969)

G. Kreytenberg: 'Hans Holbein d. J.: Die Wandgemälde im Basler Ratssaal', *Z. Kstwiss.*, xxiv (1970), pp. 181–92

R. Salvini and H. W. Grohn: *L'opera pittorica completa di Holbein il giovane* (Milan, 1971)

H. Rheinhardt: 'Ein unbekannter Holzschnitt Hans Holbeins d. J. von 1536 und Holbeins Melanchthon Bildnis', *Z. Schweiz. Archäol. & Kstgesch.*, xxxii (1975), pp. 135–40

'The King's Good Servant': Sir Thomas More, 1477/8–1535 (exh. cat., ed. J. B. Trapp and H. S. Herbrüggen; London, N.P.G., 1977–8)

Holbein and the Court of Henry VIII (exh. cat., London, Queen's Gal., 1978–9)

S. Foister: *Drawings by Holbein from the Royal Library, Windsor Castle* (London, 1983) [text vol. accompanying facsimiles of drgs]

J. Rowlands: *Holbein: The Paintings of Hans Holbein the Younger, Complete Edition* (Oxford, 1985) [with bibliog.]

Les Peintures de Hans Holbein le jeune au Louvre (exh. cat., ed. E. Foucart-Walter; Paris, Louvre, 1985)

L. Campell: 'Holbein's Miniature of *Mrs Pemberton*: The Identity of the Sitter', *Burl. Mag.*, cxxix (1987), pp. 366–71

Drawings by Holbein for the Court of Henry VIII (exh. cat. by J. Roberts, Houston, Mus. F.A., 1987)

Hans Holbein d.J.: Zeichnungen aus dem Kupferstichkabinett der Öffentlichen Kunstsammlung Basel (exh. cat. by C. Müller, Basle, Kstmus., 1988)

The Age of Durer and Holbein: German Drawings, 1400–1550 (exh. cat. by J. Rowlands and G. Bartrum, London, BM, 1988)

M. Ainsworth: ' "Paternes for Phiosioneamyes": Holbein's Portraiture Reconsidered', *Burl. Mag.*, cxxxii (1990), pp. 173–86

J. Rowlands and G. Bartrum: *Drawings by German Artists in the Department of Prints and Drawings in the British Museum: The Fifteenth Century and the Sixteenth Century by Artists born before 1530*, 2 vols (London, 1993)

SUSAN FOISTER

Holden, Charles (Henry) (*b* Great Lever, Bolton, Lancs, 12 May 1875; *d* Harmer Green, Herts, 1 May 1960). English architect. His childhood was overshadowed by the bankruptcy of his father's drapery business and the death of his mother when he was eight years old. He attended various schools and found work as a clerk in a railway store and as a laboratory assistant in a chemical works. His architectural career began when he went to work for his brother-in-law, Frederick Green, a land-surveyor in Bolton. He was apprenticed to E. W. Leeson, a Manchester architect, and studied at the School of Art and Technical College in Manchester, with such success that he soon took charge of a class. At the same period (*c.* 1896) Holden contributed designs to the *Building News* Designing Club, under the pseudonym 'The Owl', which reveal his grasp of architectural form. Among his Manchester circle of friends were the painter and etcher Francis Dodd (1874–1949) and his brother-in-law, the etcher and draughtsman Muirhead Bone. Bone and his brother, James, remained lifelong friends.

Holden worked briefly with Jonathan Simpson (1851–1937) in Bolton before coming to London in 1897 as assistant to C. R. Ashbee. He disliked the 'talk about art with a capital "A"' and in 1899 joined Percy Adams (1865–1930) as his assistant. Famous for hospital planning, Adams provided the basis of specialized expertise on which Holden constructed some of the masterpieces of Edwardian architecture. The Belgrave Hospital for Children, Clapham Road, south London (1900–03), shows Holden in his early, elemental style in brick. The King Edward VII Sanatorium, Midhurst, Sussex (1903–4), is more rural in its tile-hanging, yet tightly controlled in form, with a notable free-standing chapel. Other hospital designs included the Seamen's Hospital, Constantinople (now Istanbul), Turkey (1903–4), and the Women's Hospital, Soho, London (1908).

Holden's typical style of massed volumes and receding planes was given a classical character in the Law Society Extension, Chancery Lane, London (1902–4). He returned to a 'free Tudor' style for the Bristol Central Library (1906), won in competition. Using the topography and historical associations of the site, Holden's building is undemonstrative but full of drama and interest, with a classical interior. The formalized randomness of the rear elevation may have influenced Charles Rennie Mackintosh in the later part of the Glasgow School of Art (1905–6).

In partnership with Adams from 1907, Holden designed the British Medical Association (now Zimbabwe House), The Strand, London (1907–8; see fig.). Here classicism is reduced to geometric forms with a sense of mannerist

Charles Holden: British Medical Association building, London, 1907–8 (now Zimbabwe House)

irrationality, apparently incomplete. The controversial sculptures were commissioned by Holden from Jacob Epstein, with whom he also collaborated on the tomb of Oscar Wilde (1911–12) in Père Lachaise cemetery, Paris. This phase of Holden's career included the Royal Infirmary, Bristol (1906–12), and further hospital work. The firm became Adams, Holden & Pearson after Lionel G. Pearson (1879–1953) joined as a partner in 1913, the year in which Holden visited the USA.

While recognizably an early Modernist, having affinities even with Adolf Loos, Holden continued to use historical forms. Sutton Valence School, Kent (1914–25), is built in the tradition of Philip Webb, while King's College for Women, Kensington, west London (1914–23), is straightforwardly classical. As one of the architects to the Imperial War Graves Commission, in 1918 and 1920–26, Holden typically avoided grand gestures but produced sensitive, small-scale designs, as at Corbie, Somme, France (1918–22). He also designed the War Memorial Gateway at Clifton College, Bristol (1922).

Holden was a member of the Art Workers' Guild from 1917. Two years before, he had met Frank Pick (1878–1941), the administrator of Underground Electric Railways (later London Passenger Transport Board), with whom he was involved in the foundation of the Design and Industries Association. Pick was an inspired administrator, sharing Holden's puritanical tastes. Holden designed the new stations on the southern extension of the Northern line (1924), as variations on a theme, clad in Portland stone and without ornament, although in recognizably traditional forms. The stations were part of a consistent styling of all buildings, trains and fittings of the Underground. The underground ticket hall of Piccadilly Circus station (1926–8) was an elegant solution to the complex problem of providing exits to the many streets that converge at Piccadilly Circus. At the same time Holden began the design of a new headquarters for the Underground at 55 Broadway, Westminster, London (1927–30). Providing access to St James's Park station below, the offices rose in a cruciform shape derived from hospital planning. Sculpture by Epstein, Eric Gill, Henry Moore and others was provided on Holden's insistence.

In 1930 Holden and Pick travelled to Germany, the Netherlands and Scandinavia to see new architecture in preparation for the design of new stations on the Piccadilly line. The strong Dutch influence is apparent in Sudbury Town station (1931), the prototype design, 'a brick box with a concrete lid'. The simple masses and brick surfaces of these stations contrast with the earlier modelled shapes in Portland stone. The station at Arnos Grove (1932–3) reflects the Stockholm City Library by Gunnar Asplund with its cylindrical drum rising from a square base. The buildings originated a style that was used by all other architects working for London Transport in the 1930s.

Holden's largest commission was for the University of London Senate House, Malet Street, London (1931–8). For this major public building Holden returned to Portland stone, the weathering of which he understood particularly well. The massing of the parts of the building round a fin-shaped tower was ruled partly by the need for natural lighting and partly by the desire for a flexible shell for the building, with no risk of structural deterioration. It formed part of an unfinished scheme for London University to create a 'spine' of building extending northwards from the Senate House. The sculpture by means of which Holden wanted to humanize the otherwise impersonal building was never executed. Instead of his 'spine' scheme, Holden designed a number of brick buildings for the university in Torrington Square, Woburn Square and other places. Like other postwar products of the firm, they are well-constructed but bland. Holden also worked on planning schemes for the City of London (with William Holford) and for the South Bank of the Thames (superseded by other plans).

Holden was a man of austere habits. He twice declined a knighthood, believing that architecture was a collaborative effort. His knowledge of traditional materials and construction and his practical sympathy towards other artists stemmed from the Arts and Crafts tradition, while his large unornamented buildings reflect Modernism from outside its mainstream.

BIBLIOGRAPHY

DNB

C. H. Reilly: 'Charles Holden', *Builder*, cxli (1931), pp. 396–401

N. Pevsner: 'Patient Progress: The Life Work of Frank Pick', *Studies in Art, Architecture and Design*, ii (London, 1968), pp. 190–209

C. Hutton: 'Dr Charles Holden', *Artifex*, iii (1969), pp. 35–53

B. Hanson: 'Singing the Body Electric with Charles Holden', *Archit. Rev.* [London], clviii (1975), pp. 349–56

N. Pevsner: 'Charles Holden's Early Works', *Edwardian Architecture and its Origins*, ed. A. Service (London, 1975), pp. 386–92

G. Stamp and J. Harris: *Silent Cities* (London, 1977)

C. Barman: *The Man who Built London Transport* (Newton Abbot, Devon, 1979)

R. Cork: *Art beyond the Gallery* (London and New Haven, 1985)

E. Karol and F. Allibone: *Charles Holden, Architect, 1875–1960* (London, 1988)

ALAN POWERS

Holdermann, Georg (*b* Nuremberg, *bapt* 28 Aug 1585; *d* Nuremberg, 19 Sept 1629). German wax-modeller. He was probably first apprenticed to his father, a goldsmith. After 1614 he was referred to not as a goldsmith, but as a 'contrefecter', that is, a wax-modeller. His small-scale and medium-sized works were signed with the monogram G.H., or with *Holdermann fec*. In 1612 he produced a small wax relief with busts of the *Holy Roman Emperor Matthias and Empress Anne* in Spanish court costume (Munich, Bayer. Nmus.), probably commemorating their visit to Nuremberg in that year. His principal work is a wax relief panel with portrait medallions of seven members of the Nuremberg council of 1611 (Nuremberg, Ger. Nmus.). The seven portraits are arranged on a rectangular slate slab in pairs, with a single medallion at the bottom; this is surrounded by a richly ornamented, ivory-coloured frame, studded with numerous figures, decorated with red and white wax beads and gilded. At its base is a view of Nuremberg held by two genii. The portraits of the councillors, set in front of curtains, are enclosed by rich, delicately worked frames, resembling goldsmiths' work. About 16 years later Holdermann produced a second, similar relief panel, with the busts of the council members of 1625–7 (Nuremberg, Ger. Nmus.). A further portrait of a councillor is a relief of *Ulrich von Altenhann* (1627; London, Wallace), showing him in a detailed interior, possibly a council chamber.

BIBLIOGRAPHY

E. J. Pyke: *A Biographical Dictionary of Wax Modellers* (Oxford, 1973)
R. Büll: *Das grosse Buch vom Wachs*, i (Munich, 1977), pp. 446, 452, 482, fig. 242
C. Diemer: 'Georg Holdermann und Heinrich Kramer', *Anz. Ger. Nmus.* (1979), pp. 121–40

ELISABETH GUROCK

Hole [Holle], **William** (*b* before 1600; *d* 1624). English engraver. He was an accomplished engraver by 1607, as can be seen in his title page for a new edition, published in London, of the 'Breeches Bible' first published in Geneva in 1560. This exuberant design suggests that Hole was familiar with contemporary French work, although many of his portraits are nevertheless dreary and provincial. Hole's principal contribution to the art of engraving in England is to be found in the rare score book *Parthenia, or the Maydenhead of the First Musicke that ever was Printed for the Virginalls* (1612; example London, BL), which contains music by William Byrd, Dr John Bull and Orlando Gibbons. This is the first example in England of intaglio engraving on copperplate being used to print music, which hitherto had been carried out by means of movable type or blocks. Other work Hole undertook about this time includes the title page for Thomas Coryat's *Crudities* (1611), a popular travelogue, a *Map of Virginia* based on information and designs supplied by Captain John Smith, and a series of maps for Michael Drayton's massive topographical poem *Polyolbion* (1612, 1622). Additional literary works for which he supplied engravings include the title page for Ben Jonson's *Workes* (1616) and a frontispiece portrait bust of the poet and translator George Chapman for his *Whole Works of Homer* (1616). In 1618 Hole was appointed chief engraver for the Mint in London, a post he retained until his death; English coinage stamped during this period is of modest quality. There are examples of Hole's work as a line-engraver in the British Museum, London.

BIBLIOGRAPHY

DNB
A. M. Hind: *The Reign of James I* (1955), ii of *Engraving in England in the Sixteenth and Seventeenth Centuries* (Cambridge, 1952–64), pp. 316–40
R. T. Godfrey: *Printmaking in Britain: A General History from its Beginnings to the Present Day* (Oxford, 1979), p. 17

CHRISTOPHER FOLEY

Holford, Sir Robert Stayner (*b* 16 March 1808; *d* London, 22 Feb 1892). English patron, collector and arboriculturist. The fortune he inherited in 1838 allowed him to collect on a grand scale. In 1853 he married Mary Anne Lindsay, the cousin of Alexander, Lord Lindsay. He played a leading part in the foundation of the Burlington Fine Arts Club in 1857.

Holford bought widely from William Buchanan, William Blundell Spence and at the sale of the Aylesford Collection. Waagen thought his picture collection second only to that of the Marquis of Hertford and superior in breadth of taste. Holford acquired Renaissance and Baroque paintings from Italy and the Low Countries, for example Pesellino's *Virgin and Child with Six Saints* (*c*. 1445–50; New York, Met.) and Aelbert Cuyp's *Dordrecht on the Maas* (early 1660s; Ascott, Bucks, NT). Outstanding among his many portraits (which included five by Rembrandt) were van Dyck's *Cesare Alessandro Scaglia* (*c*. 1634–5; Viscount Camrose priv. col.) and Rubens's portrait drawing of *Isabella Brandt* (*c*. 1622; London, BM). His collection was sold between 1927 and 1929; many of the Italian paintings are in the Ringling Museum, Sarasota, FL. Holford also owned Old Master drawings, Rembrandt etchings (sold at Christie's, 11–14 July 1893) and a superb collection of medieval manuscripts, including the 14th-century *Bible historiée* (New York, Pub. Lib.), which inspired William Morris and Edward Burne-Jones.

To Holford, architecture was the first of the arts, and much of his collection was bought to suit its setting. He commissioned Lewis Vulliamy (1791–1871) to build Dorchester House (1848–63; destr. 1929), London, a vast Italianate palazzo. Holford was one of the few Victorian patrons to appreciate the genius of Alfred Stevens, who was employed from *c*. 1856 to design a complete decorative scheme for the Dorchester House dining-room (fireplace, cartoons and drawings in London, V&A; papers in London, RIBA Lib.). Holford also chose Vulliamy to build his country house, Westonbirt (1863–70), Glos, in an Elizabethan style based on Robert Smythson's Wollaton Hall (begun 1580), Notts, and he devoted much of his time to planting the famous arboretum in the gardens there.

BIBLIOGRAPHY

G. Waagen: *Treasures of Art in Great Britain*, ii (London, 1854), pp. 193–222
The Holford Collection (London, 1924)
The Holford Collection: Dorchester House, 2 vols (London, 1927)
C. Hussey: 'Dorchester House', *Country Life*, lxiii (5 and 12 May 1928), pp. 646–53, 684–90
J. Lees-Milne: 'Westonbirt House, Gloucestershire', *Country Life*, cli (18 and 25 May 1972), pp. 1226–9, 1310–13

A. N. L. Munby: *Connoisseurs and Medieval Miniatures, 1750–1850* (Oxford, 1972), pp. 147–50

OLIVER GARNETT

Holford, William (Graham) (*b* Johannesburg, 22 March 1907; *d* London, 17 Oct 1975). British urban planner and architect. He was brought up in South Africa in a Methodist family of English descent. He went to Britain in 1925, attracted by the prospectus of the Liverpool School of Architecture. Guided by the principal, Charles H. Reilly, and others, he assimilated both the classicizing and modernizing influences at work in the school; he developed self assurance and became a fine draughtsman. A short spell in the USA (1929) followed by three years in Rome on a RIBA scholarship (1930–33) deepened Holford's respect for Antiquity while quickening his appetite for a socially based approach to architecture and planning.

On Reilly's retirement in 1933 Holford secured a lectureship at Liverpool. In 1935, although inexperienced, he succeeded Patrick Abercrombie as Lever Professor of Civic Design. There were many opportunities for planners at that time, and in 1936 Holford was invited to design the Team Valley Trading Estate, Gateshead, pioneering a government-backed building programme to combat unemployment. Holford's organizational abilities and the simple symmetrical rationality of his Team Valley scheme led to his wartime appointment as head of a multi-disciplinary team to construct an ordnance factory and hostels for munitions workers (1940–42) at Kirkby. He also won a key position in the Office of Works with responsibility for planning post-World War II reconstruction.

Holford's years (1941–7) in what became the Ministry of Town and Country Planning were crucial for British planning. He brought in architectural allies and friends and set a sane but firm mark on the context for post-war urban development, including the New Towns policy. However, inter-disciplinary squabbles and inter-departmental jealousies precluded a national framework for planning. Perhaps for that reason he concentrated in his post-war career on urban layout. His longest involvement was with the City of London (from 1945), but with Myles Wright he also produced the plan for Corby, one of the more problematic New Towns, and a scheme for Cambridge. Many planning consultancies and commissions followed, in most of which Holford assumed the leading role. Two great issues in London planning exercised Holford in the 1950s and 1960s but in the long term failed to enhance his reputation: one was the layout of the environs of St Paul's Cathedral and the other, the replanning of Piccadilly Circus where Holford was called in to reconcile the interests of the speculator and the motor car with the desire for imaginative urban space. Here he valiantly upheld the civic ideal, and although his schemes were not realized, they saved Piccadilly Circus from complete destruction.

Holford's own architectural practice was divided among several offices. In those post-war projects that interested him such as the University of Exeter (from 1955), a residue of Liverpool classicism is discernible but in general Holford's production was neither distinctive nor crude and overweening. His organizational talents were deployed well in his presidency of the RIBA (1960–62), then on the threshold of reform. Holford sympathized with the demands of public-sector architects for technical and managerial reorganization, and he was brilliant at contriving compromise. In such roles he saw himself as an architect of institutions, not of buildings. However, the structures he built up enjoyed scant permanence. Holford's intelligence and breadth shine through his correspondence. Although his planning ability impressed his contemporaries, it did not outlive him.

BIBLIOGRAPHY
G. E. Cherry and J. L. Penny: *Holford: A Study in Architecture, Planning and Civic Design* (London, 1986)

□

Holgate, Edwin H(eadley) (*b* Allandale, Ont., 19 Aug 1892; *d* Montreal, 21 May 1977). Canadian painter and woodcutter. He studied under William Brymner at the Art Association of Montreal and in 1912 went to Paris, where he enrolled at the Académie de la Grande Chaumière. After serving in the Canadian army during World War I he returned to Paris, continuing his studies at the Académie Colarossi (1921–2) under Adolph Milman, from whom he gained a dedication to meticulous craftsmanship that persisted throughout his career. He then returned to Montreal, where he taught wood-engraving at the Ecole des Beaux-Arts and exhibited with the Beaver Hall Hill Group. His first recognition came in the mid-1920s with his woodcuts (e.g. *The Blacksmith*, 1928; Ottawa, N.G.). In 1926 Holgate accompanied A. Y. Jackson on a trip to British Columbia, sketching totem poles and Indian villages. He pursued his interest in West Coast native art in a commission to decorate a room at the Château Laurier Hotel, Ottawa: the Totem Pole Room (1929; destr., see Reid, fig. 3) featured totem-pole pillars and mountain-landscape murals. In 1931 Holgate became the eighth member of the GROUP OF SEVEN and with its dissolution in 1933 became a founder-member of its successor, the Canadian Group of Painters. Many of his most successful pictures were painted in the 1930s and 1940s in a figurative style that, although continuously refined, remained little changed. He is best known for his series of monumental nudes in landscape settings, begun in the 1930s. In *Nude* (1930; Toronto, A.G. Ont.; *see* CANADA, fig. 4), Holgate juxtaposed the fleshy, soft figure with the rocky lakeshore, while giving both the same treatment to create a uniform calm, controlled mood. His portraits (e.g. *Ludovine*, *c*. 1930; Ottawa, N.G.) are mostly close-up head and shoulder views and impress the viewer through their simplicity and directness. Holgate served as an Official War Artist in 1943–4 and on his return to Canada moved to the Laurentians to paint the local landscape (e.g. *Laurentian Cemetery*, 1949; Montreal, Mus. F.A.).

BIBLIOGRAPHY
Edwin Holgate: Paintings (exh. cat., Ottawa, N.G., 1975)
D. Reid: *Edwin H. Holgate* (Ottawa, 1976)

ALEXANDRA PEL

Holguín, Melchor Pérez de (*b* Cochabamba, Bolivia, *c*. 1665; *d* Potosí, *c*. 1730). Bolivian painter. In 1693 he was working in Potosí, Bolivia, the Spanish empire's largest city and most important centre of mining. He was highly esteemed and developed a characteristic style that emphasizes the facial features. His images of saints, mystics and ascetics reflect the religious ideals of the Hispano-American Baroque. He signed many of his paintings and portrayed himself in some of them, for example the *Last Judgement* (1708; Potosí, S Lorenzo).

In his early works he depicted ascetic saints famed for their acts of charity, such as *Fray Pedro de Alcántara* and *St Juan de Dios* (both La Paz, Mus. N. A.), using grey tones. At the end of the 17th century he incorporated a wider range of colours into his paintings and began to work on a larger scale, as in the *Last Judgement*, which includes scenes of the *Glory* and *Hell*. This theme became popular throughout the Viceroyalty, with compositions of this type appearing in rural highland churches, such as those at Carabuco and Casquiaviri. Holguín later began his series of *Evangelists* (Potosí, Convent of S Francisco). Among the best are the half-length *St Matthew* (Potosí, Mus. N. Casa Moneda), the series (1724) after engravings by Marten de Vos and those in the Museo Nacional, La Paz. His most famous painting, the *Entry into Potosí of the Viceroy Diego Morcillo* (1716; Madrid, Mus. América), shows a good example of the sumptuous Baroque festivals held by the imperial city. Late works depict the infancy of Christ, such as in the *Rest on the Flight into Egypt* (*c.* 1715; La Paz, Mus. N. A.). Holguín's work was extremely influential; his paintings were copied in the 19th century, and in documents he is sometimes described as 'Brocha de Oro'. Among his disciples were Gaspar Miguel de Berrío (*b* Potosí, 1706) and two later painters only known as Ecoz and Carabel.

BIBLIOGRAPHY

J. de Mesa and T. Gisbert: *Holguín y la pintura virreinal en Bolivia* (La Paz, 1977)
J. Bernales Ballesteros: *Historia del arte hispano-americano, siglos XVI al XVIII* (Madrid, 1987)
L. Castedo: *Historia del arte ibero-americano* (Madrid, 1988)
D. Bayon: *Historia del arte sudamericano* (Barcelona, 1989)

TERESA GISBERT

Holics Ceramics Factory. Hungarian ceramics manufactory. It was established in Holics (Holitsch; now Holíč, Slovakia) by Emperor Francis I in 1743. It supplied the aristocracy with faience dinner-services and ornamental table decorations. French artists and managers were employed at the factory. A variety of products were manufactured in the late Baroque, Rococo and Neo-classical styles. Enamelled tureens in the shape of cabbages and bunches of asparagus or wares decorated with scattered flowers indicate the influence from Strasbourg (e.g. coffeepot, 1750–60; Brno, Morav. Mus.). Meissen was also influential as were the high-fired wares from Castelli decorated with landscapes and figures. Chinoiseries and idyllic scenes can be attributed to the outstanding painter János Radiel (*fl c.* 1770–1806; e.g. pot-pourri vase, 1770; Budapest, Mus. Applied A.). Figures were influenced by the Vienna porcelain factories. The factory also made tiled stoves, furniture (e.g. cradle, 1775; Budapest, Mus. Applied A.) and jewellery-boxes in the shape of a chest-of-drawers. Religious figures such as the Maria Immaculata by Antal Schwaiger (?1728–?1802) were also made (*see also* HUNGARY, fig. 19). After 1792 Holics produced creamware (lead-glazed earthenware) after Viennese and English designs.

BIBLIOGRAPHY

A. Kiss: *Baroque Faience in Hungary* (Budapest, 1965)

FERENC BATÁRI

Holiday, Henry (George Alexander) (*b* London, 17 June 1839; *d* London, 15 April 1927). English stained-glass artist, painter and illustrator. He studied painting in London at Leigh's Art School and the Royal Academy Schools, where he was influenced by Pre-Raphaelitism. Contact with Dante Gabriel Rossetti's circle and the architect William Burges introduced him to the applied arts, and from 1863 he worked primarily as a stained-glass artist, particularly in collaboration with the glass manufacturers James Powell & Sons and Heaton, Butler & Bayne. After visiting Italy in 1867 he abandoned his early Pre-Raphaelite style for one inspired by Classical and Renaissance art, aiming to create a 'modern' style of stained glass no longer dependent on medievalism. His memorial window (1868) to the engineer Isambard Kingdom Brunel in Westminster Abbey and the complete glazing scheme (1869–75) of St Mary Magdalene, Paddington, London, illustrate the expressive figure drawing and feeling for monumental scale characteristic of all his mature work. In 1891, dissatisfied with the working methods of the commercial stained-glass firms, he established his own workshop in Hampstead, London, and experimented successfully with making pot-metal glass. Many of Holiday's later commissions were for American churches; his windows (1898–1925) in Holy Trinity, Manhattan, New York, reveal the influence of the Arts and Crafts Movement in their emphatic leading and use of richly textured glass. As a painter Holiday is best known for his *Dante and Beatrice* (1883; Liverpool, Walker A.G.); his most important illustrations are those for Lewis Carroll's *The Hunting of the Snark* (1876). He also produced graphics in support of such social and political causes as Dress Reform and Irish Home Rule. In 1892 he became editor of *Aglaia*, the journal of the Healthy and Artistic Dress Union, contributing articles and illustrations.

WRITINGS

Stained Glass as an Art (London, 1896)
Reminiscences of my Life (London, 1914)

BIBLIOGRAPHY

A. L. Baldry: *Henry Holiday* (London, 1930)
Henry Holiday, 1839–1927 (exh. cat. by P. Cormack, London, William Morris Gal., 1989)

PETER CORMACK

Holl (i). German family of masons, builders and architects. Jakob Holl (*b* Augsburg, 1413; *d* Augsburg, 1487) was a master mason, as was his son Sebastian Holl (*b* Augsburg, 1482; *d* Augsburg, 1545). Sebastian's son (1) Johannes Holl I worked as a master mason and master builder, and his own four sons, Johannes Holl II (*b* Augsburg, 1542; *d* before 1594), Jonas Holl (*b* Augsburg, 1546; *d* Augsburg, 1624), (2) Elias Holl I and Esaias Holl (*b* Augsburg, 1580), also became masons in their turn. Of the four, (2) Elias Holl I attained the greatest eminence. His talent, industry and skill were employed at a time when a considerable number of important new public buildings were being constructed in Augsburg, the capital city of Swabia. Elias Holl II (*b* Augsburg, 1611), son of (2) Elias Holl I, left his mason's apprenticeship to become a painter, while four of his brothers became goldsmiths: Christoph Holl (*b* Augsburg, 1619; *d* Augsburg, 1651), Johannes Holl III (*b* Augsburg, 1597; *d c.* 1615), Christian Holl (*b* Augsburg, 1627) and Jeronimus Holl (*b* Augsburg, 1614). Of the other sons of (2) Elias Holl I, Johannes Holl IV (*b* Augsburg, 1616) became a cabinetmaker, and Mattäus Holl (*b* 1620), who was released from his apprenticeship as a clockmaker in 1638, later worked as a master builder in Scandinavia. The most valuable source for the life and work of the Holl family of master builders up to the time of (2) Elias Holl I is a manuscript family chronicle, *Die Hauschronik der Familie Holl* (Augsburg, Staats- & Stadtbib., MA. 4° Cod. Aug. 82, old 899), apparently begun by (1) Johannes Holl I and continued by (2) Elias Holl I and his descendants.

(1) Johannes [Hans] **Holl I** (*b* Augsburg, 1512; *d* Augsburg, 1 Jan 1594). Obliged to supplement his income until the 1550s by working as a brewer and baker, he later received many commissions: more than 60 buildings that he executed or supervised are documented. Of those he designed for local citizens, artisans, tradesmen and even members of patrician families, few have survived. However, the vaulting on the ground floor of the Pemerhaus in what is today Maximilianstrasse and the three-bay entrance hall of the Köpfhaus in Philippine Welser-Strasse, built *c.* 1578 for the merchant Melchior Hainhofer, are surviving examples of his work. In December 1573 the brothers Markus Fugger (1529–97), Jakob Fugger and Hans Fugger, from the vastly influential family of patrons, appointed Holl as their builder. He worked principally for the Fugger family from that date while accepting other major commissions, for example the monastery church of Maria Stern (1576), on which he collaborated with Michael Herbst, who worked as a foreman, and his son Jonas Holl. The church tower combines forms of both Late Gothic and Renaissance character. At the evangelical college of St Anna (1581) Holl built a courtyard with three superimposed arcades (destr.). He was also contracted for the building of the Jesuitenkollegium (1581) under the patronage of the Fugger brothers. Most of the exteriors of his

structures, which include service buildings, follow Augsburg tradition in their lack of decoration and of individual stylistic details.

(2) Elias Holl I (*b* Augsburg, 28 Feb 1573; *d* Augsburg, 6 Jan 1646). Son of (1) Johannes Holl I. By the age of 13 he was already working on one of his father's projects, and two years later, in 1588, he collaborated with him on the Stenglinhaus. Aged 17, and a mason's apprentice, he assisted his father at the Mehrer house, Augsburg, by modelling the plaster and terracotta ornamentation on the oriel there (1590). It is not known whether he personally carved the moulds for this, or whether he cast from those supplied by others. He finished his mason's apprenticeship under his father's tutelage, but did not obtain his mastership until 25 May 1596. At the end of that year Holl was already working with six journeymen, an indication that he was being kept busy with commissions. Besides extensions and rebuilding projects for patrician families in Augsburg, he was also occupied with schemes outside the city, for example for the Ilsung family in Kissing (1595) and the Fuggers in Wellenburg (1597). In 1598–9 he completely rebuilt a large house with a courtyard for the merchant Hieronymus Harter, and in 1599 he began to build another large house of similar plan, which he decorated himself using his own hand-carved moulds, for the merchant Anton Garb, who invited Elias to accompany him on a visit to Venice. They departed on 18 November 1600, staying for a few days in Bolzano before travelling on to Venice. By 31 January 1601 Holl was back in Augsburg: 'Had a good look round Venice . . . marvellous things that will surely be useful to me in my building work', is his only recorded comment on the visit. However, an Italian influence is present in the new hall for the Beckenhaus (Augsburg bakers' guild), which Holl may have designed in 1601 (destr. 1944). His first commission, at the beginning of 1601, was the rapid rebuilding, with thick walls and broad vaults, of a foundry that had been destroyed by fire shortly before. His next project was to build a new tower for the church of St Anna (1602). Meanwhile, the rebuilding of an arsenal, which was already under way, had run into difficulties under the direction of the Civic Architect, Jacob Eschay. Holl was commissioned

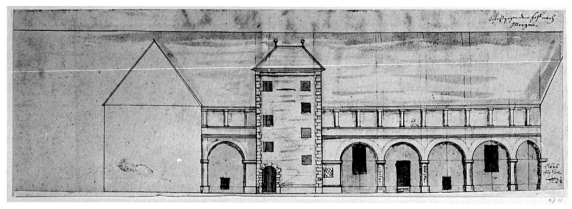

1. Elias Holl I: drawing of the south-east wing of the courtyard, Heilig-Geist-Spital, pen and ink and blue wash, 170×526 mm, *c.* 1626 (Augsburg, Graphische Sammlung im Schaezlerpalais)

to write a report on and rectify the damage: as a result of this report, on 8 July 1602, he was appointed the new Civic Architect. In this capacity, Holl was responsible for all municipal building plans in preparation, for calculations, administration, acquisition of materials and execution. He was subordinate to the Board of Works of the Patriciate, which apparently gave him frequent guidance as to the iconography and hence the formal design of municipal buildings. After his appointment, Holl built the new arsenal (1602–7), the Siegelhaus (1604–6; destr. 1809), the abattoir (1609) in the style of an Italian palazzo with a German gable, the Kaufhaus (Staple House; 1611), the Barfüsser Bridge with its shops (from 1611) and the St Anna-Gymnasium (1612–16). He supervised the heightening of the Perlachturm (1614) and the building of the Heilig-Geist-Spital (1625–30; see fig. 1), with its arcaded court-yard and groin-vaulted halls. He also directed water supply and fortification projects, notably the redesigning of the town gate-towers.

Holl's greatest achievement is undoubtedly the Augs-burg Rathaus (1615–20; see fig. 2 and AUGSBURG, fig. 2), a work with all traces of the Gothic eliminated. The nine-storey east front, divided into three vertical ranges, is articulated, save for two cornices, by the fenestration alone. This indicates at a glance the relative importance of the rooms behind: administrative offices and smaller public rooms at the sides, ceremonial halls in the middle, culminating in the Goldene Saal (destr. 1944; rest. 1982–93), which runs through three storeys and the whole depth of the building. The composition is framed by two towers, intended, in Holl's words, 'to achieve a bolder, more heroic appearance'. The *concetto* of the building in general seems to be animated by Cesare Cesariano's early 16th-century interpretation of the Vitruvian basilica. Holl also partici-pated ex officio in the planning of projects that were abandoned, including a loggia in Perlachplatz (1607–9) and the Heilig-Grab-Kapelle (*c*. 1604). He was also active in schemes outside Augsburg, including Schloss Schwar-zenberg in Franconia (1607), Willibaldsburg in Eichstätt (1609–10), with its high arcades surrounding a central court, and various monasteries and chapels. These in-cluded Mariahilf (*c*. 1602–3) at Klosterlechfeld, built on a centralized plan as a pilgrimage church and endowed by Regina Imhoff, who instructed Holl to take the Pantheon in Rome as his model. On 14 January 1631 Holl was dismissed from his post on religious grounds; he was reinstated in 1632 during the Swedish occupation of Augsburg and entrusted with work on the construction of fortifications, but he was dismissed again in 1635. For the last 11 years of his life he did little architectural work, although he still wrote reports and continued to produce his study of geometry and measurement, intended as a practical guide for prospective directors of building work.

Holl's early private buildings—the houses of the 1590s with their arcaded courtyards—are quite within the Augs-burg tradition, which Renaissance forms had begun to penetrate by the beginning of the 16th century; the Italian style of the new Fugger palaces must certainly have provided models for this process. It is probable that Holl received much stimulus and even technical advice in architectural matters from Josef Heintz I, a citizen of Augsburg from 1598 and painter at the imperial Court of

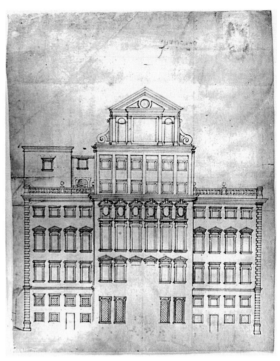

2. Elias Holl I: façade elevation of Augsburg Rathaus, pen and brown ink, 585×460 mm, 1618 (Augsburg, Graphische Sammlung im Schaezlerpalais)

Rudolf II. It was Heintz who, at the instigation of the authorities, designed the façades of Holl's first municipal work, the east front of the arsenal (1602) and the façade of the Siegelhaus (1604). He also collaborated with him on other major projects. After Heintz's death in 1609 the painter Johann Mathias Kager seems to have taken his place as a determining influence on Holl's style. Kager was, among other things, in charge of the magnificent furnishings and interior decoration of the Rathaus, and it is possible that he may have contributed ideas for the design of its architectural ornamentation.

Holl is credited with giving shape to the new Italian forms of the High Renaissance or early Baroque that his humanistically educated clients desired, to the best of his ability and on the basis of long-standing artisan tradition in Augsburg. He was the architect of one of the most superb and homogeneous town centres in Central Europe, built within two decades. For this task he made his own tools, developed new building techniques, drew up reliable structural calculations, prepared working drawings and planned and administered the execution of all building work. The 'new' architecture executed by Holl already incorporated features that are now termed early Baroque, but which were not further developed until long after the end of the Thirty Years War (1618–48).

UNPUBLISHED SOURCES
Augsburg, Schaezlerpal., MS. 11 216 [Elias Holl I: *Geometrie und Messbuch*]

WRITINGS
Hauschronik der Familie Holl (1656; pubd 1716, Augsburg, Staats- & Stadtbib., MS. 4° Cod. Aug. 82, old 899); ed. C. Meyer (Munich, 1910)

BIBLIOGRAPHY

Macmillan Enc. Architects; Thieme–Becker

J. Zimmer: 'Das Augsburger Rathaus und die Tradition', *Münchn. Jb. Bild. Kst*, xxviii (1977), pp. 191–218

B. Roeck: 'Anmerkungen zum Werk des Elias Holl: Über den Enstehungsprozess von Architektur im frühen 17. Jahrhundert', *Pantheon*, xli (1983), pp. 221–34

——: *Elias Holl: Architekt einer europäischen Stadt* (Regensburg, 1985), pp. 260–68

——: 'Der Holl-Bau des Gymnasiums bei St Anna: Sozial- und geistesgeschichtliche Implikationen eines Kunstwerks', *Nachrbl. Soc. Annensis E. V.* (1985), pp. 5–22

H.-W. Kruft and A.-R. Lepik: 'Das Geometrie- und Messbuch von Elias Holl', *Architectura*, xv (1985), pp. 1–12

Elias Holl und das Augsburger Rathaus (exh. cat., ed. W. Baer, H.-W. Kruft and B. Roeck; Augsburg, Stadtarchv, 1985)

J. Zimmer: *Joseph Heintz der Ältere* (Munich and Berlin, 1988)

JÜRGEN ZIMMER

Holl (ii). English family of artists. William Holl (1771–1838), a stipple-engraver of German origin, specialized in portrait engraving. His four sons, William Holl (1807–71), Henry Benjamin Holl (1808–84), Francis Holl (1815–84) and Charles Holl (1820–82) all practised as engravers, but William and Francis achieved greatest prominence. William, like his father, engraved many portraits for such publications as William and Edward Francis Finden's *Portraits of the Female Aristocracy of the Court of Queen Victoria* (London, 1838–9), and he also reproduced, in line and stipple, such celebrated paintings as William Powell Frith's *An English Merry-making* (exh. RA 1847; Elton Hall, Cambs), published in 1851 by the Art Union of London. Francis also engraved many portraits (after George Richmond, for example), but his outstanding achievement was the large line and mixed mezzotint plate reproducing Frith's *The Railway Station* (1862; Egham, U. London, Royal Holloway & Bedford New Coll.), declared for publication by Henry Graves & Co. in December 1862 and actually published in 1866. The most celebrated member of the family, however, was Francis's son (1) Frank Holl.

DNB

BIBLIOGRAPHY

ANTHONY DYSON

(1) Frank [Francis] **(Montague) Holl** (*b* London, 4 July 1845; *d* London, 31 July 1888). Painter and illustrator. He received his first art instruction from his father, Francis Holl. At the age of 15 he entered the Royal Academy Schools, where in 1862 he was awarded a silver medal for drawing and in 1863 the gold medal for a religious subject, *Abraham about to Sacrifice Isaac* (untraced). In 1864 he exhibited two paintings at the Royal Academy, where he continued to show his work regularly until his death. He was elected ARA in 1878 and RA in 1883.

Holl's first notable success was *The Lord Gave and the Lord Hath Taken Away* (exh. RA 1869; London, Guildhall), a dramatic social subject that depicts a bereaved family gathered at prayer in a humble cottage. The Royal Academy awarded Holl a travelling scholarship to Italy on the strength of this picture, but he remained abroad less than a year, preferring to paint British modern life rather than to study Renaissance masters. Queen Victoria, unable to purchase Holl's first exhibited success, commissioned *No Tidings from the Sea* (exh. RA 1871; Brit. Royal Col.). The morbidity of these and other works in which death

was a central theme, such as the funeral subjects *I am the Resurrection and the Life* (exh. RA 1872; Leeds, C.A.G.) and *Her First-born* (exh. RA 1876; Dundee, City Mus. & A.G.), was frequently criticized by the press. Reviewers often compared Holl's tragic impulse with that of his contemporary the Dutch painter Jozef Israëls, whose work was well known in England.

With Luke Fildes and Hubert von Herkomer, two artists with whom he worked at *The Graphic* from 1872 to 1876, Holl formed the nucleus of a school of social realism that flourished through the decade. In 1874 his 24 illustrations for Anthony Trollope's *Phineas Redux* were published in London. His social realist pictures, such as *Newgate: Committed for Trial* (exh. RA 1878; Egham, U. London, Royal Holloway & Bedford New Coll.), based on direct observation of conditions at Newgate Prison, were enormously popular with the exhibition-going public; his reputation was further enhanced by the sale of engravings after his paintings. In the late 1870s Holl turned increasingly to portraiture; in the decade preceding his death he painted an astonishing total of 198 portraits. Quilter considered him 'beyond all comparison the most popular of our living portrait painters', and his success in this genre was compared with that of Millais and G. F. Watts. His portraits, painted in the sombre hues and robust chiaroscuro of his idols Velázquez and Rembrandt, were almost exclusively of the great men of the age. Holl's financial success enabled him to commission from Richard Norman Shaw a house in Hampstead, The Three Gables (1881–2), in Old English style, and a country home, Burrows Cross (1885–6), near Comshall, Surrey. The artist's contemporaries considered that his early death from heart disease was caused by the overwork brought on by excessive portrait commissions.

BIBLIOGRAPHY

J. Dafforne: 'The Works of Frank Holl', *A. J.* [London], xxxviii (1876), pp. 9–12

W. Meynell: 'Our Living Artists: Frank Holl, ARA', *Mag. A.*, iii (1880), pp. 187–91

H. Quilter: 'In Memoriam: Frank Holl', *Univl Rev.*, i (1888), pp. 478–93

G. E. Campbell: 'Frank Holl and his Works', *A. J.* [London], li (1889), pp. 85–91

A. M. Reynolds: *The Life and Work of Frank Holl* (London, 1912)

Hard Times (exh. cat. by J. Treuherz and others, Manchester, C.A.G., 1987–8)

LEE M. EDWARDS

Holland. *See* NETHERLANDS, THE.

Holland, Henry (*b* Fulham, London, 20 July 1745; *d* Chelsea, London, 17 June 1806). English architect and designer. He was a contemporary of such architects as James Wyatt, George Dance (ii) and John Soane, yet he took little part in professional competition and concentrated on a comparatively limited number of commissions, most of which involved not only building and decoration but also the furnishing of principal rooms. Here he was to develop a distinctive style of elegant simplicity, strongly influenced by French examples. He was the eldest son of Henry Holland (1712–85), a successful builder, and received his training in the family firm, at that time engaged on several notable houses in London and the provinces. His name first appears in an account of 1767 for a house built at Sutton, Surrey. Two years later he was making drawings for additions to Hale House, Hants, and assisting his father on a number of building projects, in which he showed sufficient ability to be offered a form of partnership in 1770 by Capability Brown, the landscape gardener and architect. Brown had recently begun Claremont, Surrey, for Robert Clive, 1st Baron Clive of Passey, and required help with the interior decoration. This collaboration proved successful, and it was continued over the next few years at Benham Park (1774–5), Berks, Cadland (1775–8; destr.), Hants, and Berrington (1778–81; *see* COUNTRY HOUSE, fig. 4), Hereford & Worcs. It also led to Holland's marriage to Brown's elder daughter in 1773. Although they continued to work together from time to time until Brown's death in 1783, Holland set up an independent practice in 1776 when he designed a new clubhouse for William Brooks in St James's Street, London. This was soon to become a stronghold of the Whig aristocracy, from which Holland's future patrons were almost exclusively to be drawn.

The principal façade of Brooks's owes much to the north elevation of Claremont, with giant Corinthian pilasters set against Suffolk white brickwork, but the interior reveals the earliest example of the restraint that was to become characteristic of Holland's work. In the Great Subscription Room the walls and ceiling have minimal elaboration, and lofty pier-glasses between the east-facing windows and over the chimney-piece create an impression of lightness and space. In 1783 George, Prince of Wales (later George IV), became a member and by August had chosen Holland to remodel his new London residence, Carlton House (destr. 1827–8). Through the influence of his friend Louis-Philippe, Duke of Orléans, the Prince already had an interest in French architecture and decoration, one which he was to share with Holland. Earlier ceiling detail for Cadland indicates that Holland was by then familiar with Bernard de Montfaucon's *L'Antiquité expliquée*, but he now turned to more recent publications by such authors as Marie-Joseph Peyre, Pierre Patte (1723–1814) and Jacques Condoin. By the end of the year he had engaged two French émigrés, Jean-Pierre-Théodore Trécourt and Guillaume Gaubert, as draughtsman and clerk of the works respectively, and they were to be joined by several other French decorative painters and artisans. Holland unified the rambling exterior of Carlton House using horizontally rusticated masonry, with end blocks breaking forward on to the entrance front. The central *porte-cochère* was the first of its kind in England, and the forecourt itself was screened from Pall Mall by a low wall carrying paired Ionic columns, similar to those at the hôtels de Condé and de Salm in Paris. The interior was transformed into a sequence of rooms: those intended for state occasions were at the west end, while the private apartments, which were on a more intimate scale, faced south over the garden. The first stage was completed by 1785, when Horace William Walpole, 4th Earl of Orford, prophesied that the new palace 'will be the most perfect in Europe', though financial difficulties were to delay further work until 1787, when Parliament agreed to an additional £60,000 being spent. Meanwhile the Prince had acquired a small property in BRIGHTON, which Holland proceeded to enlarge. The 'marine pavilion' that emerged again displayed French influence, with a central dome set with columns in the manner of the Hôtel de Salm by Pierre Rousseau (1751–1810). (Holland's work was to be almost entirely obscured by the subsequent Oriental decoration by John Nash (i).) Also in 1787 Holland enlarged York (later Melbourne and subsequently Dover) House in Whitehall, London, for the Prince's younger brother, Frederick, Duke of York.

Apart from these royal commissions, Holland's major works of the 1780s were additions to Althorp House, Northants, for George, 2nd Earl Spencer (the Blue Boudoir with its wall panels was painted by T. H. Pernotin), and to Woburn Abbey, Beds, for Francis Russell, 5th Duke of Bedford. Although the Greek Doric portico, riding school and covered tennis court that he added to Woburn were demolished in 1954, his sculpture gallery and chinoiserie dairy remain. The long library (remodelled from a series of earlier rooms) with its white woodwork and ceilings is one of Holland's most successful interiors. Because Bedford also owned the land on which Drury Lane and Covent Garden theatres stood in London, Holland was chosen to remodel and redecorate them in the early 1790s. Both were burnt down some 15 years later, but surviving accounts and two sectional drawings (London, Soane Mus.) for the Drury Lane Theatre give some idea of the care Holland bestowed on the interior detailing. However, the most distinctive expression of his decorative style is Southill, Beds, remodelled for Samuel Whitbread between 1796 and 1800. Here the ceilings of the principal rooms were left unadorned or otherwise outlined with narrow borders of painted decoration. The ceiling in the boudoir was by Alexandre-Louis Delabrière, who had worked previously at Carlton House and at François-Joseph Bélanger's Bagatelle (1777) outside Paris.

In 1790 Holland was appointed Surveyor to the East India Company, in which capacity he completed the Company's new house in Leadenhall Street, London, and its extensive warehouse near by. After 1800 his only important private undertakings were Wimbledon Park House (destr. 1949), Surrey, for his previous client, Lord Spencer, and the conversion of Melbourne House (1803–4; now Albany), Piccadilly, to form residential suites, with additional apartments behind it built on either side of a long covered walk.

Concurrently with his architectural practice, Holland was involved in speculative building. Early in the 1770s he had taken a long lease on land in Chelsea from Charles, 2nd Baron Cadogan, where, in the course of the next 20 years, he was to lay out Hans Town, Sloane Street and Sloane Square. Most of the houses he built there have been replaced, including Sloane Place, the villa in a miniature landscape garden that he built for himself and where he displayed his collection of antique marbles.

BIBLIOGRAPHY

Colvin

D. Stroud: *Henry Holland* (London, 1950)

A. E. Richardson: *Southill: A Regency House* (London, 1951)

D. Stroud: *Henry Holland: His Life and Architecture* (London, 1966)

The Work of Henry Holland (exh. cat. by S. R. Houfe, Woburn Abbey, Beds, 1972) [privately printed]

DOROTHY STROUD

Holland, James (*b* Burslem, Staffs, 18 Oct 1799; *d* London, 12 Feb 1870). English painter. As a boy he was employed for seven years to paint flowers on pottery in the factory of John Davenport (*fl* 1793; *d* 1848) of Longport. In 1819 Holland moved to London, where he continued at first to work as a pottery painter but also undertook watercolours of flowers and natural history subjects, exhibiting his works at the Royal Academy from 1824. After 1828 oil paintings predominated over watercolours in the many pictures that he exhibited at the Royal Academy, the Society of Painters in Water-Colours (of which he was made an associate in 1835), the British Institution and the Society of British Artists. He travelled to Paris in 1831 and subsequently made repeated tours of the Continent. Buildings in European cities now became his favourite subject, and above all, scenes of Venice, which he first visited in 1835; his Venetian views have sometimes been confused with those by Richard Parkes Bonington. In 1837 he was commissioned by the *Landscape Annual* to make drawings in Portugal, which were engraved in the issue for 1839. He travelled again to Venice in 1845, 1851 and 1857, making sketches *en route* of the Low Countries, France, Switzerland and Austria. Other subjects favoured by Holland were Blackheath and Greenwich (both London), where he lived from 1830 to 1845. He was renowned for his fluent draughtsmanship and for his brilliant colouring in both oils and watercolours, making liberal use of gouache in the latter. The contents of his studio were auctioned at Christie's, London, on 26 May 1870.

BIBLIOGRAPHY
M. Tonkin: 'The Life of James Holland of the Old Society, 1799–1870', *Old Wtrcol. Soc. Club*, xlii (1967), pp. 35–47

PATRICK CONNER

Holland & Sons. English furniture-making firm. It was founded in 1803 by William Holland (*fl* 1803–43). From 1803 to 1843 the cabinetmakers and upholsterers William Holland and Stephen Taprell (*d* 1847) were in partnership. Their firm was called Taprell & Holland until 1835, Taprell, Holland & Son until 1843, and Holland & Sons after 1843. In 1851 the firm employed over 350 men. In 1852 it incorporated the prestigious firm of Thomas Dowbiggin (1788–1854), taking over its Mount Street premises in London. Holland & Sons received commissions for furnishing many of the government buildings and clubs built in 19th-century London, including the Athenaeum, the Reform Club, and the British Museum. The firm worked on many royal commissions, making furniture for Buckingham Palace, London, Windsor Castle, Berks, Osborne House, Isle of Wight, and Balmoral, Grampian. Holland & Sons exhibited a bookcase at the Great Exhibition of 1851, for which they won a prize, and continued to show at major exhibitions throughout the century. Best known for their Gothic Revival furniture, they also worked in other fashionable revival styles, including the Louis XV and XVI, Renaissance and Elizabethan. Holland & Sons were technical innovators, from the first using in their workshops the most modern machinery available. The firm remained under family control until it closed in 1942.

BIBLIOGRAPHY
S. Jervis: 'Holland and Sons, and the Furnishing of the Athenaeum', *Furn. Hist.*, vi (1970), pp. 43–61
E. T. Joy: 'Holland & Sons and the Furniture of Osborne House', *Antiques*, ic (1971), pp. 580–85
G. Beard and C. Gilbert, eds: *Dictionary of English Furniture Makers, 1660–1840* (London, 1986)

JULIA H. M. SMITH

Hollander, Jan de. *See* AMSTEL, JAN VAN.

Hollar, Wenceslaus [Vaclav, Wenzel] (*b* Prague, 23 July 1607; *d* London, 25 March 1677). Bohemian etcher, illustrator and draughtsman, active in Germany, Flanders and England. He was an outstanding draughtsman and etcher of landscapes and topographical views and as an etcher also excelled in still-life subjects, best exemplified by his prints of shells and of muffs dating from the 1640s. Both fields show his instinct for direct and accurate recording. However, much of his illustrative work, enormously varied in subject-matter, is of no better than workmanlike quality and has always tended to undermine his reputation. Although Hollar spent some 32 of his 52 years of working life in England and signed himself with the anglicized form Wenceslaus, he always considered himself Bohemian, appending to his signature throughout his career the name of his native country or city.

1. Background and early travels, before 1636. 2. London and Antwerp, 1636–52. 3. London and Tangier, 1652–77.

1. BACKGROUND AND EARLY TRAVELS, BEFORE 1636. His father was a Bohemian yeoman, knighted in 1600, whose social status probably enabled Hollar to become familiar with the distinguished imperial collection in Prague Castle. This then included paintings by Albrecht Dürer, Lucas van Leyden, Pieter Bruegel I, Paul Bril and Adam Elsheimer, and paintings, prints and miniatures by artists employed at the court, including Jan Breughel, Roelandt Savery, Joris Hoefnagel and Jacob Hoefnagel (1575–*c*. 1630). These works, predominantly landscapes and still-lifes, are characterized by passionate observation of nature and great attention to detail, qualities foremost in Hollar's own work. Many were reproduced by the principal court engraver, Aegidius Sadeler II, from whom Hollar may have received early instruction.

Hollar's earliest etchings (1625–7) include prints in the style of early German masters, a historical portrait of *Albrecht Dürer* (1625; Parthey, no. 1391; Pennington, no. 1391A) and a copy (Parthey, no. 457) after Heinrich Aldegrever. Much more important are the five etched views of the environs of Prague (1626; Pennington, nos 718A–E) and three drawings related to them in style and motif (*c*. 1626/7; Berlin, Kupferstichkab.; Manchester, John Rylands U. Lib.; ex-Francis Springell priv. col., Portinscale), which reveal a strong sympathy for landscape and a well-developed understanding of how to represent it naturalistically.

In 1627 Hollar left Prague, which, riven with political and religious strife, had long ceased to be an artistic centre of any consequence, and travelled to Germany. Mature topographical drawings, some with watercolour, record his subsequent presence in the Stuttgart area (1628) and at Strasbourg (1629–32), where his etchings, many based

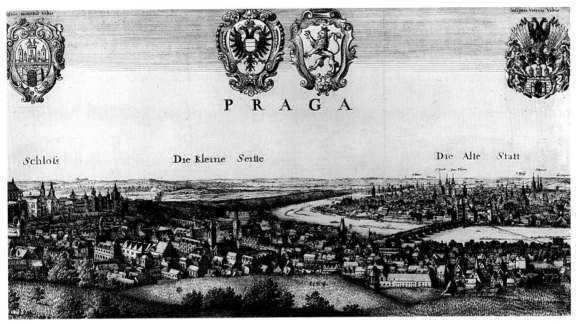

1. Wenceslaus Hollar: *Great Prospect of Prague* (detail, 276×379 mm), etching, 276×1105 mm, 1649 (Prague, National Gallery, Kinský Palace)

on drawings made locally and on trips down the Rhine to Cologne, were published by Jan van der Heyden. He became increasingly influenced by Dutch landscape prints, copying works by Jan van de Velde II. Subsequently (probably 1631–2) he worked in Frankfurt as an etcher in the workshop of Matthäus Merian (i), learning topographic and cartographic techniques and in particular the spatial construction of large topographic panoramic views in which repoussoir devices such as trees and foreground staffage are deployed to anchor the composition. These he employed in his first large city prospect, of *Mainz* (1632; Prague, N.G., Kinský Pal.). Although Merian's topographic formulae had no discernible limiting effect on Hollar's drawings, some of the prints from his later German period, such as the three related etchings depicting the *Mineral Spring*, *Thoroughfare* and *Watermill* (Parthey, nos 1238–40), show Merian's influence in composition and in the handling of foliage.

Hollar's journey through the Netherlands in 1634–5 yielded his best landscape drawings so far. These reveal a direct response to the landscape of the northern Netherlands (especially its coasts and harbours) rather than to Dutch landscape art, although in their lack of artificial repoussoir devices and bold, empty foregrounds they indirectly reflect the work of Jan van Goyen and Salomon van Ruysdael. Hollar certainly became more aware of Dutch art; in 1635 he etched a copy (Parthey, no. 1650) of Rembrandt's etching of *Saskia* (1634; B. 347). By the mid-1630s his reputation was well established. A series of 24 small landscape etchings entitled *Amoenissimae aliquot locorum . . . effigies* (Cologne, 1635; Parthey, nos 695–718), published by Abraham Hogenberg (*b c.*1578; *d* after 1653), starting with a title-page and two etchings of Prague and continuing with views of Strasbourg and Frankfurt, along the Rhine to Cologne and on to the northern

Netherlands, serves as a short topographic autobiography of his career to date and as a summary of his achievements.

In 1636 in Cologne, Hollar met the English diplomat Thomas Howard, 2nd [14th] Earl of Arundel, who was travelling on a mission from Charles I to Emperor Ferdinand II in Linz. Lord Arundel, a formidable connoisseur and collector, invited Hollar to accompany him on the mission. The drawings (Berlin, Kupferstichkab.; Chatsworth, Derbys; Windsor Castle, Berks, Royal Col.; Prague, N.G.) that Hollar made during the journey (up the rivers Rhine and Main to Würzburg, down the Danube from Regensburg to Linz and on to Vienna, and overland to Prague) mark the summit of his career as a draughtsman. Unable to practise as an etcher but secure in employment and with plenty of time to draw, he combined his skills as a topographer and his talents as a landscape draughtsman to produce drawings that are a thorough and accurate documentary record of the journey and a sensitive and personal response to what he saw. The first sketches were done on the spot, with leadpoint or quill pen and ink, sometimes with slight ink washes; later he redrew them with greater regard to spatial organization and composition, sometimes, but never obtrusively, introducing repoussoir devices to the foreground. These more finished drawings were drawn in pen and brown and black ink, with washes of coloured ink or watercolour. Many of the views were etched at a later date, and Hollar used both finished drawings and the preliminary drawings as sources for prints. During his brief stay in Prague (6–13 July 1636), he was able to replenish his stock of drawings of his native city, providing himself with motifs that he continued to use in etchings until the end of his life. Some of them were made with an immediate project in view: two drawings made on the same spot (Paris, Ecole N. Sup. B.-A.; ex-Francis Springell priv. col., Portinscale) were used for the right-hand and central portion of a large panoramic drawing of Prague seen from the Petřin Slope, the *Great Prospect of Prague* (August 1636; Prague N.G., Kinský Pal.), drawn during his stay in Regensburg on the return journey from Prague. It is arguably the greatest of Hollar's large city prospects. He etched it (Parthey, no. 880) in 1649 (see fig. 1), when he was in Antwerp.

2. LONDON AND ANTWERP, 1636–52. When Lord Arundel returned to England in December 1636, Hollar went with him. He remained closely associated with the Earl's household on the Strand in London for at least the next six years and married while in England. The migration marked a complete change in his career and, on the evidence of his surviving work, almost ended his career as a landscape draughtsman. Henceforth much of his work was reproductive and of uneven quality, although his enduring talent as an etcher recurred in work of outstanding quality at increasingly intermittent intervals. Initially at least, Hollar was employed by Lord Arundel 'draweing and copying rareties', according to John Aubrey, 'which he did etch'. Despite this, relatively few such drawn or etched copies of Arundel's collection made at this time survive, although copies of sculpture in the collection etched by Hollar when in Antwerp are known. Much of his considerable output at this period had nothing to do with Arundel or the Stuart court, although he was employed to teach drawing to the children of Charles I and did etch views of Windsor Castle (*see* WINDSOR CASTLE, fig. 1). Some of it was published by the London print-seller Peter Stent (*fl* 1640–67), with whom he had a

difficult relationship. Among his best work are three sets of etchings representing the *Four Seasons* (1641–4; Parthey, nos 606–9), published by Stent, which are thinly disguised costume studies (see fig. 2); he also drew the celebrated view of the *West Part of Southwark towards Westminster* (*c.* 1638), published in the Netherlands in 1647 (*see* THE-ATRE, fig. 8).

In 1644 Hollar moved to Antwerp, almost certainly as a result of the deteriorating prospects in England for the Royalist cause, with which he was closely associated. Also in Antwerp were the Earl of Arundel, with much of his collection, and the artist Hendrik van der Borcht I (1583–1660), who had accompanied Arundel on part of the 1636 mission. Documentary evidence of Hollar's stay in Antwerp is scanty. According to John Evelyn, he was converted to Catholicism by the Jesuits. His output during his eight-year stay there was considerable: over 350 plates etched for at least 11 different publishers, including copies of parts of the Arundel collection, landscapes and animal studies after contemporary Antwerp painters and copies after Old Masters. For his etchings he continued to use drawings that he had made earlier. A drawing of a ship (1634; ex-Francis Springell priv. col., Portinscale), made at Rotterdam during his journey in Holland, served as the basis for one of a series of eight etchings of ships entitled *Navium variae figurae et formae* (1647; Parthey, nos 1261–8). While in Antwerp, Hollar continued to produce many prints of English views and subjects, including six of the environs of Albury (1645; Parthey, nos 937–42), Lord Arundel's retreat in Surrey, which are among his best English views.

Hollar's eight years in Antwerp mark the summit of his creative talent as an etcher. His set of 12 prints of insects from Lord Arundel's cabinet, *Muscarum scarabeorum, vermiumque varie et formae* (1646; Parthey, nos 2164–75) and sundry etchings of sea shells (mid- to late-1640s; Parthey, nos 2187–2224) from the same cabinet (according to George Vertue), derive from the tradition of natural history representation established by Joris Hoefnagel in Prague, but the virtuosity with which the needle was handled has no precedent. The etchings of *Muffs* (1642–7; Parthey, nos 1945–52), Hollar's most famous production, were started in London, but most of the plates belong to the Antwerp period. They are often described as fetishistic but are the product of an obsessive interest in natural forms and are rendered with unmatched finesse.

3. LONDON AND TANGIER, 1652–77. Hollar returned to England in 1652. During the remaining years of his life he was yet more prolific than before, but the quality of his output dwindled, and he appears to have been paid less and less for his work, lacking a wealthy patron such as Arundel, so that he died a pauper. He worked extensively for the antiquary William Dugdale, providing illustrations for most of his works (e.g. *The History of St Paul's Cathedral*, London, 1658; *see* LONDON, fig. 25), and for John Ogilby (1600–76), for whose edition (London, 1654) of Virgil he provided 44 full-page plates. Much of Hollar's work during his second English period was illustrative: he etched many plates for maps after the drawings of other artists and continued to etch copies after Old Masters, many portraits and prints illustrating contemporary events. Two projects

2. Wenceslaus Hollar: *Winter*, etching, 261×185 mm, 1643 (London, British Museum)

from this period stand out. The first, never completed due to the Fire of London in 1666, was for an enormous map of London. On the evidence of what is probably the only surviving part (London, BM; Parthey, no. 1002), the project would have comprised 28 separate sheets, totalling approximately 1.5×3.0 m. The second was his set of six etchings entitled *By Islington* (1665; Parthey, nos 915–20). These prints are the best of his late work and among the most charming and unusual views of London of this time.

As a result of his appointment as 'Scenographer to His Majesty' in 1668, Hollar travelled the following year to Tangier with an expedition led by Henry Howard, 6th Duke of Norfolk (*d* 1682), grandson of his earlier patron Thomas, 2nd [14th] Earl of Arundel. He remained there nearly a year and made a series of panoramic drawings of the city and its fortifications of which *c.* 30 survive (14: London, BM). They constitute the last flowering of his talent as a topographic draughtsman and recall much earlier city prospects, such as those of Anthonis van den Wyngaerde and Joris Hoefnagel.

BIBLIOGRAPHY

J. Aubrey: *Brief Lives* (1669–96); ed. A. Clark, 2 vols (Oxford, 1898)
G. Vertue: *A Description of the Works of the Ingenious Delineator and Engraver, Wenceslaus Hollar* (London, 1759)
A. von Bartsch: *Le Peintre-graveur* (1803–21) [B.]
G. Parthey: *Wenzel Hollar, beschreibendes Verzeichnis seiner Kupferstiche* (Berlin, 1853); suppl. (Berlin, 1858) [Parthey]
A. M. Hind: *Wenceslaus Hollar and his Views of London and Windsor in the 17th century* (London, 1922)
'The Note-books of George Vertue', *Walpole Soc.* (London, 1930–55)
F. Sprinzels: *Hollar Handzeichnungen* (Vienna, 1938)
F. G. Springell: *Connoisseur and Diplomat* (London, 1963)
V. Denkstein: *Hollar Drawings* (London, 1979)
Wenzel Hollar, 1607–1677 (exh. cat. by M. van Berge, Paris, Fond. Custodia, Inst. Néer., 1979)
R. Pennington: *A Descriptive Catalogue of the Etched Work of Wenceslaus Hollar, 1607–1677* (Cambridge, 1982) [uses Parthey's classification, with *c.* 225 additions marked A, B, C, etc] [Pennington]
Wenceslaus Hollar: Prints and Drawings (exh. cat., ed. A. Griffiths and G. Kesnerova; London, BM, 1982)

GEORGE GORDON

Hollein, Hans (*b* Vienna, 30 March 1934). Austrian architect, designer and teacher. He studied (1949–53) in the Department of Civil Engineering of the Bundesgewerbeschule, Vienna, and then at the Akademie der Bildenden Künste, Vienna, until 1956, when he received his diploma. From 1958 to 1959 he carried out postgraduate work in architecture and urban planning at the Illinois Institute of Technology, Chicago, and from 1958 to 1960 at the College of Environmental Design, University of California, Berkeley, receiving his M. Arch. degree there in 1960. From 1960 to 1964 he worked in Sweden and Germany, as well as in the USA, and by April 1964 he had established his own studio in Vienna, where his design (1965) for the Retti Candle Shop rapidly established international interest. Significant early projects include the gallery (1967–9), New York, for Richard L. Feigen and Co. Inc., the staff dining facilities (1970–71) and Siemens Foundation Building (1975) for Siemens AG in Munich and the shop design (1972), Vienna, for the Schullin jewellery business. Hollein's first major project, the Städtisches Museum Abteiberg (1972–82; *see* MUSEUM, fig. 9), Mönchengladbach, marked his emergence as a leading late Modernist, rather than Post-modernist, architect. Through the 1980s he further established his reputation as a leader of the avant-garde with a series of major designs that were realized later: the Museum für Moderne Kunst (completed 1991; *see* FRANKFURT AM MAIN, fig. 3), Frankfurt am Main, the two phases of the Kohlergasse School (completed 1988 and 1991), Vienna, and the Haas Haus commercial complex (1991), opposite the Stephansdom in Vienna, which created attention in his native city.

Many of Hollein's concerns and influences emerged most clearly in the important exhibitions that he devised. In 1975 he conceived and designed the design survey exhibition *Man Transforms: Aspects of Design* at the Cooper-Hewitt Museum in New York, which displayed works that shared the principles underlying his design philosophy: that the origins of all civilized life stem directly from decisions about geometry, climatic protection and food and sustenance, expressed as basic signs and symbols of humanity. Hollein's golf club building (1991) at Schloss Ebreichsdorf, near Vienna, and the competition proposals (1990–91; unexecuted) for the Guggenheim Museum of Art at Salzburg are both imbued with this respect for man's atavistic past. Likewise in his projects within cities, Hollein always observes context, transforming it into a new relevance. His historical survey of Viennese culture, *Traum und Wirklichkeit: Wien, 1870–1930*, was shown in Vienna in 1985 and later in New York and Paris to great acclaim. He was also a notable stage designer and designer of furniture and lighting. From 1967 he was Professor of Architecture at the University of Düsseldorf and from 1976 Head of the School and Institute of Design at Hochschule für Angewandte Kunst, Vienna. He was editor (1965–70) of the influential magazine *Bau* and recipient of numerous architectural awards.

WRITINGS

'Alles ist Architektur', *Bau*, 1 (1968)
Otto Wagner (Tokyo, 1978)

BIBLIOGRAPHY

P. Cook: 'Stirling and Hollein', *Archit. Rev.* [London], clxxii/1030 (1982), pp. 53–71
C. Gable: *Hans Hollein: A Bibliography of Books and Articles* (Monticello, IL, 1983)
G. Peichl: 'Homage to Hans Hollein', *A & U* (March 1985), pp. 78–103
Hans Hollein Design: MAN transFORMS: Konzepte einer Ausstellung (Vienna, 1989)

MICHAEL SPENS

Hollemans. Dutch family of sculptors, active in England. The date of arrival of Garret Hollemans (i) (*fl c.* 1584–96) in England is unrecorded, but his earliest dated work is the memorial tablet to two daughters of the Morgan family in St Michael's, Weston under Wetherley, Warwicks, dated 1584. He established a workshop at Burton on Trent, Staffs, a flourishing centre of sculpture production. In 1593 his son Jasper Hollemans (*fl* 1593–*c.* 1630) received a payment in London for two chimney-pieces (destr.) carved by Garret at Kyre Park, Worcs. Garret returned to Worcestershire in 1594 to erect the monument to *Richard Barneby* at St Michael, Bockleton. In 1596 father and son contracted to make a tomb for *George Shirley*, installed in 1598 at SS Mary and Hardulph, Breedon on the Hill, Leics.

The influence of Hans Vredeman de Vries and Cornelis Floris is apparent in the late 16th-century tombs of the Foljambe family from the Hollemans workshop at St Mary and All Saints, Chesterfield, Derbys. In the monument to the grandparents of the Morgan daughters at SS Peter and Paul, Nether Heyford, Northants, bosses in the form of baskets appear, a detail used on Floris's rood screen of 1571–4 in Tournai Cathedral. Garret's contacts with the work of Floris and Vredeman de Vries may have been direct; in the building accounts of Kyre Park he is referred to as 'Father Garrett', suggesting that he was old enough to have had a long career in the Low Countries before emigrating.

Jasper Hollemans, described by Lord Spencer in 1615 as a 'Dutchman dwelling at Burton on Trent', was presumably born abroad. He produced tomb sculpture in a style similar to that of contemporary sculptors of the Southwark school, retaining elements of his father's work, including features from Floris and Vredeman de Vries. Jasper undertook the construction of three large monuments to the Spencer family at St Mary, Great Brington, Northants, in 1599, which are characterized by restless decoration and a strong sense of pattern. No further monuments are documented, although a series of tombs dating up to 1630 may be attributed to him. Later tombs such as those of *Sir George Bromley* (*d* 1588) and his wife, *Lady Bromley*, at St Peter, Worfield, Salop, erected in 1622, are difficult to distinguish from Southwark work. Inigo Jones produced the design for the tomb of *Sir Rowland Cotton and his Wife* at St Chad, Norton in Hales, Salop, but Jasper reduced it to Jacobean formulae. His effigies are distinguished by the use of honeycomb-patterned folds on sleeves and guilloche decoration on armour.

In 1634 Jasper's son Garret Hollemans (ii) (*bapt* 20 March 1607), under a contract witnessed by a second son Richard Hollemans (*bapt* 7 July 1611), made the effigy of *Sir Thomas Skrymsher* (*d* 1633) at All Saints, Forton, Staffs. Like other monuments of the 1630s in the area, it updates Jasper's style but is of more provincial quality.

BIBLIOGRAPHY

K. A. Esdaile: 'The Inter-action of English and Low Country Sculpture in the 16th Century', *J. Warb. & Court. Inst.*, vi (1943), pp. 80–88

M. Whinney: *Sculpture in Britain: 1530–1830*, Pelican Hist. A. (Harmondsworth, 1964); rev. by J. Physick (Harmondsworth, 1988), pp. 63–4, 434

J. Newman: 'An Early Drawing by Inigo Jones and a Monument in Shropshire', *Burl. Mag.*, cxv (1973), pp. 360–67

J. C. BAYLISS

Holliday, A(lbert) Clifford (*b* Gildersome, W. Yorks, 21 Dec 1897; *d* Manchester, 26 Sept 1960). English architect and urban planner. On graduating from the University of Liverpool in Architecture and Civic Design, he went to Palestine (1922), succeeding C. R. Ashbee as Civic Adviser to the City of Jerusalem. In 1927 he began private practice, serving also as Town Planning Adviser to the Palestine Government. In these various capacities, he was central to many major planning proposals, including the master plan (1926–30) of Jerusalem, the restoration of the walls and gates of the Old City and, together with Patrick Abercrombie, a regional plan (1933–66) for Haifa Bay, for the Jewish National Fund. His work in Jerusalem was traditional, responding sensitively to local climate, materials and culture: Barclays Bank, the 'Khan' of St John's Ophthalmic Hospital (1929–30) and his undisputed masterpiece, St Andrew's Church of Scotland (1927–30). With the Israeli architect Richard Kauffmann he planned the Reclamation Area (1929–31) in Haifa, adjacent to the new harbour; later, as consulting architect (1933–7), he set the architectural guidelines for its development: an exercise in civic design innovative in process, impressive in extent and urbane in character.

With façades to the extensive Kingsway Street frontage reminiscent of the work of Erich Mendelsohn, Holliday became a latter-day, but adept, adherent of the Modernist idiom. Leaving Palestine, he spent World War II as consultant to the colonial governments of Ceylon (now Sri Lanka), where he again collaborated with Abercrombie, on the design of the University, and Gibraltar. He returned to Britain and in 1946 joined the Stevenage Development Corporation as chief architect and planner, contributing notably to the New Towns policy and development. In 1952 he became the first Professor of Town and Country Planning at the University of Manchester.

WRITINGS

A. C. Holliday: 'Town and Country Planning in Palestine', *Palestine and Middle East Economic Review*, 7–8 (1933), pp. 290–92, 329

BIBLIOGRAPHY

O. Ahimeir and M. Levine, eds: *Modern Architecture in Jerusalem*, The Institute for Jerusalem Studies, iv (Jerusalem, 1980)

G. Herbert and S. Sosnovsky: *Bauham-on-the-Carmel and the Crossroads of Empire* (Jerusalem, 1993)

GILBERT HERBERT

Hollins, Peter (*b* Birmingham, 1 May 1800; *d* Birmingham, 17 Aug 1886). English sculptor. He trained under his father, the sculptor and architect William Hollins (1763–1843), and went to London *c*. 1822 to work for Francis Chantrey. In 1833 Hollins held an exhibition in his studio that included several portrait busts and a colossal *Murder of the Innocents* (untraced). In 1835 or 1836 he visited Italy. He returned to Birmingham in 1843 to take over his father's business and remained there for the rest of his life. His reputation has perhaps suffered, in comparison with those of such contemporaries as E. H. Baily and William Theed, because of his provincial status.

Hollins's two most impressive works are church monuments. That to Sophia Thompson (marble, 1841; Malvern Priory, Worcs), with its effigy of the deceased reclining on a couch, reflects the influence of Chantrey's Elizabeth Digby monument (1825; Worcester Cathedral). The monument to Georgina, Countess of Bradford (*d* 1842; marble, Weston-under-Lizard, Staffs), combines a reclining figure of the Countess and a relief of angels bearing her soul to Heaven, which suggests the influence of Westmacott's Duchess of Newcastle monument of 1832 (Clumber Park, Notts). Other important works by Hollins include statues of *Sir Robert Peel* (bronze; 1855; Police Training Headquarters, Birmingham) and *Sir Rowland Hill* (1868; ex-Birmingham Post Office, 1940; untraced), an ideal marble statue, *Sabrina* (1846; Quarry Park, Salop), and a church font (marble, 1862; Bodelwyddan Castle, Clwyd). He also produced many portrait busts, including those of his father *William Hollins* (marble, 1843; Birmingham, St Paul) and *Edward Grainger* (marble, 1825; London, Royal Coll. Surgeons England).

BIBLIOGRAPHY

Gunnis

Obituary, *Birmingham Daily Post* (18 Aug 1886)

N. Penny: *Church Monuments in Romantic England* (New Haven, 1977), pp. 89–92, 214

MARK STOCKER

Hollis, Thomas (*b* London, 14 April 1720; *d* Corscombe, Dorset, 1 Jan 1774). English collector, antiquary, patron and editor. He pursued humanistic and scientific studies under Dr John Ward, and in 1739/40 he was admitted at Lincoln's Inn as a law student, and lived in chambers until 1748. During a trip to Venice, in 1750 or 1751, he made the acquaintance of Joseph Smith, who became a lifelong friend and correspondent, and who may have induced him to order six of the nine paintings by Canaletto he eventually owned. These included the larger version of *Ranelagh: Interior of the Rotunda* (London, N.G.), which showed the site from a different viewpoint to the version of 1751 (priv. col., see exh. cat., p. 91), and the acclaimed *Walton Bridge* (London, Dulwich Pict. Gal.), both of which were inscribed on the back in Italian as having been painted for Hollis in London in 1754. A third, large painting, described in the catalogue of the sale of the paintings by Canaletto in 1884 as a *View of Westminster during the Building of the Bridge*, is untraced. Of the three smaller paintings commissioned, the *Capitol in Rome*, *St Paul's Cathedral*, and a capriccio of buildings at Whitehall (all untraced), only the first bore an inscription on the back which affirmed that it had been painted for Hollis in London in 1755 (*see* CANALETTO, §1(iv)). He was also a long-time supporter of Giovanni Battista Cipriani, and owned several pictures by Richard Wilson, among them a portrait of himself, painted in Rome in 1752, and a view of the Grotto at the Villa Madama in Rome, as well as Cornelius Johnson's portrait of *Milton as a Boy*.

From the time of his return from the Continent, Hollis, who was a Whig radical and a supporter of the American colonists, spent a substantial part of his income building up a collection of books and medals that illustrated his principles. He also edited a series of books, including a new edition of John Toland's *The Life of John Milton* (1761), a new edition of Sidney Algernon's *Discourses Concerning Government* (1763), *John Locke, the Philosopher, Two Treatises of Government* (1764) and *The True Sentiments of America Contained in a Collection of Letters Sent from the House of Representatives* (1768), all published in London. He also made substantial donations of books and medals to libraries in Berne and Zurich, presented a portrait of *Oliver Cromwell* by Samuel Cooper to Sidney Sussex College in 1764, and in the same year gave some Egyptian antiquities to the Comte de Caylus in Paris. He bequeathed his collection of paintings to his friend Thomas Brand, who subsequently adopted the name Brand Hollis. The paintings by Canaletto were eventually dispersed in an auction at Christie's in 1884.

DNB
BIBLIOGRAPHY
F. Blackburne, ed.: *Memoirs of Thomas Hollis*, 2 vols (London, 1780)
J. Nichols: *Literary Anecdotes of the 18th Century*, iii (London, 1812)
W. Whitley: *Artists and their Friends in England, 1700–99*, 2 vols (London and Boston, 1928)
Canaletto and England (exh. cat., ed. M. Liversidge and J. Farrington; Birmingham, Gas Hall Exh. Gal., 1994)

☐

Hollóháza Ceramics Factory. Hungarian ceramics manufactory. It evolved from a glassworks in the village of Hollóháza on the estate of Count Károlyi, in northern Hungary. Between 1860 and 1880 it was leased to Ferenc Istvánffy, who enlarged and modernized it and added stovemaking. The factory produced dinner-services, a series of ornamental plates inscribed with a line from the Lord's Prayer and ornamental dishes and bottles, which were very popular. Typical Hollóháza motifs were the cornflower and rose. After 1880 wares were decorated with new designs, which were influenced by the Zsolnay Ceramics Factory and consisted of late Renaissance and traditional Turkish motifs. The factory was very successful at the Millennial Exhibition of 1896 in Budapest and at the Exposition Universelle of 1900 in Paris. In 1915 the factory was merged with the stoneware factory of Emil Fischer in Budapest, and Fischer became the artistic and commercial director of the works. From 1918 until 1939 the factory declined under various managers, and in 1948 it was nationalized, production changing to earthenware and porcelain.

BIBLIOGRAPHY
G. Sikota: *Hollóházi kerámia* (Budapest, 1961)

FERENC BATÁRI

Hollósy, Simon (*b* Máramarossziget [now Sighet, Romania], 2 Feb 1857; *d* Técső [now Tyachiv, Ukraine], 8 May 1918). Hungarian painter and teacher. He started studying painting in Budapest but received most of his artistic training (1878–82) at the Akademie der Bildenden Künste in Munich. He then settled in Munich until 1895. The major work of his early period, *Threshing Corn* (1885; Budapest, N.G.), combines genre painting with carefully recorded naturalistic detail, very much in the spirit of Wilhelm Leibl and Jules Bastien-Lepage. He rebelled, however, against the academic tradition of history painting: in a small-scale sketch for *Zrinyi Rides Forth* (Esztergom, Mus. Christ.) the gentle style undermines the academic principles of the genre.

In 1886 Hollósy founded his own private school in Munich: his teaching methods were unrestricted by convention, and this drew a good many young artists to the school: Germans such as Otto Greiner as well as many Hungarians (István Csók, Károly Ferenczy and others). In 1896, with a group of young painters, he established a summer school for his students at Nagybánya (now Baia Mare, Romania), and this swiftly became an autonomous artists' colony (*see* NAGYBÁNYA COLONY). Here Hollósy painted *en plein air* for the first time, struggling to avoid naturalistic detail in the search to capture and convey the essential character and mood of a subject. Splendid examples of his work from this period are the sketches (1899; Budapest, N.G.) for the composition to be entitled *Rákóczi's March*, a project he never completed. Hollósy also designed grisaille book illustrations, for example for poems by József Kiss, *Ár Ellen* ('Against the current'; 1896–7).

In 1902 Hollósy left Nagybánya and moved with his pupils to Técső. In this period, lasting till his death, the primary themes of his paintings were peasants' houses, haycocks in the landscape and the River Tisza. His style varied a good deal in these late paintings: *Ricks* (1912; Budapest, N.G.) uses bold, almost Expressionist, brushstrokes; and *Self-portrait* (1916; priv. col., see Németh, 1956, pl. 72) is more precisely ordered, and sombre and contemplative in mood. Hollósy did not take part in the more official side of artistic life in either Munich or Budapest and only rarely exhibited. He held one exhibition of his collected works, in 1910 at the Könyves Kálmán Salon in Budapest. His influence on his contemporaries was mostly due to his strong personality, his passionate enthusiasm and his novel teaching methods.

BIBLIOGRAPHY
I. Réti: *Hollósy Simon* (Budapest, 1927)
L. Németh: *Hollósy Simon és kora művészete* [Simon Hollósy and the art of his age] (Budapest, 1956)
——: *Hollósy Simon műveinek jegyzéke* [An index to the works of Simon Hollósy], Művészettörténeti Tanulmányok (1960), pp. 145–68

MÁRIA SZOBOR-BERNÁTH

Holloway, Thomas (*b* Devonport, 22 Sept 1800; *d* Sunninghill, Berks, 26 Dec 1883). English manufacturer, philanthropist and collector. He was granted a patent for Holloway's Ointment and Pills and gradually amassed an immense fortune through a pioneering use of widespread advertising and judicious speculation on the stock market. He and his wife Jane had no children and lived at Tittenhurst Lodge, Sunninghill, Berks, where he assembled a collection of Old Masters (including Giovanni Bellini's *St Francis in Ecstasy*, *c*. 1480; New York, Frick) and contemporary paintings. He built the Holloway Sanatorium (1873–84), Virginia Water, Surrey, designed by W. H. Crossland (1823–1909) in the Flemish Gothic style, and the Royal Holloway College (1879–86), Egham, Surrey, a huge building in the French Renaissance style, by the same architect, at a cost of over £800,000. Holloway bought 77 contemporary paintings specifically for the College, mostly at Christie's, between 1881 and 1883 for over £83,000. Works include Edwin Long's *Babylonian Marriage Market*, Edwin Henry Landseer's *Man Proposes, God Disposes* (for both of which he paid record prices), Luke Fildes's *Applicants for Admission to a Casual Ward* (1874), William Powell Frith's *Railway Station* (1862) and John Everett Millais's *Princes in the Tower* (all at the College; now Egham, U. London, Royal Holloway & Bedford New Coll.). Three paintings by Constable, Gainsborough, and Turner were controversially sold in 1992–3 to finance repairs to the College building.

BIBLIOGRAPHY
DNB
J. Chapel: *Victorian Taste: The Complete Catalogue of Paintings at the Royal Holloway College* (London, 1982)

JEANNIE CHAPEL

Hollstein, F(riedrich) W(ilhelm) H(einrich) (*b* Wanzleben, 19 Aug 1888; *d* Amsterdam, 23 July 1957). German auctioneer and antiquarian. He trained at the firm of Amsler en Ruthardt and then joined the Berlin-based company Hollstein und Puppel as a partner to van Puppel, where he stayed until 1937, when he fled to the Netherlands. Hollstein was the initiator and first author of two series of reference books: *Dutch and Flemish Etchings, Engravings and Woodcuts c. 1450–1700* and *German Etchings, Engravings and Woodcuts c. 1450–1700*, the first volumes of which were published in 1947 and 1954 respectively. He based his work on existing publications, his personal archive and the print collection of the Rijksprentenkabinet, Amsterdam. Before his death he had completed fourteen volumes in the Dutch and Flemish series and six in the German series. Initially, the volumes

were published by Menno Hertzberger, an antiquary, library agent and auctioneer; the project was subsequently taken over by A. L. van Gendt (*d* 1986)—at one time Hertzberger's junior partner, later co-manager and ultimately head of the firm—who enabled authors working on the series to visit foreign print rooms where they could study the artists under discussion. Van Gendt also increased the number of illustrations. The volumes in both series were, in the 1980s and 1990s, being revised.

WRITINGS
Dutch and Flemish Etchings, Engravings and Woodcuts c. 1450–1700 (Amsterdam, 1947–)
German Etchings, Engravings and Woodcuts c. 1450–1700 (Amsterdam, 1954–)

BIBLIOGRAPHY
K. Boon: [review of Hollstein: *Dut. & Flem.*, i], *Oud-Holland*, lxvii (1952), pp. 167–71
J. F. Heijbroek and F. W. Kuyper: 'In gesprek met A. L. van Gendt' [Talking to A. L. van Gendt], *De Boekenwereld*, ii (1986), pp. 150–58, 167–71 [incl. review by R. E. O. Ekkart of *Dut. & Flem.*, xxix]

CHRISTIAAN SCHUCKMAN

Hollyer, Frederick (*b* 1837; *d* London, 21 Nov 1933). English engraver and photographer. He began his career as a mezzotint-engraver, reproducing two works by Edwin Henry Landseer, the *Shepherd's Grave* and the *Old Shepherd's Chief Mourner* (both London, V&A), both published by J. McQueen in 1869. In the early 1870s he was employed by Frederic Leighton to photograph paintings and drawings, which he carried out with exemplary skill. Under Leighton's patronage his clients soon included Edward Burne-Jones, Dante Gabriel Rossetti and G. F. Watts and he established himself as the leading specialist in the photographic reproduction of paintings in England. His reproductions, which sold widely in Britain and Europe, did much to popularize the artists' works. He was also a gifted portrait photographer and devoted one day a week to sitters from artistic and literary circles, producing photographs of *Camille Pissarro*, *Walter Pater* and *John Ruskin* (*see* PHOTOGRAPHY, fig. 4; all London, V&A).

BIBLIOGRAPHY
O. Mathews: *Early Photographs and Early Photographers* (London, 1973)
T. Browne and E. Parton, eds: *Macmillan Biographical Encyclopaedia of Photographic Artists and Innovators* (London, 1983), pp. 283–4

DAVID RODGERS

Holm, [Oscar William] **Bill** (*b* Roundup, MT, 24 March 1925). American painter and art historian. He received BA and MFA degrees in painting from the University of Washington in 1949 and 1951. He taught art at Lincoln High School in Seattle from 1953 until 1968. He was Curator of Northwest Coast Indian Art at the Thomas Burke Memorial Washington State Museum, Seattle; and Lecturer and later Professor in the Art History Division, School of Art, with an adjunct appointment in Anthropology at the University of Washington, Seattle, from 1968 until his retirement in 1985. After his retirement he became Curator Emeritus of Northwest Coast Indian Art at the Burke Museum and Professor Emeritus of Art History at the University of Washington. He has curated several exhibitions and published extensively on Native American art, including the classic book on northern Northwest Coast formline design (1965). He was awarded the Washington State Governor's Writer's Award five times (1966, 1977, 1981, 1984 and 1988) and has received the Lifetime Achievement Award from the Native American Art Studies Association (1991) and the University of Washington College of Arts and Sciences Distinguished Achievement Award (1994). His artistic work includes painting and carving in traditional Northwest Coast styles, beadwork and quillwork in Plains and Plateau styles, and painting in the Western art tradition. His first exhibition of paintings was held at the Burke Museum in 1992.

For general discussion of Native American painting in the 20th century see NATIVE NORTH AMERICAN ART, §IV, 2.

WRITINGS

Northwest Coast Indian Art: An Analysis of Form (Seattle, 1965)
Smoky-Top: The Art and Times of Willie Seaweed (Seattle, 1983)
Spirit and Ancestor: A Century of Northwest Coast Indian Art in the Burke Museum (Seattle, 1987)

ROBIN K. WRIGHT

Holman Hunt, William. *See* HUNT, WILLIAM HOLMAN.

Holmberg, (Gustaf) Werner (*b* Helsinki, 1 Nov 1830; *d* Düsseldorf, 24 Sept 1860). Finnish painter. He studied art in Finland under Magnus von Wright and Pehr Adolf Kruskopf (1805–52) and completed a basic architectural training at the instigation of his father. Holmberg was the first Finnish artist to study landscape painting in Düsseldorf, arriving there in the summer of 1853. From the start he was drawn to themes from nature, modelling his art on studies by Johann Wilhelm Schirmer. He was most attracted by the work of Andreas Achenbach (1815–1910), whose influence is evident in the wild romanticism of Holmberg's first work of note, *Kyrö Falls* (1854; Helsinki, Athenaeum A. Mus.). In 1855–6 Holmberg was a private pupil of Hans Fredrik Gude, the Norwegian instructor in landscape painting at the Kunstakademie in Düsseldorf. A freely romanticized style, an emphasis on light and brilliant colours give a number of his small paintings the quality of early Impressionist works. In the superb watercolour sketches he painted in the summer of 1857, he rediscovered the artistic possibilities of Finland's landscape and interpreted them in a distinctive manner (examples in Helsinki, Athenaeum A. Mus.). After a journey to Norway in the following year his style became even more painterly, and he concentrated on imbuing his work with a lyrical atmosphere.

In 1859 Holmberg produced *Rainswept Forest* (Helsinki, President's Castle), which marked a breakthrough for him in Düsseldorf; the critics placed him among Germany's foremost landscape artists. He made a journey to Finland in 1859, after which he returned to Düsseldorf to paint a number of forcefully realist works that demonstrate his complete mastery of his medium (e.g. *Cottage at Kuru*, 1860; Helsinki, Athenaeum A. Mus.). In the spring of 1860 he was invited to teach in Weimar, although the invitation was withdrawn when the Grand Duke of Saxe-Weimar decided to appoint Arnold Böcklin. Around this time Holmberg's tuberculosis worsened, he deteriorated rapidly and died in the autumn.

The last phase of Holmberg's career can be described as poetic realism. In their detail his paintings were true to life, but his religious idealism led him to aspire towards poetic beauty. In Düsseldorf he was closely linked to Gude's school. However, he rapidly surpassed his teacher in the sensitivity and youthful vitality of his style and was progressive in his treatment of light effects, which foreshadowed the style of *plein-air* painting. He was the first Finnish painter to distinguish himself internationally but, as his output was relatively small, he never significantly influenced the artistic life of Düsseldorf. In Finland he was an artist of fundamental importance; he revitalized Finnish landscape painting, turning the forest into a valid artistic subject.

BIBLIOGRAPHY

E. Aspelin: *Werner Holmberg: Elämä ja taide* [Werner Holmberg: life and art] (Helsinki, 1890)
A. Reitala: *Werner Holmbergin taide* [The art of Werner Holmberg] (Keuruu, 1986)

AIMO REITALA

Hologram. Image with the illusion of three-dimensionality, recorded on light-sensitive plates, paper or film. It is made by using a laser beam of high-intensity coherent monochromatic light. The original holographic process was discovered in the late 1940s by the British scientist Dennis Gabor (1900–77), who gave it its name; deriving from the Greek words *holos* ('whole, entire') and *gramma* ('picture'). The medium was developed only after the invention of the laser in 1960. After that, many scientists joined in perfecting variations of the process, which captured and stored all visible detail in a subject. By moving in front of a holographic plate, the viewer has the sensation of looking over and around holographed foreground objects.

Although holographic techniques differ in detail, the basic principle is to split the laser beam so that one part reflects light waves over the surfaces of the subject and from there towards a very fine-grain photosensitive surface. The second part of the reference beam comes unimpeded towards the photo-plate, where the interference pattern, made when the object waves interact with the light waves of the reference beam, is recorded. Early holograms were viewed by projecting a duplicate of the recording laser beam through the plate to reconstruct the original three-dimensional light image of the subject.

A holographic subject must remain absolutely still for all details to be accurately recorded. Many initial efforts by artists and scientists were straight holographic records of three-dimensional objects, seen floating eerily and inaccessibly within their monochromatic red, blue or green worlds. The colour was determined by the kind of laser used. Early plates were small, and an 8×10–inch plate was considered large. From a distance one saw the space visible through the frame of the holographic plate; closer, one could look obliquely behind the frame to see things hidden in the distant view. Light waves were reflected from the full-scale object, so larger subjects had to be placed some distance behind the holographic plate to 'fit' easily within the frame.

The most satisfying early holographic subjects were still-life arrangements of small-scale objects, such as the toy train (1964; see Heckman, p. 14) in a famous hologram by scientists Juris Upatnieks (*b* 1936) and Emmett Leith (*b* 1927). Developments in holography enabled portraits to be made with a pulsed laser, which froze living subjects in short bursts of light, in the same way that a strobe light captures motion. It also became possible to use larger holographic plates, to make images to be seen in incandescent light or sunlight, to produce holographic films, to design abstract works with pure colours of the spectrum or to adopt new hybrid media that combined holography with video and computer graphics.

Researchers developed new techniques to make the medium more flexible: images can be made to float in front of or behind the plate; circular holograms can provide full 360° recordings, which have been combined with image-packing techniques to create three-dimensional colour holographic films. Mass-production techniques have introduced holograms into commercial art in the form of magazine covers, credit-card logos and advertisements.

Artists were attracted to holography from the outset. Holographic pioneers, like many early photographers, had to be technicians as well as artists. Because the equipment was expensive and access was limited, practitioners such as Harriet Casdin-Silver often formed partnerships with engineers. By 1970 well-known artists such as Bruce Nauman and Salvador Dalí had experimented with the medium (e.g. Dalí's *Sardana*, see Dorra, p. 27), and holograms had been shown in New York galleries including Knoedler's and Leo Castelli. Difficulties with display and storage dampened some of the enthusiasm for collecting holograms. Although there was a decline in technical development during the 1970s, a band of dedicated holographic artists, scientists and teachers persevered.

Holography gained stature as an art medium as artists explored the expressive qualities unique to the process. Holographers such as Doug Tyler (*b* 1949) in the USA and Margaret Benyon (*b* 1940) in Britain used double exposure and collage to create impossibly co-existing multiple realities. Benyon's *Tigirl* (1985; see 1985 exh. cat., no. 2), for example, superimposes a print of a tiger with a holographic self-portrait made using a pulsed laser, interweaving two contradictory representations of spaces. Other possibilities were suggested by holographic sculpture. Doris Vila's *15 to Blue Island* (1987; Eau Claire, U. WI, Sch. Nursing) depicts an environment filled with wondrous rainbow colours, radiating from diffraction-grating holograms, activated by the shifting ambient light of the site.

Holography has also been used in museums. In Italy, for example, holographic techniques used in industry to test for metal stress were adapted for use in the conservation of 15th-century sculpture by Lorenzo Ghiberti. In the former USSR multiple holograms of works of art allowed rare or delicate objects to be shared by many museum collections. The use of holograms of works of art for special exhibitions, rather than the loan of originals, is an important development. With the establishment of holography as a medium, museums, including the Victoria and Albert Museum, London, began to acquire individual works, and many colleges, universities and art schools launched courses in holographic art. Combined with video, cinema and computer graphics, it is a potentially powerful art tool. From 1976 the Museum of Holography, New York, published the journal *Holosphere*, and in Britain from 1985 the Holographic Group of the Royal Photographic Society published the journal *Real Image*.

BIBLIOGRAPHY
W. E. Kock: *Lasers and Holography: An Introduction to Coherent Optics* (New York, 1968/*R* 1981)
E. N. Leith: 'White-light Holograms', *Sci. Amer.*, ccxxxv/4 (1976), pp. 80–95
Light Fantastic (exh. cat. by J. Wolff, N. Phillips and A. Furst, London, RA, 1977)
M. Benyon: *Understanding Holography* (New York, 1978)
Phases: A Twelve-year Retrospective of the Work of Margaret Benyon (exh. cat. by R. Jackson, J. Phipps and D. Brooks, New York, Mus. Holography, 1980)
T. H. Jeong: 'Holography', *International Exhibition of Holography* (exh. cat., Lake Forest Coll., IL, 1982)
Harriet Casdin-Silver in Collaboration with Dov Eylath: Thresholds (exh. cat., New York, Mus. Holography, 1983)
Holography Redefined (exh. cat. by D. Kirkpatrick, M. Merryman-Means, R.-P. Barilloux, A. Farkis and others, New York, Mus. Holography, 1983)
Holography Works: Application of Holography in Industry and Commerce (exh. cat. by R. Jackson, H. J. Caulfield and R.-P. Barilloux, New York, Mus. Holography, 1983)
B. Dorra: 'Holografie: Ein neues kunsthistorisches Medium?', *Kstwk*, xxviii/8 (Feb 1984), pp. 5–27
J. E. Kaspar and S. A. Feller: *The Hologram Book* (Englewood Cliffs, 1985) [tech.]
1985: The Second International Exhibition of Holography (exh. cat., Lake Forest Coll., IL, 1985)
P. Heckman: *The Magic of Holography* (New York, 1986) [tech. and hist.]
D. Kirkpatrick: 'Recent Art, Science and Technological Interactions in Chicago', *Making Waves: An Interactive Art/Science Exhibit* (exh. cat., Evanston, 1986), pp. 8–24
Light Dreams: The Art and Technology of Holography (exh. cat. by D. Tyler, Kalamazoo, MI, Inst. A., 1987)
F. Popper: *Art of the Electronic Age* (London, 1993)

DIANE KIRKPATRICK

Holscher, Knud (*b* Rødby, 6 May 1930). Danish architect. Working with Arne Jacobsen from 1960 to 1964, he planned and supervised the construction of St Catherine's College, Oxford. In 1967 he won first prize in the competition for Odense University (first phase completed 1973) for the firm Krohn & Hartvig Rasmussen, with which he then became an associate. The project was based on clear structural principles and carefully detailed industrial elements; the façade is constructed of Cor-Ten steel. After 1973, within the same firm, Holscher worked with the architect Svend Axelsson (*b* 1937). They produced a long series of buildings of distinct and polished architectural quality, many the result of competition entries. They include the swimming baths in Lyngby (1977) and Farum (1979), the extension to the Royal Theatre (1985), Copenhagen, the expansion of Copenhagen Airport (1986) in Kastrup, a commercial and domestic block on Jægersborg Allé (1988), Charlottenlund, and the Bahrain National Museum (1988) in Manama. Holscher also designed armature series and building components that won him international prizes. From 1968 to 1987 he was a professor at the Arkitektskole of the Kunstakademi in Copenhagen.

BIBLIOGRAPHY
C. Enevoldsen: 'Universitetsplanlægning og industriel design af Knud Holscher', *Arkitektur DK*, xx/8 (1976), pp. 285–91
——: 'Odense Universitetscenter', *Arkitektur DK*, xx/8 (1976), pp. 292–319
P. E. Skriver: 'Det KGL Teater: Ny-og Ombygning' [The Royal Theatre in Copenhagen], *Arkitektur DK*, xxxi/3 (1987), pp. 100–15
——: 'København Lufthavn—Finger B', *Arkitektur DK*, xxxi/7 (1987), pp. 306–17

JØRGEN SESTOFT

Holsøe, Carl (Vilhelm) (*b* Århus, 12 March 1863; *d* Asserbo, Vinderød, 6 Nov 1935). Danish painter. He studied painting from 1882 to 1884 at the Kongelige Danske Kunstakademi, Copenhagen, subsequently studying at the Kunstnernes Studieskole in Copenhagen under P. S. Krøyer. When in 1886 he made his début at the Charlottenborg December exhibition with an interior, the critic Karl Madsen stated that the painting 'almost had the character of a manifesto'. He referred to the spatial treatment of the picture, in which the objects moved 'like the fish in the sea'. Holsøe's depiction of the refraction of light is precise, and his use of colours harmonious.

Holsøe maintained this pictorial style in his later paintings. He executed many beautiful landscapes, but interiors dominated his extensive output: these often featured rooms furnished in mahogany, with a lone figure. Holsøe's themes were very close to those of his friend Vilhelm Hammershøi, whom he had met at the Kunstnernes Studieskole, and the two painters influenced each other's work, although it is not clear which was the first to paint interiors. In contrast to Hammershøi, who later achieved international recognition, Holsøe lived a secluded existence and was relatively little known. Compared with the symbolic overtones of Hammershøi's atmospheric paintings, Holsøe's works are more matter-of-fact in narrative and depiction of the natural beauty of the subject. The conception and representation of his numerous interiors (e.g. *A Lady Reading*, 1913; Århus, Kstmus.) has been compared to those of 17th-century Dutch artists.

Holsøe received a number of academic bursaries, including one to study in Italy (1897); he also received the annual Charlottenborg Academy medal in 1901 for an interior study and again in 1908 for the painting *Evening*. He took part in many exhibitions and is represented in a large number of museums in Scandinavia.

UNPUBLISHED SOURCES
Copenhagen, Kon. Bib. [letters]

BIBLIOGRAPHY
K. Madsen: 'Danish Art during the Last Year', *Nord. Tidsskr. Vet., Kst & Indust.*, i (1888), pp. 104–5
——: 'Some Exhibitions' Impressions', *Tilskueren* (1889), p. 414
S. Schultz: Obituary, *Dagens Nyheder* (8 Nov 1935)

RIGMOR LOVRING

Holst, Richard (Nicolaüs) Roland (*b* Amsterdam, 4 Dec 1868; *d* Bloemendaal, 31 Dec 1938). Dutch painter, printmaker, illustrator, writer and stained-glass artist. He trained at the Rijksakademie in Amsterdam (1886–90), under the directorship of August Allebé. Having initially painted and drawn Impressionistic landscapes, he started working in the 't Gooi region in 1892, where, influenced by Vincent van Gogh and Jan Toorop, he made a number of Symbolist drawings and lithographs. In 1896 he married the Dutch writer Henriette van der Schalk. They both devoted themselves to the recently founded Sociaal Democratische Arbeiders Partij. In the years up to *c.* 1900 Holst produced among other things a series of lithographs of political cartoons with socialist content, as well as serene landscapes and paintings of girls from the village of Huizen. His allegorical murals (1902; *in situ*), on topics such as 'Industry' or 'Commerce', in the new Koopmansbeurs in Amsterdam by H. P. Berlage (1876–1903),

marked an important point in his career as his first opportunity to construct a monumental piece of work. Partly inspired by the murals in the town hall at 's Hertogenbosch by Antoon Derkinderen, he developed a tight, stylized type of design, which he believed to be ideal for visually representing idealistic and exalted thoughts. In his murals (1903–6) in the headquarters of the Algemeene Nederlandsche Diamantbewerkers Bond (ANDB) he developed these principles into a severe system based on geometric foundations, which can be found in all his later work. This includes more murals in the ANDB's headquarters (1912 and 1936–7), a number of stained-glass windows, for example in the Amsterdam Lyceum (1920–27), in the post offices of Haarlem (1923) and Utrecht (1931) and in the cathedral in Utrecht (1926 and 1934–6), and decorated marble panels in the Supreme Court in The Hague (1937–8; destr.). In addition, throughout his career he designed sober, geometric exhibition and theatre posters, book jackets, magazine covers and programmes, mostly as lithographs. He also designed books.

Holst had an important role as professor (from 1918) and as director (from 1926) of the Rijksakademie in Amsterdam. Appointed by his friend Derkinderen to help propagate his ideal of *Gemeenschapkunst* (community art), monumental art for the benefit of the whole nation, he succeeded Derkinderen as director and allocated an even more important place in the curriculum to the teaching of monumental painting and sculpture. While Derkinderen sought his inspiration primarily in an idealized vision of the medieval guild system, Holst thought that art could only assume a central place within society again after the establishment of a socialist state. The influence of his ideas on the Dutch art world lasted until well after World War II. He put forward his views on fine art and its place within the social order not only in his lessons, but also in a number of texts, the most important being collected in *Over kunst en kunstenaars* (1923 and 1928) and *In en buiten het tij* (1940). He bequeathed a large part of his prints, drawings and designs to the print room of the Rijksmuseum in Amsterdam.

WRITINGS
Over kunst en kunstenaars—beschouwingen en herdenkingen [About art and artists—observations and obituaries], 2 vols (Amsterdam, 1923–8)
In en buiten het tij: Nagelaten beschouwingen en herdenkingen [In and outside the tide: posthumous observations and obituaries], ed. A. M. Hammacher, intro. H. Roland Holst-van der Schalk (Amsterdam, 1940)

BIBLIOGRAPHY
H. Roland Holst-van der Schalk: *Kinderjaren en jeugd van R. N. Roland Holst* [R. N. Roland Holst's childhood and youth] (Zeist, 1940)
W. Arondeus: *Figuren en problemen der monumentale schilderkunst in Nederland* (Amsterdam, 1941), pp. 58–186
B. Polak: *Het fin-de-siècle in de Nederlandse schilderkunst: De symbolistische beweging, 1890–1900* [The fin-de-siècle in Dutch painting: the Symbolist movement] (The Hague, 1955), pp. 230–71, 408–11
E. Braches: *Het boek als Nieuwe Kunst—een studie in Art Nouveau* (Utrecht, 1973), pp. 41–2, 54–60, 148–64, 272–306
Kunstenaren der idee: Symbolistische tendenzen in Nederland ca. 1880–1930 (exh. cat., ed. C. Blotkamp and others; The Hague, Gemeentemus., 1978)
P. Schatborn: 'Tekeningen van R. N. Roland Holst', *Bull. Rijksmus.*, xxvii (1979)
The Age of Van Gogh. Dutch Painting 1880–1895 (exh. cat., ed. R. Bionda, C. Blotkamp and others; Glasgow, Burrell Col., 1990–91)

L. Tibbe: *R. N. Roland Holst 1868–1938: Arbeid en schoonheid vereind: Oprattingen over Gemeenschapkunst* (diss., Nijmegen and Amsterdam, 1994) [extensive bibliog.]

JAN JAAP HEIJ

Holstein-Gottorp, House of. European dynasty of rulers, patrons and collectors, ruling in Germany, Sweden and Russia.

(1) Louisa Ulrica [Lovisa Ulrika], Queen of Sweden (*b* Berlin, 24 July 1720; *d* Svartsjö Castle, 16 July 1782). She was the daughter of Frederick William I, King of Prussia (*see* HOHENZOLLERN, (5)), and niece of George II, King of England. In 1744 she married Crown Prince Adolf Frederick of Sweden (1710–71), who became king in 1751. Intelligent and strong-willed, she tried, in vain, to play a strong political role. Her keen interest in the arts and sciences, however, made her the central personality of a refined and highly cultivated court circle, based mainly at Drottningholm (*see* STOCKHOLM, §4(ii)). She had this 17th-century castle enlarged and exquisitely redecorated by Carl Hårleman and Jean Eric Rehn. In the 1760s the theatre, and the Chinese pavilions were added by C. F. Adelcrantz.

Louisa Ulrica's extensive collections were housed at Drottningholm, but few items remain *in situ*. Among the first paintings she acquired were works by Chardin (e.g. *Domestic Pleasures*, 1747) and Boucher (e.g. *The Milliner*, 1746; both Stockholm, Nmus.), which Count Carl Gustav Tessin commissioned for her in 1745. In the same year her husband, whose collection never became as well known as hers, bought four works by Chardin, including *The Washerwoman* (1733) and the *Young Student Drawing* (both Stockholm, Nmus.), at the sale of Antoine de La Roque's collection. Louisa Ulrica's collection was spectacularly enriched in 1749, when King Frederick bought many of the pictures in the collection of Carl Gustav Tessin as a gift for her. Among them were many works by prominent contemporary French artists and 17th-century Dutch and Flemish painters. Most of her further acquisitions were made in the latter field, for example works by Nicholaes Berchem, Abraham Bloemaert, Karel Dujardin, Jan Baptist Weenix and Philips Wouwerman. Some 286 paintings are listed in an inventory (Stockholm, Riksarkv) compiled by her secretary, C. W. von Düben, in 1760, but few new purchases were made subsequently. As distinguished and renowned as her collection of paintings was Louisa Ulrica's museum of natural history; the first catalogue of her cabinet was drawn up by Carl von Linné (Linnaeus; 1707–78).

Financial difficulties forced Louisa Ulrica to sell Drottningholm and its contents to the state in 1777 on the initiative of her son, (2) Gustav III, who thereby aimed to keep the collection intact and also, eventually, to allow public access. The main part of Louisa Ulrica's collection is now in the Nationalmuseum, Stockholm; her natural history collection is owned by Uppsala University. Her husband's hardly less important collection of paintings had been dispersed after his death, but the drawings that he had acquired from Carl Gustav Tessin and about 60 out of 306 French, Netherlandish and Italian paintings (inventory, Stockholm, Riksarkv) were bought by Gustav III.

BIBLIOGRAPHY

F. Sander: *Nationalmuseum: Bidrag till Taflegalleriets historia* [National museum: contribution to the history of the picture gallery], i–iv (Stockholm, 1872–6)

F. Arnheim, ed.: *Luise Ulrike … Ungedruckte Briefe an Mitglieder des preussischen Königshauses,* i–ii (Gotha, 1909–10)

P. Lespinasse: *L'Art français et la Suède de 1637 à 1816: Essais de contribution à l'histoire de l'influence française* (Paris, 1913)

O. Jägerskiöld: *Lovisa Ulrika* (Stockholm, 1945)

B. von Malmborg, ed.: *Drottningholm* (Stockholm, 1966)

PONTUS GRATE

(2) Gustav III, King of Sweden (*b* Stockholm, 24 Jan 1746; *reg* 1771–92; *d* Stockholm, 29 March 1792). Son of (1) Louisa Ulrica. He exerted a great personal influence on cultural development in Sweden, probably due to the strong aesthetic emphasis in his education. From the age of five he learnt how to draw; later he practised both engraving and architectural design. His studies focused on French art and literature, reinforced by a visit to France in 1770–71. During the first decade of his reign he took a leading part in the creation of the Royal Academy of Music (1771) and the Royal Opera (1773) and subsequently promoted the establishment of the Swedish Academy (1786) and Royal Dramatic Theatre (1788). Literature, painting and sculpture were put to the service of the State, honouring national heroes and recording the most spectacular events of Gustav III's reign.

Gustav III's passion for architecture was greater than his interest in other arts, and his own architectural drawings (Stockholm, Nmus. and Nordiska Mus.) show that he played a significant part in the designing of such projects as the Opera House (1775–82; destr. 1892), Stockholm, and the Haga Palace (from 1783). He was familiar with the architecture of Carl Hårleman and C. F. Adelcrantz. The King's visit to Italy in 1783–4 intensified his interest in the monuments of antiquity, inspiring him to build in Stockholm a museum of antiquities (1792–4; now Museum of National Antiquities).

The GUSTAVIAN STYLE of architecture, interior decoration (*see* SWEDEN, fig. 16) and furnishings reflected Gustav III's passion for Neo-classicism. Contemporary Italian culture affected Gustav III less, but he favoured French artists in Rome with several commissions. In particular, he admired the scenography of Louis Jean Desprez, whom he succeeded in engaging in 1783–4 for the Swedish Royal Opera. Later Gustav III realized Desprez's eminence as an architect, and the latter's projects for the King reveal a fanciful approach to Neo-classicism. Gustav III's letters and architectural drawings also reveal his interest in landscape gardening; he was much involved in the creation of the English garden (*c*. 1785) at Drottningholm.

Gustav III alienated his nobility by undermining their power, and he forfeited popular support by increasing taxes; his pledge of Swedish arms against the French Revolution prompted his assassination. Political considerations have often been stressed as the essential motive behind his attitude towards the arts, but this hardly accounts for the intensity of his personal involvement. His designs do not lack originality, and his receptivity and refined taste made him an equal of the professional artists and architects.

BIBLIOGRAPHY

U. G. Johnsson, ed.: *Gustaf III: En konstbok från Nationalmuseum* [Gustav III: an art book from the National Museum] (Stockholm, 1972) [Eng. summaries]

M. Olausson: 'The Désert de Retz and King Gustavus III of Sweden', *Gaz. B.-A.*, n. s. 5, cvii (1986), pp. 181–90

——: *The Landscape Garden in Sweden: Studies on the Introduction and Development of Picturesque Gardening during the Gustavian Era* (diss., U. Uppsala, in preparation)

MAGNUS OLAUSSON

Holt, G(erard) H(endrik) M(aria) (*b* Haarlem, 16 June 1904; *d* Overveen, 14 Feb 1988). Dutch architect. He attended the School voor Bouwkunst, Versierende Kunsten en Kunstambachten, Haarlem, where his teachers included Pieter Vorkink (1878–1960). Between 1926 and 1930 Holt gained practical experience with Jan Boterenbrood, J. F. Staal, Hendrik Th. Wijdeveld and the brothers Herman Ambrosius Jan Baanders (1876–1953) and Jan Baanders (1884–1966). In 1930 he began as an independent architect. Although he was a founder-member of Groep 32, he was a functionalist-modernist and shared the Utopian views of the majority of his colleagues in De 8 en Opbouw (*see* ARCHITECTENGROEP DE 8). His design activities during the 1930s included shops in Haarlem, such as that in Anegang 33–37, major additions to a swimming-pool complex in Bloemendaal (1933–4) and various competition entries.

Between 1940 and 1958 Holt worked on the possibilities of systemizing and industrializing house production, and he was associated with the development of the Baksteen Montage Bouw and Korrelbeton systems. In 1947 Holt was appointed Professor in Design of Social Housing at the Technische Universiteit in Delft.

In 1945–6 Holt began a partnership with Bernard Bijvoet (*see* BIJVOET & DUIKER). Holt's own work at this time centred around his role in Roman Catholic church architecture. Among the churches that he designed were the St Josef church in Bos en Lommer near Amsterdam (1951; with K. P. Tholens), which retains some ornamental features in the manner of the Delft school, although its dominant image is of severe modern rectilinearity, and its exterior uses the exposed-concrete finishes that Holt subsequently favoured. By the late 1950s Holt was reflecting in his churches the liturgical need to bring the congregation closer to the altar, as in the Resurrection church in Slotervaart near Amsterdam, where the congregation is able to surround the altar on three sides. A number of theatres designed subsequently by Bijvoet's firm followed Holt's church designs in bringing the audience closer to the stage.

BIBLIOGRAPHY

H. P. G. de Boer: *Architect G. H. M. Holt (1904): Sociale woningbouw, kerken, theaters* (Amsterdam, 1983)

HILDEBRAND P. G. DE BOER

Holtzhey, Johann George [Georg] (*b* Amsterdam, 1729; *d* Amsterdam, 1808). Dutch medallist. Son of Martin Holtzhey (1697–1764), a medallist and engraver and master of the mints of Guelders and Middelburg, he trained as an engraver of coins and medals. In 1749 he took over the management of his father's medal making business in Amsterdam, producing in the same year a spectacular medal of the firework display staged in The Hague to commemorate the Peace of Aix-la-Chapelle (silver; see Scharloo, p.18). In 1752 he engraved the dies for a medal commemorating the elevation of Willem V, Prince of Orange Nassau, to the British Order of the Garter (silver; see Hawkins, Franks and Grueber, ii, no. 379). He was a prolific medallist, and his faultless classical style ensured him commissions not only from within the Netherlands (e.g. from the Temperance Society of Amsterdam and The Hague Association for the Defence of the Christian Faith) but also from the royal houses of France and Prussia, including the silver medal commemorating Prince Ferdinand of Brunswick's victory at the Battle of Minden (silver, 1759; see Hawkins, Franks and Grueber, ii, no. 432). His medals were often issued with a *verklaring*, a printed explanation of the symbolism of the reverses. From 1771 to 1776 he was Master of the Mint at Utrecht.

BIBLIOGRAPHY

Forrer; Thieme–Becker

E. Hawkins, A. W. Franks and H. A. Grueber: *Medallic Illustrations of the History of Great Britain and Ireland*, 2 vols (London, 1885)

G. van der Meer: 'Medals of the Seven Years' War by Johann George Holtzhey', *The Medal*, x (1986), pp. 11–17

M. Scharloo: 'Holtzey and Son', *The Medal*, xvii (1990), pp. 16–17

PHILIP ATTWOOD

Holy Mountain. *See* SACROMONTE.

Holy Saviour, Order of the. *See* BRIGITTINE ORDER.

Holzbauer, Wilhelm (*b* Salzburg, 3 Sept 1930). Austrian architect. He studied at the Technikum in Salzburg (1946–50) and at the Akademie der Bildenden Künste in Vienna (1950–53) under Clemens Holzmeister. In 1952 he founded the Arbeitsgruppe 4 with Friedrich Kurrent (*b* 1931) and Johannes Spalt (*b* 1920) and remained a member of it until 1964. From 1956 to 1957 he studied at the Massachusetts Institute of Technology in Cambridge, MA. As a result of his stays in the USA, he soon began to distance himself from his group's constructivist trends. He attempted to bring to mind the 'romantic realism' of his teacher Clemens Holzmeister, the semantic of monumental configurations, and the logic of surveyable space concepts with a 'pragmatic architectural notion'. His first independently created buildings were in Salzburg, the Pfarrzentrum St Vitalis (1968–73) and the Bildungshaus St Virgil (1967–76), both representing varying reactions to the manneristic Salzburg tradition. A programmatic residential building in Vienna within the framework of the 'Wohnen-Morgen' competition (1973–9) represented a successful attempt to find an adequate alternative for present-day requirements in a Viennese grid area of the late 19th century. Between 1980 and 1985 a variant of this type was realized in Berlin, at the corner of Reichenbergstrasse and Mariannenstrasse in Kreuzberg, within the framework of the Internationale Bauausstellung.

From 1970 to 1982, as one of the U-Bahn architects' group, Holzbauer designed the Viennese underground railway lines U1 and U4, which was followed by a contract for stations in Vancouver (1982–6). One of his greatest international successes was the Stadhuis (1967–77) and its opera house in Amsterdam (completed 1986), which show

Holzbauer's particular ability to transfer a complex building programme into a 'readable' configuration and to integrate it into a difficult urban location. Similarly, the University of Salzburg (Faculty of Natural Science, 1978–86; constructed with several partners), on a landscaped site, was integrated into a Baroque environment and reflected the old Salzburg city style. Holzbauer's projects of the late 1980s include Kärntnerringhof, an IBM office building, the Zentralsparkasse office building and Wien-Film residential building (all in Vienna); the Biozentrum of the Johann Wolfgang Goethe University, Frankfurt am Main, Siemens' office building in Linz, and an extension of the Landhaus in Bregenz.

BIBLIOGRAPHY

H. Hübl: *Wilhelm Holzbauer: Porträt eines Architekten* (Vienna, 1977)
Wilhelm Holzbauer, Bauten und Projekte, 1953–85, foreword F. Achleitner (Salzburg, 1985)
Wilhelm Holzbauer, Bauten und Projekte, 1985–90, foreword C. Reder (Salzburg, 1990)

FRIEDRICH ACHLEITNER

Hölzel [Hoelzel], **Adolf** (*b* Olmütz, Moravia, 13 May 1853; *d* Stuttgart, 17 May 1934). German painter. While still at school he became familiar with lithography and printing methods with the intention of joining his father's thriving publishing firm. His later decision to study art eventually met with his father's approval, and from 1876 until 1879 he trained at the Akademie der Bildenden Künste, Vienna. In 1879 he transferred to the Akademie der Bildenden Künste in Munich, where until 1881 he continued his training under Carl Barth and Wilhelm von Diez (1839–1907). After a study tour with the German painter Arthur Langhammer (1854–1901) he returned to Munich to paint.

A visit to Paris in the 1880s had a decisive effect on Hölzel's future development. He frequented the studios of Manet and Monet and was particularly impressed by the *plein-air* paintings of the Impressionists. As a direct result both his style and his technique underwent immediate change. Whereas his early work was executed in the realistic manner of Diez, and his paintings of the early 1880s (e.g. *Seamstress (Crothenburg Interior)*, 1884; Stuttgart, Staatsgal.) were similar in subject and style to those of Wilhelm Leibl, by the end of the decade his allegiance was to French Impressionist principles, as in *Beer Garden* (1890–91; priv. col., see Venzmer, p. 236).

The next important phase in Hölzel's career began in 1888 with his decision to settle in Dachau, where with Ludwig Dill (1848–1940), Fritz von Uhde and Arthur Langhammer he founded the New Dachau school of painting. In the ensuing years he became increasingly convinced that his most important function as an artist was to discover a formal language to express his inner feelings and his impressions of the external world. From *c.* 1907 his work was dominated by abstractions based on religious themes. Influenced by musical theory and inspired by the ideas of Georges Seurat, he developed a system of painting based on harmony and counterpoint, which found expression in his works from 1910, for example *Composition in Red II* (1914; Hannover, Pelican-Kstsamml.).

From 1906 until 1919 Hölzel held the post of Professor at the Staatliche Akademie der Bildenden Künste in Stuttgart where he was influential as a teacher to Oskar Schlemmer, Johannes Itten and others. The diminishing role of the subject in his work, which was subservient to the exploration of formal problems, and his ultimate concern for the integrity of the picture plane led Hölzel to be considered as one of the pioneers of abstract art in Germany.

BIBLIOGRAPHY

K. Leonhard: *Adolf Hoelzel* (Munich, 1968)
Adolf Hoelzel, 1853–1934: Gemälde, Pastelle, Zeichnungen (exh. cat., Würzburg, Städt. Gal., 1979)
W. Venzmer: *Adolf Hölzel: Leben und Werk* (Stuttgart, 1982)
Adolf Hölzel: Bilder, Pastelle, Zeichnungen, Collagen (exh. cat., ed. C. Haelein; Hannover, Kestner-Ges., 1982)

COLIN J. BAILEY

Holzer, Jenny (*b* Gallipolis, OH, 29 July 1950). American installation and conceptual artist. Her studies included general art courses at Duke University, Durham, NC (1968–70), and then painting, printmaking and drawing at the University of Chicago before completing her BFA at Ohio University, Athens (1972). In 1974 she took summer courses at the Rhode Island School of Design, Providence, entering its MFA programme in 1975 and beginning her first work with language, installation and public art. Holzer moved to New York in 1977. Her first public works, *Truisms* (1977–9), appeared in the form of anonymous broadsheets pasted on buildings, walls and fences in and around Manhattan. Commercially printed in cool, bold italics, numerous one-line statements such as '*Abuse of power comes as no surprise*' and '*There is a fine line between information and propaganda*', were meant to be provocative and elicit public debate. Thereafter Holzer used language and the mechanics of late 20th-century communications as an assault on established notions of where art should be shown, with what intention and for whom. Her texts took the forms of posters, monumental and electronic signs, billboards, television and her signature medium, the LED (light emitting diode) sign. Other works appeared on T-shirts, tractor hats, stickers, metal plaques, park benches and sarcophagi. The LED signs have been placed in high-impact public spaces such as Times Square, New York, as well as in art galleries and museums.

BIBLIOGRAPHY

Jenny Holzer: Signs (exh. cat., Des Moines, IA, A. Cent., 1986–7)
Jenny Holzer (exh. cat. by D. Waldman, New York, Guggenheim, 1989–90)
M. Auping: *Jenny Holzer* (New York, 1992)

□

Holzer, Johann Evangelist (*b* Burgeis (now Burgusio, Italy), South Tyrol, 24 Dec 1709; *d* Clemenswerth, Westphalia, 21 July 1740). German painter. His artistic talents first became apparent while he was at the monastery school of Marienberg (now Monte Maria Abbey), where he made many drawings from copper engravings after the work of Sir Peter Paul Rubens. At this time he produced an oil portrait of *Johann Baptist Murr, Abbot of Marienberg* (destr.). In autumn 1724 Murr secured for Holzer a place as apprentice with the painter Nicolaus Auer (1690–1753), in Sankt Martin, near Passau. After four years, Holzer went to Lower Bavaria to become an apprentice to Joseph Anton Merz (1681–1750). To complete his education, Holzer next moved to Augsburg. Under the guidance of

Johann Georg Bergmüller, head of the Akademie in Augsburg, Holzer produced altarpieces and devotional pictures, and he took part in commissions for façade frescoes. After a return visit to the South Tyrol, where he applied unsuccessfully for a place in the monastery of Marienberg, Holzer returned to Augsburg in August 1732.

In Augsburg, where he lived with Bergmüller, Holzer matured into an independent artist and developed a style that came to serve as a model for copyists and emulators, both in the form of finished work and through prints after Holzer's drawings. After completing various façade frescoes (he had probably learnt fresco painting under Merz in Straubing) Holzer produced his first religious ceiling fresco, for the pilgramage church of St Anton in Partenkirchen in 1736, his only fresco to have survived in its original state (see below). A year later, for the Prince-Bishop of Eichstätt, he painted the ceiling fresco of the banqueting hall at the summer residence, not far from Augsburg, for which he received the title of court painter to the Prince-Bishop. From 1737 to 1740 Holzer was principally engaged on decorations for the ceiling vault of the abbey church at Münsterschwarzach, built by Balthasar Neumann. Holzer's steadily increasing reputation is also evident in the fact that several colleagues, including Gottfried Bernhard Göz, Johann Wolfgang Baumgartner and Matthäus Günther (who later purchased parts of Holzer's artistic estate), reworked his ideas. In the summer of 1740, Holzer travelled to northwest Germany, as he had been asked to design frescoes for the hunting lodge at Clemenswerth commissioned by the Cologne Archbishop and Elector, Clemens August of Bavaria. Holzer died of a typhoid infection, however, before he was able to carry out this work.

About 110 compositions by Holzer are now known. These include oil paintings, mostly altarpanels, façade frescoes and ceiling paintings, drawings (e.g. the three fan designs of 1734; Karlsruhe, Staatl. Ksthalle), as well as etchings and mezzotint engravings made after his drawings. Most of Holzer's works are now destroyed, but copies of some are preserved, for example in the 39 engravings by Johann Esaias Nilson, made after Holzer's paintings: *Pictura a fresco in aedibus Augustae vindelic. a Joanne Holtzer pictore ingenioso* (*c.* 1765–9). One of Holzer's first works in Augsburg was a fresco *Ecce homo* (1732; destr.) on the Klinkertor, in which he independently reworked borrowings from Michelangelo and Titian found in the paintings of Bergmüller. Also from 1732 were decorations provided for the windows of the tavern Zur Goldenen Traube, with the biblical scene, *Two Spies Bring an Enormous Grape from Canaan* (1732; destr.). Here, and in the *Peasants' Dance* (1736; destr.) on the façade of another tavern, Holzer revealed his talent for combining clear drawing, warm colours and three-dimensional figure structure with decoratively rhythmic composition. In Augsburg, a centre of the German printing and publishing trades, Holzer had access to prints after a wide range of useful and stimulating sources; and the *Peasants' Dance* may have been influenced by images as varied as the work of Antoine Watteau and Hans Holbein (ii), notably the façade frescoes of the Haus zum Bauerntanz in Basle. Holzer's frescoes were much admired by Francesco Algarotti and many copies after them survive. In 1737,

Holzer carried out façade paintings for the building of the publishing house of the court copper engraver, Johann Andreas Pfeffel (1674–1748), with *Brotherly Love Shown through the Fable of Castor and Pollux* as the principal scene. For all his decorative sense, Holzer always showed an understanding of the need for clear formal structure, and of a highly contrasted use of light and shade, a technique drawn from Carlo Maratti's style, again through the work of Bergmüller. With its sensitively modified stimuli from French engravings, and from the art of contemporary Venetians such as Giovanni Battista Piazetta and Jacopo Amigoni, Holzer's fresco was a masterpiece of South German Rococo design. Holzer's ceiling fresco in the garden-room in Pfeffel's house (1737; destr.), showing the *Twelve Months Dancing to the Pipe of Time*, is especially effective. This composition survives in a watercoloured engraving by Nilson (Karlsruhe, Staatl. Ksthalle).

Outside Augsburg, the only fresco by Holzer to have survived in its original state is in the oval main cupola of the small pilgrimage church of St Anton, Partenkirchen, illustrating the *Thirteen So-called Privileges of St Anthony of Padua, Procured by him from the Christ Child* (1736; see fig.). Holzer provided *trompe l'oeil* architectural structures above the moulding, in front of which the supplicants appear in highly foreshortened perspective; the titular saint and the Christ child hover in the golden sky of the cupola above them. Vision and intercession are the central themes. Here Holzer combined the expressive values of space, light, three-dimensional form and colour with an

Johann Evangelist Holzer: cupola fresco (1736), St Anton, Partenkirchen

emotionally charged, naturalistic, popular approach to the fresco's subject-matter. Holzer was also very assured in matters of technique, and he was able to transform the appearance of his painting with the use of glazes. In this, his greatest religious work, Holzer may well have drawn on the dramatic style of Cosmas Damian Asam and the clarity of form he had observed in Bergmüller's work, as well as Venetian influences such as the work of Giovanni Antonio Pellegrini and the *sfumato* technique of Jacopo Amigoni. Holzer also painted ten small surrounding medallions.

Outstanding among Holzer's secular work is the rectangular ceiling fresco in the Sommerresidenz, Eichstätt (*in situ*, though much over-painted; small oil copy, Augsburg, Schaezlerpal.), a light, cheerful allegorical scene of *Spring*, very close to the work of Amigoni at Schleissheim (Neues Schloss). Holzer's greatest work was to be found in his frescoes at Münsterschwarzach (1737–40; destr.). In 1737, Holzer was commissioned to decorate the crossing dome (oil sketch, Augsburg, Schaezlerpal.). Again, Holzer used *trompe l'oeil* architecture to surround an open sky in which appear the Holy Trinity, and the Virgin rising towards Heaven, surrounded by the saints of the Benedictine Order. It is likely that Holzer's treatment of space would have been congenial to Balthasar Neumann's architecture, and the combination may well have influenced, for example, Matthäus Günther in planning his cupola fresco in Rott am Inn (former abbey church of SS Marinus und Anianus) in 1763. In Sept 1738, Holzer signed an additional contract for six further ceiling paintings (one each in the choir and two parts of the transept, and three in the nave). In 1739 he received the commission for the high altar panel: *The Glorification of St Felicitas*, and he completed his work at Münsterschwarzach with four ceiling frescoes in the spandrels of the crossing dome in 1740. These appear to be Holzer's last works.

BIBLIOGRAPHY

A. v. Dipauli: 'Johann Holzer', *Beiträge zur Geschichte, Statistik, Naturkunde und Kunst von Tirol und Vorarlberg*, viii (Innsbruck, 1834), pp. 272–315; repr. in *Jb. Mus. Ferdinandeum*, viii (1934)
A. Buff: 'Augsburger Fassadenmalerei', *Z. Bild. Kst*, xxi (1886), pp. 58–71; xxii (1887), pp. 275–7
E. Welisch: *Augsburger Maler im 18. Jahrhundert* (Augsburg, 1901)
A. Hämmerle: 'Der Fürstbischöflich Eichstättische Hofmaler und Augsburger Kunst- und Historienmaler Johann Ev. Holzer (1709–1740)', *Sammbl. Hist. Ver. Eichstätt*, xxiii (1908), pp. 101–55
——: 'Miscellaneen zu "Der Fürstbischöflich Eichstättische Hofmaler . . . Johann Ev. Holzer"', *Sammbl. Hist. Ver. Eichstätt*, xxiv (1909), pp. 62–3
——: 'Tätigkeit des Fürstbischöflich Eichstättischen Hofmalers . . . Johann Ev. Holzer in der Benediktinerstiftskirche Münsterschwarzach in Unterfranken', *Sammbl. Hist. Ver. Eichstätt*, xxv/xxvi (1910–11), pp. 16–32
A. Feulner: 'Süddeutsche Freskomalerei', *Münch. Jb. Bild. Kst*, x (1916–18), pp. 65–101
A. Hämmerle: 'Joh. Evangelist Holzer als Radierer', *Schwäb. Mus.* (1928), pp. 147–58
H. Ginter: *Südwestdeutsche Kirchemalerei des Barock* (Augsburg, 1930)
C. Lamb: 'Johann Evangelist Holzer: Das Genie der Freskomalerei des süddeutschen Rokokos', *Augusta 955–1955* (Augsburg, 1955), pp. 371–91
E.-W. Mick: Joannes Holzer, 1709–1740: Beiträge zur Monographie unter besonderer Rücksicht auf ikonographischen Fragen, *Cult. Atesina*, xii (1958), pp. 31–118; xiii (1959), pp. 16–54
K. Rossacher: 'Ein neuentdeckter Modello Johann Evangelist Holzers für das Hochaltarblatt von Münsterschwarzach', *Alte & Mod. Kst*, lxxvi (1964), pp. 22–4
H. Schnell: *St Anton Partenkirchen* (Munich, 1980)
H. Bauer and B. Rupprecht, eds: *Corpus der barocken Deckenmalerei in Deutschland*, ii (Munich, 1981)
E.-W. Mick: *Johann Evangelist Holzer (1709–1740): Ein frühvollendetes Malergenie des 18. Jahrhunderts* (Munich and Zurich, 1984)
Johann Evangelist Holzer, 1709–1740, zum 250. Todesjahr: Fresken in Augsburg und in Münsterschwarzach (exh. cat., Augsburg, Städt. Kstsammlungen, 1990–91)

WOLFGANG HOLLER

Holzinger, Franz Josef Ignaz (*b* Vocklabruck; *bapt* 7 Sept 1691; *d* St Florian, 14 March 1775). Austrian stuccoist. He came from a family of stuccoists and began his earliest documented work, the decoration (1718–22) of the pilgrimage church of the Holy Trinity at Stadl-Paura, near Lambach, with his father, Johann Georg Holzinger (*d* 1738), although he finished it alone. At the same time he was working at the abbeys of Lambach and St Florian (from 1719). The stuccowork (1719) in the abbot's antechamber at St Florian is typical of Holzinger's early work, in which the ribbon work usually flows out in C-shaped loops ending in scrolled acanthus leaves. The angular shape of the loops, producing squares, is also typical. From 1722 to 1724 he made the splendid atlantids in the library at Metten Abbey. The striding figures seem to carry the ceiling with ease: their fluttering garments typify south German Rococo art. Holzinger moved to St Florian in 1724 owing to an increasing number of commissions from the abbey (*see* ST FLORIAN ABBEY, §1). Other works included decoration (1730–42) of the library, imperial staircase and emperor's room at Altenburg Abbey. In 1737 he did the stucco decoration in the vestry of Reichersberg Abbey, covering the ceiling with a delicate web of stuccowork. Holzinger was one of the most important late Baroque stuccoists in Austria. He was particularly imaginative in his use of ribbon work, latticework and draped shapes in white on a pastel background, or vice versa, as in the *sala terrena* at St Florian; his mature work is characterized by finer stucco reliefs and more figurative motifs. He remained faithful to his style; the stuccowork (1768) in the observatory at Kremsmünster resembles his masterpieces of 30 years earlier.

BIBLIOGRAPHY

W. Mies van der Rohe: *Franz Josef Holzinger* (diss., Munich, Tech. U., 1945)
W. Luger: 'Barocker Stuck in Oberösterreich', *Oberösterreich Kultz.*, i (1974), pp. 14–20
——: 'Der Stukkateur Franz Josef Holzinger aus Schärfling am Attersee', *Kstjb. Stadt Linz* (1974–5), pp. 51–9
Linzer Stukkateure (exh. cat., ed. W. Luger; Linz, Stadtmus., 1977), pp. 76–9
M. Koller: 'Die Farbigkeit der Stukkatur, zu ihrer Entwicklung in Österreich vom 16. bis zum 18. Jhdt', *Kstjb. Stadt Linz* (1979), pp. 5–29

A. GERHARDT

Holzman, Malcolm. *See under* HARDY HOLZMAN PFEIFFER ASSOCIATES.

Holzmeister, Clemens (*b* Fulpmes, Tyrol, 27 March 1886; *d* Salzburg, 12 June 1983). Austrian teacher and architect. He was educated at the Technische Hochschule, Vienna, where he was made professor in 1919 at the early age of 32. Although he entered architectural practice in 1914, his reputation rests largely on an influential teaching career. After a period as professor at the Staatsgewerbeschule, Innsbruck, in 1924 he returned to Vienna, becoming professor and head of the master class in architecture at the Akademie der Bildenden Künste. He held the professorship at the Kunstakademie, Düsseldorf, from 1928 to 1932, while retaining the Viennese post until he was forced to leave Austria in 1938. In 1940–49 he was a professor of architecture at the Technical School in Istanbul, Turkey, and resumed his professorial post at the Akademie der Bildenden Künste, Vienna, in 1954. The core of his teaching method derived from the master class system, which he pursued in each post he occupied. This was particularly effective at Vienna in the 1950s. His romantic–historical approach, involving emphasis on the geographical and historical context and allowing a degree of irrationality and sensuality in his students' work, helped to lay the foundations for Austrian architecture in the 1970s and 1980s, when a new era of experimentation and innovation emerged.

Of his executed projects, Holzmeister's early buildings show the abiding influence of historicism and include the superb Eichmann country house and boathouse (1926–7), Litzelberg Seewald, and the Kreuzschwesternschule (1926), Linz. Other works include the ministerial complex and Ataturk Palace (early 1930s), Ankara; numerous ecclesiastical buildings, such as the parish church (1965), Zwolfaxing; and continuous additions (1926; 1937–8; 1956–60) to the Festspielhaus, Salzburg.

WRITINGS
Bauten, Entwürfe und Zeichnungen (Salzburg and Leipzig, 1937)

BIBLIOGRAPHY
W. Frodl: *Clemens Holzmeister, 1947–54: In Turkie und Wien* (Vienna, 1966)
M. Knofler: *Clemens Holzmeister* (Frankfurt am Main, 1975)
Clemens Holzmeister (exh. cat., Vienna, Akad. Bild. Kst., 1982)

MICHAEL SPENS

Homar, Lorenzo (*b* San Juan, 1913). Puerto Rican printmaker, painter and illustrator. He grew up in New York City and from 1937 to 1942 studied there at the Art Students League and at Pratt Institute before doing four years' military service. After World War II, he returned to New York as a designer for Cartier, the jewellers where he had been apprenticed as a student, and studied at the Art School of the Brooklyn Museum, where he met Max Beckman and Rufino Tamayo. In 1950 he returned to Puerto Rico where he was the principal founding member of the Centro de Arte Puertorriqueño and joined the staff of the Division of Community Education, becoming its Graphic Arts Director in 1951

Homar is credited as the artist most responsible for promoting printmaking in Puerto Rico. He trained other important artists, such as Antonio Martorell, José Rosa and Myrna Báez, and ran workshops at Cali in Colombia and in Havana, Cuba, helping to extend his influence further afield in Latin America.

While serving as director of the graphic workshop of the Instituto de Cultura Puertorriqueña, the most important in Puerto Rico, from 1957 to 1970, he produced more than 500 posters and several portfolios of screenprints, such as *Casals Portfolio* (1970), which were admired for their distinctive style and sophisticated technique. As many as 30 to 40 manual runs were used in the making of each poster, which were characterized also by an expressive use of typography and textures.

Screenprinted posters, woodcuts, engravings, political cartoons, book illustrations, logos and stage designs all feature in Homar's prolific production. From 1964 to 1972 he produced a series of monumental woodcuts in which he combined political or poetic texts with highly evocative images and expressive rhythmic incisions. Assimilating aspects of American Realism and German Expressionism, he also continued producing paintings on social realist themes rendered in a neat, meticulous style that suggests a printmaker's rigour and precision.

BIBLIOGRAPHY
Exposición retrospectiva de la obra de Lorenzo Homar (exh. cat. by R. Arbona, M. Benítez and M. C. Ramírez, Ponce, Mus. A., 1978)
Puerto Rican Painting: Between Past and Present (exh. cat. by M. C. Ramírez, Washington, DC, Mus. Mod. A. Latin America, 1987)

MARI CARMEN RAMÍREZ

Home, Henry, Lord Kames (*b* Berwicks [now Borders Reg.], 1696; *d* Edinburgh, 27 Dec 1782). Scottish philosopher, lawyer and judge. He wrote on a wide variety of topics including literary criticism, rhetoric, philosophy, law, natural history, education and agriculture. He played a significant role in the Enlightenment discussions of aesthetic feeling and judgement, especially the analysis of beauty and THE SUBLIME. His wide-ranging work also contributed to 18th-century debates about value and differences in the fine arts (*see also* UT PICTURA POESIS) and the development of taste. The *Elements of Criticism* (1762), his most famous work, deals with such topics as emotions and passions, beauty, grandeur, the sublime, novelty, narration and taste, and it was widely used as a textbook on criticism and rhetoric. While covering painting, sculpture, music, gardening and architecture, his views on the hierarchy of the fine arts led him to devote most of his attention to drama and the artistic use of language. The work as a whole investigates the 'sensitive part' of human nature.

Kames held that it is by determining what is naturally agreeable and disagreeable that the critic of the fine arts formulates universal critical principles. These principles are thus the basis for a rational science for the fine arts, which can be 'cultivated to a high degree of refinement'. Emotional responses, such as the perception of beauty, grandeur and the sublime, are then defined and developed as part of this process of critical judgement. Kames believed that, while beauty depends for its existence on both a perceiver and a perceived, it is not inherent in either, and he divided the perception of beauty into 'feelings' of 'intrinsic beauty', and 'sensations' of 'relative beauty'. He maintained that human psychology is such that when a train of ideas is connected in a natural order there is a feeling of pleasure (and of displeasure when the order is unnatural). Objects that give rise to pleasure are therefore characterized by simplicity, regularity, uniformity, proportion, order and completeness. 'Intrinsic beauty' is thus perceived when a person considers an ordered object in isolation and experiences this feeling of pleasure. By contrast, 'relative beauty' involves a sensation of pleasure that arises from an understanding of how an ordered object is a means properly fitted to its end. Combinations of objects can then be called beautiful by virtue of their congruity.

According to Kames, a work of art is pleasing when it is perceived as being conformable to, and imitative of, a natural order, and any work of art should therefore be judged by its success in imitating nature. He reasoned that when there is a lively and distinct image of an object, the object is ideally, though not really, present. Therefore, it is by creating the ideal presence of things mentally associated with pleasant or unpleasant emotions that art is able to give rise to pleasure or displeasure. He argued that of all the arts it is theatre, by producing its imitation through both language and action, that creates the most effective ideal presence and intense passion. To a lesser degree language alone or painting can also create vivid images and emotions; however, because passions typically require a succession of impressions, it is literature (by reiterating impressions indefinitely) that is superior to painting (which embodies a single impression of an instantaneous event). He maintained that human nature is constituted to be the ultimate standard of taste in the fine arts, that delicacy of taste can be improved and fostered through education, reflection and experience, and that it is the purpose of criticism to assist in this process.

WRITINGS
Essays on the Principles of Morality and Natural Religion (Edinburgh, 1751, 2/1758)
Elements of Criticism (Edinburgh, 1762, 11/1839)
Sketches of the History of Man (Edinburgh, 1774, rev. Glasgow, 1819)

BIBLIOGRAPHY
H. W. Randall: *The Critical Theory of Lord Kames* (Northampton, MA, 1944)
A. E. McGuinness: *Henry Home, Lord Kames* (New York, 1970)
I. S. Ross: *Lord Kames and the Scotland of his Day* (Oxford, 1972)

ALAN CODE

Homem. Portuguese family of cartographers.

(1) Lopo Homem (*b* ?Lisbon, ?pre-1500; *d* ?Lisbon, after 1565). The earliest known document to name Lopo Homem, dated 16 February 1517, indicates that he was already a master craftsman in the production of nautical charts, he was still working in 1565, when a document refers to him as a cartographer. Other documents show that he was attached to the court of John III of Portugal; he is described as a cosmographer as well as a *cavaleiro fidalgo da casa real* (knight of the royal household). It is likely that in 1524 he took part as technical adviser to the Portuguese delegation in unsuccessful discussions with representatives from Castile on the exact location of the Molucca Islands.

(2) Diogo Homem (*b* ?Lisbon, *c*. 1520; *d* ?Lisbon, after 1576). Son of (1) Lopo Homem. He worked with his father in his Lisbon workshop; of his work 12 atlases and 12 maps are known. Some of these are undated, some are unsigned; several atlases have folios containing nautical or cosmographical information.

Some time earlier than 1547 Diogo Homem was involved in the death of a certain António Fernandes, for which he was imprisoned and subsequently sentenced to a year's exile. On his release he fled to England, where his presence was recorded in 1547 and from where he sent a petition asking for a pardon from John III of Portugal. In the same year he brought an action against the Admiralty to obtain payment for a map he had drawn for a Venetian, one 'Aloisius Blancus', which was valued at between 80 and 100 ducats.

There are five known works by Diogo Homem:

Planisphere, part of an atlas of charts of the Atlantic (1519; Paris, Bib. N.). He probably collaborated with Pedro and Jorge Reinel on other maps in this atlas which are profusely decorated with drawings of people, exotic animals, trees and castles and with caravels and other ships, all carefully drawn and painted in watercolour. The scenes of daily life of the Indians of Brazil and the drawings of animals native to South America are of particular interest.

Portolan (coastal) chart (*c*. 1550; Rome, Duke Salviati di Migliarino priv. col.).

Chart of the Atlantic Ocean (*c*. 1550; Lisbon, Bib. N.).

Planisphere (1554; Florence, Mus. Stor. Sci.) containing little decoration, which suggests that, like many of the maps made by Diogo Homem, it was intended for the use of sailors and pilots rather than as a courtly gift.

Atlas (1558; London, BL) including pages of astronomical information and a roughly drawn planisphere as well as other maps decorated with depictions of cities, castles, banners and shields of various countries, one showing Prester John enthroned; others show animals that were previously unknown in Europe. The page devoted to South America is particularly rich in the variety of subject-matter and in its colouring and shows lions (which did not exist in that continent), trees, Indians engaged in rural occupations or hunting as well as a cannibal feast, as Diogo Homem imagined it. These drawings show considerable differences from those in the Homem-Reinel atlas discussed above; this supports the theory that the South American map in that earlier atlas was drawn in the workshop of the Reinel brothers.

BIBLIOGRAPHY
A. Cortesão: *Os homens: Cartógrafos portugueses do século XVI* (Coimbra, 1932)
——: *Portugaliae monumenta cartographica* (Lisbon, 1960), i, pp. 49–53; ii, pp. 3–10

LUÍS DE ALBUQUERQUE

Homer, Winslow (*b* Boston, MA, 24 Feb 1836; *d* Prout's Neck, ME, 29 Sept 1910). American painter, illustrator and etcher. He was one of the two most admired American late 19th-century artists (the other being Thomas Eakins), and is considered to be the greatest pictorial poet of outdoor life in the USA and its greatest watercolourist. Nominally a landscape painter, in a sense carrying on Hudson River school attitudes, Homer was an artist of power and individuality whose images are metaphors for the relationship of Man and Nature. A careful observer of visual reality, he was at the same time alive to the purely physical properties of pigment and colour, of line and form, and the patterns they create. His work is characterized by bold, fluid brushwork, strong draughtsmanship and composition, and particularly by a lack of sentimentality.

1. Early career, to 1872. 2. Middle years, 1873–82. 3. Late works, 1883–1910.

1. EARLY CAREER, TO 1872. Homer was the second of three sons of Charles Savage Homer, a hardware importer, and Henrietta Benson Homer, a gifted amateur watercolourist. Brought up in Cambridge, MA, where he attended school, he had an active outdoor boyhood that left a lifelong liking for the country. An independent, strong-willed young man, he showed an early preference for art and was encouraged in his interest by both parents. Like a number of self-educated American artists, Homer was first known as an illustrator. At 19 he became an apprentice at the lithographic firm of J. H. Bufford in Boston, where he developed a basic feeling for draughtsmanship and for composing in clear patterns of dark and light. When he completed his apprenticeship in 1857, he was determined to support himself as a freelance illustrator. His first illustrations—scenes of life in Boston and rural New England—appeared in *Ballou's Pictorial Drawing-Room Companion*, the noted Boston weekly. In 1859 he moved to New York and became an illustrator for *Harper's Weekly* magazine and for various literary texts, an activity that occupied him intermittently to 1887; among the authors he illustrated were the poets William Cullen Bryant, Henry Wadsworth Longfellow and Alfred, Lord Tennyson. Shortly after arriving in New York he decided to broaden his artistic training. He attended drawing classes in Brooklyn, went to night school at the National Academy of Design and for a brief time had lessons in oil painting from the French genre and landscape painter Frédéric Rondel (1826–92). During the Civil War he went south with the Union Armies, serving as artist–correspondent for *Harper's*. His illustrations, showing the daily routine of camp life, are marked by realism, firm draughtsmanship and an absence of heroics. They were among the strongest pictorial reporting of the war.

After the war Homer began to concentrate on oil painting. These early oils, inspired by wartime scenes, are sober in colour and reveal the influence of his work as an illustrator in their grasp of the simple, telling gesture and the clarity of tone. They were instrumental in his election to the National Academy at the age of 29. His masterpiece of this period is *Prisoners from the Front* (1866; New York, Met.), which shows a Union officer confronting a group of Confederate prisoners in the midst of a devastated Virginia landscape. Shown at the National Academy of Design in 1866, it created a sensation and was hailed as the most powerful and convincing painting to have come out of the Civil War; it was singled out for praise at the Exposition Universelle in Paris in 1867.

Late in 1866 Homer made his first trip to Europe, spending ten months in France. In Paris he shared a studio in Montmartre with Albert Warren Kelsey, a friend from Massachusetts, and spent time in the countryside. His paintings from this period show the influence of the Barbizon school, especially the work of Jean-François Millet. Possibly as a result of seeing the work of such progressive French landscape painters as Eugène Boudin, on his return to New York in the autumn of 1867, Homer lightened his palette, and his touch became somewhat freer (e.g. *Long Branch, New Jersey*, 1869; Boston, MA,

Mus. F.A.). Although New York was his winter home for over 20 years, he never painted it and seldom illustrated it. The outdoor world furnished the main content of his art for the rest of his life. From late spring into the autumn he worked in the country, mostly in New England but on occasion in New York state and New Jersey. These summer months provided material for almost all his early paintings and illustrations. While in a general sense he was continuing a native genre tradition initiated in the 1830s by William Sidney Mount and still being carried on by such popular painters as John George Brown, Homer's content marked a departure from the sentimentalism of the old school. Within a naturalistic style he combined authenticity of images and a reserved idyllicism. Rural children at play (e.g. *Snap the Whip*, 1872; Youngstown, OH, Butler Inst. Amer. A.) and handsome young people at leisure (e.g. a *Game of Croquet*, 1866; New Haven, CT, Yale U., A.G.) were his subjects, presented within clear, firm outlines and broad planes of colour.

2. MIDDLE YEARS, 1873–82. By 1873 Homer was at a critical point in his career. Although his ability was recognized, he sold few oils, and he derived little sense of achievement from his work as an illustrator, describing it as a form of bondage. Responding perhaps to the growing interest by collectors and critics for watercolours by American artists—undoubtedly stimulated by an immensely successful exhibition of English watercolours shown at the National Academy in 1873—Homer took up the medium. Although he had often used wash drawings in preparation for his wood engravings and lithographs, it was in the summer of 1873, spent at the fishing port of Gloucester, MA, that he explored the medium seriously for the first time. He exhibited the summer's work at the American Society of Painters in Watercolors in the spring of 1874 and became a member in 1877. Critics praised his originality, while at the same time severely criticizing him for what they called his crude colour and lack of finish. The translucency of watercolour against the white paper made an immediate difference in his colour, which attained a new clarity and luminosity. Thereafter, watercolour became an increasingly important part of his artistic expression. It became the medium in which he experimented with place and subject, and light and colour, the results of which he later embodied in oil. In time it was the medium in which he became America's undisputed master.

During the 1870s Homer's art grew steadily in strength and skill. With a growing command of *plein-air* light and its relation to form and space, his compositions became more complex and subtle. His works of the 1870s were much preoccupied with women, usually shown engaged in genteel activities. There were, however, exceptions: among them a series of paintings of black people in Virginia. Typical is the *Cotton Pickers* (1876; Los Angeles, CA, Co. Mus. A.), in which he imbues the figures with dignity and physical beauty, unlike the condescending images of blacks created by many of his contemporaries.

Unlike other American artists who flocked to Paris during the 1880s, Homer went to England in 1881 and settled in Cullercoats, a fishing village and artists' colony near Tynemouth, Tyne & Wear, an experience that had a profound effect on his art and his life. For the 20 months of his stay he devoted himself almost entirely to watercolour painting, mastering a range of academic techniques and making scores of pictures of the fisherfolk, particularly the women. The first works he produced were narrative and picturesque, closely related to the then-popular fishing subjects of the Hague school artists and to European peasant themes in general. His images gradually became more iconic, revealing a new undertone of seriousness and emotion. With such watercolours as *Inside the Bar* (1883; New York, Met.), Homer arrived at the subject that would concern him for the rest of his life: Man's struggle with Nature.

3. LATE WORKS, 1883–1910. In the autumn of 1882 Homer returned to New York City. A little more than a year later he settled permanently in Prout's Neck, ME, a lonely, rocky promontory on the Atlantic coast. He built a studio on the high shore, near the ocean, where he lived alone. His centre of interest shifted from inhabited to wild nature—to the sea and the wilderness, and the men who were part of them. From this time his art changed fundamentally; the idyllic worlds of leisure and of childhood pleasures disappeared, and women appeared less and less. The first product of this change was a series of sea paintings, among them the *Fog Warning* (1885; Boston, MA, Mus. F.A.) and *Eight Bells* (1886; Andover, MA, Phillips Acad., Addison Gal.), in which the recurring theme was the perils of the sea and the drama of Man's battle with it. Neither literary nor sentimental, their power is conveyed in purely pictorial terms. They were immediately successful, commanding high prices, and they established Homer's reputation as one of the foremost American painters. While painting his sea-pieces, Homer embarked on a new medium, etching. He etched eight

plates between 1884 and 1889, seven of which were based on his sea paintings and his English watercolours (for illustrations see Goodrich, 1968, pls 90, 92, 94, 96, 98, 100, 102–3).

Although Homer's few recorded remarks on art express a purely naturalistic viewpoint, his images are metaphors of nature, confronting the question of mortality. In one of his greatest paintings, the *Fox Hunt* (1893; Philadelphia, PA Acad. F.A.; see fig. 1), the primitive struggle for survival is played out between a fox, normally the predator, trapped in deep snow, and a flock of birds descending from the sky for the kill.

The sea had been a subject of Homer's from the time he had worked at Gloucester in the early 1870s. In 1890 he began a series of pure seascapes that became his best-known work (e.g. *Sunlight on the Coast*, 1890; Toledo, OH, Mus. A.; *The Northeaster*, 1895; New York, Met.). Critics praised these pictures for their 'virility' and 'Americanness'. Monumental in scale, they were painted with broad brushwork and great plastic strength. The power, the danger, the loneliness and the beauty of the sea are evoked with an immediacy of physical sensation that places them among the most powerful modern expressions of Nature's force. The northern wilderness was also a favourite theme, but, unlike the earlier Hudson River school painters whose approach combined spectacular Romanticism and meticulous literalism, Homer expressed the exhilarating experience of this wild and unspoiled world through expressive brushwork and resonant colour, as in his watercolour *On the Trail* (1892; Washington, DC, N.G.A.).

In his later watercolours, however, executed on vacations away from Prout's Neck, Homer attained his purest artistic values. He brought to the medium a basically new style: painterly handling and saturated colour. An outdoorsman all his life (*see* SPORTING SCENES, §4), he took

1. Winslow Homer: *Fox Hunt*, oil on canvas, 950×1712 mm, 1893 (Philadelphia, PA, Pennsylvania Academy of the Fine Arts)

2. Winslow Homer: *Deer Drinking*, watercolour, 357×510 mm, 1892 (New Haven, CT, Yale University Art Gallery)

a fishing vacation almost every year, to the Adirondack Mountains, NY, and Quebec or to Florida, the Bahamas or Bermuda. The change of scene together with the lighter medium stimulated a more spontaneous expression. In oil, his touch was powerful, exploiting the weight and density of the medium; in watercolour, it was full of sensuous nuance. His watercolours express a private and poetic vision that otherwise found no place in his art; for example *Adirondack Guide* (1894; Boston, MA, Mus. F.A.) and *Sloop, Nassau* (1899; New York, Met.) contain the pure visual sensation of nature. Painted on the spot, with fluid, audacious brushwork and full-bodied colour, composed with unerring rightness of design and linear beauty (see fig. 2), Homer's later watercolours have had a wide and liberating influence on much subsequent American watercolour painting by such diverse artists as John La Farge, John Marin and Andrew Wyeth.

Although he achieved recognition early, Homer never had the financial success of an international favourite such as John Singer Sargent. In old age he was generally regarded as the foremost living American painter, and he received many awards and honours. By the last years of his life, more of his works were in public collections than those of any other living American artist.

UNPUBLISHED SOURCES
Brunswick, ME, Bowdoin Coll. Mus. A. [Homer Archvs]

BIBLIOGRAPHY
L. Goodrich: *Winslow Homer* (New York, 1944)
P. C. Beam: *Winslow Homer at Prout's Neck* (Boston, 1966)
L. Goodrich: *The Graphic Art of Winslow Homer* (Washington, DC, 1968)
P. C. Beam: *Winslow Homer's Magazine Engravings* (New York, 1979)
G. Hendricks: *The Life and Work of Winslow Homer* (New York, 1979)
Winslow Homer: The Croquet Game (exh. cat. by D. P. Curry, New Haven, CT, Yale U., A.G., 1984)
H. Cooper: *Winslow Homer Watercolors* (Washington, DC, 1986)
Winslow Homer: Paintings of the Civil War (exh. cat. by M. Simpson, San Francisco, F.A. Museums, 1988)
Winslow Homer's Images of Blacks (exh. cat. by P. H. Wood and K. C. C. Dalton, Houston, TX, Rice U. Inst. A., Rice Mus.; Richmond, VA Mus. F.A.; Raleigh, NC Mus. A.; 1988)

HELEN A. COOPER

Homer Laughlin China Co. *See* LAUGHLIN, HOMER.

Homme–Témoin. French group of painters who held their first exhibition as a group at the Salon des Moins de Trente Ans in June 1948. Their manifesto, which affirmed their commitment to realism and to communism, was drawn up and published by the critic Jean Bouret. In the preface to the exhibition catalogue he stated that 'painting exists to bear witness, and nothing human can remain foreign to it'. The best-known artists associated with the group were Bernard Buffet and Bernard Lorjou (*b* 1908). Buffet's style, as represented by such series as *Flagellation*, *Resurrection* (both 1952) and *Horrors of War* (1954), illustrates the atmosphere of 'existential' *Angst* that characterized the work of many painters associated with Homme–Témoin. Lorjou's the *Atomic Age* (1950) is a tableau of post-war urban suffering, oppression and spiritual longing. The painters were obviously strongly influenced by the harsh and expressionistic styles of Francis Gruber and Chaïm Soutine. In content, their work developed almost into a pastiche of those contemporary artists who protested against war atrocities or political opposition to tyranny, such as Fautrier or Matisse.

BIBLIOGRAPHY

J. Bouret: *L'Age atomique de Bernard Lorjou* (Paris, 1950)
Aftermath: France, 1945–54. New Images of Man (exh. cat., London, Barbican A.G., 1982)
Y. Le Pichon: *Bernard Buffet*, 2 vols (Paris, 1986)

Hŏ Mok [*cha* Munbu, Hwabo; *ho* Misu, Taeryŏng-noin] (*b* Yangch'ŏn, Kyŏnggi Province, 1595; *d* 1682). Korean calligrapher and scholar–painter of the Chosŏn period (1392–1910). He belonged to the group of Korean calligraphers who, in the period immediately following the Japanese invasions of 1592–8 (the Imjin War) under Hideyoshi, attempted to distance themselves from Chinese influence, especially that of Zhao Mengfu, whose style had been dominant since the end of the Koryŏ period (918–1392; *see* KOREA, §V, 4 and 5). Born into a scholar–official family, Hŏ Mok became famous for his research on the *Zhou li* ('Rites of Zhou'), a Chinese text of the Warring States period (403–221 BC). However, he did not serve as an official until after the age of 50. After holding a number of local posts, he became in 1675 the Minister of the Right (one of the two ministers who worked under the Prime Minister), but in 1679 he retired to his home town to spend the rest of his life teaching and writing.

Both his clerical script and seal script were highly regarded. It is said that he studied Chinese seal script of the Han period (206 BC–AD 220), became dissatisfied with it and created a distinctive style of seal script known as *misu-ch'e* (Misu's [i.e. Hŏ Mok's] style), which is characterized by a combination of the techniques of running, cursive and seal scripts. As a result, the individual strokes of the character seem more uneven than in ordinary seal script characters, but this modulation increases its expressive quality. The impact of *misu-ch'e* was such that a contemporary high official, Yi Chŏng-yŏng (1616–86), himself a renowned calligrapher, asked the court to ban the use of *misu-ch'e* by others. A number of Hŏ's works survive both on stelae and on paper. The most representative of the former is the *Samch'ŏk tonghae pi* (Eastern Sea Stele at Samch'ŏk), composed by Hŏ when he was serving as the governor of Samch'ŏk in Kangwŏn Province on the east coast of the peninsula. The original stele was lost in a storm, but a copy, carved after a duplicate of the text prepared by Hŏ Mok himself, remains in the possession of his descendants. In this work, the peculiarity of *misu-ch'e* is clearly apparent. The vertical strokes tend to be uneven: one side, usually the right, shows a wavering contour, quite unlike the smooth, rounded strokes of the majority of seal script characters written in the technique known as 'hidden-tip' (Chin. *zangfeng*) brush. The tips of the short vertical strokes bend sharply or turn towards the left, conveying a lightness and sensitivity that contrasts with the ponderous stability expected of seal script characters. Another famous stele written by Hŏ is the Stele of Prime Minister Yi Wŏn-ik (1547–1634) in Sihŭng, Kyŏnggi Province. The colophon he wrote for a painting by Yi Sang-chwa is typical of his style (Seoul, priv. col.; see Kim, Choi and Im, pl. 125). Hŏ Mok also left some ink-bamboo and ink-plum paintings. His portrait, showing him in dignified old age, is now preserved in a copy made in 1794 by the renowned portrait painter, Yi Myŏng-gi (colour on silk, 727×611 mm; Seoul, N. Mus.; see Young Ick Lew, p. 112).

BIBLIOGRAPHY

Im Ch'ang-sun, ed.: *Sŏye* [Calligraphy] (1975), xi of *Hanguk misul chŏnjip* [The arts of Korea] (Seoul, 1973–5), p. 154, pls 91–2
Kim Ki-sŭng: *Hanguk Sŏyesa* [History of Korean calligraphy] (Seoul, 1975), pp. 600–03
Kim Won-yong [Kim Wŏn-yong], Choi Sun U [Ch'oe Sun-u] and Im Chang-soon [Im Ch'ang-sun], eds: *Paintings*, ii of *The Arts of Korea* (Seoul, 1979), p. 192, pl. 125
Young Ick Lew [Ryu Yŏng-ik], ed.: *Korean Art Tradition/Hanguk-ŭi yesul chŏnt'ong* (Seoul, 1993) [bilingual text], p. 112

YI SŎNG-MI

Homosexual art. *See* GAY AND LESBIAN ART.

Ho-mu-tu. *See* HEMUDU.

Hon'ami. Japanese family of artists. They were established in Kyoto by the mid-14th century as sword experts in the service of the military aristocracy, for whom they engaged in the decoration, maintenance and connoisseurship of swords. In the late 15th century they emerged as leaders of the *machishū*, the group of upper-class Kyoto merchants who took over control of the city in the wake of the devastating Ōnin Wars (1466–77). By 1600, however, the power of the *machishū* had been broken, and many of its members turned their energies to cultural activities. (1) Hon'ami Kōetsu played a prominent role in this movement, and, with the painter Tawaraya Sōtatsu (*see* TAWARAYA SŌTATSU, §1(i)), he formed the foundation of the school of decorative painting and design later known as *Rinpa* (*see* JAPAN, §VI, 4(v)). His grandson (2) Hon'ami Kōho continued this tradition.

(1) Hon'ami Kōetsu [Jitokusai; Tokuyūsai; Taikyoan] (*b* Kyoto, 1558; *d* Kyoto, 1637). Calligrapher, potter and lacquerware designer. He was the son of Hon'ami Kōji (*d* 1603), who had been adopted into the Hon'ami family as its intended head, but the birth of an heir displaced him, and he set up on his own as a sword expert. Kōetsu was presumably raised at the Hon'ami compound at Imadegawa-Ogawa (now Kamikyō Ward, northern Kyoto), where he remained until he moved to the nearby settlement of Takagamine in 1615. His development as a calligrapher can be traced with some certainty, but a lack of signed or dated examples makes it difficult to place in a chronological sequence the pottery and lacquerwares associated with his name. Kōetsu also contributed to garden planning and to the design of iron kettles for the tea ceremony. The esteem in which Kōetsu was held in the 19th century is demonstrated in a chapter entitled 'The Kōetsu school' that appeared in the *Koga bikō* ('Handbook of classical painting') of Asaoka Okisada (1800–56), who placed Kōetsu at the head of a line of decorative artists including Tawaraya Sōtatsu, Ogata Kōrin and Ogata Kenzan (*see* OGATA, (1) and (2)). Although this classification has been superseded by the concept of a Rinpa school of decorative painting formed under Kōetsu's influence, by bridging the gap between the artisan and the cultivated patron Kōetsu was a forerunner of the self-conscious and personally expressive artist of the early modern period.

1. Calligraphy and painting. 2. Ceramics. 3. Lacquerware.

1. CALLIGRAPHY AND PAINTING. Kōetsu was 35 years old when he began his first known activity as an artist: the study of calligraphy under Prince Sonchō (1552–97), abbot of the Shōren'in temple and a well-known exponent of the orthodox courtly style. Another student of Sonchō was SHŌKADŌ SHŌJŌ, and Shōjō, Kōetsu and the courtier KONOE NOBUTADA are together known as the Kan'ei no San'pitsu (Three Brushes of the Kan'ei era; 1624–44; see JAPAN, §VII, 2(v)). These three artists are credited with injecting new vitality into Japanese calligraphy, which had seen little innovation since the 13th century: by studying calligraphy of the Heian period (AD 794–1185) they rediscovered the importance of paper quality and design, while an interest in Chinese calligraphy of the Song period (AD 960–1279) endowed their styles with greater strength and diversity. Kōetsu himself studied ancient Japanese masters such as Kōbō Daishi and Ono no Michikaze and took a particular interest in the style of the Chinese master Zhang Jizhi (1186–1266), whose 'fat and thin' style may be the origin of the dramatic modulations in Kōetsu's script.

With the exception of a personal letter written in 1585, the earliest dated examples of Kōetsu's calligraphy are a series of poem-cards (shikishi), some of which are inscribed with the year 1606. A set of 36 poem-cards (n.d.; Berlin, Mus. Ostasiat. Kst), inscribed with poems from the Shin kokinshū ('New collection from ancient and modern times'), is thought to be from the same period. In these works the principal features of Kōetsu's style are already apparent: the contrast between large, heavily inked characters and smaller, thinly inked lettering and a pronounced sensitivity to the underlying decoration, which is usually attributed to Tawaraya Sōtatsu. These poem-cards revived the spirit of the great Heian-period poetry anthologies, which combined exquisite calligraphy with richly decorated paper. In the work of Kōetsu, however, the script is scattered across the card and selectively highlighted, suggesting a primacy of pictorial over literary intention. In the same period Kōetsu is thought to have begun inscribing horizontal poem-scrolls; an early example may be the Senzai wakashū ('Millennium of collected poems'; Tokyo, N. Mus.), which bears the seal of the papermaker Kamiya Sōji, who is presumed to have worked with Kōetsu in the first decade of the 17th century. The celebrated horizontal scrolls combining Kōetsu's calligraphy and the delicate gold and silver underpainting of Sōtatsu's Inen atelier are assigned to the period between 1605 and 1615 and include the scrolls Deer (divided between Seattle, WA, A. Mus.; Atami, MOA Mus. A.; and other cols), Flower and Grasses of the Four Seasons (Tokyo, Hatakeyama Col.; see fig. 1) and Crane (Tokyo, Agy Cult. Affairs). In each of these scrolls Kōetsu's skilful blend of Chinese and Japanese characters, including the liberal use

1. Hon'ami Kōetsu: *Flowers and Grasses of the Four Seasons*, handscroll, ink, gold and silver on paper, 337×924 mm, *c.* 1610 (Tokyo, Hatakeyama Collection)

of the variant phonetic script (hentaigana) common to classical texts, is carefully orchestrated with the decoration.

Between 1608 and c. 1624 Kōetsu's style of calligraphy became more widely available through the activities of his pupil and patron Suminokura Sōan (1571–1632), who is considered to be the initiator of the luxury publishing project known as the Sagabon ('Saga books'; see JAPAN, §IX, 2). These included anthologies of classical poetry, prose works and nō plays and were frequently printed in Japanese phonetic script with movable type. The script, generally following the manner of Kōetsu and Sōan, overlays sumptuous block-printed designs attributed to the workshops of Kamiya Sōji and Tawaraya Sōtatsu. According to the Hon'ami gyōjōki ('Annals of the Hon'ami family') compiled by Kōetsu's grandson (2) Hon'ami Kōho, the shogun Tokugawa Ieyasu (1543–1616) granted Kōetsu a tract of land in the village of Takagamine (now Kita Ward, northern Kyoto) in 1615. Kōetsu and his family are thought to have moved there from the family residence at Imadegawa-Ogawa in the same year. A map preserved at the Kōetsuji, a Nichiren Buddhist temple at Takagamine, which displays a number of artefacts connected with the master, shows a village of 55 households headed by some of the most prominent merchants and artisans in the city, including the clothier and calligrapher Ogata Sōhaku (1570–1637), the lacquerer Tsuchida Sōtaku and the mounter and brushmaker Fudeya Myōki. This has led to speculation that Takagamine was an artistic colony, but there is no other evidence for this; it is more likely that the village functioned as a religious commune, as at least two other temples of the Nichiren sect (the sect to which the Hon'ami and other machishū families belonged) were established there in or shortly after Kōetsu's lifetime.

New characteristics appear in Kōetsu's calligraphy around the time of his move to Takagamine. There is a subtle but constant tremor in his line, and he may have suffered from palsy, for he complained in a letter written from Takagamine about trouble with his hands. However, his output remained prolific, and he took an increased interest in Chinese calligraphy. In particular, his copy of the religious treatise Risshō ankoku ron ('Establishment of Buddhist orthodoxy for national peace'; Kyoto, Myōrenji) shows the influence of Zhang Jizhi. There are also a number of poem-scrolls dating from the last decade of his life, including several copies of the Wakan rōeishū ('Collection of Chinese and Japanese poems for singing'), which combine Chinese characters and the Japanese phonetic syllabary and are sometimes written on silk rather than the usual paper. About 200 personal letters attributed to Kōetsu display a marked unity of style, characterized by a relaxed cursive script with some retention of the thick and thin linear contrasts seen in the poem-cards and scrolls. In 1625 he travelled to Edo (now Tokyo), where he was received by the shogun, Tokugawa Iemitsu (1604–51), who presented him with a poem-card inscribed in his own hand.

Besides his grandson (2) Hon'ami Kōho, Kōetsu had three distinguished calligraphy pupils, Suminokura Sōan, Akiba Kōan and Ogata Sōhaku, and examples of their work appear with his own in the copybook *Kōetsu shiboku* ('Four Kōetsu-school calligraphers'; 1675). Two other prominent followers were Kojima Sōshin (1580–*c.* 1656) and Sōhaku's son Ogata Sōken 1621–87); it was Sōken's second and third sons, Ogata Kōrin and Ogata Kenzan, who took up the work of Kōetsu and Tawaraya Sōtatsu in calligraphy, painting and design and established Rinpa.

Kōetsu was recorded as a painter in early Japanese art histories, and many of the works now assigned to Sōtatsu's atelier were once thought to be from his hand. He is also said to have studied under the painter Kaihō Yūshō. However, Kōetsu himself wrote that he only dabbled in painting and had little skill. Only one attribution, a fan painting entitled *Moon and Rabbit* (Tokyo, Hatakeyama Col.), is now generally accepted.

2. CERAMICS. Kōetsu was a devotee of the tea ceremony and a pupil of the tea masters Oda Uraku (1547–1621) and Furuta Oribe, and it is in this context that he took up pottery, to which he referred, according to the *Hon'ami gyōjōki*, as an 'amusement'; it is their quality of relaxed self-expression that makes his works among the most coveted in Japan (*see also* KYOTO, §III). Kōetsu's work in ceramics is presumed to have begun after 1615, but the evidence for this is slender: some of the letters he wrote contain orders to various potters, and the style of

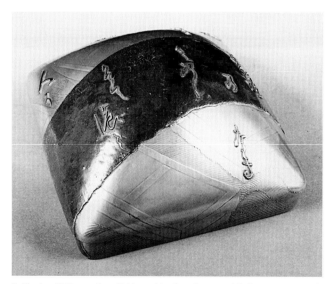

2. Hon'ami Kōetsu: *Boat Bridge*, writing-box, lacquer with decoration in gold, silver and lead, h. 242 mm, early 17th century (Tokyo, National Museum)

the calligraphy is attributed to *c.* 1615–24; the matching box for his renowned *Fujisan* ('Mt Fuji') teabowl (Tokyo, Sakai priv. col.; see Hayashiya, 1964, pl. 6) bears the artist's name Taikyōan, which he used after his move to Takagamine; and passages in the *Hon'ami gyōjōki* mention Takagamine clay. Kōetsu followed the late 16th-century tea master SEN NO RIKYŪ in commissioning wares to his own specifications from potters of the RAKU family—in Kōetsu's case, Raku Jōkei (*d* 1635) and Raku Dōn'yū (1599–1656). However, Kōetsu became much more involved in the production of his commissions than had been the case with Sen no Rikyū. He used the local red clays at Takagamine, and occasionally white clay ordered from the Raku workshop, to shape and carve his own teabowls, each of which differed in form and decoration. There are three basic shapes among the dozen or so teabowls attributed to Kōetsu: cylindrical, as in the *Fujisan* bowl; fully rounded, as in the *Otogoze* bowl (ex-Morikawa priv. col., Nagoya; see Hayashiya, 1964, pl. 9); or with a rounded bottom and a cylindrical upper half, as in the *Amagumo* bowl (Tokyo, Mitsui priv. col.; see Hayashiya, 1964, pl. 8).

Kōetsu's best work features decisive and vigorous carving, especially in the foot-ring and rim. His interest in form stands in contrast to his neglect of the finish: the glazes scale off and are discoloured, and many pieces are cracked. Kōetsu's bowls, like others in the Raku-ware tradition, are coated with a black or transparent glaze; the latter take on the red colour of the body. Notable exceptions are the half-black, half-white *Fujisan* bowl and the amber-coloured *Kamiya* bowl (priv. col., see Hayashiya, 1964, p. 72). The pieces are fired to a low temperature (approximately 800° C), but a letter from Kōetsu to a potter called Taemon contains detailed comments on the application and texture of glazes, and it may be that some pieces were fired in high-temperature kilns. Kōetsu used his ceramics to express the assertive and idiosyncratic spirit of the early 17th century in a manner akin to the underglaze-decorated Oribe wares then being produced at the MINO kilns in central Japan. By wedding that spirit to the more accessible technology of Raku-ware, Kōetsu opened up ceramics as an amateur art form comparable to painting and calligraphy. At the same time his teabowls were among the prototypes for subsequent generations of Raku potters.

3. LACQUERWARE. The 'Kōetsu-style' lacquerware (*Kōetsu makie*) survives in a select number of objects, especially writing-boxes (*suzuribako*). There is little evidence, however, of the extent of Kōetsu's participation in their manufacture. He clearly had some connection with the Igarashi family of lacquerers—his granddaughter married Igarashi Magobei (1592–1660), and he wrote letters to Magobei and his father, Igarashi Sōo (*d* 1613)—and with the lacquerer Tsuchida Sōtaku, who appears as a neighbour on the Takagamine map. It may be that these links (and his supposed skills as a lacquerer) arose out of his professional role in outfitting swords. In the 15th century, lacquerware design, especially for the writing-box, had settled on a repertory of intricately crafted poetic themes (*see* JAPAN, §X). The Kōdaiji style of the late 16th

century marked a departure towards the simplification of motifs and bolder design contrasts, and the works associated with Kōetsu continue that trend, with greater subtlety in the relationship between shape and decoration, more sophisticated thematic interpretation and a quixotic selection of materials. There are two basic types: in one Kōetsu provided the pictorial motif for a traditional shape; in the other he designed the shape, selected the materials and orchestrated the pictorial motifs. An example of the first type is a legged chest, which is traditionally considered an 'early' work, since it was made for the *Taira Family Sūtras* (Hiroshima Prefecture, Itsukushima Shrine), thought to have been restored by Tawaraya Sōtatsu in 1602. *Makie* ('sprinkled gold') designs of ivy vines, suggestive of the 'Ivy Lane' episode in the *Tale of Ise*, cascade over the chest's black-lacquer ground. The *Nenohi* bookshelf (Tokyo, Hinohara priv. col.), another 'early' work, also features simplified classical motifs—in this case references to an episode in the *Tale of Genji*—applied to a conservative form, as does a gold-lacquered flute case inlaid with designs of deer in lead and mother-of-pearl (Nara, Yamato Bunkakan), which Kōetsu is said to have made for the Komparu school of *nō* drama.

The second group is represented by the domed writing-boxes such as the *Boat Bridge* (Tokyo, N. Mus.; see fig. 2) and *Woodcutter* (Atami, MOA Mus. A.). In the former, a swelling lid decorated with boats and waves in gold lacquer is bifurcated by a broad bridge made of lead sheeting. A 25-character abstract from a classical poem on the boat bridge at Sano in Kōetsu's script has been cut out in silver and laid over the boats and bridge. The shape of the object, the motifs, the materials and the literary content achieve a full synthesis. Kōetsu also redesigned the interior of the writing-box so that the inkstone, until that time positioned in the centre of the box, was moved to the left side, closest to the writer.

Although there is little dispute over the creative brilliance of items of 'Kōetsu-style' lacquerware, the diversity of techniques suggests that they were manufactured in more than one atelier. The precise relationship between Kōetsu, the lacquer craftsman and the pieces themselves remains unclear. Both Kōetsu's designs for and his technical approaches to lacquerware spread into other Kyoto workshops in the first half of the 17th century and were revived a century later in the work of Ogata Kōrin.

(2) Hon'ami Kōho [Kūchūsai] (*b* Kyoto, 1601; *d* Kyoto, 1682). Potter, painter and calligrapher, grandson of (1) Hon'ami Kōetsu. His Raku-ware teabowls such as the deep, cylindrical *Kangetsu* ('winter moon') bowl (priv. col, see Hayashiya, 1981, p. 129) exhibit a boldness of carving and eccentricity of design rivalling that of his grandfather. Kōho also expanded the repertory to include larger vessels such as water-jars, often forcefully modelled in the gritty stoneware clay of Shigaraki. A well-known example is a cylindrical water-jar in the so-called *ubaguchi* ('hag's mouth') style incised with a paulownia crest (priv. col., see Hayashiya, 1981, p. 129). Kōho's activity as a painter and calligrapher may have earned him the honorary religious title *hōgen* (Eye of the Law) in 1641. His few surviving paintings (e.g. a set of three hanging scrolls

entitled *Lotus* (see fig.), *Maple* and *Wisteria*; Osaka, Fujita Mus. A.) depict flowering plants in the style of the atelier of Kitagawa Sōsetsu in Kanazawa. As well as carrying on the family trade of sword expert, Kōho also compiled the *Hon'ami gyōjōki* ('Annals of the Hon'ami family').

Hon'ami Kōho: *Lotus*, hanging scroll, colours on silk, 1.16×0.37 m, 17th century (Osaka, Fujita Museum of Art)

BIBLIOGRAPHY

Asaoka Okisada: *Koga bikō* [Handbook of classical painting] (n.p., *c.* 1845–53); rev. by K. Ota as *Zōtei koga bikō* [Presentation of the Handbook of classical painting] (Tokyo, 1904)

Hon'ami gyōjōki to Kōetsu [Annals of the Hon'ami family and Kōetsu] (Kyoto, 1948)

T. Hayashiya, ed.: *Kōetsu* (Tokyo, 1964)

B. von Ragué: *Geschichte der japanischen Lackkunst* (Berlin, 1967; Eng. trans., 1976)

Y. Haruna: *Kan'ei no san'pitsu* [The three brushes of Kan'ei] (Tokyo, 1971)

Y. Yamane: *Kōetsu, Sōtatsu, Kōrin*, x of *Suiboku bijutsu taikei* [Compendium of the art of ink painting] (Tokyo, 1977)

T. Masuda: *Kōetsu no tegami* [Kōetsu's letters] (Tokyo, 1980)

Exquisite Visions: Rimpa Paintings from Japan (exh. cat. by H. Link and T. Shimbo, Honolulu, HI, Acad. A., 1980)

S. Hayashiya: *Kōetsu, Kōho to Tamamizu yaki* [Kōetsu, Kōho and Tamamizu ware], v of *Nihon yakimono shūsei* [A collection of Japanese ceramics] (Tokyo, 1981), pp. 125–30

Masters of Japanese Calligraphy, 8th–19th Century (exh. cat. by J. Rosenfield and Y. Shimizu, New York, Japan House Gal. and Asia Soc. Gals, 1984–5)

RICHARD L. WILSON

Hondecoeter, d' [de Hondecoutre; de Hondekoter]. Dutch family of artists of Flemish origin. Nicolaes (Jansz.) de Hondecoutre I (*d* 1609) from Mechelen is cited in 1585–6 as a painter in Antwerp, but his work is unknown. He moved his family to Delft before 1601. Two sons became painters: Hans de Hondecoutre, otherwise unidentified, and (1) Gillis de Hondecoutre, a landscape and animal painter in Utrecht and Amsterdam. Gillis's son Gijsbert de Hondecoutre (1604–53) followed his father, concentrating on sober views of barnyard fowl, and was a member of the Utrecht Guild of St Luke (1626–32), and his daughter Josina married the landscape painter Jan Baptist Weenix. Another son, Nicolaes de Hondecoeter II (1605–?*c.* 1671), also became a painter. Gijsbert's son (2) Melchior d'Hondecoeter gained prominence for his more elegant avian themes. From the late 1620s the Dutch spelling of the family name was preferred. The relationship of other painters named de Hondecoutre in Delft and later Amsterdam is unclear.

(1) Gillis [Jelis] **(Claesz.) de Hondecoutre** (*b* Antwerp or Mechelen, ?*c.* 1575; *d* Amsterdam, 1638). Painter and draughtsman. The individuality and skill exhibited in his earliest known work, *Landscape with Music-makers* (1602; Ottawa, N.G.), suggest that Gillis was born before 1580 and initially trained by his father. In 1602 he was living in Utrecht, moving in 1610 to Amsterdam where in 1636 he became head of the Guild of St Luke.

Gillis's early paintings and pen drawings are similar to those of David Vinckboons: graceful woodland fantasies with tiny figures beneath flamboyant, swaying trees. A series of five such landscapes with biblical subjects was engraved after Gillis's designs *c.* 1614 by Johannes van Londerseel (Hollstein: *Dut. & Flem.*, nos 3, 5, 11, 14 and 29). In addition, a few open landscapes based on the Dutch countryside prompt comparison with Esaias van de Velde's contemporary work. By 1616 Gillis was painting rocky wildernesses, such as *Rocky River Valley* (1618; Kassel, Schloss Willhelmshöhe), dependent on those of his Amsterdam colleague Roelandt Savery. By 1622 he was concentrating more on animals, again inspired by Savery. These paintings represent exotic and domestic animals in a clearing, as in the typical *Orpheus Charming*

the Animals (1624; Utrecht, Cent. Mus.). Gillis also painted sober views of cattle resting in meadow settings, which, while again influenced by Savery, were still executed long before Paulus Potter took up the theme.

Although a sensitive painter, Gillis remained too loyal to the older, decorative, Flemish fantasy to have much impact on later art. Other than his son Gijsbert, only Hans Savery II (1589–1654) absorbed something of his manner.

BIBLIOGRAPHY

J. G. C. A. Briels: *Vlaamse schilders in de Noordelijke Nederlanden in het begin van de Gouden Eeuw* (Antwerp, 1987)

Masters of 17th-Century Dutch Landscape Painting (exh. cat. by P. C. Sutton and others, Amsterdam, Rijksmus.; Boston, MA, Mus. F. A.; Philadelphia, Mus. A.; 1987–8)

JOANEATH A. SPICER

(2) Melchior d'Hondecoeter (*b* Utrecht, 1636; *d* Amsterdam, 3 April 1695). Painter, grandson of (1) Gillis de Hondecoutre. His first teacher was his father Gijsbert Gillisz. de Hondecoutre, after whose death Melchior was taught by his uncle Jan Baptist Weenix. Melchior apparently became an assistant in his uncle's studio, and his earliest signed and dated work *Dog Defending Dead Game against a Bird of Prey* (1658; Le Havre, Mus. B.-A.) is in the style of Weenix.

Hondecoeter is mentioned as active in Pictura, The Hague painters' confraternity in 1659–63; his presentation piece was originally a seascape, which he withdrew and replaced with an animal painting. If the signature is correct on a painting dated 1661, *Still-life with Fish Pail* (Brunswick, Herzog Anton Ulrich-Mus.), he also experimented with a style and subject most closely associated with Abraham van Beyeren. While at The Hague he had a student, Willem Frederik van Royen (1645–1723), who became painter to the court at Potsdam.

On 9 February 1663 Hondecoeter married Susanna Tradel in Amsterdam. There is one dated picture of ducks and poultry from that year, but no further dated works are known until 1668. That year, on 16 March, he was granted citizenship of Amsterdam; he lived on the Lauriergracht there until his death. In 1668 he painted two pictures, *Animals and Plants* (Amsterdam, Rijksmus.) and *Birds, Butterflies and a Frog among Plants and Fungi* (London, N.G.), which borrow heavily from works by Abraham Begeyn. But most of the paintings dated 1668 and thereafter are either game-pieces (often confused with those of Hondecoeter's cousin Jan Weenix) or the magnificent pictures of live birds most associated with his name.

Hondecoeter's mature style owes much to Frans Snyders, the important Flemish animal and still-life painter of a generation earlier, whose work he collected. From him, Hondecoeter borrowed a compositional formula that he used consistently from the late 1660s: birds and animals seen close up in the centre of the canvas, others entering from the left or right, their bodies sometimes cropped by the frame, the middle ground blocked by a wall, fence, tree or architectural ruins across one half of the canvas, the remaining side opening to a distant vista. Hondecoeter treated the latter in a variety of ways: a hilly landscape, a seascape, an Italianate mansion, the grounds of an estate, a forest or a farmhouse. The primary subject also varied: bird fights, birds being frightened or attacked, birds at rest. A white hen crouching with a chick protected under one wing and other chicks near by was a popular subject, repeated by Hondecoeter many times, for example *Hen and her Chicks* (c. 1657; Caen, Mus. B.-A.; see fig.). In variations on this maternal theme, the hen protects her chicks from the feet of clumsy, larger birds, or from an approaching predator, or scolds them for having strayed too far from her.

Hondecoeter also painted what appear to be inventories of animals that focus on rare species, such as the pelican in the *Floating Feather* (e.g. Amsterdam, Rijksmus.). *Noah's Ark* (e.g. Brunswick, Herzog Anton Ulrich-Mus.) and Aesop's fable the *Vain Jackdaw* (e.g. The Hague, Mauritshuis) were other favourite subjects, together with occasional works based on popular Dutch proverbs or sayings. There are two extant portraits: *Anne Reijnst as a Young Woman* (c. 1680–85; Reims, Mus. St Denis) and *Johan Ortt on Horseback*, one of three equestrian subjects commissioned by Ortt in 1687 (London, Buckingham Pal., Royal Col.). Two splendid and highly unusual allegorical works, traditionally entitled the *Emblematic Representations of King William's Wars*, are in Holkham Hall, Norfolk. Both of these depict, in the upper half, battles fought in the air between birds (eagles, storks, herons and hawks), hideous monsters and demon bats, and, in the lower half, naval battles and the wreckage and destruction of war.

Hondecoeter supplied large paintings for the town houses and country mansions of rich Amsterdam burghers. Some are of such extravagant scale and sublime visual quality that they must be counted with the great mural decorations of the 17th century, for example *Park with Birds*, formerly in a house in Driemond, near Weesp (3.38×5.24 m; now Munich, Alte Pin.).

Hondecoeter does not seem to have made preparatory drawings, and there are few of certain authentication. Instead he recorded birds and animals from life in oil on canvas; he copied these whenever a certain species was required. Although 14 of these modelli were included in the inventory of his studio at the time of his death, only one is known: *Birds and Animal Sketches* (Lille, Mus. B.-A.), which is covered with detailed studies of 17 birds and a squirrel against a neutral grey ground. From 1668 throughout the rest of his career, Hondecoeter used many of these birds and the squirrel in his paintings, posed exactly as in the model. He habitually repeated entire passages from one painting to another and often made copies of compositions with only minor variations. From his vast output and its occasionally uneven quality, it appears that he was assisted in his studio. A contemporary, Adriaen van Oolen (d 1694), made a small industry of copying Hondecoeter's paintings, many of which van Oolen signed with his own name. Hondecoeter was also copied in the 18th century by Aert Schouman and many others of lesser skill. His work remained highly popular long after his death; in the 19th century he was known as the 'Raphael of bird painters'.

BIBLIOGRAPHY

Thieme–Becker

A. Houbraken: *De groote schouburgh* (1718–21), iii, p. 68

A. Bredius: 'De schilders Melchior de Hondecoeter en Johan le Ducq', *Archf Ned. Kstgesch.*, v (1882–3), pp. 288–92

——: *Künstler-Inventare*, iv (The Hague, 1921)

Melchior d'Hondecoeter: *Hen and her Chicks*, oil on canvas, 740×765 mm, *c.* 1657 (Caen, Musée des Beaux-Arts)

M. Poch-Kalous: *Melchior de Hondecoeter* (exh. cat., Vienna, Gemäldegal. Akad. Bild. Kst., 1968)

RICHARD C. MÜHLBERGER

Hondius [de Hondt] **(i).** Dutch family of printmakers and publishers of Flemish descent. There has been much confusion between this family, which was active in Amsterdam, and the HONDIUS (ii) family, who were printmakers and publishers in The Hague. The principal member of the Hondius (i) family was (1) Jodocus Hondius I, whose sister Jacomina (1558–1628) was a minor engraver. Jodocus I established a family print publishing business, which after his death was carried on by his two sons, Jodocus Hondius II (b Amsterdam, bapt 9 Nov 1593; d Amsterdam, bur 15 Aug 1629) and (2) Hendrik Hondius 'II', who is traditionally given an epithet of generation to distinguish him from the engraver and publisher Hendrik I Hondius (ii) of The Hague. The epithet 'II' is both confusing and incorrect, since no direct relationship between the families, although likely, has yet been established. The matter is further complicated by the fact that Hendrik I Hondius (ii) had a son, likewise called Hendrik, who was also a print publisher, though apparently less active than either his father or (2) Hendrik 'II' of Amsterdam.

(1) Jodocus Hondius I (b Wakken, nr Ghent, ?14 Oct 1563; d Amsterdam, ?16 Feb, bur 20 Feb 1612). Engraver, draughtsman, printer, publisher, bookseller, type-cutter, cartographer and instrument-maker. He was the son of Olivier de Hondt (d 1568), sheriff and registrar of Wakken, and Petronella d'Havertuyn. His family moved to Ghent when Jodocus was still very young; by the age of eight he had taken up drawing and engraving. In 1584, because of the war with Spain, Jodocus was staying in London as a refugee with his sister Jacomina, who was shortly thereafter married to the Flemish émigré Pieter van de Berghe (1560–1625), also from Ghent. Jodocus I married Coletta van den Keere in London on 11 April 1587, and his earliest graphic works appeared shortly thereafter. These include engravings for the English edition of Lucas Waghenaer's *Spieghel der zeevaart* (published as *The Mariner's Mirrour*, London, 1588), for *Talbot's Rose* (1589) and for two books by Hugh Broughton (1588 and 1590); he also apparently published maps of America (1589), England and Ireland (1590) and France (1591) and drew a small map of the world (1589). He then trained with the English cartographers Richard Hakluyt and Edward Wright. As with most of his early work, not much has survived of the printed segments that he engraved for English globes, such as that of Emery Molineux (1592–3; London, Middle Temple) and one that is 600 mm in diameter (Nuremberg, German. Nmus.).

In 1593 Jodocus and his wife moved to Amsterdam, where he was active for the rest of his career. The following year he compiled a calligraphic model book (*Theatrum artis scribendi*) containing one sheet engraved by his sister Jacomina, but it was mainly through his cartographic work that he made his mark in Amsterdam. During his first ten years there he published various maps of the world, including the one he made in 1596–7 according to Gerard Mercator's new method of projection. The discoveries by Sir Francis Drake and Thomas Cavendish were recorded in two hemispheres on what is known as the Broadside Map (London, BL).

New facts brought to light by Sir Walter Raleigh called for a revised map of Guyana, which Jodocus I engraved in 1598. In the Plancius globe of 1600 (Amsterdam, Ned. Hist. Scheepvaartsmus.) Hondius charted the astronomic measurements made in the southern hemisphere by the first Dutchmen sailing to the East Indies. From 1602 he studied at Leiden University. He reached a turning-point in his professional career on 12 July 1604, when he managed to purchase the copperplates used for the posthumous edition of Mercator's *Atlas* published in 1595; the separate volumes had first appeared in 1585 and 1589 respectively. Between 1605 and 1637, long after his own death in 1612, the work went through a total of 21 editions, including versions in Dutch, French, English, German and Latin (compiled with the help of, among others, Hondius's brother-in-law, van de Berghe). An edition on a smaller scale, the *Atlas Minor*, was reprinted up to six times between 1607 and 1656. Hondius engraved two further large world maps in 1608 and 1611; the second consisted of a pair of hemispheres (Swabia, Waldberg-Wolfegg priv. col.), summarizing on a single sheet the results of many exploratory expeditions.

(2) Hendrik Hondius 'II' (*b* Amsterdam, 1597; *d* Amsterdam, 16 Aug 1651). Print publisher and bookseller, son of (1) Jodocus Hondius I. In 1627 he began working in his late father's publishing house on the Dam in Amsterdam, which was then being run by his mother and the print publisher Jan Jansz., who had married Hendrik 'II's sister Elisabeth in 1612. His brother Jodocus II joined the business in 1628. By keeping the printing, publishing and selling of products firmly in one family, the company

prospered, the two brothers continuing to manage it after their mother's death in 1629 and eventually being assisted by Jodocus II's son, Jodocus III (*b* Amsterdam, *bapt* 24 July 1622; *d* Amsterdam, 1655). From 1632 the premises of Hendrik 'II' were known as De Wackeren Hondt ('The watchful dog'), a pun on the family name, which had also been used by his parents.

There is a total of *c*. 250 prints associated with either Hendrik 'II' or Hendrik Hondius I of The Hague. Stechow (see Thieme–Becker) hypothesized that Hendrik 'II' must be regarded exclusively as a publisher and bookseller. However, not all of the prints inscribed *Hondius* as the publisher can be ascribed to him (as they often have been), since some of them include the place-name *Hagae* as part of the address. Thus while there is no evidence yet that Hendrik 'II' practised as an engraver, it is known that Hendrik I of The Hague was active as both an engraver and publisher.

BIBLIOGRAPHY

Hollstein: *Dut. & Flem.*; Thieme–Becker
F. W. Hondius: *De wackere hond: Leven en werken van de kartograaf Jodocus Hondius* [The watchful dog: life and works of the cartographer Jodocus Hondius] (Antwerp, 1963)
Jodocus Hondius: Kartograaf (exh. cat., ed. H. A. J. Janssen; Nijmegen, de Waag, 1963)
C. Koeman: *Atlantes neerlandici*, 6 vols (Amsterdam, 1967–85)

CHRISTIAAN SCHUCKMAN

Hondius (ii). Dutch family of printmakers and publishers of Flemish descent. Like the HONDIUS (i) family of Amsterdam, with whom they are often confused, they fled from their native Flemish town because of the war with Spain. Guiljam Hondius, a school master in Duffel, moved his family to nearby Mechelen, but after he died his widow settled in Antwerp. Their son (1) Hendrik Hondius I married Sara Jansdochter, daughter of an Antwerp goldsmith, and they moved to The Hague, where Hendrik became one of the most important Dutch reproductive printmakers and publishers in the early 17th century. The division commonly made in the literature between prints attributed to (1) Hendrik I of the Hondius (ii) family from The Hague and Hendrik 'II' of the Hondius (i) family from Amsterdam is arbitrary and in need of revision (*see* HONDIUS (i), (2)). The two families may well have been related, but a direct connection has not yet been established. Between 1598–9 and *c*. 1616 Hendrik I and his wife had five daughters and two sons, the portrait engraver Willem Hondius (?1600–1658) and (2) Hendrik Hondius II, who became a print publisher.

BIBLIOGRAPHY

Hollstein: *Dut. & Flem.*; New Hollstein: *Dut. & Flem.* (1994); Thieme–Becker
E. F. Kossmann: 'Haagsche uitgevers van de zeventiende en achttiende eeuw' [Publishers in The Hague in the 17th and 18th centuries], *Het Boek*, xxii (1933–4), pp. 275–88
——: *De boekhandel te 's-Gravenhage tot het eind van de 18de eeuw* (The Hague, 1937), pp. 185–6
I. Fabiani-Madeyska: 'Willem Hondius en zijn poolse oeuvre, 1636–1652', *Jversl. Fund. Hondius*, xiv (1965), pp. 5–35
J. G. C. A. Briels: *Zuidnederlandse boekdrukkers en boekverkopers in de Republiek der Verenigde Nederlanden omstreeks 1570–1630* (The Hague, 1974), pp. 73, 321–2

(1) Hendrik Hondius I [the elder] (*b* Duffel, Brabant, 9 June 1573; *d* The Hague, *bur* 25 or 29 Oct 1650). Engraver, etcher, draughtsman and publisher. He trained with Godefroy van Gelder, a goldsmith in Brussels, and then with Jan Wierix, a printmaker in Antwerp. After travelling to Cologne, London and Paris, he was in The Hague by 1597. In that year he was registered in the artists' guild and obtained his first print privilege for a portrait of Prince Maurits (1597; Hollstein, Hendrik I, no. 77). He was awarded a general privilege by the States General in 1599. He left to live in Amsterdam in 1603 and Leiden in 1604–5, returning to settle in The Hague in 1605.

Hendrik I engraved landscapes and biblical and allegorical subjects after his own designs as well as those of such artists as Jan Wildens, Pieter Stevens, David Vinckboons, Pieter Bruegel I and Lucas van Leyden; he carried out about 250 prints during his long career. His earliest signed and dated print is *A Boy Blowing Bubbles* (not in Hollstein; Paris, Bib. N.) of 1594, a work that shows his early style, which is characterized by sharp series of parallel lines and curves. One of his best-known early works is the *Large View of The Hague* (1598; Hollstein, Hendrik I, no. 38) after Gillis de Saen.

Hondius also illustrated and published books on perspective and fortification by Hans Vredeman de Vries (e.g. *Perspective*; 1604) and Samuel Marolois, as well as his own books on these subjects. In 1610 he published *Pictorum aliquot celebrium praecipue Germaniae inferioris effigies*, a series of 68 engraved artist portraits for which he employed Simon Frisius, Andries Stock (*c.* 1580–*c.* 1648) and Robbert de Baudous. Besides his own activities as a printmaker, Hondius was a prolific print publisher, turning out *c.* 300 plates, which originated in his shop, and another 300 or so re-editions of plates from previous publishers. Stock was one of the main engravers for Hondius and must have been the first to work for the publisher, as early as 1601. Frisius carried out numerous etchings for Hondius mainly between 1610 and 1621. In 1614, Hondius bought a house on the Buitenhof where he produced and sold prints, drawings and books until he sold the building in 1640. By then his style was clearly influenced by Jacques de Gheyn II and such landscape artists as Paul Bril and David Vinckboons. Their influence continued into the 1620s, by which time he had developed his mature, lush forest landscapes exemplified by the *Landscape with an Elegantly Dressed Couple and a Page* (1622; Hollstein, Hendrik II, no. 27), an engraving after his own design, and such drawings as *Elijah Fed by Ravens* (London, BM) in pen and brown ink and watercolour washes.

In the 1630s Hondius reduced the number of works he engraved himself in favour of publishing, mainly official portraits and maps. He returned to printmaking in the 1640s but now turned exclusively to etching. Among his late works is the series of *Landscapes* (1644; Hollstein, Hendrik II, nos 11–16). He remained active in printmaking and drawing until the final years of his life. His late prints consist mainly of reproductive engravings after 16th-century artists, demonstrating his continued respect for these artists and the demand for their work by contemporaries. One of his last prints, the *Festival at Schellebelle* (1648; Hollstein, Hendrik I, no. 25) after Hans Bol, is proudly signed with his age, 75.

WRITINGS

Onderwijsinge in de perspective conste [Instruction in the art of perspective] (The Hague, 1623)

Korte beschrijvinge, ende af-beeldinge van de generale regelen der fortificatie [Short descriptions and illustrations of the general rules of fortification] (The Hague, 1624)

PRINTS

H. Vredeman de Vries: *Arte perspectivae formulae* (Leiden, 1604–5)
S. Marolois: *Géométrie, contenant la théorie et practique . . . à la fortification* (The Hague, 1616)
H. Vredeman de Vries: *Les Cinq Rangs de l'architecture* (The Hague, 1617)

BIBLIOGRAPHY

C. de Bie: *Het gulden cabinet* (1661), pp. 486–8
N. Orenstein: 'A View of the Court in The Hague Etched by Simon Frisius', *Delineavit & Sculp.* (1990), no. 4, pp. 24–30
——: *Hendrik Hondius (Duffel 1573–The Hague 1650) and the Business of Prints* (New York, 1992)

(2) Hendrik Hondius II [the younger] (*b* The Hague, *c.* 1615; *d* The Hague, between 27 Oct 1676 and 12 Jan 1677). Print publisher, son of (1) Hendrik Hondius I. He was a member of the Guild of St Luke in The Hague in 1635, soon after which he left the city for Brazil. Hondius married Barbara van Hoogstraten, daughter of the Dutch traitor Dirck van Hoogstraten. Hondius was taken prisoner by the Portuguese in 1645 and held at Bahias de Todos os Sanctos for five years, returning to The Hague in 1651. Like his brother Willem, he may have engraved a few early portraits for his father. After returning to The Hague, he published a few prints and books as well as numerous pamphlets, and from 1655 to 1657 he sold a paper known as *De vliegende Mercurius* ('The flying Mercury') from a shop on the Hofstraat, Westzijde.

NADINE ORENSTEIN, CHRISTIAAN SCHUCKMAN

Hondius [de Hondt], **Abraham (Danielsz.)** (*b* Rotterdam, 1625–30; *bur* London, 17 Sept 1691). Dutch painter, etcher and draughtsman, active also in England. He was the son of Daniel Abramsz. de Hondt, the city stone mason of Rotterdam. He is said to have received his first training from Pieter de Bloot (1601–58) and Cornelis Saftleven. This is confirmed by parallels between early paintings by Hondius and Saftleven, who worked in Rotterdam from 1637. Also in favour of this assumption is the fact that works by Hondius are often confused with those of Ludolf de Jongh, another pupil of Saftleven. Hondius successfully combined various stylistic influences in his compositions, without, however, developing a style of his own. More than two thirds of his paintings, etchings and drawings are animal pieces: hunting scenes, animals fighting and animal studies. He also represented landscapes, genre, religious and mythological scenes such as *Pyramus and Thisbe* (*c.* 1600–65; Rotterdam, Boymans-van Beuningen), for which there is a rare preparatory drawing of the two main figures (sold Amsterdam, Sotheby's, 26 Nov 1984, lot 16).

He lived in Rotterdam until 1659, but as early as 1651 works such as *Hunter Offered Refreshment outside an Inn* (1651; sold London, Christie's, 11 April 1986, lot 26) reveal the influence of Flemish painting, in particular animal pieces by Frans Snyders and Jan Fyt. How Hondius came in touch with these Flemish examples remains speculative. One unlikely theory is that he was inspired by Carl Ruthart, the German painter of hunting scenes who has sometimes, wrongly, been called his teacher. Another possible intermediary was Juriaen Jacobsz. (1625/6–95), a pupil of Frans Snyders, who lived in Amsterdam from

Abraham Hondius: *Hunt for Wild Boar and Deer*, oil on panel, 725×1325 mm, 1664 (Hamburg, Hamburger Kunsthalle)

1658 to 1668 (Hentzen). Yet Hondius moved to Amsterdam only in 1659, which does not explain the pictures pre-dating that year that seem to indicate the artist's familiarity with Flemish models. The most likely possibility is that Hondius knew etchings by Fyt and prints after compositions by Snyders: these he might have seen in the studio of Cornelis Saftleven, who stayed in Antwerp for some time around 1632–4. Flemish influence can also be seen in Hondius's *Bear Hunt* (1655; ex-Delaroff priv. col., 1908, see W. Bernt: *Die niederländischen Maler des 17. Jahrhunderts*, ii (Munich, 1948), no. 394), which bears resemblances to engravings after Rubens, in particular those by Pieter Soutman. The source of the Flemish elements in his *Adoration of the Shepherds* (1663; Amsterdam, Rijksmus.) is the representation of the same theme by Adriaen van Stalbemt (1622; Berlin, Gemäldegal.). Hondius was also influenced by Dutch artists, including Joachim Wtewael, Gerrit van Honthorst, Herman Saftleven (ii) and Karel Dujardin. The *Rest after the Hunt* (1662; Ansbach, Residenz & Staatsgal.) is usually considered his best work.

It is generally assumed that Hondius moved to London in 1666, where he spent the rest of his life. He painted views of London such as *A Frost Fair on the Thames at Temple Stairs* and *London Bridge* (1677; both London, Mus. London). The latest dated work is *Ape and Cat Fighting over Dead Poultry* (1690; sold London, Sotheby's, 11 July 1945, lot 151). He produced the majority of his rare 14 animal etchings in London. A series of eight appeared in 1672 (Hollstein, nos 1–8), but *A Wild Boar Attacked by Dogs* (Hollstein, no. 10) might be earlier. In the etchings and paintings of this period Hondius enlarged his animal representations in proportion to the picture surface area; the violent effect of the hunts and animal fights is thus intensified. Hondius often reused details

from his own compositions, as in the *Hunt for Wild Boar and Deer* (1664; Hamburg, Ksthalle; see fig.) where the dog lying on its back was repeated from the etching *A Wild Boar Attacked by Dogs*.

BIBLIOGRAPHY

Hollstein: *Dut. & Flem.*; *NKL*; Thieme–Becker

A. Hentzen: 'Abraham Hondius', *Jb. Hamburg. Kstsamml.*, viii (1963), pp. 33–56

CHRISTIAAN SCHUCKMAN

Hondt, de. *See* HONDIUS (i).

Honduras, Republic of. Central American country bordered by Guatemala and El Salvador to the west and south-west and by Nicaragua to the south-east. Honduras has a 640 km coastline to the Caribbean Sea in the north and a narrow access to the Pacific through the Gulf of Fonseca in the south (see fig. 1). It is the second largest republic in Central America, its area of *c.* 112,100 sq. km dominated by mountainous terrain, with narrow coastal lowlands. Because of its elevation, much of the country has a moderate tropical climate, and the vegetation ranges from pine, oak and broadleaf monsoon forests in the temperate highlands to dense mangrove thickets, open savannah and vast tropical rain-forests in the humid coastal lowlands. Communications are relatively undeveloped, particularly in the east, and the population is mainly rural, about 70% living in the mountain valleys, where Comayagua, the former capital, and TEGUCIGALPA, the present capital, are also located. Honduras was colonized by Spain after 1502, became independent in 1821 and an autonomous state in 1838. About 90% of its people are now mestizo (of mixed European and Indian descent).

For the history and art of the region before colonization *see* SOUTH AMERICA, PRE-COLUMBIAN, especially §II, 1, 2, 3 and 6(i); MESOAMERICA, PRE-COLUMBIAN, especially §§I, II, 2(i), 3(iv), 4(iv) and III,

2(ii); MAYA, especially §1; and COPÁN, an important centre of Maya culture in Honduras.

I. Introduction. II. Architecture. III. Painting, graphic arts and sculpture. IV. Patronage and institutions.

I. Introduction.

In 1502, during Christopher Columbus's fourth and final voyage to the Americas, Europeans saw for the first time the islands and north coast of what became the Republic of Honduras. At the moment of contact with Europeans, most of Honduras was inhabited by Lenca peoples (in south-west, central and east-central regions), Tolpan/Jicaque (north-central), Chorotegas (south) and intrusive Nahua groups (north-west and north-east) from central Mesoamerica, who arrived during the last centuries preceding contact. The wealth of the complex socio-political organization of these indigenous Honduran domains was based on the enormous agricultural potential of their fertile coastal valleys and well-irrigated highland basins, as well as far-reaching trade networks. For example, during Christopher Columbus's exploration of the Bay Islands (Islas de la Bahia) off the north coast of Honduras he captured a large trading canoe carrying commercial products that included cacao, cotton cloth and copper axes; when he made his first landfall on the American continent at the bay of Trujillo, some of the people he found there were dressed in cotton garments, while others were tattooed or painted or armed with flint-edged and flint-pointed weapons. In the Mosquitia region, along the coast east of Trujillo, on the other hand, the indigenous peoples were linked to Intermediate Area (Macro-Chibchan) cultures; they were semi-nomads who kept seasonal plantations of manioc and other root crops but also depended heavily on hunting and foraging for subsistence.

In 1516 a chain of slaving ships from the Antilles began to sweep the Bay Islands and adjacent Honduran mainland, beginning the process of destruction of the indigenous population that was accelerated by Spanish exploration and conquest between 1524 and 1540. During that period the indigenous populations in the areas of highest concentration—the Sula, Naco and Aguan Valleys—were hunted down to provide forced labour for the colonists in such places as Peru, their villages and plantations destroyed. This destruction reached its peak in the subsequent onslaught of European diseases. Girolamo Benzoni, an Italian traveller who passed through Honduras in 1540, calculated that the indigenous population had declined by almost 90% as a result of the wars of conquest, disease and slavery. Modern researchers agree that an estimated indigenous population of 1,200,000 in Honduras at the moment of European contact is realistic. This total was never again approached, even though some recovery took place, beginning in the 18th century. By then the population of Honduras was predominantly mestizo (of mixed Indian and European descent), and this trend was never reversed. At the end of the 20th century indigenous groups in Honduras comprised just 5% of the total population of *c.* 5 million.

Throughout the colonial period, Honduras formed part of the Spanish captaincy-general of Guatemala. Early Spanish settlements included Trujillo on the north coast, the original capital, and San Pedro Sula. Other towns were

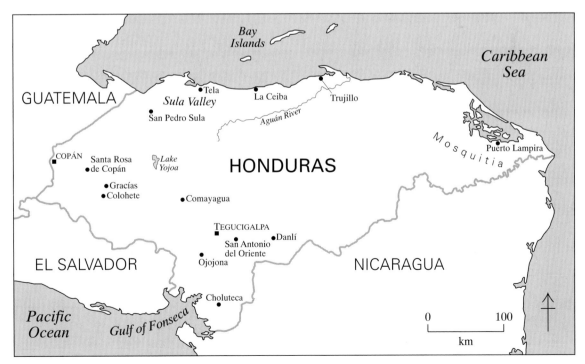

1. Map of Honduras; those sites with separate entries in this dictionary are distinguished by CROSS-REFERENCE TYPE

founded in southern and western areas occupied before the conquest, including Comayagua, which became the capital in 1573, Gracías and Choluteca. In all these centres the Roman Catholic Church and missions were the principal artistic patrons during the colonial period. The Spanish economy in the Honduran colony was initially based on cacao, sarsaparilla and silver, later including gold, cattle and indigo, and Tegucigalpa was founded *c.* 1578 as a result of the discovery and mining of silver in the region.

Traditional methods of conquest were not successful in the tropical rain-forests of the Mosquitia, and the western limits of this barrier became the frontier of Spanish colonization. In a subsequent attempt to break that barrier, the 16th-century colonial policy of conquest gave way to one of evangelism and recolonization of the indigenous groups in *reducciones* (missionary settlements). The territory of the Tolpan/Jicaque peoples was also included in the sphere of missionary activity. Ultimately, however, the mission-orientated recolonization of the largely itinerant populations had little success. By the middle of the 17th century the indigenous populations on the north-east and north-west coasts had disappeared or migrated inland. The few that remained on the Bay Islands were removed to the mainland as a guarantee against their voluntary or forced support of the pirates and privateers who swept the Caribbean. Pirate attacks in the 17th and 18th centuries led to the construction of some impressive coastal fortifications on the north coast of Honduras by the Spanish, but the depopulation of the Bay Islands allowed them to become periodic refuges and refitting ports for the Dutch, English and French until well into the 18th century. English influence in the region ultimately led to their control of the Bay Islands and the north-eastern Mosquitia region (Mosquito Coast), which lasted until 1859. In 1795-6 the English deported to the Bay Islands a contingent of several thousand belligerent Black Caribs (of mixed Carib Indian and African descent) from St Vincent Island in the eastern Caribbean. From here the Black Caribs passed almost immediately to the mainland and in a short time became, together with the Miskito, one of the predominant ethnic groups along the Caribbean coast. The Garífuna peoples of Honduras are direct descendants of the Black Caribs.

After declaring independence from Spain in 1821, Honduras joined other former colonies in the Central American Federation, an attempt by Francisco Morazán to form a united Central America; however, this was dissolved in 1838, and Honduras became an autonomous state, its politics subsequently dominated by instability. Independence did not bring advantages for the native populations. The reigning government policy included the forced integration of indigenous groups into the mestizo community, a policy accompanied by systematic discrimination against traditional lifestyles and culture. For example, in the middle of the 19th century the Tolpan/Jicaque peoples were obliged to provide manpower for sarsaparilla plantations, and the extreme abuses they were subjected to forced a number of them to seek refuge in the north-central highlands. That refuge, La Montaña de la Flor, remains the home for *c.* 600 descendants of those who fled, and they are the only Tolpan/Jicaque who still speak their native language. The Miskito and Garífuna in the Mosquitia region are the two most numerous ethnic communities in Honduras that preserve not only their language but also maintain strong cultural roots. Small populations of the Pech/Paya and Tawahka/Sumu also survive in the Mosquitia, although both groups are threatened by the uncontrolled penetration of landless peasants from the central and southern highlands of Honduras into the tropical rain-forest.

Independence resulted in some urban expansion and improvement, particularly in Comayagua and Tegucigalpa, which became the capital in 1880. A major economic stimulus was provided to the north coast by timber exploitation and the establishment of extensive banana plantations in the late 19th century and early 20th, particularly by companies from the USA, who ultimately monopolized banana production, converting Honduras into the world's largest exporter of bananas until the 1950s. This resulted in the construction of transportation networks, port facilities and new urban centres in the north. Political instability continued, however, with civil wars in 1924 and 1932. After World War II workers' strikes in the banana plantations led to the liberal agrarian and labour reforms of the government (1957–63) of Ramon Villeda Morales, but these were followed by the coup d'état of General Oswaldo Lopez Orellano and 17 years of almost continual military government. In the 1980s elected governments re-established democracy in Honduras, and in the 1990s new attempts were initiated to encourage regional economic cooperation.

BIBLIOGRAPHY
R. Chamberlain: *The Conquest and Colonization of Honduras* (Washington, DC, 1953)
C. L. Johannessen: *Savannas of Interior Honduras* (Berkeley and Los Angeles, 1963)
G. Lara-Pinto: *Beiträge zur indianischen Ethnographie von Honduras in der 1. Hälfte des 16. Jahrhunderts unter besonderer Berücksichtigung des historischen Demographie* (Hamburg, 1980)
J. Arancibia: *Honduras: Un estado nacional?* (Tegucigalpa, 1984)
A. Constenla: *Las Lenguas del Area Intermedia: Introducción a su estudio areal* (San José, Costa Rica, 1991)

GLORIA LARA-PINTO

II. Architecture.

1. 1502–1838. The first substantial colonial buildings in Honduras were constructed in Trujillo, which was formally founded as the capital of the new colony in 1524. A cathedral was completed there before 1539 and a Franciscan convent established in 1582, but here, as elsewhere in the region, earthquakes and the fragility of materials and construction resulted in the destruction of many colonial buildings of the 16th and 17th centuries, which were designed and built mostly by architects and master-builders from Guatemala and Spain. Under repeated attacks from the sea, Trujillo was abandoned in 1643 and not re-populated until the end of the 18th century. In 1573 the capital was moved to Comayagua, founded in 1537 but sacked by Indians, then re-established with city status in 1557 as a centre of silver mining; its growth was assured by its strategic location midway between the Caribbean and the Pacific. The simple rectangular church of La Merced (under construction by 1611) served as the cathedral until the early 18th century. It was designed with a single-storey, undivided stucco façade and

exemplified the 'Seismic Baroque' style, characterized by thick walls, small window openings and low towers. The present cathedral of Comayagua dates from the first quarter of the 18th century. It has a barrel-vaulted nave and side aisles culminating in a squat main dome and side domes, faced externally with local green and yellow ceramic tiles. An imposing, if simple, four-storey façade is divided into four vertical bays by single engaged columns. The church of La Caridad (1730), Comayagua, like La Merced, has a simple single-storey façade, with a crenellated gable over S-shaped cornices. However, its character was submerged under unsympathetic 20th-century restoration.

Tegucigalpa was also founded as a mining settlement in 1578. The parish church of S Miguel de Tegucigalpa (1756–82; now the cathedral), although rectangular, has side chapels adjacent to the apse, giving a cruciform effect; it is domed and has a single barrel-vaulted nave. An inscription on the façade (see fig. 2) dates that part of the building to 1765 and names the architect as Gregorio Nancianceno Quiróz. The influence of buildings in Antigua, Guatemala, is evident in the characteristic bolster pilasters applied to the two-storey façade. The cathedral

2. Tegucigalpa Cathedral, façade by Gregorio Nancianceno Quiróz, 1765

was carefully restored after earthquake damage in 1809 and 1899. Although of earlier foundation (1732), the church of Los Dolores, Tegucigalpa, which has unusually slender towers for the earthquake zone, was not finished until 1815 (restored 1910). Here the front surfaces of the bolster pilasters are flat. Inside, the church has a timber ceiling influenced by the *Mudéjar* style.

Other notable churches in Honduras include those at Gracías, La Jigua and Colohete, all in the province of Lempira in the west of the country. The stucco façade of S Manuel de Colohete (mid-18th century), for example, is covered with a network of decoration in low relief; the nave and aisles are divided by massive timber columns, bracketed to simulate *Mudéjar* arches. Typical of the mining villages around Tegucigalpa is San Antonio del Oriente, with simple single-storey houses with red-tiled roofs, and a church dedicated to La Merced (early 18th century); this boasts a single-storey façade with an undulating gable crowned with maiolica urns. A few examples of military architecture remain, such as the Fortress of San Fernando de Omoa (1759–79), the most massive Spanish fortress in Central America, built in defence against the pirates. There are also remains of Baroque civil architecture in the ruins of the Caxa Real (1739–41; designed by Don Balta Zar de Maradiaga) at Comayagua and the aqueduct at Danlí (late 18th century). Before the end of the 18th century, somewhat later than in other areas of Latin America, the Baroque style began to give way to Neo-classicism in a form imported from Spain but inspired by French architecture: a rare example in Honduras is the early 19th-century church at Danlí.

2. AFTER 1838. The demand for urban growth created by independence was less insistent in Honduras than elsewhere, owing to the agricultural base of its economy, as well as political instability. Ecclesiastical patronage also declined, and although Neo-classicism remained an influence, building activity in the 19th century concentrated largely on residential work in a colonial vernacular tradition. In 1880, however, the transfer of the capital to Tegucigalpa stimulated new development. The strongest architectural influence at the time was the work of Georges-Eugène Haussmann in Paris, but a wide range of other stylistic models from Europe was also adopted and the influence of the USA increased, especially after the 1870s, when the banana industry began to be developed. The influence of the Beaux-Arts style is apparent in such buildings as the Palacio del Distrito Central, the building of the Financiera (late 19th century; destr. 1978), both in Tegucigalpa, and the classical portals of the Cementerio (1884) at Comayagüela, the sister city of Tegucigalpa. Eclecticism in Honduran architecture continued well into the 1920s. As well as revivals of the French and Italian Renaissance, there was also evidence of the influence of the Romanesque Revival after H. H. Richardson, for example the Casa Vieja (1890s), and the Gothic Revival, for example the Casa Presidencial (1919), both in Tegucigalpa. The latter also expresses elements derived from the *Mudéjar* tradition, as does the Templo Masónico in San Pedro Sula.

As American companies expanded the fruit industry, towns on the north coast, including San Pedro Sula and the ports of La Ceiba, Tela and Trujillo, reflected the eclectic tastes of such American architects as Richard Morris Hunt (e.g. the Club Social del Banco Sogerín, San Pedro Sula); moreover, components imported from New Orleans were used in the construction of railway stations, warehouses and public buildings in the area. Art Nouveau appeared in the second decade of the 20th century in, for example, the Casa de los Muñecos (1920), Comayagüela, and in a number of buildings in San Pedro Sula and Tegucigalpa. However, acceptance of the European Modern Movement was delayed by a nostalgic return in the 1920s to colonial models involving such Mediterranean features as overhanging roofs, intricately fashioned grilles, balconies and ornamental oriel windows (e.g. the Municipalidad in La Ceiba and such houses as the Casa Cordova, 1938, in San Pedro Sula). Art Deco was also introduced in the 1920s, lasting until the 1940s (e.g. the Casa Castro, 1927–30, San Pedro Sula; by R. Bermudez). The International Style became predominant in public and commercial buildings constructed after 1935; notable examples include the Ministerio de Hacienda (1940), the Banco Central de Honduras and the Palacio Legislativo (both 1950), all in Tegucigalpa, and the Instituto Hibueras and Banco Nacional de Fomento (1950), Comayagüela. Domestic architecture was distinguished by the bungalows built by American fruit companies along the whole of the north coast after the 1920s; these were directly inspired by the California Bungalow style, and their broad eaves and spacious verandahs and porches were well suited to the informal lifestyle and tropical climate of Honduras. Architects active in the second half of the 20th century include Fernando Martínez, Leo García and Francisco Rodríguez, all of whom were influenced by international developments, particularly those originating in European countries and the USA, including Post-modernism.

BIBLIOGRAPHY

F. Lunardi: *El Tengaux y la primera iglesia catedral de Comayagua* (Tegucigalpa, 1946)

P. Kelemen: *Baroque and Rococo in Latin America* (New York, 1951), pp. 45–6, 127–32

D. Angulo Iñiguez and others: *Historia del arte hispanoamericano*, iii (Barcelona, 1956), pp. 51–60

F. Lacouture, F. Flores and R. Soto: *Edificios y monumentos históricos de Tegucigalpa y Comayagüela* (Tegucigalpa, 1977)

R. Agurcia and R. Soto: 'La casa de Don Calecho: Un ejemplo de la arquitectura vernácula en Honduras', *Yaxkin*, vii/1 (1984), p. 4

B. Dohle: *Visión de la arquitectura en Honduras según arquitectos hondureños* (San Pedro Sula, 1986)

R. Soto: 'El patrimonio cultural de Honduras', *Prisma*, ii/10 (1987), p. 20

R. C. Mejía Chacón and R. M. Ordóñez Ferrera: *Estudio preliminar para la preservación y desarrollo del casco histórico de Trujillo* (diss., Tegucigalpa, U. N. Auton. Honduras, 1989)

III. Painting, graphic arts and sculpture.

1. 1502–1838. Early colonial art in Honduras was dominated by religious painting and sculpture, which was intended to help the religious conversion of the indigenous population in addition to its use by the Spanish. At first many works were imported from Spain; particularly significant were the sculptures brought from Seville in the 17th century to the cathedral in Comayagua, then the capital city, for example the retable of the main altar (*in situ*), which contained a Crucifix commissioned by Philip IV, King of Spain, in 1620 and executed by Andrés de Ocampo. Other polychromed figures in the niches of the retable and elsewhere in the cathedral are attributed to Francisco de Ocampo (*d* 1639), the nephew of Andrés, and show the influence of Juan Martínez Montañés. The remains of a Crucifix originally sent to Trujillo (now in the monastery of S Francisco, Guatemala City) may be by Montañés himself. Other works were imported from Guatemala and Mexico, to which the Spanish Crown sent many artists. Guatemalan artists also worked in Honduras, for example the sculptor Vicente Javier (*fl* 1748–80), who arrived in Honduras *c.* 1761 and worked in a late Rococo style (e.g. the exceptionally fine main altar of Tegucigalpa Cathedral). Mestizo decoration, in which Baroque and indigenous artistic forms were combined, was executed by the Guatemalan sculptor Vicente de la Parra (e.g. the altar of *The Rosary* in Comayagua Cathedral, 1708). Guatemalan painters working in Honduras included Blas de Mesa (1740–76), who was active in the region of Comayagua at the end of the 17th century.

In the middle of the 18th century several Honduran painters gained prominence, for example Zepeda (e.g. *St Michael the Archangel*; Comayagua, S Francisco); Cubas, who worked in Tegucigalpa Cathedral; and Dardón and Antonio de Alvarez, who produced eight scenes from the *Life of the Virgin* (*c.* 1669) in Comayagua Cathedral, influenced by Francisco de Zurbarán. Perhaps the most outstanding painter of the colonial period was José Miguel Gómez (1712–1806), who was also influenced by Zurbarán. A mestizo born in Comayagua, he studied in Antigua, Guatemala. He was discovered in the middle of the century by Bishop Don Diego Rodríguez de Rivas, who commissioned from him many religious paintings now in Comayagua Cathedral. Gómez also supervised the decoration of S Miguel, Tegucigalpa (now the cathedral), and produced paintings for the hermitage dedicated to the Virgin in Suyapa (e.g. *Jesus of Nazareth*, *c.* 1777; *in situ*). His last known work, the *Divine Shepherdess* (Señora F. de Quinonez priv. col.), was signed in 1805. Gómez also produced portraits, a kind of painting that became more popular in the first decade of the 19th century. Other portraits painted towards the end of the 18th century included works by Valladares (e.g. *Bishop José de Palencia*, 1773; Comayagua, Mus. A. Relig.).

2. AFTER 1838. Political instability in the middle of the 19th century led to a decline in the production of painting, sculpture and work in gold and silver, materials that became scarce at that time. The popularity of painting also suffered from the spread of photography and lithography in Honduras, and religious commissions became particularly rare. Nevertheless, the colonial style of painting lingered into the middle of the century in the work of Toribio Torres from Comayagua. He painted religious subjects, including commissions by Bishop Compoy (e.g. a series of portraits now in the chapter room of Comayagua Cathedral); he also produced several family portraits, a genre that remained popular until the end of the 19th century. Ecclesiastical patronage also extended to Toribio Pérez (e.g. the portrait of *Monseñor Cristóbal de Pedraza*, 1850; Comayagua, Mus. A. Relig.).

In the 19th century, however, secular commissions became more important than religious ones. This trend, together with the loosening of links with Spain, opened Honduran painting to French influences, particularly history paintings and heroic portraiture of the Napoleonic era, although Honduran examples of this style were largely unremarkable. Sculpture in this period was dominated by Europeans working in Honduras, such as the Frenchman Leopoldo Morice (e.g. the equestrian statue of *General Francisco Morazán*, 1882; Tegucigalpa, Parque Central), and by the import of European works, especially from Italy. It was not until the second and third decades of the 20th century that Honduran painting and sculpture revived, led by a generation of artists who lived and studied in Spain, Italy and France. These included the sculptor Samuel Salgado, who trained in Italy, and the painter Pablo Zelaya Sierra (1896–1933). Zelaya Sierra left Honduras in 1916 and studied in Costa Rica and Madrid, where he was heavily influenced by his teacher, the Cubist Daniel Vázquez Díaz. Zelaya Sierra's works were marked by the separation of line and colour as independent elements of the picture. On his return to Honduras in 1932 he reflected the civil war of that time in the painting *Brother against Brother* or *Destruction* (Tegucigalpa, Mus. Banco Atlántida). His work, collected in the Museo Pablo Zelaya Sierra in Ojojona and in the Banco Central de Honduras in Tegucigalpa, was very influential.

Other artists of this generation who studied in Europe produced naturalistic paintings inspired by Impressionism.

They included Confucio Montes de Oca (1896–1925), a painter of luxuriant, colourful landscapes, and Carlos Zúñiga Figueroa (1892–1964), who specialized in private and public portraiture; both artists were also inspired by 17th-century Spanish painting, especially that of Diego Velázquez. Maximiliano Euceda (1891–1986) was influenced by such contemporary Spanish artists as Joaquín Sorolla y Bastida and produced landscapes and portraits with a fine sense of detail. Like Figueroa, he painted posthumous portraits of heroes of the struggle for independence, for example the portrait of *General Francisco Morazán* in the Palacio del Distrito Central in Tegucigalpa.

With the foundation of the Escuela Nacional de Bellas Artes (ENBA) in 1940 (*see* §IV below), the visual arts gained new prominence in the cultural life of Honduras. The Director, Arturo López Rodezno (*b* 1906), was an accomplished oil painter, watercolourist, draughtsman, engraver and ceramicist. He also introduced murals to Honduras, for example those in the ENBA (1942–6) inspired by Maya art, and he collaborated with Miguel Angel Ruiz (*b* 1928), who brought Mexican influences to Honduran mural painting as a result of a stay in Mexico between 1948 and 1953, when he worked with Juan O'Gorman and Diego Rivera. A later example of Ruiz's murals is the one painted in 1981 for the Banco Atlántida, Tegucigalpa, where a fine collection of late 20th-century Honduran paintings is also held (*see* §IV below). Dante

3. José Antonio Velásquez: *San Antonio del Oriente*, oil on canvas, 660×940 mm, 1957 (Washington, DC, Museum of Modern Art of Latin America)

Lazarroni Andino (*b* 1929) was also influenced by the expressionistic aspects of Mexican social realism. The foundation of the ENBA gave, in addition, a stimulus to Honduran sculpture, particularly through the work of Alfonso Henríquez and Arturo Guillen, as well as such later sculptors as Mario Zamora (e.g. statues, Tegucigalpa, Palacio Legislativo, ground floor, 1958–60), Obed Valladares and Julio Navarro.

Another influence on Honduran artists of the 1940s and 1950s was Surrealism: for example, Moisés Becerra (*b* 1926) painted highly coloured surreal representations of Honduran life, which he also depicted in his illustrations and engravings. Ricardo Aguilar (1915–51) moved from Impressionism to a Surrealist style marked by planar modelling and an esoteric symbolism. Many Honduran artists, however, persisted with a naturalistic style, for example the painter Alvaro Canales (1922–83) and the sculptor–painters Mario Castillo (*b* 1932), who painted colourful, impressionistic landscapes, and Roberto M. Sánchez (*b* 1915). As well as depicting landscapes and folkloric themes, Sánchez also continued the tradition of painting images of the heroes of independence. Another painter of rural Honduras was the amateur primitive artist José Antonio Velásquez (1903–83), whose work was widely exhibited from the 1950s (see fig. 3). His work can be compared with the naive paintings of Teresita Fortín (1896–1982), which were based on personal memories (e.g. the *Story of My Life*, 1978). Other notable artists of the period included Horacio Reina, a portrait painter and commercial artist, and Manuel López Callejas, whose activities ranged from architectural design to drawing cartoons and designing stamps.

BIBLIOGRAPHY

L. Mariñas Otero: *La pintura en Honduras* (Tegucigalpa, 1959, rev. 1977)
——: 'La escultura en Honduras', *Cuad. Hispamer.*, xlii/125 (1960), pp. 215–23
M. F. Martínez Castillo: *La escultura en Honduras* (Tegucigalpa, 1961)
El arte contemporáneo en Honduras (Tegucigalpa, 1968)
B. la Duke: *Compañéras: Women, Art and Social Change in Latin America* (San Francisco, 1985), pp. 53–6
R. Becerra and E. López: *La pintura en Honduras* (Tegucigalpa, 1989)
R. Fiallos: *Datos histórico sobre la plástica hondureña* (Tegucigalpa, 1989)

IV. Patronage and institutions.

Artistic and architectural patronage in Honduras during the Spanish colonial period was dominated almost exclusively by the Roman Catholic Church, although the Spanish Crown also played a role by sending both artists and works of art to such colonies as Honduras (*see* §III, 1 above), and the local civil and military authorities commissioned important buildings (*see* §II, 1 above). After independence in the 19th century the role of the Church declined, and patronage began to pass to the state. Official commissions celebrated independence itself, and private individuals began to commission portraits. In general, however, artistic patronage and production declined during the 19th century, largely as a result of political instability that continued into the 20th century. Although the first important institutions in Honduras were established at this time—the Biblioteca Nacional and Archivo Nacional were both founded in Tegucigalpa in 1880—Honduran artists still had to go abroad to other countries in Latin America or to Europe to receive training and patronage (*see* §III, 2 above).

This situation improved with the establishment of the Escuela Nacional de Bellas Artes in Tegucigalpa in 1940, incorporating the earlier Escuela de Artes y Oficios, founded in Comayagüela in the late 19th century. It was directed by the engineer, painter and ceramicist Arturo López Rodezno (*b* 1906), himself trained at the Escuela Libre de Pintura y Escultura in Havana and at the Académie Julian in Paris. Other teachers included the painters Maximiliano Euceda (1891–1986), Roberto M. Sánchez (*b* 1915) and Ricardo Aguilar, and the sculptor Samuel Salgado. This period was also marked by the first collective exhibitions of Honduran art, in Tegucigalpa and at the Bienal Hispanoamericana de Arte in Madrid (both 1951), and many Honduran artists became well known in the USA: for example, José Antonio Velásquez (1903–83) was discovered by the American Doris Stone and exhibited in 1953 and 1954 in Washington, DC, at the Organization of American States, and Manuel López Callejas drew cartoons for the *Washington Post*. Collecting also became more general in Honduras itself: in the 1980s the commercial popularity of such graphic arts as lithography spread to painting, which could be acquired in shopping precincts as well as commercial art galleries.

Another important feature of the 20th century in Honduras was the growth of museums, particularly those concerned with Honduran archaeology, many of which came to be administered by the Instituto Hondureño de Antropología e Historia (IHAH), an autonomous body within the Ministry of Culture that was also given responsibility for national monuments and archaeological sites. The first of these museums, the Museo Nacional, was established in Tegucigalpa in 1932 and reinstituted there by the IHAH in 1976 in a palatial neo-classical building that was once the residence of a president of Honduras, Julio Lozano Díaz. Its exhibitions cover a number of areas, including natural history, ethnology, cultural history, technology and art, but they emphasize Honduran archaeology. The Galeria Nacional de Arte is housed in the former Mercedario convent (built 1654), and the Museo Historico de la Republica is in another former presidential palace; both were opened in Tegucigalpa in 1993–4. Discoveries from the Maya ruins of Copán are displayed in the Museo Regional de Arqueología in Copán Ruinas, founded in 1940 by Dr Gustav Stronsvick and remodelled between 1984 and 1985 under the archaeologist Ricardo Agurcia (*b* 1950). Museums in the former capital, Comayagua, include the Museo Arqueología y Histórico de Comayagua, established by Colonel Gregorio F. Sanabria in 1949 to conserve and display the cultural heritage of the valley of Comayagua, particularly its archaeological remains; and the Museo de Arte Religioso, established by Monsignor Bernardino Mazzarella (1904–79) in the 1970s to exhibit liturgical objects and religious art from the region and administered by the local episcopate. Important municipal museums include the Museo del Cabildo in Danlí, founded by the engineer Gonzalo Lobo Sevilla (*b* 1920) in 1975, and the Museo de San Pedro, Cortés. Other significant historical and archaeological collections are found in private museums such as the Museo Histórico in Trujillo (belonging to Rufino Galán and opened in the

1970s); the Museo del Banco Atlántida in Tegucigalpa (founded 1988), which also has a complete gallery of paintings; and the Museo de Roatán (founded 1991) in the Bay Islands. The Museo Nacional de Historia Colonial was opened in 1990 at the colonial fortress of San Fernando de Omoa and is devoted to the history of the site.

BIBLIOGRAPHY

Escuela nacional de bellas artes, 1940–48, Ministerio de Educación (Tegucigalpa)

R. Soto: *Banco Atlántida en la historia de la pintura en Honduras* (Tegucigalpa, 1988)

El Banco Atlántida en la historia de la pintura hondureña (exh. cat., Tegucigalpa, Mus. Banco Atlántida, 1991)

ROLANDO SOTO

Hone. Irish family of artists. (1) Nathaniel Hone (i) established a fashionable practice as a miniature painter in London in the 1740s. His brother Samuel Hone (*b* Dublin, 8 Sept 1726; *d* Jamaica) was also a miniature painter, active mainly in Dublin. Nathaniel (i) trained his sons (2) Horace Hone and John Camillus Hone (*b* London, 1759; *d* Dublin, 23 May 1836), both of whom became painters, the former also an engraver. Several members of later generations of the family pursued artistic careers, notably the landscape painter (3) Nathaniel Hone (ii) in the 19th century and the painter and stained-glass artist (4) Evie Hone in the 20th.

BIBLIOGRAPHY

DNB; Strickland; Thieme–Becker

(1) Nathaniel Hone (i) (*b* Dublin, 24 April 1718; *d* London, 14 Aug 1784). Painter and printmaker. He settled in London in the 1740s and soon made a name for himself as a painter in miniature on enamel. Between 1750 and 1752 he studied in Italy. He was a regular exhibitor at the Society of Artists and, in 1768, a founder-member of the Royal Academy, where he exhibited until his death. Although Hone was a relatively successful portrait painter in oils, he was burdened by an overpowering jealousy of Joshua Reynolds and had numerous rifts with the Academy. He was, in particular, opposed to the dominant classicism based on Italian Renaissance art, preferring a more Dutch-inspired domesticity for his figures and their settings. His portraits of children, particularly his own, are considered among the best of their kind in mid-18th-century painting. They include a *Piping Boy* (1769; Dublin, N.G.), which depicts his son John Camillus and which excited great admiration at the first Royal Academy exhibition in 1769; he made an etching of it in 1771. Although Hone was primarily a portrait painter, he is especially remembered for one large subject painting, the *Pictorial Conjuror, Displaying the Whole Art of Optical Deception* (1775; Dublin, N.G.), a work that caused considerable controversy as it was a clever and detailed attack on Reynolds, the first PRA. Not only does it lampoon Reynolds's penchant for borrowings from the Old Masters but, when first displayed, it also carried the indecorous suggestion of an intimate relationship between Reynolds and the painter Angelica Kauffman. Hone was forced to paint over one section of the painting, but the picture was nevertheless rejected for exhibition at the Academy; his oil sketch (London, Tate) records its original appearance. In order to display the rejected *Conjuror*, also

in 1775 Hone arranged his own private show in London, exhibiting 70 works. This helped to initiate the trend for one-man exhibitions taken up increasingly by artists in the following century.

BIBLIOGRAPHY

Waterhouse: *18th C.*

J. T. Smith: *Nollekens and his Times*, 2 vols (London, 1829), pp. 131–44

E. Waterhouse: *Painting in Britain, 1530–1790*, Pelican Hist. A. (Harmondsworth, 1953, 4/1978), pp. 266–7

Irish Portraits, 1660–1860 (exh. cat., ed. A. Crookshank and the Knight of Glin; London, N.P.G.; Belfast, Ulster Mus.; Dublin, N.G.; 1969), pp. 47–9

A. Crookshank and the Knight of Glin: *The Painters of Ireland, c. 1660–1920* (London, 1978), pp. 86–8

J. Newman: 'Reynolds and Hone: "The Conjuror" Unmasked', *Reynolds* (exh. cat., ed. N. Penny; London, RA, 1986), pp. 344–54

FINTAN CULLEN

(2) Horace Hone (*b* London, *c.* 1754–6; *d* London, 24 May 1825). Painter and engraver, son of (1) Nathaniel Hone (i). He entered the Royal Academy Schools, London, in 1770, exhibiting at the Royal Academy from 1772 and being elected ARA in 1779. In 1782 he went to Dublin and established a practice as a miniature portrait painter. He specialized in richly coloured head-and-shoulders miniatures, as in his portraits of *Sarah Siddons* (1784; priv. col.; replica, Dublin, N.G.) and *James Gandon* (1799; Cambridge, Fitzwilliam), working mostly in watercolour and occasionally in enamel; he also produced some engravings. Appointed Miniature Painter to the Prince of Wales (later George IV) in 1795, he returned to London in 1804, also working in Bath that year. He continued to exhibit at the Royal Academy until 1822.

BIBLIOGRAPHY

Foskett

G. Reynolds: *English Portrait Miniatures* (London, 1952, rev. Cambridge, 1988), pp. 148–9

(3) Nathaniel Hone (ii) (*b* Dublin, 26 Oct 1831; *d* Dublin, 14 Oct 1917). Painter, great-grandson of Brindley Hone, a brother of (1) Nathaniel Hone (i). He studied engineering at Trinity College, Dublin, and in 1853 went to Paris to study art, first with Adolphe Yvon, then at Thomas Couture's atelier, where he was a contemporary of Edouard Manet and Pierre Puvis de Chavannes. He copied works in the Louvre, where he especially admired the Venetian masters. In 1857 Hone settled at Barbizon, meeting Jean-François Millet, Théodore Rousseau, Jean-Baptiste-Camille Corot and Henri-Joseph Harpignies. He painted village and forest scenes, at first in the manner of Courbet but then in a broader, lighter style influenced by Corot, with a harmonious use of green tones, as in *Banks of the Seine* (*c.* 1866; Dublin, N.G.). In the 1860s he lived at Bourron-Marlotte and also travelled to Brittany and Normandy, painting coastal scenes, often of fishing boats. He exhibited seven works at the Paris Salon (1865–9) and one at the Royal Academy, London (1869). After a visit to Italy he returned to Ireland in 1872, married and settled at Malahide, Co. Dublin. From 1876 he showed at the Royal Hibernian Academy, where he was elected Academician in 1880 and became Professor of Painting in 1894. In 1892 he visited Greece and Egypt, painting landscapes and archaeological subjects in watercolour and oil. His Irish marine and pastoral subjects, often scenes of cattle under cloudy skies, reveal his mature style, which is characterized by a freedom of manner and breadth of vision. Hone's widow Magdalene bequeathed a substantial collection of his oils and watercolours to the National Gallery of Ireland, Dublin. Other paintings are in the Hugh Lane Gallery of Modern Art, Dublin. Although he was a significant member of the Barbizon school and the greatest Irish landscapist of the late 19th century, Hone's work is virtually unknown outside Ireland.

BIBLIOGRAPHY

T. Bodkin: *Four Irish Landscape Painters* (Dublin, 1920)
A. Crookshank and the Knight of Glin: *The Painters of Ireland, c. 1660–1920* (London, 1978)
P. Harbison, H. Potterton and J. Sheehy: *Irish Art and Architecture* (London, 1978)
The Irish Impressionists (exh. cat. by J. Campbell, Dublin, N.G., 1984), pp. 24–9, 142–55
K. McConkey: *A Free Spirit: Irish Art, 1860–1960* (London, 1990)
Nathaniel Hone the Younger (exh. cat. by J. Campbell, Dublin, N.G., 1991)
J. Campbell: 'Nathaniel Hone's Paintings of Ancient Construction', *Irish A. Rev.* (1991–2), pp. 80–86

JULIAN CAMPBELL

(4) Evie [Eva] **(Sydney) Hone** (*b* Roebuck Grove, Co. Dublin, 22 April 1894; *d* Rathfarnham, Co. Dublin, 13 March 1955). Painter and stained-glass artist, descendant of Joseph Hone, a brother of (1) Nathaniel Hone (i). In 1905 she was crippled by infantile paralysis, and after prolonged treatment, she lived at intervals on the Continent. A visit to Assisi in 1911 made a lasting impression on her. She started training at the Byam Shaw School of Art, London, *c.* 1913, working briefly with Walter Sickert in 1918 and then with Bernard Meninsky (1891–1950); on the latter's advice she continued her studies in Paris under André Lhôte and was soon joined there by Mainie Jellett. In 1921 they persuaded Albert Gleizes to take them as pupils, working with him intermittently until 1931. During the 1920s Hone also visited Spain.

Following the critical condemnation of her exhibition with Jellett at the Dublin Painters' Gallery in 1924, Hone was received into an Anglican community in Truro, Cornwall, but left after about a year to return to painting. She persisted in her Cubist-derived abstraction in gouaches such as *Seated Woman* (*c.* 1928; Dublin, N.G.), in which indications of a head are subservient to the formal pattern of geometric and decorative colour elements. In this period of experimentation, her painting is not easily distinguished from that of Jellett, except in her occasionally more exuberant use of colour.

With her innate sense of the symbolic properties of colour, Hone turned *c.* 1933 to stained glass with the encouragement of the Irish artist Wilhelmina Margaret Geddes (1887–1955). Her first such commission was for Ardcarne church, near Boyle, Co. Roscommon, in 1934. Eventually she completed some 48 commissions in glass, the most famous being a window (1948–52) for Eton College Chapel, Windsor, Berks. In both her paintings and stained glass of the early 1930s she was strongly influenced by Georges Rouault, adapting his dominant black outline, brevity of expression and religious subject-matter in expressive oils such as *Convent at Arles* (*c.* 1935; ex-M. McEntire priv. col., Dublin). During the 1940s she developed a greater freedom of contour in landscapes such as *Snow at Marlay* (*c.* 1944; Dublin, N.G.) and *Ruin at Ardmore* (1946; Belfast, Ulster Mus.). Concurrently she

sought inspiration in medieval Irish carvings, in the stained glass of French cathedrals and in the Byzantine mosaics of Ravenna, which she visited in 1948; these influences can be seen in later works such as *Head of Christ* (gouache on paper, *c.* 1950; Dublin, Hugh Lane Mun. Gal.; see fig.). She had a strong influence on younger artists through the Irish Exhibition of Living Art, of which she was a founder-member in 1943.

BIBLIOGRAPHY

S. Frost: *A Tribute to Evie Hone and Mainie Jellett* (Dublin, 1957)
Evie Hone, 1894–1955 (exh. cat. by J. White, Dublin, U. Coll., 1958)
The French Connection (exh. cat. by H. Pyle, London and Cork, Tom Rice, 1987)
Irish Women Artists from the Eighteenth Century to the Present Day (exh. cat., Dublin, N.G., 1987)

HILARY PYLE

Hone, Philip (*b* New York, 25 Oct 1780; *d* New York, 5 May 1851). American auctioneer, patron and collector. Hone accumulated a fortune in the auction business, retiring in 1821 to devote himself to Whig politics (he was briefly mayor of New York), fashionable charities, New York's cultural life and his diary. Hone helped to make the collecting of paintings by living American artists fashionable. He was one of the first to patronize Thomas Cole, and in the early 1830s his collection (dispersed at his death) contained works by Thomas Doughty, William Dunlap, Charles Cromwell Ingham, Samuel Morse, Rembrandt Peale, John Vanderlyn and William Guy Wall (1792–after 1864), as well as Charles Robert Leslie and Gilbert Stuart Newton (then considered American painters). When in the early 1830s Hone provided Dunlap

Evie Hone: *Head of Christ*, gouache on paper, 457×343 mm, *c.* 1950 (Dublin, Hugh Lane Municipal Gallery of Modern Art)

with an annotated catalogue of his collection, he wrote with a typical mixture of pride and naivety: 'I do not know of a finer collection of modern pictures [in the United States]'.

UNPUBLISHED SOURCES

New York, NY Hist. Soc. [28-volume diary]

BIBLIOGRAPHY

W. Dunlap: *A History of the Rise and Progress of the Arts of Design in the United States* (New York, 1834/*R* 1969)
A. Nevins, ed.: *The Diary of Philip Hone, 1828–1851* (New York, 1927/*R* 1969) [contains only a portion of Hone's diary]

ALAN WALLACH

Honegger, Gottfried (*b* Zurich, 12 June 1917). Swiss painter, sculptor and printmaker. He studied (1932) at the Kunstgewerbeschule, Zurich, and first worked as a designer (1933–6). From the age of 20 he concentrated on graphic and commercial art, and it was not until 1957, with the creation of his first 'tableau-relief', that his career really began. Painting abstract works influenced by Zurich Concrete art and by contemporary American painting from 1950 onwards, Honegger developed as an artist during his stay in New York (1958–60) where his first exhibition was held at the Martha Jackson Gallery in 1960. Honegger settled in Paris in 1961, where he continued to experiment in painting and sculpture. His pictures were composed following a system and use simple, geometric forms in relief, executed in monochrome but with particular attention to technique and surface presentation. His shapes (squares, circles) are placed inside an orthogonal frame, following a pattern established beforehand and always based on numerical calculation. The paintings are made up of sharp-edged cardboard pieces placed, with strengthened backing, on to canvas and covered with several layers of paint. In this manner, the artist obtained a relief effect on the surface that catches the light and gives the composition a changeable quality (e.g. *Tableau-Relief 'Sibyl' Z 699*, 1971; Dallas, TX, Mus. F.A.). Honegger also desired to allow chance to play a role in the programming of his works. His sculpture, which he produced from 1968 onwards, uses cubes, spheres and their multiples, producing system-based structures and relationships. Numerous public commissions in Europe and the USA since 1971 enabled Honegger to apply his theories on a monumental scale (e.g. *Structure 36*, steel, h. 5 m, Cor-Ten, 1979; Blanzy, Lycée Ens. Professionel).

BIBLIOGRAPHY

K. W. Forster: *Honegger: Arbeiten aus den Jahren 1939 bis 1971* (Teufen, 1972)
S. Lemoine: *Catalogue des sculptures, 1953–1983* (Paris and Zurich, 1983)
——: *Gottfried Honegger: Tableaux-Reliefs/Skulpturen, 1970–83* (Paris and Zurich, 1983)
G. Magnaguagno and I. Fetscher: *Gottfried Honegger: Werke vor 1960/Oeuvres avant 1960* (Zurich, 1990)

SERGE LEMOINE

Honey, W(illiam) B(owyer) (*b* London, 13 April 1889; *d* 13 Sept 1956). English writer and museum curator. He won a scholarship to the Sir Walter St John's School, Battersea, London, but left at the age of 15 to pursue a career as a civil servant at the General Post Office. In 1926 he transferred from the clerical side of the Civil Service to an appointment as Assistant in the Department of Ceramics of the Victoria and Albert Museum, London.

From 1938 until his retirement in 1950, Honey was Keeper of the department and continued its interest in contemporary artists.

While at the Victoria and Albert Museum he wrote 13 monographs and numerous articles on Chinese and European ceramics, as well as works on glass, gardening, aesthetics and philosophy. He also published a collection of poems and his autobiography (1941). During the years 1947–54 Honey was contributing editor of the Faber Monograph Series on pottery and porcelain. He was among the first to challenge the correctness of the cyclical dating of Chinese porcelain, and his interpretations of reign marks and inscriptions revealed great expertise. Although some of his pioneering achievements may hold conclusions no longer valid, Honey's works are praised for their 'aesthetic sensibility and sure taste' (Gure), and some have become standard reference works within the field of ceramics.

WRITINGS

Guide to the Later Chinese Porcelain: Periods of K'ang hsi, Yung cheng and Ch'ien lung, London, V&A cat. (London, 1927)
Old English Porcelain (London, 1928, rev. 3/1977)
Dictionary of European Ceramic Art (London, 1931)
Brought out in Evidence: An Autobiographical Summing-up (London, 1941)
The Art of the Potter (London, 1945)
The Ceramic Art of China and Other Countries of the Far East (London, 1945)
European Ceramic Art from the End of the Middle Ages to about 1815, 2 vols (London, 1949–52)

BIBLIOGRAPHY

D. Gure: 'W. B. Honey', *Artibus Asiae*, xix/2 (1956), pp. 143–4

BENT NIELSEN

Honeysuckle. *See* ANTHEMION and PALMETTE.

Hongje. *See* CHŎNGJO.

Hong Kong. British crown colony located at the south of Guangzhou (Canton), China, scheduled to revert to Chinese control in 1997. The colony comprises Hong Kong Island, Kowloon peninsula and the New Territories, on the mainland, and adjacent islands. Victoria Harbour, one of the world's best deep water harbours, separates Kowloon from Hong Kong Island. The name Hong Kong, meaning 'incense harbour' or 'fragrant harbour', derives from the city's fame as a centre of the incense trade in the 19th century.

□

1. HISTORY AND URBAN DEVELOPMENT. Archaeological evidence indicates that the territory of Hong Kong was occupied during the Neolithic period (*c.* 6500–*c.* 1600 BC), and Bronze Age artefacts have also been found. Rock-carvings with zoomorphic imagery that have been found at several coastal locations probably also date to the Bronze Age. The most significant evidence of early Chinese occupation is the Han-dynasty tomb at Lei Cheng Uk (Kowloon), a brick-built structure with four chambers in a cruciform arrangement around a central domed area. Permanent Chinese settlement in the area is not mentioned in Chinese texts until the 11th century.

Most pre-colonial structures, such as the forts at Tung Chung (Lantau Island) and on Tung Lung Island, date from the Qing period (1644–1911). The New Territories contain a number of clan villages of some antiquity, and their associated ancestral halls frequently date from this period. Of note are the halls of the Tang clan near Yuen Long, where one branch of the family settled in the 13th century. The Tang Si Chung Tsz (Deng shi zong ci), built *c.* 1790, is constructed of grey brick, with three chambers and two courtyards; the roof has finely carved wooden supporting brackets. Kat Hing Wai (Jiqingwei), at Kam Tin, is the best known of the walled villages in the New Territories and was first settled in the Song period (960–1279). Tsang Tai Uk (Zengdawu), near Shatin, is a particularly distinctive example (completed *c.* 1850). Sam Tung Uk (Sandongwu; *c.* 1800), now surrounded by the town of Tsuen Wan, has been restored and opened as a museum.

The major turning-point in the history of Hong Kong, indeed, its beginning as a separate entity, was its occupation by the British in 1841. Following the ratification of the 1842 Treaty of Nanking (Nanjing) in 1843, it became a British colony; the territory was augmented by the acquisition of the southern tip of the Kowloon peninsula in 1860 and by the 99-year lease of the New Territories in 1898.

Most of the earliest British colonial buildings were erected on Hong Kong Island, alongside the harbour, then, as now, the reason for the city's existence. Many early structures belonging to the various trading companies have been destroyed, but important early non-commercial buildings do survive a little further inland. The oldest of these is Flagstaff House, built by the Royal Engineers between 1844 and 1846 as the residence of the senior British military officer. Following its restoration (1982–3) it was reopened as the Flagstaff House Museum of Teaware. St John's Cathedral, built in the Gothic style, was completed in 1849, and a new choir was added in 1872.

The gradual development of public life in the colony can be charted by noting some of the other significant colonial structures of the second half of the 19th century and the early 20th. Government House, the colonial governor's residence, was completed in 1855 but was later considerably altered. During the Japanese occupation (1941–5) a tower was added, as well as decorative elements that give the building an Eastern feel. The Supreme Court Building (now the Legislative Council Building) was completed in 1912, following plans prepared by the London architectural firm of Webb and Bell. In the same year the original building of the University of Hong Kong was finished, designed by the local architectural firm of Leigh and Orange. Now referred to as Hong Kong University's Main Building, it was extended in 1952. Only the clock-tower remains of the Kowloon–Canton (Jiulong–Guangzhou) Railway Terminal building in Tsim Sha Tsui (completed 1916); the rest was demolished in 1978.

The struggle for power in China between the Nationalist Guomindang (KMT) and the Communists, and the eventual triumph of the latter in 1949, resulted in a tide of immigration to the colony. There was a vast increase in Hong Kong's population from *c.* 600,000, when the territory was liberated from the Japanese in 1945, to approximately 2,360,000 in 1950, and extreme overcrowding led to the proliferation of squatter huts. Following a disastrous fire in 1953, a massive government-housing programme

1. Hong Kong, Bank of China Tower by I. M. Pei, 1989

began, and by 1977 nearly half the population was living in public housing. Population density remained high, however, and from 1973 several new towns, such as Shatin and Yuen Long, were constructed in the New Territories. This urban revolution was accompanied by the transformation of Hong Kong's economic life. The entrepôt role it had previously played declined in importance from the early 1950s in favour of manufacturing, which drew on a ready supply of cheap labour.

Land reclamation on both sides of the harbour has been taking place since the early 1850s, but it assumed a new pace after 1967. The location of Kai Tak Airport has restricted the height of structures on the Kowloon side of the harbour, in contrast to Hong Kong Island, where an ever-expanding forest of skyscrapers occupies the area between the harbour and the steeper slopes behind. A number of the most prominent buildings are banks, reflecting the importance of Hong Kong as a financial and service centre. Most significant architecturally are Sir Norman Foster's high-tech Hongkong & Shanghai Banking Corporation's headquarters (1981–5) and I. M. Pei's monumental Bank of China Tower (completed 1989; see fig. 1). Constructed after the Joint Declaration of 1984, in which the 1997 return of Hong Kong to China was agreed, the tower is a symbolic statement of China's stake in Hong Kong's future.

2. ART LIFE. Although cultural life was limited in 19th-century Hong Kong, artists did find their way there. The French painter Auguste Borget (1808–77) visited Hong Kong in 1838, prior to its occupation by the British. Murdoch Bruce (*fl c.* 1840–55), who was Inspector of Buildings in the early days of the colony, is also remembered as an accomplished draughtsman. The concern for topographical exactitude exhibited in his work is echoed in that of other Western artists in Hong Kong, such as the Macao-born Marciano A. Baptista (1826–96), who arrived in the late 1850s and worked as a drawing-master. GEORGE CHINNERY was the first Western artist of high technical competence and ambition to visit the territory. He had lived in MACAO since 1825 and spent the summer of 1846 in Hong Kong. Chinnery completed some 15 views of the colony during his stay (see fig. 2).

Portraits make up a significant porportion of the paintings produced by professional China coast artists (*see* CHINA, §I, 4(ii)), and Western styles had been adopted by Chinese painters prior to Chinnery's arrival, most notably by Spoilum (*see* GUAN, (1)). Chinnery's portrait style influenced Lamqua (*see* GUAN, (2)), the most significant Chinese artist working in oil during that time. Lamqua, who exhibited portraits at the Royal Academy in 1835 and 1845, ran a studio in Guangzhou (Canton), where a team of artists produced works on a production-line basis. He set up another studio in Hong Kong (1845), as did other established China-trade painters such as Sunqua (*fl c.* 1830–65) and Youqua (*fl c.* 1840–70). As the century progressed, photographic portraits largely replaced painted ones: views and images of different social types, however, constitute the main subject-matter of the photography of JOHN THOMPSON, who was a resident of Hong Kong from 1868 to 1872. As well as operating one of the many commercial photographic studios in the territory, Thomson also used it as a base for his photographic expeditions to China.

Some of the earliest Chinese artists to train in the West spent time in Hong Kong in the first half of the 20th century. Li Tiefu (1869–1952), who studied with William Merritt Chase in New York, was in Hong Kong during the 1930s and 1940s. Yee Bon (Yu Ben; 1905–95) and Lee Byng (Li Bing; 1903–94), who had studied together at the Ontario College of Art, Toronto, in the late 1920s, both returned to Hong Kong in the early 1930s. Li Tiefu's strongest works are his portraits, but landscape remained a major genre for these Western-media artists. Yee worked in oils, but Li Tiefu and Lee Byng produced many watercolours, as did LUIS CHAN, who trained in Hong Kong with the aid of correspondence courses.

More modernistic elements were introduced into Hong Kong art after 1945, with Luis Chan adopting an imagery inspired by Surrealism in works such as *Execution* (1974; Hong Kong, Mus. A.). For the most part, however, the innovative artists were those who were working within the

2. George Chinnery: *Western End of Hong Kong Island*, pen and brown ink, 215×431 mm, *c.* 1846 (Hong Kong, Hongkong and Shanghai Banking Corporation)

Chinese ink-painting tradition. The most influential of these was Lui Shou-kwan, who integrated influences from European and American gestural abstraction with elements of the Chinese aesthetic tradition in works such as *Zhuangzi* (1974; Hong Kong, Mus. A.). Among his pupils were WUCIUS WONG, IRENE CHOU, Ng Yiu-chung (Wu Yaozhong; *b* 1935), Cheng Wei Kwok (Zheng Weiguo; *b* 1920), Leung Kui-ting (Liang Juting; *b* 1945) and Chui Tze-hung (Xu Zixiong; *b* 1936). All established independent reputations within the modern ink-painting movement that gathered momentum from the end of the 1960s. Other important representatives of the more innovative side of Chinese ink painting include FANG ZHAOLING, Ding Yanyong (1902–78), LIN FENGMIAN and LIU KUO-SUNG (*b* 1932). Zhao Shaoang (*b* 1905) has been the most important representative of the LINGNAN SCHOOL in Hong Kong. Older established artists working in more clearly Western modes include the sculptors VAN LAU and CHEUNG YEE, as well as the painter Hon Chi-fun (Han Zhixun; *b* 1922). An orientation to Western modernism is the dominant tendency of the more recent generation of artists, which includes the sculptor Antonio Mak (Mai Xianyang; 1951–94) and the painter Yank Wong (Huang Renkui; *b* 1955). Many of these younger artists were born in Hong Kong (rather than having arrived as refugees from China), and many of them trained in Europe or North America. Consequently, there is less of a relationship with Chinese artistic traditions than is seen in the work of the preceding generation, with which there is little stylistic continuity.

Most 19th-century artistic activity occurred within a narrowly commercial context, and even early 20th-century artists with more elevated ambitions had to look to commercial art opportunities to make a living. Lee Byng, for instance, worked as a billboard artist for the King's Theatre upon his return from Canada. The first significant artistic organization was the Hong Kong Art Club, founded in 1935, which was, however, dominated by amateur Western artists. The first groups formed by stylistically ambitious local artists were the Circle Art Group (1963), the In Tao Art Association (1968) and the One Art Group (1970); among the many groups to emerge since are the Hong Kong Visual Arts Society (1974) and the Hong Kong Sculptors Association (1981). A thriving market in Chinese antiquities and paintings now exists in Hong Kong, but local modernist art still remains difficult to sell; the Hong Kong Arts Centre (founded 1977) has been the major promoter of contemporary art. The territory's leading museum is the Hong Kong Museum of Art. Founded in 1962 as the City Hall Art Gallery, it changed its name in 1975 and moved to a new and more spacious site in Tsim Sha Tsui in 1991.

BIBLIOGRAPHY
J. Thomson: *Illustrations of China and its People*, 4 vols (London, 1873–4); *R* as *China and its People in Early Photographs* (New York, 1982)
N. Cameron: *Hong Kong: The Cultured Pearl* (Hong Kong, 1978)
W. Meacham: *Archaeology in Hong Kong* (Hong Kong, 1980)
P. Hinterthur: *Modern Art in Hong Kong* (Hong Kong, 1985)
G. H. R. Tillotson: *Fan Kwae Pictures* (London, 1987)
S. Bard: *In Search of the Past: A Guide to the Antiquities of Hong Kong* (Hong Kong, 1988)
Ink Painting by Hong Kong Artists (exh. cat., ed. C. K. Wong and W. Y. Hung; Hong Kong, Mus. A., 1988)
Made in Hong Kong: A History of Export Design in Hong Kong (exh. cat. by M. Turner, Hong Kong, Mus. Hist., 1988)
Chung Wah Nan: *Contemporary Architecture in Hong Kong* (Hong Kong, 1989)
F. K. Chan: *The Development of Lu Shoukun's Art* (diss., U. Hong Kong, 1991)
C. L. Crossman: *The Decorative Arts of the China Trade: Paintings, Furnishings and Exotic Curiosities* (Woodbridge, 1991)
Historical Pictures: Collection of the Hong Kong Museum of Art (exh. cat., ed. K. C. Ho; Hong Kong, Mus. A., 1991)
The Art of Li Tiefu (exh. cat., ed. S. F. Ngan; Hong Kong, A. Cent., 1991)
City Vibrance: Recent Work in Western Media by Hong Kong Artists (exh. cat., ed. C. C. Tsang and others; Hong Kong, Mus. A., 1992)
D. Clarke: 'Between East and West: Negotiations with Tradition and Modernity in Hong Kong Art', *Third Text*, xxviii/xxix (double issue Autumn/Winter 1994), pp. 71–86
S. Fong, ed.: *The Art of Antonio Mak* (Hong Kong, 1995)

DAVID CLARKE

Hongren [Hung-jen; Jiang Tao; *zi* Wuzhi, Jianjiang] (*b* ?She xian, Anhui Province, 1610; *d* She xian, 1664). Chinese painter and Chan Buddhist monk. He is best known by his Buddhist name, Hongren; his secular name was Jiang Tao. Considered one of the Four Great Painter-Monks of the late Ming (1368–1644) period, he in fact reached the height of his artistic activity between 1651 and 1663, in the early Qing (1644–1911). Hongren is primarily known as the leading master of the ANHUI SCHOOL, as the creator of the distinctive angular landscapes of his mature period and as a man of great personal integrity and filial piety.

Hongren's birthplace is variously recorded as Xiuning and She xian; he probably grew up at She xian. The Jiang family was well established in the region, but the early death of Hongren's father brought hardship. Hongren supported his mother in the following years by drawing water and selling firewood; later, he may have earned an income by transcribing old texts and writing. The death of his mother so distressed him that he went into deep mourning, giving up all thought of marriage; he attempted to pay off the funeral debts as quickly as possible so as not to be 'obliged to others for one's own sake'.

As a youth, Hongren was tutored by Wang Wuyai. He studied the Five Confucian Classics and passed the local civil-service examination to become a *shengyuan*, but did not continue to further examinations or advance to an official career. When Nanjing fell to Qing troops in 1645, Hongren fled Anhui for Fujian Province with Wang Muli (1605–79), who may have been his tutor, Wang Wuyai. Both men became Chan Buddhist monks in 1646; Hongren adopted his monastic name and his sobriquet (*hao*), Jianjiang, meaning Jian River, a tributary of the Xin'an River that flowed through south-west She xian.

Hongren's antipathy to the Manchu Qing government seems to have been confined to association with various politico-scholarly groups. Among his friends, Wang Muli held a number of offices under the Ming administration and was active in resisting the Manchus; Hongren's biographer, Wang Taizheng (1600–75), and close friend Xu Chu were associated with the Fu she ('Restoration society'). Hongren became a monk only after the rapid demise of organized resistance in Fujian and may have been motivated as much by the threat of political persecution as by deep religious conviction.

Upon his return to She xian in 1651 or 1652, Hongren lived in local monasteries, including those in the celebrated Mt Huang region. He travelled frequently: to Mt Huang which is tilted towards the viewer so that a sense of both depth and volume is evoked, foreshadowing the artist's later compositions.

Few reliable paintings exist for the years between 1639 and 1651. A collaborative handscroll dated 1651 survives (see *Gean shanshui hejin juan*); another landscape album, the *Jianjiang Shangren shanshui ce*, was painted in Nanjing in 1657; a fan painting (Hong Kong, Liu Tso-chou priv. col., see Hsu, fig. 16) dates to 1655; and the *Feng River Landscape* handscroll (Kyoto, Sumitomo Col.) was painted in 1661.

Hongren reached the height of his artistic activity in 1651–63. He is often credited with having popularized the style of Ni Zan among the Anhui masters, and indeed many of his paintings are characterized by Ni's sparing arrangement of landscape forms. Typically, he used thin, light brushwork and minimal ink wash and *cun* ('texture strokes'). His landscapes often feature linear renderings of tall, flat-topped mountain bluffs. His most widely acknowledged masterpiece is a hanging scroll, *Coming of Autumn* (see fig.), dated on the basis of style to *c.* 1660. Of Hongren's works this most successfully combines the various aspects of his style. It depicts a river winding through a series of rock formations to a distant flat-topped bluff. Despite a typically linear description of forms, the use of light wash and darker accents creates a sense of volume and depth and the impression of eroded masses. Impressive tree groups provide a counterpoint to the dramatic tripartite mountains: as the trees diminish in size, the mountains loom ever larger. The central bluff and foreground pines balance each other, with the river running in between. While the contrasts, the thin, dry brushstrokes and the brittle, austere effect imitate Ni Zan's manner, the placement of small rocks between larger elements owes as much to the Yuan master Huang Gongwang. The composition itself, with its central mountain, is based on the monumental landscape paintings of the Northern Song period (960–1127), examples of which Hongren doubtless saw in Nanjing.

Hongren: *Coming of Autumn*, hanging scroll, ink on paper, 1.22×0.63 m, *c.* 1660 (Honolulu, HI, Academy of Arts)

BIBLIOGRAPHY

DMB: 'Hung-jen'

Gean shanshui hejin juan [Collaborative landscape scroll done for Ge'an] (Shanghai, 1935)

O. Sirén: *Chinese Painting: Leading Masters and Principles* (London, 1956–8), v, pp. 114–17

C. Hsu: 'Hong ren', *Shadows of Mt. Huang: Chinese Painting and Printing of the Anhui School* (exh. cat., ed. J. Cahill; Berkeley, U. CA, A. Mus., 1981), pp. 76–84

J. Cahill: *The Compelling Image: Nature and Style in Seventeenth-century Chinese Painting* (Cambridge, MA, 1982), pp. 147–68

C. Kuo: 'Hung-jen and his Followers', *Soochow U. J. Chin. A. Hist.*, xiv (1985), pp. 153–74

C. Kuo: *The Austere Landscape: The Paintings of Hung-jen* (Seattle and London, 1990)

VYVYAN BRUNST, with JAMES CAHILL

at least three times; to Nanjing, Jiangsu Province in 1658; to Yangzhou, Jiangsu, and Hangzhou, Zhejiang Province, in 1661; and to Mt Lu, Jiangxi Province, in 1663. He died in a monastery below the Piyun peak in south-west She xian. At his request he was buried in a grave surrounded by plum trees, from which is derived his posthumous name, Meihua Guna ('Old Monk of the Plum Blossoms').

The earliest surviving painting by Hongren, signed 'Jiang Tao', forms part of a joint handscroll done with four other Anhui artists (1639; Shanghai Mus.; see *Yiyuan duoying* (1987), no. 36, p. 50). Certain motifs—in particular a simple pavilion on a winding path—recall the Yuan-period (1279–1368) master NI ZAN. Two album leaves (Tokyo, Cheng Chi priv. col.) also represent the painter's early style and are probably roughly contemporary with the Shanghai scroll. Large upper areas of empty space and, in one example, a pavilion, again recall Ni Zan. The pavilion is perched precariously at the lip of a sharply jutting bluff,

Hong Se-sŏp (*b* 1832; *d* 1884). Korean painter of the Chosŏn period (1392–1910). He was born into a family of scholars and passed the examination to become an official in the central government, taking up a post in the Royal Chancellery. It appears that he did not start painting until relatively late in his life, as there are only a few extant examples of his work.

Hong Se-sŏp personified the scholar–painter. He is chiefly known for paintings of water-birds in monochrome ink, but he also painted landscapes. All his extant works are in monochrome ink on paper. In *Swimming Ducks* (see fig.) the birds are rendered in highly detailed brushwork, while the water is done in sweeping and overlapping washes of grey. The overhead perspective from which the ducks are seen is unusual. Some scholars have suggested

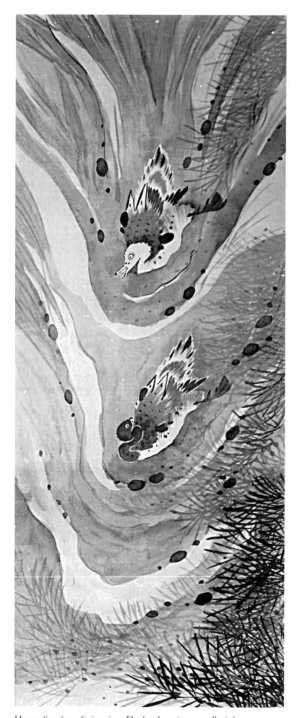

Hong Se-sŏp: *Swimming Ducks*, hanging scroll, ink on paper, 1195×480 mm, 19th century (Seoul, National Museum of Korea)

that this reflects Western influence; however, it is reminiscent of an anonymous 17th-century Korean painting of a *Swimming Duck* (album leaf, ink on paper, h. 666 mm; Seoul, priv. col.; see 1979–81 exh. cat., fig. 195, p. 125).

BIBLIOGRAPHY
5000 Years of Korean Art (exh. cat., ed. R.-Y. Lefebvre d'Argencé; San Francisco, CA, Asian A. Mus.; Seattle, WA, A. Mus.; Chicago, IL, A. Inst. and elsewhere; 1979–81)
Ahn Hwi-joon [An Hui-jun]: *Hanguk hoehwasa* [History of Korean painting] (Seoul, 1980)

HENRIK H. SORENSEN

Hongwolhon. *See* KIM (iii), (2).

Hönigsberg & Deutsch. Croatian architectural partnership formed in Zagreb in 1889 by Lav [Leo] Hönigsberg (*b* Zagreb, 1861; *d* Zagreb, 3 May 1911) and Julije Deutsch (*b* Göppersdorf, Bohemia, 1859; *d* Zagreb, 1922). Hönigsberg studied for almost a decade in Vienna, first at the Technische Hochschule under Heinrich von Ferstel and later (1883–8) in the studio of Ludwig Tischler (1840–1906). Deutsch also trained in Vienna and worked for a time in Paris with Camille Lefèvre. The partnership established between Hönigsberg and Deutsch was very productive: over 90 of their works are known, notably residential blocks constructed in the Lower Town of Zagreb after the redevelopment (1887–9) that followed the earthquake devastation of 1880. The majority are in an opulent, typically Viennese, Renaissance Revival style, while they sometimes used Baroque or Rococo elements. The Schlesinger Palace (1891), Zagreb, which they later adapted for use as the Palace Hotel (1907–8), is a good example. With their design of the Pečić Building (1899), Ilica 43, Zagreb, which was influenced by the Vienna Secession, the break with historicism became more marked: the tiled and balconied façade of the Kallin House (1903; Vjekoslav Bastl, of the Hönigsberg & Deutsch studio, is sometimes credited with the design) at the corner of Gundulićeva and Masarykova streets, with colourful depictions of typical floral and geometric motifs, represents one of the finest examples of Secessionist-style street architecture in Zagreb; and the rich *fin-de-siècle* interiors of the Croat–Slavonian Central Savings Bank (1905), Ilica 25, Zagreb, remain intact as the Café Corso. Other buildings, for example the Chamber of Commerce (1902–3; now the Ethnographic Museum) and the tall corner block at Jurišićeva 1 (1905), were shorn of their Secessionist ornament following a Modernist face-lift by Peter Behrens in 1927–8.

BIBLIOGRAPHY
L. Dobronić: *Zagrebački arhitekti Hönigsberg i Deutsch* [The Zagreb architects Hönigsberg and Deutsch] (Zagreb, 1965)

FRANK ARNEIL WALKER

Honnecourt, Villard de. *See* VILLARD DE HONNECOURT.

Honoré, Master (*b* ?Amiens; *fl c.* 1288–1300). French illuminator. He was first associated with a specific manuscript by Delisle (1902), who argued that a record of the payments for a Breviary made for Philip IV, King of France, could be matched to an extant Breviary from the turn of the 13th century (Paris, Bib. N., MS. lat. 1023). The royal accounts for 1296 show an order for the payment of 107 livres parisis 10 sous on 25 August to an intermediary, Galterus, canon of the Sainte-Chapelle. Delisle linked this record to another royal payment of 20 livres made later in 1296 (but before All Saints' Day), to 'Honoratus illuminator' for the decoration of unspecified books for the King, thus identifying Honoré with the Breviary in Paris. The internal evidence of the manuscript supports the theory of a royal origin: the calendar and offices are for the use of the Sainte-Chapelle; the manuscript was produced with exemplary care; a king kneels before a statue of the Virgin on the Beatus page (fol. 8*r*); and there are fleurs-de-lis in the background of the frontispiece (fol. 7*v*; see fig.). In addition, in the 1380 inventory of Charles V, the manuscript is listed with a binding bearing the arms of France. The date of the manuscript also appears consistent with the documents since the Office of St Louis (*can* 1297) is an added section, indicating that the rest of the manuscript must have been made before 1297. Martin (1906) associated the Honoré of the 1296 account with an illuminated copy of Gratian's *Decretals* (Tours, Bib. Mun., MS. 558) that bears a note (fol. 351*r*) stating that it was purchased in 1288 for 40 livres from the illuminator Honoré, Rue Erembourc de Brie (now Rue Boutebrie) in Paris. Martin, quoting the Parisian tax roll of 1292, noted that Honoré, his son-in-law and associate RICHARD OF VERDUN, and his assistant Thomassin were assessed at a total of 20 sous, which was more than any other workshop. On this basis he concluded that Honoré was 'probably the most able and certainly the most productive of all late thirteenth-century illuminators'. The painter's pre-eminence was endorsed by Vitzthum and was given renewed strength by Martin (1923) and the publications of Cockerell and Millar (1953), the latter of whom attributed to this illuminator a *Somme le roi* (London, BL, Add. MS. 54180; two detached folios Cambridge, Fitzwilliam, MSS 192 and 368) on the basis of the *Decretals* and the Breviary.

Four critics have voiced dissent: de Mély, Leroquais, Blum and Kosmer have questioned that the payment made to Honoré refers to the Breviary in Paris, and they have pointed to the fact that in the tax rolls of 1297, 1298 and 1300 Honoré was assessed at only a modest sum compared to some of his colleagues and was therefore not as prominent as Martin believed. A third objection is that stylistically the *Decretals* and the Breviary cannot be by the same hand. The first point, if theoretically valid, does not adequately take into account that Honoré is the sole illuminator mentioned by name in Philip's accounts, presumably a measure of his excellence. The fact that he disappears from the rolls after 1300, that a daughter of his had married probably before 1292, and that, although active for the King, he had a declining taxable income, suggests that he had grown old. In addition, with artistic recognition, Honoré was likely to be less involved with commercial trade than with princely commissions, and this often meant exemption from taxes. The third point was addressed by Millar, who saw close similarities between the first miniature of the *Decretals* and the frontispiece in the Breviary and considered the rest of the illustrations in both manuscripts to be workshop productions. Stylistic variations are also explained by the eight years that separate the two books and by their different illustrative traditions: volumes of canon law followed well-established models while the illustration of Breviaries at this period, on the contrary, was most dynamic. This accounts for the more sedate compositions and controlled palette in one volume and the greater plasticity of forms and stronger colours in the second.

While Honoré's name has been invoked freely in connection with countless late 13th-century French manuscripts, Millar (1953, 1959) and Turner, partly drawing on some of Vitzthum's work, proposed an oeuvre for the artist whose stylistic roots they saw in the Hours of Yolande of Soissons (New York, Pierpont Morgan Lib., MS. M. 729) and the St Germain-des-Prés Martyrology (1270s; Paris, Bib. N., MS. lat. 12834). Among Honoré's early works they cite the first twelve folios of an Evangeliary for the Sainte-Chapelle (London, BL, Add. MS. 17341) and two literary compendia (Paris, Bib. Arsenal, MS. 3142 and Bib. N., MS. fr. 12467). The middle period is represented by the *Decretals* in Tours and two further copies (ex-Yates Thompson priv. col.; Copenhagen, Kon. Bib., MS. Thott 160. 2²o; fragments in Boston,

Master Honoré (attrib.): *David Anointed by Saul*; *David and Goliath*, frontispiece miniature, 205×135 mm, from the Breviary of Philip the Fair, before 1296 (Paris, Bibliothèque Nationale, MS. lat. 1023, fol. 7*v*)

MA, Mus. F.A.), by a copy of Justinian's *Institutiones* (ex-Abbey priv. col.), a *Decretals* of Pope Gregory IX (ex-Dyson Perrins priv. col., MS. 33, sold London, Sotheby's, 29 Nov 1960, lot 109), a Book of Hours for the Use of Sarum (Nuremberg, Stadtbib., MS. Solger 4²o, 4), and a *City of God* of St Augustine (Cambridge, MA, Harvard U., Houghton Lib. MS Typ 228). The mature period includes the *Somme le roi* in London, which must date before 1295 since its decoration is the basis for another copy by his workshop, and bears this date and the name of the copyist Etienne de Montbéliard (Paris, Bib. Mazarine, MS. 870), and finally, the so-called Breviary of Philip the Fair (Paris, Bin. N., MS lat. 1023).

The best of Honoré's output represents the essential link between the Parisian style of the St Louis Psalter (Paris, Bib. N., MS. lat. 10525) and the innovative grisaille painting of Jean Pucelle in the early 14th century. The delicacy and mannered elegance of the inherited style were transformed by a search for plasticity through bolder forms and the use of shading, by the adoption of foreshortening and also by the interaction, through less formal gestures, of those tall swaying figures with triangular-shaped heads, curling hair and flowing beards that are hallmarks of the Honoré style.

BIBLIOGRAPHY

L. Delisle: *Notice de douze livres royaux du XIIIe et du XIVe siècle* (Paris, 1902)

H. Martin: *Les Miniaturistes français* (Paris, 1906)

S. Cockerell: 'The Parisian Miniaturist Honoré', *Burl. Mag.*, x (Oct 1906–March 1907), pp. 186–91

G. Vitzthum: *Die Pariser Miniaturmalerei von der Zeit des hl. Ludwig bis zu Philipp von Valois und ihr Verhältnis zur Malerei in Nordwesteuropa* (Leipzig, 1907)

F. de Mély: 'Le Miniaturiste parisien Honoré', *Rev. A. Anc. & Mod.*, xxxvii (1910), pp. 345–58

L. Delisle: 'Le Miniaturiste parisien Honoré', *J. Sav.*, (Sept 1910), pp. 385–90

H. Martin: *La Miniature française du XIIIe au XVIe siècle* (Paris and Brussels, 1923)

V. Leroquais: *Les Bréviaires manuscrits des bibliothèques publiques de France*, ii (Paris, 1934)

R. Blum: 'Maître Honoré und das Brevier Philipps des Schönen', *Zentbl. Bibwsn.*, lxii (1948), pp. 225–30

E. G. Millar: *An Illuminated Manuscript of La Somme le Roy Attributed to the Parisian Miniaturist Honoré* (London, 1953)

——: *The Parisian Miniaturist Honoré* (London, 1959)

D. H. Turner: 'The Development of Maître Honoré', *The Eric George Millar Bequest of Manuscripts and Drawings* (exh. cat., London, BM, 1967), pp. 53–65

E. Kosmer: 'Master Honoré: A Reconsideration of the Documents', *Gesta*, xiv/1 (1975), pp. 63–8

PATRICK M. DE WINTER

Honorius III, Pope [Cencio Savelli] (*reg* 1216–27). Italian pope and patron. He owes his fame to, among other things, the *Liber censuum* written while he was *camerarius* (chamberlain) of the Roman Church. Despite his numerous pastoral and political commitments (the first half of the 13th century was dominated by the crusade to Egypt, 1217–21, and the turbulent rule of Frederick II), he also found time to embellish the fabric of Rome. Even before he became Pope he paid for various works in the church of SS Giovanni e Paolo, of which he was Titular Cardinal.

In 1196, while Honorius III was still Cardinal Chamberlain, he supervised the casting of the two bronze doors in the cloisters of S Giovanni in Laterano and at the entrance of the oratory of S Giovanni Evangelista adjoining the baptistery of the same church. His name (*Cencius Camerarius*) can be seen carved on both doors, with that of the craftsmen, Uberto and Pietro da Piacenza. While Bishop of Rome he was responsible for enlarging the basilica of S Lorenzo fuori le Mura, the new apsidal mosaic in S Paolo fuori le Mura and renovating the church of S Bibiana, which had been built on the Esquiline Hill by Simplicius (*reg* 468–83).

Honorius considered that the church built on the Ager Veranus in 579 on the tomb of St Lawrence by Pelagius II (*reg* 579–90) was in need of radical transformation. The apse was demolished, the orientation of the building reversed and a new three-aisled basilica added, with large granite columns linked by an architrave. The body of the Pelagian church, which had an elegant old colonnade and matroneum (gallery), was preserved almost intact and transformed into a presbytery by the unusual device of raising the floor, which allowed a crypt to be formed beneath. Honorius added a portico to the front of the church (probably built by the Vassallettus family); its architrave includes a small mosaic image of the Pope himself. The church floor, one of the loveliest works of medieval Rome, and the marble liturgical fittings also date to the time of Honorius III.

At S Paolo fuori le Mura, Honorius III continued the work begun by his predecessor Innocent III, renovating the early Christian tribune. The mosaic was made by one or more Byzantine craftsmen brought from Venice, evidence for which is contained in a letter written by Honorius III to Doge Pietro Zioni of Venice on 23 January 1218; Honorius asked for two more craftsmen to be sent in addition to those already dispatched for the purpose. This very fine work, which was completed under Gregory IX (*reg* 1227–41), represents Christ enthroned in Majesty among apostles and evangelists in the upper part and the Throne of God between angels and apostles in the lower part. A tiny image of Honorius III, identified by name, kneels at the feet of the vast figure of Christ. In the mosaic as it is at present Honorius appears without his papal tiara, though this was presumably present in the original version; nonetheless the figure of the Pope is one of the few parts of the huge mosaic composition that retained its medieval characteristics in the restoration carried out after the fire in the basilica in 1823. Two other named contemporary figures are represented in the mosaic: the abbot Giovanni Caietanus, who supervised the completion of the mosaic itself as well as the building of the cloister adjoining the basilica, and the sacristan Adinulfus.

In 1224 Honorius was responsible for renovating the convent behind S Bibiana, and for various works of restoration in the church itself. We do not know exactly what the restoration work inside the church consisted of, but it must have been on a fairly large scale since, according to an inscription formerly on a side door, the building was reconsecrated that year.

From the *Liber pontificalis* we know that Honorius instigated various works of restoration in the Sancta Sanctorum in the Lateran, but any sign of this activity vanished after the large-scale rebuilding work carried out in 1278 on this same chapel at the order of Nicholas III (*reg* 1277–80). Similarly, we have no evidence to determine the nature of the work carried out for the abbey of Casamari in southern Latium and the abbey of Viterbo. Nor have we any clear picture of the ciborium he commissioned for the basilica of St Peter's, which was subsequently redesigned by Sixtus IV.

What is certain, however, is that the whole complex cultural and artistic fervour that affected Rome between the first and second decades of the 13th century undoubtedly found the necessary stimulus and support in the papal court. Honorius III, defined as *totius orbi honor* in the inscription in S Paolo, was able not only to reconcile divergent interests, but was determined above all to reinforce a type of artistic patronage typical of Rome, inspired by the desire to innovate, within traditional lines; a policy that was followed by the great popes of the end of the century, such as Nicholas III and Boniface VIII.

BIBLIOGRAPHY

A. Cianonius: *Vitae et res gestae pontificum romanorum et S.R.E. Cardinalium ab initio nascentis ecclesiae usque ad Clementem IX P.O.M.*, ii (Rome, 1677), cols 43–6
P. Pressutti: *Regesta Honorii Papae III*, 2 vols (Rome, 1888–95)
L. Duchesne, ed.: *Liber pontificalis*, ii (Paris, 1892), p. 453
J. Clauses: *Papst Honorius III* (Bonn, 1895)
H. K. Mann: *The Lives of the Popes in the Middle Ages*, xiii (London, 1925/R 1964), pp. 1–164
F. Hermanin: *L'arte in Roma dal secolo VIII al XIV* (Bologna, 1945)
G. B. Ladner: *Die Papstbildnisse des Altertums und des Mittelalters*, ii (Vatican City, 1970), pp. 80–86

MARIO D'ONOFRIO

Hontañón, Gil de. *See* GIL DE HONTAÑÓN.

Honthoir, Jean-Arnold de (*b* Liège, 1650; *d* Liège, 5 May 1709). Flemish sculptor. He was the son of a stonecutter and sculptor. Guillaume Cocquelé, his stepfather, was his first teacher. In 1672 Honthoir travelled to Italy, but by 1678 he was back in Liège, where he became the rival of Jean Delcour. During this period, Honthoir's style was indebted to the classicism of François Du Quesnoy. Among several works produced for the wealthy connoisseurs, the Surlet brothers, were the marble monument to *Jean-Ernest de Surlet* (1688; Liège, St Lambert), which contains a portrait medallion, and the marble monument to *Jean-Ignace de Surlet and his Wife* in the Dominican church. He also created the marble monument with portrait bust to the *Prince-Bishop Jean-Louis d'Elderen* (1693; Liège, St Lambert). For the high altar of the Benedictine church, Liège, he carved marble figures of *SS Benedict and Scholastica* (now Liège, St Jacques), and a white marble relief of the *Presentation of Christ in the Temple* for the Dominican church (now Liège, Mus. A. Relig. A. Mosan). The *Presentation*, together with a marble *Assumption of the Virgin* from the altar of the Brotherhood of the Rosary, also in the Dominican church, reveals a certain clumsiness in the handling of the figures and in the construction of the perspective. Honthoir also created designs for decoration, for example his drawings of swags with trophies (Liège, Cab. Est. & Dessins).

BIBLIOGRAPHY

J. Demarteau: *L'Eglise des Bénédictines de Liège, son architecte Dame Aldegonde Desmoulins (poète wallon et miniaturiste, 1640–92) et son sculpteur Arnold de Hontoire* (n.d.)
J. Yernaux: 'Les de Honthoir, artistes namurois à Liège au XVIIe siècle', *Etudes d'histoire et d'archéologie namuroises dédiées à Ferdinand Court*, ii (Gembloers, 1952), pp. 723–33

R. Forgeur: 'Trois bas-reliefs de la cathédrale de Saint-Lambert', *Bull. Soc. Royale Vieux-Liège*, clxviii (1970), pp. 441–7
P. Colman: 'Jean-Arnold de Honthoir', *De beeldhouwkunst in de eeuw van Rubens* [Sculpture in the century of Rubens] (Brussels, 1977), pp. 44–6

CYNTHIA LAWRENCE

Honthorst, Gerrit [Gérard] **(Hermansz.) van** [Gherardo delle Notti; Gherardo Fiammingo] (*b* Utrecht, 4 Nov 1592; *d* Utrecht, 27 April 1656). Dutch painter and draughtsman. He came from a large Catholic family in Utrecht, with several artist members. His grandfather, Gerrit Huygensz. van Honthorst (*fl c.* 1575–9), and his father, Herman Gerritsz. van Honthorst (*fl c.* 1611–16), were textile and tapestry designers (*kleerschrijvers*); his father is also occasionally mentioned in documents as a painter. Both his grandfather and father held official positions in the Utrecht artists' guilds, Gerrit Huygensz. from 1575 to 1579, and Herman Gerritsz. in 1616. Two of Gerrit Hermansz.'s brothers were also trained as artists. Herman Hermansz. van Honthorst (*fl* 1629–32) was trained to be a sculptor but later became a priest, and Willem Hermansz. van Honthorst (1594–1666) studied painting under Gerrit Hermansz., whose style he frequently emulated. Gerrit Hermansz. was the most successful artist in the family and the most famous member of the group of UTRECHT CARAVAGGISTI, the Dutch followers of Caravaggio. His predilection for turning the great Italian painter's dramatic patterns of natural light

1. Gerrit van Honthorst: *Christ before the High Priest*, oil on canvas, 2.69×1.83 m, *c.* 1617 (London, National Gallery)

and shadow into nocturnal scenes with cleverly rendered effects of artificial illumination won him the Italian nickname 'Gherardo delle Notti'.

1. Life and work. 2. Working methods and technique. 3. Character and reputation.

1. LIFE AND WORK.

(i) Training and visit to Italy, before mid-1620. (ii) Utrecht, mid-1620–28. (iii) England, 1628. (iv) Utrecht, The Hague and international courtly circles, 1629–56.

(i) Training and visit to Italy, before mid-1620. Gerrit trained as a painter in the Utrecht studio of Abraham Bloemaert. He must have travelled to Italy between *c.* 1610 and 1615. It is probable that he arrived closer to 1610, given his numerous surviving Italian period commissions and the fact that he attracted the attention of such important Roman art patrons as Vincenzo Giustiniani, in whose palace he lived, Scipione Borghese and, in Florence, Cosimo II de' Medici, Grand Duke of Tuscany. According to the Italian art critic Giulio Mancini, who included a biography of van Honthorst in his *Considerazioni sulla pittura* (Rome, *c.* 1619–20), the young artist attended an academy for life drawing in Rome, a fact confirmed by a dated drawing of a *Male Nude* (1619; Dresden, Kupferstichkab.). Mancini also mentioned several paintings by him with unusual light effects. These include a *Nativity* (1620; Florence, Uffizi), painted for Cosimo II, with the light source emanating from the Christ Child, and the important altarpiece of the *Beheading of St John the Baptist*, painted for the church of S Maria della Scala, Rome (1618;

in situ), in which the scene is illuminated by torchlight. The masterpiece of van Honthorst's Roman period, *Christ before the High Priest* (*c.* 1617; London, N.G.; see fig. 1), painted for Giustiniani, using a candle as light source, has been praised as an anticipation of Rembrandt's psychological insights, as well as of the works of Georges de La Tour. Not all of van Honthorst's Italian works employ artificial lighting; some, such as the striking *Liberation of St Peter* (*c.* 1616–20; Berlin, Bodemus.), also painted for Giustiniani, use the dramatic raking daylight often found in Roman period paintings by Caravaggio, for example the influential *Calling of St Matthew* (Rome, S Luigi dei Francesi), in which the light enters the composition from the right as it does in the van Honthorst painting.

(ii) Utrecht, mid-1620–28. In spring 1620 van Honthorst, together with another artist, one of the Colijn de Nole family of sculptors from Utrecht, left Rome for the northern Netherlands. His homecoming was celebrated on 26 July at the inn 'De Poortgen' in Utrecht, owned by his future mother-in-law, Bellichgen van Honthorst, a distant relative. The event was recorded in the diary of the Utrecht scholar Arnhout van Buchell; among those present were the painters Abraham Bloemaert and Paulus Moreelse, the engraver Crispijn de Passe I, the sculptors Robrecht (*d* 1636) and Jan (*d* 1624) Colijn de Nole and the artist and dealer Herman van Vollenhoven (*fl* 1611–27). In October of the same year van Honthorst married Sophia Coopmans, the daughter of a wine merchant. Several members of the Coopmans family, including

2. Gerrit van Honthorst: *Merry Company*, oil on canvas, 1.30×1.96 m, 1622 (Munich, Alte Pinakothek)

Sophia's brother Dominicus, were artists. Soon after their marriage the van Honthorsts took up residence in a house on the Snippevlucht, a small street in the centre of Utrecht where Hendrick ter Brugghen also lived. It is uncertain, however, if the two artists were actually neighbours as it is not possible to document ter Brugghen's residence on the Snippevlucht until 1627, the year van Honthorst moved to another part of Utrecht.

In 1622 van Honthorst became a member of the Utrecht Guild of St Luke, for which he served as dean in 1625, 1626, 1628 and 1629. As early as 1621, even before he had become a member of the Guild, van Honthorst began to attract international attention. A painting of *Aeneas Fleeing from the Sack of Troy* (untraced) was described enthusiastically in a letter of 1621 from Dudley Carleton, British Ambassador to The Hague, to the Earl of Arundel, in London. Van Honthorst's most important pictures of the early 1620s are his numerous artificially illuminated representations of both genre and religious subjects. Among the largest and most interesting of these is the full-length, life-size *Christ Crowned with Thorns* (*c.* 1622; Amsterdam, Rijksmus.). He also executed a number of paintings usually described as a *Merry Company* (e.g. 1622; Munich, Alte Pin.; see fig. 2). Such compositions probably represent aspects of the parable of the Prodigal Son, rather than being pure genre depictions. The earliest example of this theme (1620; Florence, Uffizi), the picture described by Mancini as a *'cena di buffonarie'* ('meal of buffoonery'), was executed in Italy for Cosimo II rather than in Utrecht. In such compositions van Honthorst, like his Utrecht compatriot Dirck van Baburen, was probably strongly influenced by Bartolomeo Manfredi's interpretation of Caravaggio's style. Van Honthorst also painted numerous genre scenes illuminated by artificial light, such as the *Young Man Blowing on a Firebrand* (*c.* 1622; Brussels, priv. col., see Judson, 1959, fig. 16), apparently a re-creation of a lost antique picture described by Pliny the elder, and the *Dentist* (1622; Dresden, Staatl. Kstsammlungen), a Caravaggesque version of the traditional Netherlandish theme, painted for George Villiers, Duke of Buckingham.

In contrast to van Honthorst's various candlelight depictions are a number of musical subjects, all executed on either panel or canvas, which utilize the steep *di sotto in sù* perspective associated with Italian ceiling and wall frescoes. The most interesting and unusual of these paintings is the *Musical Ceiling* (1622; Malibu, CA, Getty Mus.; see fig. 3), actually a fragment of what must have been a much larger ceiling decoration van Honthorst perhaps executed for one of the rooms in his own house. A piece of what was once an extremely tall, narrow canvas depicting *Venus and Adonis* (4.00×2.12 m, cut down in the early 20th century; Utrecht, Cent. Mus., where it is incorrectly attributed to Jan van Bijlert), with the same provenance as the *Musical Ceiling*, seems to indicate that as early as 1622 van Honthorst may have decorated an entire room in the Italian manner, thus anticipating the kind of large-scale painted decorative programme with which he was later to become involved for the various palaces of the House of Orange Nassau.

Although van Honthorst continued to paint Caravaggesque works, by 1624 a number of his pictures began to depart from the usual stylistic formulae of his fellow

3. Gerrit van Honthorst: *Musical Ceiling*, oil on panel, 3.08×2.16 m, 1622 (Malibu, CA, J. Paul Getty Museum)

Utrecht Caravaggisti, and artificial illumination was used less frequently in his major compositions. In such single-figure compositions as the *Merry Violinist* (1623; Amsterdam, Rijksmus.) and its pendant, the *Singing Flautist* (Schwerin, Staatl. Mus.), the subject-matter and the composition owe their origins to various related paintings by the Utrecht artists Hendrick ter Brugghen and Dirck van Baburen. Van Honthorst added a strong sense of illusionistic space, however, by providing a window-like architectural framework. Neither painting uses the dramatic patterns of light and shade characteristic of van Honthorst's earlier development.

During the mid-1620s van Honthorst's style continued to fluctuate between his typically Caravaggesque, artificially illuminated compositions, such as the large and impressive *Denial of St Peter* (*c.* 1623; England, priv. col., see Nicolson, fig. 135), which reveals the influence of the French Caravaggesque artist Valentin de Boullogne, and such pictures as the *Concert Group* (1624; Paris, Louvre), with its steep illusionistic perspective, cool daylight effects and bright colours. This work may have been executed as an overmantel for the Dutch stadholder's palace, Noordeinde, in The Hague, which would make it the first in a long series of commissions for the House of Orange Nassau. The diverse aspects of van Honthorst's style are still clearly apparent in two of his more important works from 1625: *The Procuress* (Utrecht, Cent. Mus.), a typically Utrecht Caravaggesque composition on panel, with a candle as light source, contrasting physiognomic types, a Manfredi-inspired *profil perdu* and a compact, half-length compositional format; and the full-length canvas *Granida and Daifilo* (Utrecht, Cent. Mus.), based on the first Dutch pastoral play, *Granida* (1605) by Pieter Cornelisz. Hooft (1581–1647). This pastoral theme had been introduced into Dutch art only two years earlier by another of the Utrecht Caravaggisti, Dirck van Baburen. Van Honthorst's picture seems also to have been painted for one of the stadholder's palaces, indicating the growing courtly taste for pastoral and Classical themes in Dutch art at this time. Despite their differences in subject-matter and support, both pictures from 1625 reveal a crispness in the paint surface, and sharper outlines and edges than van Honthorst's earlier works. This stylistic tendency was to dominate his later artistic production.

During the summer of 1627 Peter Paul Rubens spent several days in Utrecht and, according to Joachim von Sandrart who was then a pupil of van Honthorst, visited the studio of van Honthorst and also met other prominent Utrecht artists. The account is difficult to confirm: Rubens stayed at the Utrecht inn owned by ter Brugghen's brother rather than at 'De Poortgen', suggesting that Sandrart, in relating the facts about this visit, was biased in favour of his master. During the same year van Honthorst was paid for two paintings for the royal hunting-lodge at Honselaarsdijk: *Diana Hunting* (1627; ex-Berlin, Grunewald, Jagdschloss, untraced since 1945, see Judson, 1959, fig. 40), and probably a recently discovered *Diana Resting* (New York, priv. col.). These pictures are the earliest works that firmly document van Honthorst's association with the House of Orange Nassau, which was to play a significant part in the painter's artistic development after the mid-1630s.

(iii) England, 1628. From April until early December 1628 van Honthorst was in England. In addition to the large historiated portrait of King Charles I, his wife, Queen Henrietta Maria, and the Duke of Buckingham depicted as *Mercury Presenting the Liberal Arts to Apollo and Diana*, originally commissioned by Charles I for the Banqueting House in Whitehall, London (3.57×6.40 m; London, Hampton Court, Royal Col.), he also painted several portraits, including one of *Charles I* (London, N.P.G.), which may have served as the model for the Apollo in the Hampton Court picture. It is possible that van Honthorst's earlier contacts with the Duke of Buckingham, who appears as Mercury in the Hampton Court painting, as well as with Rubens, who later painted the ceiling in the Banqueting House and had also worked for the Duke of Buckingham, were instrumental in his obtaining this important commission. The picture was extremely well received, to judge by Sandrart's statement that van Honthorst was paid 3000 guilders and given many other costly gifts. On 28 November 1628 van Honthorst was made an English citizen and provided with a lifetime pension of £100 a year.

(iv) Utrecht, The Hague and international courtly circles, 1629–56. Van Honthorst probably received another important commission from Charles I, which he executed only after his return to Utrecht: a large historiated portrait of *Frederick V, King of Bohemia, and his Queen, Elizabeth Stuart, Daughter of James I, and their Children* (1629; Marienburg, Prinz Ernst August von Hannover). The picture may be the one that is mentioned in an early inventory of St James's Palace and is said to be based on Honoré d'Urfé's pastoral work *L'Astrée*, one of the favourite poems of Frederick V of Bohemia (1596–1632). The success of the works painted for the English court were important factors in diverting van Honthorst's talents in two new directions: towards an insipid but financially rewarding style of courtly portraiture and towards the more successful allegorical works in large-scale decorative schemes. With the death of Hendrick ter Brugghen in 1629 and van Honthorst's abandonment of Caravaggism in the early 1630s, Caravaggesque history and genre painting in Utrecht began to lose much of its vitality.

During the first half of the 1630s van Honthorst's international reputation continued to grow, especially in royal and courtly circles in England and elsewhere. In 1630, for example, his brother and assistant, Willem van Honthorst, was sent to England to deliver a group of paintings in person. When Kronborg Castle at Helsingør burnt down in 1629, Christian IV, King of Denmark and Norway, commissioned van Honthorst to paint various works including a series of four pictures based on the *Aethiopica* of Heliodorus of Emesa (*fl c.* 220–50), and four illusionistic ceiling paintings depicting flying putti carrying royal monograms for the decorations of the redesigned and rebuilt castle, all eight of which were apparently completed by 11 October 1635 (*in situ*). There are numerous other works by van Honthorst commissioned for Kronborg, some of which are dated as late as 1643.

Van Honthorst was firmly established in the courtly circles of The Hague during the early 1630s, although he continued to reside in Utrecht until 1637. He was patronized by King Frederick V and painted numerous portraits for Prince Frederick Henry and his family. Between 1636 and 1639 van Honthorst was part of a team of artists involved with painting the decoration for the palaces of Honselaarsdijk and Rijswijk. He was paid the large sum of 6800 guilders for painting the ceiling decorations (untraced) for the grand hall at Rijswijk. It is likely that his work for the House of Orange Nassau was instrumental in his decision to move to The Hague, where he became a member of the Guild of St Luke in 1637. Among the best of the portraits painted at this time is the full-length double portrait of *Prince Frederick Henry and Amalia van Solms* (The Hague, Mauritshuis), executed shortly after van Honthorst took up residence in The Hague. In 1638, when Marie de' Medici, Queen of France, made a state visit to the northern Netherlands, Frederick Henry had van Honthorst paint a portrait of her (Amsterdam, Hist. Mus.), which she presented to the burgomasters of Amsterdam during her visit to that city. Van Honthorst was elected dean of the guild in 1640.

In 1649 Constantijn Huygens, secretary to Prince Frederick Henry, and the architect and painter Jacob van Campen invited van Honthorst to help decorate the Oranjezaal of the Huis ten Bosch (*see* THE HAGUE, §V, 3), the most important extant large-scale painted hall in the Netherlands. The iconographic programme celebrated the long-awaited peace that had been concluded at the Treaty of Münster in 1648, which at last brought about official recognition of the United Provinces. Prince Frederick Henry did not live to see this historic event, having died in 1647, but in the centre of the hall's cupola, painted by van Honthorst and his workshop, he is glorified almost to the point of deification, as in *Frederick Henry's Steadfastness* (*in situ*). His widow, Amalia van Solms, who oversaw the completion of the project, also appears prominently, dressed in mourning and holding a skull. Van Honthorst's contributions to the Oranjezaal consisted only of allegorical portraiture, the best of which are the large *Allegory on the Marriage of Frederick Henry and Amalia van Solms* and the *Allegory on the Marriage of William II and Maria Henrietta Stuart* on the south wall (both *in situ*; see Judson, 1959, fig. 46).

In 1652 van Honthorst retired to Utrecht. There are relatively few works from after this date; almost all are portraits, the most interesting of which are the pendant portraits of the artist and his wife (1655; Amsterdam, Rijksmus.). The compositional and secondary elements suggest that these works celebrate the 35th anniversary of the marriage of van Honthorst and Sophia Coopmans.

2. WORKING METHODS AND TECHNIQUE.

(i) Workshop and pupils. Soon after van Honthorst joined the Utrecht Guild of St Luke in 1622 he established a large

4. Gerrit van Honthorst: drawing after Caravaggio's *Martyrdom of St Peter*, pen and brown ink and brown wash, 378×265 mm, 1616 (Oslo, Nasjonalgalleri)

and flourishing workshop and art academy, which attracted numerous students. Joachim von Sandrart, who studied with van Honthorst from *c*. 1625 until 1628, recorded that there were approximately 25 students in the studio when he was there and that each one paid 100 guilders a year for tuition, a considerable sum for the period. In 1627 van Honthorst purchased a large house on the Domkerkhof (Cathedral cemetery), apparently to house his growing atelier. Among van Honthorst's numerous pupils were Jan Gerritsz. van Bronchorst, Robert van Voerst (1597– *c*. 1636), Gerard van Kuijll (1604–73) and, according to Sandrart, the Dutch Italianate landscape painter Jan Both.

(ii) Drawings. Unlike his fellow Utrecht Caravaggisti, van Honthorst left a relatively large number of drawings. Since a number of these can be related to paintings it is clear that especially after *c*. 1625 he followed the working methods of his teacher Abraham Bloemaert rather than those of Caravaggio, who eschewed drawing in favour of direct painting. One of the most interesting surviving sheets is a signed and dated copy (1616; Oslo, N.G.; see fig. 4) of Caravaggio's *Martyrdom of St Peter* in S Maria del Popolo, Rome. Among those drawings that can be directly related to paintings is the *Prodigal Son* (Vienna, Albertina) for the *Merry Company* (1622; Munich, Alte. Pin.; see fig. 2). Most of the drawings, however, reveal similar preoccupations with Caravaggesque themes and artificial light effects, the contrasting areas of shadow being rendered in bold brown washes, as in *Brothel Scene* (*c*. 1623; Oxford, Ashmolean) and *Old Woman Illuminating a Young Girl with a Candle* (*c*. 1625; Leipzig, Mus. Bild. Kst.).

3. CHARACTER AND REPUTATION. It is surprising, given van Honthorst's early artistic and social success among the Roman aristocracy, to find him described by Mancini as 'very reserved and melancholic'; but Mancini also praised him as 'a man of his word' who could be 'trusted to deliver a painting on the date promised'. Van Honthorst was equally successful after his return to the northern Netherlands, especially in courtly circles. Constantijn Huygens, in his autobiographical notes (*c*. 1630), included the artist along with Abraham Bloemaert, Dirck van Baburen and Hendrick ter Brugghen as one of the most important Dutch history painters of the time. He was considered 'one of the most famous painters of this [the 17th] century' by Jean Puget de La Serre, a member of Marie de' Medici's French entourage, who was impressed by van Honthorst's portrait of her (Amsterdam, Hist. Mus.). The same portrait was glorified in a poem by the Dutch writer Jan Vos. When van Honthorst's brother Herman, a Catholic priest, was thrown into a Utrecht prison in 1641 for his religious activities, no less a person than Prince Frederick Henry intervened on his behalf, a clear indication of the stadholder's high personal regard for the painter. He was a natural choice for the group of artists chosen by Huygens and van Campen in 1649 to decorate the Oranjezaal of the Huis ten Bosch. But a letter Huygens wrote the same year to Prince Frederick Henry's widow, Amalia van Solms, makes it clear that van Honthorst's reputation was by then beginning to slip, especially among the other artists working on the Huis ten Bosch decorations. Despite van Honthorst's declining reputation towards the end of his career, he had already become

extremely rich through his artistic endeavours. When he sold his house to the city of The Hague in 1645, he received the princely sum of 17,250 guilders. About the same time he lent Elizabeth, Princess of Hohenzollern (1597–1660), no less than 35,000 guilders. Various other contemporary sources attest to the fact that van Honthorst lived in The Hague like a grand seigneur rather than an artist or artisan.

BIBLIOGRAPHY

M. Nissen: 'Rembrandt und Honthorst', *Oud-Holland*, xxxii (1914), pp. 73–80

G. J. Hoogewerff: 'De werken van Gerard Honthorst te Rome', *Onze Kst*, xxxi (1917), pp. 37–50, 81–92

——: 'Honthorst in Italië: Een naschrift' [Honthorst in Italy: a postscript], *Onze Kst*, xxxi (1917), pp. 141–4

A. von Schneider: 'Gerard Honthorst und Judith Leyster', *Oud-Holland*, xl (1922), pp. 169–73

G. J. Hoogewerff: *Gerard van Honthorst* (The Hague, 1924; It. trans., Rome, 1924)

A. von Schneider: *Caravaggio und die Niederländer* (Marburg, 1933)

G. Isarlo: *Caravage et le caravagisme européen* (Aix-en-Provence, 1941)

J. G. van Gelder: 'De schilders van de Oranjezaal', *Ned. Ksthist. Jb.*, ii (1948/9), pp. 119–54

Caravaggio en de Nederlanden (exh. cat. by J. G. van Gelder, Utrecht, Cent. Mus.; Antwerp, Kon. Mus. S. Kst.; 1952)

O. Miller: 'Charles I, Honthorst and van Dyck', *Burl. Mag.*, xcvi (1954), pp. 36–9

E. K. J. Reznicek: 'Een vroeg portret van Gerard van Honthorst' [An early portrait by Gerard van Honthorst], *Oud-Holland*, lxx (1955), pp. 134–6

J. R. Judson: *Gerrit van Honthorst: A Discussion of his Position in Dutch Art* (The Hague, 1959) [incl. cat. rais.]

H. Braun: *Gerard und Willem van Honthorst* (diss., U. Göttingen, 1966)

J. R. Judson: 'The Honthorst Acquisition: A First for America', *Montreal Mus. Bull.* (1970), pp. 4–7

E. K. J. Reznicek: 'Hont Horstiana', *Ned. Ksthist. Jb.*, xxii (1972), pp. 167–89

J. A. L. de Meyere: 'Nieuwe gegevens over Gerard van Honthorst's beschilderd plafond uit 1622' [New facts about Gerard van Honthorst's painted ceiling of 1622], *Jb. Oud-Utrecht* (1976), pp. 7–29

B. Nicolson: *The International Caravaggesque Movement* (Oxford, 1979); review by L. J. Slatkes in *Simiolus*, xii (1981–2), pp. 167–83

H. Peter-Raupp: *Die Ikonographie des Oranjezaal* (Hildesheim and New York, 1980)

L. Derks, M. Plomp and J. Speth: *'De dood van Seneca': Door Gerard van Honthorst?* ['The Death of Seneca': by Gerard van Honthorst?] (Utrecht, 1982)

M. J. Bok and J. A. L. de Meyere: 'Schilders aan hun ezel: Nieuwe gegevens over het schilderij van Gerard van Honthorst' [Painters at their easels: new facts about the painting of Gerard van Honthorst], *Mdbl. Oud-Utrecht*, lviii (1985), pp. 298–301

Portretten van echt en trouw [Marriage portraits] (exh. cat. by E. de Jongh, Haarlem, Frans Halsmus., 1986)

Holländische Malerei in neuem Licht: Hendrick ter Brugghen und seine Zeitgenossen (exh. cat., ed. A. Blankert and L. J. Slatkes; Utrecht, Cent. Mus.; Brunswick, Herzog Anton Ulrich-Mus.; 1986–7), pp. 30–32, 276–302, nos 60–67 [entries on van Honthorst by M. J. Bok and M. Vermeer]

LEONARD J. SLATKES

Honzík, Karel (*b* Le Croisic, 24 Sept 1900; *d* Prague, 4 Feb 1966). Czech architect, theorist, writer and teacher of French birth. In 1925 he graduated in architecture from the Czech Technical University, Prague. While still studying he became a member of *Devětsil*, the avant-garde group centred on the figure of Karel Teige. He was among enthusiastic advocates of Purism and Poetism in architecture, and with his fellow students Jaroslav Fragner, Evžen Linhart and Vít Obrtel (1901–88) he formed the Four Purists; this influence can be seen in his early works such as the block of flats (1926–8) in Starokošířská Street, Prague. In 1927 he joined the Architects' Club and later

the Left Front and Union of Socialist Architects. From 1928 to 1936 he worked with Josef Havlíček, with whom he designed a number of Functionalist projects including the *koldom* ('collective house', 1930; unexecuted), a type of low-cost residential building. Their best-known work is the General Pensions Institute building (1929–34), Prague, one of the most important examples of Functionalist architecture in the Czech Republic (now the House of Trade Unions). It was designed on a cruciform plan with slender rectangular blocks incorporating horizontal strip windows. From the mid-1930s Honzík became concerned more with theory and writing, and in 1946 he published a book on his theories, which treated architecture as the product of a living environment and lifestyle. He was increasingly critical of rigid Functionalism, and in this work he emphasized the necessity of satisfying both the practical and spiritual needs of humans in architectural design. In 1947 he was appointed Professor of the Theory of Architecture at the Czech Technical University, Prague.

WRITINGS

Tvorba životního slohu [The creation of a living style] (Prague, 1946)

Ze života avantgardy [The life of the avant-garde] (Prague, 1963)

BIBLIOGRAPHY

J. Pechar: *Architekt Karel Honzík, 1900–1966* (Prague, 1967)

'Josef Havlíček, Karel Honzík', *Tschechische Kunst der 20er und 30er Jahre: Avantgarde und Tradition* (exh. cat. by R. Sedláková, Darmstadt, Ausstellhallen Mathildenhöhe, 1988–9), pp. 113–15

Devětsil: Czech Avant-Garde Art, Architecture and Design of the 1920s and 1930s (exh. cat., ed. R. Švácha; Oxford, MOMA; London, Des. Mus.; 1990)

The Art of the Avant-Garde in Czechoslovakia, 1918–1938 (exh. cat., ed. J. Anděl, Valencia, IVAM Cent. Julio González, 1993)

RADOMÍRA SEDLÁKOVÁ

Hooch [Hoogh; Hooghe], **Pieter de** (*bapt* Rotterdam, 20 Dec 1629; *bur* Amsterdam, 24 March 1684). Dutch painter. He was one of the most accomplished 17th-century Dutch genre painters, excelling in the depiction of highly ordered interiors with domestic themes and merry companies and pioneering the depiction of genre scenes set in a sunlit courtyard. The hallmarks of his art are an unequalled responsiveness to subtle effects of daylight, and views to adjoining spaces, either through a doorway or a window, offering spatial as well as psychological release.

1. LIFE AND WORK.

(i) Early life and early work in Delft, 1629–c. 1661. De Hooch was the son of a bricklayer and a midwife. According to Houbraken, he was a pupil of the Haarlem landscape painter Nicolaes Berchem at the same time as Jacob Ochtervelt, a fellow Rotterdamer. Little or nothing of Berchem's style is detectable in de Hooch's early works, which mostly depict guardroom scenes. However, Ochtervelt went on to paint genre scenes with perspectival effects similar to those created by de Hooch. In 1652 de Hooch signed a document in Delft with the painter Hendrick van der Burgh, who subsequently became his follower and was probably his brother-in-law. De Hooch's early career as an artist seems to have required, as was commonly the case, a second career, and in 1652 he was described as both a painter and servant to a linen merchant, Justus de La Grange. An inventory of the latter's collection

completed in 1655 lists 11 paintings by the artist. In the same year de Hooch joined the Delft Guild of St Luke and he made additional payments to the Guild in 1656 and 1657. De Hooch's paintings of guardrooms have plausibly been dated to the artist's early career; they follow the tradition initiated by such artists as Pieter Codde, Willem Duyster and Anthonie Palamedesz., and they seem to reflect recent developments in the subject introduced by Gerbrand van den Eeckhout and Ludolf de Jongh. The latter's style is more fluid than de Hooch's but could have inspired not only his subjects but also aspects of his increasingly colourful palette.

De Hooch's paintings of guardrooms and peasant interiors are not as accomplished in terms of design and technique nor so sophisticated in their exploration of the expressive effects of light and space, although they often include a nascent interest in views to adjacent spaces, as in the artist's earliest dated paintings: six works from 1658, all depicting rectilinear interior genre scenes or sunny courtyard views with Delft motifs (*see* GENRE, fig. 2). These are the works of a mature master; indeed they include some of the greatest and best-known works by de Hooch, for example the *Card-players in a Sunlit Room* (London, Buckingham Pal., Royal Col.) and the *Courtyard in Delft with a Woman and Child* (London, N.G.; see fig. 1). By 1658 de Hooch was a leading practitioner of the so-called Delft school style (*see* DELFT SCHOOL (i)), the sources of which are still open to discussion; the style is characterized by a light tonality, dramatic perspectival effects and an exceptional responsiveness to natural light. Delft's greatest painter, Johannes Vermeer, who is also

associated with this school, began painting carefully composed, light-filled interior genre scenes with couples and single figures at almost the same time as de Hooch. The two artists undoubtedly knew one another, but in the early years de Hooch (who was three years older) was probably the first to master the illusion of space and subtle lighting effects; Vermeer's only dated painting from the 1650s is *The Procuress* (1656; Dresden, Gemäldegal. Alte Meister)— a life-sized genre scene in the tradition of the earlier Utrecht Caravaggisti. However, Vermeer went on to refine de Hooch's ideas, reducing the elements of his art to a single, still, three-quarter-length figure in the corner of a light-filled room. By the time that de Hooch painted his *Woman Weighing Coins* in the mid-1660s (Berlin, Gemäldegal.), it was in deliberate emulation of, possibly even in competition with, Vermeer's *Woman Holding a Balance* of several years earlier (Washington, DC, N.G.A.).

The subjects of de Hooch's mature Delft period were more conventional than their treatment. Merry companies with elegantly dressed young men and women gaming or sharing a drink (e.g. *Woman Drinking with Soldiers*, 1658; Paris, Louvre) were by this time standard themes in Dutch genre. More innovative was his contribution to the tradition of domestic subjects—images of women performing household chores, ministering to children or supervising maidservants, as in, for example, *Woman Nursing an Infant* (San Francisco, CA, Pal. Legion of Honor). De Hooch's celebration of domesticity is no doubt related to the sanctity and centrality of the home in Dutch society. In the Protestant Republic of the United Netherlands, the home rather than the church became the primary forum for moral instruction and pedagogy. By the mid-17th century the social history of the family had also changed, as the old medieval extended family was increasingly replaced by a smaller, more intimate nuclear family group. De Hooch's orderly spaces perfectly complemented this new celebration of domesticity, the walls and their light-filled windows and doorways creating a comforting framework for chores and nurturance. By the same token, his small courtyards are an extension of the home and are constructed with virtually the same spatial formulae as his interiors. Some of these scenes include identifiable buildings, for example the Oude Kerk and Nieuwe Kerk in Delft, but are in fact imaginary compositions. Although independent inventions, de Hooch's courtyards, too, are related to the rise (especially in Delft) of the TOWNSCAPE as an independent sub-genre of landscape painting.

Iconographic studies of Dutch genre paintings have often revealed 'hidden meanings', or what Erwin Panofsky called 'disguised symbolism', in outwardly naturalistic scenes. De Hooch did not share the metaphorical and highly moralizing approach of some of his contemporaries, notably Jan Steen and, closer at hand, Vermeer, but he would occasionally employ time-honoured symbolic devices, such as the painting-within-the-painting, to comment on his scenes. The meanings of his art usually arise from the associations of the subjects depicted, such as his images of domestic virtue, rather than through covertly encoded ideas. When he introduced symbols, they usually functioned as supplementary footnotes rather than the central theme of his works of art.

1. Pieter de Hooch: *Courtyard in Delft with a Woman and Child*, oil on canvas, 737×626 mm, 1658 (London, National Gallery)

2. Pieter de Hooch: *Interior with Women beside a Linen Chest*, oil on canvas, 720×775 mm, 1663 (Amsterdam, Rijksmuseum)

(ii) Amsterdam, c. 1661 and after. De Hooch had settled in Amsterdam by April 1661, or perhaps as much as 11 months earlier. There he apparently remained for the rest of his life except for a visit to Delft in 1663. Although he never abandoned his favourite domestic themes (e.g. *Interior with Women beside a Linen Chest*, 1663; Amsterdam, Rijksmus.; see fig. 2), de Hooch painted increasingly elegant subjects and wealthier households after his move. After *c.* 1663 his interior spaces, following the earlier examples of Gabriel Metsu and Jan Steen, became richer; his figures, in the manner of Gerard ter Borch, more refined; and his touch, like that of the Leiden 'Fine' painters, more minute. His simple Delft courtyards were replaced by the gardens of country villas, and his earlier cottage interiors by palatial halls, some of which are partly based on the galleries of the new Town Hall (now Royal Palace) in Amsterdam (e.g. the *Musical Company, c.* 1664–6; Leipzig, Mus. Bild. Kst.). In the late 1660s and 1670s de Hooch's palette became darker and his technique broader, and he often executed larger canvases. His address in these years suggests that he lived in a poor quarter of the town, although he continued occasionally to receive important portrait commissions (e.g. the portrait of the *Jacott–Hoppesack Family, c.* 1670; untraced, see Sutton, no. 92). The quality of his execution wavered increasingly in the late 1670s and after *c.* 1680 deteriorated alarmingly. It is unknown whether these developments were related to the painter's final illness: de Hooch died in the *Dolhuis* (Dut.: 'Bedlam'). However, the splendid twilit *Musical Party in a Courtyard* (1677; London, N.G.) proves that the artist was capable of outstanding work even late in his career.

2. INFLUENCE. Since de Hooch had no known pupils, the 'de Hooch School' is a misnomer. However, several artists worked in his style; the closest of these followers was Hendrick van den Burgh; Pieter Janssens Elinga (1623–before 1682) painted highly ordered interiors, but more rigidly than de Hooch, and he seems to have relied heavily on perspective recipes. The interest in interior perspectives exhibited by Cornelis de Man (1621–1706) probably acknowledges a debt to his younger Delft colleagues de Hooch and Vermeer. The work of Esaias Boursse and Jacobus Vrel also resembles aspects of de Hooch's paintings (and many of Vrel's paintings bear signatures altered to de Hooch's), but these two painters were essentially independent artists with no known contacts with the master. Jacob Ochtervelt was a highly accomplished painter in his own right who perhaps borrowed from de Hooch in conceiving his foyer scenes, but he ultimately created his own style, one that owes as much to Leiden and Frans van Mieris as to Delft. In the 20th century Han van Meegeren painted two 'de Hooch's', one of which was acquired in 1941 by Daniel van Beuningen, who always refused to accept that it was a forgery.

BIBLIOGRAPHY

A. Houbraken: *De grote schouburgh* (1718–21), ii, pp. 27, 34
C. Hofstede de Groot: *Catalogue of Dutch Painters*, i (London, 1908), pp. 471–570
A. de Rudder: *Pieter de Hooch et son oeuvre* (Brussels and Paris, 1913)
C. H. Collins Baker: *Pieter de Hooch* (London, 1925)
C. Brière-Misme: 'Tableaux inédits ou peu connus de Pieter de Hooch', *Gaz. B.-A.*, n.s. 4, xv (1927), pp. 361–80; xvi (1927), pp. 51–79, 258–9
W. R. Valentiner: *Pieter de Hooch*, Klass. Kst. Gesamtausgaben, xxxv (Stuttgart, 1929)
F. W. S. van Thienen: *Pieter de Hoogh*, Palet Series, v (Amsterdam, n.d. [*c.* 1945])
P. C. Sutton: *Pieter de Hooch: Complete Edition with a Catalogue Raisonné* (New York, 1980)

PETER C. SUTTON

Hood, Anthony. *See* HILDER, J. J.

Hood, Raymond (Mathewson) (*b* Pawtucket, RI, 21 March 1881; *d* Stamford, CT, 15 Aug 1934). American architect. The son of a prosperous box manufacturer in Rhode Island, he had a strict, religious and inhibiting upbringing that took some years to outgrow. He was educated locally, taking a first degree at Brown University, Providence, RI, before proceeding in 1899 to the architecture school at the Massachusetts Institute of Technology, Cambridge. In 1901 he joined the office of Cram, Goodhue & Ferguson, where he absorbed from Bertram Grosvenor Goodhue a feeling for the Gothic tradition in American architecture, which was to be an important supplement to his grounding in Beaux-Arts Classicism. In 1904 he went to study in Paris, enrolling in the Atelier Duquesne at the Ecole des Beaux-Arts. He spent much of the next seven years in Paris or travelling in Europe, apart from an interlude in 1906–8 when he worked in Pittsburgh and New York for his friend Henry Hornbostel (1867–1961). During this period he developed into a sharp, confident, ambitious, worldly and entertaining young architect of much potential, but with a conventional Beaux-Arts approach to style and planning. His early projects are impressive chiefly for their balance of Gothic and classical vocabularies.

Returning to the USA in 1911, Hood at first made slow progress. He worked for others, mainly for Hornbostel in Pittsburgh, before opening his own office in New York in

1914. His early practice and habits were mildly bohemian, earning him a certain regard but little remunerative work. Mori's Restaurant in Bleecker Street demonstrated Hood's abilities as a decorator and colourist, while the merry, boat-shaped swimming pool and pavilion (1920) to the Crimmins house, Darien, CT, revealed a gift for architectural display, fun and irreverence, which never deserted him. Hood's two later Rex Cole showrooms (1929–33) at Bay Ridge, NY, designed in the guise of refrigerators for a salesman of the product, are among the better architectural follies of the 20th century.

The turning point of Hood's career was his triumph in the *Chicago Tribune* competition of 1922, with a design for a Gothic tower (*see* COMPETITION, fig. 3). He submitted the entry in conjunction with John Mead Howells, but Hood was responsible for its development and detailing. The *Chicago Tribune* Building led to the four great sky-scrapers in New York on which Hood's fame rests: the American Radiator Building (1923–5), the *Daily News* Building (1929–30; see fig.), the McGraw-Hill Building (1930–31; *see* BUILDING REGULATIONS, fig. 3) and the RCA Building at Rockefeller Center (1931–40; for illustration *see* ROCKEFELLER). All these buildings were designed in collaboration with his partners Frederick Godley and J. André Fouilhoux (1879–1945), sometimes also with other architects (Howells at the *Daily News* Building, and two separate teams at Rockefeller Center). He excelled at this style of modern office building, and was able to stamp his individuality on each project.

In this sequence Hood exploited to the full the architectural opportunities provided for the high-rise building by the New York zoning law of 1916, progressively simplifying and refining his compositions. Working habitually from clay models, he pared down the ornament of the skyscraper, substituting a counterpoint of dramatic, colourful and subtly proportioned planes and masses. This gave the later buildings, especially the green-glazed McGraw-Hill Building, a seemingly 'modern' flavour. Hood, however, developed a distinctively American style, owing little to the European modern movement. His urban architecture is expressive, extrovert and alert to the image-consciousness of modern commerce. The unique black and gold of the American Radiator Building, symbolizing coal and flame, is the most explicit example of this; Ideal House (1929), London, a smaller and simpler building for a subsidiary of the same company, displays the same livery. Yet his architecture was also sternly practical and disciplined. As an urban planner he acknowledged the demand for maximizing rentable space and concentrating services. The varying sculptural and structural forms of his completed buildings sprang straight from this necessity.

Hood's skyscrapers are never coarse, lumpy or dependent on Art Deco ornament, in contrast to other skyscrapers in New York of the years between the two World Wars. A feeling for Gothic proportions and massing, crucial to the aesthetic development of the high-rise building, persists even in the *Daily News* and RCA buildings with their truncated tops, and this singles Hood out as the architect who did the most to develop American Gothic in the directions indicated by Goodhue.

Little else of Hood's work was executed. Apart from the idiosyncratic Patterson house of 1930 at Ossining, NY, for Joseph M. Patterson, the proprietor of the *Daily News*, his domestic architecture is not striking. His only major ecclesiastical building, the Masonic Temple and Scottish Rite Cathedral (1929), Scranton, PA, is likewise disappointing. A number of 'ideal' planning schemes, including a fantasy for skyscrapers on the bridges surrounding Manhattan, show that Hood was not untouched by the Corbusian planning mania of the inter-war years. He also had a hand in the layout of the *Century of Progress Exposition* in Chicago (1933). Yet only the challenge of the high-rise building seems to have elicited the mixture of artistic refinement, levity, novelty and practicality which was peculiar to Hood's work.

WRITINGS
'The American Radiator Company Building, New York', *Amer. Architect & Archit. Rev.*, cxxvi/2459 (1924), pp. 467–74
Raymond M. Hood, foreword by A. T. North (New York, 1931)

BIBLIOGRAPHY
F. S. Swales: 'Draftsmanship and Architecture as Exemplified by the Work of Raymond M. Hood', *Pencil Points*, ix (1928), pp. 259–69
A. Talmey: 'Man against the Sky', *New Yorker*, vii (1931), pp. 24–7
'Raymond Mathewson Hood', *Archit. Forum*, lxii (1935), pp. 127–33
W. H. Kilham, jr: *Raymond Hood, Architect: Form through Function in the American Skyscraper* (New York, 1973)
C. H. Krinsky: *Rockefeller Center* (New York, 1978)
Raymond M. Hood (exh. cat., ed. R. A. M. Stern and T. P. Catalano; New York, Inst. Archit. & Urb. Stud., 1982)
A. Saint: 'Americans in London: Raymond Hood and the National Radiator Building', *AA Files*, vii (1984), pp. 30–43

Hood, Thomas (*b* London, 23 May 1799; *d* London, 3 May 1845). British engraver and writer. During three years (1815–18) spent in Scotland because of poor health, he submitted drawings and prose to local newspapers, and

Raymond Hood and John Mead Howells: *Daily News* Building, New York, 1929–30

on his return to London he trained as an engraver. He was apprenticed to his uncle, Robert Sands (1792–1855), and then to the brothers Henry Le Keux (1787–1868) and John Le Keux (1783–1846). On completing his training he specialized in satirical engravings of his own design. In 1821 he was appointed sub-editor of the *London Magazine*, and his introduction to established authors and his marriage in 1825 to the sister of the minor poet John Hamilton Reynolds (1796–1852) encouraged his literary ambitions. His first serious verse was unsuccessful, but from 1825 with the publication of *Odes and Addresses to Great People*, on which he collaborated with Reynolds, Hood was associated with a variety of humorous magazines, many of which he edited and published himself. Hood both wrote for and illustrated *Whims and Oddities* (1826–7), for which he invented 'Picture Puns', *Hood's Comic Annuals* (1830–39) and *Hood's Monthly Magazine* (1844), all published in London. He worked for *Comic Annual* throughout the 1830s and into the 1840s; as editor he commissioned John Leach (1817–64) to produce work for it in 1842, as well as for *Whimsicalities* in 1844. On account of poverty and illness, he lived in Koblenz and Ostend from 1835 to 1840, but in 1844 his literary fame, coupled with poor health and financial insecurity, won his family a Civil List Pension.

WRITINGS

with J. H. Reynolds: *Odes and Addresses to Great People* (London, 1825)

BIBLIOGRAPHY

DNB
S. Houfe: *The Dictionary of British Book Illustrators and Caricaturists, 1800–1914* (Woodbridge, 1978)
R. K. Engen: *Dictionary of Victorian Wood Engravers* (Cambridge and Teaneck, NJ, 1985)

Hōōdō. *See under* BYŌDŌIN.

Hoogenberg. *See* HOGENBERG.

Hoogewerff, G(odefridus) J(ohannes) (*b* Amersfoort, 20 June 1884; *d* Florence, 25 March 1963). Dutch art historian. He studied medieval history at Utrecht University, specializing in medieval manuscript illumination. In 1908 he was appointed Research Assistant there to Professor W. Vogelsang, who held the first chair in the History of Art in the Netherlands. In 1909 he went to Rome, where he began studying archival documents concerning Dutch artists active in Italy. He completed his studies in 1912 with a dissertation on 16th-century Dutch painters in Italy. The same year he became the first member of staff of the Nederlands Historisch Instituut in Rome, of which he was Director from 1924 to 1950. From 1950 to 1955 he held the chair of Iconography and Iconology of Early Christian Art at Utrecht University.

Hoogewerff's publications helped to provide a historical basis for the history of Dutch art. His important research into the daily lives of Dutch artists in Rome was published in two volumes in the 1940s. He also wrote the first history of late medieval and Renaissance painting in the northern Netherlands. He contributed to the theoretical debate concerning early Christian iconography, and as early as 1928, in a lecture in Oslo, he pointed to the distinction between iconography and iconology.

WRITINGS

Bescheiden in Italië omtrent Nederlandse kunstenaars en geleerden: Rome [Documents in Italy concerning Dutch artists and scholars: Rome], 2 vols (The Hague, 1913–17)
De Noord-Nederlandse schilderkunst, 5 vols (The Hague, 1936–47)
Nederlandsche kunstenaars te Rome: Uittreksels uit der parocchiale archieven, 2 vols (The Hague, 1942–3)
De Bentvueghels (The Hague, 1952)
Via Margutta: Centro di vita artistica (Rome, 1953)
Het landscap van Bosch tot Rubens (Antwerp, 1954)

BIBLIOGRAPHY

BWN
'Festschrift Hoogewerff', *Meded. Ned. Hist. Inst. Rome*, xxxi (1961) [whole issue]
E. Kaemmerling, ed.: *Ikonographie und Ikonologie* (Cologne, 1979), pp. 81–112

JOHANNES OFFERHAUS

Hooghe, Romeyn de (*bapt* Amsterdam, 10 Sept 1645; *bur* Haarlem, 15 June 1708). Dutch etcher, draughtsman, painter, sculptor, medallist and writer. He is best known for his political caricatures of Louis XIV of France and for his prints glorifying William III, Stadholder of the Netherlands and King of England. De Hooghe is an important representative of the late Dutch Baroque. His style is characterized by strong contrasts of lights and darks and an expressive composition. In his prints he combined contemporary personalities with allegorical figures. His prints are numerous, but few of his drawings survive and his paintings are rarer still. De Hooghe's first commission for an etching probably came from Constantijn Huygens the elder, secretary to William III; this was *Zeestraet* (1667; Hollstein, no. 287). In 1668 de Hooghe was in Paris, where he produced some book illustrations, but he returned to Amsterdam, where from 1670 to 1691 he illustrated the annual newsheet *Hollandsche Mercurius*. He regularly produced such political prints as *William III Sworn in as Commander-in-Chief of the Republican Forces* (1672; Hollstein, no. 84); this event took place after Louis XIV had invaded the Netherlands, and thereafter de Hooghe was kept busy producing prints reflecting the course of the war (e.g. *Admiral de Ruyter's Victories over the English and French Fleets*, 1673; Hollstein, nos 75–6). De Hooghe also executed prints glorifying the exploits of John Sobieski, King of Poland (e.g. *John III of Poland*, 1673; Hollstein, no. 101), as well as an etching of the *Wedding of Franciscus Mollo* (1674; Hollstein, no. 388), who later became King John's representative in Amsterdam (1676–1721). In 1675 de Hooghe was created a Polish peer, possibly due to Mollo. From 1675 there are a number of prints of the new Portuguese Synagogue in Amsterdam (Hollstein, nos 116–18). On 18 February 1676 de Hooghe signed a contract to make 22 views of Delft and its surroundings for the book dealer J. Rammazijn of The Hague. Early in 1687 he was living in Haarlem following a dispute with the Amsterdam Church Council. In 1687–8 he was a Commissioner of Justice in Haarlem, and in 1688 he built a house and a drawing school. He also made a large map of the city of Haarlem.

De Hooghe commemorated the joint coronation of William III and Mary Stuart in England in 1689 (Hollstein, nos 149–51), and in the same year the King appointed him commissioner in charge of the exploration of stone quarries in the German town of Lingen in order to provide

Romeyn de Hooghe: allegorical design for a stained-glass window in the Grote Kerk, Hoorn, pen and brown ink, watercolour washes, over red chalk, 536×416 mm, 1703 (Haarlem, Rijksarchief in Noord-Holland); new windows for the church were commissioned after a gunpowder explosion (depicted at left) had destroyed all the previous ones

building material for the royal hunting lodge of Het Loo, for which he also designed garden statues and ponds (see Hollstein, nos 308–21). On 3 June of the same year he became a Doctor of Law at Harderwijk University. For the next three years (1689–91) de Hooghe, a passionate royalist, waged a pamphlet war with the Republicans in Amsterdam. He remained a dedicated Orangist and designed triumphal arches for the occasion of William III's official entry to The Hague in February 1691.

From 1692 to 1694 de Hooghe worked in Alkmaar, designing a medallion for the city corporation, a painting on panel in the Grote Kerk (the St Lawrenskerk) and ceiling and grisaille paintings for the town hall. In 1699 he made a series of 138 biblical engravings for Basagne's illustrated Bible and a ceiling painting in the Doelen building in Rotterdam. Between 1701 and 1703 he designed church windows for Zaandam and Hoorn (see fig.) and in 1707 mural paintings for the town hall in Enkhuizen. These latter were executed by others after his death. De Hooghe also wrote several political and historical treatises, including the *Spiegel van staat des Verenigde Nederlands*, for which he executed a number of allegorical illustrations (Hollstein, nos 737–52).

WRITINGS
Spiegel van staat des Verenigde Nederlands [Mirror of the state of the United Netherlands,], 2 vols (Amsterdam, 1706–7)

BIBLIOGRAPHY
Hollstein: *Dut. & Flem.*; *NKL*; Thieme–Becker
M. D. Henkel: 'Romeyn de Hooghe als illustrator', *Mdbl. Beeld. Kst.*, iii (1926), pp. 261ff and 300ff
J. Landwehr: *Romeyn de Hooghe as Book Illustrator: A Bibliography* (Amsterdam, 1970)
——: *Romeyn de Hooghe the Etcher: Contemporary Portrayal of Europe, 1662–1707* (Leiden, 1973)
W. H. Wilson: *The Art of Romeyn de Hooghe: An Atlas of Late European Baroque Culture* (diss., Cambridge, MA, Harvard U., 1974) [includes cat. of drgs]
——: 'The Circumcision: A Drawing by Romeyn de Hooghe', *Master Drgs*, xxii (1975), pp. 250–58

M. J. C. OTTEN

Hoogstraten [Hoogstraeten], **Samuel van** (*b* Dordrecht, 2 Aug 1627; *d* Dordrecht, 19 Nov 1678). Dutch painter, draughtsman, engraver and writer. His multi-faceted art and career testify amply to the unflagging ambition attributed to him as early as 1718 by his pupil and first biographer, Arnold Houbraken. During his lifetime van Hoogstraten was recognized as a painter, poet, man of letters, sometime courtier and prominent citizen of his native city of Dordrecht, where he served for several years as an official of the Mint of Holland. Today he is remembered not only as a pupil and early critic of Rembrandt, but also as a versatile artist in his own right. His diverse oeuvre consists of paintings, drawings and prints whose subjects range from conventional portraits, histories and genre pictures to illusionistic experiments with *trompe-l'oeil* still-lifes, architectural perspectives and perspective boxes. He also wrote the major Dutch painting treatise of the late 17th century, the *Inleyding tot de hooge schoole der schilderkonst, anders de zichtbaere werelt* ('Introduction to the academy of painting, or the visible world'; Rotterdam, 1678).

1. Life and work. 2. Theoretical writing.

1. LIFE AND WORK.

(i) Training and early work in Amsterdam and Dordrecht, before 1651.
(ii) Work abroad and in Dordrecht, 1651–78.

(i) Training and early work in Amsterdam and Dordrecht, before 1651. Samuel was the eldest of seven children born to Dirck van Hoogstraten (1596–1640) and Maeiken de Coninck (1598–1645). Both parents belonged to Mennonite families of skilled artisans and had emigrated from Antwerp to Dordrecht about the turn of the 17th century. Van Hoogstraten's maternal grandfather and great-grandfather were silversmiths who held hereditary titles to positions at the Mint of Holland, titles later passed on to Samuel and his brother François (1632–96). The privileges of this office helped Samuel raise his family's social and economic status. Several of van Hoogstraten's relatives, including his paternal grandfather, Hans (1568–1605), were recorded as members of the Guild of St Luke in Antwerp during the 16th century. Samuel's father Dirck, initially trained as a gold- and silversmith, later took up painting and by 1624 was registered as a painter in the Guild of St Luke in Dordrecht. His marriage in 1626 to Maeiken, daughter of the silversmith Isaac de Coninck, suggests that Dirck remained within the high artisanal milieu that his son increasingly left behind. The few surviving paintings, prints and drawings that bear Dirck's signature suggest that he specialized in figures and historical subjects.

According to his own testimony, van Hoogstraten was apprenticed to his father until Dirck's death in 1640. That

Dirck taught his son the rudiments of drawing and the technique of engraving is evident in Samuel's earliest extant work, a signed engraving of a medicinal plant, known as scurvy-grass, used in the treatment of that disease. This little print served as an illustration to the Dordrecht physician Johan van Beverwijck's medical treatise on scurvy, *Van de blaauw Schuyt* (Dordrecht, 1642).

Van Hoogstraten entered Rembrandt's studio in Amsterdam, probably in 1642, and remained there for several years. He was recorded again in Dordrecht in 1648, for his adult baptism in the Mennonite community. His years of training in Rembrandt's studio brought van Hoogstraten into contact with such diverse talents as Bernard Keil from Denmark, Juriaen Ovens from Germany, Philips Koninck, a distant relative of van Hoogstraten's mother, Abraham Furnerius and Carel Fabritius. His surviving work from the 1640s consists of paintings, etchings and drawings that imitate Rembrandt's manner so closely that in the past a number of them have been attributed to Rembrandt himself. Van Hoogstraten's earliest dated paintings, both from 1644, are the *Self-portrait Wearing a Turban* (The Hague, Mus. Bredius) and the *Young Man Reading (Self-portrait with Vanitas)* (Rotterdam, Boymans–van Beuningen). These costumed self-portraits reveal an obvious debt to Rembrandt in their richly worked paint surfaces and theatrical approach to self-portrayal and show early evidence of the interest in self-representation that van Hoogstraten retained throughout his life. Unlike his teacher, who portrayed himself in a wide variety of roles and guises, van Hoogstraten presented a relatively consistent self-image in his portraits, one that owed much to the imagery of the ideal courtier. His *Self-portrait Wearing a Medallion and Chain* (Vaduz, Samml. Liechtenstein) of 1645 is the first of several self-representations to feature those tokens of wealth and princely esteem.

The elaborately finished *Birth of the Virgin* (Paris, Fond. Custodia, Inst. Néer.) is a fine example of a van Hoogstraten drawing long thought to be the work of Rembrandt, but its typically finicky draughtsmanship, with overworked outlines and rigidly hemmed-in forms, distinguishes van Hoogstraten's style from that of his teacher. Numerous student compositional exercises and life drawings offer valuable documentation of Rembrandt's pedagogical practice in the studio. During the mid-1640s van Hoogstraten produced many fully signed drawings, resembling paintings on paper, that follow Rembrandt's practice of rehearsing narrative subjects in highly elaborated drawings. *Bileam Blessing the Israelites* (1646; London, BM) and the *Visitation* (1648; Amsterdam, Hist. Mus.) are typical of this group in their careful attention to details of setting and the combined use of ink, chalks and washes to create a wide range of textual and tonal effects. The illustrative quality of these works, which resembles that of Rembrandt's small biblical narratives of the 1630s and 1640s, also characterizes van Hoogstraten's narrative paintings of the period (e.g. *Adoration of the Shepherds*, 1647; Dordrecht, Dordrechts Mus.). Rembrandt's style dominated van Hoogstraten's art for several years after his return to Dordrecht in the late 1640s. Dated works, such as the etching of the *Jews before Pilate* (1648), a small panel of *Christ Appearing to his Disciples* (1649; Mainz, Landesmus.) and such drawings as the *Circumcision* (c. 1649;

Dresden, Kupferstichkab.) and the *Street Scene with Quarrelling Women* (1650; Amsterdam, Rijksmus.) show how strongly van Hoogstraten remained under his teacher's artistic influence during these years.

In Dordrecht, van Hoogstraten's activities were motivated by closely linked social and professional ambitions. He made his entry into Dordrecht's literary circles as early as 1649 with the publication of occasional poems and of presentation verses in books by local writers. In 1650 he published his first book, *Schoone Rosalin* ('Beautiful Rosalin'), a combined prose pastoral and epistolary novel. In 1648 and 1650 he published rhymed tributes to the House of Orange on the occasions of the Peace of Münster, the death of William II and the birth of William III, possibly in connection with court commissions he sought or had obtained. He also presented himself as a portrait painter to the court in a pen drawing of 1649 (Munich, Staatl. Graph. Samml.), which shows him holding a cartouche inscribed with verses by the Dordrecht poet Carel van Nispen, praising van Hoogstraten as painter of the princes of Orange. A letter of 1671 (Paris, Fond. Custodia, Inst. Néer.) indicates that van Hoogstraten at some time made several portraits for the court, including one of Princess Juliana Catharina of Nassau Portugal. His cultivation of court patrons went hand in hand with his adoption of certain aristocratic practices, then fashionable among Holland's wealthy urban patriciate. He was, for example, the first in his family to display a coat of arms. The family crest appears as part of a witty inscription, which he wrote in 1650, in the *album amicorum* of Johan Mulheuser (The Hague, Kon. Bib.). He also adopted the aristocratic fashion of wearing a sword, thereby alienating himself from the Mennonite community, which looked unfavourably on courtly affectations and forbade its members to bear arms of any sort. Van Hoogstraten's open defiance of the community's proscriptions ultimately led to his public reprimand.

(ii) Work abroad and in Dordrecht, 1651–78. On 16 May 1651, two weeks after his reprimand, van Hoogstraten departed for Germany, Italy and the court of Emperor Ferdinand III in Vienna and did not return to Dordrecht until 1655. The trip marked a turning-point in his career, for during this sojourn he developed the interest in the artifice of *trompe l'oeil* that would remain central to his mature art and his professional identity. He also made the acquaintance of several men well-connected in artistic circles. According to his own account, he joined the Schildersbent, an association of Dutch artists in Rome, where his host was the Dutch painter-naturalist, Otto Marseus van Schrieck. He was received by the painter-publisher Matthäus Merian (ii) in Frankfurt. In Regensburg he made the acquaintance of several clerics, including Gabriel Bucelinus, the Benedictine abbot who helped van Hoogstraten secure the commission for the *Vision of St Benedict* (Weingarten Basilica). Most decisive for van Hoogstraten's career was his decoration at the Habsburg court in Vienna in 1651, when he received a gold chain and medallion of honour from Ferdinand III in recognition of his talents as a painter of *bedriegertjes* ('little deceivers' or *trompe-l'oeil* pictures), such as the *View of the Imperial Palace* (1652) and the *Head of a Man at a Window Trellis*

1. Samuel van Hoogstraten: *Head of a Man at a Window Trellis*, oil on canvas, 1.11×0.87 m, 1653 (Vienna, Kunsthistorisches Museum)

(1653; both Vienna, Ksthist. Mus.; see fig. 1). The witty *Feigned Cabinet Door* (1655; Vienna, Gemäldegal. Akad. Bild. Kst.) is the first of several self-reflexive *trompe-l'oeil* pieces in which van Hoogstraten presents his imperial medallion and chain as a personal trademark within a display of the mimetic virtuosity it honours.

Van Hoogstraten was recorded again in Dordrecht on his investiture as master of the Mint of Holland in May 1656. His assumption of this post and its privileges, along with his marriage three weeks later to Sara Balen, the niece of the town historian Matthys Balen, situated the artist squarely within the city's most important political and social institutions. For marrying into this prominent Dordrecht family van Hoogstraten was expelled from the Mennonite community. In January 1657 he and his wife officially joined the Dutch Reformed Church. In that year, too, he enlisted the patronage of Adriaen van Blyenburgh, burgomaster of Dordrecht, in publishing *Den eerlijk jongeling, ofte de edele konst van zich by groote en kleyne te doen eeren en beminnen* ('The honourable youth, or the noble art of making oneself honoured and esteemed by one and all'), a courtier's manual, adapted from Nicolas Faret's *Honneste Homme ou l'art de plaire à la cour* of 1631. Of particular interest in this text are van Hoogstraten's remarks on 'Painting, Poetry and the Knowledge of Geography and Languages', which replace Faret's passing reference to painting with a discussion of the value of both pictorial and verbal literacy.

News of van Hoogstraten's professional successes abroad, along with his family and government connections, soon brought him several commissions for portraits,

including a large portrait of the *Masters and Officers of the Mint* (Dordrecht, Dordrechts Mus.), which he completed in 1657. He continued to paint portraits and histories as well as more experimental pictures dealing with domestic themes explored in works of genre painters like Gabriel Metsu, Gerard ter Borch (ii) and Johannes Vermeer. The haunting *Interior Viewed through a Doorway ('The Slippers')* (*c.* 1657; Paris, Louvre), which presents a covert view into a woman's boudoir, exemplifies van Hoogstraten's interest in curious perspectives. This clandestine view, which centres on a painting of a woman receiving a letter, also serves as van Hoogstraten's pictorial commentary on the images of letter reading and writing which figured so prominently in mid-century Dutch genre painting. Van Hoogstraten's experimentation with perspective's illusionistic effects culminated with his ingenious *Perspective Box of a Dutch Interior* (*c.* 1657–61; London, N.G.; *see* PERSPECTIVE, fig. 5). This device, which van Hoogstraten celebrated in his treatise for its compelling illusions of scale, offers a delightful demonstration of how the eye is deceived through the artifices of vision and painting. Experiments of this sort and instructional performances played an important part in the lessons given by van Hoogstraten in the teaching studio which he opened in his home sometime after his return to Dordrecht in the mid-1650s. His pupils, according to Houbraken, included Godfried Schalcken, Cornelis van der Meulen and Aert de Gelder.

Despite his apparent success in Dordrecht, van Hoogstraten again left his home town in 1662, this time for London. A letter that he wrote in that year to the Dordrecht merchant and writer Willem van Blyenburgh suggests that he was lured to England by the prospect of lucrative commissions at the court of the newly restored Stuart monarch, Charles II. During his stay in England, van Hoogstraten established contacts with various aristocratic patrons, for whom he painted portraits, and with members of the Royal Society, including Thomas Povey, Secretary to the Duke of York. In 1662 van Hoogstraten painted the *View down a Corridor* (Dyrham Park, Avon, NT) for Povey's house in London. This piece of perspective, admired by Samuel Pepys in his diary, was one of several large works of this kind devised for English patrons. Among the most intriguing of these pictures are the *'Tuscan Gallery'* (Innes House, Grampian) and the portraits of aristocrats set into complicated architectural perspectives, such as his *Sir John Finch Reading in a Courtyard* (Salisbury, priv. col., see Sumowski (1983), no. 898).

Van Hoogstraten remained in England until after the Great Fire of London in 1666, which he both witnessed and commemorated in verse. In January 1668 he was recorded as a member of Pictura, the painters' confraternity in The Hague, where he lived until 1671. His most impressive commission from these years was for a set of eight three-quarter-length portraits of the family of Maerten Pauw (1616–80), Receiver General of Holland, which was completed in 1671 (Zeist, Pauw van Wieldrecht, priv. col., see Sumowski (1983), nos 870–71). The aristocratic taste for elegance that these portraits display characterizes van Hoogstraten's work in other genres at this time, such as the *Woman, Nurse and Child by a Cradle* (1670;

2. Samuel van Hoogstraten: 'Trompe-l'oeil' of a Letter-rack Painting, oil on canvas, 630×790 mm, c. 1670 (Karlsruhe, Staatliche Kunsthalle)

Springfield, MA, Mus. F.A.) and the *Perspective of a Courtyard with a Woman Reading a Letter* (The Hague, Mauritshuis). During these years van Hoogstraten also celebrated his accomplishments of the previous decades in his most accomplished *trompe-l'oeil* paintings. The culmination of these is the *'Trompe-l'oeil' of a Letter-rack Painting* (c. 1670; Karlsruhe, Staatl. Ksthalle; see fig. 2). In this *tour de force* of illusionist artifice, van Hoogstraten represents his professional and social identity through the illusionistic depiction of a variety of objects—writing implements, books he has written, documents, personal insignia, including the imperial medallion and chain—all of which call attention to his status and achievements as poet, courtier and painter of highly valued deceptions.

In 1671 van Hoogstraten purchased a house in Dordrecht, where he resided until his death in 1678. As Provost of the Mint of Holland from 1673 to 1676 the artist took a more active role in the affairs of the Mint than he had during the previous two decades. His change in status is clearly reflected in his portrait of the *Officers and Masters of the Mint* (1674; Dordrecht, Dordrechts Mus.), in which he featured himself prominently displaying his medallion and chain. As his health declined during these years, so did his pictorial output. His only dated

pictures from this time, apart from a few patrician portraits, are the illustrations for his painting treatise and for Matthys Balen's monumental descriptive history of the city, the *Beschryvinge der stadt Dordrecht* ('Description of the city of Dordrecht'; Dordrecht, 1677). Both of these projects offer rich testimony to the artist's overriding concern with self-perpetuation in his later years.

2. THEORETICAL WRITING. The *Inleyding tot de hooge schoole der schilderkonst, anders de zichtbaere werelt*, van Hoogstraten's long treatise on painting (nearly 400 pp.), published just months before he died in 1678, was his last and most ambitious accomplishment. With its lively intermingling of art theoretical topoi and anecdotes of the artist's own life, the *Inleyding* is both a compendium of received knowledge about painting and a concerted effort to validate van Hoogstraten's art and the pictorial tradition to which it belongs. The treatise is of particular value for its first-hand accounts of Rembrandt and his studio, and as one of a handful of vernacular writings by Dutch artists offering keen commentary on the nature and assumptions of Dutch painting.

Van Hoogstraten compiled his text, which purports to be a step-by-step introduction to all that is known about painting, from a wide range of literary sources, both ancient and modern. Its apparent breadth of erudition owes much to the two most important vernacular compendia on painting, Karel van Mander's *Schilder-boeck* (Haarlem, [1603]–1604) and Francis Junius's *De schilderkonst der oude* ('The Painting of the Ancients'; Middelburg, 1641), from which van Hoogstraten drew most of his citations. He also incorporated material from Albrecht Dürer's writings, from the recently published Dutch treatises on painting and drawing by Willem Goeree and from a variety of other sources not specifically concerned with painting. From the standpoint of literary history, it is significant that with few minor exceptions van Hoogstraten's compilation relies entirely on vernacular writings and translations.

Van Hoogstraten was spurred in this ambitious undertaking by the formidable example of Karel van Mander, the artist-writer whose seminal *Schilder-boeck* remained the most widely-read and authoritative of the few Dutch art treatises published during the 17th century. Van Hoogstraten sought to revise his predecessor's work by reintegrating pieces of van Mander's didactic poem on painting and his biographies of the painters with numerous other texts to form an academy in book form, where 'one might learn everything pertaining to the art and through practice become a master in it'.

Van Hoogstraten linked the pedagogical and compilatory aims of his 'academy' by way of a carefully elaborated structure: he divided the work into nine books or 'classrooms', each of which he dedicated to one of the Muses, following the encyclopedic tradition that saw the Muses as the overseers of all fields of human endeavour and knowledge. He further clarified the treatise's structure by furnishing each book with an etched title-page illustration and verses of his own devising that explain the conceit of each print and announce the contents of the book it introduces.

The academic framework of the *Inleyding* and its extensive borrowings from Junius give it a superficial resemblance to the classicizing writings on art by French and Italian theorists of the 17th century. While it shares their academic preoccupation with codifying the precepts by which art can be learnt, van Hoogstraten's analysis of painting is not informed by a similarly classicist aesthetic. As its subtitle suggests, the *Inleyding* treats painting first and foremost as the means of representing the entire visible world. Both in its aims and in its encyclopedic organization, the treatise has more fundamental ties to the projects and goals of England's Royal Society. These links are most evident in van Hoogstraten's emphasis on the pedagogical importance of devising and following a clearly gradated, sequential method of instruction, and in the ways his text consistently values 'know-how' above abstract knowledge, echoing the experimental values of the new-style science.

The *Inleyding* was published in a single edition by the author's brother, François, and appeared only at the close of the great age of Dutch painting. Although it did not enjoy the popularity and influence of van Mander's *Schilderboeck* in its own time, van Hoogstraten's treatise continues to interest students of Dutch art, both for its contemporary critical appraisal of Rembrandt's art and teaching and for

its telling commentary on the specific concerns and character of 17th-century Dutch painting. The best-known passages of the treatise include van Hoogstraten's remarks on Rembrandt's *'Night Watch'*, on the use of emblems in painting, the hierarchy of pictorial subjects, the camera obscura and the perspective box. Of special interest are his lesser-known commentaries on pictorial literacy, likeness and difference in portraiture, truth and accuracy in history painting, and the symbiotic relationship of form and colour in the perception and representation of the visible world. Throughout these discussions, van Hoogstraten liberally recast the traditional rhetoric of art to emphasize the descriptive and illusionistic aspects of painting that he explored so assiduously in his own art. With this unusual focus on the imitative and deceptive properties of pictures, van Hoogstraten's *Inleyding* provides a fascinating defence of its author's artistic achievement and of the Netherlandish pictorial tradition as a whole.

WRITINGS

Den eerlyken jongeling of de edele konst van zich by groote en kleyne te doen eeren en beminnen [The honourable youth, or the noble art of making oneself honoured and esteemed by one and all] (Dordrecht, 1657); adapted from N. Faret: *Honneste Homme ou l'art de plaire à la cour* (Paris, 1631)

Inleyding tot de hooge schoole der schilderkonst, anders de zichtbaere werelt [Introduction to the academy of painting, or the visible world] (Rotterdam, 1678/*R* Soest, 1969; Ann Arbor, 1980)

BIBLIOGRAPHY

Hollstein: *Dut. & Flem.*; *NNBW*; Thieme–Becker

GENERAL

S. Slive: *Rembrandt and his Critics, 1639–1730* (The Hague, 1953)
J. A. Emmens: *Rembrandt en de regels van de kunst* (Utrecht, 1967)
Rembrandt after 300 Years (exh. cat., Chicago, IL, A. Inst., 1969)
Rembrandt and his Pupils (exh. cat., Montreal, Mus. F.A., 1969)
Tot lering en vermaak; Betekenissen van Hollandse genrevorstellingen uit de zeventiende eeuw [To instruct and delight: meanings of Dutch genre painting in the 17th century] (exh. cat., ed. E. de Jongh; Amsterdam, Rijksmus., 1976), pp. 14–20, 134–7
Stilleben in Europa (exh. cat., Münster, Westfäl. Landesmus.; Baden-Baden, Staatl. Ksthalle; 1980)
J. Bruyn and others, eds: *A Corpus of Rembrandt Paintings*, i (Boston, London and The Hague, 1982)
Still-life Painting in the Age of Rembrandt (exh. cat., ed. E. de Jongh and others; Auckland, C.A.G., 1982)
Das Stilleben und sein Gegenstand (exh. cat., ed. H. Seifertova and others; Dresden, Albertinum, 1983)
B. Haak: *The Golden Age: Dutch Painters of the Seventeenth Century* (New York, 1984)
G. Schwartz: *Rembrandt: His Life, his Paintings* (New York, 1985)
E. van de Wetering: 'Problems of Apprenticeship and Studio Collaboration', *A Corpus of Rembrandt Paintings*, ed. J. Bruyn and others, ii (Boston, London and The Hague, 1985), pp. 45–90
Masters of Seventeenth Century Dutch Genre Painting (exh. cat., ed. P. Sutton; Philadelphia, PA, Mus. A.; W. Berlin, Gemäldegal.; London, RA; 1985)
Portretten van echt en trouw: Huwelijk en gezin in de Nederlandse kunst van de zeventiende eeuw [Portraits of marriage and fidelity: marriage and household in the Dutch art of the 17th century] (exh. cat., ed. E. de Jongh; Haarlem, Frans Halsmus., 1986)
C. Brown and others: 'Samuel van Hoogstraten: Perspective and Painting', *N. G. Tech. Bull.*, ii (1987), pp. 60–85
S. Alpers: *Rembrandt's Enterprise: The Studio and the Market* (Chicago, 1988)

EARLY SOURCES

A. Houbraken: *De groote schouburgh* (1718–21), ii, pp. 155–70
W. Strauss and M. van der Meulen: *The Rembrandt Documents* (New York, 1979); review by B. P. J. Broos in *Simiolus*, xii/4 (1981), pp. 245–62

CATALOGUES RAISONNÉS

W. Sumowski: *Drawings of the Rembrandt School*, viii (New York, 1981)
——: *Gemälde der Rembrandt-Schüler*, ii (Landau, 1983)

REPRESENTATIONAL THEORY

U. Schneede: 'De wonderlijke Perspectiefkas: Hoogstraten's perfekte Tauschungen', *Artis*, xviii (1966–7), pp. 25–6

S. Koslow: 'De wonderlijke perspectyfkas', *Oud-Holland*, lxxxii/1–2 (1967), pp. 35–56

E. de Jongh: 'Realisme en schijn-realisme in de schilderkunst van de zeventiende eeuw', *Rembrandt en zijn tijd* (exh. cat., Brussels, Mus. A. Anc., 1971), pp. 143–94

F. Leeman, ed.: *Hidden Images: Games of Perception, Anamorphic Art and Illusion* (New York, 1975)

H. Vey: 'Samuel van Hoogstraten (1627–78): Augenbetrüger', *Jb. Staatl. Kstsamml. Baden-Württemberg*, xii (1975), pp. 282–3

A. K. Wheelock jr: *Perspective, Optics and Delft Artists around 1650* (New York, 1976)

S. Alpers: *The Art of Describing* (Chicago, 1983), pp. 38–9, 58–64, 76–9, 141–2

C. Brusati: *The Nature and Status of Pictorial Representation in the Art and Theoretical Writing of Samuel van Hoogstraten* (diss., Berkeley, U. CA, 1984)

H. Seifertovà: 'Augenbetrüger und ihre Motivation im 17. Jahrhundert', *Dresdn. Ksthl.*, lxxxiv/2 (1984), pp. 49–56

J. Muylle: 'Schilderkunst en kunstenaarsbiografieën als specula: Metafoor, fictie en historiciteit' [Painting and artist biographies as *specula*: metaphor, fiction and historicity], *17de eeuw*, ii/1 (1986), pp. 41–56

E. J. Sluiter: 'Beleering en verhulling? Enkele 17de eeuwse teksten over de schilderkunst en de iconologische benadering van Noordnederlandse Schilderijen uit deze periode' [Teaching and concealing: 17th-century texts on painting and the iconological approach of North Netherlandish paintings of the period], *17de eeuw*, iv/2 (1988), pp. 3–28

DRAWINGS

Rembrandt and his Century: Dutch Drawings of the Seventeenth Century from the Collection of Fritz Lugt (exh. cat., ed. C. van Hasselt; New York, Pierpont Morgan Lib.; Paris, Fond. Custodia, Inst. Néer.; 1977–8), pp. 83–5

Figure Studies: Dutch Drawings of the Seventeenth Century (exh. cat. by P. Schatborn, Amsterdam, Rijksmus.; Washington, DC, N.G.A.; 1981)

Rembrandt en de tekenaars uit zijn omgeving [Rembrandt and the draughtsmen from his circle] (exh. cat. by B. P. J. Broos, Amsterdam, Hist. Mus., 1981)

Bij Rembrandt in de leer/Rembrandt as Teacher (exh. cat. by P. Schatborn, Amsterdam, Rembrandthuis, 1984–5)

SPECIALIST STUDIES

G. H. Veth: 'Dirck van Hoogstraten', *Oud-Holland*, iv (1886), pp. 272–7

——: 'Aantekeningen omtrent eenige Dordrechtsche schilders: XVII. Samuel van Hoogstraten' [Some notes on Dordrecht painters: XVII. Samuel van Hoogstraten], *Oud-Holland*, vii (1889), pp. 125–48

A. G. van Hamel: 'François van Hoogstraten (1632–96)', *Rotterdam. Jb.*, 2nd ser., ix (1921), pp. 49–66

W. Sumowski: 'Hoogstraten und Elsheimer', *Kunstchronik*, xix (1966), pp. 302–4

E. J. Wolleswinkel: 'De portrettenverzameling van Mr Jan Willem van Hoogstraten (1722–70)', *Jb. Cent. Bureau Geneal.* (1980), pp. 68–95

M. Roscam Abbing: *Van Hoogstraten: Iconographie van een familie* (Amsterdam, 1987)

R. Schillemans: 'Gabriel Bucelinus and "The Names of the Most Distinguished European Painters"', *Hoogsteder-Naumann Mercury*, vi (1987), pp. 25–38

C. BRUSATI

Hook, James Clarke (*b* Clerkenwell, London, 21 Nov 1819; *d* Churt, Surrey, 14 April 1907). English painter. He studied with the portrait painter John Jackson and entered the Royal Academy Schools, London, in 1836, winning medals for drawing and historical painting. His Academy début was in 1839 with *The Hard Task* (untraced). In 1844 Hook was awarded a gold medal in the Houses of Parliament competition. In 1846 he won a Royal Academy travelling scholarship, enabling him to spend two years in Italy, where he was strongly influenced by the colouring of the Venetian painters. On his return his work included a series of subjects from Venetian history, including *The*

Rescue of the Brides of Venice (exh. 1851; Preston, Harris Mus. & A.G.).

Over the next few years Hook's subject-matter changed to rural, particularly coastal, genre scenes; his first major success was *'Luff, Boy!'* (exh. RA 1859; USA, priv. col., see Stephens, p. 23), much praised by Ruskin. He spent the rest of his long life painting similar canvases, showing idealized fishermen and their families in carefully painted coastal settings, ranging from the Shetlands to the Scilly Isles. *Hearts of Oak* (1875; Nottingham, Castle Mus.) is typical; painted on the rocky Aberdeenshire coast, it is a picturesque scene showing a family sitting among nets and baskets. Such works delighted the public, while Hook's technical mastery pleased the critics. Hook was elected ARA in 1850 and RA in 1860.

BIBLIOGRAPHY

F. G. Stephens: 'J. C. Hook, RA, his Life and Work', *A. Annu.* (1888), pp. 1–32

A. J. Hook: *Life of James Clarke Hook, RA*, 3 vols (London, 1929–32)

D. Bethel: *James Clarke Hook RA, 1819–1907* (diss., U. London, 1975)

R. Spencer: 'Whistler and James Clarke Hook', *Gaz. B.-A.*, n. s. 6, civ (1984), pp. 45–8

ROSAMOND ALLWOOD

Hooke, Robert (*b* Freshwater, Isle of Wight, 18 July 1635; *d* London, 3 March 1703). English architect, scientist and writer. At the age of 13 he was briefly apprenticed to the painter Peter Lely but soon transferred to Westminster School, London, after which he studied at Christ Church, Oxford. There he met Christopher Wren and others in the circle of natural scientists who in 1660 were to form the nucleus of the Royal Society. In 1662 Hooke was made the society's curator of experiments and for the rest of his career lived at Gresham College, London. He undertook research into various branches of science, including the laws of motion and gravity. After the Great Fire of London in 1666 Hooke was one of six surveyors (Wren was another) appointed by the City and the Crown to direct reconstruction. Although he is not known to have received any architectural commissions before *c.* 1669–70, this appointment suggests that by then his theoretical knowledge was considerable. In ecclesiastical architecture he played an indefinable part in Wren's rebuilding of the City churches after the Great Fire; independently he designed the charming country church of St Mary Magdalene (1680), Willen, Bucks, for Dr Richard Busby, his former master at Westminster School. Hooke's diary for 1672–80 records almost daily contact with Wren on both scientific and architectural matters; their association in the late 1660s may have developed into something akin to a master–pupil relationship with regard to architecture, although John Aubrey testified to Hooke's talent for self-instruction and invention. Hooke did not share Wren's concern for geometrical abstraction: Wren's purity and refinement (as at Trinity College Library, Cambridge) or treatment of skyline (St Paul's Cathedral, London) were beyond Hooke; nevertheless his work is often inventive in both appearance and planning. He also liked, and possibly knew at first hand, Dutch architecture.

Hooke is credited by Aubrey with the Monument to the Great Fire (1671–6), a giant Doric column in the City. Although Hooke and Wren are known to have been jointly responsible for it, the drawing that is closest to the extant structure is actually by Wren's draughtsman, Edward Woodroffe (*c.* 1622–75). Hooke was, however, solely responsible for designing Bedlam (Bethlehem Hospital; 1674–6, destr. 1815) for the Corporation of London in Moorfields. Its long north elevation, overlooking an open space, comprised two long ward blocks flanking a tall pilastered pavilion of a Dutch type and framed by similar pavilions at the extremities. Its large windows, which permitted light and airy interiors, set new standards in the care of the sick and influenced Wren's Royal Hospital, Chelsea, begun in 1682. To exclude the midday sun and traffic noise, the street side of Bedlam had only small windows. Hooke's understanding of the Classical vocabulary was evident both there and in the College of Physicians (1672–8; destr. 1879), Warwick Lane, London, for which he used superimposed orders; the oval lecture theatre he designed (destr. 1866) was built above the college gateway. These works set the standards by which attributions to Hooke of domestic buildings must be gauged. He certainly designed the first Montagu House (1674–9; destr.), Bloomsbury, London, for Ralph Montagu, later 1st Duke of Montagu, who was Ambassador to France for Charles II. It was tall and unusually well-lit and had the new sash windows, in whose invention Hooke may have been concerned. It was built on the French pattern with separate roofs for the middle and corner pavilions. All but the front screen and gate-house was burnt down in 1686 and the replacement house, made on a different plan, was by another architect. Hooke's diaries reveal several other probable domestic commissions. Some, such as Shenfield Place (*c.* 1689), Essex, are unremarkable; others have complex histories involving local builders, but their greater distinction must be taken into account. Advanced and inventive planning is their common feature: Ragley Hall (1679–83, completed by others), Warwicks, Ramsbury Manor (*c.* 1680–83), Wilts, the north range of Ralph Montagu's Boughton House (1690–94), Northants, and Burley-on-the-Hill (1696–1704), Leics.

WRITINGS

Micrographia (London, 1665)
A Description of Helioscopes, and some other Instruments (London, 1676)
Lectiones Cutlerianae (London, 1679)
H. W. Robinson and W. Adams, eds: *The Diary of Robert Hooke, 1672–1680* (London, 1935) [see also Gunther, 1935]
Posthumous Works (London, 1705)

BIBLIOGRAPHY

Colvin
J. Aubrey: *Lives* (MS., before 1693; Oxford, Ashmolean); ed. O. L. Dick as *Brief Lives* (London, 1949)
R. W. T. Gunther: 'The Life and Work of Robert Hooke', *Early Science in Oxford*, x (Oxford, 1935), pp. 69–265 [incl. diary for 1688–93]
M. I. Batten: 'The Architecture of Robert Hooke', *Walpole Soc.*, xxv (1937), pp. 83–113
M. 'Espinasse: *Robert Hooke* (London, 1956) [contains bibliog. of printed writings]
K. Downes: *English Baroque Architecture* (London, 1966)
H. A. Feisenberger, ed.: *Scientists (Sale Catalogues of Eminent Persons)*, xi (London, 1975), pp. 37–116
P. Leach: 'Ragley Hall Reconsidered', *Archaeol. J.*, cxxxvi (1979), pp. 265–8
H. J. Louw: 'New Light on Ramsbury', *Archit. Hist.*, xxx (1987), pp. 45–9
B. Cherry: 'The Devon Country House in the Late Seventeenth and Early Eighteenth Centuries', *Devon Archaeol. Soc.*, xlvi (1988), pp. 91–135
M. Hunter and S. Schaffer, eds: *Robert Hooke: New Studies* (Woodbridge, 1990)

KERRY DOWNES

Hooker, Philip (*b* Rutland, MA, 28 Oct 1766; *d* Albany, NY, 31 Jan 1836). American architect. His earliest training was with his father Samuel Hooker (1746–1832), a carpenter and builder. The family moved in 1772 to Albany, NY, the centre of Hooker's activity throughout his life. The source of his training in drawing and surveying (the latter always a second profession) is unclear: he was possibly a pupil of the French architect Pierre Pharoux (*c.* 1760–95), who spent the winter of 1794–5 in Albany. Hooker's first commission was the North Dutch Church (1796–8; now First Church of Albany). The influence of the Neo-classicism of Charles Bulfinch is strongly evident, particularly the latter's Hollis Street Church, Boston, of 1787–8. Hooker's original design is known from drawings, as the central portico of the church was destroyed during renovations in 1857. His next commission was the first New York State Capitol Building (1804–6; destr. 1883) in Albany. Few of Hooker's buildings survive, although among those that do is the Albany Academy (1814). The unremarkable exterior shows the influence of the New York City Hall (1802) by John McComb jr. The interior details, however, display a concern for impeccable craftsmanship, especially of windows and door frames. Hyde Hall (1817–35), in Otsego County, NY, part of a country estate, is a grandly proportioned structure with elements of the Greek Revival style. Hooker's most outstanding late work was the Albany City Hall (1829–32; destr.), which combines elements of French and English Neo-classicism. While not among the great innovators of his time, Hooker is important as a disseminator of contemporary architectural trends into what was then a frontier area of the USA.

BIBLIOGRAPHY

Macmillan Enc. Architects
E. Root: *Philip Hooker: A Contribution to the Study of the Renaissance in America* (New York, 1929)
W. R. Wheeler: 'The Architecture of Philip Hooker in New York State', *Antiques*, cxli/3 (1992), pp. 472–9
'A Neat Plain Modern Stile': Philip Hooker and his Contemporaries (exh. cat. by W. R. Wheeler and D. Bucher, Clinton, NY, Hamilton Coll., Emerson Gal., 1992)

□

Hooper, Basil Bramston (*b* Lahore, 17 April 1876; *d* Auckland, 3 Feb 1960). New Zealand architect. He was educated in England before emigrating to New Zealand in 1885. He was articled to the Dunedin architect J. L. Salmond (1868–1950) in 1896. From 1901 to 1904 he worked in England, first for A. Beresford Pite, then for the Housing Division of the London County Council and briefly for E. P. Warren (1856–1937) and Temple Moore. On his return to New Zealand, Hooper's knowledge and experience of recent English architecture was immediately put to use in the series of houses inspired by the Arts and Crafts Movement, which he built in Dunedin between 1906 and 1923. His best works, for example 26 Heriot Row (1911–13), Dunedin, and 319 York Place (1916), Dunedin, were strongly influenced by the work of C. F. A. Voysey, although they are more compact in form and employ a wider range of exterior finishes. Hooper's designs helped to redirect New Zealand domestic architecture away from the prevalent highly decorated, late Victorian style towards a local variant of the English Domestic

Revival. In 1923 he moved to Auckland, where he continued in practice until 1948.

BIBLIOGRAPHY

I. J. Lochhead: 'The Arts and Crafts Houses of Basil Hooper', *A. NZ*, xxxix (1986), pp. 60–63

IAN J. LOCHHEAD

Hoorn, Cornelis Cort van. *See* CORT, CORNELIS.

Hŏ Paek-nyŏn [*ho* Ŭijae, Ŭijaesanin, Ŭidoin] (*b* Chindo, South Chŏlla Province, 1891; *d* Kwangju, South Chŏlla Province, 1977). Korean painter. From the age of 11 he learnt calligraphy and painting at the Ullim sanbang (Room in Clouded Forest Mountain), a studio set up by Hŏ YU, studying particularly under Hŏ's son, Hŏ Hyŏng. In 1912, Hŏ Paek-nyŏn went to Tokyo to study law. He gave up before completing the course in favour of further painting lessons under Komuro Suiun. After his return to Korea in 1918 he was awarded several prizes in the Oriental painting section of the Korean Art Exhibition (the Japanese-sponsored Chosŏn misul chŏllamhoe). Up to the age of 40 he painted in the Japanese version of the Chinese Southern school style. In his forties Hŏ settled in Kwangju, devoting himself to creative work and to training students through the Yŏnjin Association (Yŏnjinhoe). Having cast off the Japanese elements in his style, he returned to the Southern school style as it had existed before Japanese colonization of Korea in 1910.

Disillusioned after the outbreak of the Korean War in 1950, Hŏ moved to Mount Mudŭng on the outskirts of Kwangju. He built the Ch'unsŏlhŏn (Spring Snow Eaves), began cultivating tea with his pupils and produced a number of paintings that echoed the literati style, while also reflecting both the scenery of the Korean countryside and a liberated spirituality. Many of his students became influential after graduating from the Yŏnjin Association so that his style continued to inform late 20th-century painting in Korea's southern provinces.

BIBLIOGRAPHY

Young-na Kim [Kim Yŏng-na]: 'Modern Korean Painting and Sculpture/Hanguk hyŏndae hoehwawa chogak', *Korean Art Tradition/Hanguk-ŭi yesul chŏnt'ong*, ed. Young Ick Lew [Ryu Yŏng-ik] (Seoul, 1993) [bilingual text], pp. 151–200

HONG SŎN-P'YO

Hope. English family of Dutch origin.

(1) Thomas Hope (*b* Amsterdam, 30 Aug 1769; *d* London, 2 Feb 1831). Patron, collector, connoisseur, designer and writer. He was the son of John Hope (1737–84), a Dutch merchant of Scottish extraction, and used the fortune he acquired from the family bank, Hope & Co., to influence taste in Regency England, much as the 3rd Earl of Burlington had tried to create a new style of classical purity nearly a century earlier. Hope was influenced as a collector by his father, for whom Piranesi had executed an important chimney-piece (Amsterdam, Rijksmus.). A more significant influence was his second cousin, Henry Hope (1735–1811), who built the great mansion of Welgelegen (1785–8), near Haarlem, to house his magnificent picture collection. The most remarkable feature of Hope's early life was his extended Grand Tour from 1787 to 1795, when he travelled throughout Europe and in the Near East studying art and architecture. He revisited Greece in 1799 and France and Italy in 1802–03 and 1815–17. In 1806 he married Louisa Beresford, whose father was created 1st Baron Decies in 1812.

In 1795, on the French invasion of Holland, Henry and Thomas Hope, together with several other members of the family, fled to England. Thomas began to build up an important collection of Classical sculpture and Greek vases there, and to commission such artists as Flaxman, Thorvaldsen (*see* THORVALDSEN, BERTEL, fig. 1), Canova, Haydon, Benjamin West and Richard Westall to provide works of art in related styles. He was interested in the total domestic environment, designing furniture, silverware and even his wife's costume. He put his ideals into practice in the London mansion he acquired in 1799 in Duchess Street, off Portland Place, originally built in the 1760s (destr. 1850) by Robert Adam. Hope remodelled this *c.* 1800–04 in a startlingly original way. He recorded the work in his book *Household Furniture and Interior Decoration* (1807; *see* TABLE, fig. 1) which introduced the phrase 'interior decoration' to the English language. With its outline illustrations the book owed much to Percier and Fontaine's *Recueil de décorations intérieures* (Paris, 1812), issued serially from 1801.

Hope's picture gallery at Duchess Street was one of the earliest interiors to be articulated with the baseless and fluted Greek Doric order. It was deliberately designed to recall the cella of a Greek temple, and the room became a shrine of the Muses. Hope's house was open to the public and, as a house-cum-museum, it resembled that of John Soane, who may have borrowed certain ideas from Hope, for example the display of Greek vases in tomb-like recesses. From the scenes on his Greek figured vases (bought from William Hamilton in 1801), Hope took the idea of the 'Klismos chair,' several variants of which were made from his designs for use in his Duchess Street mansion. These, like his circular library table on a three-sided concave support, exerted a wide influence on Regency furniture design.

Hope's approach to interior design and ornament was literary, poetical and narrative as well as archaeological. Thus in the Flaxman or Star Room at Duchess Street (see fig.) the decoration was related iconographically to the sculptural group that dominated it: *Cephalus and Aurora, Goddess of the Dawn* (Port Sunlight, Lady Lever A.G.). This had been commissioned by Hope from Flaxman in Rome in the 1790s. Below the vaulted ceiling of pale blue studded with stars, the walls were hung with azure, black and orange curtains edged with black velvet, parted occasionally to reveal a looking-glass behind. The intention was to recreate the effect of the sky at dawn. The house also contained an Indian Room and an Egyptian Room (for illustration *see* EGYPTIAN REVIVAL). Though the latter belonged to a tradition going back to Piranesi's interiors of the 1760s in the Caffè degli Inglesi, Rome, it boasted massive Egyptian Revival seat furniture that revealed Hope at his most inventive as a furniture designer.

With his *Observations on the Plans and Elevations Designed by James Wyatt* (1804), Hope opened a new phase in the history of the Greek Revival by successfully promoting the neo-Greek designs by the young William

Wilkins. Hope's arguments were essentially those proposed by Laugier in the 1750s in favour of truthful load-bearing architecture, stripped of unnecessary ornament. They proved influential on the numerous public buildings of such architects as Wilkins and Robert Smirke (ii). Hope, however, was to promote a very different kind of architecture at his country house, The Deepdene (destr. 1967), near Dorking in Surrey. Though he regarded the Greek Revival as suitable for an urban environment, in the country he was influenced by the theories of Richard Payne Knight and Uvedale Price in bringing pictorial considerations to bear on the design of classical buildings. The Deepdene, a substantial late 18th-century country house, was remodelled and extended by Hope with William Atkinson as his architect in 1818–19 and 1823. It emerged as one of the most picturesque houses in Britain. Its diagonal planning on a sloping site had been anticipated by Wyatville at Endsleigh (1810), Devon, but its bizarre combination of stylistic references, Pompeian, Egyptian, Gothic and Italianate, was the result of Hope's uniquely eclectic synthesis. A particularly influential feature was the loggia-topped Italianate tower as a pivot at one end of the asymmetrical building. Hope's blurring of the distinction between house and garden by means of conservatories, terraces and flights of steps adorned with oriental vases meant that the house became an incident in a dramatic landscape to which it was visually subservient. The Deepdene is well recorded in a series of watercolours made in the 1820s for an unpublished and never completed *History of The Deepdene: The Union of the Picturesque in Scenery and Architecture with Domestic Beauties*. With a text by John Britton, this book was conceived as a companion volume to *The Union of Sculpture, Architecture and Painting* (1827), Britton's account of Sir John Soane's Museum.

Hope was also important as an architectural historian. *An Historical Essay on Architecture* (1835), published posthumously, was a pioneering study of the Early Christian and Romanesque architecture of Italy. In this, Hope appears as an advocate of the *Rundbogenstil*, which emerged on the Continent in the 1830s and 1840s as a compromise between antiquity and the Middle Ages.

See also DISPLAY OF ART, §III.

WRITINGS
Observations on the Plans and Elevations Designed by James Wyatt, Architect, for Downing College, Cambridge, in a Letter to Francis Annesley, esq., MP (London, 1804)
Household Furniture and Interior Decoration Executed from Designs by Thomas Hope (London, 1807/R New York, 1971)
Costume of the Ancients, 2 vols (London, 1809/R New York, 1962)
Designs of Modern Costume (London, 1812); enlarged by H. Moses as *A Series of Twenty-nine Designs of Modern Costume* (London, 1823)
An Historical Essay on Architecture by the Late Thomas Hope: Illustrated from Drawings made by him in Italy and Germany, 2 vols (London, 1835)

BIBLIOGRAPHY
C. M. Westmacott: *British Galleries of Painting and Sculpture* (London, 1824)
J. Britton and A. C. Pugin: *Illustrations of the Public Buildings of London*, i (London, 1825)
G. F. Waagen: *Treasures of Art in Great Britain*, ii (London, 1854), pp. 112–25
A. Michaelis: *Ancient Marbles in Great Britain* (Cambridge, 1882)
E. M. W. Tillyard: *The Hope Vases* (Cambridge, 1923)
H. W. Law and I. Law: *The Book of the Beresford Hopes* (London, 1925)
S. Baumgarten: *Le Crépuscule néo-classique: Thomas Hope* (Paris, 1958)

Thomas Hope: *Flaxman Room, Duchess Street House*; from his *Household Furniture and Interior Decoration* (London, 1807), pl. vii

D. Watkin: *Thomas Hope (1769–1831) and the Neo-classical Idea* (London, 1968)
M. G. Buist: *At spes non fracta: Hope & Co., 1770–1815* (The Hague, 1974)
D. Watkin and J. Lever: 'A Sketch-book by Thomas Hope', *Archit. Hist.*, xxiii (1980), pp. 52–9
F. Collard: *Regency Furniture* (Woodbridge, 1985)
P. Thornton and D. Watkin: 'New Light on the Hope Mansion in Duchess Street', *Apollo* (Sept 1987), pp. 162–77

DAVID WATKIN

(2) A(lexander) J(ames) B(eresford) Hope [Beresford Hope] (*b* Deepdene, Surrey, 25 Jan 1820; *d* Bedgebury Park, Kent, 20 Oct 1887). Writer, collector and patron, son of (1) Thomas Hope. His family was immensely wealthy, with large merchant interests in London and Amsterdam. He succeeded to the Kent and Staffordshire estates of his step-father, 1st Viscount Beresford, in 1854, adding the name Beresford to his surname. At Trinity College, Cambridge, he formed a lasting friendship with Benjamin Webb (1819–85), co-founder with John Mason Neale (1818–66) of the Cambridge Camden Society (subsequently the Ecclesiological Society), and began a lifelong crusade for ecclesiastical Gothic and High Anglicanism. He rapidly became the Society's most important and energetic lay member, eclipsing Neale as its driving force from the late 1840s; he helped edit *The Ecclesiologist*, became Chairman of the committee after 1845 and President in 1859. Under his influence the Society advocated constructional polychromy in church building and decoration, supported the stylistic importation of foreign Gothic (although Hope also favoured the English 'Middle Pointed'), campaigned for urban mission churches and argued for a closer functional relationship between church design and contemporary High Anglican worship. All these issues received major treatment in the most important of Hope's architectural writings, *The English Cathedral of the Nineteenth Century* (1861), and all were fundamental to the development of Victorian church-building.

Hope's central influence on the architecture of mid-Victorian ecclesiology was secured on a basis of politics and patronage. He was Conservative MP for Maidstone in 1841–52 and 1857–9, for Stoke-on-Trent in 1865–8 and for Cambridge University in 1868–87. In 1842 he married Lady Mildred Cecil, sister of the future prime minister, Robert Cecil, 3rd Marquess of Salisbury. Paternalistic, antipathetic to Liberalism, rigid in defending the often embattled prerogatives of the Establishment, Hope became the recognized parliamentary spokesman of the High Church. Outside the House of Commons, he used his money to give architectural form to his religious and political convictions. In the early 1840s, at Kilndown Church on the Beresfords' Kent estate, he employed, among others, William Butterfield, Richard Cromwell Carpenter and the stained-glass artist Thomas Willement (1786–1871) to create a gorgeously decorated chancel crowded with ecclesiological fittings. Most importantly, between 1849 and 1859 he provided much of the £70,000 spent on the ecclesiological model church, All Saints', Margaret Street, London, the building that heralded the arrival of High Victorian Gothic. Hope's active and insistent involvement in work he was funding proved difficult for his architects, for he was opinionated and autocratic: All Saints', particularly, occasioned spiteful quarrelling between Hope and Butterfield.

During the completion of All Saints', Hope was at his most influential, founding the *Saturday Review* in 1855, chairing the parliamentary committee on the architectural competition for the Foreign Office in 1858 and becoming President of the RIBA from 1865 to 1867.

WRITINGS

Essays (London, 1844) [particularly pp. 1–69, 'On the Character of the English People, Regarded with a View to Present Difficulties and their Remedy']

The Church Cause and the Church Party (London, 1860)

The English Cathedral of the Nineteenth Century (London, 1861) [considers the cathedral both institutionally and architecturally; important discussion of historic plan types; illustrations of colonial and European examples]

The Art Workman's Position (London, 1864) [anti-Ruskinian]

Worship in the Church of England (London, 1874) [Hope's fullest defence of moderate High Anglican ceremonial against 1874 Public Worship Regulation Act]

Strictly Tied Up: A Novel 3 vols (London, 1880) [acerbic account of Victorian aristocracy; satiric description of *nouveau riche* architecture; i, pp. 121–4]

Worship and Order (London, 1883) [collected periodical essays]

BIBLIOGRAPHY

DNB [gives list of writings and obituaries]

R. J. E. Boggis: *A History of St Augustine's College, Canterbury* (Canterbury, 1907)

H. W. Law and I. Law: *The Book of the Beresford Hopes* (London, 1925) [the only substantial account of Hope's life]

J. F. White: *The Cambridge Movement: The Ecclesiologists and the Gothic Revival* (Cambridge, 1962)

P. Thompson: 'All Saints' Church, Margaret Street, Reconsidered', *Archit. Hist.*, viii (1965), pp. 73–9

CHRIS BROOKS

Hopewell Mounds. Prehistoric site in North America covering two terraces of the North Fork of Paint Creek, a

tributary of the Scioto River, 20 km west of Chillicothe, OH. It is the largest and most elaborate site of the ceremonial Hopewell cult or culture that spread across much of the mid-continent between *c.* 200 BC and *c.* AD 500 during the Middle Woodland period (*see* NATIVE NORTH AMERICAN ART, §I, 4(v)). The builders of the site practised a hunting, gathering and harvesting economy (if not actually cultivating native seeds and squash), and obtained ritual artefacts and raw materials by indirect trade with similar societies, who participated in the same mortuary cult.

In and around a large, non-defensive, joined earthwork rectangle and circle were 40 mounds and two smaller circular earthworks. Several sets of the small (3.0×0.5 m) mounds contained artefacts and structural remains, but few burials. Within the large Mound 23 there had been two earlier mounds, and within the larger Mound 25 (l. 150 m) there were three, of which the central contained the vast quantity of recovered remains. Burials and ceremonial floor areas occurred between and within these sub-mounds. In Mound 25 a geometrically complex single-post and in Mound 23 a circular double-set-post structure contained elaborately wrought artefacts and exotic raw materials in caches or with burial groups in log tombs, on clay altars or placed in pits after cremation. Copper (and rarely silver foil) from Lake Superior had been hammered into sheets to cover wooden or stone buttons, or folded into ear spools, celts, bracelets, rings, cut-out and repoussé zoomorphic and geometric plaques, and one fully-modelled effigy deer-antler helmet (see fig.). Reflective plates of mica from the Appalachian Mountains were cut into geometric forms or into talons, stylized human hands and heads, headless, handless trunks, or large representations

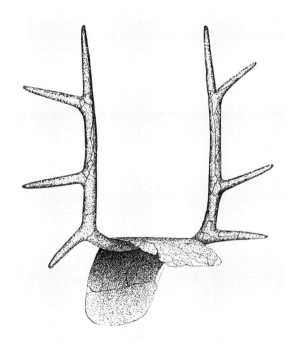

Hopewell Mounds, deer-antler helmet, copper, restored to h. 260 mm, w. 100 mm, *c.* 200 BC–AD 200 (Chicago, IL, Field Museum of Natural History)

of chipped-stone points. Many had been drilled for sewing to costumes. Other mortuary ritual artefacts included naturalistically sculptured platform smoking pipes of Ohio pipestone; cut, polished, painted and pearl-inlaid human and Rocky Mountain grizzly bear jaws and teeth; and effigy spear points of Ohio Valley cannel coal or Yellowstone Cliffs obsidian. There were also cups and dippers cut of Gulf coast conch and whelk shells. Stone beads, buttons, gorgets, troughlike containers and tubular smoking pipes or shamans' tubes had been drilled, ground and polished from minerals and ores of the lower Ohio, the upper Missouri and the Mississippi river valleys.

BIBLIOGRAPHY

D. S. Brose and N. M. B. Greber, eds: *Hopewell Archaeology: The Chillicothe Conference*, Special Papers of the Mid-Continental Journal of Archaeology, v (Kent, OH, 1979)

D. S. Brose, J. A. Brown and D. Penney: *Ancient Art of the American Woodland Indians* (New York, 1985)

N. M. B. Greber and K. Ruhl: *The Hopewell Site* (Boulder, 1989)

DAVID S. BROSE

Hopfer. German family of etchers. In 1497 (1) Daniel Hopfer married Justina Grimm (*d* between 1527 and 1530), sister of the publisher and humanist Sigismund Grimm (*fl* 1502–30; *d* by 1532). Daniel's sons Hieronymus Hopfer (*fl* 1520; *d* before 1550) and Lambert Hopfer (*fl* 1520–30) worked with him. Daniel produced more than 130 prints of various subjects for the popular market, Hieronymus 77 and Lambert 34. They placed their initials somewhere within the design on almost all of their prints (D.H., I.H., L.H.), adding a small device which might be a pinecone, from the coat of arms of the city of Augsburg, or a hop blossom, making a punning reference to the family name.

In their later years Hieronymus and Lambert, who decorated armour as well as making prints, moved to Nuremberg, taking the family's stock of plates and prints with them. In the 17th century a print dealer, David Funck, supposedly a distant relative, who owned 230 of the three Hopfers' plates, scratched a number on each plate, 91 of which were later published by C. W. Silberburg as the *Opera Hopferiana* (Nuremberg, 1802). Most of these plates still survive in private collections and museums. The early 16th-century impressions without the Funck numbers are relatively scarce today.

BIBLIOGRAPHY

Hollstein: *Ger.*

R. A. Koch: *Early German Masters*, 17 [VIII/iv] of *The Illustrated Bartsch*, ed. W. Strauss (New York, 1981)

(1) Daniel Hopfer (*b* Kaufbeuren, *c.* 1470; *d* Augsburg, 1536). In 1493 he gained rights as a citizen of Augsburg and was added to the city's roster of painters and register of taxpayers. He married in 1497. He was recorded as always financially solvent, after 1505 owning his own house. Working in Augsburg during the city's patronage as a leading humanist centre by Maximilian I, Hopfer was probably the first etcher of armour to pull impressions of etchings on paper. He was known as a designer of ornamental etchings that were applied to armour made in Augsburg, though it is not clear whether he actually etched on the armour; in most cases he probably handed his designs over to armourers who manually applied and

etched the ornament. The one surviving piece of signed Hopfer armour, a shield, dates from the year of his death (1536; Madrid, Real Armeria).

Many of the etchings on paper are ornamental, suggesting that Hopfer first made plates for prints so that he could show his armour craftsmen accurate etched designs on paper. He also etched portraits, folklore, allegorical and biblical scenes, probably for distribution to the public. Thus Hopfer seems to have quickly progressed from armourer to printmaker under the influence of Maximilian Augsburg, going from sheets pulled to facilitate ornamental design to create the first 'mass-produced' etched prints. Portraits such as those of *Emperor Maximilian* (B. 79) and *Martin Luther* (B. 86) must have had wide appeal in humanist Augsburg.

A unique characteristic of Hopfer etchings is that the plates are made of a thin iron which has shown but very slight signs of rust. Since Daniel first worked with an iron alloy used for armour which could not rust, it is likely that he used a similar metal for his plates. His technique of etching as shown in the prints is still somewhat experimental, displaying a strong, uniform line structure which does not yet fully exploit the artistic possibilities of the medium.

Hopfer's most discussed work is an etching of *Kunz von der Rosen* (B. 87; see fig.), a courtier of Maximilian. This plate was probably executed before one by Urs Graf of a young woman washing her feet, dated 1513. Hopfer's early background in graphic design for armour seems to indicate that he began etching much earlier than 1513.

Daniel Hopfer: *Kunz von der Rosen*, etching, 2nd state, 290×210 mm, probably before 1513 (London, British Museum)

Although he is recognized as the first master of a most significant new medium of printmaking, today, as in the 16th century, he is somewhat overshadowed by his contemporaries, especially Dürer. The fact that Hopfer's prints emanated from a tradition of armour-making has also discounted his reputation as a fine artist. Nonetheless, his innovation in, and impact on, the graphic arts, effected by his pulling the first etched print, should not be overshadowed by the experimental, somewhat unpolished quality of some of them.

BIBLIOGRAPHY

Hollstein: *Ger.*
E. Eyssen: *Daniel Hopfer von Kaufbeuren* (diss., U. Heidelberg, 1904)
R. A. Koch: *Early German Masters*, 17 [VIII/iv] of *The Illustrated Bartsch*, ed. W. Strauss (New York, 1981) [B.]

ROBERT A. KOCH

Hopi. Indigenous people of the Southwest region of North America (*see under* NATIVE NORTH AMERICAN ART). They are probably descendants of the Anasazi, who dominated the region before the Navajo arrived. In the late 20th century Hopi culture was one of the best preserved of all the Native American Indian cultures.

Hŏ P'il [*cha* Yŏjŏng; *ho* Yŏn'gaek, Ch'osŏn, Kudo] (*b* 1709; *d* 1768). Korean poet, painter and calligrapher. His ancestral home was Yangch'ŏn. In 1735 he passed the first level (*chinsa*) in the state examinations for civil office. He was an excellent poet and was on intimate terms with Kang Se-hwang. The two men painted and travelled together, and Hŏ P'il's criticisms of several of Kang Se-hwang's works remain. Hŏ produced mainly landscapes (Kor. *sansudo*) in the literati style of the Chinese Southern school. Among his subjects were the Kŭmgang (Diamond) Mountains in central Korea. Works attributed posthumously to him include paintings of a *Poem by Du Fu* (Seoul, Ewha Women's U. Mus.), *Landscape with Mt Umyŏn* (Seoul, N. Mus.) and, in collaboration with Kang Se-hwang, another *Landscape with Mt Umyŏn* (Seoul, Korea, U. Mus.).

BIBLIOGRAPHY

O. Se-ch'ang, ed.: *Kŭnyŏk sŏhwa ching* [Dictionary of Korean calligraphers and painters] (Taegu, 1928/*R* Seoul, 1975)
Yu Pok-yŏl: *Hanguk hoehwa taegwan* [Pageant of Korean painting] (Seoul, 1979)

PYŎN YŎNG-SŎP

Hopkins, John Henry (*b* Dublin, 30 Jan 1792; *d* Burlington, VT, 9 June 1868). American architect, designer and ecclesiastic. He was taken from Ireland to the USA by his parents in 1800 and was successively the superintendent of an ironworks, a lawyer, and an ordained minister (1824) in Pittsburgh, PA. As rector of Trinity Church, he built a new church in 1825 in the Gothic style. The design was based on publications from England of John Britton and Augustus Charles Pugin. An illustration of Trinity Church was one of 13 lithographs by Hopkins in his *Essay on Gothic Architecture* (1836), published after he became Episcopal Bishop of Vermont. This was the first book in the USA on the Gothic Revival and it preceded the main Gothic Revivalist works of A. W. N. Pugin, which in turn influenced Hopkins's later architectural designs. One of Hopkins's first acts as Bishop was to consecrate AMMI B. YOUNG's only Gothic composition, St Paul's, Burlington,

for which Hopkins designed the altar (illustrated in the *Essay*). He also designed St Thomas's, Brandon, VT (1860–63), a village church for 200 people, built, following A. W. N. Pugin's precepts, of local blue limestone. The larger Trinity Church, Rutland, VT (1863–5), accommodates 600 people, but uses wooden roof trusses, vaulting and pews similar to those in the Brandon church. Hopkins's *Essay* does not seem to have been widely distributed nor to have been influential. Most architects of the American Gothic took their cues from England, particularly from publications of A. W. N. Pugin and the Oxford Ecclesiologists.

WRITINGS

Essay on Gothic Architecture (Burlington, VT, 1836)

BIBLIOGRAPHY

J. H. Hopkins: *The Life of Bishop Hopkins* (New York, 1873)
L. Wodehouse: 'John Henry Hopkins and the Gothic Revival', *Antiques*, ciii (1973), pp. 76–83

LAWRENCE WODEHOUSE

Hopkins, Lawford & Nelson. Canadian architectural partnership formed in 1854 by John William Hopkins (*b* England, 9 Sept 1825; *d* Montreal, 11 Dec 1905), Frederick Lawford (*b* England, 1821; *d* Sherbrooke, Quebec, 11 Aug 1866) and James Nelson (*b* Belfast, 1830; *d* Arundel, Quebec, 18 Feb 1919). Hopkins arrived in Canada in 1852, Nelson in 1840 and Lawford in 1854 or 1855. Lawford trained in the office of Sir Charles Barry and was a member in the firm of Lawford & Heneker of London before settling in Canada. The firm of Hopkins, Lawford & Nelson is best known for the Post Office and the Customs House in Kingston, Ontario (both 1856–9). Two storeys high and built of the local grey limestone, these buildings reflect the influence of Barry's clubhouses in London. They have rusticated ground floors, quoins and window surrounds, prominent stringcourses, balustrades and flat roofs and are considered among the finest examples of the Italianate style in Canada. The partnership was dissolved in 1860, and Lawford and Nelson had minor practices afterwards. Hopkins became one of Montreal's leading architects and designed houses (e.g. Van Horne House, *c.* 1870, a richly decorated, Italianate building on Sherbrooke Street; destr.), churches, commercial buildings and railway stations.

BIBLIOGRAPHY

List of Public Works in Upper and Lower Canada from the Union until Confederation, Department of Public Works, Canada (Ottawa, 1868)
'The Late Mr. J. W. Hopkins', *Can. Architect & Bldr*, xviii (1905), p. 178
P. Lambert and R. Lemire: *Inventaire des bâtiments du vieux Montréal du Quartier Sainte-Anne et de la ville de Maisonneuve construits entre 1880 et 1915* (Quebec, 1977)
R. G. Hill, ed.: *The Biographical Dictionary of Architects in Canada, 1800–1950* (in preparation)

LESLIE MAITLAND

Hoppe, Emil (*b* Vienna, 2 April 1876; *d* Salzburg, 14 Aug 1957). Austrian architect. His grandfather, Anton Hoppe, was a renowned architect in Biedermeier Vienna. Emil Hoppe studied at the Staatsgewerbeschule in Vienna before going on to the 'Wagnerschule' at the Akademie für Bildenden Künste (1898–1901). He was awarded the Schwendenwein Stipendium in 1901, enabling him to travel to Italy, where he produced topographical sketches and a series of powerful drawings of heroic, imaginary architecture. These were published in the Wagnerschule yearbook of 1902 and had an influence that extended beyond the confines of Vienna; Antonio Sant'Elia was clearly indebted to Hoppe's example, and the debt may have been shared by Erich Mendelsohn.

From 1902 to 1909 Hoppe worked as an assistant in Otto Wagner's studio, together with his fellow Wagnerschule students Marcel Kammerer (*b* 1878) and Otto Schönthal. While all three worked on the major Wagner projects of the period, the Post Office Savings Bank, the am Steinhof church and the various projects for a Stadtmuseum, they also developed their own independent careers. In 1905 Hoppe and Schönthal submitted a competition scheme for a synagogue in Trieste, which incorporated many of the structural techniques used in the am Steinhof church. While working with Wagner, Hoppe also built blocks of flats (Kleine Neugasse 3, Vienna V, 1902–3; Ottakringerstrasse 82, Vienna XVII, 1906), collaborated with his brother Paul Hoppe on large-scale projects (flats, Riemergasse 8, Vienna I, 1907–8; school for the Wiener Frauen-Erwerbs-Verein, Wiedner Gürtel 68, Vienna IV, 1909) and designed glassware for the firm of E. Bakalowits. He was responsible for a small courtyard at the *Kunstschau* of 1908 in Vienna, organized by the Klimtgruppe, and was active in the design of funerary architecture.

Upon leaving Wagner's studio in 1909, Hoppe joined Kammerer and Schönthal in a group practice that played an important part in defining Viennese modernism in the years immediately preceding World War I. The new practice combined a rigorous faith in new materials and constructional techniques with a sensitive awareness of the Viennese building tradition. A convincing Neo-Biedermeier manner was achieved in a series of flats (Martinstrasse 17, Vienna XVIII, 1910; Frankenberggasse 3, Vienna IV, 1910; Rosensteingasse 73, Vienna XVII, 1911; Wiedner Hauptstrasse 126–128, Vienna V, 1912–13; Plenergasse 24, Vienna XVIII, 1912). Larger projects included office and bank buildings (Dorotheergasse 5 and 7, Vienna I, 1912–15; Zentralbank der Deutschen Sparkassen, Am Hof, Vienna I, 1913–16) and a grandstand and judges' tower for the Wiener Trabrennverband (Prater, Vienna II, 1911–13), which combined concrete technology and Baroque detailing in the most brilliant manner. Executed projects by Hoppe outside Vienna include a series of stations for the Niederösterreichische Landesbahnen and the interior of the Austrian pavilion at the Esposizione Internazionale d'Arte in Rome (1911). The outbreak of World War I halted work on a large hotel and sanatorium project at Opatija on the Istrian Riviera.

After the War Hoppe continued in practice with Schönthal, and the two-man partnership played a significant part in the social housing programme promoted by the Vienna city council in the 1920s and early 1930s. The planning ideals proposed by Otto Wagner in his book *Die Grossstadt* (1911) were applied at the Zürcher-Hof (Gudrunstrasse 145–149, Vienna X, 1928–30) and the Strindberg-Hof (Rinnböckstrasse 53–61, Vienna XI, 1930), while Camillo Sitte's more picturesque views on planning dominated at the Matteotiplatz (Sandleiten, Vienna XVI, 1925–9), the largest of all the social housing developments, on which Hoppe and Schönthal collaborated with the architects Franz Matuschek (1874–1935), Siegfried Theiss (1882–1963), Hans Jaksch (1879–1970), Franz Freiherr von

Krauss (1865–1942) and Tölk. A series of smaller industrial projects was built by Hoppe and Schönthal before the joint practice was closed in 1938. After World War II Hoppe was engaged in restoring some of his earlier buildings after war-damage.

WRITINGS
with O. Schönthal: *Emil Hoppe, Otto Schönthal: Projekte und ausgeführte Bauten* (Vienna and Leipzig, 1931)

BIBLIOGRAPHY
O. A. Graf: *Die vergessene Wagnerschule* (Vienna, 1969)

M. Pozzetto: *La scuola di Wagner, 1894–1912* (Trieste, 1979; Ger. trans., Vienna, 1980)

H. Hautmann and R. Hautmann: *Die Gemeindebauten des roten Wien, 1919–1934* (Vienna, 1980)

F. Borsi and E. Godoli: *Wiener Bauten der Jahrhundertwende: Die Architektur der habsburgischen Metropole zwischen Historismus und Moderne* (Stuttgart, 1985)

H. Weihsmann: *Das rote Wien: Sozialdemokratische Architektur und Kommunalpolitik, 1919–1934* (Vienna, 1985)

I. Boyd Whyte: *Emil Hoppe, Marcel Kammerer, Otto Schönthal: Three Architects from the Master Class of Otto Wagner* (Cambridge, MA, 1989)

IAIN BOYD WHYTE

Hoppé, E(mil) O(tto) (*b* Munich, 14 April 1878; *d* London, 9 Dec 1972). English photographer of German birth. He was educated in Paris and Vienna and moved to England in 1900, where he worked in his family's banking business and took up photography as a hobby. He joined the Royal Photographic Society in 1903, and he was encouraged by Alvin Langdon Coburn and J. C. Warburg. In 1907 the Society awarded Hoppé a fellowship, which enabled him to open his own portrait studio the same year. In 1913 Hoppé helped to found the journal *Colour*, and in 1916 he worked for the nascent British *Vogue*. During World War I and in the early 1920s Hoppé became an enormously successful society portrait photographer, especially of literary and theatrical personalities. His portraits of celebrities were sought after by such journals as the *Illustrated London News*, *The Graphic*, *The Tatler* and other stage and society magazines, which paid high prices for reproduction fees. In 1922 Hoppé held a successful one-man exhibition of over 200 portraits at the Goupil Gallery in London.

Hoppé's portraits became the hallmark of fashionable and literary Britain during World War I. Although he advocated the extensive retouching of negatives, his silver and platinum prints retained a naturalness lacking in many studio portraits of the time. Hoppé eschewed the stage props typical of Edwardian portrait studios. He dramatized faces and personalities with strong lighting and unconventional poses, and often in his portraits the sitter's face occupies most of the image. All of this made his portraits seem strikingly modern by comparison with other portrait photography. Sometimes he manipulated the surroundings in order to set the mood of the photograph. In his strongly lit, half-length portrait of *William Somerset Maugham* (1911), for example, with its wainscoting, chair spindles and Gothic panel, Hoppé established a formal grid over the surface of the image, crossed diagonally by the angle of the writer's right hand suspending the long, delicate ash of his cigarette.

By the early 1920s Hoppé had begun to tire of working exclusively in portraiture, and he began to explore other genres of photography. His work developed considerably throughout the next decade. While he kept his fashionable studio in the former house of John Everett Millais in South Kensington, London, from the late 1920s Hoppé devoted increasingly more time to travel. He pursued landscape and topographical photography, and he contributed to the Orbis Terrarum series of topographical books: *Picturesque Great Britain* (1926) studied the changing British countryside, followed by *Romantic America* (1927), which documented the American landscape. In portrait portfolios such as his *London Types Taken from Life* (1926) Hoppé brought to the ragged faces of working people the perceptive insight into personality that characterized his society portraits. In 1930 he published *Deutsche Arbeit*, a volume of studies of the German industrial landscapes; the images range from smokey, romantic photographs of forgers that borrow from traditions of early 19th-century painting, to the formalist abstractions of the machine-age aesthetic of the 1930s; some of these images would seem to anticipate landscapes of the industrial vernacular of the 1970s and 1980s. They underline the tremendous range of his photography, arising from a new period of maturity, which he continued to explore.

PHOTOGRAPHIC PUBLICATIONS

with A. St John Adcock: *Gods of Modern Grub Street: Impressions of Contemporary Authors* (London, 1913); *R* as *The Glory that Was Grub Street* (London, 1928)
Studies from the Russian Ballet (London, 1913)
with W. P. Ridge: *London Types Taken from Life* (London, 1926)
Picturesque Great Britain: The Architecture and Landscape, Orbis Terrarum (Berlin and New York, 1926; London, 1927)
Romantic America: Picturesque United States, Orbis Terrarum (New York, 1927)
Deutsche Arbeit: Bilder von Wiederaufstieg Deutschlands, intro. B. H. Burgel (Berlin, 1930)
Contributions to *Colour, The Graphic, Illus. London News, The Tatler, Vogue*

WRITINGS

Hundred Thousand Exposures: The Success of a Photographer (London, 1945/R 1975) [autobiography]

BIBLIOGRAPHY

C. Beaton: *British Photographers* (London, 1944/R 1987), pp. 33–4
Camera Portraits by E. O. Hoppé (exh. cat., ed. T. Pepper; London, N.P.G., 1978)
Pictorial Photography in Britain, 1900–20 (exh. cat., ed. J. Taylor; ACGB, 1978)

MARY CHRISTIAN

Hoppenhaupt. German family of decorators and ornamental sculptors.

(1) Johann Michael Hoppenhaupt II (*b* Merseburg, 1709; *d* Merseburg, 1778–86). He was the son of Johann Michael Hoppenhaupt I. From 1740 he worked in Prussia and contributed to the interior decoration of many of Frederick the Great's palaces. He carried out an unfinished design by JOHANN AUGUST NAHL for the concert hall at Schloss Sanssouci (1747) and for the circular study at the Stadtschloss in Berlin (*c.* 1744; destr. World War II). The decoration of Frederick's so-called Second Apartment in the New Wing of Schloss Charlottenburg (*see* BERLIN, §IV, 2), which Hoppenhaupt and his brother (2) Johann Christian carried out in 1747, also seems to derive from earlier designs by Nahl. Hoppenhaupt completed the decoration of the private audience room (1748) and the doors of the marble hall (1749) in Schloss Sanssouci. He is also believed to have decorated various noblemen's

palaces in Berlin, but there is no evidence of this. There is, however, positive evidence that Hoppenhaupt executed the designs of the master builder Johann Friedrich Friedel for Schloss Zerb (1748–50; destr. World War II). The decoration of the Porcelain Gallery, Cedarwood Cabinet and Bedroom (1753–5) in Mon Bijou (destr. World War II), the summer palace in Berlin of Frederick the Great's mother, Sophie Dorothea, was also derived from Friedel's designs. Hoppenhaupt designed some of the interiors in the Neues Palais in Potsdam (1763–9), which were executed by his brother Johann Christian (e.g. Upper Concert Room, Hunting Room, Lower Concert Room, Blue Rooms). With Nahl and Johann Christian Hoppenhaupt, Johann Michael was one of the most important craftsmen working in the Prussian Rococo style. His style is most clearly seen in 70 designs for wall decoration, ornament, furniture, clocks, stoves, coaches, sedan-chairs and coffins etched by Johann Wilhelm Meil. Hoppenhaupt's richly ornamented coach (*c.* 1745; Moscow, Kremlin, Armoury), which Frederick the Great presented to the Empress Elizabeth of Russia, is one of the finest examples of the Prussian Rococo. He also designed some book illustrations and was responsible for the title pages of the complete works of Gotthold Ephraim Lessing, published in Berlin from 1753 to 1755, which were also reproduced by Meil. Hoppenhaupt's designs are characterized by a somewhat awkward style that recalls the Baroque and that distinguishes it from the free-flowing styles of other designers of the Prussian Rococo. Hoppenhaupt lived in Mittelstrasse in Berlin until 1757 and there is no exact evidence of his whereabouts after this date.

(2) Johann Christian Hoppenhaupt (*fl* 1742; *d* Berlin, 1778–86). Brother of (1) Johann Michael Hoppenhaupt II. Hoppenhaupt represents a quite independent style of decoration in the context of the genre at the time of Frederick the Great. Typical elements of his style are naturalistically painted flowers and fruit. Hoppenhaupt is first recorded in Prussia in 1742. The ceiling of the Cedarwood Cabinet in the Stadtschloss at Potsdam (destr.) is his first independent design. Hoppenhaupt designed the decoration in parts of the Sanssouci Palace, Potsdam, including the royal bedroom (altered 1786). He also created the mirrors and overdoors in the small gallery and the encrusted marble floor and doors of the Room Maarmorsaal (marble). In 1746, with his brother Johann Michael Hoppenhaupt, he decorated the concert room in Sanssouci to uncompleted designs by Johann August Nahl. His greatest achievement at Sanssouci is the Voltaire Room (1752–3) where fruit and foliage are combined with monkeys and birds in exotically bright woodcarvings against a greenish-grey background, representing the transition into neutralism of late Rococo. The two brothers also collaborated on the extension of Frederick's second apartment in the new wing (1747) of the Palace of Charlottenburg, Berlin. In the interior decoration of the theatre in the Potsdam Stadtschloss (1748; removed 19th century) Hoppenhaupt worked solely to plans by Georg Wenceslaus von Knobelsdorff. His Oranische Kammern in the Stadtschloss (1752) and the king's writing cabinet were both destroyed in World War II. Hoppenhaupt largely controlled the interior furnishing of the Neues

Palais in Potsdam (1763–9). He designed the decoration for most of the rooms, although he often had to work from rough sketches by Frederick and used some designs by his brother (e.g. Hunting Room, Lower Concert Room, Upper Concert Room). Among Hoppenhaupt's most important works is the theatre in the Neues Palais, which shows him to be one of the most talented decorators of the European Rococo. Hoppenhaupt also worked as a decorative arts designer: in 1772 he supplied wax models for a set of five vases to be executed at the Berlin porcelain factory and it is possible that he designed many more works for this factory. Hoppenhaupt's designs are often indistinguishable from those of his brother although his style is more severe.

BIBLIOGRAPHY

NDB; Thieme–Becker

F. Nicolai: *Nachricht von den Baumeistern, Bildhauern, Kupferstechern, Malern, Stukkaturern und anderen Künstlern* (Berlin and Stettin, 1786), p. 145

H. L. Manger: *Baugeschichte von Potsdam*, 3 vols (Berlin and Stettin, 1789), p. 64

W. Kurth: *Die Raumkunst im Kupferstich des 17. und 18 Jahrhunderts* (Stuttgart, 1927), nos 218–23, 228–34

R. Sprecht: 'Die Tätigkeit des Bildhauers Johann Michael Hoppenhaupts beim Zerbster Schlossbau', *Zerbster Jahrbuch*, xviii (1933), pp. 87–96

W. Kurth: *Sanssouci: Ein Beitrag zur Kunst des deutschen Rokoko* (Berlin, 1970), pp. 153ff, 171ff

T. Eggeling: *Studien zum friderizianischen Rokoko: Georg Wenceslaus von Knobelsdorff als Entwerfer von Innendekorationen* (Berlin, 1980), pp. 15–16, 18, n. 47, 118, 188

Berliner Prunkschlitten, Kutschen und Sänften des Barock (exh. cat. Berlin, 1987), pp. 9–12, 17, nos 9–14; appendix II, nos 20–21

T. EGGELING

Hopper, Edward (*b* Nyack, NY, 22 July 1882; *d* New York, 15 May 1967). American painter, printmaker and illustrator. He was brought up in a town on the Hudson River, where he developed an enduring love of nautical life. When he graduated from Nyack Union High School in 1899, his parents, although supportive of his artistic aspirations, implored him to study commercial illustration rather than pursue an economically uncertain career in fine art. He studied with the Correspondence School of Illustrating in New York City (1899–1900). He continued to study illustration at the New York School of Art (1900–1906), under Arthur Keller (1866–1925) and Frank Vincent Du Mond (1865–1951), but began to study painting and drawing after a year. Hopper began in the portrait and still-life classes of William Merrit Chase, to whose teaching he later referred only infrequently and disparagingly. He preferred the classes he took with Kenneth Hayes Miller and especially those of Robert Henri. Hopper's skill won his fellow students' respect, as well as honours in the school where, by 1905, he was teaching Saturday classes.

In 1906 Hopper worked part-time as an illustrator for an advertising agency founded by one of his former classmates, the illustrator Coles Phillips (1880–1927). In the autumn of that year Hopper went to Paris to study works by European artists at first hand, educating himself by visiting museums and exhibitions. The many paintings that he produced in Paris were painted *en plein air*, partly through lack of studio space in his rented room and partly in emulation of the Impressionists. In response to the intense sunlight he adopted a lighter palette, the result of which can be seen in *Tugboat at the Boulevard St-Michel* (1907; New York, Whitney). In late June he went on a tour of London, Haarlem, Amsterdam, Berlin and Brussels, returning to New York at the end of August 1907. There he tried to paint while working several days a week as an illustrator for trade magazines and fiction, including *Adventure* and *Scribner's*. He detested this work and in later life was loath to discuss it, even to the point of concealing his illustrations.

Hopper first exhibited in March 1908, in a group show held in the former Harmonie Club building in New York, organized by some of Henri's former students in protest at the conservative taste of the juries of the National Academy. He returned to Paris for four months in 1909 and briefly in 1910, when he also visited Spain. Although Hopper never again went abroad, French culture had a lasting impact on him. He read French literature, particularly Symbolist poetry, and admired a number of French painters, including Degas.

From 1910 Hopper continued to work as an illustrator in New York, but he spent his summers painting in rural New England, in Gloucester and Cape Anne, MA, and Ogunquit and Monhegan Island, ME. In 1913 he moved to Washington Square, in the Greenwich Village area of New York City, which remained his permanent base. Hopper's first sale of a painting, *Sailing* (1911; Pittsburgh, PA, Carnegie Inst.), was at the International Exhibition of Modern Art, popularly known as the Armory Show (1913); he did not sell another until ten years later. Hopper was more successful with his etchings, which he made from 1915, in both sales and exhibitions. Ironically, however, it was as an illustrator that he first won fame, when he received top prize for his poster *Smash the Hun* (1918; see Levin, 1980, p. 144) in a wartime competition. In January 1920 Hopper held his first one-man exhibition, of 16 paintings at the Whitney Studio Club. He was discouraged by the failure of the exhibition to achieve either sales or critical attention, his growing reputation as a printmaker underlining his lack of success as a painter.

In 1923 Hopper re-established contact with Josephine Verstille Nivison, whom he had known at art school. She encouraged him to take up watercolour, a medium which he had used only for illustration. Working in the open air, Hopper painted his first watercolours with great facility, realistically depicting seascapes and architecture, for example *The Mansard Roof* (1923; New York, Brooklyn Mus.), one of a group of watercolours singled out for praise by the critics the following autumn. After his marriage to Jo Nivison on 9 July 1924 he painted more watercolours in Gloucester; soon after their return to New York, Hopper had his second one-man exhibition, his first in a commercial gallery, at the Frank K. M. Rehn Gallery, where he remained for the rest of his career. The exhibition was both a commercial and a critical success: all eleven watercolours exhibited, and five additional ones, were sold.

In 1925 Hopper painted *House by the Railroad*, which became the first painting by any artist to be acquired for MOMA, New York. This canvas of a solitary 19th-century Second Empire-style house, standing starkly alone against the railway tracks, has become a famous image in American art, evoking the passage of time. Nationalistic critics, who had come to view Hopper's work as typically American,

Edward Hopper: *Nighthawks*, oil on canvas, 762×1440 mm, 1942 (Chicago, IL, Art Institute of Chicago)

also praised his realism and personal content in works such as *Early Sunday Morning* (1930; New York, Whitney), depicting an empty street and shop façades. In 1933 Alfred H. Barr organized Hopper's first retrospective for MOMA, setting off a critical debate over whether Hopper was sufficiently modern to be exhibited there.

From 1930 Hopper and his wife began to spend their summers painting in Truro on Cape Cod, MA, where they built their own home in 1934. The view over the bay from this simple house designed by Hopper inspired his later canvas *Rooms by the Sea* (1951; New Haven, CT, Yale U., A.G.). During the early 1930s Hopper found ample subject-matter for both his oils and watercolours in Cape Cod, until the area became too familiar, and he was prompted to drive further afield, from Vermont to Mexico, in search of inspiration.

A feeling of loneliness and detachment pervaded Hopper's works in the second half of his career. Rarely was there any definite evidence of communication between the figures, for example in *Hotel Lobby* (1943; Indianapolis, IN, Mus. A.). He frequently depicted solitary figures in works such as *New York Movie* (1939; New York, MOMA), where the focus is not on the film audience but rather on the blonde usherette, who seems unaware of both the film and the spectator. The harsh realism of Hopper's style was underscored by his preference for bright, shadow-casting light, seen in *Office at Night* (1940; Minneapolis, MN, Walker A. Cent.), or the strange luminosity of dusk, combined with artificial light in *Gas* (1940; New York, MOMA), a painting of a solitary man in an empty petrol station, in which a long shadow is cast by the light from the building on the right. In 1942 Hopper painted *Nighthawks* (see fig.), an evocative canvas depicting people in an all-night diner.

The emergence of Abstract Expressionism meant that Hopper's style came to be regarded as illustrative, a painful comparison for a painter who had disdained illustration. His second retrospective in 1950 at the Whitney Museum, New York, was regarded by many as the work of an enduring realist maintaining an obsolete style. In 1956 *Time* magazine featured a cover story on Hopper, emphasizing his historical significance in the American Realist tradition of John Singleton Copley and Thomas Eakins. By the time of his third retrospective (1964) at the Whitney Museum, critics in a generation of Pop artists and Photorealists hailed him as the forefather of the new avantgarde. Hopper, however, viewed the entire process with much cynicism, knowing that he had consistently created realist paintings that expressed personal meaning. The Whitney Museum houses a large collection of his work.

WRITINGS
'John Sloan and the Philadelphians', *Arts*, xi (1927), pp. 168–78
'Charles Burchfield: American', *Arts*, xiv (1928), pp. 5–12
'Notes on Painting', *Edward Hopper: Retrospective Exhibition* (exh. cat. by A. H. Barr and C. Burchfield, New York, MOMA, 1933)
'Edward Hopper: An Interview', *A. Amer.*, 1 (1960), pp. 60–63 [interview with John Morse]

BIBLIOGRAPHY
G. Pène du Bois: *Edward Hopper* (New York, 1931)
L. Goodrich: *Edward Hopper* (Harmondsworth, 1949)
C. Zigrosser: 'The Etchings of Edward Hopper', *Prints*, ed. C. Zigrosser (New York, 1962), pp. 155–73
'Edward Hopper/Environment USA, 1957–1967', *São Paulo 9* (exh. cat. by W. C. Seitz and L. Goodrich, Washington, DC, Smithsonian Inst., 1967), pp. 17–28
L. Goodrich: *Edward Hopper* (New York, 1971) [incl. reprints of three statements by Hopper]
G. Levin: *Edward Hopper: The Complete Prints* (New York, 1979)
Edward Hopper as Illustrator (exh. cat. by G. Levin, New York, Whitney, 1979)
Edward Hopper: The Art and the Artist (exh. cat. by G. Levin, New York, Whitney; London, Hayward Gal.; Amsterdam, Stedel. Mus.; Düsseldorf, Stadt. Ksthalle; 1980)

G. Levin: *Edward Hopper* (New York, 1984)
——: *Hopper's Places* (New York, 1985)
——: *Edward Hopper: A Catalogue Raisonné* (New York, 1995)

GAIL LEVIN

Hopper, Thomas (*b* Rochester, Kent, 6 July 1776 or 1777; *d* London, 11 Aug 1856). English architect. The son of a lowly measuring surveyor, he was brought up in Rochester, but by 1802 he was following his father's profession in London, where he lived for the rest of his life. He was brought into the public eye at the age of 30 by his work for the picture dealer Walsh Porter and for the Prince Regent (later George IV). In 1806 Hopper fitted up the interior of Porter's Craven Cottage at Fulham, London, with a series of rooms in different styles, including Egyptian, Gothic and Persian. At Carlton House, Pall Mall, London, he redecorated some of Henry Holland's rooms and added an elaborate conservatory, apparently made of cast-iron and stained glass, in the Perpendicular Gothic style (1807; destr. 1827–8). If iron was indeed its primary material, this structure deserves recognition as a pioneering work; certainly Hopper made much use of structural and ornamental cast-iron in his later buildings, as in the handsome cast-iron colonnades he added to Woolverstone Hall, Essex, in 1823. On the strength of royal patronage, Hopper built up an extensive country-house practice; his obituary declared that 'probably no other architect . . . except James Wyatt, was so extensively employed in erecting new and extending old mansions'. At least nine new houses were built or rebuilt to his designs, but he was probably mainly occupied in making modest alterations to existing houses. Most of his known alterations, such as the austere Neo-classical staircase and drawing-room at Melford Hall, Suffolk (1813), and the dining-room at Erdigg Park, Clwyd (1827), have come to light only recently. Hopper held the post of Surveyor to the county of Essex from 1816 until his death, and though his only work of significance for the county was Springfield Gaol, Chelmsford (from 1819), with its massive Doric propylaeum, his official status brought him several private commissions in Essex. He was also Surveyor to the Atlas Assurance Company, for whom he built offices in Cheapside, London (1854–6).

Hopper competed unsuccessfully to design the new General Post Office and the new Houses of Parliament, and after both competitions he issued bitter recriminatory pamphlets, which are apparently his only published works. In one of these, *Hopper v. Cust, on the New Houses of Parliament* (1837), he issued his famous dictum that 'It is an architect's business to understand all styles, and to be prejudiced in favour of none'. Taken together, Hopper's buildings certainly reflect most of the architectural fashions of the late Georgian period: Leigh Court, near Bristol (1814), and Kinmel Park, Clwyd (1842; rebuilt 1875), were in Greek Ionic; Danbury Place, Essex (1832), and Margam Abbey, W. Glam. (1830), in Tudor Gothic; Llanover Court, Gwent (1828; destr. 1935), and Wivenhoe Park, Essex (1846), were Jacobean; and Birch Hall, Essex (1843; destr. 1954), was in the newly fashionable Italianate style. At Gosford Castle, Co. Armagh (*c.* 1820; partly rebuilt 1859), and more especially for George Hay Dawkins Pennant (1763–1846) at Penrhyn Castle, near Bangor

(*c.* 1827–40), Hopper, who always showed a marked preference for massiveness, produced the two outstanding British monuments of the Neo-Norman style, while at Arthur's (now the Carlton) Club in St James's, London (1826–7), and at Amesbury Abbey, Wilts (1834), he adopted a remarkably faithful Palladian manner. Whatever their style, most of Hopper's houses display externally his skill in picturesque massing, while all of them betray internally a liking for dramatic architectural effects, with spectacular staircases and massively heavy carved decoration. At the same time, Hopper was a competent planner and was quick to incorporate such modern additions to comfort as central heating and plate-glass windows.

WRITINGS
Hopper v. Cust, on the New Houses of Parliament (London, 1837)

BIBLIOGRAPHY
Colvin; Papworth
J. V. Hughes: *Margam Castle* (Port Talbot, 1981)
G. Jackson-Stops: 'Thomas Hopper at Erdigg and Melford', *NT Stud.* (1981), pp. 69–84
R. Evans: *The Fabrication of Virtue: English Prison Architecture, 1750–1840* (Cambridge, 1982)
N. Burton: 'Thomas Hopper and the Drama of Eclecticism', *Architectural Outsiders*, ed. R. Brown (London, 1985)

NEIL BURTON

Hoppin, Francis L(aurens) V(inton) (*b* Providence, RI, 1867; *d* Newport, RI, 10 Sept 1941). American architect and painter. After early training at the Trinity Military Institute, Providence, RI, preparing for a career in the army, he attended Brown University, Providence. From 1884 to 1886 Hoppin studied at the Massachusetts Institute of Technology and after another two years' study in Paris, he briefly joined the architectural firm of his brother Howard (1845–1940) in Providence. This was followed by an apprenticeship with McKim, Mead & White. In 1899, after eight years with this firm, he left and joined Terrence Koen (1858–1923), concentrating on projects in New York City. Luxurious country and city homes became their trademark. The James P. Lanier House (1905–06), 123 East 35th Street and the E. D. Baylies House (1905–09), 10 East 62nd Street, New York, are both in the Louis XVI style favoured by their wealthy patrons. Among his public buildings the New York City Police Headquarters (1909), 240 Centre Street, reveals the influence of the Ecole des Beaux-Arts in Paris. Most of his fire and police stations in New York were also large and extravagantly ornamented. Upon retirement he travelled and painted watercolour views in Europe and New England. He had one-man shows in New York City in 1925 and 1929, the *New York Times* in 1934 noting that his 'work is characterized by a strong architectural feel and accomplished smoothness in his use of color'.

BIBLIOGRAPHY
Withey
'Attractive Water-Colors', *New York Times* (26 April 1934), p. 21
Obituary, *New York Times* (11 Sept 1941), p. 23

DARRYL PATRICK

Hoppner, John (*b* London, 25 April 1758; *d* London, 23 Jan 1810). English painter of German descent. According to contemporary accounts, he was the most important portrait artist in Britain in the period following the retirement of Joshua Reynolds in 1789. His parents were

Bavarians employed at court in England; during his time as a chorister in the Chapel Royal he was noticed by George III as a 'Lad of Genius' for his drawing ability. As a result he was sent to live with the keeper of the King's drawings and medals and given a royal allowance. This preferential treatment led to later speculation—for which there is no evidence—that he was an illegitimate son of the King; Hoppner, who knew very well the value of publicity, never discouraged the rumours.

Hoppner entered the Royal Academy Schools in 1775, winning the Academy's silver medal for life drawing three years later. During this period he met Patience Lovell Wright (1725–86), an American sculptor in wax whose gallery was something of a fashionable meeting-place where Hoppner was to make many useful contacts. He first exhibited at the Royal Academy in 1780 and two years later won the Academy's gold medal for history painting, with a scene from *King Lear* (untraced). His marriage to Mrs Wright's daughter Phoebe in 1781 resulted in his royal allowance being withdrawn; he began to support himself by painting works that were suitable for engraving: fancy pictures and portraits of pretty women. His early pictures are well drawn and broadly painted, resembling Johan Zoffany's life-size paintings. A portrait of Phoebe, exhibited in 1783 as *Girl with Salad* (Waterville, ME, Colby Coll., Mus. A.), derives from Zoffany's *The Watercress Girl* and *The Flower Girl* (both untraced), although Zoffany, whom Hoppner may have known from court, was the only artist he ever plagiarized in so obvious a way.

Hoppner painted increasingly distinguished sitters during the 1780s: in 1785 he produced three portraits of the youngest daughters of George III (all British Royal Col.). By this time his brushwork was beginning to take on some of the freedom that was to mark his mature work: a greater reliance on scumbling and impasto is evident and his palette became purer—his paintings were noted for their colour. By 1787 he was well established as the prime successor to Reynolds and Thomas Gainsborough. In the 1790s he began painting portraits of close friends, drawing upon early 16th-century Venetian examples: penetrating, spot-lit portraits set against a rich, dark background, executed with a sensitive appreciation for the qualities of the paint. He made widespread use of *sfumato* for his treatment of hair, fur and, occasionally, foliage, and his whites are applied with considerable energy.

In 1795 Hoppner was elected RA; by then he was principal painter to the Prince of Wales (later George IV) and the most important portraitist in England: Thomas Lawrence was finding it difficult to live up to his own spectacular successes of 1790 and this continued to be the case until the end of Hoppner's life. Hoppner's portraits were known for their good likenesses; the faces of his sitters are almost anatomically and structurally built up with paint while his treatment of costume indicates a similar appreciation and understanding of the texture of each fabric. He was happiest painting simply posed portraits of sympathetic sitters; his best portraits, especially those of 1790–1810, are brilliantly executed, with vibrant brushwork and luscious colour. As an advocate of the *colore* faction of Academic dispute, his neglect of draughtsmanship was not unintentional; while his colours and

quality of execution largely compensate for this, his full-length portraits occasionally suffer as a result. Some of his quarter-length portraits are remarkable for their psychological insight, for instance those of *Sarah Franklin Bache* (New York, Met.; see fig.) and *Sir George Beaumont* (1809; London, N.G.). His landscape backgrounds are often painted with an almost abstract vigour that looks forward to the work of J. M. W. Turner. Indeed, Hoppner was instrumental in advising Turner at the beginning of the latter's career as an oil painter: Turner's first exhibited oil, *Fishermen at Sea* (London, Tate), owes more than a little to Hoppner's *Gale of Wind* (London, Tate).

Hoppner was an inveterate traveller and sketcher in England, Scotland and Wales (examples of his drawings in London, BM), but only once did he travel abroad—in 1802 to Paris during the Peace of Amiens. His exposure on this trip to Napoleon's spectacular collections in the Louvre profoundly affected his style. His work became simpler in composition (exceptions to this can invariably be blamed on the insistent whims of clients), and the execution, particularly of smaller portraits, appears often to have been frantically energetic, as in *Augustus Henry Fitzroy, 3rd Duke of Grafton* (1805; Euston Hall, Suffolk) and *Lady Caroline Lamb* (1805; Althorp, Northants). The masterpiece of his last years is *Sleeping Nymph* (1806; Petworth House, W. Sussex, NT), a reclining nude and accompanying cupid in a lush landscape, a picture highly praised for its colouring.

Hoppner took an active interest in the running of the Royal Academy. He served on the governing council and relished his occasional terms as a Visitor to the Schools. He was known for his sharp intellect, and his friendship with Joseph Farington meant that his views on any number of subjects, in addition to art, are well documented;

John Hoppner: *Sarah Franklin Bache*, oil on canvas, 762×632 mm (New York, Metropolitan Museum of Art)

Farington also chronicled the steady deterioration of Hoppner's health, which was already causing concern before 1795.

In 1785 Hoppner anonymously reviewed part of that year's Royal Academy exhibition for the *Morning Post* and when his authorship was revealed was roundly condemned by those whom he had criticized. His comments were, however, in line with the opinions of other critics and as a result, in response to Hoppner's criticisms, Benjamin West altered subsequent versions of some of his pictures. In 1805 Hoppner published *Oriental Tales*, a collection of verse fables translated from the Arabic, which is more notable for the preface of its first edition, a heated defence of his own manner of painting and a condemnation of contemporary French art, particularly that of Elisabeth Vigée-Lebrun. He also wrote several articles and reviews on topical artistic matters for *The Artist*, edited by Prince Hoare II, and the new *Quarterly Review*. Although he was known to have a horrible temper, Hoppner's opinions were sought out by artists of all levels of experience as well as by numerous connoisseurs and intellectuals.

WRITINGS

Oriental Tales (London, 1805, rev. 1806) [preface to first edn incl. disc. of ptg]

Regular contributions to *The Artist*; *Morning Post* (1785); *Q. Rev.*; *Brit. Crit.*; *The Pic-Nic*

BIBLIOGRAPHY

J. Farington: *Diaries* (1793–1821); eds K. Garlick and A. Mackintyre (i–vi) and K. Cave (vii–xvi) as *The Diaries of Joseph Farington*, 16 vols (London, 1978–84)

W. McKay and W. Roberts: *John Hoppner, R.A.* (London, 1909, suppl. 1914)

J. H. Wilson: 'The Landscape Paintings of John Hoppner', *Turner Stud.*, vii/1 (1987), pp. 14–25

J. Wilson: 'The Romantics, 1790–1830', *The British Portrait* (Woodbridge, 1991)

J. H. Wilson: *The Life and Work of John Hoppner (1758–1810)* (diss., U. London, Courtauld Inst., 1992)

JOHN WILSON

Hopton, Sir Arthur (*b* Witham, Somerset, *c*. 1588; *d* Black Bourton, Oxfordshire, 6 March 1650). English diplomat and collector. During the reign of Charles I he served first as secretary to the English ambassador in Spain, then as the English agent and finally as ambassador. A significant amount of his correspondence survives, giving important information about artistic contacts between England and Spain during the reign of Philip IV of Spain, and also about the Spanish royal collection. In 1631 Hopton sent still-lifes by El Labrador to Charles I (examples, London, Kew Pal., Royal Col.; London, Hampton Court, Royal Col.) and pictures and drawings to Thomas Howard, 2nd Earl of Arundel. According to Vicente Carducho (*Diálogos de la pintura*, Madrid, 1633), Michael Cross (*fl c.* 1633) was being supported by Hopton when he copied paintings by Titian in the Palacio Real in Madrid and the Escorial. Hopton looked after Orazio Gentileschi's son Francesco Gentileschi (*b* 1599) when he came to Spain in 1631 to present Philip IV with a *Finding of Moses* (Madrid, Prado) by his father. In a letter of 25 July 1635 Hopton claimed that it was only the death of Eugenio Cajés in 1634 that had prevented him from bringing that painter with him when he returned to England on leave. In 1640 Hopton was required to obtain moulds of some Classical busts in a gallery near the Cuarto Real at Aranjuez, writing that 'Velázquez, the King's painter, certifies that the heads sent are correct, that of Hannibal only being doubtful, there being so few statues of him existing'. On 5 August 1638 Hopton wrote of how 'the king within this 12 month had gotten an incredible number of ancient and of the best modern hands', and that Manuel de Acevedo y Zúñiga, 6th Conde de Monterrey, had brought Titian's *Bacchanal* (Madrid, Prado) from Rome to Spain. There is a double portrait by Fr. Juan Rizi entitled *Sir Arthur Hopton and Attendant* (Dallas, TX, S. Methodist U., Meadows Mus. & Gal.).

UNPUBLISHED SOURCES

London, BL, Egerton MS., 1820 [Letters from Arthur Hopton to Francis, Lord Cottington]

London, PRO, Sp. 94. 40–42 [Hopton's corr. while in Spain, 1638–41]

BIBLIOGRAPHY

M. Hume: *The Court of Philip IV: Spain's Decadence* (London, 1907)

E. du Gué Trapier: 'Sir Arthur Hopton and the Interchange of Paintings between Spain and England in the Seventeenth Century', *Connoisseur*, clxiv (1967), pp. 239–44; clxv (1967), pp. 60–64

J. Brown and H. H. Elliott: *A Palace for a King* (New Haven and London, 1980)

DAVID HOWARTH

Hopwood, Gillian (*b* Rochdale, 27 June 1927). British architect, active in Nigeria. She received her diploma in architecture from the Architectural Association School, London, in 1950. From 1955 she lived and worked in Nigeria, where she established a practice in Lagos with her husband, John Godwin (*b* London, 17 June 1928); it was amalgamated in 1989 with Tunde Kuye Associates to become Godwin Hopwood Kuye Architects, while a London practice, Godwin & Hopwood, was opened in 1987. Both firms provided a large number of multinational industrial clients with offices and factories in Nigeria, as well as building schools and housing, the latter primarily for multinational employees. Hopwood and Godwin developed the tradition established in Nigeria by Maxwell Fry and Jane Drew, disciples of Le Corbusier, in which Modernism is adapted to local conditions of climate and building technology. This heritage is clearly seen in the Christchurch Cathedral Primary School (*c.* 1960) in Lagos, a vast, horizontally orientated rectangular building of four storeys. The outer walls are organized into rectangular modules, each of which is subdivided into double rows of openings; these can be raised horizontally as sun shades, while also allowing ventilation. The housing projects for multinational industries (e.g. blocks of flats for Costain Nigeria, 1980–81, Lagos, and for Lewventis Ltd, 1981–3, Ikoyi, Lagos) are smaller in scale, while still modular in conception. In the latter, three storeys of rectangular units with flat walls alternate with broad balconies that project out from glass walls. Hopwood is a Fellow of the RIBA and in 1983 was the first woman to become a Fellow of the Nigerian Institute of Architects.

See also NIGERIA, §IV.

BIBLIOGRAPHY

B. Haigh: 'Agbara Estate: A Private Residential and Industrial Estate, Ogua State, Nigeria', *Arup J.*, xvi/3 (1981), pp. 16–24

C. Lorenz: *Women in Architecture: A Contemporary Perspective* (New York, 1990)

☐

Horadnia [Rus. Grodno]. Town in Belarus'. A regional centre and port on the River Nioman, it is first recorded in the *Ipat'yev Chronicle* for 1128 as the centre of the Grodno Principality; from 1376 it was the second capital of the Grand Duchy of Lithuania. From the 16th century it belonged to Poland, from 1795 it was in Belarus', and during 1920–39 it was again part of Poland.

The architectural heritage of Horadnia is rich and varied. In the centre of the town on Zamkovaya Gora (Castle Hill) are the palace (after 1579) of the Polish King Stephen Bathory and the New Castle (mid-18th century), but as a result of numerous rebuildings they have both lost their original appearance. The picturesque quality of Horadnia is created by its numerous Baroque monasteries and churches, including the Bernadin church and monastery (1595–1618), the Jesuit church (17th–18th centuries) and others. In the former suburb of Kolozh is the 12th-century brick church of SS Boris and Gleb. Excavations have uncovered the remains of two other old brick churches, the so-called Lower Church (*c.* 1100–50) and the Upper Church (from the late 14th century to the 15th), and ruins of 12th-century brick fortified towers.

Neo-classicism developed in the 18th century, succeeded by revivalist styles (pseudo-Russian and Style Empire) in the 19th and 20th centuries. After World War II the town went through an intensive revival and reconstruction, which preserved the old radial planning system and the historic centre. Local antiquities are exhibited in the former palace of Stephen Bathory (Horadnia, Hist. & Archaeol. Mus.).

BIBLIOGRAPHY

V. I. Kudryashev: *Grodno* (Moscow, 1960)

L. N. DROBOV

Hōrai. *See* GION NANKAI.

Horčička, František (*b* Prague, 29 June 1776; *d* Prague, 5 April 1856). Bohemian painter. He studied under Ludvík Kohl (1746–1821) and was at the Prague Academy of Arts (1800–01), studying under Josef Bergler. From 1808 he worked as curator at one of the most distinguished picture galleries of the Bohemian nobility, Opočno Castle, owned by the Colloredo-Mansfeld family. Horčička and Antonín Machek were the two leading portrait painters of the early 19th century in Prague. Horčička frequently painted learned figures in patriotic circles but also portrayed members of noble families and the clergy. His drawings and pastels reflect the stylistic changes of the period. Horčička was one of a group of artists who strove to introduce certain trends of Central European Romanticism into Czech art, and to reconcile them with the main current of an emerging national self-consciousness. Typical of the first endeavour is his gouache *Atelier with Self-Portrait* (1831–2; untraced; see Jiřík) and, of the second, an innovative altarpiece, *The Last Judgement* (*c.* 1820; Prague, St Trinity). Towards the end of his life Horčička became president of the Association of Fine Artists in Bohemia.

BIBLIOGRAPHY

Thieme–Becker

F. X. Jiřík: 'František Horčička', *Ročenka Kruhu Pěstování Dějin Umění* [Yearbook of the circle for the history of art] (1918), pp. 16–21

E. Petrová: 'Osvícenská romantika ve figurálním díle F. Horčičky' [Romanticism of the Period of Enlightenment in the figural work of F. Horčička], *Umění* (1957), pp. 241–8

ROMAN PRAHL

Hore, Somnath (*b* Chittagong, 13 April 1921). Indian printmaker, sculptor and painter. He began with visual reporting of the 1943 Bengal famine for the Communist Party organ *Jannayuddha* (People's War); he was also associated with the 1946 peasant unrest. Later, at the Calcutta Art School, he mastered traditional printmaking media. He devoted himself seriously to printmaking in the 1950s, developing viscosity printing independently in 1959, and a method for making pulp-prints in 1970. As a versatile printmaker and teacher he played a pioneering role in the printmaking movement in India. From 1974 he made expressive bronze sculptures.

BIBLIOGRAPHY

P. Ray: *Somnath Hore* (New Delhi, 1984)

Visions (exh. cat., ed. R. P. Gupta; Calcutta, 1986)

R. SIVA KUMAR

Horeau, Hector (*b* Versailles, 4 Oct 1801; *d* Paris, 21 Aug 1872). French architect and draughtsman. He studied at the Ecole des Beaux-Arts (1819–26), Paris, under Eugène-Charles-Frédéric Nepveu (1777–1862) and François Debret, and received a classical training, to which his first projects bore witness. During the 1830s and 1840s he travelled widely in Europe and beyond, and a visit to Egypt in 1837 led to the publication in 1841–7 of his *Panorama d'Egypte et de Nubie*. By the 1830s he had embarked on a long series of unsuccessful competition designs, including those for the Palais de Justice and for the prison in Lille (1827), for a new opera house for Paris (1843–5) and for Les Halles (1845), the city's new central market, which was eventually built from 1854 to designs by VICTOR BALTARD. Indeed only a few minor works by Horeau were ever executed—such as the Château des Fleurs (1847), a ballroom on the Champs–Elysées in Paris, and the Jardin d'Eté et d'Hiver (1847–8) in Lyon, neither of which has survived—and it is for a number of visionary schemes for Paris and London that he is principally remembered. Great Britain particularly attracted him, with its dynamic industry, audacious technical inventions and democratic qualities. His biggest disappointment, however, was his loss of the commission for the Great Exhibition building in London in 1850. He submitted a design that had already been rejected for the Exposition Universelle of 1849, and it won joint first prize with Richard Turner (1798–1881) of Dublin. The Exhibition Committee, however, decided to substitute their own design, which was later superseded by Joseph Paxton's last-minute submission, the 'Crystal Palace'. Horeau subsequently but unfairly thought that Paxton had cheated him of the commission, but despite this setback he moved to England *c.* 1851 and lived there intermittently until the early 1860s, when he returned to Paris. Various grandiose and unexecuted schemes of this period included a tunnel under the English Channel (1851), the redevelopment of the seafront at Brighton, E. Sussex (1858), an underground market beneath Leicester Square, London (1859), and, in the same year, designs for new government buildings between Westminster and Somerset House. The two commissions he did receive in England were probably his most substantial built works: 'The Poplars' (1855–6; destr. *c.* 1950) at 20 Avenue Road, St John's Wood, London, and Pippingford Park (1857–8; destr.), near Nutley, Sussex, both in an eclectic Second Empire style using terracotta and stone.

Although Horeau was never trained as an engineer, he produced many designs for cast-iron and glass buildings; these were essentially imaginary structures, however, and lacked any consideration of technical matters such as assembly, loading or span. For him, the mission of the architect was to create new types of buildings and improve society by the use of new materials, and to revolutionize people's lives, as well as urban and architectural aesthetics. In this respect Horeau was influenced by the ideas of FOURIERISM. For 20 years, in solitude and with little hope of seeing his plans realized, he dreamt of halls and exhibition palaces and extraordinary groupings of 'municipal' buildings such as the Infiorata, an urban complex for Paris in the Rue Rougemont linked by conservatories filled with plants (1868). Another scheme (1865–7) envisaged the enclosure of most of the older streets and boulevards of Paris with glazed roofs. In such developments, sheltered beneath light iron and glass roofs, the city dweller could be within easy reach of all the amenities of urban life. Horeau's visions for the future of mankind were as impractical as his politics; in 1870, he supported the Paris Commune, becoming its official architect, and after its fall, spent five months in prison. He passed the time by designing an iron and glass hôtel de ville for the city of Paris, to replace the one burnt down by the Communards. Horeau's visionary architecture is expressed in delicately drawn wash-drawings of muted colouring, framed by inscriptions in a small, regular hand. They are restrained images that contrast sharply with the powerful and frenzied nature of his thought. Many of his surviving drawings are in the Institut Français d'Architecture, Paris.

WRITINGS

Panorama d'Egypte et de Nobie (Paris, 1841)
'Edilité urbaine', *Gaz. Architectes & Bât.*, vi (1868), pp. 41–57

BIBLIOGRAPHY

G. Vapereau: *Dictionnaire universel des contemporains* (Paris, 1865), p. 902
N. Pevsner: *A History of Building Types* (London, 1976), pp. 241–8
Hector Horeau, 1801–1872 (exh. cat., Paris, Mus. A. Déc., 1979)
P. Dufournet: *Hector Horeau, précurseur: Idées, techniques, architectures* (Paris, 1980)
F. Boudon: 'Le théâtre dioramitisé d'Hector Horeau', *Victor Louis et le théâtre: Actes du colloque tenu … 1980 à Bordeaux* (Paris, 1982), pp. 107–20
——: 'Rêves de propriétaires, images d'architectes', *L'Architecture en représentation* (Paris, 1983), pp. 100–06 [design for a château in Tarn-et-Garonne]

FRANÇOISE BOUDON

Horemans. Flemish family of painters.

(1) Jan Josef Horemans I [le Sombre] (*b* Antwerp, 16 Nov 1682; *d* Antwerp, 7 Aug 1752). He was a pupil of the sculptor Michiel van der Voort I and then of the Dutch painter Jan van Pee (before 1640–1710), who was active in Antwerp. Horemans joined the Guild of St Luke in 1706–7. He appears to have followed in the footsteps of the 17th-century Flemish genre painters, executing a few portraits and a large number of small anecdotal pictures that were highly prized on the market. In paintings such as the *Village School* and the *Cobbler's Shop* (both 1712; Vienna, Ksthist. Mus.), the *Musical Company* (1715;

Brunswick, Herzog Anton Ulrich-Mus.) and the *Cardplayers* (Florence, Uffizi) he represented scenes from contemporary everyday life that combine observation with a certain degree of stiffness. Most of his paintings are signed. In 1746, together with his son (3) Jan Josef Horemans II, he painted the *Abbot of St Michel Visiting the Order of the Fencing Oath* (Antwerp, Kon. Mus. S. Kst.).

(2) Peter Jacob Horemans (*b* Antwerp, 26 Oct 1700; *d* Munich, 1776). Brother of (1) Jan Josef Horemans I. In 1716–17 he was mentioned as a pupil of his elder brother Jan Josef at the Guild of St Luke in Antwerp. In 1725 he settled in Munich, where he lived and worked with his compatriot, the sculptor Guillielmus de Grof. Two years later he was named court painter by Elector Charles of Bavaria, the future Holy Roman Emperor Charles VII, for whom he painted the *Musical Concert in the Presence of the Elector Charles* (1730; New York, Met.). Among other works painted for the court is a series illustrating the *Hunts of the Prince Elector* (Munich, Amalienburg). *Maximilian III Joseph with the Members of his Family from the Court of Saxony* (1761; Munich, Schloss Nymphenburg) was painted for Maximilian III Joseph, the subsequent Elector of Bavaria, for whom Horemans went to work in 1759. Horemans also worked for the Church and for private individuals. In 1765 he qualified as a master in Munich.

Peter Jacob was a talented artist and had a fertile imagination. A scrupulous recorder of everyday life in Munich during the Rococo period, he treated the most varied subjects with equal success. Besides court scenes and conversation pieces, he also painted still-lifes, for example the *Still-life with a Woman and Flowers* (Munich, Bayer. Nmus.) and *Peaches, Oranges and Grapes on a Dish* (1766; Augsburg, Schaezlerpal.), and portraits, for example a *Self-portrait* (1766) and a portrait of the bassoonist *Felix Reiner* (1774; both Munich, Bayer. Nmus.).

(3) Jan Josef Horemans II [le Clair] (*b* Antwerp, *bapt* 15 Jan 1714; *d* after 1790). Son of (1) Jan Josef Horemans I. He qualified as a master of the Guild of St Luke in Antwerp on 10 February 1767 and was dean of the Guild on two occasions (1768–9 and 1775–6). He was a placid apologist for bourgeois virtues and, following his father's example, admirably recreated the atmosphere of his age in a multitude of small paintings that are pleasantly animated and have an old-fashioned charm. He also signed in the same way as his father, but his style was more distinguished and sensitive and his palette lighter (earning him the nickname that distinguishes him from his father). Works such as the *Musical Company*, the *Interior with Figures* (both Amsterdam, Rijksmus.), *The Minuet* (Geneva, Mus. A. & Hist.) and the *Portrait of a Family* (1772; Utrecht, Centraal Mus.) combine traditional genre painting with the 18th-century conversation piece. Jan Josef II sometimes incorporated into his own compositions figures taken unchanged from David Teniers (ii) or Hieronymus Janssens, as in the *New Neighbours* (Worcester, MA, A. Mus.). He also occasionally painted interior decorations, such as the wall panels of *The Seasons* (ex-Met., New York; sold New York, Christie's, 31 May 1977), and accepted a number of official commissions, such as the *Entry of*

Charles of Lorraine into Antwerp in 1749 (Antwerp, Kon. Mus. S. Kst.). He was still exhibiting paintings in Antwerp in 1790.

BIBLIOGRAPHY

BNB; Füssli; *NKLA*; Thieme–Becker
J. N. Edler von Weizenfeld: *Beschreibung der churfürstlichen Bildergallerie in Schleissheim* (Munich, 1775), pp. 92–3, 332, 334, 420–49
F. J. Lipowsky: *Baierisches Künstler-Lexikon*, i (Munich, 1810), p. 129
C. Kramm: *De levens en werken der Hollandische en Vlaamsche kunstschilders, beeldhouwers, graveurs en bouwmeesters*, iii (Amsterdam, 1859), pp. 749–50
P. Rombouts and T. Van Lerius: *De liggeren en andere historische archieven der Antwerpsche Sint Lucasgilde* (Amsterdam, 1864–7), ii
A. Michiels: *Histoire de la peinture flamande*, x (Paris, 1876), pp. 511–12
M. Rooses: *Geschiedenis der Antwerpsche schilderschool* (Ghent, 1880), p. 159
F. J. Van den Branden: *Geschiedenis der Antwerpsche schilderschool* (Antwerp, 1883), pp. 1189–93
P. Génard: *Anvers à travers les âges*, i (1888), p. 213
München im 18. Jahrhundert (exh. cat., Munich, 1901), pp. 12–13, 36, 38–9
G. J. Wolf: 'Künstler und Künstlerleben im kurfürstlichen München', *Das Bayerland*, xxxix (1928), pp. 180–81
J. J. Delen: *Catalogue des dessins: Ecoles flamande et hollandaise*, ii (Antwerp, 1938), p. 95
F. M. Heubner: *Nederlandsche en Vlaamsche rococoschilders* (The Hague, 1943), p. 50
P. Bautier: *La Peinture en Belgique au XVIIIe siècle* (Brussels, 1945), pp. 11–12, pls ix–xii
Comte d'Arschot: *Le Portrait aux XVIIe et XVIIIe siècles* (Brussels, 1945), pp. 27–8
N. Benisovich: *A. Amer.*, xxxv (1947), p. 214
H. Gerson and E. H. ter Kuile: *Art and Architecture in Belgium*, Pelican Hist. A. (Harmondsworth, 1960), p. 170
F. B. Robinson: 'Two Scenes near Nymphenbourg', *Mus. F.A. Bull.* [Springfield, MA], xxviii/4 (1962), pp. 1–4
J. G. Prinz von Hohenzollern: *Peter Jakob Horemans: Kurbayerischer Hofmaler* (exh. cat., Munich, Alte Pin., 1974)
J. A. L. de Meyerer: 'Een herontdekt schilderij van J. J. Horemans de Jongere', *Jb.: Kon. Mus. S. Kst.* (1974), pp. 201–2
The Collector's Cabinet: Flemish Painting from New England Private Collections (exh. cat. by J. Welu, Worcester, MA, A. Mus., 1983), pp. 70–71, no. 18
Bloem en tuin (exh. cat., Ghent, Mus. S. Kst.), fig. 83

ALAIN JACOBS

Horemheb [Djeserkheprure] (*reg c.* 1319–*c.* 1292 BC). Ancient Egyptian ruler and patron of the post-Amarna period. The reign of Horemheb was rich and fascinating in terms of art and architecture, although the amount of evidence is small and the situation is confused by the large number of monuments usurped from his predecessors. It would be too simplistic to consider him merely as one who restored order and traditional religious cults after the so-called anarchy or revolution of the reign of Akhenaten (*reg c.* 1353–*c.* 1336 BC). It was during the reign of Akhenaten that he first came to prominence, perhaps under the earlier name of Paatenemheb, later appearing in the monuments of Tutankhamun (*reg c.* 1332–*c.* 1323 BC) as the general-in-chief and regent, Horemheb. He became even more powerful during the reign of Ay (*reg c.* 1323–*c.* 1319 BC), whom he eventually succeeded. It is possible that his wife Mutnodjmet was of royal descent and thus conferred on him a legitimacy that he had at first lacked.

Horemheb had two tombs built: one in the Memphite necropolis at Saqqara and the other in the Valley of the Kings at Thebes (KV 57). The Memphite tomb was constructed during the reign of Tutankhamun while Horemheb was still a general and regent. It has been excavated by a joint Anglo–Dutch expedition. Before its discovery

in 1975 the tomb was known only through fragments of relief broken up and dispersed by looters during the 19th century (now in the collections of Berlin, Ägyp. Mus.; Bologna, Mus. Civ.; London, BM; New York, Brooklyn Mus.; Cairo, Egyp. Mus.; Leiden, Rijksmus. Oudhd.; Vienna, Ksthist. Mus.). Horemheb's reign included only a few genuine military campaigns, as he attempted to regain control of the Near East, but his dream of an Egypt once again omnipotent and somehow superior to its motley crowd of restless neighbours clearly shows in the reliefs in his Memphite tomb. He was never actually buried at Saqqara although he evidently became a cult figure there. The architecture and decoration of the Memphite tomb perfectly express the characteristics and successes of the Memphite sculptural style as well as the influence of Armarna-style particularism. Horemheb's royal tomb at Thebes was also highly successful, but its decoration and appointments were much more conventional than those at Saqqara. The Theban tomb included a Book of Gates (an inscription describing the afterworld) in the chamber where Horemheb's red granite sarcophagus still stands.

Apart from Horemheb's tombs his most remarkable works included the 2nd, 9th and 10th pylons of the temple of Karnak, the imposing colonnade of the temple at Luxor, the speos at GEBEL EL-SILSILA and the rock chapel at Gebel Adda in Nubia. There are only a few surviving statues of Horemheb, of which the most beautiful and impressive is a large grey granite sculpture (New York,

Scribe statue of Horemheb, grey granite, h. 1.17 m, before *c.* 1319 BC (New York, Metropolitan Museum of Art)

Met., 23.10.1; see fig.) showing him as a scribe, before his accession to the throne. This unusual portrait probably derives from the Temple of Ptah at Memphis. The years when Horemheb ruled Egypt, whether as regent or sovereign, were a period of stability and artistic success, a meeting of influences and traditions that were diverse (indeed contradictory) but always well assimilated.

BIBLIOGRAPHY

LÄ: 'Haremheb'

B. Porter and R. L. B. Moss, eds: *Topographical Bibliography*, III/ii (1931, rev. 3/1978–81), pp. 655–61, 865

R. Hari: *Horemheb et la reine Moutnedjemet* (Geneva, 1964)

E. Hornung: *Das Grab des Haremhab im Tal der Könige* (Bern, 1971)

G. T. Martin: 'Captors and Prisoners in Horemheb's Tomb', *Illus. London News* (July 1976), pp. 61–2

——: 'The Tomb of Horemheb, Commander-in-chief of Tutankhamun', *Archaeology* [New York], xxxi (1978), pp. 14–23

J. Kruchten: *Le Décret d'Horemheb* (Brussels, 1981)

G. T. Martin: *The Reliefs, Inscriptions and Commentary* (1989), i of *The Memphite Tomb of Horemheb*, i (London, 1989–)

ALAIN-PIERRE ZIVIE

Horenbout [Horenbault; Horenbaut; Hornebolte]. South Netherlandish family of artists, active in England. After achieving some considerable success as a painter and illuminator in Ghent, in the service of Margaret of Austria, (1) Gerard Horenbout moved to England with his wife, Margaretes Vanders (*d* England, 1529), and their children; this must have occurred some time between 1522 and 1525, when the name of his son (2) Lucas Horenbout first appeared in the royal household accounts of King Henry VIII. (Gerard's name figures for the first time in the accounts only three years later.) Gerard's daughter (3) Susanna Horenbout was one of the many early women artists who were active in family workshops but whose works are no longer known. The oeuvre of her brother Lucas is also difficult to establish, and both he and his father have been linked with the anonymous MASTER OF THE BRANDON PORTRAIT, though Gerard is more generally identified with the MASTER OF JAMES IV OF SCOTLAND (for both *see* MASTERS, ANONYMOUS, AND MONOGRAM-MISTS, §I).

BIBLIOGRAPHY

H. Paget: 'Gerard and Lucas Hornebolte in England', *Burl. Mag.*, ci (1959), pp. 396–402

(1) Gerard Horenbout (*b* Ghent, ?before 1465; *d* 1541 or before). Painter, designer, scribe and cartographer.

1. LIFE. He may have been the pupil of Liévin de Stoevere (*fl* 1463), the only painter of the five artists who guaranteed his admission fee into the guild of painters and illuminators in Ghent in 1487. Horenbout became a versatile and productive artist, painting altarpieces, por-traits and illuminated manuscripts and designing tapestries and stained-glass windows. He also collaborated with the nuns of the convent of Galilee near Ghent in making a model garden with flowers made of cloth that he delivered to Margaret of Austria, Regent of the Netherlands, at her court in Mechelen. He seems to have achieved a degree of wealth commensurate with his output: in 1503 he acquired a house that may have had a façade painted with figures, which was a distinct rarity. At least three of his six children—Susanna, Lucas and another son—were active in his workshop from 1521 onwards. Pupils' places in his studio were evidently much sought after, for in each of

the years between 1498 and 1502 he engaged an apprentice on unusually exacting terms. On 1 April 1515 Margaret of Austria appointed him court painter and *valet de chambre*, with permission to maintain his workshop at Ghent. He was paid on several occasions for illuminating Books of Hours. In 1522 Margaret bought a portrait of *Christian II of Denmark* (untraced) from him. Thereafter there is no further record of him in Ghent. In 1521 Dürer met him and his daughter in Antwerp.

That Gerard moved to England at the age of nearly 60 may have been due to financial stringency at the court of Mechelen: his pension was frequently in arrears. Paget speculated that Horenbout and his family may have been Lutherans, seeking refuge at the English court at a time when Protestant influence was especially strong there. Horenbout appeared in the accounts of the royal house-hold from 1528 to 1531. It is uncertain whether he ever returned to Flanders.

2. MANUSCRIPTS. A payment to Horenbout is recorded on 17 January 1521 for 16 miniatures, 2 ornamental borders and 700 gilded letters, executed in a Book of Hours for Margaret of Austria. This is now known to relate to the Book of Hours of Bona Sforza (London, BL, Add. MS. 34294), the greater part of which was written for Bona Sforza in Milan *c.* 1490 and illuminated by Giovanni Pietro Birago. The book was not completed, however, and Bona Sforza seems to have taken it with her in its imperfect state when she returned to her native Savoy in 1495. Until her death in 1503 she remained at the court of her nephew, Philibert of Savoy, who probably inherited the manuscript from her. He died in the following year, and it passed to his widow, Margaret of Austria, who took up residence in the southern Netherlands in 1506. In 1517 the copyist Etienne de Lale was paid for setting in order and completing the sheets of a Book of Hours belonging to her, '*faictes à la mode et à painctures ytaliques que avons eu de feue madame Bonne de Millan*'. Besides the pages of text added by de Lale, the manuscript today contains six miniatures and two borders that clearly belong to a later date than the Italian miniatures and must have originated in Flanders; these are the ones for which Gerard Horenbout was paid in 1521 (see fig.). The miniature of *St Mark the Evangelist* (fol. 10*v*) is dated 1519; one of the two later borders (fol. 213*r*) bears the date 1520. This border also suggests that the complete codex may have been intended as a present, since there is a portrait of Emperor Charles V at the lower edge of the sheet.

While it is certain that these illuminations are by Gerard Horenbout, it is difficult to use them as a basis for the reconstruction of the rest of his oeuvre, as it is clear that in them he was attempting to adapt his style to that of the earlier Italian miniatures. This applies not only to motifs such as the fantastic architectural backgrounds but also to the colouring, which resembles the bright multicoloured effects of Birago, and the facial types, especially those of women. Allowances must thus be made for divergences in style in other works by Gerard. Hulin de Loo, Winkler and other scholars have suggested that a group of works provisionally referred to under the name of the Master of James IV of Scotland should be ascribed to Horenbout. The main grounds for this are the similarity in the range

Gerard Horenbout: *Raising of Lazarus*, miniature from the Book of Hours of Bona Sforza, *c*. 1519–20 (London, British Library, Add. MS. 34294, fol. 257*v*)

of types and the dramatic style of composition with crowded groups of figures. The differences as compared with the Sforza Book of Hours chiefly lie in the fact that the Master of James VI expressed himself more as a draughtsman; he tended to harden the outline of mouths, noses and especially the areas around the eyes. He also used a softened palette with broken intermediate tones such as orange and violet-grey. Those who favour identifying the Master of James IV with Gerard Horenbout ascribe these differences to the latter's 'Italianizing' style in the Sforza Book of Hours, while those who dispute the identification see it rather as a matter of personal style.

Those who definitely accept the identification (e.g. Dogaer) associate the name of Gerard Horenbout with an extensive oeuvre, including such key works as the Spinola Book of Hours (Malibu, CA, Getty Mus., MS. 83), of which Horenbout would in that case have been the chief painter; a three-volume Book of Hours (Rome, Vatican, Bib. Apostolica, Cod. vat. lat. 3768–3770); and several illuminations in a Breviary (Antwerp, Mus. Mayer van den Bergh, MS. 946) and in the Rothschild Prayer Book (Vienna, Österreich. Nbib., Cod. S. n. 2844). In the Grimani Breviary (Venice, Bib. N. Marziana, MS. lat. I, 99) Gerard Horenbout would, in this view, be the author of the famous calendar pictures and, *inter alia*, the night scene of the *Nativity* (fol. 43*v*) and the remarkable full-page illustration for the Office of the Dead (fol. 449*v*; for illustration *see* GRIMANI BREVIARY), in which the circular

field in the centre affords a view of a death chamber by night, while the remaining surface of the rectangular miniature represents an open landscape in which a fierce struggle is going on between the Three Living Men and the Three Dead. The imaginative play with the aesthetic boundaries between the miniature, the text and the often historicized border is apparently a speciality of the artist. It is already seen in the Grimani Breviary (fol. 206*r*) but is carried furthest in the Spinola Book of Hours. Sometimes the text appears, as it were, to be fastened by the miniature, on painted hinges, to the outer border (e.g. fols 56*v*–57*r*) or to be pinned like a sheet of paper on to the picture field (fols 10*v*–11*r*); sometimes the miniature and border are linked together by the architecture, showing the interior and exterior of the same building (e.g. fols 21*v*, 185*r*). Often the artist used a kind of polygonal central building, opening forwards across a corner (fol. 92*v*). The density of his pictorial creations is also noteworthy. He preferred compositions with many figures, and, when he adapted older models, he often added secondary characters. When this was not possible for iconographic reasons, he filled his miniatures with detailed depictions of the interior or of the landscape, vistas and background scenes. These owe their particular liveliness to the contrast between arrangements of a still-life character or peaceful landscapes and the often tumultuous nature of the events depicted. This is reinforced by the artist's ability to reproduce facial expressions with a few broad lines in a ruthless fashion that often verges on caricature yet is always lifelike. He was especially skilful at depicting the neckless heads of gross-looking elderly men. A regular mark of his style consists in the bulging upper and lower eyelids, outlined with powerful strokes and presenting a swollen appearance; these occur even in more delicate figures such as those of women.

Although there are no documented manuscript illuminations by Horenbout coinciding with his time in England, it seems likely that he executed three large pen drawings and a preliminary drawing for an initial in the Obituary Roll of John Islip (l. *c*. 1.63 m; London, Westminster Abbey, Muniment Room & Lib.). The subject of the roll is the death and burial of John Islip, Abbot of Westminster (*d* 1532). In all probability it was to have been illuminated, but for some reason this was not carried out. Both the historical circumstances and the elaborate detail of the drawings make it possible that Gerard Horenbout was their author. His name is also associated with a number of illuminations commissioned by Cardinal Thomas Wolsey, as well as with illuminated documents, notably an Epistolary of 1528 (Oxford, Christ Church Lib., MS. 101) and an Evangeliary of 1529 (Oxford, Magdalen Coll., MS. 223).

3. PANEL PAINTINGS. The most important panel paintings to have been attributed to Gerard Horenbout on stylistic grounds are two wings of a triptych, the centre panel of which is lost; these represent the donor Lievin van Pottelsberghe and his wife, Livina van Steelandt, with their children and protecting angels (Ghent, Mus. S. Kst.). The style of the heads, especially the long, thin faces of the angels and the children's chubby faces, with firm mouths painted in a strong red hue and with a sulky expression due to the pendant lower lip, are parallelled in

the Sforza Book of Hours and justify the attribution to Gerard Horenbout, as does the realistic portrayal of the donor, with his incipient double chin and visible growth of beard. Further supporting evidence is furnished by the two illuminated Books of Hours that lie in front of the praying couple. These are depicted in loving detail as specimens of such work as might have come from Horenbout's own studio. Two further panels, a *St Christopher* (Enschede, Rijksmus. Twenthe) and a *St Lievin* (Aachen, Suermondt-Ludwig-Mus.) were attributed to Horenbout by Wescher. All others, including the Poortakker Triptych (Ghent, Mus. S. Kst.), which is signed GERARDVS on the hem of a cloak (and was therefore formerly considered a signed work), are of markedly inferior quality.

BIBLIOGRAPHY

J. Duverger: 'Gerard Horenbault (1465?–1540): Hofschilder van Margareta van Oostenrijk', *De Kunst*, i (1930), pp. 81–90

G. Hulin de Loo: 'Comment j'ai retrouvé Horenbaut', *Annu. Mus. Royaux B.-A. Belgique*, ii (1939), pp. 3–21

F. Winkler: 'Neuentdeckte Altniederländer, II: Gerard Horenbout', *Pantheon*, xvi (1943), pp. 54–64

P. Wescher: 'Sanders and Simon Bening and Gerard Horenbout', *A.Q.* [Detroit], ix (1946), pp. 190–211

——: 'Beiträge zu Sanders und Simon Bening und Gerard Horenbout', *Festschrift Friedrich Winkler* (Berlin, 1959), pp. 126–35

A. Grote, ed.: *Breviarium Grimani: Faksimileausgabe der Miniaturen und Kommentar* (Berlin, 1973)

Gent: Duizend jaar kunst en cultuur (exh. cat., Ghent, Mus. S. Kst., 1975), pp. 190–91, 198–200

A. von Euw and J. M. Plotzek: *Die Handschriften der Sammlung Ludwig*, ii (Cologne, 1982), pp. 256–85, figs 387–468

Renaissance Painting in Manuscripts: Treasures from the British Library (exh. cat. by T. Kren, Malibu, CA, Getty Mus.; New York, Pierpont Morgan Lib.; London, BL; 1984), pp. 8–9, 63–8, 113–22

G. Dogaer: *Flemish Miniature Painting in the 15th and 16th Centuries* (Amsterdam, 1987), pp. 161–7

Lucas Horenbout (attrib.): *Henry VIII*, gouache on parchment, laid down on card, 53×48 mm, 1525–6 (Cambridge, Fitzwilliam Museum)

(2) Lucas Horenbout (*b* Ghent, ?1490–95; *d* London, 1544). Miniature painter, son of (1) Gerard Horenbout. By 1531 he was a court painter at the English court of Henry VIII, and in 1534 this office was conferred on him for life. No surviving work can be attributed to him with certainty (although Strong suggested an oeuvre of some 23 miniature portraits, all of courtiers). This is partly because, during his long career as court painter, he was paid a large fixed annuity rather than a negotiable fee for individual commissions. However, according to van Mander, it was Lucas Horenbout who introduced Hans Holbein the younger to the art of painting portrait miniatures. Lucas has been plausibly credited with the earliest of all English portrait miniatures, probably pendants representing *Henry VIII* (Cambridge, Fitzwilliam; see fig.) and *Catherine of Aragon* (Duke of Buccleuch priv. col.), both datable 1525–6. On stylistic grounds, certain other portrait miniatures as well as book illuminations may be added, for example the frontispiece of the *Liber Niger* of the Order of the Garter (Windsor Castle, Berks, Royal Lib.) or the two frontispieces in the royal book of valuations, the *Valor ecclesiasticus* (1535; London, PRO, E.344/22).

BIBLIOGRAPHY

K. van Mander: *Schilder-boeck* ([1603]–1604)

Artists of the Tudor Court: The Portrait Miniature Rediscovered, 1520–1620 (exh. cat. by R. Strong, London, V&A, 1983), pp. 34–43

(3) Susanna Horenbout (*fl c.* 1520–50). Illuminator, daughter of (1) Gerard Horenbout. Dürer mentioned her in the diary of his visit to the Netherlands in 1521, as follows: 'Master Gerard, the illuminator, has a daughter of 18 named Susanna who has illuminated a small sheet, a Salvator, for which I gave her 1 guilder. It is a great marvel that a woman should do so much'. After moving with her parents to England, Susanna married John Parker, the royal Yeoman of the Robes (*d* 1537–8); thereafter she married John Gylmyn. She is mentioned as a painter and also on several occasions as a lady-in-waiting. She was still alive in 1550. However, attempts to attribute particular portrait miniatures to her are even more hypothetical than in the case of her brother Lucas.

BIBLIOGRAPHY

D. G. Bachmann and S. Piland: *Women Artists: An Historical, Contemporary and Feminist Bibliography* (Metuchen, NJ, 1978)

BODO BRINKMANN

Horiguchi, Sutemi (*b* Gifu Prefect., 6 Jan 1895). Japanese architect and writer. He studied ancient Japanese architecture under Chūta Itō at Tokyo Imperial University; he graduated in 1920 and in that year he founded the Japan Secession Group together with other students from the university including Mamoru Yamada. This was the first movement in support of modern architecture in Japan and its members were greatly influenced by Expressionism. In 1922 he obtained a master's degree with a study of modern Western architecture and from 1923 to 1924 he travelled in Europe. Many of the works he produced after his return, for instance the Kikkawa House (1930) and the Wakasa House (1940), both in Tokyo, are statements of Rationalist architecture: white cubic designs accentuated by the horizontal lines of the eaves, they reflected his position at the leading edge of architectural theory in Japan. During this period he also taught at the Imperial

Art Institute in Tokyo (1932–8) and continued his research on the traditional architecture of Japan: he received his PhD (1944) from Tokyo Imperial University with a dissertation on *shoin* (study; *see* JAPAN, §III, 4(ii)) and *sukiya* (tea house; *see* JAPAN, §XIV, 2) styles of Japanese residential architecture, and he ultimately became one of Japan's most respected authorities on the tea house. After World War II he developed a sophisticated style of modern *sukiya* architecture, producing masterpieces that brought together the refinement of the *shoin* and the lucidity of the *sukiya* styles. Examples include the Emperor's Room (1950) at Hasshyokan Hotel, Nagoya, and the *Nakamise* (1953; rebuilt in 1967 after a fire) at the same hotel; the *ryōtei* or traditional restaurant (1955) at Uemura, Tokyo, and the Japanese Pavilion at the Biennale in São Paulo (1955). In 1949 Horiguchi was invited by Meiji University, Toyko, to become a founder member of its Architecture Department and he subsequently designed a long series of buildings for the university including campus buildings at Surugadai (1955–9), Izumi (1956–60) and Ikuta (1964–5). All these are finished in white and are characterized by the crispness typical of the best works of Rationalist architecture.

WRITINGS
Sōtei [Grass garden] (Tokyo, 1948)
Rikyū no Chashitsu [Tea rooms of Rikyū] (Tokyo, 1949)
Katsura Rikyū [Katsura Detached Palace] (Tokyo, 1952)

BIBLIOGRAPHY
I. Kurita, ed.: *Horiguchi Sutemi*, Gendai Nihon kenchikuka zenshū [Complete collection of modern Japanese architects], iv (Tokyo, 1971)

KATSUYOSHI ARAI

Horiuchi, Masakazu (*b* Kyoto, 27 March 1911). Japanese sculptor. He experimented with Constructivist sculpture in 1927 under the influence of such avant-garde sculptors as Tomoyoshi Murayama (1901–77). In 1928 he entered the sculpture department of the Higher Technical College in Tokyo; in 1929 he was accepted into the Nika-Ten exhibition and left college. At the Nikakai (Second Division Association) he studied under sculptor Yūzō Fujikawa (1883–1935). During World War II he stopped sculpting and learnt French and Latin. In 1950 he became a professor at the City College of Art in Kyoto, holding the post until 1974. From 1954 he began making sculptures from welded steel, creating such works as *Five Squares and Five Rectangles* (steel, 770 mm, 1955; Tokyo, Met. A. Mus.). In 1957 he exhibited in the fourth São Paulo Biennale. In 1963 he was awarded the sixth Takamura Kōtarō prize. In the same year an exhibition of his work was held at the Museum of Modern Art in Kamakura. In 1967 he exhibited at the ninth International Sculpture Biennale at Antwerp (Openluchtmus. Beeldhouwkst Middelheim). In the same year he exhibited *Mimichan Winking* (steel, other, h. 400 mm, 1967; Kamakura, Kanagawa Prefect. Mus. Mod. A.) at the second Gendai Nihon Chōkoku Ten (Contemporary Sculpture Exhibition, Japan) in Ube, Yamaguchi Prefecture. This work characterizes the humorous nature of Horiuchi's work. In 1969 he received the Grand Prize at the first Gendai Kokusai Chōkoku Ten (International exhibition of contemporary sculpture) at the Hakone Open-Air Museum, Hakone-machi. Thereafter he produced many sculptures of sliced spheres and fused cubes that could be described as intellectual brain teasers, for example *Ways to Slice a Sphere* (bronze, h. 450 mm, 1970; Tokyo, N. Mus. Mod. A.) and *Zigzag Cubes* (stainless steel, h. 1.06 m, 1974; Tochigi, Prefect. Mus. F.A.).

BIBLIOGRAPHY
Yamaguchi Takeo to Horiuchi Masakazu [Takeo Yamaguchi and Masakazu Horiuchi] (exh. cat., essay by K. Motoe; Tokyo, N. Mus. Mod. A., 1980)
Horiuchi Masakazu (exh. cat., essay by I. Hariu; Tokyo, Shōtō Mus. A., 1986)

YASUYOSHI SAITO

Hörmann. *See* HERMANN.

Hörmann, Theodor von (*b* Imst, Tyrol, 13 Dec 1840; *d* Graz, 1 July 1895). Austrian painter. He initially followed a career as an army officer and took part in the campaigns against Italy (1859) and Prussia (1866). From 1869 until 1875 he studied painting at the Akademie der Bildenden Künste in Vienna, and he then became a tutor in freehand drawing and in fencing at a military academy. He came to know the *plein-air* landscape painter Emil Jakob Schindler (1842–92), who had a lasting influence on his work, as seen in the impressionistic approach in the *Mill Forge* (1882; Vienna, Niederösterreich. Landesmus.). Hörmann left the army in 1884 to devote himself to painting.

In 1881–6 Hörmann travelled extensively in Hungary, producing colourful scenes of the countryside, such as *Hungarian Landscape with Cattle Drinking* (1884; Vienna, Belvedere). Between 1886 and 1890 he lived in Paris and travelled through various parts of France. His experience of French Impressionism encouraged and controlled his exploration of a freer approach to painting. During this time he produced works notable for their lively, sketchy manner, such as the *Tuileries Gardens* (1888; Vienna, Belvedere). Paintings made subsequently in Znaim (now Znojmo, Czech Republic) between 1890 and 1893 are notable for their luminosity of colour, as in the glowing pinks and greens of the vegetation in the *Field of Sainfoin near Znaim* (1893; Vienna, Belvedere).

In 1893 Hörmann became a student of Adolf Hölzel in Dachau, near Munich, where he had already produced several paintings striking for their use of vibrant colour, for example *Biergarten in Dachau* (1892; Imst, Heimatmus.). Hörmann's Impressionism brought him into conflict with the conservative members of the Wiener Künstlerhaus, who cultivated a traditional, idealizing approach. In a small publication Hörmann criticized this attitude and championed the group of young Viennese artists who were striving to follow international trends. This support encouraged the foundation, in 1897, of the Vienna Secession, which was much influenced by the advent of Impressionism.

WRITINGS
Künstler-Empfindungen: Ein Rückblick auf einige Bildwerke der XXI. Jahresausstellung im Wiener Künstlerhause, 1892 (Vienna, 1892)

BIBLIOGRAPHY
T. Braunegger and M. Hörmann-Weingartner: *Theodor von Hörmann* (Vienna, 1979)

EDWIN LACHNIT

Horn. Permanent keratinous sheath surrounding the bony outgrowth (*os cornu*) on the skulls of animals such as cattle, goats, antelope and sheep. It is a modified form of skin

Horn objects of English manufacture (clockwise, from top left): silver-mounted drinking horn, l. 300 mm, 20th century; horn beaker with glass bottom, h. 110 mm, 19th century; horn book, 110×85 mm, 17th century; engraved powder horn, l. 225 mm, early 19th century; pressed horn box, diam. 85 mm, 18th century; (centre) horn caddy spoon, l. 97 mm, 19th century (London, Museum of London)

tissue and should not be confused with the bony and deciduous antlers or 'horns' of certain species of deer. In the past most kinds of horn have been used, including, in China, rhinoceros horn (*see* CHINA, §XIII, 21), but modern application is confined to horn from European and African cattle and sheep and particularly from domestic buffalo and goats.

Once removed from its bony core, horn is more or less hollow, with only the tip being solid. The proportion of solid tip to hollow body varies from species to species or, in the case of domestic animals, with breed, as do colour and shape. The material is supremely utilitarian, being light and strong but quite easily worked with simple tools. It can be sawn, filed, drilled, carved and turned on a lathe. Pieces can be fixed together by jointing, glueing, screwing or nailing. Horn is thermoplastic and can be softened by boiling or steaming to produce flat sheets or simple shapes using dies and moulds, which can then have designs stamped or pressed on to them.

A typical kit of horners' tools contains saws for cutting the horn to size and shape and a selection of files, rasps and floats for surface preparation, shaping and finishing. Steel scrapers are used for fine finishing, gravers of various kinds for engraved decoration, chisels, gouges and knives for carved work and drills for making fixing holes or for pierced work, which can then be completed using a piercing or fret-saw. Larger equipment includes boilers or steamers for softening the horn and presses for flattening sheets or making cups, beakers or boxes and for ornamental die pressing. A lathe, together with a variety of profiled cutters and scrapers, is used for turned work.

Horn can be used virtually unmodified to produce drinking, powder and sounding horns (trumpets). The hollow portion can be cut transversely to produce beakers, cups and circular boxes; or sliced longitudinally, flattened, split and then further moulded to make knife scales, book covers, lantern (lanthorn) plates and shoe horns; or cut and filed into combs and brush backs (see fig.). The solid tip can be cut transversely to make buttons, toggles and bottle or jar stoppers. It can be used in its natural state for cutlery handles or turned to make small cylindrical objects of various types. These products can then be further ornamented by carving, engraving, hot pressing, turning and polishing. Some of the finest examples of horn-carvings are found in Japanese *netsuke* (*see* JAPAN, §XVI, 17).

BIBLIOGRAPHY
A. MacGregor: *Bone, Antler, Ivory and Horn* (Beckenham, 1941)
P. Hardwick: *Discovering Horn* (London, 1981)

FRANK MINNEY

Horn, Rebecca (*b* Michelstadt, 24 March 1944). German sculptor and film maker. She studied at the Hochschule für Bildende Künste in Hamburg (1964–70). After a period in London (1971–2), she lived for a long time in New York, with visits to Berlin and a visiting lectureship at the California Art Institute, Los Angeles, in 1974. In 1968 she produced her first body sculptures, in which she attached objects and instruments to the human body, taking as her theme the contact between a person and his or her environment. Artificial extensions of fingers and arms, antenna-like headpieces or disguises for the whole body illustrate the various sensitive functions of the human body (e.g. *Arm Extensions*, 1968; see 1983 exh. cat., p. 21).

From 1970 Horn documented her work using video and film, establishing a connection between sculpture and action. She increasingly used feathers, for example in masks or constructions that enclose the entire body, closing off the wearer from the environment. The spectator's occasional glimpses through the constructions produce a high level of intimacy; in *Widow of Paradise* (see 1983 exh. cat., p. 39), the coat of feathers becomes a cave-like container. In *Chinese Fiancées* (see 1977 exh. cat.) it is the spectator who becomes the focus of the action. In a completely darkened cabinet, which closes automatically, the spectator is exposed to the voices of two Chinese girls speaking continuously. Concentrating on these pleasant and, to him, incomprehensible sounds, the spectator is finally released into the wealth of sense impressions of the bright, lively gallery space.

In the films *Der Eintänzer* (1978) and *La Ferdinanda—Sonate für eine Medici-Villa* (1981) Horn placed her individual actions and objects within a narrative sequence. The intervals show two people or objects making contact with each other: in the tactile sense, having to cover a spatial distance or hindered by reduced mobility; verbally, through difficulties in comprehension; or, visually, through impaired vision. In the film *Buster's Bedroom* (1989–90) and in the more extensive, room-filling installations of the 1980s and early 1990s, Horn's central themes are elaborated with an increasing narrative sense.

BIBLIOGRAPHY
Rebecca Horn: Objekte, Video, Filme (exh. cat., Cologne, Kstver.; W. Berlin, Haus Waldsee; 1977)
Rebecca Horn (exh. cat., Zurich, Ksthaus; London, Serpentine Gal.; Chicago, IL, Mus. Contemp. A.; and elsewhere; 1983–4)
Nuit et jour sur le dos du serpent à deux têtes (exh. cat., Paris, Mus. A. Mod. Ville Paris, 1986)
Diving through Buster's Bedroom (exh. cat., Los Angeles, CA, Mus. Contemp. A., 1990)
Rebecca Horn (exh. cat. by J. Bruno and others, New York, Guggenheim; Eindhoven, Stedel. Van Abbemus.; London, Tate; and elsewhere; 1993–5)

BEATRICE V. BISMARCK

Horne, Sir **Herbert (Percy)** (*b* London, 18 Feb 1864; *d* Florence, 14 April 1916). English collector, art historian, designer and architect. He joined the architectural practice of A. H. MACKMURDO as an associate in 1883 and was a partner from 1885 to 1890. Together they were leading members of the CENTURY GUILD OF ARTISTS (*c.* 1883–92). At this time he developed his skills as a graphic artist, creating designs for textiles, furniture and objects (e.g. London, William Morris Gal.), as well as decorative initial letters and elegant foliar and zoomorphic motifs that appeared in the *Century Guild Hobby Horse* magazine. The Horne–Mackmurdo partnership produced plans for Brewhouse Yard at Eton College and also for a series of houses in Uxbridge Road, London (both unexecuted). In 1889 Mrs Russell Gurney commissioned Horne to design the Chapel of the Ascension in Bayswater Road, London, decorated by Frederic Shields (destr. World War II).

The turning-point in Horne's life and artistic development came when he was commissioned by the London publisher George Bell to write a monograph on Botticelli; for this reason he began making sporadic visits to Florence in 1894, settling there in 1905. During the 1890s he wrote a number of carefully researched articles on important figures in Florentine Trecento and Quattrocento art. In 1908 Horne published his volume on Botticelli, a fundamental reference work, in which the two strands of his interests, in archival research and connoisseurship, come together. It contained a wealth of new information on the artist's life and times and reveals Horne's highly developed pictorial sense, which led him to isolate in some of Botticelli's greatest works (including the *Birth of Venus*, Florence, Uffizi) elements that he believed to be by other hands. Although largely his own invention, his methods did coincide to some extent with the Morellian techniques of Bernard Berenson and the more formal visual analysis of Roger Fry.

Horne collected with extraordinary zeal and acumen, his activities as an art dealer providing him with the funds to acquire large numbers of objects of both artistic and historical interest. In 1899 he entered into an agreement with Berenson to buy and sell works of art. He was consultant to the American collector John G. Johnson, whom he encouraged to buy four predella panels by Botticelli (Philadelphia, PA, Mus. A.), and he acted together with Fry as agent for the Metropolitan Museum, New York.

In 1911 Horne bought the Palazzo Corsi in Florence to house his collection; this included paintings by Florentine and Sienese 'Primitive' and early Renaissance masters (e.g. Giotto's *St Stephen*), sculpture of the 13th to 17th centuries (e.g. *St Paul* by il Vecchietta), Italian Old Master prints and drawings of the 15th to 18th centuries (by, among others, Salvator Rosa and Giambattista Tiepolo) and works by such English artists as Alexander and John Robert Cozens and Thomas Gainsborough.

Horne sought to recapture the high ideals of civilization and rationalism expressed in the Florentine Renaissance by re-creating the interior of a Quattrocento house, gathering together furniture and everyday domestic objects, as well as assembling an extensive library and invaluable archive. He bequeathed the palazzo and its contents to the Italian State and it opened to the public as the Museo Horne.

UNPUBLISHED SOURCES

Florence, Fond. Horne, Archv, sect. III, cat. nos 1–92 [Horne papers; notes and observations on Florentine artists of the 14th to 16th c., diaries, corr., drgs and publisher's proofs]

Florence, Fond. Horne, Lib., inv. 2581 [Horne papers; proofs for the planned second vol. devoted to the school of Botticelli and his followers]

Oxford, E. Chaney priv. col. [illus. j. of visit to Italy with Frederick Shields, 7 Sept to 10 Oct 1889]

WRITINGS

'A Study of Inigo Jones', *C. Guild Hobby Horse*, i (1886), pp. 123–39

The Binding of Books: An Essay in the History of Gold-tooled Bindings (London, 1894)

trans.: *The Life of Michelangelo Buonarroti Collected by Ascanio Condivi da La Ripa Transone* (Boston, 1904)

'Andrea del Castagno', *Burl. Mag.*, vii (1905), pp. 66–9, 222–30 [on his early life and works]

Alessandro Filipepi Commonly Called Sandro Botticelli, Painter of Florence (London, 1908); *R* with preface by J. Pope Hennessy (Princeton, 1980, rev. Florence, 1986)

'A Commentary upon Vasari's Life of Jacopo del Casentino', *Riv. A.*, vi (1909), pp. 95–112; 165–84

BIBLIOGRAPHY

The Herbert Horne Collection of Drawings with Special Reference to the Works of Alexander Cozens (exh. cat., London, Burlington F.A. Club, 1916)

F. Saxl: 'Three Florentines: Herbert Horne, A. Warburg, Jacques Mesnil', *Lectures: The Warburg Institute, University of London*, i (London, 1957), pp. 331–44

F. Rossi: *Il Museo Horne a Firenze* (Milan, 1966) [inc. cat. of works, with extensive bibliog.]

I. Fletcher: 'H. Horne: The Earlier Phase', *Eng. Misc.*, xxi (1970), pp. 117–57

D. Sutton: 'Herbert Horne: A Pioneer Historian of Early Italian Art', *Apollo*, cxxi (1985), pp. 130–59 [with add. sections of letters from Horne to Roger Fry and biog. index]

L. Morozzi: *Le carte archivistiche della Fondazione Herbert P. Horne* (Florence, 1988)

——: 'Appunti su Herbert Horne, collezionista e studioso inglese a Firenze tra la fine dell'ottocento e gli inizi del novecento', *Atti del convegno l'idea di Firenze: Firenze, 1986*, pp. 211–22

I. Fletcher: *Rediscovering Herbert Horne. Poet, Architect, Art Historian* (Greensboro, NC, 1990)

B. Preyer: *Il Palazzo Corsi-Horne: Dal diario di restauro di H. P. Horne* (Rome, 1993)

E. Chaney: *The Evolution of the Grand Tour* (London, 1996)

LUISA MOROZZI

Horne, Sir William (Cornelius) van. *See* VAN HORNE, WILLIAM.

Hornel, E(dward) A(tkinson) (*b* Bacchus Marsh, Victoria, Australia, 11 July 1864; *d* Kirkcudbright, Dumfries & Galloway, 30 June 1933). Scottish painter. His parents left Australia shortly after his birth and returned to their home town of Kirkcudbright, where Hornel spent most of his life. After studying painting at the Trustees' Academy in Edinburgh (1880–83) he attended the Antwerp Academy. In 1885 he returned to Scotland and met the painter George Henry, a friend of James Guthrie and a member of the GLASGOW BOYS.

Henry joined Hornel in Kirkcudbright for the summer of 1886, and Hornel adopted the square-brush technique and naturalist manner of Henry and the Glasgow school. Gradually both painters abandoned the tonal painting of earlier years for a more full-bodied palette of strong, clear colour. The wide field of view of their naturalist paintings gave way to more restricted compositions, their experiments culminating in two pictures painted jointly, *The Druids* (1890) and the *Star in the East* (1891; both Glasgow, A.G. & Mus.). Their subject-matter increasingly relied on the theme of young girls in a woodland setting, often accompanied by farm animals. These were not the realist subjects of Guthrie and the Glasgow school, however, but were more concerned with the intertwining symbolism of subject, colour, rhythm and pattern, as in *Summer* (1891; Liverpool, Walker A.G.).

The elements of Japonisme in *Summer* were typical of both Hornel and Henry at this date. In February 1894 they began an 18-month visit to Japan (financed by the art dealer Alexander Reid) to study its art and culture by taking part in Japanese daily life rather than travelling as tourists. The many works they produced there, for instance Hornel's the *Fish Pool* (1894; Glasgow, A.G. & Mus), reflect their assimilation of the Japanese sense of colour and composition.

On his return to Kirkcudbright, Hornel gradually severed contact with Henry and other members of the Glasgow school. He returned to the theme of young girls in fields and woodland, picking flowers or chasing butterflies. He composed his works with the aid of photographs and painted in a heavy impasto which eventually obliterated the sense of pattern which had characterized similar paintings in the early 1890s. The quality of these pictures declined after 1910 but they remained popular and sold well. He also occasionally produced paintings inspired by later visits to Burma and Ceylon. He never married and devoted his growing income to his house and studio in Kirkcudbright, with its fine Japanese garden and his collection of rare Scottish books, and to foreign travel.

BIBLIOGRAPHY

W. R. Hardie: 'E. A. Hornel Reconsidered', *Scot. A. Rev.*, xi (1968), no. 3, pp. 19–21, 27; no. 4, pp. 22–6

D. Irwin and F. Irwin: *Scottish Painters at Home and Abroad, 1700–1900* (London, 1975), pp. 373, 379–93 [with excellent bibliog.]

Mr Henry and Mr Hornel Visit Japan (exh. cat., ed. W. Buchanan; Edinburgh, Scot. A.C., 1978)

Edward Atkinson Hornel, 1864–1933 (exh. cat., ed. R. Billcliffe; Glasgow, F. A. Soc., 1982)

R. Billcliffe: *The Glasgow Boys: The Glasgow School of Painting, 1875–1895* (London, 1985) [most comprehensive account and selection of pls]

ROGER BILLCLIFFE

Hornick [Hornay; Horneck;, Hörnickh; Horninck], **Erasmus** (*b* Antwerp, ?early 16th century; *d* Prague, 1583). Flemish goldsmith, printmaker and draughtsman, active in Germany. He trained as a goldsmith in Antwerp and was probably already established in Augsburg by 1555, when he married Afra Haug, who was from a prominent Augsburg patrician family. Between 1559 and 1566 he was active in Nuremberg. Because of his reputation as a goldsmith, Nuremberg's city council honoured him in 1559 with citizenship, and in 1563 he was admitted to the goldsmiths' guild. After giving up his Nuremberg citizenship in 1566, Hornick presumably returned to Augsburg, where he is recorded in 1568, in 1570 (when he remarried) and again in 1578.

Although Hornick's contemporaries held his goldsmith work in high esteem, no examples by his hand have been positively identified. His known oeuvre includes 83 etchings plus over 600 drawings attributed to him or his workshop on the basis of his prints. Most of the etchings were published as pattern books of vessels (1565; Hollstein, nos 42–59), medallions with mythological scenes

(Hollstein, nos 64–73) and other jewellery (1562; Hollstein, nos 1–20). It is not entirely clear why Hornick's workshop created so many drawings of goldsmith ornament, among them numerous variants and repetitions. Besides workshop designs, they were intended perhaps as models for patrons, other goldsmiths, or for more pattern books, or perhaps even for princely drawing collections, to which many can be traced. The prints and drawings reflect Hornick's Mannerist taste for a profusion of ornament and densely filled, complex and fanciful forms, some too bizarre or impractical for actual goldsmith work. Hornick's originality and influence are best discerned in fashionable pendants of figures within arched niches that were modelled on his designs, for example the pendant depicting *Susanna and the Elders* (1565; Hollstein, no. 29). In 1582 his appointment as imperial goldsmith to Rudolf II, Holy Roman Emperor (*reg* 1576–1612), took him to the court in Prague, where he died the following year.

BIBLIOGRAPHY

Hollstein: *Ger.*; Thieme–Becker

J. F. Hayward: *Virtuoso Goldsmiths and the Triumph of Mannerism* (London, 1976), pp. 243–51

Y. Hackenbroch: *Renaissance Jewellery* (London, 1979), pp. 156–63

JANE S. PETERS

Horny, Franz Theobald (*b* Weimar, 23 Nov 1798; *d* Olevano, nr Rome, 23 June 1824). German painter. He received his first instruction in art from his father, Conrad Horny (1764–1807), a painter and copperplate engraver, who taught at the Zeichenschule in Weimar. He attended this school from 1806 to 1816, training primarily as a painter of landscapes. In 1816, his patron Baron Carl Friedrich von Rumohr, a friend of his father, enabled him to travel to Italy. In Rome Horny became a student of Joseph Anton Koch, who introduced him to landscape composition in the classically heroic style. Through eager study, both from nature and from live models, Horny's skills developed swiftly, especially in his work in pen and watercolour (e.g. *View of Olevano with Shepherds and a Hermit*, 1817; Dresden, Kupferstichkab.). Horny was soon, however, drawn into the circle of the Lukasbrüder: Peter Joseph Cornelius persuaded him to participate in the major fresco project for the Casino Massimo in Rome. Horny completed a large number of pen and watercolour drawings (e.g. Weimar, Schlossmus.) depicting flowers, fruit and birds, and intended as wreaths and festoons to frame Cornelius's historical scenes from Dante's *Paradiso*. When Cornelius was recalled to Munich in 1818, however, this fresco was not carried out and Horny's designs were therefore not used. In the same year, Horny developed tuberculosis and moved to Olevano for his health. The rugged beauty of the Sabine Hills and their picturesque towns drew him back to the depiction of landscape. His drawings, combining Koch's classically heroic outlook with the poetic sensibility of the Lukasbrüder, often convey the impression of an earthly paradise, as in *Italian Country Life* (*c.* 1820; Lübeck, St Annen-Mus.). In his sketchbooks (e.g. Weimar, Schlossmus.; Hamburg, Ksthalle) and magnificently composed watercolours (e.g. U. Würzburg, Wagner-Mus.; Heidelberg, Kurpfälz. Mus.; Düsseldorf, Kstmus.), he may be seen as one of the principal exponents of the German school of landscape painters working in

Italy. His watercolour *Rome in the Renaissance* (1821; Heidelberg, Kurpfälz. Mus.) attests to his experiments in history painting.

WRITINGS

E. L. Schellenberg, ed.: *Der Maler Franz Horny: Briefe und Zeugnisse* (Berlin, 1925)

BIBLIOGRAPHY

M. Goltermann: *Franz Horny, 1798–1824: Ein Beitrag zur Künstler- und Kunstgeschichte der Romantik* (Frankfurt, 1927)

W. Scheidig: *Franz Horny* (Berlin, 1954)

M. Bernhard, ed.: *Deutsche Romantik: Handzeichnungen* (Munich, 1973), pp. 586–628

I Nazareni a Roma (exh. cat., Rome, G.N.A. Mod., 1981), pp. 131–41

INGRID SATTEL BERNARDINI

Höroldt [Herold; Heroldt], **Johann Gregorius** (*bapt* Jena, 6 Aug 1696; *d* Meissen, 26 Jan 1775). German porcelain painter. He probably received his initial training as a painter in Strasbourg and later as a tapestry designer in Vienna. He was brought to Dresden in the second week of April 1720 by the Meissen arcanist Samuel Stöltzel; his success was reported the following month. For the next 50 years he was the dominant figure in the decorating workshop at the Meissen Porcelain Factory. Höroldt was responsible for both the recruitment and training of a team of painters and for the development of the colours used. Between 1720 and 1731, apart from refining the underglaze blue already developed by David Köhler (*d* 1722), he created 16 new enamel colours to supplement or replace the opaque, thick tones used during the early period when Johann Friedrich Böttger was in charge. During this same decade Höroldt laid down the basis for the efficient running of his workshop, which was to be the pattern for all similar European operations.

As porcelain decoration was a completely new phenomenon in Europe, Höroldt was responsible for the establishment of the technical means of production and the creation of a new decorative vocabulary for the medium. The large collection of Japanese and Chinese porcelains, owned by Frederick-Augustus I, Elector of Saxony (*reg* 1694–1733), was accessible to Höroldt and he was encouraged to imitate their decoration. These copies, remarkable for their close adherence to their East Asian prototypes, were a blind alley artistically; the wares inspired by Japanese Kakiemon porcelain, however, were to have a profound and enduring influence on the subsequent history of porcelain throughout Europe. From them Höroldt derived a confident and fluid, floral style known as *indianische Blumen*, which was combined with amusing chinoiseries (e.g. vase, 1726; Dresden, Porzellansamml.), many of which were drawn by Höroldt and preserved in a sketchbook known as the Schultz-Codex (1725; Leipzig, Mus. Ksthandwks). These scenes were usually framed with elaborate *Laub und Bandelwerk*, cartouches in iron-red, gold and, later, puce. The workshop system established by Höroldt meant that all his painters had access to these patterns, and the different subjects from the sketchbook are found on Meissen wares by various workers over a period of 15 years.

After the arrival of Johann Joachim Kändler (1731) and his appointment as Modellmeister (1733), Höroldt's role as the dominant creative force at the factory diminished and a bitter struggle ensued between painter and modeller for control of the shape and surface decoration of the wares, which became increasingly moulded. Höroldt built up an impressive team of decorators who were anonymous but whose individual styles may be identified; certain artists left work signed with cryptic marks or even initials. Outstanding painters included Phillip Emmanuel Schindler (*b* 1695), Christian Friedrich Herold (1700–79), Bonaventura Gottlieb Hauer (1710–70) and Johann Georg Wagner (1710–97). Höroldt signed pieces made for his wife Rachel Eleonore Höroldt and father-in-law Gottfried Kiel. Examples dated 1724 for Kiel and 1726 for Beate Kiel are in the Rijksmuseum, Amsterdam, and the British Museum, London.

BIBLIOGRAPHY
S. Ducret: 'Frühmeissner Dekors', *Mittbl.: Ker.-Freunde Schweiz*, 1 (1960)
R. Ruckert: *Meissener Porzellan* (Munich, 1966)
H. Morley-Fletcher: *Meissen* (London, 1971)

HUGO MORLEY-FLETCHER

Horovitz, Bela (*b* Budapest, 18 April 1898; *d* New York, 8 March 1955). Austrian publisher, active in England; he acquired British nationality in 1946. He founded Phaidon Verlag with Ludwig Goldscheider in Vienna in 1923 and initially published bibliophile editions of literature with great attention to good design. This was followed by literary masterpieces and contemporary criticism, and in 1930 the firm began publishing classics of writing on history in large, well-illustrated and inexpensive editions. Historical biographies followed, and among them the first three of the many that Phaidon devoted to great artists: *Leben Michaelangelos* and *Velázquez und sein Jahrhundert* (both London, 1933) and *Raphael* (London, 1941, 2/?1948). In 1933 Phaidon published their first large-format monographs in several different language editions, on Van Gogh (Vienna and London, 1936), the Impressionists (Vienna, 1937) and Botticelli (Vienna, 1937), which established the firm's reputation for high quality reproduction and an international outlook. On the annexation of Austria in 1938 Sir Stanley Unwin (1884–1968) nominally took over the firm, and the company was transferred to London, where Horovitz retained control of editorial policy, and the firm of Allen and Unwin acted as distributors. At this time Horovitz was asked to publish a critical catalogue of the Old Master drawings in the British Royal collection, and the first volume appeared in 1942.

After World War II Phaidon expanded and extended its range of titles to include, for example, the series of 'pocket' classics on the history of art and civilization. E. H. Gombrich's *The Story of Art* was published in 1950, and in the early 1950s there were numerous 'colour books' devoted to great artists. In 1952 Horovitz published a very successful illustrated edition of Bernard Berenson's essays on *The Italian Painters of the Renaissance*, and in 1954 the first two volumes of Otto Benesch's complete edition of Rembrandt's drawings, *The Drawings of Rembrandt* (6 vols, 1954–7). Horovitz died the following year, having achieved his aim of successfully publishing high quality books at low prices for an increasingly large popular market worldwide.

BIBLIOGRAPHY
Phaidon Jubilee Catalogue, 1923–1973 (London, 1973)

VALERIE HOLMAN

Horovitz, Leopold [Lipót] (*b* Kassa [now Košice, Slovak Republic], 2 Feb 1838; *d* Vienna, 16 Nov 1917). Hungarian painter. After attending drawing classes in Kassa, he continued his studies at the Akademie der Bildenden Künste in Vienna. In 1860 he won a scholarship, enabling him to travel to Paris, where he settled, painting mostly portraits and genre pictures. In 1868 he moved to Warsaw, where he completed the biblical composition *Anniversary of the Destruction of Jerusalem* and painted a series of portraits of Polish and Russian aristocrats. Horovitz had his greatest success with his portraits, for which he was internationally renowned. Like Fülöp Elek László, and several other Hungarian portrait painters, Horovitz was able to travel widely in order to carry out portrait commissions. Between 1901 and 1906 he painted *Emperor Francis Joseph* five times. He also painted a number of leading figures in Hungarian political, scientific and literary circles, for example *Ferenc Pulszky* (1890; Budapest, N.G.).

BIBLIOGRAPHY
Ö. Gerő: *Müvészetről, müvészekről* [On art and artists] (Budapest, n.d.), pp. 232–40
I. Nagy: 'Lipót Horovitz', *Képzőmüveszeti Szemle* [Formative fine arts review] (1879), pp. 110–11
T. Szana: *Magyar müvészek* [Hungarian artists] (Budapest, 1889), pp. 113–28
Leopold Horovitz, 1838–1917 (exh. cat., Košice, Mus. E. Slovakia, 1938)

KATALIN GELLÉR

Horrix. Dutch furniture manufacturing company. Members of the Horrix family had been active as furniture-makers in The Hague from 1764. In 1850 the brothers Matthieu Horrix (*b* ?3 Jan 1815; *d* ?29 May 1889) and Willem Horrix (*b* ?9 Jan 1816; *d* ?17 Feb 1881), who had trained in the family workshops and completed their apprenticeships in Paris, set up the Anna Paulowna Meubelenfabriek. Although they installed steam-powered machinery, much of the furniture was still handmade. Matthieu Horrix was responsible for the artistic side of the business. He favoured French-inspired designs and a repertory of period revival styles but also used familiar motifs to produce wholly original, somewhat whimsical compositions completely unrelated to 17th- and 18th-century prototypes, for example a range of rustic furniture intended to give the appearance of having been created from branches. Horrix's designs were well thought out and well proportioned, and his submission to the Great Exhibition of 1851 in London received a bronze medal. Towards the end of the 19th century the factory was producing furniture primarily for export purposes. The Horrix factory remained the largest in the Netherlands until it closed in 1890.

BIBLIOGRAPHY
M. Horrix: 'Wat drie generaties opbouwden', *Die Hague* (1956), pp. 81–2
J. M. W. van Voorst tot Voorst: 'Haagse meubelmakers en negentiende-eeuwse meubelstijlen' [Furniture-makers in The Hague and 19th-century furniture styles], *Antiek*, iii (1974), pp. 237–62
——: 'Twee Haagse meubelfabrieken' [Two furniture factories in The Hague], *Antiek*, iv (1974), pp. 357–75
——: *Meubels in Nederland, 1840–1900*, 2 vols (Lochem, 1979)

MONIQUE D. J. M. TEUNISSEN

Horror vacui [Lat.: 'fear of empty space']. Term applied to a composition that is overcrowded.

□

Horschelt, Theodor (*b* Munich, 16 Mar 1829; *d* Munich, 3 April 1871). German painter. He trained under Michael Echter (1812–79), Hermann Anschütz (1802–80) and Albrecht Adam, in whose house he had a studio from the 1850s. Early in his career he showed a strong interest in Russian and Oriental subjects (e.g. *Arab on Horseback*, 1853; Munich, Neue Pin.) and in hunting-scenes such as *Chamois Escaping from Predators* (1852). While still based in Munich, he produced his first paintings on subjects taken from Egypt and the Caucasus. In 1853–4 he travelled to Spain and Algiers; sketches made on this journey formed the basis of many much later works, such as *Evening in the El Kantarah Oasis* and *Nomad Caravan* (bought by King William I of Württemberg). In 1858 he travelled via Odessa, Sevastopol' and Kerch to Tbilisi, observing the progress and conduct of the Crimean War. Travelling with the Russian army under General Vrefsky, he painted works for Princess Gagarin and Baroness Vrefsky, and six watercolours for Empress Maria of Russia (1824–80). In 1860 he became a member of the St Petersburg Academy. Between 1861 and 1862 he travelled widely in the Caucasus, visiting Baku, Erevan and Tbilisi, where he painted *Parade of the Tsar and his Entourage* (1862). In 1863 he returned to Munich. In 1865 he painted the *Taking of Shamy*, which includes 40 portraits, and the *Storming of an Entrenchment on Mount Gunib* (1866). In 1870 he produced studies of Strasbourg under siege from the Prussian army. His drawings and sketchbooks are in Berlin (Nationalgalerie), St Petersburg and Munich (Staatl. Graph. Samml.).

UNPUBLISHED SOURCES

Munich, Stadtarchv [letters]

BIBLIOGRAPHY

J. Albert and H. Holland: *Theodor Horschelt, sein Leben und seine Werke* (Munich, 1871)
H. Holland: *Schlachtenmaler Theodor Horschelt* (Munich, 1914)
H. Wichmann: *Bibliographie der Kunst in Bayern* (Wiesbaden, 1961) [further bibliog.]
H. Ludwig: *Münchener Malerei im 19. Jahrhundert* (Munich, 1982), ii

U. V. HASE-SCHMUNDT

Horsey, Edward (*b* Devonshire, 1809; *d* Kingston, Ont., 27 March 1869). Canadian architect of English birth. After training as a carpenter in Devonshire and a builder in London, he went to Kingston, Ontario, *c.* 1832. He worked on the Palladian-style court-house (1837–9; destr.) in Belleville by Thomas Rogers (*c.* 1780–1853), shaping four large tree trunks into Ionic columns for the portico. Returning to England in 1840, probably to acquire further training, Horsey was back in Kingston one year later listed as Architect, Civil Engineer and Master Builder and profitably engaged in building and selling terrace houses and single dwellings. For his family, Horsey built Elizabeth Cottage (*c.* 1843), 251 Brock Street, Kingston, an Early Gothic Revival residence, as a replica of the Horsey family manor house in Sherborne, Dorset. In 1848 Horsey succeeded William Hugh Coverdale as architect of the Provincial Penitentiary in Kingston. He continued Coverdale's general classical scheme for the prison and designed a dome for the main building (rebuilt 1955). His finest achievement was the Frontenac County Court-House (1855–8), Kingston. A late example of Neoclassicism in Canada, the building's composition, taken from the work of William Chambers, was standard for contemporary Ontario court-houses and was obviously influenced by George Browne's Kingston City Hall (1843–4). Horsey displayed the mastery of his art in the satisfying proportions and elegant treatment of the classical and Italianate details.

BIBLIOGRAPHY

M. Angus: 'Architects and Builders of Early Kingston', *Hist. Kingston*, xi (March 1963), p. 24

DAVID ROSE

Horsley, John Callcott (*b* London, 29 Jan 1817; *d* London, 18 Oct 1903). English painter. A nephew of the landscape painter Augustus Wall Callcott, and later Isambard Kingdom Brunel's brother-in-law, he was born into the artistic establishment. He was educated at Henry Sass's Academy and at the Royal Academy. Although he executed two frescoes for the Houses of Parliament (*The Spirit of Religion*, 1847; London, House of Lords; *Satan Wounded by Ithuriel's Lance*, 1848; London, Pal. Westminster), his career began with portraiture. Success later came with literary subjects, and in 1843 he designed the first Christmas card, for Henry Cole.

By the time of his second marriage, in 1854, to Seymour Haden's sister, Rosamund, he had met F. D. Hardy (1826–1911), through his friend Thomas Webster, and G. B. O'Neill, who married Horsley's cousin in 1855. These artists formed the CRANBROOK COLONY, meeting every summer in Cranbrook, Kent. Horsley commissioned a house, Willesley, near Cranbrook (1864–9), from Richard Norman Shaw, and his son Gerald Callcott Horsley (1862–1917) trained in Shaw's office.

The early years in Cranbrook produced Horsley's best work: informal, unpretentious paintings of contemporary subjects epitomized by *A Pleasant Corner* (1865; London, RA). Most of his output, however, consisted of period pieces derived from Dutch 17th-century genre painting, well-researched and technically accomplished but lacking in feeling. *The Banker's Private Room—Negotiating a Loan* (1870; London, Royal Holloway & Bedford New Coll.) is typical. From the 1880s, when this type of subject became unfashionable, Horsley returned to portraiture.

From 1875 to 1890 Horsley was Rector of the Royal Academy (he was elected ARA in 1855 and RA in 1864), where he agitated against French influences and the use of naked models (hence his nickname: 'Clothes Horsley'). He organized the Old Master Winter Exhibitions, an important series that contributed to public knowledge of the British aristocracy's collections (and also to their subsequent despoliation by dealers and foreign collectors).

WRITINGS

Recollections of a Royal Academician (London, 1903)

BIBLIOGRAPHY

'J. C. Horsley, ARA', *A. J.* [London] (1857), pp. 181–4
The Cranbrook Colony (exh. cat., ed. A. Greg; Wolverhampton, A.G., 1977)

ANDREW GREG

Horst [Horst P; Bohrmann, Horst Paul Albert] (*b* Weissenfels, Germany, 14 Aug 1906). American photographer of German birth. After briefly studying Chinese in Frankfurt am Main and then working for a firm of importers, he entered the Kunstgewerbeschule in Hamburg, where from 1926 to 1928 he designed and made furniture. Following this he went to work as an architectural assistant to Le Corbusier in Paris. There he met George Hoyningen-Huene, who worked as a photographer for *Vogue*, and through him Cecil Beaton. In 1931 he himself began working as a photographer for *Vogue*, at first producing images influenced by Hoyningen-Huene. His photographs soon achieved an individual style, however, characterized by their striking light effects and sensual use of the models. In 1932 he spent several months working for American *Vogue* in New York, but his employment was terminated before the end of his six-month contract. He emigrated in 1935 to the USA, again working as a photographer for American *Vogue* while continuing to contribute to the French edition until the late 1940s. He spent much of his time in New York and Paris, meeting celebrities such as the film director Luchino Visconti and the fashion designer Coco Chanel.

In 1942, the year in which he became a naturalized American citizen, Horst was drafted into the US Army, where he took photographs of fellow servicemen. It was at this time that he changed his surname from Bohrmann to Horst. After the war he returned to Condé Nast Publications, the publishers of *Vogue*, also beginning photography for *House and Garden* and advertising work. He also found time to publish *Patterns from Nature* (New York, 1946), a collection of plant and flower forms. The severe restrictions imposed on photographers in 1951 by a new editor at *Vogue* impoverished Horst's work until the arrival in the early 1960s of another editor, Diana Vreeland, who encouraged him to photograph houses and gardens for *Vogue* in addition to his fashion work. After her departure in 1971 he worked almost entirely for *House and Garden* until 1978, when he resumed his fashion photography for American, French and Italian *Vogue*. Throughout his career he also produced portraits, for example of *Luchino Visconti* (1935; see Lawford, p. 139) and *Andy Warhol* (1983; see Lawford, p. 391).

PHOTOGRAPHIC PUBLICATIONS

Photographs of a Decade (New York, 1945)
Patterns from Nature (New York, 1946)
Return Engagement: Faces to Remember, Then and Now, text by J. Watters (New York, 1984)

BIBLIOGRAPHY

Horst: Photographs, 1931–1986 (Milan, 1985)
V. Lawford: *Horst: His Work and his World* (Harmondsworth, 1985)

☐

Horta, Victor (*b* Ghent, 6 Jan 1861; *d* Brussels, 8 Sept 1947). Belgian architect and teacher. Although his work was confined almost entirely to Brussels, the ten years (1893–1903) of his active career working in the Art Nouveau style had a revolutionary effect on European perceptions of 19th-century rules of design. Apart from initiating and developing the style in Brussels, creating in particular interiors in which his furniture and decoration were remarkable for their stylistic unity and were in complete opposition to the eclecticism of 'conventional' contemporary interior decoration, he was one of the first architects to consider the potential of the open plan. He also applied the rationalist principles of Eugène-Emmanuel Viollet-le-Duc regarding the exposure of the iron structures of his buildings, and he was the first to make extensive use of cast iron in domestic architecture, combining the taste of an artist with the skill of an engineer in fashioning iron into the sinuous organic outlines characteristic of Art Nouveau. After 1903, Horta abandoned the style and his later output demonstrates a safer and more academic approach.

1. Before 1903. 2. 1903 and after.

1. BEFORE 1903. Horta studied at the Conservatoire in Ghent before moving to the Académie there in 1876 to study architecture. In 1878 he went to Paris, where he worked for the interior decorator Jules Dubuysson, before settling in Brussels in 1881 to resume his architectural studies at the Académie Royale des Beaux-Arts. In 1884 he joined the architectural office of Alphonse Balat and was soon in charge of design work on the monumental complex of conservatories that Balat was erecting for King Leopold II at Laeken, near Brussels. This project introduced Horta to the use of iron and glass, the two materials that dominated the work of his maturity: it was at Laeken that he must have appreciated for the first time the true potential of cast iron in architecture, both decorative—due to its ductile nature—and structural.

In the 1880s Horta produced some houses in Ghent in collaboration with others, as well as several competition entries. His first independent building in Brussels was the Temple des Passions Humaines (1884–9) in the Parc Cinquantenaire, intended as a permanent exhibition pavilion for sculpture by Jef Lambeaux and conceived as a small Classical temple. In 1890 Horta opened his own office in Brussels and soon began to teach at the Université Libre de Bruxelles. At this time Brussels was one of the most avant-garde cities in Europe (*see* BRUSSELS, §III, 2), with a strong native school of Symbolist painters and poets and a particular receptivity to contemporary developments in France and England, including the work of the Pre-Raphaelites and the ideals of the Arts and Crafts Movement. Two organizations founded in 1894, L'Association pour le Progrès des Arts Décoratifs and Pour l'Art, were particularly important for the development of Art Nouveau architecture, which explored the concept of the *Gesamtkunstwerk*, involving all the arts in one work. The influence on Horta of these artistic and cultural activities is unclear: he later denied having heard of Aubrey Beardsley or C. F. A. Voysey before his own style was fully established, and in 1945 he destroyed many of his original drawings. He was, however, a supporter of the ART À LA RUE movement, which believed in relating art to everyday life. He probably also visited the Exposition Universelle (1889), Paris, which was dominated by the Galerie des Machines (1889; destr.; *see* IRON AND STEEL, fig. 6) by Victor Contamin (1840–93) and Charles-Louis-Ferdinand Dutert, and the new Tour Eiffel (1887–9; for illustration *see* EIFFEL, GUSTAVE).

Nevertheless in 1892–3 Horta produced the first major work of Art Nouveau with the revolutionary Hôtel Tassel (now the Mexican Embassy), 6 Rue Paul-Emile Janson, Brussels, which was built before Henry Van de Velde—sometimes credited with the invention of the style—had built his first house. The symmetrical, stone-faced exterior of the four-storey building (*see* BRUSSELS, fig. 3) features exposed metalwork in the window mullions and lintels. The most extraordinary features of the house, however, are the exposed interior metal structure and the free plan; the latter was developed in an innovative, asymmetrical arrangement around an open staircase, with rooms of varying shapes and sizes and including a mezzanine that responded to the client's brief. The characteristic, curvilinear decoration of the interior metalwork is particularly apparent in the staircase hall (see fig. 1). Here a single free-standing column branches out to support the ceiling and landings, while organic tendrils intertwine to form the balustrade. Similar patterns are incorporated in two dimensions in the mosaic floor, and the effect was reinforced by the original painted decoration, which consisted of curvilinear patterns interweaving up the walls. Horta commented of this style that he discarded the flower and the leaf but kept the stalk, suggesting that his inspiration came from nature. The original contents (later dispersed) were also designed by Horta to match the decoration. Some elements, such as English wallpaper—probably by Heywood Sumner—in the dining room, indicate Horta's awareness of artistic developments in England that were later considered part of Art Nouveau.

The Hôtel Tassel was followed by a series of innovative Art Nouveau buildings in Brussels. In the following year Horta was commissioned to design a large house for Armand Solvay, son of the famous industrial chemist Ernest Solvay. The Hôtel Solvay (1894–1900), 222 Avenue

1. Victor Horta: staircase hall of the Hôtel Tassel, Brussels, 1892–3

Louise, was perhaps Horta's most sumptuous private commission and survives complete with its original furniture, which he also designed. The façade is almost symmetrical and is sculptural in quality, with the two end bays projecting in the first and second storeys, subdivided by thin metal colonnettes and transoms; there is elaborate abstract ironwork in the balconies. Inside, the metal structure is again exposed, and Horta's fluid organic style extended to the stained-glass windows and light fittings. Murals were painted in the house by Theo Van Rysselberghe in 1912. Another house, the Hôtel Wissinger (1895) at 66 Rue de l'Hôtel des Monnaies, was a more modest brief and its façade was designed more asymmetrically.

Perhaps the most modern of Horta's house façades is that of the Hôtel van Eetvelde (1895–7), which employed a rational iron frame decorated with mosaic panels bordered by free-flowing 'whiplash' lines. The luxurious interior, replete with marbles and gilt bronze, features a staircase and landings wrapped around a double-height octagonal hall near the centre of the plan. A shallow glass dome, which is supported by elliptical arches above a circle of iron columns, lights the hall; across the dome, long, leaf-like tendrils of coloured glass continue the sinuous curves of the structure below. Horta's own house and adjacent studio (1898–1901; now the Musée Horta) at 23–25 Rue Americaine—two independently designed buildings—have strikingly original treatments of their windows and decorative ironwork. Horta later recognized that with the completion of these two buildings his career had reached its peak. One later house in the Art Nouveau style, the Hôtel Aubecq (1899–1900; destr. 1950), with decoration by Emile Fabry, exemplified his most ingenious planning. This period was Horta's most prolific in domestic commissions: he designed 24 houses between 1890 and 1903 and only 6 between 1903 and 1915.

Horta also produced some non-residential buildings in Brussels that incorporated features of Art Nouveau design, notably the Maison du Peuple (1895–9; destr. 1964) and the department store A l'Innovation (1901; destr. 1966). The Maison du Peuple (see fig. 2) was intended as the headquarters of the recently established Belgian Socialist Party, and it was largely financed by the Solvay Company, Armand Solvay being a close friend of the militant socialist Emile Vandervelde. The building's design, with curved and angled façades, clearly reflected its irregular, partly curved site fronting on to two radial streets. The Maison du Peuple has been referred to as the Art Nouveau version of American office buildings designed by Louis Sullivan (see Hitchcock, p. 394); instead of being clad in stone or terracotta, as in the USA, however, here the iron frame was exposed, with masonry cladding used only for the end bays and around the entrance. At the top of the building, inside the high mansard roof, was an auditorium that featured Horta's most successful attempt to combine the ornamental and the structural use of iron: his exposed framework of trussed metal columns angled upwards from the floor to continue as beams across the ceiling, incorporating graceful curves and ornamental elements. The last of Horta's structures to reveal its metal structure was the department store A l'Innovation, Rue Neuve, the façade of which was the first in Brussels built entirely of iron and glass, not, as Horta wrote in his *Mémoires*, because

2. Victor Horta: Maison du Peuple, Brussels, 1895–9; destroyed 1964

of some fantasy on the architect's part but because all this glass was needed to provide maximum daylight, by which the public could clearly see the merchandise. The façade featured a giant, elliptical arch over the central section and elegant curved ornament in the iron structure.

2. 1903 AND AFTER. In his design for the Grand Bazar (1903; destr.) in Frankfurt am Main, in which the iron structure was largely concealed beneath a stone veneer, Horta signalled a change in his approach as he moved towards an increasing academicism; this was exemplified in prestigious public commissions that ultimately earned him a barony in 1932. A later store (1906) for L'Innovation in Antwerp employed terracotta made by the English Doulton ceramic factory in its façade. Much of his later professional work was concerned with two major public commissions in Brussels: the Palais des Beaux-Arts (designed 1914; built 1919–28) and the Gare Centrale (first planned 1910; begun 1937 and completed 1946–53 by Maxime Brunfaut). He also continued his teaching career and took up many official appointments. In 1912 he was appointed Professor at the Académie Royale des Beaux-Arts, Brussels. During World War I he spent time in England and in the USA, where he lectured at several universities (1916–18). In 1919, after his return to Belgium, he became Professor at the Institut Avancé des Beaux-Arts, Antwerp (becoming Head of Faculty in 1921–31). In 1925–7 he chaired an independent international jury to screen entries for the headquarters of the League of Nations in Geneva.

The achievement of Horta's earlier career was extraordinary, his skills as a decorative and structural designer and as a planner coming together to create works of rich visual and spatial experience. His buildings were highly influential, in particular for such architects as HÉCTOR GUIMARD, who met Horta in 1895. Because of his innovations in structural expression and free planning, Horta came to be regarded by many as a precursor of the Modern Movement; it is therefore curious that he did not participate in the new movements in architecture that gathered momentum after World War I and reflected many of the same preoccupations.

WRITINGS
C. Dulière, ed.: *Victor Horta: Mémoires* (Brussels, 1985)

BIBLIOGRAPHY
Macmillan Enc. Architects
R. L. Delevoy: *Monographies de l'art belge* (Brussels, 1958, 2/1964)
——: *Victor Horta* (Brussels, 1958)
H. R. Hitchcock: *Architecture: Nineteenth and Twentieth Centuries*, Pelican Hist. A. (Harmondsworth, 1958, 3/1968)
S. Giele and J. Delhaye: *Victor Horta: Son Musée* (Brussels, 1969)
F. Borsi and P. Portoghesi: *Victor Horta* (Brussels, 1970; Eng. trans., London, 1991)
Pionniers du XXe siècle: Guimard, Horta, Van de Velde (exh. cat. by R. L. Delevoy, M. Culot and Y. Brunhammer, Paris, Mus. A. Déc., 1971)
Horta (exh. cat. by S. Henrion-Giele, J. Delhaye, V.-G. Martiny and F. Strauven, Brussels, 1973)

A. Hoppenbrouwers, J. Vandenbreden and J. Bruggemans: *Victor Horta architectonographie* (Brussels, 1975)
Y. Oostens-Wittamer: *L'Hôtel Solvay*, 2 vols (Louvain-la-Neuve, 1980)
F. Loyer and J. Delhaye: *Victor Horta: Hôtel Tassel, 1893–1895* (Brussels, 1986)
Y. Oostens-Wittamer: *Horta en Amérique, Decembre 1915–Janvier 1919* (Brussels, 1986)
J. Delhaye: *La Maison du Peuple de Victor Horta* (Brussels, 1987)
P. Loze and F. Loze: *Belgian Art Nouveau: From Victor Horta to Antoine Pompe* (Ghent, 1991)

SHERBAN CANTACUZINO

Hortus deliciarum. Illustrated encyclopedia compiled by HERRAD VON LANDSBERG, Abbess of Hohenbourg, Alsace, in the late 12th century. The only copy was held in the municipal library of Strasbourg but was completely destroyed by fire in the bombardment of the city in 1870. Fortunately, records had been made of some parts of the text and copies made of some of the illustrations: Christian Moritz Engelhardt had had drawings made for his 1818 publication of the *Hortus*; the manuscript had also been lent to the French antiquary Comte Auguste de Bastard d'Estang, who had notes on the text and some coloured copies made of the illustrations by Wilhelm Stengel. Some years after its destruction Canons Straub and Keller published these and other extant drawings made from the manuscript and presented some account of its contents, but it was not until 1979 that a team of scholars published

as complete a reconstruction as possible of the text and illustration of the *Hortus deliciarum.*

The encyclopedia, made in the years from before 1176 to 1196, was almost exclusively concerned with biblical, moral and theological material, arranged according to a scheme of Christian salvation (*see* ALLEGORY, fig. 2). It had over 150 pages with miniatures comprising 346 separate scenes and diagrams, of which only about half can be reconstructed from the copies. About two thirds of the text and an even greater proportion of the illustration present the Old and New Testaments with accompanying commentary. Over 200 pictures and diagrams were interspersed in this section of the text. There follows an account of the virtues and vices with illustrations of the allegorical battle from Prudentius' *Psychomachia*. In this section a wheel of fortune and an allegorical ladder of virtue are also depicted. In the latter (*see* fig.) figures ascend the ladder assisted by angels, with devils representing the vices attempting to pull them off. A long section, also accompanied by pictures, gives an account with commentary of King Solomon and is followed!by a definition of the Church and its role in society, illustrated with six miniatures. This precedes a section on the Last Things illustrated with 20 pictures of the *Life of Antichrist*, Apocalyptic scenes and the *Last Judgement*. Other sections present excerpts from the important scholastic text the *Sentences* of Peter Lombard and material on Church history, including a list of popes. The text ends with calendar and computistical material and songs about the abbey of Hohenbourg. The latter are preceded by a double-page image of the nuns with Abbess Herrad on one page facing her predecessor, the founder of Hohenbourg, Abbess Relinde, before their patron saint, Odilia, Christ and other saints. These figures stand before a representation of the abbey's setting.

Although the text of the encyclopedia was compiled by Herrad, it is far from certain that she or any of the nuns were in any way involved in the elaborate programme of illustration. The artists had a wide knowledge of Byzantine iconography and figure style, possibly through the intermediary of Italian works, particularly from Sicily. Several of the scenes have close parallels in the mosaics of the Cappella Palatina in Palermo and Monreale Cathedral, suggesting the artists had either visited Sicily or had access to a pattern book containing drawings made from the mosaics. A fragment of such a book from this region with drawings close in style to the *Hortus deliciarum* survives (Freiburg im Breisgau, Augustinermus.).

Ladder of Virtue (fol. 215v) from the *Hortus deliciarum*, late 12th century (destr. 1870); copy of original miniature, made for Christian Moritz Engelhardt, 1818

BIBLIOGRAPHY
LM: 'Herrad von Landsberg'
G. Cames: *Allégories et symboles dans l'Hortus deliciarum* (Leiden, 1971)
——: 'La Création des animaux dans l'*Hortus deliciarum*', *Cah. Archéol.*, xxv (1976), pp. 131–42
A. Straub and G. Keller: *Herrad of Landsberg: Hortus deliciarum* (New Rochelle, 1977) [with trans. by A. D. Caratzas]
R. Green and others: *The 'Hortus deliciarum' of Herrad of Hohenbourg*, 2 vols (London, 1979) [facs. of copy of *Hortus*]
R. Will: 'La Reconstitution des miniatures de l'*Hortus deliciarum* à la recherche des sources', *Cah. Alsac. Archéol., A. & Hist.*, xxvi (1983), pp. 99–116

NIGEL J. MORGAN

Horverk, Niklas. *See under* SCHLESITZER, NIKLAS.

Hŏ Ryŏn. *See* HŎ YU.

Hōryūji [Hōryū Gakumonji; Wakakusadera; Ikaruga no Tera]. Buddhist temple complex at Ikaruga, Ikoma District, Nara Prefecture, Japan.

1. Introduction. 2. Historical development.

1. INTRODUCTION. Hōryūji is one of the oldest temples in Japan and is the head temple of the Shōtoku sect. Founded in the late 6th century AD by the regent, Prince SHŌTOKU, and refounded in the late 7th century, it became a leading centre for Buddhist scholarship and the focus of the cult of its founder. Since the early 8th century Hōryūji has been listed as the most ancient of the Seven Great Temples of Nara (Nanto Shichidaiji). The complex occupies *c.* 9 ha of flat land south-west of Nara and is divided into two precincts (*see* TEMPLE, fig. 8): the Sai'in (Western Precinct), often referred to as 'Hōryūji proper', and the Tō'in (Eastern Precinct), known officially as Jōguōden (Halls of the Lord of the Superior Palace).

The buildings at Hōryūji include wooden structures of the late 7th century AD and the early 8th, which are the oldest surviving examples of their kind in Japan and are of prime importance for an understanding of the origins of Japanese Buddhist architecture (*see* JAPAN, §III, 3(ii)). These buildings, together with those erected in the Heian (794–1185), Kamakura (1185–1333) and Muromachi (1333–1568) periods, have undergone constant restorations, especially during the Keichō (1596–1615) and Genroku (1688–1704) eras and in the period since the Meiji Restoration (1868). Reconstruction work carried out in the Sai'in since 1950 has returned the core of the precinct to what is thought to have been its disposition during the Asuka and Hakuhō periods (AD 552–710).

In 1949 fire destroyed important wall paintings of the Nara period (710–94), but their appearance is preserved in photographs and reproductions. Like many other temples in Japan, Hōryūji has in recent centuries been the setting for the staging of performing arts: a platform for *gagaku*, the traditional music of the imperial court, has been in existence at Hōryūji since the 17th century. A good deal of religious sculpture from the numerous early halls and chapels that are no longer extant are now preserved in the temple complex's museum, the Daihōzōden. This includes the gilt-wood *Kudara Kannon* (Skt Avalokiteshvara; the *bodhisattva* of mercy; *see* JAPAN, §V, 3(i) and fig. 54), the lacquered-wood Tamamushi Shrine (Tamamushi Zushi; *see* JAPAN, §VI, 3(i) and fig. 75), which bears, in miniature, the cloud-pattern bracketing (see §2(i) below) typical of architecture at the site; the gilt-bronze Lady Tachibana's Shrine (Tachibana Fujin Nenji Butsu; *see* JAPAN, §II, 3 and fig. 56); the gilt-bronze *Yumetagai* or *Yumechigai* ('dream-altering') *Kannon* (*see* JAPAN, §V, 3(i)(c)) and a Tang-period (AD 618–907) sandalwood image of *Kumen* ('nine-headed') *Kannon*. A further 300 or so items (the icons of the Hōryūji Imperial Gift; Hōryūji Kennō Gyobutsu) were given to the Imperial Household Agency in 1878 in return for a contribution to the funds needed for repairs and are now in the Hōryūji Treasure House, a separate building at the Tokyo National Museum (*see also* JAPAN, §V, 3).

2. HISTORICAL DEVELOPMENT.

(i) Before 794. (ii) 794–1185. (iii) After 1185.

(i) Before 794. According to 8th-century texts such as the *Nihon shoki* (or *Nihongi*, 'Chronicle of Japan'; AD 720), Prince Shōtoku founded Hōryūji in the last decade of the 6th century as a memorial to his father, Emperor Yōmei (*reg* 585–7), and as the tutelary temple of his family, the house of Ōe. It is thought that the buildings were constructed by Korean artisans from the kingdom of Paekche (Three Kingdoms period, 1st century BC–7th century AD; *see* KOREA, §II, 1). Constructed on the western flank of Prince Shōtoku's detached palace complex at Ikaruga (the Ikaruga no Miya, completed 601) and formally consecrated *c.* 606–7, the temple was known as the Wakakusadera or Ikaruga no Tera. It flourished until 643, when the house of Ōe was overthrown and the palace destroyed. Thereafter it sank into decline, and in 670 the entire complex was destroyed by fire. It was once thought that the ancient buildings at the heart of the Sai'in might have included those erected by Shōtoku, but in 1939 excavations along the western border of the Ikaruga palace site—south-east of the Sai'in—revealed the remains of a temple that had been attached to the palace complex. Similar in plan to the Shitennōji (*see* OSAKA, §II, 1), another temple founded by the prince, this site is now generally accepted to be the Wakakusadera, the original temple–residence of Prince Shōtoku.

The Sai'in contains an ensemble of ancient buildings that form the religious and architectural centre of the complex. Construction of these probably began soon after the fire of 670, and documents of the Heian period (794–1185) date their completion to the Wadō era (708–14). The new buildings were laid out on a north–south axis running from the Southern Main Gate (Nandaimon; *see* §(iii) below), through the Middle Gate (Chūmon) to the Main Lecture Hall (Daikōdō) to the north. The Middle Gate gives access to an inner precinct surrounded on three sides by a roofed corridor (*kairō*); the Main Lecture Hall forms the fourth side, and the two-storey Golden Hall (*kondō*; main hall) and a five-storey pagoda (*gojunotō*) stand side by side at its centre (this arrangement of *kondō* and pagoda was copied in Korea during the Koryŏ period (AD 918–1392); *see* KOREA, §II, 3(i)(a)). The *kondō* is thought to be the oldest structure at Hōryūji as there is a reference in the *Nihon shoki* to its completion in 693. Measuring 5×4 bays, it was built in the *irimoya zukuri* ('high-and-gable roof construction') format, with a tiled roof and a lean-to construction (*mokoshi*) with a plank roof surrounding the ground floor on all sides (see fig.). Notable features include the cloud-pattern bracketing (*kumogata hijiki*), found only in buildings in the Ikaruga area, and columnar entasis. The walls of the hall's outer sanctuary (Gejin) were painted with scenes of Buddhas, *bodhisattva*s and *arhat*s (Jap. *rakan*; disciples of Buddha) in various paradises (destr. 1949), and the *honzon* (the principal object of worship) is a gilt-bronze *Shaka Triad* (Skt Shakyamuni; the historical Buddha), flanked by two *bodhisattva* attendants; it is inscribed with a date equivalent to 623 and the name of the Buddhist sculptor TORI BUSSHI (*see* JAPAN, §V, 3(i) and fig. 53). The *kondō* also contains a gilt-bronze figure of Yakushi (Skt Bhaishajyaguru; the

Hōryūji temple complex, Golden Hall (*kondō*), completed AD 693

Buddha of healing), which bears the date 607 and a prayer for the Emperor Yōmei, suggesting that this may be the original *honzon* of Hōryūji; a 7th-century set of painted wooden figures of the Shitennō (Skt Lokapala; the Guardians of the Four Quarters); and a late 11th-century set of lacquered and painted joined-wood images of Bishamonten (Skt Vaishravana; the Guardian of the North) and Kichijōten (the Hindu deity Lakshmi or Shridevi who was the goddess of prosperity and the incarnation of beauty).

The pagoda, the Middle Gate and the roofed corridor were probably completed early in the 8th century, as was the Higashimuro, a dormitory to the east of the inner precinct (extensively rebuilt in 1365). All share cloud-pattern bracketing, columnar entasis and a well-ordered proportioning of their elements. The pagoda, which measures 3×3 bays and rises to a height of 30 m, is particularly noted for its balanced proportions (it is a regularly modulated structure, the fifth storey having half the area of the ground floor) and for a collection of clay figurines (*c.* 711) that line its inner sanctuary (Naijin); these depict such scenes as the famous debate between the layman Yuima (Skt Vimalakirti) and Monju (Skt Manjushri; the *bodhisattva* of supreme wisdom) described in the *Yuimagyō* (Skt *Vimalakīrtinirdeśa sūtra*). The two-storey Middle Gate, which measures 4×3 bays, was built in the *irimoya zukuri* format and has an unusual entrance two bays wide that consists of double doors on either side of the central pillars. The outer two bays contain figures of the Niō (Skt Vajradhara; the 'adamantine strengths'; temple gate guardians). The tile-roofed corridor is of the semi-enclosed type and originally ran the full length of the perimeter of the inner precinct. Now interrupted by the Great Lecture Hall, which was inserted into its northern span in the early Heian period (*c.* 9th century), it runs for 42 bays from the Middle Gate to the lecture hall on the

eastern side and for 40 bays on the west: the two east–west spans—on the eastern sides of the Middle Gate and the Great Lecture Hall—each incorporate one of the extra bays. This artifice accommodates the different sizes of the pagoda and the *kondō*, enclosed within the corridor, creating an overall harmony of proportions.

The Sai'in also contains a number of important buildings of the Tenpyō era (729–49), including the *sūtra* repository (*kyōzō*), the refectory (*jikidō*) and the Great Eastern Gate (Tōdaimon). They all have roof-support systems that feature double-rainbow beams (*nijū kōryō*) and frog-leg struts (*kaerumata*). The two-storey, 'turret-style' *sūtra* repository (3×2 bays) and the refectory (7×4 bays) were built in the *kirizuma zukuri* ('gabled-roof construction') format with tiled roofs. The refectory is thought to have been the temple's administrative office until the Kamakura period; its earthen floor (*doma yuka*) and the underside of its 'cosmetic roof' (*keshōyane*), revealed by the absence of a ceiling, give its interior a briskly functional appearance.

The Tō'in, which lies some 300 m east of the Sai'in on the site of Prince Shōtoku's palace, also originated in the Tenpyō era, when the Yumedono (Hall of Dreams), the precinct's main hall (*shōdō*), and the Denpōdō, its lecture hall, were first built. Construction of the Tō'in began in 737 or 739, when Gyōshin (*d* 750), a scholar of the Hossō sect and an early proponent of the worship of Prince Shōtoku, commissioned the Yumedono in the name of Emperor Shōmu (*reg* 724–49). It is an octagonal single-storey building with a tiled roof and an elaborate roof finial that suggests that the hall had a pagoda-like role as a memorial to Prince Shōtoku. The three-stepped bracketing of its system of bearing blocks and bracket arms is a typical feature of the Tenpyō era, but its roof-support system was extensively reconstructed in the Kamakura period. The hall's *honzon* is a gilt-wood image of the *Guze Kannon*, commonly called the *Yumedono Kannon* of the Asuka–Hakuhō period (552–710), which is housed in strict secrecy and is said to be the same height as Prince Shōtoku. Its other images include a lacquer figure of Gyōshin (8th century) and a 9th-century clay figure of Dōsen, a monk who carried out later restoration work. The Denpōdō is a single-storey structure constructed in the *kirizuma zukuri*, measuring 7×4 bays with a tiled roof and the unusual feature of wooden floors. Temple tradition holds that it was originally the residence of Lady Tachibana no Konakichi (*fl* 8th century), a consort of Emperor Shōmu, and that she donated it to Hōryūji in 761. Restorations in 1943 revealed that the building had originally measured 5×3 bays with a two-bay, roofed open area and a verandah—features appropriate to a residential building. It seems that the wooden floors were left intact when the building was remodelled for religious use. The hall has simple bracketing (*daitō hijiki*) and double-rainbow beams with frog-leg struts. The Denpōdō is an example of the *Shinden* (main hall) style of architecture (*see* JAPAN, §III, 3(iii)).

(ii) 794–1185. There are a number of important Heian-period structures at Hōryūji, most of which are in the Sai'in. These include the Great Lecture Hall (Daikōdō), the belfry and the Kōfūzō, a storehouse. The first lecture hall, erected in the early Heian period, and the original belfry both burnt down in 925 and were rebuilt during the

Shōryaku era (990–95), and it is these reconstructions that survive today. The Great Lecture Hall is a one-storey structure in the *irimoya zukuri* format with a tiled roof. Its interior has one of the earliest fully articulated examples of a 'cosmetic roof' construction. The hall was originally eight bays wide (since the Genroku era it has measured 9×4 bays) and had a six-bay façade in the 'front door' format (*tobiragamae*) and an even number of pillars—a most unusual feature. It has a very large (four-bay) altar (*butsudan*), and its *honzon* is a *Yakushi Triad* (Bhaisajya-guru with two *bodhisattvas*; gilt wood; *c.* 990–95). The Kōfūzō, to the east of the Higashimuro, probably pre-dates the lecture hall but has been repeatedly restored, most recently in 1966, when an attempt was made to recreate its form it had had in the early Heian period. Measuring 9×3 bays, the Kōfūzō was built in the *yosemune zukuri* ('hipped-gable roof construction'), with a raised floor, a tiled roof and lime-based plaster (*shikkui nuri*) applied to the exterior of the walls. It is an early example of a 'double storehouse' (*narabi kura*): the three central bays are open, while the three bays at either end serve as enclosed storage areas.

(iii) After 1185. The three most important buildings erected at Hōryūji during the Kamakura and Muromachi periods are the Saiendō, an octagonal hall on a rise just to the north-west of the Sai'in; the Shōryō'in, a shrine to Prince Shōtoku; and the Main South Gate (Nandaimon). The Saiendō is thought to be a 13th-century reconstruction of a hall commissioned in the Yōrō era (717–23) by the noblewoman Tachibana no Michiyo (*d* 733), who also sponsored the Tachibana Shrine now in the Hōryūji museum. It is considered a classic example of Kamakura-style simplicity: there are doors on four of the eight sides; latticed windows (*renji mado*) occupy the faces to each side of the main façade; and the remaining face is covered with white plaster. The Shōryō'in is a one-storey structure measuring 6×5 bays. It was built into the southern end of Higashimuro during the renovation of the latter in 1121. It was constructed in the *kirizuma zukuri* format, with a tiled roof and its main entrance under the gable. In 1284 it was rebuilt with deeper bays and double eaves (*futa-noki*). A one-bay 'open aisle' (*fukihanachi hisashi*) runs the length of the main façade, which has latticed double doors (*shitomido*) between its pillars; the one-bay front portico (*kōhai*) is roofed with cypress-bark shingles. The altar in the hall's sanctuary has the frog-leg struts and 'Chinese' ornamental gable boards (*karahafu*) typical of Kamakura-style architecture. In the shrine are 12th-century wooden figures of Prince Shōtoku and four attendants.

The Main South Gate was originally the Middle Gate of the complex and was moved to its present site in 1438 after the original gate burnt down in 1435. It is a three-bay, 'eight-legged gate' (*hakkyakumon*)—a gate with eight pillars—with one door and an elaborate roof in the *irimoya zukuri* format. The sculptural quality commonly observed in Muromachi-period architecture can be seen in elements of the roof-support system such as the head tie-beams and in the pillar brackets, among which are flower-pattern brackets (*hana hijiki*). The broad, horizontal emphasis produced by the planes of the roof is typical of the 'great

ridge-pole Japanese style' (*ōmune Wayō*) of 12th–16th-century architecture.

BIBLIOGRAPHY

K. Adachi: *Asuka Nara jidai no bukkyō kenchiku* [Buddhist architecture of the Asuka and Nara periods] (Tokyo, 1933)

C. Itō: *Nihon kenchiku no kenkyū* [Studies on Japanese architecture] (Tokyo, 1942)

A. C. Soper: *The Evolution of Buddhist Architecture in Japan* (1942/*R* New York, 1979)

H. Ōta: *Hōryūji kenchiku* [The architecture of Hōryūji] (Tokyo, 1943)

K. Asano: *Hōryūji kenchiku sōkan* [A survey of the architecture of Hōryūji] (Kyoto, 1953)

S. Mizuno: *Hōryūji*, Nihon no bijutsu [Arts of Japan] (Tokyo, 1965); Eng. trans. by R. L. Gage as *Asuka Buddhist Art: Horyu-ji* (1974), Heibonsha Surv. Jap. A., iv (New York and Tokyo, 1972–7)

M. Ōoka: *Nara no tera* [The temples of Nara] Nihon no bijutsu [Arts of Japan], vii (Tokyo, 1965); Eng. trans. by D. Lishka as *Temples of Nara and their Art*, Heibonsha Surv. Jap. A., vii (New York and Tokyo, 1973)

——: *Nanto Shichidaiji no kenkyū* [Studies on the Seven Great Temples of the southern capital] (Tokyo, 1966)

K. Asano: *Nara jidai kenchiku no kenkyū* [A study of Nara-period architecture] (Tokyo, 1969)

K. Zuzuki: *Jōdai nojiin kenchiku* [Early Buddhist architecture], Nihon no bijutsu [Arts of Japan], lxv (Tokyo, 1971); Eng. trans. by M. N. Parent and N. S. Steinhardt as *Early Buddhist Architecture in Japan*, Japanese Arts Library, ix (Tokyo and New York, 1980)

H. Ōta and others: *Hōryūji*, i–iv of *Nara rokudaiji taikan* [Survey of the Six Great Temples of Nara] (Tokyo, 1971–2)

J. Hiraoka: *Nihon jiin shi no kenkyū* [Studies in the history of Japanese Buddhist temples] (Tokyo, 1981)

MIMI HALL YIENGPRUKSAWAN

Hosaenggwan. *See* CH'OE PUK.

Hosan. *See* CHO HŬI-RYONG.

Hosenfeller [Hosenfelder; Hossenfelder], **Heinrich Christian Friedrich** (*b* Berlin, *c.* 1722; *d* Tune, 27 Oct 1805). Norwegian painter of German birth. He was probably related to the still-life painter Christian Friedrich Hosenfeller (1706–80) and probably studied at an academy of arts in Germany. Around 1760 he was working in the Herrebø Faience Factory near Fredrikshald (now Halden) in Norway as a faience painter. Some of his predominantly blue-and-white wares were decorated with blossoms, chinoiseries and magnificent shell-like motifs. In 1772 he became a citizen of Fredrikshald and with some of his inheritance money he became a portrait and decorative painter, embellishing furniture and rooms with figurative landscapes and ornaments. He devoted himself, however, to portrait painting in which he seems to have been strongly influenced by such contemporary English painters as Johan Zoffany, John Wright (1745–1820) and William Hogarth. Early works may have been painted *c.* 1776. In the Nasjonalgalleriet in Oslo there are, among other of his works, three unsigned portraits: *Lieutenant Colonel Johann Peter Vosgraff* (*c.* 1780); *Madame Vosgraff* (*c.* 1780) and *James Collett* (*c.* 1792).

BIBLIOGRAPHY

Thieme–Becker

Katalog over Norsk Malerkunst (exh. cat., Oslo, N.G., 1968)

L. Opstad: 'Alte norwegische Fayencen', *Keramos*, lviii (1972), pp. 3–14

Katalog over Norsk Malerkunst, Tilvekst, 1968–78, Oslo, N.G. cat. (Oslo, 1979)

SILVIA GLASER

Hoshikushisha. *See* NUKINA KAIOKU.

Hōshū. *See* SAKAKI HYAKUSEN.

Hosiasson, Philippe (*b* Odessa, 15 Feb 1898; *d* Paris, 13 July 1978). French painter of Ukrainian birth. He travelled to Berlin with his parents between 1910 and 1912 where he saw works by Manet and Cézanne that encouraged him to paint and draw. He later studied art history and law at the University of Odessa. In 1920 he continued his art-historical studies in Rome, where he had his first exhibition at the Casa d'Arte Bragaglia (1921). In 1922 he went to Berlin, becoming a designer for Boris Romanoff's Ballet Romantiques Russes. He accompanied the ballet in 1924 to Paris, where he settled permanently and began exhibiting at the Salon d'Automne, the Salon des Indépendants and the Galerie Percier. In 1928 he was one of the co-founders of the Salon des Surindépendants. His work of this period, such as *Italian Landscape* (1923; see Huyghe and Bazin, fig. 470), was inspired by the classicism of Poussin and David. With Christian Bérard and Eugene Berman he was part of the naturalist movement that characterized one aspect of the 'return to order' in art after World War I. In 1937 he provided mural decorations for the Martinique pavilion at the Exposition Internationale des Arts et Techniques dans la Vie Moderne in Paris.

After World War II, Hosiasson began to abandon figuration and adopted instead an informal abstract style. Initially these works were executed in sombre colours, as in *Painting* (1955; Paris, Rodolphe Stadler). From 1959 his paintings, though still abstract, became more serene and brighter in colour, as in *Painting* (1973; Paris, Pompidou).

BIBLIOGRAPHY

R. Huyghe and G. Bazin: *Histoire de l'art contemporain* (Paris, 1935/*R* New York, 1968), pp. 361–2

M. Seupher: *A Dictionary of Abstract Painting* (London, 1958), pp. 190–91

Philippe Hosiasson (exh. cat. by J. Leymarie, Paris, Mus. N. A. Mod., 1973)

Hosios Loukas, katholikon, interior looking east, ?second half of the 10th century to the early 11th

Hosios Loukas. Byzantine monastery 8 km east of Dhistomo in the foothills of Mt Helikon (nr anc. Stiris), Phokis, central Greece. Founded in the mid-10th century by the monk Loukas the younger (*d* AD 953), a healer and miracle-worker, the monastery has two unusually well-preserved churches, the Panagia or Theotokos (church of the Virgin) and the adjoining katholikon or main monastery church. The latter is famous for its lavish mosaics and wall paintings, which remain intact. Other monastic buildings of various periods survive.

The *Life of Loukas*, written after 961 by an anonymous monk, is the only record of the monastery's foundation and first building period. According to the *Life*, a church, dedicated to St Barbara, was built during Loukas' lifetime. A cruciform oratory was later erected over his grave and acted as a shrine. The translation of the saint's relics into a 'new church', which is attested by commemorative hymns, occurred under the auspices of Abbot Philotheos, the dates of whose abbacy are unknown. Although the Theotokos church has been shown to be older than the katholikon (Stikas, 1972), the identification of these two buildings with the St Barbara church and the 'new church' respectively remains controversial.

Both churches are variations on the Greek-cross plan. The Theotokos is of the cross-in-square plan (*c.* 130 sq. m in area; see CHURCH, fig. 6) with walls built in the cloisonné technique and white marble revetment around the drum of the dome. The lavish foliate and interlace sculptural ornament that appears on the capitals and templon barrier inside the church is comparable with the fragmentary marble revetment of the North Church (907) of the monastery of Constantine Lips in Constantinople (now Istanbul). The katholikon is the earliest known example of the Greek-cross-octagon plan (270 sq. m in area, excluding narthex; see fig.), with galleries on the second level. Large, reused blocks of marble from the ancient site of Stiris are incorporated into its cloisonné walling. Here, and in the Theotokos, motifs imitating kufic letters occur abundantly in the exterior masonry, a type of decoration popular in Greece in the 10th century. Inside the katholikon there is a shrine to Loukas, beneath which a large crypt houses his tomb and two others, probably those of abbots.

The mosaics and wall paintings of the katholikon are the most notable features at Hosios Loukas. A complex, hierarchical arrangement of scenes and portraits provides a comprehensive statement of Orthodox dogma. In the narthex, mosaic compositions represent the theme of death and resurrection: the *Crucifixion* and *Anastasis* frame a monumental bust of *Christ* over the entrance to the church, while the *Washing of the Feet* and *Incredulity of Thomas* appear at the north and south ends. There are standing Apostles in the soffits and medallions in the arches. The main body of the church or nave is dominated at the east by an apse mosaic of the seated *Virgin and Child*. Although wall paintings (1820) have replaced the original mosaic in the main dome, the sanctuary dome preserves an early example of the use of this space for a Pentecost scene. Three of the four squinches below the main dome retain scenes of great feasts of the liturgical year celebrating Christ's incarnation: the *Nativity*, *Presentation in the Temple* and *Baptism*. Two scenes of miraculous salvation appear in the diakonikon, the chapel to the right of the sanctuary: the *Three Hebrews in the Fiery Furnace* and *Daniel in the Lions' Den*. A great array of angels, saints, church fathers and holy men occupy all remaining vaults and lunette surfaces surrounded by lavish geometric and floral ornament in a gold ground. Notable among the portraits of saints are those in the north-east chapel, one on the south wall showing Philotheos, the founder, presenting Loukas with a model of the church, and two on the west wall of local saints, *Nikon Metanoite* and *Loukas Gurniokiotes*.

Wall paintings are also abundant and well preserved in the chapels and galleries of the katholikon and in the crypt. The funerary and baptismal connotations in the programmes of the north-west and south-west chapels, respectively, reflect their intended uses. In the north arm of the cross a remarkable painting of *Joshua*, in full armour before the archangel, survives on a wall that was part of the façade of the earlier Theotokos church, now part of the katholikon. The distinctive hieratic style of the mosaics differs sharply from the ornamental and precious quality of the mosaics at Nea Moni, Chios (*see* CHIOS, §2), and the lyrical, Hellenistic forms of DAFNI. The rather heavy-set figures have wide, staring eyes and stiff, linear draperies.

The crypt, which houses the tomb of *Loukas*, has the most complete programme of wall paintings surviving from the Middle Byzantine period (*see* EARLY CHRISTIAN AND BYZANTINE ART, fig. 42). Ten vaults of the crypt contain medallion portraits of warrior martyrs, Apostles and holy men, including three realistic portraits of contemporary abbots in the south-east vault, among whom is Philotheos. These portraits may be compared with a panel near the crypt entrance depicting three abbots standing in front of an assembly of monks. Around the walls of the crypt are eight lunettes with scenes of the *Passion* and *Resurrection*. The use of Classical proportions, white highlights and the circular stylizations of draperies encourage comparison with the 10th-century wall paintings in the New and Old Churches of Tokalı (*see* CAPPADOCIA, §2) and the Panagia Chalkion at Thessaloniki (1028; *see* THESSALONIKI, §III, 6) as well as with such manuscripts as the MENOLOGION OF BASIL II. The style is consistent with formalizing tendencies seen in the late Macedonian Renaissance. Although major differences exist between the wall paintings of the crypt and the mosaics of the katholikon, they have certain stylistic and iconographic similarities.

BIBLIOGRAPHY

Life of Loukas the Younger (after 961); ed. Migne, *PG* (Paris, 1857–66), iii, cols 441–80

R. Schultz and S. Barnsley: *The Monastery of St Luke of Phocis and the Dependent Monastery of St. Nicolas in the Fields near Skripou in Boeotia* (London, 1901)

M. Chatzidakis: 'A propos de la date et du fondateur de Saint Luc', *Cah. Archéol.*, xix (1969), pp. 127–50

E. Stikas: *To oikodomikon chronikon tis monis Hosiou Louka Phokidos* [The building chronology of the monastery of St Luke in Phocis] (Athens, 1970)

——: 'Nouvelles Observations sur la date de construction du Catholicon et de l'église de la Vierge du monastère de Saint Luc en Phocide', *Corsi Cult. A. Ravenn. & Biz.*, xxxi (1972), pp. 311–30

L. Bouras: *O gluptos diakosmos tou naou tis Panagias sto monasteri tou Hosiou Louka* [The sculptural decoration in the Panagia church of the monastery of St Luke] (Athens, 1980)

D. Mouriki: 'Stylistic Trends in Monumental Painting of Greece during the Eleventh and Twelfth Centuries', *Dumbarton Oaks Pap.*, xxxiv–xxxvi (1980–81), pp. 77–112

T. Chatzidakis-Bacharas: *Les Peintures murales de Hosios Loukas: Les Chapelles occidentales* (Athens, 1982)

D. I. Pallas: 'Zur Topographie und Chronologie von Hosios Lukas: Eine kritische Übersicht', *Byz. Z.*, lxxviii (1985), pp. 94–107

P. Mylonas: 'Domiki ereuna sto ekklisiastiko synkrotima tou Osiou Louka Phokidos' [Structural investigations of the ecclesiastical complex of Hosios Loukas in Phokis], *Archaiologia*, xxxvi (Sept 1990), pp. 6–30

C. L. Connor: *Art and Miracles in Medieval Byzantium: The Crypt at Hosios Loukas and its Frescoes* (Princeton, 1991)

P. Mylonas: 'Domiki ereuna sto ekklisiastiko synkrotimo tou Osiou Louka Phokidos: Eympliromatiki perilipsi' [Structural investigations of the ecclesiastical complex of Hosios Loukas in Phokis: supplementary summary], *Archaiologia*, xxxviii (March 1991), pp. 78–80

C. L. Connor: 'Hosias Loukas as a Victory Church', *Gr., Roman & Byz. Stud.*, xxxiii (1992), pp. 293–308

P. Mylonas: 'Nouvelles Remarques sur le complexe de Saint-Luc en Phocide', *Cah. Archéol.*, cl (1992), pp. 115–22

N. Oikonomides: 'The First Century of the Monastery of Hosias Loukas', *Dumbarton Oaks Pap.*, xlvi (1992), pp. 245–55

D. Z. Sophianos: *Hosias Loukas, ho Bios tou* [The life of Hosias Loukas] (Athens, 1993)

C. L. Connor and W. R. Connor: *The Life and Miracles of St Luke of Steiris: Text, Translation and Commentary* (Brookline, MA, 1994)

CAROLYN L. CONNOR

Hoskins. English family of miniaturists. It is difficult to distinguish between the work of (1) John Hoskins (i) and his son (2) John Hoskins (ii) in the body of miniatures signed with the monogram IH. The elder Hoskins was the uncle and guardian of Samuel Cooper and Alexander Cooper; Samuel's influence can be discerned in works from the Hoskins studio produced during the 1630s and thereafter.

(1) John Hoskins (i) (*b* c. 1590; *d* London, 1665). The earlier miniatures assigned to him are the finest produced in England between the death of Nicholas Hilliard and the maturity of Samuel Cooper. Yet little is known about his life, and it is uncertain to what extent the miniatures signed IH and assembled under his name are the work of an individual, a studio or a group of related artists. Hoskins began his career as a portrait painter in oils. So far only two documented paintings in this medium by him are known. They are head-and-shoulder portraits of Sir Hamon Le Strange of Hunstanton Hall, Norfolk, and his wife Alice. The latter's household account book records payments for them in 1617 (see Duleep Singh, and Moore and Crawley). At about this time Hoskins began to paint miniatures and became the most gifted and successful limner in England between the death of Hilliard and the emergence of his nephew and pupil Samuel Cooper. His earliest miniatures, painted c. 1615 (e.g. *Portrait of an Unknown Lady*; Windsor Castle, Berks, Royal Col.), have affinities with the style of Isaac Oliver, but works of the early 1620s, such as the miniature of *Robert Carr, 1st Earl of Somerset* (Windsor Castle, Berks, Royal Col.), show the influence of Hilliard and his successors. The accession of Charles I in 1625 led to substantial royal patronage, including commissions for miniature copies of large portraits by Daniel Mijtens, an undertaking that left its mark on Hoskins's style. He was adaptable enough to imitate other manners when called on to copy earlier portraits of the King's forebears. This eclecticism was reinforced from 1632, when Anthony van Dyck became the leading painter at the English court. It has been suggested that the breadth of handling of large miniatures of the 1630s, such as the signed *Edward Sackville, 4th Earl of Dorset* (*c.* 1632; London, V&A), may be due to the presence in the Hopkins studio of one of his nephews, Samuel Cooper or Alexander Cooper. Alexander's contact with his uncle seems to have been brief, but Samuel remained with him, first as apprentice then as partner, setting up on his own in 1641 or 1642.

(2) John Hoskins (ii) (*b c.* 1620–30; *d* after 1692). Son of (1) John Hoskins (i). He is recorded as a limner in his own right and by *c.* 1657 had his own studio. It has been suggested that he was responsible for most of the miniatures signed IH from *c.* 1645, and that his father was by then in semi-retirement. The stylistic arguments are not decisive, however, and it is remarkable that there are no works that can be assigned to him on this basis after 1658, seven years before his father's death. Whatever the answer, from the late 1630s a connected run of miniatures shows that the achievements of van Dyck were being assimilated into the tradition of English miniature painting. It is exemplified by the portraits of *Katherine Howard, Lady d'Aubigny* (*c.* 1640; London, V&A) and *Edward, 2nd Viscount Conway* (1653; London, Wallace). These are distinguished from the mature work of Samuel Cooper by their use of stippling and absence of strong accents and by their greater reticence in the interpretation of character. These works had as their successors the miniatures of Nicholas Dixon and Peter Cross.

BIBLIOGRAPHY
B. Buckeridge: 'An Essay towards an English School of Painters', *The Art of Painting, and the Lives of the Painters*, ed. J. Savage (London, 1706) [trans. of R. de Piles: *Abrégé de la vie des peintres* (Paris, 1699)]
F. Duleep Singh: *Portraits in Norfolk Houses*, ed. Rev. E. Farrer, 2 vols (Norwich, 1928)
G. Reynolds: *English Portrait Miniatures* (London, 1952, rev. Cambridge, 2/1988)
J. Murdoch: 'A. Hoskins and Crosses: Work in Progress', *Burl. Mag.*, cxx (1978), pp. 284–90
M. Edmond: 'Limners and Picturemakers', *Walpole Soc.*, xlvii (1980), pp. 60–242
J. Murdoch and others: *The English Miniature* (London and New Haven, 1981)
M. Edmond: 'Samuel Cooper, Yorkshireman—and Recusant?', *Burl. Mag.*, cxxvii (1985), pp. 83–5
A. Moore and C. Crawley: *Family and Friends: A Regional Survey of British Portraiture* (London, 1992), pp. 84–6, nos 18, 19

GRAHAM REYNOLDS

Hosmer, Harriet (*b* Watertown, MA, 9 Oct 1830; *d* Watertown, 21 Feb 1908). American sculptor. Although she was born, educated and died in the USA, Hosmer spent most of her life in Rome. Travelling with the actress Charlotte Cushman (1816–76), who formed a salon in Rome consisting mostly of women artists, Hosmer arrived in Italy in 1852. There she acquired the patronage of Russian and English nobility and became a close friend of Robert and Elizabeth Barrett Browning. She returned to the USA in 1900.

Hosmer's first piece, a bust of *Hesper* carved in the USA (1852; Watertown, MA, Free Pub. Lib.), induced John Gibson (i) to accept her as a student in Rome. Under his influence, Hosmer produced a variety of idealized marble figures, often with subjects from mythology. Her fame and most of her income were based on the frequently

copied conceits of *Puck* (marble, 1856; Washington, DC, N. Mus. Amer. A.) and *Will-o'-the-wisp* (marble, Piedmont, NY, priv. col.), but today she is admired for her sensitive and moving portrayals of doomed heroines: *Beatrice Cenci* (1853–5; St Louis, MO, Mercantile Lib.), which reveals her ability to model human form, and *Zenobia, the Queen of Palmyra* (*c.* 1857; Hartford, CT, Wadsworth Atheneum). Her highly polished, detailed and delicately restrained style reached its zenith in the monument to *Judith Falconnet* (*d* 1857), in S Andrea delle Fratte, Rome. Although Hosmer was publicly derided for using studio assistants who transferred the clay model to its marble state, a common practice in the mid-19th century, she was one of the few American sculptors of either sex who could, and at times did, carve her own work.

BIBLIOGRAPHY
R. A. Bradford: 'The Life and Works of Harriet Hosmer', *New England Mag.*, n.s., xlv (1911), pp. 265–9
W. H. Gerdts: *American Neoclassic Sculpture* (New York, 1973)
B. Groseclose: 'Hosmer's Tomb to Judith Falconnet: Death and the Maiden', *Amer. A. J.*, xii (1980), pp. 78–89

BARBARA GROSECLOSE

Hosoda Eishi [Chōbunsai] (*b* ?Edo [now Tokyo], 1756; *d* 1829). Japanese painter and woodblock-print designer. He was of samurai rank but abandoned his position to devote himself to painting and print design. Having first studied painting under Kanō Eisen'in Michinobu (1730–90), he began producing *ukiyoe* ('pictures of the floating world'; *see* JAPAN, §§VI, 4(iv)(b) and IX, 2(iii)). Early works include a series of colour prints of literary classics such as the 11th-century *Tale of Genji*. Eishi then began to produce courtesan images influenced by Torii Kiyonaga (*see* TORII, (8)) and then pictures of solitary seated women. In the print *Kasen of the Ōgiya*, from *Six Select Beauties of the Gay Quarters* (*Seirō bijin rokkasen*), Kasen is shown holding her brush over an inkstone, about to paint a fan, which she holds in her other hand. Full-bodied figures of women, depicted in activities such as letter-writing or reading, and with a few suggestions of their belongings, became part of his treatment of the theme. Later Eishi depicted standing female figures against subdued, single-colour backgrounds. Finally, Eishi elongated his women until their heads were only one-twelfth the height of the rest of the figure. The woodblock-print triptych of *A Selection of Geisha from the Green Houses* (*Seirō geisha sen*), thought to date from 1796–7 (London, V&A), is an example of this style. In his last years, Eishi nearly ceased to produce woodblock prints in favour of brush paintings of courtesans, such as he had been producing all his life, for example *Beauty Waiting for a Boat* (colours and ink on silk; *c.* 1790s; Japan, Takahashi Col.; see Neurer, p. 220). Eishi is also known as the mentor of a number of artists who produced half-length portraits, primarily during the 1790s.

BIBLIOGRAPHY
S. Kikuchi: *Ukiyoe*, Genshoku Nihon no bijutsu [Arts of Japan, illustrated], xvii (Tokyo, 1968, 19/1977)
S. Yoshida: *Ukiyoe no mikata jiten* [Encyclopedia of a view of *ukiyoe*] (Tokyo, 1977, 2/1987)
R. Neurer, H. Libertson and S. Yoshida: *Ukiyo-e: 250 Years of Japanese Art* (New York, 1979)

BRENDA G. JORDAN

Hosoe, Eikoh [Eikō] (*b* Yonezawa, 18 March 1933). Japanese photographer. He graduated from Tokyo College of Photography in 1951 and first exhibited in a one-man show *An American Girl in Tokyo* (1956; Tokyo, Konishiroku Gal.), a depiction of his friendship with an American girl. Hosoe became one of the leading photographers of the Vivo (Esperanto: 'Life') group formed in 1959 with Ikkō Narahara and Shomei Tōmatsu and others. In 1960 he published *Otoko to onna* ('Man and woman'), nude portraits of the *butō* dancer Tatsumi Hijikata and people in his group photographed in harsh contrast. His style expressed the struggle between the human body and the spirit, sometimes as fantasy, sometimes directly. He continued to evolve this style in such collections as *Barakei* ('Killed by roses'; Tokyo, 1963; rev. 2/1971/*R* 1985) for which the writer Yukio Mishima modelled; the fantasy comedy *Kamaitachi* ('A weasel's slash'; Tokyo, 1969), set in a rural village; and *Hōyō* ('Embrace'; Tokyo, 1971) which is a more abstract version of *Otoko to onna*. From 1977, he began to photograph the architecture of Antoni Gaudí and the results are collected in *Gaudí no uchū* ('The universe of Gaudí'; Tokyo, 1984).

BIBLIOGRAPHY
New Japanese Photography (exh. cat. by J. Szarkowski and S. Yamagishi, New York, MOMA, 1974), pp. 80–83
Black Sun: The Eyes of Four (exh. cat. by M. Holborn, Oxford, MOMA; London, Serpentine Gal.; Philadelphia, PA, Mus A.; 1985), pp. 17–32
M. Holborn: *Beyond Japan: A Photo Theatre* (London, 1991), pp. 57–91
Eikoh Hosoe: META (exh. cat. by C. Capa and E. Hosoe, New York, Int. Cent. Phot., 1991)

KOHTARO IIZAWA

Hosoi Kōtaku (*b* Kyoto, 1658; *d* Edo [now Tokyo], 1735). Japanese calligrapher and seal-carver. He was probably the most important Japanese master of *Karayō* (Chinese-style) calligraphy in the early 18th century. The son of a physician from Totomi Province (now in Shizuoka Prefect.), Kōtaku went to Edo as a youth to receive a Confucian education. He studied the Chinese classics with Sakai Zenken (*d* 1703) and also learnt a number of cultivated arts and skills such as poetry, painting, seal-carving, mathematics, astronomy and munitions. He also studied *Karayō* calligraphy with Kitajima Setsuzan (1636–97), who popularized in Japan the styles of Chinese calligraphers such as Wen Zhengming (*see* WEN, (1)) of the Yuan (1279–1368) and Ming (1368–1644) periods. Immigrant Ōbaku (Chin. Huangbo) Zen monks had brought this literati style, which became admired and practised partly because of the Tokugawa government's strong support for Chinese scholarly and cultural attainments (*see* JAPAN, §VII, 2(vi)). After completing his education, Kōtaku accepted a position as adviser on firearms to the shogunate councillor Yanagisawa Yoshiyasu (1658–1714). Kōtaku's primary interest, however, was in the arts, particularly calligraphy, so he eventually resigned his position and lived as a calligraphy teacher and author. His several publications on calligraphy include books showing varieties of seal-script (Jap. *tensho*; Chin. *zuan shu*) characters, but his most influential publication was *Shibi jiyō* ('Purple fern writing method'; 1724), which described the proper method of holding the brush, the fundamental brushstrokes and correct and incorrect methods of writing. Kōtaku seldom used the Japanese *kana* syllabary but mastered all five Chinese scripts—seal (Jap. *tensho*; Chin. *zuanshu*), clerical (Jap. *reisho*; Chin. *lishu*), regular (Jap. *kaisho*; Chin. *kaishu*), running (Jap. *gyōsho*; Chin. *xingshu*) and cursive (Jap. *sōsho*; Chin. *caoshu*). His writing demonstrates his thorough study of Chinese models: the brushwork is strong, bold and dramatic, with firm, thick lines and a vertical accentuation of individual characters. Kōtaku utilized every format, including pairs of six-panel screens, which were not a medium for calligraphy in China (*see* JAPAN, fig. 130). Through his teachings, his books and his personal example, Kōtaku did a great deal to spread interest in Chinese-style calligraphy in Japan.

BIBLIOGRAPHY
N. Tsuchida and others: *Gakusha* [Scholars], Sho to jinbutsu [Calligraphy and people], v (Tokyo, 1978)
S. Komatsu: *Karayō* [Chinese-style calligraphy], Nihon no sho [Japanese calligraphy], xii (Tokyo, 1983)

STEPHEN ADDISS

Hospet. *See under* HAMPI, §4.

Hospital. Institution for the care of the needy, including the poor and the elderly, but particularly for the treatment of the sick and injured. The word is derived from the Latin *hospes* ('guest') and originally denoted a place of sojourn for travellers and especially pilgrims: in medieval times, for example, the Knights of St John built a hospital for pilgrims at Jerusalem. Later, such institutions as orphanages and workhouses were referred to as hospitals, but during the 19th century the term began to be associated specifically with an environment suitable for recovery from illness. Such considerations as ventilation became important, and in the 20th century hospitals were conceived and designed predominantly as places for medical treatment. As the hospital has always been essentially a charitable institution, it has for most of its history attracted patronage by religious orders and by beneficent individuals, comprising many outstanding examples of architectural decoration.

1. Architecture. 2. Decoration.

1. ARCHITECTURE.

(i) Before 1450. (ii) 1450–1700. (iii) After 1700.

(i) Before 1450. Throughout history hospitals have adapted current architectural modes. In ancient Greece a few private patients were treated in the physician's own house (the *iatrion*), but most were housed in a stoa (the *asklepieion*). In the Roman Empire—where, as everywhere until the 20th century, most of the sick were nursed at home—two categories of patient, slaves and soldiers, because of their economic value were nursed in *valetudinaria*, the hollow square of an army barracks with small rooms. Christianity, however, saw the disadvantaged as opportunities for charitable works. Christians harboured strangers temporarily, fed the hungry, clothed the naked and tended the sick in hospitals, often in smallish rooms and with minimal attempt to segregate. The most important consideration was the salvation of the soul through confession, absolution and Mass, recited within the patients' sight (or at least hearing). An altar or chapel was thus a necessary adjunct to a ward, and in the absence of medical knowledge, hospitals were often just places to die. There were

1. Hôpital Notre-Dame des Fontenilles, Tonnerre, 1293

exceptions outside Western Europe: great Christian hospitals were founded in the Byzantine Empire from the 4th century. In 1136, for example, the hospital of the Christ Pantokrator Monastery in Constantinople had some sixty beds, one patient to a bed, roughly separated by diagnosis; there were sixteen physicians in a hierarchy, five pharmacists and only two priests (*see* CHRISTIANITY, §IV, 1). However, Byzantine practices, relayed by returning crusaders, were not implemented in the West before the 18th century.

The earliest known Western plan to include hospital arrangements is that of AD 817 (unexecuted) for St Gall Abbey. Categories of patients were to be segregated, with different rooms being allocated for sick novices, sick and aged monks, dying monks, monks routinely bled and dying lay brethren; in the hospices (for the recovery of the travel-worn) there was a further separation between pilgrims and paupers on the one hand, and distinguished rich guests on the other. At Cluny Abbey sickrooms and bleeding house were united within four large second-storey chambers of St Hugh's Infirmary, and by 1157 the monastery's basilican infirmary of Peter the Venerable included all patients save those at the travellers' hospice beside the gate. Both infirmaries at Cluny lay south-east of the church apse, a Cistercian placement that other orders sometimes followed. At Fountains Abbey the remains of two basilican infirmaries have survived, one south-west of the site for lay brethren (north wall standing with triple window openings) and one in the traditional placement for monks (room divisions marked on the earth).

Although many monastic infirmaries in France suffered during the Revolution, the infirmary of the abbey of Ourscamp (1210), south-east of the ruined apse, survived because it was used as a parish church. Significantly, it is called the Salle des Morts. Each bay of the long walls front and rear contains, 1 m above ground, a grouping of three small windows, which can be opened from within for ventilation; above them are tall twin windows, with a rose window on top, which are sealed and entirely for giving light. These expressed the dual purpose of the ward, secular (nursing) and sacred (prayer). The same duality of the ward–chapel combination is visible at the Hôpital Notre-Dame des Fontenilles (1293; west front altered 18th century; see fig. 1) in Tonnerre. The apsed chapel of the easternmost bay is vaulted in stone, with large pointed windows that once held stained glass. A considerably darker ward is barrel-roofed in wood, with smaller, round-headed clear windows that could be opened from a balcony (destr.) from which the founder, Margaret of Burgundy (1248–1308), widow of Charles I, King of Naples, could inspect the sick below in two rows of cubicles (destr.). In the barrel roof, clover-leaf ventilation holes lead to a vast reservoir of air under the hospital's peaked roof, originally tiled in the same bright local pattern still visible at the nearby Hôtel-Dieu of Beaune. The similar ward at Beaune (1443), by Jacques Wiscrère, barrel-roofed with an elaborate chapel, has been heavily restored.

Wards were combined with chapels in every possible way. At the Second Hospital of the Knights of St John (1440) on Rhodes, modelled on a Byzantine hospice, a bright chapel apse juts from the middle of the long wall, which faces east. The chapel of the Heilig-Geist-Spital (1276–86) in Lübeck inexplicably lies west of its ward. The hospital of Byloke (1201) in Ghent has, behind a double façade, a shorter three-bay chapel parallel to an eleven-bay ward, with two large arches between them for auditory connection. Already in the 13th century these arches were half filled in, anticipating the later complete separation between chapel and ward.

Two categories of patients excluded from general wards were the dangerously mad (*see* ASYLUM) and lepers, who were excommunicated from all society but had a relatively long life-expectancy during the great epidemics of the 11th–13th centuries. They might band together like monks for mutual sustenance in a cluster of small houses around a church and, to maximize almsgiving, beside a main road. One of 2000 leprosaria counted in France in 1226, the leprosarium of Meursault (before 1142), near Beaune, has survived, its stone church and individual stone cells still recognizable. The ambulatory old often lived in tiny exquisite cloisters such as God's House (1436), Ewelme, Oxon, which housed 13 poor folk (a symbolic reference to Christ and the Apostles); it had one room downstairs, one room above and steep steps. In the late 20th century the larger quadrangle (1440) of the hospital of St Cross, Winchester, Hants, continued to be used to house 35 pauper brethren and distressed gentlefolk. At the St Nikolausspital (1437) at Kues in Germany, 21 paupers lived in 2 open wards with north exposure, while 6 retired noblemen and 6 priests were given the 12 private rooms to south and east. The principle of mass accommodation for the poor and privacy for the upper classes was established at an early date.

The Ospedale degli Innocenti, Florence, the first foundling hospital in the world, was of vast architectural influence by virtue of its façade, an exterior loggia, which was the first significant work of FILIPPO BRUNELLESCHI. Yet a similar, earlier, loggia has survived at the tiny Ospedale di S Antonio (1411) in Lastra-Signa, near Florence. This has four arches, four square cross-vaulted decorated bays behind them, a central chapel with Gothic triple window, and a row of square windows on the squat upper storey. Its location just within the city gate is that of a typical hospice. In his expanded design at the Innocenti (from 1419; *see* FLORENCE, fig. 1), Brunelleschi used Corinthian columns, and he added domes to the bays of the loggia, with pilasters at the ends, but his work and its prototype are a reminder that singular outstanding hospitals always coexisted with numerous modest hospices. Some large city foundations grew from modest origins: the Hospices Civils (1143) in Strasbourg is shown on a city plan of 1548 as a two-storey house at a crossing, with an entrance door to the west and a minute four-windowed eastern apse. By the 18th century it had been enlarged four times on three different sites.

(ii) 1450–1700. Renaissance hospital planners recognized the danger of elongating a ward past the point where patients could see or hear the Mass. For the Ospedale Maggiore (1456), Milan, Filarete, architect to Francesco Sforza, Duke of Milan, designed four great wards that met in one central chapel: the first cross ward. Exhibiting the characteristic Renaissance preoccupation with centralized planning, Filarete intended two such huge crosses, one for men, one for women, to either side of a central court, but the second of these was not built for 350 years. Women were therefore given one arm of the lofty men's cross, which was inscribed in a square of two-storey but lower wings containing service rooms, private rooms and overflow wards. The central court was finally built in 1630 from a new bequest on an altered plan, and the completed double cross, extensively restored in 1972 after bomb damage in World War II, became part of the University of Milan.

Filarete solved a contemporary problem so well that the Ospedale Maggiore was imitated even before its first stage had been completed. Hospitals on Greek-cross plans were subsequently built at Como (1468), Bergamo (1458), Pavia (1449–89) and Piacenza (1471). In Florence two Roman crosses tucked one below the other formed the Ospedale di S Maria Nuova (1479). In England one very large cruciform plan was the Savoy Hospital (1509; destr.) in London, built by Henry VII. In Spain, Enrique Egas designed the Hospital de Santa Cruz (*c.* 1500; now part of the Museo de Santa Cruz) in Toledo as a Greek cross elongated at the top by a second chapel; vaults over this and the chapel at the crossing are stone and Gothic in design and contrast with *Mudéjar* coffered-wood ward ceilings. Women were accommodated upstairs lest the men look down on them. The ornate Plateresque façade is typical of Spanish hospitals and churches (see fig. 2). Egas was also responsible for the cross ward of the Hospital Real (1499; now the Hostal de los Reyes Católicos) at Santiago de Compostela. The largest surviving Greek-cross design is also in Spain: the Hospital de las Cinco Llagas (1546) in Seville. Later, in 1635, the Hospice des Femmes Incurables was built in Paris in two Greek

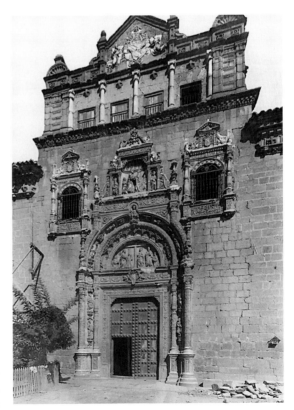

2. Hospital de Santa Cruz, Toledo, by Enrique Egas, *c.* 1500; now part of the Museo de la Santa Cruz

crosses, and in the same year Josef Furttenbach the elder, for whom the Ospedale Maggiore was 'the principal hospital of all Italy', developed a plan (1634) for a *Brechhaus* for plague victims as a Greek cross with a stairwell at the crossing.

The Lazaretto (1488) of the Ospedale Maggiore was built for plague victims, who naturally were not taken into hospitals. An immense hollow square beyond the town wall, it had 288 contiguous rooms surrounded on their inner face by an arcade, on the outer by a moat. In the centre of the plot was a small octagonal chapel 'in filigree': the whole building was arcaded, so that theoretically every patient could see the Mass, a principle taken over from the cross ward. Each room could hold eight patients but received many more during epidemics, when the central field was covered with shacks and tents for an estimated total occupancy of 14,000. Only the chapel, walled in, has survived, but the influence of this design can be seen, for example, at the Lazaretto of Mahon Harbour, Minorca, a circle of connected rooms built in 1807 around a tiny glassed-in cupola of a chapel.

A late 16th-century tendency towards regularization of differentiated forms can be seen in a print of the Julius Hospital (1576), Würzburg, designed by Georges Robin. Taller windows and a small spire at one end of the front wing indicate the chapel, but an overpoweringly ornate gate-house imposes centrality. This version of the hospital was replaced in 1789 by one of classicizing symmetry,

comprising a slightly projecting and elevated central section with long low wings to either side (destr. World War II; later rebuilt). In the 17th century some of the most imposing hospital establishments were built for those who had grown old or been disabled in the service of their country. Outstanding examples include the Hôtel des Invalides (from 1670) in Paris, designed by Libéral Bruand and Jules Hardouin Mansart (*see* PARIS, §V, 7 and fig. 41), and the Royal Naval Hospital (from 1694; *see* GREENWICH, §2, and WREN, CHRISTOPHER, fig. 4) in Greenwich, by Christopher Wren and others.

(iii) After 1700. The standard 18th-century design for hospitals, as for other buildings, was a symmetrical central block with outflung wings. The central block was used for administration and the wings for wards, with the whole edifice divided down the middle by sex. Many such hospitals survive. Among symmetrical, medium-sized three- or four-storey 18th-century hospitals modest variations can be found: the Royal Infirmary (1738; destr.), Edinburgh, which announced itself 'open to all the Cureable distressed from whatever Corner of the world they come without restriction', was a C-shape with wings facing front. A C-shape with wings running backward, the Krankenspital (1788; now a hotel), Bamberg, has a second-storey chapel revealed only by a mere oculus in the central pediment and a tiny turret on the roof. This chapel spread auditory messages to patients through windows on each side chapel wall and doors behind them in enfilade. The Pennsylvania Hospital (1755), Philadelphia, by Samuel Rhoads, a modified H-form, was built in three stages, the two wings first and the centre section last. In 18th-century Spain the standard hospital form was four wings around a court, an enlarged version of the form for large private dwellings. The hospital church typically occupied half a side wing, and its entrance from the street was very ornate, in contrast to the stark ward door beside it. Many very beautiful late 18th-century Spanish hospitals (such as those of St John of God in Granada, Antequera and Lucena) continued to receive patients into the 20th century but were gradually being replaced.

The sanitary conditions in 18th-century hospitals were such that a patient was lucky to come out alive. The worst was the Hôtel-Dieu of Paris, with a mortality rate of 25%. It had occupied the same island site, cramped between the Seine and the cathedral of Notre-Dame, since 1195, and as Paris had grown the hospital had expanded, completely without guiding plan and oblivious of ventilating courts. One ward was built on the Pont-au-Double over the Seine, and at the four-storey St Charles building smallpox and fever wards shared a wide central staircase with surgical and maternity wards. In a travesty of Christian charity all in need were accepted, and as many as seven patients would have to share a bed. In 1772 the medieval buildings burnt down, and there was discussion of relocating in four 1000-bed establishments on the outskirts of Paris. This prompted enthusiastic planning by scientists and architects, but the Revolution came before the nursing sisters could be budged from their site. Nevertheless, the plans produced at this time gave birth to the pavilion hospital.

From so terrible an example and from a better understanding of air-borne infections it was clear that 4000

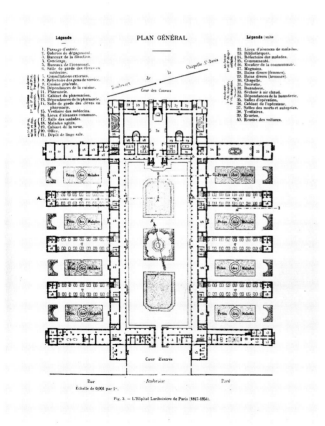

3. Plan (1789) for a hospital, by the Académie des Sciences (executed 1846)

4. Gasthuisberg Hospital, Leuven, by Richard Llewelyn-Davies, Weeks, Forestier-Walker & Born, 1985

patients should be segregated and that patients should be arranged by diagnosis and nursed in well-ventilated pavilions of limited size. One architect envisaged a colosseum of radiating pavilions, another a cross ward, but the plan preferred by the Académie des Sciences in 1789 proposed two rows of parallel pavilions not more than three storeys high, connected only by a covered walk at their ground floor, and with a large central court and space enough between units (see fig. 3). Each ward should have opposite windows down its long walls, no more than 40 beds, nursing quarters at the near (court) end, toilets and baths at the far end. During their planning the Academicians visited the Royal Naval Hospital (1756–64) at Stonehouse, near Plymouth, built by Alexander Rovehead. This housed 1250 patients in 10 separate pavilions connected by a covered walk, with a church at the head of the plan, but it deviated from the projected ideal mainly in that each block was halved by a wall parallel to the two rows of windows.

Political unrest prevented the implementation of the Académie plan in Paris until 1846, when the Hôpital Lariboisière was built. An unsuccessful forced-air ventilation experiment meant that this was in fact no more salubrious than most other hospitals, but its design exactly fulfilled the ventilation theories of Florence Nightingale, who thus enthusiastically endorsed it, publicizing the pavilion system so successfully that it became the dominant form of hospital building for 75 years. Its ascendancy meant the final demise of the cross-shaped hospital. Another late 18th-century innovation took place at the Allgemeines Krankenhaus (1783–4) in Vienna, where 2000 patients were classified financially in four categories and charged on a sliding scale for food and service. Pavilions were subsequently designed in all shapes, including circles (e.g. the Algemeen Ziekenhuis Stuivenberg, Antwerp, 1878). For lack of extension space, one famous octagonal ward was built (1885; destr.) at Johns Hopkins Hospital, Baltimore, MD. Some pavilion hospitals have no interior court: the pavilions of Herbert Hospital (1864), Woolwich, London, hang from either side of a single main corridor, and those of St Thomas's Hospital (1868–71), London, by Henry Currey (1820–1900), hang from one side only because of a narrow site. The latter remained popular with

medical staff and patients into the late 20th century. The use of pavilions spread throughout the world: the Hospital Eugenio Espejo, Quito, planned for them in 1901, although they were not built until 1933 because of lack of funds.

During the dominance of the pavilion form, there were rapid medical advances; causes were found for many diseases, and new operations became possible in a suitably designed hospital environment. New diagnostic techniques such as radiography were practical only in hospitals, and by the 1920s rich and poor alike had to go for optimum care to the hospital, which had become in itself a machine for healing. One of the most notable Modernist designs was that for the Paimio Sanatorium (1929–32) in Finland, by ALVAR AALTO, which blended Rationalism with an organic approach. More generally, however, and again assuming the dominant building form of the time, the hospital was built as a skyscraper.

Typically American, such hospitals as the Columbia Presbyterian Medical Center (1929) and the Cornell Medical Center (1933), both in New York, looked no different from any other skyscraper. As early as 1907, the Americans Albert J. Ochsner and Meyer J. Sturm had reasoned that for cities it made sound economic sense to pile pavilion upon pavilion to fit a constricted site and share utility costs. This principle was followed at the Hôpital Beaujon (1935), Paris, by Walter, Plousey and Cassan and at Westminster Hospital (1939) in London. Decades later, the inner court of an obsolete pavilion hospital came to be seen simply as available space for a rectangular highrise. When the high-rise was completed, the pavilions were torn down (e.g. at the Rigshospital, Copenhagen, 1970). Services and wards were forced into an oblong the dimensions of the garden court. The design of podium for services below with shaft for wards above (e.g. at Victoria Hospital, Kirkcaldy, Fife, 1967) or its opposite, with administrative tower and single-storey ward blocks (e.g. Wexton Park Hospital, Slough, Berks, by Powell and Moya; 1958–66) were attempts to reconcile divergent needs.

In the late 1980s changes in forms of treatment were taking place so fast and on so large a scale that the primary requirement for a hospital became flexibility. The London architects Richard Llewelyn-Davies, Weeks, Forestier-Walker & Born, who designed the Gasthuisberg Hospital (1985), Leuven, spread the high-rise over a hillside site (see fig. 4) and organized it once again around a central 'street', quite straight and level but with the ground floor of one building possibly corresponding to another floor in an adjacent building. All spaces share coordinated modules for almost immediate adaptation to other usage. Each department may not only build up to any desired height but may expand as required at right angles to the 'street'. Yet with services being consolidated, the need for patients or staff to travel is kept to a minimum.

BIBLIOGRAPHY

M. Tenon: *Mémoires sur les hôpitaux de Paris* (Paris, 1788)
F. Nightingale: *Notes on Hospitals* (London, 1859)
Hospital Plans: Five Essays (New York, 1875)
S. Wylie: *Hospitals: Their History, Organization and Construction* (New York, 1877)
C. Tollet: *De l'Assistance publique et des hôpitaux jusqu'au XIXe siècle* (Paris, 1889)
H. Burdett: *Hospitals and Asylums of the World*, 5 vols (London, 1891)
C. Mercier: 'Leper Houses and Medieval Hospitals', *Glasgow Medic. J.*, lxxxiii (1915), pp. 1–20, 81–103
J. Langdon-Davies: *Westminster Hospital* (London, 1952)
S. Spinelli: *La Ca' Granda (L'Ospedale Maggiore di Milano)* (Milan, 1958)
U. Craemer: *Das Hospital als Beautyp des Mittelalters* (Cologne, 1963)
B. Abel-Smith: *The Hospitals, 1800–1948* (London, 1964)
D. Leistikow: *Ten Centuries of European Hospital Architecture* (Ingelheim am Rhein, 1967) [excellent black-and-white photos]
L. Grassi: *Lo 'Spedale di poveri' del Filarete* (Milan, 1972)
J. Thompson and G. Goldin: *The Hospital: A Social and Architectural History* (New Haven, 1975)
N. Pevsner: *Building Types* (London, 1976), pp. 139–58
G. Goldin: 'Juan de Dios and the Hospital of Christian Charity', *J. Hist. Medic. & Allied Sci.*, xxxiii (1978), pp. 6–34
W. Horn and E. Born: *The Plan of St Gall*, 3 vols (Berkeley, CA, 1979)
T. Miller: *The Birth of the Hospital in the Byzantine Empire* (Baltimore, 1985)
D. Jetter: *Das europäische Hospital von der Spätantike bis 1800* (Cologne, 1986) [unparalleled historical survey]

GRACE GOLDIN

2. DECORATION. The largely religious nature of Western hospital patronage was reflected in the decoration of most hospitals, at least until the 18th century. One of the first Renaissance hospitals, Brunelleschi's Ospedale degli Innocenti, Florence, prompted not just some notable art, such as Luca della Robbia's *Virgin of the Innocents* (after 1450) and Domenico Ghirlandaio's *Adoration of the Magi* (1486–9) but also Andrea della Robbia's terracotta medallions of the Innocents themselves, with arms outstretched in welcome or supplication. Not to be outdone, the great hospital of S Maria della Scala, Siena, commissioned a rich array of paintings and sculpture by Francesco di Giorgio Martino, VECCHIETTA and, most notably, DOMENICO DI BARTOLO, whose fresco cycle (1440–44; *in situ*) dominates the wall of the grandest room (*see also* SIENA, §III, 2). However, Italy was not alone in the 15th century in adorning its hospitals with major paintings. For the Hôtel-Dieu at Beaune, Rogier van der Weyden was commissioned by Nicolas Rolin, Chancellor of Burgundy, to execute an outstanding altarpiece of the *Last Judgement* (completed 1451; *in situ*; for illustration *see* ROLIN, (1)). Installed in a chapel at the end of a ward, the 'Salle des Pauvres', it juxtaposes a harrowing vision of Hell with the beneficence of Heaven. The hospital of St John, Bruges,

managed to acquire some of the finest works of HANS MEMLING: the hospital sisters Jossine van Dudzele and Anna van den Moortele probably commissioned the most sumptuous of these, the gilded shrine adorned with scenes from the *Life of St Ursula* (1489; Bruges, Memlingmus). One of the most ambitious works commissioned for hospitals during the Renaissance was Matthias Grünewald's Isenheim Altarpiece (*c.* 1515; Colmar, Mus. Unterlinden; *see* GRÜNEWALD, MATTHIAS, fig. 2), a polyptych painted for a monastic hospital for skin diseases. Patients were taken to see the artist's uncompromising depiction of the crucified Christ, with his gruesome wounds and sores (although his face exudes calm and serenity), and encouraged to realize the relative insignificance of their own afflictions.

Some of the most intensely expressive images are those produced by El Greco for hospitals in Spain. At the church of the Hospital de la Caridad in Illescas he painted ecstatic interpretations of the *Annunciation, Nativity, Coronation of the Virgin* and the *Virgin of Charity* (begun 1603; *in situ*). In 1608–14, towards the end of his career, El Greco also produced some outstanding paintings, including the celebrated *Vision of St John* (New York, Met.) for the Tavera Hospital in Toledo. Later in the 17th century another Spanish artist, Murillo, executed 11 of his greatest paintings (1670–74) for the church of the Hospital de la Caridad in Seville: some of these have since been removed, such as the *Healing of the Paralytic at the Pool of Bethesda* (London, N.G.), but others remain *in situ*, such as *Moses Striking the Rock*. Near Murillo's luminous canvases hang two *vanitas* paintings by Juan de Valdés Leal (*see* VALDES LEAL, (1)). Another notable Spanish 17th-century work is a group of four eschatological scenes (1635; Barcelona, Bib. Catalunya) executed in coloured tiles at the Hospital de la Santa Creu in Barcelona. The late 17th century also saw some notable commissions for hospital decoration in Britain and France: Caius Gabriel Cibber carved two figures of *Melancholy* and *Raving Madness* (1680; London, Bethlem Royal Hosp. Archvs & Mus.), remarkable for their sense of compassion, for the entrance gateway of the new Bethlem Hospital, while the façade and courtyard of the Hôtel des Invalides in Paris were embellished with swaggering carvings (1671–5), and its dining halls were decorated with murals (1678–82) by Joseph Parrocel and Michel Corneille (ii). The most notable decoration at the Invalides, however, is to be found in the Dome, designed by Jules Hardouin Mansart, which contains frescoes by Charles de La Fosse, Louis Boullogne and others (*see* PARIS, §V, 7).

In the early 18th century there were again some notable schemes for hospital decoration in Britain. The Painted Hall of the Royal Naval Hospital at Greenwich, decorated in 1707–14 by James Thornhill, contains an elaborate ceiling painting full of robust maritime references and is perhaps the most flamboyant Baroque painted interior in Britain (for illustration *see* THORNHILL, JAMES). William Hogarth also undertook some notable hospital commissions, for example at St Bartholomew's Hospital, London, where he painted the *Pool of Bethesda* (1736) and the *Good Samaritan* (1737; both *in situ*) and at the Foundling Hospital, where he painted a splendid full-length portrait of *Captain Thomas Coram* (1740; London, Foundling

5. *View of the Sick Ward of St John's Hospital, Bruges, 1778* by Johannes Beerblock, oil on canvas, 0.76×1.52 m, 1778 (*in situ*)

Hosp.). He also supervised the decoration of the hospital's Court Room with further works by himself, Richard Wilson, Thomas Gainsborough, Michael Rysbrack and others. Around the same time Giambattista Tiepolo decorated the great hospital church of the Pietà in Venice with some soaring frescoes (*c.* 1753–5), and a little later Jacopo Guarana painted a delightful illusionistic scheme (1776) for the music room at the Ospedaletto, also in Venice. In some cases hospital life itself was the subject of paintings intended for public display (see fig. 5). In the 19th century some strikingly direct and candid works were painted in the Bethlem and Broadmoor hospitals, London, by Richard Dadd, while in the USA some notable portraits of physicians were produced, most notably by Thomas Eakins in Philadelphia (e.g. the *Gross Clinic*, 1875; Philadelphia, PA, Thomas Jefferson U., Medic. Coll.; *see* EAKINS, THOMAS, fig. 2). In the admissions hall of the John Hopkins Hospital, Baltimore, MD, is a replica of Bertel Thorvaldsen's monumental *Christus Consolator* (1838), reinforcing the hospital founder's desire to impress 'the influences of religion . . . upon the whole management of the Hospital'.

At the end of the 19th century and the beginning of the 20th, the influence of Art Nouveau was evident in the proliferation of decorated tiles in many hospitals and in the abundance of carvings and other decorations enlivening the Hospital de Sant Pau (1910) in Barcelona, designed by Lluís Domenech i Montaner. Similar influences are visible in the decoration (1904) by Kolo Moser, Richard Luksch and others of Otto Wagner's church of St Leopold 'am Steinhof' in Vienna for the patients of the Lower Austrian Institution and Sanatorium. Some of the most ambitious modern murals were produced in Mexico: these include the dramatic cycle of frescoes painted by José Clemente Orozco for the Hospicio Cabanas, Guadalajara, and the eloquent murals by Diego Rivera and David Alfaro

Siqueiros (1953) for the Hospital de la Raza, Mexico City. Around the same time Fernand Léger executed sculpture and an exterior mural (*in situ*) for the Hôpital-mémorial, France-Etats-Unis at Saint-Lô in Normandy, and between 1960 and 1962 Marc Chagall produced some of his most magnificent stained-glass windows for the synagogue of the Hebrew University Hadassah Medical Centre in Jerusalem. His 12 large panels (*in situ*) for the round-arched windows of Joseph Neufeld's hospital synagogue are based on the theme of the 12 tribes of Israel. In almost complete contrast to the figurative exuberance of Chagall's work is the abstract austerity of Naum Gabo's last public sculpture, *Revolving Torsion: Fountain* (1975), in the grounds of St Thomas's Hospital, London. The poise and grace of Gabo's work demonstrate the continuity into the late 20th century of the tradition of rich and distinguished works of art created for hospitals.

BIBLIOGRAPHY

J. Howard: *Prisons and Lazarettos* (London, 1791, 2/*R* Montclair, NJ, 1973), p. 57

M. Chagall: *The Jerusalem Windows* (New York, 1962)

D. Jetter: *Spanien von den Anfängen bis um 1500* (Wiesbaden, 1980), pp. 66–7

Patrimoine hospitalier de la Bourgogne (Dijon, 1980) [art holdings of the hosp. of one region]

F. B. Rogers: *Gallery of Portraits, Temple University School of Medicine* (Philadelphia, 1984)

H. Lobelle-Caluwé: *Memlingmuseum, Bruges* (Brussels, 1987) [excellent illus.]

G. Goldin: *Work of Mercy: A Picture History of Hospitals* (Toronto, 1994)

R. Cork: *For the Needs of their Own Spirit: A History of Western Art Made for Hospitals from the Renaissance to the Modern Period* (in preparation)

RICHARD CORK, with GRACE GOLDIN

Hostun, Marie-Joseph d'. *See* TALLARD, MARIE-JOSEPH D'HOSTUN, Duc de.

Hotan. *See* KHOTAN.

Hotel. Building designed to provide accommodation, dining, meeting and recreation facilities for the public. The modern hotel, which evolved from innovations in Europe and the eastern USA during the early 19th century, is usually distinguished from other, similar establishments, such as inns, lodges or motels, by its larger size and the provision of many guest services. By the end of the 20th century a wide range of hotel types had developed, catering largely to business travellers and tourists and varying enormously in size, site, facilities and market-orientation.

See also CLUB.

1. Before 1900. 2. 1900 and after.

1. BEFORE 1900. Lodging places for travellers have existed for thousands of years, for example as the *mansione* of ancient Rome and the CARAVANSERAI and *khān* of western Asia, but these generally offered few amenities and no assurance of quality. Medieval inns usually comprised a combined tavern and dining-room with a common sleeping area above; only occasionally were private rooms available for royalty or other distinguished guests. As roads improved and more inns were established in the 16th century, particularly in England, private rooms were added, often arranged along upper galleries encircling the stable-yard—in plan not unlike 20th-century atrium designs. By the mid-18th century assembly rooms were added to larger inns or incorporated into new designs. Despite the construction of a few lavish hotels, notably Dessin's Hotel, Calais, France, however, these establishments failed to show the architectural or operational complexity of those that developed in the 19th century.

Several important hotel and resort projects were completed soon after 1800. This expansion was due to several reasons: the introduction of the railway enhanced business and personal travel; the increased popularity of social and political functions required great banquet rooms; people with means made the 'Grand Tour' and took holidays at new spa resorts; and in the USA the remarkable expansion westwards into undeveloped regions created continual demand for new and innovative lodging accommodation. In Baden-Baden, Germany, Friedrich Weinbrenner converted a Capuchin monastery into the 50-room Badischer Hof (1807–9; destr.). In addition to a ballroom, library, reading-rooms and lounges, the building housed a magnificent three-storey skylit dining-room, surrounded on all floors by wide corridors and private guest-rooms. In England John Foulston (1772–1842) designed the Royal Hotel (1811–22; destr. 1939–41), Plymouth, combining in one complex a ballroom and theatre, a 50-room hotel including dining-room and lounges, and an adjoining literary club or Athenaeum. As in other major hotels, these were organized around a large courtyard, with provision for horses and coaches—and baths—in the rear.

While a few hotels, as distinguished from inns, had been built in the USA immediately after its independence, the first prominent one was Boston's 200-room Exchange Coffee House (1806–9; by Asher Benjamin; destr. 1818). A squarish building, with numerous dining- and assembly rooms, it was embellished with the Classical orders both on the façade and in multiple galleries. Its central domed area was used as a merchants' exchange. Often cited as the first modern hotel, the 170-room Tremont House (1828–9; by Isaiah Rogers; destr. 1895) in Boston introduced architectural monumentality (see fig. 1) as well as numerous operational and programmatic advances to the hotel. A formal portico led to a small domed rotunda and, along a lateral corridor, separate lounges and reading-rooms for men and women (for plan *see* ROGERS, ISAIAH). The hotel's innovations included a reception area—earlier hotels required registration at the bar—private and lockable guest accommodation, public spaces lit by gas, indoor baths and such amenities as pitcher, wash basin and soap. The Tremont House was immediately emulated by developers in many American and European cities, including New York, where the five-storey, 309-room Astor House (1834–6; by Rogers; destr. 1913) was faced in granite, with Greek Revival details and sumptuous public rooms. Other influential early American hotels included the St Charles (1835–6; destr. 1850), New Orleans, designed by Charles Bingley Dakin (1811–39) and James Gallier (i), which was surmounted by a large gilded dome. Hotels built in the USA in the following decades had more utilitarian exteriors but equally grand public rooms, which became central meeting places for society—both formal and informal. Dining-rooms took on greater importance, separate banqueting halls were developed (often on the top floor, with city views), suites were offered for permanent residents, retail areas filled the street frontage and many new services were added.

In Europe a similar evolution took place. The more notable hotels include the Queen's Hotel (1836–8; by Robert William Jearrad), Cheltenham, an impressive four-storey spa hotel with a giant Ionic portico and about 80 rooms, and the similar Royal Western Hotel (now Brunel House; 1837–9; by Richard Shackleton Pope) in Bristol. The expansion of the railway system in the mid-19th century led to the construction of accommodation at most terminals. Among the first in London was the Great Western Hotel at Paddington (1851–4; by Philip Charles Hardwick), designed in Renaissance Revival style, with such amenities as private toilets and electric clocks. Other examples include the Grosvenor Hotel at Victoria Station (1860–62; by James Thomas Knowles (i)), designed in a similar hybrid Italianate and French Renaissance style, and the Midland Grand at St Pancras Station; 1866–76; by George Gilbert Scott I), with Gothic Revival spires. The Danieli in Venice, converted in 1822 from a 15th-century palazzo, was among the first full-service hotels. Prominent hotels built later in Europe include the Grand Hôtel (1862; by Alfred Armand) near the Paris Opéra, and the Hôtel Continental (now the Inter-Continental; 1878; by Henri Blondel), also in Paris, which has ornately decorated and furnished public rooms, including a Grand Salon reminiscent of Charles Garnier's foyer at the Paris Opéra; the Amstel (1866; by Cornelis Outshoorn) in Amsterdam; the Frankfurter Hof (1872–6; by Karl Jonas Mylius and Alfred Friedrich Bluntschli) in Frankfurt am Main; numerous grand hotels in Vienna (1870s) on the newly constructed Ringstrasse; and others at resorts in Switzerland and on the Riviera.

In London the impresario Richard D'Oyly Carte (1844–1901) employed T. E. Collcutt to build the Savoy Hotel (1888–9), which incorporated many of the technological

1. Tremont House Hotel, Boston, MA, by Isaiah Rogers, 1828–9 (destr. 1895)

advances of the period and included balconies overlooking the River Thames. César Ritz (1850–1918), the manager, later created several luxury hotels, among them the Paris Ritz (1900; by Charles Mewès), built behind 17th-century façades in the Place Vendôme, and the London Ritz (1904–5; by Mewès & Davis), Piccadilly, using a steel frame and incorporating Louis XVI-style interiors and an elegant palm court.

Resort hotels, too, evolved in size, style and amenities as wealthy urban dwellers increasingly flocked to spas, seaside hotels and mountain hotels in the summer. Some hotels featured clusters of cottages, others were great structures with long porches, such as the Grand Hotel (1887; by George D. Mason and Zacharias Rice), Mackinac Island, MI. Timber-framed resort hotels were quickly built—the immense Royal Poinciana (1893–4; by McDonald & McGuire; destr. 1934) at Palm Beach, FL, was completed in ten months—and many burnt within a few years. The use of fire-proof materials thus developed: the Ponce de Leon (1887; by Carrère & Hastings), St Augustine, FL, was built of concrete in the Spanish Mission style, and the massive Blenheim (1905; by William L. Price and M. Hawley McLanahan), Atlantic City, was built of reinforced concrete, including the ornamental façade. Further west, resort hotels were built in widely varying styles, as in the sprawling Shingle style Hotel Coronado (1886–8; by James W. Reid), San Diego, and the Georgian colonial-style Greenbrier at White Sulphur Springs, WV (rebuilt in 1913 by F. J. Sterner).

Hotels were among the first buildings to adopt technological advances. McGinty lists the more notable advances in the USA, including gas-lighting in guest-rooms (American Hotel, 1835, New York); central heating (Eastern Exchange Hotel, 1846, Boston); electric lights in public areas (Hotel Everett, 1882, New York); upper-floor plumbing (Astor House, New York); a bath for each bedroom (Victoria Hotel, 1888, Kansas City); and guest-room telephones (Hotel Netherland, 1894, New York). Despite these innovations, many hotels became obsolete within 30 years, largely as a result of social and urban changes.

The increase in the size of hotels in the second half of the 19th century depended on two advances: the development of lifts and new structural systems. Lifts were first used for passengers in 1859 (Fifth Avenue Hotel, New York), although they had been installed two decades earlier for hauling luggage. Increased dependence on steel structures led to the design of two innovative American hotels. One, the Palace Hotel in San Francisco (1873–5; by John P. Gaynor; destr. 1906), featured a monumental glass-roofed 'Grand Court' surrounded by Italianate galleries serving as guest-room corridors. The other, the Brown Palace Hotel in Denver (1890–92; by Frank E. Edbrooke), has an elegant eight-storey atrium and is notable also for its steel frame: the brownstone exterior walls are little more than a veneer. The Chicago Auditorium Building (1886–9; by Dankmar Adler and LOUIS SULLIVAN), one of the first mixed-use projects, combined a hotel with a theatre and offices (for further discussion and illustration *see* ADLER, DANKMAR). The refinement of cast-iron and eventually steel-skeleton structures led quickly to much taller hotels, beginning with the original 17-storey Waldorf-Astoria (1893–6; by Henry Janeway Hardenbergh; destr. 1929) in New York.

2. 1900 AND AFTER. At the turn of the century there were fewer technological advances but both grand hotels for the wealthy and commercial establishments for the middle class continued to develop. Pevsner cites the Austrian architectural journalist Joseph Lux, who insisted that hotels be 'a synthesis of hospital, wagon-lits and machinery' (Pevsner, p. 192). Over the ensuing decades, increasing numbers of hotels moved away from 19th-century historicism in both form and function. After World War II several prominent changes took place in the hotel industry and its architecture. The development of motorways led to the growth of such motel chains as Holiday Inns. With none of the grandeur and few of the services of the major hotels, motels nonetheless provided the necessary comforts for middle-class families and business travellers. In some countries the government established chains, notably the Xenia group in Greece, with airy tourist motels crisply designed by ARIS KONSTANTINIDIS.

One of the most striking developments of the 1960s and after was the atrium concept developed by John Portman in his design for the Hyatt Regency Hotel in Atlanta (1966–7; for illustration *see* PORTMAN, JOHN). Portman had found much to criticize in the bland, mechanistic hotel design common in the mid-20th century; to counter this he explained (Portman and Barnett, p. 28):

> I want to explode the hotel; to open it up; to create a grandeur of space, almost a resort, in the center of the city. The whole idea was to . . . take the elevators and literally pull them out of the walls and let them become an experience within themselves, let them become a giant kinetic sculpture.

The atrium design subsequently became the predominant feature of convention hotels catering to many hundreds—even thousands—of guests. The larger hotels, such as Portman's 1800-room Marriott Marquis hotels in New York (1984) and Atlanta (1985; see fig. 2) feature atriums more than 40 storeys high, with over a dozen glass-bubble lifts. Like the atrium hotels of a century before, the guest-rooms were placed along corridors overlooking the lobby, with greatly expanded public spaces in a podium or low extension to one side.

In the 1980s, by contrast, there was an increased interest in the preservation of older hotels. Many, such as the Bellevue-Stratford (1904, expanded 1913; original architect Hewitt & Paist; rest. 1979–80 by Vitetta Group–Studio Four) in Philadelphia, once slated for demolition, were carefully restored. Moreover, hotels were adapted from other buildings; the Helmsley Palace Hotel (now New York Palace Hotel) in New York, for example, is a conversion (1978–80; by Richard Roth) of the former Villard houses (1882–6; by McKim, Mead & White) on Madison Avenue, and preserves their landmark interiors. The growth of international hotel chains transported

2. Atrium of the Marriott Marquis Hotel, Atlanta, GA, by John Portman, completed 1985

cultural standards around the world. Hilton and Inter-Continental, both connected with global airlines, established first-class hotels in major capitals. The Hilton Hotel in Istanbul (1952; by Skidmore, Owings & Merrill), an exquisite International Style slab high above the Bosporus, and the Hilton in Budapest (1978; by Béla Pintér), constructed within the ruins of a 13th-century monastery, illustrate the variety of stylistic solutions to modern hotels. In developing countries the economic importance of hotels was recognized, as in the brilliant Fragrant Hill Resort Hotel (1979–82; by I. M. Pei) near Beijing, which displays the architect's intepretation of local motifs and materials, as had Frank Lloyd Wright's Imperial Hotel in Tokyo (1917–22; destr. 1968; *see* WRIGHT, (1), §3). Resort hotels continue to provide some of the best opportunities for dramatic design. At Miami Beach the Fontainebleau Hotel (1952; rest. 1980s as the Fontainebleau-Hilton), with its sweeping lines and richly decorated interiors by noted hotel designer MORRIS LAPIDUS, is like a film set, while the Mauna Kea Beach Hotel (1962; by Skidmore, Owings & Merrill), Hawaii, is noted for its fusing of building and site; the Camino Real hotels in Cancún (1975) and Ixtapa (1981), Mexico, designed by Ricardo Legorreta, are also closely related to their environment.

BIBLIOGRAPHY
J. Williamson: *The American Hotel: An Anecdotal History* (New York, 1930/*R* 1975)
H. Weisskamp: *Hotels: An International Survey* (New York, 1968)
F. Lawson: *Hotels, Motels and Condominiums: Design, Planning and Maintenance* (London, 1976)
N. Pevsner: *A History of Building Types* (Princeton, 1976), pp. 169–92

J. Portman and J. Barnett: *The Architect as Developer* (New York, 1976)

B. McGinty: *The Palace Inns: A Connoisseur's Guide to Historic American Hotels* (Harrisburg, 1978)

J. Limerick, N. Ferguson and R. Oliver: *America's Grand Resort Hotels* (New York, 1979)

P. Boniface: *Hotels and Restaurants: 1830 to the Present Day* (London, 1981)

R. Wilson, ed.: *Victorian Resorts and Hotels* (New York, 1982)

D. Watkin: *Grand Hotel, the Golden Age of Palace Hotels: An Architectural and Social History* (London, 1984)

W. Rutes and R. Penner: *Hotel Planning and Design: A Guide for Architects, Interior Designers and Hotel Executives* (New York, 1985)

R. Jarman and W. Tabler sr: 'Hotels', *Encyclopedia of Architecture: Design, Engineering, and Construction*, ed. J. Wilkes, ii (New York, 1988), pp. 790–827

C. Donzel, A. Gregory and M. Walter: *Grand American Hotels* (New York, 1989)

A. Bangert and O. Rieswolt: *New Hotel Design* (London, 1993)

RICHARD H. PENNER

Hôtel particulier [Fr.: 'private town house']. Type of French town house, built from the mid-16th century to *c.* 1800. The history of the hôtel particulier is that of a typological system whose development over three centuries responded to changes in palatial and civic architecture and to the needs of an upwardly mobile society. This development was chronicled by some 50 contemporary building manuals and treatises that deal wholly or in part with domestic architecture. The term hôtel was originally restricted to city houses of the nobility but was appropriated by the middle classes for their town houses during the second half of the 17th century.

1. Architecture. 2. Interior decoration.

1. ARCHITECTURE. The most frequently employed layout was the *hôtel-entre-cour-et-jardin*, so called because the principal block, or *corps de logis*, was placed in the middle of the site between the forecourt and garden. Narrow wings framing the forecourt usually extended forward to the street, where the court was closed by a service wing or screen wall with a classical portico at the centre. Service courtyards were located to either side of the main court, out of view of the visitor. By the judicious placement of the parts, a building erected on an irregular urban site could be designed to appear ordered and symmetrical. The interior layout of the *corps de logis* comprised a few common rooms, such as the vestibule and salon for large gatherings, and several independent *appartements* for the habitation of individual members of the family. The basic sequence of rooms in each *appartement* always consisted of the *antichambre* or waiting-room, the *chambre* for reception and sleeping, the *cabinet* or study and the *garde-robe* functioning as dressing-room and closet. This sequence could be expanded depending on the wealth and status of the patron to include, for example, a second and third *cabinet* (*see also* §2 below).

The expatriate Italian Sebastiano Serlio was the first architect in France to combine classical principles of regularity with the French interest in practicality in his plan for the Grand Ferrare (1542–6; destr., only the gate survives), Fontainebleau. This town house marked the beginning of the first phase of hôtel development, 1544–1620, primarily during the French Renaissance. Two contemporary handbooks, the unpublished Book VI (*c.* 1550) of Serlio's treatise on architecture and Jacques

Androuet Du Cerceau (i)'s *Premier livre d'architecture* (Paris, 1559), illustrated for the first time a full range of hôtels, from simple houses to princely mansions. In general, the *corps de logis* in this first phase was only one room deep, and the rooms were rectangular. Exterior elevations were austere, often with only string courses and quoins articulating the flat walls.

During the second phase, 1620–1700, that of the Baroque period, the tradition of the illustrated building manual was continued by Pierre Le Muet in his *Manière de bien bastir pour toutes sortes de personnes* (Paris, 1623). As early as 1620 the Marquise de Rambouillet, in the design of her own hôtel in Paris, put into practice the concept of separating public from private rooms in the house. The grouping of rooms *en enfilade* in the *appartement* continued, yielding an impressive sequence of doorways and chimney-pieces facing the visitor. However, the method of placing a double zone of rooms in the *corps de logis*, as used by Louis Le Vau in the Hôtel Tambonneau (begun 1644; destr. 1844; see fig. 1) and François Mansart in the Hôtel de Jars (1645), both in Paris, made possible several *appartements* on a single floor and chambers of more specialized function, such as the dining-room. Two of the most remarkable Parisian hôtels of the period took advantage of difficult sites and featured original combinations of unusually shaped spaces: Le Vau's Hôtel Lambert (begun 1639; *see* LE VAU, (2), figs 1 and 2) and Antoine Le Pautre's Hôtel de Beauvais (1654–60). In general, exterior elevations fluctuated between severity and richness, tending in the later 17th century towards the lavish use of the orders.

The third phase of hôtel design, 1700–*c.* 1750, parallels the emergence of the Rococo. From the realm of château architecture designers drew the concept of the *corps de logis* as a free-standing block, isolated between the forecourt and garden, thus giving a suburban appearance to the hôtel. The major examples of this pavilion type, in which the service wings are largely independent, are Parisian: the Hôtel d'Estrées (1711–13) by Robert de Cotte, the Hôtel de Matignon (1722–4) by Jean Courtonne and the Hôtel de Biron (1728–30) by Jean Aubert. Germain Boffrand continued the spatial experiments of the previous period with his oval forecourt and variously shaped rooms at the Hôtel d'Amelot (1712–14). As elements in interior decoration became more curvilinear and naturalistic, the architectonic character of the exterior elevations diminished, giving precedence to decorative sculpture and wrought-iron balconies of the type evident in the hôtels of Pierre Lassurance the elder. Current housing practices were discussed extensively in the widely read second edition of Augustin Charles d'Aviler's *Cours complet d'architecture* (1710), edited by Alexandre-Jean-Baptiste Le Blond.

In the final phase of hôtel planning, *c.* 1750–1800, which occurred during the Neo-classical period, there was further development of the isolated block, now standing within an informal landscape setting. Ideal geometric configurations dominated planning. The greatest licence was given to room shapes, with an unprecedented interest in the circle. The leading figure in Paris was Claude-Nicolas Ledoux, who displayed the new formal principles in such buildings as the Hôtel d'Hallwyl (1766–7), the Hôtel

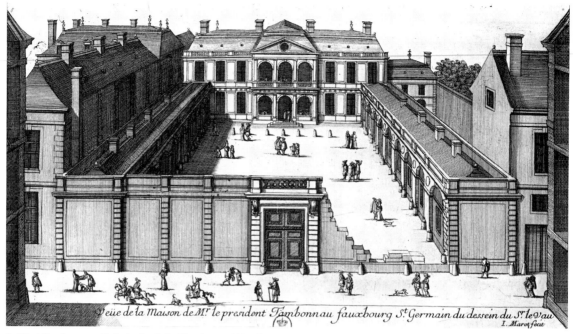

1. Hôtel Tambonneau, Paris, by Louis Le Vau, begun 1644 (destr. 1844); engraving by Jean Marot (i), 163×275 mm (Paris, Bibliothèque Nationale, Cabinet des Estampes)

d'Uzès (1767) and the Hôtel de Montmorency (1769). The Classical orders returned for the embellishment of both interior and exterior elevations. The giant order, often free-standing, was commonly used without a pediment on court façades, as at Etienne-François Legrand's Hôtel de Gallifet (1775–96), Paris. Illustrations of the houses of this last period were published by J.-C. Krafft and Pierre-Nicolas Ransonnette (1745–1810) in their *Plans, coupes, élévations des plus belles maisons & des hôtels construits à Paris . . .* (?1801–3), in which they responded to international interest by including texts in French, German and English.

The development of the hôtel particulier, in terms of new spatial configurations and the novel use of classical ornament, did not outlive Neo-classicism. However, the basic layout of the *hôtel-entre-cour-et-jardin* continued to be used during the 19th century by such architects as Louis-Tullius-Joachim Visconti in his Hôtel Pontalba (1828), Paris. Because of its suitability for urban situations, the concept survives in the planning of blocks of flats.

BIBLIOGRAPHY
L. Hautecoeur: *Architecture classique* (1943–57)
A. Blunt: *Art and Architecture in France, 1500–1700*, Pelican Hist. A. (Harmondsworth, 1953, 2/1973)
M. Gallet: *Stately Mansions: Eighteenth Century Paris Architecture* (London and New York, 1972)
W. Kalnein and M. Levey: *Art and Architecture of the Eighteenth Century in France*, Pelican Hist. A. (Harmondsworth, 1972)
J.-P. Babelon: 'Du "Grand Ferrare" à Carnavalet: Naissance de l'hôtel classique', *Rev. A.*, xl–xli (1978), pp. 83–108
M. Dennis: *Court & Garden: From the French Hôtel to the City of Modern Architecture* (Cambridge, MA, 1986)
XVIIe Siècle, xli/162 (1989) [issue dedicated to the hôtel]
M. Le Moel: *L'Architecture privée à Paris au Grand Siècle* (Paris, 1990)

ROBERT NEUMAN

2. INTERIOR DECORATION. The interior decoration of a 17th- and 18th-century Parisian hôtel particulier is characterized by comfort, privacy and civilized living. These ideas were developed from the early 17th century and codified during the next century. The major French contribution to European decoration during this period was interiors that were practical, comfortable and harmonious. The luxurious comfort first created for small, private rooms, such as *cabinets*, also effected the formality of the grander, more public rooms; these private rooms were the forerunners of the *petits appartements* of the 18th century. From about 1625 a unity in the interior decoration of a room was the dominant feature. For instance, chair covers, bed-hangings and carpets for tables were all of the same fabric. In the early 17th century the Marquise de RAMBOUILLET and her Paris town house were strongly influential (*see also* §1 above). Her use of uniformity in decoration in important rooms, often based on a single colour scheme, created a feeling of order and harmony. Her famous *Chambre bleue*, where she held her salon, was painted blue: the same colour was found in the fabric of the walls and in the *ameublement* (furnishing fabric). Particular features and the arrangement at the Hôtel Rambouillet were soon imitated in magnificent houses throughout Paris. Because of its rich interior decoration the Hôtel Lauzun, built between 1656 and 1657, probably by Louis Le Vau, was one of the most fashionable Parisian houses of the time.

A Parisian hôtel's interior decoration comprises three major elements: architectural components, such as walls, ceilings and floors; textiles; and furniture and *objets d'art*. The term *distribution*, developed by French architects and theorists, refers to the appropriate arrangement of rooms in an hôtel. There were three basic types of *appartement*: *appartement de parade*, *appartement de société* and *appartement privé*. The *appartement de parade*, on the ground floor, included the richly decorated formal state rooms, where official visitors were received. The primary rooms, preceded by a vestibule, were one or more *antichambres*, which could alternate as dining- or gaming-rooms, a *salon*, a *chambre du parade* and a *grand cabinet*. Very grand hôtels also had a separate *salle à manger*, a *galérie*, a *salle d'assemblée* and a *salle du dais*. State rooms were usually arranged *en enfilade*, so that a view through all the doorways gave a prospect of several rooms. The *appartement de société*, which usually comprised an *antichambre*, a *salle de compagnie*, a *bibliothèque*, a *salle à manger* and a *cabinet*, was where family and intimate friends met for meals, gaming, music, reading, needlework and conversation (see fig. 2). The *appartement privé* included an *antichambre*, a *chambre à coucher*, a *cabinet*, perhaps an *appartement des bains* and a *garde-robe* with a toilet or a separate *cabinet de toilette*. Both the master and mistress had their own suite of rooms for personal and domestic affairs.

Walls might be of masonry (for vestibules, anterooms and stairwells), stucco or *boiserie* (wood panelling), decorated with carving, paint, mirrors, overdoor paintings, lacquer panels, wallpaper or textiles. Some were decorated with painted scenes, such as the stairwell with *trompe l'oeil* architecture and other images executed by Gaetano Brunetti (*d* 1758) and Paolo Antonio Brunetti (1723–80) in

1747 for the Hôtel de Luynes, Paris. *Boiserie*, designed by an architect or a sculptor–ornamentalist, was the most common wall treatment. Generally of oak, but also of walnut or pine, the panels might be carved with such decorative motifs as garlands of fruit and flowers, trophies, the architectural orders or symbols specific to the owner. The panels were rarely left natural and were generally painted white or pastel, highlighted with gilding. *Boiserie* was sometimes lacquered in *vernis Martin* (*see* MARTIN (i)), as in the Green Salon (also known as the Cabinet des Fables) from the Hôtel de Soubise, Paris (now at the Hôtel de Rohan,; carving attributed to Jacques Verberckt, *c.* 1736). Wood panels were sometimes painted by well-known artists with figures, arbours, pastorals, arabesques or elaborate frames: *c.* 1750 Christophe Huet and his assistants painted the Cabinet des Singes at the Hôtel de Rohan with monkeys and pastorals (*in situ*). Painted canvases were also set into wood panelling, for example those depicting landscapes painted *c.* 1765 (Paris, Carnavalet) by François Boucher and his studio, assisted by Jean-Honoré Fragonard and Jean-Baptiste Le Prince, for the Parisian home of the engraver Gilles Demarteau. Canvases set above the doors and mirror surmounting the mantelpiece were known as *dessus de porte* (*see* OVERDOOR) and *dessus de cheminée* (overmantel). They were executed by unknown decorators, as well as by such leading artists as Charles-Joseph Natoire, Boucher, Jean-Baptiste Oudry and Nicolas Lancret. Piat, or Pieter, Joseph Sauvage (1744–

2. *Gathering in a Salon* by François Dequevauviller, engraving, 1783–4 (Paris, Bibliothèque Nationale, Cabinet des Estampes); the salon depicted is possibly the Grand Salon, Hôtel de Luynes, Paris

1818) painted simulated stucco relief overdoors; carved stucco or wood panels were also used as overdoors. Rooms were decorated with panels of Oriental or European-imitation lacquer set into wood panelling, exemplified by the Chinese red lacquer panels of the Cabinet du Laque, Hôtel du Châtelet (1771–6), Paris. Wallpaper, produced by such firms as Réveillon, Robert or Oberkampf, as well as Chinese and English imports, was also used. Chimney-pieces were of white or fine-grained grey or black marble. Coloured marble was used for the tops of commodes and console tables, and skirting-boards were of matching or painted imitation marble. Some chimney-pieces were adorned with ormolu mounts and candelabra.

Ceilings were painted in a plain colour or with decorative motifs or scenes, for example the ceiling of the Salon Doré, Hôtel Grimod d'Orsay, Paris, painted *c.* 1773 by Hugues Taraval with the *Apotheosis of Psyche*, or were embellished with wood cornices or carved stucco motifs, including scrollwork or central rosettes, often highlighted with gilding. Tiles and wood parquetry were used for floors. Marble, terracotta, limestone or faience tiles often decorated vestibules or anterooms, passages, corridors and rooms, although rooms usually had oak parquet floors laid in large squares or compartments with diagonal or chequered patterns. Examples of highly elaborate parquetry floors are depicted in the painted miniatures (*c.* 1770; Paris, priv. col.) by LOUIS-NICOLAS VAN BLARENBERGHE showing the Premier Cabinet and the Chambre du Lit of the Hôtel de Choiseul, Paris. Savonnerie, Aubusson or Oriental carpets could be laid on parquet floors.

Textiles were used in abundance for interior decoration and were often changed with the seasons. The *ameublement* of a room was generally *en suite*: wall coverings, curtains, valances, *portières*, bed- hangings and seat upholstery were made to match. For important rooms these fabrics included velvet, Lyonnaise or Genoese silks, tapestries and a variety of Oriental materials. Textiles or tapestry wall coverings could be enframed between cornice and wainscoting. The alcoves of the state bedrooms for the Prince and Princess de Rohan at the Hôtel de Soubise were decorated with tapestries. Less elaborate rooms had Indian cottons and linens or their European imitations, such as *toile de Jouy*. Window curtains and *portières*, attached to iron rods with small rings, hung straight down, were divided in two, drawn back and knotted in a number of places with elaborate tassels or were pulled up *à l'italienne* to form a billowing mass below the valance. The window-glass was covered with sun curtains of linen, embroidered Indian muslin or sheer white fabric to block strong outdoor light.

There were two types of seating, often painted to match the colour of the *boiserie* and textiles: *chaises meublantes* were symmetrically and permanently arranged against the wall; *chaises courantes* were dispersed around the room and moved when needed. Examples of both types are included in the plan (*c.* 1778–80; Stockholm, Kun. Akad. Fria Kst., Arkv) drawn by Eric Palmstedt of the salon at the Hôtel Nivernais, Paris. Tables for dining, reading, writing or serving were moved about or brought in from other rooms when they were required. Light, reflected in mirrors and gilding, emanated from the fireplace and from candles in chandeliers, wall sconces, girandoles, candelabra and candlesticks. Paintings of all sizes covered almost entire walls; chimney-pieces, pedestals and wall brackets supported small sculptures, antique bronzes, porcelain or clocks.

BIBLIOGRAPHY

M. Gallet: *Demeures parisiennes: L'Epoque de Louis XVI* (Paris, 1964)
P. Verlet: *La Maison du XVIIIe siècle en France: Société, décoration, mobilier* (Paris, 1966); Eng. trans. by G. Savage as *French Furniture and Interior Decoration of the 18th Century* (London, 1967)
P. Thorton: *Seventeenth-century Interior Decoration in England, France and Holland* (New Haven, 1978)
C. Fregnac and W. Andrew: *The Great Houses of Paris* (New York, 1979)
P. Thornton: *Authentic Decor: The Domestic Interior, 1620–1920* (London, 1984)
B. Pons: *De Paris à Versailles, 1699–1736: Les Sculpteurs ornemanistes parisiens et l'art décoratif des Bâtiments du Roi* (Strasbourg, 1986)
J. Feray: *Architecture intérieure et décoration en France des origines à 1875* (Paris, 1988)
J. Whitehead: *The French Interior in the Eighteenth Century* (London, 1992)
B. Pons: *Grands Décors français, 1650–1800* (Paris, 1995)

For further bibliography *see* §1 above.

BARRY SHIFMAN

Hotere, Ralph (*b* Mitimiti, Northland, NZ, 1931). New Zealand painter. He studied at St Peter's College, Auckland, and then at Auckland Teachers' College before specializing in art at the King Edward Technical College, Dunedin. He had his first one-man show in 1952 at the Dunedin Public Art Gallery and from 1952 to 1961 worked as a school art adviser in Northland. He was awarded a New Zealand Art Societies' Fellowship in 1961 which enabled him to study at the Central School of Art and Design in London and travel in Europe. The following year he received a residential award to paint for three months at the Michael Karolyi Memorial Foundation at Vence in France. He returned to Auckland only in 1965.

Hotere's painting developed from an Expressionist style inspired by the landscape to a hard-edged abstract style. Characteristic of the latter is the triptych *Requiem* (1973–4; Wellington, Queen Elizabeth II A. Council Col.; see Barr and Barr, pp. 112–13) which used parallel lines and concentric circles on a black background, with Maori words in the centre of the circle. Inspired by Maori language and history, he often painted works dominated by stencilled or painted words, as in *Te Taepaepatanga o te Rangi* (1972; J. Hansen priv. col.; see Cape, pl. 181), which formed part of the *Te Whiti* series of that year. He also designed stage sets and mural decorations such as the mural for the Founder's Theatre, Hamilton, NZ (1973).

BIBLIOGRAPHY

P. Cape: *New Zealand Painting since 1960* (Auckland, 1979)
J. Barr and M. Barr: *Contemporary New Zealand Painters*, i (Martinborough, 1980), pp. 106–13

Hothouse. *See under* GREENHOUSE.

Hoti-Mardan. *See* MARDAN.

Houasse. French family of painters. (1) René-Antoine Houasse was principally a decorative and religious painter in the manner of Charles Le Brun. His son (2) Michel-Ange Houasse was employed at the Spanish court of Philip V.

(1) René-Antoine Houasse (*b* Paris, 1645; *d* Paris, 27 May 1710). A pupil of Charles Le Brun, with whom he later collaborated, he was received (*reçu*) by the Académie Royale in 1673 with the portrait of *Louis XIV in the Guise of Hercules Overcoming the Hydra* (Paris, Louvre). He went on to have a brilliant career within the Académie, becoming Assistant Professor in 1675, Professor in 1680, Assistant Rector in 1695 and finally Director in 1701. He was also Director of the Académie de France in Rome between 1699 and 1704.

From 1670 René-Antoine was employed by Le Brun at the Tuileries, Paris, and on the decoration of the Grand Appartement at the château of Versailles, first in the Salon de Mars and then *c.* 1680 in the Salon de Vénus and the Salon de l'Abondance, the latter remarkable for its illusionist décor (all works *in situ*). At this time the main influences on his style were Le Brun and, through him, Raphael and Giulio Romano. He was, nevertheless, an idiosyncratic painter, whose personal style has become clearer since the restoration and reinstallation in the 1960s of the important series of mythological paintings commissioned in 1688 for the Grand Trianon at Versailles: the *Story of Minerva, Morpheus and Iris, Diana and Endymion, Mercury and Argus* and *Chione Transformed into a Fountain*. The *Story of Minerva*, for instance, combines classicizing influences, in a composition inspired by antique friezes, with elongated figures from the Mannerist canon of the school of Fontainebleau and the late paintings of Jacques Stella. This interesting style was unfortunately not always supported by draughtsmanship of adequate quality; this was perhaps due to the collaboration of his pupils. It is, however, remarkable for its freedom of execution and brushwork and delicate grey-blue and green colouring, features that had also appeared in the 1675 May of Notre-Dame de Paris (the altarpiece commissioned annually by the Paris Goldsmiths' Corporation), depicting *St Stephen Being Led to Martyrdom* (Paris, Louvre). A further example of René-Antoine's religious work is the *Battle of Joshua against the Amalekites* (Brest, Mus. Mun.), an epic work similar to the great undertakings for the crown in which he had been involved.

Surviving portraits by Houasse include an equestrian *Louis XIV* (Versailles, Château), the author *Marie-Madeleine, Comtesse de La Fayette* (Chambord, Château) and a *Portrait of a Young Woman* (Madrid, Prado) painted in Spain, where he went at the invitation of Charles II, returning in 1692. The portrait of Houasse (Grenoble, Mus. Grenoble) by François Jouvenet (1664–1749) shows the artist in front of his easel, which supports his picture of *Darius Opening the Tomb of Nicotris* (Orléans, Mus. B.-A.).

BIBLIOGRAPHY

Thieme–Becker

A.-J. Dézallier d'Argenville: *Abrégé de la vie des plus fameux peintres* (1745–52, 2/1762), iv, pp. 137–8

A. de Montaiglon and J. Guiffrey: *Correspondance des directeurs de l'Académie de France à Rome avec les Surintendants des Bâtiments (1666–1804)*, 17 vols (Paris, 1887–1908)

A. Schnapper: *Tableaux pour le Trianon de Marbre, 1688–1714* (Paris, 1967)

LAURENCE GUILMARD GEDDES

(2) Michel-Ange Houasse (*b* Paris, 1680; *d* Arpajon, 30 Sept 1730). Son of (1) René-Antoine Houasse. He trained in his father's circle, becoming familiar with the academic teaching methods then fashionable in France and also in Italy, where he went with his father. In 1706 he joined the Académie Royale de Peinture et de Sculpture in Paris, obtaining the rank of Academician in 1707 with the painting *Hercules and Lichas* (Tours, Mus. B.-A.). In Rome he probably became acquainted with the Marquis d'Aubigny, secretary to the powerful Princess Orsini, who was close to Philip V of Spain. The Spanish King already had the painter Henri de Favanne in his service in Madrid; Michel-Ange was recommended for work at the Spanish court by Count Jean Orry (1652–1719), the King's French finance minister, and arrived there in 1715. He had contact with the French artists at court and married the daughter of the French architect René Carlier.

Although he was engaged as a portrait painter, Michel-Ange was soon supplanted in this field by others, particularly Jean Ranc. However, he painted the portrait of *Luis* (see fig.) and the charming portrait of the child *Don Felipe Pedro* (Madrid, Pal. Real); the drawing of the *Family of Philip V* (Stockholm, Nmus.) is among his most interesting works. His portraits are in the style typical of late 17th-century French work and seem uninfluenced by Hyacinthe Rigaud or by other contemporaries; rather, they treat the sitters with a certain intimacy and simplicity. For the Madrid court he painted a reredos showing *St Francis*

Michel-Ange Houasse: *Luis*, oil on canvas, 1.72×1.12 m, 1717 (Madrid, Museo del Prado)

Regis Preaching and *St Francis Regis Distributing Clothing* (Madrid, Prado).

Michel-Ange produced a number of small paintings with scenes from daily life—real and invented—in which elements taken from French academic painting, *fêtes galantes*, traditional work from the Low Countries and the memory of Italy are all combined. He also executed works of allegorical–mythical content, such as *Bacchanalia* (1719) and an *Offering to Bacchus* (1720; both Madrid, Prado), and some magnificent landscapes, which include the *View of the Monastery of El Escorial* (Madrid, Prado). His use of colour, the precise detail and lightness of his brushwork, together with his remarkable powers of observation, award him a high standing among 18th-century European masters. He also produced small religious paintings and some highly original paintings depicting isolated figures. He had just completed two large cartoons depicting *Telemachus and Mentor Arriving at the Island of Calypso* and the *Banquet Held by Calypso in Honour of Telemachus and Mentor* (both *c*. 1730, Madrid, Prado) for the Real Fábrica de Tapices, when he died in France, where he had returned from Madrid because of ill-health.

BIBLIOGRAPHY

J. Held: 'Michel-Ange Houasse in Spanien', *Münchn. Jb. Bild. Kst*, xix (1968), pp. 183–206
Y. Bottineau: *L'Art de cour dans l'Espagne de Philippe V* (Bordeaux, 1969)
Miguel Angel Houasse: Pintor de la corte de Felipe V (exh. cat. by J. J. Luna, Madrid, Mus. Mun., 1981–2)
J. J. Luna: 'M. A. Houasse', *Reales Sitios: Rev. Patrm. N.*, 42, pp. 45–55; 43, pp. 33–43; 44, pp. 53–60; 45, pp. 38–48; 47, pp. 41–8; 48, pp. 65–72
——: 'Miguel Angel Houasse: Retratista', *Actas del congreso 'El arte en las cortes europeas del siglo XVIII': Madrid, 1987*

JUAN J. LUNA

Houbraken. Dutch family of artists. Although a competent artist, (1) Arnold Houbraken is best known as a writer. His three-volume *Groote schouburgh* (1718–21), the last volume of which was published posthumously, is generally regarded as one of the most important sources on the lives of 17th-century Dutch artists—despite its many omissions and errors. Houbraken's son (2) Jacobus Houbraken was a reproductive engraver, specializing in portraiture. Jacobus's sister Antonyna Houbraken (*b* Dordrecht, 30 May 1686; *d* Amsterdam, 12 Dec 1736) made topographical and portrait drawings, as well as designs for vignettes and a title-page. She married the draughtsman Jacobus Stellingwerf.

BIBLIOGRAPHY
Thieme-Becker

(1) Arnold Houbraken (*b* Dordrecht, 28 March 1660; *d* Amsterdam, 14 Oct 1719). Writer, theorist, draughtsman, etcher and painter. He began work in 1669 as a yarn-winder for the Dordrecht merchant Johannes de Haan, who also occasionally made him copy drawings and prints. In 1672 Houbraken received his first drawing lessons from Willem van Drillenburg (*c*. 1625–after 1677), and probably in the same year he was apprenticed to Jacobus Levecq (1634–75). From *c*. 1674 to 1678 he was a pupil of Samuel van Hoogstraten, whom he helped to illustrate the *Inleyding tot de hooge schoole der schilderkonst* (Rotterdam, 1678) and from whom Houbraken received his first lessons in classicizing art theory. In 1678 Houbraken entered the Dordrecht Guild of St Luke, and in 1685 he married Sara

Souburgh, a daughter of the celebrated surgeon Jacob Sasbout-Souburgh.

On the advice of the Amsterdam patron Jonas Witsen, for whom Houbraken had painted two history paintings, he moved in 1709–10 to Amsterdam, where he became a citizen on 8 October 1710. According to Jan van Gool, in 1713 Houbraken received a commission from an Englishman to draw a series of portraits of illustrious men, intended as illustrations for a book about the reign of King Charles I. However, after eight or nine months in England he returned to Holland to discover his employer had departed without paying him. Apart from his son Jacobus, Arnold's pupils included Mathys Balen (1684–1746), Adriaen van der Burgh (1693–1733) and Johan [John] Graham (1706–76), as well as the poet and draughtsman Jacob Zeeus (1686–1718). On 17 July 1720 Houbraken's artistic estate, consisting of 30 paintings, was auctioned in Amsterdam.

Houbraken was an able and prolific draughtsman who supplied countless designs and etchings for book illustrations, all strongly modelled on French examples. He also compiled several illustrated books for painters with advice on how to express emotions or render human qualities in a proper and academic way. Many of Houbraken's drawings were engraved by contemporaries (i.e. Nicolaas Verkolje). They often possess a spontaneity and vivacity lacking in his painted oeuvre, which suffered from too rigid an adherence to academic principles.

As a painter, Houbraken specialized in elegant, small figured history paintings (e.g. *Rest on the Flight into Egypt*, The Hague, Mauritshuis) and in portraits *all'antica*, both on a relatively small scale, like his contemporary Adriaan van der Werff. He also painted witty genre pictures in the spirit of the Leiden 'Fine' painters, together with several ceiling paintings and landscapes. Apart from the strong influence of Dutch classicism, Houbraken's paintings are characterized by a polished touch, subdued colouring and carefully balanced compositions; usually they are signed. Although Houbraken did not always manage to sell his work, he was fairly well esteemed as a painter during his lifetime and certainly until the mid-18th century. From then onwards the appreciation for his artistic work quickly declined, and only in the late 20th century was interest in his work slightly revived.

Houbraken's *Groote schouburgh*, begun in 1717 and intended as a sequel to van Mander's *Schilder-boeck* ([1603]–1604), consists of a series of biographies of Dutch artists from the early 16th century, occasionally interrupted by poems by Andries Pels, and general treatises about art. The greater part of the illustrations were engraved by Houbraken's son Jacobus. The *Groote schouburgh* makes use of an extensive range of written and oral sources. Houbraken's aim was twofold: to rescue certain artists from oblivion and to promote classicism, by offering directives for the beginning painter. Houbraken considered not only talent and practice of vital importance but also a sound knowledge of classicist art theory and antiquity. His most important principle was that artists should concentrate on rendering only the most beautiful and elevated of subjects, as advocated in the Classics. Naturalism and personal invention were thus rejected.

WRITINGS

Toneel van sinnebeelden geopent tot dienst van schilders, beelthouders [Drama of symbols, presented for use by painters, sculptors] (Dordrecht, 1700, rev. Amsterdam, 1723)

Verzameling van uitgelezene keurstoffen [Collection of superior material], 2 vols (Amsterdam, 1712) [also attrib. to W. Goeree]

De groote schouburgh der Nederlantsche konstschilders en schilderessen [The great theatre of Netherlandish men and women painters], 3 vols (Amsterdam, 1718–21, rev. 1753)

with G. Brit: *Stichtelijke zinnebeelden gepast op deugden en ondeugden, in LVII tafereelen vertoont door A. Houbraken en verrykt met de bygedichten van Juff, Gezine Brit* [Edifying symbols suitable for the virtuous and unvirtuous, in 57 scenes by A. Houbraken and enriched with associated poems by Miss Gezine Brit] (Amsterdam, 1723)

PRINTS

L. Schenck, ed.: *Een en veertig stuks verscheyden zinnebeelden, geinventerd en in't koper gebragt door A. Houbraken* [Forty-one pictures of various symbols, designed and engraved by A. Houbraken] (Dordrecht, 1700)

with G. Hoet and B. Picart: *Tafereelen der voornaamste geschiedenissen van het Oude en Nieuwe Testament* [Scenes from the principal stories in the Old and New Testaments], 3 vols (The Hague, 1728/*R* The Hague, 1978)

BIBLIOGRAPHY

J. van Gool: *Nieuwe schouburg der Nederlandsche kunstschilders en schilderessen* [The new theatre of Netherlandish painters] (The Hague, 1750–51/*R* Soest, 1971)

C. Hofstede de Groot: *Arnold Houbraken und seine 'Groote schouburgh'* (The Hague, 1893)

MARLIES ENKLAAR

(2) Jacobus Houbraken (*b* Dordrecht, 25 Dec 1698; *d* Amsterdam, 14 Nov 1780). Engraver, etcher and collector, son of (1) Arnold Houbraken. In the autumn of 1710 he moved to Amsterdam with his parents. Houbraken learnt how to engrave from his father and began by copying prints by Cornelis Cort, Jonas Suyderhoef and Cornelis Visscher. He etched with some skill a fine series of artists' portraits after designs by his father for the *Groote schouburgh* and also for Jan van Gool's *Nieuwe schouburg der Nederlantsche kunstschilders* (The Hague, 1750–51).

Most of Jacobus Houbraken's total of *c.* 800 prints are portraits; these were produced over a period of more than 60 years up to and including 1780. There are several individual portraits after earlier masters, such as Jan Wierix, Rembrandt and Jan Lievens, which are less fresh and fine in the use of line. The same applies to his other series of portraits, of stadholders and their families (made jointly with his pupil Pieter Tanjé; 1748–57) for example, and the 'Birch Heads' for Thomas Birch's *The Heads of Illustrious Persons of Great Britain* (in collaboration with George Vertue; London, 1747–52/*R* 1756, 1813). However, the individual portraits after drawings and paintings of contemporaries, for example such artists as Philip van Dijk, Cornelis Troost, Nicolaas Verkolje, Hendrik Pothoven, Jan Maurits Quinkhard and Aert Schouman, rank with the best examples of 18th-century portrait engraving. Houbraken's best-known acquisition as a collector was his purchase from the Six family of a collection of etchings by Rembrandt, which had been bought from the artist by Jan Six.

BIBLIOGRAPHY

A. Verheull: *Jacobus Houbraken et son oeuvre* (Arnhem, 1875, suppl. 1877)

F. Lugt: *Marques* (1921), p. 373

——: *Marques*, suppl. (1956), no. 1539a–b

CHRISTIAAN SCHUCKMAN

Houckgeest [Hoeckgeest], **Gerrit** [Geraert; Gerard] (*b* The Hague, ?1600; *d* Bergen op Zoom, Aug 1661). Dutch painter. He was a nephew of the conservative portrait painter Joachim (Ottensz.) Houckgeest (*b c.* 1585; *d* before 13 June 1644), but he was probably a pupil of the architect and architectural painter Bartholomeus van Bassen at The Hague. Houckgeest joined the painters' guild there in 1625. By 1635 he had moved to nearby Delft, where he was married in 1636; he was mentioned as a member of the local guild in 1639. In the same year he re-entered the guild at The Hague and in 1640 was cited as the designer of tapestries for the assembly hall of the States General there.

No picture by Houckgeest is known to date from before 1635, when he painted *Charles I and Henrietta Maria Dining in Public* (London, Hampton Court, Royal Col.). The composition represents a few dozen figures in an imaginary palace and is similar to van Bassen's *The King and Queen of Bohemia Dining in Public* (1634; sold London, Sotheby's, 27 March 1974). Other early works by Houckgeest, such as the *Open Gallery in an Imaginary Palace* (1638; Edinburgh, N.G.), also follow van Bassen in favouring arbitrarily arranged Baroque classical architectural elements on a monumental scale. As in the mostly imaginary Gothic church interiors painted in Antwerp by Houckgeest's near contemporary Pieter Neeffs (i), Houckgeest used a central or somewhat off-centre vanishing point to draw the eye to the deepest area of space; full-length architectural forms in the foreground act as repoussoirs, creating the impression of a self-contained and inaccessible stage set. Houckgeest continued to paint imaginary palace views and church interiors during the 1640s. The precise draughtsmanship and local colouring in his work contrast with the tonal palette and the choice of real buildings as subjects in the work of another contemporary, Pieter Saenredam. However, Saenredam's portraits of churches appear to have inspired a few of Houckgeest's less conventional compositional schemes, such as the *Imaginary Catholic Church* (1640; The Hague, Schilderijenzaal Prins Willem V). Houckgeest's church interiors of the 1640s reveal a gradual development towards more accessible space and more realistic qualities of light and atmosphere.

In 1650 Houckgeest shifted suddenly from depicting imaginary architecture to portraying the interiors of the Nieuwe Kerk and Oude Kerk in Delft. It appears likely that Houckgeest's new approach originated in a commission, probably for the large panel *Interior of the Nieuwe Kerk in Delft with the Tomb of William the Silent* (1650; Hamburg, Ksthalle). The famous monument, an Orangist (royalist) and national symbol, was depicted by van Bassen in 1620 and by Dirck van Delen in 1645, in both cases in imaginary settings. Houckgeest, by contrast, represented the monument *in situ*, within the choir of the church, taking an oblique view through the colonnade from the ambulatory. He employed an expansive perspective scheme that seems to extend beyond the limits of the picture field. The near photographic fidelity of his architectural views dating from 1650 and 1651 may indicate that he used a 'perspective frame'. This mechanical drawing device, familiar from treatises such as Samuel Marolois's *Perspectiva* (Amsterdam, 1628), could have been used both to record the view and to determine the composition. Houckgeest also introduced a lighter and more uniform

Gerrit Houckgeest: *Interior of the Nieuwe Kerk in Delft with the Tomb of William the Silent*, oil on panel, 560×380 mm, 1651 (The Hague, Koninklijk Kabinet van Schilderijen 'Mauritshuis')

colour scheme, convincingly suggesting daylight and atmosphere.

Houckgeest's new compositional scheme, consisting of a 'two-point' recession to the sides with a low horizon and usually a tall format, was applied again to the choir of the Nieuwe Kerk (e.g. two panels, both dated 1651; The Hague, Mauritshuis; see fig.); to the Oude Kerk with the tomb of Piet Hein (as recorded in a copy by Hendrick van Vliet, Amsterdam, Rijksmus.); and to views centred on the pulpits of the two Delft churches. Fewer than a dozen views of actual church interiors from the early 1650s are known, but these pictures provided indispensable models for the early works of Hendrick van Vliet and Emanuel de Witte.

From 1653 until his death Houckgeest lived in the small port of Bergen op Zoom in North Brabant, where he painted an interior view of the local cathedral (1655; Copenhagen, Stat. Mus. Kst), but this and his few late quayside scenes of imposing houses are in a distinctly retardataire style, perhaps because Houckgeest was closer to Antwerp than to any centre of Dutch art.

BIBLIOGRAPHY

L. de Vries: 'Gerard Houckgeest', *Jb. Hamburg. Kstsamml.*, xx (1975), pp. 25–56

W. A. Liedtke: *Architectural Painting in Delft: Gerard Houckgeest, Hendrick van Vliet, Emanuel de Witte* (Doornspijk, 1982)

WALTER LIEDTKE

Houdon, Jean-Antoine (*b* Versailles, 25 March 1741; *d* Paris, 15 July 1828). French sculptor. He was the foremost French sculptor of the second half of the 18th century and one of the outstanding portrait sculptors in the history of art. Although he created a number of works on Classical themes, he is best known for his remarkably vivid busts and statues of his famous contemporaries, many of which exist in several versions.

1. Paris and Rome, to 1768. 2. Paris and Gotha, 1768–79. 3. From the Salon of 1779 to the French Revolution. 4. After 1789.

1. PARIS AND ROME, TO 1768. Houdon's father was concierge to the Comte de Lamotte, whose Paris hôtel housed the Ecole Royale des Elèves Protégés. This newly established institution trained the winners of the Grand Prix of the Académie Royale de Peinture et de Sculpture before they were sent to the Académie de France in Rome. It was his proximity to some of the best artists in France that encouraged Houdon's vocation. He trained in the studios of René-Michel Slodtz, Jean-Baptiste Lemoyne (ii) and Jean-Baptiste Pigalle, and won the Académie's third prize for sculpture in 1756 and the Grand Prix (Prix de Rome) in 1761. He subsequently spent three years at the Ecole des Elèves Protégés before leaving for Rome in 1764.

Surviving works from Houdon's years in Rome attest to the variety of his interests. Like all students at the Académie de France he was obliged to make copies of antique sculptures. His plaster bust of a *Vestal* (Gotha, Schloss Friedenstein) is a severe composition with the head covered with a veil. He made a marble version of this work in 1788 (Paris, Louvre) and continued to be inspired by its source, the statue of a *Vestal* (or *Pandora*) in the Museo Capitolino in Rome, in a number of reductions produced throughout his career (e.g. bronze version, exh. Salon 1777; untraced). His bust of a *Peasant Girl of Frascati* (plaster version, Gotha, Schloss Friedenstein; later marble versions, Paris, Mus. Cognacq-Jay and St Petersburg, Hermitage) is a finely idealized head after the Antique. The plaster statuette of a *Priest of the Lupercalia* (Gotha, Schloss Friedenstein) is reminiscent of Bernini's statue of *Apollo* in the group *Apollo and Daphne* (Rome, Gal. Borghese). A commission for a statue of *St John the Baptist* for S Maria degli Angeli (plaster; Rome, Gal. Borghese) was the occasion for the production of Houdon's famous statue of a *Flayed Man* or *Ecorché au bras tendu* (plaster version, Gotha, Schloss Friedenstein; later and modified bronze version, Paris, Ecole N. Sup. B.-A.). It bears witness to Houdon's other great source of inspiration—study from nature. A statue of *St Bruno*, also for S Maria degli Angeli (marble; *in situ*), was clearly a response to René-Michel Slodtz's *St Bruno* (1744) in St Peter's. Where Slodtz's statue is dynamic, almost agitated, in character, Houdon's is sober, an image of contemplation and introspection, in which the asceticism of the face is emphasized by the striking vertical pleats of the saint's habit.

2. PARIS AND GOTHA, 1768–79. Houdon returned to Paris in 1768 and was approved (*agréé*) by the Académie Royale on presentation of a recumbent statue of *Morpheus*, god of dreams. He exhibited a monumental plaster version

of this ambitious work at the 1771 Salon (Gotha, Schloss Friedenstein) and was received (*reçu*) as a full member of the Académie in 1777 on presentation of a smaller marble version (Paris, Louvre). The 1771 Salon was also the first occasion when Houdon showed portraits of identified sitters, among them a terracotta bust of *Denis Diderot* (Paris, Louvre; *see* PARIS, fig. 19). The writer is depicted lightly idealized in the antique manner, with short hair and no draperies, his lips slightly parted. In this bust Houdon experimented with a new manner of treating the eyes, perhaps inspired by Bernini, to which he remained faithful for the rest of his career: a small isthmus of marble left within the excavated socket to catch the light represents the sparkle of the pupil.

In 1771 and again in 1773 Houdon travelled to Gotha in Saxony, where the Francophile Herzog and Herzogin were among the first collectors of his sculpture. In 1773 he showed at the Paris Salon profile medallion portraits *all'antica* of *Ernest Ludwig II, Herzog von Saxe-Gotha* and of *Maria Charlotte, Herzogin von Saxe-Gotha* (bronzed plaster; Gotha, Schloss Friedenstein). At the same Salon he also exhibited a characterful bust, made after drawings, of another important collector of his works, *Catherine the Great* (marble version, St Petersburg, Hermitage; plaster version, Schwerin, Staatl. Mus.). Russian patronage was to be important to Houdon. In particular he received commissions for four funerary monuments for members of his family from Prince Dmitry Alekseyevitch Galitzin, Russian Ambassador to France. Two of these were executed in marble (St Petersburg, Mus. Sculp., and Moscow, Don Monastery Cemetery) and were shown at the 1773 Salon. A third exists only as a terracotta model (exh. Salon 1777; Paris, Louvre). The two marbles are in the form of Neo-classical stelae with mourning figures in relief and anticipate the design of Houdon's monument for the *Heart of Victor Charpentier, Comte d'Ennery* (marble, 1781; Paris, Louvre; see fig. 1). The terracotta represents a programmatic composition of the kind advocated by Diderot, and maybe conceived as a small cenotaph, made for personal reflection—such as a Vanity—rather than a model for a large monument, never, in fact, executed.

The great series of Houdon's portrait busts began in earnest with his exhibits at the Salons of 1775 and 1777, when he showed works that are among his most successful, both from the point of view of psychological penetration and in the exceptional mastery of his handling. They included busts of the Garde des Sceaux, the *Marquis de Miromesnil* (marble versions, London, V&A, and New York, Frick), of the Contrôleur Général des Finances, *Anne-Robert-Jacques Turgot* (marble; Lantheuil, Calvados, Château), of the composer *Willibald von Gluck* (plaster; Weimar, Thüring. Landesbib.) and the singer *Sophie Arnould* (marble; Paris, Louvre), as well as Houdon's four marble masterpieces, the busts of the *Comtesse de Cayla* (New York, Frick), the *Baronne de la Houze* (San Marino, CA, Huntington A.G.) and Louis XVI's aunts *Mme Victoire* (London, Wallace) and *Mme Adélaïde* (Paris, Louvre). Also noteworthy were the terracotta busts of the children of the architect Alexandre-Théodore Brongniart (Paris, Louvre). Houdon later made portraits of his own children at different ages, such as those of *Sabine Houdon* (plaster; Paris, Louvre).

1. Jean-Antoine Houdon: monument for the *Heart of Victor Charpentier, Comte d'Ennery*, marble, 2.32×2.25 m, 1781 (Paris, Musée du Louvre)

If the Salons of 1775 and 1777 established Houdon as a portrait sculptor without rivals, he nevertheless continued to work also on a monumental scale. In 1776 he executed for the Herzog von Saxe-Gotha a large plaster statue of *Diana the Huntress* (Gotha, Schloss Friedenstein). In this, the goddess is depicted as if running forward, her bow in her hand. It is a reinterpretation of the art of antiquity in which Houdon, while choosing to depict the figure completely nude, also chose to show its anatomical details without idealization. Diana is given apparent movement by a slight twist to the torso, which gives the figure both its dynamism and its sensuality. The statue exists in a number of other large-scale versions: a marble of 1780 (Lisbon, Mus. Gulbenkian), a terracotta of *c*. 1781 (New York, Frick) and two bronzes cast by Houdon himself, one of 1782 (San Marino, CA, Huntington A.G.) and the other of 1790 (Paris, Louvre; see fig. 2 below).

3. FROM THE SALON OF 1779 TO THE FRENCH REVOLUTION. At the Salon of 1779 Houdon inaugurated his impressive gallery of portraits of famous men, modelled both from life and posthumously. This was a theme that he continued up to his last Salon in 1814, and places him firmly within the historicist current of the age of Louis XVI. Houdon's originality (he was always keen to exploit the commercial possibilities of his works) lay in creating different bust types of his illustrious subjects. Thus Voltaire, Rousseau, D'Alembert, Franklin, Washington and others were depicted in contemporary costume and hairstyles, but also with their hair dressed in the Roman manner and their shoulders naked or covered with antique drapery.

Also in 1779 Houdon received his only official commission from the Bâtiments du Roi, a statue in period costume of the 17th-century soldier the *Maréchal de Tourville* (marble; Versailles, Château). This was intended as part of the series of statues of *Illustrious Frenchmen* designed to decorate the Grande Galerie of the Louvre, Paris. The statue of Tourville was exhibited at the 1781 Salon together with one of Houdon's greatest masterpieces, his statue of *Voltaire Seated*. The latter was a private commission from the writer's niece Mme Denis. It exists in a number of versions, including the original plaster containing Voltaire's heart (Paris, Bib. N.), two marbles, shown at the Salon (Paris, Mus. Comédie Fr.), and a variant made for Catherine the Great (St Petersburg, Hermitage). The pose of the Voltaire statue, which shows him seated in a Louis XVI-style armchair, is related to the concept of the *Illustrious Frenchmen*. But the imprecise nature of the costume, a sort of dressing-gown that implies Classical drapery, and the head shown wigless but decorated with a philosopher's headband, suggest a heroization responding, but with a greater care for 'decency', to Pigalle's infamous statue of *Voltaire Nude* (1776; Paris, Louvre).

Such was Houdon's celebrity by this time that Thomas Jefferson, Ambassador of the United States to France, suggested to him a scheme for a monumental statue of *George Washington* for the Capitol at Richmond, VA. Hoping to execute a bronze equestrian statue, the apogee of the sculptor's art, Houdon went to the USA in 1785. There he executed a bust portrait of *Washington* taken from life but lightly idealized *all'antica* (terracotta; Mount Vernon, VA). Unfortunately, Washington refused to be represented in the heroic antique mode and Houdon had to content himself with making a marble standing statue showing him in contemporary costume (Richmond, VA, Capitol), which he signed in 1788. The only Classical reference is the plough behind the figure of Washington, an allusion to the retirement of Cincinnatus.

4. AFTER 1789. Houdon, who by the late 1780s had portrayed the king, the royal family and the high aristocracy as well as the men of the Enlightenment, continued his activity unabated during the early years of the Revolution. He executed busts of such political figures as *Lafayette, Necker, Barnave, Bailly, Mirabeau* and *Dumouriez*, which exist in a number of versions. Nevertheless, later he was in less demand. It is significant that he was not involved in the new sculptural decorations of the Panthéon, Paris, and he failed in his ambition to execute a monument in honour of Rousseau. He did execute a number of important works under the Empire, including a herm bust of *Napoleon as Emperor* (terracotta, 1806; Dijon, Mus. B.-A.), a statue of *Cicero* (plaster, 1804; Paris, Bib. N.) for the chamber of the Senate, and monumental marble statues of *Général Joubert* (c. 1812; Versailles, Château) and *Voltaire* (c. 1812; Paris, Panthéon), the latter this time depicted standing.

Houdon was an artist of remarkable range and calibre who dominated with ease the sculptors of his generation. His output covers all the genres, except perhaps that of the terracotta model for the consumption of private collectors. Even this taste was catered for late in his career with the half-nude female statuettes he made on the theme of *Winter* ('La Frileuse', Paris, Louvre). He executed portraits from life and posthumously, sometimes, as in the case of his busts of *Rousseau* and *Mirabeau*, using death

masks. He produced outdoor statuary, such as his fountain for the Duc d'Orléans's park at the Plaine Monceau. This consisted of a marble figure of a *Bather* (New York, Met.) on to whose shoulders water was poured by a lead *Negress* (destr. 1790s). There was also sculpture for interior settings, including marble female statues representing *Winter* and *Summer* (c. 1783–5; Montpellier, Mus. Fabre) made for the rich collector Girardot de Marigny, as well as decorative low reliefs, such as the one made for Ste

2. Jean-Antoine Houdon: *Diana the Huntress*, bronze, h. c. 2 m, 1790 (Paris, Musée du Louvre)

Geneviève, Paris (untraced). He was a superb handler of marble—perhaps only Augustin Pajou's works show a comparable finesse of touch—commercially shrewd in the production of plaster versions of his works (and equally so in the diffusion throughout Europe of copies of his portraits of the Parisian élite), and also an expert bronze-founder in the best French tradition. Although he failed in his ambition to execute an equestrian statue, he did produce bronze versions of a number of his statues, including *Winter* ('L'Hiver', 1787; New York, Met.), *Diana the Huntress* and its pendant of *Apollo* (1790; Lisbon, Mus. Gulbenkian) and the *Écorché*, as well as superb bronzes of his busts, such as that of *Rousseau* (1778; Paris, Louvre). It was of this last activity that he was most proud. In a memoir written in 1794 Houdon summed up his career thus: 'I have given myself over to only two studies, which have filled my whole life . . . anatomy and the casting of statues'.

BIBLIOGRAPHY

Lami

G. Giacometti: *La Vie et l'oeuvre de Houdon*, 2 vols (Paris, 1928)

W. Sauerländer: *Jean-Antoine Houdon: Voltaire* (Stuttgart, 1963)

L. Réau: *Houdon*, 2 vols (Paris, 1964)

H. H. Arnason: *The Sculptures of Houdon* (London, 1975) [with extensive bibliog.]

GUILHEM SCHERF

Hoüel, Jean-Pierre-Louis-Laurent (*b* Rouen, 28 June 1735; *d* Paris, 14 Nov 1813). French painter and engraver. He was born into a family of prosperous artisans and at the age of 15 was sent to the drawing academy in Rouen run by Jean-Baptiste Descamps (?1715–91). Presumably Descamps introduced him to the art of 17th-century Dutch and Flemish artists. Descamps also recommended his promising pupil to the Paris engraver Jacques-Philippe Le Bas, whose studio Hoüel entered in 1755. While in Paris Hoüel taught engraving to the celebrated amateur Blondel d'Azincourt (who had inherited a superb collection from his father Blondel de Gagny). This marked Hoüel's entry into cultivated high society, including the circle of the enlightened patron and hostess Mme Geoffrin.

Hoüel developed an interest in landscape painting early in his career. In 1758 he published a book of landscape engravings, consisting of six engravings after drawings by Boucher, and in 1764 he studied with the landscape and battle painter Francesco Casanova. In 1768 he painted six views of properties belonging to Etienne-François, Duc de Choiseul as overdoors for the music-room of his château at Chanteloup, of which four have survived (Tours, Mus. B.-A.). These works indicate his study of 17th-century northern landscape painting. Such views of estates were relatively rare in 18th-century French art.

At the suggestion of Hoüel's influential patrons, the Directeur des Bâtiments, the Marquis de Marigny, arranged a place for him at the Académie de France in Rome. He arrived in Rome in 1769 and within a month was given permission to accompany the Marquis d'Havrincourt on a trip to Naples. Hoüel became fascinated by the landscape, antiquities and customs of southern Italy, which they visited in the company of the antiquarian Baron d'Han-carville. During his Italian sojourn, Hoüel produced many gouache drawings (Paris, Louvre; Besançon, Mus. B.-A. & Archéol.), which he exhibited at the Paris Salons of the early 1770s. These exhibits aroused widespread public interest.

In 18th-century France there was relatively little demand for the non-ideal, topographical landscape painting produced by Hoüel. However, there was a market for lavishly illustrated travel books, which Hoüel hoped to exploit through writings, illustrations and engravings of his own travels. He obtained permission to make an extended trip to Sicily, Lipari and Malta from 1776 to 1779, avoiding Naples and southern Italy, already covered by the Abbé Richard de Saint-Non in his book *Voyage pittoresque ou description des Royaumes de Naples et de Sicile* (1781–7). Hoüel published four large volumes between 1782 and 1787, *Le Voyage pittoresque des isles de Sicile, de Malte et de Lipari*. They contain 264 aquatint plates and a long explanatory text. The final publication, much more than just an antiquarian travel book, is a study of the physical and human antiquity and geography of the islands. Hoüel's main intention was to render topography, but he also developed a rare sensitivity to the general effects of nature. He often employed delicate washes of watercolours to reproduce the most subtly observed effects of light and atmosphere. His preparatory drawings were generally made on the spot, while the figures and animals, which enliven the published plates, were added at the time of engraving. Hoüel helped finance his project by selling the drawings after his return to Paris in 1780: Louis XVI acquired 46 (Paris, Louvre), while Catherine II of Russia purchased over 500, of which 260 survive (St Petersburg, Hermitage).

Because Hoüel was involved in the Revolution, the period of Revolution and Empire was a less productive time for him. However, he did publish designs for a triumphal column (1802) and his entry for the competition of 1806 for a public monument at the Madeleine (pubd 1807). He also prepared two illustrated treatises on ele-phants as well as producing many drawings of animals, which suggest he had further treatises in mind.

WRITINGS

Le Voyage pittoresque des isles de Sicile, de Malte et de Lipari, 4 vols (Paris, 1782–7)

Histoire des éléphants de la ménagerie nationale et relations de leur voyage à Paris (Paris, 1798)

Histoire naturelle des deux éléphants mâle et femelle du museum de Paris, venus de Hollande en France, en l'an VI (Paris, 1803) [drgs for these two treatises on elephants repr. in Vloberg, pls XXVI–XXVII]

BIBLIOGRAPHY

M. Vloberg: *Jean Hoüel* (Paris, 1930)

PHILIP CONISBEE

Houghton, Arthur Boyd (*b* Kotagiri, Madras, India, 13 March 1836; *d* London, 25 Nov 1875). English painter and illustrator. He played a leading role in the renaissance of wood-engraved illustration during the so-called golden decade of English book illustration (*c.* 1860–75), when a new school of artists overcame the limitations of the medium. Deeply influenced by the idealism of the Pre-Raphaelite Brotherhood, he imbued both his paintings and drawings with a haunting blend of poetic realism. He was the fourth son of Captain John Michael Houghton (1797–1874), who served in the East India Company's Marine as a draughtsman.

Houghton was admitted to the Royal Academy Schools, London, in 1854 but did not pass further than the Life School. He received additional training at J. M. Leigh's academy and its convivial corollary, the Langham Artists' Society, which was then a forcing-house for young impoverished painters who wished to have a foot in both publishing and the fine arts. There, with older artists such as Charles Keene and John Tenniel, he learnt to run the race against time with a set weekly subject. Keene, already a well-known contributor to *Punch*, introduced Houghton to the master engraver J. W. Whymper (1813–1903). Houghton developed his style to suit the woodblock medium: he visualized form as a silhouette, creating compositions by juxtaposing black shapes and white spaces, and linear effects were achieved with thick and thin brushstrokes and crosshatched penstrokes. By the time he was 25 he had mastered his craft, bringing to it an intensity distilled from many sources: the Pre-Raphaelites, Adolf Menzel, Utamaro and William Holman Hunt. Despite bad eyesight he began to work on woodblock designs for the Dalziel brothers. Painting was Houghton's primary concern, but for most of his life he was condemned by family circumstances to accept commissions below the level of his talents, working on all types of subject, imaginary and real, sacred and secular.

Houghton was an illustrator of Victorian ideas and attitudes in their immense variety. His early illustrations of his own family life, *Home Thoughts and Home Scenes* (1865), rank among the finest Victorian illustration, and his designs for the Dalziel illustrated editions of *Arabian Nights* (2 vols, 1864–5) and the *Adventures of Don Quixote* (1866) inspired several illustrators of the 1890s, notably Arthur Rackham and Edmund Joseph Sullivan (1869–1933) in Britain, and Howard Pyle (1853–1911) and N. C. Wyeth (1882–1945) in the United States.

Houghton's chronicle of a raw and booming United States, made for the London weekly *Graphic* during a seven-month visit in 1869–70, established him as a narrative draughtsman. He was attracted to the vitality of American life, and a powerfully evocative series was the result: scenes of New York, Boston, a Shaker commune, the Mormon Utopia and a still wild West ('Graphic America', *Graphic*, i–xiii, 1870–75). After his return to Europe, when he depicted the blood-bath of civil war ('Paris under the Commune', *Graphic*, ii–vi, 1870–72), he turned away from modern life and towards religion as a means of making judgements on society. A large oil, *John the Baptist Rebuking Herod* (exh. RA, 1872; untraced), attracted more notice than any other work he painted. There are traces of Ford Madox Brown and John Everett Millais in Houghton's paintings of London life, for example *Volunteers* (1860; London, Tate) and *Holborn in 1861* (ex-Sir Colin Anderson priv. col., London, see Hogarth, 1981, p. 18), and in those of his family life, *Ramsgate Sands* (1862; London, Tate) and *The Family* (1861–2; ex-Sir Colin Anderson priv. col., London, see Hogarth, 1981, p. 24). But Houghton's art also reflects the satirical influence of William Hogarth, which runs through much of Pre-Raphaelite art. Van Gogh recognized this: 'He was', he wrote, 'weird and mysterious like Goya. In the same way, quite Goya-like, he also treated the American subjects in the same way, but all at once there are some that by a wonderful soberness remind one of Meryon.'

BIBLIOGRAPHY
L. Housman: *Arthur Boyd Houghton* (London, 1896)
E. Dalziel and G. Dalziel: *A Record of Work* (London, 1901)
F. Reid: *Illustrators of the Sixties* (London, 1928/R New York, 1975)
E. J. Sullivan: 'Arthur Boyd Houghton', *Prt Colr Q.*, x (1932), pp. 95–125
Arthur Boyd Houghton, 1836–75 (exh. cat. by P. Hogarth, London, V&A, 1975)
P. Hogarth: *Arthur Boyd Houghton* (London, 1981)
——: *The Artist as Reporter* (London, 1986), chaps 6 and 7
PAUL HOGARTH

Houma [Hou-ma]. City in southern Shanxi Province, China. The Eastern Zhou (771–256 BC) state of Jin had its capital at Houma (anc. Xintian) from 585 BC until the dissolution of the state in 453 BC. Archaeological work has been carried out at the site since the 1950s, and a number of major finds have been reported.

Of great historical interest are deposits of jade tablets that bear brush-written inscriptions recording oaths of allegiance pledged by vassals to their lords (*see* CHINA, §VIII, 1). More pertinent to art history is the excavation of a vast foundry site that yielded some 30,000 fragments of clay moulds (see fig.), models and other foundry debris. This debris is important partly because it throws light on

Houma, clay mould for casting tiger-shaped object, h. 185 mm, Eastern Zhou period, 771–256 BC

casting processes and partly because it exactly documents the objects and designs that the foundry produced. The Houma foundry used a highly sophisticated pattern-block mouldmaking technique (*see* CHINA, §VI, 2). Its products included not only bronze vessels but also coins, mirrors, belthooks and chariot fittings. The designs on these items are exceedingly varied, ranging from low- or high-relief dragon interlace to copper-inlaid hunting scenes. The same wide range of designs is represented in the bronzes from a tomb discovered at LIYU in northern Shanxi Province in 1923. At the time of the Liyu finds it was generally assumed that the tomb's occupant had assembled his bronzes from a number of disparate sources, but the Houma foundry debris suggests that he could have obtained almost all at Houma. Similar bronzes have since been found in tombs at many other locations, including Houma itself, Taiyuan and Changzhi in Shanxi Province and Hui xian in Henan Province. It is tempting to attribute all such bronzes to Houma workshops, but in the absence of comparable foundry remains from any other Eastern Zhou site it is difficult to estimate how large a clientele Houma served or how many other centres cast similar objects. Sixth-century tombs of the state of Chu at Xiasi in Xichuan County, Henan Province, have yielded bronze vessels and bells that, to judge by their designs, were not cast at Houma. Some of them seem to have been cast using pattern blocks, however, suggesting that the pattern-block mouldmaking technique associated with the Houma foundry was in fact more widespread.

BIBLIOGRAPHY

Li Xueqin: *Eastern Zhou and Qin Civilizations* (New Haven and London, 1985), chap. 3

'Taiyuan Jinsheng cun 251 hao Chunqiu da mu ji chemakeng fajue jianbao' [Brief report on the excavation of Spring and Autumn-period tomb and chariot burial no. 251 at Taiyuan Jinsheng cun], *Wenwu* (1989), no. 9, pp. 59–94

Houma taofan yizhi [The Houma foundry site], Archaeological Institute of Shanxi Province, 2 vols (Beijing, 1993)

Shangma mudi [The Shangma cemetery], Archaeological Institute of Shanxi Province (Beijing, 1994)

R. W. Bagley: 'What the Bronzes from Hunyuan Tell Us about the Foundry at Houma', *Orientations* (Jan 1995), pp. 46–54

Art of the Houma Foundry, Archaeological Institute of Shanxi Province (Princeton, 1996)

ROBERT W. BAGLEY

House, Harlan (*b* Vancouver, 14 Nov 1943). Canadian potter. He studied at the Alberta College of Art, Calgary (1964–9). He initially worked in stoneware making utilitarian wares but in 1975 began devoting himself exclusively to the production of individual porcelain items and was one of the first 20th-century Canadian potters to make porcelain his prime medium. Profoundly interested in the oriental tradition, particularly porcelain of the Song dynasty, he searched for self-expression within this aesthetic. His works have such glazes as celadon and temmoku and such motifs as the iris, sometimes used in three-dimensional form on vases, and are marked by technical and aesthetic standards that limit output (*see* CANADA, fig. 14). Examples of his work were shown in the Canadian pavilion at the Expo '70 World Fair in Osaka, Japan. In 1972 he taught at the University of Calgary and subsequently at selected workshops. The numerous Canadian awards he has received commend not only his own work but equally his influence in the craft community of Canada. Examples of his work are in the Glenbow–Alberta Institute, Calgary, the Montreal Museum of Fine Arts and the Royal Museum of Scotland, Edinburgh.

BIBLIOGRAPHY

G. Hickey: 'Harlan House, Ceramist', *Can. Colr*, xxii/1 (1987), pp. 38–41

ELIZABETH COLLARD

Houseman, Jacob. *See* HUYSMANS, JACOB.

Houser, Allan [Ha-o-zous] (*b* Apache, OK, 30 June 1914; *d* Santa Fe, NM, 22 Aug 1994). Native American painter and sculptor. He was the son of a Chiricahua Apache (originally from Colorado and New Mexico) family who settled in Oklahoma after release from captivity at Fort Sill in 1913. As a young boy he received a full education in Chiricahua Apache customs. He later attended the Santa Fe Indian School and studied painting with Dorothy Dunn. In 1936 he received the Arts and Crafts Award for the best work produced by a student. After graduation, he gained additional experience in oil, casein and egg tempera painting and in fresco and secco mural techniques. His early paintings were scenes of Apache ceremonial and social life in the flat, controlled style of the Santa Fe Indian school, which also revealed his skill as a draughtsman. He painted a number of murals, including the extant series illustrating Apache dancers and people on horseback for the Department of the Interior Building in Washington, DC (1939), and a buffalo hunt for the Southern Plains Indian Museum and Crafts Center, Anadarko, OK (1950). Gradually his style became more experimental, breaking away from the more conventional style associated with US Southwest Native American art. This break is particularly evident in his sculpture, which he began to produce after 1938. He was artist in residence and instructor at the Inter-Mountain Indian School, Brigham City, UT, (1951–62), and in 1962 became the first instructor in sculpture at the Institute of American Indian Arts in Santa Fe, where he was departmental head from 1971 to 1975. Houser's sculpture ranges from realistic representations to stylized images, both large- and small-scale, in steel, bronze and stone. He is recognized as a leading Native American sculptor. His works have been exhibited in the US, in Central and South America and in Europe. His major sculptural commissions include *Offering of the Sacred Pipe* (1985; US Mission at the United Nations) and *As Long as the Waters Flow* (1989; Oklahoma State Capitol). He received numerous awards, including a Guggenheim fellowship (1949), France's Palmes d'Academique (1954), State of New Mexico Governor's Award (1980), State of Oklahoma Governor's Award (1983), induction into the Oklahoma Hall of Fame (1985) and the National Medal of Arts (the USA's highest art award) in 1992. His son, Bob Haozous (*b* 1943), a Chiricahua Apache and Navajo, is a distinguished sculptor with many works on public display in Santa Fe and Tulsa.

BIBLIOGRAPHY

G. Monthan and D. Monthan: 'Allan Houser', *Art and Indian Individualists* (Flagstaff, 1975), pp. 78–85

B. H. Perlman: *Allan Houser (HA-O-ZOUS)* (Boston, 1987/*R* Washington, DC, 1991)

ARTHUR SILBERMAN

Houssaye [Housset]**, (François-)Arsène** (*b* Bruyères-sous-Laon, 28 March 1815; *d* Paris, 27 Feb 1896). French writer, theatre director and museum official. He came from an important and wealthy provincial family—his two grandfathers had been successive mayors of Bruyères, his father was a farmer and his uncle a court painter. He developed an interest in literature and the arts in the library that had been left to his grandfather by the daughters of King Louis XV. His first published works were two novels that appeared in 1836, and in 1838 he moved to Paris and wrote exhibition reviews for the *Revue de Paris*. While projecting himself as a bohemian and a liberal, he also wished to be at the centre of Parisian society and so, on arriving in Paris, he changed his name from Housset to the more aristocratic Houssaye. In 1844 he became the editor of *L'Artiste*, publishing works by such unknown contemporary writers as Charles Baudelaire and writing reviews under the pseudonym of 'Lord Pilgrim'. Among other periodicals, he wrote for *Revue des deux mondes*, *Le Constitutionnel*, *Le Journal*, *Le Gaulois* and *La Gazette de Paris*. From 1849 to 1856 he was Director of the Théâtre-Française, a post that confirmed his place in the artistic society of Paris. His friends included many artists and writers, such as Balzac, Chateaubriand, Delacroix and Gautier, as well as important figures from commerce and public life. In 1851 he took over the direction of the *Revue de Paris*, with Gautier, Maxime Du Camp and Louis de Cormenin (1821–66), and on 30th January 1856 he was named Inspecteur Général des Musées de Province—a position that was created for him by Napoleon III.

After his second trip to the Netherlands (he had been once before in 1840), in 1846 Houssaye published *Histoire de la peinture flamande et hollandaise*, which greatly enhanced his reputation as an art historian. Lavishly illustrated, the work surveys Dutch and Flemish art from the time of Jan van Eyck to that of Jan van Huysum. Houssaye saw the art of this period as characterized by a move away from religious subject-matter to that centred on man and nature. Numerous other books on art followed, covering a wide range of areas. In *Histoire de l'art français au dix-huitième siècle* (1860) he discussed both French painters and sculptors of the 18th century, opening the work with an analysis of Beauty. He dismissed the notion that there were rules in art 'because one of the rules of Beauty is variety' (p. 3). In addition to writing, Houssaye built up a significant collection of both past and contemporary art. This consisted of works in most media from many national schools, though it was dominated by French paintings. It included paintings by Lucas Cranach (i), Jean-Siméon Chardin, Jean-Baptiste Greuze, Nicolas de Largillierre and Pierre Mignard, and among contemporary artists there were works by Courbet, Delacroix, Monet (*Camille*, 1866; Bremen, Ksthalle) and Renoir. The collection was sold after Houssaye's death (Paris, Hôtel Drouot, 22–23 May 1896).

WRITINGS

Histoire de la peinture flamande et hollandaise (Paris, 1846)
Histoire de l'art en France (Paris, 1856)
Histoire de l'art français au dix-huitième siècle (Paris, 1860)
Oeuvres d'Arsène Houssaye, 8 vols (Paris, 1860–67)
Merveilles de l'art flamande (Paris, 1868)
Histoire de Léonard de Vinci (Paris, 1869)
Jacques Callot: Sa vie et son oeuvre (Paris, 1875)

Les Confessions: Souvenirs d'un demi-siècle, 6 vols (Paris, 1885–91; Eng. trans., abridged, London, 1972)
Regular contributions to *Rev. Paris* (1838–43), *L'Artiste* (1840–68), *Rev. Deux Mondes* (1840–41, 1861–6), *Le Constitutionnel* (1845–50), *Gaz. Paris* (1871–3) and *Le Gaulois* (1873–95)

BIBLIOGRAPHY

DBF
E. de Mirecourt: *Arsène Houssaye*, Les Contemporains (Paris, 1856)
——: *Arsène Houssaye*, Histoire contemporaine (Paris, 1870)
E. Lemaître: *Arsène Houssaye: Notes et souvenirs, bibliographie* (Paris, 1897)

☐

Houston. American inland port city in the state of Texas, on the flat coastal plain about 80 km from the Gulf of Mexico. It is the fourth largest city in the USA (population *c.* 1,725,000), the largest city in Texas and a centre of the USA's oil industry. Houston was founded in 1836. Its importance dates from the discovery of oil near by at Spindletop in 1901 and the construction of the deep-draught Houston Ship Channel (1902–14) linking the city to the sea. Economic and population growth followed, together with the first significant attempts at city improvements. Ralph Adams Cram designed the campus plan and initial buildings of Rice University (1912), and major urban improvements were carried out in 1916–17 by George E. Kessler (1862–1923), the landscape architect who produced a plan for Dallas in 1911.

During the 1920s Houston acquired a series of tall buildings, the highest being the 37-storey Gulf Building (1929) by Alfred C. Finn (1883–1964) and Kenneth Franzfjheim (1890–1959), as well as a public library (1926) in Spanish Renaissance Revival style by Cram and William Ward Watkin (1886–1952) that was intended to form the basis of a civic centre inspired by the CITY BEAUTIFUL MOVEMENT. The Museum of Fine Arts, the first public art museum in Texas, opened in 1924 in a Neo-classical building designed by Watkin. A system of public parks and parkway boulevards was designed by Hare & Hare from Kansas City, and the planned garden suburb of River Oaks (1923–47) was laid out by the civil engineer Herbert A. Kipp (1883–1968). Widespread use of the motor car in the 1920s caused Houston to expand outward at low population densities in a pattern of discontinuous dispersal, and rejection of a zoning code by municipal authorities in 1929 heralded the city's unusually lenient policy towards the regulation of land use and building. African Americans were compelled by racialist practices to live in separate enclaves, which were distinguished by two vernacular building types: the 'shotgun' cottage and the twin-towered church, for example Wesley Chapel African Methodist Episcopal Church (1926) by W. Sidney Pittman (1875–1968).

The International Style, introduced in a house (1950) designed by Philip Johnson for the DE MENIL family of collectors, challenged Wrightian-style modern architecture—represented by Mackie & Kamrath's temporary building (1949) for Houston's second art museum, the Contemporary Arts Museum—for local patronage. The construction of a radial network of freeways centred on the city's central business district, begun in 1946, intensified Houston's low density suburban expansion, yet between 1958 and 1983 successive episodes of tall-building construction transformed the central area (see fig.) and also created a series of suburban office centres, such as Post Oak and the Texas Medical Centre. Prominent in them are buildings by Skidmore, Owings & Merrill, I. M. Pei and Cesar Pelli. Philip Johnson produced such well-known commercial landmarks as Pennzoil Place (1975), Post Oak Central (1975, 1978, 1981), Transco Tower (1983), and the Republic Bank Centre (1984; for illustration *see* JOHNSON, PHILIP). The demand for climate-controlled public buildings accessible by car led to such typological innovations as the Astrodome (1965), an air-conditioned sports stadium by Wilson, Morris, Crain & Anderson and Lloyd, Morgan & Jones, and the Galleria (1969–86) by Hellmuth, Obata & Kassabaum and others—an extensive suburban building complex of shops, hotels, office towers and car parks.

Houston began to sustain a community of artists in the 1920s, but not until the 1950s did a distinctive artistic movement emerge, influenced by contact with such local vernacular sub-cultures as American Southern, African-American, Mexican and French Acadian. Its most extreme and influential exponent was Forrest Bess (1911–77), a painter who lived near Bay City, TX. The painters John Biggers (*b* 1924) and Dorothy Hood (*b* 1919) and the sculptor Jim Love (*b* 1927) are seminal figures. The Museum of Fine Arts, Houston, has two additions by Mies van der Rohe (completed 1958 and 1974). Its adjuncts are the Glassell School of Art (1978) by Morris-Aubry, the Cullen Sculpture Garden (1986) by Isamu Noguchi, the Museum Administration Building (1994) by Carlos Jiménez (*b* 1959) and the former home of Houston's first important collector, Ima Hogg (1882–1975): the Bayou Bend Collection and Gardens (1928) by John F. Staub (1892–1981) with Birdsall P. Briscoe (1876–1971). The Contemporary Arts Museum (1972) is the work of Gunnar Bikerts. DiverseWorks Artspace, founded in 1982, occupies a former warehouse. The Rothko Chapel (1971) by Barnstone & Aubry, was built to contain the last paintings of Mark Rothko. Adjacent to it are two buildings (1987, 1995) designed by RENZO PIANO and others to house Houston's third art museum, the Menil Collection. Other cultural buildings include the Jesse H. Jones Hall for the Performing Arts (1966) by Caudill Rowlett Scott, the Alley Theater (1969) by Ulrich Franzen, the Wortham Theater Center (1987) by Morris-Aubry and the Children's Museum of Houston (1992) by Venturi & Scott Brown. The campus of Rice University contains the first buildings in the USA by James Stirling and Michael Wilford (1981) and Ricardo Bofill (1991).

BIBLIOGRAPHY

P. C. Papademetriou: *Houston: An Architectural Guide* (Houston, 1972)
H. Barnstone: *The Architecture of John F. Staub: Houston and the South* (Austin, 1979)
C. A. Brutvan: *In Our Time: Houston's Contemporary Arts Museum, 1948–1982* (Houston, 1982)
P. C. Papademetriou: *Transportation and Urban Development in Houston, 1830–1980* (Houston, 1982)
B. Rose and S. Kalil: *Fresh Paint: The Houston School* (Austin, 1985)
J. M. Vlach: 'The Shotgun House: An African Architectural Legacy', *Common Places: Readings in American Vernacular Architecture*, ed. Upton and J. M. Vlach (Athens, GA, 1986), pp. 58–78
J. Yau: *Forrest Bess* (New York, 1988)
S. J. Barnes: *The Rothko Chapel: An Act of Faith* (Austin, 1989)
S. Fox: *Houston Architectural Guide* (Houston, 1990)

Houston, skyscrapers in the city centre

J. W. Barna: *The See-through Years: Creation and Destruction in Texas Real Estate and Architecture, 1981–1991* (Houston, 1992)

STEPHEN FOX

Houston, Richard (*b* Dublin, 1721–2; *d* London, 4 Aug 1775). Irish engraver, active in England. Together with James McArdell he was apprenticed in Dublin to the mezzotint engraver John Brooks (*fl* 1730–60). He moved to London in 1746 and soon began to publish his prints. In the 1750s he had success with a series of portraits of politicians, such as *William Pitt*, 1st Earl of Chatham (see Chaloner Smith, no. 92), after William Hoare, and with powerful mezzotints after paintings by Rembrandt. Houston's independence did not last: according to Horace Walpole, he was 'idle, capricious and extravagant'. By 1757 he was working for print-sellers, one of whom, Robert Sayer (1724–94), is said to have had him imprisoned for debt in the Fleet, so that he would know where to find him. Houston ceased to publish his own prints in 1758 with *Charles, 3rd Duke of Marlborough* (CS 77) after Reynolds. Unlike McArdell, Houston played no part in the Society of Artists, founded in 1760. After that time he worked mostly, although never exclusively, for Sayer, engraving for him, among other works, the *Death of General James Wolfe* (1772; CS 126) after Edward Penny and the *Syndics* (1775; CS 149) after Rembrandt. The latter work shows how well, despite his problems, Houston maintained his standards of work.

BIBLIOGRAPHY

Redgrave; Strickland; Thieme–Becker
J. Chaloner Smith: *British Mezzotinto Portraits*, ii (London, 1879), pp. 644–702 [CS]
J. Charrington: *A Catalogue of the Mezzotints after, or said to be after, Rembrandt* (Cambridge, 1923)
C. E. Russell: *English Mezzotint Portraits and their States: Catalogue of Corrections and Additions to Chaloner Smith's 'British Mezzotinto Portraits'*, ii (London, 1926), pp. 153–64
H. Walpole: *Anecdotes of Painting in England*, ed. F. W. Hilles and P. B. Daghlain, v (New Haven, 1937), pp. 211–15

DAVID ALEXANDER

Houte, Adriaen van den. *See under* MASTERS, ANONY-MOUS, AND MONOGRAMMISTS, §I: PSEUDO-ORTKENS.

Houzeau, Jacques (*b* Bar-le-Duc, Meuse, 1624; *d* Paris, 18 May 1691). French sculptor. A member of the Académie de St Luc from 1646, he attracted the attention of the architect Louis Le Vau who in 1656 appointed him Sculpteur du Roi. Although he also worked for private clients such as Nicolas Fouquet at the château of Vaux-le-Vicomte, Seine-et-Marne (1659–60), he was principally employed by the Bâtiments du Roi. He executed numerous decorative sculptures at the château of Vincennes, Val-de-Marne (1656–60; 1667–70), and at the Tuileries Palace, Paris (1667–70), but his largest body of work was for the château of Versailles where he was a very productive member of the team of sculptors assembled by Charles Le Brun to execute his designs for the embellishment of Louis XIV's park and palace. Among Houzeau's surviving works at Versailles are a pair of marble *Sphinxes* on the Parterre des Fleurs (1667–8), his cheerful statues of *Momus* and *Terpsichore* (stone, 1671) for the façade, fragments of the lively, naturalistic animal fountains of the *Labyrinthe* (lead, 1673–4), a powerful statue of a male nude representing the *Choleric Temperament* (marble, 1677–80), a truculent *Faun* shaped as a term (1684–7) and two dramatic bronze groups representing *Animal Fights* (1685–7). Houzeau was the brother-in-law of the sculptor Etienne Le Hongre.

Lami; Souchal
BIBLIOGRAPHY
J. Guiffrey: *Comptes des Bâtiments du Roi sous le règne de Louis XIV*, 5 vols (Paris, 1881–1901)
FRANÇOISE DE LA MOUREYRE

Hove. *See under* BRIGHTON.

Hove, Bartholomeus Johannes van (*b* The Hague, 28 Oct 1790; *d* The Hague, 8 Nov 1880). Dutch painter. He was trained by his father, who was a gilder and frame maker, by Joannes Henricus Albertus Antonius Breckenheijmer (1772–1856), a painter of stage scenery, and at the Koninklijke Academie van Beeldende Kunsten in The Hague. He succeeded Breckenheijmer as resident painter at the Hague theatre, the Koninklijke Schouwburg, where he became renowned for his beautiful sets, some of which have been preserved (Amsterdam, Theatmus.). He also produced easel paintings, chiefly townscapes. One of his best works is the *Garden at Gedempte Burgwal 34 in The Hague* (1828; The Hague, Gemeentemus.). This carefully constructed view displays skills learnt in the theatre. Later in his career, in tune with general stylistic developments in Dutch art, detailed execution and subtle use of colour gave way to a looser touch and a greyer palette. The *Gothic Gate* (1841; Enschede, priv. col. Edwina van Heek) and *View on the Zieken in The Hague* illustrate this shift. As well as his townscapes, mainly featuring complex and majestic churches, van Hove also painted church interiors (*Church Interior*, 1844; Amsterdam, Rijksmus.). He was a popular and capable teacher. The best-known of his pupils were Jan Hendrik Weissenbruch and Johannes Bosboom.

Scheen

BIBLIOGRAPHY
Op zoek naar de Gouden Eeuw [In search of the Golden Age] (exh. cat., ed. G. Jansen and L. van Tilborgh; Haarlem, Frans Halsmus., 1986)
ANNEMIEKE HOOGENBOOM

Hovenden, Thomas (*b* Dunmanway, Co. Cork, 28 Dec 1840; *d* nr Trenton, NJ, 14 Aug 1895). American painter of Irish birth. He was orphaned when he was six and was apprenticed to a frame carver and gilder at 14. His master encouraged him to enrol at the Cork School of Design. In 1863 Hovenden emigrated to New York and supported himself by colouring photographs and making frames. He attended night classes at the National Academy of Design, but was attracted to Paris in 1874, where he immersed himself in the academic painting of Jules Breton and Alexandre Cabanel and joined the artists' colony at Pont-Aven. In 1880 he returned to New York with his new wife, the painter Helen Corson (1846–1935), and the following year they settled near Philadelphia. Hovenden's favourite subjects were interiors; he is best remembered for *Breaking Home Ties* (1890; Philadelphia, PA, Mus. A.), which was voted the most popular picture at the Chicago World's Columbian Exposition in 1893. It depicts a young man leaving his rural home to make his fame and fortune in the city. The painting conveys a powerful and genuine sentimentality that is saved from excess by the solidity of the compositional structure, derived from his French training.

In general, Hovenden's output is characterized by naturalism of detail and overall clarity. Although he was primarily a genre painter, he also painted some Impressionistic landscapes, with softened forms and a lighter palette. He was elected Academician of the National Academy of Design, New York, in 1882 and succeeded Thomas Eakins as instructor at the Pennsylvania Academy of the Fine Arts in 1886. He was killed by a train while trying to save a child.

BIBLIOGRAPHY
R. Wunderlich: 'Thomas Hovenden and the American Genre Painters', *Kennedy Q.*, iii (1962), pp. 2–11
A. G. Terhune: *Thomas Hovenden (1840–1895) and Late Nineteenth-century American Genre Painting* (diss., New York, City U., 1983)
H. NICHOLS B. CLARK

Hovnat'anian [Avnatamov; Ovnatanyan; Yovnat'anyan]. Armenian family of artists active from the 17th to the late 19th century in manuscript illumination, church decoration, iconostasis painting, portrait painting and lithography. Naghash Hovnat'an (1666–1721) was a poet and artist who painted churches in Erevan. In 1720–21 he decorated the cathedral at Ēdjmiadzin; decorative fragments (tempera on dry plaster) have survived, as well as a scene showing King Trdat III (*reg* 286–330), his wife Ashkhen and his sister Khosrovidukht at prayer. Hovnat'an's sons Hakop and Harut'un (birth and death dates unknown) illuminated religious books (Erevan, Matenadaran Inst. Anc. Armen. MSS, MSS 8645, 2162, 1522), decorated churches and executed oil paintings on Gospel themes in imitation of European forms. Hakop's son Hovnat'an (1730s–1801/2) was court painter to Irakli II (*reg* 1744–98), King of Georgia. He painted a series of pictures on religious subjects, as well as portraits of prominent Armenian ecclesiastical figures. In 1786 he repainted Naghash Hovnat'an's decorative scheme in the cathedral at Edjmiadzin. Hovnat'an's son Mkrtum (1779–1845) worked in Tbilisi, where he had studied and trained apprentices. He executed religious paintings and historical portraits and decorated such churches in Tbilisi as Sion Cathedral and Norashen Church. Mkrtum's son Hakop Hovnat'anian the younger (1806–81) is the first and greatest Armenian painter of the modern period. He received his initial training from his father and in 1841 obtained his diploma from the Academy of Arts in St Petersburg. He worked in Tbilisi and is mentioned in the *Kavkazskiy kalendar* ('Caucasian calendar') as having a workshop and taking commissions for portraits. His small-scale portraits combine features from traditional Armenian miniature painting, Iranian Qajar (parade) portrait painting and European Romantic portraiture. His most accomplished works, such as the portrait of *Natalia Teumyan* (Erevan, Pict. Gal. Armenia) date from the 1840s and 1850s. His originality derives from the lyrical and distinctive presentation of the sitter and the beauty of his colours. He spent the last years of his life in Tehran. His brother Agafon Hovnat'anian (1816–93) worked in St Petersburg and was known as a lithographer.

BIBLIOGRAPHY

G. Levonyan: 'Ovnatanyany v istorii armyanskoy zhivopisi' [The Hovnat'anian family in the history of Armenian painting], *Ocherki po istorii iskusstva Armenii* [Essays on the history of Armenian art] (Moscow and Leningrad, 1939), pp. 45–55

S. Stepanyan: 'Dorevolyutsionnoye iskusstvo Armenii' [The pre-revolutionary art of Armenia], *Ocherki po istorii iskusstva Armenii* [Essays on the history of Armenian art] (Moscow and Leningrad, 1939), pp. 56–73

I. Ginzburg: 'Armyanskiye Khudozhniki pervoy poloviny XIX v.' [Armenian artists of the first half of the 19th century], *Istor.-Filol. Zhurnal Akad. Nauk Arm SSR* (1958), no. 3, pp. 106–35

R. Drampyan: *Hakop Hovnat'anian* (Erevan, 1969)

I. Dzutsova: 'Zhivopisnyye raboty Mikirtuma Ovnatanyana v Sionskom sobore v pervoy polovine XIX veka' [Mkrtum Hovnat'anian's painting in Sion Cathedral in the first half of the 19th century], *Vtoroy mezhdunarodnyy simpozium po armyanskomu iskusstvu, 1978: Sbornik dokladov* [Second international symposium on Armenian art: transactions] (Erevan, 1978), iv, pp. 219–26

N. Stepanyan: *The Fine Arts in Armenia* (Moscow, 1989), pp. 144-54

NONNA S. STEPANYAN

Howard (i). English family of patrons and collectors.

(1) Thomas Howard, 2nd [14th] Earl of Arundel [and Surrey] (*b* Finchingfield, Essex, 7 July 1585: *d* Padua, 24 Sept 1646). Politician and diplomat. Pre-eminent aristocratic patron and collector of the early Stuart period, he became known as the grandest man in England and one of the most cultured in Europe. He was the grandson of Thomas Howard, 4th Duke of Norfolk (1536–72), and the son of Philip Howard, 1st Earl of Arundel (1557–95), who was attainted in 1589 on a charge of high treason, with all his honours forfeited and his possessions confiscated by the Crown. The earldom was restored to Thomas Howard in 1604; he was granted Arundel Castle, W. Sussex, and the Norfolk estates that remained.

In 1606 the Earl married (2) Aletheia Talbot, youngest daughter of the rich and powerful Gilbert Talbot, 7th Earl of Shrewsbury (1553–1616). Thereafter he began to make his mark on an English court rapidly becoming more receptive to foreign tastes through the influence of Anne of Denmark, consort of James I, and their son Henry,

Prince of Wales. The Earl of Arundel owed much to the Earl of Shrewsbury's knowledge and encouragement, the most valuable help he received being the services of Thomas Coke, secretary and artistic adviser to the Earl of Shrewsbury, who became the first agent employed in forming the Earl's collection.

The Earl and Coke went together to the Low Countries in August 1612. It is thought that Arundel sat to Rubens, though if he did the portrait has been lost. What is certain, however, is that he encountered a far wider range of paintings than he had previously seen. He visited the collection of the Duke of Aarschet near Brussels and that of the Postmaster-General at Antwerp, where he greatly admired Sebastiano del Piombo's *Cardinal Ferry Carondelet and his Secretary* (1512–13; Madrid, Mus. Thyssen-Bornemisza), a picture he believed was a self-portrait by Raphael and which he eventually acquired in 1618.

In the autumn of 1612 Arundel and Coke left the Low Countries for Padua, intending to undertake a prolonged tour of Italy, but plans were frustrated by the death of Prince Henry, causing their return to England. By the following April the Earl had returned to Italy after accompanying Elizabeth, daughter of James I, to Heidelberg, following her marriage to Frederick V, Elector Palatine (1596–1632). Arundel and his wife, with an entourage of 35 that included Coke, INIGO JONES and WILLIAM PETTY, went first to Milan and were in Venice and Vicenza in the early autumn of 1613. In Venice the Earl commissioned Palma Giovane to paint an episode from the history of the Howard family (untraced). They then spent six weeks in the Monasteria delle Grazie in Siena studying Italian, before the Earl and Jones went on to Rome, arriving at New Year 1614.

The Earl and his entourage spent longer in Rome than anywhere else in Italy, using the city as his base for excursions down the Via Appia to Gaeta and Naples. Rome undoubtedly represented the climax of the Italian tour, a point made by the Earl in a letter to his wife, when they were temporarily separated: 'I would wish you to see Rome well, for there are no more such places'. He bought works of art extensively, but the only known purchases are four statues *all'antica* (Oxford, Ashmolean) that he ordered from Egidio Moretti. Arundel and Jones may have stayed with the Marchese Vincenzo Giustiniani, whose collection of Classical statuary, reliefs and inscriptions they would have seen. Giustiniani evidently contrived a dig in the Forum.

In June 1614 the Earl and Countess turned for home, travelling by way of Siena, where on 14 June the Earl bought a manuscript copy of Vitruvius' *On Architecture* (London, BL, Arundel MS., 122). In Florence they stayed at the Palazzo Pubblico. On this tour, the Earl gained an understanding of Italian culture such as no other Englishman had yet acquired, and his attempts to transplant Italian mores and tastes to England were to have a lasting influence.

After their return at Christmas 1614, the Earl and Countess divided the growing collection among their three houses in London: Arundel House (destr. 1678) in The Strand, with a gallery (*c.* 1615–17) designed by Jones; a property at Greenwich, remodelled by Jones (1615; destr. 1617); and a villa (destr.) at Highgate. The collection also included cabinets and tables inlaid with agate, chalcedony and lapis lazuli such as had never been seen in England. In 1616 the collection of paintings was augmented by pictures from the collection of Robert Carr, 1st Earl of Somerset, repossessed from Dudley Carleton, 1st Viscount Dorchester, and given to the Earl of Arundel by James I. The spirit of these years is evoked in two portraits by Daniel Mijtens the elder of the Earl and Countess (1617; both London, N.P.G., on dep. Arundel Castle, W. Sussex; for the portrait of the Earl *see* LONDON, fig. 16) seated against imaginary views of the south gallery at Arundel House.

At this time the Earl was pursuing what he described as his 'foolish curiosity' for the works of Hans Holbein the younger. From John Lumley, 1st Baron Lumley, a relation by marriage, he inherited works that included Holbein's *Christina of Denmark, Duchess of Milan* (1538; London, N.G.) and *Erasmus* (Longford Castle, Wilts). Such was the fame of his collection that in 1620 Cosimo II de' Medici, Grand Duke of Tuscany, begged a portrait in return for a painting of the Earl's choice from the Medici collections. Arundel sent Holbein's *Sir Richard Southwell* (1536; Florence, Uffizi), though what he received in exchange is not known. The magnificence of the Earl's Holbeins can be gauged from a reference by Joachim von Sandrart in *Teutsche Academie* (1675) to seeing a gallery full of them at Arundel House when he was in London in 1627. The collection was enriched when his brother-in-law William Herbert, 3rd Earl of Pembroke (1580–1630), gave him the series of Holbein's portrait drawings of the English court (Windsor Castle, Berks, Royal Lib.).

In the winter of 1620–21 Anthony van Dyck came to London, and it is probable that the Earl commissioned from him the *Continence of Scipio* (1620–21; Oxford, Christ Church Pict. Gal.). In 1623 Coke died, and Petty succeeded as the Earl's chief agent. In 1624 Petty was sent to Greece, where he collected a wide range of objects, from inscriptions to such bronzes as the Hellenistic head of *Sophocles* (London, BM), which at the time was thought to be the head of Homer. The inscriptions were published by John Selden (1584–1654) in 1628 as *Marmora Arundelliana*. Although by the time the book appeared Charles I and George Villiers, 1st Duke of Buckingham, had Italian pictures of equal importance to those of the Earl, neither they nor indeed any collector in England had possessions equal in diversity, number and quality to the Arundel Marbles, the fame of which had spread to continental Europe.

After the publication of the *Marmora Arundelliana*, the Earl became increasingly interested in graphic art. In 1635 it was said that his chief preoccupation was with drawings, and it is possible that Petty, in Italy on the Earl's behalf for most of the 1630s, acquired the celebrated collection of drawings that had belonged to the Florentine Niccolò Gaddi; Vasari's *Libro del disegno* may also have belonged to the Earl. In 1636, while in Germany on a mission from Charles I, the Earl met Wenceslaus Hollar, who accompanied him on the rest of the journey, making drawings on the way. Hollar then came to England with the Earl and was employed to make engravings of works of art in the Earl's collection. In 1637 it is recorded that the Earl

took an Italian connoisseur into his cabinet-room, designed for him by Jones, where more than 200 albums of drawings attributed to Leonardo, Michelangelo and Raphael were shown to him. Arundel's taste in drawings, however, was not confined to the masters of the High Renaissance; it is probable that he also owned a corpus of drawings by Annibale Carracci for the ceiling (1597–1601) of the Palazzo Farnese, Rome.

Later acquisitions by Petty for the Earl included the *Christ Crowned with Thorns* (Munich, Alte Pin.) by Titian, from the studio of Domenico Tintoretto; a Psalter by Giulio Clovio (Providence, RI, Carter Brown Lib.); and, in 1639, the collection of gems that had belonged to the Gonzaga family, the finest ever assembled. Perhaps the most important of the Earl's acquisitions of the 1630s was that of the library of Willibald Pirckheimer, an event that may have been celebrated in the portrait of *Thomas Howard, Earl of Arundel* (London, N.G.) by Rubens, with Arundel in the same pose as that in Dürer's etched portrait of Pirckheimer. An anonymous portrait of the Earl after Anthony van Dyck also dates to the 1630s (see fig.). The library contained a uniquely rich deposit of the drawings, letters and diaries of Dürer. Petty failed, however, to purchase for the Earl the obelisk that Bernini erected in 1651 in the Piazza Navona, Rome, as part of his *Four Rivers* fountain. The Earl was interested in owning not only paintings by Titian and Veronese—those favourites of the Stuart collector—but also medieval manuscripts and vestments, archaeological remains and Egyptian obelisks, as well as documents that related to the lives of artists. The collection of Charles I was largely formed by the Gonzaga family, that of the Duke of Buckingham by the eye of Rubens, but that of the Earl of Arundel depended

Thomas Howard, 2nd Earl of Arundel, after Anthony van Dyck, oil on panel, 146×127 mm, *c.* 1635 (London, National Portrait Gallery)

upon a personal vision: a breadth of interest and experience that made its creator respected, admired or resented by the great Italian collectors of the Baroque age.

The collection began to be broken up when the Earl became bankrupt in 1639, the year in which van Dyck painted *Thomas Howard, 2nd Earl of Arundel, with Aletheia Talbot, Countess of Arundel* (London, N.P.G., on dep. Arundel Castle, W. Sussex). Many major museums have pictures that belonged to Arundel: the *Man in a Red Chaperon* by Jan van Eyck (*see* EYCK, VAN, (2), fig. 2) and the *Vision of St Helena* by Veronese are both in the National Gallery, London; *St Margaret* by Raphael is in the Kunsthistorisches Museum, Vienna. Rubens's three-quarter-length portrait of *Thomas Howard, 2nd Earl of Arundel*, painted in 1629, is in the Isabella Stewart Gardner Museum, Boston, MA. The Arundel gems are dispersed: the Felix Gem is in the Ashmolean Museum, Oxford, which also houses the largest part of the collection of Arundel Marbles.

BIBLIOGRAPHY
M. F. S. Hervey: *The Life, Correspondence & Collections of Thomas Howard, Earl of Arundel* (Cambridge, 1921)
F. Springell: *Connoisseur & Diplomat* (London, 1963) [incl. most of the letters in London, BL, Add. MS., 15970]
D. Howarth: *Lord Arundel and his Circle* (New Haven and London, 1985)
Thomas Howard, Earl of Arundel (exh. cat., ed. N. Penny; Oxford, Ashmolean, 1985)

DAVID HOWARTH

(2) Aletheia [Alathea] **Talbot**, Countess of Arundel (*d* Amsterdam, 1654). Wife of (1) Thomas Howard, 2nd Earl of Arundel. She was the youngest daughter of Gilbert Talbot, 7th Earl of Shrewsbury (1553–1616), and granddaughter of Elizabeth Talbot, Countess of Shrewsbury (*see* TALBOT, (1)). She married in 1606, and her dowry, and later the inheritance of much of her father's estate, helped to finance the Earl's collecting. Although her reputation is overshadowed by that of her husband, she was clearly an intelligent and respected connoisseur in her own right. She, with her son James Howard, Lord Maltravers (*d* 1624), assisted in overseeing the development of the Arundel collection during the Earl's absences abroad. She was painted by Daniel Mijtens in 1617 (London, N.P.G., on dep. Arundel Castle, W. Sussex), the companion to his portrait of the Earl; *Aletheia Talbot, Countess of Arundel, with Attendants and Sir Dudley Carleton* (Munich, Alte Pin.) by Rubens was painted in Antwerp in 1620. She travelled extensively and in Venice in 1622 met Tizianello, son of Titian's cousin, who dedicated *Vita del insigne Tiziano Vecellio* (1622) to her. In 1639 she was painted with the Earl by van Dyck (London, N.P.G., on dep. Arundel Castle, W. Sussex). An indication of what she herself collected is to be found in an inventory made on 8 September 1641 of her 'household stuffs and goods' in Tart Hall (destr.) on the western edge of St James's Park, London, enlarged for her by Nicholas I Stone (i) in 1638–9. It contains references to family portraits, 17th-century Italianate landscapes, for example those by Josse de Momper II, with some unattributed landscapes listed as 'presented to my lady by a friend'. Works by Tintoretto and Jacopo Bassano, including a *Deo in Excelsis* by the latter, are mentioned, as is a copy after a painting by Leonardo of a *Woman and Child* and a painting of an angel by Lucas Cranach (i). The Earl and

Countess settled in Antwerp in 1643. After his death in 1646 medals and intaglios were sold to support her in exile. At the Countess's death an inventory was made of her possessions listing almost 600 paintings, including 36 as by Titian, 19 as by Tintoretto, 17 as by Veronese and over 40 works as by Holbein; many of these would have been made over to her by the Earl when he left England. Items were later dispersed by their surviving son, William Howard, Viscount Stafford.

BIBLIOGRAPHY
L. Cust: 'Notes on the Collection formed by Thomas Howard, Earl of Arundel and Surrey', *Burl. Mag.*, xix (1911), pp. 278–86; xxi (1912), pp. 256–8
C. Brown: *Van Dyck* (Oxford, 1981)
D. Howarth: *Lord Arundel and his Circle* (New Haven and London, 1985)

DIANA DETHLOFF

Howard (ii). English family of politicians, patrons and collectors. From Thomas Howard (*d* 1572), 4th Duke of Norfolk, were descended Thomas Howard, 2nd Earl of Arundel (*see* HOWARD (i), (1)), and Lord William Howard (*d* 1643) of Naworth Castle, Cumberland (now Cumbria), father of Henry Howard, 1st Earl of Carlisle (*d* 1685). In 1699 (1) Charles Howard (ii), 3rd Earl of Carlisle, built CASTLE HOWARD, N. Yorks, employing John Vanbrugh and Nicholas Hawksmoor. The house was extended by his son (2) Henry Howard (ii), 4th Earl of Carlisle, who formed important collections of antique cameos and sculpture. The family collections were greatly enriched by the activities of his son (3) Frederick Howard (ii), 5th Earl of Carlisle, patron of Reynolds. In the 19th century Frederick's great-grandson (4) George James Howard (ii), 9th Earl of Carlisle, was a painter as well as a patron. ☐

(1) Charles Howard, 3rd Earl of Carlisle (*b* 1669; *d* Bath, 1 May 1738). He was the son of Edward Howard, 2nd Earl of Carlisle, and succeeded to the earldom in 1692. His knowledge of European architecture was acquired on travels to Italy following his marriage in 1688. On his return he began to embellish Carlisle House (destr.), Soho Square, London, with furniture by Gerrit Jensen and paintings by Henry Cook (1642–1700). In 1699, following the example of his friends William Cavendish, 1st Duke of Devonshire, and Charles Seymour, 6th Duke of Somerset, who had embarked on large-scale building projects, he decided to build himself a house on the site of the ruins of Henderskelfe Castle, N. Yorks. After a disagreement with William Talman, he gave responsibility for the plans to JOHN VANBRUGH. Castle Howard (for illustration *see* CASTLE HOWARD), as it became known, was Vanbrugh's first important architectural commission, and he travelled round England looking at recently erected buildings. A model of the house was submitted to King William III in 1700. NICHOLAS HAWKSMOOR was engaged by May 1701 to supervise the work. The building of Castle Howard occupied the Earl throughout the decade following his dismissal as First Lord of the Treasury in 1702. Between 1709 and 1712 Giovanni Antonio Pellegrini executed painted decorations in the Great Hall and High Saloon (both destr. 1940). Once the main part of the house was ready for habitation the Earl turned his attention to the grounds. The Temple of the Four Winds (1724–6) was designed by Vanbrugh and the Mausoleum, the Earl's burial-place, by Hawksmoor (*see* HAWKSMOOR, NICHOLAS, fig. 4). Designed in 1728–9 and completed (1737–42) by Daniel Garrett (*d* 1753), the monument demonstrates the Earl's interest in Roman civilization.

BIBLIOGRAPHY

G. Webb: 'The Letters and Drawings of Nicholas Hawksmoor Relating to the Building of the Mausoleum at Castle Howard', *Walpole Soc.*, xix (1931), pp. 111–64
K. Downes: *Hawksmoor* (London, 1959, rev. 1979)
——: *Vanbrugh* (London, 1977)
G. Beard: *The Work of John Vanbrugh* (London, 1986)
C. Saumarez Smith: *Charles Howard, Third Earl of Carlisle and the Architecture of Castle Howard* (diss., U. London, 1986)
——: *The Building of Castle Howard* (London, 1990)

(2) Henry Howard, 4th Earl of Carlisle (*b* 1694; *d* York, 3 Sept 1758). Son of (1) Charles Howard. He was sent to Eton College, Berks, and as a fellow-commoner to Trinity College, Cambridge. In 1714 he set off on the Grand Tour and was in Genoa in November 1715. From 1715 to 1738 he represented Morpeth as a Whig in the House of Commons. In 1717 he married Frances Spencer, daughter of Charles Spencer, 3rd Earl of Sunderland. During the 1720s he was much consulted by his father on the buildings in the grounds at Castle Howard, N. Yorks, advising on Italianate models and discussing with Nicholas Hawksmoor antique precedents for the Mausoleum. In 1738, the year in which he succeeded to the earldom, he returned to Italy and in the spring of 1739 was in Rome. Correspondence (Castle Howard Archvs) from Francesco de Ficoroni in Rome and Anton Maria Zanetti (i) in Venice between 1740 and 1758 describes the Earl's purchase of important antique cameos and gems and illustrates his enthusiasm and discernment as a connoisseur and collector. The greater part of his gem-cabinet was purchased by the British Museum, London, in 1890. In Italy he also bought works by Giovanni Paolo Panini and Canaletto (e.g. Canaletto's *'Bucintoro' Preparing to Leave the Molo on Ascension Day*; Castle Howard) and the bust of *Carlo Antonio dal Pozzo* (Edinburgh, N.G.) by Bernini. At Castle Howard he commissioned his brother-in-law Thomas Robinson (i) to build the west wing (1753–9), which is Palladian in style and out of keeping with the earlier architecture. The Earl later regretted the commission. Examples of the antique statuary that were among his purchases in Italy are displayed in the Antique Passage and in the west wing at Castle Howard.

BIBLIOGRAPHY

A. Michaelis: *Ancient Marbles in Great Britain* (Cambridge, 1882)
D. Scarisbrick: 'Gem Connoisseurship: The 4th Earl of Carlisle's Correspondence with Francesco de Ficoroni and Antonio Maria Zanetti', *Burl. Mag.*, cxxiv (Feb 1987), pp. 90–104

(3) Frederick Howard, 5th Earl of Carlisle (*b* 28 May 1748; *d* Castle Howard, N. Yorks, 27 Jan 1824). Son of (2) Henry Howard. He inherited the earldom at the age of ten and was educated at Eton College, Berks, and King's College, Cambridge. He went on the Grand Tour, part of the time in the company of Charles James Fox and William Fitzwilliam, 4th Earl Fitzwilliam. In Rome he was described by Lord Kildare as 'certainly a great coxcomb; and what is worse than that [he] despises everybody, especially foreigners'. He returned to England in 1769, and his portrait (Castle Howard) was painted in May and

June of that year by Reynolds. The Earl is depicted wearing the Order of the Thistle with which he had been invested in Turin in 1768.

In the early 1770s the Earl behaved with reckless extravagance, spending money on improvements to Castle Howard, on maintaining a stud, on his political interests and, above all, on gambling. He was also purchasing works of art. In 1770 Reynolds painted a portrait of the Earl with his friend George Augustus Selwyn (Castle Howard). In February 1772 the Earl bought at Christie's, London, *Erminia Finding the Wounded Tancred* (1651; Castle Howard) by Guercino for 500 guineas and *Inspiration of the Epic Poet* (*c.* 1631–2; Paris, Louvre) by Poussin for 200 guineas, both of which had been in the Lauraguais collection. According to Reynolds, writing in April 1772, 'he buys everything that he thinks excellent . . . He is now in Paris and gone it is said purposely to buy the Duke de Choiseul's collection of pictures'. By 1775 his debt stood at £290,000, and he was forced to retrench. He retired to Castle Howard, where between 1781 and 1784 John Carr built the stables for him.

Towards the end of the 1790s the Earl was once again in a position to indulge his interest in collecting. In 1795 he acquired from the dealer Michael Bryan the *Adoration of the Magi* (*c.* 1510–12; London, N.G.) by Jan Gossart for 500 guineas. In 1798, he, with Francis Egerton, 3rd Duke of Bridgewater, and George Granville Leveson-Gower, Earl Gower (later 2nd Marquess of Stafford), was a member of the syndicate that purchased the Italian and French pictures from the Orléans collection, arranged for their exhibition in London at Bryan's gallery and the Lyceum and their subsequent disposal. The Earl of Carlisle retained for himself the *Circumcision* by the studio of Giovanni Bellini and the *Pietà* (or the *Three Marys*) by Annibale Carracci (*c.* 1604; both London, N.G.). Although he claimed to dislike contemporary painting, he continued to be a loyal friend and patron of Reynolds and was one of the pall-bearers at the painter's funeral. At Castle Howard the Earl was responsible for the 'Sheet of Water' to the north of the house, planned in the 1770s and begun in 1795. In 1801 C. H. Tatham, recently returned from Rome, redesigned the interior of the west wing for him, incorporating a sculpture and picture gallery.

BIBLIOGRAPHY

J. H. Jesse: *George Selwyn and his Contemporaries; With Memoirs and Notes*, 4 vols (London, 1843–4)
H. Ibbotson: *The Visitor's Guide to Castle Howard* (Ganthorpe, 1851)
Lord Hawkesbury [C. G. S. Foljambe]: *Catalogue of the Portraits, Miniatures &c. at Castle Howard* (Hull, 1903)
A. I. M. Duncan: *A Study of the Life and Public Career of Frederick Howard, Fifth Earl of Carlisle* (diss., U. Oxford, 1981)

CHARLES SAUMAREZ SMITH

(4) George James Howard, 9th Earl of Carlisle (*b* London, 13 Aug 1843; *d* Hindhead, Surrey, 16 April 1911). Painter, great-grandson of (3) Frederick Howard. In 1865 he went to Italy, where he studied painting under Giovanni Costa; although proficient in watercolour, under Costa, and later Alphonse Legros, he learnt to paint in oils. On his return to London he studied under the painter James Mathews Leigh (1808–60), and his circle of friends included Frederic Leighton, Edward Burne-Jones, Ford Madox Brown, Edward Lear, G. F. Watts and Dante

Gabriel Rossetti. In 1867 he and his wife commissioned Philip Webb to build their house in London, 1 Palace Green, Kensington. Completed two years later, the interiors were decorated by Morris, Marshall, Faulkner & Co. and included the frieze *Cupid and Psyche* (1872–81; Birmingham, Mus. & A.G.) designed by Burne-Jones and completed by Walter Crane. Burne-Jones carried out work at Castle Howard, N. Yorks, and at Naworth Castle, Cumbria, which also belonged to the family, he designed an overmantel. From 1881 until his death the Earl sat on the Board of Trustees of the National Gallery, London, eventually becoming Chairman. In 1889 he succeeded his uncle to the earldom and gave up his seat as a Liberal MP. He was involved in the foundation of the Tate Gallery, London, which opened in 1897, and was a member of the Society for the Protection of Ancient Buildings (SPAB). Webb described him as 'a constitutional caretaker of precious things' (Castle Howard Archv J22/64). Visits abroad, to Italy and Egypt especially, supplied the subjects for many of his landscape paintings (e.g. *Evening at Amara Lunga, Lerici*, 1878–80; Castle Howard, N. Yorks), and he exhibited oils and watercolours regularly at the Grosvenor Gallery, London, between 1877 and 1887. In 1883–4, with Leighton, William Blake Richmond, Matthew Ridley Corbet (1850–1902) and others, he founded the Etruscan school, with Costa as their acknowledged leader. Before his death the Earl negotiated the sale of the *Adoration of the Magi* (*c*. 1510–12) by Jan Gossart to the National Gallery in lieu of death-duties. He also left instructions that the Trustees of the Gallery should select 11 paintings from the collection at Castle Howard. Among those chosen was the *Pietà* (or the *Three Marys*; *c*. 1604) by Annibale Carracci, bought by (3) Frederick Howard.

BIBLIOGRAPHY

V. Surtees: *The Artist and the Autocrat: George & Rosalind Howard, Earl and Countess of Carlisle* (London, 1988)

The Etruscans: Painters of the Italian Landscape, 1850–1900 (exh. cat. by C. Newall, York, C.A.G.; Stoke-on-Trent, City Mus. & A.G.; London, Leighton House A.G. & Mus.; 1989)

CHRISTOPHER RIDGWAY

Howard, Sir Ebenezer (*b* London, 29 Jan 1850; *d* Welwyn Garden City, Herts, 1 May 1928). English social reformer, writer and shorthand-writer. He worked first as a clerk in the offices of various London merchants, stockbrokers and solicitors. In 1872 Howard emigrated to the USA where he worked as a shorthand-writer in the law courts, first in Nebraska then in Chicago. After returning to England (1877) he joined the firm of Gurney and Sons, official shorthand-writers to the Houses of Parliament, London, later becoming a partner in their successors, William Treadwell. Howard devoted his spare time to social reform, applying himself especially to problems of urban overcrowding and the depopulation of the countryside. His response was the idea of the economically self-sufficient satellite town, surrounded by agricultural land and limited to *c*. 30,000 inhabitants. In 1898 he published an influential book in support of his ideas: *Tomorrow: A Peaceful Path to Real Reform*. It set out not only his concept of the garden city but also his proposals for financing and administering it. The garden city was to consist of rural-like residential neighbourhoods surrounding a central park,

an extensive cultivable green belt to prevent urban encroachment, and facilities for shopping, cultural pursuits, community activities and recreation, the whole laid out concentrically and linked to a large town of no more than 58,000 inhabitants. No railways or highways would pass through the garden city. The scheme was anticipated by two years by that of the German political theorist THEODOR FRITSCH, as expounded in his book *Die Stadt der Zukunft* (1896); Fritsch's scheme, coincidentally, was also based on a circular plan with radial axes and ring roads, but half the area was designated as parkland.

Howard's book had a powerful impact on planning theory and practice, giving currency to the term GARDEN CITY. In 1903 the first garden city was planned according to Howard's principles by PARKER & UNWIN at Letchworth, Herts, 54 km north of London. In 1899 he formed the Garden City Association. Howard was Director of First Garden City Ltd and of Welwyn Garden City Ltd. He also served as President of the International Federation for Housing and Town Planning. Welwyn Garden City, Herts, itself, the most famous example of Howard's planning theories put into practice, was initiated in 1920. Howard's influence was widespread and long-lasting. The DEUTSCHE GARTENSTADTGESELLSCHAFT was founded in 1902, and a German translation of Howard's book (1907) had considerable impact. The first German garden city, HELLERAU, was established in 1909. In France Georges Benoît-Lévy had some limited success in propagating Howard's garden-city concept, which was assimilated and developed in Finland by Eliel Saarinen (*see* SAARINEN, (1)). (For further discussion of garden cities in an international context, *see* URBAN PLANNING, §V.)

Howard's ideas also attracted many followers with unorthodox or eccentric views on other subjects, such as diet, dress and education, which gave the garden-city movement a reputation for oddity in its initial years. It also became associated with then current propaganda promoting low-density cottage housing, conducted by publicists such as Howard's disciple Sir Frederic J. Osborn (1885–1978); it was therefore opposed by those who deplored the spread of suburbs around the fringes of towns and advocated the building of new houses to a higher density and in a more traditionally urban form. Howard did not in fact proclaim low density a virtue, but this somewhat distorted the public image of his theories. Nevertheless Howard made an important and increasingly serious contribution to urban-planning theory. Howard's views and especially his publications strongly influenced the first group of new towns to be built after World War II following the New Towns Act (1946), especially those surrounding London.

WRITINGS

Tomorrow: A Peaceful Path to Real Reform (London, 1898); rev. as *Garden Cities of Tomorrow* (1902); Ger. trans. as *Gartenstädte in Sicht*, intro. F. Oppenheimer (Jena, 1907)

BIBLIOGRAPHY

C. B. Purdom: *The Building of Satellite Towns* (London, 1925)

L. Mumford: *The Culture of Cities* (New York and London, 1938)

Barlow Report, Report of the Royal Commission on Distribution of the Industrial Population (London, 1940)

F. J. Osborn: *Garden Cities of To-morrow* (London, 1946)

R. Fishman: *Urban Utopias in the Twentieth Century: Ebenezer Howard, Frank Lloyd Wright and Le Corbusier* (New York, 1977)

R. Beevers: *The Garden City Utopia: A Critical Biography of Ebenezer Howard* (London, 1988)

J. M. RICHARDS

Howard, Henry (*b* London, 31 Jan 1769; *d* Oxford, 5 Oct 1847). English painter, illustrator and designer. He studied for seven years under Philip Reinagle, one of whose daughters he later married, and entered the Royal Academy Schools, London, in 1788. His ambitions were as a history painter in the manner of Reynolds. His *Caractacus* (untraced), which won a gold medal in 1790, was highly praised by Reynolds, then almost blind. In 1791 Howard went to Rome, where he became a close friend of John Flaxman whose Neo-classical figural style helped to form his own. In 1794, after three years study, he returned to England via Vienna and Dresden. Howard's exhibiting career began at the Royal Academy in 1794, and from 1806 to 1844 he also showed at the British Institution. His portraits and especially his historical compositions based on classical and literary themes, relatively late manifestations of the traditions of Reynolds, Fuseli and Flaxman combined in a diluted form, proved extremely popular. He was made an ARA in 1801 and an RA in 1808, his diploma work *The Sixth Trumpet Sounds* (London, RA) being typical of his version of the grand manner. He often took his subjects from Milton, particularly *Comus*. He painted some decorative schemes—such as the ceilings in the dining-room of Sir John Soane's house (now the Soane Mus.), London (1837), based on Guido's *Aurora*—occasionally collaborating with Thomas Stothard. He produced many designs for medals, Wedgwood Ceramics and book illustrations. He was secretary to the Academy in 1822 and Professor of Painting in 1833.

WRITINGS
F. Howard, ed.: *A Course of Lectures* (London, 1848)

BIBLIOGRAPHY
M. Pointon: *Milton and English Art* (Manchester, 1970), pp. 200–02

DAVID BLAYNEY BROWN

Howard, Hugh (*b* Dublin, 7 Feb 1675; *d* London, 17 March 1737). Irish painter, collector and connoisseur. In 1697 he set off on the Grand Tour. In Rome he decided to become a professional painter and remained for some time in the studio of Carlo Maratti, apparently becoming one of this favourite students. Upon his return from Italy in 1700 he spent several years in Dublin, and later in London, as a portrait painter. Although his few documented portraits, such as *Sir Justinian Isham* (1710; Lamport Hall, Northants), are not particularly distinguished, he rapidly acquired the reputation of a leading master as well as several important patrons, notably Henry Herbert, 9th Earl of Pembroke, and William Cavendish, 2nd Duke of Devonshire. Such influential connections obtained him posts that, together with a wealthy marriage, allowed him to abandon painting. He built up a collection of drawings, prints, books and medals and was regarded as one of the foremost connoisseurs of the period. His collection contained prints and drawings from such great collections as those of Thomas Howard, 2nd Earl of Arundel, Peter Lely and Prosper Henry Lankrink, which had been dispersed at the end of the 17th century. In 1728, he inherited part of the library of JAMES WEST from his brother William Howard. The prints included a large number of works by early German and Italian masters, among them a rare proof of the first state of Marcantonio Raimondi's *Portrait of Aretino* after Titian, several engravings by Martin Schongauer, notably one of the *Annunciation*, and Albrecht Dürer's *Adam and Eve* and *Melencolia I*; among the drawings was a sheet of *Studies* by Michelangelo and a *Portrait of a Young Man* by Dürer. Works by English artists included early satirical prints by Hogarth, several engravings by George Vertue, numerous mezzotints, and drawings by James Thornhill. The collection remained in the family until it was auctioned at Sotheby's in 1873 and 1874.

BIBLIOGRAPHY
F. Lugt: *Marques* (1921)
W. Whitley: *Artists and their Friends in England, 1700–1799* (London, 1928), i, p. 8; ii, p. 243
E. Waterhouse: *Painting in Britain, 1530–1790* (Melbourne, London and Baltimore, 1953), pp. 101–2, 122
I. Pears: *The Discovery of Painting* (New Haven and London, 1988), pp. 108, 145, 196–7, 244 n. 99

ANNE PUETZ

Howard, John G(eorge) (*b* Bengeo, Herts, 27 July 1803; *d* Toronto, 3 Feb 1890). Canadian architect of English birth. Born with the name John Corby, he was articled to the architect William Ford (*fl* 1820s) in London in 1824. In 1832 he moved to Canada, settling in Toronto, then still known as York, and changing his name to Howard. He was one of the first formally trained architects in the city and he became one of the busiest in Upper Canada in the 1830s and 1840s; he also held the post of Drawing Master at Upper Canada College (1839–56). Of the many buildings he completed in Toronto before his virtual retirement in 1855, only his *cottage orné*, Colborne Lodge (1836; now a museum), survives. However, he established Neo-classical architecture as the model for commercial and public buildings in Toronto in the 1830s and 1840s with such works as the city's Third Jail (1838; destr.); the Bank of British North America (1845; destr.), which revealed a knowledge of John Soane's Bank of England and its internal banking halls; and the Lunatic Asylum (1846–9; destr. 1976), the exterior of which he modelled on the National Gallery, London, by William Wilkins. Howard's most majestic surviving building is the Leeds and Grenville County Court-House (1842–4), Brockville, which follows Palladian design principles with an Ionic portico raised on a rusticated ground storey.

Howard's church designs of the early 1840s, several of which are extant in Ontario, show an evolution towards a more archaeological form of Gothic. The red brick church, Holy Trinity (1840), Chippawa, combines a rectangular plan with symmetrical classicizing quoins and emphasized keystones but has Gothic details, including pointed arches, wooden crenellation and pinnacles. Other churches, including St John's (1843), York Mills, Christ Church, Holland Landing, and Christ Church, Tyendinaga (all 1843), are in a more accurate Gothic Revival style, each with a sturdy tower and stepped buttresses, although the tracery and hood moulds are still executed in wood and the plans lack ecclesiological knowledge.

UNPUBLISHED SOURCES
Toronto, Met. Ref. Lib. [archit. drgs, pap. & office daybks]

WRITINGS

Incidents in the Life of John G. Howard (Toronto, 1885)

DCB

BIBLIOGRAPHY

E. Arthur: *Toronto: No Mean City* (Toronto, 1964, rev. 3/1986)

M. MacRae and A. Adamson: *Hallowed Walls* (Toronto, 1975)

L. Maitland: *Neoclassical Architecture in Canada* (Ottawa, 1984)

MALCOLM THURLBY

Howard de Walden, 5th Baron. *See* HERVEY, (1).

Howe, George (*b* Worcester, MA, 17 June 1886; *d* Philadelphia, PA, 16 April 1955). American architect. He entered Harvard University, Cambridge, MA, in 1904, graduating in architecture in 1907. In 1908 he passed the examination for the Ecole des Beaux-Arts in Paris; he was admitted to the studio of Victor Laloux and received the *diplôme* in 1912. He returned to the USA in 1913 and joined the firm of Furness and Evans, but Frank Furness had died in 1912, and their once noteworthy and vibrant architecture had already degenerated. Unable to improve the firm, Howe joined Mellor & Meigs (1916), which had an established reputation for work in historical styles, as well as in forms derived from traditional Pennsylvania architecture. The most important building produced during Howe's association with the firm (renamed Mellor, Meigs & Howe from 1916 to 1928) was the Newbold Estate (1921–4), Laverock, PA. Later he characterized this and other romantic designs of his early career as 'Wall Street Pastorale', indicating both the clientèle, the romantic setting and his disappointment with his early work. The Newbold design employed drooping roof lines, turrets, local stone, slate roofs, and at the arrival point a pond and a farmyard full of sheep and geese.

Dissatisfied with the romanticism of his work, like many architects in the 1920s Howe began investigating new European architectural philosophies. In the commission for the Philadelphia Savings Fund Society (PSFS; 1929–33) at 12th and Market Streets, he tried to come to terms with the needs of the modern skyscraper but found no acceptable solutions in his Beaux-Arts training. Disagreements over the design of several projects led to Howe's departure from Mellor & Meigs and his partnership with WILLIAM EDMOND LESCAZE in 1929. Lescaze's fresh approach, learnt from his training in Switzerland, particularly appealed to Howe. The contribution of each partner to the design of PSFS is controversial, but it is generally agreed that Howe produced the original concept and the details of the scheme were refined by Lescaze. The explicit identification of functional units within the buildings is characteristic of Philadelphia architecture. The building rests on a curving base of shops with a second-floor banking room above. The skyscraper shaft contains undifferentiated office floors, at the top of which is a roof-top executive suite. Even the circulation spine is separately modulated in this design. The PSFS is recognized as one of the first International Style skyscrapers, and a photograph of the unfinished building was included in the *Modern Architecture: International Exhibition* at MOMA, New York, in 1932.

Howe's partnership with Lescaze dissolved in 1932, after which he was in private practice until associating for brief periods with Louis Kahn and Oskar Stonorov, and

later with Robert Montgomery Brown (*b* 1908). Howe was a fellow at the American Academy in Rome (1947–9) and served as the chairman of the Department of Architecture at Yale University (1950–54).

BIBLIOGRAPHY

A Monograph of the Work of Mellor, Meigs and Howe (New York, 1923)

H. R. Hitchcock and P. Johnson: *The International Style* (New York, 1932)

W. H. Jordy: 'PSFS: Its Development and its Significance in Modern Architecture', *J. Soc. Archit. Hist.*, xxi (May 1962), pp. 47–83

R. Stern: 'PSFS—Beaux-Arts, Theory and Rational Expressionism', *J. Soc. Archit. Hist.*, xxi (May 1962), pp. 84–95

W. H. Jordy and H. Wright: 'PSFS', *Forum*, cxx (May 1964), pp. 124–9, 143

R. Stern: 'Yale, 1950–1965', *Oppositions*, iv (Oct 1974), pp. 35–62

——: *George Howe: Toward a Modern American Architecture* (New Haven, 1975) [complete bibliography to 1955]

J. B. Thomas: 'George Howe: Former Clara Fargo Thomas House, Mount Desert, Maine, 1937–39, A Personal Remembrance of Fortune Rock', *Global Archit. Houses*, 11 (1982), pp. 14–25

ELIZABETH MEREDITH DOWLING

Howe, Oscar (*b* Joe Creek, SD, 13 May 1915; *d* Vermillion, SD, 17 Oct 1986). Native American Sioux painter. He attended the Santa Fe Indian School (*see* NATIVE NORTH AMERICAN ART, §IV, 2), from which he graduated in 1938. Even before graduation his work was already exhibited widely in the US and Europe, and in 1940 he

Oscar Howe: *Victory Dance*, watercolour, 499×305 mm, *c.* 1954 (Tulsa, OK, Philbrook Art Center)

obtained a commission from the Works Progress Administration, the US government depression era relief programme, to decorate the ceiling of the Mitchell Library in South Dakota. After finishing his next commission, ten panels in the City Auditorium of Mowbridge, SD, he reported for military service during World War II. He earned a BA degree from Dakota Wesleyan University and an MFA degree from the University of Oklahoma. In 1957 he was appointed Assistant Professor of Fine Arts at the University of South Dakota. Howe's early work was descriptively realistic. In the early 1950s he developed a style based on Cubism. Using as subject-matter the range of Dakota philosophic and mystical experience, he sought to convey its essence through restructured planes and colouristic effects (see fig.). Although his approach was revolutionary for Native American art at the time, he stated that he had no iconoclastic intentions. On the contrary, he maintained that his purpose was to carry on the traditional and conventional in Native American art. In 1958, Philbrook Art Museum rejected his entry to their annual competition of Native American art on the grounds that it was not 'traditional Indian art'. Howe's eloquent letter of protest (1982 exh. cat., p. 19), in effect a manifesto, became a document in the history and development of Native American art. It caused Philbrook to lift its restrictions against innovative styles and affected the direction in which Native American painting developed from that time on.

BIBLIOGRAPHY

Oscar Howe (exh. cat., ed. F. J. Dockstader; Tulsa, OK, Gilcrease Inst. Amer. Hist. & A., 1982) [ess. by J. A. Day, M. Quintal, D. Dunn, F. J. Dockstader, J. A. Warner, B. Medicine and J. S. King]

ARTHUR SILBERMAN

Howell Killick Partridge & Amis [HKPA]. English architectural partnership. It was based in London and Saltash, Cornwall, and formed in 1959 by William Gough Howell (*b* London, 5 Feb 1922; *d* nr Leighton Buzzard, Beds, 29 Nov 1974), John Alexander Wentzel Killick (*b* 1924; *d* 13 Sept 1971), John Albert Partridge (*b* London, 26 Aug 1924) and joined in 1962 by Stanley Frederick Amis (*b* Egham, Surrey, 12 Jan 1924). The team from the London County Council's Architects Department that designed the Roehampton housing estate (1950–61), London, HKPA belong to the post-war generation of architects with their roots firmly in the Modern Movement despite their penchant for non-literal historicism. They described themselves as pragmatists, dogmatic only about consistency of architectural form, detailing, materials and colour. The principle of separation and articulation can be seen behind all their work. In planning this may be expressed by the separation of a larger building into several distinct parts, an approach that stems both from the Modern Movement canon of the programme as generator of form and from A. W. N. Pugin's principle of additive planning. Key examples of this discrete planning include St Anne's College, Oxford (1960–79), Christ's Hospital Arts Centre, Horsham, Sussex (1970–74), and their work for the Middlesex Polytechnic (1972–9). Spacious sites, phased construction and extendibility as well as scale, and circulation that is social and comprehensible typify the free planning of these schemes. However, separation and

articulation have been achieved where such factors as a restricted site or a need for greater formality have called for a concentrated plan. Here the solution lies in spaces grouped to form a strongly centralized whole in a way that is reminiscent of Baroque planning. The earliest example is the University Centre, Cambridge (1963–7), while later ones include the Medway Magistrates Courthouse, Chatham, Kent (1972–9), and the Hall of Justice, Trinidad and Tobago (1978–85), its plan like a section through a honeycomb.

The principle of separation and articulation is as apparent in HKPA's structural design as it is in their planning. Structure is more evident on the inside than on the exterior except in the case of the Combination Room at Downing College, Cambridge (1965–70), a witty, temple-like pavilion with a pre-cast concrete structure and stone screen walls, and the buildings for Her Majesty's Naval Base, Devonport, Devon (1971–80), where structure is manifest both externally and internally. The idea of 'the interior volume defined and articulated by. . .visible structure' can be seen at its best in the dining-hall at Cambridge University Centre. Here the trusses and steel ties, with bolts, clamps and joints, which support the roof and its lantern, are unconcealed. Moreover, they are revealed with a flourish that indicates the enjoyment HKPA took in putting structural elements and components together and showing how it is done. This is as true of their 'elementarist' furniture as it is of their buildings. According to John Partridge, 'the object of any detail (apart from its functional one) is to assist in revealing the nature of the materials and techniques employed'.

Diagonal planning and the cut-off corner are two of the more easily identified trademarks of HKPA's work, as are the 'erupted skin' (their phrase) and the erupted roof. Both are a solution to letting light into a building. The splayed pre-cast concrete window units of St Anne's College and of St Anthony's College, Oxford (1966–71), produce deep reflective surfaces that give light without glare as well as deeply modelled façades. The use of roof-lights excludes direct sunlight and again offers plenty of scope for modelling. Downing College Combination Room, the dining-halls of Darwin College, Cambridge (1964–70), St Anthony's College, Wells Hall, University of Reading, Berks (1968–73), and many other HKPA buildings have roofs with dynamic forms that contribute to the complex non-rectangular geometry that is a constant theme in their architecture.

WRITINGS

'Attitudes to Architecture', *Arena*, lxxxii (1966), pp. 95–119
HKPA (*c*. 1985) [office brochure]

BIBLIOGRAPHY

S. Cantacuzino: *Howell Killick Partridge & Amis: Architecture* (London, 1981) [incl. list of works]

JILL LEVER

Howells, John Mead (*b* Cambridge, MA, 14 Aug 1868; *d* New York, 22 Sept 1959). American architect and architectural historian. A son of the novelist William Dean Howells, he studied architecture at Harvard University (1891–4) and the Ecole des Beaux-Arts, Paris (1895–7), where his fellow students included two of his future collaborators: I. N. Phelps Stokes (1867–1944) and Raymond Hood. In 1897 Howells and Stokes formed a partnership in New York. Notable examples of their work include the Neo-classical style St Paul's Chapel (1904–7) at Columbia University, New York, a design proposal (1908) for the New York Municipal Building, and the Paint Hall (1913) music building at Harvard University. Thereafter Howells's interest in commercial skyscraper architecture came to dominate the partnership, while Stokes contributed to low-cost public housing projects in New York.

In 1922 Howells was invited to collaborate with Hood and the French engineer Jacques André Fouilhoux (1881–1934), in the *Chicago Tribune* Tower competition. Their winning skyscraper design (*see* COMPETITION, fig. 3), which was executed on Michigan Avenue, Chicago, between 1923 and 1925, consisted of a steel-framed structure overlaid with Gothic elements, including stone tracery and 13 m high decorative flying buttresses. Although a striking monument, the building was criticized as conservative in its reliance on historicist motifs, particularly in comparison with Eliel Saarinen's second-placed design. Such criticisms and the delayed impact of New York City zoning laws (1916), which required building volumes to be maximized, resulted in the cleaner, more rectangular lines of Howells's later skyscrapers. A notable example is the Panhellenic Tower (1928), Mitchell Place, 49th St, New York, which was modelled on Saarinen's *Chicago Tribune* Tower entry and has a strongly vertical composition, emphasized by simple massing and recessed windows. The *Daily News* Building (1929–30; for illustration *see* HOOD, RAYMOND), 41/42nd St, New York, also in collaboration with Hood and Fouilhoux, reflected the impact of the city's zoning laws and the client's complex requirements, which dictated the building's plan, mass and fenestration, and gave it a dominant impression of utility. Minimal decoration appears on its simple façade, except for subtly shaded vertical stripes of white stone piers and patterned red and black brick spandrels. These give a rhythm and airy lightness to its vertical structure, as well as an illusion of height in excess of its actual 37 storeys, considered remarkable in 1930.

Howells's other works include buildings at Columbia University, where he evolved a modern Byzantine style, with brick and hollow tile construction techniques, and the extension (1927) of the Pratt Institute, Brooklyn, New York. He also designed several houses, notably that for Mrs Millbank Anderson (1932; now A. J. Kobler House) at 820 6th Avenue, New York, with Adam-style detailing.

He was also an authority on early American architecture and wrote on the Pre-Columbian and colonial periods. In 1922 he had a supervisory role in the reconstruction of the University of Brussels, as part of the work of the Hoover Commission, for which he was made a member of the Belgian Légion d'Honneur.

WRITINGS

The Verticality of the Skyscraper (New York, 1928)
Lost Examples of Colonial Architecture (New York, 1931)
The Architectural Heritage of the Piscataqua (New York, 1937)
Works (New York, 1938) [cat. of bldgs and projects]

BIBLIOGRAPHY

The Chicago Tribune: The International Competition for a New Administrative Building for the Chicago Tribune, 1922 (Chicago, 1923)
T. E. Tallmadge: *The Story of Architecture in America* (New York, 1927, rev. 1936)
C. W. Condit: *The Rise of the Skyscraper* (Chicago, 1952)
K. Sabbach: *Skyscraper* (New York, 1989)

□

Howlett, Bartholomew (*b* Louth, Lincs, 1767; *d* Newington, London, 18 Dec 1827). English draughtsman and etcher. He was apprenticed to James Heath and produced plates for many topographical works, including several of his native county, such as *A Selection of Views in the County of Lincoln* (London, 1797–1801), which has 79 plates after drawings by Thomas Girtin, James Bourne (1773–1854) and others and was reissued in 1805. Among other topographical works, he provided the plates for Charles Frost's *Notices Relative to the Early History of the Town and Port of Hull* (London, 1827). He was also much employed in the preliminary sketching for aquatints and engravings.

BIBLIOGRAPHY

DNB; Thieme–Becker
W. Upcott: *A Bibliographical Account of the Principal Works Relating to English Topography*, i (London, 1818/*R* 1968), pp. 558–62

DAVID ALEXANDER

Howlett, Robert (*b* 1830; *d* Kensington, London, 2 Dec 1858). English photographer. Considered one of the most skilful photographers of his day, Howlett is best known for his portraits of Isambard Kingdom Brunel standing in front of the anchor chains of the 'Leviathan' (the *Great Eastern*). In 1857 Howlett and the publisher Joseph Cundall (1818–95) were commissioned by the *Illustrated London Times* to photograph the building and launching of Brunel's ship, the *Leviathan*. The photographs were then used to make engravings to illustrate the number devoted to the *Leviathan*, which was published on 16 January 1858. Many prints from Howlett's photographs were published posthumously by the London Stereoscopic and Photographic Company.

Howlett became associated with Cundall through the Photographic Institution in New Bond Street in 1855. They formed two companies: Cundall, Howlett & Co. and Cundall, Howlett & Downes, advertising themselves as photographers of contemporary commercial subject-matter; country houses, churches, works in progress, views, wedding groups and paintings for three guineas a day plus travelling expenses. Howlett exhibited photographs of a wide range of subjects at the Photographic Society of London, including the *Great Eastern* series, copies of paintings and engravings, portraits in historical costume, topographical views and views of renowned beauty spots. He contributed a Constable-like composition of a cart in a wide wooded stream, *The Valley of the Mole*, to the group's publication *The Photographic Album for 1857*.

In 1856 Howlett was engaged by W. P. Frith to accompany him to the Derby to photograph 'as many people as possible from the roof of the cab' (T. Sutton: 'On Some Uses and Abuses of Photography', *Photographic News*, vii (6 Feb 1863), p. 67). The photographs were used as source material for group studies in Frith's painting *Derby Day* (1858; London, Tate).

Howlett's death was possibly hastened by exposure to photographic chemicals.

BIBLIOGRAPHY
A Vision Exchanged: Amateurs and Photography in Mid-Victorian England (exh. cat. by C. Bloore and G. Seiberling, London, V&A, 1985)
G. Seiberling and C. Bloore: *Amateurs, Photography and the Mid-Victorian Imagination* (Chicago, 1986)

CAROLYN BLOORE

Howling Wolf [Honanisto] (*b c.* 1850; *d* Waurika, OK, 5 July 1927). Native American Southern Cheyenne draughtsman. He was one of the most talented and innovative of the artists imprisoned between 1875 and 1878 at Fort Marion, St Augustine, FL (*see* NATIVE NORTH AMERICAN ART, §IV, 1(iv)). The drawings in his and others' 'sketchbooks' transformed traditional Plains art and brought to it a balance, symmetry, rhythm and decorativeness seldom encountered before. Howling Wolf was arrested in 1875 after the Red River War and, charged with being a ringleader, was imprisoned without trial in Fort Marion. There, encouraged by Capt. Richard Henry Pratt (1840–1924), he filled sketchbooks for sale with drawings of life on the Plains and occasional portrayals of the journey to prison and life at the fort. He abandoned most of the old warrior art style of picture writing, suited to conveying detailed information about war deeds, and instead created a number of deliberately composed works with strong design elements (see fig.). On return from prison, he at first urged his people to follow the Bible Road. Then, disillusioned by conditions on the reservation and by his own poverty, he obtained the chieftancy of the Bowstrings, a warrior society resisting Euro-American encroachment. He also resumed attending the Sun Dance and later joined the Native American Church, the Peyote religion. After he became disillusioned Howling Wolf also resumed

depicting his war exploits and contributed drawings to at least one fellow warrior's sketchbook (untraced). The latest sketchbook known to have been produced by him was done for an ethnologist (*c.* 1881; Omaha, NE, Joslyn A. Mus.) with drawings of historical and ethnological interest. Stylistically, these are less imaginative than his work at Fort Marion.

BIBLIOGRAPHY
K. D. Peterson: *Howling Wolf, a Cheyenne Warrior's Graphic Interpretation of his People* (Palo Alto, 1968)
D. Dunn: *Plains Indian Sketchbooks of Zo-Tom and Howling Wolf* (Flagstaff, 1969)
K. D. Peterson: *Plains Indian Art from Fort Marion* (Norman, 1971)
J. M. Szabo: *Howling Wolf and the History of Ledger Art* (Albuquerque, 1994)

ARTHUR SILBERMAN

Howzer, Wolfgang (*b* Zurich, *fl* 1652–88). Swiss goldsmith, active in England. One of the most important goldsmiths working in England in the second half of the 17th century, he is noted for his exceptionally high standard of craftsmanship. He was born into a goldsmithing family and was apprenticed to his father, Hans Jacob Howzer II. He became a freeman in 1652 and had moved to England by 1657. His importance is shown by the fact that he was appointed 'Embosser in Ordinary' to Charles II and in the 1660s was employed by the Jewel House to work on several orders. He was employed directly by the Crown, but was allowed to sell his wares to other clients, due to the fact that in 1664 he, together with JACOB BODENDICK, gained permission from the King to have their wares assayed and marked by the Goldsmiths' Company. Extant objects bearing the mark attributed to Howzer (WH over a cherub) are usually of a much higher

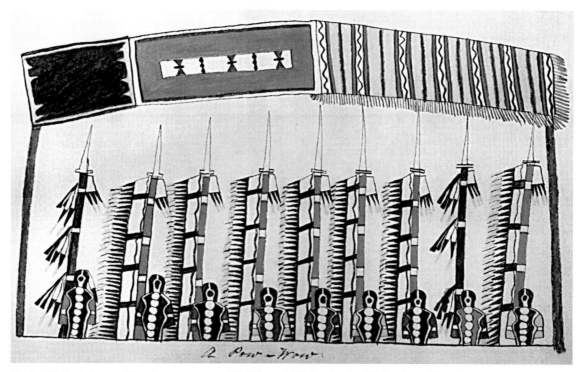

Howling Wolf: *A Pow-wow*, ink and crayon on paper, 250×150 mm, 1877 (Los Angeles, CA, Southwest Museum)

quality than plate produced by many of the native English goldsmiths of the period and are characterized by skilful embossing and chasing. Surviving objects include the large set of plate (Durham, Cathedral Treasury) for the chapel at the Bishop's Palace, Bishop Auckland, Co. Durham, of which the elaborately embossed altar dish and flagon are particularly notable. He also made altar dishes (*in situ*) for St George's Chapel, Windsor Castle, Berks, and the Chapel Royal, Whitehall, London.

BIBLIOGRAPHY
C. Oman: *Caroline Silver, 1625–1688* (London, 1970)
P. Glanville: *Silver in England* (London, 1987)
T. Schroder: *The Gilbert Collection of Gold and Silver* (Los Angeles, 1988)
EMMA PACKER

Hoyberger, Gotthard. *See* HAYBERGER, GOTTHARD.

Hoyeck, Youssef (*b* Helta, Batroun District, Lebanon, 1883; *d* Beirut, 1962). Lebanese sculptor and painter. In 1919 he went to Paris and Rome where he studied sculpture and drawing. In Paris he worked under Antoine Bourdelle and shared a studio with the poet and painter Gibran Khalil Gibran (1883–1931). In 1939 Hoyeck returned to Lebanon and opened the first sculpture studio in Beirut; he became the teacher and guide of a generation of Lebanese sculptors. In his work, mainly nudes and heads, he tried to reach a middle ground between popular taste, the influences of Rodin and Bourdelle, and the gracefulness of Italian sculpture.

BIBLIOGRAPHY
E. Lahoud: *Contemporary Art in Lebanon* (New York and Beirut, 1974), pp. 33–40
W. ALI

Høyen, N(iels) L(auritz) (Andreas) (*b* Copenhagen, 4 June 1798; *d* Copenhagen, 29 April 1870). Danish art historian and critic. He first read law at Kobenhavns Universitet, followed by theology and then history of art; since the latter was not yet an established discipline he had to compile his own education. He became friends with such notable contemporary painters as C. W. Eckersberg and familiarized himself with collections of art in Copenhagen, as well as studying drawing and perspective at the Kongelige Danske Kunstakademi. From 1822 he spent three years travelling through Germany and Italy acquiring knowledge of Romanticism as well as medieval and Italian art, which were to form the basis of his work. Back in Copenhagen he lectured on Classical art at the academy from 1826 and at the University from 1856. Between 1829 and 1833 Høyen was paid to travel throughout Denmark recording its art and architecture, and he made particularly thorough records of the collections at the National Portrait Gallery at Fredriksborg (mostly destroyed by fire in 1859) and at the Kongelige Samling, of which he became a curator and, in 1865, Director. As a critic Høyen expressed sympathy for modern movements in art and promoted the notion of an art that reflected national identity.

WRITINGS
J. L. Ussing, ed.: *Skrifter* [Collected works], 3 vols (Copenhagen, 1871–6)

BIBLIOGRAPHY
DBL
E. Drigsdahl, ed.: *N. L. Høyen i Italien, 1823–25: Rejsbreve* [N. L. Høyen in Italy, 1823–5; Letters] (Copenhagen, 1974)
JULIE HARBOE

Høyer, Cornelius (*bapt* Hellebæk, nr Helsingør, 26 Feb 1741; *d* Copenhagen, 2 June 1804). Danish miniature painter. He trained at the Kunstakademi, Copenhagen, from about 1755 to 1764, and he was particularly influenced by Carl Gustav Pilo and by Louis Tocqué, who was in Copenhagen in 1758–9. Awarded a travel grant by King Frederick V, Høyer went to Paris and received further instruction in miniature painting. From 1765 he attended the Ecole des Beaux-Arts and became the favourite pupil of Jean-Baptiste Massé. Two fine miniature portraits of an unknown man and woman (both Paris, Louvre) date from this period. He spent the years 1766–7 in Rome studying and copying miniatures by Rosalba Carriera. By then he was already a fully fledged artist. He travelled home via Dresden, where he stayed for nine months to paint the family of the Elector Frederick-Augustus III (untraced).

In 1769 at the Copenhagen Salon Høyer exhibited nine miniatures painted on the journey; Christian VII bought all of them (Copenhagen, Stat. Mus. Kst). That year he was appointed miniature painter to the court. In 1770 he was made a member of the Kunstakademi on the strength of two excellent miniatures representing *Carl Gustav Pilo* and the sculptor *Jacques-François-Joseph Saly* (both Copenhagen, Kon. Dan. Kstakad.). During the 1770s Høyer frequently painted the royal family and members of high society in Copenhagen, for example the heir-presumptive *Prince Frederick and Princess Sophia Frederica* (Copenhagen, Rosenborg Slot). His miniatures are remarkable for their striking personal characteristics and a carefully calculated but simple range of colour. He achieved brilliant effects by making use of the contrast between the translucent base of polished ivory, occasionally lightly shaded with watercolour in the flesh tones, and heavy opaque gouache colours for costume and background. His works are not unlike those of Jeremias Meyer (1735–89) and John Smart (1741–1811) in England, and they are among the most accomplished miniatures painted on the Continent during this period.

In 1781 Høyer travelled to St Petersburg via Stockholm. After painting various portraits of *Catherine II* and her entourage (Moscow, Kremlin, Armoury, and St Petersburg, Hermitage), he made his way home via Stockholm, where he stayed from 1783 to 1785 painting for Gustav III and the Swedish court (e.g. *Gustav III Walking in the Park of Haga with the Queen and Crown Prince*, 1784–5; Fredensborg Slot; and the prima ballerina *Giovanna Margareta Bassi*, 1783; Helsinki, Athenaeum A. Mus.). From 1787 to 1790 he was at work in Germany, with long stays in Berlin and Weimar, and in Paris.

Høyer spent his last years in Denmark except for a short visit to Russia in 1797–8. During the last decade of his life Høyer's style matured, and his brushstrokes grew more impastoed, partly under the influence of Peter Adolf Hall, whom he had met in Paris. A characteristic example is the portrait of *Queen Maria Sophia Frederica* (1792; Copenhagen, Rosenborg Slot), of which Jean-François Janinet executed a colour aquatint. There is no doubt that Høyer influenced the stylistic developments in portrait painting not only in Scandinavia but also in central Europe, where his work was known and valued by his contemporaries.

BIBLIOGRAPHY
T. H. Colding: *Cornelius Høyer* (Copenhagen, 1961) [with lists of works and comprehensive bibliog.]
——: *Miniature og emaillemaleri i Danmark, 1606–1850* (Copenhagen, 1991)

TORBEN HOLCK COLDING

Hoyland, John (*b* Sheffield, 12 Oct 1934). English painter and printmaker. He trained at Sheffield College of Art (1951–6) and the Royal Academy Schools (1956–60). Under the influence of Nicholas de Staël he began by 1954 to paint Sheffield landscapes and abstractions from still-life subjects. His devotion to colour began with experiments at a Scarborough summer school (1957), where tuition was provided by Victor Pasmore, Tom Hudson (*b* 1922) and Harry Thubron (1915–85). At the SITUATION exhibitions of 1960–61 he showed some of his earliest fully abstract paintings such as *Situation* (1960; Alistair McAlpine priv. col.), in which he used bands of colour to explore perceptual effects such as the relationship of image to background or to create the illusion of buckling the picture-plane. This geometric character soon gave way to sinuous lines enclosing discs of colour, and eventually to a freer and more fluid application of paint.

Hoyland's visit to New York in 1964 on a Peter Stuyvesant bursary brought him into contact with painters such as Helen Frankenthaler, Kenneth Noland and Jules Olitski and with the critic Clement Greenberg, who showed him the work of Hans Hofmann and unexhibited canvases by Morris Louis. Elements from these American developments, especially from colour field painting and Post-painterly Abstraction, feature prominently in subsequent canvases by Hoyland such as *1.11.68* (1968; London, Tate) in the use of staining techniques and acrylic paint, the interaction of unmixed colours, and an emphasis on the material weight of paint. Despite these influences, however, Hoyland came to reject the American tendency to reductivism, concentrating in later paintings such as *22.5.75* (1975; London, Brit. Council) and *North Sound* (1979; London, Tate) on the approach exemplified by Hofmann and de Staël, with varied and tactile paint surfaces and a disposition of blocks of different colours to create sensations of advancing and receding space. From the late 1960s Hoyland applied these methods also to screenprints, lithographs and later to etchings and monotypes.

BIBLIOGRAPHY
John Hoyland: Paintings, 1960–67 (exh. cat. by B. Robertson, London, Whitechapel A.G., 1967)
Marks on a Canvas (exh. cat. by A. Seymour, Dortmund, Mus. Ostwall, 1969)
John Hoyland: Paintings, 1967–1979 (exh. cat. by B. Robertson, J. McEwen and T. Maloon, London, Serpentine Gal., 1979)
John Hoyland: Recent Paintings (exh. cat. by J. McEwen, London, Waddington Gals, 1987)
M. Gooding: *John Hoyland* (London, 1990)

ADRIAN LEWIS

Hoyningen-Huene, George (*b* St Petersburg, 4 Sept 1900; *d* Los Angeles, CA, 13 Sept 1968). American photographer of Russian birth, active also in France. He came to England during the Russian Revolution of 1917 and moved to Paris in 1921. He studied painting with André Lhote, attempted fashion drawing influenced by his teacher's Cubism and collaborated with Man Ray on a fashion portfolio. After designing fashion backgrounds he began to photograph in 1925 and became chief photographer for *Vogue—France*. He was inspired by Edward J. Steichen, one of his predecessors at *Vogue*. Hoyningen-Huene very quickly developed his own sense of line and volume, utilizing back- and cross-lighting to create strong contrasts. He collaborated with Paul Outerbridge, photographing mannequins, and he made two amateur films on fashion and dance. In 1929 he came to New York where he worked for *Vogue* and was influenced by the informality of Martin Munkacsi's photographs. Hoyningen-Huene's clean sharp style is well demonstrated in the well-known photograph of a male and a female model in Izod bathing costumes (1930; for *Vogue*, see Ewing, pl. 66). He was sent by Condé Nast to Hollywood to produce a portfolio of film stars and to Berlin to make a series of portraits.

From 1935 until 1945, Hoyningen-Huene worked for Alexey Brodovitch (1898–1971) at *Harper's Bazaar*. During his tenure he travelled extensively and produced a number of books on Mediterranean and African locations. His photography began to reflect an inspiration from Classical sculpture, incorporating architectural elements in simple figure compositions and making expressive use of empty spaces (e.g. *Lisa Fonssagrives, Evening Dress by Vionnet*, 1938; see Ewing, pl. 9). He left New York in 1945 to teach at the Art Center School in Los Angeles, CA, and worked on feature films, coordinating sets and costumes, until his death.

PHOTOGRAPHIC PUBLICATIONS
African Mirage: The Record of a Journey (New York and London, 1938)
Hellas: A Tribute to Classical Greece (New York, 1943, 2/1944)
BIBLIOGRAPHY
W. Ewing: *The Photographic Art of Hoyningen-Huene* (New York, 1986)

SHERYL CONKELTON

Hoysala. Dynasty that ruled the southern Deccan, India, from the early 12th century to the mid-14th. The name refers to a story of the dynastic founder Sala (*reg* mid-11th century) killing a tiger (*hoy*) that was menacing a Jaina ascetic. Dates for the earlier rulers are uncertain. Bittiga (also known as Bittideva or Vishnuvardhana) for example reigned, according to various sources, *c.* 1106–42, *c.* 1132–41 or *c.* 1106–56. Originally feudatories of the Ganga rulers, the Hoysalas were established at BELUR and controlled the large tract between the Kaveri River and the Tungabhadra River. The Chennakesava Temple to the god Vishnu at Belur, founded by Bittiga, was completed by Narasimha I (*reg c.* 1156–73), with pierced screens and doorways being added later. The Hoysalas also built such renowned temples as the Hoysaleshvara Temple to Shiva at HALEBID and the Keshava Temple to Vishnu at SOMNATHPUR. In the late 12th century and early 13th, as the Chalukyas of Kalyana declined, the Hoysalas became increasingly powerful. Narasimha III (*reg c.* 1263–91) was able to maintain the kingdom against the forces of the YADAVA dynasty, while Ballal III (*reg c.* 1291–1342) pressed the Yadavas to near extinction. In about 1310, armies under Malik Kafur, general of the Khalji sultans of Delhi, overran Hoysala territories, but the dynasty survived through a policy of alternately submitting to the sultanate and then reasserting its power. Hoysala rule was finally ended by the sultans of Madurai in 1343.

BIBLIOGRAPHY

R. C. Majumdar, ed.: *The Struggle for Empire*, v of *The History and Culture of the Indian People* (Bombay, 1957, 2/1966), pp. 226–33

B. Sheik Ali, ed.: *The Hoysala Dynasty* (Mysore, 1972)

S. Settar: *The Hoysala Temples*, 2 vols (Bangalore, 1992)

J. MARR

Hoyte, J(ohn) (Barr) C(lark) (*b* England, *c.* 1835; *d* Mosman, Sydney, 21 Feb 1913). New Zealand painter of English birth, active also in Australia. He arrived in Auckland in 1860, worked as a school art teacher and travelled widely in search of landscape subjects for his watercolours. Apparently self-taught, he developed quickly from producing rather crude works in the early 1860s to such ambitious exhibition watercolours in the 1870s as *View of Auckland* (1873; Auckland, C.A.G.). Hoyte earned a precarious living from his art, making sketching tours and sending works to exhibitions in Sydney and Melbourne. In 1876 he moved to Dunedin, and from there to Sydney in 1879. His practice of making replicas of his more celebrated works continued in Australia, where he churned out views of such tourist spots as Milford Sound, NZ. These later works exhibit a dramatic loss of quality, and despite being the first president of the Art Society of New South Wales, Hoyte made little impact on Australian art.

BIBLIOGRAPHY

J. C. Hoyte (exh. cat. by U. Platts, Auckland, C.A.G., 1957)

ROGER BLACKLEY

Hoytema, Theo(door) van (*b* The Hague, 18 Dec 1863; *d* The Hague, 28 Aug 1917). Dutch painter, lithographer and designer. He trained at the Academie van Beeldende Kunsten in The Hague. He worked as a draughtsman at the Zoological Museum in Leiden and illustrated scientific studies, for instance *On a New Collection of Birds from S. W. Africa* by J. Büttikofer (1889) and *Zoölogische Ergebnisse einer Reise in Niederl. Ost-Indiën, von dr. Max Weber* (1890). Apart from paintings such as *Two Arabian Vultures* (Amsterdam, Rijksmus.), he made many watercolours and drawings of plants and animals, which clearly reveal his appreciation of Japanese prints: he often outlined the separate areas of flat colour in ink, in imitation of such prints, and he could describe the characteristic attitudes of animals with a masterly economy of line. Van Hoytema compiled and published two portfolios of prints of related subjects, *Dierstudies* [Animal studies] (1898) and *Bloemstudies* [Flower studies] (1905). His powerful, decorative compositions show an unmatched technical perfection.

Van Hoytema became famous for his commercial art—notably lithographed calendars—and illustrated books. With his lithographed picture books he added an entirely new element to the world of Dutch children's books. For a number of seasons he worked as illustrator for the magazine *De Kroniek*. As a decorative artist his commissions included decorating the club lounge in Gorinchem and a river ferry boat; he also decorated furniture and earthenware, and designed posters and wrapping material for the food industry.

BIBLIOGRAPHY

R. W. P. de Vries jr: 'Theo van Hoytema', *Elsevier's Geïllus. Mdschr.*, xxxviii (1909), pp. 1–11; xliv (1912), pp. 409–10

——: *Nederlandsche grafische kunstenaars* [Dutch graphic artists] (The Hague, 1943), pp. 131–8

G. Knuttel: *Theo van Hoytema* (The Hague, 1953)

A. J. Vervoorn: 'Natuur en kunst: Twee mappen litho's van Th. van Hoytema' [Nature and art: two portfolios with lithographs by Th. van Hoytema], *Antiek*, xii/5 (1977), pp. 341–56

CHR. WILL

Hŏ Yu [*ho* Soch'i; Noch'i; Hŏ Ryŏn] (*b* Chindo, South Chŏlla Province, 1809; *d* Chindo, 1892). Korean painter. He was born in the house of a ruined regional aristocrat and learnt to paint as he grew up simply by looking at albums. When he was 28 Hŏ visited a Sŏn (Chin. Chan; Jap. Zen) Buddhist master, Ch'oŭi Sŏnsa, at Taehŭng Temple in the neighbouring county of Haenam. The master became Hŏ's teacher and, under his guidance, Hŏ developed new insights into painting and calligraphy. In 1838, following the master's recommendation, Hŏ went to study under KIM CHŎNG-HŬI in Seoul, where he came into contact with the higher echelons of the literati painting world. In his later years he painted a *Portrait of Kim Chŏng-hŭi* (hanging scroll, ink and light colours on paper, 519×247 mm; Seoul, Ho-am A. Mus.; see 1984 exh. cat., pl. 255).

In 1857, the year after Kim's death, Hŏ returned to Chindo and built his own studio, which he named Ullim sanbang (Room in Clouded Forest Mountain). The studio became his base for the rest of his life. When Hŏ was in his fifties, his compositions began to change: he used larger canvases in place of the small album studies he had previously favoured, his choice of subjects became more diverse and his brushstrokes became coarser and more animated. In place of the brush Hŏ often used his fingers or nails dipped in ink, a technique known as *chiduhwa*. He focused on the Four Gentlemen, namely plum blossom, orchid, chrysanthemum and bamboo, adding peonies and oddly shaped rocks, which resulted in a plain literati style of depiction. Two examples of his work are *Landscape on a Folding Fan* (light colour on paper, 200×610 mm, 1866; Seoul, K. U. Mus.) and *Peonies* (ink on paper, 260×460 mm, *c.* 1866; Seoul, N. Mus.). Hŏ's work became the basis of the Korean modern southern painting school, known as Honamhwap'a.

BIBLIOGRAPHY

Yi Tong-ju: *Urinara-ŭi yet kŭrim* [Ancient Korean paintings] (Seoul, 1975, 2/1981), p. 240

Ho-am misulgwan myŏngp'um torok [Masterpieces of the Ho-am Art Museum] (exh. cat., Seoul, Ho-am A. Mus., 1982), pl. 233

Treasures from Korea (exh. cat., intro. R. Croepper, ed. R. Whitfield; London, BM, 1984), pl. 255

HONG SŎN-P'YO

Hozen. *See* EIRAKU HOZEN.

Hradec. Bohemian family of statesmen, patrons and collectors. Like the Rožmberk family, they were descended from the medieval Lords of the Rose. Jáchym Hradec (*b* 14 July 1526; *d* 12 Dec 1565) was educated at the Habsburg court in Vienna and in 1554 became Lord Chancellor of Bohemia. He commissioned the Italian Antonio Drizzan for the reconstruction (begun 1560) of the family's castle at Jindřichův Hradec as a large Renaissance palace; in 1560–62 Drizzan also renovated the Hradec Palace in Prague, and in 1563–6 he effected the Renaissance transformation of the large fortified castle of

Hluboká. In the old monastery of the Minorites at Jindřichův Hradec, Jáchym Hradec had a hospice built (1560)
for the poor, with two large halls vaulted on a row of
columns. The classicizing architecture of his monumental
wall tomb (begun 1570; Jindřichův Hradec, St Mary) was
inspired by triumphal arches. Jáchym's brother Zachariáš
Hradec (*b* 1528; *d* 6 Feb 1589) served in the administration
of Moravia and resided mainly at Telč. A journey to Genoa
in 1551 influenced his taste. Of three castles that he had
reconstructed, that at Telč was designed by Drizzan and
Baldassare Maggi, with Mannerist arcades on the main
courtyard. Two rooms were decorated with *sgraffiti*, the
elaborately carved ceilings of the halls with figural reliefs
and paintings, and a small chapel with stuccowork. In the
burial chapel Zachariáš had a marble tomb made and a
small marble altar with a baldacchino. He owned paintings,
works of graphic art, ten tapestries from Antwerp, a table
and armchairs made from silver from his own mines, and
German stained-glass windows dating from 1569. Jáchym's son Adam Hradec II (*b* 1546; *d* 1596), Lord
Chancellor (1584) and chief minister (1592) of Bohemia,
commissioned Maggi to complete the new palace at
Jindřichův Hradec (1580–89), with a tower and with rooms
richly decorated by Raimund Paul and Georg Widman
(*fl* 1580–94). Two Renaissance loggias were added, and
the garden was surrounded with arcades and featured a
large domed, round pavilion (1591–4). The palace was one
of the most important centrally planned buildings north
of the Alps. Adam Hradec purchased works of art in
Germany and Italy, including jewels from Augsburg,
Venetian glass, paintings and statues. The Hradec family
died out in 1604.

BIBLIOGRAPHY

F. Teplý: 'Telecké inventáře' [Inventories of Telč], *Časop. Společnosti Přátel
    Starožitností*, xxxv (1927), pp. 171–6
Knihopis českých a slovenských tisků [Bibliography of Czech and Slovak
    books], ii/2 (Prague, 1941), pp. 3–5, 28–9; iv (1948), pp. 319–34, 339;
    v (1950), pp. 86–8
J. Krčálová: *Sgrafitová výzdoba zámku v Telči* [*Sgraffiti* of the château at
    Telč] (Prague, 1954)
V. Richter: *Telč* (Prague, 1958, rev. Brno, 1976)
J. Krčálová: *Státní zámek v Jindřichově Hradci* [The national castle at
    Jindřichův Hradec] (Prague, 1959)
E. Charvátová: *Jindřichův Hradec* (Prague, 1974)
Hrady, zámky a tvrze v Čechách, na Moravě a ve Slezsku [Fortified castles,
    châteaux and small castles in Bohemia, Moravia and Silesia], i (Prague,
    1981), pp. 204, 225–30; v (1986), pp. 12, 31, 60, 70, 90–94, 96–7
J. Krčálová: *Renasanční stavby Baldassara Maggiho v Čechách a na Moravě*
    [Renaissance buildings by Baldassare Maggi in Bohemia and Moravia]
    (Prague, 1986)

J. KRČÁLOVÁ

Hrdlicka, Alfred (*b* Vienna, 27 Feb 1928). Austrian
sculptor, painter and printmaker. He studied painting at
the Akademie der Bildenden Künste (1946–52) in Vienna
with Albert Paris von Gütersloh. From 1952 until 1957 he
studied sculpture with Fritz Wotruba, but until 1961 he
lived almost exclusively on temporary work. His first
exhibition in the Zedlitzhalle, Vienna (1960), was the first
demonstration of his completely individual creative style
and made plain the great distance separating him from the
Viennese avant-garde. From that moment he attracted a
great deal of attention, winning the City of Vienna's prize
for his sculpture *Christ on the Cross* (marble, 1570×
400×400 mm, 1959; Vienna, Pal. Liechtenstein) and a

contract for a large figurative group for the city (1959–60;
destr. 1961; see Lewin, i, pp. 70–73). In 1962 he joined
the Vienna Secession.

In summer 1963 Hrdlicka ran the sculpture class at the
Internationalen Sommerakademie in Salzburg. The major
means of communication in his own sculptures was the
human body in its many forms and the changeability of its
nature. The figures, often depicted as torsos, are also the
expression of powerful curtailments of freedom by society,
suffering and destroyed people, stretching out towards the
viewer in a last revolt. In 1965 a special exhibition of his
work was held at the Grosse Kunstausstellung in the Haus
der Kunst, Munich, and from that moment he was
represented at many exhibitions of sculpture and printmaking both in Austria and abroad. In 1965 he produced
his first major print cycles, including *Hairman*, *Cornerman*
and *Noble Simplicity and Quiet Greatness*. Cruelty and
violence, fear, pain and shame are major themes in his
drawings and prints, which in their restless and nervous
lines show an extreme sensitivity to the creation of form
and colour values. During a trip to London in 1966 he
produced the *Soho Striptease* etchings, which took as their
subject prostitution. His work with the mentally ill, with
psychotherapeutic methods and drugs, was decisive for
his work as well as his experiments with LSD for the Max-
Planck-Institut in Munich. In 1969 his cycle of engravings
Randolectil, the largest and most extensive of the cycles,
was included in a presentation in the Albertina, Vienna. In
the same year he took part in a colour film about LSD for
the German television channel ZDF, and in the film
Techniken der Handzeichnung made for the Albertina.

In 1970 Hrdlicka produced designs for the *Plötzensee
Dance of Death*, 25 drawings for murals for the Evangel-
isches Gemeindezentrum Plötzensee in Berlin. From 1971
to 1973 he held a professorship at the Akademie der
Bildenden Künste in Stuttgart, and in 1973 he was
appointed to the Staatliche Hochschule für Bildende Kunst
in Hamburg. In the same year he produced his illustrations
for Thomas Mann's *Death in Venice*. In 1975 he was
reappointed to the Akademie der Bildenden Künste in
Stuttgart. In 1976–7 he worked on two large murals for
blocks of flats in Wohnpark Alt-Erlaa near Vienna, and
between 1977 and 1981 on the monument to *Friedrich
Engels* in Wuppertal. He worked as a corresponding
member of the Akademie der Künste der DDR and
exhibited his prints at the Staatliche Kunstsammlungen in
Dresden in 1978. In the 1980s he worked on themes of
sexuality and violence, associated with the French Revolution and with Fascism, which dominate the imagery of
his graphic work.

BIBLIOGRAPHY

Alfred Hrdlicka (exh. cat. by W. Schmied, Hannover, Kestner-Ges., 1974)
Alfred Hrdlicka: Skulpturen—Zeichnungen—Lithographien (exh. cat.,
    Frankfurt am Main, Städel. Kstinst., 1976)
Alfred Hrdlicka: Das plastische Werk (exh. cat., Vienna, Pal. Auersperg,
    Orangerie, 1981)
B. Buderath: *Alfred Hrdlicka: Anatomien des Leids* (Stuttgart, 1984)
M. Lewin: *Alfred Hrdlicka*, 4 vols (Vienna and Zurich, 1987)
Alfred Hrdlicka: Die grosse französische Revolution (exh. cat. by P. Gorsen,
    Vienna, Albertina, 1989)

ULRIKE GAISBAUER

Hryniewiecki, Jerzy (*b* Dorpat, Russia [now Tartu,
Estonia], 21 April 1908; *d* Warsaw, 25 Aug 1988). Polish

architect, designer and teacher. He graduated in architecture from Warsaw Technical University (1936) and then received a scholarship to study in Italy. His work in the 1930s included the design of posters in the style of Tadeusz Gronowski (*b* 1894); he also designed two tourist hostels (1933–5; with Tadeusz Sieczkowski), in Czarnohora, Ukraine, and he won first prize in a competition (1935; with others) for the development of Pole Mokotowskie, the southern quarter of Warsaw, which was not executed. Other work included interior and exhibition design, for example the interior of the Polish pavilion (1939) at the World's Fair, New York. In 1938 he began a long teaching career at Warsaw Technical University; he first taught architectural design under Rudolf Świerczyński and after 1945 he taught architectural history and industrial design there. In 1945 he also became Director of the urban planning studio at BOS, the Office for the Reconstruction of the Capital. One of his major works was the design (1954; with Marek Leykam and Czesław Rajewski) of the Tenth Anniversary Stadium, Warsaw, in the form of a Classical amphitheatre partly built from the rubble of buildings destroyed in World War II. His other important work was Supersam (1959–62; with Maciej Krasiński), a large supermarket in Warsaw; his competition-winning design incorporated a tensile roof structure. Hryniewiecki became Professor in modern architecture at Warsaw Technical University in 1968 and was a well-known teacher and lecturer both in Poland and abroad. He was also a consultant to many industrial design offices, noted for his innovative approach. After 1972 he worked in collaboration with the International Institute of Industrial Building (III) in Vienna.

WRITINGS

'Uprzemysłowienie budownictwa i jego wpływ na formy architektury współczesnej' [Industrialization of building construction and its influence on contemporary architecture], *Architektura* [Warsaw], 9 (1961)

'Jak kształcić architekta' [How to educate an architect], *Architektura* [Warsaw], 11–12 (1979), pp. 19–21

BIBLIOGRAPHY

E. Olszewski, ed.: *Politechnika Warszawska, 1915–1965* [Warsaw Technical University, 1915–1965] (Warsaw, 1965)

T. P. Szafer: *Współczesna architektura polska* [Contemporary Polish architecture] (Warsaw, 1988) [with Eng. and Rus. text]

WANDA KEMP-WELCH

Hryshchenko, Oleksa [Gritchenko, Alexis] (*b* Krolovets, 2 April 1883; *d* Vence, 28 Jan 1977). Ukrainian painter and theorist. He studied philology and biology at the universities of Kiev, St Petersburg and Moscow before turning to art. He studied painting in Moscow and established close ties with the collectors Sergey Shchukin and Ivan Morozov. In 1911 he visited Paris where he became an enthusiast of Cubist painting, which, after a trip to Italy in 1913–14, he blended with his study of early Italian Renaissance painters, creating a style that brought together the cosmopolitan and urbane with the orthodoxy of the Byzantine legacy of sacred art. Hryshchenko devoted his theoretical work to the subject of Byzantine art and its links with modern art (1912) and to an analysis of the formal and stylistic properties of Byzantine painting in terms of modernist tendencies and practice (1916). After the 1917 revolution he became a professor at the Free Art Studios (Svomas) in Moscow and a member of the Commission for the Preservation of Historic Monuments. In 1919 he left Russia by way of the Crimea for Constantinople and Greece, which marked the beginning of a distinctive and inspired period of watercolour painting. In 1921, when he arrived in Paris, 12 paintings of Constantinople were included in the Salon d'Automne. A subsequent trip to Greece resulted in works that brought him into contact with renowned dealers and distinguished collectors (Léopold Zborowski, Albert C. Barnes). After 1924 Hryshchenko lived in southern France where he painted in muted, controlled and diaphanously transparent tones. In 1937 a one-man exhibition was held at the Museum of Ukrainian Art in L'vov (now L'viv). Later, the works that had been housed in the L'viv museum were branded as 'formalist' and destroyed during the Stalinist years. To preserve his artistic legacy the Alexis Gritchenko Foundation was formed in New York in 1958.

WRITINGS

O svyazyakh russkoy zhivopisi s Vizantyey i zapadom, XIII–XX vv.: Mysli zhivopistsa [On the links of Russian painting with Byzantium and the West, 13th–20th centuries: thoughts of a painter] (Moscow, 1912)

Voprosy zhivopisi: Russkaya ikona kak iskusstvo zhivopisi [Questions of painting: the Russian icon as the art of painting] (Moscow, 1916)

'"Kryzys iskusstva" i sovremennaya zhivopis' [The 'crisis of art' and contemporary painting], *Voprosy Zhivopisi* [Questions of painting], 4 (1917)

Deux ans à Constantinople: Journal d'un peintre (Paris, 1930)

Moï roky u Tsarhorodi, 1919–1920–1921 [My years in Tsarhorod] (Munich and Paris, 1961)

BIBLIOGRAPHY

P. Kovzhun: *Gritchenko* (Léopol, 1934)

JEREMY HOWARD

Hsia dynasty. *See* XIA DYNASTY.

Hsia Kuei. *See* XIA GUI.

Hsi'an. *See* XI'AN.

Hsia Nai. *See* XIA NAI.

Hsiang Sheng-mo. *See* XIANG, 2.

Hsiang Yüan-pien. *See* XIANG, 1.

Hsiao Chao. *See* XIAO ZHAO.

Hsiao Shu-fang. *See* XIAO SHUFANG.

Hsiao Yün-ts'ung. *See* XIAO YUNCONG.

Hsia-ssu. *See* XIASI.

Hsien-yang. *See* XIANYANG.

Hsin-cheng. *See* XINZHENG.

Hsin-yang. *See* XINYANG.

Hsüeh Chi. *See* XUE JI.

Hsü Hsi. *See* XU XI.

Hsü Pei-hung. *See* XU BEIHONG.

Hsü Tao-ning. *See* XU DAONING.

Hsü Wei. *See* XU WEI.

Huaca del Loro. Pre-Columbian site in the southernmost branch of the Río Grande de Nazca drainage on the south coast of Peru, 500 km south of Lima. The site is of great importance for understanding the cultural relationship between the late Nazca culture of the coast and the HUARI culture in the adjacent Ayacucho highlands. The architecture of Huaca del Loro (round stone construction and rectilinear compounds), together with finds of pottery related to highland styles, suggests that it was established by the Huari people. This conclusion is supported by a consistent series of radiocarbon measurements that date both site and pottery to *c.* AD 700–830, the height of the expansion of the Huari empire.

When discovered in 1952 by William Strong, Huaca del Loro extended for more than 500 m along the north side of the Tunga Valley and consisted of several architectural units. One of these was a small round structure of rock and rubble set in mud mortar and coated with red-painted plaster. Rooms adjoining the round building, interpreted by Strong as a temple, contained guinea pig and whale bones. There were also two large rectilinear compounds to the north and east of the 'temple'. A third similar compound may lie on the hillside above the main site; it is surrounded by a cemetery containing many looted tombs. Since Strong's investigations the site has been badly damaged by agricultural bulldozing.

The pottery associated with the site is characteristic of Phase 8 of the relative ceramic sequence for the Nazca style. The 'Huaca del Loro' pottery, however, is technologically distinct and iconographically different from earlier Nazca pottery. Huaca del Loro pottery lacks the elaborate mythical iconography and fine, polychrome polished surfaces characterizing the classic Nazca style. It is a much heavier ware with a narrow range of vessel shapes, some of which, such as spouted bottles and cumbrous bowls, are more typical of the Ayacucho highlands than of the Nazca coast. The palette employed includes white and black pigments as well as orange and buff. The most common designs are curvilinear figures and trophyheads—derived from late Nazca motifs—and geometric shapes, several of which have strong parallels in pottery from the mountains.

BIBLIOGRAPHY

W. D. Strong: 'Paracas, Nazca and Tiahuanacoid Cultural Relationships on the South Coast of Peru', *Mem. Soc. Amer. Archaeol.*, xiii (Salt Lake City, 1957)
A. C. Paulsen: 'Huaca del Loro Revisited: The Nasca-Huarpa Connection', *Investigations of the Andean Past*, ed. D. H. Sandweiss (Ithaca, NY, 1983), pp. 98–121
H. Silverman: 'Nasca 8: A Reassessment of its Chronological Placement and Cultural Significance', *Michigan Discussions in Anthropology*, viii (Ann Arbor, 1988), pp. 23–32

HELAINE SILVERMAN

Huaisu [Huai-su; *xing* Qian; *zi* Cangzhen] (*b* Lingling County, Hunan Province; *fl c.* AD 730–80). Chinese calligrapher and Buddhist monk. He left home to become a monk while still young, taking the monastic name Huaisu, over his family name, Qian. Early devoted to the art of cursive script (*caoshu*) calligraphy, he initially imitated the style of his step-brother Wu Tong (*fl c.* mid-8th century). Huaisu probably decided to become a serious calligrapher during the 760s, after his cursive script was praised by Wei Zhi (697–761), a court official in the Board of Civil Appointments. Between AD 767 and 769 Huaisu went south to Guangzhou (Canton) to request annotations on his works from the famous calligrapher Xu Hao (AD 703–82), then provincial governor. As a result, Huaisu's reputation spread throughout southern China.

In AD 772 Huaisu went north to the capital Chang'an and the auxiliary capital Luoyang. Here, his unrestrained individualism and exquisite skill in cursive script earned him the admiration of calligraphers, including Yan Zhenqing, poets, aristocrats, officials and other figures. Huaisu received numerous poems and essays eulogizing his cursive script, some of which he rendered as calligraphy in his *Self-statement* (*Zixu tie*; Taipei, N. Pal. Mus.; *see* CHINA, fig. 92). Huaisu's wild, untrammelled cursive script broke with the sombre, classical mode that had been encouraged by the court since the beginning of the Tang period (AD 618–907). Of earlier scripts, the closest in style is the continuous cursive script of Wang Xianzhi (*see* WANG (i), (2)) and Zhang Xu (early 8th century AD). Huaisu's extant works include *Bitter Bamboo Shoots* (*Kuxun tie*; Shanghai Mus.), *Eating Fish* (*Shiyu tie*; Shanghai Mus.) and *On the Book of History* (*Lunshu tie*; Shenyang, Liaoning Prov. Mus.). His cursive script, with its characteristic alternation between thin and thick strokes, is regarded as a forerunner of cursive script calligraphy of the 11th to 17th century.

BIBLIOGRAPHY

Xuanhe shupu [Xuanhe collection of calligraphy] (preface 1120), *juan* 19 [compiled in the Qing period (1644–1912)]
Ch'en Chih-mai: *Chinese Calligraphers and their Art* (London and New York, 1966), pp. 92–6
Y. Nakata: 'Tōsō kaiso no sho' [Calligraphy of the Tang monk Huaisu], *Chū goku sho ron shu* [Collection of essays on Chinese calligraphy] (Tokyo, 1970), pp. 177–85
Weng Tongwen: 'Huaisu shengnian ershuo ji qi mingxia qianzi wen erben wenti' [On two alternative dates for the birth of Huai-su and two pieces of calligraphy attributed to him], *Soochow U. J. Chin. A. Hist.*, iii (1974), pp. 39–49 [with Eng. summary]

HO CHUAN-HSING

Huang Binhong [Huang Pin-hung] (*b* Jinhua, Zhejiang Province, 1864; *d* Hangzhou, Zhejiang Province, 1955). Chinese painter. He was the modern embodiment of the literati ideal. Huang and his contemporary Qi Baishi became known by the sobriquets Huang of the South and Qi of the North. Originally educated as a scholar–official, Huang failed the civil service examination several times. After briefly managing his ancestral estate in Shexian, Anhui Province (1901–7), he embarked on a long career of teaching, editing art books and periodicals, collecting (and occasionally dealing in) works of art, writing and painting.

Huang's works of scholarship included treatises (published 1940–42) on three artists of the late Ming (1368–1644) and early Qing (1644–1911) periods: Hongren, Kuncan and Cheng Sui (*c.* 1605–91); these laid the foundations for later fruitful study. His book *Huang shan huayuan liie* ('An account of the Mt Huang school of painting') is an indispensable guide to the ANHUI SCHOOL of painting. *Meishu congshu* ('Encyclopedia of Chinese fine art'; 20 vols), a compendium of art books first published in 1911, which Huang co-edited with Deng Shi (*d c.* 1948), is still used by scholars.

Stylistically, the paintings of Huang Binhong can be divided into four periods. In the first, up to the age of 50, the artist devoted himself to learning from both ancient and contemporary masters. In the second period, between the ages of 50 and 70, Huang travelled widely, increasing his knowledge of real landscapes. In the third, from the ages of 70 to 85, he began to establish a distinctly personal style. When he was 80 he held his first and only one-man show in Shanghai. He continued to paint until shortly before his death; during this last period his style underwent a virtual metamorphosis.

Huang took a humanistic view of a painter's role. Echoing Dong Qichang, he wrote that it is a fundamental requirement of art that the technique and skill of the artist, when he paints mountains and rivers, be invisible; consequently, these subjects, as a result of the painter's act of creation, assume a mysterious quality that cannot be found in nature. One of the most salient aspects of Huang Binhong's work was the intimate relationship between calligraphy and painting that permeated both his aesthetic theory and his practice. Huang believed that brushwork must be cultivated by means of a constant study of inscriptions on ancient bronzes and stelae (*see* CHINA, §IV, 2(viii)) and of rubbings made from these, of examples of calligraphy and even of literature. From his lifelong study of epigraphy and seal-engraving, Huang arrived at a number of principles to underpin his pictorial composition, the most important of which was to achieve 'void' (*xu*) in solid form (*shi*). Calligraphy not only suggested but embodied the inner workings of nature. Painting, like calligraphy, should accomplish 'order within disorder', 'the regularity of irregularity' and 'the resemblance of non-resemblance'. Huang also drew an analogy between composing a painting and playing a game of chess, in which the player must be constantly aware not only of the moves already made but also of those that may yet be made.

Huang constantly experimented with different ways of applying ink wash, which, when combined with his brushwork, helped him to achieve the strong stylistic effects he called *hunhou huazi* ('solidity and density in structure, and freshness and moisture in ink and brushwork'); an example can be seen in the handscroll *Lake and Mountains Before Rain* (1952; Hong Kong, Chiu Chu Tung priv. col., see 1989–90 exh. cat., p. 34, fig. 13). The album *Insects and Flowers* (see fig.) is an excellent example of Huang's brushwork, which, though strong, is apparently childlike and thus embodies the literati ideal of *zhuo* ('intentional awkwardness').

The fact that at least five types of brushwork, seven ways of applying ink and nine methods of manipulating water can be distinguished in his late work reflects Huang's sophisticated technical mastery. Indeed, the innovative use of water is one of Huang's most important contributions to 20th-century Chinese painting. In an undated album leaf depicting a landscape (336×349 mm; Hong Kong, Tao Ho priv. col., see 1989–90 exh. cat., p. 71, pl. 18D), the blending of water, ink and colour is masterful.

For the last two years of his life Huang Binhong was almost completely blind. To compensate, he relied increasingly on the intuitive use of ink and brushwork acquired through a lifetime of practice, combining his tempestuous, rough brushwork with layer upon layer of ink washes. At first glance, his late paintings appear disorderly. On close inspection, however, these works reveal a rich and complex

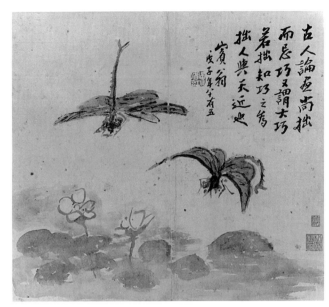

Huang Binhong: *Dragonflies and Sleepy Lotus*, leaf 10 of the album *Insects and Flowers*, ink and colours on gold-flecked paper, 318×356 mm, 1948 (New York, Metropolitan Museum of Art)

visual structure and the supramundane quality that he always sought in landscape painting.

For further discussion of early 20th-century Chinese painting *see* CHINA, §V, 1(iii) and 3(iv)(b).

WRITINGS

Binhong caotang ji [Huang Binhong's collection from the thatched cottage], 12 vols
ed., with Deng Shi: *Meishu congshu* [Encyclopedia of Chinese fine art], 20 vols (Shanghai, 1911/*R* 1947)
Ku-hua wei [Notes on Chinese painting], Wan-yu Wen-ku (Shanghai, 1929); *R* as *Guhua wei* (Hong Kong, 1961)
Yu Xiang [Huang Binhong], ed.: 'Zhejiang dashi shiji yiwen' [Anecdotes from the life of Master Zhejiang [Hongren]], *Zhonghe Yuekan*, i (1940), no. 5, pp. 26–33; no. 6, pp. 46–65
Yuan Tong [Huang Binhong]: 'Shi Shiqi shiji huibian' [Commentary on collected papers on the life of Shiqi [Kuncan]], *Zhonghe Yuekan*, iii (1942), no. 3, pp. 2–16; no. 4, pp. 75–9; no. 5, pp. 62–75
Yu Xiang [Huang Binhong]: 'Gou Daoren yishi' [Anecdotes of Gou Daoren [Cheng Sui]], *Zhonghe Yuekan*, iv (1943), no. 3, pp. 7–13
——: 'Gou Daoren yishu' [Posthumous works of Gou Daoren], *Zhonghe Yuekan*, iv (1943), no. 4, pp. 30–47

BIBLIOGRAPHY

Wang Bomin, ed.: *Huang Binhong huayu lu* [Huang Binhong's *Huayu lu* [The art of painting]] (Shanghai, 1929/*R* 1978)
Chu-tsing Li: 'Trends in Modern Chinese Painting: The Charles A. Drenowatz Collection', *Artibus Asiae*, suppl. xxxvi (1979) [whole issue]
Huang Binhong zuopin zhan/An Exhibition of Works by Huang Binhong (exh. cat. by Tao Ho; Hong Kong, A. Cent., Pao Sui Loong Gals, and U. Hong Kong, Dept F.A., 1980)
Wang Bomin: 'Huang Binhong's *Clear Lake Pavilion* and other Paintings of "Darkness, Density, Thickness and Heaviness"', *Register*, vi/3 (1986), pp. 20–31
Innovation within Tradition: The Painting of Huang Pin-hung (exh. cat. by J. C. Kuo; Williamstown, MA, Williams Coll. Mus. A., and Taipei, F.A. Mus., 1989–90)

JASON C. KUO

Huangcai. *See under* NINGXIANG.

Huang Ch'üan. *See* HUANG QUAN.

Huang Chün-pi [Huang Junbi; *zi* Junweng; *hao* Baiyuntang] (*b* Nanhai, Guangdong Province, 12 Nov 1898; *d* Taipei, 29 Oct 1991). Chinese painter and art educator. Huang studied both Chinese and Western painting, but he came to concentrate on Chinese art, studying and copying the works of old masters in public and private collections, including his own. He embarked upon an illustrious teaching career in 1923, holding key positions in major art institutions, notably the National Normal University in Taipei, where he taught from 1949, and was regarded as one of the most influential traditional painters. He was known primarily as a landscape painter, and his mature style was derived from the individualist tradition of the 17th century and the direct study of nature. He was particularly noted for his innovative representations of waterfalls and clouds rendered in vigorous brushwork and rich ink tones.

BIBLIOGRAPHY

Huang Guangnan and others: *Huang Junbi huihua fengge yu qi yingxiang* [The painting style of Huang Chün-pi and his influence] (Taipei, 1987)

Shidai yu chuangzuo: Huang Junbi jingpin zhan [Masterpieces by Huang Chün-pi] (exh. cat., Taipei, N. Taiwan A.G., 1987)

MAYCHING KAO

Huang Gongwang [Huang Kung-wang; *zi* Zijiu; *hao* Yifeng, Dachi, Jingxi Daoren] (*b* Changshu, Jiangsu Province, 1269; *d* Changshu, 1354). Chinese painter. He was designated one of the Four Masters of the Yuan, together with NI ZAN, WU ZHEN and WANG MENG. Born into a family named Lu, he was orphaned when very young. The impoverished Lu family had him adopted when he was seven or eight by a Mr Huang of Yongjia, Zhejiang Province, who was living in Changshu at the time. Since Huang was about 90 years old and without male offspring, the names Huang Gongwang and Zijiu were chosen, which together mean 'Mr Huang has desired a son for a long time'.

Huang Gongwang received a good education, and some documents suggest that he was a child prodigy. In his youth, he served as a legal clerk in the Office of Surveillance in western Zhejiang Province and was put in charge of matters related to the collection of land taxes for helping poor peasants. In 1315, when he was working in Beijing at the Investigation Bureau of the Office of the Imperial Censor, Zhang Lu, he was imprisoned for alleged involvement in mishandling of land taxes in Zhejiang. A plan to collect taxes that Zhang proposed to the court in fact had been undermined by rich landowners and corrupt officials; later, when Zhang was cleared, Huang was released. As a result of this Huang decided to give up official life, changing his name to Yifeng ('One Peak').

For a time he lived in Hauting (modern Songjiang in Shanghai Municipality), making his living as a fortune-teller. About 1329 he joined the Daoist Quanzhen sect. None of Huang's works on Daoism survive, but the *Daozang* (Daoist Canon) does include his biography. In 1334 he established a Hall of the Three Doctrines in Suzhou, Jiangsu Province. The Three Doctrines sect, which reached its height in the Yuan period (1279–1368), incorporated elements of Confucianism, Daoism and Chan (Jap. Zen) Buddhism into a syncretic philosophy; Huang's interest in it suggests the breadth of his philosophical and religious outlook. Huang was also versatile in literature and the arts. One contemporary source states: 'His learning does not rank below anyone. Of all things under heaven there is nothing that he does not know. Even regarding the smallest skill and artistry, he is in good command. He can compose long poems and short verses instantly. He is especially adept in painting. People respect him as a teacher.' Since this source is concerned with dramatists, Huang must have been a writer of plays. He wrote a volume of poetry, *Dachi Daoren ji*, no longer extant, and was also noted as a flautist. He had many literary and artistic friends, including the painters Ni Zan, Cao Zhibai, Fang Congyi, Yang Weizhen (1296–1370) and Zhang Yu (1277–1348), and the poet Yang Zai; he is said to have been a pupil of the painter Zhao Mengfu. In the Yangzi delta area Huang also lived in Quzhou, Fuyang, and, in his last years, Hangzhou and the Fuchun River area (all in Zhejiang Province). Seventeenth-century sources state that he liked to lose himself in nature, perhaps sitting all day in the mountains or staying close to the sea, watching the waves, wind and rain, or sailing a boat alone on a lake, chanting songs and drinking wine.

Some 60 extant paintings are attributed to Huang Gongwang, but only a few accepted as genuine. Huang is said to have started painting only after the age of 50

1. Huang Gongwang: *Xishan yuyi* ('Rivers and hills before rain'; detail), handscroll, 296×1065 mm, before 1344 (Beijing, private collection)

2. Huang Gongwang: *Fuchun shan ju tu* ('Dwelling in the Fuchun mountains'; detail), handscroll, ink on paper, 330×6399 mm, 1350 (Taipei, National Palace Museum)

(*c.* 1320), though none of the accepted works dates to before the 1340s. *Jiuzhu fengcui* ('Nine pearl peaks'; Taipei, N. Pal. Mus.), a hanging scroll on satin in ink, though unsigned, has a colophon indicating its dedication to Yang Weizhen and is one of Huang's earliest works. Many basic forms, such as rocks and trees, are not fully developed. *Xishan yuyi* ('Rivers and hills before rain'; see fig. 1) has an inscription of 1344 dating it to some years earlier. Elements such as patterns of trees and mountains, contrasts and variations, and freedom of brushwork are further developed. *Tianchi shibi* ('Stone cliff at the heavenly pond'; 1341; Beijing, Pal. Mus.), a hanging scroll on silk, depicts rocks making up a centralized formation of high mountains, a typical Yuan composition.

The most important painting by Huang Gongwang, *Fuchun shan ju tu* ('Dwelling in the Fuchun mountains'; see fig. 2), represents what came to be considered the most typical aspects of Huang's personal style. In ink on paper, it depicts broad stretches of the Fuchun River with free, powerful brushwork. Strokes form patterns, rhythms and movements in spontaneous ways associated with calligraphy. Although still representational, the landscape is personalized and abstracted to reflect Huang's interest in finding freedom of expression in nature, a tradition inherited from the 10th-century painter DONG YUAN. The scroll has a complex history. Originally painted for the Daoist Cheng Wuyong, in the 15th century it was acquired by Shen Zhou in Suzhou. Having passed through several hands in that area, in 1596 it came to Dong Qichang in Beijing, who brought it back to his hometown, Huating (Songjiang), where it became very influential among artists. One owner, Wu Hongyu, loved the painting so much that he ordered it to be burnt at his deathbed, and consequently, in 1650, the beginning section was damaged; total destruction was only averted by Wu's nephew. As a result, the painting exists in two sections: the main section went into the collection of the Qianlong emperor in the 18th century, and the beginning part, after repair, went through many private hands and finally into the Zhejiang Provincial Museum in Hangzhou, where it is entitled *Shengshan tu* ('The remaining mountains'). Copies of the painting include a scroll identical to the original apart from a missing last section (Taipei, N. Pal. Mus.) that is dated 1338 but was probably made in the middle part of the Ming (1368–1644) period. This version went into the

collection of the Qianlong emperor before the original did, and was at first accepted by the emperor and his staff as the genuine one. When the original was in the hands of Dong Qichang and the Wu family, copies were made by many painters, including Cheng Zhengkui, Wang Hui, Wu Li, Yun Xiang (1586–1655), Shen Hao and Zou Zhilin (*fl c.* 1610–51). Since the beginning of the 17th century, the scroll has had a great influence on Chinese painting.

Huang Gongwang's treatise on painting, *Xie shanshui jue* ('Secrets of describing landscape'), was preserved by one of his admirers, Tao Zongyi, in an edition of 1366 (*see* CHINA, §V, 3(iv)(b)). In this Huang mentions the prevalence in his time of the Dong Yuan tradition and offers many technical points in painting trees, rocks, mountains, clouds and water, emphasizing the literati tradition. He concludes, 'In doing paintings there are four words that must be absolutely expelled: perversity, prettiness, vulgarity, and derivativeness' (trans. based on Cahill), which became a guiding principle for literati painting.

See also CHINA, §V, 4(ii) and fig. 133.

BIBLIOGRAPHY

Pan Tianshou and Wang Bomin: *Huang Gongwang yu Wang Meng* [Huang Gongwang and Wang Meng] (Shanghai, 1958)
Wen Zhaotong: *Huang Gongwang shiliao* [Historical material on Huang Gongwang] (Shanghai, 1963)
The Four Great Masters of the Yuan, Taipei, N. Pal. Mus. cat. (Taipei, 1975)
J. Cahill: *Hills beyond a River: Chinese Painting of the Yuan Dynasty, 1279–1368* (New York and Tokyo, 1976), pp. 85–113
J. Hay: *Huang Gongwang's 'Dwelling in the Fu-chun Mountains'* (PhD. diss., Princeton U., NJ, 1978)
Chen Gaohua: *Yuan dai huajia shiliao* [Historical material on Yuan period painters] (Shanghai, 1980), pp. 371–90

QINGLI WAN, CHU-TSING LI

Huang Junbi. *See* HUANG CHÜN-PI.

Huang Kung-wang. *See* HUANG GONGWANG.

Huang Pin-hung. *See* HUANG BINHONG.

Huang Quan [Huang Ch'üan] (*b* AD ?900; *d* 965). Chinese painter and high official. He was one of the most important bird-and-flower painters and is sometimes regarded as the originator of the 'boneless' (*mogu*) method of painting. This was typified by the use of colours, with or without black ink in graded washes, to build up forms rather than relying on line to delineate them.

Huang Quan developed his talent for painting from an early age. In literary sources of the Song period (960–1279) it is reported that he mastered the styles of important artists in the painting of bamboo, cliffs and birds, dragons, water and pine trees, as well as landscapes. Not surprisingly, he was admitted at the age of only 17 to the imperial academy at Chengdu (now in Sichuan Province), in the then state of Shu, and made rapid progress as an official and painter, receiving honours from the academy and, when only 23, becoming its leader. During this period (Five Dynasties, AD 907–79) bird-and-flower painting was much in vogue, and Huang set about making a name for himself in this genre. By combining various older painting styles he created a new style of his own, which found particular favour in court circles.

His skill in depicting birds and insects was inordinately admired even in his lifetime, and anecdotes about the lifelike accuracy of his pictures have endured to the present. One such story concerns his picture of pheasants, painted in 953, which he presented to the emperor, who hung it in the imperial palace. An eagle, given to the emperor by a foreign guest, allegedly tried repeatedly to attack the pheasants in Huang's picture. The admiration in which the court held him was not, however, shared by the leading art critics nor by painter colleagues, especially the literati; they preferred Xu Xi, who was regarded as representing in most respects the opposite pole from Huang Quan. Xu Xi was without doubt the better painter, although he failed to achieve prominence comparable to Huang's during his lifetime. Huang painted fine images, predominantly in colours to please his aristocratic audience; Xu painted very expressively and almost exclusively in ink—characteristics that endeared him to literati, who regarded them as essential to true painting. Huang was not only a member of the academy but was also powerful enough to prevent Xu from being admitted to it; Xu thus remained an independent artist. Huang was and still is regarded as a representative of the 'detailed' style of painting (*gongbi*), while Xu represented the more impressionistic (*xieyi*; 'sketching the idea') style, a distinction that did not, however, make much impact among art critics until the Song period. (For further discussion and comparison *see* CHINA, §V, 3(v)(b).) No complete works by Huang appear to be extant, although a few fragments with pictures of insects (Beijing, Pal. Mus.), which might have come from larger pictures, are almost certainly his work.

BIBLIOGRAPHY

O. Sirén: *Chinese Painting: Leading Masters and Principles* (London and New York, 1956–8), i, pp. 174–83

FRIEDRICH ZETTL

Huang Shen (*b* Ninghua, Fujian Province, 1687; *d* 1773). Chinese painter, calligrapher and poet. His father died when Huang was young, and in order to support the family Huang was obliged to pursue a professional career in painting. Although he specialized in portraiture and figure painting, he was also skilled as a painter of landscapes,

plants and birds. His versatility was a characteristic he shared with his teacher, Shangguan Zhou (*b* 1665), a leading Fujian painter whose surviving works include *Wanxiao tang huazhuan* ('Painting record of the Wanxiao Hall'), a woodblock-printed work depicting historical characters. Huang was encouraged by his mother to aspire to a loftier goal than that of a mere craftsman, the status generally accorded professional painters. He began his education at the age of 18; asserting the oneness of painting and poetry, he studied both arts and in 1734 published the *Jiaohu shichao* ('Poetic anthology by Jiaohu'), Jiao hu being a lake to the north of Ninghua. He often included elegantly phrased inscriptions on his paintings, thereby incorporating poetry, calligraphy and painting in a single work. His calligraphy was initially modelled after the *kaishu* (regular script) of Zhong You (AD 151–230) but was later influenced by the *caoshu* (cursive script) of Huaisu. The best examples of his style are bold and sweeping, executed with an unerringly crisp and sure touch and with intricately spaced characters.

Huang is generally classified as one of the Eight Eccentrics of Yangzhou (*see* YANGZHOU SCHOOL). His association with that city began as early as 1724 and lasted for at least 30 years. At first his reception was lukewarm, but by 1730 Huang had developed individual styles of calligraphy and painting, free from an earlier dependence on Xiao Chen (*fl* late 17th century–early 18th) and Han Fan. Eventually, his cursive calligraphy and ink-play technique (*moxi*) became popular among collectors in Yangzhou and established him as a major figure in the city's art circles. His paintings were often distinguished by mannered, tremulous brushstrokes used to outline and contour forms, which were then coloured with pale vegetable pigments or ink washes. So lucrative did his painting practice become that he was able to buy a house and spend his days drinking and composing poetry with Li Shan, Gao Xiang (*fl* 1700–30) and other friends.

Huang reached the height of his success between 1723 and 1735. Documentary evidence about his life thereafter is scarcer, but extant paintings confirm that he continued to paint well into his later years. Qingliang Daoren, in his *Tingyu xuan biji* ('Notes from the Tingyu studio'), referred to a painting done by Huang in 1764 when he was 78 years old; it depicted an old man holding a chrysanthemum, a favourite subject of the artist, which he treated with gentleness, even sentimentality. Two inscriptions written by admirers and attached to *Willows in Autumn* (see fig.) confirm that he adopted various names in his youth and that he retired to Jiao hu in his eighties.

In general, Huang Shen's art developed from a meticulous style similar to that of his teacher, through an intermediary stage of relaxation, even lyricism, and finally to the spontaneous and untrammelled mode seen in *Willows in Autumn*, although some of his styles may have co-existed. He mixed the refined with the vulgar and, in historical subjects, frequently manipulated stock figures. His early landscape paintings, such as *Reminiscence from the Han River* (1729), show elements of the dense and detailed style of Guo Xi, but such influences became increasingly attenuated and then vanished altogether in the face of a far bolder approach.

Huang Shen: *Willows in Autumn* (detail), handscroll, ink on paper, 315×1500 mm, 1735 (Tokyo, National Museum)

BIBLIOGRAPHY
Liu Gangji: *Huang Shen* (Shanghai, 1979)
Yang Xin: *Yangzhou baguai* [The Eight Eccentrics of Yangzhou] (Beijing, 1981)
Cui Mingquan: 'Huang Shen *Xie sheng shanshui, shishu he ce*' [An album of landscape sketches and poems by Huang Shen], *Wenwu* (1982), no. 7, pp. 78–82
Li Wancai: *Huang Shen* (Beijing, 1982)
Liu Gangji: 'A Preliminary Enquiry into Huang Shen's *Album of Figures*', *Duoyun*, ii (1982)
Su Shiyi and Liu Liqing: 'Huang Shen's Artistic Accomplishment as Seen through an Album', *Zhongyuan Wenwu*, i (1982)
Paintings by Yangzhou Artists of the Qing Dynasty from the Palace Museum (exh. cat., Hong Kong, Chin. U., A.G., 1984–5)
Ju-hsi Chou and C. Brown: *The Elegant Brush: Chinese Painting under the Qianlong Emperor, 1735–1795* (Phoenix, 1985)
JU-HSI CHOU

Huang Tingjian [Huang T'ing-chien; *zi* Luzhi; *hao* Shangu Laoren] (*b* Fenning [modern Xiushui], Jiangxi Province, 1045; *d* Fenning, 1105). Chinese calligrapher, poet and scholar-official. He is regarded as the avant-garde figure of the Four Great Calligraphers of the Northern Song (960–1127), who emphasized individual expression in their work; the others are CAI XIANG, SU SHI and Mi Fu (*see* MI, (1); *see also* CHINA, §IV, 2(iv)). Huang was a calligraphy critic and an early theorist of literati painting (*wenren hua*; *see* CHINA, §V, 4(ii)) and is also acknowledged as the founder of the Jiangxi school of poetry. A member of an exceptionally cultured family of well-known poets, he became associated with individuals such as Su Shi, who at court opposed the reforms of the Chief Councillor, Wang Anshi (1021–86). As a result of political struggles between conservatives and reformers, Huang was exiled in 1094 to Fuzhou in Sichuan Province and only after this produced his most impressive calligraphy.

Since most of Huang's calligraphy is not dated, a chronology of his work is based on stylistic development. His early pieces in running script (*xingshu*), featuring square characters and smooth, plump brushstrokes, reveal the influence of the Tang calligrapher, YAN ZHENQING. Later, Huang's style became tighter and more irregular, and the brushstrokes, notably diagonal and vertical ones, elongated. He developed a distinctive, jerky brushwork style, created by tension in his arm movement. Huang's greatest works are in large running script (*da xingshu*) or cursive script (*caoshu*), mostly in handscroll format. One of the major stylistic sources for his large running script is the stone *Inscription for Burying a Crane* (*Yihe ming*, c. 512–14), and his works in this script include *Poem by Han Shan* (1099; Taipei, N. Pal. Mus.), *Scroll for Zhang Datong* (1100; Princeton U., NJ, A. Mus.), colophon to Su Shi's *Cold Meal in Huangzhou* (*Hanshitie*, 1100; Taipei, N. Pal. Mus.), and *Poem on Songfen Ge* (1102; Taipei, N. Pal. Mus.). Huang's mature cursive script owes much to the Tang monk-calligrapher HUAISU's *Self-statement* scroll (*Zixu tie*; Taipei, N. Pal. Mus.; *see* CHINA, fig. 92). His works in cursive script include *Li Bai's 'Recalling Past Wanderings' Poem* (Tokyo, Fujii Mus.; *see* CHINA, fig. 93) and the *Biography of Lian Po and Lin Xiangru* (*c.* 1095; New York, Met., J. Crawford col.). Among his extant works the most abundant are in small running script (*xiao xingshu*), usually in album leaf format.

Followers of Huang's style include the Southern Song (1127–1279) emperor Gaozong, the Ming (1368–1644) calligraphers Shen Zhou, Zhu Yunming and Wen Zhengming and the 20th-century artist Zhang Daqian. He also influenced Chan (Jap. Zen) Buddhist calligraphy in both China and Japan.

See also CHINA, §IV, 2(iv) and (vi).

BIBLIOGRAPHY
Huang Dian, ed.: 'Shangu xiansheng nianpu' [Chronology of Huang Tingjian] (*c.* 1199/*R* as *Shangu shi quanji* [Huang Tingjian's complete poems], 1876)
Song Huang Tingjian moji [Huang Tingjian's calligraphy], x of *Gugong fashu* [Calligraphy in the National Palace Museum] (Taipei, 1962–8)
Gugong bowuyuan cang lidai fashu xuanji [Selection of calligraphy from all periods in the Palace Museum], 26 vols (Beijing, 1963)
Yutaka Adachi: 'The Northern and Southern Song Dynasties', *Chinese Calligraphy*, ed. Nakata Yūjirō (New York, Tokyo and Kyoto, 1983)
SHEN FU

Huang Yongyu [Huang Yung-yü; Huang Niu; Huang Xingbin; Niu Fuzi; Zhang Guanbao] (*b* Fenghuang County, Hunan Province, 9 July 1924). Chinese painter and woodcut artist of the Tujia national minority. Huang learned about woodcuts in school in Fujian Province in

Huang Yongyu: *Lotus*, ink and colours on paper, 1978 (artist's collection)

1937–9 but, as a result of his expulsion for fighting, he was primarily self-taught. His parents were artists, and in 1946 he married Zhang Meixi (*b* 1928), also an artist. In Shanghai in 1947 he joined Lu Xun's anti-Guomindang (KMT) movement as a woodcut artist. In 1948 he painted and made woodcuts in Taiwan, then moved to Hong Kong, where he worked as art editor for the *Da gong bao*, a leftist newspaper. In 1953, optimistic about the new Communist government, he returned to China to teach woodcut-printing at the Central Academy of Fine Arts in Beijing. He moved back to Hong Kong in 1988, but retained his position as Professor at the Academy.

During the 1950s and 1960s Huang was well known for his woodblock portraits and his illustrations to his own witty poetry. He suffered all the humiliations of the Cultural Revolution (1966–76): beatings, incarcerations, wearing a dunce cap and placard, the destruction of his works and other personal property and more than three years of hard labour in the countryside in 1970–73. When he returned to Beijing in 1973 he was commissioned by Zhou Enlai's faction of the government to plan the decoration of the Beijing Hotel. The following year, however, Jiang Qing denounced him as a 'black painter', and he was subjected to several more years of harsh treatment. The painting by Huang that she objected to, *Winking Owl* (Laing, pl. 14), became a symbol of the ludicrous nature of the indictment of China's artists and intellectuals in the 1960s and 1970s. Jiang Qing interpreted its humorous, winking eye as an indication of Huang's opposition to the regime.

Huang recovered from the constraints of the Cultural Revolution with energy, good humour and a prolific outpouring of paintings, working in a variety of media but with traditional Chinese techniques as his foundation. He fulfilled a number of public commissions, including the design for the monumental landscape tapestry behind the seated statue of Mao in the Mao Zedong Memorial Hall

in Tiananmen Square. His preferred subjects were traditional: birds and flowers (especially the lotus flower) and landscapes. However, his use of strong colours and vivid tonal and textural contrasts was innovative. In *Lotus* (see fig.), crisp, brightly coloured petals executed in *gongbi* ('detailed strokes') stand out starkly against soft, black *pomo* ('broken ink') leaves. The combination of two opposing brush styles of Chinese painting, one precisely detailed and the other loose and impressionistic, is typical of Huang's unconventional references to the past. He drew inspiration from a variety of time-honoured techniques, but always presented a fresh perspective.

After the Cultural Revolution, Huang experimented with the Song-period (960–1279) technique of applying heavy colour (*zhongcai*) to *gaoli* paper, to achieve a more brilliant effect. This modern application of the *zhongcai* technique inspired a number of artists, including Ting Shaokuang (*b* 1939) and Zhou Ling (*b* 1941). Huang's style was rooted in his Chinese past, but his dynamic use of colours and bold contrasts conveyed an energy previously unseen in Chinese flower paintings and landscapes. Living in exile in Hong Kong in 1989–90, Huang used his vibrant flowers to protest against the Tiananmen massacre of 4 June 1989. His deep love for China is conveyed in his own summary of his art theory: 'In China, if one wants to be an artist, one must first be a genuine Chinese person'.

BIBLIOGRAPHY

Huang Miaozi: 'A Painter of Delightful Dreams', *Chin. Lit.* (1979), no. 8, pp. 71–7
P. Wilson: 'An Artist of the People: Huang Yongyu', *Chin. Lit.* (1979), no. 8, pp. 59–70
J. Cohen: 'Huang Yongyu: Dragonflies, Frogs and the Beatles', *ARTnews*, lxxix/6 (1980), pp. 69–70
Huang Yongyu huajia [The painter Huang Yongyu] (Hong Kong, 1980)
J. Cohen: *The New Chinese Painting, 1949–1986* (New York, 1987)
Huang Yongyu (Hunan, 1987)
E. J. Laing: *The Winking Owl: Art in the People's Republic of China* (Berkeley, 1988)

ANN BARROTT WICKS

Huang Yung-yü. See HUANG YONGYU.

Huánuco Pampa [Huánuco Viejo]. Pre-Columbian Inca regional capital, 150 km from modern Huánuco in north-central Peru. The well preserved city at Huánuco Pampa, which flourished during the late Imperial period (*c.* 1473–1534), consists of approximately 3500 visible structures covering an area of *c.* 2 sq. km. The city was planned according to Inca concepts of urbanism and was divided into four sectors (north, south, east and west), each of which was further subdivided into twelve sections. The centre of the city comprised a large plaza (550×350 m) with a central *ushnu* (or *usnu*; Quechua: ceremonial platform). Roads (including those to Cuzco and Quito) met at the plaza. The *ushnu* comprises a main rectangular platform (32×48×3.5 m high) set on two lower platforms, all made of stone blocks dressed on their exposed faces. The main platform included a balustrade with two entrances and a flight of steps on its southern side. The entrances were flanked by stone blocks carved in high relief with what appear to be pumas. Two small buildings on the lowest platform face east.

The plaza was the focal point for some 4000 buildings. To the east of it stood the Incahuasi (Inca's Palace) and the Acllahuasi (Palace of the Sun Virgins), both built in classic Inca imperial style. The Incahuasi was fronted by two long rectangular halls, one with nine and one with four doors facing the plaza. Both halls had gabled roofs supported by pillars set along their axes. Leading into the three courtyards and halls of the Incahuasi were three finely fitted masonry doors in the Cuzco style, aligned with the long axis of the *ushnu*. Both the Incahuasi and the Acllahuasi provided increasing privacy and variety of layout as progression was made from the plaza eastwards into the inner courts.

The northern sector included a large *kancha* (walled compound) with a single entrance from the plaza. Within were 50 similar-sized rooms. Archaeological evidence from this compound indicates that it was used for the production of cloth. Other compounds in the southern and western sectors included residential *kancha*s, structures of various, undetermined functions and *chasqui* (relay runner) posts. Most of the residential buildings were small rectangular rooms with various orientations, but over 1000 circular structures derive from the local, non-Inca building tradition. On a low hillside just south of the city stand 497 rectangular and circular storehouses with window-like doors. Arranged in neat rows and with a capacity of some 38,000 cubic metres, they were used to store tribute from adjacent regions prior to redistribution by Inca officials.

The architecture and ceramic styles found at Huánuco Pampa are often crudely executed imitations of the imperial styles of Cuzco, particularly the pottery, which lacks the precision and fine quality of Cuzco wares. Nevertheless, most of the designs and pottery shapes known in the Cuzco area are represented in local variants.

BIBLIOGRAPHY

E. Harth Terré: 'El pueblo de Huánuco Viejo', *Arquit. Peru.*, cccxx–cccxxi (1964), pp. 21–40
C. Morris and D. E. Thompson: 'Huánuco Viejo: An Inca Administrative Centre', *Amer. Anthropologist*, xxxv (1970), pp. 344–62
C. Morris: 'The Identification of Function in Inca Architecture and Ceramics', *Rev. Mus. N.*, xxxvii (1974), pp. 135–44
C. Morris and D. E. Thompson: *Huánuco Pampa: An Inca City and its Hinterland* (London, 1985)

ANN KENDALL

Huari [Wari]. Site in the Ayacucho Valley, Peru, *c.* 25 km north of modern Ayacucho, and the name given to the dominant Central Andean culture of the Middle Horizon (*c.* AD 600–*c.* 1000) period. The site was the capital of the Pre-Columbian state or empire of Huari; it was occupied in the Early Intermediate period (*c.* 200 BC–AD 600) and expanded especially during the Middle Horizon, *c.* AD 550–650, a time when many sites in the Ayacucho Valley were abandoned. Huari itself appears to have been largely abandoned by *c.* AD 800, for reasons that are unknown, and at this time too the Huari state or empire ceased to exist as an integral unit.

Although the site is estimated to cover 1000–1500 ha, it is unlikely that all of this area was occupied at any one time. Huari was first mentioned by Pedro de Cieza de León (1553), who visited the ruined city in 1550, when it was known as Viñaque, and noted its similarity to the site of TIAHUANACO in Bolivia. The exact nature of the relationship between Huari and Tiahuanaco is uncertain: both began to expand, both in size and in the spheres of their influence, from *c.* AD 500, and there was certainly contact between the two cities.

Huari, stone chambers in the Chejo Wasi sector of the city, after *c.* AD 700

1. ARCHITECTURE. Huari architecture has been used as a basis for postulating the existence of a Huari empire. Its most characteristic architectural form consists of rectangular enclosures, subdivided by avenues into rectangular units consisting of corridors surrounding large patios. The quadrangles comprise lines of corbel-vaulted rooms with finely plastered walls and floors, often associated with elaborate water-supply and drainage systems. Sites of this type may have served an administrative role, and several are of urban proportions. Excavated evidence suggests that the patios were used for serving food and drink and the corridors for preparing and storing these items. This may have been an aspect of a system of public generosity, important in the socio-economic control exercised by Huari rulers.

At Huari itself, the principal architectural component consists of a series of large rectangular structures and compounds, built of roughly dressed local stone set in mud mortar. In the Ushpa Qoto sector of the site massive rubble walls stand 5–6 m high. Large walls also survive from the Robles Moqo Hill to the Sullu Cruz sector, some reaching 200 m in length and 3 m in width at the base, tapering to 0.6 m at the top. There are few doorways in the wall remains, but many walls have rows of corbels, some of which appear to have supported upper storeys. Craft specialization at Huari is demonstrated by concentrations of distinct manufacturing areas for such activities as pottery production and the working of turquoise for use in jewellery and figurines.

Ashlar masonry was employed at Huari but did not originate in the Ayacucho Valley. It was known at CHAVÍN DE HUÁNTAR during the Early Horizon (c. 900–c. 200 BC) and may derive from there. Alternatively, the technique may have been introduced from Tiahuanaco. Examples at Huari include a number of cut stone chambers in the Chejo Wasi sector (see fig.) and a semi-subterranean temple in the Moraduchayuc sector, all of which have parallels at Tiahuanaco.

2. POTTERY. The spread of Huari influence can be most effectively traced through pottery remains. The direct origins of both Huari and Tiahuanaco styles can be traced to Pucará in the southern Peruvian highlands, although the site itself was abandoned in the 1st century BC, well before early Huari and Tiahuanaco styles began to become distinctive c. AD 500. Huari styles have many variant forms, but their main characteristics appear to have developed in the Ayacucho Valley; in addition to Tiahuanaco influence, the local Huarpa tradition and south coastal NAZCA style can be recognized. The Huarpa style, which shared features with Nazca V to VIII and possibly with earlier phases of the Nazca style, perhaps as early as Nazca II (c. 250 BC–c. AD 400), is characterized by rough-finished pottery decorated with black on white designs, which are mostly geometric. Occasionally a dark red, almost purple pigment was used. The principal vessel shapes are thick-walled, open vessels and necked jars with thickened rims; smaller shapes include cups, incurving bowls, bottles and spoons. Certain polychrome and geometric designs, including 'humped animal' and various ray designs, derive from Nazca VII and VIII (c. AD 300–c. 600).

Other early Ayacucho Valley styles include the Chakipampa, Conchopata, Robles Moqo, Black Decorated and Ocros styles. These styles constitute the component parts of a number of regional variants, which dominate, in varying proportions, the ceramic assemblages at Huari sites. Chakipampa designs and shapes were inspired by the Huarpa style and by late Nazca IV motifs. There are both fine vessels and plain, more roughly executed wares. The predominant vessel shapes are small cups, open bowls and jars. More elaborate Chakipampa wares are covered in a thick glossy red slip, with designs in white, cream and purple, outlined in black. Some motifs even appear to have derived conceptually from Nazca via Tiahuanaco. The Ocros style also derived from Huarpa pottery and incorporates late Nazca features. Its main features are a preponderance of bowl shapes and a light orange slip, frequently decorated with modelled animal heads on the lip and outlined dot-and-wavy-line designs.

Black Decorated style is distinguished by a dark brown to black background decorated with white or pink designs, including rays, dots and S-shaped motifs, on bowls and cups in particular. The Conchopata style is characterized by large bucket-shaped vessels, usually decorated on the exterior with designs similar to that carved on the Gateway of the Sun at Tiahuanaco (for illustration see TIAHUANACO). Closely related is Robles Moqo pottery, known from sites both in the Ayacucho Valley and on the coast, which differs from the Conchopata material in being decorated on both the interior and exterior; it includes various plant motifs and has a greater range of smaller, more utilitarian, shapes. Much of the Conchopata and Robles Moqo ware appears to have been primarily for ritual purposes.

Up to c. AD 650 Huari styles had spread throughout the central Peruvian highlands and central and southern coastal sites, intermingling with Nazca cultures. After c. AD 650 Huari styles achieved their greatest distribution, being taken up on the northern coastal plain. Variant types increased in number, and representations of mythical beings occur, based on Conchopata and Robles Moqo features. In the central and southern highlands the style is called Viñaque and includes polychrome designs on cups and bowls, often geometric and frequently depicting the disembodied head of the 'Staff god'. Viñaque style vessels have often been found with late Black Decorated style vessels.

In the southern coastal area the Atarco style incorporated a mixture of Viñaque, Pachacamac (see below) and late Nazca features. Necked jars, single-spouted and stirrup-spouted bottles were common. Characteristic designs include a mythical 'profiled angel' figure (anthropomorphic with feline elements) and the disembodied 'Staff god' head. Pachacamac style, named after PACHACAMAC in the Lurín Valley on the central coast, assimilated several design variants, including Robles Moqo, Atarco and Viñaque features. A common Pachacamac vessel type is a necked jar with a face and anthropomorphic body features. A winged figure in profile, with a feline body and eagle head, is also common. Much Pachacamac pottery is more crudely executed than in the other variants. Many other local variant styles existed, found alongside Huari-influenced styles in local contexts.

Some ceramics associated with Huari culture appear to have been purpose-made, exclusively for ritual contexts. The pottery tended to be placed as offerings or caches in pits and was often deliberately broken. Such caches have been found at Pacheco (Robles Moqo ware; Lima, Mus. N. Antropol. & Arqueol.), at sites in the Nazca Valley and at Conchopata (Conchopata ware; Lima, Mus. N. Antropol. & Arqueol.) and Ayapata in the Ayacucho Valley. Ceremonial pottery was typically decorated with elaborate mythical representations and may represent a Huari imperial cult of Middle Horizon date, although cache offerings were a common tradition in the Pre-Columbian Andes and continue even in modern times. In the fringe areas of Huari influence the offering tradition was occasionally 'translated' into something more local, using utilitarian pottery. From *c.* AD 800 to *c.* 1000, when a loss of central authority appears to have occurred, Huari pottery styles became even more diverse. Local designs were reintroduced, and Huari iconographic themes were added to them.

Important collections of Huari pottery include those in the Museum of Primitive Art and the Museum of the American Indian, both in New York; the Museo Nacional de Antropología y Arqueología, Lima; the Museum für Völkerkunde, Berlin; and the Musée de l'Homme, Paris.

3. SCULPTURE AND OTHER ARTS. At Huari there are numerous petroglyphs, which apparently represent plants, snakes and simple geometric designs. Eleven large sculptures (Ayacucho, Mus. Arqueol.) carved from grey volcanic tufa are also known; the first were discovered at the site in 1888. They vary in height from 0.88 m to 1.48 m. They are closely related to some examples of Tiahuanaco sculpture but are distinct enough to be regarded as a separate style. One represents a feline figure, while the others constitute human forms. Of the human figures, most are standing, though two are seated. They are carved in three dimensions in a distinctly angular manner. The figures differ in costume and headdress; the eyes are elliptical and the noses simple, flat and somewhat trapezoidal.

Huari iconographic themes also appear in textiles, metalwork, featherwork, shell-carving and wood-carving. Huari textiles demonstrate a high degree of technical expertise (*see also* SOUTH AMERICA, PRE-COLUMBIAN, §III, 6 and fig. 38). Special dress indicated status and ethnic background, as well as playing an important role in religious, political and economic life. Textiles were a major commodity in cache offerings and, to judge from Inca ethnographic records, may have constituted an important element in taxation (a good collection of Huari textiles is in the Textile Museum, Washington, DC). Much of the symbolism reflected in the Middle Horizon styles shows aspects of the social structure of the Middle Horizon ethnic groups and demonstrates the inseparability of religious and political elements within the design themes.

BIBLIOGRAPHY

P. de Cieza de León: *Primera parte de la crónica del Perú* (Seville, 1553); Eng. trans. by C. R. Markham as *The Travels of Pedro de Cieza de León* (Cambridge, 1864)
W. C. Bennett: 'The North Highlands of Peru', *Anthropol. Pap. Amer. Mus. Nat. Hist.*, xxxix (1944), pp. 1–114
——: *Excavations at Wari* (New Haven, 1953)
D. Menzel: 'Style and Time in the Middle Horizon', *Ñawpa Pacha*, ii (1964), pp. 2–105
——: 'New Data on the Huari Empire', *Ñawpa Pacha*, vi (1968), pp. 47–114
R. Ravines: 'Un depósito de ofrendas del Horizonte Medio en la Sierra Central del Perú', *Ñawpa Pacha*, vi (1968), pp. 19–45
L. G. Lumbreras: *De los pueblos, las culturas y las artes del antiguo Perú* (Lima, 1969; Eng. trans. by B. J. Meggers, Washington, DC, 1974)
G. R. Willey: *An Introduction to South American Archaeology*, ii (Englewood Cliffs, 1971), pp. 157–64
L. G. Lumbreras: *Las fundaciones de Huamanga* (Lima, 1974)
W. H. Isbell: *The Rural Foundations for Urbanism* (Urbana, 1977)
L. F. Spickard: 'The Development of Huari Administrative Architecture', *Investigations of the Andean Past*, ed. D. H. Sandweiss (Ithaca, NY, 1977), pp. 136–60
F. Kauffmann Doig: *Manual de arqueología peruana* (Lima, 1980)
R. S. MacNeish and others: *Prehistory of the Ayacucho Basin, Peru*, ii (Ann Arbor, 1981)
A. G. Cook: 'Aspects of State Ideology in Huari and Tiwanaku Iconography: The Central Deity and Sacrificer', *Investigations of the Andean Past: Papers from the First Annual Northeast Conference on Andean Archaeology and Ethnohistory: Ithaca, NY, 1983*, pp. 161–85
W. H. Isbell: 'Shared Ideology and Parallel Political Development: Huari and Tiwanaku', *Investigations of the Andean Past: Papers from the First Annual Northeast Conference on Andean Archaeology and Ethnohistory: Ithaca, NY, 1983*, pp. 186–208
M. Benavides: *Caracter del Estado Wari* (Ayacucho, 1984)
W. H. Isbell: 'Huari Urban Prehistory', *Current Archaeological Projects in the Central Andes*, ed. A. Kendall, Brit. Archaeol. Rep., Int. Ser., cxciv (Oxford, 1984), pp. 95–131
F. M. Meddens: *The Chicha/Soras Valley during the Middle Horizon: Provincial Aspects of Huari* (diss., U. London, 1985)
W. H. Isbell: 'Emergence of the City and State at Wari, Ayacucho, Peru, during the Middle Horizon', *Andean Archaeology*, ed. R. Matos Mendieta, S. A. Turpin and H. H. Eling jr (Los Angeles, 1986), pp. 189–200

FRANK MEDDENS

Huastec. Region and culture of Mesoamerica, that produced distinctive Pre-Columbian architecture, sculpture, pottery and shell ornaments. From the Middle Pre-Classic period (*c.* 1000–*c.* 300 BC) to the Late Post-Classic period (*c.* AD 1200–1521) the Huastec people occupied the Gulf Coast of Mexico; today they inhabit southern Tamaulipas, northern Veracruz, eastern San Luis Potosí and parts of Querétaro, Hidalgo and Puebla.

1. ARCHITECTURE. Few Huastec buildings survive, and these only partially. Their most common characteristic is a circular floor plan. One of the oldest is in El Ebano in Tamaulipas; it may date from the Middle Pre-Classic period and has a circular floor plan (diam. 57 m), on top of which is a sort of hemispherical cap, 3 m high. The area of the Tamuín River was the most densely populated, and among the best-known sites are Tamtok and Tamuín, both Late Classic (*c.* AD 600–*c.* 900). The former has two large pyramids and circular buildings grouped on low platforms. In Tamuín, an area of nearly 17 ha, the most important constructions are in Mound A, a complex of three connected buildings: a base supporting a temple and two altars on a platform. One altar is in the shape of a truncated cone, covered with wall paintings; the other is similar to an Aztec brazier. In all the buildings the nucleus consists of mud and stone, the facings are of sandstone bonded with mud, and the sloping walls are of ashlar blocks. Other sites with masonry architecture and circular buildings are Las Flores in Tampico, Huejutla in Hidalgo, Tancanhuitz and Tamposoque in San Luis Potosí and Cacahuatenco in the western Huastec region.

2. SCULPTURE. This is the most outstanding Huastec art form. All except one of the *c.* 400 known stone sculptures are carved from the sandstone of the region in thin, rectangular, prism-like blocks. In large sculptures of human figures the frontal and rear views are carved on the widest sides, but in figures of hunchbacks and men holding staffs the profiles are carved on the widest sides. Judging by their similarity with pottery forms and designs, these sculptures were probably carved between the 9th and 11th centuries AD. The main subjects are human figures, both male and female, some hunchbacked and old. The range of female figures varies from simple, crudely executed forms to complex and carefully carved figures, with elaborate headdresses and smooth skirts. They are always shown standing, the body and head facing forwards, the arms at the sides with hands resting on the belly. Naked torsos show the breasts, edged by a border. The form of headdress is distinctly Huastec, always with a comb and sometimes having a rectangular block and a conical cap (see fig.). Some headdresses also have such characteristically Huastec designs as circles with a central disc or discs engraved with a wavy line. Others have serpent heads or radial grooves that mimic plumes of folded paper, and some have open bird-beaks or serpent's jaws at the front, framing expressionless faces. These female figures are thought to represent the Earth Mother, Ixcuina-Tlazolteotl.

The male figures are more varied in form. Some are schematic, shown naked and with no headdress or with a tight-fitting cap that reveals a marked deformity of the skull, both at the front and back. Others are outstanding for their careful and delicate carving. Groups of designs cover their bodies, as seen in the figure of *The Adolescent*, or the loincloth, as in the figure of *Ajalpan* (both Mexico City, Mus. N. Antropol.). Both of these are shown standing; one has its arms at right angles, the other rests a hand on its belly. Body ornament frequently consists of a curved pectoral on the upper part of the figure, with typical relief designs; the lower part is trapezoidal and sometimes includes a circular hole. In one figure the ribs can be seen and beneath them, in a hollow, the heart. Many wear a conical headdress, always worn above a band, and earrings with hooks, said to be attributes of Quetzalcóatl, the Creator God. Some male sculptures consist of two figures: *The Adolescent* carries an infant on his back, and the figure of *Apotheosis* (New York, Brooklyn Mus.) carries a skeleton on its back. The latter is one of numerous finely worked sculptures in the Rio Tamuín style.

These male and female sculptures may represent gods—the female figures Ixcuina-Tlazolteotl and the male Ehecatl-Quetzalcóatl—that were later incorporated into the Aztec pantheon. Another group consists of figures of hunchbacks with deformed chests, squatting on their heels with their knees on the ground. Constituting a unique category of Mesoamerican sculpture are 40 male figures, each holding a staff or a serpent (in e.g. Jalapa, U. Veracruzana, Mus. Antropol.). Some are both hunchbacked and old and are thought to be related to phallic cults. A few free-standing reliefs exist, and they depict subjects markedly different from those of other sculptures. The local style of Huilocintla in the state of Veracruz is

Huastec female figure with a headdress, sandstone, h. 1.17 m, *c.* AD 1000–1200 (Mexico City, Museo Nacional de Antropología)

distinguished by figures performing self-sacrifice: they are shown piercing their tongues with a thorny stick.

Small terracotta figurines were made during a period of 2500 years stretching from the Middle Pre-Classic period to the Late Post-Classic. They have been described by Ekholm (1944) and MacNeish (1954). Despite their variety, they show unmistakably Huastec characteristics. They are solid cream in colour, with tar paint emphasizing breasts, eyes and eyebrows, and naked save for a brief loincloth of applied modelling technique. The heads are often flat or concave. The most common figure is a woman with a narrow waist, prominent and pointed breasts and exaggeratedly wide hips; the men are ball-players, and there are also representations of musicians (Jalapa, U. Veracruzana, Mus. Antropol.).

3. WALL PAINTING, SHELLWORK AND POTTERY. In 1946 W. du Solier discovered the only Huastec wall paintings so far known, on the altar of Tamuín, which was shaped like a truncated cone. The paintings have now almost disappeared. The main paintings are on a frieze 340 mm high that shows a series of 12 figures painted in dark red on the white background of the stucco. The figures are depicted in profile, one behind the other, all looking in the same direction. The first five are seated and carry insignia in their hands; on their faces one can see teeth serrated for beauty purposes and eyes with an appendage in the outer corner. They wear large headdresses of feathers and birds. The other seven figures are shown walking. In their hands they have fans, rattles, staffs and sticks with feathers. Their headdresses are conical hats, birds, serpents and a skull. The intricate style and the way the surface is divided into small sections show similarities to Huastec reliefs and carvings on shells. It has been suggested that the figures represent Quetzalcóatl in different manifestations.

There are fine Huastec ornaments made from conch shell, of which spiral and elongated pectorals are outstanding. Some are polished, others retain traces of paint, and the best have a carved and uneven surface (e.g. Mexico City, Mus. N. Antropol.). Complicated scenes cover these small spaces. Often two human figures occupy the upper portion, while on the lower portion are two large, coiled serpents, with their open jaws pointing upwards, acting as a support. The pectorals are between 100 and 190 mm long. Other small ornaments are earrings consisting of discs from 90 to 100 mm in diameter with a single figure surrounded by stepped frets, circles, skulls, serpent forms and other symbolic motifs.

There is evidence of Huastec pottery vessels from the 1st millennium BC; from the outset they show influences from Teotihuacán, the Maya region and the centre of Veracruz. By the Pánuco IV phase (c. AD 600–c. 900), named from the site at Pánuco in the state of Veracruz, a distinctive style had emerged; it became clearly defined by Pánuco VI (c. 1250–1521). There are plates, pots, pans and jars with handles and bridge handles (Mexico City, Mus. N. Antropol.; Tuxpan, Mus. Reg.). The forms are essentially organic: anthropomorphic, zoomorphic and vegetal. In the last case, gourds and squashes are of a monochrome cream colour, while the anthropomorphic vessels have surfaces and linear designs in dark colours: blackish brown and cherry red. The colours emphasize facial features and represent well-known symbolic designs: an inverted double 'S', a circle with discs in the centre, oblong, hexagonal or octagonal forms with points inside and a cross resembling the Maltese Cross. One type of vessel has as its only motif a human face decorated with dark colours. Vessels in hunchback form reveal the same formal solutions as the stone hunchbacks (see §2 above).

BIBLIOGRAPHY

J. W. Fewkes: 'Certain Antiquities of Eastern Mexico', *Annu. Rep. Bureau Amer. Ethnol. Secretary Smithsonian Inst.*, xxv (1907), pp. 221–96
——: 'Antiquities of the Gulf Coast of Mexico', *Smithsonian Inst. Misc. Col.*, lxx/2 (1919), pp. 81–90
W. du Solier: 'Estudio arquitectónico de los edificios huaxtecos', *An. Inst. N. Antropol. & Hist.*, i (1939–40), pp. 121–45
G. F. Ekholm: 'Excavations at Tampico and Pánuco in the Huasteca, Mexico', *Anthropol. Pap. Amer. Mus. Nat. Hist.*, xxxviii (1944), pp. 319–512
——: 'Notas arqueológicas sobre el Valle de Tuxpan y areas circunvecinas: Huastecos, Totonacos y sus vecinos', *Rev. Mex. Estud. Antropol.*, xiii (1953), pp. 413–21
R. MacNeish: 'An Early Archaeological site Near Pánuco, Veracruz', *Trans. Amer. Philos. Soc.*, xliv (1954), pp. 539–641
B. de la Fuente and N. Gutiérrez Solana: *Escultura huasteca en piedra* (Mexico City, 1981)

BEATRIZ DE LA FUENTE

Hua Yan [Hua Yen; *zi* Qiuyue, Desong; *hao* Xinluo Shanren, Baisha Daoren, Dongyuan Sheng] (*b* Shanghang, Fujian Province, 1682; *d* Hangzhou, Zhejiang Province, 1762). Chinese painter. One of the Eight Eccentrics of Yangzhou (*see* YANGZHOU SCHOOL), Hua Yan painted figures, landscapes, birds, flowers and insects. A strong sense of humour is revealed in his depictions of animals: he painted subjects such as kittens in a heap, frogs fighting, a turtle on its back and sway-backed, pop-eyed horses. His independent spirit in this genre was widely acclaimed by critics. Qin Zuyong (1825–84) even praised his paintings as comparable to those of Yun Shouping, the great bird-and-flower painter.

Autumn Scene (see fig.) is an example of his landscape painting. In the middle of the composition a scholar with a staff in his hand and his back to the viewer stands on a promontory that rises from the right corner, leading the

Hua Yan: *Autumn Scene*, album leaf, ink and colour on paper, 229×153 mm, 1729 (Washington, DC, Freer Gallery of Art)

eye towards him in a diagonal movement. Framed in a square by a tall rock to his left and a pair of spindly trees to his right, he gazes across an expanse of water at distant mountains, capped by a single peak. The brushwork is quick and sketchy, and the colours are pale: green underfoot, pink leaves, powder-blue mountains. Water is suggested only by the lines of currents in the foreground. There are only a few leaves on the trees and these are depicted almost as caricatures: as circles on one tree, brief horizontal lines on the other. The very dry, rough brushwork on the rocks and trees contrasts with the fine lines of the scholar and the grasses. A partially revealed cliff on the left is offset by two columns of calligraphy below it. Hua Yan's models in calligraphy are cited as Zhong You (AD 151–230) and Yu Shinan (558–638), but it is clear that this is not the hand of a literary man, practised in the study of early models. The characters are broad, loosely spaced and rounded, and have a naivety and awkwardness that suit the style of his painting, itself terse and somewhat gauche.

Conversation in Autumn (hanging scroll, 1732; Cleveland, OH, Mus. A.) is a far more energetic and complex painting. In the lower half of the work there are sharp, rain-drenched, near-naked trees on a foundation of pointed rocks. These craggy boulders are scribbled with energetic, lengthwise hatchmarks that lead the eye to the open window of a house, where two gentlemen can be seen within. The interior scene, framed with simple, straight, geometric lines, gives a sense of opening and expansion. The speckle of black, wet bamboo leaves and sodden, misty branches over the roof draw the eye upwards towards the narrow columns of calligraphy at the upper right, executed in a wild and agitated cursive script that echoes the effect of the trees in the foreground.

BIBLIOGRAPHY
O. Sirén: *Chinese Painting: Leading Masters and Principles* (London and New York, 1956–8), v, p. 247
Yu Jianhua: *Zhongguo huajia da zidian* [Dictionary of Chinese painters] (Shanghai, 1981)

ELIZABETH F. BENNETT

Hua Yen. *See* HUA YAN.

Hubáček, Karel (*b* Prague, 23 Feb 1924). Czech architect. He graduated in architecture from the Czech Technical University, Prague, in 1949. In 1958 he became Head of Design of Studio 2 at Stavoprojekt in Liberec. In his architectural work he aimed at the use of new materials and methods of construction, applying the principles of industrial design. In 1963 he produced a design for a television mast on Mt Ještěd, which won him the 1969 August Perret Prize from the Union Internationale des Architectes on its completion in 1969. The monumental form of the construction, determined by technical requirements, creates a majestic silhouette crowning the peak of the mountain. He continued to work mainly on technological structures such as reservoirs and power stations but also applied the principles behind their design to other buildings, including a department store (1977), Liberec, a design for a theatre for the Academy of Dramatic Art (1980; unexecuted), Prague, and the House of Culture (1986), Teplice. In 1980 a team led by Hubáček won

second prize in an international competition for a residential and recreational district in Tegel, Berlin.

BIBLIOGRAPHY
R. Sedláková, M. Benešová and S. Brož: 'Dům kultury a kolonáda v Teplicich' [Cultural centre and colonnade in Teplice], *Archit. ČSR*, xlvii/3 (1988), pp. 18–25
R. Švácha: 'Profil: Karel Hubáček', *Archit. ČSR*, xlix/1 (1990), pp. 72–5

RADOMÍRA SEDLÁKOVÁ

Hubbard, Elbert (*b* Bloomington, IL, 19 June 1856; *d* SS *Lusitania*, off Co. Cork, 7 May 1915). American designer. He was initially a successful salesman for the Illinois-based Weller's Practical Soaps. He settled in East Aurora, near Buffalo, NY, and abandoned selling soap in 1893. During a trip to England the following year, he met William Morris and admired the works of his Kelmscott Press. On returning to East Aurora, Hubbard employed his great showmanship to popularize a simplified version of English Arts and Crafts design for a wide audience. With the help of a local press he began publishing monthly biographies, *Little Journeys to the Homes of the Great* (1895–1909), the first two of which treat the lives of George Eliot and John Ruskin. Soon after he founded the Roycroft Press with the publication of *The Philistine* (1895–1915), a monthly journal combining popular philosophy, aphorisms and brief preachments with crude Art Nouveau lettering and ornament. *The Song of Songs* (1895), printed on handmade paper with rough and arty bindings, was the first of many Roycroft books. The press became the centre of the Roycrofters, a neo-medieval community of craftsmen that operated on an apprentice system. Furniture production began in 1901; this included simplified Arts and Crafts furniture in oak and adaptations of Gustav Stickley's 'Mission' furniture. Roycroft leather and metal shops produced tooled leather goods, hammered copper and wrought-iron work, and a Roycroft Inn was established at East Aurora in 1903. Hubbard's many critics, such as C. R. Ashbee, maintained that he vulgarized the Arts and Crafts movement. Commercially successful, the Roycroft shops survived Hubbard's death, existing until 1938.

BIBLIOGRAPHY
F. Champney: *Art and Glory: The Story of Elbert Hubbard* (New York, 1968)
L. Lambourne: *Utopian Craftsmen: The Arts and Crafts Movement from the Cotswolds to Chicago* (London, 1980)

E. A. CHRISTENSEN

Hubbuch, Karl (*b* Karlsruhe, 21 Nov 1891; *d* Karlsruhe, 26 Dec 1979). German painter, draughtsman, printmaker and teacher. He studied at the Staatliche Akademie der Bildenden Künste in Karlsruhe (1908–12), where he became friendly with Rudolf Schlichter and Georg Scholz (1890–1945). From 1912 to 1914 he studied portraiture and attended life classes under Emil Orlik at the teaching institute of the Kunstgewerbemuseum in Berlin. After World War I he was a postgraduate student of Ernst Würtenberger at the Kunstschule in Karlsruhe, studying etching, woodcutting and illustration. Hubbuch's concise drawings and etchings are the most significant part of his output: like those of Otto Dix and George Grosz they are full of social criticism, but they are more briskly executed. In innumerable studies he recorded situations typical of the period, particularly scenes showing human weaknesses and life in the city (e.g. *The Dream of the Tietz Girls*, etching, 1921; see 1981–2 exh. cat., p. 123). Naive narrative pictures from the immediate post-war period were followed after 1922 by the critical, objective images for which Hubbuch is best known, among them *Knowing and Blind* (etching, 1922; see 1981–2 exh. cat., p. 130), which is closely related to his 14 etchings for an edition of Goethe's *Faust* (Karlsruhe, 1924; see 1981–2 exh. cat., pp. 128–9).

In both his graphic work and his paintings Hubbuch preferred multi-figured compositions, as in the two versions of *Hilde Twice* (1923; Munich, Bayer. Staatsgemäldesammlungen, on loan to Karlsruhe, Städt. Gal. Prinz-Max-Pal.; 1929; Lugano, Col. Thyssen-Bornemisza; see 1981–2 exh. cat., pp. 206–7), in which the artist's wife appears in duplicate as a typical female figure of the 1920s. From 1925 he applied himself to an intensive study of the techniques of the Old Masters; he studied originals and specialist literature, and tried to apply traditional techniques to contemporary subjects, as in *Experimental Pictures* (1925–34). He expressed socially committed realism and unambiguous political solidarity with the working classes in the graphic series *German Concerns* (1925–7) and *La France* (40 drawings, Karlsruhe, 1931; see 1981–2 exh. cat., pp. 249–55), but his political stance led in 1933 to the Nazis dismissing him from the Akademie in Karlsruhe, where he had been a professor since 1928. He responded to the repression of the 1930s in such paintings as *Children Growing up under Stones* (c. 1933–5; Karlsruhe, Staatl. Ksthalle), in which the ominous atmosphere is expressed through the monotonous, pale colouring used to reproduce the oppressive scenario of neglected children in front of a backdrop of mid-19th-century industrial housing.

After World War II Hubbuch continued to express his political concerns in, for example, a series of pen-and-ink drawings (1945–6) for the Antifaschistische Gesellschaft. He also returned to teach at the Akademie in Karlsruhe (1948–57). In this period he responded not only to Expressionism and the art of Max Beckmann, but also to French painting, in such works as *The Painter and his Models* (1954; Karlsruhe, Staatl. Ksthalle). In the late 1950s he again reverted to the pictorial themes and stylistic forms of his most creative phase, the period preceding the Nazi seizure of power. Characteristic of his late work are large-format colour drawings. Many of these were created while he was travelling, particularly in France (e.g. *Market Street in Paris*, oil on hardboard, c. 1958–60; priv. col., see 1981–2 exh. cat., p. 295). The theme was again frequently urban life, but despite their expressiveness these pictures do not rank with his earlier works as statements of social criticism.

BIBLIOGRAPHY

R. Reister: *Karl Hubbuch: Das graphische Werk* (Freiburg im Breisgau, 1969)

Der frühe Hubbuch: Zeichnungen und Druckgraphik, 1911–25 (exh. cat. by H. Kinkel, Bremen, Ksthalle; W. Berlin, Staatl. Museen Preuss. Kultbes.; Munich, Staatl. Graph. Samml.; and elsewhere; 1973–4)

Karl Hubbuch, 1891–1979 (exh. cat. by W. Hartmann and others, Karlsruhe, Bad. Kstver.; W. Berlin, Staatl. Ksthalle; Hamburg, Kstver.; 1981–2)

W. Hartmann: '*Kinder, die unter Steinen aufwachsen*: Ein Beitrag zu Karl Hubbuchs Tätigkeit und Ikonographie nach 1933', *Jb. Staatl. Kstsamml. Baden-Württemberg*, xx (1983), pp. 161–74

——: '*Wissend und blind*: Eine "allégorie réelle" von Karl Hubbuch', *Z. Dt. Ver. Kstwiss.*, xxxvii (1983), pp. 141–55

Karl Hubbuch: Der Zeichner (exh. cat. by W. Hartmann, Hannover, Wilhelm-Busch-Mus.; Saarbrücken, Saarland-Mus.; Kiel, Kieler Stadt- & Schiffahrtsmus.; 1991)

SEPP KERN

Huber. Swiss family of artists. (1) Jean Huber, especially gifted in the art of the SILHOUETTE, is best known for his witty paintings, cut-out profiles, prints and drawings of the writer and thinker Voltaire (1694–1778). Jean Huber's son, (2) Jean-Daniel Huber, was a landscape artist. Both were important figures in the Geneva School (*see* GENEVA, §2).

BIBLIOGRAPHY

J.-J. Rigaud: *Renseignements sur les beaux-arts à Genève* (Geneva, 1876), pp. 156–62, 232–6

D. Baud-Bovy: *Les Peintres genevois, 1702–1817 (première série): Liotard, Huber, Saint-Ours, De la Rive* (Geneva, 1903), pp. 43–74, 145–6, 164–5 [excellent pls]

Dessins genevois de Liotard à Hodler (exh. cat., ed. A. de Herdt; Geneva, Mus. Rath; Dijon, Mus. B.-A.; 1984–5), pp. 22 [colour pl.], 93–7, 146–7

D. Buyssens: *Peintures et pastels de l'ancienne école genevoise* (Geneva, 1988), pp. 77–87

G. Apgar: *L'Art singulier de Jean Huber: Voir Voltaire* (Paris, 1995)

(1) Jean Huber (*b* Geneva, 13 Feb 1721; *d* Bellevue, nr Lausanne, 21 Aug 1786). Silhouettist, painter, draughtsman and printmaker. His paternal ancestors were patrician Genevese merchant bankers. As a young man he soldiered at Kassel in Germany and in Italy, where he fought for Savoy in the War of the Austrian Succession (1740–48). In 1752 he was elected to Geneva's Council of Two Hundred and served his native city as a magistrate. He had no formal artistic training, but from his youth he clipped out of paper or cards freehand profiles of a kind that later came to be called silhouettes. He also devised what he called *tableaux en découpures*, cut in vellum or parchment on the scale of large reproductive prints; these represented antique subjects, landscapes and genre scenes, such as the *Poultry Yard* (Vevey, Fond. Cuendet; for illustration *see* SILHOUETTE).

Huber's professional artistic career began in 1759, when he met Melchior Grimm, who promoted his work among the élite readership of his cultural newsletter the *Correspondance littéraire*. In the early 1760s, through Augustus Henry Fitzroy, 3rd Duke of Grafton (1735–1811), Huber presented a cut-out battle scene to the British Museum, London, and sold a set of *découpures* to George III. Another portfolio of silhouettes was bought by George Spencer, 4th Duke of Marlborough (1739–1817). These objects have disappeared, although one of 68 large cut-outs by Huber at the Fondation William Cuendet et Atelier de Saint-Prex at Vevey closely matches descriptions of the lost British Museum piece.

Also in the 1760s Huber began to paint landscapes and hunting scenes in the style of Philips Wouwerman (e.g. *Hunting Party in Savoie*, c. 1765–70; Lausanne, Pal. Rumine). Around 1770 Catherine II of Russia commissioned from him a cycle of oil paintings depicting incidents from Voltaire's domestic life; nine of these have survived (c. 550×450 mm; St Petersburg, Hermitage). Huber made several versions of the most famous of these pictures, the *Patriarch's Morning Levée* (St Petersburg, Hermitage; Paris,

Carnavalet and Inst. & Mus. Voltaire). The scene, which was engraved in 1772 and 1776, shows the writer leaping from bed into his breeches while dictating to a secretary. The cycle was finished in 1775, by which time Huber had focused his energies on launching the career of his son, (2) Jean-Daniel Huber, and on observing the natural world, an activity that culminated in the publication of a treatise on birds of prey, *Observations sur le vol des oiseaux de proie* (Geneva, 1784).

Though often imperfectly executed, Huber's oil paintings are invariably visually inventive and flawlessly designed. His invention of the *tableau en découpure* and his devotion to landscape art, both of which became important local genres, make him an important founding figure of the Geneva School. His incisive effigies of Voltaire single him out as an innovator in the art of caricature.

BIBLIOGRAPHY

D. Baud-Bovy: *Les Maîtres de la gravure suisse* (Geneva, 1935), pp. 180–83, pl. xl
G. Jean-Aubry: 'Jean Huber ou le démon de Genève', *Rev. Paris* (1 June 1936), pp. 593–626; (15 June 1936), pp. 807–21
L. Gielly: *Voltaire, documents iconographiques* (Geneva, 1948), pls 13–39
Silhouettes et découpures genevoises des 18e et 19e siècles (exh. cat., ed. A. de Herdt and G. Apgar; Geneva, Mus. A. & Hist., 1985–6)
G. Apgar: *The Life and Work of Jean Huber of Geneva (1721–1786)* (diss., New Haven, CT, Yale U., 1988)
——: 'La *Voltairiade* de Jean Huber', *Voltaire chez lui: Genève et Ferney*, ed. J.-D. Candaux and E. Deuber-Pauli (Geneva, 1994), pp. 106–35
——: *Visualizing Voltaire: The Singular Art of Jean Huber* (New Haven and London, 1995); Fr. edn (Paris, 1995)

(2) Jean-Daniel Huber (*b* Geneva, 9 Oct 1754; *d* Geneva, 31 Jan 1845). Painter and printmaker, son of (1) Jean Huber. He was trained by his father and by Nicolas Henri Joseph Fassin, a Franco-Flemish painter who exerted a seminal influence on Jean-Daniel's Romantic coevals Pierre-Louis De La Rive and Louis Ducros. In 1773 Huber went to Rome, where he compromised a cloistered daughter of the noble Ludovisi family. A wedding ensued, but the bride remained confined and the union was not consummated until Rome fell to the French in 1797.

Most of Jean-Daniel Huber's early paintings and prints (*c.* 1770–85) were landscapes. The ephemeral blue-violet atmosphere and chromatic harmonies of *Grazing* (*c.* 1782; Geneva, Mus. A. & Hist.) were inspired by such 17th-century Dutch masters as Aelbert Cuyp and Paulus Potter (i). His landscapes are subject to confusion with those of his father, since Jean-Daniel sometimes signed his pictures *J. Huber*; but his style is less virile than that of Jean, who favoured more elegant hawking or equestrian subjects. Jean-Daniel's scenes from the Bernese hinterland (*c.* 1786–94), which earned him the nickname the 'Painter of the Oberland', are harsher and more Teutonic in character (e.g. *Village of the Oberland*; Geneva, Mus. A. & Hist.). Partly due to failing vision, Huber seems to have abandoned painting within the following decade, though he etched bucolic motifs as late as 1809. Along with De La Rive and Jean-Pierre Saint-Ours, he was an important member of the Geneva School that coalesced around 1780 under the tutelage of Jean Huber, Jean-Etienne Liotard and the connoisseur François Tronchin.

BIBLIOGRAPHY

A. de Herdt: 'Dessins champêtres de Jean-Daniel Huber, 1754–1845', *Mus. Genève*, 235 (1983), pp. 5–8

GARRY APGAR

Huber, Anton (*b* Fügen, Tirol, 1763–8; *d* Fügen, 1840). Austrian sculptor, wax modeller and painter. He trained with the wood-carver Franz Xaver Nissl the elder (1731–1804) and worked under his direction on the choir-stalls and altars of the abbey church of St Josef, Fiecht, Tirol; from his own design he produced for the church a relief of the *Entombment of Christ*. The Benedictine Eberhard Zobel (1757–1837), abbot of Fiecht, a collector and patron, took an interest in Huber, encouraging him to carve and to take up modelling. For Zobel he modelled the *Sacrifice of Abraham* in wax. In 1802 he joined the Akademie der Bildenden Künste in Vienna and in 1813 went to Passau and Landshut, finally settling in Augsburg, where he modelled the first of a series of crucifixes. *Christ on the Cross*, the figure of a boy, the figures of a man and a woman and a burlesque group of a female fruit-seller in a brawl with a Jew, all modelled in wax, are in the collection of the Tiroler Landesmuseum Ferdinandeum, Innsbruck. Huber is believed to have also worked as a painter and to have executed an altarpiece, *Christ and the Woman of Samaria* (untraced), for the abbey church of Fiecht. He was one of a group of Tirolean sculptors, including Thomas Lang (1749–1812) and Franz Christian Thaler (1759–1817), who trained with Nissl and turned to classicism after attending the Akademie in Vienna.

Thieme–Becker   BIBLIOGRAPHY
E. Egg: *Baukunst und Plastik* (1970), i of *Kunst in Tirol* (Innsbruck, 1970, 2/1973)

F. FORTER

Huber, Johann-Rudolf (*b* Basle, 1668; *d* Basle, 28 Feb 1748). Swiss painter. He was probably a pupil from 1682 to 1683 of Conrad Meyer in Zurich and then from 1684 to 1685 a student at the academy founded by Joseph Werner II in Berne. He spent the years 1687 to 1693 in Italy, first in Milan, with Tempesta, then with Giandomenico Tiepolo in Venice and finally with Carlo Maratti in Rome. Back in Basle, in 1694 he executed portraits of various members of the family of Frederick V, Margrave of Baden-Durlach. In 1696 he carried out decorations (destr.) in Stuttgart, at the residence of Eberhard-Ludwig, Duke of Württemberg. Like many artists of Swiss origin, he went to a number of cities and countries in search of work. He became the portrait painter to the patrician families of Basle, Zurich and, in particular, Berne, where he lived from 1702 to 1718. In all he probably painted more than 400 portraits of the Bernese aristocracy, though he claimed to have painted more than 5000, some of which are recorded in his *Register der Contrafeit, so Ich nach dem Leben gemahldt habe* (Berne, 1683–1718). At the end of the 17th century and during the first part of the 18th, portraits by Hyacinthe Rigaud and Nicolas de Largillière were well known in Switzerland, some having been brought back by high-ranking Swiss officers serving in France. Nevertheless, portraiture in the German-speaking cantons in eastern Switzerland remained archaic and austere in style, except, perhaps, in Berne, where the influence of the Enlightenment was felt. Huber's portrait of *Hieronymus von Erlach* (1725; Berne, Stadt- & Ubib.), for example, shows his receptiveness to the new ideas, though retaining a degree of severity. In this work the Bernese magistrate and patrician is represented by Huber in front of a table laden with the symbols of his office. Numerous portraits by Huber exist, mainly in private collections, some of them less conventional in character. Huber was also a painter of miniatures and historical subjects and executed in addition some flower and animal paintings.

WRITINGS

Register des Contrafeit, so Ich nach dem Leben gemahldt habe (1683–1718; Winterthur, Kstmus.)

BIBLIOGRAPHY

H. B. de Fischer: *Le Portrait bernois à travers les siècles*, 2 vols (Basle, 1920–21)
F. Deuchler, M. Roethlisberger and H. Lüthy: *La Peinture suisse du moyen âge à l'aube du XXe siècle* (Geneva, 1975)
Johann-Rudolph Huber, 1668–1748: Ein Maler der bernischer Gesellschaft zu Beginn des 18. Jahrhunderts (exh. cat. by H. Haeberli, Jegenstorf Schloss, 1982)

VINCENT LIEBER

Huber, Jörg (*fl* 1492–6). German sculptor. He is registered as a citizen of Kraków from 22 June 1496 and had previously lived in Passau, where he may have been born. He worked as an assistant to VEIT STOSS, signing his name with that of Stoss on the tomb of *King Kasimir IV Jagiellon* (1492) in Wawel Cathedral. Huber's signature, *Jorig Huebek von Iv*, appears on the shield of *Goliath*, one of the figures of the capitals supporting the tomb's canopy. His style can be distinguished from that of Stoss; he certainly executed the capitals and probably also collaborated on the reliefs of the tombs and perhaps also helped to devise the small scenes on the capitals. Huber may have worked under Stoss on the tomb of *Zbigniew Oleśnicki, Bishop of Kraków* (*d* 1493; completed 1496), now in Gniezno Cathedral, and may have collaborated with him on the tomb of *Peter von Bnin* (*d* 1494) in Włocławek; the inscription tablet of the tomb is stylistically very similar to the capitals of Kasimir's tomb. The *Virgin and Child* in the curve of the bishop's crook and two coats of arms at either end of the tomb may also be Huber's work.

BIBLIOGRAPHY

Thieme–Becker

M. Lossnitzer: *Veit Stoss* (Leipzig, 1912), pp. 52, 58, 61–7, 69, 73, 84–5, 120, 165
S. Dettloff: 'Zur Jörg Huber-Frage', *Dawna Sztuka*, i (1938), pp. 293–304
——: 'Das Grabmal des Bischofs Peter von Bnin in Włocławek', *Aspekte zur Kunstgeschichte von Mittelalter und Neuzeit: Karl Heinz Clasen zum 75. Geburtstag* (Weimar, 1971), pp. 31–53
M. Skubiszewska: 'Program ikonograficzny nagrobka Kazimierza Jagiellończyka w katedrze wawelskiej' [The iconographic programme of the tomb of King Kazimierz Jagiellończyk in Wawel Cathedral, Kraków], *Stud. Dziejów Wawelu*, iv (1978), pp. 117–214 [with Eng. summary]   □

Huber, Michael (*b* Frontenhausen, Bavaria, 27 Sept 1727; *d* Leipzig, 15 April 1804). German translator and art historian. He began his literary career in Paris, where he arrived *c.* 1742. He was introduced to the milieu of the *Encyclopédistes* and associated with Denis Diderot, the Comte de Caylus, the Abbé Barthélemy, Claude-Henri Watelet, Jean-Georges Wille and Pierre-Jean Mariette. Towards the end of the 1750s he contributed from time to time to the famous *Journal étranger* which introduced

German works to the French public. On the advice of Caylus, Huber translated part of Johann Joachim Winckelmann's letters as *Lettre sur Herculanum* (1764). Back in Leipzig in 1765 he began teaching French literature at Leipzig University but continued to work as a translator into French of writings on art: in 1775 his translation of Christian Ludwig von Hagedorn's *Betrachtungen über die Malerei* appeared, followed by his very important translation (1781) of Winckelmann's *Geschichte der Kunst des Alterthums*. The text he used was a composite of the Dresden edition of 1764 and the Vienna edition of 1776. In spite of its complexity, it was to serve as a model for the Italian version (1783–4) by Carlo Fea and the French edition (1790–1802) by H. J. Jansen. From 1787 until his death, Huber compiled catalogues of print collections. His great work in this field was the *Handbuch für Kunstliebhaber und Sammler* (1796–1808), a large manual of art history for collectors of engravings.

WRITINGS

ed. and trans.: Letter by J. J. Winckelmann as *Lettre de M. l'Abbé Winckelmann, antiquaire de Sa Sainteté, à M. le Comte de Brühl, Chambellan du Roi de Pologne, Electeur de Saxe, sur les découvertes d'Herculanum* (Dresden and Paris, 1764)
trans.: C. L. von Hagedorn: *Betrachtungen über die Malerei*, 2 vols (Leipzig, 1762), as *Réflexions sur la peinture*, 8 vols (Paris, 1775)
Notices générales des gravures divisées par matières, et des peintres rangés par écoles, précédées de l'histoire de la gravure et de la peinture, 8 vols (Dresden and Leipzig, 1787)
trans.: J. J. Winckelmann: *Geschichte der Kunst des Alterthums* (Dresden, 1764/R 1966, rev. Vienna, 2/1776) as *Histoire de l'art dans l'antiquité*, 3 vols (Leipzig, 1781; Paris, 1789)
Catalogue raisonné du cabinet d'estampes de feu M. Brandes, 2 vols (Leipzig, 1793–4)
C. C. H. Rost and C. G. Martini, eds: *Handbuch für Kunstliebhaber und Sammler über die vornehmsten Kupferstecher und ihre Werke*, 8 vols (Zurich, 1796–1808)
with J. G. Stimmel: *Catalogue raisonné du cabinet d'estampes de feu M. Winckler*, 4 vols (Leipzig, 1801–10)

BIBLIOGRAPHY

Mariette
G. Duplessis, E. de Goncourt and J. de Goncourt, eds: *Mémoires et journal de J.-G. de Wille, graveur du roi*, 2 vols (Paris, 1857)
C. Nisard, ed.: *Correspondance inédite du Comte de Caylus avec le père Paciaudi théatin (1757–1765)* (Paris, 1877), i, pp. 409, 423
M. Reid: *Historic Studies in Vaud, Berne and Savoy* (London, 1897), ii, pp. 406, 419
H. Heiss: 'Studien über einige Beziehungen zu der deutschen und französischen Literatur im 18. Jahrhundert, I: Der Uebersetzer und Vermittler Michael Huber (1727–1804)', *Romanische Forsch.*, xxv (1908), pp. 720–800
H. Rupp and C. L. Lang, eds: *Deutsches Literatur Lexicon*, viii (Berne, 1981), pp. 189–90

PASCAL GRIENER

Huber, Wolfgang [Wolf] (*b* Feldkirch, Vorarlberg, *c.* 1485; *d* Passau, 3 June 1553). Austrian painter, draughtsman, woodcut designer and architect. A contract of 1515, for the *St Anne* altar in Feldkirch in Vorarlberg, describes him as coming from that town; Hans Huber, a Feldkirch painter mentioned in 1491, was probably either his father or uncle. He does not seem to have trained with any well-known painter of the previous generation in southern Germany or Austria. Huber has been regarded by art historians as the next most important painter in the so-called DANUBE SCHOOL after Albrecht Altdorfer; but he was a thoroughly independent artist from the outset of his career, and even later, when he did move closer to Altdorfer in his manner, he retained his individuality, distinct from any other representative of the Danube style.

His own talent was matched by a sure recognition of artistic quality that made him turn his attention when young to Albrecht Dürer and Dürer's Italian models, though not imitatively. He strove to construct calm and unified compositions with an atmosphere of lyricism and intimacy, both in his paintings—religious subjects and portraits—and in his freehand drawings—mainly landscapes. Though Italian influences are evident in Huber's work, their manner of transmission remains a mystery.

1. EARLY WORK, TO 1521. Like other painters of the Danube school, Huber produced landscape drawings virtually throughout his life; they include his first dated works. A drawing of 1510 of the *Mondsee with Schafberg Hill* (Nuremberg, Ger. Nmus.) already shows stylistic maturity. It indicates that Huber spent some time in the Salzburg region, making it likely that he saw Michael Packer's great *St Wolfgang* altar (1471–81; St Wolfgang am Abersee). Together with the drawing *Landscape with a Bridge* (?Älpelestock, nr Feldkirch, 1515; Munich, Staatl. Graph. Samml.), it provides a solid basis in the disputed chronology of this early landscape work for grouping pen drawings with dense, regular layers of strokes; the precisely observed natural forms and the views composed with almost photographic objectivity contrast with Altdorfer's passionately experienced landscapes.

In 1515 Huber concluded a contract for the *St Anne* altar in the parish church of his native town of Feldkirch; the document mentions him however as already resident in Passau, where he was to settle permanently. From an unknown date he was court painter to the Bishop of Passau, under whose protection he long remained before acquiring citizenship and, in 1539, building-land for his own house. Before the important altar-work for Feldkirch was finally executed, he seems to have taken on other

1. Wolfgang Huber: *Raising of the Cross* (detail), oil on panel, 1.15×1.56 m, *c.* 1522–4 (Vienna, Kunsthistorisches Museum)

largish projects in Passau. The memorial picture for *Jakob Endl, Burgomaster of Passau, and his Family* (1517; Kremsmünster, Benediktinerkloster; upper part untraced) indicates the social position he occupied in his adopted home town. A few drawings with scenes from the life of Christ and four woodcuts using the same format with scenes from Christ's childhood, all from before 1520, suggest both in concept and in formal terms that Huber had made an intensive study of Albrecht Dürer's woodcuts. The lovely small picture of *Christ Taking Leave of Mary* (1519; Vienna, Ksthist. Mus.) is distinguished by the same fine balancing of figure and background, whether landscape or architecture. The same noble style recurs in the *Adoration of the Magi in the Snow* (Madrid, Pal. Villahermosa) and the portraits of the *Three Children of Marx Thenn* (1516; Frankfurt, Städel. Kstinst. & Städt. Gal.), works attributed to Huber by Stange, though their authorship remains disputed.

The *St Anne* altar itself, which is actually dated 1521, is Huber's first masterpiece. (Two wings with four panels painted on both sides, rediscovered after World War II, are on loan to the Vorarlberger Landesmuseum, Bregenz; the reverse of the shrine, with a *Lamentation*, and the reverse of the predella with the *Cloth of St Veronica*, remain in the Feldkirch Pfarrkirche; the surrounding wood-carvings are untraced.) The eight scenes from the story of St Anne and her daughter Mary have superb settings, with imposing buildings receding in perspective; Huber may possibly have had Michael Pacher's *St Wolfgang* altar in mind. The breathtaking interior views of the *Presentation in the Temple*, and particularly the *Refusal of Joachim's Sacrifice* and the *Circumcision*, had already been prepared in some freehand drawings and woodcuts; they stand on their own alongside the more or less contemporaneous attempts of Altdorfer. Huber's groups of figures were, however, influenced by Albrecht Dürer's woodcuts of the *Life of the Virgin* (1511), but he succeeded in imbuing them with a unique mood of contemplation.

2. LATER WORK, AFTER 1521. Huber's next masterpiece, the result of a commission from the administrator of the bishopric of Passau, Duke Ernest of Bavaria (1517–40), opened a new chapter in his art. The *Raising of the Cross* (*c.* 1522–4; Vienna, Ksthist. Mus.; see fig. 1) is complicated in construction and richly varied in its figure types. It is accompanied by a number of studies, some dated 1522: charcoal drawings, highlighted with white, of men's heads with grotesquely exaggerated features that immediately bring Leonardo da Vinci's character heads to mind. Huber must have somehow come into contact with Italian Mannerist painting, perhaps directly after the installation of the *St Anne* altar in 1521. While at first glance the *Raising of the Cross* may appear Gothic, its closely serried groups of figures with soldiers, some in antique armour, engaged in the most diverse activities can hardly be traced back to northern Gothic traditions. Further proof that Huber was familiar with Italian painting comes from the figure composition and the perspectival landscape in the *Lamentation* (1524; Paris, Louvre), painted, according to Rose, for Huber's patron Graf Nikolaus II of Salm.

Only three pairs of panels have survived from Huber's other altar-work of the 1520s; how they relate to one another has not been definitely established. A pair of scenes from the Passion are dated 1525 (*Flagellation* and *Crowning with Thorns*, St Florian, Augustinerchorherren-stift); the others seem of similar date (*Agony in the Garden* and *Arrest of Christ*, Munich, Alte Pin.; *Visitation*, Munich, Bayer. Nmus.; and *Flight into Egypt*, Berlin, Gemäldegal.). Comparing the Marian scenes with the *St Anne* pictures for Feldkirch, there is a perceptible simplification of means and a loss of delicacy but at the same time an increase in the spiritual intensity of the characters portrayed. Of the Passion scenes the Munich pair are the more accomplished; the St Florian scenes have a certain awkwardness. In spite of the pains taken to render the grand architectural interiors, they do not ring true spatially; the emphatic physicality of the human bodies obtrudes, detracting from the overall balance.

Likewise, in the few freehand drawings of the 1520s (e.g. *Christ on the Cross*, *c.* 1525; Cambridge, Fitzwilliam; *see* GERMANY, fig. 18), Huber's interest in the human form and its expressive values increased at the expense of the illusion of depth. These preoccupations later effectively became the true subject of the picture (as in an *Agony in the Garden* of around 1545–50; Berlin, Kupferstichkab.). A strengthened linearity and an expressive recasting of nature are also characteristics of Huber's later landscape drawings. In the last of these quite unique creations, *Infernal Castle in a Ravine* (gorge in Prätigau, 1552; London, U. Coll. Slade Sch. F.A.), a carefully selected piece of nature seems to be reduced to sheer undulating energy.

Huber began painting a series of portraits in the 1520s, nearly all showing the person half-length and three-quarter face with the background barely sketched in; they are masterpieces in their own right despite the lack of inner characterization. They include *Anton Hundertpfundt*, master of the Mint to the Duke of Bavaria (1526; Dublin, N.G.; see fig. 2), and his wife *Marggret Hundertpfundt* (1526; Philadelphia, PA, John J. Johnson col.); a portrait of *An Architect* (?*c.* 1529; ex-Rohan col., Strasbourg, destr. 1947); and the remarkable portrait of *Frau Reuss* (1534; Castagnola, Col. Thyssen-Bornemisza). The portrait of the *Architect* may have been a self-portrait, referring to Huber's appointment in 1529 as an architect for Graf Nikolaus II of Salm. Although this work is not adequately documented, it must have kept him fairly busy. Between 1529 and 1531 Huber seems to have converted the Salm seat of Neuburg am Inn, a medieval fortress, into a Renaissance palace with open arcading and loggias and had it decorated with appropriate wall paintings. He probably also worked at this period on the altar tomb for Graf Nikolaus in the Dorotheenkloster in Vienna, and on the castle at Orth an der Donau (1532) for the dead count's son. Huber is also recorded in 1541 as the city architect of Passau.

Late in his career Huber worked for Prince Bishop Wolfgang I of Salm (1540–55), thus being drawn into the political upheavals of the time. His last panel painting, the *Allegory of the Cross* (or *Allegory of Salvation*, *c.* 1550; Vienna, Ksthist. Mus.), is a votive picture of Bishop Wolfgang that illustrates a theological idea and is thus

2. Wolfgang Huber: *Anton Hundertpfundt*, oil on panel, 660×420 mm, 1526 (Dublin, National Gallery of Ireland)

perhaps more interesting historically and culturally than artistically. It illustrates the words of St Peter to the high court in Jerusalem; the words (Acts, 4: 10–12) are themselves in the picture, on a tablet bearing an inscription. It shows a wide landscape with the tall cross in the centre. The Bishop, originally seen kneeling before it, was painted over not long after the work was finished. One of the standing figures on the left edge can be recognized as Huber's self-portrait. The portrait of *Jakob Ziegler von Landau* (Vienna, Ksthist. Mus.), the theologian and humanist living in exile in Passau from 1544 to 1549, is of much greater artistic merit: in fact this striking picture of an old man, full-face before a gently animated landscape, is one of the finest achievements of early German portrait art. Another striking portrait from this period is believed to represent yet another famous exile in Passau, *Elector Otto Henry of the Palatinate* (*c.* 1545–50; Merion Station, PA, Barnes Found.).

Huber seems to have had far less impact on other artists than Albrecht Altdorfer. Two important German etchers, Augustin Hirschvogel and Hanns Sebald Lautensack, can be regarded as his direct pupils. His influence can be seen mainly in the work of Georg Lemberger but also in that of Hans Leu the younger and some other followers of the Danube school.

BIBLIOGRAPHY

Hollstein: *Ger.*; *NDB*; Thieme–Becker

H. Voss: *Der Ursprung des Donaustils* (Leipzig, 1905), pp. 13–52

R. Riggenbach: *Der Maler und Zeichner Wolfgang Huber* (Basle, 1907)

H. Voss: *Albrecht Altdorfer und Wolf Huber: Meister der Graphik* (Leipzig, 1910)

P. Halm: 'Die Landschaftszeichnungen des Wolfgang Huber', *Münchn. Jb. Bild. Kst*, n. s. 1, vii (1930), pp. 1–104

M. Weinberger: *Wolf Huber* (Leipzig, 1930)

W. Hugelshofer: 'Wolf Huber als Bildnismaler', *Pantheon*, xxiv (1939), pp. 230ff

E. Heinzle: *Wolf Huber, um 1485–1553* (Innsbruck, 1953)

F. Winzinger: 'Zum Werk Wolf Hubers, Georg Lembergers und des Meisters der Wunder von Mariazell', *Z. Kstgesch.*, xii (1958), pp. 71–94

G. Künstler: 'Wolf Huber als Hofmaler des Bischofs von Passau Graf Wolfgang von Salm', *Jb. Ksthist. Samml. Wien*, lviii (1962), pp. 73–100

A. Stange: *Malerei der Donauschule* (Munich, 1962; 2nd edn 1964, rev. 1971 by L. Seghers), pp. 96–106

P. A. Rose: *Wolf Huber Studies: Aspects of Renaissance Thought and Practice in Danube School Painting* (New York and London, 1977)

F. Winzinger: *Wolf Huber: Das Gesamtwerk*, 2 vols (Munich, 1979)

W. L. Strauss, ed.: *Sixteenth-century German Artists*, 13 [VII/iv] of *The Illustrated Bartsch* (New York, 1981), pp. 180–86

Albrecht Altdorfer und der fantastische Realismus in der deutschen Kunst (exh. cat., ed. J. Guillaud and M. Guillaud; Paris, Cent. Cult. Marais, 1984), pp. 401–31

Albrecht Altdorfer: Zeichnungen, Deckenfarbenmalerei, Druckgraphik (exh. cat., ed. H. Mielke; Regensburg, Museen Stadt, 1988), pp. 315–24

JANEZ HÖFLER

Huberti, Edouard(-Jules-Joseph) (*b* Brussels, 6 Jan 1818; *d* Schaarbeek, nr Brussels, 12 June 1880). Belgian painter. He initially studied architecture at the Antwerp Academie and, subsequently, music. It was only fairly late in his life that he decided to become a painter, with the encouragement of his friend the landscape painter Théodore Fourmois, whose work he had copied. Huberti belongs to the earliest generation of Belgian landscape painters who worked outdoors and attempted to paint what they saw as realistically as possible. He showed works for the first time at the Brussels Salon in 1857, revealing his affinity to his great model, Jean-Baptiste-Camille Corot. The influence of Corot and other Barbizon painters on his work became stronger over the years. In 1868 Huberti was a founder-member of the Société Libre des Beaux-Arts in Brussels, a group of innovative young painters, principally of landscape, who regarded nature as their only master. Alfred Jacques Verwée, Louis Artan and Louis Dubois were also members.

Huberti chose simple landscape themes for his paintings, which give a strong personal and poetic impression. A single tree in a landscape, or empty, monotonous fields with large grey, unsettled skies were favourite subjects. Almost all his work has a distinctly melancholic mood. It is difficult to trace a clear development in his style because his subject-matter varied little and he rarely dated his paintings or studies. The most important development was a gradual broadening of his brushstroke, although he never adopted a fully Impressionist technique. Huberti's work remained predominantly atmospheric, as in the paintings he made for the home of the Belpaire family in Antwerp (priv. col., see 1980 exh. cat., pp. 108–9) and *Peat Bog in the Kempen* (Antwerp, Kon. Mus. S. Kst.).

Although he made trips to France, Huberti mainly worked in Belgium. He found his inspiration in the Antwerp Kempen, the Scheldepolder, the Ardennes and the area around Brussels. He was the first painter to discover Tervuren, which then became a flourishing artists' colony. Together with the influential Hippolyte Boulenger, who also worked there, Huberti was regarded by his fellow landscape painters as the founder of modern landscape painting in Belgium. In his later life, when his melancholy had turned into severe depression, he also painted flower still-lifes. These, however, lack originality and compare unfavourably with his landscapes.

BIBLIOGRAPHY

J. du Jardin: *L'Art flamand* (Brussels, 1896–1900), iv, pp. 137–44

S. Pierron: 'Edouard Huberti', *A. Flam. & Holl.*, x (1913)

M. E. Belpaire: 'Edouard Huberti, 1818–1880', *Kst- & Levensbeeld.*, ii (1919), pp. 77–106

H. Colleye: *Edouard Huberti* (Brussels, 1943)

Het landschap in de Belgische kunst, 1830–1914 (exh. cat. by R. Hoozee and M. Tahon-Vanroose, Ghent, Mus. S. Kst., 1980), pp. 104–9

SASKIA DE BODT

Hübner, (Rudolph) Julius (Benno) (*b* Oels, Silesia [now Oleśnica, Poland], 27 Jan 1806; *d* Loschwitz, nr Dresden, 7 Nov 1882). German painter and writer. In 1821 he entered the Königliche Kunstakademie in Berlin, where he began his training under Johann Gottfried Schadow. In 1823 he transferred to Wilhelm Schadow's master-class, a move that he later said was the 'most momentous event' of his life. When Wilhelm Schadow was appointed Director at the Staatliche Kunstakademie, Düsseldorf, in 1826, Hübner and his fellow students Theodor Hildebrandt (1804–74), Carl Friedrich Lessing and Carl Ferdinand Sohn moved there to be in his classes. In the next few years Hübner became one of the most celebrated painters of the Düsseldorf school and was particularly praised for his romantic history paintings. He shared the Düsseldorf painters' tendency towards an over-dependence on literary content and a coolly academic style. His first major religious painting, *Boaz and Ruth with the Reapers in the Field* (1826; ex-Residenz-Schl., Hannover), showed a classicism that was to become more marked in later years. He is chiefly remembered for his early portraits, which are often fresh and unconventional in character. An example is *Pauline Charlotte Bendemann* (1829; Berlin, Neue N.G.), which shows Hübner's fiancée, the sister of his pupil Eduard Bendemann. After their wedding in 1829, Hübner and his wife went to Rome, where they remained until the summer of 1831. They were joined there by other painters from Düsseldorf. The group portrait of the *Bendemann Family and their Friends* (*c.* 1832; Krefeld, Kaiser Wilhelm Mus.) is a collaborative work by Hildebrandt, Sohn, Wilhelm Schadow and Bendemann after a sketch done by Hübner in Rome. He himself executed the portraits of his wife and daughter, in the centre of the painting.

Hübner spent the next years alternately in Berlin and Düsseldorf, continuing his studies at the Akademie in Düsseldorf until 1838. He painted several portraits during these years, including *Johann Gottfried Schadow* (1832) and the unconventional *Young Düsseldorf* (1839; both Berlin, Neue N.G.). The latter anticipates the portrait style of Anselm Feuerbach and Arnold Böcklin. It shows the head-and-shoulder portraits of Lessing, Sohn and Hildebrandt posed before a light-blue sky behind a parapet with an inscription in the manner of Dürer. In 1839 Hübner was appointed teacher at the Königliche Kunstakademie in Dresden, and in 1842 he was made Professor. While in Dresden, he produced a large number of history paintings with subjects taken from Romantic and, occasionally,

Classical poetry, as well as from the New Testament. The *Golden Age* (*c.* 1848; Bremen, Ksthalle), reminiscent of Gottlieb Schick's work, received a gold medal in Brussels in 1851. After 1850, however, Hübner's reputation began to fade. Such later history paintings as *Luther's Disputation with Dr Eck* (1863–6; Dresden, Gemäldegal. Alte Meister) were scarcely noted by contemporary critics and were regarded as unoriginal. Perhaps to compensate for his lack of success as a painter, he devoted much of his time to composing poetry. One of his anthologies of poetry, *Helldunkel: Aus dem poetischen Tagebuch eines Malers* (1871), was also illustrated by him. In 1871 he became Director of the Gemäldegalerie in Dresden.

WRITINGS

Helldunkel: Aus dem poetischen Tagebuch eines Malers (Dresden, 1871)
'Aus meinem Leben', *Rübezahl*, 11th ser., lxxvi (1872), pp. 443–51

BIBLIOGRAPHY

E. Scheyer: 'Julius Hübner, 1806–1882: Vom Biedermeier zur Akademie', *Aurora: Eichendorff Alm.*, xxiii (1963), pp. 55–76
Die Düsseldorfer Malerschule (exh. cat., ed. W. von Kalnein; Düsseldorf, Kstmus.; Darmstadt, Ausstellhallen Mathildenhöhe; 1979), pp. 347–9
K. Renger: '"Weil ich ein Maler bin soll ich nicht dichten . . .": Zu Julius Hübner als Buchillustrator und Poet', *De arte et libris: Festschrift Erasmus, 1934–1984*, ed. A. Horodisch (Amsterdam, 1984), pp. 369–86

Hübsch, (Gottlieb) Heinrich (Christian) (*b* Weinheim an der Bergstrasse, 9 Feb 1795; *d* Karlsruhe, 3 April 1863). German architect, architectural historian, theorist, writer and teacher. He was the son of a local postmaster and was educated in Darmstadt. In 1813 he entered the University of Heidelberg to read philosophy and mathematics. There he came under the influence of Friedrich Creuzer (1771–1858), a pioneer in the field of historiography and the empirical study of history; Hübsch later used Creuzer's theories in his approach to architectural history. After only two years Hübsch decided to study architecture under Friedrich Weinbrenner in Karlsruhe, perhaps influenced to change direction by Georg Moller, whom he had met in Darmstadt. Hübsch stayed in Karlsruhe for two years and then between 1817 and 1820 made study trips to Italy, Greece and Constantinople. Throughout his life he continued to make similar journeys all over Europe, particularly to Italy, France and England. During 1823 and 1824 he again stayed in Rome, where he mixed with the German expatriate circles and particularly with the Nazarenes. In 1824 he was called to teach at the building school of the Städel'sche Institut in Frankfurt am Main, where he stayed for three years. After the death of Weinbrenner, he became Court Architect in Karlsruhe, and in 1829 he succeeded him as Director of Building for the state of Baden. He was also head of the architecture department (1832–53) of the Technische Hochschule in Karlsruhe.

During his studies with Weinbrenner Hübsch had felt dissatisfied with the current dogma of Neo-classicism. He came to believe that the architecture of antiquity was wholly inappropriate to contemporary architectural requirements. He first put this critical attitude in writing in his treatise *Über griechische Architektur* (1822), in which he rejected the contemporary belief that the forms of Greek architecture were derived from timber construction. He repeatedly attacked Aloys Hirt, the main exponent of this belief, and Hirt's standard text, *Baukunst nach den Grundsätzen der Alten* (1809), in fiercely polemical writings. In these Hübsch discussed Greek architecture as well as the relationship between function, construction and design and the concept of organic architecture. His views culminated in the treatise *In welchem Style sollen wir bauen?* (1828), which was written as a manifesto for a meeting of Nazarene artists gathered in Nuremberg for the 300th anniversary of Dürer's birth. The manifesto not only anticipated the questions that later dominated 19th-century architecture, but it also provided the theoretical basis for the so-called RUNDBOGENSTIL (round arch style) that flourished in Germany in the second half of the 19th century. Influenced by French examples and the rational theories of Jean-Nicolas-Louis Durand, Hübsch demanded that in the planning of a building its function, not the design or style, should be the prime consideration. The questions of materials, climate, construction, durability and cost were fundamental. His insistence on rationality and function was later echoed by the defenders of Gothic and in the demand for truth by theorists such as A. W. N. Pugin and Eugène-Emanuel Viollet-le-Duc. Hübsch's 1828 essay on style, and particularly its title, was later seen by many as sanctioning eclectic historicism, but this was far from his intention. He believed that every architectural style was rooted in the specific conditions of its historical circumstances and that mere imitation of earlier forms was impossible. He advocated the *Rundbogenstil*, which was inspired by the forms of Romanesque and Byzantine architecture as well as that of early Renaissance Italy. For Hübsch, however, it was not a question of repeating historical styles but of creating a new architecture by using elements that related to modern building capabilities and requirements.

Hübsch put his theories into practice in his own buildings, in which he explored new constructional techniques and introduced the use of bare, unrendered brick and rubble masonry. Most of his secular buildings were in Karlsruhe, for example the simple Finanzministerium (1829–33) and the more ornate Technische Hochschule (1833–6; altered), now part of the University. His main work was at the Botanischer Garten, with the Staatliche Kunsthalle (1837–46; partly destr. and altered), Hans-Thoma Strasse, the theatre (1851–3; destr. 1944) and the Orangerie with greenhouses (1853–7). Hübsch developed a strong interest in polychromy, in particular in the tonal effects of brick and terracotta; many of his later buildings incorporated elaborate terracotta decoration. They were also increasingly built with segmental arches instead of round ones, as these were more suitable for brickwork. His principles of the *Rundbogenstil* were best illustrated in his design for the Trinkhalle (pump room) (1837–40; see fig.) at the spa town of Baden Baden. Its monumental arcade consisted of elegant segmental arches; the design exploited the polychromy of sandstone, brick and terracotta, and Hübsch put a strong emphasis on the decorative detail. From Karlsruhe the *Rundbogenstil* spread quickly all over Germany, particularly to Munich, where it was exemplified in the work of Friedrich von Gärtner. Having effectively ended the supremacy of pure Neo-classicism, it dominated much of Germany's architecture from the 1830s to the 1850s, although it lasted much longer as a utilitarian style.

Heinrich Hübsch: Trinkhalle, Baden Baden, 1837–40

In addition to the rational logic of his functional theories, Hübsch was also deeply interested in religion, which probably inspired his interest in Early Christian architecture, and in 1850 he converted to Catholicism. He designed a great number of churches throughout his career, most of the later ones being Catholic. For churches he used a scholarly and archaeological Romanesque Revival style and mostly the basilica plan. Typical surviving examples are the Protestant churches at Mühlhausen (1829–30) and Bauschlott (1836–8), both near Pforzheim, and St Dionys (1864) at Oos, Karlsruhe. In 1854 he was responsible for the restoration and rebuilding of the west façade of the Romanesque cathedral at Speyer, Rheinland-Pfalz. In the last five years of his life he prepared his extensive research on Early Christian architecture for publication. Published posthumously, and highly influential, this work attempted to trace the development of Early Christian architecture through documentary and comparative evidence and to assess its impact on later ecclesiastical architecture.

WRITINGS
Über griechische Architektur (Heidelberg, 1822)
Über griechische Architektur: Zweite mit einer Verteidigung gegen A. Hirt vermehrte Ausgabe (Heidelberg, 1824)
Entwurf zu einem Theater mit eiserner Dachrüstung (Frankfurt am Main, 1825)
In welchem Style sollen wir bauen? (Karlsruhe, 1828/R 1984) [postscript by W. Schirmer]
Bau-Werke von Heinrich Hübsch (Karlsruhe, 1852–9)

Die altchristlichen Kirchen nach den Baudenkmalen und älteren Beschreibungen, 2 vols (Karlsruhe, 1862–5)

BIBLIOGRAPHY
A. Valenair: *Heinrich Hübsch* (Karlsruhe, 1926)
M. Bringmann: *Studien zur neuromanischen Architektur in Deutschland* (diss., U. Heidelberg, 1968)
N. Pevsner: *Some Architectural Writers of the 19th Century* (Oxford, 1972), pp. 62–7
J. Göricke: *Die Kirchenbauten des Architekten Heinrich Hübsch* (Karlsruhe, 1974)
D. Waskönig: 'Konstruktion eines zeitgemässen Stils zu Beginn der Industrialisierung in Deutschland', *Geschichte allein ist zeitgemäss: Historismus in Deutschland,* ed. M. Brix and M. Steinhauser (Giessen, 1978), pp. 93–106
Heinrich Hübsch, 1795–1863: Der grosse badische Baumeister der Romantik (exh. cat., Karlsruhe, Stadtarchv; U. Karlsruhe, Inst. Baugesch.; 1983)

CLAUDIA BÖLLING

Hudeček, Antonín (*b* Loucká u Ředhoště, nr Roudnice nad Labem, 14 Jan 1872; *d* Častolovice, nr Rychnov nad Kněžnou, 11 Aug 1941). Bohemian painter. He studied at the Academy of Fine Arts, Prague, in 1887–91 under Maximilián Pirner, in Munich in 1891–3 under Anton Ažbé and Otto Seitz (1846–1912) and again in Prague until 1894 under Václav Brožík. He spent some time studying in Italy (1902 and 1909) and had numerous one-man exhibitions from 1900 onwards. His early work concentrated on the figure, inspired by lyrical *plein-air* painting, and for a while he was influenced by Art Nouveau and Symbolism (e.g. *Spring Fairy-tale*, 1898; Prague, N.G.).

Having come into contact with the school of Julius Mařák in 1897, Hudeček devoted himself to landscapes, producing a large group of paintings of the village of Okoř. The works of this period approach the lyricism of the Glasgow School (exhibited Prague, 1903) and the sensuous impressionism of his friend Antonín Slavíček. Hudeček gradually renounced melancholy, symbolic colour harmonies and refined techniques, using his brush with greater flourish and accenting light with more striking colours (e.g. *Cottages by the Water*, 1906; Cheb, Gal. F.A.). The end of this period coincides with Hudeček's experience of Siracusa and Capri and his use of marine motives with reminiscences of Art Nouveau decorativism and Symbolism.

Hudeček's next period, marked by a lively, colourful oil painting *In the Rain* (1909; Hradec Králové, Reg. Gal.), is linked with his stay in Police nad Metují and its surroundings, to which he returned every year until 1914. He produced paintings of the forest interior and his most important works: *Machov in the Evening* (1910; Prague, N.G.), *Road* (1906; Pardubice, E. Boh. Gal.), and *Funeral* (Brno, Morav. Gal.), which have a compact compositional structure and are based on the suggestive role of, or the almost expressive stress on, colour. In later years Hudeček drew on wider-ranging landscape subjects, beyond the boundaries of Czech landscape painting, and he ranks among the most distinguished Czech painters at the turn of the century, producing work that belongs in part to the landscape lyricism of the Worpswede colony and the Dachau colony and in part to Central European sensuous impressionism.

BIBLIOGRAPHY
M. A. Brynychová: *Antonín Hudeček* (Prague, 1942)
A. Matějček: *Antonín Hudeček* (Prague, 1947)
Antonín Hudeček (exh. cat. by J. Baleka, Hradec Králové, Reg. Gal., 1957)
JOSEF MALIVA

Hudnut, Joseph (Fairman) (*b* Big Rapids, MI, 27 March 1886; *d* Cambridge, MA, 15 Jan 1968). American teacher, writer and architect. He attended Harvard College from 1906 to 1909, before qualifying as an architect at the University of Michigan, Ann Arbor, in 1912. He was head of the Department of Architecture at Alabama Polytechnic Institute, Auburn, from 1912 to 1916 and practised as an architect in New York from 1919 to 1923, designing neo-Georgian churches, country homes and commercial buildings. Around this time he became interested in the work of the Modern Movement in Europe. Resuming his academic career, Hudnut directed the McIntire School of the University of Virginia, Charlottesville, from 1923 to 1927 and was dean of the School of Architecture at Columbia University, New York, from 1934 to 1936. In the latter school he redesigned the traditional curriculum in favour of a modern system of design education. In 1936 Hudnut became dean of the Graduate School of Design, Harvard University, where he transformed the separate disciplines of architecture, landscape architecture and urban planning into a collaborative programme, whose intention was to produce thoroughly trained professionals equipped to deal with the practical exigencies of modern times.

Hudnut was also a prolific writer, who spread the ideology of modernism effectively and is credited with coining the phrase 'post-modern' in an essay of 1945. Towards the end of his career his relationship with his distinguished colleague Walter Gropius deteriorated from initial enthusiasm at the latter's appointment to an increasing belief that Gropius's views of modern architecture were too restrictive, limiting it to investigations of technology and economics at a high spiritual cost. Hudnut's retirement from Harvard in 1953 was marked by an inimical termination of their association. Although he enjoyed little public appreciation after his retirement, he was one of the most articulate, perceptive and profound proponents of modernist architecture in the USA.

WRITINGS
Modern Sculpture (New York, 1929)
'The Post-modern House', *Royal Inst. Architects Canada J.*, xxii (1945), pp. 135–40; also in *Archit. Rec.*, xcvii/5 (1945), pp. 70-84
Architecture and the Spirit of Man (Cambridge, MA, 1949)
Three Lamps of Architecture (Ann Arbor, 1952)

BIBLIOGRAPHY
Who was Who in America, 1961–1968 (Chicago, 1968)
ANTHONY ALOFSIN

Hudson, Thomas (*b* Devonshire, ?1701; *d* Twickenham, 26 Jan 1779). English painter and collector. He was one of the foremost portrait painters in England in the mid-18th century. His work combines the high-keyed colours of the Rococo with poses derived from such artists as van Dyck, Kneller and his own teacher and father-in-law, Jonathan Richardson. He painted at least 400 portraits, about 80 of which were engraved. Among his many pupils were Joseph Wright of Derby, John Hamilton Mortimer and Joshua Reynolds. Hudson was a member of the group of artists including Hogarth, Allan Ramsay, Francis Hayman and the sculptor John Michael Rysbrack who met at Old Slaughter's Coffee House in the mid-1740s and who promoted Thomas Coram's Foundling Hospital, of which they were governors, as the first public exhibiting space for artists in London.

The earliest record of Hudson as a painter is in the accounts of the Courtenay family of Devon, where he is described in 1728 as 'Mr. Hudson ye Limner'. Among his earliest recorded works were three portraits of the Courtenays (untraced) and a *St Mary Magdalene* (possibly a portrait of his wife) known from a mezzotint by John Faber. All date from the late 1720s. Until 1740, the year Richardson retired, Hudson divided his time between London and the West Country, including the fashionable spa town of Bath. His early portraits, notably that of the marine painter *Samuel Scott* (London, N.P.G.) and the series of aldermen painted for the Guildhall at Barnstaple, Devon, in 1739–40 (Barnstaple Town Council), are solidly painted and traditional in format.

In the 1740s Hudson established himself as one of the leading London portrait painters, developing the range of portrait types that he repeated with slight variations for the rest of his career. He followed the common practice of delegating much of the finishing of his pictures to drapery painters. George Vertue first mentioned his collaboration with the notable drapery painter Joseph van Aken in 1743, adding that, since van Aken worked for several portrait painters, 'it's very difficult to know one hand from another' ('The Note-books of George Vertue', *Walpole Soc.*, xxii (1934), p. 117). Hudson's technique for painting faces, in which brushstrokes follow the direction of the facial features, remains the best guide to making attributions: he used horizontal strokes for eyes, forehead, mouth and chin; vertical for nose, cheeks and edge of the face; and angular for the area of the lower cheek and near the bridge of the nose.

Hudson's style in the 1740s is well illustrated by the formal full-length portrait of *Theodore Jacobsen* (1746; London, Foundling Hosp.; see fig.) with its nonchalant cross-legged pose and mask-like features. Less typical is the Rembrandtesque bust portrait of *Charles Erskine* (*c.* 1747–8; Edinburgh, N.P.G.). *Lady Lucy Manners* (*c.* 1742–5; Marquis of Graham priv. col.), where pose and costume are derived from a portrait of Rubens's wife, thought in the 18th century to be by van Dyck, is a good example of van Aken's contribution to Hudson's output. The drapery painter used the same format and dress in reverse for Allan Ramsay's near-contemporary portrait of *Mrs Madan* (1745; Thornton Manor, Ches).

Hudson maintained his position as a fashionable portrait painter despite van Aken's death in 1749 and continued

Thomas Hudson: *Theodore Jacobsen*, oil on canvas, 2.32×1.35 m, 1746 (London, Foundling Hospital, Thomas Coram Foundation for Children)

to rely on drapery assistants. Travels to France, Holland and Flanders in 1748 (with Hogarth, Hayman, van Aken and Henry Cheere) and to Italy in 1752 (with Roubiliac) may have influenced his work. Hudson painted several group portraits; the earliest of these, *Benn's Club of Aldermen* (1752; London, Goldsmiths' Co.), was perhaps inspired by Dutch models. In addition, his face-painting technique in such portraits as *George Parker, 2nd Earl of Macclesfield* (*c.* 1753–4; London, Royal Soc.) and in the magnificent seated full-length portrait of *George Frederick Handel* in old age (1756; London, N.P.G.) became looser and more feathery, possibly influenced by works he had seen during his travels.

The return from Italy in 1752 of Hudson's former pupil Joshua Reynolds marked the beginning of an increasing rivalry between the two painters, as Reynolds began to receive commissions from Hudson's former patrons. Horace Walpole dated Hudson's decline in fashionable esteem to the period after he finished the most ambitious of his group portraits, the *Family of Charles Spencer, 3rd Duke of Marlborough* (*c.* 1755; Blenheim Pal., Oxon). Certain later paintings by Hudson, such as the richly coloured portraits of *Thomas Hardwicke* (1757–8; London, Drapers' Co.) and *Anne, Countess of Dumfries* (1763; Exeter, Royal Albert Mem. Mus.), suggest the influence of Reynolds. Hudson, who was involved in early attempts to found a royal academy of the arts, exhibited with the Society of Artists in 1761 (its first exhibition) and again in 1766, by which time he had virtually retired to his villa at Twickenham.

Throughout his career Hudson was an avid collector of Old Master drawings and paintings as well as works by his contemporaries. Only two of the more than 200 paintings he owned have been identified, but many of the drawings, which by the time he retired made his collection probably the finest in London, can be identified by his collector's mark, TH, stamped on them. His collection of drawings was concentrated on the work of Rubens, van Dyck and Rembrandt as well as the Italian 16th- and 17th-century schools, with Guercino more heavily represented than any other Italian artist. Hudson's earliest recorded purchase was in 1741, and he began collecting on a large scale in 1747 at Richardson's posthumous sale, where he apparently bought certain lots in conjunction with van Aken. At the sale of van Aken's collection in 1750 Hudson again spent heavily. In addition to such drawings as Rubens's *Self-portrait* (*c.* 1638; Paris, Louvre), van Dyck's portrait of *Orazio Gentileschi* (London, BM) and the Rembrandt-esque *Interior with a Man Reading by Lamplight at the Fireside* (U. London, Courtauld Inst. Gals), which was highly valued in the 18th century as a genuine Rembrandt, Hudson owned large numbers of drawings by his English contemporaries, including Thornhill, Vanderbank and Rysbrack. Among his small collection of terracottas was Roubiliac's model for the Vauxhall Gardens statue of *Handel* (Cambridge, Fitzwilliam). The collection was dispersed in two sales after Hudson's death in 1779 and at a third sale after the death of his wife in 1785.

BIBLIOGRAPHY

E. G. Miles: *Thomas Hudson (1701–1779): Portraitist to the British Establishment* (diss., New Haven, CT, Yale U., 1976)

Thomas Hudson, 1701–1779, Portrait Painter and Collector: A Bicentenary Exhibition (exh. cat., ed. E. Miles and J. Simon; London, Kenwood House, 1979)

Handel, A Celebration of his Life and Times (1685–1759) (exh. cat., ed. J. Simon; London, N.P.G., 1985), pp. 39–40, 43–4, 201, 204, 206

J. Boundy: 'Two Youthful West Country Sitters to Hudson', *Apollo*, cxxiii (1986), pp. 90–91

ELLEN G. MILES

Hudson River school. American group of landscape painters active in the mid-19th century. It was a loosely organized group, based in New York City. The name is somewhat misleading, particularly in its implied geographical limitation; the Hudson River Valley, from New York to the Catskill Mountains and beyond, was the symbolic and actual centre of the school but was not the only area visited and painted by these artists. Neither was this a school in the strictest sense of the word, because it was not centred in a specific academy or studio of an individual artist nor based on consistently espoused principles. The term was in general use from the late 1870s but seems not to have been employed during the 1850s and 1860s, the most important years of the school's activities. It was initially used pejoratively by younger artists and critics who considered the earlier landscape painters hopelessly old-fashioned and insular in training and outlook. Nevertheless, the name gradually gained currency and is accepted by most historians.

Landscape paintings were created in modest numbers in America from the 18th century, but the early decades of the 19th century saw a great rise of interest in the genre. Several painters, notably Thomas Doughty, in Philadelphia, PA, and Alvan Fisher, in Boston, MA, were full-time landscape painters by 1820, but Thomas Cole was the acknowledged founder and key figure in the establishment of the Hudson River school. In 1825 Cole made a sketching trip up the Hudson River, and the resulting paintings brought him immediate fame in New York, where they were seen by John Trumbull, William Dunlap and Asher B. Durand. Cole had a competent understanding of the European landscape tradition, especially the works of Salvator Rosa and Claude Lorrain, and based his interpretation of the American landscape on such 17th-century prototypes. Painting rugged mountain and wilderness scenes, such as *The Clove, Catskills* (*c.* 1827; New Britain, CT, Mus. Amer. A.), Cole gave the imprint of established art to American nature. At the same time, such writers as William Cullen Bryant (a friend and admirer of Cole) and James Fenimore Cooper were celebrating American scenery in prose and poetry, and this conjunction of artistic and literary interests provided an important impetus to the establishment of the school.

By the late 1820s Cole was the most celebrated artist in America, and he had begun to attract followers. His ambitions led him to investigate subjects other than pure landscape, such as the *Expulsion from the Garden of Eden* (*c.* 1827–8; Boston, MA, Mus. F.A.), and also to journey to Europe in 1831–2 in search of new subject-matter. For the rest of his career, Cole divided his time between allegorical and moralizing pictures, such as the *Voyage of Life* (1839; Utica, NY, Munson–Williams–Proctor Inst.; version, 1841–2; Washington, DC, N.G.A.), and pure landscapes, such as the *Notch of the White Mountains* (1839; Washington, DC, N.G.A.), establishing a dual focus for the early years of the school (for illustration *see* COLE, THOMAS).

By the early 1840s several artists, including Asher B. Durand, John F. Kensett, Jasper F. Cropsey and FREDERIC EDWIN CHURCH, had been inspired by Cole's example to take up landscape. These men regularly showed their works at the annual exhibitions of the National Academy of Design and the American Art-Union in New York, receiving praise from critics and attracting patronage from important New York businessmen and collectors, such as Philip Hone and Luman Reed.

An increasing number of artists began painting landscapes in the mid-1840s, and after Cole's death in 1848 the school burgeoned under the leadership of Durand, who became its principal spokesman and theorist. Durand's 'Letters on Landscape Painting', published in the New York art magazine *Crayon* in 1855, cogently expressed the aesthetics of the school. Addressed to an imaginary student, Durand's 'Letters' stressed the actual study of nature, the use of meticulous preparatory sketches made on the spot, and the execution of carefully conceived studio works that captured the majestic reality and special character of the American landscape.

Although Durand painted a few imaginary landscapes reminiscent of Cole, and Church and Cropsey often invested their compositions with some of Cole's high drama and intellectual content, the appeal of the allegorical mode gradually diminished in the early 1850s. Durand ultimately concentrated on pure landscape, developing two compositional types that became characteristic of the school: the expansive landscape vista, such as *Dover Plains, Dutchess County, New York* (1848; Washington, DC, N. Mus. Amer. A.), and the vertical forest interior, epitomized by *In the Woods* (1855; New York, Met.). These compositions were further developed by other painters, especially Kensett, who, in such paintings as *View on the Hudson* (1865; Baltimore, MD, Mus. A.), combined meticulously rendered foregrounds with expansive, light-filled vistas, achieving perhaps the purest, and most complete, expression of the school's aesthetic.

In the 1850s and 1860s the Hudson River school flourished, and its most important figures, Church, Cropsey, Kensett, Sanford Gifford, Albert Bierstadt, Thomas Moran and Worthington Whittredge, many of whom maintained painting rooms in the Tenth Street Studio Building in New York, created their finest works (for illustration *see* CHURCH, FREDERIC EDWIN and BIERSTADT, ALBERT). These artists travelled widely, painting in remote regions of the northern United States, Canada, the Arctic, the American West and South America. Among others Bierstadt and Whittredge studied in Europe, occasionally painting European scenes once back in America. A number of painters, especially Kensett, Gifford and Martin Johnson Heade, were, by the 1860s, working in a manner that gave light effects predominance, leading some modern historians to isolate their work within a stylistic phenomenon called LUMINISM. Although some artists that were considered luminist painters, such as Fitz Hugh Lane, had little contact with the Hudson River school, most were part of it, suggesting that Luminism was simply one aspect of the school's approach to landscape.

The school began to wane after the Civil War (1861–5), and by the 1870s it was already considered old-fashioned. American tastes gradually shifted towards more internationally current artists in general and towards Barbizon-inspired painters, such as George Inness, in particular. Although some figures of the movement continued painting into the 20th century, the school's creative energy was largely exhausted by 1880. Interest in the school revived in the 1910s, and exhibitions in the 1930s and 1940s restored it to popular attention and historical importance. By the 1960s the school's place in the history of American art had been solidly established, and by 1980 virtually every major artist had been the subject of a monographic exhibition or published study.

BIBLIOGRAPHY
The Hudson River School and the Early American Landscape Tradition (exh. cat., Chicago, A. Inst., 1945)
J. T. Flexner: *That Wilder Image: The Paintings of America's Native School from Thomas Cole to Winslow Homer* (Boston, 1962)
B. Novak: *American Painting of the Nineteenth Century: Realism, Idealism, and the American Experience* (New York, 1969)
Drawings of the Hudson River School (exh. cat. by J. Miller, New York, Brooklyn Mus., 1969)
J. K. Howat: *The Hudson River and its Painters* (New York, 1972/R 1978)
The Natural Paradise: Painting in America (exh. cat., ed. K. McShine; New York, MOMA, 1976)
B. Novak: *Nature and Culture: American Landscape Painting, 1825–1875* (New York, 1980)
American Light: The Luminist Movement, 1850–1875 (exh. cat., ed. J. Wilmerding; Washington, DC, N.G.A., 1980)
Views and Visions: American Landscape before 1830 (exh. cat., ed. E. J. Nygren; Washington, DC, Corcoran Gal. A., 1986)
American Paradise: The World of the Hudson River School (exh. cat. by J. K. Howat, New York, Met., 1987); review by A. Wilton in *Burl. Mag.*, cxxx (1988), pp. 378–9
The Catskills: Painters, Writers, and Tourists in the Mountains, 1820–1895 (exh. cat. by K. Myers, Yonkers, NY, Hudson River Mus., 1987)

FRANKLIN KELLY

Hue. City in central Vietnam on the Perfume River (Huong Giang), 100 km south of the 17th parallel and 12 km from the coast. Between the 10th and 14th centuries, Hue was part of the kingdom of Champa. In 1306, through a dynastic marriage between King Jaya Sinhavarman III (*reg c.* 1285–*c.* 1307) and the sister of Tran Anh Tong (*reg* 1293–1314), it became part of Vietnam. Under Emperor Gia Long (*reg* 1802–20) Hue became the imperial capital of Vietnam. In 1805 construction began of the Citadel to a design by the French architect Olivier de Puymanel (1767–1800), who also designed Phien An in Saigon (now Ho Chi Minh City). Inside the Citadel the Imperial City (Hoang Thanh) was built, at the centre of which is the Purple Forbidden City (Tu Cam Thanh), where the emperor and his family lived. Both the Citadel and the Imperial City suffered serious damage during the Tet Offensive in 1968, but since the end of the American War much of Ancient Hue has been restored with UNESCO assistance.

The Citadel is almost square in shape, with a perimeter of nearly 10,000 m, and it is surrounded by walls (Kinh Thanh; see fig.(a)) 6.6 m high and 21 m wide at the base. The area inside the walls covers 520 ha. There are eleven gates, four to the south, two to the north, three to the east and two to the west. Canals run along the three sides not facing the Perfume River. The Imperial City (b) is an almost exact copy of the Imperial City in BEIJING and was

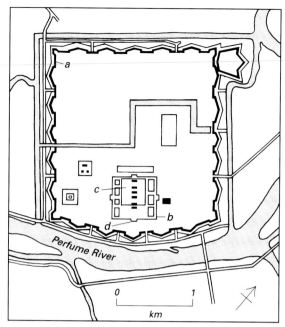

Hue, plan of the Citadel: (a) perimeter walls; (b) Imperial City; (c) Purple Forbidden City; (d) Ngo Mon gate

laid out on a site within the Citadel measuring *c.* 600×600 m in accordance with geomantic principles by virtue of which telluric and celestial powers joined harmoniously to ensure protection against evil spirits. It is surrounded by walls and defensive waterways. The walls are 4.5 m high and built of brick. They are pierced by four gates: Ngo Mon to the south, Hoa Binh to the north, Hien Nhon to the west and Chuong Duc to the east. The most important of these gates is the Ngo Mon (d), built in 1833 by Minh Mang (*reg* 1820–40). Its base of purple stone supports an elegant structure in gilded wood with three doors and a roof of glazed yellow-green tiles surmounted by the belvedere of the Five Phoenixes (Ngu Phung), where the emperor would show himself on ceremonial occasions, such as the promulgation of the lunar calendar. North of the Ngo Mon gate is the Purple Forbidden City (c), at the centre of which are the private apartments of the emperor and the Throne Room, heart of the empire and centre of imperial power. The gardens with their rocks, stunted trees and miniature lakes are representations of the mountains, forests and oceans of the cosmos. The layout of the imperial residence is in the form of an ideogram written on the ground by the emperor, for the eyes only of the emperor of heaven, from whom he was held to derive his power as universal sovereign and guardian of the cosmic order. The buildings are all arranged symmetrically on a north–south axis following the Confucian social order, with civil institutions on the left (west) and military institutions on the right (east) and men's quarters on the left and the quarters of the concubines and palace servants on the right.

The earliest temple in Hue is the Elderly Goddess (Thien Mu) Pagoda, founded in 1601 by Nguyen Hoang (*reg* 1558–1613) and situated on the Perfume River *c.* 4 km upstream from the city. Its most important building, however, is the Tower of the Source of Happiness (Phuoc Duyen), a fine brick, eight-storey, octagonal tower 21 m high, built in 1844 by Thieu Tri (*reg* 1841–7). On each storey is a Buddhist shrine, and arranged round the tower are four smaller buildings, one of which houses a great bronze bell weighing 2200 kg, cast in the early 18th century. Another building stands on a huge cosmic turtle made of marble, on which are inscribed Buddhist stelae. The Imperial Tombs lie further upstream along the Perfume River, *c.* 16 km from the city. Although the tombs are all built according to the same plan copied from the Ming Tombs, with a courtyard containing statues of mandarins, horses and elephants, a pavilion with a commemorative stele, a temple of tablets, a pleasure pavilion and a grave, each one reflects the taste of the emperor for whom it was destined.

For further discussion of the Imperial Tombs at Hue *see* VIETNAM, §II, 1(ii).

BIBLIOGRAPHY

D. Hung and Mai Ung: *Hue: Monuments of an Ancient Capital* (Hanoi, 1993)
J. Bekaert: *Vietnam: A Portrait* (Hong Kong, 1994)

NORA TAYLOR, JOHN VILLIERS

Huë, Jean-François (*b* Saint-Arnoult-en-Yvelines, 1 Dec 1751; *d* Paris, 26 Dec 1823). French painter. He was a pupil of Joseph Vernet and was admitted to the Académie Royale in 1780, his first exhibit, two years later, being *An Entrance to the Forest of Fontainebleau* (Compiègne, Château). He spent some time (1785–6) in Italy, where he painted historical landscapes in the manner of Claude Lorrain, as well as views of Tivoli and of Naples, such as *Cascade* (Tours, Mus. B.-A.) and *Tivoli* (Cherbourg, Mus. Henry). Huë's greatest claim to fame, however, was the continuation of the series of the *Ports of France*, started by Vernet; in 1791 he went to Brittany, where he painted the *Port of Brest* (three versions), the *Port of Saint-Malo* and the *Port of Lorient*, which he was to paint again when he returned there in 1801 (Paris, Pal. Luxembourg; Paris, Mus. Mar.; Cherbourg, Mus. B.-A.). He also produced historical paintings, such as the *Conquest of the Island of Grenada in 1779* (Versailles, Château) and especially depictions of Napoleonic victories on both land and sea, including the *French Army Crossing the Danube*; the *French Army Entering Genoa*; and *Napoleon Visiting the Camp at Boulogne* (all Versailles, Château). Huë was strongly influenced by Vernet, showing in his paintings the pre-Romanticism that was already apparent in his master's works; but he made even greater play with the effects of light reflected in water and the picturesque aspect of his scenes.

BIBLIOGRAPHY

Thieme–Becker

NICOLE PARMANTIER-LALLEMENT

Huelsenbeck, Richard (*b* Frankenau, Hessen, 23 April 1892; *d* Minusio, Switzerland, 20 April 1974). German writer, painter and doctor. He met Hugo Ball in 1912 and became involved with the Munich circle associated with the journal *Revolution* and Franz Pfemfert's circle in Berlin associated with *Die Aktion*. Huelsenbeck moved to Zurich in February 1916, becoming a central member of the DADA group in the Cabaret Voltaire. He returned to Berlin in late December 1916, and together with the groups involved with the periodicals *Neue Jugend*, run by Wieland Herzfelde (1896–1988), and *Die freie Strasse*, run by Franz Jung (1888–1963), he organized Berlin Dada from 1917 to 1922. His publications of this period included two versions of the *Phantastische Gebete* (Zurich, 1916 and 1920), a book of verse illustrated by Hans Arp and George Grosz, the novel *Doktor Billig am Ende* (Munich, 1921), illustrated by Grosz, and the 'Dadaistische Welt-Atlas', *Dadaco* (unpublished), as well as various polemical tracts on the movement. In 1922 he became a doctor, specializing in neuropsychiatry, and he spent much of the Weimar period as a ship's doctor. In 1936 he moved to New York, where he adopted the name of Charles R. Hulbeck and established himself as a psychiatrist, becoming involved in the neo-Freudian group of followers of the psychoanalyst Karen Horney (1885–1952). Huelsenbeck was a gifted amateur painter, producing such works as the *Lion Hunt* (oil on canvas, 1945) and a portrait of *Hans Arp* (oil on canvas, 1949; both priv. col., see W. Rubin: *Dada and Surrealism*, London, 1961, D 88 & 89, p. 428). In the period of the rediscovery of Dada in the 1960s he was a vociferous defender of the movement. Disillusionment with the USA, however, led him to return to Europe in 1969.

WRITINGS

En avant Dada: Eine Geschichte des Dadaismus (Hannover, 1920)
ed.: *Dada Almanach* (Berlin, 1920/R New York, 1966; Fr. trans., Paris, 1980; Eng. trans., London, 1993)
Mit Witz, Licht und Grütze (Wiesbaden, 1957)
ed.: *Dada: Eine literarische Dokumentation* (Reinbek, 1964)
J. Kleinschmidt, ed.: *Memoirs of a Dada Drummer* (New York, 1974)
R. Sheppard, ed.: *Zürich-Dadaco-Dadaglobe* (Hutton, 1982)
H. Kapfer, ed.: *Phantastische Gebete* (Giessen, 1993)

BIBLIOGRAPHY

R. Sheppard, ed.: *Richard Huelsenbeck* (Hamburg, 1982)
K. Füllner: *Richard Huelsenbeck: Texte und Aktionen eines Dadaisten* (Heidelberg, 1983)
U. Karthaus and H. Krüger: *Reise bis ans Ende der Freiheit* (Heidelberg, 1984)
R. Sheppard: 'Richard Huelsenbeck: Dada and Psycho-Analysis', *Litwiss. Jb.*, xxvi (1985), pp. 271–305
H. Feidel-Mertz: *Der junge Huelsenbeck* (Giessen, 1992)

RICHARD SHEPPARD

Huerta, Juan de la. *See* JUAN DE LA HUERTA.

Huet. French family of artists. (1) Christophe Huet was a painter appreciated by his 18th-century contemporaries for his animal pictures, but he is now best known for his decorative schemes in the manner of Watteau. His brother Nicolas Huet (1718–after 1788), a pupil of Jean-Baptiste Oudry, specialized in paintings of flowers and fruit. Nicolas's son (2) Jean-Baptiste (Marie) Huet I was an animal painter of some distinction, whose three sons Nicolas Huet II (*b* Paris, 1770; *fl* 1788–1827), François Huet (*b* Paris, 14 Jan 1772; *d* London, 28 July 1813) and Jean-Baptiste Huet II (*b* Paris, 29 Dec 1772) were painters and engravers.

(1) Christophe Huet (*b* Pontoise, Val d'Oise, 22 June 1700; *d* Paris, 2 May 1759). Painter. In 1734 he was admitted to the Académie de Saint-Luc; he later exhibited in the first Salons that this Académie mounted, in 1751, 1752 and 1756, showing animal paintings. In his own lifetime he was known chiefly as an animal painter, but few works by him in this genre have been identified, probably because they have been confused with those of his nephew (2) Jean-Baptiste Huet. However, his *Dog Pointing at Partridges* (1740; Nantes, Mus. B.-A.) shows the influence of François Desportes. Huet's reputation now rests entirely on the attractive interiors that he designed for various houses in and around Paris. He was responsible for the décor of a salon in the château of Champs (Seine-et-Marne), which he painted for Mme de Pompadour, and the 'Cabinet des Singes' at the Hôtel de Rohan, Paris. In 1733 he worked with Claude Audran III on the décor of the château of Anet for the Duchesse du Maine (a gilded salon, destr.). Huet is also credited with two rooms decorated with painted *singeries* in the château of Chantilly (for illustration *see* SINGERIE), which Edmond de Goncourt attributed to Antoine Watteau. In all these décors Huet featured conventional Chinese characters busily engaged in very Occidental pastimes and accompanied by monkeys imitating men. These witty scenes, painted in an alert style, without constraint and with great elegance, put Huet in the ranks of the best ornamental painters of the first half of the 18th century.

BIBLIOGRAPHY

L. Dimier: 'Christophe Huet: Peintre de chinoiseries et d'animaux', *Gaz. B.-A.* (1895), pp. 353–66, 487–96

R.-A. Weigert: 'Un Collaborateur ignoré de Claude III Audran: Les Débuts de Christophe Huet décorateur', *Etud. A.*, vii (1952), pp. 63–78

NICOLE PARMANTIER-LALLEMENT

(2) Jean-Baptiste(-Marie) Huet I (*b* Paris, 15 Oct 1745; *d* Paris, 27 Jan 1811). Painter and engraver, nephew of (1) Christophe Huet. He trained with his father, Nicolas Huet, and was then apprenticed to the animal painter Charles Dagomer (*fl* 1762–4; *d* before 1768), a member of the Académie de Saint-Luc. Huet's interest in printmaking and his acquaintance with Gilles Demarteau, who later engraved many of his compositions, both date from this period. Around 1764 Huet entered the studio of Jean-Baptiste Le Prince, where he further developed his skill as

Jean-Baptiste Huet I: *Dog Attacking Geese*, oil on canvas, 1.28×1.62 m, 1769 (Paris, Musée du Louvre)

an engraver; most of his engravings and etchings were reproductions of his own work. In 1768 he was approved (*agréé*) by the Académie Royale, and in 1769 he was received (*reçu*) as an animal painter with his painting of a *Dog Attacking Geese* (Paris, Louvre; see fig.). He first exhibited pictures at the Paris Salon in 1769. The most important of these were his *morceau de réception*, the *Fox in the Chicken-run* (San Francisco, CA Pal. Legion of Honor), and the *Milkmaid* (Paris, Mus. Cognacq-Jay). The latter is a good example of his work in the *petite manière* of genre painting popularized by François Boucher, whom he knew and admired. Huet's exhibits of 1769 were well received by the critics, especially by Louis Petit de Bachaumont and des Boulmiers in the *Mercure de France*. The quality of his animal pictures was widely praised, although Diderot made some criticisms of his draughtsmanship. Huet wanted the Académie to recognize him as a history painter, so he submitted an *Adoration of the Shepherds* to the 1775 Salon and followed this in 1779 with a painting of *Hercules and Omphale* (both untraced). Critical and academic opinion was unfavourable; however, evidence of his aspirations can be seen in his later works, an example being the Classical bas-relief in the background of the *Spaniel Attacking a Turkey* (1789; St Petersburg, Hermitage). Huet exhibited regularly at the Salon until 1789.

Wilhelm has established that between 1765 and 1770 Huet collaborated with Boucher and Jean-Honoré Fragonard on a decorative scheme for Demarteau's house in Paris. This scheme (Paris, Carnavalet), from which some elements have been lost, consists of large paintings representing landscapes and animals, against a trellis-like backdrop. From 1770 Huet published many engraved suites of his animal and compositional studies as teaching aids, himself engraving the first suite (1770). Demarteau was responsible for the second and third suites in 1772 and 1773, and thereafter various other artists undertook the rest. In 1789, at the outbreak of the French Revolution, Huet captained the town militia at Sèvres, where he had a country house. In 1800 and 1801 he again exhibited at the Salon, showing several pictures on pastoral and mythological subjects in the 'galant' mode.

BIBLIOGRAPHY

C. Gabillot: *Les Huet: Jean-Baptiste et ses trois fils, les artistes célèbres* (Paris, 1892)

D. Diderot: *Les Salons, 1759–1781*, ed. J. Seznac and J. Adhémar, iv (Oxford, 1967)

The Age of Revolution: French Painting, 1774–1830 (exh. cat., ed. F. Cummings, R. Rosenblum and P. Rosenberg; Paris, Grand Pal.; Detroit, Inst. A.; New York, Met.; 1974), pp. 494–5

J. Wilhelm: 'Le Salon du graveur Gilles Demarteau peint par François Boucher et son atelier avec le concours de Fragonard et de Jean-Baptiste Huet', *Bull. Mus. Carnavalet*, i (1975), pp. 6–20

The Age of Louis XV: French Painting, 1710–1774 (exh. cat., ed. P. Rosenberg; Toledo, OH, Mus. A.; Chicago, A. Inst.; Ottawa, N.G.; 1975), pp. 45–6

JOSHUA DRAPKIN

Huet, Bernard (*b* 14 Jan 1934). French architect, teacher and theorist. He studied at the Ecole des Beaux-Arts, Paris, but was inspired early on by the works of Le Corbusier and disliked the school's traditional approach. While on a scholarship at the Politecnico, Milan (1960), he met Ernesto Nathan Rogers, who encouraged him to rebel against Beaux-Arts architecture and in 1962 he won a scholarship to the University of Pennsylvania, Philadelphia, where he studied under Robert Le Ricolais (1894–1977) and Louis Kahn. In 1965 he ran the revolutionary teaching studio Atelier Collégial no. 1, Paris; it was run democratically by students and survived for a year. In 1968 he was asked to reform Beaux-Arts teaching. His group UP6 (Unités Pédagogiques), formed in May 1968, was based on Louis Kahn's call for an anti-monumental architecture that was responsive to local topography and materials. Finding UP6 too reductive, however, he left in 1969 to form UP8 at Belleville, Paris, later establishing the Institut d'Etude et Recherche Architecturale et Urbaine. Between 1974 and 1977 Huet was the editor of *Architecture d'aujourd'hui*, Paris, and he used his position to call for a rational reappraisal of historic buildings and planning in France. In 1981 he opened his own office, in Paris. In the same year he won a competition to convert the 19th-century Ferme du Buisson, Marne-la-Vallée, into an art and cultural centre. He placed his new building inside the restored shell of the old one, expressing his interest in conserving but not mimicking historical architecture. Another example is his restoration (1987) of the Place Stalingrad, Paris, where he designed new gardens to complement the Rotonde by Claude-Nicolas Ledoux.

Gardens held a particular fascination for him because, like cities, they develop over time. He won the Grand Prix de la Critique Architecturale in 1984.

WRITINGS
'The Teaching of Architecture in France, 1968–78: From One Reform to the Next', *Lotus Int.*, 21 (1978), pp. 36–45

BIBLIOGRAPHY
P. Davey: 'The Rebirth of the Garden', *Archit. Rev.* [London], clxxxvi/4 (1989), pp. 61–6
O. Tomasini: 'Huet: De la théorie à la pratique', *d'Architectures*, 14 (1991), pp. 28–31   □

Huet, Paul (*b* Paris, 3 Oct 1803; *d* Paris, 9 Jan 1869). French painter, draughtsman and printmaker. From an early age he painted *en plein air*, especially in Paris and its environs, in the Parc Saint-Cloud and the Ile Séguin. In 1818 he studied briefly in the studio of Pierre Guérin and from 1819 to 1822 he was tutored by Antoine-Jean Gros. In 1820 he also attended the Ecole des Beaux-Arts, and in 1822 he painted the nude figure at the Académie Suisse. Although his first works show the influence of Antoine Watteau and Jean-Honoré Fragonard (e.g. *Elms at Saint-Cloud*, 1823; Paris, Petit Pal.), the major influence was to be that of the English landscape painters, especially after

Paul Huet: *Landscape: Evening*, oil on canvas, 0.81×1.00 m, 1834 (Lille, Musée des Beaux-Arts)

his meeting in 1820 with Richard Parkes Bonington. They became close friends and often painted together in Normandy, and it is sometimes difficult to decide to whom to attribute certain of their works. At the Salon of 1824 in Paris, Huet discovered the work of Constable, and this marked a turning-point in his career: his palette became darker and his paint thicker. He quickly began to show a new sensitivity to the landscape, as is evident in *Sun Setting behind an Abbey* (1831; Valence, Mus. B.-A. & Hist. Nat.), inspired by one of Victor Hugo's poems. Huet was considered to be an innovator in the depiction of landscape in a Romantic vein, and by 1830 he had become one of the leading painters in this manner. Having made his début at the Salon in 1827, he continued to exhibit there until 1869. He also exhibited in 1834 at the Exposition des Beaux-Arts in Lille, where he received a gold medal for his painting *Landscape: Evening* (Lille, Mus. B.-A.; see fig.), an evocative composition of a woman by the bank of a stream. In 1841 he was made Chevalier de la Légion d'honneur and in 1855 showed at the Exposition Universelle in Paris, where *Flood at Saint-Cloud* (Paris, Louvre) was successfully received.

Huet travelled widely in the French provinces and was particularly fond of Normandy. In 1818, 1821, 1825 and 1828 he visited Trouville and Fécamp and, in 1829, Calais. At various times in the 1830s he was in Honfleur and Rouen, where he advised Théodore Rousseau. From 1822 he painted and sketched in the forest of Compiègne, and in 1833 he was one of the first to become interested in the region of the Auvergne. That year he also made his first trip to Avignon and Aigues-Mortes in the south of France, and he returned there in 1836. From 1838 he spent many winters at Nice, where he painted watercolours bathed in light. He also did several pen-and-ink drawings of coastal rocks (e.g. *Rocks at Nice*; Lille, Mus. B.-A.), a favourite subject of his. In 1841–3 he made an extensive tour of Italy, and in 1849 he began to paint in the forest of Fontainebleau. He returned to Normandy in the 1850s and 1860s, visiting such places as Trépont (1853) and Etretat (1868). He visited London in 1862 and Belgium and the Netherlands in 1864 to see the works of Rembrandt and Rubens. On all of his trips he painted and sketched extensively in watercolour, pastel and pencil. He was especially adept at painting in watercolour, a medium that he had mastered at an early age and to which he lent his own innovative quality. Throughout his career he was primarily concerned with interpreting variations in atmosphere, expressing the moods of nature and seeking out the contrasts of light and shade that occur in forests, storms and floods (e.g. *The Abyss: Landscape*, 1861; Paris, Louvre). He applied his paint in a thick impasto to enable him to render the play of light. His style of landscape painting influenced the work of the members of the Barbizon school, as well as that of the Impressionists. He was a close friend of Delacroix, and he also knew the writers Alphonse de Lamartine, Charles-Augustin Sainte-Beuve, Victor Hugo, Jules Michelet and the sculptor David d'Angers. He also produced wood-engravings and lithographs (e.g. *The Heron*, 1833) in which he experimented with contrasts of light and dark and of tones, and in 1831 he contributed illustrations to *Voyages pittoresques et romantiques dans l'ancienne France* (Paris, 1820–78) by Baron Isidore-Justin-Séverin Taylor and Charles Nodier. His son René-Paul Huet (*b* 1844) was also a painter and was his pupil.

BIBLIOGRAPHY
L. Delteil: *Le Peintre-graveur Paul Huet*, vii (Paris, 1911)
R.-P. Huet: *Paul Huet: D'après ses notes, sa correspondance, ses contemporains* (Paris, 1911)
P. Miquel: *Paul Huet: De l'aube romantique à l'aube impressionniste* (Paris, 1962)
Paul Huet (exh. cat., Rouen, Mus. B.-A., 1965)
P. Miquel: *Le Paysage français au XIXe siècle, 1824–1874* (Maurs-la-Jolie, 1975), pp. 194–247

LAURENCE PAUCHET-WARLOP

Huetter, Sigmund. *See under* MASTERS, ANONYMOUS, AND MONOGRAMMISTS, §I: MASTER OF THE FREISING VISITATION.

Huffel, Albert van. *See* VAN HUFFEL, ALBERT.

Hugford, Ignazio Enrico (*b* Florence, 1703; *d* Florence, 16 Aug 1778). Italian collector, dealer, painter and writer of English parentage. He studied painting with Anton Domenico Gabbiani (whose life he later wrote). Like his master, he specialized as a religious painter and copyist, but such works as *The Annunciation* (Florence, S Jacopo Soprarno) are no more than competent reworkings of Gabbiani, and Hugford enjoyed only local fame. In 1729 he became a member of the Florentine Accademia del Disegno (and in 1762 was elected its *provveditore*). He also taught at the Accademia di S Luca, where Francesco Bartolozzi and Giovanni Battista Cipriani were among his pupils. In the late 1720s Hugford began to form a collection of paintings, engravings and drawings and to act as an intermediary and dealer in art. In 1729 and 1737 he exhibited a collection of drawings that he attributed to Hans Holbein the younger. These have since been identified as French drawings of the school of François Clouet, which had been sorted and annotated by Catherine de' Medici, and which Hugford must have acquired through Gian Gastone de' Medici, Grand Duke of Tuscany; there is a large collection of these drawings in the Musée Conde, Château de Chantilly. Hugford sold many of the 'Holbein' drawings to English collectors, such as Horace Mann who in 1740 bought some of them on behalf of Horace Walpole.

Subsequently Hugford became celebrated as a dealer in and collector of Italian paintings of the Quattrocento. Although his activities in this field are not yet fully documented, he certainly owned in 1767 a *Self-portrait* by Masaccio (now thought to be by Filippino Lippi), and a *St Augustine* by Lippi (now thought to be by Botticelli; both paintings Florence, Uffizi). Some 3000 of Hugford's large collection of drawings were bought in 1779 from his executor by the Uffizi.

Hugford's elder brother, Ferdinando Enrico (Don Enrico) Hugford (1695–1771), a Benedictine monk, was also an artist, working in SCAGLIOLA.

WRITINGS
Vita di Anton Domenico Gabbiani, pittor fiorentino, descritta da Ignazio Hugford suo discepolo (Florence, 1762)

BIBLIOGRAPHY

DNB

J. Fleming: 'The Hugfords of Florence', *Connoisseur*, cxxxvi (1955), pp. 106–07, 197–206 [incl. provisional cat. of Hugford's col.]

M. Chiarini: 'Inediti de settecento fiorentino: Antonio Domenico Gabbiani, Ignazio Hugford, Gian Domenico Ferretti', *Scritti di storia dell'arte in onore di Ugo Procacci*, ed. M. G. C. D. Dal Poggetto (Milan, 1977), pp. 586–91

F. Borroni Salvadori: 'Ignazio Enrico Hugford: Collezionista con la vocazione del mercante', *An. Scu. Norm. Sup. Pisa*, n. s. 2, xiii/4 (1983), pp. 1025–56

——: 'Ignazio Enrico Hugford: Collectionneur de portraits', *Gaz. B.-A.*, n. s. 5, cii (1983), pp. 165–8

☐

Huggins, William John (*b* London, 1781; *d* London, 19 May 1845). English painter. After several years at sea in the service of the East India Company, he settled in London. His house at 36 Leadenhall Street was near East India House, and he was regularly employed to paint carefully detailed pictures of the company's ships. He exhibited 16 marine paintings at the Royal Academy between 1817 and 1844 and also showed at the British Institution and Suffolk Street. He was appointed Marine Painter to William IV in 1834, his royal commissions include three paintings of the *Battle of Trafalgar*, which now hang at Hampton Court. His daughter married Edward Duncan (1803–82), a talented watercolourist and engraver who engraved many of Huggins's paintings and sometimes acted as his assistant. The National Maritime Museum, Greenwich, has 26 of his works, mostly ship portraits of East Indiamen.

Though his seas and skies are well observed, Huggins's ships have a curiously naive quality and look more like models than real ships. They are, however, carefully drawn, and it is this precision, combined with his bright, clear colouring, which gives his best work a charming decorative appearance.

BIBLIOGRAPHY

Archibald

D. Cordingly: *Marine Painting in England, 1700–1900* (London, 1974)

DAVID CORDINGLY

Hughes, Arthur (*b* London, 27 Jan 1832; *d* Kew Green, London, 22 Dec 1915). English painter and illustrator. In 1846 he joined the School of Design at Somerset House, London, under Alfred Stevens (ii). The following year he won an art studentship to the Royal Academy Schools, where in 1849 he won the silver medal for antique drawing. In the same year he showed his first painting at the Royal Academy, *Musidora* (Birmingham, Mus. & A.G.), a conventionally painted nude. In 1850, while still a student, he saw a copy of the periodical *The Germ*, which converted him to PRE-RAPHAELITISM and led to his meeting William Holman Hunt, Dante Gabriel Rossetti and Ford Madox Brown, though he never became an official member of the Pre-Raphaelite Brotherhood. Hughes's first exhibited work in the new style, *Ophelia* (exh. RA 1852; Manchester, C.A.G.), was admired by Millais, whose own *Ophelia* (1851–2; London, Tate) was in the same exhibition. They became friends and Hughes sat for Millais's *The Proscribed Royalist* (exh. RA 1853; priv. col., see 1984 exh. cat., p. 104). From about 1852 to 1858 Hughes shared a studio with the sculptor Alexander Munro.

Hughes's paintings of the 1850s and early 1860s were heavily indebted to Hunt, Rossetti and above all to Millais for their subjects, motifs and technique. Nevertheless, in these works he expressed a mood of intimate tenderness that bore his own personal stamp. His paintings, usually on a modest scale, were often highly charged with emotion. Hughes loved the soft effects of moonlight, sunset and firelight, and he was skilled at depicting naturalistic detail and texture. His use of bright Pre-Raphaelite greens, purples and blues was particularly delicate and glowing.

Among his most memorable modern dress subjects are scenes of unhappy courtship, suggested by Millais's paintings and drawings of anguished lovers: for example, *April Love* (exh. RA 1856; London, Tate), *The Long Engagement* (exh. RA 1859; Birmingham, Mus. & A.G.) and *Aurora Leigh's Dismissal of Romney* (1860; London, Tate). All convey strong emotion heightened by the use of colour. Also inspired by Millais were subjects showing the tender feelings of childhood, often painted with a childlike delight in the details of flowers, animals and birds. They show children from humble families such as *The Woodman's Child* (1860; London, Tate), *Home from Work* (exh. RA 1861; New York, Forbes Mag. Col.) and the triptych *Bedtime* (exh. RA 1862; Preston, Harris Mus. & A.G.). Most poignant of the childhood subjects is *Home from Sea* (exh. RA 1863; Oxford, Ashmolean), showing a sailor boy weeping over his mother's freshly turfed grave while his sister, dressed in black, kneels near by.

Hughes painted a great many medieval subjects. The romantic, fairytale vision of the Middle Ages in his triptych to Keats's *The Eve of St Agnes* (exh. RA 1856; London, Tate; see fig.) owes much to Hunt and Millais. Rossetti's invitation to paint *The Passing of Arthur* at the Oxford Union in 1857 led to his interest in chivalric subjects. Most notable of these was *The Knight of the Sun* (1860; Lucerne, W. N. M. Hogg priv. col., see 1984 exh. cat., p. 187) in which an aged knight is carried out of doors for his last glimpse of a glorious sunset. Hughes also painted several pictures of dreamy figures in medieval dress making music, such as *The Rift in the Lute* (exh. RA 1862; Carlisle, Mus. & A.G.). In all these subjects the landscape settings contribute to the poetic mood. Most of Hughes's patrons came from a restricted circle of Pre-Raphaelite collectors and included William Morris, J. H. Trist of Brighton, Thomas Plint, James Leathart and Ellen Heaton of Leeds.

In the mid-1860s Hughes's art lost its intensity of vision and its precision of handling. He continued to paint subjects in medieval dress such as *Sir Galahad* (exh. RA 1870; Liverpool, Walker A.G.) and some in 16th-century costume such as *The Convent Boat* (exh. RA 1874; priv. col., see 1971 exh. cat., repr. on front cover). He also produced a number of group portraits such as *Mrs Leathart and Children* (exh. RA 1865; Newcastle upon Tyne, Leathart family priv. col., see 1968 exh. cat., pl. 8), painted after a visit to Italy in 1862. Though attractive, these portraits are in a self-consciously posed style that lacks the intimate mood of the early paintings.

Hughes continued to exhibit at the Royal Academy until 1908 but his late oil paintings are disappointingly weak. Nevertheless, much of his original delicacy of feeling survived in his many black-and-white illustrations, those for children's books being of particular charm. His first illustrations were for William Allingham's *The Music Master* (1855). He also worked for the periodical *Good*

Arthur Hughes: *The Eve of St Agnes*, oil on canvas, 710×1245 mm, 1856 (London, Tate Gallery)

Words for the Young from 1869, and among his most successful book illustrations were those for Tennyson's *Enoch Arden* (1866), Thomas Hughes's *Tom Brown's Schooldays* (1869), George Macdonald's *At the Back of the North Wind* (1871) and Christina Rossetti's *Sing Song* (1872) and *Speaking Likenesses* (1874). He also provided stained-glass designs for Morris & Co. For about ten years he was an examiner for the South Kensington art schools, and in the 1860s he had a few pupils including the watercolourist Albert Goodwin.

BIBLIOGRAPHY

DNB

F. Reid: *Illustrators of the Sixties* (London, 1928), pp. 83–95

The Leathart Collection (exh. cat. by N. Johnson, Newcastle upon Tyne, Laing A.G., 1968), pp. 19–22

R. Gibson: 'Arthur Hughes: Arthurian and Related Subjects of the Early 1860s', *Burl. Mag.*, cxii (1970), pp. 451–6

Arthur Hughes (exh. cat. by L. Cowan, Cardiff, N. Mus., 1971)

The Pre-Raphaelites (exh. cat., ed. L. Parris; London, Tate, 1984)

For further bibliography see W. E. Fredeman: *Pre-Raphaelitism: A Bibliographical Study* (Cambridge, MA, 1965)

JULIAN TREUHERZ

Hughes, John (*b* Dublin, 1865; *d* Nice, France, 1941). Irish sculptor. He entered the Metropolitan School of Art in Dublin in 1878, attending as a part-time student for ten years. His influences were mainly from the Italian Renaissance, and he retained his love for the work of Jacopo della Quercia throughout his life. In 1890 he won a scholarship to the South Kensington School of Art, London, where he studied under Edouard Lanteri. A period of study followed in Paris and Italy, and after a year teaching at Plymouth Technical School he was appointed to the Metropolitan School of Art in Dublin in 1894 and became Professor of Sculpture in the Royal Hibernian Academy Schools. *Napoli* (1900; Dublin, N. Mus.), a

small bronze also known as the *Mandolin Player*, shows his continual preoccupation with Italian models and makes particular reference to Donatello's *David*.

In 1901 Hughes resigned his teaching post to start work on two of his most successful commissions, the *Man of Sorrows* and *Madonna and Child*, for Loughrea Cathedral. In 1903, the year in which he carved his masterpiece *Orpheus and Eurydice* (marble; Dublin, Hugh Lane Mun. Gal.), he settled in Paris, but he continued to exhibit in Dublin and at the Irish exhibitions in Paris and Brussels in 1922 and 1930. He produced portrait busts of people active in Dublin's cultural life, such as *AE (George Russell)* (1885–6; Dublin, Hugh Lane Mun. Gal.), but was less original in official commissions such as the memorial to *Queen Victoria* (1901–6; ex-Dublin, Kildare Street, now Sydney, Queen Victoria Bldg).

BIBLIOGRAPHY

AE [G. Russell]: 'An Irish Sculptor: John Hughes RHA', *J. & Proc. A. & Crafts Soc. Ireland* (1898), pp. 243–8

A. Denson, ed.: *John Hughes, Sculptor, 1865–1941: A Documentary Biography* (Kendal, 1969)

Irish Art in the 19th Century (exh. cat. by C. Barrett, Cork, Crawford Mun. A.G., 1971)

A. Crookshank: *Irish Art from 1600 to the Present Day* (Dublin, 1979), pp. 60–61

Hughes, Richard (Henry) (*b* London, 4 July 1926). Kenyan architect of English birth. In 1937 he emigrated with his parents to Kenya and was educated there and in South Africa. He then studied at the Architectural Association School, London (1947–53). After working for a period in the USA with Henry J. Ludorf in Hartford, CT (1953–5), he returned to Kenya and joined Blackburn & Norburn in Nairobi (1955–7) before setting up in private practice in Nairobi (1957–76), interrupted by a brief partnership (1976–8) with Brian Arthur Smith. His earliest independent buildings were one-family houses, hospitals and schools (e.g. Alliance Girls' High School Chapel and other buildings (1957–74), Kikuyu, Kenya) produced on spartan budgets and noteworthy for their pared-down, functional design and use of local materials. In 1953 he published theories on how Kenya's three races might live together in harmony by way of new and integrated town and rural settlements, and he went on to design several examples, such as the houses (1968) at Moi Estate, Nairobi. Between 1960 and 1970 he built a number of churches, including those in the Kilifi, Embu, Meru and Kikuyu areas, whose massive quality was rigorously expressed in natural stone. Although he developed projects in other parts of Africa, the bulk of Hughes's work was executed in Kenya during an important period in the country's growth. While he retained a concern for both economic and environmental appropriateness of design, his commercial buildings in Nairobi also reveal his creative skills, from the Television Studios designed in 1962 to the giant, sculptural National Bank of Kenya building (1977), where he used just two materials, dark brown glass and concrete, and once again displayed abrasively economical construction methods. Hughes was also involved in a number of environmental projects, such as the studies in the early 1970s for the development of Lamu township and the restoration of its ancient houses and buildings.

WRITINGS

'Town Plan to Facilitate Racial Integration', *New Commonwealth* (Sept 1953)

BIBLIOGRAPHY

U. Kultermann: *New Architecture in Africa* (London, 1963)
——: *New Directions in African Architecture* (London, 1969)
J. Lawrence: 'Richard Hughes: A Man for All Reasons', *Bld Kenya*, iii/27 (June 1978), pp. 17–18

□

Hughes, Trajan (*fl* 1709–12). ?Welsh painter. He is known only by two very accomplished signed works, *Cat and Fish* (priv. col., see Waterhouse, p. 186) and *Foxglove in a Wooded Landscape* (priv. col., see 1987 exh. cat., no. 7); further examples are likely to come to light. These two works suggest Hughes, who may have been a gifted amateur rather than a professional artist, had some knowledge of the animal painter Francis Barlow.

BIBLIOGRAPHY

Waterhouse: *18th C.*
M. H. Grant: *The Old English Landscape Painters* (London, 1958), ii, p. 104
Manners and Morals: Hogarth and British Painting, 1700–1760 (exh. cat., ed. E. Einberg; London, Tate, 1987)

MARC JORDAN

Hugh of Le Puiset, Bishop of Durham and Earl of Northumberland [Hugh du Puiset, Bishop Pudsey] (*b c.* 1125; *d* 1195). English bishop and patron. A nephew of King Stephen and HENRY OF BLOIS, Bishop of Winchester, Hugh of Le Puiset probably owed his position to his high birth. In 1153 he was created Bishop of Durham, then one of the wealthiest sees in England; unusually its bishop was a great secular as well as a spiritual lord. According to a contemporary chronicler, William of Newburgh, Hugh aspired to the ranks of the greatest, but although an able administrator and one of the richest men in England, he was less successful in politics. Nevertheless, he used his wealth in a princely manner to give an impression of greatness, apparently following the example of Henry of Blois. His reputation as a patron of the arts, especially in respect to architecture, was such that local chroniclers listed his buildings before his political achievements.

The scale of Hugh's patronage has sometimes been exaggerated, but even if the list of his works is rigorously reduced it remains impressive. He can be credited with the following religious buildings: the Galilee Chapel in Durham Cathedral, the hospitals at Kepyer (a refoundation) and Sherburn, both close to Durham, and at least two parish churches, Grindon and St Cuthbert's, Darlington. His secular works include refitting Durham Castle; rebuilding the castles of Norham and Northallerton and the borough of Elvet in Durham, with part of its city walls; and building Elvet Bridge. He is also said to have refitted several of his manors, of which he had at least six, including those at Howden in Yorkshire, Gateshead, Darlington and Bishop Auckland. These works may have been carried out by a group of builders who learnt their idiosyncratic style in Yorkshire but who may also have been influenced by work carried out in the south for Henry of Blois. Within the context of Late Romanesque and Early Gothic architecture, Hugh's buildings show considerable variety of style and degree of decoration; it seems that the purpose of a building was an important factor in deciding its character. This is seen in the grandeur of the great doorway in Durham Castle and the spaciousness of the Galilee Chapel (probably executed in the late 1160s and early 1170s, respectively), in the elaborate decoration of the chancel of St Cuthbert's, Darlington, and in the simplicity of design, combined with rich materials of the hall (now the chapel) at Bishop Auckland Palace. Both these buildings were built in an Early Gothic style and were probably unfinished at Hugh's death.

Hugh may have been responsible for a stone screen in Durham Cathedral; he certainly embellished the cathedral with coloured glass and had a rich reliquary made for the bones of St Bede and the monk Girwen. These were all destroyed at the Reformation, as many of the other rich objects, provided by Hugh both for his foundations and for himself, must have been. He gave many illuminated books to the cathedral but only three volumes survive: two volumes of the Puiset Bible (Durham, Archdeacon Sharpe Lib. MS. A.II.1) in their original bindings, one of which retains its decorated clasp, and a book of the Pauline epistles (Durham, Archdeacon Sharpe Lib. MS. A.II.19). Details of the foliage patterns in the Pauline epistles correspond closely to the frieze above the figures of a knight and a bishop painted on the east wall of the Galilee Chapel; these may also have formed part of Hugh's patronage.

William of Newburgh indicated that Hugh gave much thought to his patronage, but he considered that in building on earth Hugh had neglected to build in heaven. Although many of Hugh's works are lost, the quality and scale of those that remain ensure his place among the most notable patrons of the 12th century.

BIBLIOGRAPHY

W. D. H. Longstaffe: 'Bishop Pudsey's Buildings in the Present County of Durham', *Trans. Archit. & Archaeol. Soc. Durham & Northumb.*, i (1862), pp. 1–8

R. A. Mynors: *Durham Cathedral Manuscripts to the End of the Twelfth Century* (Oxford, 1939)

G. V. Scammell: *Hugh du Puiset, Bishop of Durham* (Cambridge, 1956)

J. A. Cunningham: *The Extent of Episcopal Patronage in the North of England in the Second Half of the Twelfth Century* (MA thesis, Courtauld Inst., U. London, 1976)

——: 'Hugh of Le Puiset and the Church of St Cuthbert, Darlington', *British Archaeological Association Conference Transactions, III. Medieval Art and Architecture at Durham Cathedral: Durham, 1977*, pp. 163–9

JANE CUNNINGHAM

Hugnet, Georges (*b* Paris, 11 July 1906; *d* Paris, June 1974). French writer and collagist. He spent his childhood in Argentina, moving to Paris at the age of 16. He greatly admired Dada, which was by then largely exhausted in Paris. In 1928 he collaborated with Henri d'Arche on the film *La Perle* and soon after became involved in Surrealism, joining the group in 1930. He met many of its members, including André Breton, Paul Eluard, Miró and Yves Tanguy, who regularly gathered at his bookshop in the Boulevard Montparnasse. He was mainly occupied as a poet and writer, though he also took part in other Surrealist activities such as producing collages. He participated in the Surrealist exhibition at the Galerie Pierre Colle in Paris (1933) and also in the International Surrealist Exhibition at the New Burlington Galleries, London (1936). During his association with Surrealism, Hugnet became one of the movement's chief apologists. He contributed articles to the catalogue of the *Fantastic Art, Dada, Surrealism* exhibition at MOMA, New York (1936), and also to Herbert Read's book *Surrealism* (London, 1936). In addition he edited the *Petite Anthologie poétique du surréalisme* (Paris, 1934).

Of his several volumes of poetry, one of the most interesting is *La Septième Face du dé* (1936), of which only 294 copies were produced, some with covers by Duchamp. This comprises 90 pages of 'poèmes-découpages', in which words are cut out, often 'ready-made', from magazines and newspapers and arranged around photomontages. The title, the text and its layout owe much to Stéphane Mallarmé's 'Un Coup de dés jamais n'abolira le hasard', whilst the eroticism and reliance on imagery derive from Surrealists such as Breton and Eluard. The use of chance and the popular sources of both the words and images are Surrealist hallmarks. About 1936 Hugnet conceived the idea of the 'objet-livre', a variation on the Surrealist object. These were books whose bindings had an oblique, surreal relation to the content. For example, he bound a copy of Eluard's *Défense de savoir* (1928) in covers made of cracked glass plates (see exh. cat., p. 262). In his article 'L'Objet utile' (1935) he wrote 'There are no useless objects. Those which may seem so only prove the wretchedness of our conception of the real ... Poetry has transcended metaphor in making the object the object of its curiosity.' Like many Surrealists, Hugnet also made 'decalcomanias', produced by the smudging of paint between paper, one of which was included in *Minotaure* (1936, no. 8). In some of these he added collage elements, as in *Les Charmes des saisons* (1937; see Pierre, p. 82). Hugnet exhibited at the important *Exposition Internationale du Surréalisme* at the Galerie Beaux-Arts in Paris in 1938. This marked the high point of the Surrealists' fascination with the object and Hugnet showed the work *The Table is Set*, in which a female wax figure was sunk up to her waist in a black velvet-covered table. The same year he organized an exhibition of the same name at the Galerie Robert in Amsterdam.

Hugnet was expelled from the Surrealists in August 1938 after a dispute with Breton. The following year he founded the literary review *L'Usage de la Parole*, whose only issue was published in that December. He continued producing poetry inspired by Surrealist theory and also became increasingly interested in the historical development of Dada. In 1932 and 1934 he had published a series of articles in *Cahiers d'Art* entitled 'L'Esprit Dada dans la peinture', criticized by Tristan Tzara in 1937. With the publication of *L'Aventure Dada, 1916–1922* in 1957 he established himself as the official chronicler of the movement.

WRITINGS

'L'Objet utile: A propos d'Oscar Dominguez', *Cah. A.*, x (1935), nos 5–6, p. 139

La Septième Face du dé: Poèmes-découpages (Paris, 1936)

L'Aventure Dada, 1916–1922 (Paris, 1957)

Pleins et déliés, souvenirs et témoinages (Paris, 1972)

BIBLIOGRAPHY

W. S. Rubin: *Dada and Surrealist Art* (New York, 1968)

J. Pierre: *L'Aventure surréaliste autour d'André Breton* (Paris, 1986)

Focus on Minotaure: The Animal Headed Review (exh. cat., Geneva, Mus. A. & Hist., 1987)

H. Okun: *The Surrealist Object* (Ann Arbor, 1988)

Hugo. French family of writers and artists.

(1) Victor(-Marie) Hugo (*b* Besançon, 26 Feb 1802; *d* Paris, 22 May 1885). Writer and draughtsman. Quite apart from his vast literary output, he produced around 3000 drawings in various sizes and techniques. They constitute a fairly homogeneous body of work, comprising a mass of comic or grotesque sketches, which are not caricatures properly speaking, views of landscapes and buildings drawn from life or imagination (among them a large number of travel notes) and more delicate works typical of the artistic genres of the time. He was daringly experimental in technique, employing cut-outs, often used as stencils, impressions taken from fabric or natural objects, inkblots more or less reworked and every sort of graphic caprice.

Hugo began to draw seriously from about 1825 with some rather sketchy sheets, but he took 20 years to find a personal repertory and style. Although his taste for the picturesque and search for dramatic effects shows an affinity with Romantic imagery, his drawings go further in their energy, freedom of means and exceptionally intense sense of mystery. From about 1845 these were the dominant characteristics of his work, which persisted without major change for 30 years. Hugo's production continued at an uneven pace, often at its most intense during lulls in his writing (1850), gaining in fluidity during his exile in Jersey and Guernsey (1853–70), when he was confronted by the spectacle of sky and ocean, returning in the 1860s to the picturesque and satirical tendencies of his youth and finally dying away, as his literary output did, after 1875–7.

In Hugo's profoundly Romantic art, all is growth and metamorphosis. The unfinished nature of the forms and the floating or circulating pattern of movement in his drawings speak of an unfettered imagination attempting to come to terms with the infinite universe. The famous inkblot drawings (mostly concentrated in his notebooks of 1856–7) were dictated by chance and daydreaming. Their linear equivalents were improvised fantasies, in which jagged silhouettes were arbitrarily scribbled down and then completed with a few more intelligible details. The 'caricatures' have a less contingent relationship with reality, although they rarely concern precise models, and fantasy and the pleasure of invention probably often preceded satirical intent. A caption, usually at the expense of foolishness and authority, generally supplied the latter.

The superficially flippant turns of phrase used by Hugo to describe his 'scribbles' express his puzzlement when confronted by products that contemporary artistic concepts could only comprehend with difficulty. He spoke of 'hours of almost unconscious dreaming' in which he drew freely, liberated from the framework of rational thought as from social norms and constraints. Hugo's drawings have the emotional charge and revelatory power of 'automatic writing' before its time. Indeed, many remain unsettling and have only become legible since the aesthetic revolutions of the 20th century, especially Surrealism and *Art informel*.

Hugo's prodigious literary output provided ample material for the great French illustrators of the Romantic era. One of Hugo's favourite illustrators and a member of his circle was Célestin Nanteuil (1813–73), who etched frontispieces for *Notre-Dame de Paris* (1832), *Lucrèce Borgia* (1833) and *Marie Tudor* (1833). Outstanding later illustrated editions of *Notre-Dame de Paris* were produced in 1836 (Louis Boulanger and the Johannot Brothers), 1844 (Aimé de Lemud, 1816–87) and 1889 (Luc Olivier Merson). Hugo's own drawings were reproduced in wood- and steel-engravings in *Dessins de Victor Hugo* (1862), and they were also used, together with designs by François Chifflart and Daniel Urrabieta y Vierge (1851–1904), in the 1882 edition of *Les Travailleurs de la mer*.

WRITINGS
Oeuvres complètes (Paris, 1969–76/R 1980), xvii–xviii

PRINTS
Oeuvres complètes (Paris, 1969–76/R 1980), i–xvi

BIBLIOGRAPHY
Drawings by Victor Hugo (exh. cat. by P. Georgel, London, V&A, 1974)
P. Georgel: *Les Dessins de Victor Hugo pour 'Les Travailleurs de la mer'* (Paris, 1985)
G. Picon: *Victor Hugo, dessinateur* (Paris, 1985)
La Gloire de Victor Hugo (exh. cat. by P. Georgel and others, Paris, Grand Pal., 1985)
Maison de Victor Hugo: Dessins de Victor Hugo (Paris, 1985)
Soleil d'encre: Manuscrits et dessins de Victor Hugo (exh. cat. by J. Petit and others, Paris, Petit Pal., 1985)

PIERRE GEORGEL

(2) Charles(-Victor) Hugo (*b* Paris, 1826; *d* Bordeaux, 1871). Photographer, son of (1) Victor Hugo. He was a brilliant scholar, and after the *coup d'état* of 1851 he went into exile with his family in the Channel Islands. He took up photography when in exile in Jersey (until 1855) and continued to photograph in Guernsey (until 1870). He adopted photography largely to alleviate the boredom of life in exile. After a short course of 15 days study with his friend Edmond Bacot (1814–75) in Caen he began work on a photographic album. His associates were his brother

François Hugo (1828–73) and the poet Auguste Vacquerie, both keen photographers. His work is basically a series of family snapshots, destined to provide souvenir albums of the Hugo family for their friends in France. From a possible total of 67 albums, which were presented to friends from August 1854 onwards, only 2 remain (Rochester, NY, Int. Mus. Phot., and Paris, Bib. N.). The photographs have a romantic charm that bears witness to Hugo's enthusiastic and unselfconscious approach. Though technically poor, the images are often very striking: the photograph of *Victor Hugo Sitting on the Rock of the Exiles in Jersey* (*c*. 1853; see Gernsheim, no. 180) is a very strong and touching image. He also photographed landscapes in the Channel Islands and produced *Jersey et les Iles de la Manche* (unpubd), a collection of verses, drawings and prose, in association with his brother François and with Auguste Vacquerie.

WRITINGS
Victor Hugo photographe (Paris, 1905)

BIBLIOGRAPHY
R. Lecuyer: *Histoire de la photographie* (Paris, 1945)
H. Gernsheim: *The Origins of Photography* (London, 1982), pp. 250–51, 259, 262

PATRICIA STRATHERN

Hugo, Master (*fl* Bury St Edmunds, *c*. 1125–56). Metalworker and illuminator, active in England. The *Gesta sacristarum* of Bury St Edmunds Abbey, written in the late 13th century, mentions *magister Hugo* three times. He 'sculpted' (*insculptas*) two metal doors (*valvas*) for the church façade, surpassing even himself in this wonderful work; Hervey the sacrist, for his brother Prior Talbot (*c*. 1125–38), paid for a great Bible, which was painted by Master Hugo on parchment acquired 'in Scotiae partibus' (perhaps Ireland); and Elias, sacrist under Abbot Ordning (1148–56), commissioned the crucifix in the choir and the figures of the Virgin and St John, which were incomparably 'sculpted' by Master Hugo. A 14th-century source records the inscription on a bell that was cast by a certain Hugo during the abbacy of Anselm (1121–48). A 15th-century manuscript refers to the façade doors of the abbey church as cast (*arte fusoria*), thus confirming that Hugo's doors were indeed of metal. These references indicate that Hugo was not a monk but a professional, and they provide a unique record of the range of activities of an English Romanesque artist. It is unknown whether Hugo was resident at the abbey or itinerant.

The first volume of a giant Bible (Cambridge, Corpus Christi Coll. Lib., MS. 2) is probably, though not certainly, to be identified as part of Hervey's Bible, and thus by Master Hugo: it has a Bury pressmark, and some of its paintings are on fine vellum leaves glued on to the main folios, thus recalling the story of Hugo's search for vellum abroad (*see* BURY ST EDMUNDS BIBLE). If so, its precocious date (*c*. 1135) would make Hugo's style highly influential on the succeeding generation of English artists, not only in manuscript illumination but in wall painting (at Canterbury Cathedral), in stained glass (at York Minster), in stone carving (at the cathedrals of Durham and Winchester) and in the small-scale arts (e.g. an ivory tau and the so-called Master's enamel plaque; both London, V&A). Two other works have been attributed to Hugo: a seal of Bury St Edmunds Abbey (92×65 mm; Oxford, Bodleian

Lib., MS. Suffolk 10), probably attributed correctly, and the 'Bury St Edmunds Ivory Cross' (h. 577 mm; New York, Cloisters). There is no evidence, however, to connect the Cross with the abbey, and it is not stylistically related to the Bible.

See also BURY ST EDMUNDS, §2, and ROMANESQUE, §IV, 2.

BIBLIOGRAPHY
Gesta sacristarum monasterii S. Edmundi, [MS; late 13th century]; ed. in T. Arnold: *Memorials of St Edmund's Abbey*, ii, Rolls Ser. (London, 1892), pp. 289–90
M. R. James: 'On the Abbey of St Edmund at Bury', *Cambs Antiqua. Soc. 8vo Pubns*, xxviii (1895), pp. 7, 23, 127–8, 199
C. M. Kauffmann: 'The Bury Bible', *J. Warb. & Court. Inst.*, xxix (1966), pp. 60–81
R. M. Thomson: 'Early Romanesque Book Illustration in England: The Dates of the Pierpont Morgan *Vita sancti Edmundi* and the Bury Bible', *Viator*, ii (1971), pp. 218–24
A. Gransden: *Historical Writing in England, c. 550 to c. 1307* (London, 1974), pp. 391–5
R. M. Thomson: 'The Date of the Bury Bible Re-examined', *Viator*, vi (1975), pp. 51–8
English Romanesque Art, 1066–1200 (exh. cat., ed. G. Zarnecki; London, Hayward Gal., 1984), nos 44, 356; see also nos 88, 148, 154, 205–6, 275
NEIL STRATFORD

Hugo d'Oignies [de Walcourt] (*b* Walcourt, before 1187; *d* Oignies, *c.* 1240). South Netherlandish metalworker. According to the chronicle of Oignies (Mons, Archvs Etat), which gives the details of his birth, he had three brothers who, led by the eldest, Egidius or Gilles de Walcourt, founded the Priory of St Nicolas at Oignies on the banks of the River Sambre, in the diocese of Liège. Hugo worked in precious metals in the Meuse region and the surrounding area until *c.* 1230, when he retired to the priory, became a lay brother and continued his work in its service. It is presumed that he learnt his craft in the coin foundry at Walcourt, and the tradition that he was apprenticed to Nicholas of Verdun may be based on truth. Classicizing elements in Hugo's work give way to Gothic, however, and the influence of sculpture at Reims Cathedral can be clearly distinguished; there are also connections with the drawings of Villard de Honnecourt.

Hugo d'Oignies's three surviving signed pieces of precious metalwork (a book cover, chalice and reliquary; all Namur, Trésor Hugo d'Oignies) were produced for Oignies Priory. The book cover is richly ornamented on both front and back and dates from *c.* 1228–30. It originally contained a manuscript of the Gospels; an inscription on the back plate records that Hugo paid for the copying of the manuscript, made the cover and presented the whole to the priory. In the recessed central portion of the front plate is the *Crucifixion*; on the back is *Christ in Majesty*, with six small niello silver plaques on the outer border, one of which shows the kneeling artist (signed HUGO) offering the book to Christ (*see* GOTHIC, fig. 87). The chalice, signed clearly on the foot, was made for Hugo's eldest brother, the first Prior (*d* 1233), and is ornamented with filigree and niello. Similar forms and style of decoration as the chalice and book cover were employed for the parcel gift and niello reliquary, which was made in 1238, according to a strip of parchment accompanying the relic, a rib of St Peter. Hugo probably also made a number of other 13th-century pieces for the treasury of Oignies, most of which are preserved at Namur. The most important of these are the two double-armed reliquary crosses (one in Namur, Trésor Hugo d'Oignies; the other in Brussels, Musées Royaux A. & Hist.). A third double cross of the same type is in Walcourt (St Materne, Treasury), and a fourth, probably also by Hugo or his workshop, in London (V&A). Numerous other works are attributed to Hugo d'Oignies or to his followers, but none can be authenticated with certainty except the gold altar frontal in St Vanne, Verdun, which he delivered in 1224 for the new choir, a few years earlier than his other signed works.

BIBLIOGRAPHY
Thieme–Becker
J. J. M. Timmers: *De Kunst van het Maasland I* (Maastricht, 1971), pp. 367–72
Rhein und Maas: Kunst und Kultur, 800–1400 (exh. cat., ed. A. Legner; Cologne, Josef-Haubrich-Ksthalle; Brussels, Musées Royaux A. & Hist.; 1972–3), i, p. 344, 349–52; ii, p. 341
G. Poskin and P. Stockart: *Orfèvres Namurois* (Namur, 1982), pp. 4–6
P. Williamson: *The Medieval Treasury*, London, V&A cat. (London, 1986), pp. 176–7
A. M. KOLDEWEIJ

Hugo van der Goes. *See* GOES, HUGO VAN DER.

Hugué, Manuel Martínez. *See* MANOLO.

Huguenots. French Protestants who followed the teachings of Jean Calvin (1509–64). The name possibly derives from *Eidgenoss* (Ger.: 'confederate'), used in Geneva to describe Calvin and his followers who settled there in the mid-16th century. The Huguenots were intermittently persecuted in France from the 1530s to the late 18th century, and many went into exile in such countries as Switzerland, England and the Netherlands, where Protestantism was the official religion. During this period Huguenot exiles made a significant contribution to artistic developments in their adopted lands.

1. History. 2. Work and influence in France, the Netherlands and England.

1. HISTORY. The Reformation spread to France during the 1530s; those attracted to Protestant doctrines included some nobles but were chiefly artisans and traders. The preaching of Calvin provided theological leadership (*see* CALVINISM). In 1534 Calvin fled France and in 1536 published in Basle his *Christianae religionis institutio* (Fr. trans. 1541), which explained the doctrines of French Protestantism, and settled in Geneva, where he trained ministers who returned to preach in France.

Huguenots were able to organize a national synod by 1559 and may have formed a tenth of the French population by the late 16th century. The country's rulers, however, were determined to oppose them, resulting in the Wars of Religion that continued until 1593; thousands of Protestants were killed in the St Bartholomew's Day Massacre (1572) in Paris, instigated by Queen Catherine de' Medici. The eventual victor, Henry IV, was a Protestant prior to his accession and, in the Edict of Nantes (1598), granted the Huguenots freedom of worship and the right to maintain garrisons and distinct institutions. The right to organized self-defence was lost, however, after further civil wars in the 1620s, culminating in the surrender of the Huguenot fortress of La Rochelle in 1628.

In 1678 Louis XIV, King of France, instigated a campaign to convert the Huguenots: they were subjected to forced billeting of troops (*dragonnades*) and other repressive measures. The Revocation of the Edict of Nantes (1685) deprived the Huguenots of all their former rights, and they were commanded to abjure their faith. Some 700,000 did so; others emigrated, in the face of severe penalties, to the United Provinces (50–60,000), England (40–50,000), Germany (25–30,000), Ireland (10,000), the American colonies and the Cape of Good Hope. A small Protestant community maintained an underground existence in France in the 18th century, until a campaign supported by Voltaire's *Traité sur la tolérance* (1764) resulted in the Edict of Toleration in 1787, followed by the full acknowledgement of religious liberty in the Declaration of the Rights of Man (1789). The Reformed Church was formally recognized in 1802.

2. WORK AND INFLUENCE IN FRANCE, THE NETHERLANDS AND ENGLAND. Calvin denounced depictions of divinity but approved of artistic activity within proper limits. In France many of his followers came from families engaged in the applied arts, and the restrictions placed on political activity obliged many others, previously connected with banking and administration, to turn to craftsmanship. They formed closely knit communities, both in France and England. The ethics of Calvinism, which encouraged individuals to look for signs of salvation in their own exemplary behaviour, gave the Huguenots a reputation for industry and probity of workmanship.

(i) France and the Netherlands. (ii) England.

(i) France and the Netherlands. Notable 16th-century Huguenot craftsmen in France included ETIENNE DELAUNE, who produced engraved designs for jewellers and goldsmiths; Jacques Androuet Du Cerceau (*see* DU CERCEAU, (1) and FRANCE, fig. 75), who was highly influential in promoting classical styles through his books on architecture and ornament; and BERNARD PALISSY, who worked as a glass painter and surveyor before experimenting with tin-glazed pottery (*see* FRANCE, fig. 63). He produced a grotto at the château of Ecouen for Anne, Duc de Montmorency, Constable of France, in 1548 and another (*c.* 1567) at the Jardin des Tuileries for Catherine de' Medici. The latter commission protected him from persecution during the late 1560s. Huguenot worship placed great emphasis on preaching: the pulpit occupied a central position in their churches (also known as temples), the design of which was influenced by the need for good acoustics. The Temple de Paradis at Lyon (1564; destr. 1685; *see* CHURCH, fig. 20), probably by Jean Perrissin, and the new temple at Charenton (1606; rebuilt 1623; destr. 1685), designed by SALOMON DE BROSSE, were both distinguished by galleries used to accommodate large congregations.

Little research has been done concerning the Huguenot communities in the northern Netherlands, although the names of many artists are known, the most important of whom was Daniel Marot I (*see* MAROT, (2)). In 1686 Marot moved from France to the Netherlands and was soon employed by the Stadholder William III of Orange Nassau and his wife, Mary Stuart (*see* ORANGE NASSAU, (5) and (6)), who were interested in the latest developments in French art. In 1688 they became King and Queen

of England as William III and Mary II, and consequently many Huguenots settled there (*see* §(ii) below), resulting in the dissemination of French styles in English art. Marot, however, continued to work mainly in the Netherlands and from 1690 was involved in enlarging and refurbishing William III's palace of HET LOO, Apeldoorn, where the interiors (rest.) are typical of his unified decorative schemes on the French model: the same decorative motifs, for example lambrequins, shellwork, scrollwork and floral ornament, appear on every feature. This style was initially only popular in William's court circle (and consequently is known as the WILLIAM AND MARY STYLE), but its dissemination was facilitated by the publication of Marot's engraved designs. After William's death in 1702 Marot continued to design and refurbish houses for the wealthy citizens of Amsterdam and The Hague. A number of Huguenot silversmiths, for example Richard Musseau (*fl* 1694–1702), were also active in The Hague in the late 17th century and early 18th.

(ii) England. The first Protestant refugees came to England in the late 1540s; a Huguenot church was founded in 1550 in Threadneedle Street, London. Among those settling in London in the late 16th century was JACQUES LE MOYNE DE MORGUES, who had accompanied René de Laudonnière's Huguenot expedition to Florida in 1564 as cartographer and artist. He specialized in still-lifes and published *La Clef des champs, pour trouver plusieurs animaux, tant bestes qu'oyseaux, avec plusieurs fleurs et fruitz* (1586), a pattern book for painters, engravers and embroiderers containing 96 coloured woodcuts of birds, beasts and plants. Theodor de Bry (*see* DE BRY, (1)), worked in England from *c.* 1586 to 1589, producing engravings after the watercolours of the English artist John White that were subsequently used to illustrate his *Grands Voyages*.

Pierre Olliver (*fl c.* 1568–after 1582), a goldsmith from Rouen who had for a time lived in Geneva, arrived *c.* 1568 with his young son Isaac Oliver, who became one of the most accomplished painters of miniatures at the English courts of Elizabeth I and James I. (Isaac's son, Peter Oliver, later became a court painter to Charles I in the 1630s (*see* OLIVER).) In the 1630s JEAN PETITOT, the Geneva-born son of a Huguenot sculptor, introduced into England the art of painting miniature portraits in enamel, a technique developed by the Parisian goldsmith Jean Toutin (1578–1644). Other Huguenots patronized at the courts of James I and Charles I included the sculptor HUBERT LE SUEUR, renowned for his technical skill in bronze-casting, and the engineers and garden designers Isaac de Caus and Salomon de Caus (*see* DE CAUS).

By 1660 Huguenots in England could choose between conforming to the Anglican liturgy translated into French or maintaining the Genevan tradition. They used existing buildings for worship, although in London in 1685 Christopher Wren provided a design for an extension to the conformist chapel at the Savoy (destr. *c.* 1730), and in 1743 a new building in Church (now Fournier) Street, Spitalfields, opened for nonconformist worship. Both these churches, following the French model, were centrally planned and included galleries.

From the early 1680s a steady flow of talented craftsmen reached England, encouraged by a royal declaration of

1681 that allowed them to bring in their stock-in-trade free of import tax. The accession of the Protestant William III of Orange Nassau and Mary Stuart to the English throne in 1688 resulted in an enormous increase in the number of Huguenots settling in England. The most significant among these were the goldsmiths, gunmakers and watchmakers. Goldsmiths moved to England for economic reasons, as well as to escape religious persecution: in 1686 Louis XIV, in an attempt to finance his wars, had ordered all plate to be melted down and had forbidden the further employment of goldsmiths. Many of these craftsmen, for example DAVID WILLAUME, SIMON PANTIN, PIERRE HARACHE, DAVID TANQUERAY and PIERRE PLATEL came from provincial towns, but the quality of their work is exceptionally high. They were skilled in working with cast silver, which by this time was replacing embossed work. They also introduced new, sophisticated forms of domestic silver, for example the pilgrim-bottle, écuelle, soup-tureen, sauceboat, wine-cooler and helmet-shaped ewer, and a vocabulary of French engraved designs. Huguenot goldsmiths' work, characterized by well-proportioned forms and elegant ornament and often with fine engraving by such specialists as SIMON GRIBELIN II, captured the English market. Since the Huguenots often undercut local rates, such native English goldsmiths as Anthony Nelme regularly petitioned the Goldsmiths' Company against this unwelcome competition, although some began employing Huguenot journeymen or imitated Huguenot styles. The work of French gunmakers was also renowned; among those seeking refuge in Soho were

Noon: Huguenot Refugees Emerging from the Eglise des Grecs, Hog Lane, Soho, by William Hogarth, engraving, 450×380 mm, 1738 (London, British Museum)

Pierre Monlong (*fl* 1664–95), who arrived in 1684, and Pierre Gruché (*fl* 1680–99) from Paris. Within five years Monlong, formerly Arquebusier de la Maison du Roi, was made Gentleman Armourer in Ordinary to William III. Thus, numerous craftsmen who had been employed by Louis XIV now worked for his greatest political opponent. A pair of flintlock pistols (*c.* 1695, London, Tower, Royal Armouries) probably made for the King by Monlong are distinguished by the quality of decoration (*see* ARMS AND ARMOUR, fig. 10).

A number of Huguenot architects, sculptors, blacksmiths and designers worked in England, many of them patronized by such ambitious builders as William Cavendish, 4th Earl and 1st Duke of Devonshire, and Ralph, 1st Duke of Montagu. JEAN TIJOU was employed by Cavendish at Chatsworth, Derbys, from 1689 to 1693; between 1689 and 1699 he made wrought-iron screens, gates and balustrades (*in situ*) for William III's palace at Hampton Court, near London. Tijou's *A New Book of Drawing* (1693) was the first English book of designs for ironwork and was quickly pirated in France. The architect and designer Daniel Marot I, mainly active in the Netherlands after settling there in 1686 (*see* §(i) above), was also in England from 1694 to 1698, working on the interiors at Hampton Court. Marot's designs had considerable influence in England (as in the Netherlands), introducing the concept of the unified decorative scheme. The Huguenot furniture-maker Jean Pelletier (*fl c.* 1690–1710) and his family were among the craftsmen who worked to Marot's designs. The Pelletier family also supplied glass for window-panes, glass sconces and *verre églomisé* to Ralph, 1st Duke of Montagu. Other Huguenot architects included Samuel Hauduroy, who built the west front of Dyrham Park (1692), Glos, and Jean de Bodt, who, like Marot, was closely connected with William III's courts in the Netherlands and England.

Among Huguenot painters, Louis Chéron (*see* CHÉRON, (3)), who had been brought over to do decorative work for Ralph Montagu in the 1690s, played an influential role in England in the early 18th century. He had trained in Paris, at the Académie Royale de Peinture et de Sculpture, and in Rome, and in 1720 he helped set up the first St Martin's Lane Academy in London, introducing the innovation of a female model in 1722. Huguenot sculptors active in the early 18th century included the ivory-carver DAVID LE MARCHAND and Jean Obrisset (*fl* 1705–28), who specialized in horn and tortoiseshell. The wax modeller ISAAC GOSSET also produced carved and gilded frames for artists. The most important figure was the Protestant convert LOUIS-FRANÇOIS ROUBILIAC, who arrived in London in 1730 and taught sculpture at the second St Martin's Lane Academy from 1745. The many Huguenot printmakers included the Basire family, originally from Rouen, who were active through several generations; Paul Fourdrinier (*d* 1758), who produced engravings for the architects William Chambers and William Kent, among others; FRANCIS VIVARES; John Rocque (*d* 1762); and JEAN-BAPTISTE-CLAUDE CHATELAIN, born in London of Huguenot parents. William Hogarth, who studied at the first St Martin's Lane Academy and was instrumental in establishing the second, was among those English painters strongly influenced by the French Rococo style that early

18th-century Huguenot painters, sculptors and engravers introduced. His engraving *Noon: Huguenot Refugees Emerging from the Eglise des Grecs, Hog Lane, Soho* (1738; London, BM; see fig.) is in part an allegory on matrimony, but its allusive reference to the presence of this alien culture demonstrates that the Huguenots continued to be perceived as a distinct social group in London even at this period.

The production of decorative arts in the Rococo style was often of as high a quality as contemporary French work, as the maintenance of a separate community ensured that skills were passed on to the next generation. In the 1730s and 1740s PAUL CRESPIN, PAUL DE LAMERIE and NICHOLAS SPRIMONT were the leading makers of Rococo silver. Their English competitors, Edward Wakelin and Thomas Heming, had both trained under Huguenot masters. Second-generation Huguenots also played a crucial part in establishing the porcelain factories at Chelsea and Derby in the 1740s, as well as the short-lived enamels factory at York House, Battersea (*see* LONDON, §IV, 5), in the 1750s. At Chelsea, Nicholas Sprimont, who began a second career as a porcelain manufacturer, employed other Huguenots to produce models, as well as movements for his porcelain clock-cases. Some of these craftsmen had been trained initially in Huguenot jewellers' workshops in London, and one of them, James Giles (1708–80), who became, like his father, an independent decorator of porcelain, received considerable recognition. At Derby the first modeller was André Planché (*fl* 1750–56), a former apprentice goldsmith to the jeweller Edward Mountenay.

By the late 18th century most Huguenots in England had lost their use of the French language and had become irrevocably assimilated into English culture. Although most of the institutions set up by Huguenot refugees were gradually dissolved in the 19th century, the French Hospital (founded in London 1716; now at Rochester, Kent) continues to operate, and the Westminster French Protestant Charity School Fund (founded 1747) provides scholarships for those of Huguenot descent.

BIBLIOGRAPHY
J. Hayward: *Huguenot Silver in England, 1688–1727* (London, 1959)
W. C. Scoville: *The Persecution of the Huguenots and French Economic Development, 1680–1720* (Los Angeles, 1960)
The Quiet Conquest: The Huguenots, 1685–1985 (exh. cat., ed. T. Murdoch; London, Mus. London, 1985)
T. Murdoch: 'The Huguenots and English Rococo', *The Rococo in England*, ed. C. Hind (London, 1986), pp. 60–81
I. Scouloudi, ed.: *Huguenots in Britain and their French Background, 1550–1800* (London, 1987)
TESSA MURDOCH

Hugues, P.-F. *See* HANCARVILLE, PIERRE-FRANÇOIS HUGUES-D'.

Huguet [Ouguete] (*d* 1438). Architect, active in Portugal. His origin is unknown, but the most widely accepted hypothesis is that he was from the Mediterranean coast of Spain. Huguet was the second architect to be appointed to the construction of the monastery of Batalha, and from 1402 until his death he supervised the completion of the church, the cloisters and the chapter house, which had been begun by Afonso Domingues. Huguet was also responsible for building the Founder's chapel and beginning the mausoleum of King Duarte.

Using Late Gothic techniques, Huguet simplified the vaults, designed the main façade and crowned the construction with beautiful openwork traceried parapets. The façade is a distinct, Flamboyant design in which horizontal lines predominate and contrast sharply with the verticality of the nave. The portal with its abundance of sculptural ornament constituted a new departure for Portuguese Gothic. The chapter house is 19 metres square and covered with a single vault decorated with an eight-pointed star, a bold technical achievement. The Founder's chapel, the mausoleum of the Avis dynasty, is also square in plan but with a central octagon, again with an eight-pointed star vault; it is a complex, elegant and highly innovative structure.

The mausoleum of King Duarte is even more daring and original. Owing to its incomplete state it is known as the Unfinished Chapels. The plan comprises a large central octagon surrounded by seven squares forming the chapels; the triangular spaces in the interstices are closed on the exterior. Huguet's work at Batalha played a decisive role in the evolution of Portuguese Gothic architecture throughout the 15th century and the early 16th.

Viterbo   BIBLIOGRAPHY
F. São Luís: *Memória histórica sobre as obras do real mosteiro de Santa Maria da Victoria* [A historical record of the works of the royal monastery of S Maria da Victoria] (Lisbon, 1872)
V. Correia: *Batalha* (Oporto, 1928)
——: *Origem levantina peninsular do segundo mestre da Batalha* [The peninsular Mediterranean origin of the second master architect of Batalha] (Oporto, 1931, 2/1949)
M. Tavares Chicó: *História da arte em Portugal* (Oporto, 1942–53), ii
——: *A arquitectura gótica em Portugal* [Gothic architecture in Portugal] (Lisbon, 1954, 3/1981)
JOSÉ CUSTODIO VIEIRA DA SILVA

Huguet, Jaume (*b* Valls, *c*. 1415; *d* Barcelona, before 4 May 1492). Spanish painter. He is thought to have spent time in Saragossa in his youth (*c*. 1435–45), and he subsequently worked in Tarragona before establishing himself in Barcelona in 1448. He must, however, have had contact with painting from Barcelona before he moved there, because the centre panel of an early retable dedicated to the Virgin (Barcelona, Mus. A. Catalunya) from Vallmoll, near Tarragona, shows his awareness of the style of Bernat Martorell in the profiles of the two foreground angels, and of Lluís Dalmau's *Virgin of the Councillors* (Barcelona, Mus. A. Catalunya) in the illusionistic painting of the Virgin's jewel-trimmed garments. In other early works, such as the *Annunciation* and *Crucifixion* from a small retable (Vic, Mus. Episc.), Huguet demonstrated an interest in atmospheric perspective, but he abandoned this in his later works.

Huguet was definitely in Barcelona by 31 August 1448 and remained there until his death. With the death of Bernat Martorell in 1452, he became the leading panel painter in the city. His patrons included parish churches, prominent trade guilds (including his own Confraría de S Esteve, which encompassed both bridlemakers and painters), and Pedro, Constable of Portugal, who briefly (1464–6) ruled Catalonia. Throughout these years, Huguet maintained a large shop, training many apprentices and employing contract workers to help execute his many commissions. He also held various offices in the Confraría de S Esteve, including that of dean (*prohom en cap*) in 1488.

The retables that Huguet painted in Barcelona fitted perfectly into the aesthetic traditions of that city. The earliest documented example, the *retablo mayor* of *St Anthony Abbot* (1454) for the Confraría dels Tractants en Animals (Barcelona, S Antoni Abat; destr. 1909), shows many of the stylistic traits that characterized his work for the next 38 years. The large, frontal central effigy of the enthroned saint follows Catalan retable tradition. The patterned background, the saint's staff and his halo of concentric rings are all articulated in *embutido* (raised, gilded gesso). The same foliate-patterned ground is found in all the lateral narratives and has a tendency to flatten out the compositions, even though the tiled floors of some of these scenes, as well as the saints in the *banco* (predella), are executed in perspective.

A similar aesthetic underlies Huguet's other retables of the period, such as the *retablo mayor* of *St Vincent* (*c.* 1450–60) from the parish church of S Vicenç, Sarrià, the retable of *St Michael the Archangel* (1455–60) for the retailers' guild in S María del Pí (both Barcelona, Mus. A. Catalunya), the retable of *SS Abdon and Sennen* (1459–60; Terrassa, S Pere), and the retable of the *Epiphany* for Pedro of Portugal (Barcelona, Pal. Real Maj.). All of them have stately figures with heavily articulated drapery folds and lyrical rather than dramatic facial expressions (even when rather gruesome scenes of martyrdom are shown). The figures crowd the compositions, which tends to compress space, but such compression fits well within the demands of the multi-panelled altarpiece. All of these works were produced by Huguet with the collaboration of his large shop.

Most impressive of all is the massive *Coronation of St Augustine* (see fig.), one of two panels that Huguet himself painted for the huge *retablo mayor* (1465–86; Barcelona, Mus. A. Catalunya) of the tanners' guild for S Agostí Vell, with its life-size, symmetrically placed figures and its profusion of brocaded patterns. Huguet's style represents the last flowering of the late medieval Catalan painting tradition. Although some of his collaborators, notably Rafael Vergós (*fl* 1492–1501) and Pere Alemany (*fl* 1492–?1516), carried his manner on into the first years of the 16th century, changing styles and altarpiece configurations rendered it obsolete.

BIBLIOGRAPHY
B. Rowland: *Jaume Huguet* (Cambridge, MA, 1932)
C. R. Post: *A History of Spanish Painting* (Cambridge, MA, 1938–66), vii, pp. 46–171 [also subsequent vols]
J. Ainaud de Lasarte and J. Gudiol Ricart: *Huguet* (Barcelona, 1948)
S. Alcolea Blanch and J. Gudiol Ricart: *Pintura gótica catalana* (Barcelona, 1987)

JUDITH BERG SOBRÉ

Huhn, Carl (Theodor). *See* HÜNS, KĀRLIS.

Huie, Albert (*b* Falmouth, Trelawny, Jamaica, 31 Dec 1920). Jamaican painter. He came to the attention of the Institute of Jamaica in the late 1930s, when he also received his early training from the Armenian artist Koren der Harootian (1909–91). He was assistant to Edna Manley during her art classes at the Junior Centre, Kingston, in the early 1940s. He went on to study at the Ontario College of Art, Toronto, and at the Camberwell School of Arts and Crafts, London. He was founding tutor in painting at the Jamaica School of Art and Crafts, Kingston, in 1950. Huie is best known as a landscape and genre painter. More effectively than any other Jamaican artist he captured the shimmering, atmospheric quality of the Jamaican landscape and the rhythm of life in the rural areas. Some of his works have socio-political overtones and express nationalist sentiments and his sympathy for the working class. He also made his mark as a portrait painter; his earliest major works are portraits, among them a *Portrait of Edna Manley* (1940; Kingston, Inst. Jamaica, N.G.). His earliest works have a naive quality, while his mature work shows a strong Post-Impressionist influence. His style changed very little after the early 1940s, though in the 1960s he concentrated on the nude figure. While he usually painted in oil, his acrylic paintings are characterized by a more muted palette and a flatter design.

BIBLIOGRAPHY
Jamaican Art, 1922–1982 (exh. cat. by D. Boxer, Washington, DC, Smithsonian Inst.; Kingston, Inst. Jamaica, N.G.; 1983)
P. Archer Straw and K. Robinson: *Jamaican Art* (Kingston, 1990), pp. 7, 9–10, 24–8, 162–3

VEERLE POUPEYE

Huis ter Nieuburch, Rijswijk. *See* RIJSWIJK, HUIS TER NIEUBURCH.

Hui-tsung, Emperor. *See* HUIZONG.

Huizinga, Johan (*b* Groningen, 18 Dec 1872; *d* De Steeg, nr Arnhem, 1 Feb 1945). Dutch historian. He studied Dutch and Sanskrit at Groningen University

Jaume Huguet: *Coronation of St Augustine*, tempera on panel, 2.51×1.92 m, from the *retablo mayor* of S Agostí Vell, Barcelona, completed 1486 (Barcelona, Museu d'Art de Catalunya)

(1891–5) and linguistics at Leipzig (1895–6), returning to Groningen in 1897 to take a doctorate in Dutch literature. He taught at Haarlem from 1897 to 1905, and from 1903 to 1905 he was a private lecturer on Ancient Indian literature and cultural history at Amsterdam University. In 1905 he became professor of medieval and modern history at Groningen University, and in 1915 professor of general history at Leiden University.

In his inaugural address of 1905 Huizinga stressed the aesthetic experience of history, and later he argued against the separation of art museums from historical museums, believing instead that museums should be integrated and contain all kinds of objects, including works of art. Like Jacob Burckhardt before him, Huizinga wrote about the fine arts in the context of cultural history, but while Burckhardt treated the Renaissance as beginning in the 15th century, on the basis of Italian art, Huizinga's first broadly conceived work of cultural history, *Herfsttij der Middeleeuwen* (1919), shows, using the examples of Jan and Hubert van Eyck, the extent to which the 15th century was imbued with medieval and Late Gothic elements and could be seen as a period of transition between the medieval and modern periods.

In his theoretical treatise, *Cultuurhistorische verkenningen* (1929), Huizinga attempted to arrange his ideas under five headings. Although *Herfsttij der Middeleeuwen* comprised a balanced and extensive programme of investigation, in this later treatise Huizinga argued that cultural history was a general term embracing all branches of history, rather than a systematic science. He also held that art history could reach its full development only after the way had been mapped out by general cultural history. Decades later, this view was still being contested, notably by Gerson (1973).

In *Cultuurhistorische verkenningen* Huizinga did not prescribe any particular method of enquiry but held that '... since cultural history is to such a great extent the product of the free minds of investigators and thinkers, much care is needed in the posing of questions' (p. 16). He defined the sphere of cultural history as 'ascertaining and studying forms of life, modes of creation and modes of thought' (p. 16). 'Its true problems are always those of the form, structure and function of social phenomena' (p. 59). He distinguished two forms of culture: the external or social, and the internal or personal. The former, manifest in art and science, is central to *Homo ludens* (1938) and *Nederlands beschaving in de zeventiende eeuw* (1941). The latter, which is related to internal standards and resistance to cultural decadence, is the theme of *In de schaduwen van morgen* (1935) and *Geschonden wereld* (1945). Huizinga believed that a major cause of cultural decadence in his time was the weakening of Christian morality. Gerson deplored Huizinga's opposition to modern art in particular, and complained of a lack of discrimination in his overall picture of modern culture.

WRITINGS

'De kunst der van Eyck's in het leven van hun tijd' [The art of the Van Eycks in their contemporary context], *De Gids*, lxxx/2 (1916), pp. 440–62; lxxx/3 (1916), pp. 52–82

Herfsttij der Middeleeuwen: Studie over levens- en gedachtenvormen der veertiende en vijftiende eeuw in Frankrijk en de Nederlanden [The waning of the Middle Ages: a study of the forms of life, thought and art in France

and the Netherlands in the 14th and 15th centuries] (Haarlem, 1919; Eng. trans., London, 1924/*R* 1980)

'Het historisch museum', *De Gids*, lxxxv/2 (1920), pp. 470–84

'Het rapport der museumcommissie', *De Gids*, lxxxv/4 (1921), pp. 97–107

Cultuurhistorische verkenningen [Studies in the history of culture] (Haarlem, 1929)

In de schaduwen van morgen: Een diagnose van het geestelijk lijden van onzen tijd [In the shadow of tomorrow: a diagnosis of the spiritual distemper of our time] (Haarlem, 1935; Eng. trans., London, 1936/*R* 1964)

Homo ludens: proeve ener bepaling van het spel-element der cultuur [Homo ludens: a study of the play-element in culture] (Haarlem, 1938; Eng. trans., London, 1949/*R* 1970)

Nederlands beschaving in de zeventiende eeuw [Dutch civilization in the 17th century] (Haarlem, 1941)

Geschonden wereld: Een beschouwing over de kansen op herstel van onze beschaving [Outraged world: conditions for a recovery of our civilization] (Haarlem, 1945)

L. Brummel, W. R. Juynboll and T. J. G. Locher, eds: *Verzamelde werken*, 9 vols (Haarlem, 1948–53)

BIBLIOGRAPHY

P. Polman: *Huizinga als cultuurhistoricus* [Huizinga as a cultural historian] (Haarlem, 1946)

W. Kaegi: 'Das historische Werk Johan Huizinga's', *Schweiz. Beitr. Allg. Gesch.*, iv (1946); as booklet (Leiden, 1947)

H. Gerson: *De taal van de kunsthistorikus* [The art historian's language; inaugural address, Groningen, 22 Feb 1966] (Groningen, 1966)

——: 'Huizinga und die Kunstgeschichte', *Bijdr. Meded. Betreff. Gesch. Ned.*, lxxxviii/1 (1973), pp. 348–64

E. H. Gombrich: 'Huizinga's "Homo ludens"', *Bijdr. Meded. Betreff. Gesch. Ned.*, lxxxviii/1 (1973), pp. 275–96

H. R. Guggisberg: 'Burckhardt and Huizinga: Zwei Historiker in der Krise ihrer Zeit', *Bijdr. Meded. Betreff. Gesch. Ned.*, lxxxviii/1 (1973), pp. 297–316

A. G. Jongkees: 'Une Génération d'historiens devant le phénomène bourguignon', *Bijdr. Meded. Betreff. Gesch. Ned.*, lxxxviii/1 (1973), pp. 215–32

ANNEKE E. WIJNBEEK

Huizong [Hui-tsung], Emperor (*b* Tianshui, Gansu Province, 1082; *reg* 1101–26; *d* Wuguocheng, Yilan, Heilongjiang Province, 1135). Chinese ruler and painter. The last emperor of the Northern Song period (960–1127), he was the 11th son of the emperor Shenzong (*reg* 1068–85). Huizong is considered to be the only accomplished artist in a line of emperors who all shared an interest in the arts. The fall of the Northern Song dynasty is usually attributed to Huizong's neglect of his official duties in favour of religious and cultural pursuits. This preoccupation is described in miscellaneous notes of Deng Chun (*fl* 1127–67) in the *Hua ji* ('Painting continued'; 1167) and by Tang Hou (*fl* 1322) in the *Gujin huajian* ('Mirror of past and present painting'; 1320s), as well as in later chronicles such as the *Tuhui baojian* ('Precious mirror for examining painting'; preface dated 1365) by Xia Wenyan.

The development of Huizong's aesthetic preferences and of his painting and calligraphy was supervised by three friends. They were all of high social rank but had different interests, and their preferences are reflected in the eclectic nature of the emperor's style. Zhao Lingrang (*fl c.* 1070–1100) was a painter and connoisseur who assisted the emperor in his search for scrolls to add to the imperial collection. Wu Yuanyu (*fl c.* 1080–1104) has been described as a conservative academician. He was a pupil of Cui Bo and a conduit of the realistic tradition of painting to the emperor. The painter, connoisseur and collector Wang Shen was also an eclectic intellectual calligrapher; he introduced the emperor to the calligraphic style of Huang Tingjian. While the emperor is best known for his bird-and-flower paintings, his calligraphy is probably the most significant of his accomplishments. It is highly personal and very different from the meticulous painting attributed to him. Its unique style is described in a single reference by Tao Zongyi (*fl* 1350) in his *Shushi hui yao* ('Essentials of calligraphy'): 'The brush in Huizong's running-cursive (*xingshu*) and regular (*kaishu*) scripts is graceful and powerful. He first studied the calligraphy of Xueji (648–718), and then altered [his master's] brush method and manner to produce a style which he himself called "slender gold" script [*shoujin ti*]. The brushwork and style [of his calligraphy] evolved naturally and independently [of his master's], so that [the relationship with Xueji] cannot easily be sought.' (Chuang, p. 1.)

As a collector Huizong invoked his rank to appropriate desirable paintings from sometimes unwilling owners. They are catalogued in the *Xuanhe huapu* ('Xuanhe collection of painting'; compiled before 1119) with a preface written by the emperor and form the nucleus of the Palace Museum collection in Taipei. Huizong's artistic significance is due in great part to the influence he exerted on others. During his reign the Hanlin Painting Academy became a centre of art education as well as painting (*see also* CHINA, §V, 4(i)(c)). Members were officially graded in various ranks and were required in periodic examinations to illustrate quotations chosen by the emperor. The winning work was usually selected more on the basis of the originality of idea than on artistic merit. Huizong also maintained close supervision of paintings executed in the Baolu gong (Palace of Daoist Scriptures), where he required a flawless technique that tended to stultify painting as it emphasized craftsmanship over expression of feeling.

It is difficult to assess Huizong's true talent in painting. Early Chinese historians were anxious to elevate him to a status almost of martyrdom, and their laudatory adjectives made later objective evaluations difficult. For example, Deng Chun identifies the emperor as a genius and Tang Hou classifies his paintings as either wonderful or divine. Another problem of evaluation arises from the tradition, according to early accounts, that when the emperor painted a picture, it was immediately copied by courtiers and artists seeking to obtain his signature on their work. This would explain the discrepancies in style of the paintings with authenticated signatures generally attributed to Huizong. According to Song- and Yuan-period (1279–1368) critics, Huizong painted successfully both in colour and monochrome ink, and several extant works in these traditions are available for comparison. The monochrome ink paintings are described as following the traditions of Li Cheng and Guo Xi. Landscapes and bamboo paintings put him in competition with the contemporary literati. Re-creations of early works can be studied in his copies of past masters such as Zhang Xuan. *Ladies Preparing Newly Woven Silk* (colour on silk, 370×1450 mm; Boston, MA, Mus. F.A.) is a copy attributed to Huizong by his grandson, the Jin emperor, Zhangzong (*reg* 1190–1209), who utilizes his ancestor's calligraphic style in his inscription. Huizong is best known, however, for bird-and-flower album leaves composed in a pre-Song tradition. Carefully delineated forms drawn from life (*xiesheng*) in the tradition of Cui Bo rely on colour alone in the 'boneless' (*mogu*) technique

of the Southern Tang (AD 937–75) artist Xu Xi. They create a new synthesis using the compositional device of flattened space characteristic of Huang Quan of the Five Dynasties period (907–60). This synthesis is exemplified by the *Five-coloured Parakeet* (horizontal scroll, colour on silk, 530×1250 mm; Boston, MA, Mus. F.A.), which bears his signature but which is probably not his work. The *Dove on the Branch of a Blossoming Peach Tree* (Tokyo, Setsū Gatodo priv. col.) is similar in composition and of more acceptable authenticity. Its technical perfection makes any individuality difficult to detect, but it exemplifies the flawless technique associated with the emperor.

BIBLIOGRAPHY

Deng Chun: *Hua ji* [Painting continued] (preface dated 1167); ed. by Huang Miaozi (Beijing, 1963)
Tang Hou: *Gujin huajian* [Mirror of past and present painting] (1320s)
Xia Wenyan: *Tuhui baojian* [Precious mirror for examining painting] (preface dated 1365)
O. Sirén: *Chinese Painting: Leading Masters and Principles* (London and New York, 1956–8), v, pp. 74–86
B. Rowland: 'The Problem of Hui-tsung', *Archvs Chin. A. Soc. America*, v (1951), pp. 5–23
S. Chuang: 'The Slender Gold Calligraphy of Emperor Hui Tsung', *Gugong Jikan*, ii (1967–8), no. 4, pp. 1–6
M. Loehr: *The Great Painters of China* (New York, 1980), pp. 176–95

MARY S. LAWTON

Hulbuk [Rus. Khul'buk; Kurbanshaid]. Capital of the medieval province of Khuttal, on the Kyzyl (Akhsu) River, 7 km from the village of Vose in the Khatlon region of southern Tajikistan. The town, mentioned in medieval sources of the 10th–12th centuries, corresponds to the modern settlement of Kurbanshaid. In the 9th–10th century the town was the residence of the provincial governor under the local Banijurid dynasty, who minted coins in Khuttal and has links to the Samanids of Transoxiana. At the end of the 10th century or early 11th, Khuttal lost its independence and came under the control of the Ghaznavids, whose governor-general was based at Hulbuk.

Extensive excavations under the direction of Erkinoy Gulyamova were carried out in the 1960s to 1980s in the south-western part of the 10 ha settlement at the citadel (50×150 m). Rising 10–15 m above the surrounding area, it was the location of the governor's palace (late 9th century AD or early 10th). The palace had a central courtyard paved with fired bricks and containing a large reservoir, with rooms with iwans opening off it. Ceremonial rooms were decorated with carved stucco panels, and the walls of the iwans were decorated with paintings. Walls, built from 0.7–1 m layers of beaten clay carved in blocks to prevent cracking, were sometimes revetted with fine baked brick slabs. The floors of the palaces were also made of the same brick slabs laid out in parquet. The floor in one of the small inner courtyards had a design of inscribed rectangles and squares. Columns were also elaborately decorated. After a devastating fire, the palace was rebuilt on a different plan. In its second stage (mid-11th century–12th), the palace had two intersecting corridors dividing it into four parts with different functions (ceremonial, living quarters and service quarters). Archaeological investigation has shown that the palace was rebuilt on three separate occasions, and each time the carved stucco panels and murals were renewed.

The site has yielded more than 5000 fragments of carved stucco, including complete panels, with an exceptionally diverse range of geometric, floral and epigraphic motifs. Patterns carved before the mid-11th century were generally shallower and smaller with more detail, while the carving done in the second period after the fire was deeper. The carved plaster was often painted, including parts of the background so that the contrast between pattern and ground was heightened. Poorly preserved fragments of murals depicting warriors were found in the iwan in the northern part of the palace (late 9th century–10th). Other objects found at the site include a bronze incense burner in the shape of a cheetah with an Arabic inscription (10th–12th century), a large collection of glass vessels (10th–12th century), glazed and stamped ceramics, stone objects, chess figures and ivory objects (all finds Dushanbe, Tajikistan Acad. Sci., Donish Inst. Hist.). The artistic culture of the site differs from that found at such Transoxanian centres as Samarkand, Bukhara and Chach; rather there are links with Ghaznavid buildings in northern Afghanistan (e.g. the Ghaznavid palace at LASHKARI BAZAR) and other buildings in northern Tokharistan.

BIBLIOGRAPHY

E. Gulyamova: 'Steklo uz gorodishcha Khul'buka X–XII vv.' [Glass from the site of Hulbuk, 10th–12th century], *Izvestiya Akad. Nauk Tadzhiks. SSR*, i/24 (1961), pp. 11–64
——: 'Reznoy shtuk Khul'buka' [The carved stucco of Hulbuk], *Mat. Kult. Tadzhikistana*, iii (1978), pp. 186–202
——: 'O rabotakh khul'bulskogo i moskovskogo otryadov' [On the work of the Hulbuk and Moscow teams], *Arkheol. Raboty Tadzhikistane*, xix (1979) [1986], pp. 264–77
Drevnosti Tadzhikistana [Antiquities of Tajikistan] (exh. cat., ed. Ye. V. Zeymal'; Leningrad, Hermitage, 1985), pp. 281–91

YE. V. ZEYMAL'

Hulin, Madame (*fl* Paris, 1824; *d* 1834). French dealer and print-publisher. It has been suggested that she might be identified with a certain Madame Hulin who in January 1816 wrote to the British ambassador in Paris requesting permission for her husband to live in London (Pointon, p. 51). Her interest in the French school of young Romantic artists that developed partly under the influence of English art and literature, as well as the fact that she was co-publisher, with S. J. Fuller of London and several French colleagues, of *La Petite Normandie*, a set of ten lithographs by the English artist Richard Parkes Bonington, make it plausible that she had at least some connection with England. From 1824 to 1834 she managed a shop at 21 Rue de la Paix, Paris, and her stock catered to those buyers with a taste for the Antique and the Picturesque, exemplified by Baron Isidore-Justin-Séverin Taylor's multi-volumed topographical architectural survey *Voyages pittoresques et romantiques dans l'ancienne France* (begun 1820), fashionable at the time. Antoine-Jean Gros is said to have admired in her shop-window views by Bonington of Rouen, Caen and other French towns. As did several other dealers, she occasionally published prints; in addition to *La Petite Normandie*, she published in 1823–4 a set of four lithographs of horse subjects by Gericault. Shortly after she opened, Delacroix sold at least one picture to her, and it is possible that she sold work by Bonington,

since their names have traditionally been linked. Louis-Joseph-Auguste Coutan, an important collector of Bonington's work, is known to have frequented her shop. At her closing-down sale in 1834 (Paris, Gal. Schroth, 8–11 Dec) Claude Schroth acted as expert, and it is possible that much of her stock was bought by the dealer François-Simon-Alphonse Giroux, who well into the July Monarchy (1830–48) prolonged the vogue for Picturesque and Gothic subject-matter that had been associated with the Restoration (1814–30).

BIBLIOGRAPHY

M. Pointon: *The Bonington Circle: English Watercolour and Anglo-French Landscape, 1790–1855* (Brighton, 1985)
Richard Parkes Bonington: 'Du plaisir de peindre' (exh. cat. by P. Noon, New Haven, CT, Yale Cent. Brit. A.; Paris, Petit Pal.; 1991–2)

LINDA WHITELEY

Hulin de Loo, Georges (*b* Ghent, 10 Dec 1862; *d* Brussels, 27 Dec 1945). Belgian art historian. After studying law, philosophy and letters at the University of Ghent and abroad, he pursued further disparate studies at Ghent before concentrating on art history, principally the history of Flemish painting and manuscript illumination before 1600. He established his reputation as a brilliant young art historian through his essay 'De l'identité de certains maîtres anonymes', a section of the *Catalogue critique* (Ghent, 1902), which was published as an alternative to the official catalogue for an exhibition of early Flemish masters held in Bruges in 1902. In it he identified distinctive features in anonymous paintings, a method pioneered by Giovanni Morelli, and supported his attributions with archival documentation. By thus combining careful observation and archival research, Hulin de Loo established links between hitherto anonymous paintings and artists whose works had not yet been identified.

WRITINGS

with R. van Bastelaer: *Pierre Bruegel l'ancien* (Brussels, 1907)
Heures de Milan (Brussels, 1910–11)
Pedro Berruguete et les portraits d'Urbain (Brussels, 1942) [contains complete writings list]

BIBLIOGRAPHY

BNB
Mélanges Hulin de Loo (Brussels and Paris, 1931)
P. Bautier: 'Nécrologie: Hulin de Loo', *Rev. Belge Archéol. & Hist. A./Belge Tijdschr. Oudhknde & Kstgesch.*, xvi (1946), pp. 88–90
J. Lavalleye: 'Notice sur Georges Hulin de Loo', *Jb.: Kon. Vl. Acad. Wet., Lett. & S. Kst. België*, cxxvii (1961), pp. 15–27

R. A. D'HULST

Hull [Kingston-upon-Hull]. English port and university city in Humberside, at the confluence of the rivers Hull and Humber. Founded in medieval times, it was an important centre for the production of ceramics in the 19th century.

1. HISTORY AND URBAN DEVELOPMENT. The city was founded because Edward I recognized the strategic importance of the port and of the town of Wyke then on the site. The regular grid pattern of the street layout was started before 1293, although work did not begin on the ring of defensive walls until 1321. Bricks were made in Hull from the early 14th century, and brick buildings are characteristic of the city, for example Holy Trinity (begun *c.* 1300). The market-place was narrow, and the High Street originally had buildings only to the west, although

subsequent building on the riverbank created a new development of private merchants' houses with gardens or courts, warehouses and quays. The enclosed area was not fully built over until the mid-18th century. The island block owned by the Carmelites until the Reformation remained intact; it was progressively redeveloped in a handsome manner during the 18th century and the early 19th. In the late 14th century many of the gabled timber-framed houses were either encased by new work (often brick) or were vertically extended and refronted, thus transforming the appearance if not the underlying substance of the town. Henry VIII built the Citadel (1541) to guard the east bank of the Hull, forestalling the growth of an eastern suburb. Hull Grammar School was built in 1583.

Increased prosperity following the Restoration of the Monarchy (1660) and growing trade with the Netherlands and the Baltic states allowed many to rebuild in brick (e.g. Wilberforce House, c. 1660); externally, many buildings used a Netherlandish classical style, while the interior detailing owed more to French influence. Baltic silverwork inspired many merchants to commission local silverwork resembling it. In 1734 Peter Scheemakers the younger made the monument to *William III* situated in the market-place. An attempt to improve port facilities in the 1730s

failed, only to be revived in the 1770s, by which time Hull had improved access via river and canal to the Midlands and the West Riding of Yorkshire. The new dock, Queen's Basin (filled in), opened in 1778. The north walls had been demolished, new warehouses built and extensive storage yards added on the north (Sculcoates) side of the dock. The Dock Company's surplus land was subsequently sold off for building development flanking the new George, Charlotte and Dock streets. Many of the splendid houses were designed by the Hull architect–builder Charles Mountain the younger and were on a larger scale than previous building. Such new house owners as J. R. Pease also built suburban villas in or near the pleasant villages north and west of the town. Meanwhile, some of the former town mansions within the walled area, or Old Town, became offices. The physical division between Old and New Towns was completed with the building of two new docks after 1800. A pottery flourished in the early 19th century (*see* §2 below). The commercial depression of the late 1820s and early 1830s discouraged speculative building, but the streets of the New Town were adorned with substantial public and official buildings, something that had begun earlier with the Royal Infirmary (1784) and was continued with the Trinity House Almshouses (1828) by

Hull, Guildhall by Edwin Cooper, 1906–14

Charles Mountain. Other 19th-century public buildings included the Paragon Railway Station (1846) by George T. Andrews (1792–1869) and the town hall (1861–2; destr.) by CUTHBERT BRODRICK, which was later rebuilt as the Guildhall (1906–14; see fig.) by Edwin Cooper.

The Reform Act (1832) led one group of speculators to lay out streets and build new houses, usually Neoclassical in style, with front and back gardens, each with the minimum rateable value needed to secure a vote. There was little ingenuity in overall layout except for Pearson Park (1869), encircled by large, handsome detached villas, and, to the west of this, the Avenues district, which has tree-lined roads with big, cast-iron fountains at the principal intersections, and an emphasis on French rather than English detailing. Nearer the banks of the Hull and the Humber there was overcrowded mid- and later 19thcentury housing. Among religious work of the period, G. E. Street built the brick All Saints Church (1866–9), and Walter Crane designed two splendid stained-glass windows (1897 and c. 1907) for Holy Trinity.

In the early 20th century Henry Baines designed the Market Hall (1902–4) and Edwin Alfred Rickards the College of Art (1904). In 1954 Hull gained a university, which provided a focus for major development. Leslie Martin planned the campus (1958) and designed several buildings. The Cottingham halls of residence were largely built by Gillespie, Kidd and Coia, while the Applied Sciences and Mathematics development (1965–7) was by the Architects' Co-Partnership.

BIBLIOGRAPHY
G. Hadley: *A New and Complete History of the Town and County of the Town of Kingston-upon-Hull; With a Cursory Review of, and Observations on the Ancient Legend From its Original Foundation in A.D. 1296 By the Illustrious King Edward the First* (Kingston-upon-Hull, 1788)
J. Tickell: *The History of the Town and County of Kingston upon Hull, from its Foundation in the Reign of Edward the First, to the Present Time. With a Description of Part of the Adjacent Country Embelished with Views etc.* (Hull, 1798)
C. Frost: *Notices Relative to the Early History of the Town and Port of Hull; Compiled from Original Records and Unpublished Manuscripts and Illustrated with Engravings, Etchings and Vignettes* (London, 1827)
J. J. Sheahan: *General & Concise History and Description of the Town and Port of Kingston-upon-Hull* (London, 1864)
F. W. Brookes: 'A Medieval Brick-yard at Hull', *J. Brit. Archaeol. Assoc.*, 3rd ser., iv (1939), pp. 151–74
J. B. Fay: *Wilberforce House, Hull: History and Collections* (Hull, 1951)
A. G. Dickens and K. A. MacMahon: *A Guide to Regional Studies on the East Riding of Yorkshire and the City of Hull* (U. Hull, 1956)
N. Pevsner: *Yorkshire: York and the East Riding*, Bldgs England (Harmondsworth, 1972)
E. Gillett and K. A. MacMahon: *A History of Hull* (Birmingham, 1980)
J. Markham: *The Book of Hull* (Buckingham, 1989)

2. CENTRE OF CERAMICS PRODUCTION. Although pottery was produced in nearby Beverley, there are no known medieval potteries in Hull. In a deed dated 10 December 1802, the Humber Bank Pottery was established by the potters James Smith and Jeremiah Smith, Joseph Hapwood (a block-cutter) and Job Ridgway of Shelton, Staffs. The works produced printed cream-coloured earthenware, and in 1826 it was sold to William Bell and styled the Belle Vue Pottery. The shapes and the moulded and transfer-printed decorations deliberately imitated the Staffordshire designs, which at the time were popular in northern Europe; some items were inscribed in French or German. Twenty-nine patterns are known, printed in one of six colours on to Neo-classical or Rococo Revival shapes. Such patterns as the Chinese Marine were a reworking of other firms' designs. The firm also had a large export trade and was said to have undercut Staffordshire prices by 30%.

BIBLIOGRAPHY
J. Bartlett and D. Brooks: 'Hull Pottery', *Kingston-upon-Hull Mus. Bull.*, v (1970)

IVAN HALL

Hull Grundy, Anne. *See* GRUNDY, ANNE HULL.

Hullmandel, Charles Joseph (*b* London, 15 June 1789; *d* London, 15 Nov 1850). English draughtsman, lithographer and printer of German descent. He worked mainly in London, although he had trained in Paris as a painter and travelled extensively in Europe, making many topographical sketches and studies. In 1817 in Munich he met Alois Senefelder, who introduced him to lithography. One of the results of his travels was his *Twenty-four Views of Italy* (London, 1818), the images drawn and lithographed by himself. Dissatisfied with the way his work had been printed, Hullmandel set up his own lithographic press. His skilful production of, for instance, Giovanni Belzoni's *Plates Illustrative of the Researches and Operations in Egypt and Nubia* (London, 1820–22) did much to popularize the topographical lithograph among British artists.

Hullmandel was an indefatigable experimenter in the techniques of lithography, studying minutely the procedures of other lithographers and being particularly concerned to find ways of rendering tone with the subtlety of aquatint. He translated Antoine Raucourt de Charleville's *Mémoire sur les expériences lithographiques* (Paris, 1819) as *A Manual of Lithography* in 1820, adding extensive technical notes of another French lithographer, L.-R. Brégeaut, to the third edition (1832). In 1824 he published his own very influential *Art of Drawing on Stone* and in 1827 and 1829 pamphlets setting out further technical advances. Although an undistinguished artist, Hullmandel was a central figure in early 19th-century British lithography.

WRITINGS
ed.: *A Manual of Lithography* (London, 1820, rev. 3/1832); trans. of A. Raucourt de Charleville: *Mémoire sur les expériences lithographiques* (Paris, 1819)
The Art of Drawing on Stone (London, 1824)
On Some Important Improvements in Lithographic Printing (London, 1827)
On Some Further Improvements in Lithographic Printing (London, 1829)

BIBLIOGRAPHY
M. Twyman: *Lithography, 1800–1850* (London, 1970)

ANTHONY DYSON

Hulme, T(homas) E(rnest) (*b* Endon, N. Staffs, 16 Sept 1883; *d* Nieuport [now Nieuwpoort], Belgium, 28 Sept 1917). English writer. He studied at St John's College, Cambridge, but was 'sent down' in March 1904 for unruly behaviour. In 1906 he visited Canada and in the following year he taught English in Brussels while he studied French and German. It was also in 1907 that he first met HENRI BERGSON. Hulme was impressed above all by Bergson's criticism of 19th-century scientific rationalism and his view of reality as a 'flux of interpenetrated elements' ('Bergson's

Theory of Art', *Speculations*, p. 146) that can be comprehended as a whole only by the intuition rather than the intellect, which can grasp only discrete elements. A second part of Bergson's doctrine that he adopted was the idea that the ability to perceive reality in its complexity is weakened by the mind's practical 'orientation towards action' (*Speculations*, p. 147), and Hulme suggested that the role of the artist is precisely to pierce 'the veil placed between us and reality'.

In 1908 Hulme settled in London but began surreptitiously attending philosophy lectures at Cambridge University. In London he met Ezra Pound and A. R. Orage, the editor of the *New Age*, for which Hulme began writing articles on Bergson and other subjects in 1909. In 1911 he visited Italy and attended the Philosophical Congress in Bologna. While there he was able to visit Ravenna, where he was impressed by the Byzantine mosaics, stylistic echoes of which he thought he could see in the work of Jacob Epstein and other contemporary artists. Byzantine art seemed to him to be antithetical to the entire tradition of Western art since the Renaissance. Most importantly, its geometrical approach to form contradicted the aesthetics of humanism which, Hulme argued, had vitiated the Western artistic tradition. He condemned the art of the Renaissance for celebrating humanity, since he believed that men are by nature bad rather than good, an argument he also used as the basis for his authoritarian political opinions. Such art was therefore irreligious: 'At the Renaissance there were many pictures with religious subjects, but no religious art in the proper sense of the word' ('Humanism and the Religious Attitude', *Speculations*, p. 9). The humanism that had entered art at the Renaissance was also responsible for what Hulme saw as the remorseless decline in art up to the end of the 19th century. Nevertheless, he was hopeful that, following Cézanne, the work of a number of his contemporaries, such as Picasso, Jean Metzinger, Jacob Epstein, Wyndham Lewis and Henri Gaudier-Brzeska, represented a decisive break from the humanist tradition and the emergence of a 'new complex geometrical art' ('Modern Art and its Philosophy', *Speculations*, p. 94), characterized by a classical austerity.

In 1912 Hulme was readmitted to Cambridge, but again he did not stay long, finding the university environment unbearable, and he went to Berlin before settling once more in London. In Germany he came into contact with the work of WILHELM WORRINGER and of the aestheticians Johannes Volkelt and THEODOR LIPPS. From Worringer, Hulme adopted the distinction between vital and non-vital art, although he used it very much for his own purposes; from Volkelt and Lipps he took the idea of *Einfühlung*, or artistic empathy, which fitted well with his anti-rationalist approach.

By 1913 a number of artists in Hulme's circle, including Epstein, Lewis, Gaudier-Brzeska, Harold Gilman, Spencer Gore, Walter Richard Sickert, David Bomberg and Christopher Nevinson, had formed the London Group, and in 1913–14 Hulme wrote numerous reviews in the *New Age*, seeking to promote the work of the Group's members. In 1913 he also published a translation of Bergson's *Introduction à la métaphysique* (1903). An ardent militarist, he joined up with the Honourable Artillery Company at the beginning of World War I, and during the war he wrote articles defending militarist ideology for the *New Age* and the *Cambridge Magazine*, while also translating (1916) Georges Sorel's *Réflexions sur la violence* (1908). In addition, he had five short poems published in 1915, which were significant in the development of the Imagist movement in poetry. The same year he was wounded in France but returned to the front, to be killed in action two years later. He left a large number of notebooks containing materials for articles and lectures on aesthetic theory and other branches of philosophy, and these were later edited by Herbert Read and published as *Speculations* (1924) and *Notes on Language and Style* (1929). At the time of his death, Hulme was working on the manuscript of a book on Jacob Epstein, but this was not recovered after he was killed.

WRITINGS
trans.: H. Bergson: *Introduction à la métaphysique* (Paris, 1903) as *Introduction to Metaphysics* (London, 1913)
trans.: G. Sorel: *Réflexions sur la violence* (Paris, 1908) as *Reflections on Violence* (London, 1916)
H. Read, ed.: *Speculations: Essays on Humanism and the Philosophy of Art* (London, 1924, 2/1936/R London, 1987)
——: *Notes on Language and Style* (Seattle, 1929)
S. Hynes, ed.: *Further Speculations by T. E. Hulme* (Minneapolis, 1955)

BIBLIOGRAPHY
W. Lewis: *Blasting and Bombardiering* (London, 1937)
C. R. W. Nevinson: *Paint and Prejudice* (London, 1937)
M. Roberts: *T. E. Hulme* (London, 1938)
J. Epstein: *An Autobiography* (London, 1955)
A. R. Jones: *The Life and Opinions of T. E. Hulme* (London, 1960)

MATTHEW TAYLOR

Hülsen, Christian (*b* Berlin, 1858; *d* Florence, 1935). German architectural historian and archaeologist. He attended the University of Berlin from 1876 to 1880 and studied archaeology with Ernst Curtius and Hans Jordan, classical philology with Emil Hübner and Johannes Vahlen, ancient history with Hans Droysen and Theodor Mommsen, and epigraphy with Johann Wilhelm Adolf Kirchhoff. In 1881 he went to Rome with the aid of a grant from the German Institute of Archaeology. From then on he devoted himself to the study of Rome from the point of view of epigraphy, topography, cartography and urban development. He was especially interested in studying the ways in which Renaissance artists approached the ancient monuments of Rome. From 1887 to 1909 Hülsen held the post of second secretary of the Institute in Rome, and he was an honorary professor at the University of Heidelberg.

WRITINGS
with H. Kiepert: *Forma urbis Romae antiquae* (Berlin, 1896)
Das Forum Romanum (Rome, 1904; Eng. trans., Rome, 1906, 2/1909)
'La pianta di Roma dell'anonimo einsidlense', *Atti Pont. Accad. Romana Archeol.*, ii/9 (1907), pp. 377–424
La Roma antica di Ciriaco d'Ancona: Disegni inediti del secolo XV (Rome, 1907)
Il libro di Giuliano da Sangallo (Lipsia, 1910)
with H. Egger: *Die römischen Skizzenbücher von Marten van Heemskerck*, 2 vols (Berlin, 1913–16)
Saggio di bibliografia ragionata delle piante iconografiche e prospettiche di Roma dal 1551 al 1748 (Rome, 1915)
Le chiese di Roma nel Medio Evo (Florence, 1927)
Das Skizzenbuch des Giovannantonio Dosio im staatlichen Kupferstichkabinett zu Berlin (Berlin, 1933)

BIBLIOGRAPHY

Enc. It.; *NDB*

G. Pasquali: 'Ricordo di Christian Hülsen', *Pan: Rass. Lett., A. & Musica*, iii (1935), pp. 437–41; reprinted in *Pagine Strav.*, ii (1968), pp. 230–35

Dizionario enciclopedico italiano, v (Rome, 1956)

MASSIMILIANO DAVID

Hulsen [Hulsius; van der Hulst], **Esaias van** (*b* Middelburg, ?*c*. 1585; *d* Stuttgart, 1624). Dutch goldsmith, engraver and painter. He was the son of an emigrant family domiciled at Frankfurt am Main from 1602. By 1610 the Stuttgart Kunstkammer of Duke John Frederick of Württemberg (*reg* 1608–28) already contained naturalistic animal sculptures made of wax and feathers, which the Augsburg goldsmith Johannes Schwegler produced in collaboration with 'young Hulsio'. Similarly, Hulsen was also already engaged in the project to build a grotto for the Duke at Stuttgart before he became a court artist in 1611. Hulsen participated in the planning of the grotto, as well as furnishing it with paintings and sculptures, until the end of his life. In 1613 the engineer Gerhard Philippi (*d* 1621) had been charged with the work for the grotto and its ornamental fountains, and after his death, this reponsibility passed to Hulsen who left the project unfinished in 1624. Hulsen's technical knowledge even with regard to fortifications engineering is verified by a lost wooden model, for which he was paid by the Nuremberg council in 1617.

At his marriage in Frankfurt in 1612 Hulsen was documented as a goldsmith at Stuttgart. Almost the only evidence of his profession are his engravings for the goldsmiths' trade, some of which bear his full name, others his monogram and the dates 1606, 1609, 1616 and 1617 (e.g. *Ornament with Birds*, Holstein, nos 112–17): a series of curvilinear ornamental grotesques silhouetted in black, showing him to have been an accomplished decorative engraver. The series of engravings of the Stuttgart court festivals of 1616 and 1617, which Hulsen published in response to a ducal commission, were not executed by him, but at the most were partly based on his conception. His only known artistic involvement in the lavish festival decorations and display presentations was in the ballet productions. Painted works believed to be by Hulsen in the royal stables (the 'New Building') of the Stuttgart Altes Schloss (for which final payment was made in 1622/3) are lost, as are his paintings in the grotto.

BIBLIOGRAPHY

Hollstein: *Dut. & Flem.*; Thieme–Becker

W. Fleischhauer: *Renaissance im Herzogtum Württemberg* (Stuttgart, 1971), pp. 305–10, 334–5, 381–3, 415–16

C.-P. Warncke: *Die ornamentale Groteske in Deutschland: 1500–1650*, 2 vols (Berlin, 1979), i, p. 43; ii, pp. 98, 105–6, 108

MARION HAGENMANN-BISCHOFF

Hultén, C(arl) O(tto) (*b* Malmö, 10 Sept 1916). Swedish painter. He was self-taught as a painter, though he learnt much from his association with Max Walter Svanberg, with whom he founded the short-lived Minotaurgruppen in 1943. Three years later, with the Swedish painter Anders Österlin (*b* 1926) and others, they formed the Imaginistgruppen, which developed a specifically Swedish brand of Surrealism. Their activities, which continued until 1956, were connected from 1949 with those of the Cobra group, as was apparent from the work they exhibited at Hultén's

Colibi Gallery in Malmö in 1954. Hultén's own works at this time were painterly and were composed of fragmentary motifs of both a common and an exotic character, as in *City Woman Kissing* (1951; Malmö, Kstmus.). The poetic quality of his Imaginist works was carried through into his Abstract Expressionist period, from the late 1950s to the mid-1960s, in paintings such as *Windsign* (1961; Malmö, Kstmus.). After two extended visits to Central Africa, his work, while still surrealistic in expression, became full of allusions to exuberant tropical vegetation and to tribal culture.

BIBLIOGRAPHY

C. O. Hultén: Arbeten, 1938–1968 (exh. cat. by C. Dotremont and others, Lund, Ksthall, 1968)

A. Lundkvist: *C. O. Hultén: Fågelsyner och Urskogshot* [Views of birds and the threat to the primeval forest] (Stockholm, 1983)

C. O. Hultén (exh. cat., intro. J. Werup; Stockholm, Boibrino Gal., 1989)

SVEN SANDSTRÖM

Hültl, Dezső (*b* Felsőbánya, Transylvania [now Baia-Sprie, Romania], 6 April 1870; *d* Budapest, 11 July 1945). Hungarian architect, architectural historian and teacher. He studied (1888–92) at the Hungarian Palatine Joseph Technical University, Budapest, then joined the studio of the neo-Baroque architect Alajos Hauszmann, from whom he developed a lifelong interest in Baroque architecture. In 1902 he set up in independent practice in Budapest, producing designs in a neo-Baroque style, skilfully and tastefully adapted to modern requirements. His early buildings in Budapest, including a sanatorium, school and residential blocks, are skilfully executed, if conservative in design. The most striking is the former Piarist monastery and school (1913–18), Budapest, a vast irregular mass, based on an L-shaped plan, that nevertheless succeeds in blending in with its environment, including an 18th-century church that stands beside it. Hültl's blocks of flats of the 1920s are conventional, but his industrial buildings of the period, with the structural engineer Győző Mihailich (1877–1966), reveal a sensitivity to modern influences, for example the Corn Warehouse (1930), Csepel district, Budapest, and especially the Bus Garage (1929–30), Budapest, where his puritanical architectural outlook is embodied in a bold iron structure. During the 1930s he increasingly experimented with modernism, although without ever committing himself to it and without renouncing historicism. The galleried entrance hall of his hospital building (1934), S Peterfy Street, Budapest, is one of the most successful modernist interiors of the period. However, his blocks of flats of the late 1930s remain true to Baroque, both in form and decoration. In 1913 Hültl was made a professor in the Technical University, Budapest, where he primarily taught Renaissance and Baroque architectural history. He published a study on Bernini in 1906.

BIBLIOGRAPHY

'A piaristák budapesti építkezése' [The new building of the Piarists], *Építő Ipar-Építő Művészet*, xlii (1918), pp. 283–6, 291–3, 315–17

F. Merényi: *A magyar építészet, 1867–1967* [Hungarian architecture 1867–1967] (Budapest, 1970), p. 169 [detailed bibliog.]

FERENC VADAS

Hültz [Hiltz; Hultz], **Johann** [Jean; Johannes] (*b* Cologne, *c*. 1390; *d* Strasbourg, Aug 1449). German architect. He must have been trained in the circle of the Parler family, possibly in Cologne but far more likely in Prague, as there are close links between his work and the architecture of Prague (*see* PRAGUE, §IV, 2(i)). He is first documented as a foreman at Strasbourg Cathedral under Ulrich von Ensingen (*see* ENSINGEN, (1)), whom he succeeded as Master of the Works in 1419. He finished the octagon of the north-west tower and began the spire (*see* STRASBOURG, §III, 1).

When Hültz took over construction of the tower, the second octagonal storey was half complete, and the four stair turrets ended at the level of the first gallery. The traceried parapet of the second storey is his first identifiable work. Unlike Ulrich von Ensingen he did not use different layers of tracery but made a unified composition by using an astragal. Hültz's tracery forms, like those of Ensingen, were created by the superimposition of arch forms or by elongating them beyond the point of intersection.

A copy of Hültz's rather conventional first design for the spire survives (Strasbourg, Mus. Oeuvre Notre-Dame); the design for the spire as actually built, however, must have been ready while he was building the octagon. The spire consists of eight converging stone beams with a stairway on the outer edge of each, contained within a series of superimposed turrets. The stairway is not a simple spiral: it turns inversely from turret to turret in an undulating movement, twisting back on itself. The turrets themselves are decorated with open tabernacles, whose truncated pinnacle tops give the spire its characteristic appearance. The pinnacles have an almost smooth hexagonal section and are linked by intersecting arches. The spire terminates in a lantern; an iron cross was placed on top in Hültz's time. Hültz vaulted the second octagon storey with free-standing ribs closed in a star pattern. On every rib intersection sits a colonnette, on top of which are laid the horizontal stone slabs that form both the ceiling of the octagon and the floor of the spire.

Hültz developed new forms of construction for both the vaults and the spire, producing a practical and simple formal vocabulary quite distinct from the usual Gothic. Apparently for this reason his work was so alien to other 15th-century designers that he had no followers, even though the spire was much studied. His significance lies therefore in his structural achievements. His gravestone is decorated with his mason's mark, 3 Hs, and his motto *nit höher die Kunst* ('nothing higher than art').

BIBLIOGRAPHY

H. Reinhardt: *La Cathédrale de Strasbourg* (Grenoble, 1972)

B. Schock-Werner: *Das Strassburger Münster im 15. Jahrhundert*, 23, Veröff. Abt. Archit. Ksthist. Inst. U. Köln (Cologne, 1983)

BARBARA SCHOCK-WERNER

Humanism. Term invented in the 19th century, most commonly used to designate developments relating to the revival of Classical literature and learning in European culture from roughly 1300 to 1600. In other contexts, not covered here, it refers to post-Enlightenment programmes of educational reform promoting Classical studies in early 19th-century Germany and, broadly, to currents of opinion that accentuate the worthiness and potential of human beings either with or (often) without assistance from any religious tradition. So prominent is the 'revival of antiquity' in accounts of the transition from medieval to early modern Europe that 'renaissance' and 'humanism' are often used as overlapping, even interchangeable, concepts. Scholars in the 20th century seeking greater precision have proposed a variety of more highly differentiated definitions of the terms. None commands scholarly consensus. References to 'the humanist movement' are likewise as controverted as they are commonplace, and they highlight similarities if not direct linkages among a wide range of figures, elements and activities. Scholars routinely advise that Renaissance humanism is a broad, complex and multifaceted category embracing numerous chronological, regional, disciplinary and individual variations.

1. Humanism in 15th-century Italy. 2. The spread of humanism in Europe. 3. Humanism and the visual arts.

1. HUMANISM IN 15TH-CENTURY ITALY. The word 'humanist' (It. *umanista*) emerged in 15th-century Italy. It was apparently first applied to teachers of Classical letters devoted, following Roman precedents, to the advancement of the *studia humanitatis* (liberal arts), chiefly grammar, rhetoric, poetry, history and moral philosophy. This was a development of the tradition of Classical rhetoric, which, despite much neglect, persisted in the West. Skills (*ars dictaminis*) for the task of official letter-writing were revived in 11th-century chanceries, and the admiration for Classical writing and declamation in some legal and church circles in 13th-century Italy has been seen as proto-humanism by some scholars. From the 14th century the teacher–scholars typical of humanism sought to enlarge this course of study to include the full cycle of liberal arts and to put familiarity with the Classical heritage to new practical application. The term humanist was soon applied to others with similar interests.

Key figures in the 14th century were FRANCESCO PETRARCH, commonly called the founder of Italian humanism, and Giovanni Boccaccio. Petrarch, the first modern poet to be crowned as Poet Laureate on the Capitoline Hill in Rome (1341), was an enthusiastic and tireless advocate of Classical materials, genres and styles. He was the first to characterize the period after the fall of Rome as the 'dark ages', from which the glories of antiquity deserved to be reborn. The fame of Boccaccio, Petrarch's friend and associate, was based on his *Decameron* (*c*. 1353), a collection of vernacular short stories, his work with Classical texts and his memorials of illustrious men and women of antiquity. His compendium of Classical mythology, *De genealogia deorum gentilium* (1373), and Petrarch's *Trionfi* (*c*. 1343) were important sources for Renaissance writers and artists. Such figures inspired an increased interest in Classical antiquity, especially among the well-to-do laity of urban Italy and those aspiring to that status. This response in turn signalled a growing acceptance of the *studia humanitatis* as a pedagogical pathway leading to practical wisdom and to the perfecting of human character. The theoretical basis for humanist education beyond the university was set forth by Pietro Paolo Vergerio (1370–1444); its utility was asserted by Vittorino da Feltre and Guarino da Verona, whose schools became models for schoolmasters and tutors in Italy and then beyond. As such programmes spread, Classical studies were acknowledged as invaluable for creative endeavour in personal, civil, cultural and even ecclesiastical affairs.

A striking example of the character and effects of early humanism can be seen in the republic of Florence during the first half of the 15th century. Distinguished chancellors such as Coluccio Salutati (1331–1406), Leonardo Bruni and Poggio Bracciolini were themselves humanists by training or avocation. Around them formed coteries of patricians and others who undertook or financed humanistic pursuits. Their interests were never merely antiquarian. Classical models of eloquence in speaking and writing proved beneficial in statecraft, public policy debate and diplomacy. From Greco-Roman civilization came lessons and examples of the virtues of a free, patriotic citizenry. Their goal was to match, perhaps to excel, the public and cultural achievements of ancient Athens. Writers since Baron (1955) have portrayed Florentine civic humanism as the paradigm of Renaissance humanism. During this period humanists advocated the *vita activa*. Involvement in practical affairs and the desire to gain lasting fame by virtuous and noble deeds were encouraged; but these interests were not limited to republican Florentines. Humanists were welcomed, patronized and enrolled in service by many civic and religious leaders, some of whom were themselves humanists. Evidence of such ties include *Il principe* (1513; Rome, 1532) by Niccolò Machiavelli (1469–1517), advice to a ruler, apparently modelled on Cesare Borgia, and *Il libro del cortegiano* by Baldassare Castiglione (Venice, 1528), depicting life at the court of Guidobaldo da Montefeltro, Duke of Urbino.

Florence was also the setting for another notable development in humanism during the first half of the 15th century, the revival of Greek studies. Petrarch and Boccaccio were advocates but not masters of Greek. Florentine chancellors invited to the city scholars from Greece, most notably Manuel Chrysoloras (*c.* 1350–1415), who taught many leading humanists including Bruni, Vergerio, Palla Strozzi and Niccolò Niccoli. Bruni distinguished himself by translating the works of Plato and increasing the awareness in the West of the moral and political thought of Aristotle. Ambrogio Traversari, prior of S Maria degli Angeli, Florence, pioneered the study of Greek patristic literature. Influential in Florence and elsewhere were contacts with Byzantine scholars who came to the West in the 1430s to attempt a reunion of the Eastern and Western churches and after the fall of Constantinople (1453).

Humanism is perhaps best characterized in terms of the undertakings most typical of those who shaped it. About 1450 there were humanists throughout urban Italy, notably in Naples, Milan, Venice, Mantua, Ferrara, Rimini, Urbino and papal Rome. They were professors, schoolmasters, tutors; chancery officials, diplomats, civil servants; some were ecclesiastics; others were leisured individuals of independent means. Humanists aspired to fluency in the pure form of ancient languages—Latin, Greek and, to a lesser extent, Hebrew—rather than corrupt medieval versions. Fascination with letters extended from literacy to grammar, lexicography, rhetoric, philology and handwriting. From humanist adaptations of manuscript hands are derived typographical forms, for example the antique and italic types that remain in use. Humanists were eager to collect lost or forgotten classics, for which they often travelled far afield. Bracciolini's manuscript finds—

Ciceronian orations in Cluny, Quintilian's rhetoric in St Gall—were spectacular but not unique. Some of Europe's finest libraries were founded or enlarged in order to accommodate the texts collected by humanists. Cosimo de' Medici, a patron of humanism, established the first public library in Florence in 1444 to house the book collection of Niccoli, and popes, beginning with Nicholas V, built up the Vatican Library. Classical art and artefacts were also desired by humanists, who helped make fashionable the display of authentic and simulated antiquities. Humanists such as Bracciolini, Flavio Biondo and Cyriac of Ancona were among the first to make extensive archaeological surveys of the sites and monuments of the Classical world, both in Rome and further afield.

Collecting and surveying were rarely ends in themselves; humanists wanted to put Classical materials into public circulation. As editors, translators and commentators they laid the groundwork for much modern philological, literary and historical criticism. Lorenzo Valla (1407–57), for example, used new humanist standards of source criticism to question the authenticity of the Apostles' Creed, to expose as a forgery the Donation of Constantine—a document used to defend papal claims to temporal power—and to compare the Latin Vulgate to the Greek New Testament. Knowledge of the classics was also revealed in new literary works, both imitative and innovative. Humanists wrote letters, both public and private, and orations; novelle, aphorisms, epigrams, satires, eclogues and elegies; epic, lyrical and didactic poetry; histories of ancient and recent times; dialogues, tracts and treatises on moral philosophical concerns—human nature, the family, love, virtue and vice, politics, happiness, freedom, fortune and fate. The printing press and increased literacy opened up new markets for humanist writings: the Aldine Press, founded in 1495 by Aldus Manutius (1447–1515) of Venice, was one of the earliest and most renowned sources of such publications.

Summaries of 'humanist thought' based on samplings of these writings display certain recurring thematic emphases: human dignity, freedom and autonomy; critical reasoning; tolerance and toleration; mundane, humane and humanitarian values; appreciation of the sensory and historical world. Such listings, apt as they may be, are invariably too generalized. Humanists cared about living nobly, wisely and well; they mined the golden wisdom (*aurea sapientia*) of Classical antiquity for guidance, but they subscribed to no one philosophy or system of thought.

A development that came to fruition in the second half of the 15th century complicates any discussions of the topic. The encounter with the writings of antiquity reawakened interest in metaphysics as well as the liberal arts. The tradition of scholastic Aristotelianism was reshaped by the Paduan philosopher Pietro Pomponazzi (1462–1525) and others into a neo-Aristotelianism; Giordano Bruno (1548–1600) added elements from Neo-Platonism, the theories of Nicolaus Copernicus (1473–1543) and hermetic thought to construct a grand form of pantheism. Even more striking was the resurgence and recasting of the equally long-established (and variegated) Platonic tradition. The German philosopher Nicholas of Cusa (1401–64) identified God as the point of unity upon which all multiplicity intersects. Neo-Platonic studies flourished at the informal Platonic Academy in Florence sponsored by the Medici and led by Marsilio Ficino, whose master-works, *De religione christiana* (1474) and *Theologia platonica* (1469–74), fashioned a speculative synthesis of philosophy and theology. His associate, Giovanni Pico della Mirandola (1463–94), brought neo-Pythagorean, hermetic, mystical and cabbalistic traditions into the mix. Whether the turn to metaphysics represented a development or a deviation from the humanist movement is disputed. Neo-Platonism left such a strong imprint on later humanists that distinctions are overdrawn. Beginning with Cristoforo Landino, Angelo Poliziano and Pietro Bembo, a vast outpouring of humanist poetry and prose derived from this tradition, permeated by themes, allegories and sensibilities.

2. THE SPREAD OF HUMANISM IN EUROPE. Another critical and complicating development was the expansion of humanism throughout Europe. Its social location—in educational, courtly and church settings—remained substantially unchanged, but European humanism was far more diffuse than earlier Italian varieties. Although Classical Latinity had been the favoured (but not the exclusive) medium of expression of early humanists in Italy, vernacular eloquence by writers such as Poliziano gained increasing prominence there and elsewhere, as did interminglings of Classical with national, native and medieval materials. Northern humanists were diverse. Notable exponents included: in England, the scholar clerics John Colet (*c.* 1467–1519) and Thomas More, author of *Utopia* (Leuven, 1516); in Spain, Cardinal Francisco Jiménez de Cisneros, founder of the University of Alcalá de Henares and sponsor of the Complutensian Polyglot Bible (Alcalá de Henares, 1514–17) and Miguel de Cervantes (1547–1616), author of *Don Quixote* (Madrid, 1605–15); in France, the scholars Guillaume Budé (1468–1540) and Jacques Lefèvre d'Etaples (1455–1536), the writers François Rabelais (*c.* 1495–1533) and Michel de Montaigne; in Germany, the poet Sebastian Brant (1457–1521), author of *Das Narrenschiff* (Basle, 1494), the Dutch scholar Rudolf Agricola (1444–85), called the 'German Petrarch', Conrad Celtis (1459–1508), Poet Laureate of the Holy Roman Empire, and the Hebraist Johannes Reuchlin (1455–1522). Of international repute was Erasmus, whose travels and contacts, no less than his popular, scholarly and religious writings, made him the chief apostle of Northern humanism.

Humanists also became involved in the conflicts of the Reformation. The notion of a 'Christian humanism' in the North, as opposed to a secular, pagan or anti-Christian humanism in Italy, is largely discredited. Although humanism and scholastic Christianity have sometimes been portrayed as mutually exclusive options, popular and official Christianity were too diverse to warrant such a view, and most humanists accepted that Classical wisdom and Christian truth were harmonious. As late medieval pluralism gave way to divisions in the Church, pressures mounted for Northern humanists especially to declare themselves regarding religion and its reform. Although many, like Erasmus and More, remained Roman Catholic, many others, including Philip Melanchthon (1497–1560), Ulrich Zwingli (1484–1531) and Martin Bucer (1491–1551) associated themselves with the emerging Protestant movements. Martin Luther advocated evangelical rather than humanist faith, but he drew on humanist scholarship and backed Melanchthon's humanist reform of German education. John Calvin (1509–64) began his public career as a humanist, and this training is apparent in his thought.

3. HUMANISM AND THE VISUAL ARTS. The problems of defining humanism in relation to art are compounded by the notion of 'renaissance' art. Some scholars unhesitatingly speak of 'the arts in the age of humanism' and even 'the art of humanism'; others resolve to treat the arts in terms independent of any such associations. This division reflects a healthy suspicion about relying on broad categories such as 'humanism' and 'renaissance' in historical inquiry generally and in art history and criticism in particular. There is an increasing tendency for scholars to explore issues and employ methods that break free of traditional debates about the phases, schools and types of both 'renaissance thought' and 'renaissance style'.

Humanists were first and foremost men of letters. Insofar as they involved themselves with the visual arts, Classical or contemporary *all'antica*, they did so because of what they deemed common interests. They were often employed to devise iconographic programmes for artists. For their part, many artists and works of art displayed a familiarity with sources, tastes and ideals in favour among not only humanists but patrons and other segments of the public educated along humanist lines. Historians thus face a dilemma. It is easy to speak, at a general level, of manifold commonalities, correlations and connections between humanism and the arts; when to label any specific artist or work of art 'humanist' is another, and contested, question.

At first sight evidence of such connections appears in two fields. There are those instances in which writers and artists comment on one another with appreciation, as when Petrarch likened Simone Martini, and Ugolino Verino likened Sandro Botticelli, to Apelles. There were also various allusions to the dawning of a new age with Dante, Petrarch, Cimabue, Giotto and Duccio. Of greater moment is the inclusion of arts in humanistic memorializations of the illustrious, notably the accounts of artists' lives written by Vasari and Karel van Mander. Notoriously unreliable as histories, such testimonials are telling primary sources nonetheless. Humanism also played a part in changing the status of visual artists, a process begun by Leon Battista Alberti in the 15th century. Humanists tended to view artists as practitioners of the high-status liberal arts, rather than the mechanical, and hence to urge them to study the humanities.

By the same token, causes for which humanists laboured were treated by artists. Noteworthy examples include Taddeo di Bartolo's fresco cycle of *Cardinal and Political Virtues* (1413–14; Siena, Pal. Pub.), *Young Boy Reading Cicero* (mid-1460s; London, Wallace) by Vincenzo Foppa, the zodiacal triumphs (*c.* 1469; Ferrara, Pal. Schifanoia; see FERRARA, fig. 3) by Francesco del Cossa and others, Botticelli's *Pallas and the Centaur* (Florence, Uffizi) and *A Youth Presented to the Liberal Arts* (1491; Paris, Louvre), Raphael's *School of Athens* (1509–11; Rome, Vatican, Stanza della Segnatura), Paolo Veronese's *Triumph of Venice* (*c.* 1582; Venice, Doge's Pal.), *Pallas Protecting the Arts and Sciences* (Vienna, Ksthist. Mus.) by Bartholomeus

Spranger and *Four Philosophers* (*c.* 1612; Florence, Pitti) by Rubens. Humanists were frequently the subject of portraits. Cardinal Bessarion (?1403–72), prelate–scholar and translator of Greek texts, is portrayed in the *Vision of St Augustine* (1502–7; Venice, Scuola S Giorgio degli Schiavoni) by Vittore Carpaccio. Lorenzo Lotto's portrait of *Andrea Odoni* (1527; London, Hampton Court, Royal Col.) shows the collector surrounded by his antiquities. Raphael painted *Baldassare Castiglione* (1514–15; Paris, Louvre) as the ideal courtier. Hans Holbein the younger several times painted Thomas More and Erasmus, who was also portrayed by Albrecht Dürer (1520; Paris, Louvre) and Quinten Metsys (1517; London, Hampton Court, Royal Col.).

A second field of observation reveals instances in which writers and artists were connected by ties of patronage. Filippo Brunelleschi, Lorenzo Ghiberti, Donatello and Masaccio worked in Florence during the great era of civic humanism. Botticelli and Michelangelo were closely associated with Ficino and other leading Neo-Platonists in the circle of Lorenzo de' Medici. The Gonzagas in Mantua protected humanists including Castiglione and Vittorino da Feltre as well as the painter Andrea Mantegna. Popes Julius II and Leo X assembled a remarkable group of scholars and artists in Rome, notably Pietro Bembo, Donato Bramante, Leonardo da Vinci, Michelangelo and Raphael. Francis I patronized Budé, Leonardo, Rabelais, Sebastiano Serlio and artists of the Fontainebleau schools, such as Rosso Fiorentino and Francesco Primaticcio. The book trade too produced notable matches, for example Dürer's illustrations for Brant's *Das Narrenschiff* and prints by the Haarlem painter Maarten van Heemskerck for the publications of the Dutch humanist Dirck Volkertsz. Coornhert. Such connections suggest extensive relations between humanist men of letters and visual artists. Much of the evidence, however, is circumstantial, the relations tangential, and the extent of the impact of patrons and patronage on artists is the subject of much fresh, often revisionist, research based on archival resources and methods derived from social history.

Other connections between literary humanism and the visual arts are discernible. Humanism was demonstrated in writings as well as in works of art by, among others, Alberti, Ghiberti, Leonardo, Michelangelo, Dürer, Benvenuto Cellini and Joachim von Sandrart, the 'German Apelles'. Alberti is particularly important, as he articulated humanist views, setting the arts, and discussion of the arts, on a new, higher level, establishing the basis of academic art theory. Especially significant was his study of the rediscovered texts of Vitruvius, his appreciation of the architecture of Brunelleschi and, related to both, his reflections on proportion, balance, harmony and perspective. None of the procedures Alberti advocated was a humanist invention. He made them humanist by the adoption of mathematical, didactic and Classical principles. His thoughts on perspective were often reviewed and augmented by strains of Neo-Platonism and Neo-Pythagoreanism, later exploited in theoretical treatises by Piero della Francesca, Leonardo, Andrea Palladio and Dürer, and in such bold explorations of visual space as those of Paolo Uccello. The revival of Classical architectural forms

in the works of Bramante, Leonardo, Palladio and Serlio owed much directly or indirectly to Alberti's influence.

Humanists and artists alike were devotees of the cult of antiquity. Inasmuch as humanists led a revival of Greek and Roman literary models, it is tempting to attribute the prevalence of Classical forms and subjects in the arts to humanist influence; but the complexities of the situation justify caution. Both writers and artists drew on a far wider range of Classical forms and contents than did their medieval predecessors. For both, Classical precedents served as points of departure for creative endeavours, and these developments in letters and arts were concurrent and mutually reinforcing.

Literary humanism gave artists access to larger portions of the Classical heritage. More significantly, it helped legitimize an expanded range of artistic ventures, even those that artists undertook for reasons related to aesthetics, technique or commerce. A standard humanist notion about art was the reversal of Horace's dictum 'ut pictura poesis' ('as is painting so is poetry'; *Ars poetica* 361; *see* UT PICTURA POESIS). The rise in status of the visual arts in the Renaissance is reflected in the extension of literary comparisons to comparisons between the visual arts, such as PARAGONE, the dispute about the relative merits of painting and sculpture. Thus artists profited from humanist valuations of Classical mythology, depictions of life past and present, and the nobility and beauty of man—a theme expressed in depictions of the human figure, clothed or nude, idealized or individualized. Humanist concern for philological–historical accuracy was matched by that of many artists for the authenticity of architectural and other details in the treatment of religious as well as secular subjects. The attentiveness of Mantegna in this respect, for example in *St Sebastian* (*c.* 1480; Paris, Louvre), his frescoes (*c.* 1450; most destr. 1944) in the Ovetari chapel of the church of the Eremitani, Padua, and the *Triumphs of Caesar* (*c.* 1484–94; London, Hampton Court, Royal Col.), was a quality prized by numerous others.

Humanism also placed new emphasis on those whose virtues and deeds made a mark on human history. This was given artistic expression in various ways. It is evident, for example, in equestrian statuary: Donatello's *Gattamelata* (1447–53; Padua, Piazza del Santo; *see* DONATELLO, fig. 3), depicting the condottiere Erasmo da Narni (1370–1443), Andrea del Verrocchio's monument (*c.* 1485; Venice, Campo SS Giovanni e Paolo) to Narni's successor *Bartolomeo Colleoni* (1400–76), and Leonardo's plans (Windsor Castle, Berks, Royal Col.) for a monument in Milan to Gian Giacomo Trivulzio (1441–1518). The same impulse appears in painted equestrian portraits, such as *Sir John Hawkwood* (1436; Florence Cathedral) by Uccello, *Niccolò da Tolentino* (*c.* 1456; Florence Cathedral) by Andrea del Castagno and *Charles V at Mühlberg* (*c.* 1548; Madrid, Prado) by Titian.

Artists were also commissioned to contribute to galleries of heroes. Uccello drew on Petrarch and Boccaccio for figures (destr.) adorning the Casa Vitaliani in Padua (1444–8). Castagno featured illustrious men and women (*c.* 1450; Florence, Uffizi) in scenes for the gallery of the Villa Carducci, near Florence. Pietro Perugino memorialized figures from Livy and Plutarch in the Sala dell' Udienza (*c.* 1500) of the Collegio del Cambio, Perugia. Among other examples are Masaccio's procession of famous men of Florence (*c.* 1422; destr. 1598–1600) in S Maria del Carmine, Florence, and the portraits of 28 famous men (*c.* 1473–6; Paris, Louvre; Urbino, Pal. Ducale) that were painted for the *studiolo* of Federigo da Montefeltro's ducal palace at Urbino and are attributed to Justus of Ghent. Of similar inspiration were such distinguished funerary works of the Renaissance as the tomb of *Leonardo Bruni* (*c.* 1445–50; Florence, Santa Croce) by Bernardo Rossellino and Michelangelo's designs for the tombs of the Medici (1520–34; Florence, S Lorenzo) and *Julius II* (from 1513; Rome, S Pietro in Vincoli).

Intimacy between writers and artists is indicated by artistic renderings of humanist texts and programmes. Close investigation, however, reveals that allegations of direct dependence or collaboration are often hard to prove. Coluccio Salutati's *De laboribus Herculis* (*c.* 1391), on the meanings of Classical legends, prepared the way for many artistic renderings of the hero. Lorenzo Ghiberti's *Gates of Paradise* (*c.* 1435; Florence, Baptistery; *see* GHIBERTI, (1), fig. 4) is attributed to a programme by Traversari. Titian's mythological paintings for the *studiolo* of Alfonso I d'Este, Duke of Ferrara and Modena, were derived from the *Imagines* of Philostratus the elder. The first of the series for the *studiolo*, Giovanni Bellini's *Feast of the Gods* (*c.* 1514; Washington, DC, N.G.A.) links Bellini to Pietro Bembo, just as Mantegna's and Perugino's mythological scenes (Paris, Louvre) for Isabella d'Este's *studiolo* in Mantua link them to her artistic adviser Paride da Ceresara. Botticelli's *Calumny of Apelles* (1490s; Florence, Uffizi) follows an ekphrasis in Lucian of Samosata, while his *Primavera* (*c.* 1478; Florence, Uffizi; *see* BOTTICELLI, SANDRO, fig. 2) and *Birth of Venus* (*c.* 1485; Florence, Uffizi) are apparently based on the writings of Angelo Poliziano. They are certainly suffused with Neo-Platonism, as are Titian's *Sacred and Profane Love* (*c.* 1515; Rome, Gal. Borghese; *see* TITIAN, fig. 2) and much of Michelangelo's art. *Arcadia* (Naples, 1504) by Jacopo Sannazzaro (1456–1530) inspired innumerable pastorals in both poetry and painting.

The sources and forms of Renaissance humanism were diverse, as were its effects, including those on the visual arts. Connective links such as those suggested above show that interdisciplinary inquiries remain very much in order.

BIBLIOGRAPHY

G. Vasari: *Vite* (1550, rev. 2/1568); ed. G. Milanesi (1878–85)

K. van Mander: *Schilder-boek* ([1603]–1604)

J. Burckhardt: *Die Cultur der Renaissance in Italien* (Basle, 1860, 15/1926); Eng. trans., 2 vols (London and New York, 1929/*R* 1958)

E. Panofsky: *Studies in Iconology: Humanistic Themes in the Art of the Renaissance* (New York, 1939)

O. Benesch: *The Art of the Renaissance in Northern Europe: Its Relation to the Contemporary Spiritual and Intellectual Movements* (Cambridge, MA, 1945)

E. Garin: *Der italienische Humanismus* (Berne, 1947); rev. as *L'umanesimo italiano: Filosofia e vita civile nel rinascimento* (Bari, 1952; Eng. trans., Oxford and New York, 1965)

M. Cosenza: *Biographical and Bibliographical Dictionary of the Italian Humanists and of the World of Classical Scholarship in Italy, 1300–1800* (New York, 1952); rev., 6 vols, Boston, 2/1962–8)

M. Gilmore: *The World of Humanism, 1453–1517* (New York, 1952)

H. Baron: *The Crisis of the Early Italian Renaissance*, 2 vols (Princeton, 1955, rev. 1966)

P. O. Kristeller: *The Classics and Renaissance Thought* (Cambridge, MA, 1955); rev. as *Renaissance Thought*, 2 vols (New York, 1961–5)

E. Panofsky: *Renaissance and Renascences in Western Art*, 2 vols (Stockholm, 1960)

A. Chastel: *The Age of Humanism: Europe, 1480–1530* (New York, 1964)

P. O. Kristeller: *Eight Philosophers of the Italian Renaissance* (Stanford, 1964)

R. Weiss: *The Spread of Italian Humanism* (London, 1964)

D. Hay, ed.: *The Age of the Renaissance* (New York and London, 1967)

H. Baron: *From Petrarch to Leonardo Bruni: Studies in Humanistic and Political Literature* (Chicago, 1968)

M. Cosenza: *Checklist of Non-Italian Humanists* (Boston, 1969)

G. Holmes: *The Florentine Enlightenment, 1400–1500* (New York, 1969)

K. Clark: *The Art of Humanism* (Cambridge, 1970)

C. Trinkaus: *'In Our Image and Likeness': Humanity and Divinity in Italian Humanist Thought*, 2 vols (London, 1970)

M. Baxandall: *Giotto and the Orators: Humanist Observers of Painting in Italy and the Discovery of Pictorial Composition, 1350–1450* (Oxford, 1971)

L. Spitz: *The Renaissance and Reformation Movements*, 2 vols (St Louis, 1971)

E. Gombrich: *Symbolic Images: Studies in the Art of the Renaissance* (London, 1972)

H. Oberman and C. Trinkaus, eds: *The Pursuit of Holiness in Late Medieval and Renaissance Religion* (Leiden, 1974)

T. Brady and H. Oberman, eds: *Itinerarium Italicum: The Profile of the Italian Renaissance in the Mirror of its European Transformations* (Leiden, 1975)

P. O. Kristeller: *Renaissance Thought and its Sources* (New York, 1979)

E. Fryde: *Humanism and Renaissance Historiography* (London, 1983)

C. Trinkaus: *The Scope of Renaissance Humanism* (Ann Arbor, 1983)

B. Kohl: *Renaissance Humanism, 1300–1550: A Bibliography of Materials in English* (New York and London, 1985)

B. Cole: *Italian Art, 1250–1550: The Relation of Renaissance Art to Life and Society* (New York, 1987)

A. Rabil, ed.: *Renaissance Humanism: Foundations, Forms and Legacy*, 3 vols (Philadelphia, 1988)

A. Goodman and A. MacKay, eds: *The Impact of Humanism on Western Europe* (London and New York, 1990)

J. Henderson and T. Verndon, eds: *Christianity and the Renaissance: Image and Religious Imagination in the Quattrocento* (Syracuse, NY, 1990)

J. Monfasani and R. Musto, eds: *Renaissance Society and Culture: Essays in Honor of Eugene F. Rice, Jr* (New York, 1991)

JAMES O. DUKE

Human proportion. The quantitative relationship of the parts of the human body to each other and to the whole body. This article discusses theories of figural representation and their application in Western fine arts and architecture.

1. Introduction. 2. Painting and sculpture. 3. Architecture and cosmology. 4. The golden section.

1. INTRODUCTION. A theory of human proportion, i.e. a metrical definition of the parts of the human body in relation to each other and to the whole body, was first established and practised by the Egyptians with the measurement of the foot, forearm (ell), hand and fingers, then taken over by the Greeks and modified by POLYKLEITOS and finally concisely summarized in written form in the reign of Emperor Augustus by his military architect VITRUVIUS in *On Architecture*; it did not recover its importance until after the Migration period, when the Holy Roman Emperor Charlemagne was instrumental in reintroducing it. In his self-appointed role as Christian refounder of the Roman Empire, the Emperor and his advisers consciously wanted to renew Classical art and the Vitruvian tradition, which in France had never completely died, and were regarded as setting standards not only for architecture but subsequently for depicting people also.

Vitruvius observed with regard to human proportions (III.i.2):

> For nature has so formed the human body that the length of the face from the chin to the uppermost part of the forehead and the bottom of the hairline is 1:10; the extent of the hand from the wrist to the tip of the middle finger is likewise 1:10; the head from the chin to the apex of the crown 1:8; from the upper end of the chest with the lower part of the neck to the hairline 1:6; from the middle of the chest to the apex of the crown 1:4. From the lower part of the chin to the nostrils is a third of the length of the face itself, as is the measurement of the nose from the nostrils to the mid-point between the eyebrows. From this line to the hairline ... the height of the forehead is likewise 1:3. But the foot is 1:6 of the body height, the forearm 1:4, and the chest also 1:4. The other limbs too have their own proportions in the "symmetry".

(For the Classical meaning of 'symmetry', *see* SYMMETRY.) Vitruvius also wrote that the natural centre of the body was the navel (III.i.3):

> For if a man lies on his back with his arms and legs splayed out and the point of a compass is placed on the navel and a circle is drawn, the tips of the fingers of both hands and the tips of the toes would touch the circle. Likewise the shape of a square could be found in the body: for if you measure from the soles of the feet to the crown of the head and apply this measure to the horizontally outstretched arms, you will obtain the same breadth and height, just as on surfaces that are laid out as squares using mathematical instruments.

The linking of the human form to the circle and square is best known today through Leonardo da Vinci's drawing (see fig. 1) and referred to as '*homo ad circulum*' and '*homo ad quadratum*' in discussions relating to questions of proportion (*see also* VITRUVIUS, fig. 2).

Although these data have their real meaning in Vitruvius' work only with reference to the relevance of human proportions to the buildings built for and lived in by human beings, his remarks concerning the relationship of the human form to the circle and the square prompted cosmological interpretations and were seen as the most important proofs of human involvement in the order of the universe (which was believed to be spherical). Thus various strands of the theory of human proportion can be traced, since Vitruvius' ideas were accepted in the early Middle Ages in Europe.

2. PAINTING AND SCULPTURE. The simplest aspect concerns the practical application of Vitruvius' data to the representation of the human figure. This took the form of rules of foolproof simplicity for those employed in art workshops and studios. A simple module process based on nine face-lengths was used in Byzantine monastery workshops until the 18th century, with a single basic measure, the length of the face (excluding the hair) being a third of the length of the torso, and a single subdivision of a third of the length of the face (which also had to serve for the vault of the cranium, the length of the neck and the height of the feet). This process, with its constant divisions into three, was also held to refer to the divine Trinity, suggested by the figure of Christ. Eminent Western artists and textbooks, on the other hand, generally adhered to the eight head-lengths that Vitruvius had assigned to the human form, with the simple arithmetical proportion

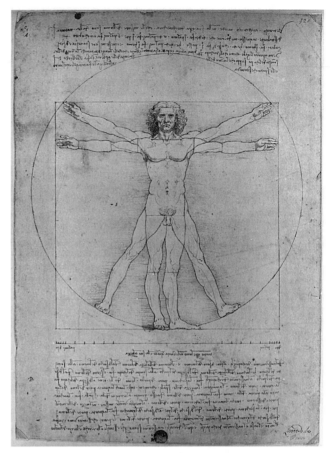

1. *Homo ad circulum*, drawing by Leonardo da Vinci, after Vitruvius, pen and ink on paper, 343×245 mm, 1485/90 (Venice, Galleria dell'Accademia)

of the parts to the whole of 4:6:8:10. Occasional minor deviations are explained by the fact that, even before Polykleitos, the Greeks had successfully made corrections to the norm once it had been established and had used these alongside the norm.

In the Renaissance a fundamental criticism of these simple rules was made by LEON BATTISTA ALBERTI. Thus for his textbook *De statua* (after 1464) he measured man from 67 positions, using a system that took the foot as its unit (based on Vitruvius' ratio of six foot lengths in the human body) and initiating a decimal system derived from human members (forearm, foot, palm etc). The foot is subdivided into 10 *unceolae* (ounces) and 100 *minutae* (so that the human height comes to 600 *minutae*); this was intended to provide a logical guide for artists. In his third textbook *De pictura* (1435) he described such measuring as a reliable and uniform record of sizes by means of which it was possible to gain and to express numerically as much knowledge of the relation of the individual parts of a body to one another as of their relation to the whole body.

Though Leonardo da Vinci began his study of proportion with a similar purpose by looking for parts of the body that were of equal length, he soon turned away from detailed measuring, which he considered unproductive, to other aspects of the science of human proportion. Albrecht Dürer (*see* DÜRER, (1)), on the other hand, followed in Alberti's footsteps and undertook a fundamental checking and correction of the simple traditional rule that presupposed a single ideal figure. Like Leonardo, he was convinced that there were regular laws according to which God had created mankind, and for 30 years he studied and investigated everything that had been written on the subject of proportion, starting with Vitruvius, in an attempt to establish by constantly repeated measurements the 'secret of the supreme beauty' that is perceived 'in creatures'. During this period Dürer measured all types of human beings, large and small, fat and thin, using the laborious measuring process evolved by Alberti. He observed that each of the various constitutions had its own beauty and its own proportion. He adopted Alberti's 'foot' as a standard, dividing it into ten 'numbers', which were again each divided into five parts, each of which was finally divided into three 'bits'. His completed project, *Die vier Bücher von menschlicher Proportion* (Nuremberg, 1528) comprised a theory of differentiated human types intended for apprentice painters. The first book introduces five male and five female types with heights of seven, eight, nine and ten face-lengths, each shown in a front, side and back view, measured in fractions of the length of the body (which are often rounded up to whole numbers and written on to the figures). It also features a child and exact measurements and pictures of a man's and woman's hand and foot. The second book increases the number of types to thirteen of either sex, measured according to Alberti's decimal system. Only occasional references to the circle into which the figures (covered with measuring data) are fitted reveal that these studies take Vitruvius as their starting-point. For Dürer as for Alberti (and in a certain sense for Polykleitos' Canon of Proportion too), the connecting link whereby proportion (according to Plato's *Timaeus*) binds together unequal parts so as to constitute beauty lay in the good relationship of each, even the smallest, individual measurement to the measured sections adjacent to it.

In the centuries that followed, the simple, traditional rules of measurement used in antiquity remained binding on painters and sculptors and were handed down in artists' studios as unquestioned lore. In 1723 Johann Georg Bergmüller published the manual *Anthropometria oder Statur des Menschen von der Geburt an nach seinem Wachstum und verschiedenem Alter nach den Regeln der Proportion* (Augsburg). Making independent use of the principles proposed by Dürer and other Renaissance writers, it draws up clear rules for representational purposes. Similar books must have been published in other European countries too after the foundation of the academies. Johann Gottfried Schadow, a sculptor at the Berlin court and later Director of the Berlin Akademie, followed Bergmüller and his inclusion of the different ages in his book *Polyklet oder von den Massen des Menschen* (Berlin, 1834), in which he produced 29 plates of children of both sexes from birth up to the age of 20 in contour outline with measurements in the 'Rhenish inch rule' for the practical use of artists.

With the advent of avant-garde, non-objective painting in the 20th century human proportions ceased to play a role even in objective painting and sculpture; art is now concerned with pursuing completely new purposes of representation and no longer sets out only to approximate nature.

3. ARCHITECTURE AND COSMOLOGY. The other two aspects of a theory of human proportion were closely bound up with one another through the entire Christian medieval period. They were its connection with architecture, emphasized by Vitruvius, and its connection with the laws governing creation, which Plato brought to light in his dialogue *Timaeus*. These aspects were ultimately interwoven, particularly in the practice and theory of architecture, with ideas concerning onto-cosmological dimensions in human existence, which were held to be made perceptible to the senses in buildings that corresponded with them.

In the early Middle Ages geometric ideal forms played an important role in painting too: the circle, the equilateral triangle symbolizing the Trinity and the square and rectangle, with their right angles symbolizing a universally 'right' order. Byzantine artists constructed not only the face of Christ but their whole picture composition using three circles or triangles or quadrangles of the above kind. In their book illustrations Christian scholars in the West developed skilful diagrams demonstrating the position of

2. Rule-of-thumb precepts of proportion from the portfolio of Villard de Honnecourt, parchment, 226×140 mm, *c.* 1235 (Paris, Bibliothèque Nationale, MS. fr. 19093)

man in the order of the world expressed in terms of geometry. Villard de Honnecourt, the 13th-century architect, produced a pattern book for painters and architects demonstrating that, even in the square grid on to which the most important points of a figure can be plotted, which had been in use as an aid to construction since the ancient Egyptian period, the relationships of squares circumscribing and conversely inscribed in a circle with the regular triangles created by their diagonals, as well as the combination of the circle with free, though symmetrical, triangular configurations, can be used as a basis not just for building but also for the composition of pictures and figures (see fig. 2). This type of practice was derived from the rules used in stonemasons' lodges, which were based on a precise knowledge of the numerical relationships existing between the lengths of the sides, heights, diagonals and inter-corner lines in polygons and polyhedrons; these can be inscribed in continually reducing dimensions in a circle or sphere, or a square or cube, and the structures thus achieved were used as the basis for the proportioning of the individual parts of a church, façade or tower. Goldsmiths also used this technique to project tower-shaped reliquaries or precious goblets, and Dürer (himself the son of a goldsmith) showed in drawings that the sculptor could rough-hew his block of wood or stone to create a correctly proportioned human figure on the basis of such a foundation plan before proceeding to detailed working.

The fact that such architectural processes were still linked to a consideration of human proportion is supported by Plato's *Timaeus*, which medieval thinkers and theologians took very seriously. It could be read there that the cosmos was constructed from a multiplicity of different polyhedrons and that within its perfect spherical form the world-soul, which animates everything, is stretched out in an X-shape, simultaneously filling the cosmos in every direction and surrounding it in a circular movement. To the Middle Ages the X meant Christ and was the image of the *homo ad circulum* that Vitruvius had described in such a matter-of-fact way as one of the measuring standards of man—although even in Vitruvius it probably had a cosmological meaning behind it. According to Plato, however, the most beautiful of all bonds, the unifying bond of proportion, prevented the various parts of the cosmos from disintegrating. Medieval scholars were convinced that man, the microcosm, was created according to the same laws as the universe, which was the macrocosm; to them the relevant proportional connections for man too were contained in these figures and length relationships.

The rediscovery and revival of Vitruvius and Plato in the 15th century, due partly to the invention of printing, led to the transformation of these old methods and speculations used by Gothic architects into a completely new theory and practice of architecture (*see also* ARCHITECTURAL PROPORTION, §II). Churches and even fortresses were now supposed to reproduce human proportions in such a way that their measurements corresponded with multiples of the measure of the head, shoulders, torso, arms or breadth or length of the body of a well-proportioned human figure. From one of his drawings Gianlorenzo Bernini appears to have seen St Peter's, Rome, with the colonnade as its arms, representing

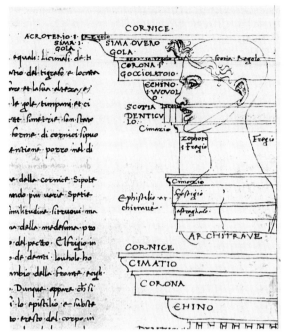

3. Cornice profile after the proportion of the human face, from the Codex Magliabechiano, mid-16th century (Florence, Biblioteca Nazionale Centrale, MS. Magl., XVII, 17, fol. 37)

the image and symbol of Christ in human form. In the Baroque period it was still known that a pilaster that served as a support would not be effective optically if it were narrower than a man's shoulders. The comparison of the various Classical orders with human forms was then adopted from Vitruvius: the Doric column with the masculine stature of nine face-lengths, the Ionic with the female stature of seven face-lengths and the Corinthian measuring eight face-lengths. Capitals and entablatures were proportioned in accordance with the human face. Drawings suggesting this could be found not only in Leonardo's work but also in architectural textbooks (see fig. 3).

In the Renaissance, Leonardo da Vinci reconsidered Plato's ideas and the meaning of the Vitruvian figures of *homo ad circulum* and *homo ad quadratum*. He perceived in the shape of the circle a correct pattern of movement for the human body that gave it a 'second form', which became visible in the circling movement round his own centre and that of his limbs round their various joints; this second form not only extended the measurements of the human body beyond the confines of the actual body to the farthest reach of the limbs but also invited comparisons with the movements of the heavenly bodies as they circle round a centre. He perceived a connection between the measurements of man and the measurements and form of space, a connection that corporeally, spiritually and aesthetically corresponds and is commensurate with the measurements of his active movement. The shape of the circle as the symbol of the form of the cosmos was the most perfect of all shapes to Renaissance Neo-Platonists; consequently it had to become the favourite figure in their architecture too, hence their predilection for centrally planned buildings. The extraordinary Codex Huygens (New York, Pierpont Morgan Lib., MS. M.39), produced in the circle of Leonardo's pupils in Milan *c.* 1570, had drawings illustrating this 'second form' of man and showing too that the most varied of polygons, even the pentagon celebrated for its relationship with the golden section, correspond to human proportions.

The introduction by Alberti of the theory of musical proportions was also important for an architecture more closely attuned to man. Vitruvius had once again provided inspiration in saying that, for certain types of building, especially the theatre, the architect required a knowledge of the laws of harmonics and their mathematical relationships. He refers to Pythagoras: the fact that the harmonies known to the Greeks arose through a string's being divided into sections with strictly defined relationships between the lengths of the sections had caused Pythagoras to recognize the close connection between sound, spatial extent and number. He thought that this connection concealed the key to the unexplored regions of the harmony of the universe, and this led him to establish geometry as a science and the basis of ancient land-surveying and architecture. In his comprehensive commentary on Vitruvius, which he likewise called *De re aedificatoria* (1485), Alberti wrote: 'The numbers which result in a harmony of voices which is pleasant to the ear are the same as those that fill our ears and souls with a wonderful feeling of well-being.' Thus the numerical relationships found in the octave (1:2), the thirds (4:5 and 5:6), the fourth (3:4), the fifth (2:3), the sixth (5:8) and the twelfth (1:3)—as well as, for the articulation of columns, the ninth (7:8)—became the basis of the architectural considerations underlying most Renaissance buildings. Alberti himself and Palladio even more after him created much-admired buildings in this way, with an increasing differentiation of the relationships of the interval numbers, producing truly musical architectural compositions in their sequences of spaces and groupings of buildings. This was the culmination of an art which corresponded to anthropological laws and was intended to place acoustic and natural laws, hitherto defined only in abstract numerical terms, on to the level of visible creation before man's eyes, making man with his innate sensitivity to proportion come into beneficent action in sympathy, at the same time as guiding his senses to worship the creator of such harmonious laws.

Time-honoured rules pertaining to the way in which human nature related to the cosmos were to some extent current as basic knowledge that was handed down as a matter of course in the Baroque period, when some architects used the mathematics of spherical bodies in the construction of vaulting. The rules were abandoned in the Age of Reason, however: in 1791 the metre was introduced, an abstract planetary measure equalling the ten-millionth part of the quadrant of the diameter of the earth.

4. THE GOLDEN SECTION. One proportion of ancient pedigree was named the GOLDEN SECTION, recognized as having a wider human application only in the 19th century. It was seldom used in the Middle Ages because it can be expressed arithmetically only in irrational numbers, while the possible geometrical construction is intricate. Renaissance mathematicians and artists, however, were especially interested in it, calling it the *divina proportione*, no doubt also because it proves constant: in plotting a series of golden sections one after the other along a line, with the next in size always arising out of the previous one, the larger of the line segments in the preceding golden section will form the smaller segment of the next one, and the complete segment of the preceding one will form the larger partial segment of the following one. When Dürer looked for constants, he found only one that could be used as an invariable rule in human proportion: the length of the torso is to the thigh as the thigh is to the lower leg. A special relationship of the golden section to the pentagon lies in the fact that the diagonals of a pentagon intersect at the golden section. They form the pentacle, considered a magic symbol in the 16th and 17th centuries.

The golden section was rediscovered in the 19th century as a morphological basic law of nature underlying the structure not only of many plants and lower forms of animal life but also of the human body. Adolf Zeising (1810–76) in his controversial book *Neue Lehre von den Proportionen des menschlichen Körpers* (Leipzig, 1854) showed that Dürer's 'rule' approximated to the golden section and that this proportion could also be demonstrated elsewhere in the human members. A modern researcher, Ernst Grassl, has been able to show that the crucial points of the structure of the brain on all horizontal planes lie in the form of a regular pentagon. A follower of Adolf Zeising, Matila Ghyka (1881–1965) spellbound Le Corbusier with the magic formula of the golden section. Le Corbusier attempted to present mankind with a 'tool' in the form of his Modulor based on the golden section (*see* ARCHITECTURAL PROPORTION, §III and fig. 8). He knew that it was really a very ancient one, as human beings, through their use as measuring tools of the ell, foot, hand etc, which are formed in the proportions of the golden section, had applied this proportion to their buildings for millennia.

See also ORDERS, ARCHITECTURAL, §I, 2(iii)(a).

BIBLIOGRAPHY

Vitruvius: *On Architecture* (1st century BC); Eng. trans. by M. H. Morgan as *The Ten Books on Architecture* (Cambridge, MA, 1914/*R* New York, 1960)

C. G. Cárus: *Die Proportionslehre der menschlichen Gestalt zum 1: Male morphologisch und physiologisch begründet* (Leipzig, 1852)

——: *Symbolik der menschlichen Gestalt* (Leipzig, 1856)

V. Mortet: 'La Mesure de la figure humaine et le canon des proportions d'après les dessins de Villard d'Honnecourt, d'Albert Dürer et de Léonard de Vinci', *Mélanges offerts à M. Emile Chatelain* (Paris, 1910), pp. 367–71

M. Ghyka: *Esthétique des proportions dans la nature et dans l'art* (Paris, 1927)

——: *Le Nombre d'or: Rites et rythmes pythagoriciens* (Paris, 1931)

E. Panofsky: *The Codex Huygens and Leonardo da Vinci's Art Theory* (London, 1940)

——: 'The History of the Theory of Human Proportions as a Reflection of the History of Styles', *Meaning in the Visual Arts* (New York, 1955), pp. 55–107

G. Hellmann: 'Die Zeichnung Leonardos zu Vitruv', *Mouseion: Studien aus Kunst und Geschichte für Otto H. Förster* (Cologne, 1960), pp. 96–101, pls 98–101

E. Grassl and H. Grassl: 'Die morphologische und harmonikale Bedeutung der Naturkonstanten 0,618', *Gegenbaurs Morph. Jb.*, iii (1971), pp. 283–92

S. Braunfels: 'Vom Mikrokosmos zum Meter', *Der vermessene Mensch, Anthropometrie in Kunst und Wissenschaft* (Munich, 1973), pp. 42–73, 181–3

E. Lorenzen: *Studies in Metrology*, 2 vols (Copenhagen, 1973–4)

S. Marinelli: 'The Author of the Codex Huygens', *J. Warb. & Court. Inst.*, xliv (1981), pp. 214ff

P. von Naredi-Rainer: *Architektur und Harmonie: Zahl, Mass und Proportion in der abendländischen Baukunst* (Cologne, 1982)

H. W. Kruft: *Geschichte der Architekturtheorie von der Antike bis zur Gegenwart* (Munich, 1985)

F. Zöllner: *Vitruv-Rezeption* (Worms, 1987)

S. Braunfels-Esche: 'Aspekte der Bewegung, Umrisse von Leonardos Proportions- und Bewegungslehre', *Festschrift Lorenz Dittmann* (Frankfurt am Main, 1994), pp. 57–72

S. BRAUNFELS-ESCHE

Humareda, Víctor (*b* Lampa, nr Juliaca, 6 March 1920; *d* 23 Nov 1986). Peruvian painter and draughtsman. He moved in 1938 to Lima, where he studied at the Escuela Nacional Superior de Bellas Artes under José Sabogal, Julia Codesido (*b* 1892) and Ricardo Grau. In 1947 he travelled to Buenos Aires, where he completed his studies at the Escuela Superior de Bellas Artes Ernesto de la Cárcova. He worked in a dramatic Expressionist style, using strong, rich colours to express his particular vision of Lima as seen from the point of view of a poor immigrant from the provinces. He was only remotely involved with commercial galleries, and his work was full of the isolation, melancholy and darkness of his life. Humareda evolved a sombre, realistic vision of the old streets of the capital and of the misery of the poor bullfighters and prostitutes, the Quixotes of his imagination. His drawings, characterized by precise and economical marks, constitute further evidence of his remarkable psychological insights.

BIBLIOGRAPHY
E. Moll: *Víctor Humareda, 1920–1986* (Lima, 1987)

LUIS ENRIQUE TORD

Humayun. *See under* MUGHAL.

Humberstone. Canadian family of potters. They were the only family in the history of Canadian ceramics active during three centuries. Five generations worked in Upper Canada (now Ontario): Samuel Humberstone (*c.* 1744–1823), Thomas Humberstone (1776–1849), Thomas Humberstone jr (1811–95), Simon Thomas Humberstone (1846–1915) and Thomas Allan Humberstone (1887–1952). Samuel Humberstone, born and trained in Staffordshire, was Upper Canada's first recorded potter. He had worked in Philadelphia before the American Revolution; as a United Empire Loyalist he subsequently received a land grant and was settled in Grenville County, Upper Canada, by 1796. His son Thomas Humberstone was the first recorded potter in York County (1798) in an area, now part of metropolitan Toronto, where the later Humberstones also worked as potters. Samuel Humberstone and Thomas Humberstone made coarse earthenware, required in the pioneer communities. Their descendants added salt-glazed stoneware to their range. Simon Thomas Humberstone was the best-known potter; a founder of the Ontario Earthenware Manufacturers Association (1872), he experimented with earthenware bodies, coloured glazes and porcelain. His notebooks (1872–1902) are a unique, first-hand account of Canadian ceramics in

the Victorian years. By the time Thomas Allan Humberstone inherited the business in 1915, production was largely dependent on stoneware churns and red flowerpots. He closed the business towards the end of World War I.

UNPUBLISHED SOURCES
Toronto, L. Humberstone priv. col. [family papers, including notebooks of Simon Thomas Humberstone]

BIBLIOGRAPHY
Elizabeth Collard: *Nineteenth-century Pottery and Porcelain in Canada* (Montreal, 1967, rev. 2/1984)

D. Badone: 'The Humberstone Potteries of North York', *Can. Colr*, xiii/6 (1978)

ELIZABETH COLLARD

Humbert de Superville, David Pierre [Giottino] (*b* The Hague, 18 July 1770; *d* Leiden, 9 Jan 1849). Dutch draughtsman, printmaker and writer. His father, Jean Humbert (1734–94), was a successful portrait painter, and David Pierre Humbert was awarded a gold medal by the art society Pictura when he was 18. The Dutch ambassador in Paris enabled Humbert to go to Italy in 1789. He stayed there until 1800, spending most of his time in Rome. He became part of the international community of artists, made working trips to Umbria and Tuscany and became a notable draughtsman, working in a highly austere, linear style, as in *Jeremiah in the Temple* (1798; Amsterdam, Rijksmus.). He was forced to leave Rome because of his support for the French Republican army defending Rome against the papal troops in 1799. He was imprisoned in Civitavecchia for three months, during which time he produced a number of drawings, such as *Gagliuffi* (1799; now Leiden, Rijksuniv., Prentenkab.).

Humbert subsequently travelled in Italy as the assistant of William Young Ottley, for whom he made drawings of 14th-century frescoes and altarpieces, such as *Sleeping Prophet* after Nicola Pisano (1792/3; Venice, Accad.). His schematic copies led to the nickname 'Giottino', which he adopted officially when he returned to the Netherlands. He was a member of the 'Accademia dei Pensieri', led by Felice Giani, where he may have developed his interest in an impersonal language of forms, fed by the subconscious. Other members of the Accademia included Anne-Louis Girodet and François-Xavier Fabre.

In 1802 Humbert returned via Paris to the Netherlands, which were currently occupied by the French. He became a teacher at the Marineinstituut in Rotterdam; in 1812, after the closure of the institute, he settled in Leiden. The university offered him a readership in French and Italian and in 1825 appointed him the first director of what was to become the Pleister- en Prentenkabinet, a position he held until his death. In Leiden, Humbert published a play called *Jésus* (1815), followed in 1817 by plans, which were never realized, for a 'Musée Classique'. He received financial support from King William I, which enabled him to publish his most important work, the *Essai sur les signes inconditionnels dans l'art*. In this essay he introduced a universal language of forms, as well as a colour theory and critical observations on art theory. He compared various civilizations, proposing that mankind recorded its experiences of the past in mythology and art. Humbert remained an active draughtsman, although his work, which ranged from strictly linear reduction to a free, directionless style, was never exhibited while he was alive. He refused to commit himself to one style only and was interested in art primarily as a universal language of forms.

WRITINGS

Essai sur les signes inconditionnels dans l'art (Leiden, 1827–32)

BIBLIOGRAPHY

D. P. G. Humbert de Superville, 1770–1849: Kunstenaar-geleerde (exh. cat. by P. Biesboer, Delft, Stedel. Mus. Prinsenhof, 1975)

B. M. Stafford: 'Arena of Virtue and Temple of Immortality: An Early Nineteenth Century Museum Project', *J. Soc. Archit. Hist.*, xxxvi/1 (March 1976), pp. 21–34

——: *Symbol and Myth: Humbert de Superville's Essay on Absolute Signs in Art* (Delaware and London, 1979)

A. F. WAGEMANS

Humboldt, von. German writers, patrons and collectors. (Karl) Wilhelm, Freiherr von Humboldt (*b* Potsdam, 22 June 1767; *d* Berlin, 8 April 1835), came from an aristocratic Prussian background. At an early age he became interested in philosophy and classical subjects and studied under the philologist Christian Gottlob Heyne at the Georg-August-Universität in Göttingen. He had a brief career in Berlin in the Kammergericht, but this ended in 1791 when he married Caroline von Dacheröden (*b* Minden, 23 Feb 1766; *d* Berlin, 26 March 1829). Together they undertook study trips to Dresden and Vienna in 1797 and lived in Paris from 1797 to 1801, where they frequented intellectual circles. They visited the Musée du Louvre many times and witnessed the arrival of the works of art plundered from Italy by Napoleon. These were subsequently installed in Alexandre Lenoir's Musée des Monuments Français, about which Humboldt wrote a long and perceptive analysis in the form of three letters to Goethe in 1799. In them he expressed the theory that the perception of history is better understood through a study of actual monuments from the past, rather than through the reading of historical texts.

From 1802 to 1809 Wilhelm von Humboldt was Ambassador to Rome. He and Caroline established a salon where such artists and architects as Karl Friedrich Schinkel, Joseph Anton Koch, Gottlieb Schick, Christian Daniel Rauch, Bertel Thorvaldsen and Carl Ludwig Fernow (1763–1808) could meet. The Humboldts also knew Canova and the art historians Séroux d'Agincourt and Conte Leopoldo Cicognara. Wilhelm commissioned from Thorvaldsen a marble figure of *Jason with the Golden Fleece* (1803; Copenhagen, Thorvaldsens Mus.), as well as his own marble portrait bust (1808; Berlin, Alte N.G.). His stay in Rome provided Wilhelm with a remarkable opportunity for study, and he began to collect antique relief sculpture. The city was for him 'the sum of all life and all history', and he felt that it was through artefacts in Rome that the historian of the Classical world should seek to form an idea of ancient Greece. He synthesized this philosophy in a poem on Rome and an essay, *Latium und Hellas oder Betrachtungen über das klassische Altertum* (both 1806).

Wilhelm and Caroline returned to Berlin in 1809. He assumed the post of Kultur- und Unterrichtswesendirektor and was responsible for the ideas behind the overall reform of Prussian universities. He was appointed Ambassador to Vienna in 1810 and negotiated on behalf of Prussia at the Congress of Vienna in 1814–15. On a mission to London in 1817–18, he had the opportunity to view the Elgin Marbles (London, BM). In 1820 he retired from public life and spent his last years writing literary and scientific works at Schloss Tegel (1822–4), his home in Berlin designed by Schinkel. The allegorical marble figure of *Hope* (1818–29; Berlin, Alte N.G.) by Thorvaldsen was executed especially for this house.

Humboldt was interested not only in the established writings on Classical art, for example those by Winckelmann, but also in the more speculative aesthetics of Kant. For Humboldt the real world and the artistic world were separate entities. He considered that the artist had to conquer Nature and recreate a new symbolic world through his imagination. The role of the artist was one of metamorphosis, enriching the mind of the spectator through his work and freeing him from the tyranny of the senses that bound him to Nature. His studies of Greek art on the basis of anthropology and sociology and his writings on the importance of language as a means of social and cultural expression are also significant. His brother Alexander von Humboldt (1769–1859) was a scientist and traveller.

WRITINGS

A. Leitzmann, ed.: *Briefwechsel zwischen Schiller und Wilhelm von Humboldt* (Stuttgart, 1900)

A. von Sydow, ed.: *Wilhelm und Caroline von Humboldt in ihren Briefen*, 7 vols (Berlin, 1906–16)

A. Flitner and K. Giel, eds: *Werke*, 5 vols (Stuttgart, 1960–81) [includes the three letters to Goethe (1799), the poem on Rome (1806) and *Latium und Hellas oder Betrachtungen über das klassische Altertum* (1806)]

BIBLIOGRAPHY

A. Wien: *Caroline von Humboldt* (Bielefeld and Leipzig, 1912)

E. Howaldt: *Wilhelm von Humboldt* (Zürich, 1944)

P. O. Rave: *Wilhelm von Humboldt und das Schloss zu Tegel* (Berlin, 1956)

P. R. Sweet: *Wilhelm von Humboldt: A Biography*, 2 vols (Columbus, 1978)

G. Wohlfart: 'Ueberlegungen zum Verhältnis von Sprache und Kunst im Anschluss an Wilhelm von Humboldt', *Dimensionen der Sprache in der Philosophie des deutschen Idealismus*, eds B. Scheer and W. Wohlfart (Würzburg, 1982), pp. 40–66

P. Quillien: *Humboldt et la Grèce: Modèle et histoire* (Lille, 1983)

W. Secker: '*Wiederholte Spiegelungen*': Die klassische Kunstauffassung Goethes und Wilhelm von Humboldts (Berne, 1985)

PASCAL GRIENER

Hume, Sir **Abraham**, 2nd Baronet (*b* London, 20 Feb 1749; *d* Wormleybury, Herts, 24 March 1838). English collector. He was the son of Sir Abraham Hume, 1st Baronet, and nephew of the founder of the family fortune, Alexander Hume, an East India merchant who acquired the estate of Wormleybury in 1739. The younger Sir Abraham succeeded his father in 1772. An MP in 1774–80 and 1807–18, Hume was a man of wide interests. A fellow of both the Society of Antiquaries and the Royal Society, and a director of the British Institution, he came to be recognized as one of the outstanding figures of the art world.

Hume had a remarkable collection of paintings; he was a pioneer in the acquisition of 15th-century Venetian pictures and was consistent in his pursuit of masterpieces of the Dutch 17th century. His catalogue, issued in 1824, records 149 pictures, to which a further 22 were subsequently added. The preface emphasizes Hume's predilection for sketches and insistence on good condition: he maintained a healthy suspicion of the restorer. Hume's earliest acquisitions seem to have been from Robert Patoun in 1778. In 1786 he acquired in Venice, Giovanni Bellini's celebrated *Portrait of a Condottiere* (Washington, DC, N.G.A.), the first of many purchases from the dealer Giovanni Maria Sasso. Hume wrote of him that 'no one deserved more the confidence that was placed in him, possessed more knowledge, or acted with greater integrity'. Their correspondence survives (partly in London, N.G.). At least 32 of Hume's 45 Venetian pictures were obtained in the following decade from Sasso, including Catena's *Adoration of the Shepherds* (New York, Met.), bought as a Bellini in 1791. Hume made further acquisitions in Florence and Rome in 1787 and secured a notable Ludovico Carracci through Armano at Bologna in 1790. In later years his Italian pictures were reinforced by such acquisitions as Titian's *Death of Actaeon* (London, N.G.), bought from the Orléans collection in 1799, and Cima's *Sacra conversazione* (Lisbon, Mus. Gulbenkian), bought in 1819 as a Bellini: Hume was the first to recognize its author.

Over 90 of Hume's pictures were Italian and, apart from most of the oil sketches, were more carefully selected than any comparable collection of the time. His northern European works included six sketches by Rubens and a notable group of van Dycks. There were only 20 Dutch pictures, but these included the superb *View of the River Maas at Dordrecht* by Aelbert Cuyp (Washington, DC, N.G.A.) and Rembrandt's *Aristotle Contemplating the Bust of Homer* (New York, Met.). The distinction of the collection is the more remarkable as Hume's means were far from unlimited.

By his marriage to Amelia, sister of the 7th and 8th Earls of Bridgewater, Hume had two daughters. The elder, Amelia, herself a gifted amateur, married Lord Farnborough, but as a result of her death, Hume's collection was inherited by his younger daughter's son, John, Viscount Alford. Following the death of Alford's son, Adelbert, 3rd Earl Brownlow, in 1921, most of the collection, then housed at Belton, Lincs, was sold at Christie's on 4 May 1923.

BIBLIOGRAPHY

DNB

A Descriptive Catalogue of a Collection of Pictures, Comprehending Specimens of All the Various Schools of Painting: Belonging to [Sir Abraham Hume] (London, 1824)

G. F. Waagen: *Works of Art and Artists in England*, ii (London, 1838), pp. 201–7

F. Russell: 'The Picture Collection of Belton' (sale cat., Belton House, Lincs, Christie's, 30 April–2 May 1984), pp. 162–5

FRANCIS RUSSELL

Hume, David (*b* Edinburgh, 28 April 1711; *d* Edinburgh, 25 Aug 1776). Scottish philosopher and historian. Although he studied and became well known in France, he lived mostly in Edinburgh and is regarded as a leading figure in the Enlightenment in Scotland. His work was influential in the development of theories based on empirical knowledge, contributing in particular to 18th-century debates about beauty, taste and judgement. In his *Treatise of Human Nature* (1739, II.i.8), Hume held that beauty is a form, or structure of parts, that produces pleasure, and can be discerned only through the operation of a sense of beauty or a faculty of taste. His *Essays Moral, Political and Literary* address, among other topics, the cultural conditions of the production of art ('Of the Rise and Progress of the Arts and Science'), the connection between art and morality ('On Refinement in the Arts'), taste ('Of the Delicacy of Taste and Passion') and also the technique and style of writing. The problem as to whether taste can be right or wrong, first raised in *A Treatise of Human Nature* (1740, II.ii.8), was explicitly tackled in his essay *Of the Standard of Taste* (1757). Although the discussion is confined to literature and oratory, Hume attempted to establish that not all sentiments of beauty or deformity are on an equal footing. After noting the great variety exhibited in taste, he provided a standard of taste in the form of a rule by means of which such sentiments may be either confirmed or rejected.

Hume observed that some philosophers held the view that because sentiments do not represent what is really in an object, but instead indicate a 'conformity of relation' between the object and the mind, then all sentiments are equally correct, and no standard of taste is possible. Although he found this plausible in certain cases, he deemed it preposterous when applied indiscriminately. While accepting the view that beauty exists in the mind and is not a quality of objects, he held that nonetheless there are rules of composition governing excellence in art. He stated that such rules are empirical generalizations 'concerning what has universally been found to please in all countries and all ages' and that there are qualities or forms present in objects that naturally produce in the human mind the feelings pertaining to sentiments of beauty or deformity. Therefore, when there is universal, or practically universal, sameness of sentiment among those whose mental faculty of internal sensation has been perfected, then that sentiment must be correct (provided that those judging are calmly attending to the object, and there are no external hindrances to the exercise of their faculty of taste).

According to Hume, the rules of composition are derived from observations of what is found to be highly pleasing, and the person of delicate taste is able to discern their operation even in cases where those pleasing qualities are less obviously present, or present to a lesser degree. He decided that four conditions must be met for a critic to be a true judge in the fine arts. Firstly, he must have a delicacy of taste improved by practice in judging works and the type of beauty appropriate to the kind of works in question. Secondly, he must perfect his delicacy through making comparisons between the different forms and degrees of excellence. Thirdly, his judgement must be free from all prejudice, and in particular the critic needs to be detached from personal feelings of friendship or enmity towards the author of the work he is judging. Finally, the critic needs reason, or 'good sense', to comprehend the relationship between a plurality of parts and the whole they constitute, and to assess them in the light of the author's purpose. Those critics possessing such delicacy of taste manifest a considerable unity of sentiment, and hence the 'general principles of taste are uniform in human nature'. However, although Hume maintained that there is a standard by reference to which questions of taste may be decided, he also concluded that even among those of delicate taste there is variation in 'humour and disposition', and variation in manners and opinions from one era to another. He thought these conditions would give rise to divergences of taste that are not due to a defect in the mental faculty, and hence cannot be amenable to adjudication by any standard.

WRITINGS

A Treatise of Human Nature, 3 vols (London, 1739–40); 1st edn L. A. Selby-Bigge (Oxford, 1888); 2nd edn P. H. Nidditch (Oxford, 1978)
Essays Moral, Political and Literary, 2 vols (Edinburgh, 1741–2)
Enquiry Concerning the Principles of Morals (London, 1751); rev. as *Enquiries Concerning the Human Understanding and Concerning the Principles of Morals*, ed. L. A. Selby-Bigge (Oxford, 1894); 3rd edn P. H. Nidditch (Oxford, 1975)
Four Dissertations: I. The Natural History of Religion. II. Of the Passions. III. Of Tragedy. IV. Of the Standard of Taste (London, 1757)

BIBLIOGRAPHY

N. K. Smith: *The Philosophy of David Hume: A Critical Study of its Origins and Central Doctrines* (London, 1941)
T. Brunius: *David Hume on Criticism* (Stockholm, 1952)
E. C. Mossner: *The Life of David Hume* (Austin, TX, 1954)
O. Brunet: *Philosophie et esthétique chez David Hume* (Paris, 1965)

ALAN CODE

Humeral veil. *See under* VESTMENTS, ECCLESIASTICAL, §1(iii).

Humfrey [Humphrey], Duke of Gloucester. *See* LANCASTER, (2).

Hummel, Johann Erdmann (*b* Kassel, 11 Sept 1769; *d* Berlin, 26 Aug 1852). German painter and writer. He studied from 1782 in the architecture class at the Akademie der Bildenden Künste at Kassel and subsequently under the Kassel court painter, Wilhelm Böttner. Hummel retained his connection with architecture, however, and this is manifested in his overpowering concern with structure and perspective. The Kassel court granted Hummel funds for travel and study in Italy and, in 1792, he went to Rome, where he joined a group of fellow Germans, including the painters Johann Christian Reinhart, Johann Martin von Rohden, Friedrich Bury and the architect Friedrich Weinbrenner. In 1796 Joseph Anton Koch joined the group. Hummel also attended the philosophical lectures given by Carl Ludwig Fernow (1763–1808) and became a friend of the archaeologist Aloys Hirt. In Rome, Hummel sketched landscapes, studied from the model and made copies of the works of Antiquity and the Renaissance, in particular of Raphael. His first, rather clumsy figure compositions reveal the influence of Asmus Carstens; and Hummel retained to the last a tendency to understand the human figure in terms of geometrical forms.

In 1794 and 1796 Hummel travelled to Naples; but when Rome was occupied by the French, and a republic was declared, he left for Germany. He returned briefly to Kassel then moved to Berlin where he remained until his death. During his first Berlin years, he was active in many fields: he worked for the theatre, designing stage sets and occasionally helping Karl Friedrich Schinkel with his own designs based on historical examples. He was also involved in archaeology, working on plans (*c.* 1805) for a reconstruction of the Temple of Diana at Ephesos. At this time he painted the *Apotheosis of Luther* (priv. col., see Hummel, 1954, p. 78), in which the main allegorical painting is surrounded by 11 scenes from Luther's life. He also produced portraits in which the rigidity of style echoes the moral stance of the artist. After being appointed Professor of Perspective and Optics at the Akademie der Künste in Berlin in 1809, Hummel painted mostly landscapes, genre scenes and architectural views. His work often combined all three, and he became known for the complex effects of light and perspective in his paintings, as in his series of four pictures from 1831 showing the finishing, erection and temporary installation of the granite bowl in front of the Lustgarten of the former Berlin Schloss (Berlin, Märk. Mus., and Staatl. Museen, N.G.). Alongside such virtuoso displays Hummel also painted very simple landscapes without any special effects, for example *In the Park at Schloss Buch* (1836; Wuppertal, von der Heydt-Mus.). Hummel's paintings were painstakingly executed, and he was not very prolific. His style showed little change as he grew older, as may be seen in comparing the two versions of his study of a candlelit interior with a moonlit view through the window, *The Game of Chess* (1818–19; Berlin, Neue N.G.; and *c.* 1845; Hannover, Niedersächs. Landesmus.). Though notably richer in detail, the second version, one of Hummel's last paintings, shows no particular advance in technique. Hummel's last years were largely devoted to a series of writings on archaeological questions and problems of perspective. In 1840 he published a study of Vitruvius, and in 1844 an introduction to perspective drawings; a posthumous publication of 1860 was devoted to problems in architectural drawing.

WRITINGS

Die Säulenordnung nach Vitruv (Berlin, 1840)
Anleitung zum Projektions—oder geometrischen Zeichnen (Berlin, 1844)
Geometrisch-praktische Construktion der Schatten für Architekten (Berlin, 1860)

BIBLIOGRAPHY

Thieme–Becker
G. Hummel: 'Johann Erdmann Hummel und sein Kreis', *Z. Ver. Gesch. Berlins*, lii (1936), pp. 1–40
——: *Der Maler Johann Erdmann Hummel: Leben und Werk* (Leipzig, 1954)
E. Schreyer: 'Johann Erdmann Hummel und die deutsche Dichtung', *Aurora: Eichendorff Alm.*, xxxiii (1973), pp. 43–62

HELMUT BÖRSCH-SUPAN

Humphrey, Jack (Weldon) (*b* Saint John, NB, 12 Jan 1901; *d* Saint John, 23 March 1967). Canadian painter. He was one of Canada's foremost painters of the 'Regionalist' school (*see* REGIONALISM (ii)) and drew much of his subject-matter from Saint John, the small maritime city where he was born. He trained at the School of the Museum of Fine Arts in Boston (1920–24) and the National Academy of Design in New York (1924–9). In New York he became aware of the realistic urban paintings of the Ashcan school and its followers, as well as the notational watercolour landscapes of John Marin. Echoes of Marin's style can be found in Humphrey's watercolour, charcoal or pencil drawings of streets and waterfronts of Saint John, such as *Untitled (Houses)* (1931; Ottawa, N.G.). In his Saint John landscapes there is a forlorn sense of a region adversely affected by the Depression of the 1930s.

In 1929 Humphrey visited France and drew extensively at La Grande Chaumière in Paris. He began to abandon a conventional academic handling of the human figure for a more sculpturally modelled style and, influenced by African sculpture and the portraits of Amedeo Modigliani, he produced such works as the strong yet sensitive *Draped Head* (1931; U. Toronto, Hart House). During a year's stay in France in 1953 he explored non-objective art more fully.

Humphrey is best known for his series of psychologically truthful portraits of adolescent children of Saint John. *Charlotte* (1939; Toronto, A.G. Ont.) is one of his most arresting works, capturing the solemn air of a little girl who seems wise beyond her years and prematurely aged due to difficult economic times.

BIBLIOGRAPHY
Jack Humphrey: A Retrospective Exhibition (exh. cat. by J. R. Harper, Fredericton, NB, Beaverbrook A.G., 1966)
Canadian Painting in the Thirties (exh. cat. by C. Hill, Ottawa, N.G., 1975)
Drawings by Jack Weldon Humphrey (exh. cat. by I. Lumsden, Fredericton, NB, Beaverbrook A.G., 1977)

KIRK MARLOW

Humphry, Ozias (*b* Honiton, 8 Sept 1742; *d* London, 9 March 1810). English painter. After training at Shipley's Academy in London from 1757 he moved to Bath in 1760 to study with the painter in miniature Samuel Collins (*fl c.* 1760–75), working there until his return to London in 1764. He exhibited miniatures at the Society of Artists from 1765 to 1771, and his sure draughtsmanship and delicate colouring can be seen in his portrait of *Queen Charlotte* (British Royal Col.). In 1772 a fall from a horse affected his eyesight and forced him to abandon small-scale works.

In 1773 Humphry went with George Romney to Rome, Florence, Venice and Naples and studied oil painting in Italy until 1777. From 1779 to 1783 he exhibited some life-size oils at the Royal Academy, such as the double portrait of *The Ladies Waldegrave* (1780; sold Christie's, London, 21 July 1944, lot 88, see Waterhouse, p. 187) which, in its use of timeless drapery and an ethereal setting, has allegorical overtones. Over-ambitious large works such as this contributed to his lack of success and his income fell sharply; the *Berkeley and Granard Families* (Berkeley Castle, Glos) show that he was better suited to miniature painting. In 1785 he sailed to India where he visited Madras, Calcutta and Lucknow. He returned to England in 1787 and attempted to paint miniatures again but his failing eyesight forced him to adopt the broader technique afforded by crayons. In 1792 he was appointed Portrait Painter in Crayons to the King. Humphry exhibited at the Royal Academy from 1788 until he went blind in 1797.

BIBLIOGRAPHY
Waterhouse: *18th C.*
G. C. Williamson: *Ozias Humphry* (London, 1918)
D. Foskett: *A Dictionary of British Portrait Miniature Painters*, 2 vols (London, 1972)
M. Archer: *India and British Portraiture, 1770–1825* (London, 1979)

HUGH BELSEY

Hundertwasser [Stowasser], **Friedensreich** [Friedrich; Fritz] (*b* Vienna, 15 Dec 1928). Austrian painter and printmaker. Born to a Jewish mother, he foiled the Nazis and was able to shield some of his relatives for a time. During Nazi rule he studied in Vienna, at public schools and at the Montessori school before briefly attending the Akademie der Bildenden Künste. His floridly patterned works with their haunting and rich colours are dependent on the decorative tradition that produced Art Nouveau. The luxurious, sinuous forms and expressive distortions affiliate him to figurative artists such as Klimt and Schiele. Hundertwasser's subject-matter modified these stylistic sources and was often influenced by his great interest in a sane environment expressed as a stable relationship between man, the built world and nature. He travelled widely and developed a pictorial vocabulary unspecific to any place or time. Hundertwasser made significant contributions to printing techniques with such works as the woodcut series *Nana Hiakv Mizu* (1973; with Japanese artists). The decorative and technical opulence of his work made him a controversial figure with the critics, while assuring him a large popular following.

WRITINGS
Verschimmelungs Manifest gegen den Rationalismus in der Architekur (Seckau, 1958)
W. Schurian, ed.: *Schöne Wege: Gedanken über Kunst und Leben* (Munich, 1983)

BIBLIOGRAPHY
W. Koschatzky: *Friedensreich Hundertwasser: Das vollständige druckgraphische Werk, 1951–1986* (Zurich, 1986 [captions have Eng. and Fr. trans.]
H. Rand: *Hundertwasser der Maler* (Munich, 1986)

HARRY RAND

Hundrieser, (Franz Richard) Emil (*b* Rastenburg, East Prussia [now Kętrzyn, Poland], 13 March 1846; *d* Berlin, 30 Jan 1911). German sculptor. In 1864 he was a pupil of Rudolf Siemering and in 1865–6 studied sculpture at the Königliche Akademie der Künste in Berlin. He was in Paris in 1867 and the following year exhibited *Bacchus* (1868) at the Akademie in Berlin. In 1873 he set up his own studio and began to produce numerous decorative sculpted figures as architectural ornament. Although initially his work was influenced by the naturalism of Siemering's sculpture, it soon began to reflect the Baroque energy inherent in the work of Reinhold Begas. For various public buildings, palaces and squares in Berlin he designed such large commemorative reliefs and statues as the coronation group (1880) for the Anhalter Bahnhof and the monument to *Andreas Schlüter* (1882–3) for the Technische Hochschule in Charlottenburg. In 1889 the large plaster model for one of his most important commissions, the *Berolina*, was installed in the Potsdamer Platz on the occasion of the visit of King Humbert I of Italy to Berlin; the final version (copper, 1895; destr.) was set up in the Alexanderplatz. In 1892 he was made a member of the Königliche Akademie and became Professor in 1895. Other significant works are the bronze statue of *Emperor Frederick III* (1894; ?destr.) in Merseburg and the marble figure of *Queen Louise* (1895; Berlin, Alte N.G.; on loan to Bad Pyrmont, Kurpark). The bronze equestrian statue of *Emperor William I* (1896; *in situ*) was commissioned for the Kyffhäuser monument in Saxony, and another statue of the emperor (bronze, 1897; destr.) was erected at the Deutsches Eck in Koblenz. The Prometheus Fountain (1897–1901; *in situ*) was designed for the Staatliche Hochschule für Bildende Künste in Berlin. In 1905 he succeeded Siemering as Director of the Rauchmuseum in Berlin, and shortly before his death his designs for the Haydn-Mozart-Beethoven monument were shown at the Akademie. His son Hans Hundrieser (1872–1929) was also a sculptor.

UNPUBLISHED SOURCES
Berlin, Akad. Kst. [personal files]

BIBLIOGRAPHY
P. Bloch and W. Grzimek: *Das klassische Berlin: Die Berliner Bildhauer-schule im 19. Jahrhundert* (Frankfurt am Main, Berlin and Vienna, 1978)
Ethos und Pathos: Die Berliner Bildhauerschule, 1786–1914 (exh. cat. by P. Bloch, S. Einholz and J. von Simson, Berlin, Hamburg. Bahnhof, 1990), pp. 123–4, 137–8, 486

BRIGITTE HÜFLER

Hunedoara Castle [Ger. Eisenburg; Hung. Vajdahunyad, Vajda-Hunyad]. Castle overlooking the mining town of Hunedoara in south-west Transylvania, Romania, *c.* 130 km south-west of Cluj-Napoca. The earliest documentary evidence of the comitat of Hunyad is from 1276, and its earliest known *ispan* (administrator) is mentioned in 1295; the first castle also dates from the second half of the 13th century, but little remains of this period, although its original plan was established by István Möller, who restored the castle in the early 20th century. As usual in Hungary at that period, it ran along the edge of a long cliff.

In 1409 King Sigismund of Luxembourg gave the castle to Vajk, the *kneaz* (leader) of the Romanian settlement, and his son John. The present building (see fig.) was commissioned by John Hunyadi, imperial regent of Hungary (*d* 1456), who built it in two stages. With its magnificent shape and careful detailing, this building gives an idea of the lost splendour of the castle of Buda, the royal capital. In the 1430s an outer ring with towers was built parallel to the old wall, preserving the basic form of the original plan. A rock-cut moat surrounds the inner castle, which was built in the second phase (1440s–50s). On the west side of the massive courtyard the two-storey Knights' Hall wing was built. Each storey has two aisles, with rib vaults supported by a single row of octagonal piers. The Gothic inscription on a capital in the lower hall gives the

Hunedoara Castle, begun *c.* 1430, view from the west

name of the patron and the year 1452. The upper hall is reached by a spiral stair. Its entrance has a pointed arch with a surround decorated with pinnacles and a tympanum containing the finely carved arms of the Hunyadi family (a raven with a ring in its beak). Opening on to the hall to the west is a vaulted passage with four polygonal bay windows, which give the west façade a particularly rich appearance. The fine castle chapel in the east range has a vault boss also decorated with the Hunyadi arms. The parapet of its west gallery has the arms of John Hunyadi's wife's family, the Szilágyi. Connected to the south end of the castle is an enclosed passage supported by massive piers, which leads to the place of ultimate refuge, called the Nebojsa (Hung.: 'Have no fear'). The north range, the Golden House, was extended in the third quarter of the 15th century by King Matthias Corvinus, son of John Hunyadi. His brick building is easily distinguishable from the earlier stone buildings. A two-storey arcade opens on to the courtyard, its upper storey ornamented with a narrative wall painting, probably representing the legendary genealogy of John Hunyadi.

In the 17th century the castle passed into the possession of the Transylvanian princes and, especially under Gabriel Bethlen (*reg* 1613–29), was embellished with new extensions and various alterations. The upper storey of the Knights' Hall was divided into three rooms by removing the vaulting and piers, and beneath the new flat roof were painted pictures of famous men. Prince Bethlen also divided the chapel with a vault. Later the castle gradually fell into partial ruin; after a serious fire in 1854 restoration work continued until 1914. The restorations undertaken in the 1960s included the return of the chapel and the upper Knights' Hall to their original state.

BIBLIOGRAPHY
L. Arányi: *Vajda-Hunyad vára. 1452. 1681. 1866. szóban és képben* [Vajda-Hunyad Castle in words and pictures, 1452, 1681, 1866] (Pozsony, 1867)
I. Möller: *A vajdahunyadi vár épitési korai* [The building periods of Vajdahunyad Castle] (Budapest, 1913)
L. Bágyuj: 'Vajdahunyad várának restaurálása, 1965–1968' [Restoration work at Vajdahunyad Castle, 1965–1968], *Korunk* (1973), pp. 1608–17
Magyarországi müvészet, 1300–1470 [Art in Hungary, 1300–1470] (exh. cat., Budapest, N.G., 1987), i, pp. 682, 684–5; ii, pp. 526–8, pls 1643–53

GÉZA ENTZ

Hung, Francisco (*b* Canton, 16 June 1937). Venezuelan painter of Chinese birth. In 1956 he entered the Escuela de Artes Plásticas 'Julio Arraga' in Maracaibo, and in 1958 he travelled to Paris to study (until 1962) at the Ecole Supérieure des Beaux-Arts. He returned to Venezuela and held his first one-man show in 1963 at the Museo de Bellas Artes, Caracas. During the 1960s he was associated with *Art informel*. His fundamentally gestural painting comprises an intensely personal calligraphy, in which Asian and American influences are blended. His murals and large-format works executed between 1964 and 1965 earned him the Venezuelan Premio Nacional de Pintura, and he was a joint representative of Venezuela in the seventh Bienale de São Paulo.

BIBLIOGRAPHY
F. Paz Castillo and P. Rojas Guardia: *Diccionario de las artes plásticas en Venezuela* (Caracas, 1973), p. 121

Based on information supplied by LELIA DELGADO

Hungary, Republic of [Magyar Köztársasag]. Country in east central Europe. It is landlocked and borders on Slovakia, Ukraine, Romania, Serbia, Croatia, Slovenia and Austria (see fig. 1). It covers 90,030 sq. km, composed primarily of a flat plain, with the capital at BUDAPEST. The rivers Danube and Tisza, which flow southward through the country, divide it into three regions: gently rolling hills in the west, the Great Plain between the Danube and the Tisza, and the Little Plain in the east. The population is *c.* 10.7 million, of which the Magyars form 98%. Around 65% of Hungarians are Catholic and *c.* 30% are Protestant. The Hungarian language belongs to the Finno-Ugric group.

I. Introduction. II. Architecture. III. Sculpture. IV. Painting and graphic arts. V. Interior decoration and furniture. VI. Ceramics. VII. Glass. VIII. Metalwork. IX. Objects of vertu. X. Textiles. XI. Patronage. XII. Collecting and dealing. XIII. Museums. XIV. Art education. XV. Art libraries and photographic collections.

I. Introduction.

1. *c.* AD 1000–*c.* 1800. In the last decades of the 9th century AD nomadic Magyar tribes crossed the Carpathians and settled in the Middle Danube basin. In AD 1000 Stephen I (*reg* AD 997–1038; canonized 1083) received a royal crown from Pope Sylvester II (*reg* 999–1003), which allowed for national autonomy in association with the Holy Roman Empire. During Stephen's reign the country was converted to Christianity. The country's churches were organized into ten bishoprics under the jurisdiction of the Bishop of Esztergom, while the Royal Castle system (comitates) formed the basis for the modern administrative divisions of the country. Across western Hungary lay an important international highway, opened in 1018, on which Székesfehérvár developed as an important city. The main aim of the ruling Árpád dynasty in the period 1000–1301 was to strengthen Hungarian sovereignty in the face of the adjacent Byzantine and Holy Roman empires, and in the late 11th century Croatia and Slovenia became autonomous regions of Hungary and remained so until 1918. The multi-ethnic, multilingual population included Slavs to the north and south, Romanians, who continued to immigrate into Hungary throughout the Middle Ages, Serbs and Walloon and German elements. The northern hills became areas of urban development, and their metal mines started to play a significant role from the 13th century. In the east the hills separated Transylvania (now part of Romania) from the rest of Hungary.

With the dominant role of the Benedictine Order at the end of the 11th century, Hungarian art developed along Romanesque lines. In the second half of the 12th century the Saxon colonization of Transylvania, French influence at the court of Bela III (*reg* 1172–96) and the establishment of the Cistercian and Premonstratensian orders led to a cultural transformation. Early Gothic court art developed before 1200 but was replaced by Late Romanesque in the 13th century. After the depredations of the Tatar–Mongol invasion (1241–2), castles were rebuilt under Bela IV (*reg* 1235–70), and a network of market towns was created.

1. Map of Hungary; those sites with separate entries in this dictionary are distinguished by CROSS-REFERENCE TYPE

In the second half of the 13th century the central European Gothic style became dominant.

In the wars that followed the end of the Árpád dynasty the House of Anjou (*reg* 1308–87) emerged victorious and consolidated the country's position. Court art began to be influenced by Italian Gothic in the mid-14th century, while Hungary's economic, political and artistic development reached a peak under Sigismund of Luxembourg (*reg* 1387–1437). Hungary became an important centre for the flowering of the Gothic court style in the first third of the 15th century. The reign of Matthias Corvinus (*reg* 1458–90) was a golden age for artistic activity: in 1470 the Late Gothic style spread, and at the same time the influence of the Italian Renaissance was felt at court. During the reign of the Jagiellon kings (1490–1526) the country was beset by feudal conflicts and in 1526 was defeated at the Battle of Mohács by the Ottoman Süleyman I (*reg* 1520–66). In the early decades of the 16th century the Late Gothic style persisted, while Renaissance influence increased alongside it. In 1541, when the Ottoman Turks captured Buda, the country's western and northern areas came under Habsburg rule; the central regions became part of the Ottoman empire, while Transylvania became an Ottoman satellite principality.

In the regions held by the Turks, Hungarian art life was destroyed; the surviving Turkish heritage consists mainly of mosques, ruins of baths and examples of ceramics and metalwork. The cultural difference between the regions under the Habsburgs and Transylvania can be attributed to their divergent political ambitions, artistic contacts and religious affiliations (Catholic Counter-Reformation in the Habsburg lands and Protestantism in Transylvania). The political and artistic golden age of Transylvania was determined by the flowering of the late Renaissance under Gabriel Bethlen (*reg* 1613–29) and George I Rákóczy (*reg* 1630–48). The Baroque style emerged in the Habsburg territories in the mid-17th century. The Turks were ousted in 1686–9 by the Habsburgs, whose harsh colonizing policies led to the revolt led by Prince Ferenc II Rákóczy from 1703 to 1711. The principality of Transylvania ceased to exist. In the 18th century Austrian influence dominated, notably in the impact of the Austrian Baroque on the rebuilding of the country and its towns. The aggressive popular response to the reforms of the enlightened absolutist Joseph II (*reg* 1780–90) put an end to his secularization of some of the religious orders and to the toleration of non-Catholics. After the Emperor's death there was a move to protect Hungarian language and culture, influenced by the Enlightenment and by national grievances.

2. AFTER *c.* 1800. In 1825 the Hungarian Parliament became a forum for demands for reform, and the Hungarian Academy of Sciences was founded. Neo-classicism was prevalent in the first half of the 19th century, but the main aim was to form a national style and to establish an independent academy of arts. The revolution of 15 March 1848 and the War of Independence was followed by a period of repression, during which Romanticism and historicizing tendencies prevailed in Hungarian art. The Compromise of 1867 between Austria and Hungary re-established a constitutional government that initiated a far-reaching modernization and building programme. Historicism dominated, reaching a peak during the celebrations of Hungary's millennium in 1896. In the late 19th century and the early 20th modernism superseded historicism; examples are the national Secessionist, Impressionist and naturalistic styles that borrowed from Western models. During the social conflicts in the early 20th century the liberal reform movement and social democratic aspirations gave rise to the avant-garde group the Eight (iii). After World War I and the collapse of the Austro-Hungarian Empire a revolution occurred in Hungary, and independence was proclaimed on 16 November 1918. The government of Mihály Károlyi resigned on 21 March 1919, superseded by a short-lived Republic of Councils (21 March–1 August 1919).

The government of Admiral Miklós Horthy (1868–1957) was in power from 1919 to 1944, and numerous Expressionist and Constructivist artists were forced to emigrate under pressure from its counter-revolutionary forces. As a result of the Versailles Treaty of 4 June 1920, Hungary lost roughly two-thirds of its territory (mainly to Czechoslovakia and Romania), which created economic and social difficulties for the series of right-wing governments that followed. The historicizing and Neo-classicist tendencies of anti-modern official art were opposed by the avant-garde: the representatives of CIAM architecture and young Surrealist artists. In the 1930s Hungary aligned itself with Nazi Germany and from 1938 to 1941 it gained territory back from Czechoslovakia, Romania and Yugoslavia. In 1941 the country entered the war alongside the Axis powers. After suffering serious defeats it began secret negotiations with the Allies, but on 19 March 1944 Germany invaded the country. The Horthy government was expelled, and the Arrow Cross (Hungarian Fascists) took power. In April 1945 the Soviet Red Army liberated the country. On 1 February 1946 a Hungarian Republic was proclaimed; during its democratic, coalition phase artistic currents, including Surrealism, that had been pushed into the background started to re-emerge. The Communist Party gradually assumed power, and by 1949 a People's Republic was proclaimed. Art was dominated by Socialist Realism, and any work that diverged from the party line was publicly denounced. The regime of János Kádár that followed the revolution of 23 October 1956 maintained the hegemony of official art, but in the 1970s a certain tolerance was displayed towards avant-garde movements, which became increasingly overt in the 1980s. In 1989 the Communists fell from power, and in 1990 multi-party elections signalled the beginning of a new era.

For further discussion *see* SLOVAKIA, §§II–V.

BIBLIOGRAPHY

A. Péter: *A magyar művészet története* [The history of Hungarian art] (Budapest, 1930)

A. Hekler: *Ungarische Kunstgeschichte* (Berlin, 1937)

L. Fülep, ed.: *A magyarországi művészet története* [The history of art in Hungary], 2 vols (Budapest, 1956–60, rev. 1970)

J. Balogh: *A művészet Mátyás király udvarában* [The art of King Matthias's court], 2 vols (Budapest, 1966)

——: *Die Anfänge der Renaissance in Ungarn: Matthias Corvinus und die Kunst* (Graz, 1975)

N. Aradi, ed.: *A magyarországi művészet története* [The history of art in Hungary] (Budapest, 1981–)

II. Architecture.

1. *c.* 1000–*c.* 1440. 2. *c.* 1440–*c.* 1520. 3. *c.* 1520–*c.* 1800. 4. After *c.* 1800.

1. *c.* 1000–*c.* 1440. The first monumental buildings in medieval Hungary were religious structures built during the reign of Stephen I (*reg* 997–1038). However, many cathedrals and monasteries have been destroyed, and those that survived have been rebuilt. Remains of the 11th-century basilica and coronation church (destr. 1601) at SZÉKESFEHÉRVÁR, where King Stephen is buried, reveal that the church was unvaulted, had a nave and aisles, no transept and a semicircular apse with square chapels. The west façade was probably similar to the westwork of German churches of the 10th and 11th centuries. The original 11th-century cathedral (destr.), at Kalocsa also had similar proportions, although it probably had an aisleless nave; at Gyulafehérvár (now ALBA IULIA, Romania) a baptistery was added to the south side of the cathedral of St Michael (destr.), with nave and aisles. From the mid-11th century many churches were built for the royal family and the aristocracy: for example, the Benedictine abbey church of St Anianus (1055; destr.) at Tihany, built by Andrew I (*reg* 1046–60), and the Salvator Benedictine abbey church (before 1060; destr.) at Szekszárd, built by Bela I (*reg* 1060–63). These early churches were built to very different plans. A church with a domed crossing was part of the plan of the abbey at Szekszárd, the foundations of which were Byzantine in style. The centrally planned parish church at Feldebrő had an 11th-century hall crypt (that still survives) located under its chancel. The Byzantine style predominated until the arrival in the later 11th century of masons from either the Balkans or Venice, who added carved stone ornament, often of figures, palmettes and interlaced designs, to the churches.

At the end of the 11th century the Benedictine Order in Hungary looked to the Upper Rhine Valley and Bavaria for designs for church building. They constructed three-apsed basilicas without transepts, as seen in the Benedictine abbey of St Giles (1091; destr.) in Somogyvár and the collegiate church of St Margaret (after 1106; destr.; crypt reconstructed) in Dömös. The second cathedral of St Adalbert (first third of the 12th century; destr.) at Esztergom was built in a style originating from Lombardy; its classical decoration of the Lombard-Comacine type was prevalent before 1156 and is also seen in the royal priory church of St Peter (completed *c.* 1148; destr.) in Óbuda (now part of Budapest). A more independent style is seen in Pécs Cathedral (begun early 12th century), which has three apses, a nave and side aisles and a crypt (*see* PÉCS, §2). Smaller 12th-century Benedictine abbeys, built chiefly by aristocratic families, such as the ones at Boldva and Ákos (now Aciș, Romania), show great diversity. The Benedictine abbey at Vasvár (late 12th century; redesigned late 17th century in Baroque style), built for the Kapor family, was a basilica with three apses, two towers and a choir at the west end, a design typical of patronal churches of the period. In ESZTERGOM monuments still survive that are examples of the court art and architecture of Bela III (*reg* 1172–96). The royal castle (reconstructed; now the Castle Museum; *see* ESZTERGOM, fig. 1) was being built at the time St Adalbert Cathedral was completed. Both buildings incorporated rib vaulting, their designs reflecting the style of the Upper Rhine Valley. In the 1190s the Early Gothic style of northern France appeared in the court chapel of the castle at Esztergom. It was also seen in such buildings as the Cistercian abbey (1184; destr.) at Pilisszentkereszt, the royal castle (in use by 1212; destr.) at Óbuda, the early 13th-century cathedral (destr.) at Kalocsa and the Premonstratensian collegiate church (1234; now the Calvinist church) at Ócsa.

In the first half of the 13th century a Late Romanesque style was seen in various forms in several buildings unconnected with the court. Building traditions popular in Esztergom, with the addition of influences from Bavaria, were found in Alba Iulia Cathedral (completed 1277) in the eastern part of the country, while in the western regions the architecture was more closely associated with the court style of Leopold VI (*reg* 1194–1230), Duke of Styria, in neighbouring Austria, as seen in the Benedictine abbey church at Ják (reconsecrated 1256; for illustration *see* JÁK ABBEY) and the Benedictine abbey church (consecrated 1224) at Pannonhalma. After 1241 this latter style also spread further into Austria. In the 1220s Bohemian and Moravian influences probably shaped the style of architecture in central Hungary, as seen in the second royal castle (begun *c.* 1226) at Óbuda and the German parish church of St Mary (now Matthias Church; 1247–65) in Buda. They were also felt in the Transdanubian region of Veszprém and in the architecture of the masons' lodges in Transylvania (now in Romania).

After the destruction caused by Mongol invasions (1241–2), Bela IV (*reg* 1235–70) initiated a new programme of building. Around 1260 a type of High Gothic architecture popular in Austria and Bohemia became the dominant style in the new towns of Buda and Pest, as seen in the Matthias Church. The style spread throughout Hungary and reached its height in the early 14th century, as seen in such buildings as the Franciscan church (first mentioned 1280) at SOPRON, the one (consecrated 1297) at Pozsony (now Bratislava, Slovakia) and the chancel of Alba Iulia Cathedral.

Many parish churches were built in villages in Hungary in the 12th and 13th centuries. They were either circular buildings ringed with apses or square ones with chancels and aisleless naves. Materials, proportions and decoration were planned on the basis of the simplest buildings erected during the Árpád dynasty (1000–1301).

In the 14th century the towns played a leading role in the development of architecture in Hungary. The most important ecclesiastical buildings extant from this time are the parish churches of St Michael (completed later 15th century) at Sopron, St James (1332–42) at Lőcse (now LEVOČA, Slovakia) and St Mary (now the Evangelical parish church; begun first half of 14th century) at Nagyszeben (now SIBIU, Romania), all of which display regional differences in design. However, their square plans and stone ornament are related to the architecture of the mendicant orders of Bavaria, Austria, Bohemia and Silesia. The buildings connected with the Anjou court at the summer palace in VISEGRÁD (e.g. the palace chapel founded in 1366), those in Buda dating from the third quarter of the 14th century (e.g. Buda Castle; *see* BUDAPEST, §IV, 1) and the royal castles in Diósgyőr (1350–75;

rest. 1960s) and the castle (1370–82) in Zólyom (now Zvolen, Slovakia) all testify to the formation of a specific Hungarian style of architecture in central Europe. The progressive style of architecture of the Hungarian court in the mid-14th century is also seen in such buildings as the collegiate church of SS Peter and Mary (before 1349) at Óbuda and the star-vaulted Collegiate Hall in the Franciscan convent at Szécsény.

The architecture of the second half of the 14th century is related to the style of the Parler workshop originating in south Germany (*see* PARLER). Sopron's architecture is similar to that in Wiener Neustadt in Austria. The plan of St Michael in Sopron is reflected in that of St Michael (begun 1349) in Kolozsvár (now Cluj-Napoca, Romania). Hall churches with ambulatories were built in many towns in the Alföld (Great Plain), among them St Andrew in Debrecen. The Stephansdom in Vienna, a hall church with three apses and a closed-off chancel, influenced the plan of the collegiate church of St Peter in Óbuda and the second Benedictine abbey church at Garamszentbenedek (now Ziár nad Hronom, Slovakia). At the end of the 14th century Viennese architecture played a leading role, as seen in the construction of several ecclesiastical buildings in Pozsony, among them the chapel of St John the Evangelist. The development of a regional style is evident in the architecture of the largest towns in Hungary at the end of the 14th century (Buda and its environs, the towns of western Hungary, Szepesség and the Saxon towns of Transylvania, particularly the centre of Nagyszeben).

At this time a distinct architectural style appeared in the centralized plan of St Elizabeth (begun end of the 14th century; completed 1507) at Kassa (now Košice, Slovakia; for illustration *see* KOŠICE); the mason of St Elizabeth was definitely a disciple of the Parler workshop of south Germany. The construction that continued until the late 1430s, when work was halted, shows the influence of Peter Parler's work in Prague (*see* PARLER, (3)), especially in the use of double curved rib vaults and tracery. The style spread from Košice to the merchant towns of Transylvania, where it can be seen in such buildings as St Michael in Kolozsvár and the former parish church of St Nicholas (completed late 15th century) in Segesvár (now SIGHIȘOARA, Romania). In Buda during the reign of Sigismund of Luxembourg (*reg* 1387–1437) the relationship with Prague played a major role in the construction and remodelling of royal buildings (e.g. the conversion of the Matthias Church into a hall church). Contemporary documents testify that the followers of Ulrich von Ensingen, architect to Sigismund, were influenced by the south German style. In 1432 French masons worked on the royal palace at Buda Castle, with its keep, gate-house and wooden barrel-vaulted Great Hall (first documented 1424). In the 1420s Sigismund began construction of a new castle (completed *c.* 1434) in Bratislava (*see* BRATISLAVA, fig. 1) in a style that overshadowed that prevalent in Buda.

2. *c.* 1440–*c.* 1520. In the 1440s there was an interregnum, and until the late 1450s civil and foreign wars disrupted the court architecture tradition. John Hunyadi (*d* 1456), the imperial regent of Hungary, modelled his castle (begun *c.* 1430) in Vajdahunyad (now Hunedoara,

Romania) after the royal palace at Buda Castle; the chapel and Knight's Hall wing at Vajdahunyad were built in 1452 (for illustration *see* HUNEDOARA CASTLE). The castle in Esztergom also had a wooden barrel-vaulted Great Hall, as at Buda. In the mid-15th century, Viennese masons had great influence; for example, before 1452 HANS PUCHSPAUM probably designed the Late Gothic vaults in the nave of St Martin (now the Cathedral), Bratislava. The town also appointed Laurenz Spenyng (*fl* 1452–76/8) as the mason in charge of building the chancel of the church. At a congress of masons in Regensburg in 1459 the Viennese lodge affirmed its right to extend its influence into Hungary. In the early 1460s the funerary chapel of the Palatine John Zápolya beside the Gothic church of St Ladislas in Csürtörtökhely (now Spišský Štvrtok) was built, possibly to a design by a pupil of Puchspaum, although this has been disputed. STEFAN, an architect active in Košice (Hung. Kassa), also worked in the Viennese style. Artistic ties with Vienna played an important role at the beginning of the 16th century, especially in the western part of Hungary, as seen in the chapel of St John the Evangelist (*c.* 1500) in the parish church of St Mary at Besztercebánya (now Banská Bystrica, Slovakia), done in the architectural style of the Danube school.

In the 1470s MATTHIAS CORVINUS (*reg* 1458–90) initiated a new court style that was Late Gothic in design and was borrowed from the Silesia–Lausitz lodge originating from the circle of ARNOLD VON WESTFALEN. Extant monuments include fragmented sections of the royal palace at Buda Castle and churches in Buda and Pest. The lodge also added the St Anne Chapel (before 1478) to the coronation church in Székesfehérvár and was responsible for such projects as the *cour d'honneur* (1484) at the palace in Visegrád and the cloisters (1486) of the Benedictine abbey at Pannonhalma. The Late Gothic court style soon appeared in buildings commissioned by noblemen: St George (1484–8; now the Calvinist church) at NYÍRBÁTOR, built by Stephen Báthory, Voivode of Transylvania, and the castle (15th century; rest. 1952–60) at Nagyvázsony, reconstructed in the 1480s by Pál Kinizsi, one of Matthias Corvinus's generals, are two examples. The style also spread throughout the country from the Transylvanian towns of Cluj (Hung. Kolozsvár) and Sibiu (Hung. Nagyszeben), resulting in a number of regional variations.

The architecture of the court of Matthias Corvinus was strongly influenced by the Italian Renaissance style, especially so after the King's marriage in 1475 to Beatrix of Aragon, daughter of Ferdinand I of Naples (*reg* 1458–94). After 1476 the royal palace in Buda Castle was rebuilt along Italian Renaissance lines, chiefly under the direction of the Florentine builder Chimenti di Leonardo Camicia (1431–before 1505), who was certainly working in Buda by 1479. *Rosso antico* marble decoration was added to the Gothic Angevin palace, a Renaissance loggia was built around the inner courtyard, and architectural mouldings were added to the coffered ceiling in the Banqueting Hall. A terraced garden was also landscaped above the cistern. The whole décor was in the style of the Florentine sculptors Benedetto da Maiano and Bernardo Rossellino and was directed by Giovanni Dalmata, who employed carvers from Dalmatia. The reconstruction of the palace was the earliest instance in central Europe in which Italian Renaissance design was used on a large scale (for further discussion *see* BUDAPEST, §IV, 1 and 2). After Matthias's death in 1490, his heir, Vladislav II (*reg* 1490–1516), continued the work on the palace and built a villa (destr.) in a similar style at Nyék, near Buda. In the 1480s the Gothic royal palace at Visegrád was also redesigned in the Italian Renaissance style. The influence of the Renaissance court style was also seen at this time in the architecture of such buildings as Vác Cathedral (destr.) and the royal palace at Esztergom.

In 1506–7 a red marble burial chapel for Archbishop Tamás Bakócz was added to St Adalbert Cathedral in Esztergom. Built on a centralized plan with a cupola, it is an early example in Hungary of Italian High Renaissance architecture. One of the most important practitioners of the style was Giovanni Fiorentino, whose known works include buildings in Menyő (now Mineu, Romania; 1514–15) and Felsőelefánt (now Horná Lefantovce, Slovakia; 1515). The second phase of the Hungarian Renaissance is represented by the decoration of the chancel of the parish church in Pest (altar fragments and tabernacles of *c.* 1506; Budapest, N.G.), Bishop György Szathmári's tabernacle in Pécs Cathedral and Canon János Lázói's chapel (completed 1512) added to the north side of Alba Iulia (Hung. Gyulafehérvár) Cathedral. Completely Renaissance buildings in Hungary are seen only in the Bakócz Chapel in Esztergom and the Lázói Chapel in Alba Iulia; others tend to consist of Renaissance ornament essentially attached to a Late Gothic structure.

BIBLIOGRAPHY

V. Mencl: *Stredoveká architektúra na Slovensku* [Medieval architecture in Slovakia], i (Prague and Prešov, 1937)

T. Gerevich: *Magyarország románkori emlékei* [Hungarian Romanesque monuments] (Budapest, 1938)

V. Vătășianu: *Istoria artei feudale în Țările Romîne* [The history of medieval art in Romania] (Bucharest, 1959)

J. Rados: *Magyar építészettörténet* [The history of Hungarian architecture] (Budapest, 1961)

J. Balogh: *A művészet Mátyás király udvarában* [The art of King Matthias's court], 2 vols (Budapest, 1966)

E. Marosí: 'Stiltendenzen und Zentren der spätgotischen Architektur in Ungarn', *Jb. Ksthist. Inst. Graz*, vi (1971), pp. 10–14

D. Dercsényi: *Románkori építészet magyarországon* [Romanesque architecture in Hungary] (Budapest, 1972, 2/1974; Ger. trans., 1975)

G. Entz: *Gotikus építészet magyarországon* [Gothic architecture in Hungary] (Budapest, 1974; Ger. trans., 1976)

J. Balogh: *Die Anfänge der Renaissance in Ungarn: Matthias Corvinus und die Kunst* (Graz, 1975)

R. Feuer-Tóth: *Reneszansz építészet magyarországon* [Renaissance architecture in Hungary] (Budapest, 1977; Eng. trans., 1981)

M. Tóth: 'Architecture et sculpture en Hongrie aux XI–XIII siècles: Etat des recherches', *A. Med.*, i (1983), pp. 81–9

E. Marosí: *Die Anfänge der Gotik in Ungarn: Esztergom in der Kunst des 12–13. Jahrhunderts* (Budapest, 1984)

E. Marosí, ed.: *Magyarországi művészet 1300–1470 körül* [Art in Hungary between 1300 and 1470] (1987), ii of *A magyarországi művészet története* [The history of art in Hungary], ed. N. Aradi (Budapest, 1981–)

ERNŐ MAROSÍ

3. *c.* 1520–*c.* 1800.

(i) Period of Turkish rule. (ii) Flowering of the Baroque style, Rococo and early Neo-classicism.

(i) Period of Turkish rule. In 1526 the Turks defeated the Hungarian army and by 1541 had occupied Buda, the capital. Hungary was then divided into three sections: the central part (including Buda) became part of the Ottoman Empire; northern Hungary and the area lying to the west of the Danube were ruled by the Habsburgs; and Transylvania and the plain stretching to Várad (now Oradea, Romania) was ruled by independent Hungarian princes. The art and architecture of the three areas diverged sharply. In Protestant Transylvania the Renaissance style was maintained (*see* §1 above), while the quickly re-Catholicizing western and northern regions (Royal Hungary) were much more open to Baroque trends. Artistic activity in the Turkish-held regions was naturally influenced by Islam. The royal court at Buda ceased to be a Renaissance centre. Instead of artists from Tuscany, Lombard artists arrived from Poland, which at that time belonged to Austria. They brought with them first a northern Renaissance style and then a Mannerist one. From 1590 Alessandro and his workshop, who came from Poland, rebuilt the castle at Sárospatak in the Renaissance style for the Perényi family. Between 1550 and 1570 many skilled Lombard architects participated in intensive fortification works in Royal Hungary, spreading a type of Renaissance castle design in which an arcaded central courtyard is surrounded by four towers, as seen in the royal castle (extended 1552–62) at Bratislava (Hung. Pozsony) by Giovanni Spazio and PIETRO FERABOSCO (*see* BRATISLAVA, fig. 1) and the Nádasdy castle (redesigned 1552–60) at Sárvár by Pietro Spazzo. Striking examples of central fortification are the pentagonal castle (1569–73) at Szatmár (now Satu Mare, Romania) by Giulio Baldigara (*fl* 1569–1608) and the hexagonal one (1583–8) at Érsekújvár by Ottavio Baldigara (*fl* 1571; *d* 1588).

Middle-class Renaissance centres were established in towns in northern and eastern Hungary in the 1520s. In 1534–6 local masons in Kolozsvár (now Cluj-Napoca, Romania) built houses in the main square in pure Tuscan style; in the 16th century Kolozsvár became the most important centre for architecture in Transylvania. In such towns as Levoča (Hung. Lőcse), Banská Bystrica (Hung. Besztercebánya) and Bratislava (Hung. Pozsony; all in Slovakia in the extreme north of Hungary), houses had arcaded loggias and porches and were decorated with sgraffito. This style, often thought of as Hungarian, was in fact influenced from the 1560s by the architecture of Moravia, Silesia, Poland and Austria, especially in the use of moulding in round-arched or dovetailed patterns for town houses and palaces, as seen, for example, in Thököly Castle (1596–1601) in Késmark (now Kežmarok, Slovakia) and later in Transylvanian architecture.

Renaissance architecture in Transylvania flourished under Gabriel Bethlen (*reg* 1613–29) and George I Rákóczy (*reg* 1630–48). Around 1620 Bethlen employed architects from Kolozsvár and from Italy—for example Giovanni Landio—to work on his palace in Alba Iulia (Hung. Gyulafehérvár) and his castle at Szamosújvár (now Gherla, Romania). At the same time István Lázár built palaces at Kisbun (1617), Alsórákos (1624; now Racos, Romania), Aranyosmedgyes (now Mediesu Aurit, Romania) and Szárhegy (now Lazarea, Romania; both *c.* 1630), the last of which has Mannerist detailing. The best example of architecture from the reign of George I Rákóczy is the late Renaissance Lorántffy wing with loggia (1642–3) of the castle at Sárospatak. His successors employed the Italian Agostino Serra to build the palace at Radnót (now

Iernut, Romania) with an arcade facing south. Besides the architecture of the nobility and the middle classes, Renaissance traditions survive in peasant wooden architecture, seen primarily in such arcaded bell-towers as the one (1640) beside St George (now the Calvinist church) in Nyírbátor (see fig. 2).

The architects active in the Turkish-occupied part of Hungary generally came from the Balkans, although Sinan (ii), architect to the Ottoman sultan, designed the mosque of Mustafa Pasha (destr.) in Buda. The most important monuments of Ottoman architecture include the square, centrally planned, domed mosques of Gázi Kasim Pasha (1543–6; now the Roman Catholic inner city parish church) and Pasha Yakovali Hassan (second half of the 16th century; rest. from the 1950s) in Pécs (*see* PÉCS, §1), the mosques in Siklos (before 1565) and Szigetvar (1588–9) and the early 17th-century minaret (rest. 1897) in Eger. Characteristically octagonal tombs (*türbe*) survive, among them the tomb (1543–8; rest. 1962) of the dervish Gül Baba in Buda. Of the nine domed Turkish baths (*c.* 1560–90) built over thermal springs in Buda, four survive (*see* BUDAPEST, §I, 1).

The Baroque style was first introduced in the 1620s and became dominant at the end of the 17th century. The first building in this style was the Jesuit church of St John the Baptist (1629–37) in Nagyszombat (now TRNAVA, Slovakia), commissioned by the Palatine Count Miklós Esterházy and executed by Pietro Spezza (*fl* 1620s–30s). Its

2. St George (now the Calvinist church), Nyírbátor, wooden bell-tower, 1640

design is based on the Jesuit church (1627–31) in Vienna and the earlier Il Gesù (begun 1568) in Rome. The plan and façade at Nagyszombat served as the model for other Jesuit churches, such as St Ignatius (1636–42) at Győr, executed by Bartolommeo Torre. The Augustinian abbey church (1655–69) at Léka, executed by Pietro Orsolino (*d* 1680), heralded a new, centrally planned church type in Hungary.

The upper extension (1630) to the royal castle at Bratislava, with its four corner towers, and the richly decorated interior, in the Baroque style by Giovanni Battista I Carlone (ii), had an effect on the development of secular architecture. It was primarily artisans engaged at the palace who were responsible for bringing the new style to castles in the western, Catholic, part of Hungary. Mainly because of their function as defensive structures at that time, only interior alterations could be made, as in the chapel (1640) by Filiberto Luchese (*see* LUCHESE) in the Batthyány castle at Rohonc (now Rechnitz, Austria), the chapel (1644) in the Esterházy castle at Frakno (now Forchtenau, Austria) and the *sale terrene* in the Esterházy castles at Vöröskő (now Červený Kameň, Slovakia) and Kismarton (now Eisenstadt, Austria). It was also in the mid-17th century that the first Baroque ornamental gardens were created, one of which was Miklós Zrínyi's garden at Csáktornya (now Čakovec, Croatia). The four-towered Baroque design (1663–72) of Schloss Esterházy at Eisenstadt, commissioned by the Palatine prince Pál Esterházy and built by Carlo Martino Carlone (1616–67) on the site of a medieval castle, was the largest secular building in Hungary at the time. It remained the only palace without fortified defences until the expulsion of the Turks at the end of the 17th century.

(ii) Flowering of the Baroque style, Rococo and early Neoclassicism. With the expulsion of the Turks, Baroque art spread through Hungary in the 1690s. As a result, Prince Pál Esterházy commissioned Francesco Martinelli (1651–1708) to build the Franciscan church of the Blessed Virgin (1695–1702) at Boldogasszony (now Frauenkirchen, Austria) in the style of the Jesuit churches. The central projection of its façade became a favoured solution for other 18th-century buildings. The Jesuit church style was also used in the palaces of the gentry; for example, the Nagy mansion (1696; now a hotel) in Bük. However, Eugene, Prince of Savoy, introduced a new plan for his summer palace at Ráckeve, built from 1701 by Johann Lukas von Hildebrandt, although its novel U-shaped design, open side wings and sinuous façade were adopted by few architects elsewhere in Hungary. The Harrach palace (*c.* 1711) in Féltorony (now Halbturn, Austria), Hildebrandt's other project in Hungary, had closed masses and a less fluid façade and was therefore more popular as a design; its plan became the characteristic choice for summer palaces in Hungary. Such buildings as the Esterházy palace (1714–33) at Cseklész (now Bernolákovo, Slovakia) have a U-shaped plan, *cour d'honneur* and articulated storeys, although the corner and multi-storey towers reflect national traditions. The hospital for disabled soldiers (begun 1716; unfinished; now the Municipal Council Building) in Pest, the execution of which was directed from 1727 to 1735 by ANTON ERHARD MARTINELLI, has

3. Joseph Gerl, Jakob Fellner and József Grossman: the Lyceum (now the Pedagogical Seminary), Eger, 1765–85

47 bays and four inner courtyards and was built in the Italian style following plans for similar buildings in Paris and Prague.

Church architecture developed chiefly in the formerly occupied territories. Giovanni Battista Carlone the younger (*d* 1747) built the Jesuit (now Cistercian) church (1717–40) in Eger, St Anne (1721–46) in Debrecen and the former Minorite church (1729–40) in Miskolc. The façades of these buildings follow the Jesuit example, although each is broken up with a sinuous pediment flanked by volutes and capped by statues. Carlone's inner spaces have depressed sail vaults (*Böhmische Kappen*), which were innovations. MARTIN WITTWER, a Carmelite monk from the Tyrol who trained in Rome, built several important ecclesiastical structures in Hungary, among them the Cistercian abbey (1739–53) at Zirc and the wings of the Benedictine abbey at Pannonhalma. His architecture was greatly influenced by the large monastery complexes built along the Danube in Austria, the plans of which are characterized by twin towers, side chapels and impressive, monumental façades with few voids. Similar designs form the basis for such structures as the Pauline church (1722–42; now the University church) in Pest and the Piarist church (1742–8) at Nyitra (now Nitra, Slovakia), neither of whose masons are known. The Austrian architect Joseph Emanuel Fischer von Erlach is credited with the plan for the cathedral (1736–74) at Temesvár (now TIMIŞOARA, Romania), while Georg Raphael Donner built the Elemosynarius Chapel (1730–32) in Bratislava Cathedral (*see* DONNER, (1)).

The greatest projects of the late Baroque period were begun in the 1740s. The largest building complex of the time was the west wing of the royal palace at Buda Castle. The original design is attributed to the court architect JEAN-NICOLAS JADOT, who joined the two square masses of the palace with wide wings, forming a U-shaped courtyard facing the Danube. His successors Nikolaus Pacassi, Ignác Oracsek and Franz Anton Hillebrandt made several modifications to his plans. Graf Antal Grassalkovich had his palace (1744–7; altered after 1867) at Gödöllő built to designs influenced by those for the royal palace in Buda and initiated a new style of palace building: its plan of two wings with a linking block featuring a central projection from which a high roof rises lends an imposing and palatial air and became the model for such buildings as the Grassalkovich palace (1754–63; now a hospital) at Hatvan by János Mayerhoffer and András Mayerhoffer. The Premonstratensian abbey church and monastery (1745–65) at Jászó (now Jasov, Slovakia), with their extraordinarily dynamic façades and their monumental scale, is the most important complex of buildings designed by FRANZ ANTON PILGRAM, a Viennese architect trained in Italy (for illustration of church interior *see* SLOVAKIA, fig. 2). He was also responsible for introducing into Hungary a church type in which the single tower is placed directly above the organ loft. His last project was the unexecuted design (1760; plans, Eger, Archbishop's Archv) for VÁC Cathedral, commissioned by Károly Esterházy, Bishop of Vác. The present cathedral (1763–72; interior completed 1777) by ISIDORE CANEVALE is very different from Pilgram's plan. With its strict proportions and huge portico of Corinthian columns, it is representative of a French-inspired form of Neo-classicism known as *architecture révolutionnaire*.

From the 1760s Rococo palaces were built in the areas close to Vienna and Bratislava. The most significant was the extension (1764–6) to Eszterháza (completed 1784; rest. 1958–9; now FERTŐD), commissioned by Prince Miklós Esterházy (*see* ESTERHÁZY, §I(3)), with a huge park in the French style and numerous garden buildings (all destr.; for interior see fig. 16 below). Other Rococo palaces designed later on a smaller scale include the Pálffy castle (destr.) at Királyfa.

The Lyceum (1765–85; now the Pedagogical Seminary; see fig. 3) at EGER was the last major project of the late Baroque in Hungary. Commissioned by Bishop Károly Esterházy, it was built to designs by the Viennese architect Joseph Gerl (*see* GERL). The architect JAKOB FELLNER modified the square plan of the three-storey building by adding central projections on all sides; its details and proportions are Neo-classical, the work was completed by József Grossman. Fellner's Episcopal Palace (1767) at Veszprém and parish church (1774–83) at Pápa also have classical influences. Other architects who worked in a Neo-classical style include MELCHIOR HEFELE, who designed the Palace of the Primate (1777–81) in Bratislava (*see* BRATISLAVA, fig. 2) and the more Baroque-looking Bishop's Palace (from 1778) and cathedral (1791–9) at SZOMBATHELY, and FRANZ ANTON HILLEBRANDT, who redecorated the choir (1773) of the parish church at SZÉKESFEHÉRVÁR and from 1765 made further modifications to the royal palace in Buda.

BIBLIOGRAPHY

J. Rados: *Magyar építészettörténet* [The history of Hungarian architecture] (Budapest, 1961)
G. Kelényi: *Kastélyok, kúriák, villák* [Palaces, country houses, villas] (Budapest, 1974)
G. Gerő: *Török építészeti emlékek magyarországon* [Turkish monuments in Hungary] (Budapest, 1976)
P. Voit: *Franz Anton Pilgram* (Budapest, 1982)

TAMÁS SAJÓ

4. AFTER *c*. 1800.

(i) *c*. 1800–1914. (ii) After 1914.

(i) c. 1800–1914. In the second half of the 18th century, when Hungarian architecture was dominated by the late Baroque style, buildings in the *architecture révolutionnaire* style were also constructed sporadically, an early and isolated example of which was Isidore Canevale's cathedral (1763–77) and Triumphal Arch (1764) at VÁC (*see* §3(ii) above). More influential were the works of KARL MOREAU, architect to the Esterházy family, who was commissioned to remodel in his patrons's houses at Eisenstadt (Hung.

Kismarton; remodelling 1795–1805) and Csákvár (1781–1823; remodelling by Moreau from 1816 in a Neo-classical style), and who created the English Garden (*c*. 1800) at Tata. He influenced several important architects: Pál Kühnel (*d* 1824), who began the archiepiscopal cathedral of St Adalbert (1822–69) in Esztergom, the largest church in Hungary (*see* ESZTERGOM, §2 and fig. 2); JÁNOS PACKH, who designed the church of St Anne (1828–31) in Esztergom, built as a large-scale model for the cathedral; and Franz Josef Engel (*fl* 1819–33), who built the Esterházy palace at Csákvár, the Benedictine abbey library (from 1819) at Pannonhalma and the Catholic church (1819–24) at Vál.

The emergence of Neo-classicism in the 1820s was prefigured by the spread of drawing schools, which led to the appearance of the first pattern books and publications on the history and theory of Hungarian architecture: *Várasi építésnek eleji* ('The origins of building in towns'; Buda, 1790) by Miklós Révai (1750–1807) and *Theorie der Säulenordnungen samt einer ungarischen Nationalsäulenordnung* (Pozsony, 1790) by Johann Nepomuk Schauff (1757–1827). All this cultivated a public taste for urban planning that was decisively felt in the development of Pest; in 1805 the town's first complete scheme for development was presented by János Hild (1761–1811), and in 1808 the Szépészeti Bizottság (Embellishment Committee) was formed, which coordinated and licensed building projects. Although Buda remained the site of the royal residence and therefore the official capital of Hungary, it was Pest, on the opposite bank of the Danube, that became the real centre of the country. Its beautification became a national affair, due mainly to the interest of Count István Széchenyi (1791–1860), the leading economic and social reformer of the day. The Chain Bridge (1839–49), the first permanent bridge between Buda and Pest, was built from public funds by the Scottish engineer Adam Clark (1811–66) and owes much to Széchenyi's efforts. The numerous public works, new building projects and renovations to existing buildings that resulted from the development of Pest

4. Imre Steindl: Parliament Building, Budapest, 1884–1904

meant that the city increasingly became the country's architectural centre. Principal architects involved in the development of Pest in the early 19th century include Mihály Pollack (*see* POLLACK, (2)), who designed the Hungarian National Museum (1836–46), and JÓZSEF HILD, who erected the buildings (one survives: Tanzer House, 3 Akadémia Street; 1836) on the wharf then undergoing development on the Pest side of the Chain Bridge. Members of guilds and less significant architects, among them JÓZSEF KAUSER and the KASSELIK and ZITTERBARTH families, were also involved in shaping the townscape (*see also* BUDAPEST, §I, 2). In towns outside Budapest, Pollack's and Hild's Neo-classical style also became popular, especially for churches, country houses and county halls. Examples are Hild's cathedral of St Michael and St John of Nepomuk (1831–7) in EGER and Pollack's Old County Hall (1828–36) in Szekszárd.

In the 1840s Romantic tendencies appeared in architecture that were to become increasingly popular in the 1850s and 1860s. A few non-Hungarian architects designed country houses in the 'Windsor Castle style', for example Franz Beer (1804–61) at Oroszvár (1841; now Rusovce, Slovakia) and Luigi Pichl (1782–1856) at Nagyugróc (1844; now Velké Uherce, Slovakia). Moreover, a Gothic Revival also took place in ecclesiastical architecture in Hungary, as seen in Pollack's rebuilding of the façade (1807–25; later altered) of Pécs Cathedral (*see* PÉCS, §2) and Hild's Hermina Chapel (1842–56), Pest. The critic Imre Henszlmann (1813–88) was an enthusiastic promoter of Romanticism and, with his architect-friends FRIGYES FESZL, Lajos Frey (1829–77) and Károly Gerster (1819–67), urged the use of this style for both public and private buildings. On the other hand, it was at this time that MIKLÓS YBL began his career working in the RUNDBOGENSTIL, as seen in the country house (rebuilt 1847) and Catholic parish church (1845–57) in Fót and the Unger House (1852) in Budapest. Other, less well-known, architects combined Romantic and *Rundbogenstil* tendencies in their works, among them Hugó Máltás (1829–1922) and Ferenc Brein (1817–79) in Budapest and Nándor HANDLER in Sopron. Feszl's Vigadó Concert Hall (1860–64; interior altered after 1945) in Pest was his most important commission and is the most significant building of the period, merging various architectural aspirations and having been designed with the deliberate intention of shaping the canon of a national architectural style.

From the 1860s on, various historicizing tendencies began to dominate (*see* HISTORICISM) that were to determine the architectural make-up not only of Budapest—as seen in such principal thoroughfares as Radial Avenue (now Andrássy Street) and the Great Ring—but also of numerous large provincial towns right up to the late 20th century. At first the Renaissance Revival played a leading role, exemplified by the work of Ybl Weber and ANTAL WEBER and also seen in such buildings as Antal Szkalnitzky's and Henrik Koch's University Library (1873–6) in Pest (*see* SZKALNITZKY AND KOCH). Slightly later, an important proponent of the Baroque Revival was ALAJOS HAUSZMANN, who rebuilt the central dome and the north wing of the Royal Palace (1895–1905; partly destr. 1945) and designed the Court of Justice (1891–6; now the

Museum of Ethnography), both in Budapest, while Ignác Alpár (1855–1928) designed several banks in Budapest in an eclectic style reminiscent of the Egyptian Revival style. The Gothic Revival had primarily two adherents: the architect and restorer of medieval buildings FRIGYES SCHULEK, who was a product of Friedrich von Schmidt's school in Vienna and whose work involved the restoration (1874–96) of the 14th-century Matthias Church and the construction of the Fishermen's Bastion (1895–1903), both in Budapest; and IMRE STEINDL, who restored (1877–96) the cathedral of St Elizabeth in Kassa (now Košice, Slovakia) and erected the Parliament Building (1884–1904) in Pest (see fig. 4). Nearly all historical styles are represented by the buildings on and around Heroes' Square at the end of Radial Avenue (now Andrássy Street), for example the Museum of Fine Arts (1899–1906) and the Art Hall (1895–6) by ALBERT SCHICKEDANZ and Fülöp Herzog (1860–1925) and the Vajdahunyad Castle (1902–7) by Ignác Alpár. These buildings grew out of an extensive architectural landscape that comprised the temporary installations of the huge exhibition of 1896 commemorating the millennium of the Magyar conquest. The work of some significant architects who used an eclectic style already reflected secessionist influence in the first years of the 20th century, notably in the Gresham Insurance Company Building (1903–6) by ZSIGMOND QUITTNER and József VÁGÓ an the Academy of Music (1904–7) by Kálmán Giergl (1863–1954) and Flóris Nándor Korb (1860–1930), both in Budapest.

The Hungarian Secessionist movement (*see* SECESSION) aspired to create a unique national architectural style that, through practising architects, was also made manifest in numerous theoretical works. Ödön Lechner (*see* LECHNER, (1)) used decorative motifs from the ancient Asian home-

5. Ödön Lechner: Postal Savings Bank, Rosenberg Street, Budapest, 1899–1902

lands of the Magyars in such buildings as the Museum of Applied Arts (1893–7), the Institute of Geology (1899) and the Postal Savings Bank (1899–1902; see fig. 5), all in Budapest. Buildings done by followers of his style include the Pannonia Hotel and Concert Hall (both 1898–1900) in Szatmár (now Satu Mare, Romania) by Zoltán Bálint (1871–1939) and Lajos Jámbor (1869–1955); the Ornate House (1902; now the Kecskemét Gallery) in Kecskemét by GÉZA MÁRKUS; and the town hall (1905) and Palace of Culture (1910) in Marosvásárhely (now Tîrgu Hureş, Romania) by KOMOR & JAKOB. Members of the following generation of architects assisted the writer and scholar Dezső Malonyai (1866–1916) in assembling information on Transylvanian folk art, which he published in five illustrated volumes, *A magyar nép művészete* ('Hungarian folk art'), Budapest, 1907–22). The material left a deep impression and provided patterns and interpretations for Secessionist architects who where eagerly hunting for motifs and ideals for the structure and decoration of their buildings. The Roman Catholic church (1908–9) at Zebegény by KÁROLY KÓS and Béla Jánszky (1884–1945) and the Sun School (*c.* 1909) at Gödöllő by EDE THOROCZKAI WIGAND, both examples of National Romanticism, brought the traditions of Transylvanian wooden architecture (in combination with early 20th-century Finnish tendencies) into the formal repertory of 20th-century Hungarian architecture. ISTVÁN MEDGYASZAY used similar forms in reinforced concrete structures, as seen in the Petőfi Theatre (1908) in Veszprém, while BÉLA LAJTA developed an increasingly Modernist language of forms in such buildings as the Parisiana Bar (1907–8; reconstructed (1987–90) in original form by art historian Ference Dávid and architects Tamás König and Péter Wagner; now Arany Janos Children's Theatre), a boys' commercial school (1910–13; now a secondary trade school) at 9–11 Vas Street and the Rózsavölgyi House (1911–12), all in Budapest.

(ii) After 1914. Neo-historicist trends were favoured by the reactionary forces prevalent after World War I, as seen in the work of GYULA WÄLDER (e.g. Cistercian secondary school, church and monastery, 1927–9; Budapest), and DÉNES GYÖRGYI and Aladár Münnich (1890–1975) (e.g. Déri Museum, 1923–9; Debrecen). However, FARKAS MOLNÁR returned to Budapest in 1925 from the Bauhaus and founded the Hungarian branch of the CIAM (Congrès Internationaux d'Architecture Moderne) group in 1929, around which Constructivist and Functionalist architects gathered in the 1930s. The left-wing orientated group, among whose members were Molnár, KÁROLY DÁVID, JÓZSEF FISCHER, FRED FORBÁT, Pál Ligeti (1885–1941), MÁTÉ MAJOR, Gábor Preisich (*b* 1909), TIBOR WEINER and Virgil Borbiró, felt that its primary task was to build small socialist flats, for example the OTI block of flats (1934) on Republic Square in Budapest. However, because of the lack of commissions, most of the group were able to design only private villas. Apart from their work, the architecture of the Constructivist LAJOS KOZMA was the most significant at that time. Béla Lajta's traditions were continued in such buildings as Kozma's Atrium Cinema and block of flats (both 1935–6) in Budapest.

During the same period, official cultural policy supported architectural *Gesamtkunstwerk*, which drew inspiration from the NOVECENTISMO movement. In this, motifs from Early Christian art were fused either with modern aspirations or with reminiscences of Transylvanian folk architecture, as exemplified by the Roman Catholic church (1932–3) in Balatonboglár by IVÁN KOTSIS, the Cathedral Square (1928–30) in Szeged by BÉLA RERRICH (see fig. 6) and St Anthony's Church and Franciscan monastery (1931–4) on Pasaréti Street, Budapest, by GYULA RIMANÓCZY. This orientation towards the *Novecentismo* movement—promoted by Tibor Gerevich (1882–1954), the most important art historian at the time—also determined the campaign in 1938 to erect monuments for the 900th anniversary of the death of the holy King Stephen I (*reg* 997–1038). Such commemorative projects included the establishment of the Garden of Ruins (1935–8) at Székesfehérvár and the reconstruction (1934–8) of the royal castle at Esztergom, both by Géza Lux (1910–45).

At the end of World War II Hungary came under the Soviet sphere of influence and was dominated by Socialist Realist architecture (*see* STALINIST ARCHITECTURE), especially after 1949 when the Communists assumed power. However, the new social order, and the fact that the country was in ruins, meant that large-scale building projects were necessary. In pursuit of this goal, architects' collectives worked to create a Socialist Realist style that would accommodate both the Functionalist principles of architects who began their careers with the CIAM and the purist and megalomaniac ideals of the *Novecentismo* architects.

With increased industrialization, factories and housing estates were built, as were such complete towns as Salgótarján (1954–5; by Győző Maróthy and associates), Komló and Sztálinváros (Stalin City; now Dunaújváros;

6. Béla Rerrich: Cathedral Square, Szeged, 1928–30

by Tibor Weiner and associates). New university buildings and whole campuses were also constructed, including Gyula Rimanóczy's 'R' Building (1951–5) of the Technical University of Budapest and the campus of the Technical University of Heavy Industry (after 1950) in Miskolc by ISTVÁN JANÁKY and associates, and large public buildings were erected, one of which was the Ministry of the Interior (1949; later the Hungarian Socialist Workers Party Central Committee Headquarters; the building now houses the offices of members of parliament) by Ágost Benkhard (1910–67), Gábor Preisich and associates. After the Revolution of 1956, the ideology of Socialist Realism was dissolved, and all that remained of its style was a form of Minimalist-Functionalism. Large housing estates built of concrete, such as Uránváros (Uranium City; 1970s) in Pécs, and major public buildings and structures, such as the Hungarotex office block (1966) by Tamás Puskás and the Erzsébet Bridge (1964) by Pál Sávoly (1893–1968), both in Budapest, were built in this style during the 1960s and 1970s. This Functionalist ethic was the guiding principle in the rebuilding of such historic monuments as the medieval royal palace on Castle Hill in Buda by László Gerő (b 1909) in 1965, the medieval keep of Visegrád Castle by János Sedlmayr (b 1932) in 1966 and the St George Chapel (1016–18) in Veszprém by Ferenc Erdei (1895–1966) in 1961; the undertaking of these projects received positive acclaim abroad.

In the second half of the 1960s the biomorphic aspects of ORGANIC ARCHITECTURE were favoured by several Hungarian architects, who rejected all Constructivist and Functionalist principles and revived the tradition of Károly Kós; their less rigid approach became a significant trend in late 20th-century Hungarian architecture. Practitioners include IMRE MAKOVECZ, who designed the Cultural Centre (1974–7) in Sárospatak, and György Csete, who built the church of St Elizabeth (1976–82) in Halásztelek. Post-modernist tendencies (see POST-MODERNISM) first appeared in the reconstruction of the centre of Pécs, primarily in houses built by Sándor Dévényi (b 1948) between 1979 and 1985. They were also seen in the 1970s in buildings begun by Gábor Bachman (b 1951), Attila Kovács (b 1938) and László Rajk (b 1949) that quoted Constructivist and Socialist Realist motifs in an ironic manner. These architects had worked as theatre designers and set designers for films because, for reasons of cultural policy, they could not get architectural commissions. Following the economic and social changes arising from the collapse of Communism in the late 1980s, a popular variation of Post-modernism became a factor in the development of entrance ways and interior spaces of businesses in the larger towns and cities. The development of a High Tech architecture with certain Functionalist and Post-modernist overtones can also be seen in the work of József Finta (b 1935; e.g. Hotel Kempinszky, 1992), Csaba Virágh (b 1933; e.g. MTI (Hungarian News Agency) Headquarters, 1990), Lajos Zalaváry (b 1923; e.g. East–West Trade Centre, 1991) and Tamás Puskás and associates (e.g. Hungarotex office block), in Budapest.

BIBLIOGRAPHY

J. Jajczay: Mai magyar egyházművészet [Hungarian ecclesiastical art of today] (Budapest, 1938; Eng., Fr. and It. trans., 1938)

H. A. Meek: 'Retreat to Moscow: Architecture in the Soviet Satellites', Archit. Rev. [London], cxiii (1953), pp. 142–51

G. Preisich: Budapest városépítészetének története [History of the urban architecture of Budapest], 3 vols (Budapest, 1960)

J. Rados: Magyar építészettörténet [The history of Hungarian architecture] (Budapest, 1961)

L. Török: 'Magyar építészet a historizmus korában' [Hungarian architecture in the age of historicism], Építés- & Építészettudomány, i (1969), pp. 131–80

J. Szendrői, ed.: Magyar építészet, 1945–1970 [Hungarian architecture, 1945–70] (Budapest, 1972); Ger. trans. as Neue Architektur in Ungarn, 1945–70 (Munich, 1978)

D. Komárik: 'Romantic Architecture in Budapest', New Hung. Rev., xiii/2 (1974), pp. 152–7

——: 'A korai gótizálás Magyarországon' [Early Gothic Revival architecture in Hungary], Művészet és felvilágosodás: Művészettörténeti tanulmányok [Art and enlightenment: art-historical studies], ed. A. Zádor and H. Szaboklcsi (Budapest, 1978), pp 209–300

L. Németh, ed.: Magyar művészet, 1890–1919 [Hungarian art, 1890–1919] (1981), vi of A magyarországi művészet története [The history of art in Hungary], ed. N. Aradi (Budapest, 1981–)

A. Zádor: A klasszicizmus és a romantika korának építészete Magyarországon [Revival architecture in Hungary: classicism and romanticism] (Budapest, 1981; Eng., Fr., Ger. and It. trans., 1985)

D. Komárik: 'A gótizáló romantika építészete Magyarországon' [Gothicizing romantic architecture in Hungary], Építés- & Építészettudomány, xiv (1982), pp. 275–319

Építészeti tendenciák Magyarországon, 1968–81 [Trends in Hungarian architecture, 1968–81] (exh. cat. by J. Gerle and G. Szegő, Budapest, Óbuda Gal., 1982) [bilingual text]

D. Komárik: 'A félköríves romantika építészete Magyarországon' [The architecture of Rundbogenstil romanticism in Hungary], Építés- & Építészettudomány, xvi (1984), pp. 139–93

S. Kontha, ed.: Magyar művészet, 1919–1945 [Hungarian art, 1919–1945] (1985), vii of A magyarországi művészet története [The history of art in Hungary], ed. N. Aradi (Budapest, 1981–)

A népi irányzat továbbélése a magyar építészetben, 1918–50 [The survival of popular tendencies in Hungarian architecture, 1918–50] (exh. cat., ed. L. Pusztai, A. Hadik and C. Fülöp; Budapest, N. Board Protection Hist. Mnmts, 1987)

J. Gerle, A. Kovács and I. Makovecz: A századforduló magyar építészete [Hungarian architecture c. 1900] (Budapest, 1990)

I. Sármány: Historizáló építészet as Osztrák-Magyar Monarchiában [Historicizing architecture during the Austro-Hungarian monarchy] (Budapest, 1990)

Architettura organica ungherese/Hungarian Organic Architecture/Magyar organikus építészet (exh. cat., ed. H. Dvorszky; Venice, Biennale, 1991) [trilingual text]

Építészet és tervezés Magyarországon, 1945–56 [Architecture and architectural planning in Hungary, 1945–56] (exh. cat., ed. S. Prakfalvi; Budapest, Hung. Mus. Archit., 1992)

L. Csorba, J. Sisa and Z. Szalay: Az Országház [The Hungarian Parliament Building] (Budapest, 1993; Eng. and Ger. trans., 1993)

A. Zádor, ed.: A historizmus művészete Magyarországon [Art and architecture in the historicist period in Hungary] (Budapest, 1993)

EDIT SZENTESI, PÉTER UJVÁRI

III. Sculpture.

1. Before c. 1520. 2. c. 1520–c. 1800. 3. After c. 1800.

1. BEFORE c. 1520. Among the few sculptures surviving from the Árpád era (1000–1301) is a recarved Roman sarcophagus (Székesfehérvár, Gdn Ruins), possibly the tomb of Stephen I (reg 997–1038); it is decorated with Romanesque interlacing work in the Friuli style with cherubim and the angel of death on the sides, following motifs from Byzantine reliefs of the Dormition. Relief fragments of figural rood screens from Dombó (now in Serbia, Novi Sad, Mus. Voïvodina) and fragments of tombstones from Aracs (Budapest, N. Mus.), as well as the Christ in Majesty tympanum above the south portal of the cathedral at Gyulafehérvár (now ALBA IULIA, Romania), all date to the late 11th century.

The most significant 12th-century sculptures are decorated reliefs on rood screens (*see also* ROMANESQUE, §III, 1(x)(d)): the relief fragments (*c.* 1148; Budapest, N.G.) from St Peter's Priory in Óbuda (now part of Budapest) were probably the work of a sculptor of the Emilian school; a provincial follower of this style carved the screen at Somogyvár, of which the *St Giles* relief survives (Kaposvár, Rippl-Ronai Mus.). The altar of the Holy Cross, the two staircases to the crypt and the screen in Pécs Cathedral were all decorated by a local workshop and are rich in relief cycles, including the *Life of Christ* and *Life of Samson* (1170s; for further discussion and illustration *see* PÉCS, §2). The Pécs workshop executed the great figural portal and the ornamental stone-carvings at Székesfehérvár Cathedral (destr.) and worked on the reliefs in the Benedictine abbey church of St Adalbert in Somogyvár. The west portal of the cathedral of St Adalbert in Esztergom was finished in marble incrustation by a workshop from northern France (before 1196).

Early 13th-century fragments from the Benedictine abbey at Somogyvár (now in Kaposvár, Rippl-Ronai Mus., and Budapest, N.G.) and column figures from the cloister of the Benedictine abbey at Pusztaszer (now Szeged, Ferenc Móra Mus.) are examples of Early Gothic work in the court style. Imported works also survive: fragments of the sarcophagus of *Queen Gertrude* (*c.* 1220; Budapest, N.G.) from the Cistercian abbey at Pilisszentkereszt indicate that it was the work of a mason trained at Chartres. The most important sculptures of the Late Romanesque—those on the west front and in the chancel of JÁK ABBEY (mainly 1230s)—are related to the 13th-century sculptures in Bamberg Cathedral.

In the second half of the 13th century and the first half of the 14th, Gothic architecture in Hungary tended not to feature sculpture, and monumental groups did not reappear until the second half of the 14th century, as in the north portal of the cathedral of St Martin in Pozsony (now BRATISLAVA, Slovakia) and the figures (before 1382) in the chancel of the parish church at Szászsebes (now Sebeș, Romania). Red marble fragments from the burial chapel of Louis I of Anjou (*reg* 1342–82) at Székesfehérvár Cathedral (now Székesfehérvár, Gdn Ruins) testify to a connection with the south German–Austrian style. During this period many red marble figural tomb carvings came from the workshops in Buda, while the earlier white marble monument to *Princess Margaret Árpád*, from the Dominican convent on Margaret Island, Budapest, was probably carved by one of Tino di Camaino's Neapolitan followers (fragments in Budapest, Hist. Mus. and N.G.). The bishop's palace at Nagyvárad (now Oradea, Romania) contains bronze sculptures by MARTIN AND GEORGE OF KOLOZSVÁR, who were active from 1360 to 1390 and produced some of the finest work of the period (largely lost).

In the early 14th century wooden sculpture of a high quality began to appear. Among the earliest examples is the Krig Altarpiece (*c.* 1320; Bratislava, Slovak N.G.). Wooden sculptures often depict the *Virgin and Child* or are crucifixes and show links with the south German–Silesian–Bohemian style. The wooden sculptures of the first third of the 15th century are related to the Soft Style of Bohemia and Austria, as in two female saints from Barka (now Borka, Slovakia), now in Budapest (N.G.; see fig. 7); a *Virgin and Child* and a *Man of Sorrows* from Toporc (now Toporec, Slovakia) are now in Veszprém (Eccles. Col.). This style is echoed in the imported stone

7. *St Dorothy*, lime-wood with traces of polychromy, h. 1.69 m, from Barka (now Borka, Slovakia), *c.* 1410–*c.* 1420 (Budapest, Hungarian National Gallery)

Pietà sculptures in the Franciscan church at Bratislava, in the church of St Giles at Bártfa (now BARDEJOV, Slovakia), at Nagyszeben (now SIBIU, Romania, Brukenthal Mus.) and the *Calvary* (1417) in the Chapel of the Cross at Nagyszeben, signed by the Austrian Petrus Lantregen. In the 1420s important sculptural works were executed to adorn the additions erected by Sigismund of Luxembourg (*reg* 1387–1437) to Buda Castle (for further discussion and illustration *see* BUDAPEST, §IV, 2 and fig. 3).

Most surviving Late Gothic sculpture is connected with the Late Gothic altarpiece type, the winged altarpiece, that originated in south Germany. The sculptures (1474–7) in the high altarpiece in the cathedral at Kassa (now KOŠICE, Slovakia) show the influence of Hans Multscher, while a *Virgin and Child* from the former high altarpiece in Bratislava Cathedral (now in Esztergom, Mus. Christ.) shows the influence of Gregor Erhart. The influence of the Veit Stoss workshop at Kraków began to spread to northern Hungary *c.* 1500, notably in the work of Pavel of Levoča (*fl* first quarter of the 16th century), who sculpted the figures in the high altarpiece (1508–17) in the parish church of St James in Lőcse (now Levoča, Slovakia; for illustration *see* LEVOČA).

At the court of Matthias Corvinus (*reg* 1458–90) the flowering of the Late Gothic style ran parallel with the introduction of architectural and sculptural ornament derived from 15th-century Italian art. Sculptural fragments from Buda and Visegrád show the influence of the Florentines Benedetto da Maiano and Desiderio da Settignano, while GIOVANNI DALMATA was employed at the Buda court from 1481. During the reign of Matthias Corvinus and after his death the Renaissance ornamental style spread to the architecture of the nobility, and in the early 16th century it played a greater role in Renaissance buildings than figural sculpture. In the same period the influence of the Danube school's Lower Austrian Renaissance style became evident in the western regions of the country, as in the sandstone high altarpiece of St George (*c.* 1527) in the parish church at Pozsonyszentgyörgy (now Jur pri Bratislave, Slovakia).

BIBLIOGRAPHY

D. Radocsay: *A középkori magyarország faszobrai* [Medieval Hungarian wooden sculpture] (Budapest, 1967)

J. Homolka: *Gotická plastika na Slovensku, 1450–1530* [Gothic sculpture in Slovakia, 1450–1530] (Bratislava, 1972)

G. Arion: *Sculptura gotică din Transilvania* [Gothic sculpture in Transylvania] (Cluj, 1974)

Árpád-kori kőfaragványok [Stone-carving of the Árpád era] (exh. cat., ed. M. Toth and E. Marosi; Székesfehérvár, King Stephen Mus., 1978)

GÉZA GALAVICS

2. *c.* **1520–*c.* 1800.** After the victory of the Ottoman Turks at Mohács (1526) and the destruction of the royal court, most Italian artists left Hungary, but stone-carving in the Renaissance style continued to develop in the provincial areas furthest from Ottoman-occupied lands, such as Márévár in County Baranya, where the rebuilding of the castle (1527–37) followed strict Tuscan ornamental models. Kolozsvár emerged in the 1530s as a significant centre of stone-carving in Tuscan style, while Tuscan stone-carvers were active in Lőcse in 1532.

The most important sculptural works in the 16th century were funerary monuments, which, untouched by the influence of the court at Buda, were in Late Gothic style, albeit of a unique nature. Throughout the 16th century and into the 17th, tombs were decorated with coats of arms or armoured warriors, as on the tomb of *István Dobó* (1575; Eger, István Dobó Castle Mus.) and the tombs of *Imre Thurzó* and *Szaniszló Thurzó* (1614 and 1625) in St James, Lőcse. Tombs in Renaissance style were commissioned from abroad and often represent the full-length figure of the deceased in a columned architectural setting, as on the tomb of *György Thurzó* (1616) in the castle at Arva (now Orava, Slovakia). Apart from their work on tombs, local stone-carvers were engaged almost exclusively on architectural decoration. The Roland Fountain (1573; by Andreas Luttringer) outside the town hall at Bratislava is an outstanding example of Hungarian late Renaissance work in an urban setting.

In the early 17th century, after a break of half a century, the stone-carving tradition in northern Hungary revived, invigorated by the numerous artists who arrived in the area from abroad, including the Kraków wood-carver Andrea Hertel, who executed the huge organcase in St James, Lőcse, and the Moravian wood-carver Christoph Kolmitz, who carved the pulpit in that church (1626). Both organ and pulpit were decorated by the Danish sculptor Hans Schmid in the spirit of the late German Renaissance. The style became popular with the middle classes and appeared in epitaphs and the new type of Renaissance altarpiece (early 17th century) as at Szepesváralja (now Spišské Podhradie, Slovakia) and Németlipcse (now Partizánska L'upča, Slovakia).

Italian architects and stuccoists played a decisive role in the development of sculptural decoration in the Baroque residences of the aristocracy in the first half of the 17th century. Philiberto Luchese, architect for the Batthyány family and later for other nobles, designed stucco decoration (1640–42) in the Batthyány castle at Rohonc (now Rechnitz, Austria); and scenes from Ovid's *Metamorphoses* (1648) in the banqueting hall at Borostyánkő (now Bernstein, Austria). The stucco decoration in the *sala terrena*, first-floor chambers and chapel in the castle at Vöröskő (now Červený Kameň, Slovakia) was executed by several Italian artists, while the 16 busts built into the walls of the first-floor chambers were carved by David Weissenburger from Wiener Neustadt (1654). By contrast, most sculpture for altarpieces was of wood and executed almost exclusively by local artists or those from neighbouring territories. One of the most influential examples is the immense four-tiered altarpiece (1637–40) in the church of St John the Baptist at Nagyszombat (now TRNAVA, Slovakia) by the Viennese wood-carver Balthasar Knillinger and Veit Stadler, a local sculptor. In the second half of the 17th century a type of altarpiece was developed that had monumental columns, applied ornament and a variety of Late Gothic and Baroque sculptures, as in the side altarpieces (1641–2) in the church of St Ignatius at Győr (see fig. 8).

While Baroque forms were readily adapted to wooden sculpture in the 17th century, reaching a wide Hungarian audience and appearing in both altarpieces and epitaphs, notably in the church of St James, Lőcse (*c.* 1650), stone-carving was slower to adapt to the new forms. The dynamic, life-size sculptures of the Apostles on the side

8. Side altarpiece with carved wood sculptures (1641–2), St Ignatius, Győr

and main façades of the church of St John the Baptist at Nagyszombat are the only surviving 17th-century examples of the style in stone. Sculptures and funerary monuments unaffected by stylistic trends continued to be made in Sopron and its environs.

Among the notable work of the period after the expulsion of the Ottomans in 1686–9 was the church decoration of the Lombard stuccoist Pietro Antonio Conti in, for example, the main nave of the church of St John the Baptist at Nagyszombat (for illustration *see* TRNAVA). During the Rákóczy War of Independence the Swedish-born medallist Dániel Warou (*d* 1729) from Selmecbánya (now Banská Štiavnica, Slovakia) designed the seals, money and memorial medals for the freedom movement between 1704 and 1707.

Stone-carvers were instrumental in the Baroque transformation of towns in the late 17th century and the early 18th. Apart from architectural sculpture, they executed numerous Marian, Holy Trinity and Pietà votive columns, either to commemorate victory over the Ottomans (e.g. the Marian Column at Győr, 1686) or to ward off plague (e.g. the Holy Trinity Column at Buda, 1715–17; rest.). More unusual monuments include the *Ark of the Covenant*, erected in 1731 at Győr after a design by Joseph Emanuel Fischer von Erlach, and the triumphal arch in Gyulafehérvár, with an equestrian statue of *Charles VI* (after 1724), commissioned by Eugene, Prince of Savoy, and executed by the Viennese court sculptor Johann König.

An important centre for sculpture in the 18th century was the court of Count Imre Esterházy, Archbishop of Esztergom, in Bratislava (*see* ESTERHÁZY, §II(1)). The Austrian Georg Raphael Donner arrived there in 1729 at the invitation of the Archbishop and decorated the Elemosynarius Chapel (1730–32) in Bratislava Cathedral (*see* DONNER, (1)). His chief work for the Archbishop was the cathedral's canopied high altarpiece (*c.* 1734), of which only the central sculptural group, *St Martin and the Beggar*, survives (*in situ*; *see* SLOVAKIA, fig. 7). Donner had a hand in two other Hungarian works, the altarpiece of the Virgin for the Trinitarian church in Bratislava (1733) and the high altarpiece (1733) in the Pauline pilgrimage church at Máriavölgy (now Marianka, Slovakia), which are on a smaller scale.

Meanwhile, Baroque wooden sculpture flowered, especially in northern Hungary. Typical are the sculptures (1695–7) in the Minorite church at Lőcse, probably by JOHANN STRECIUS, depicting the Hungarian royal saints, over life-size in dominant black-gold colours. Strecius's son, Johann Georg Strecius (1670/80–before 1742), executed the high altarpiece (*c.* 1730) for the Minorite church at Nyírbátor, while an unknown sculptor from Eperjes (now Prešov, Slovakia) carved the highly decorated Krucsay Altarpiece (1731) in the same church.

The high Baroque style was predominant after 1740 in western Hungary, notably in the work of Donner's pupils. The type of canopied high altarpiece from Bratislava appeared in Pécs Cathedral (1741; by Johann Peter Krail), in Gödöllő (1750), Gyulafehérvár (1775) and elsewhere. Donner's style was developed by Ludwig Gode from 1741 to 1759: in the decoration of the church of the Elizabethine Order in Bratislava, in the grandiose pulpits in the church of St Ignatius, Győr (1748–9), and in the Jesuit church in Bratislava (1753), among other examples. Sculptors who worked in a Baroque style that grew out of local traditions included Johann Rössler, who sculpted the high altarpiece (1743–4) in the church of St Ignatius, Győr, and the prolific Pest artists József Hebenstreit (e.g. pulpit, *c.* 1746; in the Pauline church, now the University church, Pest) and Károly Bebo, who carved the pulpit (1749) in the church of St John Nepomuk in Székesfehérvár and the sculptural decoration in Óbuda parish church (1748–51).

Surviving church sculptures in Rococo style include the rich façade stuccowork on the Minorite church at Eperjes. The workshop of József Hartmann of Kassa provided the whole of north-eastern Hungary with stone and wooden sculpture from 1744 to 1764, while the workshop of the German Philipp Jakob Straub supplied southern Transdanubia (altarpieces and other sculptures for churches at Egervár, Szécsisziget and Ercsi; 1755–7). The Veszprém sculptor Ferenc Schmidt carved the Rococo altarpieces (1742) for the church at Nagyvázsony. One of the most notable Rococo sculptors was Johann Anton Krauss, probably from Moravia, who executed the monumental sculptures (1765–70) for the Premonstratensian abbey at Jászó (now Jasov, Slovakia) and for the high altarpiece (1769–70) at the Jesuit church in Eger. Monastery workshops made a unique contribution to Rococo sculpture, as in the sacristy of the church of St John Nepomuk in Székesfehérvár (decorated 1764–7, perhaps by Johann Hyngeller) and the decoration of the library for the Pauline Order in Pest (*c.* 1775; by Antal Ruschmann). The last great sculptor of the 18th century was FRANZ XAVER MESSERSCHMIDT, who in 1777 settled in Bratislava, where he resumed work on a series of 'character' heads (Vienna,

Belvedere, and Budapest, Mus. F.A.) and carved small alabaster medallions and a portrait of *Martin Georg Kovachich* (1782; Budapest, Mus. F.A.).

BIBLIOGRAPHY

M. Aggházy: *Barokk szobrászat Magyarországon* [Baroque sculpture in Hungary], 3 vols (Budapest, 1959)
V. Gervers-Molnár: *Sárospataki síremlékek* [Sárospatak tombs] (Budapest, 1983)

TAMÁS SAJÓ

3. AFTER *c*. 1800.

(i) 19th century. Around 1800, municipal organizations, now and then already acting as commissioners of monuments, primarily employed those foreign sculptors who had been producing work for ecclesiastical buildings in the late 18th century. For example, Carlo Adami, who had previously worked on Vác Cathedral, was commissioned (1794–5) by Buda town council to sculpt a statue of *Pallas Athene* (formerly on Trinity Square; destr.), the protectress of the town; and the Bohemian FILIP JAKUB PROKOP, who had executed sculptures for the parish church at Pápa (1782; *in situ*) and for the cathedral at Szombathely (1795), sculpted the bust of Emperor *Francis I* (1803) at the behest of the Pest town council.

The spread of Neo-classicism was linked with sculptors who had studied at the Vienna Akademie der Bildenden Künste, such as JOSEF KLIEBER, who worked for both aristocracy and town councils and whose sculptures included the decoration of the Esterházy mausoleum at Nagyganna (*c*. 1825). The style was also linked with sculptors who had moved to Pest and Buda *c*. 1820, including József Huber (1777–1834), Lőrinc Dunaiszky (1784–1835), Mihály Bauer (1789–1854) and Ferenc Uhrl (1794–1862). These sculptor–entrepreneurs, who had started as artisans and then received training in Vienna and Munich, were responsible for the speed at which Neo-classical sculptural decoration of buildings spread in Pest and Buda. They also sculpted altarpieces, pulpits and tombs that were in demand throughout the country. Many of the local architects and sculptors who worked within guilds took part in the competition for the public fountain on Ferenciek Square in Pest in 1828 (executed in 1835 by Ferenc Uhrl), which was the first of numerous open competitions throughout the 19th century. Meanwhile, monumental ecclesiastical sculptural commissions were given to such foreign artists as Marco Casagrande (1804–80), who worked on the cathedrals at Eger (from 1833) and Esztergom (from 1843), and Johann Meixner (1819–72), who worked in Esztergom and Kalocsa from the 1850s onwards.

The pioneer of 'autonomous' sculpture in Hungary was ISTVÁN FERENCZY, who in 1824 returned from Rome, where he had trained in Bertel Thorvaldsen's studio. Ferenczy rejected every kind of decorative sculptural work and saw his vocation in monumental sculpture. His large-scale designs, such as *Francis I* (1839) and *Matthias Corvinus* (1840, some designs and 18 daguerreotypes depicting the artist with *bozzetti* and reliefs; Budapest, N. Mus.), were not, however, successful, partly because of lack of official support and partly because his talent did not match his ambition. His conception of creating a

national pantheon, on the other hand, received enthusiastic support.

The struggles of Rudolf Czélkúti Zűllich (1813–90), after the success of his statue of *Juno* in 1846, were due to similar causes. He made two large bronze monuments, to the dramatist *József Katona* (1857–8; Budapest, N. Mus., garden) and the poet *Sándor Kisfaludy* (1857–60; destr. 1880s), but their reception was unambiguously negative. The political repression that followed the War of Independence of 1848–9 created a climate in which monuments to national heroes were not acceptable, and this prevented any further commissions.

In the 1840s and 1850s small-scale sculpture flourished, a trend strengthened by the exhibitions organized by the

9. Miklós Izsó: *Melancholy Shepherd*, marble, h. 950 mm, 1861–2 (Budapest, Hungarian National Gallery)

Art Association of Pest, which, from 1845, included small-scale works. The dominant genre was the portrait bust, favoured not only for its low cost but also because it celebrated national heroes. Zűllich, László Dunaiszky (1822–1904), Károly Alexy (1816–80), Baron Miklós Vay (1828–86) and András Schossel (1824–74), who all belonged to the generation of Romantic artists, depicted figures from Hungarian history without depending on prior commissions, often making several dozen copies from a single bronze.

The 1860s was a fruitful decade for sculpture. From 1861 to 1863 Alexy sculpted the 16 classical female figures on the columns of the Vigadó Concert Hall in Pest, creating some of the largest and finest sculptures of Hungarian Romanticism. In 1861–2 MIKLÓS IZSÓ, who was studying at the Munich Akademie der Bildenden Künste, executed the *Melancholy Shepherd* (Budapest, N.G.; see fig. 9), which influenced the development of genre sculpture in the following decades. Before and after the 1867 Compromise competitions for monuments were held, usually by independent social organizations planning to erect monuments to political and literary figures, for example the statue of the politician *István Széchenyi* (1866–80; by József Engel (1815–1901)) and that of the writer and politician *József Eötvös* (1874–9; by Adolf Huszár (1842–85)), both in Pest. The monuments provoked widespread critical debate and were produced until the 1880s.

A historicist building phase began in the 1860s and revived decorative sculpture, as in the interior of the Vigadó Concert Hall (1860–64) and on the façade of the Opera House in Budapest (begun 1878). Caryatids, sculptures and reliefs made of stone, gypsum and stucco became an obligatory element on every building. In the 1880s salon sculpture became a favoured genre, while figural tombs were also popular, and from this time bronze became the dominant material.

In the 1890s the three outstanding exponents of academic historicism, György Zala (1858–1937), Alajos Stróbl (1856–1926) and JÁNOS FADRUSZ, received their first important commissions. Their monumental works are examples of turn-of-the-century *Gesamtkunstwerke*, as in Fadrusz's monument to *Matthias Corvinus* (1895–1902) in Cathedral Square, Kolozsvár (now Cluj Napoca, Romania), Stróbl's *St Stephen* (completed 1906) on Fishermen's Bastion, Buda, and Zala's Millenary Monument (1891–8) in Heroes' Square, Pest.

(ii) 20th century. At the beginning of the 20th century Budapest's main squares were given public monuments, providing work for the second generation of historicist sculptors, József Róna (1861–1939), Barnabás Holló (1865–1917), György Vastagh the younger (1868–1946) and Miklós Ligeti (1871–1944). Both generations of sculptors were active in the early 20th century, and several of them, most notably Ligeti, showed Secessionist elements in their work from the beginning of the century onwards. Two sculptors who were wholeheartedly part of the Secession were Ede Telcs (1872–1948) and Ödön Moiret (1884–1966).

Modernism appeared in the work of the sculptors associated with the group, THE EIGHT (iii), at the beginning of the 1910s, such as Márk Vedres (1870–1961), Fülöp Ö. Beck (ii) and his brother Vilmos Fémes Beck (*see* BECK (ii), (1) and (2)). Generally they followed the classicism prescribed by Adolf von Hildebrand, but Fülöp Beck also made roughly formed, archaicizing sculptures, while Vilmos Fémes Beck's work included Secessionist elements. The radical avant-garde grouped around Lajos Kassák did not include a sculptor, but the painter János Máttis Teutsch executed a few organic non-figurative sculptures that are similar to his paintings.

The central figure of official art and monumental sculpture in the first half of the 20th century was ZSIGMOND KISFALUDI STRÓBL, whose long life's work is a fusion of Rodinesque modelling and idealizing naturalism. The cultural ethos of the times was in accord with the Novecento Italiano and is represented by Béla Ohmann (1890–1968), who had studied in Rome, and Pál Pátzay (1896–1978). A classicizing trend was also evident in the work of such artists as Béni Ferenczy (for further discussion and illustration *see* FERENCZY, (2)). FERENC MEDGYESSY tried to establish a characteristically Hungarian art form by adopting low-life themes, while those associated with the School of Rome, among them Sándor Mikus (1903–82) and LÁSZLÓ MÉSZÁROS, were inspired by classical sculpture. Workers' themes of Ernst Barlach-like precision, on the other hand, appeared in the sculptures of Dezső Bokros Birmann (1889–1965) and György Goldman (1904–45). Of the sculptors who belonged to the EUROPEAN SCHOOL, Lajos Barta (1899–1986) worked in a geometric non-figurative style, József Jakovits (1909–94) and Iván Biró (*b* 1926) in an organic non-figurative mode and Erzsébet Forgách Hahn (1897–1984) in an Expressionist style; each produced mainly small-scale sculptures.

The Communist regime after 1948 required sculptures to be representational, and a mass of didactic monuments and friezes resulted. Numerous artists who had previously belonged to the Socialist Artists' Group or the School of Rome were able to meet the demands of SOCIALIST REALISM, among them Ferenc Medgyessy, Pál Pátzay and Sándor Mikus.

In the name of a pseudo-modernism that was favoured by the State, younger sculptors tried to renew the rigid canon of realism by roughening surfaces (József Somogyi (1916–91)), by deploying an archaic–iconic style (Jenő Kerényi (1908–75) and Agamemnon Makrisz (*b* 1913)) or by paring a design to its bare essentials (Imre Varga (*b* 1923); TAMÁS VIGH; see fig. 10). More experimental sculptors included TIBOR VILT, who had been active from the 1930s, ERZSÉBET SCHAÁR, BARNA MEGYERI and MIKLÓS BORSOS, who moved from realism to anthropomorphic abstraction in his later work.

An avant-garde emerged in the late 1960s, and Hungarian sculpture blossomed. The happening *Lunch: In Memoriam Batu Khan* (1966) was the first of a series of such events, which, along with underground classical and rock music, theatre productions, experimental poetry and films, contributed to the growth of non-official art in the 1970s, notably in the work of MIKLÓS ERDÉLY, László Najmányi (*b* 1940), László Vidovszky (*b* 1944), János Baksa-Soós, Péter Halász (*b* 1944) and István Bálint. The site of these programmes every summer was the chapel studio of

10. Tamás Vigh: *People of the Plain*, bronze, h. 530 mm, 1967 (Budapest, Hungarian National Gallery)

György Galántai (*b* 1941) by Lake Balaton, where Tibor Hajas (1946–80), who can be grouped with the Viennese Performance artists, held his first presentation. The new sculpture took two directions within the parameters of Conceptual art: satirical mobile sculpture was created by István Haraszty (*b* 1934) and György Galántai; and *objet trouvé* sculpture, an offshoot of Happenings, as in *Cooling Waters* (1965; priv. col.) by Tamás Szentjóby (*b* 1944) and *Tree Branches* by Miklós Erdély.

In the same period, more traditional sculptors made their débuts, including Gyula Gulyás (*b* 1944), who produced geometric non-figurative work, and Miklós Melocco (*b* 1935), who in his figural gypsum sculptures exploits the empty schematism of realism. György Jovánovics (*b* 1939) and Gyula Pauer (*b* 1941) introduced a theory of pseudo-sculpture, using gypsum techniques as a comment on the perennial problem of mimesis. In the second half of the 1980s they created Post-modern monuments. Contrasting sculptures in the 1980s were assemblages, as in El Kazovskij's two-dimensional figures arranged in space, mobile musical instruments constructed from *objets trouvés* by Viktor Lois (*b* 1950) and altarpieces by Lóránd Méhes (*b* 1951) and János Vető (*b* 1953).

BIBLIOGRAPHY

E. Liber: *Budapest szobrai és emléktáblái* [The monumental statues and plaques of Budapest] (Budapest, 1934)

F. Vámos: 'Alexy Károly műve a Vigadón' [Works by Károly Alexy at the Vigadó], *Művészettörténeti Értesítő*, xi (1962), pp. 265–73

L. Németh: *Modern magyar művészet* [Modern Hungarian art] (Budapest, 1968; Eng. trans., 1969)

L. Pusztai: 'Dunaiszky Lőrinc', *Művészettörténeti Értesítő*, xxi (1972), pp. 15–29

——: 'Marco Casagrande', *Acta Hist. A. Acad. Sci. Hung.*, xix (1973), pp. 91–124 [It. text]

——: 'Huber József szobrász élete és művei' [The life and works of the sculptor József Huber], *Művészet és felvilágosodás* [Art and the Enlightenment] (Budapest, 1978)

——: 'Szobrászat' [Sculpture], *Művészet Magyarországon, 1780–1830* [Art in Hungary, 1780–1830] (exh. cat., ed. H. Szabolcsi and G. Galavics; Budapest, N.G., 1980), pp. 31–6

Künstler aus Ungarn (exh. cat., Wilhelmshaven, Ksthalle, 1980)

Művészet Magyarországon, 1830–1870 [Art in Hungary, 1830–1870] (exh. cat., ed. J. Szabó and Gy. Széphelyi; Budapest, N.G., 1981) [Ger. summary]

J. Szabadi: *Jugendstil in Ungarn: Malerei, Graphik, Plastik* (Vienna, Munich and Budapest, 1982)

E. Gábor: 'Az ezredéves emlék: Schickedanz Albert Milleniumi emlékm̃ koncepciójának kialakulása' [The Millenary Monument: the genesis of Albert Schickedanz's concept], *Művészettörténeti Értesítő*, xxii (1983), pp. 202–17

K. Sinkó: 'A nemzeti emlékmű és a nemzeti tudat változásai' [The national monument and the changes in national consciousness], *Művészettörténeti Értesítő*, xxii (1983), pp. 185–201

Contemporary Visual Art in Hungary: Eighteen Artists (exh. cat., Glasgow, Third Eye Cent.; Székesfehérvár, King Stephen Mus.; 1985)

I. Nagy: 'Társadalom és művészet: A historizmus szobrászata' [Society and art: the sculpture of historicism], *Művészettörténeti Értesítő*, xxxix (1990), pp. 1–21

A. Déry: *Budapest eklektikus épületszobrászata* [Eclectic decorative sculpture in Budapest] (Budapest, 1991) [Ger. summary]

Hatvanas évek: Új törekvések a magyar képzőművészetben [The Sixties: new trends in Hungarian art] (exh. cat., ed. I. Nagy; Budapest, N.G., 1991) [Eng. summary]

K. Keserü: *Variations on Pop Art: Chapters in the History of Hungarian Art between 1950 and 1990* (exh. cat., Budapest, Ernst Mus., 1993)

A. Zádor, ed.: *A historizmus művészete Magyarországon* [The art and architecture of historicism in Hungary] (Budapest, 1993)

EDIT SZENTESI, PÉTER UJVÁRI

IV. Painting and graphic arts.

1. Before *c*. 1500. 2. *c*. 1500–*c*. 1800. 3. After *c*. 1800.

1. BEFORE *c*. 1500. Among the few paintings surviving from the Árpád era in Hungary (1000–1301) are the Romanesque wall paintings in the crypt of the church at Feldebrő (mid-12th century), which reveal similarities with south German or Salzburg styles, as do the miniatures in the Admont Bible (*c*. 1140; Vienna, Österreich. Nbib., Cods s. n. 2701–2; *see* AUSTRIA, fig. 11) which was at the Benedictine abbey of Csatár by 1263. The wall paintings of *St George* and donors (*c*. 1230s) in the church at Ják Abbey reveal Byzantine influences from northern Italy (the crypt at Aquileia), as do those in the Gizella Chapel (*c*. 1240) at Veszprém.

A Gothic linearity appeared in the second half of the 13th century, as in the wall paintings in the chancel of the Premonstratensian (now Calvinist) church at Ócsa, the painting of the *Coronation of Charles Robert of Anjou* (1317) in the cathedral at Szepeshely (now Spišská Kapitula, Slovakia) and the depiction of the *Legend of St Ladislas* in the church at Kakaslomnic (now Vel'ká Lomnica, Slovakia). This style can also be found in such Transylvanian churches as that at Őraljaboldogfalva (now Sîntămăria-Orlea, Romania). The linear style of some of the surviving 14th-century paintings, including those at Turócszentmárton (now Martin) and at Somorja (now Šamorín, both Slovakia), shows links with Austrian and Bohemian styles. The linear Gothic style also appeared in liturgical manuscripts, such as the series of 14th-century codices of the religious orders, illuminated with filigree work and initials with figures (Budapest, Loránd Eötvös U. Lib.). The import of manuscripts from the Bologna workshop, often via the Zagreb Cathedral Library, began to influence court art in the 1330s. The leader of the workshop was the so-called Pseudo Niccolò (*see* MASTERS, ANONYMOUS, AND MONOGRAMMISTS, §I: ILLUSTRATORE). His work included the *Decretals of Boniface VIII*, painted for Miklós Vásári, Bishop of Esztergom, in 1343 (Padua, Bib. Capitolare, MS. A24). The influence of 14th-century Italian art probably reached Hungary as a result of the lively relationship that developed after 1328 between the Hungarian and Neapolitan courts and through the visits of Charles Robert of Anjou (*reg* 1308–42) to Naples in 1333–4. Neapolitans probably worked on the wall painting in the palace chapel at Esztergom, copying Tuscan styles. Fragments (now in Esztergom, Mus. Christ.) from Nagyvárad (now Oradea, Romania) attest to the work of a Florentine master; the painter of St Stephen's Chapel in Zágreb was possibly from Rimini. The best-known illuminated manuscript of this period is the Illustrated Chronicle or Chronica Hungarorum (1358; Budapest, N. Szechenyi Lib., Cod. lat. 404), illuminated in the Neapolitan style for Louis of Anjou (*reg* 1342–82) by a Hungarian artist.

Italian influence is also evident in the wall paintings of the second half of the 14th century. Travelling workshops from northern Italy or the southern Tyrol often mixed Italian compositional forms with the 14th-century central European painting style, as in the work of JOHANNES AQUILA DE RAKESPURGA or the wall paintings in the Transylvanian church at Almakerék (now Mălîncrav, Romania; end of the 14th century). This style is also represented in the provinces by examples dating to the first quarter of the 15th century. Paintings showing a more direct Bohemian influence are rarer, such as those in the church of St James at Lőcse (now LEVOČA, Slovakia), in the parish church (*c*. 1415) at Pónik (now Poniky, Slovakia) and in the south chapel (1420) of the cathedral of St Elizabeth at Kassa (now KOŠICE, Slovakia).

The earliest surviving panel paintings in Hungary date to the beginning of the 15th century and show the influence of the Bohemian court: the predella from the altarpiece of *St Catherine* in St James, Lőcse; and altar fragments (*c*. 1415) from the parish church at Pónik (now in Banská Bystrica, Mus. Cent. Slovakia). The *Calvary* altarpiece (1427; Esztergom, Mus. Christ.) by Tamás Kolozsvári shows similarities with the style of the Prague court of Sigismund of Luxembourg (*reg* 1387–1437). The influence of Prague is also evident in the manuscript illumination of the period. In the 1420s, however, the Prague style, which had dominated the illumination of both books and letters patent, was superseded by influences from Austria.

11. Master MS: *Visitation*, oil on lime-wood, 1400×945 mm, 1506 (Budapest, Hungarian National Gallery)

In the mid-15th century the Soft Style began to appear in such panel paintings as the altarpiece at Mateóc (now Matejovce, Slovakia), painted by the leader of a workshop operating in northern Hungary and Lesser Poland *c.* 1450. In the 1470s new iconographic types and stylistic techniques derived from the Netherlands appeared in panel painting, such as the winged high altarpiece in the cathedral at Kassa (1474–7), that at Medgyes (now Medias, Romania) and the winged altarpiece (1470–78) in the cathedral at Szepeshely. The flowering of Late Gothic panel painting in Hungary occurred at the end of the 15th century and in the first decade of the 16th, with examples mainly in northern Hungary, in churches at Lőcse (for illustration *see* LEVOČA), Bártfa (now BARDEJOV) and Kisszeben (now Sabinov, both Slovakia); the last two are now in the Hungarian National Gallery, Budapest. The south German Danube school exerted a powerful influence on Hungarian panel painting *c.* 1500. The most prominent artist of the time was Master MS from the Upper Rhine, who worked in the mining town of Selmecbánya (now Banská Štiavnica, Slovakia). His works include the *Visitation* (Budapest, N.G.; see fig. 11) and four panels of the *Passion* (Esztergom, Mus. Christ.).

Late Gothic painting contrasts with the Renaissance works at the court of MATTHIAS CORVINUS. The most notable examples, apart from such lost works as Mantegna's portrait of *Matthias Corvinus* (*c.* 1460), are miniatures in the surviving illuminated manuscripts from the Biblioteca Corviniana (itself destr.), which testify to the operation of an illuminators' workshop in Buda in the 1480s. The work continued after the death in 1490 of Matthias Corvinus, notably in the illumination of Buda letters patent in Renaissance style.

BIBLIOGRAPHY

D. Radocsay: *A középkori Magyarország falképei* [Wall painting in medieval Hungary] (Budapest, 1954)
——: *A középkori Magyarország táblaképei* [Panel painting in medieval Hungary] (Budapest, 1955)
I. Barkovits: *Magyar kódexek a XI–XVI. században* [Hungarian codices in the 11th–16th centuries] (Budapest, 1965)
M. Toth: *Árpád-kori falfestészet* [Wall painting of the Árpád period] (Budapest, 1974)
V. Dvořáková, J. Krása and K. Stejskal: *Středověká nástěnná malba na Slovensku* [Medieval wall painting in Slovakia] (Prague and Bratislava, 1978)
M. Prokopp: *Italian Trecento Influence on Murals in East Central Europe, Particularly Hungary* (Budapest, 1983)

GÉZA GALAVICS

2. *c.* 1500–*c.* 1800. Among the few surviving examples of Hungarian early Renaissance painting from the period immediately after the death of Matthias Corvinus are the miniatures in Mme Pál Kinizsi's Magyar Benigna Prayerbook (1493–4) and the Jordánszky Codex (1516–19), in which Tuscan Renaissance motifs blend with Late Gothic elements, and the wall paintings in the castle chapel at Siklós. Most late Renaissance work perished during the Ottoman wars, including the oil painting series (*c.* 1560) by the Venetian Giulio Licino in the castle chapel at Pozsony (now BRATISLAVA, Slovakia), although his grotesque gallery paintings survive there from the same period. Also extant is the series of striking portrait engravings by the Dalmatian Martino Rota, depicting *Antal Verancsics, Bishop of Esztergom*, and several Hungarian nobles. One

of the longest-lived variations of the Renaissance style was the 'Flower Renaissance', which became nationally popular, fusing classical Renaissance elements with folk or Ottoman flower motifs, as on painted wooden-coffered church or mansion ceilings, primarily in Transylvania; late examples are found in Gyulakuta (now Fintînele, Romania; 1625) and Szentsimon (1650).

A typical genre in the early 17th century was the sharply stylized and decorative CATAFALQUE paintings that marked the beginning of portrait painting, as in the catafalque painting of *György Thurzó* in the castle at Árva (now Orava, Slovakia; 1616) and that of *Gábor Illésházy* (1648; Budapest, N. Mus.). Village churches preserved a more archaic painterly style, as in the wall painting of *St George* (1665) at Hervartó, in which late Renaissance tendencies blend with Gothic elements. In 1635 the castle at Bratislava was rebuilt. The upper chambers were decorated with 25 large ceiling paintings on canvas (completed 1643) by Paul Juvenel, celebrating Ferdinand II's victory over the Bohemian Protestants in 1620. All that survives of the paintings is an engraving that shows the series to have been a monumental expression of the ruler's apotheosis.

Baroque influences are evident in the work of Carpoforo Tencala, who worked in the Pálffys' castle at Vöröskő (now Červený Kameň, Slovakia), decorating the chapel, *sala terrena* and the ceiling of the banqueting hall. His other important work was the ceiling (1667) of the banqueting hall of Esterházy Schloss at Kismarton (now Eisenstadt, Austria). From the early 17th century a key element in the nobility's Baroque residences was the portrait gallery; those of the Batthyány, Nádasdy, Esterházy, Csáky and Zichy families survive intact or in part. The portraits were painted mainly by Hungarian late Renaissance artists. Those by Benjamin Block (1631–90), with their realistic interiors and open vistas, are among the most notable, as in *Pál Esterházy* (1655) and the pendant portraits of *Ferenc Nádasdy* and his wife (both 1656; Budapest, N. Mus.), and they were imitated until the end of the century.

Graphic work became popular in the 17th century, particularly with half-length portrait engravings of 100 Habsburg nobles by the Augsburg artist Elias Widmann, published in Bratislava (1646). Their influence was such that even 150 years later portraits of nobles followed their style. The *Mausoleum*, published by Ferenc Nádasdy in Nuremberg in 1664, comprised a series of engravings (*c.* 1610) of Hungarian kings and leaders, executed in Prague by the circle of Aegidius Sadeler II, and was an even greater success. Of especially high standard are Jesuit engravings from Nagyszombat (now TRNAVA, Slovakia), including book illustrations. György Szelepcsényi, Archbishop of Esztergom, was himself a skilled copperplate engraver (e.g. *Self-portrait*; after 1667).

The central theme of the age, the war against the Ottoman Turks, was immortalized in paintings and engravings. An early series of battle paintings is that by Hans Rudolf Miller in the banqueting hall of the castle at Sárvár, depicting the triumphant battles of the 15-year war, inspired by Johann Sibmacher's battle prints and Antonio Tempesta's late Renaissance battle engravings. Miklós Zrínyi decorated his castle at Csáktornya (now Čakovec,

Croatia) with battle scenes, as did Ádám Batthyány at Rohonc (now Rechnitz, Austria) and Archbishop György Lippay at Bratislava. Anti-Ottoman themes also appear on such allegorical altarpieces as the 'Patrona Hungariae' side altar in the church of St Ignatius at Győr (1642) or the high altarpiece (1666–7) in the church at Árpás, depicting *Leopold I* with the Hungarian nobility. These depictions influenced the 'Patrona Hungariae' type of altarpiece that became popular in the late 17th century. In it the royal saint Stephen I dedicates the country to the Virgin Mary. Religious paintings became decidedly large-scale, as in *St Anthony and the Seven Wonders of the World* (1682) in the Franciscan monastery at Sümeg and the votive picture (1683) of *Ferenc Esterházy and Katalin Thököly* in the Franciscan church at Pápa. The most notable painter associated with the Rákóczy War of Independence was ÁDÁM MÁNYOKI, who began his career with the support of the Transylvanian Prince Ferenc II Rákóczy (1676–1735). The prince sent him to study in the Netherlands in 1709. On his return in 1712 Mányoki painted his well-known portrait of Rákóczy (Budapest, N.G.; see fig. 12), possibly his most important work. Mányoki worked in the court at Dresden from 1713, spent a few unsuccessful years in Hungary in the 1720s and finally returned to Dresden in 1730.

The Jesuits played an important part in the development of Baroque art in Hungary in the 18th century. CHRISTOPH TAUSCH, architect and decorator to the order in Innsbruck, painted the ceiling of the Jesuit church at Trencsén (now Trenčín, Slovakia) from 1712 to 1715, depicting *St Francis Xavier*, after the chancel vault paintings (1680s; by Andrea Pozzo) in S Ignazio in Rome. Antonio Galli-Bibiena painted the illusionistic cupola (1744–5) in the Trinitarian

church at Bratislava. Numerous other Italian artists were active in Hungary at the time: Francesco Solimena produced five panel paintings with allegorical depictions of the Hungarian archbishops (1713; Pannonhalma Abbey); Martino Altomonte painted the altarpieces (1726–9) for the Carmelite church at Győr; Gottlieb Anton Galliardi (*fl* 1679–1720) executed the ceiling paintings (1720) for the cathedral at Nyitra (now Nitra, Slovakia); and Davide Antonio Fossati produced the emblematic wall paintings (1729) in the refectory at Pannonhalma Abbey.

Austrian painters succeeded the Italians. The Viennese painter Paul Troger executed the *Apotheosis of St Elizabeth* (1742) in the dome of the church of the Sisters of St Elizabeth at Bratislava and also decorated the chancel of the church of St Ignatius in Győr (1744) and its nave ceiling with the *Annunciation* (1747). Graduates of the Vienna Akademie who worked in Hungary include Kaspar Sambach (1715–95), who painted the interior of the church of St John Nepomuk at Székesfehérvár (1748), Josef Ignaz Mildorfer, who painted the ceiling (1764–6) of the *sala terrena* in the Esterházy palace at Fertőd and the altarpiece in the church of All Souls in Sopron (after 1760), and Johann Wenzel Bergl, who painted the ceiling of the Pauline church at Pest (1776) and in 1774 executed the *St John the Baptist* series in the church at Felsőelefánt (now Horná Lefantovce, Slovakia). The most significant Viennese artist in Hungary was FRANZ ANTON MAULBERTSCH, who decorated numerous churches and palaces in the country. Of these, the decoration of the parish church at Sümeg (1758) and the painting of the ceiling of the nave in the cathedral at Győr (1781) are among the best known. A Hungarian artist in the academic tradition was István Dorffmeister (1729–97) from Sopron, whose prolific activity between 1760 and 1800 includes the decoration of the Benedictine abbey churches at Celldömölk and Bakonybél (1760–80) and the Hungarian history paintings in the church and abbey at Szentgotthárd (1784). One of the last important painters of the Baroque age was JOHANN LUKAS KRACKER, who decorated the abbey church at Jászó (now Jasov, Slovakia) from 1762 to 1764. In 1768 he became court painter to Count Károly Esterházy, Bishop of Eger, and executed several works in Eger, including the monumental ceiling painting in the library of the Lyceum, depicting the *Council of Trent* (1777–8).

BIBLIOGRAPHY

K. Garas: *Magyarországi festészet a XVII században* [Hungarian painting in the 17th century] (Budapest, 1953)
——: *Magyarországi festészet a XVIII században* [Hungarian painting in the 18th century] (Budapest, 1954)
G. Galavics: 'Antonio Galli-Bibiena in Ungheria e in Austria', *Acta Hist. A. Acad. Sci. Hung.*, xxx (1984), pp. 177–264
Z. Szilárdffy: *Barokk szentképek Magyarországon* [Religious Baroque art in Hungary] (Budapest, 1984)
G. Galavics: *Kössünk kardot az pogány ellen: Török háborúk és képzőművészet* [Raising our swords against the heathens: Turkish wars and the fine arts] (Budapest, 1986)

TAMÁS SAJÓ

3. AFTER *c.* 1800.

(i) 19th century. There were few Hungarian artists at the beginning of the 19th century to succeed the generation of great fresco painters, as a native painterly tradition had not yet developed in Hungary. Such patrons as Count Ferenc Széchényi (1754–1820) commissioned most of

12. Ádám Mányoki: *Ferenc II Rákóczy*, oil on canvas, 755×675 mm, 1712 (Budapest, Hungarian National Gallery)

their paintings from artists in Vienna, including Joseph Kreutzinger (1767–1829), Peter Kraft and Johann Ender (1793–1854). The few Hungarian artists who could meet the criteria of the decisive figure in contemporary artistic life, Ferenc Kazinczy (1759–1831), among them Jan Stunder (1759–1811), Sámuel Czetter (1765–1819) and János Rombauer (1782–1849), found it hard to make a living; the portrait painter János Donát (1744–1830) was an exception. Even the nationalist consciousness-raising periodical literature that developed in the early 19th century usually employed illustrators from Vienna, including Joseph Fischer (1764–1822) and Vinzenz Georg Kininger (1767–1851), while such projects as costume and travel books were illustrated by amateurs (e.g. engineers, drawing teachers).

Illustrations for the literary almanac *Aurora* (est. 1821) in National Romantic mode foreshadowed the themes and styles that were to occupy painting for the next half century. Although the dominant figure in *Aurora*, the poet, painter and illustrator Károly Kisfaludy (1788–1830), painted 'Gothic' landscape fantasies in the manner of Philippe Jacques de Loutherbourg, most landscape depictions were motivated by a patriotic feeling (*see* MARKÓ (i), (1)) and were rendered in a way that is reminiscent of the style of contemporary south German masters, as is evident in the oil paintings of Miklós Barabás (1810–98) and Antal Ligeti (1823–90). Depictions of peasant life, owing much to ethnographic illustrations, show similar German and Austrian influences, as in the work of János Jankó (1833–96), while in the development of middle-class portraiture and genre painting the Viennese Biedermeier style was the determining factor (*see* BORSOS, JÓZSEF (i)).

Patriotic historical themes played a significant role in the illustrations for *Aurora*, often harking back to Baroque compositions. After the failure of the War of Independence (1848–9) they became a leading theme for Hungarian painters trained in Vienna: Henrik Weber (1818–66), Mihály Kovács (1818–92) and MÓR THAN. At the end of the 1850s the generation that had studied in Paris (e.g. VIKTOR MADARÁSZ) and Munich (e.g. BERTALAN SZÉKELY; Sándor Wagner (1838–1919); SÁNDOR LIEZEN-MAYER) expressed a mature form of National Romanticism in their work. The influential art critic and late Romantic landscape painter GUSZTÁV KELETI also trained in Munich.

The Compromise of 1867, which followed an era of political repression, affected Hungarian painting, in that the resulting economic and social recovery brought important State wall-painting commissions for artists working in Hungary, KÁROLY LOTZ among them. Their large-scale history paintings fitted in well with contemporary architectural historicism. Hungarian artists studying abroad at the time included Gyula Benczúr, MIHÁLY MUNKÁCSY, PÁL SZINYEI MERSE, LÁSZLÓ PAÁL and LAJOS DEÁK-ÉBNER. Of these, Benczúr returned home in 1883 and became a highly celebrated painter and the first Hungarian Director of Art Education (for further discussion and illustration *see* BENCZÚR, GYULA). Deák-Ebner, who regularly visited the SZOLNOK COLONY, was the first Hungarian to paint in the naturalistic style of Jules Bastien-Lepage.

The naturalistic approach became widespread in the early 1890s through the mediation of SIMON HOLLÓSY's painting school in Munich and is evident in the early work of Károly Ferenczy (*see* FERENCZY, (1)), ISTVÁN CSÓK and BÉLA IVÁNYI GRÜNWALD, whose *plein-air* tendencies were strengthened by their move in 1897 to Nagybánya (now Baia Mare, Romania; *see* NAGYBÁNYA COLONY). Impressionist painting techniques, which play a role in the work of LÁSZLÓ MEDNYÁNSZKY, approached Post-Impressionism in that of JÓZSEF RIPPL-RÓNAI, who returned from France in 1902, and occasionally appeared after 1905 in the work of ADOLF FÉNYES. The two visionary painters of the Hungarian *fin-de-siècle*, TIVADAR CSONTVÁRY and LAJOS GULÁCSY, show similarities with the European Secessionist movements in the work they executed at the GÖDÖLLŐ COLONY, founded by ALADÁR KÖRÖSFŐI-KRIESCH and Sándor Nagy.

(ii) 20th century. The members of the progressive group THE EIGHT (iii), including LAJOS TIHANYI, BÉLA CZÓBEL, ÖDÖN MÁRFFY, RÓBERT BERÉNY and KÁROLY KERNSTOK, were influenced by a range of sources, from Fauvism to Cubism. After the group's disintegration in 1912, the avant-garde ACTIVISTS emerged, with the writer and painter LAJOS KASSÁK as their driving force. Members included the expressive Cubists JÓZSEF NEMES LAMPÉRTH and BÉLA UITZ, the lyrical abstract painter JÁNOS MÁTTIS TEUTSCH, most of the later Hungarian Bauhaus activists and VILMOS HUSZÁR, who later became a member of the De Stijl movement.

After the failure of the 1919 Republic of Councils Commune, progressive artists were forced to emigrate. They included leading figures of the Eight, of the group that formed around Kassák and including SÁNDOR BORTNYIK, who had produced posters and propaganda art for the Commune, and young art historians who had rescued private collections and preserved them in the Museum of Fine Arts, Budapest (Frederick Antal (1887–1954), ARNOLD HAUSER, Johannes Wilde, Charles Erich de Tolnay, Simon Meller (1875–1949)). The revival of avant-garde organizations in the 1920s emerged with a cautious heterogeneous grouping around the New Society of Fine Artists (KÚT), including János Vaszary (1867–1939), JÓZSEF EGRY, HUGÓ SCHEIBER, Armand Schönberger (1885–1974) and Ernő Schubert (1903–60).

In the 1930s official cultural policy supported members of the so-called School of Rome (Vilmos Aba-Novák (1894–1942), Pál C. Molnár (1894–1981), Béla Kontuly (1904–83)), which was influenced by the Novecento Italiano, while the GRESHAM GROUP was united by the similarity of their aesthetic thinking rather than by any particular style. Among the members were AURÉL BERNÁTH, ISTVÁN SZŐNYI and József Egry. Artistic trends in the work of Communist worker–painters did not emerge until after World War II, the most significant painters being Gyula Derkovits and István Dési Huber, who painted in a variety of styles. The SZENTENDRE COLONY was a group of artists, including IMRE ÁMOS, who gathered around LAJOS VAJDA. Ámos and Vajda were the role models for the influential EUROPEAN SCHOOL, formed in 1945, which comprised art critics and sculptors as well as such painters as the doyen of the Hungarian avant-garde

13. Lili Ország: *Blue Gate II*, *Labyrinth* series lxxxviii, oil on wood-fibre, 1.0×0.9 m, 1975 (Budapest, Hungarian National Gallery)

JENŐ GADÁNYI, Júlia Vajda (1913–1982), ENDRE BÁLINT and DEZSŐ KORNISS. The Abstract Group, which broke away from the European School, included Tihamér Gyarmathy (*b* 1915), Tamás Lossonczy (*b* 1904), FERENC MARTYN and JENŐ BARCSAY.

From 1949 to 1957 SOCIALIST REALISM reigned supreme and influenced the work of Sándor Ék (1902–75), ENDRE DOMANOVSZKY and Rudolf Bér (*b* 1924), but several modernists continued to work in its shadow, among them LILI ORSZÁG (e.g. her series *Labyrinth*; Budapest, N.G.; see fig. 13), BÉLA KONDOR, Béla Veszelszky and Ilka Gedo, whose work was celebrated in the 1970s. The Hungarian avant-garde gradually emerged from the underground in the 1960s and was exposed to contemporary Western trends. In the early 1960s supra-naturalism appeared in the work of those who had studied under Aurél Bernáth in the 1950s, such as Tibor Csernus (*b* 1927), László Lakner and Ákos Szabó (*b* 1936), who adopted Bernáth's brilliant painting technique. The first breakthrough for the 1960s avant-garde took place at the 1968–9 expositions held in the great hall of the state industrial design enterprise. Exhibitors comprised the forceful representatives of geometrical abstraction, István Nádler (*b* 1938), Tamás Hencze (*b* 1938), Ilona Keserű (*b* 1933) and Imre Bak (*b* 1939); the lyrical abstract artists Sándor Molnár (*b* 1936) and Endre Hortobágyi (*b* 1941); the hyperrealist LÁSZLÓ LAKNER; László Méhes (*b* 1944), who developed right through to the Pop art period; and one of the initiators of Fluxus and Conceptual art, MIKLÓS ERDÉLY. In the mid-1980s a series of large-scale exhibitions was organized under the title 'New Sensibility',

displaying work by the Neo-primitive Neo-Dadaist painters working in Szentendre (András Wahorn (*b* 1953), László fe Lugossy (*b* 1947), István ef Zámbó (*b* 1950)) and by the new generation of painters who were just beginning their careers (László Fehér (*b* 1953), Gábor Roskó (*b* 1958), János Szirtes (*b* 1954)), as well as paintings by more established artists.

BIBLIOGRAPHY

É. Körner: 'Künstler der ungarischen Räterepublik', *Acta Hist. A. Acad. Sci. Hung.*, vi (1959), pp. 169–92

T. Gerszi: *A magyar kőrajzolás története a XIX. században* [The history of Hungarian lithography in the 19th century] (Budapest, 1960)

L. Németh: *Modern magyar művészet* [Modern Hungarian art] (Budapest, 1968; Eng. trans., 1969)

Á. Zibolen-Vayer: *Kisfaludy Károly: A művészeti romantika kezdetei Magyarországon* [Károly Kisfaludy: the beginnings of Romanticism in painting and graphic art in Hungary] (Budapest, 1973) [with Ger. summary]

É. Körner: *Die ungarische Kunst zwischen den beiden Weltkriegen* (Dresden, 1974)

J. Szabadi: *A magyar szecesszió művészete* [Hungarian Art Nouveau] (Budapest, 1979; Eng. trans., 1989)

Künstler aus Ungarn (exh. cat., Wilhelmshaven, Ksthalle, 1980)

J. Szabadi: 'Tradition and Modernity in the Avant-garde of the 1960s in Hungary', *Acta Hist. A. Acad. Sci. Hung.*, xxx (1984), pp. 327–55

J. Szabó: *A 19. század festészete Magyarországon* [Painting in 19th-century Hungary] (Budapest, 1985; Eng. trans., 1988)

Contemporary Visual Art in Hungary: Eighteen Artists (exh. cat., Glasgow, Third Eye Cent.; Székesfehérvár, King Stephen Mus.; 1985)

Wechsel Wirkungen: Ungarische Avantgarde in der Weimarer Republik (exh. cat., ed. H. Gassner; Kassel, Neue Gal.; Bochum, Mus. Bochum, Kstsamml.; 1986)

Neue Sensibilität: Ungarische Malerei der 80er Jahre (exh. cat., ed. K. Néray and L. Hegyi; Esslingen, Neue Gal., 1987)

K. Passuth and D. Moyer: *Les Avant-gardes de l'Europe centrale* (Paris, 1988)

G. Seregélyi: *Magyar festők és grafikusok adattára: Életrajzi lexikon az 1800–1988 között alkotó festő- és grafikusművészekről* [A biographical dictionary of Hungarian painters and graphic artists who flourished between 1800 and 1988] (Szeged, 1988)

A Golden Age: Art and Society in Hungary, 1896–1914 (exh. cat. by T. I. Berend, L. Németh and I. Sármány-Parsons, London, Barbican A.G.; Miami, Cent. F.A.; San Diego, Mus. A.; 1989–91)

P. György and G. Pataki: *Az Európai Iskola és az Elvont Művészek Csoportja* [The European School and the Abstract Group of artists] (Budapest, 1990) [Eng. summary]

S. A. Mansbach: 'Confrontations and Accommodation in the Hungarian Avant-garde', *A. J.* [New York], xlix/1 (1990), pp. 9–20

Hatvanas évek: Új törekvések a magyar képzőművészetben [The Sixties: new trends in Hungarian art] (exh. cat., ed. I. Nagy; Budapest, N.G., 1991) [with Eng. summary]

P. György and H. Turai, eds: *A művészet katonái: Sztálinizmus és kultúra* [The soldiers of art: Stalinism and culture] (Budapest, 1992); Ger. trans. as *Staatskunstwerk, Kultur und Stalinismus* (1992)

A. Zádor, ed.: *A historizmus művészete Magyarországon* [The art and architecture of historicism in Hungary] (Budapest, 1993)

EDIT SZENTESI, PÉTER UJVÁRI

V. Interior decoration and furniture.

1. Before 1600. 2. 1600–1799. 3. 1800–96. 4. After 1896.

1. BEFORE 1600. The earliest known furniture, dating from the nomadic period before the conquest of Hungary in the 10th century AD, was probably used only in the tents of the chief tribesmen. Examples include chair-thrones indicating superior rank, casket-shaped chests and cradles. Both the thrones and the cradles followed Byzantine forms, while the names used for them were Turkish in origin. After the conquest the Magyar settlers adapted such new Slav forms as square tables and probably cupboards. Textiles played a significant role when interiors

14. Bártfa Bookcase, lime- and larch-wood, h. 2.38 m, l. 4.3 m, c. 1480, from St Giles, Bardejov (Budapest, Hungarian National Museum)

were richly decorated for important social occasions. There was very little furniture in early medieval Hungarian houses, and even the houses of the nobility contained only the most basic pieces. These might be ornamented with chip-carving or painted decoration, as indicated by surviving 14th-century chests.

In the early period furniture was generally Romanesque in style. Chairs indicated status, especially thrones for those of kingly rank; it was customary for the nobility to bring their own chairs to court. Chairs with folding, X-shaped timber frames (Lat. *faldistorium*) appeared in Hungary in the 11th century; examples include the thrones of kings Béla III (*reg* 1172–96) and Emeric (*reg* 1196–1204). In the 13th century the chairs of church dignitaries were of this type when King Béla IV (*reg* 1235–70) permitted them to be seated in his presence. Chairs had either a low or high back, and so-called footchairs were provided for the lower ranks.

In the early period even noblemen usually slept on straw matting on the floor or, as depicted in the Illustrated Chronicle (1358; Budapest, N. Szechényi Lib., Col. lat. 404), on a low trestle with bedding. Tables became widely used in the 14th and 15th centuries but were not permanent fixtures in a room at this time. They were constructed of two or more boards that rested on trestle legs and were erected only for meals. Dug-out chests for storing clothes were hollowed from a single log and strengthened with iron bands. More technically advanced chests were called wardrobes; they became more widely used in the 13th century, and many were enriched with carving.

In the 15th century Gothic features appear, and several extant pieces of furniture from northern Hungary and Transylvania are datable to the second half of the century. Many were made from such soft woods as walnut, lime, sycamore or pine and decorated in low relief; bold Late

Gothic carving is also found. High-backed choir-stalls, with baldacchini, prayer stools and balusters, decorated with tracery and Gothic foliage, sometimes partly painted (and sometimes with a portrait of the donor on the baldacchino), are especially impressive. Many superb Late Gothic choir-stalls of northern and eastern Hungary (now Romanian Transylvania) survive. An exceptionally fine and well-preserved example (c. 1483; Budapest, N. Mus.) from St Giles at Bártfa (now Bardejov, Slovakia) is a five-seated choir-stall with reliefs on the back and painted coats of arms framed by foliage, among them those of King Matthias Corvinus, his wife Beatrix and the town. The Bártfa Bookcase (c. 1480; Budapest, N. Mus.; see fig. 14) originally stood in the oratory of St Giles. The front is made of lime- and larch-wood; the upper part is decorated in low relief with painted garlands of stylized flowers, and the top is crenellated. The 12 doors enclosing shelves have tin-plated fittings, lock plates and handles. One of the most important Gothic chests painted with figural ornament is the Nagyszeben Chest (Budapest, N. Mus.). The earliest surviving chest of framed-panel construction is the 15th-century Káposztafalvi Chest (Budapest, N. Mus.), which is decorated with fine foliate tracery and has tin-plated iron fittings. So-called crib tables of the 15th and 16th centuries are typically Late Gothic in style with folding lime-wood tops and oak legs. Foliage carved in low relief can often be found on the table frame and the cradle-shaped lower body; the inner part of the cradle, which had a lockable recess, was also frequently carved.

Due to the patronage of Matthias Corvinus (*reg* 1458–90), the Renaissance style appeared in Hungary by the 1480s, and both interior decoration and furniture were influenced by the new style. Matthias's marriage in 1475 to the Neapolitan Beatrix of Aragon established an Italian connection, and Italian architects and artists attached to the court assisted in the dissemination of a primarily Florentine version of the style. Although Matthias's great building projects, including the royal palace at Buda Castle, were almost completely destroyed during repeated sieges by the Turks between 1541 and 1686, excavations carried out after World War II confirmed their Renaissance character. A document of 1479 reveals that five Florentine marquetry-workers were contracted to work in Hungary for one year under the Florentine carver and marquetry-maker Chimenti di Leonardo Camicia (1431–before 1505). Camicia worked as the court architect but also took part in designing decorated timber ceilings that were executed by Baccio Cellini, the uncle of Benvenuto Cellini. Designs for marquetry door panels and coffered ceilings have been attributed to Camicia. According to Vasari, Benedetto da Maiano also supplied a pair of marquetry chests (untraced) to Matthias. The wedding of King Matthias was commemorated with richly styled built-in and free-standing credenzas. According to surviving designs in the Corvinian Antiphonal they contained many drawers, had elaborate bases and were used to display decorative vessels.

After the death of Matthias Corvinus in 1490 the Florentine trend prevailed for some time; several Italians were employed at the court of Ippolito I d'Este, the Archbishop of Esztergom, and thus the marquetry style of the Matthias period became more widespread. In 1507 Niza Fiorentinus made choir-stalls for Zagreb Cathedral that were subsequently destroyed by fire. The design was purchased by the Vicar General to Ippolito I d'Este for Eger Cathedral and executed by János, a cabinetmaker of Kassa, but the quality and style of the marquetry is indicated only by surviving fragments. The so-called Nyírbátor stalls (Budapest, N. Mus.), commissioned by the Báthory family in 1511, are signed *F. Marone*, possibly a relative of the Italian wood-carver Roberto Marone (who was also known as Raffaello da Brescia), or, if the 'F' is interpreted as 'Frater' or 'Fecit', by Marone himself. The design is Gothic but the decoration on the canopies is rich in Renaissance details. The backs are decorated with grotesques and perspective marquetry; behind the latticed doors are books, decorated jars and ecclesiastical objects depicted in the Florentine-Urbino marquetry style. The remains of the stalls from Diósgyőr Castle (Miskolc, Reformed Church) reveal the influence of Italian marquetry in their geometric ribbon inlay.

During the second half of the 16th century the Florentine-Renaissance style was modified by local traditions. A regional example of marquetry with architectural perspective is the choir-stall in the chapel of the Thököly castle in Kežmarok, Slovakia, made in 1544 by János Lang (*b* 1464). A chest from Kéžmarok also shows Italian influence but its high plinth is derived from German furniture. At the end of the 16th century this became the dominant influence on Hungarian furniture.

BIBLIOGRAPHY

J. Kovalovszky: *Gótikus és reneszánsz butorok* [Gothic and Renaissance furniture] (Budapest, 1980)

K. K. Csilléry: *A magyar népi lakáskultura kialakulásának kezdetei* [The beginnings of Hungarian folk interior design] (Budapest, 1982)

2. 1600–1799. After the Turkish conquest in 1541 the country was divided into three parts: Dunántul, northern Hungary and Transylvania. Furniture styles in these three regions developed differently. The areas closest to Austria (Dunántul and northern Hungary) were primarily influenced by south German styles, whereas in Transylvania the Italian Renaissance style was combined with Northern Mannerism and eastern influences through the Turkish connection. The quadrangular design of castles and manor houses in the last region allowed for longer wings and suites of interconnecting rooms. The apartments were painted, had carved ceilings and, according to Transylvanian sources, the furniture was often painted as well. As many 17th-century interiors have been destroyed, and few of the furnishings remain, it is possible to describe only the general character of the interior decoration and furnishing schemes.

The central room in castles and in most manor houses was the banqueting hall, where the richest furniture was on display. The floor was often made of hexagonal parquetry or flower-patterned mosaic tiles. The grandest ceilings were coffered and richly gilded, with the family coat of arms in the centre, but most ceilings were composed of finely cut beams and vividly patterned boards. The most beautiful surviving example is the banqueting hall at Szentbenedek Castle (now Hronský Beňadik, Slovakia), which is painted with Renaissance-style flower patterns. Such ceilings were executed by painter-carpenters who also decorated furniture. (For further discussion of floral decoration and the 'Flower Renaissance' *see* CLUJ-NAPOCA.)

In aristocratic households rooms were usually hung with textiles: for example, at the residence of the wife of Gábor Bethlen, Prince of Transylvania (*reg* 1613–29), the walls were covered with Flemish tapestries and Venetian woven carpets. On special occasions rooms might be hung with figured tapestries or painted canvas; the themes and styles of these followed examples imported from Flanders. A few survive from the Ferenc II Rákóczy period (1703–11). Carpets were placed on the floor only at court; elsewhere they were displayed on walls or tables. Most were imported from Asia Minor or Persia and belong to the so-called Transylvanian tradition. Tiled stoves of the 17th century were usually rectangular, their colour determined by the scheme of the room. Tin-glazed tiles with Renaissance flower patterns were popular, although in northern Hungary foliate designs were influenced by northern Mannerism. Typical of this type are the 'ankle stoves': low stoves for warming the feet and ankles made by potters from the Habáns, a German-speaking sect of Anabaptists.

During the first half of the 17th century furniture was mostly Renaissance in style. A local version of the Italian *cassapanca* is the box-seat chair; examples include those with the arms of the Garázda and Teleki families (*c.* 1600; Budapest, Mus. Applied A.). Chairs of the period usually have wooden seats without padding or upholstery, the backs and legs carved with foliage and braced with cross-bars. The backs of straddle-legged chairs were carved in low relief; examples include Mihály Teleki's armchair of 1652 and Ferenc Rákóczy's chair from the late 17th century. Armchairs generally followed northern Renaissance types, and some were upholstered in leather stitched by saddlers in scale designs. Inventories also mention velvet-covered, embroidered chairs and benches, the seats

15. Hunfalvi Chest, 535×1505×735 mm, 1692 (Budapest, Hungarian National Museum)

of which also served as beds. After 1600 the use of lavishly decorated Renaissance-style beds spread rapidly. These have turned frames and painted dome canopies hung with rich textiles, and they were nearly all imported. An example is Mária Széchy's bed of 1672. Beds without canopies were mostly painted, carved and inlaid. Tables with square or round tops and baluster-turned legs were usually covered with carpets; painted and inlaid multi-drawered letter-, jewel- or writing-cases were sometimes placed on them.

The most important item of storage furniture in the 17th century was the chest, which reflected early Italian Renaissance and northern Mannerist influences. Most examples have a low plinth and an architecturally designed front with turned columns or flat pilasters, combined with arched panels containing carved or inlaid foliate arabesque ornament. The early Renaissance geometric *tarsia a toppo*, formed by assembling thin cross-sections sliced from groups of joined polygonal rods, was superseded by *tarsia a incastro*, a technique exploiting mirror-image designs created by cutting through several layers of contrasting veneer; these could then be used on one or more pieces of furniture. This method achieved a range of intricately interlaced dark and light surface patterns and was frequently based on engraved sources and examples by Dutch and German goldsmiths. The 17th-century pattern books of the guilds of Kolozsvár (now Cluj-Napoca, Romania) record a wide range of both Italian and German Mannerist motifs. Versions of this style survive in the two-door chests from northern Hungary and Transylvania (1640, Sárospatak; *c.* 1600, Körmöcbánya, now Kremnica, Slovakia) and the choir-stalls from Körmöcbánya (1620; Budapest, Mus. Applied A.). In addition to decoration inspired by goldsmiths' ornament, 17th-century trousseau chests reveal Italian Renaissance influence in the use of coloured wooden tracery, so-called Italian pitcher motifs, angel heads and vine-leaf carvings.

Extensive trade with Dutch Protestants throughout the 17th century resulted in the introduction of new decorative elements, one being the Auricular style, which was widely used as a border on pulpits, tombstones and eventually furniture. An example is the goldsmiths' guild chest from Nagyszombat (now Trnava, Slovakia), which was signed in Hungarian (1669; Budapest, N. Mus.). A local version of this idiom is the trousseau chest (Budapest, N. Mus.) made for Katá Bethlen on her marriage to Mihály Apafi II, Prince of Transylvania, in 1695. The surface is carved, inlaid and painted with regional flower motifs and Hungarian folk-art designs. On certain chests shell-like motifs were given a local character with the addition of painted panels of women in Hungarian dress (e.g. the Hunfalvi Chest, 1692; Budapest, N. Mus.; see fig. 15). The timbers most frequently used for 17th-century Hungarian furniture were curled ash and maple, but walnut, alder and lime were also widely used. Most furniture, however, was made from cheaper softwoods, usually pine, which was then painted; green is the colour most often mentioned in sources. The late Renaissance and early Mannerist style prevailed in the eastern part of the country until the end of the century and beyond.

In the western regions the Baroque style appeared as early as the 1620s and was dominant until the end of the 17th century. Among the first to adopt this new style were the Hungarian aristocracy, the Viennese court and the Catholic Church, notably the Jesuits, who used it in church interiors and furnishings. During the second half of the century the Hungarian aristocracy in western Hungary started to employ the style for architectural projects and, subsequently, for interior decoration. Banqueting halls were decorated with stucco, ancestral portraits and prized carpets as at Sárvár Castle. The main interconnecting apartments were normally decorated with stuccowork illustrating biblical, mythological and historical scenes; these were often more representative of regional styles than the elaborate furniture that was frequently imported. The stuccowork follows northern Italian styles. The aristocracy usually acquired imported furniture for their city palaces and castles, of which over 200 were built during the 18th century; the country seats of the landed gentry were equipped with furniture made in Hungary. Most of the furniture from the castles has been destroyed, but contemporary descriptions testify to the richness of their interiors. The most important country house and garden designed and built in the 18th century was Eszterháza (now FERTŐD; see fig. 16), known as the Hungarian Versailles; its decoration and furniture were primarily imported from France, southern Germany and Austria, although some of the furniture was made locally in the court workshop by foreign craftsmen following western European designs.

Rooms in the palaces were adorned with *boiserie* framed by carpets, patterned silks or wallpapers; the elegance of the Hungarian Baroque is illustrated by the *boiserie* built into the library cupboards of the country house of the Bishop of Veszprém in SÜMEG. During the first half of the 18th century benches, tables and panelling with strapwork inlay (1732–3; Nagytétény, nr Budapest, Castle Mus.) were made for the former Jesuit house at Trencsén (now Trenčín, Slovakia), where BERNÁT BAUMGARTNER was one of the prominent craftsmen. The richly carved decoration on the Kőszeg medicine chest is the work of Jesuit monks. The influence of Baroque art can be seen in furniture made *c.* 1700, when the legs of chairs became turned spirals and high-backed chairs were upholstered with foliate and figured needlework. Towards the mid-18th century seats became smaller, backs lower and legs curved.

The Austrian Baroque style prevailed in the west of the country. Large double-doored cupboards followed the southern and central German types, with vigorously canted corners, the doors set within the frame and component parts decorated with rich strapwork or foliate inlay, pierced fretwork and coronet crestings. In the mid-18th century the so-called foliate and ribbon marquetry style spread. One of the most important examples is a sacristy cupboard in the choir of the Franciscan church at Pécs made by Lukács Jani, a lay father, in 1745. The rich marquetry surfaces portray scenes from the life of St Francis, but only fragments survive. In the mid-18th century most cupboards had double doors or drawers in the lower part, and the marquetry sometimes featured fruit trees inlaid in metal. The fashion for massive Baroque pieces declined after the mid-18th century, but two-doored cupboards were made by the guilds until the beginning of the 19th century and were often magnificent pieces. The late Baroque or Rococo style appeared in furniture design in the 1760s, when pieces became smaller and curvilinear in shape. Chairs, tables and various small pieces assumed more graceful forms. Domestic interiors were enriched with carved decoration, while delicate and costly marquetry furniture was reserved for reception rooms. New furniture types appeared, including small commodes and low writing-tables. Decoration was modest, as the Hungarian Rococo was never characterized by such elaborate and showy forms of decoration as gilding; some interiors were, however, very richly ornamented. Examples include the magnificent decoration at Eszterháza, and such work of

16. *Sala terrena*, Eszterháza, Fertőd, 1764–6

the Paulite, Franciscan and Jesuit workshops as the carvings in the Benedictine abbey at Tihany of 1760–70 by Sebestyén Stulhof, the Jesuit sacristy at Székesfehérvár of 1764–7 by János Hyngeller and the library of the Paulites in Pest (*c.* 1775) by Antal Rutschmann—all among the greatest achievements of the Rococo in Hungary.

The influence of European Neo-classicism was introduced into Hungarian furniture design in the 1780s, and the study of pattern books in the new style was obligatory in art schools from 1783 onwards. This style originated from French, Italian, German and English fashions, the strongest influences being the work of Jean-Charles Delafosse, Richard Lalonde (*fl* 1788–96) and Johann Thomas Hauer (1748–1820). In the 1780s and 1790s furniture styles were transformed throughout the country as simple bourgeois variants of the Neo-classical style appeared. Light in construction, especially the chairs, and rational in function, the furniture was characterized by pure lines and by economy and harmony of ornament. The furniture was made entirely from local woods.

BIBLIOGRAPHY

P. Voit: *Régi magyar otthonok* [Ancient Hungarian interiors] (Budapest, 1941)
M. Zlinszky Sternegg: *Renaissance Inlay in Old Hungary* (Budapest, 1966)
M. B. Nagy: *Reneszánsz és barokk Erdélyben* [The Renaissance and Baroque in Transylvania] (Bucharest, 1970)
H. Szabolcsi: *Magyarországi bútorművészet a 18–19. század fordulóján* [Hungarian furniture at the turn of the 18th century] (Budapest, 1972)

3. 1800–96. At the end of the 18th century a new type of accommodation had appeared in the form of the city apartment, and this in turn encouraged new schemes of interior decoration. During the first half of the 19th century Pest played a crucial role; it was united with Buda in 1872 and became the capital of the country. The city supported a thriving community of artists and craftsmen who developed new styles, which soon spread to other towns. Viennese tradesmen played an important role in the dissemination of the new fashions. By the early 19th century the castles and vast city palaces of the aristocracy were reflecting bourgeois tastes and a continuing preference for imported furniture. There was little difference between the interior decoration of the manor houses of the minor nobility and that of the apartments of the upper middle classes. First-floor apartments were the grandest; the central rooms at the front generally served as reception rooms leading to the drawing-room and dining-room. The domestic quarters were at the back. The floors of these elegant town houses were either patterned parquet or plain boards, made by local carpenters. The rooms were hung with carpets bought from Viennese dealers in Pest who stocked French, German and sometimes English wares; alternatively the walls might be painted with traditional carpet designs. The ceilings, decorated in imitation stucco, were ornamented with foliate designs in the centre. For curtains such light materials as muslin, lawn and cambric were favoured, although in the second half of the 19th century heavier textiles appeared. Lighting was provided by gilt-wood or bronze hanging lamps, sconces, table candlesticks and lustres or Czech cut-glass chandeliers, wall-lamps and table-lamps. Rooms were generally heated by cylindrical tiled stoves, but from about 1840 cast-iron stoves made in Hungary were widely used.

Furniture no longer had a fixed position in a formal interior but was placed where it was most convenient, often against the wall. Decorative textiles were increasingly used in domestic interiors. In the first half of the 19th century chairs were generally upholstered in leather or in fabric of one colour or striped, but in the second half they were mostly covered with plush velvet or brocade and rich braiding. In the 1830s lavish textiles appeared in aristocratic dressing-rooms, where the walls and toilet tables were elaborately hung with drapery. With the spread of Historicist styles in the second half of the 19th century floor carpets became increasingly important.

The number of cabinetmakers, active both within and outside the guilds, increased significantly at the beginning of the 19th century. New workshops appeared, and warehouses were established by the guilds, where their members' furniture was sold. In 1842 the National Trade Protection Movement founded a trade association and organized the first Hungarian trade exhibitions in 1842, 1843 and 1846, at which local furniture-makers showed their work. In 1872 the guild organizations ceased, and thereafter trade bodies represented skilled workers. In the first half of the 19th century furniture designs were produced by the craftsmen themselves, the Biedermeier style being essentially an artisan creation. Furniture-makers acquired a knowledge of currently fashionable styles while training or travelling abroad, or from German, French and English pattern books. By the 1860s most important factories employed their own designers as well as following foreign fashions; Hungarian architects and designers played a vital role in furniture design in the last decades of the century.

Until *c.* 1820 furniture perpetuated Neo-classical designs from the late 18th century; these formed the basis of the Biedermeier style in the 1820s. The Empire style was restricted to a small circle of patrons in Hungary, while a taste for Egyptian Revival furniture was allied to a Viennese version of the Empire style. Elegant furniture was mostly of mahogany or ebony embellished with composition or gilt-wood ornaments instead of gilt-bronze mounts. Chairs copied the simplest Empire patterns. Small three-legged round or oblong tables were similar to those of the early Biedermeier style, and writing desks were made in simple geometric secrétaire forms, using urn and lyre shapes. Decoration was chiefly confined to gilt or painted surfaces and composition reliefs of mythological beasts and foliage. Pianos were also designed in this style, as were many smaller pieces including mirrors, chandeliers and sconces, clock-cases, occasional tables and boxes. The greatest exponent of the Viennese Empire style was Sebestyén-Antal Vogel, the first Hungarian entrepreneurial furniture-maker.

Biedermeier furniture was made from such local light woods as walnut, cherry and sycamore, and the simple geometric forms suited the prominent grain of the timbers. In the 1830s the style became more elaborate, the inlays increasingly rich with leaf, tendril and arabesque motifs, and the forms more ornate due to the use of Rococo and Baroque elements. Upholstered sofas with exposed frames in simple shapes were popular, as were side chairs with smooth, tapered legs and fan-shaped backs (see fig. 17). The so-called globus table first appeared in the 1860s and

17. Chair with fan-shaped back by Ferenc Steindl, 910×480×420 mm, from Pest, *c.* 1840 (Győr, Czuczor Gergely Secondary Grammar School)

was fashionable until the end of the 1930s. The spherical exterior was often decorated with the signs of the zodiac, and the flat surface was revealed by sliding the upper hemisphere underneath. The most famous craftsman of the Biedermeier period was FERENC STEINDL, who designed the interiors of the first seven Hungarian Danube steamships (1837–42). The high quality of his work is apparent in the few surviving pieces of furniture that bear his name.

The economic depression following the Revolution of 1848 affected furniture manufacture, and only in the 1860s were the craft workshops again able to compete with mass production, especially of bentwood furniture. The Viennese firm of Thonet opened its third factory in Hungary in Nagyugróc in 1862, and from the 1870s until the end of the century there were 13 bentwood furniture factories operating in the country. The largest manufacturer was Endre Thék, who trained in France and opened a workshop in 1872. Austrian imports also had a significant impact. In the 1870s the achievements of Hungarian furniture-makers were recorded in the illustrated catalogue to the Weltausstellung of 1873 in Vienna and at the National Decorative Arts Exhibition of 1885, where 133 cabinetmakers showed their work. These exhibitions show that the schemes of interior decoration and furnishing produced by Hungarian factories for the new buildings in the capital in the 1870s and 1880s had reached an impressively high standard.

In the second half of the 19th century the dominant fashion was Historicism, which began with the revival of earlier furniture styles. Initially, it emerged in the increasingly ponderous Baroque Revival and Rococo Revival styles, followed by a Renaissance influence, which dominated design from the 1870s until the end of the century. Such furniture designers as Miklós Ybl, Albert Schickedanz and Alajos Hauszmann were primarily architects whose Historicism was characterized by eclecticism. By the 1890s this stylistic diversity encouraged the decoration of different rooms in various styles: the salon might be Rococo, Moroccan or Oriental, the drawing-room and the study Renaissance, the bedrooms Baroque or Louis XVI and the smoking-room Turkish. Interiors were elaborately furnished with rich timber panelling, silk wall coverings, tooled leather, plush covers, oriental carpets, rugs, brocaded curtains and collections of antique ornaments. This was the mainstream style; in progressive circles the desire to find a national style developed in the 1880s when Hungarian folk art influenced furniture decoration. The conflict between Historicism and stylistic nationalism was illustrated in the Millenial Exhibition of 1896 in Budapest, where both appeared side by side.

BIBLIOGRAPHY

H. Szabolcsi: *Régi magyar butorok* [Old Hungarian furniture] (Budapest, 1954)
M. Zlinszkyné Sternegg: 'Az első magyar "butorgyárak" Vogel Sebestyén Antal' [The first Hungarian furniture manufacturer Antal Sebestyén Vogel], *Művészettörténeti Tanulmányok* (1957), pp. 153–218
H. Szabolcsi: 'Masterpieces as Evidence of Change in Hungarian Furniture, c. 1750–1830', *Furn. Hist.*, xxi (1985), pp. 134–46

4. AFTER 1896. In addition to the search for a specifically national style, an interest in contemporary art emerged in Hungary at the end of the 19th century. The ideas of John Ruskin and William Morris and the work of English and Scottish craftsmen of the Arts and Crafts Movement were especially admired by leading Hungarian artists who wanted to create new forms to suit local needs. The Secession also had a powerful influence, primarily on interior decoration, as did Art Nouveau. In 1898 work in these styles by foreign artists was shown in an exhibition in Budapest entitled *Modern művészet* ('Modern art'), in 1898 and 1910 the work of Walter Crane was exhibited, and in 1911 the Museum of Applied Art organized a major show by British craftsmen. The strong desire for a national popular style could not be suppressed entirely, however, and a mixture of western European Secession and peasant domestic styles ultimately prevailed. This style dominated the design of the Hungarian pavilion at the Exposition Universelle of 1900 in Paris, where Ödön Faragó (1869–1935) and Pál Horti (1865–1907) won prizes for furniture and carpet designs. Both had ties to the GÖDÖLLŐ COLONY, a community of artists dedicated to Arts and Crafts principles. Faragó's work appeared at the Esposizione Internazionale d'Arte Decorativa in Turin (1902), the St Louis Exhibition (1904) and the Esposizione Internazionale del Sempione in Milan (1906) and won numerous prizes. He favoured large, austere pieces that combined national motifs with decorative fittings. He

18. Lajos Kozma: entrance to the music-room of 'Lapis Refugii', a fantasy house; from *Magyar iparművészet* (1908), p. 123

designed domestic interiors for middle-class clients in Budapest as well as the interior and furnishings of a bank (1900–10). His early work was characterized by historical eclecticism but by the turn of the century he became known for his simple national Secession style. Another important interior designer was Frigyes Spiegel, whose studio in Budapest was called Maison Moderne. He was responsible for many business and bank interiors following the style of Henry Van de Velde and became a knowledgeable intermediary for the west European Secession.

In the first decades of the century one of the most influential designers was Ede Thoroczkai Wigand, whose work included painting, architecture, interior design and furnishings. He came into contact with the Gödöllő artists, who persuaded him to study Hungarian folk art; his essays on peasant architecture and material culture were published between 1910 and 1917. His work was published in *Innendekoration* and *The Studio* and gained recognition abroad. His early furniture was Secessionist in spirit with elemental forms, sometimes crudely proportioned, that expressed the function of the piece. He preferred to work on integrated schemes, designing an apartment and all its furnishings. In 1900 he published his furniture designs, calling them *Brettstil* forms.

Pál Horti was a leading figure in the Hungarian Secession movement, and furniture design was only one of many interests. His first functional furniture dates from the 1890s and tends to be western in style although simpler

and more rustic in construction; he often used the natural beauty of the wood grain as a means of surface decoration. His designs for interior decoration were functional and Secessionist in their refined details. In 1904 Horti designed the Hungarian Manor House pavilion at the St Louis Exhibition. He was recognized in the USA as one of the most original and talented artists of his generation and helped to organize arts and crafts guilds in St Louis, New York and other American cities.

Lajos Kozma deserves recognition as the greatest Hungarian craftsman of the 20th century. A qualified architect, he was involved in many different areas of modernist applied arts. His furniture was made to his specifications by the Budapest workshop that he founded in 1913 on the model of the Wiener Werkstätte. His designs combined Secessionist, Art Deco and Hungarian folk art elements (see fig. 18). While working for the Béla Lajta Architectural Studio he created important designs for architectural and interior decoration, including those for the Rózsavölgyi Emporium. At this time his work was strongly influenced by the Hungarian Renaissance and national Baroque styles. Although dominated by carved ornament, decorative inlay, painting and gilding, his furniture was always modern in construction. His white and coloured lacquered furniture displays a wealth of western European forms influenced by Hungarian folk art. In the 1930s his style became simpler, and his interiors and furniture were Constructivist essays representing the best modern European traditions.

He founded his own school and trained many important designers between the wars. The most important was Gyula Kaesz (1897–1967), who by 1926 was a well-known designer. In the style of late 18th-century English Neoclassicism, Kaesz's furniture was light in structure, elegant in proportion and finely detailed. He also used modernized Hungarian folk forms, especially in the inlay work of cupboards designed by his wife, the graphic artist Kato Lukacs. Kaesz did much to promote interior design through his teaching and his periodical *Butor*, which was published between 1935 and 1938. His activities resulted in the establishment of the first industrial design school in Hungary. He also tirelessly promoted a specifically Hungarian style of furniture along with Zsuzsa Kovács, László Juhász and Frigyes Gabriel. The designers László Hornicsek and József Király were pupils of his.

The factories that mass-produced furniture also followed foreign designs, primarily in historical revival styles. The Endre Thék, Schmidt and Lajos Kajdy factories produced high-quality furniture in a wide range of styles, from French Renaissance through Dutch and English Baroque to the so-called Colonial style that was fashionable in the 1930s. The József Lingel furniture factory produced some of the most distinguished work in the modern style, following American designs, and it was very successful with its bookshelf-cupboard units. The Antal Nagy factory is also notable for its well-made classic modern pieces; its chief designer was Károly Nagy.

BIBLIOGRAPHY

P. Nádai: *A lakásberendezés műsvészete* [The art of interior decoration] (Budapest, 1939)

J. Koós: *Kozma Lajos munkássága* [The work of Lajos Kozma] (Budapest, 1975)

L. Nemeth, ed.: *Magyar művészet, 1885–1918* [Hungarian art, 1885–1918] (Budapest, 1981)

S. Kontha, ed.: *Magyar művészet, 1919–1945* [Hungarian art, 1919–45] (Budapest, 1985)

A Golden Age: Art and Society in Hungary, 1896–1914 (exh. cat., ed. G. Éri and Z. Jobbágyi; London, Barbican A.G.; Miami, Cent. F.A.; San Diego, Mus. A.; 1989–91)

HEDVIG SZABOLCSI

The survey of **Hungary** continues in vol. 15.

Illustration Acknowledgements

We are grateful to those listed below for permission to reproduce copyright illustrative material and to those contributors who supplied photographs or helped us to obtain them. The word 'Photo:' precedes the names of large commercial or archival sources who have provided us with photographs, as well as the names of individual photographers (where known). It has generally not been used before the names of owners of works of art, such as museums and civic bodies. Every effort has been made to contact copyright holders and to credit them appropriately; we apologize to anyone who may have been omitted from the acknowledgements or cited incorrectly. Any error brought to our attention will be corrected in subsequent editions. Where illustrations have been taken from books, publication details are provided in the acknowledgements below.

Line drawings, maps, plans, chronological tables and family trees commissioned by the *Dictionary of Art* are not included in the list below. All of the maps in the dictionary were produced by Oxford Illustrators Ltd, who were also responsible for some of the line drawings. Most of the line drawings and plans, however, were drawn by the following artists: Diane Fortenberry, Lorraine Hodghton, Chris Miners, Amanda Patton, Mike Pringle, Jo Richards, Miranda Schofield, John Tiernan, John Wilson and Philip Winton. The chronological tables and family trees were prepared initially by Kate Boatfield and finalized by John Johnson.

Habsburg, §II: (2) Philip II Museo del Prado, Madrid
Habsburg, §II: (7) Philip IV Frick Collection, New York
Hacılar Sadberk Hanım Museum, Istanbul
Hackaert, Jan Rijksmuseum, Amsterdam
Hackert: (1) Philipp Hackert Soprintendenza per i Beni Ambientali, Architettonici, Artistici e Storici per le Provincie di Caserta e Benevento, Caserta
Hadrian's Wall Cambridge University Collection of Air Photographs
Haft Tepe Photo: Ezat O. Negahban
Haggadah British Library, London (MS. 27210, fol. 6*v*)
Haghpat Monastery Photo: VAAP, Moscow
Hague, The *1, 5* Rijksdienst voor de Monumentenzorg, Zeist; *2–3* Haags Gemeentemuseum, The Hague; *4* Photo: Panorama Mesdag, The Hague
Haiti *2* Photothèque du Musée de l'Homme, Paris; *3* Photo: Robert Harding Picture Library, London; *4* Photo: Dolores M. Yonker; *5* Photo: Thomas C. Folk, Bernardsville, NJ
Hakuin Ekaku Photo: Shojuji
Halaf, Tell Editions Citadelles-Paris (from Jean Mazenod: *L'Art antique du Proche-Orient*)
Halikarnassos *2–4* Trustees of the British Museum, London
Hall (i) *1* Photo: Bildarchiv Foto Marburg; *2* Photo: Francis Woodman
Hall church *1–2* Photo: Bildarchiv Foto Marburg
Hallé: (3) Noël Hallé *1* Photo: RMN, Paris/© DACS, 1996; *2* Photo: © RMN, Paris
Hals: (1) Frans Hals *1* Hofje van Aerden, Leerdam/Museum Boymans–van Beuningen, Rotterdam; *2–3* Rijksmuseum, Amsterdam
Hals: (2) Dirck Hals Rijksmuseum, Amsterdam
Hamburg Photo: Bilderberg Archiv der Fotografen, Hamburg
Hamen y León, Juan van der National Gallery of Art, Washington, DC
Hamilton, Gavin Trustees of the British Museum, London
Hamilton, Richard © Richard Hamilton/DACS, 1996. All rights reserved
Hamilton, William (i) National Portrait Gallery, London
Hammershøi: (1) Vilhelm Hammershøi Thielska Galleriet, Stockholm
Hampton Court Palace *1* Photo: RCHME/© Crown Copyright; *2* British Library, London (no. 191.g.15)
Han Gan Metropolitan Museum of Art, New York (Dillon Fund, 1977; no. 1977.78)
Hanneman, Adriaen National Gallery of Art, Washington, DC (Andrew W. Mellon Collection)
Hannover Bildarchiv, Historisches Museum, Hannover
Hanover: (4) George IV National Portrait Gallery, London
Hansen: (2) Theophilus Hansen Photo: Anthony Kersting, London
Hansen, C. F. *1* Kunstakademiet, Copenhagen; *2* Nationalmuseum, Copenhagen

Hard-edge painting Art Institute of Chicago, Chicago, IL (Gift of Mr and Mrs Arnold H. Maremount through the Kate Maremount Foundation; no. 1962.146)/© 1996
Hardstones *1* Museo dell'Opificio delle Pietre Dure, Florence; *2* Photo: Scala, Florence; *3* National Trust Photo Library, London/Photo: Mark Fiennes; *4* Kunsthistorisches Museum, Vienna; *5* Bridgeman Art Library, London/Photo: S.J. Phillips, London
Häring, Hugo Photo: British Architectural Library, RIBA, London
Harness and trappings *1* Griffith Institute, Ashmolean Museum, Oxford; *2–3* From M.A. Littauer and J.H. Crouwel: *Wheeled Vehicles and Ridden Animals in the Ancient Near East* (Leiden and Cologne, 1979); *4* British Library, London (no. AC. 4660(9)); *5* Musée de l'Armée, Paris; *6* Photo: Archivi Alinari, Florence; *7* Board of Trustees of the Royal Armouries, London; *8* Photo: Fidelity Lancaster
Harpignies, Henri-Joseph Photo: © RMN, Paris
Harrach Photo: Robert Keyszelitz
Harris, Lawren S. National Gallery of Canada, Ottawa
Harrison, Peter Library of Congress, Washington, DC
Harrison and Abramovitz Lincoln Center for the Performing Arts, New York/Photo: William Dietz Associates
Hartley, Marsden Metropolitan Museum of Art, New York (Alfred Stieglitz Collection, 1949; no. 49.70.42)
Hartung, Hans Öffentliche Kunstsammlung, Kunstmuseum, Basle/© DACS, 1996
Hasegawa Tōhaku National Museum, Tokyo
Hashim Freer Gallery of Art, Smithsonian Institution, Washington, DC (no. 39.49R)
Hassam, Childe Toledo Museum of Art, Toledo, OH (Purchased with funds from the Florence Scott Libbey Bequest in memory of her Father, Maurice A. Scott)
Hatra *1–2* Photo: Wathiq al-Salihi
Hausa *1–2* Photo: David Heathcote
Hausmann, Raoul Tate Gallery, London/© DACS, 1996/Marthe Prèvot
Havana Photo: Paolo Gasparini
Hawaii *1* Museum of New Zealand Te Papa Tongarewa, Wellington; *2* Trustees of the British Museum, London
Hawksmoor, Nicholas *1* Photo: RCHME/© Crown Copyright; *2* Conway Library, Courtauld Institute of Art, London; *3* Photo: Kerry Downes; *4* Photo: Anthony Kersting, London
Haydon, Benjamin Robert Royal Collection, Windsor Castle/© Her Majesty Queen Elizabeth II
Hayez, Francesco *1* Photo: Bridgeman Art Library, London; *2* Photo: Scala, Florence
Hazor Israel Antiquities Authority, Jerusalem
Heade, Martin Johnson Museum of Fine Arts, Boston, MA (Bequest of Maxim Karolik)

911

Homer, Winslow *1* Pennsylvania Academy of the Fine Arts, Philadelphia, PA (Joseph E. Temple Fund); *2* Yale University Art Gallery, New Haven, CT

Hon'ami: (1) Hon'ami Kōetsu *1* Hatakeyama Collection, Tokyo; *2* National Museum, Tokyo

Hon'ami: (2) Hon'ami Kōho Fujita Art Museum, Osaka

Hondecoeter: (2) Melchior d'Hondecoeter Musée des Beaux-Arts, Caen/Photo: Martine Seyve

Hondius, Abraham Hamburger Kunsthalle, Hamburg

Honduras *2* South American Pictures, Woodbridge, Suffolk/Photo: Chris Sharpe; *3* Art Museum of the Americas (OAS), Washington, DC

Hone: (4) Evie Hone Hugh Lane Municipal Gallery of Modern Art, Dublin

Hong Kong *1* Architectural Association, London/Photo: © Petra Hodgson; *2* Photo: HSBC Group

Hongren Honolulu Academy of Arts, Honolulu, HI (Gift of Wilhelmina Tenney Memorial Collection, 1955)

Hong Se-sŏp National Museum of Korea, Seoul

Honoré, Master Bibliothèque Nationale de France, Paris

Honthorst, Gerrit van *1* Trustees of the National Gallery, London; *2* Bayerische Staatsgemäldesammlungen, Munich; *3* J. Paul Getty Museum, Malibu, CA; *4* Nasjonalgalleriet, Oslo

Hooch, Pieter de *1* Trustees of the National Gallery, London; *2* Rijksmuseum, Amsterdam

Hood, Raymond Photo: G.E. Kidder Smith, New York (from G.E. Kidder Smith: *The Architecture of the United States*)

Hooghe, Romeyn de Provinciale Atlas Noord-Holland, Rijksarchief in Noord-Holland, Haarlem

Hoogstraten, Samuel van *1* Kunsthistorisches Museum, Vienna; *2* Staatliche Kunsthalle Karlsruhe

Hope: (1) Thomas Hope British Library, London (no. 1261.f.23)

Hopewell Mounds Westview Press (from Naomi Greber and Katharine C. Ruhl: *The Hopewell Site: A Contemporary Analysis Based on the Work of Charles C. Willoughby*, 1989)

Hopfer: (1) Daniel Hopfer Trustees of the British Museum, London

Hopper, Edward Art Institute of Chicago, Chicago, IL/© 1996

Hoppner, John Metropolitan Museum of Art, New York (Catherine Lorillard Wolfe Collection; Wolfe Fund, 1901; no. 01.20)

Horemheb Metropolitan Museum of Art, New York (Gift of Mr and Mrs V. Everitt Macy, 1923; no. 23.10.1)

Horenbout: (1) Gerard Horenbout British Library, London (Add. MS. 34294)

Horenbout: (2) Lucas Horenbout Syndics of the Fitzwilliam Museum, Cambridge

Horn Museum of London

Horta, Victor *1–2* Archives d'Architecture Moderne, Brussels

Hortus deliciarum British Library, London (no. 1703.d.7)

Hōryūji Photo: Werner Forman Archive, London

Hosios Loukas Photo: Electa, Milan

Hospital *1* Photo: Ancient Art and Architecture Collection, London; *2* Photo: Ampliaciones y Reproducciones MAS, Barcelona; *3* British Library, London (no. 7687.i.9); *4* Photo: Lo Henderyckx; *5* Photo: © ACL Brussels

Hotel *1* Cornell University Library, Ithaca, NY; *2* Photo: Marriott Marquis Hotel, Atlanta, GA

Hôtel particulier *1–2* Bibliothèque Nationale de France, Paris

Michel-Ange Houasse Museo del Prado, Madrid

Houckgeest, Gerrit Mauritshuis, The Hague

Houdon, Jean-Antoine *1–2* Photo: Giraudon, Paris

Houma Photo: Robert Harding Picture Library, London

Houston Photo: Paul Hester, Houston, TX

Howard (i): (1) Thomas Howard National Portrait Gallery, London

Howe, Oscar Philbrook Museum of Art, Tulsa, OK/© DACS, 1996

Howling Wolf Southwest Museum, Los Angeles, CA

Huang Binhong Metropolitan Museum of Art, New York (Gift of Robert Hatfield Ellsworth, in memory of La Ferne Hatfield Ellsworth, 1986; no. 1986.267.204/J)

Huang Gongwang *1* Palace Museum, Beijing; *2* National Palace Museum, Taipei

Huang Shen National Museum, Tokyo

Huang Yongyu Oxford University Press (Hong Kong) Ltd (from H. Morrison: *A Photographer in Old Peking*, 1985)

Huari Photo: Beth Edelheit

Huastec Museo Nacional de Antropología, Mexico City/Photo: © Beatriz de la Fuente

Hua Yan Freer Gallery of Art, Smithsonian Institution, Washington, DC (no. 55.20h)

Huber, Wolfgang *1* Kunsthistorisches Museum, Vienna; *2* National Gallery of Ireland, Dublin

Hübsch, Heinrich Stadtarchiv, Baden-Baden

Hudson, Thomas Thomas Coram Foundation for Children, London

Huet: (2) Jean-Baptiste Huet I Photo: © RMN, Paris

Huet, Paul Musée des Beaux-Arts, Lille

Hughes, Arthur Tate Gallery, London

Huguenots Trustees of the British Museum, London

Huguet, Jaume Museu Nacional d'Art de Catalunya, Barcelona/Photo: MNAC Photographic Service (Calveras/Sagristá)

Hull Photo: James Austin, Cambridge

Human proportion *1* Galleria dell'Accademia, Venice/Photo: Soprintendenza ai Beni Artistici e Storici, Venice; *2* Bibliothèque Nationale de France, Paris; *3* Biblioteca Nazionale Centrale, Florence

Hunedoara Castle Photo: Országos Müemléki Hivatal, Budapest

Hungary *2* © Interfoto MTI, Budapest/Photo: Csaba Raffael; *3–6* Photo: © Interfoto MTI, Budapest; *7, 9–11* Magyar Nemzéti Galéria, Budapest/Photo: Mester Tibor Foto, Budapest; *8* © Interfoto MTI, Budapest/Photo: K. Matusz; *12–14* Magyar Nemzéti Múzeum, Budapest; *15* Iparmüvészeti Múzeum, Budapest (inv. no. 17.744); *16* Photo: Országos Müemléki Hivatal, Budapest; *17* János Zantus Museum, Györ; *18* Iparmüvészeti Múzeum, Budapest